£5

THE
WISDEN
BOOK OF
CRICKETERS'
LIVES

OBITUARIES FROM
WISDEN CRICKETERS'
ALMANACK

COMPILED BY
BENNY GREEN

Macdonald
Queen Anne Press

A *Queen Anne Press* BOOK

Original Wisden material © John Wisden & Co Ltd
Additional introductory material © Benny Green 1986
This Anthology © Queen Anne Press 1986

First published in Great Britain in 1986
under the title 'The Wisden Book of Obituaries' by
Queen Anne Press, Macdonald & Co (Publishers) Ltd,
3rd Floor, Hampstead Road, London NW1 7QX

a member of Maxwell Pergamon Publishing Corporation plc

Reprinted 1988

Printed in Hungary

INTRODUCTION

There are 8,614 of them. The population of a small country town, except that they come from the four corners of the earth. A marauding army, perhaps, were it not that among the ranks are to be found the occasional lady and at least one resolute quadruped. They range from crowned heads to vagrants, millionaires to beggars, reverend gentlemen to professional politicians, Gentlemen and Players, geniuses and journeymen, dukes and dustmen, those who died too young and those who perhaps lived just a little too long, like that poor Mr Filliston, knocked down and killed by a motor scooter at the age of 102. But then, who is to say when a man's time has come? The club cricketer Charles Absolon took a hundred wickets in his 81st year, while the Mackinnon of Mackinnon, generally believed to be immortal and having apparently compromised his divine status by being seen entering a local Kentish hospital in his 99th year, explained, "I am going into hospital, but only for the annual meeting, at which I shall preside". None of these veterans could be adjudged old compared to John Edward Taylor, whose wife died at the age of 103, after 68 years of marriage, and who lived on as a gentle widower until he was 105. There were pacifists and warriors, poets and peasants, professors and creative artists, bishops and music hall comics, explorers and those who were content, in the words of the Almanack, to die "at their native place". Writers and farmers, actors and generals, miners and prospectors, schoolboys and great-grandfathers, those who founded dynasties and those who finally closed some dynasty's flickering account.

The cricketers of England and her dominions have come from every walk of life, pursued every kind of path, embraced every sort of morality or no morality at all, and experienced every kind of death. They passed away in every imaginable way and one or two others besides. Being dedicated athletes every one, several of them died in mid-stroke. They took their leave while playing polo, squash, lawn tennis, golf, football, rowing, hunting, shooting, fishing, cycling, refereeing and umpiring. There is even one case recorded of death while bird-watching. Some of the very lucky ones died at the crease, like Andrew Ducat, or in the field, or even occassionally in the pavilion, like the gentleman to be found in these pages who "died in his flannels in the Bristol pavilion". At least one old cricketer would perhaps have wished to die at the ground but never quite mastered the timing; we read of A.W.Sheldon, who passed away while packing his bag for the Scarborough Festival. There have even been those who died in bed but clung to their cricketing credentials even unto the gates of Paradise. Among these was the umpire Harry Bagshot, who was laid to rest in accordance with his own carefully defined wishes, in his white coat, with six pebbles in one pocket and a cricket ball in the other, it evidently never have occurred to him that an excellent working definition of Heaven is a place where no umpiring is required. Bagshot had his colonial counterpart in the Australian who was placed in his coffin alongside a fragment of turf from the Melbourne ground.

Cricketers have died falling from windows, from horses, from express trains, and, in the case of Stanley McCabe, from cliffs. They have succumbed to earthquakes and have sometimes been incorporated in great public tragedies, like the players who went down in the *Titanic* and *Lusitania*. They have died through an unidentified virus, have been accidentlly electrocuted, been bitten to death by insects, been found floating face down in the local canal, or, like A.W.Carr, died while shovelling snow, or even, like W.Whysall, from a fall in a dance hall. One cricketing K.C. dropped dead while walking to the Law Courts, and there was an intrepid Victorian called E.E.Bowen, who died in the act of mounting his bicycle during a tour of France. Some sad cricketers took poison, or cut their throats, or blew their brains out. It may be that the most bizarre fatality of all was the one suffered by Mr Eligon, who passed away through blood poisoning caused by a nail in his cricket boot. Another cricket-related death was that suffered by the father of the Australian batsman Peter Burge, who was struck down by a heart attack while listening to a radio commentary of a Test innings by his own son. This calls to mind the heroic case of J.W.H.T.Douglas, who was drowned, with his father, while attempting to save the old boy in a boating accident. And for sheer unexpectedness, there is the case, recorded in these pages, of the young Pakistani cricketer who died at the crease on being hit in the chest by a slow off-break.

Occasionally bloody violence has spattered the pages of the Almanack, as in the case of Captain R.K.Makant, who was "murdered while on duty in Kurdistan"; the Rhodesian B.H.Williams, a victim of terrorist rockets; and the cricketing writer Jack Anderson, assassinated at his Jamaican home. From time to time the imminence of death to a cricketer has inspired gestures of sentimental affection. One Yorkshire cricketer in his last hours was awarded his Second XI cap, and there was the case of the dying Dulwich College boy appointed Head of School while lying in the coma preceding death. Most affecting of all these twelfth-hour melodramas remains the one involving the young Australian virtuoso Archie Jackson, who participated in a deathbed marriage ceremony with his childhood sweetheart. There have even been cricketing funerals brought about by cricketing funerals; Arthur H.Gregory of the great Australian cricketing dynasty, fell off a tram when returning from the burial of his cousin S.E.Gregory, and was returned to the cemetary much sooner than he or anyone else could reasonably have expected. For sheer pointlessness there is the death of Joseph Cummings, who found himself one day in the town of Pullman, Illinois, and was so overcome by the experience that he expired there from the intense heat. Nor is it generally remembered that at least one of the cricketing Graces breathed his last while participating in a match. There was even a cricketer once who died while ploughing, and another who was hanged for murder, although the Almanack decorously omitted to say so.

Extraordinary as the accumulated circumstances of the deaths of cricketers are, they might have been more extraordinary still had the editors of the Almanack not taken so long to think of the idea. When John Wisden published his first annual edition in 1864, he was so bemused by the beauty of his own invention that he had not the remotest idea what to put into it, a state of mind which caused him to fill the pages with irrelevancies so comic that to this day the researcher is vastly diverted, by tables showing the length of British canals, the dates of the principal battles of the Wars of the Roses, the date of foundation of the Antiquarian, Astronomical, Ethnological, Geological, Horticultural, Microscopical, Pharmaceutical and Philological Scoieties, and a brisk disquisition on the constitutional implications of the trial of Charles 1. Not until 1892, a generation after the first appearance of the Almanack, did obituary notices first appear, and even then consisted of little more than a name, a country and a date. This means that cricketers were dying at regular intervals for 28 years after the publication of the first Almanack without so much as a mention in its pages. But once the editors realised what a rich source of fact and anecdote might be liberated by the elaboration of death notices, this section of the Almanack quickly flowered into one of the greater glories of English sporting prose. Gradually, as the editors themselves finally qualified for inclusion in the obituary columns, the style of writing changed; the mandarin approach of the late Victorians modulates into the orotundities of the Edwardians, and then, as sensibilities readjusted in the modern age, to the functional recitation of statistics of the last 60 years, an evolution which the reader cannot help feeling has seemed likely at time to inflict permanent damage of the readability of the finished article.

Readers will also detect a glaring imbalance in the relative prestigiousness of the obituaries. The old school tended to make great play with the Old School at the expense often of professionals who played the game better and achieved more. Some forgotten Varsity hero who sacrificed his subsequent career to a footling job in the City might get twice as much space as a veteran who had been the mainstay of some ailing county side for 20 years. Certain episodes, particularly Cobden's Match, recur again and again over the years, until at last we may be forgiven for thinking that mere attendance at the match was sufficient qualification for inclusion in the obituary columns. Some references to achievements "never since surpassed" are clearly long outmoded, but to have adjusted them with editorial hindsight would have been to dilute the flavour of the original. And when the Almanack, having committed the solecism of burying someone prematurely, later relented and dug him up again in the next edition, it seemed to me worthwhile including the full text of the incident, thus endowing a few fortunate sportsmen with the rare glory of two obituaries. There is even the case of the army officer who was reported killed in one of Queen Victoria's little wars, only to turn up at his own estate just in time to enjoy his own funeral observances, which he laughingly transformed into a celebratory dance.

One aspect of the Almanack's death notices requires some comment. Of those 8,614 dear cricketing departed, about one fifth have been omitted, for a very revealing reason. I have remarked on the tendency of the old-time editors to exfloriate on the deeds of once-young gentlemen at the expense of the sometimes greater deeds of once-young players. When the Great War brought its wholesale slaughter of junior officers, the duties of the editors became at once shocking and overwhelming. In the absence of any first-class cricket, *Wisden* for four years was little more than a catalogue of death. And, understandably convulsed with grief at the endless lists of the slain pouring in from Flanders, the editors appear to have resolved to bestow on as many young men as possible a sort of immortality which bore no relationship to what they had done on the field of play. It was as though some subaltern, blown to pieces within a year or two of leaving school, must at least be endowed with the limited life to be found in the pages of the Almanack. An analysis of those 8,614 deaths discloses the appalling statistic that ever since *Wisden* began recording the deaths of cricketers, one in every eight of the obsequies was brought about by events on the Western Front. However, if the non-first-class entrants are dropped from the list, the carnage, although obscene, seems not quite as extensive. Some young men were accorded the due solemnity of an interment in the pages of *Wisden* on the strength of having once scored 50 for their school or taken six wickets in an inter-regimental match. These brave men, cheated though they were of life, hardly belong in a record-book whose avowed aim is to record the feats and fates of first-class cricketers. A few of the also-rans retain their places either by sheer force of personality or because of the one bizarre moment in their career which remains unforgettable, but for the rest, what follows is almost exclusively a register of first-class cricketers.

Some idea of what England lost through the deaths in the Great War is perhaps best conveyed by the amazing multifarious nature of the achievements enjoyed in later years by retired or retiring cricketers. Because of the predominance of cricket on the curricula of the public schools, most of these achievements fall within the orbit of the three great clearing houses of the comfortable classes, the Law, the Church and the Army. But leavening this mountainous stew of bishops and colonels and judges is the occasional professional whose ambition and abilities ran a little further than a local pub of a sports outfitters. It has sometimes been said, much to the disbelief of non-cricketing sceptics, that *Wisden,* through the sheer accumulation of facts gathered in more than a century of publication, is, in its own garbled, confused, accidental way, a sort of social history of England. However much truth there might be in the claim, it is certainly a fact that there are very few facets of English life which cannot be found somewhere in *Wisden,* only provided the researcher has the faith to persevere. In studying the contents of this anthology, the reader will encounter men who, besides distinguishing themselves at the most subtle of all team games, filled the following posts with greater or lesser distinction: Lord Lieutenant of Worcestershire; host of the Clayton Arms, Kennington; author of *The Guinea Pig;* proprietor of *The Times;* Lord Lieutenant of Buckinghamshire; Clerk of the Central Criminal Court; High Sheriff of Wiltshire; Military Secretary to the Viceroy of Ireland; County Commandant of the Hereford Boy Scouts; *Daily Express* cartoonist; Governor of the Blue Nile Province; Commissioner of Police, Shanghai; village baker; Suffragan Bishop of Knaresborough; Private Secretary to the Duke of Argyll; Acting Governor of Rhodesia; Professor of Economics at Toronto University; British Attaché at Florence; Professor of Poetry, Oxford; Chief Constable of Northamptonshire; Private Secretary to the Prime Minister (H.H.Asquith); Professor of Oriental Languages, Cambridge; Champion Archer of England; Chairman of Cunard; Resident Commissioner, Swaziland; President, Association of Headmistresses; H.M. Consul, China; Honorary Canon at Ely Cathedral; Librarian to House of Lords; Deputy Prime Minister of Fiji; Amateur Skittles Champion of Victoria; President, Corpus Christi College, Oxford; Deputy Lieutenant of Kent; Archdeacon Emeritus, Canterbury; Father of the House of Lords; bee farmer; Governor of Jamaica; Aide-de-camp to the Duke of Cambridge; Vice-Chancellor, Oxford; Chairman of the Unionist Party; inventor of the 'Aerial' Fishing Reel; Governor of Bengal; Vice-President, Royal Water Colour Society; Advocate-General, Bombay; Baron of the Cinque Ports; Secretary, Adelaide Chamber of Commerce; Commander of the British Fleet at the Battle of Jutland; Governor-General of New Zealand; Archdeacon of Timaru; High Commissioner, Trinidad and Tobago; Indian High Commissioner to Australia; Minister of Defence; President of the Poetry Society; Chief Paymaster, Australian Army; Police Inspector; Mayor of Blackpool; Registrar of Probate and Divorce Registry; Viceroy of India; bat-maker to W.G.Grace; King of England; Indian Ambassador to Holland; Bishop of Bunbury; Member of the General Gordon Relief Expedition; Klondyke prospector; Head Porter, Trinity College, Cambridge; Acting Governor-General of Australia; Commandant of Transvaal concentration camp; Mayor of Burton-on-Trent; Lord Mayor of London; Producer of *Itma;* Archdeacon of Coventry; participant in the Jameson Raid; Master of the Rolls; Music hall comedian; First Lord of the Admiralty; Gentleman Usher to the Sword; Chief Justice of the Sudan; Governor of the Gold Coast; rider of Grand National winner; Canon Emeritus, Worcester Cathedral; Serjeant-at-Arms, House of Commons; Chief Justice of the Seychelles; Secretary for the Colonies; Chief Justice, Leeward Islands; editor of *Punch;* West End musical comedy performer; breeder of Golden Retrievers; Public Prosecutor for Birmingham; Senior Priest in-Ordinary to H.M. the Queen; botanist in mountain-climbing expedition; pioneer of mink farming in England; political prisoner, Sri Lanka; member of Buffalo Bill's troupe; King of Tonga; dramatist and critic; Racing Manager to Cardiff Arms Park Greyhound Racing Club; High Sheriff of Gloucestershire; Judicial Adviser to the Khedive of Egypt; Manager of the Bombay Trading Company; organist, Magdalen College, Oxford; Private Secretary to Queen Alexandria; Secretary, the Empire Theatre, Leicester Square.

Although it must be admitted that the editors of the Almanack have never been slow in appropriating for their columns the famous, the distinguished and the ennobled, there is no question that all the blooms in the copious garland listed above are authentic enough. At first sight one or two of the crowned heads might seem faintly dubious, but certainly in the two cases of George Tubow II of Tonga and George VI of England there is irresistible evidence in favour of inclusion, of George Tubow for the knotty political problem forced upon him by the game of cricket, George VI for having achieved, admittedly in a very minor game, the most empurpled hat-trick in the history of the game, or indeed any game. Through what prevailing circumstances George as a boy was enabled to dismiss with successive deliveries Edward VII, the future George V and the future Edward VIII we remain in the dark, but no collector of the arcane could ever deny the attraction of such a feat. But even a hat-trick, or a treble century, suggest expertise rather than virtuosity, and when virtuosity is the prize, then we must look elsewhere, and settle at last on two challengers, Dave Nourse of South Africa and K.C.Gandar-Dower. At least in Nourse's case there are a few faint hints of modulation from one shift to the next, for after starting out as a drummer boy he then grew into a soldier. But then came two giant leaps, to railway guard and then billiard marker. Having veered towards the sporting life, Nourse then veered sharply away from it by becoming a saloon keeper, then a commercial traveller, then manager of an athletic outfitters, and finally a coach, in between which varied careers he managed somehow to represent South Africa in 45 consecutive Test matches. The career of Mr Gandar-Dower is altogether more chaotic, more fragmented, consisting of a series of unprepared discords leaping to improbable resolutions. Although he never aspired to the international heights achieved by Nourse, he had a much shorter life, and did at any rate play in the upper reaches of the Public School and University game. He was the Cambridge Lawn Tennis captain, won the Amateur Squash Championship, also the Amateur Fives Championship, represented Great Britain at Lawn Tennis, and also represented his university at Billiards. Gandar-Dower remains the only man ever to participate simultaneously in the Freshman's cricket match and the Freshman's Lawn Tennis tournament, "with the connivance of the tennis but not the cricket authorities". Connoisseurs of the extravagant may be interested to know how this perilous feat was achieved: "He disappeared to play off a round during the early part of his side's innings, with relays of cyclist friends to keep him informed as to the fall of wickets." After leaving University, Gandar-Dower continued to perform a succession of deeds unconnected with each other and very often with Gandar-Dower himself. It could have been said of him as it was once said of Marc Antony, the nobody knew what he would do next and neither did he. At one point he flew a private plane to India, and soon became a celebrated big game hunter and world traveller. During one of his visits to the jungles of Kenya, it was brought to his attention that cheetahs are able to travel at high speeds, at which he captured a team of the creatures and brought them home to London, where he put them to work by running them at local greyhound tracks, against dogs, dirt-track riders and each other. When not involved with the cheetahs, Gandar-Dower wrote magazine articles and published books, and altogether enjoyed a splendidly eccentric career which was curtailed by the Second World War. He became a correspondent on various battlefields, until at last he was lost at sea as a consequence of some moronic ploy by the Japanese armed forces, since which time his life's work has served as an exemplary example of enterprise and hedonism to all young men toying with the idea of going out and getting a job.

The sobering thought occurs that *Wisden* is the perfect net into which such rare and exotic butterflies may come to rest, and that had it not been for the Almanack's obituary columns the larks of Gandar-Dower might have gone unrecorded and would finally have faded into historical oblivion when the last man who knew him was himself the subject of someone's obituary compilation. Gandar-Dower is the ideal example of the man who made his own fame, but the Almanack has occasionally been confronted by the not unpleasing problem of the modest practitioner of the game who just happens to have a distinguished literary connection. Its list of late lamented has therefore incorporated Jane Austen's great-nephew, H.G.Wells' father, a decendent of John Dryden, Sir Walter Scott's godson, Edward Fitzgerald's nephew, besides those writers who earned entry by their own efforts, including Alec Waugh, P.G. Wodehouse, Sir James Barrie, Sir Arthur Conan Doyle and his brother-in-law E.W.Hornung. The Almanack also makes at least one microscopic but nonetheless significant addition to literary scholarship by including in one of its obituaries a revelatory fact concerning one of the Eminent Victorians. Frederick Gale, a cricketer-writer known as "The Old Buffer," "enjoyed the friendship of John Ruskin, and took the famous writer to the Oval in 1882 to see the Australians". The Almanack makes no further comment on this intriguing event, but it would be instructive to know if old Fred, when he led the famous critical conscience of the Victorians to the cricket, was aware that Ruskin had some years before published one of the most fatuous comments ever made about the game, in a book called *The Crown of Wild Olive:*

> "I use the test which I have adopted, of the connexion of war with other arts, and I reflect how, as a sculptor, I should feel if I were asked to design a monument for Westminster Abbey, with a carving of a bat at one end and a ball at the other. It may be there remains in me only a savage Gothic prejudice; but I had rather carve it with a shield at one end and a sword at the other."

Ruskin did not live long enough to see his feelings gratified in the Almanacks of the years covering the Great War, but it is curious that nowhere in any of the biographies or published correspondence of the Victorians is any reference made to this incongruous visit of Ruskin's to Kennington Oval. It would perhaps bear further investigation, and at any rate reduces to the proportions of mere country gossip the gallantry of George Henry Remnant one afternoon in the company of the family of Charles Dickens.

We assume that all these snippets of social history were imparted by the Almanack in the best of faith, but we cannot always be sure. Every now and again a glint of sly, straighfaced humour shines through the decorous prose of these death notices. Of the impulse to laughter there can be no doubt; the only contentious issue is whether the humour was intentional or accidental. In compiling previous *Wisden* anthologies, I have been confronted with this enigma several times before, and in restating the difficulties of assessment and reaction, I am tempted to the very apex of self-idolatry by quoting myself. Having observed that by 1900 the *Wisden* obituaries had become one of the great glories of sporting literature, I then wondered how far this glory had been calculated and how far fortuitous. How much of this glory was literary artifice and how much blimpish imperception? When diverted by the news that a Mr Ford hit a ball so hard that it disturbed some partridges, or that some worthy lived in a house called "Wickets," are we smiling at Pooter or at the Grossmiths? Whimsicality of a different kind attends the obsequies of the great footballing Alcock, who stands for all time as the exemplar of the Englishman as world leader in team games by captaining the French cricket side against Germany at Hamburg. Fame of yet another kind descended on the Reverend Arthur Butler, who one day took the doctrine of Muscular Christianity to faintly excessive lengths by becoming the only man ever to leap across the River Cherwell. We thrill to the dizzying effects of the Earl of Leicester's convoluted geneology, and laugh out loud over the notoriety of the only rowing Blue ever to be in danger of being drowned during the Boat Race. We are suitably impressed by a Kentish veteran called Banks, whose most notable accomplishment appears to have been his ability to ride a tricycle in his ninetieth year. A batsman called Fison clearly qualifies for the honour of inventing the most ridiculous mode of dismissal in the history of cricket, and one of his contemporaries, called Hemingway, stakes his claim as the holder of the record for the most runs scored off a single delivery . . .

And so it goes on, a catalogue of eccentricity, shock and surprise, of facetiousness acted out with diocesan solemnity, especially in the delicate matter of damning with faint praise. How far were the editors of *Wisden* being serious, for example, when commending a certain Chevalier Epifano Rodrigues as "the best cover point in Spain," how far frivolous in nominating one Arthur McEvoy as "probably the finest bowler in France"? Only probably? And what of Father William Ignatius Rice, whose claim to fame is that he was "the only monk whose cricketing performances are chronicled in *Wisden*"? Is the death of G.T.Groves to be included among "Killed in Action" or "Other Deaths"? *Wisden* leaves the choice to us by remarking that Mr Groves died from enemy action "when at Newmarket on duty as a racing journalist". What, one wonders, would Henry Grierson have made of the opinion stated in his obituary that as a pianist he was "better than Semprini"? And is there not a world of unspoken censure in the grudging tribute paid to H.P.Chadwyck-Healey: "as a cricketer, his enthusiasm greatly exceeded his skill, but he was quite well known as a composer of church music". Only quite well known? And would a man be content to meet his Maker where he to be aware, as one George Lacy apparently was, that he was "one of the very few men who could claim to have walked across Africa from East to West before the first Boer War". Perhaps this is the most wickedly barbed compliment to be found throughout the entire range of the Almanack's history, with its cunning implication that after the first Boer War Africa was positively congested with men walking across it from East to West, and that in any case, even before that war, hundreds of cricketers had been in the habit of walking across it from West to East.

A special case in this anthology is to be found among the gentlemen of the cloth, most of whose first-class careers were confined to their days at Oxford or Cambridge, after which they succumbed happily enough to the rusticities of some sleepy rectory. There is the Rector who was too poor to accept the invitation to represent his university at Lord's. There is the Rector who served as the model for one of the characters in *Tom Brown's Schooldays*. But nowhere does the spirit of self-sacrifice manifest itself more gloriously than in the case of the Rev. George William Gillingham, who not only cast his bread upon the waters, but cast himself in after it. To be sure, his case was exceptional, and most of the cricketing divines acknowledged by *Wisden* enjoyed what seems to have that peace with passeth all understanding. Every so often the Almanack records a tiny puff of dust as one of these ancient religious worthies breathes his last, in the first floor bedroom of some Victorian rectory whose sash windows looked down at the perfect batting wicket of the village ground, so that even in the valley of the shadow the old boy could gaze out from the plush concavities of the deep bed and follow events on the easy wicket where once he had made so many quick fifties, featherbedded in life as in death. The Rev. C.M.Sharpe was a Barnsley vicar for 34 years; Canon Evans was a rural Dean for 38; the Rev. G.H.Smith presided over the spiritual affairs of his Kentish village for more than 40 years; up in Bedfordshire the Rev. Augustus Orlebar passes his half century before taking his leave; while nearby Canon Sir John Leigh Hopkins holds on for 55 years, a mark equalled by the Venerable William Latham Bevan, vicar of Hay from 1845 to 1900. All of them must have seemed mere upstarts to Canon Upcher, ancient Rector of the Norfolk village of Kirby Cane, whose father before him had been the incumbent for 54 years, and his grandfather for 64 before that. The literary minded may be inclined to award the ecclesiastical palm either to the veteran who served under six bishops, or perhaps to the Rev. John Baird Todd, who "died after conducting evening service," a farewell so intrinsically Trollopean that we are almost shocked to find that he did not in his younger days turn out in a few matches for Barsetshire.

Politics impinged thankfully little on the lives of the cricketers, but the obituaries triumphantly record at least two instances of the game transcending the letter of the asinine law. A young Yorkshireman called Smithson lived through the ordeal of hearing his predicament debated in the House of Commons before being able to accept the highest honour available, but much more important in its effect on generations of cricketers since are the events surrounding the career of the Kent batsman James Seymour, who was granted a benefit for long service with the county, only to learn that the Inland Revenue expected a percentage of the proceeds. Seymour fought his case right up to the House of Lords, and won, since which time a professional cricketer's benefit fund is regarded as a tax-free gesture of recognition. Compared to this heroic feat, Sir Spencer Ponsonby-Fane's act of fetching from Paris the treaty which ended the Crimean War dwindles into mere diplomatic insignificance, dwarfed even by the feat of one of W.G.Grace's cousins, who one day in the New Zealand parliament embarked on a filibustering speech lasting 20 hours, or half as long again as Sir Leonard Hutton's record-breaking innings at the Oval in 1938.

The richest corpse in this collection is the ex-Surrey captain, the sixth Earl of Rosebery, who, the Almanack records with ominous clerical exactitude, left the sum of £9,650,986, a fortune which would have disgusted the old Sussex batsman Henry Hyndman, whose post-cricketing career as a gentleman-revolutionary, preaching the doctrines of Karl Marx in top hat and morning coat, are said to have constituted an act of revenge on his own class for having omitted him from the Cambridge side to play Oxford at Lord's in 1864. But even the sixth Earl would surely have deferred to the American cricketer A.J.Cassatt, whose vast fortune, even allowing for rates of exchange at the turn of the century, would have enabled him to buy up the Roseberys several times over, had they only been for sale. But for sheer style, the most opulent departure was probably Lord Willoughby de Broke's, aboard his own yacht, just as the most sordid was that of poor Private Hardy, whose last moments, in the lavatory at King's Cross Station, rank among the most horrific in the annals of the game.

Every entry in this book is self-explanatory, with perhaps three exceptions which might require a word of exposition. I was particularly touched by the case of the Rev. Archibald Hugh Conway Fargus, a Haileybury boy who played twice for Cambridge against Oxford, became a naval chaplain and went down in H.M.S. *Monmouth*, flagship of a long-forgotten admiral in the long-forgotten action in the Pacific. *Wisden* reported the death in its 1915 edition, only to retract it later. Returning from leave, the Rev. Fargus missed his train, and his death. As to those two cricketing minnows, Lieutenant Henry Webber, and Brigadier-General R.B.Bradford, they seem to me to have earned their place less for their sporting prowess than for the felicity with which they represent the plight of the sporting Englishman caught in the mud and blood of Flanders. Neither man was a particularly brilliant player. Webber had once played for Tonbridge School and run up some big scores in club cricket, while Bradford had sometimes found a place in the regimental side. What can we learn of that terrible war from two such modest men, an obscure lieutenant and a forgotten general, a young sprig of 25 and a venerable sport of 68? Nothing, except that it was the general who was 25, the lieutenant who was 68. Perhaps both of them deserved better of the providence which committed them to their sad and shocking fate. Their obituaries, being confined to their cricket, are necessarily brief, but there are times when brevity can itself be the soul of immortality.

The longest notice in this book is of course the one applying to Dr William Gilbert Grace, page after page of miracles documented with assiduous care and accuracy. But among the fleeting images of the lesser performers, what of John Jellicoe, who once captained a team of admirals? And Joe O'Gorman, the music hall star who partnered Jack Hobbs in the Surrey side, and the benign broadcaster Freddie Grisewood, who represented Worcestershire, and Captain Oates, dazzling star of the hagiography of Empire, who has been rewarded for his heroism at the South Pole by being given his place in an Almanack where he has no business to be? And for all its air of a grand pageant proceeding magisterially down the corridors of the nineteenth century, are the obsequies of Dr Grace any more sensational, any more impressive, any more praiseworthy, any funnier, any more admirable, than the single line which is the flimsy yet enduring claim to fame of an otherwise utterly obscure gentleman called Edward Rae? Let the reader decide for himself, and in all other matters referred to herein.

BENNY GREEN

ABBEY, Edwin Austin, R.A., the President of the Artists' C.C., died at Chelsea on August 1, 1911, aged 59. Although only a moderate player, he was fond of the game, and at his house at Fairford, Gloucestershire, had a private ground. He was born at Philadelphia, Pa., on April 1, 1852.

ABDUL AZIZ, who died, aged 17, during the Final of the Quaid-a-Azam Trophy, played January 16–21, 1959, was a Karachi wicket-keeper. After being struck over the heart by a slow off-break from Dildwar Awan, the Combined Services bowler, he was preparing to receive the next ball when he fell to the ground. He died on the way to hospital without recovering consciousness. This was the first incident of its kind in the Indo-Pakistan sub-continent. Abdul Aziz was a student at S.M. College and an employee of the State Bank.

ABEL, Robert, the old Surrey and England cricketer, died at his home near Kennington Oval on December 10, 1936, in his eightieth year. A great favourite at the Oval, Bobby Abel, popularly known as "The Guv'nor," began his career with Surrey in 1881, and played his last match for the county in 1904, failing eyesight causing him to drop out of the XI earlier than otherwise he need have done. Born on November 30, 1857, he was 23 when first appearing for his county. Found in club cricket in Southwark Park, he took some time to accustom himself to new surroundings and his early efforts in first-class cricket gave no idea of the skill which he steadily attained. Very keen, he overcame the handicap of being short and, while maturing his form with the bat, he attracted attention by smart fielding, especially at slip.

In his third season with Surrey he advanced rapidly as a batsman and in 1886 against the Australians at the Oval he played a remarkable innings of 144. In 1888—one of the wettest summers ever experienced—he came out first among the professional batsmen of the year, scoring in first-class matches 1,323 runs with an average of 31. Thenceforward his successful career was interrupted only in 1893 when a serious infection of the eyes interfered with his play. If late in reaching his best, he was right at the top of the tree from 1895 to 1902, scoring over 2,000 runs in first-class matches in eight successive seasons. His highest aggregate of runs, 3,309, was obtained in 1901 and his average in these eight years of conspicuous ability ranged from 56 to 41. In 1903 his eyes troubled him again, and though playing in

glasses helped him to some extent next year his first-class career then closed.

His highest innings was 357 not out against Somerset at the Oval in May, 1899; it remains a Surrey record and is second best for any county, A. C. MacLaren's 424, also off Somerset bowlers, at Taunton in 1895, still being unapproached. Besides this great score, Abel played eight innings of more than 200, and nine times in first-class matches he carried his bat through an innings. Among Surrey batsmen he ranks with Hobbs, Hayward, W. W. Read and Harry Jupp.

Extraordinarily successful in Gentlemen and Players matches at the Oval, he scored 168 not out in 1894, 195 in 1899, 153 not out in 1900, and 247 in 1901. This 247 was the biggest score ever obtained in a Gentlemen and Players match until 1925, when Hobbs made 266 at Scarborough. For Players against Gentlemen at Lord's, his highest score was 98 in a memorable match in 1900. Playing first for England against Australia in 1888, he took part in eight Test matches in this country, his best score being 94 at Lord's in 1896.

In the winter of 1887–88 when, owing to what may have been a misunderstanding between Sydney and Melbourne, but at the time was generally regarded as rivalry between the cricket authorities, two English teams visited Australia. Abel went with G. F. Vernon's side and scored 320 runs in 11-a-side matches, average 24. He was not chosen when the two bands joined forces on the occasion when Peel and Lohmann disposed of Australia for totals of 42 and 82. Abel went to Australia again in 1891–92 when W. G. Grace captained Lord Sheffield's side, and he averaged 38 for the 11-a-side games. At Sydney, in the second of the three Test matches, he accomplished the remarkable performance of carrying his bat through the first innings for 132 but Australia won the contest in which Alex Bannerman, who batted seven and a half hours for 91, received 204 balls from Attewell and scored off only five. Abel visited South Africa with Major Wharton's team in 1888–89 and scored 1,075, average 48—more than twice the aggregate and average of any other member of the side.

A batsman of great resource and patience, he rarely if ever carried caution to an extreme and for a man of his small stature he was quite a punishing player. Once at the Oval he performed the rare feat of scoring 100 runs between 12 o'clock and lunch-time. He and Brockwell enjoyed many big partnerships together for the Surrey first wicket, and against Hampshire at the Oval in August 1897, scored 379—a record for an opening stand at that time—265 against Warwickshire at the Oval in September, 1898, 231 against Sussex at the Oval in May, 1897 and 270 (unbroken) against Kent at the Oval in 1900. Other great first-wicket stands in which he shared were 364 with D. L. A. Jephson against Derbyshire at the Oval in 1900, 246 with Tom Hayward against Sussex at Hastings in 1902, and 226 with W. G. Grace for South against North at Scarborough in 1889. The biggest partnership of all in which he participated was one of 448 with Hayward for Surrey's fourth wicket against Yorkshire at the Oval in 1899, Abel scoring 193 and Hayward 273. This is the world's record for the fourth wicket.

Abel drove hard and cut well, but his special strength came in ability to get runs on the on-side. Very few batsmen have excelled him in scoring in front of short leg with brilliant and safe forcing strokes off his legs. Like many little men, he did not keep his bat perfectly straight, but accurate judgment of length of bowling and quickness on his feet compensated for this defect. A very sure field, notably at slip, Abel also bowled slow off breaks skilfully but was not often wanted in the very powerful Surrey attack. Quiet and unassuming in manner, Abel was never spoiled by success. After one of his great days at the Oval, hundreds of his admirers would gather in front of the pavilion and chant "Bob, Bob, Bob," again and again until the "Guv'nor" bowed his acknowledgements.

ABEL, William John, a capable all-round cricketer who played for Surrey 25 years ago, died in London on March 23, 1934. Born on August 29, 1887, Abel, who was the eldest surviving son of the famous "Bobby" Abel, of Surrey, first played for Surrey in 1909. His last appearance in the county team was in 1926 and, after a few games with the Second XI, he joined Accrington, the Lancashire League Club. A batsman of the unorthodox school, Abel was a pleasing, forcing player and, even though he never gained the distinction of obtaining a century in county matches, he put together many useful scores. His best season was 1923 when he had an aggregate of 957, while in 1914—when Surrey last won the County Championship—he hit up 524 runs in 16 county games with a highest score of 87. As a bowler, Abel began as fast-medium, but lessening his pace he exploited the leg-break and the "googly." In

his most successful season as a bowler, 1919, he took 37 wickets. He was a first-rate slip fielder. After serving in the War, Abel did not enjoy good health.

ABERCROMBIE, Lieut. Cecil Halliday, R.N., born in India on April 12, 1886, lost his life in the naval action off Jutland on May 31, 1916, whilst serving in H.M.S. *Defence*. He was a batsman with a delightfully free style who came to the fore in 1913 by making a series of good scores for Hampshire. On his first appearance for the county—against Oxford University at Southampton—he made 126 and 39, and subsequently obtained 144 v. Worcestershire at Dudley (where he and H. A. H. Smith (33*) added 118 for the tenth wicket) and 165 v. Essex at Leyton. His last-mentioned score was made in the second innings, when Hampshire followed-on 317 behind, and in partnership with Brown (140*) he put on 325 for the seventh wicket. In first-class matches that year he scored 936 runs with an average of 35.92. In 1914, being away on service, he was unable to assist the county, and therefore his fame rests on what he accomplished in a single season. It should, however, be added that in 1912, whilst playing at Lord's for Royal Navy v. Army, he scored 37 and 100. He had been a member of the M.C.C. since 1911, and he played Rugby football for Scotland.

ABERDARE, The Third Baron (Clarence Napier Bruce), who died on October 4, 1957, aged 72, was one of the best all-round sportsmen of his time. His death was caused by drowning after his car fell over a precipice in Yugoslavia into three feet of water in a river bed. As the Hon. C. N. Bruce, he was in the Winchester XI of 1904 and would have gained his Blue at Oxford as a Freshman but for illness. Against Cambridge at Lord's in 1907 he scored only five runs, but the following year his 46 in the Dark Blues' first innings was second top score. A fine batsman who hit the ball hard with perfect timing, due mainly to splendid wristwork, he first appeared for Middlesex in 1908 and played his last match for them in 1929. In all first-class games he scored 4,316 runs, average 28.96. Against Lancashire at Lord's in 1919 he hit 149 in two hours 25 minutes and two seasons later again trounced the Lancashire bowling on the same ground, scoring 82 not out and helping Hendren add 50 in quarter of an hour. In 1921 he also scored 144 against Warwickshire and 127 for Gentlemen v. Players at the Oval.

He won most honours at racquets, for he

was the Winchester first string in 1903–04; won the Public Schools championship in 1904; played for Oxford v. Cambridge in 1905–08; won the Oxford University Silver Racket in 1907; won the Amateur Championship in 1922 and 1931; was 10 times Doubles Champion; was Champion of the U.S.A. in 1928 and 1930; Singles Champion of Canada in 1928 and 1930 and Doubles Champion also in 1930. At tennis, Bruce was U.S.A. Amateur Champion in 1930 and of the British Isles in 1932 and 1938. He played 18 times for Great Britain in the Bathurst Cup and six times won the Coupe de Paris. He carried off the M.C.C. Gold Prize on five occasions and nine times won the Silver Prize. He also excelled at golf, playing for Oxford against Cambridge from 1905 to 1908, was a good footballer and a capital shot.

In 1937 he was appointed chairman of the National Advisory Council in connection with the Government scheme for improving the physical fitness of the nation. For 20 years he was a member of the International Olympic Executive and he played a big part in organising the 1948 Games in London. In his later years he devoted himself closely to work for the Order of St. John of Jerusalem and the St. John Ambulance Association, and was a member of the executive committee of the National Playing Fields Association. He succeeded to the title in 1929.

ABRAHAM, Dr. Arthur, who died at Whitley Bay, on June 2, 1922, aged 69, was at one time a well-known cricketer in Ireland, playing for Leinster against the South of England, when his resemblance to his twin brother led W. G. Grace to protest against him taking a second innings. He developed into a good wicket-keeper and batsman, and played county cricket for both Durham and Northumberland. In two seasons, also, he took part in the Scarborough Festival.

ABRAHAM, Jacob, believed to have been the first professional cricketer Northampton produced, died in March, 1914, at the age of 82. From 1856 until 1868 he was coach at Exeter College, Oxford. He appeared once or twice for XXII of Northamptonshire against the England XI, but without pronounced success. He was married four times, and his widow has lost four husbands.

ABSOLON, Charles, the veteran cricketer, died at his residence, Hermitage Road, Finsbury Park, on Saturday, January 4, 1908, having suffered a stroke of paralysis just a

week before. Born on May 30, 1817, Mr. Absolon was in his 91st year. He had, of course, long ago retired from the active pursuit of cricket, but he continued playing until he had reached a great age. His interest in the game remained unabated to the end, and even as recently as last June he was present at the Middlesex and Surrey match at Lord's. In his day Mr. Absolon was the most prominent figure in local cricket in and around London. An under-hand bowler of the type of the famous William Clarke, he was in such request that he has often been known to take part in two matches in the same day, his assistance, while he was at his best, generally meaning victory for the clubs he represented. The full statistics of his career as a bowler, if they had been preserved, would form very interesting reading. At one time his doings used to be published every year in the sporting papers. He took wickets literally by the hundred, some of his records in the '70s being marvellously good. He was much more than an ordinary lob bowler, having a good variety of pace and commanding, when he needed it, a comparatively fast ball. He never aimed at a big break, being content to make the ball do just enough to beat the bat. It is impossible to say how he would have got on in first-class cricket, but the batsmen who met him in club matches had every reason to dread him, his skill in finding out their weak points being so great. A kindly and genial man, Mr. Absolon made hosts of friends in the cricket field. Probably no cricketer ever played in so many matches.

ACKROYD, Alfred, born at Birkenshaw, near Leeds, on August 29, 1858, died on October 2, 1927. *Scores and Biographies* (xiii-560) said of him, "Is a good batsman, a fast, round-armed bowler, and fields generally mid-wicket off or on." He was in the Uppingham XI in 1875 and two following years, and in 1879 made one appearance for Yorkshire—v. Middlesex at Lord's.

ADAM, General Sir Ronald Forbes, B.T., G.C.B., D.S.O., who died on December 26, 1982, aged 97, was President of M.C.C in 1946. He was the oldest living member of I Zingari, to which he was elected in 1935.

ADAMS, Donald, who died at Walton-on-Thames early in 1976 aged 95, had the distinction, curious though not unique, of obtaining his only wicket in first-class cricket by bowling W. G. Grace. This he did when, on the strength of some good bowling in the

Surrey trial match in April 1902, he played a few days later for the county against London County at the Crystal Palace, opening the bowling and going in last. This was his sole appearance in first-class cricket, but he continued to play in London club cricket until well on in the 1930s.

ADAMS, Francis, who played for New South Wales v. Victoria at Sydney in 1859, died on February 10, 1911, aged 75. He was uncle of Mr. F. A. Iredale.

ADAMS, Sir Grantley Herbert, who died in November, 1971, aged 75, was a cricket enthusiast who in his younger days played for Barbados. A barrister and founder of the Labour Party there, he was Prime Minister of Barbados from 1954 to 1958 and Prime Minister of the West Indies Federation during its brief existence from 1958 to 1962.

ADAMS, Tom, died on January 20, 1894. With the death of the veteran Tom Adams there passed away one of the last connecting links between the present generation and the famous Kent XI of which Alfred Mynn, Fuller Pilch, Felix, and Hillyer were the chief members. Born at Gravesend, on May 2, 1813, Adams made his first appearance at Lord's for the South against the North in July, 1837. He did not on that occasion distinguish himself, being bowled by Cobbett for 0 and by Redgate for a single. However, he soon took a good place among the cricketers of his day, and was, so Mr. Arthur Haygarth tells us in his *Scores and Biographies* associated with the Kent XI for upwards of 20 seasons. Without in any way bearing comparison with the best of his contemporaries, Adams seems to have been a very good man on a side, being a fine punishing hitter, a straight but plain roundarm bowler, and a capital field at point, long leg, or mid-wicket. He was on the ground staff at Lord's for five seasons, commencing in 1851. Adams died at Gravesend, where, so far as we know, he had lived practically all his life.

ADAMSON, Capt. Chas. Young (Northumberland Fusiliers), killed September, 1918. Durham School XI. Durham County XI for many years. Queensland XI. English International footballer.

ADDIS, C. F., died at Northampton on August 15, 1983, aged 81. "Cherry" Addis came of a well-known cricketing family at Finedon, near Wellingborough, and for years played with success in the Kettering League. A solid cricketer, he was an old-fashioned slow left-armer who on his two appearances for Northamptonshire, both against Dublin University, in 1924 and 1926, opened the bowling and in the first made 38 in what proved to be his only innings for the county.

ADEY, F., died at Bristol on September 13, 1946, aged 87. A friend of W. G. Grace, he was connected with Bristol Umpires Association for 40 years.

AINSCOUGH, Thomas, who was born at Lancaster House, Parbold, on February 23, 1865, died there on November 20, 1927, aged 62. Although he played only occasionally for Lancashire, he rendered much service to the county's cricket both as captain of the Second XI and as a member of the Committee. Many times he appeared in big matches for Liverpool and District teams, and in games against Yorkshire made scores of 61 not out, 50 and 61.

AINSLIE, The Ven. Archdeadon Alexander Colvin, of Wells, Somerset, who died during the second week of June, 1903, presided at the meeting at Sidmouth on August 18, 1875, held after the conclusion of the match between the Gentlemen of Somerset and the Gentlemen of Devon, at which the Somerset County C.C. was formed. He was extremely devoted to the game, but his name will not be found in any matches of note.

AINSWORTH, Jerry Lionel, born on September 11, 1877, died at Falmouth on December 30, 1923, aged 46. He was a good slow left-handed bowler, who varied his pace and pitch well. In 1894 and 1895 he was in the Marlborough XI, and in the latter year was second in batting with 30.33 and first in bowling—57 wickets for 13.36 runs each. In the first innings of Rugby, at Lord's, in 1895 he took seven wickets, all bowled down, for nine runs. He did not proceed to either University, but in 1899 he appeared on a few occasions for Lancashire. Visiting America with Mr. P. F. Warner's team in 1898, he headed the bowling by taking 75 wickets for 6.33 runs each. Among his best figures were 11 for 67 (including 5 for 13) v. Gentlemen of Philadelphia at Wissahickon, 13 for 116 against the same side at Manheim, and 13 for 52 (including 6 for 17) v. 15 of Baltimore at Baltimore. He was a well-known owner of race horses and greyhounds.

AINSWORTH, Lieut.-Cdr. Michael Lionel Yeoward, died suddenly while playing cricket on August 28, 1978, aged 56. Four seasons in the Shrewsbury XI and captain in 1941, he played with considerable success for Worcestershire from 1948 to 1950. In his first innings for the county he made 71 v. Kent, a month or two later 43 and 48 v. Yorkshire and in the return match, which followed immediately, 85 and 32, while he finished the season with 100 exactly v. Warwickshire. This brought him out top of the county averages with 34.53. The next summer, playing throughout August, he made 60 and 69 not out v. Hampshire, 72 v. Middlesex and 96 v. Kent, an innings surprisingly ended by his being bowled by Ames, but which had much to do with his side winning by an innings. One match in 1950 concluded his county career, but he continued for many years to play for the Navy and for the Free Foresters against Cambridge University. His two highest scores in first-class cricket were 106 for Free Foresters v. Cambridge in 1958 and 137 in the same match the following year. A tall man, who made full use of his height, he was a fine front-of-the-wicket batsman and a particularly good off-driver. On retiring from the Navy, he joined the staff at Ludgrove School, Wokingham, under the former Yorkshire captain, A. T. Barber.

AIREY, Col. Robert Berkeley, C.M.G., D.S.O., who died on June 23, 1933, was in the Tonbridge XI in 1894. In 1911, he made three appearances for Hampshire, his highest innings being 30 against Sussex at Portsmouth.

AITKEN, Henry Mortlock, who was born at Hadley, Middlesex, on January 8, 1831, died at Eastbourne on August 12, 1915, in his 85th year. At Eton he was in the XI for four years, 1846 to 1849, being captain the last two seasons. He was a rather fast round-armed bowler with a pretty delivery, and afterwards became a good batsman. How high an opinion was formed of his play is obvious from the fact that in 1846, when only 15 years of age, he was offered a place in the Surrey XI. That season he obtained 12 wickets in the match with Harrow, and eight against Winchester; altogether, during his four years in the Eton side he took 41 wickets in the Public School games, 32 of them v. Harrow. In 1853 he was a member of the Oxford team which beat Cambridge by an innings and 18 runs, but his share in the success was not very pronounced as he took only three wickets and contributed but 18

towards a total of 297. The same season he assisted the Gentlemen at Lord's, scoring 0 and three, in the match made famous by Sir Frederick Bathurst and Mr. Kempson, who bowled unchanged throughout and caused the Players to be beaten by 60 runs. Of the 22 who took part in the game only Caffyn, in his 88th year, survives. In 1854 Mr. Aitken went to India, where for several years he was captain of the Calcutta team. On returning to England in 1871 he joined the M.C.C., and to the end of his life took the greatest interest in the game.

AKERS-DOUGLAS, Capt. Ian Stanley, who died as the result of a shot-gun accident at his home at Frant, near Tunbridge Wells, Kent, on December 16, 1952, aged 43, was in the Eton XIs of 1927 and 1928 and played for Kent between 1932 and 1937. An attractive batsman, specially skilful in off-driving and cutting, he headed the Eton batting in 1928 with 677 runs, average 52.07, hitting 42 and 158—the fourth highest innings in the series—against Harrow at Lord's. Going to Christ Church, Oxford, he put together 128 in the Freshmen's match of 1929 and 117 in the Seniors' match of the following year; but the nearest he came to receiving a Blue was when he acted as 12th man for his University against Cambridge in 1930. For Kent, his most successful season was his first. Then, scoring 557 runs, average 37.13, he made 123 and 22 against Hampshire at Portsmouth. His other first-class century came in 1934 when he hit 100 in 65 minutes from the Somerset bowling at Taunton. In 1936 he was vice-captain of Kent under A. P. F. Chapman.

Born on November 16, 1909, Akers-Douglas was a fine racquets player. He won the Public Schools competition for Eton in 1927 with K. A. Wagg and in 1928 with I. A. de H. Lyle, and others of his achievements were: Open Championship of British Isles, 1933; Amateur Championship, 1932–33–34 (he was runner-up in 1930–31–35–38–46); Amateur Doubles Championship (with K. A. Wagg), 1932–33–35.

AKROYD, Bayly Nash, born at Streatham on April 27, 1850, died in London on November 24, 1926, aged 76. He was in the Radley XI in 1866 and two following years, when it was said of him: "Is a steady batsman, and a difficult wicket to obtain, though not possessing an elegant style. Is a capital field at point, and bowls occasionally slow round-armed." In 1872 and 1873 he appeared in six matches for Surrey.

He was brother of the late Mr. S. H. Akroyd.

AKROYD, Swainson Howden, born at Streatham on February 13, 1849, died in London on December 5, 1925, aged 76. A sound batsman with excellent style, and a good field anywhere, he was in the Radley XI in 1865 and two following years. Between 1869 and 1878 he took part in 23 matches for Surrey. He made 622 runs with an average of 15.55 for the county, his highest scores being 87 v. Sussex at Brighton in 1872 and 62 v. Oxford University at the Oval in 1869. Among other noteworthy innings played by him were 76 for Gentlemen of England v. Cambridge University at Cambridge in 1870, and 133 for Southgate v. Huntingdonshire at Southgate in 1873. His brother, Mr. B. N. Akroyd, also appeared in the Radley and Surrey XIs.

ALCOCK, Charles William, J.P., who was born at Sunderland on December 2, 1842, died at Brighton on February 26, 1907. He was educated at Harrow, but, not enjoying very good health, did not obtain a place in the XI. In later years, however, he played occasionally for the Gentlemen of Essex, the Butterflies, Harrow Wanderers, and Incogniti, and once had the curious experience of captaining France against Germany in a match at Hamburg. *Scores and Biographies* describes him as "a steady bat, a fair change fast bowler, and an excellent long stop or long field." On February 6, 1872, on the strong recommendation of Mr. V. E. Walker, he was appointed secretary to the Surrey County C.C., a position he held until the time of his death. Of his work for Surrey cricket it would be difficult to speak too highly, for he was at all times both willing and anxious to do all in his power to further its welfare. He was a most voluminous writer on the game, and in 1882 founded *Cricket*, of which he was editor from the first until the day of his death. For 29 years he edited James Lillywhite's *Cricketers' Annual*, and was the chief contributor to *Surrey Cricket: Its History and Associations*, published in 1902. For many years he arranged the fixture-list of teams visiting England, and it was due principally to him that the first meeting between England and Australia in this country—at the Oval in 1880—took place. Mr. Alcock's connection with Association Football was so prominent that it is not too much to say that he more than anyone else made the game. He captained England against Scotland in 1875, and it was under his leadership that the Wanderers won the Football Association Cup in 1872 and in four subsequent years. He was hon. secretary of the Football Association from 1867 until 1890, secretary from 1891 until 1896, and a vice-president from the last-mentioned year until his death.

ALEXANDER, Frederick Russell, who died at Harrow on May 17, 1984, aged 59, made two appearances for Middlesex as a batsman in 1951 and also "played for England" in the scratch match that year, arranged when the Lord's Test against South Africa finished early. He was better known as a footballer for Queen's Park Rangers and Charlton Athletic.

ALEXANDER, George, who was born at Fitzroy, in Victoria, on April 22, 1851, died in Melbourne on November 6, 1930. He was a hard-hitting batsman, a good change fast bowler, a smart field and a sure catch. He will perhaps be better remembered as the manager of the Australian teams which visited us under the captaincy of W. L. Murdoch in 1880 and 1884. He was further identified with English cricket when he acted in the same capacity for the Hon. Ivo Bligh's side which went out to Australia in our winter of 1882–3. He took part in two Test matches, at the Oval in 1880 and at Adelaide in December, 1884. In the great contest at the Oval in 1880—the first real Test match—he joined Murdoch on the third day when Australia, with eight men out, required 84 runs to avoid a single innings defeat. Previously in 11-a-side games in this country he had scored only 10 runs in four innings but on this all-important occasion he made 33 and shared in a stand of 52. W. H. Moule, who up to then had taken part in no 11-a-side match at all in England, afterwards helped Murdoch to add 88 and England, so far from winning in an innings, had 57 to get to win and lost half their wickets for 30. For Victoria v. New South Wales at Melbourne in 1879–80 he made 75, the highest score for either side, besides taking five wickets for 64 runs. For the Australian team of 1880 during their whole tour, in England and the Colonies, he obtained 109 wickets for exactly nine runs each. In the match with XXII of Southland, at Invercargill, he took 11 in an innings for 45. Later, at Melbourne in 1883–84, he played an innings of 50 for the Australian team against The Rest.

ALEXANDER, Lieut. Harry, (Grenadier Guards) born in January, 1879, was killed on

October 17, 1915. He was in the Uppingham XI in 1897, when he made 319 runs with an average of 35.44. In 1898 he played in the Freshmen's match at Oxford, but scored only six and four. He was a vigorous batsman and a safe field. He obtained his Blue for Rugby football and was an English International.

ALEXANDER OF TUNIS, Harold Rupert Leofric George, Field-Marshal, Earl, who died on June 16, 1969, aged 77, was in the Harrow XI of 1910, taking part in "Fowler's Match", which Eton won at Lord's by nine runs. When Harrow were set 55 to win, R. St. L. Fowler bowled his off-breaks with such telling effect that he took eight wickets for 23, the innings being all over for 45. Alexander, then the Hon. H. R. L. G. Alexander, obtained three Eton wickets for seven runs in the first innings and two for 33 in the second. In 1956, he was President of M.C.C. He earned great military distinction in both World Wars, and was later Governor-General of Canada and Minister of Defence.

ALEXANDER, Henry Robert Tayler, who died in London on February 11, 1920, aged 78, was a member of the Harrow XIs of 1860 and 1861, being captain the latter year. In his two matches against Eton he was not very successful, scoring only 21 runs with an average of seven and taking five wickets for 131 runs. He was contemporary with Messrs. R. D. and I. D. Walker, A. W. T. Daniel, C. F. Buller, and W. F. Maitland. He was a capital round-armed bowler, and was unfortunate in injuring his arm just before the Lord's match in 1861. For 55 years (1865–1920) he was a member of the M.C.C.

ALEXANDER, Capt. Robert, killed during the summer of 1943 in the Far East while on active service, aged 32, played cricket for Ireland and was a brilliant heavy-weight Rugby wing forward in the British team that visited South Africa in 1938. He played 11 times for Ireland in Rugby internationals.

ALFORD, Dr. Frederick Stephen, a well-known member of the Hampstead C.C., was found dead in a small wood near the Hampstead Golf Club Links on April 18, 1906. He was in his 56th year

ALINGTON, The Rev. Henry Giles, born at Candlesby, in Lincolnshire, on July 25, 1837, died at Spilsby, on December 2, 1928, aged 91. At the time of his death he was the oldest cricket Blue. Coached by John Lillywhite, he gained a place in the Rugby XI in 1855. He was then described as "One of the best long-stops ever turned out, as well as a first-rate and attentive bat, excelling as a leg-hitter." Among his contemporaries at the School was the famous T. W. Wills. In 1859, Alington was a member of the Oxford team which, under the captaincy of C. G. Lane, lost to Cambridge by 28 runs. Later on he played for Lincolnshire, and maintaining his interest in cricket to the last, was present at every inter-University match at Lord's until 1927. He was father of the present headmaster of Eton.

ALI, Syed Nazir, who represented India in their first Test match in this country, died in Lahore in February, 1975, at the age of 68. First attracting attention by some good bowling against the M.C.C. in India in 1926–27, he then spent several years in England, making one appearance for Sussex in 1927 and playing regularly in club cricket round London. In 1930 he represented the Club Cricket Conference against the Australians at Lord's and had the distinction of getting Bradman's wicket. When he was chosen as a member of the Indian side in England in 1932, he had thus the advantage of considerably greater experience of English conditions than most of the other players. By then he had become more of a batsman than a bowler and was third in the batting averages with 1,020 runs at an average of 31.87, his highest score being 109 against Essex. He was also third in the bowling, but took only 23 wickets. A match against the M.C.C. in India in 1934 concluded his Test career. He was an attacking batsman and a particularly fine driver, and a fast-medium right-hand bowler who could move the ball both ways. In later years he was a prominent administrator in Pakistani cricket. His elder brother, Wazir, also played for India.

ALLAN, Frank Erskine ("The Bowler of a Century,"), born at Warrnambool (Victoria) December 2, 1849. Height 6ft. 1in. Died at Melbourne February 9, 1917.

Frank Allan was the first of the long line of great Australian bowlers. There were good men before his day—Sam Cosstick and others—but he was the first to develop those special qualities that made Australian bowling—when the first team came to England in 1878—the talk of the cricket world. Apart from everything else, the medium-pace bowlers were found capable of getting an amount of work on the ball that in England had only been possible to slow bowlers. Allan, who bowled left-handed and batted right, had abundant spin, but his distinctive gift was a remarkable swerve, or as it was then called a curl in the air. Batsmen who met him for the first time were bewildered by the course of the ball. Allan was a born bowler, if ever there was one. He played in his first Inter-Colonial match at Melbourne on Boxing Day, 1867, within a month of completing his 18th year, and became famous at once, taking eight wickets—five for 59 runs and three for 43—and helping Victoria to beat New South Wales by seven wickets. Thenceforward he was for years the mainstay of the Victorian XI, and the terror of the New South Wales batsmen. Midwinter, who played a great deal with Allan when both were young, said to me once: "When I began to bowl I could scarcely hit a haystack, but Allan was a bowler from the day he first took a ball in his hand."

Allan was at the height of his fame when he came to England with the famous team of 1878 and though he had not done half so well as Spofforth during the preliminary tour in the Colonies he was one of the great hopes of the side. In England, however, he did not do himself justice. Unfortunately for him the summer of 1878 was for the most part extremely cold and wet. At home no day was too hot for him, and he found our climate very trying. The result was that he failed whereas Harry Boyle—immeasurably his inferior in Australia—made a big reputation, and shared with Spofforth the triumph of the tour. Once, however, Allan revealed his powers. In the match with Middlesex at Lord's, played in glorious weather, he took three wickets for 27 runs and six for 76. Bob Thoms, who was umpiring, told me that what he did with the ball was wonderful. It was in that match that Edward Lyttelton got his famous 113—the innings of his life. Allan never paid a second visit to England, but he continued to play in Inter-Colonial matches for some time. Soon, however, his old position as Victoria's crack bowler was taken by George Palmer. Like Allan, Palmer came out when very young and jumped at once to the top of the tree, establishing his reputation in a match against Lord Harris's team in March, 1879. In comparing Allan's deeds with those of later Australian bowlers it must be remembered that in his time Australian batting was very far below the standard it has since reached, and that the wickets did not approach their present perfection. Still he was great in his day. As a batsman he played by the light of nature in a style peculiarly his own. His comrades of 1878 used to call him "the crouching panther." He was first-class

as a shot, an angler, at bowls, and as a poker player.—S.H.P.

His best performances were:—

For Victoria v. N.S.W. he took 73 wkts. for 10.52 runs each.

9 wkts. in inns. for 46 runs, Victoria v. Sixteen of Tasmania, at Hobart 1867–8

8 wkts. in inns. for 20 runs, Victoria v. N.S.W., at Sydney 1868–9

8 wkts. in inns. for 35 runs, Victoria v. N.S.W., at Melbourne 1871–2

9 wkts. in inns. for 26 runs, Australia v. Fifteen of Vict. and N.S.W., at Sydney 1877–8

11 wkts. in inns. for 57 runs, Australia v. Eighteen of Victoria, at Melbourne 1877–8

14 wkts. in match for 70 runs, Victoria v. Sixteen of Tasmania, at Hobart 1867–8

13 wkts. in match for 60 runs, Victoria v. N.S.W., at Melbourne 1871–2

14 wkts. in inns. for 84 runs, Australia v. Fifteen of N.S.W. and Vict., at Sydney 1877–8

18 wkts. in inns. for 125 runs, Australia v. Eighteen of Victoria, at Melbourne 1877–8

Took all 10 wickets in an innings for 10 runs for Warrambool v. Coranderrk Aboriginals, at Warrambool, in January, 1884.

For the 1878 team he performed thus:—
Preliminary Colonial Tour, 68 wickets
    for 428 runs
In England, 88 wickets for 995 runs
In America, 44 wickets for 131 runs
Final Colonial Tour, 17 wickets for 278 runs
    Total wickets, 217
    Total runs, 1,832

ALLCOCK, The Rev. Arthur Edmund, brother of Mr. C. H. Allcock, was born at Ravenhurst, near Harborne, in Staffordshire, on February 16, 1851, and died at Edgbaston, Birmingham, on December 23, 1924. He was educated at King Edward's School, Birmingham, but, although quite a useful batsman and a good field at mid-on and mid-off, did not obtain his Blue whilst at Cambridge. In 1874 he appeared for the Gentlemen of Warwickshire, but most of his county cricket was played for Staffordshire. In 1880 he was appointed Headmaster of the Modern Side at Wellington College, where he remained for 13 years. From 1893 until his retirement in 1908 he was Headmaster of Highgate School.

ALLCOCK, Charles Howard, died at Aberdovey on September 30, 1947, aged 92.

Educated at King Edward's School, Birmingham, he was an excellent slow bowler, but as a contemporary of A. G. Steel and C. T. Studd there was no room for him in the Cambridge XI in the late '70s. He played for the University in some matches and for Cambridge Past and Present against Australian teams; in 1882 at Portsmouth he helped in a victory by 20 runs over W. L. Murdoch's side. Allcock took six wickets for 70 runs, and in the last innings he dismissed four men for 51, sharing the honours with A. G. Steel, five for 24. Sir C. Aubrey Smith, aged 84, and S. P. Jones, opening bat for the Australians, now 86 and living at Auckland, New Zealand, are the only survivors of that match. In that Light Blue side were A. P. Lucas, C. T. Studd, A. G. Steel and the Hon. Alfred Lyttelton, who, 10 days afterwards, all played for England in the historic match at Kennington Oval when Australia won by seven runs.

ALLCOTT, Cyril Francis Walter, who died in Auckland on November 21, 1973, aged 77, was a good left-handed all-rounder who played in six Test matches for New Zealand. He visited England in 1927 and 1931 and played against England and South Africa in his own country. He also toured Australia in 1925–26. Though he achieved little in Test cricket, he did some notable performances in minor first-class cricket during a career extending from 1921 to 1946. In 1927 he (131) and C. S. Dempster (180) scored 301 for the second wicket against Warwickshire at Edgbaston and he (102 not out) and J. E. Mills (104 not out) added 190 in an unbroken eighth wicket partnership against Civil Service at Chiswick. In 1925–26 he (116) and W. R. Patrick (143) put on 244 for the second wicket against New South Wales at Sydney. As a slow to medium-pace bowler, one of his best feats was when he returned figures of five overs, three maidens, three runs, five wickets at Weston-super-Mare in 1927. Somerset, set to get 162 to win, were all out for 67 and beaten by 94 runs. For Hawkes Bay, Auckland and Otago Allcott did much excellent work.

ALLEN, Basil Oliver, who died on May 1, 1981, aged 69, rendered great service to Gloucestershire from 1932 to 1951 both as a player and as captain. Rather slow to develop, he was not outstanding at Clifton, though he was in the XI, and it was only in his third summer at Cambridge, 1932, that he attracted attention by his consistent scoring

for the county during the vacation. Next summer, 71 for the University against Yorkshire in two hours in his second match more or less assured him of his Blue, and with 53 he was top scorer for his side at Lord's. Playing regularly for Gloucestershire in 1934, he reached his 1,000 runs for the first time, but for the next two seasons little was seen of him. In 1937 and 1938 he played regularly and captained the side; in 1938 he was picked for the Gentlemen at Lord's. In 1939 and 1946 he acted as vice-captain to Hammond, but resumed the captaincy in 1947 and continued to hold it till 1950. He played a few matches in 1951, but then dropped out.

A left-hander, he was an adaptable player. His usual place was in the middle order, but he was always prepared to open if wanted. He was a remarkably consistent batsman and primarily a solid one, but he had an ample range of strokes for use when runs were wanted quickly. His highest score, 220 against Hampshire at Bournemouth in 1947, took just under six hours. He had three notable partnerships with Hammond, 233 against Leicestershire at Leicester in 1935, 269 against Worcestershire at Cheltenham in the fourth innings in 1937, which brought about an unexpected victory, and 246 against Somerset at Bristol in 1946. Altogether for Gloucestershire he scored 13,265 runs with an average of 29.47 and made 14 centuries. Moreover he was a fine field, particularly in the close positions on the leg side, which the new lbw law, introduced during his career, made so important. He was President of the Gloucestershire County Cricket Club, 1978–80, and with his wife, Joint-Master of the Mendip.

ALLEN, Charles, who died at Cirencester in May, 1958, was in the Cranleigh XI of 1894. He had a reputation as a forcing batsman in club cricket and appeared in two County Championship games for Gloucestershire in 1910, his highest score being 35 against Northamptonshire at Gloucester.

ALLEN, R. C., who died in Australia on May 2, 1952, aged 93, played in one Test match for Australia, scoring 14 and 30 at Sydney in February, 1887, when Shaw and Shrewsbury's team won by 71 runs. He also appeared against the touring side in two matches for New South Wales and one for the Melbourne Club's Australian team. He might once have toured England, but declined the invitation. He was an uncle of G. O. Allen, the England captain.

ALLEN, Sir Richard William, who died at his London home on July 17, 1955, aged 88, was in 1899 one of the founders of Bedfordshire County C.C., of which he was Hon. Secretary until 1919 and President from 1953 till his death. At one time President of the Institution of Mechanical Engineers, he was awarded the C.B.E. in 1918 and knighted in 1942.

ALLEN, W. R., who kept wicket occasionally for Yorkshire between 1921 and 1925, died on October 14, 1950, aged 57. He lived at Normanton, near Leeds, and was best known in Yorkshire club cricket as a batsman wicket-keeper. Being a contemporary of Arthur Dolphin, his opportunities of playing with the county XI were limited.

ALLETSON, Edward B., who died on July 5, 1963, aged 79, was celebrated as the batsman who hit more runs in a single over than any other player in the history of the first-class game. That was for Nottinghamshire against Sussex at Hove in 1911, when he punished E. H. Killick for 34, comprising three sixes and four fours, in an over which included two no-balls. Alletson scored 189 out of 227 in 90 minutes. Beginning quietly, he spent an hour over 50, but, by terrific driving, doubled his score in 15 minutes and added another 89 in quarter of an hour. From seven overs he obtained 115 out of 120 and in all he hit eight sixes, 23 fours, four threes, 10 twos and 17 singles.

While he never achieved another quite such punishing performance, he played 14 hard-hit innings of 50 or more for his county during a professional career extending from 1906 to 1914 in which he scored 3,217 runs, average 18.47. His most successful season was that of 1913 when he made 634 runs, average 21.13, and hit Wilfred Rhodes, the Yorkshire and England left-arm slow bowler, for three sixes from successive deliveries in the game at Dewsbury. He was also a useful fast bowler, as he showed when, with six wickets for 43 in the match with Kent at Trent Bridge in 1913, he helped to bring about the defeat of the eventual Champions. His total of wickets was 33 at 18.90 runs each and he brought off 68 catches.

ALLISTON, Cyril George Prat, who died on July 21, 1973, aged 81, was in the Repton XI in 1909. He played in one match for Kent in 1922.

ALLOO, Arthur W., died at Nelson, New Zealand, in September, 1950, aged 58. A dependable right-hand batsman and useful off-spin bowler, he played 43 times for Otago between 1913 and 1931, scoring 1,806 runs and taking 124 wickets for the Province.

ALLSOP, Capt. The Hon. Frederick Ernest, sixth son of the first Lord Hindlip, was born at Hindlip Hall, Worcestershire, on September 21, 1857, and was found dead in bed at Droitwich on December 20, 1928, aged 71. A sound bat and useful slow bowler, he was a member of the Cheltenham College XI, in 1874 and 1875, and of the R.M.A. Woolwich, in 1876. He also played much for the Royal Artillery and a little for Worcestershire.

ALLSOP, George, born at Houghton; Hampshire, on January 4, 1864, died at Johannesburg on March 27, 1927, at the age of 63. He made no mark in the game in England, for he emigrated to South Africa in 1881, living first in Cape Colony and settling in Johannesburg (where he was destined to spend the rest of his life) in March, 1888. Summed up as "A sound, defensive bat, safe catch and good field," he played several seasons for the Transvaal, and in the Currie Cup match against Kimberley in April, 1891, scored 21 and 33. It is not, however, as an active cricketer that he will be best remembered. He was Secretary of the Wanderers C.C., of Johannesburg, for 31 years (1896 until his death), he served on Selection Committees appointed to choose South African and Transvaal XIs, and he was manager—and a very popular one—of the teams which visited England in 1904, 1907, 1912 and 1924. He was also Secretary of the South African Cricket Association.

ALLSOPP, Sergt. Thomas, born at Leicester, December 18, 1882, died at Norwich of influenza on March 7, 1919. A very useful player. He had appeared for both Leicestershire and Norfolk.

ALMACK, The Rev. William, Vicar of Ospringe, died there on March 26, 1921. He contributed some very interesting recollections of cricket to Mr. W. J. Ford's *History of the Cambridge University C.C.*

ALMOND, Frederick Clarence, was born at Great Bentley, in Essex, on October 7, 1855, and died at Enfield on May 3, 1910. He was above the average as a batsman, was a useful slow bowler, and in the field generally stood point or mid-off. His first match for Essex was in 1883, and three years later he headed the county's averages with 27.25 for eight innings commenced, his highest score being 84 not out v. Derbyshire, at Leyton. In 1883 and 1884 he was engaged by Enfield, but in the following season went as coach to Elstree School, where he remained for several seasons.

ALPEN, George R., one of the best-known cricketers of Belgium, has been killed in the War, 1916, but no particulars are obtainable. He was an Australian by birth.

ALSTON, William, of Elmdon Hall, Birmingham, died June 27, 1917, aged 74. An old Warwickshire county player. Scored 51 v. Gentlemen of Notts. in 1871, and 49 v. Worcestershire in 1874. Brother of Mr. J.F. Alston, who also played for Warwickshire.

ALTHAM, Harry Surtees, who died from a heart attack after addressing a cricket society in Sheffield on March 11, 1965, aged 76, was among the best known personalities in the world of cricket—player, legislator, Test selector, historian and coach. Educated at Repton, he was in the XI as opening batsman and occasional bowler for four years from 1905 to 1908, during which time *Wisden* described him as "more the made than the natural cricketer". His best season for the School, whom he captained in 1907 and 1908, was his last, when he scored 609 runs, including an innings of 150, for an average of 46.84. At Oxford, he gained a Blue in 1911 and 1912. In his first game against Cambridge he was bowled for 0 in the first innings, being the first "leg" of a hat-trick by J. F. Ireland, the Light Blue captain; but he hit 47 in the second innings, helping Oxford to victory by 74 runs. He took part in six matches for Surrey in 1912 and, when becoming a master and cricket coach at Winchester, a post he held for 30 years, threw in his lot with Hampshire. Between 1919 and 1923, he scored 710 runs, average 22.16, for Hampshire, his highest innings and only first-class century being a faultless 141 against Kent at Canterbury in 1921 after being one of five men dismissed without scoring in the first innings.

Altham collaborated with E. W. Swanton in a book, *The History of Cricket*, and he was also the author of the *M.C.C. Cricket Coaching Book* published in 1952. Always keen on the encouragement of young players, he became chairman of the M.C.C. Youth Cricket Association and President of the English Schools Cricket Association. When appointed chairman of the Special Committee to inquire into the future welfare of English cricket in 1949, he said: "If only we can get enough boys playing this game in England and playing it right, it is quite certain that from the mass will be thrown up in some year or another a new Compton, a new Tate, a new Jack Hobbs, and when that happens we need not worry any more about our meetings with Australia."

Altham was a member of the M.C.C. Committee from 1941 till he died, Treasurer from 1951 and President in 1959. He was chairman of the Test team Selection Committee in 1954 and, on the Committee of Hampshire for over 40 years, was President of the County Club from 1946 to the date of his death.

He served in the Army during the First World War, being awarded the D.S.O. and the M.C.

ALVA, B. Chandrahasa, who died at Bangalore on November 6, 1982, at the age of 59, was a competent all-rounder, a sound right-hand batsman and a reliable medium-paced bowler. He played for Madras and Mysore in the Ranji Trophy between 1944 and 1959, captaining both teams. He scored 1,082 runs at an average of 30.33 and took 57 wickets at 23.71 apiece. In 1950–51 he played in two unofficial "Tests" against the Commonwealth team which toured India. An engineer by profession, Alva occupied influential positions in the Mysore, later Karnataka, state service.

ALVERSTONE, The First Viscount, Richard Everard Webster, who was born on December 22, 1842, died at Winterfold, Cranleigh, Surrey, on December 15, 1915. He was educated at King's College, London, and Charterhouse, and was in the latter XI in 1861, when it was said of him: "Is a good long-field, and with practice will become a fair bat." He never made a name for himself as a cricketer, but played at least once for the Gentlemen of Devonshire. In 1878 he became a member of the M.C.C., was the Club's President in 1903, served on the Committee 1904–07 and 1909–11, and in July, 1909, succeeded Mr. William Nicholson as one of the Trustees. Since May, 1895, he had been President of the Surrey County C.C., and in 1902, in conjunction with Mr. C. W. Alcock, edited *Surrey Cricket: Its History and Associations*. At Cambridge he was a notable athlete, and in 1865 won the mile and two-mile races against Oxford. He was Attorney-General 1885–92 and 1895–1900, and Lord Chief Justice from 1900 to 1913, when he retired through ill-health. With his death the title becomes extinct.

AMAR SINGH, one of the best cricketers produced by India, died at Rajkot on May 21, 1940. A very good right-hand fast-medium bowler with easy delivery, he swung the ball; and pace from the pitch made him difficult to time. Seldom failing as a taker of wickets, he seemed to reserve his most effective work for the big occasion. Tall, of athletic build, Amar Singh, besides being such a capable bowler, batted freely and fielded brilliantly. Born in December, 1910, he passed away when in his prime.

Coming to England in 1932, he stood out as a prominent member of the All-India team, dismissing 111 batsmen at a cost of 20.78 each and scoring 641 runs with an average of nearly 23. In the one match played against England he created a good impression at Lord's. Four batsmen fell to him and in an uphill struggle he played a very good innings of 51. After the tour he became a Lancashire League player for the Colne club, who released him for a few matches in 1936 when India rose to the status of three Tests. In these engagements with England Amar Singh took 10 wickets and averaged 31 with the bat. So well did he bowl at Lord's that he dismissed four of the first five England batsmen for 13 runs and altogether sent back six batsmen for 35 in 25 overs and a ball, so enabling India to lead by 13 on the first innings. England won comfortably by nine wickets, but nothing in the match was more noteworthy than the bowling of the Indian between two batting collapses by his own side. At Old Trafford he hit up 48 and was not out, while at the Oval he gave a brilliant display with the bat, making 44 out of 51 in half an hour. These exhibitions of free hitting were in keeping with his most noteworthy performance in 1932, when, going in last but one at Liverpool, he played a grand innings of 131 not out againt Lanca-shire; his chanceless hitting was remarkable. His batting average for the 1936 tour was 33.30 in 11 innings; second in the bowling list, he took 26 wickets at 23.50 each.

Against England touring teams Amar Singh met with special success, notably when Lord Tennyson led a side in the winter of 1938. In five representative fixtures, de-scribed as "unofficial Tests," he took 36 wickets at a cost of 16 runs apiece, and was largely responsible for India gaining two victories. When Tennyson's team won the rubber match by 156 runs Amar Singh took nine wickets in 12 overs—all he sent down in the two innings.

AMIR ELAHI, who died on December 28, 1980, aged 72, could lay claim to two unusual distinctions: he was one of only 12 cricketers to have played for two different countries and one of the 20 oldest cricketers to have played in a Test match. He appeared once for India, against Australia at Sydney in 1947, and five times for Pakistan, all in India in 1952–53. In his last Test match, at Cal-cutta, he was 44. Having begun life as a medium-paced bowler, he turned to leg-breaks and googlies, and it was in this latter role that he was best known. On his first tour, to England in 1936, he met with limited success (17 wickets at 42.94). In Australia, too, in 1947–48, he found wickets hard to come by (eight at 65.87), as, indeed, he did when, after partition, he went with Pakistan to India (13 at 38.76). In the Ranji Trophy, however, he was a prolific wicket-taker (193 wickets, 24.72), mostly for Baroda, whom he helped to win the competition in 1946–47, shortly before becoming a Pakistan citizen. His finest hour with the bat (he was most at home at number 11) was when he shared a last-wicket partnership of 104 (a Test rarity) with Zulfiqar Ahmed for Pakistan against India at Madras. Amir Elahi's share was a surprising 47. To meet him and talk about his cricketing days was always a pleasure.

AMPHLETT, His Honour Judge Richard Holmden, K.C., who died on November 23, 1925, aged 78, did much to keep the Worces-tershire County C.C. in existence. From 1891 until 1908 he was Recorder of Worces-ter, and in the latter year became Judge of the County Court of Birmingham.

ANDERSON, Cecil A. (Jack), who was shot to death by assailants at his home in Kings-ton, Jamaica, on April 30, 1978, was one of the most experienced and respected of crick-et writers in the West Indies. His untimely death two days after his 68th birthday caused shock throughout the Caribbean. The inci-dent occurred shortly after he had returned home after watching the third day of the Test match between West Indies and Australia at Sabina Park. For years his cricket commen-taries written with common sense and a deep devotion to the game as a whole were widely read. He became a special contributor to the *Daily Gleaner*, Jamaica in 1933, worked his way up to a sub-editor and was then trans-ferred to the *Gleaner*'s sister newspaper, the

Evening Star where he was City Editor at the time of his retirement in 1976. His writing appeared in several newspapers and magazines and, for years, he was West Indian correspondent for *Wisden*. He visited England on several West Indies tours.

ANDERSON, George, the veteran Yorkshire cricketer, died on November 27, 1902, at Bedale, his native place. Born on January 20, 1826, he was in his 77th year, and had, of course, long ceased to take any active part in the game. Indeed, to the present generation of players he was only a name. In his day, however, he was a notable figure in the cricket field, and by general consent the best of Yorkshire batsmen. He had a fine commanding style, and no one could drive harder. Standing 6 ft. high, he had great strength and a very striking presence. For many years he was a member of the All-England XI, playing first under the captaincy of William Clarke, and then of George Parr. From his early youth he was associated with Yorkshire cricket, and he had reached his highest point as a batsman before the present County Club was formed—about 38 years ago. He captained the XI for several seasons before dropping out through increasing age. The last big innings he ever played in a first-class match was 99 not out for Yorkshire against Notts, at Trent Bridge, in 1864. He went to Australia with George Parr's team in the winter of 1863–64, but, owing, perhaps, to severe sea-sickness on the voyage out, scarcely did himself justice in the Colonies. Of Parr's unbeaten side the only survivors, now that Anderson has gone, are Mr. E. M. Grace and William Caffyn. One of the most remarkable matches in which Anderson ever took part in London was the one at the Oval, in 1862, between Surrey and England, in which Willsher was no-balled by John Lillywhite, for bowling over the shoulder—an incident that led to the alteration of Law X, in 1864. Towards England's total of 503 Anderson contributed 42, the chief scorers being Tom Hayward (117), Grundy (95), and Carpenter (94). A little earlier in the season of 1862, Anderson played an innings of 57 for the North of England against Surrey, at the Oval, and made a drive for eight, which, to this day, is talked about by old cricketers. A man of kindly disposition, Anderson was always very popular among his brother professionals. He played his first match at Lord's, for North against South, in 1851.

ANDERSON, Jack, who died in the Colombo General Hospital on September 19, 1960, aged 60, was one of Ceylon's foremost batsmen. While at St. Andrew's College, Kandy, he hit 291 against St. Thomas's which still stands as the highest innings by a schoolboy in Ceylon. His opening stand of 258 with V. Fernando against Wesley is also a record. In eight matches in 1918 he obtained over 1,000 runs, scoring four consecutive centuries in inter-school matches, and averaged 92. After leaving school, he played for the Customs and was prominent in Government Service cricket.

ANDERSON, Joe, who died on June 10, 1961, aged 83, was an opening batsman for Perthshire and Scotland. He appeared against the Australians in 1909 and 1912 and against Ireland in 1909 and 1910.

ANDERSON, John Corbet, who was born at Rothesay, Isle of Bute, January 17, 1827, died at Croydon on January 3, 1907, when within a fortnight of completing his 80th year. He will always be remembered on account of the series of fine lithographs of cricketers which he published about 50 or 60 years ago. Mr. Anderson was an antiquarian of world-wide fame, and at the time of his death was the oldest ticket-holder in the British Museum Reading Room. His best known work is *Croydon Church, Past and Present*.

ANDERSON, Thomas, died in June, 1938, aged 75. While at Merchiston he played both Rugby football and cricket for Scotland, the cricket matches being against Ireland and W. L. Murdoch's great Australian team of 1882.

ANDERSON, William Burn, died at Langham Hall, Bury St. Edmunds, on January 31, 1948, aged 76. Harrow XI 1889–91. In 1891 played once for Middlesex. Was connected in business with Christie Manson & Woods.

ANDERSON, William McDougal, who died at Christchurch, New Zealand, on December 21, 1979, played for Canterbury from 1938 to 1949, scoring 1,728 runs with an average of 36.80. An attacking left-hander, in his one Test match, New Zealand's first after the War—against Australia in 1946—he opened the batting. He was perhaps unlucky not to be picked for the 1949 tour of England. Later he was for a time a New Zealand selector. His son, Robert, has played for New Zealand in recent years.

ANDREW, W., who represented Hampshire in a few matches during the seasons of 1897 and 1898, died on March 30, 1911. As he was born March 22, 1869, he had completed his 42nd year at the time of his death. A native of Bournemouth, Mr. Andrew made his first appearance for Hampshire during the Bournemouth Week of 1897, when he scored 24 and 10 against the M.C.C. and 14 and 11 against the Philadelphians. A few weeks later, after scoring 22 and 54 not out against Sussex at Brighton, he played a fine second innings of 106 against Warwickshire at Southampton, adding in partnership with Mr. A. J. L. Hill 222 runs for the fourth wicket. Their fine batting brought about a creditable draw after the game had appeared to be hopelessly lost. At the close of the season Mr. Andrew stood second in the batting averages of his county, having scored in all first-class matches 272 runs with an average of 30.2, in addition to taking 11 wickets at a cost of 34 runs each. Far from realising the promise of his first season, Mr. Andrew proved completely unsuccessful in the seven matches in which he represented the county in 1898, scoring only 43 runs in 12 innings. Twelve wickets fell to him at a cost of 21 runs apiece. He did not play for the county again.

ANDREWS, Norman Palmer, who died suddenly at Westminster School on November 5, 1971, aged 72, was in the Westminster XI in 1916 and 1917, being captain in the second season. In 1922 and 1923 he played for Northamptonshire, of whose Committee he was a member for several years.

ANDREWS, Thomas J. E., who died in a Sydney hospital on January 28, 1970, aged 79, played in 16 Test matches for Australia between 1921 and 1926. Noted for the eminently straight bat he employed, he was a skilful and attractive batsman for New South Wales and for his country. With the 1921 Australians in England, he played in all five Test matches, scoring 94 at the Oval, and on the whole tour he made 1,358 runs, average 33.95. He did not fare so well during the visit to South Africa the following winter, nor against England in Australia in 1924; but in 1926 in England, while meeting with small success on the big occasions, he reached an aggregate of 1,234 runs, average 38.56, with 164 in three hours 10 minutes from the Middlesex bowling his highest innings. "Tommy" Andrews took part in 46 Sheffield Shield games for New South Wales, scoring 3,072 runs (highest innings 247 not out) for an average of 42.08.

ANDREWS, Walter Hermann, who was born on April 17, 1865, died at Stanger, Natal, on November 26, 1908. He played in 40 matches for Sussex between 1888 and 1892, his highest score being 67 against Gloucestershire at Gloucester in his last season, and his average for 68 completed innings 13.80. He was a good left-handed batsman and an extremely fine field, and was one of the 11 sons of Mr. Henry Wyche Andrews, who played occasionally for Kent between 1852 and 1863. From 1880 to 1883 he was in the Radley XI, and from 1899 to 1902 served with the Imperial Yeomanry in the South African War. Playing for Eastbourne against Trinity Wanderers on the Saffrons ground in August, 1899, he made 119 in his first innings and 102 in his second.

ANDREWS, William, who died on December 22, 1966, aged 80, was a founder member and Past President of the Irish Cricket Union. Known as "The Grand Old Man" of Irish Cricket, "Willie" had been a member of the Northern Ireland Cricket Union for 59 years. In his playing days he appeared for Gentlemen of Ireland and for Ulster. He was at one time High Sheriff of County Down.

ANSON, Claude Esmond, who died on March 26, 1969, aged 79, played as an amateur for Yorkshire in two matches in 1924.

ANSON, Geoffrey Frank, M.C., died on December 4, 1977, aged 55. A member of the Harrow XI in 1939, he made 76 at Lord's and helped E. Crutchley to add 117 in an hour for the fifth wicket. As a Freshman at Cambridge in 1946, he had made his Blue secure by following a number of useful innings with 55 against Yorkshire and 106 in 90 minutes against Middlesex, but at this point the claims of the Colonial Service forced him to withdraw from the side and he was unable to play in the University match. However, he played a number of times that summer for Kent with fair success, his highest score being 51 v. Middlesex.

ANSON, The Hon. Rupert, who died on December 20, 1966, aged 77, was in the Harrow XI of 1908. He was dismissed for 0, but by taking five wickets in the match for 81 runs, helped in the defeat of Eton by 10 wickets. He occasionally played for Middlesex from 1910 to 1914, his best innings being 97 against Essex at Leyton in the last season. On that occasion, after Middlesex had been sent in to bat, he and F. A. Tarrant (250 not out) hit 235 for the opening stand and did much towards victory for their county in an innings with 156 runs to spare.

ANSON, The Rev. T. A., died on October 7, 1899, at an advanced age. Mr. Anson, who played his first match at Lord's for Eton against Harrow in 1835, was one of the great amateur wicket-keepers of his day. Mr. Haygarth records that with the left hand alone in the Gentlemen v. Players match in 1843 he stumped G. Butler from one of Alfred Mynn's shooters. As a batsman his style was very ugly, but on the whole he scored well. It was, however, entirely as a wicket-keeper that he earned his fame. After leaving Eton, he went up to Cambridge and kept wicket for the XI as long as he stayed at the University.

ANSTRUTHER-DUNCAN, Major Alexander William, of the Royal Horse Artillery, died October 18, 1902. He was a very good bat and an excellent field, and his name will be found twice in the Sussex XI in 1875, and five times in 1878. On the last day of the Canterbury week of 1877 he played an innings of 120 for the Gentlemen of England against the Gentlemen of Kent. He was born at Rajahmundry, Madras, October 3, 1846.

ANTHONY, George, who appeared for Nottinghamshire occasionally between 1900 and 1905, was born at Arnold on June 25, 1876, and died of consumption at his native place on May 13, 1907. He was a very useful all-round cricketer, but was handicapped by ill-health. Against Essex at Leyton in 1901 he scored 57 out of 64 in half-an-hour, reaching 50 in 16 minutes. In the following year he made 89 against Derbyshire at Derby, and 51 not out against Lancashire at Old Trafford. He was nephew of the late Alfred Anthony, of Arnold, who kept wicket for Nottinghamshire a few times in 1875 and 1876.

APPLEBY, Arthur, the once-famous Lancashire bowler, died at his residence, Clayton le Moors, on October 24, 1902. His illness—cancer of the liver—ran a very rapid course, as even during the past summer he was seen in the cricket field. Born on July 22, 1843, Mr. Appleby first appeared in the Lancashire XI in August, 1866, playing against Surrey at Liverpool. He made his mark at once, taking six wickets in Surrey's first innings at a cost of only 30 runs, and thenceforward he held his place for about 12 years as one of the greatest amateur bowlers of his day. Left-handed, with a very easy action, he was decidedly fast without approaching the tremendous speed of another left-handed bowler of the last generation—the late Mr. W. N. Powys. When Mr. Appleby came to the front the Lancashire County Club had been in existence less than two years, and while he was at his best County Cricket made nothing like its present appeal to the Manchester public.

In Gentlemen v. Players matches Mr. Appleby appeared a dozen times, taking 59 wickets for just over 17.5 runs each. He first played for the Gentlemen at Lord's in 1867, and, bowling unchanged through both innings, took six wickets for 33 runs and two for 32. The match was one of very small scores, and the Gentlemen won it by eight wickets. Mr. Appleby played for the Gentlemen pretty regularly at Lord's down to 1878, and made a final appearance in 1887, the M.C.C. committee, owing to lack of younger bowlers, sending him a special invitation. By this time, however, he was rather too old for a match of such importance, and no success rewarded him. He was essentially a natural bowler, depending on straightness, pace, and accuracy of pitch. He said of himself that though, having strong fingers, he supposed he had some spin, he never with intention made the ball break one way or the other. He was a member of the amateur team taken to Canada in 1872 by the late Mr. R. A. Fitzgerald and divided the bowling honours of the tour with the well known lob-bowler of those days, Mr. W. M. Rose. Mr. Appleby was twice invited to go to Australia—first by Mr. W. G. Grace, in 1873, and afterwards by Lord Harris in 1878—but, owing to pressure of business, he was reluctantly compelled to decline both invitations. Modest to a degree about his own great merits as a cricketer, he was, wherever he went, one of the most popular of players. He was inclined to think that the competitive spirit in cricket had been carried a little too far in recent years and he once said that for that reason the game did not afford him so much pleasure as when he was a young man. His interest in cricket, however, remained keen to the last.

APPLETON, Charles—"A fine bat, combining both hit and defence. A fair wicket-keeper"—was born on May 15, 1844, and died at Bradley Hall, Standish, near Wigan, on February 26, 1925, aged 80. He was a member of the Rossall XI of 1861, and four years later appeared in three matches for Yorkshire. He also played for the All England XI against XXII of Leeds and District in

October, 1862. For a time he was captain of the Richmond (Surrey) C.C. An all-round athlete, he excelled at running, pole-jumping and putting the stone. By profession he was a solicitor.

APPLEYARD, Francis, who died on October 11, 1971, aged 65, was a Yorkshireman nurtured in Yorkshire Council cricket. He moved south in 1932 when he first appeared for Hertfordshire for whom he excelled as a steady fast-medium bowler of impeccable length. He played for them over 60 times in the Minor Counties Championship, taking 193 wickets. His best season was in 1938 when he took 66 wickets for Hertfordshire including 17 in one match against Lincolnshire. During the war he took nearly 150 wickets for the British Empire XI and afterwards he occasionally assisted Essex for whom his best effort was five for 14 against Glamorgan at Chelmsford in 1946.

Francis Appleyard joined the Forty Club in 1959 and played regularly for them. He became Chairman in 1968 and President in December, 1970. A member of M.C.C., he was generally seen at Lord's during Test matches and twice he followed the M.C.C. team in Australia and once in South Africa. A noted farmer, he joined the N.F.U. in 1932 and made a big contribution to the industry. During the last 10 years he developed an important agricultural interest in Western Australia. His three sons, John, Roger and Peter, are all Minor Counties cricketers.

APPLEYARD, Jack, one of the best known faces in Yorkshire cricket circles, died in hospital after a long illness on August 20, 1975, aged 77. Thousands will remember him as the man who brought Sunday cricket to a sports-starved public during the Second World War. It was in 1940 that Appleyard first organised Sunday cricket in Roundhay Park, Leeds, a natural amphitheatre. The games were extremely popular with Test stars attracting as many as 70,000 to one game. Over the year Jack Appleyard's matches raised more than £20,000 for charity and cricketers' benefits. Probably the greatest team of all turned out for the Hedley Verity memorial match in 1944 when 18 Internationals played and Wilfred Rhodes and Emmott Robinson were the umpires.

The Red Cross, Leeds Infirmary, the National Playing Fields Association, Yorkshire Association of Boys' Clubs and the Cancer Research were among organisations to benefit. Among Yorkshire cricketers whose benefits received handsome donations from match proceeds were W. Barber, W. E. Bowes, T. F. Smailes, Sir Leonard Hutton, J. H. Wardle, Bob Appleyard and F. A. Lowson. Mr Appleyard began in the clothing industry at 13, putting tickets on garments and eventually owned a business that still prospers.

APTED, Samuel, born at Reigate on July 21, 1848, died there on December 21, 1916. From 1874 until 1888 he was groundsman to the Bickley Park C.C., and from the latter year until the end of 1911 (when he resigned on account of ill-health) occupied a similar position at the Oval. A painstaking and thoroughly deserving man, he gave every satisfaction during his long association with the Surrey County C.C. The excellence of his wickets had long been proverbial. They were so good as to drive even the best bowlers to despair. In 1910 the proceeds of the Surrey v. Kent match at the Oval were given to him as a benefit, with the result that he cleared upwards of £1,400. In his young days he had been a useful all-round cricketer, and as far back as 1867 had been chosen to play for the Surrey Colts. In a match against Shooters Hill he once took as many as 17 wickets. He was a man respected by all who knew him. For many years he had been an intimate friend of the veteran Surrey cricketer, William Caffyn.

ARBER, George, who died at Malvern, on June 22, 1911, aged 71, was for 39 years professional and groundsman at Malvern College. He was born at Cambridge on June 12, 1841, and played his first match at Lord's, for Colts of the North v. Colts of the South, in May, 1869, when he obtained 11 wickets for 49 runs. In *Scores and Biographies* he was described as "a fast round-armed bowler, and an average batsman." For some years he appeared occasionally in the Worcestershire XI.

ARCHER, Alfred German, a good wicketkeeper, who played for M.C.C. in 1899, for Worcestershire, and Shropshire, died at Seaford, Sussex, on July 15, 1935, aged 63.

ARGYLL, The Ninth Duke of (John Douglas Sutherland Campbell), who was born in London on August 6, 1845, died on May 2, 1913. Whilst Marquis of Lorne and Governor-General of Canada, he watched the English team play at Toronto in 1879, and had a long conversation with Richard Daft. He was patron of many cricket clubs.

ARKELL, Henry John Denham, died at Oxford on March 12, 1982, aged 83. He played a couple of matches for Northamptonshire in 1921. He also played hockey for the county.

ARKWRIGHT, Charles Leigh, who was born on June 6, 1846, died at Brighton on December 21, 1927, aged 80. His slow bowling gained him a place in the Harrow teams of 1864 and 1865, and in the former year he was very successful against Eton, his figures being five for 34 and six for 29. As he also scored 14, he had much to do with Harrow's win by an innings and 66 runs. He did not obtain his Blue for Oxford, and the most important of his subsequent cricket was played for Herefordshire. He was a younger brother of Henry Arkwright, who bowled with success for Harrow, Cambridge and the Gentlemen.

ARKWRIGHT, Lieut.-Col. Francis Godfrey Bertram, M.C., whose death, fighting in Libya, was announced early in August, 1942, played for Eton in 1922 and 1923. His one big performance came in his second year in the XI, when he hit 175 against Winchester. He and E. W. Dawson, afterwards captain of Cambridge University and Leicestershire, put on 301 for the second wicket—a record for an Eton v. Winchester match. Dawson was run out, and the next best score for Eton was 33 in a total of 433. This performance showed Arkwright as a brilliant stylish batsman with his fine physique used in front of the wicket forcing strokes, besides the powerful drive. Curiously enough, all four inter-school big matches in which Frank Arkwright took part were drawn. He headed the Eton averages with 52.44 in 1923, and, scoring a good 54, he helped Lord's Schools beat The Rest by nine wickets. He played a little for Hampshire that season, and, going to Sandhurst, showed good form for R.M.A. Service abroad with 12th Lancers limited his opportunities for cricket in England, but abroad he continued to do well, and when home on leave sometimes turned out for the Army XI.

ARMITAGE, Charles Ingram, born at Birkby Grange, Huddersfield, April 28, 1849; died at Honley, April 24, 1917. Played for Yorkshire in three matches in 1873 and one in 1878. Played also for Huddersfield and Yorkshire Gentlemen C.C. Successful left-hand fast bowler; right-handed bat. Took all 10 wickets in an innings for Scar-borough v. Holderness, at Scarborough, July, 1875.

ARMITAGE, Capt. Everard Leathley, who died in hospital on July 16, 1969, aged 68, made eight appearances for Hampshire between 1919 and 1925. He also played for the Army.
ARMITAGE, Capt. Everard Leathley, was stated in Obituary, 1969, in the 1970 edition to have played for the Army and Hampshire. This was not the case: the Hampshire cricketer was, in fact, Brigadier Edward Leathley Armitage, who died in 1957.

ARMITAGE, Thomas, who was born at Walkley, near Sheffield, on April 25, 1848, died at Pullman, near Chicago, where he had long resided, on September 21, 1922. *Scores and Biographies* (xii–656) said of him: "Is an excellent bat and field anywhere, and a straight round-armed middle-paced bowler, combined with underhand lobs, which at times have been very successful." For Keighley v. Wakefield on June 15, 1872, he took eight wickets in the first innings and all 10 in the second. Between 1872 and 1878 he assisted Yorkshire in 53 matches, making 1,074 runs with an average of 13.59, and taking 119 wickets for 14.08 runs each. His highest score for the county was 95 v. Middlesex at Sheffield in 1876, and his chief success as a bowler was to take with lobs 13 wickets for 46 runs—six for 20 and seven for 26—against Surrey at Sheffield in June, 1876. His bowling in that match made a great impression on James Southerton who thought he had never seen lobs that were so good. In the whole season of 1876 Armitage took 45 wickets for Yorkshire at a cost of 669 runs. During 1876–77 he visited Australia as a member of James Lillywhite's team and took part in both Test matches played during the tour. He was a failure in Australia, falling far below his form at home. Of the English players in the tour of 1876–77, when an England side was for the first time beaten on even terms, James Lillywhite is now the only survivor.

ARMSTRONG, Thomas, died at his native place, Keyworth, on July 5, 1938, aged 66. When on the ground staff at Trent Bridge in the early '90s he played occasionally for Nottinghamshire, and in 1895 he appeared in the Lancashire second XI.

ARMSTRONG, Warwick Windridge, one of the most famous Australian cricketers, died on July 13, 1947, aged 68. While a great all-round player, he remains in one's memory chiefly for his unequalled triumph in leading Australia to victory in eight consecutive Tests with England. After the First World War our cricket took a long time to settle down. During this period the England touring team, led by J. W. H. T. Douglas, lost all five matches, and the following summer Armstrong commanded Australia, who won the first three Tests and drew the other two. In that superb manner Armstrong terminated a remarkable career. Of colossal build at 42, Armstrong then weighed about 22 stone and bore himself in a way likely to cause offence, but he invariably carried his desires over all opposition and sometimes with good reason.

Born on May 22, 1879, Armstrong rose to prominence in the season of 1901–02, when he did well for Victoria before playing in the Tests of which A. C. MacLaren's team won the first and lost the other four. Armstrong headed the Australian Test averages, thanks to being not out four times. His bowling then was hardly wanted, but, coming to England under Joe Darling, he took 81 wickets at 17.50 runs each, besides scoring 1,087 runs, average 26. He surpassed these efforts on his second trip to England, making 2,002 runs, average 48.82, and taking 130 wickets at 17.60 apiece, being top of both averages. These figures constitute a record, no other visitor to England having scored 2,000 runs and taken 100 wickets in a season. His 303 not out at Bath was the highest innings hit on the tour, and his 248 not out contributed largely to victory by an innings and 189 runs over the Gentlemen at Lord's.

If not quite so successful in 1909 he scored 1,480 runs, average 46.39, and claimed 126 wickets at 16.23, being second in each table and by far the most effective bowler. He was absent from the Australian team that came over for the Triangular Tournament in 1912, but when he captained the 1921 side with such marked success he ranked third in batting and top of the bowling. With 1,405 runs, average 43.90, and 106 wickets, average 14.56, he for the third time accomplished the "cricketer's double," so equalling the record for any Australian in England established by George Giffen 25 years before. In four tours in England he helped Australia win the Test Rubber three times, the exception being in 1905, when F. S. Jackson won the toss in each of the five matches.

He was fortunate to lead a very powerful combination, with J. M. Gregory and E. A. McDonald, the fast bowlers, too much for England's impoverished batting, while Macartney and Bardsley headed an exceptional array of batting talent, eight men having aggregates ranging from 2,335 to 1,032, with averages from 58 to 30. The only defeats suffered by that 1921 team were at Eastbourne and Scarborough when the serious part of the tour was over. Armstrong led Australia to victory at Nottingham, Lord's and Leeds before rain ruined the Manchester match, and England recovered something of her lost prestige at the Oval.

On that occasion Warwick Armstrong acted in an extraordinary manner by way of emphasising his opinion that all Test matches should be played to a finish irrespective of time. When a draw was certain he rested his regular bowlers, went into the long field himself, an unknown position for him, and actually picked up and read a fully extended newspaper that was blown from the crowd. Clearly he was then indifferent to what happened; but he was very much alert a few weeks before at Old Trafford, where the England captain erred over a declaration. Rain prevented play on Saturday, and so the match became an affair of two days. With England's score over 300 for four wickets the Hon. L. H. Tennyson, at 10 minutes to six, went on to the field and called the players in. Ernest Tyldesley and P. G. H. Fender, the batsmen, left the field, but Armstrong demurred and sat on the turf near the stumps where he had been bowling. After a wait the Australians and umpires went to the pavilion, and Armstrong pointed out that the law, amended in 1914, showed that a closure in the circumstances of a lost first day could not be made later than an hour and 40 minutes before the time for drawing stumps. It was amazing that no England official or player in the pavilion knew enough to prevent such a lamentable blunder; that the captain should be corrected by his Australian rival was a humiliating incident. The umpires, also at fault of course, were so muddled that when, after 20 minutes delay, play was resumed, Armstrong himself was allowed to commit an error by bowling the next over—two in succession.

Armstrong established a record by playing in 42 Test matches against England—one more than Clem Hill. In these games he scored 2,172 runs, average 35.03, and took 74 wickets at an average cost of 30.91. He made four Test centuries against England—all in Australia—and in 10 Tests with South Africa he twice reached three figures. Altogether 46 centuries stand to his name in first-class cricket. With M. A. Noble, Armstrong put on 428 at Hove against Sussex in

1902—still an Australian record for the sixth wicket. In Sheffield Shield matches Armstrong scored 4,993 runs, average 49.93, and took 177 wickets at 24.16 runs apiece. At Melbourne in November, 1920, he made two centuries for Victoria against South Australia—157 not out and 245. In November, 1912, in the corresponding match, also at Melbourne, he scored 250, his highest innings in these tournaments.

Very tall and slim when first coming to England, Armstrong was of quite different build 19 years later, and his massive frame made him a dominating personality as captain, quite apart from his ability with bat and ball. If appearing ungainly at the wicket because of bent knees, almost inevitable in the case of such a big man, Armstrong was a splendid stroke player, with the drive and cut most in evidence, and his defence was untiring. Bowling slows, usually round the wicket from a great height, he did not turn the ball a lot, but his leg theory was so pronounced that on occasions he sent down over after over wide of the leg stump without being punished, because he dropped the ball with what really was deceptive flight and usually very little break. Against a field cleverly placed for catches, batsmen refrained from taking risks. In fact, Armstrong was adept at keeping down runs in emergency. John Tyldesley, at the Oval in 1905, countered this, stepping back a yard and cutting the alleged leg-breaks where no fieldsman stood.

Like many cricketers, after retiring from active participation in the game, Armstrong wrote for the Press, and his caustic Test criticisms created ill-feeling of a kind which should not be associated with cricket.—H.P.

ARNALL, Percy Joseph, died at St. Leonards, February 8, 1918, aged 47. Took a prominent part in Thames Ditton cricket 1889–1903. Good fast bowler.

ARNALL-THOMPSON, Harry Thompson, born at Belgrave, Leicestershire, on April 7, 1864, died at Anstey Frith, near Leicester, on December 28, 1916. In 1880 and two following years he was in the Rugby XI, being captain in 1882, and in his matches v. Marlborough took 22 wickets for 9.63 runs each and made 36 runs with an average of 12.00. Originally a fast bowler, it was on the advice of Mr. C.F.H. Leslie (the Rugby captain of 1880) that he took to slows, a style with which all his subsequent successes were obtained. He was left-handed with a high delivery, a useful batsman and a good field at slip or mid-off. During his last year at Rugby he bowled admirably, taking 63 wickets for exactly 12 runs apiece. In his two last matches for the School he took seven wickets in an innings for 67 runs v. Marlborough and eight in an innings for 55 v. M.C.C. and Ground, both games being played at Lord's. At Oxford he commenced well by taking seven wickets for 47 runs in the Freshmen's match of 1883, but it was not until 1886 (when he had an analysis of seven for 82 v. Lancashire at Manchester) that he obtained his Blue. On his only appearance against Cambridge he scored six and four and took four wickets for 52 runs. From 1883 until 1890 he assisted Leicestershire, and in 1888 and 1889 captained the side. Against Yorkshire at Leicester in 1883 he took 10 wickets for 112 runs and performed the hat-trick; v. Warwickshire a year later he obtained seven wickets for 19; and in 1888—when, under his leadership, the side beat both the Australians and Surrey—he had analyses of 10 for 52 v. Essex at Leyton and nine for 65 v. the Colonials. In a minor match in 1884 he took all 10 wickets in an innings, obtaining five with consecutive balls and six with seven. He had been a member of the M.C.C. since 1886. Whilst playing Shacklock's bowling in the Leicestershire v. M.C.C. and Ground match at Lord's in 1889, he had a painful and curious experience. The ball flew off the edge of his bat on to his eyebrow and rebounded to the bowler. Arnall-Thompson was momentarily stunned, and as the blood flowed freely suggested he should retire and finish his innings later. It was then gently broken to him that he was out, caught-and-bowled.

ARNEIL, John, of Auckland, New Zealand, died on August 11, 1938, aged 76. A sound, steady batsman, change bowler and capable fieldsman, he played for Auckland against early touring teams from England and Australia and at one time was captain of Auckland. A good wing forward, he also captained his Province and was president of the Auckland Rugby Union.

ARNOLD, 2nd Lieut. Alban Charles Phidias (Royal Fusiliers), killed on July 7, 1916, aged 23, was a most promising cricketer, both as batsman and wicket-keeper. After being in the XI at Twyford School, near Winchester, he proceeded to Malvern and played for the College in 1909 and 1910: in the former season he was last in the averages with 11.25, but in the latter was first with 44.33. At Cambridge he took part in the Freshmen's match in 1912 and in the Seniors' in the following year, but did not receive his Blue until 1914. Against Oxford he scored only 22 and 0, which was somewhat disappointing as he had just previously made 89 on the same ground against M.C.C. For Hampshire he played several good innings that season, among them being 54 v. Kent and 69 v. Lancashire, both at Bournemouth, and 76 v. Somerset and 51 v. Warwickshire, both at Southampton. He would probably have developed into a cricketer of very high class.

ARNOLD, Edward G., an all-round cricketer of sterling merit, died on October 25, 1942, aged 65, after a long illness from which he made periodic recoveries without regaining full health. He helped to raise Worcestershire to first-class county rank in 1899 and reached his prime in 1902, the first of four consecutive seasons in which he performed the double feat of scoring 1,000 runs and taking 100 wickets. His best year was 1903, when he made 1,157 runs and took 143 wickets. He played in eight Test matches against Australia, twice helping England to win a rubber. In the winter of 1903–04 he was in the team captained by P. F. Warner which recovered "The Ashes" after the ascendancy of Australia since 1896 when Harry Trott's team were beaten in England. Arnold in that victorious tour did better work with the ball than his figures suggest: only Rhodes, by far the most effective bowler in the side, enjoyed greater success, both in the Tests and all first-class matches. The attack was very strong with Hirst, Braund, B. J. T. Bosanquet also in form. Other bowlers new to Australia besides Arnold were Fielder and A. E. Relf, who both disappointed in 11-a-side matches; so all the more credit belonged to Arnold.

Taking four wickets for eight runs, he shared with Rhodes, five wickets for six runs, in the dismissal of Victoria for 15—the smallest score on record in first-class Australian cricket. This happened at Melbourne in February, three weeks before the fourth Test which decided the rubber. Arnold failed utterly with the bat, but avenging his first "duck", he took four wickets for 28 and, having "bagged a brace," he disposed of Trumper and Duff, Australia's opening pair—disasters from which recovery was impossible, Bosanquet and Hirst claiming the remainder of the side. Altogether in those Tests Arnold took 18 wickets at 26.38 runs apiece; Rhodes 31 at 15.74 each; Bosanquet 16 at 25.18. Perhaps because of his prolonged bowling efforts, Arnold's batting proved poor, his highest innings in the four

Tests in which he took part being 27, and in the tour 34.

In 1905, when England under F. S. Jackson won the rubber, Arnold appeared in four of the Test matches without doing himself justice. Still, the honour belonged to him of three times participating in rubbers which proved triumphant for England. In 1907, Arnold took part in the first Test match at Lord's against South Africa and claimed five wickets for 37 in the first innings, but he failed when the visitors followed-on, and was ineffective at Leeds, where his Test experience ended with England victorious in the only match of three brought to a definite finish. For some time he was a regular choice for Players and other representative sides. From 1899 to 1913 he stood out prominently for Worcestershire, making 18 centuries, the highest 200 not out against Warwickshire at Birmingham in 1909. In that match on the Edgbaston ground he and W. B. Burns added 393—a fifth wicket record in English cricket which still stands. He bowled with deadly results on many occasions. Altogether in first-class cricket Arnold scored 15,583 runs, average 29.91, and took 1,057 wickets at an average cost of 23.28.

Of good height and build, though lean, Arnold bowled right-hand above medium pace, with varied speed and spin. He brought the ball down from an exceptional height, producing lift which made him specially difficult on a lively pitch, and he could take full use of drying turf. Strong in defence, he batted with plenty of power when set, making strokes in all directions. Usually fielding in the slips, he held 163 catches.

ARNOLD, John, died on April 3, 1984, aged 76. He is apt to be thought of as something of a failure, a man who was picked for England in his second full season of first-class cricket and was never again seriously considered for a representative match. It would be fairer to remember him as a good county cricketer, for 20 years one of the mainstays of the Hampshire batting, who had the ill luck to be chosen by the selectors, faced with a difficult situation, for a task for which neither then nor later was he really suited.

An Oxford man by birth, he had a most successful season for his native county in 1929, scoring 650 runs with an average of 52.75 and securing them the Minor County Championship with a splendid innings of 62 not out in the vital challenge match against Buckinghamshire. In that season, too, he had played for Hampshire, though not yet qualified, against the South Africans, and in 1930 he became a regular member of their side, making 1,186 runs with an average of 32.05. At this time, for some years England's opening pair, Hobbs and Sutcliffe, had picked themselves automatically, but Hobbs had retired from Test cricket after 1930 and at the end of June 1931, when the side was picked to play New Zealand at Lord's, Sutcliffe was suffering from a strain. Had the opponents been Australia, Holmes or Sandham, both veterans, would probably have been called up, or the captain, Jardine, would have been put to open. But in those days Test matches against other countries were used partly to try out young players and so Arnold (who had, in fact, never played at Lord's) and Bakewell were chosen. They were not a success, and, though Bakewell was retained for the next Test and later played several times more, Arnold, who after 0 in the first innings had scored 34 in the second, was dropped and never received another chance.

Nor does his record in County Cricket suggest that he suffered any injustice, good player though he was. In 1932 he played the highest innings of his career, 227 against Glamorgan at Cardiff, and in 1934 had the splendid record of 2,136 runs with an average of 46.43, including an innings of 109 not out against the Australians, which almost certainly saved his side from defeat. After several more good seasons he had a terrible setback in 1938, when his average dropped to 20.70, and at the end of the summer he was not re-engaged. Fortunately the decision was reconsidered and how short-sighted it had been was shown when he once more headed the averages in 1939. He returned in 1946 with his powers unabated and was still going strong when, late in July, 1950, he was stricken by an illness which terminated his active career. When this occurred, he had made 1,119 runs at an average of 41.44, which again brought him out top.

By nature an attacking bat, he was especially severe on off-spinners and in-swingers, but was also a fine off-driver and hooker. For a time in the middle of his career he adopted a more defensive approach, but later he returned to his natural aggression. He batted, according to the needs of his side, as an opener or lower down the order; probably the latter position suited him better. As befitted a soccer international, he was very fast between the wickets and was also a joy to watch in the outfield. from 1961 to 1974 he was a first-class umpire. In all first-class cricket he scord 21,831 runs with an average of 32.82 and made 37 hundreds.

ARNOLD, Weller, who died in Hobart on October 28, 1957, aged 75, was Vice-President of the Tasmanian Cricket Association. He was one of the most prominent sportsmen in Tasmania during this century, his interests including cricket, Australian Rules football and horse racing. A useful right-handed batsman, he played for Tasmania againt Victoria in 1915, scoring five and 30, and in 1909–10 season headed the Tasmanian averages with 75.33, his aggregate being 453. In 1954 he received the O.B.E. for services to sport.

ARNOTT, Trevor, died at Wilton, near Ross-on-Wye, on February 2, 1975, aged 72. From 1921 to 1930 he did valuable service for Glamorgan and in 1928 captained the side. Later he played for Monmouthshire. He was a useful medium-pace swinger who generally opened the bowling, and a batsman who could hit the ball hard in front of the wicket. The highest of his three centuries was 153 against Essex at Swansea in 1928. In 1928 he went with the Hon. L. H. Tennyson's side to Jamaica.

ARROWSMITH, Isaac Frederick, who died in Bristol on November 9, 1955, shortly before his 95th birthday, was a life-long cricket lover who at one time played as an all-rounder with Dr. W. G. Grace. For many years a Gloucestershire member, he was a founder-member of the Bohemian C.C.

ARROWSMITH, James Williams, head of the well-known firm of publishers, died at Bristol on January 19, 1913. He was born at Worcester on November 6, 1839, and was always keenly interested in cricket and other sports. For many years he was on the Committee of the County Club, and he was Chairman of the Gloucestershire County Ground Company. Among the many cricket books published by his firm may be mentioned *Cricket,* by W. G. Grace; *Kings of Cricket,* by Richard Daft; *Gentlemen v. Players,* by F. S. Ashley-Cooper; *Cricket Stories,* by C. W. Alcock; and *At the Sign of Wicket,* by E. B. V. Christian. Mr. Arrowsmith played a great part in the public life of Bristol, and his death caused a gap which will be very difficult to fill.

ARUNDELL, The Rev. William Henry, who died at Bournemouth on November 29, 1912, was born at Cheriton Fitzpaine, in

Devon on May 4, 1842, and was educated at Cheltenham, where he was in the XI in 1861. In the match with Marlborough, which Cheltenham won by seven wickets, he scored 21. He was then described as "A promising bowler and fair bat." He will always be best remembered for an innings of 201 not out, made in about six hours without a chance, for Gentlemen of Cheshire v. Gentlemen of Shropshire, at Chelford, in June, 1873. His county cricket was played for Devon and Cheshire, for the latter shire whilst Curate of Chelford in 1872 and 1873. He was father of the Rev. W. R. H. Arundell and Capt. Arundell, was an enthusiastic angler, an excellent shot, and an ardent follower to hounds.

ASH, Edwin H., who acted as Manager to Mr. W. W. Read's team in South Africa in 1891–92, died at Richmond on October 25, 1911. He was born in 1844. He was closely associated with Rugby football and was the first secretary of the Rugby Union.

ASHBOLT, Alfred, the sole selector of the New Zealand team which toured Australia in 1899, died after a short illness at Wellington—his native place—on March 6, 1911, aged 63. In his early days he was an enthusiastic club cricketer and in more recent times a highly esteemed umpire. He was a life member of the Wellington Cricket Association and the father of Messrs. Frank and Leslie Ashbolt, both of whom have played for Wellington.

ASHBOLT, F., prominent in New Zealand cricket, who died at Wellington, on July 16, 1940, aged 64, was a clever right-hand slow bowler, capable of keeping a length with his leg-breaks, and a sure catch in the slips. He took many wickets for Wellington, eight for 58 against Hawkes Bay and seven for 52 against Canterbury being among his best performances. Also he did well against visiting teams on tour, dismissing six New South Wales batsmen for 52 in an innings in 1894, while in 1896, in a match against an Australian XI, captained by G. H. S. Trott, he disposed of Frank Iredale, Joe Darling and C. J. Eady. He played for North Island, and in 1898 was a member of the first New Zealand team which went to Australia.

ASHBY, David Alexander, who died at Christchurch, New Zealand, on June 2, 1934, was born at Beddington, Surrey, in 1852 and graduated to County Cricket with Croydon Amateurs. He played for Surrey for several seasons and, when only 19, turned out for All England Colts against M.C.C. He sailed for New Zealand in 1875 and for 15 years represented Canterbury. In 1878 he took five wickets for two runs and so helped to dismiss Auckland for 13, eight of which were byes—the lowest score recorded in an Inter-Provincial match. He played against various English touring teams and took part in the match of 1878 when Murdoch's Australian XI were beaten by Canterbury. In addition, he visited Australia with a Canterbury side which won three matches out of six. Ashby, besides being a dashing batsman, bowled fast round arm.

ASHCROFT, Dr. E. Maynard, who died suddenly at his home at Upton, near Chester, on February 26, 1955, aged 79, played for Derbyshire from 1897 to 1906. Shared the captaincy with A. E. Lawton in 1904 and 1905. Of his eight centuries, the highest was 162 against Leicestershire at Leicester in 1902 when he headed the Derbyshire batting figures with 843 runs, average 46.83. A free-scoring batsman, he drove and cut specially well.

ASHDOWN, William Henry, died at his home at Rugby on September 15, 1979, aged 80. For Kent between 1920 and 1937 he scored 22,218 runs with an average of 30.35 and took 597 wickets at 32.25. He made 40 centuries and twice scored over 300, being one of the very few who have accomplished this rare feat more than once in county cricket. His 332 against Essex at Brentwood, which took only six and a quarter hours, is still a Kent record; a year later he made 305 not out against Derbyshire at Dover. In 1931 he scored a hundred in each innings against Middlesex at Lord's. For years he opened the batting, first with Hardinge, and later with Fagg or Woolley. It is the beauty of his off-side strokes, his square drive and his cut that spectators will remember chiefly, though he was, too, an extremely good leg-hitter. He bowled just above medium with the easy action of a natural games player. In his best season, 1923, he took 66 wickets at 22.22. In 1914, at the age of 15, he had played for G. J. V. Weigall's XI against Oxford University and in 1947, after 10 years' absence from first-class cricket, he appeared in a festival match at Harrogate in which he scored 42 and 40 and took five for 73. He was thus the only man to take part in first-class cricket both before the Great War and after the Second. From 1938 to 1947 Ashdown was coach at Rugby, and then, after three years as a first-class umpire, was first coach and later scorer to Leicestershire. He had a quiet sense of humour, and when Kent were making 219 in 71 minutes to beat Gloucestershire at Dover in 1937, he remarked dryly to his partner—"I suppose you realise you are wasting a lot of time hitting all these sixes!". His own contribution to this unique feat was 62 not out.

J. C. Marshall, the Oxford Blue of 1953, writes:

"I was lucky enough to be coached by Bill Ashdown as a boy at Rugby—in fact I was his last captain. I shall always remember him as the best of coaches and the kindest of men. Looking back on his time at Rugby I always feel that he got his relationship with the boys absolutely right and was wonderfully understanding and helpful both in the nets and outside them. In addition to all that he did for Rugby cricket as coach, I think it is also extremely important to remember that he was head groundsman as well at a particularly difficult time and kept our grounds in wonderful condition during the War."

ASHLEY, Charles Hitchen, part proprietor of *The Sportsman,* died at Roehampton on April 26, 1914, in his 81st year. Between 40 and 50 years ago he played occasionally for the Sporting Press.

ASHLEY, Lieut.-Col. Richard, who died at Bognor Regis on August 9, 1974, played in two matches for Somerset in 1932, away to Leicestershire and Essex. In the former match he sent down his only two overs, both maidens, for the county, and by bowling W. H. Marlow, his first-class analysis stands at one wicket for no runs.

ASHLEY-COOPER, Frederick Samuel, unrivalled as an authority on cricket history, died on January 31, 1932, at his home at Milford, Surrey. He was born in London on March 2, 1877, and so had not quite completed his 55th year.

From his earliest days he was troubled with poor health and consequently did not follow any profession and yet his unvarying researches and his literary output involved an amount of labour which might well have deterred the most robust of men. His enthusiasm, however, carried him through from these early days when, helped by his friend H. T. Waghorn, an officer of the Reading Room at the British Museum, he spent several years going through, in his search for cricket matter, the newspapers and magazines printed up to to the year of 1830.

In this devotion to the history of the game, he was in the succession of the Rev. James Pycroft who, born in 1813, was author of *The Cricket Field* and of Mr. Arthur Haygarth (born in 1825) the compiler of that wonderful work *Scores and Biographies.*

Such was Ashley-Cooper's amazing energy that altogether he brought out 103 books and pamphlets on the game dealing with cricket in England, Australia, South Africa, New Zealand, India and other places, besides a very large amount of matter including 40,000 biographical and obituary notices, every production of his pen, moreover, being characterised by phenomenal accuracy to secure which he spared neither time nor trouble.

Among his works were two brought out in conjunction with Lord Harris, *Lord's and the M.C.C.* (dedicated to King George) and *Kent Cricket Matches 1719–1880* and one with P. F. Warner *Oxford and Cambridge at the Wicket.* Other products of his pen were *Cricket Highways and Byways, Curiosities of First-Class Cricket, Eton and Harrow at the Wicket, Gentlemen v. Players, E. M. Grace, Cricketer, W. G. Grace, Cricketer, Hambledon Cricket Chronicle,* a new edition of Pycroft's *Cricket Field,* and *Scores and Biographies, XV,* this last being a monumental piece of biography based in the first place upon notes left by Mr. Arthur Haygarth and by innumerable additions brought up to date.

Mr. Ashley-Cooper edited the newspaper, *Cricket* for five years and in 1920 he held the Secretaryship of the Nottinghamshire County C.C.

He was responsible for more than 30 years for "Births and Deaths" and "Cricket Records" in *Wisden,* which latter section of the *Almanack* had grown from two pages in 1887 to 61 pages in last year's edition.

In the course of his career he had gathered a unique collection of cricket books and pictures. For this fortunately he found in Sir Julien Cahn a purchaser a month or two before he died so the splendid library was not dispersed.

Early in 1931, Ashley-Cooper took a trip to the West Indies but derived no benefit from the voyage. Indeed, his health became worse and his sight failed so badly that in the autumn he had to abandon all work. A most modest and kindly man, he was always ready to give from his wonderful store of cricket history to anyone who asked his help and grudged no time spent in satisfying such requests.

To those associated in the production of *Wisden's Almanack* the passing of Ashley-Cooper is naturally felt as a personal loss.

Year by year he had spared no endeavour to make the list of "Births and Deaths" as complete as possible, conducting an enormous correspondence on the subject and searching the columns of practically every paper he could obtain to bring his information up to date and to eliminate any error. Equally zealous was he in his pursuit of any happening in the game of sufficient importance to be included in "Cricket Records". All this labour he performed with a measure of enthusiasm which never flagged even when the shadows were gathering and he knew his days were numbered. Such devotion as his to the game of cricket could not have been surpassed. It should be recognised by the powers that be in the making of arrangements such as will ensure the enlightened continuance of his life's work.

ASHTON, Acting Squadron Leader Claude Thesiger, the triple Cambridge Blue and England Association football international, was killed on active service on October 31, 1942, in a disaster which also caused the death of Squadron Leader R. de W. K. Winlaw, another Old Wykehamist and double Light Blue.

The youngest of three sons of Mr. H. S. Ashton, President of the Essex County Club from 1936, who in turn captained Cambridge cricket XIs and were together in the 1921 team, Claude became the best known. By a strange change of fortune Gilbert and Hubert each led his side to victory over Oxford by an innings, but Claude experienced extreme ill-luck in 1923. Oxford batted all the first day, and during the night a severe thunderstorm with a deluge of rain completely altered the conditions at Lord's, with the result that Cambridge were dismissed twice and beaten on the Tuesday by an innings and 227 runs, the most overwhelming defeat in the whole series of University matches and the three most decisive results to occur consecutively. In this exasperating engagement Claude Ashton, with 15, alone got double figures in the first innings of 59, while in the follow-on his 21 came next best to G. O. Allen's 28. G. T. S. Stevens and R. H. B. Bettington, the Australian Oxford captain, in turn found the drying turf exactly suited to their spin bowling. So, after two great victories under his brothers, Claude Ashton finished his University career in dismal circumstances. This was all the more regrettable because for Cambridge that season he scored 678 runs, average 28.25, and took 30 wickets. In 1921 he made 557 runs, average 46.41, with 98 against M.C.C.

at Lord's and 101 not out off the Surrey bowlers at the Oval as his best scores. His 48 against Oxford showed his form on the big occasion; next year, when rain interfered with many matches, his aggregate fell to 285, average 20.25, and he did not bat against Oxford, his brother Hubert, with his own score 90, declaring at 403 for four wickets, though less consideration for his side's prospect of victory would have allowed him the opportunity to make a second century in successive matches and so establish a record which fell to H. J. Enthoven in 1924 and 1925, only to be surpassed by A. T. Ratcliffe seven years later.

At Winchester, Claude Ashton was captain of cricket, football, racquets and fives. His best score against Harrow was 92 in 1918 and against Eton 49 in 1920. Business prevented him from giving much time to County Cricket but he played some superb innings for Essex, notably in 1934. In an astonishing match at Brentwood with Kent, who scored 803 for four wickets—Ashdown putting together the Kent record of 332—Claude Ashton, not out 71, showed that he retained his batting form. What a return to the Essex team after five years absence from County Cricket—fielding out 803 runs—but two of the wickets fell to him at a cost of 185 runs. Following immediately on this he made 118 against Surrey at Brentwood, helping O'Connor put on 287 for the fifth wicket, an Essex record, in a total of 570, which brought victory by an innings and 192. The stand occupied only two hours 20 minutes, and the fourth hundred of the innings came in 38 minutes. In those first two County Championship matches at Brentwood 2,362 runs were scored and the results were identical, Essex winning by the same margin by which they lost to Kent. In six games for Essex Claude Ashton scored 416 runs that season and headed the averages with 59.42. Altogether in first-class cricket from 1921 to 1938 he was credited with an aggregate of about 5,000 runs at an average of 25, took 139 wickets with his medium-pace bowling, and held 117 catches—he always fielded brilliantly.

Claude Ashton gained perhaps higher fame at Association football than at cricket. He could not lead his side against Oxford when captain at Cambridge in his third year in the XI, but was a grand player, and for Corinthians in Cup ties he occupied every position in the forward and half-back lines. He also appeared at full-back and kept goal for the Casuals. A prominent figure in many matches he went through some terrific Cup-tie struggles against the best professional teams, and he earned international honours as centre-forward in October, 1925, against Ireland in Belfast, where he captained England. He played in 13 amateur internationals.

For Cambridge he twice played hockey against Oxford. The three brothers occupied the inside-forward positions for Old Wykehamists in Arthur Dunn Cup ties. Born on February 19, 1901, Claude Ashton died at the age of 41, leaving a widow and three children.

ASHTON, Gilbert, M.C., who died at Abberley, Worcestershire, on February 6, 1981, was the eldest and also the last survivor of three brothers who played together for Cambridge and captained the University in three successive years, a record they share with the Studds. All three were soccer Blues (Gilbert captained Cambridge and the youngest, Claude, was a full international) and both Hubert and Claude were hockey Blues as well. A still older brother, Percy, was good enough to play for Essex after losing an eye in the Great War. Can any other family equal this record? Gilbert was in the Winchester XI in 1914 and 1915, when he was captain, and then went into the Royal Field Artillery, where he won the M.C. and was later wounded. No-one in after years watching from the boundary would have realised that he had lost his left thumb: neither in his batting nor his fielding could one detect any trace of this handicap. He got his Blue as a freshman in 1919, retained it in 1920 and was captain in 1921. This 1921 side is often spoken of as the best University side of this century, though it could be argued that the 1920 side was as strong, but in neither was Gilbert's right to a place in any doubt. He bent low over his bat in his stance, but was a fine, aggressive stroke-player and a particularly good cutter and hooker. He was also a beautiful cover-point.

Almost as soon as he went down he had, in a crisis, to take over the Headmastership of Abberley Hall, which he retained for 40 years and which was under him one of the most sought-after preparatory schools in England. For some years he used to play when possible for Worcestershire in the holidays and did enough to show what a difference he would have made could he have played regularly: his last appearance was in 1936. In 1922 he made 125 and 84 against Northamptonshire at Worcester. But probably his most notable performance was at Eastbourne in August, 1921, when A. C.

MacLaren's XI (of which he was the last survivor) inflicted their first defeat on Armstrong's great Australian side. Dismissed for 43 and going in again 131 down, MacLaren's side at once began to lose wickets and it was Gilbert who, in a brilliant little innings of 36, showed for the first time in the match that the Australian bowlers were not invincible. He paved the way for the splendid partnership of 154 between his brother Hubert and that great South African cricketer, Aubrey Faulkner, which made possible a sensational victory by 28 runs.

In addition to his work as a schoolmaster, he was a magistrate and took a considerable part in public life in Worcestershire, but he never lost his interest in cricket and in particular served for years on the committee of the County C.C., being its President from 1967 to 1969.

ASHTON, Sir Hubert, M.C., who died on June 17, 1979, aged 81, was a batsman who must have taken a high place had he been able to continue in first-class cricket. After two years in the Winchester XI, where he was captain in 1916 and had an outstanding record each year, he served in France from April, 1917, and was not demobilised until August, 1919. Going up to Cambridge he made 32 and 62 against Essex next summer in the first match, but such was the competition for places that he was not given another chance until the last home match, when he scored 236 not out against the Free Foresters in four hours; at that time a record both for Cambridge and Fenner's. This made his place secure and he retained it for three seasons, scoring 2,258 runs with an average of 64.51 and each year heading the averages and playing for the Gentlemen at Lord's. In 1921 he made 118 against Oxford, and in 1922, when he was captain, was 90 not out when he declared the innings closed, thus depriving himself of the chance of scoring a century in successive 'Varsity matches. Despite all he did for Cambridge, he is perhaps best remembered for the part he played in the famous victory of MacLaren's XI over the Australians at Eastbourne in 1921. When he and G. A. Faulkner came together in the second innings four wickets down, and 71 runs were still needed to save an innings defeat; together they added 154, and the Australians were beaten. Coming down from Cambridge in 1922 he joined the Burmah Oil Company. He was not seen again in English cricket until 1927, and rarely thereafter captured his old form. He played soccer for Cambridge for three years and hockey one.

He was one of three brothers who captained Cambridge in consecutive years; a fourth, Percy, was good enough to make runs for Essex despite the loss of an eye in the Great War. Sir Hubert was M.P. for Chelmsford from 1950 to 1964, President of M.C.C. in 1960, Chairman of Essex from 1941 to 1955, and President from 1955 to 1970. He was knighted in 1959.

ASHTON, Hubert Shorrock, father of the three Cambridge captains, Hubert, Gilbert and the late Claude T. Ashton, died on June 10, 1943, in his 82nd year. A strong supporter of cricket, he was president of the Essex County Club from 1936 until his death. Keenly interested in the welfare of the working youth of London, Mr. Ashton two years before the War secured the lease of a 50-acre area at Woodford, Essex, and was mainly responsible for having it turned into a modern sports field, with a play-ground for the younger children. The Duke and Duchess of Gloucester formally opened the ground, which is called the Ashton Playing Fields, and planted trees to commemorate the occasion. Mr. Winston Churchill and the late Mr. Ramsay MacDonald attended the ceremony.

ASHTON, Captain Percy, M.C., one of the famous brothers, died on September 18, 1934, at Rockhaven, Bigbury-on-Sea. Born on February 27, 1895, he was educated at Winchester but failed to get a place in the XI at cricket, although he played in the Association football team of 1913. He appeared once for Essex.

ASQUITH, Frederick, born at Leeds on February 5, 1870, died at Hull on January 11, 1916. For many years he played for the Hull C.C., keeping wicket well and making good scores. In 1903 he appeared for Yorkshire v. Gloucestershire at Sheffield and made two catches.

ASTILL, William Ewart, for many years one of the best all-round players in England, died on February 10, 1948, in a Leicester hospital after a long illness, aged 57. Of medium height and slight build he became a very clever slow to medium paced right-arm bowler, with spin either way, and batted in sound, orthodox style. Born at Ratby on March 1, 1890, he inherited love for cricket from his father and was engaged by the county when 15. Next season he began his first-class career, which did not end until 1939, when he rejoined the Army as an

officer after playing a few times in the previous two seasons.

Astill gained special distinction by scoring a thousand runs and taking a hundred wickets in a season nine times, his only superiors in this respect being Wilfred Rhodes, George Hirst and V. W. C. Jupp. His best period came after gaining an Army commission in the First World War. Previous to this his form varied, but from 1920, when his aggregate runs reached 708 and his wickets numbered 97, he maintained steady excellence both with bat and ball; his first "Double" came in 1921 and the last in 1930, the only year in this decade when he failed to achieve this being 1927, when he headed Leicestershire batting with 1,311 runs, average nearly 40, and took 63 wickets. For a man of moderate strength he got through an enormous amount of work season after season, with George Geary his most effective bowling partner.

Astill twice went to West Indies and once each to South Africa and India with M.C.C. teams, his only rest from competitive cricket during seven years coming in the winter of 1928. He played in five Test matches in South Africa and four in West Indies. Altogether in first-class cricket he scored 22,648 runs, average 22.78, took 2,428 wickets at 22.64 runs apiece and made 402 catches, as given in Sir Home Gordon's *Form at a Glance.*

A delightful man, Astill was equally popular on and off the field, making a name as a coach by the happy way in which he instructed and corrected faults, both with Leicestershire in 1938, when he gave up regular County Cricket, and at Tonbridge School, where he was appointed coach in 1946. An extremely good amateur billiard player, he was once champion of the British Army of the Rhine.

ASTOR of Hever, Colonel Lord (John Jacob Astor), First Baron, who died in hospital in Cannes on July 19, 1971, aged 85, was President of M.C.C. in 1937. He was in the Eton XI as an opening batsman in 1904 and 1905 and in the first year, despite an innings of 81 not out, was on the losing side against Winchester. Though he did not get a Blue at Oxford, he later assisted Buckinghamshire. A journalist, he became proprietor of *The Times* and was for years President of the Newspaper Press Fund and of the Press Club.

ATFIELD, Alfred John, a versatile cricketer of much experience, known chiefly as a very efficient umpire in first-class cricket, died at Caterham, Surrey, on New Year's Day, 1949, aged 80. Born at Ightham, Kent, on March 3, 1868, he played for the county second XI and for Gloucestershire in 1893 before being engaged by W. H. Laverton, a noted sportsman, at Westbury, in Wiltshire, for which county Atfield became prominent. Next he excelled as a coach in South Africa, being professional in Durban from 1897. A member of the ground staff at Lord's from 1901, he scored 121 not out on that ground in a Cross Arrows match after his marriage earlier in the day at Hanover Square.

ATHAWES, The Rev. John Thomas, born on December 8, 1837, died at Crown Hall, Tenbury, on October 3, 1915, having been Rector of Loughton, Buckinghamshire, since 1883. He was not in the XI whilst at Winchester, but played for Cambridge on a few occasions in 1859 and 1860, but not against Oxford. In the match against Surrey at the Oval in 1859 he made 42 in his first innings. It was said of him: "Has a very excellent defence, but does not improve in hitting."

ATKINSON, Bernard Gerard Wensley, who died in a London hospital on September 4, 1966, aged 65, played for Scotland, Northamptonshire and Middlesex. In the St. Paul's School XI from 1916 to 1919, he headed the batting averages in the last two years and while at Edinburgh Academy, where he taught for 37 years, hit many runs for Grange C.C. In 1934 for Middlesex against Surrey at Lord's, he hit a short-pitched ball from A. R. Grover for six with what was described as "an overhead lawn tennis smash". A first-rate Rugby footballer, he appeared at centre threequarter in a Cambridge Seniors' match but did not gain a Blue.

ATKINSON, George, who died on May 3, 1906, was one of the last of the brilliant professionals who represented Yorkshire in the '60s. Ephraim Lockwood and Luke Greenwood are still alive, but Slinn, Hodgson, George Anderson, Rowbotham, Roger Iddison, Edward Stephenson, John Thewlis, George Pinder, and—most famous of all—George Freeman and Tom Emmett have passed away. Born on September 21, 1830, Atkinson during his years in the Yorkshire XI, bowled first with Slinn and Hodgson, and then with Freeman and Emmett. Bowling medium pace to fast, he prided himself on his extreme straightness, as well as his accuracy of pitch, and had no belief in the "off theory" so much indulged in first by slow and

then by fast bowlers after his day. Atkinson was late in coming prominently before the public, being in his 29th year when, in 1859, he played his first match at Lord's for the United XI against the All England XI—a match that in those days was, as regards professional cricket, the event of the season. He, and the still-surviving Surrey player, William Caffyn, bowled unchanged through both innings of the All England team. Of the two bowlers Caffyn was rather the more effective, taking 11 wickets to Atkinson's eight. It may be interesting to recall the fact that in this match the late Thomas Hayward—one of the greatest batsmen of his generation, and uncle of the present player—was also seen at Lord's for the first time. After he had retired from first-class cricket, Atkinson acted as coach, first at Marlborough and then for many years at Rossall. While he was at Marlborough A. G. Steel came out of the school, and both Atkinson and his successor, the Notts batsman, Charles Brampton, took credit for teaching the new star. It is likely enough that A. G. Steel learnt much from both instructors, but he had such a genius for cricket that he probably owed more to himself than to any coaching. At any rate, when at Marlborough in 1877, he would have been quite good enough to play for the Gentlemen at Lord's if the M.C.C. committee had thought to ask him. Indeed, the late Robert Thoms, the umpire, contended that Steel never bowled quite so well as in his last year at school. One fact in connection with George Atkinson has often been referred to. He had such a fine tenor voice that, if he had been well-trained in his young days, he might easily have become a professional singer instead of a cricketer. He was buried in the Bowling Cemetery, Bradford, on May 7. Atkinson took part in the famous single wicket match at Stockton-on-Tees in September, 1862, in which Hayward, Carpenter, and Tarrant beat Five of Stockton by 22 runs. Though on the losing side Atkinson greatly distinguished himself, taking five wickets with his bowling and running out Carpenter. Atkinson was asked to go to Australia with George Parr's team in 1863, but declined.

ATKINSON, James Archibald, who died at Beaconsfield, Tasmania, on June 11, 1956, aged 60, was probably Tasmania's greatest cricket captain and was also the first batsman in that State to score 1,000 runs in three successive seasons—1928 to 1930. Born in Victoria, he found his appearances in

Sheffield Shield games limited by the necessity for concentrating upon Australian Rules football, but after migrating to Tasmania he met with considerable success. The captaincy of "Snowy" Atkinson, as he was always known, assisted in the development of many young cricketers, including the Test players, C. L. Badcock and L. Nash. Standing six feet, Atkinson was an orthodox batsman of special value on difficult pitches, a fine fieldsman close to the wicket and a useful change bowler. He retired from senior cricket in 1935, becoming a licensee at Launceston.

ATKINSON, Nigel Samuel Mitford, who died on October 24, 1966, was in the St. Paul's XI in 1916 and 1917, being second in the batting averages in the second year. His brother, B. G. W. Atkinson, who also died last year, was in the team at the same time. Sam took part in three matches for Middlesex in 1923, earning with medium-paced left-arm deliveries a match record of seven wickets for 106 runs against Cambridge University at Fenner's. He played club cricket for Hampstead for many years.

ATKINSON-CLARK, John Cecil, who died on October 2, 1969, aged 57, was in the Eton XI for three years from 1929, being captain in 1931. In 1930 against Harrow at Lord's, he hit 135 in the first innings—more than the other 10 batsmen obtained between them—and 31 in the second. He and A. G. Pelham, whose medium pace bowling brought him 11 wickets for 44 runs, were virtually responsible for victory by eight wickets. Atkinson-Clark turned out in a few matches for Middlesex between 1930 and 1932, his highest score for the county being 66 against Glamorgan at Lord's.

ATTENBOROUGH, Thomas, an old Derbyshire cricketer, was found dead at Ilkestone on January 21, 1907, aged 73. He played for the county on a few occasions, his last appearance being in 1874. His left hand bowling was often very successful, and for Derbyshire against M.C.C. and Ground at Lord's in 1870 he took four wickets for eight runs.

ATTEWELL, Thomas, younger brother of the famous William Attewell, died at Nottingham on July 6, 1937, aged 67. He played three times for his county in 1891, and was on the ground staff at Lord's from 1893 to 1925 when he received the customary gratuity of £500 in lieu of a benefit. From 1906 to 1907 he was a second-class county umpire.

ATTEWELL, William ("Dick"), born at Keyworth on June 12, 1861, died at Long Eaton, after a long illness, on June 11, 1927, one day before completing his 66th year. A right-handed medium-paced bowler of exceptional accuracy in length, he had his first opportunity to play for the county of his birth in 1881. This was the year there occurred the "Nottingham Schism," Alfred Shaw, Arthur Shrewsbury, William Barnes, Fred Morley, and James Selby refusing to comply with their engagement to play throughout the season unless the same arrangement were extended to Wilfred Flowers and William Scotton. The committee maintained their refusal to accede to the demand of those famous players, but five of them appeared in the county XI towards the end of the season. Shaw and Shrewsbury, however, remained absent after the first match. Attewell consequently strengthened the attack during this unfortunate period, playing in eight matches and taking 35 wickets at a cost of a little over 18 runs each. One performance stood out as exceptionally good—13 wickets falling to him at Brighton for 134 runs. The trouble being over next season, Attewell had to wait until Morley's health failed and then, for 16 seasons, remained a regular member of the side, while, after giving up the game in 1900, he officiated as an umpire for several years. Altogether, in first-class cricket in England, Attewell took 1,861 wickets for about 15.5 runs apiece. For the M.C.C. at Worcester in 1883 he took all of the Worcestershire wickets in the second innings. He used to mix his pace with varying flight and spin, but, like Alfred Shaw, he was renowned chiefly for a perfect length. As a batsman, Attewell often rendered useful service, and once scored 200. This occurred when he and William Gunn (who scored 219 not out), made a stand that produced 419 runs for the M.C.C. against Northumberland at Lord's in 1887. Ten years later, for Nottinghamshire, against Kent, he made 102. Attewell also did good work in the field, usually at cover-point. Among his best performances with the ball, that at Trent Bridge against Sussex in 1886, when he took nine wickets for 23 runs, deserves special mention. On eight occasions he dismissed eight men in an innings. He could bowl his accurate length for long spells without tiring, and against Sussex at Trent Bridge in 1887 26 overs from him yielded only six runs, while in another match—against Gloucestershire at Cheltenham a year later—he bowled 24 overs for five runs and three wickets. Attewell took part in three tours to Australia, going out with Alfred Shaw's team in the winter of 1884, with G. F. Vernon's side three years later, and again with Lord Sheffield's side in 1891–92. He did best with the ball on his second visit, taking 53 wickets for 11 runs each in important matches. At Melbourne he excelled against the sixth Australian team that had visited England, taking 12 of their wickets for 48 runs, and on the same ground directly afterwards, against Victoria, he took 11 wickets for 58. Against Australia, also at Melbourne, eight wickets fell to him for 55 runs. He received two benefits. In 1898 the Notts Committee gave him half the proceeds of the game with Surrey at Trent Bridge, and, although the match was ruined by rain, he received about £1,000 as the subscription lists were well filled. Five years later the M.C.C. allotted him the Middlesex v. Somerset match at Lord's, where excellent attendances were recorded on the first two days.

ATTFIELD, Dr. George Cooke, who was born at Bath on January 27, 1826, died at Hove on January 16, 1925, within 11 days of his 99th birthday. He played a little County Cricket for both Somerset and Surrey and later kept up the game in West Australia.

AUBREY-FLETCHER, Major Sir Henry Lancelot, the sixth Baronet, who died on May 30, 1969, aged 81, played with considerable success as an all-rounder for Buckinghamshire between 1921 and 1929. He was Lord Lieutenant of Buckinghamshire from 1954 to 1961. Under the *nom-de-plume* of "Henry Wade", he wrote several successful detective novels. His son, J. H. L. Aubrey-Fletcher, who succeeded to the baronetcy, also played for Buckinghamshire after the Second World War.

AUSTEN, Dr. Ernest Thomas, who died in Melbourne on June 21, 1983, aged 82, played twice for Victoria in 1928–29. He might have thought that once would have been enough, for at Melbourne in his first match, having fielded through a New South Wales innings of 713 for six declared, he became, in Victoria's second innings, one of Hooker's four victims in successive balls.

AUSTEN-LEIGH, The Rev. Arthur Henry, born at Speen, Berkshire, February 28, 1836; died at Reading, July 29, 1917. First match at Lord's for Gentlemen of England v. Gentlemen of Kent and Sussex, in 1857, when, going in first, he scored 34. Cheltenham College XI, 1853–54–55 (Captain 1855); St. John's College XI (Ox.); member of well-known brotherhood of cricketers.

AUSTEN-LEIGH, Charles Edward, the second and last surviving of seven cricketing brothers, great nephews of Jane Austen, was born on June 30, 1832, and died at Frog Firle, Alfriston, Sussex, on November 17, 1924, aged 92. After being for a time at Winchester he was sent to Harrow, where he was in the XI in 1850 and 1851. In his matches with Eton he scored eight and four, 0 and seven not out, and against Winchester made 42, 11 and 10. In his second innings in the game with Eton in 1850 he was run out by the bowler, W. P. Prest, whilst backing-up too far. He was a very steady and successful batsman, but did not obtain a place in the Oxford XI. His County Cricket was played for Berkshire. He had been a member of the M.C.C. since 1852.

AUSTEN-LEIGH, Edward Compton, a member of the well-known cricketing brotherhood, died at Eton College (where he had been a master from 1861 until 1905) on April 3, 1916, aged 76. In 1857 he played for Eton against both Harrow and Winchester, scoring 35 runs in his three innings, and he was then described as "A very useful bat, but not quite quick enough in the field." At Maidenhead in July, 1860, he played an innings of 190 for Gentlemen of Berkshire v. Gentlemen of Sussex. He represented Cambridge University at tennis and had been a member of the M.C.C. since 1869.

AUSTIN, George, who died on May 22, 1963, aged 73, served as scorer to Warwickshire for 52 years. "Chicko", as, because of his youthful appearance, he was known to cricketers, took up the position in 1911 and carried on without a break, except for the two World Wars, till he was taken ill during the match with Essex at Edgbaston a week before his death. His kindly manner made him popular, and not least with members of the Press, wherever he went. In 1954 Warwickshire granted him and E. J. Smith, the coach, a joint testimonial.

AUSTIN, Harold McPherson, who died on July 31, 1981, aged 77, was a valuable member of the Cambridge side in 1924, his only year in residence. Coming from Australia, he made his place virtually secure in the first match of the season, against Sussex, scoring 30 not out and 60 against Tate and Gilligan, the England opening pair, and he finished with the useful record of 444 runs for an average of 29.60 and 34 wickets at 23.17. Against Oxford he made 51 and took three wickets. A tall and immensely powerful man, he was essentially an attacking batsman and, with his bat impeccably straight, a fine driver on both sides of the wicket. He was a splendid field and for a man of his size a very fast runner. He bowled slow leg-breaks and topspinners which, if not always accurate, took many valuable wickets. Returning to Australia he was a member of the Victoria side which toured New Zealand in 1924–25, but he never appeared in the Sheffield Shield.

AUSTIN, Henry J. ("Harry"), who died at Cippenham, near Slough, on January 21, 1929, aged 64, had played for Hertfordshire, Bedfordshire, and Buckinghamshire, and for many years was a member of the ground staff at Eton College.

AUSTIN, Horace P., an outstanding American cricketer, died in October 1941, aged 60. He played for Pennsylvania University from 1897 to 1901, and during many years for Germantown Halifax Cup team, with which he often went on tour. He was a member of the Merion cricket club. A steady, reliable batsman, often useful in emergency, he set a good example by his safe work in the field. He came to England in 1911 with a Germantown team which showed to considerable advantage against club sides, winning five such matches, losing four and drawing two, but they suffered a heavy defeat from M.C.C. at Lord's and only just avoided a reverse from Gentlemen of Surrey at the Oval.

AUTY, Joseph Speight, who died on March 27, 1922, aged 38, was in the Mill Hill School XI in 1899 and three following seasons, being particularly successful in 1901 and 1902 as an all-round player. In 1901 he averaged 35.61 with the bat and took 58 wickets for 11.34 runs each, heading both averages, while in the following year he did great things in run-getting. Against Bishop's Stortford School he made 101 not out and v. Wellingborough Grammar School, on his opponents' ground, carried out his bat for 197 in a total of 306, which contained 22 extras. Subsequently he assisted Yorkshire Second XI on a few occasions, but he never played for the county. He had, however, appeared for Yorkshire at Rugby football.

AUTY, Karl André, who died in Chicago on November 30, 1959, aged 81, was the owner of an outstanding cricket book collection. Educated at Wheelwright Grammar School, Dewsbury, and on H.M.S. Conway Training Ship, he accomplished a Military and General course at the Sorbonne, Paris, and obtained a B.Sc. at Nottingham. He was an active participant in cricket until his late 60s in New England, B.C., and in North America. In the '30s he published a weekly newspaper, *The British American,* and for some years issued a cricket annual containing full details of Chicago cricket. He was celebrated for his Christmas cards, one of which included the following information: "It is interesting to note that a Surrey (England) team on its way to play exhibition games in Paris in 1789 was at Dover ready for the crossing, but turned back when met there by their host, the Duke of Dorset, H. B. M. Ambassador, who had fled from Paris before the coming outbreak of the French Revolution. Otherwise this would have been the first team ever to leave Britain's shores to play cricket abroad, thus depriving the 1859 team of that distinction."

AVEBURY, Lord (Sir John Lubbock), the famous scientist and well-known politician, banker and philanthropist, died at Kingsgate Castle, near Broadstairs, on May 28, 1913. He left Eton too early to be in the XI, but he was a useful left-handed batsman and a fast underhand bowler. For many years he was associated with the West Kent C.C., and occasionally he played for the Lords and Commons. He was born in London on April 30, 1834, and was the eldest of the cricketing brotherhood.

AVELING, Dr. C.T., whose name will be familiar to a great many Metropolitan cricketers, met with a tragic end on September 5, 1902. Whilst bathing at Helston, Cornwall, he was answering the appeal of a nervous lady for help, when he died of heart disease. He was well-known in connection with the Clapton Club, and had been for some years a member of the Surrey County C.C.

AVELING, Dr. E.B. (D.Sc. London University), was for several years a regular attendant at Lord's and the Oval, and often wrote about cricket. He died in August 1898.

AVORY, Henry Kemp, died at Weybridge, April 16, 1918, aged 69. An old Surrey cricketer. For many years Clerk of the Central Criminal Court.

AWDRY, Charles Edwin, who died on November 16, 1965, aged 59, was in the Winchester XI as a fast-medium bowler from 1923 to 1925, being captain in the last year. For some seasons from 1924 he assisted Wiltshire, taking nearly 300 wickets for them and scoring over 1,500 runs. He went to Egypt with H. M. Martineau's side in 1932 and 1933 and represented the Minor Counties against the 1937 New Zealanders. His father, C. S. Awdry, and his grandfather, Charles Awdry, were also in the Winchester XI of their time.

AWDRY, Col. Robert William, C.B.E., D.L., T.D., who played for Winchester, Oxford University and Wiltshire, died at Devizes in February, 1949, in his 68th year. In his only season in the Oxford XI, 1904, he opened the innings against Cambridge with J. E. Raphael, scoring 22 and 36. Most people will remember Colonel Awdry for all he did for Wiltshire cricket. A beautiful stroke player who loved to hit the ball in front of the wicket he was, with his brother, Charles, the mainstay of the Wiltshire batting before the First World War. Afterwards he became captain and for many years was the leading personality of Wiltshire cricket, for he also served the county as hon. secretary and treasurer. He delighted in training young players and was responsible for the development of giant Jim Smith, who went to Middlesex. Awdry's father owned private grounds at Shaw and Lavington where the cricket and the hospitality was of the best standard. Colonel Awdry was at one time High Sheriff of Wiltshire; he commanded the Royal Wiltshire Yeomanry and at his death was Chairman of the Wiltshire County Council as well as a Deputy Lieutenant of the county.

BABB, Commdr. Brian Osborne, who died on January 29, 1971, aged 72, was Secretary of Surrey from 1958 to 1964. During that time "Bob" Babb, as he was generally known, was also responsible for arranging the full County Championship programme each season.

BACHE, Lieut. Harold Godfrey (Lancashire Fusiliers), born at Churchill, in Worcestershire, on August 20, 1889, was killed at Ypres on February 15, 1916. He was in the XI at King Edward VI's Grammar School, Birmingham, but did not obtain his Blue at Cambridge as he did little when tried for the University. In the Freshmen's match of 1909 he made 137 and then retired, he and F. G.

Turner (98) adding 263 for the fifth wicket, and in the following year he scored 117 in the Seniors' match. Subsequently he appeared for Worcestershire. He was a left-hand bat and a fair change bowler. At Association football he played for Cambridge University, West Bromwich Albion and the Corinthians, and also obtained his international cap. He also represented his University at lawn-tennis.

BACKHOUSE, E. N., the Staffordshire professional, was killed in a motor car accident on November 1, 1936, at High Wycombe. When on the ground staff at Lord's in 1931, he came into the Yorkshire XI playing the Rest at the Oval because Oldroyd was taken ill suddenly and the champion county were without a reserve man. He was born on May 13, 1901.

BACON, Francis Hugh (Assistant-Paymaster R. N. R.), born at Colombo on June 24, 1869, was drowned off the coast of Belgium on October 31, 1915, through the patrol ship on which he was serving being mined. He was educated at St. Augustine's College, Canterbury, where he was in the XI, and afterwards settled in Basingstoke. Early in 1894, on the strength of three not-out innings of 101 for Basingstoke, he was tried for Hampshire, and in his first match for the county—against Warwickshire at Edgbaston—scored 114 without a chance in 130 minutes. He never quite realised his promise, although he made several good scores subsequently, especially one of 110 v. Leicestershire in 1907. Considering his small stature (5ft. 5in.) he was a free hitter, and for some years was one of the best cover-points in England. He was one of the comparatively few cricketers who played first as a professional and afterwards as an amateur. From 1903 until his death he was Secretary of the Hampshire County C.C., giving every satisfaction whilst in that position and making many friends by his geniality.

BADCOCK, Clayvel Lindsay ("Jack"), who died at his birthplace, Exton, Tasmania, on December 13, 1982, aged 68, was something of an infant prodigy, making his debut for Tasmania in 1929 when still under 16. A right-handed batsman, Badcock was sturdily built and a punishing driver. He was also a fine cutter of the ball, especially square of the wicket. He played 19 matches for Tasmania before transferring to South Australia for whom he played until his early retirement, owing to lumbago, in 1941. He had an insatiable appetite for runs. Playing for South Australia against Victoria at Adelaide in 1936 he made 325, his highest score. He also scored 271 not out for South Australia against New South Wales in 1938–39 and 236 against Queensland in 1939–40. His highest score for Tasmania was 274 against Victoria at Launceston in 1933–34.

For such a prolific scorer in Sheffield Shield cricket Badcock had a disappointing Test record, scoring only 160 runs in 12 innings, despite making 118 against England in only his third Test, at Melbourne in 1936–37. He toured England in 1938 and enjoyed considerable success outside the Test matches, his aggregate of 1,604 runs (average 45.82) being inferior only to those of Bradman and Brown. Self-effacing and immensely popular, he scored 7,571 runs in first-class cricket at an average of 51.54 and hit 26 centuries.

BADCOCK, Frederick Theodore, who died in Perth, Western Australia, on September 19, 1982, aged 84, played seven times for New Zealand between 1929–30 and 1932–33, though he was born in India and educated at Wellington College, Berkshire. Tall, dark and handsome, he bowled at a good medium pace, was a brilliant fielder and a good enough batsman to score 64 and 53 in successive Tests against South Africa in 1931–32. His first Test, against England at Wellington, was also New Zealand's first, and he made a "pair" in it, as well as being one of M. J. C. Allom's four victims in five balls. He ended his Test career, barely three years later, bowling to Hammond while he was scoring 227 and 336 not out in the only two Test matches which England played in New Zealand in 1932–33. Badcock's peripatetic life included a spell in England during the Second World War, when he played occasionally for Northamptonshire, some coaching in Ceylon and retirement in Western Australia. In all first-class cricket he scored 2,356 runs (average 26.47), including four centuries, and took 214 wickets at 23 apiece.

BADER, Group Capt. Sir Douglas, C.B.E., D.S.O., D.F.C., the famous airman who died on September 5, 1982, aged 72, was captain of St Edward's School, Oxford, in 1928. A good attacking bat and a useful fast-medium bowler, he later played for the RAF and in 1931 made 65, the top score, for them against the Army, a fixture which in those days had first-class status. He gained greater distinction at rugger, and at the time of the accident the following winter which cost him his legs he was in the running for an England cap.

BADGER, Henry Dixon, who died in hospital on August 10, 1975, aged 75, was in the Shrewsbury XI in 1917 and 1918 as a fast bowler and had a trial for Oxford in 1921 without getting his Blue. In that season he took six wickets for Yorkshire against Cambridge, thereby breaching the convention that an undergraduate in residence does not play against the other university except in the Varsity match. He also played one match for Yorkshire in 1922. Later he was a master at Sedbergh.

BADHAM, Peter Henry Christopher, died at Upton, near Poole, on April 10, 1983, aged 72. After a humble record in the Winchester XI in 1930, he made such rapid progress as an all-rounder that he had several trials for Oxford and in 1933 played for Leicestershire, for whom he had a birth qualification, against the University. He also played with some success for Buckinghamshire and later for Dorset. He was a fast-medium right-hand opening bowler with a high action.

BAGGALLAY, Lt.-Col. Richard Romer Claude, died on December 12, 1975, after a short illness, in his 92nd year. He was born in London on May 4, 1884. He first played for Derbyshire against the Australians in 1912 and also against Northamptonshire under his residential qualification. He captained the side in 1913 and 1914 until the outbreak of war when was recalled to his regiment as Adjutant of Yeomanry in the South Notts. Hussars. He won the D.S.O. and M.C. and was appointed joint captain with John Chapman for 1919, but only played in three matches as he was appointed Military Secretary to the Viceroy of Ireland, Lord Ypres. He was a right hand batsman and wicketkeeper. His first-class record is 31 matches, 59 innings, one not out, 688 runs, 88 highest score against Somerset at Derby in 1913, 11.86 average, 25 catches, did not bowl or keep wicket, all for Derbyshire. His brother M. E. C. Baggallay kept wicket for Cambridge University in 1911 and his cousin T. W. Baggallay (later T. W. Baggallay-Weeding) played for Surrey in 1874. R. R. C. Baggallay attained the rank of Lieutenant-Colonel, finally serving with the Irish Guards. He was the last surviving pre-First World War county captain, T. E. Manning having died three weeks earlier.

BAGGE, Thomas Edward, who was born at

Gaywood Hall, Lynn, on April 30, 1838, died at his native place on October 23, 1908, in his 71st year. He was a sound, patient batsman and a good field in the now obsolete position of long-stop. As a member of the Eton XI, in 1856 and 1857, he scored 11 and 26 in the two matches with Winchester, Eton winning on each occasion in an innings. There was no meeting with Harrow in 1856, and in the following year, when Etonians under 21 played Harrovians under 20, he made only 0 and three, the late Henry Arkwright taking his wicket in each innings. Going up to Cambridge, Mr. Bagge just missed obtaining his Blue as a Freshman, but he was in the XI in each of the three following years, being captain in his last. Although he made only 61 runs in six innings against Oxford, he was on the winning side in each year. Cambridge had several fine cricketers in residence at that period, among Mr. Bagge's contemporaries being the Hon. C. G. Lyttelton, W. H. Benthall, E. B. Fawcett, F. H. Norman, G. E. Cotterill, H. M. Marshall, Denzil Onslow, H. M. Plowden, R. Lang, and A. W. T. Daniel. In 1860, a year before he left the University, Mr. Bagge was selected for the match at the Oval between the Gentlemen and Players, and he thoroughly justified his inclusion by making 62 and 60—the highest score for his side in each innings—against the bowling of Jackson, Caffyn, Stephenson, and Hayward. His largest innings in a match of note was 81 for the University against M.C.C. and Ground at Fenner's in 1860, when David Buchanan and Grundy were among the bowlers opposed to him. Mr. Bagge was intimately associated with Norfolk cricket, and for some time was Hon. Secretary to the County Club, a position which ill-health compelled him to resign in 1865. In 1852 and 1853 his elder brother, Mr. R. S. Bagge, was a member of the Eton XI.

BAGNALL, Hamar Fraser, of Harrow, Cambridge University and Northamptonshire, died in London on September 2, 1974, aged 70. A talented batsman, he rarely did himself justice, yet on his day he was brilliant. He was in the Harrow XI of 1920, 1921 and 1922, but accomplished little in the matches against Eton, yet in 1922 when opposed to Arthur Gilligan and Maurice Tate he hit 103 for Northamptonshire at Northampton. Bagnall spent three years at Cambridge and gained his Blue as a Freshman when he scored hundreds against Free Foresters and H. D. G. Leveson Gower's XI, but he was left out of the 1924 and 1925 Light Blue sides although he still made runs for his county. Altogether in first-class cricket Bagnall had to be satisfied with 2,936 runs, average 19.31.

BAGSHAW, Henry ("Harry"), born at Foolow, Tideswell, Derbyshire, on September 1, 1861, died at Crowden, near Glossop, on January 31, 1927, aged 65, and was buried in his umpire's coat and with a cricket ball in his hand. He was a free-hitting batsman well above the average, a medium-paced bowler and a hard-working field in the slips: in batting he was left-handed, but in the other departments of the game right-handed. His first match for Derbyshire, though he had appeared for the Colts seven years earlier, was in 1887, and his last in 1902. Among his many good scores may be mentioned 96 and 90 not out v. Essex at Derby in 1893; 127 not out v. Yorkshire on the same ground in 1895; 121 v. Leicestershire and 115 v. Yorkshire, both at Derby, in 1896; 124 v. Leicestershire at Derby, 114 not out v. Surrey at the Oval, and 105 v. Hampshire at Southampton, all in 1897; and 100 not out v. Yorkshire at Harrogate in 1898. In 1900 he took five wickets for 27 runs v. Hampshire at Southampton and four for 16 v. Warwickshire at Glossop. For many years—until the end of 1923—he was an umpire in great matches. Whilst engaged by the Barnsley C.C. he scored 220 against Crofton Wanderers in August, 1888, and took all 10 wickets in an innings against Wakefield in 1891.

BAILEY, Sir Abe, so well known all over the world, who died on August 10, 1940, aged 75, was largely responsible for the great improvement brought about in cricket in South Africa during the early years of the century through his administrative and financial assistance. A number of tours, notably that of 1904 to England, were possible only as the result of his efforts, and he was largely instrumental for arranging the Triangular Tournament in England in 1912. A good right-hand medium-pace bowler in his younger days, he captained Transvaal in the Currie Cup tournament at Cape Town in March 1894, taking 11 wickets for 171 runs.

BAILEY, George Herbert, born at Colombo, in Ceylon, on October 29, 1853, died at Hobart, in Tasmania, on October 10, 1926, aged nearly 73. After being at Lichfield Grammar School, he went to Elizabeth College, Guernsey, where he was captain of the XI in 1869 and 1870. Obtaining an appointment in the Union Bank of Australia, he resided for 12 years at Launceston and for a short period at Albany, in West Australia, before settling in Hobart. In 1874 he won both batting and bowling prizes for the Launceston C.C., and it was whilst associated with that club that he was chosen as a member of the pioneer Australian team of 1878. He was then described as "A free, wristy batsman with good style; an excellent field and a good change bowler." Whilst in England he made 752 runs, with an average of 15.66, his highest score being 106 against Eighteen of Hastings. He was invited to come over again with the Australian team of 1880, but, for business reasons, was unable to do so. Of the side which visited us in 1878, only Charles Bannerman, Blackham and Garrett now survive. Almost immediately after his return home, Bailey met with a curious accident whilst fielding against Fifteen of New South Wales, at Sydney, for in throwing-in a ball he fractured his arm above the elbow. During the season of 1880–81 he played a not-out innings of 227 for Derwent v. Break-o'-Day, at Hobart, and, keeping up the game well until quite a veteran, he scored 156 out of 239 for New Town v. North Hobart, in a B. Grade match, in December, 1907. He had then completed his 54th year. He took part in many matches between North and South of Tasmania, and he particularly distinguished himself in the game at Hobart in 1892–93. The North, left with 307 to win, were successful by eight wickets, Bailey (139) and C. W. Rock (113) making 226 together for the first partnership.

BAILEY, George Keith Brooke, who died in Hobart on June 17, 1964, aged 82, played as a right-hand batsman and left-arm medium-pace bowler in two first-class matches for Tasmania in 1903–04. His father, G. H. Bailey, was a member of the first Australian team to visit England in 1878.

BAILEY, Leslie Norman, who collapsed and died at the wheel of his car on July 20, 1970, aged 66, was for 25 years cricket and boxing correspondent for the London *Star.* He had just retired from his duties as chief sports sub-editor with the *Daily Telegraph,* whose staff he joined in 1961. "Bill" Bailey reported cricket for the *Star* both in England and on tours abroad by M.C.C. teams.

BAILY, Edward Peter, died at Tupsley, Hereford, on January 21, 1941, aged 89. A very good wicket-keeper and useful batsman, he played in the Harrow XI from 1869 to 1871, finishing as captain, and was in the Cambridge XI 1872 and 1874. One of his best performances was against Eton at Lord's in 1870, when he scored 76. He appeared once for Middlesex in 1872 and for Somerset in 1881. He rowed in the Cambridge trial Eights in 1873 and did not keep his place in the cricket XI that year.

BAILY, Robert Edward Hartwell, who died on September 19, 1973, aged 88, was in the Harrow XI from 1901 to 1904, being captain in the last two years. A wicket-keeper and fair batsman, he played in a few matches for Surrey between 1904 and 1906 and gained a Blue at Cambridge in 1908. From 1939 to 1960, he was County Commissioner of Hereford Boy Scouts. His father, E. P. Baily, was a Cambridge Blue in 1872 and 1874 and also appeared for Middlesex and Somerset.

BAINBRIDGE, Herbert William, of high renown in Warwickshire cricket, died at Leamington Spa on March 3, 1940, aged 77, having been born at Assam on October 29, 1862. Standing about six feet tall and strong, he was an accomplished batsman, capable of punishing good bowling by well-controlled strokes all round the wicket; he also commanded respect for leadership. After four seasons in the Eton XI, being captain in 1882, Bainbridge was awarded his Blue at Cambridge in 1884 and helped to make University match history. He gave an exceptional display in the 1885 match at Lord's, when for the fourth consecutive time the match ended in a victory by seven wickets, this being the third such success by Cambridge. Bainbridge and Charles Wright, a stone-waller, opened the Cambridge innings with 152 runs, which gave their side a lead of 16 before Bainbridge hit a ball into mid-off's hands. His 101 was a faultless display of splendid strokes. This was at that time the best opening stand for either University; but, strangely enough, next year, when Bainbridge succeeded Lord Hawke as Cambridge captain, K. J. Key and W. Rashleigh put up 243 in starting Oxford's second innings, and this remains the first wicket partnership record for the University match. Oxford won by 133 runs. Bainbridge scored 44 and 79 in that encounter, and altogether in three meetings with Oxford he made 262 runs with an average of 43—an exceptional achievement.

Belonging to a Surrey family, Bainbridge played for that county occasionally previous to beginning his association with Warwickshire before completing the regulation period of qualification. In 1887 Leicestershire protested and the objection was upheld by M.C.C. However, Bainbridge captained Warwickshire in 1888 and kept the position until 1902, when he became hon. secretary— an office be retained when appointed chairman. In 1936 his 50 years of service received recognition by a presentation from the Warwickshire club. His highest innings for the county was 162 against Hampshire at Southampton in 1897, when he and W. G. Quaife put on 288 for the first wicket. Bainbridge played several times for Gentlemen against Players, and in the 1895 match at Kennington Oval he scored 82. That season was his most successful in first-class cricket, his aggregate runs numbering 1,162 with an average of 34. He was in the team captained by E. J. Sanders in company with W. E. Roller, K. J. Key, E. H. Buckland, Hugh Rotherham, and C. E. Cottrell, who went to America in 1886 and won seven out of eight matches, the other being drawn in their favour.

Bainbridge played Association football for Cambridge without getting his Blue, but was prominent for Old Etonians and was in the XI who lost the final tie for the F.A. Cup at the Oval in 1883, when Blackburn Olympic earned lasting fame, being the first provincial club to carry off the trophy. That was before professionalism was legalised.

BAINES, Canon Alfred George Pisani, died at Slough on May 12, 1949, aged 77. Bedford Grammar School XI. Played for Buckinghamshire and Berkshire at cricket and Association football, and was President of the Slough C.C.

BAINES, Harry, who was born at Welshpool on March 1, 1855, and died in Belfast on January 17, 1924, aged 68, was a player who, with more opportunities, might well have made a name for himself. His County Cricket, however, was played chiefly for Welsh sides—Montgomeryshire, Cardiganshire, and Merionethshire—though he appeared occasionally for Worcestershire and Shropshire, and in 1878 played at Lord's for XXII Colts of England against M.C.C.. In a match between F. C. Cobden's XI and Darrington in 1874 he took all 10 wickets in an innings, and at Darrington in the following year took five wickets in an over and sent a bail 49 yards, 7 inches. His bowling was fast round-armed. For North of Ireland against the South Africans at Belfast in 1894 he took eight wickets in an innings for 41 runs.

BAINES, John Ward, born on October 26, 1851, died at Putney on January 25, 1924, aged 72. His defensive batting gained him a place in the Marlborough XI in 1870, when he scored four and 11 v. Cheltenham and 0 and four v. Rugby. At Oxford he took part in the Freshmen's match of 1871 and played for Wadham, but did not receive his Blue.

BAISS, Reginald Sidney Habershon, who died on May 2, 1955, aged 82, played in seven matches for Kent between 1895 and 1901. A wicket-keeper, he was in the Tonbridge XI for four years from 1899 and played in trials at Oxford without gaining a Blue.

BAKER, Albert, Surrey professional from 1900 to 1907 who played again for the county in 1912, died on April 29, 1948, aged 75. A good batsman, he scored 1,257 runs in 1905 with average 31.42.

BAKER, Charles Shaw, died at St. Ives in December, 1976, aged 93. Born at Manchester, he played for Warwickshire from 1908 to 1920, scoring over 9,000 runs with an average of just under 30 and making seven hundreds. He was a solid left-hander with a good stroke through the covers. Giving up first-class cricket early to become a cartoonist, he got a contract with the *Daily Express*, but from 1925 to 1930 played with considerable success as an amateur for Cornwall, supplementing his batting with some useful off-breaks and googlies. On his first appearance for them he scored 136 not out and 93 against Surrey II and that year made 756 runs with an average of 63. Four years later he still headed both the batting and bowling averages. His death leaves E. J. Smith and Canon J. H. Parsons as the sole survivors of the Warwickshire side which won the Championship in 1911.

BAKER, Clare Vaughan, died at Betchworth, Surrey, on December 7, 1947, aged 62. Harrow XI 1905. Played for Middlesex occasionally from 1906–12. Member of London Stock Exchange. In Great War 1914–18 Lt. R.G.A.

BAKER, George Robert, a well known member of the Lancashire XI from 1887 to 1899, died at Wing, Buckinghamshire, on February 6, 1938, aged 75. He began first-class cricket for Yorkshire with little success but became a thoroughly good batsman, sound in style and strong in punishing ability. In his best season, 1897, he scored 1,219 runs in county matches, average 35.29. Lancashire were champions that year and only Albert Ward scored more runs. Baker was highest scorer with 87 for the Players at the Oval and at Lord's he made 30 and 39, being number five in a very strong batting side. Next season, Baker was awarded a benefit and, though Yorkshire won by 10 wickets on Friday afternoon, so that there was no Saturday gate, the pecuniary results were satisfactory. Of very happy disposition and popular with everyone, George Baker was coach at Harrow for 12 years.

BAKER, Graham Charsley, who died suddenly on February 21, 1977, in East London at the age of 45, produced one issue of the *South African Cricket Almanack* dated 1949/50. He was a Rhodes University student at the time. It was the first Cricket Annual production in South Africa since 1907, but although he produced only the one issue he may have sown the seed in the mind of Geoffrey Chettle whose *South African Cricket Annual* was first produced two years later and has of course been running ever since.

BAKER, James Clark, died on February 1, 1939. Regarded as one of the best forcing batsmen Otago and New Zealand have produced, he was a member of the team which toured Australia in 1899 and headed the batting averages with 41.4. His highest innings was 81 against South Tasmania, but probably 56 against Victoria, when he and D. Rees put up 135 for the first wicket, was his best display. He played several times for New Zealand against overseas teams and made 40 against the powerful 1896 Australian XI.

BAKER, Percy Charles, died on December 30, 1939, aged 65. At Uppingham and Oxford, Percy Baker failed to get a place in either XI, but his form for Beckenham warranted a trial for Kent when 26 years of age for two seasons—1900–01—he earned fame in a very strong batting side. He used good reach in powerful driving and played some brilliant forcing innings. Most memorable was his display at Trent Bridge in 1900. A great innings of 137 by William Gunn, followed by 59 in half an hour by G. J. Groves and Dench, enabled A. O. Jones to declare with five men out and good prospect of victory. Instead of playing for safety, Kent went for the runs. With six wickets in hand they wanted only 78 to complete a larger score than ever had been made in a last innings at Trent Bridge. Wass, troubled by a leg injury, then returned to the field and the whole aspect changed. Wass bowled C. J. B. Marsham; Baker was stumped off Jones; Huish run out and Wass finished the match by bowling Colin Blythe, Nottinghamshire winning by 12 runs some 25 minutes from time.

BAKER, Reginald Leslie, who died at Hollywood, California, on December 2, 1953, aged 69, was known as the greatest all-round athlete produced by Australia. He got his Blue at Sydney University for cricket and also for football, athletics and rowing. He took part in 26 different sports, representing Australia at Rugby football and taking part in international polo. "Snowy" Baker, as he was generally known, fought and lost to the late J. W. H. T. Douglas, who became captain of the England cricket team, for the Olympic middle-weight boxing championship in London in 1908. Though born in Sydney he spent most of his life in America.

BAKER, Wiri Aurunui, who died in Wellington, New Zealand, on July 1, 1966, aged 74, was the most prolific scorer in Wellington senior championship matches. A right-handed opening batsman, he hit 10,226 runs in 25 years of senior cricket. In addition, in first-class games for Wellington between 1911 and 1929, he obtained 1,835 runs, average 31.63.

BAKEWELL, Alfred Harry (Fred), who died at Westbourne, Bournemouth, on January 23, 1983, aged 74, was, from the spectator's point of view, one of the most exciting batsmen of his generation and the car smash which ended his career was as disastrous as that which finished Milburn's years later. While, as the vicissitudes of some of our modern Test match batsmen demonstrate, it is impossible to exaggerate the importance of a sound orthodox method, it is salutary that just now and again a player emerges who can defy some of what are normally considered the cardinal principles and yet completely confound the critics. Bakewell's stance was one of the most two-eyed ever seen, with the right shoulder so far round that it seemed almost to be facing mid-on: it was not helped by a slight crouch and he gripped the bat throughout with one hand at the top and the other at the bottom of the handle. Seeing this for the first time, one would have diagnosed a dull and ugly player who would score, if at all, by nudges and deflections. Yet there was in him some natural genius which enabled him to be one of the most brilliant drivers and cutters in the world, nor did he have any difficulty in getting right down the pitch to hit the ball. Naturally he was also strong on the leg side and, if in his early years his defence was a trifle suspect, especially on his off stump, he soon improved it.

If ever a batsman was a law unto himself, he was. In 1933 he scored 246 for Northamptonshire against Nottinghamshire at Northampton in just under six hours. In order to keep him quiet, Sam Staples, one of the most accurate off-spinners in England, bowled at the stumps with a packed leg side. To cut an off-break is generally a recipe for trouble: to cut an off-break on the middle stump is suicidal. Yet Bakewell, standing well clear of his leg stump, in the intervals of jumping out and driving him for four past the place where extra-cover might have been, constantly cut him. In 30 overs Staples conceded 177 runs. The innings was regarded by many as the finest they had ever seen on the ground and was a record for the county. It did not stay a record for long. In the next match Bakewell beat it with 257 against Glamorgan at Swansea. By contrast, opening for England against West Indies at the Oval later that summer, he was faced with a score-board reading 68 for four, Walters, Hammond, Wyatt and Turnbull all being out. His answer was to make 107 out of 194 in three hours, 50 minutes, a sensible, controlled innings which was just what the situation called for and which saved the side.

Born at Walsall, Bakewell learned his cricket at St. John's School, Tiffield, and later received further coaching in Oxford under the scheme organised by J. R. F. Turner. He made his first appearance for Northamptonshire in June, 1928, and immediately made his place secure not only with some useful innings, but by his brilliant fielding at short-leg. In 1929 he got his 1,000 runs and did so every season for the rest of his career. Having played his first innings of 200 in 1930, 204 against Somerset at Bath, he was picked in 1931 for the Players at Lord's and also to open the innings for England against New Zealand at Lord's and the Oval. At the Oval he made 40 and was batting well when he allowed himself to be run out rather than Sutcliffe. In 1933 his aggregate of 1,952 runs for the county was a record and in all matches he exceeded 2,000 runs, the first Northamptonshire man ever to do so. That winter he went to India with Jardine's side and was only moderately successful, and in 1934, being doubtless stale, failed to get a place against the Australians. Back in form in 1935, he played in two Tests against South

Africa without much success, but made 1,719 runs for the county, including a remarkable innings against Yorkshire at Harrogate. Those were the days when D. R. Jardine, if he wished to know how good a cricketer was, always asked, "What has he done against Yorkshire?" On this occasion someone remarked to Bakewell that he had never taken a hundred off Yorkshire: he replied, "I will do so today". The Yorkshire bowling was opened by Smailes and off his first over Bakewell hit five fours, followed by three more three overs later. In two hours he had reached 96 when Sellers just reached, one-handed at full stretch over his head at mid-off, a tremendous drive and held it. In 1936 Bakewell had another good season and ended it and his career with a great innings. At Chesterfield Northamptonshire were 65 runs down on the first innings to Derbyshire, the champions. Going in again Bakewell batted over six hours for 241 not out before his captain declared, leaving Derbyshire 347 to get. At the close they were 173 for seven. On the return journey the car in which R. P. Northway and Bakewell were travelling overturned. Northway was killed outright and Bakewell's right arm was so badly broken that he could never play County Cricket again.

In all first-class matches he had scored 14,570 runs with an average of 33.98, besides being a great short-leg. It is sometimes suggested, surely somewhat harshly, that he should, even in his short career, have achieved more than he did, but it must be remembered that he was throughout playing for a very weak county. During his nine seasons Northamptonshire won only 31 matches and lost 119; five times they were bottom of the table. So let the last word lie with his old captain, W. C. Brown: "During an all-too-short first-class career his approach to life in general may have seemed somewhat lackadaisical. Out in the middle, though, he was a splendid chap to have on the side and, when a change in the field involving someone in a long trek between overs became necessary, Fred was always the first to call out, 'I'll go skipper'."

BALDOCK, William Frederick, missing in Malaya in 1942 and subsequently presumed killed, played cricket for Winchester in 1918 and 1919, being contemporary with D. R. Jardine and C. T. Ashton. Going up to Oriel College, Oxford, he was tried in the Freshmen's match of 1920, but never in a University side. After making a few appearances for Somerset he went to Tanganyika in the

Forestry Department. He married the daughter of Mr. John Daniell, the former Somerset captain, Cambridge double Blue and Rugby football international.

BALDWIN, Charles, who died on May 2, 1947, at his home in Penn, Buckinghamshire, aged 81, was a useful batsman for Surrey from 1892 to 1898. Short and thick-set he showed good style. In his best season, 1897, he scored 1,137 runs, average 30.11, in championship matches, excelling with 234 against Kent at the Oval. He played for Suffolk from 1903, having been born at Bury St. Edmunds on December 29, 1865. He was for 17 years a very successful and popular coach at Uppingham School, so emulating the example of H. H. Stephenson, a distinguished Surrey professional, who still is referred to as the most famous of school coaches; he died at Uppingham after 25 years' service. When Fred Boyington died in 1927, Baldwin for a time took over the duty of Surrey scorer.

BALDWIN, Henry, the Hampshire professional, played for the county from 1887 to 1905. Born at Wokingham in Berkshire on November 27, 1860, he belonged to a family which could put an XI in the field. He was conspicuous in raising Hampshire to the first-class championship in 1895 and that season he took 102 wickets at 16 runs each in competition matches. Against Essex at Southampton he dismissed 13 men for 78 runs; he and Tom Soar, a splendid fast bowler on his day, were unchanged in both innings of the Derbyshire match and he was in the Players' XI against Gentlemen at the Oval. Although no more than 5ft. 6in. in height Baldwin weighed well over 12 stone. His portly figure, running to the crease for his slow right hand bowling, or standing at point, made him one of the memorable characters in a very good side captained by Dr. Russell Bencraft, now Sir Russell, President of the Hampshire club. Length and off-break with pace from the pitch made him deadly on turf affected by rain, or worn. He had no pretentions as a batsman, but in his great match against Essex, Soar and he were top scorers in Hampshire's second innings with 37 not out and 32; A. P. Lucas with 37 was highest for Essex in the whole match. The first Hampshire professional to have a "benefit", Baldwin was unfortunate in the reward received. Yorkshire were a big attraction in 1898, and so strong were they that, after a day's rain, the match was finished off between 12 o'clock and five

minutes past six. For three innings the aggregate was only 235. D. A. Steele, whose death also occurred this year, was the highest scorer with 10 in the Hampshire totals—42 and 36. Baldwin did well with four wickets for 37, but his performance came between two astonishing feats by Schofield Haigh—eight for 21 and six for 22; 14 wickets for 43 runs in the day. He died on January 12, 1935. His son, H. G. Baldwin, played for Surrey and is now a first-class umpire.

BALDWIN, John Loraine, who died on November 25, 1896, at the age of 87, will always be remembered, in conjunction wth Lord Bessborough—then the Hon. F. Ponsonby—Sir Spencer Ponsonby-Fane—then the Hon. Spencer Ponsonby—and Mr. R. P. Long, as one of the original founders of I Zingari. Mr. Baldwin had the satisfaction in 1895 of assisting at Lord's at the Jubilee of the famous club, and made some small presentations to those taking part in the match I Zingari v. Gentlemen of England. He was also a great supporter of the Canterbury Cricket Week, and is said to have never missed the week's festivities till declining health kept him away in 1896. Mr Baldwin has a further claim on remembrance as chairman of the committee that revised the laws of short whist.

BALDWIN, Thomas, for many years a member of the Suffolk XI, was born on January 18, 1832, at Bury St. Edmunds, where he died on May 7, 1907. He was a fast round-armed bowler and generally fielded at short slip. He did not appear at Lord's until 34 years of age. Charles Baldwin, who afterwards played for Surrey for some years and is now at Uppingham, is his son.

BALE, Ernest, who died at Carshalton, Surrey, on July 7, 1952, aged 65, might well have won high honours as a wicket-keeper had he not been contemporary with Herbert Strudwick, of Surrey and England fame. Born on September 18, 1878—like Strudwick at Mitcham—Bale appeared for Surrey against Oxford University in 1904, but, realising the limited possibilities with the county of his birth, commenced soon afterwards to qualify for Worcestershire. He made his debut for the Midland county in 1908, and by 1910, in which season he kept wicket for The Rest against Kent, the Champion County, definitely displaced G. Gaukrodger in the Worcestershire side. Referring to his form at that time, *Wisden* described him as "second to no one in England except

Strudwick." His career with Worcestershire continued till 1920, when, having caught 247 batsmen and stumped 82, he retired from first-class cricket.

BALFOUR, Robert Drummond, who was born at Putney on March 1, 1844, died at Welwyn on May 7, 1915. After playing in the Westminster XI, he obtained his Blue at Cambridge, appearing four times (1863–66) against Oxford at Lord's. *Scores and Biographies* said of him: "Is a safe and steady batsman, possessing an excellent style, and has distinguished himself in various matches." He was also a very good wicket-keeper, and in the University's match with Surrey at the Oval in 1866 caught three and stumped two in an innings. In his eight innings against Oxford he scored 101 runs, and was always on the losing side. In 1866, his last season in the XI, he appeared for the Gentlemen at Lord's, making 23 and four, and bringing off two catches in the second innings of the Players, who (owing chiefly to a very lucky innings of 122 not out by the late Tom Hearne) won by 38 runs. In important cricket his highest score was 82 for the M.C.C. against the University at Lord's in 1867, but a year earlier he had made 67 on the same ground off the bowling of Wootton and Grundy, and in 1863 had played an innings of 60 against Buttress and Tarrant at Cambridge. Mr. Balfour, who played for I Zingari and had been a member of the M.C.C. since 1868, was a younger brother of Mr. E. Balfour of the Oxford XI of 1852 and two following years. He was one of the men who helped to bring about the rule which prevented a cricketer from representing his University more than four times in the great match at Lord's.

BALFOUR-MELVILLE, Lieut. James Elliot (3rd Black Watch), a son of Mr. Leslie M. Balfour-Melville, was born in Edinburgh on July 9, 1882, and was killed in action in France on September 27, 1915. He was a useful hard-hitting batsman and a good wicket-keeper, and for the Malvern College XI in 1901 averaged 23.91: that year he played an innings of 51 v. Uppingham. In 1913 he was a member of the Scots side which played a few matches in England, and against Surrey at the Oval scored 32 out of 43 in 20 minutes. Among the many clubs to which he belonged were the M.C.C., I Zingari and Grange. For the last-named he averaged 57 in 1905. At Oxford he obtained his Blue for Association football, playing

from 1901 to 1905, and in the last-mentioned year being captain.

BALFOUR-MELVILLE, L. M., a remarkable all-round sportsman, died at North Berwick on July 16, 1937, aged 83. He was cricket captain at Edinburgh Academy when 15 and, playing for XXII of Edinburgh against George Parr's All-England XI, he stayed in for an hour against J. C. Shaw and Tom Emmett, making 17, the top score of the innings. When 18 he scored 150 at Raeburn Place in the first match between Edinburgh and Glasgow. In 1882 when W. L. Murdoch's Australian team were beaten by 45 runs in a one-day match, Balfour-Melville's share of Scotland's 167 for seven wickets was 73 against F. R. Spofforth, H. F. Boyle and G. E. Palmer. For Grange against M.C.C. at Lord's in 1894 he hit up 107 before lunch. Admirable in style he drove brilliantly, and maintained his form until 1913, when, nearly 60, he scored 145 for Grange v. Peebles, 149 for I Zingari against Aldershot Command and 150 for I Zingari at Stirling. An excellent wicket-keeper or slip fieldsman, he was a sound captain. In fact, during some 40 years he was the greatest cricketer in Scotland.

BALLANCE, Major Tristan George Lance, M.C., Durham Light Infantry, was killed in action during December, 1943, aged 27, three months after being awarded the M.C. for gallant and distinguished services in North Africa. For Uppingham he bowled slow left-arm effectively during a very successful 1932 season, his 76 wickets costing less than 10 runs apiece, and next year he excelled with 54 at 10.35 each, while his batting average was 21. That season Uppingham won 10 of 11 matches and were near victory over Free Foresters when time expired. At Shrewsbury, Ballance scored 31 and 26 not out and took 11 wickets for 72, his all-round work helping greatly in a victory by 58 runs. Ballance maintained this form in 1934, when Marlborough, under his encouraging lead, won nine of 12 matches and lost only one. Defeat seemed certain at Rugby, but Ballance took three of the last four wickets which fell for two runs and Uppingham won by four. Going up to Brasenose, Ballance got his Oxford Blue after taking six wickets for 41 in an innings in the Freshmen's match, but his slow left-hand bowling, delivered from a great height, proved expensive generally. He played little in 1936, but next year regained his place in the side which beat Cambridge at Lord's by seven wickets, though his share in Oxford's first victory since 1931 was slight. Ballance played for Norfolk from 1932. When the Minor Counties competition was won in 1933 he appeared seldom because of ill-health. In 1936 when he took 42 wickets at 8.11 apiece, Norfolk were unbeaten for the third successive season. He batted well next year, averaging 43.14, and in 1939 again headed the bowling averages, though playing little. He was the fourth member of the 1937 Oxford XI killed in the War.

BALOO, Palwankar, who died in India on July 4, 1955, aged 78, played for the Hindus from 1907 to 1920, doing much good work as a slow left-arm bowler. His death occurred on the day which for so long had been printed in *Wisden* "Births and Deaths" as the date of his birth, which actually was March 19. His best analysis for the Hindus was 8 wickets for 43 runs in the second innings of the Parsees in the 1919 Quadrangular Tournament.

He toured England with the 1911 All-India team, heading the bowling averages with 114 wickets, average 18.86 in all matches. During that tour his chief feats were eight wickets for 103 v. Cambridge University; seven for 83 v. Lancashire and eight for 15 in the two innings of Ulster at Belfast.

BANCROFT, Jack, who kept wicket for Glamorgan in 1922, died in January, 1942, at Swansea Hospital after a long illness. Very good at Rugby football, he played for Wales 18 times—1909 to 1914.

BANCROFT, William J., who died at Swansea on March 3, 1959, the day after his 88th birthday, was a leading batsman in Minor Counties matches for Glamorgan between 1897 and 1914, scoring a number of centuries, the highest of which was 207 in 1904. When full-back for Swansea, "Billy" Bancroft made 33 successive International appearances for Wales in Rugby football International matches, the first at the age of 18 in 1890 and the last in 1901. He claimed to have taken every penalty and every place-kick for his country during that time.

BANERJEE, Shute Nath, who died in Calcutta on October 14, 1980, aged 67, became the first Bengali to play Test cricket when he won his only cap against West Indies in Bombay in 1948. A right-arm fast-medium bowler, he took one for 73 in West Indies' first innings and four for 54 in their second. He is perhaps best remembered for having, in 1946, on the second of his two tours to England, helped C. T. Sarwate add 249 in three hours 10 minutes for the Indians' last wicket against Surrey at the Oval. This is still an Indian record and the second-highest last-wicket partnership ever made. Batting at number 11, he joined Sarwate at 205 for nine and hit 121. Sarwate finished with 124 not out. Surrey's attack included the Bedser twins, Gover, Watts, Squires, Gregory and Parker. Banerjee's best analysis in first-class cricket was his eight for 25 for Nawanagar against Maharashtra in 1941–42, his highest first-class score 135 for Bihar against Bengal in 1952–53 at Calcutta in the Raj Trophy. He captained Bihar from 1942 until 1958.

BANES-WALKER, 2nd Lieut. Cecil (2nd Batt. Devon Regiment), was killed near Ypres on May 9, 1915, aged 26. He was born at North Petherton, near Bridgwater, and came to the front as a member of the Long Ashton C.C. In 1914 he appeared in five matches for Somerset, and by aggressive batting made 172 runs with an average of 19.11, his highest score being 40 v. Hampshire at Southampton. He was also a very good hockey player, assisting Gloucestershire under the residential qualification.

BANKS, Edward, J.P., one of the oldest Kent cricketers, died at Sholden Lodge, near Deal, on January 12, 1910, aged 89. He was born in South Wales on August 12, 1820, but moved into Kent before completing his second year. Ill-health limited his appearances in County Cricket to 10 matches between 1842 and 1846. In the last-mentioned year he appeared for the Gentlemen against the Players at Canterbury, and fielded at Lord's for Alfred Mynn in the first of his single wicket matches with Felix. *Scores and Biographies* (iii–159) says of him, "Batted in a good free style, and was a most excellent field." Fuller Pilch recalled that "I found him down Sandwich way, where his property lay. He and his youngest brother, Mr. William, were the quickest between the wickets I ever did see, and Mr. Edward was one of the smartest in the long-field. He was like a thorough-bred horse, for no matter how far the ball was off he would try; and when I sang out 'Go to her, Mr. Edward! Go to her!' he would outrun himself almost, and, as sure as ever he got his hands to her, the ball was like a rat in a trap." His youngest brother, the late Mr. W. J. Banks, played occasionally for Kent in 1846 and 1848. The deceased, who was a grandson of Sir Edward Banks, the builder of London Bridge, rode a tricycle as recently as three months before his death.

BANKS, Capt. Percy D'Aguilar, Queen Victoria's Own Corps of Guides (attached 57th Rifles), was killed near Ypres on April 28, 1915. He was born in 1885 and was in the Cheltenham XI in 1902, when he made 312 runs with an average of 22.28, making 27 and 103 v. Haileybury, eight and six v. Marlborough, and 62 and six v. Clifton. In 1903 he was third in the Sandhurst averages with 33.00, and the same season played once for Somerset, scoring 0 and 278 v. Hampshire at Bournemouth. Later he did well in India, and in 1904 appeared for the Army against the Rest at Lahore. He was also well-known as a polo player. Writing of his batting in *Wisden* of 1903, the late Mr. W. J. Ford said—"Banks played a remarkable innings of 103 v. Haileybury. The pavilion critics were unanimous in calling it equal to any innings ever played by a boy at Lord's, his variety of strokes and his manipulation of the bat being quite Trumperesque. I fancied that he must be exceedingly strong in wrist and elbow."

BANKS, William John, who represented Kent on a few occasions, died at his residence, Oxney Court, near Dover, in January, 1901. He was born in 1822. *Scores and Biographies* (iii–159) describes him as "a hard hitter and an active field." He was a most entertaining old gentleman, full of cricket lore, and a regular attendant at the Canterbury Festival.

BANNERMAN, Alexander Chalmers, born in Sydney, March 21, 1859, died September 19, 1924. A member of the first Australian team in England in 1878, Alec Bannerman will be remembered as long as cricket is played. After his first trip he paid five other visits to England, coming over with the teams of 1880, 1882, 1884, 1888 and 1893. He had his most vivid experiences in England in connection with matches in which he did not personally meet with much success. He was not only on the side that in 1878 made the fame of Australian cricket for ever by beating the M.C.C. at Lord's in one afternoon, but he took part in the first Test match in this country at the Oval in 1880, and also in the unforgettable match on the same ground in 1882, when the Australians beat us by seven runs. Indeed, the catch—quite an easy one—by which he got rid of W. G. Grace in the last innings proved the turning-point of that tremendous struggle. Alec Bannerman among Australians was the most famous of all stone-walling batsmen; his patience was inexhaustible. It was said that the Sydney

public had become tired of his super-caution when Lord Sheffield's XI were out in Australia in 1891–92, and were inclined to barrack him, but that everyone spoke of him as "Good old Alec," when he took seven hours and a half to score 91 in the match that gave the Australians the Rubber against the Englishmen. In that innings of 91—spread over three days—he scored from only five off the 204 balls bowled to him by Attewell. Still, though such a slow run-getter, he made many big scores, and as a partner to great hitters like Percy McDonnell, Bonnor and J. J. Lyons he was invaluable. In Test matches with England he scored 1,105 runs with an average of 23.03, and for New South Wales v. Victoria 1,209 runs with an average of 29.29. Apart from his batting he was a superb field at mid off—fast, sure, and untiring, and a wonderfully safe catch. When his active days as a player had ended he did excellent work as coach for the New South Wales Cricket Association. Alec Bannerman took his cricket very seriously. It was said of him, not ill-naturedly, that when in the match with England at the Oval in 1888 he was out to the finest of all the catches at cover slip ever brought off by George Lohmann, he talked about his bad luck, and of nothing else, for the rest of the afternoon.—S.H.P.

His chief hundreds were:

134 Australian XI v. Rest of Australia, at Sydney, 1888–89

133 Australians v. Oxford and Cambridge Past and Present, at Portsmouth, 1893

120* Australians v. I Zingari, at Scarborough, 1882

117 New South Wales v. Victoria, at Melbourne, 1889–90

105 Australians v. Derbyshire, at Derby, 1893

101* New South Wales v. Victoria, at Melbourne, 1882–83 (In his first innings he had made 78 run out).

BANNERMAN, Charles, born at Woolwich, in Kent, on July 3, 1851, died in Sydney on August 20, 1930, aged 79. He was one of the three survivors of the 22 players who took part in what, according to records at present accepted, was the first Test match between England and Australia.

Only those whose memories go back years can recall this very fine batsman. In his day he was the best in Australia. He had a splendid style, standing well up to the ball, and was master of nearly every stroke; indeed his batting was essentially skilful and polished. He drove finely to the off, and could hit with power and accuracy to leg. Over and above his qualities as a run-getter he had another claim to fame as being a first-class field, no matter the position in which he was put. The match in which he really made his name took place in Melbourne in the middle of March, 1877. James Lillywhite's team was then touring Australia and New Zealand, and so much had the standard of cricket in Australia improved since the previous visit of an English side under W. G. Grace that when Fifteen of New South Wales twice beat Lillywhite's men and a Fifteen of Victoria also overcame them, the challenge was made to play an 11-a-side match against the Englishmen. The faith the Australians had in themselves was justified for, with England lacking the assistance of a recognised wicket-keeper, Australia won by 45 runs. In a return match a little later on the same ground Lillywhite's team won by four wickets. Charles Bannerman took part in both these matches, and in the first he had the distinction of playing an innings of 165. The runs were made against Shaw, Hill, Emmett, Southerton, Ulyett and Lillywhite, and not one of his companions was able to reach 20 in the same innings. During the first day he scored 126 of his side's 166 for six wickets. Never before had an Australian batsman scored a century against an English XI. In the second match he made 19 and 30. In 1878 there came the first visit of an Australian team to this country, and Charles Bannerman was a member of it. In the course of the tour he scored 723 runs for an average of 24. He obtained the only hundred hit by any of the Australians that summer, making 133 at Leicester against Leicestershire. (He also reached three-figures for the side in both New Zealand and Canada, and, altogether, during a tour which in all extended over 14 months, scored 2,630 runs for it with an average of 23.90). Towards the end of May he took part in the historic match at Lord's against the M.C.C., when the Marylebone Club were dismissed by Spofforth and Boyle for 19. The Australians won by nine wickets. Bannerman paid no other visit to England, illness cutting short his career as a cricketer. At various times he undertook coaching duties in Melbourne and Sydney and at Christ's College, Christchurch, in New Zealand, and later became an efficient umpire. He was elder brother of the late A. C. Bannerman of stone-walling fame.

BANNISTER, H. M., who died on June 18, 1959, aged 69, played occasionally as a medium-paced bowler for Leicestershire between 1912 and 1921.

BAPASOLA, Nasarvanji Cawasji, born in April, 1867, died at Meerut in June, 1923, aged 56. He was a member of the Parsi team which visited England in 1888, when he scored 584 runs with an average of 12.32 and took 24 wickets at a cost of 18.10 runs each. He was chosen for the first Presidency match in 1892 and for All-India against Lord Hawke's team. From first to last he played for over 30 years.

BAPTY, John, who died suddenly at his Bridlington home on December 14, 1975, aged 74, was a noted Yorkshire sports journalist. He began his professional link with Yorkshire cricket in the early days after the First World War and from 1931 until the close of the 1961 season he travelled with the Yorkshire side, being away only for Test cricket. He went to Australia with the M.C.C. teams of 1950 and 1954 and was Sports Editor of the *Yorkshire Evening Post* from 1947 to his retirement at the end of 1965. A blunt, stocky, typical Yorkshireman, John Bapty contributed to the 1969 *Wisden* a short post war history of Yorkshire—"The Top County".—N.P.

BARBER, Dr. Hugh, who died on September 7, 1969, aged 92, played in two "extra" matches outside the Championship programme for Yorkshire in 1898 against Worcestershire at Worcester and Halifax. This was the season before Worcestershire achieved first-class status.

BARBER, Richard, who was found dead in a railway-carriage at Cookham Station on June 13, 1924, whilst on his way to umpire in a match at Shoeburyness, was born at Hedsor, Buckinghamshire, on August 2, 1847. A steady batsman, a useful medium-paced right-handed bowler and a good field at short-slip, his name will be found in the Buckingham XI and, for many years, that of the Marlow C.C. In 1871 he was engaged at Lord's by the M.C.C. and later with the Royal Military College, Sandhurst.

BARBER, Wilfred, who died in hospital at Bradford on September 10, 1968, after a short illness, aged 66, rendered admirable service as a batsman and first-rate outfielder, particularly on the leg boundary, while a professional for Yorkshire between 1926 and 1947, during which period the Northern county eight times carried off the Championship. Specially strong in off-side strokes and possessing eminently sound defence, he generally exercised that restraint which one has learned to expect from Yorkshire opening batsmen. With competition so strong at the time, he did not gain a regular place in the side till 1932 when the illness of P. Holmes made way for him, and in scoring 1,000 runs "he thoroughly justified that recognition", as *Wisden* said of him.

In all first-class fixtures during his career Barber, a product of Yorkshire Council cricket, scored 16,402 runs—15,289 of them for Yorkshire—for an average of 34.38 and of his 29 centuries, he hit 27 for his county. Eight times he exceeded 1,000 runs, his most prolific season being that of 1935, when he reached an aggregate of 2,147 and an average of 42.09. His four three-figure scores that year included his highest, 285 off the Surrey bowling at Bramall Lane, Sheffield. He also hit 248 against Kent at Headingley in 1934, when he and Sir Leonard Hutton, by scoring 267 for the first wicket, saved their side from an awkward situation after facing a first-innings deficit of 148.

Barber shared in seven other opening partnerships of 100 or more for Yorkshire, four of them with A. Mitchell, with whom he became the natural successor to Holmes and Sutcliffe. He also took part in six other stands of 200, of which the largest was 346 in four and a half hours with M. Leyland, against Middlesex at Sheffield in 1932—a record for the Yorkshire second wicket which still holds good. Barber hit 162 and Leyland, despite the necessity of employing a runner because of lameness, 189.

Twice Barber appeared for England, against H. F. Wade's South African team of 1935 at Leeds and at Old Trafford; he was one of six Yorkshiremen to represent their country during the season. He toured Australasia with the M.C.C. team captained by E. R. T. Holmes in 1935–36, scoring 797 runs, average 41.94. Apart from an innings of 91 against Queensland at Brisbane, he did not altogether fulfil expectations in the Australian part of the tour, but, as senior professional, he found his best form in New Zealand. Besides 173, 93 and 60 in four representative games with New Zealand, in which he obtained 365 runs, average 60.83, he made 116 against Canterbury.

After his retirement, Barber became a coach and groundsman at a school at Harrogate.

W. E. Bowes (in an appreciation of Barber in the *Yorkshire Evening Post*) wrote: "Perhaps even more than Sir Leonard Hutton, he was a text-book player".

BARBER, Col. William Douglas, who died on April 26, 1971, aged 89, was the oldest living Nottinghamshire player. He kept wicket for the county during the 1904 season. While at Eton he took part in the match with Winchester in 1900. He later played for the Army. During the First World War, he won the M.C. and was three times Mentioned in Dispatches.

BARBER, William Henry, died in hospital in Coventry on July 23, 1981, aged 74. A fast-medium bowler and useful batsman from Nuneaton, he played five times for Warwickshire, as a professional, between 1927 and 1933. Opening the bowling against Glamorgan in 1933 he took three for 81.

BARBERY, Albert Edward, who died on May 23, 1973, aged 88, played as a fast-medium bowler for Warwickshire in 1906 and 1907 and was also a professional with Leamington C.C. One of the first professional cricketers to play in spectacles, he received a serious injury in the First World War which curtailed his active career. He later did well enough as owner of a village bakery to leave £19,000. He was a former President of the Warwickshire Old Players' Association.

BARBOUR, Dr. Eric Pitty, died at Sydney, on December 7, 1934, in his 44th year. After making a name when 17, he became so good as to score 113 not out for New South Wales against Victoria in January, 1911, and a year later 122 against South Australia. Considering the difficulties experienced in choosing the next team for England he seemed sure of a place but he was passed over. After a fine innings of 146 against Victoria in January, 1913, he made 86 against the Rest of Australia in Victor Trumper's benefit match also played at Sydney. He and Trumper in this game put on 270 together for the eighth partnership—a record for this wicket in Australia. A son of Mr. G. P. Barbour, a member of the Board of Control, Dr. Barbour also exercised considerable influence in Australian cricket and he had many English friends. During the War he played a lot of cricket in Egypt, as well as in England.

BARDSLEY, Robert Vickers, C.M.G., O.B.E., who died suddenly at Pulborough, Sussex, on July 26, 1952, aged 62, played three times for Oxford against Cambridge from 1911 to 1913. Born in 1890, he was in the Shrewsbury XI from 1905 to 1909, being captain in the last three seasons. He headed the school batting and bowling averages in 1907 and again in 1908, when he took 53 wickets, average 17.80. In his first appearance in the University match he hit 71 in 90 minutes, and in the third, despite a damaged finger which nearly cost him his place in the side, he scored 72 in the second Oxford innings, the highest and most brilliant innings of the game. This ended unluckily, for when jumping out to drive he was stumped, the ball, according to *Wisden* of the time, "rebounding from the wicket-keeper's pad or foot." Bardsley also represented his University against Cambridge at billiards in 1911–12 and at golf in 1913. From 1910 he made occasional appearances for Lancashire with little success. He served in the Sudan Political Service, and was Governor of the Blue Nile Province from 1928 until he retired in 1932.

BARDSLEY, Warren, who died in Sydney on January 20, 1954, aged 70, was one of the greatest left-handed batsmen produced by Australia. Only two of his countrymen, Sir Donald Bradman and A.L. Hassett, surpassed his record of 53 centuries—29 of them scored in England—in first-class matches. As a stylist, Bardsley compared favourably with any left-hander of his day. His upright stance and eminently straight bat never failed to exercise a special charm upon spectators, and he used his feet to perfection while employing a wide variety of strokes. If less brilliant in cutting behind point than Clem Hill, he was stronger in hitting past cover and to leg and he possessed a specially powerful straight drive.

Born at Warren, New South Wales, on December 7, 1884, he was named after his home town. Educated at Forest Lodge Superior Public School, he played as a youngster for Glebe in the First Grade Competition, displaying such skill that by 1903–04 he found a place in the New South Wales team which met Queensland at Brisbane. It was in 1907–08, however, that he first attained real prominence. Then, in the second fixture between New South Wales and the M.C.C. Touring Team, he scored a splendid 108, so that when rain, preventing cricket on the sixth day, caused the match to be left drawn, the State needed 12 runs for victory and had one wicket to fall.

Thenceforward Bardsley did not look back. In the 1908–09 season he scored in nine innings 748 runs, including 119 against South Australia, 192 against Victoria and, for the Australian XI against the Rest, 264.

Despite these feats, he was not among the first men chosen to go to England in 1909, but on that tour he at once found his finest form and retained it. When hitting 136 and 130 from the England bowling at the Oval he became the first player of a list now grown to 14 to hit two separate hundreds in a Test match. In that game, too, he and S.E. Gregory, by sharing an opening partnership of 180, set up a record for Australia against England. His total runs during the summer numbered 2,180, including seven centuries, average 46.39. When next coming to England in 1912 he did even better with eight centuries, an aggregate of 2,441 and an average of 51.98. Again in 1921, this time with nine three-figure innings among his achievements, he exceeded 2,000 runs and, as vice-captain of H.L. Collins's 1926 side, he obtained his third century against England. This was a memorable effort of 193 for which he carried his bat through an innings lasting over six and a half hours and realising 383. No higher individual score had at that time been registered in a Test match at Lord's, and of it *Wisden* said: "Had Bardsley accomplished nothing else he would have justified his selection."

Altogether Bardsley represented Australia in 41 Test matches, scoring 2,469 runs in 66 innings, average 40.47. Besides the tours of England, he visited New Zealand in 1909–10 and 1923–24, South Africa in 1921–22, and also played cricket in Fiji, U.S.A., Canada and Bermuda.

Sir Jack Hobbs said of Bardsley: "I cannot imagine a nicer type of fellow. I probably played against him as often as any Englishman and he was one of the best left-handers of the upright, classical school that I have ever seen. I would not like to choose between him and Clem Hill as the best Australian left-hander, because their styles were so different. Clem crouched more and was more aggressive."

BARDSWELL, Gerald, R., died on December 29, 1906, at New Orleans. Born on December 7, 1873, he was in his 34th year. Some months back he underwent a severe operation, but it was believed that he had completely recovered and the news of his death gave a painful shock to his many friends in Manchester where he was well-known and highly popular. Although he never took a leading position among amateur cricketers, Mr. Bardswell had a fairly long and by no means undistinguished career. He learnt the game at Uppingham, and was about the best bowler in the school XI for three years in succession, taking 55 wickets for less than 10 runs apiece in 1891, 66 wickets for 11 runs each in 1892, and 35 wickets in 1893. He then went up to Oxford, and his bowling—right-hand medium pace with a high delivery—at once gained him his Blue. He helped to win the University match for Oxford in 1894, obtaining eight wickets for 101 runs, and his season's work for the University showed an excellent result—40 wickets, with an average of 16. After 1894, however, he lost his bowling, and thenceforward he had to depend upon his batting and his exceptionally fine fielding at slip. It is not too much to say that among the short-slips of his day no one surpassed him. A damaged hand kept him out of the University match in 1895, but in the following year he had a share in gaining for Oxford a memorable victory. The match was the one in which such excitement was caused by E. B. Shine—acting under the instructions of his captain, Frank Mitchell—bowling no-balls to prevent Oxford following on. In the end Oxford had to get 330 in the last innings, and they won the game by four wickets, G. O. Smith making 132. Bardswell was in at the finish, scoring 33 not out and getting the winning hit. In 1897 he was captain at Oxford, but this time he was on the losing side at Lord's, Cambridge—much the stronger XI of the two—gaining an easy victory by 179 runs. For a little time in 1899 Mr. Bardswell was captain of the Lancashire XI, but owing to business claims he soon found himself compelled to give up County Cricket. At the time of his death he was on the Committee of the Marylebone Club, and also on the Lancashire Committee.

BARING, Frank Albert, who died in Melbourne in December, 1961, aged 69, was a prominent cricketer in Australia between 1911 and 1923 and after the death of Victor Trumper in 1915 was regarded as the best batsman in the country on bad pitches. Tall, he used his reach in playing fast bowling and drove and pulled with splendid power. He was also a useful off-break bowler. He played most of his cricket with the East Melbourne Club and represented Victoria in a number of matches, scoring 1,846 for the State at an average of 34.18 with a highest innings of 131 against New South Wales in 1918–19. He also played football for Victoria and baseball for East Melbourne.

BARKER, Kenneth Edgar Mylne, who died on August 6, 1938, aged 60, went from Uppingham to Cambridge but did not get his Blue. He played once for Surrey, was well-known in club cricket, and appeared in the London County XI with W. G. Grace.

BARLOW, Alfred, who died on May 9, 1983, aged 67, kept wicket very neatly for Lancashire in 74 matches between 1947 and 1951. He was capped in 1950, a year in which Lancashire shared the Championship with Surrey, and in the winter of 1950–51 he toured India with a strong Commonwealth side. All told he made 104 catches and 46 stumpings, most of the stumpings coming off Tattersall and Hilton. Quite a useful tail-end-batsman, he was prominent in the tied match between Lancashire and Hampshire at Bournemouth in 1947. When Hill of Hampshire began the final over Lancashire's last pair, Ikin and Barlow, were together, with the scores level. In trying a sharp single Barlow was run out.

BARLOW, Herbert Randle Brereton, who died at Bloemfontein on March 10, 1942, aged 59, was prominent as player and administrator of sport in the Orange Free State for many years. He played for the province at various times from 1904 to 1922.

BARLOW, Richard Gorton, who had been in failing health for some months, died on July 31, 1919, at his home at Blackpool in his 70th year. Unlike many famous professional players who have helped to make Lancashire great in the cricket field, Barlow belonged to the county by the closest of ties. He was born at Barrow Bridge, Bolton, on May 28, 1850. Cricket was from first to last the absorbing interest of his life. He played the game from early boyhood and long after his active career had ended—so recently indeed as 1914—he expressed his willingness to meet any man of his age at single wicket. He was then full of vigour and seemed to have many years of healthy life in store for him. He played his first match for Lancashire at Sheffield in 1871 and his last in 1891, both games, curiously enough, being against Yorkshire. Making a good start, he scarcely knew what it was to have a set-back till the time came for him to retire from the county XI. No county ever had a more zealous worker. He kept himself in such first-rate physical condition that he was always capable of doing his best and no day was too long for him. As an all-round man he was one of the best of his day. He stood first among the batsmen of the extremely steady or stonewalling school, and even if he had not been able to get a run he would for his bowling and fielding have been worth a place in almost any XI. In batting he used forward play for purposes of defence to an extent unknown in these days, but his judgment of length was so perfect, and his eye so sure that bowlers found it a terribly hard job to bowl him out. In the ordinary way he was not a batsman one would have journeyed 10 miles to see, but when he opened a Lancashire innings—as he did hundreds of times—with Mr. Hornby, he became a figure of extreme interest. His defence and his captain's brilliancy formed a combination fascinating to all lovers of cricket. Of his doings for Lancashire with bat and ball one could write pages. Some of his best feats are set out in detail below. As a bowler—left-hand medium pace—he placed implicit faith in accuracy of length and sent down very few bad balls, but he could not be described as at all mechanical. He was full of resource, he always had a fair amount of spin, and he was quick to discover a batsman's weak points.

Barlow played seven times for England against Australia in this country—at the Oval in 1882 and at Lord's, the Oval, and Manchester, in 1884 and 1886. He made no big score in these matches, but his partnership with A. G. Steel was the turning point of the game at Lord's in 1884, and at Manchester, in 1886, his steadiness pulled us through when the Australian bowlers were in deadly form on a slightly crumbled wicket. Moreover he took seven wickets for 44 runs in Australia's second innings. In 1884 at Trent Bridge, for the North of England against the Australians, Barlow played the game of his life. He scored not out 10 and 101 and took 10 wickets—four for six runs and six for 42. It is on record that when the North started their second innings on a slow and nasty wicket, Spofforth said, "Give me the ball: they won't get more than 60." As events turned out they got 255, Barlow and Flowers putting on 158 runs together after five wickets had fallen for 53. At the end of that afternoon Barlow was a very happy man. Barlow paid three visits to Australia, going out with Shaw and Shrewsbury in 1881–82, with the Hon. Ivo Bligh (now Lord Darnley), in 1882–83, and again with Shaw and Shrewsbury in 1886–87. The climate evidently suited him for in the three tours he did not stand out of a single match. A very appreciative notice of Barlow in the *Manchester Guardian* ended with the following statement: "In private life Barlow was a quiet, chatty, neighbourly man. He was thoroughly content with the world and with his own place in it, as a confession he once made shows:—'I don't think that any cricketer has enjoyed his cricketing career better than I have done, and if I had my time to come over again I should certainly be what I have been all my life—a professional cricketer'."— S.H.P.

CHIEF BATTING PERFORMANCES
(a)—Three Figure Innings

100	Lancashire v. Cheshire, at Stockport	1884
119	Lancashire v. Leicestershire, at Leicester	1884
101	North v. Australians, at Nottingham	1884
117	Lancashire v. M.C.C. and G., at Lord's	1885
108	Lancashire v. Gloucestershire, at Manchester	1885
113	Players v. Australians, at Nottingham	1886
106	Lancashire v. Cheshire, at Stockport	1889

(b)—Carrying Bat Through Completed Innings

26	Lancashire v. Kent, at Maidstone	1874
34	Lancashire v. Notts, at Nottingham	1876
34	Lancashire v. M.C.C. and G., at Lord's	1878
10	Lancashire v. Yorkshire, at Manchester	1880
66	Lancashire v. Australians, at Manchester	1882
5	Lancashire v. Notts, at Nottingham	1882
44	Lancashire v. Notts, at Liverpool	1882
58	Lancashire v. Gloucestershire, at Clifton	1882
62	Lancashire v. Gloucestershire, at Clifton	1885
29	Lancashire v. Leicestershire, at Leicester	1889
51	Lancashire v. Kent, at Maidstone	1889
29	Lancashire v. Surrey, at Oval	1890

Against Notts at Liverpool in 1882, he went in first each time, carrying his bat through the first innings and being last out in the second. He thus saw all 20 wickets fall. His scores were 44 not out and 49 run out.

(c)—Various Performances

Lancashire beat Yorkshire at Manchester in 1875 by 10 wickets, scoring 148 without loss in their second innings. Barlow made 50 of the number and A. N. Hornby 78.

In Lancashire's match with Notts, at Nottingham, in 1876, the first wicket fell at 45: A. N. Hornby 44, Barlow 0 not out, bye 1.

Scores 2 runs in 41 mins. Scores 5 runs in 150 mins.	Lancashire v. Sussex, at Manchester	1876
Scores 0 runs in 80 mins. Scores 5 runs in 150 mins.	Lancashire v. Notts, at Nottingham	1882
Scores 17 runs in 150 mins.	Lancashire v. Yorkshire, at Bradford	1874

CHIEF BOWLING PERFORMANCES
(a)—Eight or More Wickets in an Innings

8 for 22	Lancashire v. Yorkshire, at Huddersfield	1878
8 for 29	Lancashire v. Kent, at Manchester	1881
9 for 39	Lancashire v. Sussex, at Manchester	1886
8 for 26	Lancashire v. Notts, at Manchester	1887

(b)—13 or More Wickets in a Match

13 for 48	An England XI v. Cambridge University at Cambridge	1880
13 for 66	Lancashire v. Yorkshire, at Sheffield	1884

(c)—Four or More Wickets for Three Runs or Less Each

6 for 3	Lancashire v. Kent, at Manchester	1878
8 for 22	Lancashire v. Yorkshire, at Huddersfield	1878
7 for 16	An England XI v. Cambridge University, at Cambridge	1880
5 for 12	Lancashire v. Surrey, at Manchester	1880
6 for 3a 9 for 23c	Lancashire v. Derbyshire, at Derby	1881
4 for 7	Lancashire v. Somerset, at Taunton	1882
5 for 10	Lancashire v. Gloucestershire, at Manchester	1883
4 for 6	North v. Australians, at Nottingham	1884
5 for 11	Lancashire v. Surrey, at Oval	1887
5 for 13	Lancashire v. Gloucestershire, at Gloucester	1888
4 for 12	Lancashire v. Oxford University, at Oxford	1889

a Signifies 1st innings; *c* both.

(d)—Unchanged Through Both Completed Innings

With Watson, v. Derbyshire, at Derby	1883
With Briggs, v. Gloucestershire, at Liverpool	1884

(e)—Miscellaneous Feats

3 wkts. in 3 balls, Lancashire v. Derbyshire, at Derby	1881
3 wkts. in 3 balls, Players v. Gentlemen, at Oval	1884

(His victims were "W. G.", J. Shuter and W. W. Read.)

Wicket with 1st ball bowled in 1st class cricket Lancashire v. Yorkshire, at Sheffield	1871
Bowls 60 mins. for one run, Lancashire v. Sussex, at Manchester	1885

Visited Australia three times:—1881–82, 1882–83 and 1886–87.

Played for Lancashire from 1871 to 1891.

Played for Players (v. Gentlemen) from 1876 to 1885.

For England v. Australia	591 runs (aver. 22.73) and 35 wkts. (aver 21.91)
For Lancashire	9,088 runs (aver. 21.48) and 831 wkts. (aver. 12.81)
For Players (v. Gents.)	591 runs (aver. 16.88) and 41 wkts. (aver. 18.58)

Umpired for many seasons.

Author of *Forty Seasons of First-class Cricket*, and part author of *Barlow on Batting and Bowling* and *Pilling on Wicket Keeping*.

BARNARD, Thomas Henry, who died at Kempston Hoo, Bedford, on March 16, 1916, aged 50, was in the Eton XI in 1884 and 1885, in the latter year making 250 runs and being second in the averages to H. Philipson with 27.77. In his four Public School matches he scored 119 runs in five completed innings, his greatest success being to make 28 and 55 not out v. Winchester in 1885. He was described as "An erratic fast bowler, but often very useful; has a splendid old-fashioned style of hitting": he was also a good out-field and sure catch. Since 1886 he had been a member of the M.C.C. For many years he was Secretary of the Oakley Hunt.

BARNARD, The Rev. William, of the Winchester XI of 1843 and 1844, died at Stratford-on-Avon on December 2, 1908. He was born on May 21, 1825, and was therefore in his 84th year at the time of his death. In the four matches in which he appeared against Eton and Harrow he scored only 36 runs with an average of 5.14, although it was his batting which gained him a place in the side. He was a good racquet player, and won the Silver Racquet at Cambridge the year before the matches against Oxford were instituted. For 44 years, 1856 to 1900, he was Vicar of Alveston.

BARNATO, Capt. Woolf, died in a nursing home in London on July 27, 1948, aged 53. Best known for long distance motor-car racing, he occasionally kept wicket for Surrey in the seasons 1928–30. A son of Mr. Barney Barnato, the well-known diamond merchant, he was educated at Charterhouse School and Cambridge.

BARNES, J. R., M.C., died at Grange-over-Sands on July 22, 1945, aged 48. While serving in the R.A.F., pernicious anaemia caused his retirement some six months before he passed away. After leaving Marlborough he served in the R.F.C. during the First World War, being awarded the M.C. for gallantry in France. A Liverpool cotton merchant, he joined the Royal Air Force in 1941 and served as a ground staff flight-lieutenant until demobilised. He averaged 30 for Marlborough in 1914; next season, when captain, 56, and he also headed the bowling averages. Starting for Lancashire in 1919, he scored 831 runs, average 33.24 in 1921, and next year averaged 37.58. His first-class cricket aggregate reached 3,643, average 38, and he sometimes captained the county side. In Lancashire club cricket he met with great success. For Ormskirk in 1927 he averaged 70 with an aggregate of 990, and in 1932 for Liverpool he averaged 105.60 for 11 innings, being five times not out. A free batsman with good style, he was reliable in the field and in his early days bowled effectively.

BARNES, Sidney George, who died suddenly at his home in Sydney on December 16, 1973, aged 57, was both a fine cricketer and a bizarre character. He played, generally as opening batsman, in 13 Test matches for Australia, hitting three centuries, and he and Sir Donald Bradman, each scoring 234, shared a world's record partnership for the fifth wicket in Test cricket when adding 405 against W. R. Hammond's team of 1946–47.

Twice he toured England. In 1938 he was out of the game till towards the end of June, having fractured a wrist playing deck games on the voyage over. Even so, he scored 720 runs in 19 innings for an average of 42.35. His only Test that summer was that at the Oval when Sir Leonard Hutton hit his record-breaking 364.

His second English tour was in 1948, when he stood second in the Australian Test batting figures with an average of 82.25 and in all first-class matches put together an aggregate of 1,354, including three centuries, average 56.41. He hit 141 against England at Lord's. In that tour he came in for much criticism for his custom of fielding at point or short-leg some five feet from the bat and almost on the pitch. R. Pollard, batting for England in the Test at Old Trafford, ended the habit when he hit Barnes in the ribs with the ball from a full-blooded stroke, which resulted in him spending 10 days in hospital. Following that tour Barnes dropped out of cricket for two years and began writing outspoken articles for the newspapers.

Among the peculiar occurrences in Barnes's career was the occasion in 1952 when the umpires turned down his appeal for a catch. Then captaining New South Wales against South Australia at Sydney, he began to lead his side off the field. The umpire ordered their return, whereupon Barnes, though only 20 minutes remained before the tea interval, called for drinks. In 1951–52, though chosen by the selectors for the third Test against the West Indies, he was omitted at the insistence of the Australian Board of Control "on grounds other than cricket ability." He claimed £1,000 damages against the author of a letter to a newspaper on the subject, but the writer withdrew his criticism in court and paid the costs.

Next season, having been passed over by the selectors for a Test against South Africa, Barnes asked to be 12th man for New South Wales at Adelaide. There he came out with the drinks steward, attired in a grey suit with red carnation, carrying a tray with a scent spray, a portable radio and cigars which he offered to the players and umpires. He received a mixed reception from the crowd. After that season he again took to the Press Box.

In a match in England in 1948 after a strong appeal had been turned down by A. Skelding, the umpire, a dog ran on to the field. Barnes captured the animal and carried it to Skelding with the caustic comment: "Now all you want is a white stick."

He had a brief spell with Burnley, the

Lancashire League club, in 1947, but the contract was ended by mutual consent before the season ended.

SYDNEY FRANCIS BARNES
Born at Smethwick, Staffordshire, April 19, 1873; died at Chadsmoor, Staffordshire, December 26, 1967
By Sir Neville Cardus

Sydney Francis Barnes was the second son of five children of Richard Barnes who spent nearly all his life in Staffordshire and worked for a Birmingham firm for 63 years. The father played only a little cricket and Sydney Barnes averred that he never had more than three hours' coaching, but he practised assiduously to perfect the leg break after learning the off break from the Smethwick professional, Billy Ward of Warwickshire.

Most cricketers and students of the game belonging to the period in which S. F. Barnes played were agreed that he was the bowler of the century. Australians as well as English voted him unanimously the greatest. Clem Hill, the famous Australian left-handed batsman, who in successive Test innings scored 99, 98, 97 v. A. C. MacLaren's England team of 1901–02, told me that on a perfect wicket Barnes could swing the new ball in and out "very late", could spin from the ground, pitch on the leg stump and miss the off. At Melbourne, in December 1911, Barnes in five overs overwhelmed Kelleway, Bardsley, Hill and Armstrong for a single. Hill was clean bowled by him. "The ball pitched outside my leg-stump, safe to the push off my pads, I thought. Before I could 'pick up' my bat, my off-stump was knocked silly."

Barnes was creative, one of the first bowlers really to use the seam of a new ball and combine "swing" so subtly with spin that few batsmen could distinguish one from the other. He made a name before a new ball was available to an attack every so many runs or overs. He entered first-class cricket at a time when one ball had to sufffice for the whole duration of the batting side's innings.

He was professional in the Lancashire League when A. C. MacLaren, hearing of his skill, invited him to the nets at Old Trafford. "He thumped me on the left thigh. He hit my gloves from a length. He actually said, 'Sorry, sir!' and I said, 'Don't be sorry, Barnes. You're coming to Australia with me.'" MacLaren on the strength of a net practice with Barnes chose him for his England team in Australia of 1901–02. In the first Test of that rubber, Barnes took five for 65 in 35 overs, one ball, and one for 74 in 16

overs. In the second Test he took six for 42 and seven for 121 and he bowled 80 six-ball overs in this game. He broke down, leg strain, in the third Test and could bowl no more for MacLaren, who winning the first Test, lost the next four of the rubber.

Barnes bowled regularly for Lancashire in 1902, taking more than a hundred wickets in the season, averaging around 20. *Wisden* actually found fault with his attack this year, stating that he needed to cultivate an "off break". In the late '90s he had appeared almost anonymously in the Warwickshire XI.

Throughout his career he remained mysteriously aloof, appearing in the full sky of first-class cricket like a meteor—declaring the death of the most princely of batsmen! He preferred the reward and comparative indolence of Saturday league matches to the daily toil of the county tourney. Here is one of the reasons of his absence from the England XI between 1902 and 1907. He didn't go to Australia as one of P. F. Warner's team of 1903–04 and took no part of the 1905 England v. Australia rubber. The future historian of cricket may well gape and wonder why, in the crucial Test of 1902, Barnes didn't play for England at Manchester, where the rubber went to Australia by three runs only.

Barnes had bowled for England at Sheffield in the third and previous Test, taking six for 49 and one for 50. It is as likely as conjecture about cricket ever can be likely that had Barnes taken part in the famous Manchester Test of 1902 England wouldn't have lost the rubber by a hair's breadth.

He was in those days not an easy man to handle on the field of play. There was a Mephistophelian aspect about him. He didn't play cricket out of any "green field" starry-eyed idealism. He rightly considered that his talents were worth estimating in cash values. In his old age he mellowed, yet remained humorously cynical. Sir Donald Bradman argued that W. J. O'Reilly must have been a greater bowler than Barnes because he commanded every ball developed in Barnes's day—plus the "googly". I told Barnes of Bradman's remark. "It's quite true," he said, "I never bowled the 'googly.'" Then with a glint in his eye he added, "I never needed it."

Against Australia he took 106 wickets, average 21.58. Only Trumble and Peel have improved on these figures in Tests between England and Australia (I won't count Turner's 101 wickest at 16.53 because he bowled in conditions not known to Barnes and Trumble). Barnes had no opportunities to pick up easy victims. He played only against Australia and South Africa and, in all Test matches, his haul was 189 at 16.43 each. On matting in South Africa when South Africa's batsmanship, at its greatest, was represented by H. W. Taylor, A. D. Nourse, L. J. Tancred, J. W. Zulch, in 1913–14, he was unplayable, with 49 wickets in four Tests at 10.93 each. It was said he refused to play in the fifth match because he contended the South Africans had not carried out their promise of special reward if he took part in the tour. In the second Test, at Johannesburg, Barnes took 17 wickets for 159, a record which stood until 1956 when Laker laid low Australia at Old Trafford with his unique figures of 19 for 90.

Yet against Barnes's fantastically swinging, bouncing, late-turning attack on that 1913–14 tour, "Herbie" Taylor scored 508 runs, average 50.80, perhaps the most skilful of all Test performances by a batsman. Barnes was a man of character. At Sydney on the 1911–12 tour, J. W. H. T. Douglas opened the England attack using the new ball with Frank Foster. Barnes was furious. He sulked as he sent down 35 overs for three wickets and 107 runs (in the match he took only four for 179). England lost by 146 runs.

At Melbourne, Australia batted first and Barnes this time had the new ball. We all know with what results. Australia suffered defeat—and also in the ensuing three games. The destruction wreaked by Barnes, and on all his great days, was mostly done by the ball which, bowled from a splendid height, seemed to swing in to the leg stump then spin away from the pitch, threatening the off stump. Barnes assured me that he actually turned the ball by "finger twist". The wonder of his career is that he took 77 of his 106 Australian Test wickets on the wickets of Australia when they were flawless and the scourge of all ordinarily good bowlers. He clean bowled Victor Trumper for 0 at Sydney in the 1907–08 rubber; then Fielder and J. N. Crawford in the following Test dismissed Trumper for a "pair", so Trumper was out for 0 in three successive Test innings.

Barnes remained a deadly bowler long after he went out of first-class cricket. So shrewdly did he conserve his energy that in 1928 when he was in his mid-fifties, the West Indies team of that year faced him in a club match and unanimously agreed he was the best they had encountered in the season.

For Staffordshire, in his 56th year, he took 76 wickets at 8.21 each. Round about this period a young player, later to become famous in international company, was one of the Lancashire Second XI playing against Staffordshire. His captain won the toss and two Lancashire lads went forth to open the innings against Barnes. As this colt was number six in the batting order he put on his blazer and was about to leave the pavilion to watch Barnes "from behind". But his captain told him to go back to the dressing room and "get on his pads". "But," said the colt, "I'm not in until number six and I'd like to look at Barnes." His captain insisted. The young colt returned to the dressing room. "And there," he said, "there were four of us all padded up waiting. And we were all out in the middle and back again in half an hour."

Barnes had a splendid upright action, right arm straight over. He ran on easy strides, not a penn'orth of energy wasted. He fingered a cricket ball sensitively, like a violinist his fiddle. He always attacked. "Why do these bowlers today send down so many balls the batsman needn't play?" he asked while watching a Test match many years ago. "I didn't. I never gave 'em any rest." His hatchet face and his suggestion of physical and mental leanness and keenness were part of Barnes's cricket and outlook on the game. He was relentless, a chill wind of antagonism blew from him on the sunniest day. As I say, he mellowed in full age and retirement. He came to Lord's and other grounds for Test matches, even in his 95th year, leading blind Wilfred Rhodes about. And to the end of his life he worked for his living, drawing up legal and other documents for Staffordshre County Council in the most beautiful copperplate writing he learned as a boy.

As we think of the unsmiling destroyer of all the batsmen that came his way, let us also remember Barnes immortalised in that lovely verse of Alan Ross:

"Then, elbows linked, but straight as sailors
On a tilting deck, they move. One, square-
*   shouldered as a tailor's*
Model, leans over whispering in the other's
*   ear:*
'Go easy, Steps here. This end bowling'.
Turning, I watch Barnes guide Rhodes into
*   fresher air,*
As if to continue an innings, though Rhodes
*   may only play by ear."*

Other tributes to Barnes included:

Arthur Gilligan, President of M.C.C.: "He will be mourned by cricketers the world over. He was the finest bowler there ever was and a magnificent personality after his playing days."

S. C. Griffith, Secretary of M.C.C.: "The

extraordinary thing about him was that all his contemporaries considered him the greatest bowler. There was never any doubts in their minds. This must have been unique."

Wilfred Rhodes, who celebrated his 90th birthday in October, 1967, one of the greatest of cricket's all-rounders, and one of the few remaining contemporaries of Barnes in the England side: "Barnes was a very fine medium-paced bowler, the best I ever played with. He had a lovely run-up to the wicket, carrying the ball in his left hand until he was only two paces from the crease and then tranferring it to his right. He kept a perfect length and direction and, if you wanted to field close to the wicket say, at short leg, you could stand up to the batsman without any fear. He was quite a decent bat, far better than he was made out to be and too good for a number eleven. He was also a very good fielder."

Herbert Strudwick, the old Surrey and England wicket-keeper (now 88): "He was the greatest bowler I ever kept wicket to, for he sent down something different each ball of the over. He could turn it either way in remarkable fashion and I shall never forget keeping to him for the first time in a Gentle-men v. Players match at the Oval. His opening delivery pitched outside the leg stump and flew over the top of the off stump. I said to a team-mate: 'What sort of bowler have we here?' I soon found out. Sydney could do almost any-thing with the ball. On matting wickets in South Africa where I toured with him, he was practically unplayable."

Barnes took 14 wickets for 13 runs, less than one run apiece, playing for Stafford-shire against Cheshire in 1909.

Against Northumberland he took 16 for 93 in one day. Even an All-Indian team could barely muster two runs a wicket against him in 1911 when he took 14 for 29.

Fifteen years before he was selected for England he signed for Rishton in the Lanca-shire League for £3 10s. a week, which in-cluded pay for his duties as a groundsman. He received an extra 10s. 6d. for taking six wickets or more in a match, and 7s. 6d. for scoring 50.

Mr. Leslie Duckworth, in his admirable book: *S. F. Barnes—Master Bowler*, pub-lished in July 1967, states that Barnes in all cricket took 6,229 wickets, average 8.33 as follows:

SUMMARY OF ALL MATCHES

	Overs	Maidens	Runs	Wickets	Aver.
Test matches	1313.3	358	3106	189	16.43
County Cricket	1931.2	633	4456	226	19.71
Other first-class matches	2028.3	620	4600	304	15.13
For Staffordshire	5457.3	1647	11754	1441	8.15
League and Club	12802	3532	27974	4069	6.03
	23509.3	6784	51890	6229	8.33

BARNES, William. One of the best cricke-ters of his generation, passed away on Friday, March 24, 1899, William Barnes, after lying seriously ill for three weeks, dying at his home at Mansfield Woodhouse. Born on May 27, 1852, he was still a comparatively young man. His career in the Notts XI was exceptionally brilliant, and extended over a long period of time. He first found a place in the team in 1875, and did not play his last county match till 1894. His powers were then obviously on the wane, and in seven matches he only scored 137 runs. What a great player he was at his best no one who takes any interest in cricket will need to be told. It may indeed be questioned whether Notts ever possessed a more valuable man, for over and above his splendid powers as a batsman he was for many seasons one of the best change bowlers in England. He did not all at once jump to the top of the tree, but his position as one of the leading batsmen of his day was firmly established in 1880, and from that time till 1892 he kept his place in the front rank, appearing regularly for Players against Gentlemen at Lord's and the Oval, and on many occasions representing England against Australia. He took part at the Oval in 1880 in the first England and Australia match ever played in this country, and he was a member of the unhappy team that two years later lost the memorable seven runs match on the same ground.

It was not until after 1882 that it became the custom for the Australians to play three matches against England, and during the tours of 1884, 1886, 1888 and 1890 Barnes was nearly always one of our picked XI. He proved an invaluable partner to Shrewsbury in the 1886 match at Lord's, and contributed in a large degree to England's single innings victory at the Oval in 1888. He first went out to Australia with the Hon. Ivo Bligh's XI in the winter of 1882–83, but did not during that trip play in any way up to his English reputation. However, in subsequent visits to the Colonies with two of Shaw and Shrewsbury's teams he made ample amends for his previous failure, batting so finely that he once beat Shrewsbury in the 11-a-side averages. To do that, as he himself expressed it, he had to play better than he had ever played before. Of his performances for Notts as a batsman a column could be written without by any means exhausting the subject. Not so patient as Shrewsbury or so finished in style as Gunn, he was yet on his good days in quite the same class as those famous players. His method having been mainly formed against bowlers of the modern school, he was especially strong on the off-side. No one could hit harder or better than he did between cover point and mid-off. He was essentially a punishing player, and liked to keep things moving.

Once in the course of conversation at Lord's he said that some careful batsmen—he was referring especially to Mr. A.P. Lucas—were content to play just the same strict game when they had made a hundred runs as when they first went to the wickets, but that he himself always wanted to do something more than that. It may be that by acting on this principle he sometimes cut his innings short, but the spectators at Lord's, Trent Bridge, and elsewhere reaped the benefit in nearly always seeing a bright attractive display when he was in form. Though he played scores of bigger innings for Notts he rarely did anything finer, all things considered, than when he and Gunn practically won the Bank Holiday match against Surrey at the Oval in 1892. Lohmann and Lockwood were bowling their best on a far from perfect wicket and the cricket shown by Gunn and Barnes during a partnership of over an hour and a quarter will never be forgotten by anyone who was so fortunate as to be present. On both sides it was, indeed, a battle of giants.

BARNETT, Benjamin Arthur, A.M. The quiet but much liked Australian wicket-keeper of the late 1930s, whose long career covered three distinct phases as player and administrator, died suddenly at Newcastle, New South Wales on June 29, 1979, while visiting an old Army friend. A product of Scotch College, Melbourne, Barnett moved directly from the school team into the Hawthorn East Melbourne First XI in 1927, his batting at first being supplemented by

slow bowling which was soon dropped in favour of wicket-keeping. Within two years, he was in the Victorian side and scored 131 against Tasmania before succeeding J.L. Ellis in 1929 to remain the state's regular wicket-keeper until the outbreak of the Second World War. Deputy to W.A. Oldfield on the 1934 English tour and again in South Africa in 1935–36, Barnett succeeded the long-serving Oldfield on his retirement after the M.C.C. visit to Australia in 1936–37. He thus became wicket-keeper for the 1938 English tour and, although not possessed of the skill and finesse of his distinguished predecessor, Barnett performed creditably and with the efficient unobtrusive style, notably neat in taking slow bowling, which marked his long career. A useful left-hand batsman, Barnett scored 2,773 runs for Victoria at an average of 28.88, including an undefeated 104 and 92 in his second-last Sheffield Shield match before going on active service in 1940. He was a prisoner-of-war at Changi for several years, yet maintained contact and retained his position as a vice-president of the Hawthorn East Melbourne Club throughout this time. His long association with the club continued until his death, Barnett having presented it with his cricket gear only a year earlier.

Barnett returned to Hawthorn East Melbourne but did not play any post-war Sheffield Shield cricket. However, on transferring to the UK in 1940 to represent a large Australian pharmaceutical group, he entered on the two further phases of his career—as a successful playing member for Buckinghamshire and as a London administrator for major sporting and Services organisations. Barnett first played for the minor county in 1951 and continued to do so as often as business pressures permitted until final retirement in 1964, then aged 56. In one memorable season—1952—Barnett supplemented his own first-rate batting and wicket-keeping with inspiring captaincy, Buckinghamshire being the first county side, other than a Second XI, to win the Championship since 1946. Barnett then led a Commonwealth team to India in the following English winter. In all, Barnett scored 3,222 runs and five centuries for the county.

As a first-rate amateur Australian Rules footballer—his club was Old Scotch Collegians—he captained the Victorian side in the days when amateur football was at its peak. During his 20 years in London, Barnett represented Australia as its delegate to the ICC and the International Lawn Tennis Federation, of which he was president from

1969 to 1971. He also performed similar duties with the Imperial Servicemen's Legion. In 1977 he was awarded the Australian Medal for his distinguished services to sport and the community.

BARNETT, Charles Sherborne, who died on November 20, 1962, aged 78, played as a batsman for Gloucestershire from 1904 to 1926, scoring 3,666 runs, average 21.69. His best season was that of 1921 when his aggregate reached 639, average 27.78, and he hit his only two centuries in first-class cricket. His 157 against Essex at Gloucester came after a first innings of 0 and enabled Gloucestershire, after following on 194 behind, to win by 60 runs. In scoring 100 at Bristol, he shared an opening partnership of 189 with A. G. Dipper which helped substantially in the defeat of Derbyshire by 117 runs. One of his most noteworthy performances occurred in 1913 against Worcestershire at Cheltenham. He played a stubborn first innings of 67 and carried his bat for 62 in the second. His son, C. J. Barnett, the England opening batsman, played for the county from 1927 to 1948.

BARNETT, Edgar Playle, a younger brother of Mr. C. S. Barnett, was born at Cheltenham on March 22, 1885, and died at his native place, of meningitis, on January 1, 1922, aged 36. Appearing first for Gloucestershire in 1904, he made many good scores for the county, one of his best innings being 90 v. Somerset at Bristol, in 1906. A year earlier he had carried his bat through the innings for 52 against Yorkshire at Bradford. He was captain of the Cheltenham Town C.C.

BARODA, The Gaekwad of (Maharaj Kumar Shivaji Rao), second son of the Maharajah of Baroda, was born on August 31, 1890, and died in India on December 5, 1919. He was a very promising batsman at Oxford and could keep wicket. For the University in 1911 he made 51 not out v. Kent, and in 1912, after scoring 92 in the Seniors' match, made 62 and 0 v. South Africans and 17 and 12 v. Australians. When it seemed possible he might obtain his Blue, he met with an accident which resulted in concussion of the brain. For All India v. Surrey in 1911 he scored 24 and 25, this being his best performance in London.

BARRATT, Edward, born at Stockton-on-Tees April 21, 1844, died February 27, 1890. Barratt first came prominently before the public in the season of 1872, when he played for North against South in the first important match that ever took place at Prince's Ground. His slow bowling—left hand with a tremendous break—caused a great sensation, and in the South's innings he took eight wickets for 60 runs. After being attached for one season to the ground staff at Lord's, he transferred his services to the Oval, and in due course became qualified for Surrey by residence. His connection with the Surrey XI certainly formed the best and most prosperous part of his career. Playing first for the county in 1876 he remained a regular member of the team till the end of 1884; then, on the appearance of Lohmann and Beaumont, he gradually dropped out of county cricket. Perhaps his best year for Surrey was 1883, when, in the whole of the county's engagements, he took no fewer than 176 wickets. The most remarkable feat he ever accomplished was in the match at the Oval in 1878 between the first Australian team and an XI of the Players of England, on which occasion he took in the first innings of the Australians all the 10 wickets. At his best Barratt was certainly a very fine slow bowler, being able on certain wickets to get more work on the ball than almost any other cricketer of his generation.

BARRATT, Fred, fast bowler and powerful hitter, died in Nottingham General Hospital on January 29, 1947, aged 52. Playing first for the county at Lord's in 1914 against M.C.C., he took eight wickets for 91 runs, but did not bowl when the club followed-on 194 behind. He finished that season with 115 wickets at 21.80 runs apiece. After the war he was slow in finding his old form, but in 1923 he dismissed 101 men at an average of 18.54 and also became a very free scorer. In 1928 he "did the double' with 1,167 runs, average 29.17, and 114 wickets at 25.18 each. The first Nottinghamshire man to accomplish this feat since John Gunn in 1906, he punished all kinds of bowling with great freedom, thanks largely to sure driving. He excelled against Glamorgan at Trent Bridge, hitting up 110 in 85 minutes; and at Coventry 139, also not out, off the Warwickshire bowlers. W. Walker helped to add 196 in 85 minutes, a short boundary giving Barratt such an opportunity to exercise his strength that he hit seven sixes and 18 fours. Nottinghamshire declared with 656 for three wickets, then the highest total for the loss of so few men. He reached Test honours in 1929 at Old Trafford against South Africa, but did little, two wickets for 38 runs being his reward while men of less pace were supreme. Going on tour with the M.C.C. side, captained by A. H. H. Gilligan, in the winter of 1930, Barratt, with nine wickets for 93, helped to beat South Australia by 239 runs, and seven Victoria batsmen fell to him for 105, among his victims being W. H. Ponsford and H.L. Hendry, both dismissed very cheaply in each innings. He was not effective in the four Test matches in New Zealand. Altogether in first-class cricket he took 1,126 wickets at 24.27 runs apiece and scored 6,347 runs, average 15.25.

BARRETT, Capt. Edward Ivo Medhurst, one of the finest as well as one of the hardest hitters to appear for the Army, died on July 11, 1950, following an accident, at the age of 71. Born at Winchester, Barrett showed his ability at Cheltenham, where he was in the XI for three seasons, 1892–94. Even in those days he was a prolific scorer, for he made 205 against Liverpool at Cheltenham, and during his last year, when he was the College captain, he scored 69 and 224 in a House match for Bristowe. In the more important matches against Haileybury, Marlborough and Clifton, he met with only moderate success, and although he gained a place in the Sandhurst XI in 1898 his form was disappointing.

Most cricket followers will remember Barrett by his grand performances for Hampshire, for whom he first played in 1896. Besides possessing a sound defence, he always timed his forcing strokes admirably and hit with tremendous power all round the wicket. Service abroad prevented him assisting the county regularly, and when he finally appeared in 1920 his aggregate in first-class cricket was 3,793, average 32.14. Barrett's best season for Hampshire was 1912. Then he hit three of his six centuries—138 not out against Oxford University, 120 not out against Yorkshire and 119 against Derbyshire—all at Southampton. Against Oxford, Barrett and C. B. Fry (203 not out) put on 264 without being parted.

Another notable partnership was his 321 for the second wicket against Gloucestershire at Southampton in 1920 with G. Brown (120), when his score reached 215. In the same season, against Warwickshire at Portsmouth, Barrett (148) and Brown (151) added 280 together. While serving as Commissioner of Police in Shanghai he scored many runs in matches in the Far East, including games for Shanghai in Japan. Barrett was wounded while serving with the 2nd Lancashire Fusiliers in the South African War, but he came back and played for England as a Rugby footballer in 1903.

BARRETT, Dr. John Edward, born at South Melbourne on October 15, 1866, died at Peak Hill, West Australia, on February 9, 1916. He was educated at Wesley College (Melbourne), and played in turn for South Melbourne, Melbourne University and Sydney University. When only 17 years of age he appeared for XV of Victoria against the 4th Australian team, but his first match for his State XI was against South Australia, at Melbourne, in the following season, when he took five wickets for 31 runs in the first innings and six for 49 in the second. His chief scores for Victoria were 69, 56, and 55 v. New South Wales and 68 not out v. South Australia. His medical studies kept him out of cricket for some time, but he visited England with the Australian team of 1890 and was successful. His highest innings during the tour were 97 v. An England XI at Manchester, and 96 v. Oxford and Cambridge Universities at Portsmouth. In the Test match at Lord's he carried his bat through the innings for 67. As a batsman he was left-handed with very strong defence, almost invariably playing a patient game although he could hit when he chose. He was a useful change bowler, medium-paced, with a high action.

BARRETT, Peter, was killed in a road accident in Hampshire on October 28, 1983, aged 28. As a left-handed opening batsman, he played six times for Hampshire in 1975 and 1976, scoring 138 runs at an average of 12.54. His best score was 26 against Somerset at Bournemouth in 1976 when he and D. R. Turner added 85 for the second wicket. He was a prominent member of the Lymington Cricket Club and scored freely for Hampshire Second XI.

BARRIE, Sir James Matthew, Bart., O.M., who died on June 19, 1937, constantly referred in his writings and speeches to cricket. He was in the XI of the Authors Club who met the Press Club at Lord's in September 1896. In the Press Club XI were H. Vincent Jones, Hubert Preston and S. J. Southerton, all associated for many years with the production of *Wisden*.

BARRINGTON, George Bainbridge, a notable figure in Derbyshire cricket, mainly in connection with the Derbyshire Friars club, of which he was a founder, died on February 26, 1942, aged 84. Poor health prevented him playing much at Repton, but when 19 he made a name in club cricket, and remained a member of Derbyshire Friars until his death removed the last of the original members. In club cricket he scored 44,065 runs, with a highest innings of 220, 60 centuries, and an average of 31.63. He made 190 in a total of 742 by the Friars at Derby in 1881, the record total at that time. First chosen for Derbyshire in the match against W. L. Murdoch's 1880 Australian XI, he scored 24 when the county followed-on, and his was the best effort. Barrington took part in 24 matches for the county altogether, but met with only moderate success, his best innings in an aggregate of 440 being 50 and his average less than 10. He could bowl slows effectively, earned fame as a clever and considerate captain, while he often undertook the duty of umpire when compelled to give up more strenuous activities.

KENNETH FRANK BARRINGTON

AN APPRECIATION
By Robin Marlar

There should be no need for reticence in anyone paying tribute to Ken Barrington. He died of a heart attack in his hotel room at the Holiday Inn in Barbados on March 14, 1981, the Saturday night of the Barbados Test, while serving as assistant-manager on the England tour of the West Indies. As a player, as a friend, as a businessman and latterly as a leader of England's cricketers in the field, he was a man who always did what he could and, when the chips were on the table for all to see, one who could be relied upon to give of his best, his uttermost. The world and especially the cricketing world cannot ask for more. That is why Ken Barrington, master of the malaprop, the man who slept not like a log but "like a lark", commanded such affection all over the world. His widow, Ann, accompanied him on some of his later trips, and it is good that Ann is still involved in the game through the Lord's Taverners, to whom Ken gave so much.

Yet reticence there is, and the hesitation is on his family's account in recalling the circumstances of Ken's tragically premature death at the age of 50. However, *Wisden* is a book of record, and historians sometimes find that its early pages tell the facts but less than the whole truth.

To my mind, the story of Ken's death is as heroic as so many of his innings. It came as a great shock in the spring of 1969 to learn that the chest pains which had led him to withdraw from a double-wicket competition in Melbourne had in fact been a heart attack. After due reflection, taking into account not only his family but the fact that, at 38, batting in Test matches, always Ken's particular forte, was not going to get easier, Ken Barrington retired. Immediately the cares of carrying England's rickety batting through the uncertain and far from satisfying '60s slipped off his shoulders, like some leaden cloak. As he took to the village greens of charity cricket and to the golf courses where his game was good enough to be successfully competitive—and therefore a source of pleasure to a man who hated to be beaten—Ken Barrington's step seemed lighter and his stature in cricket enhanced. His admirers, both far and near, began to realise just how much private effort had gone into coping with "chuckers" and bouncers, as well as the vagaries of form and the whims of selectors.

None the less, a heart attack is a warning, a red light that never joins with amber and turns to green. Although he had managed tours to India, Pakistan and New Zealand, and indeed had had the well-deserved honour of leading the England party at the Melbourne Centenary Test, nothing in his managerial career had tested him quite like this final West Indian ordeal. As a player he had not only plundered bowlers on the great Indian sub-continent but, the son of a soldier who might well in other times have done tours of India of a different nature, he established such a good-humoured relationship there that win or lose, come triumph or disaster, the pressures of touring were easily absorbed. In Australia, where the results mattered more, his role was that of coach, so that the burdens were shared first with Doug Insole and then with Alec Bedser.

He was playing that same familiar part in the West Indies. Ironically, he had not been one of the early selections, but as an old player scarred in earlier wars against Hall and Griffith, he knew better than most the perils that a new manager, Alan Smith, and an inexperienced captain, Ian Botham, were flying into as they took on the world champions with their fast bowling quartet in the increasingly stormy Caribbean. In Guyana the heavy and persistent rain meant that the practice sessions which were his charge were suspended. They had been difficult in smaller islands like Antigua and St. Vincent in the early weeks of the tour. And then he had to take the team, badly defeated in the first Test and now with their morale increasingly affected by the start of the Jackman affair, as well as their collective lack of practice and form, to the one-day beating at Berbice, while Alan Smith began to play one of his best innings with the politicians. The events of those few days deeply disturbed Barrington. He was also worried about Ann's imminent arrival if the tour was to be cancelled.

But once the party arrived safely in Barbados he seemed to relax. My own last, long and treasured conversation with him was in the happy atmosphere of a Cunarder's bridge, a party in the harbour which he himself had organised. Whatever he felt, he was full of hope for the more distant future, his absolute faith in the ability of Botham and Gatting made more significant by the summer of '81. He knew there were gaps in the England side, but he was old enough in the ways of cricket to know that they are not easily filled.

It was a little thing, at least in the context of that global conversation, that piled all the pressure back on to this caring man. At fielding practice it was Barrington who hit the ball that split Gooch's hand. Gooch was due to bat that day, and in fact played better than anyone—as he told me, without too much discomfort. However, Ken took it badly, as he was bound to do, but it was the way in which he said to Bernard Thomas, "I didn't mean to hurt him", that in retrospect gave the party's medical superintendent the first indication that events were getting out of proportion, upsetting the nervous balance. It was that night, with the Barringtons ready for bed, that the attack struck Ken down. Ann Barrington summoned Bernard Thomas who was next door, and he knew at once that the attack had been instantaneously fatal. Next morning, when the team stood in Ken's memory, there were many tears.

My own first encounter with Ken Barrington was in 1948 when I was a boy at Harrow. Tom Barling, the new school coach, brought over from the Oval, where he had not long ceased to play for Surrey, a young leg-spinner from Reading with a West Country burr in his voice. The intention was not only to give us practice against a type of bowling that Harrow were likely to meet in the match against Eton at Lord's but also to show us what a *proper* cricketer in the making looked like. We were both 17. From then on his career in cricket progressed with its ration of setbacks until he became a record-breaking Test batsman, proudest of all in his unique achievement of scoring a century on every Test ground in England and in every Test-playing country.

As *Wisden* is a chronicle and as this was a man who rated only the best, it is not inappropriate that the essay on him as one of the Five Cricketers of the Year in the 1960 edition should have been written by Norman Preston and the piece on his retirement by John Woodcock, Preston's successor as Editor, in the 1970 edition. It is appropriate, too, to add to those assessments of his playing ability his ever-maturing skill as a leg-spinner. No-one ever bowled more enthusiastically in the nets on tour than Barrington, and whether they realised it or not the England players who faced him were getting practice against a player who might have done the double in the 1930s, a decade less demanding at Test level than the 1960s.

It is with his career in cricket during the last 10 years of his life that this eulogy is chiefly concerned. It was at Adelaide during the difficult Australian tour of 1974–75 that Barrington first began to believe that he had a contribution to make as a coach at the highest level. He was brought up in a generation which believed as an act of faith that once a cricketer had played at Test level he knew it all. How else could he have been selected? Furthermore, and this is still a more prevalent attitude than Barrington liked, a player who makes as much of a fetish about practising as Boycott is regarded as a freak. As one who had to work out his technique, to subordinate under a layer of discipline the stroke-making ability he had acquired in his early days, Barrington by the time he retired was a batsman who, if he never knew it all, was a scholar (as well as a gentleman) compared to the players he now saw trying to cope with Lillee and Thomson at their devastating best. More than once Barrington himself had had to change his approach both in style and mind, and so he was ideally suited to the task of developing younger talent and skills.

Not every captain appreciates the need for such a role; or knows how to put such available experience to its best use. Ironically, it was on his last tour that Barrington really came to fulfil himself in this the last, and to my mind, most difficult of his cricketing lives. By that time he had mastered the art of subordinating self and position without losing respect or the power to contribute. "He would get me a cup of tea, suggest something which I'd reject probably because I was tired, but then I'd do it and usually it worked." This was Ian Botham during his apprentice days as captain. To the generation that is coming to full maturity Ken Barrington had become as important as the maypole; something solid. He was the "Colonel" around whom a team of cricketers could revolve while playing no part in the dance himself.

Like the maypole he was, too, a source of great happiness, with that rare gift of turning events into comic sketches as they happened. The rat hunt in the Ritz at Hyderabad is now part of cricketing legend. Some wretched rodent, unaware of the niceties of protocol, had eaten the shoulder out of the manager's England blazer in its search for nesting materials. By the time the "Colonel's" army was assembled, the entire staff of the hotel and all its brushes and brooms were ready to go into action. The villain was struck but not apprehended, and after such a warning honour was seen to have been satisfied on all sides.

Now that he is gone, it is possible that the role he created and played may be forgotten through want of a successor. But Ken gave so much to cricket in the 1970s that he had left a few campaigners for the cause for the remainder of the 1980s. Even now as Gooch starts or finishes a drive or Gatting hooks, a memory of Barrington the batsman is stirred. For a coach there is no finer memorial that that. It is the man, though, that his contemporaries will miss; and for this one, at least, the hole that he began to dig on the Sixth Form Ground at Harrow more than 30 years ago is never going to be filled.

CAREER DETAILS

The following figures first appeared in a comprehensive analysis of the career of K. F. Barrington in the Wisden *of 1970.*

BATTING

In England

Season	Matches	Inns	Not Outs	Runs	Highest Inns	100s	50s	Avge	Ct
1953	9	14	1	237	85	0	1	18.23	4
1954	19	25	4	845	108*	3	3	40.23	16
1955	35	55	7	1,580	135*	2	9	32.91	21
1956	31	54	10	1,323	109*	2	6	30.06	20
1957	35	53	11	1,642	136	6	7	39.09	64
1958	34	45	9	1,147	101*	1	5	31.86	55
1959	32	52	6	2,499	186	6	13	54.32	45
1960	31	53	9	1,878	126	2	16	42.68	22
1961	24	42	7	2,070	163	4	15	59.14	30
1962	29	46	8	1,865	146	6	9	49.07	24
1963	28	45	7	1,568	110*	2	11	41.26	18
1964	22	35	5	1,872	256	4	9	62.40	20
1965	28	41	4	1,384	163	4	6	37.40	36
1966	20	33	6	987	117*	3	4	36.55	18
1967	28	40	10	2,059	158*	6	10	68.63	24
1968	25	43	5	920	75	0	5	24.21	23

In Australia and New Zealand

Season	Matches	Inns	Not Outs	Runs	Highest Inns	100s	50s	Avge	Ct
1962–63	17	27	5	1,763	219*	6	6	80.13	17
1965–66	11	17	3	946	158	3	9	67.57	10

In South Africa

Season	Matches	Inns	Not Outs	Runs	Highest Inns	100s	50s	Avge	Ct
1959–60	2	4	0	165	111	1	0	41.25	3
1960	4	7	0	164	66	0	1	23.42	3
1964–65	13	18	5	1,128	169*	4	4	86.76	7

In West Indies

Season	Matches	Inns	Not Outs	Runs	Highest Inns	100s	50s	Avge	Ct
1959–60	12	19	1	830	128	3	4	46.11	7
1967–68	11	16	3	591	143	2	3	45.46	6

In India

Season	Matches	Inns	Not Outs	Runs	Highest Inns	100s	50s	Avge	Ct
1961–62	10	15	5	786	172	3	3	78.60	6
1963–64	4	4	1	336	108	1	3	112.00	2

BATTING—*continued*

In Pakistan

1955–56	12	17	2	586	87	0	5	39.06	6
1961–62	6	9	1	448	149*	2	2	56.00	5

In Ceylon

1961–62	1	2	1	95	93	0	1	95.00	1

Totals	533	831	136	31,714	256	76	170	45.63	513

TEST MATCHES

In England

	Matches	Inns	Not Outs	Runs	Highest Inns	100s	50s	Avge	Ct
v. Australia	13	21	3	1,065	256	1	7	59.16	10
v. South Africa	9	16	1	481	91	0	4	32.06	5
v. West Indies	7	14	0	334	80	0	2	23.85	3
v. New Zealand	2	2	0	300 ·	163	2	0	150.00	3
v. India	8	11	0	681	97	0	7	61.90	7
v. Pakistan	7	9	3	486	148	3	1	81.00	6
	46	73	7	3,347	256	6	21	50.71	34

Abroad

In Australia	10	18	3	1,046	132*	4	6	69.73	9
In South Africa	5	7	2	508	148*	2	2	101.60	3
In West Indies	10	16	0	708	143	3	2	44.25	4
In New Zealand	3	4	0	294	126	1	1	73.50	5
In India	6	10	3	674	172	3	2	96.28	2
In Pakistan	2	3	0	229	139	1	1	76.33	1
	36	58	8	3,459	172	14	14	69.18	24

TOTALS	82	131	15	6,806	256	20	35	58.67	58

*Signifies not out.

BOWLING

In first-class matches, K. F. Barrington took 273 wickets for 8,095 runs, average 32.61. On eight occasions he took five wickets in an innings.

In Test matches, his 29 wickets were taken at a cost of 44.82 per wicket.

BARRINGTON, The Hon. Rupert Edward Selborne, who died at Forest Row on August 7, 1975, aged 97, was a useful batsman in the Charterhouse XI in 1895 and 1896 and in 1896 played for Berkshire. At the time of his death he was the oldest living member of I Zingari and may well have been the oldest living county cricketer.

BARROW, Ivan, who died in Kingston, Jamaica, on April 2, 1979, aged 68, has a place in cricket history as the first West Indian to score a hundred in a Test in England. This was at Old Trafford in 1933, and when he achieved the feat George Headley was on 99—together they added 200 for the second wicket, Barrow making 105. A year earlier the two had put on 248 against Lord Tennyson's side at Kingston for the third wicket, still a record for Jamaica; Barrow's share was 169 and he made 58 not out in the second innings. He was, at that time, the West Indians' first string wicket-keeper, a quiet and thoroughly competent performer, but in 1934 he lost his place to C. M. Christiani, who died in 1938. Barrow was recalled in 1939 for the tour to England, but after a five-year gap he was short of first-class practice. After the first Test he had to give way to his second string, J. E. D. Sealy. In all between 1930 and 1939 he played in 11 Tests.

BARTHOLOMEW, Arthur Churchill, of Oxford, the oldest cricket Blue, passed away on March 29, 1940, some five weeks after completing his 94th year. Born on February 21, 1846, at Lympstone, Devon, he was more than a year senior to the Rev. E. E. Harrison Ward, the oldest Cambridge Blue, who died on Easter Monday, five days earlier. The passing of Mr. Bartholomew, Oxford, and Mr. Ward within this brief space of time left Mr. F. A. MacKinnon, Chief of the Scottish Clan, the senior living Blue of either University. He and Mr. Ward both played for Cambridge in the "Cobden" match to which further reference will be found in the biography of Mr. Harrison Ward.

It is of interest to add here that Mr. MacKinnon, now aged 92, who went to Australia in 1878 with the team captained by Lord Harris, is the oldest living cricketer who has represented England. H. C. Maul, another member of that touring side, died early in the year; Mr. A. J. Webbe, Middlesex president for so many years, who reached the age of 86 in January, five weeks before his death, played in the only "test" of that tour.

A. C. Bartholomew went to Marlborough and appeared at Lord's against Rugby in 1865, when he was described as "a good bat with patient defence." Going to Trinity College, Oxford, he headed the University averages in 1867, but did not play against Cambridge until the following season, when, in a match of small totals, he scored seven and 11 not out. He was regarded as one of the best cover points of the day and a contemporary described his quick returns straight to the wicket, after running hard to the ball, as a pleasure to see.

For some years failing eyesight prevented him reading, but Mr. Bartholomew retained such a keen interest in the game that as recently as the summer of 1939 he listened eagerly while his daughter read the scores and descriptions of matches. He greatly prized the disc from a blotter presented to him when a master at Durham School. It is inscribed: "To A. C. B., Durham School, for

his score of 166 against Northumberland at Newcastle-on-Tyne, June 3, 1871." At one time he played for his native county, Devon, and he organised a cricket week at Reading, where he owned a private school, and coached E. H. Bray, L. P. Collins and J. F. Ireland before they gained their Blues. He founded a cricket XI and called them "Guinea-pigs"—because, he said, "they had no tail." One of his scholars was Major-General Sir Walter Kirke, Inspector-General of the Home Forces. His son, Major-General A. W. Bartholomew, was appointed Lieutenant of the Tower of London in March, 1939.

BARTLETT, E. L., who was born on March 18, 1906, died about February, 1932. Making his first appearance for Barbados when only 17 years of age, he became one of the most attractive batsmen and brilliant fielders in the West Indies in recent years. A small man, he had excellent style and was an adept at cutting. A member of the 1928 West Indies side to England, he was unfortunate as regards injury and only took part in the last Test, but he played a fine innings of 109 against Nottinghamshire—his only century in big cricket. In 1931–32, he visited Australia, but except for an innings of 84 in the first Test at Adelaide, he did virtually nothing else on the trip.

CORRECTION. Mr. E. L. Bartlett, West Indies, of whom an obituary notice appeared in last year's issue of the *Almanack*, wrote from Bridgetown in March with the assurance "that I am very much alive and fit." It is a pleasure to publish this message sent to me.—S.J.S.

BARTLETT, E. Lawson, who died in Barbados early in January, 1977, was a member of the West Indies sides to England in 1928 and Australia in 1930. His record in England, 584 runs with an average of 24.33, looks nothing much, but he was perhaps a trifle unlucky. Early in July he had just run into form with a glorious 109 against Nottinghamshire and one or two more successes then might have given him the confidence which was all he lacked to be a great batsman. Instead he broke a finger, missed several matches and failed to recover his form. His tour to Australia was a failure except for a beautiful innings of 84 out of 114 in the first innings of the first Test and after this tour he dropped out of the West Indies side. A very small man, he was quick on his feet, a powerful driver and a good cutter, whether square or late. Indeed he had strokes all round the wicket and, when he was making runs, his potentialities were obvious. It was sad that he could so seldom do justice to them.

BARTLETT, Ezra William, died on March 16, 1942, aged 80. Born at Burton-on-Trent, he was appointed to the Post Office at the age of 21, and, besides his official duties, cricket made him well known in Somerset. For many years he was president of the Taunton club and one of the best batsmen in the district. An occasional player for the county in 1895, he took part in the match in which A. C. MacLaren made 424, a record for all important cricket until W. H. Ponsford scored 429 for Victoria against Tasmania in the winter of 1922. With regard to that performance at Melbourne, A. C. MacLaren wrote strongly to S. H. Pardon as to the justice of the game with Tasmania being included in *Wisden* as first class, because Victoria's Second XI were engaged and Ponsford did not play in the highest grade inter-State cricket until later that season when at Adelaide he scored 108. Since then Ponsford himself and Bradman in turn established new records. During the Lancashire innings of 801 Bartlett went on as the ninth bowler. This prolonged innings, the highest in County Cricket at that time, came immediately after 692 by Middlesex at Taunton, making six days of first-class cricket with a Sunday intervening, which gave Bartlett an experience that only the keenest fieldsman could appreciate; his own scores in these two games were four, seven, four, six, and his highest for Somerset was 40 against Hampshire early in the 1895 season.

BARTLETT, The Rev. Gilbert Harrison, who died in a Norwich nursing home on October 10, 1958, aged 76, invented the "cradle" universally used for fielding practice. When at Cambridge he represented Corpus Christi at rowing and lawn-tennis. He was Rector of Fulmodeston, Norfolk, and had been Rector of Cley-next-the-Sea.

BARTLEY, Commdr. Edward Leslie Dayrell, who died in the Royal Naval Hospital on October 7, 1969, aged 73, kept wicket for Hampshire in three matches in 1931. When a member of the Royal Navy team, he toured South Africa with Lord—then the Hon. L. H.—Tennyson's side in South Africa in 1924–25.

BARTLEY, Thomas John, who died in a Liverpool hospital on April 2, 1964, aged 56,

stood as an umpire in six Test matches between 1954 and 1956. He played with considerable success for Cheshire from 1933 till the outbreak of the Second World War and also did well in League cricket. The best fast bowler ever to take part in the Liverpool Competition, he achieved some notable feats for Birkenhead Park, including six hat-tricks and the taking of 138 wickets in 1935—still a record for the Competition. In that season he took all 10 wickets for 37 runs against New Brighton, and during his career took nine in an innings on nine occasions. For Cheshire in 1934 he dismissed four Denbighshire batsmen with following deliveries. After one season as a second-class umpire, he was in 1948 placed on the first-class list where he remained till ill-health compelled his retirement in 1962.

BARTON, Major Charles Gerard, who died at Hatfield Peverel on November 11, 1919, of heart failure, aged 56, played for Hampshire and Bombay Presidency. He was a useful all-round cricketer, and in 1891 headed the county's bowling averages with a record of 42 wickets for 9.79 runs each. In the match v. M.C.C. and Ground at Southampton that year he took 14 wickets for 67 runs.

BARTON, Harold George Mitford, who died on July 3, 1970, aged 87, did not get into the XI when at Sherborne, but he played in eight matches for Hampshire between 1910 and 1912. He also turned out for Buckinghamshire.

BARTON, Major-General Howard James, who died at Hove on October 11, 1922, was born on July 10, 1836, and had thus reached his 87th year. At the Oval in 1857 he played for Sussex against Surrey, but made only 0 and two not out in totals of 35 and 31. He was a Crimean veteran.

BARTON, Victor, a member for 11 seasons of the Hampshire XI, died on March 23, 1906, at Southampton. Born on October 6, 1867, he was only in his 39th year. He was a bombardier in the Royal Artillery when he first became associated with County Cricket, being tried for Kent in 1889. At the end of that season he had a great share in gaining for Kent a startling victory over Notts at Beckenham. The match, even after the lapse of over 17 years, is vividly remembered, as its result caused the Championship to end in a tie between Notts, Lancashire, and Surrey. Kent had only 52 to get in the last innings, but the task, simple as it looked on paper, was in reality a heavy one, the pitch being extremely treacherous. Six of the best batsmen were out for 25, and Notts seemed to have the match in their hands, but G. G. Hearne and Barton hit off the remaining runs without further loss. The fact is worth recalling that Hearne took an hour and three-quarters to score 14 not out, his defence against the bowling of Attewell and Flowers earning him the highest praise. Though Barton started in such promising style he never established himself in the Kent team. He played in a few matches in 1890, and then transferred his services to Hampshire, for which county he appeared first in 1892. His success was immediate and pronounced, as he headed the Hampshire batting with an average of 39, and the bowling with 19 wickets for 14 runs apiece. Thenceforward he was one of the most useful members of the Hampshire XI, playing on till 1902. After that—by reason, we believe, of poor health—he dropped out. In the season of 1900 he played an innings of 205 against Sussex at Brighton, but nevertheless he was on the losing side. Barton had an attractive style of batting, and few men could drive with more power on the on-side. Fieldsmen who stood at mid-on had a wholesome dread of him.

BARTON, William Edward, died in September, 1942, at Christchurch, aged 83. In the '80s he was the finest batsman in New Zealand. An Englishman, he played at Wanganui, where he was in one of the local banks, and when transferred to Auckland he continued his good form. One outstanding innings was 44 for Wanganui versus W. L. Murdoch's team which toured New Zealand after the visit of the 1880 Australian side to England. The wickets were rough in New Zealand at that time—except at Christchurch—and runs were hard to get. The Australians scored 49 and 83; Wanganui XXII, whose first total was 48, lost 11 wickets against Spofforth, Boyle and Palmer before gaining a victory. Barton played for Wellington against Shaw's English XI of 1881–82. In New Zealand representative cricket from 1880 onwards he scored 852 runs at an average of 30.4. A good field, he was also a fine tennis player.

BASHFORD, The Rev. Alfred Myddleton, died suddenly on July 31, 1948 aged 67. Merchant Taylors' XI 1899–1900. Cambridge Seniors' match 1903. Played for Middlesex twice in 1906. Vicar of Hillingdon, Middlesex.

BASS, Harry, who had been groundsman at Canterbury for 25 years, died suddenly from heart-failure on January 24, 1904, at the age of 51. He played for Kent on a few occasions in the '70s. He was buried in the Canterbury Cemetery on January 27.

BASTARD, E. W., who was the chief bowler in the Somersetshire XI before the County became first-class, died at Taunton some time during the first week of April, 1901, in his 40th year. He played for Oxford against Cambridge in 1883 and the two following years. In 1884 he assisted in the defeat of the Australians by the University, taking five good wickets in the second innings for 44 runs. After he retired from county cricket, he frequently played for the Gentlemen of Somerset. He was educated at Sherborne, where his skill as a slow left-handed bowler was first recognised. He was born February 28, 1862.

BASTOW, John, born at Bromley-by-Bow on October 30, 1850, died in a nursing-home on June 1, 1927, at the age of 76. A useful batsman and wicket-keeper, he played for Middlesex in 1874, 1875 and 1877, heading the averages in the first-mentioned year. His highest innings were 35 v. Surrey on Prince's ground and 28 and 34 not out in the return at the Oval. Later on he assisted Essex.

BATCHELOR, Denzil Stanley, who died on September 6, 1969, aged 63, wrote on cricket and rugby football, latterly for *The Times*. Formerly Sports Editor of *Picture Post*, he was also an author, playwright and broadcaster on many other subjects.

BATCHELOR, The Rev. Wm. Jesse, born at Hayes in Kent, November 14, 1846: died at Epsom November 19, 1917. Played for Warwickshire in 1876, being a Master at Leamington College. Mr. Batchelor was a tremendous run-getter when at Cambridge, but had to decline a place in the XI as he could not spare the time to play. In 1868 he made five scores of over a hundred, besides playing an innings of 289 for the Long Vacation Club. If a man of leisure he would perhaps have been one of the famous bats of his day.

BATEMAN-CHAMPAIN, Francis Henry, who would have taken a high place among first-class cricketers but for scholastic duties as a master in turn at Wellington and Cheltenham limiting his appearances for Gloucestershire, died at Tiverton on December 29,

1942, in his 66th year. Born at Richmond in Surrey, he went to Cheltenham College and was one of five brothers in the cricket XI from 1883 to 1898. He enjoyed the remarkable distinction of playing in the XI five seasons, 1892 to 1896, being captain during the last three. Twice he headed the batting averages and, maintaining this form, he obtained his Blue as a Freshman at Oxford, where he was in the XI four years.

Captain in 1899, he earned high praise by making the first hundred hit against Joe Darling's Australian team—120 on the Christ Church ground—and Oxford led on the first innings by 38. That season, when W. G. Grace had left Gloucestershire, F. H. Bateman-Champain scored a brilliant 123 out of 182 for the first wicket against Warwickshire at Bristol; he hit all five fours in a five-ball over from S. Santall to the boundary. In 1907 he made his highest score, 149 against Surrey at the Oval, but perhaps his best display for the county was in 1897, when with little experience of first-class cricket, he stopped an utter collapse by scoring 97 in a total of 137 agaist Lancashire at Bristol. F. G. Roberts, seven not out, stayed while 74 were added for the last wicket. I saw that innings and recall how W. G. Grace and A. N. Hornby, the rival captains, congratulated the former Oxonian on his admirable style and free hitting against Hallam, Cuttell, Mold and Briggs. His liking for the Lancashire attack was shown again next year at Old Trafford in a splendid not out innings of 113, played in a great effort to get 374 for victory.

His last appearance for Gloucestershire was in 1914. He played for Gentlemen against Players at the Oval in 1897 and 1899, making 82 on the first occasion. Altogether during his much broken cricket career he scored 3,597 runs at an average of 19.42 in first-class matches. Sometimes he bowled slows, but in the field his place was at cover-point, where he was grand in the exceptional company of such a great off-side fieldsman as G. L. Jessop—his rival captain for Cambridge when the Oxford leader was known as F. H. B. Champain. He never revealed his batting form at Lord's in the University match, his best score being 34, but as a half-back for Oxford he played consistently well in the seasons 1897 and 1899. He took up fruit farming in British Columbia in 1911, and during the Great War he became captain in the Ordnance Corps.—H.P.

BATEMAN-CHAMPAIN, The Rt. Rev. John Norman, died at Westbury-on-Trym, Bristol,

on October 22, 1950, aged 70. He was in the Cheltenham XI, 1896–98, and played in various trial matches at Cambridge, but failed to win a Blue. Played twice for Gloucestershire in 1899. In 1938 he was appointed to the Suffragan Bishopric of Knaresborough, which he held till 1948, after when he became Chaplain of the St. Monice Home of Rest, Bristol.

BATES, John, who died in December, 1936, was groundsman of the Warwickshire County Club at Edgbaston for 21 years. A Yorkshireman by birth he belonged to a cricketing family. His son, Harold, a left-handed bowler, was killed in the War; a third son, Leonard, played for Warwickshire for 16 years with conspicuous success until 1935. John Bates was often called upon by county officials to give advice on the preparation of wickets.

BATES, Leonard Ashton, who died on March 11, 1971, aged 75, was born in the pavilion at the Warwickshire ground at Edgbaston, where his father was head groundsman. Len Bates played as a professional for his county from 1913 to 1935, in which time he scored 19,373 runs for an average of 27.83. He hit 116 and 144 in the match with Kent at Coventry in 1927 and altogether registered 21 centuries, the highest of which was 211 on a wearing pitch against Gloucestershire at Gloucester in 1932. He also made 200 off the Worcestershire bowling at Edgbaston in 1928. After his retirement from the first-class game, he served as coach and head groundsman at Christ's Hospital, Horsham, till he retired in 1963. His death occurred after a long and painful illness during which both his legs were amputated.

BATES, Sergeant Samuel Harold (Royal Warwickshire Regiment), born at the Warwickshire County Cricket Ground, where his father was groundsman, was killed in action on August 28, 1916, aged about 24. He was a useful all-round player, being a left-handed bowler and right-handed bat, and had played occasionally for his county. He was a member of the ground-staff at Lord's.

BATES, William, passed away on January 8, 1900, at his residence at Lipton. Born on November 19, 1855, he was still a comparatively young man. His career in first-class cricket—exceptionally brilliant while it lasted—was brought to a sudden and very painful close more than a dozen years back. He went out to Australia in the autumn of

1887 as a member of Mr. Vernon's team, and while practising at the nets, on the Melbourne ground, met with a sad accident. Several members of the English team were on the ground at the time, and a ball hit by one of them struck Bates in the eye with such terrible force that his sight was permanently injured. Thenceforward County Cricket for him was out of the question, and some little time after his return to England he attempted, in a fit of despondency, to commit suicide. He recovered his sight sufficiently to play in local matches and do some coaching, but it was of course, a painful experience for him to drop into obscurity at the age of 33, after having been for over 10 seasons one of the most popular cricketers in the country. Coming out in 1877, he quickly took a high position in the Yorkshire XI, and he was still at the height of his powers when he met with his deplorable accident at Melbourne. He will be remembered as one of the finest of Yorkshire players. As a batsman he was as brilliant as Ulyett, though he did not possess such varied resources, and, especially during his first few seasons, he was a capital slow, round-arm bowler—commanding, as he did, any amount of spin. His one weakness was in fielding, for while a genuine hard-worker, he had a way at times of missing the easiest of catches. It was only this lack of certainty in his catching that prevented him being chosen in this country to play for England against Australia. On Australian cricket fields he was always a great favourite, and during his visits to the Colonies he did many brilliant things. At Melbourne, in January, 1883, playing for the Hon. Ivo Bligh's team against the great Australian XI of 1882, he performed the hat-trick, getting rid of Percy McDonnell, George Giffen, and Bonnor with successive balls. The way in which Bonnor's wicket was obtained is amusingly described in the *Badminton Book*. All the Englishmen were desperately anxious that Bates should get his third wicket, and a council of war resulted in a very neat little plan being devised. It was said that Bonnor was sure to play slowly forward at the first ball he received, whatever its length, and on Bates promising to bowl a short-pitched ball on the leg-stump, Walter Read volunteered to stand short mid-on, and gradually creep in towards the batsman. Everything came off as had been anticipated, and Bonnor, having played the ball into Read's hands, left the wicket lost in amazement that anyone should have ventured to get so near to his bat.

BATES, William Edric, who died in a Belfast

hospital on January 17, 1957, aged 72, did much fine work as a batsman for Glamorgan in their first 11 years as a first-class county. He could not secure a regular place in the side for Yorkshire, as did his more famous father, "Billy" Bates, and after seven seasons with the county of his birth he joined Glamorgan. A consistent batsman with a variety of strokes and watchful defence, he in six summers exceeded 1,000 runs in Championship matches for the Welsh county, scoring 10 centuries. His best season was that of 1927 when his aggregate reached 1,575, average 45.00, and he reached three figures on four occasions, including 200 not out against Worcestershire at Kidderminster and 105 and 111 in the game with Essex at Leyton. Following his retirement from first-class cricket in 1931, he held several coaching engagements in Ireland.

BATHURST, Laurence Charles Villebois, died on February 22, 1939, aged 67. Of good height and build, he was best known as a clever left-handed bowler, slow to medium with varied spin. He met with much success during five seasons in the Radley XI, and finishing as captain he took 43 wickets at 8.76 each, while his right-handed, steady batting earned an average of over 40. L. C. H. Palairet gave him his Oxford Blue in 1893, but in two matches against Cambridge Bathurst did little with the bat, though by dismissing four early batsmen he was largely responsible for victory by eight wickets when C. B. Fry captained the side. Against Sussex at Lord's in 1894, he celebrated his first match for Middlesex by taking 12 wickets for 63. Among his victims was W. L. Murdoch, the famous Australian, then captain of Sussex. From 1896 he played for Norfolk, the county of his birth, but could not devote much time to county cricket, owing to scholastic duties. In 1894 Bathurst toured America with Lord Hawke's team, doing well with the bat—average 36—and he was also the best bowler—30 wickets at 6.12 runs each. He served in the Imperial Yeomanry during the South African War.

BATTCOCK, Oliver Gordon, who died in Guy's Hospital, London, on September 26, 1970, 10 days after his 67th birthday, was reputed to have taken over 6,000 wickets in club and minor county games, with bowling of medium pace, during a cricketing career spanning 50 years. Good length and late outswing played a big part in his success. He assisted Buckinghamshire from 1923 to 1952, being captain in the last three seasons, and in the Challenge Match of 1938 he dismissed 12 Lancashire batsmen for 65 runs, Bucking-hamshire winning in a single innings. He captained Datchet for 25 years, taking over 2,000 wickets for them, and for a number of years led Incogniti on tours abroad. He was a useful left-handed batsman. As Oliver Gordon, he gained distinction as an actor and producer.

BATTY-SMITH, Henry, formerly proprietor and editor of *The Sportsman*, died at Shinfield Grove, Berkshire, on May 21, 1927. In his younger days he had been a good cricketer, attaining considerable skill as a batsman and wicket-keeper, although taking part in no matches of note. He was for a time a member of the controlling body in billiards.

BAVIN, Brigadier Arthur Julian Walter, who died in hospital on August 6, 1956, as the result of a motor-car accident, aged 60, was well known in club cricket and was for some years hon. secretary of the Incogniti. Educated at Berkhamsted, he served in the Army in both World Wars.

BAWTREE, John Francis, who died on March 25, 1938, aged 64, was a good all-round club cricketer. He was in the Hailey-bury XI of 1891 and when Essex became a first-class county in 1895 he played in a few matches for them and occasionally in subse-quent seasons, but it was difficult to get a place in a very strong XI which finished third for the Championship in 1897. A. J. Turner, Percy Perrin, Charles McGahey, Harry Car-penter, C. J. Kortright, H. Pickett, F. G. Bull and Walter Mead were then in their prime and A. P. Lucas, of Cambridge Uni-versity, M.C.C., and England, who still held his own among the best batsmen, was in the Essex team after playing for Surrey and Middlesex.

BAYFORD, Robert Augustus, K.C., who was born at Albury, in Surrey, on March 13, 1838, died on August 24, 1921, surviving his wife only two months. He was educated at Kensington Grammar School, and was in the Cambridge XI in 1857 and two following years, being captain in 1859. *Scores and Biographies* (v–40) says of him: "Hits freely and well, especially to leg, and has made some capital innings in good style ... His bowling is slow round-armed, with an easy delivery, while in the field he is often wicket-keeper." Among his best scores for the University were 53 v. M.C.C. and Ground in 1858 and 60 against the same side a year

later, the former innings being played at Cambridge and the latter at Lord's. In his three matches with Oxford he did little, making only 32 runs in six innings, but in the year in which he was captain he had the satisfaction of leading his side to success by 28 runs. Among several good scores ob-tained by him in matches of note may be mentioned: 69 for Quidnuncs v. The Univer-sity in 1859, and 70 not out for S. Taylor's XI v. A. Baillie's XI and 64 for M.C.C. and Ground v. Hampshire, both at Lord's in 1861. He assisted Surrey in 1860 and 1861 and Middlesex from 1861 to 1864. He had been a member of the M.C.C. since 1858, and was the oldest surviving original member of the Middlesex County C.C.

BAYLEY-LAURIE, The Rev. Sir Emilius (Eton and Kent), born May 16, 1823, died at Maxweltown, Dumfriesshire, December 3, 1917. Having outlived nearly all his contem-poraries, Emilius Bayley, as he was called till he took in 1887 the surname of Laurie, must have been the oldest cricketer of any note in England. He was nearly five years older than the Surrey veteran, William Caffyn. On the strength of one performance he will live in cricket history. For Eton against Harrow at Lord's in 1841 he played an innings of 152, his score remaining unbeaten in the Eton and Harrow matches till D. C. Boles made 183 for Eton in 1904. Except that he got his 152 out of total of 308—with the liberal allow-ance of 63 extras—one can say nothing about Emilius Bayley's great innings. Mr. Arthur Haygarth gave no details in *Scores and Biographies*, but in his biographical note attached to the Eton and Harrow match in 1838 he described Bayley as a fine free hitter, especially to leg, and an admirable field either at long leg or cover point. Apart from his big innings Bayley's best score in the matches with Harrow and Winchester during his four years in the Eton XI was 27 against Harrow in 1838. Still he must have been an excellent bat, as he was considered good enough to play for Kent in the great days of the XI that included Fuller Pilch, Alfred Mynn, Felix, Wenman, and Hillyer. He took part in two matches for Kent in 1842, five in 1843, and two in 1844. Like many other men in his own time and in later days he gave up serious cricket on entering the Church. In the sensational match between Kent and England at Canterbury in 1842, when Kent, after leading off with a total of 278, went down for 44 in their second innings, and were beaten by nine wickets, Emilius Bayley scored not out five and not out 17. The other

10 Kent men in the second innings scored only 23 runs.—S.H.P.

BAYNTON, R. G., who was born in 1900, was killed in a motor-car accident in the King's Heath district of Birmingham on September 26, 1924. He was a medium-paced bowler and played occasionally for Warwickshire in 1921 and two following years. Most of his club cricket was played for the Moseley C.C. in Birmingham League matches.

BEADLE, Lieut.-Commdr. Sydney Wilford, R.N.(Ret.), died suddenly at Reading Street, Kent, on July 24, 1937. He played for Kent against Sussex at Portsmouth in 1911 and next year for Navy against Army at Lord's.

BEAL, Charles William, who died at Randwick, Sydney, on February 5, 1921, aged 65, was manager of the Australian teams of 1882 and 1888. He was captain of the XI whilst at Sydney Grammar School, and nephew of Mr. J. Beal, who played, in 1856, in the first of the long series of matches between New South Wales and Victoria. Mr. Beal made many friends during his two trips to England, being genial and sociable to a degree. He was extremely proud of being associated with the great team of 1882. As manager in 1888 he had to face a very awkward crisis. It was largely due to his tact that the nature of S. P. Jones's illness was so carefully kept secret. Had it become known that Jones was suffering from small-pox the tour might have been nearly ruined.

BEAN, Ernest Edward, Patron of the Victorian Cricket Association, a member of the Australian Board of Control and Test Selection Committee, died at Melbourne on March 22, 1939, aged 72. A batsman of considerable ability, he played occasionally for Victoria as far back as 1888. His best score was 103 not out against Tasmania.

BEAN, George, died at Warsop of pneumonia on March 16, 1923. George Bean was one of the many Notts cricketers who earned fame for a county other than that of his birth. His connection with the Notts XI was restricted to the season of 1885. He did not do much, and, declining the offer of half a dozen matches in the following year, he threw in his lot with Sussex for which county he had already qualified by residence. For Sussex he proved himself a most valuable batsman. Between 1886 and 1898 he took part in 219 Sussex matches and hit up 10

hundreds. The Brighton wickets were at their best in his day and they suited his style of play to perfection. He had a most brilliant cut and—the boundary being short on the pavilion side—it is no exaggeration to say that he got numberless four without running a yard. One of his performances stood out above all the rest. Playing against Notts at Brighton in 1891 he scored 145 not out and 92.

In 1891 he touched his highest point. He headed the Sussex averages and stood for the moment in quite the front rank of professional batsmen. Strictly on his merits he was picked to go to Australia with Lord Sheffield's XI in the winter of 1891–92 but somehow he never found his form and the trip detracted from his reputation. Back in England he showed a sad decline in form for one season, but in 1893 he was as good as ever and again came out at the top of the Sussex averages. Attached to Lord's for many years he was at the time of his death the senior member of the M.C.C.'s ground staff. He had his Sussex benefit in 1898 and a highly successful Whitsuntide benefit at Lord's in 1921.—S.H.P.

BEAN, Joseph, who was born at Sutton-in-Ashfield on February 16, 1876, died at his native place on January 21, 1922. He was brother of George Bean and assisted Sussex in 31 matches between 1895 and 1901, scoring 403 runs with an average of 9.37 and taking 20 wickets for 29.25 runs each.

BEARD, Donald Derek, who died on July 15, 1982, aged 62, while on a visit to England, was a member of the first New Zealand side ever to win a Test match—against West Indies at Auckland in March, 1956. He made a useful all-round contribution, scoring 31 and six not out at No. 9 and taking one for 20 in West Indies' first innings and three for 22 in 15 overs in the second. New Zealand had waited 26 years and 45 Tests for this success. An accurate, medium-paced right-hand bowler, capable of late swing, and a lively hitter of the ball, in his four Test appearances he scored 101 runs at an average of 20.20 and captured nine wickets at 33.55 apiece. In all first-class cricket (for both Central and Northern Districts) he took 278 wickets (average 21.58) and scored 2,166 runs (average 22.10).

BEASLEY, Joseph Noble, M.C., who died at Stony Stratford on January 23, 1960, aged 78, played as a hard-hitting and fast-medium bowler for Northamptonshire in 1911 and

1919. He went to Australia in 1911, returned to serve in the Army in the First World War, winning the Military Cross, and turned out again for the county in 1919. After that he devoted his attentions to farming. A fine Rugby footballer, he played as centre three-quarter for Northampton from 1906 to 1911. He also shone at lawn-tennis and hockey.

BEASLEY, The Rev. Robert Noble, who died on January 21, 1966, aged 83, played occasionally for Northamptonshire from 1907 to 1911. He was a first-class Rugby footballer.

BEATTIE, George N., who died in September, 1932, in his 64th year was one of the founders of the Scottish Cricket Union. He played in turn for Clydesdale, Pollock and West of Scotland, for which last-named club he was at various times secretary, treasurer and director. He acted as hon. secretary to the Western District of the Union and established the Western Charity Association, whilst he arranged the visits to Scotland of the Australian teams of 1905, 1909, 1919 and 1921.

BEAUMONT, John, died in South London on May 1, 1920. He was born at Armitage Bridge, near Huddersfield, on September 16, 1855. Jack Beaumont, as he was always called, appeared in his young days for Yorkshire, but failed to make a name for himself in his native county. He played once for Yorkshire in 1877 and four times in 1878. Still, he must have been a promising bowler, as when playing for a local team against the Australians—I think it was in 1880—he greatly impressed Blackham. He was practically unknown when, having duly qualified by two years' residence, he came out for Surrey in 1885. He met with immediate success, causing quite a sensation in May in his first match, he and George Lohmann getting Middlesex out on a slow pitch for a total of 25. Beaumont's record was six wickets for 11 runs. This performance made his place in the XI secure for the rest of the season and he fairly divided honours with Lohmann, taking in all matches for Surrey 123 wickets with an average of 15.26. Beaumont kept up his form for the next four seasons and, though completely overshadowed by Lohmann in 1887, had some share in winning back for Surrey—after an interval of 23 years—the first place among the counties. However, he lost his bowling in 1890 and in 1891 he dropped out of the team, playing in only one match. At his best

Beaumont was a first-rate bowler, very accurate and apt even on the best wickets to get up to a nasty height. He was quite individual in style, walking up to the crease to deliver the ball. His action was high, and, without being exceptionally fast, he could keep up a fine pace for any reasonable length of time. A big, powerful man, Beaumont retained to the end of his life all his Yorkshire characteristics. Residence in London did not in the least affect his way of speaking.—S.H.P.

His best performances were as under:

8 wkts. in inns. for 40, v. Yorkshire, at the Oval...1888
8 wkts. in inns. for 89, v. Derbyshire, at Derby...1889
6 for 11, v. Middlesex, at the Oval........1885
6 for 15, v. Hampshire, at Southampton.1885
5 for 12, v. Yorkshire, at the Oval 1886
7 for 18, v. Essex, at the Oval..............1886
4 for 11, v. Camb. Univ., at the Oval.....1886
4 for 6, v. Derbyshire, at Derby..........1886
4 for 11, v. Sussex, at the Oval.............1889

Against Kent at the Oval in 1889 he and Lohmann bowled unchanged through both innings. For South v. North, at Hastings, in 1889, he did the hat-trick.

For Surrey v. Derbyshire, at the Oval, in 1889, Beaumont (66) and Sharpe (56 not out) added 118 for the last wicket.

BECKFORD, Wilfred George, who died in July, 1959, aged 50, played as an attractive left-hand batsman for Jamaica from 1927 to 1936. Well known as "W.G.", he appeared for Jamaica before G. Headley, but by 1928 the pair became known as "The Chocolate Babes," so marked was the resemblance between them. Beckford's highest score in first-class cricket was 74 against Mr. (later Sir) Julien Cahn's XI in 1928–29; but his two finest innings were 65 and 54 from the Yorkshire bowling in 1935–36, when his off-driving was superb.

BEDFORD, Edward Henry Rilands, died in hospital at Chelmsford on October 9, 1976, aged 73, having been born at Aston, Birmingham on June 7, 1903. He was a grandson of the Rev. W. K. R. Bedford, co-founder of the Free Foresters, and was "Founder's Kin". Well known in the world of archery, he became a Woodman of Arden in 1924 and was Secretary of the Woodmen 1948–75. He played in one match for Derbyshire in 1924—against Glamorgan at Derby.

BEDFORD, Philip Ian, who died on September 18, 1966, aged 36, after collapsing while batting for Finchley at Buckhurst Hill, captained Middlesex in 1961 and 1962. While at Woodhouse Grammar School, he made his debut for the county in 1947 at the age of 17 and in his first match, against Essex at Lord's, created a highly favourable impression when, with well-controlled leg-breaks and googlies, he took six wickets. That season Middlesex won the County Championship and Ian Bedford occupied second place in their bowling averages with 25 wickets at 19.36 runs apiece. He did not fare so well in the following season and after carrying out his National Service in the Royal Air Force, for whom he played, he returned to Finchley and met with marked success. When he was called upon to lead Middlesex upon the retirement of J. J. Warr, modesty prevented Bedford from bowling as much as he might, but he still achieved an occasional useful performance. Twice he toured South America and once visited Canada with M.C.C. teams.

BEDSER, Alec, who died in June, 1981, aged 33, in a motor accident in Johannesburg, was a right-arm medium-paced bowler who played for Border in the Currie Cup in 1971–72. Like his twin brother, Eric (they were named after the famous English cricketing twins), Alec was a distinguished all-round sportsman. Another car accident, several years earlier, had curtailed his cricket career.

BEECHING, Lieut.-Col. Thomas Hugh Pitt, who died in hospital on December 31, 1971, aged 71, was in the Charterhouse XI in 1917 and played for Kent in 1920 and 1921.

BEET, George, achieved his ambition of umpiring in a Test match before he died on December 13, 1946, at his home in Derby. Appointed to the umpires' list in 1929, he stood regularly, and at length was chosen for the England and India Test at Manchester in July, 1946. On the way home by train from that game, Beet was taken seriously ill and rushed to Derby Infirmary for an operation. From this illness he never recovered. He made his first appearance as wicket-keeper for Derbyshire in 1910, and last played for them in 1922. Very dependable behind the sticks, he also gave useful help with the bat, and in 1919 was second in the Derbyshire averages with 24.80. For several seasons Fred Root was the Derbyshire fast bowler, and the junction of their names in many scores earned the pair the endearing name of "Beet-root". During the war George Beet and A. Fowler were the regular umpires in almost every match at Lord's. Beet in several

winters went to South Africa as coach. He was 60 years old.

BEEVOR, John Grosvenor, who died on May 5, 1903, will be remembered in connection with Notts cricket a generation back. Unfortunately he was not able to play much for the county, but on the few occasions on which he appeared he proved himself a batsman of high class. He played an innings of 88 against Surrey at the Oval in 1869, and scored 24 and 53 in the corresponding match a year afterwards. Standing well over six feet high he had a long reach, and was a powerful hitter. Born on January 1, 1845, he was in his 59th year at the time of his death. He was in the Uppingham School XI for four years—1859 to 1862.

BEISIEGEL, Air Commodore William Karl, who died suddenly in the Royal Air Force Hospital, Halton, on January 8, 1973, was in the Uppingham XI in 1924 and 1925, heading the batting figures each year. In 1925, when he hit 126 not out against Rugby, he obtained 539 runs at an average of 59.88. He was also a splendid fieldsman at cover point. H. S. Altham wrote of him that year in *Wisden*: "In performance Beisiegel stands out head and shoulders over his colleagues." When a Flight-Lieutenant in the R.A.F., for whom he played with considerable success, Beisiegel was called upon to captain Leicestershire in place of A. G. Hazlerigg late in the 1934 season and led them to their first victory—by 58 runs—over Yorkshire for 23 years. H. A. Smith, with six wickets for 39 runs, brought about the cheap dismissal of Yorkshire in the second innings.

BELCHER, Capt. Gordon, M.C., 3rd (attd. to 1st) Batt. Royal Berkshire Regiment, youngest son of the Rev. T. Hayes Belcher, of the Oxford XI of 1870, was killed in action in France on May 16, 1915, aged 29. He was educated at Brighton College, where he was in the XI in 1901 and three following years, leading the side in 1903 and 1904. His record there was a good one:

1901	110 runs (average 8.46) and 17	wickets (average 17.05)
1902	276 runs (average 17.25) and 36	wickets (average 16.63)
1903	216 runs (average 27.00) and 15	wickets (average 28.20)
1904	402 runs (average 28.71) and 50	wickets (average 12.14)

During his last season he made most runs, took most wickets, and headed both batting and bowling averages. In 1905 he played in the Freshmen's match at Cambridge, but did not obtain his Blue. Later he appeared frequently for Berkshire, his most successful years being 1910 and 1911, when his averages were 27.00 and 26.60 respectively. He was first in the County's bowling in 1912 and second in 1911. His highest innings for Berkshire were 112 not out v. Wiltshire at Reading in 1910, and 104 not out v. Carmarthen on the same ground a year later. In 1905 he played in one match for Hampshire—against Warwickshire at Southampton, in which he was unfortunate enough to obtain spectacles. He was born at Brighton College on September 26, 1885. In February last he was awarded the Military Cross.

BELCHER, The Rev. Thomas Hayes, died on November 26, 1919. Born at Faringdon, Berkshire, on September 12, 1847, he was in his 73rd year. Mr. Belcher will always have a place in cricket history. He was the second of the victims to F. C. Cobden's memorable hat-trick at the finish of the Oxford and Cambridge match in 1870. Of the three players he was the last survivor, S. E. Butler dying in 1903 and W. A. Stewart in 1883. As to his own share in the catastrophe, Mr. Belcher, writing to the *Globe* in August, 1901—one of the endless discussions as to the details of the sensational finish was then being carried on—declared that he was bowled off his leg. To quote his exact words he said "Mr. Cobden is right in saying that the ball which bowled me was of a good length. It entirely beat me, but it touched my right leg a little below the knee on the inside. Of this I am quite certain, but whether this slight touch turned it on to the wicket I cannot possibly say." Mr. Belcher played in the University match only in 1870. He was picked for his bowling and fully justified his selection, taking four wickets for 52 runs and two for 38. He was Vicar of Bramley, Basingstoke, Hampshire, from 1893.

BELDAM, Cyril Ashlam, who played in a few matches for Middlesex in 1896, died on September 7, 1940, aged 70.

BELDAM, George William, who died on November 23, 1937, in his 69th year, first played for Middlesex in 1900 when 32 years of age. Experience in high-class club cricket enabled him to gain a place in a very powerful side and for eight seasons he did valuable work. In 1903 when Middlesex were Champions, Beldam closely followed P. F. Warner, their most consistent batsman, in aggregate and average. He maintained his form until 1907 when he dropped out of the side. Altogether for Middlesex he scored 4,796 runs, with an average of 30.16, and took 76 wickets at 27.14 runs apiece. His highest aggregate in first-class matches was 1,158 in 1901. He also played for London County with W. G. Grace.

G. W. Beldam was restricted in effective stroke-play, depending largely on the late cut for runs, but he watched the ball carefully with unruffled patience, bowlers experiencing much difficulty in getting a ball through his defence. He bowled right hand rather slow with carefully applied swerve and though never earning real fame with the ball often broke up a partnership. He appeared several times for the Gentlemen.

In the Oval match in 1903, Beldam, with innings of 80 and 54, took a large part in beating the Players by 54 runs, G. H. Simpson-Hayward finished the match by taking the last four wickets for five runs with his underhand bowling. Opening the innings with P. F. Warner at Lord's in 1905 he made 22 out of 53 and, going in later in the second innings, scored 23 not out during a collapse, the Players winning by 149 runs. At the Oval the same year, when highest scorer for the Gentlemen with 51 and 43, Beldam again was on the losing side.

He had a liking for Surrey bowlers. In 1902 he hit 155 not out off them at Lord's and the following year made 89 and 118 at Lord's. Middlesex, in their final match at the Oval, required to escape defeat to be certain of the Championship; they won by an innings and 94 runs. Beldam played a big part in the victory, staying four hours and 40 minutes and scoring 112 after the opening pair had fallen for four runs. J. T. Hearne and Albert Trott, the only professionals in the XI, dismissed Surrey for 57, and C. M. Wells finished the match by taking five wickets for 26 with his slows.

A pioneer in action photography, George Beldam produced, in conjunction with C. B. Fry, who wrote the descriptions, a remarkable book, *Great Batsmen, Their Methods at a Glance.* He wrote also on golf and tennis.

BELL, B. T. A., who played for Canada v. United States, at Seabright, in 1886, died at Ottawa, on March 1, 1904. He was one of the very few men who have made over 1,000 runs in a single season in Canadian cricket, his aggregate during 1886 being 1,036 for 29 completed innings, average 35.21. He was invited to form one of the Canadian team which visited England in 1887, but was unable to make the journey. He was over 6ft.

in height, and was a fine forward player. He was also a splendid field at cover-point.

BELL, Geoffrey Foxton, MC, died at Haslemere on January 17, 1984, aged 87. Three years in the Repton XI and captain in the last, 1915, he played for the Gentlemen of England against Oxford in the first first-class match played after First World War and made 64. This secured him a place in the Oxford side in their next match, against P. F. Warner's XI, and he scored 34 and 40. After this he was in and out of the side, but 50 against MCC at Lord's got him his Blue. He did nothing as a batsman at Lord's, but held a great catch in the deep, running 30yds. to dismiss J. S. F. Morrison. A cousin of S. H. Evershed, the old Derbyshire captain, he made a few unsuccessful appearances for the county between 1914 and 1920. Later he was headmaster successively of Trent College and Highgate.

BELL, John Thompson, who died at Guiseley, near Leeds on August 14, 1974, aged 76, was one of the legion of Yorkshire cricketers who have made a name outside the county. Having failed to gain a regular place for Yorkshire in 1921 and then again in 1923 despite the fact that once he helped Norman Kilner put on 117 for the first wicket against Essex at Leyton, Bell found success with Glamorgan. He opened their batting from 1926 to 1931, and in his 10 years playing first-class cricket scored 8,343 runs at an average of 28.76.

His best season with Glamorgan was his first, when he hit 1,471 runs, average 38.71, to head their averages. Among four centuries that summer was 225 against Worcestershire at Dudley, during which he and Trevor Arnott put on 177 in 70 minutes. He scored another double century the next season, carrying his bat for 209 for Wales against M.C.C. He also helped to set up two Glamorgan partnership records in putting on 165 with J. T. Morgan for the fourth wicket against Nottinghamshire at Cardiff in 1927 and 167 with W. E. Bates for the first against Lancashire at Swansea in 1929.

When Bell gave up County Cricket, he returned to Yeadon, where he had first played, to serve as professional, groundsman and captain, and after similarly helping a club near Scunthorpe, he reappeared on first-class grounds as an umpire from 1948 to 1951.

BELL, Lieut. L. Clarke, one of the most prominent Canadian cricketers, fell during the Dieppe raid on August 19, 1942, within three days of completing his 32nd year. At Ridley College and for the Toronto Club he excelled as a left-handed batsman, and, coming to England in 1936 with the team that lost only once in a programme of 15 matches, he headed the averages with 45.11. Strangely enough, when the Canadians beat M.C.C. at Lord's by 76 runs, Clarke Bell failed. His highest score, 106 not out, was made at Chatham against Royal Engineers.

BELL, Percy Harrison, who died at Durban on February 4, 1956, aged 63, played in a few matches for Gloucestershire in 1911 and 1912. His highest score was 64 against Surrey at Bristol in 1911. Most of his later life was spent in South Africa, where he played in the Currie Cup competition for Orange Free State in 1912–13.

BELL, Percy Henry, who died in hospital at Hastings on July 31, 1971, aged 83, played as an amateur in a few matches for Gloucestershire in 1911 and the following season while at Cheltenham Training College.

BELL, Richard M., who died on June 11, 1953, aged 79, was a prominent slow off-break bowler for Sutton (Surrey) for more than 40 years. Born in Cumberland on New Year's Day, 1874, he was educated at Melbourne Grammar School and at The Leys School, where he was in the XIs of 1891 and 1892. He captained Surrey Second XI in 1906; played for Dr. W. G. Grace's London County side, and in 1909 went to Egypt as a member of the M.C.C. team led by Viscount Brackley. Three times he took all 10 wickets in an innings and on eight occasions performed the hat-trick.

BELOE, Gerald Harry, who died at Clifton, Bristol, on October 1, 1944, aged 66, was a useful batsman in the Marlborough XI, being captain in 1895, his fourth year. He appeared occasionally for Gloucestershire towards the end of the last century.

BELPER, The Second Lord (Henry Strutt), who was born in London, on May 20, 1840, died at Kingston Hall, Kegworth, Derbyshire, on July 26, 1914. He was in the Harrow XI of 1859, when he played an innings of 33 against Eton, and stumped R. A. H. Mitchell twice. At Cambridge he appeared in some of the Trial matches, but did not obtain his Blue, though he subsequently played for the Quidnuncs. In Lillywhite's *Companion* for 1860 he was described as "A fine hitter, with fair defence; kept wicket well to slow bowling, but was not up to Lang's pace, which required a Lockyer." He was President of the M.C.C. in 1882, and of the Notts County C.C. in 1885 and 1886, and had been a member of the former since 1863. Mr. Haygarth records that, "In December, 1865, when travelling in Greece with Lord A. Hervey and—Coore, Esq., he was taken prisoner by brigands, and had to pay (as well as the other two) £1,000 as a ransom for his release."

BENCRAFT, Sir Russell Henry William, J.P., M.R.C.S., L.R.C.P., one of the most prominent citizens of Southampton for many years, and always devoted to cricket, died on Christmas Day, 1943, at Compton near Winchester, aged 85, six months after his left leg was amputated above the knee. Born in Southampton on March 4, 1858, he lived there until his residence was destroyed by enemy action.

In the local playing fields as a boy he grew fond of the game, and at St. Edward's School, Oxford, he captained both cricket and football teams, as he did at St. George's Hospital, while as scrum-half he showed to advantage for Trojans, then the best Hampshire Rugby club.

A long biography in the *Southern Daily Echo*, of which Sir Russell Bencraft was chairman of directors, among several business offices which he held, mentioned his batting ability when a student at the Hospital. Most remarkable was the feat of playing a three-figure innings on every day of one week, including one of 243, and only being dismissed once.

No one did more towards advancing Hampshire in the world of cricket. Playing first for the county in 1876, when 18, he helped to beat Kent at Faversham by an innings and six runs. Three years later he took a prominent part in saving the County Club from extinction by becoming Hon. Secretary, and during a period of 60 years he occupied every office, including that of President, which he held when retiring from close participation in the game in 1936. He succeeded F. E. Lacey as captain in 1894 and, as the outcome of their good work, Hampshire were in the autumn ranked by M.C.C. as first-class for the season, but did not enter the championship competition until the next year, together with Derbyshire, Essex, Leicestershire and Warwickshire. So, quite appropriately, he captained the side when first taking part in the chief county tournament, but in 1896 gave way to Captain E. G.

Wynyard; and taking part in only three matches, ended his active career when 37 years old, largely because of his medical duties. Always known as Dr. Russell Bencraft in those days, his best playing years were enjoyed before Hampshire's promotion, and in 1889, when he averaged 53, his most noteworthy innings, 195 against Warwickshire at Birmingham, was the highest played for any county that season.

Russell Bencraft helped materially in the move of the county club from The Antelope to the ground still the headquarters of Hampshire cricket. Among a big store of reminiscences he found most satisfaction in recalling that he led Hampshire to victory by two wickets over Yorkshire at Sheffield in 1895; though scoring only four in each innings he was not out when the match was won.

Of medium height and robust build, he bowled fast as a youth and fielded with dash, usually at cover-point; but batting alone brought him real prominence and he was losing form when regularly facing strong opposition. As a legislator he was a valuable acquisition in all sports. For many years a member of the M.C.C. Committee; he was first president of the Southern Football League and held a similar position in the Hampshire Rugby Union and the Southampton Civil Service Sports Association, founded in 1923. He was knighted in 1924.

The Hampshire club entertained him to a Diamond Jubilee Banquet in January, 1937, Sir Stanley Jackson and many cricketers of high repute being present, while G. O. Allen, captain of the England team, cabled congratulations from Adelaide, where the fourth Test match with Australia was in progress.

BENGOUGH, Clement Stuart, a useful, free-hitting batsman and a very good wicket-keeper, who played for Marlborough College in 1879 and 1880, captaining the side in the latter year, died at Laramie, U.S.A., on November 19, 1934. Born near Bristol on January 14, 1861, he assisted Gloucestershire on a few occasions.

BENHAM, A. M., the young dramatic author, whose death in September, 1895, at the age of 23, cut short a promising career, was an enthusiastic cricketer, and played in the Rugby XI against Marlborough at Lord's in 1889.

BENHAM, Canon William, though never much of a cricketer, was very fond of the game. He was born at West Meon, Hampshire, on January 15, 1831, and died at St. Edmund's Rectory, Finsbury Square, on July 30, 1910. As a small boy he met John Nyren, who published his *Young Cricketer's Tutor* in 1833 and died four years later. He could also recall seeing Talleyrand, who died over 70 years ago, walking down Piccadilly.

BENKA, Herbert Frank, who died in hospital on April 22, 1970, aged 60, played for Middlesex between 1933 and 1937. His highest innings was 48 not out against Surrey at Lord's in 1934.

BENNETT, A. C. L. (Leo), who died on September 24, 1971, was well-known in club cricket, upon which he was the author of a book. At one time he captained the Club Cricket Conference and he played occasionally for Northamptonshire from 1947 to 1949. For a number of years he captained the B.B.C. cricket team. He played in war-time matches for the British Empire XI.

BENNETT, A. R., died in the second week in May, 1899, at the age of 30. For several seasons he was the crack bowler of the Notts Castle Club, and on various occasions he appeared in the Notts XI. He was a slow right handed bowler whose leg breaks proved highly effective in club cricket. The Notts professionals thought highly of him, and there is little doubt that it would have been to the benefit of the county if he had played more often than he did. He had the disadvantage, however, of being no batsman and not much of a field. His health had completely broken down some months before his death.

BENNETT, Cecil Tristram (Tris), who died on February 3, 1978, aged 75, enjoyed a run of eight consecutive years in the Harrow and Cambridge XIs between 1917 and 1925 and finished as captain at both places. A split hand while playing against Sussex at Hove caused him to miss the University match of 1924. He never really lived up to his youthful promise as a batsman and in 85 innings in first-class cricket—he also played for Surrey and Middlesex—his highest score was 88. Was a member in 1925–26 of the M.C.C. team in the West Indies. A brilliant slip fielder, he kept goal for Cambridge against Oxford in 1925.

BENNETT, Major Geoffrey Michael, died in Toronto on July 26, 1982, aged 72. After having a fine all-round record in the XI at

King's School, Bruton, he had a few trials for Somerset in 1928, the year he left school, and 1929, but it was not until 1932 that he gained a regular place in the side. From then until 1939 he played frequently, at one time acting as vice-captain to R. A. Ingle. His best season was 1934 when he scored 735 runs with an average of 19.86, including 71 and 73 (his highest score for the county) against Gloucestershire at Bath. Another fine innings was against Kent at Maidstone in 1939, when after seven wickets were down for 47, a brave 72 enabled his side to reach 185. He hit the ball well, especially in front of the wicket, and was a fine field. Little use was made in County Cricket of his bowling, though in 1934 he took four for 39 against Nottinghamshire at Taunton. In all he made 2,330 runs for Somerset with an average of 15.33. After the war he emigrated to Canada.

BENNETT, J. H., who died in 1947, played for Canterbury from 1898 to 1920, and for New Zealand against M.C.C. in 1906–07, Australia in 1909–10 and 1913–14. A good length medium-pace bowler, his record showed 259 wickets for 4,737 runs.

BENNETT, Capt. Richard Alexander, who died on July 16, 1953, aged 78, played in a number of games for Hampshire over the turn of the century, being contemporary with such players as E. M. Sprot, Capt. E. G. Wynyard and Major R. M. Poore. A cricketer of more than average ability, he was a steady bat and excellent wicket-keeper. He did not find a place in the XI at Eton, but played much club cricket for Eton Ramblers and Hampshire Hogs. In 1897 he toured America with Capt. P. F. (now Sir Pelham) Warner's team, which included G. L. Jessop, the mighty Gloucestershire hitter, and in 1902 led a team of amateurs which toured the West Indies. This side was got together by H. D. G. Leveson Gower, and it was expected that either he or Lord Hawke would be captain, but neither could make the trip. From 1910 he played for Thornbury Castle C.C. and continued after the amalgamation with Thornbury C.C. Chairman of Thornbury for many years, he was President from 1948 till his death, and was also a member of M.C.C. and Gloucestershire Gipsies.

BENSIMON, Alfred Samuel, who died in Cape Town on May 7, 1977, in his 91st year, had a short but very interesting first-class career. He played a single match for Western Province in 1931–32, making his debut at the advanced age of 45, and he played three more matches for them in 1933–34 when he was over 47. He was the captain on these three occasions and bowled his leg breaks so effectively that he took 17 wickets for only 177 runs. These four matches constituted his whole first-class career. As it happened he proved a statistician's nightmare, for his younger brother, Abel, had the identical initials, A.S., and he made his first-class debut in 1912–13, 20 years before his elder brother; his career ended in 1923–24. Not surprisingly, it was assumed that they were one and the same person.

BENTHALL, William Henry, one of the best-known amateur batsmen in England 50 years ago, died at St. Leonard's on January 4, 1909, in the 72nd year of his age. *Scores and Biographies* (v.–42) says of him: "Height, 5ft. 7½in., and weight about 10 st. Bats in an exceedingly pretty style, cutting beautifully to the off, and has made some capital scores in the best matches. In the field he is generally point, where he is extremely effective." As a slow bowler he was also occasionally successful, but his wickets were rather costly. He was born in Little Dean's Yard, Westminster, on July 3, 1837, and was educated at Westminster (where his father was a master), Marlborough, and Cambridge. He was only eight years of age when he left Westminster, as he was considered too young to stay after his father had retired, and it was at Marlborough that he learnt the game from Jimmy Dean, of Sussex, who was engaged to coach the boys. In 1855 and 1856 he represented Marlborough in the first two matches ever played with Rugby, and, although he made 61 runs in his four innings, he was on the losing side on both occasions. Proceeding to Cambridge he failed to secure his Blue as a Freshman owing to a damaged hand, but he played against Oxford from 1858 to 1860 and in two of the three years had the pleasure of being on the winning side. When Cambridge won by 28 runs in 1859 he played a sound and valuable second innings of 39, and in the three matches in which he appeared against Oxford he averaged 19 runs an innings. In 1858 he represented his University in the doubles at racquets, but he and his partner, J. M. Moorsom, were beaten 3–0 by W. Hart Dyke and J. P. F. Gundry. Between 1859 and 1863 he assisted the Gentlemen in seven matches against the Players, making 215 runs in 14 innings, his highest score being 45 in the match at the Oval in 1860. In County Cricket he appeared for Devonshire, Buckingham-

shire, and Middlesex, and in 1868 took part in the tie-match between the last named and Surrey at the Oval. After leaving Cambridge Mr. Benthall, owing to his duties at the India Office, where he at various times held important private secretaryships, including those to Lord Dufferin and the Duke of Argyll, found few opportunities of playing in great matches, though his name will occasionally be found in some of the matches played on Mr. John Walker's ground at Southgate. Had he been able to appear regularly he would no doubt have become famous, but, in addition to having many demands upon his time, he was handicapped by poor health. In 1874 he retired from the India Office on a pension. Since 1876 he had lived at St. Leonard's, and for many years was a familiar figure at the Hastings Festival.

BENTINCK, Bernhard W., who died on June 27, 1931, aged 53, appeared for Hampshire in 1900 and for some time was President of the Hampshire Hogs C.C. Educated at Winchester, he possessed fine driving powers. Playing for Alton in August, 1921, he had the unusual experience of being bowled by a ball (delivered by H. E. Roberts, the Sussex professional) which was deflected on to the wicket through striking and killing a swallow. Mr. Bentinck had been a member of M.C.C. for 30 years.

BENTON, Charles Henry, whose death by his own hand at Knutsford, on May 19, 1918, came as a great shock to his friends, was born on January 8, 1869. Though it cannot be said that he ever rose to much distinction as a player Mr. Benton was for many years a prominent figure in the cricket world, playing for Lancashire and Cheshire, and serving on the M.C.C. Committee.

BENTON, Capt. William Richard (Manchester Regiment), who died of wounds on August 17, 1916, played for Middlesex twice in 1913, but was best known owing to his association with the Mote Park C.C. He served throughout the South African War, and in 1915 was wounded and invalided home. Before the present War he was curate-in-charge of Bearsted, in Kent. He was in the XI whilst at Framlingham College.

BERENS, Alexander Augustus, who died in London on May 31, 1925, aged 83, appeared occasionally for Northamptonshire.

BERESFORD, Richard Augustus Agincourt, who died at Derby on July 12, 1941, aged 71, scored heavily in school and club cricket, but just failed to get his Blue at Cambridge in 1890, and next season he received a less extended trial. S. M. J. Woods and Gregor MacGregor were the captains of very strong XIs in those years. He played for Northamptonshire under the birth qualification, and also for Norfolk. When at Oundle he accomplished an extraordinary performance in scoring 102 not out and 307 not out for School House v. Laxton House in May, 1888, besides dismissing seven men in an innings. Next month he hit up 225 for the school against "The Past" and again was not out. He captained the Oundle XI in 1887 and 1888 and was in every way a good cricketer, his fast bowling getting many wickets. A capable athlete, he twice appeared at Queen's Club in the University Sports, being second in Putting the Weight, with 34ft. 8½in. in 1891, and third next year with 34ft. 11in.

BERESFORD, The Hon. Seton Robert de la Poer Horsley, who was born on July 25, 1868, and died at Cap d'Ail on May 28, 1928, aged 59, appeared for Middlesex in two games in 1909. In America he represented New York in Halifax Cup Matches and, playing for Manor Field v. Columbia Oval in 1919, he put up 228 for the first wicket with E. G. Hull. During the South African War, in which he was a special correspondent, he was the first man to enter Kimberley and notify Cecil Rhodes of the approach of the Relief Force.

BERGIN, Stanley Francis, who died in Dublin on August 4, 1969, scored more runs for Ireland than any other player. Born in Dublin on November 18, 1926, he was educated in that city at the Westland Row Christian Brothers' School. A left-hander, he made 53 appearances for his country between 1949 and 1965 scoring 2,524 runs, average 27.73. If he had chosen to do so, there is little doubt that he could have held his own in County Cricket. A journalist by profession, he wrote the section on Irish cricket for *The World of Cricket*. His brother Bernard also played cricket for Ireland in 1937.

BERKELEY, George Fitz-Hardinge, who died at Hanwell Castle, Banbury, on November 14, 1955, aged 85, accomplished many fine performances as a medium-paced left-arm bowler late last century. Born in Dublin, he was in the Wellington College XI for four years, heading the bowling averages from 1887 to 1889. In 1887 he took 63 wickets, average 10.31, and in 1889 took 47, average 8.10. He gained his Blue at Oxford as a Freshman in 1890 and played four times against Cambridge, obtaining in the big matches 27 wickets for less than 13 runs each. His best performances in the University matches were five wickets for 20 runs in the second innings in 1891, when Cambridge, having compelled Oxford to follow on 102 behind, scrambled home by two wickets, and five for 38—including the wickets of K. S. Ranjitsinhji, E. C. Streatfeild and C. M. Wells—and four for 56 in 1893. It was in the 1891 match that the Hon. F. J. N. Thesiger slipped when fielding during the opening hour, sprained his wrist and dropped out of the game. G. McGregor, the Cambridge captain, allowed T. B. Case to replace him in the Oxford team. In 1890, Berkeley distinguished himself for Oxford against the Australians by dismissing eight men for 70 runs. Two years later he appeared without success for Gentlemen against Players at the Oval. For some seasons from 1904 he played occasionally for Oxfordshire. He served in the Worcestershire Regiment from 1898 to 1901, afterwards became a barrister and author and saw service in the First World War as Brigade musketry officer in the 3rd Cavalry Reserve Regiment and on the Claims Commission in France and Italy.

BERNARD, Charles A., who died at Bristol, 1953, aged 77, was a member of the Bristol Bohemians Club and played for Somerset. He first appeared for the county in 1896, but three years elapsed before he again gained a place in the side. Then, in 12 matches, he scored 697 runs, average 33.19, and *Wisden* said of him: "He made it clear that he was a batsman of more than ordinary ability." Against Hampshire at Southampton the following season he scored 122, he and L. C. H. Palairet putting on 262 for the third wicket, and he scored another century, 101 not out, from the Gloucestershire bowling at Taunton in 1901. Strong in defence, he was particularly good in off-side strokes, but indifferent fielding prevented him from playing for Somerset more often.

BERNARD, Dr. David, who died at Bristol on July 14, 1920, aged 78, played for the old West Gloucestershire C.C. He was brother-in-law of Dr. W. G. Grace, having married the Champion's sister, Miss Alice Grace.

BERNAU, Ernest Henry Lovell, who died in January, 1966, aged 80, toured England with

T. C. Lowry's New Zealand team in 1927. In first-class matches, he took 32 wickets with left-arm medium-pace bowling for 24.21 runs each, his best analysis being six for 35 in the first innings of Glamorgan at Cardiff. "Bill" Bernau achieved some excellent performances for Wanganui, Hawkes Bay and Wellington. In 1913 he took seven South Taranaki wickets for 57 runs in the first innings and five for 45 in the second and he did the "hat-trick" in the Town v. Country game of 1923. He was also a more than useful batsman, as he showed when hitting 117 for Wellington v. Auckland in his first Plunket Shield match in 1921–22.

BERRIDGE, Dr. William Claude Morpott, who died on February 25, 1973, aged 78, was in the Malvern XI from 1912 to 1914, being captain in the last year. From 1914 to 1923 he played as an amateur for Leicestershire in occasional matches, scoring in all 455 runs, average 11.66, and taking 30 wickets at a cost of 28.80 runs apiece.

BESCH, John George Quiddington ("Daddy"), for some years one of the best known figures in Metropolitan club cricket, was born on June 30, 1861, and died at Beltinge, Herne Bay, on April 25, 1929, aged 67. At Oakham Grammar School he captained both cricket and football teams. Later on he played regularly for, and was Hon. Secretary of, the Hampstead C.C. A good batsman and an excellent organiser. When he made 98 for the club against the Stoics in August, 1886, he helped to add 214 for the second wicket with A. E. Stoddart, who scored 485. Altogether the side made 813 for nine wickets in six and a quarter hours.

BESSANT, John, who died on January 18, 1982, aged 86, played for Gloucestershire as a fast-medium bowler from 1921 to 1928. In 1921 he took 34 wickets at 25.73, but thereafter could never produce an average of under 30 and, after three seasons as a regular member of the side, had increasing difficulty in keeping his place. One of his competitors was Tom Goddard, who seeing no real future as a fast bowler, altered his style and became a great slow off-spinner. As a bat, Bessant, a useful hitter, enjoyed one triumph, against Somerset at Bristol in 1923, when he made 50, putting on 131 for the last wicket (still a Gloucestershire record) in just over an hour with W. R. Goldsworthy. Altogether for the county he scored 1,200 runs with an average of 10.26 and took 130 wickets at 35.50. For many years he was groundsman to Bristol University.

BESSBOROUGH, The Earl of, so well known to countless cricketers of former days as the Hon. Frederick Ponsonby, died on March 12, 1895. He had reached a ripe age, having been born in London on September 11, 1815. For a great number of years closely associated with the M.C.C. and perpetual vice-president of the Surrey County Club, there was no more honoured figure in the cricket world. Appearing first at Lord's for Harrow against Eton in 1832, he played in big matches till about 1845. At that date, partly owing to his profession and partly to an injury to his arm, he gave up playing at Lord's, though for several seasons he continued to take part in small matches. By cricketers of the present day Lord Bessborough will not be remembered so much for what he did in the field as for his devotion during many years to Harrow cricket, and the fact that in 1845, in conjunction with his brother, the Hon. Spencer Ponsonby-Fane, and Mr. John Loraine Baldwin, he founded I Zingari.

BESSEMER, Henry Douglas, who died on February 7, 1968, aged 73, was appointed by M.C.C. in 1937 to assist in an advisory capacity on financial questions the Commission which inquired into "the problems at present confronting the first-class counties". He was a great grandson of Sir Henry Bessemer, the inventor of the process for the direct conversion of pig-iron into steel.

BEST, William Finlay, died on August 3, 1942, aged 77. A good batsman and slow right-hand bowler, he played most of his cricket for the Preston club in Lancashire, scoring in the seasons 1890 to 1905 10,550 runs and taking 597 wickets. Educated at Folkestone, he was qualified for Kent, and at Taunton in 1891—his only match for the county that season—he did the hat-trick against Somerset, whose first season that was in the County Championship. He also appeared for Kent a few times in 1890 and 1892.

BESTWICK, Robert Saxton, who died in Jersey on July 3, 1980, aged 80, will be remembered for an incident which one can safely say is unique in first-class cricket. For Derbyshire against Warwickshire at Derby in 1922, for some 10 minutes he bowled at one end while his father, the much better known Bill Bestwick, bowled at the other, against

W. G. Quaife and his son, B. W. A fast-medium left-armer, R. S. Bestwick played five matches for the county between 1920 and 1922, but met with little success. Later he played League cricket and finally moved to Jersey where, beside being a publican, he coached and umpired at Victoria College.

BESTWICK, William, the Derbyshire professional, died on May 3, 1938, aged 62. Of good height and heavy build, he brought all the force associated with his winter occupation as a miner into his right hand bowling so effectively and with such reserve of strength, that he continued in County Cricket until his 50th year. Appointed to the list of first-class umpires, he remained a familiar figure on the field until last season when illness compelled his retirement. Bestwick first played for Derbyshire in 1898 and, gradually improving, he three times took over a hundred wickets in a season before 1909 when he preferred League cricket in South Wales. In that way he became qualified for Glamorgan, but resumed his services with Derbyshire after the War, and enjoyed his most successful season in 1921 when 147 wickets fell to him at an average of 16.72 runs apiece. All this work was done in 20 county matches, Derbyshire not having a fixture with the Australians. His best performance was, strangely enough, against Glamorgan to which county he thought of returning. In the match at Cardiff, Derbyshire were 85 behind on the first innings but then Bestwick dismissed all the home side, seven clean bowled, and 193 runs were obtained for the loss of eight men. So Derbyshire snatched a victory on the second day. Bestwick's figures read—19 overs, two maidens, 40 runs, 10 wickets. He bowled unchanged through the innings which realised 106 runs. On the first day Bestwick dismissed four men for 71, his full return in the match being 14 wickets for 111 runs—a remarkable performance for a man of his weight with 45 years old. He could bowl at full speed for long spells because he relied on a short run with the power of his arm and body giving pace to the ball and lift from the pitch. Length and spin were the mainstays of his work.

BESWICK, James, who died at Blackpool on May 1, 1951, aged 58, was at one time a wicket-keeper on the Lancashire staff and kept goal for Sheffield United.

BETHAM, John Dover, who died at his home, Rose Cottage, Sedbergh, on January 1, 1956, aged 81, was for 40 years a valued contributor to the obituaries in *Wisden.* He had been ill for some months. He was the author of *Oxford and Cambridge Cricket Scores and Biographies,* published in 1905.

BETHUNE, Major Henry Beauclerk, who played occasionally for Hampshire from 1885 until 1897, and was born on November 16, 1844, died on April 16, 1912. His highest score in County Cricket was 75 v. M.C.C. and Ground at Southampton, in 1891. In minor matches he played several long innings, including 219 for Corinthians v. United Services in 1890, 103 for Gentlemen of Hampshire v. Gentlemen of Canada in 1887, and 102 for United Services v. Parsis in 1886. He had been a member of the M.C.C. since 1888.

BETON, William, dressing room attendant at Lord's, known to M.C.C. members and first-class cricketers as "Sam," died at his home near the St. John's Wood ground on May 3, 1940, aged 69.

BETTESWORTH, Walter Ambrose, born at Horndean, in Hampshire, on November 24, 1856, died at Hampstead on February 23, 1929, aged 72. He was a sound, hard-hitting batsman, a good slow bowler and an energetic field at cover-point. He played in the Ardingly College XI—first as a pupil and later as a master—from 1871 until 1882. Assisting Sussex occasionally between 1878 and 1883, he scored 707 runs for the county with an average of 18.12 and took 36 wickets for 25.63 runs each. In 1881, when he scored 77 v. Hampshire at Southampton, he stood first in the averages and so won the silver cup offered by the Earl of Sheffield. He took part in that remarkable match between Gentlemen and Players at Hove, in 1881, arranged for James Lillywhite's benefit, when after a tie on the first innings, the Players won by a single run. Whilst a master at Blair Lodge, he made some very large scores in Scotland, among these being 227 not out v. Falkirk and 203 not out v. Stirling County. Afterwards he became a journalist and one of the best known, as well as one of the most engaging, writers on the game. He was on the staff of the *Cricket Field* 1892–95, assistant editor of *Cricket* 1896–1905, and cricket editor of *The Field* 1906–28. His books on the game were *A Royal Road to Cricket, The Walkers of Southgate,* and *Chats on the Cricket Field.*

BETTINGTON, Dr. Reginald Henshaw Brindley, who died in an accident—his car fell 100 feet on to a railway line—in New

Zealand on June 24, 1969, aged 69, was a fine all-round sportsman. He was in the Oxford cricket XI for four years from 1920, being captain in 1923; played as a forward in the University Rugby matches of 1920 and 1922 and got his Blue at golf. He appeared for Middlesex, for Gentlemen v. Players and, after returning to Australia, captained New South Wales. In addition, he won both the New South Wales and Australian amateur golf championships.

Going from King's School, Paramatta, to Oxford in 1920, "Reg" Bettington got his cricket Blue as a Freshman. He created a big impression with his leg-breaks and googlies, taking 56 wickets for the University for 15.12 runs each. In the Freshmen's match, he dismissed eight men for 48 runs in an innings, took seven for 47 and five for 42 against Somerset, five for 48 against Essex and earned a similar analysis in the match at Oxford with Warwickshire. Yet he met with little success in the University match and he did not touch the same form in the following two seasons.

In 1923, when he became the first Australian to captain Oxford, however, he reaped a rich harvest of Cambridge victims. Helped by the effects of what *Wisden* described as "the worst thunderstorm for 12 years", he took three wickets for 19 runs in the first innings and eight for 66 in the second, thus playing a leading part in victory for Oxford by an innings and 227 runs—the most substantial in the series between the Universities. Among other outstanding analyses he achieved were six wickets for 71 runs against Hampshire at Oxford and five for 22 and four for 91 against Surrey at the Oval, and his full figures for the summer were 61 wickets for 16.55 each.

From the University he went to St. Bartholomew's Hospital, where he qualified as a doctor, and in 1928 he assisted Middlesex. In 15 County Championship matches, he took 54 wickets for 29.44 runs apiece and made 605 runs at an average of 30.25. Against Somerset at Lord's, he followed an innings of 95 by sending back six second-innings batsmen for 78 runs, and he took six Somerset wickets for 78 on the same ground.

In all first-class cricket in England, he obtained 335 wickets for 22.15 runs each and, as a forthright batsman who once drove a ball into the Press Box at the Oval, he scored 3,072 runs, including five centuries, average 27.67.

For a number of years he was ear, nose and throat specialist to Hawke's Bay Hospital Board, a post he held at the time of his death.

BETTS, John Arnott, who died on July 1, 1970, aged 101, once played in a game at the Crystal Palace when Dr. W. G. Grace was on the opposing side. He appeared in a few matches for Hertfordshire.

BETTS, Morton Peto, who died on April 19, 1914, was a very useful cricketer, although he did not succeed in obtaining a place in the Harrow XI. In 1872 he appeared for Middlesex against Surrey at Prince's, and played once for Kent the same year and again in 1881, scoring altogether 83 runs with an average of 27.66. From 1887 until 1890 he was Secretary to the Essex County C.C. In club matches he made many good scores, playing frequently for Bickley Park, Streatham, the Incogniti, etc., and was very well known in the Association football world, first as a player and afterwards as a referee. He was born in London on August 30, 1847.

BEVAN, The Ven. William Latham, who died at Hay on August 25, 1908, in his 87th year, was a useful player in his Rugby and Oxford days, although he did not obtain a place in either XI. In 1838 and 1839 he occasionally represented the Sixth against the School at Rugby. He was Vicar of Hay for 56 years, 1845–1900.

BEVES, Gordon, born at Brighton on March 15, 1863, died at Johannesburg on March 22, 1927, aged 64. He learned the game at Leys School and, developing into a useful all-round player, took part in various great matches with success in South Africa, his most pleasant experience being to captain the Transvaal team which won the Currie Cup in 1895. His best innings in first-class cricket was 60 for the Transvaal v. Griqualand West at Cape Town in April, 1898. He was a well-known figure in the game, and had served as chairman of the South African Cricket Association. Before settling in South Africa he had been associated with the Notts. Forest Amateurs, heading their batting averages with 31 in 1884, when he played an innings of 177 v. Forest United, and their bowling averages a year later. He appeared a few times in the Nottinghamshire XI between 1888 and 1891, and also played Rugby football for Sussex and Old Leysians.

BEVILL, Frederick, M.A., for some years the Australian correspondent of *Cricket*, died at Randwick, Sydney, on June 2, 1911.

He was a very fair player in his younger days, and was well-known as a dramatic critic.

BEVINGTON, John Currey, twice in the Harrow XI at Lord's, scored 71 and 12 in the 1891 match when Eton were beaten by seven wickets. He played a little for Essex and Middlesex. Died on April 4, 1933, aged 62.

BEVINGTON, Timothy Arthur, who died in Vancouver in May, 1966, aged 85, was at Harrow without gaining a place in the XI. Brother of J. C. Bevington, who also played for the county, he appeared in four County Championship matches for Middlesex between 1900 and 1904. His highest innings was 27 in the last season, when he and J. H. Hunt stemmed a collapse against Gloucestershire at Lord's by adding 50 for the eighth wicket.

BEZER, Arthur, groundsman and professional to Bath C.C. died in hospital on July 11, 1944, after an accidental fall. A good all-round player, he appeared once for Somerset, but he was best known for skill in tending turf and coaching young players. He taught two sons to play cricket; both were serving in Italy at the time of their father's death, aged 68.

BICKMORE, Arthur Frederic, died in a nursing home at Tonbridge on March 18, 1979, aged 79. Four years in the Clifton XI and captain in 1917, he had a good trial for Kent in 1919, and won his Blue at Oxford in 1920. In a University match ruined by rain, his 66 on a sodden wicket was easily the highest score for his side. Later in the same season he made 104 not out for Kent v. Essex at Dover in 90 minutes. In 1921, when Oxford lost at Lord's by an innings, he was again their highest scorer with 57, and was also top-scorer for Kent against the Australians with 89, he and Hardinge adding 154 runs in two hours for the third wicket. Becoming a schoolmaster, he was after that seldom available till late in the season, and he played little after 1923, although his last appearance was not until 1929. His highest score was 120 against Essex at Tonbridge in 1922. Both for Oxford and Kent he normally opened. He was also one of the great outfields of his day and was equally good at short-leg. He was the last survivor of the 1920 Oxford side.

BIGGLESTON, Lieut. D. H., R.A., missing in July, 1942, and eventually reported killed in action, was a good wicket-keeper and useful batsman for Tonbridge School Second XI. Prominent in club cricket with St. Lawrence, Band of Brothers, Cryptics and Incogniti, he for two years before the war was captain and hon. secretary of the St. Lawrence club. For Kent Second XI he did good service until T. G. Evans replaced him as wicket-keeper.

BIGNALL, Thomas, the once well-known Nottingham batsman, dropped down dead while following his usual occupation at Nottingham on September 19, 1898. Born on January 1, 1842, he was in his 57th year. Though he had long since given up first-class cricket, Bignall in his day did capital work for Notts, playing in the XI side by side with Richard Daft, Alfred Shaw, William Oscroft, Fred Wild, J. C. Shaw, Biddulph, George Wootton, and poor George Summers. He was at his best as a batsman in the seasons 1868–69, playing an innings of 97 against Surrey at Trent Bridge in the former year, when most of the Notts players were strange to Southerton's bowling, and scoring 116 against Kent in 1869. His leg hitting in this latter innings was described at the time as not unworthy of comparison with that of George Parr.

BIGNELL, Lieut.-Col. Guy Newcome, who died on June 10, 1965, aged 78, was in the Haileybury XI in 1903 and 1904, heading the batting averages in the second year with 526 runs in 10 innings and hitting 51 against Cheltenham at Lord's. He played occasionally for Hampshire from 1904 to 1919, figuring in the last season under the assumed name of "G. Newcombe". His best score was 109 against Kent at Portsmouth in 1905.

BIGNELL, Hugh Glennie, who was born on October 4, 1882, died at Rawalpindi of enteric fever on May 6, 1907. He appeared on a few occasions for Hampshire in 1901 and 1902, his best performance being to make 49 not out and 22 not out against Somerset at Portsmouth in the former year.

BILBROUGH, James Gordon Priestley, who was fatally gassed on November 5, 1944, while engaged on rescue work during a mining accident, was a member of the Eastern Province team in the series of interprovincial matches played as trials prior to the selection of the 1929 South African team which visited England. He was 34 years of age.

BILLHAM, Frank Denis, who died at Sudbury on November 16, 1980, aged 84, played twice for Essex in 1924, against Nottingham-shire and Sussex, as a slow left-arm bowler, without taking a wicket. The first of these matches was at Ilford, for whom he played for many years. He was also on the council of the Club Cricket Conference, of which he was an Hon. Vice-President.

BINGHAM, Capt. Frank Miller (5th King's Own Royal Lancaster Regiment) was born September 17, 1874, and killed in Flanders on May 22, 1915. He was in the XI at St Peter's School, York, and in 1896 played for Derbyshire v. M.C.C. and Ground at Lord's, scoring six and 11. Up to the outbreak of war he was in medical practice at Lancaster. He was at one time a well-known Blackheath Rugby forward.

BINNEY, Edgar James, was, at the time of his death on September 9, 1978, at the age of 93, the oldest surviving Victorian first-class cricketer and a former successful bowler with the historic Essenden club in Melbourne first-grade cricket between 1907 and 1916. Personal commitments restricted his cricket after appearing for Victoria in 1910 and closed his career when he commenced in 1916—first as accountant—his 40-year as-sociation with the powerful Commercial Travellers Association of Victoria. As its secretary-manager for 25 of its most active years, Binney was widely known in Mel-bourne business and club circles for his gentlemanly bearing, noted diplomacy, and extremely friendly manner in dealing with all with whom he came in contact.

BINYON, Alfred Edwin, died at Kendal, October 4, 1948. Played for Somerset. For over 40 years a master at Ackworth School, Yorkshire, then at Stramongate School, Kendal.

BIRCH, Albert Edward, who died on November 6, 1936, aged 68, made a solitary appearance for Kent against the M.C.C. at Lord's in 1894. A useful batsman and fast-medium right-hand bowler, he played for Formby in the Lancashire League when G. R. Bardswell, the Oxford Blue, was cap-tain. He was born on August 11, 1858.

BIRCHAM, Sam, who died at Yarrowfield, Mayford, Surrey, on June 4, 1923, aged 84, had been Auditor to the M.C.C. for many years, and a member of the club since 1869. His intimate acquaintance with Parlia-mentary and Private Bill procedure enabled him, with the late Lord James of Hereford,

to procure for the M.C.C. immense and lasting advantages when it seemed possible that Lord's ground might be encroached upon by covetous railway promoters.

BIRD, Albert, born at Moseley, on August 17, 1868, died on June 17, 1927, after a very long illness, at the age of 58. Playing for Warwickshire from 1887 until 1890, and for Worcestershire from 1892 onwards in both its second and first-class days, he will be remembered as an excellent slow right-handed bowler and a safe field. For the latter county he and Mr. E. G. Bromley-Martin bowled unchanged throughout v. Hampshire at Worcester in 1897, a year later he had an analysis of four for 12 v. Glamorgan on the same ground, and at Southampton in 1901 he obtained 14 Hampshire wickets for 109 runs—seven for 53 and seven for 56.

BIRD, Lieut.-Col. Austin Carlos, died on January 4, 1938, when nearly 54 years of age. From Malvern he went into the Indian Army and made a lot of runs during his term of service in the East. He played for M.C.C. against Hampshire at Lord's in 1914, but did not often take part in first-class cricket in England.

BIRD, Rev. Frederick Nash, who died on March 3, 1965, aged 88, played occasionally as a batsman for Gloucestershire in 1899 and 1900 and for Northamptonshire in 1908 and 1909. His highest first-class innings was 61 not out for Northamptonshire against Leices-tershire at Leicester in 1908. He also played for Buckinghamshire, Devon and Suffolk.

BIRD, George, born at Hornsey, on July 30, 1849, died at Esher, Surrey, on October 28, 1930, aged 81. A member of the M.C.C. since 1870, he had played in many matches for the club. He was a sound and effective batsman with a graceful style and a good field in any position. At Lord's in July, 1873, he scored 116 not out and 30 for Fifteen Gentle-men of M.C.C. (with Rylott) against R. A. FitzGerald's Anglo-American Team of 1872, that being his best performance in a match of note. Between 1872 and 1877 he took part in some Middlesex cricket and in 1880 ap-peared for Lancashire under the residential qualification. He was father of M. C. Bird, the old Harrovian.

BIRD, Morice Carlos, whose remarkable performance of scoring two separate hun-dreds in the Eton and Harrow match in 1907 remains unparalleled, died at Broadstone,

Dorset, on December 9, 1933. Besides being famous at Harrow, whom he represented four times against Eton, he made a name as a batsman for Surrey and also played a good deal for M.C.C. Born at Liverpool on March 25, 1888, Mr. Bird was in the Harrow XI from 1904 to 1907, and was captain when he wound up his school career with his great achievement. Tall and of strong build he dwarfed the other players both in stature and skill. In Harrow's first innings he scored 100 not out in an hour and three-quarters; in the second, when fighting an uphill game, he hit up 131 in two hours and a quarter. Thanks to his fine hitting and his timely declaration, Harrow won at 20 minutes past seven by 79 runs.

The same year—1907—Mr. Bird appeared in a few games for his native county, Lancashire, but not until he played for Surrey two years afterwards did he accomplish anything of note in County Cricket. Then he was included in the M.C.C. side that toured South Africa in the winter of 1909–10, and also visited South Africa with the team of 1913–14, playing in 10 Test matches in that country. Succeeding Mr. H.D.G. Leveson Gower in 1911, Mr. Bird captained Surrey during the next two years and in 1910, 1911 and 1913 scored over a thousand runs. His best season was that of 1911, when he had an aggregate of 1,404 and an average of 30. A very fine forcing batsman, specially strong on the off side, both in driving and cutting, Morice Bird had a determined personality which often enabled him to show to most advantage on important occasions. His hitting against the Australian team of 1912 in two games at the Oval—he scored 76, 68 and 112 in dazzling fashion—is still talked about. A medium pace bowler, he took five wickets in the match with Eton which brought him such fame. In 1911, he had a record of 47 wickets for just over 20 runs apiece. He was also a capital field. After the War, he succeeded Mr. M.C. Kemp for two seasons as coach at Harrow and subsequently undertook similar duties at the Oval. He had been desperately ill for some years prior to his death.

BIRD, Percy John, who died suddenly at Freshwater Bay, Isle of Wight, in November, 1942, aged 62, took a prominent part in local cricket and occasionally played for Hampshire. He was a member of M.C.C. and well known in racing and yachting circles.

BIRD, Lieut. Wilfrid Stanley (6th Batt. King's Royal Rifle Corps.) was born at Yiewsley, Middlesex, September 28, 1883, and killed in action on April 9, 1915. He was educated at the Grange, Eastbourne, where he was captain of the cricket and football XIs, and afterwards at Malvern, where he represented the college at cricket, football and fives. He was in the Malvern XI in 1900–01–02, among his contemporaries being A.P. Day and G.N. Foster. Going up to Oxford with good credentials as a wicket-keeper he would in the ordinary course of events have stepped straight into the XI, but Oxford in 1903 had a wicket-keeper of established reputation in W. Findlay. However, he kept wicket for Oxford in 1904–05–06, being captain of the XI in his last year. As a wicket-keeper he had not the genius of Martyn or MacGregor, but he was decidedly above the average. It was his privilege to keep wicket for the Gentlemen at Lord's in 1908 and 1912. He also played on a few occasions for Middlesex. His skill was, perhaps, never seen to better advantage than when keeping to D.W. Carr's "googlies" at Scarborough in 1909. As a batsman he was only moderate, but he helped the late W.H.B. Evans to save the University match in 1904. He was a master at Ludgrove School for several years, and was gazetted to the King's Royal Rifles in January, 1915. He had been a member of the M.C.C. since 1905.

BIRKBECK, Capt. Gervase William (Norfolk Regiment), killed April 19, 1917, aged 30. 12th man at Eton; in XI at Trinity College (Camb.); good bat and field. First match for Norfolk was in 1906. Best scores for the county—111 v. Cambridgeshire, at Cambridge, 1910; 108 v. Hertfordshire, at Norwich, 1911; and 118 v. Bedfordshire, at Bedford, 1912. His father had played for Norfolk.

BIRKETT, William Norman, First Baron, who died on February 10, 1962, aged 78, was a vice-President of Lancashire County C.C. A lover of cricket, he was always in demand at functions connected with the game. He was a regular speaker at the annual dinners of the Cricket Writers' Club, where his turn of phrase, quiet humour and personal charm made him immensely popular. He wrote a little gem of an article, "The Love of Cricket," in the 1958 *Wisden*. A very distinguished member of the legal profession, he gained fame in turn as a K.C., Judge of the King's Bench Division and Lord Justice of Appeal.

BIRLEY, Francis Hornby, J.P., of the Winchester XIs of 1867 and 1868, died at Lingfield, Surrey, on August 1, 1910, aged 60. He was born on March 14, 1850. In 1868 it was said of him "Possesses excellent judgment as captain: a clever slow bowler, and an excellent field anywhere: hits freely, and, though unfortunate at first, scored largely at the end of the season." In his two matches against Eton he scored only 14 runs in four innings, but took 13 wickets. Proceeding to Oxford, he appeared in the Freshmen's match of 1869, but did not obtain his Blue. He played for Lancashire three times in 1870 and once in 1872, and in 1879 appeared for Surrey against Middlesex at the Oval. Mr. Birley was famous at Association football in the early days of the game, playing for the Wanderers.

BIRON, The Rev. Henry Brydges, who was born at Hythe on June 13, 1835, died at Derringstone, Barham, Canterbury, on April 7, 1915, in his 80th year. He was a free and attractive batsman who made several good scores for the Gentlemen of Kent. In August, 1864, he made 214 for Cambridge Quidnuncs against the Gentlemen of Sussex, at Brighton, this being the first instance of an innings of 200 or more being played in that county. "His enormous score was achieved by the most rapid hitting and judicious placing, combined with a just contempt of the wicket-keeper." The bat used on that occasion was borrowed from Mr. John Walker, the eldest of the famous brotherhood. Mr. Biron evidently had a partiality for the old Brighton ground, for he scored 59 and 68 there for the Gentlemen of Kent against the Gentlemen of Sussex in 1862, and 67 and 52 not out in the match between the same sides in the following year. Between 1857 and 1864 he represented the county in 15 matches, scoring 208 runs with an average of 9.90, and taking one wicket for 31 runs. He was educated at King's School, Canterbury, and at Cambridge, but did not obtain a place in the University XI.

BIRTWELL, Alex J., one of the great cricket characters of the Lancashire League and a well-known Burnley solicitor, died in November, 1974, aged 65. He played for Nelson, Colne, Burnley and Lowerhouse, and really made his name at Nelson in their noted side of the 1930s when Learie Constantine was the professional. A talented spin bowler, he appeared in 14 matches for Lancashire between 1937–39 when he took 25 wickets, average 39.96. He also played for Buckinghamshire.

BISGOOD, Bertram Lewis, who died on July 19, 1968, aged 87, played from time to time as an amateur for Somerset from 1907 to 1921. He enjoyed the satisfaction of hitting a century on his debut in first-class cricket when, for Somerset against Worcestershire at Worcester in 1907, he followed a first innings of 82 with one of 116 not out. Another big success came against Gloucestershire at Taunton in 1914 when he scored 116 and 78 not out.

BISPHAM, A. W. G., a native of Barbados, died at Westwood, New Jersey, on March 8, 1907, aged 28. He was secretary of the recently-formed New Jersey State Cricket League.

BISSET, Sir Murray, born at Port Elizabeth on April 14, 1876, died at Salisbury, Rhodesia, on October 24, 1931. At the time of his death he was Acting-Governor of Rhodesia. He captained Western Province for several seasons and when in 1898–99 Lord Hawke's team toured South Africa he played in two Test matches against them. In 1901, he led the South African team in England—the tour financed by J. D. Logan with Lohmann as manager. Extremely popular both on and off the field, he not only controlled the side with skill, but in all matches during the tour scored 1,080 runs with an average of 27. By brilliant hitting all round the wicket he put together, against Derbyshire, an innings of 184. Sir Murray was also a good wicket-keeper but, in view of E. A. Halliwell's consistent form that season, did not often take on these duties. His final appearance in Test cricket came in 1910 against the M.C.C. team led by Mr. H. D. G. Leveson Gower.

BISSETT, George Finlay, who collapsed and died at his home at Botha's Hill, near Durban, on November 14, 1965, aged 60, formerly played as a fast bowler for Griqualand West and for South Africa. He appeared four times against Capt. R. T. Stanyforth's M.C.C. team in 1927–28 and, in taking 25 wickets for 18.76 runs each, did much to enable South Africa to draw the Test rubber after losing the first two fixtures. In the final match at Durban, Bissett removed seven batsmen for 29 runs in the second innings, bringing about the dismissal of England for 118 and victory for South Africa by eight wickets.

BLABER, A., who was well-known in club cricket around Lewes, died on May 15, 1905.

He appeared twice for Sussex—once in 1890 and again in 1894. At the time of his death he was only 35 years of age, having been born at Ludwell Farm, Horsted Keynes, on December 15, 1869.

BLACK, Thomas Hirst, who died at Toronto on June 23, 1924, was born at Huddersfield, in Yorkshire, on October 17, 1889, and educated at Huddersfield College High Grade School and Glasgow University. About a fortnight before his death he scored 100 not out for the Yorkshire C.C. v. St. George at Toronto. He was a Professor at Toronto University.

BLACKHAM, John McCarthy, in the opinion of many people, the finest of all wicket-keepers and unquestionably a player who, in that capacity, had no superior, was born at Fitzroy, near Melbourne, on May 11, 1853, and first played cricket with the Carlton Club at Melbourne. At different times it has been urged on behalf of Blackham that in standing up to fast bowling without a long-stop he set a new fashion—indeed that he first taught Englishmen what wicket-keeping really could be. This claim is incorrect. Several English wicket-keepers—George Pinder, of Yorkshire, Tom Plumb, of Buckinghamshire and, most notably, Dick Pilling, of Lancashire—were always prepared to stand up to fast bowling without a long-stop, and often did so, but on the rough wickets of 60 years ago or more the ball flew about to such an extent that the practice of doing without a long stop was, generally speaking, ill-advised.

As a matter of fact Blackham, when he first came to England in 1878, had no really fast bowling to take except that of Spofforth, and Spofforth was more often fast-medium than really fast. Incidentally it may be recalled that, whereas Blackham, when Spofforth bowled his fastest, went back, Pilling used to say he himself could not stand back and in no circumstances did he do so. Still, as to Blackham's greatness there can be no question whatever: as to whether he was really of higher ability than Pilling, who died when only 35 years of age, opinions differed. Certainly both men were beautifully neat in all they did, and wonderfully accurate in stumping as well as in catching. Blackham stood exceptionally close to the wicket, was marvellously quick and in what was practically one action gathered the ball and whipped off the bails.

Blackham came over here with every one of the first eight teams from Australia and was captain of that of 1893. Outside his superb wicket-keeping he was a very useful bat. Like most of the early Australian batsmen he had no pretentions to style but was strong in unorthodox hitting and a very difficult man to bowl out. His highest score in England was one of 96 against Warwickshire at Birmingham in 1888.

In view of the fame to which he quickly attained after his arrival in England it is worthy to mention that previously W. L. Murdoch, the great Australian batsman, was generally regarded as the superior wicket-keeper. Indeed, *Scores and Biographies* in its remarks on what is now classed as the first Test match—that at Melbourne in 1877 when Australia won by 45 runs—states that "Spofforth refused to assist because his own wicket-keeper, W. L. Murdoch, did not play." Incidentally it may be mentioned that England—strictly Lillywhite's team—had no wicket-keeper on that occasion, Pooley, consequent upon some fracas, having been detained in New Zealand. An account of the game states that "Selby and Jupp 'kept' in turn, but neither proved equal to the job." The generally accepted belief that at the start of the tour of 1878 in this country Murdoch ranked as the leading wicket-keeper of the side is strengthened by the fact that, in the match in which the Australians made their first appearance at Lord's and proceeded to establish their fame by beating with nine wickets to spare in the course of a single day's play a most powerful team of the M.C.C., Murdoch found a place in the XI and Blackham was left out. Blackham's first appearance at Lord's was in the match against Middlesex in 1878, when, although the Hon. Edward Lyttelton made 113—the only hundred hit against the Australians that year—the Australians won by 98 runs.

In the course of the memorable tour which opened at Brisbane on November 10, 1877, and closed at Inglewood on January 10, 1879—a period of 14 months—Blackham played 90 innings and, if he averaged less than 13, only one member of the team—Charles Bannerman—averaged over 20, the average of Horan—second on the list—being 18. One of Blackham's most notable performances as a wicket-keeper was against an XVIII on a rough, bumpy pitch at Stockport in 1878 when he stumped six and caught four.

For many years a clerk in the Colonial Bank at Melbourne, Blackham was 5ft. 9½ins. in height and in his early manhood weighed only 10st. 6lb. Like several other members of the first Australian team he wore a beard as a young man of 23 and kept to it all through life.

He died at Melbourne on December 27, 1932, and so was in his 80th year.

BLACKIE, Donald J., who died in Melbourne on April 21, 1955, aged 73, played for Australia against the England team led by A. P. F. Chapman in Australia in 1928–29 when 46, being the oldest player to represent his country. He headed the Test averages with 14 wickets in three Test appearances at a cost of 31.71 runs each, six for 94 in the first innings of the third game at Melbourne being his best analysis. An off-break bowler of wiry physique who flighted the ball and allied swerve to spin and accuracy and length, he varied his pace skilfully from medium to slow-medium. Not until a late age did he enter big cricket after three years with the St. Hilda C.C., Melbourne. Then he rendered good service to Victoria, taking 159 wickets, average 23.88. In 1926–27, he bowled more balls—2,495—than anybody else in Australian first-class cricket and took more wickets—33—conceding only 816 runs.

BLACKLOCK, Carne P., who died at Wellington (N.Z.) on January 30, 1924, aged 40, was a good batsman and wicket-keeper. He was in the Wellington College (N.Z.) XI and played for Wellington in inter-Provincial matches.

BLACKLOCK, J. P., who died on January 22, 1935, aged 51, was a good forcing batsman and a smart fieldsman. He, his father, two uncles and a brother all played for Wellington. Robert and J. P. appeared for New Zealand. In 1905, J. P. was top scorer with 30 for New Zealand against the Australian team at Wellington, and he made 22 and 97 against the Melbourne club captained by Warwick Armstrong in 1906.

BLACKMAN, Arthur, who played for three counties, died on April 6, 1908, at Brighton, where he had for many years been a schoolmaster. He played in one match for Surrey in 1878, three times for Kent in 1879 and 1880, and on 15 occasions for Sussex between 1881 and 1887. He was a free and attractive batsman, a good field at cover-point, and a useful medium-paced bowler. His height was 6ft. ½in. and weight (in 1878) 13st. For Brighton and District Teachers v. Eastbourne, at Brighton, in 1881, he scored 255 not out, but in important cricket his highest innings was 73 for Sussex v. Hampshire at

Southampton in 1885. He was born at Dartford, in Kent, on October 13, 1853, and was half-brother to F. Martin.

BLACKMORE, George Patrick Maxwell, who died in hospital on January 29, 1984, aged 75, was in the Blundell's XI as a medium-paced bowler in 1925 and 1926 and played twice for Kent in 1948.

BLACKTON, Walter Reader, M.C., died in hospital at Derby on January 1, 1976, aged 80. Originally on the Notts staff, his first county match was as a professional for Derbyshire against Worcestershire in their last fixture in 1914, when he made 31 not out. He was then using the name of Reader. After the War he played a few times as an amateur in 1920 and 1921 without much success. Later he appeared occasionally for Sir Julien Cahn's side.

BLAGRAVE, Herbert Henry Gratwicke, died on March 21, 1982, aged 82. A member of the Cheltenham XI in 1917, he appeared in one match for Gloucestershire in 1922. He was a prominent figure in the horse-racing world.

BLAIR, Major-General Everard McLeod, C.M.G., R.E., died on May 16, 1939, aged nearly 73. Born at Bangalore, in India, he was educated at Cheltenham, where he was in the XI for two years before going to Woolwich. Between 1893 and 1900 he played occasionally for Kent. Strong in defence with plenty of strokes, he made 61 at Bristol in 1893 when first appearing in County Cricket, but never reproduced this form, though getting many runs in second-class cricket. He bowled slow leg-breaks and fielded admirably. He and Captain Hamilton won the Military Rackets Cup in 1895, beating the famous champion Eustace Crawley and Captain Eastwood.

BLAKE, Capt. J. P., M.C., a Royal Marine Commando, was killed in June, 1944, aged 26. A Cambridge Blue in 1939, he averaged 28.34, and also played occasionally for Hampshire, the county of his birth, from 1937 to 1939. His fielding earned much praise in the University match at Lord's, he caught J. M. Lomas, running in from the deep, and threw out R. B. Proud, so dismissing the two most successful Oxford batsmen when each seemed set for a hundred. At Aldenham School he headed the batting averages in 1935 with 41.83, but next year, when captain of the XI, he fared less well with 23.57.

BLAKER, Richard Norman Rowsell, M.C., died in Eltham Hospital on September 11, 1950, following an operation for peritonitis. Born on October 24, 1879, he captained Westminster School at cricket and Association football for four years, and, going to Cambridge, gained his cricket Blue in the three seasons, 1900 to 1902, being contemporary with such players as S. H. Day, F. B. Wilson, E. M. Dowson and E. R. Wilson. He also appeared as centre-forward in three Association football University matches against Oxford, being captain in 1901. For Kent, between 1898 and 1908, he gained a high reputation both as a hard-hitting batsman and a fine slip fielder. One of his best batting performances was against Gloucestershire at Catford in 1905, when he hit 120, including five sixes out of 194 in 75 minutes. Against Surrey at Canterbury in 1900, he and S. H. Day put on 50 in 18 minutes. He helped Kent to carry off the County Championship in 1906, and was President of the club when he died. He also captained the Butterflies. As a footballer, he was a frequent member of the Corinthian teams who achieved such great things in the early part of the century. In the first Great War, when a Lieutenant in the Rifle Brigade, he was awarded the Military Cross for bravery at Cambrai. His twin daughters, Barbara and Joan, known as the "Blaker Twins," were prominent members of the Kent women's cricket team and both played for England. During the last Canterbury Week his tent was the centre of pleasant entertainment, but he showed signs of ill-health and in little more than a month passed away.

BLAMIRES, The Rev. Ernest Oswald, who died at Takapuna, Auckland, on June 6, 1963, aged 81, represented New Zealand against New South Wales in 1925. Born in Australia, he went to New Zealand in 1903, serving as a minister of the Methodist Church for 56 years. A hard-hitting batsman, widely known as "The Cricketing Cleric", he played for Wellington and for Otago, whom he captained when in 1924–25 they won the Plunket Shield for the first time.

BLAND, Cyril H. G., the former Lincolnshire and Sussex fast bowler, was found dead in a canal at Cowbridge, near Boston, on July 1, 1950. He was 78. Bland, who took 543 wickets for Sussex between 1897 and 1904, was the only Sussex bowler to capture all 10 wickets in an innings. He performed this feat against Kent at Tonbridge in 1899, when his analysis against a side including J. R. Mason,

A. Hearne, C. J. Burnup and W. H. Patterson was 25.2 overs, 0 maidens, 48 runs, 10 wickets. Bland, in this memorable game, bowled at a great pace and made the ball kick a good deal. He was contemporary in the Sussex side with C. B. Fry and K. S. Ranjitsinhji.

BLANDFORD, J. A. R., who died in an Auckland hospital on December 24, 1955, aged 42, played for New Zealand in two "unofficial" Test matches against E. R. T. Holmes's M.C.C. team of 1935–36, scoring 40 and 36. An aggressive right-handed batsman, specially strong in off-side strokes, he was also a capable wicket-keeper and represented Wellington. When at Victoria University College, he was prominent as a Rugby football full-back and a lawn-tennis player. During service with a field ambulance unit in the Middle East and Italy in the Second World War, he contracted a severe rheumatic disease, but, settling in Auckland, became a prominent member of Middlemore C.C. side for several seasons.

BLAXLAND, Lionel Bruce, died at Temple Ewell, Kent, on April 29, 1976, aged 78. He was born at Shrewsbury on March 25, 1898, and was in the Shrewsbury XI from 1914 to 1916. He became a master at Repton in 1922, retiring in 1958, when he took holy orders and became rector of Tansley and later vicar of Doveridge, both in Derbyshire, his adopted county. "Bill" Blaxland was a fine club cricketer who hit hard and often, hooking anything short of a length with great power. As a bowler he was tireless, and always alert and sharp in the field. He first appeared for Derbyshire in 1925 and in his last match in 1947 he led the side against the South Africans at Derby when Ian Smith took six for one. His best score was 64 against Warwickshire in 1933, but most of his cricket was with The Friars and other good club sides until his career came to an end when he lost an eye playing for The Cryptics in Portugal. He was in charge of cricket at Repton for 11 years, in two spells. Blaxland played at wing half for Oxford University in 1920–21 and also for the Corinthians. In 19 matches for Derbyshire he scored 483 runs.

BLEACKLEY, Major Edward Overall, who died in a London nursing home on February 17, 1976, aged 77, was in the Harrow XI in 1915 and 1916. Particularly strong on the leg side, he made top score in each innings in one of the unofficial matches against Eton in

1916. In 1919 he played in two matches for Lancashire.

BLEACKLEY, Horace William, who died at Lausanne, Switzerland, on July 30, 1931, wrote *Tales of the Stumps, More Tales of the Stumps* and *A Short Innings.* He was educated at Cheltenham, Repton and Oxford.

BLIGH, Algernon Stuart, who died on December 27, 1952, aged 64, played for Somerset in 1925 and in one match in 1926 in the days when the county side was predominantly amateur. In 1925 he scored 433 runs in County Championship fixtures, average 19.68, his highest innings being 73 not out against Glamorgan at Cardiff.

BLIGH, The Hon. and Rev. Edward Vesey, J.P., uncle of the Earl of Darnley, died suddenly at Fartherwell, West Malling, Kent, on April 22, 1908, in his 80th year. *Scores and Biographies* (iii– 613) says of him: "A hard hitter, especially excelling in the drive, bowls slow round-armed, and fields generally middle wicket or short-slip." He was also at one time a very fair wicket-keeper. He was born in London, on February 28, 1829, and was a member of a family which had been intimately associated with Kent cricket for over a hundred years. He did not obtain a place in the Eton XI, but was more fortunate at Oxford, playing against Cambridge on Cowley Marsh in 1850, when he scored 27 and 0 and was on the winning side. During the 15 years over which his career as a county cricketer extended he assisted Kent on 23 occasions, taking eight wickets at a cost of 18 runs each and making 395 runs with an average of 11.28, his highest innings being 53 against England at Canterbury in 1862. His name will also be found in the Middlesex XI in 1862, although in that year he assisted Kent as well. From 1850 until 1855 he was in the Diplomatic Service, being successively Attaché at Hanover, Florence, and Berlin, but afterwards entered the Church. Mr. Bligh was one of the original trustees on the Mynn Memorial Benevolent Institution for Kentish Cricketers and the author of a most interesting pamphlet, printed at Maidstone in 1896 for private circulation, entitled *Former Kent Cricket.*

BLIGH, The Hon. and Rev. Henry, was born in Belgrave Square, London, on June 10, 1834, and appeared in the Kent XI once in 1854 and three times in 1860. *Scores and Biographies* (iv–490) says of him: "Hits hard and well, and also keeps wicket occasionally." In October, 1902, he resigned the living of Holy Trinity, Fareham, owing to ill-health, and retired to Winchester, where he died on March 4, 1905.

BLIGH, Ludovick Edward, son of the Rev. the Hon. E. V. Bligh and first cousin of the Hon. Ivo Bligh (the present Earl of Darnley), was born at Dover, on November 24, 1854, and died at Minehead on May 16, 1924, aged 69. He was not in the XI either at Eton or Cambridge, but he appeared for Kent in 10 games between 1878 and 1884, scoring 107 runs with an average of 7.64 and taking five wickets for 31.40 runs each. He was a useful batsman and bowled with success in club matches. He had been Master of the Minehead Harriers and M.F.H. of the Dulveston, South Berks. and East Kent packs.

BLOCK, Spencer Allan, died at Meadle, near Aylesbury on October 7, 1979, aged 71. An outstanding batsman at Marlborough, he was one of the Public Schools' side which played the Australians at Lord's in 1926. He won his Blue at Cambridge in 1929, having scored 108 in two hours against Sussex, and going in first with G. D. Kemp Welch, scored 36 and 55 against Oxford. For Surrey, for whom he played from 1928–33, his highest score was 117 v. Leicestershire in 1931 when he and Sandham put on 199 for the fourth wicket. But probably his best innings was 91 in 50 minutes with which he won the Middlesex match at the Oval in 1933. A magnificent figure of a man and hugely strong, he was a tremendous straight driver who could strike terror into the hearts of his partners; he was also a fine field and superb thrower. Apart from his cricket, he played Rugby football for Harlequins and was a hockey player of distinction.

BLOODWORTH, Bernard Sydney, who died on February 19, 1967, aged 73, served Gloucestershire as player, scorer and groundsman at Bristol from 1919 until he retired in 1965. A left-handed batsman and a natural hitter, he would have met with greater success had he been able to curb a tendency to attack the bowling too early. He scored one century in his aggregate of 3,617 runs (average 16.15)—115 against Essex at Leyton in 1925 when, during his best season, he failed by only two runs to complete 1,000. "Bernie" was also a capable wicket-keeper and though he received few chances of figuring behind the stumps for the county, he brought off 69 catches and made 24 stumpings. A fine Rugby footballer in his younger days, he captained Cheltenham R.F.C.

BLOOMFIELD, H. O. ("Blum"), a former Surrey cricketer, died on May 31, 1973, aged 82. A noted London club batsman, he scored 107 not out on his debut for the county at Northampton in 1921, but made only one other appearance for them when, in the same season, he hit nine and 53 not out from the Leicestershire bowling at the Oval. He represented Club Cricket Conference and United Banks while playing first for Cox's Bank, for whom he also gained prominence as an Association footballer, and later for Lloyds Bank. He wore spectacles and plimsolls when batting. He was son-in-law of Fred Holland, a famous Surrey player.

BLUCKE, The Rev. Robert Steuart Kidgell, Rector of Monxton, Andover, died there on March 19, 1930, aged 71. He kept wicket for Leicestershire against the Australians in 1880.

BLUNDELL, Sir Edward Denis, GCMG, GCVO, KBE, who died while on holiday in Queensland on September 24, 1984, aged 77, achieved distinction as a sportsman, a lawyer and a diplomat. From Waitaki Boys High School he went to Cambridge, where he won a cricket Blue in 1928 and 1929 and also ran in the Relays against Oxford. Called to the Bar in England in 1929, he returned to New Zealand as a barrister of the Supreme Court before becoming, in 1968, his country's High Commissioner in London and eventually, in 1972, their Governor-General.

At right-arm medium pace, he took 102 wickets in his two years in the Cambridge side, being their most successful bowler of that time and one of the best amateur bowlers in England. In 1928 he had six for 25 against Leicestershire and six for 51 against Nottinghamshire. His best figures in 1929 were six for 99 against Yorkshire. He twice represented New Zealand against E. R. T. Holmes's MCC side in 1935–36, taking four wickets against them at Wellington, two at Christchurch and dismissing Hardstaff for 0 in each match. Altogether he took 195 wickets at 25.25 apiece in 47 first-class appearances, his best performance being 11 for 130 for Wellington against Otago in 1934–35. His interest in cricket never left him, and from 1957 to 1960 he was President of the New Zealand Cricket Council.

BLUNDEN, Arthur, who died in July 1984, played a few times for Kent in the early 1930s. He took, altogether, 17 wickets at 33.88 runs apiece but was nothing of a batsman. He later became professional to Wearmouth in the Durham Senior League.

BLUNDEN, Edmund, who died in January, 1974, aged 77, was a lover of cricket and author of *Cricket Country*. A celebrated poet and writer, he was professor of English literature at Tokyo University for three years from 1924, fellow and tutor of English literature at Merton College, Oxford, from 1931 to 1943, professor of English in Hong Kong in 1955 and Oxford University professor of poetry till he resigned through ill health in 1968. He kept wicket for J. C. Squire's Invalids.

BLUNT, Roger Charles, M.B.E., who died in London on June 22, 1966, aged 65, played in nine Test matches for New Zealand between 1929 and 1931, seven against England and two against South Africa. Beginning his career as a leg-break bowler, he developed into a very fine batsman. Against A. H. H. Gilligan's England team in New Zealand in 1929, he headed his country's Test bowling averages with nine wickets for 19 runs each. In the opening Test of that tour, which marked the entry of New Zealand into the top rank of cricket, he not only gained a match analysis of five wickets for 34 runs but, with 45 not out, was top scorer in a first innings of 112. In England in 1931, his 96 helped New Zealand to a highly creditable draw with England at Lord's after being 230 in arrears on the first innings. Until B. Sutcliffe surpassed his 7,769 runs in 1953, he was the highest-scoring New Zealand batsman in first-class cricket. In a dazzling display for Otago against Canterbury at Christchurch in 1931–32, he hit 338 not out, then the highest score ever achieved by a New Zealand cricketer, though Sutcliffe many years later made 355 and 385. Well-known in business circles in England and New Zealand, he was awarded the M.B.E. in 1965.

BLYTHE, Sergt. Colin (Kent Fortress Engineers, attd. K.O.Y.L.I.), born at Deptford May 30, 1879; killed in November, 1917. Went to Australia 1901–02 and 1907–08; to South Africa 1905–06 and 1909–10; to America (with the Kent team) 1903.

The news that Blythe had been killed in France was received everywhere with the keenest regret. Inasmuch as Kenneth Hutchings had practically done with the game before joining the Army, the loss is the most serious that cricket has sustained during the

War. It is true that Blythe had announced his intention of playing no more in first-class matches, but quite possibly this decision was not final. He had certainly no need to think of retiring at the age of 38. That Blythe was a great bowler is beyond question. He had no warmer admirers than the many famous batsmen who had the satisfaction of making big scores against him. So far as I know they were unanimous in paying tribute to his remarkable powers. He was one of five left-handed slow bowlers of the first rank produced by England in the last 40 years, the other four being Peate, Peel, Briggs, and Rhodes. To place the five in order of merit is a task I shall not attempt. The best experts, if asked to give an opinion on the point, would vary considerably in their views. For example, W. L. Murdoch thought Peate far ahead of either Peel or Briggs, whereas Arthur Shrewsbury found Peel harder to play than Peate, the fast ball that Peel had at command keeping him always on the alert. Again I have heard Ranjitsinhji say that he considered Blythe a finer bowler than Rhodes, the deceptive flight of the ball making him more difficult to hit. To these views I would only add that judging by the practical test of results a good case could be made out for Rhodes as the best bowler of the five—before he turned his mind to batting. The seasons in which he did such wonderful things for Yorkshire—1898 to 1901 inclusive—were seasons of fine weather and huge scoring. Peate's great deeds were done chiefly in summers of rain and bad weather.

Blythe had all the good gifts that pertain to the first-rate slow bowler, and a certain imaginative quality that was peculiarly his own. Very rarely did he get to the end of his resources. To see him bowl to a brilliant hitter was a sheer delight. So far from being disturbed by a drive to the ring he would, instead of shortening his length to escape punishment, send up the next ball to be hit, striving of course to put on, if possible, a little extra spin. In this respect he reminded me of David Buchanan in the Gentlemen and Players matches of long ago. Blythe's spin was something quite out of the ordinary. On a sticky wicket or on a dry pitch ever so little crumbled he came off the ground in a way that beat the strongest defence. He had,

too, far more pace than most people supposed. The ball that went with his arm often approached the speed of a fast bowler and had of course the advantage of being unsuspected. On this point Fred Huish, the wicket-keeper, can be very illuminating.

Blythe was introduced to Kent cricket by Captain McCanlis, one of the best coaches the game has known. He was 20 years of age when he first played for Kent, and in 1900—his second season—he took 114 wickets in county matches alone. Illness during the winter affected his bowling in 1901, but after his visit to Australia with the team captained by A. C. MacLaren in 1901–02 he never looked back. His best season was 1909, when he took in first-class matches 215 wickets, at a cost of 14.5 runs each. A list of Blythe's feats with the ball for Kent would fill a column. Against Northamptonshire, at Northampton, in 1907, he obtained 17 wickets in one day, taking all 10 in the first innings for 30 runs, and seven in the second for 18. Test matches, owing to his tendency to epileptic fits, were very trying to him, and after having had a big share in England's victory over Australia at Birmingham in 1909 he was practically forbidden to play at Lord's. Still he was, out by himself, England's best bowler in the three matches with the famous South African team of 1907, taking 26 wickets for less than 10.5 runs a-piece. Only one of the three matches was finished, England winning at Leeds by 53 runs. Blythe on that occasion bowled himself to a standstill, but he had his reward, clearly winning the game for his country. Blythe's reputation will rest on his doings in England. His two visits to Australia scarcely added to his fame, and when he went to South Africa in 1905–06 and again in 1909–10, he did not find the matting wickets altogether to his liking. In the second of his South African tours he had a fairly good record, but as he was only picked for two of the five Test matches, he could not have been at his best. To sum up his career in a phrase, he will live in cricket history as the greatest Kent bowler of modern days. Nearly all his finest work was done for his county. It is pleasant to know that the Kent Committee have decided to put up a suitable memorial to him.—S.H.P.

Eight Wickets or More in an Innings

8 for 42	..	Kent v. Somerset, at Maidstone	..	..	..	1902
9 ,, 67	..	Kent v. Essex, at Canterbury	..	..	..	1903
9 ,, 30	..	Kent v. Hampshire, at Tonbridge	..	..	..	1904
8 ,, 72	..	Kent v. Essex, at Leyton	..	..	..	1905
10 ,, 30	..	Kent v. Northamptonshire, at Northampton	..	..	..	1907

Eight Wickets or More in an Innings—*continued*

8 for	59	England v. South Africa, at Leeds		1907
8 ,,	83	Kent v. Hampshire, at Canterbury		1908
9 ,,	42	Kent v. Leicestershire, at Leicester		1909
9 ,,	44	Kent v. Northamptonshire, at Northampton		1909
8 ,,	49	Kent v. Derbyshire, at Tunbridge Wells		1909
8 ,,	45	Kent v. Gloucestershire, at Cheltenham		1911
8 ,,	36	Kent v. Leicestershire, at Leicester		1912
8 ,,	55	Kent v. Worcestershire, at Dudley		1912
8 ,,	55	Kent v. Yorkshire, at Sheffield		1914
9 ,,	97	Kent v. Surrey, at Lord's		1914

Thirteen Wickets or More in a Match

13 for	20	Kent v. Worcestershire, at Worcester		1903
13 ,,	61	Kent v. Yorkshire, at Canterbury		1903
13 ,,	91	Kent v. Hampshire, at Southampton		1904
15 ,,	76	Kent v. Hampshire, at Tonbridge		1904
17 ,,	48	Kent v. Northamptonshire, at Northampton		1907
		(Only two clean bowled. All taken on third day of match.)		
15 ,,	99	England v. South Africa, at Leeds		1907
13 ,,	111	Kent v. Northamptonshire, at Gravesend		1908
13 ,,	123	Kent v. Leicestershire, at Canterbury		1908
13 ,,	114	M.C.C.'s Australian XI v. An England XI, at Uttoxeter		1908
16 ,,	102	Kent v. Leicestershire, at Leicester		1909
14 ,,	75	Kent v. Northamptonshire, at Northampton		1909
14 ,,	84	Kent v. Gloucestershire, at Cheltenham		1911
13 ,,	109	Kent v. Somerset, at Gravesend		1912
15 ,,	45	Kent v. Leicestershire, at Leicester		1912
13 ,,	94	Kent v. Leicestershire, at Canterbury		1913

Four Wickets or More for Three Runs or Less Each

10 for	30*a*			
7 ,,	18*b*	Kent v. Northamptonshire, at Northampton		1907
17 ,,	46*c*	*		
7 ,,	20	England v. Natal, at Pietermaritzburg		1909–10
4 ,,	12	England v. North-Eastern District, at Queenstown		1909–10
6 ,,	10	Kent v. Leicestershire, at Leicester		1911
7 ,,	9*a*	Kent v. Leicestershire, at Leicester		1912
15 ,,	45*b*			
4 ,,	10	Kent v. Surrey, at Blackheath		1912
7 ,,	21	Kent v. Worcestershire, at Stourbridge		1913
5 ,,	8	Kent v. Warwickshire, at Tonbridge		1913
7 ,,	15	Kent v. Northamptonshire, at Northampton		1914
7 ,,	20	Kent v. Worcestershire, at Canterbury		1914

a signifies 1st innings., *b* second, and *c* both.

The Following Feats were Noteworthy, Although the Figures do not Represent Work for the Complete Innings

7 wkts. for 1 run in 36 balls	Kent v. Northants, at Northampton		1907
6 ,, for 6 ,, in — ,,	Kent v. Gloucestershire, at Bristol		1909
5 ,, for 10 ,, in 10 ,,	Kent v. Surrey, at Blackheath		1910
6 ,, for 7 ,, in 48 ,,	Kent v. Worcestershire, at Stourbridge		
			1913

Bowling Unchanged Through Both Completed Innings

With—			
J. R. Mason	Kent v. Somerset, at Taunton		1901
Hearne (A.)	Kent v. Surrey, at the Oval		1903
Woolley (F. E.)	Kent v. Yorkshire, at Maidstone		1910
Woolley (F. E.)	Kent v. Notts. at Canterbury		1912
D. W. Carr	Kent v. Gloucestershire, at Dover		1912

Various Items of Interest

His first ball for Kent—It bowled F. Mitchell. Kent v. Yorks, at Tonbridge	1899
Bowls an hour for 1 run—Kent v. Sussex, at Tunbridge Wells	1904
A good day's work 17 wkts. for 48, v. Northants, at Northampton	1907
,, ,, ,, ,, 14 wkts. for 56, v. Leicestershire, at Leicester	1909
,, ,, ,, ,, 14 wkts. for 84, v. Gloucestershire, at Cheltenham	1911
Bowls 9 consecutive maiden overs—Kent v. Derbyshire, at Chesterfield	1909
Bowls 40 overs unchanged—M.C.C.'s Australian Team v. All England XI, at Scarborough	1908
3 wkts in 3 balls—Kent v. Surrey, Blackheath	*1910
3 ,, in 3 ,, —Kent v. Derbyshire, at Gravesend	1910
3 ,, in 4 ,, —Kent v. Worcestershire, at Canterbury	1914

He took four wickets in five balls.

Blythe's Bowling in First-Class Cricket

Year	Balls	Runs	Wickets	Average
1899	757	310	14	22.14
1900	5053	2106	114	18.47
1901	5273	2151	93	21.12
1901–2 Australia	1792	711	34	20.91
1902	5082	1965	127	15.47
1903	5554	1953	142	13.75
1903 America	396	168	13	12.92
1904	6146	2705	138	19.60
1905	7170	3142	149	21.08
1905–6 South Africa	2889	1046	57	18.35
1906	5321	2209	111	19.90
1907	6829	2822	183	15.42
1907–8 Australia	2360	935	41	22.80
1908	8200	3326	197	16.88
1909	7643	3128	215	14.54
1909–10 South Africa	2425	820	53	15.47
1910	6249	2497	175	14.26
1911	6238	2675	138	19.38
1912	5517	2183	178	12.26
1913	6722	2729	167	16.34
1914	6052	2583	170	15.19
	103668	42164	2509	16.80

BOARD, John Henry, born at Clifton, February 23, 1867, died April 16, 1924. The news that Board had died from heart failure on the "Kenilworth Castle," while journeying home from his annual coaching engagement in South Africa, came as a shock to all his friends. From his look of robust health no one could have seemed better assured of a long life. Board had a highly successful career, but yet did not take quite the place that in other circumstances might have been his. He was a fine wicket-keeper—fearless and untiring—but never the best in England, and for this reason his appearances in representative XIs were few. It is from his connection with Gloucestershire cricket that he will be remembered. Coming out as a wicket-keeper for Gloucestershire in 1891 he held his post right on without a break till

1914. As he succeeded Mr. J. A. Bush, who, curiously enough, died a few months after Board, we have the interesting fact that Gloucestershire depended on two wicket-keepers for over 40 years. As time went on Board developed his batting to such a remarkable extent that in six seasons—1900, 1905, 1906, 1907, 1909 and 1911—he made over 1,000 runs, his highest score being 214 against Somerset at Bristol in 1900. He had perhaps no special distinction of style, but his defence was sound, his hitting very hard, and his pluck unflinching. Board went only once to Australia, going out with Mr. Stoddart's second team in 1897–98. As wicket-keeper for that unsuccessful side he was simply the understudy to William Storer, and did not take part in any of the Test matches. He had more prominence in trips to South Africa in

1898–99 and 1905–06. For several winters he did excellent work as a coach at Hawke's Bay, New Zealand, and in matches there hit up scores of 134 and 195. In 1921 Board became one of the regular umpires in county matches, and was on the list at the time of his death. He took his benefit at Bristol in 1901, the Surrey match being allotted to him. It is an interesting fact that Board kept wicket in a first-class match before appearing for Gloucestershire, taking part in the North and South Match for Rylott's benefit at Lord's in 1891. Quite unknown at the time, he passed through a severe ordeal with great credit. The first of his appearances in Gentlemen and Players' matches was at the Oval in 1896, and his last at Lord's in 1910.—S.H.P.

BODDAM, Edmond Tudor, who died in Hobart on September 9, 1959, aged 79, was a prominent cricketer in Tasmania in the years immediately preceding the First World War. A sound, attractive batsman, he made his highest score in first-class cricket, 52, against the M.C.C. touring team of 1911–12, when P. F. Warner, the chosen captain, dropped out of the side through illness and handed over the leadership to J. W. H. T. Douglas. Boddam, also a useful medium-pace bowler, was reputed to be the first to employ "swerve" in Tasmania.

BODDINGTON, Robert Alan, who died at Fifield, Oxford, on August 5, 1977, aged 85, was in the Rugby XI in 1910 and 1911. A good wicket-keeper and a useful batsman, he was tried for Oxford without getting a Blue, but between 1913 and 1922 kept wicket frequently for Lancashire, who at that time had no reliable, professional keeper. A man of great charm, he was for years on the Lancashire Committee and was also prominent at Lord's.

BODEN, The Rev. Cecil Arthur, died at Hamstead Marshall, near Newbury, on May 31, 1981, aged 90. Educated at Christ's Hospital, where he was in the XI, and Leeds University, he showed promise for Leicestershire in 1911. In his first match he made 40 against Nottinghamshire and with Albert Knight put on 56 for the first wicket. A fortnight later against Yorkshire he helped C. J. B. Wood in a stand of 87 for the third wicket, his own share being 39, and had much to do with his side, aided by the weather, gaining a surprising victory in a low-scoring match by an innings and 20 runs. He played a few times more in 1912 and 1913, but did not repeat his success. He was

the last surviving Leicestershire player from before the Great War.

BODEN, Henry, of Derby, brother of Mr. Walter Boden, died in London on November 13, 1908, at the age of 72. He took a prominent part in the formation of the Derbyshire County C.C., and at the time of his death was the oldest member of the Meynell and Quorn Hunts. In 1862 he arranged the match at Nottingham between Gentlemen of the North and Gentlemen of the South and would have played for the former had not the death of his father prevented. He was educated at Rugby, but did not obtain a place in the XI.

BODEN, John George, born at Birstall, near Leeds, on December 27, 1848, died at Ilkley on January 3, 1928, in his 80th year. In 1878 he kept wicket for Yorkshire against the Australians at Sheffield, as Pinder was unable to play. The same year he appeared at Lord's for 22 Colts of England v. M.C.C. at Lord's, and also assisted XVIII of Scarborough against the Australians. In the latter game he stumped Murdoch and Spofforth and scored one and 28 not out.

BODEN, Timothy Walter, who died on September 5, 1969, aged 68, played for Derbyshire against Sussex at Chesterfield in 1920—a season in which the county called upon no fewer than 39 players for Championship fixtures.

BODEN, Walter, died at the Pastures, near Derby, on September 16, 1905. It was chiefly on his initiative that the Derbyshire County C.C. was established. Throughout his life he always worked in the best interests of the County Club, of which he was the first Hon. Secretary, and the President from 1895 to 1898 inclusive. His portrait formed the frontispiece to W. J. Piper's *History of the Derbyshire County Cricket Club*, published a few years ago.

BOHLEN, Francis Hermann, who died on December 9, 1942, aged 74 after being in poor health for several years, was one of the best-known American cricketers. He came to England with Gentlemen of Philadelphia teams in 1897, 1903 and 1908, and other times when in this country he played for M.C.C., London County and Free Foresters. Over six feet tall, he batted in admirable style, playing forward and driving with powerful ease. After playing against the touring team captained by Lord Hawke in

1891, he became a valuable member of Philadelphia sides. When Blackham's 1893 Australian team visited Philadelphia on the way home from England, Bohlen scored 118 in a total of 525; and 33 and 54 not out, in a total of 106, when in the return match the visitors avenged their previous defeat. Two years later he made 115, and with G. S. Patterson, 74, put up 200 for the first wicket against Frank Mitchell's University team. He seldom showed his best form for the Philadelphians in England, but averaged 27.69 for the 1903 tour. Patterson died in June, 1943.

BOLTON, Benjamin Charles, who played for Yorkshire in half-a-dozen matches in 1890 and 1891, died on November 18, 1910, from injuries sustained in falling from an express train a few miles from Hull. On his first appearance for the county—against Warwickshire at Halifax—he took 10 wickets for 64 runs, and in the six matches mentioned obtained 27 for a fraction under 15 runs each. He was born on September 23, 1862, and was a fast-medium bowler.

BOLTON, Capt. Robert Henry Dundas, who died on October 3, 1964, aged 71, was in the Rossall XI from 1909 to 1911. He played for Dorset from 1910 to 1912 and took part in seven matches for Hampshire between 1913 and 1922. Later, when Chief Constable of Northamptonshire, he became a team selector for the County Club.

BONHAM-CARTER, Lothian George, who died at Buriton House, Petersfield, on January 13, 1927, aged 69, was in the Clifton College XI in 1876, and played subsequently on a few occasions for Hampshire.

BONHAM-CARTER, Sir Maurice, who died on June 7, 1960, aged 79, was in the Winchester XI of 1898 and the following year before going to Oxford, where he gained a Blue in 1902. Against Cambridge, he was twice dismissed without scoring and took three wickets for 63 runs. He afterwards played in one or two matches for Kent. From 1910 to 1916 he was Private Secretary to the Prime Minister, Mr. Asquith.

BONNER, John Wardell, who died on November 26, 1936, played occasionally for Essex. He scored 59 in 1896 at Derby and altogether made 224 runs, average 16, in this, his first season with the county; but he could not give much time to first-class cricket.

BONNOR, George John, born at Orange (N.S.W.), February 25, 1855; died at Orange (N.S.W.), June 27, 1912. Though he was last seen on an English cricket ground more than 20 years ago, George Bonnor had not in one sense outlived his fame, his doings being constantly recalled and talked about. He was, indeed, far too striking a personality to be forgotten in less than a generation. Australia has sent to England many finer batsmen, but no other hitter of such extraordinary power. During his five visits to this country—he came here with the Australian teams of 1880, 1882, 1884, 1886 and 1888—Bonnor earned a reputation akin to that of our own C. I. Thornton, the question being often discussed as to which of the two men could make the bigger drives. Whether Bonnor ever equalled Thornton's longest hit at Brighton, or his famous drive over the old racquet court at the Oval, is a moot point, but, be this as it may, the Australian in his own particular line had only one rival. Bonnor was a splendid specimen of manhood. He stood about 6ft. 5in., but he was so finely proportioned that there was nothing ungainly in his figure or carriage. His presence contributed almost as much as his wonderful hitting to the popularity that he enjoyed wherever he played. He was not content to be a hitter pure and simple, setting himself at times to play quite an orthodox game. These efforts at steadiness afforded him some satisfaction, but they made his colleagues in various Australian XIs furious. They argued that his business was to hit, and that when he failed to fulfil his proper mission he was no use. Bonnor never met with much success as a batsman in Test matches in England but in games only slightly less important he played many a fine innings. One remembers in particular his 74 against the Gentlemen of England at the Oval in 1882. In the same season he gave a remarkable display against I Zingari at Scarborough. Nothing in Bonnor's career is more often recalled than the catch with which George Ulyett got him out in the England and Australia match at Lord's in 1884. Bonnor hit a half-volley back with all his force; Ulyett put up his right hand, and the ball stuck. Probably no harder hit was ever caught. Members of the England XI gathered round Ulyett in wonderment at what he had done. All the bowler said was that if the ball had hit his fingers he should have had no more cricket that season. Another famous catch—of quite a different kind—to which Bonnor was out was in the England and Australia match at the Oval in 1880—the first Test match in England. The ball was hit to such a tremendous height that the batsmen had turned for the third run when Fred Grace caught it. That great cricketer, who died a fortnight after the match, said he was sure his heart stopped beating while he was waiting for the ball to drop. In first-class matches Bonnor scored 4,989 runs with an average of 20.70.

BOOTH, Arthur, who died in a Rochdale hospital on August 17, 1974, aged 71, had one of the most extraordinary careers of any first-class cricketer. It began in 1931 with two matches, ceased at the end of the summer and did not continue until 1946. Then, having headed both the Yorkshire and the complete county bowling averages at the age of 43, with 84 and 111 wickets respectively, Booth appeared in only four matches in 1947, disappearing once more into the Bradford League and comparative obscurity, never to play for Yorkshire again.

That one season between the untimely death of Hedley Verity and the emergence of Johnny Wardle could not have been more dynamic. The 111 wickets taken by Booth with slow left arm bowling cost only 11.61 runs each, an average better than anything recorded in the previous 23 years, and Yorkshire retained the Championship they had won in the last season before the war.

Booth took six for 33 against the touring Indian side that year, but his best return was six for 21 against Warwickshire, a county with whom he later became associated as a scout. He never lost his love for the game; a love which prompted him to say in later life: "Just imagine, they don't even teach cricket in some schools now."

BOOTH, Clement, born at Friskney, Boston, on May 11, 1842, died at Hundleby, Spilsby, Lincolnshire, on July 1, 1926, aged 84. He was a sound free batsman, with strong back play and a fine cut, and an excellent field at long-leg and cover. At Rugby, where he was coached by Diver and Hayward and was contemporary with Messrs. E. Rutter, F. R. Evans and B. B. Cooper, he played in the XI in 1860 and 1861. In the latter year, when there was no match with Marlborough, he scored 63 v. Free Foresters and 30 v. M.C.C. Proceeding to Cambridge he obtained his Blue as a Freshman, playing against Oxford in 1862 and three following years. In 1864, when he captained the side, and made three and 22 and took a couple of wickets, Cambridge were beaten by four wickets. In his four University matches he made only 66

runs and was dismissed eight times. In his second innings in the game of 1865 he hit the ball from E. L. Fellowes to square-leg over the grandstand, and in the same match he caught R. A. H. Mitchell, left-handed on the ropes at square-leg, after running from 12 to 15 yards. It was a glorious catch, and Booth, as he held the ball, overheard a spectator ejaculate: "'Ow *could* 'e miss it? 'E's got 'ands like a 'ip-bath!" For the University in 1864 he scored 106 v. Norfolk at Cambridge and 64 and 76 v. Surrey at the Oval. He played County Cricket for Lincolnshire, Hampshire and Huntingdonshire, being Hon. Secretary of the first-named Club 1867-71 and of the Hampshire County C.C. 1874-79. Among various good innings for which he was responsible may be mentioned 78 for M.C.C. v. Oxford University at Lord's in 1876 and 77 for Hampshire v. Kent at Canterbury a year later. He never assisted the Gentlemen, but he took part in the two games of much note at Lord's—that between M.C.C. and the first Australian team in 1878 and the Veterans' match of 1887. It may be added that in both 1864 and 1865 he represented Cambridge in the Athletic Sports.

BOOTH, Frank Stanley, died at Shoreham-by-Sea on January 21, 1980, aged 72. First playing for Lancashire in 1927, he had a number of trials in the next few years, but failing to get a regular place went into League cricket. Returning to the county in 1932, he took, in 1933, 89 wickets at 27.43. In 1934, when his bowling had much to do with Lancashire winning the Championship, his figures were 101 at 23.46 and, in 1935, 89 at 19.20. After that, largely owing to injuries, he played less and his connection with the county ceased at the end of 1937. Tall and strong, he bowled fast-medium and came quickly off the pitch; he was an indefatigable trier, who revelled in long spells, and, as the quickest bowler Lancashire had at the time, he was given plenty of them. This, coupled with a long run and a slightly lumbering actions may have shortened his career.

BOOTH, 2nd Lieut. Major William (West Yorkshire Regiment), born at Pudsey on December 10, 1886, fell in action in July, 1916. His earliest cricket was played at Fulneck School, and later he was associated with Pudsey St. Lawrence and the Wath Athletic Club, which played in the Mexborough League, and of which he was captain. He appeared regularly for Yorkshire 2nd XI in 1907 and two following seasons, and in 1908 received his first trial for the county. He did not, however, secure a regular place in the team until two years later, but in 1911 he scored 1,125 runs for his county and took 74 wickets, with a highest innings of 210 against Worcestershire on the Worcester ground. He increased his reputation as a bowler in the following summer, and in 1913 made over a thousand runs and took 158 wickets for Yorkshire, his aggregate of 181 wickets in first-class matches being the highest of any bowler that season. In 1914 he was not so successful in batting, but he obtained 141 wickets for Yorkshire at a cost of 18 runs apiece. Although a fine punishing batsman, Booth's claim to fame will rest chiefly upon what he accomplished as a bowler. Possessed of a free, natural action, he made the ball come quickly off the pitch. On occasion his off-break was quite formidable, but his strong points were swerve and pace off the ground. His best feats with the ball may be summarised thus:

8 in inns. for 52, Yorkshire v.
Leicestershire, at Sheffield, 1912

8 in inns. for 47, Yorkshire v. Middlesex, at
Leeds, 1912

8 in inns. for 86, Yorkshire v. Middlesex, at
Sheffield, 1913

7 in inns. for 21, Yorkshire v. M.C.C. and
Ground, at Lord's, 1914

8 in inns. for 64, Yorkshire v. Essex, at
Leyton, 1914

14 in match for 160, Yorkshire v. Essex, at
Leyton, 1914

3 wkts. in 3 balls, Yorkshire v.
Worcestershire, at Bradford, 1911

3 wkts. in 3 balls, Yorkshire v. Essex, at
Leyton, 1912

3 wkts. in 4 balls, Yorkshire v.
Warwickshire, at Sheffield, 1913

3 wkts. in 4 balls, Yorkshire v. M.C.C. and
Ground, at Lord's, 1914

3 wkts. in 4 balls, Yorkshire v. Kent, at
Sheffield, 1914

In two consecutive matches in August 1914, he and Drake bowled unchanged throughout, Gloucestershire being dismissed for 94 and 84 at Bristol and Somerset for 44 and 90 at Weston-super-Mare. In the second innings of the latter match Booth had the very rare experience of bowling throughout without obtaining a wicket, Drake taking all 10 for 35 runs.

In 1913 Booth was chosen for the Players at Lord's, and during 1913–14 toured South Africa with the M.C.C.'s team under Douglas' captaincy. His doings abroad were somewhat disappointing, and so strong was the

side that he was left out of three of the Test matches. In the 144 games in which he appeared for Yorkshire he scored 4,213 runs with an average of 22.65 and obtair ⌐ ⌐56 wickets for 18.89 runs each. Tall of stature, good-looking, and of engaging address, Booth was a very popular figure on and off the cricket field.

BORRADAILE, Oswell Robert, the former Essex Secretary, who did great work for the club for 31 years, died at Buckhurst Hill on May 11, 1935, at the age of 76. Acting as Secretary to Essex from 1890 to 1921, when he had to retire owing to ill-health, Mr. Borradaile, with Mr. C. E. Green, saved the County Club from threatened extinction. He retained his interest in Essex cricket until the last. Born at Westminster on May 9, 1859, he was educated at Westminster School but left too early to be included in the XI. A useful batsman, a medium-paced bowler and a smart field at point, he was an outstanding figure in club cricket and played occasionally for Essex. He captained the Stoics C.C. for 10 years and acted as their Hon. Secretary for 15 years and frequently appeared for M.C.C. in minor matches. In 1889 when touring with the Marylebone Club he shared with Mr. G. F. Wells-Cole in four three-figure opening partnerships on four consecutive days. Succeeding Mr. M. P. Betts as Secretary to Essex, Mr. Borradaile served them in the days of such personalities as H. G. Owen, Carpenter, Walter Mead, C. J. Kortright, A. J. Turner, P. Perrin and C. McGahey. With the club in financial straits he worked so hard that he prevented bankruptcy and succeeded in raising Essex to great heights. They reached first-class status in 1895 and two years later the side fared so well as to make Essex cricket the feature of the season. A man of strong personality, tremendous enthusiasm and energy, Mr. Borradaile, by reason of his kindness and courtesy, made himself extremely popular. Upon his resignation from the Essex Secretaryship, the club paid him a fine tribute in the form of a testimonial and election as a life-member.

BORRETT, Robert, of Norwich, a contributor to *Wisden* for many years, died on November 22, 1947, aged 79. Sports Editor of *Eastern Daily Press* until 1945, when he retired, he held a prominent place in East Anglian sporting circles, as testified by Mr. Michael Falcon, the Cambridge Blue and captain of Norfolk County C.C. A good all-round cricketer in early manhood, Borrett played for several teams and Norfolk Club and Ground.

BORTHWICK, Cecil Hamilton, M.C., died at Burgate, Diss, Norfolk, on December 30, 1977, aged 90. He kept wicket at different times for Cambridgeshire, Norfolk and Kent II, as well as for the Gentlemen of Suffolk. His name will also be found in some of the charity matches played in Yorkshire in 1918 which included so many well-known names that the scores were recorded in *Wisden*.

BORWICK, Eric George, who died in Sydney on August 1, 1981, aged 85, was one of the best known of all Australian umpires. He stood in three Ashes series—1932–33, 1936–37 and 1946–47—and 24 Test matches, the first at Brisbane in 1931–32 and the last at Adelaide in 1948. Among his most consequential decisions, other than allowing England's bowlers to pursue, with such relentlessness, their body-line tactics in 1932–33 (no law then existed concerning the systematic use of fast, short-pitched bowling), was the one which gave Bradman not out at Brisbane in 1946–47, when England claimed a catch at slip. Borwick ruled that it was a bump ball. Bradman, 28 at the time, went on to make 187.

BORWICK, Major Peter Malise, died at Kelmarsh, Northamptonshire, on December 23, 1983, aged 70. A member of the Harrow XI in 1932, when he took seven wickets against Eton at Lord's, he played, later that summer, three matches for Northamptonshire. He was a slow left-arm bowler in the orthodox old-fashioned style, who attacked the middle and off stumps and flighted the ball well. He was also a useful school batsman. Later he was for a time Master of the Pytchley.

BOSANQUET, Bernard James Tindall, died at his home in Surrey on October 12, 1936, the day before the 59th anniversary of his birth. A capable all-round cricketer at Eton and Oxford and also for Middlesex, Bosanquet enjoyed chief claim to fame as the acknowledged inventor of the googly. In the 1925 issue of *Wisden* there was reproduced an article from *The Morning Post* in which Bosanquet described all about the discovery of what he termed in the heading "The Scapegoat of Cricket." He wrote, "Poor old googly! It has been subjected to ridicule, abuse, contempt, incredulity, and survived them all. Deficiencies existing at the present day are attributed to the influence of the

googly. If the standard of bowling falls off it is because too many cricketers devote their time to trying to master it .... If batsmen display a marked inability to hit the ball on the off-side or anywhere in front of the wicket and stand in apologetic attitudes before the wicket, it is said that the googly has made it impossible for them to attempt the old aggressive attitude and make the scoring strokes.

"But, after all, what is the googly? It is merely a ball with an ordinary break produced by an extra-ordinary method. It is not difficult to detect, and, once detected, there is no reason why it should not be treated as an ordinary break-back. However, it is not for me to defend it. If I appear too much in the role of the proud parent I ask forgiveness."

As to the "birth of the googly," Bosanquet wrote: "Somewhere about the year 1897 I was playing a game with a tennis ball, known as 'Twisti-Twosti.' The object was to bounce the ball on a table so that your opponent sitting opposite could not catch it..... After a little experimenting I managed to pitch the ball which broke in a certain direction; then with more or less the same delivery make the next ball go in the opposite direction! I practised the same thing with a soft ball at 'Stump-cricket.' From this I progressed to the cricket ball....

"I devoted a great deal of time to practising the googly at the nets, occasionally in unimportant matches. The first public recognition we obtained was in July, 1900, for Middlesex v. Leicestershire at Lord's. An unfortunate individual (Coe, the left-hander) had made 98 when he was stumped off a fine specimen which bounced four times.... This small beginning marked the start of what came to be termed a revolution in bowling....

"The googly (bowled by a right-hand bowler to a right-hand batsman) is nothing more or less than an ordinary off-break. The method of delivery is the secret of its difficulty, and this merely consisted in turning the wrist over at the moment of delivery far enough to alter the axis of spin, so that a ball which normally delivered would break from leg, breaks from the off.

"A few incidents stand out vividly. The first time it was bowled against the Australians—at Lord's late one evening in 1902—when I had two overs and saw two very puzzled Australians return to the pavilion. It rained all next day and not one of them tumbled to the fact that it was not an accident. The first googly ever bowled in

Australia, in March 1903; Trumper batting, having made 40 in about 20 minutes. Two leg-breaks were played beautifully to cover, but the next ball (delivered with a silent prayer) pitching in the same place, saw the same graceful stroke played—and struck the middle stump instead of the bat! W. Gunn stumped when appreciably nearer my wicket than his own! Arthur Shrewsbury complaining 'that it wasn't fair.' There are two or three bright patches I can recall. For instance in 1904 when in three consecutive matches I got five wickets in each innings v. Yorkshire, six in each v. Nottinghamshire, and seven in each v. Sussex (including Fry and 'Ranji').

"There was one week in 1905 in which I had 11 wickets v. Sussex at Lord's (and got 100 in each innings; the double feat is still a record); and during the next three days in the first Test match at Nottingham I got eight out of nine wickets which fell in the second innings, the last man being out just before a thunderstorm broke—and even then if Trumper could have hobbled to the wicket it meant a draw! This recalls the fourth Test, match at Sydney in March, 1904, in which at one period in the second innings I had six for 12, and then got Noble leg-before and never appealed. The last man was in, and the match won, and there were reasons!

"There is a good story of Dick Lilley, the best wicket-keeper in a big match we have known. In the Gentlemen and Players match at the Oval in 1904 I got a few wickets in the second innings. Then one of the 'Pros.' came in and said, 'Dick's in next; he's calling us a lot of rabbits; says he can see every ball you bowl. Do try and get him and we'll rag his life out.' Dick came in. I bowled him two overs of leg-breaks then changed my action and bowled another leg-break. Dick played it gracefully to fine leg and it removed his off stump! I can still hear the reception he got in the dressing room."

In that match Bosanquet took eight wickets (six in the second innings for 60 runs) and scored 145.

These performances, described personally, convey some idea of Bosanquet's ability but scarcely do justice to a splendid all-round cricketer. Quite 6ft. tall, Bosanquet brought the ball over from a great height so that flight as well as the uncertain break mystified batsmen until a whole side became demoralised. When playing a big innings, Bosanquet, in fine upstanding style, put power into his drives and forcing strokes with apparently little effort.

Born on October 13, 1877, Bosanquet was sent to Eton and profited so much by coaching from Maurice Read and William Brockwell, the famous Surrey professionals, that he got his place in the XI and against Harrow at Lord's in 1896, scored 120. In his second year at Oxford, 1898, he received his Blue from F. H. E. Cunliffe and played three times against Cambridge without doing anything exceptional. In those days he was a useful bowler, medium to fast, and gradually cultivated the leg-break.

Bosanquet played a lot for Middlesex from 1900 to 1908 and made a few appearances for the county subsequently, but did not bowl after 1908. His great year was 1904 when he made 1,405 runs, with an average of 36 and took 132 wickets for less than 22 runs apiece. Twice he put together two separate hundreds in the same match, 136 and 139 against Leicestershire at Lord's in 1900, and 103 and 100 not out against Sussex at Lord's in 1905. This was the match in which he took 11 wickets.

Among his bowling feats besides those in Test matches were:—15 wickets for 65 runs, including nine wickets in one innings, for Oxford against Sussex at Oxford in 1900; 14 wickets for 190 runs for Middlesex against Sussex at Brighton in 1904, and nine wickets in one innings for the M.C.C. against South Africans at Lord's in 1904.

Bosanquet took part in six different tours, going to America with P. F. Warner's team in 1898, and with K. S. Ranjitsinhji's team in 1899; to New Zealand and Australia with Lord Hawke's team in 1902–03; to Australia with the M.C.C. team in 1903–04. He captained sides that went to America in 1901 and to the West Indies in 1901–02.

In addition to cricket he represented Oxford University at Hammer Throwing in 1899 and 1900, and at Billiards in 1898 and 1900.

BOSANQUET, Lieut.-Col. Bernard Tindal, D.L., died at Cowley, Uxbridge, on August 5, 1910, at the age of 67. He was the father of Messrs. B. J. T. and N. E. T. Bosanquet, and in his younger days was a useful club cricketer. It has been said of him: "The father bowled exactly in the same way as the son (B. J. T.,) at whom he used to bowl from the time that he was six years old."

BOSTOCK, Herbert, who died at Ilkeston on February 20, 1954, aged 84, played in four matches for Derbyshire in 1897. A fine club player, he captained the Ilkeston Manners Colliery C.C. which, by carrying off the trophy in three successive years from 1896, won outright the Derbyshire Cricket Challenge Cup.

BOSWELL, Capt. William Gerald Knox (Rifle Brigade), born on June 24, 1892, died of wounds on July 28, 1916. In 1910 and 1911 he was in the Eton XI, and in his four Public School matches scored 95 runs with an average of 23.75 and took nine wickets for just under nine runs each. In two of these games—v. Harrow in 1910, and v. Winchester in 1911—Eton followed-on and won. At Oxford in 1912, after scoring 75 and 20 and obtaining four wickets for 47 runs in the Freshmen's match, he was tried in the XI, but he did not secure his Blue until 1913. In his two matches against Cambridge he made 93 runs in four innings and took a couple of wickets. In 1913, when he scored 101 not out against Hampshire at Southampton, he headed the University averages with 36.53, but in 1914 was fourth with 26.00. He had been Mentioned in Dispatches.

BOSWORTH-SMITH, Bertrand Nigel, died at Hove, February 19, 1947, aged 73. Harrow 1891–92. Played for Middlesex in 1895 and for Dorset. Oxford Association XI 1894–96.

BOTTING, Stephen, born at Higham in 1845, died at Shorne, near Gravesend, on January 23, 1927, aged 81. A useful batsman and a medium-paced round-armed bowler, he played for Kent twice—in 1867 and in 1875.

BOTTOM, Daniel, who died on February 16, 1937, aged 73, played for Derbyshire, the county of his birth, against Nottinghamshire in 1891. Eight years later, when qualified by residence, he appeared in three matches for Nottinghamshire. His slow bowling showed promise, when he was unchanged with Wass in Derbyshire's first innings, but he failed in the last stage of the match and did so little against Middlesex at Lord's and Kent at Trent Bridge that he was not persevered with.

BOTTOMORE, William, 60 years of age, died suddenly at Sheepshed on October 21, 1905. In 1879 and the first half of the '80s he did good service to Leicestershire as a fast bowler, and was a useful batsman. His highest innings against a first-class side was 79, v. Sussex in 1880. He also made 41 not out against Surrey in 1884.

BOUCHER, Capt. Sidney, R.N., who died on August 4, 1963, aged 73, was a left-arm opening bowler for the Royal Navy in one match for Kent in 1922.

BOUGHTON, William Albert, died at Cardiff on November 26, 1936, aged 81. He played occasionally for Gloucestershire, first appearing for the county against Middlesex at Lord's in 1879.

BOUNDY, Gerald Oscar, who died at the Royal Masonic Hospital on February 8, 1964, played as an amateur in two matches for Somerset in 1926 and 1930. He was an honorary life member of the County Club.

BOURNE, Alfred Allinson, died on July 17, 1931, aged 83. When at Rugby in 1863, he came to the fore as a slow left-arm bowler and going up to Cambridge he took part in the historic match of 1870 which Cambridge, largely owing to the splendid bowling of F. C. Cobden, won by two runs after Oxford got within five runs of success for the loss of seven wickets. Cobden took all three outstanding wickets in one over and in his own account of his historic over (in *Fifty Years of Sport*) wrote:—"Two bits of fielding by Bourne at critical moments turned the evenly-poised scale. In the penultimate over he saved an apparently certain four when fielding at short leg; and it was no ordinary catch which dismissed Butler, who hit at the ball for all he was worth and fairly got hold of it." Butler, the last man, was caught by Bourne.

BOUSFIELD, E. J. (Lancashire) died late in December, 1894, or early in January, 1895, in his 57th year. He was in his day a well-known cricketer in the North of England.

BOWDEN, John, who died at Glossop on March 1, 1958, aged 73, played for Derbyshire between 1909 and 1930, obtaining 7,615 runs, including four centuries, average 20.74, and holding 73 catches. He shared with H. Storer in a record Derbyshire opening stand of 322 v. Essex at Derby in 1929, beating the previous best in which he and W. W. Hill-Wood hit 206 from the Somerset bowling at Bath six years earlier. He also appeared for Glossop and for 20 years was a leading if careful batsman in the Central Lancashire League.

BOWDEN, M. P., whose death had some time before been incorrectly announced, died in South Africa in February, 1892. Born on November 1, 1865, Mr. Bowden was educated at Dulwich College, and made his first appearance in the Surrey XI in the season of 1883. His batting that year, especially in the Bank Holiday match against Notts at the Oval, showed enormous promise, and raised hopes which were never quite realised. In 1888, however, his last year in the county team, he did very brilliant work, scoring 430 runs in first-class county matches with an average of 30.10, and 797 in all matches with an average of 31.22. In that year also he had the honour of being chosen wicket-keeper for the Gentlemen, both at Lord's and the Oval, and also for the Gentlemen against the Australians at Lord's. At the end of the season of 1888 he went out to South Africa as a member of the team got up by Major Wharton, and there remained for the rest of his life.

BOWELL, Alec, who died at Oxford on August 28, 1957, aged 76, played for Hampshire from 1902 till 1927. An opening batsman sound in defence and specially skilled in cutting, he scored 18,510 runs, average 24.13, and was a splendid fieldsman at coverpoint. His highest innings was 204 out of a total of 377 for Hampshire against Lancashire at Bournemouth, to which venue the match was transferred from Portsmouth owing to the outbreak of the First World War. He took part in the celebrated match with Warwickshire at Birmingham in 1922 when Hampshire, after being dismissed by H. Howell and the Hon. F. S. G. Calthorpe for 15 and following-on 208 behind, put together a total of 521 and triumphed by 155 runs. Bowell was one of eight men dismissed without scoring in the first innings.

BOWEN, Edward Ernest, senior assistant master at Harrow School, met his death whilst on a cycling tour in France. He fell in attempting to mount his machine, and died almost immediately. He was enthusiastic about cricket, and will long be remembered as the author of several spirited and charming songs on the game. As a player he was a stiff bat, a superb field at long-leg, and a useful wicket-keeper. He was educated at Cambridge, but was not in the XI. Mr. Bowen, a younger son of the late Lord Bowen, was born at Wicklow, Ireland, March 30, 1836, and died April 8, 1901, aged 65.

BOWEN, M., for many years in charge of the printing office at Lord's ground, died on December 7, 1894, aged 73.

BOWEN, Major Rowland, who died suddenly at his home at Buckfastleigh, Devon, on September 4, 1978, aged 62, was one of the most learned of cricket historians. Educated at Westminster, he never claimed to have been a good player himself, but he founded in 1963 *The Cricket Quarterly* and was its Editor until he closed it down in 1971. Plenty of space in this was allotted to contemporary cricket problems, on which his views were often highly controversial, but the value of the set lies in the vast number of contributions, whether by himself or by other scholarly researchers, on abstruse points of cricket history. He himself published in 1970 *Cricket: a History*.

BOWLES, John Jesse, who died at Salisbury in November, 1971, aged 81, played occasionally for Gloucestershire from 1911 to 1920 and more frequently for Worcestershire from 1926 to 1928. A slow left-hander, his most notable performance was to take nine for 72 in the match v. Sussex at Brighton in 1926.

BOWLEY, Edward Henry (Ted), the Sussex and England cricketer, died in Winchester Hospital on July 9, 1974, aged 84. Born at Leatherhead, in Surrey, he learned his early cricket in Liss and Stodham Park, Hampshire, and qualified by residence for Sussex, for whom he made his debut in 1912. He became a regular member of the side in 1914 and for 15 successive seasons (excluding the First World War) he scored at least 1,000 runs. After serving in the Army he returned to Sussex in 1920. A sound and often brilliant opening batsman and a very useful slow right arm leg break bowler, he hit his maiden century that year, 169 against Northamptonshire at Northampton, putting on 385 with Maurice Tate for the second wicket, a Sussex record that still stands.

His best year was in 1929 when he made 2,359 runs and took 90 wickets. In 1929 he hit his highest score, 280 not out in a day against Gloucestershire at Hove and with J. H. Parks put on 368 for the first wicket, a record for the county. That was surpassed in 1933 when against Middlesex at Hove with John Langridge he engaged in a stand of 490, also still the best for the county.

A number of great batsmen stood in his way as far as England was concerned, but at the age of 39 he appeared twice for England against South Africa in 1929 before touring New Zealand and Australia with A. H. H. Gilligan's M.C.C. team. He played in three Tests in New Zealand and made 109 in the one at Auckland.

According to R. C. Robertson-Glasgow the back stroke was his glory. He wrote: "I never saw a batsman who played this stroke with his bat and elbow so high, meeting a rising ball which others would leave, with tremendous force, and hammering it straight or to the off boundary. Again, he would lean back and cut square from the off stump balls which others were content to stop. In all else his equipment was full and correct. He was a notably fine player to slow bowling, but sometimes he was too impatient perhaps, too much the pure stroke player who would rather force a good length ball for a couple past cover-point than kill it gloomily a few yards from the bat."

On his retirement he moved to Winchester, where for 23 seasons successive generations of boys profited from his coaching and enjoyed his friendship.

E. H. BOWLEY
Compiled by STANLEY CONDER
BATTING

	Inns.	Not Outs	Runs	Highest Inns.	100's	Average
In England						
1912	3	0	15	13	0	5.00
1913	7	1	204	96*	0	34.00
1914	47	3	1196	84	0	27.18
1920	55	1	1501	169	1	27.79
1921	56	1	1940	228	4	35.27
1922	54	3	1567	110*	2	30.72
1923	66	5	2180	120	2	35.73
1924	49	2	1250	106	1	26.59
1925	60	1	1690	133	5	28.64
1926	53	3	1603	106	3	32.06
1927	41	3	2062	220	4	54.26
1928	53	1	2359	188	6	45.36
1929	57	3	2360	280*	5	43.70
1930	59	3	1562	135	3	27.89
1931	41	3	1474	144	5	38.78
1932	41	3	1359	162	3	35.76
1933	50	6	1538	283	3	34.95
1934	4	0	152	63	0	38.00
In New Zealand and Australia						
1929–30	7	1	256	109	1	42.66
In South Africa						
1924–25	22	1	732	131	2	34.85
In Jamaica						
1931–32	6	0	246	115	1	41.00
In New Zealand						
1926–27	8	1	337	95*	0	48.14
1927–28	9	0	413	120	1	45.88
1928–29	5	1	167	75	0	41.75
Totals	853	46	28163	283	52	34.89

*Signifies not out

BOWLING

	Runs	Wickets	Average	Catches
In England				
1912	—	—	—	0
1913	35	0	—	5
1914	66	2	33.00	10
1920	10	0	—	8
1921	904	45	20.08	13
1922	1371	55	24.92	21
1923	1216	46	26.43	34
1924	1044	33	31.63	28
1925	1430	43	33.25	29
1926	1533	38	40.34	20
1927	1241	53	23.41	28
1928	2258	90	25.08	18
1929	1866	79	23.62	21
1930	1951	82	23.79	27
1931	772	35	22.05	17
1932	713	31	23.00	15
1933	994	39	25.48	27
1934	204	5	40.80	1
In New Zealand and Australia				
1929–30	353	12	29.41	2
In South Africa				
1924–25	113	5	22.60	18
In Jamaica				
1931–32	239	5	47.80	2
In New Zealand				
1926–27	374	19	19.68	7
1927–28	319	10	31.90	6
1928–29	257	14	18.35	2
Totals	19263	741	25.99	359

BATTING IN TEST CRICKET

	Matches	Inns.	Not Outs	Runs	Highest Inns.	100's	Aver.
v. South Africa	2	3	0	90	46	0	30.00
v. New Zealand	3	4	0	162	109	1	40.50
Totals	5	7	0	252	109	1	36.00

BOWLING IN TEST CRICKET

	Runs	Wickets	Average	Catches
v. South Africa	7	0	—	1
v. New Zealand	109	0	—	1
Totals	116	0	—	2

CENTURIES (52)

For Sussex (46)
  v. Essex (5) 188, 137, 108, 102, 110.
  v. Glamorgan (4) 146, 130, 120, 110*.
  v. Gloucestershire (4) 280*, 220, 126*, 103.
  v. Northamptonshire (4) 228, 169, 105, 104.
  v. Warwickshire (4) 176, 162, 133, 106.
  v. Cambridge University (3) 139, 121, 105.
  v. Kent (3) 135, 119, 102.
  v. Nottinghamshire (3) 173, 144, 100.
  v. Somerset (3) 134, 107, 101.
  v. Hampshire (2) 116, 102.
  v. Leicestershire (2) 127, 112*.
  v. Middlesex (2) 283, 122.
  v. Surrey (2) 146, 144.
  v. Derbyshire (1) 104.

v. Lancashire (1) 105.
v. Yorkshire (1)105.
v. South Africans (1) 106.
v. Wales (1) 107.

For Other Teams (6)
England v. New Zealand (1) 109.
Auckland v. Wellington (1) 120.
Hon. L. H. Tennyson's XI
    v. A. E. R. Gilligan's XI (1) 120.
    v. All Jamaica (1) 115.
    v. Rhodesia (1) 131.
    v. South Africans (1) 118.

E. H. Bowley shared in the following large partnerships:

For the First wicket
490 with John Langridge for Sussex v. Middlesex at Hove in 1933.
368 with J. H. Parks for Sussex v. Gloucestershire at Hove in 1929.
235 with V. W. C. Jupp for Sussex v. Leicestershire at Leicester in 1921.
226 with J. H. Parks for Sussex v. Nottinghamshire at Trent Bridge in 1928.
222 with J. H. Parks for Sussex v. Kent at Hastings in 1930.
215 with M. W. Tate for Sussex v. Kent at Dover in 1927.

For the Second wicket
385 with M. W. Tate for Sussex v. Northamptonshire at Hove in 1921.
237 with K. S. Duleepsinhji for Sussex v. Essex at Hove in 1931.
235 with K. S. Duleepsinhji for Sussex v. Surrey at Hove in 1932.
230 with K. S. Duleepsinhji for Sussex v. Hampshire at Portsmouth in 1930.
215 with W. R. Hammond for Tennyson's XI v. Gilligan's XI at Folkestone in 1925.
214 with K. S. Duleepsinhji for Sussex v. Middlesex at Hove in 1928.
201 with K. S. Duleepsinhji for Sussex v. Essex at Hove in 1930.

For the Third wicket
250 with K. S. Duleepsinhji for Sussex v. Surrey at the Oval in 1931.
200 with T. E. Cook for Sussex v. Warwickshire at Horsham in 1927.

BOWLEY, Frederick Lloyd, a leading batsman for Worcestershire during 23 years at the beginning of this century, died at Worcester on May 31, 1943, in his 68th year. Considering that his rise to fame coincided with the most brilliant seasons of H. K. and R. E. Foster, besides other brothers of the famous family, Bowley can be placed among the best batsmen of his time. Frequently he headed the Worcestershire averages, and in many partnerships he proved the heavier scorer, while in style and craftsmanship he bore comparison with his most talented colleagues. As an opening batsman, possessing strong defence and punishing power all round the wicket, he was of high value, and it seems remarkable that he never found favour for an Australian or South African tour or for an England XI at home; but at that time several distinguished opening batsmen took priority—A. C. MacLaren, C. B. Fry, R. H. Spooner, L. C. H. Palairet, Robert Abel, Tom Hayward and Len Braund come to mind, while Sir Stanley Jackson could be depended upon for any place in the batting order. So the chief honours that fell to Fred Bowley were some appearances for the Players.

Captain of his school XI when very young, Fred Bowley played for Heanor and Derbyshire Colts when only 14. Deciding to adopt cricket professionally, he qualified for Worcestershire, and in 1900, when 24 years old, he created a very favourable impression during his first full season of county cricket. H. K. Foster alone scored more runs for Worcestershire, and Bowley came fifth in the averages with 24.94 for an aggregate of 948. So well did he maintain and improve on that form that he made more than a thousand runs in 14 different seasons, while in 1922 he really completed his career, when 47, with 974 runs, before going to Glamorgan as coach, though appearing once next season. Altogether in first-class cricket he scored 21,121 runs with an average of 29.62. Anywhere in the field he proved his worth by saving runs and holding difficult catches.

Bowley gave clear evidence of ability directly he became a regular member of the Worcestershire XI, and 118 in May, 1900, against Hampshire was the first of 38 three-figure innings which he played. Three times he went into the third hundred, and in 1914 at Dudley his 276, also at the expense of Hampshire, gave him the distinction of being the highest scorer of all time for his county. He made those runs in four hours 50 minutes, beginning with 100 out of 148 in 100 minutes before lunch. Bowley showed a marked partiality for the Hampshire attack, playing altogether eight three-figure innings against that county, and his last century was hit at Southampton in August, 1922. Invariably scoring very freely when set, he enjoyed many long opening partnerships. At Derby in 1901 he contributed 140 out of 309 with

H. K. Foster, 152, in the biggest first-wicket stand for the county. Twelve years later, with F. Pearson (106), Bowley (201) again saw three hundred on the board before losing his partner at 306, and the same pair were credited with 249 against Warwickshire in 1910, while 274 came at Portsmouth in 1907 from Bowley and H. K. Foster (152). Another exceptional stand with "H. K." was 250 for the second wicket against Somerset in 1903, the runs being added in 100 minutes.

Perhaps his most wonderful effort was in 1913 at Edgbaston when none of the Fosters played and he scored 177 in two hours 40 minutes—136 out of 200 for three wickets before lunch in two hours; 38 was the only double-figure score, and in a second innings collapse he did best with 24 out of 74. Bowley often fared well against the Northern counties, and at Worcester in 1905 his 151 out of 222 in four hours off Hirst, Rhodes and Haigh, the great Yorkshire bowlers, was a grand performance, 27 being the next best effort in a total of 295 when 361 were wanted for victory. He hit 63 and 73 at Dewsbury in 1901, when the Yorkshire bowlers won a keen fight, his second effort coming out of 125; he was sixth out and the last four wickets fell for 17 runs.

At Worcester in 1907 he, with 95, and H. K. Foster, 73, hit off 170, Lancashire being beaten by 10 wickets. Besides his engagement with Glamorgan, Fred Bowley coached at different times at Repton, Hailey-bury and St. Paul's schools, and in South Africa.

BOWLEY, Thomas, who died at Sherborne on November 9, 1939, at the age of 82, was a successful fast bowler for Northamptonshire, Surrey and Dorset. He appeared for Northamptonshire between 1881 and 1884, and against Essex, at Wellingborough, in 1884, he took all the wickets, with the exception of one run out, in the first innings. Next season he joined Surrey and during seven years took 386 wickets for just over 15 runs apiece. He had a rather low delivery, but was accurate in length and direction. With George Lohmann and Jack Beaumont, he made the Surrey attack very formidable. One of his best performances was six Derbyshire wickets for 13 runs at Derby in 1889. In 1894 he was appointed cricket coach at Sherborne School, a post he held for 17 years, and assisted Dorset. He died 20 days before he and his wife would have celebrated their Diamond wedding. He was a native of Nottinghamshire.

BOWRING, Charles Warren, a native of St. John's, Newfoundland, who was educated at Marlborough College, died on November 2, 1940, aged 69. He played for Staten Island club in 1907 and 1908 and was well known in American cricket circles. A prominent shipping agent, he was a member of the American Committee of Lloyd's and a director of the British Empire Chamber of Commerce in the United States. He was one of the survivors when the *Lusitania* was sunk in May, 1915.

BOWRING, Trevor, a young cricketer of the greatest promise, died from blood-poisoning at Ditton Hill, Surrey, on August 7, 1908, in his 21st year. He learnt his cricket at a preparatory school kept by the Rev. H. C. Lenox Tindall, at Ore, near Hastings, and, proceeding to Rugby, secured a place in the XI in 1904, when he headed the batting averages with 29.38 for 13 completed innings. In 1907 he went up to Oxford and obtained his Blue as a Freshman, but scored only 12 and 18 not out in the rather low-scoring match with Cambridge. Last year he played an innings of 228 in the match at Oxford with the Gentlemen of England, and with H. Teesdale (108) scored 338 for the first wicket. He made his runs in 210 minutes, hit a six and 30 four's, and gave only one chance—to MacLaren in the slips when 156. In the University match he made only 14 runs in his two innings, but his bowling—slow with a distinct swerve—accounted for five wickets for 44. He played several times for Surrey Second XI, and in 1906, when he carried his bat through the innings for 118 against Lancashire Second XI, averaged 35.41 for 12 innings. Mr. Harvey Bowring, of the Rugby XI of 1901 and 1902, is his brother, and Mr. W. B. Stoddart, of Liverpool, his cousin.

BOXSHALL, Charles, who died at Balmain, Sydney, in November, 1924, aged 62, was for some years New Zealand's chief wicket-keeper, and he was a member of the Dominion's teams which visited Australia in 1898–99 and 1913–14. In Plunket Shields matches he represented Canterbury. By birth he was a Victorian, and before settling in New Zealand was associated with the Richmond C.C., of Melbourne.

BOYES, G. Stuart, who died on February 11, 1973, aged 74, rendered fine all-round service to Hampshire between 1921 and 1939. After one season as an amateur, he turned professional and during his career he scored 7,515 runs for the county, average 14.45 and took with slow left-arm bowling 1,415 wickets for 23.68. A splendid fieldsman at short-leg, he held 474 catches. Boyes hit two centuries, 101 not out against Lancashire at Liverpool in 1936 and 104 from the Northamptonshire bowling at Newport, I.o.W., in 1938. As a bowler able to spin and flight the ball, and deadly on helpful pitches, he three times took 100 wickets in a season, his best performances being nine wickets for 57 runs against Somerset at Yeovil in 1938, six for five v. Derbyshire at Portsmouth in 1933 and four for three v. Somerset at Southampton in 1936. Twice he performed the hat-trick, at the expense of Surrey at Portsmouth in 1925 and against Warwickshire at Edgbaston the following year. He took part in the historic game at Birmingham in 1922 when Hampshire, dismissed by H. Howell and the Hon. F. S. G. Calthorpe for 15—their lowest total—in the first innings, made such a remarkable recovery that they defeated Warwickshire by 155 runs. From 1946 till 1963, Boyes was a highly popular coach at Ampleforth.

BOYINGTON, Frederick, born at Nottingham on November 9, 1848, died in a nursing-home at Peckham on May 5, 1927. Above the average as a wicket-keeper and a good field anywhere, he was tried for the Nottinghamshire Colts, but never played for the county. Keeping wicket in an 11-a-side match for Victoria against Wilford on the Nottingham Meadow ground in or about the year 1865, he dismissed eight men in an innings by catching and stumping. In 1860, whilst still a boy, he had helped to found the Notts Castle C.C., which was known as the Castle Gate C.C. until 1875. In the early days of the organisation—there was then no Saturday half-holidays—the members used to play from six until eight o'clock in the morning, each match being spread over three days. During the long period of 44 years that he was official scorer to the Surrey County C.C., he carried out his duties in three tie-matches all at the Oval—Gentlemen v. Players in 1883, and Surrey against Lancashire and Kent in 1894 and 1905 respectively. The Surrey County C.C. voted him a pension of a pound a week early in 1925, and on the August Bank Holiday that year, on the second day of the match with Nottinghamshire, a collection made at the Oval for him realised £105 11s. He had a wonderful fund of anecdotes of cricket and cricketers.

BOYLE, Henry Frederick, who more than

anyone else, except Spofforth and Blackham, made the fame of the first Australian XI in England in 1878, died at Bendigo, Victoria, on November 21, 1907. Born on December 10, 1847, he was within three weeks of completing his 60th year. He was a Sydney man by birth, but he went to live in Victoria when only three years old, and with Victorian cricket he was always associated. He took to the game when quite a small boy, and at the age of 15 he played for XXII of Sandhurst against Victoria. When in December, 1873, W. G. Grace's XI played their first match at Melbourne, Boyle appeared for the Eighteen of Victoria, who beat the Englishmen in a single innings, and to the end of his life he recalled with pride the fact that he bowled down W. G.'s wicket. In addition to Boyle, the Victorian team included Frank Allan, Thomas Horan, B. B. Cooper—so well known in England a few years earlier as a batsman—W. Midwinter, John Conway, the manager of the Australian XI of 1878, and the once famous bowler Sam Cosstick. It is no injustice to Boyle to say that he was a far greater cricketer in England than in Australia. When he came to this country in 1878 he was not regarded as anything like such a good bowler as Allan, but whereas he enjoyed a triumph, Allan gave way before the rigours of a very ungenial summer, and only once or twice did himself justice. It is a very old story now to tell how Spofforth and Boyle on May 27, 1878, dismissed the M.C.C. for totals of 33 and 19, and in one afternoon established for good and all the reputation of Australian cricket. In the 11-a-side matches of that memorable tour Boyle took 63 wickets, coming out a very respectable second to Spofforth who took 123. Visiting England for the second time in 1880 he did not have many opportunities in first-class matches, the Australian programme that year, owing to the unfortunate incident at Sydney during the tour of Lord Harris's XI in 1878–79, being largely restricted to games with local Eighteens. Boyle, however, made the most of such chances as he enjoyed. Indeed, he perhaps never bowled better than when, towards the end of the season, Spofforth's accident threw the whole responsibility upon him and George Palmer. In the England match at the Oval the two bowlers got five wickets down for 31 runs, when England went in with 57 runs to get in the last innings. It was, however, in the great tour of 1882, that Boyle reached his highest point. He bowled down the last wicket when the Australians gained their famous victory by seven runs against England at the Oval, and in the 11-a-side matches he took 144 wickets, finishing at the top of the bowling averages with Spofforth, Palmer, and Garrett below him. The tour of 1882 was the climax of his career. From that time his powers as a bowler began to wane. In 1884, when for the first time he experienced a real English summer, he only took 67 wickets as against 216 by Spofforth, and 132 by Palmer, and in 1888, when Turner and Ferris did such wonderful things, he was quite an unimportant member of the team. He paid his last visit to England as manager of the 1890 XI. Boyle as a bowler relied mainly upon headwork and accuracy of length, and had no very remarkable break. Like Alfred Shaw, though his style did not in any way resemble that of the English bowler, he was satisfied if he could make the ball do just enough to beat the bat. No one was quicker to discover a batsman's weakness, or more persevering in turning his knowledge to account. He could peg away at the wicket for an hour without ever bowling a bad ball, and he was never afraid of pitching one up to be hit. No doubt his very high delivery helped to make him deceptive in the flight and awkward in his quick rise off the pitch. Apart from his bowling, Boyle will be remembered as perhaps the most daring fieldsman Australia has ever produced. The position he made for himself at short mid-on was not of much use on very fast wickets, but on the slow grounds in 1878, 1880 and 1882 he brought off any number of catches. Moreover, the mere fact of his standing so dangerously close in, caused many English batsmen to lose their wickets. Of course he got some ugly knocks at times, but he was quite fearless and did not mind how hard the ball was hit at him. E. M. Grace is proud of the fact that he alone gave him a fright and caused him to stand further back.

BOYTON, Harry, for many years one of the leading metropolitan cricketers, died at Crouch End on September 11, 1909, in his 49th year. He headed the Clapton averages for several seasons, and in 1887 scored 210 not out for the club against Croydon, and five years later 277 against Stoke Newington. Several times he played for Essex, and, without reproducing the form he showed in club cricket, proved a useful member of the side.

BRACEY, Frederick Robert, who died on March 28, 1960, aged 72, played as a slow left-arm bowler for Derbyshire from 1906 to 1914. Though at times expensive, he achieved one fine performance against Northamptonshire at Derby in 1907, taking five wickets for nine runs in the first innings and six for 36 in the second.

BRADDELL, Robert Lyttleton Lee, who died on March 17, 1965, aged 76, was in the Charterhouse XI from 1905 to 1907 as a hard-hitting batsman and bowler above medium-pace. In 1907, when second in the school batting figures with an average of 40.75, he shared with M. H. C. Doll a partnership of 214—180 of them scored in an hour—against Westminster. He gained a Blue at Oxford in 1910 and 1911, and though he achieved little in the matches with Cambridge, he hit 96 in the first innings against Kent at Oxford in the second year.

BRADFIELD, Arthur, who died in a North Wales nursing home on December 25, 1978, aged 86, was on the Essex staff in 1922 after making his mark as a wicket-keeper in club cricket, and he was the county's last surviving professional of that year. He made several Championship appearances and played in the game at Northampton in which Jack O'Connor hit the first of his 72 hundreds. Born at Box, Wiltshire, on January 5, 1892, he lived at Mochdre, Colwyn Bay.

BRADFIELD, Donald, who died on March 13, 1972, aged 64, played for Wiltshire when 17 years old. He then became a journalist, but was forced to give up through illness which made him a semi-invalid for 40 years. He was author of *A Century of Village Cricket* and *The Lansdown Story*.

BRADFORD, Sir Evelyn Ridley, Second Bart., Colonel of the Seaforth Highlanders, was killed in action in France in September, 1914. Born on April 16, 1869, he was thus in his 46th year at the time of his death. He was a fine batsman with good defence, a safe field and a fast bowler whose action was not approved by several first-class umpires. Whilst playing for Hampshire in 1899 he was no-balled by White and Pickett in the match with the Australians at Southampton, and by A. F. Smith at Leicester. In the last-mentioned game, however, he scored 102, the next highest score in the innings being only 39, and this was his best batting performance for his county. Against Essex at Southampton three years before he had taken six wickets for 28 runs in the first innings and five for 40 in the second. In military matches he was a heavy run-getter, and as recently as May, 1913, had played an innings of 251 for

Shorncliffe Garrison against Folkestone. For Aldershot Command v. Incogniti in May, 1895, he scored 248. His father, the Chief Commissioner of London Police, married twice, his first wife being a daughter of Edward Knight, of Hampshire and Kent, and his second a daughter of William Nicholson, of Harrow and M.C.C. Through his grandfather, Colonel Bradford was thus related to a whole host of famous cricketers, including the Jenners, Normans, Nepeans, Barnards, Bonham-Carters, Wathens, and Dykes.

BRADFORD, Brigadier-General Roland Boys, V.C., M.C. (Durham Light Infantry). Twice wounded. Born February, 1892; killed first week of December, 1917, aged 25. Played Regimental cricket for Durham Light Infantry. At the outbreak of war he was only a subaltern, and at his death the youngest General in the British Army.

BRADLEY, Walter Morris, died at his home at Wandsworth Common on June 20, 1944, aged 69. After captaining the Alleyn's School XI and doing remarkable things for Lloyd's Register—six wickets with consecutive balls at Mitcham was one effort—he was tried for Kent and became a protégé of Lord Harris, so that he found time to play County Cricket with some regularity from 1895 to 1903. No one who often watched "Bill" Bradley will forget his aggressive long run with both arms flung above his thrown-back head prior to the right-hand delivery from the full reach of his 6ft. height. Pitching at the stumps and seldom short, Bradley really personified the attack in cricket, and rarely did he fail to cause trouble among the opposition. A very hard worker, he would keep going for long spells without slackening his speed. As testimony to his worth it need only be mentioned that he played twice for England against Australia in 1899.

In the Manchester match with Joe Darling's very powerful team his great efforts in the first innings earned five wickets for 67 and a place at the Oval in one of the best sides that ever took the field: F.S. Jackson, Hayward, K.S. Ranjitsinhji, C.B. Fry, A.C. MacLaren (captain), C.L. Townsend, Lockwood, A.O. Jones, Lilley, W. Rhodes and W.M. Bradley.

By far the best amateur bowler that year, his record showed 156 wickets at 19.10 each, but after his heavy work at Old Trafford he met with no success in the Oval Test. That year at Trent Bridge his analysis showed 12 Nottinghamshire wickets for 83 runs, and at

Old Trafford in 1901 he took 14 Lancashire wickets for 134, while 12 Surrey wickets fell to him at Canterbury for 142 runs. Twice in 1899 he did the hat-trick—against Essex at Leyton and Yorkshire at Tonbridge. Altogether in his nine seasons of first-class cricket Bradley took 624 wickets at 22.64 each and made 77 catches.

Like most fast bowlers numbered last on the batting list, Bradley neither expected nor was expected to make runs, but in 1897 at Canterbury against Yorkshire he hit up 67 out of 95 in 45 minutes and was not out when Walter Wright, the left-handed bowler, fell to a catch by Hirst off F.S. Jackson. Altogether his runs totalled only 906—average 6.09, as given by Sir Home Gordon in *Form at a Glance*.

Although troubled by heart weakness, "Bill" Bradley regularly visited Lord's in these War years, and, wearing the M.C.C. tie, he stood out as a popular figure, upholding the best interests of cricket with his many friends in the Long Room.

He was buried at Elmer's End Cemetery in his own family grave, within a short distance of that of W.G. Grace. Present at the funeral were J.R. Mason, his old Kent captain, and C.J. Burnup, the old Cambridge double Blue, another prominent member of the Kent XI less than a year junior to Bradley.

For many years a volunteer with me in the First Surrey Rifles, he attended a meeting of the regimental Old Comrades Association a few evenings before his death.—H.P.

BRADSHAW, James Cecil, died at Minehead on November 8, 1984, aged 82. Playing occasionally for Leicestershire as an amateur from 1923 to 1925, he did little apart from a good innings of 68 at Gloucester in 1925. In 1926 he joined the professional staff and in 1927, without doing anything exceptional, became a regular member of the side. In 1928, however, he scored 967 runs with an average of 26.13 and scores of 140 against Hampshire and 121 not out against Sussex, when he hit Bowley for four sixes. In 1929, with 1,119 runs at an average of 25.43 and an admirable 105 not out at the Oval, he seemed likely to be for years a valuable member of the side: he had a good style with excellent off-side strokes, and was moreover a splendid fielder anywhere. However, in 1930 his average dropped to 12.80 and, though there was a partial recovery in 1931, when he made 892 runs and averaged 21.75, he lost his place in 1932 and in 1933 played his last game for the county. Altogether he scored 5,051 runs for them with an average of 18.99 and three centuries. He also represented Leicestershire at hockey. His younger brother, W. H. Bradshaw, played cricket for them on a few occasions.

BRAIN, John Heather, who died in Hobart on June 21, 1961, aged 56, was an outstanding Tasmanian player at cricket, football, golf and lawn-tennis. He opened the Tasmania innings in both matches against the West Indies touring team of 1930–31.

BRAIN, Joseph Hugh, died at his home, Bonville, near Cardiff, after a long illness, on June 26, 1914. He was born at Kingswood, Bristol, on September 11, 1863. Mr. Brain will be remembered as a brilliant batsman for Clifton College, Oxford University, and Gloucestershire, but it cannot be said that he ever took quite the place in English cricket that at one time seemed in store for him. He was in the Clifton XI in 1881–82–83, being captain in his last year, and was in the Oxford XI from 1884 to 1887 inclusive, captaining the team in 1887. As a Freshman at Oxford he shared in the memorable victory over the Australians in 1884—the match in which T. C. O'Brien scored 92 against Spofforth, Palmer, and Boyle. Mr. Brain played for Gloucestershire from 1883 to 1889, and assisted Glamorgan from 1890 onwards. For Gloucestershire against the Australians at Clifton in 1884 he played an innings of 108. Playing in a free, commanding style, with a very straight bat, he was always good to look at. In 1885 Mr. Brain experienced the most heart-breaking series of failures that one can recall in connection with a batsman of his class. When the Oxford XI came up to London he scored, in his second innings, 135 against the M.C.C. at Lord's, and was obviously in his best form. Following that fine innings, however, he was out for one and 0 against Cambridge, and in the Gentlemen and Players' matches he was got rid of for 0 and two at the Oval, and 0 and 0 at Lord's. Whether or not these failures affected his nerve, he was never the same batsman afterwards, meeting with little success for Oxford in 1886 and 1887. Still, as captain, he had the satisfaction of leading Oxford to victory at Lord's in the latter year. Apart from the two hundreds referred to, he scored 143 for Gloucestershire against Surrey at Clifton in 1884. Late in his career he hit up 144 for Glamorgan against the M.C.C. at Lord's in 1896, and 170 in an hour and a half for Cardiff against Clifton in 1899. He had been a member of the M.C.C. since 1885.

BRAIN, Michael Benjamin, who died after a long illness on August 24, 1971, aged 61, was in the Repton XI in 1928 and 1929. He played for Glamorgan in 1930.

BRAIN, William Henry, a sound batsman and first-class wicket-keeper, died on November 20, 1934. Born at Clifton, near Bristol, on July 21, 1870, he played in the Clifton College XI of 1887 and two following years, being captain in 1889. He got his Oxford Blue in 1891, and in 1893 distinguished himself in the Lord's match by catching five Cambridge men at the wicket. Mr. Brain turned out for Gloucestershire in that year but the following season he appeared for Glamorgan under the residential qualification. In 1893, when Somerset's second innings was finished with a hat-trick by C. L. Townsend, he accomplished the rare feat of stumping three men off consecutive balls. His highest score in an important match was 65 not out for M.C.C. and Ground against Somerset at Taunton in 1891. He did much to help promote Glamorgan to first-class status, and one of his sons, Capt. J. H. P. Brain, played for them. W. H. Brain kept goal for Oxford at Association football.

BRAMPTON, Charles (Notts.), who died on June 12, 1895, was born on February 5, 1828. Though only a name to the present generation, Brampton was, in his day, a capital bat, playing in many a good match for Notts 30 and more years ago in company with Richard Daft, Jackson, Grundy, Wootton, and R. C. Tinley. For a number of years he was coach at Marlborough.

BRAND, The Rt. Hon. Henry Robert, G.C.M.G., Second Viscount Hampden, was born at Devonport, on May 2, 1841, and died in London on November 22, 1906. He was in the Rugby XI in 1858 and played for Sussex once in 1860 and again in 1867. *Scores and Biographies* (vi–55) said he was "A good and free hitter, and can field well, generally at mid-wicket-off." He made some good scores for the Gentlemen of Sussex, including 56 v. Gentlemen of Hampshire, at Southampton, in 1864 and 61 not out v. Gentlemen of Kent, at Brighton, in 1867. He had been a member of the M.C.C. since 1859, and was for some years, in the '70s, a Vice-President of the Sussex County C.C. He was eldest son of the famous Mr. Brand, the Speaker of the House of Commons from 1872 to 1884, and succeeded to the title in 1892. His eldest son, Major the Hon. Thomas Walter Brand, now the Third Viscount Hampden, was in the Eton XI in 1885, 1886, and 1887.

BRANDT, Francis, who was born at Pendleton, near Manchester, on May 6, 1840, died at Cheltenham on July 17, 1925, aged 85. *Scores and Biographies* (vi–232) said he had "a great command over the ball, with a good pace and an easy delivery. As a bat he is by no means deficient, and is a dashing field, though generally short slip." He was in the Cheltenham College XI from 1856 until 1858, being coached by James Lillywhite, sen., and Grundy, and in 1857 was regarded as the best Public School bowler of the year. At Oxford he obtained his Blue in 1859 as a Freshman, and, playing three times against Cambridge, captained the XI in 1861 and was on the losing side each season. In his inter-University matches he scored 36 runs with an average of 9.00 and obtained 10 wickets for 10.10 runs each. Among his contemporaries at Oxford were C. G. Lane, W. F. Traill, J. M. Dolphin, R. D. Walker and E. T. Daubeny. Proceeding later to India, he kept up the game in Madras, where, from 1884 until 1888, he was a Judge of the High Court of Judicature. On his return to England he became Professor of Oriental Languages at Cambridge University. His portrait can be seen facing page 6 of *Annals of the Free Foresters*, 1856–94. Old James Lillywhite said that during the time he coached at Cheltenham Brandt was by far the best bowler the college turned out.

BRANN, George, who died at his home at Surbiton, Surrey, on June 14, 1954, aged 89, was a famous Sussex batsman at the turn of the century. A product of Ardingly College, where he spent 10 years, he first appeared for Sussex in 1883 and played his last match for the county in 1905, but his career really began in 1885 and ended in 1904. Originally a very free batsman and powerful hitter, he forsook his dashing methods during his last few years of County Cricket, but although becoming a far more watchful type of batsman he continued to make many runs. Born on April 23, 1865, he scored altogether 11,150 runs, average 25, and he scored 25 centuries for Sussex. He owed much to the coaching of Alfred Shaw and William Mycroft. Standing nearly 6ft., Brann was a capital fieldsman and once at Ardingly threw a ball over 115yd.

His biggest score was 219 against Hampshire at Brighton. In 1899 he and C. B. Fry opened the two Sussex innings against Middlesex at Lord's with partnerships of 135 and 148. In 1892 he enjoyed what was then the rare distinction of scoring two centuries in a match—105 and 101 against Kent at Brighton. Only Dr. W. G. Grace (three times) and W. Lambert, of Sussex, had to that point in cricket history achieved the feat. Brann went to Australia in 1887–88 as a member of Shaw and Shrewsbury's team, visited South Africa under W. W. Read in 1891–92 and America in 1899 when K. S. Ranjitsinhji was captain.

Brann was also a fine Association football forward. Fast and heavy, he did great work for that celebrated Slough club, the Swifts, and for the Corinthians and played for England against Scotland and Wales in 1886 and against Wales in 1891. After retiring from cricket he achieved some fame at golf.

BRANN, William Henry, who died at Port Elizabeth on September 22, 1953, aged 54, played as a batsman for Eastern Province from 1920 to 1934, scoring 609 runs, average 25.37, in Currie Cup games, with a highest score of 97. In 1922–23 he played for South Africa in three Test matches against England, and in the first of these, at Johannesburg, when scoring 50 in the second innings, helped H. W. Taylor in a fifth-wicket partnership of 98 which did a lot towards winning the match.

BRANSTON, George Trevor, who died on August 12, 1969, aged 84, was in the Charterhouse XI from 1901 to 1903. A good all-rounder, he was top of the bowling averages in 1901 and in his last season headed the batting figures with 708 runs, a highest innings of 144, and an average of 78.66. He got his Blue at Oxford in 1904 and the two following seasons, and from 1903 to 1913 made occasional appearances for Nottinghamshire. He toured the U.S.A. and Canada with the M.C.C. team under E. W. Mann in 1907 and also played in New Zealand. In all first-class cricket, he scored 3,301 runs, average 25.20, dismissed 144 batsmen at a cost of 26.56 runs each and held 90 catches.

BRAUND, Leonard Charles, who died at his home in Fulham on December 22, 1955, aged 80, was one of the best-known professional all-rounders of his time and between 1902 and 1907 played in 23 matches for England. He enjoyed a long and distinguished career. After appearing occasionally for Surrey during three seasons, and when qualifying for Somerset, he profited from the experience of playing for London County with W. G. Grace. In 1899 against the Australians he scored 63 for an England XI on a bad pitch at Truro; 125 for W. G. Grace's XI at the Crystal Palace, he and Alec Hearne putting on 242 for the third wicket in two hours and 40 minutes, and 82 for Somerset at Taunton.

A fine bat on all kinds of pitches, a beautiful field in the slips and a clever leg-break bowler, Braund showed such form directly he appeared in Championship matches for Somerset that in 1901 he scored 1,064 runs for them, with three hundreds and an average of 35, besides taking 78 wickets. His bowling successes included 10 Yorkshire wickets at Taunton, 11 Kent wickets at Catford—five for 23 runs in the first innings—and seven Gloucestershire wickets for 70 in the second innings at Bristol. In a memorable match at Leeds, 222 of 238 arrears were hit off by L. C. H. Palairet and Braund before a wicket fell and the Somerset total reached 630. Palairet made 173, Braund 107 and F. A. Phillips 122. Then Yorkshire, set to make 393, failed so completely that they were all out for 113, suffering by 279 runs their only Championship defeat of the summer. Sharing the bowling honours with B. Cranfield, Braund took four wickets for 41.

Braund played for Somerset until 1920, six times registering over 1,000 runs in a season and four times taking more than 100 wickets. On three occasions, from 1901 to 1903, he achieved the "cricketers' double." His bowling record in 1902 was 172 wickets for less than 20 runs each and in the following year 134 for just over 21 runs apiece, and each season he exceeded 1,400 runs. Altogether during his career he made 17,801 runs, average 25.61, took 1,101 wickets, average 27.45, and held no fewer than 508 catches.

His slip-catching was phenomenal. In the 1901 Gentlemen v. Players match at Lord's he dismissed C. B. Fry with the catch of the season and in the 1902 Test match at Birmingham he disposed of Clem Hill with a long talked-about effort which helped Rhodes and George Hirst dispose of Australia for 36—the smallest total for which they have been dismissed in a Test. Anticipating a leg-glance by the left-handed Hill off Hirst, the fast left-arm bowler, Braund darted across from slip to the leg-side and held an amazing catch. Braund played in all that series of five Test matches. At Manchester he joined F. S. Jackson when five wickets were down for 44 and shared in a partnership of 141, of which his share was 65. Wonderful bowling by

W. H. Lockwood subsequently left England on the second evening with victory in sight, but following a heavy fall of rain during the night Australia snatched a win by three runs. Had F. W. Tate caught J. Darling, whose 37 was top score in a second innings total of 86, off Braund, the result must have been different, for four wickets would have been down for 16. By holding two catches at slip off S. F. Barnes, Braund was responsible for Darling getting a "pair" in the Test at Sheffield.

With the teams led by A. C. MacLaren in 1901–02, P. F. Warner in 1903–04 and A. O. Jones in 1907–08, Braund went to Australia three times and on his first visit, when he made 103 not out at Adelaide, his batting average for the Test matches was 36 and he took 21 wickets. During the next tour he scored 102 at Sydney when R. E. Foster, with 287, created a record, but on his third trip he fared moderately. Against the famous South African attack of 1907, Braund hit 104 at Lord's, this being one of the two centuries obtained in Test matches against the bowling combination which included Aubrey Faulkner, R. O. Schwarz, A. E. Vogler and Gordon White.

After giving up active cricket, Braund became a first-class umpire, discharging his duties with marked ability until the end of the 1938 season. In 1943 it became necessary for his right leg to be amputated and three years later he lost the other, but his cheerfulness and his enthusiasm for cricket remained undiminished and for some years he watched cricket at Lord's seated in a bath chair. He was one of the 26 retired professional cricketers who in 1949 were given honorary membership of M.C.C.

C. B. Fry, the former England captain, said of Braund: "He was one of the greatest all-round cricketers—and to think that Surrey let him go! The thing about Len Braund was that he was a big-match player. I have never seen a better slip fieldsman. He had such a delicate hand. He would push it out and the ball would stick. Archie MacLaren would never take the field without him. He was a most valuable member of the England team and as cool as a cucumber."

C. T. Bennett, captain of the 1925 Cambridge University team described by Sydney H. Pardon, then Editor of *Wisden*, as "probably the best sent up to Lord's by either University since the war," said: "Braund was the greatest gentleman in cricket, either amateur or professional, I ever met. His coaching made the 1925 side, four of whom played for the Gentlemen at Lord's that year, and K. S. Duleepsinhji would be the first to admit that he owed him a lot."

BRAY, His Honoer Sir Edward, County Court Judge of Bloomsbury and Brentford, died in London on June 19, 1926, aged 77. Born at Shere, in Surrey, on August 19, 1849, he was descended from Sir Thomas More, Chancellor of Henry VIII. A capital slow bowler, he played for five years in the Westminster XI (1864 to 1868), and in 1871 and 1872 gained his Blue at Cambridge, taking in the two games against Oxford 10 wickets for exactly 12 runs each. Between 1870 and 1878 he assisted Surrey on 14 occasions, doing little with the bat but obtaining 48 wickets at a cost of 15.45 runs apiece. In the Westminster v. Charterhouse match at Lord's in 1867 he took as many as 17 wickets—nine of them for 26 runs in the first innings, and on the same ground four years later he had the great satisfaction of getting W. G. Grace caught for four in each innings in the game between Cambridge University and M.C.C. One of his sons was a Cambridge cricket Blue of 1896 and 1897.

BRAY, Sir Edward Hugh, C.S.I., who died at Rye, Sussex, on November 27, 1950, aged 76, played both cricket and Association football for Cambridge. After three years in the Charterhouse XI he got his cricket Blue in 1896, and played in the match which Oxford won with the record victorious score of 330 for six wickets. In a strong batting side Bray was number nine. He made 49 and 41, but next season, when Cambridge won by 179 runs, he did little. From 1895 to 1899 he appeared occasionally in the Middlesex XI, and toured America with P. F. Warner's team in 1898. After many years in business in Calcutta and Bengal, he became Controller of Contracts at Army headquarters with the temporary rank of Brigadier-General.

BRAYBROOKE, Henry Mellor, M.B.E., died on October 28, 1935, at Tates, aged 66. Born at Kandy in Ceylon on February 11, 1869, he went to Wellington College and was in the 1886 XI. He failed to get his Blue at Cambridge, though playing a few times for the University in 1891, but between 1890 and 1899 he met with some success for Kent, his highest score for the county being 53 against Somerset at Taunton in 1892. A free batsman, hitting specially well to the on, he played many big innings in club cricket including 256 not out for Blue Mantles against Eastbourne College in 1889, his unfinished opening partnership with J. H.

Kelsey (136 not out) producing 403. He played for Cambridge against Oxford at golf in 1890 and 1891 and gained many prizes for running.

BREARLEY, Walter, died after an operation in Middlesex Hospital on January 30, 1937. During 10 years from 1902 when he first played for Lancashire, he stood out as a conspicuous figure on the cricket field and until last season he kept up his enthusiastic love for the game, often going to the nets at Lord's for hearty practice and every April taking a prominent part in the instruction of young public schoolboys at headquarters. A fast right hand bowler of the highest class, Walter Brearley took a short run up to the crease, with a rolling gait and body swing for imparting pace. He delivered the ball in a manner not unlike that of Arthur Mold, his predecessor in the Lancashire XI.

Born on March 11, 1876, he was highly successful with the Bolton and Manchester clubs before appearing in County Cricket when 26 years of age. Altogether for Lancashire he took 690 wickets at a cost of 18 runs apiece, and in first-class cricket his record was 844 at 19.31. He met with special success in the great local struggles with Yorkshire and in the 14 matches played between these counties from 1903 to 1911 he dismissed 125 batsmen at 16 runs each.

During his most effective year in 1908, 163 wickets fell to him, but he was never in better form than in 1905 when he played for England against Australia at Old Trafford and the Oval. He found special pleasure in making extra efforts to dismiss some batsmen, and, that season, when playing for England, the Gentlemen and Lancashire, he disposed of Victor Trumper no fewer than six times. Walter Brearley also played for England against Australia at Leeds in 1909 and once against South Africa during the Triangular Tournament in 1912.

At Lord's in 1905 for Gentlemen against Players on a slow pitch that seemed unsuited to him, he prevailed to such an extent by the exercise of sheer energy that in the first innings he took seven wickets for 104 runs, and followed this by bowling 24 overs for 51 runs and two wickets. Another notable achievement that year was his 17 wickets for 137 runs against Somerset at Old Trafford—nine for 47 and eight for 90. He finished the first innings by bowling Cranfield and Bucknall with successive deliveries and when Somerset faced arrears of 77 his first two balls accounted for H. Martyn and Hardy—so in this match he was credited with four wickets in four balls. As on other occasions Brearley, by his great pace combined with excellent length, demoralised the batsmen.

Of many characteristics which delighted spectators, nothing attracted more attention or aroused more amusement than his hurried walk to the wicket when, as customary, he went in last to bat. Sometimes if, as at the Oval, he was not sure of the position of the gate on the field, he would vault the pavilion rails. It was said at Old Trafford that when Walter Brearley hurried to the wicket the horse walked between the shafts ready to drag the heavy roller for use at the end of the innings.

BREEDEN, Frank, a medium-paced right-arm bowler, who played for Warwickshire in the early years of the County Club when second class, died at his home in Moseley on April 7, 1940, aged 81. Playing for Twenty of Walsall and District in 1883, Breeden and Allan Hill, the Yorkshire fast bowler, dismissed the entire United All-England XI captained by W. G. Grace for 82 and 58. Breeden bowled "W. G." round his legs, and his record for the match was 10 wickets for 68, while Allan Hill's 10 cost 66 runs. Besides the two successful bowlers, Richard Daft and H. B. Daft, famous with Nottinghamshire, and George Pinder, of Yorkshire, a superb wicket-keeper, were in the Walsall side. W. G. Grace took 17 wickets for 135 and scored 23 and nine, but the powerful United XI were beaten.

BRETT, Patrick John, who died at Hook Heath, Woking, on December 9, 1982, aged 72, was in the Winchester XI in 1927 and 1928 and got his Blue at Oxford in 1929. For Winchester v. Eton in 1928 he scored 55 and took 12 for 115. As a batsman, at this time he was chiefly an on-side player. He bowled medium-pace right-arm, could swing the ball late both ways and came quickly off the pitch. At Oxford he was given a trial halfway through the term, largely as an opening bowler, but in that capacity was a complete failure. However, in his first match he made 30 and 75 not out against Leicestershire, in the second innings putting on 137 for the first wicket with I. Akers-Douglas. In the next match, against Middlesex, he followed this with 79, adding 143 for the fourth wicket with N. M. Ford. So strong, however, was the Oxford batting that even after this his place was in doubt: he clinched it with innings of 57 and 106 against H. D. G. Leveson Gower's XI at Eastbourne, which was for once a strong bowling side. By now he

had become a fine driver on both sides of the wicket and particularly good past extra cover. Unfortunately a bad car accident stopped him from playing cricket in 1930 and his first-class career came to an end after one season.

BREWER, Walter John, for many years groundsman at Leyton, was killed on the railway at the station there on April 23, 1928, at the age of 62.

BRICE, W. Stanley, who died in New Zealand on May 6, 1959, aged 79, was from 1902 to 1935 a noted all-round cricketer for Wellington and Petone United and five times appeared for New Zealand. In senior cricket he scored 8,349 runs, average 26.25, his highest innings being 228, and with fast bowling took 1,173 wickets for 13.65 runs each. His big hitting earned him the nickname of "Sixer". He served as a selector for both Wellington and New Zealand. As a wing-forward, he played Rugby Union football for Wellington and in 1908 he founded the Rugby League game in Wellington.

BRICKNELL, Gary A., who was killed in a train crash at Keetmanshoop, South-West Africa, on March 25, 1977, aged 22, was a slow left-hander of great promise. He had already taken 58 wickets at 21.38 for Western Province.

BRIDGEMAN, Viscount, the politician who died on August 14, 1935, aged 70, played for Eton in 1884 and three years later gained his Blue at Cambridge, his batting average for that season being 34. In the match against Sussex in 1887 he played probably the best innings of his career—162 not out. He and L. Martineau put on 193 in a splendid partnership for the seventh wicket which pulled the game round completely. A good steady bat, and a live fieldsman at point, he afterwards assisted Staffordshire. Viscount Bridgeman was President of M.C.C. in 1931 and at the time of his death was a member of the M.C.C. Committee.

BRIDGES, James J., who died in London on September 26, 1966, aged 79, bowled fast-medium for Somerset between 1911 and 1929. Before the 1914 War he played as a professional, but later he was one of the many popular amateurs who enjoyed cricket under the captaincy of John Daniell. He had a neat run-up and side-way action and took 685 wickets. When Jack Hobbs equalled W. G. Grace's record of 126 hundreds in

1925 at Taunton, Bridges had him caught at the wicket by M. L. Hill for 101. His bowling partner was usually R. C. Robertson-Glasgow, who tells in his *More Cricket Prints* how each considered himself the superior batsman; Daniell with rare judgement decided that they should toss for the last two places, a procedure which was regularly observed.

BRIDGES, John Henry, who was born at Horsham on March 26, 1852, and died at Eastbourne on February 12, 1925, was described in *Scores and Biographies* as "A free hitter and fields well, generally at long-leg, cover-point or at long-stop." He was in the Winchester XI in 1868 and three following years, but in his four matches against Eton he scored only 55 runs in seven completed innings. Whilst at Oxford he represented the University at Association football but not at cricket, and in 1876 he appeared in one match for Surrey. He was a member of the Royal Company of Archers (the King's Bodyguard for Scotland) and Champion Archer in 1905. In 1919–20 he was High Sheriff of Surrey.

BRIDGMAN, Henry H. M., who died at Torrensville, South Australia, on December 3, 1953, aged 63, was a member of the Australian Board of Control. Born on February 1, 1890, he played as a left-handed batsman for South Australia, scoring 252 runs, average 15.75, with 65 his highest innings.

BRIGGS, John, died on January 11, 1902. The last reports as to the condition of Briggs's health had been so discouraging that the news of his death did not cause much surprise. Though he rallied so wonderfully from his seizure at Leeds, during the Test match in 1899, as to bowl with nearly all his old skill and success throughout the season of 1900, it was known that his ailment—a form of epilepsy—admitted of no permanent cure, and was liable to recur at any time. He had another attack sooner than had been expected; was compelled to go back to Cheadle Asylum; and took no part in the cricket of 1901. Five or six weeks before his death it was announced that he had again rallied after a serious relapse, but this time the improvement was of very brief duration. Briggs had a long career, but at the time of his death he was only a little over 39. Like so many other famous professional crickets, he was a Nottingham man, being born at Sutton-in-Ashfield, on October 3, 1862. While still a child, however, he went to live in Lanca-

shire, and all his cricket was learnt in the county for which, during more than 20 years, he did such brilliant work. He must have shown great promise while very young, as he was given a trial in the Lancashire XI before he was 17. He played in five matches for the county in 1879, and though he met with little success his aptitude for the game was so obvious that no doubt was felt as to his future. In those early days he was played chiefly for his fielding, his quickness and energy making him from the first a special favourite with the crowds at Old Trafford. The popularity that he thus gained as a lad remained with him to the end, and wherever he went the public took the keenest interest in his doings. For two or three seasons he was not much more than a splendid field, but from 1883 his batting rapidly improved, and a little later, without much warning, he blossomed out as one of the great slow bowlers of his day. In 1885 he headed the bowling averages for Lancashire, with 79 wickets for 10.5 runs each, but, though this was a very fine record, his fame as a bowler really dated from the England and Australia match, at Lord's, in 1886—the memorable game in which Shrewsbury played his innings of 164. The opening day's cricket was interfered with by rain, and the England XI, who had won the toss, did not finish their innings till the second day, their total being 353. When the Australians went in against this formidable number, Jones and Scott scored so freely that an even match seemed in prospect. Suddenly, however, the character of the cricket underwent a complete change. Mr. A. G. Steel, who captained England, put Briggs on as first change, and the Australians, though their score stood at 45 when the first wicket went down, were all out for 121, Briggs bowling 34 overs, 22 maidens, for 29 runs and five wickets. His success caused great surprise, as he had played for England a fortnight before at Manchester without being called upon to bowl at all. When the Australians followed on, he took six wickets for 45 runs, and England won the match in a single innings. Thenceforward, Briggs's reputation as a left-handed slow bowler was firmly established and, as everyone knows, he remained in the front rank, with, of course, the fluctuations of fortune to which all cricketers are subject, till his unhappy seizure at Leeds in 1899.

He jumped to the top of the tree at a very opportune moment in 1886—Peate being then almost done with—and for many seasons his only rival in his own particular style was Peel. There is no need to go into details of his work year by year, but it is interesting to note that, according to the figures given in *Bat v. Ball*, he took in first-class matches, from 1885 to 1899 inclusive, 2034 wickets for less than 16 runs each. He had a bad season in 1898, but in 1900, after his first illness, he came out again in such form that 127 wickets fell to him for something over 17.5 runs each. During all his years of success Briggs was much more than a mere bowler. He was always a dangerous bat, likely at any time to get his 50 runs, and in the field he retained all the energy and nearly all the speed of his young days. Though the greater part of his work was done for Lancashire, he was in the truest sense of the word a representative cricketer, being picked over and over again for England and the Players, and being nearly as well known on Australian grounds as in this country. He paid six visits to the Colonies, going out with Shaw and Shrewbury's teams in 1884–85, 1886–87 and 1887–88; with Lord Sheffield's team in 1891–92, and with Mr. Stoddart's XIs in 1894–95, and 1897–98. As it happened, he went once too often, proving a sad failure for Stoddart's second team. In the other trips, however, he did himself full justice. Among all his Australian experiences the most remarkable was the famous 10 runs win at Sydney, in December, 1894, when Australia suffered defeat after playing a first innings of 586. The Australians only had to get 177 in the last innings, and at the close of the fifth day they had scored 113, with two men out. After drenching rain in the night, however, Peel and Briggs secured the eight outstanding wickets for 53 runs, gaining for Stoddart's side perhaps the most sensational victory in the history of cricket. Briggs, as a slow bowler, had nearly every good quality. His beautifully easy action enabled him to stand any amount of work; he had plenty of spin, and no one was more skilful in tempting batsmen to hit on the off-side. For a few seasons he bowled a particularly good fast ball, but in this respect he fell off in later years.

BRIGGS, John, who died at Rawtenstall on June 1, 1984, aged 68, had four matches for Lancashire, as a left-arm spinner, in 1939, when he took 10 wickets at 39.10 apiece. After the War he had two seasons back at Old Trafford, playing for the Second XI, before moving to League cricket.

BRIGGS, Joseph, an elder brother of the late John Briggs, died on November 30, 1902. His name will be found in a few Nottinghamshire matches in 1888.

BRINTON, Reginald Seymour, died at Kidderminster on February 23, 1942, aged 72. Educated at Winchester and Oxford, he failed to qualify for either XI, but played occasionally for Worcestershire from 1903 to 1909.

BRINTON, Ronald Lewis, died at Malvern on April 19, 1980, aged 77. A useful bat and medium-pace swinger, he was in the Shrewsbury XI from 1919 to 1921 and in 1924 made a couple of appearances for Worcestershire.

BRISCOE, Capt. A. W., M.C., whose death was reported, in 1941, in a Johannesburg newspaper as having occurred in the Abyssinian campaign, at the age of 30, batted well for Transvaal. Against the Australian team that visited South Africa in 1935–36 he made 60 and 18, 21 and 11 for his State, but in the second Test match his 15 and 16 were not good enough to retain his place in the side. His efforts were somewhat similar when the M.C.C. team, captained by W. R. Hammond, toured South Africa in 1938–39. Briscoe then scored 42 and 38 not out for Transvaal and for Combined Transvaal two and 12 not out, but, given a place in the second Test, he was out for two. In Currie Cup matches he played innings of 191 and 140. Awarded the M.C. for gallantry at Huberta and Ionte, he fell when again acting very bravely, regardless of danger. Bruce Mitchell and R. E. Grieveson—so well-known in South African cricket—were in action with Briscoe.

BRISTOWE, Omre Chesshyre, died of heart failure when shooting on the Norfolk Broads, on December 27, 1938. He left Eton comparatively young without getting into the XI but, going up to Christ Church, Oxford, he received his Blue as a Freshman from F. H. Knott in 1914 and took a prominent part in beating Cambridge by 194 runs. Bowling leg breaks from a good height with a googly at his command, he took five of the first seven Cambridge wickets for 70 runs and in the last innings of the match three for 30. By far the best bowler then at Oxford he, during a good season's work, had a record of 46 wickets at 16.86 runs apiece. He played occasionally for Essex in 1913 and 1914, hard hitting and sure fielding making him a very useful all-round cricketer. After the War, he devoted his spare time to golf, but a weak heart limited his activities and he died at the early age of 43.

BROCKLEBANK, Sir John Montague, Bart., died at his home in Malta on September 13, 1974, aged 59. Chairman of Cunard from 1959 to 1965, he placed the order for the construction of the *QE2*. In his younger days at Eton and Cambridge he was a talented bowler of quick leg-breaks and top spinners. He appeared against Harrow at Lord's in 1933 and took four wickets. In the Arab tour of Jersey in 1935 Hugh Bartlett recognised his possibilities and the following year caused a surprise by inviting him to tour with the Cambridge team three weeks before the University match. In nine innings he took 33 wickets, average 18.48. Bowling from a good height and keeping an accurate length, Brocklebank—a nephew of Sir Stanley Jackson—took 10 wickets for 139 in the match against Oxford at Lord's and helped Cambridge to victory by eight wickets.

On leaving Cambridge, he was apprenticed by his father, Sir Aubrey Brocklebank, in a shipyard where he found few opportunities for first-class cricket. He played in four matches for Lancashire in 1939 when he also appeared for Gentlemen against Players at Lord's. Although he took only three wickets in that match he caused such an impression that M.C.C. chose him for the tour to India, 1939–40, which was abandoned on the outbreak of war, in which he reached the rank of Major with the Royal Artillery, having joined as a Territorial. In 1943 he was taken prisoner by the Germans on the island of Cos in the Dodecanese.

BROCKWELL, William, a prominent Surrey cricketer nearly 50 years ago, died on July 1, 1935. A stylish and often brilliant batsman, strong in back play and a free hitter in front of the wicket, Brockwell also was a useful fast medium paced bowler and a smart fieldsman, notably at second slip where he succeeded George Lohmann—one of the surest catches ever seen in that position. First playing for the county in 1886, Brockwell matured slowly but it was difficult to find a place in the very powerful Surrey XI of that period. However, from 1891 to 1902 he was a regular member of the side and played his last game in 1903 when the team were declining rapidly in all round strength.

During Brockwell's career at the Oval Surrey carried off the Championship eight times and once tied for first place with Lancashire and Nottinghamshire. Needless to say Surrey were tremendously strong in those days. Brockwell played under John Shuter, K. J. Key, D. L. A. Jephson and the present president, H. D. G. Leveson Gower.

Among his contemporaries were such great batsmen as W. W. Read, Maurice Read, Robert Abel, Tom Hayward and bowlers of equal fame—George Lohmann, Tom Richardson and William Lockwood. To be in such company was an honour; and in 1894 Brockwell came out at the head of the English batting with the highest aggregate, 1,491, and best average 38.9. He was also leading scorer for Surrey with 1,091 runs and an average of 35—remarkable figures in a summer of unsettled weather.

BRODIE, James Chalmers, the oldest of Australian cricketers, died at Balwyn, Victoria, on February 19, 1912, aged 91. He assisted Victoria against Tasmania, at Launceston in 1851, in the first of the long roll of inter-colonial matches, and also played against New South Wales, scoring altogether 43 runs in six innings. In 1862 he figured in a few matches against Stephenson's team. He was a Scotchman by birth, but spent practically his whole life in Australia. He was the compiler of the *Victorian Cricketers' Guide for 1860–61*.

BROMLEY, Harry Thomas, who died at Hove in May, 1954, aged 68, expressed his love of cricket in a unique manner: he was a member of every County Club in the country. Before he retired to Hove, he was for many years a well-known personality in cricket at Slough.

BROMLEY-DAVENPORT, Hugh Richard, O.B.E., who died on May 23, 1954, aged 83, was in the Eton XI from 1886 to 1889, being captain in the last two seasons, and was described by *Wisden* of the time as "the best Public School bowler of 1887". Fast left-arm, he achieved considerable success in his first two matches against Harrow, for in 1886 he dismissed nine batsmen for 152 and the following season eight for 111.

Going up to Trinity Hall, Cambridge, he gained a Blue in 1892 and 1893 under the captaincy of F. S. Jackson. In the second meeting with Oxford he obtained a match record of five wickets for 11 runs. An incident in that game led to a change in the Laws. Convinced that Oxford intended to throw away their last wicket, which, as they were 84 behind, would have meant that they would be compelled to follow-on and thus leave Cambridge to take last innings on a deteriorating pitch, C. M. Wells frustrated any such attempt by bowling two wides to the boundary. In the end Cambridge won by 266 runs, and the following year the follow-on became compulsory only if a side finished the first innings 120 or more behind their opponents' total.

After going down from the University, Bromley-Davenport, who was born on August 18, 1870, played for his native county, Cheshire, and from 1896 to 1898 for Middlesex. In 1893 he appeared with such celebrities as K. S. Ranjitsinhji and C. B. Fry under the captaincy of W. G. Grace for Gentlemen at the Oval, where the Players won in an exciting finish by eight runs. Twice he toured the West Indies, with R. S. Lucas's team in 1894–95 and with Lord Hawke's side in 1897, visited South Africa with Lord Hawke in 1895–96 and 1898–99, and went to Portugal with T. Westray's team in 1898. A Lieutenant in the Royal Engineers during the first Great War, he was awarded the O.B.E.

BROMLEY-MARTIN, Elliot George, who died on January 23, 1946, aged 79, was principal bowler for Eton in 1884 and 1885. In the two matches against Winchester he took six wickets for 63 runs and six for 68, and at Lord's against Harrow eight for 94 and 10 for 137. He played in trial games at Oxford but failed to get his Blue. Assisting Worcestershire occasionally, he was Hon. Secretary of the County Club for some years, and went to Holland with Worcestershire Gentlemen in 1895. In 1897 he and Bird bowled unchanged in both innings against Hertfordshire, the visitors being dismissed for 75 and 116. That season Worcestershire easily headed the Minor Counties, winning seven and drawing their other three matches. Two years later Worcestershire entered the first class competition and E. G. Bromley-Martin continued to play sometimes. In 1888 he was in the Oxford Association team against Cambridge.

BROMLEY-MARTIN, Granville Edward, died at Hassocks, Sussex, on May 31, 1941, aged 65. Getting into the Eton XI in 1892, he was captain in the next two years, and played for Oxford in 1897 and 1898. A very good batsman, free and stylish in stroke play, he finished at Eton top of the averages with 38.80, but his best score in the big matches was 68 against Harrow when first playing at Lord's. Neither did he do much against Cambridge, but at Hove in 1897 he scored 137 for Oxford against Sussex. He played a good deal for Worcestershire, and in 1899, when his county was promoted to first-class rank, he made 129 in the Derbyshire match at Worcester. He and H. K. Foster added

207 in two hours. His innings finished in a curious way. A piece of his bat broke off in playing Hancock and the ball went almost straight up. L. G. Wright dashed in from point and just held the catch. A week later at Southampton he had a very different experience; the first ball he received in each innings proved fatal, C. Heseltine, the fast bowler, twice beating him completely.

BROOK, George Wilfred, who died at Bournemouth on July 24, 1966, aged 70, did fine work as a leg-break bowler for Worcestershire from 1931 to 1935. Joining the county from the Kidderminster club at the age of 35, he enjoyed marked success in his first season. With such analyses as six wickets for 30 runs against Derbyshire at Kidderminster; six for 37 v. Leicestershire, six for 80 v. Nottinghamshire and six for 89 v. Lancashire, all at Worcester, he dismissed 128 batsmen in Championship fixtures at an average cost of 21.41. Though he did not touch quite the same heights afterwards, he took 461 wickets, average 27.85, during a brief first-class career which terminated when he went to Keighley, the Yorkshire Council Club.

BROOKE, Lieut.-Col. F. R. R., who died on June 20, 1960, aged 75, played for Lancashire in 29 matches in 1912 and 1913. Military duties prevented him from appearing more frequently. A very good wicket-keeper, he stumped 11 batsmen and caught 46. Also a useful batsman, he scored 566 runs, average 16.17, his highest innings being 61 against Sussex at Old Trafford in 1912.

BROOKE, Sub-Lieut. Rupert C. (Royal Naval Division), born at Rugby on August 3, 1887, died at Lemnos of sunstroke on April 23, 1915. In 1906 he was in the Rugby XI, and although he was unsuccessful in the Marlborough match he headed the school's bowling averages with a record of 19 wickets for 14.05 runs each. He had gained considerable reputation as a poet.

BROOKES, Paul Wilson, a member of the Lord's ground staff, died in St. Mary's Hospital on January 27, 1946, from the effect of wounds received when with the Coldstream Guards in Italy. As a County of London schoolboy he headed the batting averages and played against both Eton and Harrow for selected schoolboy teams. When 16 years of age in 1938 he became famous by bowling Don Bradman in the nets at Lord's during practice before the season began.

Hooking at a left-hand delivery, Bradman missed the ball, which took his middle stump.

BROOKES, Wilfred H., who died in a nursing home at Putney on May 28, 1955, aged 60, was Editor of *Wisden* from 1936 to 1939, and for several years until the outbreak of the Second World War a partner in the Cricket Reporting Agency.

BROOKE-TAYLOR, Geoffrey Parker, who died in Buenos Aires on January 15, 1968, aged 72, was in the XI at Cheltenham from 1912 to 1914, being captain in the last season. He got his Blue as a left-handed batsman for Cambridge in 1919 and 1920. Against Oxford in the second year he scored 55 in the second innings, helping G. Ashton to put on 74 for the fifth wicket before he was run out. In that season he appeared in one match for Derbyshire.

BROOKMAN, Sidney George, who died suddenly at Bristol on May 2, 1955, aged 80, was father-in-law of T. W. Graveney, the England and Gloucestershire cricketer, who left the match with the University at Oxford upon hearing the news of his death. One of the oldest active cricketers in the country, Brookman once played against Dr. W. G. Grace. He had been a member of the Schoolmasters' C.C. since he was 18 and until 1954 played occasionally for Bristol Wayfarers C.C. of which he was a founder member. He also played Rugby football for Bristol, Saracens and United Services.

BROOKS, Edward W. J., who died on February 10, 1960, aged 61, was the regular wicket-keeper for Surrey between 1928 and the start of the Second World War in 1939. He first joined the county from Cheam C.C. in 1925 as a medium-pace bowler, but his chance came as successor behind the stumps to that great England wicket-keeper, Herbert Strudwick.

Brooks took the opportunity splendidly, and became a highly popular figure at the Oval. An able and acrobatic wicket-keeper, he helped in over 800 dismissals, and he acquired a considerable reputation as a humorist, both on and off the field. Brooks had no pretensions to first-class batting, yet he made 4,504 runs during his career, and could hit or defend dourly as the occasion demanded. He liked the role of "night watchman" at the end of the day, and was far from an easy victim when play resumed.

For some years after his first-class career ended, Brooks was a licensee at Abingdon, Berks, and later became groundsman at Littlehampton Sports Field. He lived at Lyminster, Sussex, in his last years.

BROOKS, Richard, born at Sutton-on-Sea, in Lincolnshire, on July 29, 1863, died in London on April 9, 1927. After being in the Cranleigh School XI for several seasons, he developed into one of the best wicketkeepers of the day, but his duties as a solicitor prevented him from appearing frequently in first-class matches. He played, however, for Surrey against Gloucestershire at the Oval in 1889, and later for London County, while at Lord's in 1901 he kept wicket for England v. Yorkshire and at the Oval a year later took part in the Gentlemen v. Players match. Whilst assisting London County against Worcestershire at the Crystal Palace in 1900 he did not allow a single bye in totals of 208 and 177. Being unable to spare time to appear in many three-day matches, he was obliged to content himself with taking part chiefly in good-class club games. For the Wanderers he was very successful, once obtaining as many as nine wickets in a match and several times six in succession. In one season he did not allow a single extra in nine consecutive innings. He was, too, well above the average as a batsman. It may be added that, although he was generally known as R. B. Brooks, he had only one Christian name.

BROUGHTON, Ernest Alfred, who died on February 19, 1982, aged 76, played a number of times for Leicestershire from 1928 to 1933. A useful hard-hitting batsman, against Worcestershire in 1932 he made 61 at Worcester and 52 at Hinckley. He did much valuable work for the county in captaining Second XI and Club and Ground sides, was on the Committee for many years and a Vice-President, and from 1974 to 1981 was Hon. Treasurer.

BROWN, Alfred, of Malton, died November 1, 1900, aged 46. He was for a good many years a well-known cricketer at Malton, and on September 4, 1873, he won a single wicket match for £50 a side against John Hicks of York. He was born at Malton on June 10, 1854.

BROWN, Colin E., who died at Whitby on June 25, 1936, aged 58, played for Somerset, his best score for the county being 53 in 1905.

BROWN, George, who died in hospital in Winchester on December 3, 1964, aged 77, was a great professional all-rounder for

Hampshire between 1909 and 1933—an all-rounder in the truest sense, for he was not only a top-class left-handed batsman and medium-paced right-arm bowler, but a wicket-keeper good enough to play for England and a splendid, fearless fieldsman close to the bat. He was cremated and, at his own wish, his ashes were scattered over the County Ground at Southampton.

Born at Cowley, near Oxford, he formed, with J. Newman and A. S. Kennedy, a batting and bowling backbone for Hampshire for many years. During his career, he hit 25,649 runs, average 26.71, and took 629 wickets at 29.73 runs each. As wicket-keeper, he held 485 catches and brought off 50 stumpings for his county alone. He played behind the stumps in seven Test matches for England, first when, to strengthen the run-getting, he was called upon to replace H. Strudwick in 1921 for the last three Tests with Australia—a decision by the selectors which aroused much controversy. In five innings against Warwick Armstrong's men he did much to justify his choice by scoring 250 runs. Under the captaincy of F. T. Mann, he played four times against South Africa in South Africa in 1922–23 and was selected for the final Test with Australia in 1926, but withdrew because of a damaged thumb. He also toured the West Indies in 1909–10 and India in 1926–27 and assisted Players against Gentlemen nine times from 1919 to 1930.

Tall and of fine physique, Brown was an aggressive batsman who could when the situation demanded fill a defensive role with equal skill. He shared in a three-figure stand for every Hampshire wicket except the sixth and three of them still stand as county records: 321 for the second wicket with E. I. M. Barrett against Gloucestershire at Southampton in 1920; 344 for the third with C. P. Mead v. Yorkshire at Portsmouth in 1927, and 325 for the seventh with C. H. Abercrombie v. Essex at Leyton in 1913. Twice, against Middlesex at Bournemouth in 1926 and Surrey at the Oval in 1933, he carried his bat through an innings. Of his 37 centuries, the highest was 232 not out from the Yorkshire bowling at Leeds in 1920 and he exceeded 200 on two other occasions; but the display for which he will always be remembered was that at Edgbaston in 1922. Dismissed for 15, the smallest total in their first-class history, Hampshire followed-on 208 behind and seemed destined to humiliating defeat when they lost six men for 186. Then Brown played magnificently for 172 and a maiden century by W. H. Livsey

helped the total to 521. Kennedy and Newman followed by dismissing Warwickshire for 158, carrying their side to a famous victory by 155 runs—a feat which brought considerable financial benefit to that intrepid Hampshire captain, the Hon. L. H. Tennyson, who, after the first-innings debacle, had accepted numerous bets at long odds!

Brown's best season was that of 1926 when, with the aid of six centuries, he reached an aggregate of 2,040 and an average of 40.00. Among his best bowling analyses were six wickets for 24 runs against Somerset at Bath and six for 48 against Yorkshire at Portsmouth, both in 1911. After his playing career ended he served for three seasons as a first-class umpire.

BROWN, Herbert Arthur, secretary of Nottinghamshire from 1920 to 1958, died on July 23, 1974, aged 83. His interest in Nottinghamshire covered 60 years and he was a member of the M.C.C. advisory committee in the early 1920s. A most popular personality, he was known as "Uncle Herbert" on local children's broadcast programmes and he was "Uncle Herbert" to the county cricketers. He bore a heavy burden during the bodyline dispute in 1932–33.

BROWN, James, who was born on February 7, 1864, and died at Copenhagen in December, 1916, aged 52, appeared in two matches for Sussex in 1890, scoring 31 runs with an average of 7.75. In minor cricket in the Eastbourne district he made many enormous scores. In 1889 he made 288 not out for College House v. Cliffdown, and in the following year 202 not out for the same side v. Willingdon. It has been stated that during the season of 1891 he obtained as many as 18 hundreds, the highest score being 228.

BROWN, J. T., of Darfield, who should not be confused with the great batsman of the same name, initials and county, died on April 12, 1950. Born on November 24, 1874, he played for Yorkshire as a fast bowler from 1897 to 1903, when there was a dearth of such bowlers in the county. In that time he took 102 wickets, average 20.99. His career ended when he dislocated a shoulder playing against Somerset at Taunton in 1903—a disastrous match for Yorkshire, as John Tunnicliffe split a hand and George Hirst damaged thigh muscles.

BROWN, John Thomas, died at Dr. Kingscote's Medical Home in London, on the night of November 4, 1904, of congestion of the brain and heart failure. A statement appeared a few days before his death that there were hopes of his recovery from the heart trouble which in May terminated his cricket career, but other complications set in, and despite all that medical skill could do for him, the Yorkshire batsman passed away. As he was only in his 36th year—he was born at Driffield, on August 20, 1869—he might, under happier circumstances, have gone on playing for a good many seasons to come. Still, during the time he was before the public he did enough to earn a place among the best cricketers Yorkshire has ever produced. He came out in 1889, and from the first showed such promise that no doubt was felt as to his ultimate success. Bad health checked him for a time, but in 1893 he firmly established his position, and thenceforward, allowing for the variations of form to which all batsmen are subject, he was, till his health broke down, one of the mainstays of the Yorkshire XI. Even so recently as 1903 he stood second to George Hirst in the Yorkshire averages in county matches. Short in stature, but very strongly built, he was a batsman who could get runs under all conditions of weather and wicket. He was an all-round hitter, but his best stroke was his late cut. Few batsmen since Tom Humphrey's time have been able to score with greater certainty from the short ball pitched on, or just outside, the off-stump. About half-way through his career he developed a wonderful faculty for "pulling," but this so often cost him his wicket that he to a large extent gave it up and returned to the ways of orthodoxy. Neat and finished in style, he was, whether he scored fast or slowly, an excellent bat to look at. Of his performances for Yorkshire and other teams it would be easy to write at great length. Having regard to the surrounding circumstances, his greatest day in the cricket-field was, beyond all question, March 6, 1895, when, at Melbourne, he and Albert Ward won the fifth and conquering Test match for the first of the two XIs that Mr. Stoddart captained in Australia. The Englishmen had 297 to get in the last innings, and after the second wicket had fallen for 28, Stoddart himself being out from the first ball bowled on the final morning, Ward and Brown put on 210 runs together. Their

partnership settled the matter, and in the end England won by six wickets. Brown made 140, and all the reports of the match agreed in stating that his innings was absolutely free from fault. Only those who have seen the Australians fight out a Test game can fully realise the merit of such a display. If he had done nothing else, that one innings would have been sufficient to give Brown a place in cricket history. All through the tour he was a great success in Australia, and Mr. Stoddart certainly made a mistake in not taking him out with his second team in 1897. One of the best innings Brown ever played at home was his 163 in the Gentlemen and Players' match at Lord's in 1900, when the Players, though they had to make 501 runs, won by two wickets. Brown was batting for four hours and three-quarters, and only gave one chance. His innings remains the highest ever obtained for the Players against the Gentlemen at Lord's. For Yorkshire against the Australians, at Bradford, in 1899, he made 84 and 167. His biggest scores were 311 for Yorkshire against Sussex at Sheffield, in 1897, and 300 for Yorkshire against Derbyshire at Chesterfield, in 1898. On the latter occasion he and Tunnicliffe scored 554 together for the first wicket—a record partnership in first-class cricket. At Lord's in 1896 for Yorkshire against Middlesex, he and Tunnicliffe did an extraordinary thing, making 139 for the first wicket in the first innings, and afterwards winning the game by scoring 147 together without being separated. Brown only played twice for England against Australia in this country—at Lord's and Manchester, in 1896. At Lord's he had a considerable share in winning the match for England, batting with great skill for 36 in the last innings, after a heavy shower in the morning had spoilt the wicket. Personally, Brown was a quiet, pleasant-mannered man, and did not lack the sense of humour proverbially characteristic of Yorkshire cricketers. His benefit match at Leeds, in 1901, was the biggest thing of the kind ever known prior to George Hirst's benefit at the same ground last year.

The following list of Brown's best performances in company with Tunnicliffe for the first wicket will be read with interest. It will be seen that the two batsmen scored a hundred or more runs together on 19 occasions for Yorkshire.

554, Brown (300) and Tunnicliffe (243), v. Derbyshire, at Chesterfield 1898
(A record for any wicket in great matches. On the first day Brown and Tunnicliffe scored 503 without being separated, the former making 270 not out, and the latter 214 not out).

378, Brown (311) and Tunnicliffe (147), v. Sussex, at, Sheffield 1897
(At the time a record for the first wicket in first-class cricket, but a month later exceeded by one run by Abel and Brockwell, who made 379 together v. Hampshire at the Oval).
152, Brown (80) and Tunnicliffe (85), v. Middlesex, at Lord's 1899
148, Brown (81) and Tunnicliffe (67), v. Hampshire, at Hull 1900
147*, Brown (81*) and Tunnicliffe (63*), v. Middlesex, at Lord's 1896
(In the second innings, winning the match by 10 wickets).
142, Brown (72) and Tunnicliffe (62), v. Leicestershire, at Sheffield 1895
139, Brown (203) and Tunnicliffe (62), v. Middlesex, at Lord's 1896
(In the first innings. In the last stage of the match they scored 147 together without being separated, winning the game for their side by 10 wickets).
139, Brown (131) and Tunnicliffe (79), v. Leicestershire, at Leicester 1896
138*, Brown (85*) and Tunnicliffe (51*), v. Hampshire, at Southampton 1897
(Winning the match by 10 wickets).
133, Brown (150) and Tunnicliffe (47), v. Sussex, at Brighton 1898
132, Brown (96) and Tunnicliffe (79), v. Middlesex, at Lord's 1900
131, Brown (192) and Tunnicliffe (58), v. Derbyshire, at Derby 1899
121, Brown (71) and Tunnicliffe (58), v. Derbyshire, at Glossop 1901
119, Brown (100) and Tunnicliffe (66), v. M. C. C. and Ground, at Scarborough 1898
119, Brown (84) and Tunnicliffe (36), v. Australians, at Bradford 1899
115, Brown (51) and Tunnicliffe (105), v. Notts, at Hull 1902
113, Brown (61) and Tunnicliffe (145), v. Derbyshire, at Huddersfield 1901
112, Brown (75) and Tunnicliffe (36), v. Leicestershire, at Leicester 1903
107*, Brown (53*) and Tunnicliffe (24*), v. Sussex, at Brighton 1901
Signifies without a separation being effected.

In 1894, at the Oval, Brown and Chatterton made 202 runs together for the first wicket of North v. South, Brown's score being 101, and his partner's 89.

Brown was one of the few batsmen who have scored over 10,000 runs for Yorkshire.

CORRECTION. In the biography of J.T. Brown in *Wisden* for 1905, it was stated that he only played *twice* for England against Australia in this country. This was incorrect. He played three times—at Lord's and Manchester in 1896, and at Leeds in 1899.

BROWN, Lennox Sidney, who died in Durban on September 1, 1983, aged 72, toured Australia and New Zealand with H. B. Cameron's South African side in 1931–32, playing one Test in each country. Against Australia he took one for 100 and against New Zealand at Wellington two for 89. He could bowl effectively at two paces—medium and slow. On his first-class debut, for Transvaal against M.C.C. at Johannesburg in 1930–31, he took seven wickets in the match, including Hammond's twice, and he had played only one more first-class game when at the age of 20, he was chosen for the Australasian tour. In the Currie Cup he played first for Transvaal and later for North-Eastern Transvaal, for whom, against his former province in 1937–38, he took 10 wickets in the match. He finished his career with Rhodesia, having also played Lanca-

shire League cricket for Church and professional football for Huddersfield Town and Oldham Athletic. Altogether he took 147 first-class wickets. His top score was 75, for North-Eastern Transvaal against the 1938–39 M.C.C. side.

BROWN, R. G., father of F. R. Brown, the well-known Cambridge University and Surrey slow bowler and hard-hitting free-scoring batsman, died on January 15, 1947, aged 61. When living in Peru he bowled well for Lima against the M.C.C. side in January, 1927, dismissing five men at 10 runs apiece, his victims being M. F. S, Jewell, P. F. Warner and G. J. V. Weigall—all bowled— J. C. White and T. A. Pilkington, both l.b.w. G. O. Allen took 12 wickets for 22 runs, and M.C.C. won a one-day match by an innings and 89 runs.

BROWN, Servaas van Niekerk, who died at Cape Town on June 3, 1939, aged 56, was a member of the Western Province team that won the Currie Cup competition in 1920–21.

BROWN, Thomas Austin, born at Wollaston, Nottinghamshire, on April 11, 1869, died at Dunstable on March 12, 1930, aged 60. A fair bat and a good fast right-handed bowler, he played for both Northampton-shire and Bedfordshire. Subsequently he was on the staff at Lord's until his health failed and in later years stood as umpire in many first-class matches.

BROWN, William, a notable Luton sportsman, died in January, 1940, at the age of 65. For more than 25 years he played cricket for Bedfordshire, being a prolific run-getter and medium-paced bowler. As a professional footballer he played outside-right for Luton Town and Watford.

BROWN, William Stanley Alston, who died at his home at Bristol on September 12, 1952, aged 75, was an all-round sportsman who played cricket with Dr. W. G. Grace, from whom he received instruction when a boy. A member of the Leys School XI for three seasons, he was captain in the last, 1896, when, with 1,032 runs in 12 completed innings and 57 wickets for less than 11 runs each, he headed both batting and bowling averages. As he also scored 306 in House matches and was only twice dismissed, his average for the season was 95.57. Born on May 23, 1877, he was a free and attractive right-handed batsman and a useful left-arm medium-pace bowler. He appeared for Gloucestershire and M.C.C. from 1896 to 1919, though his duties as a solicitor prevented him from playing regularly. In 1905 he figured in the Gentlemen's XI against Players at the Oval. During his first-class career he scored 4,820 runs, average 17.09, and took 169 wickets, average 33.43. His highest innings for the county was 155 against Sussex at Bristol in 1903, when he and F. G. Roberts, whose share amounted to 11, put on 104 for the last wicket. In 1898 he achieved the distinction of hitting 106 when going in No. 10 against Warwickshire at Edgbaston, he and H. Wrathall adding 156 in 90 minutes for the ninth wicket. He also represented Gloucestershire at Association football, hockey, lacrosse, golf and bowls, and played Rugby football for Bristol and Clifton. During the first Great War he served as a Lieutenant in the North Staffordshire Regiment.

BROWNE, C. R., who died at Georgetown, British Guiana, on January 12, 1964, aged 73, played in four Test matches for West Indies v. England, two in 1928 when touring with R. K. Nunes's team and two in the West Indies in 1929. A hard-hitting batsman and a bowler of medium pace, "Snuffy" Browne hit 103, including two sixes and 17 fours, in an hour from the Kent bowling at Canterbury in 1928, when his best bowling figures were eight Derbyshire wickets for 81 runs at Derby. In 1928–29 he did much to enable British Guiana to win the Inter-Colonial Cup. Against Barbados he hit 55 and 95 and took seven wickets, and in the match with Trinidad he made 83 and 24 not out and dismissed 11 batsmen. At one time a magistrate in British Guiana, he was the first West Indian to be elected an honorary life member of M.C.C.

BROWNE, Cyril Ross, died at Eastbourne, April 30, 1948, aged 55. Played for Sussex and Northamptonshire. Master at Harrow for 29 years and for some years in charge of cricket.

BROWNE, The Rev. Elliott Kenworthy, for 26 years Rector of North Stoneham, Southampton, was born at Goldington Hall, near Bedford, on October 10, 1847, and died at Bournemouth on March 10, 1915. He was in the Rugby XI in 1866, when he was described as "a fair bat, with good style and hitting; an admirable field at mid-off and long-leg, where he has made some wonderful catches." Against Marlborough he scored only two and eight, and at Oxford he did not obtain his Blue. In 1868 he appeared in the Hampshire XI, and in 1872 for Gloucestershire, for which county he made 52 v. Sussex, at Clifton.

BROWNE, Canon Francis Bernard Ross, who died on November 11, 1970, aged 70, enjoyed considerable success as a fast-medium right-arm bowler for Eastbourne College, Cambridge University and Sussex. For the school XI from 1916, he headed the bowling figures each season, taking 52 wickets for 8.71 runs each in 1917. He got his Blue as a Senior at Cambridge in 1922 when he finished top of the University bowling averages with 50 wickets for 12.80 runs each. In the big match at Lord's, he helped in victory for the Light Blues in an innings with 100 runs to spare by dismissing four Oxford batsmen for 53 runs, and against Warwickshire at Fenner's he took six wickets for 27 runs each in the second innings. His outstanding performance during a career with Sussex extending from 1919 to 1932 was a match analysis of 10 wickets for 79 against a powerful Yorkshire batting array at Bradford in 1925. It was a pity that he could not devote more time to County Cricket. In all first-class cricket he took 252 wickets for 20.66 runs apiece and brought off 35 catches.

His action was extraordinary and was once described by *Wisden* as "a weird delivery that defies description". In the act of bowling, he appeared to cross his legs and deliver the ball off the wrong foot. This earned him the soubriquet of "Tishy"—the name of a race-horse of the time who once crossed his legs in running, and was immortalised by Tom Webster, the cartoonist.

BROWNE, Franklin Doughty, died at Cobham, Kent, August 12, 1946, aged 73. Dulwich XI 1889–92 (captain). Kent County XI occasionally from 1899 to 1903. He captained Trinity College, Oxford, in 1895, but did not get his Blue.

BROWNE, Royman, who died suddenly on January 29, 1969, aged 55, was an artist with a great love of cricket whose cartoons and writings afforded amusement to readers of the *Playfair Annual, The Boundary Book* and numerous other publications. He illustrated many of his own articles and was an authority on Dr. W. G. Grace and Tom Richardson. He was Art Editor of Fleetway Publications at the time of his death. As a witty speaker on the history of the game, he was in great demand at cricket functions, his talks being enlivened by cartoons which he drew as he spoke.

BROWNLEE, L. D., who died on September 22, 1955, aged 72, represented Oxford in the 1904 University match in which J. F. Marsh (Camb.) set up a record for the highest individual innings in the big fixture by scoring 172 not out in the second innings. Brownlee also played golf for his University against Cambridge in 1905. In the Clifton XI from 1899 to 1901, he headed the batting averages in 1900. From 1901 to 1909 he appeared occasionally for Gloucestershire for whom, against Kent at Canterbury in 1902, he hit 103, his only century in first-class cricket.

BROWNLEE, W. Methven, a very great lover and supporter of the game, who will be best remembered as the author of *W. G. Grace: a Biography*, died at Clifton on July 3, 1903, at the age of 56. He was the father of Mr. L. D. Brownlee, who has played for Clifton College, Oxford University, Somersetshire, and Gloucestershire.

BROWNLEE, Wilfred Methven, son of the biographer of "W. G.," died of meningitis at Wyke Regis, near Weymouth, on October 12, 1914, whilst serving with the 3rd Dorset Regiment. He was born at Cotham, Bristol, on April 18, 1890, and was thus only 24 years of age at the time of his death. For four

seasons, 1906 to 1909, he was in the Clifton XI, for which he showed very good all-round cricket: in 1908 he headed the batting averages with 23.57, and took most wickets (49), and in 1909, when captain, averaged 32.54 with the bat and headed the bowling with 34 wickets for 15.02 runs each. In the latter year also, chosen for the Public Schools XI against M.C.C. at Lord's, he took eight wickets for 61. On his first appearance for Gloucestershire—against Worcestershire, at Worcester, in 1909—he played an innings of 64, and if he had been able to play in first-class matches at all regularly he would no doubt have developed into an excellent cricketer. In the second innings of the match with Essex at Cheltenham in 1909 he scored 49 not out, and in partnership with Langdon (38 not out) scored 91 without the loss of a wicket in 25 minutes: the innings was then declared closed, but Gloucestershire were unable to snatch a victory. Mr. Brownlee was a free hitting batsman, a fast-medium paced bowler who could make the ball swerve and a brilliant fieldsman.

BRUCE (formerly Brice), Col. Edward Archibald, born September 1, 1848; died at Hove, November 14, 1918, aged 70. Cheltenham, Gloucestershire, Gentlemen v. Players (one match); hon. secretary and chairman of committee, Sussex County C. C. In connection with first-class cricket Colonel Bruce will be chiefly remembered from the circumstance that he was chosen by the Surrey committee, for the Gentlemen and Players match at the Oval in 1872. In those days he was a very good fast bowler and in the first innings of the Players he took three wickets for 70 runs, bowling out Bob Carpenter and getting Martin MacIntyre and Emmett caught. In the second innings he met with no success and had 50 runs taken from him. He was known at that time as E. A. Brice. He owed his selection for the Gentlemen to the fact that a month before the match he took 12 wickets—six in each innings—for Gloucestershire against Surrey at the Oval.

BRUCE, William, born at South Yarra, in Victoria, on May 22, 1864, was found drowned near Melbourne on August 4, 1925. Though in later years put quite in the shade by Clem Hill, Darling, Bardsley, and Ransford, Bruce has his place in cricket history as the first left-handed batsman sent to England with an Australian team. Free and attractive in style he was a brilliant hitter, but he lacked the defence of the great batsmen who followed him. Bruce paid two visits to this country, being a member of the 1886 team under H. J. H. Scott, and coming here again in 1893 when Blackham was captain of the side. He did little during the first tour, but he played an innings of 106 against C. I. Thornton's XI, at Chiswick Park. Seven years later he met with a much greater measure of success, scoring 1,314 runs with an average of 23. He played in all three Test matches, scoring 23 at Lord's, 10 not out and 22 at the Oval, and 68 and 36 at Manchester. One of his best performances was to make 60 and 37 against Surrey at the Oval, with Richardson bowling in great form, but by those who can carry their memories back to that year he will be remembered chiefly for his great innings of 191 against Oxford and Cambridge Past and Present at Portsmouth, when the Australians put together the huge total of 843. His partnership with Trumble in that match realised 232 runs in two hours and 20 minutes. Bruce was probably at his best in the Australian season of 1891–92, during the visit of Lord Sheffield's team. In the Test matches of that tour he scored 57 and 40 at Melbourne, 15 and 72 at Sydney and, on a wicket ruined by rain, five and 37 at Adelaide. He was 61 years of age.

BRUTON, Charles Lamb, who died in hospital on March 26, 1969, aged 78, played as an amateur batsman in six matches for Gloucestershire in 1922. For three years from 1907, he was in the Radley XI, heading the batting averages in 1908. He was Resident Commissioner in Swaziland from 1937 to 1942 and Commissioner of the East African Refugee Association from 1942 to 1947.

BRUTTON, Charles Phipps, who died after a long illness on May 11, 1964, aged 65, was in the Winchester XI in 1916 and 1917. A forceful batsman, he played as an amateur for Hampshire from 1921 to 1930, scoring 2,052 runs, average 17.84. His best season for the county was that of 1927, when he hit 644 runs, average 28.00 and was one of eight Hampshire cricketers to take part in the Gentlemen v. Players match at the Oval. Against Worcestershire at Worcester in 1924, he hit his one first-class century—119, not out, which included one six and 18 fours. He and J. Newman (130) added 120 in 70 minutes. He also appeared for Denbighshire and Dorset. For 25 years he was Clerk to the Dorset County Council.

BRUTTON, Septimus, died at Southsea on September 30, 1933, aged 64. After playing

for Northumberland he appeared for Hampshire in 1904, and his son C. P. of Winchester, has played for the southern county.

BRYAN, Ronald Thurston, who died on July 27, 1970, aged 71, was one of three left-handed brothers who played as amateurs for Kent. His appearances for the county were generally limited to his annual holiday, but in 1937 he was granted three months' leave to share the captaincy with B. H. Valentine in succession to A. P. F. Chapman. Bryan made many runs in club cricket for Lloyds Bank and Beckenham and was chosen for representative Club Cricket Conference teams.

BRYANT, Frank Joseph, who died in Perth on March 11, 1984, while watching the Sheffield Shield final, aged 76, was one of three brothers who played for Western Australia on one occasion in the same match. In 32 first-class matches he scored 1,495 runs (average 26.69), including three centuries, the highest of them 155 for J. Ryder's touring team against Bombay in 1935–36. He became a popular and influential cricket administrator in Perth, welcoming many England sides there, besides managing Western Australia on numerous occasions as well as three Australian teams to New Zealand. A delegate to the Australian Cricket Board, he had much to do with Perth receiving Test status.

BUCCLEUCH, The Sixth Duke of (William Henry Walter Montague Douglas Scott), who was born in London on September 9, 1831, died at Whitehall on November 5, 1914. He was one of the oldest members of the M.C.C., having been elected as far back as 1854, and in 1888 he was President of the Club. From 1889 to 1892, and in 1896 and 1897 he served on the Committee, and since the last-mentioned year he had been one of the Trustees, succeeding the Fourth Earl of Sefton in 1897. Many years ago he presented to the M.C.C. several 18th-century bats which had belonged to the Fourth Duke, and these are still preserved in the members' writing room. Among his sons are the Earl of Dalkeith, who succeeds to the title, and was the M.C.C.'s President in 1913, and Lord George Scott, who scored 100 and 66 for Oxford in the University match of 1887.

BUCHAN, Charles Murray, who died on June 25, 1960, aged 68, while on holiday in France, played in a few matches for Durham in 1920. He was a famous Sunderland, Arsenal and England inside-forward.

BUCHANAN, David, who died on May 30, 1900, was one of the very best slow bowlers of the last generation. His career was in one respect almost unique. Though he played cricket all his life, he did not really become famous till he had reached the age of 38. Originally a fast bowler, he, some time in the '60s, changed his method, and thenceforward met with a degree of success that he had never before approached. He took hundreds of wickets in all sorts of matches, but his reputation will always rest on his really wonderful bowling for Gentlemen against Players. Beginning in 1868 and ending in 1874, he assisted the Gentlemen at Lord's and the Oval in 10 matches, and took in 19 innings 87 wickets at a cost of less than 15 runs each. For these exact statistics we are indebted to the recently published book entitled *Bat and Ball*—a collection of individual cricket records from 1864 to 1900. Bowling left-handed, Mr. Buchanan set little store on what is known as a good length. He bowled to be hit, and depended for his wickets on pitched up balls with plenty of spin on them. Whether he would have been so uniformly successful against the great professional batsmen of the present day is a question that no one can answer, but it is certain that he caused far more trouble to Daft, Jupp, and the rest of the Players than any other amateur bowler of his time. As a cricketer he was a bowler pure and simple, his batting and fielding counting for nothing. Still, as he nearly always took four or five wickets in an innings, he was worth a place in any XI. He was asked to go to Australia with Lord Harris's team in 1878, but, though much pressed, he declined the invitation. He probably felt that at 48 he was hardly equal to the fatigues of a tour in the Colonies. At the time of his death Mr. Buchanan was in his 71st year. He was born on January 16, 1830.

BUCKENHAM, Claude Percival, died on February 23, 1937, after a short illness at his home in Dundee, aged 61. Born in Surrey on January 16, 1876, he went to Alleyn School, Dulwich, but became associated with cricket at Leyton and played first for Essex from 1899. Tall and rather sparely built, Buckenham bowled very fast with a good high delivery and might have made a greater name but for his constant misfortune in seeing slip catches missed. Because of weak support in the field Buckenham often proved expensive and, in 1905 his 90 wickets cost over 32 runs apiece. Then for six seasons he ranked as one of the deadliest pace bowlers

in England. Most successful in 1911 when securing 134 wickets, he was perhaps at his best in 1910 when he dismissed 118 batsmen at an average cost of 17.66. From 1905 to 1911 he took 828 wickets at less than 23 runs each, and in the course of his county career, which closed in 1914, his record was 1,152, average 25.30.

Three times he appeared in the Gentlemen and Players' match at Lord's. In 1909, when on the ground staff, he was in the M.C.C. XI which beat Noble's Australian team by three wickets and in a second engagement between these teams he took six wickets for 98 in an innings of 434. One of his most memorable performances was taking 11 wickets for 161 runs for South against North at the Oval in 1908 in the match played for the benefit of E. G. Hayes, the noted Surrey batsman. In the second innings he made the ball break back in such disconcerting fashion that six men, five bowled, fell to him for 68 runs.

Buckenham went to South Africa with Mr. H. D. G. Leveson Gower's team in the winter of 1909 and in four of the five Tests took 21 wickets for 28 runs apiece. A hardhitting batsman Buckenham often played a useful innings when runs were wanted. He was professional to Forfarshire at the beginning of the War and after serving in the Royal Garrison Artillery he became coach at Repton.

BUCKLAND, Edward Hastings, died on February 10, 1906, at Winchester. Born on June 20, 1864, he was only in his 42nd year. Without ever reaching the top of the tree, Mr. Buckland was one of the best all-round men in the excellent XIs that represented Oxford from 1884 to 1887. He went up to Oxford with a big reputation from Marlborough, but it was not his good fortune to be in the team when the University gained their sensational victory over the Australians in 1884. He was at his best in 1886 and 1887, and in both those years was largely instrumental in beating Cambridge at Lord's. He finished off the match in 1886 with a wonderful piece of bowling, taking five wickets in 20 overs and a ball, at a cost of only 14 runs. He did not do anything so startling as this in the match of 1887, but he was the most successful bowler on the side, four wickets falling to him for 62 runs, and three for 68. A week before the University match in 1887 he enabled Oxford to beat Surrey at the Oval, playing an innings of 148 on the opening day, and in the last stage of the game taking five wickets for 25 runs. Surrey went in with 216 to get, and, though the pitch had crumbled, they seemed for a time almost sure to win, the score reaching 50 with one wicket down. Mr. Buckland then went on, and in 20 overs got rid of Maurice Read, Abel, W. E. Roller, W. W. Read, and Wood. So highly was Mr. Buckland thought of as an all-round cricketer in 1887 that he was given a place in the Gentlemen's XI against the Players at Lord's. He also played for the Gentlemen at the Oval in 1887. For a good many years past Mr. Buckland had been a master at Winchester, and the leading spirit of the school's cricket. He was an excellent golfer.

BUCKLAND, Francis Matthew, the famous Eton and Oxford cricketer of a generation ago, died at Boxhill on March 7, 1913. He was born at Laleham, Middlesex, on August 27, 1864. Mr. Buckland was in the Eton XI in 1871–72–73, and after failing to get his Blue in 1874, was in the Oxford XI from 1875 to 1877 inclusive. At Eton he was one of the best school bowlers—right hand, medium pace—of his day, but from some cause he lost the spin from leg, which had made him difficult and, though always very steady and accurate, he was too plain at Oxford to be at all formidable on hard wickets. His bowling records for Eton were remarkable. It was strange that he should have missed his Blue in his first year at Oxford, as in the Freshmen's match he played an innings of 136 and took seven wickets for 45 runs. Afterwards for the XI against the Gentlemen of England he scored 51 and 49. He played a useful part in the sensational six runs victory of Oxford in 1875, playing a first innings of 22 and taking five wickets, but as an Oxford cricketer up to the end of 1876 he was admittedly a disappointment. Then, in 1877, he jumped into fame as one of the great amateur batsmen of the season. By reason of his doings against Cambridge that year, if for nothing else, he will live in cricket history. His 117 not out was beyond all doubt one of the finest innings ever played in the University match. In face of a total of 134, Oxford lost six wickets, including those of A. J. Webbe, H. R. Webbe, and A. H. Heath, for 31 runs, the position looking absolutely desperate. At this point Buckland was joined by H. G. Tylecote, and between them the two batsmen put on 142 runs. They completely turned the fortunes of the game, and in the end Oxford won by 10 wickets. Buckland's magnificent driving that afternoon is as vividly remembered at Lord's as though the match had been played last year. Over and above his wonderful batting, he took seven Cambridge wickets—three for 21 runs and

four for 29. Ten days before the University match he had given evidence that he was in great batting form, scoring 104 at Lord's for Oxford against Middlesex. The Gentlemen were so tremendously strong in 1877 that despite his triumph in the University match, no place was found for Buckland against the Players, either at the Oval or Lord's, but for a less representative side at Prince's he was conspicuously successful both as batsman and bowler, scoring 50 and taking eight wickets. It was a misfortune that just as he had got to his best as a batsman he had to give up public cricket, little being seen of him after 1877. He was an assistant master at Winchester in 1880 and 1881, and afterwards became headmaster of a preparatory school at Laleham. As a batsman he was a fine type of the forward style of play taught at Eton by Mr. R. A. H. Mitchell.

BUCKLE, Frank ("Sandy"), who died in Sydney on June 4, 1982, aged 90, was, at the time of his death, the oldest surviving New South Wales player. A right-hand bat, he played one game for the state in 1913, in which he scored 10.

BUCKLEY, George Arthur, a director of Sheffield United Cricket and Football Club, died during an early Communion Service in St. Paul's Church, Norton Lees, in November, 1935, aged 46. An excellent cricketer, he played for Cheshire as a young man and once for Derbyshire shortly after the War. Three county clubs offered him professional engagements but he remained headmaster of a Council School in Sheffield. As a fast bowler he met with much success in Yorkshire Council League cricket and was captain of the Sheffield United XI for several seasons.

BUCKNILL, Samuel Pratt Berens, born in 1849, died in London on May 8, 1930. Whilst at Rugby, where he was coached by Diver and Hayward, he was in the XI in 1867 and 1868, in the latter year succeeding Bernard Pauncefote as captain. A hard-hitting batsman with driving his *forte*, he could also long-stop well. He played some cricket for Warwickshire and had been a member of the M.C.C. for 49 years.

BUCKSTON, Capt. George Moreton, died very suddenly on November 24, 1941, aged 61. For Eton in 1900 he scored 45 and four at Lord's in a splendid match which Harrow won by one wicket. A late choice for Cambridge in 1903, he failed, like most of his colleagues, in a one-sided encounter which Oxford won by 268 runs. A peculiar feature of the Cambridge batting was that Dowson, 54, and Keigwin, 30, in the first innings, Godsell, 59, and F. B. Wilson in the second innings, were the only scorers of double figures. Buckston played for Derbyshire in 1906, averaging 20.37 with highest innings 96, but he fared poorly next season, when Derbyshire finished last in the Championship, and did not appear again until undertaking the captaincy in 1921. Returning to important cricket after a long absence, when 40 years of age he enjoyed the satisfaction of helping Derbyshire in a great improvement on their previous season's disastrous record. He could not be persuaded to retain the position, but became chairman of the County Club Committee.

BULL, Amy, C.B.E., who died in Surrey on August 6, 1982, aged 80, learnt her cricket at Roedean, being one of three cricketing sisters, and continued to play as one of the first members of the newly founded W.C.A. In 1929, she played in the first-ever public match for London & District v. Rest of England, making 73 not out and taking three for 31. As a captain, she infected her team with determination and enthusiasm, accompanied by a keen sense of humour. Amy Bull served the W.C.A. twice as Chairman and was twice President of the Association of Headmistresses. Her services to nursing (during the War) and to education brought her the award of the C.B.E. in 1963.

BULL, C. H., who was tried for Kent before playing for Worcestershire from 1933, was killed in a road accident at Chelmsford on Whit-Sunday, May 28, 1939. He was 30 years old. This sad mishap recalled the death of Maurice Nichol at an hotel at Chelmsford when Worcestershire were playing the 1934 Whitsuntide match with Essex. Bull became a sound opening batsman, his aggregate reaching four figures each year from 1934, when his average for 1,323 runs was 30.76, until 1938, when a broken finger and a blow on the head in the first match of the season against the Australians compelled a long rest, with resultant loss of form.

BULL, Frederick George, the Essex slow bowler of a few years ago, was found drowned at St. Anne's-on-Sea, Lancashire, on September 16, 1910. He was born in Essex on April 2, 1876, played his first match for the county in 1895 and came to the front in the following year, when in all first-class

matches he obtained 85 wickets for 16 runs each. It was in 1896, when 20 years of age, that he was chosen, strictly on his merits, for the Gentlemen v. Players match at the Oval in which he took eight wickets for 94 runs in the first innings and two for 59 in the second. The same season he had an analysis of eight for 44 for Essex against Yorkshire at Bradford. In 1897 he took 120 wickets for something over 21 runs each, his best performances (all for Essex) being nine for 93 v. Surrey at the Oval, 13 for 156 v. Derbyshire at Leyton and 14 for 176 v. Lancashire on the same ground. It was in the last-mentioned match that he endeavoured to prevent Lancashire from following-on by bowling wide-balls to the boundary. Mold, however, grasping the situation, knocked his wicket down, and so enabled his side to go in again, but Essex won by six wickets. Bull was chosen for the Gentlemen at Lord's that year, but was expensive, and although he secured eight of the Players' wickets at Scarborough later in the season they were taken at rather a heavy price—a fraction under 25 runs each. In the autumn of 1897 he visited America with Mr. P. F. Warner's team and obtained 43 wickets—the largest number taken by any member of the side—at a cost of 13.86 runs apiece. In 1898 he was again successful in crediting himself with over a hundred wickets, but in the following year he proved less effective and in 1900 was so expensive that he was dropped from the side. During his four best seasons in first-class cricket he performed as follows:

Years	Overs	Mdns.	Runs	Wkts.	Average
1896	503.2	145	1360	85	16.00
1897	1007	243	2634	120	21.95
1898	952	293	2162	101	21.40
1899	798.4	249	1767	65	27.18

During most of the time that he was a member of the Essex team he filled the position of Assistant Secretary to the County Club. Upon leaving the South of England to take up a commercial appointment in Blackburn he commenced—in 1904—to play for East Lancashire, for which club he took 91 wickets that season for 12.54 runs each. Subsequently he embraced professionalism and was engaged for two seasons by Perthshire, and afterwards for the same period by East Lancashire and Rishton. Bull could make the ball break both ways and he always kept a good length and used his head well.

BULLER, Charles Francis, who died at Lyme Regis in October, 1906, will be remembered by cricketers of a past generation as one of the greatest batsman of his day.

Born at Colombo, Ceylon, on the May 26, 1846, he won his place in the Harrow XI as a boy of little more than 15, taking part in the match against Eton at Lord's in 1861. On the same occasion an almost equally famous batsman, Mr. Alfred Lubbock, was seen at Lord's for the first time, but on the opposite side. Buller was in the Harrow team for four seasons, finishing up as captain in 1864. In that year he scored 61 and Harrow beat Eton by an innings and 66 runs. Judged by the standard of these days a score of 61 does not seem anything to make a fuss about, but never did the batting of a public school boy at Lord's earn higher praise. Thanks to his great natural ability and very careful coaching, in which the Surrey player, William Mortlock, had no small share, Buller at 18 was already a finished batsman, good enough for any XI. Style in batting was thought a great deal of in the '60s, and Buller's style was as nearly as possible perfect—quite comparable to, though very different from that of Tom Hayward or Richard Daft. In the Canterbury week of 1864 Buller played for England against Thirteen of Kent, and for M.C.C. against the Gentlemen of Kent, scoring in the latter match 21 and 68. The next season he had an assured position among the leading cricketers of the day, and was picked for Gentlemen against Players both at Lord's and the Oval. His highest and best innings in 1865 was 105 not out for Middlesex against Surrey at the Oval. In 1866 he fully upheld his reputation, but in 1867, having in the meantime entered the 2nd Life Guards, he played very little owing to illness. A year later he was quite himself again, but nothing was seen of him in first-class cricket the following year and in 1870 he played in only a few big matches. Then for nearly three years he dropped out, reappearing at the close of the season of 1873 in George Bennett's benefit match at Gravesend. During 1874, 1875, and 1876 he played for Middlesex, batting in the same perfect style as ever, but his weight had gone up to over 15 st. and he was not much use in the field. During this latter part of his career two innings that he played are still vividly remembered—51 for Middlesex against Nottinghamshire on a sticky wicket at Trent Bridge in August, 1875, and 67 not out in the North v. South match for the late Tom Hearne's benefit at Lord's in 1876. The last match of importance in which he took part was, we believe, Middlesex v. Yorkshire at Lord's in 1877. He did not finish up badly, scoring 20 and 25. In *Bat v. Ball* only two hundreds and a dozen other scores of over 50

in first-class matches appear against Buller's name, but important fixtures were few in his day and any comparison of his doings with batsmen of out time would be altogether fallacious. Some idea of his merit can be gathered from the fact that the late James Southerton thought he never bowled against a better batsman except, of course, W. G. Grace. Batting was a very exact science when Buller learnt the game, and only E. M. Grace and the left-handers indulged in the pulling by which so many hundreds of runs are nowadays obtained. Buller, however, was a master of all the orthodox strokes, his cut being especially fine. Equally strong in back and forward play he had such wrist power that he could without any apparent effort block a ball to the ring. Quite late in his career he scored five runs with a stroke of this kind off a ball that Allan Hill, the bowler, thought good enough to get anyone's wicket. He was very strong indeed in dropping down on a shooter, and the last time the present writer ever met him he was rather humorous at the immunity from shooters enjoyed by modern batsmen. Curiously enough with all his ability Buller met with little success for Gentlemen v. Players. In 10 matches between 1865 and 1874 he made only 181 runs in 18 innings, his best score being 41 at the Oval in 1868. Into the scandals that marred Mr. Buller's private life and caused his social eclipse, this is obviously not the place to enter. Those whose memories go back 30 to 40 years will remember him as one of the most attractive of batsmen and, perhaps, the handsomest man the cricket field has ever known.

SYD BULLER—A GREAT UMPIRE
Born August 23, 1909; died August 7, 1970
By his colleague, Frank Lee

I feel very honoured to be invited to write this tribute to the memory of Syd Buller, for I was privileged on many occasions to officiate as umpire with him in county and Test matches.

John Sydney Buller, to give him his full name, died in tragic circumstances , on August 7, 1970, at the age of 60. He was standing as umpire in the game between Warwickshire and Nottinghamshire at Edgbaston and, during a hold-up because of rain, he collapsed and never regained consciousness.

Syd, as he became known the world over, made his first-class cricket debut in 1930, when he played in one match for Yorkshire. He left his native county in 1934 and, having qualified by residence he appeared for Worcestershire in 1936. Despite being involved in a car crash in 1939 while his new county were playing Essex at Chelmsford, when Syd was badly injured and his team-mate, Charlie Bull, was killed, he continued his playing career till 1947. Thereafter he acted as county coach and captain of the team in the Minor Counties' competition till 1951, when he gained a place on the list of first-class umpires.

I first met Syd when I was playing for Somerset against Worcestershire and he was keeping wicket and I was most impressed by his quiet efficiency, without any of that showiness or trivial appealing which some stumpers indulged in. This unobtrusiveness caused him to pass almost unnoticed. The same characteristic later showed itself in his umpiring, for he always performed his duties quietly and with no fuss.

Also, as Mr. S. C. Griffith, the M.C.C. Secretary, said in paying his tribute to Syd: "His absolute fairness earned him immense respect." Ray Illingworth, the England captain, said: "He was most courageous in his convictions as an umpire and was one of the top men in the world in this field."

He was a most worthy successor to the late Frank Chester, who was to my mind the greatest umpire of my time. Those of us who played and umpired with Chester are fully aware that he blazed a trail for other umpires to follow. His fearlessness, not only on the field, but in his dealings with the authorities, resulted in the raising of the standard of umpiring to a very considerable degree.

Syd was one of the central figures in what developed into a big controversy at Lord's in 1960, when I was his partner as umpire. This became known as the "Griffin affair". In the second Test match between England and South Africa, it became my distinctly unpleasant duty to have to "no-ball" Geoff Griffin, the South African fast bowler, no fewer than 11 times for throwing during the England innings. I should point out that Griffin had been penalised in earlier fixtures with M.C.C. at Lord's, Nottinghamshire at Trent Bridge and Hampshire at Southampton for the same offence.

As the Test match ended a quarter of an hour after lunch on the fourth day, the agreement to play an exhibition one-innings each contest came into force. In this game, Griffin bowled only one over, but what an eventful over it was, for it consisted of 11 deliveries. Syd Buller "called" him for throwing four times in his first five balls. Syd did not take such strong measures without careful study of the bowler's action; he looked at him first from square-leg and then from point before he raised a hand. Upon the advice of his captain, D. J. McGlew, Griffin decided to complete the over with under-arm deliveries—only to be no-balled immediately by me because he omitted to notify the batsman of his intention to change his action!

A vast amount of discussion and bother followed from all this, both among people directly concerned with the running of cricket and in the Press, but the inexplicable thing to me was that, despite the part I played during the actual Test, in which Buller, being at the bowler's end on each occasion that Griffin bowled, had no opportunity to penalise him for throwing, most of the unpleasant publicity fell upon him. I felt at that time, and I still do: why should a man be pilloried for conscientiously fulfilling his duty! Furthermore, the South Africans declined to agree to Syd umpiring in any of the remaining Tests, though I should say that the England authorities paid him the fees he would have received and restored him to his rightful place the following season.

I never could understand the hostility shown towards Syd in so many ways and in so many quarters afterwards. He was perfectly justified in his action and did as any right-minded umpire should have done. When asked for my version of the matter, I was naturally able to state precisely what had taken place, together with the question and answer between the fielding captain and the umpire. I added my opinion that I failed to see how anyone could have taken offence with Syd, who had correctly performed an unsavoury task. I personally felt that the whole business was unbelievable—and especially when I considered the ethics of umpiring, as I believed them to be, that an umpire should carry out his job in as quiet a manner as circumstances permitted.

Off the field as well as on it, Syd achieved much work of sterling value. On various trips abroad, including a visit to the Far East with an M.C.C. team, he instructed umpires of lesser experience. Had he lived, he would have travelled with the M.C.C. side to Australia and New Zealand last winter on a scholarship awarded to him by the Winston Churchill Memorial Trust and, of course, everybody in cricket knows that in June, 1965, he was appointed M.B.E.—the only umpire to be given such an honour.

It took time for Syd and me to know each other thoroughly and to become friends and, like most friendships of a genuine nature, ours was slow to mature. In the end, it was both sincere and lasting, based as it was upon a mutual respect for each other's opinions, especially about cricket and more particularly—and naturally—concerning umpiring. To me, Syd Buller was like a High Court Judge pronouncing judgment without fear or favour and without seeking either sympathy or understanding from others. Only a man of such determined and resolute character could have achieved what he set out to do and actually did.

A fortnight before Syd died, we umpired together in a Sunday game organised for charity by the Lord's Taverners and I well recall remarking to him on that occasion: "Syd, I've never seen you look so well and relaxed." This made it the harder for me to take the sad news of his death. He will be much missed by all lovers of cricket and will long be remembered by his contemporaries.

Quite apart from his undoubted ability, he will also be remembered by cricket-watchers for his "trade-mark": he was the umpire who regularly took the field with sleeves rolled up to the elbows, a custom followed by no other official I know.

BULLIMER, Leo, who died at Northampton on April 24, 1954, aged 78, was for 51 years scorer for Northamptonshire until retiring in 1952. His efforts in raising funds did much to keep Northamptonshire going during some of their worst financial crises. At one time he played professional Association football for Northampton Town, Stockport County, Lincoln City, Reading and Brighton.

BULLOCK, Burn W., who died suddenly on December 23, 1954, aged 58, scored many runs as a professional for Surrey Second XI between 1921 and 1925, his highest innings being 153 in 1923. As Surrey were specially strong in batting at that time, he could rarely find a place in the first team and in 1926 he became coach and cricket organiser to the late Mr. Jimmy White, the millionaire financier. He later returned to the Mitcham Club, for whom he made his first appearance at the age of 15.

BULLOCK, Thomas Lowndes, born September 27, 1845, died at Oxford on March 20, 1915. He was in the Winchester XI in 1864, and was described as a "first-rate field at long-leg; fair bat." In the match with Eton he scored 0 and 14. At Oxford he was in the New College XI, but did not obtain his Blue. He was Professor of Chinese in the University of Oxford, and formerly H.M.'s Consul in China.

BULPETT, Charles William Lloyd, who died at Nairobi, Kenya, on July 11, 1939, aged 87, played for Rugby against Marlborough at Lord's in 1891, and appeared for Middlesex against Yorkshire there in 1880. He did not gain his cricket Blue at Oxford, but enjoyed a reputation for other sporting activities. Over a level measured mile at Newmarket in 1887 he won a wager of £200 and £400 in bets by walking a mile, running a mile and riding a mile in less than 18 minutes. A year later, at the age of 35, he accomplished the feat again in better time and won a bet of £1,000 to £400. A sound bat and useful fast bowler, he succeeded A. G. Guillemard as Hon. Secretary of the Butterflies C.C. and was, in his turn, followed by C. F. H. Leslie.

BUNCE, William Newman, who died at Pill, near Bristol, on May 29, 1981, aged 70, played 14 matches for Somerset in the mid-1930s. His top score was 46. He was also a right-arm medium-paced bowler. As a professional footballer, he played for both Bristol Rovers and Bristol City.

BURBIDGE, Frederick, died on November 12, 1892, at his residence, Micklefield, near Rickmansworth, only surviving by a few weeks his old colleague in the Surrey XI, the Rev. C. G. Lane. Born at Champion Hill, Camberwell, on November 23, 1832, Mr. Burbidge had thus entered his 61st year. He played his first match for Surrey in 1854, and his last in 1866, but business always interfered more or less with his cricket, and he was never able to appear for the county so often as he could have wished. Still he had his share in the successes of the old XI often batting well when runs were wanted and being always an admirable field, more particularly at point. The highest scores he ever made for Surrey were 101 in 1863 against Sussex at Brighton, and 104 in 1864 against Thirteen of Cambridge University at the Oval. His best averages for the county were 38 in 1856, 25 in 1863, 19 in 1862 and 18 in 1864. In this last-mentioned year Surrey's batting, with Tom Humphrey, Jupp, Mortlock and H. H. Stephenson at their best, was extraordinarily strong. After his retirement from the active pursuit of the game Mr. Burbidge retained the strongest interest in Surrey cricket. He always kept his place on the committee, and even in the most severe period of depression never lost heart. To no one probably did the splendid revival of Surrey, which began in the season of 1883, afford keener satisfaction.

BURDETT, John Wilder, who died on April 16, 1974, aged 85, was in the Oundle XI before turning out in 1919 for Leicestershire, of which club his father had been secretary. He also represented the county at hockey.

BURGE, Gerard Rodon, who died in London on February 15, 1933, was born on August 9, 1857. He was in the Marlborough College XI in 1873, 1874 and 1875, and when tried in 1885 and 1886 for Middlesex, as a medium-pace bowler, took five wickets for 58 on his first appearance. Assisting Gentlemen of Sussex v. Gentlemen of Philadelphia at Hove in 1889, he performed the "hat-trick." He also played a little for M.C.C., Hertfordshire and Bedfordshire.

BURGE, Thomas John, who died at his home in Brisbane on January 7, 1957, aged 53, while listening to a radio commentary of a cricket match in which his son was batting, had been a member of the Australian Board of Control since 1952. He suffered a heart attack while his son was touring England in 1956. He was a life-member of the Queensland C.A. and managed the first Australian team to tour the West Indies in 1955.

BURKE, Daniel, born in Tipperary, Ireland, on June 26, 1827, died at Moltema, near Hobart, on August 14, 1927, aged 100. In his younger days he had been a representative Tasmanian cricketer, and he had lived for 98 years in the island where he had played a prominent part in public life.

BURKE, James Wallace, the Australian opening batsman for nearly a decade during the 1950s, died by his own hand in Sydney on February 2, 1979, aged 48. In his time, this extremely likeable personality had experienced the full circle of changing cricket fortunes at international level; he had also excelled at competitive golf, and enjoyed good company just as much as a wide circle of friends welcomed his fellowship, keen sense of humour, and a versatile musical capacity.

By the time he was 20, Jim Burke had achieved a highly successful schoolboy batting record with Sydney Grammar, played first-grade cricket with the Manly club at 15, and appeared as a New South Wales opener at 18. In his Test debut against England at Adelaide two years later, he displayed ideal temperament by scoring a maiden Test century notable for neat cuts and glances. And yet, within a year, he was dropped from the Test team—the first of five such occur-

rences—and, at 23, suffered a similar dismissal from the N.S.W. XI. A season in the Lancashire League with Todmorden started the fight back to international level where he became Colin McDonald's dogged but successful opening partner. In 1956, Burke was chosen with G. R. A. Langley as one of the two Australians featured among *Wisden*'s five Cricketers of the Year. Although his batting was becoming increasingly dour and he had put away some of his best strokes, he scored a century before lunch at Taunton. Moving on to Bombay, he scored against India—in six hours eight minutes—the slowest Test century ever put together by an Australian. India and Pakistan were followed by a successful South African tour in 1957–58 when Burke headed the averages and was the sole Australian to reach 1,000 runs (1,041 at an average of 65.06 per innings), this including a monumental innings of nine hours 38 minutes to score 189 in the Cape Town Test. Burke never fully recovered his confidence after a broken rib incurred on this tour, and his concern over the growing use of the bouncer precipitated his retirement at 28 after the England tour of P. B. H. May. His record in 24 Tests was 1,280 runs at an average of 33. In all first-class cricket, he scored 21 centuries and just over 7,600 runs at an average of 49, his record in 58 Sheffield Shield matches being 3,399 runs at 44.14 per innings. In addition, off-breaks bowled with a suggestive bent-arm action gained him 101 wickets in the first-class arena.

An honorary life member of M.C.C., Burke became a widely known and popular radio and television commentator for the Australian Broadcasting Commission cricket service. He had been due to cover the sixth Australia v. England Test which commenced a few days after his death.

BURLS, Charles William, born at Peckham on March 8, 1848, died at Datchet, Bucks., on December 17, 1923. His name will be found occasionally in the Surrey XI in 1873, 1875, 1879 and 1880, but he scored only 99 runs for the county with an average of 5.82.

BURLTON, Lieut.-Col. Arthur Temple, died at Ballochneck, Thornhill, Stirling, on February 10, 1980, aged 79. He was not in the XI at Repton, but in 1922 played five matches for Worcestershire, and against Glamorgan at Cardiff scored 32 and 35 not out, in the first innings saving the side by helping H. L. Higgins to put on 91 for the fifth wicket. He also appeared for Devon. He was author of

Cricketing Courtesy (1955), a book on cricket manners and etiquette.

BURN, Kenneth Edward, who died in Hobart, Tasmania, on July 20, 1956, aged 92, was the oldest living Test cricketer. He took part in two Test matches for Australia during the 1890 tour of England, scoring 41 runs in four innings. *Wisden* of the time termed his selection as wicket-keeper "the one serious mistake in making up the side," and described how "only when he had accepted the terms offered him and joined the ship at Adelaide was the discovery made that he had never kept wicket in his life." As a sound, painstaking batsman, Burn, popularly known as "The Scotsman," achieved many fine performances for Richmond C.C., Wellington C.C. and for Tasmania. He hit 41 centuries, two of them over 350, and headed the Tasmania C.A. averages on 11 occasions. In 1895–96 he reached three-figures in six successive innings, and set up two other Australian club cricket records by scoring 1,200 runs, average 133, in 1899–1900, and by hitting 123 not out and 213 not out for Wellington against Break O' Day in 1895–96.

BURNETT, Harold John Beverley, who died in Diego Martin, Trinidad, on December 18, 1981, at the age of 66, was, from 1974 till 1981, the efficient and affable Secretary of the West Indian Cricket Board of Control. During this time he had a difficult course to steer over the Packer Affair, which he did with his customary consideration. In 1963 he was assistant-manager of Frank Worrell's West Indian team to England, in his estimation the strongest of all West Indian sides. An outstanding games-player as a schoolboy at Queen's Royal College, Trinidad, he became for several years, as an off-spinner and middle-order batsman, a regular member of the Trinidad team. He also played football for the island.

BURNHAM, John William, died at Derby on April 20, 1914. He was born at Nottingham on June 6, 1839, and was thus in his 75th year at the time of his death. In 1863 and 1865 he appeared for Notts Colts, in 1866 for Suffolk, between 1871 and 1876 in six matches for Derbyshire, and in 1872 for Prince's C. and G. His highest score for Derbyshire was 31 v. Lancashire at Manchester, in 1871. Whilst engaged at Freston, in Suffolk, in 1866, he made 1,060 runs, then a somewhat remarkable feat. He was an all-round cricketer, and in the field was generally long-stop.

BURNS, James, who died at Hampstead on September 11, 1957, aged 92, played as a batsman for Essex from 1890 to 1895. He was in the side when the county acquired first-class status in 1894. The following season, when Essex were admitted to the Championship competition, he hit 114 against Warwickshire at Birmingham.

BURNS, 2nd Lieut. William Beaumont (Worcestershire Regiment), born at Rugeley, Staffordshire, on August 29, 1883, fell in action on July 7, 1916. Educated at the King's School, Ely, where he was in the XI, he played subsequently for Staffordshire and Worcestershire. On his first appearance for the former county—v. M.C.C. and Ground at Lichfield—he played an innings of 123 not out, and in the next year headed the averages with 57.20, his highest score being 123 v. Oxfordshire. In 1903 he began to assist Worcestershire, his appearances that season, however, being restricted to the three games played by the county outside the Championship competition as he had not yet completed his qualification. His association with Worcestershire, of course, gave him many opportunities of appearing in the best company, and in 1906, 1908, 1909, 1910, and 1911 he scored over a thousand runs in first-class cricket. His largest aggregate was 1,438 in 1911, when he averaged 31.95. His three-figure scores were as follows:

196, Worcestershire v. Warwickshire, at Edgbaston, 1909
165, Worcestershire v. Oxford University, at Worcester, 1904
165, Worcestershire v. Oxford University, at Worcester, 1906
146, Worcestershire v. Oxford University, at Oxford, 1908
125, Worcestershire v. Warwickshire, at Worcester, 1906
120, Worcestershire v. Gloucestershire, at Bristol, 1908
117, Worcestershire v. Kent, at Maidstone, 1911
109, Worcestershire v. Hampshire, at Stourbridge, 1906
108, Worcestershire v. Somerset, at Taunton, 1908
106, Worcestershire v. Warwickshire, at Edgbaston, 1911
104, Worcestershire v. Middlesex, at Worcester, 1910
102*, Worcestershire v. Gloucestershire, at Worcester, †1913
* *Signifies not out;* † *also performed the hat-trick.*

In making his 196 he put on 393 runs for

the fifth wicket with Arnold (200*).

On the Worcester ground in July, 1908, he scored 334 in four and a half hours for Gentlemen of Worcestershire v. Gentlemen of Staffordshire.

He assisted the Gentlemen against the Players at the Oval and Scarborough in 1910, and at Lord's in 1911, in the Oval match scoring 16 and 34 and taking seven wickets—three of them in four balls—for 58 runs. In 1906–07 he visited New Zealand as a member of the M.C.C.'s team, and during the tour rendered good service without doing anything remarkable. At the conclusion of the season of 1913 he settled in Canada, and was seen no more in first-class cricket in this country. He may be summed-up as a dashing, hard-hitting batsman, a useful fast bowler, and a brilliant field. His most successful years as a bowler were 1909 and 1910, when his figures were respectively 44 wickets for 25.95 runs each and 58 for 26.77 apiece. He could bowl at a great pace, but the fairness of his delivery was often questioned—and not without good reason. He had been a member of the M.C.C. since 1911.

BURNUP, Cuthbert James, who died on April 5, 1960, aged 84, was in the XI at Malvern for three years before going to Cambridge, for whom he played against Oxford from 1896 to 1898. His best season for the University was that of 1896 when he scored 666 runs in nine matches, including 80 and 11 in the big match at Lord's. W. G. Grace, junior, son of "The Champion", failed to score in either Cambridge innings. In that game E. B. Shine, acting upon his captain's orders, bowled three balls to the boundary in order to prevent Oxford following on. It was, however, for Kent, whom he captained in 1903, that Burnup enjoyed his greatest successes as opening batsman.

A careful player who took few risks, he possessed strokes which enabled him to score on all types of pitches and he showed on occasion that he could force the pace. Eight times in a county career dating from 1896 to 1907, he exceeded 1,000 runs, his best season being that of 1902 when he hit 2,048 runs, including six of his 26 centuries, for an average of 39.38. His highest innings, and at that time the highest ever made for Kent, was 200 against Lancashire at Old Trafford in 1900. He played six times for the Gentlemen against the Players, and on his first appearance hit 123 at the Oval.

Though he seldom bowled, he bore a major part in the defeat of J. Darling's Australians at Canterbury in 1899 when taking three wickets for seven runs and five for 44. He took part in tours of America (twice), Australia and New Zealand and Holland. Also a fine Association footballer, he played for Cambridge from 1895 to 1898, for England against Scotland in 1896 and for the Corinthians.

BURRELL, The Rev. Herbert John Edwin, died at Cambridge on May 22, 1949, aged 82. Charterhouse XI 1884–85. Oxford trial matches, but did not obtain his Blue. Played a little for Essex, Norfolk and Hampshire. Lawn tennis doubles for Oxford v. Cambridge 1886–87. Hon. Canon of Ely Cathedral.

BURROUGH, George Baker, who died on May 9, 1965, aged 58, did not gain a place in the XI at Wellington, but he became an accomplished spin-bowler who might have gained a reputation in first-class cricket had he been able to spare the time. He made one appearance for Somerset, against Cambridge University at Taunton in 1936. For many years he played for Street C.C.

BURROUGH, The Rev. John Wilson, who was killed in a road accident on September 11, 1969, aged 65, was in the Lancing XI before playing in occasional matches for Gloucestershire from 1924 to 1937. He was a nephew of the Rev. J. Burrough, who got his Blue for Cambridge in 1895.

BURROWS, Arthur, the oldest cricketer who had played in a match of note at Lord's, died at "The Larches," Beckenham, on September 13, 1908, in his 97th year. He was born on August 26, 1812, and played for Winchester against Eton at Lord's in 1829, when he scored 0 not out and 17. He was known as "The Father of the English Bar," being the oldest practising barrister in England, and until a short time before his death went to his chambers in Lincoln's Inn regularly two or three times a week.

BURROWS, Arthur Owen, who died in Hobart on January 4, 1984, aged 80, played 31 times for Tasmania between 1923–24 and 1936–37 and was picked for a trial match prior to the selection of the Australian team to England in 1930. An all-rounder who took 77 wickets in first-class cricket and scored 1,504 runs, he once, when playing in Hobart, bowled a ball which sent a bail 83yd. 1ft. 9in. So far as is known, this is a record distance.

BURROWS, Richard D., who helped Worcestershire rise to first-class rank in 1899 and still played for the county in 1919, died at his home, Eastwood, Nottinghamshire, in February, 1943, aged 70. Of good height and robust build, Burrows bowled fast right-hand with good action, and batted well enough to warrant the description of an all-round cricketer. In 1901 he took 96 wickets and twice exactly a hundred for the county, in 1910 at an average of 23.46 and 1913 at 21.41, being far the best man in his county's attack each year. When Worcestershire tied with Yorkshire for second place to Nottinghamshire in the 1907 championship, Burrows scored 112 against Gloucestershire at Worcester and with the bat averaged 25.28, but his bowling fell to 57 wickets at 24 runs apiece. Worcestershire twice beat Yorkshire that season, Arnold and Cuffe being their great bowlers on each occasion; Burrows was wanted in only one innings, taking three wickets for 63 runs and finishing off the match at Worcester. Arnold and Cuffe on that occasion took 16 wickets between them, and at Bradford in August they bowled unchanged throughout the match, Cuffe, by dismissing nine men in the second innings, sharing the match honours with Arnold—10 wickets each. Burrows scored his second first-class century also against Gloucestershire, 107 not out at Worcester in July, 1914, when he batted number 10. Sir Home Gordon's Form at a Glance shows that Burrows scored 5,183 runs, average 14.01, took 805 wickets at 29.32 runs apiece, and held 132 catches—mostly at the old-fashioned point position. He created a first-class record in 1911 by sending a bail 67 yards six inches from the stumps when he bowled Huddleston at Old Trafford. In 1923 he was chosen as a first-class umpire and served during nine seasons, his bulky figure bending over the stumps at the bowler's end suggesting the happiness and close attention with which he carried out his duty.

BURRUP, John, died July 29, 1900, being over 80 years of age. He was one of the 70 members of the old Montpelier Club, who joined the Surrey County C.C. on its formation in 1845. Was one of the real founders of the club, his association with Surrey cricket extending over 55 years. Succeeding Mr. W. Denison, the first Hon. Sec. of the Surrey County C.C. in 1848, he held the post till 1855, to be followed by his twin brother William. It was in a very great measure owing to his exertions during the eight years he was secretary, that the Oval was prevented from falling into the hands of the builders.

BURRUP, William, died on December 23, 1901, at the age of 81. Connected with Surrey cricket from the earliest days of the County Club, Mr. Burrup was hon. secretary from 1855 to 1872, his period of office thus covering the rise and decline of the famous XI, which, with F. P. Miller as captain, used to play England single-handed. No one, apart from the players themselves, was better known at the Oval. His interest in Surrey was not affected by lapse of time, and up to the end of his life he was a member of the committee. On Mr. Burrup's retirement from the hon. secretaryship in 1872, Mr. C. W. Alcock was appointed secretary—a post he has held ever since.

BURTON, David Cecil Fowler, who died on September 24, 1971, aged 84, enjoyed the distinction of leading Yorkshire to the County Championship in 1919, the first of three consecutive years as captain. A member of the Rugby XI in 1904, he first played for Yorkshire in 1907 while at Cambridge and he took over the captaincy after the First World War. He and W. Rhodes in 1919 shared a partnership of 254 against Hampshire at Dewsbury which remains a record for the Yorkshire seventh wicket. He toured the West Indies with the first two M.C.C. teams to visit the Islands. In all first-class cricket, he scored 2,684 runs, average 18.90. He later did valuable work as coach at Oratory School.

BURTON, George, born at Hampstead on May 1, 1851, died on May 6, 1930. A slow right-handed bowler, Burton did not play for Middlesex until 30 years of age, but in his first match—against Surrey at Lord's—he bowled Harry Jupp with the second ball he sent down and in the second innings (in which he secured five wickets for 20) he dismissed John Shuter, the Surrey captain, with his first ball. In the course of a county career which extended from 1881 to 1893 he obtained 544 wickets for Middlesex for 17 runs apiece. He enjoyed some notable successes against Yorkshire—seven wickets for 20 and seven wickets for 18 at Lord's and 16 wickets for 114 at Sheffield, this last performance following upon a match at the Oval in which he obtained 13 Surrey wickets (including all 10 in the first innings) for 78. A member of the M.C.C. ground staff from 1883 to 1904, he, in 1894 against Oxford City, again took all 10 wickets in an innings. A coachsmith by trade, Burton, even when assisting Middlesex regularly, put in, as a rule, several hours' work before taking the field. He was given two benefits—Middlesex v. Surrey in 1892 and Middlesex v. Somerset in 1905. For many years he scored for Middlesex and right up to the end he was hon. secretary to the Cricketers' Fund Friendly Society.

BURTON, Reginald Henry Markham, who died on October 19, 1980, aged 80, played for Warwickshire v. Worcestershire at Edgbaston in 1919, a match not recorded in *Wisden*. Although he made 47 and helped H. Venn to put on over 100 for the third wicket, he never represented the county again.

BURTON, Robert Claud, who died on April 30, 1971, aged 80, was in the Malvern XI from 1908 to 1910 and made two appearances for Yorkshire in 1914. He was the younger brother of D. C. F. Burton, who also assisted Yorkshire. For a number of years he was in charge of cricket at Eastbourne College, where he was a housemaster.

BURY, The Rev. Canon William, born at Radcliffe-on-Trent on October 14, 1839, died at Borough Green, Sevenoaks, on May 21, 1927, aged 87. He was educated privately, but, being a fine, free and powerful hitter and a magnificent field—he was known as "Deerfoot"—obtained his Blue for Cambridge in 1861, playing against Oxford both that year and the next. Cambridge were very strong about that time, and among Bury's contemporaries were H. M. Plowden, A. W. T. Daniel, the Hon. C. G. Lyttelton, R. Lang and Clement Booth. Both games against Oxford were won, that of 1861 by 133 runs and the one of 1862 by eight wickets. His scores in those matches were small—only two, 11, and 14—but his cricket generally was good enough to secure him a place in the Nottinghamshire team each season. In consecutive games on the Trent Bridge ground in 1862 he scored 121 for Gentlemen of North v. Gentlemen of South, and 121 for Midland Counties Diamonds v. Free Foresters, having the bowling of V. E. Walker to contend with in the former match and that of David Buchanan in the latter. Entering the Church, he early gave up playing in great matches, though he made a few fugitive appearances for Northants. He was younger brother of the late Rev. T. W. Bury, a Cambridge Blue of 1855.

BUSH, Arthur James, born July 28, 1850,

died on September 21, 1924. Mr. Bush, who had been in failing health for some time before his death, will always have a distinct place in cricket history. He was the Gloucestershire wicket-keeper in those far-off days in the '70s, when the county had its golden time and for two seasons at least—1876 and 1877—stood far ahead of all rivals. I often wonder what the class of club cricket in and around Bristol must have been that the Graces, immediately after the formation of the County Club, could find such first rate material ready to their hands. Mr. Bush was only one of many who at once enrolled themselves under W. G.'s banner. He went right through the great days—Gloucestershire never lost a match at home till the first Australian XI beat them at Clifton in 1878—and held his post for long afterwards, playing less and less as time went on and finally dropping out of the team after the season of 1890. He went to Australia with W. G. Grace's XI in 1873–74 and, quoting W. G., "It was the general opinion of the team that no wicket-keeper alive could have done better or stood the wear and tear of the task so well." In 1874 and 1875 Mr. Bush kept wicket for Gentlemen v. Players at Lord's and would very likely have been picked in later years but in 1876 Alfred Lyttelton appeared on the scene. In this connection it is interesting to recall the fact that Mr. Bush was the wicket-keeper when the Gentlemen beat the Australians at Prince's in 1878. He was a wonderfully safe catch whatever the pace of the bowling. Though originally chosen for Gloucestershire on account of his batting and fielding Mr. Bush—at any rate in first class company—had no pretensions as a batsman. Still, if he had not stuck in against Yorkshire at Cheltenham in 1876 W. G.'s famous innings would have fallen short of 318 not out. In his young days Mr. Bush was a Rugby International.—S.H.P.

BUSH, Col. Harry Stebbing, C.M.G., C.B., whose death occurred on March 18, 1942, at the age of 70, stood out as a batsman of marked ability for Surrey, when free from military duties, between 1901 and 1912. He gave an exceptionally good display at Old Trafford in 1902 when hitting 111 off the strong Lancashire attack. Other noteworthy innings for the county were 135 against Derbyshire and 101 not out against Nottinghamshire, both at the Oval in 1911, when, with an average of 41.35, he came second to Hayward in the Surrey batting. Altogether in first-class cricket he averaged 24.59 for an aggregate of 2,607 runs. A heavy scorer in

club cricket, he made 314 not out for Eastbourne against C. E. Hambro's XI in 1893 in
five hours. Also at Eastbourne that year he
scored 113 and 122 not out against Crystal
Palace. This double feat he repeated in 1909
with 114 and 134 for Army Ordnance Corps
against R.A., Woolwich; he could bowl, too,
and in that match took 12 wickets. Still more
remarkable was his all-round performance at
Folkestone against Oxford Authentics in
1909, when he scored 254, took 17 wickets
and held a catch. In his last match of
importance for the Army against Royal Navy
at Lord's in 1914 he made 34 and 36. He
excelled on fast pitches, thanks to adhering
to the custom of playing forward with full use
of his height and strength. His off-driving
was brilliant in its certainty and power. So
sure was he in timing the ball that he batted
without gloves, and seldom suffered at all
from such a daring habit that was peculiar to
himself during his own period of excellence.
Educated at Dover College, he developed
ability at Rugby football as a wing three-
quarter for Harlequins and Surrey.

BUSH, Robert Edwin, D.L., a contemporary
of W. G. Grace and one of Bristol's best
known figures, died at Stoke Bishop on
December 9, 1939, aged 84. He played for
Gloucestershire from 1874 to 1877 when
W. G. Grace was in his prime. For nearly 30
years he sheep-farmed extensively in Western Australia. During the last war he converted his home at Bishops Knoll into a
hospital for wounded Australian soldiers,
nearly 3,000 of whom were treated. He held
office for a time as chairman and president of
the Gloucestershire County C.C. While in
Australia he became a member of the legislative council.

BUSHER, S. E., who died in Australia in
1953 where he had lived for many years,
played in a few matches for Worcestershire
in 1908 and 1910. Educated at Lancing, he
appeared for Surrey in the Easter-tide game
at the Oval in 1908 against Gentlemen of
England. He scored 52 and in the match took
seven wickets for 92, twice bowling Dr.
W. G. Grace, then close upon 60 and making
his only first-class appearance of the season.

BUSWELL, Walter A., who kept wicket for
Northamptonshire and then stood as a first-
class umpire for some years, died at Lutterworth, Leicestershire, on April 24, 1950,
aged 75. In 205 games between 1906 and
1921 he helped to dismiss over 400 batsmen,
and he scored 2,670 runs, average 10.68.

BUTCHER, Douglas Harry, who died at
Wallington, Surrey, on July 4, 1945, aged 69,
played occasionally for Surrey during 1903–
13. He was a prolific scorer for Upper
Tooting.

BUTLER, The Rev. Arthur Gray, died at
Glenfinnan, Torquay, on January 16, 1909,
in his 80th year. He was in the Rugby XI in
1847 and 1848, being captain in the latter
year, and was above the average as a batsman. For some years he was an assistant
master at Rugby under Dr. Temple, and was
afterwards appointed first headmaster of
Haileybury. He was Butler of "Butler's
Leap" at Rugby and winner of the racquet
pairs at Oxford in 1855. He is said to have
been the only man who ever jumped the
river Cherwell, a tributary of the Thames at
Oxford.

BUTLER, Arthur Hugh Montagu, member
of a well-known cricketing family, died in
London on May 28, 1943, aged 69. He was in
the Harrow XI of 1890, and at Lord's against
Eton he made 19, helping his captain, A. C.
MacLaren, 76, in the only stand of the
innings, which closed for 133—a lead of 25 in
a match ruined by rain on the first day. In the
whole season Butler, 18, finished second to
MacLaren in the batting averages, the captain, with 42, being in a class by himself. He
and W. F. G. Wyndham won the Public
Schools Racquets Championship at Queen's
Club in the same year. Arthur Butler became
Librarian to the House of Lords.

BUTLER, Edward Henry, born at Hobart on
March 15, 1851, died at Lower Sandy Bay,
Tasmania, on January 5, 1928. In his time he
had been a forcing bat, a brilliant field at slip,
and a good fast bowler. He played for
Tasmania against various English teams,
Victoria and New Zealand. Bowling for
South v. North, at Hobart, he took five
wickets for seven runs in 1879–80 and six for
0 (in 19 balls) in 1881–82. For many years he
was President of the Tasmanian Cricket
Association. Whilst visiting England he took
part in the Gentlemen v. Players match at
Prince's in 1877, and also appeared for
M.C.C. and the United South of England
XI.

BUTLER, Edward Montagu, died February
11, 1948, after one day's illness, at Rogate,
near Petersfield, aged 81. Played for Harrow
1883–85 (captain), and Cambridge 1888–89;
Cambridge County 1894. Played for Middlesex two matches in 1885. Winner of the

Public Schools Racquets Championship with C. D. Buxton in 1884 and with E. Crawley 1885. Represented Cambridge at racquets in the singles 1889, doubles 1888–89, and also against Oxford in the tennis doubles 1889. Amateur racquets champion 1889 and winner of the Doubles Racquets Championship with M. C. Kemp in 1892. Assistant Master at Harrow 1892–1919.

BUTLER, Fred, a nephew of George Parr, was born at Radcliffe-on-Trent on December 29, 1858, and died at Sailor's Snug Harbor, Staten Island, on February 26, 1923. After making 43 in the Nottinghamshire Colts' match in 1881, and 47 and 34 (against Alfred Shaw and Morley) for Colts of England at Lord's, he was tried for his county, but, except for an innings of 171 against Sussex at Hove in 1890, never did quite as well as was expected. Subsequently, however, he scored well for Durham County. For about 15 years he was professional to the Sunderland C.C.

BUTLER, Robert, a nephew of George Parr, born at Radcliffe-on-Trent on March 8, 1852, died at Nottingham on December 19, 1916. He was educated at the Collegiate School, Newark, and Loughborough Grammar School, and in *Scores and Biographies* was described as "A fine free hitter, especially to leg, and in the field also he is good, generally taking mid-wicket-off and long-leg." In 1870 he began to assist Nottinghamshire, and in his first match for the county—v. Kent, at the Crystal Palace—played an innings of 60 and, in partnership with Daft, took the score to 100 after three wickets had fallen for 14. Owing to business claims he was seldom seen in first-class cricket, and he was only 25 when he made his last appearance for Nottinghamshire. In 1876 he played for the South against the North in Daft's benefit match at Nottingham and scored 20.

BUTLER, Samuel Evan. By the death at Bath, on April 30, 1903, at the age of 53, of Mr. Samuel Evan Butler, of Combe Hay, Somerset—the Oxford fast bowler—another of the famous players who made University cricket such a great thing at the beginning of the '70s passed away. During his two years at Eton and four years at Oxford Mr. Butler did a lot of good work as a bowler, but his fame rests entirely on his wonderful performance in the University match of 1871, when he took all 10 wickets in the first innings of Cambridge for 38 runs, and obtained in the whole game 15 wickets for 95 runs. His feat

remains unique, no one else in the Oxford and Cambridge match having ever taken all the wickets in one innings. He was a right-handed bowler and possessed great pace. On that one afternoon at Lord's he was unplayable, but he never afterwards approached the same form. Indeed, it has been stated that he himself declared that he never bowled really well after the day of his triumph. This, however, was an exaggeration, as when, in 1873, he played against Cambridge for the last time, he took five wickets in the first innings of the match for 48 runs. In the University match of 1870 Mr. Butler had a painful experience, as he was the first of three batsmen who, at the finish, were out to successive balls from F. C. Cobden. Mr. Butler was born in Colombo and was a man of fine physique, standing 6ft. 2in. On the strength of his great performance against Cambridge, he was chosen for Gentlemen against Players in 1871 both at Lord's and the Oval.

BUTT, Harry Rigden, born at Sands End, Fulham, on December 27, 1865, died at Hastings on December 21, 1928, a few days before completing his 63rd year. He first played for Sussex in 1890, and remained a regular member of the county side until 1912. In the following year he secured a place in the list of first-class umpires. While playing for Sussex, Butt was responsible for the dismissal of 1,202 batsmen, catching 927 behind the wicket, and stumping 274. He also made one catch while fielding at slip. In his first season for Sussex, when playing against Cambridge University at Brighton, he allowed only one bye while the University hit up a total of 703 for nine wickets. In four consecutive games, all at Hove in 1895, he allowed only six byes whilst 1,938 runs were being made. His best season as a batsman was in 1900, when he scored 652 runs for an average of 27. A year later he made his highest score in first class cricket—96 v. Worcestershire at Hove. When he carried out his bat for 74 against Cambridge University at Cambridge in 1908, he and George Cox added 156 for the last wicket. Short of stature, but very quick on his feet, Butt excelled more in catching than in stumping. His hands, unlike those of some of the most famous wicket-keepers—Blackham, Pilling, Lyttelton, McGregor, and Strudwick—were badly knocked about, but he maintained his form year after year in remarkable fashion, and he possessed an unsurpassed reputation for fairness. Against Somerset at Brighton in 1900 he made eight catches, and in the game with Kent at Tonbridge in 1899, when Bland took all 10 wickets, Butt brought off four catches in each innings. In four other matches, all for Sussex, he made six catches in a single innings. In 1894 he represented the Players against the Gentlemen at Hastings, and in 1895–96 toured South Africa as a member of Lord Hawke's team. As wicket-keeper for Sussex he followed Harry Phillips, and he was succeeded by G. B. Street, who early in 1924 met with a fatal accident when motor-cycling. As an umpire Butt ranked very high. He was quiet, but very firm, and was generally respected. Eloquent testimony to the great esteem in which cricketers held him was shown by the action of the first-class county captains at their meeting on December 10. On learning that Butt, owing to illness, did not offer himself for appointment for next season's matches, they asked the secretary of the M.C.C. to write to Butt on their behalf to express their deep regret at the cause of his retirement. He had been a member of the M.C.C.'s groundstaff since 1894, and had been accorded two benefits—Sussex v. Yorkshire at Hove in 1900 and Middlesex v. Sussex at Lord's in 1928.

BUTT, John Alec Steuart, who died on October 30, 1966, aged 74, did not get a place in the XI while at Marlborough, but played without much success in one match for Sussex in 1923.

BUTTERWORTH, Henry Rhodes Whittle, who died on October 9, 1958, aged 49, played for Lancashire from 1929 to 1937. Scoring 106 against Sussex at Old Trafford in 1932, he shared with J. Iddon in a stand of 278, a record for the county. Educated at Rydal Mount, he got his Blue at Cambridge in 1929.

BUTTERWORTH, Pilot Officer Reginald Edmund Compton (R.A.F.V.R.), the Harrow, Oxford and Middlesex cricketer, was killed in action in May, 1940. An all-rounder, he started the bowling against Eton at Lord's in 1924, and in the two innings took eight wickets for 107 runs. Although bowling well for the Freshmen and scoring 79 in an early trial, his form when first at Oxford was unreliable, and not until 1927 did he receive his Blue from E. R. T. Holmes. That season he scored 110 at the Oval against Surrey and 101 against Free Foresters, but, though always likely to prove valuable with either bat or ball, he did little against Cambridge. A good stroke player, he seldom wasted

opportunities of scoring; his medium-paced bowling was difficult when he made the ball swing late. In recent years he played many good innings for Middlesex, and in 1937 opened the batting in several matches with either Edrich or Price.

BUTTERWORTH, Wilfred Selkirk, who appeared for Lancashire on a few occasions in 1877 and 1882, died at Rochdale on April 9, 1908. *Scores and Biographies* (xiv–95) described him as "An average batsman and field."

BUULTJENS, Edward W., died in May, 1980. In 1936 he played as a bowler for Ceylon against G. O. Allen's M.C.C. side to Australia and caught and bowled Walter Hammond, his only wicket.

BUXTON, Cyril Digby, met his death by his own hand on May 10, 1892, under most distressing circumstances when suffering from severe mental depression. Born on June 25, 1866, Mr. Buxton was thus only in his 26th year, and his untimely end caused a painful sensation in cricket circles. During his all too brief career he played for Harrow, Cambridge University and Essex, appearing for Cambridge against Oxford at Lord's in 1885, 1886, 1887 and 1888. In the last year he was captain of the XI. It was only his good fortune to be once on the victorious side, Cambridge winning in 1885. Oxford won in 1886 and 1887, and in 1888 bad weather caused the match to be left drawn. Mr. Buxton perhaps never quite came up to expectations formed of him when he first went to Cambridge, but he was a punishing, dangerous batsman, and a really magnificent field. There were few better mid-offs in the country.

BUXTON, Edward North, born on September 1, 1840, died at Buckhurst Hill on January 9, 1924, aged 83. "A good forward player and effective field," he appeared for Norfolk and Essex but did not secure his Blue for Cambridge. For 61 years he was Vice-President of the Woodford Wells C.C., and at the Club's Diamond Jubilee gave £1,000 towards purchasing the freehold of the ground. For years, too, he was one of the moving spirits of the Cricket Company at Upton Park. He will, however, always be best remembered for helping to save Epping Forest for the public and to secure the Fairlop Playing Fields. His wife was sister of Sir Kenelm Digby, of the Harrow and Oxford XIs.

BUXTON, Lieut.-Col. Robert Vere, who died on October 1, 1952, aged 70, was in the Eton XI of 1902, scoring three and 74 against Harrow. At Oxford he received his Blue in 1906 and in the match with Cambridge scored 33 and 28. In 1906 and 1907 he played in a few games for Middlesex. From 1945 he was deputy chairman of Martins Bank.

BYASS, Robert William, who died at his home in London on August 22, 1958, aged 97, had been a member of M.C.C. since 1881. An enterprising batsman and useful medium-paced bowler, he was in the Eton XI in 1878 and 1879, but failed to gain a Blue at Oxford. He played in some matches for Free Foresters. He became head of the wine-shipping firm of Gonzalez, Byass and Co., who in 1954 dedicated a cask of sherry, believed to be the oldest in the world, to Sir Winston Churchill to mark his 80th birthday.

BYNG, Capt. Arthur Maitland, of the Royal Fusiliers, was killed in action in France in September, 1914. He was one of the best-known batsmen in the Army, being very sound, with a free style and plenty of scoring strokes. At Portsmouth in July, 1905, he made 204 for Hampshire Hogs v. Royal Navy, and in partnership with D. A. Steele (180) scored 335 for the first wicket. He was born on September 26, 1872, and in his two matches for Sandhurst v. Woolwich—in 1894 and 1895—scored 10 and 87 not out, and took 18 wickets. In 1905 he played in three matches for Hampshire.

BYRNE, George Robert, who died in Guernsey on May 28, 1973, aged 81, played as an amateur all-rounder for Warwickshire in 1912 and for Worcestershire from 1914 to 1921 when his duties as an Army officer permitted. In his first match for Warwickshire at Edgbaston, he enjoyed a successful spell of right-arm medium-pace bowling. He took wickets with the fourth and sixth deliveries of his opening over and with the first ball of his third over.

BYRNE, James Frederick, who died at Birmingham on May 10, 1954, aged 82, played for Warwickshire as a forcing batsman and fast bowler from 1892 to 1910, being captain for five years from 1903. Against Lancashire at Birmingham in 1905, he and S. P. Kinneir (158) set up a Warwickshire record by sharing in an opening partnership of 333, of which Byrne's share amounted to 222. Another claim to fame was that twice in a match at Crystal Palace he dismissed Dr.

W. G. Grace. He was perhaps even better known as a powerful Rugby football full-back with Moseley, for on 13 occasions between 1894 and 1899 he played for England. In all matches during the 1897–98 season he captained his country. He later became President of Moseley and of the North Midlands Union and for some years was a member of the Committee of the Rugby Football Union.

BYROM, John Lewis, born at Saddleworth, Yorks, on July 20, 1851, died at Delph, near Oldham, on August 24, 1931, aged 80. A good average batsman, a medium-pace bowler and a smart cover-point, he appeared for Yorkshire in two matches during the season of 1874.

BYRON, Charles Robert Hamilton, who died at Kingwilliamstown, Cape Province, on March 6, 1952, aged 41, first came into prominence in 1927–28, when he hit 101 for Combined South African Schools against the M.C.C. Touring Team captained by Capt. R. T. Stanyforth. He later played for Border, scoring 504 runs, average 20.16, in the Currie Cup Competition between 1933 and 1937. His highest score and only century was 135 against Transvaal at Johannesburg in 1935–36.

CADELL, Lieut. Alexander R., R. N., died in Petersfield Cottage Hospital on May 14, 1928, as the result of a motor accident the night before on Telegraph Hill. A decidedly useful cricketer, he represented the Royal Navy at Lord's and elsewhere, and in 1927 played for Hampshire against Warwickshire at Portsmouth.

CADMAN, Samuel, who died at his home at Glossop, Derbyshire, on May 6, 1952, aged 72, was for many years a prominent all-rounder for Derbyshire. Born on January 29, 1880, he joined the county staff in 1900 and, having gained a regular place in the XI four years later, held it till 1925. After one match in 1926 he was placed in charge of the Nursery at Derby with excellent results. During his long term of service, Derbyshire were generally a struggling club, both from the playing and financial viewpoints, and upon Cadman and two or three other players of all-round ability a great deal depended.

A steady, reliable batsman, he altogether scored 14,021 runs in first-class cricket and, with his medium-pace bowling, took 802 wickets. His best season as a batsman was in 1911, when he headed the Derbyshire averages with 1,036 runs, average 29.60, and appeared for Players v. Gentlemen at Scarborough; as a bowler, in 1910, when he took 67 wickets, average 23.67, and as an all-rounder, in 1908, when he stood second in batting with 942 runs, average 26.91, and headed the bowling figures with 55 wickets at a cost of 19.29 runs apiece. Among his performances in his early days was that at Derby in 1905 when Derbyshire gave a fright to J. Darling's Australian team. Cadman took five wickets for 94 in the first innings and scored 66 in the county's second, but after having 200 on the board for the loss of four wickets Derbyshire collapsed against A. Cotter and were all out for 231. The previous year Cadman took part in the match at Chesterfield where P. Perrin, though hitting 343 not out in the Essex first innings, was on the losing side! In 1913, at Derby, Cadman dismissed seven Essex batsmen for 39, the last five for 19, and followed with innings of 66 and 76. He was also a member of the Derbyshire team who in 1919 created the surprise of the season by beating H. L. Collins's Australian Imperial Forces side.

For some years after he gave up first-class cricket, Cadman assisted Glossop in the Lancashire and Cheshire League, and at the age of 70 he scored 17 not out in a Second XI match.

CADWALADER, Dr. Charles, who died in London on June 12, 1907, was for many years prominently identified with the game in Philadelphia. In 1867 he got Willsher to agree to take a team to America in the following autumn, and in 1872 he was prominent in the arrangements for the visit to Canada of Mr. R. A. Fitzgerald's team.

CAFFYN, William. Many cricket memories were revived by the announcement that the veteran Surrey player, William Caffyn, died at his home, at Reigate, on Thursday, August 28, 1919. Born on February 2, 1828, he had lived to the great age of 91. His fame rests mainly on the fact that he was the best all-round man in the Surrey XI that, with the late F. P. Miller as captain, used to meet—and twice beat—the full strength of England at Kennington Oval. Of that brilliant band the one survivor now left is Mr. E. Dowson—only 10 years Caffyn's junior, but quite hale and hearty. Many other amateurs who played with Caffyn in his prime are still living, but of the great professionals who used to make the match at Lord's between the All England and United XIs one of the events of the season, only George Wootton, the Notts bowler, remains with us.

Caffyn played his first match for Surrey in 1849, and in the following year—there were very few county fixtures in those days—he headed the batting. From that time he never looked back, becoming more and more prominent as the fame of Surrey cricket grew. He was the leading bowler in the team, as well as the finest batsman. About 1857 he reached his highest point, and right on to 1863 his powers showed no decline. Then came the end of his real career in English cricket. In the autumn of 1863 he paid his second visit to Australia as a member of George Parr's team—he had gone out two years before with H. H. Stephenson's side—and at the close of the tour he stayed behind in the Colonies, accepting a position as coach. While in Australia he played in inter-Colonial matches, but though he did much to develop young talent he scarcely, judging from the scores, added to his own reputation. He was back in England in 1872, and played several times for Surrey that year and in 1873, but it was too late to start over again. His day was done, and, though Surrey were far from strong, he could not keep his place in the XI. His long stay in Australia lost him the chance of a benefit match at the Oval, but to the end of his life the Surrey Club paid him an annuity of £39.

On the evidence of all who played side by side with him in his great days, Caffyn was a very fine batsman, free and attractive in style and master of a cut that only Tom Humphrey surpassed in brilliancy. Had he lived in these days he would no doubt have made big scores, for he needed a good wicket. The Oval and Fenner's at Cambridge were the grounds that suited him best. On the rough wickets at Lord's he was admittedly far inferior to George Parr, Carpenter, Richard Daft, and the first Tom Hayward. Still even at Lord's against Jackson, he was on two occasions seen at his best. As regards his bowling, one is rather doubtful. Right hand medium pace, he belonged to the purely round arm school—he had just settled in Australia when the law was altered—and modern wickets would very likely have been too good for him. Still on the best wickets of his own time he did wonderful things for Surrey and the United All-England XI. As an all-round fieldsman he had scarcely a superior.—S. H. P.

Lord Cobham—the Hon. C. G. Lyttelton in his cricket days, and incidentally one of the most brilliant batsmen in England—who played several times against Caffyn in Gentlemen v. Players matches, and also in matches between Cambridge University and

Surrey, has very kindly sent the following notes on the veteran as he knew him:

"My recollections of Caffyn date back 60 years, when I was captain of the Eton XI and Caffyn was our 'coach' for a few weeks. He was rather a small man, well and compactly built and very active. I do not think he was a born coach, or that he troubled himself to give much oral instruction, but his bowling, which was slow to medium, straight, and of a good length gave us excellent practice, and much could be learnt from watching his batting which was sound, graceful, and often brilliant.

"Until he left England in 1863, Caffyn was always a good man on a side. He never ceased to be a dangerous bat and he was as consistent a scorer as most of his contemporaries. He could hit hard all round, but his most notable hit was his cut, which denoted great strength and flexibility of wrist. I well remember, in a country match, his cutting an over-pitched ball of mine through a big drum, supposed to be at a safe distance from the wicket. It was said that when facing the great Jackson at Lord's, he was apt to show some 'softness' and want of nerve, but then Jackson on a characteristic Lord's wicket was a 'terror' such as is never seen in these days. Once, at all events, in the 1857 North and South match at Lord's, Caffyn made 90 against Jackson, which long ranked amongst historical innings, with those of R. Hankey, C. G. Lane and others.

"Caffyn was a good bowler, but never I think quite in the first rank. His bowling had no cunning or 'devil' in it and on present day wickets it could probably be 'pulled' or 'hooked' without much difficulty. Nevertheless he took plenty of wickets, and runs did not come easily or rapidly from him, as his analysis shows. He was a good and active field.

"At Eton, and as long as I played cricket with him, I always thought of Caffyn as a well-mannered man and pleasant to deal with, and this impression seems to me to be borne out by his book—*71 Not Out*—which is written in a modest and kindly spirit, free from jealousy or depreciation of others."

Mr. E. Dowson, now, as already stated, the only survivor of F. P. Miller's famous Surrey XI, writes:

"He was a neat, good-looking, dapper little man. As regards his bowling he bowled a medium pace ball, not difficult to look at, but he nearly always obtained his share of wickets. Curiously enough we were always glad when he had a good innings, as the more runs he made the better he bowled. His batting was always worth watching as he could hit all round, and his cutting was brilliant, especially balls off the bails. He used to get hundreds, which were very few in those days. In my opinion he would have been one of the first chosen in a Test match. He also was a good field. I must relate one case when he was really frightened. In a match v. Yorkshire at Sheffield a storm came on which deluged the ground. The captains, Mr. F. P. Miller and Mr. W. Prest, both agreed that there could be no more cricket. Poor Caffyn had dressed and got out of the ground when some of the roughs brought him back with his bag, swearing they were not going to be done out of seeing more cricket as they had paid their 3d. Chaffing then commenced and we said we were not afraid to go on. They gathered round Mr. Prest, saying 'Are you not ashamed of yourself?' He replied 'Yes, that I was born here and amongst such a lot!' The wickets were again pitched and I should imagine never on a wetter ground. The water spluttered in your face as you fielded the ball. However, Mr. Prest was so angry that he came in and won the match himself, hitting the bowling all over the place."

Mr. Herbert C. Troughton writes:

"I saw Caffyn pretty frequently during the years 1859–63. I thought him an extremely brilliant bat. He had not the defence of Carpenter or Hayward, but he was, in my opinion, far more interesting to watch, as when he made runs, he always made them quickly; he—at least whenever I saw him—acted upon what is supposed to have been the immortal Yardley's maxim—'Get runs or get out.' He was rather impetuous and was apt to get himself out by adopting hitting tactics before he had got set. Caffyn had many strokes, and all of them stylish. With perhaps the exception of Lord Cobham, better known as the Hon. C. G. Lyttelton, he was the hardest cutter I have ever seen, and his hitting to deep square leg was brilliant in the extreme. His driving powers, too, especially to the on were quite out of the common, and he had one stroke which he and W. Mortlock alone, so far as I remember, have ever regularly put in force—a huge hit between deep square leg and long on, rather nearer long-on than square leg, a stroke that earned him hundreds of runs. As a bowler he was most excellent and did many brilliant things. He seemed to love bowling, and when he did not go on first, his joy, when he was put on, was unmistakable. He had an easy and very graceful delivery, and could bowl equally well, either round or over the wicket. If the wicket gave him ever so little help he could be deadly in the extreme. He generally failed at Lord's, where Jackson's expresses were not to his liking. Indeed though I saw him at Lord's in some eight matches I can only remember his coming off in one match and that was for South v. North in 1861 when he played a beautiful first innings of 65, and supplemented this with an excellent 25 in his second innings, Jackson's bowling, for once at Lord's, having no terrors for him."

CAHILL, Keyran William Jack, who died in Launceston on March 7, 1966, aged 55, played in four first-class matches for Tasmania in 1931–32. His best performance was against H. B. Cameron's South African side when he hit 21 and 35 not out.

CAHN, Sir Julien, Bart., who died on September 26, 1944, at his home, Stanford Hall, Loughborough, Leicestershire, aged 62, was a great supporter of cricket. The XI which he captained played good matches each season at his West Bridgford ground, and he took teams on many tours, including Jamaica, 1929, Argentine, 1930, Denmark and Jutland, 1932, Canada, U.S.A. and Bermuda, 1933, Ceylon and Singapore, 1937, and New Zealand, 1939. Twice he was President of the Nottinghamshire club and defrayed the cost of building new stands at Trent Bridge; he also provided a covered practice shed so that the county players could keep in training throughout the winter. He represented Leicestershire for some years on the Advisory County Cricket Committee and attended the meetings at Lord's dealing with the post-war plans. Keenly interested in hunting, he was at different times Master of the Burton Woodland, Pytchley and Fernie Hunts. Sir Julien inherited a fortune from his father and, apart from his business interests, devoted his life to sport and philanthropy.

CAIRNS, A. S., who died on September 26, 1944, was one of the finest all-round cricketers Scotland ever produced. For over 30 years he was highly successful both as batsman and bowler, and his long career has, perhaps, never been surpassed in Scottish cricket. He made 28 centuries, and in 1894, probably his best season, he scored in all matches 1,023 runs and took 108 wickets. A real sportsman in every way, with cricket his first love, Cairns became President of the Scottish Cricket Union in 1925.

CAKOBAU, Ratu Sir Edward, who died in Suva, Fiji, on June 25, 1973, aged 64, played for Auckland and when captain of Fiji against a New Zealand touring team in 1937 he hit a century. He played for various teams when in England in 1946, turning out barefooted in the native Fiji attire. He was President of the Fiji Cricket Association and was manager of the Fiji Rugby football touring team of 1964. Son of King George of Tonga, he became Deputy Prime Minister of Fiji when the colony was granted independence in 1970.

CALDICOTT, Walter, who died at Battenhall, Worcester, on September 4, 1916, aged 70, was a useful bowler about 40 years ago, and occasionally played for Worcestershire. He was a member of the county side which met the first Australian team, at Dudley, in 1878.

CALDWELL, The Rev. Somerville, who died on January 14, 1964, played for Somerset between 1901 and 1904. His best season as a patient, watchful batsman was that of 1903 when, with the aid of innings of 101 against Leicestershire and 113 against Sussex, he hit 403 runs, average 26.86. CORRECTION. In Obituaries in the 1965 edition, the Rev. Somerville Caldwell was incorrectly stated to have played for Somerset. In fact he played for Worcestershire, for whom his highest innings was 133.

CALLAWAY, Sydney Thomas, who died in New Zealand on November 25, 1923, aged 55, after two years of ill-health, had been a splendid batsman when in form and a capital medium-to-fast bowler, with good length and pitch. He played for both New South Wales and Queensland. In the Test match with England at Adelaide in 1894–95 he took five wickets for 37 in an innings of 124 and scored 41, he and A. E. Trott (38 not out) adding 81 for the tenth wicket. He visited New Zealand with two teams from New South Wales, on each occasion heading the bowling. Later he settled in the Dominion and played for Canterbury as well as for New Zealand against English and Australian teams.

CALTHORPE, The Hon. Frederick Somerset Gough, Cambridge Blue and Warwickshire captain, died on November 19, 1935, aged 43, after a month's illness from which recovery was impossible. Born on May 27, 1892, he was one of the best all-round players of his time at Repton, being described in 1911 as "the backbone of a strong side's bowling." Going up to Jesus College,

Cambridge, he obtained his Blue as a Freshman and remained in the side for the following two seasons. During the War he served in the Royal Air Force and would have captained Cambridge in 1919 had not the letter of invitation miscarried. As it was, he played under J. S. F. Morrison in his fourth University match which Oxford won by 45 runs. The game revived the best traditions of cricket at Lord's which during the preceding four summers had been given over in various ways to the amelioration of War service.

Before the War Calthorpe appeared a few times for Sussex, but in 1919 threw in his lot with Warwickshire and next year he became captain, a position he held until 1929. Always an enthusiastic cricketer, Calthorpe reached his best in 1925 when he scored 1,404 runs for Warwickshire with an average of 34.24 and took 44 wickets. His all-round form gained him a place in the Gentlemen's team at Lord's. A most attractive batsman, who went out to the half volley or cut the short ball in true Repton style, Calthorpe usually scored freely. As a medium-paced right hand bowler, he had a peculiar corkscrew run and his swerve with the new ball often worried batsmen. One of his best performances with the ball was in 1914 when in Oxford's second innings he took five wickets for 43 runs. In 1920, when most successful as a bowler, he took 100 wickets in all matches and scored 1,025 runs. Another notable bowling feat by Calthorpe occurred at Edgbaston in 1922 when he and Howell put out Hampshire for 15. Calthorpe took four wickets for four runs in that sensational game which Hampshire won by 155 runs. He toured New Zealand and Australia in the winter of 1922 with the M.C.C. team, captained by A. C. MacLaren, and he went out to the West Indies in charge of M.C.C. teams in 1925 and 1929. Calthorpe had a lot to do with starting the Folkestone Cricket Festival. He enjoyed every minute of a game whether batting, bowling or fielding. Taking the joy of the cricket field to the golf links he became a scratch player with the Worplesdon Club, founded the Cricketers' Golf Society, and gave a cup for competition. Son of Lord Calthorpe he was heir to the title.

CALVERT, Flight-Sergt. Clive P., a very promising all-rounder of the Royal Australian Air Force team, lost his life at the age of 21 on a mine-laying expedition over the Baltic Sea on December 16, 1944. He appeared in inter-state cricket for New South Wales, and during the 1944 summer he played in the one-day matches at Lord's for Australia against England. Possessing a crisp cut and powerful drive he was an attractive batsman. His best innings was 141 in two and a half hours for the R. A. A. F. against West Indies at Birmingham. His medium-fast bowling was also a great asset to the side.

CAMERON, Horace Brakenridge, one of the finest wicket-keepers South Africa has produced and a courageous, hard-hitting batsman, died on November 2, 1935, shortly after his return home with the victorious team that toured England. Born at Port Elizabeth on July 5, 1905, he was in his 31st year when enteric fever proved fatal after only a few days' illness. Educated at Hilton College, Natal, and Jeppe High School, Johannesburg, Cameron began to take a keen interest in cricket when no more than 10 years old. He received plenty of encouragement at school to develop skill in keeping wicket, and after getting a place in the Transvaal XI he soon came right to the front both as batsman and wicket-keeper. Following his debut against the Hon. L. H. Tennyson's team in 1924–25, he was quick to establish himself as a potential Test player. He made his first hundred in important cricket—132 against Eastern Province—in 1927, and selected the same season to play for South Africa he took part, with success, in all five games against England. Coming to this country in 1929 when he began the tour with a century against Worcestershire, Cameron fully lived up to his reputation as a wicket-keeper—one of his best performances was in the game with Somerset when he caught six batsmen and stumped one. In all matches during that visit he scored 1,077 runs for an average of 32.63.

When batting in the Test match at Lord's, he met with a nasty accident. A good length ball from Larwood rose abruptly and struck Cameron on the head, rendering him unconscious; the effects of the injury prevented him playing again for three weeks or so. When the M.C.C. team went to South Africa in 1930–31, Cameron was appointed captain for the fourth Test match—the third change of leadership in four games. He marked the occasion with a splendid fighting innings of 69 not out, and at the close South Africa needed 37 runs to win with three wickets in hand. The cares of captaincy, however, appeared to weigh heavily upon him when he led the South African team in Australia the following winter. Although he maintained a high standard in wicket-keeping, he was nothing like so successful with the bat, his 10 innings in the Test matches producing no more than 155 runs and his aggregate for the whole tour being only 642. Last summer, on his second visit to England when he acted as vice-captain, Cameron stood out as one of the great personalities of the South African team. Most memorable of the many fine innings he played was that at Lord's when by his plucky batting he demoralised England bowlers who before he went in had got rid of four batsmen for 98 runs. Cameron's powerful driving and pulling captured the imagination of everyone; in the course of an hour and three-quarters he scored 90 out of 126. Against Yorkshire he hit one over from Verity for 30 runs and at Scarborough he finished the tour with another superb display of joyous batting in the innings of 160.

In no sense could Cameron be described as a mere "slogger". He combined fine technique with calculated hitting; when necessary he could adapt his game and discipline himself to the need for more restrained methods. Always a firm believer in making the bat hit the ball, he came down much harder on it that the average batsman. Blessed with power of wrist and forearms, he could drive and pull without appearing to use very much effort. In the Tests last summer he scored 306 runs (average 38) and for all games his aggregate was 1,655 and his average 41.37.

Cameron, for all his fearless hitting, will be chiefly remembered for his high place among wicket-keepers not only of South Africa but in his generation. His stumping of a batsman has been likened to the "nonchalent gesture of a smoker flicking the ash from a cigarette"—an apt simile of the speed and art of his deeds. Cameron's concentration upon his job was always evident; some of his stumping efforts dazzled the eyesight. To place him second only as a wicket-keeper to Oldfield is not undue praise. He was neither flamboyant nor noisy and he took the ball cleanly; in fact, his style may be described as the perfection of ease and rapidity without unnecessary show. Last season he stumped 21 batsmen and caught 35: in the final Test when only six England wickets fell he made two catches and stumped Hammond and Leyland beautifully. Cameron was a very fine personality, one who enriched the game and whose manliness and popularity extended far beyond the cricket field. The passing of this charming fellow was a cruel loss not only to the game but to all who knew him.

CAMERON, Dr. John Joseph, who died in Jamaica in December, 1954, aged 72, toured England with the West Indian team under the captaincy of H. G. B. Austin in 1906. Captain of Jamaica in 1910, he played for London County with Dr. W. G. Grace. He was the father of J. H. Cameron, who played for Taunton School, Cambridge University, Somerset and the West Indies.

CAMPBELL, Gerald Victor, who died in March, 1950, aged 65, was in the Eton XI of 1902 and played once for Surrey. For Sussex Martlets he took over 1,000 wickets, and, after the first World War, in which he served as a Captain in the 5th Batt., The Rifle Brigade, he acted for a time as secretary, captain and match manager.

CAMPBELL, Col. Ian Maxwell, who died at Amersham on March 6, 1954, aged 83, played under Dr. W. G. Grace for the London County XI and appeared in one match for Middlesex in 1900. For many years he was a prominent figure in the wine trade.

CAMPBELL, Ian Percy Fitzgerald, who died on December 25, 1963, aged 73, got his Blue as a Freshman at Oxford, playing in the University matches of 1911 and 1912 and playing Association football against Cambridge in the same two years. At Repton he was in the cricket and football XIs from 1906 to 1910, captaining both teams in 1909 and 1910, and also represented the school at fives. He assisted Surrey Second XI as a batsman in 1908 and made occasional appearances for the county side till 1913. Twice in 1911 he appeared against the Players, being a member of the team at the Oval deemed by Sir Pelham Warner to be the best ever to represent the Gentlemen.

CAMPBELL, Thomas, the well-known South African cricketer, was killed in the Natal railway accident which occurred to the up-mail train from Durban at Milndale early on the morning of October 5, 1924. He was born in Natal on February 9, 1882, and was thus over 42 years old at the time of his death. As a batsman he was of small account, although in a Test match against England at Durban in 1909–10 he played an innings of 48, but as a wicket-keeper he gained much note. He made his first appearance for the Transvaal in Currie Cup matches in 1906–07, and four seasons later toured Australia as a member of the South African team. With Percy Sherwell's services at command, however, he took part in none of the Test matches. In 1909–10, when South Africa won the rubber at England's expense, he took part in four games, and in 1912 he visited England. Whilst in this country rheumatism in the hands prevented him from showing his best form, and the only time he took part in one of the Triangular Tournament matches was when he played against England at Lord's. Remembering the circumstances of his death, it is interesting to recall that on December 16, 1916, he fell out of the Cape mail train from Johannesburg. He was picked up in an unconscious condition by the driver of a goods train and was found to be suffering from concussion of the brain and other head injuries. He was removed to Krugersdorp Hospital, and for some time it was doubtful if he would recover.

CANNON, James, for 65 years with M.C.C. at Lord's, died on April 20, 1949, aged 82. He started as a ball-boy for the tennis courts when 12 and held the horses for members when they visited the ground. Gradually he climbed the ladder, becoming boot-boy in the cricket dressing-rooms, and then went into the office where for many years he was chief clerk. A small, popular figure, "Jimmy" Cannon was given the title "King of Lord's," by Sir Pelham Warner. A keen gardener, he was recognised by hundreds of people by his straw-hat and button-hole of sweet-peas, rose or carnation. On his retirement in 1944, he was elected an honorary member of M.C.C.

CAPES, C. J., who was born on January 5, 1898, died in Italy on February 16, 1933. He was in the Malvern College XI in 1914 and 1915, and in the former year obtained 51 wickets, including 11 for 138 v. Repton, while in the following year, he again did well against Repton, taking five for 35 and four for 43. He played most of his cricket for Beckenham, but appeared occasionally for Kent between 1923 and 1928. Medium-pace left-hand, he often bowled really well, and in 1927, with limited opportunities, took 34 wickets at 19.64 apiece. He was a good field and though he did not accomplish very much as a batsman, he was a useful hard-hitter, a notable score being his 65 not out for Kent v. Lancashire at Maidstone in 1928. He was better known as an English International hockey player.

CARBUTT, Major Noel John Obelin, who died at Durban, Natal, on October 31, 1964, aged 68, was a leg-break and googly bowler who played much cricket for the Army. He appeared in one match for Essex in 1923,

when E. Hendren (200 not out) and F. T. Mann (122) put on 256 in a hard-hitting partnership for the fourth Middlesex wicket lasting two hours 20 minutes. Carbutt came in for punishment in the first innings, conceding 127 runs without success, but in the second innings he took two wickets for 23.

SIR NEVILLE CARDUS
Born April 2, 1889; Died February 27, 1975
C.B.E. 1964; Knighted 1967
By Alan Gibson

Sir Neville Cardus died in his sleep after a very short illness. Regular readers will remember a special tribute by John Arlott to Sir Neville which appeared in the 1965 edition.

At a Memorial Service in St. Paul's, Covent Garden, over 720 people joined in an occasion brimming over with joyous music and amusing talk.

The Royal Philharmonic Orchestra, conducted by James Loughran of the Hallé, offered Elgar—Serenade for Strings, and Mozart—the 2nd movements of both the Piano Concerto in A Major, and the Clarinet Concerto, Clifford Curzon played the former.

A Lancashire cricket match was recalled by Miss Wendy Hiller, who rose from a sick bed to read Francis Thompson's poem "At Lord's", and Dame Flora Robson read "Shall I Compare Thee to a Summer's Day".

The Service had great warmth and style, as had Cardus himself. Alan Gibson set the tone on the day with this tribute.

M. H.

Since we are in a church, I thought it proper that we should have a text. Hear then these words from the prophet Blake (I am not sure whether Blake was one of Sir Neville's favourites, though he has recalled how enthusiastically he would join in "Jerusalem" in his days with the Ancoats Brotherhood). Blake wrote, in *Auguries of Innocence*:

"Joy and woe are woven fine,
A clothing for the soul divine;
Under every grief and pine
Runs a thread of silken twine."

On an occasion such as this, joy and woe are inseparable companions: thanksgiving for such a life, sadness that it has ended. But more than that it was the mingling of joy and woe that made Sir Neville such a writer on the sensitivity to the human condition, not least his own; the ability to observe it, and to communicate what he saw, with detachment and yet with passion. His books are full of humour: rich comedy, sometimes almost slapstick, and yet he keeps us hovering between tears and laughter. For always he is conscious, and makes us conscious, of the fragility of happiness, of the passing of time. He loved the good moments all the more avidly because he knew they were fleeting.

There is no need to recite his achievement. His autobiographical books, the crown of his life's work, have done that already. His early cricket books gave him a reputation or "fancy" writing. The words "lyrical", "rhapsodical", were sometimes applied to him, usually by people who would not know a lyric from a rhapsody. These terms were still jostled about long after they had any possible justification, to Sir Neville's wry amusement. His mature prose was marked by charity, balance, and indeed by restraint, though he never shrank from emotion or from beauty. Perhaps George Orwell was as good a writer of prose; or you may think of P. G. Wodehouse, or Bernard Darwin—everyone has his own favourites—but in this century it is not easy to think of many more in the same class.

I remember clearly how I was introduced to Cardus's writing. It was in August, 1935. We were on holiday in Cornwall, at St. Ives, and my father was buying me a book, because of some small family service I had done. I said I would like a cricket book, and the choice narrowed to two: a book of reminiscences attributed to Hendren, I think it was, and "Good Days", by Neville Cardus. I doubt if I had heard of Cardus then, because it was difficult to get The Manchester Guardian in the south of England. I was inclined to Hendren, but father was inclined to Cardus. Father won. We bought "Good Days". Father read it before I did, though I have more than made up for that since. Most of us, perhaps half a dozen times in our lives, read books—not always famous books—which change us, change our thinking, books which open doors, revelatory books. That was one of mine. It was the essay on Emmott Robinson that did it—do you remember it?—when Cardus imagined "that the Lord one day gathered together a heap of Yorkshire clay, and breathed into it, and said 'Emmott Robinson, go on and bowl at the pavilion end for Yorkshire'". And then the next bit, about how Emmott's trousers were always on the point of falling down, and he would remember to grab them just in time.

All cricket writers of the last half century have been influenced by Cardus, whether they admit it or not, whether they have wished to be or not, whether they have tried to copy him or tried to avoid copying him.

He was not a model, any more than Macaulay, say, was a model for the aspiring historian. But just as Macaulay changed the course of the writing of history, Cardus changed the course of the writing of cricket. He showed what could be done. He dignified and illuminated the craft.

It was, it has occurred to me, fortunate for cricket that Bradman and Cardus existed at the same time: fortunate for them, too, since the best of batsmen was recorded by the best of critics. Each was worthy of the other.

In the music of Sir Neville's time, at least in English music, there was never one figure quite so dominant as Bradman. Elgar, Delius and Beecham were, he wrote, "the three most original spirits known in English music since Purcell, if we leave out Sullivan". He said it with a shadow of a wink, as if to say, "and take it out of that". You remember how he described Delius, when he met him in what now seem the improbable surroundings of the Langham Hotel: "His attendant carried him into the sitting-room of his suite and flopped him down on a couch, where he fell about like a rag doll until he was arranged into a semblance of human shape. There was nothing pitiable in him, nothing inviting sympathy in this wreck of a physique. He was wrapped in a monk-like gown, and his face was strong and disdainful, every line on it grown by intrepid living". There is a picture for you; there is a piece of prose for you.

As for Sir Thomas Beecham, he is always bursting out of Cardus's pages and making his own way. It was with some difficulty that Cardus stopped his splendid Aunt Beatrice from conquering his first autobiographical book. He never quite stopped Beecham, any more than Shakespeare ever quite stopped Falstaff taking charge of Henry the Fourth.

Perhaps the most remarkable episode in the life of Cardus, going by what he said himself, and one to which we should refer here, was his conversion. I think the word is properly used: I mean his conversion to music. It was achieved by one of the minor saints: Edward German. He was watching a production of a light opera, Tom Jones, at the Prince's Theatre, Manchester. He had gone there because he was reading Henry Fielding, but, he says, "the music of Edward German got past my ears and entered into my mind behind my back". Only 20 months after that first experience, he was listening to the first performance of Elgar's Symphony in A Flat, and wondering, with the other musicians in the audience, how Elgar was going to cope with such a long first subject.

He used to say that he was baffled that it should have been Edward German who had first revealed the light: yet he should not have been. It was all of a piece with the man and his thought. When Beecham and Mac-Laren, and Bradman and Ranjitsinhji, and Elgar came within the experience of Cardus, he rose to them and did them justice—but he was capable of being moved, such was his sense of humanity, by men who were no more than good county bowlers, Emmott Robinson or Edward German.

"Joy and woe are woven fine". They are not alien, they are complementary, "A clothing for the soul divine". And in another part of that poem, Blake says

"It is right it should be so,
Man was made for joy and woe,
And when this we rightly know,
Safely through the world we go."

I am not sure whether Sir Neville Cardus would approve of that as an epitaph: but he is probably too busy to bother just now, arguing with Bernard Shaw.

CARKEEK, W., died in Melbourne on February 21, 1937. Born on October 17, 1878, he was in his 59th year. When he came to England as deputy wicket-keeper to H. Carter in 1909, he did not take part in a Test match but full responsibility for this arduous task came to him in 1912 when England won the Triangular Tournament. Rather short and sturdily built, Carkeek was sound rather than brilliant. Certainly he did not approach the standard set by Blackham or Kelly; and Carter built up a much higher reputation. A moderate batsman, Carkeek averaged only nine for 29 innings during the 1912 tour and his highest score in six Test matches was six not out. He first played for Victoria in 1904 and in representative cricket for the State he averaged 13.28, for an aggregate of 1,063, with a highest innings of 68.

CARLISLE, Kenneth Ralph Malcolm, who died on July 23, 1983, aged 75, was in the Harrow XI in 1925, 1926 and 1927. In 1925 he made 45 at Lord's, in 1926 62 and in 1927, playing for Sussex in their last match against Essex at Hove, made 34, top score, in the second innings. Making 108 in the Freshmen's match at Oxford next year, he received two invitations to play for the University: the first he had to refuse through injury, the second did not reach him in time. Meanwhile his substitute had made runs in each match and his own chance was gone. He did not make runs later that year for Sussex, nor

in a trial or two for the University in 1929. He was an aggressive batsman, an attractive off-side player, with a good straight drive, who could also score well off his legs. His father captained Oxford in 1905.

CARMICHAEL, Evelyn George Massey, who died on July 14, 1959, aged 88, was educated at Harrow and Oxford without gaining distinction there at cricket. He played for Worcestershire before the county achieved first-class status.

CARMICHAEL, John, who played occasionally for Surrey between 1876 and 1881, died in America on August 24, 1914, as the result of a motor accident. He was born at Howden, in Yorkshire, on July 4, 1858, and educated at Cranleigh, where he was in the XI. *Scores and Biographies* said of him: "Is a promising batsman, bidding fair to become a valuable recruit if he is able to continue the game. He is also a fine field, generally taking cover-point or slip." In all matches for Surrey he made 241 runs with an average of 10.95, his highest innings being 47 against Notts at Trent Bridge in 1877.

CARMODY, Douglas Keith, who captained the Royal Australian Air Force cricket side in England in 1945 and was vice-captain to Lindsay Hassett in the Victory Tests, died of cancer in Sydney on October 21, 1977, aged 58. Shot down over the Dutch coast and made a prisoner of war, Carmody later led Western Australia to their first Sheffield Shield title in 1947–48 and his close-to-wicket field placings took his name as the "Carmody Umbrella".

CARPENTER, Herbert, one of the finest professional batsmen who ever played for Essex, died on December 12, 1933. He was born at Cambridge on July 12, 1869. A son of the famous Robert Carpenter, Herbert resembled his father in style. Very correct in using a straight bat, he was specially strong in back play both when defending or forcing the ball away and in late cutting. Playing first for Essex in 1888, Carpenter helped to make that county good enough to be raised to first-class status in 1895 and he became one of the mainstays in batting. He scored a thousand runs in a season seven times, his highest aggregate being 1,852 in 1901, when he put together a hundred in each innings (127 and 104) for Essex v. Kent at Leyton. He was at his best when Percy Perrin and Charles McGahey came into the county XI and as an opening batsman with his captain, H. G.

Owen, helped materially in many of the large scores made by Essex notably on the Leyton ground. Most memorable was his partnership of 328 with McGahey for the third wicket against Surrey at the Oval in 1904. Ranking with some of the best professional batsmen who never appeared in a Test match, he was chosen during his best seasons for the Players. In 1900, when the Players scored 502 in the last innings and beat the Gentlemen on time by two wickets, he did not come off, but the following year he played innings of 25 and 43 at Lord's and in 1902, 58 and 31 at Scarborough. In all first-class matches he had an aggregate of nearly 15,000 runs and his centuries numbered 25, the highest being 199 for Essex v. Surrey at the Oval in 1904. His final appearance in the game was as recently as 1920, at the age of 51. Besides being an excellent judge of the game, he did admirable service in coaching young cricketers both in Melbourne and at the Essex county ground. The Essex and Lancashire match at Leyton in 1901 was played for his benefit. Carpenter was an uncle of the present-day Essex all rounder, J. O'Connor.

CARPENTER, Robert, One by one the great professional cricketers of the last generation are passing away. Richard Daft, Thomas Hearne, and R. C. Tinley died in 1900, and on July 13, 1901, Robert Carpenter passed away. Though well advanced in years—he was born on November 18, 1830—Carpenter was in fairly good health up to a few days before his death. As an active player, he was only a name to present-day cricketers, but no one who has any knowledge of the history of the game in the last 45 years will need to be told that he was one of the really great batsmen of his time. He was very late in coming before the public, never appearing at Lord's until he was in his 28th year, but his first match—the United XI against the All England XI, in 1858—established his reputation, and he never looked back, remaining in the front rank till he was over 40. For several seasons he and the late Tom Hayward were by general consent the two best bats in England. It was difficult to say which was the better of the two, their methods being so dissimilar, but, though Hayward had an immense superiority in point of style, Carpenter was thought to be the harder man to get out. It is a curious fact that, though they were so closely associated on the cricket field, Carpenter belonged to the United XI and Hayward to George Parr's All England team. Thus, in the matches between the two

XIs, which in the early '60s were the big events of the season, they always played on opposite sides. In conjunction with George Tarrant, they made Cambridgeshire, for a few years, one of the great cricketing counties. Owing to the now half-forgotten schism between the northern and southern players which followed the season of 1862, Hayward and Carpenter did not appear at the Oval for several years, and only played on rare occasions at Lord's, most of their time being given up to matches for the travelling XIs against local Eighteens and XXIIs. If one remembers rightly, however, their complete breach with Lord's only lasted for three or four summers. The quarrel was finally made up in 1870, and great interest was excited when, in company with George Parr, Hayward and Carpenter formally returned to Lord's. All three took part in the Whit-Monday match between North and South, Hayward and Carpenter having played a few weeks before for "Righthand against Lefthanded." Carpenter was still at his best, and in the Whit-Monday match played a magnificent innings of 73 against the bowling of Southerton and Willsher, but Hayward—never a man of robust constitution—had sadly gone off, and retained little beyond his incomparable style. George Parr, playing his last match at Lord's, made a good end, staying in a long time with Carpenter and scoring 41. He had appeared first on the ground 25 years before. As a final proof that all disagreements had been healed up, the Surrey and Cambridgeshire match was revived for one special occasion at the Oval in 1871, and Hayward and Carpenter, who in their younger days had done great things together on the Surrey ground, recalled pleasant memories by their fine play. Carpenter scored 26 and 87—both times not out—and Hayward, giving at least a suggestion of his former brilliancy, made 33 and 40. The two batsmen went to America with the English XI in the autumn of 1859, and in conjunction with E. M. Grace were the great stars of the splendid XI that toured in Australia under George Parr's captaincy in the winter of 1863–64. At that time both were at the height of their fame. Carpenter was essentially a back player, and rarely went forward except when he meant hitting. No one in the old days of rough wickets at Lord's could come down on a shooter with greater certainty, and W. G. Grace himself scarcely possessed a stronger defence. Though specially noted for his skill on rough grounds, however, Carpenter keenly appreciated a good wicket when he found himself on one, and twice at the Oval he made over a hundred for Players against Gentlemen, scoring 119 in 1860, and 106 in 1861. He and Hayward were in the England team against Surrey, in the memorable match in 1862 in which Willsher was no-balled by John Lillywhite, and they contributed largely to England's total of 503, Carpenter making 94 and Hayward 117. The two cricketers were so closely connected that one never thinks of one without the other. Hayward died in July, 1876, after Carpenter had played in his last big match. Their names live on in the cricket of today, Carpenter's son being the present Essex batsman, and Hayward's nephew the great player in the Surrey XI. Of Carpenter's professional contemporaries in his younger days there are not many left, but Caffyn, George Anderson, and George Atkinson are still surviving. Alfred Shaw, William Oscroft, Tom Emmett, and others often played with him, but they only began their career after he had reached his highest point. Carpenter represented the Players on 18 occasions against the Gentlemen, making his debut in the match in 1859 and appearing for the last time in 1873. He commenced 28 innings, was not out once, and scored 723 runs with an average of 26.77. Mr. E. M. Grace says of Carpenter as a batsman that there never was a finer back player.

Carpenter's principal scores in important matches were as follows:

84, Married v. Single, at the Oval, 1858.
97, United All England XI v. the All England XI, at Lord's, 1859.
*52, H. H. Stephenson's XI v. T. Lockyer's XI, at New York, 1859.
119, Players v. Gentlemen, at the Oval, 1860.
54, Cambridge Town Club v. Cambridge University, at Cambridge, 1861.
57, Cambs. v. Surrey, at Cambridge, 1861.
100, Cambs. v. Surrey, at the Oval, 1861.
51, Players v. Gentlemen, at Lord's, 1861.
106, Players v. Gentlemen, at the Oval, 1861.
62, North v. Surrey, at the Oval, 1861.
55, All England XI v. Twenty of Yorkshire, at Barnsley, 1862.
*63, United All England XI v. All England XI, at Lord's, 1862.
*61, Cambs. v. Kent, at New Brompton, 1862.
80, Cambs. v. Surrey, at Cambridge, 1862.
*91, North v. Surrey, at the Oval, 1862.
94, England v. Surrey, at the Oval, 1862.
78, North v. South, at Manchester, 1863.
60, Cambs. v. M.C.C. and Ground, at Lord's, 1863.
52, North v. South, at Manchester, 1864.
77, Cambs. v. Cambridge University, at Cambridge, 1865.
134, The All England XI v. Yorkshire, at Sheffield, 1865.
*97, Cambs. v. Yorkshire, at Bradford, 1866.
57, Cambs. v. Notts, at Nottingham, 1866.
73, North v. South, at Lord's, 1870.
75, North v. South, at Canterbury, 1870.
*87, Cambridge v. Surrey, at the Oval, 1871.
*72, Players v. Gentlemen, at the Oval, 1871.
73, Players v. Gentlemen, at Brighton, 1871.
67, An England XI v. Cambridge University, at Cambridge, 1872.
71, North v. South, at the Oval, 1872.
57, North v. South, at Canterbury, 1872.

CARR, Arthur William, who collapsed and died after shovelling snow at his home at West Witton, Yorkshire, on February 7, 1962, aged 69, was a celebrated Nottinghamshire and England captain. Born at Mickleham, Surrey, he was educated at Sherborne where he was captain of every game except cricket. Nevertheless he earned an early reputation as a cricketer. He headed the school averages in 1910 with 638 runs at 45.47 per innings and took with fast bowling 32 wickets for 15.06 runs each; the following year, with the aid of an innings of 224, he aveaged 62. While still at school he made a few appearances for Nottinghamshire and in 1913, at the age of 18, he gave a display of that strong-driving, attacking play which always characterised his cricket when he hit 169 against Leicestershire at Trent Bridge. He and G. M. Lee (200 not out) shared in a stand of 333 in just over three hours.

Not till he took over the captaincy in 1919—a position he occupied till 1934, when he gave up, following a heart attack—did he occupy a regular place in the county XI. Then, with improved judgment allied to his forcing methods, he became a highly valuable batsman. In each of 11 seasons he exceeded 1,000 runs, his most successful being that of 1925 when, with the help of seven centuries, including his highest—206 against Leicestershire at Leicester—he aggregated 2,338 runs with an average of 51.95. That summer he hit no fewer than 48 sixes. During his first-class career he made 21,884 runs, average 31.12, took 28 wickets at 38.17 apiece and, an exceptionally alert fieldsman anywhere near the wicket, held 361 catches.

Carr played for England on 11 occasions. He toured South Africa under F. T. Mann in 1922–23, taking part in all five Test matches; he led his country in four games against Australia in 1926 till he was superseded by A. P. F. Chapman at the Oval—a decision which aroused much controversy—and in 1929 he was recalled to the leadership for the last two matches with South Africa, replacing J. C. White, captain in the first three. In 13 Test innings he hit 237 runs, with a top score of 63 at Johannesburg, average 19.75. He made a number of appearances for Gentlemen against Players between 1919 and 1929.

Of somewhat stern appearance, but kind and generous at heart and a lover of cricket, Carr was a man of forthright views. He was specially outspoken in defence of H. Larwood and W. Voce, his team-mates who were principals in the "body-line" tour of Australia in 1932–33. During his long reign as captain he led Nottinghamshire to first place among the counties in 1929—the last time they headed the Championship.

CARR, Austin Michael, who died on December 20, 1946, aged 49, played a little for Worcestershire in 1921 and 1922. A master at Abbesley Hall School, Abbesley.

CARR, Douglas Ward, who died in a nursing home at Sidmouth on March 23, 1950, at the age of 78, was one of the most remarkable cricketers at the start of the century. He was an unknown bowler when, at the age of 37, he entered first-class cricket. Originally an ordinary fast-medium bowler, Carr developed and practised the googly, then almost unknown, and his arrival with this unorthodox type of bowling created consternation among batsmen.

In his first match that season of 1909 he took seven Oxford wickets for Kent at a cost of 95 runs. So impressed were the selectors that he was invited to play for Gentlemen against Players at the Oval and Lord's. Realising that they had discovered a bowler out of the ordinary, the selectors then chose him as one of the England party to attend Manchester for the fourth Test match against Australia.

Because the ground was considered too soft for his bowling, Carr was not included in the final XI, but he won a place in the last Test at the Oval. His start was dramatic, for, opening the England attack, he dismissed S. E. Gregory, M. A. Noble and W. W. Armstrong for a combined total of 18 runs. Unfortunately for England he tired and was kept on too long. His first innings figures were five for 146 in 34 overs, and he took two for 136 in 35 overs in the second innings. Even so he showed his immense possibilities, and at the end of that season he took eight for 105 in the match and helped Lord Londesborough's XI to victory over the Australians.

Born at Cranbrook in Kent on March 17, 1872, Carr went to Sutton Valence School and then to Brasenose College, Oxford. He took part in little cricket at the University because of a football injury to his knee. He did most of his early bowling in club cricket in Kent.

Carr showed that his remarkable entry into big cricket was no mere fluke, for in 1910 he headed the Kent bowling averages. He did not join the side until the end of July, but took 60 wickets in Championship matches at an average of 12.16 runs apiece. He fully maintained his form up to 1914, when war intervened and he dropped out of first-class cricket. He enjoyed a particularly successful time in 1912, when he again headed the Kent bowling with 49 wickets for 9.59 runs each. In his brief first-class career of six years Carr took 334 wickets with an average of 16.84.

CARR, Flight Lieut. Harry Lascelles, died in a London nursing home after an operation on August 12, 1943. He and his twin brother, sons of Sir Emsley Carr, played in the Clifton XI from 1924 to 1926. They were also in the Rugby football Fifteen. In his third match against Tonbridge at Lord's, Harry Carr played a good forcing innings of 56 on a pitch recovering from rain. A useful wicket-keeper, he appeared occasionally for Glamorgan from 1931 to 1934. He excelled at golf and billiards, representing Cambridge at both these games. A member of the *News of the World* staff with his father, he joined the R.A.F. and served in the Intelligence Branch for two and a half years until incapacitated by ill-health.

CARRICK, James Stewart, one of the best batsmen Scotland ever produced, was born in Glasgow on September 6, 1855, and died at Seattle on January 2, 1923. He was a left-handed batsman, and when at the wicket took guard for the leg-stump only. He could hit freely, bowl slows (varying pitch and pace), and field well. His first appearance at Lord's was in June, 1882, for M.C.C. and Ground v. Nottinghamshire, and three years later he came suddenly into note by making 419 not out for West of Scotland against

Priory Park at Chichester, then the largest individual score on record. On that occasion he batted for 11 hours and a quarter, gave only two real chances, hit an eight (to square-leg), two sixes, two fives, 30 fours, and made 326 for the first wicket with A. D. R. Thompson (112). The total obtained by the side was 745 for four wickets. He did not take part in many matches of the first importance, but as early as May, 1871, when only 15 years of age, he represented XXII of Scotland against England at Edinburgh. Had he been identified with one of the first-class counties he would probably have performed well in the best company. His 112 for Scotland at Glasgow in 1889 was the only three-figure innings played against Nottinghamshire bowling between 1887 and 1890. He was also a capital football player, assisting Glasgow v. Edinburgh and Scotland v. England, and he excelled at golf and curling. He was educated at Glasgow Academy and subsequently joined the Caledonian C.C. Between 1876 and 1881 he played cricket but seldom. His portrait and biography appeared in *Cricket* of September 24, 1885, and the *Scottish Cricket Annual* for 1885–86.

CARRIS, Harold Edward, who died after a long illness on July 29, 1959, aged 50, was in the Mill Hill XI as an all-rounder from 1925 to 1927. He got his Blue for Cambridge in 1930, in which season he made his highest score in first-class cricket, 98, for the University against H. D. G. Leveson Gower's XI, at Eastbourne. He and F. R. Brown added 202 for the fifth wicket, a record which stood for more than 20 years. A free-scoring left-hander, Carris played a few times for Middlesex between 1928 and 1933. He played as a wing three-quarter in the University Rugby match of 1929 and also assisted Middlesex.

CARROLL, F. H., who was Hon. Secretary of Devon in 1936–37, died in June, 1950, at Sidmouth. He was the son of the Rev. S. W. Featherstone and changed his name to Carroll. A splendid batsman and wicket-keeper, he played for Devon from 1906 to 1934, his highest score being 232 against Berkshire in 1912.

CARROLL, Sidney Joseph, who died at Willoughby, his birthplace, on October 12, 1984, after a long illness, was considered by his contemporaries to be one of the best batsmen never to have played for Australia. He played 36 Sheffield Shield matches for New South Wales, thirteen as captain, and scored 2,466 runs at an average of 43.26, including six hundreds. He was one of the most attractive stroke-makers of his time, forming, with W. Saunders, a fine opening partnership for New South Wales, whom he served as a selector from 1968–72. His top score was 126 against Queensland in 1952–53.

CARROLL, Thomas Davis, who died at Hobart on June 3, 1957, following a road accident, aged 73, was one of the best-known cricketers and cricket administrators in Tasmania in the early part of the century. He played in 10 matches for the State as a fast-medium right-arm bowler between 1908 and 1922, taking 16 wickets for 48.3 runs each. He was Tasmanian member of the Australian Board of Control for two years after 1929, and was, in 1930, appointed an Australian Selector, a position he was compelled to relinquish within a year because his employment was transferred to Western Australia. Carroll was opening bowler for Tasmania in 1912 when M.C.C. scored 574 for four wickets in four and a half hours, of which F. E. Woolley made 305 not out.

CARSON, Major W. N., M.C., died of wounds in the autumn, 1944, aged 28. A hard-hitting left-handed batsman for Auckland, he failed to show his best form during the tour of the 1937 New Zealand team in England, his best scores being 85 against Surrey in the first match and 86 at Northampton; he averaged only 19 for the whole tour and did not play in any of the Tests. In January of the previous home season he, making 290, shared in a world record third-wicket partnership of 445 with P. E. Whitelaw (195) for Auckland against Otago, at Dunedin.

CARTER, Alfred S., a veteran member of the East Melbourne C.C., died on June 7, 1920. For the club he made 9,801 runs, with an average of 29.22 and took 285 wickets at a cost of 17.15 runs each. He was also a brilliant fieldsman and a useful wicket-keeper. In 1896 he won the Amateur Championship of Victoria at skittles, and a year later visited America as a member of Frank Laver's team of Australian baseballers.

CARTER, Claude Paget, who died in South Africa on November 8, 1952, aged 71, was one of the most dangerous left-arm slow bowlers on matting in the history of South African cricket. Born on April 23, 1881, he first played for Natal when 16. In all he took

155 wickets, average 16.50, a total exceeded by only four bowlers, E. P. Nupen, J. Waddington, J. H. Sinclair and J. P. McNally. He performed his best feat in 1921 when, bowling unchanged for Natal with J. L. Cox, he returned the remarkable analysis of 11—5—11—6 and so played the leading part in the dismissal of Border for 23, a total which remains the lowest recorded in the Currie Cup. Carter represented South Africa on 10 occasions, seven against England and three against Australia. He took part in the 1912 Triangular Tournament and visited England again as a member of H. W. Taylor's team, finishing top of the averages with 65 wickets, average 19.86. Following that tour he returned to England and acted as a professional in Cornwall, returning to South Africa just before the outbreak of the Second World War. In Test matches he took 28 wickets at a cost of 24.78.

CARTER, The Rev. Edmund Sardinson, died at Scarborough on May 23, 1923. Mr. Carter will be remembered not so much for what he did in the cricket field as for his personality. In whatever company he found himself he could not help being a prominent figure. Retaining as long as his health lasted the keenest interest in the game, he had a better collection of cricket stories than any of his contemporaries except, possibly, E. M. Grace, who could never be persuaded to let his be printed. No doubt the best of Mr. Carter's tales are those published in his interview in *Old English Cricketers*, but he had an inexhaustible store. Going up from Durham Grammar School Mr. Carter was a double Blue at Oxford, playing in the XI in 1866 and 1867 and rowing in the boat in 1867 and 1868. He had no chance of being in the XI in 1868, as a severe attack of pleurisy compelled him to take a sea voyage to Australia. While in Sydney he played for Victoria against New South Wales, and with scores of 16 and 63 (the highest innings on either side) helped to win the game by 78 runs. The match has, in the historic sense, a special interest. In Frank Allan, who took eight wickets for 20 runs and got New South Wales out for 37, Mr. Carter saw the first of the long line of great Australian bowlers. I have often wondered whether at the time he had any idea of what Allan's success portended.

Without being in the front rank Mr. Carter was a very useful all-round cricketer—good both as batsman and fast bowler. In his two matches against Cambridge at Lord's his scores were: four and 15 and 26 and 13.

Taking two wickets for four runs and two for 13 he had a share in Oxford's narrow win in 1866. He played occasionally for Yorkshire between 1876 and 1881, taking part in 14 matches. His best score for the county was 39 not out in 1878. A member for many years of the Yorkshire Committee he was always to be seen at the Scarborough Festival. One incident in his life must be recalled. His old colleague in the Oxford XI, Lord Loreburn, when Lord Chancellor, presented him with a living and in the accompanying letter wrote: "You broke my finger at Oxford but I bear no malice." Mr. Carter was born at Malton on February 3, 1845.—S.H.P.

CARTER, Hanson, regarded in 1909, when he took part in the first of his two tours in England as second only to the great Blackham among Australian wicket-keepers, died on June 8, 1948. Born at Halifax, Yorkshire, on March 15, 1878, he was 70 years old when he passed away at his Sydney home, having retained a close touch with cricket to the end. Altogether he played in 28 Test matches, 21 of them against England. That such a long interval as 12 years occurred between his visits here could be explained by the Triangular Test series in 1912 when Australia did not send nearly their strongest available side, many notable players preferring not to come because South Africa would provide a counter-attraction. Still in regular practice, having helped to win all five matches in the 1920–21 rubber, Carter seemed little below the top of his form and Australia, again captained by W. W. Armstrong, easily retained the honours, three victories coming before England outplayed them in drawn games at Old Trafford and the Oval. Rather short and slight in build Carter did not stand as close to the stumps as some noted keepers have done, but he took the ball with easy discretion, particularly when Cotter, of high speed, bowled his fastest. This was specially noticeable in the Test matches, very few byes swelling the England totals. Of small account as a batsman, Carter could prove useful, and at Leeds, where England were sadly handicapped by the loss of G. L. Jessop, who hurt himself when fielding, he made 30, which helped towards victory by 126 runs in a small scoring match which gave Australia the rubber by two to one, the subsequent two games being drawn. After the 1921 tour he went to South Africa, where Australia have not yet suffered defeat.

CARTER, Wilfred, who was born at Annesley (Notts.) on May 14, 1896, died at

Shrodells Hospital, Watford, on November 1, 1975. The family moved to Bolsover in Derbyshire and Carter first appeared for his adopted county in 1920. His first-class record is 65 matches, 112 innings, 10 not out, 1,812 runs, 145 highest score, 17.76 average; 16 wickets for 707 runs, 44.18 average, 26 catches. Carter's highest score of 145 was made against Leicestershire in July, 1922, when he and A. H. M. Jackson put on 182 for the eighth wicket, a record for the county which still stands. He headed the Derbyshire batting averages that year and also scored 100 not out the following year against Northamptonshire at Chesterfield. He left the staff at the end of the 1924 season but played in four matches in 1926. He was a right hand batsman and bowled slow right "donkey-drops". He joined Watford Football Club in 1920 as a wing half (left), playing in the first ever match at Vicarage Road before Watford became a member of the Football League, and played for five years. He was coach at Repton in 1929 and 1930, and also spent a few years as pro at Drumpellier.

CARTMAN, William, died at Skipton, January 16, 1935, aged 74. Born on June 20, 1861, he played cricket early and was prominently connected with the Skipton Club during many years. For Yorkshire in 1891 he scored 238 runs, average 21.

CARTWRIGHT, Philip, who died in a sanatorium at Virginia Water on November 21, 1955, aged 75, appeared for Sussex between 1905 and 1922. Born at Gibraltar, he was a steady left-hand batsman who played many valuable defensive innings. His best season for the county was that of 1909, when he scored 730 runs, average 24.33, including an innings of 101, his only first-class century, against Leicestershire at Leicester, he and C. L. A. Smith, his captain, sharing in an eighth wicket partnership of 168. *Wisden* referring to Cartwright, said: "He is far better than his somewhat peculiar style might lead one to suppose."

CARTWRIGHT, Vincent Henry, who died on November 25, 1965, aged 83, captained Rugby School at cricket and Rugby football. In the XI in 1900 and 1901, he headed the batting figures with an average of 34.31 and a highest innings of 124 not out in the second year, during which he played in three matches for Nottinghamshire. Going up to Oxford, he did not gain a cricket Blue, but played against Cambridge in the University Rugby matches from 1901 to 1904. He cap-

tained the Dark Blues and also led England, for whom he played as a forward in 14 international matches between 1903 and 1907. In 1928 he became President of the Rugby Football Union.

CASE, Cecil Charles Coles, who died on November 11, 1969, aged 74, rendered good service to Somerset as an amateur batsman between 1925 and 1935. Steady but sure, he scored in all 8,574 runs, average 22.04, and held 44 catches. Twice he exceeded 1,000 runs in a season in Championship matches, his best year being that of 1933, when his aggregate reached 1,027. In 1927 at Taunton, when he made 122 against Gloucestershire, he and J. C. White added 235 together, establishing a fifth-wicket record for the county which still holds good. The highest of Case's nine centuries was 155 against Surrey at the Oval in 1931.

CASE, Thomas (Rugby and Ox. University), born at Liverpool, July 14, 1844, died at Falmouth on October 31, 1925. Giving up the game at 24 he was only a name to the present generation of cricketers, but in his young days he was a first-rate batsman. He was in the Rugby XI in 1862 and 1863, the school being at that time very rich in cricket talent. Going up to Oxford he gained his Blue as a Freshman and was in R. A. H. Mitchell's winning teams at Lord's in 1864–65. Owing to a damaged hand—injured at Southgate two days earlier—he could not play in the University match in 1866, but he reappeared in the finely contested game—won by Cambridge by five wickets—in the following year. He did not do much in his three matches against Cambridge, his scores being 13 and five, 17 and 25, and 24 and 19. While at Rugby he hit up an innings of 170 against the Anomalies. Mr. Case was associated with Middlesex in the earliest days of the County Club, appearing on and off from 1864 to 1868. For Middlesex in 1864 he made his highest score in first-class cricket and in connection with the feat an interesting story may be recalled. Middlesex met the M.C.C. twice and in the first match—at Lord's—they were bowled out by Wootton and Jimmy Grundy for 20, suffering defeat in the end by five wickets. The second match came a week later at the Cattle Market Ground at Islington and R. A. FitzGerald, though he changed over to the Middlesex team himself, naturally chose the M.C.C. XI. According to old Tom Hearne he gave no thought to change bowling, feeling sure from what had happened at Lord's that Grundy and Wootton would do all that was necessary. He was rudely disillusioned. Middlesex scored 411, made the M.C.C. follow on, and won the game in a single innings. Tom Hearne got 125 and Mr. Case 116. As he said to me years afterwards in telling the story of the two matches, Tom Hearne had no fear of Grundy away from Lord's, where in those far-off days the most harmless-looking ball might end up as a dead shooter. All through his long life Mr. Case was a prominent figure at Oxford, being Professor of Moral Philosophy and President of Corpus Christi College. He had been both Treasurer and President of the Oxford University C.C., and his history of the club in *The Jubilee Book of Cricket* was a contribution of the first importance. In an exhaustive notice of him in *The Times* it was said that his death would be mourned by innumerable pupils of all ages. His eldest son, Mr. T. B. Case, was in the Winchester XI in 1887–89 and in the Oxford XI in 1891 and 1892. Another son—Mr. W. S. Case, who died in 1922—also played for Winchester.—S.H.P.

CASE, Thomas Bennett, died near Dublin on November 10, 1941, in his 70th year. In his third year in the Winchester XI, when captain, he scored 61 and 31 against Eton, going in first and literally leading his side to victory by 114 runs. Because of an accident to the Hon. F. J. N. Thesiger, Case completed the Oxford XI in 1891, when Cambridge won by two wickets; next year he was not out with Lionel Palairet, whose 71 was largely responsible for Oxford's victory by five wickets. M. R. Jardine did still more towards the triumph, making 140 and 39. Case scored 29 on the first day, giving useful help to Jardine and V. T. Hill. The match aroused great interest. The aggregate runs, 1,100, far exceeded any previous scoring in the University encounter; Jardine's 179 runs beat the total credited to any batsman hitherto; Cambridge in their follow-on equalled the record total of 388 made in 1872 by the Light Blues, and E. C. Streatfeild hit the third century in the match. Also J. B. Wood, a lob bowler, opened the Oxford attack and, with seven wickets in the two Cambridge innings, was surpassed in this game only by F. S. Jackson, who took eight Oxford wickets.

CASSAN, Ernest John Plantagenet, died by his own hand on December 2, 1904. A capital bowler in his day, he played for Oxford against Cambridge in 1859, taking nine wickets. He was in his 70th year.

CASSATT, Alexander Johnston, the President of the Merion C.C., of Philadelphia from 1896 until his death, was born at Pittsburg on December 8, 1839, and died at Philadelphia on December 28, 1906. His estate was valued at over a hundred million dollars.

CASTENS, Herbert Hayton, born on November 23, 1864, died in London on October 18, 1929, aged 64. A good batsman, when not handicapped by nervousness, and a first-class wicket-keeper, he was in the Rugby XIs in 1882 and 1883, being captain the latter year. In his first game with Marlborough he was clean bowled by the first ball he received in each innings. At Cape Town in 1890–91 he made 165 for Western Province v. Eastern Province, and in 1894 he captained the first South African team to visit England. His experience during the tour was, in many respects, not a happy one. The programme, which was denied first-class rank, had been badly arranged; the team failed to attract the public—the gross gate takings during the trip were less than £500— and, for financial reasons, the side was almost stranded whilst in Ireland. At Rugby football he also gained distinction, playing for Oxford v. Cambridge in 1886 and 1887, as well as for Middlesex and for South v. North.

CASTLE, Sidney, who died at Plymstock, Devon, on December 5, 1937, aged 73, played a few times for Kent from 1890 to 1893. A free scorer on fast wickets, with good style, he made many hundreds for Charlton Park and in August, 1901, he scored four consecutive centuries. In 1892 he played his highest innings, 200, against Surbiton and District.

CASTOR, Brian Kenneth, who died on October 2, 1979, aged 89, will be chiefly remembered as secretary to Essex from 1930–46 and to Surrey from 1947–57. But he was also a very useful cricketer who frequently captained Essex Second XI and made two appearances for the county v. Sir Julien Cahn's XI in 1930 and v. Cambridge in 1932. In the first of these matches his spirited 62 in the second innings undoubtedly saved his side from defeat. From 1942–45 he was a prisoner of the Japanese.

CAT, Peter, whose ninth life ended on November 5, 1964, was a well-known cricket-watcher at Lord's, where he spent 12 of his 14 years. He preferred a close-up view of the proceedings and his sleek, black form could often be seen prowling on the field of play when the crowds were biggest. He frequently appeared on the television screen. Mr. S.C. Griffith, Secretary of the M.C.C., said of him: "He was a cat of great character and loved publicity."

CATERER, T. Ainslie, who died in the last week of August, 1924, aged 65, was a left-handed bowler who had played a few times for South Australia. For many years he was Chairman of the Ground and Finance Committee of Adelaide Oval, and from 1918 to 1921 was Chairman of the Cricket Committee. He was a member of the old Kensington C.C.

CATTERALL, Robert Hector, who died in Johannesburg on January 2, 1961, aged 60, played as a right-handed batsman in 24 Test matches for South Africa against England between 1922 and 1930. In 43 Test innings he scored 1,555 runs, including three centuries, average 37.92. He toured England as a middle-order batsman in 1924, heading the South Africa Test averages with 471 runs, average 67.28. He hit 120 against England at Edgbaston when South Africa, having been dismissed for 30 by A.E.R. Gilligan and M.W. Tate, bowling unchanged, put together a total of 390 in the second innings without avoiding defeat. In the Lord's Test he also scored 120 and at the Oval was dissmissed for 95. Though he was never a good starter, his batting was delightfully free, being marked by beautiful driving and strong hitting to leg. Five years later he visited England again, this time as an opening batsman of much less attractive style. Again he did well in the Test matches, especially at Edgbaston where he played innings of 67 and 98 and shared in first-wicket partnerships of 119 and 171 with B. Mitchell. This crinkly-haired Rhodesian was also a fleet-footed and efficient deep fieldsman.

CATTLEY, Stephen Wildman, who died at Sparsholt, Winchester, on April 11, 1925, was born at Croydon on October 28, 1860. *Scores and Biographies* (xiv–692) said of him: "Is a good average batsman, hitting freely, while in the field he was at first wicket-keeper for Eton, and then cover-point or mid wicket off." He was a member of the Eton XIs of 1878 and 1879, and in his two games with Harrow scored 32 and 11, five and 29. Against Winchester in 1879—he did not take part in the match of 1878—he

made six and 13. Appearing in 24 games for Surrey between 1879 and 1883, he obtained 602 runs with an average of 14.33, his highest innings being 89 v. Sussex at Hove in the last-mentioned year. He was brother of the late Mr. A.C. Cattley of the Eton teams of 1878 and 1879.

CATTLEY, Wildman, born 1837, died December 7, 1918. Mr. Cattley was one of the most familiar figures in the Pavilion at the Oval. He followed his brother, the late Mr. Mark Cattley, as treasurer of the Surrey club and remained in office for many years, retiring after the season of 1905. Though never distinguished as a cricketer Mr. Cattley played the game in his young days and took part in many a pleasant match with the Walkers at Southgate. Fond of racing, as well as of cricket, he never missed seeing the Derby.

CATTON, James A.H., the well-known cricket and football journalist, died on August 21, 1936, aged 76. When beginning his career on the *Nottingham Guardian*, Sir James M. Barrie was a colleague. Catton's close association with the sporting side of newspaper work started in Lancashire and as Editor of the *Athletic News* he became famous for his writings under the name of "Tityrus". Always looking for the best that happened, he was absolutely fair if caustic in his criticism and "Jimmy" Catton wrote with easy clearness that made his descriptions of cricket and football delightful to read. Under his control the *Athletic News* was for many years the leading authority on Association football and in the summer Catton's reports of matches and articles on cricket never failed to interest the reader. Season after season he travelled all over the country with the Lancashire XI and when he retired from the Editorship every County Cricket Club and Football League Club subscribed to a testimonial. After leaving Manchester, Mr. Catton contributed to many papers, including the *Evening Standard* and *Observer*, until shortly before he passed away from the effects of long-standing heart trouble.

When Mr. F.S. Ashley-Cooper died early in 1932, Mr. Catton undertook the onerous duty of keeping the records in *Wisden* up to date and his desire to complete this work for the present issue was one of his last cares. A regular attendant at Test matches almost from the time that the Australians first came to England, he was steeped in cricket lore. An indefatigable worker, he kept a file of the doings of every player and in this way built up a remarkable memory which made him a walking encyclopaedia of cricket and football. At the time of his death he was President of the "25" Club—restricted to journalists who have reported at least 25 Test matches between England, Australia, and South Africa.

An ardent Freemason in recent years, Mr. Catton was a Past Master of the Alfred Robbins Lodge.

CAULFIELD, Frank, was killed in a motor accident at Blœmfontein on May 22, 1936, aged 42. He played for Orange Free State in 1925–26, and against Western Province scored 56 not out, assisting L. R. Tuckett (70) to make a South African last wicket record partnership of 129.

CAVE, Walter Frederick, who died on January 7, 1939, aged 75, was in the Eton XI of 1880 and two following seasons. He played his best innings, 49, on his last appearance against Harrow. In 1883 he appeared a few times in the Gloucestershire XI, his highest score being 42 against Surrey at the Oval. A good defensive batsman he was strong in off-side strokes. In the field he showed special smartness at long-leg. An architect of distinction, he designed many notable buildings, especially some for music, and was credited with the idea of placing candle holders on pianos. A good athlete, he won the 100 yards race and other events at Eton.

CAVE, William Francis, died at Bexhill, September 6, 1946, aged 83. Eton XI 1880–82; Gloucestershire 1883. Architect.

CAZALET, Major Peter Victor Ferdinand, who died on May 29, 1973, aged 66, was a fine all-round sportsman. In the XI at Eton as opening batsman in 1925 and 1926, he scored 100 not out against Harrow at Lord's in the second year, when he headed the averages with 53.66. Quick on his feet, he timed the ball splendidly, especially his on-side strokes, and possessed a sound defence. Though he gained a Blue at Oxford in 1927, he did not reproduce his earlier form. He also represented the University at racquets, lawn tennis and squash. Between 1927 and 1932 he turned out on occasion for Kent. He showed much promise as a steeplechase jockey till a bad fall ended his career in 1938. He then took to National Hunt training and was in charge of the horses of Queen Elizabeth the Queen Mother for 25 years. Of his 1,100 winners, more than 250 wore the Queen Mother's colours.

He was High Sheriff of Kent in 1960 and in the following year became a Deputy-Lieutenant.

CAZALET, Col. Victor Alexander, M.P., who was killed near Gibraltar on July 5, 1943, in the aeroplane accident with General Sikorski, Prime Minister and Commander-in-Chief of Poland, held a high place among games players.

For the Eton XI of 1915 he averaged 27.37 in the first war-time season and was described as "a determined player." The principal match that year was at Winchester, where the home side fell for 24 runs, C. J. Hambro taking seven wickets for six; the highest score was four and extras numbered nine. Cazalet went in first for the visitors and made 11; Eton won the match, limited to one day, by 74 runs on the first innings. He played for Oxford at tennis, lawn tennis and racquets, and excelled at "squash," winning the amateur championship four times. In 1927 he was a member of the English team which won the international squash racquets trophy.

CHADWICK, Edmund Leach, born August 31, 1847, died at Parkstone, Dorset, August 6, 1918. Mr. Chadwick, without ever rising to eminence, was in his day a very good batsman. He played for Lancashire, making his first appearance at Lord's for the county against the M.C.C. in 1875, when he scored 19 and nine. In July, 1877, in a local match between Castleton and Rusholm he made 213 not out. He was educated at Bruce Castle School, Tottenham, and Marlborough, but did not get a place in the Marlborough XI.

CHADWICK, 2nd Lieut. R. M. (R.G.A.), died of wounds on May 12, 1915. He was in the Rugby XI in 1902 and two following years, and in his three matches v. Marlborough, at Lord's, made 94 runs in five innings, his highest score being 46 in 1904. At times he bowled well, though never more than as a change.

CORRECTION. In *Wisden* for 1916 it was stated that 2nd Lieut. R. M. Chadwick (Rugby XI, 1902), died of wounds on May 12, 1915. Mr. Chadwick is happily alive and well. The mistake probably arose through some confusion of initials.

CHADWYCK-HEALEY, Hilary Philip, who died on March 30, 1976, at the age of 88, was joint-founder with Sir Henry Leveson Gower in 1924 of the Grasshoppers, of which he was

Secretary from 1924 to 1932 and President from 1954 to 1964. As a cricketer his enthusiasm greatly exceeded his skill, but he was quite well known as a composer of church music.

CHALK, Flight Lieut. Frederick Gerald Hudson, D.F.C., missing from February, 1943, was in January, 1944, officially "presumed killed." His tragic and uncertain death at the age of 32 was deplored by all who knew him and everyone interested in cricket. For Uppingham, Oxford and Kent he batted and fielded so brilliantly that he became an attractive figure whenever he played.

In 1928 he headed his school averages with 44; gained his Oxford Blue as a Brasenose Freshman in 1931 and, when captain of his University in 1934, played a brilliant innings of 108 at Lord's against Cambridge. Oxford won by eight wickets when Chalk first played against Cambridge and the next three engagements were drawn, so that he was never on the losing side in the University match. He averaged 38.84 for Kent after the Oxford term in 1934. Scholastic duties limited his appearances but his county form improved, and in 1937 he gave a splendid display in a fighting innings of 107 against Middlesex at Lord's where, on a worn pitch, he used the cut, pull and drive in delightful style; three of his strokes cleared the boundary and he hit 10 fours. Each season when county captain he scored over a thousand runs with averages of 25.34 and 30.66.

He played his highest innings, 198, at Tonbridge against Sussex in 1939 when he averaged 30.66, but perhaps his finest effort was against Yorkshire at Dover a week before the outbreak of war: making 115 not out, he carried his bat through an innings of 215 after Kent followed-on. This did not avert defeat, but five days later his 94 helped materially in victory over Lancashire by five wickets—a grand finish to a cricket career of high merit. In that last season of first-class cricket which we have known, Kent, thanks to his leadership in going for victory, drew only three of 27 games.

Of his capacity in captaincy Mr. G. de L. Hough, the Kent secretary, wrote: "Gerry Chalk will be greatly missed by his many cricket friends—especially in Kent. Apart from his ability as a batsman and fielder, he was an excellent captain in the field. The way in which he nursed the bowling in 1939 was outstanding. He nearly always managed to keep one bowler fresh for use at a pinch, and I think it is fair to say that our rise in the Championship from 12th in 1938 to fifth was largely due to this, and his example in, and placing of, the field."

Skilful defence, besides ability to score at every opportunity, made his batting especially valuable, while his speed and accuracy as an off-side fieldsman maintained the high reputation characteristic of the best Kent amateurs for generations.

Joining the Honourable Artillery Company as a gunner when war broke out, Chalk transferred to the R.A.F. as a rear gunner and won the D.F.C. in June, 1941, when returning from a raid on Hanover. As described officially, "Chalk by his cool and accurate fire undoubtedly saved his aircraft and probably destroyed the attacker—an Me. 110." Following a pilot's course he was promoted Flight Lieutenant and became a Spitfire flight commander.

Chalk married a daughter of G. N. Foster, of the Worcestershire family, who also played for Kent, as did his son, P. G. Foster, under his brother-in-law's captaincy.

CHALLEN, John Bonamy, died at Eastbourne on June 5, 1937, aged 74. In the Marlborough XI of 1879, he played for Somerset from 1880 to 1909 but could not give much time to County Cricket. He did best in 1893 when he made 108 against Sussex at Taunton in two hours by the free methods which he usually adopted; but in one of Somerset's sensational home matches which ended in the defeat of Surrey by 130 runs almost on the stroke of time he batted three hours and a quarter for 89. That was in 1891 when Somerset, quite on their merits, had reached first-class status by a diplomatic arrangement of fixtures. A clever Association forward Challen played several times for Wales and for Corinthians when the amateurs were at their best.

CHALLENOR, George, the West Indies batsman of high renown, died at Barbados on July 30, 1947, aged 59. He visited England three times, first in 1906 when only 17, and gave promise of future triumphs by scoring 108 at Nottingham. He excelled for the team which came in 1923, scoring 1,556 runs—more than twice as many as anyone else in the side obtained—average 51.86, with eight three-figure innings, the highest being 155 not out against Surrey at the Oval. With 66 out of 121, which gave his side victory by 10 wickets, Challenor made his match aggregate 221 without being dismissed; his batting in each innings was brilliant. Generally he was regarded as reaching the standard set by the best English batsmen that season, only Hendren and Mead returning higher averages. He was elected to membership of M.C.C. as a special compliment, although unable to take part in the customary qualifying matches. West Indies did not play England that season, but in 1928 they lost all three matches in the rubber by an innings. Challenor did not find his former brilliance, his highest score being 97 in an aggregate of 1,074, average 27.53, and in six innings against England his total runs reached only 101. Of medium height and powerful build, he drove to the off and cut with perfectly timed strokes, besides punishing any loose balls with pulls or non-drives. His admirable batting did much toward raising cricket in West Indies to Test match standard.

CHALMERS, Thomas, born at Glasgow on March 20, 1850, died there, in a nursing home, on May 25, 1926, aged 76. He was an excellent batsman with many strokes, a useful medium-paced bowler, and a good field either at cover or at the wicket. Besides playing for Glasgow Academy, West of Scotland, Glasgow Academicals and the Caledonian C.C., he appeared in matches of a representative nature, doing well against the All England and United South of England XIs, M.C.C. and the Australians. For the West of Scotland in 1878 he played a good innings of 38 against the bowling of Spofforth, Garrett, Allan and Boyle. Five years earlier he had scored 157 for Glasgow v. Edinburgh at Partick. As a Rugby footballer he also gained considerable fame, playing for Scotland in 1871, in the first of the series of matches against England and keeping his place in the Scotland Twenty for the next five years. He married a sister of Messrs. John and Stewart Carrick.

CHAMPION, Albert, died at Sheffield on June 30, 1909. He was born at Hollins End, near Handsworth, Yorkshire, on December 27, 1851, and between 1876 and 1880 played 25 innings for his county with an average of 7.09, and took one wicket for 17 runs. Being engaged later by the Longsight C.C. he appeared for Lancashire in 1886, but scored only four runs in two innings. *Scores and Biographies* (xiii–905) described him as "A good batsman, left-handed, but a right middle-paced, round-armed bowler."

CHAPLIN, Herbert Percy, who died on March 6, 1970, aged 87, played as an amateur batsman for Sussex between 1905 and 1914, being captain for the last five seasons. He did not find a place in the XI while at Harrow, but he obtained 6,230 runs for the county, average 24.41, hitting six centuries. His highest innings was 213 not out off the Nottinghamshire bowling at Hove in 1914, when, with 1,158 runs, average 33.08, he enjoyed his most successful season.

CHAPMAN, Arthur Percy Frank, who died in Alton Hospital, Hampshire, on September 16, 1961, aged 61, will always be remembered as a player who brought to cricket a light-hearted air seldom encountered in these days and as an England captain of great personal charm who got the best out of the men under him. He had been in ill health for some years. As a tall, polished left-handed batsman, who, excelling in the off-drive and leg-side strokes, was generally willing and able to attack the bowling, he scored 16,309 runs, average 31.97, in a first-class career dating from 1920 to 1939. Of his 27 centuries, the highest and certainly one of the best was 260 for Kent against Lancashire, that season's Champions, at Maidstone in 1927. The position when he went in was far from encouraging, half the side being out for 70 runs. Yet he and G. B. Legge (101) assailed an attack including such men as E. A. McDonald, the Australian fast bowler, Richard Tyldesley and F. M. Sibbles with such vigour that in two and a half hours they put on 284 runs. Percy Chapman's 260, scored in just over three hours and containing five sixes and 32 fours, typified his outlook on the game. A defensive policy was abhorrent to his nature, whether batting or fielding, and besides being a punishing though never reckless hitter, he made a name as a silly point, cover or slip of amazing speed and brilliancy.

Born at Reading, Berkshire, he was in the Uppingham XI for four years from 1916 to 1919, being captain in the last two, and soon attracted attention with splendid performances. In 1917 he headed the school batting figures with 668 runs in 10 innings and an average of 111.33. After an indifferent start to the season, he wound up with 66, 206, 160, 81 and 114 in five innings, being not out on four occasions and run out on the other! In those days, too, he met with success as a bowler, first slow left-arm and then fast-medium. Not surprisingly, especially as he took 118 from the Essex bowling at Fenner's on his first-class debut, he gained his Blue as a Freshman at Cambridge in 1920, scoring 27 against Oxford and being chosen for the Gentlemen at Lord's. Against Oxford in

1921 he obtained 45 and next season helped Cambridge to a handsome victory with a scintillating innings of 102 not out. In this latter season he took part in that famous match at Eastbourne where an England XI defeated Warwick Armstrong's hitherto unbeaten Australians by 28 runs, justifying the assertion of A. C. MacLaren, maintained throughout the summer, that he could pick a side good enough to overcome the touring team.

Chapman played with distinction for Berkshire before qualifying for Kent in 1924, and he became one of the few players to appear for England while taking part in Minor Counties' cricket. He turned out for England 26 times in all, 17 of them as captain, in which role he was only twice on the losing side. Twice he went to Australia, under A. E. R. Gilligan in 1924–25 and as leader of the 1928 side who, regarded as probably the best in fielding ever sent out, won the Test rubber by four wins to one. Though he played several good innings for his country, sharing stands of 116 with E. Hendren in 1926 and 125 with G. O. Allen in 1930, both at Lord's against Australia, he only once scored a century in a Test match. Then, in hitting 121 against Australia at Lord's in 1930, he achieved a triple performance never before accomplished, for on the same ground he had previously reached three figures in both the University and—in 1922—the Gentlemen v. Players match, a fixture in which he figured 19 times. He captained Kent from 1931 to 1936.

Tributes included:

S. C. Griffith, Assistant-Secretary, M.C.C.: "I will always remember him for his debonair and aggressive approach to the game and as a great fielder."

Sir John Hobbs: "I well remember the surprise caused by the appointment of Percy Chapman as the England captain for the final Test against Australia at the Oval in 1926. He was only 25 and all the team liked him. He was not a disciplinarian like his predecessors and he did not hesitate to seek advice. He often talked to me about tactics on the field and he set a great example by his brilliant catching in the slips. The Australian crowds loved him during the tour of 1928–29, when he made us a happy team."

G. Duckworth, former Lancashire and England wicket-keeper: "He was a most delightful gentleman and an ideal captain. He had such a persuasive charm as a leader that you could not help trying your utmost for him."

W. J. Fairservice, former Kent player:

"Percy Chapman and Frank Woolley, two left-handers, were two of the greatest cricketers in the game."

CHAPMAN, Horace William, died at Durban on December 1, 1941, aged 51. A useful batsman and googly bowler for Natal Currie Cup teams between 1911 and 1922, he twice represented South Africa in Test matches against England at Durban in February, 1914, and against Australia at Durban in 1921.

CHAPMAN, John, who died on April 14, 1896, at the advanced age of 82, was a very notable personage in Nottingham cricket circles in the '40s. In those now rather distant days he played against Sussex, Sheffield, the M.C.C. and more than one England XI, and met with considerable success. He died at Gainsborough, where he had for about 50 years been in practice as a veterinary surgeon.

CHAPMAN, John, who died at his home at Dunford Bridge, near Sheffield, on August 12, 1956, aged 79, captained Derbyshire for three seasons from 1910 to 1912. Educated at Uppingham, he appeared for Sheffield Collegiate and Barnsley, and captained the Yorkshire second team before joining Derbyshire, for whom he played from 1909 to 1920. An attractive batsman and excellent cover-point, Chapman (165) shared with A. R. Warren (123) in a ninth-wicket partnership of 283—a world's record—against Warwickshire at Blackwell in 1910 after Derbyshire followed-on 242 behind. They easily saved the game. Chapman's other first-class century was also against Warwickshire—198 at Coventry in 1909.

CHAPMAN, Thomas Alan, died in Marandellas, Rhodesia, on February 19, 1979, aged 59. Making his first appearance for Leicestershire in 1946, he showed promise as a batsman and was also a fine outfield. In 1947 he made the highest score of his career, 74 v. Warwickshire at Leicester; he and L. A. Hales put on 126 for the seventh wicket, and had much to do with their side's victory. He left the county at the end of the 1950 season and settled in Rhodesia, for whom he appeared in 1952.

CHAPMAN, Walter W., who died on November 23, 1931, aged 51, was partner with Victor Trumper in many rapid-scoring feats for Paddington in Sydney cricket. The two men put together 330 for the first wicket

v. Redfern at Hampden Oval in 110 minutes in 1905, Trumper scoring 215 in all and Chapman 146. Chapman's best score in grade cricket was 259 (not out).

CHARLES, Lieut.-Col. Stephen Flockton, died at Norwich on June 24, 1950, aged 91. A wicket-keeper, he was in the Harrow XI 1875–76 and played for Gentlemen against Players at Scarborough 1897–98.

CHARLESWORTH, Albert P., born at Morley on February 19, 1876, died at Hull in May, 1926, aged 50. A free-hitting batsman, he appeared occasionally for Yorkshire in 1894 and 1895 and in the latter year played an innings of 63 against Nottinghamshire at Trent Bridge. Altogether he scored 258 runs for the county with an average of 19.84.

CHARLESWORTH, Crowther, who died on June 15, 1953, aged 76, was a popular figure in the Warwickshire XI from 1898 till 1921. In that period he scored 14,309 runs for the county, average 23.61, and as a fast bowler took 295 wickets. A brilliant batsman specially strong in driving, he hit 15 centuries, the highest being 216, scored out of 338 in three hours 40 minutes, against Derbyshire at Blackwell in 1910, when he headed the Warwickshire averages. In 1914 he played a dashing innings at Dewsbury, making 206 out of 283 in less than four hours from a Yorkshire attack including such bowlers as G. H. Hirst, M. W. Booth, W. Rhodes and A. Drake. Born at Swinton, Lancashire, on February 12, 1877, Charlesworth was a member of the team who, under F. R. Foster, first won the County Championship for Warwickshire in 1911. His benefit match in 1920 realised £1,041, a sum which remained a Warwickshire record till W. E. Hollies received £4,869 in 1945.

CHARLESWORTH, The Rev. Thomas Beedham. Born May 24, 1866, died at Wirksworth Vicarage, June 5, 1917. Sedbergh School XI, 1883–85, Christ's College (Camb.) XI, Worcestershire XI occasionally.

CHARLTON, Percy Chater, who died in Sydney on September 30, 1954, aged 87, was a member of the Australian team which visited England under W. L. Murdoch in 1890, taking part in two Test matches. During the tour he scored 534 runs, average 14.30, and with fast-medium bowling took 42 wickets, average 19.04. He played his early cricket for the Ivanhoe and Belvedere clubs in Sydney, N.S.W., and first achieved prominence when, for Eighteen Sydney Juniors in 1888, he took seven wickets, including that of Shrewsbury, against Shaw, Shrewsbury and James Lillywhite's English team. Ill-health limited his first-class career.

CHATTERTON, William, one of the greatest of Derbyshire cricketers, died of consumption at Flowery Field, Hyde, on March 19, 1913, in his 50th year. For many years he occupied a high position among professional batsmen, and it was due largely to him that his county was reinstated among the first-class sides in 1894. Although he had many strokes, his batting was essentially watchful and steady. That his careful methods paid is proved by the fact that for Derbyshire alone he scored 11,619 runs with an average of 25.15. In addition, he took 199 wickets for the county at a cost of just under 23 runs each. For the M.C.C. also his all-round cricket was often most valuable, and for Mr. W. W. Read's team in South Africa in 1891–92—his only colonial tour—he was by far the biggest run-getter. His chief scores in important cricket were as follows:

113 Derbyshire v. Essex, at Leyton, 1886.
168 Derbyshire v. Essex, at Leyton, 1889.
106 Derbyshire v. Yorkshire, at Derby, 1891.
101* Derbyshire v. Yorkshire, at Derby, 1893.
127 Derbyshire v. Leicestershire, at Derby, 1895.
111 Derbyshire v. Essex, at Leyton, 1896.
104 Derbyshire v. Lancashire, at Manchester, 1896.
120 Derbyshire v. Essex, at Leyton, 1897.
142 Derbyshire v. Hampshire, at Derby, 1898.
169 Derbyshire v. Gloucestershire, at Bristol, 1901.
109* M.C.C. v. Lancashire, at Lord's, 1892.
113 M.C.C. v. Cambridge University, at Cambridge, 1894.

In Derbyshire's match with Essex at Leyton in 1896 he scored 111 and 85 not out, probably only the closure of the innings preventing him from obtaining two separate hundreds. Between 1889 and 1898 he appeared in eight matches for the Players against the Gentlemen, and, with 58 at Hastings in 1891 as his highest score, made 248 runs with an average of 20.66. He was born at Flowery Field, Hyde, December 27, 1863.

CHEALES, Col. Ralph Darby, O.B.E., who died at Vereeniging, South Africa, on December 23, 1942, aged 73, was in the Harrow XI in 1888 when Eton were beaten by 156 runs. F. S. Jackson gave a wonderful display with both bat and ball; on an occasion when many batsmen failed he scored 21 and 59 and took 11 wickets for 68 runs. It was said that before the match Jackson's father, subsequently raised to the Peerage as Lord Allerton, promised his son a sovereign for every wicket he took and a shilling for every run that he made. Congratulated after the match, young Jackson replied, "I don't care so much for myself, but it will give the guv'nor a lift." Cheales, 10th in the batting order, got only six not out and three, and did not bowl. That was better than A. C. MacLaren, 0 and four, opening batsman, who, like Jackson—so well known as Sir Stanley Jackson, P. C.—reached the highest fame in the cricket world.

CHEETHAM, John (Jack) Erskine, who died in hospital in Johannesburg on August 21, 1980, aged 60, served South African cricket with great distinction, both as player and administrator. In 15 of his 24 Test matches he captained them with a firm yet understanding touch, and after his retirement he was, from 1969 to 1972, an outstanding President of the South African Cricket Association. He was an Honorary Life President of the Transvaal Cricket Union.

Cheetham was 28 when he first played for South Africa, against F. G. Mann's side in the first Test match of the 1948–49 M.C.C. tour, and 32 when he first led them on the 1952–53 tour of Australia. It was in Australia that he made his reputation as a captain. South Africa were given no chance of holding an Australian side which was led by Hassett and included Harvey, Lindwall, Morris, Miller and Johnston. In the event the Test series was drawn, at two matches all, South Africa winning the final Test at Melbourne after Australia had scored 520 in their first innings. Much of the credit for a notable South African achievement on this tour belonged to Cheetham, not because of the runs he made (he was a batsman pure and simple) but because of the way, with the help of the manager, Ken Viljoen, himself a former Test cricketer, he welded the players into a team. There were those at the time who thought the Cheetham-Viljoen regime too authoritarian; in fact, though, it was a sign of things to come. In his attention to the fitness of his players Cheetham was the forerunner of the modern captain.

Having led South Africa to victory over New Zealand in South Africa in 1953–54, he brought them to England in 1955 for what was one of the best and most closely fought series since the War. Ironically, in the third and fourth Test matches, which South Africa won, Cheetham was prevented by injury from playing, McGlew leading the side. With the series standing at two-all Cheetham returned for the final Test at the Oval, where England clinched the series thanks to the bowling of Laker and Lock on a wearing pitch and the batting of May, who, early in his innings, survived a memorably close call for leg before wicket against Tayfield.

Cheetham was a dour batsman but a decidedly better one than a top score of 89 from 43 Test innings would suggest. He had the respect of his players and also of the opposition, knowing what he wanted and quietly setting about obtaining it. His 271 not out against Orange Free State at Bloemfontein in 1950–51 remains the highest score ever made for Western Province in the Currie Cup. In his first-class career, which lasted from 1939 to 1955, he scored 5,697 runs at an average of 42.50. In retirement Cheetham continued to give much of his time to cricket, working hard in the interests of non-white cricketers and feeling South Africa's exclusion from the Test scene as acutely as anyone. He was a devout churchman, a determined and patient administrator, a dutiful host and a conscientious senior executive in a firm of construction engineers. Two of his sons, John and Robert, have both played first-class cricket.

CHELMSFORD, Lord (The Hon. Frederick John Napier Thesiger), who died on April 1, 1933, gained some reputation as a free-hitting batsman when at Winchester and Oxford. He was in the Winchester XI in 1885 and two following years, being captain in 1887. Going up to Oxford he gained his Blue as a Freshman in 1888 and had rather a curious experience in connection with the matches against Cambridge. He took part in the 1888 fixture; did not play in 1889 because of the illness of his brother; captained the side in 1890, and the following year had to retire owing to a damaged finger after lunch time on the first day. On the last occasion, Mr. T. B. Case was allowed to take Mr. Thesiger's place in the XI. Mr. Thesiger did little of note against Cambridge. Before getting into the Winchester XI he, at the age of 16, made an appearance for Worcestershire, and between 1888 and 1892 he turned out for Middlesex in a few matches. In 1922, after he had become Lord Chelmsford, he succeeded the Hon. F. S. Jackson as President of the M.C.C. He did most valuable public service in more than one direction, being Viceroy of India from 1916 to 1921, Governor-General of both Queensland (1905–09) and New South Wales (1909–13), First Lord of the Admiralty in Mr. Ramsay MacDonald's Labour Government in January, 1924, and Alderman of the London County Council. Elected to a Fellowship of All Souls in 1892, he became Warden in 1932. He was born in London on August 12, 1868.

CHESTER, Arthur, born at Kingston-on-Thames on December 18, 1851, died in St. Thomas' Hospital on May 13, 1915, following an operation for cancer. *Scores and Biographies* said of him: "Is a good average batsman and bowler, and in the field he is generally long-leg and cover-point." He played for Surrey occasionally between 1872 and 1883, scoring 302 runs with an average of 11.61, his highest score being 54 not out against Hampshire at the Oval in 1883, the match wherein Surrey totalled 650. For nine years he was captain of the Kingston Town C.C., for which in 1888, when his average was over 54, he played an innings of 284 v. Early Rising Club at Kingston on May 21, and from 1896 to 1902 was one of the county umpires selected by the M.C.C. On April 28, 1890, a match between Surrey and Eighteen of Kingston was played for his benefit. His father, James Chester, appeared in the county XI between 1846 and 1858.

CHESTER, Frank, who died at his home at Bushey, Hertfordshire, on April 8, 1957, aged 61, will be remembered as the man who raised umpiring to a higher level than had ever been known in the history of cricket. For some years he had suffered from stomach ulcers. Often he stood as umpire when in considerable pain, which unfortunately caused him to become somewhat irascible at times, and at the end of the 1955 season he retired, terminating a career in which he officiated in over 1,000 first-class fixtures, including 48 Test matches.

The First World War cut short his ambitions as an all-rounder for Worcestershire. In 1912, at the age of 16, he joined that county's staff and in the following season he scored 703 runs, including three centuries, average 28.12, and took with off-breaks 44 wickets, average 26.88. *Wisden* said of him that year: "Nothing stood out more prominently than the remarkable development of Chester, the youngest professional regularly engaged in first-class cricket.... Very few players in the history of cricket have shown such form at the age of 17½. Playing with a beautifully straight bat, he depended to a large extent on his watchfulness in defence. Increased hitting power will naturally come with time. He bowls with a high, easy action and, commanding an accurate length, can get plenty of spin on the ball. Having begun so well, Chester should continue to improve and it seems only reasonable to expect that when he has filled out and gained more strength, he will be an England cricketer."

In 1914 he put together an aggregate of 924 runs, average 27.17, with an innings of 178 not out—including four sixes from the bowling of J. W. H. T. Douglas—against Essex at Worcester, his highest. Then came the War and, in the course of service with the Army in Salonika, he lost his right arm just below the elbow. That, of course, meant no more cricket as a player for Chester; but in 1922 he became a first-class umpire and, with the advantage of youth when the majority of his colleagues were men who had retired as cricketers on the score of *Anno Domini*, he swiftly gained a big reputation. His lack of years caused him difficulty on one occasion at Northampton for a gate-man refused him admission, declining to believe that one so young could be an umpire, and suggested that he should try the ground of a neighbouring works team!

From the very beginning of his career as an umpire, he gave his decisions without fear or favour. In an article, "Thirty Years an Umpire," in the 1954 *Wisden*, Vivian Jenkins told how, when standing in his first county match, Essex v. Somerset at Leyton, Chester was called on to give decisions against both captains, J. W. H. T. Douglas and J. Daniell, and did his duty according to his lights—Douglas lbw, Daniell stumped. "You'll be signing your death warrant if you go on like that," he was warned by his venerable colleague, but he went on undeterred.

Chester began the custom, now prevalent among umpires, of bending low over the wicket when the bowler delivered the ball, and his decisions were both prompt and rarely questioned. Yet the ruling which probably caused most discussion was one in which Chester was wrong. This occurred during the England v. West Indies Test match at Trent Bridge in 1950, when S. Ramadhin bowled D. J. Insole off his pads. Chester contended that the batsman was leg before wicket, because he (Chester) gave his decision in the brief time before ball hit the stumps, and as "lbw" Insole remained in the score. Soon after this, M.C.C. added a Note to Law 34 which made it clear beyond dispute that, where a batsman is dismissed in such circumstances, he is out "bowled."

Chester had some brushes with Australian touring players, whose demonstrative methods of appealing annoyed him, but nevertheless Sir Donald Bradman termed him "the greatest umpire under whom I played." Chester, for his part, rated Bradman "the greatest run-making machine I have ever known," and considered Sir John Hobbs the greatest batsman of all time on all pitches.

Throughout his long spell as an umpire Chester used, for counting the balls per over, six small pebbles which he picked up from his mother's garden at Bushey before he "stood" in his first match.

Tributes included:

Mr. R. Aird, Secretary of M.C.C.: "He was an inspiration to other umpires. He seemed to have a flair for the job and did the right thing by instinct. He was outstanding among umpires for a very long time."

Sir John Hobbs: "I played against him in his brief career and am sure he would have been a great England all-rounder. As an umpire, he was right on top. I class him with that great Australian, Bob Crockett."

F. S. Lee, the Test match umpire: "Frank was unquestionably the greatest umpire I have known. His decisions were fearless, whether the batsman to be given out was captain or not. There is a great deal for which umpires have to thank him."

CHETHAM-STRODE, R. Warren, M.C., who died on April 26, 1974, aged 78, was in the Sherborne XI in 1913. He became a playwright, whose most successful work was *The Guinea Pig* in 1946. When serving in the Army in the First World War, he won the M.C. His father played for New Zealand in the first team from that country to oppose an England XI, in 1879.

CHETTLE, Geoffrey Arthur, who died in Durban on May 25, 1976, at the age of 69, was the founder of the *South African Cricket Annual* in 1952, and he continued to edit and publish it, almost single-handed, for the next 24 years. The last issue, much delayed by his terminal illness, appeared in March, 1976, but he was determined that it should be published despite his background of worsening ill-health. Before Chettle's *Annual* came into being, the record of cricket annual publishing in South Africa had been, for over a century, as spasmodic as it had been in most countries, England (and *Wisden*) apart.

One issue, or perhaps a few, had appeared but there was an enormous gap of 42 years from 1907 to 1949 when a single issue appeared, three years before Chettle started his long run. Cricket enthusiasts all over the world, and particularly in South Africa, have a great deal to thank him for. Apart from this work, he was also the South African correspondent for *Wisden*, to which he contributed for 17 years, and, at the time that tours from overseas were a regular feature of the South African scene, he produced tour brochures, starting in 1953–54. Different editions were produced for each area covered by each tour, and altogether some 70 appeared.

CHICHESTER, The Earl of, whose sudden death on April 21, 1905, at Stanmer Park, Lewes, evoked so much sympathy, was in his Eton and Cambridge days a prominent figure in the cricket field, being known then as the Hon. F. G. Pelham. It was only in his last year at Eton—1863—that he secured a place in the XI. By taking eight wickets with his slow round-arm bowling he helped Eton to beat Winchester in a single innings, but in a drawn match against Harrow at Lord's he met with very little success, his only wicket costing him 44 runs. The Eton team in 1863 was an extremely strong one, including as it did Alfred Lubbock (captain), the late E. W. Tritton, J. Frederick, the Hon. G. W. Lyttelton, and the late C. A. Teape. On their form that year Lubbock and Tritton could compare with almost any school batsmen, and against both Winchester and Harrow they did great things. At Cambridge the Hon. F. G. Pelham was in the XI for four years, being captain in 1866 and 1867. He had the pleasure of taking part in some remarkable matches against Oxford, but only in 1867 was it his good fortune to be on the winning side. There was nothing surprising in this, however, the Oxford XIs of 1864 and 1865 being among the best ever sent up to Lord's. In 1864 T. S. Curteis—a fine left-handed fast bowler that season—was, with Pelham on at the other end, winning the game for Cambridge when R. A. H. Mitchell turned the scale, and by scoring 55 not out gave Oxford a four wickets' victory. Small as it looks in these days, that 55 not out was always regarded as one of the finest innings Mitchell ever played, runs being very hard to get on the bad wickets at Lord's in 1864. In the following year—Mitchell's last in the University match—Oxford won easily by 114 runs, but in 1866 they only got home by 12 runs, after a very stern fight. Then, in 1867, Pelham tasted success at Lord's, a good all-round team beating Oxford by five wickets. Pelham had a notable share in the win, taking five wickets in Oxford's second innings for 32 runs. Altogether, in his four matches against Oxford he took 26 wickets— a better record than that of the Oxford slow bowler, W. F. Maitland, in the same games. Pelham played occasionally for Sussex, and was a member of the combined Surrey and Sussex XI that met England at the Oval for Tom Lockyer's benefit in 1867. Thanks to the bowling of Emmett and W. G. Grace, England, though by no means at full strength—the leading Northern professionals keeping away from the Oval at that time—won by nine wickets. Pelham was born at Stanmer on October 18, 1844, and entered the Church in 1869.

CHICHESTER-CONSTABLE,   Brigadier Raleigh Charles, who died on May 26, 1963, aged 72, captained Yorkshire Second XI from 1926 to 1938 and later served on the County Committee. A fast bowler, he was in the XI at Stonyhurst and toured India with A. E. R. Gilligan's M.C.C. team in 1926–27. He received the D.S.O. for his services at Dunkirk.

CHIDGEY, Harry, who died in November, 1941, at his birthplace, Flax Bourton, aged 62, occupies a special place in Somerset cricket as the one professional intervening in a long reign of amateur wicket-keepers. A. E. Newton, the Rev. A. P. Wickham and H. Martyn shared the duty from 1891 to 1908, when Chidgey came to the front six years after playing once for the county as an amateur at Bath. Until the last War he lightened the work still undertaken by Newton whenever possible, and he resumed in 1919. Two years later Chidgey recorded a batting average which seldom can have had a parallel. Playing 12 innings he made 48 runs, with a highest score of 18, but 10 "not outs" gave him an average of 24: His best score for Somerset was 45 in 1909 against Yorkshire at Bath. Sent in late on the Tuesday evening, he stayed altogether 85 minutes with Len Braund and so helped Somerset draw the match very creditably. That season he averaged 13.33 for 120 runs in 15 innings, with six "not outs." After the War M. D. Lyon maintained the Somerset tradition of amateur keepers. Chidgey ranks high in this art among all the Somerset talent. He made 120 catches and stumped 50 batsmen, figures that place him for the county next to A. E, Newton, who held 250 catches and stumped 112 men. Rather small, quick and neat,

Chidgey was a very good keeper. He was given a place in his local club team when 14 and was hon. secretary when the present War broke out. As a member of the Long Ashton Urban District Council he enjoyed much popularity.

CHIGNELL, Thomas Alexander, who died in the Royal Hospital, Portsmouth, on August 25, 1965, aged 84, played occasionally for Hampshire from 1901 to 1904. A slow bowler, he played some useful innings, the highest being 29 not out against Yorkshire at Portsmouth in 1904. He assisted Havant C.C. for many years.

CHILDS-CLARKE, Arthur William, died suddenly at his home at Mevagissey on February 19, 1980, aged 74. He was a well-known London club cricketer, who played a number of times for Middlesex between 1923 and 1934, his highest score being 58 not out v. Glamorgan at Swansea in 1931; he also captained the Middlesex Second XI. In 1947 and 1948 he played for Northamptonshire, captaining the side in both seasons, playing a number of useful innings in the lower order and occasionally picking up a wicket. His highest score for Northamptonshire was 68 v. Leicestershire at Leicester in 1947, but more remarkable was his 32 not out against the South Africans in 1947, when he and L. A. Smith added 76 for the last wicket. He was in the Christ's Hospital XI in 1921 and 1922.

CHINNERY, Lieut. Harry Brodrick (King's Royal Rifles), born at Teddington, February 6, 1876, fell in action on May 28, 1916. A stylish batsman and smart field, he was in the Eton XI in 1894 and 1895, in the latter year heading the averages with 45.14. In his four Public School matches—against Harrow and Winchester—he scored 182 runs in six innings, his great triumph being to make 75 and 64 v. Harrow in 1895, in the second innings of which game he and A. B. Lubbock (66) obtained 115 for the first wicket. In 1897 he assisted Surrey and in the match with Warwickshire at Edgbaston played an innings of 149. A year later little was seen of him, but at the end of the season he scored 97 for M.C.C. v. Yorkshire at Scarborough and in 1899 began to appear for Middlesex. His greatest feat was performed in 1901 when, in consecutive innings, he made 105 and 165 for M.C.C. and Ground v. Oxford University at Oxford and 100 for Middlesex v. Gloucestershire at Lord's. He was only 26 when he made his last appearance in County Cricket. His early retirement was much to be regretted, but he continued to assist the Eton Ramblers and I Zingari. Since 1896 he had been a member of the M.C.C. He was a son of the late Mr. Walter Chinnery, the champion mile runner in the early days of amateur athletics.

CHRISTIAN, Prince Victor, who died of fever in Pretoria, on October 29, 1900, was a capable cricketer while at Wellington College, and would very likely have got into the XI at Oxford if a new wicket-keeper had been required while he was in residence. After going into the Army he made lots of runs in Military cricket, and was one of the few men who ever played an innings of over 200 in India, scoring 205 for the King's Royal Rifles v. the Devonshire Regiment, at Rawalpindi, in 1893.

CHRISTIANI, Cyril M., whose death in the West Indies occurred on April 4, 1938, toured England with the West Indies team under the captaincy of G. C. Grant in 1933. He did not take part in any of the Test matches, I. Barrow, a much better batsman, being preferred as wicket-keeper. When the M.C.C. side led by R. E. S. Wyatt visited West Indies in 1934–35, Christiani kept wicket in all four Tests. By helping to dismiss seven batsmen in the four matches he bore a useful part in winning the rubber. On that tour, the England batting failed badly against the fast bowling of E. A. Martindale, L. N. Constantine and L. G. Hylton—described by Wyatt as the best combination of its kind in the world. Christiani was in his 25th year. In February, 1937, for British Guiana Club against East India C.C. he and his brother E. S. Christiani made 296 for the first wicket—a British Guiana record for an opening stand.

CHRISTOPHERSON, Cecil, M.R.C.S., L.R.C.P., of St Leonards, who died on May 11, 1925, was a member of the well-known Kent cricketing brotherhood, who, with their father, were able to put a family XI in the field.

CHRISTOPHERSON, Douglas, C.B.E., who died on March 5, 1944, was one of 10 brothers, who, with their father, played often as a team at Blackheath from 1877 to 1880. The best known, Stanley Christopherson, the fast bowler who played for Kent from 1883 to 1890, and for England against Australia at Lord's in 1884, has been President of the M.C.C. throughout the present War years. Percy Christopherson, a younger

brother, appeared for Kent in 1888 and for Oxford without getting his Blue, but was in the Oxford Rugby Fifteen 1886–87, became captain of Blackheath and Kent, besides playing for England in 1891. He was a fine three-quarter back.

CHRISTOPHERSON, Nevill, who died on December 31, 1972, aged 78, did not gain a place in the XI at Winchester. From 1950 to 1959 he was secretary and manager of Kent and became the county President in 1962. He was one of 10 brothers in a notable Kentish sporting family. His father, Percy, gained two England Rugby International caps in 1891 when a Blackheath player and an uncle, Stanley, became President of the M.C.C. Nevill was for a time hon. secretary of Blackheath R.F.C.

CHRISTOPHERSON, Percy, born at Blackheath on March 31, 1866, died at Folkestone on May 4, 1921. In 1887 he appeared in one match for Kent, playing against Sussex at Tonbridge and scoring 27, and whilst at Oxford assisted the University in a few games, but did not obtain his Blue. He was a younger brother of Mr. Stanley Christopherson, and a member of the family XI which was composed of the father and 10 sons.

CHRISTOPHERSON, Sidney, who died at Bournemouth on September 28, 1916, aged 53, was a member of the Christopherson XI, composed of a father and 10 sons, which used to play in the Blackheath district. Only two members of the Family team—Messrs. Stanley and Percy Christopherson—now survive.

CHRISTOPHERSON, Stanley, President of M.C.C. from 1939 to 1946, the longest period anyone has held that office, died in a London nursing home on April 6, 1949, aged 87. Born at Blackheath on November 11, 1861, he earned fame as one of the best fast bowlers in the middle '80s. He was educated at Uppingham, where the celebrated H. H. Stephenson was coach. Although a splendid teacher of batting, Stephenson possessed rather lax ideas on the matter of bowling, but Christopherson's methods were beyond suspicion. Christopherson took a fairly long run, made full use of his height in bringing the ball well over and, with a natural swing, acquired a lot of pace. For a fast bowler he kept an accurate length and could send down a formidable yorker. He played a good deal for Kent for five seasons from 1883, but strained his arm in 1886 and took little active part in important cricket after 1887.

Altogether he appeared for Kent in 50 matches and against Surrey at the Oval in 1883 took eight wickets for 41. A year later his reputation was so well established that he played for Gentlemen against Players at Lord's, and Australians at the Oval, while at Lord's he was capped for England against Australia, who on that occasion suffered defeat in a single innings. For the Gentlemen against Australia's very powerful batting side, he dismissed eight men for 78 and at Canterbury, when Kent were the only county that summer to beat the Australians, he sent down in the second innings 19 overs for 12 runs and three wickets.

That season Christopherson figured in a remarkable match at Aston Lower Grounds, Birmingham, between An XI of England and the Australians. The pitch, quite bare of grass, was alleged to have been watered overnight. In these circumstances four hours of actual cricket sufficed, the Englishmen making 82 and 26 and the Australians 76 and 33 for six wickets. Spofforth took 14 wickets—seven in the second innings for three runs. Christopherson did not bowl in the first innings, but in the second disposed of Alec Bannerman, Percy McDonnell, Blackham and Spofforth in nine overs and one ball for 10 runs.

Stanley Christopherson was one of 10 sons who, with their father, used at various periods in the '70s and '80s to form a family cricket XI and play certain matches, mostly against schools in the Blackheath district. A man of great personal charm he was in his young days extremely good looking.

During the difficult War years, M.C.C. could not have possessed a better man as President. He was a big figure in the City of London and from 1943–45 was temporary chairman of the Midland Bank, yet despite the calls of business he went to Lord's on most days and rarely missed a Committee meeting. In all walks of life he always played the game.

CHRISTY, James Alexander Joseph, who died in hospital at Durban on February 1, 1971, aged 66, took part in 10 Test matches for South Africa between 1929 and 1932, scoring 618 runs, average 34.33. A tall batsman, he used his long reach to special advantage against fast bowlers. He made his first-class debut for Transvaal in 1925–26, enjoying the distinction of hitting a century in his second innings for them. In 1929 he toured England under H. G. Deane. He played in two Tests, but after an innings of 148 against Nottinghamshire he suffered a finger injury which limited his appearances.

A business appointment in London permitted him to figure in only the final Test with England in South Africa in 1930–31. In 1931–32 he visited Australia and New Zealand with H. G. Cameron's side. He hit 102 off the Western Australia bowling in his first game on Australian soil and he headed the batting averages with 1,170 runs. He also registered his one Test century, 103, against New Zealand at Christchurch, where he and B. Mitchell shared an opening partnership of 196 in two hours.

His highest innings was 175 for Transvaal against Rhodesia at Salisbury in 1927–28, one of three three-figure scores he put together in successive innings—a feat he repeated the following season. He assisted Queensland in 12 Sheffield Shield fixtures in 1934–35.

CHUBB, Geoffrey Walter Ashton, who died in East London on August 28, 1982, at the age of 71, played five times for South Africa against England in 1951 and served two terms as President of the South African Cricket Association. At 40 years 56 days he was the oldest South African to make a Test debut. It happened at Trent Bridge, and when England went in late on the second day, facing a total of 483, he had Ikin caught at slip with his third ball and finished with four for 146 off 46 overs. He and McCarthy reduced England from 375 for three to 419 all out and gave South Africa the chance to record their first win in England for 16 years. Chubb's best Test figures came at Old Trafford when he took six for 51 in England's first innings. With 21 wickets in the series at 27.47 apiece, he headed the bowling averages for South Africa. He was also their leading wicket-taker in all first-class matches on the tour, capturing 72 at 26.84 apiece and bowling over 150 overs more than anyone else.

Born in Rhodesia, Chubb began his first-class career as an opening batsman for Border in 1931–32, but on moving to Johannesburg concentrated on his bowling. He worked hard at perfecting his medium-paced seamers and developing a high degree of accuracy. Fair-haired, studious and bespectacled, he was a disarmingly effective bowler and immensely popular. After his retirement in 1951, at the end of his tour of England, he devoted his energies to cricket administration, becoming a national selector and, from 1955 to 1957 and again from 1959 to 1960, President of the S.A.C.A. In all first-class cricket he took 160 wickets at an average of 23.91, scored 835 runs (average 18.15) and held 12 catches.

CHUTE, The Rev. Theophilus Dacre, who died at Great Moulton, Norfolk, on June 15, 1926, aged 74, played with his brothers with the Vyne and Hackwood Park clubs in Hampshire, and in 1881 his name will be found in the Essex team.

CLARK, Augustus George Finnis, prominent in Hastings cricket for many years as a left-handed batsman and a bowler with a natural off-break, died there suddenly on May 7, 1928, at the age of 65. In May, 1885, he appeared at Lord's for Colts of South v. Colts of North, taking three wickets, and on the same ground a year later, against M.C.C., played in his only match for Sussex. He was born at Dover.

CLARK, Edward Winchester, inevitably known as "Nobby", who died on April 28, 1982, near King's Lynn, aged 79, possessed every qualification of a great bowler except temperament. With a lovely loose left arm, which almost brushed his left ear as it came over, he had a classic action, his right shoulder pointing straight at the batsman. He was at his best really fast and, though he was well capable of bowling, like Voce, to a leg-side field, was probably most effective round the wicket when the ball, swinging in and breaking away, would produce catches in the slips if the batsman was good enough to touch it. But he was a perfectionist and anything outside his control which interfered with that perfection—a dropped catch, an insecure foothold, a tactless word from his captain or one of his companions—was quite sufficient to put him off. It was his misfortune that his county, Northamptonshire, was throughout his career one of the weakest sides that has ever played in the Championship; not only did he have to do more than his fair share of bowling, but perhaps no fast bowler since Buckenham of Essex had so many chances dropped off him. A further annoyance to him was the rate at which his *vis-à-vis*, that splendid bowler Albert Thomas, got through his overs, an undue proportion of which were maidens, thus robbing Clark of what he considered as a rightful rest. His cricket began and ended with his bowling, neither batting nor fielding did he regard as any business of his.

Though he was born near Peterborough, it was success in League cricket in Yorkshire, where he was an engineering apprentice, that brought him to the notice of the Northamp-

tonshire authorities and he made a promising start in 1922, heading the averages with 20 wickets at 17.10. There followed two or three seasons of varying fortune, but in 1925 he came right to the front with 84 wickets at 17.79 and began to be talked of as a Test match prospect. He played in the Test trials in 1927, but in 1928, handicapped by injury, he had a poor season and he had to wait till 1929 for his first Test, against South Africa at the Oval, where he was criticised for overdoing leg-theory. A row with Northamptonshire, whom he left temporarily for League cricket, spoiled his chances of playing against the Australians in 1930. However, he returned to the county in 1932, and in 1933 he played at the Oval and Old Trafford against West Indies, bowling well without spectacular success. That winter he had a successful tour in India under D. R. Jardine and in 1934 was picked at Old Trafford and again at the Oval against Australia. At Old Trafford he bowled well without any luck, but in the second innings at the Oval he took five for 98, his victims being Ponsford, Brown, McCabe, Kippax and Chipperfield, while he twice failed by only the narrowest margin to bowl Bradman. This was his last Test, but he continued to bowl with success until 1936. In 1937, handicapped by injury, he had a poor season and dropped out of the county side, but he returned in 1946 to bowl with at least some trace of his former greatness. A few matches in 1947 concluded his career. In all first-class cricket he took 1,203 wickets at 21 runs each.

CLARK, Percy H., who died on August 12, 1965, aged 92, toured England with The Philadelphians in 1897 and 1903. A fast bowler who made the ball swerve late, he took 32 wickets for 31.28 runs each in 1897 and six years later dismissed 85 batsmen at an average cost of 20.50. He and J. B. King, who also died last year, formed the spearhead of the attack on those tours. Against a strong Australian side at Haverford in 1896, Clark took five wickets for 49 runs in the first innings and, going in at No. 10, hit 32, thus doing much to bring about defeat for the visiting team in an innings with 60 runs to spare. He was an honorary member of the Butterflies C.C.

CLARK, Ronald Disston, died at East Wittering on February 20, 1983, aged 87. Playing a few matches for Essex as a wicket-keeper at the age of 17 in 1912, the year after he left Christ's Hospital, he created a favourable impression. The county then (as indeed for many years both before and after) lacked a reliable professional wicket-keeper, and Clark would have been invaluable. Unfortunately, a match or two in 1913 and one in 1919 were all he could manage, and after that he had to confine himself to London club cricket.

CLARK, Thomas Henry, died in hospital at Luton, his birthplace, on June 15, 1981, aged 56. After heading the Bedfordshire batting averages in 1946, he moved to the Oval, but though he made 74 not out against Oxford University in 1947 on his first appearance for Surrey and for three seasons scored heavily for the Second XI, the county's batting was so strong that it was not till 1950 that he was given a proper trial in the side. That year he made 175 not out against Cambridge University in five hours. In 1952 he scored 1,000 runs for the first time and was awarded his cap, and until 1959 he remained an essential member of the side, normally opening the innings. His highest score was 191 against Kent at Blackheath in 1956, when he put on 174 in two hours with Peter May for the third wicket. Quite early, however, he began to be troubled by arthritis, and after 1959 he was no longer able to stand the strain of three-day cricket, though he continued for two more seasons to make runs for the Second XI. He was primarily a front-of-the-wicket player and a fine driver; as increasing stiffness stopped him from getting his front foot right out he took to driving the ball successfully on the rise, a stroke which calls for not only much natural ability but also an impeccably correct technique. He was, too, a useful off-spinner who in 1952 took five for 23 against Middlesex at Lord's, but with Laker and Eric Bedser in the side his opportunities were limited. In all first-class cricket he scored 11,490 runs, with an average of 26.39, including 12 centuries, and took 75 wickets at 30.85 each. Before deciding to concentrate on cricket, he had played professional football for Aston Villa and Walsall.

CLARKE, Alfred E., the founder of the East Melbourne C.C. in 1860, its first hon. secretary, and its president from 1885 to 1903, died on August 19, 1913, aged 70. A piece of turf from the club ground was lowered with the coffin, as he desired.

CLARKE, Charles Frederick Carlos, born at Welton, Northamptonshire, on April 26, 1853, died at Sunninghill on January 29, 1931. He was one of the oldest members of I Zingari, the Free Foresters and M.C.C. He started the Silwood Park Cricket Club which numbered among its players R. E. Foster, H. K. Foster, B. J. T. Bosanquet and Aubrey Faulkner and was one of the very few cricket clubs which always used white stumps. Mr. Clarke played for Surrey between 1873 and 1882 and for Berkshire but he was more attracted by the brighter atmosphere of country house and club cricket. Closely associated with the Canterbury Week and the famous band of amateur actors—the Old Stagers—he was an accomplished actor and musician. A good batsman, wicket-keeper and a first-rate field, he scored 65 for Gentlemen of England v. Oxford University at Oxford in 1883 and in the same season 63 for M.C.C. v. Kent at Canterbury. A keen all-round sportsman, he had hunted with 33 different packs of hounds.

CLARKE, Peter, who died in Dublin in December, 1915, aged about 33, came to the front suddenly in May, 1912, when he was chosen for his googly bowling for the Trial match at the Oval between England and The Rest. In his few representative games in Ireland he had done little against All India, Hampshire, and Cambridge University, and at the Oval his solitary wicket cost 68 runs. For Woodbrooke he took many wickets, but for Middlesex (for which county he had a birth qualification) he was not very successful. For three seasons he was on the ground staff at Lord's.

CLARKE, Robert Wakefield, died suddenly at Sherborne on August 3, 1981, aged 57. A fast left-armer, he did much useful work for Northamptonshire between 1947 and 1957, without ever quite fulfilling expectations. Coming into the side just as the great "Nobby" Clark, also a fast left-armer, was retiring, he must have seemed the answer to prayer, and when in his third season he took 88 wickets his prospects seemed good, even though they cost 28 runs each. Three disappointing seasons followed, but in 1953 he took 97 wickets at just under 25 runs each and hopes were revived. However, that was almost the end of his success: he became more and more expensive and finally dropped out in 1957.

His failure was certainly not due to want of trying: shortish and stocky, he was prepared to bowl all day and was indeed in temperament a complete contrast to the volatile "Nobby". But, though he could at times unleash that beautiful ball which pitches on the leg stump and whips across to the off, the real genius was lacking. He was also handicapped by cartilage trouble. Despite some fine performances, 13 for 190 against Surrey at Northampton in 1950 and eight for 26 against Hampshire at Peterborough in 1951, his career figures of 484 wickets at 34.60 runs apiece tell their own tale. Apart from his bowling he was a useful, if unorthodox, tail-end hitter and a good fielder near the wicket. Later he coached successively at the R.N.C., Dartmouth, Christ's Hospital and Sherborne.

CLARKE, W. Alfred F., of Mitcham C.C. and Surrey, died during 1935, aged 68. A very good wicket-keeper "Alf" Clarke played occasionally for the county in 1890 and the next two seasons.

CLARKE, William, who died on May 29, 1935, in his 86th year, having been born on March 17, 1850, played in a few matches for Nottinghamshire and in the neighbourhood of Kirkby, where he was born and lived, he was known as "Cricketer Clarke." A fast right arm bowler he batted left handed. In 1876 against Lancashire at Trent Bridge he took two wickets for four runs and a year later against Gloucestershire he had the satisfaction of seeing W. G. Grace caught off his bowling for three. Between 1877 and 1892 he was coach to the Royal Artillery Officers at Woolwich.

CLARKE, William Benjamin, passed away at Nottingham on August 18, 1902. He was born at Old Basford, on November 5, 1846, and was therefore in his 56th year at the time of his death. His name will be found a few times in the Nottinghamshire XI, commencing in 1874. He was not related to William Clarke, the famous slow bowler of 60 years ago, or to William Clarke, of Kirkby-in-Ashfield, who first appeared in the county XI in 1876. From 1866 to 1872 he was engaged by the Plymouth Club, and afterwards by the West of Scotland C.C., at Partick, Glasgow. In 1880, he became qualified by residence for Middlesex, and in the year named made his first appearance for his adopted county against Notts., at Lord's, and, by obtaining seven wickets for 51 runs in the first innings, raised hopes which were, unfortunately, never realised. In all Middlesex matches in which he took part, he obtained 68 wickets for 1,317 runs, and in 24 completed innings he scored 182 runs. In his day he was a useful bowler—right hand, slow to medium pace—but it would be an exaggeration to suggest that he ever occupied a very prominent place in the cricket world. For 12 years he was engaged at Harrow. In April, 1889, he became host of the Clayton Arms—a familiar landmark to all frequenters of the Oval.

CLAUGHTON, Hugh, who died in October, 1980, at the age of 88, played once for Yorkshire in 1914 and three times (including the Roses match) in 1919 as an all-rounder. For some years he was the professional at Baildon Green.

CLAY, John Charles, who died on August 12, 1973, aged 75, was one of the most dedicated cricketers ever to represent Glamorgan. He first appeared for the county when they acquired first-class status in 1921 and continued with them till 1949; was captain in six seasons and for some time hon. secretary; and at the time of his death was President of the County Club, a position he had held since 1961.

At Winchester, where he was in the XI in 1915 and 1916, "Johnny" Clay, as he was generally known in the cricket world, was a fast bowler, but eventually he took to off-breaks and possessed few equals. Not only did he spin the ball skilfully from his considerable height, but he maintained a splendid length and never wilted under punishment. In his long career he took 1,315 wickets at an average cost of 19.77, three times dismissing over 100 batsmen in a season.

His most successful summer was that of 1937, when with the aid of such analyses as nine wickets for 59 runs against Essex at Westcliff and nine for 66—17 for 212 in the match—against Worcestershire at Swansea, he obtained 176 wickets for 17.34 runs each. In 1935 at Llanelli he also took nine wickets in an innings, for 54 runs against Northamptonshire. Although he never achieved the "hat-trick", he dismissed three Northamptonshire batsmen in the course of four deliveries at Northampton in 1938.

It was a great day for Clay when in 1948 he helped substantially in a win by an innings and 115 runs over Hampshire at Bournemouth which took Glamorgan to the County Championship for the first time. His share in the victory was nine wickets for 79 runs—six for 48 in the second innings.

He played in one Test match for England, against South Africa at the Oval in 1935 when, though commanding much respect, he failed to take a wicket. He served as a Test team selector in 1947 and 1948.

CLAYTON, Richard, an enthusiastic supporter of the game in Northumberland, died at his residence, Wylam Hall, near Newcastle, on November 29, 1903, at the age of 63. He assisted Harrow against Eton, at Lord's, in 1858, and also appeared on a few occasions for Lancashire.

CLAYTON, Robert, for many years past one of the ground staff at Lord's, and formerly a member of the Yorkshire XI, died on November 26, 1901, at Gainsborough. He was born at Caley, near Otley, in Yorkshire, on January 1, 1844, and was thus nearly 58 years of age. Though he assisted Yorkshire for several seasons in the '70s, it cannot be said that he ever fulfilled the promise of his earliest performances. When he came out he made his mark at once, and was regarded on all hands as one of the best right-handed fast bowlers in the country. For a little while, indeed, his prospects were almost as good as Allen Hill's. Playing his first match at Lord's for the Colts of England against the M.C.C., on May 8, 9, and 10, 1871, in company with Richard Humphrey, the late John Selby, David Eastwood, Harry Phillips, James Phillips, and T. Hearne, jun. (the present ground-keeper at Lord's), he took six wickets—two for 49 and four for 36. A fortnight later at Lord's he played for Yorkshire against the M.C.C., and met with great success, bowling W. G. Grace in the first innings, and securing in all 10 wickets for 94 runs. His form was so good that in the Whit-Monday match, between North and South, he was, in the absence of the late George Freeman, given a place in the Northern XI. Once more he did well, for though the South scored 328 (W. G. Grace making 178), six wickets fell to him for 77 runs. His future seemed assured, but as it turned out he went back instead of forward, and though always a useful bowler, he never again reached the standard of his first season, dropping far behind Hill in the Yorkshire team. At the time of his death he was, as regards length of service, the oldest but one of the ground bowlers at Lord's, only Frank Farrands having been longer on the M.C.C. staff. It was a peculiarity of his that, though for so many years he spent every cricket season in London, his Yorkshire accent remained as strong as if he had never left his native village.

CLIFF, Alfred Talbot, who died on January 25, 1966, aged 87, played as an amateur for Worcestershire from 1912 to 1920. His highest innings for the county was 59 not out against Leicestershire at Worcester in 1914, when he and M. K. Foster shared in a partnership of 166.

CLOETE, Capt. Peter Henry Bairnsfather, a good slow bowler, who played for Western Province from 1936 to 1940, was killed in an air disaster on December 19, 1942, aged 25. His original name was Bairnsfather, but he adopted the surname Cloete in 1938 for family reasons.

CLOETE, William Brodrick, was born in 1851 and was drowned in the torpedoing of the *Lusitania* on May 7, 1915. Since 1877 he had been a member of the M.C.C., for which he played in many matches. For the club against Essex at Brentwood in 1877 he bowled unchanged throughout with Rylott, taking six wickets for 74 runs in the first innings and six for 48 in the second. In the same match he also scored 60—the highest innings played for either side—and nine. He was a well-known owner and breeder of racehorses. The best horse he ever had was Paradox—second to Melton in the Derby in 1885.

COATES, Joseph, who died on September 9, 1896, was for some time identified with New South Wales as a right-handed slow bowler, and took part in several Inter-Colonial matches in company with Spofforth and Evans. Mr. Coates came to England in 1877, and played in the Whit-Monday match at Lord's, but did not on that occasion have much chance of distinguishing himself. He was born on November 13, 1843, and was thus at the time of his death nearing the completion of his 53rd year.

COBB, Humphry Henry, who died after a long illness on December 13, 1949, played 14 innings for Middlesex in the latter part of last century, scoring 157 runs. He captained Rosslyn Park F.C. for three seasons from 1896–97 to 1898–99. Born on July 12, 1876, he was at one time President of the Bear Skating Club.

COBBOLD, John Septimus, died on July 15, 1972, aged 83, while taking off his pads after opening the innings for Old Ipswichians, of which club he was President, in a Suffolk Alliance match at Hadleigh. An active club cricketer throughout his adult life, he played for Suffolk in 1913.

COBBOLD, William Nevill, who was born at Long Melford, on February 4, 1863, died at Bournemouth on April 8, 1922. He was in the Charterhouse XI in 1881 and 1882, being captain the latter year, but although a very useful player, did not obtain his Blue whilst at Cambridge. In 1887 he appeared in one match for Kent. He could hit well all round, especially to the off, and was particularly successful in club cricket in 1891, when he played consecutive innings of 179, 163 and 104. When he made 163—for West Wratting Park v. Fitzwilliam Hostel, on May 21—he and W. R. Gray (218 not out) scored 440 together for the first wicket. It is, of course, as an Association footballer that Mr. Cobbold will always be best remembered, for his fame at that game was deservedly great and he was known as "The Prince of Dribblers". He played for Charterhouse, Cambridge (four times, 1883–86; captain in 1885 and 1886), Corinthians, England (nine times) and Old Carthusians. He also played lawn-tennis for his University.

COBCROFT, L. T., died at Wellington, New Zealand, on March 9, 1938, aged 69. Born in Sydney, he captained the New South Wales team that toured in New Zealand in 1895 and became prominent in New Zealand cricket, taking part in games against touring teams that went out under Lord Hawke, P. F. Warner, and Captain E. G. Wynyard. For the New South Wales team he scored 85 and carried his bat through the innings against Wellington. When New Zealand sent a team to Australia in 1898 he was captain; his best scores were 83 at Hobart, 53 not out at Melbourne; and in 1905 he made 49 against an Australian team at Wellington. He captained Canterbury, Wairarapa and Wellington at different times. In more recent years he often umpired in matches with overseas teams.

COBDEN, Frank Carroll, who died at Capel Curig, North Wales, on December 7, 1932, was the hero of perhaps the most sensational piece of bowling in the history of cricket.

In the Oxford and Cambridge match of 1870, Oxford, set 179 runs to win, had made 175 for the loss of seven batsmen and thus, with three wickets to fall, wanted only four runs for victory when Cobden began the over which will be for ever memorable. The first ball was hit by F. H. Hill for a single, the stroke being one which would certainly have sent the ball to the boundary had it not been brilliantly fielded by mid-wicket—as to whether this was mid-off or mid-on even those taking part in the match differ. S. E. Butler was caught off the second ball, T. H. Belcher bowled by the third, and W. A. Stewart by the fourth, with the result that Cambridge snatched an extraordinary victory by two runs.

Born at Lambley, Nottinghamshire, on October 14, 1849, Mr. Cobden was in the Harrow XI in 1866, and in the match against Eton, which Harrow won by an innings and 136 runs, he took five wickets for 37 and three for 10, or eight wickets in all for 47 runs. In the same match, W. B. Money (Harrow), afterwards captain at Cambridge, in the year Cobden accomplished his memorable bowling feat, performed the "hat-trick". Included in the Eton XI on that occasion was C. I. Thornton, the famous hitter, who in the first innings scored 46 not out. Before going to Harrow in 1864, Cobden was at Brighton College (1860–63) and at Highgate School (1863–64). He left school early, and going up to Trinity College, Cambridge, was given his Blue in 1870 and in the two following years taking, on the occasion of his great triumph, eight wickets for 76 runs. He was an excellent fast round-arm bowler and very straight, spoken of 60 years ago as "one of the best who has appeared in any XI" and described as being a better bowler at school than at any time afterwards. He stood nearly 6 ft. high, and weighed 12 st. He generally fielded at mid-on, and was a free and powerful hitter.

COBHAM, Lord (The Hon. C. G. Lyttelton in his cricket days), died on June 9, 1922. Born on October 27, 1842, he was in his 80th year. As he gave up cricket before he was 25 his deeds belonged to a distant past. The first to make the name of Lyttelton famous in the cricket field, he was one of the outstanding players of his day, stepping as a matter of course into the Gentlemen's team year after year at Lord's and the Oval, so long as he remained before the public. He was in the Eton XI from 1857 to 1860, being captain in his last two years, and in the Cambridge XI from 1861 to 1864, missing the captaincy because he was not expected to be in residence in 1864. I can only speak of him from what I have read and been told, as he had finished before I ever saw Lord's ground. Even in his school days there seems to have been no question as to his class as a batsman, but looking up the records it is curious to find how little he did for Eton as compared with R. A. H. Mitchell and Alfred Lubbock. In his seven big matches—four against Winchester and three against Harrow—his best scores were 27 and 17. Still, so much was thought of him that as a Freshman at Cambridge in 1861 he was picked for Gentlemen v. Players, both at Lord's and the Oval. In those early days at Cambridge he was in the fullest sense an all-round cricketer, as apart from his batting he was an excellent fast bowler, a fine field at point, and a very good wicket-keeper.

However, he did not care much for bowling and a strained back, I think, hampered him. He concentrated more and more on his batting and soon stood first for Cambridge with A. W. T. Daniel as his nearest rival. Like other famous batsmen before and since his time, he was never seen at anything like his best in the University match, his highest innings against Oxford being 19 not out in a match of very small scores in 1863. As a matter of fact he thoroughly disliked the rough wickets at Lord's in the first half of the '60s, and made no pretence of feeling comfortable on them. His brother, the Hon. R. H. Lyttelton, tells me that he was always fond of recalling a modest score of 28 for the Gentlemen at Lord's in 1863 against Jackson and Tarrant, saying he had never found runs so hard to get. Fenner's and the Oval were his favourite grounds and at both he did great things. He was at the top of the Cambridge batting in 1863 and 1864 with averages—very high at that time—of 38 and 41. In each of these years he played an innings of a hundred—101 against Surrey at the Oval in 1863 and 128 against the M.C.C. at Fenner's in 1864. His last experience of cricket at Cambridge had a special interest. In May, 1866, after he had gone down, he played for Eighteen of Trinity College against the All England XI and scored 90, his brother, Spencer, helping with 55. When they were firmly set George Freeman—just coming into note—went on and clean bowled them both on a perfect wicket. In the following year Freeman was beyond question the best fast bowler in England.

Lord Cobham played in 12 Gentlemen v. Players' matches, never missing one from 1861 to 1866. His average in 23 innings was 18, small scores at Lord's discounting his success at the Oval. In the match at the Oval in 1864 he played, perhaps, the innings of his life—a superb 81 which was talked about for years. At that time, be it remembered, no one except the famous Mr. Ward in 1825 had ever made a hundred for the Gentlemen, John Walker coming nearest with 98 at the Oval in 1862. Lord Cobham had a considerable share in the Gentlemen's first victory over the Players at the Oval—in 1866—scoring 45 when his side followed-on, and he was in the team that in 1865 won at Lord's for the first time since 1853. Another memorable match in which he took part was England against Surrey at the Oval in 1862—the match in which England scored 503 and

Willsher was no-balled by John Lillywhite for bowling above the shoulder. The no-balling caused a great sensation, and it is on record that when the England professionals left the field Lord Cobham stayed on the pitch with his captain, V. E. Walker. To the end of his long life Lord Cobham retained a keen interest in cricket. At the dinner given at Birmingham in September, 1911, in honour of Warwickshire having won the Championship, he proposed the toast of the Warwickshire County Club, and strongly defended the competitive spirit in county cricket.—S.H.P.

Mr. W. F. Maitland, who as an Oxford Freshman, played against Lord Cobham in the University match in 1864, and was on the Gentlemen's side several times with him against the Players, sends the following note:

"In the early middle years between 1860 and 1870, the two outstanding figures in the cricket world, amongst amateur batsmen, with the exception of E. M. Grace, the greatest run-getter of those years, were C. G. Lyttelton and R. A. H. Mitchell; the former from Cambridge, and the latter from Oxford; and I think if the question had been asked which was the greater batsman of the two, the answer from Cambridge men would have been that it was Lyttelton, and from Oxford men that it was Mitchell, and there I must leave it.

"C. G. Lyttelton's play differed from that of anyone whom I can remember. His defence, which was very strong, consisted entirely of back play—he never played forward, and when he was not hitting, he allowed the ball to practically hit his bat without any attempt to get it away in order to make a run. An over-pitched ball he hit right away with great force, especially a ball a little wide of the leg stump, which he hit very hard and clean to forward square leg. Besides these great hits, he had an exceptionally powerful wrist, which he used freely, cutting the long hops on the off side with great effect. His strokes of that description were the best, I think, I ever saw, and were famous in those days.

"In his earlier years at Eton and Cambridge he was a very good bowler, but in his later years he did not bowl so much, and became quite a good wicket-keeper. For one reason or another he gave up first-class cricket soon after he left Cambridge, to the great regret of all lovers of the game."

Old cricketers may be reminded that when the Gentlemen followed-on in 1866, and gained their first victory at the Oval, Mr. Maitland, though more famous as a slow bowler than as a batsman, made 61—the top score in an innings of 352.

The Rev. F. W. Wright, who was in the three Oxford XIs captained by R. A. H. Mitchell—1863–64–65, says: "Brilliant is the word that describes the late Lord Cobham as a bat. ('C.G.' as he used to be called by Mitchell and all of us, to distinguish him from 'Spencer', or any other 'Lyttelton'). Excellent all round, with a delightful cut: I well remember to this day a stroke of his behind point, when batting at the Gas-works end of the Oval, which rattled against the palings, and would have gone further! Stylish in the extreme, his presence on the opposite side spelt danger, and his opponents were not happy till he was out. As a wicket-keeper—well—he was good enough to keep wicket for the Gentlemen v. The Players. This was in 1863, when he stumped Willsher and caught Parr. I see that he also played for Cambridge v. Oxford in '61 and '62. His departure is the severance of one of those links with the past which are now so sadly few."

The late Sir Henry Plowden, referring in W. J. Ford's *History of Cambridge University Cricket*, to his great Cambridge XI of '62 wrote, "In my day there was, I think, more slow bowling, including 'lobs', than there is now. Many men could play slows in those days; very few honestly liked them. Among those few were certainly C. G. Lyttelton and Daniel, and perhaps Marshall. Daniel's principle was 'a run a ball', and the story is told of him that he whispered to a partner who was, he thought, scoring too rapidly, 'Don't be too greedy, or they'll take him off.' C.G. had a stroke adapted from tennis, by which he drove the ball forward (more or less in the air) at the half-bound when the ball bowled was between the half volley and good length. The stroke required extreme accuracy in timing to make the ball travel, and not merely 'loft'.

"C.G.'s theory of leg-hitting short balls was to get under the ball at the top of the bound, relatively to his own position, and help it on. To the suggestion that he risked being caught, his reply was that you deserved your fate if you did not send it over long leg's head or out of the ground. I think he did hit out of the Oval thus. He had a wonderful cut just behind the wicket, delivered from an upright attitude by wrist and arm, hard down on the ball, and I saw him thus cut Griffith, I think, for six at the Oval (not in a Varsity match). His habit was not to play good balls hard on the chance of making a run; he contented himself with just stopping them; in

appearance, just allowed them to hit his bat. Mitchell, on the contrary, played every ball hard.

"I once saw C.G. play an innings at Rickling Green in which he made 74 runs off 26 balls out of 27 delivered to him. He went in with the purpose of hitting over a big tree on the edge of the Green, on the top of which was a flagstaff, and he hit the flagstaff. His hits included an eight, without an overthrow, and not downhill; the ball was stopped in its course by a gate."

General the Hon. Sir N. G. Lyttelton writes of his brother: "Lord Cobham would have been tried for the Eton XI in 1856, before he was 14, but was prevented by mumps. He left in 1860 before he was 18, so he might have been in the XI six years and captain three and Mitchell, in my opinion the greatest boy cricketer in my time, would never have been captain at all." Speaking of Lord Cobham's magnificent cutting, Sir Neville recalls one cut for five or six against Surrey at the Oval—evidently the hit that so impressed F. W. Wright—of which H. H. Stephenson said: "It ought to be gathered up and put in a glass case." Sir Neville adds that Lord Cobham hardly ever played forward.

Sir John Horner writes: "In 1861 the Cambridge XI was so strong that it was doubtful till the last if there would be places for both C. G. Lyttelton and A. W. T. Daniel. They were captains of Eton and Harrow respectively and Daniel had in 1860 made 112 not out against Eton at Lord's. However, they both played, and Lyttelton bowled so well that he was chosen for the Gentlemen." As to Lord Cobham's fielding at point Sir John says: "He did not stand so close as the old-fashioned point and, in his time, E. M. Grace and F. W. Wright used to stand, but where he stood he stopped the hardest hits that came within reach. With regard to his batting his cutting, square leg hitting, and driving were all first rate, perhaps his cutting most of all, for he could cut an underhand lob for four or five through point, and his back defence was very sure. It was said that he played Willsher better than anyone else did, but his forward play was faulty, and this, of course, was against his success at Lord's in the old rough days."

Both Sir Neville Lyttelton and Sir John Horner say positively that Lord Cobham was a fast bowler, not a bowler of middle speed as Mr. Arthur Haygarth described him in *Scores and Biographies*. As a matter of record it may be added that Lord Cobham's highest score at Lord's was 64 for M.C.C. v. Oxford University in 1865 when, for, perhaps, the only time in his life he was out leg-before-wicket.

COBHAM, Ninth Viscount, K.C.B., died on July 31, 1949, aged 66, succeeding his father in 1922. Educated at Eton, he played as the Hon. John Cavendish Lyttelton, for the College against Winchester in 1899 when Eton won an exciting match by one wicket. Subsequently he played several times for Worcestershire County C.C., whose fortunes he always followed with the keenest interest. When he became President of M.C.C. in 1935, he emulated the example of his father, who held the office in 1886, and his uncle, Alfred Lyttelton, the England wicket-keeper of the early '80s, in 1898. He was Treasurer of M.C.C. and President of Worcestershire at the time of his death. He served with the Rifle Brigade in the South African War and was A.D.C. to the High Commissioner for South Africa, 1905–08. During the First World War, he saw service in Gallipoli, Egypt, Sinai and Palestine and in the Second he was Parliamentary Secretary of State for War, 1939–40. He had been Lord-Lieutenant of Worcestershire and of the City of Worcester since 1923 and chairman of the Council of County Territorial Associations from 1942. He represented the Droitwich Division as Conservative M.P. from 1910–16. In 1908 he married Miss Violet Leonard. He is succeeded by his son, Colonel Charles Lyttelton, a former captain of Worcestershire.

COBHAM, Charles John, Tenth Viscount, K.C., P.C., G.C.M.G., G.C.V.O., who died in hospital on March 20, 1977, aged 67, was a member of one of the greatest of cricketing families. He himself, as the Hon. C. J. Lyttelton, began to play for Worcestershire in 1932 and, after captaining them on a number of occasions in 1935 and going out to Australia and New Zealand that winter as vice-captain of the M.C.C. side under E. R. T. Holmes, was the county's official captain from 1936 to 1939. This was the more remarkable as at Eton he was nowhere near the XI. But by keenness and close study of the principles of the game he made himself first into a good club cricketer and then into a competent county one.

He never made the mistake of treating first-class bowlers with exaggerated respect. Observing that Mitchell of Derbyshire always started with a googly against an amateur, he played for it and hit it a long way out of the ground. He held that, if one used one's common sense, a great bowler could be hit as far as an ordinary one (and resented it much more), only one would not be able to hit him successfully for so long. Batting on this theory, he often made 30 or 40 in double-quick time when his companions were groping, and thus was more valuable to the side than his average suggests.

A good example is the Yorkshire match at Stourbridge in 1936, played throughout on a turning wicket of the type on which Yorkshire then were regarded as invincible. Lyttelton impressed on his side that, if they played their normal game, they stood no chance at all: if they slung their bats at the ball, one or two would probably be lucky and get a few. He himself set the example. Telling his left-handed partner, Warne, to keep Verity's bowling, he faced Ellis Robinson, an off-spinner, and in 35 minutes made 48, including four 6's and four 4's. As soon as he had to play Verity, he was out. Worcestershire won by 11 runs, their first victory over Yorkshire since 1909.

Again, against the Australians in 1938, going in first, he scored 50 and 35, being particularly severe on O'Reilly. His highest score for the county and his only century was 162 that year against Leicestershire. A medium-paced bowler who could make the ball swing, he sometimes opened the bowling and occasionally took a wicket with a very slow ball which he called his "flipper".

His County Cricket ended with the War, but he continued to play club cricket and indeed found time to play throughout his period as Governor-General of New Zealand from 1957 to 1962. It was a fitting climax to his career when in 1961 at the age of 51 he captained his own team against the M.C.C. at Auckland and made 44 in 21 minutes, including two sixes. No one ever enjoyed his cricket more or took more trouble to see that others enjoyed theirs and he amply repaid off the field the debt which he owed to the game.

As President of the M.C.C. in 1954 (a post which his father and grandfather had held before him) he was outstanding. In 1963 he became Treasurer, but had to his great regret to resign next year on becoming Lord-Lieutenant of Worcestershire. For some years he acted as chairman of the committee of the Free Foresters; he was captain of the Butterflies from 1951 to 1976 and had been Governor of I Zingari since 1956. Moreover he still managed to have an occasional country-house match on his own ground at Hagley, where among the visitors were I Zingari and the London New Zealand C.C. His death is a grievous loss not only to the cricket world, but to the public life of the country. Six days before he died, he was present at the Worcestershire County C.C. annual meeting where he was extremely gratified at being elected President, a post that was also held by his father and grandfather.

COCHRANE, Alfred Henry John, an Oxford Blue in 1885, 1886, and 1888, died on December 14, 1948, at Batheaston, Somerset, aged 83. Born in Mauritius on January 26, 1865, he went to Repton School and was three years in the cricket XI before gaining his Blue as a Freshman at Oxford in 1885. Bowling medium pace left hand, he played against Cambridge three times, injury keeping him out of the 1887 match at Lord's. The Light Blues, captained by the Hon. M.B. Hawke, won the first of these matches by 133 runs; Oxford replied with victory by seven wickets, but the third meeting in which Cochrane took part was drawn. In that game, Cochrane did his best performance for Oxford, dismissing nine men for 105 runs, but rain throughout Monday and again on Thursday, to which the fixture was extended in the hope of a finish, prevented a definite decision. He played for Gentlemen against Players at Lord's in 1886 and in turn for Derbyshire and Northumberland. Besides light verse he wrote *Repton Cricket—1865–1905* and *Told in the Pavilion*.

COCKERELL, The Rev. Louis Arthur, born on November 20, 1836, died at Oxford on March 4, 1929, aged 92. Coached, when at Rugby, by John Lillywhite, he secured a place in the XI in 1855 and played in the first match against Marlborough. He was then described as "A very rising bowler, with a good delivery: is also a neat bat." He appeared for Essex and the Gentlemen of Kent. At the time of his death he was the oldest member of the Harlequins.

COE, Samuel, who died at his home at Earl Shilton, Hinckley, on November 4, 1955, aged 82, was one of the best batsmen who ever played for Leicestershire. Between 1896 and 1923 he scored 17,438 runs, average 24.69, seven times passing 1,000 in a season. The highest of his 19 centuries, 252 not out, hit without chance in four hours when he was 41 from the Northamptonshire bowling at Leicester in 1914, remains the biggest innings ever played for the county. He represented Players against Gentlemen at the Oval in 1908. An attractive left-hand batsman, he was specially good in on-side strokes. Also a

useful left-arm medium-pace bowler, he took 336 wickets.

COGHLAN, John Cornelius, one of the Kimberley team that opposed Transvaal in the first Currie Cup match—at Kimberley in April 1890—died at Bulawayo on July 1, 1945, aged 78. Kimberley was then the strongest team in South Africa, and between 1887 and 1890 Coghlan played in many good matches, including those against the first two English sides that visited the Cape. In 1892 he showed good form against W.W. Read's team when J.J. Ferris, J.T. Hearne and F. Martin were a great bowling force.

COHEN, Pilot Officer Alec, who was killed in a flying accident in May, 1955, aged 21, joined the Glamorgan ground staff at the beginning of last summer. A wicket-keeper and batsman, he represented the Welsh Secondary Schools at both cricket and Rugby football.

COKER, The Rev. John, died on July 30, 1901. He had for 46 years been Rector of the parish of Tingewick in Buckinghamshire. He was in the Winchester XI in 1838 and 1839, and in the Oxford XI in 1840–42–43–44. He captained the Winchester XI in 1839 and the Oxford XI in 1842 and 1843. His experience of the University match was peculiarly unlucky, as Oxford did not win once in the four years he played. Among his contemporaries were Alfred Lowth, G.E. Yonge, H.M. Curteis and Walter Marcon.

COLAH, S. H. M., who played for India in two Test matches against England, in 1932 and 1933, died at Ahmedabad on September 11, 1950, aged 47. Born and educated in Bombay, Colah showed promise at school and college. He became a magnificent hitter, with a particularly effective square-cut, and a brilliant fielder who threw in beautifully. When India played their first Test match—against England at Lord's in 1932—Colah made 22 and 4, and caught Woolley and Brown in England's second innings. On that tour he scored 1,069 runs in all matches, with an innings of 122 against Lancashire at Manchester. The following year Colah scored 31 and 12 against England in the first Test match at Bombay. He played in two games against Ryder's Australian team in 1935 and once against Lord Tennyson's team in 1937. In the Ranji Trophy Tournament, Colah helped Western India States and Nawanagar, and he captained the Parsis in the Bombay Quadrangular Tournament.

COLBECK, 2nd Lieut. Leonard George, M.C. (R.F.A.). Died at sea, January 3, 1918, aged 34. Marlborough XI, King's College(Camb.) XI, Cambridge University XI, Middlesex, M.C.C. Played hockey for Cambridge.

Colbeck had a fine record as a batsman at Marlborough, but his name will live in cricket history by reason of the extraordinary innings he played in the University match of 1905. Going in for the second time against a balance of 101 runs Cambridge lost six wickets for 77, and looked to be a hopelessly beaten side. At this point Colbeck, in with the score at 44, was joined by McDonell, and in the course of 85 minutes the two batsmen put on 143 runs together, completely pulling the match round. McDonell kept up his wicket while Colbeck hit on the off side with amazing brilliancy. The partnership recalled the memorable stand made for Cambridge in the 1870 match by Yardley and J. W. Dale. Colbeck took all sorts of risks, cutting balls off the middle stump to the boundary, but his eye served him so well that he was very rarely at fault. He hit 13 fours in his 107 and was batting for two hours and a quarter. Like Yardley in 1870 he had his reward, Cambridge in the end winning the match by 40 runs. Colbeck had splendid figures for Cambridge in 1908, scoring 552 runs with an average of 42, but when tried in half-a-dozen matches for Middlesex in 1906 he did very little. He played one innings of 46 and another of 30 but on all other occasions he failed dismally. In 1906, however, he again did very well for Cambridge, scoring 63 and 44 against Oxford at Lord's, and heading the University batting with an average of 39. Against W. G. Grace's XI at Cambridge he played an innings of 175 not out.—S.H.P.

COLE, Frederick Livesay, an occasional wicket-keeper for Gloucestershire from 1879, when he first appeared at Lord's, died at Sheffield on July 1, 1941. While he would be a useful cricketer to pass muster with W. G. Grace as captain, a more interesting point than his prowess behind the stumps concerns his age. In *Scores and Biographies* the date of his birth is given as October 4, 1856. This tallied with *Wisden* until 1934, when the year was altered to 1842—a possible misprint due to re-setting "Births and Deaths". Yorkshire papers described how "he joined the Federal Army when 19 and served for four years under Generals McClellan and Phil Sheridan"; also that during the Franco–Prussian war he was in the siege of Paris and that he was with Sir Archibald Forbes, the war correspondent, in the Russo–Turkish war before being invalided home in 1876. Inquiries at the Bristol Grammar School, where he was said to have been educated, failed to trace him, neither can any mention of his name between 1837 and 1887 be found in the Registers of the Yeovil district, though his birthplace was recorded as Ilminster, together with the date, at the time of his first match at Lord's.

In response to a question in the *Bristol Evening Post*, Mr. Harry Wookey wrote that he played "with Fred Cole for Schoolmasters against Bath Association in 1880, when I was only 17 years of age. Fred Cole was born on October 4, 1856." Another Bristol cricketer confirmed that opinion. Yet it was asserted in the Yorkshire papers that "he had three centenarian brothers all living" and that he was 90 when he retired from the Sheffield Gas Company, though no one knew his exact age and thought he was 60: "George," one of the "centenarian" brothers, could not be traced in Bristol.

Fred Cole made plenty of runs in club cricket, and H. E. Roslyn, of the Gloucestershire County Committee, recalls that "Fred Cole scored the first hundred ever made on our county ground and I kept wicket while he did so"—that was the year before the formal opening in 1889.

COLE, Canon George Lamont, who died on October 14, 1964, aged 79, was in the Sherborne XI, being second in the batting averages in 1904 and 1905. Between 1909 and 1911 he played in six matches for Hampshire, his highest innings being 33 against Leicestershire at Leicester in the last season.

COLE, Terence George Owen, who died on December 15, 1944, at Stoke Court, Taunton, aged 67, scarely fulfilled the promise he showed when at Harrow. A good bat and clever left-hand slow bowler, he was in the school XI for three seasons, excelling against Eton in 1897 with 36 and 142. In the two previous seasons he met with curious experiences. Going in last, he was not out 11 and 0; then in 1896, when opening the innings, he was twice run out for six and 23. Altogether in these matches he took only five wickets, and, after being the most destructive bowler for Harrow in two seasons, he headed the batting averages with 37.50. Going up to Cambridge, he made a good 46 in the Freshmen's match, but could not find his form with either bat or ball when tried in the XI. For his college, Trinity Hall, he made 252 against St. John's in 1899, W. P. Robertson, 185, taking part with Cole in an unbroken opening partnership of 346, the runs actually being scored in two hours and a half. For Liverpool against his old University he scored 88 and 61, and 62 and 116 in consecutive years, his average in 1903 being 68.50. In succession he played for Lancashire, Denbighshire and Derbyshire with moderate results, but he continued a free scorer with Somerset Stragglers. He toured West Indies with Lord Brackley's team in 1904–05. In the First World War he was Captain in the Denbighshire Yeomanry.

COLEBROOK, The Rev. Edward Lotherington, who died on August 10, 1939, at Canterbury, aged 80, was in the Charterhouse XI three seasons and got his Oxford Blue in 1880. Going in first at Lord's, he scored only three, but the order was changed and he made 34 not out in the second innings of 151. A. G. Steel took seven wickets for 61, and Cambridge won by 115 runs. In a match between Gentlemen of Kent and England at Canterbury in 1880, he was dismissed twice for low scores by W. G. Grace.

COLEMAN, Charles Alfred Richard, who died at Market Harborough on June 14, 1978, aged 71, played for Leicestershire from 1926 to 1935 without ever quite getting a secure place in the side. He was a useful all-rounder, a hard hitting bat whose highest score and only century was 114 in two-and-a-quarter hours v. Gloucestershire at Cheltenham in 1930 and a fast-medium bowler with a high windmill action. Altogether he made 2,403 runs with an average of 15.02 and took 100 wickets at 35.76. Later he had professional engagements in Scotland and from 1946 to 1949 was one of the first class umpires and officiated more than once in Test matches.

COLEMAN, Lieut. Edward Charles (R.F.A.), killed April 2, 1917, aged 25. Dulwich College XI, 1907–08–09–10. Excellent wicket-keeper. Pembroke (Camb.) XI. Played in a few matches for Essex.

COLERIDGE, The Rev. Frederick John, died suddenly on February 20, 1906, at Cadbury, Devon, where he had been vicar for over 50 years. Born at Ottery St. Mary on December 4, 1828, he was in the Eton XI, 1844–46, and subsequently in the Oxford XI, 1847 and 1850.

COLES, Percival, born on May 2, 1865, died on February 24, 1920, at St. Leonards-on-

Sea. Although best remembered as captain of the Oxford Rugby Fifteen, in 1886, and for a few seasons secretary of the Rugby Union, he was a very useful cricketer. As a member of the XI while at Rugby, he played twice against Marlborough at Lord's, scoring 54 and four in 1883 and nine and 18 a year later. He did not obtain his Blue for cricket at Oxford, but appeared on a few occasions for the University in 1885. The same season he assisted Sussex in four matches. For Devonshire Park against G. W. Morrison's XI, at Eastbourne, in 1892, he scored 247 not out and Mr. S. Colman 209, the pair making 472 together for the first wicket.

COLLETT, William Eustace, who was born in Lambeth, September 23, 1841, died at Kennington on May 2, 1904. He was a good average batsman, could bowl fast round-armed, and in the field was generally long-stop or mid-off. He appeared for Surrey three times in 1869, and once in 1874.

COLLIER, Staff-Sergt. Charles George Alfred (Army Ordnance Corps), who was born at Banff on August 23, 1886, was killed in action on August 25, 1916. He was a useful batsman and played several good innings for Worcestershire, the best being his 72 v. Hampshire at Portsmouth in 1912. Before qualifying for Worcestershire he was on the ground-staff at Edgbaston.

COLLIER, Joseph, a survivor of the players who took the field against the first Australian touring side in 1878, died at Leicester on October 15, 1935, aged 84. For the county Collier scored 20 not out and six, the match being made memorable by Charles Bannerman getting 133—the first hundred hit in England by an Australian. Ten years later Collier was in the Leicestershire XI who beat the Australians by 20 runs. Pougher took 10 wickets for 71 and Mr. H. T. Arnall-Thompson, the county captain, nine wickets for 65.

COLLINS, Arthur, who died in July, 1945, aged 73, played for Sussex occasionally from 1895 to 1902. Like most bowlers he experienced varied fortune. At Hove in 1896, after W. G. Grace in the Gloucestershire first innings scored 243 not out, he bowled the Doctor for three in the second innings; in the return match at Bristol "W.G." made 301 before being bowled by Collins, and Gloucestershire won by an innings and 123 runs. Collins often made runs and was credited with an average of 24.48 for 1,812 runs in Sir Home Gordon's *Form at a Glance.*

COLLINS, Lieut. Arthur Edward Jeune (Royal Engineers), who was killed in action on November 11, 1914, came suddenly into note by scoring 628 not out for Clarke's House v. North Town, in a junior house match at Clifton College, in June, 1899, when only 13 years old. During the six hours and 50 minutes he was in he hit a six, four fives, 31 fours, 33 threes and 146 twos, carrying his bat through the innings, and Clarke's, who scored 836, won by an innings and 688 runs. Collins also obtained 11 wickets in the match, seven in the first innings and four in the second, and in partnership with Redfern (13) put on as many as 183 for the last wicket. In 1901 and 1902 he was in the College XI, in the former year scoring 342 runs with an average of 38.00, his highest innings being 112 against Old Cliftonians. He was a free-hitting batsman, but his military duties prevented him from taking cricket seriously: still he made many good scores in Army matches, and for Old Cliftonians v. Trojans at Southampton in August, 1913, he and F. G. Robinson made 141 without being parted for the first wicket in 38 minutes, Collins scoring 63 and his partner 77. His best performance at Lord's was to make 58 and 36 for R.E. v. R.A. in 1913. He was born in India in 1885, gazetted second Lieutenant in 1904 and promoted Lieutenant in 1907.

COLLINS, Christopher, born at Cobham on October 14, 1859, died at Gravesend on August 11, 1919. He played a few times for Kent between 1881 and 1885, and retired from the side at the age of 25 as his action was not above suspicion. He was a useful batsman and a fast round-armed bowler with a break from the off. His brother, George Collins, also appeared for the county, as well as (during his last few seasons) his son.

COLLINS, Lieut. Fred Bisset, born February 25, 1881; killed October, 1917. Scotch College (Melbourne) XI. East Melbourne C.C. XI from 1898–99 onwards, his bowling summary for the club being 15,039 balls, 5,896 runs, 422 wickets, average 13. Played for Victoria 1899–1900 to 1908–09. In inter-State games took 122 wickets for 3,267 runs, and against English sides 20 wickets for 420. Gave up cricket early owing to a strain. Excellent slip, useful bat, and bowled medium pace, with big off-break and a deceptive flight. Could bowl a really fast ball. Height 6 ft. 1 in.

COLLINS, Geoffrey Albert Kirwan, who

died suddenly on August 7, 1968, aged 59, was in the Lancing XI from 1926 to 1928. He headed the batting figures in each season, his best being that of 1928 when, as captain, he scored 863 runs, average 71.91, including four centuries, the highest of which was 212 against Lancing Old Boys. First appearing for Sussex when still at school, he played periodically for the county for seven years till 1934. Business afterwards confined his activities on the field to club cricket. As an Association footballer of ability, he assisted Lancing Old Boys and the Casuals.

COLLINS, George C., who played for Kent from 1911 to 1928, died on January 23, 1949, aged 59. His father, Christopher, and his uncle, George, both played for Kent. Born at Gravesend, G.C. Collins learned his cricket there and at Cobham, where his family had close ties. His father played at Cobham under the captaincy of the Hon. Ivo Bligh, Eighth Earl of Darnley, who captained England's successful team in Australia in 1882. A tall well-built cricketer, Collins was a splendid right-arm fast bowler and a useful left-handed batsman. His best performance for the county was in 1922 when, against Nottinghamshire at Dover, after dismissing six batsmen for 18 runs in the first innings, he took all 10 wickets for 65 runs. He kept a splendid length and came quickly off the ground. Altogether in first-class cricket he scored 6,270 runs, average 22.15, and obtained 379 wickets, average 23.60. He was a member of the M.C.C. team which visited West Indies, 1925–26.

COLLINS, George Churton, who died at Durban on August 18, 1956, aged 79, played as a batsman for Natal from 1898 to 1911, being captain for several seasons.

COLLINS, Herbert L., who died in Sydney on May 28, 1959, aged 70, took part in 19 Test matches for Australia between 1920 and 1926. First appearing for New South Wales in 1912, he was a prominent member of the Australian Imperial Forces team in England in 1919, being captain for much of the programme after C. E. Kelleway, because of some disagreement, dropped out. During that tour Collins scored 1,615 runs, including six centuries, average 38.45, and with slow left-arm bowling took 106 wickets for 16.55 runs each.

A bookmaker by profession, he was widely known as "Horseshoe" Collins by reason of his good fortune in connection with racing and in winning the toss at cricket. He was one of the great Australian team in England in 1921, when a broken thumb caused him to miss two of the Test matches, and he captained the side in England in 1926 when, handicapped by neuritis, he did not display his true form. A batsman possessing exceptionally sound defence and seemingly unlimited patience, he spent four hours 50 minutes over 40 runs in the Old Trafford Test match of 1921 when following a blank first day through rain, an England total of 362 for four wickets, declared, left Australia with nothing to hope for but a draw.

In all Test matches he scored 1,352 runs, average 45.06 and hit four centuries, the highest being 203 against South Africa at Johannesburg in 1921 and 162 against England at Adelaide in 1920–21. In 30 Sheffield Shield games for New South Wales he obtained 2,040 runs, highest innings 146, for an average of 41.63.

COLLINS, Tom, the oldest living cricket Blue, died on March 16, 1934 at his home at Newport, Salop, in his 94th year. Born on January 3, 1841, at Warwick, for which constituency his grandfather was Member of Parliament, Tom Collins went at an early age to Bury St. Edmunds, and from King Edward the Sixth School he gained an open scholarship at Christ College, Cambridge in 1859. He became Headmaster of Newport Grammar School, Salop, in 1871 and occupied the position for 32 years until his retirement. When an assistant master at King Edward School, Birmingham, Mr. Collins became a barrister of the Middle Temple in 1866 but he did not practise at the Bar.

In the cricket field Mr. Collins was remembered best for the part he took, inadvertently, in bringing about the alteration in Law 10, which until June, 1864, prevented a bowler from delivering the ball from above the height of his shoulder. In 1862 Edgar Willsher, when playing for England against Surrey at Kennington Oval, was no-balled six times consecutively by John Lillywhite for having his hand above the shoulder at the moment of delivery. On the same ground a year later Tom Collins and Mr. H. M. Plowden, who subsequently became a famous metropolitan magistrate, disposed of Surrey for 99 runs, and so took a prominent part in Cambridge beating the very powerful Surrey XI.

Directly after this came the University match at Lord's and on a wet pitch Cambridge, thanks to Plowden and Collins, gained a lead on the first innings of six runs with a total of 65. Collins disposed of such

famous batsmen as R. D. Walker and R. A. H. Mitchell early in the innings, and then, to everyone's astonishment, he was no-balled five times in succession. The occurrence was influenced by an instruction just issued directing umpires to attend particularly to the height of the bowler's hand. Collins was so upset that he did not get another wicket and failed with the bat, being dismissed for 0 and one. Oxford, set to get 68, won comfortably by eight wickets. Collins regarded his bad luck on his only appearance for Cambridge against Oxford as a distinct misfortune which he did not deserve to undergo. Still, his experience helped to make cricket history; his being "called" went a long way towards the removal of all restrictions as to the height from which a bowler delivered the ball.

Tom Collins played for Suffolk County from 1862 to 1869. Over six ft. in height, of powerful build and dark complexion, he was a conspicuous figure on the field. About medium-pace, with swerve and spin from leg, he accomplished many notable performances in those days of low scoring. In addition to his ability as an all-round cricketer he was a fine player at billiards, representing Cambridge against Oxford both in the Singles and Doubles matches.

Early in 1933, he received the very rare distinction of being elected to Hon. Membership of the M.C.C. in recognition of his being the oldest living cricket Blue. This seniority now belongs to the Rev. A. H. Winter of Westminster School and Cambridge who was born on December 4, 1844 and played against Oxford in 1865–66–67.

COLLINS, W. E. W., born in 1849, died at Heacham, Norfolk, on January 7, 1932, at the age of 83. Of this player, Mr. A. J. Webbe, the famous Oxford and Middlesex batsman, wrote a letter to *The Times*. "A very fine left-handed bowler, essentially the man for a hard wicket, as he was very fast off the pitch and came a lot with his arm. Also a great hitter. He was five years in the Radley XI, a captain in 1866 and 1867, at the same time being Head of the School. He then went up to Oxford, where he failed to get his Blue, but at that time the Oxford XI was mainly composed of Brasenose men, and Collins was at Jesus. In August, 1874, when playing at Freshwater, in the Isle of Wight, Collins actually hit up 338, not out, in about four hours, and all run out, as there were no boundaries! 'Buns' Thornton had a great opinion of Collins as a cricketer, so in 1886 he invited him to play for Lord Londesborough v. the Australians at Scarborough. Out of the huge score of 558 made by the English XI, Collins went in last, made 56 not out, scoring, I believe, off every ball he received. In 1888 he was invited to play for Oxford Past and Present v. the Australians at Leyton, and in the first innings took six wickets for 35 runs, he being then 40 years of age. What a pity that he played hardly any other first-class matches but these!"

Mr. Collins appeared at times for Shropshire and the M.C.C. He was an able writer on a variety of subjects, being for many years a frequent contributor to *Blackwood's Magazine* on cricket, animal life and other subjects. He also wrote a large part of *Annals of the Free Foresters*, published in 1895. Extremely popular and known to his intimate friends as "Colenso", Mr. Collins was a man of most generous disposition.

COLLINS, William Edward, M.B., M.R.C.S., C.M.G., born October 14, 1853, died on August 11, 1934, at Wellington, New Zealand. An excellent free-hitting batsman and a good wicket-keeper, he was in the Cheltenham College XI of 1870 and 1871. He earned greater fame as a half-back at Rugby football, playing for England against Scotland in 1874 and the next two years and also against Ireland in 1875–76. He went to New Zealand in 1878 and was a member of the Legislative Council in 1907. It was a nephew of his, A.E.J. Collins, who made the highest score on record, 628 not out, in a junior house match at Clifton College in 1899.

COLLINSON, John, who died at Hove on August 29, 1979, aged 67, appeared in two matches for Middlesex in 1939 and in his first innings for the county, against Gloucestershire at Cheltenham, was second-highest scorer with 34. In 1946, having gone as a master to Malvern, where for some years he ran the cricket, he played one match for Worcestershire. He had a solid defence, but was a very slow scorer.

COLLISHAW, William Frederick, an old Warwickshire professional, died on February 1, 1936. Born on October 2, 1860, at Hickling in Nottinghamshire, he played for Warwickshire from 1885 to 1892—three years before the county took part in the Championship. A steady batsman, he hit hard and was a useful medium-paced high delivery bowler. His highest innings, 145, in May, 1888 against Leicestershire, was the first hundred hit on the Edgbaston ground. He

made a memorable first appearance at Lord's on August 24, 1885, when, going in first wicket down for Edgbaston against M.C.C. and Ground, he scored 77 and 39, being not out at the close of each innings—so he batted while 18 wickets fell.

COLMAN, Sir Jeremiah, J.P., died on January 15, 1942, aged 82, at his home, Gatton Park, Reigate, Surrey. A year before he underwent a severe operation from which he never fully recovered, but until a few hours before his passing he attended to business and signed cheques. That was characteristic of the close interest and unflagging zeal which he applied to cricket. The game was in his blood, for his father was one of 11 brothers who played as a team in Norfolk about a century ago. He used to say that he had no chance of cricket at school, but at St. John's College, Cambridge, he learned to bowl with such good results that he became captain of the College XI in 1882.

He never played first-class cricket, but occupied his leisure watching all the best matches, particularly those between England and Australia and the Universities. A member of the Surrey club from an early age, he became President in 1916, retained the office for seven years, and remained an enthusiastic Vice-President until his end. Famous in commerce as the "Mustard Millionaire", he related that his father, one of the founders of the firm—J. and J. Colman—once said that "the family fortunes were made, not from the mustard people ate, but from what they left on their plates". He had a splendid collection of cricket pictures and was one of the best-known growers of orchids in the world.

COLMAN, Stanley, known to all cricketers in the South of England as captain of the Wanderers Club for over 50 years, died at Walton-on-the-Hill on February 27, 1942, aged 80. When a boy he founded the club, which remained his chief hobby, and changing its name from Clapham Wanderers, he conducted all its business. When at length his playing days ceased he continued as treasurer and acted as M.C. at the annual dinner—an outstanding event in cricket's social life until the War intervened. Youngest son of Mr. Edward Colman, one of 11 brothers who played cricket in Norfolk a century ago, Stanley was cousin of Sir Jeremiah, whom he outlived by only a few weeks.

An admirable bat and safe fieldsman, he played for Surrey occasionally in the '80s, his highest innings being 63—his first appearance for the county, at Trent Bridge in 1882, coincided with that of Robert Abel. He often captained the Second XI and at the Oval in 1897 carried his bat for 111 against Northamptonshire. For many years he served on the County Club Committee, and never missed watching a match at the Oval unless playing elsewhere, while, despite declining health, he maintained his attendance in 1939. A member of M.C.C., he invariably wore the club's famous red and gold tie.

During his long active career he scored over 40,000 runs and made over 100 centuries, and such was his stubborn defence that in more than 300 innings he was not out. Most memorable of his achievements was his first-wicket stand of 472 with Percy Coles for Devonshire Park against G.W. Morrison's XI at Eastbourne in 1892, a record partnership for any wicket in all grades of cricket until J. T. Brown and J. Tunnicliffe put up 554 for Yorkshire against Derbyshire at Chesterfield in 1898. While usually a steady batsman, he could use his height in fine hitting all round the wicket. S. H. Evershed (172), afterwards Derbyshire captain, and Stanley Colman (112) added 310 for the Carrow second wicket in 135 minutes at Lakenham and were not separated. Twice with D. L. A. Jephson, afterwards Surrey captain, Stanley Colman scored 300 for the first wicket. For Wanderers in 1900 he made 102 not out, 145 and 100 (retired hurt) in consecutive innings. A strange experience was his opening stand for 211 with F. E. Saunders, an England Association international half-back. Neither man hit a boundary owing to the size of the ground and long grass in "the country".

A very good sprint runner, Stanley Colman played both Rugby and Association football for Clapham Rovers. When feeling too old for the Rugby game he captained the club's Association XI. I was fortunate to play with him and N. C. Bailey. In later years he was a keen golfer until neuritis in the arm compelled him to forsake active participation in any game.—H.P.

COMBER, George, useful both as batsman and wicket-keeper, was born at Redhill on October 12, 1856, and died there on October 18, 1929. His name will be found in a few Surrey matches between 1880 and 1885. For many years he was engaged by the Reigate Priory C.C., and for that club against Guildford, at Reigate, in June, 1882, played an innings of 154, he and W. W. Read (263) adding 368 together for the third wicket.

COMMAILLE, John McIlwain Moore, who died in Cape Town on July 27, 1956, aged 73, represented South Africa at both cricket and, as outside or inside-right, at Association football. He played cricket against England in South Africa in five Test matches in 1909 and two in 1927, and took part in five in England in 1924 when vice-captain to H. W. Taylor. It was in the opening Test of this tour that A. E. R. Gilligan and M. W. Tate, bowling unchanged, dismissed South Africa at Edgbaston for 30. "Mick" Commaille also visited Australia under P. W. Sherwell in 1911, but did not appear in a Test. In 22 innings against England, he hit 355 runs, average 16.90, his highest score being 47.

Generally an opening batsman, he played for Cape Town for many years, his best season being that of 1912 when he exceeded 1,000 runs. From his early 20s till he was 47, he assisted Western Province in the Currie Cup competition and then joined Orange Free State, for whom he (186) and S. K. Coen (165) shared in a record second wicket partnership of 305. Commaille later played for Griqualand West, whom he captained. He had been Secretary of the South African Football Association and an administrator for the Western Province F.A.

COMPTON, Edward Denison, who died at Rye on October 11, 1940, aged 68, played for Somerset and Oxfordshire. Prominent in games at Lancing, he got his Association football Blue at Oxford in 1895–96.

COMPTON, Leslie Harry, died after a long period of ill-health on December 27, 1984, aged 72, at his son's home in Essex. Elder brother of Denis Compton, he was better known as a footballer, a tower of strength to the Arsenal for years at centre-half, who created a record by first gaining an international cap at the age of 38; but he was also a good enough cricketer to play for Middlesex for 19 years, during 10 of which he was a regular member of the side. After a few games in 1938 and 1939, he played more frequently in 1946, without so far having done more than attract attention by his glorious all-round fielding. However, in 1947, when Middlesex won the Championship, he gained a regular place, scoring 806 runs with an average of 21.21. Against Derbyshire at Derby he played a marvellous innings of 107, the only century of his career, adding 181 in 93 minutes for the fifth wicket with Brown and playing a notable part in a vital victory. In this season, too, he began to take over the wicket-keeping from Price, whom he succeeded next year as the regular wicket-keeper. He held this position until 1956, after which he handed over to Murray, and he played his last match in 1957.

For several years he had continued to be a valuable bat in the lower half of the order, but he never really fulfilled his promise and latterly was little more than a tailender. A big man and very strong, he was a fine, natural driver but he never became a good judge of length. On the other hand, he developed into a thoroughly reliable wicket-keeper, particularly adept at stumping off the spin bowlers and reading the googly. In all matches for Middlesex he scored 5,781 runs with an average of 16.85, caught 465 batsmen and stumped 131. Twelve wickets at 47.42 each does not suggest much of a bowler, but there were those who reckoned that, had he concentrated on his bowling, he might have been a valuable medium-pace right-armer, especially when it was necessary to keep runs down. In fact, he was a thorough cricketer. He had a benefit in 1954.

CONDER, William Stanley, who died suddenly in his garden at Kew on May 21, 1979, aged 69, spent most of his life in the City of London and devoted his spare time to cricket statistics. He was a member of his native Yorkshire, M.C.C. and Surrey, and for years compiled for *Wisden* extensive details of cricketers' careers.

CONIBERE, William Jack, who died early in September, 1982, aged 59, had a trial for Somerset as an amateur in 1950. A fast-medium left-armer, who batted right-hand, he took six wickets against Warwickshire but met with little success in his three remaining matches.

CONINGHAM, Arthur, died at Sydney on June 13, 1939, aged 73. He played for Queensland and New South Wales and in 1893 came to England but did nothing noteworthy. His highest innings was 151 for Queensland against New South Wales. In a match at Brisbane in 1891 for Stanley against Alberts in the Aitchinson Ale Trophy competition, all Stanley's 26 runs were made by Coningham. A left-hand batsman and bowler, he ranked high at home as an all-rounder. A first-class runner, rifle shot, billiards player and oarsman, he also played football.

CONSIDINE, Sidney George Ulick, died at Bath on August 31, 1950, aged 49. In first-class cricket between 1919 and 1935 he scored almost 3,000 runs for Somerset with an average of 21.33. He did not appear frequently for the county, but in 1922, when a regular member of the side, he scored 973 runs in 40 innings and finished third in the averages. His only century was 130 not out against Worcestershire at Taunton in 1921. Educated at Blundells, Considine was an all-round sportsman and played Rugby for Bath, Somerset and England. He became a solicitor, and in the 1939–45 War was a Squadron Leader in the R.A.F.

CONSTANTINE, Lebrun S., who died on January 5, 1942, at Trinidad, aged 67, came to England with the first two teams from West Indies in 1900 and 1906, and made a name for proficiency at the game, earning a reputation for zeal which his son, Laurie N. Constantine, has raised to high fame. After doing well for Trinidad as a batsman with individual style in bringing off unexpected strokes, Lebrun Constantine, under the captaincy of Mr. R. S. A. Warner, brother of Sir Pelham, averaged 30 for 610 runs on his first visit, being surpassed only by Ollivierre. Against Gentlemen of M.C.C. at Lord's, after being not out 24, he scored 113 in the follow-on, and with W. J. Burton, one of two professionals in the side, added 162 in 65 minutes for the ninth wicket, so preventing an innings defeat. On his second visit Lebrun Constantine averaged 29 for 1,025 in all matches. Besides his value as a vigorous batsman he fielded with plenty of dash.

LORD CONSTANTINE
THE SPONTANEOUS CRICKETER
By John Arlott

Lord Constantine, M.B.E. died in London on July 1, 1971. The parents of the child born in Diego Martin, Trinidad, almost 70 years before, may in their highest ambitions have hoped that he would play cricket for the West Indies. They cannot have dreamt that he would take a major share in lifting his people to a new level of respect within the British Commonwealth; that along the way he would become the finest fieldsman and one of the most exciting all-rounders the game of cricket has known: and that he would die Baron Constantine, of Maraval in Trinidad and Tobago, and of Nelson, in the County Palatine of Lancaster, a former Cabinet Minister and High Commissioner of his native Trinidad.

Learie—or "Connie" to 40 years of cricketers—came upon his historic cue as a man of his age, reflecting and helping to shape it. He made his mark in the only way a poor West

Indian boy of his time could do, by playing cricket of ability and character. He went on to argue the rights of the coloured peoples with such an effect as only a man who had won public affection by games-playing could have done in the Britain of that period.

Learie Nicholas Constantine, born September 21, 1902, was the son of Lebrun Constantine, a plantation foreman who toured England as an all-rounder with the West Indian cricketers of 1900—when he scored the first century for a West Indies team in England—and 1906. In 1923 they both played for Trinidad against British Guiana at Georgetown, one of the few instances of a father and son appearing together in a first-class match; both of them long cherished the occasion. In constant family practice the father insisted on a high standard of fielding which was to prove the foundation of his son's success.

The younger Constantine had played only three first-class matches before he was chosen for Austin's 1923 team to England when he distinguished himself largely—indeed, almost solely—by his brilliance as cover point. On that visit he learnt much that he never forgot, by no means all of it about cricket: and he recognised the game as his only possible ladder to the kind of life he wanted.

As C.L.R. James has written "he revolted against the revolting contrast between his first class status as a cricketer and his third-class status as a man". That, almost equally with his enthusiasm for the game, prompted the five years of unremitting practice after which, in 1928, he came to England under Karl Nunes on West Indies' first Test tour as an extremely lively fast bowler, hard-hitting batsman and outstanding fieldsman in any position.

Muscular but lithe, stocky but long armed, he bowled with a bounding run, a high, smooth action and considerable pace. His batting, which depended considerably upon eye, was sometimes unorthodox to the point of spontaneous invention: but on his day it was virtually impossible to bowl at him. In the deep he picked up while going like a sprinter and threw with explosive accuracy; close to the wicket he was fearless and quick; wherever he was posted he amazed everyone by his speed and certainty in making catches which seemed far beyond reach. His movement was so joyously fluid and, at need, acrobatic that he might have been made of springs and rubber.

Although he did little in the Tests of that summer he performed the double and in

public esteem was quite the most successful member of the party. He provided splendid cricketing entertainment. Everyone who ever watched him will recall with delight his particular parlour trick—when a ball from him was played into the field he would turn and walk back towards his mark: the fieldsman would throw the ball at his back, "Connie" would keep walking and, without appearing to look, turn his arm and catch the ball between his shoulder blades; no one, so far as can be ascertained, ever saw him miss.

Crowds recognised and enjoyed him as a cricketer of adventure: but the reports alone of a single match established him in the imagination of thousands who had never seen him play. At Lord's, in June, Middlesex made 352 for six and West Indies, for whom only Constantine, with 86, made more than 30, were 122 behind on the first innings. When Middlesex batted again, Constantine took seven for 57—six for 11 in his second spell. West Indies wanting 259 to win were 121 for five when Constantine came in to score 103 out of 133—with two sixes, 12 fours and a return drive that broke Jack Hearne's finger so badly that he did not play again that season—in an hour, to win the match by three wickets. Lord's erupted: and next day all cricketing England accepted a new major figure.

That performance confirmed the obvious, that Constantine was, as he knew he needed to be, the ideal League professional—surely the finest of all. He wanted a part-time living adequate for him to study law. England was the only place, and cricket his only means, of doing both. His batting could win a match in an hour; his bowling in a couple of overs, his catching in a few scattered moments. This was the kind of cricket nearest his heart: and he expressed himself through it. No man ever played cricket for a living—as Constantine needed to do more desperately than most professional cricketers—with greater gusto. Any club in the Lancashire Leagues would have been grateful to sign him. Nelson did so with immense satisfaction on both sides. Constantine drew and delighted crowds—and won matches: Nelson won the Lancashire league eight times in his 10 seasons there—an unparalleled sequence—and broke the ground attendance record at every ground in the competition. Less spectacularly, he coached and guided the younger players with true sympathy. Among the people of Nelson, many of whom had never seen a black man before, "Connie" and his wife, Norma, settled to a happy existence which they remembered with nostalgia to the end. In 1963 the Freedom of the Borough of Nelson was bestowed on the man who then was Sir Learie Constantine.

Because of his League engagements he played little more than a hundred first-class matches, in which he scored 4,451 runs at 24.32, and took 424 wickets at 20.60. In 18 Tests between 1928 and 1939 his overall figures were poor—641 runs at 19.42; 58 wickets at 30.10. On the other hand he virtually won two important Tests and shaped a third. At Georgetown, in 1930, when West Indies beat England for the first time, George Headley made a major batting contribution; but it was Constantine who twice broke the English batting with four for 35 and five for 87, figures not approached by any other bowler in the match. At Port of Spain in 1934–35 he levelled the series—which West Indies eventually won by one match—when, after scoring 90 and 31, he took two for 41 and ended his second innings three for 11 (in 14.5 overs) with the master stroke of having as great a resister as Maurice Leyland lbw with only one ball of the match remaining. In his last Test, at the Oval in 1939, when he was 37 years old, his five for 73 took West Indies to a first-innings lead.

As he grew older he grew more astute. As his pace dropped—though he was always likely to surprise with a faster ball or deal a yorker of high speed—he developed a superbly concealed slower ball; and at need he was an effective slow bowler with wrist or finger spin. He continued to play in charity matches well through his 50s when he could still make vivid strokes, bowl out good batsmen and take spectacular catches.

In his younger days some thought him bouncy or unduly colour conscious; if that were so, Nelson warmed him. It would have been strange if so dynamic and effective a cricketer had not bubbled over with confidence. Certainly, though, he gave unhesitating and helpful counsel, and generous praise to his amateur colleagues in the Nelson team. Meanwhile he fought discrimination against his people with a dignity firm but free of acrimony.

Half Learie Constantine's life was spent in England and, although his doctors had long before advised him that a lung condition endangered his life if he did not return to the warmer climate of the West Indies, he died in London. He remained in England during the Second World War as a Ministry of Labour welfare officer with West Indian workers. In 1944 he fought one of the historic cases against colour prejudice when he won damages from The Imperial Hotel in London for "failing to receive and lodge him".

He was deeply moved—and never forgot it—when the other players—all white-skinned—elected him captain of the Dominions team that beat England in the magnificent celebratory, end-of-war match at Lord's in 1946. He rose to the occasion in a fine forcing partnership with Keith Miller and his shrewd captaincy decided a narrow issue with only minutes to spare.

By then, however, his serious cricketing days were drawing to an end. He did occasional writing and broadcasting. Among his books are *Cricket in the Sun*, *Cricket and I*, *How to Play Cricket*, *Cricketers' Carnival*, *The Changing Face of Cricket* (with Denzil Batchelor), and *Colour Bar*. Years of dogged study were rewarded when he was called to the Bar by the Middle Temple in 1954. Returning to Trinidad he was elected an M.P. in his country's first democratic parliament; became Minister of Works in the government and subsequently High Commissioner for Trinidad and Tobago in London from 1962 until 1964. He was awarded the M.B.E. in 1945; knighted in 1962; made an honorary Master of the Bench in 1963; and created a life peer in 1969. He served various periods as a governor of the B.B.C., a Rector of St. Andrews, a member of the Race Relations Board and the Sports Council.

A devout Roman Catholic, of easy humour and essential patience, he lived a contented domestic life with his wife and his daughter, who is now a school teacher in Trinidad. His outlook was that of a compassionate radical and he maintained his high moral standards unswervingly.

To the end of his days he recalled with joy the great moments of his cricket and the friends he had made. His wife survived him by barely two months: and Trinidad posthumously awarded him the Trinity Cross, the country's highest honour.

CONWAY, Arthur J., who died on November 1, 1954, aged 68, played occasionally for Worcestershire between 1911 and 1919. A right-arm bowler of rather more than medium-pace who made the ball swerve appreciably, he took 54 wickets, average 34.03. Far and away his best performance was at Moreton-in-Marsh in 1914, when he took nine wickets for 38 runs in the first Gloucestershire innings and six for 49 in the second. Thanks chiefly to him Worcestershire won a match of low scoring by 180 runs.

Conway also played football for Aston Villa and Wolverhampton Wanderers.

CONWAY, John, the promoter and manager of the first Australian team (that of 1878) which visited England, died at Frankston, on August 22, 1909. He was born at Fyansford, near Geelong, on February 3, 1843, and was educated at the Melbourne Church of England Grammar School. When only 19 years of age he was chosen to appear for Eighteen of Victoria against H. H. Stephenson's team on the Melbourne ground—the first match ever played by an English side in Australia—and although he made only one run in the match he took four wickets for 60. He was then a very fast bowler. In later years he developed into a sound batsman and an able captain, and his fielding at slip was always of a high order. A week after the match mentioned he played for Victoria against New South Wales and took five wickets for 39 runs, and in the game between the same sides at Sydney in December, 1865, he took eight wickets and scored 33. He took part in a lot of club cricket in Melbourne and for many years was captain of South Melbourne. A good judge of a young cricketer, he was the first to recognise the merits of Horan and Blackham. He was also an interesting and able writer on the game, and, in addition to contributing regularly to Sydney and Melbourne newspapers, edited the *Australian Cricket Annual* which bears his name. Far beyond everything else, however, he will be remembered for his great idea—so fruitful in after results—of sending an Australian XI to England.

COODE, Arthur Trevenan, died on December 28, 1940, aged 64. A Cambridge Blue in 1898, after playing well in school cricket at Beccles, he did nothing exceptional as opening batsman with C. J. Burnup, but was much more prominent at Association football for the University and for Middlesex. In his one cricket match against Oxford he went in first and was highest scorer with 27 in the second innings of a match which ended in defeat for Cambridge by nine wickets. He played occasionally for Middlesex.

COOK, Bruce, died in Sydney in 1981, aged 66. Born in Bathurst, New South Wales, he played first-grade cricket for Manly-Warringah from the age of 16. A left-hand bat, he represented New South Wales during the time of McCabe's captaincy. A fine player of both Rugby Union and Rugby League football, he was for many years a Trustee of the Sydney Cricket Ground.

COOK, Geoffrey Glover, who died on September 12, 1982, aged 72, was a right-hand bat and medium-pace bowler who played 68 matches for Queensland between 1931 and 1947. He made 3,453 runs (average 29.76), took 125 wickets (average 35.50) and held 33 catches. His highest score, 169 not out, was made in 1946–47 against W. R. Hammond's M.C.C. team. In 1938–39 he had helped W. A. Brown make 265 for Queensland's first wicket against New South Wales in Sydney. This remained a Queensland record until 1983. Cook, who scored three first-class centuries, was the son of Barney Cook, himself a former Queensland player.

COOK, Laurence, who was born at Preston on March 28, 1885, died at Wigan on December 2, 1933. A medium-pace right-arm bowler he first played for Lancashire in 1907, but though in 1911 he took 90 wickets at 21.61 apiece, he did his best work after the War, his last four seasons (1920 to 1923) being his most successful. In 1920 he had a record of 156 wickets for 14.88 apiece. In the 1921 season, during which he was picked for the Players at Lord's, he took 151 wickets at 22.99 each, while he had 142 wickets in 1922 and 98 the following season. His seven Derbyshire wickets for eight runs at Chesterfield in 1920 was one of his best bowling feats in County Cricket. Altogether in first-class matches he took 839 wickets at an average cost of 21.20. He did little as a batsman, but in 1921 he scored 54 not out for Lancashire v. Middlesex, at Manchester.

COOK, Thomas E. R., died at Brighton on January 15, 1950, aged 48. Educated at the Brighton Municipal School, he was one of the finest all-rounders Sussex has produced. He played his early cricket and football for his native Cuckfield and, after service with the Royal Navy during the First World War, became a professional for Sussex in 1922. Thus began a long and notable career which did not end until 1937, when he accepted a coaching appointment in Cape Town. Cook was a stylish, free-scoring batsman, who played many glorious innings. *Wisden* said of him in 1935: "Cook was one of the few batsmen in England who showed a proper conception of the right way to play slow bowling. Not many players, when jumping to drive, so completely got to the pitch of the ball as he did." He made his highest score, 278, off the Hampshire bowlers at Hove, in 1930, and recorded two other scores of over 200, both against Worcestershire, 220 at Worcester in 1934 and 214 at Eastbourne in 1933. Altogether Cook scored 20,206 runs, including 31 hundreds, and held 153 catches, many of them in the outfield, where his speed and anticipation saved innumerable runs.

When the recent War started he joined the South African Air Force, and while serving with them was seriously injured in an accident at an air school in 1943. He spent nearly six months in hospital. Cook was also a fine footballer, and as a professional with Brighton and Hove Albion gained an international cap for England against Wales in 1925. After leading the Albion attack for six seasons he went to Bristol Rovers, but returned as team manager of Brighton in 1946–47.

COOK, William, who died on December 18, 1947, at Burnley, aged 65, gave promise of becoming a fast bowler of great ability when, in 1905, he took 38 wickets for Lancashire at 19.10 runs apiece; but two seasons later he made his only reappearance in the county side. After being conspicuous in Lancashire League cricket for Lowerhouse and Colne, he helped Burnley to win the League Championship in three consecutive years. After retiring from active cricket he was a blacksmith's assistant.

COOK, William Thomas, who died on September 22, 1969, aged 77, had a life-long association with Surrey cricket. A left-handed batsman of no mean skill, he captained the county's Second XI with distinction for many years and for a long time was a member of the Surrey County C.C. Committee. To him, Surrey should feel specially indebted, for it was he who swayed the Committee to appoint W. S. Surridge as captain of the county in 1952. Under Surridge, Surrey carried off the Championship for five years in succession. Cook's employment as a Civil Servant limited his opportunities for appearance in first-class cricket, but he gained his county cap between the two World Wars when the Surrey batting was immensely strong.

COOKE, Frank H., who learned his cricket at Tonbridge School and going to New Zealand played for Otago, died on June 10, 1933. A left-arm medium-pace bowler, he assisted that province for several years. Perhaps his best performance was against Canterbury in 1883 when he secured 15 wickets for 94 runs. He captained the Manawatu Eighteen which met Lord Hawke's team in 1903. By profession a barrister, he was for several years Crown Prosecutor at Palmerston North.

COOLEY, Bertram Clifford, who came to England with the 1901 South African team, died on August 17, 1935, aged 61. A sound batsman he scored 126 not out against Cambridge. In the last match he played in first-class cricket—for Natal against Western Provinces in 1907—he scored 113, helping David Nourse add 217 for the ninth wicket after eight men had fallen for 100.

COOPE, Miles, died at his birthplace, Gildersome, Yorkshire, on July 5, 1974, aged 56. A product of the Bradford League, he did useful work for Somerset as a batsman from 1947 to 1949. In 1948 he scored 1,107 runs with an average of 23.55. He made two centuries for the county, 113 against Middlesex at Taunton in 1947 and 102 against Lancashire at Manchester in 1949.

COOPER, Albert Vincent, who had a trial as a batsman for Essex against the West Indians in 1923, died at Stoke Newington on May 3, 1977, aged 83.

COOPER, Bransby Beauchamp, died at Geelong, Australia, on August 7, 1914. He was born in India on March 15, 1844, and was thus in his 71st year. Mr. B. B. Cooper will be remembered by old cricketers as one of the long line of famous Rugby batsmen that began, perhaps, with C. G. Wynch and culminated in William Yardley. He was in the Rugby XI in 1860–61, among his contemporaries being F. R. Evans, C. Booth, S. Linton, M. T. Martin, and E. Rutter. Mr. Cooper made his first appearance at Lord's for Rugby against the M.C.C. on June 27, 1860. On the two following days he was on the winning side against Marlborough, scoring 33 in an innings of 152. After leaving Rugby he did not go to Oxford or Cambridge, but he soon became a prominent figure in first-class cricket, playing for Middlesex from 1864 to 1867 inclusive, and for Kent in a few matches in 1868 and 1869. It is worthy of mention that he took part in 1864 in the first match played by the then recently-formed Middlesex County Club. His fame as a batsman in England rests, however, on what he did in representative matches. In ·1865 he was picked for the Gentlemen at Lord's and played a very fine innings of 70 against the bowling of Grundy, Wootton,

Alfred Shaw, Hayward, and George Bennett. The match was in two respects memorable. W. G. Grace, then just under 17, was, like Cooper, making his first appearance in the match, and the Gentlemen, who had a splendid team, gained their first victory over the Players since 1853, winning by eight wickets. The survivors of the match, now that Mr. Cooper has gone, are W. G. Grace, R. D. Walker, Lord Cobham (then the Hon. C. G. Lyttelton), F. R. Evans, and W. F. Maitland among the Gentlemen, and George Wootton alone among the Players. Mr. Cooper reached his highest point in 1869 when he was associated with W. G. Grace in two notable achievements at the Oval. In the Gentlemen and Players match the two batsmen scored 105 together for the first wicket in the second innings, Cooper making 40 and W. G., 83. Three weeks later, for the Gentlemen of the South against the Players of the South, they set up a record which remained unbeaten for 23 years. Going in against a total of 475 by the Players they scored 283 for the first wicket in three hours and 40 minutes. W. G. made 180 and Cooper 101, both being caught and bowled by Tom Mantle who, tried for the first time, got the two wickets in six balls. Towards the end of July, 1869, the two batsmen took part in a North and South match at Sheffield. W. G. Grace played a great innings of 122, out of a total of 173, against George Freeman—then at his very best—the only other double figure score in the innings being Cooper's 23. The record of 283 for the first wicket was first beaten in a big match when, in 1892, H. T. Hewett and L. C. H. Palairet sent up 346 for Somerset against Yorkshire, at Taunton.

Mr. Cooper left England soon after the season of 1869 and, after a short stay in the United States, settled down in Australia where he spent the rest of his life. He at once took a leading part in Australian cricket, playing for Victoria for several years in the matches with New South Wales. As regards his Australian career, two facts stand out above all others. On December 26, 27, and 29, 1873, he played for Eighteen of Victoria against W. G. Grace's England XI, and scored 84 out of a total of 266. It was the first match of the Englishmen's tour and the Eighteen won by an innings and 21 runs. A little more than three years later—in March, 1877—Mr. Cooper took part at Melbourne in the first match in which Australians met English cricketers on even terms. Australia beat James Lillywhite's England team by 45 runs, Charles Bannerman's memorable innings of 165 and Tom Kendall's splendid

bowling bringing about the unexpected result. Mr. Cooper scored 15 and three, being bowled by Southerton in the first innings and Alfred Shaw in the second. Mr. Cooper who, like most of the amateur batsmen of his day, played in very attractive style, had no lack of hitting power, but patience and sound defence were his great assets. He was a fairly good wicket-keeper without approaching the front rank.

COOPER, Charles Osborn, who died on November 23, 1943, aged 75, played a little for Kent in the seasons 1894 to 1896. He was in the Dulwich College XI, 1885–86, being a steady bat, medium-paced bowler, and good slip fieldsman, though handicapped by ill-health.

COOPER, Edwin, who died in a Birmingham hospital on October 29, 1968, aged 52, was a stylish right-handed professional batsman for Worcestershire from 1937 to 1951. During that time he scored 13,304 runs for the county, including 18 centuries, at an average of 31.90. Born at Bacup, he played for the local club in the Lancashire League before qualifying for Worcestershire, for whom he met with immediate success. He reached 1,212 runs, average 23.30, in his first season and put together a four-figure aggregate in each of the next eight summers till he left to take up a coaching appointment at the Royal Naval College, Dartmouth.

"Eddie" Cooper's highest innings for Worcestershire was 216 not out off the Warwickshire bowling at Dudley in 1938, when he batted without fault for six and a half hours and he and S. H. Martin (136) put on 245 for the fourth wicket. The following season he made the highest innings, 69, in the low-scoring "tie" game with Somerset at Kidderminster and on the same ground in 1946 hit 191 and 106 not out in the match with Northamptonshire. Generally an opening batsman, he used his height to get to the pitch of the ball, which he watched very closely; employed neat footwork against spin bowling and, with a high back-lift, put considerable power into his strokes. He was at his best on the off-side and in hooking. His most successful season was that of 1949 when, with 1,872 runs, average 46.80, he headed the Worcestershire figures. In 1951 he and D. Kenyon became what *Wisden* termed "almost the ideal opening pair", sharing seven partnerships of over 100. He was also a capital fieldsman in the deep. After leaving Dartmouth, he coached for a time at Bedford School.

COOPER, Frederick Joseph, who died at York on June 27, 1958, aged 70, played in a few matches for Essex from 1921 to 1923. He represented Shropshire at cricket and golf and played Association football for Bradford.

COOPER, William Henry, who at the time of his death in Australia on April 5, 1939, was acclaimed as the oldest Australian Test player, owned Maidstone, Kent as being his birthplace in 1849. Taken to Australia when eight he did not start serious cricket until 27, and then only on medical advice. Cooper soon gained a reputation as a slow leg-break bowler and, against England at Melbourne in the 1882 New Year's match, he took nine wickets. He came to England with W. L. Murdoch's team in 1884 but did not play in a Test. In a busy cricket life he captained Victoria, was a State Selector, and vice-president of the Victoria Cricket Association.

COPE, Henry, who was born in Philadelphia on September 16, 1850, and died there on July 26, 1924, was a very great lover indeed of the game. He was responsible for laying out the cricket grounds at Haverford College in 1875, and on that account they were named "Cope Field." He also organised and directed five teams of Haverford cricketers to England between 1896 and 1914. He was a member of the Haverford College, University, Germantown and Philadelphia clubs.

COPELAND, William, died at South Shields last week of January, 1917, aged 60. Was on the ground staff at Old Trafford about 30 years ago, when he received the appointment of professional to the South Shields C.C. Played for Lancashire in 1885 and for Durham County between 1886 and 1894.

COPPINGER, Edward Thomas, born at Bexley on November 25, 1846, died at Surbiton on February 26, 1927, aged 80. A useful all-round player and a good wicket-keeper, he was a member of a cricketing family and himself appeared in two matches for Kent in 1873. In the second innings of the game with Surrey at the Oval he had an analysis of five for 29. In 1890–91 he was Mayor of Kingston-on-Thames.

COPSON, William Henry, who died on September 14, 1971, aged 62, was a professional fast bowler for Derbyshire from 1932 to 1949. But for the General Strike of 1926, he might never have been known in the world of cricket. He showed no interest in the game when a boy and, following the normal procedure in his part of the country, duly became a coal-miner. Then came the strike and, at the age of 17, he was persuaded by fellow miners to help to fill in the period of absence from work by joining in cricket on the local recreation ground. Such success did he achieve with remarkable pace and accuracy of length that the next season he was given a place in the Morton Colliery team. From there he progressed to Clay Cross, the Derbyshire League club, and in a match with Staveley he took all 10 wickets for five runs. Not unnaturally, this attracted attention and following a trial for the county in 1931, he gained a place in the Derbyshire side for 17 matches in 1932.

The start of his career was sensational, for with his first ball in his first first-class match, against Surrey at the Oval, he dismissed no less a batsman than A. Sandham. Next season, he established a regular place in the county team and he took 90 wickets at a cost of 21.34 runs each, including seven for 62 in an innings against Gloucestershire at Cheltenham. From then on, with his late swerve and pace off the pitch, he made steady progress, despite injuries and back trouble which limited his appearances in 1935. He recovered so well that, in 1936, when Derbyshire won the County Championship, he took in all matches 160 wickets at a cost of 13.34 runs apiece, 13 times dismissing five or more batsmen in an innings. Included among his performances were analyses of five wickets for 33 and seven for 19 against Surrey at Derbyshire and five for 38 and seven for 16 against Worcestershire at Worcester.

In the following season, he performed the outstanding feat of taking four wickets in four balls against Warwickshire at Derby, his full figures for the innings being 8.2 overs, two maidens, 11 runs, eight wickets. Seven of his successes fell to him in the course of 23 balls. In 1938 and 1939 he took over 100 wickets and, despite spells of ill health, he continued in first-class cricket till retiring in 1949. Three times he performed the hat-trick, against Worcestershire and Warwickshire in 1937 and Oxford University in 1939, and altogether he took 1,094 wickets at an average cost of 18.96.

He went to Australia with G. O. Allen's M.C.C. team in 1936–37, and although he did not play in any of the Tests, he headed the bowling averages with 27 wickets for 19.81 runs apiece. In a two-day game at Canberra, he disposed of seven Southern Districts of New South Wales batsmen for 16 runs. His three Test appearances were all in England. In two games against the West Indies in 1939 he earned analyses of five wickets for 85 and four for 67 at Lord's and two for 31 and one for two at Old Trafford. In 1947, he played in the last Test with South Africa, his three wickets in the match costing 112 runs. From 1958 to 1967 he was on the first-class umpires list.

CORRECTION. In the obituary of W. H. Copson in the 1972 edition, it was stated that he performed the hat-trick against Worcestershire in 1937. This is incorrect; it was against Lancashire.

CORBETT, Alexander Merlin, died on October 7,. 1934. Born at Aston, near Rotherham, on November 25, 1854, he appeared for Yorkshire v. Gloucestershire at Bramall Lane, Sheffield, in 1881 when, in his one match for the county, he was dismissed twice without scoring. In the first innings he had an unusual experience, for he played forward to a ball which got up, went off his bat to his forehead and straight in to the hands of W. G. Grace; the bowler was W. Midwinter. A pattern maker by trade, he retired in 1929.

CORBETT, Leonard James, died on January 26, 1983, aged 85. Better known as one of the great rugger three-quarters of his day, who had 16 international caps and twice captained England, he was also a good cricketer, who, in nine matches for Gloucestershire between 1920 and 1925, made 373 runs with an average of 20.72, his highest score being 55 in the August Bank Holiday match against Somerset in 1923 at a time when the side was doing very badly. Perhaps one who well remembers fielding in a club match while he made a hundred may be allowed to say that if he had had the opportunity to play regularly he would have been invaluable to the county. Moving with all the ease of a natural games player, he had beautiful strokes and made batting look very simple; moreover he was, as one would expect, a superb field. In later life he wrote well both on rugger and cricket for the *Sunday Times*.

CORBETT, Percival Thomas, a licensee at West Malvern, who died on June 26, 1944, aged 44, played a little for Worcestershire in 1922 and 1923, and afterwards was a professional at Liverpool.

CORDEN, Charles, born at Croydon on December 30, 1874, died at his native place on February 26, 1924. He was for some time a useful member of the Surrey Second XI. In 1900 he made the first of his few appearances for Worcestershire, and against Cambridge University the next year scored 51 not out and 42 for the county on the Cambridge ground. Possibly the best innings of his career was his 102 for Fifteen of Mitcham v. T. Richardson's XI in September, 1898, when he had the bowling of Richardson, Brockwell and Braund to contend with.

CORDINGLEY, Albert, who played once for Yorkshire in 1898 and afterwards a little for Sussex, died on April 30, 1945, aged 72.

CORNFORD, Walter F., who died in a Brighton hospital on February 6, 1964, aged 63, was one of the smallest wicket-keepers to play in first-class cricket, for he stood not much more than 5ft. Born on Christmas Day, 1900, he was a regular professional for Sussex from 1921 till 1939 and was recalled in an emergency to play against Essex at Brentwood in 1947 when coach at Brighton College. In all, he helped to dismiss 953 batsmen for his county—639 caught and 314 stumped—and he scored 6,327 runs, average 14.61. His highest innings was 82 against Yorkshire at Eastbourne in 1928, when, sharing in partnerships of 83 with James Langridge and 111 with K. S. Duleepsinhji, he enabled Sussex to save the game after following-on 298 behind.

"Tich" Cornford stood right up to the wicket to all bowling, even the fast-medium deliveries of M. W. Tate, his greatest friend, and A. E. R. Gilligan, and his stumpings earned them a number of wickets. One of his happiest memories was of a match at Hastings in which he twice stumped J. B. Hobbs on the leg-side off A. F. Wensley and also took five catches off the bowling of Tate. Against Worcestershire at Worcester in 1928, he was responsible for eight wickets with four catches and four stumpings. He played in all four Tests against New Zealand when touring that country and Australia under A. H. H. Gilligan, then his county captain, in 1929–30, and in 18 matches disposed of 35 batsmen. In 1925 he took part in the first Gentlemen v. Players match to be staged at Folkestone.

One distinction which afforded him no satisfaction was that he kept wicket in the game which yielded the greatest number of extras in a Test innings. That was in the fourth meeting with New Zealand at Auckland in 1930, when extras numbered 57—31 byes, 16 leg-byes and 10 no-balls. His benefit in 1934 realised £1,200.

CORNWALL, Alan Edward Cripps, died on February 26, 1984, aged 85. A member of the Marlborough XI in 1915 and again in 1916, when he headed the batting averages, he played in one match for Gloucestershire in 1920. For many years he was a master at Marlborough.

CORNWALLIS, Capt. Oswald Wykeham, who died on January 28, 1974, aged 79, played for the Royal Navy and figured in one match for Hampshire in 1921, though he did not appear on the field of play. A brother of Lord Cornwallis, the Kent cricketer, he rose from a cadet at Osborne to Captain before retiring from the Royal Navy in 1944.

CORNWALLIS, The Right Hon. Wykeham Stanley, Second Baron, died at his home, Ashurst Park, Kent, on January 4, 1982, aged 89. A genuinely fast bowler with an easy, if slightly low and slinging action, he played for Kent from 1919 to 1926, captaining them in his last three seasons. At a time when there was a desperate shortage of fast bowling, not only in Kent but in the country as a whole, he might have been a great asset had he remained sound. But he was 27 when his first-class career started and since leaving Eton, where he was not in the XI, had been a regular soldier with only limited opportunities of playing (and none in the last five years): his muscles had not had the work and training to enable them to stand the strain of County Cricket. He was constantly breaking down, and during his three years as captain could bowl only 560 overs in all. What he could do when sound he had shown at Tonbridge in 1920 when he took five for 40 against the strong Lancashire batting side, his victims including Makepeace and Ernest Tyldesley, both clean bowled, and he bowled well next year at the start of the Australian innings at Canterbury. He was a good field and, not normally regarded as a batsman, enjoyed one triumph, against Essex at Canterbury in 1926. When he came in, Kent, facing a total of 267, were 189 for seven and Collins had retired ill. Cornwallis helped Hardinge to put on 130 and then added another 77 with Collins, who had returned; he himself made 91, largely by carefree off-side hitting, the total reached 413 and Kent won by an innings.

Later, besides holding a number of directorships, he was tireless in public life in Kent, of which he was for years Lord-Lieutenant,

but interest in the game never flagged. In 1948 he was President both of Kent and M.C.C., and only a week or two before the commencement of his last illness he was watching I Zingari, of which he was a Freeman, playing Lavinia, Duchess of Norfolk's XI at Arundel, as full of life and of cricket reminiscences as ever. A man deservedly popular wherever he went and a great public servant, he will be widely missed.

COSSTICK, Samuel, died on April 8, 1896, aged 60, in Maitland, Australia. In the early days of Australian cricket, Cosstick was considered the best bowler in the Colonies. He played first for Victoria in 1861, and took part in his last Inter-colonial match in 1876. He played against the first four English teams that visited Australia, and in 1865, as he was then residing in New South Wales, he appeared for that Colony against Victoria. Cosstick was a Surrey man and was born at Croydon, but as there is no record of his playing cricket in England, it is presumed that he went out to Australia when very young. Cosstick's fame as a bowler was eclipsed by Allan, Evans, Spofforth and others, but at his best he was a great figure in Australian cricket.

COTTER, Albert B., killed at Beersheba, October 20, 1917. New South Wales and Australia.

Albert Cotter was the successor to Ernest Jones as Australia's fast bowler, coming to England with the teams of 1905 and 1909. His first trip was not an unqualified success. It is true that in all matches he took 124 wickets for less than 20 runs apiece, but up to a certain point of the tour he had so little command over his length that his bowling was a quaint mixture of long hops and full pitches. Still, irregular as he was, his extreme pace often made him dangerous. He gained greatly in command over the ball when he shortened his run and in the last Test match, at the Oval, he bowled splendidly on a perfect wicket, his pace being terrific. In 1909 his bowling came out very badly for the whole tour, but he had a big share in winning the Test match at Leeds, taking five wickets in England's second innings at a cost of only 38 runs. For several seasons Cotter was the fast bowler of the New South Wales XI. He will never be ranked among the great Australian bowlers, but on his day he was deadly.—S.H.P.

Some of his best performances were:
4 wickets for 5 runs, N.S.W. v. Queensland, at Brisbane, 1903–04.

7 for 15 and 12 for 34, Australia v. Worcestershire, at Worcester, 1905.
Took four wickets in four balls for Glebe v. Sydney, at Wentworth Park, April 29, 1911.

COTTERILL, Major George H., died at Llanduff, October 1, 1950, aged 82. A member of the Brighton College XI for five successive seasons, he was captain in his last three (1884–86). Played seven matches for Cambridge University in 1888–89, but did not obtain his Blue. Appeared in 10 matches for Sussex between 1886–90. Cambridge Association XI, 1888–91 (captain 1890). Corinthian F.C. Represented England in five Association Internationals, 1891–93. Also an all round athlete, he won many events at Brighton and Cambridge. Excelled at Rugby football and rowed for Weybridge R.C.

COTTERILL, Sir Joseph Montague, who died in Edinburgh on December 30, 1933, at the age of 82, played his first match for Sussex when he was 18. At the time he captained the Brighton College XI of which he was a member for four seasons. A splendidly free hitter with a sound defence, he played some valuable innings for Sussex, and in 1875, against Kent at Hove, he made 191 and had a large share in the victory of Sussex by an innings and 266 runs. His best year in county cricket was that of 1873 when he headed the Sussex batting averages. In 1875 he appeared for the Gentlemen v. Players at Princes but as he went to live in Edinburgh he did not often participate in that particular fixture. Still, he played a good deal for Gentlemen of the South and the United South and more than once went in first with W. G. Grace. Standing nearly 5ft. 11in. and weighing 11st. 6lb., he was a first-rate athlete and in 1875 threw the cricket ball 121yd. As a fieldsman he excelled at cover-point or long leg. He was born at Brighton on November 23, 1851, and became a famous surgeon.

COULSON, Sydney Samuel, died at Gainsborough on October 3, 1981, aged 82. After a good trial for Leicestershire in 1923, he was a regular member of the side in 1924 and 1925, showing some promise as a steady bat who could, if wanted, open the innings. Unfortunately this promise was never fulfilled, and after a few matches in 1926 and 1927 he dropped out of the side. His highest score was 80, against Derbyshire at Leicester in 1925, when he hit 11 fours and put on 99 for the sixth wicket with Geary. In all matches for the county he scored 1,094 runs with an average of 12.43. Later he was for

some years professional and groundsman at Gainsborough.

COULTHURST, Josiah, who died on January 6, 1970, aged 76, was one of the few amateur bowlers to take 100 wickets in a season in Lancashire League cricket. His 101 victims for 9.78 runs each in 1919 for East Lancashire remains a club record. A fast bowler, he made a number of appearances for Lancashire Second XI, but played only once, in 1919, for the first team.

COVENTRY, Col. The Hon. Charles John, C.B., an old Etonian, born in February, 1867, died at Earls Croome, Worcester, on June 2, 1929, aged 62. After assisting Worcestershire, he visited South Africa with Major Warton's team in 1888–89.

COVENTRY, The Ninth Earl of (George William Coventry), born in London on May 9, 1838, died at Croome Court, Worcestershire, on March 13, 1930, aged 91. A great lover of the game, he was also "a hard slashing hitter and slow lob bowler," and had played for Worcestershire. Since 1856 he had been a member of the M.C.C. and in 1859, when 21 years of age, was the club's President. He also belonged to I Zingari and had been a member of the Jockey Club for 70 years. At the time of his death he was "Father" of the House of Lords, having been a peer for the record period of 86 years and 10 months. He was father of the Hon C.J. Coventry, who toured South Africa with Major Warton's team in 1888–89, and of the Hon. H.T. Coventry of the Eton XIs of 1886 and 1887.

COVENTRY, The Hon. John Bonynge, who died suddenly on July 4, 1969, aged 66, was in the Eton XI in 1920 and 1921, in the latter year scoring 23 runs and taking with slow left-arm bowling seven Harrow wickets for 88 runs. Though he did not get a Blue at Oxford, he played for Worcestershire from 1925 to 1935. He took over the county captaincy midway through the 1929 season, when Major M. F. S. Jewell resigned through ill health, and continued in 1930. His highest innings was 75 against Leicestershire at Kidderminster in 1929. A partner in Tattersalls, the racehorse auctioneers, Coventry was Mayor of Worcester in 1929 and 1930. He served with the Grenadier Guards during the Second World War.

COVERDALE, William, who died on October 7, 1972, aged 60, played as a professional batsman for Northamptonshire in

1931 and the following season and afterwards assisted Durham. He will be remembered as the man who took Colin Milburn, the hard-hitting England batsman, to Northampton-shire.

COWAN, Capt. Charles Frederick Roy, who died on March 22, 1958, aged 74, was hon. treasurer of Warwickshire County C.C. from 1942 until two months before his death. When serving with the Royal Navy he made occasional appearances for the county between 1909 and 1921, scoring 846 runs, average 16.92. His highest innings was 78 against Hampshire at Portsmouth in 1920. He took part in five matches in 1911 when Warwickshire won the County Championship for the first time. In the early 1930s he captained the Second XI.

COWAN, Samuel, who collapsed while re-fereeing a football match at Haywards Heath for the benefit of J. H. Parks on October 6, 1964, and died shortly afterwards, aged 65, had been masseur to Sussex County C.C. since soon after the Second World War and acted in that capacity with the M.C.C. team in Australia in 1962–63. Better known as an Association footballer with Denby United, Doncaster Rovers, Manchester City and Bradford City, he played at centre-half in three matches for England between 1926 and 1931. He captained Manchester City when they won the F.A. Cup in 1933–34 and in two other Cup Finals, afterwards became manager of the club and served as trainer to Brighton and Hove Albion.

COWARD, Cornelius, who was born at Preston on January 27, 1838, died at his native place on July 15, 1903. For many years, commencing in 1865, he was of the greatest service to Lancashire as a batsman, his cutting being especially fine. Probably the finest innings of his career was his 85 for Lancashire against Middlesex at Manchester in 1866, seeing that he obtained his score after five men had been disposed of for 16 between them. He appeared in several representative matches, such as North v. South and England v. Surrey, and on two occasions—in 1867 and 1868—took part in the Gentlemen v. Players' match at the Oval. In 1878 the match between Lancashire and Nottinghamshire was set apart as a benefit for him. Coward was a well-known county umpire up to 10 years ago.

COWIE, Capt. Alexander Gordon (Seaforth Highlanders), born at Lymington on February 27, 1889, died of wounds on April 7, 1916. He had previously been wounded in July, 1915. A fast right-handed bowler, somewhat erratic, he played a few times for Charterhouse in 1907 and upon proceeding to Cambridge obtained his Blue as a Freshman in 1910. Against Oxford he took four wickets for 67 runs, in his first over causing a sensation by bowling a couple of wides and dismissing A. J. Evans and R. Sale. That year he was the most successful of the Cambridge bowlers, his record showing 35 wickets for 20.51 runs each, but in the few matches in which he appeared for Hampshire he did little. In 1911 he failed to retain his Blue, and thereafter little was seen of him in important cricket. In 1913, however, he played at Lord's for Army v. Royal Navy.

COX, George Reuben, father of the present Sussex batsman, died at his birthplace, Warnham, near Horsham, on March 24, 1949, aged 76. One of the pillars of Sussex cricket, he played for the county from 1895 to 1928, subsequently became the official coach and, as a mark of appreciation of his long and valuable service, was made an honorary life member of the club in 1937. Only Maurice Tate had previously received a similar honour.

A splendid all-rounder, Cox was a steady right-handed batsman and a left-arm bowler, first of medium-pace from which he soon turned to slow, revealing a nice, easy action. He scored 14,650 runs at an average of 18.75, took 1,843 wickets for 22.86 runs each, and held 510 catches, mostly close to the wicket. Two Sussex records stand to his credit. In 1908 he put on 156 for the last wicket with Harry Butt at Cambridge and in 1926, at the age of 52, he took 17 Warwickshire wickets for 106 runs at Horsham. When Cox played his highest innings, 167 not out against Hampshire at Chichester in 1906, he and Butt added 116 for the last wicket.

Down the years his most effective work was as a bowler. Beside the feat of obtaining 17 wickets in one match, he took five wickets for no runs in six overs against Somerset at Weston-super-Mare in 1921. Beginning in 1900, Cox was a member of the M.C.C. ground staff for many years and, playing for them against Royal Navy in 1907, took all 10 wickets in an innings for 117 runs. He was given the match against Surrey at Hove in 1914 as his benefit, but as it was cancelled owing to the War, Sussex allotted him the game with Yorkshire at Hove in 1920. A genial character, Cox was popular wherever he went. He paid four visits to South Africa and one to India as coach.

COXON, Henry ("Harry"), born at New Lenton on August 12, 1847, died at West Bridgford on November 5, 1929, aged 82. For very many years he was the Nottinghamshire scorer, undertaking the duties for the first time in 1867 and, except during the "Cricket Schism" of 1881, carrying them out regularly from 1870 until the end of 1923. His activities thus extended from the time of George Parr to that of A. W. Carr, and he claimed to have noted every run made for the county by Arthur Shrewsbury—to whom he was distantly related—during that batsman's long and successful career. He was a great authority on angling, on which subject he wrote a treatise, and he invented the "Aerial" fishing-reel. In 1898 the Notts team gave him a gold pin surmounted with a jewelled fly. He wrote much on sporting subjects, especially cricket and fishing, beginning his journalistic work with the *Nottingham Review.* In 1924 the match at Trent Bridge between the Second XIs of Nottinghamshire and Lancashire was given to him as a benefit.

COY, Arthur H., O.B.E., who died at Port Elizabeth on May 15, 1983, was a prominent member of the South African Cricket Association during the days of strictly segregated cricket, being its President from 1953 to 1955 and again from 1957 to 1959. He had captained Eastern Province before the Second World War, in which he served with the Royal Engineers, and was much in the news at the time of the D'Oliveira affair in 1968.

CRABTREE, Harry Pollard, M.B.E., died at Great Baddow, Essex, on May 28, 1982, aged 76. A Yorkshireman by birth, he came south as a schoolmaster to Westcliff-on-Sea, where he was a prolific scorer in club cricket. He had made a stray appearance for Essex in 1931, but most of his cricket for the county was played in the summer holidays of 1946 and 1947. In 1946 he made 793 runs with an average of 49.56, including three centuries. In 1947, though he scored 117 against the South Africans, he was less successful and he did not appear for the county after that year. A sound opening bat, he had an impeccable technique and was especially strong on the leg side. For many years he served on the Essex Committee. He will be particularly remembered for the work he did to encourage cricket coaching in state schools and as the instigator of the M.C.C.'s highly successful group coaching scheme. His friendliness and enthusiasm reassured and inspired many a young cricketer.

CRABTREE, Herbert, who died at his home in Colne in March, 1951, aged 70, was one of the finest all-round cricketers the local club has produced. A tall, commanding figure at the crease, with a glorious straight drive off the back foot, Mr. Crabtree scored 50 at least twice on every ground in the Lancashire League. Through perseverance, he made himself the most consistent length bowler in the League and his slip-fielding was unsurpassed. Apart from spells as a professional with other League clubs and five appearances for Lancashire, including one against Yorkshire in 1902, nearly all his 27 years in active cricket were with Colne. He was a leading member of Colne's Championship-winning teams in 1902, 1905 and 1910, and in his last season, 1924, he helped the club to win the Worsley Cup.

CRADDY, W.H., who died at Westbury-on-Trym in January, 1979, aged 73, had a brief trial as a batsman for Gloucestershire in 1928, and in his first innings for the county made 29 against Glamorgan at Bristol, helping Dipper to put on 99 for the fifth wicket.

CRADOCK, Thomas Tresillian, who died at Durban on June 27, 1948, aged 71, played in Currie Cup matches for Transvaal in 1904–05 and for Natal against M.C.C. in 1909–10.

CRAIG, Albert, "The Surrey Poet," died after a long illness at 8, Mayflower Road, Clapham, on July 8, 1909, in his 60th year. A Yorkshireman by birth and up-bringing, he started life as a Post Office clerk in Huddersfield, but was still a young man when, discovering that verse-making was his forte, he decided to devote his time and energies to celebrating the doings of cricketers and footballers. He was a familiar and welcome figure on the chief grounds in all parts of the country, but especially those of Surrey and Kent. He was possessed of much humour and it was seldom indeed that anyone had the best of him in a battle of wits. His pleasantries, which were never ill-natured, served to beguile many a long wait occasioned by the weather.

CRAIG, John, one of the best cricketers in Scotland about 30 years ago, died on April 7,

1910, *en route* for South Africa, aged about 60. He was a right-handed bowler, but batted left, and he and his brother Robert were always referred to by cricketers as the "Dalkeith Craigs". For Gentlemen of Scotland against the Australian team of 1880 he took six wickets, including those of Murdoch, McDonnell, Palmer and A. H. Jarvis, for 60 runs.

CRANFIELD, Beaumont, the Somerset left-handed slow bowler, died at Bristol on January 20, 1909, of pneumonia, the result of a chill contracted while watching a football match four days before. He was born at Bath, on August 25, 1874, and first appeared for his county in 1897. At one time it seemed likely that he would develop into a very fine player, but although he rendered his county excellent service he never quite took the position which had been expected. Between 1900 and 1904 he bowled as follows in first-class matches:

Year	Overs	Mdns.	Runs	Wkts.	Aver.
1900	554	107	1751	74	23.66
1901	852	197	2534	122	20.77
1902	869.3	192	2618	141	18.56
1903	723.1	147	2351	121	19.42
1904	597.4	101	1978	74	26.72

There was a distinct falling-off in 1905 and he was never again particularly effective. At his best he had good command over the ball and considerable spin, and when the ball was new was able to impart a pronounced curve to it: at times the curve was so great that he would place almost all his fieldsmen on the leg-side. Among his best feats with the ball may be mentioned his 14 wickets for 126 runs against Lancashire at Manchester in 1902, and his 13 for 102 against Gloucestershire on the Gloucester ground in the following season. He was a member of the ground-staff at Lord's from 1899 to 1906, and in his great year of 1902 was chosen for the first of the matches played between M.C.C. and Ground and the Australians: later in the same seaon he was picked for the Gentlemen v. Players match at Scarborough. Had Cranfield belonged to a stronger bowling side he would no doubt have done better.

CRANSTON, James, so well known years ago as a member of the Gloucestershire XI, died at Bristol on December 10, 1904. Though his career in first-class matches had for some time been over, Mr. Cranston was a comparatively young man—not quite 46. He was born on January 9, 1859, and played first for Gloucestershire in 1876. In his early days

he was an extremely fine field, as well as a good bat. After the season of 1883 he left Bristol, and except for a few appearances for Warwickshire—the county of his birth—nothing more was seen of him till 1889, when he returned to his old place in the Gloucestershire team. Owing to greatly increased weight, his old brilliancy in the field had quite left him, but he was a better bat than ever. Indeed, in 1889 and 1890 he was one of the best left-handed players before the public. Unfortunately, however, his renewed connection with Gloucestershire soon ended. He was seized with a fit during a match in 1891, and although he recovered, he did not after that year take part in county cricket again till 1899 when he played four times, these being his last appearances. His greatest distinction in the cricket field came to him in 1890, when, owing to some difficulties in making up the side, the Surrey committee offered him a place in the England XI against Australia at the Oval. The match—played from first to last on a pitch ruined by rain—was a memorable one, England winning, after a tremendous finish, by two wickets. As a batsman, Mr. Cranston proved quite worthy of the honour conferred on him. He only made 16 and 15, but his defence under very trying conditions against the bowling of Turner and Ferris, was masterly. In the last innings, in which England went in to get 95, he and Maurice Read turned the fortunes of the game after the four best wickets had fallen for 32 runs. Mr. Cranston played a very stubborn game, while Read hit, Turner's break—coming, of course, the reverse way—seeming to cause far less trouble to him than it did to any of the right-handed batsmen. He and Maurice Read took the score to 83, and looked like finishing the match, but four more wickets were lost before the end was reached. In 1890 Mr. Cranston had a brilliant season for Gloucestershire, being very close to Mr. W. G. Grace, both in aggregate of runs and average. The two batsmen were mainly instrumental in winning a wonderful match against Yorkshire at Dewsbury. Gloucestershire were 137 behind on the first innings, and when they went in for the second-time three wickets were lost for 19. At this point Mr. Cranston joined his captain, and by flawless cricket 188 runs were added to the score in two hours and 20 minutes. Mr. Cranston made in all 152—the highest innings he ever played in a big match. Gloucestershire won the game by 84 runs. Earlier in the same season he scored 101 against Yorkshire at Bristol, but in that match Gloucestershire suffered defeat by eight wickets. Strong defence and powerful driving were the chief characteristics of Mr. Cranston's batting. Few left-handed men have ever played with such a uniformly straight bat.

CRAPP, John Frederick, who died at his home in Bristol on February 15, 1981, aged 68, had 42 years' association with first-class cricket, broken only by the Second World War. He played for Gloucestershire from 1936 to 1956, 15 seasons of cricket, in only one of which did he fail to make his 1,000 runs, and then for 21 years, until ill-health caused his retirement after 1978, he was a first-class umpire, several times officiating in Tests.

A solidly built left-hander, he was a reliable rather than a spectacular bat and in his early years was sometimes criticised for being too unenterprising—not that in a side containing Hammond and Barnett there was much danger of getting behind the clock. But with experience he learned to use with discretion his natural powers of hitting, and in the latter years of his career he was quite capable of forcing the pace when required. He was always a fine field, especially in the slips. In all he scored 23,615 runs with an average of 35.03, including 38 centuries.

Born at St. Columb and said to be the only Cornishman ever to have played for England, he qualified for Gloucestershire by residence and at once adapted himself to first-class cricket, passing 1,000 runs in his first season. By 1938 he was already being talked of as a potential England player, but, the War intervening, he had to wait until 1948, when he was 36, for his chance. Then, after making 100 not out for his country against the Australians, he played in the third Test and followed a valuable first innings of 36 at a crisis with 19 not out in the second. This secured him a place in the two remaining Tests, in which, however, he did little. That winter he was a member of F. G. Mann's M.C.C. side in South Africa where, without achieving anything sensational, he was a distinct success. He played in the last four Tests, his scores being 56, 35, 54, 51, 5, 4 and 26 not out; in the second innings of the fifth Test, some fine strokes at the end just enabled his side to win a match which a few minutes before had looked like a draw. He made centuries against Orange Free State and Eastern Province. Despite this and although he continued to score consistently for Gloucestershire, he never played for England again. He had a benefit in 1951 and in 1953 became the first professional captain of the county. But he did not enjoy the position. It affected his play (1954 was the only season in which he failed to score 1,000 runs), and after two years he was glad to hand over to his friend, George Emmett.

CRAWFORD, Capt. Alexander Basil (West Yorkshire Regiment), who was born in Warwickshire on May 24, 1891, fell in action in May, 1916, aged 24. In 1907 and 1908 he was in the Oundle XI, and in 1911 appeared a few times for Warwickshire, making 140 runs in seven innings and taking 13 wickets for 23.84 runs each. Against the West Indians he made 24 not out and took six wickets for 36 runs. Subsequently he appeared for Nottinghamshire, and in the match with the Australians in 1912 played an innings of 51.

CRAWFORD, Andrew, born at Edinburgh on January 27, 1826, died at Wimbledon on May 31, 1926, in his 102nd year. Although never gaining note as a player, he was a useful club cricketer, especially as a bowler. He was father of the Rev. J. C. and the late Major F. F. Crawford, and grandfather of Messrs. V. F. S., R. T., and J. N. Crawford.

CRAWFORD, Major Frank Fairbairn, who occasionally assisted Kent, under the residential qualification, died on January 16, 1900, at the base hospital, Pietermaritzburg, of dysentery. At the time of his death he belonged to the Veterinary Department of the Royal Artillery, which he entered in 1873. His military duties caused a great part of his life to be spent in India and Natal, and both countries found in him a hearty supporter of cricket. In *Scores and Biographies* he is described as "a splendid field, generally at long-leg or cover-point, and a good average batsman". Mr. Crawford was born at Hastings, June 17, 1850.

CRAWFORD, The Rev. John Charles, M.A., died at Wimbledon on February 21, 1935, aged 85. Born on May 29, 1849, at Hastings, he was the oldest surviving member of a remarkable cricketing and athletic family. "Parson" Crawford, as he was always called when well known as a cricketer, played occasionally for Kent from 1872 to 1877 and for Leicestershire in 1878; also for Gentlemen of Sussex and Gentlemen of Surrey, and for Surrey Second XI; but he never appeared for the county. Large framed and powerfully built, he could bowl very fast right hand or slow left. It is on record that Willsher, the famous umpire, said that Crawford was the fastest bowler he had ever seen.

In a match at Dunkirk in 1867 he sent one bail 51 yards and the other 49 yards. He hit very hard and against weak bowling would sometimes bat left-handed, particularly in club cricket in which he was a familiar figure around London for many years. He loved the game so much that all his children played from an early age. More than once a team of 11 Crawfords, including grandfather, his two sons, the Parson's two sons, daughters and a nephew took the field. One of the oldest and most respected members both of the M.C.C. and of the Surrey club, he had numberless friends both at Lord's and the Oval, where he was constantly in the pavilion watching cricket very late in life.

His father, who lived to the age of 101, played for Gentlemen of England in the days when cricketers wore top hats. His brother, Major F. F. Crawford, who died in the South African War, captained Kent in the early '70s and played for M.C.C. in South Africa, India and elsewhere. Parson Crawford was the father of R. T., J. N. and the late V.F.S. Crawford, all of whom played first-class cricket with distinction. J. C. Crawford took his degree from University College, Oxford, and for 36 years was Chaplain to Cane Hill Mental Hospital in Surrey.

CRAWFORD, John Neville, who died on May 2, 1963, aged 76, was one of the best all-rounders of his era, although he habitually played in spectacles. Son of the Rev. J. C. Crawford and nephew of Major F. F. Crawford, both of whom played for Kent, he created such a reputation as a batsman and a bowler of varying pace at Repton that he was invited to play for Surrey in 1904 at the age of 17. He was an immediate all-round success and he and H. C. McDonell bowled unchanged through both innings of Gloucestershire at Cheltenham, Crawford taking 10 wickets for 78 and his fellow amateur 10 for 89.

Jack Crawford appeared regularly for Surrey from 1906 till 1909. Twice in succession he completed "the cricketers' double" and in 1908 failed to do so a third time by two wickets. During this period he made 12 appearances for England, going to South Africa in 1905–06 and to Australia in 1907–08, when he headed the Test bowling averages with 30 wickets for 24.79 runs each. After a mid-season dispute with Surrey in 1909 he settled in Australia, playing with distinction for South Australia and paying a visit to New Zealand with an Australian XI, in 1914. In the course of this tour he played an extraordinary innings in a two-day fixture

with a South Canterbury XI at Temuka. Of a total of 922 for nine wickets, he obtained 354—264 of them from 14 sixes and 45 fours—in five and a half hours. He and Victor Trumper put on 298 in 69 minutes for the eighth wicket and he and M. A. Noble at one point added 50 in nine minutes.

Crawford returned to England following the First World War, and, the disagreement having been settled, played again for Surrey from 1919 till he retired in 1921. A hard-hitting batsman, he shared a match-winning stand of 96 in 32 minutes with J. B. Hobbs against Kent in 1919 and the same season played what was described as the innings of his life. Going in at number eight against the Australian Imperial Forces side at the Oval, he hit 144 not out. When Tom Rushby, the last man, reached the wicket, Surrey needed 45 to avoid a follow-on; but Crawford attacked the bowling with such ferocity that 80 runs were added in 35 minutes, Rushby's share in this partnership amounted to two runs. Of Crawford, *Wisden* of the time recorded: "The way in which he drove Gregory's fast bowling was magnificent." In all first-class cricket, Crawford hit 7,005 runs, average 30.19, dismissed 600 batsmen at a cost of 20.50 runs each and brought off 117 catches.

CRAWFORD, Lieut.-Col. Proby Edward Payne, died at Reading on April 11, 1949, aged 86. Former Sussex County Cricketer and he played in the same M.C.C. team as W. G. Grace. Late Royal Sussex Regiment and a survivor of the Gordon Relief Expedition.

CRAWFORD, R. T., died on November 15, 1945, in hospital at Swiss Cottage, London, after a long illness, aged 63. He appeared for Leicestershire when able to give the time from 1901 to 1911. His elder brother, V. F. S., who played for Surrey and Leicestershire, and younger brother, J. N., a prominent all-rounder for Surrey and South Australia, earned far more renown than R. T., who, however, by some good judges was considered the most stylish of the three sons of Rev. J. C. Crawford, connected with both the Kent and Surrey County Clubs. R. T. enjoyed most success for Leicestershire in 1902 when 19 years of age, scoring 852 runs, average 25.05, and taking 40 wickets at 23.70 each. A fine, free batsman he used the drive with great effect and withstood the best bowlers on any kind of pitch.

CRAWFORD, Thomas Alan, who died suddenly on December 5, 1979, aged 69, rendered notable service to Kent cricket. A member of the Tonbridge XI for four years and captain in 1929, he made 12 appearances for the county between 1930 and 1951 without particular success. But he scored many runs for Kent's Second XI, including an innings of 175 against Wiltshire in 1931, and captained them from 1950 to 1955, a task for which he was well suited. He had a good knowledge of the game; moreover, at a time when the over rate was already becoming a problem, he insisted on 20 overs an hour from his bowlers. He was primarily an attacking batsman and a good driver; he also picked up occasional wickets with slow spin. For many years Crawford served on the Kent committee, being President of the club in 1968. He was later appointed Chairman of the Committee, but had to resign almost immediately for reasons of health.

CRAWFORD, Vivian Frank Shergold, died on August 21, 1922, at the age of 43. He was born on April 11, 1879. Coming out for Surrey in 1898 he took part in 12 matches, his best scores being 73 against Gloucestershire and 83 against Oxford University—both at the Oval. His first hundred for Surrey was 129 against Somerset at the Oval in 1899. In June that year he put his knee out at Chesterfield and could play no more for Surrey during the season. He was appointed secretary to Leicestershire in 1903 and having a birth qualification for the county was able to step into the XI at once. At the Oval in 1909 he hit up a score of 172 against Surrey, and in the following season he finished with County Cricket. For some years before the War he was living in Ceylon. He died, after two or three days' illness, from pneumonia, the War having left him with a much-impaired constitution.

Mr. D. L. A. Jephson has written the following tribute to his old colleague in the Surrey XI: "To those of us who love the clean, straight bat, the full-faced drive, the low, clean, golf-tinged shot, or the shoulder swing that cleared the ground, minimum of effort, maximum of accomplishment, his passing in the very prime of manhood, came as a blow—delivered in the face. From his earliest school days he showed a wonderful aptitude for the game, in all its branches, though as quite a youngster his bowling overshadowed his batting—he was always a splendid field. Educated at Whitgift Grammar School he was for years the brain and backbone of their cricket side. It is impossible here for me to give a full list of his astonishing performances. These can be found in *Wisden's Note Book* for 1900, and strangely pleasant is the reading of them to those of us who knew him. To those who did not, their perusal must be a continual source of surprise at the startling success of so young a player.

"In 1895 he made 1,780 runs and took 200 wickets. Playing for Richmond and District v. Surrey he took eight wickets for 35 in 17 overs, his victims being Abel, Lockwood, Holland, Ayres, Thompson, Mills, Clarke, and Richardson. In his second innings he made 25 out of 48 for eight wickets down. In 1896 he scored 218 before lunch, for the Young Amateurs v. Young Professionals at the Oval—218 out of a total of 296, the sort of innings many of us would tramp long, weary miles to see. For years I had the privilege of playing on his side; I played with him in club games and I played with him for Surrey. As a batsman Frank Crawford possessed many strokes, he was strictly orthodox in all his methods of attack or defence, and the straightness of his bat was a thing to marvel at, considering the wonderful power behind what seemed, and was, an effortless stroke. He will go down to posterity as one of the greatest straight-drivers the game has known: at any rate this is the opinion of players like Ranjitsinhji, C. B. Fry and G. W. Beldam. He was essentially a scientific *hitter* not a *slogger*. Here are a few of the many memories that are always with me of Frank Crawford at his best.

"In his prime he was the personification of athleticism at its zenith. I shall never forget at Bradford once when Surrey had lost five wickets for 30, he made a lightning hundred against Hirst and Rhodes, then in the heyday of their fame. The football pavilion at Bradford is opposite the cricket pavilion; its two ends are ornamented with flagstaffs and it has a slate roof. Crawford hit six sixes—the right-hand flagstaff was struck, and the ball rebounded 20 yards into play. An over afterwards, and the left-hand staff returned the compliment, and on two occasions the slates went upwards in a cloud of dust. And there was one fierce low drive, off Wilfred Rhodes, that Denton, great outfield that he was, would not touch; it laid out a parson first hop.

"Again, at Bristol I saw him carry the pavilion. We were all seated on top of the old-time structure—Paish was bowling, Champain, the old Oxford Blue, was in the out-field on the edge of the cinder track. Crawford took one step and the ball soared upwards. 'He's out,' I cried, and we watched

Champain; there was so little fuss about the shot. Out, not a bit of it—it cleared Champain, it cleared the track, it sailed 20 yards over our heads on top of the pavilion, to fall nearly 170 yards from the crease. It was the greatest drive I have ever seen. I watched him make a hundred against Lancashire at the Oval in less than an hour: at 50 he was caught by E. M. Dowson on the top of the ladies' pavilion, and before he was out he had planted Mold, at his fastest, into the football stand from a wicket well to the right of the members' enclosure. Space forbids me to tell many an anecdote I should love to tell, many an innings of his that would well bear allusion, but in conclusion I will say this, that I have seen and appreciated the punching of C. I. Thornton, the firm-footed fireworks of J. J. Lyons, and the wonderful hitting of Gilbert Jessop, whirling a leviathan weapon; but I have never seen a drive to the rails, a drive over the rails, or a drive that cleared the pavilion equal to the driving of Frank Crawford; he never 'drove furiously', but he drove uncommonly straight! His physical equipment was magnificent, his heart was in the right place and he played the game in the great spirit—the spirit that strives not for itself but for the side."

CRAWLEY, Leonard George, a member of a notable games-playing family and himself one of the most versatile games-players of his day, died on July 9, 1981, aged 77. Though he was perhaps best known to the general public as for years golfing correspondent of the *Daily Telegraph* and one of the select body of Englishmen who have won a single in the Walker Cup, in which he appeared four times, he might well have been no less distinguished in the cricket world if he had been able to give the time to the game; in addition he had been first string for Cambridge at racquets and he was a fine shot.

Three years in the Harrow XI, he played a memorable innings of 103 at Lord's in 1921, and, getting his Blue at Cambridge as a Freshman in 1923, played three years also for them. In 1925 he was 98 not out at lunch against Oxford, needing only two runs to equal the record of his uncle, Eustace Crawley, the only man who had made a century in both the Eton and Harrow and the Varsity match; unfortunately he was out to the first ball after lunch. In 1922, his last year at school, and again in 1923, he had headed the Worcestershire batting averages, in 1923 actually averaging 86, but Lord Harris discovered that neither he nor the leading Worcestershire professional batsman, Fox,

was properly qualified and M.C.C. declared both ineligible for the county. This led to a famous scene in the Long Room at Lord's between Lord Deerhurst, the Worcestershire President, and Lord Harris, with J. W. H. T. Douglas, unseen it is thought by the protagonists, mimicking the actions of a boxing referee in the background.

In 1925–26 Crawley went on an M.C.C. tour of the West Indies, then quite a minor affair, and from 1926 to 1937 played for Essex, though never for more than a few matches a season and sometimes not for that. However, in 1932 he averaged 51.87 for them and was asked whether he would be available to go to Australia that winter if wanted. Again in 1937 against Glamorgan at Pontypridd, on his first appearance of the season, he made 118, including five sixes, two of them out of the ground; noone else made 20. But the effort left him so stiff that he was unable to take any further part in the match. A few weeks later he featured in a bizarre incident against Worcestershire at Chelmsford. The visiting captain, the Hon. C. J. Lyttelton, seeing him coming out to open and knowing that, given a chance, he would try to drive the first ball over the screen, instructed the bowler, Perks, to give him one slightly short of a length on the middle stump. Perks produced just the right ball and Crawley's bat struck it when its face was pointing straight upwards to the sky. The ball rose vertically to an astronomical height. A. P. Singleton in the gully put his hands in his pockets and said "I'm not taking that". Lyttelton looked round in desperation and finally said to Singleton, "Sandy, you've got to take it", whereupon Singleton took his hands out of his pockets and held what in the circumstances was a fine catch.

CREBER, Harry, cricket professional and groundsman to the Swansea Cricket and Football Club for 40 years, died on March 27, 1939, aged 65. A left-hander, he was one of the stock bowlers when Glamorgan became first-class in 1921. In the August Bank Holiday match at Cardiff in 1902 against the Australians he took four wickets for 65 runs for a combined Glamorgan and Wiltshire side, and twice enjoyed the distinction of dismissing Clem Hill, the great left-hand batsman. Joe Darling's team had to fight for victory by six wickets, the match ending on the second day with 10,000 people looking on.

CREEK, Frederick Norman Smith, M.B.E., M.C., who died at Folkestone on July 26,

1980, aged 82, was a good bat and a useful change bowler. When available, he played for Wiltshire for some years between the Wars, his highest score being 124 not out against Dorset in 1930. He was better known as a footballer: he won a Blue at Cambridge in 1919 and 1921, played constantly for Corinthians in the F.A. Cup and gained five amateur international caps and one full one—against France in 1923. Later, besides doing much valuable work as a coach, he became well known as a broadcaster on football as well as a regular correspondent for the *Daily Telegraph*.

CREESE, William Leonard Charles, who died in hospital at Dover on March 9, 1974, aged 66, played as a professional all-rounder for Hampshire from 1928 to 1939. A hard-hitting left-hander born in South Africa, he scored most of his runs by drives and leg-side strokes. He scored six centuries, the highest in his last season, when he took 241, including 37 fours, from the Northamptonshire bowling at Northampton.

After the Second World War, he served as groundsman at the Central Ground at Hastings for some years, during which he suffered the agonising experience of seeing his small grandson, whom he idolised, killed by a heavy roller in the interval between innings in a Festival match. He later became head groundsman at the Sussex county ground at Hove.

Len Creese was the son of W. H. (Bill) Creese, whose family were curators, caterers and even secretaries at the famous Newlands Ground, Cape Town, for nearly 60 years. The reign ended on August 30, with the death of Ronnie Creese at the age of 57. He was the son of Frank Creese, brother of Bill, who was baggage-master to J. W. H. T. Douglas's team in 1913–14 and went to Newlands in 1915. Frank joined him in 1923 and was in charge of the ground and secretary till 1958. It was an extraordinary devotion to the game by two sons and two fathers, but Len alone made his name first as a cricketer. His father did play once for Transvaal in 1897–98 and once for the M.C.C. team in a minor engagement against Border at King Williamstown in 1913.

BATTING

	Inns.	Not Outs	Runs	Highest Inns.	100s	Aver.
1928	5	0	18	12	0	3.60
1929	30	2	425	50*	0	15.17
1930	34	4	385	87	0	12.83
1931	32	4	369	53	0	13.17
1932	39	6	723	74	0	21.90
1933	41	5	1275	165*	2	35.41
1934	41	2	909	93	0	23.30
1935	49	4	1153	130	1	25.62
1936	50	7	1331	94*	0	30.92
1937	30	1	684	74	0	23.58
1938	54	4	1421	103	1	28.42
1939	49	3	1240	241	2	26.95
Totals	455	42	9933	241	6	24.05

BOWLING

	Runs	Wickets	Average	Catches
1928	28	0	—	1
1929	370	12	30.83	6
1930	606	14	43.28	15
1931	345	10	34.50	14
1932	182	5	36.40	13
1933	788	21	37.52	15
1934	1660	52	31.92	15
1935	1643	58	24.16	17
1936	2179	95	22.93	31
1937	1456	57	25.54	13
1938	937	39	24.02	24
1939	959	31	30.93	19
Totals	11153	404	27.60	183

CREGAR, Edward Mathews, born in Philadelphia on December 28, 1868, died, in his native place, of cancer, after a long illness, on May 6, 1916. He was a fair batsman and fast bowler, and a brilliant field, who played in turn for Tioga, Belmont, and Philadelphia. In 1897 his figures for the Philadelphian team in England were 320 runs (average 16.00) and 23 wickets (average 27.13): during the tour of 1903 they were 219 (average 10.95) and 26 (average 24.07) respectively. In 1908 he was Manager of the Philadelphian side which visited us. His best performance was undoubtedly to take eight wickets in an innings for 35 runs against Warwickshire at Coventry in 1903. He was a fine type of sportsman, genial and popular, and stood 6ft. 3in. He it was who induced J. B. King to take to cricket.

CRESSWELL, George Fenwick, who was found dead with a shot-gun at his side on January 10, 1966, aged 50, did not play in first-class cricket till he was 34. After only one trial match, he was chosen for the 1949 tour of England by New Zealand, and he did so well with slow-medium leg-theory bowling that he took 62 wickets in the first-class fixtures of the tour for 26.09 runs apiece. He played in one Test match that season, the fourth, disposing of six batsmen for 168 runs in an England total of 482. He also took part in the two Tests against F. R. Brown's England team of 1950–51. He played for Marlborough, Wellington and Central Districts.

CRESSWELL, Joseph, born at Denby, near Derby, on December 22, 1866, died in July, 1932. A medium-paced bowler for Warwickshire in the '90s when the county secured promotion to first-class rank, he assisted that county from 1889 until 1899, his most successful season being that of 1890 when he took 40 wickets for 13 runs apiece.

CRICK, Flight-Lieut. Harry, who was killed in a car crash on February 10, 1960, aged 49, was formerly wicket-keeper for Yorkshire Second XI and took part in a few games for the Championship side between 1937 and 1947. He participated in over 70 bombing sorties with the R.A.F. during the Second World War and returned to the service as recruiting officer after the end of his cricket career.

CROCKETT, Henry Laurence, who died at Durban on January 22, 1964, aged 86, was a life President of the South African Cricket Association. As Secretary of the Natal C.A., he was mainly responsible for the introduction of turf pitches in South Africa. A turf pitch was used for the first time in the game between Natal and Border at Kingsmead in December, 1926, and after A. P. F. Chapman's England team engaged in the first Test match on turf at Newlands in 1930–31, matting pitches steadily disappeared. Born in Surrey, Crockett settled in Durban in 1902.

CROCKETT, Robert W., the Australian umpire, died on December 12, 1935, aged 72. Born in Melbourne, he was closely connected with Melbourne cricket for many years, and was at work on the club's famous ground when he contracted a chill, as the result of which he passed away. "Bob" Crockett "stood" in most of the Test matches during a long period when England teams visited Australia, and was held in high regard by everyone for his accurate decisions. Recognised by cricketers the world over as one of the finest umpires of his time, his quiet demeanour, unfailing good humour and strict impartiality endeared him to all players with whom he came in contact. When failing sight compelled him to give up umpiring, he became a director in a company to make cricket bats at Melbourne out of Tasmanian willow. This experiment proved fairly satisfactory, and provided Crockett with a livelihood for many years. The bats are still being made. So many times did Crockett umpire at the end from which Blackie, the Victorian, bowled, and so many decisions did he give in favour of Blackie, that their combination gave rise to many jests. When the two met in the street, "Rocketty" would welcome Crockett with "How's that, Bob?" and the umpire answered with the "out" signal, raising his hand high in the air. J. B. Hobbs coupled him with Frank Chester as the best umpires he knew, and the Surrey batsman had good opportunities of forming an opinion, because when he was in the M.C.C. team captained by A. O. Jones in 1907, Crockett already held an honoured name for his unfailing care and accuracy. Crockett came to England with the Australian team in 1926 and umpired in one match—Public Schools Fifteen v. the Australians, at Lord's.

Mr. P. F. Warner, when asked about Bob Crockett, said: "A very fine umpire: one of the best I have ever seen. He commanded the respect of everyone, and gained a reputation with English cricketers who, even if they doubted whether they were out, were quite satisfied when they realised that Crockett had made the decision."

CROMB, Ian Burns, was killed in a car accident in Christchurch, New Zealand, on March 6, 1984, aged 78. He made his first-class debut for Canterbury in 1929–30 and his last appearance 17 years later. A right-hand bat and a useful swing bowler, he toured England in 1931 with T. C. Lowry's New Zealand side, playing in all three Tests and reducing England, in the first of them, at Lord's, to 31 for three by taking the wickets of Arnold, Bakewell and Hammond. He played only two further Tests, both against South Africa in New Zealand in 1931–32, when he bowled the famously obdurate Bruce Mitchell for a duck at Wellington, a match in which he scored 51 in New Zealand's first innings. After he had taken six for 46 against MCC at Lord's in 1931, Jardine, who played in the match, said that he "made the ball come at you so quickly that it hit the bat before the bat could hit the ball". His 58 wickets on the tour, a comparatively disappointing return, cost 26.3 runs apiece. In 1935–36 Cromb captained New Zealand in three of their four representative matches against E. R. T. Holmes's MCC side, with character but limited personal success. In senior club cricket he had a long career, which lasted well into his 50s, scoring over 13,000 runs and taking nearly 700 wickets.

His playing days over, he became involved with the administration of Canterbury cricket, being President of the association from 1973–75, as well as a selector and coach. The competitiveness of his playing days manifested itself in forceful argument. His overall record in first-class cricket was 3,950 runs at 29.04, including three centuries, the highest of them 171 for Canterbury against Wellington in 1939–40, and 222 wickes at 27.7. He was also a low handicap golfer, winning the South Island title and several Canterbury championships, and helping to launch Bob Charles, New Zealand's most successful golfer, on his career.

CROMMELIN-BROWN, John Louis, who died suddenly at Minehead, Somerset, on September 11, 1953, was in the Winchester XIs of 1906 and 1907. At Trinity College, Cambridge, he participated in Freshmen's and Seniors' matches without gaining a Blue. From 1922 to 1926 he appeared irregularly for Derbyshire, for whom he was an hon. secretary from 1945 to 1949. He also played Association football for the Corinthians, and was a fine billiards player. Between 1911 and 1949 he was assistant master and house master at Repton, where he was in charge of cricket for many years.

CROOKE, Frederick James, born on April 21, 1844, died at Southsea on August 6, 1923. He was in the Winchester XI of 1860, when he scored five and 14 against Eton. He was described as "A very fine hitter, and patient in defence; a very good thrower from long-leg." He appeared in one match for Lancashire in 1860 and a few times for Gloucestershire in 1874 and 1875.

CROOM, Arthur J., who died on August 16, 1947, aged 50, played for Warwickshire from 1922 to 1939. Sound and stylish, he steadily improved from a modest start and became opening batsman with such success that he scored over 1,000 runs each season from 1927, except in 1936, the year of his benefit match, which unfortunately was ruined by rain. He played his highest innings, 211, against Worcestershire at Edgbaston in 1934, Norman Kilner helping in a first-wicket stand of 272. That season Croom's 1,402 was the highest aggregate for the county. The most regular playing member of the team in 1939, he scored 1,112 runs averaging over 30; only Dollery and R. E. S. Wyatt gained higher averages. Born on May 23, 1897, he was too old to resume his place in the side when the War ceased.

CROOME, Arthur Capel Molyneux, born at Stroud, Gloucestershire, on February 21, 1866, died in a nursing-home at Maidenhead on September 11, 1930, aged 64. A good hard-hitting batsman and an energetic field at mid-off, he was in the Wellington XI in 1883 and 1884, played for Oxford against Cambridge in 1888 and 1889, and appeared for Gloucestershire between 1885 and 1892, and for Berkshire from 1895 until 1901, being captain of the last-mentioned side 1895–1900. Among his good innings in first-class cricket were 81 for Oxford v. M.C.C. at Lord's in 1889, 71 for Gloucestershire v. Lancashire at Clifton in 1890, and 66 for Past and Present of Oxford v. Australians at Leyton in 1888. Whilst fielding against Lancashire at Manchester in 1887, he impaled himself on the railings; one of the points entered his neck, and for some time his life hung in the balance, but after a severe illness he regained his health. His highest score for Berkshire was 158 v. Hertfordshire at St. Albans in 1897. In September, 1890, he made 120 in 37 minutes for A. S. Winterbotham's XI at Thornbury. As a golfer, hurdler and skater he gained many honours, and he took part in the inter-University Sports from 1886 to 1889 inclusive, winning the hurdle race in 16⅖ seconds in 1886 and being second in the same event two years later. For many years, from 1889 onwards, he was an assistant-master at Radley College but later on became an author and journalist by profession.

CROSFIELD, Sydney Morland, the well-known Lancashire cricketer, died at Las Palmas on January 30, 1908, in his 47th year. He was born at Warrington on November 12, 1861, and was educated at Wimbledon School, Surrey, where he was in the XI in 1878 and 1879. Originally a fast bowler, he, upon returning to the north, changed to slow as he found that pace far better suited to the slower wickets. He was a hard-working field and a very useful batsman, his best efforts invariably being made when runs were of moment to his side. His first appearance for Lancashire was against Oxford University in 1883 when, by making 43 and 49, he proved the greatest run-getter in the team. Although he scored 176 runs in 10 innings for the county that season he was not, curiously enough, accorded another good trial for five years. During that period he became associated with Cheshire cricket, with no small credit to himself and with distinct advantage to the county. In 1885, when he played for two counties, he appeared for Lancashire against Oxford University and for Cheshire against Lancashire. To state that he scored 1,886 runs in first-class cricket with an average of 17.33 is to give no idea whatever of his worth to a side, for the greater need there was for runs the better he seemed to play. He was, too, a very good captain. His highest score was 82 not out which he made against Yorkshire at Bradford in 1891 and against Notts at Trent Bridge a year later, but beyond doubt his best innings was 57 on a difficult wicket against Surrey at the Oval in 1891. After retiring from first-class cricket Mr. Crosfield kept in the closest touch with the game, and many players are only too glad to acknowledge how much they owe to his encouragement. He was a fine shot with the gun and two years in succession won the Grand Prix de Casino at Monte Carlo.

CROSSE, E. M., who died on June 28, 1963, aged 81, was in the Cheltenham XI of 1900, scoring 56 not out and 14 in the match against Haileybury. From 1905 to 1910 he assisted Northamptonshire, whom he captained in 1907, playing in 48 matches and scoring 1,166 runs, average 13.55. His highest innings was 65 from the Hampshire bowling at Southampton in 1905. He was a member of M.C.C. for 60 years.

CROSSLAND, Andrew, who was born at Dalton, in Yorkshire, on November 30, 1817, died at Hull, on November 17, 1902, and was buried in the Hessle Road Cemetery, at Hull. He was a very fine batsman, a medium-paced, round-armed bowler, and a useful wicket-keeper. He was the "crack" of the famous Dalton XI when that club was in its prime. He made his first appearance for Yorkshire in 1844 and his last in 1855, but continued to participate in minor matches until almost 70 years of age. His death was not noted by any newspaper.

CROSSLAND, John. The death on September 26, 1903, of Crossland—at one time the most talked-off bowler in England—recalled a very lively controversy that disturbed the cricket world in the '80s. A Nottingham man by birth, Crossland qualified for Lancashire by residence, and appeared first for that county in 1878. Three years later, when Lancashire stood at the head of the counties, he began to assert himself, and in 1882 he was beyond doubt the most effective fast bowler in England. His pace was tremendous, and even the best batsmen rather dreaded him. Outside Lancashire, however, his delivery was generally

condemned, the majority of experts having no hesitation in describing him as a rank thrower. But for this feeling as to his action he would in all probability have been picked for England in the memorable match at the Oval when the Australians—thanks to Spofforth and Boyle—won by seven runs. Crossland was passed by the umpires, but all through the season of 1882 his bowling was the subject of discussion, among those who thought him unfair being Thomas Horan and other members of the Australian XI. At the same time there were other Lancashire bowlers who did not escape criticism, and the upshot was that Middlesex in 1883 and Notts in 1884 declined to make fixtures with Lancashire. Naturally, a great deal of ill-feeling was aroused, and on one occasion at the Oval a demonstration against Crossland so enraged Mr. Hornby that he was with difficulty persuaded to finish the match. The climax of the controversy was reached in 1885, when Kent, after appearing at Manchester, refused to play their return match with Lancashire on the ground that that county employed unfair bowlers. In taking this step Kent were guided by their captain, Lord Harris, who explained his position in a letter to the Lancashire committee. So far as Crossland was concerned the quarrel suddenly came to an end on a different issue altogether, it being ruled by the M.C.C.—after full inquiry—that by living in Nottinghamshire during the winter he had broken his qualification, and had no longer any right to play for Lancashire. This ended his career in first-class cricket, but he continued to play in small matches, and only gave up the game about four years ago.

CROUCH, George Stanton, who died at Brisbane on August 21, 1952, aged 74, was a London-born cricketer who represented Queensland in five Inter-State matches between 1904 and 1906. He served for a time on the executive of the Queensland Cricket Association. A useful right-hand batsman, he made his highest score in first-class cricket, 68, against New South Wales in 1905. In 1912 he was manager of the Australian team which took part in the Triangular Tournament in England. He also played lawn tennis for his State. For many years prominent in Australian Red Cross circles, he was chairman of the Queensland Division.

CROWDY, The Rev. James Gordon, born at Farringdon, in Berkshire, on July 2, 1847, died at Winchester on December 16, 1918. He was in the Rugby XI in 1866, when he scored 44 not out and 17 v. Marlborough at Lord's, and subsequently played for Hampshire. *Scores and Biographies* (ix–439) said of him: "Is a good hitter and fields generally at point or cover-point."

CROWE, George Lawson, who died on June 23, 1976, at the age of 91, played several useful innings for Worcestershire between 1906 and 1913, the two highest, both against Hampshire, being 78 in 1906 and 56 in 1909. In all he scored 584 runs for the county with an average of 16.22. An attacking batsman, he was in the Westminster XI in 1903. He was for nearly 40 years a master at Bromley County Grammar School, Kent, and a prominent member of Bickley Park C.C.

CRUICKSHANKS, Wing Commander George Lawrence, D.F.C., a South African, who was killed in action, 1942, played for Eastern Province in two Currie Cup matches at Johannesburg before joining the R.A.F. A powerful left-handed batsman and sound wicket-keeper, he played for All Egypt when stationed in the East against H. M. Martineau's XI in 1936 and the two following years. His best scores were 62 and 59; while at Lord's in 1939 he made the highest score in each innings for R.A.F. against the Royal Navy—run out 90 and 70 not out. He was posthumously awarded the D.F.C.

CRUTCHLEY, Gerald Edward Victor, who died on August 16, 1969, aged 78, was a capital right-handed batsman. In the Harrow XI in 1908, he did much to win the fixture with Eton by 10 wickets, scoring 74 runs and, with outswingers of varying pace, disposing of eight batsmen in the two innings for 46 runs. Though he achieved little as a batsman on the big occasion the next year, he took seven wickets for 33 runs and enabled Harrow to enjoy the best of a drawn game.

Going up to Oxford, he did not gain a Blue till 1912 and in that year against Cambridge he set up a curious record. Having scored 99 not out, he was found at the end of the day to be suffering from measles and had to withdraw from the match.

Business prevented Crutchley from appearing for Middlesex as often as he would have liked, but he turned out for the county whenever possible from 1910 to 1930. Among his chief feats for them was the scoring of 145 in an opening partnership of 231 with H. W. Lee (243 not out) in two and a quarter hours off the Nottinghamshire bowling at Lord's in 1921, in which season Middlesex carried off the County Championship. He held another distinction, for he was the last man to play cricket during the Canterbury Week and to act at night for the Old Stagers.

A batsman of delightfully free style, specially skilled in driving to the off, he hit 4,069 runs, including five centuries, average 22.23; took 60 wickets for 34.56 runs each and held 53 catches during his first-class career. For five years from 1957 he was President of Middlesex. As a Lieutenant in the Scots Guards during the First World War, he was wounded and held prisoner of war in Germany for almost four years.

CUDWORTH, Harry, a member of the Burnley C.C. for 20 years and one of the best-known players in Lancashire League cricket, died at Burnley early in April, 1914. In 1900 he appeared in a couple of matches for Lancashire, against the West Indians playing an innings of 102.

CUFF, L.A., who died at his home in Launceston, Tasmania, on October 9, 1954, aged 88, was one of the founders of the New Zealand Cricket Council in 1894–95. Between 1893 and 1897 he played as a tall, strong and aggressive batsman for New Zealand against New South Wales, Queensland and Australia, being captain in 1895–96. In 1893–94 he and J. D. Lawrence, by scoring 306 for the first Canterbury wicket against Auckland, set up a New Zealand record which stood for 57 years. Cuff's share in this partnership was 176. A prominent sports administrator, he helped to form the New Zealand Amateur Athletic Association and when taking up residence in Tasmania continued his activities there, appearing on several occasions in Tasmanian representative cricket teams.

CUFFE, John Alexander, born at Toowoomba, Queensland, on June 26, 1880, was found drowned at Burton-on-Trent on May 16, 1931. A right-hand batsman, and a left-arm bowler on the slow side of medium pace, he appeared for New South Wales twice before coming to England where he played for Worcestershire regularly from 1905 until 1914. His highest innings was 145 v. Hampshire in 1905 and he had some fine bowling performances to his credit including the following: nine for 38 v. Yorkshire at Bradford, 1907; nine for five v. Glamorgan at Cardiff, 1910, when he hit the stumps eight times and Glamorgan were out for 36; eight for 41 v. Gloucestershire at Dudley, 1911; and a "hat-trick" against Hampshire at

Bournemouth in 1910. In 1911, he scored 1,054 runs and took 110 wickets while his record in all first-class matches was 7,512 runs (average 22) and 739 wickets (average 25). After playing in Lancashire League cricket, he was on the first-class umpires list from 1925 to 1927 and just before his death had taken up a post as coach at Repton School.

CUMBERLEGE, Barry Stephenson, who died on September 22, 1970, aged 79, was in the Durham school XI before going up to Cambridge, where he got his Blue in 1913. He played for Durham and Northumberland, and for Kent in 1923 and 1924 he scored 288 runs in nine innings, his highest score being 76 against Essex at Leyton. His chief claim to fame was as a Rugby footballer. In the Fifteen at school he got his Blue as a Freshman in 1910 and held his place at scrum-half for the next three years, the last as captain. After the First World War he became full-back for Blackheath and in that position he appeared for England in eight International matches between 1920 and 1922. He was later a noted referee.

CUMMING, Bruce Leonard, who died in Johannesburg in May, 1968, was educated at Michaelhouse, South Africa. He did not gain a Blue at Oxford, but played in a few matches as a batsman for Sussex from 1936 to 1938.

CUMMINGS, Joseph, who died from the heat at Pullman, Ill., on June 15, 1913, was born at Durham on July 10, 1861. He went to Chicago in 1886, and, after playing for the Wanderers, identified himself with the Pullman C.C. He was a punishing bat and a good fast bowler. His highest score was 162 for Milwaukee v. Racine College.

CUNLIFFE, Major Sir Foster Hugh, Sixth Bart. (Rifle Brigade), born at Acton Park, Wrexham, on August 17, 1875, died of wounds on July 1, 1916. As a batsman he had a fine, free style, and he excelled as a left-handed medium-pace bowler, having a good length and sending down a difficult ball that came with his arm. He was in the Eton XI in 1893 and 1894, and in his four Public School matches obtained 35 wickets for 10.17 runs each: he took 11 for 74 v. Winchester in 1893 and 13 for 94 v. Harrow in 1894. At Oxford he obtained his Blue as a Freshman and in 1898, his last year in the XI, was captain. In his four games against Cambridge he scored 99 runs in five complete innings and took 26

wickets for 22.88 runs each. Against Surrey, at Oxford, in 1896, he obtained eight wickets in an innings for 26 runs. In 1897, when he began to appear for Middlesex, he was chosen for the Gentlemen at Lord's, and took three wickets in each innings of the Players. In 1895 he became a member of the M.C.C., serving on the committee from 1903 until 1906. He was a Fellow of All Soul's, Oxford, and a distinguished military historian.

CURGENVEN, Gilbert, died on May 26, 1934, aged 51. A free batsman with attractive style he headed the Repton averages in 1901 when he started playing for Derbyshire and continued helping his county intermittently until 1922. In 1904 he scored 822 runs in all matches, with an average of 24, his best innings being 124 against Surrey at Derby. He also did well in 1921 with 765 runs, average 20. Altogether in first-class cricket he made 3,568 with an average of over 20.

CURGENVEN, Dr. William Grafton, M.D., who was born at Plymouth on November 30, 1841, died at Fareham, in Hampshire, on March 18, 1910. His early cricket was played in Devonshire, and it was for the Gentlemen of Devon that he made his first appearance at Lord's—against M.C.C., in June, 1864. Removing later to Derby, he served for many years on the Committee of the County Club, and, except in 1877, played every year for Derbyshire from 1872 until 1878 inclusive. He was described as "A brilliant bat, hitting well all round, and on a lively wicket a fast run-getter; a good field at long leg and cover-point." In 1873 he scored 39 of a total of 70 against Lancashire at Manchester, and in the following year made 34 and 74 in the match with Yorkshire on the Derby ground, while in 1875 he obtained 71 against Kent, also at Derby. Two of his sons have played for Derbyshire during recent years.

CURLE, Gerald, died at Budleigh Salterton on March 4, 1976, aged 83. He was in the XI at King Edward's, Birmingham, and in 1913 had a trial for Warwickshire as a batsman, his highest score being 34 against Sussex. His younger brother, A. C. Curle, also appeared for the county.

CURRIE, Sir Donald, K.C.M.G., the famous shipowner and philanthropist, who was born at Greenock on September 17, 1825, died at the Manor House, Sidmouth, on April 13, 1909. He was the donor of the Currie Cup, which has been the means of greatly increasing the popularity of the game in South Africa.

CURSHAM, Henry Alfred, who died on August 6, 1941, aged 81, earned chief fame in sport at Association football in the Notts County XI and for England in the early '80s; but he was a good cricketer and, during a long career with Notts Amateur C.C., twice appeared for the county. Against Surrey in 1880 William Gunn also was taking his first trial in the side; a small-scoring match was drawn. In 1904, when A. O. Jones rested, Cursham captained the county against the South Africans in a very different kind of game. He scored 12 and 25 not out in totals of 320 and 242, but Notts were weak and suffered defeat by an innings and 49 runs. Cursham was on the Nottinghamshire Club Committee for several years.

CURTEIS, Robert Mascall, born at Windmill Hill, near Hailsham, on October 12, 1851, died at Uckfield on January 21, 1927, at the age of 75. A free-hitting batsman and a good field, he was a member of the Westminster XI in 1867 and three next years, being captain in 1870, and played in half-a-dozen matches for Sussex between 1873 and 1878. His highest score for the county was 41. At Eastbourne on May 22, 1875, he played an innings of 200 not out for Devonshire Park against the 5th Batt. R.A.

CURTIN, John, Prime Minister of Australia, a cricket enthusiast, died on July 4, 1945, aged 60. Notwithstanding his many national activities he maintained a close interest in cricket and often mentioned the game in his speeches. Last year's *Wisden* quoted his memorable remarks regarding Lord's when he became a Freeman of London.

Early in the War he declared that games were not detrimental to the War effort, but a refresher, and he recommended that a series of Test matches between Australia and England should be played immediately after the War as an effective way of demonstrating to the world the characteristics of the British race. Mr. Curtin visited Lord's in 1944, and just before the first "Victory Test" last May he sent a message to M.C.C. conveying his best wishes for the reopening of a series which he hoped would never again be interrupted.

Flight-Lieut. K. Johnson, a member of the Australian Board of Control, who was in England when the news came that Mr. Curtin was dead, said that although a very busy man at Canberra, the headquarters of Australian politics, a long way from cricket centres, Mr. Curtin seldom missed an opportunity of watching the game. He was often a spectator at West Australia matches. By his death, cricket in England and Australia lost a very valuable friend and supporter.

CURTIS, C. B., who died in January, 1899, was an old Essex cricketer who frequently assisted the county when the headquarters were at Brentwood. He is described as having been a good steady bat and a useful bowler. While digging in his garden at Bexley he injured his leg. Blood-poisoning set in, and this, in conjunction with pneumonia, caused his death.

CURTIS, John Stafford, who died on March 8, 1972, aged 84, played for Leicestershire intermittently from 1906 to 1921. An accurate medium-pace off-spinner and an attacking batsman, he would have been valuable had he played regularly, but he preferred League cricket and only in 1919 did he appear at all frequently. Analyses that year of five for 67 v. Lancashire and seven for 75 v. Nottinghamshire showed what he could do: in 1912 he had taken six for 32 v. Hampshire. His highest score was 66 v. Hampshire in 1911.

CURZON, Major Francis (Derbyshire Yeomanry), died March 3, 1918, aged 58, at Lockington Hall, Leicestershire. A former Hon. Secretary of the Derbyshire County C.C. Better remembered as F. C. Newton. He assumed the name of Curzon on succeeding to the Lockington Hall estates.

CUTTELL, William, who died on June 10, 1896, was an old Yorkshire professional, who played for the county in 1862 and occasionally in some later seasons. He was born on January 28, 1835, and was thus at the time of his death in his 62nd year. He was the father of W. Cuttell, the Nelson bowler, who was tried for Lancashire two or three times last season.

CUTTELL, Willis Robert, born at Sheffield on September 13, 1864, died at Nelson on December 9, 1929, aged 65. The son of William Cuttell, who appeared occasionally for Yorkshire between 1862 and 1871, Willis Cuttell played twice for that county when engaged in Lancashire League cricket, and, under the residential qualification, he assisted Lancashire from 1896 to 1906. A rather slow right hand bowler, Cuttell had good command of length and made the ball turn either way. An excellent field and a sound batsman with strong defence and good hitting powers, he became under the captaincy of A. C. MacLaren a first rate all-round cricketer. In first-class cricket during the season of 1898 he scored 1,003 runs and took 114 wickets, being the first Lancashire player to qualify for a place in the list of "All-Round Cricketers." Of Lancashire players only J. Hallows in 1908 has enjoyed equal prominence by scoring 1,000 runs and taking 100 wickets. Altogether Cuttell dismissed 755 batsmen for 19 runs each and his aggregate scores in England numbered 5,667 runs. In the winter of 1898 he went to South Africa with the team captained by Lord Hawke and did well as a bowler, though the chief honours went to Albert Trott and Schofield Haig. Among many good performances, Cuttell took four wickets for eight runs against Sussex at Hove in 1897, and at Old Trafford a year later eight Gloucestershire batsmen fell to him in one innings for 105 runs. In 1901, at Derby, he took seven wickets for 19 runs, and in 1904, at Old Trafford, four Kent wickets for three runs. Playing for the North against the South at Hastings in 1897 he took four wickets at three runs apiece. His highest score was 137 against Notts at Old Trafford in 1899. Appointed coach at Rugby School in 1907 he retained his duties there for 20 years and then, for two seasons, acted as a first-class umpire. In July, 1903, he and Charles Smith had, as a joint benefit, the match between Lancashire and Essex at Old Trafford. A portrait and biography of Cuttell appeared in *Wisden's Almanack* of 1898.

DACRE, Cecil Charles, who died in Auckland, New Zealand, on November 2, 1975, aged 76, was for some years one of the most exciting batsmen in the world, if never one of the heaviest scorers. A stocky, strongly built man, and a fine driver, he scored at a great pace and was capable of doing so against good bowling, but was too uncertain a starter to be consistent. Though he had played in first-class cricket in New Zealand before he was 16, had scored 45 and 58 for a representative New Zealand side against MacLaren's M.C.C. team in 1923 and had made two hundreds in a match for Auckland, his name was unknown to the general public in this country when he arrived as vice-captain of the first New Zealand side in England in 1927. After two matches everyone was talking about him. He started by making 101 in an hour against H. M. Martineau's XI at Holyport (the match was not first-class) and

followed this with 107 in an hour and a half against a strong amateur M.C.C. bowling side at Lord's. When he went in four wickets were down for 106 and another 137 were needed to save the follow-on: in the end New Zealand led by 68. After this, apart from a brilliant 176 at Derby, his form was rather disappointing.

At the end of the tour, entirely on his own initiative, he stayed behind to qualify for Gloucestershire, with which he had family links. In his first match for them, while he was qualifying, he made 69 and 50 not out against Oxford in 1928. By 1930 he was qualified and for five seasons was a valuable member of the side, without ever making quite the number of runs hoped for. His highest score was 223 against Worcestershire in 1930 and it was against Worcestershire too that he made a hundred in each innings in 1933. After poor seasons in 1935 and 1936 he dropped out of the side and returned to New Zealand. Apart from his batting, he was a fine field whether in the deep or at cover and could keep wicket if required. He was a right-handed bat, but bowled and threw left-handed. His career was shortened by muscular rheumatism.

DAFT, Charles Frederick, elder brother of the late Richard Daft, died at Nottingham on March 10, 1915, aged 84. He was born at Nottingham on June 8, 1830, and was described in *Scores and Biographies* as "A good and steady batsman ... in the field is generally mid-wicket on and long-stop." His career in County Cricket was short, extending only from 1862 to 1865. One of his best innings was his 46 v. Kent, at Trent Bridge, in 1864, "slowly but well played for." As a cricketer he was somewhat late in coming to the front, and he had almost completed his thirty-second year when he appeared at Lord's for the Colts against M.C.C. In that match he scored 26 and 13 and took five wickets for 34, an all-round feat for which he was called up to the pavilion and presented with a prize bat. For several years he was secretary of the Nottingham Commercial C.C., as well as one of the most useful players in the team.

DAFT, Richard, died on July 18, 1900. His death, which took place at Radcliffe-on-Trent, removed from amongst us one of the greatest cricketers of the last generation. As late as the summer of 1899 he seemed to have years of life before him, but some time afterwards his health completely broke down, and for several weeks before his death he was lying ill without any hope of recovery. He was born on November 2, 1835, and was thus in his 65th year. Coming out as an amateur, he made his first appearance at Lord's, for North against South, in 1858, and quickly established a reputation as one of the best batsmen of his day. He took to cricket as a professional in 1859, but played again as an amateur when his career in public matches was nearly over. It is a noteworthy fact that he and the Warwickshire cricketer, Diver, are the only men who have played on both sides in the Gentlemen and Players' match. Beginning in 1858, he was a regular member of the Notts XI for over 20 years, succeeding George Parr as captain, and not retiring until the season of 1881. After he had done with first-class matches he still kept up his cricket, and in 1891 he made so many runs in local matches that for one special occasion he reappeared in the Notts XI—as a substitute for Shrewsbury—playing against Surrey in the August Bank Holiday match at the Oval. He was at his best as a batsman from perhaps 1861 to 1876. He came before the public at about the same time as Robert Carpenter and the late Thomas Hayward, and for three or four seasons it was a disputed point as to which of the three was the finest bat in England. George Parr was on the wane, and they had no rival until E. M. Grace appeared on the scene. Whether Daft was as good or better than Hayward or Carpenter is purely a matter of opinion, but there can be no question that in their day all three were very great indeed. It is a fair criticism to say that while Daft and Hayward were far ahead of Carpenter in point of style, Carpenter's was, perhaps, the hardest wicket to get. Daft batted in exceptionally fine form, utilising every inch of his height, and being very strong in back play. Like nearly all the batsmen of his time, he learnt most of his cricket against fast bowling, and was, perhaps, never seen to better advantage than when facing such bowlers as Willsher, Emmett, and George Freeman. The finest innings he ever played in his young days was 118 at Lord's for North against South in 1862, and the highest of his whole career in first-class matches was 161 for Notts against Yorkshire at Trent Bridge in 1873. His best performance in Gentlemen and Players' matches was at Lord's, in 1872, when against the bowling of Appleby, Powys, and David Buchanan, he scored 102. Scores were far smaller all round in his day than they are now, and grounds by no means so true, and, allowing for these facts, his records were wonderfully good. In the history of Notts

cricket his name as a batsman will stand with that of George Parr in the past, and those of Arthur Shrewsbury and William Gunn in our own time.

DAFT, Richard Parr, the elder son of the celebrated "Dick" Daft—most elegant of batsmen—who died on March 27, 1934, in his 70th year, played once for Nottinghamshire in 1886 against Surrey at Trent Bridge being caught by Wood at the wicket off Beaumont for five runs.

DAILY, Charles Edwin, who died suddenly at his home at Ockley, on June 30, 1974, aged 74, was a sound steady batsman who played for Surrey between 1923 and 1929, but his opportunities in the county side were infrequent owing to the galaxy of batting talent at that period at the Oval. His hobbies were cricket and singing and he was a stalwart of Capel Choral Society. Until his death he sang in the Guildford Cathedral concerts with the Surrey Festival Choir under its conductor, Ralph Nicholson. For many years Daily was coach at St. Paul's School, West London.

DALE, J. W. (Tonbridge School, Cambridge University and Middlesex), died at the end of June, 1895. He was born at Lincoln on June 21, 1848, and had thus only just completed his 47th year. His premature death was, we believe, due to an attack of pneumonia following influenza. Though he had for some time dropped entirely out of first-class cricket, Mr. Dale will be remembered as one of the best amateur batsmen of his day. He was in the Tonbridge School team from 1863 to 1866 inclusive, and, on going up to Cambridge, played in the University match in 1868, 1869 and 1870. In the last-mentioned year he was one of the heroes of the memorable match which F. C. Cobden's bowling won for Cambridge by two runs. He scored on that occasion 15 and 67, his partnership with Mr. Yardley in Cambridge's second innings completely turning the fortunes of the game. In 1870, indeed, Mr. Dale was quite at his best as a batsman, appearing for the Gentlemen against the Players both at Lord's and the Oval. In the second innings of the Oval match he went in with Mr. W. G. Grace and helped to make 164 runs for the first wicket, his own score being 55. Mr. Dale's style of batting was extremely finished and elegant. His abilities in the world of sport were by no means restricted to the cricket field. He rowed in the Cambridge eight in 1869 and 1870, with Mr. J. H. D.

Goldie as stroke, and was a first-rate fisherman.

DALES, Hugh Lloyd, who died at Whitley Bay on May 4, 1964, aged 75, played as an amateur batsman for Middlesex from 1920 to 1930, frequently opening the innings. In all first-class cricket he scored 4,635 runs, average 26.63, his best season being that of 1923 when his aggregate reached 1,138, his average 29.17 and he registered the highest of his eight centuries—143 against Somerset at Taunton. "Horace" Dales, as he was generally known in cricket circles, was a member of the Hon. F. S. G. Calthorpe's M.C.C. team in the West Indies in 1925–26 and made one appearance for Gentlemen against Players, at the Oval in 1924. A left-handed batsman specially strong in defence and an occasional slow left-arm bowler, he assisted Durham from 1911 to 1913.

DALLAS BROOKS, General Sir Reginald Alexander, who died on March 22, 1966, aged 69, was in the Dover XI from 1912 to 1914 as a batsman and medium-paced bowler. In his last season he headed the school batting figures with 939 runs, of which he scored 187 in an innings against King's School, Canterbury, at an average of 62.62, and was also leading bowler with 36 wickets at 12.94 runs each. In 1919 and 1921 he appeared in a few matches for Hampshire, hitting 107 from the Gloucestershire bowling at Southampton in the first year. A fine all-round sportsman, he captained the Combined Services against touring teams from Australia, South Africa and New Zealand, led them at hockey, at which he played for England against Ireland and France and captained the Royal Navy at golf. Joining the Royal Marines on his 18th birthday, he earned the D.S.O. in the First World War for his part in the St. George's Day raid on Zeebrugge in 1918. He was Governor of Victoria from 1949 to 1963.

DALMENY, Lord, who died from blood poisoning on November 11, 1931, aged 21, won considerable distinction as a cricketer at Eton. In addition to being a free hitter, he was very effective with his fast medium bowling and could make the ball come back or swing away. Playing against Harrow in 1928, as the Hon. A. R. Primrose, he scored four and 19 and took four wickets for 87. The following season at Lord's, by brilliant driving mainly to the off-side, he hit 65 out of 116, including 12 fours, off the Harrow bowlers, this score following upon an innings

of 65 and a bowling record of four for 91 in the Winchester match. He finished the season with 299 runs, average 33.22 and 38 wickets at a cost of 28.88 apiece. Lord Dalmeny made a few appearances in the Middlesex XI and played in one match for Oxford in 1930. He became Lord Dalmeny in May, 1929.

DALTON, Eric Londesbrough, who died in Durban on June 3, 1981, aged 74, was one of the finest all-round sportsmen produced by South Africa between the wars. Considered fortunate to have been picked for the 1929 South African cricket tour to England, with only nine first-class matches behind him, in which he had limited success, Dalton, by late-summer, was giving every sign of developing into a very good, attacking, middle-order batsman. Against Kent at Canterbury, towards the end of August, he scored 157 and 116 not out, followed by 102 and 44 not out against Sussex at Hove and 59 against Sir Julien Cahn's XI at West Bridgford. On returning to South Africa, Dalton quickly established himself as an extremely fine cricketer. He was an automatic choice for the South African tour to Australasia in 1931–32, where he averaged 32.41 with the bat, his best score being 100 against Tasmania at Launceston. He played in two Tests in Australia and two in New Zealand, in the first of which, at Christchurch, he made 82. By the end of the 1934–35 season he had become one of South Africa's most reliable batsmen, having averaged 54.76 in first-class matches since returning from New Zealand. His bowling, too, came on tremendously during this period: in 1934–35 he captured 25 wickets at 19.08 each with his leg-breaks.

The value of having taken him to England in 1929, when only 22, was reflected in his performances on his return there in 1935. So well did he play that by the end of the tour he had scored 1,446 runs at an average of 37.07, including his first Test hundred at the Oval. With the wickets of Wyatt and Hammond in England's first innings he also contributed valuably to South Africa's famous victory at Lord's, their first over England in England. Despite a decline in form over the next couple of years, he was back to his best for the visit of W. R. Hammond's M.C.C. side to South Africa in 1938–39, averaging 44 in the Test series, including 102 in the first Test at Johannesburg (the last Test hundred to be scored by a South African at the old Wanderers Ground), and, for good measure, hitting 110 for Natal against the Englishmen at Pietermaritzburg and three times taking the important wicket of Hammond, once in the first Test and twice (stumped) in the "timeless" fifth. His ninth-wicket partnership of 137 with A. B. C. Langton, against England at the Oval in 1935, still stood as a record when South Africa last played Test cricket.

After two post-War seasons for Natal, Dalton concentrated on golf, a game which he also played with great distinction for many years, winning the South African Amateur Championship in 1950 and representing them in the first Commonwealth Tournament at St. Andrew's in 1954. He had taken to golf in Australia in 1931–32 when, having had his jaw broken in the match after making his hundred against Tasmania, he was unable for some weeks to play cricket. His mentor at the time was Ivo Whitton, who, as an amateur, won a record number of Australian Open Championships. Dalton was also a fine bowls player, hard to beat at both tennis and table tennis, an accomplished pianist and the possessor of a fine baritone voice. He led many a sing-song on board the *Kenilworth Castle*, bound for England in 1929. A lovable character, he made the most of his many talents.

He scored 5,333 first-class runs at an average of 33.12, with 13 centuries. His batting average in Tests, from 698 runs, was 31.72.

DALTON, George Londesbrough, who died at Durban on July 12, 1946, aged 70, was a regular member of Natal teams in Currie Cup and other inter-provincial matches from 1897 to 1908. His highest score was 40 against Transvaal. His son, E. L. Dalton, has played for South Africa in Test matches, and he himself represented South Africa at Association football.

DANIELL, John, who died on January 24, 1963, aged 84, rendered splendid service to cricket and Rugby football over many years as player and administrator. He was in the Clifton XI—and the Fifteen—in 1895, 1896 and 1897, heading the batting averages in the last year. Though he created little impression as a cricketer when he went up to Emmanuel College, Cambridge, S. M. J. Woods, the Somerset captain, included him in the county team for six games in 1898. When, the following season, Daniell hit 107 against such a powerful bowling side as Lancashire, G. L. Jessop felt compelled to award him the last place against Oxford. Daniell also played in the following two University matches and, as a lively and enthusiastic Rugby forward, he

represented Cambridge from 1898 to 1900. In 1899, "The Prophet," as he was then usually known, was first chosen for England at football and he gained seven caps between then and 1904, twice being captain. A member of the Rugby Football Union Selection Committee from 1913 to 1939, he was chairman for the last eight years; he became a Vice-President of the Union in 1938, was acting-President from 1940 to 1945 and President from 1945 to 1947.

After going down from Cambridge, he was a schoolmaster for a brief spell and then took up tea-planting in India till, in 1908, he returned to England and accepted the captaincy of Somerset. A keen and highly popular leader, intolerant of "slackers", he possessed a forcefully picturesque vocabulary when things did not go as he expected; but because he was always scrupulously fair, his sometimes caustic criticism left no ill-effects. He remained Somerset captain for four seasons and then retired, but after serving in the Army in the First World War, he responded to an appeal by the county and resumed the position from 1919 to 1926.

Altogether Daniell, a hard-driving batsman at his best against off-spin bowling, scored 10,415 runs in first-class cricket, average 21.12, but it is as a fearless fieldsman at silly point, where he brought off the vast majority of his 222 catches, that he will be best remembered as a cricketer. However hard the hit, Daniell generally seemed able to hold any catch within reach. Of his nine centuries, he obtained two in one match at the age of 46—174 not out and 108 against Essex at Taunton in 1925.

When his playing days finally ended, Daniell served as an England cricket selector and also, to help his county in a financial crisis, acted for a time as hon. secretary to Somerset.

DANN, The Rev. John Walter, M.A., brother-in-law of the late Dr. W. G. Grace, was born at Fermoy, County Cork, on November 20, 1842, and died at Downend, of which parish he had been Vicar for 47 years, on July 22, 1915. He was never much of a cricketer, but took a keen interest in the game, and played occasionally for the Thornbury and Downend clubs. He took a very active part in the formation of the Gloucestershire County C.C., undertaking practically all the correspondence in the matter for the late Dr. H. M. Grace. In his younger days he was an excellent lawn-tennis player, and he played quite a good game until he was 70.

DARK, Francis, formerly of Lord's Ground, died at Gunnersbury on February 14, 1906, aged 86.

DARLING, Joseph, died on January 2, 1946, at Hobart, Tasmania, aged 75. His passing recalls some of the most stirring times of cricket in England and Australia. A left-handed batsman of medium height and robust build, Darling invariably opened the innings. Possibly he did not show the same style as Warren Bardsley or Clem Hill, but he seldom failed, and could defend with stubborn steadiness or pull a game round by determined forcing tactics. Besides his run-getting powers, Darling in the field, notably at mid-off, held opposing batsmen in check, and as a captain he inspired his men to reveal their best form. Joseph Darling first came to England in 1896, and he captained the Australian sides that visited us in 1899, 1902 and 1905.

Starting cricket when very young, he revealed remarkable ability just before his 15th birthday, when, in a two-day match for St. Peter's College on the Adelaide Oval, he scored 252 out of 470, so beating 209 by George Giffen—then the highest innings in the State. Farming occupied him for some years, and not until the 1893–94 season did he play for South Australia. Then he found his form, and next season against the England team, captained by A. E. Stoddart, he made 117 and 37 not out, so helping materially in a victory for South Australia by six wickets. He averaged 38 against the Englishmen, and, coming to England in 1896, he started at Sheffield Park with 67 and 35. In the Test matches of that tour he was not fortunate, but his value was established, and altogether he played in 31 matches for Australia against England and three against South Africa. Altogether in Test matches against England he made 1,632 runs, average 30.79. His highest score in England was 194 at Leicester in 1896, and an aggregate of 6,305 runs, average 33, for the four tours included a dozen centuries. Most successful in 1899, he made 1,941 runs, including five centuries, average 41.29. At Cambridge after a tie—436 on the first innings—he and Worrall hit off 124, the last 74 runs coming in 28 minutes.

His side won the rubbers in 1899 and 1902, the second of these series being memorable for the tense finishes at Old Trafford, where Australia won by two runs, and Kennington Oval, where England won by one wicket. Under P. F Warner, England regained the Ashes in the 1903 winter, and F. S. Jackson

led England to a great triumph in 1905, when England were victorious in the only two finished games.

Jackson won the toss in each of those five Tests, and it was related that when they met again at the Scarborough Festival at the end of the tour, Darling, with a towel round his waist, waited in the dressing-room, and received Jackson with the remark, "I'm not going to risk the toss this time except by wrestling." But the spin of the coin again favoured Jackson, and he scored 123 and 31 not out in a match unfinished because of rain.

By a remarkable coincidence Sir Stanley Jackson and Joseph Darling were born on the same day, November 21, 1870. So Darling passed on at the age of 75.

In 1908 Darling left Adelaide and settled in Tasmania as a farmer, and continued making many runs in club cricket until well over 50. He became a member of the Legislative Assembly, being awarded the C.B.E. in 1938. So he followed the example of his father, the Hon. J. Darling, who, when a member of the Legislative Council of South Australia, was responsible for inaugurating a central cricket ground, famous for many years now as Adelaide Oval.

CORRECTION. An advice from Australia states that Joe Darling made 252 for Prince Alfred College, not for St. Peter's, in the annual match of 1885 between the two colleges. The team's total, 500, on that occasion was a record for the Adelaide Oval.

DARNLEY, The Eighth Earl of (Ivo Francis Walter Bligh), born in Bruton Street, London, on March 13, 1859, died peacefully in his sleep of heart failure at Puckle Hill, Cobham, Kent, on April 10, 1927, aged 68. It was in October, 1900, that he had succeeded to the Earldom. As a small boy he received some coaching from "Farmer" Bennett, and at Cheam, where he had some of the Studds among his companions, his bowling gained him a place in the XI. Naturally, he developed his cricket considerably whilst at Eton, and in his four matches against Harrow and Winchester—in 1876 and 1877—made 106 runs with an average of 26.50, his highest innings being 73 against the latter side in 1876. Eton won three of the four games with an innings to spare: the other, against Harrow in 1877, was drawn with the position fairly open. A feature of Mr. Bligh's batting was his driving—he was 6ft. 3in. in height—and, until ill-health handicapped him, he was a capital long-field and point. At Cambridge he gained his Blue as a Freshman, being the last choice, and so was a member of the famous team of 1878, which played eight matches and won them all—that against the Australians, at Lord's, by an innings and 72 runs. In his four games with Oxford he was on the winning side three times, Cambridge (when he was captain) losing by 135 runs. His scores in those matches were 14 and 24 not out, one, 59 and 13, 37 and six—an aggregate of 154 with an average of 25.66. In his University's match with Surrey at the Oval in 1879 he carried out his bat for 113, and in Kent's game against the same county on the same ground a year later (when he probably reached his full powers) he made 105. His association with the Kent XI, owing to ill-health, extended only from 1877 to 1883, during which period he played in 47 matches, scoring 1,490 runs with an average of 18.86 and occasionally, during the absence of Lord Harris, leading the side. There can be little doubt that, had he remained in full vigour, he would have developed into a really great batsman, for he was only 21 when his breakdown occurred. In 1879 and 1880 he had represented the Gentlemen against the Players three times, and, although he played no large innings in the matches, he showed consistent cricket in making 55 runs for three times out. The most interesting episode of his short career was his visit to Australia in 1882–83 as captain of a team in an endeavour to regain for England the laurels lost in the historic Test at the Oval the previous summer. The Australians, under W. L. Murdoch's captaincy, had then, it will be remembered, won, after a thrilling finish, by seven runs—a result which led to the term "The Ashes" being coined. The said Ashes were supposed to have been taken to Australia, and hopes ran high that Mr. Bligh's team would recover them. As it happened, Mr. Bligh was successful in his quest, for, meeting Murdoch's men in three matches the Englishmen, after losing the first by nine wickets, won the second by an innings and 27 runs and the third by 69 runs. It is true that in a fourth game later in the tour, Australia—not solely Murdoch's men—were successful by four wickets: still, the rubber having been gained against the side which had defeated us at the Oval, honours were considered to have been won by the Englishmen. Mr. Bligh's interest in cricket remained as great as ever after he had dropped out of first-class matches, and he was President of the M.C.C. in 1900 and of the Kent County C.C. in 1892 and 1902. Apart from cricket, he had whilst at Eton distinguished himself greatly at racquets,

having been champion in the singles in 1876 and one of the champions in the doubles in both that year and the next; while he represented Cambridge at tennis in the singles in 1879 and 1880, and in the doubles in 1878 and two following years. Later on he played a fair amount of golf, but his great love was always cricket—the game with which his family had been associated for nearly 150 years. Lord Darnley was one of the most genial and kind-hearted of men. Only a short time before he passed away he penned some interesting reminiscences of Mr. F. R. Spofforth for publication in *Wisden*.

DASTUR, M. P., one of the most gifted of Parsi cricketers, was killed in a motor-cycle accident at Karachi on November 2, 1926, aged 30. Only a few days before he had appeared in a couple of matches against the M.C.C. team, scoring 32 and 38 for Parsis and Moslems, and one and 61 for All Karachi. In representative Parsi games he had made 157 not out v. Rest, at Karachi, in 1920, and 142 v. Europeans, at Nagpur, two years later.

DAUBENY, The Rev. Edmund Thomas, died at Southacre Rectory, Swaffham, on August 20, 1914, aged 74. He was born in London on July 14, 1840, and educated at Bromsgrove School. At Oxford, where he was contemporary with R. D. Walker, R. A. H. Mitchell, T. P. Garnier and F. G. Inge, he was in the XI in 1861 and 1862, in which years, in his matches against Cambridge (both of which were lost by Oxford), he made 14 runs with an average of 4.50, and took nine wickets at a cost of 17.55 runs each. Mr. Haygarth has recorded in *Scores and Biographies* that "his bowling was very straight, and on dead ground considered difficult to play". He was, in addition, a severe hitter, though sometimes lacking confidence. In 1862 he assisted Sixteen of his University in their famous tie-match with the All England XI on the Christchurch ground, and certainly no-one had better reason than he to look back upon the game with satisfaction, seeing that in the first innings he took eight wickets for 14 runs, and in the second, whilst fielding at first slip, caught out the first three men off Mr. Reade's bowling. His chief batting success was an innings of 78 for Eighteen of Lansdown against England in June 1864. Mr. Daubeny was 6ft. 1½in. in height, and weighed 12st. 7lb.

DAUGLISH, Maurice John, who was born in London on October 2, 1867, died at Hunton

Bridge, King's Langley, on April 20, 1922. He was in the Harrow XI in 1884 and two following years, being captain in 1886, and played for Oxford in the University matches of 1889 and 1890. Of his play whilst captain of Harrow it was said: "Has good hitting powers, but requires rather more defence, an excellent wicket-keeper, and a brilliant field anywhere; bowls lobs fairly well; worked hard as captain, and the good fielding of the team at Lord's was chiefly owing to his exertions." In his three matches v. Eton he scored 46 runs in five completed innings, and on his two appearances against Cambridge made 0 and 0, nine and four. He appeared for Middlesex from 1886 to 1890 and subsequently for Berkshire. He was the youngest of six brothers, all keen and exceedingly loyal Harrovians, and whilst at the school he obtained his colours for football as well as for cricket.

DAVENPORT, George, whose death took place at Nantwich on October 4, 1902, was for many years a well-known member of the ground staff at Lord's. A capable batsman and a wicket-keeper of some merit, he was born in May, 1860, and thus was in his 43rd year at the time of his death. He had dropped out of prominence for some time, but in 1890 he scored 158 not out for M.C.C. against Derbyshire. He did capital work for Cheshire in the '80s, one of his most notable successes being an innings of 119 not out against the M.C.C. and Ground in 1885, the club bowlers on that occasion including William Mycroft, George Hay, and Pickett. Other good scores he made—at a time when run-getting was not so heavy as it has been of late years—were 52 not out for Cheshire against the M.C.C. and Ground at Lord's in 1884, 64 for Cheshire against Lancashire at Manchester in 1886, when he had Briggs, Barlow and Watson against him, and 57 for M.C.C. and Ground v. Essex, at Lord's in 1896.

DAVEY, Darnton Charles, a member of the South African team which visited England in 1894, died suddenly at Durban on October 7, 1911. He was born at Mansfield on July 7, 1856, and educated at Colchester, where he learned the game. Emigrating to South Africa when about 24 years of age, he soon made his mark in the cricket world there, and in March, 1883, played the highest innings of his career, making 177 not out for Winburg v. Brandfort. He was a fine free bat, an excellent field anywhere, and in his younger days a slow bowler of considerable

ability. In more than one Currie Cup Tournament he scored well for Natal, and he was third in the averages for the South African side in England in 1894.

DAVID, Major Rodney Felix Armine, who died in hospital on July 2, 1969, aged 62, was in the Wellington XI from 1923 to 1925. He headed the batting averages in his last season when captain and made a few appearances for Glamorgan between that year and 1929.

DAVIDSON, George, Derbyshire cricket sustained a heavy blow in the death from pneumonia on Wednesday morning, February 8, 1899, of George Davidson. For some years he had been the best all-round man in the team, and, with the exception of William Storer, the county has never produced a player of finer powers. By reason of his superiority as a bowler, he was of greater use on the side than even Chatterton. Born on June 29, 1866, he was just in his prime, and but for the illness which—following on influenza—had such a sad termination, he might have assisted Derbyshire for a good many seasons to come. Had he been associated with a stronger county, it is likely that he would have enjoyed a still more brilliant career, the fact of being so often on the beaten side having naturally a somewhat depressing effect on his cricket. It is a fair criticism to say that, though never quite the cricketer one would choose for England against Australia, he only fell a little below the highest class. He reached his best in the season of 1895, when he was the only man in first-class matches to score over 1,000 runs and take over 100 wickets. To be quite exact, he made that year 1,296 runs, with an average of 28, and took 138 wickets at a cost of less than 17 runs each. Derbyshire had, perhaps, a stronger all-round XI in 1895 than at any time before or since, and so well did they play that, though bad weather robbed them of victories over Surrey and Lancashire, they came out fifth among the counties. Davidson did much of his best work that year in county matches, being fourth in the batting averages and top in bowling. As a batsman he fared even better for Derbyshire in 1896, when, against Lancashire at Old Trafford, he scored 274—the highest innings of his life. In 1898 with very little assistance, he bowled finely for the county, but his batting fell below its best standard. A man of barely medium height, Davidson had an appearance that suggested great strength both of muscles and constitution. As a batsman he combined hit and defence in no common degree, and his fast bowling was marked by a really wonderful accuracy of pitch.

DAVIDSON, Joseph, who died in the first week in December, 1901, was the father of the famous Derbyshire player George Davidson, whose premature death so weakened the county XI. Joseph Davidson assisted Derbyshire in 1871 and 1874, taking part in the first match played by the present County Club. He was chiefly known as a right-handed medium-pace bowler. In one season, while engaged with the Carlisle club, he took 143 wickets for less than two runs each.

DAVIDSON, Kenneth R., who was killed in an airplane crash at Prestwick Aerodrome on December 25, 1954, the day after his 49th birthday, played as a batsman for Yorkshire on a number of occasions from 1933 as amateur and professional. In 1934 he scored 1,053 runs, including an innings of 128 against Kent at Maidstone. Previously he appeared for the Second XI, for Bingley in the Bradford League and for Scotland. Better known as a badminton player, at which he displayed remarkable ability, he went to America in 1935 and was returning to his New York home after a world tour with a U.S.A. team when he met his death.

DAVIES, Dai, who died at Llanelli on July 16, 1976, was a man who held a very special place in the hearts of Glamorgan supporters. Not only was he for many years an indispensable member of the county side, but he and his namesake, Emrys, who was no relation, were the first home-born professionals to find regular places in it. Moreover, Dai was a typical Welshman and could never have passed for anything else; indeed, when batting he was happiest if he had a partner with whom he could call the runs in Welsh. Though he had plenty of scoring strokes, chiefly in front of the wicket, he was primarily a solid and determined batsman; he was moreover a useful medium-paced off-spinner and a superb cover.

Between 1923 and 1939 he scored over 15,000 runs, including 16 hundreds, for the county, his highest score being 216 v. Somerset in his last season, and took 275 wickets. Summoned at the very last moment to play against Northamptonshire at Swansea at the age of 27, and scoring on his first appearance 58 and 51, besides taking some wickets, he at once made his place secure and it remained so until 1939 when he was 43 and the

Committee decided to terminate his engagement at the end of the season. So when he reappeared in 1946 it was as an umpire. He remained on the first-class list until 1961 and during that time umpired in 23 Tests. As might be expected, he was firm and decisive and was as much respected in this second part of his career as he had been in the first. In his later days he was much crippled with arthritis.

DAVIES, Emrys, died at Llanelli on November 10, 1975, aged 71. In the course of a career of 30 years, he played a big part in raising Glamorgan from an habitual position near the bottom of the table to Champion county. His success gave particular pleasure to the county's supporters as he and his namesake, Dai, were the first home-born pros of any consequence to win places in the side after its promotion. Emrys was not a natural cricket genius. He reached the top only by hard work and his progress was very slow. Indeed, but for the insistence of that fine judge, J. C. Clay, the county would have let him go.

He first appeared in 1924 and it was not till 1932 that he made his place secure by scoring over 1,000 runs, a feat he was to repeat for the next 15 seasons. It was in this year also that he started his long association with Dyson as the county's opening bats: they were soon recognised as one of the most formidable and consistent pairs in England and in 1937 beat the Glamorgan record by putting up 274 against Leicestershire. An even more prolific stand was against Essex in 1948 when Emrys and W. E. Jones added 313 for the third wicket. In 1935 he became the first Glamorgan player to achieve the double, taking his 100th wicket with the last ball of the season. Two years later he went one better by making 2,000 runs as well as taking 100 wickets. His highest score, 287 not out against Gloucestershire in 1939, is still a record for the county.

Left-handed in both departments, he was essentially a sound and imperturbable batsman and a good player of fast bowling, but he was also quick on his feet, a fine driver whether straight or to the off and by no means deficient in leg-side strokes. He bowled slow, sometimes over the wicket and sometimes round, kept a good length, flighted the ball skilfully and was never afraid to toss it up, but, lacking the vicious spin which makes his type dreaded when the ball is turning, he was primarily a hard-wicket bowler. A good field, usually at a distance from the wicket, he had a remarkably safe pair of hands and it was quite an event when he dropped a catch.

Retiring in 1954, Emrys Davies was on the first-class umpires' list from 1955 to 1960 when ill-health forced him to resign. He had twice officiated in Test matches. Later he coached at Llandovery College and also in Johannesburg. He was a man universally loved and respected, not least by shy young players whom he went out of his way to help and put at their ease. One of his contemporaries in the Glamorgan side writes, "He was an example to all both on and off the field in everything. No one could have had higher standards of conduct, thought or belief than Emrys."

BATTING

	Matches	Innings	Not Outs	Runs	Highest Innings	100s	Average
1924	2	3	0	19	14	0	6.33
1925	9	18	0	150	21	0	8.33
1926	17	25	4	302	50	0	14.38
1927	24	34	6	344	44	0	12.28
1928	20	29	4	388	61	0	15.52
1929	24	46	4	671	89	0	15.97
1930	27	44	7	629	58*	0	17.00
1931	30	44	10	401	45*	0	11.79
1932	29	48	2	1134	175	2	24.65
1933	26	43	4	1068	85	0	27.38
1934	27	46	3	1595	127	2	37.09
1935	28	50	3	1326	155*	2	28.21
1936	28	51	9	1479	159*	4	35.21
1937	31	52	2	2012	140	3	40.24
1938	27	48	1	1408	100	1	29.95
1939	28	45	3	1714	287*	3	40.80
1946	27	45	5	1382	119	2	34.55
1947	28	47	1	1615	177	5	35.10
1948	30	48	1	1708	215	2	36.34
1949	31	54	1	1366	158	2	25.77
1950	33	50	3	1516	110	2	32.25
1951	31	52	2	1307	146	2	26.14
1952	29	52	1	1678	97	0	32.90
1953	27	43	2	1174	77	0	28.63
1954	9	16	1	180	27	0	12.00
Totals	622	1033	79	26566	287*	32	27.84

* *Signifies not out.*

BOWLING

	Balls	Maidens	Runs	Wickets	5 wkts. in Inns.	Average	Catches
1924	84	3	39	1	0	39.00	0
1925	653	27	273	11	0	24.81	5
1926	1215	60	445	17	0	26.17	3
1927	2267	92	955	28	0	34.10	13
1928	2312	107	990	20	0	49.50	7
1929	1986	75	775	28	1	27.67	5
1930	2323	84	982	26	2	37.76	8
1931	3351	124	1419	43	2	33.00	14
1932	5420	168	2441	70	0	34.87	19
1933	4417	187	1835	31	1	59.19	12
1934	3131	109	1456	45	1	32.35	15
1935	5744	279	2107	100	4	21.07	12
1936	3691	174	1491	50	1	29.82	7

1937	6243	274	2373	103	2	23.03	8
1938	4196	135	1862	72	5	25.86	7
1939	4091	62	1948	60	4	32.46	6
1946	3621	144	1528	68	4	22.47	10
1947	3720	141	1589	50	2	31.78	9
1948	264	8	117	0	0	—	3
1949	330	8	143	2	0	71.50	12
1950	2478	132	923	57	3	16.19	8
1951	1323	73	449	15	0	29.93	9
1952	526	22	254	6	0	42.33	8
1953	84	1	46	0	0	—	4
1954	24	1	18	0	0	—	3
Totals	63494	2490	26458	903	32	29.30	207

DAVIES, Eric Quail, who died at Port Alfred on November 11, 1976, aged 67, was perhaps a slightly unlucky cricketer. Picked for South Africa for the fourth Test against Australia in 1935–36 on the strength of having taken six for 80 for Eastern Province against them, he took four for 75 in an innings of 439, his victims including Fingleton, McCabe and Richardson, a notable performance which might have been a sensational one had his catches been held as they should. This ensured his place in the final Test, in which he was a failure. However, in 1938–39, playing for the Transvaal against M.C.C., he felled Hutton with the third ball of the innings, which rolled from his head on to the wicket, and finished with six for 82. This got him a place in the first three Tests, but he was again a failure, his three wickets costing 352 runs. After the War he represented North Eastern Transvaal, but, as he was a schoolmaster, his opportunities for first-class cricket were limited and he never again played in a Test. A tall athletic man, who swung the ball away, he was regarded as faster than R.J. Crisp, South Africa's regular fast bowler in the '30s.

DAVIES, Capt. Geoffrey Boisselier (11th Essex Regiment), born on October 26, 1892, fell in action near Hulluch, France, on September 26, 1915. In 1909 and three following years he was in the Rossall XI, being captain in 1912. His most successful season there was his last, when he made 468 runs with an average of 33.42, scoring 117 v. Shrewsbury and heading the averages, and took 41 wickets for 14.75 runs each. He had been second in the batting averages in 1910 with 31.07, and first in 1911 with 27.57: in the latter year he also obtained 37 wickets at a cost of 12.67 runs apiece. Proceeding to Cambridge, he at once made his mark, scoring 81 and 18, and

taking five wickets for 19 in the second innings of the Freshmen's match of 1913. Both in that year and the next he played against Oxford, but hardly did as well as was expected, his four innings producing but 19 runs and his six wickets costing 132 runs. In 1912, 1913 and 1914 he assisted Essex, and there can be little doubt that, but for the War, he would have developed into an England player. In all first-class matches in 1914 he made 852 runs (average 21.30) and took 83 wickets (average 19.72): he twice reached three-figures, scoring 118 v. Somerset at Weston-super-Mare, and 100 v. Northamptonshire at Leyton. He had good strokes on both sides of the wicket, and was an excellent slip fieldsman. He was an all-round athlete.

DAVIES, George A., who died in Melbourne on November 27, 1957, aged 66, was manager of the Australian team who toured England under A.L. Hassett in 1953. In a few appearances for Victoria in the early 1920s, Davies scored 143 runs, average 20.42, and took five wickets for nearly 18 runs each. He was a member of the executive committee of the Victorian Cricket Association.

DAVIES, Harry Donald, who was killed in the Munich air crash on February 6, 1958, aged 65, when returning from a football match in Belgrade with the Manchester United team, played in 11 games for Lancashire in 1924 and 1925. His best score was 46 against Kent in the first match. After the War he became a member of the Lancashire County Committee and also a vice-president. He played football for Bolton Wanderers and gained an Amateur International cap for England. For nearly 30 years he wrote for the *Manchester Guardian* under the nom de plume of "Old International."

DAVIES, Capt. Philip Havelock, M.C., born at Brighton on August 30, 1893, died at the Catholic Military Hospital, Yorkshire, on January 30, 1930, aged 36. A useful batsman and a good fast bowler, quick off the pitch, he was in the Brighton College XI in 1909 and three following seasons. In 1910 he took 67 wickets for little more than 10 runs each, and in his last year was first in both batting and bowling, his respective averages being 31 and—for 78 wickets—less than 11. Obtaining his Blue for Oxford in 1913, he played twice against Cambridge, taking in the two games eight wickets for 132 runs. In the University's match with Middlesex at Oxford in 1914 he did the hat-trick. His County Cricket was played for Sussex.

DAVIS, Private Arthur Edward (Royal Fusiliers), born on August 4, 1882, fell in action in November, 1916. He was educated at Mill Hill, where he was in the XI in 1898 and 1899, in the latter year being second in the batting averages with 24.43. Subsequently he appeared for Leicestershire, his best season being that of 1903, when, besides catching 22 men and stumping four, he played several useful innings. In 1905, when he took part in only a few games, he made his highest score for the county—55 v. Sussex at Brighton. He was a very good wicket-keeper and in local cricket was associated with the Leicester Ivanhoe C.C.

DAVIS, Joseph, who died in Sydney on May 18, 1911, aged 52, was at one time one of the best-known cricketers in New South Wales. His best innings was probably his 85 for New South Wales against the Hon. Ivo Bligh's team in December, 1882, when he made his runs off the bowling of Barlow, Barnes, Bates, Morley, A. G. Steel and C. T. Studd. On a few occasions he appeared in the matches against Victoria, and on the Melbourne ground in December, 1881, made 11 in his first innings and 53 in his second. He was a member of the N.S.W. teams which visited New Zealand in 1890 and 1894, and in the former tour headed the batting averages with 30.55, scoring 275 runs in nine completed innings.

DAVIS, Thomas, who died on May 30, 1898, at Nottingham, was in the Notts XI in the early 60s. At the time of his death he was in his 71st year.

DAWSON, Edward William, who died at Idmiston, Wiltshire, on June 4, 1979, aged 75, was a cricketer who by sheer application and strict adherence to the basic principles of batting reached a higher place than many players of greater natural ability. In his last year at Eton, where he was in the XI in 1922 and 1923, he made 159 against Harrow. He had already made 113 v. Winchester, the first boy to make a century in both matches in the same year, and he finished with an average of over 50. In both those seasons he had a few trials for Leicestershire. At Cambridge he won his Blue as a Freshman and retained his place as an opening batsman throughout his four years, being captain in 1927. His performances for Leicestershire showed him to be by now fully up to county standard, and coming down he took over the captaincy and held it in 1928, 1929, 1931 and 1933. He himself always paid a most generous tribute to the help and kindness he received from George Geary. He proved himself, as he had at Cambridge, an outstanding captain, besides being one of the county's most reliable bats. He played for the Gentlemen at Lord's in 1925 and 1927 and was a member of the M.C.C. sides to South Africa in 1927–28 and to New Zealand in 1929–30. He also toured the West Indies with Sir Julien Cahn in 1929. In his first-class career he scored 12,597 runs with an average of 27.09, and made 14 hundreds. His last innings for Leicestershire in 1934 was a faultless 91 against the Australians. He was a splendid field, especially on the off side.

DAWSON, Gilbert, who died in Paisley on May 21, 1969, aged 55, played for Hampshire from 1947 to 1949. Taken ill while umpiring in a club game, he was later found dead in his crashed car. Of Yorkshire birth, "Gerry" Dawson assisted East Bierley, Windhill and Pudsey St. Lawrence in the Bradford League before coming south, where he did good work as opening batsman for Hampshire. The first of his four centuries for the county was against Yorkshire at Bournemouth in 1947. The highest, 158 not out off the Nottinghamshire bowling at Trent Bridge, came in 1948 when, with 935 runs, average 33.39, he stood second in the batting figures and enjoyed his best season. He was well-known in Scottish cricket circles.

DAWSON, Harold Littlewood, died in Northern Nigeria on November 16, 1909, at the early age of 34. He made some capital scores for Streatham, and in 1900 played for Surrey at the Oval against the West Indians.

DAWSON, Major John Miles, died at Wetherby, Yorkshire, on December 3, 1948, aged 77. Educated at Eton and Cambridge, but not in either XI. Played for Yorkshire Gentlemen. In 1894 he proved the best batsman in the first British team, captained by R. Slade Lucas, to visit West Indies; scored 138 against Barbados. In 1896 he was a member of Lord Hawke's team in West Indies. A Vice-President of Yorkshire County Club, he served on the Committee from 1911.

DAY, A. G., who was born at Dewsbury on September 20, 1864, died at his native place on October 16, 1908. He played in 11 matches for Yorkshire between 1885 and 1888, making 163 runs in 17 innings with an average of 9.58. His highest score was 63 against Leicestershire at Huddersfield in 1888.

DAY, Arthur Percival, who died on January 22, 1969, aged 83, played as an amateur for Kent from 1905 to 1923. In the XI at Malvern from 1901 to 1904, he was captain in the last two seasons. In 1904, with the aid of an innings of 201 not out, he headed the school batting figures with 880 runs, average 67.69. His first summer with Kent was his most successful as a batsman, for he hit a century in each of the two matches with Gloucestershire and reached an aggregate of 1,050 runs, average 35. In 1908, when he scored 118 against Somerset at Taunton, he and E. Humphreys added 248, which remains a record for the Kent seventh wicket.

One of his most remarkable achievements occurred in 1921 when, playing only eight innings for the county, he made 555 runs—including his highest score, 184 not out against Sussex at Tonbridge—for an average of 111.00. An enterprising batsman, he enjoyed the distinction of reaching three figures in 55 minutes off the Hampshire bowling at Southampton in 1911. He appeared in three Gentlemen v. Players games, being on the winning side when the Gentlemen triumphed at Lord's by 134 runs in 1914.

In all first-class cricket, Day scored 7,175 runs, including 13 centuries, average 32.31. Though for some years rarely employed as a bowler by Kent, he took 137 wickets for 26.56 runs each and he held 21 catches. He was the younger brother of S. H. and S. E. Day, also Malvern and Kent cricketers.

DAY, Capt. D. A. S., killed in action in Burma in February, 1944, gained prominence as a batsman for Tonbridge in 1933 and the next season doing especially well against Clifton at Lord's. He scored 27 and 60 in the first of these matches, and in 1934, when he headed the school batting averages with 62.18, played two fine innings—71 and 130 not out. He also took four wickets for 52 runs and, as an all-rounder, gave promise of following the example of his father, A. P. Day, who excelled for Malvern and Kent. This difference marked their bowling: the father was right-arm medium-paced with admirable delivery, the son lured opponents to destruction with left-hand lobs—a very rare type of attack.

DAY, Harold Lindsay Vernon, who died suddenly on June 15, 1972, aged 73, played for Bedfordshire after leaving Bedford School. In 1922 he began an association with Hampshire which lasted till 1931, scoring 3,166 runs, average 25.73. A batsman possessing a variety of strokes and the ability to suit his methods to the needs of the occasion, he scored 56 and 91 against Kent in his first county game and in all he put together four centuries. He used to tell many amusing stories concerning Lionel Tennyson, under whose captaincy he played, particularly in regard to that remarkable match in which he participated at Edgbaston in 1922 when Hampshire, having been dismissed for 15 and compelled to follow on 203 behind, defeated Warwickshire by 155 runs. Tennyson accepted tremendous odds against his side winning following their complete collapse and won a lot of money.

As a burly, strong-running wing three-quarter, very good at goal-kicking, he played Rugby football for Leicestershire, the Army and in four International matches for England between 1920 and 1922. His kicking skill in borrowed boots saved England from defeat in the match with France at Twickenham in 1922—after which he was dropped from the side! He was also a noted Rugby International referee before he became a cricket and Rugby journalist of repute. He wrote an article, "Happy Hampshire", for the 1962 *Wisden* after Hampshire won the County Cricket Championship.

DAY, Samuel Hulme, died at Chobham, Surrey, on February 21, 1950, aged 71. Captain of the Malvern College XI in 1897 and 1898, he obtained his Blue at Cambridge as a Freshman and played in the four Varsity matches of 1899 to 1902. In 1901 he led Cambridge, and in 1902 he made 117 not out against Oxford. A stylish batsman, who cut and drove to the off with special skill, Mr. Day played for Kent from 1897 to 1919 and scored 5,893 runs. While still at Malvern

College he scored a century, 101 not out, against Gloucestershire at Cheltenham in his first county match, a unique feat. Sammy Day was also an excellent inside-forward at Association football. He played for Cambridge University in 1901, and in 1903 he helped Corinthians beat Bury, the Cup holders, by 10 goals to three and win the Sheriff of London Charity Shield. In 1906 he played in three Internationals for England.

DAY, Sydney Ernest, who died on July 7, 1970, aged 86, played from 1922 to 1925 for Kent, of which county he was President in 1954. He was a brother of S.H. and A.P. Day. Educated at Malvern, he did not find a place in the XI. A capital Association footballer, he played at outside-right for Old Malvernians and the Corinthians.

DEAN, Harry, who died at his home at Garstang, near Blackpool, on March 12, 1957, aged 71, was one of the most successful bowlers who ever played for Lancashire. He first appeared for the county in 1906 and before he left them at the end of the 1921 season he took, with left-arm bowling, 1,301 wickets in all first-class matches for 18.14 runs apiece. He suited his methods to the conditions, bowling fast-medium with deceptive swerve or slow according to the state of the pitch. He made an auspicious start, for in his first season he dismissed 60 batsmen, and in each of the next seven summers he took over 100 wickets, as he did also in 1920. Six times he obtained nine wickets in an innings, his best analysis being 15.1 overs, eight maidens, 31 runs, nine wickets against Somerset at Old Trafford in 1909.

The performance which afforded Dean most satisfaction, however, was against Yorkshire at Aigburth in 1913 in an extra match arranged to mark the visit to Liverpool of King George V. He took nine wickets for 62 in the first innings and eight for 29 in the second, bringing his match figures to 17 for 91. There is no recorded instance of greater success by a bowler in a "Roses" match. In his best season, 1911, Dean secured 183 wickets, average 17.43. He played for England in two Test matches against Australia and one against South Africa in the 1912 Triangular Tournament, his 11 wickets in these three games costing 153 runs. After the end of his first-class career, he played for some years for Cheshire and from 1926 to 1932 was coach at Rossall School.

DEANE, Hubert Gouvaine (Nummy), one of South Africa's great captains, died suddenly at Johannesburg on October 21, 1939, after a heart attack. He will always be remembered for his fine leadership of the young teams of 1927–28 and 1929, and there can be no doubt that his inspiration and careful team-building were chiefly responsible for the improvement in South African cricket of recent years. Born at Eshowe, Zululand, on July 21, 1895, Deane, an attractive batsman, who scored fast when set, and a brilliant fieldsman, especially at cover, played for Natal for a few seasons after the First World War and for Transvaal from 1923. A member of the 1924 team in England he played in all five Test matches, but did nothing outstanding. After captaining the Currie Cup-winning Transvaal teams of 1925–26 and 1926–27, he was appointed captain of South Africa against the English touring team of 1927–28, and, after the first two Tests had been lost, and the third drawn, the last two were won largely owing to his fine tactics. Deane won the toss in all five Tests, which were played on matting, and in the 2nd, 4th and 5th games, he sent England in first, so that his young team would know what they had to beat, and he triumphantly justified his policy. In the third match he scored 77 and 73, putting up a record Test partnership with E.P. Nupen in each innings. His leadership of the young and inexperienced side that toured England in 1929 increased his reputation, and the team did much better against the chief sides than expected. In the fifth Test match at the Oval Deane won the toss and sent in England, who could make only 258. With three wickets down for 25 runs Deane joined H.W. Taylor, and they added 214, the captain scoring a courageous 93. England recovered well, but the honours went to South Africa. Deane retired from first-class cricket after this tour, in which he scored 1,239 runs, average 34.41. Persuaded to captain South Africa again, in 1930, he found himself so much out of form that he resigned after playing in the second and third Tests. In the Currie Cup competitions, Deane scored 1,082 runs, average 37.31, his highest three scores being 165 for Transvaal against O.F.S. in 1923–24. He took a prominent part in the administration of the game, and was a member of the committees that selected the South African teams of 1929, 1930–31 and 1931–32.

DEARNALEY, Irvine, who died after being involved in a road accident on March 14, 1965, aged 88, was a great run-getter for Glossop for many years and became captain.

He first played as a professional for Derbyshire against the West Indian touring team of 1900, but in a few matches in 1905 and 1907 he played as an amateur. His highest score for the county was 34—the best of the innings—against Essex at Glossop in 1905.

DE BROKE, Lord Willoughby, who died on his yacht in December, 1902, at the age of 57, was a great supporter of cricket and held the position of President of the Warwickshire County Club.

DE CRESPIGNY, Philip Augustus Champion, who played for Hampshire v. Somerset at Bournemouth in 1880, scoring two and three, was born on July 22, 1850, and died on September 4, 1912, at Round Hill, Lyndhurst. As a naval lieutenant, he served in Her Majesty's ship *Galatea* under the Duke of Edinburgh in his voyage round the world in 1871.

DEED, John Arthur, who died on October 19, 1980, aged 79, did useful work for Kent as a batsman from 1924 to 1930. A made rather than a natural player, he had been for two years a wholly undistinguished member of the Malvern XI, but had proved a solid and reliable second string to a brilliant stroke player in a winning racquets pair at Queen's. Much the same qualities appeared in his cricket. He was never in the running for a Blue at Cambridge, and owed his trial for Kent to an innings of 252 for the Second XI at the Oval in May, 1924. In those days the county had no shortage of attacking bats, but, especially in the early part of the season when most of the amateurs were not available, there was a lack of solidity and Deed's steadiness was often valuable. In all he scored 1,996 runs at an average of 23.76, with two centuries, both against Warwickshire at Birmingham, 103 in 1928 and 133 in 1930. He retained to the end his interest in Kent cricket and was President in 1965.

DE KLERK, Theo, who died in Durban on July 2, 1982, aged 75, was a useful all-rounder who scored 791 runs at an average of 17.57 and took 89 wickets for Western Province in 33 matches between 1925 and 1936. He made his first-class debut in 1925–26, for Western Province against Orange Free State, making what was to remain his highest first-class score, 79, in Western Province's first innings. His best season was 1931–32 when his 33 wickets cost 16.42 apiece. In later years he became one of South Africa's leading racehorse trainers, saddling over 1,000

winners. A versatile sportsman, he also played first league rugger and first league soccer. He had a vivid personality and was a sought-after speaker.

DELACOMBE, William Barclay, by whose death at Derby on October 15, 1911, the Derbyshire County C.C. sustained a great loss, was born at Ascension on July 20, 1860. From 1889 until 1907 he was the Hon. Secretary of the County C.C., and for over 30 years he showed his interest in Derbyshire cricket in a variety of ways. When necessary he would play and captain the XI, and would frequently accompany the team on out-matches and keep the score. His appearances for Derbyshire covered the period from 1891 to 1900, and although he was not a great cricketer, he was certainly a useful one. He was a good outfield and a sure catch, and useful with both bat and ball. For Incogniti v. L. C. R. Thring's XI, at Dunstable, in 1897 he took all 10 wickets, in doing which he performed the hat-trick. He was captain of the Bruton School XI in 1878, in which year he became one of the original members of the Derbyshire Friars. He was 6ft. 5in. in height.

DE LASAUX, Robert Augustus, died at Canterbury on December 7, 1914, aged 80. He was born at Canterbury, where his father was Coroner for East Kent for 64 years, on November 24, 1834, and was educated at Canterbury and Kennington (London). He was a good fast-medium round-armed bowler, breaking both ways, a fine cutter, and in the field, where he was very smart, either point or long-stop. He was one of the founders of the St. Lawrence C.C. and one of the original members of the Band of Brothers. His name will be found in several matches played by the Gentlemen of Kent, but he appeared only once for the county—against England at Canterbury in 1858—when he was unfortunate enough to obtain spectacles. He was a pupil of Fuller Pilch.

DELME-RADCLIFFE, Arthur Henry, who died on June 30, 1950, was a native of South Tedworth, Hampshire. A member of the Sherborne XI before going to Oxford, he headed the school's batting averages in 1889. Subsequently he played for Hampshire and Berkshire. While batting for Hampshire against Somerset at Southampton in August, 1889, he was concerned in a curious incident. Thinking he was out stumped, Delme-Radcliffe began to walk towards the pavilion, but the appeal had not been upheld. Then a fieldsman pulled up a stump and he was given out "run out", but in the meantime the other umpire had called "over," so the batsman continued his innings.

DEMPSEY, General Sir Miles Christopher, who died on June 5, 1969, aged 72, was in the Shrewsbury XI for three years from 1912 to 1914. In the third year, when scoring 662 runs, average 44.13, and taking 23 wickets with slow left-arm bowling for 14.43 runs apiece, he led the school to victory over Uppingham for the first time. He played for Sussex against Northamptonshire in 1919 and later appeared for Berkshire. He served with great distinction in both World Wars and commanded the Second Army in the invasion of Normandy in 1944. Sir Miles was godfather to E. D. R. Eagar, the present Hampshire Secretary.

DEMPSTER, Charles Stewart, who died in Wellington, his birthplace, on February 13, 1974, aged 70, was one of the greatest batsmen produced by New Zealand. He played in 10 Test matches between 1929 and 1932, scoring 732 runs, average 65, and hitting two centuries, both against England—136 at Wellington in 1929–30, when he and J. E. Mills shared an opening stand of 276 which remains a New Zealand record, and 120 at Lord's in 1931. It was difficult to realise that such a stylish, gifted batsman never enjoyed the benefit of coaching.

He toured England on two occasions, in 1927—when he said that he really learned cricket—and in 1931 when, despite missing several matches because of a leg strain, he registered 1,778 runs, average 59.26. Of his seven centuries during the latter tour, he made 212 from the Essex bowling at Leyton.

In 1935 "Stewie" Dempster made his first appearance as an amateur for Leicestershire and from 1936 to 1938 he both captained the county and headed the batting averages each season. Of his 35 centuries, he obtained three in successive innings in 1937: 110 v. Sussex at Leicester and 133 and 154 not out v. Gloucestershire at Gloucester, and he repeated the feat the following year with 105 against the Australians at Leicester, 110 v. Hampshire at Southampton and 187 v. the University at Oxford. Later he played occasionally for Warwickshire. In a career extending from 1921 to 1948, he hit 12,267 runs, average 45.43, many for Wellington in State cricket.

DENCH, Charles Edward, who died at Nottingham on June 30, 1958, aged 84, played as an all-rounder for Nottinghamshire from 1897 to 1910. In that time he scored 2,660 runs, averge 21.80, and with medium-paced bowling took 77 wickets, average 28.46. A steady batsman he hit 150 for Nottinghamshire Colts against Yorkshire Colts in 1897 and in the same season took nine M.C.C. wickets for 50 runs at Lord's. His highest innings in first-class cricket was 88 against Yorkshire at Bradford in 1899, in which year he also performed the hat-trick against Gloucestershire at Bristol. In 1901 he was a member of the Nottinghamshire side dismissed by the Yorkshire bowlers, Rhodes (six for four runs) and Haigh (four for eight) on a sticky pitch at Trent Bridge for 13, at that time the lowest total in County Cricket history. Dench was one of four batsmen who failed to score. For a time after retiring from County Cricket, he was coach to Dublin University and also stood as a first-class umpire, officiating in a Test match.

DENNETT, George, the Gloucestershire slow left-arm bowler, died at Cheltenham on September 14, 1937, aged 57. After an engagement with the Grange Club, Edinburgh, he played regularly for the county from 1903 until 1925 and subsequently made occasional appearances.

G. L. Jessop discovered Dennett in Bristol club cricket, the scorer of a century and the taker of many wickets in one match. Tried at Lord's, Dennett began with a hard experience. Middlesex, who won the Championship that year, scored 502, P. F. Warner and L. J. Moon making 248 for the first wicket. Jessop in *A Cricketer's Log* wrote: "Despite the rare pasting he received, Dennett lost neither his head nor his length; nor did he seem the slightest bit dismayed by our infernally bad fielding."

A consistently hard-working and earnest cricketer, Dennett had one particularly brilliant performance to his credit. In 1907 at Gloucester, Northamptonshire were put out for 12 runs—the lowest in first-class cricket—and Dennett took eight wickets for nine runs, including the hat-trick. His record in the match was 15 wickets for 21 runs, a feat which he accomplished in the course of one day.

Dennett's bowling was an outstanding feature of Gloucestershire's cricket that season when, with practically everything depending upon him, he rarely failed his side; dismissing 184 batsmen for less than 16 runs each in County Championship matches he was the only cricketer to take 200 wickets in first-class matches. Dennett, like Parker, another slow left-hander, had the distinction of taking all 10 wickets in an innings—against Essex at Bristol in 1906—a feat no other Gloucestershire player had achieved until Goddard, last season, dismissed the whole Worcestershire side at Cheltenham for 113 runs.

In an extraordinary day's cricket at Dover in 1912, when 30 wickets fell for 268 runs, Dennett in 20 balls dismissed the last six Kent batsmen without conceding a run.

Dennett served throughout the South African war with the Somerset Light Infantry, played cricket for the Army at Pretoria and kept goal for the Army at Cape Town. In the Great War he rejoined the Colours, gained a commission and retired with the rank of Captain.

He was an all-round games man, having, in addition to cricket and football, distinguished himself at fives, billiards and shooting. On retiring from County Cricket Dennett succeeded W. A. Woof, the former Gloucestershire slow left-hand bowler who died earlier in the year and whose biography also appears in this issue, as coach at Cheltenham College.

DENTON, David, one of the liveliest of batsmen and a superb field, died suddenly at his home at Wakefield on February 17, 1950. He was 75. Denton made his first appearance for Yorkshire in 1894 and concluded his career as an active cricketer in 1920. He did little as a batsman when he first played with the county, but in the following year, coming off early in the summer against both Cambridge University and Lancashire, he made his place secure. For 21 seasons his record exceeded 1,000 runs, his aggregate reaching 2,000 in five summers, and in 1905 amounting to 2,405, with an average of 42. For 20 years this stood as the highest Yorkshire aggregate until surpassed by Herbert Sutcliffe.

Possessed of very flexible wrists, Denton made strokes all round the wicket with considerable hitting power, while he played forward so hard that he always made the ball travel. On fast wickets he seized every opening to score on the off side, cutting in particularly brilliant fashion, and when the ground was slow he employed the pull and the hook with fine effect. The force of his strokes was surprising as he was below medium height and lightly built. He batted in exceptionally good style and never lost any time in getting to work. Going out for runs immediately he arrived at the wicket, he naturally gave many chances and was some-

times referred to as the luckiest of cricketers. Certainly he often enjoyed a liberal share of good fortune, but if let off he would settle down to hitting as clean and well-timed as it was continuous.

Brilliantly as he batted, Denton attained to even higher excellence as a fieldsman, especially in the deep and at third man. Indeed, he held a place almost alone as an outfield, no one chasing the ball at a greater speed, picking it up more clean or returning it more quickly. A rare judge of a high catch in the long field, he established among his colleagues such a firm belief in his abilities that on one memorable day at Lord's when he committed two blunders the whole Yorkshire team were upset.

In the course of his career he scored 36,520 runs in first-class matches with an average of 33. He put together 69 three-figure innings—61 of these for Yorkshire—his highest being 221 against Kent at Tunbridge Wells in 1912, 209 not out against Worcestershire at Worcester in 1920, and 200 not out against Warwickshire at Birmingham in 1912. Three times he registered two separate hundreds in the same match—107 and 109 against Nottinghamshire at Trent Bridge in 1906, 131 and 121 against the M.C.C. at Scarborough in 1908, and 139 and 138 against the Transvaal and Johannesburg for the English team which went out to South Africa in 1909–10. These last two scores he immediately followed with 104 against South Africa, and so played three successive three-figure innings. This feat was accomplished on the occasion of his second visit to South Africa, where he went first in the winter of 1905–06. Denton never went to Australia. Presumably it was feared he might not enjoy at the hands of the Australians the luck which generally favoured him in this country and that the match-winning qualities he possessed in being able to score so rapidly would lose their value in games played without a time limit. On the other hand, his fielding must have been an asset to any side. On his one Test appearance against Australia at Leeds in 1905 he accomplished little, but he played in 10 Tests in South Africa.

Denton figured in many Gentlemen and Players' matches, and for the professionals at Scarborough in 1906 he scored 157 not out. Twice he took part in a stand of more than 300 runs, putting on 312 in company with George Hirst against Hampshire at Southampton in 1914 and 305 with J. W. Rothery against Derbyshire at Chesterfield in 1910. As his benefit he was given the Yorkshire v. Lancashire match at Leeds in 1907, and the contest yielded a profit of nearly £2,000. Following upon his retirement from active participation in the game, Denton fell into bad health and for a time acted as scorer for Yorkshire, but, undergoing an operation performed by Sir Berkeley Moynihan, he recovered so completely that from 1925 onwards he found himself able to perform the duties of an umpire in first-class cricket.

Born at Thornes, near Wakefield, on July 4, 1874, Denton played for several years for Hodgson and Simpson, for whom in olden days quite a number of famous Yorkshire cricketers qualified to play in local competitions. Among these was Edmund Peate, the greatest left-handed slow bowler of his day. Denton left £10,533.

DENTON, John Sidney, who died in hospital on April 9, 1971, aged 80, was in the Wellingborough XI before playing as an amateur for Northamptonshire from 1909 to 1919. He scored 3,298 runs, including two centuries, for an average of 21.69, took with leg-break and googly bowling 67 wickets for 18.11 runs each and held 56 catches. He and his twin brother, W. H. Denton, extraordinarily alike in appearance, opened the innings for the county during the 1914 season.

DENTON, William Herbert, the last survivor of three brothers who played together for Northamptonshire, died on April 23, 1979, aged 88. He and his identical twin, J. S., who between them caused endless confusion to spectators and scorers, first appeared in 1909. By 1912, when the county, calling upon only 12 players in the Championship, came second, they had become essential members of the side. In 1913 both exceeded 1,000 runs and, from August that year until cricket was stopped by the War, they formed the regular opening pair. Both were taken prisoner in the closing months of the War and J. S. played little County Cricket afterwards but W. H., after a few appearances between 1919 and 1923, resumed a regular place for the season of 1924. Unfortunately his spell as a prisoner had taken its toll of his health and, though he did much useful work, he was not the player he had been. He did not play for the county again. A small man, he had a sound defence and his footwork was neat, a large proportion of his runs were scored behind the wicket. His highest score was 230 not out, at that time a record for the county, against Essex at Leyton in 1913. Going in first he carried his bat through an innings of five hours 40 minutes and was on the field throughout the match. Apart from his bat-

ting he was a fine mid-off. When Northamptonshire played Somerset in 1914, the Denton twins opened for Northamptonshire and the Rippon twins, A. D. E. and A. E. S., for Somerset—an occurrence unique in first-class cricket.

DE SARAM, Frederick Cecil (Derrick), died in Colombo on April 11, 1983, aged 70. Strange things happened in the world of cricket at Oxford in the 30s, few stranger than that De Saram, one of the finest bats at either University between the Wars, should have had only one trial in The Parks in his first two years. Coming up from Royal College, Colombo, he played in the Freshmen's match in 1932 without success and was not seen again until the Seniors' match in 1934, when he probably owed his place to a fine record for Hertfordshire the season before. Making 64 in this match, he was picked for the University's opening fixture against Gloucestershire, in which, on his first-class debut in England, he made 176 in three hours. A few weeks later he scored 128 against the Australians, treating Grimmett with a disrespect of which few Test batsmen had shown themselves capable; the Oxford total was 216 and the next highest score 16. In all for Oxford that summer he scored 1,119 runs with an average of 50.86, his highest score being 208 against a weak bowling side of H. D. G. Leveson Gower at Eastbourne. Like some other outstanding batsmen, he failed against Cambridge. In 1935 Schools prevented him from playing regularly or getting into form, but in the first innings at Lord's, when things were going badly, he got 85 in two and a half hours, easily top score in a total of 221, and, when he was out, he received an ovation. That was the end of his first-class cricket in England, but for Hertfordshire in the vacation he had an aggregate of 904 runs and an average of 90.40, figures believed at that time to be a record for Minor County Cricket. He continued to play with great success in Ceylon, whom he captained from 1949 to 1954: indeed in 1954 he made 43 against M.C.C. on their way to Australia. He also did much for the game off the field as an administrator and selector. A complete batsman with lovely wrists, all the strokes and at the same time a strong defence, he was a fierce competitor who, had he been born 50 years later, would have been a godsend to the present Sri Lankan side—unless politics had intervened. In 1962, as formidable in public life as on the cricket field or lawn tennis court (a game at which he also represented Oxford), he was sentenced to a long term of imprisonment for conspiring against the Government of the day.

DE SILVA, Deva Lokesh Stanley, died in a motor cycle accident on April 12, 1980, aged 22. A regular opening bowler on Sri Lanka's tour of England and Ireland in 1979, he was not related to the other two, more successful, de Silvas in the team: all three were Sinhalese. No batsman, he was a medium-fast right-arm swing bowler of real promise. His part in Sri Lanka's impressive win over India in the Prudential Cup match at Old Trafford in 1979 was the capture of the valuable wickets of Gaekwad and Kapil Dev for 36 runs. He came from Mahinda College, Galle, and was an official of the Ceylon Tobacco Company. His early death is a heavy loss to Sri Lanka with their aspirations to be granted full Test status.

DE SILVA, J. A. ("Bertie"), who has died in Sri Lanka in 1982 at the age of 84, was one of his country's best all-rounders between the Wars. Coming up to Oxford in 1924, he played twice for the University, once that year and once in 1925, without getting a Blue. A left-handed batsman, he was 14 not out when Oxford beat Kent by six wickets in The Parks in 1924. The Kent side included Chapman, Freeman, Woolley, Ashdown and Hardinge.

DEVEY, John Henry George, died in a Birmingham nursing home on October 13, 1940, aged 73. If better known as a fine forward for Aston Villa and a director of the club for 33 years, John Devey was a very useful cricketer, doing good service in the Warwickshire XI from 1888 to 1907. A hard hitting batsman with plenty of strokes, he helped his county obtain promotion to the first class in 1895. Altogether he scored 7,659 runs for Warwickshire—average 25.31. Particularly good in defence on rain-affected pitches he improved in value with increased experience, excelling in 1906 when he made 1,237 runs—average 41.23. That was his benefit year and, unlike most professionals, he excelled when in the public eye, scoring 106 and taking a prominent part in Warwickshire getting within 52 of Surrey's 562 at Edgbaston. The match brought Devey about £400. Strangely enough he lost his form next season, doing little in a few games. In the highest innings he played, 246 against Derbyshire at Edgbaston in 1900, Devey gave a wonderful display of powerful driving—a characteristic of his batting when set.

DEVONSHIRE, The Tenth Duke of (Edward William Spencer), K.G., M.B.E., T.D., died suddenly at Eastbourne on November 26, 1950, aged 55. He had been President of Derbyshire County C.C. since 1938, when he succeeded his father, and in turn was succeeded by his son, the former Marquis of Hartingdon, M.C., now the 11th Duke of Devonshire.

DEWFALL, Ernest George, who died in November, 1982, aged 72, played two matches for Gloucestershire in 1938 as a fast bowler without much success.

DEXTER, Joseph, who played occasionally for Leicestershire about 1887 and 1888, died at Nottingham on March 2, 1915, aged 52. He was of no account as a batsman, but was a good wicket-keeper, and when he played for the Nelson C.C. was regarded as the best taking part in Lancashire League matches. For a time he was engaged on the groundstaff at the Oval.

DE ZOETE, Herman Walter, who died in March, 1957, aged 80, played for Cambridge against Oxford in 1897 and 1898. He bore a big share in victory by 179 runs in the first of these University matches, helping C. E. M. Wilson in an eighth wicket stand of 56 and, with medium-pace bowling, dismissing four men for 26 runs in the Oxford second innings. He also represented Cambridge at golf in 1896, 1897 and 1898. He was in the Eton XI of 1895 and in 1898 appeared once for Essex.

DICKENS, Henry Charles, who died in November, 1966, aged 83, was the last surviving grandson of Charles Dickens. A keen cricketer, he was a member of M.C.C.

DICKENS, Walter, who died at Kimberley, South Africa, on January 11, 1951, aged 67, kept wicket for Griqualand West on numerous occasions between 1904–05 and 1923–24. He was captain of the Currie Cup team in his last season, when he also made his highest score of 68 against Western Provinces. His brother, William Dickens, and his son, C. J. Dickens, have also played for Griqualand West.

DICKINSON, Arscott William Harvey, who died at his home at Bude, Cornwall, on January 21, 1952, in his 93rd year, captained the Lincoln College, Oxford XI in 1882, but was not tried for the University. Though never participating in first-class cricket, he was for many years a prominent figure in West Country Cricket, playing for both Devon and Cornwall in the same season before the Minor Counties competition was officially organised. A hard-hitting batsman with a powerful straight drive, he liked to recall that he had in his prime been referred to by the local press as "The Plymouth Bonnor." A dangerous medium-paced bowler with pronounced finger spin, he in later years bowled slow off-breaks, which to an advanced age earned him many wickets in local cricket. Blessed with exceptionally large hands, he seldom missed a catch which came within his reach. He kept up the game till nearly 80, and claimed that he had played cricket for 70 consecutive seasons without a break.

DICKINSON, George Ritchie, who died in April, 1978, aged 74, played for New Zealand in the first two Tests against Harold Gilligan's side in 1929–30. A genuinely fast bowler, he took in these five wickets for 134 runs and had the distinction of dismissing Woolley twice. His only other Test appearance was two years later v. South Africa, when he took three for 111. He played for Otago.

DICKINSON, Patrick John, who died in hospital in London on May 28, 1984, aged 64, will be remembered for his innings in the University Match of 1939, which no less a judge than Sir Pelham Warner described as one of the finest in the history of the match. Set to make 430 in the fourth innings, Cambridge were 155 for five when Dickinson joined A. H. Brodhurst. They put on 84 in under an hour before Brodhurst was out for 45. Two more wickets fell quickly and at 249 for eight the match seemed over, especially as the incoming batsman, J. Webster, had a batting average of under six. However, he defended staunchly. Dickinson continued playing glorious strokes all round the wicket and the pair had added 95 when he was caught immediately after reaching his hundred. Even then the last wicket added 40, Webster eventually making 60, and Cambridge lost by only 45 runs.

After a brilliant career at King's College School, Wimbledon, where he twice exceeded 1,000 runs in the season, Dickinson at once made his mark at Cambridge. In the Freshmen's match in 1939 he took seven for 42 in the second innings and then, going in first, carried his bat for 60 not out in a total of 92. This secured him a trial in the side and, without doing anything exceptional before

the match at Lord's, he kept this place with a number of useful performances, becoming one of the team's opening bowlers. Indeed, his medium-paced in-swingers probably did more to secure his Blue than his batting. Late in the summer he had a good trial for Surrey, but accomplished little. He did not return to Cambridge after the War, but played some first-class cricket in India.

DICKINSON, Stanley Patrick, died at Dolbenmaen, near Criccieth, on June 25, 1972, aged 82. He was born at Norton, then part of Derbyshire, on March 7, 1890, and played for the county in two matches in 1909. He was in the Haileybury XI in 1906–07.

DIFFORD, Capt. Archie (South African Dept. Units), killed September, 1918. A very useful cricketer, who played for Western Province and, later, for the Transvaal. In 1906–07 he scored 103 for the former v. Griqualand West; in 1908–09, he made 94 for Rest of South Africa v. Wanderers C.C., and in the same season 91 for Transvaal v. Border.

DILLON, Edward Wentworth, whose death at the age of 60 occurred on April 26, 1941, was a brilliant left-handed batsman when at Rugby and Oxford University before doing splendid service for Kent, his county experiences extending altogether from 1900 to 1913. He practically finished his county career by leading Kent to the Championship, so repeating an achievement which stood to his name in 1909 and 1910. In this way Dillon surpassed the efforts of any of his Kent predecessors. In fact, not until C. H. B. Marsham succeeded J. R. Mason—an outstanding personality in the game for several years—did Kent first secure the honours in 1906. Yet Mason resumed as leader for the last month of the 1909 season, when Dillon stopped playing for business reasons—often a preventive of continuous cricket for him. These great cricketers had with them K. L. Hutchings—a superb batsman and fieldsman—the brothers S. H. and A. P. Day, Frank Woolley, Humphreys, Colin Blythe—taker of 178 wickets at 14 runs apiece—Arthur Fielder, Fresh Huish and D. W. Carr.

Dillon earned early fame by heading the Rugby averages in 1899 and 1900, the second time with 56.36 for 620 runs and a highest innings of 157. He made 110 not out when 190 were hit off in two hours at Lord's and Marlborough were beaten by nine wickets within 15 minutes of time. He also took six wickets for 84 runs with his slow left-hand bowling. Described in *Wisden* as the best school batsman of the year "having also covered himself with glory for Kent"—his average was 36.50 in eight innings—Dillon maintained his form and seldom disappointed his side when returning to the game after an interval with little practice. A notable example of this was at the Oval in 1913 when he scored 135 in a vain attempt to save his county from defeat.

When he got his Blue as a freshman the University match was drawn, and his best effort was 143 against Somerset when Oxford were hopelessly placed. He proved very useful for Kent, being second in the averages to Mason, with 103 not out his highest score. Despite his fine displays for 85 and 59, Oxford lost at Lord's next year, S. H. Day, his Kent colleague, batting grandly for 117 not out and helping largely towards the Cambridge triumph. After being the chief batsman at Oxford in his second year, Dillon went into business and gave his spells of leisure to Kent cricket. His best years were 1905, average 48.51, and 1906, average 43.23, and he played many of his highest innings as opening batsman. The powerful Yorkshire attack suffered from Dillon's onslaught at Dewsbury in 1910, a grandly hit 138 starting Kent on the road to victory by nine wickets. In the return at Maidstone his vigorous 49 paved the way for triumph by 178; Colin Blythe and Woolley bowled unchanged in both Yorkshire innings. Altogether in first-class cricket Dillon scored 10,353 runs, average 28.20.

Very free in style, Dillon used his long reach to the best advantage. Going in to meet the ball, he drove straight and to the off with great power and placed his forcing strokes skilfully. He made two tours abroad—to West Indies with B. J. T. Bosanquet's side in 1902 and next year with the Kent team to America.

Dillon took the highest honours in Rugby football. Developing into a splendid three-quarter when playing for Blackheath, he was capped against Scotland, Ireland and Wales in 1904 and next season against Wales.

DISNEY, James, born on November 20, 1861, died on June 25, 1934, at Ripley, Derbyshire. A good wicket-keeper he was in the county XI from 1881 to 1890 before Derbyshire ranked as first-class, though most of their fixtures were with the more important counties. He did good service until replaced by the famous William Storer.

DIVER, Edwin James, born at Cambridge, March 20, 1861, died at Pontardawe, near Swansea, on December 27, 1924. Edwin Diver who, without realising all the bright promise of his early days, played a prominent part in the cricket field for many years, was found dead in his bed. He will always be best remembered on account of his short but brilliant connection with Surrey. He became qualified for the county by residence through holding a mastership at Wimbledon School, and made his first appearance in the XI in 1883. A most attractive batsman in point of style, with splendid hitting power on the off side, his success was immediate. Indeed, he created such an impression that in the following year he was given a place in the Gentlemen's XI against the Australians at Lord's. As things turned out the match was, perhaps, the most memorable in which he ever took part. The Australians had to follow on, but they set the Gentlemen 128 to get in the last innings and against Palmer and Giffen, bowling at the top of their form on a worn pitch, the task proved a formidable one. Indeed, the Australians looked to be winning when, with six wickets down and 45 still required, Diver joined A. G. Steel. Rising to the occasion, they hit off the runs without being separated. One can remember the finish as well as if the match had been played last season. Except that Diver put one ball up—it dropped out of reach over Boyle's head at short mid-on—the batting was flawless.

It cannot be said that Diver ever improved upon his earliest efforts for Surrey, but he held his own, playing many a fine innings—the highest of them 143 against Oxford University at Oxford in 1885. After playing for Surrey three years as an amateur he declared himself a professional in 1886, and at the end of that season his association with the county came to an end. Following a rather long interval he qualified by residence for Warwickshire, and played for them from 1893 till 1901. Always more or less successful, he had an especially good season in 1899, when he scored 1,010 runs in county matches, hit up a score of 184 against Leicestershire at Birmingham, and averaged 31. After finishing with Warwickshire he kept up his cricket in a modest way for Monmouth from 1903 onwards. Diver had the very rare experience of playing for both sides in Gentlemen v. Players matches. He was in the Gentlemen's team at the Oval in 1884, and assisted the Players at the same ground in 1886 and 1899. In all he scored 2,962 runs for Surrey with an average of 21, and 5,931 runs

for Warwickshire with an average of 26.—
S.H.P.

DIXON, Sub.-Lieut. Eric J. H., R.N.V.R.,
was presumed killed on active service in
April, 1941, aged 25. From St. Edward's
School, Oxford, he went to the University,
and captained the Dark Blues in his third
year 1939 with such success that Cambridge
were beaten at Lord's by 45 runs. After
showing sound defence and good stroke play
in making 75, the highest score in a total of
313, he revealed clever strategy in managing
his bowling and wisdom in letting his side bat
again 156 ahead rather than enforce the
follow-on. His declaration with three men
out proved so well timed that, despite a
grand 100 by P. J. Dickinson, Cambridge
were dismissed at five minutes past seven in a
splendid finish. Oxford won the 1937 match
by seven wickets and the next game was
drawn, so that Dixon could look back on his
experiences at Lord's with justifiable pride.
He averaged 33.43 for Oxford in 1939, his
best performance concluding his University
cricket. For Northamptonshire he then came
out strongly. Averaging 27.15, he played a
best innings of 123 against Somerset—exactly half his side's total—being ninth out to a
fine catch at long leg after batting four hours
and a quarter. He possessed the ideal temperament for an opening batsman, patient,
optimistic and dour, in conformity with his
county characteristics—he was born in Yorkshire—and he set a splendid example in the
field.

DIXON, John Auger, who captained Notts
from 1889 to 1899, died at Nottingham on
June 8, 1931, after being ill for a month.
While Notts, like Yorkshire, always make a
point of playing men born in the county, Mr.
Dixon, as was the case with Lord Hawke,
Yorkshire's leader for 28 years, first saw the
light in Lincolnshire.
  Born at Grantham on May 27, 1861, Mr.
Dixon, building up a great reputation in club
cricket, was tried for Notts in 1882, but failed
to justify that distinction. Nervousness appeared to prevent him from reproducing for
the county the ability he displayed in minor
cricket. Indeed, he continued to disappoint
expectations, but in 1887, called upon in an
emergency to play for Notts against the
M.C.C. at Lord's, he scored 89 against
several of the finest bowlers of the day.
Having at length done himself justice, he
never looked back, playing with much consistency for 16 seasons.
  A fine free batsman, with the off-drive and

the cut as his best strokes, he timed the ball
admirably, and when occasion demanded he
could also play quiet, sound defensive
methods. He was always a good hard-working field and as a bowler of medium pace
with a high delivery he proved quite skilful.
Against Lancashire at Trent Bridge in 1887
he performed the hat-trick.
  His biggest innings—268, not out, against
Sussex at Trent Bridge in 1897—extended
over part of three days. In the same summer
he made 102 and 91 in a match with Kent at
Gravesend and finished the season with an
aggregate of 1,100 and an average of 44.
Another fine score to his credit was 165
against Kent at Canterbury in 1898. He
appeared 11 times for the Gentlemen in
opposition to the Players.
  Mr. Dixon also made a name for himself in
Association football, and appeared for England against Wales at Blackburn in 1885. As
a club player he assisted Notts County.

DIXON, Joseph Gilbert, who died on
November 19, 1954, aged 59, played as an
all-rounder for Essex from 1914 to 1922. His
best season for the county was that of 1921,
when he scored 810 runs, average 22.50, and
took 67 wickets, average 34.47. The highest
of his three first-class centuries was 173,
made out of 296 in two and a half hours
against Worcestershire at Leyton in 1922. A
strong driver, he hit one six and 24 fours. In
the Felsted XI in 1912 and two following
years, he headed the school batting figures in
1914 with 646 runs, average 58.72, and took
29 wickets.

DIXON, Thomas James, born in London on
October 6, 1843, died at Potchefstroom
(Transvaal) on April 23, 1915. For some
years he was one of the leading cricketers in
South Africa. At Kroonstad in 1883 he
scored 158 not out for Home-Born v. Colo-
nial-Born, and at Kimberley in April, 1890,
represented the Transvaal against Kimberley
in the first Currie Cup match.

DOBSON, Arthur, who died on September
17, 1932, appeared in two matches for Yorkshire in 1879. *Scores and Biographies* described him as "a moderate batsman, a
medium-pace bowler, generally fields at
cover-point." He was born at Ilkley on
February 22, 1854.

DOBSON, Fred, died at his home in Hampshire on October 15, 1980, aged 82. He was
an amateur who played three matches for
Warwickshire as a slow left-arm bowler in

1928 and, taking seven wickets for 38 runs, came out top of their averages. However, he decided that he preferred club cricket.

DOBSON, Kenneth William, who died on March 3, 1959, aged 59, played as a fast bowler in three matches for Derbyshire in 1920.

DOCKER, Cyril Talbot, M.B.E., who died in Sydney at the age of 91 on March 26, 1975, started his first-class career by taking nine for 132 for New South Wales v. Queensland in 1909, but New South Wales then had Cotter and there was no room for him in the Sheffield Shield side. During the First World War he served with the Australian Forces and took part in several matches at Lord's and in 1919 was a member of the A.I.F. side in England. Before the tour began he was listed in the press as the team's fast bowler, Gregory being strangely put down as fast medium, and in their first match, v. Lionel Robinson's side at Attleborough, he opened the bowling in the first innings with Kelleway and took five for 34, while Gregory did not bowl at all. A week later he took five for 41 and made 52 not out against Cambridge, but by now it was apparent that Gregory was far the more formidable proposition and Docker's opportunities became fewer and fewer: after mid-July he did not play at all. He reappeared for the side in South Africa, where he took five for 20 against the Transvaal, and in their matches in Australia, but after that dropped out of big cricket, though he retained his interest in the game to the end. His two younger brothers also played for New South Wales.

DOCKER, Ludford Charles, of Derbyshire and Warwickshire, died on August 2, 1939, aged 79. He played for Derbyshire from 1881 to 1886, being captain for a time, and then went to Warwickshire, for whom he appeared regularly until 1894. He became President in 1915, retiring in 1931. In August 1886 he made 132, 112 and 110 in consecutive innings—the first and third of these centuries for Smethwick in cup-tie matches and the other for Warwickshire against M.C.C. at Edgbaston. His highest score in County Cricket was 163 at Edgbaston against Cheshire in 1891, while three years later his average, 37.20, was the best by any gentleman in first-class cricket. He went to Australia in the winter of 1887 with Shrewsbury's team, but met with little success, his best innings being 48 in 11-a-side matches. Owing to an unfortunate muddle two teams visited

Australia during that season. They joined forces to play Combined Australia and won by 126 runs, thanks mainly to the bowling of Peel, 10 wickets for 58, and Lohmann, nine wickets for 52. Docker did not take part in that match, but he was in Shrewsbury's XI twice against Australia, making 21 and being not out four when the first ended in a victory by five wickets, while in the second, won by 158 runs, he scored 33 valuable runs, so helping to stop a first-innings collapse caused by C. T. B. Turner.

Powerfully built and over 6ft. tall, Docker played a strong, lively game, with special freedom in driving; he bowled fast, fielded well, and generally was a valuable member of any side.

DODDS, Norman (son of the Lord Chief Justice of Tasmania), died at Hobart on December 13, 1916. Excellent wicket-keeper and a good bat with many strokes. Played District cricket for Wellington, Derwent, North Hobart and New Town, and headed the averages in 1902–03 and 1906–07: he averaged 90.16 in 1906–07, 75.33 in 1902–03, 63.20 in 1909–10 and 63.16 in 1908–09. Scored 81 for Tasmania v. Victoria, at Melbourne 1907–08 and 80 not out for the Australian XI v. Rest of Australia at Melbourne the next season, hitting 15 fours in the latter innings, which lasted only 65 minutes and was chanceless. That year he was nearly chosen for the visit to England. He and W. Ward added 122 for the 10th wicket of Tasmania v. Victoria, at Hobart, in 1898–99.

DOGGART, Alexander Graham, who died while occupying the chair at the annual meeting of the Football Association on June 7, 1963 aged 66, played both cricket and Association football for Cambridge University. Educated at Bishop's Stortford College, he saw service in the Army during the First World War before going to the University, where he got his Blue at cricket in 1921 and the following season. With innings of 45 and 71 he helped in substantial victories over Oxford. He also assisted Middlesex and Durham on occasion and in first-class matches between 1919 and 1930 he scored 1,790 runs, average 30.33, took 88 wickets for 31.14 runs each and held 48 catches. He was a member of the Sussex Committee and of the full M.C.C. Committee. As an inside-left, he appeared in the Cambridge football XI in 1920 and 1921, gained a full International cap for England against Belgium in 1924 and took part in four Amateur Internationals. He was a leading forward for the famous Corinthians, scoring the goal by which they defeated Blackburn Rovers in the F.A. Cup in 1924, and played for Bishop Auckland and the Casuals.

Tributes included:

Mr. S.C. Griffith, Secretary of M.C.C.: "This is a heavy blow to me, for he was a personal friend of mine for many years. With his death we have lost not only a great cricketer, but a splendid committee-man and administrator whose services meant more to us at Lord's than I can say."

Mr. Denis Follows, Secretary of the Football Association: "Graham was a man of high principles and tremendous sense of duty. He never spared himself in the interests of the Association and was punctilious in his attention to his duties. In spite of his health, he never gave up and died serving the game he loved and which he had adorned for so long both as a player and as an administrator."

DOGGART, Arthur Peter, who died in Epsom District Hospital on March 17, 1965, aged 37, was in the Winchester XI as a batsman and medium-paced bowler in 1944 and 1945. A son of A.G. Doggart and younger brother of G.H.G. Doggart, the Cambridge Blues, he played occasionally as an amateur for Sussex between 1947 and 1951. He was on the staff of *The Cricketer*, for whom he wrote on public schools cricket.

DOIG, Jack, who died at Invercargill on November 24, 1951, aged 81, was for many years a noted sportsman in New Zealand. Born in Victoria, Australia, he went to New Zealand at an early age. As a youth he made a name as a bowler and during his career he was credited with no fewer than 50 hat-tricks. On five occasions he took all 10 wickets in an innings, and he would have performed the feat a sixth time but for a dropped catch. A member of the Invercargill Club for 46 years, he represented Southland for 20 years, playing his last game for them at the age of 63. His interest was not confined to cricket, and he did much for Rugby football, hockey, athletics, basketball, boxing and golf in Southland.

DOLDING, Desmond Leonard, who died in hospital on November 23, 1954, aged 31, as the result of injuries received in a motor-car accident, was a member of the M.C.C. staff for seven years. He played only once for Middlesex, in 1951, but as a right-arm leg-break bowler took part in many games for M.C.C. A brilliant fieldsman, he acted as 12th man for England in the second Test match with New Zealand at Lord's in 1949 and was summoned to Leeds to stand by as substitute in the fourth Test with Australia in 1953. An Association footballer of ability, he played as a wing forward for Queen's Park Rangers, Chelsea and Norwich City and was on the books of Margate at the time of his death. In the Second World War, he served as a bomb-aimer with the R.A.F., where, as in sport, his quiet and likeable personality made him very popular.

DOLIGNAN, The Rev. J. W., who died on June 15, 1896, was in the Eton XI in 1832, and with a score of 52, contributed in no small degree to Eton's single innings victory over Harrow at Lord's. He appeared for the Gentlemen against the Players at Lord's in 1844.

DOLL, Mordaunt Henry Caspers, who died at Devizes on June 30, 1966, aged 78, was a hard-hitting batsman. In the Charterhouse XI from 1905 to 1907, he hit 195 against Westminster in the last season, when he and R.L.L. Braddell put on 214 together—180 of them in an hour. From 1912 to 1919 he played occasional matches for Middlesex and against Nottinghamshire at Lord's in 1913, scored 102 not out in an unfinished stand of 182 in two hours with H.R. Murrell. He toured the West Indies with the M.C.C. team captained by A.F. Somerset in 1912–13 and also appeared for Hertfordshire.

DOLLING, Dr. C.E., died at Adelaide on June 11, 1936, aged 49, having been born on September 4, 1886. He played a good deal for South Australia, scoring 1,168 runs for the State with an average of 37.67 and 113 as his highest innings in Sheffield Shield matches. A sound judge of a cricketer he was on the committee who chose the Australian team for the 1934 tour in England.

DOLPHIN, Arthur, the well-known wicket-keeper and Test match umpire, died at his home in Bradford on October 24, 1942, in his 56th year. Yorkshire wicket-keepers have been noted for long and effective service, and Dolphin followed Ned Stephenson, George Pinder, Joe Hunter and David Hunter, while Arthur Wood, his successor, came as the sixth who, taken together, did splendid service for their county during nearly 80 years.

First appearing for Yorkshire in 1905, Dolphin became the regular keeper in 1910, and held the position until he retired at the end of the 1927 season. Contemporary with Herbert Strudwick and E. J. Smith, Dolphin only once played for England—in the fourth Test match at Melbourne in February, 1921, when Australia, captained by W. W. Armstrong, won the rubber with five victories over the team led by J. W. H. T. Douglas. During a career extending over 23 seasons, Dolphin held 488 catches and stumped 231 men, and scored 4,191 runs in first-class matches, average 10.76.

As a batsman he often defended well in a crisis, and perhaps his best performance was against Essex at Leyton in 1919, the season of two-day matches; he scored 62 not out, and with E. Smith put on 103 for the last wicket, so saving their side from following-on when Yorkshire were in danger.

One of his most notable feats behind the stumps was against Hampshire at Leeds in 1921, a match which provided a genuine sensation. Hampshire declared at 456 for two wickets, Dolphin having conceded only two byes. Two England left-handers, George Brown 232, and C. P. Mead, 122, both not out, severely punished the Yorkshire bowling and the northern county were beaten by an innings and 72 runs. In his benefit match in 1892 at Leeds against Kent, which realised £1,891, he scored two, and 20 out of 24 without being dismissed, he having the honour of hitting off the runs required by Yorkshire for victory by 10 wickets.

When his playing days were over, Dolphin became an efficient and popular umpire, known as "the man who never wore a hat." Even on the hottest day he stood bareheaded in the middle.

DONNELLY, Desmond Louis, who was found dead in a London hotel bedroom on April 4, 1974, aged 53, founded in 1940 the British Empire XI which, including many famous cricketers, all unpaid, raised much money for the Red Cross. In the first season over 80,000 people watched the Empire XI's 37 matches, the Red Cross benefiting by £1,239. Donnelly afterwards joined the R.A.F., serving with the Desert Air Force, and following the end of the Second World War became a Member of Parliament, firstly with the Labour Party and then as an Independent. A journalist, he was the author of 11 books.

DOOLAND, Bruce, who died in Adelaide, his birthplace, on September 8, 1980, aged 56, was one of the last great leg-spinners in first-class cricket. As early as 1940–41, when

only 17, he had been asked to play for South Australia, but his employers refused leave. War service with the Australian commandos had intervened before he made his first appearance for them in 1945–46 and, against Victoria, performed the first hat-trick in post-War Australian cricket. In 1946 he was a member of W. A. Brown's team to New Zealand and in 1946–47 was picked for the third Test against England at Melbourne. Taking four for 89 and one for 84 and helping McCool to put on 83 useful runs for the ninth wicket, he did not do badly, especially as his victims were Washbrook (twice), Hammond and Ikin; he was retained for the fourth Test, in which he took three for 133 (Washbrook, Edrich and Ikin) and made 29. For the last Test he was replaced by Tribe. His only other Test was against India at Melbourne in 1948. For the 1948 tour of England, McCool and Ring were preferred to him: his later records suggest that in time he became a better bowler than either, but leg-spinners tend to mature slowly learning from experience, and both were considerably older. The immediate consequence was that he came to England to play in the Lancashire League. In 1950–51 he went with the Commonwealth side to India and made two hundreds in the unofficial Tests. In 1953 he was registered to play for Nottinghamshire. He continued to play for them for five seasons during which he scored 4,782 runs with an average of 24.52 and took 770 wickets at 18.86. Twice he did the double and once he missed it by only 30 runs. He played twice for the Players at Lord's. His batting figures show remarkable consistency as they include only one hundred—115 not out v. Sussex at Worthing in 1957—a match in which he also took 10 for 102. Perhaps his most remarkable bowling performance statistically was 16 for 83 v. Essex at Trent Bridge in 1954. Against Somerset in 1953 he took 10 for 49 in the match at Weston-super-Mare and later in the month 10 for 48 in the return at Trent Bridge. Standing over 6 ft. he was taller than most leg-spinners and had a long strong arm which had helped him to become one of the best baseball pitchers in his state. Delivering the ball usually with his front foot behind the bowling crease, he was a trifle quicker than many of his predecessors, but like them relied mainly on the leg-break and the topspinner, keeping the googly in reserve. Probably the chief difference between his bowling in 1948 and in 1953 was that he had become more skilled at varying his pace and his flight. As a batsman, he could cut and drive well and he was also a good fieldsman near the wicket. After 1957 he returned to Australia, as he wished his son to be brought up as an Australian.

DORMAN, The Rev. Arthur William, of the Cambridge XI of 1886, died at Hinton Charterhouse, near Bath, on January 7, 1914, aged 51. He was educated at Dulwich, where he was in the XI in 1879 and 1880, being captain in the latter year, when he was described as "A first-rate left-handed bowler, with a high delivery and good break; a good straight bat, playing the ball very hard; a good judge of a run; fields well, especially at slip." His best performance in first-class cricket was to take nine wickets for 103 runs—four for 48 and five for 55—for his University against Yorkshire at Cambridge in 1886. Later in the season he appeared for the Gentlemen at the Oval, where his bowling proved expensive, his one wicket costing 48 runs. He was born on October 24, 1862.

DOUGLAS, Col. Archibald Philip, who died at Taunton on January 24, 1953, aged 85, was one of four brothers—the others were James and Robert Noel, both Cambridge Blues, and Captain Sholto—who played for Middlesex. In the Dulwich XI from 1882 to 1884, he headed the batting averages in the last season, and did the same at Woolwich the next two years. On a few occasions in 1886 and 1887 he assisted Surrey, and afterwards appeared for Middlesex, the county of his birth. He also played much military cricket in India. During the first Great War, when serving as Colonel of Royal Artillery (Indian Army), he was Mentioned in Dispatches and awarded the C.M.G. and the Serbian Order of the White Eagle (Fourth Class).

DOUGLAS, Cecil Herbert, who died at Frinton-on-Sea in September, 1954, aged 68, was the younger brother of J. W. H. T. Douglas, the Essex and England captain. Cecil, generally known as "Pickles," played for Essex in a few matches from 1912 to 1914, his highest innings being 78 against Lancashire at Old Trafford in 1919. He was a celebrated boxing referee.

DOUGLAS, James, who died at Cheltenham on February 8, 1958, aged 88, played for Cambridge in the University matches of 1892 and the two following years. As a capital right-handed batsman and left-arm slow bowler, he was in the Dulwich XI for five years from 1885. In 1889, when captain, he hit 166 against Brighton College, finishing the season with a batting average of 58.66. He became a master at Dulwich College and later had his own school at Godalming, Surrey. From 1893 till 1913 he assisted Middlesex during the school summer holidays. As opening batsman he proved of immense value to the county, first as partner to A. E. Stoddart and later to P. F. Warner. In 1896 he and Stoddart shared in three three-figure opening stands in a fortnight—178 v. Yorkshire at Bradford, 158 v. Nottinghamshire at Trent Bridge, and 166 v. Kent at Lord's. His highest innings for Middlesex was 204 against Gloucestershire at Bristol in 1903. Four years later at Taunton, when scoring 180 from the Somerset bowling, he helped in three big partnerships—110 in 50 minutes with Warner for the first wicket, 103 in 55 minutes with H. A. Milton for the second, and 155 in 65 minutes with F. A. Tarrant for the third. He was a member of the Gentlemen's team who beat the Players at Lord's by an innings and 39 runs in 1894, when F. S. Jackson and S. M. J. Woods, bowling unchanged in both innings, gained match-figures of 12 for 77 and six for 124 respectively. In all first-class cricket, Douglas scored 9,099 runs, average 29.67.

DOUGLAS, John William Henry Tyler, born at Clapton, Middlesex, on September 3, 1882, was drowned on December 19, 1930, in a collision which occurred in the Cattegat between the steamships *Oberon* and *Arcturus*. Together with his father, Mr. J. H. Douglas, Mr. Douglas, when the accident occurred, was a passenger on the *Oberon* returning to England from a business trip.

Johnny Douglas, as he was known in nearly every country where cricket is played, had a remarkable career. He was not only a fine cricketer but an even greater boxer and he attained some fame at Association football, appearing for the Corinthians and the Casuals and gaining an A.F.A. international cap. While it was as a cricketer that he made his name a household word in so many parts of the world, he came to the front as a boxer when still at Felsted by his doings in the Public Schools' Championship. Later on, as he developed physically, he reached the highest class as a middle-weight and in 1905 won the Amateur Championship while in 1908 he carried off the Olympic Middle-Weight Championship by beating in a memorable encounter the Australian "Snowy" Baker. So level were the men at the end of three rounds that neither judges nor referee could arrive at a decision and after an extra round the margin was of the narrowest.

Douglas learned his early cricket at Moulton Grammar School, Lincolnshire. He was in the Felsted XI in 1898, 1899, 1900 and 1901 and captain in the last of these years. It is curious, in view of the stolid batsman Douglas became, that when at Felsted he was coached by T. N. Perkins, a notable hitter in his Cambridge days. Douglas first appeared for Essex in 1901—the year he left school—and had a most disheartening experience in his opening match being bowled in each innings by George Hirst's "swerver" without making a run either time. He saw little of County Cricket during the next year or two and for some time afterwards was merely a useful all-round player. By 1908, however, he had thoroughly established his position in the Essex XI and three years later he showed he had about him the possibilities of an international player. He became captain of Essex in 1911 and continued to hold that post until the close of the season of 1928. In that summer of 1911, he enjoyed a great personal triumph in the Gentlemen and Players match at Lord's, scoring 72 and 22, not out, and taking seven wickets. This performance suggested he was the man for the big occasion and that he often proved in subsequent years. He had been out to New Zealand as a member of the M.C.C.'s team in the winter of 1906–07, distinguishing himself there with both bat and ball, and in the autumn of 1907 he had formed one of the sides Marylebone sent out to the United States and Canada.

Heavy responsibility was soon thrust upon his shoulders for P. F. Warner, who had been appointed captain of the team which went out to Australia in 1911–12, falling ill after the opening contest, the duties of leadership devolved upon Douglas. The first Test match was lost but, the side enjoying the services of those exceptionally fine bowlers, S. F. Barnes and F. R. Foster, the other four were won and so Douglas returned home with his reputation as a captain established. Strangely enough in the following summer—the season of the Triangular Tournament—when he might well have played for England in all six Tests, Douglas did not get a chance until the last match with Australia. For all that further honours soon fell to him as he was chosen to captain the M.C.C. team in South Africa in 1913–14 when four Test games were won by England and the other drawn. After the War, in the course of which, getting a commission in the Bedfordshire Regiment, he reached the rank of Lieutenant-Colonel, Douglas was appointed captain of the M.C.C. side that visited Australia in 1920–21 and lost all five Test matches. He played for England against Australia in the five Test contests of 1921 —in the first two as captain and in the remainder under the leadership of Tennyson. Finally he accompanied to Australia the team sent out under A. E. R. Gilligan in 1924–25 but played a very small part in that tour. His record in Test match cricket was as follows:—

	Innings	Not outs	Most in an Innings	Total Runs	Average
v. Australia	28	2	75	696	26.76
v. South Africa	7	0	119	266	38.00

Possessed of exceptional defensive skill and inexhaustible patience, Douglas was a batsman very hard to dismiss. Sometimes, so intent was he upon keeping up his wicket, that he carried caution to excess and became tiresome to watch. Indeed, with his rather cramped style and limited number of strokes, he could never be described as an attractive player. Still there could be no question about his ability to face an awkward situation or about the soundness of his methods and, although so chary of investing his play with enterprise, he was able to hit with plenty of power on either side of the wicket. As a bowler he was a much more interesting figure. Distinctly above medium pace, he could keep at work for hours without losing either speed or length and to a new ball he imparted, late in its flight, a very awkward

swerve to leg. Always extremely fit, Douglas, even at the end of the hottest and longest day, scarcely knew what fatigue was and, if—strangely enough for a first rate boxer— by no means quick on his feet in the cricket field, and therefore apt to miss the chance of making a catch, he never spared himself. As to his abilities as a captain on the field, opinions differed and he certainly was more brusque of manner than might be wished in a leader, but eloquent testimony in his favour was always forthcoming from players, professional as well as amateur, who had served under him on tours in other lands. To balance any lack of restraint in expressing his views about a blunder, he possessed that saving grace of humour which enjoyed tales against himself. How thoroughly he realised his limitations was shown by his remark "An optimist is a man who batting with Johnny Douglas, backs up for a run." On one occasion Douglas batted an hour and a half for eight, not out, against Kent at Canterbury but, in so doing, he saved his side from defeat. His highest score was 210, not out, for Essex against Derbyshire at Leyton in 1921. In company with A. E. Knight of Leicestershire, he put on for An England XI against the Australians at Blackpool in 1909 no fewer than 284 for the first wicket.

Among his many achievements in taking wickets, the following were the most striking:—

5 bowled in 8 balls for 0 runs, including hat-trick, Essex v. Yorkshire, Leyton, 1905.

8 for 83, Essex v. Leicestershire, Southend, 1906.

13 for 155, Essex v. Kent, Leyton, 1907.

3 in 4 balls, Gentlemen of South v. Players of South, Hastings, 1909.

13 for 172 (including 9 for 105), Gentlemen v. Players, Lord's, 1914.

6 for 18, Essex v. Sussex, Southend, 1914.

Unchanged through both innings with Tremlin for Essex in 1914 v. Surrey, Oval, and v. Derbyshire, Derby.

8 for 49, Gentlemen v. Players, Lord's, 1919.

8 for 39, Essex v. Derbyshire, Derby, 1920.

Hat-trick, England v. New South Wales, Sydney, 1920–21.

14 for 156, Essex v. Worcestershire, Leyton, 1921.

14 for 91 (including 7 for 17), Essex v. Hampshire, Bournemouth, 1921.

9 for 47, Essex v. Derbyshire, Leyton, 1921.

8 for 45, Essex, v. Gloucestershire, Cheltenham, 1922.

4 in 6 balls (including hat-trick), Essex v. Sussex, Leyton, 1923.

13 for 150, Essex v. Somerset, Colchester, 1923.

6 for 14, Essex v. Northamptonshire, Southend, 1923.

DOUGLAS, The Rev. Robert Noel, who died at Colyton, Devon, on February 27, 1957, aged 88, played both cricket and Rugby football for Cambridge. He went to the University from Dulwich College in 1889 and for the three following years appeared against Oxford at Lord's, scoring as opening batsman an aggregate of 97 runs in the six innings. Twice he assisted Gentlemen against Players and he later turned out first for Surrey and then for Middlesex. Altogether he hit 2,661 runs in first-class cricket, average 23.13. He played as a forward in the University Rugby match of 1891 and also helped the Harlequins. He was a master at Uppingham

before serving as headmaster of Giggleswick from 1910 to 1931.

DOUGLAS, Stanley, who died in December, 1971, aged 68, played occasionally for Yorkshire from 1925 to 1934. In first-class matches he took, with slow left-arm bowling, 49 wickets for an average of 26.73 runs apiece. He was one of the few bowlers to dismiss 1,000 batsmen in Bradford League cricket.

DOUTHWAITE, Harold, who died in hospital on July 10, 1972, aged 72, scored over 1,000 runs, average 112, for Lancaster Grammar School in 1919, his highest innings being 180 not out against Sedbergh. Between 1919 and 1949, he hit more than 8,000 runs for Lancaster C.C. In 1920 and 1921 he made several appearances for Lancashire. He gained an Association football Blue at Cambridge in 1923, in which year he took part in the Amateur International match for England against Wales and he toured Europe with the Corinthians. Later he played at stand-off half for Vale of Lune R.F.C.

DOVEY, Raymond Randall, the Kent off-spin bowler, died suddenly at his home in Tunbridge Wells on December 27, 1974, aged 54. He appeared for Kent in a few matches before the 1939–45 War and when he retired in 1955 he had taken 777 wickets in first-class cricket at 27.53 runs each and scored 3,827 runs, average 11.59. Born at Chislehurst, Dovey was tall and lean and wore glasses. He was a reliable stock bowler who could turn to medium pace and when he accomplished his best performance, eight wickets for 23 runs in 19.2 overs for Kent at Blackheath in 1950, he opened the attack with J. W. Martin. On a rain-affected pitch, he turned the ball sharply into the batsmen and many fell to leg-side catches. As he took five for 52 in the second innings, his match figures were 13 for 75 and Kent won for the first time in 16 years in the then traditional Surrey fixture at the Rectory Field. On his retirement, Dovey went first as coach to Sherborne, playing for a time for Dorset. He then moved to Tonbridge where he was responsible for the high standard of cricket for many years. Colin Cowdrey paid a special tribute to Dovey for his work at Tonbridge, where he also ran the school shop.

DOWER, Robert Read, who died at Cape Town, where he was an attorney, on September 16, 1964, aged 88, was the oldest surviving South African Test cricketer. He played in the first two Tests with Lord

Hawke's team in 1898–99 at Johannesburg. He assisted Cape Colony and Eastern Province.

DOWLING, Capt. Geoffrey Charles Walter (7th King's Royal Rifle Corps), was killed in Flanders on July 30, 1915, aged 23. He was in the Charterhouse XI in 1908 and two following years, averaging 25.90 in 1908 and 28.60 in 1910. In Public School games his highest scores were 78 not out (going in tenth) v. Westminster in 1908, 57 v. Haverford in 1910, and 31 v. Wellington in 1908. At Cambridge, where he did very well indeed in college cricket, he made 60 in the Freshmen's match in 1911, but obtained spectacles in the Seniors' two years later. He appeared for Sussex three times in 1911 and once in 1913, his largest innings being 48 v. Cambridge University at Cambridge, and 33 v. Kent at Tunbridge Wells, both in the former season. In 1913 he became a member of the M.C.C., and playing for the club at Rye that year against Rye he scored 138, he and R.D. Cochrane (184) adding 294 together for the second wicket.

DOWNES, Alec, died at Dunedin, New Zealand, on February 10, 1950, aged over 80. One of the leading New Zealand bowlers of his time, Mr. Downes represented Otago from 1888 until 1914. A slow bowler who turned the ball considerably from the off, he took 322 wickets in first-class cricket for an average of 15.77, and for many years formed a formidable pair of bowlers with A.H. Fisher. He represented New Zealand six times and many notable feats stand to his credit. Among them were 14 wickets in a match for Otago against St. Hawke's Bay at Dunedin in 1893–94, and in the same season he took four wickets with successive balls against Auckland at Dunedin. On more than one occasion Mr. Downes bowled throughout the two innings of a match. Mr. Downes was also a noted Rugby centre three-quarter and represented Otago 13 times, also playing for South Island in 1888. In later years he refereed International Rugby games and also stood as umpire in several Test matches.

DOWNES, Frank, who died in Little Bay Hospital, Sydney on May 20, 1916, aged 51, was a left-handed bowler formerly well-known with the old Oriental C.C., in junior cricket, and with the Carlton (Sydney) in senior. He appeared occasionally for New South Wales, and in his matches v. Victoria took eight wickets for 329 runs and had a batting average of 10.

DOWSON, Edward, one of the oldest of Surrey cricketers, died at Surbiton, on April 29, 1922, aged 84. He was born at Camberwell on February 17, 1838, and was educated at Shrewsbury. *Scores and Biographies* (ix–43) says of him: "Is a capital field at long-leg and cover-point, being able also to throw in well, and from a considerable distance. As a batsman he is a fine, hard hitter, especially forward and to leg, having made most excellent scores, principally on the Oval and for his county." His chief innings for Surrey were—94 (Surrey Club) v. Middlesex in 1862, 87 v. Sussex in 1863, 80 v. England in 1861—all at the Oval—and (at Cambridge) 73 v. Cambridgeshire in 1862. He also scored 87 for Gentlemen of the South v. Players of Surrey at the Oval in 1863. His name will be found in the Surrey XI from 1860 to 1867 and in 1870, and in the Gentlemen's XI from 1861 to 1863. Mr. Dowson took the greatest interest in cricket to the last, and was full of most entertaining reminiscences of the players of 60 years ago. He was father of Mr. E.M. Dowson. Outliving Caffyn, Mr. Dowson was the last survivor of F.P. Miller's famous Surrey XI—photographed at the Oval after their victory over Notts in 1861. His 80 against England in 1861 could fairly be described as the innings of his life.

DOWSON, Edward Maurice, the former Harrow and Cambridge University captain, died at Ashburton, Devon, on July 22, 1933. The son of Mr. Edward Dowson the old Surrey cricketer, he went to Harrow in the autumn of 1894 and next year, at the age of 15, created a great surprise when he appeared against Eton at Lord's. Bowling left-arm slow he kept his length perfectly during long spells of work and made the ball do a great deal, and although Harrow had the worst of a drawn match Dowson, who opened their bowling, took five wickets for 90 and three for 105. He stood no more than five feet and bowled extremely slow. Given, owing to his stature, the nickname of "Toddles" he was called this by his friends for the rest of his life. Coming into the match at such an early age, he played no fewer than five times against Eton (1895–99) and was captain in the last two years. In 1898, when Harrow won by nine wickets, he scored 47 and took nine wickets; the following season he scored 87 not out and was mainly responsible for his school gaining the lead. Going up to Cambridge, he took part in all four Varsity matches from 1900 to 1903 and led the side to victory in his last year. He proved a valuable all-rounder, especially in 1902 when he took five wickets in each innings and scored 40 and 29. In his last three years at Cambridge, he exceeded a four-figure aggregate, and in 1903 obtained 1,343 runs, average 34.43. Mr. Dowson, had he played regularly in the Surrey team, would, unquestionably, have taken a high place among amateurs, but the cricket field saw little of him after he came down from Cambridge. He assisted Surrey a few times in 1900 and visited America and the West Indies, while during the tour of Lord Hawke's team in Australia and New Zealand of 1902–03 his batting created a very favourable impression. Moreover, besides finishing second to Mr. P. F. Warner in the batting averages, he took 40 wickets for 8.20 runs apiece. Representing the Gentlemen at Lord's in 1902 and 1903, he in the second game had the distinction of clean bowling Tom Hayward in each innings. In first-class cricket, E. M. Dowson made eight centuries, his highest being 135 against Sussex at Brighton in 1903, and the same year for Cambridge against Worcestershire he narrowly missed the achievement of a hundred in each innings, his scores being 94 and 122 not out. He was a sound batsman, correct in style and generally to be relied upon at a crisis.

DOYLE, Sir Arthur Conan, M.D. (Edin.), the well-known author, born at Edinburgh on May 22, 1859, died at Crowborough, Sussex, on July 7, 1930, aged 71. Although never a famous cricketer, he could hit hard and bowl slows with a puzzling flight. For M.C.C. v. Cambridgeshire at Lord's, in 1899, he took seven wickets for 61 runs, and on the same ground two years later carried out his bat for 32 against Leicestershire, who had Woodcock, Geeson and King to bowl for them. In *The Times* of October 27, 1915, he was the author of an article on "The Greatest of Cricketers. An Appreciation of Dr. Grace". (It is said that Shacklock, the former Nottinghamshire player, inspired him with the Christian name of his famous character, Sherlock Holmes, and that of the latter's brother Mycroft was suggested by the Derbyshire cricketers.)

DRAKE, Alonzo. The death took place on February 14, 1919, of this well-known Yorkshire cricketer at his home at Westgate, Hanley, near Huddersfield. He was in his 35th year. Drake—left-handed both as batsmen and bowler—first found a place in the Yorkshire team in 1909, having previously played for the Second XI. Tried in five matches, he showed distinct promise, but in the following season he fell below expectation, and it was not until 1911 that he firmly established himself in the side. In that season he had a batting average of 35 in county matches, and took 61 wickets. Thenceforward, until the outbreak of the War put a stop to first-class cricket, he was one of the best men in the Yorkshire XI. In 1913 he came right to the front as a bowler, taking 102 wickets and heading the Yorkshire averages with the late M. W. Booth next to him. Finally, in 1914, he bowled better than ever, taking 135 wickets and being again practically at the head of the averages. Eclipsing everything he had previously done, he took all 10 Somerset wickets in one innings at Weston-

Drake – Bowling Performances

8 in inns. for 59	Yorkshire v. Gloucestershire, at Sheffield	..	..	1913
10 in inns. for 35 ⎱ 15 in match for 51 ⎰	Yorkshire v. Somerset, at Weston-super-Mare	..	..	1914
5 for 10	Yorkshire v. Western, at Glasgow	..	..	1910
4 for 4a ⎱ 7 for 7c ⎰	Yorkshire v. Somerset, at Bath	..	..	1913
5 for 6	Yorkshire v. Derbyshire, at Chesterfield	..	..	1914
3 wkts. in 4 balls ⎱ 4 wkts. in 6 balls ⎰	Yorkshire v. Middlesex, at Leeds	..	..	1909
3 wkts. in 3 balls ⎱ 4 wkts. in 7 balls ⎰ †	Yorkshire v. Essex, at Huddersfield	..	..	1912
4 wkts. in 4 balls	Yorkshire v. Derbyshire, at Chesterfield	..	..	1914
3 wkts. in 4 balls	Yorkshire v. Lancashire, at Hull	..	..	1914

a signifies 1st innings; *c* both.

†*In this match he at one period took 5 wickets for 0 runs.*

Bowling Unchanged Through Both Completed Innings

With Booth, for Yorkshire v. Gloucestershire, at Bristol	..	..	1914
With Booth, for Yorkshire v. Somerset, at Weston-super-Mare	..	..	1914

The above were consecutive Yorkshire matches.

super-Mare, his analysis for the full match being 15 wickets for 51 runs. For some little time before his death he was in a bad state of health. On a wicket that helped him he was a very difficult bowler, and in 1914 he seemed likely to have a big future. He was born at Parkgate, near Rotherham, April 16, 1884.

DRAKE, The Rev. Edward Tyrwhitt, who was born at Bucknall, Bicester, in Oxfordshire, on May 15, 1832, died on June 20, 1904, in his 73rd year. In *Scores and Biographies* (iv – 380) he is described as follows: "Is a very fine, energetic, and most active field anywhere, generally, however, taking long-leg and middle-wicket. Bowls slow under-hand "lobs," twisting in from the leg to the off. At times they are very telling, but the analysis shows that they receive a good deal of punishment. As a batsman (using a bat of great weight) he is one of the most slashing that has yet appeared, hitting at almost everything, and generally sending the ball all over the ground." He was educated at Westminster, and in 1852, 1853, and 1854 assisted Cambridge against Oxford. He appeared for the Gentlemen against the Players on eight occasions, his first match being in 1854 and his last in 1864. In the match at Lord's in 1857—rendered memorable by Reginald Hankey's superb innings of 70— Mr. Drake made a great and most praiseworthy effort to win the game for his side. The Gentlemen were set 128 runs to win, but only Drake and Hankey (13) reached double figures, the former scoring 58 against the bowling of Wisden, Willsher, Jackson, Caffyn, and Parr. The Players won by 13 runs, Willsher obtaining five wickets for 26 runs. Mr. Drake's highest scores in great matches were:

75*, Oxfordshire v. Surrey, at the Oval, 1856.
51*, Gentlemen of England v. Gentlemen of Kent and Sussex, at Lord's, 1856.
57*, M.C.C. and Ground v. Sussex, at Brighton, 1856.
58, Gentlemen v. Players, at Lord's, 1857.
62, I Zingari v. Gentlemen of Hampshire, at Southampton, 1857.
88, M.C.C. and Ground v. Cambridge University, at Lord's, 1858.
57, M.C.C. and Ground v. Middlesex, at Lord's, 1862.
63*, M.C.C. and Ground v. Middlesex, at Lord's, 1862.
59, M.C.C. and Ground (with G. Parr and E. Willsher) v. Cambridgeshire, at Lord's, 1863.

79, M.C.C. and Ground v. Cambridge University, at Lord's, 1865.
**Signifies not out.*

Like many contemporaries of his he retired from first-class cricket on taking Holy Orders, many bishops considering it improper for their clergy to take part in games on the result of which there was heavy betting. His fame as a cricketer was chiefly due to his skill as a lob bowler, he being ranked as second only to V. E. Walker—*longo intervallo*, however. Still, a careful perusal of scores leads one to believe that he was of more assistance to a side as a batsman than as a bowler.

DRAPER, H., the well-known umpire, died on December 31, 1896. Born at Penshurst on February 12, 1857, he was in his 50th year. Draper played in the Kent XI during the '70s, and was at one time engaged as coach at Tonbridge school. By trade he was a cricket ball maker.

DRUCE, Eliot Albert Cross, born June 20, 1876, died on October 24, 1934. He was educated at Marlborough but, unlike his famous cousins, W. G. and N. F., he failed to get a place in the college XI and at Cambridge was not a Blue although sometimes tried in the XI. He appeared in a few matches for Kent. Played hockey for Cambridge against Oxford in 1897–98.

DRUCE, Norman Frank, who died at Milford, Surrey, on October 27, 1954, aged 79, was a celebrated batsman and slip fieldsman towards the end of the last century. Like his elder brother, W. G. Druce, he captained both Marlborough and Cambridge University. From 1891 to 1893 he was in the Marlborough XI, leading the side in the last season, and he played in the University match in 1894 and the three following years, being captain in 1897. He averaged 66 for Cambridge in 1897, an unprecedented performance, and *Wisden* said of him: "He plays his own game without any rigid over-adherence to rule, scoring on the on-side from straight balls in a fashion only possible to a batsman with genius for timing." In that season he hit 227 not out—the highest innings to that date at Fenner's—against C. I. Thornton's team. Twice in 1895 he appeared for Gentlemen against Players, and in 1895 he assisted Surrey without achieving anything of note. When playing for the county in 1897 he did better, though never reproducing the form he showed for his University. He visited America with Frank Mitchell's team in 1895 and went to Australia under A. E. Stoddart in 1897–98, when he scored 109 against New South Wales at Sydney.

DRYDEN, Sir Alfred Erasmus, Eighth Bart. —a direct descendant, though on the distaff side, of the famous John Dryden—was born October 14, 1821, and died at Canons Ashby, Byfield, Northamptonshire, on April 2, 1912. He was in the XI both at Winchester and Oxford, playing for the former in 1839 and 1840, and against Cambridge in 1841 and two following years. In his four Public School matches he made 40 runs in eight innings, and in his three University matches 56 in six, his highest score being 28 in 1841.

DRYDEN, Charles Henry, died at Russell, Auckland, on July 1, 1943, aged 81. A right-hand slow bowler, he helped the Star Club twice win the senior championship in Wellington, and thus secure the silver cup presented by Colonel Edward Pearce. One of his best performances was against Nelson in 1886. When the game seemed lost, he and Arthur Motley, a Yorkshireman, added 72 runs, and Nelson were left with 64 to win. As W. J. Ford, the famous hitter, then Principal of Nelson College, led the Nelson team, this seemed well within reach, but Dryden dismissed seven men for 24 and Wellington won by 13 runs. In December, 1889, Dryden took 12 wickets for 93 against Canterbury, and in 1891, against the same side, 11 for 56. Dryden played for Wellington against the Australian XI of 1886 and the English team of 1888.

DRYSDALE, John, who died in February, 1923, was associated with the Fitzroy C.C., of Melbourne, and played a few times for Victoria, the first occasion being against New South Wales in 1888–89. He was an all-round cricketer.

DU BOULAY, Brevet Lieut.-Col. Arthur Houssemayne, D.S.O. (Royal Engineers), Mentioned in Dispatches six times. A.Q.M.G. Born June 18, 1880, died in hospital abroad after influenza, October 25, 1918. Cheltenham College; R.M.A. (Woolwich); Kent XI; Gloucestershire XI; Army XI; R.E. XI.

Du Boulay to a large extent learnt his cricket at Cheltenham being in the XI in 1895, 1896, 1897. In his last year he was captain and finished up with an excellent record, scoring 309 runs with an average of 30 and heading the bowling with 33 wickets at a cost of something over 17 runs each. He

played five matches for Kent in 1899 and got on remarkably well, making 250 runs in eight innings. In minor cricket Du Boulay was a great run getter. In one week, playing for the Royal Engineers, he made scores of 204, 153 and 175 and in 1907 for the School of Military Engineering against the Royal Navy and Royal Marines at Chatham he played an innings of 402 not out.

DUCAT, Andrew. The sudden death at Lord's, on July 23, 1942, of Andrew Ducat, Surrey batsman of high talent and effective execution, England international Association footballer, captain of a cup-winning Aston Villa team, and in recent years cricket coach at Eton, came as a shock to countless friends and admirers. A man of delightful disposition, quiet and unassuming, he endeared himself to all who met him and as a reporter of games, after giving up activity in the field, he revealed his character in unbiased, accurate descriptions of matches and criticisms of the high-class players who were his successors. The last time I saw Ducat he sat a few feet from me in the Press box at Lord's. He passed a pleasant remark as he joined his fellow writers and we watched the cricket, intent on the players in the field. Next thing I heard of him, a few days afterwards, was his final and fatal appearance at the crease, where we had seen other cricketers play the game with all the energy of keen sportsmen such as always identified his own efforts.

That Ducat should collapse and die, bat in hand, was the last thing anyone would have expected of such a well-set-up, vigorous, healthy-looking and careful-living man. Evidence of those in the field proved clearly that he expired directly after playing a stroke and as he prepared to receive another ball, for he was dead when carried to the pavilion. The medical report gave the cause of death—failure of a heart that showed signs of definite weakness.

The loss of Ducat in this way may be attributed to the War, but for which there would not have been the Home Guard for him to join. His Surrey Unit were playing their Sussex brothers-in-arms, and Ducat was not out at lunch-time. On resuming, he raised his score from 12 to 29 before the catastrophe occurred.

Class Company

Born on February 16, 1886, at Brixton, in South London. Ducat died at the age of 56, cut off when apparently in the full glow of health. In his youth and subsequently he lived at Southend, and there he played cricket well enough to induce him to become a member of the Oval staff in 1906. Good batting for the Surrey Second XI soon took him to the first-class rank in which he stood out conspicuously from 1909 to 1931. In his first full season he gave proof of his ability by scoring a century at the Oval against Somerset and averaging 27 for an aggregate of 1,080. From that form he never looked back. At a time when Surrey possessed a wealth of attractive fast run-getting batsmen anyone might have failed to shine in the splendour revealed by Tom Hayward, Jack Hobbs, Ernest Hayes, Alan Marshal the Australian giant, and J. N. Crawford; but Ducat bore comparison with all this array of talent. In 1910, a summer of indifferent weather, he played the highest innings for Surrey—153 against Yorkshire at the Oval. He got the runs, in his best display so far, in less than three hours, his driving, pulling, leg-hitting and cutting being brilliant. In 75 minutes he and Hobbs put on 121, and Hitch helped in such a hurricane of hitting that 127 runs came in an hour. That performance, typical of Ducat at his best, was the forerunner of many grand displays. Naturally, and by preference, a forcing batsman, he used his height, 5ft. 10in., in perfect forward strokes which brought the drive into action with a minimum of effort, such was the accuracy in timing of his pendulum swing of the bat propelled by strong arms and shoulders.

Highest Innings

Altogether he put together 52 three-figure innings, all for Surrey, the highest being 306 not out against Oxford University at the Oval in 1919. This really sumptuous display, at the expense of a by no means poor bowling side, was not the only proof that he had not suffered from lack of first-class cricket during the four years of War. In fact, that season he scored 1,695 runs, entirely for Surrey, and his 52.96 placed him sixth in the batting averages for the whole country. Before this happy resumption of cricket, accidents caused serious checks in Ducat's career. An injured knee kept him out of several matches in 1912, and when football began that winter a broken leg incapacitated him completely. It seemed that he might be a permanent cripple, but a silver plate in the shin bone enabled him to recover so thoroughly that the loss of 1913, so far from prejudicing his prospects, preceded a prosperous season, for in 1914 he hit four centuries in Championship matches and with 42 came out second to Hobbs—in superb form—in the Surrey averages. Again

misfortune overtook him when in net practice prior to the start of the 1924 season a ball from Hitch fractured a bone in his arm, and "Mac," as he was called by all his friends, could not play during that summer.

Meanwhile the highest honour of the game rewarded Ducat. For the good reason of his skill and resolution in playing fast bowling and his unfailing courage he was picked for the Leeds Test match against Australia in 1921, when J. M. Gregory and E. A. McDonald struck terror into the hearts of many batsmen. Speed and sure hands in deep fielding also influenced his selection. Honoured with the distinguished place of number four, Ducat still found himself dogged by ill-luck, for, in playing McDonald, the shoulder of his bat was broken and the ball went to the slips, where Gregory held the catch, while the splinter of wood fell on the stumps, shaking off a bail. So Ducat was doubly out. Carter, the Australian wicket-keeper, handed to Ducat the piece of wood —a souvenir which could not compensate the batsman for such an unfortunate dismissal; and he stumped Ducat in the second innings! That was in keeping with the lamentable way in which everything went against England in that series of Tests against W. W. Armstrong's team, the first three wickets falling very cheaply in each of three consecutive defeats which cost England the rubber.

A Great Sequence

When incapacitated in 1924, Ducat became manager of the Fulham football club, and while holding that appointment he was not always available for Surrey, but he invariably resumed full of runs. Sometimes Hobbs was kept idle by strains, and during one such period in 1928 Ducat scored 119 at Old Trafford, 179 not out against Warwickshire at the Oval, 101 not out and 42 at Horsham against Sussex, and 208 off the Essex bowlers in consecutive matches—649 runs for twice out. His chief partners were Sandham, 282 retired ill, who helped to add 299 in three hours and a half against Lancashire, and Shepherd, 145 not out, who hit so finely at Leyton that 317 runs came for the third wicket in two hours and three-quarters. All this happened in 17 days; and with a fifth century, 121 against Somerset, Ducat, although not playing in every engagement, made 994 runs in less than six weeks.

Until the end of the 1930 season, in which he scored 1,593 runs, average 45.51, in Championship matches, and 2,067, average 49.21, in all engagements, with 218 against Nottinghamshire at the Oval, the best of five three-figure innings, Ducat maintained his full value as batsman and fieldsman in the Surrey team; but he fell off next year and, his agreement with Surrey having expired, he was called upon to retire. So he said farewell to first-class cricket, at the age of 44, carrying with him the good will of colleagues and the satisfaction of having gained the highest honours at both cricket and Association football. Altogether in first-class cricket he scored 23,373 runs at an average of 38.31.

At Eton

No wonder that when a vacancy occurred at Eton for a coach that choice should fall upon a professional who himself might have been modelled on the style associated with R. A. H. Mitchell, the Lytteltons, the Studds, and carried on through succeeding generations on Agar's Plough—the forward stroke with the bat kept straight by the left elbow pointing to mid-off. Certainly the controlled off-drive, the square and late cut could be shown by this capable coach for young talent to copy, and the quiet, explanatory manner of Ducat during five years earned popularity which will make his place on the Eton cricket staff difficult to fill. In the Public School section, Mr. C. H. Taylor, master of cricket at Eton, Oxford Blue from 1923 to 1926, who played for Leicestershire, pays a tribute to Andrew Ducat.

Just as at cricket so at football Ducat prospered during a long career which reached its climax in the years immediately following the protracted War break. When with Woolwich Arsenal in the old days at Plumstead he played right-half for England in all three internationals in the spring of 1910, and 10 years later, when he was with Aston Villa, I saw him in two of the most remarkable matches ever played. On the day Wales visited Highbury in March, 1920, pools of water stood on the sodden mud to which the turf was reduced, and the Welshmen literally splashed their way to victory by the odd goal in three. With Arthur Grimsdell on the left and Barson in the centre, Ducat completed a grand half-back line. A month later, on a sea of mud at Hillsborough, Sheffield, England, when apparently losing, fought back so valiantly that they beat Scotland by the odd goal in nine. Games of that kind live in the memory even if, by force of circumstance, they do not provide a display of perfect football. Ducat played his last international in 1921 against Ireland, England winning by two clear goals at Sunderland, and that summer came his England honour at cricket. Yet, of all his distinctions,

Ducat must have prized most that April afternoon in 1920 at Stamford Bridge, when, as captain of Aston Villa, he received the Football Association Cup as reward for a hard-fought victory by the only goal scored over Huddersfield Town. In this way Aston Villa won the Cup for the sixth time, a record which Blackburn Rovers equalled in 1926.

So far as I have seen, no one has mentioned any parallel case to the suddenness of the Ducat tragedy, with death of a first-class cricketer occurring on the field of play, but in 1870, at Lord's, John Platts, the Derbyshire fast bowler, playing for M.C.C. against Nottinghamshire, bowled a ball which caused the death of George Summers. The batsmen received so severe a blow on the head that he died from the effects of the accident a few days afterwards. Pitches at Lord's at that time were notoriously bad, and, as the outcome of this accident, far more attention was paid to the care of the turf. Over the grave of George Summers at Nottingham the M.C.C. erected a memorial tablet "testifying their sense of his qualities as a cricketer and regret at the untimely accident on Lord's ground."

Ducat Hit 52 First-Class Hundreds

1909 (1)
114	v. Somerset, at the Oval.

1910 (1)
153	v. Yorkshire, at the Oval.

1911 (2)
104	v. Gloucestershire, at the Oval.
101*	v. Somerset, at Taunton.

1912 (2)
137	v. Gloucestershire, at the Oval.
124	v. Worcestershire, at the Oval.

1913
Did not play owing to a broken leg.

1914 (4)
118	v. Worcestershire, at the Oval.
108	v. Hampshire, at Portsmouth.
105	v. Nottinghamshire, at Nottingham.
102	v. Middlesex, at the Oval.

1919 (4)
306*	v. Oxford University, at the Oval.
271	v. Hampshire, at Southampton.
190	v. Sussex, at the Oval.
134	v. Middlesex, at the Oval.

1920 (3)

203	v. Sussex, at the Oval.
149	v. Northamptonshire, at Northampton.
104*	v. Warwickshire, at Birmingham.

1921 (5)

290*	v. Essex, at Leyton.
204*	v. Northamptonshire, at Northampton.
134	v. Northamptonshire, at the Oval.
131	v. Warwickshire, at the Oval.
120	v. Warwickshire, at Birmingham.

1922 (1)

| 108* | v. Essex, at the Oval. |

1923 (5)

134	v. Oxford University, at the Oval.
126	v. Glamorgan, at the Oval.
120	v. Sussex, at Hastings.
115	v. Cambridge University, at the Oval.
114	v. Essex, at the Oval.

1924

Did not play owing to a broken arm.

1925 (1)

| 128 | v. Somerset, at the Oval. |

1926 (4)

235	v. Leicestershire, at the Oval.
130*	v. Warwickshire, at Birmingham.
121	v. Essex, at the Oval.
116	v. Lancashire, at Manchester.

1927 (4)

166	v. Warwickshire, at the Oval.
142	v. Gloucestershire, at the Oval.
100	v. New Zealanders, at the Oval.
100	v. Middlesex, at the Oval.

1928 (5)

208	v. Essex, at Leyton.
179*	v. Warwickshire, at the Oval.
121	v. Somerset, at the Oval.
119	v. Lancashire, at Manchester.
101*	v. Sussex, at Horsham.

1929 (4)

171	v. Hampshire, at the Oval.
168*	v. Cambridge University, at the Oval.
134	v. Oxford University, at the Oval.
105	v. Essex, at the Oval.

1930 (5)

218	v. Nottinghamshire, at Nottingham.
125	v. Worcestershire, at the Oval.
104*	v. Warwickshire, at the Oval.

| 102 | v. Yorkshire, at Sheffield. |
| 100* | v. M.C.C., at Lord's |

1931 (1)

| 125 | v. Warwickshire, at the Oval. |

Signifies not out.

DUCK, George Nixon, born at Ridgeway House, Bristol (where "W. G." was educated), on February 9, 1831, died at Wallington, in Surrey, on February 10, 1919. He played in many matches with Dr. H. M. Grace, and later for Yorkshire Gentlemen, Roxburghshire, Yorkshire United, and Redcar and Cotham, of which team he was for some years the captain. He was interested in the game to the last, and for many years had been a Vice-President of the Beddington C.C.

DUCKWORTH, George, who died on January 5, 1966, aged 64, was an outstanding character in first-class cricket in the period between the two World Wars, a time when the game possessed far more players of popular personality than at the present time. Small of stature, but big of heart and voice, Duckworth used an "Owzat" shout of such piercing quality and volume that his appeal alone would have made him a figure to be remembered.

But Duckworth possessed many other qualities. He was one of the finest wicketkeepers the game has produced; as a batsman he could be relied upon to fight in a crisis; he possessed wit and good humour which made him an endearing companion, and he was a sound judge of a player, an ability which served his native Lancashire well as a committee man in recent years.

Duckworth, born and resident in Warrington all his life, joined Lancashire in 1922. He made his debut a year later and ended his first-class career, perhaps prematurely, in 1938. He took up journalism, but hardly had time to establish himself before war broke out in 1939. Then he spent spells in hotel management and farming before his post-War career, which included journalism, broadcasting, and acting as baggage-master and scorer to M.C.C. teams abroad, and for touring countries here. He also took Commonwealth sides to India.

Duckworth received a trial with Warwickshire before arousing the interest of his native county with whom he quickly showed his talent by the confident manner in which he kept to such varied and demanding bowlers as the Australian fast bowler, E. A. McDonald, and the spin of C. H. Parkin and R. Tyldesley. By 1924 he had gained the first of 24 Test caps for England, a total which undoubtedly would have been much higher but for the competition of L. E. G. Ames of Kent, who in the 1930s usually gained preference because of his batting prowess. In his later days with Lancashire, Duckworth also faced strong competition from Farrimond, which he resisted successfully.

In Test cricket, Duckworth claimed 59 wicket-keeping victims, and he also hit 234 runs, with 39 not out as his highest. For Lancashire his number of victims was a record 921, and his highest score 75. In all first-class matches he helped in 1,090 dismissals, 751 catches and 339 stumpings. He dismissed 107 batsmen, 77 caught and 30 stumped, in his best season, 1928.

That season completed three Championship successes for Lancashire, captained by Leonard Green, who described Duckworth as "One of the smallest, but noisiest of all cricketing artists—a man born to squat behind the wicket and provide good humour and unbounded thrills day by day in many a glorious summer."

Lancashire won the Championship again in 1930, and 1934, so that Duckworth gained the honour of being a member of five Championship teams. In 1949–50 Duckworth, a man of administrative ability, took his first Commonwealth team to India, Pakistan and Ceylon, and repeated the successful venture in 1950–51 and 1953–54. Then followed his duties as baggage-master and scorer, at home and abroad, where his jovial personality, wise counsel and experience were of benefit to many a team and individual cricketer. His radio and television commentaries, typically humorous and forthright, became well-known, both on cricket and on Rugby League, in which game he was a devoted follower of Warrington.

Among many tributes were:

H. Sutcliffe (Yorkshire and England): "George was a delightful colleague, a great man on tours particularly. He had a vast knowledge of the game and he was always ready and willing to help any young player. As a wicket-keeper he was brilliant."

C. Washbrook (Lancashire and England): "He was a magnificent wicket-keeper and a fighting little batsman. In his later years he became one of the shrewdest observers of the game and his advice was always available and eagerly sought by cricketers of every class and creed."

DUFF, Reginald Alexander, died in Sydney, December 13, 1911. R. A. Duff had for some time dropped out of first-class cricket in Australia, but in his day he ranked among the best batsmen. Born in New South Wales on August 17, 1878, he ought to have had a longer career. He came to England with the Australian teams of 1902 and 1905, and was highly successful in both tours. In 1902 he scored over 1,500 runs with an average of 28, and in 1905 over 1,400 runs, his average, curiously enough, being the same as before. Thanks largely to an innings of 146 at the Oval, he came out first of the Australian batsmen in the Test matches in 1905, making 335 runs with an average of 41. He was never the same man after his second visit to this country, quickly losing his form. For a few years in Australia he did brilliant things, being scarcely inferior to any batsman in the Commonwealth, except Trumper, Hill, Noble, and, for one season, Mackay. In 1902–03, at Sydney, for New South Wales against South Australia, he and Trumper scored 298 together for the first wicket, and in the same season, on the same ground, they sent up 267 for the first wicket against Victoria. A year later they scored 113 together for the first wicket against Victoria, and in the second innings hit off, without being separated, the 119 runs required to win the match. In the same season of 1903–04, Duff, for New South Wales against South Australia, at Sydney, played an innings of 271, Noble scoring 230. Further back, in 1900–01, when he was becoming famous, Duff contributed 119 to New South Wales's record total of 918 against South Australia, at Sydney, four other batsmen getting over a hundred each. Duff was a very punishing player, with splendid driving power.

DUFF, William Dick, who died at Johannesburg on October 7, 1953, aged 63, was a leg-break and googly bowler who played on occasion for Transvaal between 1919 and 1925. In 1924–25 he represented South Africa in two of the unofficial "Test" matches against the English team captained by the Hon. L. H. Tennyson.

DUFFIELD, John, who died suddenly at Worthing on September 7, 1956, aged 39, played as a fast-medium bowler for Sussex in a few matches between 1938 and 1947. He also represented his county at Association football and later became a professional with Portsmouth F.C.

DUGDALE, John Stratford, K.C., Recorder of Birmingham, died at Barford, Warwickshire, on October 27, 1920, aged 85. He had played for the Free Foresters and Warwickshire.

DUGGAN, Mary Beatrice, who died on March 12, 1973, aged 48, played for Worcestershire, Yorkshire and England, whom she captained for several years. She toured Australia with the England teams of 1948–49 and 1957–58 before being given the captaincy, retiring after ending her career in 1963 with innings of 101 not out and 32 and bowling figures of seven wickets for 72 runs which helped England to victory by 49 runs over Australia at the Oval and so deciding the Test rubber. She bowled fast-medium left-arm. For 10 years before her death she was vice-principal of Dartford (Kent) College of Education. She left £500 to the Women's Cricket Association "to assist in the coaching of young women cricketers."

DULEEPSINHJI, Kumar Shri, who died from a heart attack in Bombay on December 5, 1959, aged 54, was among the best batsmen ever to represent England and certainly one of the most popular. Ill-health limited his first-class career to eight seasons, but in that time he scored 15,537 runs, including 49 centuries, at an average of 50.11. A remarkably good slip fieldsman, he brought off 243 catches. "Duleep" or "Mr. Smith," as he was affectionately known in cricket circles, was in the Cheltenham XI from 1921 to 1923, and when captain in the last year headed the batting figures with an average of 52.36, his highest innings being 162. He also met with considerable success as a leg-break bowler and in 1922 was top of the averages with 50 wickets at 13.66 runs each, but he rarely bowled after leaving school. During this time H. S. Altham, the present President of M.C.C., wrote of him in *Wisden*: "In natural gifts of eye, wrist and footwork he is certainly blest far above the ordinary measure ... there is no doubt about the judgment and certainty with which he takes toll of straight balls of anything but the most immaculate length. His late cutting is quite beautiful and there is a certain ease and maturity about all his batting methods that stamps him as of a different class from the ordinary school batsman." The accuracy of this estimate of his qualities was borne out when in 1925 he went up to Cambridge. He got his Blue as a Freshman, scoring 75 in the University match, and also played against Oxford in 1926 and 1928. Illness kept him out of the side for most of the 1927 season.

His career with the Sussex, whom he captained in 1932, began in 1926 and he headed the county averages in every season until 1932, when doctors advised him not to take further part in cricket. In 1930 he hit 333 in five and a half hours against Northamptonshire at Hove, which still stands as the highest individual innings played for Sussex and beat the biggest put together by his famous uncle, K. S. Ranjitsinhji—285 not out against Somerset at Taunton in 1901; three times he reached three figures in each innings of a match, 246 and 115 v. Kent at Hastings in 1929, 116 and 102 not out v. Middlesex and 125 and 103 not out for Gentlemen v. Players, both at Lord's the next summer; and in 1931 he registered 12 centuries, four of them in successive innings.

He made 12 appearances for England and in his first against Australia at Lord's in 1930 he obtained 173. Of this display a story is told that, when Prince Duleepsinhji was at last caught in the long field from a rash stroke, his uncle remarked: "He always was a careless lad." His one tour abroad was with the M.C.C. team in New Zealand and Australia in 1929–30, when he scored more runs than any other member of the side. A. H. H. Gilligan, the captain, rated him the best player of slow bowling on a wet pitch that he ever saw. "Duleep" had to withdraw from the team for D. R. Jardine's "body-line" tour of 1932–33.

He joined the Indian foreign service in 1949 and became High Commissioner for India in Australia and New Zealand. Upon returning to India in 1953 he was appointed chairman of the public service commission in the State of Saurashtra.

When he retired from cricket through recurring illness, *Wisden* wrote of him: "Of singular charm of character; extremely modest of his own wonderful ability; and with a love for the game which transcended his joy in all other pastimes, Duleepsinhji will always be remembered as one of the outstanding personalities during his period in first-class cricket." So he remained to the end.

Tributes included:

Sir John Hobbs: "He was an extremely popular personality and did not have an enemy on the field. He was a brilliant player."

R. Aird: "He was not only a very great cricketer, but he also possessed a charming and gentle nature which endeared him to all his many friends."

H. Sutcliffe: "There was no better man to play with. He was never out for personal glorification, his great concern being for the success of the team. He was a real joy to watch and was, above all, a first-class man."

DUMINY, Dr. Johannes Petrus, who played in three Tests for South Africa against England between 1927 and 1929, died in hospital in Cape Town on January 31, 1980, aged 82. "J.P.," as he was known, went as a Rhodes Scholar to Oxford in 1921, where he won a Harlequin as a left-handed batsman and a slow right-arm bowler. Scoring 95 not out, 55 and 74 not out for Transvaal against the 1927–28 M.C.C. team, he was chosen for two of the five Test matches of that series, though without success. Having missed selection for the South African tour to England in 1929, he was holidaying in Switzerland when he was sent for to join a team beset with injuries. He played in the third Test at Headingley, scoring two and 12. A distinguished academic, and a man with many friends, he became Vice-Chancellor of the University of Cape Town in 1959. Duminy worked as devotedly as anyone towards the establishment of multi-racial cricket in South Africa.

DUNCAN, D. W. J., died in December, 1919. Though he never took a high position in the cricket world Mr. Duncan was in his day quite a prominent batsman in the Hampshire XI. He was at his best in the seasons of 1876–77, making scores—all against Kent— of 68, 58 and 75. His highest innings for the county, however, was 87 not out against Somerset at Southampton in 1884. Hampshire on that occasion ran up the huge total of 645, Mr. E. O. Powell getting 140 and Mr. F. E. Lacey 100. Born on July 8, 1852, Mr. Duncan was in his 68th year at the time of his death. After he had given up cricket he became a well-known writer on golf.

DUNELL, Owen Robert, born at Port Elizabeth on July 15, 1856, died suddenly at Lyons, France, on October 21, 1929, aged 73. Although useful as a batsman and a good field, he was not in the XI whilst at Eton, nor did he gain his Blue at Oxford. In 1888–89 he appeared for South Africa in what have come to be regarded as the first two Tests with England, at Port Elizabeth and Cape Town. He had been a member of the M.C.C. for 56 seasons—since 1874. Whilst at Oxford, he played full back at Association football against Cambridge in 1877 and 1878, and also represented the University in both singles and doubles at tennis in the latter year.

DUNLOP, C. E., who died in London in the last week of August, 1911, was born on June 25, 1870, and had therefore only recently completed his 41st year. He was educated at Merchiston and Oxford, and played occasionally for Somerset between 1892 and

1902. His most successful season was 1893, when he scored 213 runs with an average of 26, his highest innings being 64 v. Gloucestershire, 62 v. Middlesex—both played at Taunton—and 53 not out v. Kent at Tonbridge. He was an excellent fieldsman.

DUNNING, John Angus, who died suddenly in Adelaide on June 24, 1971, aged 68, played as an off-break bowler in four Test matches for New Zealand against England between 1932 and 1937. He was a member of the Australian Cricket Board of Control. Though given a trial for Oxford in 1928 when a Rhodes scholar, he did not get a Blue.

His wickets in Test cricket were few and costly, but he achieved some note-worthy successes in other first-class games when touring England with M. L. Page's New Zealand team in 1937. He took 10 wickets for 170 runs in the match with Essex; nine for 64 v. Cambridge University and six for 67 v. Middlesex. Additionally, in the first innings of a two-day fixture at Stoke, he dismissed eight Staffordshire batsmen for 26 runs. In the three-day matches on the tour, he took 83 wickets at a cost of 30.10 runs each, sending down more overs than any other of his colleagues. He did good work in Plunket Shield games for Otago.

DURLACHER, Patrick Neville, who died suddenly while fishing in Ireland on February 26, 1971, aged 68, was in the Wellington XI as opening batsman from 1919 to 1921. In 1919 and 1920, he was partner to G. J. Bryan and in the latter year at Haileybury the pair scored 258 in two and a half hours for the first wicket, Bryan making 147 and Durlacher 124. Durlacher did not get a cricket Blue when at Cambridge, but after a successful season for Buckinghamshire in 1920, he turned out in a few matches for Middlesex during the next three years. A versatile athlete, he was first string in the Wellington racquets pair who won the Public Schools Championship in 1921 and he gained a Blue as a cross country runner for Cambridge.

DURSTON, Frederick John, who died in hospital at Southall on April 8, 1965, aged 71, played as   bowler for Middlesex from 1919 to 19   l first-class cricket, he dismissed 1,3⁵   men for 21.94 runs apiece, scored 3,⁵⁵1 runs at an average of 12.16 and held 227 catches. Born at the village of Clophill, Bedfordshire, he learned his cricket with the local club before becoming, like so many illustrious cricketers, a ground-staff boy at Lord's in 1914. Tall and powerfully built, "Jack" Durston showed greater control of length as his career progressed and he took many wickets on the hard pitches at Lord's with a speedy break-back. He helped Middlesex win the County Championship in 1920 and 1921 after service in the Royal Engineers during the First World War.

In 1919, his first year in the county side, his success was limited to five wickets in five matches, and those at 74.20 runs each. Yet in each of the next two seasons his victims exceeded 100. As *Wisden* of the time recorded, "he improved out of knowledge". His performance in taking seven wickets for 84 in the first innings and four for 65 in the second for Middlesex against Warwick Armstrong's Australians in 1921 helped to gain him a place for England in the second Test match at Lord's; but though he disposed of five men in the match for 136, he was never again chosen. Still, he toured the Argentine with Julien Cahn's team in 1929 and again with Sir Theodore Brinckman's side in 1937–38. His best season was that of 1921 when he took 136 wickets, average 19.50, and made his one appearance for the Players against the Gentlemen at Lord's.

Six times he took over 100 wickets in a season and twice he performed the "hat-trick"—against Cambridge University at Fenner's in 1922, when obtaining six wickets for 29, and against Oxford University at Oxford the following season, when his second innings analysis was eight for 27. Of negligible value for a long time, his batting steadily improved. In 1927 he and E. Hendren (201 not out) set up a Middlesex record which still stands, punishing the Essex bowling for 160 in 80 minutes. Durston's highest innings was 92 not out against Northamptonshire at Lord's in 1930 which followed 51 in the first innings.

In his younger days he was a goal-keeper of ability, playing for Brentford F.C.

DURY, Theodore Seton, late Chief Master of the Supreme Court (Taxing Office) died on March 20, 1932, in London. Born on June 12, 1854, he appeared in the Harrow XI against Eton at Lord's in 1870 and six years later played for Oxford against Cambridge. He also represented Oxford in the racquets singles in 1876, and, partnered by Mr. A.J. Webbe, in the doubles in 1875–76. From 1878 to 1881 he played occasionally for Yorkshire. He was a free hitter, an admirable field at either long-leg or cover-point and a medium-pace round-arm bowler. His grandfather, the Rev. Theodore Dury, was in the Harrow team of 1805 that opposed Eton in the first match between those schools.

DUTHIE, Col. Arthur Murray, who died on June 3, 1973, aged 91, did not gain a place in the XI at Marlborough, but he played for Hampshire in 1911.

DUTNALL, Frank, who died on October 24, 1971, aged 76, played occasionally as a professional for Kent in 1919 and 1920. He later met with success in the Lancashire League. His brother, W.M. Dutnall, also appeared for Kent.

DWYER, John Elicius Benedict Bernard Placid Quirk Carrington (always referred to as E.B. Dwyer), died on October 19, 1912, at Crewe, where he had been engaged during the season. He was born on May 3, 1876, at Sydney (N.S.W.), where all his early cricket was played, first with the Redfern Wednesday C.C. and afterwards with Redfern. On P.F. Warner's suggestion he came to England in the spring of 1904, and early that year, whilst engaged temporarily at Lord's, came under the notice of C.B. Fry, who persuaded him to qualify for Sussex. His first match for the county was in 1906 and his last three season later, when, owing to lack of form, he dropped out of the side. In 1906 he took 96 wickets for 26.80 runs each, and in the following year 58 at an average cost of 27.65. Although having good pace, he was an unequal bowler, but deadly on his day. In 1906 he took nine wickets in an innings for 35 runs against Derbyshire, at Brighton, and 16 for 100—the first time for 80 years so many had been obtained by a bowler for Sussex in a match—v. Notts. on the same ground. In 1907, by taking six for 25 against the South Africans, he had a great deal to do with the Colonials being dismissed for 49, their smallest total during their tour. At times he hit hard and well, and at Brighton in 1906 scored 63 out of 82 in 50 minutes against Surrey. Dwyer was a great-grandson of Michael Dwyer, the Wicklow chieftain, who was one of the boldest leaders in the Irish insurrection of 1798. He held out for five years in the Wicklow mountains and was exiled in 1804 to Australia, where he died in 1826.

DYSON, Arnold Herbert, died at Goldsborough in Yorkshire, his native county, on June 7, 1978, after a short illness, aged 72. Playing for Glamorgan from 1927 to 1948, he contributed his full share to raising them from a side normally near the bottom of the table to Champion County in his last year. Few things are more important to a team than a reliable opening pair and this Glamorgan had for the first time in Dyson and Emrys Davies. On 32 occasions they put up more than a 100 for the first wicket and in 1947 actually did so in three consecutive innings. Altogether Dyson scored 17,922 runs with an average of 27.15. He made 24 hundreds, five times carried his bat through a completed innings and in 10 seasons exceeded 1,000 runs. His highest score was 208 v. Surrey at the Oval in 1932. In his young days he was a good outfield and later was outstanding at slip or short leg; moreover he was a shrewd thinker whose advice was often valuable to his captain. He was always immaculately turned out and his batting was as neat and tidy as his appearance. A radically orthodox player, he was a particularly good driver and cutter and was never bothered by pace. Though he was not normally regarded as a quick scorer, he could go fast enough when necessary, In 1937 on the first day of the season he made a hundred before lunch against Kent and in 1947 he and Emrys Davies put on 116 for the first wicket in 47 minutes to beat Sussex. He was an admirable runner between the wickets, quick off the mark and always on the look out for that second run, especially to third man, which so many batsmen miss. Essentially a county player, he made 305 consecutive appearances in the Championship between 1930 and 1947. Later he was for many years coach at Oundle.

EADIE, William Stewart, who was born at Burton-on-Trent on November 2, 1864, died at Barrow Hall, Derby, on September 20, 1914, aged 49. He began to appear for Derbyshire in 1885, but although he continued to play for the county until 1899, claims of business prevented him from assisting the side regularly. It was said of him: "At the nets is one of the finest bats in the county, but does not do himself justice in matches, playing quite a different game." His best feats were to score 62 v. Lancashire at Manchester in 1885, and 51 v. Notts, at Trent Bridge four years later.

EADY, Charles John, died on December 23 1945, in Tasmania, aged 75. Of exceptional build, 6ft. 3in. tall and weighing 15st., he excelled in Tasmanian club cricket, but during his one visit to England in 1896 he failed to reveal his powers either as batsman or bowler. He scored only 10 not out and two at Lord's in the first Test, but showed to advantage with the ball, on that occasion taking four wickets for 69 runs in 32 overs. Ill-health handicapped him and in the whole tour his appearances were limited to 16 matches in which he scored 290 runs, average 13.17, and took 16 wickets at 25.8 runs each. For Tasmania against Victoria at Hobart in January, 1895, he made 116 and 112 not out, but was best known for his 566 scored out of 908 in less than eight hours for Break-o'-Day against Wellington in March, 1902. For Tasmania against Victoria at Melbourne in 1895 he took eight wickets in an innings for 35 runs and all 10 wickets for 42 for South Hobart v. East Hobart in January, 1906.

In *Scores and Biographies* it is related that "When a Wellington bowler was ordered by K. E. Burn, the captain, to send down no-balls to prevent a follow-on, Eady declared the Break-o'Day innings closed—a skilful and legitimate move, but one which, unfortunately, caused the match to come to an abrupt conclusion." A solicitor by profession, Charles Eady was at one time President of the Australian Board of Control, and, like Joseph Darling, who died on January 2, 1946, he was a member of the Tasmanian Legislative Council.

EAGER, Edward Desmond Russell, who died suddenly on holiday in Devon on September 13, 1977, aged 59, will always be remembered for his services to Hampshire cricket. He started as captain and joint-secretary in 1946, and remained captain to the end of 1957 and secretary until his death. A good attacking batsman and a fine field, especially at short leg, he was an inspiring captain and there can be no doubt that the seed sown under him had much to do with the county winning the Championship for the first time in 1961. As secretary he worked tirelessly, even after a serious operation early last summer, and did much to increase the membership and to place the finance on a sound basis.

He was in the Cheltenham XI from 1933 to 1936 and captain of it for two seasons and while there, apart from his batting, met with considerable success as a slow left-hand bowler. From 1935 to 1939 he played a number of times for Gloucestershire. Having gone up to Oxford, he was 12th man at Lord's in 1938 and having made over 600 runs for the University, was distinctly unlucky to miss his Blue. He got it in 1939, when he headed the averages and was clearly the most dangerous, if not the soundest, bat in the side.

In all first-class cricket he scored 12,178

runs with an average of 21.86 and made 10 centuries, the highest being 158 not out for Hampshire v. Oxford University in 1954. In 1958–59 he was Assistant Manager of the M.C.C. side in Australia. A considerable authority on cricket history and bibliography, he wrote much and well for E. W. Swanton's *World of Cricket* and was one of the joint-authors of the official history of Hampshire County Cricket. At Oxford he also had a Blue for hockey and, had the War not intervened, might well have got an international. Later he was hockey correspondent of the *Sunday Telegraph*. His son, Patrick, has made a great reputation as a cricket photographer.

EALES, Cyril C., who died at Northampton on August 16, 1926, aged 57, was a fast right-handed bowler and a hard-hitting batsman: also a very good field at point. Although a member of the Surrey County C.C. ground-staff at the Oval in 1888, he played his County Cricket for Northamptonshire.

EARLE, Guy Fife, who died at his home at Maperton, Wincanton, on December 30, 1966, aged 75, was a batsman who, while by no means a stylist, used his considerable physique to hit the ball tremendously hard. From 1908 to 1911 he was in the Harrow XI chiefly as a fast bowler, and he captained the school in the famous "Fowler's Match" of 1910 when Eton, only four runs ahead with nine wickets down, won by nine runs. He played two games for Surrey in 1911, but did not reappear in first-class cricket till turning out in 1922 for Somerset, with whom he stayed till 1931. In all first-class games he hit 6,303 runs, average 20.59 and took 109 wickets for 30.11 runs each. His highest innings for Somerset was 111 against Gloucestershire at Bristol in 1923; his biggest in first-class cricket was 130 for A. E. R. Gilligan's M.C.C. team against Hindus at Bombay in 1926, when he displayed his punishing powers to the full by hitting eight sixes and 11 fours. He and M. W. Tate (50) put on 164 in 65 minutes. Earle was also a member of the first M.C.C. team which met New Zealand in official Tests in 1929–30 under the captaincy of A. H. H. Gilligan. His highest score on that tour was 98 in 40 minutes, including three sixes and 11 fours against Taranaki. On the way to New Zealand he punished Clarrie Grimmett for 22 in an over, including three sixes when M.C.C. met South Australia at Adelaide. Earle struck 59 in 15 minutes against Gloucestershire at Taunton in 1929.

EASBY, John William, who died at Dover on February 8, 1915, was born at Appleton-upon-Wiske, Yorkshire, on August 12, 1867. He learned his cricket under Major L. A. Hamilton in the King's Own York and Lancaster Regiment, and gave such promise that he was persuaded to leave the Army and accept the position of groundsman to the St. Lawrence C.C., of Canterbury, so as to qualify for Kent. This he did, and the very first time he played on the famous ground he scored 172 not out against Chatham House. That was on June 27, 1892, and six weeks later he made 202 (retired), again for St. Lawrence, v. Holborn. In the following season he punished the South Hampstead bowling for 213. It cannot be said that he accomplished all that was expected of him in County Cricket, for in the 62 games wherein he played for Kent between 1894 and 1899 he scored only 1,851 runs with an average of 18.32, his highest innings being 73 not out v. Philadelphians at Maidstone in 1897, and 73 v. Middlesex at Tonbridge in 1895. He had sound defence and many strokes, was a fine field, and could keep wicket well.

EAST, William, born at Northampton on August 29, 1876, died at his native place on December 19, 1926, aged 50. A good bat and a capital medium-paced right-handed bowler, he did much excellent work for his county in both its second-class and first-class days. He took his place in the side at the age of 19 and kept it for over 20 years, his retirement then being caused by broken health. Owing largely to his efforts and Thompson's, Northamptonshire gained admission to the first-class rank. In Minor Counties cricket East had a bowling average of 15.35 for 426 wickets and a batting average of 26.59 for 2,789 runs. In first-class games his figures were 493 wickets (average 20.77) and 3,913 runs (average 17.31). Against Lancashire at Northampton, in 1911, he had an analysis of seven for 11.

EASTMAN, Lawrence C., the Essex all-rounder, who was born at Enfield, died in Harefield Sanatorium on April 17, 1941, following an operation, at the age of 43. His end was hastened through a high-explosive bomb bursting close to him while he was performing his duties as an A.R.P. warden. This caused him severe shock.

For many years Eastman did not enjoy the best of health, otherwise there can be no doubt he would have been seen to much greater advantage on the cricket field. He intended to take up medicine as a profession, but the Great War, in which he won the D.C.M. and M.M., forced him to give up the idea, and he became interested in cricket. Those great Essex stalwarts, J. W. H. T. Douglas, Percy Perrin, Charles McGahey, A. C. Russell and Bob Carpenter, helped in his development. Eastman began playing for the county as an amateur and, in his first match, against Gloucestershire at Bristol in 1920, he took three wickets in four balls. Next he appeared at Lord's, and going in number 10 when Russell had hit 100, he scored 91, the pair adding 175 before stumps were drawn for the day. In 1922 Eastman was appointed Assistant-Secretary at Leyton and became a regular member of the county team. He gave up the position in 1926 and turned professional.

Standing 6ft. he was a natural hitter and proved most successful when opening the innings. Indeed, in 1925 against Lancashire at Leyton, he and Cutmore made opening stands of 115 and 172. Eastman never hesitated to use the straight drive, which, beautifully executed, often earned him six, and he also hooked well. In his early days he bowled medium pace, but served Essex best when he changed to spin; he could turn the ball each way and was particularly deadly with the leg-break. He naively remarked that he gained more pleasure from slow bowling and delighted in pitting his brains against batsmen with flight and spin instead of relying solely on pace and swerve. Against Somerset at Weston-super-Mare in 1934 his first-innings analysis was four wickets for no runs, when he dismissed A. W. Wellard, R. A. Ingle, G. M. Bennett and H. L. Hazell in 13 deliveries and ended the innings.

Altogether in first-class cricket Eastman scored 12,481 runs and took 967 wickets. His highest score was 161 at Derby in 1929, but he considered his best performance was against Sussex at Leyton in 1922, when, besides taking 12 wickets for 82 runs, he went in last but one and made 37 not out.

Eastman used to say that he had batted in every position except number 11; but curiously enough, in his benefit match with Middlesex at Southend in 1939, which realised £1,200, he was lamed by water on the knee and so compelled to go in last; otherwise Essex might have won instead of losing by five runs.

He paid three visits as coach to New Zealand, besides rendering similar service at Kimberley, South Africa, and in 1937 he was a member of the team which toured the Argentine. When war broke out, Eastman helped London Counties, and was particularly proud of being captain when the side first appeared at Lord's.

EASTWOOD, David, a well known cricketer of a previous generation, passed away on May 17, 1903, at Huddersfield, in his 56th year. He was born at Lascelles Hall on March 30, 1848, and made his first appearance for Yorkshire in 1870. Considering how useful an all-round player he was, it is surprising that he did not participate more in County Cricket, for he assisted his county on but 29 occasions despite the fact that he played successfully in several North v. South matches. The best innings of his career was his 68 against Middlesex in 1877, which was the chief cause of the success of his side by 35 runs. As a bowler he was frequently utilised, and his most successful performance with the ball was accomplished in the North v. South match at Prince's in 1877, when, going on first with Morley, he obtained six wickets for 69 runs in the South's innings of 459 (W. G. Grace, 261). In a minor match in 1874—when playing for Durham County against Yorkshire United—he obtained four wickets in four balls. In 1877 Eastwood assisted the Players against the Gentlemen at Prince's, this being his only appearance in the classic match.

EATON, Jack, who died on December 31, 1972, aged 68, played for Sussex from 1926 to 1946. A useful wicket-keeper, he would have played more for the county but for the excellent form of W. ("Tich") Cornford. As it was, Eaton's appearances in the first team were strictly limited, he being called upon only when Cornford was unable to play or in first-class friendly matches. Even so, he was awarded his county cap in the mid-1930s. He helped in the dismissal of 76 batsmen, 49 caught and 27 stumped. Towards the end of his career with Sussex he served as county coach for one year. In 1954 he was elected as honorary life member of the County Club.

EBDEN, Charles Hotson Murray, died at Elvanfoot, Lanark, on May 24, 1949, aged 68. Cambridge Blue 1902–03. Played a little for Sussex and Middlesex. Member of Lord Brackley's team in West Indies 1905. Cambridge hockey XI 1901–03 and England XI 1903. Served in the First World War 1914–18, Lieutenant R.N.V.R.

EBELING, Hans Irving, M.B.E., who died on January 12, 1980, aged 75, was a member of the 1934 Australian side in England and was later prominent in administration. It was he who conceived the idea of the 1977

Centenary Test and who, by his persistence, got it carried out. Though he had a long career for Victoria and captained them when they won the Sheffield Shield twice in four years, he lost four seasons to the claims of work in his early days: otherwise he might have gone further than he did. No less a judge than Jack Hobbs thought highly of his bowling and was surprised that he was ever omitted from a representative side. A tall man, he bowled medium-pace with a sharp in-swing, but he could also make the ball run away. Moreover, he was a useful attacking bat and a particularly good driver and hooker. He owed his selection in 1934 largely to a good performance against Jardine's side in 1933, when his three wickets, which included those of Sutcliffe and Wyatt, combined with an innings of 68 not out, had much to do with Victoria tying the match. In England he was a distinct success: in a side which relied heavily on spin he took 62 wickets with an average of 20.80, and in the final Test at the Oval, the sole Test appearance of his career, took three wickets, including Hammond, and in an admirable second innings of 41 put on 56 in 40 minutes with O'Reilly for the last wicket. At the time of his death he was President of the Melbourne C.C.

EBERLE, Victor Fuller, who died in Bristol, in 1974, aged about 90, claimed fame as the man who in 1899 dropped A. E. J. Collins when he had scored 20. It was in the House match at Clifton College in which Collins went on to score 628 not out!

ECCLES, Alexander, born at Preston on March 16, 1876, died suddenly at Bilsborough Hall, near Preston (Lancs.), while ploughing on March 18, 1919. He was in the Repton XI in 1893–94–95, being captain the last two years, and appeared for Oxford v. Cambridge in 1897–98–99, playing an innings of 109 in 1898. Playing for Lancashire between 1898 and 1907, he scored 3,771 runs with an average of 24.25, and occasionally captained the side. Good bat as he was, Mr. Eccles never quite fulfilled the hopes at one time entertained of him. His 109 against Cambridge was such a splendid display that it suggested great things.

ECCLES, Joseph, died on September 2, 1933, aged 70, at Barton near Preston in Lancashire. Born at Accrington on April 13, 1863, he played for the county from 1886 to 1889. In 1887 he scored 677 runs in all matches with an average of 33, his best score

being 113 at Cheltenham. In the following season, when he made 184 against Surrey at the Oval and 97 against Middlesex at Lord's, he headed the Lancashire averages with 27 for an aggregate of 525 runs. He was in the Gentlemen's XI which won at Lord's by five runs, the last four Players—Attewell, Peel, Lohmann and Flowers—falling at one total to C. Aubrey Smith and S. M. J. Woods.

ECKERSLEY, Lieut. Peter Thorp R.N.V.R., M.P., died on August 13, 1940, at the age of 36 as the outcome of an accident when flying. Known as the "cricketer-airman," he often flew his own plane to matches. In 1928, when prospective candidate for the Newton division of Lancashire, he announced the compulsion of deciding between politics and cricket and that he chose cricket. Experience at Rugby and Cambridge University, where he did not get his Blue, equipped Eckersley so well in batting and fielding that after one season in the XI he was appointed captain of the Lancashire County Club when only 24. This difficult position, with little amateur companionship, he held with honour for six years and led his side to the Championship in 1934.

In the seasons 1923 to 1936 Eckersley often played well when his side were badly placed, and he scored 5,730 runs, including a very good century against Gloucestershire at Bristol. A first-rate fieldsman, he set his team a splendid example, notably at times when some slackness was apparent. Still, he retained a liking for politics and, reversing his previous decision, he contested the Leigh division in 1931 before he achieved his ambition by becoming Unionist Member of Parliament for the Exchange Division of Manchester in 1935. He consequently resigned the captaincy of Lancashire, but his restless nature, known so well to intimate friends, influenced him to join the Air Arm of the R.N.V.R. when war broke out. Despite indifferent health he was always keen for duty until his strength became overtaxed.

ECKHOFF, A. D., who died at Wellington, New Zealand, on April 1, 1949, aged 73, played in 14 matches for Otago between 1899 and 1915. He appeared against Lord Hawke's touring team of 1902–03 and the M.C.C. side of 1906–07.

EDE, Edward Lee, died suddenly at Southampton on July 7, 1908. He was educated at Eton but, although a good all-round cricketer, did not obtain a place in the XI. A batsman of considerable skill, he also kept wicket and bowled lobs with success on many occasions; he learnt to bowl through watching old Clarke coaching the boys at Eton. His chief scores in matches of note were—all for the Gentlemen of Hampshire against the Gentlemen of Sussex—95 at Brighton in 1863, 73 at Southampton in 1864, and 66 at Brighton in 1865. In 1864, as he was fond of recalling, he was one of the XIV of Hampshire who, at the Oval, gained the only victory obtained over Surrey that season. He had a considerable share in the success as, in addition to scoring 25, he took six wickets for 60 runs in an innings of 233, dismissing Tom Humphrey, E.W. Tritton, Caesar, Edward Dowson, Lockyer and Tom Sewell, junr. Mr. Ede was closely associated with Hampshire cricket all his life, and to the day of his death took the keenest interest in the fortunes of the county. For many years he was editor of the *Hampshire County Cricket Guide*, and for almost a quarter of a century, commencing in 1882, was hon. scorer to the county team. He was born at Southampton on February 22, 1834, and at one time was prominently identified with the turf, having several horses in training. His twin brother, Mr. G.M. Ede, was a very well-known gentleman jockey: he won the Grand National on The Lamb for Earl Poulett in 1868, and was killed two years later when riding Chippenham for the same owner in the Sefton Steeplechase at Liverpool.

EDEN, Ebenezer Zachariah, who died at Westcliff-on-Sea, Essex, on September 15, 1975, aged 72, spent a life-time as a sports journalist. Eb Eden joined the now defunct *Cricket Reporting Agency* in 1922 when one of his first tasks was to take down on the typewriter the Notes by the Editor, dictated by the famous Sydney Pardon. His connection with the compilation of *Wisden*, including the Obituary section in latter years, continued until November, 1974, when he was stricken by illness and defective eyesight. A born humorist, Eden was a splendid colleague to work with and a true craftsman. He travelled the British Isles covering Rugby Union football for the Press Association and besides writing under his own name he also used the pen-names Peter Jardine and E. Adams Holme whom he portrayed as a crusty old down-to-earth critic of cricket matters. Eden was also responsible for forming the Ludgate Ramblers C.C. which between the Wars had regular Sunday fixtures.—N.P.

EDGSON, Charles Leslie, died suddenly in

hospital on June 28, 1983, aged 67. A heavy scorer at Stamford School, he played occasionally for Leicestershire from 1933 to 1939 and against Derbyshire at Chesterfield in 1934, when only 19, played two invaluable innings of 49 and 43. Going up to Oxford he made 57 in the Freshmen's match in 1936, but did not get a trial for the University. Altogether for Leicestershire he scored 321 runs with an average of 13.38. Later he was for years a master at Brentwood School, where he was in charge of the cricket.

EDRICH, Arthur, who died at Reymerston, Norfolk, early in February, 1979, aged 84, was a member of the famous cricket family and had himself played for Norfolk.

EDRICH, William, who died at his home in Salham, Norfolk, on November 16, 1979, at the age of 89, was the father of Bill (Middlesex and England), Geoffrey (Lancashire), Eric (Lancashire) and Brian (Kent). John Edrich (Surrey and England) is the son of William's brother, Fred. William himself was a keen Norfolk club cricketer, who kept wicket and scored his first hundred when he was 40.

H.M. KING EDWARD VII died at Buckingham Palace on May 6, 1910. As a small boy he received tuition at Windsor from F. Bell, of Cambridge, but it cannot be said that he ever showed much aptitude for the game. He played occasionally during his Oxford days, however, and, while he was staying at Madingley Hall, a special wicket was reserved for his use at Fenner's. He showed his interest in the game in many ways. When funds were being collected to pay off the pavilion debt at Fenner's, he contributed £10, at the same time promising to make up any amount required at the end of the term, and during one of the critical moments in the history of the M.C.C. was the largest contributor to the fund raised to pay for the freehold of Lord's. Furthermore, as Duke of Cornwall his late Majesty was for many years landlord of the Oval, and in several ways he showed his interest in the Surrey County C.C. His Majesty was born at Buckingham Palace on November 9, 1841, and was therefore in his 69th year at the time of his death.

EDWARDS, Col. Charles William, D.S.O., late R.A.S.C., died on May 22, 1938, aged 54. He played occasionally for Gloucestershire in 1911 and 1912, his best score being 42.

EDWARDS, Frank, who died suddenly on

July 10, 1970, aged 85, rendered splendid service to Buckinghamshire as a professional left-arm bowler and useful batsman, between 1921 and 1945. He helped them to carry off the Minor Counties' Championship on five occasions. Altogether he took 1,082 wickets for the county at a cost of 10.91 runs each—104 of them in 10 matches in 1923 at an average of 9.99. Originally a bowler above medium pace, he turned to spin with such success that, as Sir Pelham Warner wrote in 1924, he was regarded by many as the best slow left-hander in the country. Chosen for Players against Gentlemen at the Oval on one occasion, he represented the Minor Counties against Australia, South Africa and the West Indies, and at Lord's in 1933 he took eight West Indies wickets for 98 runs. For Slough, he three times dismissed all 10 batsmen in an innings—the last being when, at the age of 63, his analysis against the Royal Navy at Devonport was 10 wickets for 15 runs in 16 overs. While professional for Haslingden in the Lancashire League from 1925 to 1929, in each of four seasons he obtained over 100 wickets. From 1906 to 1911 he was on the Surrey staff, his services, and those of several other players, being dispensed with when Surrey encountered financial problems. Edwards was a popular coach at Eton, Uppingham and for 16 years at Millfield.

EDWARDS, H. I. P., who died on September 24, 1946, did not get into the Winchester XI, but was good enough a batsman to play for Sussex against Kent at Canterbury in 1908.

EDWARDS, John Dunlop, a member of the Australian team of 1888, died on July 31, 1911, through a complication of ailments. He was born in Melbourne on June 12, 1861, and was educated at Wesley College, where the fine form he showed gained him a card of honorary membership for two years of the Melbourne C.C. For several years he was chosen to represent Victoria against New South Wales, but after his removal to Sandhurst (in 1885) he could seldom obtain the necessary leave of absence. For the Sandhurst C.C. during the 1884–85, 1885–86 and 1886–87 seasons he averaged 53, 101—for 22 innings, 10 of which were not out—and 95 respectively. In 1887–88, too, he was again well to the fore, and in each of the last two innings he played for Sandhurst before leaving Australia he was not out, with 254 against North Bendigo and 104 v. Castlemaine. An injury to his hand compelled him to retire in

the first match of the Australian tour in England, and his first appearance was at Sheffield, where he showed good steady cricket for 24 against Yorkshire. Though there was nothing brilliant about his batting, he was often of great use to the team. He had good defence as well as hitting powers, and was when set a very difficult wicket to get. In all first-class matches during his career he scored 1,005 runs with an average of 14.35, his highest innings being 65 for Victoria against Shaw's team at Melbourne, in December, 1881.

EDWARDS, Major Reginald Owen, born on October 17, 1881, died at Bishop's Stortford, on November 16, 1925. A great cricket enthusiast Major Edwards went to big matches in any part of the country whenever possible, and had a large circle of intimate friends among county cricketers. A Yorkshireman, he supported the Champions zealously without undue prejudice; his chief interests for many years were largely in the South. He played occasionally for Norfolk and Cambridgeshire, and in 1921 for Rest of England v. Royal Air Force at Eastbourne. He played for the M.C.C. in Germany in 1922; for Incogniti in Holland, and often captained Surrey Club and Ground in recent seasons. He spent a considerable time in Africa, and years ago found solace during solitary days up country reading *Wisden* to which he frequently contributed. During the War he was gassed badly, and in a later expedition to Southern Russia he lost all his baggage except his set of *Wisden*, which accompanied him on all his travels. Major Edwards never tired of retailing stories of first-class cricketers.

EDWARDS, 2nd Lieut. Wm. Armine (Yeomanry), died of wounds, November 1, 1916, aged 25. Swansea C.C. and Glamorgan County XI.

EGGAR, John Drennan, who died aged 66 on May 3, 1983, while playing lawn tennis, was three years in the Winchester XI and captain in 1935, but neither then, nor in his first two years at Oxford, did he do anything outstanding, though his friends knew him to be a good player. However, in 1938 he followed a hundred in the Seniors' match with 51 not out early in May out of a total of 117 against the Australians. As he had Schools that summer, he could not play again for the University until the match against Lancashire in the Parks six weeks later, when an innings of 125 made it clear that he must be in the side, even though it meant relegating to 12th man E. D. R. Eagar, who had a good record. At Lord's Eggar, who had meanwhile made 98 against Sussex, justified his selection: a stubborn second innings of 29 ensured that Oxford saved a match that they could easily have lost. Later that summer he appeared twice for Hampshire, but after the War, being a master at Repton, he played for Derbyshire in the summer holidays, regularly until 1950 and occasionally until 1954. His record of 1,385 runs with an average of 31.48 shows how valuable he was. In 1947 he and C. S. Elliott put on 349 for the second wicket against Nottinghamshire at Trent Bridge, still the highest partnership ever made for the county. He was essentially a sound player, whose bat in defence could look unnaturally broad, but he did not lack strokes, and, though the highest of his three centuries for the county, 219 against Yorkshire at Bradford in 1949, took over seven hours, it included 27 fours. On that occasion he was battling in vain to save his side from defeat. Well-taught at Winchester by H. S. Altham and E. R. Wilson, he was himself a successful coach at Repton. Later he was for 16 years headmaster of Shiplake College, where he was greatly respected and achieved a considerable success, more than trebling the numbers of what, when he went there, was a school with an uncertain future.

EGLINGTON, Richard, died in hospital at Winchester on March 20, 1979, aged 70. Captain of Sherborne in 1926 and 1927, he headed the batting averages in both years with averages of over 50. He did not get a Blue at Oxford, but in 1938 and 1939 he captained Surrey Second XI, and in 1938 appeared twice for the county.

ELAM, Fred W., who died on March 19, 1943, aged 71, scored 28 when playing once for Yorkshire in 1900. He appeared a few times in the next two seasons, while during the last War he showed his batting skill when making 86 for the county against an England XI—the first match of the Bradford holiday week in August, 1918; he and Percy Holmes opened for Yorkshire with a stand of 107. He was then captain of the Leeds club.

ELERS, Major Charles George Carew, born at Lyme Regis on January 2, 1868, died at Torpoint, Cornwall, on December 11, 1927. An excellent wicket-keeper and a good batsman, with strong driving power, he played for both Devon and Glamorgan. For the latter county against Carmarthenshire at Swansea in 1910 he made a score of 151.

ELFORD, Lionel H., a well-known umpire in the Hastings district of Sussex, was killed on August 17, 1904, through being thrown out of a brake (the horse, frightened by a traction-engine, having bolted) near Cranbrook, in Kent, whilst on tour with the Hastings Rovers. He was in his 65th year.

ELIGON, Donald, died at Port of Spain, Trinidad, on June 4, 1937, aged 28. After playing for Shannon C.C. he joined the Trinidad inter-colonial team in 1934 and quickly became one of the outstanding bowlers in West Indies. Last season he took seven wickets for 63 runs in the second innings against British Guiana, and five for 39 against Grenada. His death was due to blood poisoning caused by a nail in his cricket boot.

ELLIOTT, George Frederick, who was born at Farnham on May 1, 1850, died at his native place on April 23, 1913. He was a sound batsman, a useful change bowler, and in the field was generally mid-off or cover point. In 1874 he played twice for Kent, but in the following year began to assist Surrey. Against Notts, at Trent Bridge, in 1876, he played a very patient innings: at one period he was in 55 minutes for two runs, and he took 85 minutes to increase his score from 12 to 16.

ELLIOTT, Harry, who died at Derby on February 4, 1976, aged 84, was born at Scarcliffe on November 2, 1891. It was whilst he was with Sir Joseph Laycock, at Wiseton Hall in Nottinghamshire that Sir Archibald White, formerly captain of Yorkshire, recommended him to Derbyshire, and he first played and kept wicket in 1920 against Essex. Immediately he made his place secure, displacing George Beet, but his early promise as a batsman never matured, though he was an excellent man in a crisis. He appeared in 194 consecutive Derbyshire matches up to 1928, when the Test match against West Indies broke the sequence; subsequently he made 232 consecutive appearances up to 1937 when injury intervened.

Chosen to tour South Africa with M.C.C. under G. R. Jackson in 1927–28, when the latter had to withdraw and was replaced by R. T. Stanyforth (himself a wicket-keeper), Elliott's chances were greatly reduced, though in the final Test at Durban he allowed only four byes in an aggregate of 401. He also toured India under D. R. Jardine in 1933–34, playing in two Tests, when he caught six and stumped three.

Elliott played in 532 first-class matches,

764 innings, 220 not out, 7,578 runs, 13.93 average; 904 catches, 302 stumpings. His total of 1,206 dismissals had, at that time, been exceeded by only four other 'keepers. He holds several Derbyshire wicket-keeping records—most dismissals (a) in a season—90, (b) in a match—10, (c) in an innings—6 (three times); most stumpings in a season—30. He led the side on a number of occasions, the most notable being at Loughborough in 1933 when he made his best score of 94, sharing a stand of 222 with L. F. Townsend to set up a new record for the third wicket, and allowed no byes in the match, which was won by an innings. In 1935 he allowed no byes in 25 completed innings.

In 1946 he became an umpire but retired when he was appointed coach for 1947, re-appearing to keep wicket in four matches at the age of almost 56, though it was not until 1967, at the reunion of the Championship winning side of 1936, that he disclosed that he had been born in 1891. He returned to the umpires' list in 1952 and continued until 1960. He was the uncle of C. S. Elliott.

ELLIOTT, Herbert Denis Edleston, who died on April 26, 1973, aged 86, was educated at Newport School, Salop, and in 1913 appeared for Essex.

ELLIS, John Leslie, who died on July 28, 1974, aged 83, was one of those unfortunate cricketers destined to live under the shadow of the famous. He never played for his country because he had a contemporary in Bert Oldfield, who kept wicket for Australia from 1920 to 1936. Ellis made one tour to England with H. L. Collins' 1926 side and distinguished himself with 21 catches and 23 stumpings, but Oldfield played in all five Tests. His career with Victoria stretched from 1918 to 1931 when he gave way to Ben Barnett. In one of his 48 Shield games, Ellis, batting number 10, scored 63 against New South Wales in 1926–27 and took the side past the thousand and on their way to 1107, still the highest total in first-class cricket. Ellis certainly was no mean batsman; he once hit a century against South Australia. His final recognition came in 1935 when at the age of 44 he went to India with a veteran Australian team led by Jack Ryder.

ELLIS, Reginald Newnham, who died in Melbourne on May 26, 1959, aged 68, played in six Sheffield Shield matches for Victoria between 1928 and 1930. In his second game he hit 107 not out against Queensland. As a young man he played with Victor Trumper

for Gordon C.C., Sydney. He also represented Victoria at bowls.

ELMHIRST, The Rev. J., who died in November, 1893, was at one time considered one of the best amateur wicket-keepers in England. He was associated with Leicestershire cricket from 1842 to about 1860, when the then county ground was sold for building purposes. When the Leicestershire County Club was re-established in 1876 his cricket days were over. He was born at Bag Enderby, in Leicestershire, on November 26, 1811, and appeared first at Lord's in July, 1844, for the North, with Alfred Mynn, against the M.C.C. and Ground with Fuller Pilch. It was a close match of small scores, the M.C.C. winning by 13 runs. Mr. Elmhirst scored 16 and eight. He took part in the Gentlemen and Players match in 1848, but according to *Scores and Biographies*, he was rarely seen at Lord's except in that year. He was in the Cambridge XI in 1834.

ELTHAM, Lieut. Keith (Australian Expeditionary Force), born at Hobart, October 10, 1886, killed December 31, 1916. Representative Tasmanian player. Scored 78 v. New South Wales, at Sydney, 1910–11; 58 v. Victoria, at Melbourne, 1912–13; 51 v. South Africans, at Hobart, 1910–11. Played in district cricket for Wellington and (later) West Hobart, scoring 2,589 runs with an average of 33.62, his highest innings being 146 for West Hobart v. New Town, in 1905–06. A useful bowler.

ELWORTHY, Frank William, who died in Johannesburg on March 15, 1978, at the age of 84, was one of the dwindling band who played first-class cricket in South Africa before the First World War. He made his debut for Transvaal in 1912–13 at the age of 19 and was a fairly regular member of the team until 1921–22, making one final appearance eight years later in 1929–30. A googly bowler, he was good enough to be selected for one of the unofficial Tests against the Australian Imperial Forces XI in 1919–20.

EMERY, Raymond William George, who died in Auckland on December 18, 1982, aged 67, played twice for New Zealand as a right-hand opening bat in their inaugural series against West Indies, in 1951–52. He was already 36 when he did so, though it was during his best season (433 runs at 72.16 for Canterbury in the Plunket Shield). He also bowled, at medium pace, and in a West Indian total of 546 for six in the second Test at Auckland took the wickets of Worrell and Walcott. In all first-class cricket he scored 1,177 runs (average 29.42), including three centuries, and took 22 wickets at 34.27 apiece.

EMMETT, George M., died on December 18, 1976, aged 61. Born in India, he started his career on the ground staff at Lord's and then, after several successful seasons for Devon, began to qualify for Gloucestershire in 1936. The soundness of his method at once made it clear that he had great possibilities, but it was not until 1947 that he really fulfilled expectations. From then until 1959 he was one of the mainstays of the side, which he captained from 1955 to 1958. In all he made for Gloucestershire 22,806 runs with an average of 31 and scored 34 hundreds. A fine player on a turning wicket, he could also hit the ball astonishingly hard for so small a man and was always prepared to adapt his game to the needs of the side. In 1954 against Somerset at Taunton he scored the fastest century of the season, reaching his hundred in 84 minutes. Highly though he was rated for years, he played only once for England, against Australia at Old Trafford in 1948, when Lindwall's pace was too much for him. After his retirement from the Gloucestershire side he served the county further as groundsman and coach.
CORRECTION. Mrs. J. McMurray, sister of the late George Emmett whose obituary appeared on page 1039 in the 1977 *Wisden*, points out that on his retirement as coach to Gloucestershire County C.C. he was appointed General Secretary of the Imperial Athletic Club in Bristol, and that never at any time was he a groundsman.

EMMETT, Tom, died suddenly on June 30, 1904, in his 63rd year. He had long ago dropped out of the public gaze, his connection with the Yorkshire XI ending in 1888, but he had assuredly not been forgotten. There was never a more popular professional, his cheery nature, and the inexhaustible energy with which he played the game, making him a prime favourite wherever he went. His closing days were, unhappily, rather clouded, but on this point there is no need to dwell. He was, perhaps, the only instance of a great fast bowler who was skilful enough to remain effective after he had lost his pace.

Those who only saw him bowl in the latter part of his career, when his main object was to get chances on the off side, can have no idea of what he was like when he first won fame on the cricket field. His speed for five or six years was tremendous, and every now and then he would send down an unplayable ball that pitched on the leg stump and broke back nearly the width of the wicket. Born in September, 1841, he was rather late in coming forward, being a man of nearly 25 when he first found a place in the Yorkshire team. Once discovered, however, he jumped almost immediately to the top of the tree, playing for England against Surrey and Sussex in Tom Lockyer's benefit match at the Oval, in 1867—his second season. A still greater bowler—the late George Freeman—was getting to his best at the same time, and from 1867 to 1871 inclusive, the two men did wonderful things together. How they would have fared on the more carefully prepared wickets of these days is a question difficult to answer. The important point is that under the conditions prevailing in their own time they were irresistible. It is quite safe to say that a more deadly pair of purely fast bowlers never played on the same side. After 1871 business took Freeman away from first-class cricket, but Emmett found another excellent colleague in Allen Hill, and in later years he shared Yorkshire's bowling with Ulyett, Bates, Peate, and Peel. As time went on his pace left him, and he became the clever, dodgy bowler—full of devices and untiring in effort—whom men still young well remember. The charm of Emmett as a cricketer lay in his keen and obvious enjoyment of the game. No day was too long for him, and up to the end he played with the eagerness of a schoolboy. He was full of humour, and numberless good stories are told about him. He went to Australia three times, and was the mainstay in bowling for Lord Harris's team in 1878–79. During the first of his three visits he took part at Melbourne, in March, 1877, in the first match in which the Australians ever met an English XI on even terms. Charles Bannerman scored 165, and the Australians won by 45 runs. No one in this country had any idea in those days of what Australian cricket would become, but Emmett, on his return home, spoke very highly of the Colonial bowling.

Some of Emmett's Most Notable Bowling Feats Were:

Wkts.		Runs					
6	for	7	Yorkshire v. Surrey, at Sheffield..	..	..	..	1867
8	,,	22					
6	,,	13	Yorkshire v. Lancashire, at Holbeck	..	..	..	1868

9	,,	34	Yorkshire v. Notts., at Dewsbury	1868
7	,,	15 ⎫	Yorkshire v. Cambridgeshire, at Hunslet	1869
9	,,	23 ⎭		
8	,,	31	Yorkshire v. Notts., at Sheffield	1871
4	,,	8	North v. South, at Huddersfield	1875
8	,,	54	North v. South, at Hull	1875
6	,,	14 ⎫	England v. XXII of South Australia, at Adelaide . .	1876–77
6	,,	11 ⎭		
8	,,	46	Yorkshire v. Gloucestershire, at Clifton . .	1877
8	,,	16	Yorkshire v. M.C.C. and Ground, at Scarboro' . .	1877
5	,,	3 ⎫	Yorkshire v. Gents' of Scotland, at Edinboro'	1878
8	,,	24 ⎭		
6	,,	12	Yorkshire v. Derbyshire, at Sheffield	1878
7	,,	9	Yorkshire v. Sussex, at Brighton	1878
8	,,	51	England v. Gloucestershire, at the Oval	1878
9	,,	45	England v. XVIII of South Australia, at Adelaide . .	1878–79
8	,,	47 ⎫	England v. New South Wales, at Sydney	1878–79
6	,,	21 ⎭		
4	,,	9	Yorkshire v. Surrey, at Hull	1879
7	,,	7 ⎫	England v. XXII of Canada, at Toronto	1879
14	,,	36 ⎭		
8	,,	22	Yorkshire v. Surrey, at the Oval	1881
5	,,	10	Yorkshire v. Australians, at Bradford	1882
8	,,	52	Yorkshire v. M.C.C. and Ground, at Scarboro' . .	1882
8	,,	39	Mr. C. I. Thornton's XI v. Cambridge University, at Cambridge	1884
8	,,	32	Yorkshire v. Sussex, at Huddersfield	1884
7	,,	20	Yorkshire v. Derbyshire, at Derby	1884

In the match between Yorkshire and Surrey, at the Oval, in 1881, Emmett, at one time in the second innings of Surrey, took five wickets in three overs without a run being made from him.

In July, 1868, Emmett and the late George Freeman, playing for Yorkshire, at Holbeck, dismissed Lancashire for totals of 30 and 34. Emmett's analyses were two for 11 and six for 13; Freeman's eight for 11 and four for 12.

Emmett bowled in 22 matches for the Players against the Gentlemen, delivering 2,399 balls for 1,128 runs and 38 wickets, average 29.68.

In all matches for Yorkshire he obtained 1,269 wickets at a cost of 12.68 runs apiece.

ENGLISH, Edward Apsey, who died on September 8, 1966, aged 102, was the oldest surviving county cricketer. He played as an amateur for Hampshire from 1898 to 1901. In the first season, "Ted" English hit his highest first-class innings, 98 against Surrey at the Oval, when he and A. Webb, by putting on 164 for the fifth wicket in the second Hampshire innings, rescued their side from a precarious position. He continued playing club cricket till 65 and remained an active sportsman till 1957. When 82 he holed in one on the Alton golf course and was 91 when he played his last game of golf. At 93 he reached the final of the Alton Conservative Club snooker championship. For 36 years he was Registrar at Alton.

ENTHOVEN, Henry John, who died at his home in London on June 29, 1975, aged 72, had a distinguished career for Harrow, Cambridge, Middlesex and the Gentlemen. After four years in the Harrow XI in which he twice played a big part in bowling out Eton, he got his Blue as a Freshman in 1923 and in 1924 caused some surprise by making 104 at Lord's, a performance far in advance of anything he had done before. When on the other hand he followed this next year with 129, thus becoming the second player to make a hundred twice in the University match, there was no surprise. That year he topped the Cambridge batting with 779 runs at an average of 51.93, was second in the bowling with 50 wickets at 22.14 and was one of four Cambridge players picked for the Gentlemen at Lord's.

As captain of Cambridge in 1926, he made 51 and 23 and took in the two innings six for 79, thus having a considerable share in his side's victory by 34 runs. Playing again for the Gentlemen, he finished the first innings of the Players by doing the hat-trick—the first Gentleman ever to perform this feat at Lord's in the long history of the match.

For Middlesex he played frequently, though never regularly, from 1925 to 1936, and in 1933 and 1934 shared the captaincy with Nigel Haig. Among many good performances three stood out. In 1927 Middlesex, faced with a total of 413, were in grave trouble against Lancashire at Lord's: Macdonald was then probably the most dangerous bowler in the world, eight wickets were down for 209 and Enthoven had reached a brave but rather unconvincing 50 in two hours and 25 minutes. At this point he started to attack, adding 89 out of 110 in 55 minutes and dealing especially severely with Macdonald. As Nigel Haig wrote years afterwards, "Better hitting of high-class fast bowling can rarely, if ever, have been seen." In 1930 he scored a hundred in each innings against Sussex at Lord's: in the first innings the last wicket put on 107 in 75 minutes of which his share was 102. Finally in 1934 he did the hat-trick against the Australians.

He never had the style or elegance of the typical Public School and University batsman of his time, but he was a courageous player with a strong defence, who took full toll of anything loose and when he was set could disrupt any bowling. An accurate medium-paced bowler who moved the ball chiefly from the off, he opened the bowling for Cambridge in his last two years, but in County Cricket was used simply as a change. By profession he was a stockbroker.

EVANS, Alfred Henry, died on March 26, 1934, at the age of 75. He collapsed when playing golf near Barnstaple.

Born at Madras on June 14, 1858, Mr. Evans was educated at Rossall, Clifton and Oriel College, Oxford. One of the best fast bowlers of his time he took 36 wickets for 471 runs in the four University matches from 1878 to 1881. In the first game he claimed 12 wickets at a cost of 141, among his opponents being such notable batsmen as A. P. Lucas, the Hon. Alfred Lyttelton, the Hon. Edward Lyttelton, A. G. Steel and the Hon. Ivo Bligh. During the first innings, by holding two catches at slip he had a hand in the dismissal of seven batsmen consecutively, and at one period four wickets fell to him in 11 deliveries.

In the following year he did little, but in 1880 he again bowled so well as to take 10 wickets for 133 runs. Next year, when captain, Mr. Evans, on a pitch that just suited his type of bowling, proved most destructive, securing 13 wickets at an average of 10 runs

apiece, and led his side to victory, after a sequence of three Cambridge wins. It was confidently expected that Cambridge would then repeat their previous three triumphs as they included in their team seven of the successful side of 1880. Mr. Evans, however, upset all calculations, for when Cambridge, after leading on the first innings by 48, went in to get 259 runs, his pace had most of the batsmen in such difficulties that the Light Blues were all out for 123, Evans taking six wickets for 56. Besides bowling Ivo Bligh, G. B. Studd, C. T. Studd, A. G. Steel and C. P. Wilson, he caught H. Whitfield and J. E. K. Studd in the first innings.

Whilst at Oxford, Evans had the distinction of assisting the Gentlemen against the Players. Occasionally he played for Somerset and Hampshire. A clever half-back, Evans got his Rugby Blue in 1877 and 1878, and was elected captain in 1879, but resigned at Christmas before the match with Cambridge took place, frost having compelled a postponement. An assistant master at Winchester College for six years, he was subsequently appointed headmaster of Horris Hill Preparatory School, Newtown, Newbury.

EVANS, Alfred John, who died in London on September 18, 1959, aged 71, was a fine all-round sportsman. Educated at Winchester, where his father, A. H. Evans, a former Oxford cricket Blue and captain, was a master, he won both the schools racquets and the golf in 1905 and the two succeeding years, and played at Lord's for three years. Going up to Oxford he won his cricket Blue as a Freshman in 1909, scoring 79 and 46. He also played against Cambridge in the three following seasons, doing good work as a hard-driving batsman and medium-paced bowler. He led the side in 1911. In 1910 he represented his University at racquets and in 1909 and 1910 at golf. He played cricket for Hampshire in 1911 and, after serving with distinction in the Royal Flying Corps during the First World War, when he earned fame for his escapes from enemy prison-camps, he assisted Kent and M.C.C. In 1921, on the strength of an innings of 69 not out for M.C.C. against the Australians, he was chosen for England in the Test match at Lord's, but was not a success.

EVANS, Charles, who died in a Chesterfield hospital in January, 1956, aged 89, played as a fast bowler and useful batsman in a few matches for Derbyshire between 1889 and 1895. He spent his entire working life of over 50 years with a Chesterfield engineering firm, who gave him leave of absence to appear for the county. His best first-class performance was at Derby in 1894 when, in scoring 27 not out and taking five wickets for 67 runs, he helped in a surprise win by 10 wickets over Warwickshire.

EVANS, David Linzee, died at West Down, near Bristol, on November 12, 1907, aged 38. He was born in Gloucestershire in 1869, and was educated at Loretto, where he was in the XI for three years, commencing in 1887. He was an aggressive batsman, a hard-working field, and a useful medium-paced bowler. In 1889, his last year at Loretto, he played a few times for Gloucestershire and with a not-out innings of 50 against Sussex, at Brighton, as his highest score, made 70 runs in five completed innings. During the next two seasons he did little in the few county matches in which he appeared and then, after an absence of two years from first-class cricket, he appeared under the residential qualification for Somerset. Against Surrey at the Oval in 1894 he played an innings of 60, and for the county that season scored 172 runs with an average of 17.20. The following year he did little, and then dropped out of the game, though he continued to take part in minor matches.

EVANS, Col. Dudley McNeil, who died on December 18, 1972, aged 86, was in the Winchester XI from 1902 to 1904. At Eton in 1903, he took six wickets for 42 runs in the first innings and four for 24 in the second and yet was on the losing side, Eton winning by 43 runs. From 1904 to 1911, he played for Hampshire, scoring 382 runs, average 14.69, and taking 55 wickets for 26.23 runs each.

EVANS, Edwin, the once-famous Australian cricketer, died at the Walgett's Hospital, New South Wales, on July 1, 1921. It was a thousand pities that Evans did not visit England while he was in his prime. If he had come over with the first team in 1878, or with the great side of 1882, there is every reason to think he would have justified the reputation he enjoyed at home. As it happened he delayed too long. When at last he came here, in 1886, his powers were obviously on the wane. He was still a very accurate bowler, but he had lost much of his spin and in a summer of hard wickets he had no terrors for English batsmen. More than that, circumstances were against him. The members of the 1886 team were not a happy family. Disagreements began during the opening match at Sheffield Park and the late

H. J. H. Scott, the captain, had anything but a pleasant time. Still, nothing that Evans did during the tour suggested the bowler about whom we had heard so much. His great days were over. Born in March, 1849, he was in his 38th year—rather an advanced age at which to seek a new reputation. His record as a bowler for the whole tour was 30 wickets for something over 20 runs apiece and his batting average was 12. These were poor figures for one who only a few years before had been the best all-round man in Australia. He took part in 30 of the 39 matches, but bowling in 22 of them he delivered only 506 overs, Scott evidently having little faith in him. At home Evans had a brilliant career. He played his first match for New South Wales against Victoria in March, 1875, and helped materially to win it, taking in Victoria's second innings six wickets for 25 runs. This performance established him and for years he went on from strength to strength. He and Spofforth did great things together, once getting Victoria out for 37. More often than not Evans had the better average of the two. He was at his best against James Lillywhite's team in 1876–77, and Lord Harris's team in 1878–79 found in him one of their stoutest opponents. I remember asking Mr. Hornby when he came back from the latter tour what he thought of Evans. His reply—I cannot after all these years vouch for the exact words—was something like this, "He is a very good bowler, the sort of man who can pitch on a sixpence, but he is not a Spofforth."—S.H.P.

EVANS, Canon The Rev. Frederic Rawlins (a nephew of George Eliot), born at Griff House, near Nuneaton, on June 1, 1842, died at Bedworth Rectory, Warwickshire, on March 4, 1927, aged 84. *Scores and Biographies* said of him: "Is a good bat, having patient defence, combined with great power of hitting; and is also a sure field, often (when not bowling) at long-leg. Is most noted, however, as a high and fast round-armed bowler, occasionally difficult to play." It was at Rugby, where he was coached by Alfred Diver and Tom Hayward (of Cambridge), that he began to distinguish himself. He was in the XI there in 1860 and 1861, having been previously at Cheltenham College. In 1863 and two following seasons he was in the Oxford XI under R. A. H. Mitchell, and in his three matches against Cambridge, all of which were won by Oxford, he scored exactly 100 runs with an average of 20. Very little bowling indeed fell to his share in those games, the reason being that Mr. Mitchell was not quite sure whether his action would satisfy the umpires. Umpires' decisions were then apt to vary; in the 1863 match Mr. Collins was no-balled for getting his hand above his shoulder. When Mr. Evans assisted the Gentlemen at Lord's, in 1865, on his only appearance against the Players, he obtained seven wickets for 83 runs, the Gentlemen, after losing 19 matches off the reel, winning by eight wickets. After leaving Oxford Mr. Evans played most of his important cricket for the Free Foresters, Warwickshire, and Worcestershire. He was for 38 years Rural Dean of Monks Kirby and for nearly 21 years an Honorary Canon of Worcester. He had been Rector of Bedworth since 1876.

EVANS, Harry, who died at Spondon on July 30, 1920, aged 63, played occasionally for Derbyshire in 1878, 1881 and 1882. He was a straight, fast bowler, a useful batsman and an excellent field. In the course of a week in 1881 he took six wickets for 60 runs v. Sussex at Brighton, performing the hat-trick, and seven for 47 v. Kent at Maidstone.

EVANS, James, who died on August 26, 1973, aged 82, played as a professional for Hampshire between 1913 and 1921.

EVANS, Ralph du Boulay, born on October 1, 1891, was killed in a motor accident at Los Angeles, California, on July 27, 1929, aged 37. He was in the Winchester XI in 1909, when bowling right-hand medium he was second in the averages with 36 wickets for 10.75 runs each. Later on he played some County Cricket for Hampshire, and also appeared for Cambridge, but not against Oxford.

EVANS, Lieut. Richard J., who was killed in an air crash at Cape Town on May 29, 1943, aged 29, played for Border from 1934 to 1940. A good spin bowler, he would probably have been a member of the South African team due to visit England in 1940 but for the War. In 1937–38 in five Currie Cup matches he took 36 wickets at an average cost of 13.11 runs, including eight wickets for 64 runs in an innings against Transvaal. A promising batsman, he played a fine innings of 88 against the M.C.C. touring team in January, 1939.

EVANS, Royston, who played for Western Australia from 1906 to 1924, died at Perth in March, 1977, aged 93.

EVANS, Victor J., died at Barking on March 28, 1975, aged 63. He played for Essex as a medium-pace off-spinner from 1932 to 1937, without ever winning an assured place in the side. His best season was 1935 when his 56 wickets cost 25.42 runs each.

EVANS, William Henry Brereton, whose tragic death at Aldershot in August, 1913, when flying with Colonel Cody, caused such a painful shock, was one of the best all-round amateur cricketers of his day. Indeed, if he had been able to keep up his cricket regularly after he left Oxford, it is quite likely that he would have had the distinction of playing for England. He was a batsman of very high class, and one of the best amateur fast bowlers seen in University cricket since Woods. He was in the Malvern XI from 1898 to 1901, being captain in his last year. He must have been about the best Public School cricketer in 1901, as he headed the Malvern batting with an average of 51, and took 53 wickets. Going up to Oxford with a big reputation, he won his Blue as a Freshman. His bowling for Oxford in 1902 was disappointing, but he did very well in batting, scoring 16 and 67 against Cambridge at Lord's, and playing a great innings of 142 against Sussex at Brighton. In the following year he was less successful as a batsman, but he bowled better than at any time in his life. He had a great share in beating Cambridge at Lord's, taking 11 wickets (seven for 52 runs and four for 34) and scoring 21 and 60. In 1904, when he was captain at Oxford, his bowling practically left him, but he was, perhaps, a better bat than ever. With two splendid innings of 65 and 86 not out, he saved his side from defeat at Lord's, and his average for Oxford was 54. He finished his Oxford career in 1905. In that year he to some extent recovered his bowling, but for the first time he failed as a batsman in the University match, scoring only 21 and eight. Evans was first selected for the Gentlemen at Lord's in 1903, and again in 1905. Going into the Egyptian Civil Service, he had not much chance of playing first-class cricket in recent years, but he was in the Gentlemen's XI, both at the Oval and Lord's, in 1909, batting very well at the Oval. He was born on January 29, 1883.

Mr. Evans was in the Oxford Association football team from 1902 to 1905, and in company with Mr. B. S. Foster, he won the Public School Racquet Championship in 1900. He was a nephew of Mr. A. H. Evans, the Oxford fast bowler of 1878–81.

EVERARD, Sir William Lindsay, D.L., J.P.,

died at Torquay on March 11, 1949, aged 57. Harrow XI 1908. Played twice for Leicestershire. Hon. Secretary of Leicestershire Gentlemen's Club 1914–35. President of County Club 1936 and 1939; member of the M.C.C. Committee 1938–45. One of the pioneers of private flying at his own aerodrome near his Leicestershire home, Ratcliffe Hall. Vice-President and former Chairman of Royal Aero Club, M.P. for Melton 1924–45; Knighted 1939.

EVERETT, Samuel Charles, who died on October 10, 1970, aged 69, represented New South Wales as a fast bowler in 16 Sheffield Shield matches and toured England as a member of the 1926 Australian team. He was chosen for that tour after the Australian Board of Control gave the selectors authority to pick an extra player, provided he was a young bowler. Of splendid physique, he possessed fine pace and although he did not appear in a Test, he took part in 18 matches on the tour and took 31 wickets, average 23.83.

EVERITT, Russell Stanley, who died in May, 1973, aged 91, did not find a place in the XI at Malvern, but played occasionally as an amateur right-handed batsman for Worcestershire in 1901 and Warwickshire between 1901 and 1909. He also turned out for Mosely in the Birmingham League and for Richmond, Surrey. He captained Warwickshire against Surrey at the Oval in 1909 when in hitting 38, his highest first-class score, in the second innings, he helped S. P. Kinneir to add 99 for the seventh wicket.

EVERSHED, Frank, died in London, March 18, 1945, aged 79. Educated at Amersham and Oxford he played a little for Derbyshire, 1889–94. Younger brother of S. H. and W. W. Evershed. Derbyshire were not then a first-class county. In 1890 he scored 111 against Norfolk at Norwich.
CORRECTION. In the 1946 *Wisden* there occurred an error. The inclusion of Mr. Frank Evershed in the obituary notices was incorrect. Mr. Henry Ellis, of Burton-on-Trent, informed me of the mistake, to which I call attention, with the hope that Mr. Evershed long may remain an active partner with Messrs. Talbot & Co.

EVERSHED, Sir Sydney Herbert, Kt., of high renown in Derbyshire cricket, died on March 7, 1937, at Burton-on-Trent, aged 76. A good, free batsman at Clifton College, S. H. Evershed played in the Derbyshire XI when 19 years of age, became captain in

1889, helped the county to rise to first-class rank in 1895 and altogether led the side for 10 years. Afterwards chairman of committee and President in 1908, he always kept up close interest in the county's doings.

Of middle height and very strongly built, S. H. Evershed crouched as he awaited the ball, which he met with all his weight behind powerful arms. He excelled in offside hitting, but often pulled his drive and generally got himself out in the endeavour to score quickly. His last match for Derbyshire was his one appearance of the season in 1901, against Hampshire at Southampton, and he hit up 123 out of 170 for the first wicket.

His best year was in 1898, when he scored 729 runs, with an average of 33. That was the season when, at Chesterfield, J. T. Brown and John Tunnicliffe made 554 for Yorkshire's first wicket, a record which stood until Holmes and Sutcliffe went one run better against Essex at Leyton in 1932. Born on January 13, 1861, Sir Sydney was one of four brothers who played for Derbyshire.

Elected captain of the Burton club in 1880 he held the position until his death. In 1913, at the age of 52, he headed the batting averages with 59.

A very good Rugby football half-back, he captained the Burton Club and Midland Counties and twice played for North against South—1883 and 1884—besides being chosen as reserve half-back for England.

EVERSHED, Wallis, a younger brother of Mr. S. H. Evershed, died on May 8, 1911, aged 47. He was in the Clifton XI in 1880 and two following seasons, being captain in 1882, when he was described as "A good bat, hitting and playing back very hard, and has improved in defence; he lost his command of the ball at the beginning of the season, but bowled well on several occasions later on; a good field; won the fielding prize." In 1881 he played an innings of 185 against University College, Oxford. In 1882, 1883 and 1884 he appeared occasionally for Derbyshire, scoring 357 runs with an average of 14.87. His best form was shown at the end of 1883, when in successive matches he scored 92 v. Surrey at the Oval and 56 v. Sussex at Brighton. He was born on May 10, 1863, and played for the Kendal Club from 1885 until 1903.

EVETTS, William, who died on April 6, 1936, at the age of 88, was the last survivor of the Harrow XI of 1865. Standing 6ft. tall he was a free hitter and a brilliant fieldsman. A very sure catch, he was concerned in a strange coincidence. In the 1864 match with

Eton at Lord's he caught W. B. Barrington at long leg; Harrow won in a single innings. Precisely the same ending came to the 1865 match, Evetts at long leg again catching Barrington the last Eton batsman, and the Light Blues being beaten by an innings. Barrington became the Ninth Viscount Barrington and until his death in 1933 he and Evetts were the sole survivors of those taking part in those two games. In the Harrow XI were W. B. Money, a very famous lob bowler, and A. N. Hornby who for many years led Lancashire and captained England at the Oval in 1882 when Australia won by seven runs. When playing for Oxford against Cambridge Evetts was twice on the losing side, but he scored 102 in an hour and 50 minutes against Surrey at the Oval in 1868 and during that season made three other centuries in matches of less importance. He was in the Brasenose College Sixteen who, in 1871, beat the All-England XI captained by George Parr. The match aroused very great interest. Mr. Evetts was born on June 30, 1847, at Tackley Park, near Thame in Oxfordshire and he died there. Mr. A. C. Bartholomew is now the only survivor of the 1868 Oxford XI.

FABER, Canon Arthur Henry, of the Winchester XI of 1847 and 1848, was born in India on February 29, 1832, and died at Doncaster, on November 29, 1910. In his four Public School matches he scored 54 runs in eight innings, took 10 wickets, and on every occasion was on the beaten side. He did not obtain his Blue at Oxford, although he was a far better batsman than his scores against Eton and Harrow would lead one to suppose. In July, 1862, he played an innings of 100 at Lord's for Gentlemen of the North v. Gentlemen of the South, and a fortnight later, at Leamington, he made 79 for Sixteen Free Foresters v. the All England XI, who had Wootton, Jackson, Tinley, and Tarrant to bowl for them. *Scores and Biographies* described Canon Faber as "A most excellent batsman," and added that he played frequently under the name of St. Fabian.

FABIAN, Aubrey Howard, died on September 26, 1984, aged 75. Captain of Highgate in 1928, when he headed both the batting and the bowling averages with fine figures, he got his Blue at Cambridge in 1929 and played three years at Lord's. A slow-medium bowler who could turn the ball both ways, he was as a rule expensive in first-class cricket, but against a full Yorkshire side at Fenner's in 1930 he took eight for 69.

Granted that the wicket helped him, this was a notable performance for an undergraduate. His highest score for Cambridge was 76 against Free Foresters in 1930. He also captained Cambridge at soccer and won several amateur international caps and was one of the finest Eton fives players of his day. At all games he was a determined competitor, and it was typical that in his Varsity cricket matches, Oxford never got him out: he made 86 runs against them in five innings.

FAGG, Arthur Edward, died at Tunbridge Wells on September 13, 1977, aged 62. Although in a career which extended from 1932 to 1957 he scored 27,291 runs with an average of 36.05, made 58 centuries and played five times for England, it cannot be said that he ever fulfilled expectations. In the middle '30s Sutcliffe was dropping out of Test cricket and England was looking for a new opening pair. Fagg and Hutton were at once recognised as obvious candidates and Fagg, a year the senior and by some considered the better prospect, got the first chance, playing in two Tests v. India in 1936 and being picked for the Australian tour that autumn. Halfway through the tour he was invalided home with rheumatic fever, a great setback to his career, and he missed the entire season of 1937. Naturally, in 1938 the selectors were cautious about playing him and, though he had a splendid season, it was not until the final Test that they picked him and then he was one of those left out.

That his health was not fully trustworthy was shown when he refused an invitation for the South African tour that winter. In 1939 he played in one Test v. West Indies. Unfit for the Services during the War, he went as coach to Cheltenham and, when first-class cricket was resumed in 1946, felt so doubtful whether he could stand the strain that he decided to stay there.

In 1947 Kent persuaded him to return, but already at 32, he was moving like a veteran. Hutton and Washbrook were established as England's opening pair and his days of Test cricket were clearly over. Still, for 10 years more he did splendid work for Kent and no one watching him could fail to see that he was far more than a good county bat. Very sound, he had strokes all round the wicket and, being a fine hooker, was particularly severe on fast bowling. Against spin he was less impressive.

One record which he holds may well never be equalled. In 1938 against Essex at Colchester, he scored 244 and 202 not out, the second innings taking only 170 minutes. His fielding was never on a par with his batting and after his early years, it was difficult to place him anywhere save in the slips, where he held his share of catches without being outstanding. In the Second XI he had been trained to keep wicket and was good enough to keep on a few occasions for the county when neither Ames nor Levett was available.

From 1959 to his death he was one of the First-Class umpires and from 1967 to 1976, when he retired for reasons of health, was on the panel of Test-match umpires. His long tenure of this appointment is sufficient testimony to the respect in which he was held and, when at Birmingham in 1973 he threatened to withdraw after the second day because of the behaviour of some of the West Indian side who had disagreed with one of his decisions, he could be sure of public sympathy. He did not indeed appear on the field on the third morning until the second over, Alan Oakman, the Warwickshire coach, having stood during the first.

BATTING

Season	Matches	Innings	Not Outs	Runs	Highest Inns.	100s	50s	Average	Catches
1932	4	6	0	72	30	0	0	12.00	4
1933	12	20	0	221	50	0	1	11.05	7 & 7 st
1934	24	43	5	1235	111	1	6	32.50	19
1935	31	58	2	1835	122	2	15	32.76	15
1936	28	52	3	1927	257	4	9	39.32	15
1938	30	53	6	2456	244	9	6	52.25	34
1939	27	51	6	1851	169*	5	6	41.13	31
1945	1	1	0	131	131	1	0	131.00	0
1946	2	3	0	270	109	1	2	90.00	1
1947	29	56	5	2203	184	5	13	43.19	41
1948	27	48	3	2423	203	8	10	58.84	35
1949	25	46	2	1774	129	3	11	40.31	28
1950	29	54	3	2034	156	6	8	39.88	37
1951	28	51	1	2081	221	6	11	41.62	29
1952	24	46	1	1519	143	3	6	33.75	25
1953	24	44	1	1377	269*	1	7	32.02	21
1954	16	30	0	841	130	1	5	28.03	14
1955	29	56	1	1375	106	1	7	25.00	37
1956	26	48	4	977	90	0	4	22.20	15
1957	10	20	2	290	45*	0	0	16.11	8
In Australia									
1936–37	10	17	1	399	112	1	1	24.93	6
Totals	436	803	46	27291	269*	58	128	36.05	422&7st.

Signifies not out.

TEST CRICKET

		Tests	Inns.	Not Outs	Runs	Highest Inns.	Average	Catches
1936	v. India	2	3	0	69	39	23.00	2
1936–37	v. Australia	2	3	0	42	27	14.00	2
1939	v. West Indies	1	2	0	39	32	19.50	1
Totals		5	8	0	150	39	18.75	5

A. E. Fagg has shared in the following large partnerships:
For the First Wicket

295   with C. J. Barnett for M.C.C. v. Queensland at Brisbane, 1936–37.
251   with L. J. Todd for Kent v. Leicestershire at Maidstone, 1949.
230   with L. J. Todd for Kent v. Northamptonshire at Tunbridge Wells, 1948.
221   with W. H. Ashdown for Kent v. Indians at Canterbury, 1936.
204   with F. E. Woolley for Kent v. Worcestershire at Tonbridge, 1938.

For the Second Wicket
275 with F. G. H. Chalk for Kent v. Worcestershire at Dudley, 1938.
260 with F. E. Woolley for Kent v. Northamptonshire at Northampton, 1934.
228 with L. E. G. Ames for Kent v. Sussex at Hastings, 1948.
219 with F. E. Woolley for Kent v. Surrey at Blackheath, 1934.
218 with F. E. Woolley for Kent v. Somerset at Taunton, 1934.
211 with F. E. Woolley for Kent v. Hampshire at Southampton, 1936.

For the Fourth Wicket
236 with R. Mayes for Kent v. Nottinghamshire at Trent Bridge, 1953.

FAIRBAIRN, Gordon Armitage, who died on November 5, 1973, aged 81, was educated at the Church of England Grammar School, Geelong, before going up to Cambridge, where he gained his Blue in 1913, 1914 and 1919. In the last year he also played for Middlesex.

FAIRBANKS, Walter, who was born at Luton, near Chatham, in Kent, on April 13, 1852, died at Guildford on August 25, 1924, aged 72. A capital batsman and a very good field at point, he was in the Clifton College XI from 1869 to 1871, in his last year making 129 not out against Sherborne. He did not obtain his Blue for Cambridge, but he played Rugby football for the University. His name will be found occasionally in the Gloucestershire team between 1877 and 1884, but he never did himself justice for the county. At Portsmouth in 1885 he played an innings of 219 for Old Cliftonians v. United Services. For some time he was a master at Clifton College.

FAIRBROTHER, Jim, had just retired as head groundsman at Lord's when he died on October 4, 1984, aged 65. After working as a ground-keeper in a Nottingham park, he moved to Trent Bridge as a member of the groundstaff in 1952 and to Lord's in 1968. With a temperament ideally suited to the job, he tackled with disarming patience the problems peculiar to Lord's, not least the slope of seven and a half feet from the Grand Stand to the Tavern boundary, but to do also with such things as bomb scares during Test maches. With his gentle smile and love of the job, he became a popular figure at headquarters, twice winning the award as Groundsman of the Year (1981 and 1982) and rarely taking offence, whatever might be said about his pitches. Written in conjunction with Reginald Moore, his book, *Testing the Wicket*, was published the month before he died.

FAIRFAX, Alan G., who died in London on May 17, 1955, aged 48, played as an all-rounder in 10 Test matches for Australia from 1929 to 1931. He had been in indifferent health following a serious injury received during the Second World War, after which he joined the staff of a London Sunday newspaper. Progressing through grade cricket, Fairfax reached Inter-State rank following an innings of 107 for New South Wales Colts against Queensland Colts in 1928–29 and he made his first appearance as a steady and somewhat restrained stroke-player for Australia in the fifth Test match against A. P. F. Chapman's team that season. In the first innings he scored 65, sharing in a stand of 183 with D. G. Bradman (123) which set up a record for the fifth Australian wicket. He visited England under W. M. Woodfull in 1930, taking part in four of the Test matches. With 53 not out his best innings, he averaged 50 against England, and in all first-class games during the tour scored 536 runs, average 25.52, and, with right-arm medium-pace bowling from a good height, took 41 wickets for 29.70 runs each. Next season in Australia he played in all five Test matches against West Indies, being third in the batting averages with figures of 48.75 for six innings. He returned to England in 1932 as professional to Accrington in the Lancashire League and afterwards until the outbreak of War ran an indoor cricket school in London.

FAIRSERVICE, William John, who died on June 26, 1971, aged 90, played as a professional off-break bowler of medium pace for Kent from 1902 to 1921. In normal circumstances, he could well have achieved greater fame; but, with such noted bowlers as Colin Blythe and Frank Woolley as teammates, his opportunities were limited. Not till after the First World War, indeed, did he command a regular place in the county side and the only season in which he took 100 wickets was that of 1920. That summer he dismissed 113 batsmen at a cost of 17.46 runs apiece, showing his ability on rain-affected pitches by earning match-figures of 10 wickets for 58 runs against Surrey at Blackheath and nine wickets for 62 runs against Worcestershire at Tonbridge.

His first victim in first-class cricket was no less a person than Dr. W. G. Grace, whom he bowled twice in a match with M.C.C. at Lord's in 1903, and altogether he took 750 wickets at an average cost of 25.64 runs and brought off 112 catches. He was also a useful tail end batsman, averaging 15.23 for 4,920 runs. For a few years after leaving Kent, he played for Northumberland and then coached at Tonbridge, Malvern and Lancing before becoming scorer to Kent Second XI, a position he occupied till he retired at the age of 87. When over 80, he often bowled in the nets at King's School, Canterbury, where his son, who played for Kent, was sports master.

FALCK, Ernest Dyson, who died at Bridport on February 19, 1982, aged 74, played four matches for Somerset in the mid-1930s with a top score of 28.

FALCON, Michael, who died suddenly at his home in Norwich on February 27, 1976, aged 87, was a cricketer who might well have played in Test matches had he been qualified for a first-class county. As it was, there were those who thought that he would have strengthened the deplorably weak English bowling in 1921 and their opinion was confirmed when, by taking six for 67 in the first innings, he had much to do with the sensational victory of MacLaren's XI over the Australians at Eastbourne. He had moreover a knack of producing his best form on important occasions.

A fast bowler who swung the ball away late and could get considerable lift, he took six for 58 for the Gentlemen against a strong Players' side at the Oval in 1913, six for 41 for the Gentlemen against the 1919 A.I.F. side and, perhaps most remarkable of all, seven for 42 for H.M. Martineau's XI against the Australians at Holyport in 1926 in the first match of their tour. By then at 38 he had slightly shortened his run and moderated his pace, at the same time gaining something in subtlety, so that the very dead wicket was not the handicap to him that it would have been a few years earlier.

Strangely enough, he did not start to bowl seriously until his last year at Cambridge. As a member of the Harrow XI in 1906 and 1907 he was primarily a batsman and at Cambridge, where he got his Blue as a Freshman and was captain in 1910, he hardly bowled at all in his first three years, but scored plenty of runs. After he came down, he was regarded in first-class cricket mainly as a bowler, but for the Gentlemen at the Oval in 1924, after taking seven for 78 in the first

innings, he made 34 not out in the second going in last and helped Arthur Gilligan to put on 134 for the last wicket in an hour.

A fine fieldsman, he was indeed a thorough cricketer. His name will always be especially associated with Norfolk. He had the astonishing record of playing for them for 39 years, 1907 to 1946, and captaining them from 1912 to 1946. In all he scored 11,340 runs for them with an average of 32.87, his highest score being 205 against Hertfordshire in 1920, and took 727 wickets at 16.13. Nor was he a passenger in his last season, when at the age of 58 he headed the batting averages. Later he was Chairman of the Norfolk Committee from 1950 to 1969 and President from 1969 to 1972, after which he and his wife were elected Hon. Vice-Presidents. He had sat in the House of Commons as M.P. for East Norfolk and had also been High Sheriff of the county.

FALLOWS, Jack, who collapsed and died on January 20, 1974, aged 67, rendered excellent service to Lancashire as captain in 1946 when the county were in the process of building a new side after the Second World War. Though he scored only 171 runs at an average of 8.14 in his one season of first-class cricket, he proved an able leader and under him the team blended harmoniously. He played for Cheshire for a time before that and gained prominence in club cricket. For a number of years till retiring in 1971 through pressure of business, he served on the Lancashire Committee and was chairman of selectors.

FANE, Frederick Luther, who died on December 9, 1954, aged 79, was a prominent figure in the cricket world for some 20 years before the First World War. Born at the Curragh Camp on April 27, 1875, he was educated at Charterhouse, where he was in the XI from 1892 to 1894, and Oxford and played a lot for Essex, whom he captained from 1904 to 1906. Though he did not quite realise expectations at the University, he gained a Blue in 1897 and the following year.

Meanwhile in 1905 he began his long association with Essex, for whom he exceeded 1,000 runs in each of five years. His best season was that of 1906, when he scored 1,572 runs, average 34. In 1899 he hit his highest innings, 207 against Leicestershire, in which he showed all his attractive style and sound judgment. In 1905, when Essex beat the Australians by 19 runs, Fane finished the match with a truly remarkable catch, not for any exceptional excellence as a piece of fielding, but from the place where it was made.

With a close finish clearly in sight and Buckenham bowling at great pace, Fane, to save a possible boundary from byes, took up a position practically in line with the wickets and just inside the Pavilion rails—in short, that of very deep long-stop. Frank Laver, sweeping the ball right round with a curious stiff-armed stroke from the shoulder, lifted it high and straight to where Fane was standing. Though not as a rule the safest of fieldsmen, Fane did not fail his side on that occasion.

In the winter of 1907–08, when going to Australia as a member of the side under A. O. Jones, Fane led the Englishmen in the first three Test matches when his captain fell ill. During the tour he scored 774 runs, average 33, his first notable innings being 101 against New South Wales. In the four Test matches in which he played, he averaged 24. Fane also visited South Africa twice, in 1905–06 and in 1909–10, New Zealand in 1902–03 and the West Indies in early 1902.

CORRECTION. Owing to an unfortunate error, the 1956 *Wisden* reported the death of Mr. F. L. Fane, the former Essex and England cricketer.

The error occurred because of a similarity of initials. The Mr. F. L. Fane who died in December, 1954, was Mr. Francis L. Fane, a cousin of the cricketer, Mr. Frederick L. Fane. By a coincidence, Mr. Fane informs us, his father also once read his own obituary!

FANE, Frederick Luther, who died on November 27, 1960, aged 85, was a prominent figure in cricket for some 20 years before the First World War. Owing to a similarity of initials, *Wisden* reported his death when he was 79. The man concerned was Francis L. Fane, his cousin. By a coincidence, Mr. Fane's father also read his own obituary.

FARGUS, The Rev. Archibald Hugh Conway, who went down in the *Monmouth*, Admiral Cradock's flagship, in the action in the Pacific on November 1, 1914, was born at Clifton, Bristol, on December 15, 1878, and was educated at Clifton, Haileybury and Cambridge. He left Clifton too young to be in the XI, but played for Haileybury in 1897 and 1898, making seven, 78 and 17 and taking 11 wickets for 123 runs in his two matches v. Cheltenham, and scoring one, 48, 0, and one v. Wellington. He appeared for Cambridge in the drawn games with Oxford in 1900 and 1901, in which he made eight and 17 not out and obtained six wickets for 260 runs. He assisted Gloucestershire in 1900

and 1901 and Devonshire in 1904, and had been a member of the M.C.C. since 1901. In first-class cricket his highest score was 61 for Cambridge University v. Sussex at Brighton in 1901, and his best performance with the ball to take 12 Middlesex wickets for 87 for Gloucestershire at Lord's in 1900. He was described as a stout hitter, a good hammer and tongs bowler, and a hardworking field. Since 1907 he had been a Chaplain in the Royal Navy, and in 1913 was appointed Vicar of Askham Richard, York. At the beginning of the War he became temporary Acting-Chaplain to the *Monmouth*, on which he went down.

CORRECTION. He was not lost, as stated in the Press, in Admiral Cradock's flagship, the *Monmouth*, on November 1, 1914. Missing a train, he was prevented from re-joining the ship just before it left for the Pacific and was appointed to another.

FARMER, Wilfred, who died in Barbados in February, 1976, at the age of 54, was a former captain of Barbados and was credited with having discovered Gary Sobers.

FARNES, Pilot Officer Kenneth (R.A.F.), the Cambridge, Essex and England fast bowler, was killed during the night of October 20, 1941, when the plane in which he was pilot crashed. His death at the age of 30 came as a great shock to countless friends and the whole world of cricket. After training in Canada he desired to become a night-flying pilot, and within four weeks of his return to England he met his disastrous end.

Discovered when 19 years of age by Mr. Percy Perrin in an Essex Club and Ground match against Gidea Park in 1930, Kenneth Farnes took five Kent wickets for 36 runs in his second county match and was welcome in the Essex team whenever available. After three years in the Cambridge XI, he went as a master to Worksop College, and consequently his appearances in first-class cricket were limited. His University experiences brought continuous improvement. In 1933 his work for Cambridge showed 41 wickets at 17.39 runs apiece, and he was by far the most effective amateur bowler in the country with a record of 113 wickets at 18.38 each. In a drawn match with Oxford seven wickets fell to him at a cost of 71 runs. His best performance that season—11 wickets for 114 runs, seven for 21 in the second innings—enabled Essex to beat Surrey by 345 runs at Southend, their first success against these opponents since 1914. In 10 matches for the county, Farnes claimed 67 wickets at an average cost of 16.07, and this form brought him the honour of representing England in the first Test against Australia in 1934. Despite his fine performance—10 wickets for 179 runs—England lost by 238 runs. Strangely enough, when England won by an innings and 38 runs at Lord's, Farnes did not meet with any reward, Verity taking the honours. Farnes was not called upon again in that series, but in 1938 he took most wickets in Tests against Australia—17 at 34.17 each.

In 1934 he was largely responsible for the first victory of Essex over Yorkshire since 1911 by taking 11 wickets for 131, Southend again proving a favourable ground for him. Thanks to Farnes dismissing seven men for 59 in the final stage, Essex brought about a great triumph by an innings and 46 runs. After a tour in West Indies knee trouble prevented Farnes from playing in 1935, but next season, for the Gentlemen at Lord's, he created a sensation by bowling Gimblett, Hammond and Hardstaff in quick succession, a stump being sent flying in each case. With four men out for 33, the Players were in danger of defeat, but, after the complete loss of Wednesday owing to rain, there was not time to reach a finish in two days. This fine work influenced the choice of Farnes to tour Australia with the team captained by G. O. Allen in the winter of 1936. Never did he bowl better than in the last Test, when he took six wickets for 96 runs in a total of 604; Australia won by an innings and 200—a result that decided the rubber.

Farnes bowled well in Test trials at Lord's. In 1938 he gave special proof of being in great form by dismissing eight Players for 43 runs in the first innings and three in the second for 60, so doing a lot towards the Gentlemen winning by 133 runs—their second victory in this encounter since the last War. In the following winter he went with the England touring team to South Africa, where he was second in Test bowling to Verity. His 16 wickets cost 32.43 each, while in the whole tour 44 wickets fell to him at 27.43 apiece. He did the best bowling of the third Test, the only one brought to a definite finish, which gave W. R. Hammond's side the rubber. With four wickets for 29, Farnes was mainly instrumental in making South Africa follow on, and he dismissed three men for 80 in their second innings of 353, which left England still 13 runs to the good after a declaration with only four men out. Paynter, 243—a South African record—and Hammond, 120, were the great batsmen on that occasion; their stand realised 242.

Farnes made his first appearance of the season in 1939 for the Gentlemen, and showed his fondness for Lord's by disposing of the last three Players in the course of six balls. This final effort by Farnes at headquarters recalls how well he bowled in University matches; but in 1932 he disfigured an analysis of five wickets for 98 runs by being "called" 21 times. The discipline then brought to bear was effective in correcting a faulty approach to the crease. Nearly 6ft. 5in. tall, Farnes, taking a comparatively short and easy run, brought the ball down from a great height with the inevitable effect of sharp lift, which made him extremely difficult to time when retaining a good length. Altogether in first-class cricket Farnes took 720 wickets at an average of 20.55 each.

A very good field near the wicket, Farnes reached many catches that would have been impossible for a man of medium height. He had no pretensions as a batsman, but in 1936, at Taunton, hit up 97 not out in two hours, Wade helping to add 149 for the last wicket; dismissing six men in the match, Farnes was largely responsible for Essex winning by an innings and 66 runs. He laughed at just failing to get a century—the ambition of every batsman.

Farnes wrote a very interesting book—*Tours and Tests*, published in 1940; among his hobbies were painting and music.

FARRANDS, Frank Henry, born at Sutton-in-Ashfield on March 28, 1835, died at Mansfield on September 22, 1916. *Scores and Biographies* said that he was "a most excellent fast round-armed bowler, a tolerable bat, and can field well, generally at slip." He appeared occasionally for Nottinghamshire in 1871 and 1873, but, considering his skill, was seen all too seldom in matches of note. In 1870, at Lord's, he came into the Players' team at the last moment as a substitute and took 10 wickets for 88 runs, but never again had an opportunity of appearing against the Gentlemen. Twice during 1873 he took all 10 wickets in an innings—for M.C.C. and Ground v. Gentlemen of Worcestershire at Worcester for 36 runs, and for Lord Huntly's XI v. M.C.C. and Ground at Aboyne Castle. In 1881 the match at Lord's between Over 30 and Under 30 was set apart as a benefit for him. He became a member of the ground-staff at Lord's in 1868 and remained there until 1908, becoming head of the staff. He was extremely well-known as a capable umpire, especially at Lord's, and it was estimated that in 40 years he officiated in 2,000 matches.

FARRIMOND, William, who died at home at Westhoughton, near Bolton, on November 14, 1979, aged 76, had the rare experience of being an England wicket-keeper who had been playing for 14 years for his county before getting a regular place in the side. This was the more exasperating as for 35 years Lancashire had hardly had a reliable professional 'keeper, merely a succession of men who had to give way when a competent amateur was available. In 1923 they found that great 'keeper, Duckworth, and in 1924 Farrimond appeared. It was only Duckworth's premature retirement at the end of 1937 that gave him an assured place, and after two seasons his career was ended by the War. It speaks volumes for Farrimond's loyalty that during this long period he never accepted any of the offers he received to qualify for another county.

Meanwhile he had kept four times for England, twice in South Africa in 1931, when Duckworth fell ill, once in the West Indies in 1935 and again later that year v. South Africa at Lord's. On the last two occasions Ames was playing as a batsman and fielder. In technique Duckworth and Farrimond were poles apart. Duckworth was flamboyant, spectacular and a shrill and tireless appealer. Farrimond was quiet and unobtrusive, but immensely sound and particularly good on the leg. Against Kent at Old Trafford in 1930 he equalled what was then the world's record by claiming seven victims in an innings. He was a considerably better batsman than Duckworth. He scored heavily for the Second XI, and though he never made a century for the county, in 1934 he hit 174 for the Minor Counties against Oxford University. On his tour to South Africa he averaged 30.70. His long and useful service was recognised by a benefit in 1939.

FARTHING, F. Hadfield, a very capable club cricketer, died from heart failure while taking part in a match at East Dulwich on September 1, 1928. After sending down two overs, in each of which he obtained a wicket, he moved to his place in the slips and there collapsed. Born in Yorkshire on July 30, 1875, he was a well-known and popular journalist, and at the time of his death occupied the post of night editor of the *Daily Express*, to which paper he contributed a weekly article on cricket.

FAULKNER, Major George Aubrey, D.S.O. born at Port Elizabeth on December 17, 1881, died of gas poisoning at the Faulkner School of Cricket, Ltd., on September 10, 1930, at the age of 48. During the South African War and whilst living in Cape Town, he received some coaching from Walter Richards, of Warwickshire, then engaged by Western Province, and later became not only one of the dominating figures in South African cricket but also one of the finest of all-round players. One of the earliest exponents of the googly, he differed from other bowlers of that type because of his ability to send down quite a fast ball, almost a yorker, and when at his best, with faultless length, skill in turning the ball either way and a puzzling variation of flight, he proved too much for some of the world's greatest batsmen.

Many will remember his fine bowling at Leeds in 1907 when, playing for South Africa in the second Test match of that series against England, he dismissed six men in the course of 11 overs for17 runs. His career was full of remarkable performances. In that same season of 1907 he, in all matches for the South Africans, scored 1,288 runs and took 73 wickets. He was probably at his best in 1909–10 when his doings with both bat and ball against the English team were magnificent. When South Africa visited Australia in the season of 1910–11, Faulkner headed the Test match batting averages with 732 runs and an average of 73.20. In all matches during that tour he scored 2,080 runs, taking 60 wickets, and in the Test match at Melbourne he hit a splendid 204. For the team of 1912 he made 1,075 runs and obtained 163 wickets. Although at the beginning of his career, particularly at the time when he first became prominent in South African Inter-State cricket in 1906, he was of little value as a batsman, he became as the years passed, almost as great a batsman as he was a bowler. His style rather conveyed the impression of awkwardness and he could not, at any time, be described as a free, forcible bat. Nevertheless, very few men made runs with more assurance than Faulkner, and he was a most difficult batsman to get out. After settling down in England he had a great season in club cricket in Nottinghamshire, making 12 hundreds in scoring 2,868 runs with an average of 84.35, besides taking 218 wickets, including all 10 in an innings on two occasions. Still, his finest innings in this country was at Eastbourne in 1921 when by a wonderful 153 against the Australians—up to that point an unbeaten side—he virtually gave victory to A. C. MacLaren's XI. Faulkner was also a first-rate field.

When the time came for him to retire from the game, he gained much distinction as a coach. He followed theory entirely his own when he established the first cricket school known in London and at the time of his death the school had earned world-wide fame. Faulkner devoted the greater part of his time to the school, though he found opportunity to write many articles on the game. During the European War he served with distinction with the R.F.A. in Salonika, Egypt and Palestine, gaining the D.S.O. in 1918 and the Order of the Nile.

FEAR, H. P., who played twice for Somerset in 1934 and was in the Taunton School XI, died early in 1943.

FEARNLEY, Michael C., died while playing cricket at East Bierley on July 7, 1979, aged 42. An accurate fast-medium swing bowler with a good action, he played a few times for Yorkshire between 1962 and 1964, but was better known as assistant-coach to the county for the last 13 years, in which capacity he was greatly respected, and as one of the most successful bowlers in the Bradford League. He was the elder brother of C. D. Fearnley of Worcestershire.

FELLOWES, Col. James, born at the Cape of Good Hope on August 25, 1841, died at Dedham, in Essex, on May 3, 1916. *Scores and Biographies* said of him: "Has been successful in the matches in which his name is found, being a very hard hitter, and a fast round-armed bowler, while in the field he can take any place with effect, except long-stop or wicket-keeper." Between 1873 and 1881 he appeared in nine matches for Kent, and in later years for Hampshire (of which club he was for some seasons co-Secretary with Dr. Russell Bencraft) and Devon. The county grounds at Southampton and Exeter were laid down under his supervision, and he was founder of the Hampshire Hogs and Devon Dumplings.

In strictly first-class cricket his greatest feats were to take seven wickets for 24 runs for Kent against Surrey at Maidstone in 1873, and 13 for 100 for Kent v. Lancashire on the same ground in 1874. He had been a member of the M.C.C. since 1869, and at Lord's in 1887 took part in the Centenary match between Eighteen Veteran Gentlemen and XI Gentlemen of the M.C.C. As a curious occurrence it may be recalled that, when playing for M.C.C. v. Woolwich at Lord's in 1871, he hit his foot with his bat in playing the ball and broke one of his toes. When playing for North Kent Eighteen v. United South of England XI, at Gravesend in 1875, he made 20 runs—three sixes (all

over the pavilion) and a two—off a four-ball over delivered by "W.G." He was father-in-law of Col. W. C. Hedley.

FELLOWS, Harvey Winson, who was born at Rickmansworth, in Hertfordshire, on April 11, 1826, died at his native place on January 13, 1907, in his 81st year. He was in the Eton XI in 1841 and 1842, and in each year played against Harrow and Winchester. In 1841, when Emilius Bayley played his historic 152 and Eton won by an innings and 175 runs, George Yonge and Walter Marcon obtained all the wickets between them, but in the following year, when the tables were turned and Harrow proved successful by 65 runs, Harvey Fellows went on and bowled three wickets. In the latter match, although the Harrow totals were only 141 and 121, there were 53 extras (38 byes and 15 wides) in the first innings and 32 (28 byes and four wides) in the second. It is interesting to recall that of the Eton XI of 1841 three members, all octogenarians, still survive—Cyril Randolph, now Rector of Chartham, and the brothers Emilius and L. H. Bayley. In the Winchester match of 1841, which Eton lost by 109 runs, Mr. Fellows made three and 26 not out and took six wickets, whilst in the following year he scored 24 and dismissed eight men, thereby contributing in no small measure to the defeat of Winchester by seven wickets. Mr. Haygarth, in *Scores and Biographies* (iii – 41), said of him: "As a batsman, at first he was a hard slashing hitter, but he afterwards became steadier. At Himley (Lord Ward's) September 19, 1848, in the match I Zingari v. Gentlemen of Worcestershire, he hit a ball off Nixon 132 yards to the pitch. Is, however, most famous as a bowler, though his great success only lasted three or four seasons, commencing in 1847. The pace was then terrific (by some thought quite dangerous to bat against), very straight, and with a good deal of 'spin' on the ball, which, in its progress, often has been heard to hum like a top. The delivery was low—so much so, indeed, that by some it was called underhand, which, however, was quite a mistake. He afterwards got his arm higher, and this is supposed to be the reason that he soon lost his tremendous speed, and also some of his straightness. His bowling against the Players in 1848 and 1849 was quite different from that in 1850 and 1851.

'And Fellows, whose electric speed with due precision blends.'

Messrs Marcon, H. Fellows, W. Fellows, Osbaldeston, and G. Brown, sen., are supposed to be the fastest bowlers that have ever yet appeared. T. Brett, A. Mynn, Esq., T. Sherman, Tarrant, J. Jackson, Wisden, and R. Lang, Esq., ranking next as to speed. In the field Mr. Fellows is generally cover-point, where he is very active, notwithstanding his great bulk."

After leaving Eton Mr. Fellows quickly made his mark, being chosen for practically all the great matches of his time, including Gentlemen v. Players from 1847 to 1851. His swift bowling on the rough wickets which were general in his time was frequently destructive, though often expensive to his own side on account of the number of byes that resulted. Mr. E. S. E. Hartopp was considered to long-stop to his bowling more successfully than anyone else, and for that reason was called "Mr. Fellows' long-stop." Fuller Pilch, it has been said, has been known to play his bowling at Lord's with his head turned away, whilst Parr admitted that he was the only bowler he could not hit to leg. In a match at Lord's in 1850, he and Mr. Jones G. Nash bowled unchanged through both innings for Gentlemen of England v. Gentlemen of Kent, while for M.C.C. and Ground v. Hampshire at Lord's in 1861, he bowled 33 balls for two runs and four wickets. Playing for I Zingari v. Gentlemen of Warwickshire at Leamington in 1849, he bowled down the first nine wickets in the first innings and caught the 10th. He frequently appeared at Canterbury for the Gentlemen of England v. the Gentlemen of Kent; in 1847 he played an innings of 51 there, and in 1853 one of 61, while, when bowling Mr. G. M. Kelson in the M.C.C. v. Gentlemen of Kent match of 1864, he knocked all three stumps out of the ground. Mr. Fellows had often served on the Committee of the M.C.C., to which he was legal adviser, and of which he had been a member since 1859. In 1867 he played in Paris for the M.C.C. and I Zingari in the first matches those clubs ever played outside the United Kingdom. He was elder brother of the late Rev. Walter Fellows of the Oxford XI of 1854 and three following years.

FELLOWS, The Rev. Walter, who was born at Rickmansworth, in Hertfordshire, on February 23, 1834, died at Toorak Parsonage, near Melbourne, July 23, 1901. He was educated at Westminster and Oxford, and is described in *Scores and Biographies* (iv – 471) as "a hard slashing hitter, and a tremendous fast round-armed bowler." He was younger brother of Mr. Harvey Fellows, who still, happily, survives. For Westminster against Rugby, at Westminster, in 1852, he obtained nine wickets in the first innings and six in the second, but was on the losing side, Westminster making only 19 and 11, against Rugby's scores of 114 and 129. Although Mr. Fellows' bowling was effective, it was certainly expensive, as there wre 15 byes in the first innings, and 27 in the second. Moreover, he bowled 30 wides, thereby giving away as many runs as Westminster made in their two innings combined. For four years he assisted Oxford against Cambridge, namely from 1854 to 1857, and made scores of 33, 0 and five, 35 and 30 (the highest in each innings), 24 and three. In the 1855 match he bowled 12 overs for six runs and two wickets. In 1855 and the two following years he appeared for the Gentlemen against the Players, at Lord's, participating in the match in which Reginald Hankey played his historical innings of 70. Whilst at practice on the Christ Church Ground, at Oxford, in 1856, Mr. Fellows hit a ball, bowled by Rodgers, a distance of 175 yards from hit to pitch, the length of the drive being carefully measured by E. Martin, the ground-keeper. In 1863 he emigrated to Australia and joined the Melbourne Club the following year. He was interested in the game to the last. Height, 5ft. 11in., and playing weight as much as 17st. 4lb.

FENNER, F. P.'s death, on May 22, 1896, destroyed one of the few remaining links between the cricket of the present day and the generation of Mynn and Fuller Pilch. Born at Cambridge on March 1, 1811, Mr. Fenner had reached a ripe old age. In his day he was a capital cricketer, taking his part with no little distinction in big matches, but his fame rests not so much upon what he did in the field, as on the fact that he laid out the beautiful ground at Cambridge, which, though now the property of the University, is nearly always spoken of by old cricketers as Fenner's. The ground was opened in 1846, and is still, after 50 years' play, one of the best in the world. Mr. Fenner played his first match at Lord's in 1832, appearing for the Cambridge Town Club against the M.C.C. On that occasion Fuller Pilch played for the Cambridge Club as a given man and with scores of 50 and not out 41, won the match.

FERGUSON, William Henry, who died at Bath on September 22, 1957, aged 77, was the best-known cricket scorer in the world. For 52 years, from the time he first visited England with Joe Darling's Australian side of 1905, he acted as scorer and baggage-master for England, South Africa, West

Indies, New Zealand and, naturally, Australia, in no fewer than 43 tours. In all that time his boast was that he never lost a bag. "Fergie," as he was affectionately known in the cricket world, scored in no fewer than 208 Test matches in every country where big cricket is played. He liked to relate how he first took up the job. The office in Sydney, his birthplace, where he was employed as a clerk, overlooked the harbour and he often felt the urge to travel. So in 1905 he "thought up a nice toothache," went to see his dentist, M. A. Noble, the Test batsman, and brought up the question of scoring. Amused at the ingenious method of approach, Noble put forward "Fergie's" name to the authorities, with the result that this short, slightly-built man began his travels which totalled well over half a million miles. His salary for the 1905 tour was £2 per week, from which he defrayed his expenses, and he paid his own passage.

For all his long connection with it, "Fergie" never took much active part in the game, but figures, for which he always had a passion, fascinated him, and he loved to travel. Besides actual scoring, he kept diagrams of every stroke played, with their value, by every batsman in the matches in which he was concerned, and could account for every ball bowled—and who fielded it. Touring captains, including D. G. Bradman and D. R. Jardine, employed his charts to study the strength and weaknesses of opposing batsmen.

When in England with the Australian team of 1948, "Fergie" was presented to King George VI. That summer Bradman scored 2,428 runs. Said the King: "Mr Ferguson, do you use an adding-machine when the Don is in?"

"Fergie," who received the British Empire Medal in 1951 for his services to cricket, emerged from two years' retirement to score for the West Indies last summer. A fall at an hotel in August prevented him from finishing the tour, and he spent some time in hospital, returning home only two days before his death. His autobiography, titled *Mr. Cricket*, was published in May, 1957.

FERNANDES, Maurius Pachaco, who died in Georgetown on May 8, 1981, aged 84, had the distinction of leading West Indies to their first Test victory—against England at the Bourda Oval, Georgetown, in February 1930. In spite of this, it was the only Test in that series in which he played, the West Indian custom in those days being to appoint a different captain in each match, usually from the colony in which the game was to be played. Fernandes was a right-hand batsman who usually filled a high place in the order. After making a name for himself as a teenager with the Demerara C.C., he captained British Guiana many times between 1922 and 1932, scoring two inter-colonial centuries, 141 against Barbados and 124 against Trinidad. On the first of his two tours to England, in 1923, he scored 110 against Leicestershire, "cutting and driving," as *Wisden* put it, "with equal facility"; on his second, in 1928, he batted at number three in West Indies' first Test match, at Lord's. He was an obdurate batsman, and a quietly spoken man, who scored 2,087 first-class runs at an average of 28.20.

FERNS, Charles Samuel, who died at his home at Clapham Common on December 19, 1954, aged 75, was a member of the staff of the Cricket Reporting Agency for 56 years till he retired in 1952. He served under six Editors of *Wisden*.

FERRIS, J. J., died on November 17, 1900, at Durban, where he was serving with the British forces. Mr. Ferris, though only in his 34th year, had for some time dropped out of first-class cricket, and had to a certain extent outlived his fame. Still, though his career ended early, he will always be remembered as one of the finest left-handed bowlers—either English or Australian—that ever appeared. Having in the two previous winters done great things against English teams in the Colonies, Ferris first came to this country in 1888 as a member of the Australian XI captained by the later Percy McDonnell. Much was expected of him, and he more than fulfilled the most sanguine anticipations. No one who can recall the cricket season of 1888—one of the wettest on record—will need to be told what a sensation he and Charles Turner created. They were the mainstays of a team which, after a brilliant start, suffered many defeats, but the shortcomings were not in any way due to the two bowlers, who made their names famous wherever cricket is played. The XI being deficient in change bowling, they had far too much to do, but they never seemed to tire, keeping up their form in a really wonderful way. Turner was the more successful of the two, taking in the whole tour 314 wickets for little more than 11 runs each. Ferris, however, also has a splendid record, 220 wickets falling to him for something over 14 runs apiece. The two men formed a perfect contrast, Turner being right hand, with an off-break perhaps never equalled at his speed, and Ferris left hand, with great accuracy, fine variety of pace, and a lot of spin. The weather flattered them, the wickets day after day giving them immense assistance, but it may be questioned if two finer bowlers ever played on the same side. One would not say that they were better than Spofforth and Palmer in 1882, but by reason of one being right-handed and the other left they were a more effective combination. As to the relative merits of Spofforth and Turner, cricketers have always been divided in opinion, the balance—among English players, at any rate—being in Spofforth's favour on account of his better head and more varied resources. In Ferris's case no question of comparison arose, as he was the first great left-handed bowler produced by Australia since the days of Frank Allan and Tom Kendall. Ferris and Turner came to England for the second time in 1890, and though associated with the least successful of all the Australian XIs, they fully sustained their reputations. This time Turner could only show a fractional superiority over his comrade. In the whole tour each man took 215 wickets, and there was a difference of less than a run a wicket in their averages. The summer was very wet, but there were more hard wickets to bowl on than in 1888, and under conditions favourable to run-getting Ferris perhaps did better work than Turner. That, at least, was the general opinion while the tour was in progress. With the tour of 1890 Ferris's career as a representative Australian cricketer came to an end. He agreed to qualify for Gloucestershire, and when the Australians came here in 1893 he played for the county against his old friends. For Gloucestershire, however, he proved as a bowler—not to mince matters—an utter failure. It was thought that he would be invaluable to the XI, but he rarely showed a trace of the skill that had made him so famous, and when we last saw him bowl in a Gloucestershire match—in 1895—he had lost his pace, his spin, his action and everything. In the autumn of 1895 he returned to Australia, but his efforts to recover his old position in Colonial cricket met with no success, and little was heard of him till it was announced that he had gone to South Africa to try his fortune at the war with the Imperial Light Horse. We must not forget to add that he went out to South Africa with Mr. W. W. Read's team in the winter of 1891–92. He had a brilliant tour, taking 235 wickets, but he never bowled in the same form afterwards.

FEWIN, Henry, who died on August 25, 1980, aged 94, played one game for Queensland (against Victoria) in 1929–30 as a right-

hand batsman. He fell in each innings to Ironmonger, for seven and 11.

FIDDIAN-GREEN, Charles Anderson, who died on September 5, 1976, aged 77, was a batsman who added to the gifts of a fine natural games player an impeccable style and a solid defence. Going up to Cambridge University from The Leys at the age of 21 in 1919 because of the War, he did not get a trial for the Varsity in his first year, but in 1921, coming into the side on the tour, he scored so heavily as to put his claims beyond doubt and got a Blue in a year in which batsmen like T. C. Lowry, G. O. Shelmerdine, W. W. Hill-Wood, T. E. Halsey and H. D. Hake had to be passed over. He had already gained valuable experience for Warwickshire in 1920. In 1922 he came second in the Cambridge averages with 49.21 and represented the Gentlemen at Lord's.

Becoming a master at Malvern, where he ran the cricket, he continued to play at times for Warwickshire in the holidays till 1928, in which year he headed their averages with 50.71. He played no more first-class cricket till 1931, when in his first match for Worcestershire he scored a hundred, and he continued to play spasmodically for them till 1934. He was a batsman who must have taken a high place had he been able to play regularly after he came down. He also represented Cambridge at hockey (he was an international) and golf. In his one Varsity golf match he won his single seven and six and his foursome four and two, thus contributing substantially to Cambridge's victory by one match.

FIELD, Edwin, died at Bromley, Kent, on January 9, 1947, aged 75. Clifton XI 1888–91 (captain 1890 and 1891). Cambridge XI 1894. Berkshire 1895. He played for Middlesex from 1904 to 1906, his best performance being 107 against Sussex at Lord's in 1895. A Cambridge Rugby Blue 1892–94, he played for England v. Wales and Ireland in 1893. Solicitor.

FIELD, Frank E., died on August 25, 1934, at his home in Droitwich. Born near Alcester on September 23, 1875, he played first for Warwickshire in 1897 and steadily improved as a fast bowler, but not until 1908, at the age of 32 did he accomplish anything out of the ordinary. In that season Field took 106 wickets in county matches at a cost of 20 runs apiece, and three years later, in company with his captain, F. R. Foster, he played a leading part in carrying off the County

Championship—the only time that this honour has come to Warwickshire. That was Frank Foster's first year as captain, and his fast left-hand bowling round the wicket, coupled with Field's extra pace, with good easy right-hand delivery and off-break, caused many sides to collapse. Proving slightly more effective than did Foster, Field took 122 wickets at 19 runs apiece in Championship matches. He met with special success against Yorkshire at Harrogate, where in the second innings he dismissed seven men for 20 runs. He was unchanged with Foster, Yorkshire, on a worn pitch, failing so completely before the two fast bowlers, that they were all out for 58, and suffered defeat by 198 runs. Rather above medium-height, Field did not always deliver the ball at the full extent of his arm above his head, but ability to impart spin made him very fast off the pitch, and in the hot season of 1911 the dry turf suited his style perfectly. He and Foster kept up their form with remarkable energy day after day in the heat and never seemed to tire. Each sent down more than 700 overs, and as a combination they were invariably effective.

Field accomplished a remarkable feat in the match between Worcestershire and Warwickshire at Dudley on June 1, 2 and 3, 1914. In the second innings of Worcestershire he went on to bowl with the score at 85 for four, and took the six remaining wickets in eight overs and four balls, seven maidens, at a cost of two runs, the only scoring stroke made off him being lucky from the second ball of the second over before he had taken a wicket. While finishing off the Worcestershire innings in this startling fashion Field delivered five no-balls, with one of which he clean-bowled M. K. Foster. In taking these six wickets Field received no assistance, three batsmen being bowled, two caught and bowled, and one leg-before-wicket.

For the Players at Scarborough in 1911 he dismissed eight of a powerful side of Gentlemen in the first innings for 94 runs. Field was very smart in stopping hard return strokes from his own bowling. When he ceased to play for Warwickshire in 1920 he had taken in first-class cricket 1,024 wickets at a cost of 23 runs each. He made no pretensions to being a batsman. In recent years he acted as a first-class umpire, until chronic rheumatism ruined his health.

FIELD, 2nd Lieut. Oliver (Durham Light Infantry), was killed in action in France on July 18, 1915, aged 42. A steady batsman and good field, he was in the Clifton College XI

in 1890, when he scored 113 runs with an average of 14.12. Proceeding to Oxford, he played for Trinity in 1892 and 1893, averaging 29.00 in the former year and 27.50 in the latter. His highest innings for the College was 100 not out v. Malvern College in 1893. He was a direct descendant of Oliver Cromwell.

FIELDER, Arthur, Kent fast bowler for 12 years immediately prior to the First World War, died in St. Thomas's Hospital, London, on August 30, 1949, aged 71. He enjoyed a distinction possessed by no other cricketer: in a Gentlemen v. Players match at Lord's, he took all 10 wickets in an innings. This feat he accomplished in 1906 when, despite his great achievement, the Gentlemen won a fine game by 45 runs. Taking in first-class matches that season 186 wickets for 20 runs apiece, Fielder did much towards enabling Kent, for the first time, to carry off the Championship. His success was the more remarkable as, after showing capital form in 1903 and 1904, his first two years in the Kent XI, he fell off so badly in 1905 that, taking comparatively few wickets, and those at heavy cost, he lost his place in the side.

Fielder did big things in 1907, taking 172 wickets for only 16 runs each, and he continued to render fine service for the next seven seasons till the War. Over 40 years old when County Cricket was revived in 1919, he played no more for Kent. Altogether he took 1,221 wickets for less than 21 runs apiece. While never regarded as much of a batsman, he shared at Stourbridge in 1909 in what is still, as regards purely domestic cricket, a record stand for the last-wicket in England. Nine Kent wickets were down for 320 when he joined Frank Woolley and the two players added 235, Woolley making 185 and Fielder 112 not out.

Born at Plaxtol, near Tonbridge, on July 19, 1878, Fielder fulfilled engagements at Tonbridge and Canterbury before he found a place in the county team, succeeding W. M. Bradley as fast bowler. Despite a wet summer he acquitted himself well enough to be taken to Australia in the autumn of that year as a member of the first team led by P. F. Warner, but he accomplished little and figured in only two of the five Test matches. In 1907, he again went to Australia under A. O. Jones and in four of the Tests he took 25 wickets for just over 25 runs each.

Very strong, Fielder undertook a rare amount of work without sign of fatigue. As a rule he bowled well outside the off-stump and at times made the ball break back, but his best delivery was one which swung away.

This made him very dependent upon the smartness of his slips where, in their famous year of 1906, Kent were specially well served by such men as J. R. Mason, K. L. Hutchings, Woolley and Seymour, with the almost infallible Huish as wicket-keeper.

FIELDING, Felix, who played for Surrey in seven matches between 1889 and 1891, died at Surbiton on February 4, 1910. He was born on February 24, 1858, and was educated at Malvern, where he was in the XI in 1875. Later he became prominent in connection with the Incogniti, M.C.C., and Richmond C.C., and for some years was captain of the Surbiton C.C. In his second match for Surrey—against Oxford University at the Oval, in 1889—he scored 75, and with Abel (138) added 183 runs for the second wicket: the county made 614, and won by an innings and 367 runs. He was well above the average as a wicket-keeper, and in 1889 took part in the North v. South match at Manchester. As a batsman he possessed strong defence, but it was his skill behind the wicket which obtained him a place in first-class cricket.

FILGATE, Charles Roden, born at Cheltenham on October 16, 1848, died at Northwood, Middlesex, after a prolonged period of ill-health, on September 1, 1930, in his 81st year. *Scores and Biographies* said of him: "Has a strong defence, combined with fine hitting powers, besides being a brilliant field anywhere (though generally at long-leg or cover-point) with a quick return." At Cheltenham College, where H. W. Renny-Tailyour and George Strachan were among his contemporaries, he was coached by James Lillywhite, senior and junior, and was in the XI four years, 1865 to 1868 inclusive. In each of his last two seasons there he made over 1,000 runs, his aggregate in 1868 being 1,027 with an average of 54. Beginning his County Cricket in 1870, he took part in many Gloucestershire triumphs. Against Surrey at the Oval in 1873 he carried out his bat for 58, and in the match with Sussex at Clifton three years later he scored 93. He also took part in much cricket in Ireland and, for County Louth in 1868, at the age of 18, he made 158 v. Navan. For the long period of 62 years—since 1869—he had been a member of the M.C.C. When playing for the club against Yorkshire at Lord's, in 1870, he had the unusual experience of seeing all his three stumps sent out of the ground when bowled by Freeman.

FILLISTON, Joseph W., who died in hospital on October 25, 1964, aged 102, five days after being knocked down by a motor-scooter, acted as umpire to the B.C.C. Cricket Club for many years. "Old Joe" stood in the Old England v. Lord's Taverners match at Lord's when over 100. In his younger days he played cricket with Dr. W. G. Grace and he helped Gentlemen of Kent defeat the Philadelphians by six wickets at Town Malling in 1889. He also played as a professional in the Staffordshire League. He liked to tell of the occasion when he gave "W. G." out leg-before in a London County game at the Crystal Palace. The Doctor, he said, refused to leave the crease and, as nobody had the courage to contradict him, he continued his innings.

FINDLAY, William, who died at his home at Tenterden, Kent, on June 19, 1953, aged 72, following a heart attack, was Secretary of M.C.C. from 1919 to 1926 and President in 1951–52. A wicket-keeper and batsman of considerable ability, he captained Eton in 1899 and, going to Oxford, gained his Blue in 1901 and the two following years. He led the Dark Blue side who beat Cambridge by 268 runs in 1903. From 1902 he played irregularly for Lancashire till 1906, helping to win the County Championship in 1904. In first-class cricket he held a batting average of 20.28 and dismissed 157 batsmen, 132 by catches.

He began important secretarial duties in 1907, when succeeding C. W. Alcock as Secretary of Surrey. Going to Lord's as assistant to F. E. (later Sir Francis) Lacey in 1929, he became Secretary of M.C.C. in 1936, a position he held for 10 years, and for which his genial, diplomatic manner and never-failing courtesy suited him admirably. During his term of office at Lord's the new Grand Stand, with the famous "Father Time" weather-vane, was erected. In 1937 he made one of his biggest contributions to cricket legislature when heading a Commission appointed by M.C.C. to explore the question of the difficulties of counties taking part in the County Championship and which is always referred to as "The Findlay Commission."

A member of the Committee and a Trustee of M.C.C., he at one time served on the Committee of four separate County Clubs, including that of Lancashire, of whom he was President in 1947 and 1948. His services to the game received recognition in the way of presentations from the Boards of Control of Australia, South Africa, New Zealand, the West Indies and India.

His calm efficiency earned him a glowing tribute from the M.C.C. President of 1929,

Field Marshal Lord Plumer, who said of him: "If Findlay had been a soldier, I should like to have had him on my staff."—E. E.

FINGLETON, John Henry Webb ("Jack"), O.B.E., died on November 22, 1981, at the Royal North Shore Hospital in Sydney. He was 73. Born at Waverley in Sydney's Eastern Suburbs, Fingleton was educated firstly by the Christian Brothers at St Francis's School, Paddington, and then at Waverley College. Leaving school at the age of 15, he embarked on a career as a journalist which commenced with a cadetship at the *Sydney Daily Guardian*. Later, he was to move to the *Telegraph Pictorial* where he worked for several years prior to the Second World War. At the outbreak of War, he joined the Army before being seconded to the former Prime Minister, Billy Hughes, as Press Secretary. From this time onwards, he lived and worked in Canberra. Fingleton achieved no particular distinction on the cricket field while at school, but, on joining Waverley, he quickly graduated to the first XI of a club which included Kippax, Carter, Hendry and Mailey within its ranks. A right-hand opening batsman, Fingleton was noted more for his stubborn defence than for his aggression. The one epithet unfailingly used to describe his batting was "courageous." He was also an outstandingly gifted fieldsman, whose reputation was made in the covers but who was later to win fame with Vic Richardson, and sometimes with W. A. Brown, in South Africa in 1935–36 as part of the "O'Reilly leg-trap." Neville Cardus, for whom Jack had the greatest regard, once described the Fingleton-Brown combination as "crouching low and acquisitively, each with as many arms as an Indian God."

In 1930, when 22, Fingleton won his first cap for New South Wales and within 12 months (after only five first-class matches) he was selected for Australia. In the home series against South Africa in 1931–32, he was thrice 12th man and he eventually won his place in the side for the final Test only because Ponsford was forced out of the selected side by illness. In a game notable for its low scoring Fingleton was second top-scorer with 40. In the following summer came the "Body-line" series. Early in the season, Fingleton scored a brave century for New South Wales against the Englishmen, which was sufficient to ensure his selection for the first Test. He started the series in fine form, with scores of 26, 40 and 83, and seemed as well equipped as any to handle the novel tactics of the opposition. However, the

third Test at Adelaide was a disaster for Fingleton. Australia were beaten by 338 runs, Fingleton made a "pair," and he was blamed for leaking to the newspapers details of the exchange between Woodfull and Warner which took place in the Australian dressing-room and almost led to the abandonment of the Test series. Perhaps as a repercussion, Fingleton was a surprise omission from the Australian side selected to tour England in 1934.

He was restored to the Test team for the tour of South Africa in 1935–36, a tour that was to mark the apogee of his career. Against Natal at Durban he scored 167 (the highest innings of his first-class career), during the tour he had several mammoth opening partnerships with Brown, and he concluded the series with centuries in each of the last three Test matches—112 at Cape Town, 108 at Johannesburg and 118 in Durban. Australia won each of these games by an innings. In the following season in Australia, against an M.C.C. side captained by G. O. Allen, he created history by scoring a fourth consecutive Test hundred at Brisbane. The achievement was later equalled by Alan Melville (whose four consecutive Test hundreds were scored between 1939 and 1947) and then surpassed by the West Indian, Everton Weekes (1948–49). In the 1936–37 series, Fingleton achieved another place in the record book by sharing with Bradman, in the third Test in Melbourne, a sixth-wicket partnership of 346, a record which still stands. In 1938, Fingleton was selected in the Australian team which toured England, a Test series in which he had only moderate success. This, he was later to say, was "because I couldn't play the pull shot, I was never suited to English pitches." His Test career ended at the Oval in "Hutton's Match." For Fingleton it was a disappointing end: in the course of England's marathon innings of 903 for seven declared he sustained a leg injury which was sufficiently serious to prevent him from batting in either Australian innings.

After the Second World War Fingleton retired from first-class cricket and divided his time between Canberra, where for 34 years until his retirement in 1978 he was political correspondent for Radio Australia, and the coverage of Test matches. In Canberra he was a close friend of several Prime Ministers. Typical of these relationships was that which he enjoyed with Sir Robert Menzies, who provided him with a handsome and laudatory foreword in his book, *Masters of Cricket*. Fingleton's coverage of Tests resulted in publication of a number of books which secured for the writer a place at the forefront of Australian cricket writers. The books included *Cricket Crisis* (which involved itself principally with the Body-line series of 1932–33), *Brightly Fades the Don* (England 1948), *Brown & Company: The Tour in Australia* (Australia 1950–51), *The Ashes Crown the Year* (England 1953), *Masters of Cricket, Four Chukkas to Australia* (Australia 1958–59), *The Greatest Test of All* (Brisbane 1960), *Fingleton on Cricket* and

The Immortal Victor Trumper. His final book—*Batting From Memory*—was to have been launched in Australia during the week of his death. In addition to his writing, Fingleton was a witty, good-humoured and perceptive commentator for the BBC and at various times a contributor to *The Times*, the *Sunday Times*, the *Observer*, and various newspapers in Australia, South Africa and elsewhere. In 1976, he was appointed O.B.E. for services "to journalism and to cricket".

TEST RECORD

	Tests	Inns.	Not Outs	Runs	Highest Inns.	Avge.	100s	Ct.
1931–32 v. South Africa	1	1	0	40	40	40.00	0	2
1932–33 v. England	3	6	0	150	83	25.00	0	3
1935–36 in South Africa	5	7	1	478	118	78.33	3	4
1936–37 v. England	5	9	0	389	136	44.22	2	2
1938 in England	4	6	0	123	40	20.50	0	2
Total	18	29	1	1,180	136	42.46	5	13

In his first-class career, J. H. Fingleton batted in 166 innings, was not out 13 times, and scored 6,816 runs (average 44.54), including 22 hundreds. His highest score was 167 v. Natal, Durban, in 1935–36. He held 82 catches, effected two stumpings, and took two wickets (average 27.00).

Other tributes:

Bill Bowes: "Like all good opening batsmen, Jack Fingleton did not have much back-lift. He kept the bat close to his left foot and was rarely surprised by the quicker long half-volley or yorker. He had what could be described as a 'good fault' in that he tended to overdo his positioning and get too far in front of the ball instead of keeping bat and left leg side by side. This meant he had to bring the bat round the left leg to play the ball. In recent years Colin Cowdrey did the same thing, sometimes to such an extent that he occasionally had his leg stump knocked down behind his legs. It is the reason why Geoffrey Boycott takes so many knocks on the knuckles when the ball lands on the seam and lifts more than expected. When the pitch is a good one, though, this overdoing of position can bring many benefits. There are runs to be had for pushes to the on-side. And, more effectively than Boycott, Fingleton would steer the ball with accuracy through the gaps on the off-side. On true surfaces, like those found in Australia and South Africa in the 1930s, he was a dangerous opponent, full of guts; against the leg-theory bowling of Larwood during the famous "Body-line tour" of 1932–33 he

never retreated. He was a reliable fieldsman in any position, especially at short leg, and possessed a strong arm. He was also a good team man. That he thought deeply about the game was evinced by his distinguished writings on cricket and cricketers."

E. W. Swanton: "The number of Test cricketers whose reputations as writers on the game have come near to matching their skill on the field is very small. In this select category Jack Fingleton comes straight away to mind; but he differed from all such in that he entered first-class cricket as a well-qualified journalist rather than making his name first as a player. To a fellow cricket-writer this distinction was regularly in evidence. It was not only that his training quickened his observation and eye for detail. His judgements were always informed by careful first-hand evidence. Equally his nose unerringly sniffed a story, big or small, serious or funny. His work was lightened by various aspects of humour; it could be sly, sardonic or side-splitting. These qualities were equally appreciated by listeners on sound radio and television.

"If he was not exactly an easy professional companion he was certainly a stimulating one. Some of those who, unwittingly perhaps, stepped on his corns, remained wary of him ever after. But if he was a bad enemy he was a devoted friend to a wide and diverse circle. Among his contemporaries on the field and in the press box, perhaps Bill O'Reilly, Lindsay Hassett and Ian Peebles stood at the peak of his esteem. An affectionate profile of O'Reilly for *The Cricketer* was one of his last articles. He served the *Sunday Times* most ably for many years as their Australian cricket correspondent. In his own country he wrote all too little about the game, concentrating on his duties as a lobby correspondent from his base at Canberra and serving newspapers in many countries.

"The first of his 10 books, *Cricket Crisis*, published 13 years afterwards in 1946, is far the best story of the Body-line tour of 1932–33, in which he was a participant and victim. There were five tour books, all lively, entertaining, wherein cricket is often merely the continuing narrative thread. It was sad that he died of a heart attack immediately upon publication of his autobiographical *Batting from Memory*—though not before he had read a highly appreciative review of it in the Melbourne *Age*, the paper whose opinion he would have valued most. In this book, as in most of his others, one had to discount an incompatibility of temperament with Sir Donald Bradman (as a man, not as a cricketer) which was damaging both to Australian cricket and even, in some degree, to their own reputations. Sir Donald, characteristically, has borne it all in silence. This qualification notwithstanding, Jack Fingleton remains surely, as cricket writer and broadcaster, the best his country has produced."

FIRTH, Jack, died at his home near Bradford on September 7, 1981, aged 63. He played a few times for Yorkshire, his native county, as a wicket-keeper in 1949 and 1950 but had no chance of displacing D. V. Brennan, although an innings of 67 not out against Gloucestershire in his last match for the county saved his side from collapse and showed that his value was not confined to his 'keeping. Moving to Leicestershire, where he replaced Corrall, in 1951 he at once made a name for himself, being especially skilful, indeed almost infallible, at taking the extremely difficult left-arm chinamen and googlies of Walsh. In 1952 he set up a record for the county with 85 dismissals. He had besides Walsh two more orthodox spinners in Jackson and Munden and thus had plenty of opportunities of standing up. Moreover, in both 1951 and 1952 with an average of just under 20 he helped the batting considerably. After that his batting fell off, though his highest score, 90 not out against Essex, was not made till his last season. However, he maintained his reputation as a wicket-keeper who would not, had the chance arisen, have been out of place in a higher sphere of cricket. In 1958 he was awarded a benefit and retired at the end of the season.

FISCHARDT, Charles Gustav, one of three cricketing brothers, was born at Bloemfontein on March 20, 1870, and died after an operation on May 30, 1923, aged 53. He was educated at Grey College (Bloemfontein), in Scotland, and at Hamburg, and was a useful lob bowler and a vigorous batsman. He played for the Orange Free State against three English teams and in Currie Cup matches, and also for South Africa against England in 1891–92 and 1895–96. In 1895–96, when he captained the Free State XVI against the Englishmen, he took six wickets for 93 runs in the first innings. In a small match at Bloemfontein he and L. Richardson once added 401 together for the second wicket. His portrait can be seen on page 61 of *The History of South African Cricket*.

FISHER, Arthur H., who died in Dunedin on March 23, 1961, aged 90, was well known in New Zealand cricket circles. He joined the Carisbrook C.C. in 1887 and played for them with distinction for many years. He also rendered good service to Otago, for whom, with fast-medium left-arm bowling, he took 253 wickets, average 13.40, achieving his best performance in 1896–97 when taking nine wickets for 50 against Queensland at Dunedin. He appeared several times for New Zealand, with whom he toured Australia.

FISHER, Lieut. Charles Denis (R.N.V.R.), born at Blatchington Court, Sussex, on June 19, 1877, was lost in H.M.S. *Invincible* on May 31, 1916. A safe and steady batsman, and a bowler who could keep a good length and had a considerable off-break, he was in the Westminster XI in 1893 and three following years, being captain in 1895 and 1896.

He headed the batting during his last year, and in bowling was first in 1893, second in 1894 and 1896 and fourth in 1895.

At Oxford he obtained his Blue in 1900, and in the match with Cambridge scored 26 and took three wickets for 42 runs. In 1898 he began to assist Sussex, and his highest score for the county was 80 v. Worcestershire at Brighton in 1901. Since 1904 he had been a member of the M.C.C. He was 6ft. 3in. in height.

FISHER, Horace, a left arm slow bowler, who played infrequently for Yorkshire, 1928–36, died at his home at Overton, near Wakefield, on April 16, 1974, aged 70. A contemporary of Hedley Verity, Fisher seldom played unless Verity was on Test duty. In first-class cricket he took 93 wickets, average 28.18. He was also a useful batsman at a crisis and a splendid close-to-the wicket fieldsman. A careful man, he bowled with a low trajectory, just short of a length and he counted his overs, his maidens and the runs that were hit off him.

Fisher was the first bowler to register a hat-trick of lbw victims when he took five wickets for 12 runs against Somerset at Sheffield in 1932. The story has often been told that when umpire Alec Skelding having given out Mitchell-Innes and Andrews lbw, stared up the wicket at Luckes when the third appeal was made, uttered almost in disbelief, "As God's my judge, that's out, too," and he lifted his finger. Earlier in that same week in August, Fisher had taken six wickets for 11 runs against Leicestershire at Bradford. In 1934, Fisher toured West Indies with the Yorkshire team. A League professional for 20 years, Fisher played for various clubs in the Bradford, Huddersfield, Lancashire and Central Lancashire Leagues.

FISHWICK, Tom Silvester, died at Sandown, Isle of Wight, on February 21, 1950, aged 73. A strong batsman with plenty of strokes, he was joint captain of Warwickshire in 1902 and 1907. Between 1900 and 1909 he scored 12 centuries for the county, and in 1904 and 1905 exceeded 1,000 runs. In 1905 he established a Warwickshire record by bringing off 40 catches and, except for wicket-keepers, this is still unequalled for the county.

FISON, Thomas Arthur, a well-known figure in Metropolitan cricket circles about a quarter of a century ago, died at Hampstead, on April 14, 1911. For years he was captain of the Hendon C.C., and was in local cricket one of the hardest hitters of his day. Against Highgate School in August, 1879, he scored 264 not out in three hours and a half, hitting a seven, two fives, nine fours, 23 threes, and 40 twos. All the hits were run out, and in the score-sheet it was recorded that he "retired to catch a train for the Continent." In a match between the same sides at Hendon in 1884 he made 201. Mr. Fison, was 6ft. 2in. in height, and was a good wicket-keeper. He was born at Romsey, in Hampshire, on October 7, 1853, and was educated at Mill Hill School.

FITZGERALD, James, a fast bowler and useful batsman of Queensland between 1902 and 1905, died at Brisbane in August, 1950. He played for his State against the M.C.C., captained by Sir Pelham Warner, in 1903–04, and was a contemporary of Henry, Queensland's first aboriginal bowler.

FITZGERALD, Brigadier General Percy Desmond, D.S.O., who died on August 17, 1933, aged 61, played for M.C.C. in first-class matches, the last in 1897.

FITZMAURICE, Desmond Michael John, who died on January 19, 1981, aged 63, played twice for Victoria in 1947–48 as a medium-paced bowler. He toured India in 1949–50 with a strong Commonwealth team, opening the bowling in two of the five unofficial Tests, and played for a while as a professional in the Central Lancashire League. He also took a coaching appointment in Kimberley, South Africa. In all he played in 17 first-class matches, scoring 272 runs at an average of 17 and taking 28 wickets at 28.50 apiece. He was the younger brother of D. J. A. Fitzmaurice, who also played for Victoria.

FITZROY NEWDEGATE, Commander The Hon. John Maurice, who died in hospital on May 7, 1976, aged 79, captained Northamptonshire as Commander J. M. FitzRoy from 1925 to 1927. A tall man with enormous hands, he was a fine slip and a most energetic chaser of the ball in the field; he did much to improve his side's fielding and was a splendid captain to play under. His premature retirement owing to a knee injury was greatly regretted. As a bat he was a fierce hitter who might have made more runs had he not tried to clear the boundary quite so often. As it was, he sometimes made useful scores when more esteemed batsmen had failed. In the few matches he was able to play in his last season, he made 50, the highest score of the innings and of his career, against Kent, and against Worcestershire he and T. B. G. Welch scored 86 in 52 minutes in an unbroken partnership to win the match with eight minutes to spare.

FITZSIMMONS, Edward, a good slow bowler for Wellington 50 years ago, died at Wanganui on January 29, 1942, aged 73. He used the off-break with effect and his accurate length made him difficult to punish. A smart slip fieldsman, he completed his value as an all-rounder by causing trouble late in the batting list.

FLAMSON, William Henry, who died in January, 1945, in his 40th year, was a useful bowler for Leicestershire during the three seasons immediately preceding the outbreak of the Second World War.

In 1936 he took 59 wickets but never played regularly owing to injury. Of powerful build, he bowled fast-medium with plenty of life, but want of good length often made him expensive. He showed little skill in batting.

FLEETWOOD-SMITH, Leslie O'Brien, who died in a Melbourne hospital on March 16, 1971, aged 60, played in 10 Test matches for Australia between 1935 and 1938, taking 42 wickets. A left-arm spin bowler who changed his style after breaking his right arm as a schoolboy, he often exploited the googly and the "chinaman" with effect. In all first-class cricket his record was 597 wickets, average 22.00. "Chuck," as he was known, first toured England in 1934 when he obtained 119 wickets—including three in four deliveries against Oxford University—for 18.06 runs apiece, but failed to gain a Test place against such formidable rivals as C. V. Grimmett and W. J. O'Reilly.

In 1936–37, however, after faring moderately in South Africa the previous year, he helped Australia to carry off the Ashes following the loss of the first two Tests, in which he did not play, to G. O. Allen's England team. Fleetwood-Smith did specially well in the fourth Test at Melbourne, his match analysis being 10 wickets for 239 runs. Again in England in 1938, he took part in four Tests and at Leeds earned match figures of seven wickets for 107 runs, he and O'Reilly (10 for 122) bearing a major part in the victory which decided the rubber.

In the final match of the series at the Oval—his last Test appearance—however, he, in company with the other Australian bowlers, came in for a mauling. It was in that game that Leonard Hutton put together his record-breaking 364 and England won by the overwhelming margin of an innings and 579 runs. Fleetwood-Smith's analysis in a total of 903 was one wicket for 298 runs from 87 overs.

For Victoria, Fleetwood-Smith took 246 wickets for 24.56 runs each in 40 Sheffield Shield fixtures. Twice he enjoyed the distinction of dismissing nine batsmen in an innings—for 36 runs against Tasmania in 1932–33 and for 135 runs against South Australia five seasons later—at Melbourne in each case. He fell on hard times some years ago and was "living rough," but his friends rallied round him and latterly he was his old self again.

FLEMING, James M., who, after a long illness, died in an Edinburgh hospital on September 4, 1962, the eve of his 61st birthday, played for Scotland against Ireland and H. L. Collins's Australian team in 1926, when he was one of the best all-rounders in Scottish cricket. An excellent wicket-keeper

and a good batsman, he was also a useful slow bowler. He founded the Cricket Society of Scotland in 1952. An accomplished curler, he was a member of the winning rink of the world championship in 1949, only a year after he took up the game. He organised many tours of Scottish cricketers and after one of these wrote an amusing book entitled *Through Wales With Bat and Bottle*.

FLETCHER, Thomas, who died at Derby on September 29, 1954, aged 73, played for Derbyshire against H. B. G. Austin's West Indian team of 1906, scoring 28 and sharing in a win by six wickets. In his youth, he played Association football as an amateur for Derby County F.C. and toured America and the Continent with amateur sides.

FLETCHER, William, a fast bowler who played in 12 matches for Yorkshire during the seasons of 1891 and 1892, died in June, 1935. Born on February 16, 1866, he was in his 70th year.

FLINT, Joseph, who died on November 2, 1912, was born at Wirksworth, near Glossop, on May 12, 1844, and was thus in his 69th year at the time of death. He was a good slow round-armed bowler, with a break-back, a useful batsman and a good field at slip or point. His career as a county cricketer was short, for his first match for Derbyshire was in 1872 and his last in 1879, and he did not appear for the side in 1876 or 1877. His greatest feat was for Sixteen of Derbyshire against Notts at Wirksworth in 1873, when he and W. Mycroft, bowling unchanged, got the visitors out for 14, the former taking six wickets for seven runs and the latter four for six. Among his other good performances for the county may be mentioned his 11 for 87 v. United XI in 1874, his four for 14 v. Lancashire at Manchester in the same year, and his six for 28 v. M.C.C. and Ground at Lord's in 1879.

FLINT, William A., who died in Nottingham on February 5, 1955, aged 64, was one of the most prominent all-round sportsmen of his time. From 1919 till 1928 he played cricket for Nottinghamshire, scoring 3,345 runs and taking 237 wickets; from 1908 to 1926 he appeared as wing half-back for Notts County F.C., becoming captain. In his first game for Nottinghamshire he took six wickets for 53 and two for 34 against Middlesex at Lord's and in the return game he hit 98, sharing with John Gunn in a last wicket stand of 111. His best season as an all-rounder was that of 1924, when he scored 412 runs and was second in his county's bowling figures with 58 wickets, average 19.74. That summer against Surrey at the Oval he scored 103, the highest of his three-figure innings, he and W. Walker adding 178 for the seventh wicket. When scoring a hard-hit 100 not out from the Northamptonshire bowling at Trent Bridge in 1927, he helped W. Payton in an unfinished partnership of 247 in three hours.

FLOQUET, Bertram Harold, who died at Johannesburg on June 16, 1953, aged 69, was a punishing batsman who appeared for Transvaal from 1902 to 1913. His highest innings in the Currie Cup competition was 104 against Griqualand West at Durban in 1910–11. He was an elder brother of C. E. Floquet, who played against England in 1909.

FLOWERS, Wilfred, the last survivor of the Notts XI that in 1878 played the opening match with the first Australian team to visit this country, died on November 1, 1926, at Nottingham, in his 70th year. A steady slow bowler with an offbreak, which rendered him extremely difficult on a soft wicket, a fine resolute batsman, and a capital field, Flowers was one of the best all-round cricketers of his time. Born at Calverton on December 7, 1856, but soon associated with Sutton-in-Ashfield—the great nursery of Notts cricket for many years—he was first engaged by the Worksop club when only 17. Three seasons later he was given a place in the Notts Colts match, and he at once made his mark by taking the wickets of five members of the County XI at a cost of only eight runs. This performance naturally led to his appearance in the game between the M.C.C. and the Colts of England—at that period and for a long while afterwards the recognised test for the most promising of young professional cricketers. Again Flowers seized his chance for, if in the first innings he disposed of only one batsman, that player was none other than W. G. Grace, and in the second innings, when he obtained four wickets, he again enjoyed the distinction of dismissing the great man. In the same season—1877—Flowers found his way into the Notts XI, and the association then started lasted for a period of 20 years. A year later he joined the staff at Lord's, and one of his first matches

for the M.C.C. was that memorable struggle on May 27, 1878, when the Australians—previously beaten in a single innings at Nottingham—startled the cricket world by defeating the powerful side got together to represent the premier club, by nine wickets. M.C.C. made 33 and 19, and the Australians 41 and 12 for one wicket, the game being over in the one day. Flowers was not called upon to bowl, Alfred Shaw and Fred Morley being unchanged, and in the first innings Spofforth disposed of him without scoring, but in the second Flowers made 11 of the 19 runs for which the whole Marylebone team were dismissed. Flowers in the course of his long career had several notable successes against the various Australian teams. In 1884 he made 90 for the North of England, at Trent Bridge, and two years afterwards, on the same ground, he shared in a wonderful partnership with Richard Barlow, of Lancashire. Barlow scored 113 and Flowers 93, the pair adding no fewer than 172 for the ninth wicket. A third notable display of his against Australian bowling was at the expense of the side captained by Blackham, in 1893. The game took place at Lord's' Blackham, sending the M.C.C. in to bat. The club put together a total of 424, to which Flowers contributed 130 and Frank Marchant 103. Flowers's best year was probably 1883, when he scored 1,144 runs, with an average of 24—no mean record in those days—and in addition took 113 wickets for less than 15 runs each. In 1893 he made over 1,000 runs, and in 1896—his last season with Notts—he put together in his last match for the county an innings of 107 against Sussex at Trent Bridge. Altogether he appeared for different Players' XIs on 18 occasions. He went out to Australia in the winter of 1884–85 with a team led by Arthur Shrewsbury, and again in 1886–87 under the same captain. Once he played for England in this country—at Lord's against Australia in 1893. Two of his notable all-round performances for the M.C.C. were as follows:

v. Derbyshire, 1883. Made 131 and took 10 wickets for 87.

v. Cambridge University, 1884. Made 122 (out of 160) and took 14 wickets for 80.

Among many bowling feats he accomplished were:

7 wickets for 16 runs, Notts v. Middlesex, at Lord's	1879
8 wickets for 23 runs, Notts v. Gloucestershire, at Clifton	1881
8 wickets for 25 runs, M.C.C. v. Cambridge University, at Cambridge	1883
8 wickets for 31 runs, England v. Victoria, at Melbourne	1884–85
8 wickets for 22 runs, M.C.C. v. Cambridge University, at Lord's	1885
5 wickets for 11 runs, England v. New South Wales, at Sydney	1886–87

In the matter of benefits, Flowers has a strangely unhappy experience. Notts, in 1895, gave him the match with Lancashire, at Trent Bridge, but so completely did the home batsmen fail against Arthur Mold, that, with 15 wickets falling to that bowler, the contest was over early on the second day. An even greater blow occurred in 1899, when the M.C.C. arranged with Middlesex for the Whitsuntide match with Somerset to be given to Flowers as a reward for his long and excellent service to the club. To the general dismay, rain fell so continuously on the Bank Holiday that not a ball could be bowled, and next day on a drying wicket little more than three hours' play sufficed to finish off the game. In view of these misfortunes Notts in 1904 awarded Flowers part of the proceeds of a match at Trent Bridge, but still Flowers' experience of benefits bordered on the tragic. When his connection with the Notts XI ended in 1896, Flowers acted as a first-class umpire, but failing eyesight prevented a satisfactory performance of the duties attaching to that calling and he soon abandoned the position. At the end of his cricket career, Flowers returned to the lace trade, and pursued that employment for many years, while at the time of his death he was employed by a hosiery manufacturer. He naturally never lost interest in the game in which he had attained such prominence, and last summer was a spectator at the Australians' matches at Trent Bridge. Modest about his achievements, quiet in manner and well-spoken, Flowers was generally popular and bore the ups and downs of life with much philosophy.

FOLEY, Lieut.-Col. Cyril Pelham, born on November 1, 1868, died on March 9, 1936, aged 67. He enjoyed the very special distinction of being in the Eton XIs of 1886–87 when both matches with Winchester and Harrow were won, and then helping Cambridge beat Oxford three times—1889 to 1891. Patient and sound in defence he scored freely to the off side. Usually going in first he seldom failed. Against Harrow in 1886 he made 114 and 36. His scores next year were 37 and eight while against Winchester he played innings of 38 and 23 and 23 and seven. For Cambridge he was equally consistent with 22, 26 and one not out, 12 and 41.

He appeared for Worcestershire in 1888, played for Middlesex from 1893 till 1906, and in the winter of 1904–05 toured the West Indies as a member of Lord Brackley's team. At Lord's in 1893 he was the centre of an unusual incident. In the match between Middlesex and Sussex he picked up a bail which had fallen and, on appeal, Henty, the umpire, gave him out; but, at the request of W. L. Murdoch, the Sussex captain, Mr. Foley continued his innings. As a soldier, he had much experience abroad and his exploits in the Jameson raid of 1895 earned for him the nickname of "The Raider."

He served with distinction in the Boer War and came home in temporary command of the 3rd Royal Scots. During the European War he commanded the 9th East Lancashire Regiment.

FOLEY, Harry, died in Brisbane on October 16, 1948, at the age of 42. Born in Wellington, Foley went to Wellington College and in 1923 he joined the staff of the Commercial Bank of Australia. He continued his studies at Victoria College and obtained his B.A. and B.Com. degrees. As a cricketer he developed into an exceedingly good left-hand opening batsman with limitless patience and there were few better slip fieldsmen. He played many fine innings for Wellington in 1931–37 and represented New Zealand in the first Test against the 1929–30 M.C.C. team at Christchurch. He probably would have played more regularly for his country had he not suffered from ill-health.

FOLEY, Paul Henry, born in London on March 19, 1857, died there suddenly on January 21, 1928, aged 70. He played for Worcestershire, commencing in 1878, and in 1895 visited Holland as captain of a Gentlemen of Worcestershire team. In one of the matches during that tour his lobs accounted for eight wickets in an innings. He batted left-handed, bowled right, and fielded point. For many years—up to 1908—Hon. Secretary of Worcestershire, he was a most generous supporter of the county's cricket. He was 6ft. 3in. in height, and a cousin of the well-known Etonian cricketers of the same surname.

FOLJAMBE, Lieut.-Col. George Savile, C.B., V.D., who died in London on September 13, 1920, aged 63, played for Notts five times in 1879 and twice in 1881. He was not in the XI at either Eton or Oxford, but was a good free hitter, and in 1881 played an innings of 99 for M.C.C. and Ground v. Oxford University at Oxford.

FONTAINE, Frederick Ernest, who died on October 24, 1982, aged 69, was a right-hand opening batsman who scored 118 for Victoria against Tasmania on his first-class début at Hobart in January 1931. He played 10 first-class innings in all for the state, scoring 379 runs with an average of 37.90.

FOORD-KELCEY, William, who was born at Smeeth on April 21, 1854, died at Woolwich on January 3, 1922. He was educated at Chatham House (Ramsgate) and at Oxford, and in 1874 and 1875 appeared against Cambridge at Lord's. He was a hard-hitting batsman, a round-armed bowler of great pace, and a capital field at mid-off. Between 1874 and 1883 he played for Kent in 64 matches, having a batting average of 14.79 and taking 202 wickets for 19.35 runs each. In a match at Oxford, in 1875, between the University and the Gentlemen of England he bowled Mr. W. H. Hadow with a ball which sent a bail 48 yards. For Oxford in 1875 he took six wickets for 12 runs v. M.C.C. and Ground, seven for 15 v. Gentlemen of England, and 13 for 128 v. Middlesex at Prince's. For Kent he obtained eight wickets in an innings for 49 runs v. Lancashire at Gravesend in 1876, and eight for 53 in an innings v. Yorkshire on the same ground six years later. His highest score in an important match was 105 for Kent v. Hampshire at Tunbridge Wells in 1878.

FORBES, Walter Francis, who was born at Malvern Link, January 20, 1858, died on March 31, 1933. He made a reputation at Eton, being as a schoolboy cricketer contemporary with Alfred and Edward Lyttelton, Ivo Bligh, W. H. Long, W. H. Grenfell, A. J. Webbe and others who were either renowned in cricket or in the larger world. Endowed with powerful physique he made the most of his height and strength. He appeared in the Eton XI at Lord's against Harrow in 1873 (when 15 years old), 1874, 1875 and 1876 (when captain). In 1873 he was not prominent though one of the first-wicket pair. In 1875 he was—very unkindly—credited with the "worst innings ever played at Lord's"—45 minutes for nine runs, all off the edge of the bat and behind the wicket, but he took five wickets for 21 runs with his fast round-arm bowling. In 1875 his 47 against Harrow prepared the way for feats during the following summer. He won the toss against Harrow, shouted with joy, took J. E. K. Studd in with him and scored 113 out of 150. The pitch was perfect, and the temperature tremendous, but Forbes revelled in the conditions, was only at the wicket one hour and 45 minutes, and hit 22

fours. This 1876 was his *annus mirabilis*, as apart from such a memorable hundred he had the satisfaction of leading Eton victories over both Harrow and Winchester, and threw a cricket ball exactly 132yd., 10yd. further than his throw of 1875; and also hurled the hammer 78 feet. If then only 18 years old he stood 6ft. 1½in., and weighed 12 stone. For the Yorkshire Gentlemen he made high scores and he also assisted I Zingari. Although he played for the Gentlemen at Lord's and at the Oval in 1883 (the tie match) he took little part in first-class cricket as he became steward to the Duke of Richmond at Goodwood.

FORD, Augustus Frank Justice, born on September 12, 1858, died on May 20, 1931, aged 72. *Scores and Biographies* describes him as "a capital and effective batsman, a middle paced round-armed bowler with a curious preliminary hop, and in the field good, though taking no particular place". At Repton, he was in the XI in 1874–75–76–77, being captain in the last two years. Going up to Cambridge, he got his Blue as a Freshman in 1878 and played the next three seasons. His best performance in the Varsity match was in 1881 when he scored 34 and 24 and took two wickets. In that season he made his highest score in first-class cricket—102 v. Surrey at the Oval. For Middlesex, whom he assisted from 1879 to 1882, he showed himself a first-rate slip fieldsman and caught seven men in a match against Gloucestershire at Lord's in 1882. His best bowling feat in first-class matches was accomplished in 1880 when at the Oval he took 13 Surrey wickets for 82.

FORD, Francis Gilbertson Justice, the youngest of seven brothers, all good cricketers at Repton, and nephew of G. J. Ford, who played for Oxford at Lord's 100 years ago, died on February 7, 1940, aged 73, at Burwash, Sussex. After four years in the Repton XI, being captain in the last two seasons, Francis Ford was the third of the brothers who played for Cambridge, receiving his Blue as a Freshman. In his first year Oxford won by seven wickets, the next match was drawn, and then he took part in two handsome victories. When captain, he led his side to a great triumph by an innings and 105 runs, and, playing again, he helped Cambridge to win by seven wickets, this being the sixth time in nine consecutive seasons on which that margin settled the trial of strength between the Universities at Lord's.

Standing 6ft. 2½in., he used his height with such effect that despite spare physique he put exceptional force into his left-hand strokes. Elegant in style, standing upright, he made many good-length balls into half volleys, and when the bowler pitched shorter he forced the ball away at a great rate on either side of the wicket. He failed to show his best form in the University match except in 1890, when on a treacherous pitch ruined by rain he made the highet score, not out 32, which won the game. Under similar conditions he took Middlesex to victory over Yorkshire at Headingley in 1898. With Hirst, Rhodes and F. S. Jackson in their prime, 60 in the last innings meant a difficult task, but Ford, going in number four with the total 26, hit up 29, finishing the match by driving Haigh over the far away off boundary—as Sir Pelham Warner, the first batsman to fall, has described.

Probably Francis Ford never gave a more brilliant display than in scoring 191 at Hove against Sussex in 1890. Gregor McGregor, the Cambridge captain, 131, and C. P. Foley, 117, also contributed centuries to the Cambridge second innings total of 703 for nine wickets—then a record score in English first-class cricket. Ford, going in when the bowling was mastered, scored almost as he pleased. His drives, either kept down or lifted over the bowler's head, were dazzling, and his cuts the perfection of timing. He revelled in these strokes when fast bowlers lost their length because of his punishment, and at Lord's the crowds grew enthusiastic over the way he scored from the best fast bowlers—Arthur Mold of Lancashire, Tom Richardson and Bill Lockwood of Surrey, suffered specially at his hands.

In 1893 he was second to A. E. Stoddart in the Middlesex averages when scoring generally was moderate, and in the winter of 1894 was in the first team captained by Stoddart which won the Test match at Sydney by 10 runs. He scored 48 when England followed-on in face of Australia's 586, so helping Albert Ward and J. T. Brown to pull the game round and set their rivals to get 177, a task which Peel and Briggs rendered impossible of achievement.

He headed the first-class batting in 1897, when he averaged 53 for an aggregate of 805. He excelled for the Gentlemen at Lord's, playing two grand not-out innings of 50 and 79. The second, on worn turf, was superb, only W. G. Grace and G. L. Jessop of the other batsmen doing much.

Poor health compelled Francis Ford to give up County Cricket at the finish of the 1899 season, with an aggregate of 7,293 runs, average 27.21. A good slow left-handed bowler, he often caused trouble by dropping the ball an accurate length from a great height with plenty of spin and curl; in first-class cricket he took 198 wickets, average 22 runs. A capable goalkeeper, he got his Blue, captained the Cambridge Association XI, and played sometimes for the Corinthian club. Always closely in touch with cricket, Francis Ford held strong views regarding "leg before," and his influence was largely responsible for bringing about the recent addition of the last phrase to Law 24.

FORD, Percy H., born on July 5, 1880, died at Gloucester in November, 1920, after an illness of three days, septic pneumonia following scarlet fever. For many seasons he played with Gloucester City and occasionally for the county. As a fast bowler he was very useful making the most of his height (6ft. 7in.), but unfortunately for Gloucestershire he was not often available. At Cheltenham in 1906 he and Dennett bowled unchanged through both innings of Sussex, Mr. Ford's figures being five for 29 and six for 84. Against Somerset at Bristol the same year he took nine wickets for 67 runs.

FORD, Reggie Gilbert, who died in Bristol in October, 1981, aged 74, played in 57 matches for Gloucestershire between 1929 and 1936. At the outset of his career he was expected to develop into a sound bat and, as a medium-pace right-armer, was often given the new ball. But as his final record for the county was 496 runs, with an average of 10.55, and a highest score of 37 not out, and as his 10 wickets cost him 49.30 runs each, he can hardly be said to have fulfilled his promise.

FORD, William Justice, the eldest and probably the best-known of the famous brothers, died in London on April 3, 1904. He was in the Repton XI in 1870, 1871 and 1872, and in the following year assisted Cambridge against Oxford, being put into the team at the last moment, and scoring 51 not out and 11. He was a tremendous hitter, a good field at point, a useful wicket-keeper, and a slow round-arm bowler. Height 6ft. 3in., and weight (in 1871) 15st. 4lb., which by 1886 had increased to 17st. 4lb. He occasionally appeared for Middlesex, and it was when assisting that side against Kent, at Maidstone, in 1885, that he made 44 in 17 minutes and 75 out of 90 in three-quarters of an hour. His longest *measured* hit was 143yd. 2ft. He hit out of almost all the grounds upon which he played, including Lord's and the Aigburth ground at Liverpool. Playing once for M.C.C. and Ground v. Eastbourne, at the Saffrons, he hit J. Bray over the trees, the ball pitching 60yd. beyond them. On another occasion, when playing at Torquay, he hit a ball out of the ground (above the ordinary size), across a road, and so far into another field that it put up a brace of partridges. He made many large scores for the M.C.C., Nondescripts, and Incogniti, his most productive innings being 250 for M.C.C. v. Uxbridge, in 1881. At various times he was a master at Marlborough, Principal of Nelson College, N.Z., and head master of Leamington College. Once, in a match at Marlborough, he had made 92 when the last man came in, and, wishing to make sure of his hundred, hit the very next ball with such hearty good will that he and his partner ran 10 for the stroke! Of recent years he had been a prolific writer on the game, his best-known books being the histories of the Middlesex County and Cambridge University Clubs, the latter of which will probably become a classic. His article on Public School Cricket had some years been a feature of *Wisden's Almanack*, Mr. Ford must be regarded as one of the greatest hitters the world has ever seen, having been equalled by few and surpassed only by Mr. C. I. Thornton. He was born in London November 7, 1853.

FORESTER, Tom, D.S.O., who died on December 27, 1927, after a long illness, played first for Warwickshire and afterwards for Derbyshire. A useful left-handed bat, he was better known as a right-handed medium pace bowler. He had a peculiar action which made him appear at times as though he delivered the ball with his right foot in front. He made the ball swerve and got on an appreciable amount of spin. His best season was in 1911. At the outbreak of War he enlisted, and subsequently reached the rank of Major, being awarded the D.S.O. Born on September 21, 1873, he was in his 55th year at the time of his death.

FORMAN, The Rev. Arthur Francis Emilius, who was born at Gibraltar on July 26, 1850, died of consumption at Repton on February 13, 1905. He was a good all-round cricketer, but will be better remembered as a coach than as a player. For 30 years he was a master at Repton School, and, while he was there, many cricketers, who afterwards took part with success in the best matches of the day, passed through his hands. The best

known of his pupils are Lionel Palairet, F. G. J. Ford, and C. B. Fry, and J. N. Crawford, who has played so well for Surrey during the last two seasons, bids fair to make a great name for himself both as batsman and bowler. Mr. Forman was in the Sherborne XI from 1866 to 1869, being contemporary with W. H. Game, but although he afterwards proceeded to Trinity College, Oxford, he did not succeed in obtaining his Blue. In 1877, 1878, 1879, and 1882 he occasionally appeared in the Derbyshire team, but did not meet with much success, his highest score being 32 against Sussex in 1882. He wrote many articles on Public School Cricket, a subject in which he was greatly interested and one which he dealt with most skilfully. He was a man of fine physique, standing 6ft. and weighing 13st. 8lb.

FORMAN, Frank Gerald, who died on December 8, 1960, aged 76, played in one match for Derbyshire in 1911. He achieved much all-round success in club cricket in which he continued till he was 62. A fine hockey player, he captained the county team for some time.

FORMAN, Frederick Gerald, whose death was recorded in the 1961 edition was inadvertently stated to be Mr. Frank Gerald.

FORMAN, Humphrey, born at Repton on April 26, 1888, died at Bangkok, after an operation, on May 21, 1923. He was a batsman with good defence and some effective strokes, bowled slow-medium and fielded well. During his last year at Shrewsbury he was captain of the XI, but he did not secure his Blue for Cambridge though he was tried for the University in 1910. In the year mentioned his name will be found in the Somerset team. In the First World War he was taken prisoner whilst serving as Lieutenant in the South Wales Borderers.

FORSTER, Lord, of Lepe, P.C., G.C.M.G., died on January 15, 1936, when nearly 70 years of age. During three years in the Eton XI H. W. Forster did not meet with much success in the important school matches but he scored, in irreproachable style, mainly by off-drives and cuts, 60 not out for Oxford against Cambridge in 1887. Essentially a fast wicket batsman he often got out disappointingly after rain, but on true turf he showed most attractive stroke play. He was a member of the Hampshire XI for several seasons until 1895, mostly under F. E. Lacey. In 1919, before being raised to the Peerage, he became President of M.C.C., his former Hampshire captain then being Secretary at Lord's. As Governor-General of Australia, Lord Forster took special interest in cricket in the Commonwealth and entertained the M.C.C. touring teams. In 1925, during the third Test match at Adelaide, when Arthur Gilligan's team lost the rubber, he unveiled a portrait of George Giffen, who came to England in 1882, helped Australia to victory by seven runs in "The Ashes" match, and paid several other visits. Lord Forster, who was born on January 31, 1866, stood over 6ft. high and, with powerful physique, had a commanding figure. A strong right-handed batsman, a slow left-hand bowler and a splendid field at mid-off, he was a very useful all-round cricketer.

FOSTER, Basil S., who died in Hillingdon Hospital on September 28, 1959, aged 77, was one of the brothers who did so much for Worcestershire in the early part of the century that the county became known in cricketing circles as "Fostershire." He also appeared on occasion for Middlesex. As an actor, he gained prominence on the London stage and later took up theatrical management.

FOSTER, Christopher Knollys, who died on December 4, 1971, aged 67, did not gain a place in the XI while at Malvern, but he played in two games for Worcestershire in 1927. He was the son of H. K. Foster.

FOSTER, Major Derek George, died at Chipping Camden on October 13, 1980, aged 73. He played for Warwickshire from 1928 to 1934, but only in 1929 and 1931, when he opened the bowling for the Gentlemen at Lord's, was he able to appear at all frequently. A fast-medium bowler with a good action in which he made full use of his height, he could, on a pitch that gave him any help, make the ball lift unpleasantly. His career figures of 150 wickets at 27.47 are not impressive and a better idea of how dangerous he could be is given by some of his analyses—six for 11 v. Glamorgan at Cardiff and five for 39 v. Kent at Tunbridge Wells in 1929, seven for 42 v. Surrey at the Oval in 1930 and seven for 68 v. Kent at Folkestone in 1931. Not highly regarded as a batsman, he occasionally hit well and in 1931 made 70 v. Somerset at Taunton in under an hour, including five sixes. He had been in the Shrewsbury XI in 1924.

FOSTER, Frank Rowbotham, who died at Northampton on May 3, 1958, aged 69, was one of the most prominent all-rounders of his day—a fine left-arm fast-medium bowler and a forcing right-hand batsman. His career in first-class cricket was brilliant but all too brief, for it began in 1908 and terminated with the outbreak of war in 1914.

Nothing was known of him outside local cricket until 1908, when he played in five matches for Warwickshire, but his natural aptitude for the game was such that he at once jumped into front rank and two years later figured in Gentlemen v. Players matches at Lord's, the Oval and Scarborough. In all three games he showed such ability that several famous cricketers unhesitatingly described him as obviously a man who would play for England. Indeed, J. T. Tyldesley, after batting against him the previous year, expressed the view that a new left-arm bowler of exceptional ability had been discovered. In 1910, Foster made nearly 600 runs and took 91 wickets for his county, but up to that time he was regarded as little more than a bowler.

The summer of 1911, however, found him by general consent the best all-rounder of the year. Soon after being elected captain of Warwickshire, he announced his impending retirement, but he was induced to reconsider his decision. Such wonderful cricket did he play, making 1,383 runs, average 44, and taking 116 wickets for just over 19 runs apiece, that his individual efforts constituted the chief factor in gaining the County Championship for Warwickshire for the first time in their history. The magnitude of this achievement may be understood when it is mentioned that 1911 was the only year since 1872 that the title had not been carried off by one of the "Big Six"—Yorkshire, Lancashire, Nottinghamshire, Surrey, Kent and Middlesex. Heading the batting and bowling figures and setting a fine example in the field, Foster, as a match-winner, stood out as the best young captain seen since W. G. Grace in the early days of Gloucestershire. During that memorable season, Foster played a three-figure innings in each match with Yorkshire and one of 200 against Surrey at Edgbaston.

The following winter he formed one of the team to Australia taken out by P. F. Warner but, owing to the captain's illness, led on the field by J. W. H. T. Douglas. England lost the first Test match, but won the other four largely owing to the splendid bowling of Sidney Barnes and Foster. In the series, Foster obtained 32 wickets for less than 22 runs each.

Returning home, Foster appeared for

England in the ill-starred Triangular Tournament, but, except in the first engagement with South Africa, when he took eight wickets for 60 runs, accomplished little worthy of his reputation, all the bowling honours going to Barnes. During that very wet summer Foster scarcely maintained his form—possibly three strenuous seasons in the course of 16 months were too much for a man of 23. Early in 1913, when he seemed to have lost much of his fire and spin, he had to take a rest and although he obtained 91 wickets, these cost 24 runs each. Yet he was quite himself again in 1914, making 1,396 runs, average nearly 35, with a highest innings of 305 not out—scored in four hours 20 minutes—against Worcestershire at Dudley, and dismissing 117 batsmen, average just over 18. Then came the First World War, during which he met with a motor-cycle accident that left him lame and destroyed any possibility of him ever again being an effective bowler.

Distinctive and individual in bowling method, Foster possessed an easy, natural action, commanded considerable swerve and imparted so much spin to the ball that he generally gathered pace from the pitch. He was one of the originators of leg-theory and often employed only three men on the off-side. As a batsman he was brilliant as well as confident and if he did not play with quite a straight bat and took many risks, he was the personification of youthful energy and so a most attractive figure on the field. In the course of his first-class career, he took 721 wickets for a little over 20 runs each and scored 6,510 runs, average 26.

FOSTER, Geoffrey N., who died on August 11, 1971, aged 86, was one of seven brothers who played for Worcestershire and at one time earned the county the soubriquet of "Fostershire." All the brothers were at Malvern, where Geoffrey was in the XI from 1902 to 1904. Going up to Oxford, he was not only awarded his cricket Blue from 1905 to 1908, but also took part in the University Association football matches of 1905–06–07–08, being captain in the last·season, and gained Blues for golf and racquets. He earned an amateur International Cap for England against Holland in 1907. Though his appearances for Worcestershire were restricted by business claims, he scored in all first-class fixtures 6,551·runs for an average of 26.84 and, an excellent fieldsman, held 151 catches.

Specially skilled in off-side strokes, particularly drives through the covers, he could score very quickly, as he proved when hitting 101 in 60 minutes for Oxford against Gentlemen of England at Eastbourne in 1908 and when he and W. B. Burns put on 181 in 65 minutes for Worcestershire against Hampshire at Worcester in 1905. His highest score was 175 off the Leicestershire bowling in 1913, and the Worcestershire sixth-wicket record of 195 established by him and J. A. Cuffe in that game still stands. After the First World War, Foster turned out occasionally for Kent. He played football for the Corinthians, of which club he was for a number of years hon. secretary. He was the father-in-law of F. G. H. Chalk, of Kent.

FOSTER, Henry ("Harry") Knollys, M.B.E., who died at his home near Hereford on June 23, 1950, in his 77th year, was the eldest of seven brothers who played for Worcestershire, but he was not the most famous member of the family. That distinction belonged to his brother, R. E. Foster, who at Sydney in 1903 put together for England against Australia the memorable score of 287 which stood as the record individual score in International matches until Sir Donald Bradman beat it at Leeds in 1930. Still, H. K. Foster was a very fine batsman who—at his best—would not have been out of place in a Test match, and, furthermore, he was a truly great racquets player.

Born on October 30, 1873, he received his education at Malvern College, and in his last year there, and his fourth season in the XI, 1892, headed the batting averages of an XI which included W. L. Foster, W. W. Lowe and C. J. Burnup. Curiously, on going up to Oxford he was never given a trial for the XI in 1893, but he did very well a year later when the only match the Dark Blues won was that against Cambridge.

His reputation as a first-rate batsman dated from 1895, when he gave a memorable display in the second innings against Cambridge. Set 331 to win, Oxford were all out for 196, but of this number Foster made 121 out of 159 in little more than two hours without a real blemish beyond a sharp chance when 45 to cover-point's left hand. The pace at which his cuts and off-drives went to the boundary was always recalled with admiration by those who witnessed the match. Foster was also a member of the Oxford XI that in 1896 made 330 runs and beat Cambridge by six wickets.

After his Oxford days, Harry Foster was for many years the mainstay of the Worcestershire XI, captaining the side when the county secured promotion to first-class rank in 1899, and—apart from the summer of 1901, when he played no important cricket —he led the team until the end of the season of 1910. Five times in the course of a brilliant career which extended in all over about 20 years he averaged more than 40 runs an innings—with one of 48 in 1908 his highest. Even in 1913, when he looked to have finished with first-class cricket, he came out once more for Worcestershire, made nearly 1,000 runs, and averaged 35. Six times he appeared for the Gentlemen against Players, and altogether in first-class matches he made 29 separate hundreds, all of which, except that against Cambridge, were played for Worcestershire. His highest scores were 216 against Somerset in 1903 and 215 against Warwickshire in 1904.

As a batsman he was quite a master of style, few men indeed playing in more attractive form, and while essentially an off-side run-getter he could pull with great effect. A brilliant field at short slip, he stood 6ft. high and in his Oxford days weighed less than 10½ st. In 1907, when South Africa sent over such a remarkable set of bowlers— Vogler, Schwarz, Faulkner and White— Harry Foster and C. H. B. Marsham assisted Lord Hawke in choosing the England XIs. Five years later, on the occasion of the ill-starred Triangular Tournament, Foster, John Shuter and C. B. Fry were responsible for the selection of England's representatives, and in 1921, when in this country cricket had not recovered from the War, Foster, R. H. Spooner and John Daniell shared the thankless task for picking England's XIs.

At racquets Foster carried off numerous honours. He and his brother, W. L. Foster, won the Public Schools Championship for Malvern in 1892. In the next four years he represented Oxford and proved victorious in both Singles and Doubles. Several times, efficiently partnered, he carried off the Doubles Championship, and from 1894 to 1900 and again in 1904 he won the Singles Championship.

FOSTER, Capt. Jack Heygate Nedham, died on November 16, 1976, aged 71. A good stylist, quick on his feet, with a beautiful pair of wrists, he was in the Harrow XI in 1923 and played an outstanding innings of 75 at Lord's in the course of which he and G. O. Brigstocke put on 92 for the last wicket. In 1925 he scored 108 for Kent Second XI v. Norfolk and in 1930 had a couple of trials for the county without success.

FOSTER, Maurice Kershaw, sixth of the seven brothers who played for Worcestershire, died at Lichfield on December 3, 1940. All these sons of the Rev. H. Foster, of Malvern College, in turn were prominent in school games and stepped, naturally, into the atmosphere of University and County Cricket. When promoted to first class in 1899, Worcestershire included three Fosters in the XI and promptly the new addition to the front rank of the game became known as "Fostershire." Maurice first played for the county in 1908, but business abroad permitted only occasional appearances until 1923, when he became captain and led the side for three seasons. In 1926 he was available still, and in each of these four years his aggregate in Championship matches exceeded 1,300 runs. Of good height and well proportioned, "M. K." was typical of his famous family in the strength of stroke play produced by the powerful wrists and forearms always associated with those proficient at racquets—and all the brothers excelled also at this game. His forcing strokes on either side of the wicket were brilliant. Invariably reliable, he enjoyed periods of special success. In June, 1924, he came out strongly with 157 not out against Sussex, 128 against Kent, and 125 against Somerset; he finished that season with 111 and 42 not out at Taunton off the Somerset bowlers.

He enjoyed special success in 1926, when he scored 141 and 106 at Worcester against Hampshire, and in the whole season made 1,615 runs with an average of 32.95. After appearing for the county occasionally in 1927 and 1934, he turned to Birmingham League cricket, helping Walsall win the Championship three times, and he played for the team in 1940. M. K. Foster could field anywhere, saving many runs and holding the most difficult catches. Chosen for the Gentlemen against Players at the Oval and Lord's, in 1924, he failed to do himself justice in either match. He died within a month of completing 52 years.

FOSTER, Neville John Acland, who died at Malvern on January 8, 1978, aged 87, was the youngest and the last survivor of seven brothers who did so much for Worcestershire that the side got the nickname of "Fostershire." He did not get into the XI at Malvern and, as he spent most of his life in Malaya, his County Cricket was confined to three matches in 1914 and five in 1923. In 1914 he did little, but in 1923 showed clearly in a series of useful innings, the highest of them being 40 not out against Derbyshire, that he had his share of the family eye and wrists. Unfortunately he was kept out of several matches by a strain. Later he captained the Federated Malay States. In 1908 with his brother M. K. he won the Public Schools racquets for Malvern: he was the fifth of the brothers to play in a winning pair, a record which no other family has approached.

FOSTER, Reginald Erskine, died at his home in London on May 13, 1914. He was born at Malvern on April 16, 1878. Mr. Foster's death from diabetes at the age of 36 came as a great shock to the cricket world, but was no surprise to his intimate friends. His health broke down in the summer of 1913, and a visit to South Africa did him no permanent good. He had not reached the age at which, by means of rigid dieting, diabetes can sometimes be kept in check. He was one of the pre-eminently great batsmen of his day, ranking with MacLaren, Fry, Jackson, Tom Hayward and Tyldesley, among those who stood nearest to Ranjitsinhji. Of all the fine batsmen who learnt the game at Malvern he was incontestably the best and his record for Oxford in 1900 has never been equalled in University cricket. Three of his feats stand out above all the rest—his 171 against Cambridge at Lord's in 1900, his 102 not out and 136 for the Gentlemen against the Players at Lord's 10 days later, and his 287 for the M.C.C.'s England XI against Australia at Sydney in December, 1903. This 287 remains the record innings in Test match cricket. Mr. Foster was the first batsman to make two separate hundreds in a Gentlemen and Players' match, and the feat has only once been repeated—by J. H. King for the Players at Lord's in 1904. Curiously enough, both Mr. Foster and King were playing in the big match for the first time. It is a strange fact that Mr. Foster never played for England against Australia in this country. The Australians were not here in either 1900 or 1901 —his two great seasons. This was very unfortunate for him, as in both those years he would have been one of the first men chosen for Test matches. After 1901 he could not, except in 1907, when he captained England against South Africa, spare much time for first-class cricket. When the Australians came here in 1905 he played very little, and in 1909 he was not seen at all. It may not be generally known that Mr. Foster had the refusal of the captaincy of the M.C.C. team that visited Australia in the winter of 1907–08. He would have liked above all things to bat again on the Sydney and Melbourne wickets, but he could not arrange to be away from England

for the length of time required. His last big match was for Worcestershire against the Australians at Dudley in 1912 when he scored 26. A week before that he had hit up 127 at Lord's for the M.C.C. against the Public Schools, playing, after the first few overs, with undiminished brilliancy. It was characteristic of Mr. Foster that, like C. J. Ottaway and W. H. Patterson, he could at any time return to first-class cricket and play as well as if he had been in full practice all the season. A case in point occurred in 1910. He only played once for Worcestershire that year, but he scored 133 against Yorkshire.

A striking parallel can be drawn between Mr. Foster's career as a batsman at Oxford and that of F. S. Jackson, at Cambridge. Both were very good bats at school, but in their early days of University cricket there was little suggestion of the heights they were destined to reach. Steadily improving for three seasons, each in his last year—Jackson in 1893 and Foster in 1900—blossomed out as an England batsman of the first rank. In his position at the wicket—he stood with both eyes turned full on the bowler—and his general style of play, Mr. Foster was quite modern but, in adapting himself to swerving bowlers, he did not, like so many batsmen, lose his brilliancy on the off-side. Nothing could have been finer than his hitting past cover-point, and his late cut was a model of safety and clever placing. After his two hundreds for the Gentlemen in 1900, C. B. Fry said of him that no one, except Ranjitsinhji, could wield a bat with greater quickness. One of seven brothers who have been seen in the Malvern School and Worcestershire County XIs, he was beyond doubt the best of them all. This may be said without in any way disparaging H. K. Foster's skill and commanding style. Apart from his splendid batting, R. E. Foster was one of the finest slip fieldsmen of his day. Tall, slim, and lithe, he brought off catches that would have been impossible to ordinary men. Mr. Foster was in the Malvern XI 1893–96, and in the Oxford XI 1897–1900. He was on the M.C.C. Committee at the time of his death, having previously served from 1904 to 1907. Without approaching his brother H. K.'s class, he was a good racquet player, and at Association football he won International honours, playing for England three times against Wales, and once each against Scotland and Ireland. He was twice in the Oxford Association team against Cambridge, and did brilliant things for the Old Malvernians.

FOSTER, Thomas W., who played for Yorkshire occasionally from 1893 to 1896, died at Dewsbury, on January 31, 1947, aged 75. A fast-medium bowler, he took nine wickets for 59 against M.C.C. at Lord's in 1894, this being his best performance, but he did good steady work, taking altogether 68 wickets at 16.25 apiece, and with the bat he averaged 10.11, his aggregate being 182 runs.

FOSTER, Major Wilfred Lionel, who died on March 22, 1958, aged 83, was the second of seven brothers who all played for Worcestershire. After being in the Malvern XI for three years from 1890, he represented the Royal Military Academy, Woolwich, in 1893 and 1894, heading the batting averages in both seasons. Only in 1899 was he able regularly to assist Worcestershire, and then he finished at the top of the batting figures with an average of 42.57. His aggregate of 894 runs included 140 and 172 not out against Hampshire at Worcester. In the same match his younger brother, R.E., hit 134 and 101 not out. Major Foster was a member of the Corinthian F.C. from 1892 to 1898. He and H.K. Foster won the Public Schools Racquets Cup in 1892 and the Amateur Racquets Doubles Championship in 1898, and in 1907 he and B.S. Foster carried off the latter title. Major Foster served in the Boer War and in the First World War won the D.S.O.

FOULKE, William, born at Dawley (Salop) on April 12, 1874, died in a private nursing home in Sheffield on May 1, 1916. In 1900 he played in four matches for Derbyshire, making 65 runs with an average of 10.83, his highest innings being 53 v. Essex at Leyton. He was the famous goal-keeper of Sheffield United, was 6ft. 2½in. in height and very heavy—at least 25st., but always active.

FOWKE, Major G.H.S., captain of Leicestershire from 1922 to 1927, died on June 24, 1946, aged 65. He learned the game at Uppingham, where he was in the XI, and played for the county in 1908. Altogether he made 4,663 runs, average 19.75, in first-class cricket, faring best in 1922 with 922 runs in Championship matches, and next year hitting 104 at Northampton, his first century for Leicestershire.

FOWKE, John Nicholls, died at Christchurch, New Zealand, on April 25, 1938, aged 78. The best wicket-keeper of his day in New Zealand, he represented the Dominion against New South Wales in 1895–96 and the Melbourne Club team in 1900. A steady batsman he often helped in a useful stand.

He played in 42 representative matches, mostly for Canterbury, but he toured New Zealand with the Auckland side.

FOWLER, Archibald John Burgess, who died on May 7, 1977, in London, aged 86, had many trials for Middlesex as a slow left-hander between 1921 and 1931 and received his County Cap. He never quite made his place secure, but must have been fairly near it in 1924 when he took five for 29 against Lancashire, then a very strong side. Later in the mid-'30s he succeeded George Fenner as head coach at Lord's. Those of us who regard Fenner as one of the finest coaches we have ever known realise what it means that Fowler was in his turn regarded as outstanding. He constantly umpired at Lord's and finally for many years acted as scorer, his connection with the ground extending in all for over half a century. He was a Life Member of the Middlesex County C.C.

FOWLER, Edwin, died at Armadale on May 31, 1909, in his 69th year. He learnt the game in England and was a batsman with a capital style, and a very good wicket-keeper. In December, 1865, he played at Melbourne for Victoria against New South Wales and distinguished himself by an innings of 37. In a drawn single-wicket match which was played immediately afterwards he scored 51 against Caffyn, Lawrence, Cosstick, and Thompson.

FOWLER, Gerald, brother of Mr. W. Herbert Fowler, was born in Essex on July 27, 1866, and died at Trull, Taunton, on May 24, 1916, after an operation for appendicitis. In 1883 and two following years he was in the Clifton XI, being captain in 1885, when he scored 235 runs with an average of 18.07, his highest innings being 128 v. Old Cliftonians, and headed the bowling with a record of 63 wickets for 10.50 runs each. He had been first in the bowling figures the previous year, taking 51 wickets at a cost of 17.00. It was said of him in 1885: "Is a good medium-paced bowler with considerable break and spin: and sometimes very deceptive; a fine, hard-hitting bat, but rather wanting in patience and defence; a good field: the XI was very successful under his captaincy." At Oxford he obtained his Blue in 1888, and in the drawn match with Cambridge scored 0 not out and took five wickets for 48 runs. He assisted Essex between 1884 and 1889, after which he appeared for Somerset. His highest score in County Cricket was 118 for Somerset v. Gloucestershire at Bristol in 1895, when he and L.C.H. Palairet (80) scored

205 for the first wicket: this was the match in which "W.G." obtained his historic 288, his 100th century in first-class cricket. Mr. Fowler was the Hon. Treasurer of the Somerset County C.C. from 1896 until 1916, and also for many years captain of the Taunton C.C.

FOWLER, Howard, died on May 6, 1934, aged 75. Born on October 20, 1857, he was in the Clifton College XI in 1874–76, being captain in his last year. Going up to Oxford he at once got his Blue but did little against Cambridge until 1880 when he scored 43. He assisted Essex in 1886–87–88. A noted Rugby forward he captained the Oxford Fifteen in 1878 and also played for England.

FOWLER, The Rev. Richard Harold, who died on October 27, 1970, played in a few matches for Worcestershire in 1921. After taking five Gloucestershire wickets for 33 runs at Stourbridge, he was told that only his cloth had saved him from being no-balled. This doubtless accounted for the brevity of his first-class career.

FOWLER, Capt. Robert St. Leger, M.C., born on April 7, 1891, died at Rahinston, Enfield, County Meath, on June 13, 1925, aged 34. Owing to his profession, he was not very well-known to the general cricket public, but he was the hero of a match which may, without exaggeration, be described as the most extraordinary ever played. The story of the Eton and Harrow match in 1910 has been told over and over again, but it can never grow stale. No victory in a match of widespread interest was ever snatched in such a marvellous way. As captain of the Eton XI Fowler—it was his third year in the big match—found his side for about a day and a half overwhelmed. On the first day Harrow scored 232, and Eton, before bad light caused stumps to be drawn, lost five wickets for 40 runs. This was bad enough, but worse was to come. Eton's innings ended on the Saturday morning for 67, and in the follow-on five wickets were lost for 65. Fowler, scoring 64, played splendidly and received valuable help, but, in spite of all his efforts, the game reached a point at which the odds on Harrow could not have been named. With one wicket to fall Eton were only four runs ahead. But the Hon. J.N. Manners—killed in the War in 1914—hit so fearlessly and had such a cool-headed partner in Lister-Kaye that the last wicket put on 50 runs. Honour was in a measure saved, no one imagined that Harrow would fail to get the 55 runs

required. Then came the crowning sensation. Fowler bowled his off-breaks with such deadly accuracy that he took eight wickets—five of them bowled down—and won the match for Eton by nine runs. No one who was at Lord's on that eventful Saturday evening will ever forget the scene at the finish. Old Harrovians, bearing their sorrow with as much fortitude as could be expected, said sadly that a grievous blunder had been committed in putting the heavy roller on the rather soft pitch, and there was a good deal in their contention. Still, nothing could detract from Fowler's achievement. Something heroic was demanded of him, and he rose to the height of his opportunity. From one point of view it was a pity he went into the Army. In Oxford or Cambridge cricket he would assuredly have played a great part.

In his three matches against Winchester he scored 113 runs for twice out and took 15 wickets for 136 runs: altogether in his six big Public School matches he made 238 runs with an average of 29.75 and obtained 39 wickets for 10.10 runs each. For Eton he was first in bowling in 1909, and first in both batting and bowling the following year. For Sandhurst v. Woolwich in 1911 he carried out his bat for 137 and took seven wickets for nine runs in a total of 63, and in a small game at the R.M.C. that year, for C.Co. v. E.Co., he scored 112 in his first innings and 132 in his second. When he made 92 not out for Army v. M.C.C. at Lord's in 1920 he and Capt. W. V. D. Dickinson (150) put on 237 together for the eighth wicket in 90 minutes, and on the same ground four years later he took seven wickets for 22 runs for Army v. Royal Navy. With the Incogniti he toured America in 1920, making 142 v. All Philadelphia at Haverford, and with the Free Foresters he visited Germany the same year and Canada in 1923. When it was contemplated sending an M.C.C. team to the West Indies in 1924–25, he was offered, and accepted, the captaincy. In 1924 he appeared in two matches for Hampshire. In the First World War he served as Captain in the 17th Lancers and gained the Military Cross.—S.H.P.

FOWLER, Corpl. Theodore Humphry (Honorable Artillery Company), died in the London County Hospital, Epsom, on August 17, 1915, after an operation for hernia. He was born on September 25, 1879, and was thus in his 36th year at the time of his death. In 1894 and three following seasons he was in the Lancing XI, being captain in 1897. His most successful year was 1896, when he made 457 runs with an average of 45.70. He could hit hard when necessary, and was a useful wicket-keeper, and for two seasons he won all the long-distance races at the College. Between 1901 and 1914 he played cricket for Gloucestershire (by birth) and Dorset, his most noteworthy feat being to make 114 for the former against London County at the Crystal Palace in 1903, when he and Wrathall (160) scored 277 together for the first wicket. He was twice wounded in action, and twice declined a commission.

FOWLER, William Herbert, died on April 13, 1941, aged 84. Educated at Rottingdean and Grove House School, Tottenham, he played for Essex in 1877, and two years later appeared for Somerset with marked success, averaging 23 and doing the best bowling. Over 6ft. 3in. in height and more than 14 st. in weight, he put great force into his strokes. One hit off W. G. Grace at Gloucester carried 154yd., and also in 1882 at Lord's he drove a ball from George Hay 157yd., as measured by Tom Hearne, head of the ground staff. This was a remarkable match, M.C.C. winning by one wicket after Fowler had done the hat-trick in the club's first innings. When M.C.C. visited Taunton later in the season, Fowler scored 139, and for M.C.C. against Oxford University at Lord's in 1884 he made the large proportion of 60 runs out of 68 while he was at the wicket.

An accomplished golfer, he played for England against Scotland in 1903 and two following years. He designed the Walton Heath and many other well-known courses in England and America. Maintaining a close connection with Somerset, he was a trustee of the County Ground at Taunton.

FOX, C. J. Macdonald, died suddenly from heart failure on April 1, 1901, in a hospital at Albury, New South Wales. He was born at Dum Dum, near Calcutta, on December 5, 1858, and was educated at Dufton College, Calcutta, and Westminster School, where he was in the XI. He first came into notice in 1874 by playing an innings of 87, out of a total of 220, against Charterhouse. In 1876, being qualified by residence, he appeared for Surrey against Gloucestershire, at the Oval, and his fine fielding was one of the features of the match. A return to India restricted his connection with Surrey to this one match, and it was not until 1885 that he reappeared with any prominence in English cricket. By 1888 he had become qualified for Kent, and it is with that county that his name will always remain associated. In his first season

for Kent he played a splendid innings of 93, at Huddersfield, against Yorkshire, on a wicket drying under the sun and playing very queerly. His highest score for his adopted county was 103 against Notts, at Tonbridge, in 1891. As a batsman he possessed plenty of hitting power, and was, on occasion, a very fast scorer. He was also a useful bowler—keeping a good length and using his head well—and a splendid field. In minor cricket Mr. Fox made runs by the thousand, and his record in 1887 for the Crystal Palace Club was remarkable, even for him. That year, in consecutive innings, he scored 66 v. United Hospitals, 54 v. Reigate Priory, 58 v. Incogniti, 177 not out v. Surrey Club and Ground, 65 v. Gipsies, 243 not out v. Hampstead, and 185 not out v. H. E. Burrell's XI (at Littlebury). In four completed innings he thus scored 828, giving an average of 207. He exceeded the 200 on three occasions for the Crystal Palace, making 261 not out v. Charlton Park, in 1887, 255 v. Incogniti, in 1891, and 243 not out v. Hampstead, in 1887. In the last mentioned match, he and F. W. Janson (252) added 351 runs whilst together for the third wicket, the total of 650 for five wickets taking only six hours to get. A curious accident, which might have proved serious, occurred to Mr. Fox in the match between Kent and Gloucestershire at Bristol, in 1890. In the first innings of the latter county, whilst fielding at point, he dislocated his shoulder in stopping a hard cut, and was prevented from taking further part in the game.

FOX, John, a left-handed batsman and left-arm slow bowler who played for Warwickshire and Worcestershire, collapsed and died on a Birmingham bus on his way home from work on November 15, 1961. He was 57. Small in stature and of frail physique, Fox appeared for Warwickshire from 1922 to 1928, scoring 2,827 runs, average 17.45, and taking 31 wickets at 41.45 runs each. He assisted Worcestershire from 1929 to 1933, making 2,438 runs, average 17.06, with 73 against Northamptonshire at Worcester in 1931 the highest first-class innings of his career. He took 31 wickets for Worcestershire, average 40.00. He continued to be well known in the Midlands, as he umpired for a number of seasons in the Birmingham and District League.

FOX, Lieut.-Col. Raymond Wodehouse (Royal Warwickshire Regiment). died at Ticehurst, Sussex, August 21, 1948, aged 75. In the Wellington XI 1889–91, he was wicket-keeper for Oxford University 1897–98 and sometimes for Sussex.

FOX, Capt. Ronald Henry, M.C., who died at Bloxham on August 27, 1952, aged 72, was in the Haileybury XI of 1898. As a wicket-keeper he was a member of the M.C.C. team who, under Capt. E. G. Wynyard, toured New Zealand in 1906–07.

FOX, William V., the former Worcestershire batsman, died in Manchester following an operation on February 18, 1949, aged 51. He made his debut in first-class cricket in 1923, when he scored 981 runs, average 32.70, with a highest innings of 178 not out against Northamptonshire at Worcester. A native of Yorkshire, he was the type of player Worcestershire badly needed, but M.C.C. decided that both he and L. G. Crawley were not properly qualified and Fox could not play again for the county until 1926, being compelled to go through the full two years necessary for qualification. On his return he scored 1,010 runs, including three hundreds in 1926 and for four seasons, when the side were generally weak in batting, he served them admirably. His most successful summer was 1929 when his aggregate reached 1,331 runs, average 29.13, and that year he made the highest score of his career, 198 against Warwickshire at Birmingham. He never reproduced the same form and after appearing in four matches in 1932 he did not play again for the county. Fox was also a fine footballer and played for Middlesbrough, Wolverhampton Wanderers and Newport County.

FOY, Phillip Arnold, who died in the British Hospital, Buenos Aires, on February 12, 1957, aged 65, was for many years prominent as a bowler in Argentine cricket. He distinguished himself against the M.C.C. touring side captained by Lord Hawke in 1912. Educated at Bedford School, Foy played for Bedfordshire and when on leave assisted Somerset, for whom, in 1920, he took 31 wickets, average 22.48, and scored 352 runs, with 72 against Essex at Leyton his highest innings in first-class cricket

FRANCIS, Charles King, born at Upminster, Essex, on February 3, 1851, died on October 24, 1925. Though his active days in first-class cricket dated back half a century, Mr. Francis retained to the end a keen interest in the game and was constantly at Lord's. Old cricketers will remember him as one of the best amateur fast bowlers of his day. It cannot be said, however, that he lived up to his early reputation. The work that made him famous was done before he was 20. At Rugby, when Pauncefote and Yardley had raised the school's cricket prestige to its highest point, he was in the XI from 1867 to 1869. He wound up with a performance that has perhaps never been surpassed in a Public School match, taking in 1869 17 wickets against Marlborough at Lord's—all 10 (nine of them bowled) in the second innings. On the strength of this astonishing form he went up to Oxford with a great flourish of trumpets. In his first year he fulfilled all expectations, taking 12 wickets in the University match—the sensational match that Frank Cobden's hat-trick won for Cambridge by two runs—and being chosen for the Gentlemen. He was in the Oxford XI for three more years but against Cambridge, though he had one effective little spell in 1873, he never reproduced his form of 1870 or anything like it. Very possibly he was overbowled at school, but on this point I cannot speak with any certainty. He went to Canada in 1872 with R. A. Fitzgerald's famous team and played for Middlesex from 1875 to 1877, appearing, however, in few matches after the first year. Called to the Bar in 1876 he was a Metropolitan Police Magistrate from 1896 till the end of his life.—S.H.P.

FRANCIS, G. M., a bowler of exceptional merit, as county batsmen discovered in 1923 when a team from West Indies visited England, died in January, 1942, aged 44. Avoiding any theory, such as many fast bowlers have overdone, he bowled at the stumps. A groundsman in Barbados, he attracted the attention of H. B. G. Austin, captain of the side, and by his influence Francis came to England. He took 96 wickets at 15.32 apiece, and in first-class matches with 82 at 15.58 each he far surpassed the efforts of any of his colleagues. He did not maintain this form in 1928 when West Indies received Test status, and generally faced stronger opposition than on their previous tour. To Francis only 56 batsmen fell at an average cost of 31.96, chief honours going to L. N. Constantine and H. C. Griffith. These three were described at one time as the strongest combination of fast bowlers in any Test side, but they accomplished far more at home than when in England. In January, 1926, for Barbados, Francis took nine wickets for 56 runs, and the M.C.C. team captained by the Hon. F. S. G. Calthorpe were beaten in an innings—the only defeat suffered. Directly afterwards England enjoyed full revenge in the first representative match, but when

Barbados were faced again—these three games being played in the course of a fortnight—Francis, with seven wickets for 50 and two for 41, helped to outplay the Englishmen, who, with eight wickets down after following-on, narrowly escaped defeat on a pitch damaged by rain. When West Indies lost at Port of Spain, Francis did little, but again was the best bowler at Georgetown, where England had to fight to avoid defeat. In the Australian season of 1930–31 West Indies contested a full series of five Tests, and Francis, without accomplishing anything exceptional, was prominent in an attack which helped to gain a victory by 30 runs, after two declarations by G. C. Grant, in the final match of the series at Sydney. They lost four times, and this first success over Australia, though largely due to changed conditions by rain, showed that West Indies were making rapid progress in the cricket world. Francis had no pretensions in batting, but fielded in the dashing style associated with teams representing West Indies. In 1933 Francis, then engaged in English League cricket, played in the first Test at Lord's, but failed and did not appear again.

FRANCIS, Howard Henry, died at Cape Town on January 7, 1936, aged 65. Born at Bristol he played for Gloucestershire from 1890. His highest score was 55 against Middlesex at Clifton in Jack Painter's benefit match in 1894; he and Jack Board put on 137 for the ninth wicket. He then went to South Africa and from 1895 to 1902 often appeared for Western Province. In 1899 he played for South Africa in both Test matches against Lord Hawke's team.

FRANCIS, Percy Thomas, who died on September 8, 1964, aged 89, played in a few matches for Worcestershire in 1901 and 1902 and later assisted Suffolk.

FRANCIS, Thomas Egerton Seymour, who died suddenly in Bulawayo, Rhodesia, on February 24, 1969, aged 66, played for Cambridge at both cricket and Rugby football. As a batsman of correct style, he was in the Tonbridge XI from 1919 to 1921, gaining a batting average of 51.50 in the second year and 68.15 in the third. He got his cricket Blue in 1925. He was stand-off half-back in the University Rugby matches of 1922 and the two following winters, being partner to the famous A. T. Young, and in 1925 figured in the centre against Oxford. In the 1925–26 season he earned four International caps for England. From 1921 to 1923 he assisted Somerset as an amateur from time to time and later played cricket in South Africa for Eastern Province.

FRANCIS, Dr. William, died at Forest Gate, April 28, 1917, aged 62. Did good service for Essex 30 years ago.

FRANCOIS, Air Sergt. Cyril Matthew, was killed in a motor accident near Pretoria on May 26, 1944. A hard-hitting batsman and right-arm fast-medium bowler, he was a regular member of Griqualand West teams from 1920 to 1928. In Currie Cup matches he scored 610 runs, average 17.94, and took 76 wickets at 25.98 each. He came into prominence in the 1922–23 season with seven wickets for 114 runs for Griqualand West against the M.C.C. team and played in all five Test matches. Selected as a bowler, he took only six wickets in the series, three of these for 23 runs in England's first innings in the first Test match, but he batted consistently well, scoring 252 runs at an average of 31.50, including scores of 72, 43 and 41. He was unlucky not to be selected to tour England in 1924 with the South African team, but he played in one of the unofficial Test matches against the English team led by the Hon. L. H. Tennyson the following season, scoring 0 and 35. His last two appearances in first-class cricket were in the 1927–28 season, when he scored 54 v. M.C.C. and 97 and 54 against Orange Free State. In all first-class games he scored 1,232 runs, average 22.81, and took 101 wickets at 28.44 apiece. Born in London on June 20, 1897, Francois, who went to South Africa when very young, was 46 at the time of his death.

FRANCOIS, Hugh August, who died in Johannesburg on July 17, 1982, aged 77, played 16 times for Border from 1923 to 1928, scoring 484 runs at an average of 18.61 and taking 26 wickets at 41.26 apiece. Born at Tsolo in Transkei, he was one of three brothers to play first-class cricket, the others being C. M. and S. H. (C. M. played in all five Tests against England in 1922–23.) A middle-order batsman and off-spin bowler, H. A. turned in several useful performances for Border: his top score was 61 against Orange Free State, his best bowling analysis seven for 79, also against the Free State, two seasons later. In his last first-class match, against R. T. Stanyforth's M.C.C. side, he made a top score of 40 and in an M.C.C. innings of 362 for five declared claimed the wickets of Holmes, E. Tyldesley and Dawson for 114 runs.

FRANK, Joseph, a Yorkshireman, who did not fulfil expectations, died on October 22, 1939, aged 82. When playing for Eighteen of Scarborough against W. L. Murdoch's first Australian team in 1880, his very fast right-hand bowling received strong criticism for doubtful action, and he appeared only once for the county—at Scarborough in 1881 against I Zingari. Two seasons later he played at Kennington Oval in the Gentlemen and Players match, which ended in a tie. He used his height and strength in left-handed batting and was a useful slip fieldsman.

FRANK, Robert Wilson, a notable personality in Yorkshire cricket, died at Pickering on September 9, 1950, aged 86. From 1900 he was captain of Yorkshire Second XI, and between 1889 and 1903 he appeared in 33 matches for the First XI. He made many large scores in minor matches, the highest being 309 for Middlesbrough against Scarborough. He was Senior Vice-President of Yorkshire County C.C. and served on the Committee and Selection Committee. For 64 years he attended the Scarborough Festival until 1949.

FRANK, William Hughes Bowker, who died at Durban on February 2, 1945, played for South Africa in March, 1896, against Lord Hawke's team. The visitors won easily. That was the only match of note in which Frank took part.

FRANKISH, F. Stanley, at one time one of the best-known cricketers in New Zealand, died at Wanganui on May 30, 1909, at the early age of 35. His first match for Canterbury was in 1896, against Wellington, and for almost 10 years he continued to represent the Province. He played for New Zealand against Queensland in 1896, against the Melbourne Club in 1900, and against Lord Hawke's team three years later. In 1898–99 he visited Tasmania and Australia with the New Zealand team, but did not meet with much success. His bowling was fast left-hand.

FRANKLIN, Walter Bell, who died suddenly on March 5, 1968, aged 76, was a regular member of the Buckinghamshire side from 1911 to 1946, holding the position of captain from 1919 till his retirement from the game. Under his leadership, the county carried off the Minor Counties' Championship on five occasions. In the Repton XI for three years from 1908 to 1910, Franklin was a first-rate wicket-keeper and as such gained a Blue at Cambridge in 1912. He lost his place against

Oxford next year because the Harrovian, A. H. Lang, possessed greater ability as a batsman. Though he rarely took part in first-class cricket, Franklin's ability behind the stumps was rated so highly that he was chosen to play for the Gentlemen against the Players at Lord's in 1926 and the two following years, doing surprisingly well as a lower-order batsman. His class may be gauged from the comments of Sir Pelham Warner in his book, *Lord's*. Of Franklin's 1926 performance, Sir Pelham wrote that he "kept superbly" and of that of 1928 that he was "almost as good as Duckworth." Franklin became President of the Minor Counties C. A. and of Buckinghamshire and he contributed a chapter on wicket-keeping to the Lonsdale volume.

FRAZER, John Ewan (Winchester, Oxford University and Sussex). Cricketers and many others must have been shocked by the tragic death of Jack Frazer (aged only 25), the result of a ski-ing accident on January 2, 1927, at Davos Platz. Few of his generation can have equalled the promise shown by him for all-round genius and ability. A double Blue (for cricket and Association football), a Balliol Exhibitioner, and a first-class in the the Schools. At Winchester he was, until his last year, a really fine left-handed bowler above medium pace, an invaluable forcing batsman with all the typical left-hander's shots, and a fine fieldsman. In the XI three years, he had the satisfaction of playing in sides which beat Eton in 1919 and 1920. It is safe to say that had not his bowling almost mysteriously deserted him—possibly a result of gymnastics—he would have been in the first flight of all rounders. As it was he got his Blue (in 1924) as a batsman in spite of trouble with his eyes, and in that as in the two previous seasons, he rendered useful service to Sussex after the Oxford term. In 1924 on the East Grinstead ground he scored 228 not out, in two hours and a quarter, for the local club against Sussex Martlets. He was born at Lydney, on April 22, 1901.— D.R.J.

FREEMAN, Alfred Percy, who died on January 28, 1965, aged 76, was one of the finest slow bowlers the game has known. He played as a professional for Kent from 1914 to 1936 taking 3,776 wickets at an average cost of 18.42 runs each and between 1924 and 1929 appeared in 12 Test matches for England. Only one man, W. Rhodes with 4,187 wickets, has met with greater success. Freeman's wonderfully well controlled leg-breaks, with a skilfully disguised googly or top-spinner interspersed, his well-nigh perfect length and cunning flighting frequently puzzled the most experienced opponents and on no fewer than 17 occasions he dismissed 100 or more batsmen in a season.

His most triumphant summer was that of 1928, when his victims totalled 304 for 18.05 runs each, a feat without parallel in first-class cricket, and five years later he took 298. His wickets exceeded 200 in five other seasons: 276 in 1931, 274 in 1930, 253 in 1932, 212 in 1935 and 205 in 1934. Three times—a feat unequalled by any other bowler—this short but stockily-built man, known in the cricket world as "Tich," took all 10 wickets in an innings, against Lancashire for 131 runs at Maidstone in 1929, and that despite an innings of 126 by F. Watson; against Essex for 53 runs at Southend in 1930 and against Lancashire again, this time at Old Trafford, for 79 runs in 1931. Additionally, at Hove in 1922, he disposed of nine Sussex batsmen in the first innings for 11 runs, bringing about the dismissal of the side for 47, of which E. H. Bowley obtained 24. This was one of two matches in which Freeman was responsible for 17 wickets, his second innings analysis being eight for 56; the other was against Warwickshire at Folkestone 10 years later. Three times he achieved the hat-trick, for Kent against Middlesex at Canterbury in 1920 and against Kent at Blackheath in 1934 and for M.C.C. against South Australia at Adelaide in 1922–23.

"Tich" seldom reached in Test cricket the phenomenal success he attained in the county sphere. He toured Australia and New Zealand with A. C. MacLaren's M.C.C. team in 1922–23 and made his first appearance for England in Australia in 1924–25.

Though he did reasonably well in other matches, he took only eight wickets in two Tests and conceded 519 runs. Nor did he achieve anything of note when visiting South Africa in 1927–28, his total wickets in four Tests amounting to 14 at an average cost of 28.50. In home Tests he fared better. Against the West Indies in 1928 he headed the averages with 22 wickets at 13.72 runs apiece, including 10 for 93 at Old Trafford. For Kent against the West Indies team at Canterbury he took nine wickets in the second innings for 104 runs. He also topped the England bowling figures against South Africa the following season, dismissing 12 men for 171 runs at Old Trafford and seven for 115 in the first innings at Leeds.

When Kent, who gave him two benefits, dispensed with his services at 1936, Freeman played for a time as professional for Walsall in the Birmingham and District League. In 1949 he became one of the 26 cricket personalities to be elected to honorary life membership of M.C.C.

Two celebrated leg-break bowlers paid these tributes:

D. V. P. Wright (Kent and England): "I always held him to be one of the finest leg-break bowlers I ever saw. The more I bowled, the more I realised how great 'Tich' was."

R. W. V. Robins (Middlesex and England): "Against other than the greatest of batsmen, he was the most effective bowler I ever saw. We will never see his like again as a consistent wicket-taker. Under Percy Chapman, Freeman sometimes opened the bowling, which is astonishing in itself and almost unheard of for a leg-break bowler these days."

First-Class Record

	Runs	Wkts.	Average	Five Wkts. an Inns	Ten Wkts. a Match
1914	799	29	27.55	2	—
1919	1,209	60	20.15	4	2
1920	1,790	102	17.54	4	—
1921	3,086	166	18.59	14	6
1922	2,839	194	14.63	16	8
1922–23	1,654	69	23.97	5	2
1923	2,642	157	16.82	9	1
1924	2,518	167	15.07	13	2
1924–25	1,209	40	30.22	2	—
1925	2,544	146	17.42	14	4
1926	3,740	180	20.77	18	5
1927	3,330	181	18.39	18	5
1927–28	965	50	19.30	4	2
1928	5,489	304	18.05	36	15
1928–29	1,136	35	32.45	3	—

1929	4,879	267	18.27	29	13
1930	4,632	274	16.84	34	15
1931	4,307	276	15.60	35	13
1932	4,149	253	16.39	28	13
1933	4,549	298	15.26	40	17
1934	4,753	205	23.18	23	7
1935	4,562	212	21.51	25	9
1936	2,796	110	25.41	10	1
	69,577	3,776	18.42	386	140

FREEMAN, Edward Charles, died at Sherborne in his 79th year on October 16, 1939. He played occasionally when Essex were promoted to first-class rank in 1895, but became prominent in the cricket world for making the Leyton ground suitable for important cricket. In the effort to improve the pitches and prolong the matches, he asked Sam Apted, the Surrey expert, how he kept the Oval turf so impervious to wear. Freeman was advised to apply a liquid mixture "three days before the match." Surrey were the next visitors to Leyton, and Essex winning the toss, expected a perfect pitch, but on a real "sticky dog," their powerful batting side fell for 37 before Lockwood and Brockwell. The most attractive match of the Essex season ended on the second afternoon. Freeman had applied the mixture on each of the three days, instead of only on the third day before the match! Afterwards he produced pitches equal to any in the country and Essex prospered. Several of his family were players of repute, the chief being his nephew, A.P., "Tich," whose slow bowling for Kent earned records season after season—notably 304 wickets in 1928. He was succeeded as coach and groundsman at Sherborne School by one of his six sons, E.J. Freeman.

FREEMAN, Edward John, who died on February 22, 1964, aged 83, played as a professional wicket-keeper and batsman for Essex from 1904 to 1910. He did not reach expectations as a batsman and of his 1,280 runs, he made 564 in 1907, when he hit his highest score, 84 against Nottinghamshire at Trent Bridge. He later played for Dorset and was for many years coach at Sherborne School. As an Association footballer he gained 27 Essex County medals and was immensely proud of the Corinthian Shield finalists' medal he won when captaining Leyton schoolboys against South London schoolboys at the Crystal Palace in 1896. Son of E.C. Freeman (Essex), he was cousin of J.R. Freeman (Essex) and A.P. Freeman (Kent).

FREEMAN, George, the famous Yorkshire cricketer, died at Thirsk on November 18, 1895, in his 52nd year. He was by general consent the finest fast bowler of his generation. His career was short, but quite dazzling in its brilliancy. Coming before the public when Jackson was done with, and Tarrant on the wane, he jumped to the top of the tree and remained unapproachable so long as he devoted himself to the game. A profitable business as an auctioneer, however, soon drew him away from the cricket field, and after playing for Yorkshire, if we remember rightly, from 1867 to 1871 inclusive, he practically retired, his powers being almost unimpaired. He bowled against Mr. W.G. Grace in a benefit match at Sheffield in 1872 (the great batsman on that occasion scoring 150), but for some years after that he was a stranger to first-class cricket. Having in the meantime prospered in business, he reappeared for Yorkshire at Lord's in 1878 playing as an amateur, and in 1880, at Huddersfield, he assisted his county against the second Australian XI. These, however, were merely fugitive efforts, and cannot be regarded as belonging to his real career. In 1882 he was invited by the Surrey Club to play for the Gentlemen of England at the Oval against the greatest of all the Australian teams, but he did not think himself quite good enough for such a match, and politely declined the honour. He was a member of the English professional team that, under Willsher's captaincy, went to America in the autumn of 1868, and met with extraordinary success, his spin and tremendous pace being altogether too much for the American batsmen. Mr. W.G. Grace has always described Freeman as the best of the fast bowlers he met in his younger days, and he remembers especially an innings he played against him and Emmett, with Mr. C.E. Green as his partner, on a terribly rough wicket at Lord's in 1870. Mr. Grace scored 66, but when he had finished he was covered with bruises from shoulder to ankle. Mr. Green made 51, and to this day Mr. Henry Perkins, the secretary of the M.C.C., says the batting was the best he ever saw. George Freeman was a man of singularly fine presence, and in the Yorkshire XI of his day was by many degrees the most striking and picturesque figure.

FRIEND, Major-General The Right Hon. Sir Lovick Bransby, K.B.E., C.B., died in a London nursing home on November 19, 1944, aged 88. He showed good batting form at Cheltenham without getting into the XI, and nearly 60 years ago he played three times for Kent. In 1885 he made 198 for Royal Engineers against Band of Brothers, and 10 years later he and Captain Johnson put on 200 in an hour for Southern District against Connaught Rangers, but his best performance was in 1897, when he hit up 208 for United Services (Portsmouth) against Aldershot Division. He was a good wicket-keeper and sometimes fielded at cover-point.

FRITH, Charles, who died at Dunedin in April, 1919, had played for Canterbury many years earlier, and later for Otago, as a right-handed, medium-paced bowler.

FROST, George, the old Derbyshire cricketer, died at Wirksworth in the first week of February, 1913, aged 64. His county career extended from 1872 to 1880, and for Derbyshire during that period he scored 776 runs with an average of 11.58.

FROWD, George William, of Messrs. Lillywhite, Frowd and Co., died at Forest Hill on November 13, 1914, aged 70. For many years he was proprietor of *James Lillywhite's Cricketers' Annual*.

CAPTAIN CHARLES BURGESS FRY
By Neville Cardus

Captain Charles Burgess Fry, who died at his home at Hampstead, London, on September 7, 1956, aged 84, was probably the greatest all rounder of his or any generation. He was a brilliant scholar and an accomplished performer in almost every branch of outdoor sport. Fry was the perfect amateur; he played games because he loved them and never for personal gain. He captained England in Test matches, and the Mother Country never lost under his captaincy. He played Association football for England against Ireland in 1901; he was at full-back for Southampton in the F.A. Cup Final of 1902; and he put up a world's long-jump record of 23ft. 5in. in 1892 which stood for 21 years. But it was at cricket that his outstanding personality found its fullest expression. The following tribute by Mr. Neville Cardus first appeared in the Manchester Guardian.

Charles Fry was born into a Sussex family on April 25, 1872, at Croydon, and was known first as an England cricketer and footballer, also as a great all-round athlete who for a while held the long-jump record, a hunter and a fisher, and as an inexhaustible virtuoso at the best of all indoor games, conversation.

He was at Repton when a boy, where at cricket he joined the remarkable and enduring roll of superb young players emanating from the school—Fry, Palairet, Ford, J.N. Crawford, to name a few. At Oxford he won first-class honours in Classical Moderations at Wadham, and it is a tribute to his calibre as a scholar and personal force that most of the obituary articles written after the death of Viscount Simon named Fry in a Wadham trinity with Birkenhead. Not the least doughty and idealistic of his many-sided achievements was as a Liberal candidate for Brighton, where he actually polled 20,000 votes long after he had ceased to live in Sussex and dominate the cricket field.

With all his versatility of mind and sinew Fry himself wished that he might be remembered, as much as for anything else, by his work in command of the training-ship *Mercury*. For 40 years he and his wife directed the *Mercury* at Hamble, educating youth with a classical sense of values. He once invited the present writer to visit Hamble and see his boys play cricket and perform extracts from "Parsifal"! Hitler sent for him for advice during the building-up of the "Youth Movement" in Germany. He was a deputy for the Indian delegation to the first, third, and fourth Assemblies of the League of Nations, edited his own monthly magazine more than half a century ago, and was indeed a pioneer in the school of intelligent and analytical criticism of sport. He wrote several books, including an autobiography, and a *Key Book to the League of Nations*, and one called *Batsmanship*, which might conceivably have come from the pen of Aristotle had Aristotle lived nowadays and played cricket.

Fry must be counted among the most fully developed and representative Englishmen of his period; and the question arises whether, had fortune allowed him to concentrate on the things of the mind, not distracted by the lure of cricket, a lure intensified by his increasing mastery over the game, he would not have reached a high altitude in politics or critical literature. But he belonged—and it was his glory—to an age not obsessed by specialism; he was one of the last of the English tradition of the amateur, the connoisseur, and, in the most delightful sense of the word, the dilettante.

As a batsman, of course, he was thoroughly grounded in first principles. He added to his stature, in fact, by taking much thought. As a youth he did not use a bat with much natural freedom, and even in his period of pomp he was never playing as handsomely as his magnificent physical appearance seemed to suggest and deserve. He was, of course, seen often in contrast with Ranjitsinhji, who would have made all batsmen of the present day, Hutton included, look like so many plebeians toiling under the sun. Yet in his prime Fry was a noble straight-driver. He once said to me: "I had only one stroke maybe; but it went to 10 different parts of the field." But in 1905, when the Australians decided that Fry could make runs only in front of the wicket, mainly to the on, and set the field for him accordingly, he scored 144 in an innings sparkling with cuts.

In his career as cricketer, he scored some 30,000 runs, averaging 50, in an era of natural wickets, mainly against bowlers of great speed or of varied and subtle spin and accuracy. From Yorkshire bowling alone he scored nearly 2,500 runs in all his matches against the county during its most powerful days, averaging 70, in the teeth of the attack of Hirst, Rhodes, Haigh, Wainwright and, occasionally, F. S. Jackson. In 1903 he made 234 against Yorkshire at Bradford. Next summer he made 177 against Yorkshire at Sheffield, and 229 at Brighton, in successive innings. Ranjitsinhji's performances against Yorkshire were almost as remarkable as Fry's; for he scored well over 1,500 runs against them, averaging more than 60 an innings. In 1901 Fry scored six centuries in six consecutive innings, an achievement equalled by Bradman, but on Australian wickets and spread over a season. Fry's six hundreds, two of them on bowler's wickets, came one on top of the other within little more than a fortnight.

The conjunction at the crease of C. B. Fry and K. S. Ranjitsinhji was a sight and an appeal to the imagination not likely ever to be repeated; Fry, 19th-century rationalist, batting according to first principles with a sort of moral grandeur, observing patience and abstinence. At the other end of the wicket, "Ranji" turned a cricket bat into a wand of conjuration. Fry was of the Occident, "Ranji" told of the Orient.

Cricket can scarcely hope again to witness two styles as fascinatingly contrasted and as racially representative as Fry's and Ranjitsinhji's. Between them they evolved a doctrine that caused a fundamental change in the tactics of batsmanship. "Play back or drive." "Watch the ball well, then make a stroke at the ball itself and not at a point in space where you hope the ball will presently be." At the time that Fry was making a name in cricket most batsmen played forward almost automatically on good fast pitches, frequently lunging out full stretch. If a ball can be reached only be excessive elongation of arms and body, obviously the pitch of it has been badly gauged. Fry and Ranjitsinhji, following after Arthur Shrewsbury, developed mobile footwork.

It is a pungent comment on the strength of the reserves of English cricket half a century ago that Fry and "Ranji" were both dropped from the England team at the height of their fame. In 1901 Fry scored 3,147 runs, average 78.67; in 1903 he scored 2,681 runs, average 81.30. In 1900 Ranjitsinhji scored 3,065, average 87.57. Yet because of one or two lapses in 1902, both these great players were asked to stand down and give way to other aspirants to Test cricket.

As we consider Fry's enormous aggregates of runs summer by summer, we should not forget that he took part, during all the extent of his career, in only one Test match lasting more than three days, and that he never visited Australia as a cricketer. For one reason and another Fry appeared not more than 18 times against Australia in 43 Test matches played between 1899, when he began the England innings with W. G. Grace, and 1912, in which wet season he was England's captain against Australia and South Africa in the ill-fated Triangular Tournament. By this time he had severed his illustrious connection with Sussex and was opening the innings for Hampshire. The general notion is that Fry was not successful as an England batsman; and it is true that in Test matches he did not remain on his habitual peaks. None the less, his batting average for Test cricket is much the same as that of Victor Trumper, M. A. Noble, and J. T. Tyldesley. The currency had not been debased yet.

Until he was no-balled for throwing by Phillips—who also "called" Mold at Old Trafford—Fry was a good fast bowler who took six wickets for 78 in the University match, opened the Gentlemen's bowling against the Players at the Oval, and took five wickets. Twice he performed the hat-trick at Lord's

He played Association football for his University, for the Corinthians, Southampton, and for England.

In his retirement he changed his methods as a writer on cricket and indulged a brisk impressionistic "columnist" style, to suit the running commentary needed by an evening paper: "Ah, here comes the Don. Walking slowly to the wicket. Deliberately. Menacingly. I don't like the look of him. He has begun with a savage hook. He is evidently in form. Dangerously so. Ah, but he is out . . . ." Essentially he was an analyst by mind, if rather at the mercy of an impulsive, highly strung temperament. He sometimes, in his heyday, got on the wrong side of the crowd by his complete absorption in himself, which was mistaken for posing or egoism. He would stand classically poised after making an on-drive, contemplating the direction and grandeur of it. The cricket field has seen no sight more Grecian than the one presented by C. B. Fry in the pride and handsomeness of his young manhood.

After he had passed his 70th birthay, he one day entered his club, saw his friend Denzil Batchelor, and said he had done most things but was now sighing for a new world to conquer, and proposed to interest himself in racing, attach himself to a stable, and then set up "on his own." And Batchelor summed up his genius in a flash of wit: "What as, Charles? Trainer, jockey, or horse?"

It is remarkable that he was not knighted for his services to cricket, and that no honours came his way for the sterling, devoted work he did with the training-ship *Mercury*.

Mr. Hubert Preston writes: "Charles Fry secured a place in the Repton XI in 1888 and retained it for the next three years, being captain in 1890 and 1891. In his last season at school his average reached nearly 50.

"When he went up to Oxford, Fry was captain of the cricket and Association football XIs and president of the athletic club, acting as first string in the 100yd. and the long-jump.

"He also played a good deal of Rugby football, and his friends insisted that but for an unfortuanate injury he would have added a Rugger Blue to his other honours. Charles Fry was also a fine boxer, a passable golfer, swimmer, sculler, tennis player and javelin thrower. But it was on the cricket field that he achieved his greatest triumphs. He represented three counties—Sussex, Hampshire and Surrey—scoring altogether 30,886 runs in first-class matches, average 50.22. His total of centuries reached 94 and five times he scored two separate hundreds in a match.

"Fry's best season was 1901 when his aggregate reached 3,147, average 78.67. In that summer he scored 13 hundreds and made six in successive innings—a feat equalled only by Sir Donald Bradman. In 1899, 1901, and 1903, Charles Fry hit a century for the Gentlemen against the Players at Lord's, his 232 not out in 1903 remaining the highest individual score for the Gentlemen at Headquarters.

"His one three-figure Test innings against Australia was 144 at the Oval in 1905, when the rubber had already been decided. Two years later he made his only other hundred for England, 129 against the South Africans, also at the Oval. Fry shared with Vine (J.) in 33 opening partnerships of 100 for Sussex.

"Considering the very high rank he attained among batsmen, Fry, at the outset, was a stiff ungainly performer and was still somewhat laboured in stroke-production when he went up to Oxford. But from the time he began playing for Sussex with 'Ranji' his game improved. He was a natural on-side batsman with a powerful straight drive and many useful leg-side strokes.

"The records contain very few details of Fry's achievements as a bowler. Yet he figured in a somewhat heated controversy in the '90s about 'unfair deliveries.' Cricket writers generally regarded him as a 'thrower.' Fry was equally insistent that all his deliveries were scrupulously fair.

"In his writings, Fry recalled how Jim Phillips, an Australian heavy-weight slow bowler turned umpire, was sent to Hove specially to 'no-ball' him.

"'A bright move,' commented Fry, 'because, of course, I rolled up my sleeve above my elbow and bowled with my arm as rigidly straight as a poker. The great Jim, sighting himself as a strong umpire, was not deterred. Large as an elephant, he bluffly no-balled me nine times running. It was a farce and the Sussex authorities and players were very angry.

"'However, I bowled often afterwards unscathed, even in Gentlemen v. Players at Lord's and in a Test match.'

"Outside sport, Fry's greatest work was accomplished as director of the training ship *Mercury*, which he saved from extinction and to which he devoted 42 years of unsparing effort entirely without remuneration. He was assisted by his wife, formerly Miss Beatrice Holme-Sumner, who died in 1941. In recognition of their work, Charles Fry was given the honorary rank of Captain in the R.N.R. and Mrs. Fry was awarded the O.B.E.

"In his absorbing autobiography, *Life Worth Living*, published in 1939, Fry told of how he 'very nearly became the King of

Albania.' His association with Ranjitsinhji led him to occupy the position of substitute delegate for India at the Assemblies of the League of Nations at Geneva, where he composed a speech delivered by Ranji which 'turned Mussolini out of Corfu.'

"The Albanians sent a delegation and appointed a Bishop, who bore a striking resemblance to W. G. Grace, to find 'an English country gentlemen with £10,000 a year' for their King. Fry had the first quali-fication but not the second; but Ranji certainly could have provided the money. 'If I had really pressed Ranji to promote me,' said Fry, 'it is quite on the cards that I should have been King of Albania yesterday, if not today.'

"In collaboration with his wife, he wrote the novel *A Mother's Son* which was pub-lished in 1907."

Other tributes included:

Sir Pelham Warner: "His style was stiff, but he had a cast-iron defence and played well off his pads. He put his great mental powers into improving his cricket, and that he developed into a very great batsman there can be no question. Ranjitsinhji's opinion was that he was 'the greatest of all batsmen of his time on all wickets and against every type of bowling.' ... Perhaps his greatest innings was his 129 at the Oval in 1907 against the famous South African googly bowlers—Vogler, Faulkner, Schwarz and White—on a wicket which *Wisden* says 'was never easy' and on which 'the South African bowling was very difficult and the fielding was almost free from fault.'"

Sir John Hobbs: "I played with 'C. B.' in my first Test against Australia in this coun-try. The year was 1909 and we both got blobs in the first innings. 'C. B.' persuaded Archie MacLaren, our captain, to let him go in first with me in the second innings, and we knocked off the 105 runs wanted for victory. ... Later he was my skipper and we always got on well together. He was a great racon-teur and my wife and I have spent many happy hours just listening to him. I saw him at Lord's this season."

Sir Leonard Hutton: "He was a fine judge of a cricketer and he always took the keenest interest in the progress of young players. I had a number of letters from him when I was still in the game. They were kindly, en-couraging letters which contained much sound advice which I greatly appreciated."

Frank Woolley: "He was one of the most solid batsmen I ever bowled against. He had a tremendous amount of determination, es-pecially on difficult pitches, and the patience

to play the type of game required. I remem-ber once bowling to him on a 'sticky' when the ball was tunring a lot. I beat him several times in one over without getting his wicket. Next over, to my surprise, he demonstrated that I was not pitching the ball on the right spot and it was going over the stumps. That was typical of him. He was a great theorist."

FRY, K. R. B., who died in June, 1949, was a cousin of C. B. Fry. Born on March 15, 1883, he was in the Cheltenham XI before going to Cambridge, for whom he played against Oxford in 1904, scoring 28 and 57 (10 fours). A big hitter, he scored 235 for Sussex Mart-lets against Cuckfield in 1907. He played in two matches for Sussex.

FRY, Stephen, died on May 18, 1979, aged 78. A son of C. B. Fry, and father of C. A., who played for Oxford, Hampshire and Northamptonshire, he himself played for Hampshire from 1922 to 1931. As a batsman he tried to follow his father's dictum—"Attack, attack, always attack"—but lacked his father's rare qualities to implement this philosophy. He could keep wicket in an emergency, and occasionally captained Hampshire in the absence of Lord Tennyson.

FRYER, William Henry, born at Greenwich on March 29, 1829, died at Loose, near Maidstone, on January 23, 1919. At his best he was a free and hard-hitting batsman and an excellent wicket-keeper. He played for Kent from 1852 to 1872, taking part during those years in 74 matches. In 49 of those games he kept wicket, catching 48 men and stumping 22. His highest score was 65 against Sussex at Brighton in 1864. In September, 1862, he met with a most unfortunate acci-dent, being thrown out of a trap and, as the result, losing the sight of his right eye. He continued to appear for the county, how-ever, batting successfully, but seldom keep-ing wicket. He was also useful as a change-bowler, and against England at Lord's in 1864 took eight wickets in an innings for 40 runs. Two matches were played for his benefit—Kent v. Eighteen of Mote Park in 1862 and Kent v. Surrey, also at Maidstone, in 1870. For some years he proved himself an excellent umpire, and he was in every way a worthy man.

FULCHER, Edward Arthur, died at Quest, Sidmouth, February 2, 1946. Made many runs for Devon between 1905 and 1930.

FULCHER, Major Eric Arthur, who died on

August 15, 1973, played as an opening bats-man for Devon for a number of years from 1923.

FULCHER, Major Eric Arthur, stated in the 1974 edition to have died on August 15, 1973, was not the Devon player, who was Edward Arthur Fulcher, whose death was reported in the 1947 edition.

FULLER, Lancelot Grahame, who died at Bloemfontein on February 7, 1946, aged 43, was a very useful all-rounder for Orange Free State from 1924 to 1929. His best season was 1925–26, when his performances in-cluded seven wickets for 41 against a strong Natal team and a hard-hit 84 against Western Province, when he went in last and with L. R. Tuckett put on 115. In this match Tuckett shared in a century last-wicket part-nership in each innings. Prominent in the administrative side of the game, Fuller, at the time of his death, was President of the Orange Free State Cricket Union.

FULLER-MAITLAND, William, at the time of his death the oldest surviving Oxford Blue, was born at Stansted, Bishop's Stort-ford, on May 6, 1844, and so, when he passed away at Brighton on November 15, 1932, had completed his 88th year. A hard hitting batsman, an excellent field and a remarkably fine slow bowler, he stood out among the leading amateurs of the day in the later '60s. Going up to Oxford after four years in the Harrow XI, he, as a Freshman in 1864, obtained a place in the University team. In that same season he appeared for the Gentlemen against the Players at the Oval and in the following summer he assisted the Gentlemen at Lord's. Indeed for some six years he was a fairly regular participant in the great match of the season but, after the summer of 1869, when he once again figured in the Gentlemen's team at the Oval, the cricket field saw him no more. Thus his career was almost as brief as it was brilliant. In answer to an enquiry early last year as to the cause of retirement from the game when, with his fame solidly established, he was at the height of his powers, Mr. Fuller-Mait-land wrote "One reason was that I always suffered badly from hay-fever in the months of June and July. Another reason—that I had a great wish to see as much of the world as I could. In my travels I spent three years in America, India and Spain and had no hay-fever at all. When three years more were over, I went into Parliament."

At Harrow, where he first secured a place in the XI in 1860, he had among his collea-gues I. D. Walker, for so many years captain of Middlesex, and in the opposing Eton team of that year was James Round, the best amateur wicket-keeper of his day, who, when up at Oxford, was not given his Blue and yet in the same year appeared for Gentlemen against Players at Lord's. Fuller-Maitland apparently developed his bowling only towards the close of his school-days, four wickets for 52 runs rewarding his efforts in the first innings of his last match against Eton, but in 1862, although on the losing side, he put together a score of 73. Strangely enough, considering the fame he afterwards obtained as a bowler, Fuller-Maitland's as-sociation with the Harrow XI was identified with the first three unfinished Eton and Harrow matches.

Fuller-Maitland had a happy experience of the University match as, with eight wickets for 53 in 1864 and eight wickets for 76 in 1865, he took more wickets than anyone else on his side and in the two subsequent years, with scores of 51 and 45, he proved to be the most successful run-getter. In all he obtained 21 wickets for Oxford against Cambridge at a cost of 10 runs apiece and in six completed innings registered 157 runs with an average of 26. His personal success, however, was discounted to some extent by the fact that while during his first three years in resi-dence—the first two under R. A. H. Mitch-ell—Oxford gained the victory, Cambridge won when Fuller-Maitland was captain in 1867. In 1864 against Surrey— a most for-midable combination at that time—he se-cured 12 wickets for 138 runs and in the following summer 12 wickets for 135 runs.

He first appeared for Gentlemen v. Play-ers at the Oval in 1864 and at Lord's in that contest a year later. The match in which he assisted the Gentlemen at Lord's in 1865 was that in which W. G. Grace first appeared for the Gentlemen. W. G. Grace taking 11 wick-ets and F. R. Evans seven, Fuller-Maitland enjoyed little opportunity on that occasion of displaying his abilities as a bowler.

A very slow bowler, Fuller-Maitland added to a fine command of length and skill in "flighting" the ball—what *Scores and Biographies* described as a "great curve, getting many wickets"—a fine leg-break and, at times, according to a famous old enthusiast, a phenomenal one. This admirer of Fuller-Maitland remembered that in the University match of 1867 J. S. E. Hood was bowled by a ball which came right round his legs. The ball pitched so wide that Hood left it alone, only, much to his chagrin, to find himself bowled. The enthusiast used to say that in the course of half a century, he had seen only three other balls which did so much. According to the same authority, Fuller-Maitland was the best slow bowler that has ever appeared in the University match except A. G. Steel as that great cricketer was in 1878. He further insisted that, with the exception of V. E. Walker, there was no one so clever in making a catch off his own bowling. Mr Fuller-Maitland had been a member of the M.C.C. since his days at Harrow—nearly 70 years ago.

An all-round athlete, Fuller-Maitland showed great ability at the High Jump as well as at the Long Jump and took part in the University Sports from 1865 to 1867. In 1866 he appeared for Oxford at racquets in both the Singles and Doubles. He entered Parliament as member for Breconshire in 1875 and held the seat until 1895 when he retired.

FURLEY, John, born at Oakham on March 24, 1847, died suddenly at his native place on June 30, 1909. His first appearance at Lord's (under the assumed name of "A. Yorker, Esq.,") was for Northamptonshire v. M.C.C. and Ground in July, 1873, when he made 0 and 24 and took eight wickets for 93 runs. In 1877, when he made several large scores for Burghley Park, he was chosen to play for England against Gloucestershire at the Oval. *Scores and Biographies* (xii–781) described him as: "A fair bat, a good and fast round-armed bowler, fielding generally at short slip."

FURNESS, Frederick, one of the Pavilion clerks at Lord's, and a most respected and popular servant of the M.C.C.; died of pneumonia on January 21, 1892. Mr. Furness was most courteous and obliging to everyone with whom he came in contact, and his loss was much regretted by the staff at Lord's. In addition to his work for the Marylebone Club he usually scored in the out matches of the Middlesex XI.

FURNISS, Harry, the well-known artist and caricaturist, was born at Wexford on March 26, 1854, and died at Hastings on January 14, 1925. He contributed the Preface and a hundred sketches of W. G. Grace to *How's That?* published by Messrs. Arrowsmith, of Bristol.

GAINFORD, Lord, who died at Headlam Hall, near Darlington, on February 15, 1943, aged 83, captained Durham County Club from 1886 to 1891, and continued playing cricket until he was 74, when, as he wrote to

Mr. Bulmer, secretary of Durham County C.C., "Inability to take a quick run forced me to give up the game." His last innings was nine not out. Joseph Albert Pease, known as "Jack," joined the County Club on its formation in 1882 and was the oldest member. He played for the county until 1892, having a batting average of nearly 19, and he kept wicket. In 1878 he went to Cambridge, captained Trinity College cricket XI, played in the polo team, was master of the drag hounds, and sometimes played Rugby for the University without getting his Blue. One of the proudest moments of his life, he used to relate, was when "I took a catch in the outfield off W. G. Grace, who shook me by the hand." That was in a match for M.C.C., of which he was a member for many years.

During 34 years in the House of Commons he became Postmaster-General, President of the Board of Education, Chancellor of the Duchy of Lancaster, and Chief Liberal Whip. He was raised to the Peerage in 1916 and took an active part in the House of Lords debates. Shortly before his death he recalled an occasion in the Commons some 50 years ago when a fray arose over the Home Rule for Ireland Bill, and he used the rugby tackle to keep Dr. Tanner out of the "maul" until John Burns separated the combatants.

GALE, Frederick, well known to thousands of cricketers under his nom de plume "The Old Buffer," died on April 24, 1904, in the Charterhouse. Born in 1823, he had lived to a ripe old age. He was in the Winchester XI in 1841, and appeared at Lord's that year against both Harrow and Eton. Winchester suffered a single-innings' defeat at the hands of Harrow, but beat Eton by 109 runs. The victory was one to be proud of, as the Eton team included Emilius Bayley, Walter Marcon, George Yonge, and Harvey Fellows. Mr. Gale did not win fame as a player, but no one loved cricket more than he did, or supported it more keenly. He kept up his enthusiasm to the end, and even so recently as the season of 1903 he was to be seen at the Oval—bent in figure, but still full of vivacity. As a writer on the game he was prolific, several books and numberless magazine and newspaper articles coming from his pen. He lived for a good many years at Mitcham, and in those days took the liveliest interest in young Surrey players, delighting in the triumphs of Jupp, Tom Humphrey, and, a little later, Richard Humphrey. A special protegé of his was George Jones, who bowled for Surrey more than 20 years ago, when the county's fortunes were at a low ebb. Mr.

Gale had a high ideal of the way in which cricket should be played, and in his various writings always insisted on the necessity of good fielding. His particular aversion was the batsman who played for his average rather than for his side. Like many old men, he had an abiding regard for the heroes of his youth, and nothing pleased him better, when he found a congenial listener, than to talk about Fuller Pilch, Hillyer, and Felix. Still, he could be just as enthusiastic when discussing the batting of W. G. Grace and the bowling of Alfred Shaw. He enjoyed the friendship of John Ruskin, and took the famous writer to the Oval in 1882 to see the Australians.

His best known books were:

Echoes from Old Cricket Fields, 1871 (Re-issued by David Nutt in 1896 at 1/-).

The Game of Cricket, 1887.

Memoir of Hon. R. Grimston, 1885.

Public School Matches and those we meet there, 1853 & 1867 (Re-issued by David Nutt in 1896 at 1/-).

Ups and Downs of a Public School, 1859.

Modern English Sports, 1885.

Sports and Recreations, 1885.

GALE, Harold Frederick, who died at Croydon on April 15, 1954, aged 74, was for 58 years a sports journalist. He commenced his career with the *Pall Mall Gazette* in 1896, and for 42 years was associated with the *Observer*, of which he was Sports Editor from 1939 till his death. A great lover of cricket, he played in matches with Dr. W. G. Grace, whom he claimed to have bowled on three occasions. In his younger days a fine billiards and snooker player, he wrote on those games for *The Times* for many years. Courteous and always ready to extend a helping hand to young journalists, he was a most popular figure in Fleet Street.

GALE, Norman Rowland, the "Cricket Poet," who played the game with the Rugby Club, died on October 7, 1942, aged 80. Among his many beautiful publications were *Cricket Songs*, 1890 and 1894; *More Cricket Songs*, 1905; and *Close of Play*, 1936, with which he ended:

"Run out:

To cricket played without a crease,

Its scorers, umpires and police,

A harrowing farewell:

All that I had to sing is sung,

And now, being very far from young,

I have no more to tell."

GALE, Percival George, who played with W. G. Grace in the London County team,

died on September 7, 1940, aged 75. As captain of Walham Green he made a name in club cricket. For the powerful Wanderers club he showed to advantage, and became a Vice-President. After the last war, during which he rose to the rank of Chief Inspector in the Special Constabulary, he took up golf. He was Chairman of the Tooting Bec Club which bought the course and renamed it South Lodge Club.

GALLICHAN, Norman M., who died at Taupo, New Zealand, on March 25, 1969, aged 62, played in one Test match for New Zealand. A slow left-arm bowler who stood over 6ft., he was called upon after the original 14 players for the 1937 tour of England had been selected, and though he scarcely encountered helpful conditions, he took 59 wickets in first-class games for 23.92 runs each. Against Scotland at Glasgow, he earned first-innings figures of six wickets for 46 runs and in the match with Minor Counties at Gainsborough analyses of five for 52 and five for 20. He took part in the second Test with England at Old Trafford, scoring 30 and two and taking three wickets. Most of his cricket in New Zealand was for Manawatu in the Hawke Cup competition, in which he dismissed 177 batsmen for 11.59 runs apiece and, as a right-handed batsman, hit 1,409 runs with a highest innings of 142 and an average of 32.76. Though rarely chosen to assist Wellington in Plunket Shield fixtures, he appeared in 1928 for New Zealand against V. Y. Richardson's Australian XI at Auckland.

GAME, William Henry, a famous Oxford and Surrey batsman in the '70s, died at Brancaster, Norfolk, on August 11, 1932, in his 79th year.

Mr. Game enjoyed the unique distinction of having hit a ball from Spofforth, the great Australian bowler, out of the Oval. The occasion which furnished this memorable feat was the match between Surrey and the Australians early in the tour of 1878. The Australians, a week or two earlier, had made their name in sensational fashion by beating in the course of a single day's cricket at Lord's a most formidable team of Marylebone, so Surrey's defeat by five wickets occasioned no surprise. Game was dismissed without getting a run in the first innings and in the second made only 10, but that small score included the mighty square-leg hit off Spofforth.

A fine free hitter, if rather lacking in defensive skill, and an exceptionally brilliant out-field, W. H. Game was born at Stoke Newington on October 2, 1853. Educated at Sherborne, he captained the XI there in 1871 when he reached three-figures upon four occasions, his great triumph being an innings of 281, put together against Motcombe School, in four hours and a half. Three years later at the age of 20, when in residence at Oxford, he hit up, for Wadham against Oriel, a score of 234, not out, in two hours and a quarter. He first appeared for Surrey in 1871 when only 17 years old.

Going up to Oxford in 1873, Game was in the XI four years, captaining the Dark Blues in 1876 when in the second innings he made 109. For all that, Oxford suffered defeat by nine wickets, Game's hundred—the first ever hit for Oxford against Cambridge—having been preceded by a score of 105, not out, on the part of W. S. Patterson in the first innings of Cambridge. Prior to that year the only three-figure scores registered in the Universities' match had been those of William Yardley, the great Cambridge batsman, who made 100 in 1870 and 130 in 1872. These four innings, together with 117, not out, by F. M. Buckland in 1877 and 107, not out, by W. H. Patterson in 1881, were the only individual hundreds recorded in the course of the first 47 matches between Oxford and Cambridge. In the same season that he enjoyed his notable success against Cambridge, Game made 141 for Oxford against Middlesex. He did not play a great deal for Surrey, but in 1875 averaged 22 runs an innings—no small achievement in those days.

An all-round athlete, Game not only distinguished himself on the cricket field but, in 1873 at Cambridge and the two following years, when Oxford and Cambridge tried conclusions at Rugby football on the Oval, he formed one of the Dark Blues' team. At that time 20 players figured on each side. The varying formations which then obtained are strongly emphasised by Game's records, which show that in the match decided in February, 1873, he was one of the *two* backs, in that of 1873–74 the *one* three-quarter, and in the contest of 1874–75, one of *three* backs.

In the Oxford University sports of 1873, when 19, he threw the cricket ball 127yd. 1ft. 3in. and, at the Oval in 1875, after throwing the cricket ball 111yd. he at once threw it back the same distance.

GAMLIN, H. T., most famous as a Rugby full back, who died at Cheam, Surrey, on July 12, 1937, aged 59, played a few times for Somerset as a professional. In 1895 A. C. MacLaren, after making 424, the highest

score by an Englishman in first-class cricket, was caught off Gamlin, who, in Lancashire's innings of 801—then the highest total in County Cricket and made in only eight hours—bowled 26 overs for 100 runs and two wickets.

GANDAR-DOWER, Kenneth Cecil, was lost at sea through Japanese action in February, 1944, at the age of 36. He played for Harrow against Winchester in 1927, but not in the Eton match. At Cambridge he did well in the Freshmen's match and was a Crusader, but his time was mainly given up to tennis, at which he captained the University team. One of the most versatile players of games of any period, he was amateur squash champion in 1938, won amateur championships at fives, and played lawn tennis for Great Britain. In all, he represented Cambridge at six forms of sport: tennis, lawn tennis, Rugby fives, Eton fives, squash racquets and billiards. In fact, time hardly sufficed for their rival calls. He probably created a record when he played simultaneously in the Freshmen's match and Freshmen's tournament, with the connivance of the tennis but not the cricket authorities; he disappeared to play off a round during the early part of his side's innings, with relays of cyclist friends to keep him informed as to the fall of wickets! He flew a private aeroplane to India. In spite of other demands he continued to find time for cricket, making some 10 appearances for the Frogs each season almost to the outbreak of war, and got many runs and wickets.

Famous as a big game shot, and extensive traveller, he introduced a team of cheetahs from Kenya jungle to London and on greyhound tracks they set up speed records. A writer of articles and books, he acted as a War Correspondent in various theatres of operations up to the time of his death.

GANGE, T. H., a right-arm fast bowler who appeared for Gloucestershire from 1913 to 1920, died in March, 1949, in his 58th year. During the four seasons he appeared in first-class cricket he scored 571 runs, average 10.01 and took 103 wickets, average 31.69. His best year was 1913 when he obtained 54 wickets at a cost of 25.68 runs each.

GANNON, Brigadier Jack Rose Compton, C.B.E., M.V.O., who died at Midhurst on April 25, 1980, aged 97, was one of the oldest of first-class cricketers. Elected a member of M.C.C. in 1908, he kept wicket a number of times for the club in that and the two following seasons in first-class matches.

Later he was better known in the polo world.

GARDINER, Dr. Ivor Burberou, who died at East London, South Africa, in July, 1951, aged 48, was a steady, slow left-arm bowler and useful batsman who played for Western Province from 1926 to 1929 and for Border from 1933 to 1938. He frequently captained both sides. In all Currie Cup matches he scored 616 runs, average 17.60, and took 48 wickets, average 21.14. His best performances were 107 against Eastern Province at Port Elizabeth in 1934–35 and seven wickets for 28 against Orange Free State at East London in 1937–38.

GARDNER, Fred Charles, who died at Coventry, his native place, on January 13, 1979, after a long illness, aged 56, did valuable work for Warwickshire as an opening bat. In his first match, against Gloucestershire at Birmingham in 1947, he scored 53 and 42, sharing with Hill in first-wicket stands of 81 and 111, and next year made his first hundred, 126 v. Kent. It was not until 1949 that he won a regular place in the side and was awarded his cap. In 1950, when he made 1,801 runs with an average of 48.67 and headed the county averages, he obtained his highest score, 215 not out against Somerset at Taunton, and also scored a century in each innings against Essex at Ilford. Probably his most memorable feat was in 1953 against the Australians, when he scored 110, the first hundred ever made by a Warwickshire batsman against an Australian touring side. Essentially a solid defensive player, he was very strong on the leg side, was a good runner between the wickets, and an excellent field. He had a benefit in 1958, his last regular season, and played his last match in 1961. In all he scored 17,826 runs for Warwickshire, with an average of 33.83, and made 29 centuries.

GARDNER, James, of Saxon Hall, near Newmarket, died on March 1, 1910, in his 61st year. A steady batsman and a useful slow bowler, he played occasionally for Suffolk and Leicestershire. Several times 11 members of the Gardner family formed a side in the cricket field.

GARNETT, Capt. Harold G., born November 19, 1879, killed on the Italian front at the beginning of December, 1917. Harold Garnett will be remembered as a distinguished member of the Lancashire XI. Tried twice for his county towards the end of the season of 1900, he jumped into fame the following year, playing so finely that he seemed likely to become the best left-handed bat in England. His style was attractive and his hitting very brilliant. Against Sussex at Manchester he scored 110 and 89, and in two other matches—against Leicestershire at Leicester and Middlesex at Lord's—he made over a hundred, his scores being 139 and 114. As the result of his season's work he came out second to Tyldesley in the Lancashire averages. On the strength of this performance he was chosen to go to Australia with Mr. McLaren's team, but he failed, doing next to nothing during the tour. He was so obviously out of form that he was given a few chances. For several seasons, till business took him to the Argentine, Garnett batted exceedingly well for Lancashire, but he never quite equalled his efforts in 1901. Returning to England in 1911 and again in 1914 he renewed his connection with the Lancashire XI. In 1914 he had developed into a first rate wicket-keeper, and strictly on his merits he was picked for Gentlemen v. Players at Lord's. He proved fully worthy of the distinction, and had no small share in winning the match. The way in which he stumped Hitch in the Players' second innings would have been wonderful even if done by Blackham at his best. Garnett volunteered at the outbreak of the War, and soon obtained a commission.—S.H.P.

GARRARD, Wilson Roziere, who died at Auckland on June 2, 1956, aged 56, played as wicket-keeper for New Zealand in 1924–25. Unfortunate to be contemporary with R. W. Rountree, who kept wicket for New Zealand, he made only 11 appearances for Auckland. A member of the legal profession, he was compelled by business claims to end his representative cricket career at the age of 26.

GARRETT, Lieut. H. F. (9th Service Batt. East Yorkshire Regiment) was killed in the Dardanelles in July, 1915. He was an excellent bat and effective googly bowler, but did not obtain a place in the Cambridge XI. In the Eastbourne Week of 1913 he bowled very effectively for Mr. H. D. G. Leveson-Gower's XI., his analyses against Cambridge University being three for 31 and five for 39, and against Oxford six for 60 and four for 32. In all first-class matches that season he made 209 runs with an average of 13.06 took 32 wickets for 20.93 runs apiece. He was well-known in Eastbourne club cricket, and appeared occasionally for Somerset.

GARRETT, Thomas William, the oldest surviving Australian Test player, died at Sydney on August 6, 1943, aged 85. A very fine hard-wicket bowler, a capital field, and a punishing if not dependable batsman, he took part in the two matches against James Lillywhite's all-professional team in March and April, 1877, after which he came to England with the first Australian team in 1878, and also in 1882 and 1886. Thus he served under three different captains—David Gregory, W. L. Murdoch and H. J. H. Scott. When Australia in March, 1877, won by 45 runs what years after was styled the first Test match, he scored 19 not out and 0, and took two wickets for 81, while in the return, which Lillywhite's team won by four wickets, he scored 12 and 18 but earned no success with the ball. Really his first experience of meeting the full strength of England was in the historic 1882 encounter at the Oval where Australia won by seven runs, but his share in "The Ashes" triumph was small—12 runs for once out and one wicket for 32 runs.

The 1878 team altogether played as a touring side for 14 months. Opening with a series of matches in Australia, they went through the season in England, then followed with a trip to America, while a second series of games in Australia concluded the enterprise before the side disbanded. The huge programme of 77 engagements was gone through by practically 11 men, for Midwinter, who they hoped would assist them regularly in England, had signed an agreement with Gloucestershire, and, after appearing for the Australians on a few occasions, was carried off from Lord's to the Oval by W. G. Grace and J. A. Bush, and he did not take the field again as a member of the touring side. For that combination in England Garrett claimed 38 wickets for 10 runs apiece in 11-a-side games—20 of the fixtures were against odds. His record during the 14 months in all matches showed 291 wickets for five runs each.

Four years later—1882—when contests with Eighteens and XXIIs no longer figured on the programme arranged for the Australians, Garrett took 128 wickets for under 14 runs apiece, and in 1886 his record was 123 wickets for something over 18 runs each. Possessed of a nice easy action, he made good use of his height—nearly 6ft.—and so came fast off the pitch. He bowled above medium-pace and under favourable conditions could turn the ball either way, while he sent down a very telling "yorker," but got most of his wickets with the ball which pitched just outside the off-stump and went

away slightly. On hard ground many good judges regarded him as more effective than Spofforth or Boyle.

In the 1878 tour he took 10 Middlesex wickets at Lord's for 82 runs, and at Prince's he disposed of seven Players of England for 41 runs. Four years later among his best performances were seven Surrey wickets for 31 runs and 12 Kent wickets for 120, while in four matches which the Australians played with Yorkshire 27 wickets fell to him for nine runs apiece. In 1886 his successes included seven wickets for 40 against Lord Sheffield's XI, seven for 47 in the first of two games with Gentlemen of England, seven for 84 against Yorkshire and seven for 82 at Bradford against the Players. In 19 matches for Australia against England he took 36 wickets and scored 340 runs.

During his three visits to England Garrett's highest innings was 59 against Northumberland in 1882; at Sydney in 1885 his 51 not out contributed largely to Australia beating England by six runs. In his 35th year, when the Sheffield Shield was instituted in 1892, he appeared for New South Wales in only 17 competition matches, scoring 776 runs, highest innings 131, average 26.75 but taking only five wickets at the very high cost of 62 runs apiece.

Born at Woolongong, near Sydney, on July 26, 1858, Garrett was educated at Newington College, Sydney, and at Sydney University, where he earned distinction as a sprinter. A solicitor by profession, he held the position of Public Trustee in Sydney. On the occasion of his diamond wedding celebration on March 25, 1939, the M.C.C. sent him a congratulatory message on behalf of all cricketers in England, where he enjoyed great popularity, as he did in Australia.

GARRETT, William T., who died at Loughton, where he was a licensee, in February, 1953, aged 76, played as a batsman in 16 matches for Essex between 1900 and 1903. His chief successes were achieved at the expense of Warwickshire. In 1900 at Leyton, after Essex followed-on 394 behind the Midland county's first innings total, Garrett stayed nearly four hours for a match-saving 64 not out. The following season he hit 92 at Edgbaston and 76 in the return game at Leyton. Born on January 9, 1877, he also assisted Surrey Second XI in 1904 and 1905.

GASKIN, Berkeley McGarrell, died in Georgetown, Guyana, on May 2, 1979, aged 71. A medium-pace opening bowler, he played for British Guiana from 1929 to 1953, and in 1948, when nearly 40, was picked for the first two Tests against G. O. Allen's side. Later he served frequently as Guiana's representative on the West Indies Board, and as a selector. At the time of his death he was president of the Guyana Cricket Association. He was manager of the West Indies sides to India and Pakistan in 1958–59, to England in 1963, and to Australia and New Zealand in 1968–69.

GASTON, Alfred James, so well-known in connection with cricket literature, records and curios, was born on October 14, 1854, and died at Brighton on October 31, 1928, aged 74. A zealous collector of cricket books, photographs and other things concerning the game, in the sale of which he had built up a considerable business. Mr. Gaston was, of course, particularly interested in Sussex cricket and cricketers and of late years had worked very hard for the county. Among his many activities in that direction was the giving of lectures, illustrated by lantern slides, in various parts of Sussex and in these he generally enjoyed the help of Mr. Arthur Gilligan or Mr. W. L. Knowles. He was the author of *History of Cricket in Sussex*, and other publications and to *Wisden's Almanack* he contributed articles on the *Bibliography of Cricket* to the issues of 1892, 1894, 1900 and 1923. For many years he had written regularly for the *Sussex Daily News*, in which as "Leather Hunter" he provided an immense amount of interesting cricket information drawn from the books and records he had gathered so diligently and for so many years. A kindly veteran, he will be greatly missed next summer by cricketers generally when attending the Hove ground.

GAULD, Dr. George Ogg, former captain of Nottinghamshire County C.C. and hon. secretary of the club from 1922 to 1935, died in Nottingham on June 16, 1950, aged 76. A useful batsman, he first played for the county in 1913, and in 1914 he made his highest score—90 out of 115 in 65 minutes against Derbyshire at Trent Bridge.

GAUNT, The Rev. Canon Howard Charles Adie, who died at Winchester on February 1, 1983, aged 80, was a successful bat at Tonbridge, but did not obtain a Blue at Cambridge. However, he played in 11 matches for Warwickshire between 1919 and 1922, his highest score being 32 against Somerset at Edgbaston in 1922. From 1937 to 1953 he was Headmaster of Malvern and once, batting for Free Foresters, won the admiration of Arthur Povey, the much-loved pro at Tonbridge, who exclaimed, "He may be a Headmaster, but he can hit them to square leg all right!" He represented Cambridge at hockey and lawn tennis.

GAY, Major Leslie Hewitt, who played in a Test match in Australia in the winter of 1894–95 and kept goal at soccer for England, Cambridge University Corinthians and Old Brightonians, died at Sidmouth on November 1, 1949, aged 78. A cousin of Mr. K. J. Key, captain of Surrey, Gay, who was born at Brighton on March 24, 1871, kept wicket for Cambridge against Oxford in 1892 and 1893. He helped Hampshire and Somerset between 1888 and 1900, and appeared for Gentlemen v. Players at the Oval in 1892. In 1894, when a member of the Somerset team, he toured Australia with A. E. Stoddart's team but played only in the first Test. At football, Gay kept goal in the University match in 1892 and was capped for England against Scotland in 1893, and against Scotland and Wales the following year.

GEARY, Alfred, who played in four matches for New South Wales against Victoria between 1877 and 1881, died in Brisbane on October 14, 1911, aged 62. In the matches referred to he scored 39 runs in seven innings, and took two wickets for 41. He was a left-handed bowler.

GEARY, George, who died at the age of 87 on March 6, 1981, after a long period of ill-health, had been in his day one of the best bowlers in the world and was also one of the last survivors of those who were playing regular County Cricket before the Great War. A tall, powerful man, he bowled fast-medium well within his strength, with a short run and a beautifully easy action. His stock ball moved naturally from the off and could be deadly if the wicket helped him, as when he ruined his second benefit, against Warwickshire at Hinckley in 1936, by taking 13 for 43 (the match produced him £10). This was varied by a delivery which came straight through and, a far more dangerous ball, the leg-cutter which pitched on middle-and-leg and left the bat sharply. This was the one which the experts dreaded and which secured the all-important wicket of Bradman, caught at slip for 29, in the Nottingham Test of 1934. Apart from this he could make full use of the shine to swing the new ball. Yet with all these gifts, he will probably be remembered chiefly as a stock bowler who would peg away cheerfully all day if need be, keeping the situation under control whether or not he was getting wickets. As a batsman he never claimed to be a stylist, but he was typically effective: the more runs were needed, the more resolutely he would set himself to get them, not least by punishing ruthlessly anything which fell short of his very high standards of what first-class bowling should be. In his last season, at the age of 45, when an injury prevented him from doing his full share of the bowling, he scored three centuries. He was a fine slip, but in fact his vast hands were equally tenacious anywhere: in the Oval Test of 1926, besides two blinding slip catches off Larwood, he caught a brilliant one low at mid-off off Rhodes to dismiss Arthur Richardson.

Making a few appearances for Leicestershire in 1912, he gained a regular place in 1913, and in 1914, when he took over 100 wickets, he was picked for his first representative match, the Centenary at Lord's, the Rest of England against M.C.C.'s South African team. This should have given him his one chance of seeing the great Sydney Barnes bowl, but, when he arrived in the dressing-room, he found Barnes urging the others not to play unless they received more money. *Wisden* says Barnes was prevented from playing by a strain. At this point Geary's career suffered a serious setback. Serving in the Air Force in the Great War, he was lucky not to have his leg severed by a propeller; but the damage was such that, after an unsuccessful season in 1919, he decided that he was not for the moment strong enough for County Cricket and went into the Lancashire League. It was not till 1922 that he resumed a regular place in the Leicestershire side.

In 1923 he appeared in a Test trial and in 1924–25 made his first tour abroad, for Lord Tennyson's unofficial side in South Africa, where he was an outstanding success as a bowler. In 1924 he had been picked for his first Test, against South Africa, and in 1926 he played against Australia at Leeds, where Carr put his opponents in with disastrous results. According to Geary his captain's great mistake was taking his batsmen, not his bowlers, out to inspect the wicket. At any rate, when Geary came in the score, in face of a total of 494, was 182 for eight. He and Macaulay added 108, Geary making 35 not out, and, though he could not save the follow-on, he may well have rescued England from defeat. He played again in the final Test at the Oval. That winter he went with M.C.C. to India and in 1927–28 was a member of their side in South Africa, where

he took 12 for 130 in the first Test and was reckoned by the South Africans to be, on a matting wicket, the finest bowler of his type since Barnes. Unfortunately, in the second Test his right arm, which had troubled him intermittently for some years, became so bad that he could not play again until the last match, and further he missed most of the 1928 season. Indeed his career was in jeopardy. He was saved by Lord Harris, who enquired into his case and insisted upon his having the best medical treatment. An operation was performed on his elbow and was so successful that he was not only able to accept an invitation to go to Australia in 1928–29, but, with 19 wickets at an average of 25, headed the bowling averages in the Tests. At Sydney in the second Test he followed five for 35 with an innings of 66, and in the final Test at Melbourne he had in the first innings the astonishing analysis of 81–36–105–5. In 1929 he played in the last two Tests against South Africa; in 1930 he played against Australia at Leeds, and in 1934, also against Australia, at Nottingham and Lord's. At Nottingham, coming in at 165 for six, he scored 53, including 10 fours, and helped Hendren to put on 101 in 110 minutes. In 1932 he had gone with Lord Tennyson's team to the West Indies and, as he also once took a coaching appointment in South America, he was one of the most widely travelled cricketers of his time.

His last season for Leicestershire was 1938 and then he became the professional at Charterhouse. He showed himself a great coach and in particular was one of the few who could really teach bowling. Feeling that at 65 he would be rash to undertake another three-year contract, he left Charterhouse in 1959 with great reluctance on both sides, but Rugby were desperate for help and persuaded him to come and stand behind their nets. Before the end of the first net he could bear it no longer, had his coat off and continued to bowl for another 11 years.

Few professionals have been more popular and more respected, and deservedly. No-one ever saw him out of temper; he was always cheerful and smiling and had a wonderful sense of humour which made him a splendid raconteur. E. W. Dawson said that, when he took over the Leicestershire captaincy immediately after coming down from Cambridge and utterly inexperienced, he owed everything to Geary, who, though not yet the senior professional, looked after him like a father.

In all first-class matches he made 13,500 runs (including eight centuries) with an average of 19.80 and took 2,063 wickets at 20.03.

Peter May, who was coached by Geary at Charterhouse, writes: "George really fired me with the enthusiasm and ambition to play first-class cricket and to get to the top. When he told me of his great experiences in Australia and India and the wonderful friends he had made, I knew that this was something which I really wanted to follow. 'You will be judged by your scores. Never give your wicket away.' I shall always have the happiest memories of this great man."

GEESON, Fred, who was born at Redmile, in Leicestershire, on August 23, 1862, died in Johannesburg on May 4, 1920. He will be best remembered as a medium-paced bowler, but he was, too, a very useful batsman. After his action had been condemned by the county captains at Lord's in December, 1900, he cultivated leg-breaks and with such success that in the following season he obtained as many as 125 wickets at a cost of 26.64. In 1902, however, he showed such a decline—his record showed only 17 wickets for 47.23 runs each—that he lost his place in the Leicestershire team. Among his best feats may be mentioned 13 wickets for 102 runs v. Derbyshire at Leicester in 1898, eight in an innings for 110 for M.C.C. and Ground v. Cambridge University at Lord's in 1900, five for 17 for Leicestershire v. Hampshire at Southampton in 1900 and seven for 33 for Leicestershire v. South Africans at Leicester in 1901. For his county against Derbyshire at Glossop in the last-mentioned year he carried out his bat for 104 and obtained a dozen wickets. In a small match at Grantham in September, 1902—for Sixteen of Grantham v. A. Priestley's XI—he took all 10 wickets in an innings for 69 runs. Geeson joined the ground-staff at Lord's in 1891, and was a member of it for 28 seasons.

GEHRS, D. R. A., who died in June, 1953, aged 72, was a prominent batsman for South Australia in the early part of the century. In all he scored 3,387 runs for his State, average 39.38. He took part in one Test match against England in 1903 and one when visiting this country with J. Darling's team in 1905, showing disappointing form. During the tour he scored 675 runs in all matches, average 21.77. In 1910, when South Africa went to Australia, "Algy" Gehrs did better, making four Test appearances and hitting 67 at Sydney and 58 at Melbourne.

GENTRY, Jack Sydney Bates, C.I.E., C.B.E., died at Loxwood, Sussex, after years of ill-health, on April 16, 1978, aged 78. He had the distinction, rare until recent years of representing three first-class counties. After being in the XI at Christ's Hospital, he made one appearance for Hampshire in 1919, eight for Surrey in 1922 and two in 1923 and one for Essex, the county of his birth, in 1925. For Surrey in 1922 he took 31 wickets with an average of 21.54 and came second in their averages. A slow left-hander, he was extremely accurate, but lacked the spin of the great bowlers and was in fact more effective on hard wickets than on soft. The consistency of his performances suggested that he could have been valuable had he been able to play regularly.

GEOGHEGAN, J. P. A., died in Swansea Hospital during the second week of April, 1916, after an operation, aged 49. He was educated at St. Charles College and played for the Middlesex Colts, St. Thomas' Hospital, and various clubs in the Metropolitan district. About 30 years ago he went as professional to Swansea for two seasons, and subsequently played for Glamorgan as an amateur. He was a useful all-round cricketer.

H.M. King GEORGE V, died at Sandringham on January 20, 1936. As Duke of Cornwall, when Prince of Wales, His Majesty was ground landlord of Kennington Oval, and remained Patron of the Surrey club until his death. King George was also Patron of M.C.C., and the book *Lord's and The M.C.C.* by Lord Harris and F. S. Ashley-Cooper, published in 1914, was dedicated by gracious permission to His Majesty.

He habitually visited Lord's when Colonial teams were playing against England, and on such occasions the match was invariably interrupted in order that all the players and umpires could be presented to His Majesty in front of the pavilion, an informal ceremony which the spectators watched with keen interest marked by expressions of loyalty.

H.M. King GEORGE VI, died at Sandringham on February 6, 1952. He was Patron of the Marylebone, Surrey and Lancashire clubs. When Prince Albert he performed the hat-trick on the private ground on the slopes below Windsor Castle, where the sons and grandsons of Edward VII used to play regularly. A left-handed batsman and bowler, the King bowled King Edward VII, King George V and the present Duke of Windsor in three consecutive balls, thus proving himself the best Royal cricketer since Frederick, Prince of Wales, in 1751, took a keen interest in the game. The ball is now mounted in the mess-room of the Royal Naval College, Dart-mouth. King George VI, like his father, often went to Lord's when Commonwealth teams were playing there, and invariably the players and umpires were presented to His Majesty in front of the pavilion. He enter-tained the 1948 Australian team at Balmoral, and in his 1949 New Year's Honours Donald Bradman, the captain, received a Knight-hood.

GEORGE TUBOW II, King of Tonga, the last of the independent kings in the Pacific, died April, 1918, aged 46. Very fond of cricket, gaining his love of the game while at school in Auckland. His subjects became so devoted to the game that it was necessary to prohibit it on six days of the week in order to avert famine, the plantations being entirely neglected for the cricket field.

GEORGE, William, who was born on June 29, 1874, died on December 4, 1933. As a forcing batsman, he played a few times for Warwickshire in 1901, 1902 and 1907, his highest innings being 71 in the last year against Hampshire, at Basingstoke. He was better known as the Aston Villa and English International Association goal-keeper, and played against Scotland, Wales and Ireland in 1905.

GERMAN, Arthur Clive Johnson, who died in an Aberdeen hospital in February 2, 1968, aged 62, was in the Repton XI in 1922 and 1923. He did not get a cricket Blue at Oxford, but represented the University against Cambridge at Association football from 1925 to 1927, becoming captain. He was also a noted half-back for the Corin-thians. He played in a few matches for Leicestershire in 1923 and the following season.

GERRARD, Major Ronald Anderson, D.S.O., an exceptionally good all-round ath-lete, besides being so brilliant a three-quar-ter that he played in 14 Rugby internationals for England, was killed in the Middle East on January 22, 1943, aged nearly 31. After showing outstanding ability at Taunton School, he played Rugby for Bath and Somerset. Tall and strongly built, he won the Public Schools weight-putting at Stamford Bridge in 1929 and 1930. An opening bats-man, he headed the Taunton School aver-ages three times; in 1929 with 38.40, highest innings 130, and next year he did still better

with an average of 43.25, his best display being 123. J. H. Cameron was then the school's great bowler. Gerrard was a forcing player, and his hitting against M.C.C. and other visiting teams brought him special distinction. He appeared three times for Somerset in 1935 without showing his form. Lawn tennis, table tennis, and Fives cham-pion, he also played water polo for the school and was a first-class rifle shot. A Royal Engineer, he won the D.S.O. for clearing mines and booby traps during the advance from El Alamein.

GHOPADE, Jaysingh, who died in Baroda on March 29, 1978, aged 47, was for some years regarded as one of the best all-rounders in India, a beautiful stroke player, who was always looking for runs, a useful leg-spinner and a magnificent field in the covers. But it must be said that, for a player of this reputation, his performances in the highest class were disappointing. A member of the sides in the West Indies in 1952–53 and in England in 1959, he played in eight Tests between 1953 and 1959, and in these his batting average was only 15 and his highest score 41 against England at Lord's, when he helped Contractor to add 83 for the fourth wicket. Moreover, India being rich at that time in leg-spin, he was seldom given a bowl and never took a wicket in a Test. Indeed on the 1959 tour of England his total record was only 833 runs with an average of 23.80, highest score 70 against Derbyshire, and he took only two wickets. However such was his reputation as a fieldsman that he was almost always 12th man in any match in which he was not playing. He always played in specta-cles. At the time of his death he was chair-man of the Indian Selection Committee.

GHULAM, Mohamed, who died in Karachi on July 21, 1966, aged 68, toured England with the Maharajah of Porbandar's All India team in 1932. He proved a big disappoint-ment, taking only three wickets in first-class matches at a cost of 95.33 runs each, but on the matting pitches of his own country he achieved much success with left-arm de-liveries of medium pace. He played for the Mohammadans in the Sind Pentangular and Bombay Quadrangular tournaments.

GIBB, Dr. J. M., the captain of the Kensing-ton C.C., perished in the earthquake in Jamaica, on January 14, 1907. He rep-resented Jamaica against Mr. R. S. Lucas' team in 1895, Mr. A. Priestley's in 1897, and Mr. Bosanquet's in 1902.

GIBB, Paul Anthony, who died suddenly at Guildford on December 7, 1977, at the age of 64, was a cricketer who should be judged by the figures he achieved. It would have needed a shrewd critic to discern, when watching him play a long innings, that he was more than a determined and solid University and county batsman. Never did one catch a glimpse of that spark of genius which normally marks the Test player. The figures tell a very different story. In his first innings for Yorkshire he made 157 not out. For his four University matches he averaged 54, making a century in his last year and in the previous year being stupidly run out for 87. His average for his eight Tests was 44.69. In his first, against South Africa, he scored 93 and 106; in the final Test of that series 120. In the first Test after the War, against India, he made 60 and helped Hardstaff to add 182 badly needed runs for the fifth wicket. In his early days a tendency to overdo the hook was often fatal, but once he had conquered this it was indeed a problem to get him out. He was quite happy to rely on his immensely strong back play and to let the runs come at their own rate: his patience seemed inexhaustible. Two Gibbs on a side could have been difficult and three intolerable: one was often invaluable.

With his wicket-keeping it was different: not even his best friends would have claimed that he was anywhere near the best of his day. Yet after playing purely as a batsman for Cambridge in his first year while S.C. Griffith, a far better performer, kept and keeping himself in his second year when Griffith was injured, in his third year he was given the preference completely and Griffith did not play at all. This aroused considerable criticism, but not as much as when in the next season, Ames being injured, Gibb was selected for the third and fourth Tests over the heads of a number of better keepers including Arthur Wood, who was almost always preferred to him by Yorkshire. In fact the third Test was completely washed out by rain and by the fourth Gibb was injured and so had to wait for the South African tour that winter before actually taking the field for England.

On that tour he was second-string to Ames, but in 1946 he kept in the first two Tests against India and the following winter in the first Test in Australia, before on each occasion making way for Evans.

To summarise his career, he was in the XI at St. Edward's, Oxford, played for Cambridge from 1935 to 1938 and for Yorkshire from 1935 to 1946. After returning that winter from Australia, he was seen no more in first-class cricket until 1951 when he appeared for Essex as a professional, the first cricket Blue ever to turn professional. Though now no longer a candidate for Tests, playing for Essex for six seasons he made a thousand runs in four of them, besides proving a serviceable keeper. He dropped out of the Essex side in 1956 and from 1957 to 1966 was a first-class umpire. At the time of his death he had for some years been a bus-driver in Guildford.

GIBBES, William R.L., who died in November, 1918, had played with the Waverley C.C., of Sydney, and for Wellington (N.Z.). He was left-handed both as batsman and bowler, and once in a match in New Zealand scored 220 for the first wicket with W.A. Baker.

GIBBONS, Harold Harry Ian, who died in a Worcester hospital after a long illness on February 16, 1973, aged 68, was one of the best batsmen of his time who failed to gain a cap for England. Born in Devon, he served on the ground-staff at Lord's till, seeing little hope of getting a place in the Middlesex team, he qualified for Worcestershire via the Birmingham League. Between 1927 and 1946 he scored 21,087 runs, average 34.34, the highest of his 44 three-figure innings being 212 not out for Worcestershire against Northamptonshire at Dudley in 1939.

His most successful season was that of 1934. Then, with eight centuries—four of them in five successive innings—to his name, he hit 2,654 runs at an average of 52.03, figures unsurpassed by any other Worcestershire batsman. Generally known as "Doc"— a nickname he earned when he arrived at Worcester at the start of his career carrying his playing attire in a little black bag—he was a batsman of polished style and even temperament with strokes all round the wicket, and an exceptionally good fieldsman. He shared three Worcestershire records which still hold good. Against Kent in 1933 and Glamorgan in 1934, both at Worcester, he and the Nawab of Pataudi hit 274 for the second wicket; he and B.W. Quaife made 277 for the second wicket against Middlesex at Worcester in 1931 and he and R. Howorth added 197 for the seventh wicket against Surrey at the Oval in 1938. Twice in 1934 Gibbons and that equally gifted batsman, C.F. Walters, joined in massive opening partnerships, taking 279 from the Essex bowling at Chelmsford and 278 without being parted against Leicestershire at Worcester.

After the Second World War, Gibbons became a director of a Fleet Street advertising firm. He eventually served as President of the West Midlands Newspaper Advertisers' Association.

GIBBS, Glendon L., died at Georgetown, Guyana, on February 21, 1979, aged 53. A left-handed opening bat with a sound defence and a slow left-arm bowler, he played for British Guiana throughout the West Indies, and is chiefly remembered for an innings of 216 against Barbados at Georgetown in 1952 when he and L. Wight, who scored 262, put on 390 for the first wicket; still a record for first-class cricket in the West Indies. In 1955 he played in the first Test against the Australians. He was, until his death, Secretary of the Guyana Cricket Board of Control and represented it on the West Indies Board of Control.

GIBSON, Clement Herbert, who died in Buenos Aires after a short illness on December 31, 1976, aged 76, will always be remembered for the part he played in helping Maclaren's XI to beat the Australians at Eastbourne in 1921. After failing to get a wicket in the first innings, he took six for 64 in the second, including the opening pair, Bardsley and Collins.

He had a wonderful record at Eton, where in four years in the XI he had taken 122 wickets at an average of 10.50. He was captain in 1918 and 1919 and in 1919 took six for 18 and three for 12 at Lord's. Later that summer he played a few times for Sussex. He was a member of the very strong Cambridge sides of 1920 and 1921, when he and C.S. Marriott were one of the most formidable pairs of bowlers either University has ever had and provided a perfect contrast. On coming down he went out to the Argentine, where he spent the rest of his life.

In the winter of 1922–23 Gibson was a member of Maclaren's side in Australia and New Zealand and, though his record does not look much, must have bowled well, as it is said to have been largely on Maclaren's recommendation that he was asked to go with the M.C.C. to Australia in 1924. This invitation he had to refuse, perhaps fortunately, as, when he was home for the summer in 1926 and played for Sussex, he met with little success, though he could still produce at times a good ball: at the Oval he clean bowled Hobbs with a beauty in each innings.

This was the end of his County Cricket, but in 1932 he captained a South American side on a brief tour of England. With a good run up and a beautifully easy action, he bowled fast-medium, kept at his best a good length and made the ball swing very late. His best one would pitch on the leg stump and hit the off. He was also an extremely useful bat in the lower half of the order. Had he been able to continue regular first-class cricket after coming down, he would probably have taken a high place. Gibson was one of the Five Cricketers of the Year (schoolboys) in 1918.

GIBSON, George, a native of Jamaica, died at Carlton, Melbourne, on September 5, 1910, aged 83. His first appearance in a match of note was for Victoria v. New South Wales, on the Melbourne ground, in December, 1865, and his highest innings in a first-class game 41—against the same colony in March, 1872—for playing which, he was presented with a bat made from a willow-tree grown in his own garden. In addition to being a capable batsman, he was a good wicket-keeper.

GIBSON, Dr. Ian, who died on May 3, 1963, aged 26, played for Oxford University from 1955 to 1958, his best score against Cambridge being 63 in the second innings in 1957. In that season he took part in six matches for Derbyshire, hitting 66 not out from the Nottinghamshire bowling at Ilkeston. An excellent batsman especially strong in strokes off the back foot, a fine fieldsman and a useful leg-break bowler, he was in the Manchester Grammar School XI from 1951 to 1954, being captain in the last two years when he also appeared in representative school matches at Lord's. In 1953 he headed his school's averages with 760 runs in 19 innings, including three centuries. After going down from Oxford, he played much cricket for Guy's Hospital.

GIDDY, Lennox Llewellyn, died at Pretoria in June, 1942, aged 73. He batted well for Eastern Province teams from 1887 to 1906. For Grahamstown XXII in March, 1889, against the first English team to tour South Africa he scored 45, and played against each of the next four English teams. In Currie Cup cricket his best performance was 62 and 71 for Eastern Province against Griqualand West at Port Elizabeth in April, 1903. An outstanding tennis player, he was the South African singles champion from 1894 to 1898.

GIFFEN, George, born in Adelaide on March 27, 1859, died in a private hospital at his native place, after a long illness, on November 29, 1927, aged 68, thus surviving his old comrade, J. J. Lyons, a few months only. As a batsman Giffen possessed a wonderfully fine defence. He stooped a little but had a great variety of strokes, with great freedom in his use of the bat, and was exceptionally strong in driving. He bowled right-hand, rather below medium-pace, with considerable spin and well-concealed change of flight and pace. He used to send down with much effect a slow ball, very high-tossed, which, seeming to be coming well up to the batsman, pitched short, and resulted in many a "caught and bowled." It was expected that Giffen would have charge of the Australian team which toured England in 1886, but his merits as a leader were not commensurate with his merits as a player. Giffen first visited England in 1882 as a member of the team which beat England at the Oval by seven runs. As the side included Spofforth, Boyle, Garrett, and Palmer—four of the finest bowlers of the time—Giffen was overshadowed, and while they averaged 150 wickets at a cost of less than 13 runs each, he had to be content with taking 32 wickets for 22 runs each. Still, he had a brilliant success against the Gentlemen of England at the Oval, where he took 11 wickets for less than 10 runs each—eight in the first innings for 49 runs—and contributed largely to a memorable triumph. Nor had his batting powers at that period fully developed, but his record of 873 runs with an average of 18 was a vastly bigger thing than it would be regarded on the easy wickets of to-day. He showed a marked advance in 1884, and two years later, headed both batting and bowling averages, scoring 1,454 runs, for an average of 25, and taking 162 wickets for 16 runs each. Giffen declined invitations to join the Australian teams of 1888 and 1890, but was a member of the side captained by Blackhan in 1893, and also of that led by Harry Trott in 1896. In these years, however, though he came out with a fair record for the whole of each tour, he accomplished little in the representative games. Giffen, indeed, in England scarcely reproduced his Australian form, which was of so high a class that he used to be referred to as the "W. G. Grace of Australia." As a member of the five teams mentioned he visited the United States three times, New Zealand twice, and Canada once, besides taking part in two small games in Ceylon.

His 18 three-figure scores in first-class cricket—six in England and a dozen in his own country—were:

113   Australians v. Lancashire, at Manchester, 1884. (Also the hat-trick).
119   Australians v. Cambridge University Past and Present, at Leyton, 1886.
203   South Australia v. G. F. Vernon's England XI, at Adelaide, 1887–88.
166   South Australia v. Victoria, at Adelaide, 1887–88. (And 14 for 125).
135   South Australia v. Victoria, at Melbourne, 1888–89. (And 13 for 159).
237   South Australia v. Victoria, at Melbourne, 1890–91. (And 12 for 192).
271   South Australia v. Victoria, at Adelaide, 1891–92. (And 16 for 166).
120   South Australia v. New South Wales, at Sydney, 1891–92. (And 12 for 150).
181   South Australia v. Victoria, at Adelaide, 1892–93. (And 11 for 235).
180   Australians v. Gloucestershire, at Bristol, 1893. (And 7 for 11).
171   Australians v. Yorkshire, at Bradford, 1893.
205   South Australia v. New South Wales, at Adelaide, 1893–94.
103   South Australia v. Victoria, at Melbourne, 1893–94.
161   Australia v. England, at Sydney, 1894–95.
115   Australians v. South, at Eastbourne, 1896.
130   Australians v. Hampshire, at Southampton, 1896.
104*   South Australia v. New South Wales, at Sydney, 1896–97.
115   South Australia v. Queensland, at Brisbane, 1898–99.

Signifies not out.

On three other occasions he obtained over 100 runs and more than 10 wickets in a match, each time for South Australia:

20 & 82 and 17 for 201 v. Victoria, at Adelaide	..	..	..	..	1885–86
64 & 58* and 11 for 224 v. England, at Adelaide	..	..	..	..	1894–95
81 & 97* and 15 for 185 v. Victoria, at Adelaide	..	..	..	..	1902–03

He trained specially for the last mentioned game, being then within a week or two of completing his 44th year. Most remarkable of all, perhaps, was his all-round performance in scoring 161 out of a total of 586, and 41 in a total of 166 for Australia v. Stoddart's team at Sydney in December, 1894, as in that match he also took eight wickets, and yet was on the losing side. The bowling of Peel and Briggs on a ruined pitch won the match for England by 10 runs. In the winter of 1883, at Sydney, for the fourth Australian team against the Rest of Australia, Giffen took all 10 wickets in an innings for 66 runs. He had his great success as a bowler in England during the season of 1886, when 16 Derbyshire wickets fell to him for 101 runs, and in five consecutive innings he dismissed 40 batsmen at a cost of 222 runs. He did the "hat-trick" three times—for South Australia, against G. F. Vernon's team, at Adelaide, in 1887–88; against Lancashire, at Manchester, in 1884; and against an England XI, at Wembley Park, in 1896. Altogether in first-class matches, Giffen scored 12,501 runs, at an average of 29, and took 1,109 wickets at a cost of 21 runs each. In matches between Australia and England he made 1,238 runs, and took 103 wickets. In 1922–23 the match at Adelaide between South Australia and Victoria was played for his benefit, and the resulting sum, £2,020, was vested in trustees. After being a Civil Servant in the General Post Office at Adelaide for 43 years, he retired on pension in March, 1925, thereafter finding the chief delight of his life, whilst health permitted, in coaching young boys in a purely honorary capacity.

GIFFEN, Walter Frank, a brother of George who appeared in 31 Tests for Australia, and who himself played in three Tests against England, died in Melbourne in June, 1949, aged 87. W. F. Giffen was a member of the Australian team of 1893 which visited England, but accomplished nothing out of the ordinary. He was a sound batsman and concentrated mainly on defence. He hit many hundreds in Adelaide club cricket and played for South Australia. As a fieldsman he excelled in the deep and like the majority of Australians he possessed a capital return to the wicket. In 1886 he met with an accident at the Brompton Gasworks, Adelaide, where he got his left hand between a pair of cogwheels and lost the tops of two of his fingers.

GIFFORD, George Cooper, who died on September 16, 1972, aged 80, played as a batsman for Northamptonshire between 1923 and 1929. In his first match for the county he made 98 against Worcestershire at Northampton, an innings which occupied five hours.

GILBERT, Edward, who was the best remembered aboriginal cricketer to play first-class cricket in Australia, had been long absent from the scene of his sometimes sensational fast bowling feats of the 1930s and in ill health for many years before his death in the Wolston Park Hospital near Brisbane on January 9, 1978, aged 69. Nevertheless, this notably quiet but well spoken product of Queensland's Cherbourg Aboriginal Settlement has remained a legend down through the years. After successfully graduating through the Queensland Colts XI in 1930, Eddie Gilbert quickly reached the headlines in the 1931 Sheffield Shield match against N.S.W. in Brisbane by his first over dismissals of Wendell Bill and Bradman without scoring. Both were caught by wicketkeeper Len Waterman within seven deliveries, but not before one ball rising from a green top had flicked off Sir Donald's cap and another knocked the bat from his hands! Sir Donald has since recalled that the six deliveries he faced on this occasion were the fastest experienced during his career.

Lightly built and only a little over 5ft. 7in. in height, Gilbert possessed exceptionally long arms and could bowl at great pace off a run sometimes no longer than four paces. It was this, allied with a somewhat whippy forearm action, which led to suggestions that his right arm bent on occasions during a pronounced arc action which finished with his hand almost touching the ground and his head at knee level. Strong advocacy for Gilbert's Test selection was nullified by the suspect action, a view several times shared and acted on by senior umpires. Nevertheless, the same officials completely accepted his delivery on most other occasions. Several films were taken without conclusive decision and controversy continued throughout Gilbert's career which was undoubtedly affected by the publicity. He faded out of the game in 1936 after showing fine form while taking six wickets in his final match—against Victoria at the Brisbane Cricket Ground in 1936. In 19 Shield matches, he took 73 wickets at an average of 29.75, while a further 14 wickets were gained in Queensland matches against touring M.C.C., West Indies and South African sides.

GILBERT, George, who died at Summer Hill, N.S.W., on June 16, 1906, at the age of 78, was a cousin of the Graces, and in his time played no mean part in the cricket field. He was born in Gloucestershire, and appeared several times for the Gentlemen of Surrey, and, in 1851, for the Gentlemen against the Players at Lord's. He went to

Australia in 1852, and four years later captained New South Wales in the very first match that State ever played against Victoria. He also played for the New South Wales XXII against the first English team which visited Australia—in 1861–62—and to the last took a great interest in the game. At the Oval, in 1851, he played a single-wicket match against Mr. F. P. Miller, the Surrey captain, in which a curious occurrence took place. The latter cut a ball which went round the boundary stump. Gilbert threw the ball at the wicket but, as it did not pass within bounds, was told to fetch it back and try again. During the argument Mr. Miller ran 13 for the hit.

GILBERT, Humphrey Adam, who died on July 19, 1960, aged 74, was in the XI at Charterhouse in 1904 and 1905 and, as a medium-pace bowler able also to spin the ball, he got his Blue at Oxford in 1907 and the two following years, heading the University bowling figures in the last two seasons. In the first innings against Cambridge in 1907 he took six wickets for 36 runs and in the 1909 University match his first innings analysis was six wickets for 52. Against M. A. Noble's Australian team of 1909 he distinguished himself by dismissing eight batsmen for 71 runs, a feat which resulted in him being asked to travel to Birmingham in case he should be required by England for the first Test match. From 1921 to 1930, "Barmy" Gilbert played for Worcestershire; between 1908 and 1910 he made four appearances for the Gentlemen, his six wickets for 112 runs in the second innings of the Players at the Oval in 1908 doing much towards victory by six wickets. He also turned out for M.C.C., Monmouthshire, Radnorshire and the Free Foresters. In all first-class cricket, he took 476 wickets, average 23.67. His qualities as a batsman may be gauged from the fact that in his five innings against Cambridge he scored one run. He was a barrister by profession.

GILBERT, John, the veteran Sussex cricketer, died at the end of November, 1896, aged about 66. For many years Gilbert was employed by Lord Sheffield, and on May 27, 1884, he played a remarkable innings of 250 not out for the Sheffield Park XI against Newick. He was only batting one afternoon, and it is reckoned that he ran out nearly 400 runs, the boundaries on the ground being very few. He was much liked and respected at Sheffield Park, and indeed by everyone with whom he came in contact.

GILBERT, Walter Raleigh, was born in London on September 16, 1853, and died at Calgary, in Alberta, Canada, on July 26, 1924, aged 70. A steady batsman, a very useful slow round-armed bowler, and a very good field at long-leg and cover-point, he played for Middlesex by birth in 1873 and 1874, for Gloucestershire by residence 1876 to 1886, and four times for the Gentlemen v. Players between 1874 and 1877. He also appeared in a few stray matches for Worcestershire and Northamptonshire. In 1873–74 he toured Australia under the captaincy of his cousin, W. G. Grace, and he took part in a very large number of minor matches, especially for the United South of England XI, which he "managed" after the death of G. F. Grace in 1880. His fielding at deep-leg to W. G. Grace's bowling was always excellent, for he covered much ground and was a sure catch. Although overshadowed by his famous cricketing cousins, he played a prominent part in the victories gained during Gloucestershire's greatest years. For Thornbury v. Sneyd Park in 1874 he made 254 not out, but in a match of note his highest innings was 205 not out for An England XI at Cambridge against the University in 1876, when he batted for about seven hours without a mistake and carried his bat through; he hit a five, nine fours, and as many as 66 singles, and batted on each of the three days. At Canterbury later in the same season he scored 143 for Kent and Gloucestershire against England, and at Gloucester in 1885 made 102 v. Yorkshire. In the match with Nottinghamshire at Clifton in the last mentioned year he took 70 minutes to obtain four runs in his first innings, and two hours and three-quarters to score 21 in his second. Against Sussex at Brighton in 1878 he took four wickets for 12 runs and in the return, at Cheltenham, four for eight, while in the match with Lancashire at Clifton in 1878 he and W. G. Grace bowled unchanged through both innings. At the beginning of 1886 he became a professional, and the season was not far advanced before his career in first-class cricket ended abruptly. He then left England for Canada. He kept up the game in the Dominion and made hundreds in both Halifax and Montreal.

GILL, G. C., a fast bowler and hard-hitting batsman, died at Leicester on August 21, 1937, aged 61. He played for Somerset from 1897 to 1902, for Leicestershire from 1903 to 1906, under birth qualification, and also for London County. In his last season with the western county he scored 804 runs, average

19.60, and took 79 wickets at 18.60 each in all matches. Next year, when with Leicestershire, he averaged 21.36 for 641 runs and dismissed 52 batsmen at 23.78 apiece in all matches; he made 100 against Sussex at Leicester and a fortnight later took nine Surrey wickets, both matches having very close finishes.

GILLER, James Frederick, who died on June 13, 1947, at his home at Albert Park, Melbourne, aged 77, was one of Victoria's best all-round cricketers of his time and narrowly missed a place in the Australian team. For South Melbourne Club from 1893 to 1913 he scored 6,654 runs at an average of 35, and took .531 wickets at 15 runs each. A strong-driving batsman with good defence and a right-hand medium-pace bowler, he made for Victoria in Sheffield Shield matches 878 runs in 29 innings, average 33.76, and captured 37 wickets at a cost of 23 runs each. His best scores were 145 against New South Wales at Sydney in 1905 and 116 against South Australia at Adelaide in 1898.

GILLESPIE, Capt. Francis Sydney (Royal Sussex Regiment) died of wounds on June 18, 1916, aged 26. He was not in the XI while at Dulwich, but afterwards played with success for London County, Surrey and the Wanderers. He was a left-handed batsman and in 1912 and 1913 headed the Surrey Second XI averages: in the former year he made 105 v. Wiltshire at the Oval, and in the latter 57 and 55 not out v. Glamorgan on the same ground. Tried for Surrey in 1913, he made 249 runs with an average of 22.62, his highest score being 72 against Gloucestershire at the Oval.

GILLESPIE, Hector Donald, who died in Auckland on October 12, 1954, aged 53, was a member of the New Zealand team which toured Australia in 1925–26. He represented Auckland in Plunket Shield matches between 1920 and 1932 and for some years captained Eden C.C., for whom in 1924–25 he and J. E. Mills shared in an opening stand of 441 against University at Eden Park. Educated at Auckland Grammar School, Gillespie was also a keen Rugby footballer. A law clerk for 38 years, he became a Justice of the Peace.

GILLIGAN, Albert Herbert Harold, A.F.C., who died on May 5, 1978, aged 81, was the youngest and the last survivor of three distinguished cricketing brothers. Frank, the

eldest, captained Oxford and played for Essex, Arthur was a notable captain of Sussex and England, Harold was in the Dulwich XI for three years and captain in the last, 1915. In 1914 he made the highest score then recorded for the school, 190 v. Bedford Grammar School. Coming into the Sussex side in 1919, he played for them continuously until 1931 and, after often captaining them in his brother's absence, was the official captain in 1930. In 1924–25 he was a member of S. B. Joel's unofficial side to South Africa, captained by the Hon L. H. Tennyson, and in 1929–30, when his brother Arthur, after accepting an invitation to captain the M.C.C. team to Australia and New Zealand, had to withdraw owing to ill-health, he was appointed to take his place.

One can pay him no higher compliment than to say that as a leader he was no less popular than his brother both with his own side and with the opposition: moreover he showed himself a shrewd captain on the field. This, though stronger than any previous English side in New Zealand, was still far short of an England side: it contained only three players who took part in the Tests in England in 1930. The captain himself had a good tour, batting particularly well in the preliminary matches in Australia. But it must be admitted that, taking his career as a whole, he was a disappointing batsman. A beautiful stylist, he would constantly through impetuosity get out to a terrible stroke just when he seemed set for a big score and, though as time went on, with much help from Albert Relf, to whose coaching he admitted a great debt, he became sounder and more consistent, he never wholly cured himself of this fault.

His figures tell their own tale. His average for his career with Sussex was only 17, he made only one century, 143 v. Derbyshire at Hove in 1929, and only in three seasons, 1923, 1927 and 1929, did he score 1,000 runs. His figures for 1923 must constitute some kind of record: in 70 innings he scored 1,186 runs with an average of 17.70 and a highest score of 68. At this period he was regularly opening the batting with Bowley. Apart from his batting he was one of the great cover-points of his day and in his early years did useful work as a slow leg-spinner. After the Second World War he became active behind the scenes in Surrey cricket. He served on the Committee, was for a time Hon. Treasurer and later was a Vice-President. His daughter, Virginia, married Peter May.

ARTHUR EDWARD ROBERT GILLIGAN
Born in London, December 23, 1894
Died at Pulborough, September 5, 1976
By R. L. Arrowsmith

Arthur Edward Robert Gilligan who died at his home at Pulborough, aged 81, was one of the most popular and inspiring captains that England or Sussex ever had. Those whose memories go back that far will always feel that his tour of Australia in 1924–25, although England won only one Test, was the moment when we first had cause to hope that the dark days were ending, that soon we would be once more competing with Australia on level terms. In two or three seasons by his insistence on fielding and on attacking cricket and by his own superb example he raised Sussex from being nothing in particular to one of the biggest draws in England.

For all too short a span, before injury reduced his effectiveness, he was himself an exciting cricketer—the best really fast bowler we had produced for many years—though even then we did not quite put him among the great, a batsman of whom one might say that, however low he went in, no match was irredeemably lost until he was out for the second time, and one of the finest mid-offs anyone could remember.

But even at the height of his career his services to cricket did not stop there. Unless he was touring abroad in the winter, he was touring Sussex, speaking at dinners, lecturing and doing all he could to spread the enthusiasm for the game that he himself felt; and this continued for years after his retirement. His first-class career ended in 1932—indeed he played little cricket of any kind afterwards—but he went on working tirelessly for Sussex cricket and, when opportunity offered, for England.

He had been Chairman of Sussex and in 1967 was President of the M.C.C. He remained fit and active to the end. Throughout the summer of 1976 he might be found watching at Hove or Lord's or Arundel, as clear in mind and alert as ever, endlessly appreciative of good cricket and showing the utmost kindness and encouragement to the young, but equally uncompromising in his condemnation of anything which savoured of sharp practice or ill temper. In between he was still playing golf regularly at Pulborough, where he had gone round in under his age, and in the winter he was off to follow an England side in Australia or the West Indies, or to ski on the continent.

At Dulwich, where he also distinguished himself as a runner and a hurdler, he was four years in the XI and captain in the last two, 1913 and 1914, in both of which seasons he played for Surrey Second XI in the holidays. The War stopped his cricket till 1919, when he got his Blue at Cambridge and in the second innings against Oxford took six for 52. This was widely acclaimed as the best fast bowling seen in the match for many years. For Cambridge against Sussex that year he created some sensation by making 101 going in last; he and J. N. Naumann, who like himself later played for Sussex, put on 177 in 65 minutes. However it must be admitted that Sussex had, as not infrequently at this time, a very weak bowling side.

Later Gilligan played three matches for Surrey, but in 1920, after again playing for Cambridge, he transferred to Sussex, for whom he continued to play till 1932, captaining them from 1922 to 1929. At first he was only a useful county player, but in 1922 he jumped right to the front, taking 135 wickets with an average of 18.75 and playing for the first time for the Gentlemen. That winter he went with the M.C.C. to South Africa and next summer for the only time did the double.

In 1924 he was picked to captain England and in the first Test at Edgbaston he and Tate bowled out South Africa on a good wicket for 30, Gilligan's share being six for seven; in the follow-on he took five for 83. There can be no doubt that just at that period these two were the most formidable combination in the world. A week or two earlier in consecutive matches for Sussex they had bowled out two of the strongest batting sides in England, Surrey for 53 at the Oval and Middlesex for 41 at Lord's, Gilligan on this occasion taking eight for 25. At the end of June that year he had taken 74 wickets at 15 runs each.

At the beginning of July, batting for Gentlemen v. Players at the Oval, he was struck over the heart by a rising ball from Pearson of Worcestershire, a medium pace off-spinner and a man universally liked and respected. It was clear that he was badly hurt, but no one guessed how badly. He undoubtedly increased the damage by insisting on going on playing and even more by scoring 112 in the second innings in an hour and a half and adding 134 for the last wicket with Michael Falcon. As he himself wrote some years later, "That was probably the worst thing I ever did." He was never able to bowl really fast again and indeed was never more than a change bowler. When he captained England in Australia that winter, his 10 wickets in the Test cost him 51.90 runs each and his highest score was 31. Except for his brilliant fielding and inspiring captaincy he was a passenger. In 1926 he was a Selector and the following winter made his last tour abroad, captaining the M.C.C. in India, not then a Test-playing country.

At his best, Gilligan was a genuinely fast bowler, who bowled at the stumps or for catches in the slips. His action may have been slightly low, but he was accurate and regarded it as a cardinal sin to bowl short. He was an attacking batsman, who believed especially that fast bowlers needed hitting. His 12 centuries in first-class cricket must have been scored at an average rate of over a run a minute. Nearly all of them he made going in late, when runs were desperately wanted. Moreover, they were usually against strong sides—two against Lancashire, two against Kent, one each against Yorkshire, Nottinghamshire, Surrey and the Players. At mid-off he has had few rivals.

As a captain, he may not have been in the top rank of tacticians, but no one excelled him in getting the best out of his side and inspiring them in the field. From every point of view he was a cricketer with whom England could well do now.

After he retired from active cricket he became a popular radio commentator on Test matches and will be especially remembered for his partnership with another much loved cricketer, Victor Richardson. Gilligan was, as may be imagined, a master of the diplomatic comment if any tiresome incident occurred.

He was prominent too in the golfing world, being President of the English Golf Union in 1959 and also, up to the time of his death, of the County Cricketers' Golfing Society. His two brothers were only less distinguished as cricketers than himself. F.W., the eldest, who played against him in his two Varsity matches, captained Oxford and kept wicket for Essex for many years in the holidays, while the youngest, A.H.H., succeeded him as captain of Sussex and took an M.C.C. side to Australia and New Zealand in 1929; his daughter married Peter May.

The three brothers were in the Dulwich XI together in 1913. Well might a newspaper of that day say, "The Gilligans of Dulwich seem destined to become as famous in sports as the Fords of Repton, the Lytteltons of Eton and the Fosters of Malvern." Indeed their only rivals among their contemporaries were the Ashtons of Winchester and the Bryans.

Career Figures
BATTING AND BOWLING

Season	Inns.	Not Outs	Runs	Highest Inns.	100s	Aver.	Runs	Wkts.	Aver.	Catches
In England										
1919	19	6	231	101	1	17.76	1,105	35	31.57	7
1920	39	3	624	66	0	17.33	1,908	81	23.55	13
1921	49	8	640	77*	0	27.58	2,758	90	30.64	11
1922	58	5	916	69	0	17.28	2,532	135	18.75	17
1923	56	0	1,183	114*	2	21.12	2,853	163	17.50	16
1924	44	4	864	112	1	21.60	1,995	103	19.36	11
1925	37	1	542	66	0	15.05	168	8	21.00	8
1926	39	5	1,037	126	4	30.50	1,556	75	20.74	9
1927	36	6	828	103	1	27.60	715	29	24.65	19
1928	40	5	942	144	2	26.91	1,997	76	26.27	10
1929	18	0	130	26	0	7.22	275	4	68.75	7
1930	2	0	51	46	0	25.50	68	3	29.33	1
1931	11	2	190	75*	0	21.11	220	2	110.00	5
1932	4	0	9	5	0	2.25	87	0	—	1
In Australia										
1924–25	24	4	357	138	1	17.85	1,075	28	38.39	8
In South Africa										
1922–23	12	4	143	39*	0	17.87	573	26	22.03	5
In India and Ceylon										
1926–27	22	2	453	73	0	22.65	234	10	23.40	12
Totals	510	55	9,140	144	12	20.08	20,139	868	23.20	160

Signifies not out.

GILLIGAN, Frank William, who died at Wanganui, New Zealand, where he had been headmaster of the Grammar School for 19 years, on May 4, 1960, aged 66, was brother of two England captains, Arthur and Harold. Educated at Dulwich, Frank Gilligan was an excellent wicket-keeper and a better batsman than his style suggested. He got his Blue at Oxford in 1919 and, with innings of 70 and 14, contributed substantially to victory by 45 runs over a Cambridge team including his brother Arthur. He captained the University the following season. From 1919 to 1929 he made a number of appearances for Essex, against whom in 1920 he obtained his one first-class century, 110 at Oxford. In all cricket he scored 3,024 runs, average 23.62, and brought off 150 catches. For services to education, he was awarded the O.B.E. in 1955.

GILLINGHAM, Canon Frank Hay, who died on April 1, 1953, aged 77, was a great personality in the Church and on the cricket field. Born in Tokyo on September 6, 1875, he came to England when eight, gained a place in the Dulwich XIs of 1891 and 1892, and appeared with much distinction for Durham University. When ordained in 1899, he became a curate at Leyton and so qualified for Essex. During this period he showed his love of the game when making his rounds of the parish by joining in street cricket with local boys.

After a few appearances for the second XI, he first played for the Essex Championship side in 1903, and he appeared whenever his clerical duties permitted till 1928. Altogether he scored 9,942 runs, average 30.49, and brought off 102 catches. Tall and powerfully built, he was a strong believer in hitting the ball hard in front of the wicket, and, though the first to admit that he was not at ease against spin, he dealt firmly with bowlers of pace. His best season for the county was that of 1908, when he scored 1,033 runs, average 39.73, and hit four centuries; his highest innings was 201 against Middlesex at Lord's in 1904. He appeared three times for Gentlemen against Players, and in 1919 bore a considerable part in the defeat—their first—by an innings and 133 runs of the Australian Imperial Forces XI at the hands of the Gentlemen of England at Lord's. Gillingham scored 83 and made four catches. He was also a member of the Essex XI who, in 1905 at Leyton, beat J. Darling's Australians by 19 runs, and he went on tour to Jamaica with the Hon. L. H. Tennyson's team in 1927.

A fine preacher who filled his churches to overflowing, he was appointed Chaplain to the King in 1939. He was also an after-dinner speaker with a wonderful sense of humour; his supremely funny anecdotes, told without the vestige of a smile, frequently convulsed listeners. As Sir Pelham Warner wrote of him in *The Cricketer:* "Gillingham was a man with a charming individuality who exerted a powerful and beneficial influence over people of various types and characteristics. He was a very human being, kind, gentle and understanding, who was the last to condemn. No one ever came to him in trouble without going away comforted. His friends and admirers were numerous indeed."

GILLINGHAM, The Rev. George William, who died on June 11, 1953, after a ministry of 52 years, played cricket for Gentlemen of Worcestershire before the First World War. Though never attaining to first-class standards, he was a great cricket enthusiast who did much good work for Worcestershire. When becoming Rector of St. Martin's, Worcester, he revived and managed the Worcestershire Club and Ground matches, and in 1923 he organised a bazaar which realised £2,300 for the County Club. From 1929 he acted for some seasons as honorary secretary to Worcestershire in order that the secretary, C. F. Walters, could play for the county. During this period when, during the winter the River Severn flooded the county ground at Worcester, Gillingham swam across the ground to gain access to the Pavilion and returned with the account books. He was author of *The Cardinal's Treasure,* a romance of the Elizabethan age, part of the proceeds from which he devoted to the Worcestershire County C.C. and the R.S.P.C.A. When Vicar of St. Mark's, Coventry, he was for four years tenant of a condemned public house, "The Barley Mow", which he transformed into a "Hooligans' Club" where boxing and Bible classes went hand-in-hand.

GILMAN, Major James, died on September 14, 1976.

R. L. Arrowsmith writes: James Gilman was the oldest living cricket Blue and probably the oldest first-class cricketer of any standing and the last man to open the batting in an important match with W. G. Grace. This he did for London County against the West Indies at the Crystal Palace in 1900: the match was not first-class and was the first-ever played by the West Indies in England. Gilman's share of a first-wicket stand of 136 was 63. He had been in the XI at St. Paul's, but it was undoubtedly the experience of playing constantly in the next few years for London County with W.G. that made him into a good enough player to get his Blue at Cambridge in 1902, his fourth year. His record for the University was not outstanding, but he fully justified his selection at Lord's. Set 272 to get in the fourth innings, Cambridge were 197 for five when Gillman came in to join that great batsman, S. H. Day, and they hit off the runs between them, Gilman's share being 37. He had played a few times for Middlesex in 1900 and 1901 but his first-class career ended when after 1904 London County confined themselves to club cricket. Later he played for Northumberland. He had been first-string for Cambridge in the half and had also represented them in the mile. In the last years of his life he was a constant spectator at Hove. His death leaves C. A. L. Payne, the Oxford Blue of 1906 and 1907, who has lived for many years in Vancouver, as the oldest surviving Blue.

GIMBLETT, Harold, who died at his home at Verwood, Dorset, on March 30, 1978, aged 63, was the most exciting English batsman of his day. Years ago, C. B. Fry wrote of MacLaren: "Like all the great batsmen, he always attacked the bowling!" If that view was once shared by the selectors, they had abandoned it by Gimblett's time. They preferred soundness and consistency. Watching our batting in Australia in 1946–47, Macartney expressed amazement that both Gimblett and Barnett had been left at home. Gimblett played in three Tests only, two against India in 1936, the first of which at Lord's he finished with a dazzling 67 not out, culminating in five consecutive boundaries, and one against the West Indies in 1939. Those of us who saw the inexpressibly feeble English batting against Ramadhin and Valentine at Lord's in 1950 shown up for what it was by the bold tail-end batting of Wardle, longed for an hour of Gimblett, and indeed he was picked for the next Test, but was unfortunately ill and unable to play.

The start of his career was so sensational that any novelist attributing it to his hero would have discredited the book. Given a month's trial on the Somerset staff in 1935 after a number of brilliant performances in local matches, he was told before the period had expired that there was no future for him in County Cricket and was sent home. Next day there was a last minute vacancy against Essex at Frome and he was recalled to fill it,

mainly as a young man who could chase the ball in the field and perhaps bowl a few overs of mild medium pace. In fact, coming in to face Nichols, the England fast bowler, then at his best, with six wickets down for 107, he reached his 50 in 28 minutes and his 100 in 63, finally making 123 out of 175 in 80 minutes with three sixes and 17 fours. The innings won him the Lawrence Trophy for the fastest 100 of the season. In the next match, against Middlesex at Lord's, though lame and batting with a runner, he made 53 against Jim Smith, Robins, Peebles and Sims, three of them England bowlers. It was hardly to be expected that he could keep this up and his record at the end of the season was modest, but his second summer dispelled any notion that his early successes had been a fluke, as he scored 1,608 runs with an average of 32.81. People sometimes talk as if after this he was a disappointment. In fact his one set-back apart from being overlooked by the selectors, was when in 1938, probably listening to the advice of grave critics, he attempted more cautious methods and his average dropped to 27. But can one call disappointing a man who between 1936 and his retirement in 1953 never failed to get his 1,000 runs, who in his career scored over 23,000 more than any other Somerset player, and 50 centuries, the highest 310 against Sussex at Eastbourne in 1948, and whose average for his career was over 36? Moreover after his first season he habitually went in first and yet he hit 265 sixes, surely a record.

Naturally, as time went on, his judgment improved with experience, he grew sounder and in particular became the master of the hook instead of its slave, though he never abandoned it, as did Hammond and Peter May. To the end, he might have said, as Frank Woolley used to, "When I am batting, I am the attack." Apart from his hook he was a fine cutter and driver, his off-drives often being played late and going past cover's left-hand, and like nearly all great attacking bats he freely employed the pull-drive, with which he was particularly severe on Mahomed Nissar at Lord's in 1936. Early in his career, on the fallacious grounds that a great games-player must be a great slip, he was put in the slips where he was only a qualified success. Elsewhere, a fine thrower and a good catch, he was far more successful and many will remember the catch at cover with which he dismissed K. H. Weekes in the Lord's Test in 1939.

For 20 years after his retirement he was coach at Millfield.

Career Figures
BATTING

Season	Matches	Inns.	Not Outs	Runs	Highest Inns.	100s	50s	Average	Catches
In England									
1935	17	30	2	482	123	1	2	17.21	4
1936	29	54	5	1,608	160*	5	4	32.81	27
1937	27	52	1	1,558	141	3	10	30.54	10
1938	29	51	3	1,304	112	2	7	27.16	21
1939	30	50	3	1,922	129	5	10	40.89	18
1945	1	2	0	41	30	0	0	20.50	0
1946	25	41	2	1,947	231	7	8	49.92	24
1947	26	47	2	1,539	118	2	9	34.20	19
1948	24	45	1	1,857	310	4	10	42.20	13
1949	27	52	4	2,093	156	5	12	43.60	24
1950	27	49	1	1,819	184	2	12	37.89	6
1951	27	50	2	1,475	174*	4	5	30.72	21
1952	29	55	1	2,134	169	5	11	39.51	24 &1 st.
1953	27	53	4	1,920	167*	4	11	39.18	27
1954	2	4	0	39	29	0	0	9.75	1
In India with Commonwealth Team									
1950–51	21	38	6	1,269	111	1	8	39.65	5
Totals	368	673	37	23,007	310	50	119	36.17	244 & 1 st.

Signifies not out.

TEST CRICKET

	Tests	Inns.	Not Outs	Runs	Highest Inns.	Average	Catches
1936 v. India	2	3	1	87	67*	43.50	0
1939 v. West Indies	1	2	0	42	22	21.00	1
Totals	3	5	1	129	67*	32.25	1

Signifies not out.

CENTURIES (50)

In England (49)

All of Harold Gimblett's 49 centuries in England were scored for Somerset.

123	v. Essex at Frome, 1935.
160*	v. Lancashire at Old Trafford, 1936.
143	v. Northamptonshire at Bath, 1936.
106	v. Northamptonshire at Kettering, 1936.
103	v. India at Taunton, 1936.
102	v. Sussex at Weston-super-Mare, 1936.
141	v. Hampshire at Wells, 1937.
129*	v. Glamorgan at Newport, 1937.
100	v. Gloucestershire at Bristol, 1937.
112	v. Kent at Folkestone, 1938.
105	v. Northamptonshire at Kettering, 1938.
129	v. Worcestershire at Taunton, 1939.
108	v. Lancashire at Old Trafford, 1939.
108	v. Leicestershire at Leicester, 1939.
108	v. Gloucestershire at Taunton, 1939.
103*	v. Sussex at Taunton, 1939.
231	v. Middlesex at Taunton, 1946.
135	v. Surrey at Weston-super-Mare, 1946.

133	v. Gloucestershire at Bristol, 1946.
118	v. Leicestershire at Wells, 1946.
114	v. Cambridge University at Bath, 1946.
102	v. India at Taunton, 1946.
101	v. Surrey at the Oval, 1946.
118	v. Nottinghamshire at Trent Bridge, 1947.
113*	v. Northamptonshire at Northampton, 1947.
310	v. Sussex at Eastbourne, 1948.
119	v. Leicestershire at Frome, 1948.
107	v. Northamptonshire at Kettering, 1948.
105	v. Nottinghamshire at Bath, 1948.
156	v. Essex at Clacton, 1949.
115 } 127* }	v. Hampshire at Taunton, 1949.
110	v. Nottinghamshire at Trent Bridge, 1949.
101	v. Worcestershire at Kidderminster, 1949.

184	v. Kent at Gravesend, 1950.		132	v. Kent at Gravesend, 1952.
106	v. Glamorgan at Cardiff, 1950. (Friendly.)		104	v. Northamptonshire at Glastonbury, 1952.
174*	v. Worcestershire at Taunton, 1951.		167*	v. Northamptonshire at Taunton, 1953.
108	v. Worcestershire at Worcester, 1951.			
110	v. Surrey at the Oval, 1951.		151	v. Northamptonshire at Northampton, 1953.
103	v. Sussex at Weston-super-Mare, 1951.		146	v. Kent at Bath, 1953.
169	v. Worcestershire at Worcester, 1952.		109	v Surrey at Taunton, 1953.
146⎱ 116⎰	v. Derbyshire at Taunton, 1952.			

In India (1)
111 for Commonwealth Team v. Madhya Pradesh Governor's XI at Nagpur, 1950–51.

*Signifies not out.

GIMSON, Christopher, C. I. E., who died at Leicester on November 8, 1975, aged 88, had an outstanding record as a batsman at Oundle and in 1908 played for Cambridge University against Yorkshire without getting his Blue. Entering the I.C.S., he played a number of times for Leicestershire when home on leave in 1921 and against Kent at Gravesend, when he was acting-captain, scoring 40 out of 41 in 20 minutes. He was an attacking batsman and a fine outfield.

GLADWIN, Joseph, who died in September, 1962, aged 72, played as a fast bowler in two matches for Derbyshire in 1914. He was the father of Clifford Gladwin, the Derbyshire and England bowlers.

GLOVER, Alfred Charles Stirrup, died at Kenilworth on May 22, 1949, aged 77. Repton XI 1890–91. Played for Staffordshire and Warwickshire, hitting seven centuries. In all scored 5,142 runs with an average of 25.83. Enjoyed fair success also as a bowler taking 49 wickets at a cost of 32.20 runs apiece.

GLOVER, George Keyworth, a member of the first South African team that visited England in 1894, died at Kimberley on November 15, 1938, aged 68. A slow right hand bowler, he took 56 wickets at a cost of 17 runs apiece and scored 377 runs by steady batting. He played for South Africa at Cape Town in March, 1896, against Lord Hawke's team but did nothing of note. In 1894 in a Currie Cup match for Griqualand West against Eastern Province, he took 15 wickets for 68 runs and his highest scores in this Competition were 78 and 76. Born at Wakefield, Yorkshire, on May 13, 1870, he was taken to South Africa when a child.

GOAD, Francis Edward, who died at Godstone, Surrey, on May 19, 1951, aged 82, played for Eton in 1888 when, thanks to the all-round work of F. S. Jackson and R. B. Hoare, nephew of Sir Samuel Hoare, Harrow won by 156 runs. In the Eton second innings of 52, Goad scored 22. Jackson scored 21 and 59 and took five wickets for 28. Before the match commenced, his father promised him a sovereign for every wicket he took and a shilling for every run he made. Congratulated afterwards upon his efforts, Jackson is said to have replied: "I don't care so much for myself, but it'll give the guv'nor such a lift!" Goad was for many years principal fur auctioneer for the Hudson Bay Company.

GOATLY, Edward Garnet, who died at his home at Brighton on February 12, 1958, aged 75, played for Surrey from 1901 to 1914. A very sound if unattractive batsman, he was too slow in the field to command a regular place in the county side. Altogether he obtained 4,400 runs, average 25.08, his best season being that of 1913, when he scored 884 runs, average 23.26. His highest innings was 147 not out against Derbyshire at the Oval in 1905, when he batted brilliantly for 2 hours 50 minutes. Between the First and Second World Wars, he was dressing-room attendant at the Oval.

GODAMBE, Shankarrao Ramachandra, who died on December 6, 1969, aged 70, was a member of the India team who toured England in 1932 under the captaincy of the Maharajah of Porbandar, scoring in all matches 200 runs, average 10.52, and taking with swing bowling 28 wickets for 25.46 runs apiece. He represented Bombay in the Ranji Trophy competition and the Hindus in the Quadrangular Tournament, in the 1925 final of which he hit 61 and 51 not out. For the Hindus against A. E. R. Gilligan's 1925–26

M.C.C. team at Bombay, he (58) partnered C. K. Nayudu while the last-named hit 153, including 11 sixes and 13 fours, in 100 minutes.

GODDARD, Thomas William John, who died at his home in Gloucester on May 22, 1966, aged 65, was one of the greatest off-break bowlers the game has known. A big man, standing 6ft. 3in., with massive hands, he spun the ball to a remarkable degree and on a helpful pitch was almost unplayable. He bowled mostly from round the wicket and had such a command of length and flight that even on easy surfaces he kept batsmen apprehensive. His height enabled him to make the ball lift more than most spinners and the Gloucestershire combination of Goddard and the slow left-hander, Charlie Parker, was probably the most feared in Championship cricket.

The early days of Goddard's career gave no hint of the success he was later to achieve. Born on October 1, 1900, he first played for Gloucestershire in 1922 as a fast bowler. Despite his strong physique he made little progress and in six years took only 153 wickets at a cost of 34 runs each.

At the end of the 1927 season he left the county and joined the M.C.C. ground staff at Lord's. There he decided to experiment with off-breaks and his long, strong fingers were ideally suited to this type of bowling. Beverley Lyon, the Gloucestershire captain, saw him in the nets at Lord's and, immediately struck by Goddard's new-found ability, persuaded Gloucestershire to re-engage him. The effect was immediate and dramatic. In 1929 Goddard took 184 wickets at 16 runs apiece and he never looked back.

When he finally retired in 1952, at the age of 51, Goddard had taken 2,979 wickets, average 19.84 and in a period when off-break bowlers were not fashionable in Test cricket, he played eight times for England. He finished with six hat-tricks, the same number as his colleague, Parker, and only one less than the all-time record of seven, by D. V. P. Wright of Kent.

One of the hat-tricks came in a Test match, against South Africa at Johannesburg on Boxing Day, 1938. His victims were A. D. Nourse (caught and bowled), N. Gordon (stumped) and W. W. Wade (bowled). This is still the only hat-trick achieved in Test cricket in Johannesburg. That match was drawn, but it also included two other remarkable performances by Englishmen, a century in each innings from E. Paynter, and 93 and 106 on his Test debut by P. A. Gibb.

Goddard appeared three times for England on that tour. His other Test appearances were once against Australia in 1930, twice against New Zealand in 1937 and twice against West Indies in 1939, all in England. His success was limited to 22 wickets, costing 26.72 runs each, but he enjoyed one fine performance, bowling England to victory by 130 runs against New Zealand at Old Trafford in 1937 with six for 29 in the last innings. He was among the 13 England selected for Old Trafford against Australia in 1938 when rain prevented a ball being bowled.

On 16 occasions Goddard took 100 or more wickets in a season, four times reaching 200. His most successful year was 1937 when he claimed 248 victims. Two years later he achieved the wonderful feat of taking 17 wickets in a day, against Kent at Bristol, nine for 38 and eight for 68. Only two other bowlers have equalled this, H. Verity of Yorkshire and C. Blythe of Kent.

In his big year, 1937, Goddard took all 10 Worcestershire wickets in an innings for 113 at Cheltenham. He also obtained six for 68 in the first innings of that match. On seven occasions he finished with nine wickets in one innings.

One of the matches which gave Goddard most pleasure came at Bristol where Gloucestershire tied with the formidable Australian side of 1930. He played an important part in that thrilling match by taking three wickets in five balls at one stage and ended it by taking the final wicket, that of P. M. Hornibrook.

During the Second World War, Goddard obtained a commission in the R.A.F. He was back at his best when first-class cricket resumed, but because of ill-health he announced his retirement in 1951. To help the county out of difficulties he returned in 1952 and despite his age he took 45 wickets in 13 Championship matches.

When he eventually gave up Goddard established a successful furniture shop in Gloucester in which he was active until about a year before his death.

His final tally of wickets places him fifth in the order of bowlers the game has known. Only W. Rhodes, A. P. Freeman, C. W. L. Parker and J. T. Hearne have taken more. Umpires over the years got to know Goddard's frequent and loud appeals. His first benefit, in 1936, brought him £2,097 and from his second, in 1948, he received £3,355.

GODSELL, R. T., who died in March, 1954, aged 74, played in the 1903 University match for Cambridge. Dismissed without scoring in the first innings, he was first in and last out for 59 in the second. In the Clifton XI in 1898, he assisted Gloucestershire on occasion from 1903 to 1910. His best season for the county was that of 1905, when he scored 356 runs, average 22.25. That year, against Nottinghamshire at Bristol, he carried his bat through an innings of 269 with 98 not out.

GOLDIE, Major Kenneth Oswald, died at Madras of pneumonia, on January 14, 1938, in his 56th year. When 13 years of age, for his school at Rottingdean he showed exceptional promise in an innings of 239 not out, and did so well at Wellington that in 1899 he averaged 59, an innings of 140 not out against Free Foresters, who included B. J. T. Bosanquet and two other Oxford Blues, being a brilliant display. That season he scored two separate hundreds in a match at Hove for Gentlemen of Sussex against Old Cliftonians and this prepared the way for a place in the county XI when free from Army duty. He distinguished himself with several fine innings in Championship matches and in 1901 scored 950 runs, average 32.75. Against Gloucestershire at Hove he made 140, K. S. Ranjitsinhji's 65 being the only other score of note for Sussex. He again excelled in 1907 with 131 against Surrey at Hove—a grand innings which helped towards an average of 26. An attractive, punishing batsman and a dashing fieldsman, K. O. Goldie when home on leave from the Indian Army was always welcome in the Sussex XI during the period when Ranjitsinhji, C. B. Fry, Joe Vine, Albert Relf, and E. H. Killick, the present county scorer, were at their best. He went to America with an M.C.C. amateur team for a brief tour in 1907 and headed the batting averages with 34.50.

GOLDSMITH, Louis K. C., at one time one of the best-known cricketers in Victoria, died at East Melbourne on September 15, 1911. He was born at Melbourne on September 14, 1846, and was a brilliant, though somewhat uncertain, bat, and a fine field. He played for Victoria in four matches against New South Wales, four against Tasmania, and three against Mr. W. G. Grace's team, scoring in the 11 games 154 runs with an average of 9.05. For many years he was a prominent member of the East Melbourne C.C., for which, between 1867 and 1879, he scored 2,915 runs in 149 innings, averaging 19.56. He was one of the first Australian batsmen to cultivate the pull stroke.

GOODFELLOW, James Edward, born in

Surrey on August 21, 1850, died in Adelaide in July, 1924, aged 73. A good medium-paced bowler and a capital field, especially at slip and to his own bowling, he played occasionally for South Australia and often for the South Adelaide C.C. He was a member of the firm of Goodfellow and Hele, which published a *Cricketers' Almanack* for 1878–79.

GOODHEW, William, who died in April, 1897, will be remembered as a regular member of the Kent XI in the days of Edgar Willsher, George Bennett, W. H. Fryer, Mr. G. M. Kelson, and Mr. South Norton. Without ever being in the front rank of professional cricketers, Goodhew was a very fair bat and rendered useful service to Kent at a time when the fortunes of the county were at rather a low ebb. Born on May 24, 1828, he was in his 69th year at the time of his death.

GOODMAN, Clifford Everard, the greatest bowler the West Indies ever produced, and a member of a famous cricket brotherhood, died in Barbados on February 15, 1911, at the early age of 40. He was educated at the Lodge School, Barbados, and subsequently joined the Pickwick C.C., which he helped to make the strongest club in the island. In the 14 important matches—inter-colonial and against teams from England—in which he appeared his fast bowling accounted for as many as 122 wickets. He used his head well, varied pace and pitch with good judgment, had a deadly yorker at his command, and broke in from the off in disconcerting fashion. His height was 6ft. 4in.

GOODMAN, Sir Gerald Aubrey, a member of the well-known cricketing family of Barbados, was born on September 6, 1862, and died in England on January 21, 1921. He was educated at the Lodge School and Harrison College, of Barbados, and University College, London. He was the first of the brotherhood to make his mark in important cricket, and was one of the founders of the Pickwick C.C.

GOODMAN, Percy Arnold, died at Barbados on April 25, 1935, aged 60. With his death there came to an end a cricket quartette of Goodmans. Sir Gerald Aubrey captained the Pickwick Club; Evan was the fastest scorer in Barbados; Clifford the best bowler and Percy the best all-rounder. Percy Goodman played against all the English touring teams from 1895 to 1911 and he came to England with the West Indies sides of 1900 and 1906. He hit a century against Lord

Brackley's team in 1905; in 1900 he made 104 not out against Derbyshire and in 1906 he scored 102 not out against Yorkshire and 107 against Northamptonshire. He had a good defence and hit the loose ball very hard.

GOODWIN, Harry Smyth, who died on November 13, 1955, aged 85, played 50 innings for Gloucestershire between 1896 and 1907, scoring 546 runs, average 12.40. His highest score was 46 against Somerset at Taunton in 1899. For some years he was President of Horsham C.C.

GOODWYN, Canon Frederick Wildman, was born on January 20, 1850, and died at St. Leonards-on-Sea on April 23, 1931, in his 82nd year. He was in the Clifton College XI 1866–68 and afterwards assisted Gloucestershire occasionally.

GORDON, Herbert Pritchard, who died on October 17, 1965, aged 68, did not gain a place in the XI while at Malvern, but played a few games as an amateur for Worcestershire in 1923 and the following season. On his first appearance for the county, he followed 0 in the first innings with 68 not out against the West Indies touring team at Worcester.

GORDON, Sir Home Seton Charles Montagu, Twelfth Baronet Gordon of Embo, Sutherlandshire, who died suddenly at his home at Rottingdean on September 9, 1956, aged 84, was celebrated as a cricket historian. Always immaculately dressed and wearing a red carnation, he was known on grounds all over the country. He began a journalistic career immediately he left Eton in 1887 and at one time was the sole proprietor of the publishing house of Williams & Norgate Ltd. He used to say that the ideal publisher was the man who builds upon three rocks—the Public, the Press and the Bookseller.

Among his books on cricket were *Cricket Form at a Glance, A Biography of W. G. Grace, Background for Cricket,* and *A History of Sussex Cricket*; he did much work in connection with annuals for county clubs and contributed to the *Encyclopaedia Britannica.* As a young man he played for M.C.C. amateur sides, but never took part in first-class cricket, though, for his services to Sussex, he was awarded a county cap—an old one belonging to A. E. R. Gilligan.

His memory of the game went back to 1878 when, not seven years old, he was taken to the Gentlemen of England v. Australians match at Prince's. He first went to Lord's on Whit-Monday, 1880, being presented to W. G. Grace. In that season he watched the first England v. Australia Test match at the Oval and saw Alfred Lyttelton keep wicket for Middlesex against Gloucestershire at Clifton "in a hard straw hat." During his long life he attended no fewer than 70 Oxford v. Cambridge games.

He was on terms of intimate friendship with such great figures of the past as K. S. Ranjitsinhji, with whom he drove in a silver coach to the Delhi Durbar, Lord Hawke and Lord Harris. He was President of the London Club Cricketers' Conference in 1917–18; chairman of the Sports Conference in 1919, and had held practically every honorary position for Sussex, becoming President in 1948. He was also captain of the Rye Golf Club.

He succeeded his father in the Baronetcy in 1906, but, as there were no children of either of his two marriages, the title, created by King Charles I in 1631, becomes extinct.

GORDON, John Harvey, who died on April 23, 1933, at Charlottenville, U.S.A., aged 46, was in the Winchester and Oxford XIs and also played for Surrey. Cambridge won both the matches 1906–07 in which he appeared at Lord's. In 1907 he hit the only century for Oxford—117 against Surrey at the Oval.

GORDON-STEWARD, Brigadier-General Charles Steward, C.B.E., who will be better remembered by cricketers as C. S. Gordon, was born at Oakleaze, Gloucestershire, on September 8, 1849, and died at Nottingham House, Weymouth, on March 24, 1930, aged 80. He was described as "An effective batsman, possessing great freedom of play. In the field is good anywhere, while his bowling is slow underhand." He could also keep wicket, if required. He was acknowledged to be the most useful member of the Marlborough XIs of 1867 and 1868, his batting average in the latter year being a fraction under 31. His first appearance in first-class cricket was in February, 1870, at Melbourne, where he was stationed for a time with the 14th (Buckinghamshire) Regiment of Foot, and with which he returned to England a few days after the match. Playing for Victoria v. New South Wales he made in his second innings 121 out of 255 in four hours and three-quarters without a mistake. After playing County Cricket for Dorset he appeared for some seasons for Gloucestershire, for whom he scored 96 v. Sussex at Clifton in 1874, he and G. F. Grace (103) adding 209 for the fourth wicket. His cutting on that occasion was described as "superb." He also made 53 v. M.C.C. at Lord's in 1870 and 68 v. Surrey at the Oval a year later. For Marlborough College v. C. L. Bell's XI in June, 1868, he made a hit to square leg for 10 without an overthrow, and for Aldershot Division v. Royal Artillery at Woolwich in August, 1874, he took 16 wickets.

GORE, Charles St. George, for several years one of the most useful batsmen in New Zealand, died at Wellington on December 11, 1913, at the early age of 42. His highest score in a match of note was 57 for Wellington v. Canterbury at Christchurch, in January, 1897.

GORNALL, Capt. James Parrington, D.S.O., R.N. (Retd.), who died at Lower Froyle, Hampshire, on November 13, 1983, aged 84, was a good club batsman who played several times for the Navy and made one appearance for Hampshire in 1923.

GOSCHEN, George Joachim, First Viscount Goschen, of Hawkhurst, was born on August 10, 1831, and died at his seat, Seacox Heath, Hawkhurst, on February 7, 1907. He was educated at Rugby and Oxford, but did not obtain a place in either XI. He was a great lover of the game, and at the Centenary dinner of the M.C.C. in 1887 made a very interesting speech when returning thanks for the House of Commons.

GOSLING, Robert Cunliffe, born on June 15, 1868, died at Hossobury Park, Bishop's Stortford, on April 8, 1922. He was in the Eton XI in 1885 and two following years, and in the Public School matches was most successful, averaging 35.50 against Harrow and 39.33 v. Winchester. It was clearly his innings of 56 not out against the former in 1887 that enabled his side to win by five wickets. At Cambridge he obtained his Blue as a Freshman, and in his three inter-University matches he was dismissed only once, his scores being 29 not out and 18 not out in 1888, 22 not out in 1889, and 1 in 1890. His highest innings for the University was 61 v. Yorkshire, at Cambridge, in 1888, and for Essex, the county he assisted from 1888 to 1896, 57 v. Surrey at Leyton in 1889. He was one of four brothers who played for Eton against Harrow, and they were cousins of E. D. Gosling who, as 12th man, came into the team in 1889. As an inside forward at Association football, Mr. R. C. Gosling made a great name for himself, obtaining his

Blue in 1890 and also playing for England (five times), the Corinthians and Old Etonians.

GOTHARD, Edward James, died in Birmingham on January 17, 1979, aged 74. In 1947 and 1948 he captained Derbyshire, and was later the county's Hon. Secretary and Hon. Treasurer. Between the Wars he made a number of appearances for Staffordshire.

GOULD, John, at one time a prominent cricketer in New South Wales, died at Lewisham Hospital, Sydney, on December 4, 1908, in his 40th year. He appeared occasionally for his State and in 1892 took part in the return match with Lord Sheffield's team. In January and February, 1894, he toured New Zealand with the New South Wales team and played so well that he headed the batting averages and was second in the bowling: he made 337 runs in 12 completed innings and took 33 wickets at a cost of 12.93 runs each. He was a wonderful boy cricketer, but did not quite fulfil his early promise.

GOULDSWORTHY, William R., who died in February, 1969, aged 76, played as an amateur for Gloucestershire between 1921 and 1929. A medium-paced bowler, he took 62 wickets at an average cost of 27.88. Though he generally achieved little as a batsman, he played one memorable innings of 65 not out. That was against Somerset at Bristol in 1923, when he and J. G. Bessant (50) shared a stand of 131 which remains a record for the Gloucestershire last wicket. Despite the efforts of this pair, Somerset triumphed by an innings and 70 runs. Bill Gouldsworthy did much for Packer's team, which he captained.

GOULY, Lionel, a well-known West Australian cricketer, died of cancer at Perth on April 15, 1911. He played a fine not-out innings of 69 against Mr. J. J. Lyons' South Australian team in 1905–06, and made useful scores against the English team in 1907–08.

GRABURN, William Turbett, well known in connection with the Surrey County Club, died on December 13, 1944, at his home at East Molesey, aged 79. Born at Filey in Yorkshire, he was in the Repton XI of 1884, and three years later appeared in London playing for Scarborough at Lord's against M.C.C., as told in *Scores and Biographies*. He captained the Yorkshire Colts in 1886 and played for Yorkshire Gentlemen before being chosen from many candidates to be instructor to the young players at the Oval, where he was called "Teacher." Besides his work as coach, he regularly led Surrey Club and Ground sides, and he played once for the county in 1894. A sound bat, he made plenty of runs in club cricket, mostly for Thames Ditton, and was a member of East Molesey for many years. He could bowl slows with effect and set a good example by his smart fielding.

GRACE, Agnes Nicholls, widow of "W.G.," died at Hawkhurst, Kent, on March 23, 1930, aged 76. Mrs. Grace possessed a rare fund of reminiscences of the game. Her memory will be cherished by many cricketers.

GRACE, Dr. Alfred, the last of the famous brotherhood, who was born at Downend on May 17, 1840, died in a nursing home in Bristol on May 24, 1916, and was buried at Chipping Sodbury. He never appeared at Lord's, but was a very useful cricketer, his usual post in the field being long-stop. As a player he at no time ranked with his brothers, but in local cricket he scored several hundreds, and when only 15 years of age formed one of the Gloucestershire XXII which met the All England XI at Bristol. Although he was not in the front rank of cricketers, he stood out as one of the finest horsemen in England, and for many years followed the Duke of Beaufort's hounds three or four times a week. He was known as "The Hunting Doctor." For many years he practised as a surgeon at Chipping Sodbury, Gloucestershire. He never got over the tragic death of his son, Dr. Gerald Grace, in South Africa.

GRACE, Dr. Alfred Henry, born at Chipping Sodbury on March 10, 1866, died at Iron Acton, near that town, on September 16, 1929, aged 63. He was son of Dr. Alfred Grace and, therefore, nephew of W.G., E.M., and G.F. Grace. His appearances for Gloucestershire were very few, although in good-class club cricket he was a free and successful bat, often going in without pads against all types of bowling and playing a dashing innings. He was also a good change bowler, similar in style to "W.G.," and an excellent field. For Thornbury, Chipping Sodbury and British Medicals he made many hundreds. He was educated at Epsom College, where he gained a place in the XI.

GRACE, Charles Butler, the last surviving son of W.G. Grace, died while playing in a cricket match at Hawkhurst, on June 6, 1938, aged 56.

GRACE, Dr. Edgar Mervyn, of Hilltop, Alveston, Bristol, who died on November 24, 1974, aged 88, was the son of Dr. Edward Mills Grace, known in his cricketing days as "The Coroner". He was a nephew of W.G. Grace and G.F. Grace, Dr Edgar made his first appearance for the Thornbury club at the age of nine when he came in as a substitute against Cinderford and took six wickets for 24 with innocent-looking lobs. He went on to become captain of Thornbury for 37 years and altogether served the club for 79 years. In 1920, his best season, he scored well over 1,000 runs and took 146 wickets for only 7 runs each. Dr. Edgar's son, Gerald (G.F.) and grandson, (E.M.) now carry on the family association with Thornbury.

GRACE, Edward Mills, died on May 20, 1911, after a long illness at his residence, Park House, Thornbury, Gloucestershire. But for the accident that his own brother proved greater than himself, E.M. Grace would have lived in cricket history as perhaps the most remarkable player the game has produced. Barring W.G., it would be hard indeed to name a man who was a stronger force on a side or a more remarkable match winner. Primarily, he was a batsman, but his value in an XI went far beyond his power of getting runs. As a fieldsman at point—at a time when that position was far more important than it is in modern cricket—he never had an equal, and, though he did not pretend to be a first-rate bowler, he took during his career thousands of wickets. In his young days he bowled in the orthodox round-arm style, but his success in club cricket was gained by means of old-fashioned lobs. Fame came to him early in life. Born on November 28, 1841, he made his first appearance at Lord's in 1861, and a year later he was beyond question the most dangerous bat in England. It was in the Canterbury Week in 1862 that, playing as an emergency for the M.C.C. against the Gentlemen of Kent, he scored 192 not out, and took all 10 wickets in one innings. This was a 12-a-side and one man was absent in the second innings when he got the 10 wickets. He reached his highest point as a batsman in 1863, scoring in all matches that year over 3,000 runs.

After the season was over he went to Australia as a member of George Parr's famous team, but it cannot be said that in the Colonies he did all that was expected of him. He was handicapped by a bad hand, but, as he himself stated, there was another reason for his comparative lack of success. At the start of the tour he fell into rather a reckless style of batting, and, try as he would, he could not get back to his proper method. Still, he did some good things, scoring, for example, 106 not out in a single-wicket match. He had not been back in England more than two years before W.G., as a lad of 18, began to put him in the shade. The two brothers were in the Gentlemen's XI together in 1865— W.G.'s first year in the representative match—and had a share in gaining for the Gentlemen their first victory at Lord's since 1853. While he was qualifying as a surgeon E.M. Grace to a certain extent dropped out of first-class cricket, but he came very much to the front again on the formation of the Gloucestershire County Club in 1871. He was secretary from the start, and held his post without a break till his resignation in 1909.

In Gloucestershire's early days he renewed the successes of his youth, batting especially well in August, 1872, when W.G. was away in Canada with the amateur XI captained by the late R.A. Fitzgerald. It is matter of common knowledge that chiefly through the efforts of the three Graces—G.F. died in 1880— Gloucestershire rose to the top of the tree, being Champion county in 1876 and again in 1877. Not till the first Australian team played at Clifton in 1878 did the Gloucestershire XI know what it was to be beaten at home. One of the greatest triumphs of E.M. Grace's career came in 1880, when, strictly on his merits, he was picked to play for England at the Oval in the first Test match with Australia in this country. After an extraordinary

game England won by five wickets, the task of getting 57 runs in the last innings against Palmer and Boyle costing the side five of their best batsmen. E.M. and W.G. opened England's first innings, and scored over 90 runs together. W.G. made 152, and in Australia's second innings W.L. Murdoch just beat him by scoring 153 not out. Never has a finer match been seen.

E.M. Grace continued to play for Gloucestershire for many years, dropping out of the XI after the season of 1894. Thenceforward his energies were devoted to club cricket, chiefly in connection with his own team at Thornbury. Lameness gradually robbed him of his old skill as a run-getter, but even in 1909, 119 wickets fell to his lobs. As a batsman E.M. Grace was unorthodox. Partly, it is thought, through using a full-sized bat while still a small boy, he never played with anything like W.G.'s perfect straightness, but his wonderful eye and no less wonderful nerve enabled him to rise superior to this grave disadvantage. He was perhaps the first right-handed batsman of any celebrity who habitually used the pull. In his young days batting was a very strict science, but he cared little for rules. If an open place in the field suggested runs the ball soon found its way in that direction. Personally, E.M. was the cheeriest of cricketers—the life and soul of the game wherever he played. It was a great misfortune that he could never be induced to write his recollections of the cricket field. His good stories could be numbered by the hundred, and in conversation he told them with immense vivacity.

E.M. Grace's scores of 70 and over in first-class cricket:

Runs		Year.
192*	M.C.C. v. Gentlemen of Kent, at Canterbury	1862
73	South v. North, at Lord's	1863
75	M.C.C. v. Gentlemen of Kent, at Canterbury	1863
112	Fourteen Gentlemen of South v. XI Players of South, at Southampton	1863
78	England v. Surrey, at the Oval	1864
111	Gents. of England v. Gents. of Middlesex, at Islington	1865
71	Gentlemen v. Players, at the Oval	1867
115	The World v. Surrey, at the Oval	†1867
108	Gloucestershire v. Notts, at Clifton	1872
70	Gloucestershire v. Surrey, at the Oval	1873
76	Gloucestershire v. Sussex, at Brighton	1873
73	Gloucestershire v. Sussex, at Cheltenham	1873
71	Gloucestershire v. Sussex, at Cheltenham	1875
89	Gloucestershire v. Notts, at Nottingham	1877
77	Gloucestershire v. Surrey, at the Oval	1881
108	Gloucestershire v. Somerset, at Gloucester	1882
122	Gloucestershire v. Lancashire, at Clifton	1882
71	Gloucestershire v. Surrey, at the Oval	1883

84	Gloucestershire v. Lancashire, at Manchester	..	..	..	..	..	1887
70	Gloucestershire v. Kent, at Clifton	..	..	..	..	..	..	1887
96	Gloucestershire v. Kent, at Gloucester	..	..	..	..	..	1890
77	Gloucestershire v. Surrey, at Bristol	..	..	..	..	..	..	1890
78	Gloucestershire v. Sussex, at Bristol	..	..	..	..	..	..	1890
70	Gloucestershire v. Somerset, at Bristol	..	..	..	..	..	1892

*Signifies not out.

†This was a scratch match, on the third day of Tom Lockyer's benefit.

GRACE, Captain Edward Mills, (R.A.M.C.), a grandson of the great hitter and lob bowler, Dr. E.M. Grace, "The Coroner," of Gloucestershire and England after whom he was christened, died of typhoid fever on March 14, 1944, the illness being caught when on active service in Italy. A useful cricketer, left-handed with both bat and ball, he played for Wrekin College and Bristol University, for whom he did well in a good innings of 96 against Birmingham University. In 1935, when a substitute for Worcestershire Gentlemen against Gloucestershire Gipsies, a club of which his father, Dr. Edgar Mervyn Grace, was captain, he made 82 not out at Cirencester, and in recognition was elected a member of the club! In build he resembled his illustrious grand-uncle W. G. Grace, and fielded finely close to the wicket—a characteristic of his grandfather as described in *The Cricketer*. He was aged 28.

GRACE, Edward Sidney Henry, who died at his home at Cheltenham in April, 1953, aged 79, was the eldest son of Dr. E. M. Grace, a nephew of the famous Dr. W. G. Grace. E. S. H. Grace appeared with his father and "W.G." in a team composed entirely of members of the Grace family.

GRACE, Dr. Henry, the eldest member of the famous cricket family, died on November 13, 1895, from an attack of apoplexy. He was born on January 31, 1833, and was thus in his 63rd year. Though never coming prominently before the public, like his younger brothers, E.M; W. G. and G. F.; Dr. Henry was, in his young days, an excellent cricketer, and but for the calls of his profession would probably have played more frequently in important matches. He is described as having been a vigorous bat, a medium pace round-arm bowler, and an excellent field, mostly at point. He appeared at Lord's for the first time on July 18 and 19, 1861, and, with a first innings of 63 not out, materially helped the South Wales Club to beat the M.C.C. by seven wickets. The match is a historical one, in as much as it introduced Mr. E.M. Grace to Lord's ground. Dr.

Henry Grace was from the formation of the county club an enthusiastic supporter of Gloucestershire cricket, and was never absent from the county matches played at home.

GRACE, Capt. Norman Vere, (R.N.), (retired), who died on February 20, 1975, aged 80, was a son of the famous E. M. Grace and thus a nephew of W.G. A useful all-rounder, he was a member of the Free Foresters and had played for the Royal Navy.

GRACE, Lieut. T. M. (New Zealand Expeditionary Force), killed on August 8, 1915, played in inter-Provincial matches in New Zealand for Wellington. He was a useful all-round cricketer. Against Otago, at Dunedin, in 1913–14 he took four wickets for six runs.

W. G. GRACE
William Gilbert Grace, born at Downend, near Bristol, July 18, 1848
Died at his home, Fairmount, Eltham, Kent, October 23, 1915

In no branch of sport has anyone ever enjoyed such an unquestioned supremacy as that of W. G. Grace in the cricket field. In his great days he stood alone, without a rival. Not even George Fordham and Fred Archer as jockeys, or John Roberts as a billiard player, had such a marked superiority over the men who were nearest to them in point of ability. Whatever may be in store for the game of cricket in the future it seems safe to say that such a player will never be seen again. A rare combination of qualities went to the making of W. G. Grace. Blessed with great physical advantages, he united to a strength of constitution that defied fatigue a devotion to the game which time was powerless to affect. When he was in his prime no sun was too hot and no day too long for him. It is on record that when, for a cricketer, he was no longer young, he spent the whole night by the bedside of a patient, and on the following day stepped on to the Clifton College ground and scored over 200 runs.

Mr. Grace's career in the cricket field—almost unexampled in point of length—can be sharply divided into two portions. His early fame as a batsman culminated in the season of 1876, when in the month of August he scored in three successive innings, 344 against Kent at Canterbury, 177 against Notts at Clifton, and 318 not out against Yorkshire at Cheltenham. Soon after that, having passed his examination at Edinburgh as a surgeon, he thought of gradually retiring from cricket and settling down, like his elder brothers, to the busy life of a general practitioner. As a matter of fact, he did for many years hold a parish appointment at Bristol, a locum tenens doing his work in the summer months. There can be little doubt that his change of plans was mainly due to the appearance in England in 1878 of the first Australian XI. Those whose memories go back to that now somewhat distant time will remember the tremendous sensation caused by the victories of that XI, and in particular by Spofforth's bowling, and Blackham's wicket-keeping. Englishmen realised, with an excusable shock of surprise, that in the cricket field there were serious rivals to be faced.

Mr. Grace had never been in such poor batting form as he was in 1878, and on the few occasions that he met the Australian bowlers he did nothing in the least degree worthy of his reputation. I have no exact knowledge on the point, but I feel tolerably certain that the success of the Australians revived Mr. Grace's ambition. At any rate, the fact remains that, though the most brilliant part of his career had ended before the invasion of 1878, the Australians found him for the best part of 20 years the most formidable of their opponents. This second part of his career as a batsman began towards the end of the season of 1880. Following some fine performances for Gloucestershire he played, as everyone will remember, a great innings of 152 at the Oval in the first match in this country between England and Australia. Even then, however, though only in his 33rd year, he laboured under one serious disadvantage. In the four years following his triumphs of 1876, he had put on a lot of weight and was very heavy for so young a man.

He said himself at the time that he was never in better form than in those closing weeks of the season of 1880, and that, but for lack of condition, he would have made many more runs. Against increasing bulk he had to battle for the rest of his cricket life. For a long time he retained his activity to a surprising extent, but as the years went on his once splendid fielding gradually left him. He kept up his batting, however, in a marvellous way, the success of what one may call his second

period in the cricket field reaching its climax when in 1895 he scored a thousand runs in first-class cricket in the month of May. His batting at that time has never been approached by a man of the same age; he was nearly 47. In 1896 he was still very good, but after that the years began to tell on him, and in 1899, when he moved from Bristol to the Crystal Palace, he played at Trent Bridge his last match for England against Australia. Still, though he had now done with Test matches, he went on playing first-class cricket for several seasons, his career practically ending with the Gentlemen and Players' match at the Oval in 1906. The finish was worthy of him as, on his 58th birthday, he scored 74, batting up to a certain point with much of the vigour of his younger days.

Of Mr. Grace's cricket from the time of his first appearance at Lord's in July, 1864, for the South Wales Club against the M.C.C. down to the end of 1876, columns could be written without exhausting the subject. He was picked for the Gentlemen, as a lad of 17, both at Lord's and the Oval in 1865, the honour being conferred upon him quite as much for his medium-pace bowling as for his batting. A year later, however, he proved himself, beyond all question, the best batsman in England, two wonderful innings at the Oval establishing his fame. He scored 224 not out for England against Surrey and 173 not out for Gentlemen of the South against Players of the South. An attack of scarlet fever interfered with his cricket in 1867, but after that he never looked back. His best seasons as a batsman were, I fancy, 1871, 1873, and 1876. His play in 1871 far surpassed anything that had ever been done before.

In his whole career he scored in Gentlemen and Players' matches 6,008 runs with an average of 42 and took 271 wickets for a trifle under 19 runs each. He made seven hundreds for the Gentlemen at Lord's, four at the Oval, and one each at Brighton, Prince's, Scarborough, and Hastings. The first of his seven hundreds at Lord's was obtained in 1868, and the last, after an interval of 27 years, in 1895. Of these seven innings the first was, perhaps, the most remarkable. Going in first wicket down for a very strong side he took out his bat for 134, the total only reaching 201. As Lord Harris has pointed out the wickets at Lord's in those far-off days were by no means so true and easy as careful attention made them in later years. A score of a hundred at Lord's in the '60s against the best bowling was an incomparably bigger feat than it is at the present time.

No mention has yet been made of Mr. Grace's connection with Gloucestershire cricket. With his two brothers, E. M. and G. F., and other fine, though less gifted, players to help him, he built up a team of remarkable strength in batting and fielding. The County Club was established in 1871, and in 1876 and 1877 the XI stood ahead of all rivals. Until beaten at Clifton by the first Australian XI in 1878 the team never lost a match at home. After G. F. Grace's death in 1880, Gloucestershire never seemed quite the same as before, but in 1885, and again in 1898, there was, thanks to W. G.'s batting and C. L. Townsend's bowling, a brief revival of old glories. The Gloucestershire matches at Clifton and Cheltenham in the old days were delightful, the Gloucestershire XI being quite a family party. Like other families they had their little differences of opinion, but there was a great feeling of comradeship among them, and they played cricket with tremendous zest.

Mr. Grace's venture in connection with the London County at the Crystal Palace did not add to his fame. He was in his 51st year when he left Bristol, the experiment being made far too late. Many pleasant matches were carried through in too leisurely a spirit to appeal to a public brought up on cricket of a much sterner character. If tried 15 years earlier the project might have proved a success. As it was the London County faded out when Mr. Grace's contract with the Crystal Palace Company came to an end.

With Mr. Grace's characteristics as a batsman I must deal rather briefly. He was, in the main, quite orthodox in style, his bat being as perfectly straight as Fuller Pilch's, but he greatly enlarged the domain of orthodoxy, playing a far more aggressive and punishing game than any of the classic batsmen who came before him. It should be explained here that E. M. Grace, who first made the family name famous, played a game of his own and was a little outside comparisons. W. G. developed the art of batting to an extraordinary degree, but he was not, like E. M., a revolutionist. There is his own authority for stating that he did not indulge in the pull till he was 40. A splendid all-round hitter, he excelled all his predecessors in his power of placing the ball on the on-side. A story is told of a cricketer who had regarded Fuller Pilch as the last word in batting, being taken in his old age to see Mr. Grace bat for the first time. He watched the great man for a quarter of an hour or so and then broke out into expressions of boundless delight. "Why," he said, "this man scores continually from balls that old Fuller would have been thankful to stop." The words conveyed everything. Mr. Grace when he went out at the ball did so for the purpose of getting runs. Pilch and his imitators, on the other hand, constantly used forward play for defence alone.

When the wicket was difficult and the ball turning, Mr. Grace trusted for defence to that strong back play which, even in his boyhood, convinced his people at home that he would be a greater batsman than his brother, E. M. Mr. Grace's batting from 1868 onwards quite overshadowed his bowling, and yet during his career he took many hundreds of wickets. Indeed, old Bob Thoms, the umpire, always contended that if he had not been such a wonderful batsman he would have been the best slow bowler in England. Even as it was he held his own very well with such masters as Alfred Shaw and Southerton. He bowled medium pace with a purely round arm action in his young days, but slackened his speed about 1872.

His superb strength and health enabled him to stand any amount of cricket, but in his best two years as a bowler—1875 and 1877—his batting fell off 50 per cent. He did not rely much on break, only turning in a little from leg, but he had great command over his length and very seldom indeed pitched short. His chief strength lay in head work. No one was quicker to find out the weak points of a batsman or more certain to lure an impetuous hitter to his doom. In Gloucestershire's great days he was much helped by brilliant fielding, Fred Grace in particular, at deep square leg, being invaluable to him. When he first appeared for the Gentlemen, Mr. Grace was a splendid outfield, capable of throwing the ball 100yd., but as time went on he took to fielding near the wicket and for many years he had no superior at point except his brother E. M.

Personally, W. G. struck me as the most natural and unspoiled of men. Whenever and wherever one met him he was always the same. There was not the smallest trace of affectation about him. If anything annoyed him he was quick to show anger, but his little outbursts were soon over. One word I will add. No man who ever won such world-wide fame could have been more modest in speaking of his own doings. Mr. Grace was married in 1873 to Miss Agnes Day. His domestic life was unclouded except by the death of his only daughter in 1899 and of his eldest son in 1905. Mrs. Grace and two sons—Captain H. E. Grace, R.N., and Captain C. B. Grace, K.F.R.E.—survive him.—S.H.P.

W. G. GRACE IN FIRST-CLASS CRICKET

Inns.	N.O.	Most	Total	Aver.		Balls	Runs	Wkts.	Aver.
8	1	48	189	27.00	**1865**	630	268	20	13.40
13	2	224*	581	52.81	**1866**	1,215	434	31	14.00
6	1	75	154	30.80	**1867**	799	292	39	7.48
13	2	134*	625	56.81	**1868**	1,384 / —	686 / —	48 / 1	14.29 / —
24	1	180	1,320	57.39	**1869**	3,138	1,255	73	17.19
38	5	215	1,808	54.78	**1870**	1,817	782	50	15.64
39	4	268	2,739	78.25	**1871**	3,060	1,346	79	17.03
32	3	170*	1,561	53.82	**1872**	1,835 / —	736 / —	62 / 6	11.87 / —
38	8	192*	2,139	71.30	**1873**	2,727 / —	1,307 / —	101 / 5	12.94 / —
32	0	179	1,664	52.00	**1874**	4,101	1,780	140	12.71
48	2	152	1,498	32.56	**1875**	6,757	2,468	191	12.92
46	4	344	2,622	62.42	**1876**	6,321	2,458	129	19.05
40	3	261	1,474	39.83	**1877**	7,170	2,291	179	12.79
42	2	116	1,151	28.77	**1878**	6,680	2,204	152	14.50
29	3	123	993	38.19	**1879**	4,420	1,491	113	13.19
27	3	152	951	39.62	**1880**	4,062	1,480	84	17.61
25	1	182	917	38.20	**1881**	2,434	1,026	57	18.00
37	0	88	975	26.35	**1882**	3,404	1,754	101	17.36
41	2	112	1,352	34.66	**1883**	4,417	2,077	94	22.09
45	5	116*	1,361	34.02	**1884**	4,150	1,762	82	21.48
42	3	221*	1,688	43.28	**1885**	5,738	2,199	117	18.79
55	3	170	1,846	35.50	**1886**	6,102	2,439	122	19.99
46	8	183*	2,062	54.26	**1887**	5,094	2,078	97	21.42
59	1	215	1,886	32.51	**1888**	4,390	1,691	93	18.18
45	2	154	1,396	32.46	**1889**	2,313	1,014	44	23.04
55	3	109*	1,476	28.38	**1890**	3,048	1,183	61	19.39
40	1	72*	771	19.76	**1891**	2,364	973	58	16.77
11	1	159*	448	44.80	**1891-92**	385	134	5	26.80
37	3	99	1,055	31.02	**1892**	2,128	958	31	30.90
50	5	128	1,609	35.75	**1893**	1,705	854	22	38.81
45	1	196	1,293	29.38	**1894**	1,507	732	29	25.28
48	2	288	2,346	51.00	**1895**	900	527	16	32.93
54	4	301	2,135	42.70	**1896**	2,768	1,249	52	24.01
41	2	131	1,532	39.28	**1897**	2,971	1,242	56	22.17
41	5	168	1,513	42.02	**1898**	2,378	917	36	25.47
23	1	78	515	23.40	**1899**	1,220	482	20	24.10
31	1	126	1,277	42.56	**1900**	1,759	969	32	30.28
32	1	132	1,007	32.48	**1901**	2,815	1,111	51	21.78
35	3	131	1,187	37.09	**1902**	2,917	1,074	46	23.34
27	1	150	593	22.80	**1903**	798	479	10	47.90
26	1	166	637	25.48	**1904**	1,308	687	21	32.71
13	0	71	250	19.23	**1905**	510	383	7	54.71
10	1	74	241	26.77	**1906**	506	268	13	20.61
2	0	16	19	9.50	**1907**	—	—	—	—
2	0	25	40	20.00	**1908**	12	5	0	—
1,493	105	344	54,896	39.55	Totals	126,157 / —	51,545 / —	2,864 / 12	17.99 / —

Signifies not out.

The above figures, which have been checked most carefully throughout, will be found to differ in several instance from those given in the cricket publications of the '60s and '70s; but, considering that the handbooks of that period frequently contradicted each other, and that the averages given in one seldom, if ever, agreed with those tabulated in another, this is not surprising. One instance of the loose manner in which statistics were compiled in those days may be cited. In 1873, when "W.G." 's scores in the M.C.C. matches v. Hertfordshire and Staffordshire, and in the North v. South game at the Oval on July 26, were included in his first-class aggregate for the season, his bowling in the same matches was ignored completely.

MR. W. G. GRACE'S PERFORMANCES IN GENTLEMEN v. PLAYERS MATCHES, 1865–1906.

Matches Batted in.	Innings.	Times not out.	Highest Score.	Total.	Average.	Ground And Date Of First Appearance	Matches Bowled in.	Balls.	Runs.	Wickets.	Average.
35	66	5	215	2,582	42.38	**Oval,** 1865	34	5,831	2,403	110	21.84
35	62	3	169	2,398	40.64	**Lord's,** 1865	29	4,867	1,863	108	17.25
1	2	0	217	217	108.50	**Brighton,** 1871	1	324	123	7	17.57
5	8	0	110	281	35.12	**Prince's,** 1873	5	1,322	473	39	12.12
1	1	0	174	174	174.00	**Scarborough,** 1885	1	159	60	3	20.00
7	12	2	131	356	35.60	**Hastings,** 1889	5	295	171	4	42.75
84	151	10	217	6,008	42.60	**Totals**	75	12,798	5,093	271	18.78

THE SIDES FOR WHICH W. G. GRACE OBTAINED HIS RUNS.

	Date of First Match.	Inns.	Times not out.	Most in an Inns.	Total.	Aver.
Anglo-American XI	1873	2	0	152	157	78.50
England	1865	54	5	224*	1,930	39.38
,, (*in Australia*)	1891–	11	1	159*	448	44.80
England XIs	92	50	2	92	1,267	26.39
Gentlemen v. Players	1875	151	10	217	6,008	42.60
Gentlemen of England	1865	43	2	165	1,595	38.90
Gentlemen of South	1865	37	2	180	1,625	46.42
Gloucestershire	1865	618	49	318*	23,083	40.56
Gloucestershire and Kent	1868	6	1	121	346	69.20
Gloucestershire and Yorkshire	1874	2	0	110	162	81.00
Grace's XI, Mr. W. G.	1877	15	4	81*	511	46.45
Kent (with "W. G." and A. W. Ridley)	1871	2	0	58	108	54.00
London County	1877	103	1	166	3,483	34.14
M.C.C.	1900	13	2	344	904	82.18
M.C.C. and Ground	1869	211	15	196	6,876	35.08
Non-Smokers	1869	1	0	10	10	10.00
Non-University Gentlemen	1884	1	0	12	12	12.00
Orleans Club	1874	1	0	34	34	34.00
Over 30	1882	8	0	51	193	24.12
Right-handed	1879	1	0	35	35	35.00
Single	1870	1	1	189*	189	*189.00
South	1871	137	8	268	5,130	39.76
South, United	1866	15	1	126	492	35.14
South of Thames	1870	7	1	130	260	43.33
United XI	1866 1882	3	0	23	38	12.66
Totals	1865	1,493	105	344	54,896	39.55

Signifies not out.

THE PREVIOUS TABLE ANALYSED.

For	Date of First Match.	Innings.	not out.	Most in an Innings.	Total.	Aver.	Scores of 50 or more.
Anglo-American XI v. XV of M.C.C. (with Rylott)	1873	2	0	152	157	78.50	152
England— v. Australia	1880	36	2	170	1,098	32.29	152, 170, 75*, 50, 58, 68, 66
v. XIII of Kent	1878	4	1	63*	101	33.66	63*
v. Kent & Sussex	1902	2	0	70	79	39.50	70
v. Lancs. & Yorks.	1903	2	0	28	30	15.00	
v. M.C.C. & Ground	1868	2	0	66	95	47.50	66
v. Middlesex	1867	1	0	75	75	75.00	75
v. New South Wales	1891–92	3	0	45	79	26.33	
v. Notts & Yorks.	1872	1	1	170*	170	170.00*	170*
v. South Australia	1891–92	1	0	2	2	2.00	
v. Surrey	1865	3	1	224*	277	138.50	224*
v. Surrey & Middlx.	1868	2	0	24	43	21.50	
v. Surrey & Sussex	1867	5	0	40	97	19.40	
v. Victoria	1891–92	2	1	159*	203	203.00	159*
v. Yorkshire	1902	1	0	29	29	29.00	
England XIs— v. Anglo-Australian XIs	1885	7	1	58	161	26.83	51, 58
v. Australians	1884	26	0	92	679	26.11	92, 74, 64, 63
v. Camb. Univ.	1875	11	0	54	282	25.63	54, 52
v. England XI†	1892	2	0	63	65	32.50	63
v. Home Counties	1899	2	1	21*	36	36.00	
v. Yorkshire	1901	2	0	24	44	22.00	
Gentlemen— v. Players	1865	151	10	217	6,008	42.60	134*, 83, 215, 109, 50, 217, 77 & 112, 117, 163, 158, 70, 110, 152, 90, 169, 63, 90, 100, 66, 89, 76, 174, 65 & 50*, 67, 54, 57 & 68, 71, 56, 131, 118, 53*, 54, 66, 50, 60, 78, 58, 57, 54, 82, 74.
Gentlemen of England v. Australians	1878	13	0	165	656	50.46	61, 107, 148, 165
v. Camb. Univ.	1871	3	0	162	181	60.33	162
v. Gents. of Kent	1879	3	0	54	61	20.33	54
v. Gents. of Middlsx.	1865	2	0	48	82	41.00	
v. I Zingari	1885	9	1	101*	390	48.75	68, 73, 58, 101*
v. Oxford Univ.	1866	5	0	71	111	22.20	71
v. Players of South	1904	2	1	6*	8	8.00	
v. Surrey	1905	6	0	32	106	17.66	

†Lord Sheffield's Anglo-Australian XI v. Rest of England.

For	Date of First match.	Innings.	Times not out.	Most in an innings.	Total.	Aver.	Scores of 50 or more.
Gentlemen of South—							
v. Gents. of North ..	1870	5	1	118	270	67.50	77, 118
v. I Zingari	1866	2	0	50	80	40.00	50
v. Players of North ..	1873	10	0	145	399	39.90	145, 104, 72
v. Players of South ..	1865	20	1	180	876	46.10	173*, 55, 180, 66, 134, 150
Gloucestershire—							
v. Australians ..	1878	30	4	116*	856	32.92	77, 116*, 110, 51, 92, 66
v. Derbyshire ..	1886	2	0	20	22	11.00	
v. England	1877	4	0	31	94	23.50	
v. Essex	1898	3	0	126	195	65.00	126
v. Kent	1887	41	6	257	1,680	48.00	101 & 103*, 64, 109*, 257 & 73*, 64, 56*, 58, 71
v. Lancashire ..	1878	75	8	112	2,154	32.14	58*, 75*, 106, 86, 112, 53, 50, 94, 90, 51 & 102*, 56
v. M.C.C. & Ground	1868	5	1	172	20	73.00	172
v. Middlesex	1879	68	7	221*	2,848	46.68	85 & 81*, 69, 64, 80, 89, 85, 94, 69 & 54, 221*, 113, 63, 101, 127*, 57, 72*, 72*, 89, 96, 68, 169, 60 & 56, 51, 55.
v. Nottinghamshire ..	1871	84	5	182	3,276	41.46	78 & 55, 79 & 116, 67, 119, 60, 177, 116, 102, 51 & 182, 55, 92*, 84, 113*, 59, 70*, 61, 119, 55, 126, 131, 63, 168
v. Philadelphians ..	1897	1	0	113	113	113.00	113
v. Somerset	1879	33	0	288	1,373	41.60	113, 80, 75 & 58, 288, 186, 109
v. Surrey	1870	97	7	160*	2,815	31.27	143, 83, 160*, 123, 67, 50*, 55, 88 & 51, 66, 55, 104, 58, 94, 54, 64, 61*, 51
v. Sussex	1872	73	6	301	3,172	47.34	51, 179, 53, 77, 104, 78, 52, 56*, 51 & 57, 51, 215, 70, 84, 58, 99, 75, 88, 91, 243*, 301, 116, 93*
v. Warwickshire ..	1894	15	1	70	392	28.00	52, 70

For	Date of First Match.	Innings.	Times not out.	Most in an Innings.	Total.	Aver.	Scores of 50 or more.
v. Yorkshire	1872	87	4	318*	3,801	45.79	150, 79, 167, 127, 111, 57, 318*, 84, 71, 62, 89 & 57*, 56, 51, 54, 132, 92 & 183*, 97, 148 & 153, 50, 52, 98, 53, 61, 54, 70, 55.
Gloucestershire & Kent—							
v. England	1874	6	1	121	346	69.20*	94 & 121, 91
Gloucestershire & Yorks.—							
v. England	1877	2	0	110	162	81.00	52 & 110
Grace's XI, Mr. W. G.							
v. Australians ..	1899	1	0	25	25	25.00	
v. Camb. Univ. ..	1906	4	1	64	109	36.33	64
v. England XI ..	1883	2	0	81	132	66.00	81 & 51
v. Kent	1871	4	3	81*	194	194.00	81*, 69*
v. Surrey	1907	2	0	16	19	9.50	
v. West Indians ..	1906	2	0	23	32	16.00	
Kent (with "W.G." & A. W. Ridley)—							
v. England	1877	2	0	58	108	54.00	50 & 58
London County—							
v. Australians ..	1902	1	0	1	1	1.00	
v. Camb. Univ. ..	1900	13	0	93	533	41.00	86 & 62, 93, 72, 59
v. Derbyshire ..	1900	16	0	87	307	19.18	87
v. Gloucestershire ..	1903	3	0	150	179	59.66	150
v. Ireland	1902	2	0	32	51	25.50	
v. Lancashire ..	1903	2	0	22	28	14.00	
v. Leicestershire ..	1901	12	0	83	313	26.08	83, 73 & 54
v. M.C.C. & Ground	1900	15	0	166	674	44.93	110, 132, 131, 166
v. South Africans ..	1901	4	0	37	47	11.75	
v. Surrey	1900	17	0	97	595	35.00	71 & 80, 97, 61, 81, 52
v. Warwickshire ..	1900	14	0	129	523	37.35	82, 76, 76, 129
v. Worcestershire ..	1900	4	1	110*	232	77.33	72 & 110*
M.C.C.—							
v. Kent	1869	11	2	344	871	96.77	127, 117, 57*, 123, 344
v. Yorkshire	1889	2	0	27	33	16.50	
M.C.C. & Ground—							
v. Australians ..	1878	19	0	101	489	25.73	101, 75, 50
v. Camb. Univ. ..	1869	28	3	196	993	39.72	55, 54*, 116*, 139, 196
v. Derbyshire ..	1877	6	1	74*	210	42.00	74*
v. England	1877	6	0	47	115	19.16	
v. England XI ..	1891	2	0	19	21	10.50	
v. Herts.	1872	4	0	75	148	37.00	75
v. Ireland	1902	1	0	44	44	44.00	
v. Kent	1871	20	2	128	649	36.05	51, 80, 128, 125
v. Lancashire ..	1869	17	1	73	312	19.50	73, 61*

For	Date of First Match.	Innings.	Times not out.	Most in an Innings.	Total.	Aver.	Scores of 50 or more.
v. Leicestershire	1901	2	0	15	26	13.00	
v. Middlesex	1871	4	0	88	113	28.25	88
v. North	1874	2	0	43	55	27.50	
v. Nottinghamshire	1869	12	1	121	492	44.72	121, 117*, 52, 63
v. Oxford Univ.	1869	23	1	117	1,058	48.09	117, 54 & 73*, 62, 65, 67, 104, 95, 72, 79
v. South	1869	4	0	44	92	23.00	
v. South Africans	1901	3	0	27	47	15.66	
v. Staffordshire	1873	1	0	67	67	67.00	67
v. Surrey	1869	14	2	181	771	64.25	51, 138*, 84, 181, 146
v. Sussex	1871	15	2	103	516	39.69	59, 81*, 73, 103, 65
v. Yorkshire	1870	28	2	101	658	25.30	66, 98, 101, 71
Non-Smokers—							
v. Smokers	1884	1	0	10	10	10.00	
Non-University Gentlemen—							
v. University Gents.	1874	1	0	12	12	12.00	
Orleans Club—							
v. Australians	1882	1	0	34	34	34.00	
Over 30—							
v. Under 30	1879	8	0	51	193	24.12	51
Right-handed—							
v. Left-handed	1870	1	0	35	35	35.00	
Single—							
v. Married	1871	1	1	189*	189	189.00*	189*
South—							
v. Australians	1884	19	2	84	617	36.29	53, 84, 66, 53
v. North	1866	118	6	268	4,513	40.29	122, 96, 178, 268, 87, 114, 68, 192*, 98, 82, 92 & 73, 114*, 69 & 50*, 58, 261, 54, 61, 77, 64, 69, 154, 61, 54, 104, 126.
South, United—							
v. England	1876	2	0	19	27	13.50	
v. North, United	1871	11	1	126	435	43.50	51*, 65, 126 & 82
v. Yorkshire	1874	2	0	15	30	15.00	
South of Thames—							
v. North of Thames	1866	7	1	130	260	43.33	130 & 102*
United XI—							
v. Australians	1882	3	0	23	38	12.66	
Totals	1865	1,493	105	344	54,896	39.55	*See above.*

*Signifies not out

W.G.'s SCORING ON THE CHIEF LONDON GROUNDS.

	Date of First Match.	Matches.	Innings.	Times not out.	Highest Score.	Total.	Aver.
Lord's	1865	208	364	19	196	12,690	36.78
Oval	1865	122	209	18	268	8,261	43.25
Prince's.. ..	1872	17	28	0	261	1,321	47.17
Crystal Palace ..	1899	40	60	1	166	2,535	42.96

It should be remembered that the Doctor had completed his 50th year when he appeared at the Crystal Palace for the first time.

W. G. GRACE'S BATTING AVERAGES FOR GLOUCESTERSHIRE.

Year.	Innings.	Not out.	Highest Score.	Total.	Average.
1868	2	0	24	37	18.50
1870	4	0	172	366	91.50
1871	8	1	116	435	62.14
1872	6	0	150	284	47.33
1873	11	3	160*	497	62.12
1874	7	0	179	594	84.85
1875	14	0	119	541	38.64
1876	12	1	318*	890	80.90
1877	13	1	84	367	30.58
1878	21	2	116	605	31.84
1879	15	2	123	709	52.53
1880	18	2	106	614	38.37
1881	19	1	182	720	40.00
1882	22	0	88	666	30.27
1883	22	0	112	871	39.59
1884	22	4	116*	672	37.33
1885	26	2	221*	1,034	43.08
1886	26	2	110	714	29.75
1887	27	5	183*	1,405	63.86
1888	28	1	215	1,068	39.55
1889	26	2	127*	884	36.83
1890	29	2	109*	930	34.44
1891	22	1	72*	440	20.95
1892	25	3	99	802	36.45
1893	30	3	96	747	27.66
1894	33	1	88	633	19.78
1895	29	1	288	1,424	50.85
1896	36	3	301	1,693	51.30
1897	30	2	131	1,192	41.84
1898	28	4	168	1,141	47.54
1899	7	0	33	108	15.42
Totals	618	49	318*	23,083	40.56

Signifies not out.

W. G. GRACE'S HUNDREDS IN FIRST-CLASS CRICKET.

Score	For	Against	Ground	Year.
224*	England	Surrey	Oval	1866
173*	Gents. of South	Players of South	Oval	1866
134*	Gentlemen	Players	Lord's	1868

W. G. Grace's Hundreds—*Continued*.

Score	For	Against	Ground	Year
130 ⎫ 102* ⎭	South of Thames	North of Thames	Canterbury	1868
117	M.C.C. & Ground	Oxford Univ.	Oxford	1869
138*	M.C.C. & Ground	Surrey	Oval	1869
121	M.C.C. & Ground	Notts	Lord's	1869
180	Gents. of South	Players of South	Oval	1869
122	South	North	Sheffield	1869
127	M.C.C.	Kent	Canterbury	1869
117*	M.C.C. & Ground	Notts	Lord's	1870
215	Gentlemen	Players	Oval	1870
109	Gentlemen	Players	Lord's	1870
143	Gloucestershire	Surrey	Oval	1870
172	Gloucestershire	M.C.C. & Ground	Lord's	1870
181	M.C.C. & Ground	Surrey	Lord's	1871
118	Gents. of South	Gents. of North	West Brompton	1871
178	South	North	Lord's	1871
162	Gents. of England	Camb. Univ.	Cambridge	1871
189*	Single	Married	Lord's	1871
146	M.C.C. & Ground	Surrey	Oval	1871
268	South	North	Oval	1871
117	M.C.C.	Kent	Canterbury	1871
217	Gentlemen	Players	Brighton	1871
116	Gloucestershire	Notts	Nottingham	1871
101	M.C.C. & Ground	Yorkshire	Lord's	1872
112	Gentlemen	Players	Lord's	1872
117	Gentlemen	Players	Oval	1872
170*	England	Notts. & Yorks	Lord's	1872
114	South	North	Oval	1872
150	Gloucestershire	Yorkshire	Sheffield	1872
145	Gents. of South	Players of North	Prince's	1873
134	Gents. of South	Players of South	Oval	1873
163	Gentlemen	Players	Lord's	1873
158	Gentlemen	Players	Oval	1873
152	Anglo-American XI	XV. of M.C.C. (with Rylott)	Lord's	1873
192*	South	North	Oval	1873
160*	Gloucestershire	Surrey	Clifton	1873
179	Gloucestershire	Sussex	Brighton	1874
150	Gents. of South	Players of South	Oval	1874
104	Gents. of South	Players of North	Prince's	1874
110	Gentlemen	Players	Prince's	1874
167	Gloucestershire	Yorkshire	Sheffield	1874
121	Kent & Glouces.	England	Canterbury	1874
123	M.C.C.	Kent	Canterbury	1874
127	Gloucestershire	Yorkshire	Clifton	1874
152	Gentlemen	Players	Lord's	1875
111	Gloucestershire	Yorkshire	Sheffield	1875
119*a*	Gloucestershire	Notts	Clifton	1875
104	Gloucestershire	Sussex	Brighton	1876
169	Gentlemen	Players	Lord's	1876
114*	South	North	Nottingham	1876
126	United South	United North	Hull	1876
344	M.C.C.	Kent	Canterbury	1876
177	Gloucestershire	Notts	Clifton	1876
318*	Gloucestershire	Yorkshire	Cheltenham	1876
261	South	North	Prince's	1877

W. G. Grace's Hundreds—*Continued*.

Score	For	Against	Ground	Year
110	Glouces. & Yorks.	England	Lord's	1877
116	Gloucestershire	Notts	Nottingham	1878
123	Gloucestershire	Surrey	Oval	1879
102	Gloucestershire	Notts	Nottingham	1879
113	Gloucestershire	Somerset	Clifton	1879
106	Gloucestershire	Lancashire	Clifton	1880
152	England	Australia	Oval	1880
100	Gentlemen	Players	Oval	1881
182	Gloucestershire	Notts	Nottingham	1881
112	Gloucestershire	Lancashire	Clifton	1883
101	M.C.C. & Ground	Australians	Lord's	1884
107	Gents. of England	Australians	Oval	1884
116*	Gloucestershire	Australians	Clifton	1884
132	Gloucestershire	Yorkshire	Bradford	1885
104	Gloucestershire	Surrey	Cheltenham	1885
221*	Gloucestershire	Middlesex	Clifton	1885
174	Gentlemen	Players	Scarborough	1885
148	Gents. of England	Australians	Oval	1886
104	M.C.C. & Ground	Oxford Univ.	Oxford	1886
110	Gloucestershire	Australians	Clifton	1886
170	England	Australia	Oval	1886
113	Gloucestershire	Middlesex	Lord's	1887
116*	M.C.C. & Ground	Camb. Univ.	Lord's	1887
183*	Gloucestershire	Yorkshire	Gloucester	1887
113*	Gloucestershire	Notts	Clifton	1887
101 ⎫ 103* ⎭	Gloucestershire	Kent	Clifton	1887
215	Gloucestershire	Sussex	Brighton	1888
165	Gents. of England	Australians	Lord's	1888
148 ⎫ 153 ⎭	Gloucestershire	Yorkshire	Clifton	1888
101	Gloucestershire	Middlesex	Lord's	1889
127*	Gloucestershire	Middlesex	Cheltenham	1889
154	South	North	Scarborough	1889
109*	Gloucestershire	Kent	Maidstone	1890
159*	England	Victoria	Melbourne	1891–92
128	M.C.C. & Ground	Kent	Lord's	1893
139	M.C.C. & Ground	Camb. Univ.	Cambridge	1894
196	M.C.C. & Ground	Camb. Univ.	Lord's	1894
131	Gentlemen	Players	Hastings	1894
103	M.C.C. & Ground	Sussex	Lord's	1895
288b	Gloucestershire	Somerset	Bristol	1895
257	Gloucestershire	Kent	Gravesend	1895
169	Gloucestershire	Middlesex	Lord's	1895
125	M.C.C. & Ground	Kent	Lord's	1895
101*	Gents. of England	I Zingari	Lord's	1895
118	Gentlemen	Players	Lord's	1895
119	Gloucestershire	Notts	Cheltenham	1895
104	South	North	Hastings	1895
243*	Gloucestershire	Sussex	Brighton	1896
102*	Gloucestershire	Lancashire	Bristol	1896
186	Gloucestershire	Somerset	Taunton	1896
301	Gloucestershire	Sussex	Bristol	1896
113	Gloucestershire	Philadelphians	Bristol	1897
126	Gloucestershire	Notts	Nottingham	1897
116	Gloucestershire	Sussex	Bristol	1897

W. G. Grace's Hundreds—*Continued*.

Score	For	Against	Ground	Year
131	Gloucestershire	Notts	Cheltenham	1897
126	Gloucestershire	Essex	Leyton	1898
168	Gloucestershire	Notts	Nottingham	1898
109	Gloucestershire	Somerset	Taunton	1898
126	South	North	Lord's	1900
110*	London County	Worcestershire	Crystal Palace	1900
110	London County	M.C.C. & Ground	Crystal Palace	1900
132	London County	M.C.C. & Ground	Crystal Palace	1901
131	London County	M.C.C. & Ground	Crystal Palace	1902
129	London County	Warwickshire	Crystal Palace	1902
150	London County	Gloucestershire	Crystal Palace	1903
166	London County	M.C.C. & Ground	Crystal Palace	1904

Signifies not out.
a His 50th century in first-class cricket; *b* his 100th.

The above 126 scores were obtained thus:—

For England...................................... 5
,, England, Gents. of 6
,, Gentlemen (v. Players) 15
,, Gloucestershire 51
,, Glouces. & Kent 1
,, Glouces. & Yorks. 1
,, London County 7

For M.C.C. 4
,, M.C.C. & Ground 15
,, Single 1
,, South 10
,, South, Gents. of 7
,, South, United 1
,, South of Thames 2

TWO SEPARATE HUNDREDS IN A MATCH.

130 & 102* South of Thames v. North of Thames, at Canterbury   1868
101 & 103* Gloucestershire v. Kent, at Clifton   1887
148 & 153   Gloucestershire v. Yorkshire, at Clifton   1888

The following feats are also noteworthy:

94 & 121   Kent and Gloucestershire v. England, at Canterbury..   1874
92 & 183* Gloucestershire v. Yorkshire, at Gloucester 1887
126 & 82   United South v. United North, at Hull 1876

Signifies not out.

THREE SEPARATE HUNDREDS IN SUCCESSION.

118	Gentlemen of South v. Gentlemen of North, at West Brompton	
178	South v. North, at Lord's	1871
162	Gentlemen of England v. Camb. Univ., at Cambridge	
112	Gentlemen v. Players, at Lord's..	
117	Gentlemen v. Players, at the Oval	1872
170*	England v. Notts & Yorkshire, at Lord's	
134	Gentlemen of South v. Players of South, at the Oval	
163	Gentlemen v. Players, at Lord's	1873
158	Gentlemen v. Players, at the Oval	
121	Kent and Gloucestershire v. England, at Canterbury	
123	M.C.C. v. Kent, at Canterbury	1874
127	Gloucestershire v. Yorkshire, at Clifton	
344	M.C.C. v. Kent, at Canterbury	
177	Gloucestershire v. Notts, at Clifton	1876
318*	Gloucestershire v. Yorkshire, at Cheltenham	

Signifies not out.

For Gloucestershire in 1874 he played consecutive innings of 179 v. Sussex at Brighton, 167 v. Yorkshire at Sheffield, and 127 v. Yorkshire at Clifton.

In consecutive innings for Gentlemen v. Players in 1871–72–73 he scored 217, 77 and 112, 117, 163, 158, 70.

In May, 1895, when in his 47th year, he made the following scores in succession for Gloucestershire: 288 v. Somerset at Bristol, 257 and 73 not out (winning the match by nine wickets) v. Kent, at Gravesend, 169 v. Middlesex at Lord's, and 91 v. Sussex at Brighton.

CARRYING BAT THROUGH A COMPLETED INNINGS.

Some	For	Against	Ground	Season
138	M.C.C. & Ground	Surrey	Oval	1869
117	M.C.C. & Ground	Notts	Lord's	1870
189	Single	Married	Lord's	1871
81	W. G. Grace's XI	Kent	Maidstone	1871
170	England	Notts & Yorks.	Lord's	1872
192	South	North	Oval	1873
318	Gloucestershire	Yorkshire	Cheltenham	1876
221	Gloucestershire	Middlesex	Clifton	1885
81	M.C.C. & Ground	Sussex	Lord's	1887
113	Gloucestershire	Notts	Clifton	1887
37	Gloucestershire	Lancashire	Bristol	1889
127	Gloucestershire	Middlesex	Cheltenham	1889
109	Gloucestershire	Kent	Maidstone	1890
159	England	Victoria	Melbourne	1891–92
61	Gloucestershire	Surrey	Oval	1893
243	Gloucestershire	Sussex	Brighton	1896
102	Gloucestershire	Lancashire	Bristol	1896

LONG PARTNERSHIPS FOR FIRST WICKET. (69).

283 W.G. (180) & B. B. Cooper (101): Gents. of South v. Players of South, at the Oval   1869

238 ,, (150) and T. G. Matthews (85): Gloucestershire v. Yorkshire, at Sheffield   1872

226 ,, (154) and R. Abel, (105): South v. North, at Scarborough   1889

203 ,, (152) and A. J. Webbe (65): Gentlemen v. Players, at Lord's   1875

175 ,, (73) and C. I. Thornton (107): Gents. of England v. I Zingari, at Scarborough   1887

172* ,, (101*) and A. Sellers (70*): Gents. of England v. I Zingari, at Lord's ..   1895
(Made in 105 minutes, winning the match by 10 wickets.)

170 ,, (170) and W. H. Scotton, (34): England v. Australia, at the Oval ..   1886

169 ,, (109) and W. Troup (127): Gloucestershire v. Somerset, at Taunton ..   1898

168 ,, (71) and A. Marshal (94): Gents. of England v. Oxford University, at Oxford   1905

164 ,, (215) and J. W. Dale (55): Gentlemen v. Players at the Oval   1870

163 ,, (72) and W. G. Quaife, (108): London County v. Camb. Univ., at the Crystal Palace   1901

161 ,, (88) and John Smith, of Cambridge (81): M.C.C. & Ground v. Middlesex, at Lord's   1871

161 ,, (85) and W. R. Gilbert (99): Gloucestershire v. Middlesex, at Clifton ..   1879

160 ,, (93) and C. J. B. Wood (88): London County v. Camb. Univ., at the Crystal Palace   1900

158 ,, (165) and J. Shuter (71): Gents. of England v. Australians, at Lord's ..   1888

156 ,, (83) and E. M. Grace (70): Gloucestershire v. Surrey, at the Oval ..   1873

156 ,, (92) and W. H. Scotton, (71): Lord Londesborough's XI v. Australians, at Scarborough   1886

154 ,, (98) and H. Jupp, (80): South v. North, at Canterbury   1873

154 ,, (73) and W. L. Murdoch (74): London County v. Leicestershire, at the Crystal Palace   1904

LONG PARTNERSHIPS FOR FIRST WICKET.   (69).—*Continued*

151	W. G.	(68) and A. E. Stoddart (83): England v. Australia, at the Oval	1893
151	,,	(118) and A. E. Stoddart (71): Gentlemen v. Players, at Lord's	1895
150	,,	(104) and A. E. Stoddart (71): South v. North, at Hastings ..	1895
149	,,	(123) and I. D. Walker (37): M.C.C. v. Kent, at Canterbury	1874
146	,,	(64) and Marshal, A. (75): W. G. Grace's XI v. Cambridge University, at Cambridge ..	1906
142	,,	(80) and C. J. B. Wood (70): London County v. Surrey, at the Crystal Palace (*Second innings*.)	1901
140	,,	(79) and G. J. Mordaunt (55): M.C.C. and Ground v. Oxford University, at Lord's	1897
139	,,	(172) and C. S. Gordon (53): Gloucestershire v. M.C.C. and Ground, at Lord's	1870
139	,,	(90) and E. M. Grace (69): Gloucestershire v. Lancashire, at Clifton	1890
137	,,	(127) and E. M. Grace (51): Gloucestershire v. Yorkshire, at Clifton ..	1874
134	,,	(96) and H. Jupp, (63*): South v. North, at Canterbury	1869
134	,,	(78) and E. M. Grace (65): Gloucestershire v. Notts, at Clifton	1871
131	,,	(71) and C. J. B. Wood (66): London County v. Surrey, at the Crystal Palace (*First innings*)	1901
130	,,	(52) and A. E. Stoddart (84): A. J. Webbe's XI v. Camb. Univ., at Cambridge	1895
130	,,	(61) and C. B. Fry (82): London County v. Surrey, at the Oval	1902
127	,,	(117*) and I. D. Walker (48): M.C.C. and Ground v. Notts, at Lord's	1870
127	,,	(101) and E. M. Grace (7): Gloucestershire v. Kent, at Clifton ..	1887
126	,,	(169) and C. J. Ottaway (42): Gentlemen v. Players, at Lord's	1876
122	,,	(82) and E. G. Arnold, (58): London County v. Warwickshire, at Edgbaston	1900
121	,,	(114) and H. Jupp, (40): South v. North, at the Oval	1872
121	,,	(83) and F. L. Fane (54): London County v. Leicestershire, at the Crystal Palace	1901
120	,,	(45) and A. E. Stoddart (74): M.C.C. and Ground v. Australians, at Lord's	1893
120	,,	(61*) and W. L. Murdoch (68): M.C.C. and Ground v. Lancashire, at Lord's	1902
119	,,	(152) and C. J. Ottaway (52): Anglo-American XI v. XV of M.C.C. (with Rylott), at Lord's ..	1873
119	,,	(54) and A. O. Jones (105): Gentlemen v. Players, at Hastings ..	1901
119	,,	(82) and G. W. Beldam (57): Gentlemen v. Players, at the Oval	1902
118	,,	(57) and J. J. Ferris (60): Gentlemen v. Players, at the Oval	1893
118	,,	(54) and H. H. Burton (59): London County v. Leicestershire, at the Crystal Palace	1904
118	,,	(166) and W. L. Murdoch (51): London County v. M.C.C. & Ground, at the Crystal Palace	1904
117	,,	(46) and E. M. Grace (78): Gloucestershire v. Sussex, at Bristol ..	1890
116	,,	(67) and C. Booth (78): M.C.C. and Ground v. Oxford University, at Lord's	1876
115	,,	(121) and Lord Harris (33): Kent and Gloucestershire v. England, at Canterbury ..	1874
114	,,	(49) and A. E. Stoddart (94): Shrewsbury's XI v. Australians, at Nottingham	1893
113	,,	(51) and E. M. Grace (73): Gloucestershire v. Sussex, at Cheltenham ..	1873
113	,,	(40) and A. C. MacLaren (72): England v. Surrey and Sussex, at Hastings	1898
111	,,	(29) and A. E. Stoddart (115): South v. North, at Lord's ..	1890
111	,,	(76) and W. L. Murdoch (55): London County v. Warwickshire, at the Crystal Palace	1900
107	,,	(117) and J. W. Dale (36): M.C.C. v. Kent, at Canterbury ..	1871
106	,,	(70) and J. J. Ferris (53): Gloucestershire v. Warwickshire, at Bristol	1895
106	,,	(63) and R. W. Rice (42): Gloucestershire v. Notts, at Bristol	1898
106	,,	(168) and W. Troup (37): Gloucestershire v. Notts, at Nottingham ..	1898
105	,,	(83) and B. B. Cooper (40): Gentlemen v. Players, at the Oval	1869

LONG PARTNERSHIPS FOR FIRST WICKET. (69).—*Continued*

105	W.G.	(101) and O. G. Radcliffe (55): Gloucestershire v. Middlesex, at Lord's ..	1889
104	,,	(80) and E. M. Grace (52): Gloucestershire v. Somerset, at Bath ..	1881
104	,,	(148) and W. H. Patterson (44): Gents. of England v. Australians, at the Oval	1886
103	,,	(162) and A. J. A. Wilkinson (19): Gents. of England v. Camb. Univ., at Cambridge	1871
103	,,	(73) and F. Hearne, (34): M.C.C. and Ground v. Sussex, at Lord's ..	1888
101	,,	(114*) and A. J. Webbe (41): South v. North, at Nottingham	1876
101	,,	(63) and A. Shrewsbury, (62): Lord Sheffield's XI v. Australians, at Sheffield Park	1893
100	,,	(36) and A. E. Stoddart (71): South v. North, at Hastings	1891

*Denotes an unfinished partnership *or* not out.

In three consecutive innings which they opened together against the Australians in 1893, W. G and A. E. Stoddart made 120, 114 and 151 in partnership.

LONG PARTNERSHIPS FOR OTHER WICKETS. (12).

281	for 2nd.,	W.G.	(261) and J. M. Cotterill (88): South v. North, at Prince's ..	1877
281	,, 3rd.,	,,	(132) and L. Walker (222): London County v. M.C.C. and Ground, at the Crystal Palace	1901
261	,, 5th.,	,,	(318*) and W. O. Moberly (103): Gloucestershire v. Yorkshire, at Cheltenham	1876
256	,, 2nd.,	,,	(139) and W. Chatterton, (113): M.C.C. and Ground v. Camb. Univ., at Cambridge	1894
255*	,, 3rd.,	,,	(160*) and E. M. Knapp (90*): Gloucestershire v. Surrey, at Clifton	1873
248	,, 7th.,	,,	(243*) and E. L. Thomas (109): Gloucestershire v. Sussex, at Brighton	1896
241	,, 2nd.,	,,	(217) and G. F. Grace (98): Gentlemen v. Players, at Brighton	1871
234	,, 2nd.,	,,	(143) and F. Townsend (89): Gloucestershire v. Surrey, at the Oval	1870
227	,, 5th.,	,,	(344) and P. C. Crutchley (84): M.C.C. v. Kent, at Canterbury	1876
223	,, 3rd.,	,,	(288) and C. L. Townsend (95): Gloucestershire v. Somerset, at Bristol	1895
211	,, 2nd.,	,,	(301) and R. W. Rice (84): Gloucestershire v. Sussex, at Bristol	1896
200	,, 3rd.,	,,	(196) and K. S. Ranjitsinhji (94): M.C.C. and Ground v. Camb. Univ. at Lord's	1894

*Denotes an unfinished partnership
or not out.

MEN WHO HAVE CLEAN-BOWLED W. G. GRACE IN FIRST-CLASS CRICKET.

20 *Times*.

Shaw (A.)

14 *Times*.

Richardson (T.)

13 *Times*.

Barlow (R. G.)

11 *Times*.

Morley (F.)

10 *Times*.

Briggs (J.)

Emmett (T.)
Hill (A.)

9 *Times*.

Peate (E.)
Shaw (J. C.)

8 *Times*.

Flowers (W.)
Southerton (J.)

7 *Times*.

Lohmann (G. A.)
Spofforth (F. R.)
Turner (C. T. B.)

6 *Times*.

Bates (W.)
Hearne (J. T.)
Martin (F.)
Palmer (G. E.)
Peel (R.)
Steel (A. G.)
Wootton (G.)

5 *Times*.

Attewell (W.)
Barnes (W.)
Giffen (G.)
Lillywhite (Jas., jun.)
Mold (A.)
Wainwright (E.)

EIGHT OR MORE WICKETS IN AN INNINGS.

W.	R.		Year
8 for 40	Gentlemen of South v. Players of South, at the Oval	.. .. ..	1865
8 ,, 25	Gentlemen v. Players, at Lord's	..	1867
8 ,, 33	Gloucestershire v. Yorkshire, at Sheffield	..	1872
10 ,, 92	M.C.C. v. Kent, at Canterbury (12 a-side)	..	1873
9 ,, 48	South v. North, at Loughborough	..	1875
8 ,, 69	Gloucestershire v. Notts. at Clifton	..	1876
8 ,, 36	South v. North, at Lord's	..	1877
8 ,, 54	M.C.C. and Ground v. Derbyshire, at Lord's	..	1877
9 ,, 55a 8 ,, 34b }	Gloucestershire v. Notts, at Cheltenham	..	1877
8 ,, 23	M.C.C. and Ground v. Derbyshire, at Lord's	..	1878
8 ,, 81	Gloucestershire v. Surrey, at Cirencester	..	1879
8 ,, 31	Gloucestershire v. Somerset, at Gloucester	..	1882
8 ,, 93	Gloucestershire v. Australians, at Clifton	..	1882
9 ,, 20	M.C.C. and Ground v. Notts, at Lord's	..	1885
10 ,, 49	M.C.C. and Ground v. Oxford Univ., at Oxford ..	..	1886
8 ,, 37	M.C.C. and Ground v. Sussex, at Lord's	..	1889

THIRTEEN OR MORE WICKETS IN A MATCH.

13 for 84	Gentlemen of South v. Players of South, at the Oval ..	.. ..	1865
15 ,, 79	Gloucestershire v. Yorkshire, at Sheffield	..	1872
15 ,, 147	M.C.C. v. Kent, at Canterbury (12 a-side)	..	1873
14 ,, 66	Gloucestershire v. Surrey, at Cheltenham	..	1874
13 ,, 98	Gloucestershire v. Yorkshire, at Clifton	..	1875
14 ,, 108	South v. North, at Loughborough	..	1875
14 ,, 109	M.C.C. and Ground v. Derbyshire, at Lord's	..	1877
17 ,, 89	Gloucestershire v. Notts, at Cheltenham	..	1877
13 ,, 106	Gloucestershire v. Sussex, at Cheltenham	..	1878
15 ,, 116	Gloucestershire v. Surrey, at Cirencester	..	1879
16 ,, 60	M.C.C. and Ground v. Notts, at Lord's	..	1885
13 ,, 110	London County v. M.C.C. and Ground, at Lord's ..	.. ..	1901

FOUR WICKETS OR MORE FOR THREE RUNS OR LESS EACH.

6 for 10	M.C.C. and Ground v. Lancashire, at Lord's	.. ..	1869
7 ,, 19	M.C.C. and Ground v. Hertfordshire, at Chorleywood ..	..	1873
7 ,, 18	Gloucestershire v. Surrey, at Cheltenham	..	1874
8 ,, 23	M.C.C. and Ground v. Derbyshire, at Lord's	..	1878
6 ,, 18	Gloucestershire v. Sussex, at Cheltenham	..	1878
6 ,, 16	Gloucestershire v. Middlesex, at Lord's	..	1879
9 ,, 20	M.C.C. & Ground v. Notts, at Lord's	..	1885

BOWLING UNCHANGED THROUGH BOTH COMPLETED INNINGS.

With			Year.
I. D. Walker	Gentlemen of South v. Players of South, at the Oval ..	.. ..	†1865
Wootton (G.)	M.C.C. and Ground v. Staffordshire, at Lord's ..	.. ..	1873
W. R. Gilbert	Gloucestershire v. Lancashire, at Clifton	..	1878

† Aged 16.

A THREE-FIGURE INNINGS AND TEN WICKETS OR MORE IN ONE MATCH.

Scores.		Bowling.
134*	Gentlemen v. Players, at Lord's, 1868	10 for 81
117	M.C.C. v. Kent, at Canterbury, 1871	†12 ,, 146
114	South v. North, at the Oval, 1872 ..	11 ,, 126
150	Gloucestershire v. Yorkshire, at Sheffield, 1872 ..	15 ,, 79
179	Gloucestershire v. Sussex, at Brighton, 1874	12 ,, 158
23 110 }	Gentlemen v. Players, at Prince's, 1874	10 ,, 119
167	Gloucestershire v. Yorkshire, at Sheffield, 1874 ..	11 ,, 101
94 121 }	Gloucestershire & Kent v. England, at Canterbury, 1874	‡10 ,, 160
123	M.C.C. v. Kent, at Canterbury, 1874	..†‡11 ,, 129
127	Gloucestershire v. Yorkshire, at Clifton, 1874	‡10 ,, 121
7 152 }	Gentlemen v. Players, at Lord's, 1875	12 ,, 125
261	South v. North, at Prince's, 1877	11 ,, 139
221*	Gloucestershire v. Middlesex, at Clifton, 1885	11 ,, 120
104	M.C.C. & Ground v. Ox. Univ., at Oxford, 1886	12 ,, 109

(*Including all 10 wickets in second innings.*)

*Signifies not out.
†12 a-side   ‡Consecutive matches

FIRST-CLASS CRICKET MEMORABILIA.

1865.—Appeared for the first time, at the age of 16, for Gentlemen v. Players—at the Oval. He scored 23 and 12* and took seven wickets for 125 runs.

1866.—His first match for the South—v. the North, at Lord's. He made 19, and took one wicket for 33 runs.

Aged 18, he scored 224 not out for England v. Surrey at the Oval, and 173 not out for Gentlemen of South v. Players of South on the same ground, thereby earning the title of Champion.

1868.—His first match for Gloucestershire—v. M.C.C. and Ground, at Lord's. He scored 24 and 13, and took five wickets.

Scored 134 not out, whilst only 57 other runs were made, of a total of 201 for Gentlemen v. Players at Lord's. The runs were obtained on very bad and difficult ground, and the only other double-figure score for the side was 28 by B. B. Cooper, and the next highest in the match 29 not out by Grundy.

For North of Thames v. South of Thames, at Canterbury, he scored 130 and 102 not out, this being the first occasion since 1817 on which two separate hundreds had been made by anyone in a match of note. W. G. was then 20 years of age, and he obtained his runs off Wootton, Howitt, Grundy, and Hearne (T.)

1869.—W. G. was elected a member of the M.C.C., being proposed by T. Burgoyne (Treasurer) and seconded by R. A. FitzGerald (Secretary). In his first innings for the club— v. Oxford University, at Oxford—he scored 117.

In making 283 for the first wicket of Gentlemen of South v. Players of South, at the Oval, W. G. (180) and B. B. Cooper (101) established a record for first-class cricket.

For North v. South, at Sheffield, he scored 122 of the total of 173, the next highest innings for the side being 23 by B. B. Cooper.

1870.—W. G. scored 117 not out, for M.C.C. and Ground v. Notts at Lord's, but when he had made about 60 he played-on hard from a ball from Shaw (J. C.) without a bail falling.

In his innings of 109 for Gentlemen v. Players, at Lord's, were as many as 54 singles, but the fieldsmen were placed deep.

1871.—In match between Gentlemen of England and Cambridge University, at Cambridge, W. G. (162) and A. J. A. Wilkinson made 103 runs before the first wicket fell, the latter scoring only 19 of the number, so fast did the Champion obtain his runs.

In first-class cricket this year "W. G." scored 2,739 runs, this being the first time that any batsman obtained as many as 2,000 in a single season in such matches.

1873.—For Gentlemen v. Players, at the Oval, W. G. scored 158, but when 44 had his wicket hit by a ball bowled by Emmett without a bail being disturbed.

1876.—For Gloucestershire v. Yorkshire, at Sheffield, the three brothers Grace had a hand in getting out the whole of the Yorkshire XI in both innings.

In first innings of United South v. United North, at Hull, W. G. scored 126 out of 153 in 165 minutes: the only other score above four in the completed innings of 159 (five extras) was 14 by Pooley.

By making 344 for M.C.C. v. Kent, at Canterbury, the Doctor set up a fresh record for first-class cricket, exceeding William Ward's 278 for M.C.C. v. Norfolk (with E. H. Budd, T. Vigne, and F. C. Ladbroke) at Lord's in 1820. In his two following innings he made 177 for Gloucestershire v. Nottinghamshire at Clifton, and 318 not out for Gloucestershire v. Yorkshire at Cheltenham, thus obtaining 839 runs in three innings, once not out, in 10 days.

1877.—In the course of his innings of 261 for South v. North, at Prince's, his own score was 202 with the total 300.

For Gloucestershire v. Nottinghamshire, at Cheltenham, W. G. obtained 17 wickets, nine in the first innings and eight in the second. With the last 41 balls he delivered he took seven wickets without a run.

1878.—As W. G. was running between the wickets in Gloucestershire's match v. Surrey, at Clifton, the ball was thrown in and it lodged in his shirt. After running six runs—three with the ball in his possession—he was stopped, and Jupp asked him to give up the ball, but this he wisely declined to do, as he might have been adjudged out for handling the ball.

1879.—On the second day of the match at Lord's between Over 30 and Under 30, W. G. was presented, in front of the pavilion, with a national testimonial in the form of a handsome clock, of the value of 40 guineas, and a cheque for £1,458. The list was headed by the M.C.C. with 100 guineas, and H. R. H. the Prince of Wales was among the subscribers. In the absence in America of the Duke of Beaufort, the presentation was made by Lord Fitzhardinge. It had been arranged that the Over 30 v. Under 30 match should be a complimentary one for the Doctor, and the proceeds added to his testimonial fund, but with great liberality he suggested that it should be played for the benefit of Alfred Shaw, whose match earlier in the season—between North and South—had been ruined by the weather.

1885.—For Gentlemen v. Players, at Scarborough, W. G. scored 174 out of 247 in 235 minutes on a treacherous wicket. The next highest score in the completed innings of 263 (six extras) was 21 by T. C. O'Brien.

For an XI of England v. Shaw's Australian team, at Harrogate, he scored 51 of the first 53 runs.

1886.—For M.C.C. and Ground v. Oxford University, at Oxford, W. G. scored 104 and took all 10 wickets in the second innings for 49 runs.

For England v. Australia at the Oval, W. G. made 170 out of 216 in four hours and a half. With Scotton, who scored 34, he obtained 170 for the first wicket.

1888.—For M.C.C. and Ground v. Sussex, at Lord's, he scored 73 out of 103 in 70 minutes.

1889.—This year his portrait was painted for the M.C.C. at the cost of £300 by Archibald Stuart Wortley. Private subscriptions for the same were limited to £1. In the following year the portrait was exhibited at the Royal Academy in Gallery X, No. 1003.

1890.—In the second innings of the North v. South match at Lord's, A. E. Stoddart (115) at one period of his innings made 50 runs whilst W. G. was obtaining three.

1895.—Aged 46, W. G. scored 1,016 runs during the month of May with an average of 112:

13 & 103	M.C.C. & Ground v. Sussex, at Lord's.
18 & 25	M.C.C. & Ground v. Yorkshire, at Lord's.
288	Gloucestershire v. Somerset, at Bristol.
52	A. J. Webbe's XI v. Cambridge Univ., at Cambridge.
257 & 73*	Gloucestershire v. Kent, at Gravesend.
18	England v. Surrey, at the Oval.
169	Gloucestershire v. Middlesex, at Lord's.

At lunch-time on the third day of the match at Gravesend only an innings each had been completed, yet Gloucestershire won by nine wickets. W. G. was on the field during every ball of the game. In appreciation of his wonderful rejuvenescence, a National Testimonial was organized, the *Daily Telegraph* collecting £5,000 (by means of a shilling subscription) and the M.C.C. £2,377 2s., less £21 8s. 10d. expenses. He was entertained at banquets both in London and Bristol, that at the latter place being organized by the Gloucestershire County C.C.

Gentlemen of England, set 172 to win v. I Zingari, at Lord's, made the runs without loss of a wicket in 105 minutes, W. G. scoring 101* and A. Sellers 70*. It was the Zingari Jubilee match.

1898.—The Gentlemen v. Players match at Lord's was commenced on W. G.'s 50th birthday, and every man who took part in it was presented by the M.C.C. with a medal struck in honour of the occasion. The Champion scored 43 and 31 not out and took a wicket. On the second day of the match he was entertained at dinner by the Sports Club, Sir Richard Webster (Lord Alverstone) presiding.

In the second innings of Gloucestershire's match v. Sussex, at Bristol, W. G. declared when he had made 93, thereby crediting himself with having obtained every number from 0 to 100 in first-class cricket.

1899.—In January, W. G. formed the London County C.C., with headquarters at the Crystal Palace.

His last match for Gloucestershire—v. Middlesex, at Lord's. He scored 11 and 33 and bowled 20 balls for 10 runs and one wicket.

His last Test match—v. Australia, at Nottingham. He made 28 and one, and delivered 110 balls for 37 runs without obtaining a wicket.

In December he was elected a life-member of the M.C.C. on the suggestion of Lord Harris.

1900.—In scoring 169 for Oxford University v. London County, at Oxford, R. E. Foster made four sixes from consecutive balls from W. G.

Aged 52, he scored 72 and 110 not out for London County v. Worcestershire, at the Crystal Palace.

In the first innings of South v. North, at Lord's, P. F. Warner drove back a ball to E. Smith, who turned it on to the broad back of W. G. who was batting at the other end. Off the rebound Smith made the catch, Warner thereby being caught and bowled.

1902.—In the second innings of M.C.C. and Ground v. Lancashire, at Lord's, W. G. made a hit to leg off Hallows, the ball going over the grand-stand and out of the ground into an adjoining garden.

For London County v. Ireland, at the Crystal Palace, W. G. (32) and W. L. Murdoch (41) made 75 for the first wicket, but the whole side were out for 92.

1904.—His last match (in first-class cricket) for M.C.C. and Ground—v. South Africans, at Lord's. He scored 27.

1905.—Playing for Gentlemen of England v. Surrey, at the Oval, W. G. pulled a ball from J. N. Crawford right out of the ground, scoring six, and sent the next delivery from the same bowler almost as far for four.

His last match for the South—v. Australians, at Hastings. He scored two.

1906.—A. E. Harragin, for West Indians v. W. G. Grace's XI, at the Crystal Palace, scored three sixes and a two off an over from W. G.

At the Oval W. G. made his 85th, and last, appearance for Gentlemen v. Players. He made four and 74, obtaining the latter number on his 58th birthday.

1908.—His last appearance in first-class cricket—for Gentlemen of England v. Surrey, at the Oval. He scored 15 and 25, and bowled 12 balls for five runs without taking a wicket.

SPECTACLES.

XXII of Lansdown v. The England XI, on the Sydenham Field, Bath, May 28, 29, 30   1863
   (c Clarke (A.), b Thinley 0; c Anderson b Tinley, 0.)
Clifton v. Lansdown, on the Sydenham Field, Bath, August 7, 8   1863
   (lbw, b E. M. Grace, 0; b E. M. Grace, 0.)

U.S.E.E. v. XXII of the Cadoxton C.C. (with Howitt), in Knoll Park, Neath, May 21,
22, 23   1868
   (c Struve b Howitt, 0; c and b Howitt, 0.)
Bedminster v. Great Western Railway (Swindon), at Bedminster, May 7   1870
   (c and b Laverick, 0; c Dormand b Laverick 0).

The Doctor never performed this easy feat in a first-class match.

AN AGGREGATE OF 3,000 RUNS IN A SEASON.

Year.											Average
1870	3,255	runs in 67 completed innings		..	..	..	..	..	..	..	48.58
1871	3,234	,, ,, 48	,,	,,	..	..	..	..	..	..	67.37
1872a	3,030	,, ,, 63	,,	,,	..	..	..	..	..	..	48.09
1874b	3,505	,, ,, 74	,,	,,	..	..	..	..	..	..	47.36
1876	3,908	,, ,, 72	,,	,,	..	..	..	..	..	..	54.27

a Including the trip to America; and *b* the tour through Australia.

The runs obtained in first-class matches are included in the above totals.
In 1874, 1875, 1877, and 1878 he took over 300 wickets during the season.

HUNDREDS IN MINOR MATCHES (91).

Score.		Year.
170	South Wales v. Gentlemen of Sussex ..	1864
126	Clifton v. Fowne's XI ..	1864
157	Clifton v. Belmont	1866
150*	Clifton v. Clifton College	1866
101	Bedminster v. Lansdown	1866
118	W. Absolon's XI v. Eastern Counties Club ..	1866
111	Bedminster v. Lansdown	1868
210	Clifton v. Civil Service ..	1868
100	Bedminster v. Lansdown	1869
172*	Stapleton v. Knowle	1869
111	Stapleton v. Swindon	1869
108	W. G. Grace's XI v. Lillington's XI (Bedminster) ..	1870
197	Gloucestershire v. Glamorganshire ..	1870
109	Frenchay v. Thornbury	1870
115	United South E.E. v. XXII of Sleaford and District	1870
112	United South E.E. v. XXII of Glasgow and District	1872
142	R. A. FitzGerald's Team v. XXII of Toronto	1872
126	England v. XXII of Ballarat ..	1873–74
126	England v. A Victorian XI	1873–74
259	Thornbury v. Clifton ..	1874
109	M.C.C. and Ground v. Gentlemen of Herefordshire	1874
153	United South E.E. v. XXII of Leinster	1874
110	Thornbury v. Knole Park	1875
112	United South E.E. v. Eighteen of Trinity College, Dublin ..	1875
152	United South E.E. v. Eighteen of North Kent	1875
210	United South E.E. v. Eighteen of Hastings and District	1875
400*	United South E.E. v. XXII of Grimsby and District	1876
133	United South E.E. v. XXII of Stockport	1876
109	United South E.E. v. Eighteen of Grange, Edinburgh	1877
124	United South E.E. v. XXII of Stockport and District	1877
110	Lord Westmorland's XI v. Burghley Park	1877
126*	Married v. Single (Clifton)	1880
152	Bedminster v. Lansdown	1880
168*	Bristol Medicals v. Thornbury	1880
140	Lansdown v. Clifton	1880
128	Thornbury v. Old Sneed Park ..	1880
196*	Thornbury v. Jas. Thorne's XI	1881
203	Bedminster v. St. George's	1881

Score.		Year.
109	Clifton v. Newport	1881
124	Bedminster v. St. George's	1881
144	Thornbury v. Baker, Baker & Co.	1882
126	Lansdown v. Western Wanderers	1882
130	Thornbury v. Bath Association	1882
177*	Thornbury v. Chepstow	1882
122*	United XI v. XXII of Market Bosworth	1882
111	Thornbury v. Lansdown	1883
142	Bedminster v. Swindon	1883
151*	Thornbury v. Newport	1883
111	Gloucestershire v. Twenty-four Colts	1884
131	Clifton v. Taunton	1884
136	Thornbury v. Chepstow	1884
107	East Somerset v. Cardiff	1884
166	Bedminster v. St. George's	1885
100*	O. G. Radcliffe's XI v. Cardiff	1885
182	Thornbury v. St. George's	1889
174	Thornbury v. St. George's	1891
204*	Thornbury v. Bath Association	1893
135	W. G. Grace's XI v. W. W. Read's XI	1893
129*	Gloucestershire v. South Africans	1894
101*	Gloucestershire v. XXII Colts	1895
108	Gloucestershire v. XXII Colts	1896
121	W. G. Grace's XI v. Dublin University	1897
146*	Gloucestershire v. XXII Colts	1898
175*	London County v. Worcestershire	1899
109	London County v. Croydon	1899
130	Crystal Palace v. Beckenham	1899
100*	London County v. Ealing	1899
103*	London County v. Sydenham	1899
110*	London County v. Gravesend	1900
151*	London County v. Wanderers	1900
116*	London County v. Northern Nomads	1900
100*	London County v. Oundle Rovers	1900
111	London County v. H.M.S. *Wildfire*	1901
114	Worcester Park Beagles v. London County	1901
100	London County v. H.M.S. *Wildfire*	1901
188*	London County v. Wiltshire	1901
174	London County v. Croydon	1901
103*	London County v. Nineteen of Sydenham Park	1902
101*	London County v. Anerley	1902
137*	London County v. Heathfield	1902
127	London County v. Wiltshire	1902
119	London County v. Bradford	1903
104*	London County v. Belgrave	1903
103*	London County v. Clapham	1904
104*	London County v. Clare College Rovers	1905
120	London County v. Kensington	1906
147	London County v. Beddington	1906
140	London County v. Forest Hill	1907
102*	London County v. Cyphers	1907
118	London County v. Catford	1907
110*	London County v. Whitgift Wanderers	1908

Signifies not out.

NOTE.— In the match v. XXII of Stockport, in 1876, W. G., in his second innings, was bowled by Randon (F.) for 13, but later was asked to go in again with the result that he ran up a score of 133.

MEMORABILIA OF MINOR CRICKET.

1857.—His first match—for West Gloucestershire v. Bedminster, at Rodway Hill, July 19. He scored three not out.

1860.—Makes his first half-century—51 for West Gloucestershire v. Clifton, on Durdham Down, July 19, 20.

1862.—Aged 14. Plays for Gentlemen of Gloucestershire v. Gentlemen of Devon, at Teignbridge, and scores 18 and one.

1864.—Aged 15, makes 170 and 56 not out for South Wales v. Gentlemen of Sussex, at Brighton. He also obtained two wickets.

Made his first appearance at Lord's—for South Wales v. M.C.C. and Ground—and scored 50 and two, and took a wicket.

1868.—At the athletic sports at the Oval, during the visit of the Australian Aboriginals, W. G., in three successive attempts, threw the cricket ball 116, 117, and 118yd., and also threw it 109yd. one way and back 105. He once threw it 122yd. at Eastbourne.

W. G. and G. F. Grace, playing for Clifton v. Gloucester, at Bristol, obtained all 20 wickets of their opponents, W. G. taking nine of them.

1870.—In a single-wicket match—for V of the United North E.E. v. XI of Northampton-shire, at Northampton—W. G. made only three singles in a score of 63.

1872.—Visited the United States and Canada as a member of Mr. R. A. FitzGerald's team.

1873.—In a practice-match, for United South E.E. v. Eighteen of Edinburgh, at Raeburn Place, W. G. made a hit of 140 yards.

For United South E.E. v. Seventeen of Coventry (with Greenwood, L.) he took 25 wickets (14 and 11) and made five catches off other bowling, thus claiming 30 wickets in a match.

1873–74.—Captained a team in Australia, which played 15 matches (all against odds), winning 10, losing three, and drawing two.

1874.—In match, W. G. Grace's XI v. F. Townsend's XI, at Cheltenham, the arrangement was that W. G. should use a broomstick, each of the other players being allowed a bat. Even so handicapped, he made the second largest score (35) in the game.

1875.—Col. (then Capt.) J. Fellowes, R. E., playing at Gravesend for Eighteen of North Kent v. United South E.E., made 20 runs (three sixes—all over the pavilion—and a two) off a four-ball over from W. G.

1876.—For United South E.E. v. XXII of Grimsby, at Grimsby, he scored 400 not out, batting 13½ hours against 15 bowlers, hitting four sixes and 21 fours, and offering no chance until 350. This is the record score against odds. *Scores and Biographies* (xiv–cvii): "Of this match it was subsequently stated that Mr. W. G. Grace's score was 399, not 400, one being added to make the enormous total."

1879.—For Kingsclere v. Newbury, at Kingsclere, he took all 10 wickets in an innings.

1880.—In the 13 a-side match between Thornbury and Lansdown, at Alveston, W. G. took 17 wickets for the former and E. M. Grace six: the other wicket was run out.

1881.—For Thornbury v. Bath Association, at Bath, W. G. (eight) and E. M. (10) again obtained all the wickets between them: one man was absent and another run out.

1889.—W. G. and E. M. Grace, playing for Thornbury, dismissed Wotton-under-Edge for 35 and eight, each taking 10 wickets.

1899.—Founded the London County C.C., of which he was secretary, manager and captain. The club's first match was v. Wiltshire, at Swindon, May 5, 6. W. G. scored 1,092 runs for the club that season with an average of 84.

1900.—In all matches for London County W. G. made 2,273 runs (average 55.43) and took 133 wickets.

1901.—In all matches for London County, W. G. made 2,457 runs (average 58.50) and took 142 wickets.

1902.—In minor games for London County, W. G. made 1,200 runs (average 100) and took 100 wickets (average 13.52).

1904.—For London County v. Oundle Rovers, at Crystal Palace, he went in last man and made 80* of the 118 added for the wicket with G. R. Ryan (29).

In all matches for London County C.C. he scored 1,405 runs (average 31.22) and took 121 wickets (average 18.03)

1905.—When playing for Strutt Cavell's XI v. Eighteen of Twickenham, at Twickenham, W. G. was hit for 28 off six consecutive balls by R. Hiscock.

In all kinds of cricket this year, W. G. made 1,038 runs (average 32.43) and took 105 wickets (average 16.97)

1906.—In all kinds of cricket he made 1,096 runs and took 65 wickets.

1907.—In all kinds of cricket he scored 1,051 runs (average 47) and took 104 wickets (average 13).

1908.—His last hundred—110* for London County v. Whitgift Wanderers, at the Crystal Palace, June 26. He made 26 hundreds in Minor Matches for London County, 1899–1908, between the ages of 51 and 60.

In all matches this season he made 724 runs (average 33) and took 116 wickets (average 13). On August 19 he injured his foot at Lord's, and played only once or twice afterwards: otherwise he would undoubtedly have made over 1,000 runs as usual.

This was the last season of the London County C.C.

1913.—His last match for M.C.C.—v. Old Charlton, at Charlton, June 26. He scored 18.

It is estimated that during his career W. G. made about 80,000 runs and took about 7,000 wickets.

Signifies not out.

GRACE, William Gilbert, Jun., eldest son of the greatest cricketer, died suddenly at three o'clock on the morning of March 2, 1905, at East Cowes, after an operation for appendicitis. As he was born on July 6, 1874, he was under 31 years of age at the time of his death. He was in the Clifton College XI in 1891–92–93, being captain in his second year, and assisted Cambridge against Oxford in 1895 and 1896. His first pronounced success was gained in the Reigate Festival of 1894, when he played a not out innings of 148 for his father's XI against Mr. W. W. Read's XI. At Cambridge on June 1, 1896, he and G. S. Graham-Smith made 337 together for the first wicket of Pembroke College v. Caius College, and at the Crystal Palace on September 16, 1901, he and W. L. Murdoch (who carried out his bat for 200) put up 355 for the first wicket of London County v. Erratics. In these matches his scores were respectively 213 and 150. As a bowler he frequently did well, and for London County v. Bromley Town, at the Crystal Palace, on August 25, 1902, he obtained all 10 wickets in an innings. From 1897 until 1903 he was an assistant-master at Oundle, and during the last two years of his life he occupied a similar position at the Royal Naval College, Osborne. He was buried at Elmers End Road Cemetery on March 6.

GRAHAM, Harry, born at Carlton, Melbourne, November 29, 1870, died at Dunedin, New Zealand, February 7, 1911. Graham did many brilliant things as a batsman but scarcely gave himself a fair chance. Had he ordered his life more carefully he might have had a much longer and more successful career in first-class cricket. His natural powers were great. He did not play with quite a straight bat but he was a splendid hitter with any amount of dash and vigour. When he came to England for the first time in 1893 he was at his best, playing the innings of his life against England at Lord's. No one who saw the match will forget the way in which he and Gregory knocked off the England bowling after Australia had lost five wickets for 75. Graham was very successful all through the tour and headed the averages in all matches, just beating Lyons. However, he was not the same man in 1896 and had to be left out of many matches. He recovered his batting form at home and for a couple of seasons was almost as good as ever, playing two innings of over a hundred for Victoria against South Australia. Taking his career as a whole he was a player of immense possibilities only half fulfilled.

Graham's performances in first-class cricket:

	Inns.	Times not out.	Most in an inns.	Total runs.	Average.
In Australia, 1892–93	7	2	86*	262	52.40
In England, 1893	53	3	219	1,435	28.70
In America, 1893	4	0	25	30	7.50

In Australia, 1893–94 to 1895–96	25	0	105	691	27.64
In England, 1896	32	2	96	547	18.23
In America, 1896	3	0	5	5	1.66
In Australia, 1896–97 to 1899–1900	38	1	124	1,081	29.21
In New Zealand, 1899–1900	6	0	169	373	62.16
In Australia, 1900–01 to 1902–03	23	1	120	842	38.27
In New Zealand, 1903–04 to 1906–07	29	0	86	688	23.72
Total	220	9	219	5,954	28.21

Signifies not out.

Graham's 100s in important cricket:—

Runs.		Year.
219	Eighth Australian Team v. Derbyshire, at Derby	1893
169	Melbourne C.C. Team v. Canterbury, at Christchurch	1899–1900
124	Victoria v. New South Wales, at Sydney	1898–99
120	Victoria v. South Australia, at Melbourne	1900–01
118	Victoria v. South Australia, at Adelaide	1899–1900
107	Australia v. England, at Lord's	1893
105	Australia v. England, at Sydney	1894–95
103	Victoria v. New South Wales, at Melbourne	1895–96
101	Victoria v. Queensland, at Brisbane	1902–03

GRAINGER, George, died in hospital at Chesterfield on August 17, 1977, in his 90th year, having been born on November 11, 1887, at Morton. A left hand batsman and bowler, he played for Derbyshire in 1909, 1910 and 1921 in a total of five matches.

GRANT, Edward A., who died in January, 1953, aged 78, played for Wiltshire as a spin bowler and made two appearances for Somerset in 1899. He was born on June 16, 1874.

GRANT, George Copeland ("Jackie"), who died in hospital in Cambridge on October 26, 1978, aged 71, first captained West Indies when they sent a side to Australia for the first time in 1930–31 and achieved an historical triumph, winning the last Test by 30 runs on a rain-affected wicket. At Cambridge, he played for the University against Oxford at Association football in 1928–29–30 and at cricket in 1929 and 1930. He proved himself to be a sound tactician and an admirable captain, probably at this best when R. E. S. Wyatt took a weakened M.C.C. side to the West Indies in the winter of 1934–35 and their weaknesses were exposed by Grant's men, who won the series.

GRANT, Rolph Stewart, who died on October 18, 1977, aged 67, was the younger of two brothers, both Cambridge Blues, to captain the West Indies. Not a distinguished player at Cambridge, he owed his selection for one of the last places in 1933 largely to his superb fielding: he was a soccer Blue and an Amateur International goalkeeper. But he was also a useful bat in the lower half of the order and a useful bowler of slow off-spin round the wicket and fully justified his place. He dismissed three of the first four Oxford batsmen for 44 runs and made an astonishing catch at short leg to get rid of F. G. H. Chalk, a very dangerous player. Returning to the West Indies, he played in the Tests against the M.C.C. side in 1934–35 and in the fourth made his highest Test score, 77. Appointed captain of the West Indian side in England in 1939 and faced by mid-June with the awkward problem of finding an opening partner for J. B. Stollmeyer, he solved it with characteristic courage by going in first himself and continued to do so until the end of the tour with very fair success. Against Lancashire he made 95, his highest score of the season, but certainly his best innings was in the Old Trafford Test when, opening after England had declared at 164 for seven on a wicket which was not easy and likely to become rapidly more difficult, he scored 47 out of 56 in 38 minutes including three sixes off Goddard. When he was out the whole crowd rose to him, a tribute seldom paid to so short an innings. Earlier that day he had taken the wickets of Hutton and Hardstaff for 16 runs. Though he was obviously short of the experience which most Test captains have, he proved himself in other ways an admirable leader.

GRANVILLE, Richard St. Leger, who died on August 8, 1972, aged 65, was not in the XI while at Eton. He took part in one match for Warwickshire in 1934.

GRAVES, Nelson Zwingluis, Jun., born in Philadelphia, August 10, 1880, died March 31, 1918, at Germantown, aged 37. He was educated at Pennsylvania University and visited England with the Philadelphian teams, in 1903 and 1908. For the former team he made hundreds against Lancashire and Scotland, hitting so fiercely, in the Lancashire match, as to score 60 out of 70 in half-an-hour. In 1898 he hit up 128 for United States v. Canada. He scored well, too, for Germantown C.C.

GRAY, Cyril Douglas, who died on February 20, 1969, aged 73, did not find a place in the XI while at Harrow, but he played as an amateur in 14 Championship matches for Middlesex between 1925 and 1927. A strong driver whose style was not altogether ortho-dox, he began his county career with an innings of 79 against Worcestershire at Worcester. His highest score was 81 off the Warwickshire bowling at Lord's in 1927, he and E. H. Hendren (156) adding 214 runs in less than two hours. He was a fine golfer and played for England on a number of oc-casions.

GRAY, Laurence Herbert, died at Langdon Hills, Essex, after a long illness, on January 3, 1983, aged 67. Born at Tottenham, he was that comparative rarity, a Middlesex crick-eter with a birth qualification. After a few matches in 1934 and 1935, he began to make his mark as a fast bowler in 1936, when he and Jim Smith bowled out Nottinghamshire at Lord's in the second innings for 41, his own share being four for 26. From then until 1949 he was a regular and valuable member of a side which depended largely on slow spin, the other quick bowlers being Jim Smith (until the War), Edrich and G. O. Allen, when available. It was a glorious period in the county's history: in those eight seasons they won the Championship twice, were second five times and third once. To this impressive record Gray made a con-siderable contribution, though after doing much good work in 1937 and 1938 he fell off sadly in 1939. At this period he was apt to lose his length and bowl short, faults which were less evident after the War. In 1946 he took for Middlesex 95 wickets at 19.06 and in all matches, for the only time, exceeded 100 wickets, while in 1947 his record for the county was 92 at 22.46. He continued to bowl with some success for two more years, but, losing a regular place in 1950, played his last match in 1951. An arthritic hip shortened his career. In 1946, when he took 11 for 34

against Hampshire at Lord's, he appeared for the Players at Lord's and in a Test trial. It will be seen that the War robbed him of six seasons when he might reasonably have expected to be in his prime. Even so it may be doubted whether he would ever have been more than a good county bowler. He had not quite the physique or the speed to attain greatness. In all first-class matches he took 637 wickets for 25.14. A batting average for his career of 7.38, with a highest score of 35 not out, suggests no great ability in that line, but he played at least one memorable innings. Against Essex at Lord's in 1939 he helped Denis Compton to put on 83 in three-quarters of an hour for the last wicket, his own share being one not out. To Compton he later owed a great debt. As the senior of the two, Compton was due for his benefit in 1948, but waived his claim in Gray's favour. Gray's benefit raised over £6,000, a sum which, low though it may seem by modern standards, had then only once been ex-ceeded. From 1953 to 1970 Gray was a first-class umpire, standing in four Test matches.

GREATOREX, The Rev. Canon Theophilus, of the Harrow XIs of 1882 and 1883, died suddenly in London on July 27, 1933. In 1883 he was awarded the Ebrington Cup for his batting. He appeared in a couple of matches for Middlesex the same year, and played for Cambridge University in 1884, 1885 and 1886, but did not get his Blue. His highest score in County Cricket was 44 not out in his first season for Middlesex, for whom he made isolated appearances in 1892 and play-ed for the county's Second XI as far on as 1896. He had a fine, free style of batting, but whilst practising at Cambridge early in 1884 broke a finger and this greatly interfered with his play. After his cricketing days he became Rector of Guildford, Western Australia. He was born in London on December 14, 1864.

GREEN, Charles Ernest, died at his home near Epping on December 4, 1916. To the present generation Mr. Green was chiefly known as the leading spirit of the Essex County Club, but lovers of cricket whose memories go back to the '70s will remember him as one of the most brilliant batsmen of his day. He learnt the game at Uppingham, being, indeed, one of the first men who earned for that school any cricket reputation. In later years he rendered the school an incalculable service by inducing the late H. H. Stephenson to take up the duties of cricket coach. That step, as everyone knows, produced astounding results, Uppingham during Stephenson's reign turning out a succession of remarkable players. On leaving Uppingham Mr. Green went to Cambridge, and was in the University XI from 1865 to 1868 inclusive, captaining the team in his last year. Of the four matches in which he took part against Oxford, Cambridge lost those of 1865 and 1866, but won the other two. It was Mr. Green's good fortune to have an exceptionally strong side under his command in 1868, the XI including W. B. Money, H. A. Richardson, J. W. Dale, C. A. Absolom, George Savile, J. M. Richardson (afterwards so famous as a gentleman rider), and W. S. O. Warner. Of those seven players only Money and H. A. Richardson are now alive. Cambridge gained an easy victory over Oxford by 168 runs, Mr. Green, with 44 and 59, heading the score in each innings. Three years later, in the Gentlemen and Players match at the Oval, he played the innings of his life. His score was only 57 not out, but the way in which he won the game against time will never be forgotten by those who were so fortunate as to be present. He made his last 27 runs in seven hits, and at the finish he had just three minutes to spare. As different statements have appeared in print it is only right to state that the Gentlemen in that memorable match were left to get 144 runs in an hour and three-quarters. Their victory has been made to appear even more remarkable than it was.

At Lord's, in 1870, for the M.C.C. and Ground against Yorkshire, Mr. Green played a great innings of a different kind, he and W. G. Grace standing up to Freeman and Emmett on a wicket so rough as to be quite unfit for a first-class match. Mr. Grace made 66 and Mr. Green 51, but they paid a high price for their runs, being covered with bruises from ankle to shoulder. The late Mr. Henry Perkins said, after the lapse of over 30 years, that the batting that day was the pluckiest he ever saw, and Freeman and Emmett used, in talking about the match, to wonder how the batsmen escaped serious injury, so dangerously did the ball fly about on the rough ground. Mr. Green played in his young days for both Middlesex and Sussex, and became identified with Essex long before that county took a prominent place in the cricket world. He was fond of recalling the fact that two Cambridge cricketers who threw in their fortunes with Essex —A. P. Lucas and the late C. D. Buxton— followed him at the University at intervals of 10 and 20 years respectively, and, like himself, played four times against Oxford. Lucas was in the Cambridge XI from 1875 to 1878,

and Buxton from 1885 to 1888. Mr. Green was a partner in the firm of F. Green and Co. and a director of the Orient Steamship Company. He was President of the M.C.C. in 1905. Master for a long time of the Essex Hunt, he was even more devoted to hunting than to cricket, being out four days a week every season for years.—S.H.P.

GREEN, John Pugh, who died in Philadelphia, his native place, on March 9, 1924, aged 85, will be remembered as the author of *Tour of the Gentlemen of Philadelphia in Great Britain, 1884. By One of the Committee.* He played for the Merion C.C. and was for some years President of the Pennsylvania Railroad Company. He was also one of the founders and for a long time President of the Belmont C.C., whose history he has written.

GREEN, Col. Leonard, M.C., who died on March 2, 1963, aged 73, captained Lancashire when they won the County Championship in the three years from 1926 to 1928. Though not himself a brilliant cricketer, he possessed the strength of will and good-natured tact to weld a team of individual talent into a title-winning combination. A useful batsman, besides a reliable fieldsman, he scored 3,575 runs for his county between 1922 and 1935, average 24.65. His highest innings, 110 not out against Gloucestershire at Gloucester in 1923, played a big part in a win for Lancashire by 75 runs after being 26 in arrear on first innings.

He took part in the game with Essex at Colchester in 1928 when Lancashire, needing four runs to win at the close of the second day, had to wait till the third morning to essay the task. That match led to the extra half hour being allowed on the second day if a result could thereby be achieved. It was in this fixture that the late J. W. H. T. Douglas, captaining Essex, flung up his bat, lost his grip on it and fell headlong when a short-pitched delivery from E. A. McDonald rose head-high. Anxious fieldsmen, fearing that he had been hurt, clustered around the batsman, but beat a hasty retreat as Douglas expressed his views in loud and virulent terms. When at length he arose and resumed his stance at the crease, he was informed that he was out, for the ball had struck the handle of the bat and glanced into the hands of H. Makepeace at short-leg!

After leaving Bromsgrove School, Green joined the East Lancashire Regiment, earning the Military Cross during the First World War. For many years a member of the Lancashire Committee, he became President in 1951 and 1952. He also represented the county at hockey and Rugby football.

GREEN, Brigadier Michael Arthur, who died on December 28, 1971, aged 80, possessed a remarkable sporting record. He played for Gloucestershire, Essex, the Army, and M.C.C.; Association football for the Army, Casuals and Surrey; Rugby football for the Army, Harlequins and Surrey and racquets and squash for the Army. He was secretary of Worcestershire from 1945 to 1951, manager of the M.C.C. team in South Africa in 1948–49 and joint manager with J. H. Nash, of Yorkshire, of the M.C.C. team in Australia in 1950–51. His services on these tours promoted M.C.C. to elect him a life member. He saw service in both World Wars.

GREENE, Alan Douglas, born at Brandeston, Suffolk, on April 15, 1856, died at Tunbridge Wells on June 18, 1928. A steady bat and a good field at mid-off and long-leg, he was in the Clifton XI in 1874 and three following years. In 1876 he won the average bat with 59.28. For Oxford he gained his Blue as a Freshman, and in his fourth season, 1880, captained the team. In his four inter-University matches A. D. Greene made only 84 runs, but his 35 not out in 1878 was the highest effort for his side, and a year later, when he scored 20, he alone reached double-figures during the innings. His largest score in first-class cricket was 93 not out in Oxford's match with Middlesex at Lord's in 1877. He assisted Gloucestershire many times between 1876 and 1886, appeared occasionally for Somerset, and also represented the former county at Rugby football.

GREENFIELD, The Rev. Frederick Francis John, born at Gornekpoor (Bengal), May 10, 1850, died in Cape Colony in November, 1900. *Scores and Biographies* (xiii–156), sums him up as follows: "Is a very free hitter, bowls slow round-armed, and in the field is generally point." He was educated at Hurstpierpoint School, in Sussex, and whilst there, made 216 not out against Bolney, on May 20, 1871, going in first and carrying his bat through the innings. He represented Cambridge against Oxford in 1874, 1875 and 1876, being captain in the last-mentioned year. For a period of 11 years, commencing in 1873, his name is found in the Sussex XI. He twice exceeded the hundred for Sussex, making 126 v. Gloucestershire, at Clifton, in 1876, and 107 v. Kent, at Gravesend, in 1882. In 1883 he scored 1,210 runs for the Gravesend Club, his highest

innings being 203 not out, against the South Essex Wanderers, on August 28, and 189 against the West Kent Wanderers, on June 16.

GREENHILL, Major Hubert McLean (Dorsetshire Regiment.), born on September 18, 1881, was found dead on January 22, 1926, in a small wood at Bockhampton, near Dorchester. He was a hard-hitting batsman with a long reach and a good style, and a useful left-handed medium-paced bowler. Educated at Wimborne Grammar School and Sherborne, he was in the latter XI in 1898 and two following years, having in his third season a batting average of 20.14, besides heading the bowling with 29 wickets for 11.48 runs each. For many years, commencing in 1900, he played for Dorset, and he also appeared for Hampshire in 1901, besides taking part in much Regimental cricket.

GREENING, Tom, who died at Leamington on March 25, 1956, aged 74, played cricket for over 50 years. A member of the Coventry and North Warwickshire C.C. for many years, he took 100 wickets season after season with left-arm swing or spin bowling. On one occasion he obtained all 10 wickets against a Leicestershire XI. He appeared a few times for Warwickshire in the early 1920s, but declined a professional engagement with the county.

GREENWOOD, Frank E., who died on July 30, 1963, aged 59, suffered a cerebral haemorrhage while watching the fourth Test match between England and the West Indies on television at the Huddersfield Conservative Club. Educated at Oundle, Greenwood played as an amateur for Yorkshire from 1929 to 1932, when he gave up the game because of business commitments. In all first-class cricket, he scored 1,558 runs average 26.86, his highest innings being 104 against Glamorgan at Hull in 1929. He led the side to the County Championship in 1931, when he was involved in the first of the "freak" declarations of that season. After two blank days through rain at Sheffield, he and B. H. Lyon, the Gloucestershire captain, each agreed to declare his first innings after four byes had been given away, so making it possible for a definite result to be reached.

GREENWOOD, Henry William, who died in hospital in Horsham on March 24, 1979, aged 74, was a batsman who just failed to make the grade in first-class cricket. A short, stocky man, he was not a natural stroke-player, but had limitless patience and a strong defence and could cut well. After playing a few games for Sussex in 1933 and 1934, he helped John Langridge to put on 101 for their first wicket against Oxford in 1935, going on to make 77, and a few weeks later the two shared in an opening partnership of 305 in four hours against Essex at Hove, to which he contributed 115. For the county that season he scored 404 runs with an average of 36.72, but even so failed to get a regular place and next year did not play in a single Championship match. Perhaps his fielding did not help as, though an adequate slip, he was a slow mover elsewhere. Moreover, the Sussex batting was strong at the time. So he left the county and on his own initiative qualified for Northamptonshire, then the weakest side in the competition, playing meanwhile first for Forfarshire and then for Stoke. In 1938 he was available for Northamptonshire only in mid-week, but did fairly well, scoring 573 runs with an average of 26.04. However, in 1939 he was disappointing, though he made his highest score for the county, 94 against Warwickshire at Edgbaston. After serving in the R.A.F. in the War, he returned to the side in 1946, but had a poor season, not helped by being required to act as wicket-keeper in the absence of anyone better. This concluded his first-class career.

GREENWOOD, Leonard Warwick, who died at Astley, near Stourport-on-Severn, on July 20, 1982, aged 83, was a good opening bat in the Winchester XI in 1916 and 1917. In 1917 he played a fine innings of 141 against Harrow. In 1919 he played for Oxford against the Gentlemen of England (the first first-class match to be played after the Great War), but failed to get a Blue. However, he represented Somerset against the University in 1920 and between 1923 and 1926 appeared three times for Worcestershire without much success. For many years he was a master at Abberley Hall, near Worcester.

GREENWOOD, Luke, one of the last of the famous Yorkshire players of the '60s, died on November 2, 1909. Born on July 13, 1834, he was in his 76th year. He played his first match for Yorkshire in 1861 and his last in 1875. At the beginning of his career he shared the bowling with Slinn, Hodgson, and George Atkinson, and it was afterwards his good fortune to be in the XI with George Freeman and Tom Emmett. Greenwood, himself, was a right-handed bowler—medium pace to fast—and very straight. By far his best season for Yorkshire with the ball

was 1867, when he took 33 wickets for less than 10 runs each. In that year at the Oval, bowling unchanged, he and Freeman got rid of Surrey for totals of 92 and 62, Yorkshire winning the match in a single innings. Greenwood was more an all-round man than a bowler pure and simple. For the Players against the Gentlemen at the Oval, in 1866, he played an innings of 66, and in 1870, at Lord's, he helped to win a memorable match for Yorkshire against the M.C.C., scoring 44 in the last innings. The wicket on that occasion was very dangerous, and even now, after the lapse of over 40 years, the way in which W. G. Grace and C. E. Green played the tremendously fast bowling of Freeman and Emmett is vividly remembered by old cricketers. After his active days as a player were over, Luke Greenwood did a lot of umpiring. He was retained by some of the early Australian XIs, and stood with Bob Thoms in the great match with England at the Oval in 1882. Greenwood and the late John Thewlis were the first of the Lascelles Hall players who earned more than a local reputation.

GREGORY, Arthur H., born at Sydney on July 7, 1861, died at Chatswood, Sydney, on August 17, 1929, aged 68. Returning from the funeral of S. E. Gregory he fell from a tramcar, and blood-poisoning supervened as a result of injuries to arm. He was a member of the most famous of Australian cricket families, and, although perhaps better known as a graceful and well-informed writer on the game, was a sound batsman, a good field and a fair leg-break bowler and had himself appeared for New South Wales. He was younger brother of E. J., D. W., and C. S. Gregory, and uncle of S. E., C. W. and J. M.

GREGORY, Charles S., died at Sydney on April 5, 1935, aged 88 years. One of the famous Gregory family of seven brothers, five of whom represented New South Wales, he played for his State against Victoria in 1871 and 1872 and figured with his brothers, David and Edward, in the historic single wicket match on the Albert Ground, Sydney, in April, 1871, when the three brothers defeated the Victorians, T. W. Wills, Sam Cosstick and John Conway, by five runs.

Father of J. M. Gregory, Australia's fast bowler.

GREGORY, Charles W., died at St. Vincent's Hospital, Darlinghurst, New South Wales, on November 14, 1910. Born on September 13, 1878, he was only in his 33rd year. At one time it was confidently expected that he would rival his brother, Sydney Gregory, and make a great name for himself, but, though he did many brilliant things, he proved, on the whole, a disappointment and was never thought quite good enough to be picked for a tour in England. From some cause or other he generally failed on big occasions. One performance will cause his name to be remembered. For New South Wales against Queensland at Brisbane in November, 1906, he scored 383—the second highest innings on record in a first-class match and the highest in Australia.

GREGORY, David William, who died at Sydney on August 4, 1919, will be for ever famous in cricket history as the captain in 1878 of the first Australian team that came to England. The victory of that team in one afternoon at Lord's over a very powerful M.C.C. XI marked the beginning of a new era. English cricketers realised that day that their supremacy was no longer unchallenged. It was a rude shock, but the game received a tremendous impetus. One of a family of cricketers, David Gregory in 1878 was only 33, though with his full beard he looked considerably older. He was born at Woolloongong, New South Wales, on April 15, 1845. Except as a tactful leader, who readily accommodated himself to strange conditions, Gregory did not earn much distinc-

tion on English cricket grounds. It was a dreadfully wet summer, and no doubt the slow, treacherous wickets were too much for him. His best score in the 11-a-side matches was 57 against the Players at Prince's towards the end of the tour, and his average only 11. Like many Australian batsmen in those early days he had no grace of style to recommend him, but his defence was stubborn and he lacked neither pluck nor patience. When for once—against Middlesex at Lord's—he found himself on a good wicket he got on very well, making 42 in each innings. Both before and after his visit to England Gregory was a regular member of the New South Wales XI. In the Inter-Colonial matches with Victoria he scored 445 runs in 28 innings, three times not out, with an average of 17.80. His best innings were 85 at Melbourne and 74 at Sydney. In his time, be it remembered, Australian wickets did not approach their present perfection. It was Gregory's privilege to play for Australia at Melbourne in March, 1877, when Australia beat James Lillywhite's team—the first victory over England on even terms—and also in the return match, when the Englishmen were successful. He had no share in the victory, but in the second match he scored one not out and 43. For some years he was hon. secretary of the New South Wales Cricket Association.— S.H.P.

Short Genealogical Table of the Gregory Family

Edward J. ("Ned") (B. 29/5/39; d. 14/4/99. N.S.W. & Australia.)	David Wm. ("Dave") (B. 15/4/45; d. 4/8/19. N.S.W. & Australia. Capt. of 1878 Team.)	Charles S. (B. 5/8/47. New South Wales.)	Arthur H. (B. 7/7/61. New South Wales. Cricket Writer.)
Sydney E. (B. 14/4/70. N.S.W. & Australia.)	Charles W. (B. 30/9/78; d. 14/11/10. New South Wales.)	J.M. (B. 14/8/95. Sydney Church of England Grammar School. Australian I.F. team 1919.)	Warwick (North Sydney C.C.)

The Gregory and Donnan families inter-married

GREGORY, E., who died at Sydney, New South Wales, on April 22, 1899, was the father of the famous Australian batsman, S.E. Gregory, and brother of David Gregory, who captained the first Australian XI in England in 1878. He was an excellent player in the early days of Australian cricket, and in the latter part of his life was custodian of the Association ground at Sydney.

GREGORY, J.C., who died in June, 1894, was in his day perhaps the most successful and industrious of local cricketers in and about London. In association with his old

friend, Mr. Charles Absolon, he took part in numberless matches in the '60s. In 1870 he was connected with the Surrey Club, acting on some occasions as captain of the XI. He had perhaps had too much cricket against inferior bowling to do himself justice in first-class company, but once at least he was seen to great advantage for Surrey, an innings of 70 that he played against Notts at Trent Bridge on August 25, 1870, contributing in no small degree to Surrey's victory by 53 runs. Mr. Gregory was a most punishing batsman in local matches and a very brilliant field. An unfortunate accident by which he injured a tendon in his leg compelled him to give up cricket while at the height of his powers.

JACK GREGORY, CRICKETER IN EXCELSIS
Born in Sydney, August 14, 1895
Died at Bega, N.S.W., August 7, 1973
By Sir Neville Cardus

Jack Morrison Gregory, of a famous Australian cricket family, had a comparatively brief Test match career, for although he played in 24 representative games, his skill and his power were as unpredictable as a thunderstorm or a nuclear explosion. He was known mainly as a fearsome right-arm fast bowler but, also, in Test matches he scored 1,146 runs, averaging 36.96 with two centuries. He batted left-handed and gloveless.

As a fast bowler, people of today who never saw him will get a fair idea of his presence and method if they have seen Wes Hall, the West Indian. Gregory, a giant of superb physique, ran some 20 yards to release the ball with a high step at gallop, then, at the moment of delivery, a huge leap, a great wave of energy breaking at the crest, and a follow-through nearly to the batsman's door-step.

He lacked the silent rhythmic motion over the earth of E.A. (Ted) McDonald, his colleague in destruction. Gregory bowled as though against a gale of wind. It was as though he *willed* himself to bowl fast, at the risk of muscular dislocation. Alas, he did suffer physical dislocation, at Brisbane, in November, 1928, putting an end to his active cricket when his age was 33.

My earliest vivid impression of his fast bowling was at the beginning of the first game of the England v. Australia rubber, at Trent Bridge, in 1921. The England XI had just returned from Australia after losing five Tests out of five (all played to a finish). Now, in 1921, England lost the first three encounters, taking long to recover from Gregory's onslaught at Trent Bridge.

He knocked out Ernest Tyldesley in the second innings with a bouncer which sped from cranium to stumps. Ernest's more famous brother J.T. had no sympathy; he bluntly told his brother, "Get to the off side of the ball whenever you hook, then, if you miss it, it passes harmlessly over the left shoulder." At Trent Bridge, that May morning in 1921, "Patsy" Hendren arrived with runs in plenty to his credit, largesse of runs in county matches. Gregory wrecked his wicket with an atom bomb of a breakback. Yes; it *was* a ball which came back at horrific

velocity, not achieved, of course, by finger-spin, but by action.

Gregory, like Tom Richardson, perhaps the greatest of all fast bowlers ever, flung the upper part of his body over the front left leg to the offside as the arm came over, the fingers sweeping under the ball. Herbert Strudwick once told me that in the first over or two he took from Richardson he moved to the offside to "take" the ball. It broke back, shaving the leg stump, and went for four byes. Gregory, at Trent Bridge, took six wickets for 58, in England's first innings of 112; next innings McDonald took five for 52. Only once, at Lord's, in 1921, did Gregory recapture the Trent Bridge explosive rapture.

In the South African summer of 1921–22 he renewed his batteries and regained combustion. Next, in Australia 1924–25, he was able to take 22 wickets in the Tests against England at 37.09 runs each. But the giant was already casting a shadow; in 1926, in England, his three Test wickets cost him 298 runs. He was not a subtle fast bowler, with the beautiful changes of pace, nuance and rhythmical deceptions of Lindwall or McDonald (at his best). But as an announcement of young dynamic physical power and gusto for life and fast bowling, there has seldom been seen on any cricket field a cricketer as exciting as Jack Gregory.

In 1921 certain English critics made too much ungenerous palaver about Gregory's "bouncers." These "bouncers," no doubt, were awesome but not let loose with the regularity of, say, a Hall, a Griffith, not to mention other names, some playing today. In fact, no less an acute a judge of the game as A.C. MacLaren declared, in 1921, that Gregory's bowling during the first deadly half hour at Trent Bridge was compact of half-volleys.

His baptism in English cricket was in 1919, with the Australian Imperial Forces team. He was already a menacing shattering fast bowler, but at Kennington Oval he was subjected to treatment such as he never afterwards had to suffer. Surrey faced a total of 436 and got into hopeless trouble. They wanted 287 to save the follow-on and five wickets went down for 26. Soon J.N. Crawford came in at number eight—a catastrophic moment—and he smote Goliath. He smote Gregory as any fast bowler has not often been smitten, except by Bradman and Dexter. Crawford actually drove a ball from Gregory, that immortal afternoon at Kennington Oval, into the pavilion, cracking and splintering his bat. When Rushby, the last man, went in Surrey still required 45 to save the follow-on. Crawford went on hitting magnificently and they added 80 in 35 minutes, Rushby's share being a modest two. In some two hours Crawford scored 144 not out having hit two sixes and 18 fours. And Gregory applauded him generously.

He was a generous and likeable Australian. He gave himself to cricket with enthusiasm and relish. He enjoyed himself and was the cause of enjoyment in others. At Johannesburg in 1921 Gregory scored a century in 70 minutes v. South Africa—the fastest hundred in the long history of Test cricket. He was a slip fielder of quite unfair reach and alacrity, a Wally Hammond in enlargement, so to say, though not as graceful, effortless, and terpsichorean. Gregory was young manhood in excelsis. All who ever saw him and met him will remember and cherish him.

J. M. GREGORY
Statistics by Stanley Conder

TEST CRICKET
Batting

	Tests	Inns.	Not Outs	Runs	Highest Inns.	100s	Average	Catches
v. England	21	30	3	941	100	1	34.85	30
v. South Africa	3	4	0	205	119	1	51.25	7
Totals	24	34	3	1,146	119	2	36.96	37

Bowling

	Tests	Balls	Maidens	Runs	Wickets	Average	5 wkts. in Inns.
v. England	21	4,887	109	2,364	70	33.77	3
v. South Africa	3	694	29	284	15	18.93	1
Totals	24	5,581	138	2,648	85	31.15	4

Batting in ALL First-Class Matches

	Innings	Not Outs	Runs	Highest Inns.	100s	Average
1919 (England)	36	4	942	115	1	29.43
1919–20 (South Africa)	11	0	410	86	0	37.27
1919–20 (Australia)	6	1	375	122	2	75.00
1920–21 (Australia)	18	4	844	130	2	60.28
1921 (England)	33	2	1,135	107	3	36.61
1921–22 (South Africa)	6	0	266	119	1	44.33
1921–22 (Australia)	4	0	11	6	0	2.75
1924–25 (Australia)	14	1	261	45	0	20.07
1925–26 (Australia)	7	0	254	100	1	36.28
1926 (England)	30	6	843	130*	2	35.12
1926–27 (Australia)	1	0	44	44	0	44.00
1927–28 (Australia)	5	0	231	152	1	46.20
1928–29 (Australia)	2	0	45	38	0	22.50
Totals	173	18	5,661	152	13	36.52

Bowling in ALL First-Class Matches

	Runs	Wickets	Average	5 wkts. in Inns.
1919 (England)	2,383	131	18.19	10
1919–20 (South Africa)	613	47	13.04	5
1919–20 (Australia)	283	19	14.89	2
1920–21 (Australia)	962	43	22.37	2
1921 (England)	1,924	116	16.58	8
1921–22 (South Africa)	445	30	14.83	3
1921–22 (Australia)	252	11	22.90	1
1924–25 (Australia)	1,132	33	34.30	2

1925–26 (Australia)	678	18	37.66	0
1926 (England)	1,158	36	32.16	0
1926–27 (Australia)	99	3	33.00	0
1927–28 (Australia)	318	12	26.50	0
1928–29 (Australia)	332	5	66.40	0
Totals	10,579	504	20.99	33

GREGORY, Robert James, who died suddenly on October 6, 1973, aged 71, was a valuable all-round cricketer while a professional for Surrey from 1925 to 1947. An attractive batsman, he scored 19,495 runs at an average of 34.32, with leg-break bowling took 437 wickets and held 281 catches. In addition, he had few equals in his day as a deep fieldsman. He reached 1,000 runs in nine seasons. Of his 39 centuries, the highest was 243 against Somerset at the Oval in 1938.

As the playing career of Sir John Hobbs neared its end, "Bob" Gregory often opened the county innings in his place and in 1934 he scored 2,379 runs, including eight hundreds, average 51.71, following with 2,166 (seven centuries), average 46.08, in 1937. Popular with players and spectators alike, Gregory went to India with D. R. Jardine's M.C.C. team in 1933–34, and though he did not gain a place in the side for any of the three Test matches, he hit 148 against Bombay Presidency. After leaving Surrey, he became secretary of Watney Mann's Sports Club, a position he filled till his death.

GREGORY, Sergt.-Observer Ross G. R.A.A.F., who stood out prominently among Australian batsmen during three seasons before the War, died when on air operations as announced on June 24, 1942. Born on February 26, 1916, Ross Gregory became one of the youngest cricketers to play in a Test, sharing in recent years with A. A. Jackson, S. J. McCabe and D. G. Bradman the distinction of playing for Australia before coming of age; but Clem Hill still holds the record of appearing in a Test for Australia in his youth—19 years three months—against England at Lord's in June, 1896. The untimely end of Ross Gregory removed a batsman showing promise of a long career for Australia. After doing brilliant things as a boy, he was chosen for Victoria when still at school. Continuing to improve, he established himself in his State XI and against G. O. Allen's 1936–37 M.C.C. team he made 128 for Victoria, his stand with I. Lee for 262 being a fourth wicket record against an England team. In State matches that season he averaged over 39, with 85 against South Australia his best

score, and he helped Victoria carry off the Sheffield Shield. So it was no surprise that during that season he rose to Test match fame, playing in the last two engagements against England with marked success. He scored 23 and 50 (run out) at Adelaide, where Australia won by 148 runs, and 80 in the deciding encounter at Melbourne, where victory by an innings and 200 runs brought success in the rubber for Don Bradman's side. Only Bradman and S. J. McCabe recorded higher averages in that series of Tests, and Ross Gregory clearly possessed strong claims for a place in the team that came to England in 1938, but for some reason he was passed over.

In 1938–39 he gave further evidence of consistency by averaging 44.72, with top score 77, for Victoria. That finished his cricket career; he joined up for the War directly on the declaration of hostilities, and his Air Force training in England took place during the next winter, so he never played in this country. Below medium height, Ross Gregory used his strong arms in brilliant front-of-the-wicket forcing strokes and pulled in confident style. His cut also earned praise, and quick footwork enabled him to defend with high skill. A slow leg-break bowler, deceptive in flight and varied pace, Ross Gregory took five wickets for 69 runs for Victoria against the M.C.C. team captained by E. R. T. Holmes, which toured Australia and New Zealand in 1935–36. With limited opportunities for taking part in the attack, he failed to maintain that form with the ball, but sure hands made him valuable in the field.

GREGORY, Sydney Edward, born on the site of the present cricket ground at Sydney, on April 14, 1870, died at Randwick, Sydney, on August 1, 1929, aged 59. It is given to few men to enjoy such a long and successful career in international cricket as that which fell to his lot, but he had cricket in his blood, for what the Graces and the Walkers were to the game in England, the Gregory family, it could be urged, was to that in Australia. Twelve years after his Uncle Dave had come to England, as captain of the pioneer side of 1878, S. E. Gregory paid his first visit here as a member of the 1890 team under W. L. Murdoch, and he was chosen for every side up to and including that of 1912. On his first two visits here he did not quite realise expectations as a batsman—he completed his 20th year on his way here in 1890—but he jumped to the top in the Australian season of 1894–95, and when in England in 1896 he batted brilliantly, scoring over 1,400 runs in all matches and coming out at the head of the averages. Altogether he played in 52 Test matches for Australia, a larger number than any other Australian cricketer. In the course of these he made four three-figure scores and obtained 2,193 runs with an average of 25.80. He captained the Australian team of 1912—the year of the Triangular Tournament—but had a somewhat thankless task in filling that office. Dissatisfied with the financial terms offered, several of the leading Australian cricketers refused to make the trip and the side, as finally constituted, included, in the regrettable circumstances, several players who had little claim to figure as representatives of the best in Australian cricket. He himself scored over 1,000 runs but the team, although beating South Africa twice, had only a moderate record.

Pronounced and numerous as were his triumphs in batting, Sydney Gregory will probably be remembered more for what he accomplished as a fieldsman for, while several men have equalled and some have beaten his achievements as a run-getter, the cricket field has seen no more brilliant cover-point. Clever in anticipation and quick to move, he got to and stopped the hardest of hits, gathered the ball cleanly and returned it with deadly accuracy. His work, indeed, was always an inspiration to his colleagues and a joy to the spectators. Small of stature—he was little more than 5ft. in height—Gregory overcame this disadvantage in a batsman by splendid footwork. He possessed a very finished style, strong wrists and a keen eye. Particularly attractive in his strokes on the offside, he also, thanks to his quickness of movement, used to take balls off the middle stump with remarkable facility. The latter stroke, no doubt, cost him his wicket on many occasions but it brought him a lot of runs and, when successful, had a demoralising effect upon the bowler. He could stonewall when the situation called for those methods but his natural tendency was always to attack and, even when the ball turned a lot, his dashing game often knocked a bowler off his length. In short his cricket, both as batsman and fieldsman, suggested the bright

and happy temperament which Sydney Gregory possessed in such full measure.

On the occasion when he made 201 against A. E. Stoddart's team, Australia put together a total of 586, England scoring 325, and, when they followed on, 437. Australia were thus left with 177 to get to win, and at the drawing of stumps on the fifth day had obtained 113 of these for the loss of only two wickets. The match was as good as over, but a drenching downpour of rain in the night, followed by bright sunshine, altered the whole aspect, and Peel and Briggs bowled with such effect that the side were all out for 166, England gaining a memorable victory by 10 runs.

In addition to his eight tours in England he visited America three times as well as South Africa and New Zealand. His benefit match, New South Wales v. Rest of Australia at Sydney in 1906–07, brought him in about £630. At Lord's in June, 1912, he was presented with a silver cup and a purse of £200 to mark his 50th appearance in Test cricket against England.

GREIG, Canon John Glennie, who died at Milford-on-Sea on May 24, 1958, aged 86, served Hampshire as player, secretary and President. He first appeared for them in 1901 when a captain home on Army leave from India. In that season he scored 1,125 runs, including five centuries, average 41.66. Opening the innings at Worcester four years later, he took 115 and 130 from the Worcestershire bowling and in the return match at Bournemouth hit 187 before retiring hurt. Altogether he scored 4,375 runs for the county, average 34.17. His three-figure innings numbered 10, the highest being 249 not out against Lancashire at Liverpool in 1901.

Though of slight physique, he possessed strong wrists which enabled him to employ a variety of attractive strokes, with the cut predominant. He played his last game in 1921, when he became secretary, a position he held till 1930. He was President in 1945 and 1946. In 1935 he was ordained a Catholic priest in Rome and 12 years later was made an honorary Canon of the Diocese of Portsmouth.

GRESSON, Francis Henry, a left-handed batsman and bowler, who played for Winchester, Oxford University and Sussex, died on January 31, 1949, at Eastbourne, aged 80. A native of Worthing, he was in the Winchester XI of 1885 and 1886 and when the following year he made 91 and 95 in the Freshmen's match, he immediately won his

Blue and figured in three matches against Cambridge. He accomplished little against the Light Blues, but opening the innings for Oxford against Lancashire at Manchester in 1888 he hit 114. He helped Sussex for the first time in 1887, but between 1890 and 1899 did not play at all for the county. In 1901 he took part in Fred Tate's benefit match at Brighton but was not called on to bat. Sussex, with C. B. Fry scoring 209 and E. H. Killick 200—their partnership realised 349—made 560 for five wickets declared against Yorkshire whom they dismissed for 92. Gresson, a medium-paced bowler, took the last wicket for a single. Occasionally Gresson, a schoolmaster, appeared for M.C.C., and *Scores and Biographies* records that in 1905 "whilst batting for M.C.C. against Littlehampton at Littlehampton, he cut a ball hard which bounced once ere reaching the pavilion, where a retired elderly gentleman named Lee was sitting in the front row. Mr. Lee had an eye knocked out and literally smashed by the ball."

GRESWELL, William Territt, who died on February 12, 1971, aged 81, was reputed to be the first bowler to introduce the in-swinging delivery to first-class cricket. Gaining his colours at the age of 15, he was in the Repton XI from 1905 to 1908, heading the bowling figures in the last season with 59 wickets for 12 runs each. He began playing for Somerset in 1908 and continued to do so from time to time until 1933. Meantime he represented Gentlemen against Players three times.

In first-class matches in England, he took 525 wickets for 20.77 runs each with bowling of slow to medium pace, deceptive flight and spin. His best analysis was nine wickets for 62 for his county against Hampshire at Weston-super-Mare in 1928. As a batsman, he hit 2,499 runs, including a century against Middlesex at Lord's in 1909, for an average of 14.95, and he held 91 catches, mostly in the slips, where his fielding reached a high standard. He became President of the County Club in 1962.

It came as a blow to Somerset when Greswell left for Ceylon in 1909 to take up a position with the family tea and rubber estates, though he continued to turn out for the county when on leave. In Ceylon cricket he achieved great things and he became known as the best European player to appear there. Between 1909 and 1923, he disposed of 1,016 batsmen for 8.72 runs each, nearly all of them in first-class fixtures. Twice he took all 10 wickets for Colombo C.C.—for 26 runs against Malay C.C. in 1911 and for 21 runs against Mercantile XI 10 years later—and on no fewer than 29 occasions obtained at least eight wickets in an innings. He dismissed four men with consecutive balls against Galle C.C. and three other times in first-class cricket he performed the "hat-trick." In 1911, he set up a Ceylon record with 232 wickets for just over eight runs apiece.

Besides his cricketing ability, Greswell showed aptitude at other ball games. He played hockey for Somerset and the West of England and captained hockey and Association football teams in Ceylon. He also won the Ceylon A.A.A. half-mile championship.

GRIBBLE, Herbert Willis Reginald, died at Teddington on June 12, 1943, aged 82. He captained Clifton in 1878, his second season in the XI, and played for Gloucestershire from 1878 to 1882 without doing anything of note, though at school he opened the batting and showed good free style. He played Rugby football for Gloucestershire.

GRIERSON, Henry, who died on January 29, 1972, aged 80, was in the XI at Bedford Grammar School, being captain in 1910, and gained a Blue as a Freshman at Cambridge in 1911. From 1909, when still at school, till 1924, he regularly assisted Bedfordshire, whose side he led for four seasons. In 1936 he founded the Forty Club, membership of which has included numerous celebrated cricketers. He figured prominently with a number of teams in club cricket. A fine all-round athlete, he was in the Rugby XV at school, appeared in University trial matches and turned out for Bedford, Rosslyn Park and Leicester. At golf, he was a low handicap player and was also a capital racquets exponent who once won the Kilbey Cup. Besides being an after-dinner speaker of unusual merit, he was a pianist of considerable skill and broadcast on occasion during the 1930s. So good was he that, while staying with H. E. H. Gabriel, the hon. secretary of the Forty Club, he excited the admiration of his host's schoolgirl daughters. Some days later a then new performer, Semprini, broadcast. The comment of the two girls was that he was good, "but not as good as that chap Daddy brought home last week-end."

GRIFFITH, Bernie, who died in Wellington on September 29, 1982, aged 72, played as a leg-break and googly bowler for New Zealand in the last two unofficial Tests against

E. R. T. Holmes's M.C.C. side in 1935, having earlier helped Wellington to a famous victory over the tourists by 14 runs. In 14 first-class matches he took 50 wickets at 26.88 apiece.

GRIFFITH, Herman C., died at Bridgetown, Barbados, on March 18, 1980, aged 86. He was late in coming to the front, being 35 when he appeared in England in 1928 with the first West Indian team to be granted Test status, but he had played for Barbados as early as 1921, and in 1926 had taken nine for 96 for them against the Hon. F. S. G. Calthorpe's M.C.C. side. In 1928 his final record was not impressive, his 76 wickets costing 27.89 runs each, but there were those who reckoned him the best bowler on the side. Not as fast as Constantine, indeed really fast-medium, he was more of a stock bowler and was an indefatigable trier, a quality less common then in West Indian sides than it has since become. Getting plenty of pace off the pitch and swinging away sharply, he relied greatly on catches in the slips. His best performances were in the final Test at the Oval where, in an innings of 438, he took six for 103 (with a spell of five for 21) and 11 for 118 against Kent at Canterbury, where he was largely responsible for the innings defeat of a strong batting side. In 1930 he took eight wickets against an unrepresentative England side at Port-of-Spain and in the fifth Test at Sydney in 1931 he played an important part in the first West Indian victory over Australia by bowling Bradman for a duck with a slower ball, which he tried to turn to leg and made into a yorker. His second visit to England at the age of 40 in 1933 was perhaps a mistake: he was naturally not the bowler he had been, his 44 wickets costing him over 37 runs each, and he played in only two of the Tests. He continued, however, to play in first-class cricket at home until 1941. Apart from his bowling he had a safe pair of hands in the field.

GRIFFITHS, John Vesey Claude, died at Wedmore, Somerset, on February 18, 1982, aged 50. A left-handed bat and a slow left-arm bowler, he had a number of trials for Gloucestershire between 1952 and 1957 but met with little success and failed to secure a regular place in the side.

GRIMSDELL, Arthur, who died on March 13, 1963, aged 68, though more celebrated as a footballer, served Hertfordshire as an amateur wicket-keeper and batsman from 1922 to 1947. In Minor Counties' cricket he hit 3,458 runs, average 19.00, for Hertfordshire, his highest innings being 107 in 1934. He played Association football for St. Albans City before becoming professional with Watford, his native town. From there he joined Tottenham Hotspur, for whom he played as left half-back from 1912 to 1929. He gained an F.A. Cup-winners' medal in 1921 and played in six full and two "Victory" international matches for England.

GRIMSHAW, Irwin, of the Yorkshire XI of the middle '80s, died at Farsley on January 19, 1911, aged 53. He was born at the same place on May 4, 1857, and always had his home there. Without ever quite reaching the standard expected of him, he was for a few years—1884 to 1886—one of the best batsmen on the Yorkshire side.

GRIMSHAW, B/S/M James William Travis, H.A.C., was killed in action in September, 1944, aged 32. He went from King William School, Isle of Man, to Cambridge and was in the 1934 and 1935 XIs. A slow left-hand bowler, he played for Kent in a few matches.

GRINTER, Trayton Golding, who died on April 21, 1966, aged 80, played for Essex as an amateur in occasional matches between 1909 and 1921. While serving with the Artists' Rifles in the First World War, he was severely wounded in the left arm. Nevertheless he continued to play cricket for South Woodford and Frinton-on-Sea with marked success while virtually batting one-handed, and he put together more than 200 centuries in club matches. At the age of 50 he turned his attentions to golf and within a few weeks became a seven handicap player. Joining Cockburn and Co., the wine merchants, as office boy on Mafeking Day, 1900, he became chairman 33 years later.

GRISEWOOD, Frederick Henry, who died in a Hindhead nursing home on November 15, 1972, aged 84, was in the Radley XI before playing for Worcestershire against the University at Oxford in 1908. He later became famous as a B.B.C. broadcaster.

GROSS, Frederick Albert, died at Birmingham on March 11, 1975, aged 72. A leg-break and googly bowler, he had a good many trials for Hampshire as an amateur between 1924 and 1929 and got his county cap, but never became a regular member of the side. Turning professional, he played for Mitchell and Butler in the Birmingham

League from 1930 to 1947 and in 1934 made one appearance for Warwickshire.

GROUBE, Thomas Underwood, born at Taranaki, New Zealand, on September 2, 1857, died at Glenferrie, Victoria, on August 5, 1927, aged 69. He was a steady batsman, a medium-paced bowler, and a very good field at cover-point and long-on. As a member of the Australian team of 1880, he had the distinction of taking part in the first Test match ever played in this country. His highest innings in England was 61 in the match with Yorkshire at Huddersfield. For the East Melbourne C.C. he had a batting average of 155.33 for the season of 1879–80, and for that side against South Melbourne on the latter's ground in March and April, 1884, he scored 101 and 98, in the second innings adding 174 for the last wicket with Mr. G. Gordon.

GROUT, Arthur Theodore Wallace, who died in hospital in Brisbane on November 9, 1968, aged 41, kept wicket for Australia in 51 Test matches between 1957 and 1965. He entered hospital only two days before his death. A Brisbane doctor was afterwards reported as saying that Grout knew that he might collapse at any time during the last four years of his Test career and that he took part in the Australian tour of the West Indies only a few months after a heart attack in 1964. Yet "Wally's" unfailingly cheerful demeanour gave no inkling that there might be anything amiss with him.

Few chances escaped the agile Grout behind the stumps. In Test cricket he dismissed 187 batsmen, 163 of them caught and 24 stumped. Of these, 23 fell to him in the series with the West Indies in Australia in 1960–61; 21 in England in 1961 and 20 against England in Australia in 1958–59. Only T. G. Evans, who played in 40 more Test matches for England, possesses a better record. On two occasions Grout claimed eight victims in a Test match and his six catches in one innings against South Africa at Johannesburg in 1957–58 set up a world record which has since been equalled by J. D. Lindsay for South Africa and J. T. Murray for England. On five other occasions Grout disposed of five batsmen in an innings. Outside Test cricket, his greatest achievement was when he exceeded all previous wicket-keeping feats in first-class cricket; for Queensland in the Sheffield Shield match at Brisbane in 1960, he sent back eight Western Australia batsmen, all caught, in one innings. That world record still stands.

In addition to his wicket-keeping ability, Grout was also a distinctly useful late-order batsman, as he proved in that Test at Johannesburg in which he brought off his six catches. He and R. Benaud, in adding 89, set up a new record for the Australian eighth wicket against South Africa.

Tributes to Grout included:

S. C. Griffith (M.C.C. Secretary): "Among cricketers, he was regarded as one of the most kindly and generous of men. Speaking as a former wicket-keeper myself, I regarded him as among the most consistent performers behind the wicket I have ever played with or seen."

Sir Donald Bradman: "He was one of the finest wicket-keepers of all time."

R. B. Simpson: "He was the greatest wicket-keeper I ever saw."

R. Benaud: "He was able to read a match as well as any captain and was always of tremendous value to me in captaining the Australian side."

W. W. Hall: (West Indies fast bowler who played for Queensland in two Sheffield Shield series): "He was the finest wicket-keeper I either played with or against in my 10 years of big cricket."

B. N. Jarman (successor to Grout as Australian wicket-keeper): "I could not speak too highly of Wally as a wicket-keeper. He was one of the game's greatest characters. I never begrudged playing second fiddle to him."

GROUT, Herbert, Dunmow, Essex, died on September 25, 1895, aged 40. Grout was at different times engaged as a bowler at Cambridge and in the early days of the Essex County Club he played once or twice in the XI.

GROVE, Charles William, who died at Solihull on February 15, 1982, aged 69, did much good work for Warwickshire between 1938 and 1953. He showed promise before the War, but then came an eight-year gap and he did not resume his place in the side till 1947 when, with 98 wickets, even if they were somewhat expensive, he showed himself a very useful member of the attack. Again in 1949 and 1950 he topped 90 wickets and in 1950 had much to do with Warwickshire being the only county to beat the West Indians, taking eight for 38 in the first innings. However, it was in his last three years for the county that his best work was accomplished. In 1951, his benefit year, with 110 wickets at 18.52, he played a big part in Warwickshire winning the Championship, and he followed it with 118 at 17.53 in 1952 and in 1953 with 83 at 18.50. A big man, he was an extremely accurate fast-medium opening bowler, who could move the ball both ways, and a useful tail-end hitter, whose big performance was an innings of 104 not out in 80 minutes against Leicestershire at Leicester in 1948. Leaving Warwickshire, the county of his birth, at the end of 1953, he played in 1954 for Worcestershire with only moderate success and then went into the Birmingham League. In his first-class career he took 744 wickets at an average of 22.67. From 1974 to 1981 he was the Warwickshire scorer.

GROVES, George Jasper, died on February 18, 1941, as the result of a wound suffered through enemy action when at Newmarket on duty as a racing journalist. Born on October 19, 1868, in Nottingham, where his Yorkshire parents were on a visit, he had a county qualification which was discovered by a friend watching him make many runs for the Richmond club, and a recommendation obtained for him a trial when 30 years of age in the 1899 August Bank Holiday match at the Oval. At that time he ran a sports reporting business, founded by his father, and he was well known in the Press world. I was one of several in the Press box anxious for his success, and we were delighted at the way he overcame the ordeal of facing Lockwood, Richardson, Hayward, Brockwell and Lees before a 20,000 crowd. He said to me afterwards, "Tom Richardson gave me a short one on the leg side and the four, that was a gift, quietened my nerves." He made 42, helping A.O. Jones in a stand that stopped a collapse of Notts. Against Middlesex at Trent Bridge his 51, the highest score in the Notts second innings, could not stave off defeat by 10 wickets, brought about mainly by the all-round play of C.M. Wells, who batted grandly for 244 and took nine wickets for 111 runs with his slows. Next year at Lord's, going in first with A.O. Jones, Groves batted soundly for 28 and not out 36 which brought victory over M.C.C. by eight wickets. His highest innings in County Cricket, 56 not out, after a grand 137 by William Gunn, helped towards a dramatic victory over Kent. So well did P.C. Baker bat that a Trent Bridge record for runs hit off was expected. Tom Wass, the fast bowler, had retired lame, but when victory for Kent seemed inevitable he returned. The last six wickets fell for 66 runs, and Nottinghamshire won within 25 minutes of time by 12 runs, the innings closing for 346—one of the best finishes that I ever saw. Very consistent,

Groves averaged 23.36 during two seasons in county matches, but journalistic duties compelled him to give up first-class cricket. A small man of rather light build, Groves used the hook stroke and cut well. He fielded very smartly, usually at third man.

He learned games at school in Sheffield, and played Association football for that city against London—a great match for amateurs. He was a useful member of Sheffield United before his family settled in London. Then he captained Woolwich Arsenal in the old days at Plumstead. A full-back at one time, and then centre-half, he was a strong skilful player, and I enjoyed many games in his company for mid-week amateur teams. Good at billiards, he often acted as referee in professional matches.—H.P.

GRUNDY, George Graham Stewart, died on March 4, 1945, at Hunstanton, aged 84. He played in the Harrow XI of 1875 and 1876, but, though opening the bowling, and batting second wicket down, he did little in the big matches at Lord's. For Sussex he appeared occasionally.

GUARD, David Radclyffe, who died suddenly at Hartfield, Sussex, on December 12, 1978, aged 50, was four years in the Winchester XI, and in the last, 1946, when he was captain, headed the batting averages with excellent figures. Between 1946 and 1949, played a number of times for Hampshire, his most notable performance being an innings of 89 which saved them from probable defeat against Glamorgan at Cardiff in 1949.

GUARD, Ghulam Mustafa, died at Ahmedabad on March 13, 1978, aged 52. A left-hand medium pace bowler, who represented Bombay, he played for India in the first Test against the West Indies in 1958–59 and in the third Test against Australia in the following season. He opened the bowling on both occasions, but met with no particular success.

GULLAND, Robert George, died on October 27, 1981, aged 81. A good bat and an opening bowler, he had a remarkable record at Highgate, where he was in the XI all his four years in the school and captain in the last two, 1917 and 1918. On the strength of an innings of 57 in the Surrey trial match at the Oval, he was asked to play for the county in their first match in 1919. However, he had to refuse, and in fact never did play for them, though he appeared for the Second XI. He did not get a Blue at Cambridge. Later he was for many years a master at Berkhamsted School.

GUNARY, William Charles, who died on January 26, 1969, aged 73, played in one match for Essex in 1929.

GUNASEKARA, Dr. Churchill Hector, who died on May 16, 1969, aged 74, created a high reputation as a cricketer at Royal College, Colombo, which he captained in 1912. A good all-round sportsman, he also won his colours at Association football and athletics. He went up to Cambridge, where his chances of a Blue disappeared with the outbreak of the First World War. Afterwards he played a number of times for Middlesex in 1919 and when they won the County Championship in the two following years. In 1919 against Essex at Leyton he scored 58 and took five wickets for 90 runs, and in the game with Lancashire at Old Trafford dismissed five men for 15. Returning home after completing his medical studies, he represented Ceylon on 12 occasions, nine of them as captain, and he led Ceylon touring sides in India in 1932 and Malaya in 1938. He also played lawn tennis for Ceylon, carrying off both the singles and doubles championships.

GUNASEKERA, L. D. S. (Chippy), who died in January, 1974, aged 69, was a former Ceylon captain who led the team against Jack Ryder's Australians in 1935. He had a successful career at Royal College, Colombo, which he captained in 1925. A fine left-handed opening batsman he took part in many three-figure partnerships with M. K. Albert for the Sinhalese Sports Club when he was a splendid cover fieldsman. Toured India in 1932 and he had the best analysis with his leg-spinners in 1938 against Bradman's Australians. A shrewd tactician, eminent coach and one of the Island's leading criminal lawyers.

GUNN, Archibald, born at Taunton on October 11, 1863, died in New York City on January 16, 1930, aged 66. Educated at Tettenhall College, he was a very hard hitter and an excellent field at point. On settling in America he took part in much good-class cricket and in 1896 played against the Australian team. He was a well-known artist. The cricket menu cards he designed are much valued by collectors.

GUNN, George, who died in his sleep at Tylers Green, Sussex, on June 28, 1958, aged 79, was probably the greatest batsman who played for Nottinghamshire. Had he possessed a different temperament he would doubtless have improved upon his splendid records, for his skill and judgment were such that he made batting successfully against first-class bowlers appear the easiest thing imaginable. Not only did he show complete mastery in the art of back-play, but he frequently got right in front of his wicket and walked down the pitch to meet the ball no matter what type of bowler he was facing. Rarely when he left his ground in this way did his skill betray him and yet, though obviously so completely at home that he could have done almost anything with the ball, he would make a stroke which sent it tamely to the bowler, to mid-off or to mid-on. In match after match this practice of merely "killing" the ball was indulged in to such an extent as to become almost an obsession. It appeared to furnish Gunn with complete satisfaction, but it occasioned considerable annoyance to spectators who knew that, if he wished, he could score both without undue effort and as rapidly as anybody.

A younger brother of John Gunn and a nephew of William Gunn, George Gunn first appeared for Nottinghamshire in 1902. He met with no special success to begin with, but displayed such good style and powers of defence that there could be little doubt about his class. He steadily improved, but a haemorrhage of the lungs late in July ended his cricket for the summer. Happily a winter in New Zealand did him so much good that in 1907 he took the field again and, finishing at the top of the averages, bore a big part in winning the Championship for Nottinghamshire. Although his health was thus obviously re-established, his friends decided that he should spend the next winter in Australia. There went a team sent by M.C.C. and the illness of A. O. Jones, the captain, necessitated a call upon Gunn's services. The young professional made full use of his chance, making 119 and 74 in the first of the five Test matches, 122 not out in the fifth and for the whole tour heading the batting figures with an average of 51.

Visiting Australia again in 1911–12 under J. W. H. T. Douglas, Gunn again showed to marked advantage, batting so consistently that he averaged 42 in the Test matches. While he enjoyed a well-earned reputation for Test cricket in Australia, he had a tragic experience in England, where only once, at Lord's in 1909, was he called upon to play for his country. Upon his form at the time, his selection was a mistake; he himself thought he should not have been chosen and, playing without his usual confidence, he was dismissed for one and 0.

Apart from that failure upon what might have been a big occasion in his life, Gunn enjoyed a wonderfully successful career. For Nottinghamshire before the First World War he made over 13,000 runs in the course of 12 full seasons, his best summer being that of 1913 when he hit 1,697, average nearly 50. On cricket being resumed, he made five separate centuries in 1919, gaining an average of 65. For 12 consecutive seasons he registered over 1,000 runs, his aggregate amounting to nearly 1,800 in 1927 and again in 1928. Among his triumphs was a first-wicket stand of 252 with W. W. Whysall against Kent at Trent Bridge in 1924. He and Whysall altogether associated in 40 three-figure opening partnerships. Three times Gunn put together two hundreds in a match at Nottingham: 132 and 109 not out v. Yorkshire in 1913; 169 and 185 not out v. Surrey in 1919; and 100 and 110 v. Warwickshire in 1927 when aged 48. Characteristic of the man was the game with Yorkshire. He batted six hours for 132, but, with no occasion for anxiety, he followed with 109 out of 129 in less than 90 minutes. He celebrated his 50th birthday by hitting 164 not out against Worcestershire at Worcester and in the West Indies next winter he and A. Sandham obtained 322 for the first wicket against Jamaica at Kingston.

In the course of his career, Gunn played 62 three-figure innings and registered 35,190 runs, average 35.90. Of these runs 1,577 came in Australia, where he averaged 52. He was an excellent field at slip, where he brought off most of his 438 catches. He shared in one rare, if not unique, performance in 1931 against Warwickshire at Edgbaston when he and his son, the late G. V. Gunn, each scored a century in the same innings.

GUNN, George Vernon, who died in hospital at Shrewsbury on October 15, 1957, aged 52, as the result of injuries received in a motorcycle accident, played for Nottinghamshire from 1928 to 1939, scoring in that time just over 10,000 runs and taking close upon 300 wickets. In 1931 he scored 100 not out—his first century—against Warwickshire at Edgbaston and in the same innings his father, George Gunn, then 53, hit 183. This, it is believed, is the only instance of a father and son each reaching three figures in the same first-class match. G. V. Gunn's best season as an all-rounder was that of 1934 when he

obtained 922 runs and, with slow leg-breaks, dismissed 77 batsmen. In that summer he achieved his best bowling performance, taking 10 wickets for 120 in the game with Hampshire at Trent Bridge. He exceeded 1,000 runs in each of his last five seasons with the county, his highest aggregate being 1,765, average 44.07, in 1937. His biggest innings was 184 against Leicestershire at Nottingham the following year, a display featured by brilliant driving. After giving up County Cricket, he coached in the north of England and later at Wrekin College and for Worcestershire County C.C.

GUNN, John, who died in hospital at Nottingham on August 21, 1962, aged 87, was a member of a celebrated Nottinghamshire cricketing family. Nephew of William Gunn and elder brother of George, he was uncle of G. V., all of whom, like himself, played for the county. A fine all-rounder, John Gunn made his first appearance for Nottinghamshire in 1896 and continued his professional career with the county till 1925. In that time he scored 24,601 runs, average 33.19, took 1,243 wickets at 24.50 runs each and held 233 catches.

A left-hander possessing both sound defence and well-varied powers of hitting, he registered 41 centuries, the highest being 294 in less than four and a half hours against Leicestershire at Trent Bridge in 1903 when he and William Gunn, in adding 369, established a Nottinghamshire third-wicket record which still stands. That season was the first of four in succession in which John Gunn scored over 1,200 runs and took more than 100 wickets. Two years later, against Essex at Leyton, he and A. O. Jones added 361 for the fourth wicket, which also remains a record for the county.

As a left-arm slow-medium bowler with skilful variation of flight and spin, he achieved some notable successes, among them 14 wickets for 132 runs (eight for 63 and six for 69) against Surrey at the Oval and 14 for 174 runs (six for 53 and eight for 121) against Essex at Leyton, both in the same week in 1903, his most notable summer as an all-rounder with 1,665 runs (average 42.69) and 118 wickets (average 19.34). He performed the hat-trick at the expense of Derbyshire at Chesterfield in 1904 and of Middlesex at Lord's in 1899 and in 1921 at Nottingham he dismissed three Lancashire batsmen, all leg before, in four balls. He excelled as a fieldsman at cover-point, where, clever in anticipation, he had few superiors.

He made six appearances for England. His one visit to Australia was in 1901–02 with that unfortunate team led by A. C. MacLaren which, after winning the first of the Test matches in a single innings, suffered defeat in the other four. He played once against Australia in England, at Trent Bridge under F. S. Jackson in 1905. He represented Players v. Gentlemen on 13 occasions.

After leaving Nottinghamshire he played for Retford in the Bassetlaw League, heading the League batting averages when 54, and later acted as head groundsman at the ground owned by Sir Julien Cahn.

GUNN, William. After a long illness, the nature of which left no hope of recovery, William Gunn died at his home at Nottingham on January 29, 1921. Born on December 4, 1858, he was in his 63rd year. Few batsmen of his own or any other day were so well worth looking at as William Gunn. He carried his great height—he must have been nearly if not quite 6ft. 3in.—without the least stoop, and there was a natural grace in his every movement. Wherever he played he was the most striking figure in the field. As a batsman he represented the orthodox—one might even say the classic—school at its best. With his perfectly straight bat and beautifully finished style, he was a model to be copied. Not for him the hooks and pulls of present-day run-getters. He may at times have indulged in a pull, but as a general rule he hit the off ball on the off side, and hit it with tremendous power. Blessed with a splendid pair of wrists, he excelled in the hit past cover-point, the ball travelling along the ground at a pace that might have beaten Mr. Vernon Royle, whom Gunn himself described as the best cover-point he had ever seen.

It was sometimes urged that, considering his advantages of height, reach and strength, Gunn played too restrained a game, but he had a good answer to his critics. He said once to the writer of these lines "I can make as big hits as anyone if I like, but if I begin to lift the ball I never score more than 40." As an innings of 40 would in his prime have fallen far short of his desires, he did well to go his own way, and keep the ball down. While batting with complete self-control, he was often brilliant enough to satisfy the most eager lovers of fine hitting, and even when he had a quiet half hour or so he was still a delight to the eye.

His was no sudden jump to fame. Outside Nottingham the public knew nothing of him till he was over 21, and his first efforts in the Notts XI in 1880 gave little suggestion of the career that was before him. In 20 innings he scored scarcely more than 160 runs. At that time his outfielding was a greater asset than his batting. He could run 100 yd. inside 11 seconds, and he judged the lofty catch unerringly. He learned the game in face of some difficulties. Employed in Richard Daft's shop in Nottingham, he had not much spare time, but, determined to make himself a cricketer, he used to get some practice at unearthly hours in the morning. During the strike of the leading professionals that demoralised Notts cricket in 1881, he stuck to his place in the XI, and improved so much that he had an average of 24. He was greatly encouraged that season when the old Notts fast bowler, John Jackson, who stood umpire in one of the matches, told him he had never seen a colt who batted so well. The next two years were years of marked progress—he was second to Shrewsbury in the averages in 1884, when Notts had a wonderful season—and in 1885, with an innings of 203 for the M.C.C. against Yorkshire at Lord's, he took the position among English batsmen that was his till, in the ordinary course of nature, time began to tell upon him. At his very best from 1889 to 1898, he remained a fine player till 1903, when he scored 998 runs for Notts with an average of 38. Then, with a big and rapidly-growing business to look after, he thought he had done enough. He played in only four matches in 1904, and from that time he was an onlooker, content to see the name of Gunn in Notts cricket worthily kept before the public by his two nephews, George and John.

During his long career William Gunn played many innings that have become historical. His 228 for the Players at Lord's in 1890 is the highest score ever made against the Australians in this country. The Australians as a team were not strong in 1890, but they had Charles Turner and Ferris to bowl for them. With regard to this particular match rather a good story has been told. Asked in an interview whether he had ever felt tired of cricket, Sydney Gregory said he thought not, except, perhaps, when he heard Billy Gunn say "No" at Lord's for seven hours and a half. Another great innings that Gunn played was his 139 for the Players against the Gentlemen at Lord's in W. G. Grace's jubilee match in 1898. Just after he went in Gunn was beaten and all but bowled by one of Kortright's fastest. Then he played magnificently, till at last, deceived in the pace, he lunged forward at a slow ball from Woods and was bowled all over his wicket.

Between 1888 and 1899, Gunn played in nine matches for England against Australia. He did best in 1893—when, incidentally, he just beat Stoddart in the season's averages—scoring 77 at Lord's and 102 not out at Manchester. Though he made bigger scores without number, Gunn never played finer cricket than in the memorable match between Notts and Surrey at the Oval in 1892. His 58 against the superb bowling of George Lohmann and Lockwood on a far from easy wicket was a veritable masterpiece of batting. For an hour and a quarter on the second afternoon he and William Barnes withstood a tremendous onslaught. It was cricket that no one who saw it could ever forget.

In his young days Gunn was a famous forward at Association football, combining skill with great speed. He was a mainstay of Notts County and played for England in 1884 against Scotland and Wales.—This notice of Gunn appeared, almost as it stands, in *The Times*.—S.H.P.

In strictly first-class cricket Gunn made 48 centuries:

For England (1):
  v. Australia, 102*.
For England XI (1):
  v. Yorkshire, 137.
For M.C.C. and Ground (6):
  v. Australians, 118.
  v. Somerset, 188.
  v. Sussex, 124, 138.
  v. Worcestershire, 110.
  v. Yorkshire, 203.
For Non-Smokers (1):
  v. Smokers, 150.
For North (1):
  v. South, 125*.
For Notts (34):
  v. Derbyshire, 135, 207*, 152, 230, 273, 120, 101.
  v. Essex, 127.
  v. Gloucestershire, 119.
  v. Kent, 109, 129, 137.
  v. Lancashire, 116.
  v. Leicestershire, 111, 139.
  v. Middlesex, 138, 120.
  v. Somerset, 121*, 101.
  v. Surrey, 118, 125, 236*, 112.
  v. Sussex, 122, 205*, 196, 161, 109, 156, 219, 125, 150.
  v. Yorkshire, 150, 110.
For Players (4):
  v. Australians, 228.
  v. Gentlemen, 169, 103, 139.
  For Notts he also made 161 v. West Indians, in 1900, in a match not counted first-class.
  His eight scores of over 200 were obtained thus:
273   Notts v. Derbyshire, at Derby, 1901.
236*   Notts v. Surrey, at the Oval, 1898.
230   Notts v. Derbyshire, at Trent Bridge, 1897.
228   Players v. Australians, at Lord's, 1890.
219   Notts v. Sussex, at Trent Bridge, 1893.
207*   Notts v. Derbyshire, at Derby, 1896.
205*   Notts v. Sussex, at Trent Bridge, 1887.
203   M.C.C. & G. v. Yorkshire, at Lord's, 1885.
  His longest partnerships:
398 for 2nd, Gunn (196) and Shrewsbury (267): Notts v. Sussex, at Trent Bridge, 1890.
367 for 3rd, Gunn (139) and Gunn, J. (294): Notts v. Leicestershire, at Trent Bridge, 1903.
330 for 4th, Gunn (203) and Barnes (140*): M.C.C. and G. v. Yorkshire, at Lord's, 1885.
312 for 2nd, Gunn (161) and Shrewsbury (165): Notts v. Sussex, at Brighton, 1891.
310 for 3rd, Gunn (150) and Shrewsbury (236): Non-Smokers v. Smokers, at East Melbourne, 1886–87.

* *Signifies not out*

At Lord's in 1889, for M.C.C. & Ground v. Northumberland, he carried out his bat for 219, and, in partnership with Attewell (200), put on 419 for the second wicket. On the same ground against the same county in the following year he scored 196 and Flowers 99 not out.

GUTTERIDGE, Frank H., born at Nottingham April 12, 1867; died there June 13, 1918. Played his early cricket with the Notts Incogniti, and for a time was professional at Cape Town. His first match for Notts was in 1889. Played later for Sussex: made 114 v. Oxford University in 1894. Re-appeared for Notts in 1896. Good all-round cricketer; bowled fast right-hand. For some years umpired in first-class cricket.

GWYNN, Lucius H., died at Davos Platz, on December 23, 1902. He was born on May 25, 1873, and was thus in his 30th year. A few seasons back he was the best batsman in Ireland, showing in 1895 such remarkable form for Dublin University, that the Surrey committee asked him to appear for Gentlemen against Players at the Oval. He met with brilliant success, scoring 80 and 0. In getting his 80 he was at the wickets for three and a quarter hours, the bowlers opposed to him including Richardson and the late George Lohmann. He again played for the Gentlemen at the Oval in 1896, but this time he did not do nearly so well as before, being out to J. T. Hearne's bowling for scores of 24 and one. There can be little doubt that if he had had regular opportunities of playing in first-class matches in England he would have earned a high place among the batsmen of his day. In Rugby football circles he was very well known. Playing in ordinary matches for Monkstown, he also had the distinction of representing Ireland in International matches, being one of the side that defeated England at Richmond in 1898. He was a centre three-quarter, and if not comparable with the great exponents who have filled that position, he was a thoroughly dependable player. Like most of the Irish three-quarters, his methods were more in accord with the old three-quarter days than with those demanded from a centre under the present system.

GWYNN, The Rev. Robert Malcolm, of Trinity College, Dublin, who died in Dublin on June 10, 1962, aged 85, was a member of a well-known Irish cricketing family. He played for Gentlemen of Ireland and the Phoenix C.C. and once in a match at College Park, Dublin, enjoyed the distinction of bowling Dr. W. G. Grace first ball.

HACK, A. T., who died on February 4, 1933, at the early age of 27 from appendicitis, did useful work for South Australia from 1927–28 to 1931–32. Captain of the Glenelg Club near Adelaide he was a son of Mr. F. T. Hack, a famous South Australian batsman. Before Walker came into the State side, Hack was played as wicket-keeper but also distinguished himself as a good batsman of the steady type and made a century against Queensland in 1928.

HACKER, Stamford, who died at Bristol on December 8, 1925, was a useful fast-medium bowler, introduced into the Gloucestershire team by W. G. Grace in 1899. He appeared seldom for that county, however, and after playing a little for Herefordshire he helped Glamorgan to gain promotion, meeting with some success when the Welsh county became first-class. He headed the Glamorgan bowling averages in 1910, 1912, 1913 and 1922 and was second in 1909, 1911, 1914 and 1921. He appeared in several matches for South Wales and in the game with All India at Cardiff in 1911 he had an analysis of six wickets for 17.

HADOW, E. M., who died at Cannes, February 20, 1895, was the youngest of the four brothers Hadow who at different times appeared in the Harrow XI. Born on March 13, 1863, he was within a few weeks of completing his 32nd year at the time of his premature death. Though he did some good work for Middlesex it can scarcely be said that Mr. Hadow, as a man, fulfilled the hopes formed of him in his schooldays. At Harrow he was a brilliant batsman, playing admirably against Eton at Lord's in 1880 and 1881. In the former year, when he was ninth on the batting order, he scored 28 not out and 49, while in 1881 he made 11 and 94, one of the best innings that had for some years been played for Harrow in the Schools' match. Mr. Hadow, who had for some time before his death dropped out of first-class cricket, was one of the best amateur racquets players of his time.

HADOW, Patrick Francis, died at Bridgwater on June 29, 1946, aged 91. One of the seven sons of P. D. Hadow, himself an old Harrovian, he and three brothers played in the Harrow XI, W. H., who died in 1898, being specially famous. P. F. took a large share in the victory over a powerful Eton XI in 1873, when he patiently scored 54 not out, and Harrow, getting 167 in the last innings, won by five wickets. He played a little for Middlesex before going to Ceylon where he settled down as a tea planter. Three of the brothers played racquets for Harrow in the Public Schools Challenge Competition, and P. F., with F. D. Leyland, won the Cup in 1873. Five years later he won the Lawn Tennis Amateur Championship at Wimbledon, beating S. W. Gore, who was in the Harrow XI from 1867–69.

HADOW, Walter Henry, passed away at Dupplin Castle on Thursday, September 15, 1898, after a long illness. The eldest and most distinguished of several brothers who earned fame on the cricket field, Mr. Hadow was born in London on September 25, 1849, and thus had not quite completed his 49th year. Educated at Harrow, he soon displayed the possession of remarkable ability as a cricketer, and it is told of him in *Scores and Biographies* that when only 13 years of age he played an innings of a hundred. He made his first appearance at Lord's in the Schools' match of 1866—the same year that C. I. Thornton, the wonderful hitter, came out from Eton—and scored 31. Earlier in the same season he had attained great celebrity among his school fellows by making against the Household Brigade 181 not out—at that time the highest innings ever played at Harrow. In the following year he was not successful against Eton at Lord's, and going up to Oxford, he, curiously enough, never came off against Cambridge, although he obtained his Blue in 1870 and in the two subsequent years. Despite these failures for his University, he gave plenty of evidence of his skill as a batsman, and in 1871 he was included in the Gentlemen's team against the Players at Lord's, where, only a few weeks previously, he had scored 217 for Middlesex. This was an especially notable achievement, as no innings of over 200 had been hit in a good match at Lord's since the memorable 278 by Mr. Ward so far back as 1820. Mr. Hadow did little against the professionals at Lord's, wet weather spoiling the game, but at the Oval, a few days later, he made 97 against J. C. Shaw, Alfred Shaw, Lillywhite and Southerton, and thereby had a large share in the Gentlemen's victory by five wickets. In the autumn of 1872 he was invited to form one of the splendid team of amateurs Mr. R. A. FitzGerald took out to Canada, the side including W. G. Grace, the late C. J. Ottaway, A. N. Hornby, the Hon. George Harris (Lord Harris), Alfred Lub-

bock, Edgar Lubbock and Arthur Appleby. Unfortunately, Mr. Hadow had a finger put out, and, handicapped in this manner, he did nothing to add to his reputation. He played for Middlesex during the '70s, and after dropping out in 1877, he reappeared with considerable success a year later. Although only taking part in half a dozen matches, he made more than 300 runs. His chief success was against Notts on the occasion of Bob Thoms' benefit, when, against Alfred Shaw, Morley, Barnes and Flowers, he put together 140 and 44. A free and most polished batsman, Mr. Hadow had the habit, like another famous Harrovian, A. J. Webbe, of standing with his legs very wide apart, and thus did not make quite the most of his height, which was over 6ft., but he was a very attractive player to watch, possessing remarkable power of wrist, his cut being an exceptionally fine stroke. Although known chiefly as a cricketer, Mr. Hadow distinguished himself in other branches of athletics. He was a skilful player at racquets and tennis, representing his University in the former game both in 1871 and 1872; while in the two previous years he pulled in his college (Brasenose) boat. Of the four brothers, all of whom played for Harrow, A. A. Hadow died four years ago, at the age of 41; E. M. Hadow passed away at Cannes, in 1895, at the still earlier age of 31; the one survivor being P. F. Hadow—a contemporary at Harrow of A. J. Webbe. Mr Walter Hadow left a widow—Lady Constance Hadow—and three children. At the time of his death he was one of Her Majesty's Prison Commissioners for Scotland.

HAIG, Nigel Esme, who died in a Sussex hospital on October 27, 1966, aged 78, was a celebrated amateur all-rounder between the two World Wars. He did not gain a place in the XI while at Eton, but from 1912 until he retired from the game in 1934 he rendered splendid service to Middlesex, whom he captained for the last six years of his career. He was a member of the Championship-winning sides of 1920 and 1921. In addition, he played for England against Australia in the second of the disastrous Test series of 1921 and four times against the West Indies for the Hon. F. S. G. Calthorpe's M.C.C. team of 1929–30 without achieving much success. In all first-class cricket, Haig hit 15,208 runs, average 20.83, and with swing-bowling above medium pace he obtained 1,116 wickets for 27.47 runs each.

Six times he exceeded 1,000 runs, five times he took 100 or more wickets in a season and in 1921, 1927 and 1929 he did the "cricketers' double." An agile fieldsman, he held 218 catches. His batting style was scarcely classic, but a quick eye stood him in good stead and, despite his not very powerful physique, he could hit the ball hard. The highest of his 12 centuries was 131 against Sussex at Lord's in 1920, when he, P. F. Warner, H. W. Lee and J. W. Hearne, the first four Middlesex batsmen, each reached three figures—an unprecedented occurrence in first-class cricket which was repeated for the same county by H. L. Dales, H. W. Lee, J. W. Hearne and E. Hendren against Hampshire at Southampton three years later.

Seemingly built of whipcord, Haig, a nephew of Lord Harris, bowled for long spells without apparent signs of fatigue. Among his best performances with the ball was the taking of seven wickets for 33 runs in the Kent first innings at Canterbury in 1920. This was another eventful match for Haig, for he scored 57 in the Middlesex first innings and became the "second leg" of a hat-trick by A. P. Freeman in the second. In 1924 Haig took six wickets for 11 runs in Gloucestershire's first innings on Packer's Ground at Bristol, a game rendered specially memorable by the fact that C. W. L. Parker, the slow left-hander, twice accomplished the hat-trick at the expense of Middlesex. Haig was also a fine real tennis player, could hold his own with lawn tennis players of near-Wimbledon standard and was equally good at racquets, squash and golf. While serving with the Royal Field Artillery during the First World War, he won the M.C.

HAIGH, Schofield, died at Berrybrow, Huddersfield, on February 27, 1921. He was born at Berrybrow on March 19, 1871, and thus passed away at just under 50 years of age. He had been in failing health for some time, but to the great body of cricketers the news of his premature death came as quite a shock. After retiring from first-class cricket he took up an appointment as coach at Winchester, and seemed to have a very pleasant time before him. A thorough sportsman, who obviously loved the game, Haigh will live in cricket history as one of the most valued members of Lord Hawke's famous Yorkshire XI. In two of the three years—1900–02—in which Yorkshire carried off the Championship and put up such wonderful records, he was at his very best. In 1900 he divided the bowling honours with Rhodes, taking in County Championship matches 145 wickets

for little more than 14 runs apiece, and after a set-back in 1901 he was again at the top of his form in 1902, taking 123 wickets in purely county fixtures, and beating Rhodes in the averages. It was in 1901, when Haigh proved comparatively ineffective, that George Hirst discovered his swerve, and became the deadliest bowler of the season.

Haigh began to play cricket as a schoolboy, and when 18 joined the club at Armitage Bridge. Before long he came under the notice of Louis Hall, who at that time was in the habit at the close of each season of taking teams up to Scotland. On Hall's recommendation Haigh was engaged by the Aberdeen club, and after three years with that body he went to Perth. A little later came the turning-point of his career. He met with great success for a Scotch team against Lancashire, and the Yorkshire authorities realised that he might be a first-rate county bowler. He settled down at Leeds, and after a brilliant trial against Durham at Barnsley in 1896 he was given his first opportunity in big cricket, playing for Yorkshire against Australia at Bradford. Yorkshire lost the match by 140 runs, but in the Australians' second innings Haigh took eight wickets—five of them bowled down— and his position was established. Thenceforward till his career ended Haigh, as everyone knows, was one of Yorkshire's mainstays. A right-handed bowler, medium pace to fast, he had a good variety of speed in combination with an off-break that on sticky wickets often made him practically unplayable. In his early days he took a great deal out of himself, finishing his delivery with a tremendous plunge, but as time went on he modified his style and economised his strength. When the conditions helped him he was beyond question one of the most difficult bowlers of his generation, but on hard, true wickets he did not rank with Hirst and Rhodes. He was first and last a county cricketer, all his best work being done for Yorkshire. He played four times for England against Australia—at Lord's and Leeds in 1905, at Lord's in 1909, and at Manchester in 1912—but these matches did not add to his reputation. Indeed, at Lord's in 1905, he proved ineffective on a wicket that was expected to suit him to a nicety. Apart from his special gifts as a bowler Haigh was a thorough cricketer—keen to a degree in the field and quite capable of making runs when they were wanted. If he had been less of a bowler he might easily have made a name for batting. In a memorable match against Surrey at Bradford in 1898 he went in 10th and scored 85, he and Hirst putting on 155 runs together. Haigh retired from the Yorkshire XI after the season of 1913.—S.H.P.

Schofield Haigh's chief performances in important cricket may be summarised as follows:

Eight or More Wickets in an Innings

8 for 78, Yorkshire v. Australians, at Bradford	1896
8 for 35, Yorkshire v. Hampshire, at Harrogate	1896
8 for 21, Yorkshire v. Hampshire, at Southampton	1898
9 for 36, England v. Fifteen of Rhodesia, at Bulawayo	1898–99
9 for 44, England v. Fifteen of Griqualand West, at Kimberley	1898–99
8 for 34, England v. Cape Colony, Cape Town	1898–99
8 for 33, Yorkshire v. Warwickshire, at Scarborough	1899
9 for 25, Yorkshire v. Gloucestershire, at Leeds	1912

Thirteen or More Wickets in a Match

14 for 50, Yorkshire v. Durham, at Barnsley	1896
14 for 43, Yorkshire v. Hampshire, at Southampton	1898
13 for 44, England v. Fifteen of Rhodesia, at Bulawayo	1898–99
13 for 94, Yorkshire v. Middlesex, at Leeds	1900
13 for 40, Yorkshire v. Warwickshire, at Sheffield	1907
14 for 65, Yorkshire v. Gloucestershire, at Leeds	1912

Four Wickets or More for Three Runs or Less Each

7 for 17, Yorkshire v. Surrey, at Leeds	1897
6 for 18, Yorkshire v. Derbyshire, at Bradford	1897
8 for 21, Yorkshire v. Hampshire, at Southampton	1898
4 for 8, England v. XV of Border, at King William's Town	1898–99
6 for 11, England v. South Africa, at Cape Town	1898–99
4 for 8, England v. Fifteen of Rhodesia, at Bulawayo	1898–99
4 for 12, Yorkshire v. Warwickshire, at Scarborough	1899
4 for 8, Yorkshire v. Notts, at Nottingham	1901
4 for 10, Yorkshire v. Gloucestershire, at Cheltenham	1902
5 for 13*a* 8 for 24*c* } Yorkshire v. Essex, at Sheffield	1903
4 for 12, Yorkshire v. Gloucestershire, at Cheltenham	1904
4 for 11, Yorkshire v. Somerset, at Bath	1906
4 for 3, Yorkshire v. South Wales, at Cardiff	1906
5 for 13, Yorkshire v. Cambridge University, at Cambridge	1906
5 for 9, Yorkshire v. Essex, at Leyton	1907
7 for 13, Yorkshire v. Warwickshire, at Sheffield	1907
6 for 13, Yorkshire v. Surrey, at Leeds	1908
4 for 11, Yorkshire v. Surrey, at Sheffield	1909
7 for 20, Yorkshire v. Sussex, at Leeds	1911
5 for 14, Yorkshire v. Somerset, at Dewsbury	1912
6 for 14, Yorkshire v. Australians, at Bradford	1912
9 for 25, Yorkshire v. Gloucestershire, at Leeds	1912

a Signifies 1st innings; *c* both.

Bowling Unchanged Through Both Completed Innings

With Rhodes, Yorkshire v. Worcestershire, at Bradford	1900
With Rhodes, Yorkshire v. Cambridge University, at Sheffield	1903
With Rhodes, Yorkshire v. Hampshire, at Leeds	1904
With Hirst, Yorkshire v. Northamptonshire, at Northampton	1908

Various Feats

4 wkts. in 4 balls, England v. Army XI, at Pretoria	1905–06
3 wkts. in 3 balls, Yorkshire v. Derbyshire, at Bradford	1897
3 wkts. in 3 balls, Yorkshire v. Somerset, at Sheffield	1902
3 wkts. in 3 balls, Yorkshire v. Kent, at Leeds	1904

(Obtained with leg-breaks. The match was not reckoned first-class as the wicket was tampered with after the first day's play.)

3 wkts. in 3 balls, Yorkshire v. Lancashire. at Manchester   1909

3 wkts. in 4 balls, Yorkshire v. Worcestershire, at Stourbridge   1906

Twice whilst appearing for Yorkshire Haigh, at one period of an innings, obtained five wickets without a run being made off him—v. Derbyshire at Bradford in 1897, and v. Somerset at Sheffield in 1902.

HAIGH, William Henry, probably the finest wicket-keeper ever identified with American cricket, died in Boston, U.S.A., on March 21, 1905, at about the age of 70. He was born at Halifax, in Yorkshire, and, prior to emigrating to America, earned a name for himself in this country as a wicket-keeper of more than average ability. It was said indeed that he could take the bowling of Tarrant, of Cambridge, better than any other man in England, which was certainly high praise. The late R.A. Fitzgerald, too in, *Wickets in the West*, spoke of him as by far the best man behind the sticks he saw during the tour of the Englishmen through America in 1872. He was interested in the game to the last.

HAIGH SMITH, Hamilton Augustus, who died in St. Mary's Hospital, London, following an operation on October 28, 1955, aged 71, made occasional appearances as batsman and slow bowler for Hampshire from 1909 to 1914. His highest score was 43 not out against Worcestershire at Worcester in his first season. He also represented the county at Rugby football and hockey. Educated at Marlborough, he was best known for his activities in football circles. As a forward he played for Trojans, Blackheath and the famous Barbarians before the First World War, and for some years was Hon. Secretary of the Barbarians, of which club he was also President at the time of his death. In 1938 he was Hon. Assistant-manager of the British Rugby team which toured South Africa and became Hon. Treasurer of the Four Home Unions Tours Committee. For a number of seasons he acted as touch-judge for England in international matches.

HAINES, Claude Vincent Godby, who died on January 28, 1965, aged 59, was in the King's, Canterbury, XI and played for Kent Second XI in 1924. He played as an amateur in a few matches for Glamorgan in 1933 and 1934, his highest first-class innings being 59 against Sussex at Cardiff in the first season. He also turned out for the British Empire XI which raised funds for the Red Cross during the Second World War. His father, A.H.J. Haines, played for Gloucestershire.

HAKE, Herbert Dengo, O.B.E., died in Australia on April 12, 1975, aged 80. He was in the Haileybury XI for five years, 1910 to 1914, and captain for the last three. After serving in the War he went up to Cambridge in 1919, but the University batting at that time was crushingly strong and, though he had a number of trials, he did not get his Blue. However, between 1920 and 1925 he played some valuable innings for Hampshire, notably 94 against Leicestershire and 72 against Warwickshire, both in 1921, and 81 not out against Lancashire in 1923, made when runs were badly needed. A tall man, he was a fine striker of the ball and could score very fast. He was also a beautiful field and could keep wicket if required. He represented Cambridge at both hockey and racquets and was runner-up in the Amateur Racquets singles in 1929. After many years as a master at Haileybury, he was Headmaster of King's School, Paramatta, from 1939 to 1964.

HALE, Walter H., who died in August at Bristol, 1956, aged 86, enjoyed a long and varied sporting career, for he played cricket and, as a forward, Rugby football for both Gloucestershire and Somerset. From the age of 17 he turned out for Knowle C.C., and in 34 years' association with them scored over 25,000 runs. After appearing in nine matches for Somerset and for Burnley in the Lancashire League, he accepted the invitation of Dr. W. G. Grace to turn out for Gloucestershire, the county of his birth. Between 1897 and 1909 he played in 57 County Championship games for Gloucestershire, twice hitting centuries. In 1901 he scored 109 not out against Essex at Leyton when C. J. Kortright was bowling at his fastest. "He was the fastest ever," said Hale of Kortright, "He hit me black and blue!" That season Hale headed his county's averages above G. L. Jessop. In 1902 he obtained 135 from the Nottinghamshire bowling at Bristol. As a footballer he assisted Bristol R.F.C. for many years.

HALL, Alfred Ewart, who died at Johannesburg on January 1, 1964, aged 67, played seven times as a fast bowler for South Africa against England between 1923 and 1931, taking 40 wickets for 22.15 runs each. His first Test match, against F. T. Mann's team at

Cape Town in 1922–23, was sensational. England needed 173 to win, but Hall bowled so effectively, taking seven wickets for 63 runs, that, despite a stand of 68 by Mann and V. W. C. Jupp, they got home by no more than one wicket. In the match Hall gained figures of 11 wickets for 112 and he was carried shoulder-high from the field at the end. In 1927–28 he played a big part in South Africa's success by four wickets at Johannesburg when he obtained nine wickets for 167. In seven seasons for Transvaal he took 128 wickets in Currie Cup fixtures, his best being that of 1926–27 when, with a chief performance of 14 for 115 against Natal, he dismissed 52 batsmen in six games. After that he returned for a time to his birthplace, Bolton, Lancashire. He appeared as a professional for Lancashire nine times in 1923 and 1924.

HALL, Charles H., who died in December, 1976, aged 70, had a number of trials for Yorkshire as a fast bowler between 1928 and 1934. When he and Bowes bowled out Leicestershire in 1932 for 72, Hall's share was five for 27.

HALL, Derek, who was killed in a car crash in Canada in late April, 1983, played for Derbyshire from 1955 to 1958. Standing well over 6ft., he had a good trial in 1955 and, without any notable performance, showed promise, taking 24 wickets at 26.41. Given another good trial in 1956, he was disappointing and after a match or two in 1957 and 1958 he left the county. Altogether he took 48 wickets at 28.88. As a batsman he did not contribute much, his highest score in 20 matches being 10 not out.

HALL, John Bernard, died in Retford Hospital on May 27, 1979, aged 75. Educated at Bloxham, he was a useful bat and a good medium-pace right-arm bowler who played a good deal for Sir Julien Cahn, with whom he toured Ceylon in 1937. Between 1935 and 1946 he made a few appearances for Nottinghamshire. Since 1968 he had been chairman of the Bassetlaw League. His son, M. J. Hall, also played for Nottinghamshire.

HALL, Louis, the famous Yorkshire batsman, died at Morecambe on November 19, 1915. He was born at Batley on November 1, 1852. Hall played his first match for Yorkshire at Prince's Ground against Middlesex in 1873, but his real career in the county XI dated from 1878. He had been almost forgotten when an innings of 78 for a local Eighteen against the first Australian XI revealed

his full powers. Few English batsmen had up to that time met with much success against the great Australian bowlers, and this one performance established Hall's reputation. He went back at once to the Yorkshire team and kept his place without a break till 1892. For a few seasons he did nothing exceptional, but in 1883 he took a big step to the front, scoring 911 runs for the county and, with 10 not outs to help him, averaging 43. His best season of all was 1887—a summer of sunshine and hard wickets—when he made 1,544 runs with an average of 41. Hall was in the strict sense of the words an old-fashioned batsman, trusting as much for defence to forward play as the men of Fuller Pilch's day. It cannot be said that he was an attractive bat to watch—he was at times a veritable stonewaller—but in the Yorkshire XI which included George Ulyett and William Bates his stubborn defence was of priceless value. In match after match he kept up his wicket while one or other of those brilliant hitters demoralised the bowling. He and Ulyett on 11 occasions sent up the hundred for Yorkshire's first wicket. Once—against Sussex at Brighton in 1885—they scored the hundred together in both innings. Hall made 15 hundreds during his career—all but two of them for Yorkshire—and 17 times he carried his bat right through an innings. His greatest success was in the Yorkshire and Middlesex match at Sheffield in 1884 when he scored 96 and 135. He was not often chosen for Players against Gentlemen, but he played at Lord's in 1883, 1884, and 1885, and at the Oval in 1884. Not much success rewarded him in these games, his best score being 32 at Lord's in 1883. He was given the Surrey match for his benefit at Sheffield in 1891, and profited to the extent of £570. A quiet man of very careful habits, Hall enjoyed the good opinion of everyone who knew him. After his active career in the cricket field had come to an end he was for some time coach at Uppingham School.

HALL, Thomas Auckland, who died suddenly on April 21, 1984, aged 53, was a tall fast-medium bowler who did useful work for two counties. Captain of Uppingham in 1948, he played one match for Derbyshire in 1949 and for the next two seasons was a fairly frequent member of the side, taking 36 wickets in 1951 at 23.69. After playing a few matches in 1952, he moved to Somerset for whom in 1953 he took 58 wickets at 32.46. A few matches in 1954 concluded his county career. Besides his bowling, he played two notable innings. In his second match for

Derbyshire, against Surrey at the Oval in 1950, he made 52, the highest score in a total of 147, only two others reaching double figures, and for Somerset against Northamptonshire, coming in when the side were 129 behind with two wickets to go, he scored 69 not out and had an unfinished partnership with Gimblett. A fine sportsman, he was a member of the crew of the original *Crossbow*, which broke the world sailing speed record, and also a splendid golfer.

HALLAM, Thomas Haydn, who died at Christchurch, New Zealand, on November 24, 1958, aged 77, played in 10 matches for Derbyshire in 1906 and 1907. His highest innings was 68, in a total of 162, against Warwickshire at Edgbaston. Going to New Zealand in 1920, he appeared for Wellington and Wairarapa and for 25 years from 1923 was groundsman at Lancaster Park.

HALLAS, Charles Edward Whestley, of Huddersfield, shot himself in a London hotel on August 20, 1909. He was a good left-handed slow bowler and had played occasionally for Yorkshire Second XI. He was only 32 years of age.

HALLEY, Russell, once a prominent cricketer in New Zealand, died at Wellington (N.Z.) on July 6, 1909, in his 50th year. His first appearance in a representative match was for Canterbury against Wellington in 1886–87, when he and Dunlop, bowling unchanged, dismissed Wellington for 66 and 34. Halley took nine wickets in the match for 52 runs, at one period bowling 50 balls for one run and five wickets. He never did so well again in an important match, although he took six wickets for 50 for Eighteen of Canterbury against Shrewsbury's team at Hagley Park in March, 1888. He was a left-handed medium-paced bowler and a fair bat.

HALLIWELL, Ernest Austin, the famous wicket-keeper, an Englishman by birth, who died at Johannesburg in October, 1919, after an operation for gangrene of the leg, made his name as a cricketer in South Africa, and was associated almost exclusively with South African cricket. His reputation dated from 1894, when he returned to this country as a member of the first South African XI. The team as a whole did not attract any large amount of public attention, but it was generally agreed that Halliwell as a wicket-keeper ranked among the very best men of the day. When he came here again in 1901 with the second team from South Africa he was found

to be even better than before. By that time the old plan of standing up to fast bowling had been to a large extent abandoned, but Halliwell stood up to Kotze, and the manner in which he took that bowler of tremendous pace aroused general admiration. Visiting England once again, in 1904, he stood up to Kotze for a few matches, but afterwards fell in with the prevailing fashion and went back. While of opinion that on the matting wickets of South Africa, on which the ball comes along at much the same height all through the day, standing up was preferable, he eventually came to the conclusion that on English wickets the plan of going back, resulting as it did in a greater number of catches, paid best. Still he retained a strong liking for the old method.

Having a birth qualification for Middlesex—he was the son of R. Bissett Halliwell, who kept wicket for Middlesex in the old days at the Cattle Market ground at Islington—he made one appearance for that county towards the end of the season of 1901. He also appeared for Gentlemen v. Players at Hastings. His was a clear case of inherited talent. Making full allowance for the vastly better wickets on which he played, it is not unfair to say that he was a much finer wicket-keeper than his father, though the latter was good enough to be chosen for Gentlemen v. Players. In addition to being a superb wicket-keeper, E. A. Halliwell was more than useful as a batsman. In September, 1892, at Johannesburg, in a match between the Mother Country and Colonial Born, he and T. Routledge scored 289 together, this being for some years the first wicket record in South Africa. Halliwell made 139 not out and Routledge 147 not out. They were together only an hour and three-quarters, their side having been set the impossible task of getting 347 in that time. Born at Ealing on September 7, 1864, Halliwell had completed his 55th year.—S.H.P.

HALLOWS, Charles, the cricketer who refused to grow old, died suddenly at his Bolton home on November 10, 1972, and the fact that he was aged 77 must have surprised all but the older generation of Lancashire cricket followers. They remembered Hallows as a stylish left-hander who in 1928 hit a thousand runs *in May*—a feat performed by only two other players, Dr. W. G. Grace and W. R. Hammond—and scored more than 20,000 runs for his county between 1914 and 1932 ... yet played only twice in Test matches for England.

A member of the Lancashire side which

won the County Championship three years in succession, in 1926–27–28, Hallows was an opening batsman who, with Harry Makepeace, gave their county the kind of starts which Herbert Sutcliffe and Percy Holmes used to provide for Yorkshire and Sutcliffe and Jack Hobbs did for England. Tall, slim and handsome with a head of sleek black hair always perfectly groomed, Hallows spanned two World Wars in his cricketing career, and when he retired from the first-class game at the age of 37, he resumed in other circles.

He earned the unique distinction of holding professional posts in leagues in England, Scotland, Ireland and Wales, and when he finished stroking his way to runs galore in week-end cricket, he qualified as one of the leading coaches in the game. He held appointments as chief coach with Worcestershire for five years and then with Lancashire, ending his career where it began, at Old Trafford. He was 74 when he finally declared his innings over, but any stranger would have argued that he was at least 20 years younger. His figure was still the upright one of old; his weight never varied from the day he first took guard to the last. His hair showed only a faint tinge of grey and the spirit of the man was remarkable.

Yet he was within a month of celebrating his golden wedding when he returned from the local library, sat in front of the fire and passed away complaining only that he was "a little short of breath."

Hallows hit 55 centuries, 52 of them for Lancashire, and every one of them was a classic example of batsmanship at its best. His highest innings was 233 not out against Hampshire at Liverpool in 1927 when, with an aggregate of 2,343 runs, he averaged 75.58. Twice, at Ashby-de-la-Zouch against Leicestershire in 1924 and off the Warwickshire bowling at Edgbaston in 1928—in which season he reached three figures on 11 occasions—he scored two centuries in a match. I recall him hitting a Nottinghamshire fast bowler over mid-on for six at Old Trafford. The ball dropped on to the platform at Warwick Road Station; and the shot was made with effortless ease.

In the field he was a fast mover and one of the stars of a team that included Parkin, Dick Tyldesley, McDonald and Ernest Tyldesley. His pairing with Makepeace at the opening of any Lancashire innings provided the perfect blend of defence from the dour Makepeace and attack from the stylish Hallows when the ball was new and the bowlers fresh.

When last I saw Hallows he was as enthusiastic as ever about cricket and the way Lancashire were playing it. His death leaves only Len Hopwood, Frank Watson and Eddie Paynter to sustain the legend of Lancashire at their mightiest best in the glorious days of the 1920s and I can pay no greater tribute to the delightful player than to say that Charlie Hallows—some called him Charles—was the youngest old cricketer of my time!—J.K.

HALLOWS, James, one of the best all-round cricketers ever produced by Lancashire, died at Farnworth, near Bolton, on May 20, 1910, after an illness of six weeks. As he was born at Little Lever on November 14, 1875, he was in his 35th year at the time of his death. Ill-health—he was subject to epileptic fits—interfered greatly with his cricket, but he did enough during his comparatively short career to stamp himself as one of the best players of his time. He was left-handed both as batsman and bowler. In addition to possessing a sound defence he had several good strokes on the off side, while as a bowler he could make the ball break either way and had a deceptive flight. His early cricket was played with Little Lever Temperance C.C., and afterwards with Little Lever, whose batting and bowling averages he headed the first season he was a member of the First XI. In 1896, on the strength of his doings in club cricket, he was chosen for the Lancashire Colts match at Old Trafford, and at once made his mark by scoring 133 in his first innings and 77 not out in his second. On the advice of the late Mr. S. M. Crosfield he forsook fast bowling in favour of the medium-pace style, and never had cause to regret the decision. In his first year at Old Trafford he took 84 wickets and had a batting average of 25, and in the following season he played his first match for Lancashire. It was, however, not until 1901 that he became a regular member of the side, and he then batted so well that he would have been worth a place in the team if he had not been able to bowl at all. His great season was that of 1904, when his all-round cricket enabled Lancashire to carry off the Championship. Barnes had thrown in his lot with Staffordshire, and a very successful season had not been anticipated. Hallows, however, rose to the occasion, and in Championship matches alone scored 1,058 runs and took 108 wickets. In all first-class cricket during the season his record was 1,071 runs and 108 wickets. In more recent years he failed to show such form, ill-health being chiefly responsible, and in 1907—against Essex at Manchester—he appeared for his county for the last time.

His hundreds in first-class cricket were

137* v. Middlesex, at Manchester, in 1904; 130* v. Sussex, at Brighton in 1905; 130 v. Essex at Leyton in 1901; 125 v. Essex at Leyton in 1904; 111 v. Derbyshire at Derby in 1904; 110 v. Derbyshire at Manchester in 1906; 109 v. Somerset at Bath in 1902; and 103* v. London County at Manchester in 1903. At Leyton in 1901 he and Broughton (99) added 207 together for the sixth wicket and on the same ground three years later he remained with Mr. R. H. Spooner (215) whilst 296 runs were put on for the third partnership. Appended is a list of his chief bowling feats in first-class matches:

4 for 15	Lancashire v. Warwickshire, at Manchester	..	..	..	..	..	1901
3 " 12	Lancashire v. Surrey, at Manchester	..	..	..	..	..	1901
3 " 11 3 " 6	Lancashire v. Essex, at Manchester	..	..	..	..	..	1901
6 " 42 7 " 29	Lancashire v. Kent, at Tonbridge	..	..	..	..	..	1902
7 " 46 5 " 49	Lancashire v. Notts, at Manchester	..	..	..	..	..	1903
2 " 15 9 " 37	Lancashire v. Gloucestershire, at Gloucester	..	..	..	..	..	1904

(In the second innings he took his first five wickets for seven runs).

| 8 for 50
4 " 40 | Lancashire v. Gloucestershire, at Liverpool | .. | .. | .. | .. | .. | 1904 |
| 7 " 84 | Lancashire v. Worcestershire, at Manchester | .. | .. | .. | .. | .. | 1904 |

(The last two feats were performed in consecutive matches in one week.)

In the second innings of Lancashire's match with M.C.C. and Ground at Lord's in 1902, one of his deliveries was hit to leg over the grandstand and out of the ground into an adjoining garden by W. G. Grace.

In County Championship matches he scored 4,702 runs with an average of 29.20 and took 268 wickets at a cost of 22.89 runs each.

HAMBLING, Montague L., who died in August, 1960, aged 66, played on occasion for Somerset from 1920 to 1927. A fast bowler and hard-hitting batsman, he achieved his best all-round performance at Worcester in 1920. He hit 58, sharing in a third wicket partnership of 101 with J. Daniell, and in the second Worcestershire innings took six wickets for 31, thus playing a big part in victory by an innings and 45 runs. A prominent club cricketer, he three times took all 10 wickets in an innings. He was also a very good footballer and golfer.

HAMMOND, Charles, a cricketer of the very old school, died in the middle of July, 1901, at Storrington, in Sussex. His father was John Hammond, who participated in all the great matches at the end of the 18th and the commencement of the 19th century, whilst Ernest Hammond, whose name is found in the Sussex XIs of 1870, 1874 and 1875, was nephew to the deceased. *Scores and Bio-* *graphies* says of Charles: "Was a fine and powerful hitter, and very successful for his county during the few seasons he played. After 1849, however, he seldom was engaged in a match, owing to (at least the compiler was so informed) his being a bad field, but could throw in well at the distance of 70 or 80 yd." His batting averages for Sussex are appended.

Year	Matches batted in	Innings	Not out	Highest score	Total	Average
1841	1	2	1	2*	2	2.00
1842	4	8	0	43	127	15.87
1843	6	11	1	92	177	17.70
1844	4	7	0	58	161	23.00
1845	4	8	1	31*	78	11.14
1846	5	10	1	32*	102	11.33
1847	5	9	0	24	117	13.00
1848	5	9	2	22*	86	12.28
1849	4	7	1	28	74	12.88
	38	31	7	92	924	14.43

His highest scores in important cricket were 92 v. Notts, at Nottingham in 1843; 58 v. M.C.C. and Ground, at Lord's in 1844; and 57 v. M.C.C. and Ground, at Brighton, also in 1844. He made his score of 92 against the bowling of William Clarke and Samuel Redgate; and he was unfortunate to be dismissed when so near his hundred. In the same match two other players missed their century by a few runs only, C. Hawkins making 95 for Sussex, and John Gilbert 92 for Notts. One of Hammond's bats can be seen in the collection at Wisden's, in Cranbourn Street. Hammond was born at Storrington, on September 6, 1818, and was, therefore, in his 83rd year at the time of his death. In the famous Sussex v. Kent engraving, issued by Mason, of Brighton, and other publishers, Charles Hammond is to be seen fielding at cover-point.

HAMMOND, Ernest, who was born at Storrington on July 29, 1850, died in August, 1921, aged 71. He was a useful all-round player, but was handicapped by ill-health. Between 1870 and 1875 he assisted Sussex in five matches, but accomplished nothing of note. He was nephew of Charles Hammond and grandson of the famous John Hammond, both of whom had played for the county.

HAMMOND, Ernest Robert ("Wally"), who died in Kimberley on February 13, 1977, after a long illness at the age of 65, was the second serious loss to cricket administration in South Africa in just over a month, the President of the S.A.C.A., W.C.B. Woodin, having died in office on January 11. Just as Billy Woodin had had a long association with Eastern Province cricket, so Wally Hammond was the pillar of cricket in Griqualand West. He was Chairman of the Griqualand West Cricket Union for more than 30 years.

WALTER REGINALD HAMMOND
Born at Dover, June 19, 1903
Died at his home at Durban, South Africa, July 2, 1965
By Neville Cardus

When the news came in early July of the death of W. R. Hammond, cricketers everywhere mourned a loss and adornment to the game. He had just passed his 62nd birthday and had not played in the public eye for nearly a couple of decades, yet with his end a light and a glow on cricket seemed to go out. Boys who had never seen him said, "Poor Wally"; they had heard of his prowess and personality and, for once in a while, youth of the present was not sceptical of the doings of a past master.

"Wally" indeed was cricket in excelsis. You had merely to see him walk from the pavilion on the way to the wicket to bat, a blue handkerchief peeping out of his right hip pocket. Square of shoulder, arms of obvious strength, a beautifully balanced physique, though often he looked so weighty that his sudden agility in the slips always stirred onlookers and the batsmen to surprise. At Lord's in 1938, England won the toss v. Australia. In next to no time the fierce fast bowling of McCormick overwhelmed Hutton, Barnett and Edrich for 31. Then we saw the most memorable of all "Wally's" walks from the pavilion to the crease, a calm unhurried progress, with his jaw so firmly set that somebody in the Long Room whispered, "My God, he's going to score a century." Hammond at once took royal charge of McCormick, bouncers and all. He hammered the fast attack at will. One cover drive, off the backfoot, hit the palings under the Grandstand so powerfully that the ball rebounded half-way back. His punches, levered by the right forearm, were strong, leonine and irresistible, yet there was no palpable effort, no undignified outbursts of violence. It was a majestic innings, all the red-carpeted way to 240 in six hours, punctuated by 32 fours.

I saw much of Hammond in England and in Australia, playing for Gloucestershire on quiet west country afternoons at Bristol, or in front of a roaring multitude at Sydney. He was always the same; composed, self-contained, sometimes as though withdrawn to some communion within himself. He could be changeable of mood as a man; as a cricketer he was seldom disturbed from his balance of skill and poise. His cricket was, I think, his only way of self-realisation. On the field of play he became a free agent, trusting fully to his rare talents.

His career as a batsman can be divided into two contrasted periods. To begin with, when he was in his 20s, he was an audacious strokeplayer, as daring and unorthodox as Trumper or Compton. Round about 1924 I recommended Hammond to an England selector as a likely investment. "Too much of a 'dasher'," was the reply. In May, 1927, in his 24th year, Hammond descended with the Gloucestershire XI on Old Trafford. At close of play on the second day Lancashire were so cocksure of a victory early tomorrow

(Whit Friday) that the Lancashire bowlers Macdonald, Richard Tyldesley and company, arranged for taxis to be in readiness to take them to the Manchester races.

Macdonald opened his attack at half-past 11 in glorious sunshine. He bowled his fastest, eager to be quick on the spot at Castle Irwell to get a good price on a "certainty." Hammond, not out overnight, actually drove the first five balls, sent at him from Macdonald's superbly rhythmical arm, to the boundary. The sixth, also, would have counted—but it was stopped by a fieldsman sent out to defend the edge of the field, in front of the sight-screen—a straight deep for the greatest fast bowler of the period, bowling his first over of the day and in a desperate hurry to get to the course before the odds shortened....

That day Hammond scored 187 in three hours—four sixes, 24 fours. He hooked Macdonald mercilessly, yes, "Wally" hooked during the first careless raptures of his youth.

As the years went by, he became the successor to Hobbs as the Monument and Foundation of an England innings. Under the leadership of D. R. Jardine he put romance behind him "for the cause," to bring into force the Jardinian theory of the Survival of the Most Durable. At Sydney, he wore down the Australians with 251 in seven and a half hours (on the 1928–29 tour); then, at Melbourne, he disciplined himself to the extent of six and three-quarter hours for 200, with only 17 fours; *and* then, at Adelaide, his contributions with the bat were 119 (four and a half hours) and 177 (seven hours, 20 minutes). True, the exuberant Percy Chapman was "Wally's" captain in this rubber, but Jardine was the Grey Eminence with his plotting already spinning fatefully for Australia's not distant future. In five Tests of this 1928–29 rubber, Hammond scored 905 runs, average 113.12.

Walter Reginald Hammond was born in Kent at Dover on June 19, 1903, the son of a soldier who became Major William Walter Hammond, Royal Artillery, and was killed in action in the First World War. As an infant, Walter accompanied the regiment with his parents to China and Malta. To the bad luck of Kent cricket when he was brought back to England he went to Portsmouth Grammar School in 1916 and two years later moved with his family to Cirencester Grammar School, rooting himself for such a flowering as Gloucestershire cricket had not known since the advent of W. G. Grace.

In all first-class games, Hammond scored 50,493 runs, average 56.10, with 167 centuries. Also he took 732 wickets average 30.58. In Test matches his batting produced 7,249 runs, average 58.45.

As a slip fieldsman his easy, lithe omnipresence has not often been equalled. He held 78 catches in a single season, 10 in one and the same match. He would stand at first slip erect as the bowler began to run, his legs slightly turned in at the knees. He gave the impression of relaxed carelessness. At the first sight, or hint of, a snick off the edge, his energy swiftly concentrated in him, apparently electrifying every nerve and muscle in him. He became light, boneless, airborne. He would take a catch as the ball was travelling away from him, leaping to it as gracefully as a trapeze artist to the flying trapeze.

Illness contracted in the West Indies not only kept him out of cricket in 1926; his young life was almost despaired of. His return to health a year later was a glorious renewal. He scored a thousand runs in May, 1927, the season of his marvellous innings against Macdonald at Whitsuntide at Old Trafford. I am gratified that after watching this innings I wrote of him in this language: "The possibilities of this boy Hammond are beyond the scope of estimation; I tremble to think of the grandeur he will spread over our cricket fields when he has arrived at maturity. He is, in his own way, another Trumper in the making."

Some three years before he thrilled us by his Old Trafford innings he astounded Middlesex, and everybody else on the scene, by batsmanship of genius on a terrible wicket at Bristol. Gloucestershire, in first, were bundled out for 31. Middlesex then could edge and snick only 74. In Gloucestershire's second innings Hammond drove, cut and hooked no fewer than 174 not out in four hours winning the match. By footwork he compelled the bowlers to pitch short, whereupon he massacred them. He was now hardly past his 20th year.

Like Hobbs, he modulated, as he grew older and had to take on heavier responsibilities as a batsman, into a classic firmness and restraint. He became a classical player, in fact, expressing in a long innings the philosophy of "ripeness is all." It is often forgotten that, on a bad wicket, he was also masterful. At Melbourne, in January, 1937, against Australia, on the worst wicket I have ever seen, he scored 32 without once losing his poise though the ball rose head-high, or shot like a stone thrown over ice.

He could, if he had given his mind constantly to the job, have developed into a bowler as clever as Alec Bedser himself with a new ball. Here, again, he was in action the embodiment of easy flowing motion—a short run, upright and loose, a sideway action, left-shoulder pointing down the wicket, the length accurate, the ball sometimes swinging away late. I never saw him besmirching his immaculate flannels by rubbing the ball on his person, rendering it bloody and hideous to see.

He was at all times a cricketer of taste and breeding. But he wouldn't suffer boredom gladly. One day at Bristol, when Lancashire were scoring slowly, on deliberate principle, he bowled an over of ironic "grubs," all along the ground, underhand.

As a batsman, he experienced only two major frustrations. O'Reilly put him in durance by pitching the ball on his leg-stump. "Wally" didn't like it. His batting, in these circumstances, became sullen, a slow but combustible slow fire, ready to blaze and devour—as it did at Sydney, in the second Test match of the 1936–37 rubber. For a long time Hammond couldn't assert mastery over O'Reilly. For once in his lifetime he was obliged to labour enslaved. In the end he broke free from sweaty durance, amassing 231 not out, an innings majestic, even when it was stationary. We could always hear the superb engine throbbing.

The other frustration forced upon "Wally" occurred during this same 1936–37 rubber. At Adelaide, when victory at the day's outset—and the rubber—was in England's reach at the closing day's beginning, Fleetwood-Smith clean bowled him. Another of "Wally's" frustrations—perhaps the bitterest to bear—befell him as England's captain. At a time of some strain in his life, he had to lead in Australia, in 1946–47, a team not at all ready for Test matches, after the long empty years of World War. Severe lumbago added to Hammond's unhappy decline.

Those cricketers and lovers of the game who saw him towards the end of his career saw only half of him. None the less they saw enough to remain and be cherished in memory. The wings might seem clipped, but they were wings royally in repose. "Wally" had a quite pretty chassé as he went forward to drive; and, at the moment his bat made impact with the ball his head was over it, the Master surveying his own work, with time to spare. First he played the game as a professional, then turned amateur. At no time did he ever suggest that he was, as Harris of Nottinghamshire called his paid colleagues, "a fellow worker."

"Wally" could have batted with any Prince of the Golden Age at the other end of the pitch—MacLaren, Trumper, Hobbs, Spooner, "Ranji"—and there would have been no paling of his presence, by comparison.

Tributes to Hammond included:

A. V. Bedser (Surrey and England): "I rate him the greatest all-rounder I have ever known."

C. J. Barnett (Gloucestershire and England): "I played with Wally for 20 years and consider him the greatest athlete I ever knew."

W. E. Bowes (Yorkshire and England): "Wally was a naturally-gifted player of most games. Tennis, golf, swimming, boxing, soccer and billiards all came alike to him."

Sir Donald Bradman (Australia): "I have never seen a batsman so strong on the off-side and as a slip fieldsman he ranked as one of the greatest. He was usually too busy scoring runs to worry about bowling, but when he did take a hand at it he caused plenty of concern. He was a much better bowler than he was given credit for."

Sir Learie Constantine (West Indies): "Those of us who were fortunate enough to have watched him and played against him will always remember him."

G. Duckworth (Lancashire and England): "He hardly played in a game without leaving his imprint as batsman, fielder or bowler."

T. W. Goddard (Gloucestershire and England): "He was the greatest batsman of them all, ahead of Bradman and the rest. A brilliant bowler, he was incomparable as a fielder."

H. Larwood (Nottinghamshire and England): "He was a magnificent cricketer. We used to expect a 'ton' from him every innings and more often than not he seemed to get it."

S. J. McCabe (Australia): "Everything he did he did with the touch of a master. One could refer to him as the perfect cricketer."

A. Melville (South Africa): "He was the greatest all-rounder I ever played against. He was a magnificent fielder and as a bowler I think he underestimated his capabilities."

W. A. Oldfield (Australia): "Wally was majestic on the field—the perfect batting artist."

W. J. O'Reilly (Australia): "He was certainly the greatest English batsman of my time, tough, hard, but always a brilliant player."

At the age of eight or nine Hammond first played cricket in Malta. He can be termed a self-taught cricketer. Even at Cirencester there was no systematic coaching, but he gave indication of his ability by hitting 365 in a boarders' match.

On becoming associated with Gloucestershire he received valuable advice from George Dennett, the old left-arm slow bowler.

Hammond first played for the Gloucestershire club in 1919 at the age of 16 on the same day as B. H. Lyon, later his captain, made his debut.

After he retired from first-class cricket in 1947, Hammond settled in South Africa where he invested all his savings in the motor trade which has been the ruin of others with far more experience than he had; in a few years his capital had vanished and he was glad to be employed as Coach-Groundsman at Natal University.

His death at the age of 62 was from an illness due in great part to severe injuries suffered in a motor accident five years earlier. He left a widow with two daughters and one son.

Mrs. M. Hammond, his mother, attended the Memorial Service in Bristol Cathedral on July 17 and she was accompanied by B. H. Lyon. The Bishop of Malmesbury officiated and the Duke of Beaufort, President of Gloucestershire County C.C., read the lesson. Viscount Cobham, former Worcestershire captain, in his address said it was hard to evaluate the sum of human happiness created by the majesty and power of "Wally" Hammond's cricket.

W. R. HAMMOND
Career at a Glance
Compiled by Stanley Conder

BATTING

In England

Season	Matches	Inns.	Not Outs	Runs	Highest score	100s	50s	Average	Catches
1920	3	4	1	27	18	—	—	9.00	—
1921	2	3	–	2	1	—	—	0.66	—
1922	5	9	–	88	32	—	—	9.77	8
1923	29	55	4	1,421	110	1	8	27.86	21
1924	27	45	4	1,239	174*	2	4	30.21	30
1925	33	58	5	1,818	250*	3	9	34.30	65
1926			(did not play owing to illness)						
1927	34	47	4	2,969	197	12	12	69.04	46
1928	35	48	5	2,825	244	9	15	65.69	78
1929	28	47	9	2,456	238*	10	8	64.63	36
1930	27	44	6	2,032	211*	5	8	53.47	31
1931	32	49	7	1,781	168*	6	5	42.40	46
1932	30	49	4	2,528	264	8	9	56.17	50
1933	34	54	5	3,323	264	13	8	67.81	54
1934	23	35	4	2,366	302*	8	5	76.32	23
1935	35	58	5	2,616	252	7	12	49.35	54
1936	25	42	5	2,107	317	5	10	56.94	13
1937	33	55	5	3,252	217	13	15	65.04	38
1938	26	42	2	3,011	271	15	7	75.27	33
1939	28	46	7	2,479	302	7	7	63.56	35
1945	6	10	–	592	121	3	2	59.20	11
1946	19	26	5	1,783	214	7	9	84.90	19
1950	1	2	1	107	92*	—	1	107.00	1
1951	1	1	—	7	7	—	—	7.00	—
In Australia and New Zealand									
1928–29	13	18	1	1,553	251	7	1	91.35	10
1932–33	14	20	2	1,511	336*	5	5	83.94	16
1936–37	14	23	2	1,242	231*	5	4	59.14	11
1946–47	13	19	–	781	208	2	2	41.10	12

Signifies not out.

BATTING *(continued)*

In South Africa

1927–28	14	21	2	908	166*	2	4	47.78	13
1930–31	13	19	2	1,045	136*	3	7	61.47	18
1938–39	15	18	1	1,025	181	4	4	60.29	15
1942–43	1	2	–	78	60	—	1	39.00	2

In West Indies

1925–26	10	18	3	732	238*	2	2	48.80	15
1934–35	10	17	3	789	281*	3	—	56.35	15

All First-Class

Matches	633	1,004	104	50,493	336*	167	184	56.10	819

MODE OF DISMISSAL

Bowled	..	..	..	263
Caught	..	..	..	444
Lbw	..	..	..	100
Stumped	..	..	..	67
Hit Wicket	..	..	..	9
Run Out	..	..	..	17
Total	..	..	..	900

Signifies not out.

BOWLING

In England

Season	Overs	Maidens	Runs	Wickets	Average	5 wkts. Inns.	10 wkts. Match
1921	10	0	76	0	—	-	-
1922	1	0	8	0	—	-	-
1923	232	41	742	18	41.22	1	-
1924	307.3	69	775	29	26.72	-	-
1925	680.1	146	2,003	68	29.45	1	-
1926			(did not play owing to illness)				
1927	274	55	884	20	44.20	-	-
1928	720.3	168	1,941	84	23.10	6	2
1929	345	84	978	28	34.92	-	-
1930	406	105	928	30	30.93	1	-
1931	591.3	138	1,457	47	31.00	1	-
1932	627.5	176	1,483	53	27.98	-	-
1933	532.4	115	1,375	38	36.18	2	1
1934	395.1	94	1,059	21	50.42	-	-
1935	617	142	1,636	60	27.26	-	-
1936	423.2	108	1,047	41	25.53	1	-
1937	420.1	68	1,094	48	22.79	2	-
1938	343.2	82	847	14	60.50	-	-
1939	9	1	39	3	13.00	-	-
1945	—	—	—	—	—	-	-
1946	6	3	14	1	14.00	-	-
1950	11	3	25	0	—	-	-

In Australia and New Zealand

1928–29	229.6	50	661	11	60.09	-	-
1932–33	211	38	597	20	29.85	1	-
1936–37	196.3	27	577	27	21.37	2	-
1946–47	3	—	8	0	—	-	-

In South Africa

1927–28	250	58	644	27	23.85	2	-
1930–31	221.4	51	494	15	32.93	-	-
1938–39	97	23	260	7	37.14	-	-
1942–43	2	1	5	0	—	-	-

BOWLING *(continued)*

In West Indies

1925–26	198	42	573	20	28.65	2	–
1934–35	57	11	161	2	80.50	–	–
Totals for all First-Class Matches			22,391	732	30.58	22	3

Note: Overs in Australia, South Africa in 1938–39, and England in 1939 were of eight balls.
    In Test matches W. R. Hammond took 83 wickets for 3,140 runs, an average of 37.83 per wicket. He took five wickets in an innings, once against Australia and once against South Africa.

AGGREGATES

	Matches	Inns.	Not Outs	Runs	Highest Inns.	100s	50s	Average	Catches
In England	516	829	88	40,829	317	134	154	55.09	692
In Australia	47	70	4	4,340	251	17	11	65.75	43
In West Indies	20	35	6	1,521	281*	5	2	52.44	30
In South Africa	43	60	5	3,056	181	9	16	55.56	48
In New Zealand	7	10	1	747	336*	2	1	83.00	6
Totals	633	1,004	104	50,493	336*	167	184	56.10	819

TEST MATCHES

	Matches	Inns.	Not Outs	Runs	Highest Inns.	100s	50s	Average	Catches
Australia	33	58	3	2,852	251	9	7	51.85	43
West Indies	13	20	2	639	138	1	1	35.50	22
South Africa	24	42	7	2,188	181	6	14	62.51	30
New Zealand	9	11	2	1,015	336*	4	1	112.77	9
India	6	9	2	555	217	2	1	79.28	6
Totals	85	140	16	7,249	336*	22	24	58.45	110

COUNTY CHAMPIONSHIP MATCHES

	Matches	Inns.	Not Outs	Runs	Highest Inns.	100s	50s	Aver.	Catches
1920	3	4	1	27	18	—	—	9.00	—
1922	5	9	0	88	32	—	—	9.77	8
1923	26	50	4	1,313	110	1	8	28.54	21
1924	24	41	4	1,085	174*	2	3	29.32	24
1925	28	51	2	1,571	250*	2	8	32.06	55
1926			(did not play owing to illness)						
1927	25	38	3	2,522	197	10	10	72.05	38
1928	25	35	5	2,474	244	9	12	82.46	57
1929	19	31	5	1,730	238*	7	4	66.53	30
1930	16	27	4	1,168	199	3	3	50.78	23
1931	23	36	6	1,389	168*	5	5	46.30	38
1932	23	37	4	2,039	264	6	9	61.68	44
1933	26	44	4	2,578	239	10	8	64.45	41
1934	13	20	4	2,020	302*	8	3	126.25	8
1935	25	42	3	1,803	252	5	6	46.23	37
1936	20	33	3	1,432	317	3	7	47.73	7
1937	23	40	4	2,393	217	10	10	66.47	30
1938	17	28	2	2,180	271	13	2	83.84	23
1939	23	36	5	2,121	302	6	7	68.41	30
1946	12	16	3	1,404	214	6	7	108.00	16
1951	1	1	0	7	7	—	—	7.00	—
Totals	377	619	66	31,344	317	106	112	56.67	530

Signifies not out.

FOR GLOUCESTERSHIRE AGAINST TEAMS IN ENGLAND

	Matches	Inns.	Not Outs	Runs	Highest Inns.	100s	50s	Aver.	Catches
Derbyshire	24	37	3	2,158	237	6	11	63.47	40
Essex	26	44	6	1,888	244	6	4	49.68	48
Glamorgan	28	42	7	2,774	302*	10	6	79.25	28
Hampshire	26	44	2	1,576	192	3	11	37.52	31
Kent	26	48	3	2,352	290	6	14	52.26	35
Lancashire	29	47	4	2,823	271	10	6	65.65	33
Leicestershire	17	27	2	1,460	252	5	4	58.40	24
Middlesex	27	49	5	2,398	178	8	9	54.50	47
Northants	9	13	3	796	193	3	3	79.60	15
Nottinghamshire	20	28	3	1,935	317	10	1	77.40	38
Somerset	28	43	9	2,483	214	10	11	73.02	41
Surrey	22	37	3	2,066	205*	11	3	60.76	35
Sussex	24	42	2	1,627	168*	4	10	40.67	24
Warwickshire	20	32	4	1,545	238*	3	8	55.17	22
Worcestershire	27	44	5	1,946	265*	6	7	49.89	45
Yorkshire	24	42	5	1,517	162*	5	4	41.00	24
Total for County Championship Matches	377	619	66	31,344	317	106	112	56.67	530

*Signifies not out.

OTHER MATCHES FOR GLOUCESTERSHIRE

	Matches	Inns.	Not Outs	Runs	Highest Inns.	100s	50s	Aver.	Catches
Oxford Univ.	11	16	2	915	211*	2	6	65.35	9
Cambridge Univ.	2	3	1	228	113*	2	—	114.00	1
Australians	4	6	—	169	89	—	2	28.16	1
South Africans	2	4	1	232	123	1	1	77.33	2
West Indians	4	7	2	399	264	1	—	79.80	5
Indians	3	6	2	194	81	—	1	48.50	2
New Zealanders	2	3	—	183	108	1	—	61.00	1
Totals	405	664	74	33,664	317	113	122	57.05	551

OTHER MATCHES

	Matches	Inns.	Not Outs	Runs	Highest Inns.	100s	50s	Aver.	Catches
Gentlemen v. Players	23	33	2	1,183	138	3	6	38.16	29
For Other Teams	120	167	12	8,397	281*	29	32	54.17	129
Totals	143	200	14	9,580	281*	32	38	51.50	158

BATTING ON ENGLISH GROUNDS

Ground	Matches	Inns.	Not Outs	Runs	Highest Inns.	100s	50s	Aver.	Catches
Bath	1	1	—	53	53	—	1	53.00	1
Birmingham	9	16	3	744	238*	2	3	57.23	9
Blackpool	2	3	—	58	48	—	—	19.33	4
Bournemouth	3	4	—	58	27	—	—	14.50	5
Bradford	3	6	2	346	147	1	2	86.50	3
Brentwood	2	2	—	168	154	1	—	84.00	6
Brighton	6	10	2	290	168*	1	1	36.25	3
Bristol	114	180	24	9,633	302*	33	38	61.75	146
Burton-on-Trent	3	6	1	384	123	2	1	76.80	4
Canterbury	3	5	1	414	163	2	1	103.50	7
Cardiff	5	7	—	249	156	1	1	35.57	5

*Signifies not out.

BATTING ON ENGLISH GROUNDS (Continued)

Ground	Matches	Inns.	Not Outs	Runs	Highest Inns.	100s	50s	Aver.	Catches
Chelmsford	1	1	—	244	244	1	—	244.00	5
Cheltenham	50	87	12	3,631	231	10	16	48.41	88
Chesterfield	3	5	—	221	81	—	3	44.20	4
Clacton	2	4	—	146	51	—	1	36.50	3
Clifton	6	8	2	400	119	2	—	66.66	12
Colchester	1	2	1	93	72*	—	1	93.00	2
Derby	4	7	—	325	134	1	1	46.42	6
Dewsbury	1	2	—	28	17	—	—	14.00	2
Dover	2	4	—	233	123	1	2	58.25	4
Dublin	1	2	1	107	92*	—	1	107.00	1
Dudley	2	3	1	294	265*	1	—	147.00	2
Eastbourne	1	1	—	52	52	—	1	52.00	1
Folkestone	21	32	1	1,697	184	5	11	54.74	27
Gillingham	1	2	—	24	23	—	—	12.00	2
Gloucester	47	76	5	3,583	317	13	·6	50.46	57
Gravesend	1	2	—	143	80	—	2	71.50	—
Hinckley	1	2	—	34	30	—	—	17.00	3
Horsham	2	4	—	350	160	1	2	87.50	4
Hove	2	4	—	164	73	—	2	41.00	—
Hull	2	4	1	207	162*	1	—	69.00	1
Ilkeston	1	—	—	—	—	—	—	—	2
Kettering	1	1	—	37	37	—	—	37.00	2
Leeds	6	10	1	496	113	1	4	55.11	7
Leicester	5	9	1	682	252	2	1	85.25	8
Leyton	4	7	—	239	127	1	—	34.14	5
Liverpool	1	1	—	264	264	1	—	264.00	—
Lord's	56	89	5	3,903	240	12	14	46.46	70
Maidstone	4	8	—	236	121	1	—	29.50	5
Manchester	22	31	2	1,704	250	6	6	58.75	24
Newport	2	3	1	486	302	2	1	243.00	2
Northampton	2	4	1	154	92*	—	2	51.33	5
Nottingham	13	20	1	634	153	3	—	33.36	30
Nuneaton	1	1	—	40	40	—	—	40.00	1
Oxford	9	13	1	799	211*	2	5	66.58	4
Peterborough	1	2	—	152	131	1	—	76.00	—
Pontypridd	1	1	—	1	1	—	—	1.00	3
Portsmouth	3	6	—	236	112	1	—	39.33	1
Preston	1	2	—	81	65	—	1	40.50	1
Scarborough	6	8	—	244	81	—	3	30.50	13
Sheffield	6	10	1	324	100	1	1	36.00	7
Southampton	8	13	2	619	192	1	6	56.27	11
Southend	1	2	1	6	4	—	—	6.00	1
Stourbridge	1	2	—	47	38	—	—	23.50	2
Swansea	5	10	1	401	177	1	1	44.55	3
Taunton	11	18	2	1,038	197	4	4	64.87	18
The Oval	29	44	8	2,159	217	9	5	59.97	34
Tunbridge Wells	2	3	—	300	290	1	—	100.00	1
Westcliff	2	4	1	436	207	2	—	145.33	4
Weston-super-Mare	1	1	—	51	52	—	1	51.00	—
Worcester	8	12	2	646	160	3	2	64.60	9
Worthing	1	2	—	41	33	—	—	20.50	2
Totals	516	829	88	40,829	317	134	154	55.09	692

Signifies not out.

BATTING ON AUSTRALIAN GROUNDS

Ground	Matches	Inns.	Not Outs	Runs	Highest Inns.	100s	50s	Aver.	Catches
Adelaide	10	15	1	1,101	188	6	1	78.64	11
Brisbane	8	14	1	262	44	—	—	20.15	10
Hobart	1	1	—	7	7	—	—	7.00	2
Launceston	1	1	—	43	43	—	—	43.00	3
Melbourne	11	20	—	1,086	203	3	6	54.30	7
Perth	6	6	—	627	208	3	2	104.50	6
Sydney	10	13	2	1,214	251	5	2	110.36	4
Totals	47	70	4	4,340	251	17	11	65.75	43

BATTING IN WEST INDIES

Ground	Matches	Inns.	Not Outs	Runs	Highest Inns.	100s	50s	Aver.	Catches
Bridgetown	6	10	3	679	281*	2	—	97.00	10
Georgetown	6	10	2	388	111	2	—	48.50	9
Kingston	3	5	—	81	34	—	—	16.20	3
Port of Spain	5	10	1	373	116	1	2	41.44	8
Totals	20	35	6	1,521	281*	5	2	52.44	30

BATTING ON SOUTH AFRICAN GROUNDS

Ground	Matches	Inns.	Not Outs	Runs	Highest Inns.	100s	50s	Aver.	Catches
Benoni	1	1	—	61	61	—	1	61.00	—
Bloemfontein	3	3	—	118	48	—	—	39.33	3
Bulawayo	2	3	1	63	49*	—	—	31.50	1
Cape Town	7	10	—	514	181	2	2	51.40	7
Durban	8	12	2	834	140	4	3	83.40	12
East London	2	2	1	292	166*	2	—	292.00	5
Johannesburg	12	20	1	853	132	1	8	44.89	13
Kimberley	3	3	—	99	53	—	1	33.00	3
Pietermaritzburg	2	2	—	63	41	—	—	31.50	1
Port Elizabeth	1	1	—	52	52	—	1	52.00	1
Pretoria	1	2	—	64	48	—	—	32.00	1
Salisbury	1	1	—	43	43	—	—	43.00	1
Totals	43	60	5	3,056	181	9	16	55.56	48

BATTING ON NEW ZEALAND GROUNDS

Ground	Matches	Inns.	Not Outs	Runs	Highest Inns.	100s	50s	Aver.	Catches
Auckland	1	1	1	336	336*	1	—	—	—
Christchurch	3	4	—	338	227	1	1	84.50	3
Dunedin	1	2	—	37	33	—	—	18.50	1
Wellington	2	3	—	36	26	—	—	12.00	2
Totals	7	10	1	747	336*	2	1	83.00	6

INNINGS BY INNINGS IN TEST CRICKET

	No. of Tests	Inns.	Not Outs	Runs	Highest Inns.	100s	50s	Aver.	Catches
v. Australia	33	58	3	2,852	251	9	7	51.85	43
v. West Indies	13	20	2	639	138	1	1	35.50	22
v. South Africa	24	42	7	2,188	181	6	14	62.51	30
v. New Zealand	9	11	2	1,015	336*	4	1	112.77	9
v. India	6	9	2	555	217	2	1	79.28	6
Totals	85	140	16	7,249	336*	22	24	58.45	110

Bowling—83 wickets (average 37.83)

Signifies not out.

Season		Innings	Runs	Average
1927–28	(S.A.)	51, 43, 14, 90, 1*, 28, 25, 66, 3	321	40.12
1928	(W.I.)	45, 63, 3	111	37.00
1928–29	(A.)	44, 28, 251, 200, 32, 119*, 177, 38, 16	905	113.12
1929	(S.A.)	18, 138*, 8, 5, 65, 0, 17, 101*	352	58.66
1930	(A.)	8, 4, 38, 32, 113, 35, 3, 13, 60	306	34.00
1930–31	(S.A.)	49, 63, 57, 65, 136*, 75, 15, 29, 28	517	64.62
1931	(N.Z.)	7, 46, 100*, 16	169	56.33
1932	(Ind.)	35, 12	47	23.50
1932–33	(A.)	112, 8, 23, 2, 85. 20, 14, 101, 75*	440	55.00
1932–33	(N.Z.)	227, 336*	563	563.00
1933	(W.I.)	29, 34, 11	74	24.66
1934	(A.)	25, 16, 2, 4, 37, 20, 15, 43	162	20.25
1934–35	(W.I.)	43, 29*, 1, 9, 46, 1, 11, 34	175	25.00
1935	(S.A.)	28, 27, 27, 63, 87*, 29, 63*, 65	389	64.83
1936	(Ind.)	167, 217, 5*	389	194.50
1936–37	(A.)	0, 25, 231*, 32, 51, 20, 39, 14, 56	468	58.50
1937	(N.Z.)	140, 33, 0, 31	204	51.00
1938	(A.)	26, 240, 2, 76, 0, 59	403	67.16
1938–39	(S.A.)	24, 58, 181, 120, 1, 61*, 24, 140	609	87.00
1939	(W.I.)	14, 30*, 22, 32, 43, 138	279	55.80
1946	(Ind.)	33, 69, 8, 9*	119	39.66
1946–47	(A.)	32, 23, 1, 37, 9, 26, 18, 22	168	21.00
1946–47	(N.Z.)	79	79	79.00

CENTURIES IN TEST CRICKET (22)

Lord's	Leeds	Birmingham	Manchester
140 (1937)	113 (1930)	138* (1929)	167 (1936)
240 (1938)			

Oval	Adelaide	Melbourne	Sydney
101* (1929)	119* (1929)	200 (1929)	251 (1929)
100* (1931)	177 (1929)		112 (1932)
217 (1936)			101* (1933)
138 (1939)			231* (1936)

Durban	Cape Town	Christchurch	Auckland
136* (1931)	181 (1939)	227 (1933)	336* (1933)
120 (1939)			
140 (1939)			

In each of his first two Test matches—v. South Africa in 1927—W. R. Hammond scored 50 runs and took five wickets.

Against Australia in 1928–29 he scored 779 runs in five consecutive Test innings—251, 200, 32, 119 not out, and 177.

In 1930–31, v. South Africa, he had five consecutive innings each over 50—63, 57, 65, 136 not out and 75. Immediately preceding these innings he had scored 49 (v. South Africa) and 60 (v. Australia).

Hammond is the only cricketer who has scored over 700 runs in four consecutive Test innings: 101 and 75 not out (v. Australia), 227 and 336 not out (v. New Zealand)—all in 1933.

In Test cricket Hammond's record is unparalleled. No other cricketer has played 140 innings, scored over 7,000 runs (including 22 hundreds), taken over 80 wickets, and made over 100 catches.

TWO HUNDREDS IN ONE MATCH

Innings		For	Against	Ground	Year
108	128	Gloucestershire	Surrey	Oval	1927
139	143	Gloucestershire	Surrey	Cheltenham	1928
119*	177	England	Australia	Adelaide	1929
122	111*	Gloucestershire	Worcestershire	Worcester	1933
104	136	M.C.C.	South Australia	Adelaide	1936
110	123	Gloucestershire	Derbyshire	Burton-on-Trent	1938
121	102	England XI	Dominion XI	Lord's	1945

Signifies not out.

FIFTY AND HUNDRED IN ONE MATCH

Innings		For	Against	Ground	Year
110	92	Gloucestershire	Surrey	Bristol	1923
99	187	Gloucestershire	Lancashire	Manchester	1927
123	55	Gloucestershire	Kent	Dover	1927
197	58	Gloucestershire	Somerset	Taunton	1927
50	134	Gloucestershire	Middlesex	Lord's	1929
147	71*	Gloucestershire	Yorkshire	Bradford	1932
70	133	Gloucestershire	Middlesex	Lord's	1932
101	75*	England	Australia	Sydney	1933
160*	57	Gloucestershire	Somerset	Bristol	1936
108	62	Gloucestershire	Surrey	Cheltenham	1936
86	100*	South	North	Lord's	1937
121	63*	Gloucestershire	Glamorgan	Newport	1937
121	56	Gloucestershire	Glamorgan	Bristol	1937
110	55	Gloucestershire	Somerset	Bristol	1937
121	75	Gloucestershire	Lancashire	Manchester	1937
86	101*	Gloucestershire	Somerset	Bristol	1938
214	52*	Gloucestershire	Somerset	Bristol	1946

TWO FIFTIES IN ONE MATCH

Innings		For	Against	Ground	Year
58	82	Gloucestershire	Somerset	Taunton	1925
56	52	M.C.C.	Trinidad	Port of Spain	1926
76	63	Gloucestershire	Lancashire	Bristol	1927
55	68	Gloucestershire	Kent	Folkestone	1928
66	61	Gloucestershire	Sussex	Bristol	1928
64	65	Gloucestershire	Hampshire	Southampton	1928
57	65	England	South Africa	Cape Town	1931
53	92*	Gloucestershire	Northants	Northampton	1932
59	95	Gloucestershire	Sussex	Horsham	1932
59	64	M.C.C.	Victoria	Melbourne	1933
55	51	Gloucestershire	Worcestershire	Worcester	1933
63	87*	England	South Africa	Leeds	1935
66	71	Gloucestershire	Oxford Univ.	Oxford	1935
50	63	An England XI	New Zealanders	Folkestone	1937
71	56	Gloucestershire	Hampshire	Southampton	1937
66	64	Sir P. F. Warner's XI	England Past and Present	Folkestone	1938
60	71	Gloucestershire	Middlesex	Lord's	1939
80	63	Gloucestershire	Kent	Gravesend	1946

TEN WICKETS IN A MATCH

Analysis	For	Against	Ground	Year
15 for 128	Gloucestershire	Worcestershire	Cheltenham	1928
10 for 134	Gloucestershire	Sussex	Brighton	1928
12 for 74	Gloucestershire	Glamorgan	Clifton	1930

CENTURIES (167)
For Gloucestershire (113)

v. Surrey (11): 205*, 199, 143, 139, 135, 128, 120, 113, 110, 108, 108.
v. Glamorgan (10): 302*, 302, 239, 218*, 177, 156, 140, 121, 121, 120.
v. Lancashire (10): 271, 264, 250*, 187, 164, 155, 134, 126, 121, 120.
v. Nottinghamshire (10): 317, 217, 211*, 153, 140, 119, 118*, 116, 111, 103.
v. Somerset (10): 214, 197, 160, 140, 120, 116, 110, 104, 101*, 100.
v. Middlesex (8): 178, 174*, 166, 134, 124, 116, 113, 104*.
v. Derbyshire (6): 237, 231, 134, 134, 123, 110.
v. Essex (6): 244, 207, 164*, 154, 127, 105*.
v. Kent (6): 290, 163, 153*, 136, 123, 121.
v. Leicestershire (5): 252, 217, 206, 114, 113.

Signifies not out.

CENTURIES *(Continued)*

v. Yorkshire (5): 162*, 147, 143, 135, 124.
v. Sussex (4): 168*, 160, 137, 116.
v. Hampshire (3): 192, 112, 112.
v. Northamptonshire (3): 193, 131, 102.
v. Warwickshire (3): 238*, 192*, 142.
v. Cambridge University (2): 113*, 110.
v. Oxford University (2): 211*, 132.
v. West Indies (1): 264.
v. South Africans (1): 123.
v. New Zealanders (1): 108.

Other Matches (54)

England v. Australia (9): 251, 240, 231*, 200, 177, 119*, 113, 112, 101.
England v. Australia (Victory Match) (1): 100.
England v. South Africa (6): 181, 140, 138*, 136, 120, 101*.
England v. New Zealand (4): 336*, 227, 140, 100*.
England v. India (2): 217, 167.
England v. West Indies (1): 138.
M.C.C. v. South Australia (4): 188, 145, 136, 104.
M.C.C. v. Victoria (2): 203, 114.
M.C.C. v. Western Australia (2): 208, 141.
M.C.C. v. New South Wales (1): 225.
M.C.C. v. W. Australia Combined XI (1): 107.
M.C.C. v. Border (1): 166.
M.C.C. v. Transvaal (1): 132.
M.C.C. v. Natal (1): 122.
M.C.C. v. Cape Province (1): 126.
M.C.C. v. Western Province (1): 100.
M.C.C. v. British Guiana (2): 111, 106*.
M.C.C. v. West Indies XI (1): 238*.
M.C.C. v. Barbados (1): 281.
M.C.C. v. Trinidad (1): 116.
Players v. Gentlemen (3): 138, 110, 106.
South v. North (2): 130, 100*.
England v. The Dominions (2): 121, 102.
England v. The Rest (1): 107.
England XI v. West Indies (1): 133.
South of England v. M.C.C. (1): 184.
L. H. Tennyson's XI v. A. E. R. Gilligan's XI (1): 120.

DOUBLES CENTURIES

Innings	For	Against	Ground	Year
336*	England	New Zealand	Auckland	1933
317	Gloucestershire	Nottinghamshire	Gloucester	1936
302*	Gloucestershire	Glamorgan	Bristol	1934
302	Gloucestershire	Glamorgan	Newport	1939
290	Gloucestershire	Kent	Tunbridge Wells	1934
281*	M.C.C.	Barbados	Bridgetown	1935
271	Gloucestershire	Lancashire	Bristol	1938
265*	Gloucestershire	Worcestershire	Dudley	1934
264	Gloucestershire	West Indies	Bristol	1933
264	Gloucestershire	Lancashire	Liverpool	1932
252	Gloucestershire	Leicestershire	Leicester	1935
251	England	Australia	Sydney	1929
250*	Gloucestershire	Lancashire	Manchester	1925
244	Gloucestershire	Essex	Chelmsford	1928
240	England	Australia	Lord's	1938
239	Gloucestershire	Glamorgan	Gloucester	1933

Signifies not out.

DOUBLES CENTURIES *(Continued)*

Innings	For	Against	Ground	Year
238*	M.C.C.	West Indies XI	Bridgetown	1926
238*	Gloucestershire	Warwickshire	Birmingham	1929
237	Gloucestershire	Derbyshire	Bristol	1938
231*	England	Australia	Sydney	1936
231	Gloucestershire	Derbyshire	Cheltenham	1933
227	England	New Zealand	Christchurch	1933
225	M.C.C.	New South Wales	Sydney	1929
218*	Gloucestershire	Glamorgan	Bristol	1928
217	England	India	Oval	1936
217	Gloucestershire	Leicestershire	Gloucester	1937
217	Gloucestershire	Nottinghamshire	Bristol	1934
214	Gloucestershire	Somerset	Bristol	1946
211*	Gloucestershire	Oxford University	Oxford	1930
211*	Gloucestershire	Nottinghamshire	Bristol	1946
208	M.C.C.	Western Australia	Perth	1946
207	Gloucestershire	Essex	Westcliff-on-Sea	1939
206	Gloucestershire	Leicestershire	Leicester	1933
205*	Gloucestershire	Surrey	Oval	1928
203	M.C.C.	Victoria	Melbourne	1933
200	England	Australia	Melbourne	1929

WHERE THE CENTURIES WERE MADE

ENGLAND

Bristol 33	Clifton 2	Horsham 1
Gloucester 13	Leicester 2	Hull 1
Lord's 12	Newport (Mon.) 2	Leeds 1
Cheltenham 10	Oxford 2	Leyton 1
The Oval 9	Westcliff-on-Sea 2	Liverpool 1
Manchester 6	Bradford 1	Maidstone 1
Folkestone 5	Brentwood 1	Peterborough 1
Taunton 4	Brighton 1	Portsmouth 1
Nottingham 3	Cardiff 1	Sheffield 1
Worcester 3	Chelmsford 1	Southampton 1
Birmingham 2	Derby 1	Swansea 1
Burton-on-Trent 2	Dover 1	Tunbridge Wells 1
Canterbury 2	Dudley 1	

ABROAD

Australia: Adelaide 6, Sydney 5, Melbourne 3, Perth 3.
South Africa: Durban 4, Cape Town 2, East London 2, Johannesburg 1.
West Indies: Bridgetown 2, Georgetown 2, Port of Spain 1.
New Zealand: Auckland 1, Christchurch 1.

Number of Grounds in England	..	38
Number of Grounds abroad	.. ..	13
Total	.. ..	51

ONE THOUSAND RUNS IN MAY
(May 7–31, 1927)

	Innings	
	1st	2nd
For Gloucestershire		
v. Yorkshire at Gloucester	27	135
v. Surrey at the Oval	108	128
v. Yorkshire at Dewsbury	17	11
v. Lancashire at Manchester	99	187
v. Leicestershire at Leicester	4	30

Signifies not out.

ONE THOUSAND RUNS IN MAY *(Continued)*

							1st	2nd
v. Middlesex at Bristol	..	..	..	..	..	..	83	7
v. Hampshire at Southampton	..	..	..	..	..	..	192	14

Innings ..	..	..	..	..	..	14
Runs ..	..	..	..	..	..	1,042
Average	..	..	..	..	..	74.42

In 1927 Hammond scored over 1,800 runs in May and June, and owing to bad weather he had only one innings in the last two county matches in June.

LARGE PARTNERSHIPS IN WHICH W. R. HAMMOND SHARED

SECOND WICKET
251 with C. J. Barnett: Glos. v. Sussex at Cheltenham 1934
225* with C. C. Dacre: Glos. v. Worcs. at Worcester 1933
221 with H. Sutcliffe: England v. South Africa at Birmingham 1929
221 with R. E. S. Wyatt: M.C.C. v. Western Australia at Perth 1936–37
216 with A. E. Dipper: Glos. v. Middlesex at Lord's 1929
215 with E. H. Bowley: Tennyson's XI v. A. E. R. Gilligan's XI at Folkestone 1925
211 with R. A. Sinfield: Glos. v. Glamorgan at Cardiff 1931
204* with D. C. H. Townsend: Glos. v. Surrey at Bristol 1933

THIRD WICKET
336 with B. H. Lyon: Glos. v. Leics at Leicester 1933
330 with A. E. Dipper: Glos. v. Lancs. at Manchester 1925
273 with B. O. Allen: Glos. v. Leics. at Leicester 1935
269 with B. O. Allen: Glos. v. Worcs. at Cheltenham 1937
264 with L. Hutton: England v. West Indies at the Oval, 1939
262 with D. R. Jardine: England v. Australia at Adelaide 1928–29
245 with J. Hardstaff: England v. New Zealand at Lord's 1937
242 with E. Paynter: England v. South Africa at Durban 1938–39
226 with A. E. Dipper: Glos. v. Surrey at the Oval 1927
220* with A. E. Dipper: Glos. v. Essex at Bristol 1927
209 with C. J. Barnett: Glos. v. Glamorgan at Bristol 1937
208 with B. O. Allen: Glos. v. Essex at Brentwood 1937
205* with C. J. Barnett: Glos. v. Yorks. at Sheffield 1936
204 with B. O. Allen: Glos. v. Warwicks. at Gloucester 1937

FOURTH WICKET
333 with E. Hendren: M.C.C. v. New South Wales at Sydney 1928–29
321 with W. L. Neale: Glos. v. Leics. at Gloucester 1937
266 with T. S. Worthington: England v. India at the Oval 1936
226 with E. Hendren: Players v. Gentlemen at Folkestone 1927
222 with E. Paynter: England v. Australia at Lord's 1938
208 with W. L. Neale: Glos. v. Glamorgan at Gloucester 1933
202 with J. F. Crapp: Glos. v. Yorks. at Gloucestershire 1938

FIFTH WICKET
242 with L. E. G. Ames: England v. New Zealand at Christchurch 1932–33
242 with B. O. Allen: Glos. v. Somerset at Bristol 1946
214 with J. F. Crapp: Glos. v. Glamorgan at Newport 1939
205 with A. E. Dipper: Glos. v. Somerset at Taunton 1924

SIXTH WICKET
285 with B. H. Lyon: Glos. v. Surrey at the Oval 1928
243 with James Langridge: M.C.C. v. South Australia at Adelaide 1946–47
226* with G. M. Emmett: Glos. v. Notts. at Bristol 1946
218 with T. O. Jameson: M.C.C. v. West Indies XI at Barbados 1925–26
Signifies not out.

LARGE PARTNERSHIPS (Continued)

SEVENTH WICKET
195   with C. C. Dacre: Glos. v. Kent at Tunbridge Wells 1934
177   with W. J. Edrich: England XI v. Dominion XI at Lord's 1945

EIGHTH WICKET
239   with A. E. Wilson: Glos. v. Lancs. at Bristol 1938

NINTH WICKET
133   with V. J. Hopkins: Glos. v. Notts. at Bristol 1936

TENTH WICKET
122   with C. I. J. Smith: M.C.C. v. Barbados at Barbados 1934–35

W. R. Hammond also shared in a first-wicket partnership of 180 with A. E. Dipper for Gloucestershire v. Surrey at Bristol in 1923, and with R. E. S. Wyatt at Durban in 1930–31 put on 160 for the first wicket, each time his own contribution being over 100. Thus Hammond had the unique distinction of sharing in a century partnership for all 10 wickets and scoring a hundred himself in each such partnership.

HIS MOST NOTABLE ACHIEVEMENTS

W. R. Hammond in his career broke and set up many records, the following being a selection of the more important ones:

IN TEST CRICKET

1. He scored most runs (7,249).
2. Most runs in a series of Test matches by an English batsman (905 v. Australia in 1928–29).
3. Twice he scored double centuries in consecutive Test innings—251 and 200 v. Australia in 1928–29, and 227 and 336 not out v. New Zealand in 1932–33.
4. The only cricketer who has scored 700 runs in four consecutive innings in Test cricket—101 and 75 not out v. Australia at Sydney, and 227 and 336 not out v. New Zealand at Christchurch and Auckland, all in 1933.
5. He has made (a) most catches (110) and (b) played most innings (140).

IN FIRST-CLASS CRICKET

1. Most catches in a season (78 in 1928) and most in a match (10 v. Surrey at Cheltenham in 1928).
2. The quickest century of centuries on record—Hammond scored his first hundred in 1923 and his 100th in 1935.
3. 13 hundreds in a season for Gloucestershire in 1938.
4. Twice in Australia, 1936–37 and 1945–46 he scored four hundreds in succession.
5. He scored separate hundreds in a match on seven occasions which is more than any other batsman.
6. His average of 56.10 per innings is the highest of any batsman who has scored over 30,000 runs.
7. In May, 1927, Hammond scored 1,000 runs in 22 days.
8. In Gloucestershire matches in 1938 he scored seven hundreds in eight successive innings.
9. Hammond is the only English batsman who has scored four innings of over 300 runs.
10. Playing for Gloucestershire v. Surrey and Worcestershire at Cheltenham in 1928 Hammond obtained the following figures in the two matches:

	Batting	Bowling	Fielding
v. Surrey	139	1 wkt. for 71	10 catches
	143		
v. Worcestershire	80	9 wkts. for 23	1 catch
		6 wkts. for 105	
Totals	362	16 wkts. for 199	11 catches

Probably this all-round feat is without parallel for one week's cricket.

Signifies not out.

HAMPDEN, David Francis, Fifth Viscount, who died at Glynde on September 4, 1975, aged 73, was better known to cricketers as the Hon. D. F. Brand. He was three years in the Eton XI and captain in 1921. In 1919 at Lord's he played a very valuable innings of 50 not out, in 1920 he took five for 38 in the second innings and in 1921, besides doing useful all-round work, he was especially praised for his management of the bowling. He had a trial for Cambridge in 1922 without getting a Blue, but was a member the following winter of MacLaren's side to Australia and New Zealand. With 469 runs at an average of 21 and 41 wickets for 21 runs each he justified the choice, his best performance being an innings of 60, made when runs were badly wanted, off a New South Wales side who had Kelleway, Hendry, Mailey and J. D. Scott to bowl for them. An attractive, attacking batsman and a useful fast-medium bowler, he showed abundant promise, but unfortunately played no first-class cricket after his return. His family had had a long connection with cricket and his elder brother and his father had both been in the Eton XI. Moreover he was related by marriage to the Freeman-Thomas and Hill-Wood families.

HAMPTON, William Marcus, who died suddenly on April 7, 1964, aged 61, was a sound batsman in the Clifton XI from 1919 to 1922, being captain in the last year when he headed both batting and bowling averages. In 1922 he played for Warwickshire against Northamptonshire, scoring 34, and in 1925 and 1926 he appeared for Worcestershire. He was a master at Winchester.

HANCOCK, William Ilbert, of 27, Anne Street, Cavendish Square, died on January 20, 1910, aged 36. He was a useful cricketer and appeared on a few occasions for Somerset.

HANDFORD, Alick, who died at Tavistock on October 15, 1935, aged 66, played for Nottinghamshire from 1894 to 1898 without ever holding a regular place in the XI. He was also on the ground staff at Lord's. A right hand medium paced bowler with a good easy action he caused a sensation at the end of July, 1894, in the second innings of Gloucestershire at Trent Bridge. Starting the bowling with William Attewell, he sent down 13 overs, 11 maidens, for three runs and five wickets—including those of W. G. Grace, clean bowled, J. J. Ferris, the Australian, and E. M. Grace. His success ended there but his complete analysis showed 26 overs, 18 maidens, 25 runs, five wickets. A year later he took five Leicestershire wickets for 23 runs in the course of 17 overs of which 10 were maidens. Failing to get a permanent place in the county XI Handford devoted himself to coaching at schools.

HANDLEY, Morton, an old Nottinghamshire professional cricketer who in the '60s played for local XXIIs against All England XIs, died on November 14, 1933. *Scores and Biographies* said of him: "He is a good average batsman, a fast round-armed bowler and fields generally at short slip." Although born in Nottinghamshire, he never played for that county.

HANDS, Kenneth Charles Myburgh, who died in Paris on November 18, 1954, aged 62, was the youngest of three brothers who played cricket for South Africa, though his own appearance was in one of the "unofficial" Test matches against the Hon. L. H. Tennyson's English team of 1924–25. After gaining a Blue at Rugby football in 1912, he was tried for the Oxford University cricket XI before returning to South Africa, where he played regularly for Western Province from 1921 to 1931. In all first-class matches, he scored 1,543 runs, average 29.11. Of his three centuries, the highest was 171 not out against Natal in a Currie Cup match at Cape Town in 1925–26.

HANDS, Philip Albert Myburgh, who died at Parys, Orange Free State, South Africa, on April 27, 1951, aged 61, was a batsman noted for his fearless hitting who represented South Africa in seven Test matches, scoring 300 runs, average 25.00. His best Test innings was a chanceless 83 against England at Port Elizabeth in 1913–14, scored out of 98 and 105 minutes. In Currie Cup cricket he played for Western Province from 1912–13 to 1926–27, scoring 899 runs, average 29.00, including three centuries, his highest score being 119 against Transvaal at Johannesburg in 1923–24. In 1924 he was a member of the South African team which toured England, but he scored only 436 runs in 26 innings in first-class matches. Previously, like his two brothers, R. H. M. and K. C. M., who were also well-known South African cricketers, he won a Rugby Blue at Oxford University (1910), but he did not play for the University at cricket. During the First World War he was awarded the D.S.O. and M.C.

HANDS, William Cecil, one of four survivors of Warwickshire's 1911 Championship side, died on August 31, 1974 aged 87. An amateur, business prevented his full-time participation in County Cricket. Hands played in eight of Warwickshire's 20 Championship matches in 1911 when Frank Foster (116 wickets) and F. E. Field (122 wickets) were the big men in the attack. Right hand, medium pace with an easy action, Hands claimed only 17 victims that year; he was so lean in body that he could not make a sustained effort. His best performance was five for 10 against Surrey at the Oval in 1912 on a hard, fast pitch. Altogether, between 1909 and 1920, Hands took 142 wickets, average 24.71, and he held 35 catches. He averaged 12.96 with the bat.

HANSELL, John (Norfolk), died at North Elmham, in Norfolk, January 19, 1900, aged 49. Bowled fast to medium (right hand), and batted left-handed, with good hitting powers. In the match at Lord's in July, 1885, Hansell was one of the three batsmen (the brothers Jarvis being the two others) who scored a hundred in the Norfolk innings against the M.C.C. The total of 695 by the county remained a record for Lord's ground for over 10 years.

HARBEN, Sir Henry, D.L., J.P., died at Warnham Lodge on December 2, 1911, in his 89th year. He was a keen supporter of Sussex cricket and President of the County Club in 1901 and 1906. It was largely through him that Bland qualified for Sussex, and that Cox was tried in the county XI. He was born at Bloomsbury on August 24, 1823, and was a cousin of the Rt. Hon. Joseph Chamberlain.

HARBEN, Major Henry Eric Southey, who died suddenly in Malta on October 1, 1971, aged 71, did not gain a place in the XI while at Eton, but played in eight matches for Sussex in 1919.

HARDCASTLE, The Venerable Edward Hoare, died at Brighton on May 20, 1945, aged 83. Winchester XI, 1880. A fast left-handed bowler, he played once for Kent in both 1883 and 1884, and occasionally for Worcestershire. Archdeacon Emeritus of Canterbury.

HARDCASTLE, Frank, who played on a few occasions for Lancashire in 1867 and 1869, but with little success, died at 87 Lancaster Gate, London, on November 6, 1908, in his 65th year. He was educated at Repton and from 1885 to 1892 was M.P. for the Westhoughton Division of Lancashire.

HARDING, Kenneth, died on November 30, 1977, aged 85. A member of the XI at St. Edward's, Oxford, he lost part of his right hand in the First World War, but even with this handicap made so many runs for Eastbourne that in 1928 he played three matches for Sussex and against Essex at Leyton scored 55 not out.

HARDING, Norman Walter, the Kent fast right-arm bowler, died on September 25, 1947, of infantile paralysis in a Berkshire isolation hospital after less than a week's illness; he was only 31. Of good height and graceful build, he bowled with an easy action and, besides making the ball swing, he could use the off-break with some effect. Born in Southampton, he learned cricket at Reading School, and played for Berkshire before joining the Kent staff at Canterbury in 1936, when for the Second XI against Wiltshire at Swindon he accomplished the extraordinary feat of taking 18 wickets in the match—nine wickets for 39 and nine for 61— regarded as unique in County Cricket. His first County Championship match was at Dover in 1937, and in the two seasons before the War he met with considerable success. Subsequently he took chief part in the county's pace attack and was regarded as the fastest Kent bowler since W. M. Bradley. Last season he took 64 wickets at an average cost of 25 runs. In August, 1945, for Kent in a one-day match against the Rest of the County at Canterbury, Harding took all 10 wickets for 32 runs in a total of 89, and his side won by 104 runs. He bowled seven men and got one leg-before.

HARDINGE, Harold Thomas William, who died at Cambridge on May 8, 1965, aged 79, was one of a very small number of men who played for England at both cricket and Association football. A sound and reliable opening batsman at a time when cricketers of ability in that place in the order were plenti ful, he played for England in 1921 at Leeds in a match against Australia from which J. B. Hobbs had to withdraw on the opening day because of appendicitis. As a centre-forward, Hardinge represented his country against Scotland at Glasgow in 1910 and he also played for Sheffield United and Arsenal.

"Wally" Hardinge rendered great service to Kent as a professional from 1902 to 1933 and he took part in six Gentlemen v. Players matches between 1911 and 1924, making 127 at the Oval in 1921. During a career lasting

31 years, he scored 33,519 runs in first-class cricket at an average of 36.51 per innings, dismissed 371 batsmen with slow left-arm bowling for 26.37 runs each and held 293 catches. He hit 75 centuries, the highest being 263, scored in six hours against Gloucestershire at Gloucester in 1928. That summer was his most successful in run-getting, for he reached an aggregate of 2,446 average 59.65. Altogether he passed 1,000 runs in a season on 18 occasions, five times exceeding 2,000. He put together two separate centuries in a match four times: 153 and 126 v. Essex at Leyton in 1908; 175 and 109 v. Hampshire at Southampton in 1911; 117 and 105 not out v. Hampshire at Dover in 1913 and 207 and 102 v. Surrey at Blackheath in 1921. In 1913 he reached three figures in four successive innings—154 not out against Leicestershire at Canterbury; 117 and 105 not out v. Hampshire and 107 v. Northamptonshire at Dover. As a bowler, his most outstanding analysis was achieved at Tunbridge Wells in 1929 when, on a pitch responsive to spin, he took six Warwickshire wickets in 11.5 overs at a cost of nine runs. For many years he was on the business staff of John Wisden and Co., Ltd.

HARDSTAFF, Joseph, senior, died suddenly at his Nottingham home on April 2, 1947, aged 66. Rather short and strongly built, he played for Nottinghamshire from 1902 to 1924, scoring altogether in first-class cricket 17,146 runs, average 31.34. He toured Australia in 1907–08, when A. O. Jones, his county captain, led the English side, and he met with marked success, averaging over 51 in all matches, with much the highest aggregate—1,384, and his three centuries surpassed the efforts of all his colleagues. His average in the five Tests was 31.10, only George Gunn and Jack Hobbs doing better. Free in stroke play all round the wicket, he could put up a stout defence in a way quite in keeping with the best of Nottinghamshire batsmen. He helped Nottinghamshire to carry off the Championship in 1907, and, by scoring 124 not out and 48 against the South African team, influenced his choice for the tour in Australia; Nottinghamshire won the match by five wickets. A brilliant field, especially in the deep, he occasionally bowled rather fast but with moderate success. Sir Home Gordon credits him with 182 catches.

Hardstaff soon became a favourite with the Australian spectators, who showed their appreciation by calling him "Hot Stuff." He died while his son was on the way home from Australia. The Hardstaffs provide the only case of a father and son representing England in Australia; but Fred Tate played in one Test match in England against Australia 22 years before his son, Maurice Tate, first went to Australia in 1924. After retiring from the Nottinghamshire team, Hardstaff senior became a popular first-class umpire and stood in several Test matches. He would probably have officiated in many more but for the fact that he was not allowed to umpire when young Hardstaff was playing in such games. Of course, he could not officiate when Nottinghamshire were engaged, and so he saw comparatively little of his son as a player.

HARDSTAFF, Richard Green, who was born on January 12, 1863, at Selston, Nottinghamshire, died there on April 18, 1932. A left-arm medium-pace bowler, he rendered good service to Rawtenstall, the Lancashire League club, for several years and between 1893 and 1899 he played occasionally for his county. Altogether he took 99 wickets for Notts at an average cost of 19. He put together his highest score in 1896 in W. Chatterton's Benefit match at Derby when Notts made 466 runs, of which W. Gunn obtained 207 not out. Going in last Hardstaff hit up 60 before being run out and, taking eight wickets for less than seven runs apiece, was mainly responsible for Derby's small total of 93. In the Notts Colts' match at Trent Bridge in April, 1896, he disposed in the course of one day of 14 batsmen at a cost of only 38 runs. In the same year on the same ground he took for Notts against Yorkshire 10 wickets for 94 runs—seven in the first innings for 44 runs.

HARDY, Private Frederick Percy (County of London Yeomanry), born at Blandford on June 26, 1881, was found dead on the floor of a lavatory at King's Cross station (G.N.R.) on March 9, 1916. His throat was cut and a blood-stained knife was by his side. He was on the Oval ground-staff in 1900 and 1901 and began to appear for Somerset in 1903. In consecutive innings for the Surrey Colts in 1901 he made 141 v. Wandsworth and 144 not out v. Mitcham Wanderers. In 1910 he played two excellent innings at Taunton, making 91 v. Kent and 79 v. Surrey. He was a left-handed batsman and a useful right-handed medium-paced change bowler.

HARDY, Norman, who died suddenly of heart failure at the age of 31 whilst playing football on November 17, 1923, had appeared occasionally for Somerset since 1912. He was a fast-medium bowler, and in 1919 took 18 wickets for 13 runs each.

HARDY, Silas, who played for Nottinghamshire a few times in 1893 and 1895, died in June, 1905. He was born at Kimberley on April 30, 1868, and was therefore only 37 years of age at the time of his death. He was a good free bat and fast bowler, but never appeared regularly for the county.

HARDY, Major W. Eversley, for some years a member of the Committee of the M.C.C., died in April, 1908. (He was buried at Bath on April 11.)

HARE, Stericker Norman, C.B.E., who died at Meadle, near Aylesbury, on September 30, 1977, aged 77, played in three matches for Essex in 1921. In his first innings for the county against Derbyshire at Leyton, batting at number 10, he scored 98 and helped J. W. H. T. Douglas to add 251 for the ninth wicket. Captain of Chigwell in 1918, he played club cricket for Ilford.

HARFORD, Herbert Merrick, when at his best a dashing batsman with sound defence and a capital out-field, died of pneumonia at Bushey on December 29, 1916, aged 43. He played frequently for Hertfordshire between 1898 and 1911, and captained the side with sound judgment. His most successful season was 1908, when he scored 182 runs with an average of 22.77, his highest innings being 82 v. Bedfordshire at Watford, where he and W. H. Marsh (47 not out) added 127 for the last wicket. He had been a member of the M.C.C. since 1901.

HARFORD, Noel Sherwin, who died in Auckland on March 30, 1981, aged 51, played eight times for New Zealand between 1955 and 1958, his double of 93 and 64 in his first Test match, against Pakistan at Lahore, being much his best effort. He was a "sparkling" (*Wisden* 1959) driver of the ball, but without a defence to match. He was one of four players to score 1,000 runs on New Zealand's somewhat unsuccessful tour to England in 1958, his 158 in the Parks at Oxford seeing him at his best. He played Plunket Shield cricket for both Central Districts and Auckland. In Test matches he scored 229 runs at an average of 15.26. In all first-class cricket his aggregate was 3,149 runs and his average 27.62.

HARGREAVE, Samuel, born at Longsight, near Manchester, September 22, 1876, died at Stratford-on-Avon on January 2, 1929, aged 52. Before qualifying for Warwickshire he played for Lancashire Second XI and was a member of the ground-staff at Old Trafford. From 1899 until 1909 he did good work as a left-handed, slow-medium bowler, keeping an excellent length and varying his pace well. He was also a very smart field, especially to his own bowling. But for a strain sustained in 1907 which had a permanent effect upon his cricket, his career in great matches would undoubtedly have been longer. Among his many good feats with the ball were: (see below)

14 for 115 (including 8 for 66), v. London County, at Edgbaston	1901
8 for 62 v. Gloucestershire, at Edgbaston	1901
14 for 109 (including 8 for 52), v. Lancashire, at Manchester	1902
6 for 12	1902–03
8 for 42 Lord Hawke's Team v. South Island, at Dunedin	1903
15 for 76 v. Essex, at Leyton	1903
(including 9 for 35), v. Surrey, at the Oval	
(He and Santall, (S.) were on unchanged throughout).	
5 for 12 v. Oxford University, at Oxford	1905
13 for 102 v. Derbyshire, at Derby	1906
(At one time he took five for five in 31 balls).	

On his first appearance for the Players, at the Oval in 1902, he had an analysis of six for 53: his other matches against the Gentlemen were at Lord's in 1903 and at the Oval in 1904. In 1902–03 he was a member of Lord Hawke's team to New Zealand and Australia.

HARGREAVES, James Henry, who played occasionally for Hampshire as "J. Smith," died at Portsmouth on April 11, 1922. He had been a useful batsman, was President of the Portsmouth Cricket Association and for nearly 40 years coached at the Portsmouth Grammar School. His first match for Hampshire was in 1884, and his highest score for the county 72 not out v. Sussex at Southampton in 1889.

HARGREAVES, Reginald Gervis, born at Oak Hill, Accrington, on October 13, 1852, died at Lyndhurst on February 12, 1926, aged 73. He was described as: "A good hitter, fields well at cover-point, and bowls slow under-hand." He appeared for Hampshire, commencing in 1875, and was always interested in the welfare of the County Club, of which he was a Vice-President at the time of his death.

HARGREAVES, Tom Knight, who died in hospital at Rotherham on November 19, 1955, aged 61, was a prominent all-rounder in Yorkshire Council cricket from 1921 till 1951. He played for Wath till he was 57, scoring many runs and proving successful as a slow bowler. A forcing batsman, he scored 191 in 90 minutes against Brampton in 1935. He brought off one of the biggest hits in cricket on one occasion when playing at the Wath Athletic Ground. A mighty six sent the ball soaring out of the ground and into a wagon of a goods-train on the nearby railway line. The ball was carried on to Scunthorpe.

HARPER, Leonard Vyse, born at Balham, in Surrey, on December 12, 1880, died at his native place on January 13, 1924, aged 43. A free-hitting batsman and a brilliant field at mid-off, he was in the Rossall XI in 1896, 1897, 1898 and 1900, being captain in the two last mentioned years. (He was absent during 1899.) At Cambridge he obtained his Blue as a Freshman, and in 1901 played a beautiful, if lucky, innings of 84 against Oxford. In 1904, when he appeared for Surrey in half-a-dozen games, he came into the Gentlemen v. Players match at the Oval as a substitute, but failed to distinguish himself. He represented his University at hockey as well as at cricket.

HARRAGIN, Col. A. E., captain of the Trinidad team over a long period, died in the spring of 1941, aged nearly 64. He took a prominent part in the tour of the West Indies team in 1906, scoring 639 runs with an average of nearly 32; highest 86 in all matches. Of good height and build, he put plenty of power into his drives and generally was attractive in applying the bat to the ball. He did specially well against Kent at Catford, making 31 and 51, but despite his second effort the touring team were beaten in an innings. In the match against Minor Counties at Ealing he scored 68 and 63, so largely helping in victory by 215 runs—the first success of West Indies in England.

HARRIS, Charles, a left-hand batsman and bowler, who played occasionally for Northamptonshire before they became first-class, died at Knottingley, Yorkshire, on February 16, 1951, aged 83. He was a prominent player for Keighley in the early days of the Bradford League.

HARRIS, Charles Bowmar, who died in Nottingham General Hospital on August 8, 1954, aged 45, played as opening batsman for Nottinghamshire from 1928 till 1951, in which time he scored nearly 20,000 runs. A fine batsman, capable of strong hitting or dour defence, and a capable spin-bowler, he did not gain a regular place in the county side till 1931, when he got his chance as a result of a motoring accident involving three Nottinghamshire players. So well did he seize the opportunity that in 12 games he scored 456 runs, headed the county averages with 50.66 and earned his county cap. Next season, for the first of 11 times, he exceeded 1,000 runs and established himself in the XI.

In 1933 he made 234 against Middlesex at Trent Bridge, he and W. W. Keeton sharing in a first wicket stand of 277. He and Keeton steadily became one of the best opening pairs in the country and in 1950 they joined in two three-figure partnerships against Northamptonshire at Northampton. Harris's best season was that of 1934, when he obtained 1,891 runs, average 38.59, and hit five centuries. His highest innings was 239 not out in 1950 when he carried his bat against Hampshire at Trent Bridge. His benefit match, against Yorkshire in 1949, realised £3,500— a county record—despite the loss through rain of the opening day. Troubled by ill-health for some years, Harris appeared to have recovered when he was appointed a first-class umpire last season, but after standing in a few matches he broke down and was compelled to resign.

Well known as one of cricket's humorists, he habitually greeted the fieldsmen when going in to bat at the start of a day with the remark: "Good morning, fellow workers." On one occasion when the light was far from good, he made his way from the pavilion carrying a flare and headed straight for square-leg!

HARRIS, Dennis Frank, who died on December 17, 1959, aged 48, played in one match for Warwickshire in 1946. In the King Edward's Grammar School, Camp Hill XI in 1925 and 1926, he became a leading batsman for Moseley, whom he captained from 1949 to 1951 and helped to the Birmingham League Championship in 1938.

HARRIS, Lieut.-Colonel Frank, who died at Tunbridge Wells on July 2, 1957, aged 91, was for 35 years captain of Southborough C.C., for whom he first played when 16. In his younger days an enthusiastic runner, he walked from Bidborough to London on his seventieth birthday because his father did the same thing and had told him that he would not be able to do so when he was 70. The journey occupied him just over 13 hours. He served in the Royal Engineers during the First World War, being Mentioned in Dispatches.

HARRIS, Henry Edward, born at Brighton on June 8, 1854, died at Littlehampton on November 8, 1923. He was educated privately at Brighton, and was a useful batsman and fielded generally at point. In 1875 and 1876 he was Hon. Secretary of the Brighton Club, but, living in Hampshire from 1877 until 1881, he appeared in a few matches for that county in 1880. For many years, commencing in 1887, he was Hon. Secretary of the Littlehampton C.C., and he had served on the Committee of the Sussex County C.C.

HARRIS, Stanley Shute, born at Glenavon House, Clifton, Bristol, on July 19, 1881, died at Farnham, in Surrey, on May 4, 1926, aged 45. A batsman who could hit all round hard and clean, he was second in the Westminster averages in 1899 with 41.62, his highest innings being 111 v. Incogniti. At Cambridge he played for the Freshmen in 1901 and for the Seniors in 1902 and 1904, but was not awarded his Blue, although tried in the XI in 1902 and two next years. He appeared, however, for Gloucestershire and Surrey, though very seldom, and at the Crystal Palace in 1904 scored 76 for London County against the South Africans. He played most of his cricket with Old Westminsters, Butterflies, Free Foresters, Quidnuncs, Incogniti and Crusaders. Better known in the world of Association football, he was a great forward, playing for Cambridge in 1902 and two following seasons— he was captain in 1904—for the Corinthians, and for England on two occasions each against Scotland, Wales and Ireland. Since 1904 he had been Headmaster of St. Ronan's Preparatory School, West Worthing.

HARRISON, Frederic, the well-known publicist, was born in London on October 18, 1831, and died at Bath on January 14, 1923. As a bowler he played for King's College, London, from 1847 until 1849, and for Wadham College, Oxford, in 1850 and two following years. Between 1846 and 1849 he took part in small matches at Lord's, where the famous William Lillywhite bowled to him. He had many most interesting reminiscences of Pilch, Parr, Box, Alfred Mynn, Clarke, Sir Frederick Bathurst, and other giants of the past, and he must have been one of the last survivors of those who saw Alfred Mynn defeat Felix at single-wicket at Lord's in 1846.

HARRISON, George Pickering, a typical Yorkshireman of the old school, died, aged 78, at Scarborough, his home, in September, 1940. He came to the front when first given a trial in 1883, and his career ended almost as suddenly in 1892 from the effects of injury. A right-handed fast bowler, he appeared for Colts of the North at Lord's and clean bowled nine Colts of the South—five of them in six balls—at the low cost of 14 runs. Chosen for the Yorkshire XI without delay, he excelled in his first county match at Dewsbury against Kent; he bowled unchanged through both innings with Ted Peate, the slow left-hander. Harrison came out with 11 wickets for 76 runs as his share in disposing of the visitors for totals of 65 and 79, so surpassing the work of his England colleague. The distinction of being chosen for Players against Gentlemen at Lord's followed, and in the whole season he took 100 wickets at an average cost of 13 runs, his Yorkshire record being 88 at less than 12 runs each.

After such an exceptional start, Harrison suffered an injury when throwing in from the deep field. This accident occurred when he was acting as substitute, and it necessitated the abandonment of fast bowling. Reducing his speed, he met with some success, but could not retain his place in the county XI.

In Yorkshire Council cricket for Bowling Old Lane he took 878 wickets, and in three seasons for Idle 215 fell to him, the average cost for all this effective work being about nine runs a wicket. He enjoyed a day of great success for the North and East Ridings of Yorkshire touring in the South, taking 15 Chiswick Park wickets for 38 runs.

Known familiarly as "Shoey," an abbreviation of his trade as shoemaker, Harrison often umpired in first-class cricket, and at every Scarborough Festival in recent years his favourite corner in the pavilion was alive with humour and reminiscences. Of many tales told of him, one mentioned in *The Cricketer* goes back to his first match at Lord's. When accepting the invitation to play for the Colts he asked Mr. Henry Perkins, the M.C.C. Secretary, to meet him at King's Cross as he had never been to London.

HARRISON, Harry S., who died on December 10, 1971, aged 88, played as a professional for Surrey from 1906 to 1922. With the county then so richly endowed with batting talent, he could not command a regular place in the side, but in 1913 he and A. Sandham shared a partnership of 298 against Sussex at the Oval which remains the highest for the sixth Surrey wicket. During this stand Harrison obtained one of his two first-class centuries. Altogether he scored 5,237 runs, average 23.59, by very steady batting marked by extremely sound defence. His large hands—he was a bricklayer before he joined the Oval staff—stood him in good stead in the slips where he held 116 catches. After leaving Surrey he coached first at Charterhouse and for many years at Corfe School in Kent.

Of him, A. Sandham said: "He was a very correct batsman—so correct that he played his shots mostly to the fielders! I should say that he would get into most county sides today."

HARRISON, Isaac Marshall, who played in seven matches for Nottinghamshire in 1901, died at Calverton, his native place, on February 25, 1909, at the early age of 29. He was a stylish batsman and a brilliant field, but was obliged to give up the game owing to ill-health.

HARRISON, William Philip, who died on September 7, 1964, aged 78, ended a brief first-class career on a glorious note when, in his last innings, he hit 156 for Middlesex against Gloucestershire at Gloucester, where he and E. S. Litteljohn added 131 for the third wicket. In the XI at Rugby in 1902 and 1903, he hit 55 in the match with Marlborough at Lord's in the first year and 76 in the next, when he headed the school averages. He gained a Blue at Cambridge in 1907, but achieved little on the big occasion. He took part in seven matches for Kent in 1904 and 1905 and from 1906 to 1911 he played for Middlesex. In 1906–07 he toured New Zealand with the M.C.C. team.

HARRY, Frank, who was born at Torquay on December 22, 1878, died at the North Malvern Hotel, Malvern, on October 27, 1925. Becoming a member of the ground staff at Old Trafford in 1900, he played for Lancashire from 1903 until 1908. He was a medium-paced bowler with an easy action and a break both ways. Among his good figures for the county were 15 for 70 (six for 26 and nine for 44) v. Warwickshire at Manchester in 1906, five for 14 v. Worcestershire at Stourbridge in 1907, and six for 18 v. Leicestershire at Manchester in 1908. Against Sussex at Eastbourne in 1907 he bowled eight consecutive maiden overs, and he repeated the feat the next year in the match with Oxford University at Oxford. After his connection with Lancashire he accepted an engagement with the Kilmarnock C.C., and later appeared for Durham County through residence at South Shields. In 1915 he settled in Malvern and after the War played occasionally for Worcestershire as an amateur. In his day he was a prominent Rugby football player of the Northern Union school, being attached to the Broughton Rangers.

HARRY, John, of Victoria, Australia, was born on August 1, 1857, and died at Canterbury (Victoria), October 27, 1919. At his best he was an excellent all-round cricketer, being well above the average as a batsman, a useful change bowler, a good wicket-keeper, and a brilliant fieldsman at mid-off. Several times he was nearly chosen as reserve wicket-keeper to tour England, and in 1896 was actually selected, but at the last moment was discarded owing to an injury to his knee which it was considered would hamper his play. He thereupon proceeded to England on his own responsibility and joined the ground-staff at Lord's but was only fairly successful, his best performance being an innings of 56 for M.C.C. against the University at Oxford. For Victoria he made many good scores, the chief being 114 v. Western Australia at Melbourne in 1892–93 and 107 v. South Australia at Adelaide in 1895–96. He generally did well as Adelaide, and in March, 1894, made 82 and 50 in the inter-State match there. In club cricket he scored 6,970 runs for East Melbourne with an average of 37.15 and took 107 wickets for 16.17. For Bendigo he made 4,308 runs and took 143 wickets, his respective averages being 28.15 and 14.42. In the inter-State match at Adelaide in 1891–92 he had the unusual experience of bowling both left and right hand. At Easter, 1919, a match played at Bendigo for his benefit realised over £200. Harry was also a capital skittles player and gained inter-State honours at Baseball.

HARTIGAN, Gerald Patrick Desmond, who died in a Durban hospital on January 7,

1955, aged 70, played for South Africa at both cricket and Association football. As a right-handed batsman and fast-medium bowler, he appeared for Border in the Currie Cup competition from 1903 to 1927, his highest innings being 176 not out against Eastern Province in 1910–11. In 1912 he was a member of the South African team who figured in the Triangular Tournament in England, but he played in only 12 matches, including two Tests, for, in returning a ball from the deep field, he fractured an arm. In 1913–14 he took part in the first three Test matches against the England touring side led by J. W. H. T. Douglas and at Johannesburg in the second was top scorer in the first innings with 51.

HARTIGAN, Roger Joseph, who died in Brisbane on June 7, 1958, aged 78, played for Australia in two Test matches against A. O. Jones's England team in 1907. Born at Sydney, he took part in one game for New South Wales before moving to Brisbane, where he earned a big reputation as a batsman for Queensland. After scoring 59 for his State and 55 not out for an Australia XI against the M.C.C. side, he was chosen for the third Test at Adelaide in 1907 and enjoyed the distinction of hitting a century in the second innings. He (116) and Clem Hill (160) added 243 for the eighth wicket, an Australian record which still stands. He toured England with M. A. Noble's Australians in 1908, but never found his true form, his one century being against Western Union at Glasgow, and he averaged no more than 18.84 for 33 innings. When his playing career ended, he served on the Australian Board of Control for 35 years and was chairman of the Brisbane Cricket Ground Trust. He represented New South Wales at baseball and Queensland at lacrosse.

HARTINGTON, Harry E., died at Pontefract, West Riding, in February, 1950, aged 67. He played for Yorkshire as a fast bowler in 1910 and 1911. He also assisted Featherstone until 1929, when he became chairman of that club.

HARTLEY, Lieut. Alfred (R.G.A.), born 1879, killed in October, 1918. Lancashire XI. Alfred Hartley could not be classed among the greatest of Lancashire batsmen, but during his few seasons for the county he was invaluable to the XI, his strong defence making him a worthy successor to Albert Ward. He was given three trials for Lancashire in 1907 having shown fine form that

summer for the Second XI. He justified the committee's action in selecting him, scoring 126 runs in six innings. Having found a place in first-class cricket he improved from year to year, scoring 1,053 runs for Lancashire in 1908, and 1,129 runs with an average of 36 in 1909. Then in 1910 he left all his previous form behind. Scoring 234 against Somerset at Manchester, 126 not out against Somerset at Bath, and 168 against Leicestershire at Leicester, he had a record for his county of 1,511 runs with an average of 38. On the strength of his fine cricket he was deservedly chosen for Gentlemen against Players, both at Lord's and the Oval. The Gentlemen failed dismally at Lord's, going all to pieces on a difficult wicket, but Hartley himself played very well—24 and 35. In his second innings he received two dead shooters in succession from George Thompson. He stopped the first one but the second bowled him. In 1911 Hartley fell off a great deal in his batting, and in the following year he practically retired from first-class matches.— S.H.P.

HARTLEY, Charles R., born at New Orleans, U.S.A., on February 13, 1873, died at Brooklands, Cheshire, on November 15, 1927, aged 54. He was an elder brother of Mr. Alfred Hartley and, being a sound batsman with plenty of strokes, he played frequently for Lancashire, his first appearance for the county being in 1897 and his last in 1909. His best season was that of 1900 when, in all first-class matches, he obtained 1,084 runs with an average of 30. That year he played three three-figure innings, making 139 v. Gloucestershire at Bristol, where he and Albert Ward added 211 together for the sixth wicket, 104 v. Leicestershire at Leicester, and 109 v. Derbyshire at Glossop. In 1901, when he scored 112 against Gloucestershire at Gloucester, he and Mold put on 101 together for the 10th wicket. C. R. Hartley was also for some time a prominent figure in the Rugby football world, playing for Cheshire and, in 1900 and 1901, at full back for North against South.

HARTLEY, Frank, who died on October 20, 1965, aged 69, did good all-round work as an amateur for Oxfordshire between 1922 and 1931. His first season was his best, for he scored 353 runs, with a highest innings of 139, average 29.41, and took 32 wickets for 12.08 runs each. Better known as an Association footballer, Hartley played with distinction at inside-left for Oxford City and the Corinthians and took part in seven Amateur

International matches between 1923 and 1926. He also gained a full England cap against France in 1923. When joining Tottenham Hotspur, he became the first Corinthian player to sign professional forms.

HARTLEY, Col. John Cabourn, who died on March 8, 1963, aged 88, played as a slow-medium bowler for Oxford University and England. In the Tonbridge XI of 1893, he gained a Blue at Oxford in 1896 and the following year. In the first match against Cambridge he bore a leading part in a victory by four wickets, scoring 43 and taking 11 wickets for 239. When dismissing eight men on the opening day for 161 runs, he bowled W. G. Grace, junior, son of the great Doctor, for the first of his two "ducks" in the match. Hartley went to America with Frank Mitchell's team in 1893 and, as a member of P. F. Warner's M.C.C. side in South Africa in 1905–06, took part without much success in two Test matches. He later played occasionally for Sussex. He served in the South African War and the First World War, being twice wounded and four times Mentioned in Dispatches.

HASLIP, Shearman Montague, who died on July 4, 1968, aged 71, was in the Rugby XI in 1914 and 1915 as a fast-medium bowler and batsman. He played in a few matches for Middlesex in 1919, heading the bowling averages with 12 wickets at a cost of 21.08 runs each.

HASTILOW, Cyril Alexander Frederick, C.B.E., died at Moseley, Birmingham, on September 30, 1975, aged 80. In 1919, when for Moseley he scored 1,000 runs and took 100 wickets, he had a brief trial for Warwickshire and was captain of their Second XI from 1935 to 1947. He had been Hon. Secretary, Chairman and President of the County C.C., and had also served on the M.C.C. Committee.

HASTINGS, E. P., formerly of the Victoria XI, died in June, 1905, at the age of 57. In *Conway's Cricketers' Annual* for 1876–77 he was described as "Perhaps the nattiest, and certainly one of the most painstaking crick-eters of the day. For his club he has often shown splendid batting form, and a few seasons ago he made a series of brilliant scores. His *forte* is batting, and he has a *penchant* for cutting, which he executes very neatly. ... As a field he is untiring, and throws in beautifully from long-leg and cover." For some years one of his innings (250) ranked as the highest ever made in the Colonies. Playing for East Melbourne against Civil Service, at East Melbourne, in January, 1877, he and C. G. Allee scored 44 runs off two overs—a remarkable performance, although achieved in a match of little note. The brilliant manner in which he once caught out Ulyett on the Melbourne ground is still recalled by old followers of the game.

HATFEILD, Capt. Charles Eric (Eton, Oxford University and Kent), born March 11, 1887, was killed on September 21, 1918. Though his plucky hitting won the University match for Oxford in 1908, Hatfeild did not as a man fulfil on the cricket field the hopes formed of him while he was at Eton. When in 1903 he played his first match against Harrow at Lord's, he gave promise of developing into a first-rate slow bowler. Bowling left-handed he had a nice easy action and for a boy a remarkable command over his length. No doubt the slope at Lord's ground helped him to make the ball go with his arm, but be that as it may, he took 12 Harrow wickets at a cost of 91 runs, and had a big share in gaining for Eton a single innings victory—their first win since 1893. On that early form, however, Hatfeild never improved. While he remained at Eton he steadily went off in bowling, and it was his batting rather than his bowling which gained him his Blue at Oxford in 1908. He played for Kent whenever he was wanted, but though always an enthusiastic cricketer he was not good enough to secure a regular place in the county team.—S.H.P.

HATHORN, Maitland, who was born at Pietermaritzburg on April 7, 1878, died in Johannesburg on May 17, 1920. At his best he was a good and sound batsman and during his first two visits to this country was very successful. During his three tours he batted as follows in all matches:

Year.			Innings.		Not out.		Most.		Total.		Average.
1901	..	..	39	..	3	..	239	..	1261	..	35.02
1904	..	..	38	..	2	..	139	..	1339	..	37.19
1907	..	..	40	..	4	..	117	..	584	..	16.22

It was on the recommendation of Lohmann that he was included in the 1901 team, for which he scored 103 on his first appearance and headed the averages. His hundreds in great matches were as follows:

Score.						Year.
103	South Africans v. Hampshire, at Southampton	..	..	..	..	1901
239	South Africans v. Cambridge University, at Cambridge	..	..	..	1901
139	South Africans v. Sussex, at Brighton	..	..	..	..	1904
130	South Africans v. London County, at the Crystal Palace	..	..	..	1904
128	South Africans v. Leicestershire, at Leicester	..	..	..	1904
102	South Africa v. England, at Johannesburg	..	..	..	..	1905–06
117	South Africans v. Warwickshire, at Edgbaston	..	..	..	1907

His other averages in leading cricket were:

	Innings.	Not out.	Most.	Total.	Average.
Currie Cup	.. 13	.. 0	.. 91	.. 303	.. 23.30
Tests v. England	.. 12	.. 1	.. 102	.. 188	.. 17.09
Tests v. Australia	.. 8	.. 0	.. 45	.. 137	.. 17.12

Owing to ill-health, he did practically nothing during his trip to Australia in 1910–11.

HATTERSLEY-SMITH, The Rev. Percy, born May 19, 1847, died at Cheltenham, January 1, 1918. Hattersley-Smith spent practically the whole of his active life at Cheltenham, being on the teaching staff of the college for 44 years. As a cricketer he will be remembered as a useful batsman years ago in the Gloucestershire XI. He was at his best in 1878, scoring 56 against Notts at Trent Bridge and 51 not out against Sussex at Cheltenham.

HAVEWALLA DADY RUSTOMJI, who died in Bombay on July 21, 1982, aged 70, was a big-hitting left-handed batsman. His innings of 515, including 32 sixes and 55 fours, for the BB and CI Railway against St. Xavier's College in the Times of India Shield in December, 1933, was for a long time a record in any class of Indian cricket. He was always keen to derive the utmost enjoyment from his tenure of the crease and was very popular with the crowds. C. G. Macartney's tribute to him when he scored a rapid 71 against Ryder's Australian team in 1935–36 was fulsome. "I can truly say," wrote the great Australian, "that I have seldom seen finer hitting than that by Havewalla." Another notable effort was his 106 in 93 minutes for the Maharaja of Patiala's team against Lord Tennyson's at Patiala in 1937–38. This effort earned him a place in the Indian team for the fourth and fifth unofficial Tests at Madras and Bombay. In the Madras match, which India won by an innings, he made 44, the second highest score for the side. Havewalla played for Bombay in the Ranji Trophy from 1934–35 to 1941–42, his best score being 103 against Western India in 1935–36. He had started his career as a left-arm medium

bowler, and took 27 wickets in the Ranji Trophy.

HAVILAND, 2nd Lieut. John Boria (Royal Fusiliers), born in 1882, died of wounds on July 16, 1916, aged 34. He was in the Marlborough XI in 1900, when he made 77 runs with an average of 12.83 , and in 1903 played in one match for Northamptonshire. He had also been wounded in September, 1915.

HAWKE, Martin Bladen, Seventh Lord, died on October 10, 1938, in an Edinburgh nursing home after an operation, aged 78.

THE LATE LORD HAWKE
by Sir Stanley Jackson

There can be few, if any, whose services to cricket have more deserved acknowledgement and reocrd in the pages of *Wisden* than the late Lord Hawke. What service he may have rendered to cricket and cricketers was for him a labour of love. He gained his greatest pleasure from playing cricket and doing what he believed to be best in the interests of the game.

For 50 years he was closely associated with the M.C.C. and as a member of the Committee, President and Treasurer, he took an active part in the administration and the consideration of the various problems and controversies which arose from time to time. It is, however, for his long association with Yorkshire County Cricket that Lord Hawke's name will be best remembered. During 57 years in connection with the club, 28 years as captain and 40 years as president, he saw it progress to its present flourishing position.

Lord Hawke will also be remembered far and wide as the leader of those amateur teams which he organised to visit various parts of the Empire. When at Cambridge, he was selected as a regular member of the Yorkshire County XI—in those days a completely professional side including players whose names became famous in cricket history. The Hon. M. B. Hawke, as he was then, was appointed captain of Yorkshire in 1883. He soon realised that such a team of fine natural cricketers, under sympathetic management and firm leadership, would develop into a most formidable and attractive county side.

This happened: public interest and support throughout Yorkshire followed and continued to increase until to-day the Yorkshire County C.C. with its fine county side, receives, probably, the most generous and loyal support of any in the country, Hawke's initiative, with the co-operation of an enthusiastic and competent committee, laid the foundation of Yorkshire County Cricket upon which the present position has been built.

A personal interest in each individual player and his welfare, which was then begun and lasted to the end, gained for "His Lordship" a respect and loyalty from every member of the team which I think must have been unique.

Leaving a tour in Australia when he succeeded to the title owing to the death of his father, Lord Hawke was captain of a team of amateurs who went to India in 1889. During the next years he took teams to America, New Zealand, India, West Indies, South Africa, Canada and America and the Argentine. He personally organised each tour from start to finish with remarkable ability and the fact that in all these tours there was not one instance of discord speaks for itself.

Hawke's hope that the visits would help to create enthusiasm for cricket amongst the inhabitants and a desire to play the game and excel at it would appear to have been realised—now four of these countries send teams here and claim matches with our best on equal terms.

It was my good fortune to go to India with Lord Hawke's side in 1892–93. We found Lord Harris as Governor of Bombay and Lord Wenlock Governor of Madras—cricket certainly received every encouragement from them; but I think I am right in saying that the only two Indian sides we met were the Parsees at Bombay and a team at Madras. My later experiences in India left no doubt in my mind that those early visits of Hawke's teams did much to rouse enthusiasm for cricket in India and helped it on its way to a high standard.

In 1928—35 years later—I had the plea-sure of entertaining Lord and Lady Hawke at Government House, Calcutta. On going to a cricket match at Eden Gardens on Christmas Day we saw in a pavilion a photograph of Lord Hawke's team of 1892–93 and also a photograph of Lord Hawke himself. I am told that photographs of Hawke hang in the pavilions of numerous grounds he visited throughout the Empire where he is always respected as a benefactor.

There are many other reasons why Martin Hawke will be long remembered by all who knew him—cricketers and others alike. He was a generous and loyal friend; he had the gift of good fellowship, which, he maintained, was acquired on the cricket field. An admirable host, he was never more happy than when he and Lady Hawke, a lady of great charm and kindliness, dispensed hospitality to their innumerable friends.

A straightforward and honourable gentleman, he had a long innings, played it well and enjoyed it. He leaves behind a record as creditable to himself as it is an example for others to follow.

By Sir Francis Lacey

Since the history of cricket was first written, there have been chapters in which certain men have been outstanding figures. Another chapter seems to have closed with the death of Lord Hawke, who was certainly one of the most prominent in his day. Besides being a great cricketer in the highest sense of the word, he was an administrator who not only aimed at the general welfare of the game, but sought to preserve in it an untarnished ethical code. To him cricket was more than a game. It was a philosophy that coloured his dealings with people and things. His anxiety that English cricket should not fall below the high standard that he thought it should maintain led him to give expression to the wish that the captain of England should always be an amateur. He was unfairly misrepresented for holding this view, as after Hammond changed his status to that of amateur, he gave it as his opinion that a wise selection had been made when the Selection Committee appointed Hammond captain of England.

His cricket career is a well known matter of history. It may not, however, be generally known how the strength of his character was tested when, as a young man on leaving Cambridge, he undertook the responsibility of captaining the Yorkshire side, composed at that time of elements that were not entirely harmonius. Owing to his tact, judgment and integrity, he moulded the XI into the best, and probably the most united County Cricket team in England. He regarded Yorkshire as his home by adoption and wherever he went he hailed Yorkshiremen as his friends. He always played to win, but whatever the game, he was a generous opponent and never harboured resentment. The writer recollects running him out when Cambridge University were playing Surrey at the Oval—a bad run out—the offence was forgiven but it is doubtful if it was forgotten.

Through the long and anxious years during the Great War, Lord Hawke was president of M.C.C. The ground was being used for military purposes, training and recreation. Problems frequently arose, and he was the greatest help in giving wise counsel towards their solution. After the War he followed Lord Harris as Treasurer of M.C.C. and only resigned shortly before his death. Like Lord Harris, he was devoted to the M.C.C. and believed that the well-being of cricket depended on the allegiance given to the club by its members, by the County Clubs, and by the judicial and impartial administration of its Committee.

Lord Hawke was a member of the I Zingari Committee, and in recent years many of its meetings were held at his house in Belgrave Square, where the Committee had the privilege of accepting his hospitality—a great experience. It has been said that candidates for election had a better chance of being selected after luncheon than before.

And so has passed a kind and loyal friend, and one who has contributed much that is valuable to our national game.

By Hubert Preston

When first a Cambridge Light Blue cap caught my eye it was worn by the Hon. M. B. Hawke fielding for Yorkshire in front of the Oval pavilion. A prominent figure then, with his speed and sure picking-up, he became the dominant personality during many years to those who made frequent journeys to report matches in which Yorkshire were engaged. That was my good fortune when Lord Hawke captained the team which, under his firm, friendly leadership, had already become the strongest of the counties—a position retained with him as President.

Personally, throughout his active career, he experienced all the vicissitudes inseparable from cricket and never seemed to lose the joy of the game as played in the best sporting spirit. Some occurrences come to mind with the vivid memory of a close watcher and reporter of all that happened. One of the strangest was in August 1898 when at Chesterfield, John Brown, of Driffield, and John Tunnicliffe, of Pudsey, scored over 500 on the first day. For some reason Lord Hawke put himself down number three, the place usually given to F.S. Jackson; the captain wore his pads from 12 o'clock until the drawing of stumps and again on the Friday morning until the opening stand ended for 554. Sir Stanley will remember the occasion—not without a chuckle—a reference to the score shows him the best Yorkshire bowler with seven wickets for 78 in the two Derbyshire innings.

During the impregnable period from August 1899 to July 1901, when Yorkshire went unbeaten, Hirst, Rhodes and Haigh made a bowling combination perhaps never surpassed on all kinds of pitches. After seeing them supreme very often, it came as an astonishing change to find Hirst toiling in the deep at Headingley, while Somerset ran up a score of 630, and then gain an amazing victory by 279 runs after being 238 behind on the first innings. Lord Hawke was powerless; not one of his bowlers could stop the flow of runs that came from the bats of Lionel Palairet, Len Braund, F. A. Phillips and S. M. J. Woods, whose cogent word "Magnum" expressed the delighted feelings of Somerset on returning to their hotel victorious over the Champions.

With so many superb players under his command, Lord Hawke could afford to take a risk though this was seldom necessary. The opposition so often fell easy victims that, no doubt, he considered the position quite safe when he declared at Bradford in August 1908 and sent Middlesex in after lunch, wanting 269 wins to win with two hours 40 minutes left for cricket. To everyone's surprise Middlesex went for the runs. James Douglas stood away from the stumps and used the cut or drive in grand style when Hirst bowled inswingers to a packed leg-side field. F. A. Tarrant often ran down the pitch and got the bowlers off their length so that he could drive, pull or cut with impunity. The task was reduced to 51 wanted with 20 minutes remaining. Albert Trott, another Australian of exceptional ability, was the man to do this, but, attempting a run for a stroke to the unguarded off-side, he collided with Newstead, also a heavyweight, dashing across the pitch from short leg. Both men fell; Hirst returned the ball and Trott, to his disgust, was given run out—a doubtful decision after an absolute accident when the batsman was obstructed! Lord Hawke's judgment in the powers of his side at least to avoid defeat proved sound, for Middlesex finished 36 behind with two wickets in hand. Such an afternoon makes the game great.

In 1896 Lord Hawke scored 166 towards the 887 made by Yorkshire at Edgbaston against Warwickshire, the record total for any first-class match in England until the 903 for seven wickets in the Oval Test last August. He and Robert Peel put on 292— still the highest eighth wicket partnership by English batsmen. The best last wicket stand for Yorkshire was by Lord Hawke and David Hunter, 148 against Kent in 1898.

In another record of a very different kind, Lord Hawke was concerned closely, for he chose F. S. Jackson to open the bowling with George Hirst in the second innings against the Australians at Leeds in 1902 and the total—23—remains the smallest by an Australian side apart from the 18 for which Harry Trott's XI were sent back by the M.C.C. at Lord's in 1896. The preference for Jackson to start the bowling was the more noteworthy because that distinction usually belonged to Wilfred Rhodes who, four days before, when sharing England's attack with Hirst at Birmingham, had taken seven Australian wickets for 17 runs. Jackson dismissed the last four batsmen in five balls—match record nine wickets for 42 runs.

Thoughtful interest for the general welfare of his players was apparent even in the stern measures which Lord Hawke found necessary to take when he turned out of the side one of the best all-round cricketers of the time. Such strong discipline, exercised for the second time by Lord Hawke, sufficed to curb any player's possible lack of self control in the future.

While Lord Hawke, from 1883 until the time of his passing, became more famous as captain and president than he ever was as a batsman, he played many a fine innings and, late in the batting order, he frequently turned the scale in favour of his side by sound defence and hard clean hitting— notably the powerful off drive for which his height and robust figure were well suited.

He did little in the Eton and Cambridge XIs at Lord's but his three University matches each resulted in victory for his side by seven wickets; curiously enough in 1884, when he stood down, Oxford proved superior to the same extent. This remarkable series of identical margins was continued both in 1887, Oxford winning, and in 1890, Cambridge being successful. Six similar results in the course of nine annual encounters!

For many years Lord Hawke's speeches at the annual general meeting of the Yorkshire County Club contained outspoken comments on current cricket which always commanded attention. At other times his caustic remarks were wrongly construed in some quarters; notably when he expressed the fervent hope that England would never be captained by a Professional. This was not derogatory of the players for whom he had done so much and always held in high esteem, but expressed his strong desire that there would always be a Gentleman good enough a cricketer for the high position as leader of our XI. No one knew better than did Lord Hawke the heavy responsibilities of captaining a cricket XI.

HAWSON, Reginald J., born on September 2, 1880, died at Hobart on February 20, 1928. He was an attractive and skilful batsman. Against Victoria he made 139 at Hobart in 1908–09, and 199 not out at Melbourne in 1912–13. In other matches against the same State he played innings of 96.90 not out, 90, 79, 74 and 56, and he also scored 76 for South Tasmania v. New Zealand at Hobart in 1898–99 and 82 v. South Africa on the same ground in 1910–11. In January, 1904, whilst playing for Derwent v. Wellington, at Hobart, he made 135 in his first innings and 121 not out in his second.

HAWTIN, Alfred Powell Rawlins, who died at his home in Northampton on January 15, 1975, aged 91, did splendid work for Northamptonshire and was a batsman who must have taken a high place had he been able to devote his life to cricket. As it was, for many years his only regular cricket was one half-day match a week on early closing day in club cricket of very moderate standard. From this he would emerge to hold his own in a county side which was normally desperately in need of runs. This was in later years a source of embarrassment at times to his colleagues on the county committee, who had difficulty in convincing him that players of lesser natural ability could not adapt themselves to the big change involved as easily as he had done. A tremendous enthusiast and a great student of the game, he was a sound defensive batsman whose footwork could hardly have been bettered. He could never be tempted into a rash stroke and was quite imperturbable: the bowler never felt any nearer to getting him out just because he had beaten him once or twice. His first match for Northamptonshire was in 1902, when they were still second-class. He did not appear again until 1908 and, after playing several times in that and the three following seasons, was seen no more till the War. In 1919 an invitation to play reached him while he was still overseas and, after having hardly touched a bat for five years, in his first match he made 135 against Sussex, the highest of his three centuries for the county and also the first. He continued to play when he could until 1930 and in his last innings made 79 against Middlesex at Lord's. He had to refuse the captaincy in 1927. After his retirement he continued to work for the county off the field and during the Second World War was almost solely responsible for keeping the club going. After the War he became Chairman. His elder brother had also played for Northamptonshire.

HAWTIN, Roger William Rawlins, born at Bugbrook, September 30, 1880; died at Northampton, September 7, 1917. Northamptonshire XI. Highest score: 65 v. Warwickshire, at Peterborough, 1910. Useful all-round. Steady bat. Could not play often. Brother of A. P. R. Hawtin.

HAY, George, died at Staveley, his native place, on October 24, 1913. As he was born on January 28, 1851, he was thus in his 63rd year at the time of his death. It was as a fast round-armed bowler that he came to the front, but he was also a fair bat and a good field at cover-point and short slip. His first appearance at Lord's was in 1875, for Colts of the North v. Colts of the South, when he and Watson dismissed the latter in their first innings for 33, Hay taking four wickets for 10 runs and Watson six for 21. The same season Hay made his debut for Derbyshire, but his county career was short as he played seldom after 1881. He did some very good things during that time, however, his best feats being to take five wickets for 15 v. Kent at Derby in 1875, and six for 16 v. Sussex at Brighton in 1880. In 1882 he joined the ground staff at Lord's, of which he was subsequently the head, and in 1902 was given the Whit-Monday match between Middlesex and Somerset for his benefit. His highest innings in a match of note was 49 for Derbyshire v. Lancashire, at Manchester, in 1880.

HAY, John, a younger brother of George Hay, of Lord's, was crushed to death on February 4, 1908, whilst at work in the Ireland Colliery of the Staveley Company. He was born at Staveley, in Derbyshire, on May 13, 1854, and was a very steady batsman and a useful fast right-handed bowler. He played for the Derbyshire Colts on one occasion but never appeared for the county, although in and about 1880 he was fully

entitled to a trial. During his athletic career he won 122 prizes.

HAYCOCK, Daniel M., who died at Cambridge on February 2, 1953, aged 87, was elder brother of Tom Hayward, the Surrey and England cricketer. In his younger days a medium-pace bowler for Cambridgeshire, "Dan" was groundsman for more than 25 years at Fenner's, headquarters of Cambridge University cricket and athletics.

HAYCRAFT, James Samuel, died in London on March 26, 1942, aged 77 years. A prolific scorer for the Stoics, Nondescripts and Pallingswick clubs, he played once for Middlesex—against Surrey at the Oval in 1885. Going in first, he was bowled by George Lohmann for 0 and five. On a drying pitch Middlesex, in their first season under A. J. Webbe, dismissed for 25 and 77, were beaten by an innings and 64 runs. W. (Billy) Williams, still a familiar figure at Lord's, also was making his first appearance for Middlesex and retained his place as wicket-keeper during that summer; but the dismal experience satisfied Haycraft.

HAYES, Ernest George, who died at his home at Norwood on December 2, 1953— the date of the Surrey dinner to celebrate the winning of the County Championship at which he was to have been an honoured guest—aged 77, was among the finest batsmen of his day.

Born at Peckham on November 6, 1876, he first appeared for Surrey in 1896 and ended his first-class career 30 years later. Altogether he scored 27,325 runs, average 32.18, hitting 48 centuries; with leg-breaks he took over 500 wickets, and held 605 catches. His most successful season as a batsman was that of 1906 when he scored 2,309 runs, average 45.27, and reached three figures on seven occasions. The highest of his 48 centuries was 276 against Hampshire at the Oval in 1909 when he and Hobbs shared in a wonderful second wicket stand of 371. Specially strong in driving, he also pulled fearlessly and was always attractive to watch. In 1909, when a member of the Surrey team who, by five runs, inflicted upon M. A. Noble's Australians the first defeat of the tour, he made his only Test match appearance against Australia, though he toured that country with A. O. Jones's side two years previously. He played four times for England against South Africa, three when touring the Union in 1905 and the other during the 1912 Triangular Tournament. He represented

Players v. Gentlemen on many occasions, being captain at the Oval in 1914.

Until the First World War, in which he served with the Sportsman's Battalion and received the M.B.E., he played regularly for Surrey, but, after re-appearing as an amateur, he left the county in 1919. Damaged hands contributed to his decision to retire. In his early days Tom Richardson and Bill Lockwood were in their prime, and fielding in the slips to these two great fast bowlers led to the curling up, because of nerves put out of action by frequent bruising, of the third and little fingers of Hayes's right hand. As a consequence he for some years experienced difficulty in gripping a bat, but nevertheless in his last season for Surrey he scored 153 against Hampshire at Southampton, where he and Ducat joined in a third wicket partnership of 353 in 165 minutes.

From Surrey he went to Leicestershire as coach, taking part in matches for the Second XI with such success that, in 1926, he was persuaded to turn out for the Championship side. At the age of 50 he headed the Leicestershire averages, obtaining in seven innings 254 runs, average 36.28, and failing by one run to complete a century against Nottinghamshire at Trent Bridge. He returned to the Oval in 1929 as coach, a position he held till 1934, when he became a licensee at West Norwood.

HAYES, W.B., who died early in November, 1926, was a good batsman and leg-break bowler who had played a prominent part in Queensland cricket. Against New South Wales at Brisbane in 1907–08 he scored 98, and in the match with the same State at Sydney in the following season he scored 52 and 31 and took eight wickets for 124 runs. In making 143 for South Brisbane v. Valley, at Brisbane in October, 1905, he and T.B. Faunce scored 290 for the first wicket in two hours and a quarter, 100 going-up in 35 minutes and 200 in 75.

HAYGARTH, Arthur. By the death of Mr. Arthur Haygarth at his London residence on May 1, 1903, at the age of 77, there passed away a famous cricketer, whose name will always be gratefully recalled as long as the game continues to be played. Although a very capable exponent of the game which he loved so much, he will always be chiefly known to fame as the compiler of the *Cricket Scores and Biographies*. In 1842, while still at Harrow School, he commenced his labour of love, being but 16 years of age at the time, and it says much for his enthusiasm for his

work that to the day of his death his interest in the subject remained as great as ever. When he began to collect facts concerning the history of cricket and the chief players, it was merely as an amusement, and with no idea of his notes ever being published. In 1852, however, Mr. F.P. Miller, the captain of the famous Surrey team of which Caffyn, H.H. Stephenson, Lockyer, Mortlock, Griffith, and Caesar were the leading lights, asked Mr. Haygarth to lend him his manuscript with a view to publication. To this the latter readily consented, but Vol. I. did not appear until 10 years later. In 1873, the M.C.C. invited Mr. Haygarth to continue his work, with the result that the last 10 volumes of the *magnum opus* have been published through the instrumentality of the premier club. Altogether the work consists of 14 volumes, every line of which was penned by Mr. Haygarth, the statement inserted at the commencement of the first volume that the Lillywhites assisted in the compilation being altogether inaccurate, and inserted merely to suit their own ends. It would be impossible to overestimate the value of Mr. Haygarth's labours, while to state that his death has left a gap which it will be impossible to fill is a fact of which every student of the game is fully conscious. For a period of over 60 years he worked loyally at his self-imposed task, never losing heart when meeting with a rebuff, nor becoming weary in seeking out unexplored fields that promised to contain any records or novelties connected with the game. With reference to his great work, Mr. Haygarth wrote: "There is certainly one great mistake, or rather oversight, which I made during the 50 years and upwards in which I was engaged on the *Cricket Scores and Biographies*, and it is this—I preserved too many matches of an inferior calibre by far. If I had not done this the 14 volumes already published would have reached a date much further than they do now, namely, to the end of 1878."

The last volume issued was the 14th, in 1894, the M.C.C. declining to continue publication owing to the fact that it was not a success financially. This action on the part of the club caused Mr. Haygarth much distress, but did not result in his enthusiasm for the game lessening in the slightest degree. A short time before his death Mr. Haygarth said to the writer of this memoir, "I can truly affirm that if, when I began the collection, I had known the trouble and expense I have been put to for so many years, I should never have undertaken the work. I am wise too late." He was a voluminous writer and frequently contributed articles and paragraphs to *Cricket* under the *nom de plume* of "An Old Harrovian."

Mr. Haygarth was born at 29, Wellington Square, Hastings, on August 4, 1825, and received his early education at Temple Grove School, East Sheen, Surrey, where he remained from 1833 until 1837, and here it was he first became interested in the game. He entered Harrow in September, 1839, and left in July, 1843. In 1843, and again in the following year, he appeared at Lord's against Eton and Winchester, exhibiting even then defence of a very powerful nature. In 1844 he became a member of the M.C.C., on the proposal of the Earl of Bessborough (then the Hon. F. Ponsonby) and the Hon. Robert Grinston, who had taught him his cricket whilst at Harrow. He appeared at Lord's from first to last, for 20 seasons, playing in over 150 matches, and in his last innings, against Hampshire in 1861, scoring 46 before being bowled off his legs by Holmes. The defence he exhibited on the rough and bumpy wickets which were used at Lord's in his time was remarkable. By his extreme steadiness he frequently wore down the bowling, and so did great service for the side on which he appeared. When asked what his average was, he would reply, "One hour," which was about the time he generally stayed at the wicket. Between 1846 and 1859 he assisted the Gentlemen against the Players on 16 occasions, and one of the incidents of his long life which he was fond of recalling concerned the match between the two sides at Lord's in 1857. In the first innings Mr. Reginald Hankey, after stating to the Players that he did not feel very well and probably should not trouble them long, played the innings of his life (70), hitting the bowling of Willsher, Wisden, H. H. Stephenson and Jackson all over the ground, a display to which the veterans are never tired of referring. During all the time Mr. Hankey was at the wicket, Mr. Haygarth was in with him, and in after years he always spoke with the greatest enthusiasm respecting Hankey's batting upon that occasion. Mr. Haygarth, going in first wicket down, carried out his bat for 53, for which he was in over four hours. His chief innings at Lord's in great matches were:

57, Gentlemen of England v. Gentlemen of Kent	..	..	..	..	..	1847
71, Viscount Mountgarret's XI v. Earl of Winterton's XI		..	..	..	..	1849
50, M.C.C. and Ground v. Cambridge University		..	..	..	..	1851
58, Gentlemen of M.C.C. v. Gentlemen of England		..	..	..	..	1853
97, M.C.C. and Ground v. Surrey Club and Ground		..	..	..	..	1855
58, Gentlemen v. Players	..	..	..	..	..	1857
81, Gentlemen of England v. Gentlemen of Kent and Sussex		..	..	..	..	1857
71, M.C.C. and Ground v. Cambridge University		..	..	..	..	1858

In 1864, on being made a life member of the M.C.C., he severed his connection with the Surrey club, which he had joined in 1850. In the field he was very active, and was occasionally of use as a change bowler. His best performance with the ball was for M.C.C. and Ground against Sussex at Lord's in 1860, when he and the late J. Grundy bowled unchanged throughout the match.

Mr. Arthur Haygarth, who was buried at Brompton on May 5, was the youngest of three brothers, the others being the Rev. Canon Henry William Haygarth, who died on December 31, 1902, aged 81, having been vicar of Wimbledon since 1859 and Col. Francis Haygarth, late adjutant of the Scots Fusilier Guards, who was most severely wounded at the battle of the Alma, and who survives. Mr. Arthur Haygarth was the only one of the three brothers who participated in the game. Three cousins, however, earned distinction on the cricket field, Mr. J. W. Haygarth playing for Winchester in 1858, 1859, 1860 and 1861, being captain in the last two years, and for Oxford in 1862, 1863 and 1864; Mr. Frederick being in the Winchester XIs of 1864, 1865 and 1866; and Mr. E. B. appearing for Lancing College in 1868, 1869 and 1870. The three last-named were brothers, of whom a fourth, Mr. G. A. Haygarth, was also a good player, although not known to fame.

HAYLEY, Harry, who was born on February 22, 1860, and died on June 3, 1922, played for Yorkshire in 10 matches between 1881 and 1898, scoring 186 runs with an average of 11.62 and taking two wickets for 55 runs apiece. He was for many years a well-known figure in club cricket in Yorkshire.

HAYMAN, The Rev. Canon Henry Telford, died in his 88th year on February 8, 1941, at Cheltenham. After being in the Bradfield XI he went to Cambridge, but did not get his Blue. Born at West Malling, he played for Kent in two matches, one in 1873 being the only fixture kept in connection with the Cup offered by M.C.C. for competition among invited counties at Lord's. Sussex were beaten by 52 runs. Although on that occasion bowled in each innings for one run by James Lillywhite, Jnr., Hayman was described as a fine batsman; also a good long-stop.

HAYMAN, Herbert B., born on October 5, 1873, died on July 31, 1930, at the age of 56. A capital hard-hitting bat and an excellent outfield, he began to assist Middlesex in 1893, and in all matches for the county made 3,518 runs with an average of 25. His highest scores for the side were 152 v. Yorkshire at Lord's in 1896 and 110 v. Gloucestershire on the same ground in 1901: in the former game he made 218 for the first wicket with A. E. Stoddart and in the latter 200 with P. F. Warner. Against Kent at Catford in 1898 he carried his bat through the innings for 104, and twice at the Oval—in 1896 and 1901—took part in the Gentlemen v. Players match. For the Hampstead C.C., 'for whom he played with Stoddart, Spofforth and other first-class cricketers, he did some remarkable things. When the club made 273 for two wickets in 95 minutes v. Eltham, at Hampstead in 1901, he and B. Everett took the total from 100 to 178 in 20 minutes; on that occasion he carried out his bat for 164, at one period of his innings making eight fours and a six in successive scoring hits. Four years later, also on the Hampstead ground, he made 201, run out, after Upper Tooting had declared at 377 for seven, leaving the home side two and half hours in which to bat. In that time 348 were made for the loss of four men, Hayman, hitting three sixes and 30 fours, and obtaining his runs in 80 minutes.

HAYNES, R. W., died suddenly in October, 1976, while playing golf at North Oxford. He was 63. He appeared for Gloucestershire from 1930 to 1939, but did not get a regular place until 1936 when he showed promise as an opening batsman. This promise he failed to fulfil in the next three seasons. His highest score was 89 v. Hampshire in 1936 when he and Barnett put on 183 for the first wicket. In 1929 and again between 1946 and 1952 he played occasionally for Oxfordshire. He was a forcing bat with a good square cut and a moderate change left-arm bowler, who thoroughly enjoyed his cricket. He was also a first-class hockey player.

HAYWARD, Daniel, brother of the famous Tom Hayward, of Cambridge, and father of the present-day Surrey batsman, died at Cambridge on May 30, 1910. He was born at Chatteris on October 19, 1832, and was thus in his 78th year at the time of his death. In 1854, owing to the mistaken notion that he was born in the county, he played in one match for Surrey—the Haywards were a very old Mitcham family—and in 1860 he began to appear for Cambridgeshire. He was a good long-stop and bat.

HAYWARD, Thomas Walter, who died on July 19, 1939, aged 68, at his Cambridge home, was one of the greatest batsmen of all time. He afforded a notable instance of hereditary talent. A son of Daniel Hayward, a player of some repute, he was a nephew of Thomas Hayward, who in the '60s was by common consent the leading professional batsman in England.

Born at Cambridge on March 29, 1871, he belonged to a family which lived for many generations at Mitcham; both his father and grandfather appeared in the Surrey XI. Like his famous uncle he played in beautiful style. Using a straight bat he possessed all the qualities essential for success at the wicket—unlimited patience, admirable judgment, watchfulness and strong defence. While he scored all round the wicket, his chief strokes were the cut and off-drive. It may be questioned whether anyone ever surpassed him in making the off-drive, the stroke being executed delightfully and so admirably timed that the ball was rarely lifted. Of good height and build Hayward had remarkable powers of endurance. He first appeared for Surrey in a county match in 1893 and in 1898 played his greatest innings—315 not out against Lancashire at the Oval.

Equal in merit was his 130 for England when badly needed in the fourth match against Australia at Old Trafford in 1899. At the Oval that season Hayward and F. S. Jackson, the best batsmen in the earlier Tests, were chosen by A. C. MacLaren to open the England innings and they made 185, the amateur's share being 118. England put together 576, so beating the 551 by Australia on the Surrey ground in 1884. Hayward altogether played in 29 Tests against Australia, which he visited three times, and he also played in six matches against South Africa. An automatic choice for the Players, Hayward, in 29 matches against the Gentlemen at Lord's and the Oval, scored 2,374 runs with an average over 47.

For 20 years in succession, 1895–1914, he scored over 1,000 runs each season in first-class cricket. In 1904 he made 3,170, and in 1906, 3,518, which still stands as the record aggregate in first-class cricket. Hayward,

273, and Abel, 193, made a world record for the fourth wicket, 448 against Yorkshire at the Oval in 1899. Before the War—1905 to 1914—Hayward and Hobbs, also born at Cambridge, became the most notable opening pair in the game. They put up 100 or more for the first wicket on 40 occasions. In 1907 they accomplished a performance without parallel in first-class cricket by making 100 for Surrey's first wicket four times in one week: 106 and 125 against Cambridge University at the Oval; 147 and 105 against Middlesex at Lord's.

Hayward was the first batsman after W. G. Grace to complete 100 centuries, and altogether he reached three figures on 104 occasions, 58 times at the Oval and 88 for Surrey. In three matches he scored a hundred in each innings, excelling in 1906 by doing this twice in six days—144 not out and 100 at Trent Bridge off the Nottinghamshire bowlers, 143 and 125 at Leicester. He carried his bat through the first innings for 225 at Nottingham, the next best score being 32. That season Hayward made 13 centuries, equalling the record set up by C. B. Fry in 1901. Eight times he carried his bat through an innings; achieved the double event in 1897 with 1,368 runs and 114 wickets; and another distinction he enjoyed was scoring 1,000 runs before the end of May in 1900.

When at the height of his fame as a batsman, Tom Hayward also was worth his place in the Surrey XI as a bowler. In 1897 Tom Richardson took 238 wickets at 14.55 runs each in County Championship matches, Hayward coming next with 91 with an average of 19.28. Hayward, bowling medium paced off-breaks, contrasted with Richardson, whose expresses often whipped back from off to leg stump. Leicestershire experienced the strength of this combination in 1897 on the Aylestone Road Ground where they were twice dismissed for exactly the same total—35. Hayward took seven wickets for 43 and Richardson came out with the astonishing figures of 12 wickets for 20 runs. They bowled unchanged in each Leicestershire innings and the match was all over in a day. Between the two collapses, Surrey made 164, Hayward being top scorer with 26. In 1899 Hayward twice performed the hat-trick—against Gloucestershire at the Oval and Derbyshire at Chesterfield.

Putting on weight, he became rather slow in the field, though playing to the end of season 1914 but, 43 years of age when the War broke out, he did not attempt to return to active participation in the game when cricket was resumed in 1919.

Altogether in first-class cricket Tom Hayward scored 43,409 runs with an average of 41.69 and took 481 wickets at a cost of 22.94 each. Complete statistics of his career were supplied by the late Major R. O. Edwards for the 1921 issue of *Wisden*. By a strange oversight the compiler missed one century. He mentions specially the 100th in June, 1913. Hayward made two other hundreds that season and two more in 1914 when Surrey last won the Championship. His 116 against Yorkshire at Lord's where Surrey played two matches during the early weeks of the War, was Hayward's last century.

HAYWOOD, Robert A., a batsman who did good service for Northamptonshire from 1910 to 1921, died in Edinburgh on June 1, 1942, aged 54. The opportunity of becoming coach at Fettes College influenced him to give up County Cricket when at the height of his form. Born at Eltham, in Kent, he played for Northamptonshire against Philadephians in 1908, and next season, with 39, he was the highest scorer in the second innings against M. A. Noble's Australian team during the county qualifying period. He started modestly when appearing in most of the Championship matches in 1910, and, rising to number three in the list, he became the most prolific batsman next season, with 153 against Gloucestershire—his first century, made by brilliant hitting all round the wicket. He joined G. J. Thompson when six wickets were down for 69, and they added 222 in two hours and a half. Victory by 10 wickets resulted. The same pair put on 230 at a slow pace against Yorkshire at Dewsbury earlier in the season, and their steadiness helped to beat Yorkshire by 44 runs in the return match. Curiously enough, when in 1912 Northamptonshire finished a close second to Yorkshire for the Championship, Haywood declined more than other batsmen in a wet summer, and bowling accounted for the county doing so well. Usually a hard hitter, Haywood sometimes avoided risks, but was always good to watch. In 1920 the visit of Surrey to Northampton produced the record aggregate for a county match—1,475 for 27 wickets—Haywood contributing 15 and 96. Next season, his last, he scored 1,887 runs, average 43.88, and was by far the most valuable batsman for the county. He hit eight of the 11 centuries scored for the side, his highest, 198 against Glamorganshire, a splendid display of hard, safe stroke play, marred by only one chance when 168. Altogether in first-class cricket his aggregate reached 8,225 at an average of 28.66 an innings.

HAZLERIGG, Lord Arthur Grey, Lord Lieutenant of Leicestershire, died in London on May 25, 1949, aged 70. Without any practical knowledge of first-class cricket he took over the captaincy of Leicestershire in 1907 and continued to 1910. He did little as a batsman, scoring 866 runs, average 9.84, but he was a popular leader. His heir, Major A. G. Hazlerigg, played for Eton, Cambridge University and Leicestershire.

HAZLITT, Gervys R., who was born in New South Wales on September 4, 1888, died on October 31, 1915, aged 27. A very useful all-round cricketer, he made his first appearance for Victoria in 1905–06, when only 17, and during the next few seasons was one of the most promising players in Australia. In 1906–07 he made 52 for Rest of Australia v. New South Wales, and in the following season appeared in a couple of Test matches against England, and by an innings of 34 at a critical period helped largely to gain a victory by two wickets for his side at Sydney. He also bowled well for his State that year, taking seven wickets for 127 runs v. England, and six for 134 v. South Australia at Melbourne. In 1908–09 he obtained eight for 99—three for 19 and five for 80—v. South Australia on the last-mentioned ground, and later in the season scored 62 for Rest of Australia v. The Australian Team at Sydney. His form at that time was so good that he only just failed to be chosen for the trip to England. In 1909–10 he took part in only two big matches, but in one of them—v. South Australia at Adelaide—scored 82 not out, adding 126 for the eighth wicket with Dr. N. L. Speirs (49) after seven had fallen for 140. At Melbourne in 1910–11 he made 77 v. South Australia at Melbourne, and a year later, upon accepting a mastership at The King's School, Parramatta, assisted New South Wales, for which State he was qualified by birth. During 1911–12 he took nine wickets for 104 v. South Australia at Sydney, and, on the same run-getting paradise, six for 140 v. Victoria and seven for 95 v. England: he also played in the fifth Test match, in which his four wickets cost 31.75 runs each. He visited England in 1912, and although his batting was disappointing—his highest score was only 35 not out v. Cambridge University—he took 101 wickets for slightly under 19 runs each. For some time he had eye trouble, being obliged to undergo an operation, and doubtless this militated against his success. His great feat was performed in the Test match against England at the Oval, when he

took seven wickets for 25 runs in the second innings, at one period taking five for one in 17 balls (including four without a run in 10). But for this very pronounced success it is certain that Australia would have saved the game, for within half-an-hour after England had won the rain descended in torrents and further play would have been impossible. In the same match he made a most brilliant catch at short-leg which dismissed Spooner. During the early part of the tour he undoubtedly threw a good deal, but he bowled with a straighter arm later. His visit to England practically marked the end of his career in first-class cricket. His bowling was medium-paced, right-hand, with a useful off-break and much swerve. In the field he was excellent. Before appearing in first-class cricket he was coached by Carpenter, of Essex.

HEAD, John Reginald, died at Folkestone on May 15, 1949, aged 80. Clifton XI 1885 and 1886 when he was captain. Played occasionally for Middlesex in 1892 and 1898.

HEADLEY, George Alphonso, M.B.E., who died in Jamaica on November 30, 1983, aged 74, was the first of the great black batsmen to emerge from the West Indies. Between the Wars, when the West Indies batting was often vulnerable and impulsive, Headley's scoring feats led to his being dubbed "the black Bradman." His devoted admirers responded by calling Bradman "the white Headley"—a pardonable exaggeration. In 22 Tests, when the innings could stand or fall on his performance, Headley scored 2,190 runs, including 10 centuries—eight against England—with an average of 60.83. He was the first to score a century in each innings of a Test at Lord's, in 1939, and it was a measure of his ability that from 1929 to 1939 he did not have a single bad Test series. By the start of the Second World War he had totalled 9,532 runs in first-class cricket with an average of 72.21. Afterwards, though not the power that he had been, he extended his aggregate to 9,921 runs, with 33 centuries and an average of 69.86.

Born in Panama, where his father had helped to build the Canal, Headley was taken to Jamaica at the age of 10 to perfect his English—Spanish had been his first tongue—and to prepare to study dentistry in America. At school he fell in love with cricket, but he might still have been lost to the game had there not been a delay in getting his passport for the United States. While he was waiting, Headley was chosen to play against a visiting English team captained by the Hon. L. H. Tennyson.

Though not yet 19, he had innings of 78 in the first match and 211 in the second, and dentistry lost a student. Surprisingly he was not chosen for the 1928 tour of England immediately afterwards, but in the home series against England in 1929–30 he scored 703 runs in eight Test innings, averaging 87.80. His scores included 21 and 176 in his first Test, 114 and 112 in the third and 223 in the fourth. In 1930–31 in Australia he scored two more Test centuries and ended the tour with 1,066 runs. Clarrie Grimmett described him as the strongest on-side player he had ever bowled against. In 1932, in a single month, he hit 344 not out (his highest-ever score), 84, 155 not out and 140 against another English side to visit Jamaica. Against sterner opposition and in more difficult conditions in England in the following year, he averaged 66 for the tour, scoring a century on his first appearance at Lord's and taking 224 not out off Somerset. In the second Test at Manchester he made 169 not out, a score he improved upon with 270 not out at Kingston in the 1934–35 series.

Headley was of medium build, compact, balanced and light on his feet. Like most great batsmen he was a superb back-foot player and seldom made a hurried shot. Sir Leonard Hutton, who saw him at his best in 1939, declares he has never seen a batsman play the ball later. It was hard to set a field for him, such was his genius for collecting runs with his precise placement of the ball. In League cricket in England Headley also excelled. At every level of the game, in fact, he scored an avalanche of runs with a style and brilliance few of any age have matched. His contribution to the strength and power of modern West Indies teams cannot be exaggerated.

One of his sons, R. G. A., an opening batsman for Worcestershire and Derbyshire, played twice for West Indies in England in 1973.

HEALING, John Alfred, M.C., who died on July 4, 1933, aged 59, went to Cambridge from Clifton College, but did not get his Blue. He played for Gloucestershire occasionally.

HEANE, George Frank Henry, who died on October 24, 1969, aged 65, was an amateur left-handed batsman and right-arm medium pace bowler for Nottinghamshire. His election to the county captaincy came as something of an echo of the "body-line" tour of

D. R. Jardine's M.C.C. team in Australia in 1932–33. At Trent Bridge in 1934 for Nottinghamshire against W. M. Woodfull's Australians, W. Voce, the left-hander, caused a controversy by bowling fast leg-theory to a packed leg-side field, contrary to an agreement by the first-class captains. As a consequence of this, an apology by the Committee to the ~~touring team~~ and several stormy meetings of county members, Heane and S. D. Rhodes were appointed joint captains for 1935. From the following season till 1946, Heane was in sole charge of the team on the field.

He became a prominent member of the side, and in Championship matches he hit 5,587 runs, including seven centuries, the highest of which was 134 against Worcestershire at Trent Bridge in his last season, and took 182 wickets. His most successful season was in 1946, for he obtained 1,530 runs, average 40.26, and took 40 wickets for 34.27 runs each, so that it came as rather a surprise when, without explanation, he was replaced in the captaincy by W. A. Sime in 1947. A veterinary surgeon and farmer by profession, Heane did well for Sir Julien Cahn's XI before first appearing for the county in 1928. After leaving Nottinghamshire, he assisted Lincolnshire.

HEAP, J. S., the graceful Lancashire left-arm slow bowler, who played for the county from 1903 to 1921, died at Stoneclough, near Bolton, on January 30, 1951, aged 67. During his career with Lancashire, Heap took 400 wickets at an average of 23.75 runs each, and scored over 5,000 runs. Unfortunately he was handicapped through periodical attacks of lumbago, otherwise his full county record would have been more imposing. At Northampton in 1910 he dismissed 14 Northamptonshire batsmen for 93—nine for 43 in the second innings. Twice he took 11 wickets in matches against Yorkshire—one occasion being at Manchester in 1913, when he had the remarkable figures of six for 16 and five for 23. As a batsman he could defend stubbornly or hit hard as the occasion demanded. His benefit in 1921 realised £1,804. For some time he was coach at Shrewsbury School.

HEARN, William, the well-known cricketer and umpire, died at Barnet, after a short illness, on January 30, 1904. As he was born at Essendon, in Hertfordshire, on November 30, 1849, he was in his 55th year at the time of his death. In *Scores and Biographies* (xi – 278) he is described as "An excellent batsman, a middle-paced, round-armed bowler, and fields generally at cover-point, being extremely good in the latter department of the game, and a dead shot at the wicket." In 1878, on the suggestion of Mr. V. E. Walker, he was engaged on the M.C.C. staff at Lord's, and retained the post until the day of death. His highest innings for Hertfordshire was his 167 against M.C.C. at Lord's, in 1887, while for M.C.C. and Ground he made scores of 177 not out against Notts Castle, 160 against Uppingham Rovers (including Hugh Rotherham and Stanley Christopherson), and 149 against Suffolk. In August, 1893, the match at Watford, between Hertfordshire and Bedfordshire, was played for his benefit, and four years later the M.C.C. showed their appreciation of his services by handing him the proceeds of the match between Middlesex and Somerset, at Lord's. Hearn was an enthusiastic cricketer, as well as a genial man, and his death at a comparatively early age, was regretted by all with whom he had come in contact. He was buried in the Christ Church Cemetery, High Barnet, on February 4, several prominent cricketers, including Mr. Henry Perkins, George Burton, J.T., G.F., and G.G. Hearne being present. At the conclusion of the burial service, Canon Trotter, an Old Harrovian, and a keen devotee of the game, referred to the prestige deceased had gained as a cricketer and umpire, and spoke in laudatory terms of cricket as a game.

HEARNE, Alec, who died at Beckenham on May 16, 1952, aged 88, was one of the best cricketers who never played for England. A younger brother of George and Frank, both Kent cricketers, he was born at Ealing on July 22, 1863. He derived his qualification for Kent from the fact that his father, "old George Hearne," held the post of groundsman at Catford Bridge, where, in 1875, Kent decided all their home county matches. When first tried for the county in 1884, Alec Hearne was no batsman, but a clever leg-break bowler slightly above normal pace, with a good command of length, deceptive flight and plenty of spin. More than once in his early years he proved a thorn in the side of Yorkshire, enjoying a particular triumph at Bramall Lane in 1885 when taking 13 wickets, including five for 13 in one innings, at a cost of 48 runs. The strain upon his elbow entailed in imparting a leg-break troubled him so much that after a few seasons he took to bowling off-breaks, which he did with considerable success. Still, his great ambition was to become a good batsman,

and by 1889 he established himself as the skilful run-getter that he remained for nearly 20 years.

Neat in method, he was strong in back-play and cut with precision, getting well over a rising ball or, if it got up particularly high, "upper-cutting" it over the slips. On slow pitches he was quick and accurate in hooking. Altogether Hearne played in first-class cricket for 23 seasons, scoring 16,380 runs, average 21, and taking 1,167 wickets for 19 runs each. Most of his work was done for Kent, for whom he scored 11 of his 15 centuries, but he played four times for Players against Gentlemen and in the winter of 1891–92 formed one of the team which, under W. W. Read, went to South Africa. Among his big scores were 162 not out against Nottinghamshire at Trent Bridge in 1899 when he and J. R. Mason (181 not out) put on 351 and established a Kent third-wicket record which stood for 35 years, and 155 against Gloucestershire at Gravesend in 1895—the match in which W. G. Grace, hitting 257 and 73 not out, was on the field while every ball was bowled. Other notable innings were 154 not out against Worcestershire at Worcester in 1906 and 152 not out from the Essex bowling at Leyton in 1901.

His most remarkable bowling analyses for Kent were: five wickets for 15 runs v. Hampshire at Tonbridge, four for 0 v. Somerset at Taunton, five for 13 v. Warwickshire at Maidstone, eight for 36 v. Middlesex at Lord's, four for 10 v. Gloucestershire at Tonbridge in 1902 and eight for 15 against the same county on the same ground the following year. Twice he performed the hat-trick, for M.C.C. v. Yorkshire at Lord's in 1888 and for Kent v. Gloucestershire at Clifton in 1900.

That Hearne should never have taken part in a Test match was the more remarkable because he accomplished several fine feats in games with various Australian teams. In 1884, in which summer Kent were the only county side to beat Murdoch's third team, he took seven wickets for 66, and two years later, when Kent triumphed by 10 wickets at Canterbury, he dismissed four batsmen for 37 runs. In 1890 he helped to a further Kent victory with scores of 24 and 35, and in 1893, when the Australians lost on the St. Lawrence ground, he made 20 and 39 and took eight wickets. In 1893 he averaged 38 against the Australians, with a highest score of 120 for the South at the Oval, and obtained 17 wickets for 12 runs apiece. He played another three-figure innings against the Australians in 1899, getting 168 for W. G.

Grace's XI at the Crystal Palace.

Kent gave him the match with Lancashire in 1898 as a benefit, and the M.C.C. awarded him the Middlesex v. Hampshire game at Lord's in 1913. For some years he was coach at the Kent Nursery at Tonbridge, and after the death of his cousin, Walter Hearne, in 1925 became scorer to the county, a post which, though latterly crippled by rheumatism, he fulfilled until 1939. Like all the other Hearnes, Alec was quiet of speech and manner, modest, and an excellent judge of cricket.

HEARNE, Frank, who died in July, 1949, at the age of 90, had the rare experience of playing in Test matches for England against South Africa and also for South Africa against England.

Born on November 23, 1858, he was one of three brothers who gained fame with Kent. The others were George Gibbons and Alec Hearne. Only 5ft. 5in. tall, he was a batsman with a sound defence and many fine off-side strokes. He first played for Kent in 1879 and up to 1889 scored 3,426 runs and took 41 wickets with fast round-arm bowling before ill-health made him give up County Cricket.

He toured South Africa with Major R. G. Wharton's team in 1888–89 and played in two Test matches for England. Subsequently he settled in South Africa and was engaged by the Western Province Cricket Club. In 1891 he appeared for South Africa when England went to that country and also played in three Tests in the 1895 English tour. In 1894 he was a member of the first South African team to visit England.

Probably the best display of his career was the 111 he made for South of England against the Australians in 1886. His highest innings was 144 for Kent against Yorkshire in 1887. The previous year he and his brother, G. G. Hearne, added 226 for the second Kent wicket against Middlesex at Gravesend, Frank scoring 142 and George 126.

All three brothers figured in Kent's great victory over the Australians at Canterbury in 1884 when they were the only county that summer to lower the colours of the touring team. Frank Hearne played a notable part in this performance. He opened the batting and in the second innings his 45 was second highest score in a total of 213. Alec Hearne, with five wickets for 36 and two for 30, also helped considerably towards the overthrow of W. L. Murdoch's men. Stanley Christopherson, who died a few weeks before

Frank Hearne, was another member of that Kent side.

Frank Hearne retained his interest in the game long after his career ended, and a few months before his death he was present at the Test between England and South Africa at Cape Town in 1949.

HEARNE, George Alfred Lawrence, who died at Barberton in the Eastern Transvaal on November 13, 1978, at the age of 90, was a member of the 1924 South African team to England and appeared in the fifth Test. He was the son of Frank Hearne (1858–1949) and was born at Catford, Kent, on March 27, 1888. In November of that year Frank Hearne sailed as a member of Major Wharton's team (the first English team to visit South Africa) which played in the two "Test matches" which marked the start of first-class cricket in South Africa. Thus George Hearne's lifetime exactly spanned this era. His father stayed on to coach in South Africa and subsequently played for South Africa in several Test matches. Both father and son lived to the age of 90, which must be unique in Test match history. George, at the time of his death, was not only the senior South African Test player (on an age basis) but second only to E. J. ("Tiger") Smith in the world. It was the season of 1921–22 which brought him into prominence. That year he made 541 runs at an average of 45. His highest score of 138 was made in his last season—1926–27.

HEARNE, George Francis, born at Stoke Poges on October 18, 1851, died on May 29, 1931, aged 79. A member of the famous cricket family he played in M.C.C. matches for 32 years and altogether his service with M.C.C. extended over 46 years. A useful bat and bowler, he once hit a hundred for Ealing and District v. M.C.C. at Lord's. As pavilion clerk at Lord's from 1873 to 1908, he was well known to all first-class cricketers and during that time was captain of the St. John's Wood Ramblers (now Cross Arrows C.C.) for 36 consecutive seasons.

HEARNE, George Gibbons, the eldest of three brothers—Frank and Alec were the others—all of whom played with much distinction for Kent, was born at Ealing on July 7, 1856, and derived his qualification for Kent through his father having charge of the Private Banks Ground at Catford Bridge. George Hearne's chance of appearing in the county ranks was, no doubt, materially increased by the fact that in 1875—the first year of Lord Harris's captaincy—all Kent's home matches with other counties were contested at Catford Bridge. Playing first for Kent in that summer of 1875 when less than 19 years of age, George Hearne kept his place in the XI for 21 seasons. Primarily a bowler, left-hand round arm, fast medium in pace, he afterwards developed into a capable left-handed batsman. He used to get on a decided natural break and off his bowling many catches were given in the slips where C. A. Absolom seldom missed a chance. He always batted in correct style and, improving as he increased in strength, played many fine innings, some of which, as Lord Harris wrote, would have been larger but for his captain running him out so often. Smart if not brilliant in the field, George Hearne, as a rule, stood point or mid-wicket. Following upon his first season for Kent, he was engaged at "Prince's" and in 1877 began a connection with the M.C.C. which continued for nearly half a century.

"G. G.," as he was known to all cricketers, took in the course of his 21 seasons of County Cricket, 577 wickets for Kent at a cost of 16½ runs each and scored 7,344 runs with an average of 18. As a result of his labours as bowler in 1877 and 1878 he had 201 wickets for 12 runs apiece and in 1886—his most successful season as a batsman—he made 987 runs for the county with an average of 41. His aggregate in all first-class matches that year was 1,125, among his big performances being: 126 against Middlesex at Gravesend, when he and his brother Frank shared in a partnership of 226, and 117 against Yorkshire at Canterbury, where he and Cecil (afterwards Bishop) Wilson added 215 while together. Three years later at Gravesend he put together 103 against Sussex, a stand with Frank Marchant, who scored 176, producing 249 runs.

Among George Hearne's bowling feats were: eight wickets for 46 against Lancashire at Old Trafford, when he performed the hattrick; four for nine against Hampshire at Winchester; 14 for 130 against Derbyshire at Derby; 13 for 75 against Hampshire at Southampton; 14 for 45 against M.C.C., at Lord's, and eight for 53 against Lancashire at Canterbury—all in the '70s.

In 1889, when Notts, Lancashire and Surrey tied for the Championship, Notts entered upon their concluding engagement apparently assured of first honours but in this match—at Beckenham—they were dismissed in their second innings for 35. Kent, set 52 to win, lost six wickets for 25 but hit off the remaining runs without further loss, George Hearne batting with rare skill on a diabolical pitch for an hour and three-quarters and being not out 14 at the finish.

Hearne participated in May, 1878, in the match at Lord's which established the reputation of Australian cricket, the tourists on that occasion, after dismissing a most powerful M.C.C. team for 33 and 19, putting on 41 and 12 for one wicket and finishing the game off in a single day.

Of the Kent XI that defeated the Australians in 1884—Lord Harris, F. A. MacKinnon, W. H. Patterson, Cecil Wilson, M. C. Kemp, Stanley Christopherson, F. Lipscombe, George Hearne, Frank Hearne, Alec Hearne and James Wootton—George Hearne was the first to pass away—more than 47 years after that memorable triumph. He died on February 13, 1932.

HEARNE, Herbert, who assisted Kent on 25 occasions between 1884 and 1886, was born at Chalfont St. Giles, Buckinghamshire, on March 15, 1862, and was a fast round-armed bowler and a fair bat and field. He retired early from the game owing to an injury, and died at his native place on June 13, 1906. He was a brother of the better-known J. T. and Walter Hearne.

HEARNE, John Thomas, one of the finest bowlers the game has ever known, who played for Middlesex and England, died on April 17, 1944, after a long illness at Chalfont St. Giles in Buckinghamshire, the place of his birth on May 3, 1867. From 1891 to 1914 he held a prominent place among the very best bowlers, and finished his career with a record of 3,060 wickets, an aggregate surpassed only by W. Rhodes, 4,188, A. P. Freeman, 3,775, and C. W. L. Parker, 3,274.

Right-hand medium-pace, he took a fairly long run up to the wicket, and it would be difficult to recall a bowler with a more beautiful delivery, made as his left hand pointed down the pitch. Standing nearly 5ft. 11in., he brought the ball over with a perfectly straight arm, and such was his command of length that a batsman might wait many overs for a ball from which he was certain to score. Even on the best of wickets he got on quite an appreciable off-break, and, varying his pace cleverly, he used at times to send down a fast ball which swung with his arm. On a bowler's wicket he could dismiss the strongest sides, and on one of the crumbling pitches which occasionally bothered batsmen 40 years ago he was simply unplayable. The leading bowler, not only for Middlesex but for the M.C.C. in the days when the club programme included quite a number of first-class matches, he was called upon for an amount of work which would have tired out most men in a very few years, but his splendid methods served him so well that a career in first-class cricket, which opened in 1888, did not close until the First World War, and in 1923 at Edinburgh he took six wickets for 64 for Middlesex against Scotland.

Jack Hearne came of famous cricket stock. A nephew of old Tom Hearne and of George Hearne, both of whom played for Bucks and Middlesex, before the latter went to Catford Bridge, he was a cousin of G. G. Hearne, Frank Hearne and Alec Hearne, all distinguished professionals for Kent. His brother, Walter Hearne, also a good Kent bowler, broke down through knee trouble when he looked to have many years of success before him and then became scorer, as did Alec Hearne when his cousin died.

J. T. used to relate how chance helped him into first-class cricket. "I was born and bred in Buckinghamshire, which, in my young days, did not have a county club or I might have got no further than that," but A. J. Webbe, having watched him on the Evelyn School ground, where Hearne coached, asked him to play in a Middlesex Colts match, and then against the Australians in 1888. He took two cheap wickets, but a further invitation for the next match against Surrey could not be accepted, one of the masters advising him that he was not qualified. By living with his brother in London this difficulty was overcome, but he still worked at Evelyn School during the summer, and in June, 1890, he received a telegram asking him to play for Middlesex that very day.

"I turned over my pitch-mowing job to someone else, dashed to the station, and from a newspaper found that Middlesex were playing Notts. When I arrived at Lord's just before lunch-time I saw 99 for no wicket on the score-board. Not until reaching the dressing-room did I learn that my side were batting. If Notts had been at the wickets I should not have played in that match. I remember Mr. Webbe leaning out of the pavilion window as I passed down the little alley to the players' room and saying, 'It is quite all right but I nearly left you out.'

"When Notts batted near the end of the day I bowled J. A. Dixon with a real beauty, and as we left the field the great Arthur Shrewsbury said to me, 'Well bowled, young 'un. If you bowl like that you will get someone else out to-morrow'—and I did— six for 62. That is how I began my connection

with Middlesex and, barring a couple of matches missed through a strained arm, I went on playing for the county without a break until I retired from County Cricket in 1914."

Next season at Lord's he took 14 Yorkshire wickets for less than five runs apiece, and in 14 matches the capture of 118 wickets for 10 runs each put him top of the first-class averages. From that proof of ability he went steadily ahead, and in 1893 the fine reward of 212 wickets fell to him, while his aggregate rose to 257 wickets at 14.72 each in 1896; only Tom Richardson with 246 at 16.79 each fared nearly as well. In fact, that was Hearne's greatest year. He appeared for the Players against the Gentlemen at the Oval and Lord's, but those matches were comparatively of small importance in view of his doings against the Australians. With 56 wickets at 13.17 runs apiece he far surpassed the work of any other bowler during the summer against the touring team, though his rivals for fame included Robert Peel, George Lohmann, John Briggs, Tom Richardson and A. D. Pougher. He finished at Hastings for South of England by taking six Australian wickets for eight runs in 17 overs, 13 of them maidens. He also made 29 not out, the next highest score of his side to 53 by W. G. Grace. In the three Test matches that season he took 15 wickets at 14.1 each, dividing the honours with Tom Richardson, whose 24 wickets cost 18.7 each. At Lord's his bowling was not required until the second innings, when he sent down 36 overs for 76 runs and five wickets; but at the Oval, where Australia scored only 119 and 44, he took six wickets for 41 and four for 19—10 in all for six runs apiece, so having a large share in winning the rubber match by 66 runs.

An even more memorable game that season was at Lord's in June when M.C.C. avenged the disaster of 1878 by dismissing the Australians for 18, one less than the club fell for 18 years previously. On that occasion Spofforth and Boyle brought undying fame to our visitors—in fact, made a name for Australian cricket in England. The revenge performance earned most renown for A. D. Pougher, who, going on to bowl with three wickets down for 18, disposed of five batsmen without a run being scored off him and the innings ended without addition. Yet Hearne took a greater part than did the Leicestershire bowler in gaining a single innings victory for M.C.C. In the first innings he sent down 11 overs for four runs and four wickets, and in the second, when the Australians put together a total of 183, he took, at a cost of 73 runs, all nine wickets that fell—the visitors batted one man short, Giffen being ill.

In the winter of 1897 he went to Australia with A. E. Stoddart, and his nine wickets for 141 in the first Test at Sydney helped materially in England's only win in the rubber of five matches, which all told yielded him no more than 20 victims. He took part in three Test matches in 1899—the first experience of a rubber of five in England—and at Leeds set up a record that still stands by doing the only hat-trick against Australia in a Test match in England. His victims were those formidable opponents Clem Hill, Sidney Gregory and M. A. Noble. He did three other hat-tricks; and another big achievement when meeting Australians occurred nine years earlier for Middlesex at Lord's, where he bowled W. L. Murdoch, the Australian captain and great batsman, for nought in each innings.

Besides coaching during several winters in India for the Maharaja of Patiala, Jack Hearne went to South Africa in 1891–92 and, with the two left-handers, J. J. Ferris and "Nutty" Martin, as colleagues, he claimed 163 wickets for less than seven runs each. South African batting was very weak at that time, and Ferris, the Australian, then qualified for Gloucestershire, with 235 wickets at 5.91 each, eclipsed Hearne's performance.

In 15 different seasons Jack Hearne took over 100 wickets; three times more than 200. From 1891 to 1904 the only exception was 1901, when the number fell to 99, partly, no doubt, because that was his best batting year with 522 runs, average 20.88. In addition to his exceptional effectiveness with the ball, Hearne scored 7,137 runs, average 11.04, and held 382 catches, mostly close to the wicket, where he was a dependable and often a brilliant fieldsman. Statistics vary as to J. T. Hearne's total wickets, but the runs scored and catches held are from Sir Home Gordon's *Form at a Glance*.

From 1891 to 1924 Hearne was engaged at Lord's, and the M.C.C. voted him, in lieu of a benefit, the sum of £500. Middlesex gave him the match with Somerset in 1900 as a benefit, and in 1920 he was elected a member of the Committee of the Middlesex County Club, an honour for a professional previously awarded only to William Gunn by Nottinghamshire in 1906. When acting as coach during many seasons at Oxford, Jack Hearne endeared himself to the University undergraduates in the same way that all who met him were impressed by the modest kindliness that marked his whole life.

To be on friendly terms with "J. T." for 50 years, as I was, meant an education in cricket and good fellowship.—H. P.

HEARNE, John William, who died on September 13, 1965, aged 74, rendered admirable service as a professional for Middlesex from 1909 to 1936 and took part in 24 Test matches for England between 1912 and 1926. Joining the Lord's staff as a ground-boy in 1906, he became one of England's greatest all-rounders. In his early days he drove hard and though ill-health impaired his ability in that direction, his impeccable style and artistry in placing the ball, combined with sound defence, in which he employed a remarkably straight bat, brought him many runs. At his best on difficult pitches, he altogether scored 37,252 runs in first-class cricket, average 40.98, including 96 centuries; with skilfully-controlled leg-break and googly bowling from what surely must have been the shortest of run-ups, he took 1,839 wickets for 24.42 runs each and he held 329 catches.

"Young Jack," as he was known, was a cousin of J. T. Hearne, also of Middlesex and England fame. He received his first trial for the county in 1909, when he created a highly favourable impression with an innings of 71 against Somerset at Taunton. The following summer he hit two centuries and occasionally bowled with marked success, as against Essex at Lord's where he distinguished himself by disposing of seven men in just over five overs for two runs. Thenceforward, Hearne was an established cricketer in the world of cricket and undoubtedly one of the most immaculately attired. Five times he achieved the "cricketer's double" of 1,000 runs and 100 wickets—in 1911, 1913, 1914, 1920 and 1923—the most successful being that of 1920 when he hit 2,148 runs and dismissed 148 batsmen; in 19 seasons his aggregate runs exceeded 1,000 and four times he passed 2,000. His highest innings was 234 not out against Somerset at Lord's and on 10 other occasions he put together scores of more than 200, two of them in 1912. From the Glamorgan bowling at Lord's in 1931, he reached three-figures twice in the match. Often in company with his great friend and ally on the field, "Patsy" Hendren, who in their day formed the highly valuable combination for Middlesex that D. C. S. Compton and W. J. Edrich were in later years to become, Hearne shared in many a big stand. The largest between him and Hendren was 375 for the third wicket against Hampshire at Southampton in 1923 and 325 against the same opposition at Lord's in 1919. For the second wicket,

Hearne and F. A. Tarrant added 380 against Lancashire at Lord's.

Hearne began his long Test career in 1911–12, P. F. Warner successfully pressing his claims when some members of the Middlesex Committee considered him too young for so arduous a trip. In that tour he hit his only Test century, 114 at Melbourne, where he and Wilfred Rhodes joined in a second-wicket stand of 127. In the same tour Hearne and Frank Woolley put on 264 for the third M.C.C. wicket against Tasmania at Hobart. Illness prevented him from playing in all but the opening Test in Australia in 1920–21. His full Test record was 806 runs, average 26.00, and 30 wickets for 48.73 runs apiece.

For all his comparatively frail physique, Hearne did not flinch from the hardest of hits in the field. At Lord's in 1928, for instance, when L. N. Constantine, with innings of 86 and 103 and a second-innings analysis of seven wickets for 57 runs, did so much towards a sensational victory by three wickets for the West Indies over Middlesex, Hearne instinctively grabbed at a return of intense ferocity from Constantine with resultant damage to his hand which put him out of the game for the remainder of the season.

Always immensely popular, with his quiet manner and subtle sense of humour, Hearne acted as coach at Lord's for many years after retiring from the field of play. In 1949 he was one of 26 former professional players honoured with life membership by the M.C.C.

HEARNE, Thomas, died at Ealing on May 13, 1900, in his 74th year. Born on September 4, 1826, he was late coming before the cricket public, little being known of him outside local circles until he was over 30. His reputation, however, was firmly established in 1859, when for the United against the All England XI at Lord's he and Carpenter scored 149 for the first wicket. Carpenter made 97 and Hearne 62. From that time till his retirement from the Middlesex XI in the '70s Tom Hearne played regularly in the best matches, proving himself a first-rate bat, and by no means a bad bowler. One of his best innings was 122 not out for Players against Gentlemen at Lord's in 1866. He was in particularly good form that year, and largely helped to place Middlesex first among the counties. Against Surrey he scored 146. His career as an active player terminated in 1876, in which year he had a very severe stroke of paralysis. He made a remarkable recovery, however, and for more than 20 years afterwards kept his post as chief of the ground staff at Lord's, only resigning after the season of 1897. In personal character no professional cricketer stood higher, and all through his life he enjoyed the respect of everyone who knew him. Lovers of cricket who have reached middle-age will remember him particularly in connection with the Middlesex matches more than 30 years ago at the Cattle Market Ground. He went to Australia with the first English XI in 1861, but could not do himself justice in the Colonies. He was perhaps the last batsman who played the old-fashioned "draw." His eldest son, Thomas Hearne, junior, is now the Ground Superintendent at Lord's, and his second son, George F. Hearne, has for years been Pavilion Clerk at Lord's. Tom Hearne was very proud of the success gained in the Kent XI by his three nephews—G. G., Frank and Alec Hearne.

HEARNE, Walter, the old Kent cricketer, who was for many years scorer to the Kent County Club, died at Canterbury on April 2, 1925, at the age of 61. His active career in first-class cricket was cut short by an injury to his knee that would not yield to surgical treatment. In more fortunate circumstances he might have played nearly as long for Kent as did his more famous brother, J. T. Hearne, for Middlesex. He, also, was a right-handed medium-pace bowler with a fair amount of spin and great accuracy of length. Hearne was given his first trial for Kent in 1887, but made little impression at that time, and it was not until five years later that he gained a regular place in the county XI. In the match with Lancashire at Manchester in 1893 he took 15 wickets for 114 runs, and against the same side at Tonbridge a year later he did the hat-trick. He reached the top of his form in 1894, when in first-class matches he took 116 wickets—99 in county fixtures—at a cost of 13.34 runs each. He had a wonderful spell of success in July, taking in three successive matches, 13 wickets for 61 runs against Gloucestershire, 12 wickets for 72 runs gainst Nottinghamshire and 13 for 98 against Surrey. His position among the leading bowlers of the day seemed assured, but in the following May his knee gave way so badly that he was kept out of the field for the whole season, and on starting afresh in 1896 he finally broke down against Yorkshire at Leeds. He then became official scorer for Kent—a position he held for the rest of his life. He was born at Chalfont St. Giles, in Buckinghamshire, on January 15, 1864.

HEASMAN, Dr. William Gratwicke, who

died on January 25, 1934, when 71 years old, played occasionally for Sussex between 1885 and 1895. A useful hard-hitting batsman, he had the good average for those days of 21.17 with 66 against Oxford in 1893 as his best score. In club cricket he stood out as a most capable all-round player. He scored 207 for United Hospitals against Chiswick Park, 200 for Arundel against a scratch side and 236 not out for Aldborough against Gunton Park in 1890. Dr. Heasman played sometimes for Berkshire and Norfolk, and in 1907 went with a Philadelphian team to Bermuda. A fast bowler, he was very keen in the field and a safe man at point. Born at Angmering in Sussex on December 9, 1862.

HEATH, Col. Arthur Howard, born at Newcastle-under-Lyme, Staffordshire, on May 29, 1856, died in London on April 21, 1930, in his 74th year. He was summed-up as "A free-hitting bat, strong on the off-side, fielded well at long-leg or cover-point, bowled fast-round and lobs." In 1873 and two next years he was in the Clifton XI, making 120 not out v. Sherborne in 1874 and a faultless 164 v. Cheltenham in 1875—in each case on his opponents' ground. He also played for Gloucestershire in 1875. Going up to Oxford, he played in the XI in 1876–77–78–79, but hardly did himself justice against Cambridge, though in 1878 he took two wickets for four runs with five deliveries and in 1879 played an innings of 45. Among his notable scores for Oxford were: 1876, 71 against Middlesex and 50 against M.C.C.; 1879, 61 against Middlesex. He played for Middlesex in 1878 against Yorkshire at Sheffield, and against Notts at Trent Bridge. Col. Heath had a long active and official association with the Staffordshire C.C. He played for the county from 1879 to 1898 and was captain from 1884 to 1893, hon. secretary from 1886 to 1888, and for many years hon. treasurer. He was chiefly a bat and a safe field but could bowl on occasion. His highest scores for the county were 217 v. Lincolnshire at Stoke in 1889—made in four hours—and 155 not out v. Cheshire in 1882. Whilst bowling for M.C.C. in Surrey's second innings at Lord's in 1876, he sent down a curious over. The first ball was a wide, the second jumped over long-stop's head and five byes resulted, the third knocked Elliott's middle stump out of the ground, the fourth nearly bowled R. Humphrey, the fifth was a wide for which two were run, and the sixth was played. Col. Heath was also well known as a Rugby footballer in the '70s. He was in the Oxford University Fifteen v.

Cambridge in 1875, 1877, 1879, and 1880, and appeared for England against Scotland in 1876, the last occasion on which 20-a-side was played in International games. He represented Hanley and, later, Leek in Parliament in the Conservative interest.

HEATH, Walter H. G., who died suddenly on December 4, 1965, the day following his 68th birthday, played for Surrey as an amateur in two matches in 1919. A wicketkeeper-batsman, he held four catches and against Essex at the Oval hit 58 not out. He also played for the Royal Air Force.

HEDGES, Lionel Paget, who died on January 12, 1933, at the early age of 32, was a brilliant schoolboy batsman and a fine coverpoint when at Tonbridge. In the school XI from 1916 to 1919, he, in his last year at Tonbridge, when captain, enjoyed a veritable triumph. The XI that season included four other players who later took part in firstclass cricket—E. P. Solbé and C. H. Knott of Kent, H. C. A. Gaunt of Warwickshire and T. E. S. Francis (Somerset). Hedges surpassed them all by scoring 1,038 runs—a record for the school—with the fine average of 86.50. He hit up 193 against Westminster, 176 v. Lancing, 111 v. M.C.C., and 163 against Clifton at Lord's. In the Lancing match, he and C. H. Knott added 290 runs together, all but 60 of them actually being obtained in an hour. Hedges got his Blue as a Freshman at Oxford in 1920 and played against Cambridge in the next two seasons, but although his fielding remained uniformly good his batting fell away considerably. Assisting Kent from 1919, he enjoyed his best season in County Cricket two years later, obtaining 1,138 runs with an average of 34. Perhaps the finest innings he ever played was against Yorkshire at Maidstone in 1920, when he hit up 130 runs in two hours and a half, and by his dashing batting helped materially to a Kent victory by 121 runs. Adopting the profession of schoolmaster, Hedges joined the staff at Cheltenham College and thus gained a residential qualification for Gloucestershire. He turned out for that county in several matches and his firstclass career extended until 1929. He was born on July 13, 1900.

HEDLEY, Col. Sir Walter Coote, K.B.E., C.B., C.M.G., who died on December 27, 1937, was a free batsman with good style, a fast right-handed bowler and smart fieldsman. He went to Marlborough and played for Kent in 1888, but when he took 14

Middlesex wickets for 109 runs at Lord's doubts were expressed about his delivery. Naturally with Lord Harris striving to stamp out unfair bowling, Hedley did not get a regular place in the Kent XI, but from 1890 he met with conspicuous success for Somerset. In 1895 at Leeds he took eight wickets for 18 runs in Yorkshire's first innings and six for 52 in the second. He was in the Gentlemen's XI against Players at Lord's in 1890 and at the Oval in 1892. When the county captains held a special meeting in 1900 to discuss the growing evil of unfair bowling, Hedley came under their notice.

A splendid soldier, Major Hedley was then serving in the South African War and he played little more first-class cricket though occasionally appearing for Devon and Hampshire. As batsman he showed to most advantage in scoring 102 for Somerset against Yorkshire at Taunton in 1892 after L. C. H. Palairet and H. T. Hewett had made the then record first wicket stand for 346. His only other century was 101 against Hampshire at Bournemouth in 1898.

HELE, George, who died in Australia, in 1982, at the age of 91, umpired 16 Test matches between 1928 and 1933, 10 of them between England and Australia. He stood in all five Tests in the 1932–33 Bodyline series, subsequently expressing his disapproval of the leg-theory tactics employed by some of the English fast bowlers. Himself one of the best umpires produced by Australia, his father, Andy, was also a first-class umpire, as was his son, Ray.

HELMORE, John Harold, who died at Bath in January, 1954, aged 80, played on a number of occasions for Somerset representative teams under the captaincy of the late S. M. J. Woods. He also represented Somerset at bowls and at one time was West of England table-tennis champion.

HEMINGWAY, George Edward, a brother of Messrs. W. M'G. and R. E. Hemingway, died at Rangoon on March 11, 1907. He was born at Macclesfield in 1872, was in the Uppingham XI in 1888, and in 1898 appeared for Gloucestershire against Yorkshire, at Sheffield. He was a free batsman and in the field generally stood mid-off or cover-point, but business and weak sight handicapped his play considerably. On one occasion, when playing a single-wicket match against his two brothers, he hit the ball into a bed of nettles; the fieldsmen quarrelled as to who should recover it, and during the argument the batsman ran about 250.

HEMINGWAY, 2nd Lieut. Ralph Eustace (8th Sherwood Foresters), was born on December 15, 1877, and killed in action in France on October 14, 1915. He was not in the XI whilst at Uppingham, but subsequently made some good scores by hard hitting for Nottinghamshire. Perhaps it was in 1904 that he was seen at his best, for that season he scored 300 runs in first-class cricket with an average of 23.07. Against the South Africans he made 85 and 30, he and George Gunn (143) obtaining 165 together for the opening partnership in the first innings. A year later, when he played more frequently, he scored 84 against Sussex at Brighton, and in the course of a week at the end of that season had the curious experience of assisting the North v. South at Blackpool and the Gentlemen of the South v. Players of the South at Bournemouth.

HEMMING, Sir Augustus William Lawson, G.C.M.G., was born in London on September 2, 1841, and died at Cairo on March 27, 1907. *Scores and Biographies* (viii.–60) described him as "a good average bat, but has been principally noted as a fast round-armed bowler. Fielded at first generally at short-slip, and afterwards as long-stop." He was educated at Epsom College, being a member of the first XI ever formed there, and at Godolphin School, and frequently played for Richmond, Civil Service, M.C.C., Kensington Park, Surrey Club and Ground, etc. In 1869 he joined the M.C.C., and afterwards served on the Committee. Occasionally he appeared for the Gentlemen of the South, and he took part in the match at the Oval in 1866 wherein "W. G." carried out his bat for 173. His best feat with the ball was for Eighteen Gentlemen of the Richmond Club against a strong scratch team in the Old Deer Park at Richmond in 1866 when he took eight wickets, namely those of T. A. Raynes, Jupp, Tom Hearne, Mantle, Tom Humphrey, Griffith, Pooley, and Willsher, for only 33 runs. Sir Augustus will always be best remembered on account of his association with the Incogniti, of which he was one of the original members, and for many years, commencing in 1871, the hon. secretary. In 1896 and 1897 Sir Augustus Hemming was Governor of British Guiana, and from 1898 to 1904 Governor and Commander-in-Chief of Jamaica.

HEMUS, L. G., a member of the New Zealand team that visited Australia in 1913–14 under the captaincy of Mr. D. Reese, died on October 28, 1933, aged 49. Up to the commencement of the War in 1914, he had made more centuries in Plunket Shield cricket than any other New Zealand player. A stylish and graceful batsman, he used to exploit with great success the art of late-cutting, by which stroke he obtained a large proportion of his runs. Appearing first for Auckland in 1903, he retired from representative cricket in 1922. In Plunket Shield cricket he scored over 2,000 runs, including four hundreds.

HENDERSON, Matthew, who died on June 17, 1970, aged 74, was a member of the first New Zealand team who, under the captaincy of T. C. Lowry, toured England in 1927. A fast left-arm bowler, he took 33 wickets for 24.21 runs each in the first-class fixtures. He played in one Test match, at Christchurch against A. H. H. Gilligan's England side of 1929–30. In representative games for Wellington between 1927 and 1932, he took 70 wickets and in Wellington senior championship cricket dismissed 333 batsmen at an average cost of 21.90.

HENDERSON, R. G., who died on September 22, 1895, will be remembered for the excellent service he rendered to Middlesex as a bowler during several seasons in the '70s. He was one of the few cricketers who, despite the enormous disadvantage of having to play in glasses, have met with success in first-class matches. He was a right-handed bowler, slow to medium pace, and, without ever being great, was decidedly above the average among amateurs. Mr. Henderson was educated at Harrow, and was considered very unfortunate in just missing a place in the XI. He was only 44.

HENDERSON, Robert, a member of the Surrey XI during the great years of the side when led by Mr. John Shuter, first played for the county in 1883 at the age of 18. He was an excellent batsman, generally able to give of his best when most was required of him, a useful slow bowler in his early years of first-class cricket and a thoroughly sound, if scarcely brilliant, fieldsman. In his first season with Surrey he scored 581 with an average of 15 and took 35 wickets at a cost of 18 runs apiece. Against Gloucestershire that summer, in a match which W. W. Read and Maurice Read finished off by hitting up 141 runs in 65 minutes, Henderson took six wickets in the second innings for 17 runs.

Bad health prevented Henderson from playing regularly until the season of 1887 and, though he was occasionally called upon in 1896, his last season before losing his form was that of 1893. Altogether during the period that Henderson was a member of the county XI Surrey won the Championship seven times, and in 1889 tied with Lancashire and Notts for first place, this being the only break of uninterrupted headship of the tournament during six consecutive seasons. So powerful were Surrey at that time that it was a great distinction to belong to the side. Henderson kept his place because of his consistent scoring and splendid nerve. As an example of his ability to do himself full justice at a crisis may be mentioned his innings of 59 not out against Yorkshire at the Oval, in what is still known as the "Gaslight Match," the gas-lamps in the road circling the Oval having been lighted for some time before the end was reached. Thanks to Henderson's determined batting, Surrey won by two wickets, Henderson finishing the match with a cut to the boundary when it was difficult to see the ball. Again, in 1893, when Surrey twice beat the Australians at the Oval, Henderson scored 28 and 15 in a small scoring game which the county won by 58 runs, and in the return match he made 60 not out and 14 not out.

Altogether, between 1883 and 1896, he made 5,061 runs for Surrey with an average of 19, among his scores being three separate hundreds at the Oval—106 v. Somerset, 105 v. Hampshire and 133 v. Scotland. During one winter he went to India to coach the Parsees, was paid great honours on his departure, and on his return was given—by his Surrey colleagues—the name of "Framjee." Born at Newport, in Monmouthshire, on March 30, 1865, Robert Henderson went to live at Beddington as a boy, and in local cricket for his choir he scored many runs and took wickets very cheaply. Always maintaining his association with church work, Henderson for many years was Warden of Beddington Parish Church, and chorister and churchwarden over a period of 56 years. He died on January 28, 1931, at Wallington.

HENDREN, Dennis, who died in hospital on May 30, 1962, aged 79, played for Middlesex from 1905 to 1908 in the days when the county side was predominantly amateur. His career with them ended a year before his younger and more famous brother, E. ("Patsy") Hendren, made his first appearance for Middlesex. Dennis Hendren afterwards threw in his lot with Durham, whom he assisted in the Minor Counties' competition from 1910 to 1914. He stood as a first-class umpire for a number of years between 1931 and 1949.

HENDREN, Elias, who died in a London hospital on October 4, 1962, aged 73, was one of the most famous batsmen to play for Middlesex and England. Only one cricketer, Sir John Hobbs, in the whole history of the first-class game hit more centuries than Hendren's 170; only two, Hobbs and F. E. Woolley, exceeded his aggregate of runs, 57,610 scored at an average of 50.80 per innings.

"Patsy," as, because of his Irish ancestry, he was affectionately known the world over, joined the Lord's ground-staff in 1905 and from his first appearance for Middlesex in 1909 he played regularly till 1937. Not always orthodox in style, this short, stockily-built batsman was celebrated for the power with which he invested his driving, for his cutting and for his courage in hooking fast bowlers. On pitches helpful to bowlers, he used his feet with consummate skill. His ability as a deep fieldsman is illustrated to some extent by the number of catches he brought off, 725, but the number of runs he saved cannot be gauged.

Apart from his achievements, "Patsy" was a "character" of a type sadly lacking in modern cricket. No game in which he was engaged could be altogether dull. If it looked like becoming so, Hendren could be relied upon at one time or another to produce some antic which would bring an appreciative chuckle from the onlookers. Furthermore, he was a first-rate mimic and wit, qualities which made him an admirable member of teams on tours, of which he took part in six—three in Australia, one in South Africa and two in the West Indies. Altogether he played in 51 Test matches, 28 of them against Australia, scoring 3,525 runs.

Of his seven centuries in Tests the highest was 205 not out against the West Indies at Port of Spain in 1930, when he and L. E. G. Ames (105) shared a fourth wicket stand of 237. "Patsy's" aggregate of 1,766, average 126.14, in that tour remains a record for a season in the West Indies. His highest innings in first-class cricket was 301 not out from the Worcestershire bowling at Dudley in 1933; on four occasions he put together a hundred in each innings of a match and he reached three-figures for Middlesex against every other first-class county. His best season was that of 1928 when he hit 3,311 runs, including 13 centuries, at an average of 70.44. In three summers he exceeded 3,000 runs; in 12 he made more than 2,000 and in

10 over 1,000. Among many big partnerships with his great friend and county colleague, J. W. Hearne, that of 375 against Hampshire at Southampton in 1923 was at the time a world record for the third wicket.

In 1933 Hendren caused something of a sensation at Lord's when he batted against the West Indies' fast bowlers wearing a special cap. Fashioned by his wife, this cap had three peaks, two of which covered the ears and temples, and was lined with sponge rubber. Hendren explained that he needed protection after being struck on the head two years earlier by the new-fashioned persistent short-pitched bouncers.

Following his retirement from the field, he succeeded Wilfred Rhodes as coach at Harrow School and for four years held a similar post with Sussex. He was elected a life member of M.C.C. in 1949 and also served on the Middlesex Committee. In 1952 he became scorer for Middlesex, continuing till ill-health compelled him to give up in 1960. In his younger days he was a fine Association football wing forward, playing in turn for Brentford, Queen's Park Rangers, Manchester City and Coventry City, and he appeared in a "Victory" International for England in 1919.

Tributes included:

Sir John Hobbs: "Patsy was a great cricketer and a great companion. He was the life and soul of the party on all our tours. In my opinion he was as good a player as anyone. He had beautiful strokes and he did get on with the game. I do not know of any bowlers who could keep him quiet on a good pitch and he was not so bad on the stickies. He was at his best after the 1914–18 War when he and Jack Hearne carried the Middlesex side."

Mr. S. C. Griffith, Secretary of M.C.C.: "Patsy was coaching Sussex while I was Secretary of the county and I also played with him. Apart from being a great cricketer, and perhaps more important, he brought a tremendous amount of fun and happiness to everything associated with the game. We at Lord's shall miss him terribly."

HENERY, Perceval Jeffery Thornton, died on August 10, 1938, at Washford, Somerset, aged 79. He twice played in the Harrow XI against Eton, the second time in 1878, when, thanks largely to his 45 and seven wickets for 106 runs, Harrow won a splendid match by 20 runs. Twice in the Cambridge XI when Oxford were beaten, each time by seven wickets, he scored 61 on his first appearance for the Light Blues in 1882 but did not bowl.

Of medium height, he was a hard hitting batsman, slow round-arm bowler with decided break and a brilliant fieldsman. Regarded as the best all-rounder of his time at Harrow, Henery played for Middlesex from 1879 to 1894, his best year being 1892 when he averaged 23.12.

HENFREY, Arthur George, who died at Finedon, Northamptonshire, on October 17, 1929, aged 61, was a successful batsman and a keen field. In 1883 and the next four years he was in the Wellingborough Grammar School XI, being captain his last three seasons. Each time he led the side he was first in batting, his average being 35 in 1885, 79 in 1886, and 42 in 1887. For some years he assisted Northamptonshire, and in 1893 and the following season captained the team. As an Association footballer he obtained his Blue for Cambridge, played for England six times, and assisted the Corinthians.

HENLEY, Francis Anthony Hoste, who died on June 26, 1963, aged 79, was in the Forest School XI before going to Oxford, for whom he played against Cambridge in 1905. A fast bowler, he took one wicket for 40 runs and three for 39 and scored one and 11. He experienced an extraordinary piece of good fortune during the second innings, when a ball touched his leg stump without removing a bail. In 1905, too, he was a member of the M.C.C. team who, under the captaincy of E. W. Mann, visited the U.S.A., where he scored 207 runs, average 20.70, and headed the bowling figures with 42 wickets for 8.40 runs each. He took part in three matches with Middlesex in 1908 and also appeared for Suffolk.

HENRY, A., the Queensland aboriginal fast bowler, died of consumption at Yarrabah, Queensland, on March 13, 1909. In the seven matches in which he appeared for his State between 1901–02 and 1904–05 he took 21 wickets for 674 runs, his only marked successes being when he obtained five wickets for 40 in the second innings of New South Wales at Brisbane in December, 1902, and when he took four for 49 against the same side at Sydney 13 months later.

HENSON, Lieut.-Col. Hugh Arnold, who died following a heart attack at Bournemouth on November 17, 1958, aged 74, was secretary of Gloucestershire from 1935 to 1956 and from 1942 till the end of the war acted as deputy assistant-secretary of M.C.C. Educated at Malvern, he was for

some years an actor appearing in several popular musical comedies in London. He served in the First World War, being twice Mentioned in Dispatches, and afterwards took a regular commission in the R.A.S.C. and then with the Indian Army. He rejoined his old regiment at the outbreak of the Second World War till he retired on grounds of health.

HENTY, Edward (Kent), born at Hawkhurst, in Kent, August 11, 1842; died January, 20, 1900. *Scores and Biographies* (xii–156) says: "Is a very efficient wicket-keeper, and as a bat he is above the average, being very steady, perhaps indeed a trifle too much so." For United South v. XXII of Swansea, May 25, 1876, he stumped six and caught five in the match. Height 5ft. 8½in., and weight at the start of his cricket career, 10st. 11lb. A great match—England v. Thirteen of Kent, at Canterbury, in 1881—was played for his benefit.

HERBERT, Eric James, who died in a Wellingborough hospital after a long illness on October 14, 1963, aged 55, played as a professional in 35 matches for Northamptonshire from 1937 to 1939. A medium-pace bowler, he took 69 wickets, average 33.65.

HERBERT, The Hon. Mervyn Robert Howard Molyneux, born November 27, 1882, died at the British Embassy, in Rome, on May 26, 1929, aged 46. He was in the Eton XI in 1901. The same year he made the first of his six appearances for Notts and marked the occasion by scoring a capital 65 v. M.C.C. at Lord's. From 1903 onwards he assisted Somerset occasionally. One especially good innings he played for that county was 78 v. Middlesex at Lord's in 1909. A remarkable performance in which he had a share whilst at Eton—it was in a House-match, for A. C. Benson's v. H. V. Macnaghton's in 1901—deserves mention. He made 201 not out and the Hon. G. W. Lyttelton 260 not out, the pair, after one man was out, adding 476 together without being separated. The two also shared between them all 15 wickets which fell of their opponents.

HERCY, John Eustace, who for many years assisted with the Births and Deaths and Obituary sections in *Wisden*, died on January 30, 1950, aged 82, after a long illness.

HESELTINE, Lieut.-Col. Christopher, O.B.E., D.L., J.P., President of Hampshire

County Club and in several years a member of the M.C.C. Committee, died on June 13, 1944, at Lymington, aged 74. He failed to get a place in the Eton XI and, going up to Trinity Hall, did not find favour at Cambridge in the cricket field, but played in the Association football XI against Oxford in the winter of 1891. He began County Cricket when Hampshire were second-class, and was 27 years old before making a name as a fast bowler in the best company. Fully utilising his height, he brought the ball over at the extreme extent of his arm with deadly effect at times, but he was inconsistent and required careful nursing because apt to tire. He showed to most advantage in 1897 when he took 41 wickets at 17.12 apiece, his best performance being in a drawn game with Surrey at Southampton, nine wickets falling to him for 61 runs. Among his victims was Robert Abel without scoring in each innings. In July next year at Portsmouth, Heseltine again dismissed Abel for 0, the famous Surrey professional thus failing three times in succession when facing the Hampshire express. He went to India, South Africa and West Indies with teams captained by Lord Hawke. Joining the Imperial Yeomanry, he saw active service in the South African campaign, and in the last European war, when in the Royal Fusiliers, he was twice Mentioned in Dispatches.

HETHERTON, Walter, died at Hexham on April 19, 1938. A good bowler, he helped Northumberland to head the Minor Counties in successive seasons. The second occasion in 1925 was notable for Hetherton dismissing 91 batsmen at 9.25 runs apiece, his most notable performance being all 10 wickets for 52 runs in Yorkshire's second innings at Horsforth. Next year he was in the Minor Counties XI for the opening match of the Australian tour and dismissed the captain, H. L. Collins.

HEVER, Harold Lawrence, who died in October, 1971, aged 74, was a professional slow left-arm bowler for Kent from 1921 to 1925. Though his appearances in the Championship team were limited, he accomplished much good work for the Second XI. CORRECTION. H. L. Hever died in 1970, not 1971 as stated in the 1972 Obituaries.

HEWETSON, Edward Pearson, died in hospital on December 26, 1977, aged 75. In the early 1920s there was a desperate shortage of fast bowlers in this country and Hewetson was one of the few who could be called genuinely fast. A tall and hugely strong man and a fine natural athlete, he had the physical attributes of a great fast bowler, but unfortunately not the technique. There was too much arm in his action and too little body, with the result that he was inaccurate and was also prone to bowl no-balls, nor did he, though fast, generate the speed that he might have done. Indeed in his last year at Oxford, E. R. T. Holmes, who shared the new ball with him, was with his much smoother action on the testimony of the wicket-keeper for a few overs the faster of the two.

Hewetson's best bowling performance was in 1924 against a strong Kent batting side in the Parks, when he followed five for 16 with five for 26. Four years in the Shrewsbury XI, in 1919, his second year, he appeared for Warwickshire and in the next two played for the Public Schools at Lord's, taking in 1920 nine for 33 for the Rest against the Lord's Schools. In the Freshman's match at Oxford in 1922 he scored 106 in 80 minutes and later headed the University bowling averages, but failed to get his Blue. He played against Cambridge however for the next three years. In these matches his most notable performance was to make 57 in 25 minutes in 1923 going in ninth, a fine bit of hitting but one that reflected little credit on the Cambridge bowling tactics. Hitting firm footed and usually with a cross bat, he thrust his left foot out as far as he could to anything reasonably well up and swung with all his might. A few days before in an innings of 34 he had hit three sixes into the pavilion at the Oval.

He continued to play for Warwickshire off and on until 1927, but with only moderate success. Apart from his cricket he represented Oxford in the three miles in 1923 and in the mile for the next three years and in 1924 was in their hockey side. After coming down he was for some years a master at St. Edward's, Oxford, and later for many years a preparatory school master in the Lake District.

HEWETT, Herbert Tremenheer, died at Brighton on March 4, 1921. Born on May 25, 1864, he was nearly 57 years of age. Giving up first-class cricket whilst still a young man, Mr. Hewett had long been out of the public eye, but he will be vividly remembered as one of the most remarkable left-handed batsmen we ever had, and also for the dominating part he played in establishing Somerset as a first-class county. In his early days he did little to suggest the fame that was in store for him. In 1882–83, in his two matches for Harrow against Eton at Lord's, he only scored seven runs in three innings.

Going up to Oxford he only secured his Blue in 1886, and in the University match circumstances were rather against him. He was bowled without getting a run on the first day, and in Oxford's second innings he was one of the batsmen who, with disastrous results, obeyed rather too literally H. V. Page's injunction to play a free game after K. J. Key and W. Rashleigh had made their memorable stand of 243 runs for the first wicket. In the meantime Hewett had begun to play for Somerset, then a second-class county of modest pretensions, and it is with Somerset cricket that his name will always be associated. The County Club was formally established in 1886. In 1890 Somerset won all their matches, and at the meeting of secretaries in December they secured the requisite number of fixtures, and passed automatically into the front rank. They could not have started under happier circumstances. S. M. J. Woods was still at the top of his form as a fast bowler, and L. C. H. Palairet was getting to his very best as a batsman. The Somerset XI became a great attraction both at home and away, the climax being reached when, at Taunton in 1892, Hewett and L. C. H. Palairet scored 346 together for the first wicket against Yorkshire, beating a record—by W. G. Grace and B. B. Cooper—that had stood since 1869. In 1892 Somerset came out third among the nine leading counties, Hewett getting an average of 40. There seemed every reason to think that he would remain for a long time connected with Somerset, but after the season of 1893 he resigned the captaincy of the XI and gave up County Cricket. There is no doubt that he was largely influenced by an incident that occurred during the match with the Australians at Taunton. Owing to the wretched weather it was agreed in the morning to abandon play for the day, but late in the afternoon the players were gathered together and the game started. Some of Mr. Hewett's friends thought he made far too much of the matter, but he was very angry, considering that his authority had been unwarrantably overruled. As a batsman he was individual to a degree. Playing his own game, he could not be imitated. Very daring, and blessed with an unfailing eye, he could demoralise bowling just as Jessop did, and was capable of hitting up 50 runs on impossible wickets. Apart from his batting he was, on the evidence of those who played under his leadership, one of the very best county captains of his day. Though he was not seen very often after severing his connection with Somerset, Mr. Hewett played in several

matches in the next three seasons and kept up his batting form, getting 110 for A. J. Webbe's XI against Oxford in 1894, and 109 against Cambridge, and 102 against Oxford for the Gentlemen of England in 1895. His scores of 50 or more in *Bat v. Ball* from 1885 to 1896 number 38, by far his biggest innings being his 201 in the memorable match at Taunton in 1892.—S.H.P.

HEWSON, Robert, who died in Melbourne in October, 1972, kept wicket for Western Australia between 1924–25 and 1931–32. He appeared in 13 first-class matches and captained his State against the South African touring team in 1931–32.

HEYGATE, Harold John, who died at Guildford on June 27, 1937, aged 53, was in the Epsom College XI and played occasionally for Sussex in 1903 and 1905. A sound stylish batsman he opened at Tonbridge against Kent in 1905 by scoring 80 and in the second innings made 68 not out.

HEYMANN, William Goodall, who died on November 27, 1969, aged 84, was in the Haileybury XI from 1902 to 1904, being captain in the last year. He appeared for Nottinghamshire in 1905.

HICKLEY, Anthony North, who died suddenly on September 5, 1972, aged 66, did not gain inclusion in the XI at Winchester, but he played for Middlesex against Yorkshire at Bramall Lane in 1930.

HICKMOTT, Edward, was groundsman at The Mote, Maidstone, for 27 years. Born on March 20, 1850, he died on January 7, 1934, at the age of 83. He played 11 times for Kent between 1875 and 1888 with 44 as his best score. A hard-hitting, right-handed batsman, he was tried as a wicket-keeper by Lord Harris.

HICKMOTT, Lieut. R. G. (New Zealand Reinforcements), born on March 19, 1894, died of wounds in September, 1916. He was educated at Christchurch High School, where he was in the XI for five seasons and captain for three. He came to the fore in November, 1911, by scoring 235 without a mistake for Fifteen Colts v. the Canterbury XI on the Christchurch ground, and the same year was tried for Canterbury. His first four innings in inter-Provincial cricket were 30 and 39 v. Wellington at Wellington and 52 and 33 in the return match at Christchurch. He was then only 17 years of age, and his form that season was so good that to February 17 he had made 1,466 runs with an average of 81.44. In 1912–13 he scored 77 v. Otago at Christchurch; in 1913–14 he toured Australia as a member of the New Zealand team; and during 1914–15 he made 63 and 56 v. Auckland at Auckland and 109 v. Hawke's Bay at Hastings, besides taking four wickets for five runs against Otago at Christchurch. In club cricket he played for the St. Alban's C.C., of Christchurch. He was probably the most promising young cricketer in the Dominion, and his early death will be felt severely when the game is resumed.

HICKMOTT, William Edward, who died on January 16, 1968, aged 72, played as a professional left-arm bowler for Kent between 1914 and 1921 and for Lancashire in 1923 and 1924. In his first year with Lancashire he took 57 wickets, average 23.96, including five for 20 against Leicestershire at Old Trafford. *Wisden* said of him at that time: "He bowled medium to rather slow and sometimes caused a lot of trouble without doing steady enough work to fulfil expectations." As a professional with Rochdale, he set up a Central Lancashire League record in 1927 by taking 140 wickets during the season. Nephew of E. Hickmott, the old Kent player who served for so long as groundsman at The Mote, Maidstone, he afterwards became celebrated as a breeder and trainer of golden retrievers.

HICKS, John, who played in 15 matches for Yorkshire between 1872 and 1876, died of pneumonia at York on June 10, 1912. He was born December 10, 1850, and was therefore in his 62nd year at the time of his death. He scored 313 runs for his county with an average of 14.22, his highest innings being 66 v. Surrey at the Oval in 1875. In the Whit-Monday match at Lord's in 1875 between the North and the South, he scored nine in each innings, being bowled by Southerton in his first innings and lbw to "W. G." in his second. Southerton took 16 wickets for 52 runs, and the match was completed in a day.

HICKTON, William, who died at Lower Broughton, February 27, 1900, did good service for Lancashire 30 years ago. He was a good batsman and a fast round-armed bowler, being altogether a cricketer above the average, and fielding generally at slip. His first appearance at Lord's was for Lancashire v. M.C.C. and Ground, June 3, 4, 5, 1867, and it was a curious fact that none of the Lancashire XI (except C. Coward, who

appeared as a colt in 1862) had ever before played at Lord's. The match was seriously interrupted by the weather, and mops and pails were used to clear the pools of water from the pitch, and by this means the match was finished. Hickton's bowling proved very successful, accounting in the first innings for five wickets for 69 runs, and in the second for six for 22. Hickton will chiefly be remembered for obtaining all 10 wickets for 46 runs in the second innings for Lancashire v. Hampshire, at Manchester, in July, 1870. He only represented the county from 1867 to 1871, and during that time obtained 144 wickets for 2,022 runs. On July 20, 1883, a match between Lancashire and Eighteen of the Manchester Broughton Club, was played for his benefit. He was born at Hardstaff, near Chesterfield, in Derbyshire, December 14, 1842. Assisted the Players on one occasion only—at the Oval, in 1867, when he bowled eight balls for six runs and one wicket, and 216 balls for 63 runs and two wickets.

HIDDLESTON, John Sydney, one of the ablest all-round cricketers Wellington and New Zealand have produced, died suddenly at Wellington on October 30, 1940, in his 50th year. In Plunket Shield matches he created several records: he scored for Wellington, 2,523 runs in 46 innings with an average of 56; in each of the seasons 1923–24 and 1925–26, when he played innings of 204 and 212, his aggregate exceeded 500 runs. This double performance and also his eight centuries—three each against Auckland and Otago, and two against Canterbury—are New Zealand records. Hiddleston also played for Otago, and his complete aggregate falls only 30 short of the 2,597 scored by Roger Blunt, who represented both Canterbury and Otago and holds the New Zealand record in Plunket Shield games. An able slow break bowler, Hiddleston was also an excellent fieldsman. By many Wellington cricketers he was compared favourably with C. S. Dempster. He played in representative sides against teams visiting New Zealand from 1920 to 1925.

HIDE, Arthur, a medium paced left-hand bowler, who fielded well at short slip, and also batted left-hand low on the list, died at Bexhill-on-Sea, his home, on November 5, 1933. Born on May 7, 1860, he was 22 when first playing for Sussex and he kept his place in the side until 1890 when he became coach at Marlborough College. Altogether, in 124 matches for Sussex, he took 459 wickets at

18.10 runs apiece and scored 1,289 runs—average 7.76. At Hove in 1882 he took nine Yorkshire wickets for 112 runs. In 1888, his best season, he took seven Surrey wickets for 44 runs in one innings, and against Lancashire six for 34, nine in the match for 86, both at Brighton.

HIDE, Jesse Bollard, who was born at Eastbourne on March 12, 1857, died at Edinburgh on March 19, 1924, aged 67. A useful steady batsman and fast bowler and a good field at point and long-stop, he played his first match for Sussex in 1876 and his last in 1893, but he did not assist the side between 1878 and 1883, being engaged at Adelaide, in Australia. For the county he made 4,691 runs with an average of 16.12 and took 460 wickets for 20.87 runs each. Against Kent at Hove he scored 112 in 1884 and 173 in 1886, and on the same ground he also made 115 v. Cambridge University in 1887 and 130 v. Gloucestershire in 1888. Against Lancashire at Manchester in 1885 he had eight wickets in an innings for 47 runs, and in the match with M.C.C. at Lord's in 1890 took four wickets —those of Flowers, W.J. Ford, C.W. Wright and J.S. Russel—with consecutive balls. For Fifteen of South Australia against The Australian XI of 1882, at Adelaide in 1882–83, he bowled 64 balls for one run—a remarkable feat against so strong a team. In minor matches for Eastbourne he accomplished several noteworthy performances. Thus, in 1883 he took all 10 wickets for 11 runs v. M.C.C., and two years later, against Bexley, his figures were eight for 43 and all 10 for 39. In the latter match he also played an innings of 115. For Sussex Club and Ground v. Seventeen Colts in 1890 he had an analysis of 14 overs for one run and one wicket. His benefit match was Sussex v. Nottinghamshire at Hove in 1894. Commencing in 1896, he assisted Cornwall for a few seasons, and for that county he obtained 14 wickets v. Glamorganshire at Swansea in 1897, and 12 v. Dorset at Truro a year later, also playing an innings of 84 in the latter match.

HIGGINS, Harry Leonard, who died at Malvern on September 15, 1979, aged 85, did good work for Worcestershire as a batsman. After being in the XI at King Edward's, Birmingham, and then being severely wounded in the First World War, he played for the county from 1920 to 1927, exceeding 1,000 runs in 1921 and 1922 and making a couple of centuries in each year, his highest being a particularly fine innings of 137 not

out v. Lancashire at Worcester in 1922. In 1922 he was picked for a fairly strong side of Gentlemen at the Oval. His elder brother, J.B. Higgins, also played with some success for Worcestershire.

HIGGINS, James, who died at Wibsey in July, 1954, aged 77, kept wicket for Yorkshire in several matches early in the century. For many years afterwards he captained Featherstone till retiring from the game in 1932.

HIGGINS, John Bernard, who died in a Malvern nursing-home on January 3, 1970, aged 84, played as an amateur for Worcestershire between 1920 and 1930, scoring 3,832 runs, average 19.85, and holding 54 catches. He was in the XI at King Edward's School, Birmingham. Not till late in his career did he reach his best form for the county, his most successful year being 1928, when he obtained 1,041 runs, including 101 against Yorkshire at Worcester, for an average of 30.61. The highest of his three centuries was 123 in a total of 227 off the Glamorgan bowling at Kidderminster in 1927.

HIGGS, Geoffrey, the Dulwich College cricket captain of 1950, died at the age of 18 on April 29, 1951, following an injury received while playing for the First Fifteen on November 18, 1950. For over five months he lay paralysed in hospital. Throughout his illness he set a magnificent example of courage. In the words of the College Chaplin, the Reverend A.W. Brown, "It is easy to talk of courage and fortitude when all is going well, but it is a very different matter to exhibit those shining qualities when the test comes." Three years after entering the school, Higgs became a member of the XI, and in the following year he was chosen for the athletics team. During 1950 he was made captain of Marlowe, captain of athletics and captain of cricket, and finally gained a place in the First Fifteen. He was made captain of the school while in hospital.

HIGGS, Kenneth Alan, who died at Haywards Heath on January 21, 1959, aged 72, achieved the rare feat of hitting a century, 101, for Sussex against Worcestershire at Hove in 1920, upon the occasion of his first appearance in a first-class match. He played for Sussex from 1920 to 1924, scoring 1,693 runs, average 26.65. His highest innings was 111 from the Warwickshire bowling at Hove in 1921, he and W.J. Malden scoring so freely that they put on 188 for the third wicket in two hours. He was a Vice-President of the County Club.

HIGGS-WALKER, James Arthur, died at Midhurst on September 3, 1979, aged 87. A useful fast bowler in the 1911 Repton side, he played one match for Worcestershire in 1913 and another in 1919. From 1925 to 1953 he was headmaster of Sevenoaks School.

HIGSON, Thomas A., who died at his home at Grange-over-Sands on August 3, 1949, was a former Test selector and the chairman of Lancashire County C.C. He played in first-class cricket for Lancashire and Derbyshire, and also appeared for Cheshire and Rossall School. A member of the Lancashire Committee for 49 years, Mr. Higson succeeded the late Sir Edwin Stockton as chairman in 1932 after serving as hon. treasurer for eight years. He became an M.C.C. member in 1897, and served from 1931 to 1934 as a member of the M.C.C. Selection Committee, together with Sir Pelham Warner and Mr. P. A. Perrin.

At Rossall, Mr. Higson captained the school cricket team for two years; he also led the hockey XI and was Fives champion. While at New College, Oxford, where he took an M.A. degree, he played for the University at both cricket and Association football, but did not gain a Blue. In the soccer side he played with Mr. G. O. Smith.

When 17, Higson played cricket for Cheshire, and in 1890 he captained Derbyshire. From 1905 onwards he made a number of appearances for Lancashire, and his last first-class appearance occurred in 1923, when he led the Lancashire team which beat the West Indies.

A Manchester solicitor, Mr. Higson gave great service to cricket as an administrator. He helped to choose the M.C.C. side which visited Australia in 1932–33, and when the "body-line" controversy arose concerning that tour, he expressed the view that such bowling was detrimental to cricket. He was an advocate of brighter cricket, and in 1934 urged two-day single innings county matches.

In first-class cricket he scored 537 runs at an average of 12.78 and with right-arm slow bowling took 39 wickets for 28.23 each.

HILDER, Alan Lake, who died on May 2, 1970, aged 68, headed the batting averages in 1920 when in the Lancing XI. He enjoyed the distinction of hitting a century on his first appearance for Kent, for whom he played occasionally between 1924 and 1929, but he never afterwards approached that form. The big occasion was against Essex at Gravesend,

where he scored 103 not out and he and C. Wright added 157 together—a record for the eighth Kent wicket which still stands.

HILDYARD, The Rev. Lyonel D'Arcy, M.A., who died suddenly at Rowley Rectory, Hull, on April 22, 1931, aged 70, was in the Oxford XI in 1884–85–86. He was a Freshman in 1884, when a remarkable entry of first-class young cricketers made the Oxford team, under M. C. Kemp, the most successful that ever represented the University before or since. Assisted by T. C. O'Brien, K. J. Key, J. H. Brain, E. H. Buckland, H. O. Whitby, and others, Oxford won seven matches out of eight, among their defeated opponents being the Australians, who lost to them by six wickets. No Australian XI since then has been beaten by either University. Hildyard was fortunate to get his Blue, for he only came into the side at the last minute, mainly owing to the failure of A. R. Cobb who, coming up with a great reputation from Winchester, could make no runs at Oxford. In 1885, when Oxford fared very badly, Hildyard came to the front and, though he did little against Cambridge, headed the batting averages with an aggregate of 262 runs and an average of 29. In 1886 without doing anything special he was well worth his place in the team. He also played occasionally for Somerset and for Lancashire. A useful player with a sound defence, he was also an excellent field at point, standing close in and making many fine catches. He was at one time a minor canon of Windsor and afterwards rector of Rowley, East Yorkshire, where members of his family have been rectors for several centuries.

HILL, Allen, born at Kirkheaton, near Huddersfield, November 14, 1845, died at Leyland in Lancashire on August 29, 1910. Although he played his last match for Yorkshire so long ago as 1883, Allen Hill is still vividly remembered as one of the best right-handed fast bowlers of his day. It is a curious fact that, though he did not come out until long after the alteration in 1864 of Law 10, he bowled in the old fashioned style with a purely round-arm action, the hand at the moment of delivery being very little above the shoulder. Great as was the reputation, he would probably have been thought still more of if it had not been his fate to follow George Freeman in the Yorkshire XI. He proved an admirable substitute for that famous bowler but he had not Freeman's wonderful spin and, as the late Mr. William Yardley, among others, contended, his lower action made him easier to see. His delivery was one of the best of its kind that can be recalled and with a far shorter run up to the wicket than most modern fast bowlers find necessary he had great pace. He sprang into fame in 1871, when against Surrey at the Oval he took 12 wickets—six in each innings and all of them bowled down—at a cost of only 57 runs. For this fine performance he was presented by a supporter of Yorkshire cricket resident in London with a silver cup. The match was played on August 21 and 22 and from that time forward Hill's position was secure. He was at his very best in the summer of 1874, when just at the height of the season an accident interfered with his cricket. He was indeed curiously unfortunate in meeting with mishaps. His knee gave way when he was bowling as well as ever in 1879 and finally a broken collar-bone cut short his career. In the Gentlemen and Players' match at Lord's in 1874 he did the hat-trick in the Gentlemen's second innings, bowling I. D. Walker, and catching and bowling A. W. Ridley and A. N. Hornby. Personally Hill was one of the most popular of professional cricketers—a man of kindly nature and gentle manners. When his cricket days were over he found an excellent friend in the late Mr. Stannard of Leyland who gave him an engagement that he retained to the day of his death. Hill went to Australia in the winter of 1876–77 with James Lillywhite's team and took part in the first matches in which the Australians met England on level terms.

Among Hill's most noteworthy bowling performances in great matches were the following:

Wkts.	Runs		Year.
8 for	73	An England XI v. Cambridge University, at Cambridge	1874
8 ,,	48	North v. South, at Prince's	1874
13 ,,	116	All England XI v. Fourteen of Oxford University, at Oxford	1874
6 ,,	9	Yorkshire v. United South of England XI, at Bradford. (United South of England, set 66 to win, were got out for 39. (W. G. Grace (15) alone made double figures.)	1874
4 ,,	11	Yorkshire v. Lancashire, at Manchester	1874
10 ,,	9	England v. XXII of South Australia, at Adelaide	1876–77
4 ,,	11	England v. New South Wales, at Sydney	1876–77
7 ,,	14	Yorkshire v. Surrey, at Hull	1879
5 ,,	16 }	Yorkshire v. Derbyshire, at Sheffield	1879
4 ,,	9 }		
4 ,,	11	Yorkshire v. I Zingari, at Scarborough	1880
6 ,,	18	Yorkshire v. M.C.C. and Ground, at Lord's	1881
4 ,,	8	Yorkshire v. Middlesex, at Lord's	1881

In the North v. South match, at Tunbridge Wells in 1875, he opened the bowling for the former and in his first over dismissed W. G. Grace with the first ball, Charlwood with the second, and G. F. Grace with the fourth.

On his first appearance in the Gentlemen v. Players match—at the Oval in 1874—he took nine wickets for 150 runs and in the 10 matches in which he bowled against the Gentlemen between 1874 and 1882 he obtained 40 wickets at a cost of 21.25 runs each.

In Yorkshire matches his yearly records were as under:

	Matches.	Balls.	Runs.	Wickets.	Average.
1871	3	603	201	19	10.53
1872	10	1,529	564	32	17.62
1873	12	2,910	993	82	12.10
1874	8	1,853	657	60	10.95
1875	13	3,433	1,072	81	13.23
1876	12	2,215	705	62	11.37
1877	12	1,288	464	27	17.18
1878	18	2,020	636	48	13.25
1879	7	814	198	29	6.82
1880	14	1,647	643	43	14.95
1881	7	1,081	340	36	9.44
1882	18	1,803	561	30	18.70
1883	2	499	117	14	8.35
Totals	136	21,695	7,151	563	12.70

In the same matches he scored 1,786 runs with an average of 8.79.

For Yorkshire against Surrey at the Oval in 1880 he did the hat-trick.

On five occasions he and Emmett bowled unchanged through both completed innings of a match for Yorkshire—twice against Surrey and Lancashire, and once against Notts—and he also performed the same feat for the County with Ulyett Armitage and Peate.

In July, 1884, Hill was given the Yorkshire v. Lancashire match at Sheffield for his benefit, but it yielded him only £376 15s. 7d.

HILL, Arthur James Ledger, a fine all-round cricketer who played for Marlborough College, Wiltshire, Cambridge University and Hampshire, died on September 6, 1950, aged 79. Born at Bassett, near Southampton, he was by profession a banker, and excelled at most games. Tall and stylish, Hill was a splendid batsman with a free, natural approach to the game. He was also a useful fast bowler before taking to lobs, and in addition he was a reliable field, notably at short slip. In first-class cricket Hill hit 20 hundreds, scoring altogether 9,995 runs, averaging 27.91, and he took 278 wickets, average 29.60. He went with Lord Hawke's team to India in 1892–93, America 1894, and South Africa 1895–96, and with M.C.C. to Argentine 1911–12. He played in three Tests in South Africa, scoring 124 at Cape Town.

Hill made his first appearance as a player at Lord's in 1887, a day after completing his 16th year, for he was in the Marlborough XI three seasons, during which time he also turned out for Wiltshire (1888). Going to Cambridge, he played four times against Oxford, 1890–93, and in May, 1891, he performed the hat-trick for the University against Next Sixteen—a feat he also achieved the following year for Lord Hawke's team against Madras Presidency at Madras. Altogether his cricket career covered 30 years and finished with him appearing with his son in the Hampshire side.

His best score for the county was 199 against Surrey at the Oval in 1898. In 1904, at Worcester, for Hampshire Hill made 98 not out and 117, and in 1905 at Southampton, in the match between Hampshire and Somerset, he hit 124 and 118 not out. In the second innings he was engaged in a remarkable stand of 150 with Major E. G. Wynyard. Hill was lame and, owing to a damaged thumb, Wynyard could bat with only one hand. Yet Hill made his runs in two hours hitting one six, one five and 22 fours. He scored 80 while his partner made seven; in fact Major Wynyard spent over an hour getting his first two runs. Hill captained Hampshire teams at Rugby football and hockey, and he was also good at racquets and boxing.

HILL, Clement, the Australian left-handed batsman, ranked among the finest cricketers in the world during a long period, died on September 5, 1945, aged 68. Born at Adelaide on March 18, 1877, the son of H. J. Hill, who scored the first century on Adelaide Oval, Clem Hill excelled his brothers—all good at the game—and when 16 he put together the remarkable score of 360 in an Inter-College match at Adelaide. This was the highest innings hit in Australia at that time, 1893, and young Clem Hill gave clear indication of the skill which matured without a check.

Soon after completing his 18th year he scored 150 not out and 56 for South Australia against A. E. Stoddart's team in 1895, and a year later, with Harry Trott as captain, he made the first of four visits to England. Third in the averages, he established himself as being worthy of a place in any XI, and when next Stoddart took a side to Australia Hill exceeded the highest expectations by scoring 829 runs in 12 innings, his average of 75 far surpassing that of both K. S. Ranjitsinhji and A. C. MacLaren, the chief batsmen in the touring side. That season he scored 200 for South Australia against the visiting team, and his 188 at Melbourne in the fourth Test, when Australia began so badly as to lose six men for 57, was largely responsible for a victory by eight wickets. This innings was considered the finest that Clem Hill ever played.

Coming to England with the side under the captaincy of Joe Darling, another fine left-handed batsman, in 1899, he showed splendid form until taken ill early in July. He and Victor Trumper each scored 135 at Lord's, sharing the chief honours in beating England by 10 wickets, and so helping largely to win the rubber: for this was the only decisive result in the five Tests. He headed the averages for the tour with 60.20. To prove that even such a splendid batsman may fail it is interesting to recall that in the second innings of the third Test at Leeds, the order of batting being altered, he fell the first victim of a hat-trick by J. T. Hearne; Hill was clean bowled, S. E. Gregory and M. A. Noble were both caught in the slips. From 1896 to 1912 he played in 49 Test matches, 41 against England, eight against South Africa;

he captained Australia when South Africa were the visitors in 1910, and in the following season against the England touring side, led by J. W. H. T. Douglas owing to the illness of P. F. Warner.

As a rule Clem Hill, going in first wicket down, was at his best on the important occasion and in Test matches he scored 3,412 runs; average 39. He hit seven centuries against South Africa and four against England, besides 96, 99, 98 and 97. The innings of 98 and 97 were the highest scores for Australia at Adelaide in January, 1902, and, with Trumble's all-round work, brought about the defeat of England by four wickets. These displays followed his 99 which helped in a victory by 229 runs at Melbourne—three consecutive scores just short of the century in Tests with England.

A specially brilliant batsman on hard pitches, Clem Hill scored 6,274 runs, average 52.28 in Sheffield Shield matches—a record until beaten by Don Bradman. His highest innings was 365 not out for South Australia against New South Wales at Adelaide in December, 1900, his average that season being 103.33. In similar matches he made 206 not out at Sydney in 1895 and 205 at Adelaide in 1909.

While able to drive hard to the off or straight, usually with the ball kept down, Clem Hill scored chiefly on the leg side by skilful strokes perfectly timed and placed, the way in which he turned straight balls clear of fieldsmen being exceptional. Brilliant square and late cutting made Hill delightful to watch and in defence his style claimed admiration while his patience was unlimited. A splendid field particularly in the deep, Clem Hill brought off one catch that will never be forgotten by the spectators at the third Test match at Old Trafford in 1902. When England wanted eight runs for victory with two wickets in hand Dick Lilley made a square-leg hit which looked like carrying the pavilion rails, but as Hill ran from long-on the wind seemed to check the force of the hit. The ball fell almost straight and Hill, racing across its flight, with outstretched hands, held it, so accepting a chance that few fieldsmen would have thought worth attempting. Australia won by three runs, and the victory, following success at Sheffield, where Hill scored 119, by far the highest innings in the match, gave them the rubber, a triumph to which Hill's amazing catch contributed to an unknown degree. Rain ruined the first two Tests and England won the last by one wicket.

Two Australian Test match partnership records stand to his name—165 for the seventh wicket with H. Trumble at Melbourne in January, 1897, and 243 for the eighth wicket with R. J. Hartigan at Adelaide in January, 1908. On that second occasion an attack of influenza prevented Hill from fielding, but he batted five hours 20 minutes for 160, and Australia, after being 78 behind on the first innings, won by 245 runs.

Besides Clem Hill, two other members of the 1896 team in England died within a period of four months, C. J. Eady on December 3 and Joseph Darling on January 2, 1946.

HILL, Lieut.-Col. Denys Vivian, who died on May 15, 1971, aged 75, played as an opening bowler for Worcestershire in 1927 and 1928, taking in County Championship engagements 75 wickets for 29.99 runs apiece. He also represented the Army.

HILL, H. J., a younger brother of Clement Hill, died at the end of October, 1906, at the early age of 28. He was a very useful allround cricketer, and accomplished several good performances in club matches in Adelaide and (afterwards) Melbourne. For South Australia against the M.C.C.'s England team, at Adelaide, in March, 1904, he took three wickets for 27 runs. Like his famous brother, he was educated at Prince Alfred College.

HILL, H. John, father of the well-known Australian cricketing brotherhood which included Clement Hill, died in Adelaide on September 18, 1926. A good player in his day, he will be remembered chiefly for having been the first batsman to play a three-figure innings on the Adelaide Oval—102 not out for North Adelaide v. Kent C.C. on January 26, 1878. A trustee of the South Australian Cricket Association for many years and a vice-president of that body since 1893, Mr Hill was also a famous whip and in 1874 he drove W. G. Grace's team to Kadina in one of his four-in-hands. Born in Adelaide on March 16, 1847, he was, at the time of his death, in his 80th year.

HILL, Henry, who played occasionally for Yorkshire from 1887 to 1891, died at Headingley, Leeds, on August 14, 1935. Business prevented him from giving much time to first-class cricket or he might have played regularly in the county XI during the early years of Lord Hawke's captaincy. A free batsman, fond of driving, he scored 565 runs in all matches for the county at an average of

15.09 for 36 completed innings before York-shire ever carried off the Championship. When first appearing for the county against Leicestershire, then second class, at Dews-bury, he made 65, the highest score in the match. Very fond of fielding in the deep, he brought off some remarkable catches. He captained the Savile club at Dewsbury for several seasons and played local cricket until 70 years old. Henry Hill represented Dews-bury, his native town, on the Yorkshire Committee up to the time of his death at the age of 76.

HILL, Henry Grosvenor, died at Hands-worth, Birmingham, on June 4, 1913, aged 51. He was educated at King Edward's School, and was founder of the Birmingham and District Cricket League, of which he was at various times President, Hon. Secretary and Treasurer. On three occasions whilst playing for Handsworth Wood he took all 10 wickets in an innings, and for the club in 1895 obtained 239 wickets. His appearances for Warwickshire extended from 1888 to 1900, and among his best feats with the ball were three wickets for five runs v. Derbyshire, five for 14 v. Durham, three for 15 v. Gloucester-shire, five for 28 v. M.C.C., five for 28 v. Durham, and five for 54 v. Lancashire. He bowled left-hand and batted right. He was born in the Old Square, Birmingham, on July 23, 1861.

HILL, J. Ernest, who died in a Birmingham nursing home on December 2, 1963, aged 96, enjoyed the distinction of hitting the first century registered for Warwickshire after they attained first-class status in 1894—139 not out against Nottinghamshire at Trent Bridge. His position as Public Prosecutor for Birmingham allowed him to play only oc-casionally for the county between 1894 and 1898, in which time he scored 791 runs, average 25.

HILL, John Charles, who died in Melbourne on August 11, 1974, at the early age of 51, played all his Test cricket for Australia overseas. His first-class career with Victoria amounted to just 15 games when the selec-tors picked him along with two other leg spinners, Benaud and Ring, for the 1953 trip to England. He took 63 wickets, average 20.98 in all matches that tour, though like the other two bowlers of his type, left little impression in the Tests.

Nevertheless, Hill's seven England victims were not inconsiderable, consisting as they did of Graveney, May, Bailey and Kenyon at Trent Bridge and Bill Edrich, Bailey and Laker at Old Trafford. To these he added Holt of the West Indies on his only appearance for his country, at Bridgetown in 1955.

Always known as Jack, Hill was not the most elegant of leg spinners in his approach to the wicket and he was apt to make life difficult for the wicket-keeper by his constant attack on or about the leg stump. He took 121 wickets in all for Victoria, taking over from another Test cricketer, Jack Iverson. A civil servant by profession, Hill also excelled at football, playing for St. Kilda until he twice fractured his skull. He served with the Royal Australian Air Force during the War.

HILL, Col. Joseph, C.B., died at Wollaston Hall, Wellingborough. May 16, 1918, aged 68. At one time captain of the Northants XI.

HILL, Mervyn Llewellyn, who died in London on February 28, 1948, aged 45, was a wicket-keeper of considerable ability. He helped Eton beat Harrow by nine wickets at Lord's in 1920; also played for Lord's Schools and in several trial games at Cam-bridge, but did not get his Blue. He played for Somerset from 1925 for some years. In the winter of 1926 he was a member of the M.C.C. team captained by A. E. R. Gilligan that went through the tour of India without suffering defeat.

HILL, Richard Hamilton, who died on Oc-tober 5, 1959, aged 58, was in the Winchester XI in 1918 and 1919, being contemporary with such players as D. R. Jardine and C. T. Ashton. An opening batsman, he headed the averages in 1918, scoring 362 runs at 51.71 per innings. Though taking part in trials, he did not get a cricket Blue at Cambridge, but he represented the University at royal tennis and, from 1920 to 1922, at racquets. He appeared for Middlesex for several seasons, his highest score being 50 against Gloucester-shire at Bristol in 1927, he and J. W. Hearne sharing in a sixth-wicket stand of 147. For many years he reported racquets, lawn tennis and cricket for *The Times*.

HILL, Vernon Tickell, the Oxford Univer-sity, Somerset, and Glamorgan cricketer, died on September 29, 1932, at his home near Weston-super-Mare. Born at Llandaff, South Wales, on January 30, 1871, he was in his 62nd year.

A left-hand batsman who drove with tremendous power and a man who could throw a cricket ball over 120 yd., Hill was a useful cricketer in the Winchester XI in 1887 and the two following years. At Oxford he gave a remarkable display of hitting in the Varsity Match of 1892. When, on the opening day of this fixture, Hill joined M. R. Jardine, Oxford had lost half their wickets for 157, but the two men stayed together for an hour and 40 minutes and added 178 runs. Hill scored 114 of these, the style of the two men affording a very strong contrast. Jardine played a sound game, running no risks, while his partner hit with a freedom that was amazing. Hill's straight drives were admirably kept down and 72 of his runs came from strokes to the boundary.

A batsman who by his free hitting often completely altered the fortunes of a game, Vernon Hill put together many useful scores for Somerset, whom he assisted from 1890 to 1902 and also in 1908. Against Kent at Taunton in 1898 he made 116. Later on he appeared in the Glamorgan XI.

He visited America twice—in 1895 with Frank Mitchell's team and three years later with the side led by P. F. Warner—and in 1922 played for the M.C.C. team in Denmark.

Although over age, he joined the Army during the First World War and served in France, receiving promotion as Major in the King's Royal Rifles. He was president of the Somerset County C.C. in 1930.

HILLIARD, Harry, one of the oldest Australian cricketers, and the last survivor but one of the first match between New South Wales and Victoria—at Melbourne in March, 1856—died in Sydney (his native place) on March 19, 1914. He was born on November 7, 1826, and was thus in his 88th year. Altogether he played in five games against Victoria, with 20, at Sydney in January, 1857, as his highest score. Few men followed cricket more closely, and for very many years he watched the matches between the two States both in Melbourne and Sydney. In 1878 he visited England and saw the Australian team of that year win their memorable match with the M.C.C. at Lord's—an event, almost needless to add, which occasioned him the greatest satisfaction.

HILLS, Henry Francis, who had played a few times for Essex, died at Earls Colne on March 24, 1930, aged 91. Against Suffolk at Ipswich in 1881 he took five wickets for 17 runs.

HILLS, Joseph John, who died in October, 1969, aged 72, played as a professional batsman for Glamorgan from 1926 to 1931, scoring 3,252 runs, average 20.58, for the county and bringing off 92 catches. He hit six centuries, the highest being 166 against Hampshire at Southampton in 1929. From 1939 to 1956 he was on the list of first-class umpires and he stood in the fourth Test match between England and South Africa at Leeds in 1947. A popular personality, he was also a good Association football goal-keeper, playing as a professional for Cardiff City, Swansea Town and Fulham before injury compelled him to give up the game. In the First World War he won the Military Medal while serving with the Royal Engineers.

HILL-WOOD, Denis John Charles, M.C., died on May 4, 1982, aged 75. Never in the XI at Eton, he got a Blue at Oxford in 1928, owing his place to the need for finding a solid rather than a stroke-playing opening partner for A. M. Crawley, and, though the side's batting that year was so strong that the Nawab of Pataudi failed to get in, he fully justified his choice. In his first match he helped Crawley to put on 197 against the Free Foresters, of which his share was 44, and at the Oval they put on 153. His contribution at Lord's was a useful 23 in each innings. Altogether he made 286 runs with an average of 26, his highest score being 62 against Essex at Colchester. In both 1928 and 1929 he appeared for Derbyshire without success. In 1928 he was also a member of the Oxford soccer side and since 1959 had been Chairman of the Arsenal. He was one of four brothers (three of them Blues) who had played for Derbyshire: their father had captained the county.

HILL-WOOD, Sir Samuel, Bart., D.L., J.P., one of the most prominent figures in sport in the last half-century, died at his home in London on January 4, 1949, aged 57. Undoubtedly Association football was his greatest love. Before the First World War he built up his own club of Glossop, which reached the First Division of the Football League. Although most of the players were amateurs the venture was estimated to have cost him over £30,000. He became chairman of Arsenal in 1927 and was still in office at the time of his death. As a cricketer he was no more than a moderate player scoring 758 runs, average 17.22, in the three years, 1899 to 1901, in which he captained Derbyshire. A curiosity was that his four children, all boys, followed his footsteps in going to Eton and also gaining a county cap for Derbyshire. Sir

Samuel represented the High Peak Division of Derbyshire as a Conservative from 1910 to 1929.

HILL-WOOD, Sir Wilfred William Hill, K.C.V.O., died in London on October 10, 1980, aged 79. He was one of the many amateurs who were compelled to give up serious cricket before they had had a chance to fulfil their promise. When his county career for practical purposes ended at 22, some good judges already reckoned him a possible future candidate for England. In technique he was the antithesis of the traditional amateur. With a crouching stance, which he had adopted early in his life to counteract a tendency to move away, he was unattractive to watch though he had a good range of strokes: his strength lay in his defence. At Eton, where he was in the XI for three years and captain in 1921, he was an all-rounder and at Lord's in 1919 his leg-breaks, which later in first-class cricket often broke an awkward partnership, brought him four for 40 and seven for 29. Though he played for Derbyshire as early as 1919, he did not get his Blue at Cambridge until his second summer, 1922, and then only secured the last place. He fully justified his selection, going in first on a sodden wicket and batting four and threequarter hours for 81. When the total at lunch was 60 for no wicket after two hours' play, he and his partner, C. A. Fiddian-Green, came in for some criticism: in the end, however, they could justifiably feel that they had made a substantial contribution to an innings victory. That winter Hill-Wood was a member of A. C. MacLaren's M.C.C. side to Australia and New Zealand and accomplished the feat for which he is best remembered. In the return against Victoria at Melbourne, the touring side had been out for 71 and Victoria had declared at 617 for six. Defeat seemed certain, but Hill-Wood and Geoffrey Wilson, later captain of Yorkshire, batted out the rest of the match and after four and threequarter hours were undefeated with 122 and 142 respectively. In 1923 he played throughout the season for Derbyshire, heading their averages with 961 runs at 34.32 and making 107 v. Somerset at Bath. He played a few matches in the next two or three seasons and indeed made one appearance as late as 1936, but his serious career was over. Later he served for many years on the M.C.C. Committee. He was one of four brothers who played for Derbyshire, three of them also being awarded Blues. Their father had captained the county at the turn of the century.

HILLYARD, The Rev. Arthur, who died at Upton Pyne, near Exeter, on May 31, 1919, aged 65, played for Pembroke College (Ox.) and Free Foresters, and occasionally for Warwickshire. In 1867 and 1868 he ran in the Hurdles for Oxford v. Cambridge.

HILLYARD, Commander George Whiteside, R.N., died on March 24, 1943, aged 79. Of high fame in the lawn tennis world, he enjoyed success at many games, and if able to give more time to cricket would have taken a prominent place among fast bowlers over 50 years ago. After captaining the *Britannia* training ship cricket XI, he played in turn for Middlesex, Hertfordshire and Leicestershire, while for the Gentlemen at the Oval in 1895 he took five wickets for 152 runs in the two Players innings of a drawn match. At Boston in 1894 he took 10 wickets for 15 runs against Fifteen of Massachusetts during the second tour of America he made with teams captained by Lord Hawke. At Cannes he played golf with great skill, notably when beating Harold Hilton in 1903 in a club match. Swimming, pigeon-shooting and billiards afforded Hillyard opportunities to win prizes, besides the many honours that came to him on the tennis courts. For many years he acted in official capacities at Wimbledon.

HILLYARD, Major Jack Montagu, who died on February 16, 1983, aged 92, was in the Harrow XI in 1909 and 1910. A son of G. W. Hillyard, who, besides bowling fast for Middlesex and Leicestershire, was a first-class lawn tennis player and golfer, he had inherited much of his father's ability and was a fine natural games player. In 1910 at Lord's, in "Fowler's Match," he made 62 very well in the first innings, which was top score, and also took five wickets.

HILTON, Philip, who was born at Selling on March 10, 1840, died in a nursing home on May 26, 1906. He was a good batsman and a fine field, especially at mid-off and mid-wicket. He played for Kent 25 times between 1865 and 1873, and rendered good service to the county, being for many years on the committee, and becoming captain of the Kent Second XI when, in 1884, it was decided to form a Second XI to encourage latent talent. He was educated at Cheltenham, but was not in the XI. For many years he was prominently identified with the Incogniti C.C. His highest score in a match of note was 74 for Kent against Surrey, at the Oval, in 1871.

HILTON, Robert, at one time engaged on the Ground Staff at Hove, died on February 11, 1905. He was 6ft. 7in. in height, and, according to his own statement, was no less than 6ft. 9in. when he held himself fully upright.

HIME, Charles Frederick William, who died on December 6, 1940, aged 71, was a reliable batsman and effective medium-paced bowler. Born on October 24, 1869, he was only 19 when he took six wickets for 40 runs for Pietermaritzburg XXII against the first English team that visited South Africa. In January, 1896, he scored 62 against Lord Hawke's English team, adding 184 for the second wicket with R. M. Poore (112). As a result of this he played for South Africa against the tourists at Port Elizabeth; dismissed for 0 and eight, and taking one wicket for 31 runs, he was not chosen for either of the other two Tests. Hime played for Natal until January, 1906, when he captained the team against P. F. Warner's M.C.C. team and took five wickets for 18 runs in the first innings; a keen match ended in a victory to the visitors by four wickets.

HIND, Alfred Ernest, who died at Leicester on March 22, 1947, aged 68, went from Uppingham to Cambridge, where he was in the XI from 1898 to 1901, and also played a little for Nottinghamshire without doing anything exceptional. He represented Cambridge against Oxford for three years in athletics; was in the Rugby Fifteen; a member of the England team which visited South Africa in the winter of 1902, and played for England in 1906.

HINDLEKAR, D. D., one of the best wicket-keepers ever produced by India, died at Bombay on March 30, 1949, aged 40. He was one of the small band of cricketers who opened an innings and went in last in separate Test matches. Hindlekar toured England in 1936 and 1946 and altogether played in four Test matches. At Manchester in the second Test in 1946 he and Sohoni, the last pair, stayed together for the last 13 minutes of the match and warded off defeat. During the 1936 tour he opened the innings in the first Test at Lord's, but subsequently chipped a bone in a finger and also was troubled by blurred vision. Ten years later a strained back kept him out of several matches.

His choice for the 1946 visit to England was unexpected, for he was then 37, but such was his form in the Bombay Pentangular final of 1945–46 that he could not be over-looked. Never spectacular, but always sound, both behind the stumps and when batting, Hindlekar was a cheerful personality and an extremely popular member of the touring parties.

HINE-HAYCOCK, The Rev. Trevitt Reginald, who died on November 2, 1953, aged 91, was the last survivor of the Oxford University team who, under M. C. Kemp, beat W. L. Murdoch's Australian side by seven wickets at Oxford in 1884. Never before or since had Oxford won against the Australians. Born at Little Heath, Old Charlton, Kent, on December 3, 1861, he was in the Wellington XI for three years from 1878, being captain in 1880, and he gained a Blue as a steady opening batsman at Oxford in 1883 and in 1884 when he was hon. secretary. He could also keep wicket. In the University match of 1883, after Hine-Haycock and J. G. Walker scored 29 for the first wicket, Oxford collapsed on difficult turf against the bowling of C. T. Studd and C. A. Smith, losing their last nine wickets for 26. Next year Hine-Haycock, by scoring 40 and 35 not out, helped exactly to reverse a defeat by seven wickets. From 1882 to 1884 he assisted Devon, and in 1885 and 1886 played for Kent. He assisted Gentlemen v. Players at the Oval in 1884, and visited America in 1885 and 1886 as a member of E. J. Sanders's teams. He was vicar of Christ Church, Greyfriars, which was bombed during the War, and a year or so before his death was appointed senior priest-in-ordinary to the Queen.

HINLEY, Joseph, of the Worcestershire XI of 1905 and 1906, died at Birmingham of consumption on November 21, 1907, in his 29th year. He was born in Yorkshire on October 28, 1879, and before qualifying for Worcestershire was for some time engaged on the ground staff at Edgbaston. In the 18 matches in which he appeared for Worcestershire he caught 26 and stumped four. He was a poor bat.

HIPKIN, Augustus Bernard, who died in a Lanarkshire hospital on February 11, 1957, aged 56, did much excellent work as a slow left-arm bowler for Essex from 1923 to 1931. A "discovery" of J. W. H. T. Douglas, then Essex captain, "Joe" Hipkin took in all first-class matches 528 wickets at an average of 25.56. He flighted the ball cleverly with a high action and spun it considerably. His best season was that of 1924 when, in dismissing 109 batsmen for 20.34 runs each, he headed the Essex averages. That year he performed the "hat-trick" against Lancashire at Blackpool. He was also a capital fieldsman and a useful batsman, scoring 4,446 runs, average 16.40. When Essex did not renew his contract, he went to Scotland, meeting with marked success as professional with the Uddingstone and West of Scotland clubs.

HIPPISLEY, Lieut. Harold Edwin, of the 1st Gloucestershire Regiment, was killed in action in October, 1914. He was in the XI at King's School, Bruton, whose batting averages he headed in 1909 with 62.90, his highest score being 113. The same season he made 40 not out for Somerset against Worcestershire on the Worcester ground. He was born at Wells on September 3, 1890, was a brilliant hockey-player, and was married on the day his regiment was ordered to France. In scoring 150 for Old Brutonians v. Sidmouth, at Sidmouth in July, 1911, he and P. W. Vasey (282 not out) added 396 for the third wicket.

HIRD, Sydney Francis, died in Bloemfontein on December 20, 1980, aged 70. He was one of five brothers, a member of a family that in the 1930s was something of a sporting institution in the Sydney suburb of Balmain. He played first-grade cricket from the age of 15 and was 21 when first selected for New South Wales. In 14 first-class games in Australia, he scored 797 runs at an average of 38. He hit two centuries—101 in just over two hours against the 1931–32 South African touring side (his third first-class match) and 106 against Queensland. As a bowler of leg-breaks and googlies, he took 31 wickets at 30 apiece, his best performance being against the 1932–33 M.C.C. side. In 1934, unable to find employment in Australia, he decided to try his luck in England: when Ramsbottom failed to entice Bradman to the Lancashire League, they signed Hird as their professional instead. For the remainder of the decade, he played cricket in England, an undoubted loss to the game in Australia. He enjoyed much success in the Lancashire League but was only once selected to play for Lancashire, in 1939 in a rain-affected match against Gloucestershire in which there was so little cricket that he had the opportunity neither to bat nor bowl. After the War he moved to South Africa where he lived for the remainder of his life. In 1946 he was chosen to play for Eastern Province and, at the age of 36, made 130 against Griqualand West. In 1947 he was made captain of Eastern Province. Hird ended his cricketing days as a

successful coach of Eastern Province and Orange Free State.

HIRSCH, John Gauntlett, who died in Cape Town in March, 1958, aged 75, made a few appearances for London County under Dr. W. G. Grace early in the century. Educated at Shrewsbury, "Baron" Hirsch played Association football there, but took up Rugby with marked success when going up to Cambridge. Returning to South Africa, he played for Eastern Province and toured the British Isles as centre three-quarter with Paul Roos's Springbok side of 1906.

HIRST, Edward Theodore, the old Oxford Blue, died at Llandudno on October 26, 1914. He was born at Huddersfield on May 6, 1859, and was in the Rugby XI in 1874 and two following years, being contemporary with G. F. Vernon and C. M. Cunliffe. In 1875, when he played an innings of 151 against the Old Rugbeians, he headed the averages with over 31 runs an innings, and in the following season he was captain. During his last year he greatly distinguished himself by scoring 100 not out v. M.C.C. and Ground at Lord's against the bowling of William Mycroft. In his three matches against Marlborough, however, he did little, making only four, 19, 0, eight and 0. Proceeding to Oxford, he played against Cambridge in 1878, 1879, and 1880, making in the three matches 114 runs with an average of 22.80. In 1878 he scored 114 against M.C.C. and Ground at Lord's. Between 1877 and 1888 he appeared in 23 matches for Yorkshire, and, with 87 not out against the Australians at Bradford in 1888 as his highest score, made 387 runs with an average of 11.38. He was a free batsman, with good defence, and very useful in the field, and in May, 1887, scored 200 for Huddersfield against Leeds Clarendon. From 1877 to 1880 he was in the University Fifteen.

HIRST, George Herbert, who died at his Huddersfield home a few miles from his birthplace, Kirkheaton, on May 10, 1954, aged 82, was one of the most illustrious cricketers who graced the Golden Age. On the 24 occasions on which he played for England, Hirst achieved only a few noteworthy performances, but such was his prowess with bat and ball for Yorkshire in a career spanning 40 years that Lord Hawke described him as the greatest county cricketer of all time. Certainly this blunt, outspoken man of extreme buoyancy and cheerfulness brought such a tenacity to the game that no match in which he figured was won or lost till the last ball was bowled. Small wonder, therefore, that in Yorkshire he was an unchallenged hero, and throughout the length and breadth of England his popularity stood unrivalled.

Figures alone tell only part of the story of Hirst, but they show unmistakably his supreme prowess as an all-round cricketer in the fullest meaning of the phrase. Between his first county game for Yorkshire in 1889 and his last in 1929, Hirst scored 36,203 runs, average 34.05, and took 2,727 wickets, average 18.77; at his peak friends and opponents alike recognised him as the best mid-off in the country, with a pair of hands so sure that a considerable proportion of his 550 catches were made from scorching drives in a period when strong driving was an essential component in every batsman's game. The measure of Hirst's ability is best reflected in that he accomplished the double feat of 1,000 runs and 100 wickets 14 times, a number surpassed only by his renowned contemporary, Wilfred Rhodes (16), and that he alone made 2,000 runs and took 200 wickets in a season, which he did in 1906. His figures were 2,385 runs and 208 wickets. Years afterwards, when asked if he thought his record might be broken, Hirst made an answer typifying his whole approach. With a twinkle in his eye, he replied: "I don't know, but whoever does it will be very tired." Yet, through the years, he himself showed little evidence of fatigue. Only a very fit man, such as he was, could have reached 1,000 runs in 19 seasons and taken 100 wickets in 15 different years.

The people of Kirkheaton and the surrounding areas almost lived for cricket and from an early age Hirst, born on September 7, 1871, showed that he would be a player of more than ordinary skill. He became associated with Huddersfield when 18 and before his 19th birthday his first ambition, that of playing for Yorkshire, was realised. Hirst was fond of recalling that in those days his equipment, which he carried to the ground in a canvas bag, was worth no more than 10 shillings, that he wore a shilling cap, a sixpenny belt and brown boots. Success in County Cricket came slowly, but after some seasons of quiet progress, he established himself in 1896 by scoring 1,122 runs and taking 104 wickets. Thenceforward he gathered strength as he went along. Of his 60 first-class centuries, all but four were played for Yorkshire, his highest being 341—still a county record—against Leicestershire in 1905. Leicestershire suffered particularly from his bowling as well as from his batting.

Twice he did the hat-trick against them, once in a match in 1907 in which he took 15 wickets, his greatest success in one game. Five times Hirst bowled unchanged through a match, Rhodes being his partner on three occasions and Schofield Haigh on the other two, and twice he took three wickets in four balls.

The combination of Hirst and Rhodes was feared as much by batsmen as that of Peel and Briggs, Gregory and McDonald and, in later years, Grimmett and O'Reilly. In the 1902 Test match at Birmingham, Hirst and Rhodes bowled out Australia for 36 runs, their lowest total in any Test. Rhodes took seven wickets for 17, and Hirst three for 15. This was the most memorable joint feat of Hirst and Rhodes, but in the next match the Australians met Yorkshire, who put them out for 23 (Hirst five for nine runs and F. S. Jackson five for 12). Another Yorkshire bowling triumph in which Hirst played a notable part occurred in 1908 when he and Schofield Haigh dismissed Northamptonshire for 27 and 15, Hirst taking 12 wickets for 19 runs and Haigh six for 19.

On his two tours to Australia, with A. E. Stoddart's team in 1897–98, and P. F. Warner's side in 1903–04, Hirst did not realise English hopes but he played a conspicuous role in a dramatic victory over Australia at the Oval in 1902. When Hirst, who scored 58 not out in the final innings, was joined by the last man, his lifelong friend and colleague, Rhodes, England required 15 to win. The story has been passed on that, as Rhodes met him on the way to the wicket, Hirst confidently murmured: "We'll get 'em in singles, Wilfred"—which they proceeded to do. Whether true or not, that is the type of remark Hirst would have made. One last instance of his versatility; in 1906 he scored two centuries and took 11 wickets in the match against Somerset at Bath.

Essentially a self-taught batsman, Hirst frequently gave of his best when the pitch afforded help to bowlers. His remarkable quickness of eye and feet enabled him to develop the hook and pull strokes so well that some bowlers complained that they found exceeding difficulty in bowling to him anything except a yorker which he did not treat as a long-hop. His liking for the hook was costly only in Australia. By contrast to his right-handed batting, Hirst was a natural left-arm bowler, a shade faster than medium. After a long bounding run, he delivered with a free, easy action and he often made the new ball swerve and dip into the batsman so late that many of his victims confessed themselves as suspecting that they had been thrown out from cover. Hirst, in fact, has been described as the father of all modern seam and swing bowling. Before he showed its possibilities, bowlers rubbed the new ball in the dirt to take off the polish.

Hirst, short and thick-set, found perpetual pleasure in every game he played and captains such as Sir Pelham Warner have testified that they could not have wished for a better man to be in their teams. Both as a player and as a personality, none could speak too highly of him. Sir Pelham has said that when things were going wrong on tour Hirst was first to come to the aid of everybody with his ready wit.

When Hirst was given a benefit by Yorkshire in 1904 he received a sum of £3,703, a remarkable figure in those days. Seventeen years later a testimonial for him produced £700. Virtually that came at the finish of his active career, for he became coach at Eton College in 1921, but he played occasionally for Yorkshire for another eight years. During his 18 years at Eton, Hirst endeared himself to hundreds of young cricketers who benefited from his kindly guidance, and nothing was more fitting than that M.C.C. should include him in the 26 professionals whom they honoured in 1949 with Honorary Life Membership.

Cricket was George Hirst's life and less than a year before his death he sat with Rhodes, now sightless, while England recovered from a seemingly hopeless position against Australia at the Leeds ground on which he himself so often stood in the breach.

HISCOCK, E. J., a member of the Adelaide Club, died on December 16, 1894, at the age of 26. He played for South Australia in intercolonial matches on more than one occasion.

HITCH, John William, the Surrey and England right-arm fast bowler, died in Cardiff Hospital on July 7, 1965, aged 79. A firm favourite at the Oval, where he was loved as much for his big hitting and brilliant fielding as for his bowling, he was a devoted cricketer who always displayed tremendous energy and enthusiasm. Born at Radcliffe, Lancashire, on May 7, 1886, he played his first serious cricket with Cheveley, just south of Newmarket. Upon the recommendation of Tom Hayward, whom he had impressed in a minor match in Cambridgeshire, he joined the Oval staff in the spring of 1905 and made his first-class debut in 1907. Soon he established himself as one of the fastest bowlers in

the country. He had an unusual hesitant run-up in which his approach to the crease was punctuated by two or three hops. More than once he broke a stump, and at the Oval in 1921 he sent a bail 55 yd. 1 ft. in bowling A. R. Tanner of Middlesex.

His most successful season was that of 1913 when he took 174 wickets at 18.55 each, including eight for 48 in an innings at the Oval against the powerful Kent side, that year's Champions. At Scarborough, in September of that year, he received a souvenir from Lord Londesborough for his performance in taking nine wickets for Players against Gentlemen and scoring not-out innings of 53 and 68, hitting seven sixes. He represented Players against Gentlemen 10 times (twice at Lord's) between 1912 and 1923, taking three wickets in four balls on his final appearance at the Oval in 1923. Twice he did the hat-trick—against Cambridge University in 1911, when taking four wickets in five balls, and against Warwickshire in 1914, both at the Oval.

He toured Australia without marked success with the M.C.C. sides of 1911–12 and 1920–21, playing for England on both tours, as well as appearing in Tests in England in 1912 and 1921. He played in seven Tests in all, though his bowling record was modest. Against Australia at the Oval in 1921, however, he scored one of the fastest innings recorded in Test cricket, 51 not out in 40 minutes. Always a spectacular hitter he more than once hit a ball clean out of the Oval. At Trent Bridge in 1919, he scored 74 out of 84 in 35 minutes, and in the following year at Scarborough he batted 32 minutes for 68 out of 87 for C. I. Thornton's XI. He received only 12 balls when scoring 32 in 17 minutes against Glamorgan at the Oval in 1924, three hits off F. Ryan landing in the pavilion seats. In his benefit match against Kent at the Oval in 1921, he reached 71 in 50 minutes.

As a fielder, Hitch was quite outstanding at short-leg, where he stood often perilously close to the bat: but in any position he fielded magnificently. In his first-class career, which ended in 1925, he took 1,398 wickets, average 21.48, scored nearly 8,000 runs and held over 200 catches. The highest of his three centuries was 107, hit in 70 minutes, against Somerset at Bath in 1922.

For four seasons from 1926 he was professional for Todmorden in the Lancashire League, where his younger brother, R. Hitch, was an amateur with Rawtenstall. In his first year he took six wickets for five runs against Lowerhouse and did the hat-trick against Colne. From 1926 to 1929, during which Todmorden won the Championship once and were twice runners-up, he took 289 wickets at 11.62 each, one of his best performances being eight for 45 against Rishton in 1927.

He later became coach to Glamorgan before taking a position with a South Wales firm, for whom he played in annual matches until he was 60.—I.R.

SIR JOHN BERRY HOBBS
Born at Cambridge December 16, 1882
Died at his home, at Hove, December 21, 1963
Knighted for his services to cricket 1953
By Neville Cardus

John Berry Hobbs, the great batsman whose first-class cricket career spanned 30 years and brought him fame everywhere as a player second to none, was born in humble surroundings at No. 4 Rivar Place, Cambridge, quite close to Fenner's, Parker's Piece and Jesus College.

Christened John Berry Hobbs because his father's name was John and his mother's maiden name Berry, John—or Jack as he was always known—was the eldest of 12 children, six boys and six girls. His father was on the staff at Fenner's and also acted as a professional umpire. When Hobbs senior became groundsman and umpire to Jesus College, young Hobbs took immense delight in watching cricket there. During the school holidays he used to field at the nets and play his own version of cricket with the College servants, using a tennis ball, a cricket stump for a bat and a tennis post for a wicket on a gravel pitch. This primitive form of practice laid the foundations of his skill. Little more than 10 years old at the time, young Jack tried to produce the strokes which he had seen players employ in college matches. The narrow straight stump helped him to appreciate the importance of a straight bat, and with the natural assets of a keen eye and flexible wrists he learned to hit the ball surely and with widely varied strokes. Hobbs was self-taught and never coached, but he remembered all his life a piece of advice which his father gave him the only time the pair practised together, on Jesus College Close. Jack, facing spin bowling from his father, was inclined to stand clear of his stumps. "Don't draw away," his father told him. "Standing up to the wicket is all important. If you draw away, you cannot play with a straight bat and the movement may cause you to be bowled off your pads."

When 12, Jack joined his first cricket team, the Church Choir XI at St. Matthew's,

Cambridge, where he was in the choir, and the first match in which he ever batted was for the choir of Jesus College who borrowed him, on their ground. He helped to form the Ivy Boys Club and they played both cricket and football on Parker's Piece.

Ranjitsinhji practised there, and Hobbs watched his beautiful wrist-play wonderingly, but the hero of Jack's boyhood was Tom Hayward, son of Dan Hayward who looked after the nets and marquees on Parker's Piece. Cricket became Jack's passion and his supreme ambition was to be good enough to play for one of the leading counties, preferably Surrey, the county of his idol, Tom Hayward. Hobbs practised morning, noon and night, and when he knew that he would be busy during the day he rose at six and practised before he went to work.

Tom Hayward first saw him bat when the noted Surrey player took a team to Parker's Piece for the last match of the summer in 1901, the season in which Jack played a few times for Cambridgeshire as an amateur.

In 1902, Hobbs obtained his first post as a professional—second coach and second umpire to Bedford Grammar School—and in the August of that year he helped Royston, receiving a fee of half a guinea for each appearance. He hit a fine century against Herts Club & Ground, so bringing immense joy to his father, but Mr. Hobbs was not destined to see further progress by his son, for he died soon afterwards.

Tom Hayward was instrumental in Jack going to Surrey. A generous man, Hayward arranged a benefit for the widow Hobbs, and another friend of the family, a Mr. F. C. Hutt, asked Hayward to take a good look at Jack. Hobbs was set to bat for 20 minutes on Parker's Piece against William Reeves, the Essex bowler, and Hayward was so impressed that he promised to get Jack a trial at the Oval the following spring. Mr. Hutt thought that Hobbs should also try his luck with Essex, but they declined to grant him a trial, and so, in April, 1903, Hobbs went to Surrey. Immediately they recognised his budding talent and engaged him. A two years' qualifying period had its ups-and-downs for Hobbs—he began with a duck when going in first for Surrey Colts at the Oval against Battersea—but soon his promise was clear for all to see. In his first Surrey Club & Ground match he made 86 against Guy's Hospital, and in his second qualifying year—1904—when he played several matches as a professional for Cambridgeshire, he scored 195 in brilliant style against Hertfordshire. His apprenticeship over,

Hobbs commenced in 1905 the long and illustrious career with Surrey in first-class company which was to make his name known the world over and earn him a knighthood from the Queen—the first professional cricketer to receive the honour.

From the time he was awarded his county cap by Lord Dalmeny, afterwards Lord Rosebery, following a score of 155 in his first Championship match against Essex, Hobbs built up the reputation of the "Master" cricketer—a reputation perpetuated by the Hobbs Gates at the Oval and by his other permanent memorial, the Jack Hobbs Pavilion, at Parker's Piece. The tables of his achievements, given here, tell eloquently how thoroughly he deserves remembrance by cricket enthusiasts, but comparisons with "W.G." will still be made.

From this point of view, Hobbs was, without argument, the most accomplished batsman known to cricket since W. G. Grace. In his career, Hobbs scored 61,237 runs with an average of 50.65 and scored 197 centuries. He played in 61 Test matches. Other players have challenged the statistical values of Hobb's cricket. None has, since Grace, had his creative influence.

Like "W.G.," he gave a new twist or direction to the game. Grace was the first to cope with overarm fast bowling, the first to mingle forward and back play. Hobbs was brought up on principles more or less laid down by "W.G." and his contemporaries—left leg forward to the length ball. Right foot back to the ball a shade short, but the leg hadn't to be moved over the wicket to the off. Pad-play among the Victorians was not done. It was caddish—until a low fellow, a professional from Nottingham, named Arthur Shrewsbury, began to exploit the pad as a second line of defence—sometimes, in extremity, a first.

When Hobbs played his first first-class match for Surrey on a bitterly cold Easter Monday (April 24) in 1905, the other side, captained by "W.G." was called "The Gentlemen of England". Hobbs, then 22 years and four months old, scored 18 and 88—taking only two hours making the 88. Grace contemplated the unshaven youth from his position of "point." He stroked the beard and said: "He's goin' to be a good 'un." He could not have dreamed that 20 years later Hobbs would beat his own record of 126 centuries in a lifetime—and go on to amass 197 before retiring, and receive a knighthood for services rendered.

Hobbs learned to bat in circumstances of technique and environment much the same as those in which Grace came to his high noon. The attack of bowlers concentrated, by and large, on the off stump. Pace and length on good pitches, with varied flight. On "sticky" pitches the fast bowlers were often "rested," the damage done by slow left-hand spin or right-hand off breaks. Leg breaks were called on but rarely, then as a last resort, though already Braund, Vine and Bosanquet were developing "back-of-the-hand" trickery. Swerve was not unknown in 1905; there were Hirst, Arnold, Relf, Trott, and J. B. King "swinging" terrifically. But in those days only one and the same ball was used throughout the longest of a team's innings. And the seam was not raised as prominently as on balls made at the present time.

In 1907, two summers after Hobbs's baptism of first-class cricket, the South Africans came to this country, bringing a company of "googly" bowlers as clever as any seen since—Vogler (quick), Gordon White, Faulkner and Schwarz. Hobbs faced them only twice, scoring 18 and 41 for Surrey and 78 and 5 for C.I. Thornton's XI at Scarborough. J.T. Tyldesley, Braund, Jessop and Spooner also coped with the new witchcraft, so did George Gunn, who could cope with anything. Partly on the strength of his showing against the South Africans, Hobbs was chosen for his first overseas tour: 1907–08 in Australia.

But it was two years later, when the M.C.C. visited South Africa, that Hobbs demonstrated quite positively that he had found the answer to the problems of the back-of-the-hand spinners. The amazing fact is that he made his demonstration on the matting wickets then used in South Africa. What is more, it was Hobbs's first taste of the mat, on which the South African spinners were at their most viciously angular. South Africa won this rubber of 1909–10 by three wins to two. In the Test Hobbs scored 539 runs, average 67.37; double the averages of England's next best four run-makers: Thompson (33.77), Woolley (32.00), Denton (26.66) and Rhodes (25.11). It was Hobbs who first assembled into his methods all the rational counters against the ball which turned the other way. Moreover, on all kinds of pitches, hard and dry, in this country or in Australia, on sticky pitches here and anywhere else, even on the "gluepot" of Melbourne, on the matting of South Africa, against pace, spin, swing, and every conceivable device of bowlers Hobbs reigned supreme.

His career was divided into two periods,

each different from the other in style and tempo. Before the First World War he was Trumperesque, quick to the attack on springing feet, strokes all over the field, killing but never brutal, all executed at the wrists, after the preliminary getting together of the general muscular motive power. When cricket was resumed in 1919, Hobbs, who served in the Royal Flying Corps as an Air Mechanic after a short spell in a munition factory, was heading towards his 37th birthday, and a man was regarded as a cricket veteran in 1919 if he was nearing his 40s. Hobbs entering his second period, dispensed with some of the daring punitive strokes of his youthful raptures. He ripened into a classic. His style became as serenely poised as any ever witnessed on a cricket field, approached only by Hammond. He scored centuries effortlessly now; we hardly noted the making of them. They came as the hours passed on a summer day, as natural as a summer growth. An astonishing statistical fact about "The Master" is that of the 130 centuries to his name in County Cricket, 85 were scored after the First World War; that is, after he had entered "middle-age." The more his years increased the riper his harvests. From 1919 to 1928 his seasons' yields were as follows:

1919	..	2,594 runs average 60.32
1920	..	2,827 runs average 58.89
1921	..	312 runs average 78.00
		(a season of illness)
1922	..	2,552 runs average 62.24
1923	..	2,087 runs average 37.94
1924	..	2,094 runs average 58.16
1925	..	3,024 runs average 70.32
1926	..	2,949 runs average 77.60
1927	..	1,641 runs average 52.93
1928	..	2,542 runs average 82.00

From the time of his 43rd to his 46th birthday, Hobbs scored some 11,000 runs, averaging round about the 60s. Yet he once said that he would wish to be remembered for the way he batted before 1914. "But, Jack," his friends protested, "you got bags of runs after 1919!" "Maybe," replied Hobbs, "but they were nearly all made off the back foot." Modest and true to a point. "The Master" knows how to perform within limitations. Hobbs burgeoned to an effortless control not seen on a cricket field since his departure. The old easy footwork remained to the end. At Old Trafford a Lancashire "colt" made his first appearance against Surrey. He fielded at mid-off as McDonald, with a new ball, opened the attack on Hobbs. After a few overs, the "colt" allowed a

forward stroke from Hobbs to pass through his legs to the boundary. His colleagues, notably burly, redfaced Dick Tyldesley, expostulated to him—"What's matter? Wer't sleepin'?"—with stronger accessories. The "colt" explained, or excused his lapse. He had been so much "mesmerised" watching Hobbs's footwork as he played the ferocious speed of McDonald that he could not move.

It is sometimes said that Hobbs in his harvest years took advantage of the existing leg-before-wicket rule which permitted batsmen to cover their wickets with their pads against off-spin pitched outside the off-stump. True it is that Hobbs and Sutcliffe brought "the second line of defence" to a fine art. By means of it they achieved the two wonderful first-wicket stands at Kennington Oval in 1926 and at Melbourne two years later, v. Australia, each time on vicious turf. But, as I have pointed out, Hobbs's technique was grounded in the classic age, when the bat was the main instrument in defence. Always was the bat of Hobbs the sceptre by which he ruled his bowlers. In his last summers his rate of scoring inevitably had to slacken—from 40 runs an hour, the tempo of his youth, to approximately 30 or 25 an hour. In 1926, at Lord's for Surrey v. Middlesex, he scored 316 not out in six hours 55 minutes with 41 boundaries—a rate of more than 40 an hour, not exceeded greatly these days by two batsmen together. And he was in his 44th year in 1926, remember. It was in his wonderful year of 1925 that he beat "W.G.'s" record of 126 centuries, and before the summer's end gathered at his sweet will 3,024 runs, with 16 hundreds, average 70.32. He was now fulfilled. He often got himself out after reaching his century. He abdicated.

Those of us who saw him at the beginning and end of his career will cherish memories of the leaping young gallant, bat on high, pouncing at the sight of a ball a shade loose, driving and hooking; then, as the bowler desperately shortened his length, cutting square, the blow of the axe—a Tower Hill stroke. Then we will remember the coming of the regal control, the ripeness and readiness, the twiddle of the bat before he bent slightly to face the attack, the beautifully timed push to the off to open his score—the push was not hurried, did not send the ball too quickly to the fieldsman, so that Hobbs could walk his first run. I never saw him make a bad or a hasty stroke. Sometimes, of course, he made the wrong good stroke, technically right but applied to the wrong ball. An error of judgment, not of technique.

He extended the scope of batsmanship, added to the store of cricket that will be cherished, played the game with modesty, for all his mastery and produce, and so won fame and affection, here and at the other side of the world. A famous fast bowler once paid the best of all compliments to him—"It wer' 'ard work bowlin' at 'im, but it wer' something you wouldn't 'ave missed for nothing." Let Sir Jack go at that.

Other tributes:

Andrew Sandham: "Jack was the finest batsman in my experience on all sorts of wickets, especially the bad ones, for in our day there were more bad wickets and more spin bowlers than there are to-day. He soon knocked the shine off the ball and he was so great that he really collared the bowling. He could knock up 50 in no time at all and the bowlers would often turn to me as if to say 'Did you see that?' He was brilliant. Despite all the fuss and adulation made of him he was surprisingly modest and had a great sense of humour."

Herbert Strudwick: "On any type of wicket, he was the best batsman in my experience, a first-class bowler if given the chance, and the finest cover point I ever saw. He never looked like getting out and he was just the same whether he made 100 or 0. I remember G. A. Faulkner after an England tour in South Africa, saying to Jack: 'I only bowled you one googly.' 'Why,' said Jack, 'I did not know you bowled one.' Faulkner said, 'You hit the first one I bowled for four. If you did not know it how did you know it would turn from the off?' 'I didn't,' answered Jack. 'I watched it off the pitch.'"

Herbert Sutcliffe: "I was his partner on many occasions on extremely bad wickets, and I can say this without any doubt whatever that he was the most brilliant exponent of all time, and quite the best batsman of my generation on all types of wickets. On good wickets I do believe that pride of place should be given to Sir Don Bradman. I had a long and happy association with Sir Jack and can testify to his fine character. A regular church-goer, he seldom missed the opportunity to attend church service on Sunday mornings both in England and abroad. He was a man of the highest integrity who believed in sportsmanship in the highest sense, teamwork, fair-play and clean-living. His life was full of everything noble and true."

Percy Fender: "Jack was the greatest batsman the world has ever known, not merely in his generation but any generation and he was the most charming and modest man that anyone could meet. No-one who saw him or met him will ever forget him and his legend will last as long as the game is played—perhaps longer."

George Duckworth: "My first trip to Australia in 1928 was Jack's last and I remember with gratitude how he acted as a sort of father and mother to the young players like myself. Always a boyish chap at heart, he remained a great leg-puller. When 51 he promised to come up and play in my benefit match in 1934 and despite bitterly cold weather he hit the last first-class century of his career. He told me he got it to keep warm!"

Frank Woolley: "Jack was one of the greatest sportsmen England ever had, a perfect gentleman and a good living fellow respected by everyone he met. I travelled abroad with him many times to Australia and South Africa, and I always looked upon him as the finest right-handed batsman I saw in the 30 years I played with and against him."

Wilfred Rhodes: "He was the greatest batsman of my time. I learned a lot from him when we went in first together for England. He had a cricket brain and the position of his feet as he met the ball was always perfect. He could have scored thousands more runs, but often he was content to throw his wicket away when he had reached his hundred and give someone else a chance. He knew the Oval inside out and I know that A. P. F. Chapman was thankful for his advice when we regained the Ashes from Australia in 1926."

JACK HOBBS—THE MASTER

Statistics by Leslie Smith
BATTING (ALL FIRST-CLASS MATCHES)

	Inns.	Not Outs	Runs	100s	50s	Highest Inns.	Aver.
1905	54	3	1317	2	4	155	25.82
1906	53	6	1913	4	10	162*	40.70
1907	63	6	2135	4	15	166*	37.45
1907–08 (M.C.C. in Australia)	22	1	876	2	6	115	41.71

Signifies not out.

BATTING *(continued)*

	Inns.	Not Outs	Runs	100s	50s	Highest Inns.	Aver.
1908	53	2	1904	6	7	161	37.33
1909	54	2	2114	6	7	205	40.65
1909–10 (M.C.C. in S. Africa)	20	1	1194	3	7	187	62.84
1910	63	3	1982	3	14	133	33.03
1911	60	3	2376	4	13	154*	41.68
1911–12 (M.C.C. in Australia)	18	1	943	3	2	187	55.47
1912	60	6	2042	3	14	111	37.81
1913	57	5	2605	9	12	184	50.09
1913–14 (M.C.C. in S. Africa)	22	2	1489	5	8	170	74.45
1914	48	2	2697	11	6	226	58.63
1919	49	6	624	8	14	205*	60.32
1920	50	2	2827	11	13	215	58.89
1920–21 (M.C.C. in Australia)	19	1	924	4	2	131	51.33
1921	6	2	312	1	1	172*	78.00
1922	46	5	2552	10	9	168	62.24
1923	59	4	2087	5	8	136	37.94
1924	43	7	2094	6	10	211	58.16
1924–25 (M.C.C. in Australia)	17	1	865	3	5	154	54.06
1925	48	5	3024	16	5	266*	70.32
1926	41	3	2949	10	12	316*	77.60
1927	32	1	1641	7	5	150	52.93
1928	38	7	2542	12	10	200*	82.00
1928–29 (M.C.C. in Australia)	18	1	962	2	7	142	56.58
1929	39	5	2263	10	8	204	66.55
1930	43	2	2103	5	14	146*	51.29
1931	49	6	2418	10	7	153	56.23
1932	35	4	1764	5	9	161*	56.90
1933	18	0	1105	6	3	221	61.38
1934	18	1	624	1	4	116	36.70
Totals	1315	106	61,237	197	271	316*	50.65

AGGREGATES

	Inns.	Not Outs	Runs	100s	50s	Highest Inns.	Aver.
In England	1179	98	53,984	175	234	316*	49.93
In Australia	94	5	4570	14	22	187	51.34
In South Africa	42	3	2683	8	15	187	68.79
Totals	1315	106	61,237	197	271	316*	50.65

TEST MATCHES

	Tests	Inns.	Not Outs	Runs	100s	50s	Highest Inns.	Aver.
Australia	41	71	4	3636	12	15	187	44.26
South Africa	18	29	3	1562	2	12	211	50.07
West Indies	2	2	0	212	1	1	159	106.00
Totals	61	102	7	5410	15	28	211	56.94

	Matches	Inns.	Not Outs	Runs	100s	50s	Highest Inns.	Aver.
1907–08 (Australia)	4	8	1	302	0	3	83	43.14
1909 (Australia)	3	6	1	132	0	1	62*	26.40
1909–10 (S. Africa)	5	9	1	539	1	4	187	67.37
1911–12 (Australia)	5	9	1	662	3	1	187	82.75

Signifies not out.

BATTING *(continued)*

	Matches	Inns.	Not Outs	Runs	100s	50s	Highest Inns.	Aver.
1912 (Australia)	3	4	0	224	1	1	107	56.00
1912 (S. Africa)	3	5	1	163	0	2	68	40.75
1913–14 (S. Africa)	5	8	1	443	0	4	97	63.28
1920–21 (Australia)	5	10	0	505	2	1	123	50.50
1921 (Australia)†	1	—	—	—	—	—	—	—
1924 (S. Africa)	4	5	0	355	1	1	211	71.00
1924–25 (Australia)	5	9	0	573	3	2	154	63.66
1926 (Australia)	5	7	1	486	2	2	119	81.00
1928 West Indies)	2	2	0	212	1	1	159	106.00
1928–29 (Australia)	5	9	0	451	1	2	142	50.11
1929 (S. Africa)	1	2	0	62	0	1	52	31.00
1930 (Australia)	5	9	0	301	0	2	78	33.44
Totals	61	102	7	5410	15	28	211	56.94

TEST INNINGS
v. Australia (41 matches)

1907–08 in Australia	Second Test (Melbourne) ..	..	..	..	..	..	83 and 28
	Third Test (Adelaide)	..	..	..	..	..	26 and 23*
	Fourth Test (Melbourne) ..	..	..	..	..	..	57 and 0
	Fifth Test (Sydney) ..	..	..	..	..	..	72 and 13
1909 in England	First Test (Birmingham)	..	..	..	..	..	0 and 62*
	Second Test (Lord's)	..	..	..	..	..	19 and 9
	Third Test (Leeds) ..	..	..	..	..	..	12 and 30
1911–12 in Australia	First Test (Sydney) ..	..	..	..	..	..	63 and 22
	Second Test (Melbourne) ..	..	..	..	..	..	6 and 126*
	Third Test (Adelaide)	..	..	..	..	..	187 and 3
	Fourth Test (Melbourne) ..	..	..	..	..	..	178
	Fifth Test (Sydney) ..	..	..	..	..	..	32 and 45
1912 in England	First Test (Lord's) ..	..	..	..	..	..	107
	Second Test (Manchester) ..	..	..	..	..	..	19
	Third Test (The Oval)	..	..	..	..	..	66 and 32
1920–21 in Australia	First Test (Sydney) ..	..	..	..	..	..	49 and 59
	Second Test (Melbourne) ..	..	..	..	..	..	122 and 120
	Third Test (Adelaide)	..	..	..	..	..	18 and 123
	Fourth Test (Melbourne) ..	..	..	..	..	..	27 and 13
	Fifth Test (Sydney) ..	..	..	..	..	..	40 and 34
1921 in England	Third Test (Leeds) ..	..	..	..	..	..	Absent ill
1924–25 in Australia	First Test (Sydney) ..	..	..	..	..	..	115 and 57
	Second Test (Melbourne) ..	..	..	..	..	..	154 and 22
	Third Test (Adelaide)	..	..	..	..	..	119 and 27
	Fourth Test (Melbourne) ..	..	..	..	..	..	66
	Fifth Test (Sydney) ..	..	..	..	..	..	0 and 13
1926 in England	First Test (Nottingham)	..	..	..	..	..	19*
	Second Test (Lord's)	..	..	..	..	..	119
	Third Test (Leeds) ..	..	..	..	..	..	49 and 88
	Fourth Test (Manchester) ..	..	..	..	..	..	74
	Fifth Test (The Oval)	..	..	..	..	..	37 and 100

Signifies not out.   †Retired ill.

TEST INNINGS *(continued)*

1928–29	First Test (Brisbane)	49 and 11
in	Second Test (Sydney)	40
Australia	Third Test (Melbourne)	20 and 49
	Fourth Test (Adelaide)	74 and 1
	Fifth Test (Melbourne)	142 and 65
1930	First Test (Nottingham)	78 and 74
in	Second Test (Lord's)	1 and 19
England	Third Test (Leeds)	29 and 13
	Fourth Test (Manchester)	31
	Fifth Test (The Oval)	47 and 9

v. South Africa (18 matches)

1909–10	First Test (Johannesburg)	89 and 35
in	Second Test (Durban)	53 and 70
S. Africa	Third Test (Johannesburg)	11 and 93*
	Fourth Test (Cape Town)	1 and 0
	Fifth Test (Cape Town)	187
1912	First Test (Lord's)	4
in	Second Test (Leeds)	27 and 55
England	Third Test (The Oval)	68 and 9*
1913–14	First Test (Durban)	82
in	Second Test (Johannesburg)	23
S. Africa	Third Test (Johannesburg)	92 and 41
	Fourth Test (Durban)	64 and 97
	Fifth Test (Port Elizabeth)	33 and 11*
1924	First Test (Birmingham)	76
in	Second Test (Lord's)	211
England	Third Test (Leeds)	31 and 7
	Fifth Test (The Oval)	30
1929 in England	Fifth Test (Oval)	10 and 52

West Indies (2 matches)

1928 in	Second Test (Manchester)	53
England	Third Test (The Oval)	159

DETAILS AGAINST OPPONENTS IN ENGLAND

	Inns.	Not Outs	Runs	Highest Inns.	Aver.
Surrey v. Derbyshire	26	4	922	133	41.90
Surrey v. Essex	67	6	3045	215*	49.91
Surrey v. Glamorgan	19	2	986	137	58.00
Surrey v. Gloucestershire	50	2	2518	143	52.45
Surrey v. Hampshire	57	3	3017	205	55.87
Surrey v. Kent	70	5	2697	155	41.49
Surrey v. Lancashire	57	5	2178	142	41.88
Surrey v. Leicestershire	51	5	2272	145	49.39
Surrey v. Middlesex	70	7	3510	316*	55.71
Surrey v. Northamptonshire	39	3	1446	136*	40.16
Surrey v. Nottinghamshire	73	7	3378	226	51.18
Surrey v. Somerset	47	5	2274	204	54.14
Surrey v. Sussex	61	2	2044	117	34.64
Surrey v. Warwickshire	63	5	3742	215	64.51
Surrey v. Worcestershire	42	5	2008	184	54.27
Surrey v. Yorkshire	73	3	2915	202	41.64

Signifies not out.

DETAILS AGAINST OPPONENTS IN ENGLAND *(continued)*

	Inns.	Not Outs	Runs	Highest Inns.	Aver.
Surrey v. Oxford Univ.	17	0	944	261	55.52
Surrey v. Cambridge Univ.	19	1	894	143*	49.66
Surrey v. M.C.C.	10	2	563	100*	70.37
Surrey v. Australians	19	3	904	205*	56.50
Surrey v. South Africans	9	1	230	79	28.75
Surrey v. West Indies	3	1	357	221	178.50
Surrey v. New Zealanders	2	0	146	146	73.00
Surrey v. Scotland	4	2	240	150*	120.00
Surrey v. Gents of England	5	1	220	88	55.00
Total for Surrey	953	80	43,450	316*	49.77
Players v. Gentlemen	79	5	4050	266*	54.72
Rest v. Champion County	21	2	1218	215	64.10
Other First-Class Matches (excluding Tests)	86	8	3331	153	42.70
England v. Australia	26	2	1143	119	47.62
England v. South Africa	12	1	580	211	52.72
England v. West Indies	2	0	212	159	106.00
Totals in England	1179	98	53,984	316*	49.93

DETAILS AGAINST OPPONENTS ABROAD

	Inns.	Not Outs	Runs	Highest Inns.	Aver.
England v. Australia	45	2	2493	187	57.97
England v. South Africa	17	2	982	187	65.46
M.C.C. v. New South Wales	11	0	369	112	33.54
M.C.C. v. Victoria	13	1	599	131	49.91
M.C.C. v. South Australia	11	1	455	101	45.50
M.C.C. v. Western Australia	2	0	57	40	28.50
M.C.C. v. Queensland	5	0	142	51	28.40
M.C.C. v. Tasmania	3	0	227	104	75.66
M.C.C. v. An Australian XI	3	1	151	67*	75.50
M.C.C. v. A Victorian XI	1	0	77	77	77.00
M.C.C. v. Western Province	5	0	335	114	67.00
M.C.C. v. Natal	2	0	229	163	114.50
M.C.C. v. Transvaal	8	1	376	131*	53.71
M.C.C. v. Border	4	0	164	70	41.00
M.C.C. v. The Reef	2	0	70	39	35.00
M.C.C. v. Eastern Province	1	0	79	79	79.00
M.C.C. v. XI of Transvaal	1	0	137	137	137.00
M.C.C. v. Griqualand West	1	0	141	141	141.00
M.C.C. v. Cape Province	1	0	170	170	170.00
Totals	136	8	7253	187	56.66
Totals in England	1179	98	53,984	316*	49.93
Totals Abroad	136	8	7253	187	56.66
Totals	1315	106	61,237	316*	50.65

MODE OF DISMISSAL

Bowled	..	..	..	286
Caught	..	..	..	695
Lbw	..	..	..	125
Run out	..	..	..	31
Stumped	..	..	..	66
Hit Wicket	..	..	..	6
Total	..	..	..	1209

Signifies not out.

BATTING GROUND BY GROUND

Ground	Inns.	Not Outs	Runs	Highest Inns.	Aver.
Adelaide	21	2	1056	187	55.57
Aldershot	4	1	75	32	25.00
Attleborough	1	1	85	85*	—
Bath	9	1	257	116	32.12
Beckenham	2	0	22	16	11.00
Birmingham	35	4	1920	215	61.93
Blackheath	37	2	1497	150*	42.77
Bournemouth	8	1	304	162	43.42
Bournville	2	0	129	84	64.50
Bradford	13	0	523	100	40.23
Bray	4	1	142	56	47.33
Brentwood	2	0	33	33	16.50
Brisbane	8	0	228	51	28.50
Bristol	16	0	708	139	44.25
Cambridge	8	0	174	93	21.75
Cape Town	8	0	523	187	65.37
Cardiff	5	1	182	128	45.50
Cheltenham	6	1	253	96	50.60
Chesterfield	5	0	126	105	25.20
Derby	8	1	308	133	44.00
Dudley	1	0	21	21	21.00
Durban	6	0	529	97	88.16
Eastbourne	5	0	131	39	26.20
East London	3	0	154	70	51.33
Folkestone	5	0	179	64	35.80
Glasgow	2	1	79	50*	79.00
Gloucester	2	0	90	52	45.00
Hastings	20	0	716	106	35.80
Hobart	1	0	58	58	58.00
Horsham	12	0	502	79	41.83
Hove	12	0	208	70	17.33
Hull	2	0	72	64	36.00
Johannesburg	14	2	759	131*	63.25
Kimberley	1	0	141	141	141.00
King Williamstown	1	0	10	10	10.00
Launceston	2	0	169	104	84.50
Leeds	23	1	708	172*	32.18
Leicester	25	1	1212	145	50.50
Leyton	27	3	1377	215*	57.37
Liverpool	2	1	27	25	27.00
Lord's	89	8	4900	316*	60.49
Loughborough	2	0	49	42	24.50
Maidstone	1	0	77	77	77.00
Manchester	33	2	1148	116	37.03
Melbourne	31	2	1777	178	61.27
Northampton	20	2	964	136*	53.55
Nottingham	41	5	1757	203*	48.80
Oval	567	51	27,006	261	52.33
Oxford	4	0	189	60	47.25
Perth	2	0	57	40	28.50
Pietermaritzburg	1	0	66	66	66.00
Port Elizabeth	4	1	293	170	97.66
Portsmouth	5	0	120	56	24.00
Pretoria	1	0	1	1	1.00
Scarborough	52	4	2725	266*	56.77
Sheffield	13	1	465	112	38.75

Signifies not out.

BATTING GROUND BY GROUND—*continued*

Ground	Inns.	Not Outs	Runs	Highest Inns.	Aver.
South Melbourne	1	0	77	77	77.00
Southampton	9	0	695	200	77.22
Southend	4	0	94	52	23.50
Stourbridge	3	0	124	54	41.33
Swansea	2	0	42	21	21.00
Sydney	28	1	1148	115	42.51
Taunton	14	2	612	101*	51.00
Uttoxeter	2	1	54	29	54.00
Vogelfontein	3	0	207	137	69.00
Weston-super-Mare	2	0	182	134	91.00
Worcester	13	1	721	184	60.08
Totals	1315	106	61,237	316*	50.65

HOBBS HIT 244 HUNDREDS IN ALL MATCHES
197 In First-Class Matches

1905 (2)

155   Surrey v. Essex, at the Oval
102   Surrey v. Essex, at Leyton

1906 (4)

162*   Surrey v. Worcestershire, at the Oval
130   Surrey v. Essex, at Leyton
125   Surrey v. Worcestershire, at Worcester
103   Surrey v. Middlesex, at the Oval

1907 (4)

166*   Surrey v. Worcestershire, at the Oval
150*   Surrey v. Warwickshire, at the Oval
135   Surrey v. Hampshire, at Southampton
110   Surrey v. Worcestershire, at Worcester

1907–08 (2)

115   M.C.C. Team v. Victoria, at Melbourne
104   M.C.C. Team v. Tasmania, at Launceston

1908 (6)

161   Surrey v. Hampshire, at the Oval
155   Surrey v. Kent, at the Oval
125   Surrey v. Northamptonshire, at Northampton
117*   Surrey v. Notts, at Nottingham
106   Surrey v. Kent, at Blackheath
102   Surrey v. Oxford University, at the Oval

1909 (6)

205   Surrey v. Hampshire, at the Oval
162   Surrey v. Hampshire, at Bournemouth
160 }
100 }   Surrey v. Warwickshire, at Birmingham
159   Surrey v. Warwickshire, at the Oval
133   Surrey v. Gloucestershire, at Bristol

1909–10 (3)

187   England v. South Africa, at Cape Town
163   M.C.C. Team v. Natal, at Durban
114   M.C.C. Team v. Western Province, at Cape Town

1910 (3)

133   Surrey v. Derbyshire, at Derby
119   Surrey v. Oxford University, at the Oval
116   Surrey v. Leicestershire, at Leicester

Signifies not out.

1911 (4)

154* Players v. Gentlemen, at Lord's
127 Surrey v. Leicestershire, at Leicester
117* M.C.C.'s Australian XI v. Lord Londesborough's XI, at Scarborough
117 Surrey v. Lancashire, at the Oval

1911–12 (3)

187 England v. Australia, at Adelaide
178 England v. Australia, at Melbourne
126* England v. Australia, at Melbourne

1912 (3)

111 Surrey v. Lancashire, at Manchester
107 England v. Australia, at Lord's
104 Surrey v. Notts, at Nottingham

1913 (9)

184 Surrey v. Worcestershire, at Worcester
150* Surrey v. Scotland, at the Oval
144* Surrey v. Middlesex, at the Oval
136* Surrey v. Northamptonshire, at Northampton
122 Surrey v. Warwickshire, at Birmingham
115 Surrey v. Kent, at the Oval
113 Surrey v. Gloucestershire, at the Oval
109 Surrey v. Hampshire, at Southampton
107 Surrey v. Gloucestershire, at Bristol

1913–14 (5)

170 M.C.C. Team v. Cape Province, at Port Elizabeth
141 M.C.C. Team v. Griqualand West, at Kimberley
137 M.C.C. Team v. XI of Transvaal, at Vogelfontein
131* M.C.C. Team v. Transvaal, at Johannesburg
102 M.C.C. Team v. Transvaal, at Johannesburg

1914 (11)

226 Surrey v. Notts, at the Oval
215* Surrey v. Essex, at Leyton
202 Surrey v. Yorkshire, at Lord's
183 Surrey v. Warwickshire, at the Oval
163 Surrey v. Hampshire, at the Oval
156 Players v. Gentlemen, at the Oval
142 Surrey v. Lancashire, at the Oval
141 Surrey v. Gloucestershire, at the Oval
126 Surrey v. Worcestershire, at Worcester
122 Surrey v. Kent, at Blackheath
100 Surrey v. Yorkshire, at Bradford

1919 (8)

205* Surrey v. Australian Imperial Forces, at the Oval
120* Players v. Gentlemen, at the Oval
116 Players v. Gentlemen, at Scarborough
113 Players v. Gentlemen, at Lord's
106 Surrey v. Lancashire, at the Oval
102 Surrey v. Kent, at Blackheath
102 Surrey v. Lancashire, at Manchester
101 Rest of England v. Yorkshire, at the Oval

1920 (11)

215 Rest of England v. Middlesex, at the Oval
169 Surrey v. Hampshire, at Southampton
138 Players v. Gentlemen, at Scarborough
134 Surrey v. Leicestershire, at Leicester

Signifies not out.

132   Surrey v. Kent, at the Oval
122   Surrey v. Warwickshire, at the Oval
115   Players of the South v. Gentlemen of the South, at the Oval
114   Surrey v. Northamptonshire, at Northampton
112   Surrey v. Yorkshire, at Sheffield
110   Surrey v. Sussex, at the Oval
101   Surrey v. Warwickshire, at Birmingham

1920–21 (4)

131   M.C.C. Team v. Victoria, at Melbourne
123   England v. Australia, at Adelaide
122   England v. Australia, at Melbourne
112   M.C.C. Team v. New South Wales, at Sydney

1921 (1)

172*   Surrey v. Yorkshire, at Leeds

1922 (10)

168   Surrey v. Warwickshire, at Birmingham
151*   Surrey v. Notts, at Nottingham
145   Surrey v. Leicestershire, at Leicester
143   Surrey v. Gloucestershire, at the Oval
140   Players v. Gentlemen, at Lord's
139   Surrey v. Gloucestershire, at Bristol
126   Surrey v. Middlesex, at Lord's
112   Surrey v. Middlesex, at the Oval
102   Surrey v. Essex, at the Oval
100   Rest of England v. Yorkshire, at the Oval

1923 (5)

136   Surrey v. Middlesex, at the Oval
116*   Surrey v. Somerset, at Bath
105   Surrey v. Notts, at the Oval
105   Players v. Gentlemen, at Scarborough
104   Surrey v. Lancashire, at the Oval

1924 (6)

211   England v. South Africa, at Lord's
203*   Surrey v. Notts, at Nottingham
118*   Surrey v. Derbyshire, at the Oval
118   Players v. Gentlemen, at Lord's
105   Surrey v. Gloucestershire, at the Oval
105   Surrey v. Notts, at the Oval

1924–25 (3)

154   England v. Australia, at Melbourne
119   England v. Australia, at Adelaide
115   England v. Australia, at Sydney

1925 (16)

266*   Players v. Gentlemen, at Scarborough
215   Surrey v. Warwickshire, at Birmingham
189   Surrey v. Notts, at Nottingham
143*⎫
104 ⎭   Surrey v. Cambridge University, at the Oval
140   Players v. Gentlemen, at Lord's
129   Surrey v. Essex, at Leyton
120   Surrey v. Warwickshire, at the Oval
111   Surrey v. Somerset, at the Oval
109   Surrey v. Glamorgan, at the Oval
107   Surrey v. Essex, at the Oval
106   Rest of England v. Yorkshire, at the Oval

Signifies not out.

105	Surrey v. Kent, at Blackheath
104	Surrey v. Gloucestershire, at the Oval
101* 101 }	Surrey v. Somerset, at Taunton

1926 (10)

316*	Surrey v. Middlesex, at Lord's
261	Surrey v. Oxford University, at the Oval
200	Surrey v. Hampshire, at Southampton
176*	Surrey v. Middlesex, at the Oval
163	Players v. Gentlemen, at Lord's
119	England v. Australia, at Lord's
112	Surrey v. Gloucestershire, at the Oval
108	Surrey v. Cambridge University, at the Oval
102	Surrey v. Yorkshire, at the Oval
100	England v. Australia, at the Oval

1927 (7)

150	Surrey v. Yorkshire, at the Oval
146	Surrey v. New Zealanders, at the Oval
131	Surrey v. Notts, at the Oval
121	Surrey v. Kent, at Blackheath
119	Players v. Gentlemen, at Scarborough
112 104 }	Surrey v. Hampshire, at the Oval

1928 (12)

200*	Surrey v. Warwickshire, at Birmingham
159	England v. West Indies, at the Oval
150	Rest of England v. Lancashire, at the Oval
124	Surrey v. Gloucestershire, at the Oval
123*	Surrey v. West Indies, at the Oval
119*	Mr. H. D. G. Leveson Gower's XI v. West Indies, at Scarborough
117	Surrey v. Northamptonshire, at Northampton
114	Surrey v. Notts, at Nottingham
109	Surrey v. Kent, at the Oval
105	Surrey v. Yorkshire, at the Oval
101	Surrey v. Leicestershire, at the Oval
100*	Surrey v. M.C.C., at Lord's

1928–29 (2)

142	England v. Australia, at Melbourne
101	M.C.C. v. South Australia, at Adelaide

1929 (10)

204	Surrey v. Somerset, at the Oval
154	Surrey v. Hampshire, at the Oval
151	Mr. C. I. Thornton's XI v. South Africans, at Scarborough
150*	Surrey v. Kent, at Blackheath
134	Surrey v. Somerset, at Weston-super-Mare
128	Surrey v. Glamorgan, at Cardiff
118	Surrey v. Kent, at the Oval
115*	Surrey v. Leicestershire, at the Oval
111	Surrey v. Middlesex, at Lord's
102*	Surrey v. Essex, at the Oval

1930 (5)

146*	Surrey v. Australians, at the Oval
137 111* }	Surrey v. Glamorgan, at the Oval
106	Surrey v. Sussex, at Hastings
100	Surrey v. Leicestershire, at the Oval

Signifies not out.

1931 (10)

153	Mr. H. D. G. Leveson Gower's XI v. New Zealanders, at Scarborough
147	Surrey v. Warwickshire, at the Oval
144	Players v. Gentlemen, at Scarborough
133*	Surrey v. Yorkshire, at the Oval
128	Surrey v. Somerset, at the Oval
117	Surrey v. Sussex, at the Oval
110	Players v. Gentlemen, at the Oval
106	Surrey v. Glamorgan, at the Oval
105	Surrey v. Derbyshire, at Chesterfield
101*	Surrey v. Somerset, at Taunton

1932 (5)

161*	Players v. Gentlemen, at Lord's
123	Surrey v. Somerset, at Taunton
113 } 119* }	Surrey v. Essex, at the Oval
111	Surrey v. Middlesex, at Lord's

1933 (6)

221	Surrey v. West Indies, at the Oval
133	Surrey v. Nottinghamshire, at the Oval
118	Surrey v. Cambridge University, at the Oval
117	Surrey v. Somerset, at the Oval
101	Surrey v. Kent, at Blackheath
100	Surrey v. Warwickshire, at the Oval

1934 (1)

116	Surrey v. Lancashire, at Manchester

MINOR MATCHES

1901 (1)

102	Ainsworth v. Cambridge Liberals

1902 (1)

119	Royston v. Hertfordshire Club and Ground

1903 (1)

100	Southwark Fire Brigade v. Enfield Depot

1904 (3)

195	Cambridgeshire v. Hertfordshire
129	Cambridgeshire v. Hertfordshire
110	Putney v. Fulham Palace

1906 (2)

116 } 105* }	South Kensington v. Luton

1909–10 (1)

110	M.C.C. Team v. Western Province Colts

1911 (1)

175	Sir E. Walker's XI v. J. Bucknell's XI

1912 (1)

172	Surrey Club and Ground v. Godstone

1913–14 (1)

107	M.C.C. v. South-Western Districts (Cape Town)

1915 (1)

120	Deptford A.S.C. v. Catford

*Signifies not out.

1916 (1)

131   Idle v. Windhill

1917 (2)

132   Idle v. Saltaire
111   Hounslow Garrison v. The Guards, Windsor

1918 (4)

153*   R.A.F. v. Guards Depot, Caterham
118   R.A.F., Uxbridge v. R.A.F., Reading
125   R.A.F., Kenley v, Honor Oak
109   R.A.F., Uxbridge v. Northolt

1919 (3)

102   Oval Ground Staff v. "L" Division Metropolitan Police
106⎫
118⎭ Surrey Trial game

1920 (1)

120   P. G. H. Fender's XI v. A. C. MacLaren's XI

1920–21 (1)

138   M.C.C. team v. Geelong

1921 (1)

119   Oldlands Hall v. Maresfield

1924 (1)

129   J. B. Hobbs' XI v. Cambridge and District

1924–25 (1)

114   M.C.C. Team v. Australian Juniors

1926 (2)

159   P. G. H. Fender's XI v. Portland Cement S.C.
102   W. Cook's XI v. Sidmouth

1930 (6)

103   J. B. Hobbs' XI v. Cambridge Eighteen
101   J. B. Hobbs' XI v. Wimbledon Eighteen
100*   Vizianagram XI v. Allahabad at Benares
117   Vizianagram XI v. Singalese XI at Colombo (three days)
161   Vizianagram XI v. Up Country XI at Ceylon
144*† Vizianagram XI v. All Ceylon at Colombo (three days)

1931 (1)

107   Witney v. Oxford City

1933 (3)

118   L. A. T. Pritchard's XI v. City of London School
101   L. G. Crawley's XI v. H. B. Rowan's XI at Moffat
110   A. Sandham's XI v. Surbiton Eighteen

1934 (2)

181   F. T. Gauntlett's XI v. Ewell Castle School
115   Witney v. Oxford City

1935 (1)

102   J. B. Hobbs' XI v. Merton

1936 (2)

104   H. B. Rowan's XI v. Combined Schools, Glasgow
100   Letchworth v. Three Counties Mental Hospital

1939 (1)

106   H. G. Occomore's XI v. Eltham College

1941 (1)

116   Father's XI v. Kimbolton School

Signifies not out.   †Retired hurt.

FIRST WICKET SUCCESSES

In no fewer than 166 innings Hobbs shared a partnership that brought 100 runs and upwards on the score-board before the fall of the first wicket. His partners on such occasions were T. Hayward 40 times, A. Sandham 66, H. Sutcliffe 26, W. Rhodes 13, D. J. Knight six, A. Russell five, G. Gunn and Percy Holmes each two, and C. B. Fry, A. Baker, E. Hayes, M. Howell, A. Ducat and R. Gregory each once.

Particulars of these performances which produced upwards of 200 runs are appended, with the name of each partner:

428	A. Sandham, Surrey v. Oxford University, Oval	1926†
352	T. Hayward, Surrey v. Warwickshire, Oval	1909
323	W. Rhodes, England v. Australia, Melbourne	1911–12**
313	T. Hayward, Surrey v. Worcestershire, Worcester	1913
290	T. Hayward, Surrey v. Yorkshire, Lord's	1914
283	H. Sutcliffe, England v. Australia, Melbourne	1924–25
268	H. Sutcliffe, England v. South Africa, Lord's	1924
264	A. Sandham, Surrey v. Somerset, Taunton	1932
253	A. Sandham, Surrey v. West Indies, Oval	1928
244	A. Sandham, Surrey v. Middlesex, Oval	1923
243	H. Sutcliffe H. D. G. Leveson Gower's XI v. New Zealand, Scarborough	1931
242	E. G. Hayes, Surrey v. Lancashire, Oval	1911
234	T. Hayward, Surrey v. Kent, Blackheath	1914
233	A. Sandham, Surrey v. Gloucestershire, Oval	1922
232	A. Sandham, Surrey v. Warwickshire, Oval	1925
231	A. Sandham, Surrey v. Somerset, Oval	1931
227	H. Sutcliffe, Players v. Gentlemen, Scarborough	1931
221	W. Rhodes, England v. South Africa, Cape Town	1909–10
219	T. Hayward, Surrey v. Worcestershire, Worcester	1907
216	A. Sandham, Surrey v. Essex, Leyton	1925
212	H. Sutcliffe, The Rest v. Lancashire, Oval	1928
211	W. Rhodes, M.C.C. v. Transvaal, Johannesburg	1913–14*
210	A. Sandham, Surrey v. Glamorgan, Cardiff	1929
209	A. Sandham, Surrey v. Glamorgan, Oval	1931
207	W. Rhodes, M.C.C. v. Natal, Durban	1909–10
203	A. Sandham, Surrey v. Nottinghamshire, Oval	1927
203	H. Sutcliffe, Players v. Gentlemen, Oval	1931
203	A. Sandham, Surrey v. Middlesex, Lord's	1932

**Record for first wicket of England v. Australia.*
Partnership unfinished.
†*Record for first wicket of Surrey.*

NOTABLE ACHIEVEMENTS

Hobbs scored 61,237 runs in his first-class career, more than any other batsman in history, despite the loss of four years during the First World War.

His 197 centuries is 27 better than the next best. From the time he began in 1905 to the end of his career in 1934 he scored at least one century in each English season and on each tour. He obtained 132 centuries following the War, after his 36th birthday. He made 175 centuries in England.

In 1925 he played 16 three-figure innings which remained unsurpassed until D. Compton made 18 in 1947.

Hobbs completed his 50th hundred—170

v. Cape Province at Port Elizabeth on November 21, 1913, his 100th hundred, 116* against Somerset at Bath on May 8, 1923, his 150th, 114 v. Notts at Trent Bridge on May 28, 1928, and his 197th, v. Lancashire at Old Trafford on May 28, 1934.

On August 28 and 30, 1926, Hobbs scored 316* for Surrey v. Middlesex, the highest individual innings ever made in a first-class match at Lord's. On September 3 and 4, 1925, he made 266* for The Players against The Gentlemen at Scarborough—the highest ever made on either side in the long history of these matches.

Hobb's 100th hundred, at Bath, was his

first against Somerset. Two years later (1925), against the same county, at Taunton, he reached 101 and 101 not out on successive days, August 17 and 18, equalling and beating W. G. Grace's record of 126 hundreds in the same match. Six times he obtained a century in each innings of a match.

On July 12, 1927, he made 121 for Surrey v. Kent at Blackheath, his 100th three-figure innings for Surrey.

In 1907 Hobbs and T. W. Hayward shared four three-figure opening stands in one week.

On average Hobbs shared in a three-figure opening once in every eight times he batted.

Hobbs and A. Sandham, his regular opening partner for Surrey for many years, made a first-wicket stand of 428 against Oxford University at the Oval in 1926.

Hobbs and H. Sutcliffe (Yorkshire) his regular opening partner for England in later years, shared three successive first-wicket stands of over 100 in Tests against Australia in 1924–25. Hobbs and Sutcliffe altogether made 26 opening three-figure stands, 15 in Tests.

Hobbs and Sandham shared 66 opening three-figure stands and Hobbs and Hayward made 40.

During his career Hobbs helped to make 100 or more for the first wicket 166 times, 117 of them for Surrey.

Hobbs and W. Rhodes (Yorkshire) opened with 323 against Australia at Melbourne in 1911–12.

D. G. Bradman, alone, has made more centuries and more runs than Hobbs on either side in Tests between England and Australia.

Hobbs, like W. G. Grace, was never dismissed twice in first-class cricket in the same match for a duck. The nearest Hobbs came to performing "this easy feat" was against Notts at Trent Bridge in 1907, when his scores were 0 and one.

Early in his career Hobbs fielded at third man and in the long field, but he became a cover-point of universal renown for accuracy and speed. In 11 matches during the tour in Australia (1911–12) his returns to the wicket brought about the dismissal of 15 batsmen.

In 1909–10 Hobbs opened the bowling for England in three Tests against South Africa. A lively medium-paced bowler in his early days, he took just over 100 wickets in first-class cricket.

Hobbs scored 3,024 runs in 1925, made over 2,000 runs in 16 other seasons and over 1,000 in nine seasons. Only W. G. Grace and

F. E. Woolley (each 28 times) and C. P. Mead (27 times) obtained 1,000 or more runs in a season on a greater number of occasions.

Against Hampshire at the Oval on May 6, 1909, Hobbs and Hayes played the major role in helping Surrey to reach 645 for four wickets in five hours and 20 minutes—the record score in one day in the Championship. Hobbs (205) and Hayes (276) shared a dazzling second-wicket stand which produced 371 in only two and three-quarter hours. Hobbs played a chanceless innings, despite his tremendous scoring rate. Surrey's ultimate total of 742 took them only six hours and 20 minutes.

Twice, in 1920 and 1925, Hobbs obtained four hundreds in successive innings.

In 1919 Hobbs (47) and J. N. Crawford (48) made 96 in 32 minutes for the unbroken first wicket at the Oval after Kent left Surrey to get 95 to win in 42 minutes.

Hobbs often captained The Players against The Gentlemen. Otherwise he was never an official captain of a first-class side, but he led England during the fourth Test match against Australia at Old Trafford in 1926 when A. W. Carr retired with tonsillitis.

Hobbs made his last appearance for Surrey at the end of August, 1934, when he was dismissed for 0 by Glamorgan at Cardiff. Then going to the Folkestone Festival he played his last two matches in first-class cricket, scoring 38 for An England XI against the Australians and 24 and 18 for Players against Gentlemen.

On his retirement on February 25, 1935, Surrey elected Hobbs an Honorary Life Member of the club. It was the highest honour they could pay him. Hobbs also became an active member of the Surrey County C.C. Committee which he served up to the time of his death.

When M.C.C. first granted Honorary Cricket Membership to former England professionals in 1949, the name of Hobbs was in the list of 26.

Special *Wisden* features on Hobbs are: 1909—Portrait and Biography, 1926—Portrait and Special Article, 1935—The Hobbs Era (By Hobbs), 1936—Twenty-five Years of Triumph, 1963—One of Six Giants in the Wisden Century.

Hobbs received three benefit matches from Surrey. The first in August, 1914, against Kent was spoiled by the War and was transferred to Lord's. The second, also against Kent, was in the two-day season of 1919 and brought in £1,671 and was reckoned a big success. The third was the August Bank Holiday match of 1926 against Nottinghamshire and yielded £2,670. Hobbs used the money to finance his sports outfitter's business in Fleet Street.

Jack Hobbs was married at St. Matthew's Church, Cambridge, in 1906. He had three sons, Jack, Leonard and Ivor, and one daughter, Vera.

Hobbs always said that he owed much of his success to his wife. Lady Ada Hobbs died in March, 1963, and he survived her by only a few months. Both were buried in Hove cemetery.

Hundreds of Surrey members, together with past and present cricketers, and admirers, paid a last tribute to Sir John Hobbs at a Memorial service in Southwark Cathedral, London Bridge, on February 20, 1964.

HOBSON, Thomas E. C., died on September 2, 1936, aged 56, at Hopetown, South Africa. He played for Western Province in the Currie Cup Tournament of 1906–07. A well-known Rugby football player, he appeared for South Africa against the British touring team of 1903.

HODGES, Edward, a nephew of the famous John Willes, was born at Bellringham, Sutton Valence, on February 11, 1819, and died at Southsea on February 20, 1907. His name will be found in the match between the Gentlemen of Kent and I Zingari at Canterbury in 1853. He was a useful batsman, a good medium-paced bowler, and generally fielded at point. It was his mother who gave her brother, Mr. John Willes, the idea of round-armed bowling by *throwing* to him in practice in a barn at Fonford, near Canterbury.

HODGKINSON, Capt. G. F., of the Sherwood Foresters, was reported wounded and missing in July, 1940. When 22 he played first for Derbyshire against the South African team of 1935, and was the highest scorer with 44 in the County's first innings.

HODGKINSON, Wing-Commander Gerard William, who died on October 6, 1960, aged 77, played occasionally for Somerset from 1904 to 1911. His highest innings was 99 not out against Gloucestershire at Taunton in 1910.

HODGSON, Gordon, who died at Stoke-on-Trent after an illness lasting two months on June 14, 1951, aged 47, played as a fast bowler for Lancashire from 1928 to 1933. In that time he took 107 wickets in competition matches at a cost of just over 28 runs each.

His best season was that of 1932, when he dismissed 50 batsmen. In 1928 he made the winning hit at Colchester when Lancashire went in on the third morning to score two runs for victory and Essex fielded without changing into flannels. This game resulted in the rules of County Cricket being altered to permit an extra half-hour on the second day if necessary to finish a match. Hodgson, born of English parents in South Africa on April 16, 1904, came to England to join Liverpool F.C., with whom he gained three International "caps" as inside-right for England in 1931. He afterwards played for Aston Villa and Leeds United, became coach at Leeds, and in 1946 was appointed to the managership of Port Vale F.C., a position he held at the time of his death.

HODGSON, The Rev. Richard Graves, born at Winchester on March 9, 1845, died at Canterbury on November 1, 1931, aged 86. A good average batsman, he made several appearances in the Kent XI under the captaincy of Lord Harris but did little of note. When playing for St. Lawrence Club against Cavalry Depot in July, 1888, he hit up 245 and carried his bat. He stood over 6ft. Joining the staff of the King's School, Canterbury, in 1868 he in 1879 became first head master of the Junior King's School, holding that office until 1908. Altogether he was on the Cathedral foundation for over 60 years.

HOLBECH, Lieut. William Hugh, of the Scots Guards, died of wounds on November 1, 1914, aged 32. He was educated at Eton, but was not in the XI, but subsequently appeared with some success for Warwickshire. He was born in Canada on August 18, 1882, and had been a member of the M.C.C. since 1903.

HOLBERTON, Lieut.-Col. P. V. (Manchester Regiment, attd. Lancashire Fusiliers), killed March 26, 1918, aged 38. Shrewsbury XI; Sandhurst Second XI. Received Serbian Order of the White Eagle, 4th Class.

HOLDEN, Cecil, who died at Claughton, in Lancashire, on August 22, 1928, aged 63, was a free right-handed batsman, a useful medium-paced bowler, a very good slip, and could keep wicket well. Most of his County Cricket was played for Cheshire, for whom he made 109 not out v. Warwickshire at Edgbaston in 1894, but he also appeared for Lancashire in 1890. At Liverpool in 1897 he scored 172 for Liverpool and District v. Cambridge University, that being his highest innings in a match of note. From 1893 until 1912 he captained Birkenhead Park, scoring 19,028 runs and taking 650 wickets for the side. For that club in July, 1896, he obtained 202 of a total of 261.

HOLDSHIP, A. R., who was born in New Zealand, died in Sydney on January 28, 1923, aged 55. A sound batsman and useful medium-paced bowler, he played for the Freshmen in 1887 and the Seniors in 1889 whilst at Cambridge, in the latter match taking four wickets for 21 runs in the first innings and three for 48 in the second. As a member of the Caius College XI he averaged 33.66 in 1888 and 35.69 in 1889, in the former year scoring hundreds against Clare and Queen's. In 1890 he did particularly well for the Surbiton C.C., his highest innings being 175 v. Wimbledon. Returning to New Zealand, where he practised as a solicitor, he played for both Auckland and New Zealand, rendering useful service without doing anything remarkable.

HOLDSWORTH, Frank, well known in New Zealand cricket towards the close of last century, died at Wellington on August 4, 1941, aged 69. A forcing batsman and medium-paced bowler who made the ball lift, he helped towards many victories for Wellington. In 1895 he took seven wickets against Canterbury, and two years later he dismissed six Hawkes Bay batsmen in each innings. He also enjoyed success against touring teams, notably Harry Trott's Australian side in 1896 and the Melbourne club in 1900.

HOLDSWORTH, Romilly Lisle, died at Blagdon Hill, Taunton, on June 20, 1976, aged 77. Three years in the Repton XI and captain in 1917, he went up to Oxford in 1919 and, getting his Blue both for cricket and soccer as a Freshman, played for four years against Cambridge at cricket and three at soccer. From 1919 to 1921 he played for Warwickshire and from 1925 to 1929 for Sussex. His highest innings in first-class cricket was 202 for Oxford against the Free Foresters in 1921, but undoubtedly his most notable performance was to score 159 for Sussex against Lancashire at Eastbourne in 1927 in five hours, 40 minutes. He and Arthur Gilligan, who made 103, put on 188 in two and a half hours for the eighth wicket, and this, coupled with splendid bowling by the Rev. F. B. R. Browne, resulted in Lancashire, the champion county, suffering their only defeat of the season.

Altogether in first-class cricket he made 4,716 runs with an average of 26.20, including seven centuries. Essentially a sound batsman, he was a beautiful stylist and also a glorious field with a wonderfully safe pair of hands. Apart from his playing ability, his charm and his quiet sense of humour made him a welcome member of any XI. After some years as a master at Harrow, he went on to become Headmaster of the Doon School, Dehra Dun. In 1931 he was botanist to the Kamet Expedition, climbed Kamet, the first peak of over 25,000 ft. ever to be climbed, and brought back plants of considerable scientific interest.

HOLLAND, Frederick Charles, who died on February 5, 1957, five days before his 81st birthday, played as a batsman for Surrey from 1894 to 1908, scoring 10,384 runs, including 12 centuries, average 25.57. Four times he exceeded 1,000 runs in a season. Encouraged by his seven elder brothers, he played cricket from the early age of three, and when 17 joined the the Oval ground staff. Of graceful style, he showed to special advantage in cutting and hitting to leg, and he was also a very good short slip. His highest innings was 171 against Cambridge University at the Oval in 1895, when he and R. Abel (165) added 306 for the third Surrey wicket. Next season he hit 153 from the Warwickshire bowling at Edgbaston. Following his retirement from first-class cricket, he became coach at Oundle.

HOLLAND, John, who was born at Nantwich on April 7, 1869, died on August 23, 1914. He was a good, steady batsman with a pretty style and many strokes, and played during his comparatively short career for three counties—Leicestershire, Lancashire, and Cheshire. Probably his best innings was 72 for Leicestershire against Notts at Leicester in 1893: for Lancashire his largest score was 63 v. Essex at Manchester in 1901. As a curiosity it may be recalled that in the Leicestershire v. Hampshire match at Leicester in 1894, he was given out for "handling the ball."

HOLLIES, William, who died in March, 1968, aged 84, was father of W. E. Hollies, the former Warwickshire and England leg-break and googly bowler. In his playing days "Will" earned a reputation in the Midlands as a skilful bowler of lobs for Old Hill and in 1940 he and his son helped the club to win the Birmingham League Championship.

HOLLIES, William Eric, who died suddenly on April 16, 1981, aged 68, was almost the last of the long line of leg-break and googly bowlers who played such a notable part for 50 years in English cricket. He bowled, as was then becoming fashionable, a trifle faster than many of his predecessors and turned the ball a bit less: what he lost in spin he gained in accuracy and he could well be used as a stock bowler. Like most of his type, he relied for his wickets mainly on his leg-break and top-spinner. Coached by his father, a well-known bowler in the Birmingham League, he made a modest start for Warwickshire in 1932, but in 1933 gained a regular place, which he retained until his retirement in 1957. By 1934 he had shown such promise that he was picked for the M.C.C. side to the West Indies where, taking seven for 50 in the first innings of the third Test, he headed the Test match bowling averages. In 1935, when he took 100 wickets for the first time, a feat he accomplished on 14 occasions, he was picked for the third Test against South Africa but was forced by injury to withdraw. After this, despite his fine record in County Cricket, he was overlooked by the selectors until 1947, when he played in three Tests against South Africa. In 1948, after taking eight for 147 for Warwickshire against the Australians, he played in the final Test at the Oval and performed the feat by which he is best remembered. Bradman, coming in to prolonged applause for his last Test innings, received for his first ball a leg-break, which he played with a dead bat: the second, a perfect googly, bowled him.

But even apart from this Hollies, taking five for 131, fully justified his selection, his other victims being Barnes, Miller, Harvey and Tallon. In 1949 he played in four Tests against New Zealand and in 1950 in two against West Indies, in the first of which he took five for 63 in West Indies' first innings. That winter he was one of the M.C.C. side to Australia and New Zealand, but the pitches did not suit him and his 21 wickets in first-class matches cost him over 40 runs each. However, in 1951 he did much to help Warwickshire win their first Championship for 40 years and he was still bowling with unabated skill in his last season, 1957, when he took 132 wickets at 18.94. Only in 1956, when he had to captain the side, did he fall below his usual standard. When he retired, he had taken far more wickets for his county than any other bowler. His most sensational performance for them was to take all 10 wickets for 49 runs, against Nottinghamshire at Edgbaston in 1946 without any assistance from the fieldsmen: seven were bowled and three lbw. In 1958 he played a few times for Staffordshire, his native county, and he continued to bowl with success in the Birmingham League until he was over 60. No doubt his short run and easy action helped him to last, but he possessed also one of the greatest assets a bowler, and especially a bowler of his type, can have, an endlessly cheerful temperament.

In all first-class cricket this immensely popular player took 2,323 wickets at 20.94 and scored 1,673 runs with an average of 5.01, his wickets thus easily exceeding his runs. His highest score was 47 against Sussex at Edgbaston in 1954.

HOLLINS, Sir Frank Hubert, who died on January 31, 1963, aged 85, was in the Eton XI of 1896 and gained a Blue at Oxford in 1901. Between 1902 and 1904, he made a few appearances for Lancashire and in 1903 against Worcestershire at Worcester hit his one century in first-class cricket, 114, he and A. C. MacLaren putting on 233 for the third wicket.

HOLLOWAY, Capt. Bernard Henry (9th Battalion Royal Sussex Regiment), brother of Mr. N. J. Holloway, the Cambridge Blue, was born in Surrey on January 13, 1888, and killed in France on September 27, 1915. In 1904 and three following years he was in the Leys School XI, being a very useful all-round player, and proving himself a good captain. He was third in the batting averages in 1904, second in 1905 and 1906—in the latter year with 35.81—and top in 1907, when his figure was 35.75. In the last-mentioned season he also took 22 wickets for 14.59 runs each. At Cambridge, where he did not obtain his Blue, he did little in the trial games save in 1911 when, in the Seniors' match, he scored 52 and made 133 for the first wicket with C. G. Forbes-Adam (78). During 1910–11 he visited the West Indies as a member of the M.C.C. team and, making 443 runs with an average of 24.61, rendered excellent service: his highest score was 100 v. British Guiana at Georgetown. In 1911 and three following seasons he appeared occasionally for Sussex, for which side his best performances were against his old University, on the Cambridge ground, in 1913 and 1914, his scores being 58 not out and 32 not out, and 54 and 15. He played half-back at Rugby football for Cambridge v. Oxford in 1907, and centre three-quarter back in 1909. He was also in the University Lacrosse XII in 1908–09–10, being captain in 1910, in which year he played at the game for England.

HOLLOWAY, George James Warner, who died on September 24, 1966, aged 82, was in the Clifton XI of 1903. From 1908 to 1911 he played a few times for Gloucestershire.

HOLLOWAY, Norman James, who died on August 17, 1964, aged 74, was in the Leys XI from 1906 to 1908, heading the batting averages in the last season, with 220 not out against M.C.C. his highest innings, and taking 47 wickets for 16.36 apiece. At Cambridge he concentrated mainly upon fast bowling and he got his Blue in 1910, 1911 and 1912. In the third match against Oxford he and R. B. Lagden put on 58 for the ninth wicket, enabling the Light Blues, who eventually won by three wickets, to tie on first innings at 221. From 1911 to 1925 he appeared for Sussex, for whom he took 13 Warwickshire wickets for 156 runs in the match at Hastings in 1914, being largely responsible for victory by 259 runs. In all first-class cricket he dismissed 322 batsmen for 24.49 runs each. His highest innings for the county was 55 against Surrey at Hove in 1911.

HOLLOWAY, Reginald Frederick Price, who died in Bristol on February 12, 1979, aged 74, played occasionally for Gloucestershire as a batsman from 1923 to 1926. He was in the Clifton XI in 1922. He served after the War on the county's management committee and as a selector, and was President from 1974–76.

HOLLOWOOD, Albert Bernard, editor of Punch from 1957 to 1968, died on March 28, 1981, aged 70. The son of an ex-Staffordshire professional, he himself played for the county as a batsman frequently before and occasionally after the War. Later he was well known in club cricket in Surrey. He was author of Cricket on the Brain.

HOLMES, Group Capt. Albert John, A.F.C. and Bar, died suddenly at his home at Burwash after a heart attack on May 21, 1950. Born at Thornton Heath, Surrey, on June 30, 1899, he was a member of the Test Match Selection Committee in 1939, became Chairman for the first four seasons following the War, and was appointed for 1950, but resigned through ill-health upon the advice of his doctor. Generally known among cricketers as "Jack," he was educated at Repton, where he did well as a batsman. After service in the First World War, in the Royal Field Artillery and then with the Royal Flying Corps, he made his first appearance for Sussex in 1923, scoring over 1,000 runs, but in 1925 he rejoined the Royal Air Force, and not until 1935, when he transferred to the Reserve, was he able to play again for the county. Then, when A. Melville resigned the position before returning to South Africa, Holmes took over the Sussex captaincy, which he held till the outbreak of the last War, when he returned to the R.A.F. His most successful season was that of 1937, when he scored 1,108 runs, average 25.76. In 1940, when a Wing Commander, he was awarded the Air Force Cross and received a Bar to the decoration in 1942. His genial personality made him very popular and contributed largely to his success as manager of the M.C.C. team which toured South Africa in 1938–39. He was a pioneer of mink farming in England.

HOLMES, Errol Reginald Thorold, the Oxford University, Surrey and England cricketer, died in a London hospital after a heart attack on August 16, 1960, aged 54. He was one of the most gifted amateur batsmen of his day and his passing at such a comparatively early age was widely felt in cricket circles. He had been a most valuable member of both the M.C.C. and Surrey County C.C. committees.

Born at Calcutta on August 21, 1905, Holmes soon showed an aptitude for cricket at Andrew's School, Eastbourne, before becoming one of the greatest cricketers Malvern has produced. Coached by Charles Toppin, he was in the school XI for four years, 1921–24, and at 16 had a batting average of 60 as well as heading the bowling averages. Definitely fast for a schoolboy, he took all 10 wickets in an innings for 36 runs. The next year, when captain, a strain hampered him in bowling but his batting improved out of all knowledge and, scoring 730 runs, he averaged 60.83 per innings. After being captain of cricket for his last two years, he went up to Oxford, promptly gained his Blue and for three seasons was a prominent member of the side, being captain in his final year. He also gained his Association football Blue as a centre-forward and in due course captained the side.

Although having one or two triumphs with his medium-fast bowling, it was by his batting that Holmes made such a fine impression on his introduction to first-class cricket. For Oxford, against the Army in 1925, he scored 238 runs for once out—a performance that had much to do with his season's aggregate of 553 runs, average 34.56 which placed him second in the batting to G. B. Legge, his

Malvern captain of 1922 with whom during 1926 he was involved in a motor accident. This incapacitated Holmes for a time as a damaged foot handicapped him in batting and fielding. He finished his Oxford career brilliantly in 1927 when he was captain. Against Cambridge he stood far above the rest of the team. They were set to make 379 in the fourth innings and the opening pair, A. M. Crawley and P. V. F. Cazalet, went for nothing, but Holmes and A. T. Barber put on 183 in just over two and a half hours, Holmes' share being 113. He hit all round the wicket in delightful style, timing his strokes admirably and while at first particularly strong on the leg-side, he afterwards excelled in clean driving. Altogether he hit 17 fours.

That innings was typical of the way Holmes approached cricket all his life. He believed that everyone should enjoy the game. A marked characteristic about his batting was the ease and certainty of his strokes; a very strong forward player he drove really hard, especially to the off and so good was his footwork and power of wrist that he had no need to exploit the modern method of leg-side play, but even so he was no mean exponent of such strokes. With left shoulder forward and firm right knee, Holmes convinced one directly he went in that he was there to make runs. And never did he change his methods.

For all his brilliance Holmes did not figure on the winning side against Cambridge. One of his three matches was drawn and the other two lost, but in those games he himself made 289 runs, average 48 and he took seven wickets. Holmes made his first-class debut in 1924 when in his only innings he failed to score for Surrey against Somerset at Taunton, but in the following year he took part in that historic match on the same ground when J. B. Hobbs hit two centuries and passed W. G. Grace's then world record of 126 centuries.

On going down from Oxford, Holmes, due to business reasons, dropped out of first-class cricket for seven years, but the break did not harm his batting. He returned to Surrey (1934) at a time when the affairs of the club were unsettled. The long reign of P. G. H. Fender had ended and his successor, D. R. Jardine, following the "body-line" controversy, had given up the leadership after only two seasons. The appearance of Holmes marked the beginning of a new era for Surrey. He entertained the idea that County Cricket generally required some vitalising influence. Modern methods accounted for the loss of much of the real spirit of the game—life and enjoyment. There had crept in a tendency by many leading batsmen to "play for keeps." Holmes, holding strongly to the opinion that County Cricket would benefit from a touch of the country house spirit, applied himself to the task of installing these precepts into the minds and consequently the play of those under him. Although he had in A. R. Gover one of the best fast bowlers in the country he set his face resolutely against the employment to any great extent of the short-pitched ball—not that Gover himself wished to do otherwise than bowl a full length.

Holmes was always attractive to watch. He made the most of his height and hit strongly in front of the wicket. For a few seasons he was undoubtedly one of the best batsmen of his day. Scoring 1,925 runs he finished 10th in the country's batting in 1935 when he played in the second Test against South Africa at Lord's. He was vice-captain of the M.C.C. team in West Indies in 1934–35 and the following winter he led the side to Australia and New Zealand on a good-will tour.

Again in 1936 he was in fine form and was chosen to go with M.C.C. to Australia under G. O. Allen, but business compelled him to decline and his place was taken by R. E. S. Wyatt. Holmes announced his retirement from first-class cricket in 1938, but after the War when Surrey were again hard-pressed for a responsible leader he returned as captain in 1947 and 1948. From 1949 to 1953 he was a member of the M.C.C. Committee. In his preface to his book *Flannelled Foolishness* he wrote, "What success I had can, I think, be attributed to my natural desire to hit the ball. I hated being kept quiet." The modern professional might well take this as a maxim.—N.P.

Sir John Hobbs writes:

"Little did I think when I was walking with Errol Holmes to Victoria Station after the funeral of Donald Knight at St. Michael's, Chester Square, that within a few months I would be bidding Errol farewell. He was a true sportsman and a lovable fellow. He was captain of Surrey in 1934 when I scored my last century, the 197th, against Lancashire at Old Trafford.

"Errol was a fine all-round cricketer. He had the ability and the right approach to the game. He followed in the steps of the real amateurs of my early days; men like Lord Dalmeny, Lord Tennyson, Ranjitsinhji, MacLaren, Spooner and later Greville Stevens and Nigel Haig. We used to enjoy our cricket. Though doughty opponents on and off the field, we laughed and joked about it.

"As a captain Holmes was always popular with the professionals, but he never shirked his duty. As a player he was a fine attacking batsman with an excellent style—a true Malvernian. He was a keen opening bowler of the tearaway type and he set a fine personal example in the field. He played in only five Tests and it was a pity he could not find more time to play because I am sure he would have appeared more often for England.

"In recent years I saw a good deal of Errol Holmes. We were together on the Surrey Committee until the time of his death. As Chairman of the cricket committee he proved very efficient and I know he was a tower of strength on the M.C.C. committee at Lord's. He had the pulse of cricket at his finger tips and he always led Surrey the right way. A purist, he would not tolerate anything shady or underhanded and being a God-fearing man he was against Sunday play in the big-match sense.

"When difficult questions cropped up, he used to look at me and say, 'What does Sir John think?' Perhaps I should have backed him up more than I did. I feel his loss very much."

HOLMES, Henry, who died on January 6, 1913, was born at Ramsey on November 11, 1833, and was thus in his 80th year. He will be remembered chiefly as one of the best players in the Hampshire team in the '60s. He was included in the Fourteen of Hampshire who beat Surrey at the Oval in 1864— the only match that Surrey lost that season. He then scored 17 and not out 38. In the return game, at Southampton, which ended in a draw, he did still better, making 42 and 63, and heading the score in each innings. Perhaps the best innings he ever played was 77 for the Players of the South against the Gentlemen of the South at the Oval in 1868. The Players hit up a total of 413, winning the match by an innings and 91 runs. Of the Hampshire cricketers who played with Holmes in 1864 there are still a few survivors, including Mr. H. Maturin, who, though now in his 72nd year, still takes an active part in the game.

PERCY HOLMES—A TRUE YORKSHIREMAN
Born at Oakes, Huddersfield, November 25, 1887
Died September 3, 1971
By Sir Neville Cardus

Over decades a Yorkshire batsman has been one of the two opening an England innings in Test matches, Rhodes with Hobbs, Sutcliffe with Hobbs, Hutton with Washbrook; now Boycott sustains the great tradition. But one of Yorkshire's most accomplished Number One (or Number Two) batsmen only once raised the curtain of an England innings v. Australia; his name Percy Holmes, a name as famous in Yorkshire during the 1920s and early 1930s, as Brown or Tunnicliffe, or Sutcliffe or Rhodes, or Boycott.

Holmes opened for England at Trent Bridge against Gregory and McDonald, the fearsome bowlers of Warwick Armstrong's rough-riding team, which arrived in England in 1921, having defeated J. W. H. T. Douglas's hapless England contingent five times in five Test matches, in Australia, each played to a finish. And in 1921, blessed by a glorious English summer, Armstrong's conquerors proceeded to annihilate England in the first three Test matches, three-day engagements. And the victories were settled well within the allotted time span.

Percy Holmes walked jauntily to the wicket at Trent Bridge on May 28, 1921, accompanied by D. J. Knight. England were all out for 112 and Holmes defended stoutly for 90 minutes, making top score, 30. Next innings he made no more than eight. The match was all over on the second afternoon. And this was the end of his Test match appearances until the South African season of 1927–28. He then went in first with Sutcliffe in five consecutive Test matches, at Johannesburg, Cape Town and Durban; his scores were 0 and 15 not out; nine and 88; 70 and 56; one and 63; and in the fifth game of this rubber 0 and 0.

In 1932, 10 days after Holmes and Sutcliffe had made 555 together at Leyton, Holmes once again, and for the last time, received recognition from the English Selection Committee; he went in first with Sutcliffe at Lord's v. India, scoring only six and 11. So, altogether this superb batsman played for England on seven occasions, and his modest record of 14 innings, 357 runs, average 27.46, is a complete falsification of what manner of cricketer and what manner of Yorkshire character Percy Holmes was, season after season.

His name was household in Yorkshire, as closely and proudly linked with Sutcliffe's as Tunnicliffe's with Brown's. As everybody knows—or should know—Holmes and Sutcliffe surpassed the first-wicket stand and aggregate of 554, incredibly achieved by Brown and Tunnicliffe v. Derbyshire, at Chesterfield in 1898. Holmes was 44 years and troubled with lumbago in 1932, when he and Sutcliffe belaboured the Essex attack and after what the politicians call a recount, went beyond the Brown–Tunnicliffe scoreboard marathon.

Holmes, seven years to the day older than Sutcliffe, technically was perhaps Sutcliffe's better. His range of strokes was wider; he was the more versatile and impulsive batsman of the two. But Sutcliffe knew that very rare secret, which is revealed to few men, whatever their vocation. Mastery comes to him who knows his technical limitations. Again, Holmes, as a temperament, was at Sutcliffe's extreme; he was volatile, unpredictable of mood, always alive by instinct, so to say, intent on enjoyment on the cricket field, or off it. He was always first to admit that, like the rest of humans, he was fallible.

Sutcliffe seldom, if ever, admitted, as batsman, to ordinary mortal frailty. In other words, Sutcliffe found it hard to imagine that any bowler could get him out, whatever the state of the game or the wicket. One day, I saw Maurice Tate clean bowl Sutcliffe, at a game's outset—Yorkshire v. Sussex. The ball was good enough to overwhelm Bradman. As Sutcliffe returned to the pavilion, I commiserated with him. "Unlucky, Herbert, to get such a ball at the beginning of the morning." But Sutcliffe reacted to my sympathy in high dudgeon. "I could have played it," he asserted, "but a man moved in the stand, unsighting me." "I could have played it," he repeated. I felt that I had offended Sutcliffe family pride.

Holmes, as I say, was different. At Lord's, in 1925, he actually accumulated 315 v. Middlesex, in 10 minutes under seven hours, with 38 boundaries, as comprehensive an exhibition of stroke play as well could be imagined, all round the wicket, brilliant with late cuts and enchanting flicks to leg. Yet, when later he talked of this innings—it broke a century-old record at Lord's—and a year afterwards it was beaten by the Master Batsman of All (Sir Jack Hobbs)—Holmes could not account for it, at least not for the first half hour of it. He exaggerated by reckoning he was "morally out" half-a-dozen times in the first few overs. One of the Middlesex bowlers who had to cope with Holmes, in "these first few overs," confessed to me that he hadn't "so and so noticed" Holmes's insecurity. "He never missed a ball he intended to play."

Holmes was a great Yorkshire cricketer in one of the most historical periods of the county's many triumphant summers. From 1919, his real baptism to top-class cricket, till his last year of 1933, Yorkshire won the County Championship eight times. And in his prime, Yorkshire were more or less invulnerable—1922 to 1925. These were the halcyon years, when Old Trafford, Leeds, Bradford and Sheffield would close gates at noon for a Yorkshire v. Lancashire match. Nearly 80,000 people watched Lancashire v. Yorkshire at Old Trafford, in 1926.

Holmes was one of the "characters," identifiable as soon as he took guard, twiddling his bat. Robertson-Glasgow, brilliant as observer as with his wit, rightly discerned in Holmes a certain aspect of "an ostler inspired to cricket." There was a curious "horsey" stable-boy air about him; he seemed to brush an innings, comb it, making the appropriate whistling sounds. He was not of the broadly soily nature of Emmott Robinson and Rhodes. I doubt if Rhodes, in his heart of hearts, really approved of Holmes's delight in a late-cut. "Cuts were never business strokes," quoth Wilfred. Roy Kilner, lovable as Maurice Leyland, would describe Percy as "a bobby-dazzler." (By nature's law of compensation, there are usually one or two rich genial spirits in the Yorkshire XI, to allow cheerfulness occasionally to creep in.)

Holmes really played cricket for fun. In a word, he was an artist, revelling in his batsmanship for its own sake. If he was furthering "The Cause"—the Yorkshire will-to-win, all very well. But he set himself to drink deeply from the sparkling wine distilled in most innings he played. In his career he scored 30,574 runs, average 42.11, including 67 centuries; and I'm pretty certain that the bulk of them, the ripe bin of them, were vintage stuff.

Holmes and Sutcliffe made a most fascinating conjunction and contrast of character and technical method: Holmes was as spruce and eager to begin a Yorkshire innings as a jockey to mount his horse, using his bat as a sort of pliant persuasive whip to urge his innings along the course to the winning-post of a first-wicket century partnership.

Sutcliffe was all relaxed as he took guard. Then, very likely, he would wave, with his bat, some obtrusive member in the pavilion, even at Lord's, out of his way, wave him into crawling oblivion—and the poor exposed movable spectator could easily have been our Lord Chancellor. But, as soon as the bowler began his attacking run, Sutcliffe became almost stiff and angular with concentration. He scored with the air of a man keeping an appointment with a century, and must not be late.

Holmes often appeared to improvise; he could change stroke whenever his first glance at a ball's length had deceived him. He might move forward anticipating a half-volley; if the ball dropped shorter than its first flight advertised, he would, on swift feet, move back and cut late exquisitely. There was a certain light-footedness in his batsmanship; he could defend as obstinately as most Yorkshiremen, but even then, he gave the impression that he was defending by choice, not compulsion. He was an artist, as I say, expressing himself through cricket.

Sutcliffe, of course, was also an artist expressing himself in a different temperamental way. Never let it be thought that Sutcliffe was a tedious batsman; whether or not he was moving the score ahead, he remained an individual, lord of all that he surveyed. He was the image of supreme confidence, basking in it.

Holmes was prepared to risk the mercy and indulgence of fortune. Sutcliffe was not only surprised but scandalised, if he was bowled; Holmes accepted such a downfall as part of the common lot of cricketers and of human nature in general.

Some 69 times Holmes and Sutcliffe rounded the hundred mark for Yorkshire's first wicket. Undoubtedly Holmes would, but for the omniscient presence of Hobbs, have opened for England with Sutcliffe against Australia, not once but perennially.

Most of the achievements batsmen dream about came to Holmes—a century in each innings v. Lancashire at Old Trafford in 1920; 1,000 runs in a single month, June 1925, average 102.10; 2,000 runs in a season seven times, over 30,000 runs in his career.

But the scoreboard could not tell of his personal presence and animation. He seldom seemed static; he was always in the game. Between overs, and in the field, he was, as they say, eye-catching; but not self-consciously "producing" himself. He was as natural as could be, not aware that, as Percy Holmes, he "signed" everything he did.

His end as a cricketer arrived with an abruptness which, I am sure, tickled his mellow sense of humour. In 1932, he took part in the gigantic 555 first-wicket stand. The summer following, in 1933, he batted for Yorkshire 50 innings, scoring only 929 runs, average 19.25. This was the fall of the curtain for him. True, he was in his 46th year; but somehow none of us suspected that age was on his heels and shoulders. He is a permanent chapter, not to say a whole volume, of Yorkshire's cricket history.

He had the talent—not always nurtured in the North country—to play hard for Yorkshire and, at the same time to spread over our cricket fields flashes of pleasure by his batsmanship, his nimble fielding and—best of all—by his infectious, though not demonstrative, Yorkshire nature.

PERCY HOLMES—CAREER AT A GLANCE
Compiled by Stanley Conder
BATTING

In England

Season	Matches	Inns.	Not Outs	Runs	Highest Inns.	100s	50s	Aver.
1913	8	16	3	170	36	0	0	13.07
1914	12	17	3	222	61	0	1	15.85
1919	32	48	5	1,887	140	5	6	43.88
1920	34	51	6	2,254	302*	7	7	50.08
1921	29	43	2	1,577	277*	3	6	38.46
1922	35	51	5	1,776	220*	5	4	38.60
1923	36	54	3	2,001	199	3	11	39.23
1924	36	55	6	1,954	202*	5	10	39.87
1925	37	52	9	2,453	315*	6	10	57.04
1926	36	50	4	2,006	143	4	11	43.60
1927	35	47	9	2,174	180	6	11	57.21
1928	33	43	5	2,220	275	6	14	58.42
1929	31	46	4	1,724	285	4	8	41.04
1930	34	52	6	2,003	132*	4	11	43.54
1931	34	43	4	1,506	250	3	8	38.61
1932	21	31	4	1,208	224*	2	8	44.74
1933	34	50	2	929	65	0	1	19.35
1935	1	2	0	65	59	0	1	32.50

Signifies not out.

CAREER AT A GLANCE—*continued*

Season	Matches	Inns.	Not Outs	Runs	Highest Inns.	100s	50s	Aver.
In South Africa								
1924–25	12	20	1	536	81	0	4	28.21
1927–28	14	22	3	1,112	279*	3	4	58.52
In West Indies								
1925–26	10	17	0	797	244	1	6	46.88
Totals	554	810	84	30,574	315*	67	142	42.11

MODE OF DISMISSAL

Bowled	224
Caught	404
Lbw	60
Stumped	9
Hit Wicket	4
Run Out	25
Total	726

CENTURIES (67)
For Yorkshire (60)

v. Middlesex (7): 315*, 179*, 149, 133, 129, 128, 105.
v. Lancashire (6): 143, 132, 126, 125, 123, 111*.
v. Derbyshire (5): 150, 125, 107, 104, 100.
v. Glamorgan (5): 138, 130, 130, 118*, 107.
v. Nottinghamshire (5): 285, 133, 112, 101†, 100.
v. Northamptonshire (4): 277*, 145*, 133, 110*.
v. Warwickshire (4): 275, 250, 220*, 209.
v. Essex (3): 224*, 141, 136.
v. Gloucestershire (3): 180, 132*, 122*.
v. Hampshire (3): 302*, 159, 108.
v. Leicestershire (3): 194, 140, 110.
v. Somerset (3): 199, 126, 102.
v. Kent (2): 107, 105*.
v. Surrey (2): 142, 127*.
v. Cambridge University (1): 126*.
v. Oxford University (2): 110, 107*.
v. M.C.C. (1): 134.
v. New Zealanders (1): 175*.

OTHER MATCHES (7)

Players v. Gentlemen (1): 127.
North v. South (1): 127*.
C. I. Thornton's XI v. South Africans (1): 202*.
M.C.C. v. Orange Free State (1): 279*.
M.C.C. v. Transvaal (1): 184*
M.C.C. v. A South African XI (1): 128.
M.C.C. v. Jamaica (1): 244.

TEST MATCHES

	Matches	Inns.	Not Outs	Runs	Highest Inns.	100s	50s	Aver.
v. Australia	1	2	0	38	30	0	0	19.00
v. South Africa ...	5	10	1	302	88	0	4	33.55
v. India	1	2	0	17	11	0	0	8.50
Total	7	14	1	357	88	0	4	27.46

*Signifies not out.   †Retired hurt.

TEST MATCHES—*continued*

P. Holmes scored a century in each innings for Yorkshire v. Lancashire at Old Trafford in 1920, his scores being 126 and 111*.

He scored over 2,000 runs in a season on seven occasions.

In June 1925 he scored 1,021 runs in 12 innings (twice not out) for an average of 102.10.

He carried his bat through a completed innings on three occasions.

With H. Sutcliffe, P. Holmes made 100 or more runs for the first wicket of Yorkshire on 69 occasions. Their highest first-wicket partnership was 555 against Essex at Leyton in 1932. This is the best first-wicket stand in first-class cricket.

Four times this pair put on 300 or more runs for the first wicket.

In bowling P. Holmes took two wickets at a cost of 183 runs.

Signifies not out.

HOLMES, The Rev. R.S., who died on January 13, 1933, was the author of *The History of Yorkshire County Cricket 1833–1903*. He was a great collector of and an authority on cricket literature.

HOLT, John Kenneth, who died in Kingston, Jamaica, on August 5, 1968, aged 83, played as an all-rounder for Jamaica. He toured England as a member of H. B. G. Austin's West Indies side in 1923, his highest innings being 56 against Somerset at Weston-super-Mare.

HONE, Sir Brian, O.B.E., who died in Paris on May 28, 1978, aged 70, was the noted Australian educationalist who enjoyed a brief but successful first-class cricket career between 1928 and leaving his home city, Adelaide, as its 1930 Rhodes Scholar. In that time, Sir Brian scored 860 runs at an average of 50.58, including three excellent Sheffield Shield centuries. A determined player, possessed of a good defence, he won cricket and tennis Blues at Oxford and, on joining the staff of Marlborough College as head of the English Department, he played with success for Wiltshire in the Minor Counties Competition when the opportunity presented itself, topping the side's batting averages between 1937 and 1939. Returning to Australia as Headmaster of Sydney's Cranbrook School in 1940, Sir Brian became Headmaster of Melbourne Grammar School in 1950, a post he filled with distinction until retirement in 1970. He was later to be Deputy Chancellor of Monash University in 1973–74 and Chairman of the Commonwealth Secondary Schools Libraries Committee between 1971 and 1974.

HONE, William Patrick, M.C., a member of the famous Irish cricketing family, died at Clondalkin, Co. Dublin, on February 28, 1976, aged 89. A good batsman and wicket-keeper, he had played for and captained Ireland and was a member of the Gentlemen of Ireland's side in Canada in 1908. He had been in the XI at Trinity, Dublin, and for years played for the Phoenix Club, but he will probably be best remembered for his book *Cricket in Ireland*, published in 1955, which is the standard history of the game in that country.

HOOD, Rear-Admiral The Hon. Horace Lambert Alexander, R.N., C.B., D.S.O., M.V.O., born 1870, lost in his flag-ship, the *Queen Mary*, in the Battle of Jutland, May 31, 1916. Was a very keen, if not very distinguished cricketer. When in command of a battleship he always endeavoured to secure good cricketers as the officers of his ward and gun-rooms. When in command of the *Hyacinth* he was captain of the officers' team, which included C. H. Abercrombie (who perished with him), and Lieut. F. W. B. Wilson, who had played at Lord's for the Navy, and was the all-round 'star' player.

HOOKER, John Edward Halford ("Hal"), died in Sydney on February 12, 1982, aged 83. A right-arm medium-paced bowler, capable of swinging the ball both ways, he was regarded by many as one of the best bowlers never to play for Australia. He made his first-class debut for New South Wales against Victoria in Melbourne in 1924–25 and in his 17 first-class matches, including one Test Trial, took 63 wickets at 29 apiece. He is best remembered for having partnered Alan Kippax in what still stands as the world record 10th-wicket partnership of 307 against Victoria at Melbourne in 1928. He joined Kippax late on Christmas Eve, when New South Wales were 113 for nine in reply to Victoria's first-innings total of 376. On Christmas Day a sparse crowd gathered to see Victoria capture the remaining wicket and enforce the follow-on. But by lunch Hooker was still there, on 18, and by tea he had advanced to 22. When eventually, on

Boxing Day morning, he was dismissed for 62 (caught Ryder bowled A'Beckett), he had batted for 304 minutes, New South Wales had scored 420 and Kippax was 260 not out. The match was drawn. A month later, the return match was played at Sydney, and again Hooker made a remarkable contribution. Batting first New South Wales declared at 713 for six; Victoria were then dismissed for 265, Hooker finishing off the innings with a hat-trick (Ebeling, Gamble and Ironmonger). When Victoria followed on Hooker took a wicket (Austin) with his first ball, thus becoming the only person ever to have claimed four wickets with consecutive balls in Sheffield Shield cricket. Three of his victims were bowled, the other caught and bowled. Hooker had one other claim to cricketing fame. After a long and unsuccessful stint, bowling at Ponsford, he complained light-heartedly to the umpire that Ponsford's bat exceeded the legal width. The bat, when measured later, was found to be fractionally in excess of the regulation size of four and a quarter inches. On his retirement from first-class cricket Hooker worked for almost 20 years as a sporting commentator for the Australian Broadcasting Commission.

HOOMAN, Charles Victor Lisle, who died in a nursing home at Palm Beach, Florida, on November 20, 1969, aged 82, was a fine all-round sportsman. In the Charterhouse XI from 1903 to 1906, he was captain in the last year when he headed the batting with an average of 85.71. A splendid batsman, he played for Oxford against Cambridge in 1909 and 1910, being top of the University averages in each season and scoring an attractive 61 in the big match at Lord's in 1910. He also gained his Blue at golf and at racquets. He turned out for Devon before assisting Kent in 1910, scoring 567 runs, average 28.35, in 14 matches and helping in the winning of the County Championship. In 1910, he represented Gentlemen v. Players at Lord's and played golf for England against Scotland. He also appeared for England in the first of the series of Walker Cup matches.

HOOPER, The Rev. Robert Poole, died at Hove, September 12, 1918, in the 92nd year of his age. Played for Cambridge University v. Harrow in 1848; and was asked to play v. Oxford, but "had already made previous promises for matches which I could not honourably throw over." Stroke of the first Trinity boat for two years. Norfolk County Cricket XI. Considered the finest left-hand tennis player of his generation.

HOPKINS, Albert J., born at Sydney on May 3, 1875, and died there on April 25, 1931. A right-hand slow-medium bowler with a pronounced swerve and break from the off, a brilliant field and a forceful batsman, he was one of several good all-round cricketers who came to England in 1902 under the captaincy of Joseph Darling. During that tour he scored 1,192 runs (average 25.91) and took 38 wickets (average 17.60). He made two other visits—in 1905 and 1909—but in the latter tour did not show anything like such good ability in batting as when previously in England, his aggregate runs amounting to only 432. Altogether he took part in 17 Test matches, scoring 434 runs and taking 21 wickets. On one occasion he earned great distinction. In the second Test match at Lord's in 1902, when play was restricted to an hour and three-quarters on the opening day, Darling, to everyone's surprise chose Hopkins to open the bowling from the Pavilion end, although such capable men as Saunders, Armstrong and Noble were there to share the attack with E. Jones. As it happened, C. B. Fry made a wretched stroke to short-leg and Ranjitsinhji was bowled off his pad, both these famous batsmen failing to get a run. A. C. MacLaren and F. S. Jackson took the score to 102, and that was the extent of the cricket in that game.

As it happened Hopkins did not get another wicket in Test matches during that tour. His highest innings in this country was 154 against Northamptonshire in August, 1905, when the Australians ran up the great total of 609. He usually went in first for New South Wales, and against South Australia at Adelaide in December, 1908, he played a great innings of 218, his partnership with Noble yielding 283 runs for the second wicket in two hours and 50 minutes. This brilliant display was characteristic of his forcing game. His record in Sheffield Shield cricket was 1,594 runs at an average of 30.65 and 96 wickets, average 22.57.

HOPKINS, Dr. Herbert Oxley, who died suddenly at Milverton, Somerset, on February 23, 1972, aged 76, was at St. Peter's College, Adelaide, before going to Oxford. He gained a Blue in 1923, hitting 42 against Cambridge. Just before the University match he scored 100 not out off the M.C.C. bowling. He turned out for Worcestershire from 1921 to 1927, making two centuries—137 v. Nottinghamshire at Trent Bridge in 1924 and 122 v. the University at Oxford the following summer. He went to the Malay

States as a doctor and when on leave played in nine Championship games for Worcestershire.

HOPKINS, Jesse, born at Birmingham, on June 30, 1875, died at Southampton, on January 16, 1930, aged 54. A right-handed bowler with a high action, he played for Warwickshire between 1898 and 1903 and against Kent at Edgbaston in the first of those seasons took five wickets for 10 runs. In 1904 he went to Southampton and became one of the best-known groundsmen in the country. He qualified automatically for Hampshire and made a few appearances for that county.

HORAN, Thomas Patrick, who died at Malvern, Melbourne, on April 16, 1916, was in his time the crack batsman of Victoria. He visited this country with the first Australian team in 1878—a very wet season—when he made as his best score in 11-a-side matches 64 against C. I. Thornton's XI at the Orleans Club, Twickenham. Mr. Horan did not come in 1880, but two years later, with an aggregate of 1,175 and an average of 25, he ran second to W. L. Murdoch, for the ever-famous team that beat England by seven runs at the Oval. His highest innings that summer were 112 against the United XI at Chichester and 141 not out against Gloucestershire at Clifton. His career extended from the middle of the '70s to the late '80s. He enjoyed the distinction of being chosen for the memorable match at Melbourne in March, 1877, when, for the first time, an Australian side playing an English team on level terms proved victorious. Like Charles Bannerman he formed his method and earned high distinction as a batsman before enjoying the advantage of a trip to England. He had no special grace of style, but his defence was very strong, and he excelled against fast bowling. Even after an interval of nearly 35 years one recalls the masterly way in which he played Crossland at Liverpool in 1882, getting him away again and again on the leg side. Among his most notable innings at home were 124 for Australia against Alfred Shaw's First Team at Melbourne in 1882 and 117 not out for Victoria against Shaw's Third Team at Melbourne in 1886. A splendid judge of the game, Horan wrote on it for a great many years under the signature "Felix" in the columns of the *Australasian*. It may not be generally known that he was a native of Ireland. He was born in Dublin on March 8, 1855, but emigrated to Australia when quite a small boy.

In Test matches he played 27 innings, twice not out, highest score 124, total runs 471, average 18.84, and took 11 wickets for 143 runs, average 13.00.

For Victoria v. New South Wales he played 50 innings, twice not out, highest score 129, total runs 1,295, average 26.97; and took 12 wickets for 372 runs, average 31.00.

His big innings in first-class matches were:

141*	Australians v. Gloucestershire, at Clifton	..	..	..	..	..	1882
129	Victoria v. New South Wales, at Melbourne	..	..	..	..	..	1882–83
126	Victoria v. New South Wales, at Melbourne	..	..	..	..	..	1883–84
124	Australia v. England, at Melbourne	..	..	..	..	..	1881–82
117*	Victoria v. England, at Melbourne	..	..	..	..	..	1886–87
113	Victoria v. South Australia, at Melbourne	..	..	..	..	..	1880–81
112	Australia v. United XI, at Chichester	..	..	..	..	..	1882
102	Victoria v. New South Wales, at Sydney	..	..	..	..	..	1881–82
95	Victoria v. New South Wales, at Melbourne	..	..	..	..	..	1881–82

Signifies not out.

The highest innings of his career was 250 not out for East Melbourne v. Tasmania at East Melbourne in December, 1879: he batted about 10 hours and gave no chance. It was a two-day match: East Melbourne scored 742, and the Tasmanians had no innings.

HORDERN, Dr. H. V., who died on June 17, 1938, aged 54, was a googly bowler of exceptional merit. Medical studies limited his appearances in first-class cricket and he could not spare time to visit England with an Australian side but the cables of his doings against the team that went to Australia in the winter of 1911–12 caused a sensation. In the Test matches he took 32 wickets at an average cost of 24.37, an achievement little less remarkable than that of Sidney Barnes who, with 34 wickets at 22.88 apiece, was largely responsible for England winning four matches and the rubber. In the first encounter which England lost on the sixth day by 146 runs Hordern took 12 wickets for 195 runs. By wonderful batting, Hobbs, Rhodes, Hearne and Woolley mastered Hordern for long periods in the subsequent Tests, but the sudden rise of this bowler created a great impression on the players whom J. W. H. T. Douglas led on the field because of the illness of P. F. Warner, who went out as captain of the side. A useful batsman, Hordern averaged 21.62 in these five matches. In a few Sheffield Shield games for New South Wales Hordern took 18 wickets for less than 14 runs apiece. In 1907 Hordern came over with the Pennsylvania University team and met with great success against the English Schools. He had a bowling average of 9.68 for 110 wickets and scored 391 runs, average 21.72.

HORLICK, Lieut.-Col. Sir James Nockells, Bart., who died on the Isle of Gigha on December 31, 1972, aged 86, was in the Eton XI in 1904, taking six wickets for 90 runs against Harrow at Lord's. Though he did not get a Blue at Oxford, he played for Gloucestershire between 1907 and 1910. He served with the Coldstream Guards during the First World War in France, the Balkans and South Russia, being four times Mentioned in Dispatches and awarded the Military Cross, the Legion of Honour and the White Eagle of Serbia.

HORNBY, Albert Henry, who died at North Kilworth, near Rugby, on September 6, 1952, aged 75, captained Lancashire from 1908 to 1914. Born on July 29, 1877, the son of A. N. ("Monkey") Hornby, of England cricket and Rugby football fame, he first appeared for the county in 1899, and during his career he scored 9,541 runs, average 24.78, with 129 against Surrey at the Oval in 1912 his highest innings. Also in 1912, Hornby (96) shared in a partnership of 245 in two and a half hours with J. Sharp (211) against Leicestershire at Old Trafford, a Lancashire seventh-wicket record which still stands. Another noteworthy performance of this free-hitting batsman occurred in 1905 when, going in No. 9, he hit 106 from the Somerset bowling at Old Trafford, he and W. Findlay who afterwards became Secretary of M.C.C., adding 113 in half an hour for the ninth wicket.

The following appreciation by Mr. Neville Cardus appeared in the *Manchester Guardian*: "Those who were boys at Old Trafford just before the War of 1914 will wish to express gratitude for the pleasure given by the cricket of A. H. Hornby. He was no mere chip from the old block; any metaphor suggestive of solidity, woodenness, or any object or body not endowed with spirit and volition is out of place in a discussion or description of the Hornbys. Albert, like his father, played the game for fun, and would have been as ashamed to refuse the challenge of a good ball as the challenge of a stiff jump on the hunting field.

"A batsman so constituted and sharing his ideas might easily seem eccentric and anachronistic nowadays. He was known as a dashing batsman. We used strange categories in those old-fashioned years so as to get our players in their right degree and pedigree. There were also stonewallers; one in every county XI but not more than one as a rule, though Warwickshire boasted two, Quaife and Kinneir, each of whom scored his centuries at the rate of 25 runs an hour, which is the speed of our contemporary "Masters."

"Albert Hornby for years was content to go in for Lancashire number seven or eight in the batting order; and usually he sustained an average of round about 23–28 an innings. Considering the quality of first-class bowling then and first-class bowling now, Hornby's figures can safely be raised in the present currency to 32 an innings. He played for the Gentlemen against the Players at Lord's in 1914, went in first, and in the second innings, in spite of a nasty wicket, scored 69 ("hitting brilliantly," says *Wisden*) against the attack of Barnes, Hitch, Tarrant, Kennedy and J. W. Hearne—and what an attack! He batted in the manner of C. S. Barnett and H. Gimblett, not as good and as well organised as either maybe, but he was in the same class. We could always be sure that if he stayed at the wicket half an hour he would for certain show us every time at least six great and thrilling strokes. Only of Gimblett can as much as this be said in 1952.

"He was a gallant and purposeful captain for Lancashire, and a superb fieldsman. To this day I can see his catch near the off-side boundary at Old Trafford in June, 1906; he ran yards like a hare to hold a really magnificent hit by E. W. Dillon of Kent. It was in this same match that on Whit Thursday J. T. Tyldesley scored 295 not out and was fielding at third man at six o'clock; Lancashire had made 531 at more than 100 an hour. This was Woolley's first game in County Cricket; he missed one or two catches—one of them gave Tyldesley a second innings at about 130; he was bowled by Cuttell for none and took one wicket for a hundred odd. But in Kent's second innings he drove and cut in a way that heralded the coming of a new and incomparable star.

"Perhaps Hornby himself would wish to be remembered most of all at Old Trafford for his innings of 55 not out against Nottinghamshire in June, 1910. On the third day—a Saturday—Nottinghamshire, all out second innings, left Lancashire 403 to get to win in five and a quarter hours. Tyldesley and Sharp attacked ruthlessly and scored 191 in two and a half hours. But there was work to do after they had both got out, and Hornby, so we thought, would not bat because of lameness. At the pinch he hobbled to the field on invisible crutches. He scarcely needed his runner; he drove right and left—off the back foot, an unusual position for any Hornby to be seen in during the act of belabouring a bowler. Lancashire won the match—403 in a fourth innings in less than five and a quarter hours. On this occasion—and I can remember no other—the crowd rushed across the field to cheer the conquering heroes near the pavilion. One small boy remained gazing in awe at the wicket on which only a few moments ago his heroes had stood and walked and run and played. He was mightily impressed by the depth of the holes made by the bowlers. ... O my Hornby and my Tyldesley long ago!"

HORNBY, Albert Neilson, the famous batsman who captained Lancashire for nearly 20 seasons, and whose association with that county as a player extended over a period of 33 years, was born at Blackburn on February 10, 1847, and died at Parkfield, Nantwich, on December 17, 1925. Going up to Harrow in 1862, he played against Eton at Lord's in 1864 and 1865, his first appearance there taking place 13 days before that of W. G. Grace. At that time, Hornby was of such slight physique that he weighed ("bat and all," according to one account) less than 6st. He took part in a match between Lancashire and Yorkshire at Whalley in 1867, but two more years elapsed before that close and active connection with the Lancashire XI, that only ceased in 1899, really commenced.

For many seasons one of the leading English batsmen, Hornby had an attractive forward style, and possessed splendid punishing powers which he used freely. In addition, he was a magnificent field, and as a captain so firm, keen and genial that he could always get the best out of the men under his charge. His dashing methods, coupled with his obvious enthusiasm—he appeared thoroughly to enjoy every moment he was on the field—made him a general favourite wherever he went.

The extent to which he dominated matters as a run-getter during his prime may be gauged from the fact that during the 12 years, 1870 to 1881 inclusive, he was the only batsman to reach three-figures for Lancashire, and that during that period he did so on seven occasions—three times in 1881, in which season he was credited with the largest aggregate and highest average of any player in the country, his figures being respectively, 1,531 and 41.38. Of the hundreds he made for Lancashire the highest was his 188 v. Derbyshire at Old Trafford in 1881, but of more merit was his 161 against Surrey at Liverpool in 1886. He and R. G. Barlow formed perhaps the most famous first-wicket pair of their time, and although Hornby's impulsiveness often led to Barlow being run out, they enjoyed many memorable successes. Among these were the putting on of 191 against Oxford University at Manchester in 1886, 180 against Middlesex at Lord's in 1882 and 157 against Derbyshire at Manchester in 1881. Their greatest triumph, however, was achieved in the match with Yorkshire at Manchester in 1875, when Lancashire, set 146 to win, scored 148 without loss, Hornby making 78 of the number and his partner 50. The performance, which would have been a noteworthy one even on the smoother grounds of more recent years, made quite a sensation at the time, such a feat being without parallel.

In the course of his career, Hornby put together 17 hundreds in first-class matches—10 of these being for Lancashire, and two for the M.C.C.—while in 1873 he made 104 for Gentlemen against Players at Prince's and four years later 144 for Gentlemen against Players at the Oval. Between 1869 and 1885 he represented the Gentlemen against the Players on 31 occasions, scoring 1,221 runs in those matches and, only once not out, having an average of 24.42. Hornby played twice for England against Australia, captaining the side that at the Oval in 1882 lost by seven runs, and also figuring in the Test match at Manchester in 1884. He went out to America in August, 1872, with the side got together by Mr. R. A. Fitzgerald, at that time the Secretary of the M.C.C., and also formed one of the team that Lord Harris took to Australia in the winter of 1878–79. For many years he was President of the Lancashire County Club and also a member of the M.C.C. Committee.

Hornby figured in that memorable match at Lord's in May, 1878, when a very powerful M.C.C. XI lost to the Australians by nine wickets, 31 wickets going down for an aggregate of 105 runs and the game being all over in a day. In the second innings of the M.C.C. Hornby in playing Spofforth met with an injury of so severe a description that it compelled his retirement and would certainly have kept most men out of the field for a week or so, but such was his indomitable pluck that with his side faring disastrously— they were all out for 19—he came out to resume his innings. The painful experience, however, probably shook even his splendid nerve, for, although he remained one of England's leading batsmen for several years afterwards, his only notable score against Spofforth was one of 94 for the North in 1884.

Another incident in Hornby's career was that on the Sydney ground when Lord Harris's team played there in February, 1879. Annoyed with an umpire's decision the crowd burst on to the field and a "larrikin" struck Lord Harris with a stick. Hornby seized the offender and although hit in the face and having his shirt nearly torn off his back he conveyed his prisoner to the pavilion.

A characteristic tale of the famous batsman concerned the Gentlemen and Players match at the Oval in 1881. Hornby and W. G. Grace had given the amateurs a capital start when, from a powerful drive, Hornby was magnificently caught high up in the long field by William Gunn, who stood some 6ft. 3in. in height. "Bad luck, Monkey" said a friend as Hornby passed into the pavilion. "Yes," answered Hornby, "no one but a damned giraffe would have got near it."

In addition to being one of the most famous cricketers of his day, A. N. Hornby took high rank as a Rugby football player in the late '70s and early '80s. He appeared five times for North v. South, and nine times for England—on four occasions against Scotland and on five against Ireland. All through his life he was a keen rider to hounds, and after his football days he spent most of the winter in the hunting field, but of late years lameness prevented him from enjoying any form of activity.

HORNBY, Edgar Christian, who was born on September 14, 1863, died on April 2, 1922. He was a cousin of Mr. A. N. Hornby, and was educated at Winchester, but was not in the XI whilst there. From 1885 to 1887, however, he played several times for Lancashire, making 82 against the University at Oxford in 1886 and 64 v. M.C.C. at Lord's in 1885. For years he was associated most

prominently with the Liverpool C.C., succeeding Mr. Arthur Kemble in the captaincy and being invariably included in the district teams against Yorkshire, the Australians and other important sides. Like his father, Mr. H. H. Hornby, he became President of the club, and many times he took part in the Liverpool Public Schools' tour. Against Marlborough he scored 100 in 1892 and 127 in 1888. He was left-handed both as batsman and bowler.

HORNER, Charles Edward, born at Dulwich on April 9, 1857, died at Gloucester Terrace, Regent's Park, on September 4, 1925, aged 68. Cricketers, and more especially Surrey cricketers, learned with sincere regret of Mr. Horner's death. His illness was very brief, extending over scarcely a week. He had a short career in the Surrey XI—practically only four seasons—but as a member of the committee he remained to the end closely connected with the club. His interest in cricket never declined, and on most afternoons in the summer he was to be found at the Oval or Lord's. He came out for Surrey in 1882. The county's fortunes were then at a low ebb, but the great revival, with the late John Shuter as captain, was close at hand. As a right-handed bowler—medium-pace to fast—Horner did excellent work. He was at his best in 1884, taking in that season over 100 wickets for a trifle less than 15 runs apiece. A persevering bowler whom nothing perturbed, he could by the hour keep a length on or just outside the off stump. He had no pretensions as a batsman but his nerves were strong and at Gravesend in 1885 he helped George Lohmann to win a sensational match for Surrey against Kent by one wicket. Thirty-two runs were wanted when he went in and the game looked all over. At this distance of time there can be no harm in saying that the Kent team felt sure he was out when an appeal for a catch by the wicket-keeper was answered in his favour. Mr. Horner took a keen interest in billiards and, for an amateur, played a very good game. In his later years he was prominently associated with the Billiards Control Club.— S.H.P.

HORNIBROOK, Percy M., who died at Brisbane on Agusut 23, 1976, aged 77, was a bowler of whom Australia probably ought to have made more use in the 1920s. Possibly the fact that his State, Queensland, was not admitted to the Sheffield Shield until 1926 made it harder for him to gain recognition. A tall slow-medium left-hander with a loose arm and a good action, he was prepared to open the bowling with swingers and then after a few overs would reduce his pace and begin to spin and flight the ball. He first attracted attention by taking 81 wickets at an average of nine, on a tour of New Zealand in 1920 and many thought he should have been included in the 1921 side to England, which was distinctly weak in slow-wicket bowling, though in the event it did not require it.

There was far greater surprise when he was omitted from the 1926 side, and no less a judge than M. A. Noble advocated his inclusion. He would at least have saved Macartney from being bowled to death in the early weeks of the tour and in the vital last Test on a rain-affected pitch he might easily have tipped the scales in Australia's favour. It was not until he was 30 in 1929 that he got a place in the fifth Test against A. P. F. Chapman's side: he was given the new ball and bowled well without spectacular success.

Chosen at last to go to England in 1930, he came second in the bowling averages with 96 wickets at 18.77, but did nothing in the Tests until the last one. Then in the second innings on a turning wicket, his analysis read 31.2—9—92—7 and he had much to do with England losing the match and the Ashes after making 405 in the first innings. But his figures suggest, what good critics confirm, that he bowled far too many bad balls: one indeed said that "bogey" for a good slow left-hander on that wicket would have been seven for 30. Perhaps had he had longer experience of English conditions he would have been better. At any rate by then he was past his peak—his arm had dropped and he was more full-chested. At the end of the tour he retired from first-class cricket.

HORNUNG, Ernest William, who died at St. Jean-de-Luz, Basses-Pyrénées, on March 22, 1921, aged 54, was a keen cricketer, but was not in the XI whilst at Uppingham. He married a sister of Sir A. Conan Doyle.

HORSFALL, Richard, died on August 25, 1981, aged 61. Born at Todmorden, he had played League cricket for them before joining Essex in 1947. In his first season he showed great promise, especially in an innings of 170 against Hampshire at Bournemouth, and in 1948, when he scored 1,407 runs with an average of 31.97, this promise seemed likely to be fulfilled. Unfortunately in 1949 he could play little owing to back trouble and he was still labouring under the handicap in 1950. In 1951 his aggregate was 1,665, his average 35.21, and against Kent at

Blackheath he made 206, the highest score of his career, in four and half hours and added 343 for the third wicket with Paul Gibb, an Essex record. He followed this with an aggregate of 1,560 (average 33.91) in 1952 and in 1953 with 1,731 runs (average 37.63). His five centuries in the latter year included one against Warwickshire at Edgbaston made in 85 minutes, which was the fastest of the season. This season was the climax of his career. In 1954 he was again handicapped by his back and the slow wickets did not suit him. In 1955 his form was so poor that he was not re-engaged, and although in 1956 he played a match or two for Glamorgan without success, a career which had been so full of promise ended disappointingly at 36. A fine driver and cutter, he was always primarily a fast-wicket bat, though his play on slow wickets improved as time went on. He was a good field.

HORSFIELD, Gordon Cameron, who died in Sydney in September, 1982, aged 69, was a left-handed batsman who played five times for New South Wales between 1934–35 and 1941–42, though with modest success.

HORSLEY, James, was born at Melbourne, Derbyshire, on January 4, 1890, and died at Derby on February 13, 1976, aged 86. He lived in Nottingham for some years where he came to the fore as a fast medium bowler, playing for Nottinghamshire in three matches in 1913 with little profit. Horsley was an immediate success when appearing for his native county in 1914, taking four or more wickets in an innings on eight occasions in 13 matches to head the county's bowling averages. In addition he shared a record last wicket stand of 93 with Humphries in his fourth match, which remains the club record. Horsley reappeared in 1919 and took six for 55 (including the hat-trick) and six for 62 when Derbyshire was the only county to defeat the Australian I.F. XI. He played for Burnley for the next three years, but returned in 1923 and took 170 wickets in three seasons, showing he was still a more than useful bowler, especially on helpful pitches. He went back to League cricket in Lancashire before spending two summers with Aberdeenshire and then became professional to several clubs in Northern Ireland up to the outbreak of war. During his county career he was almost invariably given in initial W. in *Wisden*. His complete first-class record in 87 matches: 132 innings, 32 not outs, 1,367 runs, 66 highest score, 13.67 average; 267 wickets, 5,412 runs, 20.26; 47

catches. He was related to J. H. Young who played for the county 1899–1901.

HORSPOOL, Ernest, who died at Auckland on June 21, 1957, aged 65, was a dependable batsman for Auckland and played for New Zealand in an "unofficial" Test match with the Australian touring side of 1913–14. In a first-class career extending over 19 years, he scored 1,686 runs, average 24.43, his highest innings being 143 out of 212 added with N. C. Sneddon for the second Auckland wicket against Victoria, on tour in New Zealand, in 1924–25.

HORTON, Thomas, who died at Bilton House, near Rugby, on June 18, 1932, at the age of 61, was born on May 16, 1871. A member of the Repton School XI in 1889 and 1890 and in his playing days a fine forcing batsman and keen fielder, he captained Northamptonshire in 1905 and 1906—the first two seasons of their career as a first-class county. From 1921 to 1924 he was President of the County Club.

HOSIF, Alec L., who died on June 11, 1957, aged 66, played periodically for Hampshire between 1913 and 1935 when on leave from India. He was educated at St. Lawrence College, Ramsgate, and Magdalen College, Oxford, where he gained Blues for hockey, lawn tennis and Association football. A quick-footed, hard-hitting batsman, he scored 4,176 runs in first-class cricket, average 26.10. His best season for the county was that of 1928, when, with 1,187 runs, average 31.23, he stood third in the Hampshire averages. That summer he made his highest score, 155 against Yorkshire at Southampton, and he also hit two centuries against Middlesex—132 at Portsmouth and 106 at Lord's.

HOSKIN, Worthington Wynn, who died at East London, South Africa, on March 4, 1956, aged 71, appeared in five matches for Gloucestershire in 1912. While at Oxford University he received only one trial in the cricket XI, but played as a forward against Cambridge in the Rugby football matches of 1904–05–06–07.

HOSKYNS, Canon Sir John Leigh, Ninth Bart., died suddenly at Bournemouth on December 8, 1911. Born on February 4, 1817, he was the oldest Rugbeian, and had played for the Sixth and the School as far back as 1835. He had been Rector of Aston Tyrrold, Berkshire, since 1845. His golden wedding was celebrated in 1906, and he was survived by his wife, then in her 95th year.

HOTHAM, Admiral Sir Alan G., who died on July 10, 1965, aged 88, played for Hampshire against Lancashire at Portsmouth in 1901. He also assisted Devon.

HOUGH, Capt. Gerald de Lisle, who died on September 29, 1959, aged 65, played for Kent in 1919 and 1920. In the XI at Winchester from 1911 to 1913, he was captain in the last year. After service in the First World War with the Royal West Kent Regiment, he appeared for the county before becoming a master for 10 years at Bradfield College. In 1936 he took over the position first of manager and later secretary to the Kent club, continuing till ill-health compelled his resignation in 1949. An aggressive batsman and slow off-break bowler, he took a wicket with the first ball he sent down in first-class cricket, but that was his only success for, handicapped by a war-time wound in the arm, he rarely bowled afterwards. It was suggested on occasion that his name should be included in *Wisden* in the list of those who have scored a century upon debut in first-class cricket, for he hit 30 not out and 87 not out for Lionel Robinson's XI against the Australian Imperial Forces team of 1919.

HOUSTON, Richard, who died in Melbourne in November, 1921, was a very good wicket-keeper but, being contemporary with Blackham, did not appear frequently in the Victoria XI. He was captain of North Melbourne and, later, played for Williamstown.

HOWARD, Charles, born at Chichester, September 27, 1854, died there on May 20, 1929, aged 74. Well above the average as a batsman, he was for many years a well-known figure in Sussex cricket, though his appearances for the county itself were restricted to 25 matches between 1874 and 1882. In those games he made 647 runs, his highest innings being 106 v. Hampshire at Hove in 1880. In June, 1886, the match at Chichester between Lord March's XI and the Australians was given to him for his benefit. In club cricket he obtained many large scores including one of 300 not out for Goodwood Park v. Westbourne on the former's ground in August, 1884: he went in first wicket down, at eight, and carried out his bat when the innings closed for 476. He also made 219 for Priory Park v. City Ramblers at Chichester in August, 1885. In later years he owned some race horses of which the most famous was Priory Park.

HOWARD, H. C., who died on September 18, 1960, was at one time a fine opening batsman for Western Australia, of whose Cricket Association he became a vice-president. In 1908 at Perth, "Tim" Howard and H. Rowe shared a first-wicket stand of 175 against the M.C.C. touring team, then a record for the State.

HOWARD, Nigel David, died suddenly in the Isle of Man, where he had lived since his retirement from business three years earlier, on May 31, 1979, aged 54. He headed the Rossall batting averages in 1941 and 1942 and, making his first appearance for Lancashire in 1946, obtained a regular place in 1948 when he made the highest score of his career, 145 v. Derbyshire at Old Trafford. In 1949 he took over the captaincy, which he retained until he retired from first-class cricket after the season of 1953 in order to devote himself to the family textile business. He was the youngest player ever to captain Lancashire. However, greatly helped by Washbrook, his senior professional, he led the county to the top of the table in 1950, captaining the Gentlemen at Lord's in 1951 and taking the M.C.C. side to India and Pakistan at the end of that year. Unluckily he missed the latter part of this tour through illness. An attractive bat with a good range of strokes, especially when runs were wanted quickly, he did much valuable work for his county. His best seasons were 1948, when he scored 944 runs with an average of 36.30, and 1950, when his aggregate was 1,124 and his average 36.68. Later he served on the Lancashire committee and was for a time chairman of the cricket committee. He also represented Cheshire at hockey and golf. He came of cricketing stock; both his father, for some years secretary at Old Trafford, and his younger brother played for Lancashire.

HOWE, Lieut. Gilbert (New Zealand Reinforcements), born at Wellington (N.Z.), killed January, 1917. Left-hand bat and good wicket-keeper. Played for Wellington (N.Z.) in inter-Provincial matches. In 1913–14 season had a batting average of 15.44 for Wellington in representative games, and in the four matches caught five and stumped four.

HOWELL, Harry, a famous fast bowler, died at Birmingham on July 9, 1932. Born at Birmingham on November 29, 1890, Howell first played for Warwickshire in the season of 1913 when, at the age of 22, he appeared for the county in three matches. A year later he had fully established himself as a member of the team, participating in 17 matches and helping to form, in company with F. R. Foster, F. E. Field and P. Jeeves, as strong an attack as that of any first-class county. Taking a fairly long run and bowling with a nice easy action, Howell was distinctly a fast bowler, without, however, possessing the special gift of extra pace off the pitch.

After the War, he met with much success for several years. In 1920, he obtained 161 wickets in all matches for just under 18 runs each and in 1923 he secured 152 wickets for Warwickshire for less than 20 runs apiece. In the latter season he enjoyed the distinction at Edgbaston of taking all 10 Yorkshire wickets in the first innings of that county for 51 runs. A year later on the same ground he and Calthorpe between them dismissed Hampshire for 15. Howell in the course of four overs and five balls, took six wickets for seven runs, the other four falling to Calthorpe for four runs. This was one of the most amazing of matches, for Hampshire, after following on 208 in arrear, hit up a total of 521 and in the end won by 155 runs.

Howell played four times for England against Australia—twice at Melbourne and once at Adelaide for the team led by J. W. H. T. Douglas in 1920–21, and also at Nottingham in the first Test match of 1921. He accomplished nothing of note in these matches, but must have had a very different record had he been given proper support in the field. From all accounts the slip fieldsmen, early in each of the three matches in Australia, failed him wretchedly. Chosen to assist the Players against the Gentlemen in 1920, he secured six wickets for 40 runs in the second innings of the Oval match and at Lord's took six wickets in all for 13 runs apiece. He dropped out of first-class cricket in 1929.

As an Association football player he appeared at times for Wolverhampton Wanderers, Port Vale and Stoke.

HOWELL, 2nd Lieutenant John (King's Royal Rifle Corps), was killed in Flanders on September 25, 1915. Among all the young cricketers who have fallen in the War not one of brighter promise than John Howell can be named. Judging from his wonderful record at Repton it is not too much to say that he was potentially an England batsman. But for the War he would have been at Oxford last year and would no doubt have been seen in the Surrey XI at the Oval. Born on July 5, 1895, he was only 20 when he lost his life. He was in the Repton team for four seasons—1911 to 1914—being captain in 1914. From the first he showed great promise as a batsman, his style having obviously been modelled on that of Tom Hayward. He did well in 1911 and 1912, and in the next two years he was probably the best school bat in England. In 1913 he scored 737 runs for Repton, with an average of 56, and in 1914, 686 runs with an average of 52. He took some little time to find his form in school cricket in 1914, but he scored 202 not out against the Old Reptonians and 202 against Uppingham. In a trial match at the Oval at the beginning of the season he played an innings of 109. In 1913 he scored 108 and 114 against the Old Reptonians, and 144 for Young Surrey Amateurs against Young Essex Amateurs. Towards the close of the season in 1913 he journeyed up to Walsall with Surrey's Second XI for the express purpose of playing against Barnes's bowling and had the satisfaction of scoring 45.

HOWELL, Leonard Sidgwick (Winchester and Surrey), who died on September 7, 1895, was a valuable member of the Surrey XI at a time when the fortunes of the county were at a very low ebb. He was born at Dulwich on August 6, 1848, and after playing in the Winchester XI in 1864, 1865 and 1866, played first for Surrey in 1869. He was a fine, free hitter and, without ever making a great name for himself, scored well so long as he kept up the game. He appeared first at Lord's for Surrey against the M.C.C. on May 14, 1872. The match, in which play was impossible on the first day owing to rain, was finished off on the second day in very sensational fashion. The M.C.C., who went in first, lost seven wickets without a run, and were all out for 16. In the end Surrey won the game by five wickets.

HOWELL, Miles, who died at his home at Worplesdon on February 23, 1976, aged 82, went up to Oxford after having a fine record as captain of Repton in 1913, and at once made his Blue safe by scoring 121 in the Freshmen's match and following this with 123 against Kent in his second match for the University. After serving through the War and being wounded, he returned to Oxford in 1919 and captained them at both cricket and football. He headed their batting averages with fine figures and in the Varsity match played a great innings of 170. Cambridge were strong favourites, but when Oxford won the toss on a sodden ground and

batted, Howell and Donald Knight made 70 for the first wicket. From then on wickets fell steadily until Frank Gilligan contributed a cheerful 70 at number eight. Everything depended on Howell; he was in no position to take risks and his innings lasted five hours and 40 minutes. He scored largely on the leg, which was inadequately guarded, and the slowness of the outfield can be gauged from the fact that he hit only three fours as against 15 threes and 66 singles. It was probably fatigue from the amount of running involved that caused him to be stumped when three short of the record. As in the second innings he threw out Brooke-Taylor brilliantly just when he looked like winning the match for Cambridge, he was largely responsible for Oxford's victory by 45 runs.

From 1920 to 1925 he played for Surrey whenever they could get him, though it usually meant that some pro whom other counties would have welcomed with open arms had to stand down for him. Apart from his batting, his brilliant out-fielding was a strong point in his favour. After 1925 his first-class cricket was largely confined to playing for the Free Foresters at Oxford, which he continued to do until 1939 with no apparent diminution of skill.

A small man, of the typical soccer forward's build, who always played in spectacles, he was a good defensive player, particularly strong on the leg-side, but he had all the strokes and was never dull to watch. Indeed in club cricket he would often bat brilliantly. Cricket was in his blood. His father and his uncle had both played for Surrey and his younger brother, John, who was killed in action in 1915, was regarded by good judges as a future England player.

Miles Howell played for The Corinthians and gained several Amateur international caps. Apart from his own achievements as a cricketer and footballer he deserves to be remembered for the wonderful work he did in getting both games going again on the right lines at Oxford in 1919.

HOWELL, Reginald, who played in three matches for Surrey in 1878 and 1879, died at Esher on August 3, 1912. He was born at Streatham on April 16, 1856, and was educated at Tonbridge, but, leaving at the age of 15, was not in the XI. *Scores and Biographies* (xiv–886) says of him: "Is a good batsman, bowls slow round-armed, and fields generally at cover-point." He had served on the Committee of the Surrey County C.C.

HOWELL, William P., the Australian

bowler, died on July 14, 1940, aged 70, at Sydney. No one has made a more sensational first appearance in England than did "Bill" Howell when, in the third match of Darling's team in 1899, he dismissed the whole Surrey XI. His analysis, 23.2 overs, 14 maidens, 28 runs, 10 wickets, indicates this exceptional performance as being quite out of the ordinary, no matter what the state of the pitch. As the natural effect of this achievement, Howell, after being left out of the first two engagements, became a regular member of the side. He did little in the five Tests, taking only eight wickets at 43 runs apiece, but if unable to live up to such a start, Howell for the whole season came out with a record of 117 wickets at 20.35 apiece, his average placing him between Hugh Trumble and Ernest Jones, who each dismissed more batsmen.

Visiting England with the next two Australian teams, Howell took fewer wickets but at smaller cost—68 for 17.86 each and 79 for 19.34 each.

He began Test cricket by bowling A. C. MacLaren in both the Adelaide matches in the season of 1898–99, when the Lancashire amateur averaged 54. Altogether Howell appeared on 16 occasions for Australia without accomplishing anything exceptional, though bowling wonderfully well at Melbourne in 1904. At a time when the Australian attack was very strong, his Test record showed 35 wickets at an average cost of 35.57. For New South Wales in Sheffield Shield matches he claimed 159 wickets, average 23.55.

Of good height and heavily built, Howell made full use of his strong wrist and fingers in spinning the ball at medium pace. Usually, command of length gave him special ability, and he was deadly against batsmen unaware that his simple-looking delivery imparted unexpected life from the pitch. Howell showed this merit for New South Wales in November, 1894, when he clean bowled five of A. E. Stoddart's team, including the captain and J. T. Brown, the Yorkshireman, while yielding only 44 runs—a happy introduction to his experiences against English cricketers.

A left-handed batsman, he sometimes startled the bowlers and the crowd by tremendous hitting. A notable case was at Sydney against Stoddart's team in 1898. Going in last for New South Wales, he hit up 48 in three-quarters of an hour and eclipsed this in the second innings with 95 in less than an hour, 76 of these runs coming in boundaries. For the most part in England, as well

as in all Test matches, Howell did little with the bat, but in Sheffield Shield matches he averaged 22.86 for an aggregate of 1,029 runs, with 128 his best score.

In Test matches against South Africa, Howell took 14 wickets at 12.42 runs apiece. He turned the ball a lot on the matting pitches.

A bee farmer in Penrith, New South Wales, Howell was a local celebrity alike for his cricketing ability and genial character.

HOWLETT, Brigadier Bernard, D.S.O. and Bar (Royal West Kent Regiment), was killed in action in November, 1943, aged 44. Educated at St. Edmund's School, Canterbury, he played occasionally for Kent under the residential qualification from 1922, and for the Army. Bowling fast right-hand, he took 46 wickets at 41.50 runs apiece in first-class cricket.

HOWORTH, Richard, died in hospital on April 2, 1980, aged 70. A slow left-arm bowler, who kept an immaculate length and could spin and flight the ball, an attacking left-handed batsman, who usually appeared in the middle of the order but was prepared to open if wanted, and a good field close to the wicket, he did great service for Worcestershire from 1933 to 1951, scoring for them 10,538 runs at an average of 20.20, taking 1,274 wickets at 21.36 and holding 188 catches. Three times, in 1939, 1946 and 1947 he achieved the double in all matches, and he played five times for England. Born at Bacup, he appeared for Worcestershire in 1933 against the West Indians while qualifying and in the first innings was top scorer with 68. Qualified in 1934, he was disappointing, but in 1935 he jumped right to the front, heading the bowling averages with 121 wickets at 18.94, and from that time he never looked back. In 1936 he played an important part in Worcestershire's sensational victory over Yorkshire, their first since 1909: in the second innings he took five for 21. Later that summer he made the first and highest of his three centuries in County Cricket—114 in two hours and 10 minutes v. Kent at Dover, scored out of 180 for the first wicket—and followed it by taking, in the two innings, eight for 91. Before the War, with Verity available, there was little chance in the England side for any other slow left-armer, but in 1947 Howorth was picked for the final Test v. South Africa at the Oval and proved a great success. He took six wickets in the match, including one with his first ball, and was described in *Wisden* as "far the best

England bowler"; he also scored 23 and 45 not out and made two fine catches in the gully. That winter he went with M.C.C. to West Indies under G. O. Allen and played in all four Tests: so important was his steadiness to a weak attack that he was not left out of a single match. But the West Indies is not the ideal place for left-arm spin and his wickets were costly.

In his early days Howorth owed much to his captain, the Hon. C. J. Lyttelton, later Lord Cobham, who, whenever he showed signs of shortening his length and bowling too fast, insisted that he should pitch the ball up and flight it more. When in 1951, at the age of 42, he announced his retirement after a season in which he had headed the Worcestershire bowling averages with 118 wickets at 17.97 and appeared to be bowling as well as ever, Lord Cobham, upon asking him why he was retiring, received the reply, "Because it's not as much fun as it was." Howorth played later for Stourbridge in the Birmingham League, served for many years on the Worcestershire Committee and ran a newsagent's shop across the river from the Worcester ground. He was much liked and respected, though the partial disenchantment which prompted his retirement from the firstclass game was never quite thrown off.

HUBBARD, George Cairns, who died suddenly at Eltham on December 18, 1931, aged 64, was a member of the Tonbridge cricket XI in 1884 and following year and played three times for Kent in 1895. The mainstay of the Blackheath Cricket and Football Clubs for many years, he secured, like his son "J. C.," England International honours at Rugby football.

HUBBLE, John Charlton, who died on February 26, 1965, aged 84, was one of a trio of great wicket-keepers, who, playing in succession for Kent, spanned well over half a century. He succeeded F. H. Huish and was succeeded by L. E. G. Ames. Hubble served his county as a professional from 1904 to 1929, helping them on the last occasion they carried off the County Championship in 1913. In that time he scored over 10,000 runs and helped in the dismissal of more than 500 batsmen.

A beautiful exponent of off-side strokes, he was played until 1919 chiefly for his rungetting ability and it was not until after the First World War that he took over as regular wicket-keeper. Though a consistent batsmen, he hit only five centuries in his long career, the highest being 189, put together in

less than three hours, against Sussex at Tunbridge Wells in 1911. His best performance as a wicket-keeper was at Cheltenham in 1923, when he disposed of 10 batsmen in the match, six in the first innings and four in the second. He held nine catches and brought off one stumping. He took part in the match with Yorkshire at Harrogate in 1904 which was declared void because the pitch had been tampered with. Holes, clearly obvious at the close of play on the first day, had been filled in before the second morning, and though play continued so that the crowd should not be disappointed, the match was not allowed to count in the Championship. Schofield Haigh, the Yorkshire and England medium-pace bowler, tried his hand at slow leg-breaks in the Kent second innings and performed the hat-trick.

For a number of years Hubble acted as coach in South Africa.

HUDDLESTON, William, who died on May 22, 1962, aged 87, did capital service to Lancashire as a medium-paced off-break bowler between 1899 and 1914, taking in that time 684 wickets at an average cost of 17.58. For some years a League engagement prevented him playing in as many matches for Lancashire as they would have liked; yet when he did become fully available he was often omitted from the county XI. As *Wisden* recorded in 1910: "He has suffered from the notion of the Committee that, although almost unplayable on sticky wickets, he was no good at all on firm turf." Certainly most of Huddleston's best performances were achieved on rain-affected pitches and on one occasion at Tunbridge Wells in 1908 the conditions were such that A. H. Hornby summoned him specially to the ground by telegram after he had been left out of the team. At the same time he was rarely easy to punish.

His best analysis in a single innings was nine wickets for 36 runs against Nottinghamshire at Liverpool in 1906, when his match-figures of 13 for 41 were also his best. He was a member of the side which in 1904 carried off the Championship without suffering defeat. Lancashire looked like losing at the Oval where Surrey, set 337 to get to win, obtained 206 for two wickets by lunchtime on the last day. Then, with sunshine following a shower, the last eight batsmen were dismissed for 60, Huddleston coming out with figures of seven wickets for 72 runs.

Three times he dismissed 12 batsmen in a match: for 82 runs v. Surrey; for 186 v. Warwickshire in 1907, and for 89 v. Leicestershire in 1913, all at Old Trafford. His most successful season as a bowler was that of 1913, when he took 113 wickets at a cost of 19.68 runs each. No mean batsman, he played his biggest innings, 88, against Yorkshire at Sheffield in 1914, he and James Tyldesley (62 not out) putting on 141 in 90 minutes, which fell only one short of the record for the Lancashire ninth wicket. His benefit that season yielded £896.

HUDSON, John Lambert, who died on March 16, 1961, aged 78, played in seven first-class matches for Tasmania between 1907 and 1912. A solid right-handed batsman, he scored 308 runs, average 31.80. He made his highest score, 94, against New South Wales in 1910–11, when he shared a record fourth-wicket stand of 163 with W. K. Eltham. Next season he hit 51 from an M.C.C. attack including S. F. Barnes and F. R. Foster. In domestic cricket in 1908–09, he hit 1,052 runs, average 85.63. His partnership of 348 with R. J. Hawson for South v. North Tasmania in 1910 was a record for any wicket in this fixture.

HUGGINS, Harry J., a Gloucestershire professional from 1901 to 1921, died on November 19, 1942, at Stroud, aged 65. He started when G. L. Jessop made the Western county an attraction wherever they played, and some of his remarkable performances with the ball helped in victories over presumably more powerful sides. Born at Oxford in 1877, Huggins was 24 when his residential qualification enabled him to appear in County Cricket, and, taking 63 wickets, he at once showed his value, but was expensive. Relying less on swerve, he concentrated on length and spin next season, with such good results that his medium-paced bowling, gathering pace from the turf, brought startling results in two matches. At Hove in May, in the Sussex first innings he bowled 21 overs and five balls, 15 maidens, for 17 runs and seven wickets—a grand achievement that paved the way to a substantial victory. He also clean bowled Ranjitsinhji in the second innings, and formed a strong contrast to Fred Roberts, the last left-hander, who claimed in the match seven wickets for 57. In August, at Worcester, Huggins returned figures almost as good—21.1—8—37—7.

Two years later, 1904, he surpassed these efforts in the August Bank Holiday match at Bristol by taking nine Sussex wickets for 34 runs in 26 overs and two balls—15 maidens. If less successful in the second innings, he again bowled C. B. Fry, so repeating one deadly ball bowled at Hove in May, when his match record showed 10 wickets for 132 runs. In that first innings at Bristol, Huggins clean bowled eight men and caught his other victim from a return. No wonder that the Sussex captain described Huggins as "equal to any bowler that Sussex played against during that summer." Fry spoke from personal experience, besides critical observation from the pavilion. George Dennett then had succeeded Roberts as the stock left-handed bowler, and to his clever slows the speed of Huggins proved a most valuable foil, quite apart from the ability of the faster bowler to dismiss the best batsmen. Unfortunately Huggins put on weight for a middle-height man and his brilliant days grew infrequent. His full record in first-class cricket, 584 wickets at 29.03 runs apiece, showed clearly that he often proved expensive.

As a batsman also he was fitful. He looked like developing into a great all-rounder when in 1904 at Nottingham he contributed 53 to the highest total made by any county that season, 636; Jessop hit 206 and Gloucestershire won in a single innings. But his rise in the batting order did not last, and his best year, 1906, brought him no more than 465 runs, average 22.14 in county matches, with 91 his best display. His record in 16 seasons totalled 4,375 runs, average 14.43. After retirement as a player he scored for the county during several seasons. For over 40 years he was associated with the Stroud club, for whom his ability as a forcing batsman brought many runs.

HUISH, Frederick Henry, who died at Northiam, Sussex, on March 16, 1957, aged 87, was the first of a line of exceptional Kent wicket-keepers which L. E. G. Ames and T. G. Evans continued. First appearing for the county in 1895, he continued until the outbreak of war in 1914, accounting in the meantime for no fewer 1,328 batsmen—952 caught and 376 stumped. Yet, unlike Ames and Evans, he was never chosen to play for England and only once, at Lord's in 1902, for Players against Gentlemen.

It was a curious fact that while Huish, born at Clapham, was a Surrey man who played for Kent, H. Wood, from whom he learned much of his skill, was Kentish by birth and assisted Surrey. One of the ablest and least demonstrative wicket-keepers of his generation, Huish was among the few to assist in the taking of 100 wickets in a season. This performance he achieved twice, for in 1911 he obtained 100 victims (62 caught, 38 stumped) and in 1913 raised his tally to 102

(70 caught, 32 stumped). In 1911 he enjoyed his greatest triumph in a single match when, against Surrey at the Oval, he caught one batsman and stumped nine, thus dismissing 10 in the two innings. On five other occasions he disposed of eight men in a game. Four times he helped Kent to carry off the County Championship, in 1906, 1909, 1910 and 1913.

Huish showed his readiness and resource in memorable if lucky fashion in a match between Kent and the Australians at Canterbury in 1902. He was standing far back to W. M. Bradley, the famous amateur fast bowler, when R. A. Duff played a ball a few yards behind the wicket and the Australian's partner called for a run. To get to the ball, Huish had to move so far that he realised that he would not have time to gather it before the batsmen got home. Accordingly he attempted to kick it on to the stumps at his end. The ball missed its immediate objective, but Huish put so much power into his effort that the ball went on and hit the wicket at the other end before Duff could make the necessary ground.

Though not generally successful as a batsman, Huish scored 562 runs in 1906, his best innings being 93 against Somerset at Gravesend. When Huish became the Kent senior professional, he was reputed to exercise remarkable control over his colleagues. Indeed, it used to be alleged that, unless he appealed, no brother professional dared to ask for a catch at the wicket!

HULTON, Campbell Arthur Grey, born on March 17, 1846, died in London on June 23, 1919. He was not in the XI while at Rossall, but played a few times for Lancashire between 1869 and 1882. In 1888 he was elected a member of the M.C.C., and for many years he managed the Sussex Schools Tours. He was appointed to the Committee of the Club in 1913.

HUMAN, Capt. Roger H. C. (Adjutant Oxford and Bucks L.I.), died on active service in November, 1942, aged 33. Very good in games at Repton, he gained cricket and Association football Blues at Cambridge. Captain of Repton in 1928, when he averaged 37.27 as a free batsman and took 32 wickets at 19.62 each with medium-paced bowling, he looked like becoming a great all-rounder, but failed to maintain this form. A late choice for Cambridge in 1930, he did little towards beating Oxford, who threw the match away by bad fielding and poor batting. Next year, when Oxford, winning by eight wickets, gained their first victory over Cam-

bridge since 1923, Human again failed, and generally he proved disappointing in University cricket but always fielded well. At different times he played for Berkshire, Oxfordshire and Worcestershire when a master at Bromsgrove School. Altogether in first-class cricket he was credited with 1,869 runs, average 24.92, and 48 wickets at 37.87 each.

HUMBLE-CROFTS, The Rev. Prebendary William John, born at Sutton Rectory, near Chesterfield, on December 9, 1846, died (Rector of Waldron, Sussex) on July 1, 1924, aged 77. A useful batsman and good cover-point, he played for Derbyshire in 1873, 1874 and 1877, as well as for the Yorkshire Gentlemen C.C. and Free Foresters. He did not obtain his Blue whilst at Oxford.

HUMPHERSON, Victor William, who died on October 19, 1978, aged 82, played a number of times for Worcestershire from 1921 to 1923. A right-hand medium pace bowler, he took five for 50 in the first innings against Gloucestershire at Clifton in 1921.

HUMPHREY, Richard, was found drowned in the Thames, and was buried in St. Pancras Cemetery, East Finchley, on February 28, 1906. He had for a long time been in poor circumstances and no doubt his mind became unhinged. He was a batsman who did not accomplish half of what was expected from him. Gaining a high reputation very early in his career, he no sooner reached the top of the tree than he began to decline in power. Born on December 12, 1848, he learnt his cricket at Mitcham—the training ground of many of Surrey's best players—and came out when his more famous brother, the late Tom Humphrey, was on the wane. He first found a place in the Surrey XI in 1870, and with an innings of 82 against Cambridge University gave clear proof of his class. His record for the season was a modest one, but no doubt was felt that he would make a name. In the following year he improved enormously, his best scores being 116 not out against Kent, 80 against Yorkshire, and 70 against Gloucestershire, and in 1872 he reached his highest point, standing on a level that season with the best professional batsmen in England. Picked for Players against Gentlemen at Lord's and the Oval, he came off in both matches, his success being the more noteworthy from the fact that at Lord's the Gentlemen's bowling was exceptionally strong. At the Oval he scored 96 in his first innings, opening the batting with Jupp and being the ninth man out. A few weeks later, for Surrey against Yorkshire at the Oval, he made 70 in each innings, with Emmett and Allan Hill bowling at him, this being perhaps the best performance in his career. He headed the Surrey averages for the season, and a very bright future seemed in store for him. From this time, however, he steadily fell off. In 1873 he was nothing like the batsman he had been 12 months before, and though he continued to do good work for Surrey, playing for the county till 1881, he never regained the position that had once been his. After his career as an active player was over, he did a good deal of coaching, being engaged at one time at Clifton College, and recently he had acted as umpire, giving great satisfaction in 1904 and 1905 in the matches played by the Minor Counties. Old cricketers will remember him as a batsman who was worth going a long way to see, his style being very finished and correct.

HUMPHREY, Stuart Harold Guise, who died at Dallington, Northampton, on June 9, 1975, aged 81, was in the XI at Oakham for five years, 1909 to 1913, and played for Northamptonshire from 1913 to 1926, though never regularly. A big man and a formidable centre three-quarter at Rugger, he was a tremendous hitter and the highest of a number of useful innings he played for the county, 61 not out against Leicestershire in 1925, took only 35 minutes and included five straight drives for six over the sight-screen off Astill. For St. Thomas's Hospital against the Middlesex Hospital in 1920 he scored 286 and took nine wickets. By profession he was an eye-specialist in Northampton.

HUMPHREYS, Edward, one of the best-known figures in Kent cricket, died at his Maidstone home on November 6, 1949, aged 68. Thus ended an association with began 53 years before when "Punter," as he became known, joined the Kent staff. Two years later, when 17, he made his first appearance, as a left-arm slow bowler, for the county, but he soon gained greater prominence as a right-hand opening batsman. An especially strong back player, he showed particular skill when the ball was turning. No little testimony to his skill was contained in the fact that he retained his place in the Kent side in their halcyon years when they won the Championship four times, from 1906 to 1913, the only occasions when they carried off the honours. One of his best feats occurred in 1908 when he shared with A. P. Day in a seventh wicket stand of 248 for Kent against Somerset at

Taunton. In 1912–13 he went to West Indies as a member of the M.C.C. team captained by A. F. Somerset and enjoyed a successful tour with 461 runs, average 40.07, and 40 wickets for 16.75 runs each.

In his playing career, which extended from 1899 to 1920, Humphreys played under five Kent captains, J. R. Mason, C. J. Burnup, C. H. B. Marsham, E. W. Dillon and L. H. W. Troughton. Altogether he scored 16,603 runs, average 27.95, hit 20 centuries, and took 342 wickets, average 24.49. He also earned distinction for his magnificent fielding at mid-on and short-leg.

"Punter" Humphreys was a good coach as well as a fine player. During his playing days he went to Jamaica five times to impart his knowledge to the young players out there, and before that he coached in New Zealand. After finishing first-class cricket Humphreys became coach at Uppingham School where he played a large part in the development of two Kent captains, A. P. F. Chapman and F. G. H. Chalk. His engagement at Uppingham had four years to run when at the request of Lord Harris he returned to Kent. Humphreys was appointed chief Kent coach at Canterbury and saw the rise of such present-day players as A. E. Fagg, D. V. P. Wright, and T. G. Evans. On all Kent grounds he was a familiar and a respected figure.

In the First World War Humphreys served in the Royal Navy and took part in the raid on Zeebrugge.

HUMPHREYS, George T., who died on December 19, 1894, was an elder brother of Walter Humphreys, the famous lob bowler. Born in 1845, he played from time to time for Sussex, but though he was a fair bat and wicket-keeper, it cannot be said that he ever met with any great success in first-class cricket.

HUMPHREYS, Walter Alexander, the famous lob bowler, died at Brighton on March 23, 1924. He was born at Southsea on October 28, 1849, but lived in Sussex from the time he was three weeks old. Humphreys came out for Sussex in 1871, being then a fairly good young cricketer with no special qualifications. He could bat and field and, in an emergency, keep wicket. Not till nine years later did he develop the lob bowling which gained him his celebrity. Having taken up the study of lobs, he did not have to wait long for success, as when the Australians played Sussex at Brighton towards the end of the season in 1880 he did the hat-trick, getting rid of Groube, Alec Bannerman and Blackham. This, however, proved quite an isolated performance, and for Sussex in the next three seasons he did nothing out of the common. Then in 1884 against the Australians at Brighton he had another hat-trick to his credit, the batsmen who fell to him this time being Percy MacDonnell, George Giffen and Scott. To the fast-footed Australian batsmen of those days, Humphreys caused so much trouble that I have often wondered whether, at some sacrifice to the team in run-getting power, it would not have been wise in 1884 to play him for England at the Oval. When for the first and only time Sussex, in 1888, had the satisfaction of beating the Australians, Humphreys had a big share in the victory, taking five wickets for 21 and four for 19. On that occasion, Arthur Hide divided honours with him. Humphreys' career as a lob bowler culminated in 1893 when, in all matches for Sussex, he took 148 wickets for less than 17½ runs each. As he played so much of his cricket at Brighton, with easy boundaries on the Pavilion side of the

ground, these were indeed remarkable figures. Mr. Stoddart took Humphreys to Australia with his team in 1894–95, but the experiment was not a success. The lob bowler was past his zenith. He had no terrors for the class batsmen, and though he did well in the up-country games he was left out of all the Test matches. At his best Humphreys could do a great deal with the ball, and was very clever in disguising his intentions. In this connection, W. L. Murdoch, who played an innings of 286 not out for the Australians against Sussex at Brighton in 1882, paid him a high compliment. He said, "Even when I had made 200 runs I could not tell from watching his hand which way he meant to turn the ball." Humphreys retired from the Sussex XI after the season of 1896, having taken for the county during his career 767 wickets for just under 20 runs apiece. He turned out in 1900 for Hampshire but his day was so obviously over that he quickly retired from the public gaze. He had his benefit at Brighton—Sussex v. Gloucestershire—in 1891.—S.H.P.

SOME BOWLING FEATS

In Important Matches—

8 wickets for 89	v. Lancashire, at Manchester	.. .. ..	1892
8 wickets for 83	v. Middlesex, at Hove	.. .. ..	1893
8 wickets for 121	v. Somerset, at Taunton, 1893	(In match 15 for 193)	
8 wickets for 98	v. Yorkshire, at Hove	.. .. ..	1893
8 wickets for 121	v. Cambridge University, at Hove	.. .. ..	1895
4 wickets for 9	v. Hampshire, at Hove	.. .. ..	1884
5 wickets for 10	v. M.C.C., at Lord's	.. ..	1891

Other Matches—

For Heron's Ghyll v. Nutley, at Heron's Ghyll on April 6, 1888, he took eight wickets for 0 in 33 balls in the first innings (doing the hat-trick), and four for two in 32 balls in the second. Nutley were dismissed for four and six.

For Brighton Brunswick he took all 10 wickets in an innings v. Ardingly College in 1882, v. Lower Clapton in 1888, and v. Yarra C.C., in 1889.

HUMPHRIES, Gerald Harvey, who died on February 3, 1983, aged 74, played one match for Worcestershire in 1932 and another in 1934. In the second, against Glamorgan at Cardiff, he scored 31 going in first. He had captained the Kidderminster side before the War and again in 1946, when they headed the Birmingham League, and had also served on the Worcestershire committee. He was one of three brothers who played for Worcestershire.

HUMPHRIES, J., one of the best of the famous wicket-keepers who have appeared for Derbyshire, died at Chesterfield on May 8, 1946, within 10 days of reaching 70 years of age. First playing for the county in 1899 as understudy to William Storer—then still at

his best—Humphries gradually became the regular keeper, and from 1902 steadily improved until he went out to Australia in the winter of 1907. It proved an ill-fated tour; an attack of pneumonia kept A. O. Jones, the captain, out of the first three Tests, and in the first match R. A. Young of Cambridge and Sussex, who wore spectacles, was preferred as wicket-keeper—no doubt because of his batting. As a matter of fact Young scored only 27 runs in four Test innings, while Humphries, replacing him until the fifth Test, made 44 in six innings. Sir Home Gordon, in *Form at a Glance*, credited Humphries with 545 catches and 103 stumpings up to 1914, when the War finished his first-class career. His runs numbered 5,436, average 14.15.

HUNT, George, who died on January 22, 1959, aged 62, played as an all-rounder for Somerset from 1921 to 1931, scoring 4,952 runs, average 15.42, and taking with right-arm spin bowling 386 wickets, average 32.88. A hard driver, he hit his one century against Glamorgan at Weston-super-Mare in 1928, scoring 101 out of 138. That was his most successful season as a run-getter, for in all matches he registered 997 runs. Though often expensive as a bowler, he dismissed seven Sussex batsmen for 61 runs at Bath in 1926. A splendid fieldsman at short leg, he held 188 catches. In his first season with the county he had the experience of being in the side when J. C. White took all 10 Worcestershire wickets for 76 runs at Worcester and when T. Rushby, for Surrey at Taunton, obtained all 10 Somerset wickets at a cost of 43 runs. After leaving first-class cricket, he joined Kilmarnock C.C.

HUNT, J. H. (Middlesex), born November 24, 1874, killed 1916(?). Details with regard to the death of Mr. Hunt have never been published. Place and date are unknown, but his friends have long given up hope that he is still alive. Mr. Hunt was a very good all-round cricketer and so full of enthusiasm for the game that he was more valuable on a side than many players of greater natural gifts. He was a very plucky punishing bat, a useful change bowler—right hand fast—and a brilliant fieldsman wherever he was placed. He played his first match for Middlesex in 1902 —a disastrous year for the county—making his first appearance in the Whit-Monday fixture against Somerset. After an interval of over 15 years one recalls his undisguised delight when on being tried as second change, he took a wicket with the first ball he bowled. In his second innings he hit up 60, but in his four subsequent matches for Middlesex in 1902 he did next to nothing with either bat or ball. In 1903, however, when Middlesex won the County Championship he proved his worth as a batsman, getting an average of 27 with 57 as his highest score. It cannot be said that during his connection with Middlesex he improved as a batsman on his early efforts, but he headed the bowling in 1908, taking 13 wickets in five matches with an average of 19 runs a wicket. His highest innings in first-class cricket was 128 in the Gentlemen v. Players match at the Oval in 1904—the very unsatisfactory match in which two changes were made in the Gentlemen's team after the first day.—S.H.P.

HUNT, Robert Norman, died in hospital at Chichester on October 13, 1983, aged 80. A good bat and a useful fast-medium right-hand bowler he was for years a prominent member of the Ealing side and between 1926 and 1928 made a few appearances for Middlesex. Though his total record was only 138 runs with an average of 19.71 he had one good performance, scoring 81 not out against Worcestershire at Lord's in 1926.

HUNT, William Alfred, who died in Sydney on December 31, 1983, at the age of 75, played once for Australia, against South Africa at Adelaide in 1931–32, when Bradman scored 299 not out and Hunt, as a slow left-arm bowler, took 0 for 39 in 16 overs, made 0 in his only innings and held a catch. His Sheffield Shield cricket, between 1929 and 1932, was played for New South Wales: in 17 matches he took 62 wickets (22.37), scored 301 runs (15.05) and took 11 catches. He played Lancashire League cricket for Rushton and took over 500 wickets for Balmain in club cricket in Sydney.

HUNTER, Charles Herbert, who died on April 2, 1955, aged nearly 88, played in two matches for Kent in 1895 when with Bickley Park C.C. One of these games was that in which Dr. W. G. Grace, hitting 257 and 73 not out for Gloucestershire at Gravesend, was on the field for the whole of the three days. In that season "W. G." became the first batsman in history to score 1,000 runs in May. A good wicket-keeper, Hunter played for Uppingham in 1885 and 1886, but did not get a Blue when going up to Cambridge, where he was overshadowed by Gregor MacGregor, of Middlesex and England fame.

HUNTER, David, born at Scarborough on February 23, 1860, died suddenly at his native place on January 11, 1927, aged 66. In 1888 he succeeded his brother Joseph as the Yorkshire wicket-keeper and he retained the position until 1909, taking in all matches for the county during that period 1,272 wickets—920 caught and 352 stumped. He was quiet, sure and neat in his methods and his hands never sustained any deformity or serious injury, notwithstanding the great amount of work he got through. In Hall's benefit match—against Surrey at Sheffield in 1891— he caught five men and stumped one in an innings; in a game with the same county at Bradford seven years later he claimed eight of the 20 wickets, catching two and stumping six; while in his last season, 1909, he made six catches in the course of an innings against

Surrey at Leeds. Although he appeared several times for the Players, he was never chosen for a Test match or a tour abroad. Without ever being a great batsman, he often played a most useful innings and in county games took part in stands of 153, 148, 121, 118 and 102 for the 10th wicket. In eight different seasons he assisted Yorkshire to win the Championship, and when he was accorded his benefit match—v. Lancashire at Bradford in 1897—he received £1,975. He always played the game in the best possible spirit, and was deservedly popular.

HUNTER, George James, of Staines, who died on July 14, 1943, aged 84, left his *Wisden Almanacks* from 1880 to 1942 to his Stock Exchange friend Mr. Jon Keeble Guy. Mr. Hunter was a keen club cricketer and an enthusiastic follower of the game. Mr. Guy ran the Reigate Priory club for 10 years and played also for Essex Second XI.

HUNTER, Joseph, who was for several seasons a regular member of the Yorkshire XI, died on January 4, 1891. He was only in his 34th year, having been born on October 21, 1857. Joseph Hunter followed George Pinder as the regular wicket-keeper in the Yorkshire team, and was in turn succeeded by his brother David. Though never taking the same rank as Pilling and Sherwin, Hunter, at his best, was good enough for any county team, and it is a matter for regret that his career should have been so short. For some little time before his death he had completely dropped out of first-class cricket, but continued to make occasional appearances for the Scarborough Club. He visited Australia in the winter of 1884–85 as wicket-keeper to Shaw and Shrewsbury's second team.

HURST, Christopher Salkeld, who died on December 18, 1963, aged 77, was a free-scoring batsman specially strong in driving. In the Uppingham XI from 1903 to 1905, when he was captain, he headed the batting averages in each season, hitting 167 not out against Malvern in 1904. Going up to Oxford, he played against Cambridge in the matches of 1907, 1908 and 1909, being captain the last year. With innings of 61 and 46, he bore a big part in an Oxford victory by two wickets in 1908. He also represented the University at hockey from 1906 to 1909. He subsequently appeared occasionally for Kent and in 1922, after an absence from the county side of 10 years, distinguished himself by hitting centuries against Lancashire,

Essex and Leicestershire during the month of June, scoring 383 runs in seven innings and finishing first in the batting figures with an average of 76.70.

HURT, Colin Noel, who died on December 31, 1972, aged 79, played for Derbyshire in 1914.

HURWOOD, Alexander, who died in Brisbane on September 26, 1982, aged 80, was a right-hand bowler who could spin the ball appreciably at near medium pace, and a fine slip fielder. He played 18 matches for Queensland between 1925–26 and 1931–32 and won two caps for Australia against West Indies in 1930–31. In January, 1930, he took six for 179 for Queensland against New South Wales in Sydney in the innings in which Bradman made the then world record individual score of 452 not out. When Bradman had made 80, Hurwood bowled a ball which hit Bradman's wicket without dislodging a bail. He toured England in 1930 with W. M. Woodfull's side, but without appearing in a Test match. He took 28 wickets on the tour and had a top score of 61 against Sussex. After taking 11 wickets in the first two Tests against West Indies in 1930–31 he somewhat unluckily lost his place. All told he scored 575 runs in first-class cricket (average 11.27) and took 113 wickets (average 27.62).

HUSKINSON, Geoffrey Neville Bayley, died at Hinton Waldrist on June 17, 1982, aged 82. In the Oundle XI from 1915 to 1917, he did not get a Blue at Oxford but played for Nottinghamshire in their first two matches in 1922 and in the second made 33 against Glamorgan. He also appeared a number of times for Nottinghamshire Second XI, occasionally acting as captain. He was a useful bat and a good field at slip or cover and was related by marriage to the great Richard Daft. A member of the County Committee from 1943 to 1958, he was President in 1959 and 1960 and a Vice-President from 1961. At his home, Langar Hall, he used to grow cricket bat willows. He had also been a first-class rugger player, and, when advancing years forced him to give up cricket, he made himself into a good enough croquet player to represent Nottinghamshire at that game too.

HUSSAIN, Syed Mahmud, who died at Hyderabad on July 2, 1982, at the age of 80, was a sound and attractive stroke-player who proved himself against three visiting teams. He scored 90 against the first official M.C.C. team to visit India in 1926–27 at Madras, 73

ior Moin-ud-Doela's XI against Ryder's Australian team at Secunderabad in 1935–36, and in 1937–38, for the same team, 55 against Lord Tennyson's team, also at Secunderabad. About his performance against Ryder's team, C. G. Macartney wrote: "The best innings of the day was played by Hussain, who had the misfortune to be run out when his valiant display deserved the coveted century." Hussain played in one unofficial Test against Ryder's team at Calcutta, but failed on a rain-affected pitch. He was a member of the Indian team to England in 1936, when his best effort was an innings of 55 against Worcestershire. He was captain of Hyderabad in the Ranji Trophy from the start in 1934–35 to 1941–42 and had the distinction of leading the side to its only Championship victory in 1942–43. He belonged to the landed classes.

HUTCHEON, John Silvester, C.B.E., Q.C., who died at Brisbane on June 18, 1957, aged 75, represented Queensland at cricket and lacrosse. He was a member of the Australian Board of Control for International Cricket from 1919 onwards and at one time chairman. He was called to the Bar by Lincoln's Inn in 1914 and became a member of the Queensland Bar in 1916.

HUTCHINGS, Frederick Vaughan, was in Tonbridge School XI and played occasionally for Kent in 1901 and 1905. Born on June 3, 1880, he was 54 when he died suddenly at Hamburg on August 6, 1934.

HUTCHINGS, Lieut. K. L. (King's Liverpool Regiment, attached to Welsh Regiment), was killed in action during the first week in September, 1916. He was struck by a shell, death being instantaneous. Of all the cricketers who have fallen in the War he may fairly be described as the most famous.

Kenneth Lotherington Hutchings did not fulfil all the hopes formed of him, but at his best he was one of the most remarkable batsmen seen in this generation. Those who follow cricket will not need to be reminded of the sensation caused by his play in 1906—the year in which Kent, for the first time in modern days, came out as Champion

County. To the triumph of the side no one contributed more than Hutchings. It is true that he fell a little below C. J. Burnup in the averages, but he played with amazing brilliancy, getting four 100s in county matches, and scoring 1,358 runs. His success astonished the public, but it was scarcely a surprise to those who had watched him from his school days. He had a great career at Tonbridge, being in the XI for five years, and heading the batting for three seasons in succession. The first evidence of his ability in County Cricket was given when, in 1903, he scored 106 for Kent against Somerset at Taunton. His batting in 1906 took him at once to the top of the tree, and on all hands he was regarded as an England cricketer. Unfortunately he never again reached quite the level of his great season. From time to time he did brilliant things, playing especially well in 1909 and 1910, but in 1912 he lost his form and dropped out of the Kent XI.

In 1909 he was chosen twice for England against Australia, scoring nine at Manchester and 59 at the Oval. He paid one visit to Australia, being a member of the M.C.C.'s team in the winter of 1907–08. Taking the tour as a whole, he did not meet with the success expected, but at Melbourne, in the only Test match the Englishmen won, he played a very fine innings of 126. Hutchings was quite individual in his style of batting, recalling no predecessor. His driving power was tremendous, and when at his best he could score from good length balls with wonderful facility. It was said in 1906 that when he played for Kent against Yorkshire, even George Hirst—most fearless of fieldsmen at mid-off—went back several yards for him, so terrific being the force of his hitting. Like most modern batsmen, Hutchings trusted for defence wholly to his back play. When he went forward it was always for the purpose of scoring. Playing the daring game that he did, he could only do himself full justice when physically very fit. His fielding was on a par with his batting. In the slips or in the deep field he was equally brilliant. He was born at Southborough, near Tunbridge Wells, on December 7, 1882.—S.H.P.

The following records of Hutchings' career speak for themselves:

Tonbridge School

Year	Inns.	Times not out	Most in an innings	Total Runs	Average
1898	11	2	41	185	20.55
1899	11	0	60	218	19.81
1900	15	2	127	743	57.15—1st. Made 127 v. Band of Brothers.

Tonbridge School—*continued*

Year	Inns.	Times not out	Most in an innings	Total Runs	Average
1901	13	2	101*	522	47.45—1st. Made 100 v. Free Foresters.
1902	12	2	205	633	63.30—1st. Made 205 v. West Kent, 178* v. Free Foresters, and 120 v. Old Cliftonians.

For Kent—1st played for the County in 1902

Year				Innings	Times not out	Most in an innings	Total Runs	Average
1902	..	..	..	2	0	10	11	5.50
1903	..	..	..	17	1	106	454	28.37
1903†	..	..	..	6	1	16	48	9.60
1904	..	..	..	2	0	66	96	48.00
1905	..	..	..	4	0	31	87	21.75
1906‡	..	..	..	28	4	176	1,454	60.58
1907	..	..	..	31	2	109*	955	32.93
1908	..	..	..	36	0	132	953	26.47
1909‡	..	..	..	36	1	155	1,368	39.08
1910‡	..	..	..	36	2	144	1,461	42.97
1911	..	..	..	34	2	103*	938	29.31
1912	..	..	..	10	0	53	178	17.80
Totals				242	13	176	8,003	34.94

Hundreds in First-Class Cricket

106	Kent v. Somerset, at Taunton	..	..	..	..	1903
125	Kent v. Middlesex, at Tonbridge	..	..	..	..	1906
131	Kent v. Yorkshire, at Sheffield	..	..	..	..	1906
176	Kent v. Lancashire, at Canterbury	..	..	..	..	1906
124	Kent v. Hampshire, at Bournemouth	..	..	..	..	1906
101	Kent v. Hampshire, at Tonbridge	..	..	..	..	1907
109 / 109*	Kent v. Worcestershire, at Worcester	..	..	..	..	1907
108	Kent v. Lancashire, at Canterbury	..	..	..	..	1907
126	England v. Australia, at Melbourne	..	..	..	..	1907–08
132	Kent v. Northamptonshire, at Gravesend	..	..	..	..	1908
102	Kent v. Derbyshire, at Derby	..	..	..	..	1908
120	Gentlemen v. Players, at Scarborough	..	..	..	..	1908
100	Kent v. Gloucestershire, at Catford	..	..	..	..	1909
155	Kent v. Somerset, at Gravesend	..	..	..	..	1909
116	Kent v. Hampshire, at Bournemouth	..	..	..	..	1909
104	Kent v. Northamptonshire, at Northampton	..	..	..	..	1910
112	Kent v. Derbyshire, at Derby	..	..	..	..	1910
109	Kent v. Leicestershire, at Tonbridge	..	..	..	..	1910
144	Kent v. Sussex, at Hastings	..	..	..	..	1910
114	M.C.C. & Ground v. Yorkshire, at Scarborough	..	..	..	..	1910
103*	Kent v. Hampshire, at Canterbury	..	..	..	..	1911

In Gentlemen v. Players Matches

1906	At Lord's	2 and 10	
1906	Scarborough	36 and 14*	13 inns., 0 not out, 120 highest score, 339 total, 26.07 aver.
1908	Scarborough	3 and 120	
1909	Oval	0 and 59	
1909	Scarborough	11	(He made his 120 out of 164 in 100 mins.)
1910	Scarborough	19 and 42	
1911	Scarborough	18 and 5	

*Also took 4 wickets for 15.

*Signifies not out.   †American Tour.   ‡Champion County.

In England v. Australia Matches

1907–08	At Sydney	42 and 17	
1907–08	At Melbourne	126 and 39	
1907–08	At Adelaide	23 and 0	
1907–08	At Melbourne	8 and 3	12 inns., 0 not out, 126 highest
1907–08	At Sydney	13 and 2	score, 341 total, 28.41 aver.
1909	At Manchester	9	
1909	At Oval	59	

HUTTON, Norman Harvey, who died in Adelaide on June 7, 1980, aged 67, was a member of a well-known cricketing family. As a fast-medium bowler he played twice for South Australia in 1934–35. His father, Percy, had played for the state in 1905–06, as did his two brothers, Maurice and Mervyn, in 1928–29 and 1930–31 respectively.

HYDE, Sir Charles, Bart., O.B.E., LL.D., President of the Warwickshire County C.C. from 1931, died on November 26, 1942, aged 66. At the annual meeting of the club in March 1940 he made a memorable speech regarding money-making sports. Sir Charles said that "when County Cricket started again something would have to be done about the entertainment tax. Cricket was one of the few sports which had not degenerated into a gambling and money-making concern. Racing, football, dog-racing and other sports could afford the tax, but it was slowly killing County Cricket. He was sorry to see that the Football Association and the football coupon businesses were now extending their activities right into the summer and this had to be watched carefully." He also denounced "freak declarations" and said, "They are not good for cricket. There were some curious happenings last season, and under the present system of scoring in the County Championship a club appears to need the services of a skilled mathematician to advise whether an innings should be declared or whether a side should bat at all!"

Unmarried, Sir Charles did not leave any heir, and with his death the Baronetcy, bestowed on him in 1922, became extinct.

HYLAND, Frederick J., who died in February, 1964, aged 70, played as a professional in one match for Hampshire in 1924. Cricket in this game, at Northampton, was limited by rain to two overs from which Northamptonshire scored one run without loss. Hyland later earned a reputation as a nurseryman in Cheshire.

HYLTON, Leslie G., died in Jamaica on May 17, 1955, aged 50. He played in six Text matches for West Indies. A fast bowler for Jamaica, he helped in the winning of the rubber against R. E. S. Wyatt's team in the West Indies in 1934–35 when, in four Tests, he dismissed 13 batsmen at an average cost of 19.30. In 1939, he visited England under the captaincy of R. S. Grant, being chosen for two of the Test matches, but met with moderate success.

HYLTON-STEWART, Bruce Delacour, who died on October 1, 1972, aged 80, was in the Bath College XI before playing for Somerset as an all-rounder from 1912 to 1914, scoring 989 runs and taking 55 wickets. Against Essex at Leyton in 1914, he hit 110 in 105 minutes. He later assisted Hertfordshire for some years.

HYMAN, William, who died in February, 1959, aged 83, earned fame as a hard-hitting batsman who, for Bath Cricket Association against Thornbury at Thornbury in 1902, hit 359 not out in 100 minutes in a total of 466 for six wickets. He was specially severe upon E. M. Grace, brother of "W. G.," whom he 32 times hit for six and punished for 62 runs in two following overs. "Billy" Hyman made 27 appearances for Somerset between 1900 and 1914, his highest innings being 110 against Sussex at Bath in 1913 when he and P. R. Johnson added 159 for the second wicket. He and his three brothers all played Association football for Radstock Town and he also turned out for Bath City and Somerset.

HYNDMAN, Henry Mayers, died at his home in Hampstead on the morning of November 22, 1921. Mr Hyndman, so well known as a Socialist leader, had some claim to be remembered for his powers in the cricket field. While up at Cambridge he only just missed getting his Blue in 1864. In his first book of recollections he admitted that in later life many things of greater moment caused him far less disappointment. He was very pleased one night at his club to hear the opinion expressed that he ought to have been chosen. Still, Cambridge were rich in run-getters in 1864, and Mr. Hyndman's best score in the three trial matches in which he took part was 35 against the Free Foresters.

He was one of the Thirteen of Cambridge who played against Surrey at the Oval, a drawn game producing 1,104 runs—a huge aggregate in those days. Mr. Hyndman kept up his cricket for several years, playing a good deal for Sussex and the Gentlemen of Sussex. He was clearly at his best in 1864. In August that year he scored at Brighton 58 against Hampshire and 62 against Middlesex, the latter innings enabling Sussex to gain a hard-won victory by three wickets. In his first book of recollections Mr. Hyndman had a good deal to say about cricket, paying a high tribute to Buttress, the famous slow bowler. Born on March 7, 1842, he was in his 80th year at the time of his death.

HYNES, Sir Lincoln Carruthers, died during the year, 1977, at the age of 65. As a fast left-hander, he did useful work for New South Wales in the 1930s. His proudest moment was when he had Bradman caught at leg-slip for 0. He was knighted in 1971 in recognition of his work for broadcasting, charities and hospitals.

HYSLOP, Hector Harry, who died by his own hand at Cosham, near Portsmouth, on September 11, 1920, was born in Australia on December 13, 1840. He was a useful batsman and wicket-keeper, and appeared for Hampshire in 1876 and for the Australians in a few of their matches in 1878. Always devoted to cricket he was a great enthusiast. He had close friends among the members of the earlier Australian teams in England.

I'ANSON, John, a very useful all-round cricketer, who played for Lancashire with varying success from 1896 to 1908, died at Eccleston near Chester on September 16, 1936, aged 66. For some 15 years, he had been head gardener on the Duke of Westminster's estate at Eaton Park. A medium-paced bowler and steady batsman, he never fulfilled expectations, though in 1902 he averaged 26.23 for 341 runs and took 49 wickets at 19.12 apiece. His best innings was 110 not out against Surrey at Old Trafford. He was not required often in 1904 when Lancashire's very powerful side carried off the Championship.

IDDON, John, the Lancashire all-rounder, was killed in a car accident at Crewe on April 17, 1946, when returning home from a business visit to the Rolls-Royce works. Born at Mawdesley, near Ormskirk, on January 8, 1903, he came of a cricketing family, his father being professional to the Lancaster club for 14 years. After doing well for Leyland Motors, Jack Iddon made his first appearance for Lancashire against Oxford University in 1924, and played for the county for 15 seasons prior to the War. He represented England in five Test matches, four against West Indies during the M.C.C. tour of 1934–35, and once against South Africa at Nottingham the following summer.

A right-handed, hard-driving batsman, Iddon reached 1,000 runs in 11 successive seasons up to 1939, obtaining 2,261 in 1934, when Lancashire were Champion County for the fifth time during Iddon's career. Altogether he scored 22,679 runs in first-class cricket and took over 500 wickets. His first century came against Surrey at Old Trafford in 1927, and two years later he played his highest innings, 222 against Leicestershire at Liverpool.

Iddon bowled slow left-arm and was particularly effective when the wicket showed signs of wear. On such a pitch at Sheffield in 1937 he accomplished his best performance, taking nine wickets in the Yorkshire second innings for 42 runs and enabling Lancashire to beat their great local rivals after a lapse of five years. In 1936 his benefit realised £1,266.

Iddon did not rejoin Lancashire for the 1946 season, but hoped to play occasionally as an amateur. From 1929 to the time of his death he was technical representative to a firm of brake-lining experts in Manchester. He left a wife and two children. Damages totalling £9,801 were awarded at Stafford Assizes to Mrs Iddon as compensation.

Iddon was the second Lancashire cricketer who met his death in a road accident in recent years. E. A. McDonald, the Australian and Lancashire fast bowler, was knocked down and killed by a motor-car on the Manchester-Chorley Road in 1937.

IKIN, John Thomas (Jack), who died at home at Bignall End on September 15, 1984, aged 66, played in 18 Tests for England between 1946 and 1955, scoring 606 runs with an average of 20.89 and taking three wickets at 118 runs each. These figures naturally suggest the question, why was he picked so often and so long? The answer is that, though at the time England had such bats as Hutton, Washbrook, Compton and Edrich and, at the end of the period, May and Cowdrey, there was not the depth of batting there had been before the War: two or three reliable players were wanted to support the stars and crises were frequent. One gets the impression that the selectors, at a loss to fill the gap, constantly fell back on Ikin.

He was essentially a sound player, though in his young days stronger on the off than on the leg. He was determined and could be trusted not to throw his wicket away stupidly. He was left-handed, he was adaptable and equally happy to open or to go in six or seven. Above all he was a superb field, whether at short leg or in the slips. Though he never made a big score for England, he often played bravely when runs were wanted. At Sydney in 1946–47 his 60, made in three hours, was the second-highest innings in a total of 255, while at Melbourne in a desperate situation he made 48 and helped Yardley to put up 113 in two hours. In 1951 against South Africa at Trent Bridge his 33 was top score in the second innings, at Lord's he made 51 and at Old Trafford, where he faced bravely a fierce battering from McCarthy, his 22 and and 38, made as Hutton's opening partner, were important contributions in a low-scoring match. In 1952 he made 53 against India at the Oval. In 1955, after a three-year absence, he was recalled as one of five left-handers to counter Goddard's leg-theory, but the experiment was not a success.

Born at Stoke-on-Trent, he played for Staffordshire in 1934 at the age of 16, gained a regular place in the side in 1936 and in 1938, when he headed the batting, was picked for the Minor Counties against Oxford University. In 1939 he appeared in four matches for Lancashire and took his first wicket in first-class cricket, that of the great George Headley. Playing regularly for Lancashire in 1946, he was picked for England before he had got his county cap and that winter went with MCC to Australia, where he played in all the Tests. In 1947-48 he was a member of G. O. Allen's side to the West Indies, but was a failure. His only other tour was with a Commonwealth team to India in 1950–51. Here he had the most prolific season of his career, heading the averages in the unofficial Tests with 625 runs and an average of 89.28. An injury forced him to refuse the MCC tour to India the following winter. For Lancashire he did splendid work as a batsman and was also useful as a leg-break and googly bowler. Against Somerset at Taunton in 1949 he did the hat-trick. His highest score was 192 against Oxford University at Oxford in 1951. Latterly he missed a good deal of cricket through ill health and injury and it was this that caused him to retire at the end of 1957.

However, his career was far from over. He rejoined Staffordshire and continued to play for them until 1968, scoring heavily and captaining them from 1957 to 1967. In 1965–66 he was assistant manager on the MCC tour to Australia and New Zealand, and after retiring from active cricket he did much coaching in the North and Midlands. Gentle, generous and friendly, he perhaps lacked the toughness to make quite the most of a considerable natural talent. In all first-class cricket he scored 17,968 runs with an average of 36.81 and took 339 wickets at 30.27. In eleven seasons he reached his 1,000 runs and he made 27 centuries.

IMLAY, Alan Durant, who died on July 3, 1958, aged 74, captained Clifton before gaining a Blue as wicket-keeper for Cambridge in 1907, in which season he played for Gentlemen against Players at the Oval. From 1905 to 1911 he made occasional appearances for Gloucestershire. He had been an assistant master and bursar at Clifton.

INGELSE, Ray G., one of the leading personalities of his time in Dutch cricket, died on May 18, 1976, aged 78. He was the originator of the fund set up in 1965 to maintain the grave of W. G. Grace at Elmers End.

INGRAM, Edward A., who died in a Basingstoke hospital on March 13, 1973, aged 62, played for Ireland 48 times between 1928 and 1955, being captain on eight occasions. He scored 1,628 runs, average 20.09, and dismissed 151 batsmen at a cost of 20.11 runs each. He also played for Leinster. His name was always linked in Irish cricket circles with that of J. C. Boucher, with whom he was at Belvedere College and played for Ireland for 25 years. Coming to England, Ingram joined the Ealing Club in 1936 and altogether took over 3,000 wickets for them with varied bowling of impeccable length besides regularly scoring 1,000 runs a season. A great character of Pickwickian girth, he also gained a cap for Middlesex.

INNES, Gerald Alfred Skerten, who died in Cape Town after a long illness on July 19, 1982, aged 50, was a widely respected and much-liked figure in South African cricket. Born in Cape Town, he was educated at Diocesan College, Rondebosch, and the University of Cape Town. An outstanding schoolboy cricketer, he captained the "Bishop's" XI in his last two years at school, as well as the Western Province Nuffield Shield side, which he had the rare distinction of representing for four consecutive seasons. He also captained the South African Schools representative side. In January, 1951, he was given a trial for that year's South African tour to England, batting competently for 49 but failing to make the team. After a fine season for Western Province in 1951–52, in which he completed his first first-class hundred, 139 against Eastern Province, he toured Australia with J. E. Cheetham's side in 1952–53. His best score was 109 against Victoria at Melbourne. Although he never played in a Test match, he was chosen by the *South African Cricket Annual* as one of its cricketers of the year in 1958–59, having made hundreds for Western Province against both Natal and Transvaal. In 1959 he assumed the captaincy of Western Province. Having transferred to Johannesburg in 1963, he played for Transvaal in 1963–64, making 140 not out against Natal at Durban. After retiring from first-class cricket in 1965, he became a Transvaal selector, and upon returning to Cape Town he served Western Province in the same capacity. His warmth, friendliness and good humour made him popular wherever he went and with cricketers of all ages.

INSOLE, John Herbert, who died on February 23, 1974, aged 74, was father of D. J. Insole, of Cambridge University, Essex and England. "Jack" Insole served on the Essex Committee from 1959 to 1970. As a member of the Festival Committee at Leyton from 1963 till 1973, he called upon every member of his family, including grandchildren, to lend a hand at matches there. When Essex finances were at a low ebb, he instituted the collecting of trading stamps, the sale of which raised several hundreds of pounds for the county funds. Though never a prominent player, he took part in club cricket in East London in his younger days.

INVERARITY, Mervyn, a stalwart figure in the development of Western Australian cricket for well over half a century, died in Perth on March 17, 1979. A leading all-rounder with Scotch College in the early 1920s, he moved quickly into a successful grade career, made good use of the then infrequent first-class opportunities for his State's players, and maintained his form at a high level until the Second World War. A regular member of the State team during the years its matches were practically confined to those against visiting international sides or the Australia XI en route to Britain, he scored 748 runs and took 50 wickets, first with leg-breaks and later with slow-medium-pace deliveries. He captained

the Fremantle club for more than 15 years and also the State side before moving into administration. Attention to detail and meticulous dress on the field were among the memorable characteristics of Mervyn Inverarity and they have been very much in evidence with his son John, the successful captain of the State's Sheffield Shield team.

IREDALE, Francis Adams, the famous New South Wales cricketer, died at North Sydney on April 15, 1926. As he had been born on June 19, 1867, he was in his 59th year at the time of his death. A resourceful batsman, he combined sound defence with good hitting; he could also cut gracefully and vigorously, while in the long-field he was excellent, covering much ground and being a sure catch. He made his first appearance for New South Wales at the age of 21, but it was not until the season of 1894–95 that he began to make a name for himself. Then he did very well against Mr. Stoddart's team, and, maintaining his form, was one of the first men chosen for the trip to England in 1896. Until the latter part of June he did not during that tour perform up to his reputation, but then in quick succession he scored 94 not out v. Notts, 114 v. Yorkshire, 106 v. Hampshire, 171 v. Players, 108 in the Test match at Manchester, 73 v. Derbyshire and 62 v. M.C.C. During the tour only S. E. Gregory, Darling and Hill had better records, his average of 1,328 runs being 27.32. Coming to England again three years later he made 1,039 runs and averaged 29.68, his largest innings being 115 v. W. G. Grace's XI at the Crystal Palace and 111 v. Middlesex at Lord's. In all Test matches, both at home and abroad, against England he scored 807 runs with an average of 36.68, his highest effort being 140 against Stoddart's team at Adelaide in 1894–95. In Australia he made six centuries in big matches, the largest of them—both for New South Wales—being 196 v. Tasmania in 1898–99 and 187 (he scored 80 not out in his second innings) v. South Australia in 1895–96. Playing his last game for his State in 1901–02, he had a short though brilliant career in great matches. From early in 1922 until his death he was Secretary of the N.S.W. Cricket Association, and he also did much journalistic work besides being the author of a very interesting book entitled *Thirty-three Years' Cricket*. At Sydney in February, 1922, a match between The Australian XI and the Rest of Australia was played in his honour, and it brought him in £1,740 10s. 9d.

IREMONGER, Albert, who died on March 9, 1958, played for Nottinghamshire between 1899 and 1914, his best score being 60 not out against Sussex at Trent Bridge in 1909. He was a younger brother of the more celebrated Nottinghamshire batsman, James Iremonger. Albert Iremonger's chief claim to fame was as an Association footballer. He stood nearly 6ft. 6in. and, as a goalkeeper for Notts County, with whom he was associated for 24 years, and later for Lincoln City, could throw the ball as far as most men could kick it.

IREMONGER, James, who died at Nottingham on March 25, 1956, aged 80, was one of the finest batsmen ever to play for Nottinghamshire. While it could not be said that he was a player of particularly graceful style, his skill as a run-getter was beyond doubt. Standing over 6ft, he watched the ball closely and could hit hard in front of the wicket, being specially good in on-driving.

Though of Yorkshire birth, he came of a Nottingham family and played from 1897 till 1914 for the county, for whom he scored 16,328 runs, average 35.33, including 32 centuries. His best season was that of 1904 when, with the aid of six centuries, he scored in 34 innings 1,983 runs, average 60.09. In that summer he hit the highest of his four scores of 200 or more, 272 against Kent at Trent Bridge, in the course of which he shared three partnerships exceeding 100. He and A. O. Jones began Nottinghamshire innings with as many as 24 stands of three figures—twice in a match (134 and 144) against Surrey at the Oval in 1901 and (102 and 303) against Gloucestershire at Trent Bridge in 1904.

Iremonger was chosen for Players v. Gentlemen on eight occasions, three times at Lord's and five times at the Oval, and he toured Australia with Pelham Warner's M.C.C. team of 1911–12 without taking part in a Test match.

Besides his ability in batting, he developed into a capital medium-pace bowler, bringing the ball down from a good height and making it break back from the off. He took 616 wickets for Nottinghamshire, average 22.25. Among his performances was the dismissal of eight Gloucestershire batsmen for 21 runs in the first innings at Trent Bridge in 1912.

Against M.C.C. and Ground at Lord's in 1902, he was the central figure of an unusual incident. For the first time in a big match, white enamelled stumps were being used—and the enamel was not quite dry. Iremonger received a ball which moved a stump to which the bail adhered! He went on to score 100.

At the end of the 1921 season he was appointed coach to Nottinghamshire, holding that post till he retired in 1938. To him belonged much credit for the early development of that celebrated pair of England fast bowlers, H. Larwood and W. Voce.

Besides his cricketing ability, Iremonger was an Association footballer of class. During 15 years with Nottingham Forest as left full-back, he gained England International honours three times; against Scotland and Germany in 1901 and Ireland the following season. He later served as player-coach to Notts County.

IRONMONGER, Herbert, who died in his sleep in Melbourne on May 31, 1971, 10 days before his 89th birthday, was, at 45 years 237 days, the fourth eldest cricketer to make a Test debut when, against England at Brisbane in 1928–29, he made the first of 14 appearances for Australia. A slow-medium left-arm spin bowler, he achieved some remarkable performances during his brief Test career, chief among them being that in 1931–32 when he earned a match analysis of 11 wickets for 24 runs on an awkward pitch at Melbourne and was mainly responsible for the dismissal of South Africa for totals of 36 and 45. His full figures in the two innings are worth recording. They were:

Overs	Maidens	Runs	Wickets
7.2	5	6	5
15.3	7	18	6

In four matches of that Test series, he took 31 wickets for 9.67 runs each.

He also achieved great things against G. C. Grant's West Indies team in 1930–31. For Victoria against the tourists, his figures were five wickets for 87 in the first innings and eight for 31 in the second, and in four Test matches he obtained 22 wickets at a cost of 14.68 runs each, heading the Australia averages. In the last Test at Melbourne, his analyses were seven wickets for 23 runs and four for 56. In the same season, he helped Victoria to carry off the Sheffield Shield, his main feats being seven wickets for 135 runs against Queensland and five for 60 against South Australia.

Though not meeting with such phenomenal success against England he dismissed in six meetings with Australia's oldest cricket rivals—including four in D. R. Jardine's "body-line" tour of 1932–33—21 batsmen for an average of 33.90. His figures for all Test matches were 74 wickets, average 17.97.

"Dainty" Ironmonger did the hat-trick

once, against A. E. R. Gilligan's 1924–25 M.C.C. team at Melbourne, where for Victoria he ended the innings by disposing of the last three batsmen with successive balls. In 42 Sheffield Shield matches for Victoria, his wickets numbered 215, average 24.74, and he also bowled with marked success for the Melbourne and St. Kilda clubs.

His achievements were the more remarkable because he had lost the forefinger of his left hand.

IRVINE, Col. Leonard George, who died suddenly on April 27, 1973, aged 67, was in the Taunton School XI before he went up to Cambridge in 1926 and created something of a sensation by taking 11 wickets for 42 runs in the Freshmen's match. That season for the University he took with slow leg-breaks 52 wickets at an average cost of 19.59. He got his Blue that year and in 1927, when he took part in one match for Kent.

ISAAC, Lieut. Arthur Whitmore (Worcestershire Regiment), born on October 4, 1873, fell in France on July 7, 1916. He was not in the XI at either Harrow or Oxford, but rendered the greatest service to the game in Worcestershire. He played in the county team over a long period, being a hard-hitting bat and excellent field, served on the Committee many years, and for a time was Treasurer of the County Club. He was captain of Worcester St. John's C.C., and in club matches obtained almost a hundred centuries. Since 1907 he had been a member of the M.C.C. His brother and brother-in-law, Major Wodehouse, were killed at Neuve Chapelle.

ISAAC, Capt. John Edmund Valentine, D.S.O. (2nd Batt. Rifle Brigade), was born in February, 1880, and killed in action in France on May 9, 1915, having previously been Mentioned in Dispatches, and wounded on October 24. He was not in the XI whilst at Harrow, but played occasionally for Worcestershire in 1907 and 1908, and had been a member of the M.C.C. since 1903. His name will occasionally be found in Free Foresters matches. During the South African campaign he was severely wounded at Nooitgedacht in December, 1900. He was a well-known gentleman jockey, and in 1911 rode the winner of the Cairo Grand National.

ISHERWOOD, Lieut.-Col. Lionel Charles Ramsbottom, who died on September 30, 1970, aged 79, did not gain a place in the XI while at Eton, but he played occasional

matches for Hampshire between 1919 and 1923 and from 1925 to 1927 assisted Sussex.

IVERSON, John Brian, who died in Melbourne on October 24, 1973, aged 58, was an unusual bowler who created something of a sensation during a brief career in Australian cricket. He bowled fast when at school, but took no part in cricket for 12 years afterwards. While on Army service in New Guinea, "Big Jack," as he was known, developed a peculiar method of spinning the ball, which he gripped between his thumb and middle finger. This enabled him to bowl a wide variety of deliveries, including offbreaks, leg-breaks and googlies, without any change of action. He first attracted attention in big cricket in 1949–50 when he took 46 wickets for Victoria at an average cost of 16.12. In the following autumn with W. A. Brown's team in New Zealand, he, in all matches, disposed of 75 batsmen at a cost of seven runs each and in the next Australian season, at the age of 35, he was chosen for his country against the England team captained by F. R. Brown. So perplexing did the visiting batsmen find the bowling of this tall man that in the Test series he obtained 21 wickets for 15.73 runs apiece, including six for 27 in the second innings of the third Test at Sydney. During the fourth Test at Adelaide he suffered an ankle injury when he trod on the ball. He played in only one game in each of the next two seasons and then gave up cricket altogether.

JACKSON, Alfred Louis Stuart, who died on July 23, 1982, aged 79, was captain of Cheltenham in 1922, when he headed the batting averages and played for the Lord's Schools. Going out to South America, he played for both Chile and the Argentine and was a member of the South American side which toured England in 1932 and played a number of first-class matches. He himself came out top of the batting averages, making 674 with an average of 39.64. Against a strong side of Sir Julien Cahn's he and D. Ayling put on 102 and 113 for the first wicket, the second of these partnerships taking only 65 minutes. Jackson's scores were 62 and 78. The touring side, facing a total of 413, won by five wickets. He was a younger brother of J. A. S. Jackson of Somerset.

JACKSON, Archibald, the New South Wales and Australian Test cricketer, died at Brisbane on February 16, 1933, the day that England defeated Australia and regained the

Ashes, at the early age of 23. His passing was not only a very sad loss to Australian cricket in particular but to the cricket world in general. A native of Scotland, where he was born on September 5, 1909, he was hailed as a second Victor Trumper—a comparison made alike for his youthful success, elegant style and superb stroke play. Well set up, very active on his feet, and not afraid to jump in to the slow bowlers and hit the ball hard, he accomplished far more in big cricket than Trumper had done at his age. He first attracted attention when at school at Balmain, Sydney, and later at the Roselle School. So quickly did he mature that, at the age of 17, he gained an assured place in the New South Wales team. In his first season of Sheffield Shield cricket he scored 464 runs at an average of 58; next year he achieved a feat no other batsman of his age had performed, by making two centuries in a match—131 and 122 against South Australia. For a time Jackson had something of a reputation of being a second innings batsman, for often he failed at his first attempt and then made a good score in the second innings. This weakness, however, he overcame and he soon established himself as an opening batsman for New South Wales. Given his place in the Australian team when the M.C.C. side, under the captaincy of Mr. A. P. F. Chapman, toured Australia in 1928–29, Jackson, on his first appearance in Test cricket against England, made a hundred—the youngest player to do so. This was at Adelaide where in the fourth Test match, which England won by 12 runs, he scored 164. For sheer brilliance of execution his strokes during this delightful display could scarcely have been exceeded. He reached three figures with a glorious square drive off Larwood in the first over after lunch and was one of the very few Australian batsmen who during that tour could successfully jump in and drive J. C. White. An innings of 182 in the Australian Test Trial—regarded as the finest he ever played—made certain of his inclusion in the team which visited England in 1930. Unfortunately, English cricket lovers did not in that tour see Jackson at his best, for although he scored over 1,000 runs he failed to reveal his true form until towards the end of the summer. Then, in the final Test match at the Oval, he put together a score of 73, and helped Bradman in a partnership of 243 for the fourth wicket which still stands as a record in a Test match between Australia and England. Jackson, of course, never saw Trumper play, but Kippax, in style and stance and in some strokes, was not unlike

Trumper; and Jackson, consciously or unconsciously, and while giving full play to his natural tendencies, took Kippax as his model. He had a splendid return from the deep field and, if not so fast a runner as Bradman, covered ground very quickly. His later years were marred by continued ill-health and his untimely end was not unexpected. While lying in hospital on what was to prove his death-bed he was married.

JACKSON, Arthur Kenneth, who died in Germany on May 31, 1971, aged 67, had been on the Warwickshire Committee since 1959. In his younger days a good fast bowler, he played twice for the county in 1928 and 1931.

JACKSON, Arthur Kenneth, included in the 1973 edition, should read **JACKSON, Arnold Kenneth**.

JACKSON, Dirk Cloete, who died on his farm near Pretoria on September 17, 1976, at the age of 91, was almost certainly the Senior first-class cricketer in South Africa measured by length of service. He made his debut for Western Province in 1908–09 and after playing for them for three seasons, he moved to the Transvaal for whom he made a couple of appearances in 1912–13. He had been the scrum-half in the first Springbok Rugby team to tour the United Kingdom in 1906 and was the last survivor of that team.

JACKSON, Capt. Guy R., who died in a Chesterfield hospital on February 21, 1966, aged 69, was a left-handed batsman who captained Derbyshire for eight years. While at Harrow, he appeared against Eton at Lord's, scoring 59—his highest innings of the season. After serving in the First World War, during which he was twice Mentioned in Dispatches and awarded the M.C. and the Legion d'Honneur, he played for Derbyshire from 1919 to 1936, becoming captain in 1922. In four seasons he exceeded 1,000 runs. In all first-class cricket until his retirement from the game he scored 10,153 runs, including nine centuries, for an average of 23.07, and held 109 catches. He was joint managing director of the family iron and steel business, the Clay Cross Co., Ltd.

JACKSON, John, died in Liverpool Workhouse Infirmary on November 4, 1901, in his 69th year. His career, which extended from 1855 to 1866, was terminated, as regards big matches, by a serious accident sustained whilst playing against Yorkshire. Inasmuch as his connection with first-class cricket ended 35 years ago, John Jackson had long outlived his fame, but no one acquainted with the history of the game will need to be told that in his day he was the best fast bowler in England. Born in Suffolk on May 21, 1833, he was taken to Nottingham in infancy, and with Notts cricket he was associated all the time he played. He first appeared at Lord's in 1856, and soon went to the top of the tree. Cricket in those days was very different from what it is now. Wickets were not prepared with the excessive pains now taken over them, scores were naturally far smaller, and bowlers met with a measure of success that in this generation would be impossible. It is fruitless to inquire what rank John Jackson would have taken in the cricket world if he had been born 30 years later. The important fact is that under the conditions prevailing in his own time he was great. He was past his best when the accident occurred that cut short his career, but as he was then only 33 he would probably have lasted several seasons longer. In style he belonged to the old round-arm school, all his best work being done before the restriction as to the height of the arm was removed, but as he was a man of fully 6ft. the ball came from a good elevation. He had tremendous pace, and, like most of the right-handed fast bowlers of his time, but unlike Tarrant, made the ball go a little with his arm. Tarrant at times broke back but, on the evidence of Caffyn and others who played against him, was not so straight or so accurate in length as Jackson. The two bowlers went to Australia with George Parr's team in 1863–64, and met with great success. Jackson was then at the height of his fame, but he began to decline when he returned to England. He was a member of the England XI that in 1859 visited America. He assisted the Players in their matches against the Gentlemen from 1859 to 1864, bowling in 12 matches (23 innings) 2,139 balls for 827 runs and 69 wickets, average 11.98. At Lord's in 1861 he and the late Edgar Willsher bowled unchanged through both innings of the Gentlemen, Jackson obtaining 11 wickets for 99 runs, and Willsher six for 70. During the greater part of the time he was before the public he was one of the stars of the All England XI, taking any number of wickets against local XXIIs all over the country. Some years after his retirement from the county XI the Notts Committee gave him a benefit at Trent Bridge, but in his later days he felt the pinch of poverty severely.

A famous cricketer of the last generation, who played occasionally against Jackson, and often saw him bowl, writes: "It always struck me that he had a greater command over the ball than any other very fast bowler, and was able to vary pitch and pace with great judgment." By reason of his command and variety, this gentleman considers that Jackson was far better than Tarrant on a good wicket, and superior even to George Freeman. Mr. E. M. Grace, writing of Jackson's bowling, differs from other authorities in saying that he broke both ways, and adds that except Bickley and the Hon. Wingfield Fiennes, he cannot recollect any bowler who came quicker off the pitch.

JACKSON, Samuel Robinson, was closely devoted to the welfare of the Yorkshire County Club from early manhood until his death at Leeds on July 19, 1941, soon after entering his 83rd year. He played a few matches for Yorkshire in 1891, then represented Leeds on the Committee, and was a Vice-President for many years. When the Scarborough ground was opened, on the occasion of a match between the Leeds and the Scarborough clubs, he received the first ball bowled.

SIR STANLEY JACKSON
The passing of Colonel The Honourable Sir Francis Stanley Jackson, P.C., G.C.I.E., on March 9, 1947, in his 77th year, came as a shock, not only to all who knew him personally, but also to every lover of cricket who had watched and enjoyed his wonderful prowess on the field of play. From the time that F. S. Jackson at Lord's by his remarkable all-round success helped Harrow gain a victory over Eton by 156 runs in 1888, he went on from strength to strength, until he became one of the finest cricketers ever seen in England. Unfortunately he could not go on any tour to Australia owing to business reasons, and the presence of Lord Hawke in command of Yorkshire until 1910 prevented him from ever being the county captain, though occasionally in charge of the side. He reached the zenith of fame in 1905 when captain of England against Australia. In all five Tests he won the toss; made 492 runs with an average of 70, among his scores being 144 not out at Leeds, 113 at Manchester, 82 not out at Nottingham, 76 and 31 at the Oval; took 13 wickets at 15.46 each, surpassing the efforts of all his colleagues and opponents. Of the five contests, England won that at Nottingham by 213 runs—after declaring with five men out—and that at Manchester by an innings and 80 runs, while they held much the stronger position in each

of the three matches left unfinished. By a curious coincidence Stanley Jackson and Joseph Darling, then the Australian captain, were exactly the same age, both having been born on November 21, 1870. That was Darling's third visit as captain and his last tour in England. He died on January 2, 1946, and his obituary in last year's *Wisden* contains some of his experiences in opposition to Jackson.

Regarding his luck in winning the toss in those 1905 Tests and as captain of M.C.C., for whom he scored 85 in a rain-ruined match at Lord's, Jackson said that at Scarborough, when captain for the seventh time against the Australians: "I found Darling stripped to the waist. He said, 'Now we'll have a proper tossing, and he who gets on top wins the toss.' So I said to George Hirst, 'Georgie, you come and toss this time.' Darling then said, 'All right, we'll toss in the old-fashioned way!'" Again winning the toss, Jackson scored 123 and 31 not out, rain preventing a definite result.

Born at Chapel Allerton, near Leeds, Stanley Jackson showed remarkable batting ability when at a preparatory school before he went to Harrow, where he was in the XI for three years, being captain in 1889. He did little on the first occasion, and his father, then the Rt. Hon. W. L. Jackson, a member of the Cabinet in Lord Salisbury's second Government, promised Stanley a sovereign for each wicket he took and a shilling for each run he made. Stanley scored 21 and 59 and took 11 wickets for 68 runs; Harrow won by 156 runs. His father's generosity over cricket ceased with that match. Stanley's only comment was that he was glad he had come off, as it would "do father so much good."

Next year, when captain, five wickets fell to him, and his vigorous 68, best score in the match, accounted largely for victory by nine wickets. Proceeding to Cambridge, Jackson gained his Blue as a Freshman, and in 1892 he headed both the batting and bowling averages, and in first-class matches came out third among the amateur bowlers with 80 wickets for less than 19 runs apiece.

Re-elected captain, he led Cambridge to victory by 266 runs in 1893, showing such convincing form that he was given a place in the England team for the first Test at Lord's. He followed a splendid innings of 91 with 103 at the Oval, but when, late in August, the time came for the third Test—at Manchester—he and other Yorkshiremen who might have been included in the side turned out for their county against Sussex at Brighton. He was one of "Five All-Rounders" given prominence in 1894 *Wisden*.

Describing his first Test innings of 91 in 1893 at Lord's, Sir Stanley smiled and then related that, in the second Test at the Oval, W. G. Grace, the England captain, said, "With all these batsmen I don't know where to put you." "Anywhere will do." "Then number seven." "Thanks. That's my lucky number; I was the seventh child." "And that match brought my first hundred for England. Mold came in last when I was 99. He nearly ran me out, so in desperation I jumped in and drove Giffen high to the seats, reaching 103. Then the bewildered Mold did run me out."

Jackson figured in all the 1896 Test matches, also in the next visit of Australia when the "rubber" was extended to five fixtures, being credited with 118 at the Oval in 1899. In the great games of 1902 Jackson was England's best batsman. He did little at Sheffield, but at Birmingham, when three wickets fell for 35, he scored 53 and with J. T. Tyldesley saved England from collapse. At Lord's Fry and Ranjitsinhji were dismissed without a run, but Jackson and A. C. MacLaren, contemporaries at Harrow, raised the total to 102 without being separated before rain washed out the match. In the memorable Manchester struggle, which Australia won by three runs, five England wickets went down for 44 in reply to a total of 299, but Jackson and Braund pulled the game round with a partnership of 141, Jackson himself going on to make 128. At dinner in the evening of that great day a lady sitting next to him said, "I was so disappointed that Ranjitsinhji failed"—and this remark was made to the man who had played the innings of his life. He was fond of telling this little yarn against himself. At the Oval Jackson scored 49, sharing in a partnership of 109 with G. L. Jessop, whose wonderful innings of 104 paved the way to England's one-wicket victory. Altogether Jackson scored 1,415 runs in Test matches against Australia—all in this country—with an average of nearly 49, and took 24 wickets at an average of 33.

Jackson played first for Yorkshire in 1890, and his last appearance for the side was in 1907. During that period he scored 10,405 runs for the county, averaging nearly 34 an innings, and dismissed 506 batsmen for 19 runs apiece. In 1898, the only season when he appeared regularly for his county, he scored 1,566 runs and took 104 wickets. His highest scores for Yorkshire were 160 against Gloucestershire, 158 against Surrey, and 155 against Middlesex. He appeared on many occasions for Gentlemen against Players, and in those games made over a thousand runs, average 31.50, and took 50 wickets. His aggregate for all first-class matches was 16,251 runs, average 33, and 834 wickets at 19 runs each.

Among his bowling triumphs were eight Lancashire wickets at Sheffield in 1902 for 13 runs, and the last four Australian wickets in five balls at Leeds in the same year, his analysis being five wickets for 12; he and George Hirst dismissed the Australians for 23. This happened directly after England in a drawn Test match had disposed of Australia for 36; Rhodes, who took seven wickets for 17, did not bowl in the more remarkable collapse of the Australians for the second lowest total ever recorded by an Australian side in England. When in 1896 Harry Trott's team fell for 18 before M.C.C. at Lord's, Jackson scored 51 on a treacherous pitch. In the Gentlemen and Players match at Lord's in 1894 he and S.M.J. Woods bowled unchanged. Jackson took 12 wickets for 77 and, in addition, made 63—the highet score of the match, which the Gentlemen won by an innings and 37 runs before four o'clock on the second day.

Going to India with Lord Hawke's team in the winter of 1892–93, Jackson took 69 wickets at 10.27 runs apiece and tied for first place in the batting averages with A.J.L. Hill, a Cambridge contemporary. When again captain of the Light Blues in 1893, Jackson gave Ranjitsinhji his Blue. At Lord's he instructed C.M. Wells to bowl wides in order to prevent Oxford from getting a desired follow-on, and Cambridge won by 266 runs. This set an example followed by Frank Mitchell three years later, when Oxford won by four wickets, and so primarily led to an alteration in the laws, making the follow-on an optional choice for the side holding the upper hand.

President of the Marylebone Club in 1921, the highest honour that a cricketer can enjoy, Sir Stanley Jackson was chairman of Test Match Selection Committee in 1934, and in 1943 presided over the special committee appointed by M.C.C. to consider Post-war Cricket.

Well-built and standing nearly 6 ft. high, Stanley Jackson was equipped with special physical advantages for cricket; to these were added fine judgment, perseverance, and, above all, exceptional courage which amounted to belief in his own abilities. Free and stylish in method, he drove splendidly on either side of the wicket and was perhaps the finest forcing on-side batsman of his time. While essentially a forward player on hard wickets, he had at his command on sticky wickets a strength and science of back play to which few men have attained. His great stroke sent a good-length ball through the covers; he cut square or late and turned the ball cleverly on the leg side with similar precision. Nothing was better than the way he jumped in and drove the ball over the bowler's head, as shown in the life-like picture at Lord's, and as I saw at Bradford, where he sent the ball high over the football stand.

A right-handed rather fast-medium bowler with a nice easy action and plenty of spin, he kept a good length and often got on a sharp off-break. On a difficult wicket he was a bowler who might dispose of any side. While always a keen and smart field, especially at cover-point, he was not in his early days a sure catch, but steadily improved in this respect and made himself in every sense a great player.

At Bradford on one occasion he was out to a brilliant catch in the long field, whereupon he tucked his bat under his arm and joined vigorously in the applause which greeted the fieldsman's splendid effort.

On the same ground, where there is a stone wall in front of the pavilion, a ball bowled by Jackson was sent by a low skimming drive with such force that it rolled back from the wall into the middle of the field, coming to rest practically at the bowler's feet. Jackson, in appreciation of the remarkable occurrence, made the ball a dignified bow.

In the South African War Jackson served with the Royal Lancaster Regiment of Militia, and in the First World War, he was Lieutenant-Colonel of a West Yorkshire Regiment battalion which he raised and commanded. He entered Parliament in 1915 and remained Unionist member for Howdenshire Division of Yorkshire until 1926. One day in the House of Commons dining-room Mr. Winston Churchill, who had been his fag at Harrow, said, "Let me introduce you to Mr. Lloyd George." There came a quick exclamation, "I have been looking all my life for the man who gave Winston Churchill a hiding at school."

When he wanted to make his maiden speech the debate went unfavourably, and he received a note from the Speaker: "I have dropped you in the batting order; it's a sticky wicket." Then, at a better opportunity, he sent this hint: "Get your pads on; you're next in."

In 1922 he was appointed Financial Secretary to the War Office, and next year he succeeded Lord Younger as Chairman of the Unionist Party Organisation. In 1927 he went out to India as Governor of Bengal. There he proved equal to the most trying situation, behaving with splendid nerve and authority when he nearly fell a victim to attempted assassination by a Calcutta girl student who fired five shots at close range, narrowly missing Sir Stanley when presiding at a meeting. His London home was bombed in 1940, and in August 1946 he was run over by a taxi, receiving a severe injury to his right leg: a climax to unpleasant experiences which no doubt contributed to his last illness and hastened the end of this very distinguished Englishman.

H.P.

TRIBUTES

In *Wisden*, 1932, Lord Hawke, in an article—"Fifty Years of Yorkshire County"—wrote:

"Our greatest amateur was undoubtedly Stanley Jackson, who was 'Jacker' to everyone from his Harrow days. He was a great batsman, great bowler, fine fielder—a great cricketer to the core. Few who remember him as a batsman know that he was once No. 10 in the batting order for Yorkshire! This is how it happened. Though he had just taken seven for 42 against Middlesex, somebody had run him out for a song and he did not seem keen to play in the next match at Chesterfield.

"'Why,' I argued with him, 'you've just got seven of 'em out at six apiece! You must come.' So he came all right. Next day as I was writing out the order I asked him where he'd like to go in, so he said, 'Oh, don't know. Treat me as a bowler.' So I wrote him down No. 10. Brown and Tunnicliffe then proceeded to make 554 for the first wicket. I was No. 3 that day in Jackson's place. As they walked out to bat I put on my pads. I took them off for the lunch interval; I put them on again and took them off again for the tea interval. Again I put them on, and sat another couple of hours. Such is cricket!

"I have never seen 'Jacker's' equal at bowling for his field. I remember one occasion when we were 'in the cart' at Bradford against Surrey how precisely he bowled for his field, and how he apologised to me for having bowled a ball not intended. Though his grand batting for England is probably best remembered, he was a bowler of the very highest class, with a graceful, flowing delivery of a kind but rarely seen nowadays.

"Since those happy days 'Jacker' has passed through more serious times in Bengal. There, a couple of years ago, he and I were the guests of honour at the dinner to us of the Calcutta Cricket Club given at the Bengal Club. We both made speeches, and when he got up to speak first he said across the table to me, 'I've got first innings to-day, old man. You bossed me often enough in the past, but I'm boss here!'"

Sir Pelham Warner, in a letter to *The Times*, wrote:

"I had known Sir Stanley Jackson since 1889, when Harrow met Rugby at Althorp Park. On that evening began a friendship which grew with the years, and which I prized greatly. 'He was my friend, faithful and just to me,' and though we all have to face the Pale Horseman there is no need to be afraid of him, and I am certain Sir Stanley faced him with the same calm courage as he showed in the great matches of his day. He was a splendid all-round cricketer—one of the finest in the history of cricket—and never was he finer than in a crisis; it was a stirring sight to see him come down the pavilion steps to set right any early failures there may have been; immaculate in his flannels and his beautifully cleaned pads and boots, with his neat trim figure every inch a cricketer. No English cricketer had a finer record in England against Australia. And then, when he gave up, he sat on the Woolsack of Cricket, as President of the M.C.C., and at the time of his death he was a trustee of Lord's, chairman of the Cricket Committee, and president of the Yorkshire County C.C. To the end he took the greatest possible interest in M.C.C. Never a week passed, even during the winter, that he was not at Lord's, and in the summer he was the best known of all the men who delight in the charm and atmosphere of the famous ground. He was busy with every avenue and aspect of the game and his enthusiasm never flagged. That he had been seriously ill for some time was obvious, but only a few days before he died he telephoned asking me to come to see him. I found him in good spirits, saying that he felt so much better that he had good hopes of coming to Lord's for a committee meeting.

"As a batsman he was soundness itself, with all the strokes—what I call a 'complete' batsman. His style was easy and natural and he inspired confidence. Bowling medium pace, with a beautifully easy action, he kept a length. At cover point, his usual position, he was not a Hobbs or a Jessop, but active and quick, missing few chances. In a gallery of great players it is impossible to have a fixed order of merit, but he was in the first class of an honours school of cricket both as a batsman and an all-rounder. When you have known and been very fond of a man for nearly 60 years it is not easy to write exactly what you feel about him, but this I will say, that his manner was always easy and pleasant, and in the cricket world, by young and old alike, he was welcomed, appreciated and respected. His absence leaves a big void."

Wilfred Rhodes, now 70 years of age, wrote: "In paying a modest tribute to the late Sir Stanley Jackson it is difficult for me to find words that would express my appreciation of such a great cricketer with so fine a personality. From 1898 to the close of his first-class cricket career I was fortunate to play on the same side for Yorkshire and under his captaincy several times for England, chiefly in Tests against Australia, and had a great admiration for his ability. He was one of England's greatest captains and played many splendid innings during this period. It was a pity he never toured Australia, as I think he would have been very successful with his style of play on their fast wickets.

"A model all-round cricketer if ever there was one, he was immaculately dressed, flannels always neat and trim even at the end of a long innings, and whether batting, bowling or in the field, his movements were stylish and graceful. He was a great batsman and possessed the gift of a fine temperament, with plenty of confidence and pluck, and always appeared at his best on great occasions, especially when fighting with his back to the wall. Many times he pulled the game around for England and helped to put them on the way to victory. His batting was stylish, orthodox and very copy-book, with strokes all round the wicket, and particularly strong to the off.

"As a bowler he used spin and variation of pace with a clever slow one. On one occasion, when bowling to G.L. Jessop at Cambridge, he sent up his slower ball, which was hit out of the field over the trees. Schofield Haigh, fielding mid-on, was laughing, and F.S., turning round, said to him, 'What are you laughing at?' Haigh replied, 'Your slow ball, sir.' F.S.: 'It was a good one, wasn't it?'"

George Hirst, the famous Yorkshire cricketer, now in his 77th year, wrote at the time of Sir Stanley's death:

"I am deeply grieved to learn of the death of my friend and colleague. He was one of the most graceful of all cricketers, whether he was batting, bowling or fielding, and he was a

perfect gentleman in everything he did, both on and off the field.

"In him young cricketers had a perfect model. Many are the times I have seen him with a beautifully rolled umbrella in his hand demonstrating strokes to schoolboys. He loved to help the youngsters, and that was possibly why he was always so keenly interested in my work as coach to the County Club. I have indeed lost a good friend."

Mr. H.D.G. Leveson Gower said: "As a Test match player Sir Stanley never has been excelled in temperament or skill. I served with him on many M.C.C. committees, and his views on the game always commanded attention. I played against him for Oxford in the Varsity match of 1893, and consider the Cambridge XI he captained one of the most powerful to represent that University. His name will always live in the annals of cricket, the game he adorned."

Mr. Stanley Christopherson, President of M.C.C. for several years until 1946: "I held the greatest admiration for Sir Stanley both as a cricketer and for his great work for the game; he was most painstaking and did splendid work on many committees and as a selector."

Mr. T.L. Taylor, an old Cambridge Blue who was elected the new president of Yorkshire in the autumn, a contemporary player with Sir Stanley, described his death as a very serious loss to county and international cricket and the game in general, and said: "He was one of Yorkshire's greatest all-rounders, and one of England's most redoubtable Test captains."

The King was represented by Lord Chorley at the London memorial service for Sir Stanley Jackson. Canon F.H. Gillingham, the former Essex cricketer, who conducted the service, said:

"The first time I ever played with him I was impressed with his strength of character and control. He always seemed to have that extra reserve of strength to compete with any cricket crisis, however severe.

"He was the most honest man I ever met—in fact he was too honest. I never heard him say an unkind word about anyone, and he always had excuses for anyone who spoke an unkind word to him.

"So we say farewell to a great English gentleman, but we will retain with us for ever the remembrance of all that he meant to us and to the country he served so well."

JACKSON, Victor Edward, who was killed in a motor-car accident in Australia on January 28, 1965, aged 48, played for New

South Wales in 1936 before qualifying by residence for Leicestershire. He played in two non-Championship matches for the county in 1938 and 1939, when he toured New Zealand with Sir Julien Cahn's team, and when war broke out returned to Australia. Back in England, he appeared as a professional for Leicestershire from 1946 to 1956. An all-rounder, he scored 15,698 runs, average 28.43, and took with off-breaks 965 wickets for 24.73 runs each. The highest of his 21 centuries was 170 against Northamptonshire at Leicester in 1948 and he completed 1,000 runs in each of his 11 seasons. He often coached in South Africa during the English winter and in 1957 and 1958 was professional for Rawtenstall in the Lancashire League.

JAGGER, Samuel Thornton, who died suddenly on May 30, 1964, aged 59, was a Cambridge Blue who, between 1922 and 1931, assisted Worcestershire, Sussex, Bedfordshire, Denbighshire and Wales. He headed the Malvern batting averages in both years he was in the XI, 1921 and 1922, and played as a medium-pace bowler in the University matches of 1925 and 1926. His four wickets for 34 runs in the second innings at Lord's in 1926 helped Cambridge to success by 34 runs. He also represented the University at fives. His best batting effort in first-class cricket was 41 for Worcestershire against Hampshire at Worcester in 1923, when he and the Hon. J. Coventry added 67 in three-quarters of an hour for the ninth wicket. His career with the county ended when it was found that he was not qualified to play for them. Jagger later became a house-master at Lancing.

JAI, L.P., who died on January 29, 1968, aged 66, was in his day among the leading Indian batsman. He scored 1,278 runs, average 31.95, for Hindus in the Quadrangular (later Pentangular) Tournament, with 156 against the Muslims in 1924 the highest of his three centuries; and he captained the side when they won the Pentangular Tournament in 1941. He hit 774 runs, average 43.00, in Ranji Trophy matches for Bombay, whom he led to victory in the competition in 1934–35. His one Test match appearance for India was against A. E. R. Gilligan's England team in 1933, and he toured England with little success in 1936. He had been vice-president of the Bombay Cricket Association and a Test selector.

JAMES, 2nd Lieut. Burnet G. (R.F.A., attached to Flying Corps), fell in action in France at the end of September, 1915. For five years he was captain of the Bristol Imperial C.C., for which his batting average in 1914 was over 100. In the season mentioned he appeared on a few occasions for Gloucestershire, but with small success, scoring only 27 runs with an average of 5.40. He also represented Gloucestershire at hockey.

JAMES, Kenneth C., died at Palmerston North, N.Z., on August 21, 1976, aged 71. When he came to England with the first New Zealand team in 1927, he was expected to be second-string keeper to his captain, Tom Lowry. He soon disposed of this theory, keeping in a large proportion of the matches and, in a side which was clearly not yet ready for Test cricket, being accepted as one of the players of Test class. This impression he strengthened on his second visit in 1931. Qualifying for Northamptonshire, he played for them from 1935 to 1939 and then, after serving in the R.N.Z.A.F. during the War, returned to New Zealand. In a career for Wellington which started in 1923 he had scored several centuries and came to be regarded as a reliable bat, but, though he often showed valuable determination in a crisis, he did not, in England, live up to this reputation until his third regular season for Northamptonshire, 1938, when he exceeded 1,000 runs and made two hundreds. As a wicket-keeper he ranked high, but, in as much as he was one of the first to make a habit of standing back to medium-pace bowling, he must be regarded as partially responsible for one of the most questionable developments in modern cricket. He excelled in dealing with the spin of W. E. Merritt his New Zealand colleague who joined him at Northampton.

JAMES, Ronald Victor, who died on April 28, 1983, aged 62, was a right-hand batsman and agile field who played 33 Sheffield Shield games—20 for New South Wales and 13 for South Australia. For South Australia he scored 85 against W. R. Hammond's M.C.C. team in 1946–47 and in the following season made his best score, 210, for South Australia against Queensland. In 1949–50, by when he had returned to Sydney, he took over the captaincy of New South Wales from Keith Miller who had been called to reinforce the Australian team then in South Africa. New South Wales won the Shield. At the end of a career in which he scored 2,582 runs (average 40.34), James became a New South Wales selector.

JAMESON, Tom Ormsby, who died in a Dublin hospital on February 6, 1965, aged 72, was in the Harrow XI in 1909 and 1910, taking part in the historic "Fowler's Match" in the second year. In that game Eton, dismissed for 67 and following on 165 behind, had lost five men for 65 before R. St. L. Fowler came to the rescue with an innings of 64. Even so, Harrow were left only 55 runs to get for victory, but they collapsed against the off-breaks of Fowler, who took eight wickets for 23, and Eton snatched a remarkable win by nine runs. In the match, Fowler scored 85 runs and earned bowling figures of 12 wickets for 113 runs.

"Tommy" Jameson was a great player of ball games. He played cricket for Hampshire as an all-rounder between 1919 and 1932; he represented Gentlemen against Players on four occasions; he played twice for Ireland and made three tours abroad—with the Hon. L. H. Tennyson's team to South Africa in 1924–25, with the Hon. F. S. G. Calthorpe's M.C.C. team to the West Indies in 1925–26 and P. F. Warner's M.C.C. side to South America in 1926–27, when he obtained two centuries and headed the batting averages with 42.11. In all first-class cricket he hit 4,631 runs, average 31.71, with leg-break bowling took 241 wickets for 23.92 runs each and, chiefly at slip, held 86 catches.

A fine racquets player, he won the Army Singles Championship in 1922, 1923 and 1924; was one of the winning pair in the Inter-Regimental Doubles Championship in 1920, 1921 and 1922 and reached the final of the Amateur Singles Championship in 1924. He also won the Amateur Squash Racquets Championship in 1922 and 1923.

JAQUES, Capt. Arthur (12th West Yorkshire Regiment), who was born at Shanghai on March 7, 1888, fell in action in France at the end of September, 1915. In 1905 and two following years he was in the Aldenham XI, in 1907 having a batting average of 20, and heading the bowling with a record of 43 wickets for 10.74 runs each. Subsequently he appeared with pronounced success for Hampshire. In 1913, his first season as a regular player for the county, he did nothing remarkable, but in 1914 in Championship matches alone he obtained 112 wickets for 18.26 runs each. Doubtless his unusual methods contributed much to his success, for, placing nearly all his field on the on-side, he pitched on the wicket or outside the leg-stump, and, swinging-in and getting on an off-break, cramped the batsmen so much that many of them lost patience and suc-

cumbed. That year he assisted the Gentlemen both at Lord's and the Oval, but took only two wickets in the two games for 73 runs. His best analyses during the season—all for Hampshire—were 14 for 105 (including eight for 67) v. Derbyshire at Basingstoke; 14 for 54 (including eight for 21) v. Somerset at Bath (he and Kennedy bowling unchanged throughout), and seven for 51 v. Warwickshire at Southampton. In all first-class matches during 1914 he obtained 117 wickets for 18.69 runs each. It is interesting to recall that at Cambridge he was never tried in the XI, although he played for the Freshmen in 1908 and the Seniors in 1909 and 1910, and that when he went to the West Indies in 1912–13 as a member of the M.C.C. team his five wickets cost 29 runs each. He was 6ft. 3in. in height.

JARDINE, Douglas Robert, who died in Switzerland on June 18, 1958, aged 57, was one of England's best captains and a leading amateur batsman of his time. He caught tick fever while visiting Southern Rhodesia in 1957 and thenceforward had been in poor health.

Son of M. R. Jardine, himself an Oxford Blue, Douglas Jardine was born at Bombay and educated at Winchester, where he was in the XI for three years, being captain in the last, 1919, when he headed the batting figures with 997 runs, average 66.46. Going up to New College, Oxford, he got his Blue as a Freshman and played against Cambridge in 1920, 1921 and 1923 without achieving anything out of the ordinary. He missed the 1922 University match because of a damaged knee. In 1923 he began to play for Surrey and in 1932 took over the captaincy from P. G. H. Fender.

He went to Australia in 1928–29 with the M.C.C. team under A. P. F. Chapman, taking part in all five Test matches. To England's success by 12 runs in the fourth Test he made a big contribution when scoring 98 and sharing with W. R. Hammond in a third-wicket partnership of 262. He also enjoyed the distinction of hitting three centuries in successive innings, against Western Australia, Victoria and New South Wales.

Four years later he captained the M.C.C. side in Australia in what was probably the most controversial tour in history. England won four of the five Tests, but it was the methods they employed rather than the results which caused so much discussion and acrimony. H. Larwood and W. Voce, the Nottinghamshire fast bowlers, exploited "leg-theory," or what came to be known as "body-line" bowling to a packed leg-side field. The Australians and others considered this means of attack placed batsmen at a grave disadvantage because they had either to risk being struck on the head or body by persistently short-pitched balls or, if they attempted to play them, were virtually certain to be caught by the close-set field.

Strongly-worded cables passed between the Australian Board of Control, who asserted that "body-line bowling has assumed such proportions as to menace the best interests of the game, making protection of the body the main consideration," and the M.C.C. The Australians threatened to call off the projected tour of England in 1934. M.C.C. at length agreed that "a form of bowling which is obviously a direct attack by the bowler upon the batsman would be an offence against the spirit of the game." Jardine always defended his tactics and in a book he wrote about the tour described allegations that the England bowlers directed their attack with the intention of causing physical harm as "stupid and patently untruthful."

Finally in 1934 M.C.C. issued a ruling: "That the type of bowling regarded as a direct attack by the bowler upon the batsman, and therefore unfair, consists in persistent and systematic bowling of fast and short-pitched balls at the batsman standing clear of his wicket." That was the end of body-line bowling.

Meanwhile in 1933, however, fast leg-theory had been employed by both England and the West Indies in the second Test match at Old Trafford. Jardine, who always held that this type of attack could be successfully countered by a resolute batsman, set out to prove the accuracy of his contention. For nearly five hours he faced the hostile pace of L. N. Constantine and E. A. Martindale and he hit 127, his first and only century in a Test match. In the process, he took much physical punishment, but "The Iron Duke," as he was sometimes called, had proved his point to his own satisfaction.

Jardine captained the M.C.C. team in India the following winter, but thereafter his appearances on the field became fewer till in 1937 he dropped out of first-class cricket altogether. At the same time he maintained his interest in the game, being President of the Oxford University C.C. from 1955 to 1957 and making occasional contributions to the Press. In 1953 he became the first President of the Association of Cricket Umpires.

Six feet tall, he possessed a very strong defence and was specially skilful in on-side strokes. In 22 Test match appearances he hit 1,296 runs, average 48, and held 26 catches. During his career his runs numbered 14,821, average 46.90, the highest of his 35 centuries being 214 not out against Tasmania in 1928–29. Extremely proud of his Oxford associations, he always wore a Harlequin cap.

Tributes included:

Sir Pelham Warner: "In my humble opinion, Jardine was a very fine captain, both on and off the field, and in the committee-room he was also extremely good. If ever there was a cricket match between England and the rest of the world and the fate of England depended upon its result, I would pick Jardine as England captain every time."

Sir Jack Hobbs: "I played with him a lot in the Surrey side and I feel that he will be chiefly remembered as a splendid skipper. As a captain, I would rank him second only to P. G. H. Fender. He was a great batsman—how great I do not think we quite appreciated at the time. I remember that he was the first man to refer to me as 'The Master.'"

W. E. Bowes: "To me and every member of the 1932–33 M.C.C. side in Australia, Douglas Jardine was the greatest captain England ever had. A great fighter, a grand friend and an unforgiving enemy."

R. Aird: "Jardine was a great player and captain and a man of character who, like all men of character, was not liked by everybody. He did what he set out to do, as when his side won the 'Ashes' in Australia in 1932–33, even if the method he adopted did not meet with general approval. His sound, solid batting inspired confidence in his colleagues."

JARDINE, Malcolm Robert, who died on January 16, 1947, aged 77, gained two great honours in the cricket world. In 1892, by scoring 140 and 39 against Cambridge at Lord's, he created an individual record for the highest aggregate in a University match; and his son, D. R. Jardine, captained England during the Australian tour of 1932–33 when the Ashes were recovered in the series of five matches made memorable by the "body-line" description of specially fast bowling, introduced with leg-side fieldsmen in a manner since copied by Australian teams without objection by England and adverse criticism. Malcolm Jardine began cricket at Fettes, and when captain in 1888 he went ahead of all the other boys by averaging 77 with the bat and taking 24 wickets at 6.3 each.

Getting his Oxford Blue as a Freshman, he

was captain in his third year, and finished his University career gloriously, although studies kept him out of all the home matches. He found his best form at Lord's, making 83 runs in the game with M.C.C. and then taking the principal part in a win by five wickets for the side captained by Lionel Palairet, and including C. B. Fry, then a Freshman. F. S. Jackson led Cambridge, who could look back on handsome victories in the three previous matches, and were again favourites. A good off-side player, Malcolm Jardine excelled with the off-drive, but on this occasion leg glances earned him most praise, and he adopted the unusual role, for him, of defensive player, because two wickets were down without a run scored when he joined Fry. During four hours and three-quarters he did not give a chance, and his 140 was only three less than the record of K. J. Key for the match at that time.

When at school he bowled fairly fast, but subsequently used his fielding energy in saving runs by quickness after the ball and sure picking-up. He played a little for Middlesex.

Born in Simla, Malcolm Jardine returned to India with honours gained at Balliol College and the Middle Temple. After practising at the Bombay Bar, he advanced to various appointments until he rose to Advocate-General of Bombay. Returning to England, he was a prominent member of the Surrey club, of which his son became a distinguished captain, and was a Vice-President for several years up to the time of his passing.

JARRETT, Harold Harvey, died on March 17, 1983, aged 75. A leg-break and googly bowler, who took a longer run than most of his type, he came out for Warwickshire at the beginning of August, 1932, and, playing in their last seven matches, took 36 wickets for an average of 29.63, showing distinct promise. On his first appearance he also played a valuable innings of 45. Next year his chances were limited by the rapid rise of Eric Hollies and his career for the county ended. Moving to South Wales, he later edited the *South Wales Cricketers' Magazine* and in 1938 made an appearance for Glamorgan. In his first-class career he took 51 wickets at 32.35. His son represented Wales at rugger as a full-back and also played cricket for Glamorgan Second XI.

JARVIS, Arthur Harwood, who ranked as one of Australia's best wicket-keepers, died at Adelaide on November 15, 1933. Unfortunately for him the exceptionally brilliant form shown by J. Mc. C. Blackham at the time when Jarvis visited England limited his opportunities of distinguishing himself in Test cricket. Some Australian judges claimed that Jarvis was distinctly as good, if not better than Blackham behind the wicket, but no one who saw the two men in England could possibly agree with that opinion. Still Jarvis remained a good second among Australian wicket-keepers for many years. Born at Hindmarsh near Adelaide on October 18, 1860, he made his debut in the South Australian XI in 1877, and the visit of Lord Harris's team at the end of the following year gave him fresh opportunities. Although only 18 at the time, he proved successful both with the bat and in wicket-keeping, and against the touring team at Adelaide caught three batsmen and stumped one in the two innings. To the recognition of his ability on that occasion he owed his place in the second Australian team to visit England in 1880. Though there were no high figures attached to his name in the records of that tour he often batted well in dogged fashion. He never reached three figures in first-class cricket, although at Adelaide in 1894–95 he made 98 not out for South Australia v. New South Wales, and 82 in the Test match with England at Melbourne in 1884–85. One of his best feats as a wicket-keeper was also achieved against Shaw's team when, in February 1885, playing for the XI of Australia at Sydney, he had a hand in the downfall of six English wickets, catching five batsmen and stumping one. Lillywhite asserted after the match that the effective wicket-keeping of Jarvis was the principal cause of the defeat of Shaw's team on that occasion. Jarvis played for South Australia until the season of 1900–01. Altogether he took part in 11 Test matches against England—seven of them at home—and visited England in 1880, 1886, 1888 and 1893.

JAYASUNDERA, Don Summigen, who died on October 11, 1964, aged 53, was one of Ceylon's fastest bowlers. He took 10 wickets in an innings three times, his best performance being 10 for 14 against Panadeira, and performed the hat-trick on five occasions. Coached by "Razor" Smith, the Surrey bowler, he played for Ceylon against D. R. Jardine's team of 1933–34.

JAYAWICKREME, S. S. ("Sargo"), M.B.E., who has died, 1983, at the age of 72, was one of Sri Lanka's leading batsmen in the days when, as Ceylon, they were taking their first tentative steps beyond their own shores. As a member of C. H. Gunasekera's side to India in 1932–33 he scored the first century (130) on the Ferosha Kotla in New Delhi, the ground being inaugurated with an unofficial "Test" between the two countries. In 1940–41, as captain of the second Ceylon side to visit India, he scored 138 against an Indian XI in Calcutta. Jayawickreme made many runs for the Sinhalese Sports Club and is the only Sri Lankan cricketer to have been decorated for his services to the game in the island.

JAYES, Thomas, the Leicestershire cricketer, died on April 16, 1913, at Ratby, from consumption. A fine right-handed fast bowler, who, despite his pace, at times made the ball turn considerably, Jayes first played for Leicestershire in 1903, but it was not until two years later, when the temporary disablement of King gave him his chance, that he became a regular member of the XI. In that season he took 95 wickets, and in the following summer 93, while in 1909 he obtained 102 wickets for less than 20 runs apiece. His health broke down early in the summer of 1911, when his appearances for Leicestershire were only two in number. The Leicestershire County Club sent him out to Switzerland to try what a change of climate would do for him, but there was never much hope of his recovery. Tremendously keen in the field, Jayes was one of the finest mid-offs of his generation, and by his inspiring example he did much to encourage his colleagues. A hard hitting batsman, he once made 100 against Warwickshire at Birmingham, and another time 74 against Derbyshire, in the latter match also taking nine wickets and catching the 10th man in one innings. Against Notts at Leicester, in 1910, he scored 87 out of 112 in 55 minutes and in the same year he and Shipman added 59 in 17 minutes v. Yorkshire, at Leeds. Jayes was one of the men originally picked for the Test match between England and Australia at Lord's, in 1909. At the last moment, however, it was decided to leave him out, and England, going into the field without a right-hand fast bowler, suffered defeat by nine wickets. Jayes did the hat-trick twice for Leicestershire—v. Northants at Leicester in 1906, and v. Kent at Maidstone in 1907. Born at Ratby on April 7, 1877, Jayes was just over 36 years of age at the time of his death. He was an uncle of Astill, the Leicestershire bowler.

JEACOCKE, Alfred, who died in Lewisham

Hospital on September 25, 1961, aged 68, rendered able service to Surrey as a right-handed batsman between 1920 and 1929. In 1921, when J. B. Hobbs, first because of an accident and then through illness, could play in only one county game, Jeacocke formed a splendid opening partner to A. Sandham, scoring in all matches 1,056 runs, average 42.24. An enterprising batsman specially strong in driving, he hit eight centuries for Surrey, the highest being 201 not out (22 fours) against Sussex at the Oval in 1922, and altogether obtained 6,228 runs, average 28.83. A capital slip fieldsman, he held 106 catches. Among his six appearances for Gentlemen against Players was that at the Oval in 1927 when A. Kennedy, of Hampshire, took all 10 wickets in the Gentlemen's first innings at a cost of 37 runs. His first-class cricket in 1922 came to an abrupt end when *Wisden* records: "Jeacocke . . . dropped out of the team in August under circumstances that gave rise to some friction and discussion, the M.C.C. ruling, after an enquiry asked for by Kent, that his qualification was not valid." The reason was that the house where he lived came within the boundary of Kent; the other side of the road was in the county of Surrey! From 1929 onwards, Jeacocke confined his activities to club cricket, chiefly with Forest Hill.

JEEVES, Percy (Royal Warwickshire Regiment), was killed on July 22, 1916, England losing a cricketer of whom very high hopes had been entertained. Jeeves was born at Earlsheaton, in Yorkshire, on March 5, 1888. He played his first serious cricket for the Goole C.C., and became a professional at Hawes. He took part in Yorkshire trial matches in 1910, but presumably failed to attract much attention. Soon afterwards he went to live in Warwickshire, playing for that county, when not fully qualified, against the Australians and South Africans in 1912. No special success rewarded him in those matches, but in 1913 he did brilliant work for Warwickshire, both as bowler and batsman, and firmly established his position. He took 106 wickets in first-class matches that season at a cost of 20.88 each, and scored 765 runs with an average of 20.13. In 1914 he held his own as a bowler, taking 90 wickets in first-class matches, but in batting he was less successful than before. He was chosen for Players against Gentlemen at the Oval, and by his fine bowling helped the Players to win the match, sending down in the Gentlemen's second innings 15 overs for 44 runs and four wickets. Mr. P. F. Warner was greatly impressed and predicted that Jeeves would be an England bowler in the near future. Within a month War had been declared. Jeeves was a right-handed bowler on the quick side of medium pace, and with an easy action came off the ground with plenty of spin. He was very popular among his brother players.

JEFFREYS, The Rt. Hon. Arthur Frederick, P.C., M.P., marked his first appearance at Lord's by an innings of 91 for M.C.C. and Ground v. Rugby School, in 1871. He was born in London on April 7, 1848, and was educated at Eton and Oxford, but was not in either XI. He was a very good batsman, and for several years played for Hampshire. His death occurred at Burkham House, Alton, on February 15, 1906. An excellent portrait of him appears in the recently-issued *Cricket in North Hants*.

JELF, Commander H. F. D., R.N., who played for Derbyshire occasionally in the 1910 and 1911 seasons, died at Southport on April 18, 1944.

JELLICOE, Admiral of the Fleet, Earl, OM., G.C.B., G.C.V.O., who died on November 20, 1935, aged 75, was a member of M.C.C. and I Zingari. He captained a team of Admirals on the cricket field against the Nautical College at Pangbourne in 1930. Born on December 5, 1859, he was a very good fieldsman at cover. In 1919 Admiral Jellicoe was elected at the Annual General Meeting an Honorary Member of the M.C.C.

JELLICOE, The Rev. Frederick Gilbert Gardiner, born at Southampton on February 24, 1858, died in Guy's Hospital, London, on July 29, 1927, aged 69. It was said of him: "An average batsman, right-handed, but excels principally as a middle-paced left round-armed bowler, while in the field he is often short-slip or short-leg." After being in the Haileybury XI in 1875 and 1876, he obtained his Blue for Oxford as a Freshman and played against Cambridge in 1877 and 1879. In the two matches he took five wickets for 25.60 runs each. For his University v. Gentlemen of England at Oxford in 1879 he had an analysis of eight for 36, and for Hampshire (whom he assisted from 1877 until 1880) he took five for 14 v. M.C.C. at Southampton in 1880. He was elder brother of Admiral of the Fleet, Earl Jellicoe.

JENKINSON, Cecil Victor, died late in 1980 at the age of 89. Keeping wicket for Essex on

a few occasions in 1922 and 1923, he created a favourable impression and might have been invaluable had he been able to play more frequently, as the side at that time lacked a reliable wicket-keeper until Frank Gilligan was available in August.

JENNER, F. D., who died on March 31, 1953, aged 59, played as a batsman for Sussex in the first three seasons after the First World War. Meeting with little success, he could not gain a regular place in the team. His best innings was 55 at Cardiff in 1921, when Glamorgan, by 23 runs, won their first match after acquiring first-class status. Jenner and E. H. Bowley (146) put on 166 for the fourth wicket but could not save Sussex from defeat.

JENNER-FUST, Herbert, the oldest of cricketers, passed away on July 30, 1904. The veteran, who played his first match at Lord's for Eton against Harrow in 1822, was born on February 23, 1806, and was thus in his 99th year. He was the last survivor of the first Oxford and Cambridge match in 1827, and, owing to the calls of his profession, retired from first-class cricket the year before Queen Victoria came to the throne. Still, though nothing was seen of him in great matches after 1836, he played cricket in a more modest way for a long time, and made his last appearance in the field very late in life. It is interesting to recall the fact that when, in 1877, a dinner was given to celebrate the Jubilee of the University Match he was one of the chief speakers, and referred to the changes that had come over the game in 50 years. In his cricket days he was known simply as Herbert Jenner, the additional name of Fust being taken after he had in a practical sense done with the game. How good a player he was in comparison with men of a later date one cannot tell, but in his own generation he ranked high as batsman and bowler, and was still more famous as a wicket-keeper. Up to a short time before his death he was in such excellent health and had preserved his faculties so well—nothing but deafness troubling him—that there seemed every reason to think he would live to complete his hundred years. A letter from him towards the end of 1901 revealed no sign of extreme old age, the hand-writing being quite firm and clear. Herbert Jenner, to speak of him as he will always be known in cricket history, was President of the M.C.C. in 1833, and was for many years President of the West Kent C.C., holding this position to the end of his long life. It is a curious fact that though he retained a keen interest in cricket he never took the trouble to see W. G. Grace play.

JENNINGS, C. B., who played six times for Australia in the 1912 Triangular Tournament in England, died in Adelaide in July, 1950, aged 66. He was South Australian correspondent of the British Department of Overseas Trade and until 1937 secretary of the Adelaide Chamber of Commerce. In 1938 he was appointed a delegate to the Australian Cricket Board of Control. A batsman of considerable ability, Jennings played for South Australia from 1902 to 1907 and for Queensland from 1910 to 1912. During the Triangular Tournament he opened the innings for Australia several times. Although he preferred fast pitches he showed adaptability, and in all matches in that season scored 1,060 runs, average 22.55, with a highest innings of 82.

JENNINGS, Corpl. David William (Kent Fortress Engineers), was born on June 4, 1889, died in hospital at Tunbridge Wells in August, 1918, after an illness due to shell-shock and gas. As a cricketer Jennings was a trifle unfortunate. Had he belonged to a weaker county than Kent he would no doubt have taken a more prominent position. All the time he was playing Kent was so rich in batsmen that he could not secure an assured place in the XI. Still, of the chances that came his way he made good use. He first played for Kent in 1909 and in 1911, when only tried in a few matches, he headed the averages. In 1912, playing six times, he came out second, scoring 100 against Hampshire at Southampton, and both in 1913 and 1914 he did very well without rising to quite the first-class. In 1914 he hit up an innings of 106 against Essex at Tunbridge Wells.

JENNINGS, George A., who died in July, 1959, played occasionally as a slow left-arm bowler for Warwickshire from 1923 to 1925. He later succeeded his father as coach at Marlborough, a position he held for more than 30 years.

JENNINGS, Thomas Shepherd, who died at Tiverton on September 7, 1972 aged 76, played as a slow left-arm bowler for Surrey from 1921 to 1924. The pitches at the Oval at that time provided little encouragement for a bowler of his type and he was never a regular member of the side. His best season was his last, when he took 23 wickets for 18.52 runs each. After that, Jennings, a member of a

well-known Devon cricketing family, became coach and head groundsman at Blundell's School and he assisted Devon from 1926 to 1933. In 1936 he was appointed to the Minor Counties' list of umpires, on which he served for 26 years.

JEPHSON, Digby Loder Armroid, born at Clapham, in Surrey, on February 23, 1871, died at Cambridge on January 19, 1926, in his 55th year. For many seasons a familiar and popular figure in the game, Jephson was a most useful all-round cricketer, fit, when at the height of his powers, for inclusion in any team except those of an international character. He learned the game whilst at Manor House School, Clapham, and, with more opportunities, developed his skill at Cambridge. As a batsman he possessed many strokes and could hit very hard indeed, while in the field he always worked hard. He will, however, always be best remembered for his lob bowling, a style he cultivated after employing fast over-arm for some years. In 1890 he obtained his Blue for Cambridge, but in his three matches against Oxford he scored only 31 runs in three completed innings. It was for Surrey that most of his best feats in first-class cricket were performed. He assisted that county from 1891 until 1904, and in two seasons, 1901 and 1902, captained the side. His highest of the nine three-figure innings he played for Surrey was 213 against Derbyshire at the Oval in 1900, when he and R. Abel (193), going in against a total of 325, made 364 together for the first wicket. In the match with Sussex at Hove a year later the same pair twice made over a hundred together for the opening partnership—114 in the first innings and 109 in the second, Jephson's scores being 95 and 85. In 1900 he had an excellent all-round record, for, besides making 1,952 runs with an average of 41.53, he took 66 wickets for 23.40 runs each. In the Gentlemen v. Players match at Lord's in 1899 his lobs gained him an analysis of six for 21—a splendid performance against a strong batting side. For Surrey he took five wickets for 12 runs against Derbyshire at Chesterfield in 1899, and performed the hat-trick v. Middlesex at the Oval in 1904. In club cricket he did many remarkable things, especially for the Wanderers. For Crystal Palace v. Seaton in 1894 he and Stanley Colman made 300 together for the first wicket, and for Wanderers v. Tonbridge in 1900 the same pair put up 349 together, his own contribution on the latter occasion being 226. Other large innings played by him were 261 for Crystal Palace v. Eastbourne in 1893 and 301 not out—made in three hours and a quarter—for Wanderers against Norwood two years later. With his fast bowling he took five wickets in eight balls for Crystal Palace v. Eastbourne in 1888, and twice his lobs accounted for all 10 wickets in an innings—for Wanderers v. Chiswick Park in 1894 and for G. E. Bicknell's XI v. Streatham in 1902. For some time he was on the London Stock Exchange, but later he took to journalism and coaching on the Cambridge University Cricket Ground. He was the author of a book of verse entitled *A Few Overs*.

JERVIS, The Hon. William Monk, J.P., D.L., M.A., B.C.L., brother of the third Viscount St. Vincent and uncle of Lord Harris, was born in London on January 25, 1827, and died at Quarndon Hall, near Derby, on March 25, 1909. He helped to establish the Derbyshire County C.C. and was its President from 1871 until 1887. In his younger days he was a very useful cricketer, but was past his best when the County Club was formed, and in consequence his play for Derbyshire was restricted to a single match—that v. Lancashire at Derby in 1873, in which he scored 0 and six. Since 1860 he had been a member of the M.C.C., and he had also been identified with the Band of Brothers, the Oxford Harlequins and other well-known clubs.

JESSON, Major Robert Wilfred Fairey (Wilts. Regiment), born at Southampton, June 7, 1886; killed February, 1917. Sherborne XI, 1903–04–05. At Oxford he played in the Freshmen's match, 1907; Seniors' match, 1908 and 1909. Merton College (Ox.) XI but not a Blue; Hampshire XI occasionally. Good all-round, hard hitter; bowled right-hand slow leg-breaks. In his last year at Sherborne he took 40 wickets and had a batting average of 30. Had been wounded in Gallipoli.

JESSOP, Gilbert Laird, who died at St. George's Vicarage, Dorchester, on May 11, 1955, aged 80, was famed as the most remarkable hitter cricket has ever produced. He had lived with the Rev. Gilbert Jessop, his only child, from 1936 till his death.

Born at Cheltenham on May 19, 1874, he enjoyed a memorable career in first-class cricket which, dating from 1894 to the start of the First World War, extended over 20 years. There have been batsmen who hit the ball even harder than Jessop, notably C. I. Thornton and the two Australians, George Bonnor and Jack Lyons, but no one who did

so more often or who, in match after match, scored as rapidly. Where Jessop surpassed all other hitters was in the all-round nature of his scoring. At his best, he could make runs from any ball, however good it might be. Although only 5ft. 7in. in height, he bent low as he shaped to play, a method which earned him the sobriquet of "The Croucher." Extraordinarily quick on his feet, he was ready to hit firm-footed if the ball were pitched well up and equally, when it was of shorter length, to dash down the pitch and drive. When executing leg-side strokes, he almost lay down and swept round with the bat practically horizontal, putting great power behind the ball as, thanks to strong, supple wrists, he also did when bringing off the square cut. Lightness of foot allied to wonderful sight made it possible for him to run out to the fastest bowlers of his time—Richardson and Mold—and at the peak of his form pull or straight-drive them with almost unerring certainty. No one ever approached him in this particular feat; indeed, nobody else could have attempted it with reasonable hope of success.

At times Jessop sacrificed his wicket through trying to hit before he got a true sight of the ball or judged the pace of the turf and, not unnaturally in view of the liberties he took with good length bowling, the ball which kept low often dismissed him. A batsman with such marvellous gifts that in half an hour he might win a game seemingly lost, he was a wonderful personality on the field and the idol of spectators who always love a fearless batsman.

Jessop's claims to distinction were not limited to the brilliancy of his run-getting. For a number of years he ranked high as a fast bowler and for a man of his pace he showed surprising stamina. Far more remarkable than his bowling, however, was his fielding, which might fairly be termed as phenomenal as his hitting and which was a matter of great pride to him. No hit proved too hard for him to stop and his gathering and returning of the ball approached perfection. In his early days he fielded at cover-point; later he specialised in the position of extra mid-off, standing so deep that with almost anyone else a run would have been a certainty. Jessop's presence deterred the boldest of batsmen from making any attempt. In short, such a fine bowler and such a superb fieldsman was he that, even without his batting ability, he would have been worth a place in almost any team. A man of engaging manner, he was a charming companion and, like most truly great men, modest to a degree.

First tried for Gloucestershire in 1894, Jessop established his reputation a year later when, among other performances, he hit 63 out of 65 in less than half an hour from the Yorkshire bowling at Cheltenham. He continued to assist Gloucestershire till the end of his first-class career and for 13 years from 1900 he captained the side. By 1897 he had become one of the great players of the day, making 1,219 runs in first-class matches and taking 116 wickets for less than 18 runs each. In that summer he hit two particularly noteworthy innings—140 for Cambridge University against the Philadelphians in 95 minutes and 101 out of 118 in 40 minutes against Yorkshire at Harrogate. In the course of the latter display he hit the ball six times out of the ground and some dozen times over the ropes. Until 1907 a hit over the ropes counted four; only a hit out of the ground earned six. Except in 1898 he regularly made over 1,000 runs every season until 1909, when a bad back injury sustained while fielding in the Test match at Leeds in early July kept him out of the game for the rest of the year. In 1900 he scored 2,210 runs and took 104 wickets and next summer his aggregate amounted to 2,323, including 157 out of 201 in an hour against West Indies at Bristol.

Among his 53 centuries were five of more than 200: 286 out of 335 in 175 minutes for Gloucestershire against Sussex at Brighton, 1903 (he and J. H. Board adding 320 for the sixth wicket); 240 out of 337 in 200 minutes for Gloucestershire v. Sussex at Bristol, 1907; 234 out of 346 in 155 minutes for Gloucestershire v. Somerset at Bristol, 1905; 233 out of 318 in 150 minutes for An England XI v. Yorkshire at Lord's, 1901; and 206 out of 317 in 150 minutes for Gloucestershire v. Nottinghamshire at Trent Bridge, 1904.

Four times for Gloucestershire he reached three figures in each innings of a match: 104 and 139 v. Yorkshire at Bradford, 1900, when the newspapers stated that, in the two innings he cleared the ropes more than 20 times; 143 and 133 not out v. Somerset at Bath, 1908; 161 and 129 v. Hampshire at Bristol, 1909; and 153 and 123 not out v. Hampshire at Southampton, 1911. He achieved the feat on another occasion, against Somerset in a friendly game organised for the opening of a new club pavilion. S. M. J. Woods termed this a remarkable performance on a pitch far from true and against professional bowling. Altogether in first-class cricket he hit 26,058 runs, average 32.60.

His bowling successes included eight wick-ets for 34 runs v. Hampshire, 1898; five for 13 v. Lancashire, 1895; eight for 54 v. Lancashire, 1898; eight for 29 v. Essex, 1900; eight for 58 v. Middlesex, 1902. All these were achieved for Gloucestershire except that against Hampshire, on which occasion he was playing for Cambridge. His wickets in first-class cricket totalled 851, average 22.91.

Jessop took part in 18 Test matches between 1899 and 1909, 13 against Australia and five against South Africa, and would probably have appeared in others but for the back strain he suffered in 1909. He disappointed in Australia except for his fielding, and in most of the contests in England met with moderate success; but he earned undying fame in the Oval Test of 1902. There, under conditions considerably helpful to bowlers, England, set 273 to make to win, lost their first five wickets for 48. Australia looked to have the match in hand, but Jessop joined F. S. Jackson and in marvellous fashion hit 104 out of 139 in an hour and a quarter, paving the way to victory by one wicket for England. Twice he sent the ball on to the roof of the Pavilion and from another big hit was caught on the Players' Balcony by H. K. Foster.

Jessop went to Cambridge in 1896 and played for the University for four seasons, being captain in 1899. He accomplished little of note against Oxford in the way of batting, two innings of over 40 being his best scores on the big occasion, but he bowled to good purpose in two of the games, taking six wickets for 65 in the first innings in 1897 and six for 126 in the first innings a year later.

Besides his cricketing ability, Jessop was an all-round athlete of note. He got his Blue as a hockey goalkeeper, but fell ill and could not play in the University match; came near getting an Association football Blue and played for the Casuals as half-back or goalkeeper. He also appeared as a wing three-quarter for Gloucester R.F.C. He would have played billiards for Cambridge against Oxford, but was "gated" and could not take part. In one week he made two breaks of over 150. He could run the 100 yards in 10.2 seconds and frequently entered for sports meetings. A scratch golfer, he took part in the Amateur Championship in 1914, was Secretary of the Cricketers' Golfing Society and for some years Secretary of the Edgware Club.

In addition to the visit he paid to Australia in 1901–02 under A. C. MacLaren, he went to America with the team captained by P. F. Warner in 1897, and again in 1899 when K. S. Ranjitsinhji led the side.

For Beccles School in 1895, when a master there, Jessop scored 1,058 runs, average 132, and took 100 wickets at a cost of less than two and a half runs apiece.

He served as a captain in the Manchester Regiment during the First World War from 1914 till he was invalided out with a damaged heart in 1918. Married in October, 1902, he first met his bride a few months earlier during his visit to Australia. She died in 1953.

Tributes paid to Jessop include:

Sir Pelham Warner: "He was a wonderful cricketer. It was a great pleasure to play with or against him. It has been said that he was unorthodox, but no one watched the ball more closely."

Sir John Hobbs: "He was undoubtedly the most consistently fast scorer I have seen. He was a big hitter, too, and it was difficult to bowl a ball from which he could not score. He made me glad that I was not a bowler. Gilbert Jessop certainly drew the crowds, too, even more than Bradman I should say."

JESSOP, Hylton, born in 1868, died in a nursing home at Cheltenham on July 19, 1924. A good forcing bat and an adherent of the old-fashioned donkey-drop bowling, he played much for the East Gloucestershire C.C. and occasionally for Gloucestershire. He was a cousin of Mr. G. L. Jessop.

JESSOP, Osman Walter Temple, younger brother of G. L. Jessop of free-scoring fame for Cambridge, Gloucestershire and England, died on May 25, 1941, aged 63. He showed promise at Cheltenham and appeared twice for Gloucestershire in 1901 and 1911, but could give very little time to first-class cricket.

JEWELL, Major Arthur North, who died at Selsey on September 8, 1922, aged 34, after a long period of ill-health, was educated at Felsted and played for the Orange Free State in 1910–11, but did not appear in first-class cricket in England until 1919. For Worcestershire his chief innings were 123 v. Mr. H. K. Foster's XI at Worcester in 1919, and 110 v. Hampshire on the same ground and 110 v. Gloucestershire at Gloucester, both in 1920. He was a first-class wicket-keeper and a good free batsman. At the Oval in 1920 he kept wicket for the Gentlemen against the Players.

JEWELL, John Mark Herbert, who died at Durban on October 28, 1946, played in two matches for Worcestershire in 1939, his highest score being 24 v. West Indies. Born at Bloemfontein in 1917, he was the son of J. E. Jewell, who played for Orange Free State from 1911 to 1926, and nephew of M. F. S. and A. N. Jewell. Joining the R.A.F. in 1938, he served throughout the War and was released with the rank of Squadron-Leader and awarded the M.B.E. He was for two years a prisoner of war.

JEWELL, Maurice Frederick Stewart, C.B.E., who died on May 28, 1978, aged 92, did notable work for Worcestershire cricket. Those whose memories start in 1946 or later have no conception how much some counties at the bottom of the Championship before 1914 and between the Wars owed to certain amateurs, often only moderate players who could never have kept a place in a good county side, but who year after year gave up their summer to keeping their county going, captaining it themselves and somehow collecting an XI for each match, being rewarded at the end with perhaps two or three wins, perhaps less. It was due largely to the devoted labours of such as these that no first-class county ever had to pack up, though some in those days came pretty near it. In this category Jewell stood high. Far his best summer personally was 1926 when he was 41 and made 920 runs with an average of 27.05, including the only two centuries of his career, oddly enough one in each match against Hampshire. A better indication of his status is given by the figures for his full career of 24 years—4,014 runs, average 18.37 and 104 wickets at 33.15. He was a batsman disposed to attack, but with a fair defence, and a useful slow left-hand change bowler. Another indication of the services he rendered is that he was captain of the side in 1920–21, 1926 and 1928–29— in other words he was prepared to step into the breach when no one else would. A shrewd captain and a disciplinarian, he was also tireless in raising money for the club during the winter. Later he was President from 1950 to 1955 and had been a Life Member since 1956. He had a curious career. Born in Chile, he played for Worcestershire first in 1909. In 1911 he played a few matches for Surrey Second XI and in 1914 and 1919 for Sussex. In 1919 he also played for Worcestershire, who did not that year enter for the Championship, and thus provides one of the few instances in modern times of a man representing two counties in one season. He continued to play for Worcestershire till 1933 and in his last innings scored 55 v. Oxford University. Two brothers of his attained some distinction— A.N. played for Worcestershire and the

Orange Free State and kept for the Gentlemen at the Oval in 1920; J.E. played for Surrey Second XI and the Orange Free State, and his son, J.M.H., played for Worcestershire in 1939. Maurice Jewell himself and W.H. Taylor, who preceded him as captain of the county side, married sisters.

JILANI, M. Baqa, who came to England with the team from India in 1936, died on July 2, 1941, within 28 days of completing 30 years. A useful bat, he averaged 18.52 in three-day matches, with 113 at Leicester his one really big innings. He played in one Test, the third at the Oval, presumably for his bowling, but he did not take a wicket, and, batting last but one, he scored not out four and 12. Altogether in three-day matches he took 11 wickets at the high cost of 40.72 runs apiece.

JOBSON, Edward Percy, who played fairly regularly for Worcestershire for over 20 years, died at Himley on April 20, 1909, after an operation for appendicitis. He was born at Wallheath House, near Dudley, on March 20, 1855, and first came into prominence as a member of the Dudley C.C. *Scores and Biographies* (xiii–251) said of him: "Is a good batsman and a middle-paced round-armed bowler, fielding generally at cover-point or mid-wicket-off. He learnt most of his cricket when quite young from John Platts." His average for Worcestershire in 1886 was as high as 45.30 and in 1891 it was 30.25, while at least seven other seasons it exceeded 20. His last appearance for the county was as recent as 1903. In 1881 he made 103 against Warwickshire and 12 years later played an innings of 102 v. Devon. He had been a member of the M.C.C. for exactly a quarter of a century.

JOHN, George, who died at Port of Spain, Trinidad, on January 14, 1944, was a prominent fast bowler in the West Indies. He toured England in 1923, and came out with the best average in all matches played by the touring team—90 wickets at 14.68 each. But G.N. Francis, a bowler of still more pace, did much better work in the first-class matches. This was five years before West Indies were accorded Test match status by playing England three times in this country.

The chief feature of the 1923 season was the batting of G. Challenor. Thanks to him, with an aggregate of 221 without being dismissed, and the bowling of Francis, Surrey were beaten by 10 wickets, and in the last match John helped Francis to cause a panic among a strong batting side at Scarborough, six wickets falling for 19 runs before John Douglas and P.G.H. Fender enabled H.D.G. Leveson Gower's team to scramble home for four wickets when set no more than 28 runs to get in the last innings.

JOHNS, Alfred E., who was born on January 22, 1868, and died in February, 1934, had as contemporaries such great wicket-keepers as J.J. Kelly and A.H. Jarvis. Consequently he never played for Australia in a Test match. He succeeded the famous J. McC. Blackham as Victoria's wicket-keeper in 1896, and did good service as a left-handed batsman when in 1897 he went in last with J. O'Halloran and added 136 against South Australia at Melbourne. This partnership stood as an Australian record for the 10th wicket during 15 years. Then M. Ellis and T. Hastings put on 211 in the corresponding match. He came to England with the Australian teams in 1896 and 1899 as reserve wicket-keeper to Kelly. In 1922 he was appointed a trustee of the Melbourne cricket ground.

JOHNSON, C.L., at one time one of the best-known Irish cricketers, died at Maraisburg, in the Transvaal, on May 31, 1908, in his 38th year. He was born in County Kildare and educated at Dublin University, where he was in the XI from 1889 to 1893. Playing against Cambridge University at Dublin in 1892 he scored 49 and 56 against the bowling of E.C. Streatfeild, F.S. Jackson, C.M. Wells and H.R. Bromley-Davenport, and later in the year visited America as a member of the Gentlemen of Ireland's team. In 1893, owing to ill-health, he left his native country and settled in the Transvaal, and in the following year came to England as a member of the first South African team. During the tour he scored 508 runs with an average of 14.32 and took 50 wickets at a cost of 17.27 runs each. He made 112 against Liverpool and District and 79 against the Gentlemen of Ireland. He afterwards represented the Transvaal, and in March, 1896, was included in a South African XI which met Lord Hawke's team at Johannesburg. He was a fast right-handed bowler and a good bat.

JOHNSON, Frederick, born at Rolvenden, in Kent, on March 14, 1851, died on November 24, 1923. A useful medium-fast left-handed bowler, he played in 21 matches for Surrey between 1878 and 1883, taking 55 wickets for 25 runs each. He never appeared for his native county, except in a match against Seventeen Colts at Maidstone, in 1877.

JOHNSON, George Harry, who died on January 20, 1965, aged 70, kept wicket as an amateur in 18 matches for Northamptonshire between 1922 and 1932. He served on the County Committee from 1926 to 1939.

JOHNSON, The Hon. George Randall, who died at Fenton Court, Honiton, on November 24, 1919, had reached the advanced age of 86. He was born at Lavenham, Norfolk, on November 7, 1833. He was captain of the Cambridge University XI in 1855 and kept his place—under the leadership of Joseph McCormick and J. M. Fuller—in the two following years. In 1856—when Joseph Makinson's all-round cricket determined the result—he was on the winning side, but Oxford won in 1855 and 1857. His best score against Oxford was 24 in 1855, but in the three matches he took 12 wickets. His bowling would seem to have left him in 1857 as he was not put on in Oxford's first innings and only sent down eight overs and a ball in their second innings though the total reached 261—a big score at Lord's in those days. In *Scores and Biographies* he is described as a quick and lively hitter, a good field, generally at point, and a middle-paced round-arm bowler. His best scores were 73 for the University v. Gentlemen of Cambridgeshire (with Arnold and Reynolds) in 1857, 60 for Past (with Jackson and Parr) v. the University in 1858, 51 for M.C.C. and Ground v. Oxford University in 1859, and 66 for M.C.C. and Ground v. Cambridge University in 1860. At Lord's, in 1855, he took four wickets for seven runs for Sixteen of Cambridge University Past and Present v. the United All England XI. He was a distinguished member of I Zingari and played a great deal for the club. Mr. Johnson lived in New Zealand for many years, and was a member of the Legislature from 1872 to 1890. He was the father of the brilliant Somerset batsman, P. R. Johnson.—S.H.P.

JOHNSON, Joseph Leonard, who died in Ipswich on April 20, 1977, aged 57, came out for Queensland after the War and continued to be one of the mainstays of their bowling until 1953, by which time he had taken 171 wickets in Sheffield Shield matches. He was a useful tail-end hitter. A fast-medium right-hander, analyses of six for 83 against the Indian side in Australia and seven for 114 against South Australia, secured him a place in the last Test in 1947–48. As he took six for 74 in the two innings and made 25 not out, he must have been in the running for a place in the 1948 side to England. In the event this was his sole appearance for Australia.

JOHNSON, Peter Randall, who died on July 1, 1959, aged 78, was in the Eton XI in 1897 and appeared for Cambridge against Oxford at Lord's in 1901. A stylish batsman of upright stance, specially strong in off-side strokes, he assisted Somerset from 1902 to 1927 and toured Australia and New Zealand with Lord Hawke's team captained by P. F. Warner in 1902–03. During his first-class career he obtained 12,041 runs, average 24.82. Five times he headed the Somerset batting averages, his best season being that of 1921, when he hit 961 runs, average 30.03, and in scoring 163 against Worcestershire equalled his feat against the same county on the same ground 15 years earlier. He enjoyed a wonderful run of success in 1908 when, in successive matches, he made 164 and 131 against Middlesex at Taunton, 117 and 19 v. Hampshire at Southampton and 31 and 126 v. Kent at Taunton.

JOHNSTON, Col. Alexander Colin, D.S.O., M.C., who died suddenly at his home at Woking on December 27, 1952, aged 68, was a leading personality in Army sport during 40 years' service. Born on January 26, 1884, he played as opening batsman and leg-break bowler in the Winchester XIs of 1901 and 1902. His second match with Eton, in which he dismissed eight batsmen for 56 runs, was rendered memorable by the fact that G. A. Sandeman took all 10 wickets for 22 runs in the Winchester first innings. From Winchester, Johnston went to Sandhurst, and he spent a year as a cowboy in Colorado and New Mexico before joining the Worcestershire Regiment. He was later attached for four years to the Northern Nigerian Regiment. During the First World War he served three years in France as a member of the original Expeditionary Force, being four times wounded, five times Mentioned in Dispatches, and rising to the rank of Brigadier General. Though left with a permanent limp, he continued his activities as soldier and sportsman. He played cricket for Hampshire over a period of 12 years and three times appeared for Gentlemen against Players, making top score for his side in the Lord's match of 1912. In all first-class games he scored 5,996 runs, average 30.91, hitting 10 centuries. He also represented the Army at Association football and hockey and played polo for Western Nigeria.

JOHNSTONE, Conrad Powell, who died suddenly at his Eastry home on June 23,

1974, aged 78, had spent the previous three days at Lord's watching the Test with India in which country he had spent much of his life. He was awarded the C.B.E. for his efforts on behalf of cricket in Madras. A talented left-handed batsman, Johnstone was in the Rugby XI in 1912, 1913, being captain the second year and he played in both schools matches at Lord's. Going up to Cambridge after the War, he gained his Blue in 1919 and 1920 when he usually opened the Light Blues innings. He played for Kent between 1919–33 and later served many years on the County Committee, being President when Kent first won the Gillette Cup in 1967. In 1920 he led Cambridge to a surprising golf victory against Oxford despite being opposed to C.J.H. Tolley and R.H. Wethered.

JONES, Arthur Owen, died on December 21, 1914, at his brother's house at Dunstable. He played in a few matches for Notts at the beginning of the past season, but his condition was very bad, and his friends knew he would not be able to go on for long. During the summer he spent some time at a sanatorium in the New Forest, but nothing could be done for him, consumption being too far advanced. He went home, given up as incurable, and the end came as a release from his sufferings. Born on August 16, 1872, Mr. Jones played his first match for Notts against Lancashire at Trent Bridge in 1892. Helping Notts to a victory by six wickets, he at once gave proof of his brilliant qualities as a cricketer. The match was a remarkable one. Notts—a great side that season—had 222 to get to win. As he had made 17 not out in the first innings, Jones was selected to go in with Shrewsbury, and between them the two batsmen scored 75 for the first wicket, putting their side on the high road to victory. They might have done more, but a brilliant run out ended the partnership. Jones was then up at Cambridge, but he only played once against Oxford at Lord's, being on the winning side in 1893. He was rather slow to develop as a batsman, his full powers being, perhaps, first revealed in a superb innings of 98 in the Whit-Monday match between Notts and Surrey in 1896. Richard Daft said of that innings that he had never seen anyone play Tom Richardson so well. Jones's great days began three years later, and from 1899 to 1907 he was, except in one season, at his very best. In the winter of 1907–08, when in Australia as captain of the M.C.C.'s team, he had a severe illness, from the effects of which he perhaps never wholly recovered.

However, he was able to resume his career in England in 1908, and continued to play as much cricket as ever. Early in the season of 1913 he contracted a violent chill, playing on a bitterly cold afternoon at Manchester. This kept him out of the field for more than two months, and no doubt brought on the illness which ended in his premature death.

It is essentially as a Notts cricketer that Mr. Jones will be remembered. Nearly all his best work was done for his county. He only played five times for England against Australia in this country, and when he paid his first visit to Australia as a member of Mr. MacLaren's team in 1901–02, he failed to do himself justice as a batsman. Always rather eager and impetuous, he had not quite the right temperament for Test match cricket. All through his career his fielding was even finer than his batting. Indeed it may be claimed for him that a better all-round fieldsman has never been seen. Unequalled in his favourite position in the slips—a sort of short third man—he was almost as brilliant in the deep field, and in the England v. Australia match at Birmingham in 1909 he made a catch at short-leg that has become historical. As an orthodox slip fieldsman he was seen at his highest pitch in the England v. Australia match at Trent Bridge in 1905, and the Gentlemen v. Players match at Lord's in 1907. He succeeded Mr. J.A. Dixon as captain of the Notts team in 1900, and held that position until he had to give up cricket last summer. Under his leadership Notts won the County Championship in 1907. As a batsman he was essentially a brilliant player, his hitting on the off-side being wonderfully fine. His position at the wicket, with legs wide apart and both knees bent, was rather cramped and ungainly, but once the ball had left the bowler's hand all awkwardness vanished. In hitting he was always free and graceful. He and Iremonger put up the hundred together for the first Notts wicket 24 times. In his young days Mr. Jones excelled in Rugby football, and of late years, in connection with that game, he was, by general consent, one of the best of referees.

JONES, Charles J. E., who died in hospital on September 1, 1966, aged 73, founded the London Counties war-time team of professional cricketers who played at Lord's and many other grounds around the Metropolis. Always a keen club cricketer, he was a Vice-President of Forest Hill after acting for many years as fixture secretary as well as being a most efficient umpire. Jones, who possessed an astute business brain—he was connected with the Inland Revenue—sponsored the first Sunday benefit match. It was for Harold Larwood, following the "bodyline" tour of over 30 years ago. It took place at Forest Hill before a crowd of 5,000 and later that evening when Larwood was presented with a cheque for £100 he was so surprised that he showed his appreciation by giving back £25 to the club's funds. More recently, Jones sent to Lord's a scheme to bring all the Test match playing countries to England in the same season, embracing the Counties in a Championship as well as a full series of Test matches. He even drew up a list of fixtures with dates and grounds and stated that he felt sure that, if approached, big business firms would be willing to sponsor the whole affair. Now that firms like Gillette, Rothman's, Horlicks, Carreras and Charrington's are supporting cricket it seems that Jones was not, after all, far off the mark.

JONES, Charles Langton, was born at Liverpool, November 27, 1853, and was educated at Carlton House in that city. He died most suddenly on April 2, 1904, at 41, Falkner Street, Liverpool, of heart seizure. He and Mr. E. Roper (who assisted both Yorkshire and Lancashire) were a great first-wicket pair, especially as members of the Sefton XI. The two men put up over 100 runs for the first wicket more than 30 times during their career. On one occasion they ran up over 200 together against Formby, and in two successive years scored over 150 for the first wicket against Manchester, in whose ranks were Watson and Crossland. In 1876 Mr. Jones assisted Lancashire against Notts, at Old Trafford, scoring 0 and 12, and played once more for the county in 1882. He was a very fair bowler in his younger days, and bowled with success against the first Australian team on August 8 and 9, 1878, taking four wickets for less than 30 runs.

JONES, Ernest, who died in Adelaide on November 23, 1943, aged 74, is considered to have been the best fast bowler ever produced by Australia. During three visits to England in the course of seven years his great pace caused many a collapse on hard pitches, but on soft turf he earned less reward, as was natural enough in our variable climate. Still, he took 121 wickets in 1896, 135 in 1899, and 71 in 1902 at an average cost of 19 runs apiece in the three tours.

As a fresh opponent our batsmen experienced difficulty in timing his expresses, particularly on turf which tended to make the ball lift. His first effort in England was rewarded by the dismissal of W. G. Grace, F. S. Jackson, Arthur Shrewsbury, William Gunn, K. S. Ranjitsinhji, C. B. Fry and George Davidson—seven wickets for 84 runs at Sheffield Park in Sussex. He gained a still better analysis, eight wickets for 39 runs, against an England XI at Crystal Palace, the last four wickets falling to him without cost, but on that occasion the beaten batsmen were of far less class. He proved specially effective against Yorkshire, dismissing six men for 74 in an innings at Sheffield and seven for 36 runs at Leeds. Four wickets for 13 at the Oval and six for 33 at Edgbaston helped in decisive victories for Harry Trott's team over Surrey and Warwickshire, but in the three Tests his record showed only six wickets at 34.4 runs each.

For South Australia at Adelaide against A. E. Stoddart's side in March, 1898, he took 14 wickets at a cost of 237 runs, his victims including such famous batsmen as K. S. Ranjitsinhji, J. R. Mason, N. F. Druce, Tom Hayward, George Hirst, William Storer and Ted Wainwright. That performance remains a record against an England team on the Adelaide Oval. His Test match work in that tour earned 22 wickets at 25.13 runs each.

In 1899, when first Tests were first played in England, Jones proved more destructive than either Hugh Trumble or M. A. Noble with 26 wickets at 25.26 and in the only one of the series brought to a definite conclusion, Australia winning at Lord's by 10 wickets, his analysis showed 10 wickets for 164—seven for 88 in the first innings—so that he stood out prominently in winning the rubber. Three years later, when Joe Darling for the second time led Australia to victory over England, Jones declined in form and his three wickets in Test matches cost 107 runs, but that season of wet weather told against fast bowlers generally.

The *South Australian Year-Book* gives Jones as taking 248 wickets at 26.19 runs apiece in matches in Australia. Among his best performances, besides those mentioned already, were six wickets for 15 at Melbourne against Victoria and seven for 103 against New South Wales at Adelaide, both in 1896. Altogether in 19 matches against England his full return was 60 wickets at an average cost of 29.28 runs.

Besides his right-arm deadliness with the ball, Jones fielded splendidly at mid-off. Some good judges thought there was never a superior in that position and as a hard-hitting batsman he sometimes did good service late in an innings, but it is as a bowler that Jones remains in one's memory.

Rather below medium height and of very powerful build, Jones put all his bodily strength behind the delivery after a comparatively short run for a fast bowler, and the intense force often made the ball rise unpleasantly for the batsman, especially if pitched at all short. Although his action came in for criticism, it went through the 1896 tour unchallenged, but in the Australian season of 1897–98 James Phillips, himself an Australian, who played for Middlesex, twice no-balled Jones for throwing when playing against A. E. Stoddart's team. Phillips as a resolute umpire took a prominent part in stopping the epidemic of "doubtful delivery" in England. Subsequently Jones reduced his run, concentrated on length and ball control with good effect. When Jones first came to England, W. L. Murdoch, captain of Australian teams, was captain of Sussex, and the county offered Jones £350 a year for five years to qualify by residence, but the invitation was declined.

JONES, Percy Sydney Twentyman, who died on March 8, 1954, aged 77, following a serious operation, played for South Africa at both cricket and Rugby football. Born on September 13, 1876, he appeared as a batsman for Western Province from 1898 to 1905. Against the Australian touring team of 1902, he was, with 33 and 50, top-scorer in each innings for Western Province on a bad pitch. This performance earned him a place in the third Test match at Cape Town, but he was twice dismissed without scoring. He represented South Africa at football in 1896. In later years he became a well-known sports administrator. He was formerly Judge President of the Cape of Good Hope Division of the Supreme Court.

JONES, Richard Stoakes, died on May 9, 1935, aged 78, at Dymchurch, Kent, where he was born on March 14, 1857. From Chatham House, Ramsgate, he went to Trinity College, Cambridge, and played in the XI in 1879 and 1880. Although on the winning side in each match he failed completely. Often playing for Kent from 1877 to 1886 he scored 1,412 runs, average 17.43, his highest innings being 83 against Lancashire at Manchester in 1883. He made 124 for the University against Gentlemen of England at Cambridge in 1880. A stylish bat with admirable defence he was a fine leg hitter. A very good deep field.

JONES, Samuel Percy, who died at Auckland, New Zealand, on July 14, 1951, in his 90th year, was then the oldest Test cricketer and the last survivor of the side which beat England in the Ashes Test match at the Oval in 1882, Australia's first victory in England.

Educated at Sydney Grammar School and Sydney University, he toured England four times, in 1882, 1886, 1888 and 1890. A sound batsman with good defence, he was also a brilliant fieldsman and useful change bowler. Before he reached the age of 20, he made a century for New South Wales against Victoria. His most successful tour was that of 1886, when he finished second in the averages and made 151 at the Oval against the Gentlemen, a feat for which he was presented in the Committee Room at Lord's with a gold watch and chain as a souvenir from Australian friends. In 12 Test matches against England he scored 428 runs with an average of 21.40.

Having settled in Queensland, Jones toured New Zealand with that State's team in 1896–97. In 1904 he went to live in New Zealand, playing for Auckland in 1904–05 and 1905–06. He afterwards paid only one brief visit to Australia and he never saw Bradman bat.

During the 1882 Oval Test, Jones was concerned in an incident which caused great controversy. In the Australian second innings Murdoch played a ball to leg and with Jones, his partner, ran a single. The Hon. A. Lyttelton, the English wicket-keeper, chased the ball and returned it to the striker's end, where Dr. W. G. Grace, who had moved up from slip, took it. Jones, apparently thinking the ball was dead, moved out of his ground to pat the soft pitch, and Grace put down the wicket, the umpire giving Jones out. Several of the Australians felt very bitter about Grace's action, and many people thought that the ball should have been considered dead, since it had settled in the hands of Grace, who might for the moment have been considered to be in the position of wicket-keeper. Others maintained that Grace's action was quite justified and within the law and spirit of cricket.

That the affair left Jones without ill-will was illustrated a few years before his death. Of W. G. Grace, whom he described as a great sportsman and cricketer, he said: "I never saw him leave alone any ball outside the off stump. He either cut or drove them."

He liked to recall his early days in cricket, comparing the comparatively meagre expenses then allowed in inter-Colonial cricket with those received by modern players. "Yet," he said, "I am game to wager that we had more real enjoyment during those times than the financed ones have to-day. Twice daily we practised, with no restrictions as to 'a modest quencher.' I shall always remember breakfasting at Magdalen College before our first match of the 1882 tour. Champagne cup was sent round with monotonous regularity, with old Oxford Ale as a sort of topper to the function."

JORDAN, Cortez, who died in Barbados on September 8, 1982, aged 61, umpired in 22 Test matches between 1953 and 1974. He was the only man to no-ball Charlie Griffith for throwing in a first-class match. It happened on the day when, playing for Barbados against the Indian touring team at Bridgetown in 1962, Griffith had inflicted serious injury on Nari Contractor, the Indian captain, whom he hit over the right ear with a bouncer. Jordan's appointment to the Georgetown Test of 1964–65 between West Indies and Australia broke new ground. Until then no umpire had stood in a Test match in West Indies outside his home territory. In protest at this new departure, the local umpire, Cecil Kippins, who had been appointed to stand with Jordan, was ordered by the British Guiana Umpires Association to withdraw from the match. This led to Gerry Gomez, a former Test player and then a West Indian selector, having to officiate. Although the holder of an umpiring certificate, Gomez had not previously stood in a first-class match. Quiet and efficient Jordan always umpired in a white panama hat and dark glasses.

JORDAN, Lieut.-Col. Henry Guy Bowen, died in hospital at Tonbridge on October 5, 1981, aged 83. A member of the Marlborough XI from 1914 to 1916, he played as a batsman for Derbyshire against Essex in 1926, but was unfortunate enough to make a pair.

JORDON, Thomas Carrick, the greatest wicket-keeper America has yet produced and a useful batsman, was born on February 10, 1877, and died on March 28, 1925, aged 48. It was testimony to his skill that he was able to take the very fast bowling of Mr. J. B. King with great ease. He was seen in England with the Philadelphian teams of 1903 and 1908 and with the Germantown C.C. in 1911, and had represented the United States against Canada besides taking part in many other great games in America against visiting sides. In 1911 he played an innings of 106 against the Gentlemen of Liverpool at Aigburth.

JOSE, Dr. A. D., who died on February 3, 1972, aged 42, was at Adelaide University before gaining a Blue at Oxford in 1950 and 1951. A fast-medium bowler, he played for South Australia and in 1951 and the following season for Kent, in occasional matches.

JOY, Frank Douglas Howarth, who died in a Winchester nursing home on February 17, 1966, aged 85, was in the Winchester XI in 1895 and from 1897 to 1899. A fast-medium left-arm bowler, he took 5 Eton wickets for 21 runs in 1897. At Oxford, he played in the Freshmen's match of 1900, but did not gain a Blue. From 1909 to 1912 he occasionally turned out for Somerset, then predominantly amateur, his best match analysis being seven wickets for 72 runs against Yorkshire at Taunton in 1910, and he appeared for Bombay Presidency in 1908. As a captain in the Army, he was Mentioned in Dispatches during the First World War. His daughter, Nancy, was author of *Maiden Over*, the standard history of women's cricket.

JOY, Col. Ronald Cecil Graham, D.S.O., who died in hospital at Ditchingham, Norfolk, on December 12, 1974, aged 76, was in the Winchester XI in 1916, and appeared a number of times for Essex between 1922 and 1928, besides playing for the Army. A fast-medium right-hander with a high action and a useful bat, he was a good club player, but never accomplished much in County Cricket. His wife was a daughter of Frank Penn, who played for England in the Test match at the Oval in 1880.

JOYCE, Ralph, who was born at Ashby-de-la-Zouch on August 28, 1878, died suddenly at Ashbourne, in Derbyshire, on March 12, 1908. Educated at the Ashby and Bedford Grammar Schools, he assisted Leicestershire two years prior to proceeding to Brasenose College, Oxford. In the Oxford Freshmen's match of 1898 he made 82, and two years later scored 37 and 25 in Trial matches, but he never appeared in the University XI. His first match for Leicestershire was against Essex at Leicester in 1896 and his last against Kent on the same ground in 1907. He was a free and stylish batsman, a splendid field, and a useful slow bowler. In 1902 he headed the county's averages with 38.00 for seven completed innings. His largest score in a match of note was 102 v. Notts at Trent Bridge in 1905.

JUPP, Vallance William Crisp, who collapsed and died in the garden of his home on July 9, 1960, aged 69, was one of the rare cricketers who began as a professional and later became an amateur. A splendid all-rounder, who played eight times for England, he was one of the best players in the country between the two World Wars. Born at Burgess Hill, Sussex, on March 27, 1891, Jupp was educated privately and later went to St. John's School, Burgess Hill, where he became captain of the XI. In his last year there he averaged over 100 with the bat and his achievements attracted the attention of the county authorities. He started with Sussex as a professional and made steady progress. In 1914 he played an innings of 217 not out against Worcestershire at Worcester and averaged over 36 for the season. With 51 wickets, he headed the county bowling averages that year.

During the War Jupp served with the Royal Engineers before being transferred as a cadet to the R.A.F. On demobilisation in 1919 he appeared for Sussex as an amateur and quickly showed that the absence of four years from the game had not reduced his skill. In 1921 he scored 2,169 runs in first-class matches and took 121 wickets.

At the end of the 1920 season he was invited to tour Australia with the M.C.C. but could not accept. Two years later he went to South Africa under the captaincy of F.T. Mann. His Test appearances were against Australia twice, in 1921, against South Africa, four times on the 1922–23 tour, and against West Indies, twice, in 1928. At the end of 1921 he accepted the position of secretary with Northamptonshire and then qualified for the county, giving them valuable service as captain and player until he retired in 1939. He decided to give up the captaincy in 1931, having taken that course twice previously, only to be pressed into service again.

As a batsman, Jupp could vary his style to suit the occasion. He watched the ball with extreme care and was able to play a rigidly defensive game, but on true, fast pitches he scored with easy freedom, being strong in driving. Before the 1914 War and for a time afterwards he bowled slightly above medium-pace, but later he turned to off-spin and few bowlers of his day were able to turn the ball to the same extent. Again, as a bowler, he showed himself adept at varying his methods, depending on the condition of the pitch. He was also a first-class fieldsman, especially at cover.

In his career he scored just over 23,000 runs for an average of almost 30 and he took more than 1,600 wickets for about 23 runs apiece. Ten times he achieved the "double" and in 1932 he took all 10 wickets in an innings against Kent at Tunbridge Wells. Jupp performed the hat-trick five times, three for Sussex and two for Northamptonshire. His best season with the ball was in 1928 when he took 166 wickets, average 20.15.

KANNANGARA, Richard Lionel, who died in Colombo in August, 1972, was a stylish left-handed batsman celebrated for his driving in which he rarely lifted the ball. While at Wesley College, whom he captained in 1917, he hit three centuries and in 1927, as the only Ceylonese included in an Up-Country XI, he took five wickets for 60 runs against A. E. R. Gilligan's M.C.C. team.

KAYE, Lieut.-Col. Harold Swift, who died on November 6, 1953, aged 71, played for Yorkshire when a Lieutenant in 1907 and 1908, scoring 243 runs, average 10.12. Born on May 9, 1882, he was in the Harrow XI in 1899 and 1900. His 60 in the Harrow first innings helped considerably towards a victory by one wicket over Eton in 1900. In the second innings he was the second victim in a hat-trick performed by the Eton right-arm slow bowler, E. G. Whateley, whom Kaye had twice dismissed. He was awarded the D.S.O. and M.C. during the First World War, when he rose to the command of the 4th K.O.Y.L.I. and was five times Mentioned in Dispatches.

KEATING, Mr. James Leslie, who died suddenly in Melbourne on March 6, 1962, aged 70, the day after watching an exciting game between Richmond and Collingwood, played for Victoria from 1918 to 1925. His best score in first-class cricket was 154 for Victoria against New South Wales at Sydney in his first season with the State. He also represented Victoria at baseball.

KEEBLE, Frank Henry Gamble, who died in New York City on August 19, 1925, was a fair batsman who played with the Staten Island C.C. He was a well-known art critic, and was born in London on June 10, 1867.

KEENE, John William, who played for Surrey, Worcestershire and Scotland, died on January 3, 1931. A useful left-hand bowler on the slow side of medium pace, he used, when playing for Mitcham, to make the ball come back sharply and on a pitch which helped him meet with considerable success in club cricket. After appearing for Surrey in 1897, he represented Worcestershire, but his career with that county extended over only three seasons—1903–05. His best year was 1903, when he took 36 wickets for 17.88 runs each. Keene, who was born on April 25, 1874, held the post of coach at Loretto School.

KEETON, William Wallace, who died on October 9, 1980, aged 75, was a great servant of Nottinghamshire and one of the many candidates for a place in the England side as an opening bat in the years immediately before the Second World War. In fact he played in only two Tests, v. Australia at Leeds in 1934 and v. West Indies at the Oval in 1939. Probably most people would reckon that the selectors were right, that he was a good county player but not quite Test class. He had a sound defence, was a fine cutter and also had a good cover drive, but what spectators will chiefly remember is his legside play and in particular his mastery of that difficult and neglected stroke, the on-drive. Moreover, he was, as befitted a first-class soccer forward, a fine outfield. He first played for his county in 1926, but the Nottinghamshire batsmen of that era retained their skill almost undiminished to a patriarchal age and it was not until 1931 that the premature death of Whysall secured him a serious trial. He made the most of his opportunity, scoring his thousand runs with an average of 30 and making two centuries. For most of the season he had the valuable experience of opening with George Gunn. From then for 20 years his career was interrupted only by illness or injuries, of which he had more than his share; in January 1935 he was knocked down by a lorry and was lucky to be able to resume his place in the side late in June. But despite all this and the loss of six seasons in the War he reached his thousand runs on 12 occasions and made 54 hundreds. His highest score, 312 not out in seven and three-quarter hours v. Middlesex at the Oval (Eton were playing Harrow at Lord's) in 1939, remains the only innings of 300 ever played for Nottinghamshire, and he is also one of the few batsmen to have scored a century against every county. From 1932 to 1948 his regular partner was that eccentric player, Charlie Harris, and a notable pair they were. On 45 occasions they put up three figures, 14 times they exceeded 150 and five times 200. Twice they put up 100 in each innings. Their highest stand was 277 v Middlesex at Trent Bridge in 1933. Keeton was

still as good as ever after the War, but Hutton and Washbrook had now established themselves as England's opening pair. As late as 1949 he scored 2,049 runs with an average of 55.37. In 1951, at 46, he lost his regular place in the side but against Kent at Trent Bridge helped Simpson to put on 269 for the first wicket. A single match in 1952 concluded his career. In all he had scored 24,276 runs with an average of just under 40. After retiring he had a sports shop for a time and later worked for the National Coal Board.

KEIGWIN, 2nd Lieut. Henry Daniel (Lancashire Fusiliers), born in Essex in 1881, fell in action on September 20, 1916. After playing successfully in St. Paul's XI in 1899 and 1900, he proceeded to Cambridge but did not obtain his Blue. For Peterhouse, however, he made many excellent scores, and in 1901 and again in 1904 made over 1,000 runs by the end of May. On the Amalgamation ground on April 26, 1904, he scored 140 not out and his brother, Mr. R. P. Keigwin, 124 not out for Peterhouse v. Fitzwilliam Hall, the pair making 318 together for the first wicket without being parted. Nine days later, on the same ground, the same pair scored 244 without being separated for Peterhouse v. Trinity Hall after the latter had declared with five wickets down for 242, H. D. making 160 not out and R. P. 72 not out. Mr. H. D. played a few times for Essex, and (whilst Director of Music at Glenalmond) appeared in representative matches for Scotland, and assisted the Grange C.C. At the Oval in 1906 he scored 77 and 27 for Gentlemen of England v. Surrey. Later he settled in Bulawayo. He had many strokes, and was a useful left-hand medium-paced bowler.

KEIGWIN, Richard Prescott, who died on November 26, 1972, aged 89, captained Clifton in 1901 and 1902 before going up to Cambridge, where he won his Blue at cricket from 1903 to 1906. He also represented the University at Association football, hockey and racquets. He later played cricket and football for Essex and Gloucestershire; hockey for Essex and England and lawn tennis for Gloucestershire. When in France for a time, he became an expert at pelota. He did much good work as a coach at the R.N.C., Osborne, and while a master at Clifton for 16 years and afterwards as Warden of Wills Hall, Bristol University. Rated one of the foremost translators of Danish writings into English, he became an authority on the works of Hans Christian

Andersen and was made a Knight of the Danish Order of the Dannebrog.

KEITH, Geoffrey Leyden, died on December 26, 1975, aged 38. After playing a number of times for Somerset from 1959 to 1961, he returned to his native county, Hampshire, in 1962 and in his first match made 82 against Oxford. But though he was a correct batsman and a good slip he could never command an assured place in the side and at the end of the 1967 season left at his own request to live in South Africa, where he played for Western Province. He returned in 1971 to succeed Leo Harrison as the Hampshire coach, a position he held until his death. His highest score in first-class cricket and his only hundred was 101 not out against the South Africans in 1965, when after a stubborn innings he reached his century in the last over of the day with an on-drive for six into the pavilion. His early death was particularly tragic as he was a man who took great pains to keep himself physically fit.

KELAART, Mervyn, who died in Victoria, Australia, on February 2, 1968, aged 60, was a member of a celebrated Ceylon cricketing family. A stylish left-hand batsman and right-arm medium-pace spin bowler, he headed both sets of averages for St. Joseph's College, Colombo, when 16. He represented Ceylon against the M.C.C. team of 1932 and also against New Zealand and was an outstanding success in the Ceylon side that toured India in 1932–33, when he scored 101 off the All India bowling at Lahore. He again visited India in 1940, and, as a member of Dr. C. H. Gunasekara's touring team in Malaya, took six wickets for 19 runs and two for 20 against Malaya.

KELAART, Thomas, who died in Colombo on May 25, 1950, aged 79, was a leading cricketer in Ceylon. A left-arm bowler, he once took nine wickets for 71 runs against Lord Hawke's team. He bowled W. G. Grace when playing against Lord Sheffield's XI in 1891.

KELLEWAY, Charles E., who played in 26 Test matches for Australia in the years 1910 to 1928, died in Sydney on November 16, 1944, after a long illness, aged 55. He made his name with New South Wales, most successful of the States in the Sheffield Shield Tournament, and, starting Test cricket when South Africa first visited Australia in 1910, he might have enjoyed a more remarkable career but for ill-health and some differences with team selectors. A very sound batsman, invaluable for opening the innings or facing a crisis, he possessed unlimited patience combined with high skill in scoring strokes; he also bowled well above medium pace with length and swerve which kept the best batsman on the alert for unexpected trouble.

He first played against England in the 1911–12 season, when the team captained by P. F. Warner won four of the five Tests. Kelleway's best effort in eight innings was 70 and six wickets cost him 41.50 apiece: but coming to England in 1912 he made 360 runs in six Test matches, with 114 at Manchester and 102 at Lord's both against South Africa. His achievement compared favourably with the work of Warren Bardsley, his only superior for the side on our pitches that were often treacherous during that season of the Triangular Tournament. This England won with four victories and two draws—both when meeting Australia. Kelleway in the whole tour averaged 30.95 and took 47 wickets.

After the 1914–18 War Kelleway stopped in England and captained the Australian Imperial Forces team during the early part of the tour. In nine innings he scored 505 with an average of 56.11, but then for some undisclosed reason he left the side, the captaincy devolving upon H. L. Collins. He did not come to England again as a player, but in the Australian season of 1920–21 he was a prominent member of the very powerful side captained by W. W. Armstrong which beat England under J. W. H. T. Douglas in all five Tests. Kelleway averaged 47.14 in the series and took 15 wickets at 21.00 apiece, the lowest cost for either side.

In the third encounter at Adelaide, England gained a lead of 93 on the first innings, but then Kelleway, missed before scoring, stayed nearly seven hours for 147, a display that earned him the nickname of "Rock of Gibraltar." This display of solid defence in an uphill struggle for his country ranks with the 90 in five and three-quarter hours by William Scotton, who saved England from collapse at the Oval in 1884; the supremacy of M. A. Noble during eight hours and a half for Australia at Manchester in 1899 when he scored 60 not out and 89 in the follow-on, his patience being so controlled that during one spell of three-quarters of an hour he did not get a run; H. L. Collins proved equally imperturbable at Old Trafford in 1921 when 40 runs was his reward for four hours 50 minutes at the wicket. These three were saving efforts that proved effective; Kelleway paved the way for victory by 119 runs on the sixth day. In all five Tests against Arthur Gilligan's team he averaged 28 and took 14 wickets. Four years later he finished his Test career, falling ill during the first match at Brisbane, where England won by the record margin of 675 runs before losing the other four contests in the rubber. According to the New South Wales Year-Book Kelleway's figures were 874 runs, average 31.21; 37 wickets, average 31.29 against England; 548 runs, average 54.80; 15 wickets, average 35.20 against South Africa.

In Sheffield Shield matches for New South Wales Kelleway scored 2,304 runs at an average of 40.42. He played his highest innings, 168, in December 1920 at Sydney against South Australia, and in partnership with Warren Bardsley, 235, put on 397, which remains a world record for the fifth wicket. When South Australia followed-on 611 behind, heavy rain flooded the ground, and they asked that the match should be abandoned and a victory credited to New South Wales. This was done—the first time that a Sheffield Shield match was left unfinished. For his State Kelleway took 126 wickets at 27.73 each.

In the biography of C. E. Kelleway in the 1945 issue the reference to the 1928–29 Tests should have emphasised that England won the first four Tests and lost only the last match of the series.

KELLY, Gustavus Noel Blake, died at Castlebar, Co. Mayo, on March 14, 1980, aged 80. A tall, right-hand batsman and fast-medium right-arm bowler, he was educated at Stonyhurst and Clongowes Wood College and made seven appearances in first-class cricket for Dublin University and Ireland from 1922 to 1926, scoring 275 runs, average 30.56, and taking 17 wickets at 23.35 apiece. He played little cricket after leaving University. His father, G. W. F Kelly, was an Oxford Blue, while a brother, A. W. B. Kelly, and an uncle, A. D. Comyn, also played for Dublin University and Ireland.

KELLY, James Joseph, died in Sydney on August 14, 1938, aged 71. A wicket-keeper of pronounced ability he went from Victoria, where J. McC. Blackham held sway, to Sydney, and appeared for New South Wales two seasons before he made, in 1896, the first of his four visits to England. He was highest scorer with eight when the Australians were dismissed for 18, M.C.C. having revenge for their own fall for 19 in 1878 at Lord's. As successor to Blackham, comparison with this greatest keeper of all time was bound to tell unfavourably for the newcomer, but Kelly was extremely good in the very exacting experience of continually taking such very fast and erratic bowlers as E. Jones and A. Cotter. With the bat he was capable of forcing the game or defending as needed. In the Old Trafford Test of 1896 he and Hugh Trumble batted an hour for the last 25 runs, Australia winning by three wickets after a terrific struggle against the superb fast bowling of Tom Richardson. Kelly made 103 at Edgbaston in 1899 and 74 out of 112 in an hour for the last wicket at Bristol in 1905. His average in first-class cricket for an aggregate of 4,411 runs was 20. In 33 Test matches against England he scored 613 runs, average 17.51, and dismissed 55 batsmen, 39 caught, 16 stumped. He gave up first-class cricket after his visit to England in 1905, because of a damaged finger and heart weakness due to a blow from a ball bowled by Walter Brearley. A benefit match at Sydney in the following January brought Kelly £1,400. By a strange coincidence he died on the same day as Hugh Trumble. There was a difference of only 14 days in the ages of these two very popular Australians who were colleagues on the tours to England in 1896, 1899 and 1902.

KELLY, John Martin, died in hospital at Rochdale on November 13, 1979, aged 57. Born at Bacup on March 19, 1922. Kelly joined the Lancashire staff in 1947, making his debut in the final home match that year. However, he played in only five more games in the two succeeding years, failing to gain a regular place in a strong batting side. He joined Derbyshire in 1950 and soon became a reliable early-order batsman along with Arnold Hamer, who came from Yorkshire at the same time. Despite his slight build Kelly was a fine, graceful player, possessing all the strokes, which were marked by the use of his wrists. A little hesitant perhaps in his approach, he tended to play each ball on its merit, and his real ability was sometimes evident only when an aggressive lower-order batsman like George Dawkes was his partner. In 1957 he scored four of his nine hundreds, making 127 against Leicestershire at Chesterfield when he added 246 with D. B. Carr for the third wicket—a new Derbyshire record, and still the county's best stand against Leicestershire. When making his debut for Derbyshire at the Oval in 1950 he scored 74 in the second innings, this then being the highest score for the county on a first appearance. Like Hamer's, his last season was 1960, when he was granted a benefit which realised £2,263, and since then he had been coach and groundsman at Thornleigh College, Bolton.

KELLY, T. J. D., (Victoria) died in Melbourne in July, 1893. Mr. Kelly played for Victoria for many years in the Inter-Colonial matches, and was regarded as by far the best fieldsman at point Australia has yet produced.

KELLY, William L., who died in Melbourne in December, 1968, aged 92, was manager of the Australian team in England in 1930—Sir Donald Bradman's first tour. Kelly played for Victoria in 1908. An amusing story is told of his visit to England. During a match at the Oval, he was said to have placed a notice on the door of the Australian dressing-room which read: "Nobody admitted without manager's authority." The Oval, of course, forms part of the Duchy of Cornwall, which provided a source of revenue to the then Prince of Wales, now the Duke of Windsor. The Prince attended the match, saw the notice and told Kelly: "You can't keep me out. I'm your landlord!"

KELSON, George Mortimer, died on March 29, 1920, in his 85th year. He was born on December 8, 1835. Mr. Kelson retired from first-class cricket so long ago that to the present generation he was not even a name, but in his day he held a prominent place, being at one time beyond question the best bat in the Kent XI. Kent cricket in the '60s was in a very depressed condition, but Mr. Kelson took part in many a hard-fought game side by side with Willsher and George Bennett. The irony of the position at the end of the '60s was that Kent, with their full strength in the field, would have had about the strongest batting side in England. Some of the amateurs avoided county matches, but were seen during the Canterbury Week. Mr. Kelson played his first match for Kent in 1859 and his last in 1873. He was at his best in the seasons of 1863–64–65. In 1863 he played at Kennington Oval the innings of his life—122 against Surrey. He was on the losing side in an extraordinary match, Surrey with 192 to get in the last innings hitting off the runs for one wicket. To the best of my knowledge the feat was, at that time, without parallel in first-class cricket. H. H. Stephenson made 78 not out, and Jupp, then just coming to the front, 74 not out. There used to be a little harmless betting on cricket in those days and the task looked so formidable that Caffyn who had backed Surrey hedged all his money. Mr. Kelson did not do a great deal outside Kent cricket, but he was picked for Gentlemen against Players at the Oval in 1864 and 1866, and when, after 1862, the notorious schism kept Hayward, Carpenter, and George Parr away from the Oval he played two or three times for England against Surrey, scoring 26 and 40 in 1864 and 40 in 1865. Appearing for the Gentlemen in 1866 when, for a very strong side, he was put in last, he had the satisfaction of taking part in a game in which the Players were beaten at the Oval for the first time, the match dating from 1857. I cannot recall Mr. Kelson's batting, though I saw him play, but from all accounts he was a fine punishing player with a free attractive style. Mr. Kelson was a great fisherman and wrote much on the gentle art, being at one time fishing editor of "Land and Water."—S.H.P.

KEMBLE, Arthur Twiss, a member of the well-known theatrical family of that name, was born in Cumberland on February 3, 1862, and died at Park Cottage, Crawley Down, Sussex, on March 13, 1925, aged 63. He was a useful batsman—he made many very good scores for Liverpool, including one of 172 v. Tu Quoques—and was much above the average as a wicket-keeper. He first took to wicket-keeping whilst at Appleby Grammar School, in Westmorland, and it was his skill in that position which enabled him to appear for Lancashire from 1885 until 1894. He had no easy task in following such a man as Pilling, but he acquitted himself well, standing close up to the wicket even against Mold. He kept wicket for the Gentlemen against the Players at Hastings, in 1891, 1892 and 1894 and at the Oval in 1893. For Lancashire v. Surrey at the Oval in 1892 he made 50, and for Liverpool and District v. Cambridge University at Aigburth in 1895 he played an innings of 59. His earliest County Cricket was played for Cumberland, commencing in 1889. In 1899 he took a team to the Canaries which played three matches and won them all, and he had served on the Committees of the Lancashire and Sussex County Clubs. He distinguished himself at Rugby football as well as at cricket, and besides representing Lancashire at that game played also for England against both Ireland and Wales.

KEMP, Arthur Fitch, a slow bowler and sound batsman, one of four brothers who were in the Harrow XI during the period 1874 to 1885, died on February 14, 1940, at Virginia Water, aged 76. Twice he was on the winning side against Eton. In 1880, when

Manley C. Kemp was captain, Harrow won by 95 runs, and next season A. F. Kemp led the XI to victory at Lord's by 112 runs. In the first match Arthur Kemp, opening the innings, scored 33 and took five wickets for 61 runs. When captain he made 28 runs, but did not meet with any success as a bowler. He played for Kent, the county of his birth, three times in 1884. In partnership with E. M. Hadow, he won the Public Schools Racquets Championship in 1881.

KEMP, Harold Fitch, youngest of the four brothers who played for Harrow, died at Harpenden, Hertfordshire, on March 2, 1942, in his 75th year. In the XI two years, 1885 and 1886, he was unfortunate in his experiences at Lord's.

KEMP, Sir Kenneth Hagar, Twelfth Baronet of Gissing, died at Sheringham on April 22, 1936, aged 83. Born on April 21, 1853, at Erpingham, Norfolk, he went to the Clergy Orphan School, Canterbury, where he was coached by Fuller Pilch, and in 1866 received a bat inscribed "with Fuller Pilch's love." Although scoring 52 in the Cambridge Freshmen's match of 1872 and next season making 50 and 20 for "Next Sixteen," besides 14 and 25 for M.C.C. against the University, he did not get his Blue. He captained Sandhurst against Woolwich at Lord's in 1876, and scored 49. He played for Norfolk from 1877 to 1884 and was Hon. Secretary of the County Club for some years until 1889.

KEMPIS, George Stephen, died at Scottburgh, Natal, in March, 1948. He played a few times for the Transvaal in Currie Cup matches and was a member of the first South African team that toured England in 1894. Born at Port Elizabeth on November 25, 1871, he was a younger brother of G. A. Kempis, who played in the first England and South Africa match, but died shortly afterwards.

KEMPSON, Matthew, died on June 20, 1894. Cricketers whose memories extended back 40 years learnt with great regret of the death in his 63rd year of this once famous amateur bowler. He was merely a name to the present generation, as he went out to India while still a young man, and, staying there many years, did not return to this country until his cricket career had long been over. Educated at Cheltenham, where he was captain of the XI, in 1848–49–50, he made his first appearance at Lord's for Cambridge against Oxford in 1851. He does not seem, from the score-sheet, to have bowled much on that occasion, but with a score of 48 he contributed in some measure to the victory of Cambridge by an innings and four runs. Mr. Kempson was a good hard hitter, but it was his medium pace round-arm bowling that made him celebrated. If he had done nothing else his name would be remembered for the performance accomplished by him in conjunction with Sir Frederick Bathurst in the Gentlemen v. Players match at Lord's in 1853. The two bowlers were unchanged through the two innings, and owing to their efforts the Gentlemen won the match by 60 runs. This feat of bowling unchanged through a Gentlemen v. Players match had never been done before, but it has since been performed by Edgar Willsher and George Tarrant at Lord's in 1864, by Mr. A. G. Steel and Mr. A. H. Evans at the Oval in 1879, and at Lord's in 1894 by Mr. F. S. Jackson and Mr. S. M. J. Woods.

KEMPSTER, John Frank, died at Kilteman, County Dublin on April 21, 1975, in his 83rd year. A noted authority on the game in Ireland, he made two first-class appearances for his country v. Scotland 1920–22 scoring 55 runs average 13.75 and taking none for 18. He played for the Leinster club, as did his father F. G. Kempster, also an octogenarian, a noted Irish batsman of the 1870s.

KEMPTON, Andrew, who died in a London hospital on November 17, 1957, aged 72, did much good work over nearly 50 years for Surrey. He was the "Father" of the Surrey Colts team, whom he captained up to last season. In his younger days he played as an excellent wicket-keeper-batsman for Catford and Richmond. It was while he was President of Catford that J. C. Laker, now the England off-break bowler, returning from military service overseas, turned out for the club, and Kempton brought him to the notice of the Surrey authorities. A great friend of Sir John Hobbs, Kempton was a founder-director of his sports-outfitters firm in 1919.

KEMP-WELCH, Capt. George Durant, died in June, 1944, as the outcome of enemy action which destroyed the Guards Chapel. He gave up important business connections when war broke out and joined the Grenadier Guards. As a soldier he carried the same compelling force that made him prominent as a games player at Charterhouse and Cambridge, while, with more time available, he might have become invaluable in the Warwickshire cricket XI.

He progressed steadily in batting, after showing more prominence as a fast-medium-paced bowler at school, and, though in 1929 doing little at Fenner's, he found his form at Cheltenham against Gloucestershire as an opening batsman and gained his Blue when a Freshman. The big occasion provided the opportunity for Kemp-Welch to produce his best skill and admirable style: in his three matches against Oxford he played six innings, scoring 270 runs with an average of 45—an exceptional level of consistent batting under the trying conditions that always prevail at Lord's.

In 1930 Kemp-Welch helped E. T. Killick in an opening stand for 139, and he took two wickets for 10 runs in a collapse, Cambridge winning by 205 runs. When captain next year he batted admirably for 87 and 28 against Oxford, beginning the match in a partnership of 149 with A. Ratcliffe, who went on to create a score of 201 which the Nawab of Pataudi immediately excelled by making 238 not out. The great innings, which mainly accounted for Oxford winning by eight wickets, still heads the list of three-figure scores made in inter-University matches. Continuing the habit begun in 1927 of playing for Warwickshire in the summer vacation, Kemp-Welch finished the summer with a remarkable experience of travelling and good batting: in the course of two weeks he played for Warwickshire at Taunton, for the Gentlemen both at Folkestone and Scarborough, and then back to Folkestone for the Rest of England match against the M.C.C. South African team. Opening the batting, he scored in these games 56, 12, 51, 28 and 40. In that year he also played for the Gentlemen at Lord's, and altogether that season scored 1,561 runs, average 37.16.

In February 1932 Kemp-Welch went to Jamaica with a team captained by Lord Tennyson, and again was associated with a record by an opponent, G. Headley, scoring 344 not out, the highest individual innings played by a West Indies batsman. Kemp-Welch made 105 in the same match and 186 in the return encounter with All Jamaica. Brilliant fielding helped to make him a valuable member of any side.

After playing well for three years in the Charterhouse team, Kemp-Welch gained his Association football Blue at Cambridge as centre-forward and became captain of the XI.

In 1934 he married Mrs. Richard Munro, daughter of Mr. Stanley Baldwin, subsequently Lord Baldwin of Bewdley.

KENDALL, Thomas, died at Hobart on the August 17, 1924, at the age of 72. He had lived in Hobart for forty-three years, being employed all that time by the *Mercury* newspaper, but he was born in Bedfordshire. Tom Kendall may be described as, perhaps, the best Australian bowler who never came to England. Indeed in his young days, though his opportunities in first-class company were few, he ranked as a left-handed bowler, slow to medium pace, with the famous Frank Allan. From all accounts he had a wonderful command over his length and could break either way. He was regarded as one of the certainties for the trip to England in 1878 but for some reason he was dropped after the preliminary tour. Still though so little was seen of him in big matches he did enough for fame. Next to Charles Bannerman he had the biggest share in beating James Lillywhite's team at Melbourne in March 1877—the first victory gained by Australia over an England side on level terms. In that match Kendall took eight wickets for 109 runs and in the return—won by the Englishmen—six for 106. Writing home to the *Sportsman* at that time James Southerton said how greatly Australian cricket had improved since his visit with W. G. Grace's team three years before and expressed a positive opinion that if Kendall were in England, no representative side would be complete without him. Such praise from such an expert should have prepared us for the class of bowling we were to see in 1878. Kendall was past his best when Ivo Bligh's team toured Australia in 1882–83 but, as one reads in the first *Badminton Book*, he greatly impressed A. G. Steel. Two incidents in Kendall's career deserve record in *Wisden*. Playing at Melbourne for Fifteen of Victoria in 1874 he got W. G. Grace caught off his bowling for eight and in March 1892, when Lord Sheffield's team visited Hobart, he bowled the great man for 27.—S.H.P.

KENDLE, The Rev. William James, died on January 30, 1920, aged 73, at Woodsford, Dorset, of which place he had been Rector for 33 years. A very useful batsman, he had been in the XI at Sherborne, and had appeared occasionally for Hampshire. In 1867 he took park in the Freshmen's match at Cambridge, but did not obtain his Blue.

KENNAWAY, The Rev. Charles Lewis, who died on April 23, 1940, at the advanced age of 92, was probably the last survivor of the

Norfolk team which in 1885 made 695 against M.C.C. at Lord's, the record score up to that time. With Jack Hansell, Mr. Kennaway put on 155 for the third wicket. Another notable occasion in his cricket career was the victory of Norfolk at Norwich in 1882 over the professional side run by Shaw and Shrewsbury. His highest score for the county was 147 against Free Foresters at Norwich in 1882. Besides being a sound, attractive batsman he was an excellent cover-point. For many years he played at Garboldisham, where he was Rector until 1914. He then went as Vicar to Tarrant Crawford in Dorset.

KENNEDY, Alexander Stuart, who died on November 15, 1959, aged 68, was prominent as an all-rounder for Hampshire between 1907 and 1936, in which time he took 2,874 wickets—2,549 for his county, a record—for 21.24 runs each, scored 16,496 runs, including 10 centuries, average 18.54, and held 500 catches. He made his first appearance for the county when 16, but did not gain a regular place in the team till 1909. Sturdily built, he bowled at medium pace with a high delivery and in-swing which, combined with spin and a marked accuracy of length, made him difficult to master.

In 15 seasons, "Alec" Kennedy dismissed over 100 batsmen, his best summer being that of 1922 when his victims numbered 205. For many years he and J. Newman formed the backbone of the Hampshire attack and this pair each performed the "cricketer's double" five times. Among Kennedy's best performances were all 10 wickets for 37 runs for the Players, for whom he appeared in 16 matches, in the first innings of the Gentlemen at the Oval in 1927; nine for 33 v. Lancashire at Liverpool, 1920; nine for 46 v. Derbyshire at Portsmouth, 1929; eight for 11 v. Glamorgan at Cardiff, 1921; and seven for eight v. Warwickshire at Portsmouth, 1927, when he disposed of six men in 14 balls while conceding four runs. Forty-four times he took 10 or more wickets in a match and against Somerset at Bath in 1922 earned figures of 14 wickets for 116 runs. He achieved three hat-tricks—v. Gloucestershire in 1920 and 1924, both at Southampton, and v. Somerset at Bath in 1920.

A sound batsman, he hit his highest innings, 163 not out, from the Warwickshire bowling at Portsmouth in 1923 and as he also obtained nine wickets for 77 runs, played a big part in success for Hampshire by 244 runs. In the game with Nottinghamshire at Trent Bridge two years earlier, he carried his bat through the innings for 152.

He took part in all five Test matches in South Africa for F. T. Mann's team of 1922–23, heading the bowling with figures of 31 wickets, average 19.32. With analyses of two for 46 and five for 76 he, together with A. C. Russell, of Essex, who came from a sick-bed to play his second century of the match, had much to do with victory in the final Test and the rubber. After his retirement he was for a time coach at Cheltenham College and from 1947 to 1954 coached in South Africa.

H. L. V. Day, who played with him in the Hampshire team, in a tribute, said: "There was never a greater hearted trier than Kennedy, nor was there a fairer bowler."

KENNEDY, Charles Marshall, who was born at Brighton on December 15, 1849, died at Tunbridge Wells in the first week of February, 1906. He was educated at Blackheath and Cambridge, but never gained a place in the University XI. Between 1872 and 1879 he assisted Sussex on 22 occasions, his highest score being 37 against Surrey, at Brighton, in 1874. He was a fair batsman and a useful wicket-keeper.

KENNEY-HERBERT, Edward Maxwell, who died at Ealing on January 24, 1916, was born at Bourton Rectory, Rugby, December 10, 1845. Fifty years ago he was a good all-round cricketer and was then known as E. M. Kenney simply, not assuming the additional name of Herbert until 1875. As a member of the Rugby XI of 1864 he scored 74 v. Marlborough on the old Cattle Market ground at Islington, and averaged over 25 runs an innings for the season. Proceeding to Oxford, he obtained his Blue in 1866 and in his three matches against Cambridge took 22 wickets for 235 runs: in the 1868 game, which Oxford lost by 168 runs, he obtained six for 51 in the first innings and eight for 68 in the second. His bowling was fast left-hand round the wicket, but he batted right-handed and was a good and free hitter. In 1868 he scored 68 for his University against Surrey at the Oval. Between 1864 and 1869 he appeared occasionally for Warwickshire, but unfortunately was not seen in first-class cricket as frequently as his skill entitled him. He was elected to the M.C.C. in 1882 and was a member of the Free Foresters. It may be added that he was also a very good racquets player, and that in 1866 he declined the honour of representing his University at that game against Cambridge.

KENT, Kenneth Gwynne, who died on December 29, 1974, aged 73, played a few times for Warwickshire between 1927 and 1931 as a fast-medium right-hand bowler, but without much success. He was in the XI at King Edward's School, Birmingham.

KENTFIELD, R. W., who was born at Bognor, in Sussex, died in Manchester at the end of October, 1904. He was a left-hand medium-paced bowler, who, with more opportunities, would probably have made a name for himself in first-class cricket. He appeared for Lancashire on four occasions during 1888, and for Sussex once in 1894 and once in 1896. For Lancashire against Cheshire, at Stockport, in July, 1888, he took eight wickets for 52 runs, and for Sussex v. Middlesex, at Lord's, in July, 1894, he obtained seven for 94.

KENYON, Myles N., who died on November 21, 1960, aged 73, captained Lancashire from 1919 to 1922 and in 1936 and 1937 was President of the County Club. He enjoyed his best season in 1921, when he scored 635 runs, average 22.67, and hit his highest innings, 61 not out against Surrey at the Oval. In the match with Warwick Armstrong's Australian team at Liverpool that year, he scored 24 in a first innings of 100. E. A. McDonald took eight wickets for 62 runs, of which Kenyon punished him for 18 in an over—one six and three fours. At one time Kenyon was High Sheriff of Lancashire and a Deputy Lieutenant.

KERMODE, Alexander, died at Sydney on July 17, 1934, aged 58. Discovered by M. A. Noble when playing junior cricket, Kermode was chosen for New South Wales in 1901 and during the same season A. C. MacLaren, captain of the English touring team, was so impressed with his form that he induced him to come to England and qualify for Lancashire. From 1904 to 1908 Kermode remained with Lancashire but his fast bowling against first-class batsmen never reached the standard expected. He met with most success in 1905 when 107 wickets fell to him at 21.43 runs apiece as compared with Walter Brearley's 121 at 18.64. Of tall and ungainly build Kermode ended his term with Lancashire as his ability suddenly deteriorated. When in League cricket moderate batsmen fell ready victims to his speed and off-break. The importation of Kermode to qualify for Lancashire received severe criticism in many quarters. The case of Albert Trott—one of the best all-round cricketers ever produced by Australia or England—coming to Middlesex was cited as a precedent, but the example of Yorkshire and Nottinghamshire relying entirely upon native talent was urged as desirable to be copied by all counties.

KERR, John, one of Scotland's greatest cricketers, died in a Greenock hospital on December 27, 1972, aged 87. An opening batsman, he gained fame in 1921 when in two matches at Perth and Edinburgh he scored 222 runs against Warwick Armstrong's formidable Australian team. In the first match he made 15 and 60 not out, and he batted all of one day in the next at Raeburn Place for 147, *Wisden* stating that until he reached three figures he played a rigidly defensive game.

Jack Hobbs ranked him among the world's best batsmen. He was capped 39 times and scored 2,096 runs for his country with his highest innings 178 not out against Ireland in 1923. Between 1901 and 1940 when he retired, John Kerr made over 40,000 runs in club matches. Kerr was also a brilliant slip fielder and skilful slow bowler.

Mr. Kerr, whose father and brother, and cousin J. Reid Kerr (Scottish cricketing and rugby internationalist) all played for Greenock, became the club's first Hon. President in 1956, an office he held until his death.

After retiring from cricket, Mr. Kerr took up bowling and was a member of Greenock's Ardgowan Club, of which he was a past president.

He was an elder in Greenock Presbytery for 27 years and served on several committees of the General Assembly of the Church of Scotland. He also had a long association with the Boys' Brigade and was captain of the 7th Greenock Company for nearly 40 years.

KERR, Simon, who was found stabbed to death in a flat in Bristol on March 17, 1974, performed the extraordinary feat of scoring, when 19, five not out centuries in six innings for St. George's College, Salisbury, in 1972. The following year he paid his own fare from Rhodesia, joined the Gloucestershire ground staff and lived in the pavilion on the Bristol ground. He played for the Second XI. He was recommended to the county by M. J. Procter, the South African Test match all-rounder.

KERSHAW, John Edward, who assisted Lancashire in 1877 and the three following seasons, died of consumption on November 30, 1903. He was a capital batsman and field, and occasionally acted as wicket-keeper in the absence of Pilling. He was born at Heywood, in Lancashire, on January 12, 1854, and was educated at Eccleshall College, near Sheffield. He was captain of the Heywood Club from its formation in 1878 until 1898, when he removed to Burnley. His greatest success as a batsman was when he played an innings of 66 against Sussex, in 1877.

KETTLEWELL, Lieut.-Col. Henry Wildman, who died on April 28, 1963, aged 88, was in the Eton XI from 1890 to 1892. He played for Somerset at Portsmouth in 1899 in the match made memorable by the feat of Major R. M. Poore, who played innings of 104 and 119 not out for Hampshire.

KEY, Sir Kingsmill James, Bart, died on August 9, 1932, at his residence Wittersham, Kent, from blood-poisoning, the result of an insect bite. An Oxford double Blue and captain of Surrey from 1894 (when he succeeded John Shuter) until 1899, he was born at Streatham on October 11, 1864, and so at the time of his death had not quite reached the age of 68.

He first made his name by a notable performance which he achieved in company with W. E. Roller. Tried for Surrey in 1882 at the age of 17, he had accomplished nothing of special note up to the time he and Roller found themselves engaged in August, 1883, in a match against Lancashire. Surrey were set 234 to make against Crossland, Watson, Barlow and Nash, and late on the second afternoon had lost seven wickets in putting together a score of 122 and so looked doomed to defeat. At that point, Key joined Roller and so ably did these two young men bat that before the drawing of stumps 56 runs had been obtained without further loss. Next morning Key and Roller, with 56 more still required, again played with such skill and confidence that, without being separated, they hit off the remaining runs and so not only gained for Surrey a notable victory but established their individual reputations. Key made 60 and Roller 55. Key in later years had many fine batting performances to his credit but nothing was more remarkable than this memorable display at the age of 18.

Educated at Clifton, Key was in the XI there from 1881 to 1883. As a boy he not only showed much promise as a batsman but, as a slow bowler with an off break, met with considerable success. Indeed, in his last year at school he scored 90 and one and took five wickets against Cheltenham and against Sherborne, in addition to making 59, secured

in the first innings five wickets for 31.

At Oxford he obtained his Blue as a Freshman and played four times against Cambridge. His great triumph in the University match was an innings of 143 in 1886, when he and W. W. Rashleigh put on 243 for the first wicket. Another memorable performance was his partnership with H. Philipson in a match between Oxford University and Middlesex at Chiswick Park in 1887. Key made 281 and Philipson 150, the partnership of 340 being at the time the largest on record in first-class cricket.

Key's connexion as an active player with Surrey extended altogether over 17 years before D. L. A. Jephson succeeded him in the captaincy. During this period he scored 12,928 runs in first-class matches with an average of 26. He appeared for Gentlemen against Players between 1885 and 1889 and, while making in club games several scores of over 200, had one of 179 against Kent in 1887 as his highest in County Cricket. He went to America with E. J. Sanders's team in 1886 and with Lord Hawke's team in 1891 and himself captained a side of Oxford Authentics in India.

A fine, free, powerful batsman, Key also possessed a very strong defence and had at his command all sorts of strokes. He played back with a dead straight bat and could force the ball away with great power. He was never more in his element than in times of difficulty. Indeed, a position of anxiety or disaster brought out his highest skill. Finally, he was a man of most original views, an always philosophic cricketer and an imperturbable captain. As the years rolled by he put on much weight and turned slow in chasing the ball, yet he could generally be trusted to bring off anything which came his way in the shape of a catch.

In addition to the distinction he gained at cricket Key attained some excellence as a Rugby football player and appeared for Oxford against Cambridge in 1885 and in 1886. On the first occasion he figured as one of the three three-quarters and in the following year he filled the post of full-back.

KEY, Laurence Henry, who died on April 18, 1971, aged 75, played occasionally as an amateur for Somerset between 1919 and 1922.

KEYSER, Charles Edward, born in London, September 10, 1847, died at Aldermaston Court, Berkshire, May 23, 1929, aged 81. It was said of him, "A steady bat, bowls fast round-armed, and fields in no particular place." He captained Hertfordshire for some years up to the end of 1883 and was Hon. Secretary of the County Club, 1876–1883. He died worth £788,255.

KIDD, Eric Leslie, died on July 2, 1984, aged 94. Four years in the Wellington XI, he got his Blue at Cambridge as a Freshman and played four years against Oxford, being captain in the third, 1912, when he had much to do with leading his side to a three-wicket victory after they had tied on the first innings. He himself scored 46 and 45 and took in the match eight for 143. The impression he made as an outstanding Varsity captain was confirmed when later in the season he captained Middlesex in the absence of Sir Pelham Warner. In the next year, 1913, he headed the Cambridge batting averages with exceptional figures, scoring 866 runs with an average of 72.16, including three hundreds. In both 1912 and 1913 he represented the Gentlemen at Lord's, in 1912 with conspicuous success. He took four for 97, his victims being Hobbs, Hayes, Mead and "Tiger" Smith, and then played a valuable innings of 37. Meanwhile he had, since 1910, been playing for Middlesex in the vacations, his outstanding feat being to score 150 not out in two and a half hours against Hampshire at Lord's in 1911.

Unfortunately, as with many fine amateurs, his regular first-class cricket ended when he came down, though he continued to play a few matches for Middlesex most years till 1928, coming over from Dublin, where he worked, to do so. As a batsman he had a strong defence and opposing bowlers saw little of his stumps: at the same time he could hit powerfully and was far from being a slow scorer. He bowled slow leg-breaks with a high action, at his best with great accuracy, and was a superb field, especially in the gully. Neither in batting nor fielding did he appear to be handicapped by always playing in spectacles. In all first-class cricket he scored 5,113 runs with an average of 24.94 and made six centuries: he also took 186 wickets at 24.63. His highest score was 167 for Cambridge against Sussex at Fenner's in 1912. It was against Sussex at Fenner's, too, that he achieved his best bowling performance, taking eight for 49 in the second innings in 1911.

KIDD, Dr. Percy Marmaduke, who died on January 21, 1942, aged 90, was in the Uppingham XI for three seasons from 1867, being captain in the last two years. He played once for Kent in 1874.

KIDDLE, P/O Horace Peter Harvard, aged 20, Dulwich College fast bowler, died on active service in April, 1944. Kiddle was one of a celebrated bowling trio with T. E. Bailey and A. W. H. Mallett, who took their side to victory on numerous occasions. Kiddle used his height to full advantage and kept a splendid length besides varying his pace skilfully. Against King's College School, Wimbledon, in 1941, when he took 50 wickets, average 7.86, he dismissed eight batsmen for three runs, including the hat-trick—a feat regarded as a record in Public School cricket.

KIERNAN, Christopher, who died at North Fitzroy, Melbourne, in December, 1925, was a good batsman, a useful change bowler and a brilliant field at cover and mid-off. His chief scores for Victoria—all made in Melbourne—were 58 v. Tasmania in 1912–13, 61 v. New Zealand in 1913–14, and 59 v. Tasmania in 1914–15.

KILBY, Len, physiotherapist and medical attendant to Kent County C.C. for the last five years, died on July 22, 1974, the day set for his second marriage. He was 69 and a widower. His wedding was set two days earlier, but he put it back in case Kent got into the final of the Benson and Hedges Cup. He retired as chief physiotherapist at Canterbury Hospital some years ago and was a very popular figure on all the Kent grounds. He was also well known in the athletic world and accompanied many British teams abroad, including the Olympic Team to Melbourne.

KILLICK, The Rev. Edgar Thomas, who died while taking part in a cricket match between the diocesan clergy of St. Albans and Coventry at Northampton on May 18, 1953, aged 46, played for Cambridge University, Middlesex and England. He first showed his ability as a sportsman while at St. Paul's School, where he won his colours as a Rugby three-quarter and captained the cricket XI. In 1925 his batting average was 104.44, and the following summer he led the Public Schools Fifteen against the Australians at Lord's.

H. L. Collins, the Australian captain, objected to the Schools fielding 15 players and Killick had the unenviable duty of deciding which four had to leave the field. Happily, Collins relented and the four boys returned. Killick made 31 on a difficult pitch.

Everyone predicted that he would be an automatic choice as a Freshman for the 1927 Cambridge XI, but for some reason he failed to do himself justice and did not obtain his

Blue that year. For a time during the early part of the next season it looked as if the distinction might again elude him, but an innings of 82 for Middlesex against Essex ensured him a further trial. He seized the opportunity, taking 100 off the Surrey bowlers at the Oval and 161 from the Sussex attack at Hove. He made another hundred for Cambridge v. M.C.C. at Lord's and in the Varsity match hit 74 and 20.

One of his finest innings was the 206 he scored for Middlesex against Warwickshire in 1931, his opening stand with G.T.S. Stevens producing 277 runs. Curiously, this was the only time he played for the county that season. Moreover, play was possible only on the first day because of rain. He twice played for England against South Africa in 1929, going in first with H. Sutcliffe, but his appearances in first-class cricket subsequently became more infrequent because of his work. Nevertheless, he continued to play as often as possible in club matches. E. Hendren once described Killick as "the prettiest forward player since Lionel Palairet." Certainly, there was grace in his stroke-play and few batsmen executed the off-drive and square-cut with such ease of movement. As a fieldsman he delighted onlookers by his anticipation, swift running and clean picking up of the ball in the deep.

Perhaps it was not altogether surprising that he showed a natural aptitude for games, for he came from a sporting family. A brother, G.S. Killick, represented Great Britain at rowing in the Olympic Games. Another brother was a wing three-quarter, and Stanley, the youngest, also played rugby and cricket. E.T. Killick was for a time chaplain at Harrow School. Later he became rector of Willian, near Letchworth. During the War he went to West Africa as Senior Padre (Church of England) of the R.A.F. West Africa Command. He had been Vicar of Bishop's Stortford since 1946.

KILLICK, Ernest Harry, who died at Hove on September 29, 1948, was closely connected with Sussex County Cricket from 1893 until the time of his death. Born at Horsham on January 17, 1875, he learned cricket from uncles and Alfred Shaw, the famous slow bowler who played for Sussex after leaving Nottinghamshire. Short and of rather slight build—5 ft. 6 in. and weighing 10 st.—he batted freely with all the best strokes of a left-hander and steadily improved from his first appearance for the county when 18. Although having to wear spectacles in 1897 he became accustomed to

what seemed a handicap and in 1905 he "did the double," scoring 1,392 runs and taking 108 wickets; his highest aggregate came next season—1,767, average 36.06. From July 1898 he played in 389 matches for Sussex without a break; altogether he scored 18,768 runs and took 729 wickets in first-class cricket before retiring during the 1913 season.

With great batsmen, like C.B. Fry, K.S. Ranjitsinhji and W. Newham, as contemporaries the diminutive Killick naturally suffered somewhat by comparison, but he accomplished notable performances. The highest of his 22 three-figure innings was 200 against Yorkshire at Hove in 1901, when his second-wicket stand with Fry realised 349 runs. He showed freedom in strokes all round the wicket, especially in cutting, and excelled in 1899 against the Australians with admirable innings of 106 and 57.

In bowling he experienced extremes of fortune, taking four Nottinghamshire wickets for two runs, five Hampshire wickets for two runs, seven Essex wickets for 10 runs and five for 14 against Nottinghamshire at Hove in 1910, the other deadly spells being on foreign soil. For a set off to these successes may be mentioned his help to Alletson, the Notts giant, who at Hove in 1911 occupied only 40 minutes in scoring 142 out of 152 added for the last wicket. In an over from Killick, including two no-balls, Alletson made 34 runs with three sixes and four fours the scoring strokes. Scorer for Sussex for many years, he sometimes did duty after the War.

KILNER, Norman, died on April 28, 1979, aged 83. A younger brother of the famous Roy, he was severely wounded in the Great War and then from 1919 to 1923 played frequently for Yorkshire. Though he played many useful innings, including two centuries, he was competing for a place with Oldroyd and Leyland and, much though he would have preferred to stay with his own county, naturally accepted an offer from Warwickshire. After one match for them in 1924 while qualifying, he played regularly from 1926 to 1937, scoring his thousand runs each year and making 23 hundreds. His best season was 1933, when he scored 2,159 runs with an average of 44.97; his highest score was 228 v. Worcestershire at Worcester in 1935, in the course of which he made a hundred before lunch. In all, he made 16,075 runs for the county at an average of 31.90. At one time he regularly opened the innings, and late in his career, as senior professional, sometimes captained the side. On his retirement he had one season on the first-class umpires' list and in 1939 became coach at Edgbaston. During the War, he also acted as its groundsman. After another season as a first-class umpire, he was from 1946 to 1965 head groundsman and coach at Birmingham University. To the end of his life he was a regular spectator at Edgbaston.

KILNER, Roy, born at Low Valley, Wombwell, near Barnsley, on October 17, 1890, died of enteric in the Barnsley Fever Hospital on April 5, 1928, aged 37. By his early death English cricket lost, not only a notable exponent of the game, but a man of rare charm. Few modern professionals commanded such a measure of esteem and kindly regard from his own immediate colleagues and his opponents in the cricket field as did Roy Kilner. He was modest to a degree concerning his own abilities, and generous in his estimate of those he played with and against. Kilner's cricketing life consisted of two separate and distinct periods. Before the War he was essentially a batsman, Yorkshire having such a wealth of bowling talent that the need for him to exploit this part of the game did not really arise. The death of M. W. Booth—killed at the Battle of Lens, just before which Kilner himself was wounded in the right wrist—followed, after hostilities had ceased, by that of A. Drake, and the retirement of George Hirst, brought about a considerable change in Yorkshire's strength in attack. Without neglecting his batting, Kilner turned his serious attention to bowling, but the season of 1922 had dawned before he became one of the leading left-handed bowlers in the country and an all-round player of marked ability. His powers as a batsman were a little slow to ripen, for, although he gained a place in the Yorkshire XI in 1911, not until two years later did he firmly establish himself. Left-handed, as in bowling, Kilner could, if necessary, play a

dogged game, but that was foreign to his temperament, and he will always be remembered by his rather aggressive methods. He drove with considerable power on the off-side and pulled very hard. For Yorkshire he put together 15 100s, and in all matches for his county scored 13,014 runs with an average of 29.91. Four times in his career he accomplished the double feat of making 1,000 runs and taking 100 wickets in a season.

In 1927, although he scored 1,004 runs with an average of over 33, his bowling seemed to have lost some of its former deadliness, even in favourable conditions. At his best, however, he was a fine slow bowler, spin and accuracy of length making him at times almost unplayable. To a close student of the game he afforded the greatest interest. His admirable length enabled him to keep on for long spells without undue punishment, and he never ceased during these to try all sorts of experiments in the way of variation of flight and pace. In his hands the spinning ball, just a trifle faster than usual with no apparent change of action, proved most effective. He took part in seven Test matches against Australia, three when a member of the M.C.C. team under Mr. A. E. R. Gilligan in the winter of 1924–25 and four in England in 1926. He achieved little of consequence in the latter matches and did not appear in the Oval match when England regained the Ashes, but he accomplished useful work in Australia, where in all games he had a batting average of 31 and obtained 57 wickets for less than 20 runs apiece. At Adelaide, on a treacherous pitch, he and Woolley finished Australia's second innings by getting down the last seven wickets in an hour for 39 runs, Kilner taking four for 14. But Australia, after a great struggle, won the match by 11 runs. Kilner's benefit—against Middlesex at Leeds in 1925—realised £4,016—a record. The play was watched by 71,000 persons.

His most successful years in batting were:—

					Innings	Not outs	Highest Innings	Runs	Average
1913	..	..	..	..	..	50	4	104	1586	34.47
1914	..	..	..	..	..	44	1	169	1329	30.9
1920	..	..	..	..	..	38	2	206*	1316	36.55
1923	..	..	..	..	..	49	8	79	1404	34.24
1925	..	..	..	..	..	39	4	124	1068	30.51
1926	..	..	..	..	..	35	3	150	1187	37.0
1927	..	..	..	..	..	41	11	91*	1004	33.46

*Signifies not out.

His best years in bowling were:—

	Overs	Runs	Wickets	Average
1922..	1081.1	1797	122	14.73
1923..	1259.5	2040	158	12.91
1924..	1159.4	1927	145	13.28
1925..	1228.2	2348	131	17.92
1926..	1199.5	2410	107	22.52

In the winter of 1924–25 he went to Australia, where he scored 448 runs, average 24.88, and took 40 wickets for 25 runs each, and in the West Indies in 1925–26 he averaged 22.63 for 249 runs, with 34 wickets at a cost of less than 30 each.

During his career, his record was:—

Batting	Innings	Not outs	Highest Innings	Runs	Average
	540	55	206*	14,422	29.73

Bowling	Runs	Wickets	Average
	18,321	991	18.48

The highest of his 15 three-figure innings for Yorkshire was 206 not out v. Derbyshire at Sheffield in 1920. He also made 113 in the Gentlemen v. Players match at Lord's in 1920 and 103 for England v. West Australia at Perth in 1924–25. Among his many good feats for his county as a bowler were the following:—

5 for 14, v. Notts., at Trent Bridge	1922
6 for 13, v. Hampshire, at Bournemouth	1922
8 for 26, v. Glamorgan, at Cardiff	1923
6 for 14, v. Middlesex, at Bradford	1923
5 for 12, v. Hampshire, at Portsmouth	1923
6 for 15, v. Hampshire, at Portsmouth	1924
3 in 4 balls, v. Leicestershire, at Hull	1925
5 for 14, v. Lancashire, at Sheffield	1925
5 for 14, v. Sussex, at Bradford	1925
6 for 15 in 38 balls, v. Middlesex, at Bradford (in innings, 8 for 40)	1926

*Signifies not out.

In other matches he took five for 11 for North v. South at Eastbourne, in 1922, and six for 16 in first innings and eight for 23 in second for Europeans v. Hindus at Lahore in 1922–23. For the Players at Lord's, in 1924, besides scoring 113, he took six for 20 in the second innings (not bowling in the first), five of these being obtained in the course of five overs for two runs. During the last winter in which he accepted an engagement in India, he played an innings of 283 not out for Rajendra Gymkhana v. Gurgaon at Delhi, in November, 1927, hitting six sixes and 40 fours. He was a nephew of the late Irving Washington, of Yorkshire, and brother of Norman Kilner, of Warwickshire. His portrait appeared in Wisden's Almanack of 1924.

KINCH, Tom, who died on June 22, 1944, at Leeds, played cricket for West Hartlepool and Durham County from 1906 to 1926. He captained the county side with distinction from 1920 to 1923, and also Durham County Pilgrims. In all matches for the county he scored 2,843 runs, average 24.30. In 1919 he made 105 against the Australian Imperial Forces team, a specially fine performance because only five centuries were scored against the Australians during their successful tour. A brilliant cover-point, he played in several matches for M.C.C., of which he was a member. In 1919 he was in the Minor Counties XI against M.C.C. at Lord's. A very fine golfer, he played for Seaton Carew Club and Durham County.

KING, Benjamin Philip, who died following a heart attack on March 31, 1970, aged 54, was a Yorkshire-born player who in 1946 hit 122 for Lancashire at Old Trafford against his native county. At his best an aggressive batsman, Phil King played for Worcestershire from 1935 till the outbreak of the Second World War, enjoying the distinction of hitting a century before lunch off the Hampshire bowling at Worcester in 1938, when he scored 1,177 runs, average 22.63. After the War he again offered his services to Worcestershire on the condition that he received no payment till after he scored

1,000 runs. After that, he required £1 per run. The offer was declined and King joined Lancashire, for whom in 1946 he again hit 100 before lunch, this time against Gloucestershire at Gloucester. He gave up first-class cricket after 1947 and became cricket and Rugby League football columnist for the *People*. He was preparing for his third tour of Australia with a Great Britain Rugby League team at the time of his death.

KING, Donald, who died in hospital in Toronto on October 2, 1977, aged 59, was the man to whom in recent years Canadian Cricket owed more than to any other. He re-established the Canadian Cricket Association and was its Secretary for over 20 years, was Canada's delegate to the I.C.C. from 1972 to 1975, and had rightly been elected an Hon. Member of the M.C.C. He wrote on Canadian cricket for many years in *Wisden*.

KING, Edmund Hugh, who died in a car accident near Worcester on November 25, 1981, aged 75, was in recent years an influential administrator of the first-class game. He played a few games for Warwickshire from 1928 to 1932, as a middle order batsman and a slow off-spinner, and was a notable player on the Midland club scene. He joined the Warwickshire county committee in 1936, became Hon. Treasurer in 1959 and was Chairman from 1962 to 1972. At a national level he was a key figure in the formation and establishment of the Test and County Cricket Board. As a prominent accountant in Birmingham, he was well suited to becoming Chairman of the Test and County Cricket Board's Finance and General Purposes Sub-Committee from 1968 to 1980. A kindly and genial man, he was widely respected and greatly liked.

KING, G. L., who played a little for Sussex some sixty years ago after being three years in the Rugby XI, died at Brighton in July, 1944, aged 87. A good bat in club cricket, he retained a close interest in Sussex. Sir Home Gordon mentioned in *The Cricketer* that King's father played for Sussex at Brighton in 1842 when the county beat England by six runs. G. L. King was a cousin of Mr. A. Miller-Hallett, President of the Sussex club.

KING, Horace David, who died on March 7, 1974, aged 59, played as amateur wicketkeeper for Middlesex between 1936 and 1946.

KING, John Barton, who died in a Philadelphia nursing home on October 17, 1965, aged 92, was beyond question the greatest all-round cricketer produced by America. When he toured England with the Philadelphians in 1897, 1903 and 1908, Sir Pelham Warner described him as one of the finest bowlers of all time. Very fast and powerfully built, King made the ball swerve late from the leg, demonstrating that what could be done with the ball by a pitcher at baseball, at which he was expert, could also be achieved with a ball half an ounce heavier. In 1897 he took 72 wickets, average 24.20, and hit 441 runs, average 20.10. His best analysis that season was seven wickets for 13 runs at Hove where, on a good pitch, he bowled K. S. Ranjitsinhji first ball for 0 and Sussex were disposed of for 46. Six years later "Bart" King dismissed 93 batsmen for 14.91 runs each and scored 653 runs, average 28.89. At the Oval, where the Philadelphians defeated Surrey by 110 runs, he distinguished himself by scoring 98 and 113 not out and taking six wickets. Against Lancashire at Old Trafford, he followed an analysis of five wickets for 46 in the first innings by sending back nine men in the second—eight of them bowled—for 62, the remaining batsman being run out. In 1908 his record was 87 wickets in first-class games for 11.01 runs each, the best average in England that year, and he scored 290 runs, average 16.11. When Kent made a short tour of America in 1903, King played innings of 39 and 41 for Philadelphia against them and in the first county innings took seven wickets for 39 runs. He played 11 times for the U.S.A. against Canada from 1892, rarely being on the losing side, and in 1902, 1904, 1908 and 1911 held the Childs Cups for the best batting and bowling in Philadelphia cricket.—J.I.M.

KING, John Herbert, one of the best left-handed players of his day, died on November 21, 1946, aged 75. Born on April 16, 1871, he first appeared for Leicestershire in 1895, but did not assist the side regularly until 1899. As a batsman he displayed much confidence against fast bowling, being particularly effective in cutting and driving. A slow or medium-paced bowler, with a puzzling flight and good length, he required careful watching, while his slip fielding often reached a high standard. In first-class cricket he made over 25,000 runs and took more than 1,200 wickets; in 1912 his aggregates were 1,074, average 22.85, and 130 average 17.63. In the match against Northamptonshire at Leicester in 1913 he made 111 in the first innings and 100 not out in the second. A year later he carried out his bat for 227 against Worcestershire, and in the game with Hampshire at Leicester in 1923, when 52 years of age, he scored 205. He may be said to have been unlucky not to have appeared for England in more than one Test—that against Australia at Lord's in 1909, when he scored 60 and four and took only one wicket when opening the bowling with George Hirst. Perhaps his best performance was for the Players at Lord's in 1904. Substitute for J. T. Tyldesley, injured, because, as a member of the ground staff, he was at hand when the game was due to start, he played two great innings, 104 and 109 not out, the only instance of a professional making two separate 100s in this match at Lord's, as R. E. Foster and K. S. Duleep-sinhji did for the Gentlemen. Two years later at the Oval for the Players he scored 89 not out and 88 and took two wickets. Among his best bowling feats were eight wickets for 17 runs (including seven without the cost of a run in 20 balls) against Yorkshire in 1911, and two hat-tricks—against Sussex at Hove in 1903, and against Somerset at Weston-super-Mare in 1920.

An unusual experience befell King at the Oval in May 1906 when playing against Surrey. Having hit the ball a second time in defence of his wicket, he ran, and on appeal was given out "hit the ball twice." For some years he was a first-class umpire.

KINGSCOTE, Col. Henry Bloomfield, born at Kingscote (Gloucestershire), on February 28, 1843, died in London on the August 1, 1915. He was nephew of the famous Henry Kingscote, and was described in *Scores and Biographies* as "An excellent wicket-keeper and a fine, free hitter, his scores being very large." He entered the Royal Artillery in 1862 and kept wicket for them from 1864 until 1881, but his military duties prevented him from assisting Gloucestershire more than very occasionally. He joined the M.C.C. in 1864, and when playing for the club against Kent at Canterbury in 1877 caught three and stumped five. Between 1882 and 1889 he took part in many matches in India and was interested in the game to the last, being a regular visitor both at Lord's and the Oval, at the former ground especially. In the Army v. Bar matches at Lord's he generally chose the former team and Mr. R. D. Walker the latter.

KINGSTON, The Rev. Frederick William, who was born at Oundle on December 24, 1855, died at Willingdon, Bedfordshire, on January 30, 1933. The eldest of nine members of a family all of whom represented Northamptonshire, he led that side in its second-class days. Educated at Abingdon House School, of which his father was principal, he played for Cambridge University against Oxford in 1878; a capable bat, he was also a good wicket-keeper.

KINGSTON, The Rev. George Herbert, who died in a Rugby hospital on February 17, 1959, aged 94, was one of several brothers who played cricket for Northamptonshire and Rugby football for Northampton late in the 19th century. A story was told of him that, at the age of 11, he once bowled W. G. Grace and received a shilling from the Doctor in recognition of the performance.

KINGSTON, H. E., who died on June 9, 1955, aged 78, took part in the first match for Northamptonshire when they were accorded first-class status in 1905. In that game, against Hampshire at Southampton, he scored 33 and 68. He played in 12 matches altogether during 1905 and the following season.

KINGSTON, James Phillips, the second of nine brothers who played cricket and Rugby football for Northamptonshire, was born at Northampton, July 8, 1857, and died in Italy, where he had lived for 25 years, in March, 1929, aged 71. He was described as "A good bat, a slow round-armed bowler with a break from the leg, and in the field takes the wicket and also cover-point." Beginning to assist Northamptonshire in 1875 he captained the team from 1877 until 1887 and in 1891. In 1892 and 1893 he was the County Club's Hon. Secretary. He also appeared, under the residential qualification, for Warwickshire on a few occasions. At Northampton in September, 1887, he carried out his bat for 223 for Northamptonshire Club and Ground v. Grammar School Rovers.

KINGSTON, William H., who died on March 28, 1956, aged 81, was one of six players named Kingston who appeared for Northamptonshire. He enjoyed the distinction of playing the first ball after Northamptonshire attained first-class status in 1905 and in 77 appearances between that year and 1909 he made 2,596 runs, average 18.81. He was also a Rugby footballer of note, and for three years captained Northampton, for whom he scored 206 tries.

KING-TURNER, Dr. Charles John, who died on April 4, 1972, aged 67, was in the Cheltenham XI in 1921 and played in a few matches for Gloucestershire the following season.

KINNEIR, Septimus Paul, born at Corsham,

Wiltshire, on May 13, 1873, died on October 16, 1928, whilst motor-cycling on his way home from playing golf. His death at the age of 55 removed one of the finest batsmen who ever played for Warwickshire. After assisting Wiltshire he, in 1898, threw in his lot with the Midland county, then moderately strong, and remained one of their most consistent run-getters until the break caused by the War. Of considerable experience at the age of 25, he found first-class cricket quite congenial. Possessing exceptional grace of style without any of the exaggeration of pull that so often marks a left-handed batsman, Kinneir for the most part contented himself with patient defence and orthodox stroke play in which cutting and off-driving stood out prominently. Occasionally he departed from his usual custom and hit with freedom that made him most attractive to watch. He played specially well against fast bowling. For many seasons he rivalled Willie Quaife at the head of the Warwickshire batting averages and altogether was credited with 15,721 runs and an average of nearly 33 for a period of 19 years. Against Leicestershire, at Leicester, in 1907, he carried his bat through both innings, making 70 not out and 69 not out. When Warwickshire won the County Championship in 1911 under the captaincy of F. R. Foster, Kinneir had the highest aggregate, 1,418 runs, averaging 44, and with 268 not out, against Hampshire at Birmingham, he established a batting record for Warwickshire while he scored two separate hundreds in the match against Sussex, at Chichester. On this form he was chosen for the Players at the Oval—and scored 158 and 53 not out, showing such steadiness that he was selected as the third left-handed batsman to go to Australia that winter under P. F. Warner. After opening the batting with Hobbs in the first Test match—this was lost—Kinneir did not take part in any of the four games which under the command of J. W. H. T. Douglas—the official captain having been overtaken by illness during the first match of the tour—were won.

F. R. Foster and Barnes with the ball, Hobbs, Rhodes and Woolley with the bat, were the great match-winning factors that had most to do with bringing home the Ashes. As Warner himself said when the team came home: "Kinneir, I am sure, would have made a lot of runs had he played regularly, but there was no room for him in the best XI, his fielding being so moderate."

KINNERSLEY, Kenneth Charles, who died in hospital at Bristol on June 30, 1984, was four years in the Clifton XI and captain in 1932, when he made 702 runs, with an average of over 50, and took 26 wickets. Later in the season he played three matches for Somerset and his slow-medium spinners created a good impression, especially when he dismissed three of the first five Indian batsmen for 40. He was unable to play much for the county after that, but reappeared for a few matches in 1937 and 1938 without much success.

KIPPAX, Alan Falconer, who died in Sydney on September 5, 1972, aged 75, was a brilliant and prolific batsman for New South Wales. During nearly 20 years in first-class cricket, he took part in 22 Test matches for Australia between 1924 and 1934, 13 of them against England, hitting 1,192 runs, average 36.12. He toured England under W. M. Woodfull in 1930 and 1934. The first of his two Test centuries was 100 against A. P. F. Chapman's England team of 1928–29; the other was 146 against South Africa at Adelaide in 1930–31.

A man of personal charm, he was a cultured stroke-player whose graceful style was regarded by many judges of long memory as being the nearest approach to that of Victor Trumper. For New South Wales, whom he captained for some years following the retirement of H. L. Collins, he scored 6,096 runs at an average of 70.88, his highest innings being 315 not out off the Queensland bowling at Sydney in 1927–28. In the following Australian season he (260 not out) and J. E. H. Hooker (62) set up a world's record for the tenth wicket which still stands by adding 307 in five hours for New South Wales against Victoria. Of those runs, Kippax obtained 240.

KIRK, Ernest Charles, who, from 1905 until the outbreak of the War, played for Surrey whenever he could find the time and also appeared on a few occasions in 1919 and 1921, was a skilful left-handed bowler rather above medium-pace. He kept a good length, often made the ball go with his arm and kept the batsman constantly playing at him. Of his work in 1908 when, among other performances he dismissed six Worcestershire batsmen for 41 runs, *Wisden* said of him: "In E. C. Kirk, who could only spare time for half a dozen matches, there was found possibly the left-handed bowler Surrey have been waiting for for so many years. Exception was taken to him by some critics on the ground that his delivery was too low, but he made the most of his limited opportunities, taking

30 wickets for little more than 14 runs each. Bowling at the Oval in fine weather is such thankless work that these figures are much better than they look." Born on March 21, 1884, Mr. Kirk died in a London hospital after an operation for appendicitis on December 19, 1932, and so was in his 49th year.

KIRK, Lionel, who died in Nottingham on February 27, 1953, aged 68, was Chairman of Nottinghamshire County C.C. A member of the Committee for 30 years, he was President of the County Club in 1951. Born on November 1, 1884, he captained the Second XI for several years, and also led the Championship side on occasion between 1920 and 1929. He captained Nottinghamshire in the sensational match at Swansea in 1927 when, needing only to draw with Glamorgan to make certain of carrying off the County Championship, they collapsed on rain-damaged turf against the bowling of Mercer and Ryan and, all out for 61, suffered defeat by an innings and 81 runs. This gave Lancashire the title. A noted Rugby footballer, Kirk once played in an England International Trial match.

KIRTON, Harold Osborne, who died at Holland-on-Sea, Essex, on May 9, 1974, aged 80, played as an amateur in two matches for Warwickshire and made 82 runs in three innings. Against Surrey at Edgbaston in 1925 he went in first and scored 12 and eight, and five years later at number three he made top score, 52 against Middlesex at Lord's in a patient display of three hours on a difficult pitch.

KIRWAN, The Rev. J. H., died on June 13, 1899, at a very advanced age. He played his first match at Lord's for Eton against Harrow in 1834. Mr. Kirwan's name will live in cricket history if only by reason of one performance. In the match between the M.C.C. and Eton on July 9, 1835, he bowled down all the 10 wickets in the M.C.C.'s second innings. After leaving Eton he went up to Cambridge, and in a match between the Town and University on May 24, 1836, he took 15 of the Town Club's wickets—all being bowled down. He took six wickets in the first innings and nine in the second. He was in the Cambridge XI, but was unable to play against Oxford at Lord's in 1836. He was a round arm bowler of tremendous pace, with a very low delivery which, Mr. Haygarth says, approached a jerk but was allowed.

KISSLING, H. P., who was born in 1869, died at Auckland, New Zealand, on May 11, 1929. A stylish batsman, he played for Auckland 1886 to 1890, and in the season of 1889–1890 scored 51 against the visiting New South Wales team.

KITCAT, Sidney Austyn Paul, an accomplished batsman for Marlborough in 1885 and 1886, and for Gloucestershire when able to appear in County Cricket until 1904, died at Esher, aged 73, on June 17, 1942. In 1896, at Bristol, he scored 77 not out, helping W. G. Grace, who made 301, put on 193 for the ninth wicket against Sussex. Another good display was in 1897, when his 93 not out off the Middlesex bowling was largely responsible for his inclusion in the Gentlemen's XI against Players at the Oval. Business prevented him from playing much first-class cricket, but he was very prominent in the Esher XI for many seasons, and when over 70 years of age he captained the veterans against the colts in their annual match. He went to Portugal in 1895 and 1898 with teams captained by Mr. T. Westray.

When captain of Marlborough in 1886, his second season in the XI, and Rugby won by 37 runs, Kitcat was the victim of an irregularity which certainly influenced the result. At that time Law 14 read:

> "The bowler may not change
> ends more than twice in the
> same innings, nor bowl more
> than two overs in succession."

The Rugby bowlers and the umpires were responsible for the error, C. W. Bengough, the Rugby captain, went on to bowl twice at each end, and in his first over when bowling a second time from the pavilion end, Kitcat, when well set, was caught at cover-point for 27. The umpires after discussion gave Kitcat out, and Mr. Perkins, the M.C.C. secretary, supported the verdict; but Bengough, after completing the over, was not allowed to bowl another ball in the innings. Much argument and correspondence ensued, and largely because of this incident the law was amended in 1889, allowing a bowler "to change ends as often as he pleases provided that he does not bowl two consecutive overs in one innings." Kitcat played Rugby football for the college and Marlborough Nomads; also hockey for Marlborough, Moseley, Middlesex, Surrey, the South and England.

KITTERMASTER, Frederick James, who died at Rugby on July 2, 1952, aged 83, was in the Shrewsbury XI of 1887. While at

King's College, Cambridge, he gained an Association football Blue as full-back in 1892—a considerable achievement considering that in the final of the College Cup Ties he had ordered M. H. Stanbrough, the University captain, off the field! He was a master at Clifton, Uppingham and, for many years, at Rugby.

KNAPP, Charles Arthur, born in Lincolnshire on November 27, 1845, died in Wellington (N.Z.), on September 8, 1927, aged 81. He had lived in New Zealand for over 56 years, and played for Wellington in representative matches. Against Hawke's Bay in 1873–74, he took four wickets for 14 runs. He was a member of the Management Committee of the Wellington C.A., and for a long period acted as its chairman. He was educated at Lancing and Oxford.

KNELLER, Arthur Harry, who died on July 19, 1969 aged 75, was in the Ardingly XI in 1911 before playing in eight matches for Hampshire between 1924 and 1926. For many years afterwards he gained much prominence in Kenya and East Africa. He was for some years Deputy Commissioner of Labour in Kenya.

KNIGHT, Albert E., who died in April 1946, aged 72, was a sound batsman and an excellent field at cover-point. He did fine service for Leicestershire from 1895 to 1912, when he went to Highgate School as coach. During that period he scored nearly 20,000 runs at an average of 29.24. Knight possessed no exceptional gifts as a cricketer, but, studious and painstaking, made himself a first-rate batsman of the old style. Driving particularly well to the off and using the square-cut with good effect, he pulled or hooked scarcely at all. In 1899—his first big year—he made 1,246 runs, and for eight consecutive seasons reached his thousand. At his best in 1903, when, sixth in the general first-class averages, his aggregate was 1,835, average 45. Among his most notable successes were 229 not out at Worcester, 144 not out at Trent Bridge, 144 at the Oval, 127 against Surrey at Leicester, and a faultless 139 for Players against Gentlemen at Lord's. Curiously enough, during that summer Leicestershire gained only one victory in the County Championship. In the autumn of 1903 Knight went to Australia in the M.C.C. team captained by P. F. Warner. Figuring in three of the five Test matches, Knight scored 70 not out at Sydney in the fourth game of the series, and on the same ground made 104 against New

South Wales, but, on the whole, scarcely realised expectations. The following summer found him again in great form with an aggregate of 1,412, an average of 40, and five separate three-figure innings to his credit, including 203 against M.C.C. at Lord's. He wrote a book entitled *The Complete Cricketer*, grandiose in style, containing much startling metaphor.

KNIGHT, Bruce, who died on December 5, 1966, aged 93, played as a young man with W. G. Grace and G. L. Jessop for Witney Town C.C., Oxfordshire. He was formerly proprietor and Editor of the *Witney Gazette*.

KNIGHT, Donald John, who died on January 5, 1960, aged 65, was one of the most stylish batsmen of his day. In five seasons, two of them as captain, in the Malvern XI from 1909 to 1913 he displayed such ability that he hit 2,860 runs at an average of nearly 47, and during his schooldays he appeared for Surrey. At Oxford he gained his Blue as a Freshman in 1914, played innings of 11 and 64 and, following the First World War, he made 35 and 78 in the match with Cambridge in 1919, being on the winning side on each occasion. In the latter season he enjoyed special success, sharing in a number of splendid opening stands for Surrey with Jack Hobbs and scoring altogether 1,588 runs, average 45.37. His nine centuries included 114 and 101 in the match with Yorkshire at the Oval and he obtained 71 and 124 for Gentlemen against Players at Lord's. He became a master at Westminster in 1920, in which season he received a heavy blow on the head when fielding at short-leg and never again recovered his old form. All the same he played in two Test matches for England against Warwick Armstrong's Australians in 1921. Thenceforward he could spare little time for cricket, but in 1937, at the age of 43, he was persuaded to take part in 12 matches for Surrey, scoring 584 runs, including 105 against Hampshire at the Oval, average 24.33.

KNIGHT, George, who occasionally appeared for Sussex between the years 1860 and 1874, died at Petworth, on January 8, 1901, but his death was not noticed in any of the sporting papers. He was a good batsman and a useful slow under-hand bowler, but his strong point was wicket-keeping, in which department of the game he was most proficient. He was born at Petworth, on March 28, 1835, and practically spent the whole of his life in that town, being one of the leading figures in the Petworth Club, then one of the strongest local organisations in the South of England.

KNIGHT, Robert Francis, who died in January, 1955, aged 75, was a member of the team which played against Hampshire at Southampton in Northamptonshire's opening game as a first-class county in 1905. He made occasional appearances for the county till 1921. He was in the Wellingborough School XI and though not very successful in County Cricket, enjoyed considerable success in club matches. For Wellingborough Amateurs in 1910, he scored 98 and took ten Burton-on-Trent wickets for 62. He also achieved distinction at hockey, golf, Rugby and Association football.

KNIGHTLEY-SMITH, William, who collapsed and died on July 31, 1962, the eve of his 30th birthday, while playing tennis in Edinburgh, was for four years in the Highgate School XI, being captain in 1951, in which year he led the Public Schools side to victory over Combined Services at Lord's. Next season he assisted Middlesex, scoring 814 runs in Championship matches and gaining his county cap. Going up to Cambridge, he received a Blue in 1953, scoring 20 and 10 against Oxford, and he represented the University at Association football in 1953 and 1954. In 1955 he became assistant-secretary for Gloucestershire, for whom he was specially registered as a player, and appeared for them for three seasons without achieving much success apart from an innings of 95, his highest, against his old University in his first match. He afterwards became an insurance executive first at Liverpool and then at Edinburgh.

KNOTT, Frederick Hammett, who died on February 10, 1972, aged 80, was in the Tonbridge XI from 1908 to 1910. In the last season, when captain, he scored 1,126 runs at an average of 80.43 for the school and distinguished himself by hitting 155 for Public Schools against M.C.C. at Lord's. He turned out for Kent late in that summer and, as a free scoring opening batsman, hit 114 in 135 minutes from the Worcestershire bowling. Going up to Oxford, he failed to get a Blue as a Freshman, but did so in 1912 and the next two years, being captain in 1914, though he never showed for the University the form he displayed as a schoolboy. His appearances in first-class cricket afterwards were few. As a half-back, he played in four University matches from 1910 to 1913.

KNOWLES, Robert George, who died in Auckland on March 13, 1981, aged 61, had been Secretary of the New Zealand Cricket Council for 22 years, and was still in office at the time of his death. Not himself an especially good player—though his first victim in senior-grade cricket was Walter Hadlee—he was one of the game's most efficient and popular administrators. He was President of the Canterbury Cricket Association during its centennial year and twice went to Lord's to represent New Zealand at the annual meeting of the International Cricket Conference. He was also in Bombay, not long before he died, as one of New Zealand's representatives at the Silver Jubilee Test match between India and England.

KNOWLES, William Lancelot, J.P., for 22 years Secretary of Sussex County Club, died on December 1, 1943, aged 72. During the autumn he resigned the position owing to bad health, but did not live long enough to realise the full appreciation of his services as shown by the response to the testimonial raised in recognition of the high regard in which he was held. Born at Twineham Grange, near Haywards Heath, he went to St. John's College, Hurstpierpoint, where he played in the cricket XI, the football team, and was captain of Fives. From 1892 to 1902 he appeared at intervals for Kent, showing himself a skilful batsman, notably on slow pitches, and fielding with dash and certainty. Strong in forward play and driving, he enjoyed special success in 1900, making 127 at Blackheath against Somerset, and 124 against Surrey at the Oval, where he and J. R. Mason put on 248 for the fourth wicket in 160 minutes. Abel and Brockwell surpassed this effort with 270 in an unfinished opening stand which raised the aggregate of the match to 1,245, including five centuries, for 30 wickets. Knowles averaged 41.11 for nine innings that season; altogether in first-class cricket his figures were 1,388 runs, average 23.52. His only appearance for Sussex was in 1905 against Northamptonshire, scores of 37 and 29 affording further evidence of his ability. Could he have given more time to cricket, he might have been a leading amateur batsman. He made many runs for Gentlemen of Sussex.

Master of the Brighton foot beagles during several years, he also used his untiring efforts for many winters in organising, with A. E. R. Gilligan and Maurice Tate, whist drives and dances on behalf of the County Club funds. His happy manner helped in the enjoyment of the Sussex Weeks, and his influence went far towards County Cricket being a success at Worthing.

KNOX, Major Neville Alexander, died at Surbiton, Surrey, on March 3, 1935, at the age of 50. His cricketing career was brief but brilliant. Born on October 10, 1884, he played both cricket and Rugby football for Dulwich College. He appeared for Surrey against Lancashire in 1904 and took four wickets. Next season he rose to fame in remarkable fashion and had a big share in winning back for Surrey, after a year of extreme depression, a high position among the counties. For the county he took 121 wickets, and in all matches dismissed 129 batsmen at an average of less than 22 runs apiece. In the following year he did even better, taking 144 wickets for 19.63 runs each and achieving a notable triumph for the Gentlemen against the Players at Lord's. By taking 12 wickets for 183, he had a large share in a victory for the Gentlemen by 45 runs; seven of his victims were clean bowled. It was astonishing how H. Martyn, the Oxford and Somerset wicket-keeper, stood up to his tremendously fast bowling. In the same game Arthur Fielder, the Kent fast bowler, performed the feat—never previously accomplished in this fixture—of taking, at a cost of 90 runs, all 10 wickets in the Gentlemen's first innings.

The first-class career of Knox ended in 1910. He developed an acute form of shin soreness, and had to struggle against chronic lameness. He often played when he ought to have been resting, and only sheer pluck and resolution enabled him to get through the work he did. Loose limbed and standing well over six feet, Knox made full use of his physical advantage. His long and peculiar run, starting from near deep mid-off, made the length and direction of the ball difficult to judge. He bowled at a great pace with undeniable off-break, and his good length deliveries often reared up straight.

In 1907 he played for England against South Africa in the second and third Test matches at Leeds and Kennington Oval, without, however, achieving much success. In last year's Almanack Hobbs, referring to fast bowlers, said:—"Being a member of the same county side, I only played against N. A. Knox in Gentlemen and Players matches and games of a similar description, when he was probably past his best, but I think he was the best fast bowler I ever saw."

Knox joined the R. A. O. C. as a lieutenant in 1915 and was promoted captain in 1919.

KORTLANG, Bert J., who died in Western Australia on February 15, 1961, aged 80, played cricket in many parts of the world. He took part in Sheffield Shield matches for Victoria before going to New Zealand. For Wellington v. Auckland in 1925–26, he hit his highest score, 214 not out. In 1923–24 he played for New Zealand against New South Wales.

KORTRIGHT, Charles Jesse, the old Essex cricketer and probably the fastest bowler in the history of the game, died at his Brentwood home on December 12, 1952, aged 81. He played County Cricket from 1889 to 1907 and was contemporary with such other noted fast bowlers as Knox and Richardson of Surrey and Brearley and Mold of Lancashire. Kortright who also played for Free Foresters never appeared in a Test match, but he accomplished many fine feats and William Gunn, the famous Nottinghamshire batsman, said after Kortright had bowled him in a Gentlemen v. Players match at Lord's that the ball which beat him was a yard faster than any he had ever played against. The late Sir Stanley Jackson in an article in the 1944 edition of *Wisden* on "The Best Fast Bowler" wrote, "Kortright was generally regarded as the fastest bowler of his time in this country. Not only was he a very fast bowler, but also a very good one."

Against Surrey at Leyton in 1895 he took six wickets, including those of Hayward, Abel and Lohmann, for four runs. In another game against Surrey, at Leyton in 1893, he dismissed 13 men for 64 runs. Another splendid achievement was his eight for 57 against the powerful Yorkshire batting side of 1900 at Leyton. In 1893, also at Leyton, he and Walter Mead bowled unchanged through both completed Surrey innings.

A man of splendid physique, standing six feet and possessing abundant stamina, Kortright took a long run and hurled the ball down at a great pace. He was fond of recounting the tale of a club match at Wallingford where, so he declared, he bowled a ball which rose almost straight and went out of the ground without a second bounce. This, he asserted, made him the first man to bowl a six in byes! He also claimed to have bowled Brockwell of Surrey with a yorker which rebounded from the bottom of the stumps and went back past Kortright almost to the boundary. With the bat, Kortright was at times an effective hitter. Against Hampshire at Southampton in 1891 he scored 158 in an hour and three-quarters, and he hit 131 out of 166 off Middlesex at Leyton in 1900.

In later life Kortright turned his sporting activities mainly to golf, and he was for many years a devoted and popular member of the Thorndon Park club in Essex. He always retained the keenest interest in cricket and was a vice-president of the Essex County Club, at whose matches he was frequently to be seen until recent years. When interviewed for *Wisden* of 1948, Kortright advocated plenty of hard work in practice as the secret of producing a fast bowler, and he deprecated the modern cults of swing and spin. He believed that length and direction at the stumps should be the aim of fast bowlers, with much more use than seen today of the yorker, especially against newly arrived batsmen. He also stressed the need for good fielding and its effect in encouraging the bowler to give of his best. Kortright did not agree that present-day pitches were less favourable to fast bowlers than those of his playing days, and pointed out that the bowler of today enjoyed such advantages as a slightly smaller ball, wider crease, bigger stumps, and an l.b.w. law allowing a batsman to be given out to a ball pitching outside the off stump.

KOTZE, J. J., whose death in Cape Town occurred on July 8, 1931, was born on August 7, 1879. He was thus within a month of completing his 52nd year.

The fastest bowler who ever played in important cricket in South Africa, Kotze paid three visits to this country—in 1901, 1904 and 1907. He did very well in his first season in England, taking 79 wickets in all matches with an average of 20.58 and 49 in first-class matches with an average of nearly 25. His best year was his next, however, when in first-class matches he dismissed 104 men for 20.50 runs apiece, and in all matches 117 at a cost of 19.34. On the occasion of his third visit, when the season was very wet and South Africa had those four wonderful bowlers R. O. Schwarz, A. E. Vogler, G. A. Faulkner and Gordon White, Kotze was not called upon to do anything like the same amount of work. He played in only one of the Test matches—the first time representative engagements between England and South Africa took place in this country. In first-class matches he took 25 wickets and 37 in all matches.

Kotze could with perfect justice be included among the first half-dozen of the fastest bowlers seen. On the hardest pitches he was able to make the ball turn, for he possessed that great and essential attribute of a fast bowler—a fine body swing. Having

regard to the very long run he took, it was quite remarkable how he maintained his pace, and often when he had been bearing the brunt of the attack for considerable periods during the day, he would go on again late in the afternoon and bowl as fast as ever.

It is doing him no injustice to say that he did not like being punished, and on more than one occasion he got a little disheartened when he had catches missed off him in the slips. The ball, however, always went at terrific speed to the fieldsmen, and it is likely that had it been possible for him to field to his own bowling his opinions on the catching of his colleagues would not have been quite so scathing. Despite Kotze's tremendous pace, Halliwell, in "keeping" to him, used to stand up to the wicket. Of all cricketers in this country who played him with ease, K. S. Ranjitsinhji, turning the ball to fine leg in masterly fashion, stood out by himself. On one occasion—in the concluding match of the 1904 tour at Hastings—G. L. Jessop scored 159 out of 237 and hit Kotze to all parts of the field. Actually, at one time, Kotze had four men fielding deep.

Kotze was nothing of a batsman while his fielding was clumsy. He played in the second and third Test matches against Australia in South Africa in 1902.

KREEFT, Charles Vaughan, who died at Wellington (N. Z.) on August 1, 1924, was a fast bowler and aggressive batsman. It was his bowling which obtained him a place in the Wellington team against Auckland in December, 1882.

KUYS, Frederick, who died at Oudtshoorn, Cape Province, on September 12,1953, aged 84, played in one Test match for South Africa against England in 1898–99. During the last few seasons before the South African War he appeared as an all-rounder for Western Province.

KYLE, James H., a good length bowler and useful batsman, died suddenly of heart failure in Melbourne, on January 11, 1919, just after batting in a junior match between Middle Park and Brunswick. He played senior cricket for Hawksburn and South Melbourne, and was a member of the latter's team to New Zealand in 1912–13, when he was the best bowler and third in batting. At Melbourne in 1910–11 he played an innings of 50 for Victoria v. New South Wales. In a club match in 1906–07 he took part in a 10th wicket stand of 220.

LACEY, Sir Francis Eden, who died on May 25, 1946 aged 86, will be remembered chiefly for his work as Secretary of the Marylebone Club. Appointed in 1898 on the retirement of Henry Perkins, Sir Francis held office for 28 years. A barrister by profession, Mr. Lacey used keen perception and business instincts in changing for the good all the easy-going methods obtaining for many years before he accepted the position. Drastic methods were necessary and were forthcoming in no uncertain manner. Under the new regime a strictly business tone prevailed during all matches and any slackness on the part of the employees disappeared. The new broom swept a little too clean perhaps, but in the end the Marylebone Club benefited enormously in having as their executive officer a man so able, so masterful and so painstaking. As the years went on, with the spread of cricket in so many parts of the world, big questions arose for decision and in the preparation of these for the deliberations of the M.C.C. Committee, the County Cricket Council Boards of Control and Imperial Conferences, Francis Lacey rendered splendid service to the game of cricket.

Born on October 19, 1859, at Wareham, Dorset, Francis Lacey went to Sherborne, and was in the XI there from 1876 to 1878. He captained the school at football as well as at cricket. In 1878, when he made six separate hundreds for Sherborne, he appeared for Dorset, and next year he began an active association with Hampshire cricket which lasted until 1897, and included a continuous period of six seasons—1888 to 1893—during which he captained the county. Among a number of notable performances for Hampshire were innings of 157 and 50 not out, as well as 11 wickets, against Sussex at Hove in 1882, and of 211 and 92 not out against Kent at Southampton in 1884, while in 1887 at Southampton against Norfolk he made 323 not out, which at the time was the highest score on record in a county match. After leaving Sherborne he went up to Cambridge, and there played an innings of 271 for Caius College against Clare. In 1881 he was in the Cambridge football XI against Oxford, but not until 1882 did he get his Blue for cricket.

Rather over 6ft. in height, F. E. Lacey was a stylish bat hitting with plenty of power especially in front of the wicket, a capital field, and a slow round-arm bowler with deceptive flight. On retirement from the office of Secretary in 1926, he received the honour of knighthood and was elected a trustee of the Marylebone Club. Mr. Perkins held office for over 22 years and Sir F. E. Lacey for over 28 years, so that there were only two M.C.C. sec-

retaries in half a century prior to the election of Mr. William Findlay, who served until June 1936, when Col. R. S. Rait Kerr took office.

LACY, George, a great lover of cricket, and at one time a well-known critic, died on November 3, 1904, at Grafton House, East Sandgate, Kent. He was born in Surrey in 1844, and had followed the game closely in many parts of the world. His articles on "Present-Day Cricket," which appeared in *Cricket* in 1897, attracted much attention. He was one of the very few men who could claim to have walked across Africa from East to West before the first Boer War. He was best known in the literary world as the author of *Liberty and Law*.

LAIDLAY, William James, F.R.G.S., of the Grange C.C., died at Glenbrook, Isle of Wight, on October 25, 1912, aged 66. About 35 years ago he was one of the best and most effective bowlers in Scotland, and frequently did well in representative matches. In 1873 he took seven wickets in an innings for Edinburgh v. Glasgow and five for 18 for Eighteen of Edinburgh against the United South of England XI. At times, too, he scored well, and for Edinburgh v. Glasgow in 1877 was the most successful batsman in the match, with 35 not out and 32. He was a member of the English and Scottish Bars, a founder of the New English Art Club, and for a number of years a constant exhibitor at the Salon, the Royal Academy, and the New Gallery.

LAING, John M., who died in Toronto on November 1, 1947, aged 74, was probably the best all-round cricketer who ever played for Canada. During 10 years, from 1891, no team was representative without him. At a time when hundreds were comparatively rare he scored 11 centuries, and used his height— 6ft. 4in.—as a very effective bowler. In nine matches for Canada against United States, 63 wickets fell to him for 653 runs, his best performances being in 1895, seven wickets for 21 runs, in 1896 six for 17 runs and eight for 37—14 for 54 runs in the match. He played against many touring teams, including Lord Hawke's sides in 1891 and 1894, Ireland in 1892, Australians in 1893, Oxford and Cambridge XI in 1895. While living in Chicago in 1903, he scored 249 for Wanderers against Douglas Park. He was a barrister by profession.

LAINSON, Major John Arthur, who died on December 31, 1930, within a few weeks of his 86th birthday, was the oldest member of the Bury and West Suffolk C.C. for which he played in a memorable match when W. G. Grace was in the visiting M.C.C. team. Educated at Harrow and University College, Oxford, he had been a member of M.C.C. since 1873.

LAMASON, John Ryder, who died on June 25, 1961, aged 55, was a member of the New Zealand team which visited England in 1937. He failed to produce the batting form he showed for Wellington, whom he captained, and did not play in any of the three Test matches. He scored 395 runs, average 15.80, his highest innings being 71 against Somerset at Taunton, where he shared in a stand of 160 with M. W. Wallace (115) for the fourth wicket. As a loose forward, he also captained Wellington at Rugby football. His wife, Ina, represented Wellington and New Zealand at cricket and hockey.

LAMB, Arthur, of Cheltenham, died at Margate on July 26, 1908, aged 40. He played for Gloucestershire against Yorkshire at Bradford in 1895 and against Lancashire at Bristol in 1896, but was not on the winning side on either occasion. He was a useful all-round cricketer and met with considerable success in club matches.

LAMBERT, George, born on May 31, 1842, died in London on August 1, 1915. For many years he was Tennis Master at Lord's, and as a player was unrivalled from 1871 to 1885, being at his best in 1872–73–74. He was a useful cricketer, being a hard hitter to leg— he once hit a ball over the roof of the old Tennis Court at Lord's—and a good slow bowler. He was the chief promoter of the old St. John's Wood Ramblers C.C., the membership of which was composed of those employed at or connected with Lord's.

LAMBERT, Reginald Everitt, who died on January 23, 1968, aged 85, was in the Harrow XI in 1901, making top score, 71, and helping in victory by 10 wickets over Eton at Lord's. He played in one match for Sussex in 1904, against Cambridge University, when C. B. Fry (150) and J. Vine (82) shared an opening partnership of 220 for the county.

LAMBERT, Robert H., who died on March 24, 1956, aged 81, was the best all-rounder produced by Ireland, for whom he played 52 times between 1893 and 1930, scoring 1,995 runs, including four centuries, average 27.70, taking 179 wickets for 18.35 runs each and holding 41 catches. He captained his country

on 13 occasions. He enjoyed his greatest success towards the close of the last century when in each of three successive seasons he scored over 2,000 runs and took more than 200 wickets. He hit his 100th three-figure innings at the age of 59. At the invitation of Dr. W. G. Grace he made several appearances for London County. After his playing days ended, Lambert served for many years as an Irish selector and was twice President of the Irish Cricket Union. He was also an International badminton player and held the Irish Championship in 1911.

LAMBERT, Sidney J., who died suddenly in Wellington (N. Z.) during the last week of September, 1916, had played on a few occasions for Otago. He was a fast-armed bowler, and against Canterbury at Dunedin in 1873–4 took three wickets for four runs. Later he was a well-known umpire in Wellington.

LAMBERT, William, born at Hatfield, Hertfordshire, on April 19, 1843, died at St. Fagan's near Cardiff, on March 4, 1927, aged 83. It was said of him, "Is an excellent batsman, bowls middle-paced round-armed, and fields generally at slip." He played occasionally for Middlesex in 1874, 1875 and 1877 and in the first-mentioned year made 34 not out v. Surrey at the Oval and 28 v. Yorkshire at Scarborough. He also appeared for Hertfordshire. His brother, George Lambert, was tennis champion of England.

LAMPARD, Albert Wallis, who died in Victoria on January 11, 1984, aged 98, was the last survivor of the Australian Imperial Forces (AIF) team of 1919–20. He also played for Victoria from 1908 to 1922, his first match for them being Victor Trumper's last. As a member of the AIF side, which toured England, South Africa and Australia after the First World War, he scored 112 against Surrey at the Oval, and took nine for 42 against Lancashire, 12 for 100 against Western Province and seven for 99 against Victoria. He also toured South Africa with Vernon Ransford's Australian side in 1920–21. After starting as a wicket-keeper, he turned to leg-spin bowling and was a good, forceful batsman. In 63 first-class matches, between 1908 and 1921, he scored 2,597 runs (30.91), including three hundreds, took 134 wickets (26.06), held 30 catches and stumped four batsmen.

LANCASHIRE, Oswald Philip, who died on July 23, 1934, was in the Lancing College XI from 1873 to 1877 and captain in the last three years. Going to Cambridge he played against Oxford in 1880 and with 29 in the second innings helped in a victory for a very powerful side by 115 runs. For Lancashire he scored over 2,000 runs with an average of 14, his highest innings being 119 against Cheshire in 1884 when of his colleagues Dick Barlow alone got as many runs in an innings for the county. He was the Lancashire president in 1923 and 1924. Although a short man Mr. Lancashire hit very hard and was a fine fieldsman in any position. He played Association football against Oxford three times, finishing as captain, and on each occasion Cambridge won. Born on December 10, 1857, Mr. Lancashire reached the good old age of 76.

LANCASHIRE, Walter, died on July 7, 1981, aged 78. A Yorkshireman by birth, he played in 18 matches for Hampshire, as an amateur, between 1935 and 1937, scoring 471 runs with an average of 16.82. His most notable performance was against Essex at Southampton in 1936, when he followed a first innings of 32 with 66 out of 83 in the second innings, made in 50 minutes and containing a six and 10 fours. Later in the season he made a valuable 54 against Middlesex at Lord's.

LANCASTER, Thomas, who played for Lancashire with some success as a bowler in the '90s, died on December 12, 1935, aged 72. Yorkshire tried him in 1891 but, though taking five wickets for 87 runs in the match, he did not appear again. He played most of his cricket in the Lancashire League.

LANDON, Charles Whittington, was born at Bromley, in Kent, May 30, 1850, and died at Ledstone Hall on March 5, 1903. He was in the Bromsgrove School XI in 1866 and 1867, and appeared for Lancashire in 1874 and 1875 and for Yorkshire in 1878, 1879, 1881 and 1882. He was a good all-round player, and in inter-club matches met with very great success. He will always be remembered in connection with the Yorkshire Gentlemen's Club, for which he had played regularly since 1876. As a bowler he was medium-paced, right-hand round-arm. He was buried at Ledsham on March 7.

LANE, A. F., who played at different periods from 1919 to 1929 for Warwickshire and Worcestershire, was killed near Stratford-on-Avon on January 29, 1948, when his car mounted the grass verge of the roadway and crashed into a hedge. His most valuable

performance in first-class cricket was at Leyton in May 1929; going in number 10, he scored 70 and 60 not out, his good batting gaining the first victory for Worcestershire since June 1927. One of the best amateur cricketers in the Midlands, he was known familiarly as "Spinney."

LANE, The Rev. Charlton George, who died on November 2, 1892, at the Rectory, Little Hoddesdon, Hertfordshire, was scarcely more than a name to the present generation, but in the days of the old Surrey XI he was one of the most popular cricketers in the country. Born on June 11, 1836, in the Parsonage at Kennington, then a market garden, Mr. Lane was connected by the closest of ties with the county with which his cricket fame was associated. He played in the Westminster XI in 1849 when only 13 years of age, and afterwards went up to Oxford, where he had the greatest distinction of being a double Blue, rowing in the eight in 1858 and 1859, and playing in the XI at Lord's in 1856, 1858, 1859 and 1860. Like many other famous batsmen before and since his time, however, Mr. Lane did very little in the University match, his best score in four games being only 21. Mr. Lane appeared first for Surrey in the season of 1856, and his connection with the county practically ceased after the season of 1861, when he only played in one match. Six years later, however, he emerged from his retirement to take part in Tom Lockyer's benefit match at the Oval— Surrey and Sussex v. England. An examination of his scores makes it rather difficult for present-day cricketers to understand how he should have gained so great a reputation, but there can be no doubt that he was considered by competent judges one of the best batsmen of his day, and he was also a superb field, especially at long-leg. Mr. Lane's last public appearance in the cricket field was in 1887, when in the M.C.C. Centenary Week at Lord's he appeared for the Veterans against the leading club. On that occasion he scored double figures in each innings, and proved that the praise bestowed in former days on his style was not undeserved.

LANE, George, born at Kimberley, Notts., July 25, 1853; died on the Merion ground, Philadelphia, July 31, 1917. In 1878 played for XXII Colts of Notts. v. The County XI; and in 1881 played in three matches for Notts. A left-hand bowler and bat. Professional to the Staten Island A.C. 1879–80, and for many years was engaged by the Merion C.C. His highest innings was 140 not out for Single v. Married (Professionals) at Philadelphia, 1885.

LANE, J. K., who died on August 4, 1958, aged 71, was President of Nottinghamshire. He served on the County Committee for 30 years, being chairman from 1953 to 1957. For a time he captained the Second XI and played on a number of occasions for M.C.C. A solicitor, he was educated at Rossall.

LANE, John Henry Hervey Vincent, of King's Bromley Manor, Lichfield, died February 22, 1917, aged 49. A keen cricketer and a member of M.C.C. since 1900. A direct descendant of Mr. Thomas Lane, the country gentleman who assisted Charles II to escape after the Battle of Worcester.

LANE-JOYNT, Lieut. A. W., (Motor Machine-Gun Service) was killed on February 26, 1916. He played in the Radley XI in 1913, scoring 66 runs with an average of 13.20 and taking 12 wickets for 19.17 runs each, and also for Surrey Club and Ground. In 1914 he edited a publication on Public School Cricket during 1913.

LANG, Andrew, one of the most charming writers on the game, was born at Selkirk on March 31, 1844, and died at Banchory, Deeside, on July 21, 1912, aged 68. Among the books to which he contributed were *Imperial Cricket*, *Kings of Cricket*, and the Badminton *Cricket*, but he wrote innumerable articles and some most graceful poems on the game. He was an elder brother of the late Mr. T.W. Lang, and had been a member of the M.C.C. since 1875.

LANG, 2nd Lieut. Arthur Horace, (Grenadier Guards, attached to Scots Guards) was born at Bombay on October 25, 1890, and was reported "Missing, believed killed" on or about January 26, 1915. Since then no news has been received, and his family and friends have abandoned hope. He was in the Harrow XI in 1906 and three following years, being captain in 1908 and 1909, in each of which seasons he was chosen for the Public Schools v. M.C.C. match at Lord's. In addition to being a sound batsman—he averaged over 20 in three of the four years mentioned—he was an excellent wicket-keeper, and in the game with Eton in 1907 made four catches in each innings. At Cambridge he did not receive his Blue until 1913, when he scored 28 and four against Oxford and stumped three. From 1907 to 1911 he assisted Suffolk, and in 1912 and 1913 Sussex,

in the last-mentioned year scoring 141 v. Somerset at Eastbourne, and 104 v. Cambridge University at Cambridge. He had been a member of the M.C.C. since 1910.

LANG, Capt. John (T. F.), killed April or May, 1917. Loretto XI, 1865 and 1866. Author of "Cricket Across the Border" in *Imperial Cricket*. Brother of Messrs. Andrew and T. W. Lang. Obtained his commission at the age of 65.

LANG, The Rev. Robert, who was born at Jessore, in India, on April 6, 1840, died at Woodham Walter, in Essex, of which place he was rector, on March 23, 1908, in his 68th year. Mr. Haygarth, in *Scores and Biographies* (v-90), said of him:—"His round-armed bowling at the commencement of his cricketing career was slow, but afterwards (about 1858) the pace was tremendous, being one of the fastest bowlers that has ever appeared, and with a break-back from the off. If he had only been a little straighter, he would have been excelled by none, though he was by no means a wide bowler, and was at times most effective. As a batsman he was a fine and hard hitter, and in the field he was an admirable short-slip. ... When quite young and bowling in practice (August, 1854) at Canterbury during the Week, William Lillywhite, the famous old bowler, gave him some advice, and prophesied his future excellence." This was probably the veteran's last appearance on a cricket ground, for two days after the conclusion of the week mentioned he was dead. Mr. Lang was a member of the Harrow XI from 1855 until 1859, being captain in the last two years. In the matches with Eton he scored 37 runs in two completed innings and took 12 wickets for 89 runs; the two sides did not meet in 1856 and in 1857 the match which took place was not a regular one between the two XIs. Mr. Lang, therefore, played against Eton three times, and on each occasion Harrow won by an innings. Proceeding to Cambridge, he secured his Blue as a Freshman, and was for three seasons a member of the University XI. Again he was fortunate enough to be on the successful side each season in the most important match, Oxford being beaten by three wickets in 1860, by 133 runs in 1861, and by eight wickets in 1862. It was on account of his bowling for Cambridge that he will always be remembered. His pace was terrific—by some deemed greater than that of Tarrant and Jackson—and his hand below the shoulder in delivery in accordance with the wording of Law X, as it stood until June

10, 1864, when all restriction as to height of hand was abolished. Had not Cambridge possessed an excellent long-stop in Mr. Herbert Marshall, his bowling would have been very expensive to the side owing to the number of byes which would have resulted. In the three matches in which he played for the University in London in 1860 he was most successful, averaging nine with the bat and obtaining 19 wickets at a cost of four runs each. Against England at Lord's he took three wickets for 20 runs; against Surrey at the Oval 10 for 37 (four for 14 and six for 23), and in the University match six for 19 (one for nine and five for 10). In the following year he was ineffective, but in 1862 he closed his University career in great style by taking 10 wickets for 26 runs (six for 21 and four for five) against Surrey at the Oval, and nine for 35 (five for four and four for 31) against Oxford at Lord's. He had just before obtained three wickets in an over for one run against the Gentlemen of Cambridgeshire; therefore in his last three matches for the University he took 22 wickets for 62 runs. He was a useful batsman, and twice exceeded the half century, making 63 against Cambridge Town Club in 1861 and 59 v. Surrey at the Oval in 1862. He was a broad-shouldered and powerfully built man, and could hit very hard when set. Mr. Clement Booth, the captain of the Cambridge XI of 1864, wrote:—"Bob Lang was certainly the fastest bowler I have ever seen in a Varsity XI, while the prettiest sight I ever witnessed was to see Herbert Marshall long-stopping to him. Remember in those days the grounds were not so perfect as they are now, and Bob was a little erratic at times; but Marshall hardly ever let a bye, and his return was wonderfully pretty, a sort of underhand jerk back to the bowler, the wicket-keeper standing short-slip, as nobody could 'take' Bob Lang, half of his balls never leaving the ground at all." Lord Cobham, perhaps better known to cricketers as the Hon. C. G. Lyttelton, had also testified to his skill. "I do not recollect seeing him, Booth, Daniel, Marshall, or Bury ever miss a catch," he wrote; and again, "He was in his day perhaps the best University bowler ever seen, being very straight for a bowler of his great pace." In the opinion of the Hon. Robert Grimston he was the finest short-slip in England. In 1860 Robert Lang was chosen for the Gentlemen v. Players match at Lord's. The Gentlemen had won only once since 1849, and nobody was surprised to see them beaten again in an innings. Lang took two wickets, those of Caffyn and John Lillywhite, for 64 runs, and

had the pleasure of seeing Hayward playing an innings of 132. Two years later he appeared in the Oval match, which witnessed the late Mr. John Walker's fine innings of 98. The match ended in a draw, the Players, with two wickets in hand, requiring 33 runs to win. In the second innings of the Players Mr. Lang's bowling was ineffective, but in the first he disposed of Caesar, Griffith, and Caffyn for 99 runs. Ten days later he took part in the match at Lord's, in which the sides were restricted to cricketers under 30 years of age; he took three wickets, including Daft's, for 98 runs, and the Gentlemen were beaten by 157 runs. Owing to his profession, the Church, he did not keep up the game after 1862. His elder brother, Mr. G. L. Lang, was the fast bowler of the Harrow XI in 1854 and 1855.

LANG, Thomas William, died on May 30, 1902. Mr. Lang (a brother of Mr. Andrew Lang, the well-known writer) had long ago dropped out of first-class cricket, but during his brief career he earned great distinction. Born at Viewfield, Selkirk, in Scotland, on June 22, 1854, he was educated at Clifton and Oxford, proving himself in both XIs a capital bowler—right hand, medium pace. He made a most successful first appearance at Lord's, on August 7 and 8, 1871, for Clifton College against the M.C.C., taking in all 14 wickets, and being largely instrumental in winning the match for his side by an innings and 81 runs. While still at Clifton he played under the residential qualification for Gloucestershire, and in August, 1872, during the absence in Canada of Dr. W. G. Grace, who was touring with the late Mr. R. A. Fitzgerald's team, he helped to win for the county, on the Clifton College Ground, a remarkable match against Sussex. Gloucestershire followed on against a majority of 101, and won the game by 60 runs. Sussex only wanted 153 in the last innings, but poor Fred Grace and Mr. Lang, bowling unchanged, got them out for 92, the former taking seven wickets for 43 runs and Lang the other three for 42. Mr. Lang played for Oxford against Cambridge, at Lord's, in 1874 and 1875, and had the satisfaction on both occasions of being on the victorious side, Oxford winning by an innings and 92 runs in the first year, and, after a tremendous finish, by six runs in the second. In both matches Mr. Lang did great things, taking 10 wickets for 74 runs in 1874, and taking seven wickets for 68 runs and scoring 45 and two in 1875. However, he somewhat marred his otherwise brilliant work in the latter year by missing two catches in the last innings. He was eligible to play for Oxford in 1876, but preferred to rest content with what he had already done. Judging him by his doings for Oxford and Gloucestershire he was certainly one of the best medium-pace amateur bowlers of his day.

LANGDON, The Rev. George Leopold, died at Craysfoot Rectory in January 1894. Mr. Langdon was born at Winchester on February 11, 1818, and became associated with Sussex cricket by reason of his residence in Brighton. He was a left-handed batsman, and in the field generally stood point or mid-wicket. Owing to the fact of his entering the Church his career as a public cricketer was very short, terminating when he was only 24. In 1839 he was hon. secretary of the Sussex County Club, and in that year appeared for the county at Lord's against the M.C.C., which had Fuller Pilch and Wenman as given men. On that occasion Mr. Langdon scored only two and one not out. In 1841 he played for the Gentlemen against the Players at Lord's, when he scored 11 and 25 against the bowling of Redgate, Cobbett and William Lillywhite. In 1840 he was a member of the Sussex XI when they met England at Brighton.

LANGDON, Thomas, who played for Gloucestershire from 1900 to 1914 scoring 10,729 runs with an average of 21.24, died on November 30, 1944, aged 65. Despite steady improvement from a modest start, he lost his form so completely in 1906 that he was dropped from the side, but, strangely enough, next year proved his best. Only G. L. Jessop, his captain, scored more runs, and his 1,219 in the County Championship came as the result of consistent, if rugged, cricket, his highest innings being 97 and average 29.02. He accomplished one performance unequalled that season. In the match with the strong South African side—particularly good in bowling—he and Board hit up 95 in an hour at the start of the match, the most valuable first-wicket stand against the touring team. Otherwise the batting was so poor that the county began their second innings 189 behind. Then Langdon, giving another admirable display, set up a personal record by carrying his bat for 78 in a total of 151, the next best effort being 20 by Jessop. In playing through the innings and remaining unbeaten Langdon accomplished what no other batsman did against that South African team. In this match he showed his ability both as a free scorer and patient defensive

player without forsaking his skill in making strokes of all kinds. He exceeded the thousand in two subsequent seasons and made 824 runs, average 20.09 in 1914, the War finishing his first-class career. An occasional bowler, left-hand medium pace, he took two wickets for eight runs against Middlesex in 1907, but altogether is credited with only 19 at 43.94 apiece by Sir Home Gordon, who also has 197 catches to Langdon's credit in *Cricket Form at a Glance.*

LANGFORD, W., who died in Faversham Hospital on February 20, 1957, aged 81, played as a fast-medium bowler for Hampshire between 1902 and 1908, taking during that time 215 wickets, average 26.88. He headed his county's averages in 1904 with 42 wickets at a cost of 13.95 runs each, his most successful match being against Warwickshire at Southampton that season. In the first innings he dismissed five men for 30 runs and in the second six for 41. After retiring from first-class cricket, he served for some years as coach at Tonbridge School.

LANGLEY, Colin Kendall, died at Leamington, June 26, 1948, aged 59. In the Radley XI 1905. Trial matches at Oxford 1909. A fast bowler, he played occasionally for Warwickshire 1908–14. In 1912 at Edgbaston he took eight Worcestershire wickets for 29 runs. Chairman of Committee and Hon. Secretary of the County Club at the time of his death.

LANGRIDGE, James, of Sussex and England fame, died at his home in Brighton on September 10, 1966, aged 60. An all-rounder in the truest sense of the word he could compare for both his left-hand batting and his slow left-arm bowling with the best in either field. He played for Sussex from 1924 until 1953, winning an England place on eight occasions. In his career he scored 31,716 runs, average 35.20, and took 1,530 wickets at 22.56 runs each, achieving the "double" feat of 1,000 runs and 100 wickets six times. He hit over 1,000 runs in 20 seasons, a total exceeded by only nine batsmen, and compiled 42 centuries.

James Langridge—his Christian name was always employed to distinguish him from his brother, John, who opened the batting for Sussex for many years—was born at Newick on July 10, 1906. His early cricket was played first at the local school and then for the local club, where he displayed such potential that in 1923 he went to the Sussex Nursery on the county ground. The coach, A. Millward, rapidly realised that he had in his charge a batsman of considerable ability, though at the time his bowling skill had yet to manifest itself. Langridge appeared three times for the county in 1924, but could not gain a regular place until 1927. In that season he missed by eight scoring 1,000 runs and fell four short of a maiden hundred against Middlesex at Brighton. Next season he managed both targets comfortably.

Meanwhile his bowling made swift advances. His 35 wickets in 1928 proved expensive, but in the following year he took 81 wickets for less than 21 runs apiece. At the beginning of the 1930s his batting aggregate fell away, but his bowling proved immensely useful to Sussex, and in recognition of his promise as much as his achievements *Wisden* chose him as one of the Five Cricketers of 1931. He amply justified the choice with a remarkable spell of bowling the following summer at Cheltenham, where he took seven Gloucestershire wickets for eight runs.

A year later came his first Test match, against the West Indies at Manchester. In the second innings of a drawn game he took seven wickets for 56 runs, including that of George Headley, whom he caught off his own bowling. This feat kept him in the side for the final Test and also earned him a place in the M.C.C. team in India that winter. He scored 70 in a draw at Calcutta when batting number four, and took five wickets for 63 runs in the last Test at Madras. His other three appearances on the Test field were in the home series of 1935, 1936, and 1946, and he went abroad again with E. R. T. Holmes' team to Australasia in 1935–36 and to India with Lord Tennyson in 1937–38.

Langridge would undoubtedly have been chosen more frequently for England but for the presence of Hedley Verity, of Yorkshire. After the Second World War, during which Langridge served with the National Fire Service, the England selectors, left without a left-arm spin bowler of Test class by the untimely death of Verity, turned to Langridge, then aged 40, for the tour of Australia.

He was one of several players to spend an unhappy time there in the cricketing sense. Chosen for the third Test at Melbourne, he injured a groin muscle at practice and thus missed his life's ambition. That virtually ended his tour and his representative career, though he continued to render splendid service to Sussex.

In 1950 he became only the second professional cricketer in recent years to be appointed the captain of a county side, the first being H. E. Dollery, of Warwickshire. He led Sussex for three seasons. His last match was against the 1953 Australians and he gained some slight consolation for the disappointment of Melbourne by materially assisting in preventing the tourists bringing off a win, when he batted for almost two hours in scoring 46.

Langridge could perhaps be cited as the typical professional of the pre-War era, skilled in all departments of the game to which he devoted his whole life. His batting style was as modest and unobtrusive as the man himself, most of his longer innings being patiently compiled. His bowling seldom troubled the best batsmen on good pitches, but, conversely, he was rarely heavily punished, so accurate was his length.

After his playing career ended, he continued to dedicate himself to the county he had served for 30 years, being coach from 1953 until 1959. In his later years he coached at Seaford College. His son, Richard, maintains the family's traditional link with Sussex cricket. Also a left-hand batsman, Richard has played for the county since 1957, gaining his cap in 1961.

LANGTON, Flight-Lieut. Arthur Beaumont Chudleigh, killed on active service in November, 1942, aged 30, was a member of the team which in 1935 gained the first triumph for South Africa in England, their victory by 157 runs at Lord's being the only definite result in the rubber. In that match he took six wickets for 89—four for 31 in England's second innings, after helping Bruce Mitchell (164 not out) add 101 in two hours. This stand enabled H. F. Wade to apply the closure when Langton returned a catch to W. R. Hammond. The wonderful bowling of X. Balaskas contributed perhaps more than anything else to that success, but in the five Tests, Langton, with 15 wickets, came second to C. L. Vincent in effectiveness, while his batting average of 30.25 showed his all-round value. In the whole tour he excelled among the bowlers with 115 wickets at 21.16 each, and scored 537 runs—average 21.48. He played his highest innings of the tour, 73 not out, at the Oval, where he and E. L. Dalton, 117, added 137 in 70 minutes, a ninth wicket record for matches between England and South Africa. Such valuable batting late in the innings was characteristic of Langton, and he concluded the tour at Scarborough by making 20 and 68 when runs were wanted badly, so helping to remove fear of defeat from H. D. G. Leveson-Gower's powerful side in a very keen match.

The youngest member of the team of 15

players who came over, Langton also was the tallest, and he made the most of his 6 ft. 3 ins. by bringing the ball well over at good medium pace. Accurate in length, with late swerve and spin, if the pitch helped, he did not require the new ball to trouble batsmen, but could go on at any time, and always needed careful watching for lift, break or change of speed. With the bat he showed ability in defence, but was at his best when forcing the game with pulls, drives and cuts. He was a worthy member of a fine fielding side, and altogether proved a most capable all-round cricketer.

Immediately after this tour he played in all five Tests when Australia first sent a team direct to South Africa. Like many of his colleagues, Langton seemed as if suffering from the effects of the heavy work in England. The Australians went through 16 matches without defeat and won four of the Tests, the other being cut short by rain. Langton made 45 and 20, and twice took four wickets in an innings for Transvaal, but could not find his form in the Tests; his 12 wickets—most for South Africa—cost 44.33 runs apiece, and his batting average fell to 6.88. Against England's successful team captained by W. R. Hammond in 1938–39, Langton went through another trying experience without adequate reward. His 13 Test wickets cost 51 runs apiece, and seven innings brought him only 115 runs, while in the final match, which remained unfinished after 10 days, he bowled 91 overs for 203 runs and four wickets.

Langton first earned notice in March 1931, when, after coaching by Wainwright, the old Yorkshire professional, he played for the Public Schools XV against the England team captained by A. P. F. Chapman. In 1934 he appeared for Transvaal in the Currie Cup competition, and so graduated to the highest class cricket. Born on March 2, 1912, Arthur Langton passed away in the pride of manhood; his name will live in South African cricket history.

LANIGAN, Joseph, who died in Perth, Western Australia, in December, 1972, played as a leg-break bowler for his State just after the First World War. In 1922 against Victoria he scored 64 not out, he and F. Buttsworth, after the fall of nine wickets for 91, sharing a partnership of 154.

LARKIN, Gerald Michael, died suddenly in Johannesburg on May 9, 1976, at the age of 61. He was better known as an administrator and team manager than as a player. He was the Local Manager of several Springbok Test teams, also Transvaal teams on tour, and was the Manager of the South African Invitation XI which played the International Wanderers in Johannesburg only a month before his death. A useful wicket-keeper and opening bat, he appeared three times for Western Province between 1935 and 1938. His opportunities were limited as the wicket-keeping position was securely held by A. B. Glantz in the decade before the War. In 1942–43 he appeared in two matches in Johannesburg, in one of which the late Wally Hammond made his only domestic first-class appearance in South Africa.

LATHAM, Percy Holland, who was born at Llandudno on February 3, 1873, died at Haileybury, where he had been a master since 1895 and in charge of the cricket, on June 22, 1922. A free batsman with beautiful cuts and drives, he was also a useful slow bowler, a splendid field at cover-point, a good and energetic captain and a good judge of the game. He played for Malvern in 1887 and four following years, being captain from 1889 until 1891. In his last season, besides taking 28 wickets for 15.07 runs each, he scored 600 runs in 10 innings, making 214 v. Rossall and 116 v. M.C.C., who had Wootton (of Kent) and Pickett to bowl for them. Proceeding to Cambridge with a deservedly high reputation, he obtained his Blue as a Freshman and was captain in his last season there, 1894. His scores against Oxford were five and 69, 21 and 54, 21 and 16. He commenced to play for Worcestershire in 1892 and for Sussex in 1898, and in 1893 appeared in the Gentlemen's XI at the Oval, scoring 37 and 0. For his University he made 116 v. M.C.C. at Lord's in 1894: for Worcestershire 106 v. Surrey Second XI at the Oval in 1893; and for Sussex 117 v. Hampshire at Portsmouth in 1898; 103 v. Lancashire at Brighton in 1899, and 172 v. Middlesex on the last-mentioned ground in 1901. On his first appearance for Sussex, against Lancashire at Brighton in 1898, he made 93 in his first innings and carried out his bat for 29 in his second. Mr. Latham has a special claim to remembrance. He was the first Malvern cricketer seen in the Oxford and Cambridge match.

LAURIE, Augustine Gaviller, died on September 13, 1937, aged 52. He was a fine all-rounder in West Indies and American cricket and in 1912 headed the New York and New Jersey bowling averages. He afterwards went to South America where he was presented with a silver mounted ball for scoring 300 not out in an afternoon game. Standing 6 ft. 5½ in., he was a powerful hitter and a good fast bowler.

LAVER, Frank, who died in Melbourne on September 24, 1919, was probably a better batsman on Australian wickets than he ever proved himself in this country. Otherwise he would hardly have secured a place in the great team that came here in 1899, as at that time he was not regarded as more than just a change bowler. During the tour he scored 859 runs, and, with 10 not-outs to help him, had an average of 30, but his style of batting was so ungainly that even when he did well very little was thought of him. No serious demands were made upon him as a bowler in 1899, the side being so strong, but he came off on the last day of the Test match at Lord's, when England for the moment seemed to have a chance of making something like a fight after having been hopelessly outplayed. With tempting balls on the off-side he got Hayward, Tyldesley, and Jessop caught in quick succession, this surprising bit of work making Australia's victory absolutely certain.

In 1905 and 1909 Laver's experiences were altogether different. He came over as man-ager in 1905, and only expected to play now and then, but circumstances forced him to the front, and for fully a month he was the best bowler in the team, his success culminating in the Test match at Nottingham, when in England's first innings he took seven wickets. After that, probably from overwork, he fell off, but he was recovering his form towards the end of the trip. A tall, powerful man, he bowled medium pace, with an excellent command of pitch, and no doubt his height helped to make the flight of the ball deceptive. English batsmen considered him a very good but not an exceptional bowler, and often wondered why they fared so badly against him. Some of them thought that on fast wickets he ought generally to have been punished as MacLaren punished him at Trent Bridge in 1905, but perhaps his bowling was not so easy to hit as it looked to be. In 1909, when Australia won the rubber of Test matches by two to one and had all the best of two drawn games, Laver headed the bowling averages with a record of 70 wickets for just under 15 runs apiece, but he played in less than half the matches. He had a great day against England at Manchester, taking eight wickets and having only 31 runs hit from him. He was born on December 7, 1869.—S.H.P.

HIS CHIEF SCORES IN FIRST-CLASS CRICKET WERE:—

Score						Year
104	Victoria v. South Australia, at Adelaide ..	..	..	..	..	1892–93
137*	Victoria v. South Australia, at Melbourne	..	..	..	..	1898–99
136	Rest of Australia v. Australian XI, at Sydney	..	..	..	..	1898–99
143	Australians v. Somerset, at Taunton	..	..	..	..	1899
105*	Victoria v. South Australia, at Melbourne	..	..	..	..	1901–02
164	Victoria v. South Australia, at Adelaide ..	..	..	..	..	1904–05

Signifies not out.

LAVIS, George, who died at Pontypool on July 29, 1956, aged 47, after an illness lasting two years, joined the Glamorgan staff when 17 and had been with them ever since apart from two years in Scottish cricket. He played in a number of matches for the county between 1928 and 1949, his best season as a batsman skilled in driving and pulling being that of 1936 when he scored 810 runs, average 24.84. Of his three centuries, the highest was 154 against Worcestershire at Cardiff in 1934 when, although he was suffering from a severe chill, he and C. Smart (128) set up a fourth-wicket record for their county by adding 263. Lavis had been coach to Glamorgan since the War.

LAW, Alfred, born at Birmingham, on De-cember 16, 1862, died at Handsworth, on May 19, 1919. He made 4,500 runs for Warwickshire with an average of 18.55, his highest innings being 106 not out v. Somerset at Taunton in 1889 and 101 not out v. Cheshire at Birmingham six years later. Probably the most meritorious innings of his career was his 89 against Yorkshire at Bradford in 1895. He was a sound batsman and a smart long-field.

LAWLEY, The Rt. Hon. Beilby, Third Lord Wenlock, was born on May 12, 1849, and died at Portland Place, London, on January 15, 1912. Although an enthusiastic cricketer, he was not in the XI at Eton or Cambridge, but in 1870 he became a member of the M.C.C. and 15 years later was President of the Club. Whilst Governor of Madras, he and Lord Harris (then Governor of Bombay) more than once opened the innings together, especially for Ganeshkhind, whose ground had been made by the latter.

LAWRENCE, Chas., born at Hoxton (Middlesex), December 16, 1828; died at Melbourne January 6, 1917. Surrey XI, 1854 and 1857—qualified by residence at Mitcham. Played for Middlesex by birth. He went to Australia with H. H. Stephenson's XI, 1861–62. At the end of the tour he settled in Sydney and accepted an engagement with the Albert Club. Played for New South Wales in five games v. Victoria, taking 25 wickets (aver. 10.84) and averaging 10.22 with bat. For XXII of N.S.W. v. England in 1863–64 he took 10 wickets for 90—four for

Lord Wenlock was one of the three critics upon whose advice Lord Harris asked W. C. Hedley to stand out of the Kent team owing to his doubtful delivery in bowling.

42 and six for 48. He coached the Aboriginal team and came to England with them in 1868. As far back as 1846 he was engaged by the Perth C.C., and in 1851 by the Phoenix C.C. of Dublin. While in Dublin he was Secretary of the United All Ireland XI, which body he formed. For many seasons—to the end of 1898—he was coach to the Melbourne C.C.

For 24 years was in the service of the New South Wales Government, retiring at the age of 63 through ill-health. His best performances as a bowler were:—

(All)				b	22 of Scotland v. All England
	10 wkts. in inns. for	53 runs		c	XI, at Edinburgh, 1849*
	13 wkts. in match for	112 runs			Ireland v. M.C.C., at Lord's, 1858,
	8 wkts. in inns. for	32 runs			England v. XXII of N.S.W. and
	9 wkts. in inns. for	36 runs			Victoria, at Sydney, 1861–62
					N.S.W. v. Victoria, at Sydney (7 for
	14 wkts. in match for	73 runs			48 and 7 for 25) 1862–63

He and V. E. Walker bowled unchanged throughout for Middlesex v. M.C.C. and Ground, at Lord's   1861
* Bowled Felix with a shooter which sent all three stumps out of the ground.
Lawrence was an excellent judge of the game and keen on it to the last.
He played a single-wicket match against a Bendigo man, who had 11 to field. Each man made 0 and 0, but, the Bendigo man bowling a wide Lawrence won by one run. The score is not given in *Scores and Biographies* or Hammersley's *Guide*.

LAWRENCE, Lieut.-Col. Hervey Major, D.S.O., O.B.E., died at Ely on September 17, 1975, aged 94. In 1899 he played in four matches for Kent as a fast-medium bowler, but met with little success. In all matches that year he took 209 wickets for 1953 runs. Later he played for Kent Second XI and for the Army. He was the last known survivor of those who played first-class County Cricket before 1900.

LAWRENCE, Sir Walter, founder of the Lawrence Trophy for cricket, died on November 15, 1939, at his home at Hyde Hall, Sawbridgeworth, Herts., aged 67. An enthusiastic sportsman, who kept his own cricket field at Hyde Hall, Sir Walter in 1934 introduced his trophy and a 100 guineas order on a London store for the cricketer who hit the fastest hundred in a first-class match. It discouraged senseless stonewalling and was an inducement to enterprising players to try for the annual prize. The winners have been: Woolley, Gimblett in his first match for Somerset, Ames, Hardstaff, H. T.

Bartlett and again Ames, who in 1939 scored the fastest hundred of the season for the second time. Hardstaff made his hundred at Canterbury in 51 minutes.

LAWTON, Albert E. who died in a Manchester nursing home on Christmas Day, 1955, aged 76, played for Derbyshire from 1900 to 1909. Very tall, he was a prodigious hitter. He captained Derbyshire in 1902 when he hit three of his first-class centuries—149 (in two and a quarter hours) against London County, captained by W. G. Grace; 146 v. Hampshire and 126 (in just over two hours) v. Warwickshire, all at Derby. In all matches that season he scored 1,044 runs, average 27.47. He continued to lead the county side the following season and for the next two shared the captaincy with E. M. Ashcroft. When his activities in the cotton industry took him to Manchester, he appeared for Lancashire from 1912 till the outbreak of the First World War in 1914. In all he scored 7,254 runs in first-class cricket, average 25.10, took 112 wickets, average 30.85, and held 118 catches.

LAWTON, Joseph Clement, who died on January 20, 1934, at the age of 76, played regularly for the Blackpool club until 65. A native of Moseley, Birmingham, he appeared occasionally for Warwickshire, in company with three of his brothers, before going to New Zealand whence he returned in 1906. On his 57th birthday, playing for Blackpool against Fylde, he took seven wickets for one run, five men falling to consecutive balls. Against Burnley Crusaders he dismissed the whole side by taking nine wickets and catching the other batsman. As a professional for Otago in a New Zealand interprovincial match all 10 wickets fell to him at a cost of 71 runs. He was also a good free batsman.

LAYNE, Oliver H., a member of the West Indies team that toured England in 1906, died in August, 1932. An all-rounder, he began that tour by taking six wickets for 74 in the second innings against Mr. W. G. Grace's XI at the Crystal Palace, and in the second match—against Essex at Leyton—scored 106. He finished sixth in the batting list, scoring 465 runs and averaging 23.25, and came out second in bowling with a record of 34 wickets for 24.08 runs apiece. He was born on July 2, 1876.

LEA, Sir Thomas, Bart., died at Kidderminster on January 9, 1902. He was, in his day, a capital player, identifying himself with the Worcestershire County C.C. At the time of his death he was in his 61st year.

LEACH, George, who died at Rawtenstall, Lancashire, on January 10, 1945, aged 63, played for Sussex from 1903 to 1914, and then in Lancashire, Bradford and Bolton League cricket. A very useful all-round cricketer—fast right-arm bowler and free-hitting batsman—he took 412 wickets at an average cost of 27.98 and scored 5,874 runs, average 18.77, in first-class cricket. His best year with the bat was 1906, when in all matches he made 1,016 runs, average 24.78, but his bowling suffered, whereas in 1909 when 100 wickets fell to him at 19.24, and Sussex finished fourth in the Championship, he scored 572 runs. By making 113 in an unfinished stand with C. L. A. Smith, the captain, realising 179 in 80 minutes, he helped materially in a victory over Derbyshire by an innings and 274 runs at Hove, while at Lord's Leach, taking seven wickets for 27, and A. E. Relf dismissed Middlesex for 47, no one reaching double figures on a good pitch, and Sussex on the Monday led by

296, but rain prevented a ball being bowled on the Tuesday and Wednesday.

LEACH, William Edmund, who, born on November 7, 1851, died on November 30, 1932, was one of 10 brothers who were at Marlborough. Eight of them appeared in the XI during a period—1863–1879—and another was 12th man. W. E. secured his place in 1868 and following season and was a good all-round player, combining fast scoring with sound defence. He was a destructive lob-bowler and could field well anywhere. He assisted Lancashire in one match in 1874.

LEAF, Major Henry Meredith, D.S.O., born at Scarborough on October 18, 1862, died in London on April 23, 1931. He played for Marlborough at cricket, tennis and racquets. A batsman above the average, a slow round-arm bowler and a good field at point, he appeared in the Marlborough XI in 1880 and 1881. Subsequently he played a good deal for Free Foresters and also for Wiltshire and Essex. He had a splendid record in the Great War.

LEANEY, E. J., who kept wicket for Kent on a few occasions in 1892, died on September 1, 1904, in the Seamen's Hospital, Greenwich, as the result of an operation. He was well known in Metropolitan Club cricket, and has been for many years identified with the Old Charlton C.C. In 1891–92 he accompanied the English Team to South Africa under the captaincy of Mr. W. W. Read.

LEAR, The Venerable Francis, late Archdeacon of Sarum, who died at Salisbury on February 19, 1914, was born at Dounton, Wiltshire, on August 23, 1823, and was thus one of the oldest cricketers. At Winchester, where he was contemporary with V. C. Smith and Fred Gale, he was in the XI in 1841, scoring 0 and one v. Harrow, and one and 11 v. Eton. In 1843 and 1844 he played for Oxford against Cambridge, scoring one and six in the former year and six in the latter. He lived practically all his life in the Salisbury diocese and served under six bishops.

LEATHAM, Albert Edward, died at Christchurch, New Zealand, on July 13, 1948, aged 88. Educated at Eton, he did not play in the XI, but occasionally for Gloucestershire. Member of G. F. Vernon's team in India 1889–90 and of Lord Hawke's team in India three years later. He also went to New

Zealand in 1902–03. Played for Yorkshire Gentlemen, East Gloucester and Incogniti clubs.

LEATHAM, Gerald Arthur Buxton, was born at Hemsworth Hall, Pontefract, April 30, 1851, and died at Padstow on June 19, 1932, aged 81. Although he failed to secure a place in the Uppingham XI and was only a moderate batsman, he developed into a fine wicket-keeper and played for Gentlemen v. Players at Lord's in 1882. He made occasional appearances in the Yorkshire team between 1874 and 1886 and in other first-class fixtures.

LEATHER, Rowland Sutcliffe, who was born at Leeds on August 17, 1880, died at Heliopolis on January 3, 1913. He was in the Marlborough XI in 1898, making 22 v. Rugby, but did not obtain his Blue for Oxford. He played, however, for the Authentics and, from 1904 to 1906, for Yorkshire Second XI, in the year first named scoring 108 v. Nottinghamshire Colts at Trent Bridge. His only appearance for Yorkshire was against the West Indians, at Harrogate in 1906, when he made five and 14.

LE COUTEUR, Philip Ridgeway, who died in Australia on June 30, 1958, aged 73, did fine work as an all-rounder for Oxford University, where he was a Rhodes scholar, in the early part of the century. From Melbourne University he went to Oxford in 1908 and appeared in the XI in the three following seasons. He fared moderately in his first match against Cambridge, but in 1910 enjoyed pronounced success. He played an innings of 160 and, in taking six wickets for 20 and five for 46, bore a leading part in the dismissal of the Light Blues for 76 and 113 and their defeat in an innings with 126 runs to spare. Next season he took eight wickets for 99 in the second innings and helped Oxford to victory by 74 runs. In 1910 and 1911 he made six appearances for Gentlemen against Players. A batsman who excelled in back-play and on-side strokes, he also bowled leg-breaks skilfully with deceptive variation of pace. After leaving Oxford, he studied psychology for two years at the University of Bonn, returning in 1913 to Australia, where he became lecturer in philosophy at the University of Western Australia. He made two or three appearances for Victoria without achieving distinction.

LEDWIDGE, Reginald Ross, one of Australia's most proficient umpires, died in a Sydney hospital on December 10, 1977, less than a week before he was due to stand in the Second Australia v. India Test in Perth. A Sheffield Shield umpire from 1972, Ledwidge officiated in two Tests, against the West Indies in 1975–76 and Pakistan in 1976–77. A firm and imperturbable umpire, Ledwidge earlier excelled as a most successful all-round Grade Cricketer for the Randwick Club, scoring 8,084 runs and capturing 507 wickets between 1946 and 1961.

LEE, The Rev. Arthur George, born on August 31, 1849, died in London on July 11, 1925. As a batsman he was described as "An excellent wrist player, hits freely and well all round," and he was also a useful wicket-keeper. At Westminster, where he was in the XI in 1865 and 1866, he was coached by Mantle, Holmes and Tom Hearne. Whilst at Oxford he played for the Freshmen and Seniors and was tried for the University, but did not obtain his Blue. His County Cricket was played for Berkshire, Worcestershire and Suffolk. Two of his brothers, Messrs. H.W. and F.H. Lee, were in the Marlborough XI.

LEE, His Honour Judge Arthur Michael, D.S.O., died in hospital at Midhurst on January 14, 1983, aged 69. A useful bat and slow spinner, he was captain of Winchester in 1932 and had a trial for Hampshire in 1933. His father, an Oxford Blue, had also played for the county.

LEE, Edward Cornwall, an old Wykehamist and Oxford Blue, died at Petersfield on June 16, 1942, aged 64. A very good bowler of medium pace with easy action, his most memorable performance was at Lord's in 1898, when taking seven wickets for 57 (five for 31 in the Cambridge first innings), he was largely responsible for Oxford winning by nine wickets. For Winchester in 1896 he dismissed five Etonians for 98 in a total of 343, but next year, when Winchester avenged the previous defeat, his share of the 20 Eton wickets was only two. He made occasional appearances for Hampshire from 1896 to 1909, but seldom caused serious trouble to county batsmen. He played golf for Oxford—1898 to 1900—and ice hockey against Cambridge in 1900. He went to America with P.F. Warner's team in 1898, and to West Indies with B.J.T. Bosanquet's side in 1902.

LEE, Frank Stanley, who died suddenly on March 30, 1982, was the youngest of three brothers who attained distinction in first-class cricket. The eldest, Harry, went in first for Middlesex for years. Jack and Frank, seeing no opening in Middlesex, migrated to Somerset, where they opened the innings together for several seasons and on one occasion put up a hundred together thrice in four days. Jack was killed in action in Normandy, Frank had a couple of trials for Middlesex in August 1925, but although in his first innings he scored a valuable 42 in two hours against Worcestershire, was not persevered with. He started to play for Somerset in 1929 and within a few weeks had shown his value with innings of 62 and 107 against Hampshire. He finished the season with 852 runs and an average of 19.81. After a disappointing year in 1930, he got his thousand runs for the first time in 1931; indeed, the three Lees provided the first instance of three professional brothers achieving the feat in the same season. It was in that year, too, that Luckes, the regular wicket-keeper being out of action, Frank Lee, always a good fielder, took over his position and emerged from the ordeal without discredit. His great season was 1938, when he became the first Somerset player to score 2,000 runs in a summer and also the first to make three hundreds in successive innings: his final figures were 2,019 runs with an average of 44.86. His highest innings by the county was 169 against Nottinghamshire at Trent Bridge in 1946. Somerset went in 209 runs in arrears, but Lee, batting for six hours, averted any danger of defeat. One of his best performances was against the Australians in 1934, when he went in first and carried his bat for 59 out of a total of 116 against O'Reilly on a damp wicket. In 1947 he had a record benefit for the county, but his own form was poor and he retired at the end of the season.

He and his brother were, apart from Braund and A. Young, almost the first professionals to play for the county mainly as batsmen, but they were certainly not in the adventurous Somerset tradition. Frank was a solid rather than an entertaining left-hander, but, as his record shows, there could be no doubt about his value. In his first-class career he scored 15,310 runs with an average of 27.93, including 23 centuries. Not normally regarded as a bowler, he took five for 53 against Warwickshire at Taunton in 1933 and in the next match was given the new ball. He bowled right-arm medium-pace. From 1948 to 1963 he was a first-class umpire and quickly became recognised as one of the best and most respected on the list, standing in 29

Tests. He will be especially remembered for his fearless no-balling of Griffin, the South African, in the Lord's Test in 1960, the first time a member of a touring team had been no-balled in England.

LEE, Fred, once such a prominent member of the Yorkshire XI, died in September, 1896. Born November 18, 1856, he was thus a little short of completing his 40th year. Lee had first-rate powers as a batsman, and for a time did brilliant work, but his career for Yorkshire was unhappily a short one. He first found a place in the county XI in 1884. Playing in 10 matches he scored 334 runs, with an average of nearly 21, and was at once recognised as a batsman of high promise. A year later he reached the front rank, scoring for Yorkshire 818 runs, with an average of 31, and being only second to Ulyett. In 1886 he showed a sad falling off, his batting being so unsuccessful that he only took part in 11 of the best county matches, but the season of 1887 found him in good form again, with an average in first-class county matches of 29. He did fairly well for Yorkshire in all matches in 1888, but his batting largely deserted him in 1889, and then he gradually dropped out of the XI, playing in only 16 matches out of 30 in 1890, and not appearing at all in 1891. At his best he was a very brilliant bat, with fine hitting powers.

LEE, Frederick, died at his home at Streatham on November 13, 1922. Born in Finsbury Square on August 11, 1840, he was in his 83rd year. Mr. Lee was in the Rugby XI in 1858 and 1859, and in the Cambridge XI in 1860. He appeared for Surrey in 1861–62, but did not secure a regular place in F. P. Miller's famous team. It cannot be said that he did anything remarkable in first-class cricket, but he was good enough—on the strength of his batting and fine fielding—to be picked for Gentlemen v. Players at the Oval in 1861 and 1862. The second of the two matches has secured him a modest place in cricket history. Outliving Mr. Edward Dowson and Lord Cobham, he was the last survivor of the memorable game which was left drawn in 1862, the Players at the close requiring 33 runs to win with two wickets to fall. Perhaps no other drawn match has been so often talked about in the Pavilion at the Oval. Mr. Dowson referred to it the last time I met him in the summer of 1920. Curiously enough the not-outs for the Players—George Anderson and H. H. Stephenson—scored 33 each. The man left to go in was Tom Lockyer, and he was in a very disturbed state in the old players' gallery, because he so dreaded V.E. Walker's lobs. Mr. Lee played a distinguished part in the match, getting 35 in his first innings. He and F.P. Miller gave such help to John Walker—whose 98 was the innings of his life—that the Gentlemen scored 276 after having had six wickets down for 70. Never losing his keen interest in cricket, Mr. Lee was a member of the Surrey Committee till nearly the end of his long life, resigning in 1922. He served on the M.C.C. Committee from 1878 to 1882 and again from 1883 to 1887.—S.H.P.

LEE, Garnet Morley, died at Newark on February 29, 1976, in his 89th year, having been born at Calverton on June 7, 1887. A sound right-hand batsman who also bowled leg-breaks and googlies, he joined the Nottinghamshire staff in 1905 but had to serve an apprenticeship of five years before making his debut against Sussex. In 1911, he made his place secure, and he was believed to be the sole surviving member of the Nottinghamshire XI when Alletson scored 189 out of 227 in 90 minutes at Hove that year. Lee helped Alletson in an eighth wicket stand of 73 in 40 minutes. In 1913 Lee scored 200 not out in five hours against Leicestershire, adding 333 for the second wicket with A.W. Carr. This was the only year in which he reached 1,000 runs for Nottinghamshire and in 1922 he lost his place to W. Whysall.

He spent two years qualifying for Derbyshire where he was an immediate success, scoring 1,000 runs in his first year, and six times in all. In 1926 he hit 191 against Kent and in the following year made 100 not out and took 12 for 143 against Northamptonshire, and headed the bowling averages. Early in 1928 he toured Jamaica with the Hon. L.H. Tennyson's side and played for North v. South at Bournemouth. In 1931 at Northampton he hit Jupp for eight sixes, three off successive balls, in an innings of 141 not out, and in 1932 added 212 for the sixth wicket with Worthington against Essex—still a club record. He was an umpire from 1935 until 1949, and coached at Repton 1941–45. It was during this period, and when L.B. Blaxland was in charge of cricket, that D.B. Carr developed into one of the best schoolboy cricketers of all time. Lee's complete first-class record is 373 matches, 623 innings, 47 not outs, 14,846 runs, 200 not out highest score, 25.77 average; 397 wickets, 11,133 runs, 28.04 average; 153 catches; 22 centuries.

LEE, George, died on October 29, 1894, at Portland Town, St. John's Wood. George Lee held for many years a prominent position as an umpire, being regularly engaged by the M.C.C.; also at the Oval, and by different colleges and public schools. Lee, who was in his 86th year at the time of his death, had for a long time suffered from ill-health, and received in his later days a weekly allowance from the Marylebone Club.

LEE, Harry William, for many years a reliable opening batsman for Middlesex, died in hospital on April 21, 1981, aged 90. Born in Marylebone, he had a number of trials for the county between 1911 and 1914 without any notable success, but on the outbreak of war several of the amateurs on whom the county were relying joined the forces and Lee got his chance. He took it with a faultless innings of 139 against Nottinghamshire. As soon as the season was over he joined up and in May 1915 was reported killed in action. Fortunately the report was untrue; he had in fact a badly broken thigh and was a prisoner. A few months later he was repatriated with one leg shorter than the other and was told he would never play cricket again. Happily this too proved wrong and by the summer of 1916 he was playing for M.C.C. against schools and making runs: when first-class cricket was resumed in 1919, no one watching him bat, bowl, or even more, chase the ball in the field would have known he had been wounded. Meanwhile he had spent 18 months in India, coaching and playing for the Maharajah of Cooch Behar.

He speedily made his place in the Middlesex XI secure and against Surrey at the Oval scored a hundred in each innings. In 1920, with 1,473 runs at an average of 44.63, 40 wickets at 24 runs each, and a century in the vital match against Surrey at Lord's, he played a considerable part in the county winning the Championship. Against Sussex at Lord's the first four, including himself, all made hundreds, a unique performance, and he took 11 for 68 as well. Consequently he was seriously considered for the M.C.C. side to Australia. In 1921 he was less successful as a batsman—though he played the highest innings of his career, 243 not out against Nottinghamshire at Lord's in rather over six hours—but he had his best season as a bowler, taking 61 wickets at 21.25, including six for 53 against the Australians. Although for years he remained a valuable member of the county team, his best years were now over. Only in 1928, when he averaged 41.64, did he produce consistently his form of the first two or three seasons after the War. In 1929 for the second time he scored two hundreds in a match, on this occasion against the formidable Lancashire attack. His winters he spent usually coaching in South Africa and it was there in 1930–31, when A. P. F. Chapman's M.C.C. side was sorely stricken with illness and injury, that he was roped in to play in the fourth Test, his sole appearance for England. In 1934 he was dropped from the Middlesex side in an endeavour to encourage younger players, but with a hundred for M.C.C. against Oxford University and another which saved the county against Warwickshire, when he was recalled for a match or two in August, he showed that there was still a lot of cricket in him.

With an exaggerated crouch at the wicket and a tendency to score mainly on the leg side, he was not an effective bat, but there could be no doubt of his value in a team which seldom lacked fast scorers lower in the order. He bowled slow-medium off-spinners and could also float the ball away: at one time he quite often took the new ball. He kept a good length and on a hard wicket got plenty of pace off the pitch. Against Gloucestershire at Cheltenham in 1923 he took eight for 39. From 1935 to 1946 he was a first-class umpire and from 1949 to 1953 coach at Downside. He was also author of *Forty Years of English Cricket*, an interesting book of reminiscences. Two younger brothers, Frank and Jack (who was killed in action in 1944) after starting with Middlesex did valuable work for years for Somerset. At Lord's, in 1933, the scorecard for Middlesex's first innings in their match against Somerset read "H. W. Lee *c* F. S. Lee *b* J. W. Lee 82."

LEE, Herbert, who was born at Lockwood, in Yorkshire, on July 2, 1856, died at his native place on February 4, 1908. He came into note in May, 1885, through scoring 141 for Yorkshire Colts v. Notts Colts at Trent Bridge. In the year named he played in five matches for Yorkshire, but made only 20 runs in six innings, his highest score being 12 against Middlesex at Lord's. G. H. Lee, who played for the county once in 1875, is his brother.

LEE, Jack W., serving as a private in the Pioneers, was killed in action during the early part of the Normandy campaign in July, 1944. A brother of F. S., the Somerset opening batsman, and H. W. Lee, the former Middlesex professional, Jack Lee was a reliable batsman and useful spin bowler during a first-class career from 1923 to 1936, when he accepted the post of head groundsman and coach at Mill Hill School. In 1934 he scored 1,433 runs in Championship matches, with an average of 32.56. He and Frank Lee, the two most reliable of the regular Somerset players, engaged in a three-figure partnership for the first wicket in three successive innings in August, 213 against Surrey at Weston-super-Mare, 119 and 146 against Sussex at Eastbourne. These stands took place in the course of four playing days, Jack Lee making 86, 60 and 100 not out. Both matches were drawn. He hit his highest score—193 not out—against Worcestershire at Weston-super-Mare in 1933. Altogether in first-class cricket he scored 7,856 runs, average 21.23, and took 494 wickets at 29.80 apiece. London club cricketers knew him well through his war-time games for London Counties. Like his two brothers, he played for Middlesex before he appeared in the Somerset XI. Born on February 1, 1904, he died in his 41st year.

LEE, The Rev. John Morley, who died on January 20, 1903, at the age of 77, was born in London in 1825, and was educated at Oundle and Cambridge. He was a good hitter, a brilliant field anywhere, and one of the fastest runners between wickets there has ever been. He played for Cambridge in the University matches of 1846, 1847 and 1848, and in 1847 and 1850 was chosen to assist the Gentlemen at Lord's against the Players. In the Inter-University matches he took 20 wickets in six innings, and in all first-class matches for Cambridge University obtained 93 wickets in 27 innings. In 1848 he scored 196 runs in nine innings for the University, his largest score being 110 against the Gentlemen of Kent at Canterbury. He represented Surrey on a few occasions in 1849, being second in the batting averages. Owing to his profession—the Church—he abandoned the game while in his prime, the Gentlemen in consequence losing one of their best men in their matches against the Players. Mr. Lee had been Rector of Botley, near Southampton, of which the patronage was in his own gift, since 1855, rural dean of Bishop's Waltham since 1858, and a surrogate for Winchester diocese from 1872. In 1877 he was appointed an honorary canon of Winchester Cathedral. His half brother, Mr. F. Lee, appeared for Rugby in 1859, for Cambridge University in 1860, and for Surrey in 1861 and 1862. Mr. J. M. Lee was buried at Botley on January 24.

LEE, Philip Keith, who died in Adelaide on August 9, 1980, at the age of 75, played twice for Australia—against South Africa in 1931–32 and against England at Sydney in the body-line series of 1932–33. His four for 111 in England's first innings of 454 included the wickets of Hammond for 101, Paynter for 9 and Allen for 48, in spite of ill-luck with catches. In Australia's first-innings, batting at number eight, Lee scored 42. For South Australia in 1930–31, his first innings of 106 (his only first-class century) and five for 57 in the West Indians' second innings had much to do with South Australia gaining an exciting victory. Bowling off-breaks at a slow-medium pace, he had good control of length and his flight could be deceptive. With Wall and Grimmett, he formed the nucleus of a useful South Australian attack. Like Victor Richardson, the great South Australian sportsman, Lee was also a talented footballer and baseball player. In 1933–34 he played in both Test trials, held as a guide to the selection of the Australian side to England in 1934, but although he scored a 50 in the second of them he was never chosen to tour. His 152 first-class wickets cost him 30.16 apiece and he scored 1,669 first-class runs at an average of 18.54.

LEE KOW, Eric Nicholas, who died at Port of Spain, Trinidad, on April 7, 1961, aged 49, was one of the best-known umpires in the West Indies. He officiated in the second Test match between the West Indies and England at Port of Spain in 1960 when many members of a crowd of 30,000—a record for any sporting event in the Islands—objected to a run-out decision by him and invaded the playing area.

LEES, Walter Scott, born at Sowerby Bridge near Halifax, in Yorkshire, December 25, 1876, died at West Hartlepool of double pneumonia on September 10, 1924. Though perhaps never in quite the front rank of bowlers—he was very good without being great—Walter Lees had a long and distinguished career. He won nearly all his fame for Surrey, playing his first match for the county in 1896 and lasting on till 1911. His best days were from 1903 to 1910. In those eight seasons he took in first-class cricket in England 1,031 wickets for 20.5 runs each, being especially successful in 1905 when 193 wickets fell to him. Always on the quick side of medium pace he was very accurate and, with a delivery that seemed part of himself, made the ball come off the pitch with plenty of life. Hard wickets suited him much better than soft ones. He was picked for Players against Gentlemen at the Oval in 1904, at Lord's in 1905 and at both grounds in 1906. The 1906 match at Lord's remains vividly in memory. Not often in modern days has English fast bowling been so deadly, Fielder for the Players and Knox and Walter Brearley for the Gentlemen doing wonders. In the second innings of the Gentlemen Walter Lees took six wickets and seemed stirred to emulation. Never perhaps did he put on quite so much pace. Incidentally, in getting 51 on the last day he faced Knox and Brearley with far more confidence than any of the Players except Hayward and Hayes. He was more than a useful batsman, twice hitting up a hundred for Surrey—130 against Hampshire at Aldershot in 1905 and 137 against Sussex at the Oval in 1906. He was never picked for a tour in Australia but he went with the M.C.C.'s team to South Africa in 1905–06. It was a disastrous tour, the Englishmen—baffled by novel bowling of very high quality—winning only one of the Test matches and losing the other four. Lees had his benefit at the Oval—Surrey v. York-shire—in 1906 and profited to the extent of £1,356. During the three days 66,923 sixpences were taken at the gates. Lees' best performances as a bowler were as under.—S.H.P.

8 or more wickets in an innings

9 for 81	Surrey v. Sussex, at Eastbourne	..	..	..	..	.. 1905
8 for 31	Surrey v. Hampshire, at the Oval	..	..	..	..	.. 1900
8 for 16	Surrey v. Hampshire, at the Oval	..	..	..	..	.. 1904
8 for 58	Surrey v. Cambridge University, at Cambridge		..	..	..	.. 1904
8 for 66	Surrey v. Derbyshire, at Derby	..	..	..	..	.. 1904
8 for 91	Surrey v. Hampshire, at the Oval	..	..	..	..	.. 1905
8 for 45	Surrey v. Nottinghamshire, at the Oval		..	..	..	.. 1905

13 wickets in a match

13 for 75	Surrey v. Cambridge University, at Cambridge			..	..	.. 1903
13 for 123	Surrey v. Cambridge University, at Cambridge			..	..	.. 1904
13 for 109	Surrey v. Nottinghamshire, at the Oval		..	..	..	.. 1905
13 for 93	Surrey v. Gloucestershire, at the Oval		..	..	..	.. 1907

He did the hat-trick v. Hampshire at Southampton, in 1897, and bowled unchanged with Rushby through both innings v. Lancashire at Manchester in 1908.

Against London County at the Oval in 1904 he took five wickets for seven runs in 42 balls, his victims including W. G. Grace, W. L. Murdoch, A. C. MacLaren and Poidevin. The same season he took five for seven runs in 55 balls v. Hampshire on the same ground.

LEESE, Charles Philip, died on January 19, 1947, aged 57. After showing to advantage as a batsman at Wellington School, he played a little for Lancashire from 1908 to 1911; and at Oxford in the Freshmen's match of 1908 he made the highest score, 49, but was tried only twice in the XI. In 1909 he did well in the Seniors' match with 68 and 29, but the competition was too severe for him to reach the Blue class.

LEESE, Sir Joseph Francis, Bart., K.C., died at Sutton Park Cottage, Guildford, on July 29, 1914. He was born at Manchester on February 28, 1845, and appeared occasionally for Lancashire between 1865 and 1877. In matches of note his highest scores were 72 for Gentlemen of Lancashire v. Gentlemen of Yorkshire at Manchester in 1867 and 62 for XVIII Veterans v. M.C.C. in the Centenary match at Lord's in 1887. His sons were all useful cricketers, and his brother, Mr. Ernest Leese, also appeared for Lancashire. Sir Joseph was M.P. for Accrington from 1892 until 1909 and was created a baronet in 1908. Since 1878 he had been a member of the M.C.C.

LEESE, Lieut.-General Sir Oliver, Bart., K.C.B., C.B.E., D.S.O., who attained great distinction as a soldier in the Second World War, died on January 20, 1978, aged 82. In 1914 he was 12th man for Eton, having played for the side as a batsman with only very moderate success throughout the season. Later he played much I Zingari, Eton Rambler, Butterfly and Regimental cricket. In 1965 he was President of the M.C.C. and had the unenviable task of presiding at the acrimonious General Meetings called to consider the ambitious rebuilding schemes in which the club was then involved. He was also President of Warwickshire from 1959 to 1976 and had been President of Shropshire since 1962. From 1968 to 1973 he was President of the Cricket Society.

LEESTON-SMITH, Frederick Aitken, who had played for Brecknockshire and Somerset, died during 1903. He was a powerful hitter, a middle-paced round-armed bowler, and generally fielded at point. In 1881 he played an innings of 204 for Weston-super-Mare v. Clevedon. He was educated at Malvern, but did not obtain a place in the XI, leaving there at the age of 14. He afterwards went to Christ College, Brecon, where he was in the XI. He was born in London, May 10, 1854, was 5ft. 10½ins. in height and weighed 12st. 4lbs. In 1880 he assumed the name of Leeston. In a match between Weston-super-Mare and Thornbury, he once hit E. M. Grace for four sixes from consecutive balls, a performance which the latter has described as follows: "F. L. Cole made one off my first ball, F. A. Leeston-Smith six off the second, six off third, six off fourth, six off fifth, when the umpire said, 'I am afraid it is over, Doctor.' I said, 'Shut up, I am going to have another,' and off this one he was stumped. Weston-super-Mare had to follow their innings. Leeston-Smith came in first, and the first ball I bowled him he hit for six. The second also went for six, but off the third he was stumped again."

LE FLEMING, John, M.A., a valuable batsman at Tonbridge School in 1882–84 and, when available, for Kent from 1889 to 1899, died at Montreux in Switzerland on October 9, 1942, within a few days of completing 77 years. Of medium height and build, he showed good style in defence and hitting. He played his best innings for the county in 1892 at Hove, scoring 134 off the Sussex bowlers while 188 were added to the score. Using the drive and cut with effect, he could play a punishing game, but was inconsistent. He fielded well in the deep. In 1884 he went to Holland with Tonbridge Rovers and made many runs for the Tonbridge Club, a notable innings being 228 against Southborough in 1889. At Cambridge he did not appear in the cricket XI, but speed as a three-quarter back got him his Rugby football Blue in 1884. He appeared altogether three times against Oxford, the last two of these matches being won by the Light Blues. In 1887, when a member of Blackheath, he took part in a drawn match between England and Wales. A very good athlete, he won the hurdles for Cambridge and the amateur championship 120 yards hurdle race in 1887. A year later, when representing Cambridge for the third time, he again proved victorious in the hurdles. He also excelled as a skater, and he won the Challenge Bowl and Shield given by the Davos Platz Club for figure competitions in 1893.

LE FLEMING, Lieut.-Col. Lawrence Julius (East Surrey Regiment), born at Tonbridge, June 3, 1879, was killed March 21, 1918, after having been wounded twice during the War. He was twice Mentioned in Dispatches. Le Fleming was in the Tonbridge XI in 1896, when he headed the batting with an average of 28. He played for Kent in one match in 1897, and seven matches in 1898, but did not meet with much success for the county.

LEGGAT, John Gordon, who died suddenly in Christchurch on March 10, 1973, aged 46, was chairman of the Board of Control of the New Zealand Cricket Council and six days before his death presided at the meeting where the team to visit England last summer was selected. He played nine times for New Zealand as a batsman between 1951 and 1956, touring Pakistan and India in 1955–56. He was manager of the New Zealand team in South Africa in 1961–62 and was a Test team Selector from 1959 to 1965.

LEGGATT, Lieut.-Col. William Murray, R.A., D.S.O., died in London on August 11, 1946, aged 46. Winchester XI 1917 and 1918, when he averaged 22.50, and was the best bowler with 33 wickets at 8.26 each. He played occasionally for Kent, scoring 393 runs at an average of 30.23.

LEGGE, Lieut. Geoffrey Bevington, (R.N.V.R., Fleet Air Arm) suffered death while flying in November, 1940, aged 37. Legge played little first-class cricket since 1930, when he resigned the Kent captaincy. After batting up to the high form associated with Malvern School, where he was captain, particularly in off-driving and cutting, Legge gained his Oxford Blue in 1925 and captained the University XI next season. Each year he headed the batting averages, and scored 83 in four innings, against Cambridge, the first of two good matches ending in a draw and Oxford losing the other by 34 runs. In this 1926 match R. G. H. Lowe did the fifth hat-trick, all by Cambridge bowlers, in the University match. In 1928 he succeeded A. J. Evans as Kent captain, and managed the side so well in the field that Lancashire, winners of the Championship, alone came out with a superior record. He went to South Africa in the winter of 1927, and also toured New Zealand and Australia when A. H. H. Gilligan captained the M.C.C. team in 1929. At Auckland in the specially arranged fourth Test match, Legge excelled by making 196, the next highest score in a total of 540 being 75 by M. S. Nichols. Legge bowled slows with some success. Usually fielding in the slips, he seldom dropped any catch within reach, and in everything he attempted showed skill at the game. He was in the Malvern football XI and also represented the School at racquets.

LE GROS, Lieut.-Col. Philip Walter, died at the Star and Garter Home, Richmond, on February 27, 1980, aged 87. A good all-rounder, he was in the Rugby XI of 1910, being at that time a dangerous fast bowler who, in the second innings against Marlborough, took nine for 49. From 1911 to 1930 he played for Buckinghamshire and, though he bowled little after the War, was one of their leading batsmen when they won the Minor Counties Championship in 1922, 1923 and 1925. Despite a distinct stoop at the wicket, he was a stylish batsman and a strong hitter. For many years there hung in the High Wycombe pavilion a photograph of a row of cars standing by the pavilion, their windscreens smashed by Le Gros's hits. He was also a first-class squash player.

LEICESTER, Second Earl of, Thomas William Coke, was born at Holkham, in Norfolk, on December 26, 1822, and died there on January 24, 1909, in his 87th year. He became a member of the M.C.C. in 1847 and in the following year was elected President of the Club. He played for Norfolk on several occasions as well as for the Houses of Parliament against I Zingari, and for many years entertained an M.C.C. team at Holkham. In minor matches he made some capital scores and in 1850 was credited with an innings of 123. He was one of the greatest of British agriculturalists and at the time of his death was Father of the House of Lords. He survived the birth of his father by no fewer than 155 years; he had a half-sister who married Viscount Anson as far back as 1794; and he married for the second time in 1875, exactly a century after his father's marriage. His eldest son was born in 1848 and his youngest in 1893.

LEIGH, The Rev. Augustus Austen, a member of the well-known cricket brotherhood, and a great-nephew of Jane Austen, the novelist, died suddenly at Cambridge on January 28, 1905, aged 64. He was born in Berkshire on July 17, 1840, and educated at Eton and King's College, Cambridge. From 1893 to 1895 he was Vice-Chancellor of the University, and, at the time of his death, was President of the Cambridge University C.C. and Provost of King's College, having filled the latter position for 15 years.

LEIGH, The Hon. Sir Edward Chandos, **K.C.B., K.C.,** late Counsel to the Speaker, who was born at Stoneleigh Abbey, Warwickshire, on December 22, 1832, died in London on May 18, 1915. His death followed very closely on that of his elder son, while his younger son had also earlier in the year met a soldier's death at the front. He was in the Harrow XI in 1849 and two following years, being captain in 1851. In his first two seasons he did little in the Public School matches, apart from his long-stopping, which was very good indeed; but in 1851 he scored eight and 11 v. Winchester, and 42 v. Eton. In the last-mentioned year it was said of him: "The captain of the XI, and certainly he appeared a most excellent and popular one. His style of batting is awkward, but he is a fine hitter forward and to leg. He played remarkably well in the matches at Lord's. We noticed him last year as one who in the field will let a ball go through him rather than by him, and the same steady determination was evident this year." He was right-handed as a batsman, but fielded left, and was excellent at long-stop. At Oxford he obtained his Blue as a Freshman and played against Cambridge in 1852, 1853 and 1854. In the three matches Sir Edward made only eight runs, but Oxford won each game by an innings. In important cricket his highest score was 62 for M.C.C. v. Gentlemen of Kent at Canterbury in 1861. He was one of the founders of the Oxford Harlequins, and for many years Secretary of I Zingari. Between 1853 and 1856 he assisted Oxford-shire. He joined the M.C.C. in 1852, served on the Committee 1866–69, 1877–79, 1888–91, and was President in 1887. He was brother-in-law of Mr. R. A. FitzGerald and uncle of Mr. H. D. G. Leveson-Gower. He was Recorder of Nottingham from 1881 to 1909 and Counsel to the Speaker from 1883 to 1907.

LEIGH, James, who was born in December, 1862, died at Shepperton-on-Thames on September 25, 1925, aged 62. A hard-hitting stylish batsman and a good field, he was a member of the Uppingham XI of 1880 and played a few times for Lancashire between 1887 and 1889. He also appeared for the Uppingham Rovers and the M.C.C., and in 1896–7 visited the West Indies as a member of Mr. A. Priestley's team.

LEIGH, Spencer Austen, a member of the well-known cricket brotherhood, died at Alfriston, Sussex, on December 9, 1913. He was born at Speen, near Newbury, in Berkshire, on February 17, 1834, and was in the Harrow XI of 1852, among his contemporaries being A. H. Walker, R. A. Fitz-Gerald, and Kenelm Digby. Against Winchester he made only four and 19, but in the match with Eton he played a very fine first innings of 85 not out. *Scores and Biographies* (iv–398) described him as "A splendid and free hitter and a capital field, either at point, cover-point, or long leg." Unfortunately, he played but seldom in the great matches of the day, but for the Gentlemen of Berkshire and the Gentlemen of Sussex he made many large scores, among them being:

133*	Gentlemen of Berkshire v. Gentlemen of Sussex, at Reading	..	1858
112	Gentlemen of Berkshire v. Gentlemen of Sussex, at Reading	..	1859
119	Gentlemen of Berkshire v. Gentlemen of Sussex, at Maidenhead	..	1860
162	Gentlemen of Sussex v. Gentlemen of Wiltshire, at Brighton	..	1863
173	Gentlemen of Sussex v. Gentlemen of Kent, at Brighton	..	1865
132	Gentlemen of Sussex v. Gentlemen of Hampshire, at Brighton	..	1865

Signifies not out.

He assisted Sussex in 10 matches between 1862 and 1866 and, with 42 as his highest score, made 155 runs with an average of 11.07.

LE ROUX, Frederick Louis, who died on September 23, 1963, captained Transvaal for several years and played in one Test match for South Africa against England in 1914.

LESLIE, Charles Frederick Henry, died on February 12, 1921. Mr. Leslie did not, in the cricket field, do all that was expected of him, but for a couple of seasons he was quite in the front rank. As a public school batsman he was perhaps the best of his day. The long line of famous Rugby batsmen that began, I think, with C. G. Wynch, seemed to have ended with Pauncefote and Yardley, but Leslie restored the ancient glories. He was in the Rugby XI from 1877 to 1880 inclusive, being captain the last three years, and had a truly remarkable record for the school. In his first match against Marlborough at Lord's he found A. G. Steel's bowling too good for him, and was out for 28 and five, but in 1878 he scored 98 and had the chief share in a single innings victory. He scored 16 and 80 in 1879, Rugby winning by 97 runs, and in 1880 he finished his school career in triumph with a finely hit 91, Rugby gaining an easy victory in one innings. In his four matches against Marlborough Leslie made 315 runs in six innings, averaging just over 52. Naturally he went up to Oxford with a tremendous reputation. In his first year at the University he more than realised expectation. He came off in every match and stood out by himself among the Oxford batsmen with an aggregate of 519 runs and an average of 57. The story has often been told of how in his innings of 70 against Cambridge at Lord's he left the wicket after scoring eight, under the impression he had been caught and bowled, and was called back when his partner, W. H. Patterson, appealed to the umpire. As things turned out the season of 1881 marked the highest point in Leslie's career. He was never as good afterwards. In 1882 he again headed the Oxford batting, but his average dropped to 28. He went to Australia as a member of Ivo Bligh's team in the winter of 1882–83, but only twice in the big matches did he do himself full justice, scoring 144 against New South Wales and 54 in the second of the three games with the great Australian side that had beaten England by seven runs at the Oval. In 1883 Leslie nearly finished with first-class cricket. He played very little and was in no form, failing in the University match and also for the Gentlemen at the Oval. As late as 1888, however, he scored 62 for Past and Present at Oxford against the Australians at Leyton, playing the splendid bowling of Turner and Ferris with much of his old skill. At his best he was a batsman of very high class, combining wonderfully strong defence with his powerful hitting. I remember being struck one afternoon when he and A. P. Lucas were in together at Lord's by the contrast in their back play. Lucas came down very hard on the ball every time, but Leslie adopted a sort of hanging guard and almost allowed the ball to hit his bat. Both were watchful to a degree, but Lucas was much the better to look at. Leslie played five times for Gentlemen v. Players, his best score being 59 at the Oval in 1881.—S.H.P.

LESLIE, Sir John, First Bart., born on December 16, 1822, died in London on January 23, 1916, aged 93. He was the last surviving original member of I Zingari, the oldest Blue, and (since the death of Sir Spencer Ponsonby-Fane) the oldest member of the M.C.C.: he had been elected to the Club on May 31, 1841, on the proposal of the Hon. E. H. Grimston, seconded by the Hon. Robert. He was not in the XI whilst at Harrow, but played for Oxford against Cambridge, at Oxford, in 1843, scoring eight and 12: Cambridge won by 54 runs, R. Blaker (grandfather of Mr. R. N. R. Blaker) and B. S. T. Mills bowling for them unchanged throughout. Sir John was a cousin of the great Duke of Wellington, and could recall having seen George IV and Talleyrand.

LESTER, John Ashby, one of the great figures in American cricket, died on September 3, 1969. Born at Penrith, Cumberland, on August 1, 1872, he thus reached the age of 97. He was playing cricket at Ackworth, Yorkshire, in 1892 when he met Dr. Sharpless, President of Haverford College, who invited him to the United States. Lester captained Haverford on their first overseas tour, scoring 105 against M.C.C. on his first appearance at Lord's. He was the leading batsman of the Gentlemen of Philadelphia on their tour of England in 1897 when they met the first-class counties, scoring 891 runs, average 37.12. He captained the Philadelphians in 1903 and 1908 on their tours to England. His highest score in first-class cricket was 126 not out for Philadelphians v. Leicestershire in 1903.

He is one of the few American cricketers noticed in *Scores and Biographies* which said: "a watchful batsman who could hit well and had plenty of strokes and strong defence." A biography of him appeared in *Cricket* for July 23, 1903. He kept up his interest in cricket to the end of his life. In 1952 he was the author of *A Century of Philadelphia Cricket*, the definitive history of the game in that city. In 1966 he was an honoured guest of the American members of the Forty Club at a dinner at Philadelphia. On that occasion he made an interesting speech recalling that youth needs heroes and that his hero was George Lohmann of Surrey . . . a great cricketer and a great man. In 1969 he made his final public appearance at a cricket function when the C. C. Morris Library was opened at Haverford. He presented the Library with a pair of gold cuff-links given to him by K. S. Ranjitsinhji. Dr. Lester received his Ph.D. for education from Harvard in 1902 and for many years was head of the English Department at the Hill School, Pottstown, Pennsylvania.—J.I.M.

LETCHER, Charles, died in West Australia, November, 1916. Left-hand bowler, just over medium pace—the best for some years in "Boyle and Scott" matches in Melbourne. Later he headed the East Melbourne averages, and altogether for that club he took 224 wickets (average 11.87). Took five wickets for 63 runs for Sixteen of East Melbourne v. Lord Sheffield's team, 1891–92.

LEVERS, Walter Charles Sidney, who died in Auckland, New Zealand, on November 10, 1922, aged about 56, was a good, hard-hitting batsman and an excellent wicket-keeper. He played for Wellington against the Australian team of 1896, Auckland, Hawke's Bay, etc., and was at one time Hon. Secretary of the Wellington Cricket Association. A Nottingham-born man, he played for the XXII Colts against the county at Trent Bridge in 1886, but met with no success.

LEVESON GOWER, The Rev. Frederick Archibald Gresham, died at Folkestone, October 3, 1946, aged 75. In the Winchester XI 1889–90; and at Oxford he was tried a few times for the University but did not obtain his Blue. For Hampshire XI from 1891 to 1909 he appeared at times without getting many runs, but was a useful wicket-keeper.

LEVESON GOWER, Sir Henry Dudley Gresham, who died in London on February 1, 1954, aged 80, was associated with M.C.C., Surrey and Scarborough Festival cricket for over 50 years. Known wherever cricket is played as "Shrimp," a nickname given him, presumably because of his slight physique, during his schooldays, he was born at Limpsfield, Surrey, on May 8, 1873, the seventh of 12 sons of Mr. G. W. G. Leveson Gower. At Winchester, where he was one of three brothers to gain colours at cricket and where, according to him, he really learned the game, he was in the XI for three years from 1890. In 1892 he led the school to their first victory—by 84 runs—at Eton since 1882. He and J. R. Mason, later famous with Kent, took chief honours in that success. Mason hit 147 and 71 and took eight wickets for 139; Leveson Gower made 16 and 83 and dismissed eight batsmen for 33 runs.

At Magdalen College, Oxford, he got his Blue as a Freshman in 1893 and figured in the team in the three following years, being captain in 1896 when E. B. Shine bowled three balls to the boundary in the University match in order to prevent Oxford from following-on as, according to the Laws prevailing at the time, they would otherwise

have been compelled to do. His highest innings against Cambridge was 73 in 1895, when he also took seven wickets for 84 runs. In that season, too, began the association with Surrey which continued till his death. A skilful right-handed batsman and a keen field, usually at cover-point or mid-off, he hit his biggest innings for the county, 155 against his former University at Oxford, in 1899, and he captained Surrey from 1908 to 1910. Several times he appeared for Gentlemen against Players, and besides regularly getting together teams to meet the Universities at Eastbourne, he was responsible from 1899 till 1950 for the selection of the sides taking part in the Scarborough Festival. Recognition of his work in this direction came in 1950 when he was made a Freeman of the Borough of Scarborough.

Leveson Gower also had considerable experience of cricket outside England. He went to South Africa with M.C.C. teams in 1905–06 and 1909–10, being captain on the second occasion; visited the West Indies under Lord Hawke in 1896–97, and in the autumn of 1897 toured in America with the side captained by P. F. (now Sir Pelham) Warner. During the American trip some of the newspapers experienced difficulty over Leveson Gower's name, and he found himself referred to in print as "The Hyphenated Worry" and "The Man with the Sanguinary Name." Between 1928 and 1934, he also played with teams in Malta, Gibraltar and Portugal. Altogether in first-class cricket he scored 7,662 runs, average 22.88.

Aside from his playing ability, probably his best service to cricket, for which he was knighted in 1953, was rendered as a legislator and Test Selector. For many years a member of the Committee of the M.C.C. and Treasurer of Surrey from 1926 to 1928, he succeeded G. H. Longman as President of the County Club in 1929. In 1909 he became a member of the Test Team Selection Committee, of which he was chairman in 1924 and from 1928 to 1930. During the First World War he served in the Army, attaining the rank of major and being Mentioned in Dispatches. He contributed articles to *Wisden*, in 1937 on "Recollections of Oxford Cricket," and in 1946 on "100 Years of Surrey Cricket" and also wrote a book, *On and Off the Field*.

LEWIS, A. E. ("Talbot"), who died in March, 1956, aged 79, did splendid work as an all-rounder for Somerset between 1899 and 1914, scoring 7,745 runs, average 21.39, taking with medium-pace bowling 515 wickets, average 22.96, and bringing off 87 catches. The highest of his eight centuries was 201, scored in four and a half hours with only one chance, against Kent at Taunton in 1909. As a goalkeeper, he saw service with several Football League clubs, including Sunderland, and he was a highly skilled billiards player.

LEWIS, Arthur Hamilton, who died on August 23, 1978, played one match for Hampshire in 1929 and later, for several seasons, did useful work for Berkshire. A cross-bat hitter with a wonderful eye and a magnificent cover-point, he was credited with some remarkable scoring feats in club cricket.

LEWIS, Esmond Burman, who died at Dorridge on October 19, 1983, aged 71, created a Warwickshire record on his first appearance for the county, against Oxford University at Edgbaston in 1949, catching eight batsmen and stumping one. He continued to keep occasionally for the county until 1958, but his opportunities were limited because the regular wicket-keeper, Spooner, was a far better batsman and so Lewis only kept in 43 matches in all. In 1957 he was picked for the Gentlemen at Lord's and kept very well. His highest score was 51 against the Combined Services in 1949.

LEWIS, Percy, born at Hamilton, in Tasmania, on March 14, 1864, died in Melbourne on November 29, 1923. He was a sound batsman and good wicket-keeper, but, being contemporary with J. McC. Blackham, had few opportunities of distinguishing himself in great matches. For the East Melbourne C.C. he scored 5,408 runs with an average of 38.50, his largest innings being 237 against Fitzroy in 1883–84. At the early age of 14 he was chosen for XXII of Ballarat against Lord Harris's England team and scored 21 and 28.

LEWIS, Percy Tyson (Plum), who died in Durban on January 30, 1976, at the age of 91, was the oldest Springbok and the last survivor of the South Africans who played in the 1913–14 series. Following a splendid innings of 151 for Western Province against the M.C.C. in the opening match of that tour, he was selected for the first Test match in Durban, but failed to score in either innings, being "caught Woolley b Barnes" in both innings. He first appeared for Western Province in 1907–08 and, at the conclusion of the M.C.C. tour of 1909–10, he was a member of the team picked by H. D. G. Leveson Gower to tour Rhodesia.

Lewis served in France as a Lieut.-Col. in the First World War and won the M.C. and Bar. He was severely wounded in the leg and played no more first-class cricket, but continued to play some club cricket, and in one match, despite his crippled leg, scored a century using a runner. A lawyer, he was for a brief period an acting judge. He volunteered for service again in the Second World War, and was the Officer-in-Charge of demobilisation at South Africa House in London when the War ended.

LEWIS, Lieut.-Col. Richard Percy (Manchester Regiment), born March 10, 1874 (according to the *Winchester and Oxford Registers*), died of wounds, September 9, 1917. Had previously been wounded. Winchester XI, 1891, 1892; Surrey XI, 1892; Middlesex XI, 1898; Oxford University XI, 1894–95–96. Went with Priestley's team to West Indies, 1897. Played much Military cricket, for Devon Regiment, King's African Rifles, Egyptian Army, etc. Lewis seemed likely at one time to be a great wicket-keeper. At Winchester he was spoken of as a coming MacGregor, but it cannot be said that he quite fulfilled his early promise. His ability was beyond question, but his hands would not stand the hard work of first-class matches, and when they went wrong he had bad days. He had no pretensions as a batsman, and in the University match in 1894 he was very pleased that he managed to stay for a couple of overs, enabling Charles Fry to add 17 runs and complete his hundred. Served in the South African War. Member of M.C.C. since 1893.

LIARDET, Col. C. A., one of the greatest supporters there has ever been of Indian cricket, died at Ootacamund (Madras Presidency) early in March, 1903. He took part in the first Inter-Presidency match—played 40 years ago—arranged in India, when a Madras team went up to Calcutta.

LIDDELL, Alan G., who died on February 17, 1970, aged 62, played as a professional for Northamptonshire between 1927 and 1934. A batsman strong in defence and adept at driving and hitting to leg, he did not altogether fulfil early expectations. His most successful season was that of 1933 when, in scoring 626 runs, average 20.19, he hit centuries against Worcestershire and Nottinghamshire. He played his highest innings, 120, against Essex at Northampton in 1930.

LIDDICUT, Arthur Edward, who died in Melbourne on April 8, 1983, aged 91, toured New Zealand with Vernon Ransford's Australian team in 1920–21. An all-rounder, who often opened the bowling at right-arm medium-pace and went in usually at number eight or nine in a strong Victorian batting side, he started his first-class career in 1911–12 and retired in 1932. He scored three centuries and achieved his best bowling figures of seven for 40 for Victoria against Tasmania at the age of 39. Against A. C. MacLaren's M.C.C. team in 1922–23 he was one of four Victorians to score a century in a total of 617 for six declared. In the same match he took four for 16 in M.C.C.'s first innings. In 62 first-class games he took 133 wickets (average 27.56) and scored 2,503 runs (average 31.28). On his retirement from active cricket Liddicut was for many years a delegate to the Victorian Cricket Association.

LIDDLE, James Richard, who died at Cape Town on January 15, 1959, aged 29, after a long illness, was the finest left-arm slow bowler produced by South Africa since N. B. F. ("Tufty") Mann. When 14, he distinguished himself by taking 52 wickets for 364 runs during Nuffield Week and he three times represented South African Schools. During his first-class career he played for Eastern Province, Orange Free State and Western Province. In eight seasons he dismissed 181 batsmen, taking on three occasions seven wickets in an innings. He achieved his best bowling figures, 12 wickets for 212 runs, and his highest innings, 77, in the same match, for Orange Free State against Rhodesia. During his most successful season, 1951–52, when he took 40 wickets in six Currie Cup games, he was unlucky in missing through injury the final trial before the selection of the side to tour Australia and New Zealand. He was at one time Eastern Province junior lawn-tennis champion.

LIGHT, W., born at St. Faith's on March 1, 1880, died suddenly at Exeter on November 10, 1930, aged 50. Summed up as "Good bowler, fair field and bat," he played for Hampshire whilst quite a boy and, after being engaged at Marlborough College, became professional to the Devon County C.C. He assisted the latter county under the residential qualification.

LILLEY, Arthur Augustus ("Dick"), born at Birmingham on November 18, 1867, died at Brislington, near Bristol, on November 17, 1929, within a day of completing his 62nd year. For many seasons he kept wicket for Warwickshire, the Players and England, and in 31 Tests against Australia he obtained 84 wickets—65 caught and 19 stumped. In those games he also scored 802 runs with an average of 20, batting particularly well at Manchester in 1896 for 65 not out and at Leeds three years later for 55. When he gave up County Cricket in 1911 he settled in Bristol, and after the War was a member of the special advisory committee which helped to re-establish the Gloucestershire County C.C. Playing for Warwickshire first in 1888 when the county had not been admitted to first rank, Lilley kept wicket continuously for 23 years. Even in those years, he was recognised as one of the best wicket-keepers in the country. In the course of his career he caught out 705 batsmen and stumped 200. For Warwickshire v. Yorkshire at Edgbaston in 1889 he caught three men and stumped four, and for the county v. M.C.C. at Lord's in 1896 he caught eight. He was also a fine forcing batsman, and could generally be relied on for runs. In first-class matches he scored 15,746 runs, including 16 centuries, and averaged 26. In three seasons he made over 1,000 runs. For his county against Surrey at the Oval in 1898 he, despite a broken finger, batted 85 minutes for 57 runs. He first appeared in a Test against Australia at Lord's in 1896. In that year he played in three of those matches; in 1899 in four, and in 1902, 1905, and 1909 he represented England in all five Tests against Australia. He went out to Australia with touring teams in 1902–02 and 1903–04. As a wicket-keeper he was most consistent and so pronounced an artist that at the end of his career his hands and fingers showed scarcely a trace of the heavy strain to which they had been subjected in taking bowling of all descriptions. Other wicket-keepers may have appeared more brilliant but there was none more sure in making a catch. Lilley, outside his powers as wicket-keeper and batsman, was an exceptionally fine judge of cricket and so well did captains, even of international teams, recognise his special qualities in this direction that they often consulted him during a match.

In the course of his many games for England, Lilley was intimately associated with two dramatic finishes at Old Trafford. In the match of 1896 in which Ranjitsinhji played his great innings of 154 not out and Tom Richardson bowled so wonderfully, Lilley when Australia, with three wickets to fall, wanted nine runs for victory, missed Kelly in curious fashion. He took the ball cleanly enough but as he did so, pulled his arm back and struck his thigh, the impact being so sharp that it shook the ball out of his hands. Six years later on the same ground, England, with two wickets to fall, were within eight runs of victory when off a splendid square leg hit, Lilley was out to a marvellous catch by Clem Hill. As the stroke was made a four looked absolutely certain but the wind held the ball and Hill, running at top speed some 30 yd. or more, took the ball one hand close to the boundary. Rain then delayed the progress of the game for nearly an hour and on resuming Australia snatched a three runs victory.

Lilley's benefit match—Warwickshire v. Yorkshire—at Birmingham in 1901 realised £850.

LILLEY, Aubrey Roy, who died in an air crash near Johannesburg on August 10, 1979, at the age of 28, was a left-arm seam bowler who took 132 first-class wickets for Natal and Transvaal, four times taking five in an innings. Born at Grahamstown, he was educated at Maritzburg College and played for both the Natal and South African Schools in 1969. He toured England with the Kingsmead Mynahs in 1976. It was after he had had one season for Transvaal that he was killed. When Natal were bowled out for 71 by Transvaal in the Currie Cup of 1978–79, Lilley took four for nine.

LILLEY, Ben, who kept wicket for Nottinghamshire between 1921 and 1937, died at his home at Nottingham on August 4, 1950, aged 55. He was licensee of the Forest Tavern, Mansfield Road, Nottingham, and had been in failing health for some years. A native of Kimberley, a village in Nottinghamshire, Lilley first played for the county against Essex at Leyton in 1921, but he could not find a regular place in the team until 1925. Then, as successor to Tom Oates, he set up a Nottinghamshire record by becoming the first wicket-keeper to score over 1,000 runs in a season. He achieved the feat again in 1928. Lilley was considered one of the best wicket-keepers in the country, but Test honours eluded him.

For several years he "kept" to Larwood and Voce the England fast bowlers. He retired in 1937 following injury to a thumb. During his first-class career Lilley scored 10,479 runs, including seven centuries, made 645 catches and stumped 132 batsmen. In a Second XI match he scored 200 not out against a Staffordshire side including S. F. Barnes.

LILLYWHITE, James, Jun., born at West Hampnett, Sussex, on February 23, 1842, died at Westerton, Chichester, on October 25, 1929, aged 87. He was the last survivor of the team which, under his captaincy, went to Australia in the winter of 1876–77, and played what is now known as the first Test match against Australia. There had been previous combinations to tour that country, but not until March, 1877, did the Australians regard themselves as strong enough to engage an English XI on level terms. That their faith in themselves was justified is proved by the fact that they won by 45 runs, but in the return match played just afterwards England, who on the previous occasion had been compelled to take the field without a regular wicket-keeper, were successful by four wickets. Of the 22 men who took part in that historic game there are now only three left, and they are all in Australia —Charles Bannerman, J. McCarthy Blackham, and Tom Garrett. James Lillywhite came of a great cricketing family, of whom the best known was his uncle, William, the "Nonpareil." He bowled, as he batted, left-handed, was rather slow with a high delivery, and like others of the same period was exceptionally accurate in his pitch. His first appearance at Lord's was in June, 1862, in a match between Sussex and the M.C.C. when he took 14 wickets for 57 runs—nine in the second innings for 29 runs. A curious feature of the contest was that there was no change of bowling in any one of the four innings, Lillywhite and Stubberfield bowling unchanged for Sussex and Jimmy Grundy and George Wootton for Marylebone. Many other remarkable bowling feats stand to Lillywhite's credit, among them being the following:

8 for 29, Players v. Gentlemen, at Lord's	1862
13 for 95, Players of South v. 13 Gentlemen of South, at Southampton	1864
13 for 97, Sussex v. Kent, at Hastings	1865
3 wickets in 4 balls, South v. Surrey, at Oval	1865
(Tom Humphrey, Stephenson, Pooley)	
15 for 55 (8 for 29), Players of South v. 14 Gentlemen of South, at Southampton ..	1866
5 for 5 Single v. Married, at Lord's	1871
(Including 4 in 4 maiden overs)	

All 10 for 129, South v. North, Canterbury	..	..	..	..	..	1872
14 for 172 (8 for 114), South v. North, at Canterbury		..	..	..	..	1873
13 for 70, Sussex v. Kent, at Brighton	..	..	..	..	..	1875
8 for 43, Sussex v. Kent, at Brighton	..	..	..	..	..	1879

(1st innings. In second he sent down 108 balls for 2 runs)

For Sussex he bowled unchanged through a match 12 times—once with Stubberfield, on five occasions with Southerton, and six times with Fillery. Three of the instances with the last-named were in consecutive matches in 1873—v. Surrey at the Oval, v. Kent at Lord's, and v. Gloucestershire at Brighton. In two other big games he and Southerton were on unchanged throughout—for Players of South v. 14 Gentlemen of South at Southampton in 1865 and for South v. North at Liverpool in 1872. Playing against odds in Australia, during the tour of 1873–74, he took 18 for 72 v. 15 off New South Wales and Victoria at Sydney and 12 for 61 v. 18 of Victoria at Melbourne. Three seasons later he obtained nine for 23 v. 22 of South Australia at Adelaide. In 1872 he took 94 wickets for 13 runs each; in 1873, 101 at the same cost; and in 1876, 91 wickets for 14 runs each. He was, in his early days, a smart field, either at slip or mid-on, and, like most left-handers, a vigorous batsman. Twice he reached three figures for Sussex, making 105 against Hampshire at Brighton in 1864, and 126 not out against Middlesex on the Old Cattle Market Ground at Islington. His first match for Sussex was played in 1862, and his last against Yorkshire, in 1883, and for the county he took 917 wickets for 14.75 runs apiece. For 20 seasons, 1862 to 1881 inclusive, he appeared in every game played by the side.

He visited the United States and Canada in 1868 as a member of Willsher's team and paid six visits to Australia, first as a member of the side W. G. Grace took out in 1873–74, next as captain of the team in 1876–77, and four times afterwards when he joined in undertakings with Alfred Shaw and Arthur Shrewsbury, but devoted himself mainly to the business side of those enterprises, not all of which proved successful pecuniary speculations. For a time he was Secretary of the United South of England XI and, after his playing days, he proved an efficient umpire. His first benefit match, at Brighton in 1881, produced a memorable struggle, the Players making 204 and 112 and the Gentlemen 204 and 111. (He himself had taken part in several games between such sides, and in them had obtained 35 wickets for 20 runs each.) His second benefit was North v. South at Chichester in 1889. He arranged the fixture lists of the first two Australian teams which visited England—those of 1878 and 1880.

LINCOLN, Robert, died at Grimsby, May 15, 1918, aged 63. Played for the XXII in the match, in 1876, in which W. G. Grace made 400 not out. A useful bat.

LINDLEY, Tinsley, died on March 30, 1940, aged 74. A barrister living in Nottingham, Tinsley Lindley was known in sport chiefly as an outstanding centre-forward for England and Corinthians besides his local clubs. A very useful cricketer, he made 40 and seven for Nottinghamshire against Surrey at Trent Bridge in the Whitsuntide match of 1888, and he was in the county XI which beat the Australians by 10 wickets.

LINDSAY, Neville Vernon, who died in Pietermaritzburg on February 2, 1976, at the age of 89, made one appearance for South Africa against Warwick Armstrong's Australians in 1921–22, and he also appeared in one of the unofficial tests against S. B. Joel's XI in 1924–25. He was then nearing the end of his career, which began in 1906–07 for Transvaal when he was 19, and he played for them during almost the whole of his career. A fine batsman, he scored a total of 2,030 runs at an average of 33 and made five centuries. In his last season, 1926–27, he was a member of an immensely strong Transvaal team which included H. W. Taylor, M. J. Susskind, J. A. J. Christy, H. B. Cameron, H. G. Deane, A. D. ("Dave") Nourse, A. E. Hall, E. P. Nupen, D. P. Conyngham and Bruce Mitchell, then at the outset of his career, almost a Springbok side in itself. They won each of their six matches, four of them by an innings. In 1922–23, Lindsay with G. R. McCubbin set up a new South African ninth wicket record of 221 playing for Transvaal against Rhodesia, at Bulawayo, and this record still holds. Lindsay was a fine all-round sportsman and made his name also at rugby, hockey, golf and bowls. With the death of P. T. Lewis (noted above), Lindsay became the oldest Springbok, on an age basis, but held that position for less than a week.

LINDSAY, William, born in India on August 3, 1847, died in the middle of February, 1923, in his 76th year. He was in the Winchester XI in 1864 and 1865, and in his three innings against Eton scored 11, two and 43. As a batsman he had a first-rate style and he was brilliant in the field, especially at cover-point and long-leg. Between 1876 and 1882 he made 987 runs for Surrey with an average of 17.31, his highest innings being 74 against Middlesex at the Oval in 1877. At Association football he appeared for England against Scotland in 1877 and also played at back for the Wanderers when they won the Cup three years in succession.

LINDSAY, Sir William O'Brien, K.B.E., who died in Nairobi on October 20, 1975, aged 66, was three years in the Harrow XI as a batsman and wicket-keeper, averaging 55 in the last. At Oxford he got a Blue in 1931, his third year, as an opener, though his average was only 13.50 and his highest score 25. D. C. G. Raikes was preferred to him as a wicket-keeper. Later in the season Lindsay made a couple of appearances for Kent, for whom he had a birth qualification, and in the first of them kept wicket in the absence of Ames. In 1932 he failed to retain his place in the Oxford side, despite a brave innings of 63 against Lancashire. He had no grace of style, but was a determined player with a good defence and one who seldom let off the leg-ball. Later he had a distinguished career in the Sudan, becoming Chief Justice.

LINTON, George Constantine, who died in Jamaica on January 20, 1960, aged 84, played for Jamaica before the First World War. A powerful hitter, he was known as "the local Jessop."

LIPSCOMB, Robert, died on January 8, 1895, aged 57. He will be remembered as one of the fastest and straightest amateur fast bowlers of his day. Commencing about 1862, he played regularly for Kent for several years, sharing the honours of many a good match with Willsher, Bennett and Mr. G. M. Kelsom.

LIPSCOMB, William Henry, born November 20, 1846, died in London, April 9, 1918. Marlborough XI, 1865; Oxford XI, 1868; Hampshire, 1866–67. A well-known oarsman. He earned a place in the Oxford XI in 1868 but did not have the luck to be on the victorious side, Cambridge winning by 168 runs. At this distance of time it is not easy to say why he was given his Blue. As he went in last he was presumably chosen for his bowling but in Cambridge's second innings of 236 he only sent down seven overs. In the first innings E. M. Kenny and E. L. Fellowes

bowled so well that there was no need to call on his services.

LISSETTE, Allen F., who died suddenly in Hamilton, N.Z., on January 24, 1973, aged 53, played in two Test matches for New Zealand during the 1955–56 tour by the West Indies. A slow left-arm bowler, he assisted the Hamilton and Waikato clubs for many years after the Second World War, in which he served in the R.N.Z.A.F., and was awarded the M.B.E. for work in forming the 7th Squadron of the Air Training Corps in Hamilton. He represented first Auckland and then Northern Districts in the Plunket Shield competition. He played cricket up to the 1972–73 season when he suffered a heart attack during a match in October.

LITTLE, Charles William, born at Tonbridge on May 22, 1870, died at Southgate Hill, Winchester, on May 20, 1922. A good bat, cutting particularly well, and an excellent wicket-keeper, he was in the Winchester XI in 1888 and 1889, scoring in his two matches against Eton four and 37, 30 and 40. He did not obtain his blue whilst at Oxford, but in 1893 he appeared in five matches for Kent, for whom he made 50 runs in six innings. He had been a master at Winchester College since 1904.

LITTLEJOHN, Arthur Rieusett, died in a nursing home in London on December 8, 1919. His connection with first-class cricket did not last long, his medical work leaving him little time for three-day matches, but he made a very distinct mark. Indeed, when he played for Middlesex in the early part of the season in 1911, his bowling (right-hand slow to medium pace) caused something approaching a sensation. In five matches he took 37 wickets: his greatest success was against Lancashire, 15 wickets falling to him, and Middlesex winning the game in a single innings. Helped by no peculiarity of delivery, and breaking to a very small extent from leg, he did not look to be at all a difficult bowler, but he had one sovereign merit. His command of pitch was so great that one could have counted quite easily the number of bad-length balls he sent down in an innings of normal duration. The result was that even the most adventurous batsman treated him with considerable respect. His skill had been acquired by long and assiduous practice. He had to give up playing as soon as he had established a reputation, and when he reappeared for Middlesex in 1912 he did not repeat his success, proving ineffective and very expensive. Probably he was not in the same form as before, but he had to bowl a good deal on slow wickets and they did not suit him. He was always at his best on a lively pitch. In Metropolitan club cricket he obtained many large scores, and in making 160 for Ealing v. Pallingswick on the Ealing ground on July 8, 1905, he and his brother, Dr. E. S. Littlejohn (191 not out), added 322 together for the second wicket. Born at Hanwell on April 1, 1880, he was in his 40th year at the time of his death.—S.H.P.

LITTLEWOOD, George H., born May 12, 1882, at Friarmere (Yorkshire), died at Oldham, December 20, 1917. Played for Lancashire a few times, and v. Australians at Liverpool in 1902 took 12 wickets for 98. Bowled slow left-hand. Useful bat. Played later as a professional for Accrington, and as an amateur for Crompton.

LIVESAY, Brigadier-General R. O'H., D.S.O., died on March 23, 1946. He played for Kent on occasions between 1895 and 1904. His best score, 78, was against the South Africans at Canterbury in 1904. A member of the Wellington XI for three years, he subsequently showed fine batting form for Sandhurst, making 169 against Woolwich in 1895 and 128 the following year. An attractive bat, he fielded admirably. A splendid Rugby footballer for the Blackheath club, he played for England against Wales in 1898–99.

LIVSEY, Walter H., who died at Merton Park on September 12, 1978, aged 84, was one of the best county wicket-keepers of the '20s. Born at Todmorden, Yorkshire, he was originally on the staff at the Oval, but with Strudwick in his prime there was no opening for him, and he was persuaded to move to Hampshire. While qualifying, he played in 1913 against Oxford and gave an immediate sign of his class, allowing only three byes in an innings of 554. In 1914 he succeeded Stone as regular 'keeper, and his stumping of Jack Hobbs off a sharply lifting ball from Kennedy wide of the leg stump created quite a sensation. Not being demobilised in time, he missed the season of 1919, but from 1920 continued as the county's regular wicket-keeper until a breakdown in health caused his retirement at the end of 1929. Despite his wicket-keeping he is now perhaps better remembered for the part his batting played in one of the most sensational county matches in history. At Edgbaston in 1922, Warwickshire made 223 and then on a plumb wicket bowled Hampshire out for 15. In the follow-on, six wickets were down for 186, and when Livsey came in at number 10, Hampshire were only 66 ahead. He and George Brown put on 177, and then Boyes helped him to add 70 for the last wicket. Livsey's share was a faultless 110 not out and Hampshire won this incredible match by 155 runs. His only other century was 109 not out in 85 minutes against Kent at Dover in 1928, but in 1921 against Worcestershire he helped Bowell to put on 192 in 110 minutes for the last wicket, his own contribution being 70 not out.

LLEWELLYN, Charles Bennett, who died at Chertsey, Surrey, on June 7, 1964, aged 87, was a great all-rounder in his day. A forcing left-hand batsman, a slow to medium left-arm bowler and a splendid fielder, particularly at mid-off, Llewellyn, who was born at Pietermaritzburg, appeared in 15 Test matches for South Africa, five against England and 10 against Australia, between 1895 and 1912, scoring 496 runs, average 18.37, and taking 48 wickets at 27.27 runs each. It was as a professional for Hampshire that he did his best work, however, and between 1899 and 1910 he hit 8,772 runs for the county, average 27.58, took 711 wickets for 24.66 runs apiece and brought off 136 catches. Five times he scored over 1,000 runs and five times dismissed more than 100 batsmen in a season, achieving the "double" in 1901 and repeating the performance in all matches in 1908 and 1910.

He created a stir in his first match before he had qualified for Championship games by hitting 72 and 21 against the 1899 Australian touring side and taking eight wickets for 132 in the first innings on a true pitch. That performance gained him a place in K. S. Ranjitsinhji's team who toured America the following winter. One of his best all-round feats was against Somerset at Taunton in 1901 when he played an innings of 153 in 100 minutes and took 10 wickets at a cost of 183 runs. Against the South Africans at Southampton the same season he reached the highest of his 15 centuries, 216, put together in three hours and including 30 boundaries, and followed by sending back six batsmen for 105 runs and holding three catches. Twice he registered two centuries in a match: 102 and 100 against Derbyshire at Derby in 1905 and 130 and 101 not out against Sussex at Hove in 1909. His second innings at Hove occupied only an hour.

A bowler skilled in variation of pace and spin, he gained his best match-analysis at

Southampton in 1901, dismissing 14 Worcestershire batsmen for 171 runs.

A disagreement over terms resulted in him severing his connection with Hampshire, but after touring Australia with P. W. Sherwell's South African team in 1910–11, he returned to England and played in League cricket. Incidentally, he might once have assisted England, for he was among the 14 players from whom the team who met Australia in the first Test at Edgbaston in 1902 was selected.

LLOYD, Edward Wynell Mayow, born on March 19, 1845, died at Hartley Wintney, Hampshire, on September 27, 1928. *Scores and Biographies* (vii–295) says of him: "Was a very painstaking batsman, having a good defence, besides being an admirable hitter. Also an excellent field." In 1864, his third and last season as a member of the Rugby XI, he scored 139 not out v. Marlborough at Islington and 95 v. M.C.C. at Lord's. He played some County Cricket for both Shropshire and Somerset. From 1876 until 1910 he was headmaster of Hartford House School, Winchfield.

LLOYD, John, born in 1833, died in London on June 8, 1915. He was a sound batsman and above the average as a wicket-keeper. For some years he was Hon. Secretary of the South Wales C.C., with which the brothers Grace were prominently associated. It was for that club that W. G. obtained his first great success as a batsman, making 170 and 56 not out against the Gentlemen of Sussex on the old ground at Brighton. In the same match Mr. Lloyd scored 82 and four not out and caught one and stumped three. As a memento of the occasion Mr. Lloyd presented "W.G." with an appropriately inscribed bat. He was the founder of the Brecknockshire County C.C., and was most keenly interested in the game to the last. He will always be chiefly remembered for the very prominent part he played in obtaining a system of county government for London.

LLOYD, Neil, who died at Wakefield, of an unidentified virus, on September 17, 1982, aged 17, was a left-handed batsman of great promise. He had played for three years for Yorkshire Second XI and barely a fortnight before his death had gone in first for Young England against Young West Indies in the third of last season's "Test" matches. He was awarded his Yorkshire Second XI cap posthumously.

LLOYD, Richard Averil, who died in hospital in Ireland on December 23, 1950, aged 59, played for Lancashire on a few occasions in 1921 and 1922, scoring 100 runs, average 20.00. A celebrated Ireland Rugby football half-back, he gained 19 caps between 1910 and 1920, being renowned for his dropped goals. He also played for Ulster, Liverpool and Lancashire. Educated at Armagh Royal School, Portora Royal School and Dublin University, he served in the First World War as a Captain in the Liverpool Scottish.

LOCK, Herbert Christmas ("Bert"), who died on May 18, 1978, aged 75, will be remembered as groundsman for years at the Oval and as the man who in the winter of 1945–46 accomplished the superhuman task of getting the ground fit again for cricket after six years of disuse and maltreatment. A medium-pace right-hander, he had many trials for Surrey between 1926 and 1932, but, though he took lots of wickets for the Second XI, could never make the grade in the First. From 1934 to 1939 he bowled with great success for Devon. He was a member of the Hon. L. H. Tennyson's side to Jamaica in 1926–27, but achieved very little there. He finished his career as Official Inspector of Pitches for the T.C.C.B.

LOCKER, William, who died at Derby on August 14, 1952, aged 85, appeared in 16 matches for Derbyshire between 1894 and 1902. His highest innings was 76 in 1901 at Derby, scored out of a first-wicket partnership of 140 with L. G. Wright in reply to a Nottinghamshire total of 661, of which William Gunn obtained 273. Locker played football for Notts County and in 1891 took part in the F.A. Cup Final won by Blackburn Rovers.

LOCKETT, Aaron, who died in February, 1965, aged 71, was a professional with Oldham in the Central Lancashire League from 1929 to 1940, and also played for Staffordshire and the Minor Counties. An all-rounder, he once took all 10 Royton wickets for 53 runs and five times dismissed 100 or more batsmen in a season. He shone particularly as a batsman in the game against the West Indies at Exeter in 1928. He hit 22 and 154 and the Minor Counties, after following-on 181 behind, won by 42 runs. As an Association footballer, he played at inside-forward for Port Vale and Stoke City.

LOCKHART, John Harold Bruce, who died in London on June 4, 1956, aged 67, was headmaster of Sedbergh from 1937 to 1954 and one of the school's most distinguished old boys. He won a scholarship at Jesus College, Cambridge, and after taking 12 wickets for 187 with slow leg-breaks in the Freshmen's match of 1909, gained his cricket Blue that summer. Against Oxford at Lord's he distinguished himself by dismissing six batsmen for 96 runs in the first innings and three for 82 in the second, and he headed the Cambridge bowling figures with 49 wickets, average 17.97. In the University match of the following year, he was by no means so successful. Thanks to the all-round play of P. R. Le Couteur, who hit 160 and took 11 wickets for 126 runs, Oxford triumphed in an innings with 126 runs to spare. Bruce Lockhart's analysis was two wickets for 72 runs and he was out for "a pair." Also a splendid Rugby footballer, he represented Cambridge against Oxford at fly-half in 1910. He played football for Scotland, for whom he also appeared at cricket, against Wales in 1913 and, after service throughout the First World War with the Intelligence Corps and being Mentioned in Dispatches, against England in 1920. He was a master at Rugby and at Cargilfield, near Edinburgh, before his appointment at Sedbergh.

LOCKHART, W. P., died in the latter part of the summer, 1893. In his time Mr. Lockhart was the best amateur wicket-keeper in the north of England. He was born at Kirkcaldy, N.B., on October 15, 1835. He never appeared at Lord's, but in 1859 he was one of the Gentlemen's XI against the Players at the Oval.

LOCKTON, John Henry, who died in hospital on June 29, 1972, aged 80, was a very good cricketer and Association footballer. In the Dulwich XI from 1906 to 1909, he won his purples for both cricket and football at London University. From 1919 to 1926 he assisted Surrey as a fast-medium bowler with a curious loping run-up to the crease and a hard-hitting batsman, receiving his county cap in 1920. He took part in the game against Somerset at Taunton in 1925 when J. B. Hobbs equalled and beat Dr. W. G. Grace's record of 126 centuries.

From 1910 to 1927, he turned out for Honor Oak C.C. and in 1920 he took all 10 Guy's Hospital wickets for 50 runs. Five years later, for Arthur Thorpe's XI against Britannic House, he put together an innings of 105 out of 182 and took all 10 wickets for 23 runs.

As a footballer, he played at inside-left as an amateur for Nottingham Forest and Crystal Palace and at various times for London, Surrey, Ilford, Nunhead, the Corinthians and Casuals. When his playing career ended, he became a referee, officiating in the University match in 1935 and the F.A. Amateur Cup final.

LOCKWOOD, Ephraim, died on December 19, 1921. Playing his last county match in 1884 Lockwood was only a name to the present generation, but middle-aged people will remember him as the finest Yorkshire batsman of his day. He rose to fame at one bound, and for 15 years he was in the front rank, never looking back. His career had a brilliant climax, followed almost immediately by eclipse. In August, 1883, against Kent at Gravesend, he scored 208—the highest, and in some respects the best innings of his life—but in the following year he lost his form so completely that he had to be left out of the Yorkshire XI, and, except for a match in Scotland in 1888, no more was seen of him. Never in the history of Yorkshire cricket did a young batsman make a more remarkable first appearance for the county. It is an old story, but one that will bear retelling. When in August, 1868, Lockwood stepped on to the Oval to play against Surrey he was unknown to the general public. At the beginning of the season he had played at Lord's for the Colts of England, but as he made very few runs his doings attracted no attention. As the result of the Surrey match he suddenly found himself a celebrity. Trained in a stern school at Lascelles Hall he was not troubled by nerves. Rather late in the afternoon he was sent in with his uncle, John Thewlis, and when next day Yorkshire's first wicket fell the score stood at 176. Lockwood got 91, and the Oval critics could not say too much in his praise. Success did not in any way turn his head, and in the following season he took his place among the best batsmen in England, being chosen for the Players against the Gentlemen at Lord's. He failed in that match, but against Surrey at the Oval he confirmed his previous form, scoring 103 and 34 not out. This time he and Joe Rowbotham sent up 166 for the first wicket. From 1869 to 1883 Lockwood was one of Yorkshire's mainstays, knowing no rival among the county batsmen till George Ulyett came to the front. Looking up the statistics in *Bat v. Ball* I find that, including six 100s, Lockwood made for Yorkshire 37 scores of 50 or more. His average year by year would look small in comparison with the records of present-day batsmen, but run-getting in his time was not what it is now. The wickets were not so carefully prepared. Lockwood took part, between 1869 and 1883, in 28 Gentlemen and Players matches, and enjoyed marked success, especially in the middle '70s, his highest innings being 97 at the Oval in 1877. In the old North and South matches of which we at one time had so many, he nearly always did well. Rather clumsily built Lockwood was not exactly a stylist, but he played with a perfectly straight bat, he had an ever-watchful defence, and his cutting was superb—a model combination of brilliancy and safety. The short ball he sent like a flash behind point and when he could trust the wicket he did not scruple to cut balls off the middle stump. His eye in his best days was unfailing. More than once Lockwood was asked to go to Australia, but he resolutely declined. The sea had no charm for him. When he went to America with Richard Daft's team in 1879 he was always wishing himself safely back at Lascelles Hall.—S.H.P.

Lockwood's scores of a hundred in first-class cricket were:

103	For Yorkshire v. Surrey, at the Oval	1869
121	For Yorkshire v. Surrey, at the Oval	1872
108	For United North v. United South, at Hull	1876
103	For North v. South, at Hull	1877
107	For Yorkshire v. Gloucestershire, at Sheffield	1878
109	For Yorkshire v. Surrey, at Huddersfield	1881
104	For Yorkshire v. I. Zingari, at Scarborough	1882
208	For Yorkshire v. Kent, at Gravesend	1883

LOCKWOOD, William Henry, the famous fast bowler, died at his home, at Radford, Nottingham, on April 26, 1932, at the age of 64. He had been in failing health for about five years. In his day one of the finest fast bowlers the game of cricket has ever known, Lockwood had a somewhat chequered career. Born at Old Radford, Nottinghamshire, on March 25, 1868, he was given a trial for Notts in 1886, but accomplished nothing of note and in the following year he accepted an engagement on the ground staff at Kennington Oval. He duly qualified for Surrey and although Notts were anxious to secure his services in 1889, he preferred to stay with his adopted county, and that season signalised his association with Surrey by an innings of 83 against Notts in the August Bank Holiday match at the Oval.

Not until two years later did he make his mark as a bowler, his great performance that summer being 11 wickets for 40 runs against Kent at the Oval, but in 1892 when Surrey had George Lohmann and Tom Richardson as well as Lockwood, the last-named headed the averages for all matches, taking 168 wickets for less than 12½ runs apiece. Lockwood continued a great bowler during the next two seasons but, going out to Australia in 1894–95, he failed deplorably and, on his return home, went down the hill so steadily that in 1897 he lost his place in the Surrey team.

Happily in the ensuing winter he was at great pains to get himself fit, and in 1898 obtained 134 wickets and scored nearly 1,000 runs in first-class matches. He remained a splendid bowler for several years after this, but finally dropped out of the Surrey team in 1904.

In 1902 he appeared for England against Australia in four of the five Test matches, and in the contest at Manchester, securing 11 wickets for 76 runs, accomplished one of the greatest bowling performances ever witnessed. To begin with, the pitch proved so soft that not until the score reached 129 was Lockwood given a trial but still, in an innings of 299, he disposed of six batsmen for 48, the last five wickets falling for 43 runs. In Australia's second innings Lockwood got rid of Trumper, Hill and Duff while the score was reaching 10. Fred Tate, at deep square leg, missing Darling off Braund the fourth wicket, which should have gone down at 16, did not fall until 64. For all that Lockwood dominated the game, taking five wickets for 28 and the tourists were all out for 86. England had only 124 to make but a night's heavy rain placed batsmen at a big disadvantage and Australia, despite Lockwood's magnificent work, won by three runs.

Lockwood took no such long run as his famous colleague, Tom Richardson, and did not appear quite so fast through the air, but when he was at the top of his form, no one ever came off the pitch much faster than he or—with his off-break also a distinguishing quality of his bowling—was more difficult to play under conditions favourable to batting. He had, too, at his command a slow ball which in his early days he sent down without any perceptible change of delivery. After he "came back" in 1898 he did not bowl this ball quite as well as before but it was still a very useful part of his equipment.

In addition to being one of the most famous bowlers of his generation, Lockwood was also a first-rate batsman and, had he not been compelled to concentrate his energies upon the taking of wickets would, no doubt, have gained high rank as a run-getter. Among his many triumphs was one for the Players against the Gentlemen at Lord's in 1902, when in addition to taking nine wickets for less than 12 runs apiece, he put together an innings of 100.

LODGE, Lewis Vaughan, born December 21, 1872, was found drowned in a pond near Buxton, in Derbyshire, on November 21, 1916. He was in the XI at Durham School and played for both Durham County and Hampshire, being a useful batsman. Apart from making 48 and 55 in the only two innings he played for Durham in 1897, he did little in County Cricket. At Cambridge he played for the Freshmen in 1892 and for the Seniors in 1893. He was a well-known Association footballer, being a Cambridge Blue and an international.

LOGAN, C. J., one of the finest bowlers Canada has ever produced, died at Galt, Ontario, on December 21, 1906. He was educated at Trinity College School, and appeared for Canada against the United States in 1880, 1881, and 1883. He was a very fine field and a useful batsman. In 1879 he played with success against the England team which visited America that year, taking seven wickets for 35 runs for XXII Canadian-born cricketers at Toronto, and six for 39 for Seventeen of Hamilton, at Hamilton. His portrait can be seen in *Sixty Years of Canadian Cricket.*

LOMAS, John Millington, an Oxford Blue at cricket and Association football, died suddenly on December 4, 1945, aged nearly 28. Joining the Royal Navy for war service he was invalided out and returning to Oxford became a Fellow of New College. He made a name as an opening batsman at Charterhouse, and in 1936, when captain of the school XI, he averaged 55. That year Charterhouse did not lose an inter-school match and inflicted the first defeat suffered by Eton from a school since 1920. Lomas, when captain of The Rest against Lord's Schools, made a brilliant 83, and he also led the Public Schools against the Army at Lord's, both matches being drawn.

He began at Oxford in 1938 with 32 and 45 against Yorkshire and maintained this form so consistently that he averaged 45.40, his final effort, 94, against Cambridge in a drawn match, following 97 and 50 against M.C.C. Such batting at Lord's created a very favourable impression, which he increased in 1939 by making 138 off the M.C.C. bowlers and 91 in the University match, Oxford winning by 45 runs, after a great struggle. Cambridge totalled 384 in the last innings, thanks to P. J. Dickinson, whose 100 was the first three-figure innings by a freshman for the Light Blues in this match since 1887 when Eustace Crawley scored 103 not out.

In 1942 Lomas made 123 not out and 73 in Oxford Authentic matches, but poor health prevented him from playing any more serious cricket. Of medium height and light build he batted with easy skill, close concentration helping him to meet any form of attack by sure defence and every stroke at his command. In the field speed and sure hands enabled him to save many runs.

LONERGAN, Roy, who died at Adelaide after a long illness on October 22, 1956, aged 46, rendered excellent service as a batsman to South Australia from 1929 to 1935. Strong in strokes all-round despite his slight physique, he enjoyed his best season in 1931–32, scoring 586 runs in 12 Sheffield Shield innings, average 48.83. In that season he went near to hitting two centuries in a match, being dismissed for 95 and 97 against Queensland at Brisbane, and he achieved the feat with 115 and 100 in 1933–34 against Victoria at Melbourne when, despite his performance, South Australia lost by five wickets. Lonergan played six innings for a total of 105 runs against D. R. Jardine's M.C.C. team of 1932–33—the "body-line" tour. In 72 innings for South Australia, he reached an aggregate of 3,002 runs, average 43.50. Of his nine centuries, the highest was 159 against Victoria at Adelaide in 1930–31.

LONEY, Escott Frith, who died in Toronto on June 19, 1982, aged 78, played for Derbyshire between 1925 and 1927, scoring 511 runs (average 17.03) and taking 20 wickets at 32.50 apiece.

LONG, Herbert James, who died on October 6, 1964, aged 85, was a London sports journalist for 50 years till retiring in 1955. Between the two World Wars he reported county cricket for the *Cricket Reporting Agency* and the *Press Association* and also assisted in the preparation of *Wisden.* Through his own sports news agency, he reported football in London for many provincial newspapers. A first-rate organiser, he excelled himself at the first Wembley Cup Final in 1923 when the gates were closed on an attendance estimated at 150,000. Thousands of people remained outside the ground, but Long persuaded the police to form a path through the huge crowd so that his army of messenger boys were enabled to convey running reports of the game to the many telephones he had hired. As a fast bowler and aggressive batsman, "Bert" Long was on the Essex County C.C. staff in his youth and he was fond of recalling the occasion when he bowled Dr. W. G. Grace in the nets at Leyton. He also played Association football for Woolwich Arsenal before they changed their name to Arsenal.

LONG, The First Lord, of Wraxall, P.C., who was born at Bath, on July 13, 1854, died at Rood Ashton, Trowbridge, on September 26, 1924. As Walter Hume Long he was in the Harrow XI in 1873, when, by scoring 36 and 17, he contributed to Eton's defeat by five wickets. He was a good, free-hitting batsman and an excellent field at coverpoint. Mr. R. P. Long, of the Harrow teams of 1843-44, was his father. Lord Long entered Parliament in 1880 and held various offices, the last time being from 1919 to 1921 as First Lord of the Admiralty. In 1906 he was President of the M.C.C. His name will be found in the Wiltshire and Devonshire XIs.

LONG, Robert, born at Richmond on November 9, 1846, died at Enfield on August 6, 1924. It was at one time thought he might do well as a fast bowler, but in his two matches for Surrey in 1870 he met with no success. At various times he was engaged by Christ College (Finchley), Winchester College, and Beaumont College (Old Windsor).

LONGBOURNE, Capt. Hugh Richard, D.S.O. (Queen's Royal West Surrey Regiment), killed May, 1916. Repton XI, 1901-02-03. Received the Russian Order of St Stanislaus with Swords.

LONGDEN, Arthur, who died at Christchurch (his native place), New Zealand, in July, 1924, played several times for Canterbury and against Wellington in January, 1884, made a score of 42.

LONGFIELD, Thomas Cuthbert, died on December 21, 1981, aged 75. Five years in the Aldenham XI, he played for Cambridge

at Lord's in 1927 and 1928. In 1927, when his match return of eight for 93 and his second innings of 48 played a considerable part in his side's victory over Oxford, he was second in the batting averages with 504 runs, average 42.00 and third in the bowling with 46 wickets at 30.93. In 1928 he made 519 runs, average 28.83, and took 44 wickets at 29.18. An orthodox, old-fashioned medium-pace bowler, he possessed a beautiful action, kept a good length, and could move the ball both ways. He was a fine field. A good stroke-player who could score quickly, mostly in front of the wicket, he made two centuries for Cambridge: 114 not out against Gloucestershire at Bristol in an hour and three-quarters in 1927, and 120 against Leicestershire at Fenner's in 1928, when he and J. T. Morgan put on 214 in two and a half hours for the sixth wicket. Going out to India when he came down from Cambridge, he was available for his county, Kent, only when on leave in England, and so between 1927 and 1939 managed only 29 matches for them. He played some useful innings, with a highest score of 72 against Surrey at Blackheath in 1927, but he was curiously ineffective as a bowler: indeed his 23 wickets cost 66.26 each. He was the father-in-law of E. R. Dexter.

LONGHURST, The Rev. Canon William Henry Roberts, who died at Budleigh Salterton on September 3, 1943, within eight days of completing 105 years, played in the 1856 Marlborough XI. At Lord's against Rugby, in the second match between these schools, he made four run out and 10; earlier in the season at Cheltenham he scored 35 in a total of 84 and 18. That was the first meeting of Cheltenham and Marlborough. In each game Longhurst was on the losing side. When at Pembroke College, Oxford, he showed to advantage in several sports and won the "hurdles" in 1861 and 1862. During his first curacy at Savernake he was classical master at Marlborough—1865 to 1876. For over 50 years he took a prominent part in philanthropic work in Worcester, and, after being an honorary canon, he became Canon Emeritus of Worcester Cathedral in 1936 when 97 years of age. At the time of his death Canon Longhurst was the oldest clergyman in Britain, the oldest member of Oxford University, and senior Old Marlburian.

LONGMAN, George Henry, died on August 19, 1938, aged 86. An enthusiastic cricketer, he retained a close interest in the game until the end of his life. At Eton he was in the XI for four years, 1868 to 1871; captain in his last year. At Cambridge, Longman got his Blue as a Freshman and played against Oxford four times from 1872 to 1875. With a score of 80 he helped to beat Oxford by an innings and 166 runs in his first University match. Longman and A. S. Tabor, another Eton Freshman, put up the 100 for the first wicket, then a record for this engagement.

Mr. Longman writing about "My Years at Cambridge" in the 1929 *Wisden* said regarding that match—"An ardent Oxonian was sitting in the pavilion and up to him came another Oxonian with the eager question: 'Well, how is it going?' 'Going,' replied his friend, 'There are two —— little Freshmen in, and they've got the 100 up without a wicket.'"

Oxford were very strong at that time and in the three following years, twice as Cambridge captain, Longman was on the losing side.

Longman played for the Gentlemen at Lord's in 1875 and on subsequent occasions. He was an excellent batsman, possessing beautiful style. Very keen on fielding, he enjoyed the reputation of having greatly improved this important part of the game at Cambridge. No doubt he was influenced in this effort by the fact that in his first match for Eton at Lord's he was run out twice, while his big performances for Cambridge came to a similar end. How good he was in the field may be imagined from the following description given in *Wisden* of the catch which dismissed Allan Hill, the Yorkshire fast bowler, in the Gentlemen and Players match at Prince's in 1876. "The innings was ended at long-field-on by 'the catch of the season' made by Mr. Longman, who was then fielding at deep long-off, close up to the people in front of the new road in course of formation. With body bent back over some of the visitors, and right arm extended still farther over, he caught and held the ball with that right hand in such grand style that a roar of admiring cheers rang out, and all who witnessed it agreed it was the finest catch they had seen that season. It was hard lines for Hill to suffer defeat from so fine a drive but his consolation must be he suffered from a catch in a thousand." Longman himself described how "A. P. Lucas and I both went for it. I called out 'Mine' just in time to prevent a collision. The ball came fairly into my right hand."

After leaving the University he played cricket for Hampshire for some years. He joined the Surrey club in 1894, became

president in 1926, a position he held for three years, after which he exchanged offices with Mr. H. D. G. Leveson Gower, and remained hon. treasurer until his death, which came in his sleep. He played golf on the previous day.

LONGMAN, Lieut.-Col. Henry Kerr, who died on October 7, 1958, aged 77, was the son of the late G. H. Longman. Like his father, H. K. Longman played for Eton and Cambridge. In the Eton XI of 1899 and the two following years, he enjoyed considerable success against Harrow and Winchester as a batsman specially skilled in strokes in front of the wicket. In 1899 he shared in an opening partnership of 167 against Harrow at Lord's with F. O. Grenfell, who won the Victoria Cross and was killed in the First World War. Longman gained his Blue as a Freshman at Cambridge, scoring 27 and 34 in the University match of 1901 and hitting 150 from the Yorkshire bowling at Fenner's. He then took a Commission in the Army and afterwards played occasionally for Surrey and Middlesex. During the First World War he won the D.S.O. and M.C. and rose to the rank of Major in the Gordon Highlanders.

LONGRIGG, Edmund Fallowfield, who for 50 years rendered great service for Somerset cricket as a sound left-handed batsman, captain, chairman and president, died at his home in Bath on July 23, 1974, aged 68. Educated at Rugby, he was in the XI for four years, finishing as captain in 1925. He was a Cambridge Blue in 1927 and 1928 and he played for Somerset from 1925 to 1947.

Altogether in first-class cricket, Longrigg scored 9,416 runs, including 10 centuries for Somerset, average 24.64 and he held 134 catches. His best season was 1930, when he made 1,567 runs and hit 205 against Leicestershire at Taunton. A solicitor by profession, he did not play regularly between 1931 and 1937, but he captained Somerset in 1938, 1939 and 1946 when he led them to fourth position in the Championship and their best at that time since 1892. Longrigg served on several M.C.C. Committees and was a member of two sub-committees of the Test and County Cricket Board. A well-known golfer and county hockey player, he was an R.A.F. officer during the Second World War and for 18 years he was president of Frome R.A.F.A. He will be remembered for his unfailing courtesy, goodwill, and understanding, especially in some very heated county committee debates.

LORD, Albert, who died in March, 1969, aged 80, played as a professional batsman and occasional bowler for Leicestershire from 1912 to 1926. He scored 3,809 runs, including one century, took 39 wickets and held 67 catches.

LOUDEN, George Marshall, who died on December 28, 1972, aged 87, was a fine fast bowler from the Ilford club who played for Essex from 1912 to 1927. Of splendid physique and standing over 6 ft., he possessed a high easy action. During his first-class career he took 451 wickets at a cost of 22.35 runs each and held 50 catches. Never reckoned to be much of a batsman, he hit by far his highest innings, 74, against Sussex at Leyton, in 1913. His best season was that of 1919 when he dismissed 66 batsmen. He was a frequent member of Gentlemen's teams against Players at Lord's, the Oval, Scarborough and Folkestone between 1919 and 1923.

It was a pity he could not appear more often for his county, or more honours would probably have come his way. As it was, he never played for England. He might well have got his chance in 1921, when England fared so disastrously against the Australian team led by Warwick Armstrong and called upon no fewer than 30 players in the five Test matches. Sir Pelham Warner, writing later about the Test series, said that the omission of Louden had been a mistake.

LOUGHNAN, Austin, who died in the last week of October, 1926, had played for Victoria and been prominently associated with the Melbourne C.C. He was in the Stonyhurst XI in 1868 and 1869, and in the latter season it was written of him: "The neatest and most correct bat in the XI, his fine upright play and strong defence were the admiration of all; a distinctive medium-paced bowler and good coverpoint."

LOVE, H. S. B., who died from a heart attack in Sydney on July 22, 1969, aged 73, kept wicket for Victoria and New South Wales. "Hammy" Love played in one Test against England in 1932–33. W. A. Oldfield, having been struck on the head by a ball from H. Larwood during the third Test of D. R. Jardine's "body-line" tour, was unable to take part in the Test at Brisbane and Love acted as deputy. Earlier in the tour, Love, though not chosen even as 12th man, was permitted by Jardine to keep wicket for New South Wales when Oldfield fell ill, and he stumped two M.C.C. batsmen and caught one.

LOVE, Harry, who played sometimes for Sussex in 1892 and 1893, died at Hastings on March 27, 1942, aged 70.

LOVELOCK, Oswald H., who died in Perth on August 1, 1981, was a wicket-keeper and middle-order batsman who played 20 matches for Western Australia between 1932 and 1940, scoring 731 runs (average 27.07) and claiming 33 victims behind the stumps.

LOWE, Wing-Commander John Claude Malcolm, who died on July 27, 1970, aged 82, was in the Uppingham XI for three years from 1904 to 1906, being captain in the last season. A fast-medium bowler who was able to make the ball swerve appreciably, he gained his Blue as a Freshman at Oxford and also took part in the University matches of the next two seasons; but loss of form cost him his place in 1910. He was also a hockey Blue and a good golfer. He played for Warwickshire in 1907.

LOWE, William Walter, died at Hartley Witney on May 26, 1945, aged 72. In the Malvern XI, 1890–93, he got his Cambridge Blue in 1895, and, taking five wickets for 48 runs with his right-hand fast bowling in the Oxford second innings, contributed largely to a victory by 134 runs, despite a great innings of 121 by H. K. Foster, his school contemporary. For Worcestershire from 1898 to 1911 Lowe showed useful all-round form and was a member of Frank Mitchell's XI in America, 1895. A Cambridge association Blue in 1895–96, he often played for Corinthians. For some years a master at Malvern.

LOWNDES, William Geoffrey Lowndes Frith, died at Newbury on May 23, 1982, aged 84. A member of the Eton XI in 1915 and 1916, he got a place in the strong Oxford batting side of 1921, of which he was the last survivor. He was a late choice. Playing for the Free Foresters against the University in the last match but one of the term, he scored 29 and 21 and took three wickets, with the result that he was picked for the next match against the Army. An innings of 88 secured him a further trial and he clinched his place by making 52 at Hove and 216 against H. D. G. Leveson Gower's XI at Eastbourne, where he and H. P. Ward put on 218 in just over 90 minutes. Though he failed at Lord's, he finished second in the University averages. He first appeared for Hampshire in

1924, but played little more first-class cricket until he was persuaded to succeed the Hon. L. H. Tennyson as captain of the county in 1934. Though the side, then in a state of transition, did not meet with great success, he was a popular captain and had no reason to be dissatisfied with his own efforts. He made three centuries, the most notable being 140 against the 1934 Australians. On this occasion he reached his 100 in 75 minutes and with Mead added 247 in under three hours for the fourth wicket. In 1935 he made 118 before lunch against Kent in two hours on the first day of the season, but scored very few runs thereafter and resigned at the end of the year. In fact, he found a full season's cricket rather more than he wanted, and in neither of his years as captain did he play in more than two-thirds of the matches. He was a natural cricketer: an attacking batsman and a particularly fine driver, at his best on fast wickets; a useful fast-medium away-swinger, who sometimes took the new ball and might perhaps have used himself more; and a good mid-off. In his attitude to the game he was typical of the amateur of his own and earlier periods—to him it was fun and he tried to make it fun for others.

LOWRY, Thomas Coleman, who died at Hastings, New Zealand, on July 20, 1976, was born at Wellington, New Zealand, on February 2, 1898. The importance of this fact lies in the tradition that his sole qualification for Somerset in later years was, as P. R. Johnson's had been before him, "born at Wellington." He was at school at Christ's College, served in the R.F.C. at the end of the First World War and, going up to Cambridge in 1921 made 183 in the Freshmen's match, but neither in that year nor the next did he get his Blue, although in both seasons he did valuable work for Somerset when term was ended. So strong was Cambridge cricket then that, if one looks at the 1921 side, it is impossible to see who could have been left out for him.

In the winter of 1922 he went with Mac-Laren's side to Australia and New Zealand. In 1923 an innings of 161 against Lancashire in the first match scored in two hours, 50 minutes made his place in the Cambridge side secure; he got over 1,000 runs for the University and played for the Gentlemen at Lord's. After captaining Cambridge in 1924 he went back to New Zealand, but returned in 1927 and again in 1931 to captain the first two New Zealand sides in England.

An outstanding captain, he aimed at winning, not drawing, insisted on absolute punctuality and abhorred waste of time. On both tours he was one of the team's most reliable bats. In 1937 he came again, this time as manager to play when wanted, and an innings of 121 in 105 minutes against Nottinghamshire showed that he was still worth a place. Altogether he hit 18 first-class 100s. A very strong man, he was a thorough cricketer—a fine attacking bat, always at his best in a crisis, a splendid field close to the wicket, a competent wicket-keeper if required, and a useful slow bowler, who was not afraid to give the ball plenty of air. In later life he was President of the New Zealand Cricket Council. One of his sisters married R. H. Bettington, another A. P. F. Chapman.

LOWRY, William Chalkley, born on June 11, 1860, died at Moorestown, N.J., on June 29, 1919. An excellent slow bowler, he played for Haverford College, the Gentlemen of Philadelphia, and the United States. For many years he played with success with the Merion C.C. During his visit to England in 1884, when he took 110 wickets for 12.79 runs each, his bowling was the feature of the tour.

LOWSON, Frank Anderson, died at Pool-in-Wharfedale on September 8, 1984, aged 59. In a career of only 10 years he made 15,321 runs with an average of 37.18, including 31 centuries, and played in seven Tests. Few players have made a better start. Trained in the Yorkshire League, he played his first match for Yorkshire in May 1949 against Cambridge and made 78. Within a month he had opened in a Test trial and scored 64. At the end of the season his record was 1,799 runs with an average of 35.98, which, with only one century, 104 against Middlesex at Sheffield, showed rare consistency. In his second season his aggregate was 2,152 and his average 42.19. In 1951 he was picked for the fourth and fifth Tests against South Africa and at Leeds scored 58, putting on 99 with Hutton for the first wicket. That winter he went with MCC to India and Pakistan, but, though he scored over 1,000 runs, he was a disappointment in the Tests. His last Test match was against South Africa at Leeds in 1955: he was unlucky to be called on at the last moment when he was himself out of form to deputise for Watson, who was injured, and he did nothing. However, he made 1,000 runs that year for the seventh time running and did so again in 1956. In 1957 he was batting well when leg trouble ended his cricket for the summer in mid-June. In 1958 he never refound his form, and after being left out of the side was not re-engaged at the end of the season.

Slightly built, he was a stroker of the ball rather than a striker: yet his highest score, 259 not out against Worcestershire at Worcester in 1953, though it took almost six hours, include 36 fours. At a time when there was a predominance of in-swing and off-breaks, he was especially strong on the leg, but he had all the strokes and, when opportunity offered, could cut and drive as well as anyone. Technically very correct, he was a good player of the moving and turning ball. He was perhaps unlucky that his opening partner through almost the whole of his career was Hutton, for he was inevitably over-shadowed. The crowd had come to see Ajax the Great, not Ajax the Less. On the other hand he must have learned technical lessons from studying, at such close quarters, so great a player. Given more physical strength and a little more fire, Lowson could have reached greater heights than he did. An adequate field, he eventually made himself an expert close catcher in the leg trap to bowlers such as Appleyard. After retiring from first-class cricket he made a successful career in insurance.

LOWTH, The Rev. Alfred James, who was born at Grove House, Chiswick, on July 20, 1817, died at Winchester on February 5, 1907, being at the time senior Wykehamist. He was left-handed both as batsman and bowler, but did not continue the game long after taking Holy Orders. *Scores and Biographies* (ii–278) states that his delivery was "round-armed, fast, with a beautiful, easy delivery." He played for Winchester from 1834 to 1836, for Gentlemen v. Players in 1836 and 1841, and for Oxford against Cambridge in 1838, 1840 and 1841. For Winchester against Harrow, in 1835, he took 10 wickets and scored 23 in each innings and in the same year bowled down eight wickets in the first innings, of Eton. In the three matches in which he played against Cambridge he obtained 24 wickets, his most successful appearance being that of 1840, when he took 11, and when he was, curiously enough, on the losing side for the only time. It is testimony to his greatness that in 1836 a deputation from the M.C.C. went down to Winchester to see him bowl and, as a result, asked him to assist the Gentlemen against the Players at Lord's. He accepted the invitation and took nine wickets. Mr. Lowth was at Eton from 1826 to 1828, but was elected to a scholarship at Winchester in 1829. He was one of a family of 13, and grandson of the

Right Rev. Robert Lowth, Bishop of London.

LUBBOCK, Alfred, died at Kilmarth Manor, Par, Cornwall, on July 17, 1916. Cricketers whose memories go back to the early '70's will recall Alfred Lubbock as one of the greatest batsmen of those days. Mr. Lubbock had a short career in first-class cricket, practically giving up the game before he was 28, but so long as he appeared in public he was in the very front rank. There were no Test matches in his time, but in his best seasons he would have had every right to play for England. Indeed, it was for England against Middlesex at Lord's, in 1867, that he made his highest score in a big match—129. W. G. Grace, then a lad of under 19, was on the same side, and scored 75. There was something appropriate in the two young men doing so well together. In the pages of *Scores and Biographies*, it is stated that, with the exception, perhaps, of W. G. Grace himself, no one ever did so much with the bat up to the age of 20 as Alfred Lubbock. This is a sweeping claim, but there is abundant evidence to support it.

Lubbock was in the Eton XI for three seasons, captaining the side in 1863. Bearing in mind the comparatively small scoring at that time, it is safe to say that in the whole history of Eton cricket his batting for the school in 1863 has never been surpassed. He scored 174 not out against Winchester, nought and 80 against Harrow, and he had, if one remembers rightly, an average of 58. Even R. A. H. Mitchell—generally regarded as the best of all Eton batsmen—never had a school season so brilliant. Leaving Eton before he was 18, Lubbock played a little first-class cricket in the next three years, but did nothing exceptional. In club matches, however, he made hundreds of runs, playing in 1866 an innings of 220 against the Royal Engineers. Then in 1867 he revealed his full powers against the best bowling, following up his 129 for England at Lord's with 107 not out for Gentlemen against Players at the Oval. For the moment he threatened to be W. G. Grace's most formidable rival. In subsequent years, however, he was not seen very often, but whenever he cared to play he was sure of his place in the Gentlemen's XI at Lord's. He was, indeed, one of those rarely gifted batsmen who could at any time step into a big match and play as well as if he had been in full practice for months. He finished with Gentlemen and Players matches in 1871, failing in the wonderful match that C. E. Green won for the Gentlemen at the Oval, but scoring 42 and 21 against George Freeman's bowling at Lord's and nought and 41 in John Lillywhite's benefit match at Brighton. Altogether he played eight times for the Gentlemen between 1866 and 1871, scoring 396 runs, with an average of 30—a very fine record at that time.

Alfred Lubbock was a member of the team that R. A. FitzGerald took to Canada and the United States in the autumn of 1872, and in *Wickets in the West*—FitzGerald's account of the tour—there are many references to him. In those vivacious pages he is always spoken of as Alfred the Great. The travelling team played a match at Lord's in 1873 against Fourteen of the M.C.C., with Rylott. In that match—his last at Lord's, or, at any rate, his last of any consequence—Lubbock showed that his skill as a batsman had in no way left him. Getting 46 not out, he kept nearly all the bowling to himself, scoring six or seven times from the last ball of the over—a remarkable feat with 15 men in the field.

Those who remember Alfred Lubbock in his great days will agree that no batsman was better worth looking at. For grace of style he held his own with the first Tom Hayward, Richard Daft, and C. F. Buller. An enthusiastic American critic said of him that he carried batting into the region of the fine arts. In the field he was very brilliant at long leg and cover point. Born in London on October 31, 1845, Alfred Lubbock was in his 71st year.—S.H.P.

LUBBOCK, Edgar, LL.D., a younger brother of Mr. Alfred Lubbock, was born in London on February 22, 1847, and died at 18, Hans Court, Chelsea, on September 9, 1907. He was in the Eton XI in 1864 and two following years, and in 1872 visited America as a member of Mr. R. A. FitzGerald's team. Only once—against M.C.C., at Canterbury, in 1871—did he appear for Kent, and as he then scored 11 and 54 it is surprising that he never assisted the county again. He was a right-handed batsman with an awkward style, and bowled left underhand fast. He had been a member of the M.C.C. since 1869.

LUBBOCK, Sir Nevile, K.C.M.G., the third son of Sir John William Lubbock, Bart., F.R.S., and a member of the well-known cricketing brotherhood, died very suddenly at Oakley, Bromley Common, in Kent, on September 12, 1914. Born in London on March 31, 1839, he was in his 76th year. He left Eton too young to be in the XI, but was a good steady batsman, and usually fielded at point, and was associated with F. H. Norman as keeper of "Sixpenny." In 1860 he appeared in two matches for Kent, scoring 24 runs with an average of eight. His life and work were devoted chiefly to West Indian interests.

LUCAS, Alfred Perry, died at his home at Great Waltham, on Friday, October 12, 1923. Though his career in the cricket field began half a century ago, Mr. Lucas played so long—he captained the M.C.C. at Lord's against the Australian XI of 1902, and played his last match for Essex in 1907—that his doings will be fresh in remembrance. He was one of the finest of batsmen—almost unique in his combination of perfect style and impregnable defence. As regards the early development of his powers he belonged to a very select band. Like Mr. R. A. H. Mitchell, Mr. Alfred Lubbock, Mr. C. F. Buller, Mr. A. J. Webbe, and, in later days, Mr. MacLaren and Mr. Spooner, he was good enough while still at school to play for the Gentlemen. One is thinking only of public school batsmen. Mr. W. G. Grace—outside all comparisons—actually played for the Gentlemen at Lord's before he was 17, and had no small share in winning the match. Mr. Lucas did not appear for Gentlemen v. Players as a schoolboy, but he came very near it. In 1874—the year he left Uppingham—he was picked for the Gentlemen of the South against the Players of the North at Prince's, and scored 48 and 23. His form in those two innings—against Alfred Shaw and Morley at their best—left no doubt as to his class. It was felt by all good judges that a new star had been discovered. Mr. Lucas had been most carefully coached at Uppingham by H. H. Stephenson—he was by far the best of all Stephenson's pupils—and throughout his career he never tired of saying how much he owed to his teacher. When he jumped into fame at Prince's, Mr. Lucas was under $17\frac{1}{2}$; to be quite exact he was born on February 20, 1857. He never looked back. Going up to Clare College, Cambridge, he won his Blue as a Freshman and was in the XI for four years—1875 to 1878. He shared in all the other victories of the great team of 1878, but illness kept him out of the crowning triumph at Lord's against the first Australian XI. In his four matches against Oxford he was twice on the winning and twice on the losing side, his own record being wonderfully good. His scores in the four matches were 19 and five; 67 and not out 23, 54 and eight, four and 74. In the Cambridge averages Mr. Lucas was fourth in 1875 with 23, first in 1876 with 50 and first again in 1877 with 33, but in 1878, despite his success in the big match, he dropped to the sixth place and averaged only 20.

In County Cricket Mr. Lucas had a varied experience. He came out in 1874 for Surrey, played some years later for Middlesex, and finally in 1889, with the view of helping his life-long friend, Mr. C. E. Green, threw in his lot with Essex. While in his prime he was chosen, as a matter of course, year after year for Gentlemen v. Players. In these matches he played some of his best cricket, scoring 91 at Lord's in 1878 and 107 in 1882.

For England against Australia he appeared four times—at the Oval in 1880 and 1882 and at Manchester and Lord's in 1884. Possibly he could recall nothing in his career more vividly than the last innings of the disastrous match at the Oval in 1882 when England, after seeming certain of victory, lost by seven runs. He stopped any number of Mr. Spofforth's terrible break-backs, but at last played one of them on to his wicket. The misfortune was that, while showing such superb defence, he could not relieve the tension by a hit to the boundary.

Mr. Lucas was in the truest sense of the word a classic batsman. A master of both back and forward play, he represented the strictest orthodoxy. No doubt if he had allowed himself a little licence he might have made more runs, but his method served him so well that right into middle age he kept up his form. It may fairly be said of him that no defensive batsman of any generation was more worth looking at. He played the ball so hard and his style was so irreproachable that one could watch him for hours without a moment of weariness. Having played against all the great Australian bowlers from Spofforth and Frank Allan to Hugh Trumble, he thought Spofforth and George Palmer the best of them. Mr. Lucas was not much of a traveller, but he went to Australia with Lord Harris's team in 1878–79. During that tour he had to do far more bowling than he had expected, the side being almost wholly dependent on Emmett and George Ulyett. How with such limited resources they ever managed to get their opponents out remains to this day a marvel.

This notice of Mr. Lucas appeared, almost as it stands, in *The Times*.—S.H.P.

Mr. Lucas's best scores in first-class cricket were as under:

145	For England v. Cambridge University, at Cambridge	1882
142	For Gentlemen of England v. Cambridge University, at Cambridge	1881
135	For Essex v. Somerset, at Taunton	1895
115	For Surrey v. Notts, at the Oval	1877
110	For Surrey v. Kent, at Maidstone	1877
107	For Gentlemen v. Players, at Lord's	1882
105	For Cambridge University v. England, at Cambridge	1876
103	For Essex v. Derbyshire, at Leyton	1902
97	For Middlesex v. Gloucestershire, at Lord's	1883
95	For Cambridge University v. M.C.C., at Lord's	1877
91	For Gentlemen v. Players, at Lord's	1878
90	For Cambridge University v. Gentlemen of England, at Cambridge	1877

LUCAS, Charles James, of Warnham Court, Horsham, born at Clapham, in Surrey, on February 25, 1853, died in London on April 17, 1928. He was a member of the well-known cricketing family—brother of Messrs. M.P., H.T., and F.M. Lucas. According to *Scores and Biographies* "A good batsman, bowls fast round-armed, and in the field prefers mid-wicket off." For Middlesex he played twice in 1876 and once in 1877 and for Sussex he appeared in eight matches between 1880 and 1882. He was a member of the Lucas Family XI which took the field at Horsham.

LUCAS, Morton Peto, who was born at Clapham on November 24, 1856, died in London on July 9, 1921, having been taken ill whilst attending the Eton v. Harrow match the day before. He was educated at Harrow and Cambridge, but, although quite a useful cricketer, was not in either XI. Between 1877 and 1890 he appeared in 23 matches for Sussex, making 837 runs, with an average of 20.41, and taking seven wickets for 33 runs each. Against Hampshire at Brighton in 1881 he scored 131, and on the same ground that year took part in the Gentlemen v. Players match, won by the latter by one run after the game had been a tie on the first innings. Subsequently he was seen occasionally in the Warwickshire XI, having qualified for that county by residence at Leamington. Probably the innings of which he felt most proud in his career was 66 for Sussex against the

Australians at Brighton in 1880. Palmer and Boyle at that time were at the top of their bowling form.

LUCAS, Robert Slade, who died on January 5, 1942, aged 74, was a valuable batsman for Middlesex during 10 years at the end of last century. Perhaps his best innings in first-class cricket was 97 against Surrey at the Oval in 1894, when Lockwood and Richardson were at the top of their form. Next season he was good enough to play in every match for the powerful Middlesex batting side. His highest innings came in a heavy scoring match at Hove in June 1895. The aggregate amounted to 1,259 for 28 wickets, a high figure at that time. Lucas made 185, and with T. C. O'Brien (202) put on 338 at the rate of 100 runs an hour for the fifth wicket; the Middlesex total reached 566. That season he played for Gentlemen against Players at the Oval. R. S. Lucas went to America with Lord Hawke's team in the autumn of 1894, and he captained the first English team that visited West Indies. In a remarkable match during that tour, Barbados in their first innings scored 517 and gained a lead of 206; but the touring side won by 25 runs. Prominent for Richmond and Teddington in London club cricket, Lucas also played for Old Merchant Taylors', and in 1891, in a not-out innings of 141 at Charterhouse Square against the school, which he had captained in 1885, he hit the ball out of the ground seven times, twice in succession through the same window of a private house. He played hockey for England.

LUCKES, Walter Thomas, who died at Bridgwater on October 27, 1982, aged 81, kept wicket for Somerset from 1924 to 1949. When he first appeared, the bulk of the keeping was done by M. D. Lyon and M. L. Hill, and it was not till 1927 that Luckes (pronounced Luckies) gained a regular place. Hardly had he done so than his career was nearly terminated by ill-health. In 1929 and 1930 he could play little, in 1931 not at all, and it was not until part way through 1932 that he was fit to resume his place. Condemned then by the doctors to bat at No. 11, he came second in the batting averages, mainly owing to 15 not out innings. However, one of these was 58 against Yorkshire. As far back as 1927, an innings of 45 against McDonald at his best had shown what he could do, and later, in his benefit year, 1937, being allowed for some reason to go in at No. 5 against Kent at Bath, he made 121 not out, driving in great form. For the most part,

however, he had to resign himself to causing unwelcome delay to the opposition just when they thought the innings was as good as over. As a wicket-keeper he ranked high, higher indeed than the general public ever realised. Quiet in method and, except in appealing, wholly undemonstrative, he made the job look so easy that only the experts or those out in the middle could see how often he brought off as a matter of course what was in fact a brilliant catch or stumping. To others he might seem only one who seldom made an obvious mistake. Fortunately, after 1932 he suffered no interruptions on account of his health and it was only in 1949, when he was 48, that he made way for Stephenson. His first-class cricket was confined to Somerset, for whom he caught 586 batsmen and stumped 241, besides making 5,640 runs with an average of 16.02.

LUCKIE, Martin Maxwell Fleming, O.B.E., a Wellington cricketer and civic administrator, died at Wellington, New Zealand, on July 2, 1951, aged 83. He played lower grade cricket when his senior days were over and did not retire from active play until he was 70 years old. He was a useful left-arm slow bowler. Mr. Luckie gave splendid service as President of the Wellington Cricket Association and President of the Wellington C.C., for whom he played between 1891 and 1913. The Wellington City Council named a park, with playing fields for cricket and football, after him.

LUCKIN, Maurice William, died at Johannesburg on March 8, 1937, aged 61. Born in Essex, he went to South Africa in 1895 and in 1910–11 played for Transvaal in the Currie Cup tournament. He was best known for compiling *The History of South African Cricket* (which covered the period 1876 to 1914) and *South African Cricket, 1919–27*. From 1914 to 1918 he was secretary of the South African Cricket Association.

LUFF, Henry ("Harry"), proprietor of *Wisden's Cricketers' Almanack* and of the firm of Messrs. John Wisden & Co., of Cranbourn Street, died on July 18, 1910. Born at Petersfield, in Hampshire, on January 26, 1856, Mr. Luff was in his 55th year at the time of his death. For some time his health had been precarious, and although he benefited to some extent by a visit to Australia during the winter of 1907–08, the improvement was only temporary, and last year he suffered another breakdown which proved to be the beginning of the end. For many years he acted as secretary of the Cricketers' Fund Friendly Society, and only within a fortnight of his death did he resign the position.

DE LUGO, Señor Anthony Benitez, Marquis de Santa Lusana, a well-known member of the Surrey County C.C., died at Pau on March 16, 1907, aged about 50. He was author of three booklets published in Madrid for private circulation—*Surrey at the Wicket, 1844–1887. The Surrey Champion: A Complete Record of W. W. Read's Performances, 1873–1894,* and *A Summary of Surrey Cricket, 1844–1899.*

LUGTON, Lance-Corpl. Frank (Australian Expeditionary Force), killed July 29, 1916, aged 22. Northcote C.C., of Melbourne; for Victoria v. Tasmania, at Launceston, in March, 1914, he scored 94 not out and 20. For Victoria that season his batting figures gave him an aggregate of 218 runs and an average of 31; and he took nine wickets for 34.11 runs each.

LUMB, Edward, of Huddersfield, died on April 5, 1891, aged 38. Owing to delicate health Mr. Lumb had for several seasons fallen out of public matches, but at one time he was one of the best-known amateurs in Yorkshire. During the season of 1883 he played with great success for the county, and seemed likely to prove a most valuable acquisition to the team, but unfortunately he was soon afterwards compelled by the state of his health to give up cricket. At his best he was an admirable batsman of the defensive school, and was seen to the utmost advantage against fast bowling.

LUPTON, Major Arthur William, died suddenly at Carlton Manor, Yeadon, near Leeds, on April 14, 1944. The unusual experience fell to him of captaining a county for the first time when 46 years of age, and he celebrated the notable choice of the Yorkshire club by leading them in 1925 to their fourth consecutive Championship. He retained the office for two more years and altogether scored 668 runs with an average of 10.27, but did not take a wicket. Yorkshire were not champions again until 1931. Lupton was a fast bowler and free left-handed batsman at Sedbergh School and he played once for the county in 1908. Born on February 23, 1879, he died in his 66th year.

LUSK, Harold Butler, who died on February 14, 1961, aged 84, represented New Zealand against Melbourne C.C. in 1906 and the Australians in 1910. Making his first Plunket Shield appearance in 1899, he played for Auckland, Canterbury and Wellington before retiring in 1921. He was New Zealand golf champion in 1910.

LUTHER, Major A. C. G., who died in June, 1961, aged 80, was a member of the Rugby XI in 1897 and 1898. He later played for the Army, Yorkshire Gentlemen and Sussex. He was at one time Secretary of Berkshire County C.C. and assistant secretary at the Oval. At racquets, he won the Army Singles in 1911 and 1913, the Army Doubles in 1912 and 1914 and was runner-up in both the Amateur Singles and Doubles in 1907.

LYLE, Capt. Robert Charles, M.C., died on September 27, 1943, aged 56. Sporting Editor of *The Times,* he reported all games and made a great name as racing correspondent. At Felsted School he played cricket with some success, but showed his best skill in the hockey field, as he did when at Corpus Christi College, Cambridge, until concentrating more on golf. During the First World War he served with the R.A.S.C. in France and was awarded the M.C. and Bar. In the Second World War he acted as war correspondent with the Royal Navy in the Mediterranean until invalided home in June 1941. Having recovered, he continued his energetic journalism until death occurred suddenly at his home.

LYNN, George Henry, who died suddenly on September 21, 1921, aged 73, played for Sussex six times in 1872 and twice in 1873, scoring 128 runs with an average of 9.84 and taking one wicket for eight runs. He was born at East Grinstead on March 31, 1848.

LYON, Beverley Hamilton, who died on June 22, 1970, aged 68, was one of the most astute captains of his era. Of Surrey birth, he was in the Rugby XI in 1917 and 1918, heading the batting averages in the second year, when his highest innings was 98 not out and he represented Lord's Schools against The Rest. Going up to Oxford in 1920, he gained a Blue in 1922 but failed to score in either innings in the University match, which Cambridge won by an innings and 100 runs. On the big occasion the following season, he gained some recompense, for although he scored no more than 14, an immensely powerful Oxford team this time triumphed in two days with an innings and 227 runs to spare.

In 1921, Lyon began his association with Gloucestershire. He became captain in 1929, a position which he filled for four seasons, and under his inspiring influence the county enjoyed greater success than for many years. T. W. Goddard, whose services as a fast bowler had been dispensed with by Gloucestershire, had joined the ground-staff at Lord's and become an off-break exponent. Lyon recalled him to the county and between them Goddard and the left-arm C. W. L. Parker developed into the most effective spin-bowling combination in the Championship.

Lyon also played his part as a hard-hitting batsman. He hit 1,397 runs, including three centuries, in 1929 for an average of over 33 and next season obtained 1,355 runs, average 41.00. In 1930 he hit two of his total of 16 centuries—115 and 101 not out—in the match with Essex at Bristol, and he enjoyed the distinction of helping his county to a tie with W. M. Woodfull's Australian team.

Lyon, known as an apostle of brighter cricket, was revolutionary in his cricket outlook. He was the originator in 1931 of the scheme by which a declaration by each side with only four byes scored in the first innings enabled maximum points to be available to the winning county after the loss of the opening two days of a Championship match through rain. This caused the Advisory County Cricket Committee to revise the regulations.

In all first-class cricket, Lyon made 10,615 runs for an average of 25.15, four times exceeding 1,000 runs in a season. He was also an excellent fieldsman, either at short-leg or in the slips.

He was the first to suggest first-class county games on Sundays, an idea which it took 36 years for the authorities to adopt. He also advanced the scheme for a knock-out competition, which came into being over 30 years afterwards.

His elder brother, M. D. Lyon, preceded him in the team at Rugby, got his Blue for two years at Cambridge and also assisted Somerset.

There was no funeral for Beverley Lyon, for he bequeathed his body to the Royal College of Surgeons.

LYON, Admiral Sir George H. D'Oyly, K.C.B., died at Midhurst, Sussex, on August 20, 1947, aged 63. He played cricket for Royal Navy and a little for Hampshire. At Rugby football he played for United Services, the Navy, and for England in 1908 and 1909. He was very good at tennis and golf.

LYON, George Seymour, who died at Toronto on May 11, 1938, in his 80th year, played for Canada against Frank Mitchell's University team in 1895, also against United States, and in other representative matches. In 1894 he created a Canadian record by scoring 238 not out for Rosedale against Peterborough and in the same match took five wickets for 17 runs. In 1896 he scored 1,075 runs, average 53.75. A splendid golf player he won the Canadian Amateur Championship eight times between 1898 and 1914 while he gained the Canadian Senior title five years consecutively from 1918.

LYON, Malcolm Douglas, who died after a long illness at Hastings on February 17, 1964, aged 65, was one of the best-known amateur cricketers of his time and, indeed, was considered by many to be among the best batsmen who never gained a cap for England. Brother of B. H. Lyon, for so long captain of Gloucestershire, "Dar" Lyon was in the Rugby XI from 1914 to 1916, being captain the last year when he hit 77 and 45 not out in the game with Malvern and also played for Lord's Schools against The Rest. Going up to Cambridge, he kept wicket in the University matches of 1921 and 1922, being on the winning side on each occasion. He attracted the attention of Somerset before receiving his Blue and his career with the county extended from 1920 to 1935. During that time he scored 6,506 runs, including 14 centuries, at an average of 30.68 and helped in the dismissal of 169 batsmen, 128 caught and 41 stumped. His highest innings was 219 for Somerset against Derbyshire at Burton-on-Trent in 1924 and he took 210 from the Gloucestershire bowling at Taunton in 1930. This latter innings, scored out of a total of 372, occupied him three hours and 50 minutes and included three sixes and 23 fours. His driving, as always, was superb on that occasion. Attack was his watchword, as he showed in one of his best-remembered displays. That was when he hit 136 against the 1926 Australians at Taunton, a brilliant innings in the course of which that great Australian slow bowler, C. V. Grimmett, came in for specially heavy punishment.

As a wicket-keeper, Lyon could reach the highest class, but his nonchalant outlook prevented him from being consistent and could well have resulted in him being passed over for Test honours. He appeared for Gentlemen against Players in six matches between 1923 and 1930. In the first, at Lord's, he distinguished himself by making 120 against an attack comprising H. Howell,

M. W. Tate, C. H. Parkin, R. Kilner, J. W. Hearne and F. E. Woolley, he and G. T. S. Stevens (122) putting on 219 for the second wicket.

Called to the Bar in 1925, Lyon was appointed as a magistrate in Gambia in 1932 and he did not again play for his county till 1935. Then, against Middlesex at Lord's, he was twice dismissed without scoring and that ended his first-class career. After service in the Second World War, he became Resident Magistrate in Kenya from 1945 to 1948; from then till 1957 he was Chief Justice, Seychelles, and afterwards till 1961 Puisne Judge, Uganda.

A mistake has been pointed out in *Wisden* for 1965, where it states in the obituaries that M. D. Lyon's last appearance for Somerset was in 1935. In fact, having returned to England, he played throughout the season of 1938, though, not surprisingly after so long an absence from regular first-class cricket, was a shadow of his former self. He did, however, play a valuable innings of 122 not out against Northamptonshire at Frome. His figures for his career should read 7,294 runs with an average of 29.18, and he made 14 hundreds.

LYONS, Aidan T., the best all-round cricketer of the Eastern Province, died at Queenstown on February 12, 1910, at the early age of 31. He was a good batsman, a fast-medium right-hand bowler, and a sound captain. For just over 10 years he played with success against visiting teams and in Currie Cup matches.

LYONS, John James, born at Gawler, in South Australia, on May 21, 1863, died in Adelaide on July 21, 1927, aged 64. He visited this country on three occasions—in 1888, 1890, and 1893. Those whose cricket memories go back over 30 years will remember him as a very fine hitter indeed. He was not, perhaps, so famous as George Bonnor, nor did he have the same capacity for scoring on all sorts of wickets as Percy McDonnell. In fact, when the ball was turning he generally proved an easy victim to a spin bowler. On a hard, true wicket, however, he was a most dangerous bat, and likely to demoralise the best of bowlers. Before coming here first he had established his reputation, and in the winter of 1891–92 he played an innings of 134 in a Test match at Sydney against Lord Sheffield's team, captained by W. G. Grace. It was in 1893 that people in England saw him at his best, when in all matches he had an aggregate of 1,605, a highest score of 149, and an average of over 28. He again headed the batting in representative matches, 23 innings yielding him 761 runs and an average of 33. In May, 1893, at Lord's, Lyons played probably the most brilliant innings of his career. The Australians had to go in a second time against a powerful M.C.C. team 181 runs behind. Yet these were hit off before a wicket fell by Lyons and Alec Bannerman, and of this number Lyons obtained no fewer than 149. At such a terrific pace did he score that he completed his 100 in an hour, with the total at 124. The strokes of Lyons's innings were 22 fours, three threes, 20 twos, and only 12 singles, and to this day people who saw that day's play describe his batting as the greatest display of fast-footed driving ever given at Lord's.

His chief innings in great matches in Australia were:

101	The Australian Team v. New South Wales, at Sydney	1888–89
134	South Australia v. Victoria, at Adelaide	1889–90
104	South Australia v. Victoria, at Adelaide	1891–92
145	South Australia v. New South Wales, at Sydney	1891–92
134	Australia v. England, at Sydney	1891–92
124	South Australia v. New South Wales, at Adelaide	1892–93
101	South Australia v. Victoria, at Adelaide	1893–94
135	South Australia v. Victoria, at Melbourne	1894–95
110	South Australia v. Victoria, at Melbourne	1896–97
113	South Australia v. Victoria, at Adelaide	1896–97

Among his best free-hitting displays were the following:

99 out of 117 in 75 mins., v. M.C.C., at Lord's		1890
55 out of 66 in 45 mins., v. England, at Lord's		1890
53 out of 64 in 45 mins., South Australia v. Victoria, at Melbourne		1890–91
51 out of 64 in 50 mins., Australia v. England, at Melbourne		1891–92
134 out of 175 in 2¾ hours, Test v. England, at Sydney		1891–92
149 out of 181 in 90 mins., v. M.C.C., at Lord's		1893
75 out of 102 in 70 mins., v. North, at Manchester		1893
83 out of 117 in 100 mins., v. M.C.C., at Lord's (return)		1893

Lyons's batting overshadowed the rest of his cricket but he was at times distinctly useful as a bowler. Against one of the English teams at Adelaide in 1887–88 he took seven wickets for 94 runs for South Australia, and in the Test match at Lord's in 1890 he had an analysis of five for 30 besides being chief scorer for his side with 55 and 33. As a benefit he received part proceeds of the match between South Australia and New South Wales at Adelaide in 1925–26, when, from all sources, the sum realised was £1,252.

LYTTELTON, The Rev. The Hon. Albert Victor, born in London on June 29, 1844, died there of influenza on April 4, 1928, aged 83. He was a member of the famous cricketing brotherhood, and but for illness would probably have been in the Eton XI of 1861.

He was summed up as "A good average batsman, field and thrower, besides being a middle-paced round-armed bowler." He played for Worcestershire, and also for the Lyttelton XI, which beat Bromsgrove School at Hagley in 1867.

LYTTELTON, The Hon. Alfred, K.C., was born in London on February 7, 1857, and died after a brief illness, following an operation, on July 5, 1913. As fitting tribute is paid to Alfred Lyttelton below by the Earl of Darnley—his colleague in the Cambridge XI in 1878 and 1879—it will be sufficient here to give briefly the chief facts of his remarkable career. He was one of those cricketers about whose greatness there was never any question. From his school days he seemed destined to take a very high place. He was in the Eton XI from 1872 to 1875, and in the Cambridge XI from 1876 to 1879, finishing up in each case as captain. The best amateur wicket-keeper of his day, he was picked for Gentlemen against Players at Lord's in his first year at Cambridge and he kept wicket for England against Australia at the Oval in 1880 and 1882 and at Lord's and the Oval in 1884. As a batsman he represented, in its highest development, the forward style of play taught by Mr. R. A. H. Mitchell at Eton. Owing to the claims of his work at the Bar, he gave up first-class cricket when he was little more than 28. He played his last match for Middlesex in 1887. He was President of the Marylebone Club in 1898, and served on the Committee from 1881 to 1885, and from 1899 to 1903. Apart from his cricket Mr. Lyttelton was the best amateur tennis player of his time, excelled also at racquets, and played for England at Association football. No one, perhaps, has ever had a greater all-round genius for ball games. A few statistics of his cricket career are appended.

His 100s in first-class cricket were:

101	M.C.C. v. Lancashire, at Lord's					1877
100	Middlesex v. Notts, at Nottingham	..	..	..	..	1877
102	Middlesex v. Notts, at Nottingham	..	..	..	..	1879
120	Gents. of England v. Gents. of Kent, at Canterbury	..	..	..	..	1880
115	XI of England v. Camb. Univ., at Cambridge	..	..	..	..	1883
181	Middlesex v. Gloucestershire, at Clifton	..	..	..	..	1883
103	Gents. of England v. Camb. Univ., at Cambridge	..	..	..	..	1883

He made his 101 at Lord's in 1877 out of 158 while in, the next highest score of the innings being Wheeler's 15. One six and 21 fours were included in his big score at Clifton, when he and I. D. Walker (145) added 324 for the second wicket.

His scores in the University match were:

1876	..	..	43 & 47	
1877	..	..	4 & 6	234 runs, aver. 33.42
1878	..	..	5 & 64	
1879	..	..	53 & 12*	

For Middlesex, 1877–87, he made 1,656 runs with an aver. of 27.15
For Camb. Univ., 1876–79, he made 1,224 runs with an aver. of 29.14
For Gentlemen v. Players, he made 269 runs with an aver. of 18.21
In all first-class cricket, he made 4,432 runs with an aver. of 27.87
For Gentlemen v. Players, at the Oval, in 1877, he caught six and st. one.

A TRIBUTE TO ALFRED LYTTELTON

By the Earl of Darnley

Having been asked by Mr. Pardon to write a few lines in memory of my old friend and playmate of former years, Mr. Alfred Lyttelton, my recollection travels back some 41 years to the summer of 1872, when as a lower boy in my first half at Eton, I waited on him, the guest of my fagmaster, Mr. Evan Hanbury, at Mr. Joynes' house, and attended to him, I have no doubt, with all the respect and hero worship that the new boy would naturally give to one lately raised to the proud position of a place in the Eton XI. Even at that first moment of our acquaintance I can recall the cheery smile, the generous kindly consideration to the younger boy, so thoroughly characteristic of the man in after life. The physical impression remaining in my mind is of a tall, chubby faced, bustling youth, giving brilliant promise of future excellence at all the Eton games, cricket, football, racquets, and fives.

The next three years, as every Etonian of that day remembers, abundantly fulfilled these expectations, and by 1875, the year of his captaincy of the cricket XI, he had arrived at a position of gladly acknowledged supremacy in every phase of Eton life that might well have turned the head of anyone possessing a less modest and well-balanced disposition. As his old friend and contemporary, Lord Curzon of Kedleston, justly said in his eloquent appreciation in *The Times* newspaper, "no boyish hero was ever quite such a hero." Such matchless brilliancy in every athletic game, such wise and unquestioned leadership among boys and elders alike, and this without neglect of the more serious side of school life, for our friend was among the ablest students of history, both at school and University. And then the personality of the hero of all this boyish achievement. Tall, vigorous, muscular, athletic grace characteristic of every movement, the merriest eye, the most engaging smile that ever gladdened the heart of a friend—were ever so many brilliant and attractive qualities blended in one youthful person? I fancy many of his contemporaries will be at one with me when I say that for us there was and will be this one inimitable hero of our youthful days.

His chief distinctions as a cricketer, as all the cricket world knows, were as batsman and wicket-keeper. His style of batting was bright, vigorous, and very straight, driving and playing back with great force. Curiously enough, although he especially admired the stroke, and had an excellent wrist for racquets and tennis, his cutting of the more horizontal sort behind the wicket was never specially good, and his runs were mostly made well in front of the wicket. He was strong also on the leg-side both in defence and on-side driving, and altogether a batsman of very high class in any company. If I am not mistaken I have seen his style described as the champagne of cricket, a not inapt simile for the lively attractiveness of his methods. As a wicket-keeper a very sure and brilliant catcher, not taking the ball quite so near the wicket as one or two others, Blackham and Pilling for instance, but very reliable and sure, with a strong safe pair of hands that stood the work of that arduous position with unusual freedom from accident. As a brilliant fieldsman, fine runner and thrower, he used frequently towards the end of a long innings to opt for the comparative freedom of the outer field, and very good he was in any position.

The first innings of his that I can remember was a brilliant 20 or so not out, which finished the Eton and Harrow match of about 1872, and from that time in Eton, Cambridge, Middlesex, and other matches, I saw many brilliant innings of his, and fielded out through some of them between 1875 and 1884.

He was essentially one of those natural players who could take up the game again after a long spell of retirement and almost at once find his best form: he went on playing occasionally in first-class cricket for several years after he had given up regular play. Between 1878 and 1888 it was a considerable source of strength to a representative English side to have such first-class wicket-keepers and brilliant batsmen combined in one person, as in Mr. Lyttelton and Mr. E. F. S. Tylecote, and I am inclined to think the English team of that date was, partly through that fact, as strong as any we have seen.

When the writer went with an English team to Australia in 1882, it was our great hope that A. L. would come as captain, but, although he was very anxious to come, it was a time when serious work at the Bar was just beginning, and the plan had to be abandoned to our infinite regret and, I think, his.

The years 1878 and 1879 will be remembered as remarkable years for Cambridge cricket. The captains were the brothers Edward and Alfred Lyttelton successively, and the XI was unbeaten either year. Probably the 1879 XI was not so good as the 1878, which not only did not lose a match, but actually won all eight matches, including the Australian—won in an innings. This 1878 XI has been often quoted as, perhaps, the strongest University XI we have seen, though the difficulty of accurate comparison of XIs at widely distant dates must always involve a certain amount of guesswork.

Looking back to Eton school-days, no more striking athletic picture comes back to my mind than Alfred at Eton football. The rules of the game offered more opportunity for brilliant individual performance than any other rules, and I can see, as it were yesterday, the dashing vigorous figure scattering his adversaries like nine-pins, the ball apparently glued to his "flying" feet, till, the last enemy swept away, a characteristic triumphant shout proclaimed the rare achievement of a run-down goal of the whole length of the field.

At Hagley, the Worcestershire home of the Lytteltons, there was an annual match with Birmingham, and, when the family was at its best, the number of recumbent Birminghamites on the field after one of these rundowns was a sight to be remembered. But, be it said, though his football feats were so splendidly vigorous, it was all done with such good temper and enjoyment that no trace of resentment was left with the defeated foemen.

At racquets and fives he was almost equally pre-eminent and successful and, although he gave up racquets after his third year at Cambridge in order to keep more closely to tennis, he always derived intense enjoyment from the pace and vigour of the game and the wonders of the half-volley or volley half an inch above the line, and used to relieve his feelings by loud and characteristic exclamations that seem to ring even today in the ears of his friends.

I well remember the last single game at racquets with him at Cambridge about 1879. After one good rally when we had both hit harder and harder till we could hit no longer, we both sat on the floor and laughed for sheer enjoyment of the fun and exhilaration of it all.

One particular feature of his play at all games was a very remarkable generosity to an opponent whom he was beating easily—so characteristic was this of our friend that he was not always quite so reliable in a match in which he had rather the best of the odds. As many game-players know, however much start a player may have of his opponent, to slacken the game so as to let up the adversary is always dangerous, and the player who does it will very likely find it impossible to find his best game when he wishes to put on full steam again. In his third year at Cambridge,

A. L. finally gave up match play at racquets, and soon reached the position of head amateur at tennis, after a historic series of matches with that wonderful veteran Mr. J. M. Heathcote. Those who were fortunate enough to see those encounters were able to see an interesting study in contrasts of physique, style, and method. The almost emaciated, but tirelessly active physique of the older player against the muscular strength and vigour of the younger; the careful painstaking accuracy and judgment against the more brilliant and dashing style, the shrewd and masterly adaptation of natural resources against the athletic grace and classic method.

Until very recent years the foremost amateurs in the tennis world were young men who had left off their racquets at about the University age of 18 or 19 to take up tennis. In the last few years, Mr. Jay Gould and others have taken up the game as boys, and, if this becomes the rule, the advantage of the rapid powers of imitation and assimilation at the earlier age is likely to bring about a higher standard of amateur tennis than that to which we have been accustomed. We may perhaps look on A. L. as the equal of any amateur of the earlier type.

The only game perhaps at which he did not reach the front rank was the game of his later years, golf. Though he was devoted to the game and played with boundless zest and enthusiasm, he had taken up this highly technical game somewhat late in life for a beginner, between the age of 30 or 40, I think. I remember playing with him at Muirfield, about the time when he became Secretary for the Colonies, and thinking what a sound golfing style he was developing at that time, but afterwards, through the increasing demands of work and the diminishing opportunities for play and practice, he developed some curious eccentricities of play, which rather detracted from its efficacy. Not that he was by any means a weak player even then, far from it; within the last three or four years I remember a score of 82 or 83 of his in the Autumn Medal at St Andrews, as an emphatic piece of evidence to the contrary. I feel convinced that another year or two in his 1905 style would have made him a good scratch player. At all times a game with him was a rare treat from the contagious zest and vigour of his boyish enthusiasm.

In these few lines I have touched on but one aspect of his full and busy life, the game-playing side of it.

Far abler pens have in many places dealt with its more serious sides, as lawyer, politician, and constant worker in many useful and philanthropic spheres.

Forty years of cheery comradeship, intermittent of later years, but always on the same delightful footing, may possibly enable me to give some slight picture of my old friend on his lighter side.

Brilliant as were his performances at almost everything that he took up, it was the charm of his generous, eager personality, and the fascination of his unselfish nature that will leave so affectionate a recollection of him in the hearts of the countless friends who mourn his loss.

LYTTELTON, The Rev. The Hon. Charles Frederick, born on January 26, 1887, died in London on October 3, 1931. Although a really good fast bowler he missed getting into the XI at Eton but at Cambridge, in 1908, met with more success and in a very close match which Oxford won by two wickets he took five wickets for 85. In a drawn game at Lord's next season he did not get a wicket. He occasionally assisted Worcestershire.

LYTTELTON, The Rev. The Hon. Dr. Edward, youngest but one and last survivor of eight sons of the fourth Lord Lyttelton, seven of whom played for Eton during the period 1857 to 1875, died on January 26, 1942, at Lincoln. Born on July 23, 1855, he was 86 years old. Less tall than some of his brothers, he was nearly 6 ft. and well proportioned—in fact the ideal build for sport. Great at the Field and Wall games at Eton, he played Association football for England against Scotland in 1878. He excelled at Fives and did well at the Long Jump and Weight Putting, but his great triumphs came on the cricket field. He played for Eton 1872 to 1874, finishing as captain, when his 58 went a long way towards beating Harrow by five wickets at Lord's, and there followed more brilliant achievements during four years in the Cambridge XI. Alternately he knew defeat and victory, the second success over Oxford coming when he led his side to victory by 238 runs; he contributed 53 and 10. His average of 29 for the season was remarkable in those days. That match came in the course of a wonderful experience for Edward Lyttelton at Lord's. With scores of 44 and 66 he helped the Gentlemen to beat the Players by 206 runs; the match produced 1,066 runs, the only aggregate of four figures that season. Then E. Lyttelton led Cambridge to victory by an innings and 72 runs over the Australian team. This concluded the Cambridge programme of eight matches, all won decisively against powerful opponents, four with an innings to spare. Edward Lyttelton was unlucky for, after hitting three fours and a three, he was run out. Before these three games Edward Lyttelton scored the only hundred hit against that first Australian team captained by D. W. Gregory. The match holds a special place in the history of the game for several reasons. It took place soon after the dismissal of M.C.C. for 19 runs by the Australians, who in a victory attained in one day placed themselves in the front rank of cricket. On the morning of the Middlesex match the brothers Grace came to Lord's and fetched W. Midwinter, a member of the Australian team, to play at the Oval for Gloucestershire, the county of his birth, for whom he had appeared in the previous season. Then I. D. Walker, captain of an entirely amateur Middlesex team, took the unusual course in those days of putting the Australians in to bat—the weather was fine after much rain. The county replied to a total of 165 with 111 for the loss of four men, A. J. Webbe making 50; but the innings closed for 11 more runs, T. W. Garrett altogether taking seven wickets for 38 runs. The Australians maintained their advantage, and Middlesex, wanting 284 to win, fared lamentably, losing four wickets with the total 14. Edward Lyttelton at this crisis scored 37 before stumps were drawn with the total 79 for six wickets.

Wisden describes how "on the Saturday, in weather so hot that the glass stood at 105 in the sun, Edward Lyttelton hit so brilliantly that he made 10 runs in an over (four balls at that time) from Allan and 12 in an over from Spofforth, 31 runs in 14 minutes, and 57 out of 69 in 41 minutes, before Spofforth bowled H. R. Webbe for 17. E. Lyttelton went on hitting in superb style until last out to a catch at slip for 113, his 76 runs that morning having been made in 74 minutes. The very finest hitting display made in 1878. The Australians won by 98 runs."

In 1882 he was in the Cambridge Past and Present team that beat the Australians at Portsmouth by 20 runs.

Splendid in style, Edward Lyttelton cut both late and square and drove to the off in the true Etonian manner with great power, and was a dashing field at long-leg or "middle wicket off." He played sometimes for Worcestershire, and continued to assist Middlesex and other sides until 1882, when he gave up first-class cricket. He hit many 100s in minor cricket, and in 1877 for Cambridge Long Vacation Club made 228 against M.C.C.

After being an assistant master at Wellington and Eton, he became headmaster at Haileybury until he returned to Eton in 1905, remaining headmaster until 1916, when he retired.

LYTTELTON, The Hon. George William Spencer, fourth son of Baron Lyttelton, died at his residence, Hill Street, W., on December 5, 1913, in his 67th year. He was born in London on June 12, 1847. Spencer Lyttelton, as he was generally called, had the family devotion to cricket, and though he did not earn the fame in the field that was won by three of his brothers—Charles, Edward, and Alfred—he had a good record, both at Eton and Cambridge. He was in the Eton XI in 1863, 1864, and 1865, making his first appearance at Lord's against Harrow as a member of a brilliant team, which included Alfred Lubbock—the finest school batsman of 1863—E. W. Tritton, the Hon. F. G. Pelham (afterwards Earl of Chichester), and J. Frederick. The match was drawn, Tritton scoring 91 and 58, and Lubbock 0 and 80. In the two following years Harrow were overwhelmingly strong, beating Eton by an innings and 66 runs in 1864, and by an innings and 51 runs in 1865. Spencer Lyttelton was the most successful batsman for the beaten side in 1864, playing a second innings of 50 against some admirable bowling, but he failed in 1865. His best score for Eton was 96 not out, against Winchester in 1864, he and W. S. Prideaux winning the match in great style by nine wickets. At Cambridge Mr. Lyttelton was in the XI for two seasons—1866 and 1867. He did nothing against Oxford in his first year, but in 1867 he was one of the heroes of an intensely interesting finish. Cambridge required only 110 to win, but five of their best wickets were down for 54, E. M. Kenney's left-handed fast bowling being very difficult. However, Cambridge won the game without further loss, W. S. O. Warner—a fine bat and still finer racquet player, who died at the age of 27—scoring 34 not out and Lyttelton 20 not out. Spencer Lyttelton was clearly at his best as a batsman in 1867, as in that year he scored 114 at Fenner's for the University against Cambridgeshire. Mr. Lyttelton in public affairs was best known as chief private secretary to Mr. Gladstone, 1892–94. An excellent musician, he was on the Executive Committee of the Royal College of Music.

LYTTELTON, Lieut. John Anthony, of the Grenadier Guards, killed in action during February, 1944, aged 22, was a member of the family so well known in cricket for over 100 years. The fourth Lord Lyttelton played for Cambridge in 1838. The father of J. A., the Hon. and Rev. C. F. Lyttelton, played for Eton, Cambridge University and Worcestershire. J. A. Lyttelton was in the Eton XI of 1939, when for the first time since 1908 Harrow were victorious in the great schools match at Lord's. He scored 28 runs and took two wickets. Next season, in the one-day wartime match at Harrow, he brought off three catches but did nothing with either ball or bat to help in an exciting victory for Eton by one wicket. Eton did not suffer defeat that season.

LYTTELTON, General Rt. Hon. Sir Neville Gerald, P.C., G.C.B., G.C.V.O., born at Stourbridge on October 28, 1845, died July 6, 1931, aged 85. A good free hitter, he did not greatly distinguish himself at Eton where he was in the XI in 1862–63–64. His best performance against Harrow was in 1863 when in the second innings he scored 26. A member of M.C.C. from 1868, he played occasionally for Worcestershire.

LYTTELTON, The Hon. Robert Henry, died at North Berwick on November 7, 1939, aged 85. Educated at Eton and Cambridge, he excelled as a student and critic of the game rather than as a player. With A. G. Steel he edited the *Badminton Library* volume in 1887, and in particular he was a foremost advocate of reform of the leg-before-wicket rule. Trained in the earlier school, which regarded putting the legs in front of the wicket for the purpose of defence as not only bad play but unsportsmanlike, he strove hard for over 30 years to bring about such alteration in the law as would penalise batsmen backing up with their pads. He went so far as to urge that a batsman should be given out "if the ball hit any part of his person (except his hand) that is between wicket and wicket." In *Crisis in Cricket and the "Leg-Before" Rule,* he expounded his views on the subject and also on the artificial preparation of wickets. His dramatic account in the *Badminton* volume of the University match at Lord's in 1870 ("Cobden's match") was honoured by inclusion in *The Oxford Book of English Prose.* "Bob" Lyttelton, sixth son of the fourth Lord Lyttelton, and one of eight brothers, seven of whom played for Eton between the years 1857 and 1872, was nearly 6 ft. 3 in. tall. A useful bat for Eton he failed to get his Blue at Cambridge but represented the University in the doubles tennis match of 1874.

LYWOOD, Lewis William, who died at Caterham on October 31, 1971, aged 64, was a fast bowler who had short spells as a professional with Surrey and then Essex. One of his few first-team appearances for Surrey was against Gloucestershire at the Oval in 1928, when he suffered severely from W. R. Hammond. Surrey made 418, but Hammond 205 not out, and his captain B. H. Lyon, 131, put on 285 in three and a half hours, the total reaching 544. Not being retained in first-class cricket, Lywood returned to work in Croydon Town Hall and thereafter played for Croydon Municipal Officers, performing many remarkable fast bowling feats in South London club cricket circles where he was well known.

MACARTNEY, Charles George, who died in Sydney on September 9, 1958, aged 72, was one of the most brilliant and attractive right-handed batsmen in the history of Australian cricket. Daring and confident, he possessed a quickness of eye, hand and foot, a perfection of timing which made him a menace to the best of bowlers. Sydney H. Pardon, then Editor of *Wisden*, wrote of him in 1921 as "a law to himself—an individual genius, but not in any way to be copied. He constantly did things that would be quite wrong for an ordinary batsman, but by success justified all his audacities. Except Victor Trumper at his best, no Australian batsman has ever demoralised our bowlers to the same extent."

Of medium height and stocky build, "The Governor-General," as Macartney came to be known, was specially good in cutting and hitting to leg, though there was no stroke, orthodox or unorthodox, of which he did not show himself master. Intolerant of batsmen who did not treat bowling upon its merits, he was quoted as giving, not long before his death, as the reason why he had ceased to be a regular cricket spectator: "I can't bear watching luscious half-volleys being nudged gently back to bowlers." Yet in regard to his own achievements this man with the Napoleonic features could not have been more modest; he had no regard at all for records or averages, nor was he ever known to complain about an umpire's decision.

How punishing a batsman he could be was never more fully demonstrated than in 1921 when, at Trent Bridge, he took such full advantage of a missed chance when nine that he reached 345 from the Nottinghamshire bowling in less than four hours with four sixes and 47 fours among his figures. This still stands as the highest innings put together by an Australian in England and, furthermore, no other batsman in first-class cricket has scored as many runs in a single day. It was also the third of four centuries in following innings, the others being 105 v. Hampshire at Southampton, 193 v. Northamptonshire at Northampton and 115 v. England at Leeds, where he performed the rare feat of getting to three figures before lunch.

From the time that he made his first appearance for Australia in 1907 till he ended his Test career in 1926, Macartney represented his country 35 times, scoring 2,132 runs, including seven centuries, average 41.80. His highest Test innings was 170 against England at Sydney in 1920–21. He headed the Australia averages with 86.66 that season and also figured at the top in England in 1926 when, with the aid of innings of 151, 133 not out and 109, his average was 94.60. He took part in 12 Test partnerships of 100 or more, the biggest being 235 with W. M. Woodfull for the second wicket against England at Leeds in 1926.

For all the batting prowess he revealed later, it was as a slow left-arm bowler that Macartney did his best work when first visiting England in 1909. During the tour he took 71 wickets at a cost of 17.46 runs each, and he played a big part in the overthrow of England at Leeds by dismissing seven batsmen for 58 runs in the first innings and four for 27 in the second. In an unofficial Australian tour of America in 1913, his ability as an all-rounder reached such heights that he hit 2,390 runs and took 180 wickets, finishing at the top of both sets of averages. As a fieldsman, particularly at mid-off, he had few equals.

He accomplished much fine work for New South Wales, for whom he first played in 1905, scoring 2,443 runs, average 42.12, with 201 against Victoria in 1913–14 his highest innings. Twice he got two separate centuries in a match—119 and 126 for his State against the South Africans in 1910–11 and 142 and 121 for the Australians against Sussex at Hove in 1912. In all cricket his runs numbered 15,003, average 45.87, and he hit 48 hundreds.

Of him, Sir Jack Hobbs said: "I saw him begin his Test career in Australia and we thought him a very unorthodox player, but we soon realised he was brilliant. He hit particularly hard through the covers and frequently cut even fast bowlers off his stumps. He certainly had a wonderful eye. He was a charming fellow and a highly confident cricketer."

MACAULAY, Pilot Officer George Gibson, one of the chief Yorkshire bowlers during a career lasting from 1920 to 1935, died on active service, as announced in December, 1940. Born at Thirsk on December 7, 1897, he did not take part in County Cricket until 23 years of age, when he appeared for Yorkshire as a fast bowler. Under the influence of George Hirst and Wilfred Rhodes, he reduced his speed to medium pace, developing spin and controlling his length with such effect that on June 2, 1921, at Hull, six Derbyshire batsmen fell to him at a cost of only three runs, his match record being seven wickets for 12 runs. That success set Macaulay on the road to fame. Forsaking his position in a bank, he became a valued member of the county side.

In 15 seasons, when a regular member of the Yorkshire XI, he took 1,773 wickets for the county at 17.08 runs apiece, and altogether in first-class cricket, 1,838 at 17.64. He reached the top of his form in 1925, when in County Championship matches he claimed 176 wickets at 15.21 runs each, and his full record showed 211 wickets, average 15.48. Under suitable conditions for using the off-break, batsmen seemed at his mercy. Four times he did the hat-trick, more often than any other Yorkshire bowler, and for the county only Rhodes, Hirst, and Schofield Haigh have proved more successful with the ball. Not only did he often send down the unplayable delivery, but he could keep batsmen on the defensive for long periods; such an instance occurred at Kettering against Northamptonshire in 1933, when he bowled 14 overs for nine runs and dismissed seven batsmen. Like others capable of turning the ball a lot from the off, Macaulay often bowled round the wicket; short steps to the crease and easy delivery were characteristics that earned him a distinct place among contemporaries. In the field he excelled close to the batsman, particularly when Emmot Robinson, his chief supporter in the Yorkshire attack, was bowling. These two were unchanged in the 1927 match with Worcestershire.

Macaulay soon met with recognition from the England selection committee, and, after appearing for the Players at Lord's, he was chosen to go to South Africa with the team captained by F. T. Mann in 1922. Macaulay took a wicket with his first ball in Test cricket; then, in a sensational finish to this match at Cape Town, he made the stroke which brought England victory by one wicket. In his only match for England against Australia—at Leeds in 1926—he did little

with the ball, but, joining George Geary, he scored 76, the ninth wicket realising 108 runs. This stand went a long way towards enabling England to make an honourable draw in the face of a total of 494 by Australia.

If this was his most noteworthy performance with the bat, Macaulay frequently gave useful help, and his runs for Yorkshire totalled 5,759, average 18.11. An injury to his spinning finger in 1934, when attempting to hold a return catch in the match with Leicestershire at Headingley, no doubt hastened Macaulay's retirement from the county. He left Yorkshire at the end of the next season and then played for League clubs in Wales, Lancashire and Yorkshire.

Educated at Barnard Castle, Macaulay regularly each season brought an XI of noted players to meet his old school. During the First World War Macaulay served in the Royal Field Artillery, and early in 1940 he joined the Royal Air Force.

His benefit was a small reward for a Yorkshire professional, realising no more than £1,633, but the county made him a special grant of £250 on his retirement.

MacBRYAN, John Crawford William, who died on July 14, 1983, a few days before his 91st birthday, was England's oldest surviving Test cricketer. Captain of cricket at Exeter School, he was in the XI at the RMC Sandhurst when he played for Somerset in their last two matches in 1911 and against Surrey at the Oval was second-top scorer with 20 in a total of 97. In the next three years he made a few appearances for the county and in 1914 scored 61 against Gloucestershire. But in August that year he was wounded in the right arm at Le Cateau and spent the rest of the War as a prisoner, latterly in Holland, where he was able to play plenty of cricket. In 1919 he was up at Cambridge, but, though he scored 90 against the Navy, was only 12th man at Lord's. However, he topped the Somerset averages and indeed did so in six of the eight seasons 1919–26. He duly got his Blue in 1920. His two best years for Somerset were 1923, when he made 1,507 runs for them with an average of 37.67, and 1924, when his aggregate was 1,355 and his average 43.70. By now he was near the England side. In 1923 he made top score, 80, for The Rest against England in the Test trial at Lord's and in 1924 was picked for the Gentlemen at Lord's, and again made runs in a Test trial. As a result he was selected for the fourth Test against South Africa at Old Trafford, but the match was ruined by rain and he did not bat. Many expected him to be in the side for Australia, but his chance was probably lost when the doctors passed J. W. Hearne as fit. In any case, the team was overweighted with openers: in addition to Hobbs and Sutcliffe, there were Sandham, Whysall and J. L. Bryan. Instead MacBryan went with the Hon. L. H. Tennyson's unofficial side to South Africa, where he was only moderately successful. Two more seasons for Somerset virtually concluded his career. Though he continued to play occasionally until 1931, he was never after 1926 in sufficient practice to do himself justice, and so, like many other amateurs, he dropped out just when he was at his best. Short but strongly built, he was primarily a back-foot player and a fine cutter and hooker. He also played well off his legs and was a far better bat on a turning wicket than most amateurs. Moreover, lack of inches did not stop him countering Tate at his best by playing forward and getting well over the ball. In all his movements he was neat and elegant. In the field his wounded arm prevented him throwing far, but he was good near the wicket, especially at short-leg. A rich character, he was in his element in a side captained by John Daniell and containing R. C. Robertson-Glasgow, G. F. Earle and J. C. White, with the great Sam Woods, to whom he acknowledged a special debt for teaching him to play Tate, in support off the field. In all first-class cricket he scored 10,322 runs with an average of 29.50, including 18 centuries, the highest of them 164 against Leicestershire at Taunton in 1922.

MacDONOGH, Capt. James J., who visited Bermuda with the Philadelphian teams of 1908, 1910, and 1911, and Jamaica with the team of 1909, died in Pennsylvania Hospital, Philadelphia, on January 26, 1912, aged 40. He was a free-hitting, attractive batsman, and a very good change bowler. In a match against Jamaica in 1909 he played fine cricket for 86 and 59. He represented the United States against Canada in 1909 at Montreal and in 1911 at Toronto. Capt. MacDonogh was one of the participants in the Jameson Raid: he had also served with distinction in the Boer War and had seen service in Egypt.

McGIRR, Herbert M., who died in Nelson, New Zealand, on April 14, 1964, aged 73, was one of the most noted all-rounders to appear for Wellington. In a first-class career extending from 1914 to 1932, he scored 3,992 runs, average 28.71, and took 239 wickets with fast-medium bowling for 27.04 runs

each. He toured England with T. C. Lowry's team of 1927, hitting 809 runs in all matches at 21.86 per innings and dismissing 69 batsmen for 23.98 runs apiece. McGirr played for New Zealand in two Tests against A. H. H. Gilligan's England team of 1929–30, scoring 51 in the fourth at Auckland. When he retired from first-class cricket he continued in club matches till, after making 70 at the age of 67, he slipped after taking in the milk the following morning and had to give up the game.

MacGREGOR, Gregor. It was a shock to all lovers of cricket to learn on August 20, 1919, that Mr. Gregor MacGregor was dead. Still in early middle-age, he would had he lived another week have completed his 50th year. To be quite exact, he was born in Edinburgh on August 31, 1869. He was a prominent figure in first-class cricket for, roughly speaking, 20 seasons, playing his last matches for Middlesex in 1907. Fame came to him before he was 20. After two years in the Uppingham team he went up to Cambridge, and as soon as he was seen at the University ground in the spring of 1888 it was realised that a wicket-keeper of extraordinary ability had been found. He gained his Blue at once, and during his four years at Cambridge he was one of the stars of the XI. Alfred Lyttelton had left behind him the reputation of being the best wicket-keeper Cambridge had ever possessed, but even his warmest admirers— among them A. G. Steel—were forced to admit that MacGregor surpassed him, his superiority lying chiefly in the fact that he took the ball much closer to the wicket, and was in consequence the quicker stumper. In catching there was little to choose between the two men.

It was MacGregor's good fortune to be associated all through his Cambridge career with S. M. J. Woods. In those days Woods was the fastest amateur bowler in England and a terror to the Oxford batsmen at Lord's. The fashion of standing back to fast bowling had not then become general among wicket-keepers, and it is difficult to say how much Woods owed to MacGregor's fearless skill. To see the two in the University match was something never to be forgotten. Putting on all his pace, Woods was apt to be a little erratic in pitch, but MacGregor—quite imperturbable—was equal to every emergency. Their first match together against Oxford had to be left drawn—even a fourth day was of no use in the dreadful summer of 1888—but in the three following years Cambridge had a succession of victories. Woods was captain in 1890, and in 1891 he played under MacGregor. Their cricket skill was not greater than their personal popularity. They held high rank among the heroes of the cricket field. Cambridge days over, their paths diverged, Woods playing for Somerset and MacGregor for Middlesex, but they were associated for many a year in the Gentlemen v. Players matches at Lord's.

MacGregor was a brilliant wicket-keeper as long as he played cricket, but he was at his very best in his early years, when he had no English superior except Pilling. He kept wicket for England against Australia at Lord's and the Oval in 1890, and at Lord's, the Oval, and Manchester in 1893, doing himself full justice on all occasions. When the Australians came here in 1896 he gave place to Lilley, and Test matches knew him no more. Still, he remained a force in County Cricket, following A. J. Webbe as captain of the Middlesex XI. His most exciting experience for England against Australia was in the Oval match in 1890. He was in at the finish with Jack Sharpe, the Surrey bowler, and England scrambled home by two wickets. A desperately short run settled the business, the ball being returned to the middle of the pitch. Had the ball been thrown to either end a run-out would have been inevitable. MacGregor went once to Australia, going out with Lord Sheffield's team in the winter of 1891–92. That tour did not add to his fame. He was not up to his highest standard as a wicket-keeper and Australian critics, having expected so much, were disappointed.

MacGregor's interest in cricket did not decline in even the slightest degree when he dropped out of the public eye. A few weeks before his death he followed the Gentlemen and Players match at Lord's as eagerly as if he had been taking part in it himself. For some time and up to the end of his life he was honorary treasurer of the Middlesex County C.C.

While not attaining as a football player to the exceptional excellence which characterised his skill as a wicket-keeper, Gregor MacGregor earned much fame on the rugby field. In 1889 and 1890 he appeared as full back for Cambridge against Oxford, showing himself a fine tackler and very accurate kick. In the same season that he first appeared for Cambridge, international honours fell to his share. Indeed, he was chosen by the Scottish Union to appear for Scotland in all three International matches. A similar distinction befell him in 1891 and 1893—he was out in Australia with Lord Sheffield's cricket team in 1892—and in 1894 he played against England and Wales, his final appearance in an international game being in that between Scotland and England, decided at Hampden Park, Glasgow, in 1896. Although he began and finished his career in great matches as a full back, MacGregor played mostly in those games as a centre three-quarter—those were the days of the three three-quarter system—and, thanks to his fine turn of speed and a safe pair of hands, he ranked with the foremost rugby men of his day. In the course of his career he appeared on several occasions for Middlesex. On one of these, when the four three-quarter system had come into vogue, he had for his colleagues A. E. Stoddart, A. J. Gould, and G. T. Campbell—all also internationals. One glorious bout of passing these famous four brought off, but for all that Yorkshire proved victorious.—S.H.P.

MACHIN, Reginald Stanley, who died on November 3, 1968, aged 64, was in the Lancing XI as wicket-keeper in 1922 and 1923. He got a Blue at Cambridge in 1927 and, with one catch and three stumpings, helped in the defeat of Oxford by 116 runs. From 1927 to 1930 he made occasional appearances for Surrey. In all first-class cricket "Rex" Machin brought off 55 catches and 14 stumpings. For 32 years he was headmaster of Bilton Grange Preparatory School, Dunchurch, near Rugby.

MACKAY, 2nd Lieut. Claude Lysaght (2nd Worcestershire Regiment) died on June 7, 1915, at Boulogne, of wounds received in action on May 28, aged 20. In 1912 and 1913 he was in the Clifton XI, in the latter year making 400 runs with an average of 36.33—his highest score was 71 v. Cheltenham—and taking 20 wickets for 15.45 runs each. He was essentially the all-round man of the side, being second in batting and first in bowling. He had a good reach and would undoubtedly have made a name for himself had he been able to devote himself to first-class cricket. On his only appearance for Gloucestershire—v. Kent at Maidstone in 1914—he scored 13 and 15. He won the Challenge Cup in the Athletic Sports at Clifton and the Public Schools heavyweight Boxing Competition at Aldershot in 1913.

MACKAY, James Rainey Munro, who died in Walcha Hospital, New South Wales, on June 13, 1953, aged 71, was one of Australia's greatest cricketing sons. Only a magnificent constitution enabled him to live so long, for his doctor told him 15 years before that he might pass away at any time. Born on September 9, 1881, he never came to England, and so was not so well known as some of the Australians who did. Yet he batted brilliantly for New South Wales in Inter-State games, and in 1905–06 was wonderfully successful. In successive innings he hit 90 v. South Australia, 194 v. Victoria, 105 and 102 not out v. South Australia, 18 and 50 v. Victoria. When the 1905 Australian team returned from England, they played a match for Jim Kelly's benefit against New South Wales, for whom Mackay scored 4 and 136. Against Queensland, not then in the Sheffield Shield tournament, he made 203.

Wisden of 1907 stated of this performance: "The sensation of the season was the wonderful batting of J. R. M. Mackay ... who scored in six innings, once not out, 559 runs. In face of such form it would seem that a great mistake was committed in not bringing him to England in 1905.... It was the general opinion that, for brilliancy, his batting has never been surpassed in Australia except by Trumper."

Shortly after, Mackay accepted a lucrative position in Johannesburg and was very successful in South African cricket. The question arose as to whether he should be a candidate for selection in the 1907 South African team to tour England, but it was felt that he had not lived long enough in the Union to qualify. This was a great disappointment to him, for he thus had the hard luck of just missing two visits to the Mother Country. He was known by the nick-name of "Sunny Jim," a tribute to his disposition on and off the cricket field.—G.A.B.

MacKAY, Kenneth Donald, M.B.E., who died on June 13, 1982, aged 56, was one of the best and most popular cricketers ever produced by Queensland. As a left-handed middle-order batsman, he possessed a highly distinctive style, this endearing him to crowds which otherwise might have found his rate of scoring unendurably slow. At the crease he stood impassively, cap at a rakish angle, knees slightly bent, chewing compulsively. He employed negligible backlift and was an uncanny judge of line, often leaving balls that seemed to make the bails quiver. When a stroke was required, his most prolific were a deflection wide of cover-point's right hand and a type of "shovel" shot past midwicket. He was more often a match-saver than a match-winner. Very occasionally he would play an innings of remarkable and unexpected aggression and unorthodoxy, one such being at Lord's against Middlesex

in 1961 when he made a whirlwind 168. As a right-arm medium-paced bowler, he became in the early '60s a useful member of the Australian attack, possessing the ability to contain batsmen for long periods and often taking good wickets. He had a stealthy, almost apologetic approach to the wicket, but the innocuous appearance of his deliveries masked subtle variations of pace and swing.

"Slasher" MacKay first played grade cricket in Brisbane at the age of 15. By 1946 he had won a place in the Queensland side, the start of a first-class career that lasted for 18 years and included 100 appearances for his state and 37 for Australia. He became captain of Queensland in 1954–55 and in 1956 toured England with Ian Johnson's side. He made his Test debut at Lord's, in the only Test won by Australia that summer, batting for more than seven hours in the match, yet scoring only 38 and 31. In his second innings, which lasted for 264 minutes, he fulfilled what was to become a familiar sheet-anchor role while Benaud played a brilliant innings of 97. MacKay's performance in the next two Tests threatened his international career: at Headingley he made two and two, at Old Trafford Laker dismissed him for a "pair". He was dropped for the last Test at the Oval and was not an original selection for Ian Craig's team to tour South Africa in 1957–58. However, he was added to Craig's side at the last moment and, with Test scores of three, 65 not out, 63, 32, 52 not out, 83 not out and 77 not out, he justified his selection.

MacKay's best Test performances were achieved on a tour of Pakistan and India in 1959–60. On a matting wicket at Dacca he helped Australia to gain their first Test win in Pakistan, recording in the second innings the remarkable bowling figures of 45–27–42–6. Against India at Madras he made his highest Test score, 89—ended, somewhat surprisingly, when he was stumped. His best remembered Test innings must have been against West Indies at Adelaide in 1961, the series of the tied Test. With 100 minutes of the game remaining Australia, trailing by many runs, lost their ninth wicket. As Lindsay Kline joined MacKay a West Indian victory seemed assured. However, dour defence by both batsmen frustrated all the efforts of Worrell's side and the game ended with Australia's last pair still together, MacKay undefeated with 62, made in almost four hours. He played his last Test against England at Adelaide in January, 1963, and not long afterwards announced his retirement from first-class cricket, his final appearance being for Queensland against Victoria in 1964. "In affection and gratitude," the people of Brisbane contributed some £20,000 to a "bob in for Slasher" campaign, conducted by the city's morning paper. For 15 years after his retirement MacKay was a state selector, and in 1977 he was appointed state coach for Queensland. In 1962 he was made an M.B.E. for his services to cricket.

MACKAY, William Gilfellow, who died on August 8, 1962, aged 70, was from 1920 to 1939 a regular opening batsman for Northumberland, whom he captained on several occasions. In Minor County Cricket during that period this fearless hooker and courageous fieldsman close to the wicket hit nearly 7,000 runs and held more than 200 catches. His highest innings was 173 against Warwickshire Second XI at Jesmond in 1932. In that season against Lancashire Second XI at Warrington, he helped H. Robson to a "hat-trick" by taking three consecutive catches at close point.

MACKINNON of Mackinnon, The (35th Chief of the Mackinnon Clan), the title to which Mr. Francis Alexander Mackinnon succeeded on the death of his father in 1903, passed away at his home, Drumduan, in Forres, Morayshire, on February 27, 1947. He would have been 99 years old on April 9. As it was he reached a greater age than attained by any other first-class cricketer, surpassing that of Herbert Jenner-Fust, Cambridge captain in the first match with Oxford in 1827, who died in 1904 when his exact age was 98 years five months and seven days. Mackinnon was within 40 days of 99 years at his passing.

Born at Acryse Park, in Kent, he went to Harrow without getting into the XI, but at Cambridge he played in the historic match of 1870 when Cobden did the hat-trick by dismissing the last three Oxford batsmen and gaining for the Light Blues a dramatic victory by two runs. He played 10 years for Kent, and in 1884, going in first, he helped, with scores of 28 and 29, in the only victory gained by a county over the Australians. Of the winning side, Mr. Stanley Christopherson, President of M.C.C. during the war years, who finished the match by taking three wickets for 12 runs, Mr. M. C. Kemp, wicket-keeper, and Alec Hearne, seven wickets for 60, are three survivors of that XI.

During that year he scored 115 against Hampshire and 102 against Yorkshire, his average being 33, second to 41 by Lord Harris. He was President of the Kent County Club in 1889.

In the winter of 1878 he went with Lord Harris to Australia. A strong batting side included only two professionals, George Ulyett and Tom Emmett, the Yorkshiremen. Mackinnon was a victim of F. R. Spofforth in a hat-trick in the only match with the full strength of Australia, who won by 10 wickets.

Born on April 9, 1848, three months before W. G. Grace, he married in 1888 the eldest daughter of Admiral, first Baron Hood, the Hon. Emily Hood, who died in 1934. There survive a son and a daughter, who accompanied her father on his cricket visits to the South.

The oldest Harrovian, University Blue and Test cricketer, he was also the senior member of M.C.C., to which he was elected in 1870. Until the last he retained a keen interest in the game he loved so well by following the reports of the matches played by the England team in Australia.

Although he gave up County Cricket 62 years ago, he maintained to a remarkable extent a close touch with the game, as his memory and good physique gave evidence. Using two sticks, he walked firmly, and enjoyed meeting old friends on Kent grounds as well as at Lord's. During the Tunbridge Wells Cricket Week in 1946 he watched the cricket from the Band of Brothers' tent or from the pavilion. One afternoon, accompanied by his daughter and the Marchioness of Abergavenny, he visited Rose Hill School and examined the old desk where he used to sit as a pupil 89 years before. He gave a talk to the whole school, besides inspecting the Sea Scout Troop.

Several opportunities occurred for me to speak to the Mackinnon, and he related some of his experiences in the happiest way. He liked Canterbury better even than Lord's, his second love. An amusing tale was how, at the Oval when playing for Kent, Lord Harris put him to field at a particular spot—"'Mac, by that worm cast.' After some hits just out of reach, my captain said: 'You have left your cast.' 'No, George, I haven't. That's another worm's cast.'"

Referring to "Cobden's Match," he said with a smile, "I really won the match, for I scored two" (the margin of victory). That was his second innings, after a useful 17 not out at a time when runs were never more difficult to get than at Lord's on the big occasion.

Among those who chatted with him in the Lord Harris Memorial garden, where he enjoyed a picnic lunch with his daughter during the University match, was the Rev. T. R. Hine Haycock, an Oxford Blue in 1883, who played for Kent when Mackinnon was finishing his active cricket career and is now 85 years old.

Mackinnon wore an I Zingari tie, and on his watch-chain showed with pride a gold medallion bearing the insignia of crossed bats presented to all the team captained by Lord Harris in Australia. His wonderfully clear conversation and strong handshake revealed his hearty enjoyment in meeting any cricket acquaintance. Among the last active signs of his fondness for the game was the presentation to Canterbury of a picture of the Kent and Sussex match at Hove 100 years ago, in which the players, among them Alfred Mynn, "the Lion of Kent," and Fuller Pilch, are wearing tall hats.

When 98 years of age, in reply to a question by telephone from London as to his health, he said: "I am going into hospital tomorrow—but only for the annual meeting at which I shall preside. I am very well in health—very well indeed. I still do a lot of work in the garden: weeds don't like me at all."—H.P.

MACKLEY, Alan, who died in Perth, in 1982, aged 69, was the first Western Australian to stand in a Test match, officiating in the fourth Test between England and Australia at Adelaide in 1962–63. He became, subsequently, a member of the Western Australian Cricket Association Appeals Board and also of the Umpires Appointments Board.

MACKRORY, Henry Alfred, who died at Durban on November 22, 1947, aged 61, kept wicket for Natal regularly from 1919 to 1930. Not usually of much account as a batsman, he scored 78 not out against Griqualand West in 1926–27 when batting number 10.

MacLAREN, Archibald Campbell, very prominent in cricket during a long career lasting altogether from 1887 to 1923, died on November 17, 1944, when nearly 73 years of age. An immaculate batsman possessing the grand manner, he would have gained still higher renown on the playing field but for periods of poor health and the calls of business. Expert knowledge, obtained by careful study of every intricacy of the game, besides experience in leading his school, his county, the Gentlemen and England, might have made him supreme as captain, but he lacked the buoyant optimistic temperament

so necessary for complete success in cricket and was easily upset by disagreement with selectors in being given players whom he did not consider suitable to the occasion.

To satisfy his own exacting ideas of perfect play and leadership, as described in his book *Cricket Old and New,* he required the position of dictator in order to pick his own XI and control them with expectation of ready response to his every word or gesture. Unfortunately for MacLaren, such idealistic conditions were never forthcoming on the big occasion, but the responsibility for this rested partly with him more than once, when he was one of the selectors. Facts bear this out, as will be seen; but in batting he accomplished much, and will remain a magnificent figure in the eyes of all who saw him making runs.

He will always be remembered for his 424 for Lancashire against Somerset at Taunton in 1895, a first-class score that stood unbeaten for nearly 30 years and has been exceeded only by Don Bradman, who now holds the record with 452 not out, and W. H. Ponsford in Australia. For choice as a Test captain he remains unrivalled, having in the course of 11 years led England in 22 matches, and his 35 appearances against Australia have been surpassed only by Hobbs and Rhodes during far longer periods. Often unfortunate when commander in these big events, he never led England to victory in a rubber, but showed his exceptional knowledge of the game when, having asserted that he could pick a side capable of beating the all-conquering Australian team of 1921, he fulfilled his prophecy by selecting and captaining 11 amateurs, who, at Eastbourne at the end of August, gained a victory by 28 runs after being 130 behind on the first innings. In that climax to his career in England he retained his superb figure, though white hair suggested more age than the approach of his 50th birthday. He finished his intimate association with first-class cricket by acting as manager to S. B. Joel's team that toured South Africa in 1924–25.

Son of Mr. James MacLaren, for many years Hon. Treasurer of Lancashire C.C., Archie MacLaren was born on December 1, 1871, at Manchester, and began his important cricket life auspiciously when only 15 years of age by scoring 55 and 67 for Harrow against Eton in 1887. He finished four years in the XI as captain, and with 76 in a total of 133 off the Eton bowlers at Lord's, showed such form that a month later he appeared in County Cricket, and in his first match for

Lancashire played a fine innings of 108 against Sussex at Hove.

His obvious powers took some time to ripen, but within a few years he reached the front rank of batsmen. Possessed of great resource, he could, according to circumstances, play a cautious or a brilliant game that made him splendid to watch from the ringside. Standing erect with bat raised well behind him, he was ready to receive any kind of delivery and would force the ball away with every sort of powerful stroke.

Captain of Lancashire from 1894 to 1896, and again from 1899 to 1907, he reasserted himself in 1921 as described, and in the winter of 1922–23, at the age of 51, when leading an M.C.C. side in New Zealand, he scored 200 not out at Wellington in a representative match. Besides his record 424, he three times exceeded 200 for his county, 226 at Canterbury against Kent in 1896, next year 244 in the same fixture, and 204 at Liverpool against Gloucester in 1903. From 1893 to 1909 he frequently appeared for Gentlemen against Players, making 728 runs in these games with an average of 45; in 1903, when he and C. B. Fry added 309 in three hours for the third wicket without being separated, he scored 168.

Eight times in England and once in Australia he obtained over 1,000 runs in a season, his largest aggregate being 1,886 (average 42) in the summer of 1903. He enjoyed pronounced success on the Sydney ground, where in the winter of 1897–98 against New South Wales he scored 142 and 100 in one match, 109 and 50 not out a month later against Australia, 61 and 140 in another match with New South Wales, and 65 in the last Test. He also got 124 against Australia at Adelaide and 181 at Brisbane, altogether six centuries on that tour, in which he made 1,037 runs, average 54.57, in first-class matches. No wonder that MacLaren is still talked of in Australia, and especially at Sydney, for his wonderful batting as an object lesson for everyone.

In Test matches between England and Australia he made 1,931 runs, four times reaching three figures and averaging nearly 34. Twice in the '90s he toured Australia with teams led by A. E. Stoddart, and in the winter of 1901–02 he himself took out a side; but in Test matches this team, like the second captained by Stoddart, suffered four defeats and gained only one victory. In three home seasons—1899, 1902 and 1909—England, captained by him, won only two of 14 engagements and lost each rubber. MacLaren visited America with K. S. Ranjitsinhji's team in 1899, and the Argentine in 1911–12 with the M.C.C. side led by Lord Hawke, and he also played in India.

He astonished everyone by taking S. F. Barnes, of small experience in first-class cricket, on the 1901–02 tour in Australia. Yet he could not keep that wonderful bowler in the Lancashire county XI, and in 1909 he failed to persuade his county colleague, Walter Brearley, then the best of our fast bowlers, to accept a last-moment invitation to play for England at Lord's.

Opinions differ as to the ability of MacLaren as a captain. Everyone agrees that he held strong views and was loath to depart from them even if his leadership actually suffered. In fact, it appeared more than once that he pursued ways that showed up some curious decision of selection committees in carrying out their duties.

Undoubtedly he found occasional brilliant inspirations, born of his exceptional knowledge of cricket, but he committed some blunders difficult to understand in a man of his experience. A notable illustration of his erratic disposition occurred at the Oval in the Test match of 1909. To begin with, having the final word in the composition of the XI, he decided, despite fine weather and a hard wicket, that England should take the field without a good fast bowler, John Sharp, of Lancashire, being preferred to Buckenham, of Essex. Then, with the score nine and one man out, he took Sidney Barnes off in favour of Sharp, mainly a batsman, and kept D. W. Carr, a googly bowler, aged 37, on at one end for an hour and a half, an action for which it would have been difficult to excuse anybody. That was the match in which Warren Bardsley made 136 and 130.

Another lapse from wisdom was at Old Trafford in 1902, when he sent to deep square leg Fred Tate, always a short slip: and that historic dropped catch brought about England's defeat in a match upon which the rubber depended—only victory in that engagement could have prevented the honours going to Australia. Yet such was his knowledge of the game that at Leeds in 1904 he gave Yorkshire first innings, and Lancashire, by avoiding defeat in George Hirst's benefit match, went through the season unbeaten and were champions for the only time under MacLaren's captaincy.

An incident in which MacLaren took strong action was of a kind without precedent or repetition, so far as known, and it aroused severe criticism. In July 1907 at Lord's on the second day the paying public were admitted although saturated turf showed no sign of drying and any cricket was extremely unlikely. Yet the stumps were set, and when pulled up at quarter to five some of the crowd, after demonstrating in front of the pavilion, walked across the pitch. After prolonged discussion between the captains—Gregor MacGregor led Middlesex—and umpires, this statement was handed to the Press by A. C. MacLaren himself: "Owing to the pitch having been deliberately torn up by the public, I, as captain of the Lancashire XI, cannot see any way to continue the game, the groundsman bearing me out that the wicket could not be again put right.—A. C. MacLaren." As described in the 1908 *Wisden*, the match was accordingly abandoned. Rolled next morning for the regulation 10 minutes, the pitch showed little trace of the damage.

Naturally such a cricketer received many tributes to his ability. In January 1896 the Lancashire club elected him a life member and presented him with a gold watch and chain in recognition of his record score and of three successive 100s hit in the course of eight days at the end of August that same season—152 at Old Trafford against Nottinghamshire, 108 at Lord's against Middlesex, and 135 at Leicester. Ten years later Lancashire made him a special presentation. In September 1921 he accepted an appointment to coach young players of the county, but an injured knee compelled his resignation early in the 1923 season.—H.P.

MacLAREN, Geoffrey, who died on September 14, 1966, aged 83, played, like his elder brothers, A. C. and Dr. J. A. MacLaren, for Harrow and Lancashire. Against Eton in 1901, though taking four wickets for 84 runs, he was dismissed for 0; next year he helped in a win by eight wickets by hitting 41 and nine and again dismissing four men for 84. He played in two matches for Lancashire in 1902 under the captaincy of A. C. MacLaren.

MacLAREN, Dr. James Alexander, M.D., who died as the result of a fall at Salisbury on July 8, 1952, aged 82, was in the Harrow XI from 1886 to 1888, being captain on the last occasion. He was the eldest of three brothers who played for the school, the most famous of them being A. C. MacLaren, of Lancashire and England. J. A. MacLaren, who was born on January 4, 1870, also made a few appearances for the county.

MacLEOD, Alastair, who died at Broomfield, near Colchester, on April 24, 1982, aged 87, made 12 appearances for Hampshire between 1914 and 1938. Four years in the Felsted XI, he came into the county side the month after leaving and crowned several useful scores with a fine innings of 87 in two hours against Essex at Bournemouth. He played a couple of matches in 1920 and made 48, top score, against Sussex at Brighton and, had he been able to play more frequently, would probably have been valuable. However, his next appearance was not till 1935 and a few matches in 1938 concluded his first-class career. A fine driver, he made altogether 271 runs with an average of 15.05. From 1936 to 1939 he was Secretary of the Hampshire County C.C.

MacNUTT, Howard, born near Stirling, in Scotland, on June 13, 1859, died at Miami, Florida, on December 27, 1926. For many years he was a prominent figure in American cricket, being a very good fast bowler, straight with a sharp rise from the pitch, and an excellent field, covering much ground and throwing-in particularly well. He visited England with the Gentlemen of Philadelphia's team in 1884, and against the Gentlemen of Leicestershire bowled unchanged throughout with Mr. W. C. Lowry. In the following year he took five wickets for 10 runs for United States v. Canada at Toronto. Twice, whilst associated with the Oxford C.C. he won the Childs Cup for bowling in the Halifax Cup matches, taking 25 wickets for 4.96 runs each in 1882 and 22 for 9.68 in 1885.

MADDEN-GASKELL, Major John Charles Pengelley, O.B.E., died on February 4, 1975, aged 78. After making one appearance for Glamorgan in 1922 and scoring 32 against Yorkshire, he played a few times for Somerset from 1928 to 1939. In 1928 he made 42 and 63 against Northamptonshire at Taunton, driving Larwood, then in his prime, in a way that suggested considerable possibilities if he could have played more frequently.

MAKANT, Capt. Robert Keith, who was born on June 28, 1895, was murdered whilst on duty in Kurdistan on June 18, 1922. He was in the Harrow XI in 1913 and 1914, and in his two matches with Eton scored four and 46, four and 14 and obtained five wickets, but on each occasion was on the losing side. He bowled slow from a great height, and in 1913 headed the averages with a record of 23 wickets for 16.06 runs each. During the First World War he was wounded, and he gained the M.C. and Bar whilst serving with the

Royal North Lancashire Regiment.

MAKEPEACE, Harry, who died at his home at Bebington, Cheshire, on December 19, 1952, aged 70, was one of the few men who played both cricket and Association football for England. Born at Middlesbrough, Yorkshire, on August 22, 1882, he was associated with Lancashire County C.C. for 46 years. His playing career with the county commenced in 1906 and he held a place in the side until 1930. Altogether he scored in first-class cricket 25,745 runs, average 36.15, including 43 centuries, the highest of which was 203 against Worcestershire at Worcester in 1923. In the same summer he hit 200 not out from the Northamptonshire bowlers at Liverpool. Ten times he obtained more than 1,000 runs in a season, his best being in 1926 when his aggregate reached 2,340 and his average 48.75. An excellent cover-point and a batsman who, strong in defence, relied chiefly upon placing the ball and seldom put much power into his strokes, he carried his bat four times through a Lancashire innings. He shared in five partnerships of over 200 for the county, the largest of which was 270 for the first wicket with C. Hallows against Worcestershire at Worcester in 1922. In the match with Nottinghamshire at Trent Bridge in 1912 he and A. H. Hornby engaged in a century opening stand in each innings—141 and 196. As a member of J. W. H. T. Douglas's M.C.C. team in Australia in 1920–21, he took part in four Test matches, and in the fourth, at Melbourne, he hit 117 and 54.

For 20 years, Makepeace was coach to the Lancashire club, who, upon his retirement in 1951, made him an honorary life member. His benefit in 1922 realised £2,110, small reward by current standards. As a footballer he played right half-back for Everton, and he represented England against Scotland in 1906, 1910 and 1912, and against Wales in 1912. He was a member of the Everton team which won the F.A. Cup Final at the Crystal Palace in 1906 and lost that of 1907.

MAKINSON, Joseph, died at his home, Roundthorne, Sale, in Cheshire, on March 21, 1914. Born on August 25, 1836, he was thus in his 78th year. Only a name to the present generation, Mr. Makinson was one of the great cricketers of his day. Had he been able to devote more time to the game he would, beyond doubt, have earned a still higher reputation. Even as it was, he did more than enough for fame. After his schooldays at Huddersfield College and Owen's College, Manchester, he was for three years—1856–57–58—the bright particular star of Cambridge cricket. In those three years he was only once on the victorious side against Oxford at Lord's, fairly winning the 1856 match by his splendid all-round play. He took eight wickets—three for four runs and five for 36—and scored 31 and 64. Cambridge had 123 to get in the last innings and only won by three wickets, no one except Makinson and J. W. Marshall, who made 16 not out, being able to do anything with the Oxford bowling. A score of 64 at Lord's in 1856 was, of course, a vastly greater feat than it would be in these days. It was no fault of Makinson's that Cambridge lost the match in 1857 as he took 10 wickets—seven for 38 and three for 65—and scored four and 30, being run out in his first innings. In 1858 he finished his Cambridge career with a failure. It is true that three wickets fell to him, but he was bowled out for six and five, Oxford winning the match in a single innings. Among many good innings at Fenner's he hit up two 100s, scoring 126 in 1857 against the Gentlemen of Cambridgeshire, with Arnold and Reynolds, and 136 in 1858 against the Professionals of Cambridge with four Gentlemen. This latter innings was the more remarkable of the two, as the professionals' side included the great bowler Buttress, then at his very best. Thirteen years after he had left the University, Mr. Makinson appeared once at Fenner's. In June, 1871, he played for the Gentlemen of Lancashire against Cambridge and, as if to show the new generation how fields were won, scored 64 and 65 against the bowling of Powys, Bray, and Cobden. It is, however, upon two performances against the travelling XIs that Mr. Makinson's fame as a batsman really rests. He was one of the very few men who ever made 100 against the All England XI, scoring, in 1860, 104 on the Broughton ground at Manchester. This was a great feat against the bowling of Jackson and Wilsher, both in their prime. Seventeen years later, also on the Broughton ground, he scored 104 not out against the United South of England XI. Mr. Makinson was associated with Lancashire in the earliest days of the County Club, and took part in July, 1865, in the first county match at Old Trafford. His scores were 45 and 0, Lancashire beating Middlesex by 62 runs. He played on and off for Lancashire till 1868, and again appeared in the XI in 1873 and 1874. He kept up his cricket by playing for the Broughton club, of which he was for years the life and soul. In the Gentlemen and Players matches he was only seen on three or four occasions. He did well at the Oval, scoring 49 in 1860 and 64 not out in 1864, but at Lord's in 1860 Jackson's bowling was too much for him. W. G. Grace in his book on cricket, published in 1891, and the late Richard Daft in *Kings of Cricket*, have both paid warm tributes to Mr. Makinson's powers as a batsman. A man rather below medium height—he was not quite 5 ft. 7 in.—he was a brilliant player of the forward school, going out of his ground to hit in a way quite foreign to the style of modern players. Of his fast bowling it is said in the Badminton book that he was quite as successful against Oxford as his merits justified. Mr. Makinson was for many years Stipendiary Magistrate at Salford. On retiring from the Bench, he spoke with some pride of the very few cases in which his decisions had been reversed. He never lost his interest in cricket, and was for some time Chairman of the Lancashire Committee.

MALDEN, Eustace, died at Rottingdean on December 3, 1947, aged 84. He played for Haileybury 1881–82, Hertfordshire County 1887–88 and for Kent 1892–93.

MALLETT, R. H., known throughout the British Empire as a prominent cricket legislator, died on November 30, 1939, aged 81, at his home, Ickenham, in Middlesex. Hon. Secretary of the Durham County Club, he played for the county from 1884 to 1906; captain in 1897. He took a leading part in the formation of the Minor Counties Cricket Association in 1895 and was the Hon. Secretary from 1897 to 1907, afterwards becoming Chairman and President. Mr. Mallett retained the Presidency until 1938 and in recent years he served two periods on the M.C.C. Committee, but was best known for his work in connection with touring teams. He was responsible for the programmes of several teams that came to England. In this way he was closely associated with the Australian visiting teams of 1926 and 1930 and the South African team of 1929. The West Indies were specially indebted to Mr. Mallett. He managed their tours to England in 1906, 1923 and 1928. In 1929–30 he managed the M.C.C. tour in the West Indies and next autumn he was in charge of the West Indies team that went to Australia. When a young man, he was so fit that on one day he played at wing three-quarter for Hartlepool Rovers and in an Association Cup-tie.

A charming man in every way, he always worked to the advantage of cricket. Keeping in close touch with the game and a great authority on the laws, Mr. Mallett was appointed a member of the Commission, with Mr. W. Findlay and Mr. R. C. N. Palairet, which in 1937 after lengthy inquiries, issued a report as to the best ways and means of conducting the County Championship.

MALLINCKRODT, Kelsey Warner, who died in New York City, on October 23, 1911, aged 37, played for the United States against Canada in 1903. For XVI of Baltimore against Mr. P. F. Warner's XI in 1897 he took nine wickets for 103 runs.

MALTHOUSE, Samuel, who died on February 7, 1931, was born at Whitwell, Derbyshire, on October 13, 1857. He played for Derbyshire between 1890 and 1895 and scored 74 (not out) v. Leicestershire at Derby in the first-mentioned year. He was a free-hitting left-handed batsman and medium-paced bowler.

MALTHOUSE, William Norman, who died on June 4, 1961, aged 70, played in four matches for Derbyshire in 1919 and 1920. Son of Samuel Malthouse, who assisted the county between 1890 and 1895, William was a member of the Derbyshire team who, by 36 runs at Derby, inflicted upon the Australian Imperial Forces team of 1919 the one defeat suffered from a county.

MANGOLD, Charles August, who died at Port Elizabeth on August 6, 1954, aged 78, played for Eastern Province in the Currie Cup competition. In 1896, for XVIII of Port Elizabeth against Lord Hawke's team, he performed the "hat-trick", his victims being A. J. L. Hill, Lord Hawke and H. R. Bromley-Davenport.

MANJREKAR, Vijay Laxman, who died in Madras, where he had gone for a sportsmen's gathering, on October 18, 1983, aged 52, was a conspicuously good player of fast bowling in an era when India had few of them. Having played in the first of his 55 Tests in 1951–52, against England at Calcutta, he soon showed his quality by making 133 in his first Test in England (at Headingley) in June, 1952, when only 20. Coming in at 42 for three on the first morning, with Trueman and Bedser on the war path (and Laker to follow), he and his captain, Hazare, rescued India's innings with a fourth-wicket partnership of 222, which still stands as a record between the two countries. If, as the years passed, problems of weight slowed him down, he had sufficiently nimble footwork and enough natural ability always to be a dangerous opponent and often a joy to watch. Like many of the best Indian batsmen, he was small and a fine cutter and hooker. Within nine months of his 133 at Headingley he scored 118 against West Indies at Kingston, sharing on that occasion a record second-wicket partnership with Pankaj Roy. His two best Test series were against New Zealand in India in 1955–56 (386 runs, average 77.20) and against England in India in 1961–62 (586 runs, average 83.71). He made seven Test centuries, the highest his 189 against England at Delhi in 1961–62 and the last of them in his final Test innings, against New Zealand at Madras in February 1965. At Bombay in 1964–65 his two innings of 59 and 39 were invaluable contributions towards India's first Test victory over Australia. An occasional off-spinner, a serviceable wicket-keeper and in his early days a fine cover fielder, he played at different times for no fewer than six sides in the Ranji Trophy—Bombay, Bengal, Andhra, Uttar Pradesh, Rajasthan and Maharashtra. In Test matches he scored 3,208 runs (average 39.12), took one wicket, held 19 catches and made two stumpings. In the Ranji Trophy he scored 3,734 runs (average 57.44) and hit 12 100s.

MANKAD, Mulvantrai, affectionately known to cricketers throughout his life by his schoolboy nickname of "Vinoo," died in Bombay on August 21, 1978, aged 61. He was the greatest all-rounder that India has yet produced. In Tests he scored 2,109 runs with an average of 31.47 and took 162 wickets at 32.31. He made five centuries and twice took eight wickets in an innings. Against New Zealand at Madras in 1955–56 he scored 231, still a record for India in a Test, and with P. Roy put on 413 for the first wicket, a record for any Test. His average for that series was 105. When India at Madras in 1952 gained their first victory over England, his bowling was almost wholly responsible. On a wicket which gave him little assistance he took eight for 55 and four for 53. His most famous feat was v. England at Lord's in 1952 when going in first he scored 72 and 184. In the second innings he went straight to the wicket after bowling 31 overs that day. In the whole match he bowled 97 overs and took five for 231. England won by eight wickets, but Mankad's performance must surely rank as the greatest ever done in a Test by a member of the losing side. Indeed in assessing his record one must remember that of the 44 Tests between 1946

and 1959 in which he played India won five only.

His first-class career started in 1935, but it was against Lord Tennyson's team in India in 1937–38 that he came into real prominence. With a batting average in the unofficial Tests of 62.66 and a bowling average of 14.53, he headed both averages, and Tennyson is reported to have said that he would already get a place in a World XI. In 1946 for India in England he made 1,120 runs and took 129 wickets. He remains the only Indian ever to have accomplished this feat and no member of any touring side has achieved it since. In 1947 he went into League cricket and, though he remained available in India during the winter, when they came to England in 1952, he was released for the Tests only. Indeed the Lord's Test was his first first-class match that season. He captained India in Pakistan in 1954–55. In his first-class career, which ended in 1962, he scored 11,480 runs with an average of 34.78 and took 774 wickets at 24.60.

As a batsman, he had great powers of concentration and a strong defence. His record stand with Roy lasted over eight hours and they were not separated till after lunch on the second day. At the same time, if a ball wanted hitting, he hit it. Many will remember how at Lord's in 1952 the match had barely been in progress half an hour when he hit Jenkins high over the screen at the Nursery End. He had a fine cover-drive and hit well to leg. Like many players of great natural ability he did not in attack worry overmuch about the straightness of his bat. In fact he was essentially a practical batsman who was prepared to go in cheerfully whenever his captain wanted and adapt his tactics to the state of the match.

As a bowler, he was a slow left-hander of the old-fashioned orthodox type, varying his natural leg-break with a faster one which came with his arm and got him lots of wickets. His figures in 1946 are the more creditable when one realises that for most of the tour he was suffering from an injury which made this ball tiring and difficult to bowl. As a boy he had experimented with the chinaman but was fortunately persuaded by that shrewd coach, Bert Wensley, to abandon it. For some years he was undoubtedly the best bowler of his type in the world.

His son, Ashcock, played for India in 15 Tests as a batsman. The pair provide one of the rare instances of father and son both representing their country.

TEST CAREER
BATTING AND FIELDING

Season	Opponents	Tests	Inns	Not Outs	Runs	Highest Inns	100s	50s	Average	Catches
1946	England	3	5	0	124	63	0	1	24.80	3
1947–48	Australia	5	10	0	306	116	2	0	30.60	2
1948–49	West Indies	5	9	0	143	29	0	0	15.88	6
1951–52	England	5	8	1	223	71*	0	2	31.85	6
1952	England	3	5	0	271	184	1	1	54.20	0
1952–53	Pakistan	4	5	1	129	41	0	0	32.25	4
1952–53	West Indies	5	10	2	229	96	0	2	28.62	2
1954–55	Pakistan	5	6	1	51	33	0	0	10.20	6
1955–56	New Zealand	4	5	0	526	231	2	0	105.20	4
1956–57	Australia	3	6	0	82	27	0	0	13.66	0
1958–59	West Indies	2	3	0	25	21	0	0	8.33	0
Totals		44	72	5	2,109	231	5	6	31.47	33

Mode of dismissal: Bowled 22; caught 35; lbw 7; run out 3. Total 67.

BOWLING

Season	Opponents	Tests	Balls	Maidens	Runs	Wkts	5 wkts/ Inns	10 wkts/ match	Avge
1946	England	3	839	40	292	11	1	0	26.54
1947–48	Australia	5	1,392	21	630	12	0	0	52.50
1948–49	West Indies	5	1,635	52	744	17	0	0	43.76
1951–52	England	5	2,224	151	571	34	1	1	16.97
1952	England	3	1,038	68	386	9	1	0	42.88
1952–53	Pakistan	4	1,592	100	514	25	3	1	20.56
1952–53	West Indies	5	2,070	102	796	15	1	0	53.06
1954–55	Pakistan	5	1,581	130	399	12	1	0	33.25
1955–56	New Zealand	4	1,003	66	328	12	0	0	27.33
1956–57	Australia	3	754	29	313	11	0	0	28.45
1958–59	West Indies	2	558	18	262	4	0	0	65.50
Totals		44	14,686	777	5,235	162	8	2	32.31

How wickets were taken: Bowled 36; caught 77; lbw 28; stumped 19; hit wicket 2. Total 162.

TEST CENTURIES (5)

116   v. Australia at Melbourne, 1947–48.
111   v. Australia at Melbourne, 1947–48.
184   v. England at Lord's, 1952.
223   v. New Zealand at Bombay, 1955–56
231   v. New Zealand at Madras, 1955–56.

CENTURY PARTNERSHIPS

First Wicket
413   with P. Roy v. New Zealand at Madras, 1955–56.
124   with C. T. Sarwate v. Australia at Melbourne, 1947–48.
106   with P. Roy v. England at Lord's, 1952.
103*   with P. Roy v. England at Calcutta, 1951–52.

Second Wicket
124   with H. R. Adhikari v. Australia at Melbourne, 1947–48.

Third Wicket
211   with V. S. Hazare v. England at Lord's, 1952.

Signifies not out.

CENTURY PARTNERSHIP—*continued*

Fourth Wicket
167   with A. G. Kripal Singh v. New Zealand at Bombay, 1955–56.

Seventh Wicket
153   with M. L. Apte v. West Indies at Port-of-Spain, 1952–53.

FIVE OR MORE WICKETS IN INNINGS

Five for 101	v. England at Old Trafford, 1946.
Eight for 55	v. England at Madras, 1951–52.
Five for 196	v. England at Lord's, 1952.
Five for 72	v. Pakistan at Bombay, 1952–53.
Eight for 52	v. Pakistan at New Delhi, 1952–53 (First Innings).
Five for 79	v. Pakistan at New Delhi, 1952–53 (Second Innings).
Five for 228	v. West Indies at Kingston, 1952–53.
Five for 64	v. Pakistan at Peshawar, 1954–55.

MANN, Eric William, who died at Rye on February 15, 1954, aged 71, was in the Harrow XI from 1899 to 1901, being captain in the last year when his innings of 69 helped in a victory by 10 wickets over Eton. A hard-hitting batsman with free style and special strength on the leg-side, he was also a useful change bowler. Going up to Trinity College, Cambridge, he gained a Blue in 1903 and two following seasons, leading the side in 1905. His highest score in the three University matches was 42 in 1904, but he played a number of fine innings in other games. In 1902 and 1903, Mann appeared six times for Kent with little success. He captained the M.C.C. team which engaged in a short tour of America and Canada in 1905.

MANN, Francis Thomas, who died suddenly on October 6, 1964, was among the most forceful batsmen in the history of cricket. In the Malvern XI from 1904 to 1907, he was captain in the last year. Going up to Cambridge, he played in the University matches of 1909, 1910 and 1911 without achieving anything of note. Though he played Association football at Malvern, he gained a Rugby Blue as a forward in 1910.

In 1909 "Frank" Mann began his association with Middlesex, for whom he played till 1931. He soon became celebrated for his powerful stroke-play, and particularly for his tremendous driving. Once against Yorkshire he drove the ball four times on to the roof of the Pavilion at Lord's. At Trent Bridge in 1925 he helped Middlesex to score 502, the highest fourth-innings total in the County Championship, and beat Nottinghamshire by four wickets. His contribution amounted to 101, he and Hendren (200) hitting off the last 271 runs in three and a quarter hours without

being parted. Altogether Mann scored 14,182 runs at an average of 23.67 and brought off 165 catches, most of them at mid-off where he was an eminently safe fieldsman. The biggest of his eight three-figure innings was 194 from the Warwickshire bowling at Edgbaston in 1926. His best season for Middlesex was that of 1922, when he hit 935 runs, average 24.60.

A highly popular personality on and off the field, he captained Middlesex from 1921 to 1928, also acting as hon. secretary for most of that time, and he led them to the County Championship in the first season. He captained England in South Africa in 1922–23; one of his sons, F. G. Mann, also a Cambridge and Middlesex cricketer, followed suit 26 years later. Frank Mann represented Gentlemen against Players in 14 matches between 1914 and 1930, distinguishing himself at Scarborough in 1922 by hitting 82 and 100. In 1930 he served as a member of the Test Selection Committee. As an officer in the Scots Guards during the First World War, he was three times wounded and three times Mentioned in Dispatches.

MANN, Norman Bertram Fleetwood, died in a Johannesburg nursing home on July 31, 1952, aged 30. The untimely death of this modest and likeable man, known throughout the cricket world as "Tufty," was yet another grievous blow to a country which has lost so many fine cricketers in their playing prime. Taken ill soon after the fourth Test in England in 1951, he underwent an abdominal operation and stayed in England for three months before flying home. He bore his troubles with the steadfastness and patience which characterised him in all things, but another operation became necessary midway through 1952 and he died some six weeks later.

Born at Brakpan, Transvaal, on December 28, 1921, Mann was first educated at Michaelhouse College. He represented Natal Schools at cricket, and, at the age of 16, won the Natal Amateur Golf Championship. Subsequently he went to Cambridge. Although bowling well in the Freshmen's match there in 1939 he did not gain a place in any of the University games, but, turning his attention again to golf, he won his Blue. Going back to South Africa, he played for Natal in the 1939–40 season. His first experience of big cricket could have been anything but encouraging, for Mann was a member of the Natal attack against which Transvaal scored 608 runs for six wickets. E. A. Rowan's 306 not out still remains a South African batting record. With two wickets for 106 in 45 overs, Mann did not suffer so much from Rowan's flogging as did his colleagues.

During the War Mann was captured in Italy, but he escaped and was hidden by peasants. On his return to South Africa he settled in Port Elizabeth and began his association with Eastern Province. He quickly made his mark by impeccable length, direction and control of spin, and in December 1946, against Transvaal at Johannesburg, he established a then world record by bowling 542 balls (67.6–38–69–6) in an innings.

The selectors merely confirmed the opinion of all South African cricketers when they chose him as the left-arm slow bowler to make the tour to England in 1947.

In a high-scoring series of Tests, Mann headed the South African bowling averages with 15 wickets, average 40.20 Making his international debut on a typically docile pitch at Nottingham, Mann conformed so successfully to the tactics required by his captain that he opened with eight successive maiden overs against such punishing batsmen as Denis Compton and Edrich—in their peak year—and in the match sent down 80 overs for 104 runs. More accurate bowling on an unhelpful pitch scarcely could be imagined. Another good performance was his four for 68 in 50 overs in the fourth Test. Throughout the tour he completely fulfilled the two main functions of a left-arm slow bowler—to seal up one end when conditions favoured batsmen and to extract full advantage when they offered him the slightest assistance. Although indifferent eyesight compelled Mann to wear glasses and also handicapped his batting, he occasionally delighted spectators with powerful hitting made with a free swing of the bat. That season he trounced the Glamorgan bowling for 97 out of 122 in a stand with A. M. B. Rowan lasting 55 minutes. He fell to a catch in the deep when trying a big hit which would have completed his only century in first-class cricket.

From the time of his entry into Test cricket, Mann became an automatic choice for South Africa and, until illness forced him to withdraw from the fifth Test at the Oval in 1951, he played in 19 consecutive Tests, 14 against England, five against Australia. Earlier in that 1951 season Mann's four for 24 in the second innings at Nottingham helped South Africa to gain their first Test victory for 16 years and the second in all visits to England.

Few better illustrations of Mann's accuracy could be provided than the fact that, on seven occasions when he bowled 50 or more overs in Test cricket, only once did he give away more than 100 runs. Two of his best feats were eight for 59 against Western Province at Cape Town in 1947–48 and six for 59 against F. G. Mann's M.C.C. team in the Durban Test of 1948–49. His record in Currie Cup games bore comparison with any bowler of his type in the Union. In the 12 games in which he participated he took 75 wickets, including 12 for 102 against Rhodesia in 1950–51.

MANNING, Cardinal, died on January 14, 1892, aged 83. It may seem a little strange to include Cardinal Manning's name in a cricket obituary, but inasmuch as he played for Harrow against Winchester at Lord's in 1825, in the first match that ever took place between the two schools, his claim cannot be disputed.

MANNING, James Lionel, who died in King's College Hospital, London, on January 18, 1974, aged 60, had been troubled with indifferent health for some years, but as a campaigning writer and broadcaster for all that was good in sport he kept going right to the end. A member of M.C.C., cricket was his favourite sport. He had been Sports Editor on the *Sunday Chronicle, Sunday Dispatch* and *Daily Mail* and was for some years a columnist on the *Evening Standard.* He wrote many reviews on *Wisden.* His father, L. V. Manning, wrote his first sports column in 1919 and the father's attitude to sport and the philosophy of sport had a marked influence on the son.

MANNING, Thomas Edgar, who died on November 22, 1975, aged 91, was easily the senior surviving captain of a first-class county. His death left Lieut.-Col. R. R. C.

Baggallay, captain of Derbyshire in 1914, the sole survivor of those who captained a county before the First World War. After averaging 61 in his last year in the Wellingborough XI, Manning went up to Cambridge, where he played in some trials and might perhaps have got a Blue as a wicketkeeper had he not been contemporary with M. W. Payne. He had first appeared for Northamptonshire in 1903 and from 1908 to 1910 captained the side. Promoted in 1905, the county had hitherto shown little claim to justify it. The turning-point came under Manning's captaincy when in 1909, after losing seven of their first eight matches, they won eight out of the next nine and finished seventh. Next year, they were ninth and in 1912 second. Reappearing in 1919 after nine years' absence, he headed the batting averages and made his highest score for the county, 57 against Derbyshire. A match in 1922 concluded his career. From 1948 to 1955 he was President of the County C.C.

MARCHANT, Francis, who died April 13, 1946, was closely connected with the Kent XI over a period of 23 seasons—1883 to 1905—and captain of the side from 1890 to 1897. He was a brilliant and stylish batsman. Born at Matfield, Staplehurst, on May 22, 1864, Frank Marchant, after one term at Rugby, went to Eton, and was in the XI there in 1882 and 1883. In his second match with Harrow at Lord's he gave a delightful display, making, mainly by cutting and square-leg hitting, 93 out of 115 in 95 minutes. At Cambridge he gained his Blue as a Freshman, but his cricket career at the University was rather disappointing for a player of such promise. Had he exercised a little more restraint on first going in, he must, with his gifts, have attained the highest honours. Still, he did some great things for Kent, scoring 111 out of 150 in 95 minutes against Yorkshire at Sheffield in 1901, and in the same year 100 out of 141 on a bad wicket in 75 minutes against Middlesex at Lord's. In the match with Yorkshire at Leeds in 1896 he narrowly missed two separate 100s, making 128 in the first innings and 88 in the second. His highest score for Kent was 176 against Sussex at Gravesend in 1889, when he and G. G. Hearne (103) put on 249 for the fourth wicket.

Marchant's most famous performance was an innings of 103 for the M.C.C. against the Australians at Lord's in 1893, when he and Flowers (130) put on 152 runs in 70 minutes.

MARDER, John Israel, died in London on August 27, 1976, aged 67. Born at Nottingham and educated there and at Boston University, U.S.A., he did much to revive interest in cricket in America and was founder in 1961 and first President of the United States Cricket Association. Two years later he was largely responsible for reviving the old fixture between Canada and the United States. His writings on cricket included a history of the contest, 1884–1967, entitled "The International Series," an article on United States cricket in *The World of Cricket* and a number of contributions to various cricket periodicals. He covered cricket in the U.S.A. regularly in recent years for *Wisden* and in the 1975 edition in *Buying Back One's Past* he drew attention to the old advertisements.

MARINDIN, Col. Sir F. A., C.M.G., K.C.M.G., born May 1, 1838; died April 21, 1900. Batted steadily, and in the field was generally point. Height, 6 ft. 1 in.; weight, 12 st. Frequently played for the Royal Engineers. In 1884 he was elected Vice-President of the Kent County C.C. In 1889 he resigned the Presidency of the Football Association.

MARKS, Alexander Edward, who died on July 28, 1983, aged 72, played 33 times for New South Wales between 1928 and 1937 as a left-handed batsman, scoring 1,837 runs at an average of 36.01. When still only 18 he played in a Test trial, scoring 83 and 14; but the Australian side went to England in 1930 without him. Of his three 100s, the highest was 201 against Queensland at Sydney in 1935–36. His sons, Neil and Lyn, both also played for New South Wales.

MARKS, Geoffrey, C.B.E., who died on August 25, 1938, was at Whitgift School and kept wicket for Middlesex occasionally in 1894 and 1895.

MARLOW, Francis William, who scored a century on his debut in first-class cricket, died at Brighton on August 7, 1952, aged 84. He also enjoyed the distinction of hitting a century when first appearing for Players v. Gentlemen at the Oval in 1895, scoring 27 and 100. Born at Tamworth, Staffordshire, on October 8, 1867, he was taken to live at Brighton when a month old, and returned to play for his native county from 1887 to 1890, heading the batting averages in the last season when making 133 v. Northamptonshire at Stoke. In 1891 "Billy" Marlow began to qualify by residence for Sussex, being contemporary with such famous players as "Ranji", C. B. Fry and Sir Aubrey Smith. Against M.C.C. and Ground at Lord's in that season, his first match for his new county, he hit 144, and as a stylish, forcing opening batsman and brilliant fieldsman at mid-off and third man he continued till he retired from the game in 1904. Later he became a first-class umpire.

His highest innings for Sussex was 155 against Somerset at Hove in 1895, when he and K. S. Ranjitsinhji added 226 for the second wicket, and he hit 130 from the Oxford University bowling on the same ground when sharing in an opening stand of 303 with G. L. Wilson. Next year, also at Hove, he and George Bean made 211 for the first wicket against Gloucestershire. Altogether he scored 7,855 runs, average 22.44.

MARLOW, William Henry, died on December 16, 1975, aged 74. A slow left-hander, he provided some useful variety to the Leicestershire attack between 1931 and 1936. But, though he could flight the ball and spin it, he needed help from the pitch to be really dangerous and his 261 wickets cost 29.17 runs each. He was a good all-round field with a safe pair of hands and a useful tail-end batsman who against Gloucestershire in 1933 helped Astill to put on 157 for the last wicket, a record for the county. His own share of the partnership was 49.

MARR, Alfred P., who died at Sydney in March, 1940, aged 77, played for the Combined XI of Australia in one of four such matches against Arthur Shrewsbury's side in 1885. A useful batsman and bowler for New South Wales, he was chosen three times to come to England, but was never able to accept the invitation. So well did he maintain his ability that when 67 years of age, in a grade competition match at Sydney, he scored 101.

MARRIOTT, Charles, born at Cotesbach, Leicester, on October 18, 1848, died July 9, 1918. Mr. Marriott was for a long period a very prominent and popular figure in the cricket world, being captain of the Leicestershire XI about 15 years—1872 to 1887—and doing much for the county in its early days. He was three times President of the club. Though quite a good bat at Winchester, he did not till his last year at Oxford succeed in getting his Blue. He was on the winning side against Cambridge at Lord's, but in his only innings was bowled without getting a run. He won his place for Oxford, however, strictly on his merits, scoring consistently in the trial matches at home. After his Oxford days he played a lot of cricket for I Zingari, and in later years served several times on the Committee of the M.C.C.

MARRIOTT, Charles Stowell, who died on October 13, 1966, aged 71, was one of the best leg-break and googly bowlers of his era. He learned his cricket in Ireland, where he was educated at St. Columba's, and gained a Blue at Cambridge in 1920 and 1921, meeting with remarkable success in the University matches. In 1920, when rain prevented play on the first two days, he took seven wickets for 69 runs and in the following season he played a leading part in a triumph for the Light Blues in an innings with 24 runs to spare by dismissing seven Oxford batsmen in the match for 111 runs.

In all first-class cricket he took 724 wickets at an average cost of 20.04 runs and his bowling skill so far outreached his ability as a batsman that his victims exceeded his aggregate of runs by 169. Cunning flighting, allied to the ability to turn the ball sharply, made him a menace to batsmen even on good pitches, and when the turf gave him help he could be well-nigh unplayable. His action was high with a free, loose arm which he swung behind his back before delivery in a manner reminiscent of Colin Blythe. From 1919 to 1921 he appeared for Lancashire and when beginning a long association with Dulwich College as master-in-charge of cricket, he threw in his lot with Kent, whom he assisted during the school holidays from 1924 to 1937.

In his first season with the southern county he distinguished himself by taking five wickets for 31 and six for 48 in the game with Lancashire at Dover, and against Hampshire at Canterbury he returned figures of five for 66 and five for 44, and he achieved many other notable performances in later years.

He met with great success on the occasion of his one appearance in a Test match for England. That was at the Oval in 1933, when he so bewildered the batsmen that he took five wickets for 37 runs in the first innings and, with second innings figures of six for 59, hurried the West Indies to defeat by an innings and 17 runs—a feat described by *Wisden* of the time as one of the best accomplished by a bowler when playing for England for the first time.

"Father" Marriott, as he was popularly known, engaged in two tours abroad. In 1924–25 he was a member of Lord—then the Hon. Lionel—Tennyson's side in South

Africa and in 1933–34 he went with D. R. Jardine's M.C.C. team to India, where, against Madras, he did the hat-trick for the only time in his first-class career. During the Second World War he served as an anti-aircraft gunner in the Home Guard.

MARRIOTT, The Rev. George Strickland, a younger brother of Messrs. C. and J. M. Marriott, died on October 21, 1905. He was in the Winchester XI in 1872, 1873, and 1874, and in 1878 assisted Oxford against Cambridge. *Scores and Biographies* described him as "A good batsman, bowls fast round-armed, whilst in the field he is generally point." From 1874 until 1885 his name will occasionally be found in the Leicestershire XI. He was born at Cotesbach, near Lutterworth, on October 7, 1885.

MARRIOTT, Harold Henry, died in London after a heart attack on November 15, 1949, aged 74. Malvern XI 1893–94. Played for Leicestershire 1894–1902 and four times for Cambridge, his best effort against Oxford being 50 in 1897. Toured America with F. Mitchell's team in 1895 and P. F. Warner's in 1897.

MARSDEN, Lance-Corpl. Arthur (Manchester Regiment) was born at Buxton and died in July, 1916, of wounds received near Fricourt. He was captain of Chetham's School, Manchester, and in 1910 played for Derbyshire v. Kent at Derby, scoring 0 and six. He was associated with the Longsight and Levenshulme clubs.

MARSDEN, Capt. Edmund (64th Pioneers, Indian Army) died of malarial fever in Burma in September, 1915, aged 34. In 1909, when he averaged 42.09 for the East Gloucestershire C.C., he played in two matches for Gloucestershire, scoring seven and 11 v. Notts and 38 and 23 v. Northamptonshire, both games taking place at Gloucester. (Owing to an oversight, his initial was given as G. in *Wisden* for 1910.)

MARSDEN, Edward L., died at Hampstead, July 2, 1946, aged 75. Played for Hampstead for many years and for Middlesex against Philadelphia in 1897. Served in the First World War as 2nd Lieut., Bedfordshire Regiment.

MARSH, Edward Caldecot, who died at Kendal on November 27, 1926, aged 61, was a useful batsman with strong strokes to leg. Obtaining a place in the Malvern XI in 1883, he was second in the averages with 28.58. In 1885

and 1886 he appeared on a few occasions for Somerset, but in 1887 began to assist Devonshire, which side he captained for a time.

MARSH, John, the well-known aboriginal fast bowler, died in hospital at Orange (N.S.W.) on May 26, 1916. He played Grade cricket for the South Sydney and Sydney clubs, and also appeared for New South Wales. In the match with Victoria at Sydney in February, 1901, he was no-balled 17 times for throwing by R. Crockett, of Melbourne: the other umpire, S. P. Jones, however, allowed his bowling as fair. A few seasons later he had a six months' tour through the Commonwealth with a Hippodrome company, being exhibited in the role of a fast bowler and demonstrating his skill to any countrymen who were anxious to stand up against him.

MARSHAL, Alan (15th Batt. Australian Imperial Forces) who was born at Warwick, in Queensland, on June 12, 1883, died of enteric at Imtarfa Military Hospital, Malta, on July 23, 1915, after serving in Gallipoli. He was a cricketer of unfulfilled promise. He had it in him to be great, but somehow he missed the position that at one time seemed to be within his reach. A hitter of greater natural powers has seldom been seen. The son of a Lincolnshire man who had emigrated to Australia, he took to cricket while quite young, playing both at the South Brisbane State School and the Brisbane Grammar School. He learned much through watching Boyle, McDonnell, S. P. Jones, and others, and at the early age of 14 began to play in Grade cricket. Later he played for a time in Grade matches in Sydney, and had represented Queensland a few times before coming to England. He always showed distinct talent, his batting improving rapidly from the time he had the advantage of playing on turf wickets. On arriving in England he soon made his mark, his form being so good that before he had been here long he was asked to qualify for Surrey. For London County in 1905 he made 2,752 runs with an average of 56.16 and took 118 wickets at a cost of 16.41 runs each, and in the corresponding fixtures of the following year his aggregates were 3,578 (average 76.12) and 167 (average 14.10) respectively. In *all* matches in 1906 he scored 4,350 runs, making 14 100s, and took 210 wickets. Against Croydon he made 300 not out at the Crystal Palace, and 171 in the return: he also scored 245 v. Egypt at the Crystal Palace, 219 v. Norbury at Norbury, and 204 not out v. Cyphers at the Palace. Having qualified by the necessary two years' residence, he duly appeared for the county. Everything suggested that Surrey had found a prize. At first, however, Marshal did not do himself full justice in his new surroundings. In the season of 1907 he made over 1,000 runs for Surrey, but there was a certain restraint in his play. For the moment he was feeling his way. In 1908 he showed all that he could do. He had a splendid season for Surrey, scoring 1,884 runs with an average of 40 in all matches for the county and finishing second only to Hayward. Five times he exceeded 100, an innings of 108 against Middlesex at the Oval being a marvel of powerful driving. When the season ended his place among the great players of the day seemed assured. Apart from his batting, he was a good change bowler and in the field he had scarcely a superior. He could fill any place with credit and no catch, if reasonably possible, escaped his hands. The future looked bright indeed for him, but he never again reached the same level. At the height of the season of 1909 the Surrey committee suspended him for a time and in the following year they terminated his engagement. Marshal returned to Queensland and played cricket there, but without doing anything exceptional. He sailed for Australia on September 12, 1910, and on the day before his departure played a magnificent innings of 259 not out for Whitcomb Wanderers v. W. Jones' XI, at Acton, hitting 13 sixes and 36 fours. Earlier in the season—at Ashford (Middlesex) on July 7—he had taken all 10 wickets in an innings for 28 runs for A. H. Marriott's XI v. Ashford. Marshal's 100s in first-class cricket were as under:

111	Surrey v. Worcestershire, at Worcester	..	..	..	..	..	1907
176	Surrey v. Worcestershire, at Worcester		..	..	..	..	1908
143	Surrey v. Northamptonshire, at Northampton			..	..	..	1908
103	Surrey v. Philadelphians, at the Oval	..		..	..	..	1908
108	Surrey v. Middlesex, at the Oval	..	..	..	..	..	1908
167	Surrey v. Kent, at the Oval	..	..	..	..	..	1908
110	Surrey v. Yorkshire, at the Oval	..	..	..	..	..	1909
106	An Australian XI v. South Africans, at Brisbane		..	..	..	1910–11

In the second innings of Queensland v. New Zealand, at Brisbane, in December, 1913, he went in first and carried his bat through the innings for 66.

As a bowler he had two great successes for Surrey at the Oval in 1908, taking five wickets for 19 against Nottinghamshire in the August Bank Holiday match, and in the match with Derbyshire at one period dismissing five men in 13 balls without a run being made off him.

MARSHALL, Allan George, who died on March 14, 1973, aged 77, was a noted all-round cricketer when in the Taunton School XI for five years. During that time he once scored centuries in following matches, twice took all 10 wickets in an innings, became captain and turned out for Somerset. He went up to Cambridge, but the First World War broke out and he joined the Army, being twice wounded. In 1921 he returned to his old school as a master and continued till retiring in 1955. In holiday time he played for Somerset and in 1929 became second wicket-keeper. He appeared for the county till 1931. He also played much club cricket.

MARSHALL, Charles, of the Rugby XIs of 1860, 1861 and 1862, died on February 25, 1904. As he was born at Cricklewood, in Middlesex, on February 20, 1843, he was in his 62nd year at the time of his death. He was a sound batsman, a particularly fine field at long-leg and cover-point, and could throw the ball over 100 yd. with ease. He was contemporary at Rugby with C. Booth, B. B. Cooper, F. R. Evans, E. Rutter, M. T. Martin, G. P. Robertson, J. S. E. Hood, and T. Case. After leaving Rugby he appeared for Cambridgeshire, Middlesex, Huntingdonshire, M.C.C., Free Foresters, etc. He assisted Middlesex on two occasions only, both times in 1866, scoring 33 against Cambridgeshire, at Cambridge, and 50 against Surrey, at the Oval.

MARSHALL, Edwin Alfred, who died on January 28, 1970, aged 63, was President of Nottinghamshire in 1964 and 1965, and for many years before that a member of the county committee. He collapsed and died at the annual meeting while making a plea for support for the club. He was a pace bowler for Notts Amateurs and when appearing for the county against the Australians at Trent Bridge in 1938 he enjoyed the distinction of dismissing Sir Don Bradman. He bore a leading part in the signing by Nottinghamshire of the celebrated West Indies all-rounder, Garfield Sobers. He was chairman of the Nottinghamshire County Cricket Supporters' Association, of which he was a founder member, for 15 years, and had been a City councillor.

MARSHALL, Lieut.-General Sir Frederick, K.C.M.G., born at Godalming, July 26, 1830, died at 9, Eaton Place, London, June 8, 1900, aged 69. *Scores and Biographies* (v–156), says of him: "Height 6 ft. 3 in., and weight 13 st. 4 lb. Is a powerful hitter forward and to leg, and in the field is generally cover-point or long-leg. Has not, however, participated in many quite first-rate contests, his performances being principally with I Zingari and in regimental matches. In 1859 he became President of the United All England XI, which office, however, he resigned at the end of the season of 1863, and was succeeded in May, 1864, by Mr. George Mason, of Bradford. In May, 1867, he became President of the Surrey County C.C. in place of his uncle, Mr. Henry Marshall, who had held that office for 14 years. Was educated at Eton, but was not in the XI while there, and at Sandhurst. His brothers, Messrs. Alexander and Harry Marshall, also excelled in the game. Was Lieut.-Col. in the 2nd Life Guards, but in March, 1873, he retired on half-pay, and was appointed aide-de-camp to the Duke of Cambridge." *Scores and Biographies* (xiii–22), adds: "In February, 1879, he assumed the command of the cavalry at the Cape of Good Hope in the Zulu War." *Scores and Biographies* (xiv–36), says: "On December 2, 1889, he was presented with a portrait of himself by the members of the Chiddingfold Hunt, of which he was (1889) master. In 1890 he was appointed Colonel of the 1st Dragoon Guards. His portrait and biography appeared in *Baily's Magazine*, of January, 1891." In 1854, Surrey played Nottinghamshire on Mr. Marshall's ground at Godalming, instead of at the Oval, owing to a dispute with W. Houghton, the proprietor of the Surrey ground. For many years previous to his death he was Vice-President of the Surrey County C.C.

MARSHALL, Herbert Menzies, who died at South Kensington on March 2, 1913, will be chiefly remembered as the long-stop in the Cambridge XI to the late Robert Lang's tremendously fast bowling in the University match of 1862. Cambridge won the game by eight wickets, Lang taking five wickets for four runs and four for 31. The long-stop has disappeared from modern cricket, but 50 years ago the position, more especially at Lord's, was one of great importance. Perhaps for the reason that he had Lang's bowling to deal with, Mr. Marshall was

generally considered the best long-stop of his day. However, he had other qualifications as a cricketer, being a brilliant bat, though, according to *Scores and Biographies*, rather careless in the matter of defence. He was in the Westminster School XI in 1858–59–60, captaining the team in his last year, and was in the Cambridge XI for four years, 1861–64 inclusive. In 1861 he scored 76 not out and two, and in 1862, 31 and 0 not out against Oxford, but he failed as a batsman in 1863 and 1864. Mr. Marshall, who was born at Outwood Hall, near Leeds, on August 1, 1841, was picked for Gentlemen against Players both at Lord's and the Oval in 1861 and 1862. He met with no success in batting in these four matches, but he had the pleasure of taking part in the wonderful drawn game at the Oval in 1862, when the Players, at the finish, had 33 runs to get with two wickets to fall. An artist of no small distinction, Mr. Marshall was at one time Vice-President of the Royal Water-Colour Society. He was Professor of Landscape Painting at Queen's College, Harley Street, from 1904.

MARSHALL, Howard Percival, who died on October 27, 1973, aged 73, earned a place in cricket history as the first man to broadcast reports of the game for the B.B.C. He was an Authentic while at Oxford. His voice was also known to thousands for his descriptions of boxing, Rugby football and events in North Africa and Western Europe, including the D-Day landings. He also wrote cricket and rugby reports for the *Daily Telegraph* for some years.

MARSHALL, Joseph, who played occasionally for Derbyshire from 1887 to 1890, died at Derby on January 15, 1913, aged 50. He was an excellent slip, and a good scorer in club cricket, but for the county his highest innings was only 31 v. Surrey, at Derby, in 1887.

MARSHALL, Leslie Phillips, M.D., died on February 28, 1978, aged 84. Eleven appearances for Somerset, spread over 18 years, 1913–31, did not give him much chance of acclimatising himself to first-class cricket and his most successful match was his last, when he contributed 29 and 37 against New Zealand, both at a time when runs were badly needed. He and his brother, A. G., who also played for the county, were a very formidable pair in the Taunton School XI shortly before the First World War.

MARSHALL, Murray Wyatt, a member of a family identified prominently with the Surrey

County C.C. since its formation, died at Godalming on July 28, 1930, at the age of 77, as the result of a chill caught whilst umpiring in a match at Haslemere. He was in the Wellington College XI in 1870, played much good class club cricket, and was Hon. Secretary of the Broadwater C.C. for well over 50 years. Since 1873 he had been a member of the Surrey club, on whose committee he had served frequently.

MARSHALL, Walter, who held a high place in active connection with Nottingham cricket for over 60 years, died on January 15, 1943, aged 89. Born at Hyson Green on October 27, 1853, he made a name as a capable batsman with Notts Castle club, but did not play for the county until 1891, when 36 years old. He was not successful in two matches for a side rich in batting, but was chosen to manage the ground staff in 1897, when Nottinghamshire adopted the club and ground scheme for fostering local talent, of which Mr. Marshall possessed special knowledge. As expected by the county committee, the young professionals derived great benefit under his able supervision, and he held the position for 25 years. Subsequently he earned higher and more widely known fame as chief groundsman at Trent Bridge, where, under his care, the pitches and the whole playing area became a cause for admiration by all cricket lovers—except perhaps bowlers unable to derive any help from the turf. Marshall retired to well-earned rest at the end of the 1935 season when over 80 years of age, and passed away near to the ground which he knew during nearly all his long life.

MARSHAM, Charles Jacob Bullock, a member of the family of the Earl of Romney, and brother of the Rev. C. D. Marsham, once the best amateur bowler in England, died on August 20, 1901, at Suffolk Street, Pall Mall, after a short illness, at the age of 72. He was uncle to Mr. C. H. B. Marsham, who played an historical innings of 100 not out in the University match of 1901, and of his capabilities as a cricketer *Scores and Biographies* (iv–267) has the following: "Is a fine and powerful hitter, especially forward, and has made some capital scores for the Marylebone club and for Oxford.... In the field is generally short slip." In 1857 he assisted the Gentlemen against the Players at the Oval. His highest scores in important matches were 50 for M.C.C. and Ground v. Kent, at Gravesend, in June, 1856, and 50 for M.C.C. and Ground v. Kent, at Gravesend, in July, 1857. Mr. Marsham was born at Merton College, Oxford, January 18, 1829.

An old friend of Mr. Marsham—a famous cricketer—writes about him as follows: "Numbers of Oxford men will have heard of the death of Mr. Charles Marsham with great regret, and Oxford University cricket has lost one of its keenest, if not its keenest, supporter. The eldest son of the Venerable Warden of Merton, Mr. Marsham lived at Oxford for many years after taking his degree, during which time he rarely missed a match on the Varsity ground, and thus developed that strong Oxford partisanship which only ended with his life. Mr. Marsham was one of the original members of the Harlequins, and used to get up the teams to play against the Royal Artillery and Royal Engineers till quite late in life. He was president of the club for years and years, and never failed to take the chair at the annual meeting held at Oxford in the May term; indeed, only this last season he came up specially from Wales in order to preside. But it was not only Oxford cricket in which Mr. Marsham delighted. There was no more constant frequenter of Lord's (he was several years a member of the M.C.C. Committee) and the Oval. Unlike the majority of old cricketers, Mr. Marsham kept up with the times, and never contrasted the cricket of the present day unfavourably with that of bygone years. By generations of Oxford men he was affectionately spoken of as 'Charlie', and his disappearance leaves a gap that cannot be filled."

MARSHAM, The Rev. Cloudesley Dewar Bullock, died at Harrietsham, near Maidstone, of which parish he had been rector for 27 years, on March 2, 1915. Born at Merton College, Oxford, on January 30, 1835, he had completed his 80th year, outliving his famous Cambridge contemporaries Joseph Makinson and Joseph McCormick. Mr. Marsham retired from first-class cricket so long ago that to the present generation he was merely a name, but in his day he was the best amateur bowler in England. Playing all his serious cricket before the alteration of Law X, he bowled—right-hand on the fast side of medium pace—with a purely round arm action, but as he stood 6 ft. 1 in. the ball was delivered from a good height. He was very straight, with great accuracy of length, and came off the pitch with plenty of life. It has been said that he had a quick break from the leg side, but a famous cricketer who remembers him perfectly well says that he did not with intention make the ball turn, such break as he got on now and then being due to the ground.

What Mr. Marsham would have done in these days of carefully prepared wickets and the heavy roller it is futile to conjecture. It is sufficient that on the wickets of his own time he was brilliantly effective as long as he remained before the public. He said himself that flexibility of wrist was the chief cause of his success. He played five times for Oxford against Cambridge—1854 to 1858—and even if he had done nothing else his record in the University match would have made him famous. In the Gentlemen and Players matches he appeared 10 times, playing every year at Lord's from 1854 to 1862, but it was never his good fortune to be on the winning side. Still he took 48 wickets against the Players for just under 18 runs apiece. In 1860 he had the honour of being chosen captain at Lord's of the first XI of England against the Next Fourteen. Mr. Marsham did not play much important cricket after entering the church, but he took part in a few matches for Bucks between 1864 and 1868. He played for I Zingari and Free Foresters and had been a member of the M.C.C. since 1868. It was under the leadership of his son, C. H. B. Marsham, that Kent won the Championship in 1906.

MR. C. D. B. MARSHAM'S PERFORMANCES IN THE UNIVERSITY MATCH

Year	Scores	Bowling	Result
1854	.. 2	3 for 37 & 6 for 19	.. W. Inns. & 8 runs.
1855	.. 0	2 for 47 & 3 for 36	.. W. 3 wkts.
1856	.. 10 & 13 ..	5 for 38 & 2 for 37	.. L. 3 wkts.
1857†	.. 36 & 17 ..	5 for 31 & 3 for 58	.. W. 81 runs.
1858†	.. 0	5 for 42 & 6 for 17	.. W. Inns. & 38 runs.

This shows a record of 40 wickets for 9.05 runs each.

CHIEF BOWLING FEATS IN IMPORTANT CRICKET

(a) 8 or more wickets in an innings:

9 for 64	Gents of England v. Gents of M.C.C., at Lord's	1855
8 for 19	Oxfordshire v. Oxford University, at Oxford	1858
9 for 30	16 of Oxford University v. England, at Lord's	1858
8 for 37	Past v. Present (Oxford University), at Oxford	1861
8 for *	Past v. Present (Oxford University), at Oxford	1862

(b) 13 or more wickets in a match:

16 for 93	Gents of England v. Gents of M.C.C., at Lord's	1855
13 for *	Oxford University v. Players Engaged at Oxford, at Oxford	1857
15 for 63	16 of Oxford University v. England, at Lord's	1858
14 for *	Past v. Present (Oxford University), at Oxford	1862

(c) 4 or more wickets for 3 runs or less each:

8 for 19	Oxfordshire v. Oxford University, at Oxford	1858
6 for 17	Oxford University v. Cambridge University, at Lord's	1858
5 for 15	England v. Kent (with Jackson, Caffyn, and Parr), at Lord's	1858

(d) bowling unchanged through both completed innings:

With Stephenson (H. H.), for England v. Kent (with Jackson, Caffyn, and Parr), at Lord's 1858

* Signifies analysis not preserved.
† Captain of the XI.

In the 10 matches in which he bowled for Gentlemen v. Players he delivered 2,563 balls for 862 runs and 48 wickets, average 17.95.

MARSHAM, Cloudesley Henry Bullock, born at Stoke-Lyne, Bicester, on February 10, 1879, died at Wrotham on July 18, 1928, at the early age of 49. He was the son of the late Rev. C. D. B. Marsham, the best Gentleman bowler of his day, and went to Eton in 1892, to the house of Mr. R. A. H. Mitchell, the famous nurse of young cricket-ers. He made his first appearance at Lord's for Eton against Harrow in 1897, and played again the following season. Going up to Oxford, he was in the XI in 1900, 1901, and 1902, being captain in his last year. Born with cricket in his blood and enjoying such an auspicious beginning to his career, he was obviously marked down as a future Kent captain, and in 1904 on the retirement of C. J. Burnup he succeeded to that post, having under his command such famous players as J. R. Mason, E. W. Dillon, S. H. Day, Blythe, Fielder, Huish, Humphreys, and Fairservice. Marsham played his first match for Kent in 1900, and in 1906 he enjoyed the satisfaction, while acting as captain, of seeing his side carry off the County Championship for the first time in the history of the County Club. He did not have a particularly long career, for after 1908 he dropped out of first-class cricket, playing only twice in the following season, once in 1910, and a few times after the War. In this sterner field he was a captain in the West Kent Yeomanry, being attached to the Buffs and the R.A.F., and serving in Egypt, Gallipoli, and Palestine.

A good, but not a great batsman, Cloudesley Marsham will be remembered more probably for his ability to rise to the occasion at critical times than by any pronounced or consistent skill. Scores of 53 and 31 for Eton against Harrow in 1898 showed that, if necessary, he could play a dogged game but, if rather slow, his methods were sound in helping H. C. Pilkington to put on 85 for the first wicket when Eton followed on. In the University match, his great year was in 1901, when Oxford saved the game after losing seven wickets for 145 in an attempt to make 327 to win in the last innings. On that occasion Marsham played an invaluable innings of 100 not out, Oxford, in drawing the game, owing nearly everything to him. Apart from a possible chance when 13, he did not make a mistake of any kind. He batted for three hours, made his runs in 33 hits—20 fours, two threes, three twos, and eight singles, and obtained his last 50 runs in an hour. He was essentially an off-side player, and in this particular innings he cut and drove in a manner perfectly delightful to see. A hard worker and keen trier himself in the field, he inspired his men by fine example. As a captain, he secured unfailing support and unswerving loyalty from those under him, while a charming and courteous disposition endeared him to all opponents. His family have been associated with Kent cricket for about 150 years.

MARSHAM, George, born at Allington Rectory, near Maidstone, on April 10, 1849, died at Hayle Cottage, Maidstone, on December 2, 1927, aged 78. He gained no note as a player whilst at Eton, but later developed into a useful batsman and a good wicket-keeper. He could also bowl slow underhand. Playing for Oxford Harlequins against Royal Engineers at Chatham in 1874,

he caught four men and stumped three. He was tried for Kent—once in 1876 and twice in 1877—and was President of the County Club in 1886. For many years he was a most enthusiastic supporter of the game in Kent as well as one of the Trustees of the Mynn Memorial Benevolent Institution for Kentish Cricketers and President of the Mote C.C. He was, too, a prominent figure in the tents of I Z., B.B., and Old Stagers during the Canterbury Week. His family had been associated with the game for very many years, and had produced many good players: Messrs. C. J. B., R. H. B., and C. D. Marsham were his cousins and he was uncle of Mr. C. H. B. Marsham. To *Wisden* of 1907 he contributed a very interesting article on Kent County Cricket history.

MARSHAM, The Rev. The Hon. John, born at Boxley House, Maidstone, on July 25, 1842, died at Roehampton on September 16, 1926, aged 84. A fast bowler, he played for Kent in two matches in 1873.

MARSHAM, Robert Henry Bullock, the well-known Metropolitan magistrate, died at Bifrons, Canterbury, on April 5, 1913. Though he never took anything like the position in the cricket field gained by his younger and still surviving brother, the Rev. C. D. Marsham—one of the most famous of amateur bowlers—Mr. Marsham in his young days was a good player. At Oxford he was in the XI only one year, being on the losing side in 1856. Mr. Marsham had the distinction of being picked for the Gentlemen against the Players at Lord's in 1859 and 1860, and also for the Gentlemen under 30 against the Players under 30 in 1862. His best score in these three matches was 24 in 1862, when he opened the Gentlemen's first innings with the late Mr. E. M. Grace. The Players won all three matches very easily. Mr. Marsham played with great success for the M.C.C. against the Surrey club (with Caffyn, Tom Lockyer, and H. H. Stephenson), at Lord's, in July, 1859, taking four wickets for 40 runs and eight for 27. The M.C.C. were the weaker team, but Mr. Marsham's bowling won the match for them by 119 runs. His bowling was rather slow round-armed with a twist in from leg. He made a lot of runs for I Zingari, and was fond of recalling that he took part in the double-tie match between Cranbury Park and I Z. in 1864. In 1860 he was chosen to play for England against Kent, at Canterbury. He was born at Merton College, Oxford, September 3, 1833 From 1853 until 1864 he assisted Oxfordshire, and in the last-mentioned year he also assisted Buckinghamshire, playing an innings of 59 against Middlesex at Newport Pagnell.

MARTIN, Austin Walter, who died on December 23, 1952, aged 80, was from 1924 to 1940 head groundsman at the Oval, in which time he was responsible for the preparation of many Test match pitches, including that upon which in 1938 Hutton scored his record 364 against Australia. He was a member of the Surrey County C.C. ground staff for 51 years. Well known to all in the cricket world as "Bosser," he was an authority upon the subject of the destruction of insect pests. In 1935, when the turf at Lord's suffered so considerably from a plague of "leather-jackets," he was called in with successful results to act as general in the "war." His son is head groundsman at Lord's.

MARTIN, Eric, M.C., R.A.F., born on May 20, 1894, was killed in a flying accident at Duxford Aerodrome, near Cambridge, on May 2, 1924. He was educated at Christ's College, Finchley, and played on various occasions for Middlesex between 1919 and 1923, his best feat for the county being to score 64 against Essex at Leyton in 1919, when he and Murrell added 152 for the ninth wicket in an hour and a quarter. He was captain of the Finchley C.C. and a prominent member of the Casuals Football club.

MARTIN, Commdr. Evelyn George, R.N.V.R., O.B.E., died of heart failure on April 27, 1945, aged 64. Two years in the Eton XI he took part in a very exciting match with Winchester in 1899, Eton winning by one wicket, a success to which he contributed eight not out and 23, two wickets for 24 and six for 45. Mr. W. Findlay, so well known as M.C.C. secretary from 1926 to 1936, who captained both Eton and Oxford and kept wicket when Martin was in the sides, has described that Martin bowled fast right-hand, usually round the wicket with splendid length. Receiving his Blue in 1903 from Findlay, Martin played for Oxford in four seasons without doing anything exceptional, and a little for Worcestershire, altogether in first-class cricket taking 107 wickets at an average of 23.51.

MARTIN, Frank C., captain of Western Province, who scored two centuries in Currie Cup cricket, was drowned off Cape Town on May 24, 1933.

MARTIN, Frederick, died at his home at Dartford on December 13, 1921. On the previous day he had seemed in his usual health, but he had a sudden seizure in the night and never recovered consciousness. Born on October 12, 1861, he was a trifle over 60 years of age. Martin had a fairly long career for Kent, playing his first match for the county in 1885—he had only one trial that year—and his last in 1899. For three seasons—1889 to 1891—he was one of the best left-handed bowlers in England. After that, though he retained his command of length, he had not the same spin and batsmen naturally found him easier to play. In those three years, according to his figures in the History of Kent Cricket, he took for Kent alone 315 wickets—87 in 1889, 116 in 1890, and 112 in 1891. In 1894 he had a very good season, bowling with astonishing success on soft wickets for the M.C.C. at Lord's in May. He bowled medium pace with a high easy action that seemed part of himself. Most of his work was done for Kent and the M.C.C., but he once took part in a Test match, playing for England against Australia at the Oval in 1890. His selection came as a surprise. Yorkshire would not let Peel off from a county match, Briggs was more or less disabled, and a left-handed bowler was a necessity. Martin rose to the occasion. On a pitch ruined by rain he was deadly, taking 12 wickets for 102 runs—six for 50 and six for 52. The Australians were very weak in 1890, but Turner and Ferris made them formidable on slow grounds, and England only just scrambled home by two wickets. Martin appeared four times for Players against Gentlemen and went to South Africa as a member of W. W. Read's team in 1891-92. During that tour, though quite overshadowed by Ferris and to some extent by J. T. Hearne, he took 109 wickets at a cost of less than 8½ runs apiece. Martin was never much of a batsman, but he played an innings of 90 for Kent in 1897 and one of 70 not out in 1896. Some of his best bowling performances, apart from the England match, were:

7 wickets for 18 runs	Kent v. Notts, at Beckenham	.. ..	1889
5 wickets for 8 runs	M.C.C. and Ground v. Notts, at Lord's	..	1894
6 wickets for 18 runs	Kent v. Surrey, at Catford	.. ..	1896
4 wickets for 11 runs	Kent v. Notts, at Maidstone	.. ..	1894
11 wickets for 29 runs	(seven for 12 and four for 17). M.C.C. and Ground v. Sussex, at Lord's	.. ..	1894

Against Surrey at the Oval in 1890 he did the hat-trick, getting rid of Abel, Maurice Read, and K. J. Key.—S.H.P.

MARTIN, Geoffrey William, who died in Launceston on March 7, 1968, aged 72, played in 22 matches for Tasmania between the 1922–23 and 1931–32 seasons. An aggressive right-hand batsman, strong in off-side strokes, he excelled in matches with M.C.C. teams, scoring 121 at one a minute against A. E. R. Gilligan's 1924–25 side and 92 against that led by A. P. F. Chapman in 1928–29. On the latter occasion he was bowled by the Nottinghamshire fast bowler, H. Larwood, the bail travelling 67 yd. 6 in., or equal to the world record distance for a bail set up by R. D. Burrows, of Worcestershire, in 1911. Martin's career in Senior Grade cricket in Launceston extended over 44 years and in his last season at the age of 60 he played an innings of 63.

MARTIN, Marcus Trevelyan, died on June 5, 1908, in Portland Place, W., after an operation for appendicitis. He was born at Barrackpore, in India, on April 29, 1842, and was educated at Rugby, where he was in the XI from 1858 to 1861. During his last year at the school he was chosen to assist the Gentlemen of the North against the Gentlemen of the South at the Oval, and he thoroughly justified his selection by playing an innings of 63. He obtained his Blue as a Freshman in 1862, but made only 13 against Oxford, although earlier in the season he had played an innings of 103 not out against a Cambridgeshire side which included the famous Buttress. In 1864 he made 53 v. M.C.C. at Fenner's and 90 v. Surrey at the Oval, but again proved a disappointment in the Lord's match, scoring only three runs in his two innings. He appeared for Middlesex in 1870 and occasionally assisted Warwickshire. In addition to being a good and safe bat he was a fair wicket-keeper.

MARTIN, Sir Richard Biddulph, First Bart., who was second cousin of the brothers Norman, of Eton, was born in Eaton Square on May 12, 1838, and died at Overbury Court, Tewkesbury, on August 23, 1916. Like his father and brothers, he was an enthusiastic member of the West Kent C.C., and played occasionally for the club. He was not in the XI either at Harrow or Oxford. His family's love of cricket was commemorated in a poem by Benjamin Aislabie.

MARTINDALE, Emanuel A., who died at

Bridgetown on March 17, 1972, aged 63, played as a fast bowler in 10 Test matches for the West Indies between 1933 and 1939, taking 37 wickets for 21.72 runs each. During his tour of England, in 1933, he and L. N. Constantine caused a sensation by bowling the type of leg-theory in the Old Trafford Test which had aroused such acrimony in Australia the previous winter. D. R. Jardine, instigator of this method of attack, despite receiving heavy punishment, put together 127, his only Test century. In that tour Martindale took 103 wickets—14 of them in the three Tests—his performances including eight wickets for 32 runs against Essex; eight for 39 against Sir Lindsay Parkinson's XI and eight for 66 against Nottinghamshire. His pace was remarkable in view of the fact that he stood no higher than 5 ft. 8½ in.

"Manny" Martindale spent a number of years in League cricket in the north of England, where he earned much popularity and respect, both on and off the field. On returning to his native Barbados, he became a coach.

MARTINEAU, Gerard Durani, who died in hospital at Lyme Regis on May 28, 1976, aged 79, was not in the XI at Charterhouse and was never more than a moderate club cricketer, though he was for a short period a Holiday Coach at the Faulkner School of Cricket, but he was a great lover of the game and a copious writer on it. He was a considerable contributor to E. W. Swanton's *World of Cricket*, wrote for years for *The Cricketer* and was author of a number of books, of which the most important to the cricket historian are *Bat, Ball, Wicket and All*, a history of cricket implements, and *The Valiant Stumper*, a history of wicket-keeping. But in general his books were not works of much original research. Pleasantly written, they were ideally calculated to arouse the interest of the novice and spur him on to try for himself the masterpieces of Nyren and Pycroft. His other books included a *History of the Royal Sussex Regiment*, in which he had served in the First World War.

MARTINEAU, Hubert Melville, who died on September 11, 1976, aged 84, was a very great lover and patron of cricket. On his private ground at Holyport Lodge, near Maidenhead, club cricket of a high standard was played throughout the summer from 1923 to 1939, and four touring sides, the Australians in 1926, the New Zealanders in 1927, the West Indies in 1928 and the Indians in 1932, started their programme there. In addition every year from 1929 to 1939 he took a side largely consisting of first-class players on a tour to Egypt in April. He was not in the XI at Eton, but made himself into a useful slow left-arm bowler.

MARTINEAU, Lionel, who was born on February 19, 1867, died at Esher on November 17, 1906. He was in the Uppingham XI in 1883 and two following years and assisted Cambridge against Oxford, at Lord's, in 1887. His highest score in an unportant match was 109 for Cambridge University v. Sussex, at Brighton, in 1887. He was a good batsman, having strong defence and possessing strokes all round the wicket, a useful slow bowler with a high delivery, and a fine field at mid-off.

MARTINGELL, William, died September 29, 1897, at Eton Wick. This famous old cricketer, one of the last of the Mynn and Fuller Pilch era, was born at Nutfield, in Surrey, on August 20, 1818, and was thus within a few weeks of completing his 79th year. He retained his interest in cricket to the end of his life, and was always to be seen on the St. Lawrence ground in the Canterbury week. During his later years he had a permanent engagement at Eton College, where he was originally engaged as coach in 1853–54–55. To the present generation Martingell was of course only a name, but in his day he was one of the best bowlers in England. Forming his style under the old law, he delivered the ball a little below the shoulder and depended like the late Frank Silcock—a younger bowler of the same school—on his bias from the leg-side. Mr. Arthur Haygarth in *Scores and Biographies* mentions that he was very prone to get over the crease and that in 1858 alone he bowled from this cause no fewer than 30 no-balls. In his young days Martingell played for Kent, his connection with that county lasting from 1841 to 1852. As Surrey gradually became famous, however, he threw in his fortunes with the county of his birth and at the Oval in the '50s shared the pleasant labours of many a capital match with Caffyn, Tom Lockyer, Tom Sherman, and H. H. Stephenson. The Surrey club gave him a benefit at the Oval in 1860, from which he cleared upwards of £260. The match was between the two great travelling XIs, the All England and United All England, then at the height of their popularity. Martingell was always full of talk about cricket and cricketers, and among modern batsmen he had an especially strong admiration for the Hon. Alfred Lyttelton. A few weeks after the veteran's death Lord Harris wrote to the papers making an appeal for Mrs. Martingell, who was unfortunately left in very straitened circumstances.

MARTYN, Henry, born at Lifton, Devon, on July 16, 1877, died at Dawlish on August 8, 1928. In style and execution he was one of the finest wicket-keepers ever seen in first-class cricket. Tall, and possessed of long arms and a beautiful pair of hands, he almost invariably stood close up to the fastest bowlers, and, even so, made singularly few mistakes. Going up to Oxford from Exeter Grammar School, he played in the Freshmen's match in 1897. He was in the Oxford XI in 1899 and 1900, and then it was obvious that a great wicket-keeper had been discovered. In 1900 he enjoyed the distinction of playing for the Gentlemen at Lord's, in the match in which R. E. Foster, his captain, scored 102 not out and 136, and the Players, set to make 501 in the last innings, won by two wickets. He played his first match for Somerset in 1901, and was a regular member of the county XI until 1906. After that he played only one more match for Somerset, when in fulfilment of a long-standing promise he turned out in 1908 in Braund's benefit match against Surrey at Bath. He did great work for Somerset, developing into a very good batsman, but his chief claims to remembrance rested on his appearances for the Gentlemen against the Players at Lord's. He was in the team in 1903, 1905 and 1906, and on this last occasion stood up to W. Brearley and N. A. Knox when those two famous fast bowlers were really terrifying in their pace. Bowling quite so fast as that of Knox had not been seen in a Gentlemen and Players match since C. J. Kortright appeared in 1898. Martyn had no hand in the disposal of any of the Players, but he kept wicket magnificently, taking Knox's bowling on the first afternoon with the ease and certainty of a Blackham or a Pilling. Splendid wicket-keeper though he was, Martyn never had the good fortune to play in a Test match, Lilley, of Warwickshire, being in his prime when the Australians were here in 1902 and 1905. In his two inter-University matches he scored 27 and nine not out in 1899, and 94 and 35 a year later. In making his 94, he hit 16 fours, reached 50 in 25 minutes, and with J. W. F. Crawford added 60 in 20 minutes. When Somerset followed-on against the Australians at Bath in 1905, he made some splendid on-drives in scoring 130 not out; he and Braund obtained 146 for the first wicket in an hour and a half. Before beginning to assist

Somerset, Martyn had played for both Devon and Cornwall.

MASON, Frederick Richard, died on May 11, 1936, aged 54, at Auckland, New Zealand. A free bat and excellent fieldsman, either at cover point or in the country, he played for North Island and New Zealand. Against P.F. Warner's M.C.C. team in December, 1902, he made the top score of 26 in one innings, for Auckland. One of his best performances was 79 against Cotter, Noble, Armstrong, Hopkins and McLeod, who were in the Australian visiting team of 1905.

MASON, James Ernest, who died on February 8, 1938, aged 61, played once for Kent in 1900. A younger brother of John Richard Mason, captain of Kent for several years, James did not fulfil the promise as a batsman shown when at Tonbridge School, but he was a capital field at cover point.

MASON, John Richard, who died on October 15, 1958, aged 84, was one of the finest amateur all-rounders to play for Kent since the days of Alfred Mynn. Yet he never appeared for England against Australia in a home Test match. As one of A. E. Stoddart's second team who toured Australia, he took part in all five Test matches in 1897–98, but in England his nearest approach to a "cap" came in 1902 when he was one of 14 from whom the final selection for the Birmingham Test was made. Still, he ranked as a very great player. Well over 6 ft., Mason made full use of his height and played with so straight a bat that he was always worth watching.

Essentially a forward player, possessing a drive scarcely surpassed for cleanness and power and a most effective cut, he could also bat to good purpose on slow turf, as many leading bowlers of his time found to their cost. In addition he was a right-arm fast-medium bowler of considerable skill and few excelled him as a slip-fielder.

Educated at Winchester, Mason showed even in his schooldays that he would take high rank in the cricket world. Against Eton in 1892 he scored 147 and 71, dismissed eight batsmen and brought off three catches, and in the corresponding fixture the following season he hit 43 and 36 and again took eight wickets. His record for the school in 1892 was 777 runs, average 48, and 48 wickets for 18 runs each; in 1893 his aggregate was 719, average 55, and he obtained 45 wickets for under 17 runs apiece.

In the same summer that he left Winchester, he was tried for Kent and figured in the game in 1893 when the county defeated the Australians by 36 runs. He failed to realise expectations in 1894, but the next summer jumped to the front and for several seasons afterwards rendered splendid all-round service. He succeeded Frank Marchant as Kent captain in 1898 and not only held that office with distinction for five years, but would doubtless have continued to lead the side for far longer had not the calls of his profession as a solicitor compelled his resignation. So heavy were the claims upon his time that he played no first-class cricket after 1906.

If comparatively brief, his career was brilliant. For Kent in 1900 he scored 1,662 runs, average 53, and took 78 wickets, average 19; the following year he made 1,467 runs, average 39, and secured 92 wickets, average 20. Altogether he hit 13,363 runs for the county, average 33, and obtained 675 wickets at a cost of 21 runs each. His highest innings were 183 v. Somerset at Blackheath and 181 not out v. Nottinghamshire at Trent Bridge, where he and Alec Hearne (162 not out) shared in a third-wicket partnership of 321. Against Surrey at the Oval in 1900, he scored 98 and 147, and four years later hit three successive centuries—138 v. Yorkshire, 126 v. Somerset and 123 v. Essex. He appeared for Gentlemen v. Players in 1894 and 1895 and from 1897 to 1902. In the Lord's match of 1899 he and W. G. Grace put on 130. The Doctor, then 51 years old, hit 78 and appeared set for his hundred when, called for a short run, he lost his wicket, Mason forgetting for the moment his partner's age and weight!

MASSIE, Hugh Hamon, died at Point Piper, Sydney, on October 12, 1938, at the advanced age of 83. A remarkably free and attractive batsman, he took a prominent part in the seven runs victory gained by Australia at the Oval in 1882—the first defeat of England in this country which caused such a sensation that it inspired "The Ashes" memorial. Bowlers always held the upper hand in the match except when Australia batted a second time 38 behind. Then Massie, by hitting up 55 out of 66 for the first wicket on wet turf paved the way for the ultimate triumph brought about by the bowling of Spofforth and Boyle. Between showers Australia made only 56 runs after Massie was bowled by A. G. Steel, but England, wanting 85 to win, were dismissed for 77 on the drying pitch.

Nearly 6 ft. in height and very active,

Massie was a wonderful forcing batsman with drives and cuts his most effective strokes in hitting bowlers off their length. He went to the pitch of the ball whenever possible and did not mind lifting his drives—he was invaluable on treacherous turf. He fielded brilliantly anywhere, and held the most difficult catches in amazing style. He began his England experience by scoring 206 out of 265 against Oxford University, getting his second hundred while his partners contributed 12 runs between them. Altogether in first-class matches during the tour, Massie scored 1,403 runs, average 24. He played many fine innings for New South Wales, but his position in a Sydney bank prevented him from accepting invitations for other tours to England. When on a private visit in 1895 Massie was made an honorary member of M.C.C. He then played for the club against Kent, and in the match celebrating the Jubilee of I Zingari he was in the Gentlemen of England XI.

MASSIE, Robert John Allwright, who died on February 14, 1966, was, as a 6 ft. 4 in. fastish left-hander for New South Wales, regarded as Australia's bowler of the future in 1914. Unhappily a wound received while on Army service during the First World War ended his cricket career. He represented New South Wales at cricket, Rugby football, athletics and rowing and was also amateur boxing champion of the State.

MASTERMAN, Sir John Cecil, sometime Provost of Worcester and Vice-Chancellor of Oxford University, died in an Oxford nursing home on June 6, 1977, aged 86. A man of distinction in many walks of life, he was a remarkable games player, who had played hockey and lawn tennis for England, won the high jump in the University sports and reached a high standard at cricket, golf and squash. "Cricket," he wrote, "was my first and most enduring passion" and, though never near a Blue at Oxford, he became a formidable club player, good enough to be elected a Harlequin many years after he went down and to play for both Harlequins and Free Foresters against the University, to do valuable work for Oxfordshire from 1922 to 1925 and, to be a member of the M.C.C. side to Canada in 1937. He was a sound left-handed bat and, being a good fighter, one whom one was always glad to have on one's side when things were not going well, and a right-hand medium pace bowler with a rather low and clumsy action, but very steady and reliable. For many years he was on the

committee of both I Zingari and Free Foresters. He enjoyed writing on the game and did so delightfully, but a busy life left him little time for this. His novel, *Fate Cannot Harm Me*, contains one of the best descriptions extant of a country house match and there is an interesting chapter on cricket in his autobiography, *On the Chariot Wheel*. Besides these there is a sketch of W. E. W. Collins in *Bits and Pieces* and a fascinating article contributed to Blackwood in June 1974 on that remarkable character, Capt. E. G. Wynyard.

MATHER-JACKSON, Sir Anthony Henry, Bart., who died suddenly on October 11, 1983, aged 83, was in the Harrow XI in 1916 and 1917: in 1917 he took six for 43 in the one-day match against Eton at Eton. Between 1920 and 1927 he played fairly frequently for Derbyshire, but only in 1922 was he able to appear regularly. In that season he made 580 runs with an average of 18.12 and played a number of useful innings, including 75 against Leicestershire, his highest score in first-class cricket, and 69 against Worcestershire. He was an attacking batsman and a good field and bowled fast-medium swingers. In all for the county he scored 1,199 runs with an average of 14.80 and took 44 wickets at 30.89. He was a cousin of G. R. Jackson, the Derbyshire captain.

MATHEWS, John Kenneth, who died on April 6, 1962, aged 78, played occasionally as a forcing batsman for Sussex from 1920 to 1930, his highest innings being 58 against Gloucestershire at Hove in 1927, when he and W. Cornford put on 60 for the last wicket. In the Felsted XI early in the century, he became a Vice-President of Sussex. He was a former hockey international.

MATON, Leonard James, who died at Bath on April 15, 1932, was a member of the Rugby School XI in 1863 and 1864 and, while still at school, played for Wiltshire. He was much more widely known in connection with the Rugby game. A fine powerful forward, he captained the once famous Wimbledon Hornets. An original member of the Rugby Union Committee, he was one of three men to whom was delegated the task of drafting the first Rugby Union Laws. As he was confined to his room at the time owing to an accident, the two other members of the committee appointed to do the work left the matter to him as some employment during his illness. So well did he execute the task that his Laws were unanimously accepted by the full committee of the Union and they remained unchanged for many years.

MATTHEWS, Austin David George, who died in hospital on July 29, 1977, aged 72, had a career which was almost unique. Born at Penarth and educated at St. David's, Lampeter, he played for Northamptonshire from 1927 to 1936 and at that time was merely a useful member of one of the weakest county sides, who could not on his performances have kept his place for a leading county. His 567 wickets had cost him 26.45 runs each and he had made a couple of centuries. In 1937 he went to coach cricket and rugby at Stowe and threw in his lot with Glamorgan, making his first appearance at the end of July.

In little more than a fortnight his bowling had created such an impression, particularly at Hastings, where on a perfect wicket he had taken 14 for 132, that he was picked for the final Test at the Oval against New Zealand. Here, on an unresponsive pitch, he bowled respectably and by no means disgraced himself, but met with little success. He continued to play for Glamorgan until 1947 and his 225 wickets for them cost only 15.88 apiece, an astonishing contrast to his figures for Northamptonshire. In 1946 he took in all 93 at 14.29. For a short time after the War he was the county's Assistant Secretary.

A tall man, who bowled fast-medium with a high action, he was accurate and had the cardinal merits of keeping the ball on the wicket and making it run away. He was also a useful bat in the lower part of the order, and hit two first-class 100s, both for Northamptonshire, in 1929 and 1934.

Between 1934 and 1950 he coached Cambridge University. Apart from his cricket he was a first-class rugby forward; he captained Northampton R.F.U. club, also played for East Midlands and Penarth and gained a Final Welsh Trial Cap. He refereed the first Combined Oxford and Cambridge R.U. tour to Argentina in 1948 and was also a Welsh Table Tennis international. He had strong views on the subject of coaching and in *Wisden 1966* wrote *Cricket a Game—Not a Subject.*

MATTHEWS, Frank Cyril, who died at Willoughby-on-the-Wolds on January 11, 1961, aged 67, enjoyed a brief but successful career as a fast bowler for Nottinghamshire. After achieving some noteworthy performances in Army cricket when serving with the Northumberland Fusiliers during the First World War, Matthews, who stood 6 ft. 4 in., joined the staff of the County Club for whom he played from 1920 to 1926. In all matches he took 314 wickets, average 22.29. His best season was that of 1923 when he dismissed 115 batsmen in Championship engagements for 15.30 runs each and, against Northamptonshire at Trent Bridge, earned the remarkable analyses of eight wickets for 39 runs and nine for 50. When bowling A. J. B. Wright he sent a bail 41 yd. The next season at Canterbury, where he played as a last-minute replacement for F. Barratt, injured, he disposed of eight batsmen for 33 runs, Kent being all out in the first innings for 67, of which H. T. W. Hardinge obtained 35. At one point, Matthews's figures read: six wickets for one run.

MATTHEWS, T. J., who earned everlasting fame at Old Trafford by doing the hat-trick twice in one match for Australia against South Africa in the 1912 Triangular Tournament, died on October 14, 1943, in Caulfield Military Hospital, Melbourne, aged 59. His feat, unparalleled in Test cricket, occurred in the first match of the competition. Matthews with his slow right-arm bowling dismissed the last three batsmen in South Africa's first innings, and in the follow-on, when five wickets were down for 70, he repeated the feat of dismissing three men with successive balls. That was the extent of his effectiveness in that encounter, and the series of six matches, which all three countries contested, brought him no more than 15 wickets altogether; but his average of 17 was less than that for the 25 taken by W. J. Whitty and for the 19 by G. R. Hazlitt. During the whole of that tour in England his bowling earned 85 wickets at 19.37 each, while he scored 584 runs, average 18.25. A wet summer certainly did not help the team, captained by S. E. Gregory, and far from representing the full strength of Australia, but Matthews played up to his reputation as a very useful all-round cricketer. England easily won the three-cornered rubber with four victories and two draws.

The Victorian handbook shows that for his State Matthews scored 1,334 runs, average 30.31, and took 79 wickets at 29.50 each during a short career in first-class cricket. After serving in the First World War he became Curator of the Williamstown ground, the home of the club for which Matthews played most of his cricket. At the time of his death three of his sons were on active service.

MATTHEWS, Thomas Gadd, probably the last survivor of that famous band of amateurs—W. G. Grace, E. M. Grace, G. F. Grace, J. A. Bush, W. O. Moberley, Frank Townsend, R. F. Miles, W. R. Gilbert, F. G. Monkland and C. R. Filgate—who gained the Championship for Gloucestershire twice during the first seven years of the existence of that County Club, was born on December 9, 1845, and died on January 6, 1932, at the age of 86. He first played for Gloucestershire in 1870, and a year later, making 201 against Surrey on the Clifton College ground, enjoyed the distinction of being the first player to put together a score of over 200 in County Cricket. Like many of his contemporaries, Mr. Matthews excelled in the big square leg hit over the ring—a stroke so rarely attempted in these days. In what may perhaps be described as his finest display of batting—an innings of 76 against Yorkshire—he hit Allen Hill, a very fast bowler, high over the square-leg boundary and right out of the ground. He was eventually stumped off Hill by George Pinder who, on the very dangerous wickets of those times, used to stand close up to the fastest of bowling and on one occasion stumped A. W. Ridley off a leg-shooter from Hill. Mr. Matthews made his last appearance for Gloucestershire in a match against Surrey at the Oval in 1878. Until over 80 he hunted regularly with the Badminton and the Berkeley Hounds.

MATURIN, Dr. Henry, M.R.C.S., L.R.C.P., who was born at Clondevaddock, Co. Donegal, on April 5, 1842, died at Hartley Wintney, in Hampshire, on February 24, 1920. He played for Middlesex in 1863 and later for Hampshire, being a good batsman and field and a useful fast round-armed bowler. His career in great matches was short, but he kept up his cricket in village games until well past 70, often obtaining wickets. He played for Fourteen of Hampshire at the Oval in the only match lost by Surrey in the season of 1864.

MAUDE, Frederick William, born at Plumstead, in Kent, on February 28, 1857, died in London on February 9, 1923. His height was 6 ft. 3 in. and weight 12 st. 4 lb. He never played for his native county, and his first match at Lord's was for M.C.C. v. Northamptonshire in August, 1882. He was educated in Germany and was a fine and free hitter, a useful medium-paced bowler and a good field at short-slip. Playing for M.C.C. v. Wiltshire at Lord's in August, 1886, he

scored 146 in his first innings and 143 in his second. Between 1885 and 1895 he stood four times for Parliament as a Liberal and a Liberal-Unionist, but was not returned. He was a Baron of the Cinque Ports.

MAUDE, John, died on November 17, 1934, aged 84, having been born on March 17, 1850. Going to Eton when 10 as a colleger he was there for nine years under three headmasters—Goodford, Balston, and Hornby. His tutor was the Rev. J. E. Yonge. In his time he had three future Bishops as fags—Welldon (Calcutta), Ryle (Liverpool) and Harmer (Rochester).

He played in the Eton XI at Lord's as a medium left-hand bowler in 1868 and 1869. In the former year, when Harrow won, he took three wickets for 20 runs. Lord Harris, who was also a member of the team, wrote in his recollections of the match, "Our best bowler was John Maude, who probably did not bowl nearly enough." In 1869 Maude, by taking seven wickets for 36 in the second innings, contributed largely to Eton's victory by an innings and 19 runs. Of that famous match Mr. H. S. Salt, in his "Memories of Bygone Eton", wrote: "C. J. Ottaway made a century. Thanks mainly to his patient and skilful batting and to some fine left-hand bowling by John Maude, the match ended in a single innings victory for Eton. Old Stephen Hawtrey is said to have stopped Maude in the street and asked to be allowed to shake 'that noble hand,' which by a wonderful 'caught and bowled' had disposed of Harrow's most formidable batsman. We all believed the story. It seemed exactly what Stephen Hawtrey would have done. But 57 years later I was told by Maude that he had no recollection of the incident. It *ought* to have happened, anyhow." Maude also played in the Mixed Wall and Field XIs in 1868, and won the school fives in 1869. He went up to Oxford, and got his cricket Blue in 1873. At Lord's he took six Cambridge wickets for 39 runs in the second innings. On the first day he caught F. E. R. Fryer, the Light Blue captain, in sensational fashion. He was a member of the Harlequins, and played for the Gentlemen of Warwickshire in 1874.

MAUDSLEY, Professor Ronald Harling, who died in San Diego, California, on September 29, 1981, aged 63, was in the Oxford side in 1946 and 1947, played for Warwickshire from 1946 to 1951, and also had Blues for golf and Rugby fives. Yet he was not one of the great natural games-players to whom success comes easily: rather he was one who, typically of his attitude in other walks of life, by study and concentration made the maximum use of the obviously considerable gifts with which he had been endowed. At Malvern, where he was in the XI from 1934 to 1936, he had a comparatively modest record. It was in the Oxford side of 1946 that he made his name. He was the ideal partner for Martin Donnelly, who with him solidly entrenched at the other end could attack the bowling without worrying too much about what there was to come. Maudsley himself would have been the first to acknowledge how much he owed to his partner's help and example. Together they took part in three century stands in successive innings, 171 unfinished against the Indians and 218 and 134 against Lancashire. That year Maudsley came second in the Oxford averages with 719 runs and an average of 35.95 and, though he was afterwards very useful to Warwickshire, he never improved on this form. In 1947 exams kept him out of the Oxford side during the term and he played little part in their season's cricket. In 1948, when already a Fellow of Brasenose, he shared the Warwickshire captaincy with Dollery, taking it over when the vacation set him free. His last first-class match was for Warwickshire against Oxford in 1951 and he finished his career with a hundred, his fourth in first-class cricket and his second for the county.

In all first-class cricket he made 2,676 runs with an average of 24.10 and took 52 wickets at 28.27. He was a medium-pace swinger, with one or two good performances to his credit. Sometimes, in a shortage, he took the new ball for his county and in fact headed their averages in 1947, as he had done the Oxford averages in 1946.

MAUL, Henry Compton, died on October 10, 1940, aged 90, at his home, Banbury, Oxfordshire. A free-hitting batsman, he played several innings of over 200, the most praiseworthy being 267 for Warwickshire against Staffordshire on August 17, 1888. He was then captain of the county side, seven years before Warwickshire became first class, and he headed the averages with 42. He went to Australia in the winter of 1878 in the team captained by Lord Harris, but did not take part in the one representative match, which Australia won by 10 wickets. Of that side F. A. Mackinnon now alone survives him. Mr. Maul was a Major in the Oxfordshire Militia. Three of his sons are serving in the present War.

MAULE, The Rev. Dr. Ward, of the Cambridge XI of 1853, died at Boulogne-sur-Mer on September 23, 1913. He was born on September 1, 1833, was educated at Tonbridge, and appeared occasionally for the Gentlemen of Kent. At Tunbridge Wells in 1854, whilst bowling at practice to Fuller Pilch before the match between Kent and Eighteen of Tunbridge Wells, he took the single stump three times in successive balls. "Oh! sir," said Pilch; "I should not have believed it possible." In his one match against Oxford he scored seven and 14 not out, and took three wickets. "He *wards* his own wicket, while he *mauls* those of others," once said a well-known cricketer.

MAXWELL, Cecil R., who died in October, 1973, aged 59, made a reputation as a fine wicket-keeper and hard-hitting batsman when in the Brighton College XI from 1929 to 1931. Captain in the last year, he distinguished himself by heading the batting figures with 1,037 runs, including six centuries—the highest was 180 not out against Lancing—average 69.13 and helping in the dismissal of 35 batsmen. He later played occasionally for Nottinghamshire, Middlesex and Worcestershire and twice appeared for Gentlemen v. Players at Lord's. Most of his cricket, however, was with Sir Julien Cahn's XI, with whom he toured Denmark, North America and Bermuda, Ceylon and Malaya and New Zealand. His biggest innings was remarkable. Against Leicestershire at Nottingham in 1935, he hit 268 out of 398 in three hours 10 minutes, registering four sixes and 44 fours. He and F. C. W. Newman put on 336 in two hours 10 minutes for the seventh wicket.

MAY, Frank Boyd, died by his own hand at the Old Malt House, Hurley, near Marlow, on June 1, 1907, in his 46th year. Earlier in the day, to the regret of his many friends, he had been declared a defaulter on the Stock Exchange. He had been a member of the M.C.C. since 1888, and also played for the Free Foresters and Old Cliftonians. At the conclusion of the Annual General Meeting of the M.C.C. at Lord's on May 2, 1906, Mr. May proposed the following resolution, which, after some discussion, was carried: "That in a two-day match, the captain of the batting side has power to declare his innings closed at any time, but such declaration may not be made on the first day later than one hour and 40 minutes before the hour of drawing stumps."

MAY, Percy Robert, who died on December 6, 1965, aged 81, was in his day a fast bowler of repute. He appeared occasionally for Surrey from 1902 to 1909, taking six wickets for 88 in the Worcestershire first innings at the Oval in 1906, and played with Dr. W. G. Grace for London County in the early part of the century. May got his Blue at Cambridge in 1905 and 1906, in which seasons he also played at full-back in the University Association football matches. In his second season for Cambridge, he distinguished himself by taking 12 Yorkshire wickets for 76 runs and six for 28 against Gloucestershire, both at Fenner's. He toured New Zealand with Capt. E. G. Wynyard's M.C.C. side of 1906–07, dismissing 56 batsmen in all matches, average 14.73. He was author of *M.C.C. in New Zealand*. His one match for Gentlemen against Players was at the Oval in 1906, the last of its kind in which Dr. Grace took part. Later well-known in Ceylon cricket, he took, during his first-class career, 247 wickets at a cost of 24.46 runs each.

MAYER, Joseph Herbert ("Danny"), who died on September 6, 1981, aged 79, was a fine example of a county servant. Between 1926 and 1939 he played in 333 first-class matches, 332 of them for Warwickshire. Not only was he a tremendous worker: he was a model of consistency. From 1928 to 1939 his highest aggregate of wickets was 126 in 1929, his lowest 70 in 1928, when he missed eight matches through injury. His average varied from 19.09 in 1936 to 24.61 in 1933. Only twice did he reach 100 wickets, but on four other occasions he took over 90 and on three he was in the 80s. In all these seasons he would almost certainly have topped the hundred had a reasonable proportion of slip catches been held. But whether they were held or not, he never ceased to put everything into his bowling and, as throughout his career there was a grave lack of pace bowling to help him, he had to be over-bowled. In all he took 1,145 wickets at 22.15, figures which in the circumstances are not a true index of his class or of his value to the county. As early as 1928 he had shown what he could do when he took eight for 62 in the first innings against Surrey at Edgbaston, dismissing the first seven batsmen—Hobbs, Sandham, Ducat, Shepherd, Barling, Peach and Fender, indeed a notable bag.

Strongly built he bowled fast-medium, kept the ball well up, obtained considerable pace off the pitch and moved a bit both ways. Batsmen had always to treat him with respect. Against Gloucestershire at Edgbaston

in 1937 he took 13 for 70 and in the corresponding match a year later, besides capturing 11 for 78, he scored 52 not out, adding 78 for the last wicket with Hollies. In view of the amount of bowling he had to do, he did not normally trouble much about his batting, but two innings in 1927 showed clearly that he could bat and that, being the genuine cricketer he was, he could adapt his tactics to the situation. Against Surrey at the Oval, going in last, he scored 74 not out, including 14 fours, and put on 126 in 75 minutes with Wyatt. In the same season, rain having reduced the home match against Yorkshire to a struggle for first innings points, Mayer coming in last again with 35 needed for the lead presented a dead bat to everything, until his partner, Santall, had scored the necessary runs. He was then caught off his first attempt to score, having been in 35 minutes for 0. This against Macaulay, Robinson, Kilner, Rhodes and Jacques was no mean feat.

MAYES, Dr. Alexander Dunbar Aitken, who died on February 8, 1983, aged 81, played 10 times for Queensland between 1924 and 1927, taking 21 wickets and scoring 297 runs.

MAYNARD, Edmund Anthony Jefferson, who died on January 10, 1931, was a useful bat and change slow bowler when in the Harrow XI of 1879. He assisted Derbyshire from 1880 to 1887, being captain in 1885. Against Surrey at the Oval in 1883, he hit a score of 84. He was born at Chesterfield on February 10, 1861.

MAYNE, Edgar Richard, who died in Melbourne on October 27, 1961, aged 78, was one of the best opening batsmen produced by Australian cricket. A tall, stylish player, he excelled in the cut and the drive. He captained Victoria and South Australia in the Sheffield Shield competition, in which he scored 3,464 runs, average 34.64. First appearing for South Australia in 1906, he joined Victoria in 1917, and in 1923 he (209) and W. H. Ponsford (248) set up a first-wicket record for the State by scoring 456 against Queensland at Melbourne. Mayne played in four Test matches for Australia, one each against England and South Africa in the 1912 Triangular Tournament in England, and two in South Africa in 1921, and he also visited America and New Zealand with Australian teams.

MAYNE, Henry Blair, of Westminster School and Oxford University, died at

Brighton on January 20, 1892. On leaving Oxford he became a member of the Marylebone club and I Zingari, and it is worth mentioning that in addition to his connection with cricket he was one of those who helped to frame the rules of Short Whist.

MAYO, H. E., born in South Lambeth, November 13, 1847, died on October 31, 1891. Mr. Mayo played for Surrey in 1869, and, without ever taking a high position, was a very fair all-round cricketer.

McALISTER, Peter A., died at Melbourne on May 10, 1938, in his 69th year. When vice-captain to M. A. Noble in 1909, it was said that he should have come to England 10 years before. Certainly it was asking a lot of a batsman to reveal his best form under fresh conditions at the age of 40, and, though showing signs of stylish skill, he scored no more than 816 runs on the tour with a highest innings of 85 and an average of 29. As opening batsman he played in the second and third Tests, both of which Australia won, but 22 was his best of four innings. These two victories after an England success at Birmingham decided the rubber, the matches at Manchester and the Oval being drawn, and it is interesting to recall that Noble was so troubled about opening batsmen that he called upon Cotter, the fast bowler, Warren Bardsley, Frank Laver and S. E. Gregory besides McAlister to go in first against England. McAlister scored 2,398 runs with an average of 32 in Sheffield Shield matches for Victoria, but even in Australia he did little in representative games either in 1903–04, when P. F. Warner's team won the rubber, or four years later when A. O. Jones led an unsuccessful side.

McALPINE, Kenneth, born at Leamington on April 11, 1858, died at Loose, near Maidstone, on February 10, 1923. He was educated at Haileybury but, leaving young, was not in the XI. In 1885 and 1886 he played for Kent three times, and in 1891 and 1894 visited America with Lord Hawke's teams. For years he was associated most prominently with the Mote Park C.C., and for the club at Maidstone in June, 1886, played an innings of 226 against Royal Marines, he and C. Lake (137) making 346 together for the first wicket. He was, too, a splendid worker on behalf of the Kent County C.C., and in 1922 was President of the club. He was a very great lover indeed of the game.

McAULAY, Donald M., died in Barbados on January 27, 1912, aged 46. He appeared for the West Indies against the American team at Georgetown in 1888, and represented Barbados in Intercolonial tournaments, and against the English teams of Mr. R. S. Lucas, Lord Hawke, and Sir A. Priestley. He was a free bat, a useful change bowler and an excellent field.

McBEATH, Daniel J., who died at Timaru on April 13, 1963, aged 66, appeared for New Zealand in nine matches and was a member of the touring team in Australia in 1925–26. A left-arm medium-pace bowler, he played from 1917 to 1927 for Otago, Canterbury and Southland, taking 170 wickets, average 20.83. For Canterbury in the 1918–19 season, he distinguished himself by dismissing 15 batsmen in the Plunket Shield game against Auckland—nine for 56 and six for 113.

McBRIDE, Walter Nelson, who died on January 30, 1974, aged 69, was in the Westminster XI from 1922 to 1924, being captain in the last season. Going up to Oxford, he gained a Blue in 1926, being the first victim in a hat-trick with which R. G. H. Lowe, who was in the Westminster side with him, finished off the Dark Blues' first innings. He later played for Hampshire. McBride also got a Blue at Association football, keeping goal in 1927 when Oxford won by 6–2 at Stamford Bridge.

McCABE, Stanley Joseph, who died on August 25, 1968, aged 58, following a fall from a cliff at his home in Sydney, was one of Australia's greatest and most enterprising batsmen. In 62 Test innings between 1930 and 1938 he scored 2,748 runs, including six centuries, for an average of 48.21. During a first-class career lasting from 1928 to 1942, he obtained 11,951 runs, average 49.39, reaching three figures on 29 occasions. Short and stockily built, with strong arms, flexible wrists and excellent footwork, he was at his best when facing bowlers of pace. Though he scored most of his runs by strokes in front of the wicket, with the drive his speciality, he also hooked splendidly. In addition, he was a useful change bowler above medium pace, with the ability to send down the occasional ball which came back from the off at disconcerting speed, and an energetic and accurate fielder.

He displayed an early aptitude for cricket when, after a month in the second team at St. Joseph's College, Hunter Hill, Sydney, he gained a place in the first XI as an all-rounder at the age of 14 and held it for three years. After leaving school, he assisted Grenfell Juniors, a country district club, and in 1928 made the first of many appearances for New South Wales. His form for the State was such that he earned a place in W. M. Woodfull's team which visited England in 1930 when, having taken some time to become accustomed to unfamiliar conditions, he averaged 35 in the five Test matches and in all first-class fixtures reached 1,012 runs without hitting a century. In 1931–32 he enjoyed remarkable success in his three innings for New South Wales, scores of 229 not out against Queensland at Brisbane and 106 and 103 not out from the Victoria bowling at Sydney giving him the phenomenal Sheffield Shield average of 438. That season, too, he averaged 33.50 in five Tests with South Africa.

Against D. R. Jardine's team in 1932–33, in what is often called "the body-line tour," when England employed fast leg-theory bowling to a packed leg-side field, McCabe distinguished himself by hitting 385 runs in the five Tests, average nearly 43. His 187 not out in the first match of the series at Sydney was a remarkable exhibition of both craftsmanship and courage. He made his runs out of 278 in less than four and three-quarter hours, after his earlier colleagues failed, with 25 fours among his figures. His hooking of short-pitched deliveries by H. Larwood and W. Voce, the Nottinghamshire pair, was something which will for ever hold a place in Australian cricket history. In England again in 1934, he put together eight centuries—more than any of his team-mates—including 240, the highest of his career, against Surrey at the Oval and 137 in the third Test at Old Trafford. As *Wisden* of the time said of him: "He blossomed forth as an almost completely equipped batsman of the forcing type and was probably the best exponent—Bradman himself scarcely excluded—of the art of hitting the ball tremendously hard and safely."

Next season at home he became captain of New South Wales and on tour in South Africa in 1935–36 he enjoyed more success, heading the Test batting figures with 420 runs, average 84. He hit 149 in the first Test at Durban, sharing a second-wicket partnership of 161 with W. A. Brown, and 189 not out in the second meeting with South Africa at Johannesburg, where he and J. H. Fingleton put on 177 together. At Johannesburg he showed his fast-scoring ability to the full by reaching 50 in 42 minutes.

Perhaps McCabe's most famous innings was his 232 not out in the opening Test against England at Trent Bridge in 1938 which, scored at the rate of one a minute, prompted Sir Donald Bradman, his captain, to greet him on his return to the pavilion with the words: "If I could play an innings like that, I'd be a proud man, Stan."

S. C. Griffith, Secretary of M.C.C., commented upon this innings when paying a tribute to McCabe, calling it one of the best batting displays ever seen. "McCabe was a very great cricketer and a wonderful friend to all cricketers," said Mr. Griffith.

Other tributes included:

Sir Robert Menzies, former Prime Minister of Australia: "One of his great points was that he never bothered about averages; he enjoyed his batting. He was one of the two or three greatest batsmen I ever saw."

Sir Leonard Hutton: "I knew him well. It would be hard to think of a greater Australian batsman. He had qualities that even Bradman hadn't got. I always liked to watch him bat and he was a most likeable fellow."

McCANLIS, Capt. William, born at Woolwich on October 30, 1840, died at Blackheath on November 19, 1925, in his 86th year. He was a sound, hard-hitting batsman, driving particularly well, and a good field; and between 1862 and 1877 assisted Kent in 46 matches, making 1,123 runs with an average of 14.73, with 67 v. Lancashire at Gravesend in 1873 as his highest score, and taking 18 wickets for 27.55 runs each. In the county's first innings against Surrey at the Oval in 1873 he and his younger brother, George McCanlis, made 99 between them and all the other players only eight. Capt. McCanlis kept up the game, in minor matches, until far advanced in years, and was for many seasons in charge of the coaching of the young players at Tonbridge. Among the cricketers he turned out were Blythe, Frank Woolley, Hardinge, James Seymour, Humphreys and Hubble. He continued the duties until 1912, when he resigned and was succeeded by Mr. G. J. V. Weigall.

McCASKIE, Norman, who died suddenly on July 1, 1968, aged 57, was in the XI at Winchester in 1928 and 1929, but did not gain a Blue at Oxford. He made one appearance for Middlesex at Lord's in 1932, when he formed the third "leg" of a hat-trick by G. Paine, the Warwickshire left-arm slow bowler, who took seven wickets for 14 runs.

McCAUGHEY, S., who died at Deniliquin, New South Wales, on January 29, 1955, played as a fast bowler in two games for Cambridge University in 1913. In the first innings of Middlesex at Fenner's, he took seven wickets for 46 runs.

McCORMACK, Vincent Charles, who died on April 8, 1966, aged 74, was a one-time Jamaican cricketer and former President of the Jamaican Cricket Board of Control. He was financial controller of the Jamaica Tourist Board.

McCORMICK, Edward James, a well-known Hastings sportsman, specially prominent at cricket, died in Ireland in January, 1941, aged 79. He began young, playing when 15 for Hastings and District against the first Australian team in 1878. Appearing first for Sussex in 1880 and finishing County Cricket in 1890, he scored 1,345 runs, average 15.63, and, bowling medium-paced, took 18 wickets. He fielded well at third man and in the deep. In 1889 he scored 20 and 25 not out for Gentlemen against a powerful team of Players in the Hastings festival and so helped largely to win the match by one wicket. As a memento of the occasion the Mayor of Hastings presented Mr. McCormick with a bat and said it was a great thing for the town that, among the many great players, a local man had been able to carry off the honours. For an XI which he captained he hit 212 in 1885 on the Hastings ground, and when 56 years of age he made over 100 in a single-wicket match on the same ground.

McCORMICK, The Rev. Canon Joseph, rector of St. James's, Piccadilly, died in London on April 9, 1914. Born in Liverpool on October 29, 1834, he was thus in his 80th year. Canon McCormick's fame as a cricketer belongs, of course, to a day long gone by. He ranked among the best men of his generation, and would undoubtedly have earned a bigger name if he could have spared more time for the game. A man of great height and strength—he stood considerably over 6 ft.—he was a fine, punishing batsman of the forward school, *Scores and Biographies* describing him, when he played his first match at Lord's, for Cambridge University against the M.C.C., in 1854, as one of the hardest hitters seen up to that time. He was also an excellent slow round-arm bowler, very deceptive with plenty of spin from leg. As a bowler he no doubt learned much at Cambridge from the once-famous William Buttress, upon whose style he largely modelled his own. Canon McCormick was

in the Cambridge XI in 1854 and 1856, being captain in the latter year. He ought to have played in 1855, but could not stay in London for the match. Oxford won by an innings and eight runs in 1854, but in 1856, thanks to Joseph Makinson's all-round cricket, Cambridge won by three wickets. Canon McCormick did not do much in the two matches. His scores were 0, 12, five, and 0. He only appeared once for Gentlemen against Players, taking part in the 1857 match at Lord's, made memorable by Reginald Hankey's innings of 70. After leaving Cambridge and going into the Church, Canon McCormick could not find time for much cricket, but in the Canterbury Weeks of 1866–67–68 he proved that he retained all his old skill, both as bowler and batsman. In 1866, for I Zingari against the Gentlemen of the South, playing under the name of J. Cambridge, he had the satisfaction of bowling out W. G. Grace, and in 1868, for North of the Thames against South of the Thames, he played the innings of his life, scoring 137 against the bowling of Willsher, James Lillywhite and R. Lipscomb. Up to the end of his life he retained a keen interest in cricket, being always seen at Lord's at the University match. In *Wisden's Almanack* for 1895 he wrote, under the *nom de plume* of "An old Cambridge Captain," a most interesting article on "Cricketers Past and Present:" and to the issue for 1913 he contributed some recollections of John Wisden. Apart from his cricket he had great athletic powers. He was in the Cambridge boat in 1856, and, on the testimony of his sons and others competent to speak on the point, he was a wonderful boxer.

McCRAITH, Sir Douglas, who died on September 16, 1952, aged 74, was President of Nottinghamshire County C.C. in 1937 and was chairman of the committee. He was educated at Harrow and Cambridge without gaining distinction at cricket. He bore an active part in bringing to a satisfactory conclusion the controversy over the bowling of Harold Larwood. He was a noted personality in civic and political affairs in Nottingham.

McCUBBIN, Major George Reynolds, D.S.O., who died at Johannesburg on May 9, 1944, aged 46, took part in two first-class matches, both for Transvaal against Rhodesia in March 1923. In the second of these, at Bulawayo, batting No. 10, he scored 97, adding 221 for the ninth wicket with N. V. Lindsay (160 not out), a South African record for that wicket which still stands. A pilot in the R.F.C. in the First World War, he was awarded the D.S.O., and won fame in June 1916 when he shot down the famous German ace, Max Immelmann. He served with the South African Air Force in North Africa in the Second World War, but had to retire owing to ill-health.

McDONALD, Edgar Arthur, famous with Australia and Lancashire, was killed on the road near Bolton after being concerned in a motorcar collision early in the morning of July 22, 1937.

Born in Tasmania on January 6, 1892, McDonald went to Melbourne in his youth and became a good fast bowler in Pennant matches. He played once for Victoria against the M.C.C. team captained by P. F. Warner in February 1912 but not until 1919 did he become prominent by taking eight wickets, six bowled, for 42 runs at Sydney under conditions favourable to batsmen, in the first innings of New South Wales.

McDonald did Australia splendid service in Test matches. He played in three against the M.C.C. team that went to Australia in the winter of 1920 with J. W. H. T. Douglas as captain. Mailey, Gregory and Kelleway were the bowlers mainly responsible for the five defeats than inflicted on England. McDonald's six wickets cost 65 runs apiece, but he was picked for the ensuing visit to England and in the Tests he took 27 wickets for 24 runs apiece.

In the Test at Nottingham McDonald took eight wickets for 74 and at Lord's and Leeds he was mainly responsible for the fall of England's first three wickets so cheaply that defeat became inevitable. The Australians thus won the rubber and so beat England eight times in consecutive engagements.

At the end of the tour McDonald decided to accept an engagement as professional with the Nelson club and in due course became qualified for Lancashire. Naturally enough, a bowler capable of such devastating work against the flower of England's batting accomplished remarkable things in County Cricket and from 1924, when he was available only in mid-week matches, until 1931, when his ability suddenly declined, he took 1,040 wickets for Lancashire. In his best season, 1925, he dismissed in all matches 205 batsmen at an average cost of 18.67. During this period Lancashire won the County Championship four times. One of his best performances was at Dover in 1926 when Kent, wanting 426 to win, got within 65 of victory for the loss of five wickets. McDonald then performed the hat-trick and Lancashire

triumphed by 33 runs. In the match he took 12 wickets for 187 runs.

Of good height and loosely built, McDonald ran with easy grace to the crease and his rhythmical action with accurate length and off-break surprised every batsman when first facing him and often afterwards. In these particulars he was very different from Gregory with a longer, faster run and leaping delivery; but in Australian cricket the names of these two fast bowlers must be coupled as the terrific force which humiliated England in the first years of Test cricket after the First World War. Ordinarily of small account as a batsman, McDonald hit up a century not out in 100 minutes against Middlesex at Old Trafford in 1926. His benefit match with Middlesex at Old Trafford in 1929 brought him nearly £2,000.

After giving up County Cricket, McDonald returned to the Lancashire League with the Bacup club as successor to Arthur Richardson, another Australian. McDonald played for Victoria at both Rugby and Association football.

McDONALD, John Archibald, who died on June 4, 1961, aged 79, played three matches for Derbyshire in 1905 and 1906.

McDONELL, Harold Clark, who died on July 23, 1965, aged 82, was in the Winchester XI from 1899 to 1901. A leg-break bowler and a splendid fielder to his own bowling besides being a fair bat, he captained the school in the last two years. Against Eton in 1900, he gained match figures of 11 wickets for 111 runs. He got his Blue at Cambridge in 1903, 1904 and 1905, being top of the University bowling averages in the first and last years. In 1904 he took nine wickets for 125 runs in the University match. Next season at Lord's, though achieving little as a bowler, he played an innings which completely altered the course of the game. Facing first-innings arrears of 101, the Light Blues seemed destined to be beaten when they lost six wickets and were still 24 behind. Then McDonell (60) and L. G. Colbeck (107) added 143 in 85 minutes and, as A. F. Morcom (six wickets for 41 runs) followed with a remarkable spell of bowling, Cambridge snatched victory by 40 runs. McDonell's best bowling performance was in 1904 at Cambridge, where he took 15 Surrey wickets for 138 runs—and was on the losing side. He turned out occasionally for Surrey in 1903 and 1904, heading their County Championship averages in the first season with 24 wickets in five matches at a cost of

17.87 runs each. From 1908 until 1921 he rendered good all-round service to Hampshire. He also represented Gentlemen v. Players in 1903 and 1904.

McDONNELL, Percy Stanislaus, the announcement of whose death at Brisbane at the end of September, 1895, caused a painful shock in English cricket circles, will always be remembered as one of the most brilliant of Australian batsmen. He came to England with the teams of 1880, 1882 and 1884, and paid his fourth and last visit in 1888, when he was captain of the XI. It seems he had been ill for some little time, and that his death was not so sudden as was at first supposed. A splendid bat and under all circumstances a dangerous run-getter, McDonnell was in proportion a finer bat on bad wickets than on good ones. Indeed it may be questioned if on a pitch thoroughly ruined by rain he has ever been equalled. Time after time during his visits to England his fearless hitting under almost impossible conditions turned the scale in favour of his side, his greatest achievement being the memorable innings of 82 with which he won the match against the North of England at Old Trafford in 1888. Mr. McDonnell was born in London on November 13, 1860, but inasmuch as he was taken out to the Colonies while quite a child, his early cricket associations were entirely Australian.

McELHONE, Frank Eric, who died on July 23, 1981, aged 94, was the oldest surviving New South Wales cricketer and one of the last to have played with Victor Trumper. He played twice for New South Wales in the Sheffield Shield, both times in 1910–11, his four innings, all against Victoria, being 26, 23, 101 and 34. In the same season he scored 94 for New South Wales against the touring South Africans. In 1911–12 he failed to score in his one first-class match, against P. F. Warner's M.C.C. side. He was a nephew of W. P. McElhone, a founder member of the Australian Cricket Board.

McEVOY, Arthur, probably the finest bowler in France, died at 1, Place de l'Ecole, Paris, on July 21, 1904, aged 33, and was buried at Ivry, near Paris, on July 24. For many years he was a member of the Albion C.C., and had several times accompanied Paris teams on tour in England.

McEWAN, John William, whose name will be found in the Middlesex XI in 1884, died suddenly in February, 1902, at the age of 39.

McGAHEY, Charles Percy, the famous Essex batsman, died in Whipps Cross Hospital on January 10, 1935. His death was the result of an accident on Christmas Day when, slipping on a greasy pavement, he fell and damaged a finger. Septic poisoning ensued and proved fatal. Born on February 12, 1871, Charles McGahey first appeared for Essex in 1893 when the county was second-class and not until 1921 did he retire. He was assistant secretary of the club for several years and captained the county XI from 1907 to 1910, while from 1930 onwards he acted as official scorer for Essex.

Just a natural hitter in club cricket when given a trial by Essex, he advanced slowly, but profited so much from practice against professional bowling provided by Mr. C. E. Green before each season at Leyton and experience in match play, as his form improved, that he became one of the best batsmen of his time. During his long career he scored 20,723 runs with an average of 30 in first-class cricket and as a slow right-hand leg-break bowler he took 328 wickets at 31 runs each. Ready application of what he saw to his own use enabled McGahey to overcome his early faults and for some 10 seasons he was one of the mainstays of the Essex team. Standing well over 6 ft., he played forward with great power and used this stroke even in defence of his wicket rather than wait to see what the ball would do. Essentially a hitter, he showed great strength in driving either to the off or the on and he punished any short ball with severity. Seldom did he cut. He was a good field in the slips or in the deep.

Charles McGahey and Percy Perrin—a still taller man—were known as the "Essex Twins" and they enjoyed many long partnerships together. McGahey reached the height of his form in 1901 when he headed the Essex batting with an aggregate of 1,627 runs and an average of 47. His five centuries included one for London County against Warwickshire at the Crystal Palace and two in the match against Gloucestershire at Leyton—114 and 145 not out. Altogether that summer he scored 1,838 runs with an average of 48.36, and took 52 wickets at 28.50 each. Such was his play that season that he was chosen as one of the "Five Cricketers of the Year" for the *Almanack* and he went out to Australia with the team which A. C. MacLaren captained. He took part in two Test matches without success and generally on the tour he failed to produce anything like his full ability.

Usually going in second wicket down

McGahey shared in three very prolific stands for Essex. In 1900 against Kent at Leyton he and Perrin scored 323 together, setting up what at that time was a record for the third wicket. Four years later at the Oval he and Herbert Carpenter hit up 328 off the Surrey bowlers and at Leyton in 1912 he and Perrin added 312 against Derbyshire. McGahey's highest innings was 277 against Derbyshire at Leyton in 1905, but probably the best display of batting he ever gave was at Old Trafford in July 1898. Essex wanted 336 in the last innings and the previous best total of the match was 254, but thanks to McGahey, who scored 145, they won by four wickets. McGahey's partnership of 191 with Perrin for the third wicket practically decided the result of a memorable game. In 1908 at Leyton he drove a ball from Hallam, the Nottinghamshire bowler, over the pavilion and into the road. In minor cricket he played many big innings. In 1901 he and Perrin made 309 for Tottenham's first wicket at Clapton without being separated. In 1896 he made 205 for Leyton against Clapton and in 1906 at Llanelly for an Essex XI he played the highest innings of his career—305 not out.

More than once indifferent health threatened to cause his premature retirement from cricket, but during a trip to Australia in the winter of 1897 he threw off the danger of a breakdown. At that time and for many years Charles McGahey was a splendid full-back at Association football. He played for City Ramblers, Tottenham Hotspur, Clapton, Woolwich Arsenal and Sheffield United besides captaining both London and Middlesex when representative XIs often included famous Corinthians.

Mr. Percy Perrin, the best batsman in England who never played Test cricket, and still well known as one of the present Selection Committee, gives this appreciation of his old colleague:

"Charles McGahey, in my view, was one of the most popular and kindest-hearted players ever seen in first-class cricket; certainly he was most encouraging to any young player. I have known him on many occasions go out of his way to give a youngster good advice. Dry humour was an outstanding feature of his attractive characteristics. Having played with him more or less for 25 years I consider McGahey one of the very best cricketers Essex ever had. Really a magnificent cricketer he was undoubtedly the hardest hitter I ever faced. The opposite batsman had to keep his eyes open, as McGahey used to jump to the ball and drive back very straight. On one occasion he drove the ball back so hard that he broke his partner's arm!

I well remember one instance of his quick thinking wit when I was in at the other end. McGahey was 99, he played at the next ball, said 'Come one' but failed in his stroke and was bowled. As he passed by on the way to the pavilion he said to the bowler, 'Lucky for you I wanted a drink.'

I think one of his greatest innings was 277 against Derbyshire in 1905. He and I had many long stands together. Two come to mind readily. Kent, having fielded out 270 runs at the Oval without taking a Surrey wicket in the last stage of a drawn match, came to Leyton, and lost the toss; they got two men out before lunch, then McGahey and I batted the rest of the day and altogether added 323. The other was 312 against Derbyshire seven years later. McGahey was then 41 and I, 36. We made the runs in about three hours, his share was 150.

A very useful change bowler McGahey got us out of many a difficulty. He was a self-made cricketer without any tuition whatever. We were 'dubbed' 'Essex Twins' by Joe Armour, the Essex scorer for 44 years—a living volume of Essex cricket history. When I started Joe Armour, in his quaint way, complained that he could not distinguish one from the other. McGahey's height was 6 ft. 2 in., mine 6 ft. 3 in. He suggested that one of 'the twins' should wear a scarf round his waist so that he could get the runs down to the right man."

McGAW, Lieut.-Col. Alfred Joseph Thoburn, who died in hospital in Jersey on February 8, 1984, aged 83, was not in the XI at Charterhouse, but later attracted attention by scoring many runs in Army cricket in India; particularly by an innings of 300 (said to have taken only three hours) for the Rifle Brigade against the 60th Rifles at Rawalpindi in 1925–26. Later he played for the Army and appeared twice for Sussex in 1928. A tall man he had an immaculate style as a bat and was a fine fieldsman, with a lovely, accurate wrist-flick to the top of the stumps. He was also a leg-spinner, who bowled fewer loose balls than most of his type. Some will remember the delightful weeks of country-house cricket organised by his father on his beautiful ground at St Leonard's Forest, Horsham.

McGREGOR, William, died on October 5, 1980, aged 92. He was a wicket-keeper from the Victorian country town of Benalla and, although he never played first-class cricket for Victoria, he was the last surviving member of Sir Arthur Sims's 1913–14 Australian team which toured New Zealand. Others on this tour included Trumper, Noble, Armstrong, Ransford and the Englishman J. N. Crawford. McGregor's share of an Australian total of 922 for nine against a South Canterbury Fifteen at Temuka was 74; Crawford's was 354 (14 sixes and 45 fours) and Trumper's 135.

McILWRAITH, John, a member of the fifth Australian team which visited England in 1886, died at Melbourne on July 13, 1938, aged 81. A hard-hitting batsman at his best, he was not particularly successful on that tour, making 533 runs, average 15. He played in one Test. Just before coming to England he hit 133 for Victoria against New South Wales—his first appearance for the State—and 125 for the Australian team against Victoria. In first-class cricket in Australia he scored 947 runs with an average of 32. In the 1883–84 season his aggregate exceeded 1,500 runs for the Melbourne C.C. alone.

McINTYRE, William, who died on September 13, 1892, will be remembered for his long and honourable connection with the Lancashire County C.C. Born at Eastwood, Nottinghamshire, on May 24, 1844, he came out for his native county and made his first appearance at Lord's for North v. South in Whitsun week, 1876. Curiously enough, his first match at Lord's was George Parr's last. Quite early in his career McIntyre transferred his services to Lancashire, and with the latter county he was connected so long as he remained before the public. He was a very fast right-handed bowler, extremely straight, and in his best day very effective. For a good many seasons he shared the Lancashire bowling with Watson and Mr. Appleby, and the best testimony to the general efficiency of the three will be found in the comparatively small scores made against them. William McIntyre had two brothers who were cricketers, one, the famous Martin McIntyre, who for two or three seasons did such brilliant things for Notts; and the other Michael McIntyre, who appeared about the year 1863, but soon dropped out of notice.

McIVER, Colin D., died suddenly, aged 73, when on a visit to Worcester College, Oxford, on May 13, 1954. Born at Hong Kong on January 23, 1881, he was in the Forest School XI from 1897 to 1901 and in the last season attracted special attention by scoring 1,003 runs, average 100.30. He gained a Blue at Oxford in 1903 and 1904 and in his first match against Cambridge helped towards a win by 268 runs by scoring 51 in the second innings and sharing with K. M. Carlisle in a stand of 109. When a Freshman, he made his first appearance for Essex in 1902 and he played a number of times for the county after leaving the University. As an efficient wicket-keeper, he played until over 60 for M.C.C., the Grasshoppers and the local club at Ashtead, Surrey, where he lived for so long. As an Association footballer, he got a Blue as centre-forward in 1904, and in 1906, when a member of Old Foresters, played at wing half-back for the England amateur team who beat France in Paris by 15 goals to nil.

McKENZIE, Douglas, who died at Perth on July 1, 1979, aged 73, was captain of both the Western Australian cricket and hockey teams and later applied his wide business experience as a member of the W.A.C.A. executive committee for 15 years from 1946. He was Association vice-president from 1960 until his retirement because of ill health in 1976. In a career covering both sides of the Second World War, he was a high-scoring batsman with the Claremont-Cottesloe club, and his first-class career extended from 1935 until 1945, a year in which he captained the side. Until War service with the A.I.F. interrupted his career, he was a prominent hockey player from 1932, his association with that sport being recognised by life membership of the W.A. Hockey Association.

McKIBBEN, Thomas Robert, died at the close of 1939, aged 69. He came to England with Harry Trott's team in 1896, and his delivery raised such criticism that it was written "there can be little doubt that he continually threw when putting on his off-break"—an opinion often expressed in Australia also. Very powerfully built, of medium height, he accomplished deadly work with his right-hand slow to medium bowling when he kept a length. Perhaps most remarkable was his performance against Lancashire on the Aigburth ground, Liverpool, where he took 13 wickets at a cost of only 38 runs. The county fell for 28 in their second innings, McKibben's analysis being seven wickets, including the hat-trick, for 11 runs. Frank Sugg did not attempt to play one ball that came back a prodigious amount on to the stumps. In the two innings McKibben and Trumble were unchanged.

Playing in two of the three matches against England, McKibben took 11 wickets at 14.8 apiece, and his season's record showed 101 at 14.27—figures that put him at the top of the Australian averages above Hugh Trumble, Ernest Jones and George Griffen, who all claimed over 100 wickets. A left-handed batsman, he made few runs. In Sheffield Shield matches for New South Wales 136 wickets fell to him at 20.50 runs each. Twice he took 14 wickets in a match, and once 15— at Adelaide in 1896. He was seldom needed in Test matches, and altogether in five such encounters his tally showed 17 victims, average 29.17. A visitor with the team captained by Don Bradman in 1938, McKibben renewed many friendships in England, where his frank, happy character made him deservedly popular.

McKINNON, Atholl Henry, who died in Durban on December 2, 1983, aged 51, played eight times for South Africa between 1960 and 1967, taking 26 Test wickets at 35.57 apiece. As portly as he was affable, he belonged to the classical school of slow orthodox left-arm bowlers, length, line and flight playing at least as much a part as spin. Born at Port Elizabeth and educated, like the Pollock brothers, at Grey High School, McKinnon began his first-class career, in 1952–53, with Eastern Province and ended it, in 1967–68, with Transvaal.

He toured England twice, in 1960 and 1965, being the only member of the 1965 team to have also been in the previous side. In 1964–65, when England were last in South Africa, McKinnon was brought into the South African side for the fourth Test. His four for 128 in 51 overs in England's first innings and three for 44 in 35 overs in the second showed him at his best, his control being excellent, his line off stump and outside. In South Africa in 1966–67 when, amid nation-wide excitement, the home side won a series against Australia for the first time, he played in the first two Tests. He was a burly tail-ender, who batted right-handed and had a top score of 62. After retiring he was a patient and popular cricket coach. His death, from a heart attack, came when he was managing the unofficial West Indian team touring South Africa. All told he took 470 first-class wickets (average 21.14) and scored 1,687 runs (average 15.06).

McLAREN, J. W., born on December 24, 1887, died of diabetes in November, 1921, at the early age of 33. As a fast bowler he

gained his place in the Australian team which visited England in 1912, the year of the Triangular tournament, but, playing comparatively seldom, he took only 27 wickets for 22.96 runs each. He was not chosen for any of the Test matches. In his own country he performed well for Queensland, and he was captain of the Valley C.C., of Brisbane, when the club won the premiership three years in succession.

McLEOD, Charles, born October 24, 1869, died November 26, 1918. While *Wisden* was passing through the press the news came from Melbourne by mail that Charles McLeod died on November 26 at his home at Toorah. Though never a great force in Australian cricket he was an excellent all-round man, good enough for a place in almost any XI. He came to England with the great Australian team of 1899, and paid us a second visit in 1905. In both tours, without doing anything startling, he justified his selection. In 1899 he was overshadowed by the many finer batsmen on the side, but he scored 545 runs, with an average of 17. The Australians were so strong that he was given a chance in only one of the five Test matches, but against England at the Oval he scored 31 not out and 77. He was always a batsman of the ultra-careful school, very strong in defence, but undistinguished in style. Bowling fairly well in 1899 he took 81 wickets at a rather heavy cost. The tour of 1905 found him much the same cricketer as before; he scored 722 runs and took 91 wickets. This time he played in all five Test matches, but did little or nothing. For many seasons—1893 to 1905—McLeod was a member of the Victorian XI in the Inter-State matches. He played an innings of 112 against England at Melbourne in 1898 and scored 100 against New South Wales in 1896.

McLEOD, D., who died at Melbourne, on November 25, 1901, in his 30th year, was a member of the well-known cricketing family, of which R. W. and C. E. were the best exponents. In March, 1891, when but 19 years of age, he played an innings of 204 not out for the Scotch College against Geelong Grammar School. His first appearance in inter-State cricket was for Victoria against Tasmania, at Hobart, in January, 1895, and he celebrated the occasion by making a score of 107. In inter-club matches in Melbourne, he made thousands of runs, his chief scores being obtained for Port Melbourne and the University.

McLEOD, Robert, who died on June 14, 1907, will be remembered in England as a member of the Australian team of 1893. This was his first and only visit to this country. He proved himself a fairly good all-round cricketer but it cannot be said that he came up to the reputation he enjoyed at home. In the course of the tour he scored 638 runs with an average of 17 and took 47 wickets for something over 24 runs apiece. On this record he was hardly good enough for a representative Australian team. However, he played a very creditable part in the memorable match against the M.C.C. in which Lyons made his great score of 149. Following-on against a balance of 181 runs, the Australians set the M.C.C. 167 to get. Up to a certain point the club looked to have an easy victory in prospect, but in the end they were only saved from defeat by Attewell's defence, wanting 14 runs to win at the finish with two wickets to fall. McLeod in this innings bowled better than on any other occasion in England, taking five wickets in 19 overs for 29 runs. His better-known brother came to England in 1899 and again in 1905. He was born on January 19, 1868.

McMASTER, Joseph Emile Patrick, who died suddenly in London on June 7, 1929, aged 68, was a member of the English team which went to South Africa in 1888–89.

McMICHAEL, Sam, who died at Brighton, in Victoria, on April 21, 1923, aged 53, was a good batsman and fine field. He was born on July 18, 1869. Several times he played for his State, and possibly his most meritorious innings was his 97 against South Australia at Melbourne in 1897–98. For the East Melbourne C.C. he was a prolific scorer, and in 1898–99 his average for the club was as high as 82. In making 246 not out that season against St. Kilda, he added 295 for the third wicket with F. Laver (126 not out), while two years earlier he (211) and Val Thompson (228 not out) put on 315 together for the fifth wicket against Richmond, the latter, who died young, being then only 18 years of age. Mr. McMichael was also a good footballer and amateur boxer.

McMILLAN, 2nd Lieut. N. W., who played for Auckland in the Plunket Shield competition, was killed in the Middle East in 1942.

McMILLAN, Quintin, died at Randfontein, Transvaal, on July 3, 1948, aged 44. A slow leg-spin and googly bowler and free-scoring batsman, he played in 13 Test matches for South Africa at home and in England, Australia and New Zealand, scoring 306 runs, average 18.00 and taking 36 wickets, average 34.52. Born near Johannesburg on June 23, 1904, he played for Transvaal in 1928, when he scored 61 and took nine wickets in his first match, and then scored 185 not out against Orange Free State, setting up a South African fourth wicket record of 265 with H. B. Cameron. Chosen for the 1929 South African team to England, he enjoyed a successful tour, scoring 749 runs, average 26.75 and taking most wickets—91, average 25.45—in first-class matches. After playing in all five Test matches against A. P. F. Chapman's M.C.C. team in South Africa in 1930–31 he toured Australia and New Zealand the following season, taking 71 wickets in all first-class matches, including nine for 53 in an innings against South Australia. At the end of this tour McMillan retired for business reasons from first-class cricket. His career, which lasted for little more than three years, consisted of two overseas tours and only nine first-class matches (five of them Tests) in South Africa. His final record in big cricket was 1,607 runs, average 26.78 and 189 wickets, average 26.63.

McMURRAY, Thomas, who died in his native Ireland on March 24, 1964, aged 52, made occasional appearances as a professional for Surrey between 1933 and 1939, having joined the staff while playing for Millwall F.C. A good all-rounder, he could keep wicket and he excelled with his speed in the outfield. He fielded as substitute for England against Australia at the Oval in 1934 when L. E. G. Ames and W. E. Bowes were injured. From 1945 he was in charge of P.T. and helped with cricket and soccer at Campbell College, Belfast, where his modesty and efficiency made him a deservedly popular member of the staff.

McRAE, Temp. Surgeon Lieut. F. M., R.N.V.R., was killed when H.M.S. *Mahratta*, a destroyer, was lost in February, 1944. Playing first for Somerset in 1936, he steadily improved in batting, although not finding time for regular participation in first-class cricket, and in 1939 he averaged 30.40, his best innings being 107 against Hampshire at Taunton—his only century for the county. He fielded very smartly. At St. Mary's Hospital he made a name as a dashing three-quarter and appeared in a Rugby international trial. His death at the age of 28 was a great loss to Somerset, as expressed by

Brigadier Lancaster, Hon. Secretary to the county.

McVITTIE, Charles Arthur Blake, who died on September 4, 1973, was in the Bedford School XI before going up to Cambridge. In 1929 he kept wicket in three matches for the University, but did not get a Blue, and in the same season he assisted Kent against Derbyshire at Dover.

MEAD, Charles Philip, who died in hospital at Bournemouth on March 26, 1958, following an operation for internal haemorrhage, aged 71, was for 30 years a mainstay of the Hampshire batting. A left-hander of the highest class, he scored in that time 55,060 runs—a number exceeded only by Sir Jack Hobbs, F. E. Woolley and E. Hendren—at an average of 47.87. He hit a century against every other county, totalling 153 in all, with 280 not out against Nottinghamshire at Southampton in 1921 the biggest.

Though he often appeared to the uninitiated to be a slow run-getter, he could, by clever placing of the ball, take singles which many another batsman could not have obtained. His defence was remarkably sound, he was excellent in hitting to leg and in driving on either side of the wicket, and his quick-footedness made him specially capable of dealing with slow spin bowling. He also bowled slow spinners which brought him 277 wickets, average 34.46, and by nimble slip-fielding surprising in a man of his large build he held 647 catches.

One of his mannerisms when preparing to receive the bowling was to place his bat in the block-hole, shuffle his feet towards the bat and then touch the peak of his cap. Born at Battersea, he first joined the Surrey staff, but deeming his opportunities of advancement slight, decided to throw in his lot with Hampshire. While completing two years of qualification by residence, he appeared for his new county against the 1905 Australians and afforded evidence of his capabilities by making 41 not out against A. Cotter at his fastest. He played his first County Championship match the following year and his value to the county is shown by the fact that in no fewer than 27 seasons he scored over 1,000 runs. He exceeded 3,000 twice and 2,000 nine times.

On three occasions Mead hit a century in each innings of a match: 109 and 100 not out v. Leicestershire at Leicester, 1911; 102 and 113 not out v. Leicestershire at Southampton, 1913, and 113 and 224 v. Sussex at Horsham, 1921, when he headed the English

averages with an aggregate of 3,179 runs at 69.10 per innings. That last season, a disastrous one for England, Mead played in the last two Tests against Australia, putting together innings of 47 and 182 not out and helping in two drawn games after three defeats. These performances suggested that he might with advantage have been called upon earlier to break the stranglehold on batsmen gained by that deadly pair of fast bowlers, E. A. McDonald and J. M. Gregory. That innings of 182 stood as the highest against Australia in England for 17 years. He took part in 17 Test matches in all, involving visits to Australia in 1911 and 1928 and South Africa in 1913 and 1922. While he achieved nothing out of the ordinary in Australia, he proved a distinct success in South Africa and in the third Test at Durban in 1922–23 he showed his most dogged tactics when staying eight hours 20 minutes for 181.

Other of Mead's achievements were the scoring of three 100s in following innings in 1921, 1922, 1923 and 1933, and record stands for Hampshire of 344 for the third wicket with G. Brown against Yorkshire at Portsmouth, 1927, 259 for the fourth wicket with the Hon. L. H. Tennyson v. Leicestershire at Portsmouth, 1921, and 270 for the seventh wicket with J. P. Parker v. Kent at Canterbury, 1926.

After leaving Hampshire, he turned out for Suffolk in the Minor Counties' Championship competition in 1938 and 1939, meeting with considerable success. For the last 10 years of his life he was totally blind, but his interest in cricket endured and he often attended Hampshire matches.

MEAD, Harold, son of Walter Mead, died at Epping in April, 1921, at the early age of 25. He played for Essex occasionally before the First World War. Whilst serving with the Essex Regiment he was wounded severely in 1915, and it cannot be said that he ever really recovered.

MEAD, Walter, who died in hospital at Ongar on March 18, 1954, aged 84, was in his day one of the most notable of slow-medium right-arm bowlers. With an easy delivery and remarkable command of length, he possessed exceptional powers of spin and could make the ball turn on the best of pitches. While generally employing the off-break, he sent down an occasional leg-break with good effect, this ball bringing him many of the 1,906 wickets he took at an average cost of 19.08 runs during his first-class career. Twice he performed the rare feat of taking 17 wickets in a match, an achievement equalled only by A. P. Freeman, of Kent. The first of these was in 1893 against the Australians, when Mead dismissed nine men for 136 in the first innings and eight for 69 in the second. Two years later against Hampshire at Southampton he took eight for 67 and nine for 52.

Born at Clapton, in Middlesex, on March 25, 1869, Mead was invited by Bob Thoms, a celebrated umpire, to take part in a colts' match for the county in 1885 but declined and five years later, having qualified by residence, made his first appearance for Essex. He continued to play for the eastern county until 1913, except for the seasons of 1904 and 1905 when, because of a dispute over the question of winter pay, he took no part in County Cricket. During those two summers he played for M.C.C. and London County without achieving much success. His best season for Essex was that of 1895 when he took 179 wickets for less than 15 runs apiece and gained fifth place in the first-class bowling averages. In three successive innings he disposed of 24 batsmen for 192 runs.

Mead rarely distinguished himself as a batsman, but at Leyton in 1902 he hit 119 against Leicestershire. At Sheffield in 1893, when no other Essex player exceeded 20, he went in at No. 10 and scored 66 not out, followed by taking four wickets for eight runs in the first Yorkshire innings and six for 73 in the second and so bore a leading part in a victory by seven wickets. As a fieldsman, Mead generally occupied the cover-point position with distinction.

His sole appearance for England was against Australia at Lord's in 1899 when, though bowling 53 overs, 24 of them maidens, he took only one wicket for 91 runs. From 1891 to 1918, he was a member of the M.C.C. staff at Lord's.

MEAD-BRIGGS, Richard, who died on January 15, 1956, aged 54, played in two matches for Warwickshire in 1946. For 36 years until ill-health compelled his retirement in 1954, he was a notable all-rounder for Harborne C.C., Birmingham, and for some seasons captained the club.

MEADE, Spencer, a fast left-hand bowler with a peculiar spin, was born at Philadelphia (Pa.) on January 19, 1850, and died there on April 3, 1911. He figured prominently in the international matches against Willsher's team in 1868 and Mr. Fitzgerald's in 1872, as well as in the Halifax tournament of 1874.

MEHER-HOMJI, Khurshed Rustomji, who died in Bombay on February 10, 1982, aged 70, toured England as a wicket-keeper with the Maharaj Kumar of Vizianagram's Indian team in 1936, playing in the second Test match at Old Trafford. That was his only appearance for India. At home he played for the Parsis in the Bombay tournament and for West India and Bombay in the Ranji Trophy. His uncle, Rustomji Meher-Homji, toured England with the 1911 All-India side.

MEHRA, Ramprakash, who died in Delhi on March 7, 1983, aged 65, was a batsman of more than average ability who became closely associated with the growth of cricket in Delhi and was President of the Board of Control for Cricket in India in 1975–76 and 1976–77. For Northern India and Delhi, in the early days of the Ranji Trophy, he scored 1,202 runs with an average of 30.82, many of them with a flourish. In 1940–41 he scored 209 against Maharashtra.

MEHTA, Dhanji S., who died on June 2, 1928, aged 63, toured England with the Parsi team of 1888. He was regarded as the best batsman in the side, but his form here was most disappointing.

MELLE, Dr. Basil George von Brandis, who died on January 8, 1966, aged 74, was among the earliest of leg-theory bowlers. He played in first-class cricket in South Africa, helping Western Province carry off the Currie Cup in 1908–09, before going up to Oxford, where he gained a Blue as a Freshman in 1913. High right-arm medium-pace in-swing to three short-leg fieldsmen so confounded Cambridge that he took six wickets for 70 runs in their first innings and two for 46 in the second. "A genuine discovery" *Wisden* wrote of him, and indeed he was for, with little support, he headed the University averages that season with 55 victims for 15.90 runs each. Next year he broke a finger in an early game and the consequent loss of practice meant that he never became even a shadow of his previous self, though he again took part in the University match. From 1914 to 1921—the War intervened—he played for Hampshire, and though his bowling declined so much that he was seldom employed in the attack, his batting improved out of all knowledge. In 1919 he finished third in the county averages with 927 runs—110 of them in an innings against Gloucestershire at Bristol—for an average of 33.52. He was also a keen fieldsman.

MELLOR, His Honour Judge Francis Hamilton, C.B.E., was born in London on May 13, 1854, and died in Paris, after an operation, on April 27, 1925, aged 70. He was in the Cheltenham XI in 1871 and two following years, and in 1873, when he played an innings of 187 against Old Cheltonians, he was described as "The most correct bat of the XI, his play on the leg side being especially brilliant; an excellent out-fielder, and useful underhand slow bowler." He was a Cambridge Blue of 1877, and against Oxford scored five and 15 not out. In 1877 and 1878 he appeared in four games for Kent. In 1898 he became Recorder of Preston and he held that office until made a County Court Judge in 1921.

MELLUISH, Gordon Christopher, who died on April 14, 1977, aged 70, had a few trials for Essex as a slow left-hander in 1926. For years he was well known in club cricket in the south-east and during the Second World War for Northamptonshire.

MELVILLE, Alan, who died in the Kruger National Park on April 18, 1983, aged 72, was arguably the most elegant batsman of his generation. Those who were lucky enough to see it still remember after 50 years his innings of 114 in two and a half hours for Sussex against the West Indies at Hove in 1933. It was the summer after the body-line tour and the fast bowlers, Griffith and Martindale, assailed him with vicious bouncers. They might have been serving up by request something to amuse him and the spectators. They were mercilessly hooked and, if they pitched the ball up, they were driven. Even granted the placid Hove wicket, it was a remarkable display. Years afterwards, meeting him at Lord's at a time when short-pitched fast bowling was being constantly discussed, I asked him if he had ever ducked to it. He smiled sweetly and said, "I don't think so. I think either I hit them or they hit me!" From what I saw of him I doubt if he was ever hit by anything that rose high enough to be hooked.

Standing 6 ft. 2 in. and slightly built, he was a wonderful timer of the ball; his methods were a model for the young cricketer and reduced every risk to a minimum. The drive, the hook and the cut all seemed to come equally easily to him and he was, besides, a good player off his legs. Moreover, he was a fine field anywhere and in his younger days a serviceable change bowler, first with leg-breaks and later with off-breaks and swingers.

Picked for Natal at 17, while still a boy at Michaelhouse, he scored a century next season in a trial to select the 1929 side to England and his father was asked whether he would allow him to go. But he was anxious to follow his elder brother, Colin (also a stylish batsman who had a trial for the University), to Trinity, Oxford, and it was thought wiser to refuse. In the Freshmen's match in 1930 he made 132 not out and took eight for 72. Naturally he was picked for the first match, against Kent, in which he scored 78 and put on 148 with N. M. Ford for the fourth wicket before being run out. In the next match he made 118 against Yorkshire. These innings were the more remarkable as he had had little experience of playing on grass. Unfortunately in the Varsity match he was hampered by a knee so weak that it was only a few minutes before the start that it was decided to play him and he did nothing. In 1931 D. N. Moore fell ill and Melville was appointed captain in his place. In 1932 he was captain in his own right, but missed much of the season owing to a collar-bone broken by a collision while batting. In 1933, when he played a fourth time, he had to stand out of many matches in order to work. Although his cricket for Oxford during these years left no one in any doubt about his class, he was, like some other notable Varsity bats, a disappointment in the match at Lord's: his highest score was 47 and his six innings produced an average of 16 only. As Oxford had Peebles in 1930 and Owen-Smith for the next three years, comparatively little use was made of his leg-breaks, but in 1932 he did the hat-trick against Leveson Gower's XI at Eastbourne and headed the averages.

He had been playing for Sussex since 1932 and continued to do so with great success until 1936, captaining them in 1934 and 1935. In 1935 and 1936 he headed their batting averages and in 1935 the bowling averages too, though he took only 12 wickets. It will not surprise the friends of so charming and modest a man that he was criticised for not bowling himself more. In 1935, though suffering from a very sore thumb, he made 101 in 90 minutes against Larwood, then admittedly past his best, and Voce at Hove, and his last innings for the county, against All India in September 1936, was the highest he ever played for them, 152, including 100 before lunch on the second morning.

Returning home at the end of that season and joining a firm of stockbrokers in Johannesburg, he became captain of the Transvaal side and then captained South Africa in 1938–39 against England. He did little himself in the first two Tests, but in the third promoted himself to open and shared in stands of 108 and 131 for the first wicket, and in the notorious timeless Test which concluded the tour scored 78 and 103, though he was handicapped throughout these three matches by a bad leg which finally forced him to move himself down the order.

Not physically very strong, he had never fully recovered from a back injury sustained in a car smash before he went up to Oxford, and a fall while training with the South African forces in the Second World War caused a recurrence of the trouble. For nearly a year he was in a steel jacket, and it was feared that his career was at an end. Luckily the fears proved false and by 1947, after various vicissitudes, he was fit to undertake the captaincy of the South African side in England. The earlier part of the tour was a personal triumph for him, culminating in innings of 189 and 104 not out in the first Test at Nottingham, followed by 117 in the first innings of the Lord's Test. He thus became the first batsman to score four consecutive 100s against England in Tests. Moreover, at Nottingham his stand of 319 with Nourse, made in exactly four hours, was at the time the highest for the third wicket in any Test. After this and in view of his inspiring captaincy, it was disappointing that his side should lose three of the Tests and draw two. He himself was, not surprisingly, completely worn out by the end of June: he had lost a lot of weight and the food rationing still in force did not help him. After a brave 59 in the second innings of the third Test, he accomplished, by the high standards he had set himself, comparatively little, though an innings of 114 not out against his own county at Hove must have given him much pleasure. At the end of the tour he announced his retirement from first-class cricket. However, in the autumn of 1948 he was persuaded to reappear and an innings of 92 for Transvaal against F. G. Mann's M.C.C. side brought him an invitation to play in the first Test. This he had to refuse owing to an injured wrist, but played in the third Test, in which he ended his international career with two useful innings. Later he was for many years a South African selector.

MENZIES, Dr. Henry, a very good wicket-keeper, was up at Cambridge with Gregor McGregor and so had no chance of getting his Blue. A well-known Free Forester, he played a few times for Middlesex in the early '90s. He died on March 7, 1936, aged 68.

MENZIES, Sir Robert Gordon, the famous Australian statesman, who died at his home in Melbourne on May 15, 1978, aged 83, was a very great lover of cricket indeed and had much to say in his autobiography, *Afternoon Light,* on how much it had meant to him. A close friend of many of the Australian players, between 1965, when he was appointed Lord Warden of the Cinque Ports, and the breakdown of his health in 1971, he spent much of each summer in England and was constantly to be found watching, specially on Kent grounds. He was President of the Kent County C.C. in 1968 and was a member of I Zingari and of the Band of Brothers.

MERMAGEN, Patrick Hassell Frederick, died on December 20, 1984, aged 73. Four years in the Sherborne XI and captain in the last two, he had in his final season the splendid record of 863 runs with an average of 66.38 and 40 wickets at 13.80, heading both tables. After representing the Public Schools at Lord's in 1930, he played for Somerset in their last eight matches but with somewhat disappointing results. His fast-medium bowling was hardly used and his 10 innings produced only 114 runs; though in the last match, against Hampshire at Taunton, he scored 35 and helped R. C. Robertson-Glasgow add 81 for the eighth wicket. This was, however, the last match of his first-class career. Going up to Cambridge, he failed to make his mark at Fenner's and never received a trial for the University. For many years a master at Radley, he later became headmaster of Ipswich School.

MERRICK, H. J., who died in August, 1961, aged 73, played in 14 matches for Gloucestershire between 1909 and 1911. His highest innings was 58 against Essex at Leyton in 1909. He was at one time a master at Clifton College.

MERRITT, William E., died at Christchurch, New Zealand, on June 9, 1977, aged 68. A leg-break and googly bowler, he was under 19 when picked for the first New Zealand team to England in 1927 and had played only four first-class matches. The experiment was a triumphant success. In a weak bowling side, he was by far the most successful bowler, taking in first-class matches 107 wickets at 23.64 and in all matches 169 at 19.54, figures which would obviously have been better had he had more help. He never fulfilled this early promise. Against A. H. H. Gilligan's side in New Zealand in 1929–30 his eight wickets in the

Tests cost over 50 runs each and in England in 1931 his 99 wickets averaged 26.48 and he was again a complete failure in the Tests. However, it was on this tour that he accomplished the best performance of his career, taking seven for 28 in the second innings against a strong M.C.C. side at Lord's and securing an innings victory.

After that season he went into League cricket, and from 1938 to 1946 played for Northamptonshire. Here he suffered from dropped catches and his bowling was expensive, but he supplemented it by many useful hard-hitting innings, the highest of them 87 in 57 minutes against Sussex at Kettering in 1939. As a bowler, when hit he tended to try to spin the ball more and his length naturally suffered. At times too he was inclined to bowl the googly too much in preference to the more dangerous leg-break. In 1946, owing to a League engagement, he played in mid-week matches only and after that season left first-class cricket, but continued to play in the League as well as being in business in Dudley. He returned to New Zealand in 1966.

MERRY, Cyril A., who died at Port of Spain on April 19, 1964, aged 53, played for Trinidad and toured England with the 1933 West Indies team. He took part in the first and third Test matches with little success. In all first-class fixtures that season, he hit 856 runs, average 28.53, his highest score being 146 against Warwickshire at Edgbaston when, by brilliant batting, he and G. Headley added 228 in two hours for the fifth wicket.

MERRY, Deputy Flight Commdr. D., a younger brother of the West Indies Test player, was killed in Canada on May 4, 1944, when doing a night flying trial. A very useful batsman, he made 135 in three completed innings for Trinidad in 1941 and went to England directly afterwards. He was only 21.

MESTON, Samuel Paul, who died at Vancouver, British Columbia, on January 9, 1960, aged 77, played in three matches for Gloucestershire in 1906. The following year he appeared for Essex, for whom his 130 against Lancashire at Leyton was the highest innings of the season. He and C.P. Buckenham put on 186 for the sixth wicket and he and A.P. Lucas 118 for the seventh.

METCALFE, Evelyn James, who died on June 14, 1951, aged 87, was a member of the M.C.C. for 60 years. Soon after leaving Eton

he went to Australia, where he lived for 25 years, and played for Queensland against New South Wales, Victoria and South Australia, being referred to as one of the best slip fieldsmen in Australia. He also represented the State at lawn tennis. On occasional visits home he appeared for Hertfordshire and, when finally returning to England, took teams to Philadelphia and Canada. Born on September 29, 1865, he was a member of I Zingari, Free Foresters, Eton Ramblers, Butterflies and Incogniti.

M'EVOY, Frederick E., a Victorian State player, died at Brighton (V.) on November 5, 1913. On his only appearance against New South Wales—at Melbourne in December, 1877—he opened the innings and scored five and 16. He was regarded as a good batsman but slow in the field.

MEYER, William E., who died on October 1, 1953, aged 70, played 16 innings for Gloucestershire in 1909 and 1910, scoring 136 runs. His highest score was a hard-hit 43 against Kent at Catford.

MEYERS, Harry A., who was born at Hamilton, Bermuda, on November 24, 1888, died at Brooklyn, N.Y., on April 1, 1925, at the early age of 36. A skilful wicket-keeper, he developed into a useful fast bowler and batsman, and, after playing in Bermuda against the Gentlemen of Philadelphia, the Australians and other touring teams, he settled in New York and became associated with Columbia Oval, King's County, Brooklyn, Manhattan, the Crescent A.C., and various other clubs. In 1919, 1920 and 1921 he was the most successful bowler in the Metropolitan District League and in 1914 he won the batting prize. His highest score was 116 for Brooklyn v. Prospect Park in 1911.

MEYRICK-JONES, The Rev. Frederic, died at Shaftesbury on October 25, 1950, aged 83. A hard-hitting batsman, he was in the Marlborough XI 1884–85, and three years later, when a Senior, he was given his Cambridge Blue on the day of the match against Oxford. Although he did not go in until last but one, he made 16 and 36 and took part in two useful stands. In turn he assisted Hampshire, Kent and Norfolk. An antiquarian of some note, he was also head of the Rugby School Mission from 1898 until his retirement in 1905.

MIAN MOHAMMED SAEED, who died suddenly in Lahore on August 23, 1979, aged

68, did splendid work for Pakistan cricket. Playing originally for Northern India in the Ranji Trophy and later for Punjab in the Qaid-E-Azam in Pakistan, he captained Pakistan before they received Test status in their first representative match against West Indies at Lahore in November 1948 when he made 101 in the second innings, and with Imtiaz Ahmed put on 205 for the second wicket. Later he helped to organise the Pakistan Eaglets' visit to England and at the time of his death was chairman of Pakistan's selectors. He was the father-in-law of Fazal Mahmood.

MIDDLEBROOK, William, the well-known fast bowler, who was born at Morley, on May 23, 1858, died suddenly on April 26, 1919. He played in 23 games for Yorkshire in 1888 and 1889, taking 77 wickets for 16.49 runs each and making 139 runs with an average of 5.14. At different times he was associated with the Morley, Preston, Bradford and Leeds Buckingham clubs. In May, 1891, he and Amos Marshall, playing for Bradford, dismissed Dewsbury and Savile for two runs.

MIDDLETON, The Earl of, President of the Surrey club in 1923 and for many years a vice-president and trustee, died on February 13, 1942, aged 85. Among his many activities he found time for much committee work and generally in furthering the interests of the County C.C., besides constantly attending matches at the Oval. Objecting to excessive preparation of pitches, he preferred the kind of turf on his private ground at Peper Harow, Godalming, where he said that a match of four innings could be played to a finish between 11.30 and 6.30.

MIDDLETON, James, the leading South African left-handed bowler from 1894 until 1906, died at Newlands, Cape Town, on December 28, 1913, aged 48. He was born at Chester-le-Street, Durham, and was bought out of the Army by the Cape Town C.C., who engaged him as their professional. Against visiting teams from England and in Currie Cup matches he obtained many wickets, his best feat being to take 12 for 100 for Western Province v. Transvaal at Cape Town, in 1897–98. In 1894 and 1904 he toured England with the South African teams of those years. In the former season, when he took 83 wickets for 15.79 runs each, his best analyses were seven for 45 v. Surrey, 12 for 83 v. M.C.C. and Ground, and eight for 48 v. Leicestershire, against whom he and

F. Rowe were on unchanged throughout. Ten years later, when he was overshadowed by Schwarz, Kotzé, Sinclair and White, he obtained only 35 wickets and at a cost of 24.97 runs apiece.

MIDGLEY, C. A., who played in four matches for Yorkshire in 1906, died in Bradford in June, 1942, aged 68. A useful bat, he scored 115 runs in those few games with an average of 28.75, and took eight wickets at 18.62 apiece. Actually, he was placed fourth in batting to Hirst, 2,164 runs, Denton, 1,905 runs, and Rhodes, 1,618 runs, while only Schofield Haigh and Hirst had better bowling averages—but their wickets were 161 and 201 respectively. Hirst accomplished his unique double record, and Rhodes also did the double that season.

MIGNON, Edward, born at Kilburn on November 1, 1885, died in Guy's Hospital on May 14, 1925, of pneumonia aggravated by malaria. His fast bowling gained him a place in the Middlesex team from 1905 until 1913, and for the county he took 410 wickets for 25.99 runs each and scored 977 runs with an average of 8.42. Against Kent at Tonbridge in 1907 he had an analysis of 12 for 90. In the First World War he saw service as a lance-corporal in the Army Service Corps.

MIGNON, William, who died in Grenada on November 30, 1965, aged 95, was the last surviving member of the West Indian cricket team to tour England in 1900 under the leadership of R. S. A. Warner, brother of Sir Pelham Warner. A professional bowler, Mignon made the trip when by no means fit and did not produce his best form. During the tour, he took 30 wickets for 29.43 runs each, his best analysis being 10 wickets for 117 runs against Lancashire at Old Trafford.

MILDMAY, Major Sir Henry Paulet St. John, Sixth Bart., born on April 28, 1853, died at Dogmersfield Park, Winchfield, Hampshire, on April 24, 1916. He was a good, steady bat and safe field, who had played occasionally for Hampshire and also for the Household Brigade. He had been a member of the M.C.C. since 1875, and was formerly in the Grenadier Guards.

MILES, Eric Victor, who died in 1982, aged 83, represented Border in 12 matches between 1920 and 1930. A left-handed batsman and right-arm bowler he scored 419 runs in first-class cricket, took four wickets, and held four catches. His highest score, 69, was made against Eastern Province in 1925–26. Against S. B. Joel's English touring team in 1924–25 he made top score in each innings, 44 and 33. His brother, Lawrence, had a longer career in provincial cricket. Once, after spending the night in Cathcart, before a league match, they turned up at the ground to find themselves the only members of the Whittlesea team present, the others having been delayed by a river in flood. Unabashed, they went in to bat, and when their team-mates arrived had made a century apiece and were still going strong.

MILES, Robert Fenton, born at Bingham, Notts, on January 24, 1846, died at Clifton, Bristol, on February 26, 1930, aged 84. He was one of the last survivors of the famous Gloucestershire XI which between 1870 and 1880 took so high a place in County Cricket. Miles went from Marlborough to Oxford, and in his second year was given his Blue by W. F. Maitland. This was in 1867, when Oxford's chances in the University match were ruined by the illness of E. L. Fellowes, their best bowler. Miles did little that season but in 1868 and 1869 he retained his place, bowling slow left-hand with good effect in many of the University games. Perhaps his best performance was to take six for 65 against the All-England team when they played Sixteen of Oxford in 1869. He also got seven wickets in his last year against Cambridge and in the match with M.C.C., at Oxford, in 1868 he took five for 14. A Nottinghamshire man by birth, Miles lived all his life in Bristol, where he was a banker. He played in three matches arranged by W. G. Grace in 1870, before the Gloucester-shire County C.C. was formed and after the club was started in the following season he became a regular playing member of the side until 1879. In those days the strength of the county team was centred largely in the per-sonal efforts of W. G. Grace and his two brothers, but there was some good outside talent. Matthews, Frank Townsend, and Moberly were all capital batsmen, J. A. Bush was an excellent wicket-keeper, and Miles a most useful bowler. Quite slow, left-hand, Miles owed much to a brilliant fielding side and took a lot of wickets. He exploited the off theory to such an extent that he bowled numerous wides, in the process of tempting indiscreet batsmen, and in 1878, his best summer, when he took 31 wickets for 447 runs, he also had 48 wides against his name. Against Yorkshire at Clifton, in 1877, he had an analysis of four for 10. He was not much of a bat (right-handed) but in 1871, going in

10th against Surrey, he knocked up 79 in dashing style. In the Gloucestershire and Surrey match of 1872 he had a distressing experience for the last Surrey batsman came in with two runs to win, and put up his first ball from W. G. Grace into the hands of Miles at mid-on. Victory, the chronicler says, was literally in the grasp of Gloucestershire but unfortunately it did not stay there and Surrey won by one wicket. At that time Gloucestershire cricket was entirely amateur and no professional appeared for them until Midwinter, the Australian, came to England in 1877. In 1876 the county won the Cham-pionship—and won it with ease—without the assistance of any professional. That per-formance, in which Miles played a valuable part, has not been repeated since.

MILLAR, Charles Christian Hoyer, founder and for 55 years president of Rosslyn Park Rugby football club, who died on November 22, 1942, aged 81, deserved mention in *Wisden* for a very special and unique reason. He undertook on his own initiative to "weed" Lord's turf, and Sir Francis Lacey, secretary of M.C.C., signed a deed of ap-pointment making him "Honorary Weedkil-ler to G.H.Q. Cricket." From 1919 to 1931 he kept up his task, being particularly busy on summer evenings after stumps were drawn, and his zeal often received comment from pressmen walking to the exit when their duties were done. Mr. Millar, according to his own reckoning, accounted for 624,000 "victims," having spent 956 hours in his war against plantains and other "unwanted vege-tation."

MILLER, Audley Montague, who died on June 26, 1959, aged 89, was a capital all-rounder who captained Wiltshire for 25 years and also was hon. secretary. He played in a number of matches for M.C.C. and in 1895–96 was a member of the M.C.C. team in South Africa captained by Lord Hawke, playing in one Test match.

MILLER, James H., born on February 3, 1868, died suddenly in Glasgow on April 23, 1926, aged 58. He was for a long period associated prominently with the West of Scotland C.C., of which his father was for many years hon. secretary. A good hard-hitting, left-handed batsman, he often headed the club's averages, and once played an innings of 167 against Edinburgh Aca-demicals. His bowling, too, proved useful on occasion and he gained some distinction from the fact that he got C. B. Fry out twice in the match between West of Scotland and Sussex in July, 1903. His name will be found several times in representative Scottish teams.

MILLER-HALLETT, Alexander, for 10 successive years until 1946 President of Sussex, died at Brighton on February 14, 1953, aged 97. His cricketing connections with Sussex went back as far as 1866, and in the years before the Second World War he did much to increase the membership of the County Club. Known as "The Grand Old Man of Sussex Cricket," he was also a celebrated breeder of Jersey cattle. While he was watching cricket nothing else mattered. Once during a wartime match at Hove a German aircraft dropped a bomb on the ground. Without moving from his seat, Miller-Hallett remarked to his neighbour: "Fancy disturbing our game like that!"

MILLES-LADE, The Hon. H. A., died at Faversham, on July 30, 1937, in his 70th year. He went to Eton and Cambridge but did not get into either XI; played twice for Kent and toured America with Lord Hawke's team in 1891.

MILLIGAN, Lieut. Frank W. (Yorkshire). Born at Aldershot, March 19, 1870, died whilst with Colonel Plumer's force (endeavouring to relieve Mafeking), March 31, 1900. An excellent all-round player, a splendid field, fast bowler, and hard hitter. Represented the Gentlemen v. the Players in 1897 and 1898. He made a successful first appearance for the Gentlemen—at the Oval in 1897—scoring 47 and 47, and obtaining two wickets for three runs in the second innings of the Players. In the Scarborough match in 1898, he took in the second innings seven wickets for 61 runs.

MILLS, Corpl. A. E. (New Zealand Expeditionary Force), who was killed in July, 1916, was for some years a well-known player in senior cricket in Auckland.

MILLS, Edwin, the Notts and Surrey player, died on January 26, 1899. He was born on March 6, 1857, and was thus nearly 42 years of age. At the outset of his career Mills was regarded as an all-round cricketer of great promise, but he never fulfilled the hopes that had been formed of him. Like William Attewell and C. Shore, the left-handed bowler who has for years past done such great things for Norfolk, Mills came to the front during the strike of the leading Notts

players in 1881. He did well for Notts that season, taking 32 wickets in eight matches and scoring 197 runs with an average of 15, but he did not prove good enough to keep his place in the XI when the chief Notts players had made up their differences with the committee. He afterwards took an engagement at the Oval and qualified for Surrey by residence, but here again, though he made some appearances in county matches, he fell short of the standard demanded. He was a left-handed bowler of medium pace, and a very hard hitter. He was associated with Barnes in a wonderful finish at Lord's, in a match between Notts and the M.C.C. in June, 1882. Notts went in on the second afternoon at 10 minutes past five to get 164 to win, and it was arranged to play on until half-past seven if there was a chance of finishing, and afterwards to go on still later if the light remained fit for cricket. Notts lost seven wickets for 54 runs and the match seemed all over. However, on Mills becoming Barnes's partner, 99 runs were added before Mills was bowled. In the end Notts won by one wicket, the match finishing in semi-darkness at eight minutes to eight.

MILLS, George, died at Auckland on March 13, 1942, aged 74. Very good both as a slow bowler and batsman, he kept his form for many years. In 1887 he showed his ability by taking 10 wickets for 70 runs and scoring 39 not out against Wellington; nine years later he made the first century for Auckland, carrying his bat through the innings for 106, against the same opponents. He met various touring sides from Australia and Lord Hawke's team, captained by P. F. Warner, which went to New Zealand in the winter of 1902. His son, J. E. Mills, toured England with New Zealand teams in 1927 and 1931.

MILLS, Isaac, who died at Auckland on August 16, 1956, aged 87, was a member of the first New Zealand representative team to tour Australia in 1898–99. Born in Kent, he was taken to New Zealand in his sixth year. He and three of his brothers played for Auckland and he and his brother, George, for New Zealand.

MILLS, John, born at Coddington, near Newark, on January 28, 1855, collapsed in his seat during an interval in the match between Derbyshire and Notts at Ilkeston on June 27, 1932, and when carried into the pavilion life was found to be extinct. He and Arthur Shrewsbury appeared at Trent Bridge for the first time for the Colts on

Easter Monday, 1873, and were top scorers against the county XI with 24 and 35 respectively. A couple of seasons later both were introduced into the county side, for which Mills played occasionally for eight years. He made the record hit on the Wollaton ground and assisted Lenton United until an accident caused his retirement from active participation in the game.

MILLS, John, who died at Basle on April 14, 1935, aged 86, was the last surviving member of the celebrated Gloucestershire team of the early '70s. He played in 1870 when Gloucestershire first met Surrey. E. M., W. G., and G. F. Grace were in an entirely amateur XI and, as told in *Wisden*, "The Shire" beat "The County" by 52 runs on Durdham Down, Bristol. In the return at the Oval W. G. scored 143 and Frank Townsend 89. W. G. also took eight wickets for 55 and Surrey were beaten by an innings and 129 runs.

MILLS, John E., who died on December 12, 1972, aged 67, was a capital opening batsman for Auckland and for New Zealand, for whom he appeared in seven Test matches between 1929 and 1932. On the occasion of his Test debut, he hit 117 against England at Wellington in 1929–30, he and C. S. Dempster scoring 276 for the first wicket—a New Zealand record which still stands. In his one visit to England, under T. C. Lowry in 1931, Mills was one of six batsmen to exceed 1,000 runs for the touring side, but achieved little in his three Test matches.
CORRECTION. The New Zealand left-handed batsman was incorrectly stated in the 1973 edition to have visited England only once. In fact, he toured England twice, in 1927 and 1931, scoring over 1,000 runs on each occasion.

MILLS, Percy T., the medium-paced bowler who was one of the mainstays of the Gloucestershire team from 1902 to 1929, died at his home at Abingdon, Berkshire, on December 8, 1950, at the age of 67. A slight figure, he was precise and neat. His best performance occurred at Bristol in 1928 when, against Somerset, he took five wickets without conceding a run. This was only the fourth time that the feat had been achieved and no one has done it since that day. After his retirement when 45, he went to Radley College as coach, but he returned to first-class cricket in 1947 as an umpire. Last summer Mills helped in the coaching at the County Ground, Bristol, where he paid particular attention to the juniors. During his career he took 823 wickets for Gloucestershire at an average cost of 25.20.

MILLS, Walter George, who died in January, 1902, was an all-round player of more than average ability. He was especially well known in Lancashire cricket circles, and represented the county on a few occasions in 1871, 1875, 1876, and 1877. His highest score in a great match was 26 for Lancashire v. Sussex, at Brighton, in 1876. He bowled with success in a match against the Australians, at Longsight, in 1880.

MILTON, Sir William Henry, C.M.G., K.C.M.G., late Administrator of Southern Rhodesia, was born on December 3, 1854, and died at Cannes on March 6, 1930, aged 75. He was in the Marlborough XI in 1871 and 1872 and in the latter year the *Marlburian* said of him: "Possesses tremendous hitting powers and good defence; hits equally hard to all parts of the field. Has a wonderful power of punishing loose bowling. A splendid field anywhere, and throws in beautifully: very quick at the wicket." For many years he was a prominent figure in the game in South Africa. He captained the Western Province C.C. for 11 years, 1885–96, and had much to do with the visit of Major Wharton's team in 1888–89. Whilst at Marlborough he was in the Football Twenty, and later was captain of the Marlborough Nomads. He played half-back for England against Scotland in 1874 and against Ireland in 1875.

MISSEN, E. S., who died on November 17, 1927, was for many years the best bat in the Colchester district, and made heaps of runs for the Colchester and East Essex club. He also bowled (right-hand medium) with much success for that club of which he was for many years either captain or vice-captain. He played for Essex against Hampshire at Colchester in 1921.

MISTRI, Col. K. M., who died on July 22, 1959, aged 84, was a splendid left-handed batsman and useful bowler. Most of his first-class cricket in India was for the Parsees, for whom he first appeared in 1893 in the annual Presidency matches, but he was a member of the India team who visited England in 1911. He had been chairman of the Indian selection committee.

MITCHELL, Arthur, who died in hospital in Bradford on Christmas Day, 1976, aged 74, was a typical Yorkshire cricketer of one of the county's great periods, unpretentious, unspectacular, but immensely effective and always prepared to adapt himself to the needs of the side—a wonderful man at a crisis. No match was ever lost until the opposition had got him out. Spectators probably remember him primarily as a dour, on-side player, but if runs were wanted quickly he could get them and would start producing off-side strokes which they never dreamed he possessed: he was in fact an especially good cutter. On his one appearance for the Players at Lord's in 1934 he took two hours and five minutes over his first 50 and an hour later was out for 120.

Summoned from his garden at the last minute to take the place of Leyland, stricken by lumbago, in the Test against South Africa at Leeds in 1935, he took over three hours to score a valuable 58 in the first innings, but in the second, sent in first with D. Smith, made 72 in under two hours and helped in an opening stand of 128. In the final Test of the same series, again going in first, he made 40 in three hours. His third and last appearance in a Test in this country was against India at Lord's in 1936. As a member of the M.C.C. side in India, he had played in three Tests there in 1933–34.

In the course of his career he scored 19,523 runs with an average of 37.47, including 44 centuries, four of them in consecutive matches in 1933. He had played for Yorkshire as early as 1922, but competition was fierce and in the next three years he had few chances. An innings of 189 against Northamptonshire in 1926 revealed his possibilities, but it was not until two years later that he at last got an assured place. So strong was the county's batting that in 1930 he was one of five members of the side who averaged over 50. In those days he went in three, four or five, but after the retirement of Holmes in 1933 more often opened.

Apart from his batting, he was one of the greatest fieldsmen of his day, specialising close to the wicket, whether on the leg or the off. He continued to play regularly up to the War, but in 1945 became the county's coach, a post he held until 1970, doing splendid work not only by his teaching, but by going about talking on the game.

Brian Sellers, Yorkshire captain in the latter years of Mitchell's career, said: "Cricket has lost a great personality and I have lost a very great friend and old team-mate. Arthur was a loyal supporter and hard worker for Yorkshire and he did extraordinarily good work as coach. He will be greatly missed by the club. He was a dedicated cricketer who worked hard at the game and became a resolute and determined player. His determination is shown in that he was a poor fielder in league cricket at first but he practised so much that he became one of the best in the world."

MITCHELL, Clement, who died at Hove in October, 1937, aged 75, played occasionally for Kent, first appearing in 1890. A left-handed batsman, he scored many runs when at Felsted School, but did little in County Cricket. He scored 246 for Calcutta against Ballygunge in 1887 and for Crystal Palace in 1892 he made 210 not out at Chiswick Park. He played centre-forward for England in several Association matches from 1881 to 1885 when his club, Upton Park, had one of the strongest sides in the south.

MITCHELL, Frank, died at his home at Blackheath, London, on October 11, 1935, aged 63. ·A triple Blue, representing Cambridge University at cricket, Rugby football and putting the weight, Frank Mitchell enjoyed the distinction of playing cricket for both England and South Africa. He gained six caps for England as a Rugby forward and captained his University in both these games against Oxford. So readily did he adapt himself to all sports that he kept goal at Association football for Sussex.

Born on August 13, 1872, at Market Weighton, Frank Mitchell went to St. Peter's School, York, where he captained the XI in his last two seasons before going to Brighton as a schoolmaster. During some two years at Brighton he played good club cricket and made many runs. Going up to Cambridge, an older man than most undergraduates, he soon attracted attention with innings of 143, 203 and 136 for Caius College. He did well in the Freshmen's match of 1894 and on first appearing for the University scored 67 against C. I. Thornton's team and a little later made 75 and 92 against Yorkshire. Gaining his Blue he remained in the side four seasons, but never did himself full justice against Oxford, his aggregate for seven innings in the University match at Lord's being 136. Cambridge were very weak in bowling when Mitchell went up and, fairly fast, he came out at the head of the averages with 21 wickets at 21 runs apiece. Fifth to go on in Oxford's first innings, he dismissed four batsmen for 44 runs but after that season he was seldom called upon.

In 1896, when captain of Cambridge, he helped to make cricket history by instructing

E. B. Shine, his fast bowler, to give away extras so that Oxford should not follow-on. Three years before F. S. Jackson, in the great match at Lord's, acted in the same way with the aid of C. M. Wells and then Rule 53 was altered to 120 runs instead of 80 for the follow-on. The second case of a Cambridge side avoiding the ordinary course of the game as defined by the Laws caused a storm of protest. Members in the pavilion stood up and shouted "Play the game" and "Play cricket." Frank Mitchell himself said that one irate gentleman threw a pair of field glasses at him. Such was the effect on the nerves of the Cambridge XI that they began their second innings most disastrously and, despite a recovery, they eventually suffered defeat by four wickets. G. O. Smith—still more famous as an Association centre-forward—by scoring 132, took the chief part in hitting off 330 runs, which at that time was a most exceptional performance. In commenting upon the match *Wisden* said: "We defended F. S. Jackson and C. M. Wells for what they did and, believing that even in its amended form Law 53 is ill adapted to modern cricket, we think Mitchell was quite entitled in the interests of his side to take the course he did." Opposite views were expressed during correspondence in *The Times* but the authorities eventually changed the Law so that the side batting first and leading by 150 runs should have the option of enforcing the follow-on or themselves going in a second time.

Frank Mitchell first appeared for Yorkshire in 1894 and, though he met with limited success following his fine play at Fenner's, most good judges, including W. G. Grace, had strong faith in his future. Lord Hawke took him to South Africa in the winter of 1898 and so well did he play that he was given a regular place in the Yorkshire XI next summer; then he proved a model of consistency. Scoring 1,502 runs in county fixtures he finished up a good third to F. S. Jackson and George Hirst. At Leicester in 1899 he and Wainwright put on 329 for the fifth wicket when Yorkshire had made a bad start, his score of 194 being his best for the county. After a year in South Africa, Mitchell in 1901 headed the Yorkshire batting with an average of 46.17 for an aggregate of 1,801, including seven centuries, four of them, two not out, in consecutive matches. He far surpassed George Hirst, T. L. Taylor, J. T. Brown, Denton and Tunnicliffe, all of whom scored over 1,200 runs. This form brought him recognition as one of the "Five Cricketers of the Year" in *Wisden*. His last

appearance for Yorkshire was in 1904; altogether for the county he scored 4,090 runs with an average of 34.35. If not very polished in style, he had great qualities and became an accomplished batsman on any kind of wicket. Essentially an off-side player, he drove with tremendous power. Altogether during his first-class career in England and for England touring teams in South Africa he scored 8,438 runs with an average of 32.45.

After his first experience of South Africa he served in the Yorkshire Dragoons during the Boer War and following his best season in England he was almost lost to Yorkshire. Returning to South Africa he became secretary to Sir Abe Bailey and played for the Transvaal. In 1904 he captained the South African side which came to England and eight years later he was in charge of the side that took part in the Triangular tournament. Broken as it was by various changes in his life, Mitchell's first-class cricket career then ended, but two years later he played for M.C.C. in one match, scoring 17 and 66 at Fenner's against his old University. So Cambridge was the scene of the start and finish of Mitchell as a first-class cricketer.

Mitchell played Rugby football for Cambridge University from 1893 to 1895 and for Blackheath. He gained international honours in 1895 and 1896 as a forward when England put in the field particularly strong packs. Frank Mitchell took a team to America in 1895; two years later he went there with a side captained by B. J. T. Bosanquet and in 1901 made his third visit to the United States under P. F. Warner.

During the First World War, he rose to the rank of Lieut. Col. in the West Riding R.F.A. and was Mentioned in Dispatches. He wrote *Rugby Football*, in the Badminton Library, and did considerable journalistic work.

MITCHELL, Horace, who played occasionally as a professional for Sussex between 1882 and 1891, was within a few days of his 93rd birthday when he died at West Tarring on January 4, 1951. A bowler of considerable repute in club cricket, he did equally well on his few appearances for the county, taking 19 wickets at 16.79 runs apiece.

MITCHELL, Richard Arthur Henry, died at his residence, at Woking, on April 19, 1905. Born at Enderby Hall, near Leicester, on January 22, 1843, he was in his 63rd year. In 1866—the year after he left Oxford—Mr. Mitchell became an assistant master at Eton, and for over 30 years he was the ruling spirit of Eton cricket, acting as chief coach down to 1897, when he retired from duty. In recognition of his invaluable services, he was presented with a silver bowl bearing the inscription "Presented to Mr. R. A. H. Mitchell by the Captains of the Eton Elevens, 1866–1897." The bowl was presented to Mr. Mitchell, in the pavilion at Lord's, on the second day of the Eton and Harrow match, in 1898. Lord Harris, speaking on behalf of the subscribers, drew attention to the fact that, with the one exception of Mr. E. O. H. Wilkinson—captain in 1872—who was killed in the Zulu War, all the captains were then living. A portrait and biography of Mr. Mitchell appeared in *Baily's Magazine*, for July, 1865—the last season in which he was able to play regularly in first-class matches. After he became a master at Eton he practically restricted himself to the Canterbury Week, but it is worthy of mention that he took part in the Gentlemen and Players match, at Brighton, for the benefit of the late John Lillywhite, in 1871 and, being practically as good a bat as ever, scored 50 and 37 against the bowling of J. C. Shaw, Martin McIntyre, and Southerton. Playing in his young days against Jackson, Tarrant, and Willsher, Mr. Mitchell at the end of his career once met Spofforth. The match was I Zingari against the Australians, at Scarborough, in 1882, and Mr. Mitchell scored 32.

MITCHELL, Robert, who died in September, 1926, was for long a familiar figure in Melbourne cricketing circles. A member of the Fitzroy C.C. for 26 years, he joined Northcote in 1907, and he served on the Victorian Cricket Association. Several times he played for Victoria, and among his best innings for the State were 52 v. West Australia in 1892–93, and 92 v. Tasmania in 1899–1900.

MITCHELL, William, who died at Leeds on April 19, 1938, aged 62, was an effective fast bowler in Lancashire club cricket and for Yorkshire Second XI. In a game at Pateley Bridge he did the hat-trick by dismissing such noted county players as George Hirst, Schofield Haigh and David Denton with successive balls while taking five wickets for one run.

M'LACHLAN, Norman, born at Darlington on October 12, 1858, died at Torquay on February 18, 1928. He was only moderate as a batsman, but a good fast-medium-paced bowler and an active field, generally at long-

leg or long-off. At Loretto he was in the XI for four years, being captain his last two—1877 and 1878—and at Oxford he obtained his Blue as a Freshman, playing four times against Cambridge—1879 to 1882—and leading his side in the last-mentioned season. Mr. M'Lachlan was also a member of the Oxford University Fifteen, in 1879 and 1880. In those days teams were composed of two backs, two three-quarters, two halves and nine forwards. Mr. M'Lachlan was one of the backs.

MOBERLY, John Cornelius, born on April 22, 1848, died at Bassett, Southampton, on January 29, 1928, aged 79. In 1866 he was in the Winchester XI, and in the following season he took part in the Oxford Freshmen's match. Later he played for Hampshire, but the best work he did for the county was off the field. For some years he was the club's treasurer, for many its chairman of committee, and from 1913 to 1918 its president. Besides being useful as a batsman, he was "A steady and painstaking bowler, varying the pitch considerably, and was sometimes very successful."

MOBERLY, William Octavius, who was born at Shoreham, Sussex, on November 14, 1850, died at Mullion, Cornwall, on February 2, 1914. He was in the Rugby XI in 1868 and 1869, scoring 17, six, and 24 in his matches with Marlborough, and was one of the best players ever eligible who has failed to obtain his Blue for Oxford. In 1870 he scored 52 in the Freshmen's match, and in the following year 66 in the Seniors', but received very few trials in the XI. There can be no doubt that even then he was a first-rate batsman, his late-cutting especially being good. For Gloucestershire, between 1876 and 1887, he made many excellent scores, including 121 v. Somerset at Taunton in 1883, 103 v. Yorkshire at Cheltenham in 1876, 101 not out v. Nottinghamshire at Trent Bridge in 1877, and 99 v. Middlesex at Clifton in 1880. He was, too, a fine fieldsman and could keep wicket. In December, 1913, he resigned his position at Clifton College, after a connection with the school which lasted nearly 40 years, during which period he had done much to encourage athletics. At Rugby football also he gained high honours, playing for Oxford at the Oval in December, 1873, and for England v. Scotland in 1872.

MOFFAT, Douglas, who played for Middlesex v. M.C.C. and Ground on the Cattle Market ground at Islington in 1864, died on

March 29, 1922, aged 78. In his time he played much for various leading clubs, including the M.C.C., Oxford Harlequins and Incogniti. Whilst at Oxford he distinguished himself as a boxer.

MOFFATT, Norman John Douglas, who died in hospital on October 11, 1972, aged 89, played as an amateur batsman for Middlesex from 1921 to 1926. His highest innings was 55 not out against Nottinghamshire at Trent Bridge in 1924 when Middlesex, after following on 209 runs behind, won a remarkable victory by 27 runs. G. O. Allen took six Nottinghamshire wickets for 31 runs in the second innings.

MOLD, Arthur, died, after a long illness, on April 29, 1921, at Middleton Cheney, near Banbury, his native village, where he had resided since his retirement. Arthur Mold had been out of first-class cricket for nearly 20 years, but he remained fresh in the memory of all who follow the game at all closely. He was one of the deadliest fast bowlers of his day, but right through his career the fairness of his delivery formed the subject of lively discussion. This may be said without doing him the smallest injustice. Born in Northamptonshire on May 30, 1865, he came out for his native county, but quickly qualified for Lancashire by residence. He gained a place in the Lancashire XI in 1889, and remained associated with the team until he gave up public play. Season after season he met with brilliant success, keeping at his best until 1895 or 1896. After that he began to decline, but he was still a bowler to be feared. Even while he was at the height of his fame his delivery was, in private, spoken of in strong terms by many famous batsmen, but nothing happened until 1900, when in the Notts and Lancashire match at Trent Bridge, he was no-balled by James Phillips, and sent down only one over in the whole game.

A little later the county captains took up the question of unfair bowling, and at their famous meeting Mold's delivery was condemned by 11 votes to one. The climax came when at Manchester in July, 1901, in the Lancashire and Somerset match, Mold was no-balled by James Phillips 16 times in 10 overs. Mold played for England against Australia at Lord's, the Oval, and Manchester in 1893, but he was never picked for a tour in Australia. It has been urged in some quarters that Mold was an ill-used man, and that there was no ground for the severe criticisms passed upon him. I should say, on the other hand, that he was extremely lucky to bowl for so many seasons before being no-balled. To pretend that a perfectly fair bowler could have been condemned as he was is absurd. I happen to know that a famous batsman who played against him in his Northamptonshire days said: "If he is fair he is the best bowler in England, but I think he is a worse thrower than ever Crossland was." This opinion—expressed before Mold had been seen in a first-class match—and the vote of the county captains towards the close of his career, surely dispose of the notion that Mold was unjustly attacked. He did wonders for Lancashire, but personally I always thought he was in a false position.—S.H.P.

The following statistics of Mold's career will speak for themselves.

Eight or more wickets in an innings:

8 for 38	Lancashire v. Yorkshire, at Manchester	1890
9 for 41	Lancashire v. Yorkshire, at Huddersfield	1890
9 for 43	Lyric Club v. Australians, at Barnes	1890
8 for 72	Lancashire v. Somerset, at Taunton	1891
8 for 51	Lancashire v. Gloucestershire, at Bristol	1891
9 for 29	Lancashire v. Kent, at Tonbridge	1892
8 for 50	Lancashire v. Middlesex, at Manchester	1892
8 for 87	Lancashire v. Kent, at Tonbridge	1893
8 for 49	Lancashire v. Sussex, at Brighton	1893
8 for 76	Lancashire v. Notts, at Manchester	1893
8 for 67	Lancashire v. Sussex, at Brighton	1894
8 for 84	Lancashire v. Sussex, at Manchester	1895
9 for 62	Lancashire v. Kent, at Manchester	1895
8 for 20	Lancashire v. Notts, at Nottingham	1895
8 for 64	Lancashire v. Warwickshire, at Liverpool	1895
8 for 61	Lancashire v. Warwickshire, at Edgbaston	1895
8 for 33	Lancashire v. Surrey, at Manchester	1896
8 for 69	Lancashire v. Gloucestershire, at Bristol	1899

Thirteen or more wickets in a match:

13 for 111	Lancashire v. Yorkshire, at Huddersfield	1889
13 for 76	Lancashire v. Yorkshire, at Huddersfield	1890
15 for 131	Lancashire v. Somerset, at Taunton	1891
14 for 95	Lancashire v. Gloucestershire, at Bristol	1891
13 for 91	Lancashire v. Kent, at Tonbridge	1892
13 for 123	Lancashire v. Middlesex, at Manchester	1892
14 for 159	Lancashire v. Sussex, at Brighton	1892
13 for 114	Lancashire v. Middlesex, at Liverpool	1894
13 for 167	Lancashire v. Kent, at Tonbridge	1894
13 for 60	Lancashire v. Somerset, at Manchester	1894
13 for 123	Lancashire v. Gloucestershire, at Manchester	1894
15 for 87	Lancashire v. Sussex, at Brighton	1894
16 for 111	Lancashire v. Kent, at Manchester	1895
15 for 85	Lancashire v. Notts, at Nottingham	1895

Four wickets or more for three runs or less each:

7 for 21	Lancashire v. Kent, at Manchester	1890
5 for 11	Lancashire v. Sussex, at Manchester	1891
5 for 13	Lancashire v. Essex, at Leyton	1891
7 for 17	Lancashire v. Sussex, at Manchester	1894
7 for 10	Lancashire v. Somerset, at Manchester	1894
7 for 20	Lancashire v. Sussex, at Brighton	1894
4 for 9	Lancashire v. Middlesex, at Manchester	1897
7 for 19	Lancashire v. Derbyshire, at Glossop	1899
5 for 15	Lancashire v. Sussex, at Hastings	1900

Bowling unchanged through match:

With Watson	Lancashire v. Yorkshire, at Huddersfield	1890
With Briggs	Lancashire v. Sussex, at Brighton	1891
With Briggs	Lancashire v. Kent, at Tunbridge Wells	1892
With Briggs	Lancashire v. Sussex, at Brighton	1892
With Briggs	Lancashire v. Notts, at Nottingham	1895
With Briggs	Lancashire v. Middlesex, at Lord's	1895
With Briggs	Lancashire v. Leicestershire, at Leicester	1895

Various feats:

Four wickets in four balls—Lancashire v. Notts, at Nottingham, 1895.

Hat-trick—Northamptonshire v. Staffordshire, at Northampton, in 1887, and Lancashire v. Somerset, at Manchester, in 1894.

Bail sent 63 yd. 6 in.—Lancashire v. Surrey, at the Oval, in 1896 (in bowling Lohmann).

At one period of the match v. Derbyshire, at Manchester, in 1900, he took four wickets without a run, and at one portion of Lancashire match v. Somerset, at Manchester, in 1894, his analysis was 20 balls, no runs and seven wickets.

During 1895 he obtained 213 wickets for under 16 runs apiece, having in the previous year taken 207 for something over 12 each. During the four seasons 1893–96 he took 736 wickets.

For Manchester v. North and East Ridings, at Castleford, in June, 1893—a 12-a-side match—he took all 11 wickets in an innings for 50 runs.

In minor matches he took all 10 wickets for 61 runs, and 17 for 112 in the match for Manchester v. Uppingham Rovers in 1887, and all 10 for St. Helen's Recreation v. Club Moor in 1891.

For Manchester v. Longsight in 1887, he bowled a bail off the wicket 53 yd.

For Middleton Cheney v. Culworth in 1910 he took five wickets in five balls, his analysis for the innings being eight wickets for no runs.

He obtained eight wickets for 11 runs and 15 for 29 (doing the hat-trick in each innings) for Manchester v. North and East Ridings in 1889, and the same year took 12 for 16 for Barlow's XI v. XXII of Blackpool and District.

As a batsman Mold was not of much account, but occasionally he made a good score. In obtaining 57 against Leicestershire, at Manchester in 1895—his highest innings for

Lancashire—he helped Albert Ward to put on 111 for the last wicket, and six years later, against Gloucestershire, at Gloucester, when he carried out his bat for 31, he and Mr. C. R. Hartley added 101 for the last wicket.

MOLINEUX, Capt. George King (2nd Batt. Northumberland Fusiliers), born on April 15, 1887, was stated to have fallen in France about the beginning of June, 1915, having previously been officially reported missing. He was in the Winchester XI of 1906, when he scored 343 runs with an average of 26.38, and took 39 wickets for 24.25 runs each. Against Eton he played an innings of 35 and took five wickets for 157. That season he and J. Leslie were the best all-round men in the side. He was elected a member of the M.C.C. in 1912.

MOLONEY, Lieut. D. A. R., who died of wounds while a prisoner of war in 1942, aged 32, played for New Zealand in representative matches from 1935 to 1939. A reliable batsman for Wellington, he came to England in 1937 and met with considerable success. He averaged 26 in the three Tests, and in all matches scored 1,463 runs, average 34.83, with best innings 140 against an England XI at Folkestone. His value as a bowler was shown by 57 wickets at 26.68. He scored 60, once out, for a New Zealand XI against G. O. Allen's team in March 1937 at Wellington.

MONAGHAN, Harold Wyatt, who died on October 15, 1958, aged 72, played as a right-arm medium-paced bowler and left-handed batsman for Wellington and Canterbury in the early part of the century, and in 1905–06 was a member of the New Zealand team against Melbourne C.C. In Wellington's first match with the 1907–08 M.C.C. touring team, he took seven first-innings wickets for 50 runs. Educated at Wellington College and Victoria University, he had been Archdeacon of Timaru and of Rangitiki.

MONCKTON, Walter Turner, First Viscount of Brenchley, who died on January 9, 1965, aged 73, kept wicket for Harrow against Eton in "Fowler's match," to which fuller reference has been made in the obituary of T. O. Jameson. Going up to Oxford at a time when the University was unusually rich in wicket-keepers, he did not gain a Blue, though he was awarded a Harlequin cap in 1912. From 1919 to 1946 he kept wicket for the Bar, became President of M.C.C. in 1956 and was President of Surrey from 1950 to 1952 and from 1959 until his death. He gained great distinction as a bar-

rister and was in turn Attorney-General—a post he held at the time of the abdication of King Edward VIII in 1936—Solicitor-General, Minister of Defence, Paymaster-General and Minister of Labour.

MONEY, The Rev. Walter Baptist, who was born at Sternfield in Suffolk on July 27, 1848, died suddenly at Edgbaston on March 1, 1924. As Walter Money retired from first-class cricket directly he entered the Church, only people whose memories go back more than 50 years will recall him in the field, but for a few seasons he was in the first flight of amateur cricketers—a dominating figure at Harrow and Cambridge. Few men have ever had a pleasanter experience of Lord's ground. In the matches there that specially appealed to him, he was never on the losing side until in 1871, Butler—taking all 10 wickets in the first innings—brought about the downfall of the Cambridge XI. Money was in the very strong Harrow teams that beat Eton in one innings in 1865 and 1866 and was captain in the drawn game of 1867. In those days he was essentially an all-round player and more to be feared for his lob bowling than his batting. He took in the three matches 21 Eton wickets, doing the hat-trick in 1866. By the way Canon McCormick, who saw all the lob bowlers from William Clarke to Walter Humphreys, thought that Money in his prime was always rather underrated.

Going up from Harrow with a big reputation, Money stepped straight into the Cambridge XI as a Freshman in 1868 and played the regulation four years. He does not seem to have been in residence in 1871, as he only took part in the London matches, and to judge from his scores he could scarcely have been in full practice. Cambridge beat Oxford by 168 runs in 1868 and by 59 runs in 1869. Then came the two runs victory in 1870—Cobden's match—when Money was captain. In 1871 Oxford won by eight wickets. Of the many stories that have enshrouded the Cobden match—the Balaclava Charge of the cricket field—Money himself contributed one of the best, telling how Jack Dale, when reproached for allowing a simple catch at point to go unheeded, apologised by saying, "I'm awfully sorry, Walter, I was looking at a lady getting out of a drag."

Money's record at Cambridge was curiously uneven. Only in 1868 was he in form both as batsman and bowler—he had a batting average of 31 that year and took 30 wickets for less than 10½ runs each. In 1869 he bowled better than ever, but for the time he lost his batting, his best score for Cambridge in six matches being 23 not out. Then in 1870 there was a great change. His skill in bowling lobs deserted him but he batted as he had never batted before, scoring 165 against Birkenhead Park Club and Ground at Cambridge and 134 against Surrey at the Oval. He failed in the University match, but his average for Cambridge was 53—very high indeed in those days. He was at the top of his form and for Gentlemen against Players at the Oval he enjoyed the biggest success of his cricket life, scoring 70 and 109 not out. Fenner's and the Oval were the grounds that suited him best. Like two of his brilliant contemporaries at Cambridge—H. A. Richardson and F. E. R. Fryer—but not to the same extent, he found the wickets at Lord's rather too difficult for him. In a word, with all his fine qualities as a batsman, he had not the defence of Yardley or Ottaway.—S.H.P.

MONKLAND, Francis George, born at Trichinopoly on October 8, 1841, died in London on January 15, 1915. As a batsman he was a good hitter, while in the field he excelled at long-stop and mid-on. He was educated at Repton, where he was in the XI in 1872 and 1873, during which season he scored 403 runs for the School with an average of 21, and took 46 wickets. His first appearance for Gloucestershire was in 1874, and three years later he was chosen for the Gentlemen v. Players match at Prince's. In first-class cricket his highest score was 59 against Surrey at Clifton in 1875. By profession he was a solicitor.

MONKS, Clifford I., of Downend, Bristol, who died on January 23, 1974, aged 62, played for Gloucestershire as an amateur in 1935 and concluded his county career in 1952. A sound batsman, a fine fielder and a useful change bowler, he would have been at his best during the War years. In 101 innings for the county he hit 1,589 runs and his highest score was 120 against Cambridge University at Bristol in 1948. He will be remembered for a miraculous catch against Middlesex at Cheltenham in August 1947 during the match which virtually decided the County Championship. Middlesex, with a slight lead of 27 on the first innings, were collapsing in their second until R. W. V. Robins attacked the bowling vigorously and

collected 45 in 49 minutes. Then he made a huge leg-side hit off Goddard which looked a certain six, but a record crowd of 14,500—the gates were closed—saw Monks race round the boundary edge and without any hesitation in his stride, make a perfect catch head high. It gave Gloucestershire a chance of victory which they did not take and they were beaten by 68 runs, being dismissed for 100. Middlesex eventually won the Championship and Gloucestershire finished runners-up.

MONTEATH, 2nd Lieut. A. P., an Otago player in Plunket Shield matches, was killed in the Middle East in 1942.

MONTGOMERY OF ALAMEIN, Field Marshal Lord, who died at Islington, Hampshire, on March 24, 1976, at the age of 88, was in the XI at St. Paul's School in 1905 and 1906 as an opening batsman. His election to I Zingari in 1967 gave him very great pleasure. Before the battle of El Alamein he told his troops to hit Rommel's Corps for six. And they did.

MOON, 2nd Lieut. Leonard James (Devon Regiment), born in London on February 9, 1878, died of wounds on November 23, 1916. He was in the Westminster XI in 1894 and two following seasons, heading the averages with 25.71 in 1895 and being second in 1896 with 46.69. In the last-mentioned year he played an innings of 57 against Charterhouse. Proceeding to Cambridge, he obtained his Blue and both in 1899 and 1900 played against Oxford. In the former year, when he scored 138 v. the Australians, he was second in the averages with 28.07, and in the latter fifth with 27.09. In his two matches against Oxford he made 154 runs in four innings, and in 1900 (when his scores were 58 and 60) scored 101 for the first wicket in the second innings with J. Stanning (60). In 1898 he had become a member of the M.C.C. and in the following season began to play for Middlesex.

Against Gloucestershire at Lord's in 1903 he and P. F. Warner made 248 together for the first wicket, and five years later the same pair scored 212 for the opening partnership v. Sussex on the same ground. In the autumn of 1905 he was second in the averages for the M.C.C.'s team in America with 33.00, and before the next season opened toured South Africa with another M.C.C. side. During the latter tour he made 826 runs with an average of 27.33. He was a vigorous batsman who could cut well, and a useful wicket-keeper.

At Association football he gained high honours, obtaining his Blue for Cambridge and playing for the Corinthians.

MOON, William Robert, a well-known solicitor, died on January 9, 1943, aged 74. He headed the Westminster School averages with 28.62 in 1885, his second season in the XI, and six years afterwards played in two matches for Middlesex, scoring 17 not out in the only innings he played for the county. Surrey were beaten by an innings and 20 runs, and the other game was ruined by rain. A free, hard-hitting batsman, he fielded finely in the deep, earning fame as a sure catch. He also was good behind the stumps, and it was as wicket-keeper that he received his trial for Middlesex. Taking a more prominent part in Association football, he kept goal four times for England against Scotland, 1888 to 1891, and in three matches against Wales. He excelled for Old Westminster and Corinthians.

MOORE, Francis, who died at Nottingham on January 14, 1900, played for Notts against Surrey at the Oval in 1862. He only made a few appearances for his county, however, being tried as wicket-keeper when he was between 30 and 40 years of age. It is said of him in *Scores and Biographies* that he was not much of a batsman, and that no long score will be found to his name. He was born at Nottingham on July 18, 1827. Was a very short man, standing only 5 ft. 3½ in. He came out for the Colts of Nottingham against the county XI at Trent Bridge in August, 1861, among those who were on the same side with him being Charles Daft, Samuel Biddulph and Sir H. Bromley. Biddulph rose to fame so quickly as a wicket-keeper that a year later he played for England against Surrey at the Oval, in the famous match in which England scored 503, and Willsher was no-balled by John Lillywhite for bowling over the shoulder.

MOORE, George, who was born at Ampthill, in Bedfordshire, on April 8, 1820, died at Maitland (N.S.W.) on September 29, 1916, in his 97th year. He went to Australia in 1852, and played against the English teams taken out by Stephenson, Parr and W. G. Grace. In his matches v. Stephenson's side he was very successful as a bowler, taking three wickets for 10 runs and five for 20 for XXII of New South Wales on the Sydney Domain, and four for 22 and six for 39 for a combined XXII of N.S.W. and Victoria on the same ground. He played in three of the

matches between New South Wales and Victoria: at Melbourne in 1871–72 he took six wickets for 56 runs, and at Sydney in the following year three for 17. He was grandfather of C. G. Macartney.

MOORE, Jack, who died in June, 1980, at the age of 89, was tried for Hampshire as a batsman between 1910 and 1913; but in 15 matches his highest score was 30 and he never got a regular place in the side.

MOORE, William, who died at Sydney in February, 1956, aged 90, played occasionally as wicket-keeper for New South Wales in 1893 and 1894. Moving to Western Australia at the end of last century, he became captain of the State team.

MOORHOUSE, Robert, born at Berry Brow on September 7, 1866, died at Huddersfield on January 7, 1921. For some years he was a prominent member of the Yorkshire team, and between 1888 and 1899 scored 6,232 runs for the county with an average of 18.77 and took 65 wickets for 26.93 runs each. He was a very useful all-round cricketer, but he never reached the front rank. His highest innings was 113 v. Somerset at Taunton in 1896. He was an excellent fieldsman. For several seasons he was engaged as coach at Sedbergh School.

MORDAUNT, Eustace Charles, died on June 21, 1938, aged 67. He headed the Wellington College averages with 35.10 in 1889, having played previously for Hampshire when 16. In subsequent years he appeared occasionally in the Middlesex and Kent XIs without doing anything exceptional. In 1914 he went to Egypt with I Zingari. A prominent fast bowler in club cricket he bowled down all 10 wickets of Kensington Park Hockey Club at a cost of only nine runs on April 28, 1894, in St. Quentin Park, London.

MORDAUNT, Gerald John, who died on March 5, 1959, aged 86, played for Oxford against Cambridge from 1893 to 1896, being captain in 1895. He got his colours at Wellington when 15 and was in the XI from 1888 to 1892, captaining the side for the last three years. A free-scoring batsman, specially skilled in off-side strokes, he hit 264 not out in four and a half hours for Oxford against Sussex at Brighton in 1895, a match which yielded 1,410 runs—at that time an English first-class record. He was a magnificent fieldsman anywhere. In 1894 he made two appearances for Gentlemen against Players and also played in the Lord's match the following season. He visited America with Lord Hawke's team in 1894 and between 1895 and 1897 took part in 16 matches for Kent, his highest score for the county being 81 not out against Surrey at the Oval. He and R. H. Raphael won the Public Schools Racquets Challenge Cup in 1891 and he represented his University in the long jump against Cambridge in 1896.

MORDAUNT, Sir Henry John, Twelfth Baronet, died on January 15, 1939, aged 71. An all-round athlete of exceptional ability he took a prominent part in the sports at Eton and was in the cricket XI three seasons, finishing as captain in 1886. Making the best of the material under his command H. J. Mordaunt led Eton to victory over Harrow at Lord's for the first time since 1876. His name stands high at Eton also for having thrown a goal in the Wall Game in 1885, thus repeating the feat of Mr. Walter Marcon in 1842. He did not play a big innings in the important matches for Eton, but was always useful with the ball and when his side beat Winchester by eight wickets he dismissed six men in each innings at a total cost of 65 runs. Winchester's totals were 233 and 59. This was 12 days before Harrow were defeated by six wickets. Bowling a good pace he relied on length with the extra fast ball which made batsmen cautious about attempting risky strokes. Getting his Blue at Cambridge in 1888 he did little in a drawn game but next year, when Oxford were beaten by an innings and 105 runs, he made 127, the third highest score in University encounters up to that time. Going in first he was fourth out at 250 and only 50 more runs were added. By taking two wickets for 11 runs Mordaunt gave useful help in dismissing Oxford a second time for 90, but S. M. J. Woods was the great bowler of the match with 11 for 82 runs. Mordaunt scored 78 for Cambridge against the Australian team of 1888 and was largely responsible for the University leading on the first innings by 66, the match being drawn. H. J. Mordaunt played a little for Hampshire in 1885 and 1887 and occasionally for Middlesex from 1889 to 1893. Six feet tall and well built he was a powerful driver with good style.

MORDAUNT, John Murray, born on December 30, 1837, died in London on December 21, 1923. A good all-round cricketer, he was in the Eton XIs of 1854 and 1855, playing each year against both Harrow and Winchester. In the four matches he scored 69 runs in eight innings and took 11 wickets. He

did not obtain his Blue at Oxford, but played subsequently for I Zingari, Warwickshire and Free Foresters. His portrait can be seen facing page 68 of *Annals of the Free Foresters*. Three of his sons—Messrs. E. C., H. J. and G. J. Mordaunt—became cricketers of note.

MORE, Richard Edwardes, of the Egyptian Civil Service, who died at Cairo on November 24, 1936, was a good all-round cricketer. He captained the Westminster School XI and at Oxford received his Blue from R. E. Foster in 1900. In the match at Lord's against Cambridge, More scored 20 not out towards the total of 503, which remains a record for the University engagement. A year later, More, with 76, helped Oxford to gain a small first innings lead, and, opening the bowling, he took three wickets in each Cambridge innings.

He then began playing for Middlesex and made 101 not out against Sussex at Hove, his brilliant display staving off defeat. During the 1901 season he scored 830 runs, with an average of 24.41, including 133 for Oxford against Surrey, and he took 67 wickets at 30.59 runs each. In the following autumn he toured Canada and America with B. J. T. Bosanquet's team and, bowling consistently well, headed the averages with 43 wickets at a cost of 11.20 runs each. His best season with Middlesex was 1904, when he scored 120 not out against Yorkshire at Sheffield. Going in last but one he helped B. J. T. Bosanquet put on 128 in 48 minutes. In all More got his runs out of 219 in 100 minutes, and the Middlesex total, 488, occupied no more than four hours and a half. Altogether for the county More scored 1,010 runs in 56 innings with an average of 21.04 and took 55 wickets at 30.96 each. An unreliable batsman, More hit brilliantly in front of the wicket when set and was a better medium-paced bowler than his figures suggest.

He captained the Westminster School football XI, but did not get his football Blue at Oxford.

MORGAN, Charles, who was born at Greenwich, in Kent, on January 29, 1839, died on July 17, 1904. He was a fast left-hand round-armed bowler, but a right-handed batsman, and fielded generally at short-slip. He appeared for the Gentlemen of Kent on a few occasions, and for Surrey four times in 1871. He was well known in Metropolitan cricket circles in connection with the Civil Service, Richmond, Wimbledon, and Streatham clubs. When assisting Streatham v. Buckhurst Hill, at Streatham, on June 2, 1888, he bowled all through the first innings of the latter (which amounted to 33) delivering 50 balls for four wickets, without a single run being obtained from him. His son, Mr. C. L. Morgan, appeared for Surrey a few times in 1889 and 1890.

MORGAN, Edward Noel, died suddenly in August, 1975, aged 70. At Christ College, Brecon, he was an outstanding batsman who in 1923 averaged over 50. Later he made one appearance for Glamorgan in 1934. He was elder brother of W. G. Morgan (later Stewart-Morgan), who played frequently for Glamorgan and captained Wales at Rugby.

MORGAN, John Hinds (Jack), the noted Welsh cricket journalist, died on April 8, 1978, a few weeks before his 80th birthday. He had reported Glamorgan county matches since their entry into first-class cricket in 1921, not only for *Wisden*, but the old Cricket Reporting Agency and the Press Association. As Alderman J. H. Morgan he was Lord Mayor of Cardiff in 1957–58 and during his year in office Glamorgan presented him with a county player's tie and made him the first honorary playing member of the club. In the 1949 *Wisden* Jack Morgan told of Glamorgan's March of Progress and in the 1970 edition he again looked back into Glamorgan's past.

MORGAN, John Trevil, who died suddenly at Bristol on December 18, 1976, aged 69, was the hero of a few performances so remarkable as to leave his friends wondering why he did not score more consistently. At Charterhouse in 1922, when just 15, he came in against a particularly strong Harrow side at 20 for five and made 148 not out. In 1929 before the Varsity match his average for Cambridge was 11 and he would hardly have retained his place had he not been required to keep wicket, but at Lord's, coming in at 137 for five, he scored 149 out of 208 in three and a half hours, an innings described as one of the best ever played in the match. Older spectators compared it to H. K. Foster's famous 100 in 1895. At one time C. K. Hill Wood, a fastish left-hander, had three men on the boundary behind him. Later that season he made a brilliant 103 not out in a total of 237 for Glamorgan against the South Africans. For Cambridge at the Oval in 1930 he and F. R. Brown put on 257 for the seventh wicket.

Five years in the Charterhouse XI, he never fulfilled his early promise there and

owed his place in the Schools' match at Lord's largely to his unexpected development as a bowler. However, after narrowly missing his Blue in 1927, he secured it in 1928 and was captain in 1930, when he led Cambridge to a sensational victory at Lord's. He declared, leaving an exceptionally strong Oxford batting side 307 to get in two hours, 20 minutes. They were out in two hours for 101. Some critics praised him for a brilliant declaration. He himself with typical honesty admitted that it never occurred to him that Oxford would attempt to get the runs, still less that they would be got out. He merely thought it indecent to go on batting.

For Glamorgan he did useful work from 1925 to 1934 and later captained the Second XI and served on the committee. At the time of his death he was President of the South Wales Hunts C.C. A left-handed batsman, of the build and style of Leyland rather than of Woolley, he was a brilliant driver, who was never afraid to lift the ball if necessary, a fine cutter and played well off his legs. In club cricket he was a good medium-paced right-hand off-spinner, but just lacked the venom to be dangerous in first-class cricket. Though he kept wicket three years for Cambridge, he never regarded himself as more than a stop-gap and after coming down always left his gloves at home for fear he should be asked to keep. He was a reliable slip. His elder brother, A. N. Morgan, played a few times for the county: they were not related to any other Glamorgan cricketers of the same name.

MORGAN, Samuel, Warwickshire's first regular wicket-keeper upon the re-establishment of the County Club in 1882, died at the Crown Inn, Edgbaston, in February, 1913. He was a poor batsman, and did not take part in County Cricket after 1886.

MORGAN, W., who died at Bath on October 22, 1914, aged 52, had played for Glamorgan, M.C.C., and the Lansdown C.C. He was a member of the Somerset County C.C. committee. Since 1891 he had been a member of the M.C.C.

MORKEL, Denys Paul Beck, died suddenly in hospital at Nottingham on October 6, 1980, aged 74. He first appeared for South Africa against Capt. R. T. Stanyforth's M.C.C. side in 1927–28, when he played in all five Tests, but, though he made some useful scores, he met with no particular success and his bowling was hardly used. It was on the tour of England in 1929 that he showed his real possibilities. In first-class matches he scored 1,443 runs with an average of 34.35 and took 69 wickets at 26.01. In the Tests he came second both in batting and bowling: at Lord's he made 88 and 17 not out and took seven wickets, at Old Trafford he scored 63 out of a total of 130 and at the Oval 81. Tall and well built, he bowled fast-medium away-swingers with an easy action and plenty of pace off the pitch, and was probably the best bowler in the team. A fine driver on both sides of the wicket, he was inclined to be impetuous but had, as he showed at Lord's, a solid defence when required. He was also a good slip. A great future seemed in store for him and that winter he helped S. S. L. Steyn to put on 222 for the eighth wicket for Western Province v. Border, still a South African record. But he had already decided to settle in England and so was not available to play against the M.C.C. side in 1930–31. However, he was a member in 1931–32 of the South African team to Australia, where he was a sad disappointment. As a batsman he could never get going in the Tests and his bowling was a complete failure. Only in the last match against Western Australia, not then the power they have since become, did he show his best form, scoring 150 not out and taking eight for 13 in the second innings. In extenuation it must be said that he was in poor health at the beginning of the tour and that he also had trouble with his bowling action. This was the end of his Test career. In 1932 Sir Julien Cahn helped him to establish a business in the motor trade in Nottingham, which became a flourishing concern. For Sir Julien between 1932 and 1939 he made nearly 10,000 runs and took over 400 wickets. During the War he served in the Army. His brother, Ray, also played for Western Province and at one time showed promise of being the better bowler of the two.

MORLEY, Haydn Arthur, who died at Hathersage in May, 1953, aged 91, played for Derbyshire against Nottinghamshire in 1891. A very good club batsman, he captained Belper Meadows C.C. from 1891 to 1893, succeeding F. R. Spofforth. He was the first player to be signed by Derby County F.C. after their formation in 1884.

MORRIS, Christopher C., one of the most brilliant American cricketers in history, died at his home in Villanova, Pennsylvania, on June 17, 1971, at the age of 88. He was one of the last of the talented group of Philadelphia cricketers who played first-class cricket.

As a group they were long-lived to an extraordinary extent, and F. C. Sharpless and H. A. Furness still happily survive. "Christy" Morris's enthusiasm for cricket was deep and long-lived: his playing days extended from the '90s to at least 1933 as a regular player, and he turned out for the Haverford Alumni as late as 1951. He was a beautiful bat, up to the best English first-class county form. He first appeared for the United States against Canada in 1900 and also played in the games of 1902, 1905, 1906 and 1912.

He toured England with the Gentlemen of Philadelphia in 1903 and 1908. In 1903 he scored 164 v. Nottinghamshire at Trent Bridge, the highest score made by an American in first-class cricket. In later life he took to bowling, and took many wickets with his slow flighted deliveries. He was one of the first American players to experiment with the googly. In 1904 he toured with Haverford College in England and scored 147 against Winchester. Christy's club was Merion C.C. for whom he performed many great batting and bowling feats during his long career.

His enthusiasm and devotion to the game never flagged. He was one of the older generation who helped in the modest revival of American cricket after the Second World War. In October 1966 the American members of the Forty Club held a dinner in Philadelphia to honour him and other members of the old Philadelphia XI, and cricket enthusiasts from all parts of the United States travelled to Philadelphia to honour him. The new Cricket Library and Collection now housed in a special wing of the Library at Haverford College was named in his honour, and is a collection of cricket memorabilia of special and enduring interest. Christy's photograph appeared in *Cricket* for May 12, 1904, one of the few American cricketers to be thus honoured.—J.I.M.

MORRIS, Col. John, who died at Glebe Point, Sydney, on December 9, 1921, aged 91, played for New South Wales against Victoria on the Domain as far back as 1859 and also appeared against Parr's team. He excelled as a long-stop.

MORRIS, Leonard John, who died at Dorridge, near Birmingham, on March 9, 1984, aged 85, was a left-hand bat and right-arm medium-paced change bowler who played a few matches for Warwickshire in 1925 and 1926. He had one considerable success. Against Glamorgan at Swansea in 1926 he was top scorer in the first innings with 53, only one other batsman, J. H. Parsons, with whom he put on 89, reaching double figures. In the second innings he scored 76 and put on 132 in 70 minutes for the seventh wicket with F. R. Santall. He had also represented Brazil against Argentina. Altogether for Warwickshire he scored 262 runs with an average of 23.82.

MORRIS, Percy, died at Swansea in July, 1975, aged 94. Primarily a batsman, he did useful work for Glamorgan in their second-class days, and in their first first-class match against Sussex at Cardiff in 1921 when they gained a surprising victory, he opened the bowling. He continued to play occasionally until 1925 and in his last match, going in first with N. V. H. Riches against Essex at Swansea, made 30. He played for Swansea for many years and maintained his interest in cricket to the end of his life.

MORRIS, Philip E., died at Hove on July 10, 1945, aged 67. He played a little in County Cricket for Essex, and in 1923 at Leyton his slow bowling accounted for seven Gloucestershire wickets for 72 runs in an innings of 204. He scored 418 runs, average 10.71, and took 83 wickets at 22.26 apiece in first-class cricket. Subsequently he captained Sussex Martlets.

MORRISON, Charles S., a member of the West Indies team which toured England in 1906, died at Kingston, Jamaica, on November 25, 1948.

MORRISON, John Stanton Fleming, who died in Farnham Hospital on January 28, 1961, aged 68, captained Cambridge University at both cricket and Association football. He was in the cricket XI at Charterhouse in 1910 and 1911, being captain in the second year when he headed the averages with 52.53 for 683 runs with a highest innings of 173. Going up to Cambridge, he got his Blue as a Freshman in 1912 and, after being passed over the following season, appeared again at Lord's in 1914, hitting 54 in the first innings against Oxford. He served with the Royal Naval Air Service during the First World War and returned to the University, becoming cricket captain in 1919. His best season for Cambridge was that of 1914. A strong driver, he scored 717 runs, average 35.85, hitting 233 not out against M.C.C. at Fenner's—then the biggest innings ever put together on the historic ground. The same season he made 231 in the Seniors' match. As a full-back, he represented Cambridge in

1913, 1914 and, as captain, in 1920 and he also played with distinction for the Corinthians and for Sunderland. After leaving the University, he became a golf-course architect of high repute.

MORROW, G. A., one of Ireland's best all-round cricketers, died in a nursing hospital in Dublin on November 16, 1914, aged 37. He played in many representative Irish matches, generally with success, although against the South Africans in 1907 he was unfortunate enough to make spectacles. A year later, however, he scored 14 and 49 for Ireland against Yorkshire, who had Rhodes, Brown (of Darfield), Booth and Newstead to bowl for them, and in 1909 was seen at his best when visiting America as a member of the Gentlemen of Ireland's team. His best performance was to carry his bat through the innings for 50 against the Gentlemen of Philadelphia at Haverford, and at the end of the tour he headed the batting with 288 runs (average 32) and was second in the bowling with 12 wickets for 11.50 runs each.

MORTON, Arthur, died at Stockport, after a long illness, on December 19, 1935. Last summer, he had to relinquish his engagements as umpire owing to ill-health, but he was again on the list for first-class matches for next season. A very good official, he umpired in several test matches. During many years Morton stood out as a very useful all-round player in the Derbyshire XI. In 1910, he was by far the best bowler for the county, taking 116 wickets for 22 runs each, and in batting he had only two of his regular colleagues above him. Four years later, he headed the batting averages with 27.64 for an aggregate of 1,023 runs, and he took 50 wickets. He again took 100 wickets in 1922. Gaining a regular place in the side in 1904, he continued playing for the county until 1926. Born on May 7, 1884, he was tried for Derbyshire when 17 years old, and so his career with the county extended over 25 years. Of stocky build, he bowled right-arm medium pace, with length as his chief asset. A steady bat, he could hit hard. He had been on the ground staff at Lord's for many years. He scored six separate centuries for Derbyshire, and four of these were made at Leyton off the Essex bowlers in consecutive seasons 1922 to 1925.

MORTON, Cecil Howard, who died at Lexden on April 3, 1945, aged 86, was the last survivor of the Norfolk XI of 1885 which made cricket history at Lord's by scoring 695

against M.C.C. Bowling slow left he dismissed three of the best opposing batsmen. He earned nothing like the fame of his elder brother, Philip H. Morton, the right-hand fast bowler, Cambridge Blue from 1878 to 1880, contemporary with A. G. Steel in very powerful Light Blue sides. Both Mortons were in the Rossall School XI with Vernon Royle, the great cover-point of Oxford and Lancashire fame, and their housemaster was the Rev. S. C. Voules, an Oxford Blue from 1863 to 1866. Cecil Morton, as described in *Eastern Daily Press*, Norwich, played on and off for Norfolk for 20 years. He took 15 wickets for 113 runs against Hertfordshire at Bishop's Stortford, and five for 57 against Derbyshire when F. R. Spofforth, the Australian "Demon," was in the opposing team. Three weeks after being elected a member of M.C.C. in 1891 he took all 10 wickets for the club against Colchester Garrison. He played for Free Foresters, Iceni, and often took part in country house cricket.

MORTON, Frank L., who died on October 14, 1971, aged 70, was a fast bowler for South Australia in 1921–22. He moved to Victoria in 1926–27 and in his second match for his new State Victoria put together a total of 1,107—a world record—against New South Wales at Melbourne. Morton's share was "run out 0!" He played for Victoria until 1931–32, being captain in four games. His 74 wickets for 30.18 runs each included a hat-trick against Tasmania in his last match. He was a member of the Australian team who toured New Zealand under V. Y. Richardson in 1927–28.

MORTON, Philip Howard, who will always be remembered as a member of the great Cambridge XI of 1878, died suddenly at Bournemouth on May 13, 1925, after an operation. He was born at Tatterford Rectory, near Fakenham in Norfolk, on June 20, 1857, and was thus in his 68th year at the time of his death. He may be summed up as having been a first-rate fast bowler, a useful batsman and a good field at slip and short-leg. His fame rests on his bowling, for he had a formidable off-break and a good yorker at his command and could make the ball nip quickly off the pitch. He gained his Blue for Cambridge in 1878, during his second year of residence, and he contributed much to the unchecked series of successes the side gained that season under the captaincy of the Hon. Edward Lyttelton. The team worked together splendidly throughout, and won all the eight matches played, four of them—

against M.C.C., the Gentlemen of England, Surrey and the Australians (at Lord's)—with an innings to spare. Although they beat Oxford by 238 runs, their greatest triumph was to defeat the Australians, before lunch on the second day, by an innings and 72 runs. Owing to illness, neither A. P. Lucas nor F. W. Kingston was able to play, yet 10 members of the side reached double figures, and Morton himself had the chief share in the victory, taking 12 wickets—nine bowled, one leg-before, one caught-and-bowled, and one caught at the wicket. On a perfect pitch this was an extraordinary performance. His break, at such a pace, astonished the Australians. In the second innings of the inter-University match he and A. G. Steel, in wonderful form that year, dismissed Oxford for 32, Morton's figures during that second innings being five for 20. Seven men failed to score. In his three matches against Oxford he scored 54 runs with an average of 13.50 and obtained 12 wickets for 15.66 runs, being on the winning side each year and performing the hat-trick in the game of 1880. In 1875 and 1876 he had been in the Rossall XI, and in the latter year, when he was captain, had bowled down all 11 wickets in an innings in a 12-a-side game against the Masters. After leaving Cambridge little was seen of him in great matches, but he appeared for the Gentlemen against the Players at the Oval in 1880, when he took 12 wickets for 91 runs, and at Lord's in 1882 (five for 94), and assisted Surrey in a couple of games in 1884 under the family-home qualification. He continued to represent Norfolk until 1886, and for that side at Norwich in 1883 had analyses of five for 19 v. Northants and 11 for 40 v. Leicestershire. He was founder of the Northern Nomads, and was hon. secretary of the club for eight years. For many years he was in the scholastic profession, and after being an assistant-master at Elstree from 1880 until 1889, was headmaster in succession of Bracewell Hall School, Skipton; of Scaitcliffe School, Englefield Green; and of Wixenford School, Wokingham.

MOSES, Harry, was one of the best Australian cricketers who never came to England. This misfortune could be attributed to the fact that, no matter how well he played for New South Wales and other sides against English touring teams, his highest scores for Australia against England were 33 and 31 in the six matches for which he was chosen. English players regarded his left-handed batting as of the highest class and regrets were expressed that English lovers of the game did not have an opportunity of seeing him. The 1888 team under P. S. McDonnell might have found such a capable run-getter invaluable during a somewhat disastrous tour, and his omission two years later also was criticised. He died on December 7, 1938, in Sydney, aged 80.

MOSS, John, who died at Keyworth, Nottinghamshire, in July, 1950, aged 84, was for many years one of the best-known first-class umpires in England, and he officiated at four of the five Test matches between England and Australia during the summer of 1921. A useful batsman, he served for a long period on the M.C.C. ground staff and played in one match for Nottinghamshire during 1892. In 1904–05 he went as umpire to the West Indies with Viscount Brackley's team and played there in two matches.

MOSS, Sam, reputed to have been at one time the fastest bowler in England, was killed on the railway line whilst walking to a match at Featherstone on August 7, 1923. He was in his 56th year. He was very successful for Bacup in the Lancashire League in 1899 and at least twice during his career he obtained all 10 wickets in an innings—for 19 runs for Padiham in 1908 and for 32 runs for Barnsley v. Huddersfield. At various times he was also on the Old Trafford ground staff and with the Batley C.C.

MOTT, Charles Cheape, born at Rugby on April 6, 1865, died in Liverpool on November 27, 1930. A useful batsman, he was in the Rugby School XI in 1884, and later on played for Warwickshire, Staffordshire and Denbighshire. His highest innings for Warwickshire were 84 v. Somerset at Edgbaston in 1887 and 80 v. Hampshire at Southampton two years later.

MOULDER, J. W. H., who was born on September 29, 1881, died in October, 1933. He played a few times for Surrey from 1902 to 1906, and for Transvaal from 1909 to 1911. In 50 innings he made 682 runs, with an average of 15.50, his highest score being 48 for Surrey against Notts at the Oval in 1903. His slow bowling took 13 wickets at 30 runs apiece.

MOULE, W. H., a Judge in Australia, died in Melbourne in September, 1939, aged 81. He played for Victoria, and in 1880 was a member of the second Australian team that visited England, with W. L. Murdoch as captain. He scored 75 runs in six 11-a-side

matches and took four wickets for 69 runs. Moule played at the Oval in the hastily arranged first match between fully representative sides of England and Australia and proved a valuable substitute for "the Demon," F. R. Spofforth, who was indisposed. Moule did by far the best bowling for Australia, three wickets for 23, in a total of 420 and when Australia followed-on he helped W. L. Murdoch in a last wicket stand which saved the innings defeat and enabled the Australian captain to finish 153 not out, one more than W. G. Grace scored for England. All who played in the match are dead now.

MOULT, Thomas, a poet and author, who reported cricket extensively before the Second World War, died in Essex, where he had retired to Finchingfield, on November 19, 1974, aged 89. In 1931 he edited Jack Hobbs' autobiography *Playing for England* which Sir Leonard Hutton said inspired him as a lad of 15. Among 40 books he wrote or edited were also two books of verses, *Bat and Ball* and *Willow Pattern*. He became President of the Poetry Society in 1952, an office he held for 10 years, and he was chairman of the editorial board of the Poetry Review from 1952 to 1962.

MOUNSEY, Joseph Thomas, who died at Godalming, April 6, 1949, aged 77, played in 108 matches for Yorkshire from 1890 to 1897. A skilful batsman and medium-paced bowler he scored 2,357 runs, average 16.71, and took 19 wickets at 30.63 each. From 1899 he was for many years coach at Charterhouse School.

MOUNTENEY, Arthur, who was born on February 11, 1883, died on June 1, 1933, at Leicester. As a batsman of the forcing type and a good field, he did most useful work for Leicestershire from 1911 to 1924, but never quite established himself in the county XI. His highest aggregate in a season was 836 in 1922, and his best average of 32.05 was obtained in the previous year, when he scored 545 runs. He hit six centuries in first-class cricket—all for Leicestershire. He was also a good Association football player, and represented Leicester Fosse, Preston North End, Grimsby Town and Birmingham.

MOYES, Alban George, M.C. who died suddenly at his home in Sydney on January 18, 1963, aged 70, was a celebrated cricket radio-commentator and author. "Johnny" Moyes, as he was generally known, played for South Australia in Sheffield Shield matches from 1912 to 1915, scoring 104 against Western Australia in the first season and, after service with the Australian Forces during the First World War, in which he won the M.C., assisted Victoria in 1920–21. As a team-selector for New South Wales in 1926–27, he helped Sir Donald Bradman to get his first chance in State cricket. His services to sport earned him the M.B.E. At one time he was news editor of the *Sydney Daily Telegraph*.

M'SHANE, P. G., one of the leading players of Victoria a few decades ago, died in Melbourne on December 11, 1903, in his 46th year. In Boyle and Scott's *Cricketers' Guide* he is described as a "Very fine left-hand bowler, with great command over the ball; splendid batsman, and has made some fine scores; good field." He did excellent service for Victoria in inter-State matches for a number of years. While engaged as curator to the St. Kilda club he had to be removed to Kew Asylum, suffering from a mental ailment, and though he was able to be removed temporarily, a relapse occurred from which he never recovered.

MUFASIR-UL-HAQ, who died in Karachi on July 27, 1983, aged 38, played his one Test match, for Pakistan against New Zealand, at Christchurch in February 1965, taking three wickets and scoring eight not out. A left-arm medium-paced bowler, he played for Karachi, P.W.D. and National Bank in first-class cricket. He was only the second Pakistani Test cricketer to die, the first being Amir Elahi.

MUGLISTON, Francis Hugh, who died on October 3, 1932, in his 47th year, represented Cambridge University at cricket, Association football and golf and played cricket for Lancashire and football for the Corinthians. He was educated at Rossall where he captained the cricket team in 1904—his fourth year in the XI—and also played for the School at football, hockey, racquets and fives. In 1904 he represented Rossall in the Public Schools racquets championship and he also assisted the Public Schools XI against the M.C.C. at Lord's. Going up to Cambridge, he played against Oxford in 1907 and 1908, making in the latter year 109 and 56 against Lancashire for which county he afterwards appeared on occasion without achieving much success. Playing left-back, he took part in the Association football match against Oxford in 1907, and in the

following year captained the XI. As a Corinthian player he toured South Africa in 1907 and in 1908 was a member of the University golf team. From 1920 until his death he represented Cambridge on the Council of the Football Association, and also served on the committee of the Surrey County C.C. He joined up on the outbreak of the War and, after being badly wounded, was invalided out.

MULHOLLAND, Sir Henry George Hill, Bart., D.S.O. who died on March 5, 1971, aged 82, was in the Eton XI of 1917 and gained a Blue at Cambridge in 1911, 1912 and 1913, being captain in the last year. In all first-class cricket he scored 1,493 runs, including three centuries, average 28.16, took 51 wickets for 23.00 runs apiece and held 36 catches. After the First World War, in which he was awarded the D.S.O., he entered politics and became a member of Parliament. He was speaker of the Northern Ireland House of Commons from 1929 to 1945 and Lieutenant for County Londonderry from 1961 to 1965.

MULLAGH, John, died in August, 1891. Mullagh was the best batsman in the Aboriginal XI which visited England in 1868. He played on one or more occasions for Victoria against New South Wales in the inter-Colonial matches.

MUNCER, Bernard Leonard, died suddenly on January 18, 1982, aged 68. When he left Middlesex in 1946 at the age of 33 after 13 seasons, his career seemed a failure. Nor had a spell on the Burma–Siam Railway, as a prisoner-of-war, improved his prospects. He had played fairly regularly in 1934 and 1935 with moderate success, but since then he had failed to keep his place: his highest score was 85 against Northamptonshire in 1937 and his 23 wickets had cost over 28 runs each. Yet when he retired in 1954 after eight seasons with Glamorgan, he had five times taken over 100 wickets, once being the first in England to reach that target, he had made four centuries, he had had much to do with his county winning the Championship in 1948, and in 1952 he had done the double. Moreover, at one period some regarded him as the best slow spinner in England and in 1948 he had played for the Players at Lord's. The main reason for this dramatic development was that he had switched from leg-breaks and googlies to off-breaks. With these, besides the cardinal gifts of length, flight and spin, he had the rarer virtue of making the batsman play six balls an over. To add to his value he was a good slip. His highest score was 135 against Somerset at Swansea in 1952. Later the emergence of McConnon, also an off-spinner, restricted his opportunities and, having been awarded a benefit in 1954, he left the county at the end of the season and returned to Lord's, where he eventually became head coach. A cheerful, friendly man, he was deservedly popular.

MUNDS, Raymond, who died on July 30, 1962, aged 79, played as wicket-keeper in three matches for Kent between 1902 and 1906. He did much good work for the Second XI.

MUNNION, Henry, who appeared once for Sussex in 1877 and once in 1880, died at Ardingly on June 24, 1904. He was a useful bowler, being left-hand, medium-pace. For some years he was engaged at Ardingly College, in Sussex. He was born at Ardingly, January 23, 1849.

MUNT, Col. Harry Raymond, who died as the result of a motor car accident on December 27, 1965, aged 63, headed the Westminster batting figures in 1921 with 554 runs, average 51.36, and also took 35 wickets. He used his height to advantage as a hard-hitting batsman and fast bowler. In 1923 he played for Middlesex against Essex at Lord's, but did not bat, and he also assisted Sir Julien Cahn's XI.

MURCH, William, born at Bristol on November 18, 1867, died at his native place on May 1, 1928, aged 59, being at the time ground manager there to the University. His chief asset was his medium-paced bowling, though he could field well at third man and at a distance from the wicket. From 1889 until 1899 he assisted Gloucestershire, and he also played for London County as well as occasionally for Wiltshire. His best season was that of 1893, when he took 69 wickets in first-class cricket for 22.85 runs each. Against Surrey at the Oval that year he had an analysis of eight for 74. A curious hit at his expense was made at the end of the Gloucestershire v. Middlesex match at Lord's the same season, J. E. West sending one of his deliveries full pitch on to the roof of the covered stand near the scoring box, the ball travelling between point and cover.

MURDIN, John Vernon, who died on April 11, 1971, aged 79, played as a professional fast bowler for Northamptonshire from 1913 to 1927. In that time he dismissed 444 batsmen for 27.86 runs apiece and brought off 102 catches. His most successful season was that of 1922, when he took 91 wickets at an average cost of 18.47, his analyses including six wickets for 38 runs against Yorkshire and seven for 44 against Kent, both at Northampton, where in 1920 he performed the hat-trick in the game with Kent. For a number of years after giving up first-class cricket, he was coach at Wycliffe College.

MURDOCH, William Lloyd, born at Sandhurst, Victoria, October 18, 1855, died at Melbourne, February 18, 1911. Present at the Test match between Australia and South Africa, he was seized with apoplexy during the luncheon interval and passed away later in the afternoon. Murdoch had a long career as a cricketer, but his fame will rest mainly on what he did for the Australian teams of 1880, 1882, and 1884. He captained the three XIs, and in all three he was incontestably the finest batsman. Within the last 10 years his performances have been to some extent eclipsed by Victor Trumper, but comparison between the two men would hardly be fair, their methods being so different. Sufficient that in his own day Murdoch had no serious rival among Australian batsmen, and except for W. G. Grace, scarcely a superior in England. It is no injustice to him, however, to say that, depending far more than present-day batsmen upon forward play, he did not rise to great heights on wickets spoilt by rain. The daring pulls and hooks by which bowlers are now so often demoralised were not within his range, and when the ball turned a great deal he was reduced to defence. To be seen at his best, he needed sunshine and a lively pitch. Then he could be great indeed, as those who remember his famous 153 not out at the Oval in 1880 in the first Test match in this country, and his 211 on the same ground in 1884 will not need to be told.

Few batsmen have been better worth looking at, his style leaving no loophole for criticism. He was essentially an off-side player, his cut and drive being equally fine. Nothing in his play was more skilful than the quickness of foot by which in getting forward at the ball he made up for a limited reach. It could not be urged against him that he was a slow scorer, but if the occasion demanded caution he had inexhaustible patience. In a word, he was in the domain of orthodox batting a complete master. His method served him well, his perfectly straight bat enabling him even at the end of his career to defy lack of condition and get 100s. So recently as 1904 he scored 140 in the Gentlemen and Players' match at the Oval.

In his early days in Australia, Murdoch was a first-rate wicket-keeper, and it was chiefly as a wicket-keeper that he secured his place in the Australian team of 1878. He kept wicket in the memorable match against the M.C.C. at Lord's—the match that once and for all established the fame of Australian cricket—but he soon found that he could not hold his own with Blackham, and thenceforward batting became his exclusive study. He had to do some wicket-keeping years afterwards for the ill-starred XI he captained in England in 1890, but little of his old skill remained, and he found the task distasteful. So great was his reputation as a wicket-keeper in his young days that Spofforth declined to play in the first big match against James Lillywhite's team in 1877 because Blackham had been chosen in preference. In the light of after events this scarcely seems credible, but it is strictly true.

Murdoch's career was sharply divided into two parts. Soon after the season of 1884, and following his marriage, he gave up first-class cricket, and little was seen of him in the field until 1890 when he paid his fifth visit to England. It cannot be said that in that year he quite lived up to his reputation, but he played very well, and headed the Australian averages. His doings when he settled in this country, captaining Sussex for several seasons, and afterwards playing for London County, will be fresh in recollection. A man of fine physique and splendid constitution, he ought to have lived to a far greater age than 55. His remains were embalmed, and brought to England for burial at Kensal Green.

W. L. Murdoch in first-class cricket:

	Inns.	Times not out	Most in an inns.	Total runs	Aver.
In Australia	61	9	321	2249	43.25
In England (with Australians)	223	17	286*	5336	25.90
In England (1891–1904)	411	21	226	9685	24.83
In South Africa (1891–92)	1	0	12	12	12.00
In America (1878)	2	1	37	37	37.00
Totals	698	48	321	17319	26.64

W. L. Murdoch's 100s in important cricket:

Runs		Year
321	New South Wales v. Victoria, at Sydney	1882–83
286*	Australians v. Sussex, at Brighton	1882
279*	Fourth Australian team v. Rest of Australia, at Melbourne	1883–84
	(He batted on each of the three days for this score.)	
226	Sussex v. Cambridge University, at Brighton	1895
	(During this innings he took part in three separate stands of over 100.)	
211	Australia v. England, at the Oval	1884
172	Sussex v. Hampshire, at Southampton	1894
158	New South Wales v. Victoria, at Melbourne	1883–84
158	Australians v. Sussex, at Brighton	1890
155	London County v. Lancashire, at Manchester	1903
153*	Australia v. England, at the Oval	1880
153	First Australian team v. Fifteen of Victoria, at Melbourne	1878–79
144	Sussex v. Somerset, at Brighton	1896
140	Gentlemen v. Players, at the Oval	1904
132	Australians v. Cambridge University, at Cambridge	1884
132	London County v. Leicestershire, at the Crystal Palace	1902
130	Sussex v. Gloucestershire, at Bristol	1897
129	Australians v. Cambridge University Past and Present, at Leyton	1890
	(He and G. H. S. Trott (186) added 276 for the third wicket.)	
121*	Sussex v. Notts, at Nottingham	1898
107*	Australians v. Orleans Club, at Twickenham	1882
105	Sussex v. Cambridge University, at Cambridge	1897
104	Gentlemen of South v. Players of South, at Lord's	1894

* Signifies not out

MURDOCH-COZENS, Lieut.-Col. Alan James, who died on July 23, 1970, aged 76, was in the XI, as A. J. Murdoch, while at Brighton College. He played seven innings for Sussex in 1919, scoring 124 runs, average 17.71. He was one of 27 amateur players who appeared for the county in that season.

MURDOCK, Major E. G., born on November 14, 1864, died in his flannels in the Bristol pavilion in the third week of May, 1926. A good wicket-keeper, he played for both Somerset and Gloucestershire, and was associated prominently with the Bedminster C.C.

MURRAY, Athol Leslie, who died on January 10, 1981, aged 79, had a good trial for Warwickshire as a batsman in 1922, but his highest score was only 33 against Surrey and his average 9.47. Educated at St. George's, Harpenden, he was better known as a golfer, playing for Oxford in 1922 and again in 1923, when he had the distinction of beating E. F. Storey in the University match.

MURRAY, Ronald McKenzie, died on April 8, 1951, from injuries received when he fell accidentally while visiting a sick friend at Hanmer Springs, Canterbury, New Zealand. Aged 23, he was a right-arm medium-pace bowler and promising batsman who would probably have represented New Zealand but for his tragic death. He first played for Wellington against Auckland in February 1947, and the following month took three wickets for 43 and five for 85 against W. R. Hammond's M.C.C. touring team. His second innings victims were Fishlock, Edrich, Compton, Hammond and Evans. He again appeared for Wellington in 1947–48 and took 13 wickets in Plunket Shield matches, but the following year he did not do well and, though taking part in the last two trials, failed to win a place in the New Zealand team for England. He achieved a hat-trick against Otago in 1949–50. Murray was a member of the journalistic staff of the *Evening Post*, Wellington.

MURRAY-WOOD, William, who died in hospital on December 21, 1968, aged 51, enjoyed remarkable success as a hard-hitting batsman and leg-break bowler while in the Mill Hill XI from 1932 to 1935. Three times he headed both sets of averages and in 1935, when captain, held a batting average of 48.50 and took 61 wickets for 9.49 runs each. He got his Blue as a Freshman in 1936 at Oxford, where he distinguished himself by scoring 106 not out against Gloucestershire in his first first-class match. Unfortunately he could not maintain this form and against Cambridge failed to score in either innings. He made his debut for Kent that season and played occasionally until he was appointed county captain in 1952 and 1953.

In August, 1953, his first-class career came to an abrupt end. During the closing match of the Canterbury Festival in August, the Kent committee announced that he was being replaced forthwith as captain by D. V. P. Wright, a professional. Murray-Wood, clearly upset by this decision, made it plain that he had not resigned. Not until the Kent annual meeting the following February was it stated that the committee's unprecedented action came as a result of representations by the club's amateur players, who had said that they would not continue under Murray-Wood's leadership.

A farmer by profession, Murray-Wood toured Jamaica with the Combined Oxford and Cambridge team in 1938 and Bermuda with W. S. Surridge's XI in 1961.

During the Second World War he worked with the Special Operations Executive which trained men and women to parachute into occupied territory and work with patriot forces.

MURRELL, Harry Robert, who died at his home at West Wickham, Kent, on August 15, 1952, aged 71, was for 46 years associated with Middlesex, first as wicket-keeper and afterwards as scorer. Born at Hounslow, Middlesex, on November 19, 1880, "Joe" Murrell, as he was always known, began his first-class career with Kent, playing for them in 27 matches between 1899 and 1905. As Fred Huish was then in his prime, Murrell found the opportunity to keep wicket on only six occasions during that period, but he caught 17 batsmen and stumped three. He took part in the "tie" between Kent and Surrey at the Oval in 1905, of which match Lord Harris, in his *History of Kent County Cricket*, wrote: "To show the coolness of some of our team, when the match was a tie and Smith skied the ball to Murrell"—at third man—"the latter quietly rubbed his hands on his trousers and then caught it, while I am told that Blythe said, before the ball was in Murrell's hands, 'This is the first tie-match I have ever played in!' "

The following season Murrell joined Middlesex, and he retained his place in the county side until 1926. In that time he helped in the dismissal of 749 batsmen for the county. A first-class wicket-keeper, specially good on the leg-side because he was left-handed, he would undoubtedly have gained higher honours had he not been contemporary with E. J. Smith and H. Strudwick. Twice he helped Middlesex to win the County Championship, in 1920 and 1921, and of him *Wisden* of the time said: "In Murrell, Middlesex had one of the best of wicket-keepers—never estimated at quite his real value."

His best performance was when, in 1926, he dismissed six batsmen in the second innings of Gloucestershire at Bristol, catching four and stumping two. Sir Pelham Warner, the former Middlesex captain, paid a high tribute to Murrell's loyalty, judgment and advice in critical situations, particularly when in 1920 Middlesex beat Kent at Canterbury by four runs and Yorkshire at Bradford by five runs. A fast-footed, tall and lean right-handed batsman, Murrell could hit extremely hard. For M.C.C. and Ground against Kent in 1905, he scored 67 out of 89 in 40 minutes, and, going in No. 9 for Middlesex at Leeds in 1906, he punished the Yorkshire bowling for 63 in just over an hour.

MURSELL, The Rev. Arthur, one of the oldest members of the Surrey County C.C., and a life-long lover of the game, died at St. John's Wood on May 23, 1914, aged 82. When quite a small boy he was included as a substitute in a local XXII against the All-England XI, and distinguished himself by hitting the only ball he received from William Clarke for four—a feat which so pleased Sir Henry Bromley that he presented him with a half-crown, which was treasured for many years. At the General Meeting of the Middlesex County C.C. in 1913 he made a delightful speech, in the course of which he said that he had visited Lord's ground for over 70 years.

MUSGROVE, Henry, who died at Sydney in November, 1931, came to England in 1896 as manager of the Australian team captained by Harry Trott. The tact and courtesy of the manager in carrying out the arrangements contributed largely to a very pleasant tour. Mr. Musgrove was not in any way distinguished as a player.

MUSSON, Francis William, A.F.C., C.M.G., who died on January 2, 1962, aged 67, played in 16 matches for Lancashire between 1914 and 1921. Educated at Tonbridge, he was in the XI there from 1910 to 1913, being captain in the last year when heading the batting averages with 44.25. Also a very good wicket-keeper, he took part in the Cambridge Freshmen's match of 1914. For Lancashire he scored 510 runs, average 19.61, his highest innings being 75 against Hampshire at Southampton in 1920. In the First World War he served with the Loyal North Lancashire Regiment and the Royal Flying Corps, being wounded in France in 1915. He was awarded the A.F.C. in 1918 and created C.M.G. in 1958.

MYCROFT, Thomas, for 22 years a much respected member of the M.C.C.'s ground staff at Lord's, and for several seasons a well-known umpire, died on August 13, 1911, at Derby. He was born at Birmingham on March 28, 1848, and was therefore in his 64th year at the time of his death. A brother of the once famous bowler, William Mycroft, he never took a prominent position in the game, but he played occasionally for Derbyshire. He was of use chiefly as a wicket-keeper, but as he was contemporaneous with A. Smith and Disney he did not appear regularly for the county. His benefit, at Lord's, was favoured by fine weather and realised over £1,000.

MYCROFT, William, died on June 19, 1894. The famous left-handed bowler, who for several seasons was the mainstay of the Derbyshire XI, had impaired health for so many months that the announcement of his death caused little surprise amongst cricketers. Born at Brimington, near Chesterfield, on February 1, 1841, he was very late in coming before the public, little or nothing being known of him until September, 1873, when he and Flint, bowling for Sixteen of Derbyshire, dismissed the Notts XI for 14 runs. This performance at once directed attention to his powers, and by the season of 1875 he had secured a position as one of the best left-handed bowlers in the country. Possessing great physical strength, he combined pace and spin in a remarkable degree. There is little doubt that his fast yorker with which he used to get so many wickets was open to serious question on the score of fairness, but on this point there is now no occasion to dwell. His career in first-class cricket was naturally shorter than it would have been if his ability had been discovered earlier in life. Appearing at Lord's for the first time in 1876, he was promptly engaged by the M.C.C.; and even as recently as 1893 he was still a member of their ground staff.

MYERS, Lance-Corpl. Edward Bertram (Surrey Rifles), born at Blackheath on July 5, 1889, was killed on September 15, 1916. He was a useful all-round cricketer and had been a member of the Oval staff since 1908. He played for the Surrey Second XI from 1909 until 1914, and in 1913, when his batting average was 30.33, played an innings of 142 v. Yorkshire Second XI at the Oval. He was tried occasionally for the county between 1910 and 1914. His highest score in club and ground matches was 196 v. Honor Oak in 1911.

MYERS, Hubert, an old Yorkshire professional, died at Hobart, Tasmania, on June 12, 1944, aged 67. First tried for the strongest of our counties in 1901 when 24 years old, Myers played intermittently until the end of the 1910 season, when he was dropped in company with Rothery and Wilkinson. A very useful all-round player, Myers would have been welcome in many counties, but Yorkshire could not find room for all the talent available, and Myers, like others, suffered from being in such high-class cricket. During his 10 years' connection with County Cricket Yorkshire were champions four times, Myers helping to the extent of 282 wickets at 25.15 apiece and averaging 18.31 an innings for 4,450 runs. After some experience as coach he settled down with the Tasmanian Cricket Association, played in many representative matches, and headed the Association batting averages. His medium-paced bowling remained good, if not difficult, on extra easy pitches, and Mr. E. A. Eltham, brother of Lieut. W. Keith Eltham—killed in France in 1916—describes how well Myers batted against New South Wales. Also how "Myers had a fleeting return to the stage when captaining Tasmania against Arthur Gilligan's side at Hobart in January 1925. As recorded in *Wisden*, he top-scored for the locals (40). I can still picture his gratification when the English players, out on the ground prior to the commencement of the match, were recognising his old faded 'White Rose' cap and fraternising with him."

MYERS, Matthew, born at Yeadon on April 12, 1851, died suddenly at his native place on December 8, 1919. Useful all-round, he played 23 times for Yorkshire between 1876 and 1881, scoring 586 runs with an average of 15.42.

NAGEL, Lisle Ernest, who died on November 26, 1971, aged 66, was a tall fast-medium swing bowler for Victoria, for whom his twin brother, Vernon, also played. Lisle was chiefly responsible for the dismissal of D. R. Jardine's powerful M.C.C. team in 1932–33 at Melbourne for a total of 60, for he took eight wickets for 32 runs for an Australian XI. This feat gained him a place in the first Test match, but his two wickets cost 110 runs and he was never chosen again for Australia, though he toured India with J. Ryder's team in 1935–36. In 1939–40 he established a Melbourne Pennant record by taking 86 wickets for 13.45 runs each.

NAOOMAL JEOOMAL, who died in Bombay on July 18, 1980, aged 76, served the game of cricket for many years, first in India and, after partition, in Pakistan. As a member of the Indian side to England in 1932 he opened their innings at Lord's in their first-ever Test match, scoring 33 and 25, and played twice more against England, in India in 1933–34. His highest score in England was 164 not out against Middlesex in 1932 and in India 203 not out against Nawanagar in 1938. In the 1950s he became Pakistan's national coach. He lived to enjoy the Jubilee Test match between India and England in Bombay in February 1980.

NAPIER, Lieut. Guy Greville (35th Sikhs), born on January 26, 1884, died in France on September 25, 1915, of wounds received earlier that day. Mr. Napier will live in cricket history as one of the best medium-pace bowlers seen in the University match in his own generation. Playing four times for Cambridge—1904 to 1907—he took 31 wickets for 544 runs. Considering the excellent condition of the ground in the first three of these matches his figures will bear comparison with the finest records of old days when scores were far smaller than they are now. He was nearly always seen to great advantage at Lord's, the slope of the ground no doubt helping him. At Lord's for the Gentlemen in 1907 he took six wickets for 39 runs in the Players' second innings, this, having regard to the class of the batsmen opposed to him, being the best performance of his life. It is scarcely an exaggeration to say that he did not bowl a bad ball in the innings. He fully retained his skill after his Cambridge days were over. When home from India, where he held a Government appointment at Quetta, he bowled with marked success for the M.C.C. against Yorkshire at Scarborough in 1913, taking eight Yorkshire wickets in one innings for 44 runs. Bowling with a fairly high and very easy action he had great command of length and made the ball go with his arm. Quick off the ground, he nearly always looked hard to play. He was in the Marlborough XI for three years—1899, 1900, and 1901—taking nine wickets in his last match against Rugby. For Cambridge in first-class matches he took 67 wickets in 1904, 64 in 1905, 77 in 1906, and 75 in 1907. He was thus consistently successful for four seasons, but most of his best work was done at Lord's. In 1904 he played for the Gentlemen for the first time and made his first appearance for Middlesex. His figures against Oxford were:

1904	..	5 wickets for 121 runs
1905	..	7 wickets for 160 runs
1906	..	10 wickets for 159 runs
1907	..	9 wickets for 104 runs

He was on the winning side three times, the match in 1904 being drawn. In 1905 he helped A. F. Morcom to get Oxford out in the last innings for 123, Cambridge gaining a sensational victory by 40 runs.

NAPIER, The Rev. John Russell, who died on March 13, 1939, aged 80, accomplished two remarkable performances for Lancashire in 1888. Against P. S. McDonnell's Australian team he made 37, the highest score in Lancashire's second innings and then, with John Briggs, the slow left-hander, dismissed the visitors for 66. Napier took seven wickets in the match and Lancashire won by 23 runs. At Sheffield in July he took four wickets without conceding a run, Yorkshire's last five wickets falling at the same total, 80. A fast round-arm bowler, he was captain of the Marlborough XI in 1878 and played occasionally for Cambridge University. In 1881 when sure of his Blue he ricked his back and was compelled to rest when the match with Oxford was played at Lord's.

NAPPER, Edwin, who died on March 18, 1895, was one of the best known of the old school of Sussex cricketers. Born on January 26, 1815, he had entered his 81st year. He made his first appearance at Lord's for Sussex (with Fuller Pilch) against England on June 8, 1840, and played regularly in the Sussex XI for upwards of 20 seasons. He was that somewhat unusual combination, a left-handed bat and right-handed bowler. Mr. Arthur Haygarth, in *Scores and Biographies*, says of him that, like all left-handed batsmen, he was a fine, free hitter, making splendid cuts and drives, and that his round-arm bowling was of middle speed, with a

pretty and easy delivery. Other authorities have also described him as one of the best left-handed batsmen of his day among the amateurs. He was born in Leigh Parish, Pulborough, Sussex, and was senior by little over a year and a half to his brother, Mr. William Napper, equally well known in connection with Sussex cricket.

NAPPER, William, died at Brighton on July 13, 1897, not having for very long survived his elder brother Mr. Edwin Napper, who died on March 18, 1895. William Napper was born at Wisborough Green, August 25, 1816, and like his brother was intimately connected all his life with Sussex cricket. Like his brother, too, he was a left-handed bat and right-handed bowler. He played his first match at Lord's, for Sussex versus the M.C.C. and Ground with Fuller Pilch, on June 2–3, 1845. The Sussex XI on that occasion included Tom Box, Jimmy Dean, and C. G. Taylor. Mr. Napper retained the keenest interest in cricket until the end of his life and rarely missed a match at Brighton.

NARAYAN SINGH, Prince Kumar Hitendra, who died of influenza at Darjeeling on November 7, 1920, aged 30, was brother of the Maharajah of Cooch Behar, and was educated at Eton and Cambridge and played a few times for Somerset. He was a good batsman and in 1908 made several large scores for Somerset Stragglers, among them 104 and 103 not out v. Devon Dumplings at Taunton and 99 and 91 v. Incogniti on the same ground.

NASH, Albert Jack, who died in a London hospital on December 6, 1956, aged 83, played for Glamorgan from 1903 to 1922. A medium-pace bowler, he headed the Glamorgan averages in 1921, the season they were accorded first-class status, taking in County Championship matches 90 wickets— more than twice as many as any other player for the county—at an average cost of 17.34. He dismissed 15 Worcestershire batsmen for 116 runs at Swansea, bearing a major part in a victory by an innings and 53 runs. Altogether he took 136 wickets in first-class cricket for 22.48 runs each.

NASH, George, who died of paralysis at Aylesbury on November 13, 1903, will be chiefly remembered from his association with Lancashire cricket in the early '80s. A contemporary of Alec Watson and the late John Crossland, Nash was a slow left-handed bowler, to whose method of delivering the ball, as well as to that of his two colleagues, great exception was taken. By reason of his moderate pace, Nash did not excite such strong opposition as Crossland, but the belief in the unfairness of his delivery was quite as generally entertained. He first appeared for Lancashire in the season of 1879, but only assisted the county in two matches that summer. In the following year he took 37 wickets. His best seasons were 1881 and 1882, when he obtained 52 and 62 wickets respectively at a cost of just over 10 runs apiece. He dropped out of Lancashire cricket in 1885. In recent years he played regularly for Buckinghamshire.

NASH, The Rev. William Wallace Hayward, who died on July 24, 1971, aged 86, was in the King's Bruton XI before turning out occasionally for Gloucestershire in 1905 and 1906.

NASON, Capt. John William William (Royal Flying Corps), born at Corse Grange, Gloucestershire, on August 4, 1889, was killed in December, 1916. He was educated at University School, Hastings, and Cambridge, where he obtained his Blue in 1909. As a lad he was regarded as a player of unusual promise, but, although he made some useful scores both for the University and Sussex, it cannot be said that he did as well as was expected. In his two matches against Oxford—in 1909 and 1910—he scored only 32 runs with an average of 10.66. His first appearance for Sussex, against Warwickshire at Hastings in 1906, was marked by a curious incident, for he was allowed to replace Dwyer after that player had bowled five overs, and in his second innings carried out his bat for 53. In 1913 he began to assist Gloucestershire, and in that season played an innings of 139 against Nottinghamshire on the Gloucester ground. This was his highest score in first-class cricket. When playing for University School v. Hastings Post Office in 1908, he opened the innings and when he was bowled after batting for half an hour the score-sheet read: J. W. W. Nason b Cox, 97; L. Inskipp not out, 1; bye, 1; total (1 wkt.) 99. He obtained all the first 64 runs and hit three sixes and 14 fours.

NAUMANN, Major Frank Charles Gordon, M.C., who died on October 30, 1946, aged 55, played for Oxford in the University match of 1919, when his brother, J. H. Naumann, was in the Cambridge team and the brothers F. W. Gilligan (Oxford) and A. E. R. Gilligan (Cambridge) also were on opposing sides. Two brothers facing two brothers in a University match set up a case without parallel. A medium-paced bowler, Frank Naumann, taking 11 wickets for 157 runs, was largely responsible for Oxford winning by 45 runs. In 1914 he helped Oxford to victory by 194 runs, finishing the game by taking four wickets for 10 runs, the last three men falling to him in four balls. He excelled in 1919, being top of the Oxford bowling with 29 wickets at 23.82 each, and scoring 451 runs, average 34.69. In the match with M.C.C. at Oxford he was run out for 84, and in the second innings made 102 not out, the game producing altogether 1,409 runs while 29 wickets fell. The brothers Naumann played for Malvern in 1911, and both appeared occasionally for Surrey.

NAUMANN, John Harold, who died in New York on December 6, 1964, aged 72, played for Cambridge University before and after the First World War. He did good all-round work when in the Malvern XI in 1911, his slow-medium left-arm bowling enabling him to head the averages with 51 wickets at 18.33 runs apiece. Gaining his Blue as a Freshman, he bore a leading part in a Cambridge win by four wickets over Oxford in 1913, dismissing eight batsmen in the match for 94 runs. In that season he played in one match for Surrey Second XI. In 1919, when he headed the Cambridge batting figures with an average of 45.88 and hit 134 not out against Sussex at Hove, he lost his bowling skill and achieved little in the University match. His elder brother F. C. G. Naumann—his captain at Malvern—took chief honours in the big game when, with swing bowling, he paved the way to victory by 45 runs for Oxford by taking five wickets for 76 runs in the first innings and six for 81 in the second. John was bowled by his brother in the second innings. The match was noteworthy for the fact that two pairs of brothers took part, for F. W. Gilligan appeared for Oxford and A. E. R. Gilligan for Cambridge. John Naumann played in 15 Championship matches for Sussex in 1925, his highest innings being 74 against Worcestershire at Hove.

NAVARANTA, Benedict, Sri Lanka's greatest wicket-keeper, died on June 9, 1979, in Kandy, aged 63. He was of strong build, a physical culturist, agile and confident behind the stumps, and a capable batsman. He played against M.C.C., Australia, West Indies and Commonwealth teams of 1949–50 and 1950–51.

NAWAB IFTIKHAR ALI of PATAUDI, who died after a heart attack while playing polo at New Delhi on January 5, 1952, at the age of 41, will always be associated with Ranjitsinh-ji and Duleepsinhji as three great Indian batsmen who became leading figures in English cricket. Pataudi, known as "Pat" throughout the world, achieved the rare distinction of representing England and India in Test cricket.

Born at Pataudi in the Punjab on March 16, 1910, he went to Chiefs' College, Lahore, and received cricket coaching from M. G. Salter, the Oxford Blue. Going to England in 1926, he obtained further guidance from Frank Woolley, the Kent and England left-hander. In October 1927 Pataudi went to Oxford, but had to wait until 1929 before gaining his Blue. That season he accomplished little with the bat until the University match, when his innings of 106 and 84 went a long way towards saving the game. The following year he disappointed against Cambridge, but on his third appearance in 1931 he reached the height of his powers. In form from the start of the season, he scored 1,307 runs in 16 innings and finished top of the Oxford batting with the splendid average of 93. In successive innings he made 183 not out against the Army at Folkestone, 165 and 100 against Surrey at the Oval and 138 and 68 against H. D. G. Leveson Gower's XI at Eastbourne. Even this he overshadowed with a remarkable 238 not out against Cambridge at Lord's, the highest individual score ever made in the University match.

On the previous day A. Ratcliffe, of Cambridge, made 201, beating the previous best University score of 172 not out made by J. F. Marsh of Cambridge in 1904. Ratcliffe's record lasted only a few hours and it was said that before going in Pataudi declared his intention of trying to pass that figure. That was typical of the man—a great fighter who was at his best when a definite challenge was at hand. The innings caused him so much physical and nervous strain that he collapsed on his return to the pavilion.

His health was never strong and he was not always fit when touring Australia with D. R. Jardine's team in 1932–33. Nevertheless, he added another great triumph to his name by scoring a century in his first Test match and helping England to victory by 10 wickets at Sydney. He played in the next Test but did little, and was left out for the remaining three games.

Pataudi did not allow his disappointment to upset him, and on returning to England he was again in fine form for Worcestershire, his adopted county. In 1934 he was once more chosen for England against Australia, but scored only 12 and 10 at Nottingham in the first Test, and ill-health handicapped him afterwards. Although making occasional appearances for Worcestershire, he virtually dropped out of the game, but surprised everyone by returning to England as captain of the Indian touring team in 1946. He showed glimpses of his class, notably when becoming one of four batsmen to score 100 in the same innings against Sussex at Hove, and finished third in the averages, but he was again handicapped by ill-health and he failed in the three Test matches.

After that tour, Pataudi again dropped out of cricket, but he made one more attempt to return. In November 1951 M.C.C. approved an application for Pataudi to be regarded as still qualified to play for Worcestershire, and it was expected that he would appear occasionally for the county, despite his age of 41. He died a few weeks later.

A quick-footed batsman with a splendid eye, Pataudi possessed a wide variety of strokes, but did not have the fluency of his Indian predecessors, Ranjitsinhji and Duleepsinhji. He was also a fine hockey and billiards player and an accomplished speaker, although some considered his wit to be sharp and cynical. After the partition of India and Pakistan, Pataudi, a Moslem, found himself without a State to rule, but preserved his ruling status and was employed in the Indian Foreign Office in New Delhi. He left three daughters besides an 11-year-old son, who has shown promise of developing into a good cricketer.

NEALE, William Legge, who after a long illness died in hospital at Gloucester on October 26, 1955, aged 51, played for Gloucestershire from 1923 until 1948, scoring 14,752 runs, average 23.75. Educated at Cirencester Grammar School, he appeared as an amateur for six years before becoming a professional. Of his 14 centuries, the highest was 145 not out against Hampshire at Southampton in 1927. His best summer as a steady right-handed batsman was that of 1938 when, reaching three figures on five occasions, he scored 1,488 runs, average 29.76. Six times he exceeded 1,000 runs in a season. In 1937 he (121) and W. R. Hammond (217) set up a Gloucestershire fourth wicket record by adding 321 against Leicestershire at Gloucester. Though not often called upon to bowl, he occasionally broke a stubborn stand when the regular members of the attack had failed to do so, and at Bristol in 1937 he distinguished himself by dismissing six Somerset batsmen for nine runs. As a fieldsman he excelled near the boundary.

NEED, Philip, who died of pneumonia on November 23, 1924, aged 76, had been well known to hundreds of cricketers as the pavilion attendant at Lord's, where he had been engaged for 45 years. By birth he was a Nottinghamshire man, and before going to the M.C.C. had been in the service of the late Mr. Arthur Walker, of Southgate, for about seven years. The North v. South match at Lord's in 1900 was given to him for his benefit. Need, who was a vice-president of the Cross Arrows C.C., always carried out his duties most conscientiously and was much respected by all who knew him.

NEEDHAM, Ernest, did not play first-class cricket until 28 years of age, but Derbyshire might have tried him earlier with advantage. His first innings for the county was 57 against the South Africans in 1901, and three years later he got his first century (131) against Hampshire at Derby. He showed rather in and out form until enjoying his most successful season in 1908, when he scored 1,122 in Championship matches with an average of 28.76—by far the best record for the county—and he made three of the five individual 100s hit for Derbyshire that summer. Strangely enough his three big innings were played against Essex. He scored 104 and 37 in the home match, and victory was gained by seven wickets, but at Leyton, where a month later he hit up two separate 100s, Essex won by six wickets. Needham carried his bat through the first innings of 195, his share being 107 and he was at the crease nearly as long—three hours and a quarter—while scoring 104 of the second total of 255. A left-handed bat with sound defence if not very graceful in style, Needham drove and cut well and was a very useful member of the Derbyshire XI until 1912. He earned the highest honours at Association football with Sheffield United as a half-back. He played 16 times for England and took part in three final ties for the Association Cup. Twice he was on the winning side and in 1902, when Southampton were beaten after a drawn game, his opponents included C. B. Fry. Born on January 21, 1873, Needham died after an operation in Chesterfield Hospital on March 7, 1936, aged 63.

NEILL, Robert, who died at Auckland on August 27, 1930, aged 65, had gained considerable reputation as a slow right-handed bowler. Against Canterbury at Auckland he took nine wickets in an innings twice—for 75 runs in 1891–92 and for 86 in 1897–98. In matches with Wellington on the same ground he obtained 12 for 136 in 1895–96 and 11 for 54 in 1899–1900 as well as 12 for 132 at Wellington in 1893–94.

NELSON, Guy Montague Blyth, who died on January 13, 1969, aged 68, was in the Rugby XI in 1918. In 1921 and the following season he played as an amateur for Warwickshire.

NELSON, Robert Prynne, became a 2nd Lieut. in the Royal Marines and was killed in October 1940. His death at the age of 28 brought grief to his many cricket associates. A free left-handed batsman with good style, he made many runs when at St. George's School, Harpenden, where he became a master. He got his Cambridge Blue in 1936, and, scoring 91 at Lord's, gave a delightful display. Controlling his lively strokes by clever placing, he cut and drove to the off in beautiful style. He was unfortunate, when so near a century, to fall to a remarkable catch at short leg. Walford knocked up the ball over his shoulder and, turning round, held the catch an inch from the ground as he fell full length. His stand of 113 with N. W. D. Yardley contributed largely to the Cambridge total of 432 and the eventual victory by eight wickets. He got only a single while the 17 runs wanted were knocked off, but his highest score of the season was the best in the match. After a few appearances for Middlesex, Nelson joined Northamptonshire, and captained the XI with such good effect in the last two seasons of first-class cricket that in 1939 a decisive win at Cambridge was followed by victory in a county match after a prolonged spell of misfortune extending over three years. The success over Leicestershire enabled Northamptonshire to rise from the bottom of the Championship, a position which they had occupied in five consecutive seasons.

Besides exercising the heartening influence of a buoyant personality, Nelson stood out as one of the chief batsmen for the county, scoring 1,031 runs, average 27.13, in 1938, and 1,078, average 32.66, next season. He showed skill in managing his attack and knew when to use his own slow left-hand bowling. His possibilities as an all-rounder were seen at the Saffrons in 1937, when for M.C.C. he scored 183 not out and dismissed six Eastbourne batsmen for 13 runs.

He appeared for the British Empire XI several times, heading the averages with

49.83, and played also for Club Cricket Conference at Lord's last summer.

D. L. Donnelly, who organised the British Empire XI, received this tribute to Nelson from W. C. Brown, the Northamptonshire captain from 1933 to 1935, and present hon. secretary of the County Club:

"Robert Nelson's death is a tragedy. Having known him, you will appreciate what his loss means to this county. His own prowess allied to his patience with, and encouragement to, those under him worked wonders. At the end of 1937 the Northamptonshire side was a disorganised rabble. In two seasons he quietly and imperceptibly moulded them into a team which it was impossible to recognise as the same lot who had done duty before he took over the captaincy. His promise to carry on for at least one season after the War had been the

mainspring of the committee's exertions to keep the club together since County Cricket lapsed. His loss has left a great gap."

Donnelly himself wrote: "Robert Nelson was a source of inspiration to us this summer. In our efforts to raise funds for the Red Cross and in our desire to provide attractive, keen cricket on the field he was always eager to help. From his quiet, unassuming manner it was impossible to gather that he was a personality in the cricket world. We who played with him admired him immensely."

From the time of his first match for St. George's School, Harpenden, at the age of 12, R. P. Nelson kept a record of his performances without a break. He played for his school for seven years, from 1925 to 1931 inclusive, and his figures, comprising his complete cricket career, were:

Batting		Innings	Not Outs	Runs	Highest Innings	Average
All games	.. ..	795	118	26,008	183*	38.41
First-class matches	..	136	12	3,394	123*	27.37

Bowling		Overs	Maidens	Runs	Wickets	Average
All games	.. ..	6,479	1,580	17,958	1,423	12.61
First-class matches	..	6,794	208	2,202	6	35.51

Signifies not out

NEPEAN, The Rev. C. E. B., who died on March 26, 1903, was born on February 5, 1851. Mr. Nepean had since 1876 been vicar of Lenham, in Kent. As a cricketer he did not gain so much distinction as he deserved, fortune being somewhat unkind to him. After four seasons in the Charterhouse team he went up to Oxford with a good reputation as a batsman, and was 12th man in 1870, missing his Blue, but playing against Surrey at the Oval immediately after the memorable Oxford and Cambridge match which F. C. Cobden's bowling won at the finish for Cambridge by two runs. His future at Oxford seemed assured, but from some cause he did not get a place in the XI until his last year—1873. Then, however, he made up for lost opportunities, scoring 22 and 50 against Cambridge, and helping the late C. J. Ottaway to gain for Oxford a well-deserved victory by three wickets. On the strength of this excellent performance he was picked three weeks later for the Gentlemen in the first Gentlemen and Players match ever decided at Prince's ground, Hans Place. He was an admirable batsman, with a very neat and business-like style. Nothing was seen of him in good class matches of late years, but as a member of the

Kent committee he kept in close touch with the game.

NEPEAN, Evan Alcock, the Oxford University and Middlesex cricketer, died after a brief illness on January 20, 1906. Born on September 13, 1865, he was only in his 41st year. Mr. Nepean learnt his cricket at Sherborne School, and on going up to Oxford was in the University XI in 1887 and 1888. In the former year he had a considerable share in gaining for Oxford a seven wickets victory against Cambridge, taking five wickets and in the last stage of the game scoring 58 not out. He did nothing in the University match in 1888, and had a poor record for Oxford that season, both as batsman and bowler. For Middlesex, however, in the same year he got on very well, taking 13 wickets in four matches for a little over 16 runs each, and having a batting average of 25. He reached his highest point as an all-round cricketer just after he left Oxford, being highly successful in 1889, when he came out third for Middlesex in batting and first in bowling. That year he appeared for Gentlemen against Players, both at Lord's and the Oval, scoring at the Surrey ground 21 and 39 not out. He also played for the Gentlemen in 1887 at the

Oval, and in taking four wickets had the satisfaction of getting Arthur Shrewsbury out for two runs. Altogether he took part in six Gentlemen v. Players' matches. A slow leg-break bowler, he could get a lot of spin on the ball, but his pitch was always rather uncertain. After being called to the Bar, he gradually dropped out of first-class cricket, but he had a good season as a bowler for Middlesex in 1891, and played for the M.C.C. against the Australians at Lord's in 1893.

NESBITT, Capt. Arnold Sterns, of the 3rd Batt. Worcestershire Regiment, who was killed in action on November 7, 1914, kept wicket at Lord's earlier in the season for Worcestershire v. Middlesex. He was in his 36th year, and was a member of the Bradfield XI of 1895.

NESER, Mr. Justice Vivian Herbert, who died in Pretoria on December 22, 1956, aged 62, played both cricket and Rugby football for Oxford University. From South African College, Cape Town, he went to Oxford as a Rhodes Scholar just after the First World War, during which he served in the Royal Field Artillery. He represented Brasenose College at cricket, Rugby and Association football, lawn tennis and hockey. In the 1921 University cricket match he, with such celebrities as D. R. Jardine, R. H. Bettington, G. T. S. Stevens and R. C. Robertson-Glasgow, was a member of the Oxford XI beaten by an innings and 24 runs. He scored two and 10. As a Rugby footballer, he appeared against Cambridge as a forward in 1919 and in the following season, following injury to F. A. Waldock, was pressed into service at the last moment as fly-half against Cambridge. So well did Neser play in this, the last University match to be played at Queen's Club, that he "made" one try and scored another, and Oxford won by 17 points to 14. Returning to South Africa, he played cricket for Transvaal, turning out for his Province against F. T. Mann's M.C.C. team of 1922–23. He practised law in Pretoria for many years, became acting Judge of the Transvaal Provincial Division of the South African Supreme Court, and was raised permanently to the Bench in 1944.
CORRECTION. Regarding the obituary which appeared in the 1957 *Almanack*, Mr. A. S. Frames, Secretary of the South African Cricket Association, writes: "The late Mr. Neser captained South Africa in all five Test matches in 1924–25 against Mr. S. B. Joel's touring side. Colours were not granted, but this was probably the most outstanding feature of Mr. Neser's cricket career in South Africa."

NEVILE, Capt. Bernard Philip (Lincolnshire Regiment) fell on February 11, 1916, aged 27. He captained Lincolnshire in the Minor Counties Championship competition and also played for Worcestershire—in 1913 for both counties. In the second innings of the Seniors' match at Cambridge in 1912 he took four wickets for 27 runs. He obtained his Blue for golf.

NEWCOMBE, Lieut. Charles Neal (7th Batt. King's Own Yorkshire Light Infantry) fell in action in December 1915, aged 24. He was a useful left-handed slow-to-medium bowler, who made the ball swing, and in 1910 played for Derbyshire v. Yorkshire at Chesterfield.

NEWCOMBE, Harry C. E., who appeared for New South Wales against Victoria in 1861 and two following years, died at Randwick, Sydney, on October 26, 1908, in his 74th year.

NEWELL, Andrew L., the well-known Australian cricketer, left home over a year ago and has not been seen or heard of since. He had been in indifferent health for some time and had been advised to take a month's holiday. It is probable that he lost his life over the sea cliffs in the vicinity of Ben Buckler, near Bondi, in 1908. He was born on November 13, 1870, and was a very useful all-round player identified with the Glebe Electorate C.C. of Sydney. He will be best remembered on account of his innings of 68 not out for New South Wales in the return match with Stoddart's team at Sydney in February, 1898. He added 169 for the eighth wicket with S. E. Gregory (171) and 109 for the last in 63 minutes with Howell, who claimed 95 of the number. New South Wales, who had made 415 in their first innings, scored 574 in their second, and won by 239 runs.

NEWHALL, George Morgan, a member of America's most famous cricketing family, died in Baltimore Hospital on January 25, 1921. He was born on June 22, 1845, and so had completed his 75th year. His early cricket was played with the Young America club, and he captained sides against the English teams of 1868 and 1872. In 1880 he appeared for the United States against Canada. The highest innings of his career was 180 not out for Young America v. Baltimore in 1880. A delightful writer on cricket, he was author of

Germantown Cricket Grounds, and contributed the introduction to *Cricket and Cricketers*.

NEWHALL, Robert Stuart, who was born at Philadelphia, on September 16, 1852, died at his native place on December 9, 1910. He was one of the best exponents and most generous supporters the game ever had in America, and in 1884 captained the Gentlemen of Philadelphia during their tour in England. For many years he was prominently identified with the Young American club, which amalgamated with the Germantown C.C. in 1889. He was a skilful captain and a fine batsman. His highest innings was 126 v. Gentlemen of Cheshire in 1884, but his best was probably played against the Australians in 1878.

NEWHAM, William, died on June 26, 1944, aged 83, when still in harness as assistant secretary of Sussex County C.C., with which his official connection dated back to 1889. That season, when both secretary and captain, he headed the batting averages with 30.20 for 31 completed innings. Educated at Ardingly, he remained at the college as a master until 1887, and two years later became secretary of Sussex, a post he resigned in 1907, when, with Col. E. A. Bruce, hon. secretary, he was appointed assistant secretary, an office which enabled him to retain his connection with the County Club until his death.

He first appeared for the county in 1881, and his 63 years as amateur player, captain, and in secretarial duties are regarded as constituting a cricket record. Although in a few summers he played little because of his other activities, he did not give up playing until late in the 1905 season, when in first-class cricket his total runs numbered about 14,500 with an average of 24.

At his best Billy Newham stood out in the front rank among batsmen, and excelled as a fieldsman "in the country." Of middle height and well built, he displayed exceptional skill against fast bowling. He drove hard on either side of the wicket, cut brilliantly, and earned special fame when playing back with forcing strokes past mid-on or turning the ball to leg.

In his second year with Sussex he headed the averages, a feat he repeated in 1884 and 1889. Of 19 three-figure innings he played his highest, 201, against Somerset at Hove in 1896. In company with C.B. Fry, K.S. Ranjitsinhji and George Brann, his junior at Ardingly, Newham made the Sussex batting very strong, particularly at Hove, a fast-scoring ground. Yet some of his best performances were away from home. In 1902 at Leyton he and "Ranji" (230) put together 344, which still stands as a world record for the seventh wicket; Newham made 153. Perhaps his most meritorious achievement took place at Old Trafford in 1894, when he carried his bat through an innings of 174, his 110 not out being described at the time as a remarkable combination of resolute hitting and skilful defence against deadly bowling by Mold and Briggs. Alfred Shaw, then nearly 52 years of age, making his first appearance for Sussex under the residential qualification, went in last and alone of the other Sussex batsmen reached double figures with 16. Following-on, Sussex fell for 38, Newham with nine being exceeded only by C. Aubrey Smith, 10.

Newham in his only match at Lord's for Gentlemen against Players made 25, the highest score for his side, who won an exciting struggle by five runs. Four times he appeared for the Gentlemen at the Oval and three times at Hastings. In the winter of 1887, when touring Australia with the team organised by Shaw and Shrewsbury, he played in the side combined with that led by W. W. Read against Australia, who were beaten in the one representative match by 126 runs.

A very good Association football player, Newham was a member of the Corinthian club.

NEWLAND, Philip M., born at Adelaide on February 2, 1876, died on August 11, 1916. In Australia he ranked high as a wicket-keeper, but when he visited us as second wicket-keeper in the team of 1905 he found the varying pace of our pitches too much for him. During the tour not much work fell to his lot, but this was owing partly to the fact that he was not very robust. For South Australia, for which he appeared for the first time during the season of 1899–1900, he played several useful innings, among them 77 v. New South Wales and 50 v. England, both at Adelaide in 1903–04. By profession he was a solicitor.

NEWMAN, Douglas Leonard, who died in a London hospital on September 11, 1959, aged 39, captained Middlesex Second XI from 1954 to 1958, his best season being that of 1954 when he hit 465 runs, average 31.00, with 132 his highest innings. He made occasional appearances in County Championship matches in 1950 and 1951. A well-known club cricketer, he was captain of Winchmore Hill.

NEWMAN, F. C. W., who died early in 1966 following a long illness, aged 72, played a few matches for Surrey in 1919 and 1921. A free-scoring batsman from his schooldays at Bedford Modern, he scored something like 30,000 runs in club cricket and hit over 60 100s. He made many runs for the Dulwich club and appeared in the Minor Counties competition before the First World War for Bedfordshire. In 1926 he became private secretary to Sir Julien Cahn, for whose side he played regularly for many years. He also organised Cahn's tours to West Indies, South America, Denmark, Canada, U.S.A., Bermuda, Malaya and New Zealand.

NEWMAN, George Christopher, who died on October 13, 1982, aged 78, had the unusual experience of getting into the Eton XI so late in his last year at school, 1923, that he played two innings only, against Winchester and against Harrow. He owed his selection to the advice of R. A. Young, then master-in-charge of cricket, who had spotted, beneath a style which did not wholly conform to the strict Eton canons of orthodoxy, possibilities of a fine attacking batsman. His judgement proved, as so often, right: Newman, after making 22 at Winchester, did at Lord's exactly what was wanted—going in No. 9, he hit some erratic Harrow bowling all over the ground to score 82 not out. This early success was typical of his later career, even though it did not secure him any kind of trial in the Parks during his first two years at Oxford. He had to wait until his third year when, given a chance on the tour, he made his place secure with an innings of 66 at the Oval, where he helped C. H. Taylor to add 141. He failed at Lord's, but in 1927, after starting with 92 against the full bowling strength of Lancashire, that year's champions (an innings described as "one of the best played in the Parks since the War"), he came second in the Oxford averages with 481 runs at an average of 40.08. Again he failed at Lord's and so it came as a surprise to many when, given a trial by Middlesex in 1929, he played a brilliant innings in his third match, 112 out of 168 in just over two hours against Gloucestershire at Lord's. He should have been stumped off Parker first ball, but immediately retaliated by hitting Goddard for two sixes off consecutive balls with pulled drives towards the Tavern. The match was, in fact, otherwise notable as the occasion on which Goddard, taking 13 for 120, first demonstrated that an indifferent fast bowler had in one season's absence from County Cricket changed himself into a great slow off-

spinner. Newman made two more fine centuries in 1930, against Warwickshire and Essex, and continued to play for the county until 1936, though never regularly; indeed after 1931 for a match or two a year only. In 1937 he captained an M.C.C. side in Canada. A tall man, who made full use of his reach, he was a fine striker of the ball in front of the wicket, but also a good cutter and a glorious off-side fieldsman with a beautiful return. He was a natural athlete who had represented Oxford in the high jump and the low hurdles and been president of the O.U.A.C. He had also played in the first two squash matches against Cambridge. In later life he did valuable work on the M.C.C. committee and had been one of the club's trustees since 1970. He was also, from 1963 to 1976, president of Middlesex.

NEWMAN, John Alfred, who died in a Cape Town hospital on December 27, 1973, aged 89, rendered splendid all-round service to Hampshire for 25 years. He began with them in 1906 and continued until 1930. In that time he hit 15,333 runs, including nine centuries, for an average of 21.65, took 2,032 wickets at 24.20 runs apiece and held 296 catches. This lean but wiry player performed the "cricketers' double" five times between 1921 and 1928, being first to do so—on July 31—in 1921.

For a number of years he and A. S. Kennedy virtually comprised the Hampshire bowling. Against Sussex in 1921 and in opposition to Somerset two years later, both at Portsmouth, the pair bowled unchanged through both innings. Newman, like Kennedy, of medium pace, could make the ball swing when it was new and afterwards turned to off-breaks of equally excellent length. He took 100 wickets in a season on eight occasions, his best year being 1921, when his victims numbered 177 at 21.56 runs each. He did the hat-trick against M. A. Noble's Australian side at Southampton in 1909; dismissed three Sussex batsmen in the course of four balls at Hove in 1923 and at Weston-super-Mare against Somerset in 1927 obtained 16 wickets for 88 runs in the match. His best all-round feat was in 1926 when he hit 66 and 42 not out and took 14 Gloucestershire wickets for 148 runs. Next summer he scored 102 and 102 not out from the Surrey bowling at the Oval when Jack Hobbs also hit two separate 100s in the same match—a rare double performance in those days.

In 1922 Newman was the central figure in an unhappy incident at Trent Bridge, where he refused to bowl while the crowd engaged in barracking. The Hampshire captain, the Hon. L. H. (later Lord) Tennyson ordered him from the field—upon which Newman kicked down the stumps, a most unusual display of petulance from a likeable man. He continued later after an apology.

For nine seasons after retiring as a player, Newman stood as a first-class umpire and then went to live in Cape Town, where he coached for a number of years.

CORRECTION. John Newman of Hampshire, died on December 21, 1973 and not December 27, the day of his funeral, as stated in the 1974 *Wisden*.

NEWMAN, Leonard William, who died on March 21, 1964, aged 82, was a fine forcing batsman for many years in club cricket, scoring over 80,000 runs and hitting 250 centuries. A former captain of Alexandra Park C.C., he was president of the Club Cricket Conference in 1953.

NEWMAN, William, the last surviving member of the old Montpelier C.C., which played so prominent a part in the formation of the Surrey County C.C., died in London on November 21, 1919, in his 100th year. He probably saw more cricket at the Oval than any other spectator.

NEWNHAM, Lieut.-Col. Arthur Tristram Herbert, died in Newton Abbot Hospital on December 29, 1941, aged nearly 81. After three years in the Malvern XI he went to Sandhurst, and served mostly in the Army abroad or he would have made a big name in English cricket. Playing first for Gloucestershire in 1887 at Lord's, he scored 25 not out, helping W. G. Grace to add 84 for the ninth wicket before the champion was leg-before to A. J. Webbe for 113. Rain ruined the pitch, but Newnham, with 20, was best scorer in the second innings, and then he and W. G. dismissed A. E. Stoddart, A. J. Webbe, S. W. Scott and T. C. O'Brien, the four best Middlesex batsmen, for 25 before the match was left drawn. At Gloucester against Yorkshire, when W. G. Grace scored 92 and carried his bat through the second innings for 183, Newnham, 56, took part in an eighth-wicket stand for 143. Played primarily as a fast bowler, Newnham appeared for Gentlemen against Players at the Oval that season. For many years he was prominent in cricket abroad, particularly at Bombay.

NEWTON, Col. Alan Colin, Paymaster-in-Chief of the Australian Army when he retired from the Commonwealth Department of Defence, and probably Tasmania's most gifted all-round athlete, died in Sydney on March 27, 1979, aged 85. "Picker" Newton achieved early fame in 1908 when he shared an undefeated opening partnership of 400 for Queen's College, Hobart, with the (later) Tasmanian Rhodes Scholar, John Barnett; their record still stands. As a schoolboy, Newton took seven wickets for 33 in his first "A" Grade match, and gained initial representative honours with a score of 68 in the same season, despite the expressed objection of selectors to his "wearing knickerbockers" at the time. Originally associated with East Hobart, Newton helped to form the harbourside Sandy Bay club in 1926 and was its captain and committee chairman for most of the time until his Defence Department duties took him first to Perth in 1936 and then to the Royal Military College, Duntroon. He was honoured with Tasmanian Cricket Association life membership a year later. During his 22 years as the outstanding all-round player in the Tasmanian XI, his highest score was 117 at Launceston in 1922 against Victoria when, batting No. 10, he established a new state record partnership of 148 with H. C. Smith. In all, he scored 1,108 runs and took 66 wickets for Tasmania. He was a most attractive right-hand batsman, and his left-arm bowling ranged from fast-medium in-swing to leg-breaks.

A keen tennis player, he won eight major championships, including the Tasmanian singles titles of 1924 and 1925 and the state doubles championship on three later occasions between 1930 and 1933.

This true amateur gave much time as a committeeman of the T.C.A., its Executive Cricket Council, and as a state selector, as well as being honorary treasurer of the Lawn Tennis Association. He wrote with authority on both sports as a local Hobart press correspondent, using the noms-de-plumes "Willow" and "Volley."

NEWTON, Arthur Edward, who died at his home at Trull, Somerset, on September 15, 1952, three days after his 90th birthday, was a famous wicket-keeper who continued his activities in club cricket until the age of 81. When 74, having cycled to the Taunton ground to turn out for Somerset Stragglers, he demonstrated that his ability had not seriously declined by stumping five batsmen. While at Eton in 1880 he began an association with Somerset which lasted for 34 years. "A.E.", as he was affectionately known to so many, helped S. M. J. Woods to take a wicket with the first ball he bowled for Somerset. This was at Edgbaston in 1886. C. W. Rock, batting for Warwickshire, missed a very fast yorker on the leg-side, and Newton stumped him brilliantly.

Born on September 12, 1862, he played against Harrow at Lord's in 1879 and the two following years. The matches of 1880 and 1881 were noteworthy for the fact that, though P. J. de Paravacini took 12 Harrow wickets on each occasion, he was twice on the losing side. When at Pembroke College, Oxford, Newton gained a Blue in 1885, and he appeared for Gentlemen against Players at the Oval in 1897, conceding only two byes in a total of 431, and at Lord's in 1902. He took part in two tours abroad. In 1885 he was a member of a team of amateurs who went to the U.S.A. under E. J. Sanders, finishing second in the batting averages, and in the winter of 1887–88 he visited Australia with G. F. Vernon's side. Cricket grounds in the Antipodes in those far-off days left much to be desired. Newton used to relate how one of his team-mates refused to field in the deep during a match in Tasmania because he had seen a snake wriggle into a hole close to where he was placed! Altogether in first-class cricket Newton caught 297 batsmen and stumped 119. Until the last 10 years of his life he hunted regularly with the Taunton Vale Foxhounds and the Taunton Vale Harriers. He was a member of the M.C.C. from 1884.

NEWTON, Frederick Arthur, born at Denaby Main, Yorkshire, on September 16, 1887, was killed by a fall of roof on August 8, 1924, whilst at work at the Staveley Coal and Iron Company's Warsop Main Colliery. He was a good batsman and field, and a fair change leg-break bowler, right-hand. He played occasionally for Derbyshire, commencing in 1909, and against Warwickshire at Blackwell—the match in which Warren and Mr. J. Chapman put on 283 for the ninth wicket—scored 87 in an hour and three-quarters without a mistake, hitting 15 fours.

NEWTON, Stephen Cox, born at Nailsea, Somerset on April 21, 1853, died in a nursing-home at Ipswich on August 16, 1916, after an operation. *Scores and Biographies* described him as "A fine and free hitter, and a most excellent field." At cover-point he was one of those who came nearest in excellence to the incomparable Vernon Royle. At Victoria College, Jersey, where he once threw the ball 120 yd. in the Sports, he was in the XI for as many as seven seasons,

1866 to 1872 inclusive, heading the averages in 1867, 1868, 1869, 1870, and 1872, when he played an innings of 117 v. Elizabeth College, Jersey. He was captain during his three last years at the College. At Cambridge he obtained his Blue in 1876, but made only seven in the match with Oxford. Between 1876 and 1890 he assisted Somerset, and captained the side from 1880 until 1884. In 1885 he appeared, under the residential qualification, for Middlesex. For some years he was Headmaster of Loudon House School, St. John's Wood. Since 1878 he had been a member of the M.C.C. He was not related to Mr. A. E. Newton, also of Somerset.

NICE, E. H. L., a useful all-rounder, who played intermittently for Surrey from 1897 to 1905, died in June, 1946, aged 70. In 1904, his best season, he took 48 wickets at 29 runs apiece and was helped to a batting average of 24.60 by being not out five times in the course of 20 innings.

NICHOL, Maurice, the Worcestershire cricketer, died suddenly at Chelmsford, where Essex were playing Worcestershire on May 21, 1934. Born at Hetton, Durham, on September 10, 1905, Nichol was in his 29th year. He played as an amateur for Durham in the Minor Counties competition and had a trial at the Oval for Surrey before qualifying for Worcestershire in 1929. During his period of qualification Nichol had the distinction of making 100 on his first appearance in first-class cricket—104 for Worcestershire against West Indies in 1928. Playing regularly for the county in 1929 he scored 1,442 runs and the following season he registered the highest innings of his career, 262 not out against Hampshire at Bournemouth. Nichol possessed a neat style and, as he proved himself a consistent run-getter, hopes were entertained that he would become an England cricketer. In 1931 he acted as 12th man for England in the Test match against New Zealand at Lord's, and after faring moderately the following season, he jumped into his best form in 1933 when he concluded the summer with three successive 100s: 116, against Hampshire at Bournemouth; 165 not out against Glamorgan at Worcester and 154 against Yorkshire at Worcester, he and Martin adding 243. Altogether hitting eight centuries he finished third in the county's batting averages with an aggregate of 2,085 runs and with C. F. Walters, who got nine 100s in an aggregate of 2,165, broke run-getting records for Worcestershire which had been held by R. E. Foster since 1901. Nichol made 17 centuries during his all too brief first-class career.

While his end came unexpectedly, Nichol, in recent years, had not enjoyed the best of health. During the winter of 1931–32 he spent several weeks in Sunderland Royal Infirmary where he was very seriously ill with pneumonia. The following summer he failed to regain his real form, a long day in the field or an effort to put together a big innings being too exacting for his physical resources. Strangely enough during the Whitsuntide fixture of 1933, played at Leyton, he was taken ill at Stratford station and had to retire from the game, so that his death a year later while the Essex match was in progress came as a dramatic coincidence.

NICHOLAS, F. W. H., who died on October 20, 1962, aged 69, was at Forest School before going up to Oxford, where he failed to gain a Blue after playing in trial matches in 1913 and 1914. He first played for Essex in 1912, but the following year assisted Bedfordshire with much success. After the First World War, he returned to Essex, playing as batsman–wicket-keeper from 1922 to 1929. His best season for the county was 1926 when he scored 729 runs, including 140, his only century, against Surrey at Leyton. In 1924–25 he toured South Africa with the Hon. L. H. Tennyson's team and in 1928–29 and 1929–30 visited Jamaica and Argentina with teams raised by Sir Julien Cahn, for whose XI he appeared frequently in England.

NICHOLLS, Benjamin Ernest, died at Kirdford, Sussex, on June 5, 1945, aged 80. After playing two years for Winchester he got his Blue at Oxford in 1884 and appeared for Sussex in four matches between 1883 and 1888. Reappeared in first-class cricket in 1901. In the match against Australia at Oxford in 1884 he made seven catches at short-slip.

NICHOLLS, Charles Omar, who died on January 4, 1983, aged 81, was a very tall all-rounder who gained a Test trial in 1928–29 after making 100 for New South Wales against Victoria and taking nine wickets in a match against South Australia.

NICHOLLS, Richard William, died at Eastbourne, January 22, 1948, aged 72. Rugby XI, 1892–93; played occasionally for Middlesex, 1896–1904. In June 1899 he and W. Roche, an Australian, made 230 for the last wicket against Kent at Lord's—then the best

10th-wicket stand in first-class cricket. Nicholls scored 154. Nine men were out for 55 when he was joined by Roche. Middlesex won the match by 118 runs; J. T. Hearne and A. E. Trott each took eight wickets in a remarkable game.

NICHOLLS, Sidney, who died at Wellington, New Zealand, on April 27, 1929, aged 65, had captained Wellington at both cricket and football. A good wicket-keeper and a free bat, he represented the Province in 18 games between 1882 and 1894.

NICHOLS, George Benjamin, who was born at Fishponds, Bristol, on June 14, 1862, died of pneumonia at Dublin on February 19, 1911. Playing originally as an amateur for Gloucestershire, he was subsequently for 14 years a useful all-round professional member of the Somerset XI. In first-class cricket his highest innings was 74 not out, but in minor matches he was a prolific run-getter, and in 1891 he ran up 311 not out for Somerset Club and Ground v. Glastonbury. After dropping out of the Somerset team he played in a few matches (in 1900 and 1901) for Devonshire.

NICHOLS, Morris Stanley, who died on January 26, 1961, aged 60, was, in an era of a good many all-rounders, one of the best. An Essex player from 1924 to 1939, he scored 17,789 runs, average 26.39, as a left-handed batsman strong in strokes in front of the wicket and with right-arm fast bowling took 1,834 wickets for 21.66 runs apiece. Of his 20 centuries the highest was 205 against Hampshire at Southend in 1936. He was first recommended to Essex solely as a batsman, but Percy Perrin, observing his height and strong physique, encouraged him as a pace bowler. How successful this proved is shown by the fact that in each of 11 seasons "Stan" Nichols dismissed over 100 batsmen, his best being that of 1938 when he took 171 wickets at a cost of 19.92 runs each. He could bowl for long spells without fatigue or loss of accuracy.

He enjoyed perhaps his greatest triumph as an all-rounder in 1935 when at Huddersfield he played the leading part in the overthrow by an innings and 204 runs of Yorkshire, the ultimate Champions, whose one defeat in the competition this was. In the two innings he gained an analysis of 11 wickets for 54 runs and he hit 146. Three years later at Gloucester, he played an innings of 159 and gained full bowling figures of 15 wickets for 165 runs, his first-innings analysis being nine wickets for 37 runs in 15.2

overs. On three other occasions he took nine wickets in an innings—for 59 runs v. Hampshire at Chelmsford in 1927; for 32 runs v. Nottinghamshire at Trent Bridge in 1936 and for 116 runs v. Middlesex at Leyton in 1930. Twice he disposed of four batsmen in four deliveries—v. Sussex at Horsham in 1929 and v. Lancashire at Chelmsford in 1935—and he also achieved the hat-trick against Yorkshire at Leeds in 1931.

Eight times he performed the "cricketers' double"—five in succession from 1935 until the War ended his first-class career in 1939—a number exceeded by only four men, W. Rhodes, G. H. Hirst, V. W. C. Jupp and W. E. Astill. He played 14 times for England between 1929 and 1939, took part in M.C.C. tours of Australasia in 1929 and India in 1933, also visited Jamaica on two occasions and appeared in nine matches for Players v. Gentlemen. He played in Birmingham League cricket after the War.

As modest as he was popular, Nichols was once asked if he had found any batsman particularly difficult. He replied: "Old George Gunn, I think. He used to walk down the pitch to me. I always felt a fool trying to bowl him out."

In his footballing days a useful goalkeeper, Nichols played for Queen's Park Rangers.

NICHOLSON, Frank ("Nipper"), who died in Port Elizabeth on July 30, 1982, aged 72, kept wicket four times for South Africa against Australia in 1935–36. From 1927 until 1947 he represented Griqualand West, captaining them for several seasons. A neat wicket-keeper and more than adequate batsman, he accounted for 64 victims and scored 2,353 runs at an average of 24.76 in a first-class career of 52 matches. His highest score of 185 was made against Orange Free State. His best season was 1933–34 when, in four Currie Cup matches, he scored 353 runs for an average of 44.12, caught seven batsmen and stumped 15. On the death of H. B. Cameron he took over briefly as South Africa's wicket-keeper, in a losing series against Australia. With K. G. Viljoen he established what still stands as the third-wicket record for Griqualand West—212 against Western Province in 1929–30—and his total of 54 wicket-keeping victims for Griqualand West in Currie Cup matches is unsurpassed.

NICHOLSON, Walter, who was born on April 13, 1861, died at Mexborough on September 18, 1914. On his only appearance for Yorkshire—v. Durham, at Darlington in 1892—he scored 48 and 16 and took one wicket for 12 runs; in the previous month he had made 53 and 29 and taken four wickets for 25 for Yorkshire Second XI v. Lancashire Second XI at Manchester. He was one of the founders of the Mexborough and District Cricket League.

NICHOLSON, William, D.L., J.P., of Basing Park, Hampshire, a Trustee of Lord's Cricket Ground, and one of the oldest members of the M.C.C., died at 2, South Audley Street, London, on July 25, 1909. He was born at Upper Holloway on September 2, 1824, and was in the Harrow XI for three seasons, commencing in 1841, and captain in his last. *Scores and Biographies* (iii.–39) says of him: "Height, 5 ft. 10 in., and weight, 11 st. 7 lb. Has been a most successful batsman for several years, getting his runs exceedingly fast and well in the best matches, especially about 1852, when he was not to be excelled. Is one of the best wicket-keepers in England, standing up pluckily to the fastest bowling, and has at that important post in the field received many a severe blow. Also an exceedingly fast runner between wickets, a capital judge of a short run, and is altogether an energetic cricketer. Was captain of the Harrow XI in 1843, when, by his strict management and fine play, he helped much to win both against Winchester and Eton. His elder brother, Mr. John Nicholson, played for Harrow in 1840 and 1841, and for Cambridge in 1845." Among his contemporaries at Harrow were E. M. Dewing, Arthur Haygarth, and J. Marshall. In the matches with Eton he scored four and nine, seven and 35, 11 and 0, while against Winchester his innings were four, one and 52, 21 and six. He became a member of the M.C.C. in 1845, and appeared for the Gentlemen against the Players from 1846 to 1858, and in the Canterbury Week from 1847 to 1869. For many years he played for the celebrated Clapton club, of which Messrs. Craven, Gordon and Key, and the Walker brothers were great supporters.

His most successful season was that of 1852 when he made the highest score (39 and 70) in each innings for England v. Kent at Lord's, and made 86 for Gentlemen of England v. Gentlemen of Kent at Canterbury. In the former match his side were set 156 to win and obtained them for three wickets, which was exceptional scoring for those times, especially against such bowlers as Mynn, Martingell and Willsher. Few men attended the Canterbury Week more regu-

larly than did Mr. Nicholson, who was an
enthusiastic Old Stager and one of the oldest
members of I Zingari. As a curiosity it
may be mentioned that, when keeping
wicket for M.C.C. and Ground v. Cambridge University at Fenner's in 1853, he
stumped the first three men off Mr. F.
Walker's bowling.

Great as Mr. Nicholson's skill as a player
undoubtedly was, it is probable that he will
always be best remembered for the unstinted
support he was ever ready to accord the
game. In *Cricket* of January 1886, it was told
how, when the fate of Lord's was almost in
the balance, before the sudden increase of
wealth from Eton and Harrow and University matches, Mr. Nicholson stood in the gap,
and after all England had been drawn for
subscriptions to save the ground—for few
escaped Mr. Roger Kynaston and his red
book—he advanced the money as mortgage
on a security which the outside public would
not take. Little was said about it, as men who
do such things do not talk about them, but
there is no doubt he saved Lord's from the
builders. The celebrated Mr. William Ward
did a similar thing many years before. He
drew a cheque for £5,000, and gave it to
Lord's for the lease, and as it happened this
turned out a good investment as indeed did
Mr. Nicholson's mortgage also, though he
ran the risk for the love of cricket, and the
sum advanced was a large one—a very long
way into five figures. This action on his part
should cause his name always to be gratefully
remembered, not only by members of the
Marylebone club, but by all English cricketers in whatever part of the world they may be
domiciled. His generosity enabled the old
club to purchase the freehold of Lord's: but
for him the ground might have been built
over and the M.C.C., the recognised head of
the game, have been rendered homeless. In
1879 Mr. Nicholson was elected to the presidency of the club. Although he led a very
busy life his interest in the game and his old
school was always of the strongest: in fact 50
years after he had led the Harrow XI, he
purchased a large piece of ground at Harrow
and presented it to the school.

Mr. Nicholson became M.P. for
Petersfield, Hampshire, in 1866. He lost his
seat at the General Election in 1874, but
regained it in 1880, only, however, to be
unseated again five years later. At first he
was a Liberal in politics, but subsequently a
Conservative. His portrait can be seen in the
large picture published in 1908 by Messrs.
Dickinson, of New Bond Street, entitled
"Eton v. Harrow."

NICOLSON, John Fairless William, died at
Kilkeel, County Down, Ireland, on December 18, 1935, aged 36. He had been on
the staff of Mourne Grange School for three
years. Born on July 19, 1899, he came to
England in 1921, and went up to Oxford,
where he played in the Seniors' match of
1923, and appeared for the University
against the West Indies, but failed to get his
Blue. He made a lot of runs for Oxford
Authentics and Blue Mantles, the famous
Kent club. Returning to South Africa, Nicolson became famous by scoring with I. J.
Siedle 424 for Natal's first wicket against
Orange Free State, at Bloemfontein, in the
match which extended over New Year's Day,
1927. This opening partnership set up a
record which still stands in the Currie Cup
competition, and Nicolson's 252 not out was
the highest innings at the time; but it has
been beaten since in this contest. During the
next season, Nicolson played in three Test
matches against the England XI led by Capt.
R. T. Stanyforth, his best score being 78. An
excellent left-handed bat, Nicolson had
sound defence, and when hitting freely his
best stroke was on the leg side.

NISSAR, Mahomed, who died at Lahore on
March 11, 1963, aged 52, played as a fast
bowler in six Test matches for India against
England. Tall and well-built, he was specially
dangerous with the new ball, possessing the
ability to make it swing and break back. He
twice visited England. In 1932, under the
captaincy of the Maharajah of Porbandar, he
headed the India bowling averages for first-
class matches with 71 wickets, average 18.09,
and in the only Test match that year dismissed five batsmen for 93 and one for 42. Other
good performances by Nissar on that tour
were six wickets for 32 v. Oxford University;
six for 45 v. Somerset; six for 92 v. Kent and
six for 26 in the match with Yorkshire. As a
member of the Maharaj Kumar of Vizianagram's team in 1936, he topped the Test
averages with 12 wickets at a cost of 28.58
runs each and, with 66 wickets for 25.13
apiece, proved the most successful Indian
bowler in all first-class games. He took part
in two Tests against D. R. Jardine's side in
India in 1933, taking five wickets for 90 runs
in the first innings of the opening match of
the series.

**NITSCHKE, Holmedale Carl ("Jack" or
"Slinger"),** who died in Australia on September 29, 1982, aged 77, was an attacking
left-hand batsman who played twice for Australia against South Africa in 1931–32, scor-

ing six in the first Test and 47 in the second. For several years he made enough runs for South Australia to have been chosen considerably more often for a weaker Australian side, but his best years coincided with those of Bradman, Ponsford, Woodfull, Jackson, McCabe and Kippax. In 1932–33, in two matches for South Australia against D. R. Jardine's M.C.C. side he scored 67, 28, 38 and 87 with a dash and confidence which caused the Englishmen to believe he would have done better in the Test matches than some of those who played. For four successive seasons he scored centuries for South Australia against New South Wales, carrying his bat in the last of them, at Sydney in 1933–34, for 130 out of a total of 246. In 1934–35 he was one of four batsmen—the first four in the order—to score centuries for South Australia against Queensland in Adelaide, the others being V. Y. Richardson, Lonergan and Badcock. In all first-class cricket he scored 3,320 runs (average 42.03), including nine centuries. He became, after his retirement, an outstandingly successful racehorse breeder.

NOEL, Evan Baillie, born on January 23, 1879, died in London on December 22, 1928, aged 49. A useful and orthodox batsman and slow bowler, right-handed in both respects although ambidextrous. He was in the Winchester XI in 1896 and two following years, being second in batting with 25.23 in 1897 and first with 31.64 next season. In his three matches against Eton he made 149 runs for five times out, his scores being 61 and 24, three and 51, one and nine not out. Winchester won by eight wickets in 1896 and by 51 runs a year later, but the game of 1898 was drawn. His chief success in later times was obtained for the Gentlemen of M.C.C. v. Gentlemen of Holland at Lord's in 1906, when he took 17 wickets—eight for 89 and nine for 77: one man was run out in the first innings. In the second he bowled unchanged with "W.G." whose analysis was one for 69. But for ill-health, with which he had to contend for many years, he would doubtless have made his mark in matches of note. In 1926 he was the author of *Winchester College Cricket*, a most interesting and authoritative work. He was an expert player at many ball games, about which he wrote in delightful fashion, both during the time, 1903 to 1909, that he was Sporting Editor of *The Times* and later. At racquets he represented both Winchester and Cambridge, and, by beating B. S. Foster, won the Amateur Championship in 1907, while at Royal Tennis he played

for Cambridge and also won the M.C.C. Silver Prize in 1908 and the Manchester Invitation Handicap in 1912. Since 1914 he had been secretary of Queen's Club.

NOEL, Jack, who made 18 of the 23 runs scored in the first innings of the match between South Australia and Victoria at Melbourne in 1883, died on January 9, 1938, in his 80th year.

NOONAN, David James, born on January 8, 1877, died in Sydney on March 8, 1929, aged 52. Useful both as batsman (left-handed) and bowler, he played for New South Wales. He was a member of the N.S.W. team which visited New Zealand in 1895–96, when he had a batting average of 35.50 and was second in bowling with 20 wickets for 16.45 runs each.

NORDEN, Richard Watts, who died at Johannesburg on February 20, 1952, aged 73, played as a slow left-arm bowler for Transvaal between 1904 and 1907. In a Currie Cup match against Rhodesia at Johannesburg in 1905 he took 12 wickets for 33 runs, his second innings analysis reading 12—8—12—8.

NORMAN, Frederick Henry, born at Bromley on January 23, 1839, died in London on October 6, 1916. He belonged altogether to a cricketing family, his father, two brothers and a son having (like himself) all been in the Eton XI: he was, too, a nephew of the famous Mr. Herbert Jenner-Fust and related by marriage with the Barnard, Bonham-Carter, Dyke, Nepean and Wathen families. He was in the Eton XI in 1854 and three following years, being captain in 1857, and in that of Cambridge for three seasons, commencing 1858, and captain in 1860. In his matches against Harrow and Winchester he made no long scores, but against Oxford in 1858, when he obtained his Blue as a Freshman, he played a first innings of 43. He was a free and attractive batsman, hitting well and successfully, and making many large scores. At Cambridge in 1858 he made 100 for the University v. Cambridge Town club, and at Lord's, in 1859, 103 for Gentlemen of Kent v. Gentlemen of England. He played in excellent style, perhaps rather too much forward for the rough wickets of his time, when the ground at Lord's was fiery and dangerous. On modern wickets he would doubtless have been a great success. He had been coached by Martingell. In the field he was generally long-leg and cover-point. He was a member of the original committee of the Kent County C.C., formed at Maidstone in 1859, and also one of the original trustees of the Mynn Memorial Benevolent Institution for Kentish cricketers. Between 1858 and 1864 he appeared in 10 matches for Kent, and at Lord's in 1858 assisted the Gentlemen against the Players. He used sometimes to play for the Home Circuit—he was admitted a barrister, Inns of Court, in 1863—which had some very good cricketers, Robert Marsham, R. A. Bayford, etc., and some famous men like Sir George Honyman, A. L. Smith and the Hon. A. F. Thesiger, who all became judges. In one of the Home Circuit's matches, at Maidstone, Mr. Norman got over 100 and to commemorate the event Honyman (with whom he read law) gave him some law books: a bat would perhaps have been more appropriate. Mr. Norman had been a member of the M.C.C. since 1863 and served on the committee of the club from 1866 to 1868.

NORNABLE, Charles Ernest, who died in hospital on April 21, 1970, took five wickets for 72 runs for Derbyshire against Sussex at Derby in 1909, but was prevented by business claims from making further appearances for the county.

NORRIS, Oswald Thomas, who died at Tilgate, Sussex, on March 22, 1973, aged 89, was for two years captain at Charterhouse—in 1901 and 1902. Going up to Oxford, he was asked to play against Cambridge in his second year, largely on the strength of a fine 87 against Surrey at the Oval, but, being injured just before the match, had to stand down. Next year, 1905, he started well, but struck a bad patch and lost his place. He was thus one of the few who have been "given their Blue" and never played in the Varsity match. He did, however, captain Oxford at Association football. He was father-in-law of M. J. C. Allom.

NORTH, T. H., well known in New Zealand cricket, died at Christchurch in October 1942. He played for Canterbury from 1893 to 1897, being specially useful as a fast-medium bowler. Against Otago in 1896 he took five wickets for 13 runs, but in a low scoring match Canterbury were beaten by nine wickets. For his club—Lancaster Park—he did many good performances. His son is chairman of the Canterbury Cricket Association management committee.

NORTHCOTE, Dr. Percy, played occasion-ally for Middlesex in 1888 and for Kent in 1889 and 1895. A prominent member of the Beckenham club. A good free right-handed batsman, he bowled slow left. In 1894 against the first South African team to visit England he made 42 not out and took 12 wickets at less than 7 runs each for Chatham and District. Born on September 18, 1866, he died on March 3, 1934, in his 68th year.

NORTHWAY, Reginald Philip, aged 27, was killed in a motorcar accident when travelling with Bakewell, his Northamptonshire colleague, after the match with Derbyshire at Chesterfield, on August 25, 1936. It was the last engagement on their county's programme and the victims of the accident were Northamptonshire's opening batsmen. Bakewell, who scored 241 not out in the second innings, received serious injuries from which he made a remarkable recovery; Northway was found dead in a ditch by the roadside, near Kibworth, Leicestershire. A good, steady bat, Northway also excelled as a fieldsman in the country. This was his first season with Northamptonshire. Previously he assisted Somerset.

NORTON, Dr. Selby, who played as an emergency man for Kent v. Nottinghamshire, at Trent Bridge, in 1863, was born at Town Malling on September 13, 1836, and died at Brixton on November 11, 1906. Two of his brothers, Messrs. W. S. and Bradbury Norton, and a first cousin, Mr. W. O. J. Norton, also played for Kent on various occasions.

NORTON, William South, born at Town Malling on June 8, 1831, died in the Charterhouse, London, on March 19, 1916. *Scores and Biographies* said: "He is a very steady batsman, combined with occasional hard hitting, especially to square-leg. Bowls round armed of middle speed also, and in the field is often point." He played for Kent in 63 matches between 1849 and 1870, scoring 1,378 runs with an average of 13.50 and taking 20 wickets at a cost of about 22 runs each. His two highest innings for the county were in 1866—120 not out v. Sussex and 59 v. Surrey, both at Gravesend. He was captain of the side for some years, and in 1859 became joint hon. secretary with Lord North to the old Kent County club, formed that year at Maidstone: the latter position he retained until the re-formation of the county club in December, 1870, but Lord North resigned after holding office for one season only. For the Gentlemen of Kent Mr. Norton's best score was 96 not out v. Gentlemen of Sussex at Brighton in 1864, and in a match between the same sides at Tunbridge Wells in 1861 he took seven wickets for 19 runs. Two of his brothers, Messrs. Bradbury and Selby Norton, and two cousins (Messrs. W. O. J. Norton and Thomas Selby) also appeared occasionally for Kent. Mr. Norton wrote an important chapter in the *History of Kent County Cricket*.

NOTHLING, Dr. Otto Ernst, who died on September 26, 1965, at Brisbane, aged 65, played for Australia as a medium-paced bowler at Sydney in the second Test of the 1928–29 series against the England team led by A. P. F. Chapman, but did not take a wicket. He made 14 appearances for New South Wales in Sheffield Shield engagements, scoring 678 runs, average 27.12, and taking 24 wickets for 44.79 runs each. He had been president of the Queensland Cricket Association. When at Sydney University, he achieved a reputation as an athlete and, as a Rugby Union full-back, played against New Zealand.

NOURSE, Arthur David, known as the G.O.M. of South African cricket, died at Port Elizabeth on July 8, 1948, aged 70. During a first-class career extending from 1897 to 1936, Nourse scored over 14,000 runs and took 305 wickets. He made 45 consecutive appearances in Test matches for South Africa from 1902 to 1924 and also represented his country against the Australian Imperial Forces in 1919–20 and against S. B. Joel's touring team in 1924–25.

Born at Croydon, Surrey, on January 26, 1878, Nourse went to South Africa as a drummer-boy with the West Riding Regiment in 1895 and two years later made his first appearance in first-class cricket in a Currie Cup match at Johannesburg, scoring 61 for Natal against Eastern Province. He was a little over 24 when he first played in a representative match, scoring 72 against the Australians, who made a short tour of South Africa on the way home from England in 1902. Nourse toured England with South African teams in 1907, 1912 and 1924 and also visited Australia in 1910–11. In his own country he represented Natal from 1897 to 1925, Transvaal in the next two seasons and Western Province from 1927–28 to 1935–36. In his last big match, when 58, he scored 55 for Western Province against an Australian side which included O'Reilly. A left-hander, both with bat and ball, Nourse possessed enormous hands which helped considerably

to establish his reputation as a brilliant slip fieldsman. He occasionally did well with slow to medium bowling, but made his great reputation as a batsman. He hit seven double hundreds, with a highest innings of 304 not out for Natal against Transvaal at Johannesburg in the season 1919–20. This stood as a South African record for 20 years. When almost 55 he scored 219 not out for Western Province against Natal at Cape Town in 1931–32. Despite his large number of appearances he met with surprisingly little success in Test matches, hitting only one hundred—111 against Australia at Johannesburg in November 1921. Probably his best Test innings was in 1906 at Johannesburg, where he played the leading part in the first victory by South Africa over England. South Africa needed 45 to win when Sherwell, the last man, joined Nourse. Between them they knocked off the runs and South Africa won an exciting match by one wicket, Nourse being 93 not out.

His great achievements were carried on by his son, Dudley Nourse, the present captain of South Africa. "Dave" Nourse was not christened "David," but was always known by that name and ultimately adopted the initial "D." During a varied career he was a soldier, a railway guard, billiard marker, saloon keeper, commercial traveller, manager of an athletic outfitters and finally coach to Cape Town University. He also represented Natal at Association and Rugby football and rowed for the Durban Rowing club.

NOURSE, Arthur Dudley, who died in Durban on August 14, 1981, aged 70, made with his father A.W., popularly known as "Dave," perhaps the greatest of all father and son cricketing combinations. "Dave" played 45 times for South Africa between 1902 and 1924 and Dudley 34 times between 1935 and 1951. Of South Africa's 100 Test matches between the first and the last of these years there were only 21 in which there was not a Nourse in their side.

Dudley first appeared for Natal in 1931 and quickly established himself as a batsman of outstanding promise. Thickset (like his father), with immensely strong forearms, he was as capable of superb stroke-play, as when he scored 231 in only 289 minutes against Australia at Johannesburg in 1935–36, an Australian side that contained Grimmett and O'Reilly at the height of their powers, as of unyielding defence, as when, in the "timeless" Test at Durban in 1938–39, he took six hours to make 103. With the Second

World War coming when it did, Dudley Nourse never toured Australia. The first of his three visits to England was in in 1935 when, although finishing the tour with an aggregate of 1,681 (only E. A. B. Rowan scored more) he made a slow start to his Test career. After failing at Nottingham and Lord's he was dropped for Headingley, before coming back and scoring 29, 53 not out, 32 and 34 in the last two Tests. That winter came the first of his two Test double-hundreds. Against W. R. Hammond's M.C.C. team in South Africa in 1938–39 he scored 422 runs for an average of 60.28. Following war service in the Middle East he was back in England in 1947, when his contribution to a golden summer was a Test aggregate of 621 runs at an average of 69 and a record third-wicket partnership of 319 with his captain, Alan Melville, in the first Test at Trent Bridge. For England's next visit to South Africa, under F. G. Mann in 1948–49, he captained South Africa for the first time, Melville having retired and Nourse being his natural successor. In no way did the extra responsibility affect his form: if anything the reverse was so. With centuries in the third Test at Cape Town and the fourth at Johannesburg he scored 536 runs in the series for an average of 76.57, the best figures on either side. The following season, when Australia visited South Africa, he scored 114 against them in the second Test in Cape Town and once again headed South Africa's batting averages.

Nourse's last Test series was when he took the South African side to England in 1951 and, within a few months of his 41st birthday, enjoyed perhaps his finest hour, scoring 208 in the first innings of the first Test, against an attack comprising Bedser (then in his prime), Bailey, Brown, Wardle and Tattersall. This great effort led to South Africa gaining their first Test victory since 1935. Although England won three of the next four Tests, Nourse, upon his retirement soon afterwards, could look back upon a playing career of outstanding distinction.

Not only was he one of the most gifted and successful of all South African cricketers; before and after the War he would have had a place in a World XI as well. His special glory was the square-cut; but there was no shot that he could not play and he was as nimble and punishing against spin bowling as he was fearless against speed. In all first-class cricket he scored 12,472 runs, including 41 100s, at an average of 51.37. His Test figures were 2,960 runs, average 53.81. He hit six double-hundreds, one fewer than his father, who holds the South African record. Quietly spoken, firm of purpose and a man with the highest personal standards, Dudley Nourse was a figure of national respect in South Africa. After his retirement as a player, he was a selector for some years and managed D. J. McGlew's side to England in 1960. An autobiography, *Cricket in the Blood*, appeared in 1949.

CAREER FIGURES

	Matches	Innings	Not Outs	Runs	Highest Innings	Average	100s	Catches
1931–32	7	11	0	525	105	47.72	1	2
1932–33	5	7	1	232	77	38.66	0	1
1933–34	5	7	0	268	110	38.28	1	9
1934–35	5	7	1	322	114	53.66	1	2
1935	30	46	5	1,681	160*	41.00	4	21
1935–36	7	14	2	653	231	54.41	2	0
1936–37	5	6	1	846	260*	169.20	4	4
1937–38	6	9	1	464	120	58.00	2	2
1938–39	7	12	2	510	120	51.00	2	2
1939–40	5	7	0	453	136	64.71	1	4
1942–43	1	2	1	171	141*	171.00	1	0
1945–46	4	5	1	195	81	39.00	0	4
1946–47	9	12	0	775	192	64.58	2	8
1947	23	36	2	1,453	205*	42.73	4	26
1947–48	8	11	2	864	214*	96.00	4	12
1948–49	9	16	3	877	129*	67.46	3	5
1949–50	9	16	2	607	114	43.35	2	5
1950–51	6	7	0	514	124	73.42	4	7
1951	18	28	2	673	208	25.88	1	11
1952–53	6	10	1	389	155	43.22	2	9
Totals	175	269	27	12,472	260*	51.37	41	134

* Signifies not out.

NUGAWELA, Major Edward A., who died on July 5, 1972, aged 82, was a member of the Royal College XI in 1917 and 1918. He played under the captaincy of L. C. Khoo, the only Burman to play cricket in Ceylon. Nugawela became a member of the State Council and after Independence a Minister of Education in the first Ceylon Parliament.

NUNES, Robert Karl, who died in St. Mary's Hospital, London, on July 22, 1958, aged 64, captained West Indies in England in 1929, the year in which they were accorded Test match status. In the three games against England he scored 87 runs and in all first-class matches during the tour he hit 798 runs, average 23.47, with 127 not out from the Glamorgan bowling at Swansea his highest innings. Educated at Dulwich College, he was a member of the Jamaican Board of Control from its inception in 1926 and president of the West Indies Board of Control from 1945 to 1952. In 1951 he was made a C.B.E. for public services, chiefly as chairman of the Agricultural Societies Loan Board.

NUPEN, Eiulf Peter, always known as "Buster," died in Johannesburg, his native place, on January 29, 1977, aged 75. Although in a Test match career for South Africa which extended from 1921 to 1935, his 50 wickets cost him 35.76 runs each, he was regarded at his best as one of the greatest bowlers on a mat there has ever been. So ineffective, however, was he on turf that when the M.C.C. were in South Africa in 1930–31, although in the first Test he took 11 for 150 and in the second innings of the fourth, when admittedly the English batsmen were hitting recklessly in a vain endeavour to force a win, six for 46, he was omitted from the third and fifth Tests, the first two ever to be played on grass in South Africa.

Similarly in this country in 1924, when, after his record at home, he was expected to be one of the main match winners, he was a complete failure. It is true that he was handicapped by injury, but the general impression was that, even when fit, he was n(formidable. He never toured abroad aga' What he could do in his own country ' shown against the Hon. L. H. Tenny' unofficial side in 1924–25, which was a' a strong England "A" side: in four resentative matches he took 37 wi(11.45.

In Currie Cup matches Nupen extraordinary record for the Trans' wickets at 12.75. In nine of his 28

them he took over 10 wickets and against Griqualand West in 1931–32 took nine for 4P in an innings and 16 for 136 in the match. H first attracted attention by taking six for for the Transvaal against the great Aus' lian side of 1921. Handicapped by havin(an eye at the age of four, he wa' normally regarded as a serious ba' However, in the third Test against F in 1927–28, he made 51 and 69, he captain, H. G. Deane, putting on (eighth wicket in the first innings a the seventh in the second.

Tall and strongly built, he ' medium right-hand round the ' the mat his off-break spun came off very quick and lift' leg-cutter, with which he va obvious and less accura Geary's, but none the less

When England were 1930–31, Deane, a gr' tired, and though, reappeared, did not enough practice for captained the side a ing his biggest per' captained in the r resigned, being and for the fc Cameron, dou' Nupen would a grass wick'

NUTTER, in the L Novemb He was shire a

OAF Au' sp' h'
'

College XI, he was described as "A fine bat, with a good defence; and a good straight bowler."

OATES, Archer Williamson, who died on December 31, 1968, aged 60, played as a right-arm fast bowler for Nottinghamshire in a few matches between 1931 and 1933. His opportunities were limited by the presence in the county team of the England pair, H. Larwood and W. Voce, and he left the staff to join the Nottingham City Police Force. He retired with the rank of inspector in 1964. He was a nephew of T. W. Oates, the long-serving Nottinghamshire wicket-keeper.

OATES, Capt. Lawrence Edward Grace, who died on March 17, 1912, his 32nd birthday, whilst returning from the South Pole with Capt. Scott's ill-fated party, played cricket for his House as a lower boy at Eton.

OATES, Thomas William, who died at his home at Eastwood, Nottinghamshire, on June 18, 1949, aged 73, gave Nottinghamshire splendid service as a player for 28 years, from 1897 to 1925. For some years afterwards he was the county scorer and subsequently he became a first-class umpire. In wicket-keeping Oates was directly responsible for the dismissal of 989 batsmen (756 catches and 233 stumpings), his best performance being against Middlesex at Trent Bridge in 1906 when he caught nine, six in an innings, and stumped one. Never more than an ordinary batsman, he scored 6,091 runs, average 12.08, but at times he played valuable innings, such as his highest, 88 against Kent, in 1920. Oates was chosen for Players against Gentlemen at Lord's in 1907.

OATES, William, who played a few times for Yorkshire in 1874 and 1875, died on December 9, 1940, aged 88.

OATES, Lieut.-Col. William Coape, D.S.O., died in a nursing home on February 20, 1942, aged 79. Twelfth man for Harrow in 1879, he played a few times in 1881 and 1882 for Nottinghamshire, a very powerful side at that period.

OATLEY, James N., who died in Sydney in December, 1925, aged 80, played against the second English team which visited Australia, in 1863–64, and for many years was identified with the Warwick C.C. He was described as: "A very fair bat with plenty of style and wrist play, but wants confidence: is a good long-stop and fair field." He

appeared twice for New South Wales v. Victoria.

O'BRIEN, Robert, who had played for Queensland as a medium-paced right-hand bowler, died in October, 1922.

O'BRIEN, Sir Timothy Carew, Third Bart., who at the time of his passing was the Senior Test player in England against Australia, died in the Isle of Man on December 9, 1948, aged 87. Born in Dublin on November 5, 1861, he was educated at Downside, always a good cricket school, and he became qualified for Middlesex when at St. Charles College, Notting Hill, but he did not reveal his full batting ability until going up to Oxford in 1884. Taking this step for the purpose of cricket, he fulfilled his ambition by at once being given his Blue by M. C. Kemp, his senior by about two months.

He started against the Australians and, playing a brilliant innings of 92, was largely responsible for defeating the visitors by seven wickets, the only victory gained by Oxford over an Australian team. With 72 for M.C.C. at Lord's he showed to equal advantage and again helped to beat the Australians, but when he played for England against Australia at Manchester that season and at Lord's four years later, he did little in low scoring matches.

During a long career lasting until 1898, O'Brien was one of the most attractive and valuable amateur batsmen in the country. He used his height and powerful build with great effect in forcing the game and played many notable innings for Middlesex, M.C.C. and Gentlemen. He went to Australia with the team captained by G. F. Vernon in 1887–88 and to South Africa with Lord Hawke's side in the winter of 1895.

Strangely enough he failed utterly in his first University match, being bowled in each innings without scoring; yet Oxford won by seven wickets, but next year, 1885, when Cambridge won by a similar margin, O'Brien made 44 and 28. By a remarkable coincidence Sir C. A. Smith, who died 11 days after O'Brien, played in the same matches. He failed to score in 1884, being twice not out, and took two wickets; next year Smith scored 23 in a valuable last-wicket stand and with six wickets for 81 assisted materially in the Cambridge victory.

For Middlesex O'Brien scored 7,222 runs at an average of 30, with highest innings 202 against Sussex in 1895 at Hove, where he and R. Slade Lucas put on 338 in three hours 20 minutes. A more notable performance was against Yorkshire at Lord's in June 1889, when Middlesex were set to make 280 in little more than three and a half hours. For a time everything pointed to a tame finish, but with about 90 minutes left and 151 wanted, O'Brien went in and hit up 100 in 80 minutes; the last 83 runs came in 35 minutes and Middlesex won by four wickets, 10 minutes from time. This brilliant display followed 92 by O'Brien in the first innings. That match created a record for heavy scoring in England, the aggregate being 1,295 runs; there were then five balls to the over.

I saw O'Brien play a fine innings of 110 not out at Taunton against Somerset in August 1894 and Middlesex won a great match by 19 runs—that was the first occasion on which P. F. Warner appeared for Middlesex. Some years after giving up first-class cricket, O'Brien, when nearly 53 years of age, played for Lionel Robinson's XI against Oxford at Attleborough in 1914 and scored 90 and 111 in splendid style.

Sir Timothy married in 1885 Gundrede Annette Teresa, daughter of Sir Humphrey de Trafford, and there were two sons and eight daughters of the marriage. The elder son, Timothy John Aloysius, was killed in action during the First World War, and the baronetcy passed to the younger son Robert Rollo Gillespie O'Brien.—H.P.

O'BRIEN, Lieut. Timothy John Aloysius (R.F.A.), killed on August 7, 1916, aged 23, was elder son of Sir T. C. O'Brien, Bart. He was in the Beaumont College XI and also played for I Zingari and Free Foresters.

OCHSE, A. L., died at Middlebury, South Africa, in May, 1949, aged 49. A fast bowler, he played for Eastern Province and in 1929 visited England with H. G. Deane's team. During the tour he took 52 wickets and headed the Test bowling averages with 10 wickets at a cost of 31.70 runs apiece. He played in three Test matches, one of them against England in South Africa in 1927. He bore the leading part in the dismissal of the M.C.C. side for 49 by Eastern Province at Port Elizabeth in 1928, taking five wickets for 31 runs. This effort was not enough to bring victory, M.C.C. winning by 10 wickets.

O'CONNOR, J. A., who toured England in 1909 with M. A. Noble's Australian team, died at Sydney in November, 1941, aged 66. A rather slow bowler, he relied on speed from the pitch and did not find the comparatively slow turf in England suitable to his methods. He played only in the first of the five Test matches, and that was the one which England won before Australia recovered and carried off the honours. Until late in the season he seldom accomplished anything notable against any strong batting side, but on the whole tour O'Connor took 85 wickets at 19 runs apiece. He sometimes played for Australia at home, and altogether in Test cricket his bowling record showed 13 wickets, average 29 runs each. He played for both New South Wales and South Australia. His best performance was seven wickets for 36 runs at Melbourne in January 1909; thanks to his effort, South Australia, after being 219 runs behind on the first innings, snatched a victory by 15 runs.

O'CONNOR, Jack, who died in the Forest Hospital, Buckhurst Hill, on February 22, 1977, aged 79, was a very good county cricketer who was for years on the edge of Test cricket. He played once against South Africa in 1929 and that winter took part in three matches for the M.C.C. in the West Indies, which *Wisden* then called "Representative matches," but which are now included in the Test records, though the English side could not possibly be described as more than England "A." After a modest start for Essex in 1921, O'Connor gained a fairly regular place next year and scored his first 100, but it was in August 1923 that he first attracted much attention; in four consecutive matches he played innings of 111 not out, 128, 93 and 99. He remained one of the mainstays of the side until 1939. In all first-class cricket he made 28,575 runs with an average of 34.95, scored 72 centuries, including at least one against every other county and both Universities, reached his 1,000 on 16 occasions and in 1926, taking 93 wickets as well, narrowly missed the double.

He bowled slow leg-breaks and off-breaks mixed and had the advantage of looking a good deal simpler than he was. At any rate in his career he took 557 wickets. A small man, very quick on his feet, he was a good driver on both sides of the wicket and a fine hooker, but he was more liable to spells of failure than a top-class batsman should be and had moreover an unconcealed distaste for fast bowling, nor was he outstanding in the field. He was a great player of slow spin, but the popular theory that he was Freeman's master is hardly borne out by figures. Certainly when set he made Freeman look very ordinary, but in his 52 innings against Kent between 1922 and 1936, though he made seven centuries, his average was only 31 and on 15 occasions Freeman had him out under 30.

After his retirement he was for many years coach at Eton and in 1946 and 1947 played for Buckinghamshire. Later he coached at Chigwell. He came of good cricket stock. His father had played with success for both Cambridgeshire and Derbyshire and bowled for many years in the nets at Fenner's. His uncle, Herbert Carpenter, was for years one of the mainstays of Essex batting and represented the Players, while his great uncle, Robert Carpenter, had been one of the leading batsmen in England in the 1860s.

JACK O'CONNOR—Season by Season
By STANLEY CONDER

Season			Matches	Innings	Not Outs	Runs	Highest Innings	Average
In England								
1921	..	..	4	6	2	25	13	6.25
1922	..	..	24	33	7	414	102*	15.92
1923	..	..	28	52	3	1,218	128	24.85
1924	..	..	27	47	5	997	78	23.73
1925	..	..	29	50	3	1,070	142	22.76
1926	..	..	32	55	4	1,402	84	27.49
1927	..	..	32	49	3	1,357	139*	29.50
1928	..	..	31	53	4	2,325	157	47.44
1929	..	..	32	54	3	2,288	168*	44.86
1930	..	..	29	45	7	1,601	138	42.13
1931	..	..	30	47	3	1,634	129	37.13
1932	..	..	21	36	8	1,350	119	48.21
1933	..	..	30	52	5	2,077	237	44.19
1934	..	..	30	49	7	2,350	248	55.95
1935	..	..	30	55	4	1,603	139	31.43
1936	..	..	28	47	3	1,343	127	30.52
1937	..	..	28	52	3	1,475	192	30.10
1938	..	..	30	50	3	1,839	152	39.12
1939	..	..	30	48	2	1,716	194	37.30
Hon. L. H. Tennyson's XI in Jamaica								
1926–27	..	..	3	5	0	296	154	59.20
Sir Julian Cahn's team in Jamaica								
1928–29	..	..	3	6	0	154	63	25.66
M.C.C. team in West Indies								
1929–30	..	..	10	15	1	341	67	24.35
Totals	..	..	541	906	80	28,875	248	34.95

J. O'CONNOR IN TEST CRICKET

			Tests	Innings	Not Outs	Runs	Highest Innings	Average
v. South Africa								
1929	..	..	1	2	0	11	11	5.50
v. West Indies								
1929–30	..	..	3	5	0	142	51	28.40
Totals	..	..	4	7	0	153	51	21.85

Centuries (72)

102*	Essex v. Northamptonshire at Northampton, 1922.
128	Essex v. Gloucestershire at Cheltenham, 1923.
111*	Essex v. Hampshire at Leyton, 1923.
142	Essex v. Leicestershire at Leicester, 1925.
111	Essex v. Glamorgan at Leyton, 1925.
139*	Essex v. Leicestershire at Leyton, 1927.
124	Essex v. Nottinghamshire at Trent Bridge, 1927.
107	Essex v. Kent at Gravesend, 1927.
101	Essex v. Worcestershire at Leyton, 1927.
157	Essex v. Oxford University at Colchester, 1928.

*Signifies not out.

J. O'CONNOR, Centuries (72)—*continued*

130*	Essex v. Yorkshire at Leyton, 1928.
124	Essex v. Gloucestershire at Chelmsford, 1928.
123	Essex v. Leicestershire at Leyton, 1928.
123	Essex v. Middlesex at Leyton, 1928.
101	Essex v. Somerset at Chelmsford, 1928.
168*	Essex v. Cambridge University at Cambridge, 1929.
157	Essex v. Hampshire at Leyton, 1929.
151	Essex v. Surrey at Leyton, 1929.
123	Essex v. Warwickshire at Chelmsford, 1929.
116	Essex v. Kent at Folkestone, 1929.
110	Essex v. Leicestershire at Southend, 1929.
109	Essex v. Glamorgan at Colchester, 1929.
106	Essex v. Surrey at the Oval, 1929.
102	Essex v. Kent at Leyton, 1929.
138 } 120* }	Essex v. Gloucestershire at Bristol, 1930.
119	Essex v. Warwickshire at Leyton, 1930.
104	Essex v. Middlesex at Lord's, 1930.
101	Essex v. Derbyshire at Derby, 1930.
129	Essex v. New Zealanders at Leyton, 1931.
122	Essex v. Lancashire at Clacton, 1931.
119	Essex v. Kent at Colchester, 1931.
118*	Essex v. Northamptonshire at Northampton, 1931.
108	Essex v. Leicestershire at Leyton, 1931.
100	Essex v. Kent at Gravesend, 1931.
119	Essex v. Sussex at Eastbourne, 1932.
115	Essex v. Surrey at Leyton, 1932.
112*	Essex v. Glamorgan at Cardiff, 1932.
104	Essex v. Surrey at the Oval, 1932.
237	Essex v. Somerset at Leyton, 1933.
140	Essex v. Gloucestershire at Clacton, 1933.
130	Essex v. Hampshire at Bournemouth, 1933.
122*	Essex v. Warwickshire at Edgbaston, 1933.
115	Essex v. Hampshire at Leyton, 1933.
102*	Essex v. Lancashire at Leyton, 1933.
248	Essex v. Surrey at Brentwood, 1934.
174	Essex v. Leicestershire at Leicester, 1934.
143	Essex v. Surrey at the Oval, 1934.
112	Essex v. Sussex at Hove, 1934.
106	Essex v. Middlesex at Lord's, 1934.
105*	Essex v. Kent at Brentwood, 1934.
103	Essex v. Northamptonshire at Northampton, 1934.
102*	Essex v. Gloucestershire at Westcliff, 1934.
101	Essex v. Hampshire at Portsmouth, 1934.
139	Essex v. Kent at Ilford, 1935.
127	Essex v. Sussex at Hove, 1936.
111	Essex v. Nottinghamshire at Clacton, 1936.
100	Essex v. Kent at Southend, 1936.
192	Essex v. Northamptonshire at Colchester, 1937.
111	Essex v. Cambridge University at Brentwood, 1937.
107	Essex v. Somerset at Ilford, 1937.
152	Essex v. Sussex at Hove, 1938.
130	Essex v. Gloucestershire at Brentwood, 1938.
129	Essex v. Yorkshire at Ilford, 1938.
122	Essex v. Middlesex at Lord's, 1938.
115*	Essex v. Northamptonshire at Rushden, 1938.
113	Essex v. Kent at Gravesend, 1938.
194	Essex v. Nottinghamshire at Trent Bridge, 1939.

* Signifies not out.

J. O'CONNOR IN TEST CRICKET Centuries (72)—*continued*

128	Essex v. Middlesex at Lord's, 1939.
122	Essex v. Hampshire at Brentwood, 1939.
118*	Essex v. Worcestershire at Chelmsford, 1939.
154	Tennyson's team v. Jamaica at Sabina Park, Kingston, 1927.

J. O'Connor has shared in the following large partnerships:

For the Second Wicket

219	With J. A. Cutmore for Essex v. Derbyshire at Derby, 1930.
211	With D. F. Pope for Essex v. Warwickshire at Leyton, 1930.
206	With J. A. Cutmore for Essex v. Surrey at the Oval, 1929.
203	With C. Bray for Essex v. Middlesex at Leyton, 1928.

For the Third Wicket

333	With R. M. Taylor for Essex v. Northamptonshire at Colchester, 1937.
250	With A. C. Russell for Essex v. Leicestershire at Leyton, 1927.
233	With A. C. Russell for Essex v. Gloucestershire at Chelmsford, 1928.
225	With A. V. Avery for Essex v. Middlesex at Lord's, 1939.
216	With J. A. Cutmore for Essex v. Surrey at Leyton, 1932.
206	With M. S. Nichols for Essex v. Kent at Southend, 1936.
203	With J. A. Cutmore for Essex v. Hampshire at Bournemouth, 1933.

For the Fourth Wicket

271	With T. N. Pearce for Essex v. Lancashire at Clacton, 1931.
210	With M. S. Nichols for Essex v. Hampshire at Leyton, 1929.
202	With E. Hendren for M.C.C. v. British Guiana at Georgetown, 1929–30.

For the Fifth Wicket

287	With C. T. Ashton for Essex v. Surrey at Brentwood, 1934.
207	With R. M. Taylor for Essex v. Nottinghamshire at Trent Bridge, 1939.

For the Sixth Wicket

206	With J. W. H. T. Douglas for Essex v. Gloucestershire at Cheltenham, 1923.

In bowling, J. O'Connor took 557 wickets at a cost of 18,335 runs with an average of 32.91 per wicket.
Twice he took 10 wickets in a match as follows.
10 for 103 v. Leicestershire at Leicester in 1926.
10 for 160 v. New Zealanders at Leyton in 1927.

*Signifies not out.

ODD, Montagu, who died at Sutton, Surrey, on June 11, 1951, aged 82, used to make cricket bats by hand for Dr. W. G. Grace at a guinea apiece. He was at work in his little shop a few days before his death.

ODELL, 2nd Lieut. William Ward (Sherwood Foresters), born November 5, 1885; missing, believed killed, October, 1917.

Military Cross. Had been wounded. For several seasons Odell was one of the best bowlers in the Leicestershire XI. He was right-handed and bowled medium-pace. He met with marked success for Gentlemen against Players at the Oval in 1905, taking four wickets for 86 runs and six for 54. Some of his best performances were:

8 wkts. for 20 runs, Leicestershire v. M.C.C. and G., at Lord's	.. ..	1906
8 wkts. for 40 runs, Leicestershire v. Yorkshire, at Hull	.. .. ..	1907
6 wkts. for 15 runs, Leicestershire v. Derbyshire, at Chesterfield	.. .. ..	1905
8 wkts. for 20 runs, Leicestershire v. M.C.C. and G., at Lord's	.. ..	1906
4 wkts. for 9 runs, Leicestershire v. Northamptonshire, at Northampton	..	1907
5 wkts. for 10 runs, Leicestershire v. Essex, at Leyton	.. .. ..	1908
3 wkts. in 3 balls, London County v. M.C.C. and G., at Lord's	.. ..	1904
3 wkts. in 3 balls, Leicestershire v. Northamptonshire, at Leicester	.. ..	1908

For London County v. M.C.C. and G., at Lord's, in 1904, he at one period took seven wkts. for nine runs in 58 balls.

OGDEN, Dr. Edward Russell, who died on May 15, 1913, at Chicago, was born at Oakville, Canada, June 17, 1862, and educated at Upper Canada College, Toronto, where he was in the XI four years, commencing 1876, and captain the last three. He played for Canada against the United States in 1881, 1883, and 1884, captained the Canadian team which visited England in 1887, and led the Chicago team for a number of years. Whilst on tour in this country he scored 701 runs with an average of 23.37, his highest innings being 133 v. Gentlemen of Hampshire, and took 91 wickets for 16 runs apiece. He was clearly the best all-round player in the side, and bowled medium-pace righthand and batted left.

O'GORMAN, Joe G., who died at Weybridge on August 26, 1974, aged 84, was famous as the other half of a comedy act with brother Dave, but he always delighted in his cricket adventures with Surrey, which included batting with Jack Hobbs. This gave him as much pleasure as seeing his name in lights on Broadway. An all-rounder, he might well have made his mark in the game had he chosen. He played in three Championship matches for the county in 1927, sharing with Andy Sandham a partnership of 119 in 65 minutes, against Essex. O'Gorman hit 42 of those runs, with Sandham scoring altogether 230. A slow bowler, he took a wicket with his first ball in County Cricket against Glamorgan at the Oval when he dismissed W. E. Bates, the opening batsman. For many years he and his brother played club cricket for Richmond for which club he took over 1,500 wickets.

O'HANLON, William J., who died at Sydney in July, 1940, aged 77 years, kept wicket for New South Wales from 1884 to 1886, showing good form in inter-colonial matches.

OHLSON, F. H., for many years a prominent figure in Auckland cricket and Rugby football circles, especially on the administrative side of these games, died on May 20, 1942, aged 74. In representative cricket his best efforts were 59 not out against the New South Wales side which toured New Zealand in 1896, and 49 the same season against Wellington. He played also against other touring teams from Queensland, Melbourne, and Lord Hawke's side captained by P. F. Warner in 1902–03. He made many runs for the Parnell club.

O'KEEFFE, Frank Aloysius, born at Waverley, Sydney, on May 11, 1896, died on March 26, 1924, at the New End Hospital, Hampstead, of peritonitis, at the early age of 27. A brilliant batsman and field as well as a very useful slow right-handed bowler, a great future seemed in store for him. He had performed splendidly in Australia before coming to England, and had he lived, would have been qualified for Lancashire by residence last June. Our climate, unfortunately, did not suit him, and he was never in the best of health while in this country. After playing for Waverley C.C. he appeared for Paddington for two years under M. A. Noble's captaincy, and for New South Wales against Queensland in 1920–21 he scored 83 at Sydney and four and 72 at Brisbane. Settling in Melbourne, where he thought his skill would be better appreciated, he enjoyed a most successful season in 1921–22. In succession he made 87 and 79 for Victoria v. New South Wales at Sydney, 177 and 144 for Rest of Australia v. the Australian XI of 1921 in Iredale's benefit match on the same ground, and 180 for Victoria v. South Australia at Adelaide, where he and E. R. Mayne (85) put up 144 for the first wicket. Accepting an engagement with the Church C.C., in the Lancashire League, he was disappointing in 1922, but for the club a year later he scored 650 runs with an average of 40.62 and took 50 wickets for 14.38 runs each. He was a man of much personal charm, and his early death was regretted by a very large number of friends.

OLDROYD, Edgar, who died in Cornwall on December 27, 1964, aged 76, played as a professional batsman for Yorkshire from 1910 to 1931. Generally at No. 3 in the batting order, he scored 15,929 runs during his first-class career for an average of 35.16 and held 115 catches. Strong in defence and possessing seemingly limitless patience, yet capable of powerful hitting, Oldroyd obtained 38 centuries, seven in 1928, the highest being 194 put together in four and a half hours from the Worcestershire bowling at Worcester in 1923. His best season was that of 1922, when his aggregate reached 1,690, average 43.33, and in nine other summers he exceeded 1,000 runs. On 10 occasions he shared partnerships of over 200 for his county, the biggest being 333 with P. Holmes against Warwickshire at Edgbaston in 1922—then a record for the Yorkshire second wicket—and in 1927 he took part in 10 three-figure stands. Seven times between 1912 and 1931 he helped Yorkshire to carry off the County Championship. His benefit match at Bradford in 1927 realised £1,700.

OLIFF, Caleb, who died at Auckland on May 21, 1961, aged 78, played for New Zealand against the Australians in 1909–10 as opening batsman and slow bowler. He appeared for Auckland for 10 seasons from 1903. His best performance was against Wellington in 1913, when he took six wickets, including the hat-trick, for 62 runs in the first innings and seven for 42—the first six for three runs—in the second.

OLIPHANT, John Stuart, born at Hyderabad on February 17, 1837, died at Grafton, Highfield, Southampton, on July 21, 1924, aged 87. As a wicket-keeper he was well above the average and in 1861 was chosen for the Gentlemen v. Players match at Lord's, the game in which Jackson and Willsher bowled unchanged through both innings of the Gentlemen, who were beaten by an innings and 60 runs. Mr. Oliphant never took part in County Cricket, but for many years he was associated very prominently with the Wimbledon C.C. He was one of the founders of the club on May 20, 1854, and played for it for about 20 seasons, and he was also its first hon. secretary, resigning the office at the end of 1859, when he was succeeded by his brother, Mr. A.C. Oliphant. His batting average for the club was 12.

OLIVER, Charles Joshua, the New Zealand cricketer and Rugby footballer, died at Brisbane after a very short illness on September 25, 1977, aged 71. A Canterbury man, he became one of his country's most famous sportsmen. As a cricketer he toured Australia twice and England once in the mid-1920s. Then his Rugby took precedence. He played at home for New Zealand in 1928, toured Australia with the teams of 1929 and 1934 and was vice-captain and star player of the 1935 All Blacks in Britain. He was a strong-running and imaginative centre-threequarter. Eventually he and his family went to live in Australia.

OLIVER, Charles Nicholson Jewel, C.M.G., born in 1848, died in June, 1920. A useful batsman in his time, he appeared in three matches for New South Wales against Victoria, scoring six not out and 29 at Melbourne in 1865–66, three and 0 on the same ground in 1869–70, and six and 10 at Sydney in 1872–73. He also played for the State against W. G. Grace's team in 1873–74.

Later he became chairman of the Sydney Cricket Ground Trust.

OLIVER, Leonard, born at Glossop on October 18, 1886, died suddenly there on January 21, 1948. A forcing left-hand batsman, he played for Derbyshire from 1908 to 1924, and on a number of occasions in 1919 and 1920 he captained the team. In 1919 he led the side when Derbyshire were the only county to beat the Australian Imperial Forces XI. Playing as he did when Derbyshire were weak in batting, he often had to curb his free style or he would probably have made more runs. Altogether he scored 6,303 runs for the county, average 20.39. The highest of his six centuries was 170, including two sixes and 18 fours, against Nottinghamshire at Trent Bridge in 1920. His best season was 1913, when in 36 innings he obtained 957 runs, average 28.14. He was a vice-president of the County Club at the time of his death. Educated in Manchester, he played for the Manchester club while at school, and as late as 1931 he headed the Lancashire and Cheshire League batting averages.

OLIVIER, Eric, born on November 24, 1888, died in Cape Town on June 1, 1928. After taking 38 wickets for 19.05 runs each for Repton in 1906, he proceeded to Cambridge and took part in the matches with Oxford in 1908 and 1909. In those two games he scored 25 runs for two completed innings and obtained 13 wickets for a fraction under 20 runs each. In 1908, when his analysis was 10 for 141, he was the best of the Cambridge bowlers. He was fast-medium right-hand with a swerve. In 1911 he appeared for Hampshire and afterwards for South-Western Districts, in South Africa. In the First World War he served as a trooper in German South-West Africa in 1914–15, and later as 2nd Lieut. (T.) in the R.F.C. Whilst at Cambridge he was also an Association football Blue.

OLIVIER, Capt. Sidney Robert, C.M.G., R.N. (retired), who played for Hampshire in 1895, died on January 21, 1932.

OLLIVIERRE, Charles Augustus, died at Pontefract, West Riding, on March 25, 1949, aged 72. Born in Kingston, Jamaica, he toured England with the first West Indies team in 1900 and headed the batting averages. He and P. F. Warner, playing his only innings for the touring team, shared in an opening stand of 238 against Leicestershire. Ollivierre scored 159.

He stayed in England and qualified for Derbyshire in 1902. That year he made 167 against Warwickshire, but his most memorable innings occurred in 1904 when he was the dominating figure in a remarkable match. Percy Perrin scored 343 not out in a total of 597 for Essex at Chesterfield in July. Ollivierre responded with 229 out of 548 and after an Essex collapse for 97 he hit 92 out of 149, Derbyshire winning by nine wickets— an unprecedented performance for a side after facing so large a score in a three-day match. Never before in first-class English cricket could any team claim anything approaching such an achievement.

Because of eye trouble, he retired from first-class cricket after 1907, but took part in Yorkshire club games. From 1924 to 1939 he went each year to Holland to coach schoolboys.

OLLIVIERRE, Helon, a member of the well-known cricketing brotherhood of St. Vincent, died on February 23, 1907, at the early age of 25. In the only two innings he played in the West Indies against Lord Brackley's team he scored 45 and 47.

OLLIVIERRE, Richard Cordice, died in New York on June 5, 1937, aged 57. A good all-round cricketer for St. Vincent he was a member of the second West Indies team which visited England in 1906. In first-class matches he scored 480 runs, average 20, and took 58 wickets, average 21.56. The best performance of the side was at Harrogate where West Indies dismissed a mixed Yorkshire XI for 50 runs on a fast pitch, and, after a declaration with six wickets down, won the match by 262 runs. In Yorkshire's first innings Ollivierre took seven wickets for 23 and in the match his record was 11 for 125. Ollivierre bowled very fast right-hand and when accurate in length, as on this occasion, he fully tested the defence of the best batsmen. His father and three brothers were all good cricketers. Charles, who came to England in 1900 and afterwards played for Derbyshire, ranked among the finest batsmen of his time.

O'NEILL, William Paul, who died on December 8, 1966, at Philadelphia, Pennsylvania, aged 86, had a notable career in cricket. He was a native Philadelphian and a graduate of Penn Charter School and the University of Pennsylvania. He came out in big cricket when he appeared for Philadelphia Colts v. Ranjitsinhji's touring team in 1899, taking six wickets for 70 with his slow off-spinners. He appeared on five occasions for the United States against Canada. O'Neill has a minor place in cricket history as the last American to get W. G. Grace's wicket! This occurred in 1911 when he toured England with the Germantown C.C. In a match against Blackheath, the famous W.G. appeared for the Kent club. O'Neill also toured England with the Philadelphia Pilgrims in 1921 but never found time to participate in any first-class tours with the Philadelphians. In 1913 he appeared for a Germantown Twelve v. Australia in which the American team snatched a famous victory by three wickets. In that match "Pete" O'Neill's fielding was legendary. He held 10 catches during the game, one catch at second slip being held 18 inches from the ground as he fell forward and reached out flat for the ball.

ONGLEY, Arthur Montague, an outstanding personality in New Zealand sport, both in cricket and Rugby football, who became New Zealand president in each sphere, died at Palmerston North on October 17, 1974, aged 92. He played for Hawke's Bay, Westland and Manawatu and in 1902–03 he appeared for a Westland Seventeen against Lord Hawke's English team and captured eight wickets for 36 in an innings of 69 with his leg-spinners. Sir Pelham Warner in *Cricket Across The Seas* wrote, "Ongley, a boy of 19, who had some coaching from Albert Trott, bowled slow right-hand with a break both ways, the ball coming off the matting very quickly, but he derived much assistance from his 16 fielders." Ongley was the pioneer in establishing, after years of effort, the interests of the Minor Associations from 1923 until finally, in 1950–51, Central Districts was admitted to the Plunket Shield. Ongley was honoured with the C.B.E. and was president of the New Zealand Cricket Council in 1954–55.

ONSLOW, Denzil Roberts, who was a member of the Surrey committee for over a quarter of a century, died suddenly at Little St. James's Street, S.W., on March 21, 1908. He was born at Chittore, Madras, on June 12, 1839, and was educated at Brighton College, where he was in the XI, among his contemporaries being Messrs. E. B. Fawcett, G. E. Cotterill, and A. E. Bateman. *Scores and Biographies* (vi—393) says of him: "Height 6 ft., weight 12 st. Fields anywhere, except as wicket-keeper or long-stop, and is a very hard hitter indeed." He was also a useful change bowler. In 1860 and 1861 he was a member of the Cambridge XI and on each occasion was on the winning side: in the two matches he took four wickets for 41 runs and scored 77 runs in four innings. Residence for some years in India, where he was private secretary to three successive Finance Ministers of India and where he identified himself with the Calcutta and Simla clubs, kept him out of first-class cricket for some years, but when opportunity offered he played occasionally for Sussex, for which county he was qualified by living at Brighton. In the 12 innings he played for that county between 1860 and 1869 he scored 75 runs, and in addition took six wickets at a cost of 13.83 runs each: five of the wickets were taken against Surrey at the Oval in 1869 for 28 runs in an innings of 233, among his victims being Jupp, Griffith, and Pooley. His best innings in a match of note was 53 for M.C.C. and Ground v. Surrey at the Oval in 1871, when he made his runs against Southerton, Marten, and Street. Mr. Onslow, whose grandfather played in his day first for Kent and afterwards for Surrey, represented Guildford in the House of Commons in the Parliaments of 1874 and 1880, and continued to do so until the borough was disfranchised under the last Reform Act.

OPENSHAW, William Edward, of the Lancashire County C.C., died on February 15, 1915. In 1869 and 1870 he was in the Harrow XI, being described as "A very neat and careful bat, and frequently makes good scores; is also a good field, especially at cover-point." In his two matches with Eton he scored 45 runs with an average of 11.25 and took two wickets—Mr. G. H. Longman's was one of them—for 24 runs. Between 1879 and 1882 he appeared a few times, but without much success, for Lancashire, and he also played for the Gentlemen of Cheshire. In 1869 he was in the Harrow football XI, and 10 years later represented England v. Ireland at rugby.

ORCHARD, D. A., who died in April 1947, aged 71, first played for Canterbury against the Fijian touring team of 1894–95 and last played for the province in 1913. He was a selector and manager of the 1913–14 side in Australia. A left-handed batsman and bowler, he hit very hard. A noted Rugby football player he was in the New Zealand sides of 1896 and 1897.

ORLEBAR, The Rev. Augustus, the last survivor of the Rugby School v. M.C.C. match of June, 1841, immortalised in *Tom*

Brown's School Days, died on September 30, 1911, aged 88, at Willington, Bedfordshire, of which place he had been vicar 54 years. He entered Rugby School in 1838 and was in the XI in 1841, 1842, and 1843, being captain the two last seasons. In the match referred to against the M.C.C. he scored only 12 and one, but in the first innings of his opponents he made a remarkably fine left-handed catch at cover-point which dismissed F. Thackeray, a former Cambridge Blue. His highest score at Rugby was 53 for the school against the Sixth in 1842, but in the following year he did a far better thing in making 23 against Nottingham, who had Redgate to bowl for them. In later years he played occasionally for Bedfordshire. It is of interest to recall that Mr. Orlebar was the original of Tom Brown in his fight with "Slogger" Williams, who still survives in the person of the Rev. Bulkeley Owen Jones.

ORMSBY, George, who died in a New York hospital on April 14, 1968, aged 67, was a noted American cricketer. Born in British Honduras, he first appeared in New York cricket in 1919 and continued until heart trouble caused his retirement in the '50s. He hit 28 centuries, a New York record, the highest being 179 not out, and while on tour with a club side in Canada in 1937 obtained five within a week. During a visit to England in 1939, he played for the Buccaneers and was invited by Sir Pelham Warner to turn out for Middlesex, but business claims prevented him accepting.

ORR, Herbert Richard, perhaps the most prominent personality connected with Bedfordshire cricket, passed away on May 22, 1940, at the age of 75. Getting into the Bedford School XI when 15, Herbert Orr finished five years in the side as captain in 1884, and actually played his first game for the county in 1882. From that time his interest in the Bedfordshire club remained undiminished.

His devotion to the game found lasting proof in his will, by which he left "the cricket picture, Sussex v. Kent, to his friend, Dr. Alfred F. Morcom, of Belgrave Square, S.W., in memory of many pleasant days spent together in the cricket field, £100 to the Bedfordshire County C.C., and £50 to the Bedford Town C.C., in memory of my dear friend Reginald William Rice, with which clubs we have enjoyed so many pleasant games together." Also in his gift was a fielding trophy to Bedford School, for award in the First XI. Appropriately enough, this was won two years ago by the son of Mr. Frank Crompton, the present hon. secretary of the Bedfordshire County Club. He was a member of M.C.C.

After leaving Cambridge, where he just failed to get his Blue, Herbert Orr went to Australia. His ability was recognised very soon; he played for the Melbourne club and captained the first Western Australia team in 1892. Returning to England in 1899, he resumed his association with Bedfordshire and captained the side until 1915. With him at one period was A. F. Morcom, a fast bowler, the Cambridge Blue of 1905 to 1907. In the match against Suffolk at Luton in 1908 Morcom created a record, which still stands in English cricket, by sending a bail 70¼ yd. Also in the Bedfordshire XI at that time was R. W. Rice, the former Oxford University and Gloucestershire batsman.

After the First World War Herbert Orr invariably visited Australia to see the Test matches, and on one return trip to England with the Australian team he won "The Ashes" at deck quoits. A small silver urn containing cigarette ash was inscribed with the names of the players—W. H. Ponsford and W. A. Oldfield were of the party.

OSBORN, F., who died on October 12, 1954, aged 64, played in two matches for Leicestershire in 1911 and 1913.

OSBORNE, George, for over 30 years professional to the Upper Clapton C.C., died on March 1, 1913. He was a fast bowler, and in the three games in which he was tried for Middlesex in 1881 took four wickets for 102.

OSCROFT, Percy William, who was born on November 27, 1872, at Nottingham, died in London on December 8, 1933, after three months' illness. A useful defensive batsman with a good style, he did little on the few occasions he represented Nottinghamshire between 1894 and 1900, his highest innings being 40 against Middlesex at Nottingham in 1896. He was, however, a very fine fielder. For 22 years he had been a science master at Uppingham.

OSCROFT, William. The death took place on October 10, 1905, after an illness from which there was never any hope of recovery, of the once-famous Notts batsman, William Oscroft. Born on December 16, 1843, Oscroft first came prominently into notice when playing at Lord's in May, 1864, for the Colts of England against the M.C.C. and Ground. Never, perhaps, did a young batsman make a more brilliant first appearance. The wickets at Lord's in those days were not by any means what they are now, and heavy scores were quite exceptional. Oscroft had to face the bowling of George Wootton and the late James Grundy—both at their very best in the season of 1864—but he scored 51 and 76, his play creating a genuine sensation. It was seen that Notts had discovered a batsman of the class of George Parr and Daft, and a great future for the young cricketer was predicted. Oscroft at once found a place in the Notts XI, and in 1865 he went to the top of the tree, beating Daft in the Notts averages. From that time forward he played regularly for Notts until the end of the season of 1882, after which a breakdown in his health brought his cricket career to a close. Fine batsman as he often proved himself, it can scarcely be said that the hopes entertained of him in his early days were quite realised. His form varied a great deal from year to year, and despite his natural gifts he will not in the history of Notts cricket rank so high as Parr, Daft, Shrewsbury, Barnes, and William Gunn. Probably his best seasons after 1865 were those of 1873 and 1879. He paid one visit to Australia, going out with Mr. W. G. Grace's XI in the winter of 1873–74, and in the autumn of 1879 he was a member of the powerful professional team taken to Canada by Richard Daft.

Having a commanding style of play, Oscroft at his best was a most attractive bat to look at, and certainly no finer square-leg hitter has been seen in modern days. At the outset of his career he was a fairly good fast bowler, but as time went on he became a batsman pure and simple. After his active days as a cricketer were over, he was a regular attendant at Trent Bridge, his interest in the game being maintained to the last. A better judge of cricket it would have been hard indeed to find.

Oscroft's highest scores in first-class cricket were:

140 for Notts v. Kent, at Canterbury, in 1879.
107 for Notts v. Sussex, at Brighton, in 1865.
98 for North v. South, at the Oval, in 1879.
96 for An England XI v. Cambridge University, at Cambridge, 1873 (May 19).
90 for An England XI v. Cambridge University, at Cambridge, 1873 (May 26).
86 for The All-England XI v. The United, at Lord's, in 1866.

84 for Notts v. Sussex, at Nottingham, in 1873.
84 for Notts v. Gloucestershire, at Clifton, 1876.
80 for Notts v. M.C.C. and Ground, at Nottingham, in 1880.
78 for Notts v. Cambridgeshire, at Manchester, in 1865.
77 for Notts v. Middlesex, at Lord's, in 1878.
76 for Notts v. Gloucestershire, at Nottingham, in 1879, and
73 for Players v. Gentlemen, at the Oval, in 1873.

OSTLER, Harold, who died at Algiers in December, 1910, was for many years a prominent member of the Hull Town C.C. He was a successful left-handed batsman, but on his only appearance for Yorkshire—against Durham, at Sunderland, in 1891—made but six runs in his only innings and had 13 runs scored from his bowling without taking a wicket. From 1891 to 1905 he represented Hull on the committee of the Yorkshire County C.C. He was born on May 17, 1865.

OVER, John, died on December 20, 1939, aged 89. Cricket and football grounds were his special care. When he helped to prepare the pitch at Kennington Oval for the first fully representative match between England and Australia in September 1880, soot was the only "dope" used on the Surrey ground. Water and the roller brought the turf to perfection—a description given to this pitch at the time of the match. W. G. Grace scored 152 and, when Australia followed on, W. L. Murdoch went one better with 153 not out. For some 30 years John Over kept the Tottenham Hotspur ground at White Hart Lane in good order.

OVER, William, for some years one of the best players of the Richmond club, Melbourne, died in South Africa in November, 1910. He played four times for Victoria—twice against Tasmania and once against South Australia and New South Wales. His best performance was to make 91 in the match with Tasmania at Hobart in 1889–90.

OWEN, Hugh Glendower Palmer, for nearly 20 years a member of the Essex XI, was born at Bath on May 19, 1859, and died at Landwyck, Southminster, on October 20, 1912. He was educated privately and at Corpus Christi, Cambridge, where, although he did well in College matches—in 1882 he averaged 52 for 16 innings—he did not obtain his Blue. On the strength of a score of 44 for the Sixteen against the XI in 1882, he was chosen for the match with the M.C.C. at Cambridge, but, scoring only nine and five, was not tried again for the University. His earliest success in County Cricket was an

innings of 51 for Essex v. M.C.C. and Ground at Lord's in 1881, but his career as a county player really dates from 1885, in which year he scored 64 not out v. Hertfordshire and 52 v. Northamptonshire. His steady and sound batting was for years of the greatest value to the side, but it will be by his captaincy that he will always be chiefly remembered. He took over the leadership in 1895 and retained it until his retirement from first-class cricket in 1901, proving himself during that period a most cheerful, popular, and able captain. Of the many fine innings he played mention may be made of his 153 against Leicestershire at Leyton in 1889, when he went in first and carried out his bat, and his 109 and 86 not out in the match with Oxford University on the same ground five years later. At one time Mr. Owen was qualified for three counties—Somerset by birth, Derbyshire by residence, and Essex by family home, but the last-named was the only side of the three for which he ever played. In club cricket he did many notable things: thus, for the Bradwell and Tillingham C.C. in 1885 he averaged 185 for six innings, and in 1887 for Trent College, where he was a master for nine years, made five 100s and scored 1,809 runs. In 1888, between June 16 and July 19 he made 35, 104, 205, 31, 119, 55, and 23 in successive innings, and was dismissed only once—when he obtained 55. In 1889 he scored 1,839 runs and took 108 wickets with his right-hand medium-paced deliveries, and in a match against Tibshelf in July, 1890, carried his bat through *both* innings of Trent College for 27 and 46. In one season his figures for Notts Forest Amateurs were quite a curiosity, being 5—4—61 not out—244—244.00. Mr. Owen had been a member of the M.C.C. since 1885.

OWEN, Canon Robert, a great cricket enthusiast, died in October, 1904, just before celebrating his 81st birthday. He was educated at Repton and Cambridge, and played occasionally for Staffordshire and Derbyshire. He was an excellent amateur wicketkeeper, and for many years was actively identified with the Yorkshire Gentlemen's C.C. In his young days, before wicketkeeping gloves had been invented, he kept wicket to the tremendous bowling of Samuel Redgate, of Nottingham. While vicar of Boroughbridge, in Yorkshire, the Canon was the cricket tutor of the famous George Freeman. He was born in Staffordshire on October 23, 1823.

OXENHAM, Ronald K., who died at Brisbane on August 16, 1939, aged 48, made a name in first-class cricket comparatively late, but became the best all-rounder produced by Queensland. A right-arm medium-pace bowler, noted for accuracy of length and skill in flighting, he was a good bat and smart slip field. He played in three Tests against A. P. F. Chapman's team in Australia, and also represented the Commonwealth against South Africa and West Indies. In Sheffield Shield matches, he took 167 wickets, average 22.14, and scored 2,314 runs, for an average of 30.72. He suffered serious injury in a car accident in 1937 and, never fully recovering, took no further part in first-class cricket.

OYSTON, Charles, who played occasionally for Yorkshire in the seasons 1900 to 1909, died during the summer of 1942, aged 73. Chosen first for the county when approaching middle life—31—his chance in the powerful side captained by Lord Hawke depended upon an accidental vacancy. With his bowling of varied pace he took 22 wickets at 29.86 runs each, and as batsman he scored 84 runs, average 7.63.

PABST, Dr. J. C., who died suddenly at Wellington (N.Z.) on May 19, 1924, aged 55, was a useful batsman and wicket-keeper. He was an Australian by birth and played for Melbourne University and, between 1895 and 1898, for Auckland.

PACKE, Major Charles William Christopher, killed in Normandy in July, 1944, aged 35, played intermittently for Leicestershire from 1932. When he first appeared for the county the committee could not find a regular captain, and Packe was one of six amateurs who undertook the duty during the season. A fair batsman, he never found his best form in County Cricket, but for the Army in 1938 he scored 176 at Cambridge against the University, and another fine innings was his 145 for the Army against R.A.F. at Aldershot in 1938. He was a fine, free-hitting batsman.

PACKE, Michael St. John, who died in Alderney on December 20, 1978, was the youngest of three brothers who played for Leicestershire. Captain of Wellington in 1934, he went up to Cambridge and in his first innings for the University scored 65 against Essex but failed to win a Blue. He played for Leicestershire from 1936 to 1939 (captain in 1939), scoring a brilliant 118 against Glamorgan at Leicester in 1936—his only century.

PACKER, Sidney Charles, who died on January 29, 1961, aged 87, was secretary of Leicestershire County C.C. from 1910 to 1932. He invented the modern type of pitch-covering now in use on the majority of county grounds.

PAGE, Charles Carew, who was born in London on April 25, 1884, died suddenly at Woking on April 10, 1921. A very free and stylish batsman, he played with success for Malvern, Cambridge University and Middlesex. In his two matches against Oxford, however, he made only 12 and four, six and 46, and, so far as first-class cricket was concerned, it was for Middlesex he was seen at his best. In 51 completed innings for the county he made 1,423 runs with an average of 26.84, his highest score being 164 not out v. Somerset at Lord's in 1908, made out of 262 in 110 minutes, and including 28 fours. Of greater merit, however, was his 117 against Lancashire on the same ground three years earlier. He was a very good outfield, but was seen all too seldom in first-class cricket. At Association football he also gained honours, playing for Cambridge, Old Malvernians, the Corinthians, and England.

PAGE, Dallas Alexander Chancellor, captain of Gloucestershire, died in Cirencester Hospital on September 2, 1936, as the result of injuries received in a motor accident, which occurred when he was returning to his home, after leading his county to victory in an innings over Nottinghamshire, at Gloucester, on the last day of the County Championship season. He finished the match by catching Wheat. Born on April 11, 1911, Mr. Page was in the Cheltenham XI of 1928–29, and in Rugby football gained distinction as a stand-off half. He played first for Gloucestershire in 1933 and two years later he scored 1,059 runs when taking over the duties of leadership from B. H. Lyon. Last summer, the second year of his captaincy, he proved most astute in directing his XI, and scored in all matches 826 runs for an average of 18.35. Against Kent at Gloucester in May he hit 116—the only three-figure score of his career. Son of H. V. Page, the Cheltenham and Gloucestershire cricketer who played for Oxford University between 1883 and 1886 and was captain for the last two years of that period, he saw Gloucestershire rise from 15th to fourth position in the Championship. A hard-hitting batsman who drove particularly well, he looked most convincing when attacking the bowling. He fielded brilliantly, usually at cover point. His tragic end at the age of 25 came as a shock to all cricketers with whom he was very popular.

PAGE, Herbert Vivian, born on October 30, 1862, died in a nursing-home at Cheltenham on August 1, 1927, at the age of 64. In *Scores and Biographies* (xv—288) it was written of him: "A capital batsman, possessing strong defence and good hitting power. He was also a medium-paced bowler with a curl from leg and a break from the off, could keep a good length and was to be relied on. In the field he was hard-working and excellent, being safe in any position." As a member of the Cheltenham College teams of 1881 and 1882, he was very successful in his two matches with Clifton, taking five wickets for 11 runs in the former year and 12 for 34 (including seven for six) in the latter. At Oxford he secured his Blue as a Freshman and played against Cambridge in 1883 and the three next seasons, being captain in 1885 and 1886. His batting in those four games was consistently good, his scores being six and 57, 25 and 38, 22 and 78 not out, 20 and two. Twice he was on the winning side and twice on the losing. He assisted Gloucestershire many times between 1883 and 1895, his highest score for the county being 116 v. Somerset at Moreton-in-Marsh in 1885, but his best innings, taking into consideration the bowling with which he had to contend, was his 93 in the match with Nottinghamshire at Cheltenham in 1883. His name will be found in various Gentlemen v. Players matches between 1884 and 1894. He was asked to visit Australia with Mr. G. F. Vernon's team in 1887–88 but was obliged to decline the invitation. In a match at Oxford in May, 1886, he took all 10 wickets in an innings for Mr. M. C. Kemp's XI against Hertford College. He played Rugby football for Oxford University (in 1884 and 1885) and Gloucestershire, and was captain of the East Gloucestershire Hockey club for 22 years. From 1888 until 1923 he was a master at Cheltenham College.

PAGE, Thomas, a well-known cricketer in the Windsor district, died at Eton on March 28, 1908, in his 59th year. In 1888, when playing at Windsor against Ascot, he was hit on the head by a full-pitch delivered by Mr. W. A. Tobin. Page ducked down to avoid the ball, as he thought, but instead got into the way of it, and was given out leg-before-wicket by old Tom Hearne's eldest son, who said that the ball would have hit the wicket about four inches from the top. He was born at Apsley Guise, in Bedfordshire, in 1849.

PAGE, William, who played for the Derby Midland C.C. for 24 years (from 1872 to 1896), died on September 27, 1904. In 1881 and 1882 he was tried several times for the county, but without being able to do himself justice. An accident a few years ago deprived him of the sight of one eye, a circumstance which compelled him to abandon the game.

PAINE, George Alfred Edward, who died at Solihull on March 30, 1978, aged 69, was for a short time pretty near the full England side as a slow left-hander and would probably have been picked had anything happened to Verity. In 1934, a season not on the whole helpful to bowlers of his type, he headed the first-class averages with 156 wickets at 17.07. His father and grandfather had both been employed at Lord's and he himself, born at Paddington, was engaged on the Lord's staff and in 1926 played five matches for Middlesex. In only one of these did he meet with any success taking five for 77 and three for 25 against Warwickshire, who were so much impressed with his possibilities that, with the consent of Middlesex, they invited him to qualify for them. As a result of this he was a regular member of their side from 1929 to 1938.

In his earlier years though useful he was often expensive, but he wisely concentrated on improving his length, the first essential in a slow left-hander, and gradually acquired more spin, though he never became one of the great spinners and was always a little too inclined to bowl defensively. Still in 1931 for Warwickshire he took 127 wickets at 19.20 and in 1932 136 at 18.93 and after a slight setback in 1933, when his wickets were more expensive, reached his peak in 1934. That winter, going with the M.C.C. to the West Indies, he played in four Tests and had for a bowler of his type there, a highly respectable record, but on his return his decline was as steady and as rapid as his advance had been. He began to be troubled with rheumatism. In 1935, 115 wickets cost him 22.27 each and averages of 28, 30 and 28 in the next three seasons tell their own tale. In 1936 he was in fact kept out of the side for much of the summer by ill-health. At the end of 1938 he failed to agree with the county on terms and left them for League cricket, only reappearing for one match in an emergency in 1947.

Considerably slower than Verity, he stood over 6ft. and made the most of his height. Altogether in first-class cricket he took 1,021 wickets at an average of 22.85. A right-handed batsman, he made himself into a useful seven or eight and was a good field whether in the slips or to his own bowling. For many years he was groundsman and coach at Solihull School and later became a leading authority on non-turf wickets. He was also a skilled woodworker and photographer, who made considerable contributions in these lines to the adornment of the County C.C.'s buildings at Edgbaston. Above all he was a man of whom one never heard anybody say an unkind word.

G. A. E. PAINE
CAREER FIGURES
BATTING

Season	Matches	Inns	Not Outs	Runs	Highest Inns	Average	Catches
In England							
1926	5	7	3	23	16*	5.75	3
1929	29	44	11	434	38	13.15	28
1930	25	30	8	111	20	5.04	15
1931	30	29	12	102	15*	6.00	14
1932	26	29	4	258	70	10.32	13
1933	29	37	5	570	79	17.81	15
1934	26	36	5	613	75	19.77	16
1935	24	36	2	301	45	8.85	11
1936	11	18	3	167	41	11.13	6
1937	23	37	5	353	56	11.03	14
1938	19	29	0	348	38	12.00	8
1947	1	2	1	25	21	25.00	0
In West Indies							
1934–35	10	15	3	125	49	10.41	12
Totals	258	349	62	3,430	79	11.95	155

BOWLING

Season	Balls	Maidens	Runs	Wickets	5 wkts/ Inns	10 wkts/ match	Average
In England							
1926	702	20	356	11	1	0	32.36
1929	4,581	248	1,776	61	3	0	29.11
1930	4,897	236	1,977	75	7	1	26.36
1931	5,731	228	2,439	127	11	2	19.20
1932	6,620	320	2,575	136	11	2	18.93
1933	8,281	462	3,075	125	8	1	24.60
1934	7,715	463	2,664	156	13	4	17.07
1935	6,384	299	2,562	115	9	1	22.27
1936	2,083	73	994	36	4	1	27.61
1937	5,272	246	2,107	70	1	0	30.10
1938	4,350	179	1,777	64	2	0	27.76
1947	214	8	75	5	1	0	15.00
In West Indies							
1934–35	2,214	103	957	40	3	1	23.92
Totals	59,044	2,885	23,334	1,021	74	13	22.85

HAT-TRICKS (2)

Warwickshire v. Middlesex at Lord's, 1932.
Warwickshire v. Glamorgan at Cardiff, 1933.

Signifies not out.

G. A. E. PAINE—*continued*
TEST CRICKET

			BATTING			BOWLING			
		Not		Highest					
West Indies	Tests	Inns	Outs	Runs	Inns	Average	Runs	Wickets	Average Catches
1934–35	4	7	1	97	49	16.16	467	17	27.47 5

PAINTER, John, Gloucestershire. Born at Bourton-on-the-Water, November 11, 1858, died at Clifton, September 16, 1900. At various times coach at Cheltenham, Sherborne and Clifton. A hard-hitting batsman, and a fair change bowler. His bowling in a few matches in May, 1895, met with astonishing success, so much so, in fact, that for a short time he occupied first place in the bowling averages of the whole country. Played his first match for Gloucestershire in 1881, and his last in 1897.

PAISH, A., died August 15, 1948. Playing for Gloucestershire County C.C. from 1898 to 1903, this short, sturdily built, slow left-arm bowler possessed an easy action and for the county took 364 wickets at an average cost of 23.65. His best year was 1899 when he captured 125 wickets, average 18.93. He scored 967 runs. Paish was born in 1874.

PALAIRET, Henry Hamilton, who died at Dorchester on March 20, 1923, aged 78, was not in the XI whilst at Eton, but played for Exeter College, Oxford, as a wicket-keeper. He was a good shot, a keen fisherman, took part in rowing, cricket, and hunting, and excelled at archery. Five times—in 1876, 1878, 1880 to 1882—he was champion archer of England. He was father of Messrs. L. C. H. and R. C. N. Palairet.

PALAIRET, Lionel Charles Hamilton, a famous batsman with a singularly graceful style who played for Oxford University, Somerset and England, died on March 27, 1933. Somerset by close association—he received his early education at a school at Clevedon—he was born on May 27, 1870, at Grange-over-Sands in Lancashire. It was rather curious that, while above all remembered for his graceful and virile batting, he achieved a remarkable bowling performance at the age of 10 when in a school match he took seven wickets with consecutive balls. Proceeding to Repton, he was in the XI there in 1886 and the three following seasons, being captain in 1888 and 1889. In his last year he had a batting average of 29 and took 56 wickets for a little more than 12 runs apiece. Going up to Oxford in the autumn of 1889 he sprang into prominence as soon as he

appeared by his strikingly beautiful and effortless batting. He played four times in the Varsity match (1890–93) and was captain in the last two years. The most interesting part of Lionel Palairet's history, however, consisted in his career with Somerset, for whom he first played in 1890. The county had not attained first-class rank at that time, but the following season they were admitted to the County Championship. Palairet that season scored 560 runs, with an average of 31, and in 1892 he ranked as one of the great batsmen of the day by scoring 1,343 runs with an average of 31 and appearing for Gentlemen against Players at Lord's. Late in August he and H. T. Hewett—a formidable opening pair—put up a record opening partnership of 346 runs against Yorkshire at Taunton. The two batsmen were together only three and a half hours. Right up to 1907 Palairet—if not always able to play a great deal—remained a leading member of the Somerset XI. He never went to Australia but played twice for England in 1902. Those games were two of the most thrilling Test matches in history, Australia winning at Manchester by three runs and England getting home at the Oval by one wicket. In first-class games Palairet hit 27 centuries, his highest innings being 292 against Hampshire in 1896. His best season was that of 1901 when he scored 1,906 runs with an average of 57; he and L. C. Braund made 222 for the first Somerset wicket in the second innings against Yorkshire at Leeds, Palairet obtaining 173. That was a remarkable match, Somerset, going in a second time 238 behind, hitting up a score of 630 and beating Yorkshire by 279 runs. Palairet's cricket for Somerset will never be forgotten. His drives into the river and the churchyard at Taunton are still remembered by those who had the good fortune to see him in such form. He had almost every good quality as a batsman; combining strong defence with fine cutting and driving on either side of the wicket he always shaped in classic style. Essentially a forward player he was handicapped on a soft pitch, but under any conditions he made the off drive in a manner few have approached and no one has surpassed. He represented Oxford in the Three Miles, and played Association football for Combined Universities, London, and Corinthians. In addition he was at one period an ardent follower of hounds. .He was president of the Somerset County C.C. in 1929.

PALAIRET, Richard Cameron North, who died at his home at Budleigh Salterton, Devon, on February 11, 1955, aged 83, played, like his more famous brother, Lionel, for Repton, Oxford University and Somerset. Born at Grange-over-Sands, Lancashire, on June 25, 1871, Richard was the more consistent of the two brothers during three seasons in the Repton XI from 1888, hitting 172 against Malvern. An injury received while playing as inside-forward at Association football at Oxford prevented him from rivalling Lionel in more important cricket, for he was a graceful batsman, strong in forward play and possessing a fluent drive. As it was, a damaged knee handicapped him in running and batting and ended his activities as an athlete at which he excelled at school. Even so, he gained his Blue in 1893 and 1894 as an opening batsman. Among his best performances was that against Lancashire when, with Briggs and Mold bowling for the county, he scored 70 out of 94 in 65 minutes. He also played in the Association football match against Cambridge in 1891.

From·1889 to 1902 he appeared frequently for Somerset, his highest innings being 156 against Sussex at Taunton in 1896. In the winter of 1896–97, he formed one of the team taken to the West Indies by Sir Arthur Priestley. Soon after the outbreak of the First World War in 1914 he took a commission in the Devonshire Regiment at the age of 43 and rose to the rank of Staff Captain, seeing much service in India. In 1920 he became secretary of Surrey, a post he held until 1932, and in the winter of 1932–33 he

and Sir Pelham Warner were joint managers of D. R. Jardine's M.C.C. team in Australia on what became known as "The Bodyline Tour." From 1937 to 1946, he was president of Somerset. After service as an air-raid warden in the Second World War, his health steadily failed.

PALIA, Phiroz Edulji, who died in Bangalore on September 9, 1981, aged 71, played twice for India, each time at Lord's, in 1932 and 1936. Having pulled a hamstring in the field in the 1932 match, he batted at No. 11 in the second innings in a vain attempt to save the match for India. Palia was a left-hand batsman, wristy and attractive, and a useful bowler of the orthodox slow left-arm type. More was expected of him in England, certainly as a batsman, than he achieved. Despite batting high in the order, in 37 first-class innings his top score was 63 against Oxford University in 1936. His highest first-class score, 216, was in the Ranji Trophy for United Provinces against Maharashtra in 1939–40. After his retirement he kept in touch with the game as a Test selector and radio commentator.

PALLET, Henry James, born at Birmingham, January 2, 1863; died June 18. 1917. His earliest feats of note were for the Aston Unity C.C. Played for Warwickshire 1883 to 1898: slow to medium pace bowler, and excellent on slow wickets. Towards the end of the '80s Pallet was very good indeed, he and Shilton forming a capital combination. The two bowlers, together with Lilley as wicket-keeper, did much to secure Warwickshire's promotion to the first-class. Pallet had a nice easy action, great accuracy and, when at his best, a lot of spin. Some of his best bowling feats were:

6 wkts for 8 runs	.. Warwickshire v. Somerset, at Edgbaston	1887
11 wkts for 51 runs	.. Warwickshire v. Yorkshire, at Halifax	1888
8 wkts for 20*a* runs ⎱ 13 wkts for 46*b* runs ⎰	.. Warwickshire v. Somerset, at Bath†	1888
9 wkts for 27 runs	.. Warwickshire v. Leicester, at Edgbaston	1889
9 wkts for 52 runs	.. Warwickshire v. Somerset, at Edgbaston	1889
13 wkts for 144*b* runs	.. Warwickshire v. Somerset, at Taunton	1889
8 wkts for 49 runs	.. Warwickshire v. Kent, at Edgbaston	1890
9 wkts for 55*a* runs ⎱ 14 wkts for 100*b* runs ⎰	.. Warwickshire v. Essex, at Leyton	1894
7 wkts for 13*a* runs ⎱ 13 wkts for 78*b* runs ⎰	.. Warwickshire v. Kent, at Edgbaston	1894
8 wkts for 69 runs	.. Warwickshire v. Derbyshire, at Edgbaston ..	1895
7 wkts for 19 runs	.. Warwickshire v. Leicestershire, at Edgbaston ..	1895
14 wkts for 141 runs	.. Warwickshire v. Hants, at Southampton	1896

a—1st inns.; *b*—1st and 2nd inns.

† Pallet and Shilton bowled unchanged throughout.

He was also useful as a batsman. In his later years he became coach to Mitchell and Butler's, West Bromwich, and Dartmouth and Nettlefold's (Birmingham). Altogether he took 958 wickets for Warwickshire—296 of these in first-class matches for 21.50 runs each.

PALMER, Lieut.-Col. Cecil Howard (9th Royal Warwickshire Regiment) who was born in July, 1873, was killed in the Dardanelles on July 26, 1915. He was fourth in the Radley College averages in 1890 and third in 1891. In 1899 he made his first appearance for Hampshire, his chief success for the county that year being an innings of 64 v. Yorkshire, at Bradford. Four seasons later— in June, 1903—when assisting the Gentlemen of Worcestershire v. Gentlemen of Warwickshire, on the Edgbaston ground, he made 102 in his first innings and 127 not out in his second. In July, 1904, he scored 41 and 75 not out for Worcestershire v. Oxford University, at Worcester, and later in the same season played in three matches for Hampshire, in that with Somerset at Taunton making 37 and 49. He served in the South African War, being Mentioned in Dispatches and receiving the Queen's medal with four clasps.

PALMER, George Eugene, one of the greatest of Australia's many famous bowlers, died at Badaginnie, near Banalla, Victoria, on August 22, 1910. Born at Albury, New South Wales, on February 22, 1860, he was in his 51st year at the time of his death. Few bowlers have reached the top of the tree so early in life. His fame was established when at Melbourne, in March 1879, playing for Victoria against Lord Harris' XI, he took six wickets, all bowled down, for 64 runs, and three wickets for 30. Among the batsmen who fell to him were Lord Harris and George Ulyett, twice each, Tom Emmett, and Vernon Royle. His bowling astonished the English team, but to one fine judge of cricket in Melbourne his success did not come as a surprise. Mr. Hedley, of the *Melbourne Age*, has told the story of how the late Mr. T. W. Wills—for many years the moving spirit of Victorian cricket—asked him one morning

on the Melbourne ground if he would like to go out to the nets and see a better bowler than Frank Allan. From the day of his success against Lord Harris' team there was no doubt as to the position Palmer would take in Australian cricket, and for the next six years he had no superior except Spofforth. As all who follow cricket will remember he paid four visits to England, coming over with the teams of 1880, 1882, 1884, and 1886. Many English batsmen of those days maintain that they never met a bowler who was more difficult on a hard true wicket. In one way his effectiveness in fine weather told against him, as on soft wickets he did not get the same opportunities as Spofforth and Harry Boyle. During the latter part of the season of 1880, however, when Spofforth was laid aside by an injured hand, he had a chance of showing what he could do under all conditions, and his success was great. Still he was not so accurate as Spofforth, and afterwards Turner, on a sticky wicket, often doing too much and missing the stumps after beating the batsman. Palmer had many gifts as a bowler. His delivery was one of the best and most natural ever seen, he had a fine off-break and a good variety of pace, and his yorker was deadly. Moreover he bowled a quick leg-break with extraordinary skill. This leg-break, however, proved to some extent his undoing. While he kept it strictly in reserve it was an invaluable servant to him, but as time went on he bowled it more and more and his accuracy of pitch suffered. When he came to England for the last time in 1886 he was not nearly so good a bowler as he had been in his three previous visits. It must be said, however, that while his bowling declined, he developed into an excellent batsman. Following his return to Australia after the unsuccessful tour of 1886, he had the misfortune to fracture his knee-cap and not much more was seen of him in first-class cricket. The latter part of his life was the reverse of prosperous, but on this point there is no need to dwell. He married a sister of Blackham, the great wicket-keeper.

Among Palmer's best performances with the ball in England may be mentioned the following:

Wkts	Runs							Year
5 for	16	v. Derbyshire, at Derby	..	..	..	..	..	1880
5 for	24	v. Yorkshire, at Dewsbury	..	..	..	..	..	1880
7 for	44	v. Sussex, at Brighton	..	..	..	..	..	1880
11 for	89	v. Players, at Crystal Palace	..	..	..	..	..	1880
14 for	110	v. Sussex, at Brighton	..	..	..	..	..	*1882
5 for	15	v. Leicestershire, at Leicester	..	..	..	..	..	1882
6 for	22	v. Northamptonshire, at Northampton	..	..	..	..	1882

Wkts	Runs							Year
3 for	9	v. Middlesex, at Lord's	..	..	..	..	..	1882
6 for	21	v. Northumberland, at Newcastle	..	..	..	..	1882
5 for	6							
10 for	72	v. Lord Sheffield's XI, at Sheffield Park		..	..	..	1884
3 for	10	v. Surrey, at the Oval	..	..	..	..	..	1884
11 for	54	v. Yorkshire, at Bradford	..	..	..	..	..	1884
7 for	31	v. Gloucestershire, at Cheltenham	..	..	..	..	1884
5 for	10	v. South of England, at the Oval	..	..	..	..	1884
3 for	9	v. North of England, at Manchester	..	..	..	..	1886
5 for	22	v. Warwickshire, at Edgbaston	..	..	..	..	1886

Including the hat-trick.

In Test matches between England and Australia he scored 296 runs with an average of 14.09 and took 78 wickets for 21.51 runs each. In 11-a-side matches for the Australians in England, Palmer took 80 wickets in 1880, 138 in 1882, 132 in 1884, and 110 wickets in all matches in 1886.

PALMER, Richard, died on March 2, 1939, at his home near Sittingbourne, aged 88, having been born at Hadlow in Kent on September 13, 1850. On the recommendation of William Yardley, the Cambridge captain in 1871, Palmer took a professional engagement at Fenner's ground. He played occasionally for Kent from 1873 to 1876 and again in 1882. Described as a good batsman and medium-paced round-arm bowler he was most useful as wicket-keeper. In 1875 for Kent against M.C.C. during the Canterbury Week he showed his skill behind the stumps by dismissing six men —four caught, two stumped, and Kent won by six wickets. W. G. Grace scored 35 and took six wickets in the match. In 1873 Palmer played in a match unique in its way. The Marylebone club had offered a Champion County Cup for competition at Lord's. Several counties, after deciding to compete, declined to enter the contest and M.C.C. withdrew the offer, but Kent and Sussex agreed to play "their round" at Lord's. Kent won by 52 runs, as described in *Wisden*, "on dangerous and bad wickets. A new and very fast bowler, Mr. Coles, battering and bruising several of the Sussex men and finally disabling George Humphreys. Mr. Coles had 10 Sussex wickets— eight bowled." This was the only match played for the Cup. "Subsequent to this match the preparation of wickets at Lord's was left to the superintendence of the Umpires who were selected a week previous to the match being played; the result was good wickets for the remainder of the season."

PANTER, George, once so well-known in connection with the Leicestershire XI, died on April 19, 1896. Born on September 27, 1837, he was in his 59th year. After giving up active cricket, Panter was nominated by Leicestershire as one of the regular umpires in county matches.

PAPENFUS, Air Sergt. Christian F. B., killed in action in Libya on November 18, 1941, aged 27, bowled fast for Orange Free State in provincial matches during the 1939– 40 season; he took 23 wickets at 18.82 each. Besides taking six wickets against North-Eastern Transvaal, he played a very good innings of 60, although normally of little account as a batsman.

PARAVICINI, Percy John de, died on October 12, 1921, having undergone a surgical operation. Mr. Paravicini's numberless friends were shocked at the news of his death, no mention of his illness having appeared in any of the newspapers. Few men personally more popular have ever been seen in the cricket field. His career was in one respect peculiar. He was in proportion a far greater force in his schooldays than he ever became in first-class matches. At Eton he was quite a dominating figure, bowling with a success that he never approached for Cambridge or Middlesex. He was in the Eton XI for four years, getting his place in 1878 and being captain in 1880–81. In those four seasons he was on the winning side three times against Winchester, but never against Harrow. His greatest triumph was the match against Winchester in 1881, when he scored 27 and 32 and took 10 wickets—five for 25 runs and five for 46. Thanks mainly to his efforts Eton beat Winchester—a side composed of abnormally tall and powerful young cricketers—by six wickets. Going up to Cambridge after the season of 1881 Paravicini was in the University XI for four years. He was on the winning side three times at

Lord's, Cambridge winning in 1882, 1883, and 1885, but losing by seven wickets to M. C. Kemp's splendid XI in 1884. In these four matches Paravicini's best score was 37. His quick bowling, so formidable at Eton, had quite left him, and in the four matches he was only put on in three innings, meeting with no success. Though a failure as a bowler and only a partial success as a batsman, Paravicini was one of the finest outfields ever seen in the University match—very fast, untiring, and a sure catch. In this connection I remember hearing J. A. Turner say in the pavilion, when Cambridge had won the 1885 match by seven wickets, "Para, we didn't get any runs, but we fielded damned well." For Middlesex Paravicini played some good innings, but in County Cricket, as for Cambridge, his value lay chiefly in his splendid fielding. As a man Paravicini earned far more distinction at Association football than at cricket. One of the best backs of his day, he was for several seasons a mainstay of the Old Etonians, and in the season of 1882–83 he played for England against Scotland, Wales, and Ireland. He was a member of the Old Etonians' team that won the Association Cup in 1882. He was born on July 15, 1862.—S.H.P.

PARDON, Edgar Searles, died on July 16, 1898, in his 39th year. From the time he left school until within about a month of his death Mr. Pardon was constantly engaged in the task of reporting cricket matches and it is no exaggeration to say that he was a familiar figure on nearly every county ground. He was in peculiarly close touch with the Australians, travelling all over England with David Gregory's team in 1878 and being present at every England and Australia match in this country. His association with *Wisden's Almanack* commenced in 1886 and during recent years he had taken a very large share in the preparation of the annual. He was buried at Highgate Cemetery on July 20.

PARFITT, His Honour Judge James John, K.C., born at Slwch Villa, near Brecon, on December 23, 1857, died at The Grange, Wimbledon, on May 17, 1926, aged 68. He was educated at Prior Park College, Bath, and London University, and whilst playing for the former side on May 20, 1874, he and his brother, John Parfitt, dismissed Downside for nine runs, which included a leg-bye. A good fast bowler in addition to being a useful batsman he, on his first appearance for Surrey—against Yorkshire at the Oval in 1881—bowled Ulyett with the first ball he

delivered. In 1883 he began to assist Somerset, and later played occasionally for Warwickshire. He was County Court Judge on the Leeds and Wakefield Circuit from 1918 until 1921, and since the latter year had presided at Clerkenwell.

PARK, Alfred Heath, who played for New South Wales against the early English teams which visited Australia and also in three of the games with Victoria, died on January 16, 1924, aged 83. He was born at Oatlands, in Tasmania, on April 15, 1840.

PARK, Dr. Roy L., who died on January 24, 1947, aged 54, scored 2,714 runs, average 40.54, for Victoria. In the season 1919–20 he averaged 83.71, with aggregate 586 and highest score 228 in the Sheffield Shield competition revived after the War. Only New South Wales, Victoria and South Australia competed and Park was described as the best batsman in Australia. In 1921 at Melbourne in his only Test match against England he was bowled first ball by H. Howell. He was father-in-law of Ian Johnson of the 1948 Australian team in England.

PARKE, Elliott Anderson, born in London on July 19, 1850, died on June 22, 1923. He was a good batsman, a fast round-armed bowler and generally fielded at long-slip and mid-on. In 1874 he played for Kent against Derbyshire at Tunbridge Wells, and scored nine and 47. He was educated at Harrow and Oxford, but did not obtain a place in either XI. He played much cricket for M.C.C., Richmond, Incogniti, Blue Mantles, Devonshire Park (Eastbourne) and other clubs.

PARKER, Charles Warrington Leonard, who died on July 11, 1959, aged 74, was for many years one of the finest slow left-arm bowlers in first-class cricket. Recommended to Gloucestershire by Dr. W. G. Grace, he joined the county staff in 1903, but not until after the First World War did he achieve real prominence. Then in every summer from 1920 to 1935, when he retired, he took over 100 wickets. In five of these seasons his victims numbered more than 200, for in 1922 he dismissed 206 batsmen; in 1924, 204; in 1925, 222; in 1926, 213; and in 1931, 219. His full figures during a distinguished career were 3,278 wickets—a record surpassed only by W. Rhodes and A. P. Freeman—at a cost of 19.46 runs each; he hit 8,197 runs, average 10.33, and brought off 235 catches.

When pitches favoured him he could be well-nigh unplayable and by virtue of his command of spin and flight and, above all, his accuracy of length, he was rarely easy to hit. His bowling feats were too numerous to be chronicled in full, but they included six hat-tricks, three of them in the 1924 season and two in the game with Middlesex at Bristol. He took all 10 wickets for 79 runs in the first Somerset innings at Bristol in 1921 and on eight different occasions obtained nine wickets in an innings. One of his most remarkable performances was at Gloucester in 1925 when he played an outstanding part in the crushing defeat of Essex. He disposed of nine batsmen—A. C. Russell was run out—for 44 runs in the first innings and eight for 12 in 17 overs in the second, achieving a match analysis of 17 wickets for 56 runs.

In his benefit match at Bristol in 1922 when, on rain-damaged turf in the first Yorkshire innings, he took nine wickets for 36 runs—eight without assistance from the field—he hit the stumps five times with consecutive deliveries, but the second was a no-ball. He took part in the historic "tie" match at Bristol between Gloucestershire and W. M. Woodfull's Australian side of 1930. When the touring team, set to make 118 to win, scored half the runs for the first wicket, they appeared assured of easy victory. Then Parker, erratic at first, exploited a worn spot with such success that the last nine wickets fell for 58. Parker came out with figures of seven wickets for 54 runs, a feat which doubtless afforded him the more satisfaction as in the previous Australian fixture, the fifth Test, he had attended at the Oval but was not included in the England XI beaten by an innings and 39 runs. It was from Parker's bowling that W. R. Hammond held eight of the 10 catches he brought off in the game with Surrey at Cheltenham in 1928.

Despite his consistently fine performances, Parker played only once for his country, against Australia at Old Trafford in 1921 when, in a weather-spoiled match, he earned an analysis of 28—16—32—2. He toured South Africa and the West Indies with teams led by the Hon. L. H. (later Lord) Tennyson. For two seasons after his retirement he served as a first-class umpire and for a time later as coach at Cranleigh School. Besides his cricketing skill, he was well known in the West Country for his prowess at golf.

PARKER, Gunner Ernest F. (Australian Expeditionary Force), killed May 2, 1918, aged 33. Perth High School XI; St. Peter's College, Adelaide, XI. For some years the "star" batsman of Western Australia. Scored 76 and 116 v. South Australia at Fremantle in 1905–06; 26 and 69 v. New South Wales at Perth in 1906–07; and one and 117 v. Victoria at Perth in 1909–10. For Rest of Australia v. Australian XI, at Melbourne, in 1908–09, he made 65 and eight. In club cricket he made many 100s, and in 1902–03 made 1,003 runs, 14 complete innings for the East Perth C.C., including 246, 199, 172, and 105. He also scored 204 not out for St. Peter's College Old Boys v. Prince Alfred College Old Boys in 1904–05; and 222 not out for Wanderers v. North Perth in 1906–07. He was a great lawn tennis player, and gave up cricket on account of failing eyesight.

PARKER, John Frederick, who died on January 26, 1983, aged 69, played for Surrey from 1932 to 1952, his career spanning the last days of Jack Hobbs to the early days of Peter May. For years he was an essential member of the side, a consistent bat and a fine driver whose instinct was to attack and many of whose best innings were played in a crisis, a medium-paced bowler who could open if required and who, without many sensational performances, was always getting wickets, and a safe catcher in the slips. A tall man, he would have done even better but for a troublesome back. He was almost solely a county player and, though he had been picked for the tour of India in 1939 which never took place, one may doubt if he would have established himself in Test cricket. It is, however, fair to point out that the War deprived him of his cricket between the ages of 26 and 33, when he might have expected to be at his best. He had a good trial in 1932 and 1933 and, without doing anything exceptional, showed promise, but then came a setback: in 1934 he lost his place and did little more until 1937, when he scored 915 runs with an average of 27.72 and took 65 wickets at 28.36. In 1938 came his first century and in 1939 he surpassed anything he had done before with 1,549 runs and an average of 37.78 and 56 wickets at 22.83. This improvement was partly due to health, while in bowling he concentrated more on length and on always aiming at the stumps. But on the whole his best years were after the War. In 1946, despite further trouble with his health, he headed the bowling averages with 56 wickets at 15.58 and followed in 1947 by heading the batting. In 1949 he made the highest score of his career, 255 against the New Zealanders, made out of 568 in six and a half hours, and he continued to be a valuable member of the Surrey side until 1952, when, although he was unable to bowl, he still got his 1,000 runs as usual, but retired at the end of the season, having had the satisfaction of playing in the first Surrey team to win the Championship since 1914. He had had a benefit in 1951. In all first-class cricket he scored 14,272 runs with an average of 31.58, including 20 centuries, took 543 wickets at 28.87 and caught 331 catches.

PARKER, John Palmer, who died suddenly on August 9, 1984, deserves a place in cricket history as perhaps the only inexperienced and unknown batsman to get the better of "Tich" Freeman at his best. When he came in for Hampshire at Canterbury in 1926 in the second innings, he had been playing County Cricket for two months only and his average for 11 innings was 20.70. Hampshire, going in on the second afternoon 268 behind, had lost six for 57 on a perfect pitch by four o'clock. True, Mead was still there, but there was little to come and the match seemed likely to end soon after tea. In fact, when stumps were drawn, the score was 251 for six, Parker was 119 and Mead 84. Next morning the two settled down as if there had been no break and added another 77 before Parker was caught off a skyer at cover for 154. They had put on 278 in under three hours. Livesey, one of the heroes of Hampshire's historic win over Warwickshire in 1922, helped in a partnership of 86 and it was 3.45 pm when the innings closed. Mead was 175 not out and Kent had just two hours in which to make 172. Thanks to a splendid partnership between Woolley and Chapman they got them in an hour an a half. Parker's technique was simple. Straight balls he played with a straight bat: at almost anything else he took a full-blooded swing. Had his leg-side method been a little btter, he would have scored even more: at balls outside his legs he often swished one-handed. When his luck was in he deserved every bit of it. The Kent fielding that day became distinctly ragged and Freeman tried to bowl defensively, a role for which he was ill suited. Unfortunately Parker was never able to play enough to do justice to his possibilities. He continued to appear spasmodically until 1933, towards the end sometimes captaining the side. His total record from 44 matches was 1,094 runs with an average of 18.54. In 1927 he was a member of Lord Tennyson's team to Jamaica.

PARKIN, Cecil Henry, who died on June 15, 1943, in a Manchester hospital, earned the description of cricket's chief comedian. Of medium height and rather slim, eccentric in character and in action, he brought every known device besides his own special jugglery into his right-arm bowling. For variation of pace and spin he ranked with the cleverest of attackers, his high-pitched very slow ball being specially deceptive. He chiefly used the off-break, but overdid experiments, so that the most experienced captain found it difficult to place a field able to check run-getting when punishing batsmen faced Parkin. Yet a well-known amateur said in the Oval pavilion that he would like Parkin on his side because he took wickets quickly and left his batsmen plenty of time in which to get runs.

League cricket occupied much of Parkin's time before he started for Lancashire by taking 14 Leicestershire wickets at Liverpool in 1914, and after the First World War his Saturdays were engaged similarly; but in 1919 at Old Trafford he helped materially in the defeat of Yorkshire by taking 14 wickets at exactly 10 runs apiece, the margin, curiously enough, being 140 runs—precisely the number hit off Parkin in 60 overs. Chosen for the Players at the Oval and Lord's, he did nothing exceptional, but next season at the Oval he dismissed nine Gentlemen, six clean bowled, in the first innings for 85 runs, a performance which influenced his choice for the team which visited Australia that winter. Except at Adelaide, where five wickets fell to him for 60 in the first innings, Parkin, like other England bowlers during that ill-fated tour, suffered severely in the Tests; but he took most wickets, 73 at 21 runs apiece during the whole campaign. Next summer he again proved the most effective bowler when appearing in four of the five Tests, but England were still far below their best, and altogether Parkin was on the losing side eight times without knowing the satisfaction of victory when playing for his country against Australia.

Of the drawn match at Old Trafford, where he took five wickets for 38 runs, he told a story well suited to his own character. "H. L. Collins, the Australian, batted seven hours for 40 runs. A spectator shouted to our skipper, Lord Tennyson, 'Eh, Tennyson, read him one of your poems!'—and with the very next ball I got Collins l.b.w." When England batted a second time, 187 runs ahead, Parkin went in first, and so could claim the proud privilege of being one of the few men who have opened both the bowling and batting for England.

He was in the XI which beat South Africa by an innings and 18 runs at Edgbaston in 1924. Arthur Gilligan, six wickets for seven runs, and Maurice Tate, four for 12, dismissed the visitors for 30—the lowest Test match total—and again shared the honours when South Africa, following-on, scored 390.

Parkin was at his best about that time, being the most effective Lancashire bowler both in 1923 and the following season, with records of 209 wickets at 16.94 runs apiece, and 200 at the low cost of 13.67 each. His deadliness declined in 1925, when his analysis showed 121 wickets at 20.79 each. E. A. Macdonald and Richard Tyldesley were then his superiors in the powerful Lancashire attack. His benefit match with Middlesex that season realised £1,880. In 1926 he played in 11 county matches, taking 36 wickets at 15.13 apiece, and so shared in Lancashire gaining the Championship for the first time since 1904; but his finish in important cricket in his 40th year was regrettable—due to a breach with the Lancashire authorities. Altogether in first-class cricket Parkin was credited with 1,060 wickets at an average cost of 17.49.

As a batsman he was useful at times and showed good style, but his average of 11.47 denotes uncertainty to a high degree. Parkin told his early cricket life in a very vivacious book and, in conformity with his cricket gestures, was a conjuror of no mean ability. Born on February 18, 1886, he was 57.

PARKIN, Durant Clifford, who came to England in 1894 with the first South African team, died on March 20, 1936, aged 65. A medium-paced right-arm bowler, he played for Eastern Province, Transvaal and Griqualand West. Against W. W. Read's team of 1891–92 he took five wickets for 27 runs and in the only representative match, which was played at Cape Town, he took three wickets for 82 in a total of 369.

PARKINSON, Sir Kenneth Wade, who died on June 20, 1981, aged 73, was president of Yorkshire from 1974 until the time of his death. Despite having lost a leg when only 16, he took an active part in many forms of sport, becoming M.F.H., a good grouse shot and an accomplished conjuror. A useful opening batsman, he played an innings once for the Free Foresters in which he faced five balls, all against the fast bowling of Philip Utley: the first sped to the boundary and was signalled four runs, the fifth bowled him. In the dressing-room afterwards, four large dents were to be seen in his tin leg. Although he had many commitments, being chairman of the *Yorkshire Post* among other things, he

was an excellent host at Headingley, where his humility and sense of humour were much appreciated.

PARKINSON, Leonard W., who died on March 16, 1969, aged 60, played as a professional all-rounder for Lancashire from 1932 to 1936. In that time he scored 2,132 runs, average 21.53, and, with leg-break bowling, disposed of 192 batsmen at a cost of 29.44 runs each. His highest innings was 93 against Nottinghamshire at Old Trafford in 1934. Also a sound fieldsman, he held 49 catches.

PARKINSON, Sir Lindsay, Kt., died at Blackpool on February 3, 1936, within three weeks of his 66th birthday. From 1890 he played cricket for his native town and joined his brother in giving the cricket ground, with pavilion, on which Lancashire play county matches. He was president of the Blackpool C.C. and chairman of the Blackpool F.C. A very good Association player for Blackpool, then known as South Shore, and Blackburn Rovers, he was approached by several League clubs, including Aston Villa, to sign as a professional. He became Mayor of Blackpool, Member of Parliament for the Borough and head of the firm of government contractors bearing his name.

PARKS, Henry William, who died at Taunton on May 7, 1984, aged 77, was the younger brother of Jim Parks and thus a member of a notable cricket family. If one were asked what was meant by "a good *county* player", he might well serve as an illustration. For 20 years he was a valuable member of the Sussex side; six of those years were lost to the War, but he made 1,000 runs 14 times, scored 42 hundreds and his total aggregate for the county was 21,721 with an average of 33. Moreover, until the years overtook him, he was a fast and safe outfield. Yet he never represented England nor the Players at Lord's, and it may be assumed that his selection was never seriously considered. The adjectives most frequently applied to him were "consistent" and "reliable". He did not for the most part make enormous scores or do sensational performances and it is probable that after 50 years few spectators have a vivid memory of any innings they saw him play. Yet there is no disputing the evidence of the figures. Probably his finest feat was to score 114 not out and 105 not out against Essex at Leyton in 1933, thus saving a match which, in face of a total of 560 for nine, Sussex could easily have lost. His highest score was also against Essex, 200 not out at Chelmsford in 1931, in the course of which he put on 239 for the third wicket with Duleepsinhji in 160 minutes.

His career began with a few matches in 1926. In 1927 he had a good trial and showed distinct promise; in 1928 he made his first century and reached his 1,000 runs. After a bad setback in 1929, when he lost his place, he again scored 1,000 runs in 1930 and continued to do so every season up to his retirement. Until the War he was a middle-order batsman, but after it he became John Langridge's opening partner and in that capacity enjoyed two of his best seasons, heading the averages in 1946 and in 1947 scoring for the only time over 2,000 runs. He again reached 1,000 in 1948 and shared a benefit with John Langridge, but he was now getting slow in the field and his contract was not renewed. In 1949 and 1950 he stood as a first-class umpire and later coached for many years at Taunton School. A strongly built man, he was an attractive bat and a good driver, at his best a fast pitch.

PARKS, James Horace, who died on November 21, 1980, aged 77, will be remembered for his feat of scoring 3,003 runs and taking 101 wickets in 1937, a record which, unless the whole pattern of County Cricket is radically changed, cannot possibly be equalled. First appearing for Sussex in 1924, he created a sensation by taking seven for 17 in his third match, in the second innings against Leicestershire at Horsham. Naturally, great things were hoped of him, but he was slow to develop and it was not until 1927, when he made 1,036 runs with an average of 23.54 and took 44 wickets at 26.93, that he began to justify the confidence which the county had placed in him. From then until the Second World War he was an indispensable member of the side. In 1928 he made the first of his 41 100s and in 1929 helped Bowley to put up 368 in three hours, at that time a Sussex record, for the first wicket against Gloucestershire; his share was 110. In 1935 he did the double and appeared for the Players at Lord's; that winter he was a member of E. R. T. Holmes's M.C.C. side to Australia and New Zealand, which did not play official Tests. His one Test appearance was against New Zealand at Lord's in 1937, when he opened the batting with Hutton, also making his Test debut, but, though he scored 22 in the first innings and bowled well, he can never have been a strong candidate for a place against Australia. His first-class career ended in 1939. After the War he went

to the Lancashire League and later, for a time in the 1960s, was the county coach at Hove. He was essentially a county player, immensely dependable, but lacking the touch of genius which marks the top class. Indeed, after 40 years it is difficult to have any vivid picture of his cricket, except perhaps of his brilliant close fielding. As a batsman he was sound and a particularly good cutter, not very attractive to watch, but capable of scoring fast if wanted. Stockily built, he was for years a formidable opening partner for John Langridge, and had the considerable merit that no fast bowler was likely to intimidate him. He bowled slow-medium in-swingers, which, if there was any bite in the wicket, often moved away after pitching; but again he was normally reliable rather than deadly. He was first of a distinguished cricket family. His younger brother was for years one of the mainstays of the Sussex batting; his son, at one time captain of Sussex, played many times for England both as a batsman and as a wicket-keeper, and his grandson has recently been playing for Hampshire.

PARNHAM, Charles, who died at Radcliffe-on-Trent on November 12, 1922, aged 79, was for over half a century a very well-known cricketer in the Nottingham district. He played much with Richard Daft, and in 1864 was given a trial in the All-England XI by George Parr.

PARNHAM, John, who was born at Bottesford, Leicestershire, on September 6, 1856, died at Church, near Accrington, on February 18, 1908. He was a left-handed, slow-to-medium-paced bowler with a high delivery, and on a wicket to his liking was very destructive. His two best performances with the ball were against the strong Australian team of 1882, when he took 15 wickets for 129 runs for his county at Leicester, and 12 for 126 for the United XI at Tunbridge Wells. It was on account of these performances that he was engaged the following year on the ground staff at Lord's, where he remained 11 seasons. He was a vigorous and, at times, successful batsman. His highest score in a first-class match was 90 not out for XI of the North v. XI of the South at Lord's in 1886. He went in when nine wickets had fallen for 148, and, in partnership with J. White (62), a young wicket-keeper from Nottinghamshire, added 157 for the last wicket in 115 minutes. Parnham played his last county match in 1886 and afterwards took to umpiring.

PARR, George (Notts) died on June 23, 1891. As he was born at Radcliffe-on-Trent on May 22, 1826, he had, at the time of his death, completed his 65th year. Readers of *Wisden's Almanack* will not need to be told that George Parr for many years occupied an undisputed position as the best bat in England, succeeding Fuller Pilch in that enviable distinction, and holding his own until he, in turn, was supplanted by Hayward and Carpenter. His career as a public player was a very long one, commencing in 1844 and not coming to an end until 1871. He lived all his life in his native village, and the attendance at his funeral there showed the respect in which he was held. With the wreaths on his coffin was placed a branch from the tree at the Trent Bridge ground which has for a generation past been known as "George Parr's Tree." This name it acquired in connection with the great batsman's leg-hitting. Parr was for many years captain of the Notts county XI, a post which, on his retirement, was given to Richard Daft, and he was also for a long period captain of the old All-England XI, a position in which he succeeded William Clarke, the first organiser of the team. George Parr went to America with the English team in 1859, and he was also captain of the splendid XI which journeyed to Australia in the winter of 1863–64. Among the many brilliant innings that he played for his county, the highest, and the one most often referred to, was 130 against Surrey at the Oval in 1859.

PARR, Henry Bingham, born at Grappenhall Hayes, near Warrington, on June 5, 1845, died in Liverpool on March 24, 1930, aged 84. *Scores and Biographies* said of him: "He is a good hitter, with stubborn defence and the patience of Job; fields generally at long-leg and bowls 'when required'." He was in the Cheltenham College XI in 1863 and 1864, and played for Gentlemen of Cheshire, Lancashire, and for North v. South. For Lancashire he made 61 v. Derbyshire at Manchester in 1873 and 52 v. Leicestershire at Leicester two years later. For Liverpool v. Dingle in 1874 he scored 202. He became "Father" of the Liverpool Stock Exchange which he joined in 1866.

PARRINGTON, William Ferguson, who died at Northallerton on May 7, 1980, aged 90, played a few matches for Derbyshire as a bat in 1926, his highest score being 47 against Warwickshire at Derby. He had been in the Rossall XI in 1907 and 1908 and in 1914 had appeared for Durham, the county of his birth.

PARRIS, Frederick, a medium-paced bowler for Sussex during the '90s and a first-class umpire for some years, died on January 17, 1941, aged 74. He rose to fame in County Cricket under the captaincy of W. L. Murdoch, the famous Australian, and no doubt he learned much from Alfred Shaw, who resumed first-class cricket in 1894 when engaged by Lord Sheffield after retiring from the Nottinghamshire side. Then 52, Shaw retained his accuracy of length and power in spinning the ball so well that he headed the Sussex averages with 41 wickets at 12.24, Parris coming next with 63 at 13.44 runs apiece. Off-break and slightly varied pace made Parris deadly on a pitch giving any help. Seizing such an opportunity at Bristol, he took 15 Gloucestershire wickets—including that of W. G. Grace twice—at a cost of 98 runs in one day. Another very good performance was at Catford, 10 Kent wickets for 58 runs, and a handsome victory again resulted. Fred Tate, after some decline from his early effectiveness, became the best Sussex bowler in the following season, with Parris next in general utility if expensive, his 40 wickets costing 31 runs apiece. Parris never fulfilled expectations, his moderate days coming too frequently. Of medium height and sturdily built, Parris batted left-handed, but runs were seldom wanted from him in a side containing C. B. Fry, K. S. Ranjitsinhji, as they came from the Universities, W. Newham, still on the list of Sussex officials at the age of 81, George Brann, also of Ardingly, Killick and Marlow, besides the captain.

In club cricket Parris did some remarkable things, once taking 18 out of 20 wickets in a match; and at Bexhill in 1903 he hit 23 fours in an innings of 105.

PARSONS, The Rev. Canon John Henry, M.C., who died in a Plymouth nursing home on February 2, 1981, aged 90, had a unique career. He played for Warwickshire from 1910 to 1914 as a professional: commissioned in the First World War and continuing in the Army after it, he appeared in 1919 and 1923 as Capt. J. H. Parsons; in 1924 he resumed his professional career. In 1929 he was ordained and from then to his retirement in 1934 he played again as an amateur. But for this almost complete gap of 10 years, when he would normally have been in his prime, he might well have played for England. In that dismal season of 1921, when most of the batsmen who did play were cowed by the pace of Gregory and McDonald and when more slip catches were dropped than held, he would have been a strong candidate. A tall man, who made full use of his height, he was a superb driver of fast bowling, which he believed in attacking, and one of the safest slips of his day. By the time he resumed his career, English batting was fast recovering, a younger generation, Hammond, Leyland, Jardine, Chapman, was knocking at the door, and his opportunity was gone.

Born at Oxford and qualified by residence in Coventry, he had a brief trial for Warwickshire in 1910, and in 1911, with 568 runs at an average of 22.72, was a useful member of the side which so unexpectedly won the Championship. After a bad setback in the wet season of 1912, he got his 1,000 runs in 1913 and in 1914 was picked for the Players at the Oval, then an important match, a sign that he was regarded as potentially more than a mere county player. His few matches in 1919 and 1923 showed clearly what a loss he was and, when he returned to regular cricket in 1924, he did not disappoint expectations. In 1926–27 he was one of the leading batsmen on Arthur Gilligan's M.C.C. side in India, not then a Test country, and in 1927 he had the splendid record for Warwickshire of 1,671 runs with an average of 50.64. This included the highest score of his career, 225 against Glamorgan at Edgbaston. Even this record he surpassed in 1931 when he averaged 63.72 in 18 matches. In 1930 he had represented the Gentlemen at Lord's, thus joining the select band of those who played on both sides in these matches. The finale came in 1934, and perhaps no cricketer has made a more glorious exit. At Hull, under his captaincy, Warwickshire were dismissed for 45; they had to get 216 in the last innings and, thanks to Parsons who made 94 out of 121 in under two hours with three sixes and 12 fours, they won by one wicket. It was his last match for the county.

In all first-class cricket he scored 17,983 runs with an average of 35.69, including 38 centuries. Shortly before his death a biography of him, *Cricketer Militant*, appeared written by Gerald Howat.

PARTRIDGE, Norman Ernest, who died at Aberystwyth on March 10, 1982, aged 81, was an outstanding schoolboy cricketer. For Malvern in 1918 he scored 514 runs with an average of 102.80 and in 1919 took 71 wickets at 12.98. In 1919 he and G. T. S. Stevens of University College School were both asked to play for the Gentlemen, Stevens at Lord's and Partridge at the Oval.

They are believed to have been the first schoolboys so honoured since R. A. H. Mitchell in 1861. Stevens played, but, the match being in term-time, Malvern refused leave to Partridge, just as Eton had to Mitchell. Going up to Cambridge, Partridge duly got his Blue in a very strong side, but, though his final record of a batting average of 25 and 38 wickets at 21.60 was respectable, he hardly achieved as much as had been hoped of him. This was his only summer in residence, but between 1921 and 1937 he played for Warwickshire, for a few seasons frequently but later seldom for more than a match or two. Yet he generally did something either as a batsman or a bowler that showed what a loss it was that he could not play regularly. In all he scored 2,352 runs for the county with an average of 18.52 and took 347 wickets at 22.27. His highest score and his only century was 102 against Somerset at Edgbaston in 1925, made in 100 minutes: he and R. E. S. Wyatt put on 138 in an hour and a half for the seventh wicket. Bowling fast-medium in-swingers, he had, like many of his type, a rather ugly action which, though he was never no-balled, was regarded by some as slightly suspect. It is said that a batsman whom he had comprehensively bowled said indignantly to "Tiger" Smith behind the wicket, "He threw that." "Yes," said "Tiger". "And bloody well too."

PATERSON, Lieut.-Col. Arthur Sibbald, D.S.O., who died in 1937 at Burnham-on-Sea, aged 59, played twice for Somerset in 1903.

PATERSON, Robert Fraser Troutbeck, died in Edinburgh on May 29, 1980, aged 63, after a long illness. He headed the Brighton College averages in 1933 and 1934, when he played for the Public Schools at Lord's, and, making his first appearance for Essex in 1946, was for that season a regular and valuable member of the side. He played many useful innings—the highest of them 80 against Yorkshire, the Champion County, at Harrogate—occasionally picked up a wicket as a medium-paced change bowler and in one match at least kept wicket creditably in the absence of T. H. Wade. Apart from one appearance in 1948, this ended his first-class career, though from 1947 to 1950 he was the county's secretary. He then moved to Scotland where he continued to make many runs and also did notable work as a coach. He was a particularly good off-driver.

PATIALA, The Maharajah of, who died in

November, 1900, was a great supporter of cricket in India, and had, during several winters, engaged W. Brockwell and J. T. Hearne to coach and play for his XI.

PATIALA, The Maharajah of, president of the Cricket Club of India, died on March 23, 1938, at the age of 46. At the opening of the Brabourne Stadium, Bombay, when Lord Tennyson's team played there in December 1937, the Maharajah expressed the hope that "the Stadium will become to India what Lord's ground is to England." That was typical of his keen interest in cricket when poor health compelled him to give up active participation in the game at which he was proficient as a free-scoring batsman and keen field. His successor, the Yuvarajah of Patiala, playing for India, was top scorer with 24 and 60 in the third representative match against D. R. Jardine's team at Madras in 1934, and also did well against Lord Tennyson's side.

PATIALA, The Maharajah of, latterly **Lieut.-Gen. Yadavindra Singh,** died on June 17, 1974, in The Hague where he had been Indian Ambassador to Holland since November 1971. He was 61. In his only Test match, against England at Madras in February 1934, he made India's top score, 60, but his side were beaten by D. R. Jardine's team by 202 runs. A tall, graceful batsman, he played for the Hindus in the Quadrangular tournament and captained Southern Punjab in the Ranji Trophy, scoring 132 against Rajputana in 1938–39. He was chosen for the 1936 tour of England but State business caused him to decline. The Yuvraj played in many representative matches against touring sides from overseas and in minor cricket he hit about 50 100s, including 284 against a Bombay XI at Patiala in 1938. His father was a noted patron of cricket, besides being a first-class player and was donor of the Ranji Trophy.

PATRICK, C. W., died at Coogee on November 29, 1919. He played for New South Wales v. Queensland at Sydney in March, 1894, making 12 and one, and was later identified with the game in the latter State, which he represented several times.

PATRICK, W. R., who died in August 1946, aged 58, represented Canterbury from 1905 to 1927, except in the season 1917–18, when he played for Otago and captained Canterbury for several years. After captaining the 1925–26 New Zealand team in Australia, he helped to select the 1927 team for England.

A stylish batsman, he was especially strong in off-side strokes.

PATTERSON, George Stuart, one of the best all-round cricketers ever produced by America, died in June, 1943, aged 74. Over 6ft. tall and of slim build, he batted in good style and bowled right-arm medium-pace. For Haverford College and Pennsylvania University he made a name when young and played for Germantown club when only 15. He came to England with the Gentlemen of Philadelphia team in 1889 and, scoring 529 runs, average 40.69, he headed the batting figures, besides taking 42 wickets at 23 runs apiece.

In 1897 he captained a similar side, and with 33 was second in the averages, his chief innings being 162 at Trent Bridge against Nottinghamshire. In America he played many big innings, the highest being 271. Four times he exceeded 1,000 runs in a season, and in 1891, besides making 1,402 (average 50), he took 112 wickets at 7.97 each. With F. H. Bohlen, who passed away in December 1942, Patterson made 200 for the first wicket against Frank Mitchell's University team that visited Philadelphia in 1895.

PATTERSON, The Rev. John Irwin, exactly a year younger than his brother W. H., far more famous in the cricket world, died on September 22, 1943, aged 83. A defensive batsman and good field, he made a name as a left-hand slow bowler, playing six times for Kent in 1881 and 1882, besides getting his Blue at Oxford in 1882, when Cambridge won by seven wickets—the first of four consecutive results by the same margin, Oxford in 1884 varying the run of Cambridge victories. At Maidstone in 1881 he took five Derbyshire wickets for 12 runs, and in 1880 for St. Lawrence he dismissed seven Dover batsmen, three bowled and four caught, in seven balls, as recorded in *Scores and Biographies*.

PATTERSON, William Harry, almost a life-long figure in Kent cricket, died on May 3, 1946, aged 87. An exceptionally sound and skilful batsman, he could produce his best form without previous practice in first-class cricket. For many years, owing to the calls on his time as a solicitor, he got practically no County Cricket until late in the season, but then he was as likely as anyone to make a big score. He was elected captain of Kent for the second half of the season four times. Playing with a very straight bat and watching the ball carefully, he surpassed most of his amateur contemporaries on the sticky turf so often experienced in the days before pitches underwent over-elaborate preparation.

Born at the Royal Military College, Sandhurst, on March 11, 1859, Harry Patterson, after some years at school in Ramsgate, gained a place in the Harrow XI, and, proceeding to Oxford, played a big part in a victory over Cambridge by 135 runs in 1881. The Light Blues, very strong with three Studds and A. G. Steel, were expected to gain a fourth consecutive victory, but the Oxford fast bowler, A. H. Evans, took 13 wickets for 10 runs apiece. His second effort came after Patterson, going in first, played so admirably for five hours, despite having a finger broken, that he carried out his bat for 107. Besides this heroic display, Patterson gave further help. Early in the innings C. F. H. Leslie played a ball back to A. F. J. Ford, who, over 6ft. in height, reached up, took it with one hand, and threw the ball up. Leslie walked towards the pavilion, but Patterson, not satisfied that it was a catch, appealed to Farrands, the umpire, who decided in favour of the batsman. Leslie raised a score of eight to 70.

During 20 years, from 1880, Patterson made 6,902 runs for Kent, and in three seasons his average exceeded 40, the best being 49 in 1885. His highest innings was 181 against Somerset at Taunton in 1896; he and Lord Harris—who scored 119—put on 220 for the second wicket. Patterson shared in another stand of 220 against Somerset at Taunton two years later, when he made 111 and Alec Hearne 112, while against Gloucestershire at Gravesend in 1898 he and J. R. Mason (152) added 213 for the third wicket. He appeared for Gentlemen against Players four times in the '80s, and took part in Kent's victory over the Australians at Canterbury in 1884, the only success by a county against the touring teams of that season and 1882. At the time of Patterson's death, F. A. Mackinnon, Stanley Christopherson, M. C. Kemp and Alec Hearne were survivors of that triumphant XI. Often serving on the M.C.C. committee—first in 1893—he for some years was an auditor. After being Kent president he became a vice-president and trustee of the County Club, retaining these offices until the end.

PATTERSON, William Seeds, of Fulwood Park, Liverpool, died at his home at Woking on October 20, 1939, aged 85. An outstanding cricketer in the '70s, he was educated at Uppingham and was one of many players who established the cricket fame of that school. He captained the XI in 1873; played in the Cambridge Freshman's match in 1874, scoring 147, and in the next three seasons appeared against Oxford. In the 1876 University match he scored 105 not out and took seven wickets. He captained Cambridge in 1877 when Oxford, led by A. J. Webbe, won by 10 wickets. F. M. Buckland played a great innings of 117 not out and in the two Cambridge innings took seven wickets for 52. A. J. Webbe and his brother, H. R. Webbe, hit off 47 runs wanted by the Dark Blues for victory.

That year both University captains played for the Gentlemen in a memorable match against the Players at Lord's. The Gentlemen were set to get 143 to win and the task appeared light for a team so strong in batting that I. D. Walker, the captain, put himself in last. The order was changed in the second innings and when Patterson joined G. F. Grace nine men were out for 97, but the runs were obtained amidst tremendous excitement, the Gentlemen winning by one wicket and was described as "The Glorious Match." Now, A. J. Webbe, for many years captain and president of Middlesex, alone remains of 22 noted cricketers, the flower of the game at that time.

Patterson was an excellent all-round cricketer, an attractive batsman and a reliable slow bowler. After his University days he played little first-class cricket, though he turned out occasionally for Lancashire, the last time, as he said, being about 1882. Asked if he were ever president of the county, he replied: "Lancashire had rather a strong amateur representation, two or three Steels, two or three Hornbys as well as Vernon Royle. The management was always jealously retained at Manchester. I lived in Liverpool!"

PATTESON, Thomas Charles, who played for Canada against the United States in 1859, 1860, and 1865, was born at Patney, in Wiltshire, on October 5, 1836, and died at Toronto on September 21, 1907. He was educated at Eton and Oxford, but, although a good cricketer, did not obtain a place in either XI. He settled in Toronto in 1858, and was the promoter of the visit to America of Mr. Fitzgerald's team in 1872. He was a very fine wicket-keeper, and a keen supporter of the game. John Coleridge Patteson, who played for Eton and Oxford, was his cousin.

PATTISSON, Walter Badeley, who died at Beckenham on November 6, 1913, entered Tonbridge School at the age of nine, and was a member of the school XI in 1869, 1870, and 1871, being captain in the last year and always keeping wicket. He left school at the age of 16, and eventually became a partner in Messrs. Hores, Pattisson, and Bathurst, solicitors. It was in consequence of his business engagements that he was unable to play regularly for his county. He was playing for Kent when Mr. W. G. Grace made his famous score of 344 at Canterbury. His first appearance for the county was in 1876, when he played at Brighton against Sussex and made 36 in the second innings. He continued to play occasionally for the county until 1887, sometimes captaining the team. Altogether he appeared for Kent in 12 matches, making 214 runs with an average of 10.70, and occasionally playing under the name of W. Batt. After giving up first-class cricket in 1888 he was elected to the committee of the Kent County C.C. From 1872 to 1880 he was the hon. secretary of the Tonbridge C.C., and from 1886 to 1888 the hon. secretary of the Bickley Park C.C., for which he made many 100s. Mr. Pattisson was also prominent as a Rugby Union player, and at three-quarter he took part in some of the international trials in 1874, 1875, and 1876. He was not only one of the many first-class cricketers, but also one of the finest athletes produced by Tonbridge School. He was born at Witham, in Essex, on August 27, 1854.

PAUL, Arthur George, who died at his home at Didsbury, Manchester, in January, 1947, aged 82, played for Lancashire from 1889 to 1900. Tall and robust, he was a batsman of high skill, excelling at Taunton in 1895 when A. C. MacLaren played his great innings of 424—still a record for first-class cricket in England. Paul on that occasion made his highest score for the county, 177, and with his captain put on 363 for the second wicket. Lancashire totalled 801—still their highest innings. In that his best year Paul scored 829 runs for an average of 25.12, being third in the county to MacLaren and Albert Ward. A coach at Old Trafford after retiring from the XI because of ill-health, Paul was given a benefit in 1913, the Lancashire club contributing £400.

Born in Belfast, son of an Army Colonel, he became a good club cricketer with Notts Castle before qualifying for Lancashire when with the Nelson club. He also excelled at Rugby football, playing for Swinton at fullback or in the three-quarter line, and was a member of the team which toured Australia in 1888 under A. E. Stoddart's captaincy. In 1899 he was a good goalkeeper for Blackburn Rovers.

PAWLEY, Tom Edward, born at Farningham on January 21, 1859, died suddenly at Canterbury on August 3, 1923. He was educated at Tonbridge, but, although a very useful cricketer whilst there, did not obtain a place in the XI. He assisted Kent twice in 1880 and once in 1882 and again in 1887, in the last-mentioned game—v. Sussex at Tonbridge—taking three wickets for 11 runs. For many years he was captain of the Tonbridge C.C., and also hon. secretary from 1881 until his death. He was a good batsman and useful bowler, being originally fast, but afterwards taking to lobs. In 1911–12 he was manager of the English team which visited Australia. He will, however, always be best remembered for the splendid work he did for Kent County Cricket, his official association with the club extending from 1898 to 1923. As manager of the team he rendered capital service, and his assistance in the arrangement of the various Kent festivals had much to do with their smooth working. He was the founder of the Tonbridge Week.

PAYNE, Alfred, died of consumption at Leicester, his native place, on May 7, 1908. He kept wicket for his county on five occasions, catching six and stumping one. He was only a moderate bat. His first match for Leicestershire was against the West Indians in 1906.

PAYNE, Arnold C., who died on February 13, 1973, aged 75, served on the Northamptonshire committee for 40 years and was president of the County Club in 1969. He kept wicket in three first-class matches between 1931 and 1933.

PAYNE, Charles, who played for Sussex from 1857 until 1870, and for Kent from 1863 until 1870, died at Tonbridge on February 18, 1909. He was born at East Grinstead on May 12, 1832, and played for Sussex by birth and for Kent by residence. In *Scores and Biographies* (v—326) he was described as: "A fine, free, but very steady forward player, having a great reach, besides being a good hitter, and he has made many long scores in the best matches; also a splendid field at short-leg, in fact he was considered the 'best out' at that post." In a match against Hastings at Tunbridge Wells in 1863 he hit a ball from the late John Sands for which 13 were run, but when he scored 122 against XXII of Richmond in 1867 his first 26 runs were all singles. His highest score for Sussex was 137 v. M.C.C. and Ground at Brighton in 1867, and for Kent 135 not out v. Surrey at Gravesend in 1866. He played for England and for the South of England XI, but never, curiously enough, for the Players. When England met Surrey at the Oval in 1866 he was sent in first and made 86; "W.G.", then 18 years old, scored 224 not out, he and Payne adding 135 for the fourth wicket. For several seasons Payne, who belonged to a well-known cricketing family, umpired in first-class matches and gave the greatest satisfaction.

PAYNE, Charles Arthur Lynch, died in hospital in North Vancouver on March 21, 1976, aged 90. A member of the Charterhouse XI in 1903 and 1904, he first appeared in first-class cricket for M.C.C. v. Derbyshire at Lord's in 1905 and scored 101 in 110 minutes, following it a few days later with 52 for Middlesex v. Essex. He continued to play occasionally for Middlesex until 1909 and in 1906 and 1907 represented Oxford at Lord's. For Oxford his highest score was 78 against Sussex, though in 1907 in the first innings v. Cambridge he was top scorer with 38, but probably his most notable performance in first-class cricket was for Middlesex v. Kent at Tonbridge in 1906, when in a needle match he made 40 and 81, in the second innings putting on 182 with Sir Pelham Warner, who to the end of his life spoke highly of Payne's batting on that occasion. Joe Mounsey of Yorkshire, pro at Charterhouse from 1898 to 1926, always regarded Payne as the best batsman he ever taught there, although, like most Carthusians and unlike most Yorkshiremen, he was apt to give considerable encouragement to the slips. About 1910 he went out to Vancouver, where for years he did much to help and encourage young players, and in 1939 published a book entitled *What Matters in Batsmanship*. He played billiards for Oxford in 1906 and 1907, was Amateur Billiards Champion of Canada in 1927 and 1928 and had been Amateur Golf Champion of British Columbia. A cousin of M. W. Payne, against whom he played in his two University matches, he was at the time of his death the oldest living Oxford cricket Blue.

PAYNE, Joe, died at Luton on April 22, 1975, aged 61. He played for Bedfordshire from 1937 to 1951. In his second game for the county he took seven for 30 and six for 56 against Oxfordshire. His highest score was also against Oxfordshire—58 in 1938. He was better known as a footballer, playing successively for Luton, Chelsea and West Ham and gaining one international cap for England. By scoring 10 goals for Luton against Bristol Rovers in 1936, he established a League record.

PAYNE, John, who died at Glebe Point, Sydney, in May, 1928, at the age of 84, had played for XXII of New South Wales against Parr's team in 1863–64. He became a well-known umpire, and stood in a Test match with England.

PAYNE, Meyrick Whitmore, who died on June 2, 1963, aged 78, was a brilliant hitter and a first-rate wicket-keeper. A member of the Wellington XI from 1902 to 1903, he gained his Blue at Cambridge in 1904 and played for the University until 1907. His highest innings was 178 against Surrey at Cambridge in 1905, but that for which he will be most remembered was his 64 on the opening day of the University match the following summer. He hit the first 45 runs of the game in 20 minutes, taking 34 from the first two overs bowled to him by N. R. Udal, and altogether made 64 out of 73 in just over half an hour. Another notable display was 129 in two hours 25 minutes from the Lancashire bowling at Fenner's in 1907, in which year he captained Cambridge. Between 1904 and 1909, he made 25 appearances for Middlesex and he represented Gentlemen against Players on five occasions, being on the winning side at both Lord's and the Oval in 1904. He also toured America and Canada with E. W. Mann's all-amateur team in 1905. In all first-class cricket he scored 3,524 runs, average 24.30, and helped in the dismissal of 152 batsmen—120 caught and 32 stumped.

PAYNE, Richard, who was born at East Grinstead on June 9, 1827, died at Tunbridge Wells on April 11, 1906. He was elder brother of the "crack," Charles Payne, and himself played for Sussex occasionally between 1853 and 1866. He was a very fair all-round cricketer.

PAYNE, William, a member of the well-known cricketing family, died at East Grinstead on June 25, 1909. Between 1877 and 1883 he played in 19 matches for Sussex, scoring 214 runs with an average of 7.92 and taking 26 wickets for 19.42 runs each. He was born at East Grinstead on August 6, 1854, and was a nephew of Charles Payne.

PAYNTER, Edward, who died at Keighley on February 5, 1979, aged 77, was a left-handed batsman who averaged 84.42 for his seven Tests against Australia, a figure which no other Englishman can approach. This in itself would entitle him to a place among the great, but his figures become even more remarkable if his innings are analysed. In three of these matches he came to the rescue at a grave crisis. On the first occasion, the third Test in 1932–33, he came in at 186 for five, not a good score by the standards of Tests in Australia in those days, and made 77, adding 96 with Verity for the eighth wicket. In the fourth Test at Brisbane, he was taken to hospital with tonsilitis and doubtless, had all gone well with England, would not have batted. But all did not go well, and at 216 for six he emerged from the pavilion, refused Woodfull's offer of a runner, was still there at the close, and returned to bed in hospital. Next morning, he was not out until he had scored 83 in nearly four hours. On this occasion he and Verity put on 92 for the ninth wicket. Normally quick on his feet and a fine driver, he had conserved energy by waiting for opportunities to hit the ball to leg, preferably to the boundary. Few innings in history have so captivated the imagination of the public. Moreover, Paynter insisted on fielding for a couple of hours before retiring and then, as if to show that he was none the worse, in a brief second innings he finished the match with a six.

In 1938 at Lord's, he came in at 31 for three and helped Hammond in a stand of 222, of which his own share was 99. In the previous Test at Nottingham he had broken the record for England against Australia in this country with an innings of 216 not out. In all Tests, Paynter's average was 59.23. In the series in South Africa in 1938–39 he averaged 81.62, scoring a hundred in each innings of the first Test, and 243 in the third. Yet Paynter was 24 when he first made a hundred

for Lancashire Second XI, and between 1926 and 1929 he appeared only 11 times for the county without any success. It was not until 1931, when he was 30, that he made his first century against Warwickshire at Old Trafford, gained a regular place, and reached his 1,000 runs. In 1932 he was inconsistent, but on the strength of some notable innings was selected for the M.C.C. side to Australia. He had been picked for the third Test against New Zealand in 1931 but scored only three.

It was four years after the 1932–33 tour before Paynter played for England again. Meanwhile, he had made plenty of runs for Lancashire, and in 1936 actually scored 964 runs in August; unfortunately the side for Australia had already been picked. In 1937, however, he could be denied no longer. He scored 2,904 runs with an average of 53.77, including 322 in five hours against Sussex at Hove, and 266 against Essex at Old Trafford, and played in two Tests against New Zealand, missing the third because of injury. Two years later the War virtually ended his career. He resisted pressure to return to the county side at 45, but in 1947, in a couple of festival matches at Harrogate, played innings of 154, 73, and 127, the last taking only 85 minutes.

A small man, Paynter was by instinct an attacking batsman, particularly effective against slow spin, but also a fine hooker and cutter who did not spare the fast bowler if he pitched short. He was one of the great outfields of his day and almost equally good at cover—a beautiful thrower with a safe pair of hands. This was the more remarkable as early in life he had lost the top joints of two fingers in an accident. At Lord's in 1938, when Ames had broken a finger, Paynter kept wicket through the Australian second innings of 204, and though he had little or no experience of wicket-keeping conceded only five byes and held a catch. A wonderful cricketer.

CAREER FIGURES

Season	Matches	Inns	Not Outs	Runs	Highest Inns	100s	50s	Average	Catches
In England									
1926	2	4	0	10	8	0	0	2.50	1
1927	1	1	0	4	4	0	0	4.00	0
1929	7	10	2	100	21	0	0	12.50	3
1930	19	26	2	547	66	0	3	22.79	5
1931	31	49	6	1,235	102	2	6	28.72	12
1932	34	55	1	2,035	159	5	9	37.68	14
1933	34	41	4	1,342	176	1	8	36.27	15

Signifies not out.

CAREER FIGURES—*continued*

Season	Matches	Inns	Not Outs	Runs	Highest Inns	100s	50s	Average	Catches
In England									
1934	29	45	8	1,501	157*	5	4	40.56	12
1935	32	48	6	1,542	208*	3	7	36.71	13
1936	33	54	10	2,016	177	4	13	45.81	18
1937	34	58	4	2,904	322	5	18	53.77	20
1938	31	52	6	2,691	291	8	10	58.50	8
1939	31	50	4	1,953	222	4	7	42.45	13
1945	1	2	1	57	47*	0	0	57.00	0
1947	2	3	0	354	154	2	1	118.00	4
In Australia									
1932–33	11	16	3	538	102	1	3	41.38	4
In South Africa									
1938–39	11	14	0	1,072	243	5	4	76.57	4
In New Zealand									
1932–33	2	2	0	36	36	0	0	18.00	0
In India									
1950–51	2	2	1	86	75*	0	1	86.00	1
Totals	347	532	58	20,023	322	45	94	42.24	147

TEST CAREER

Season		Tests	Inns	Not Outs	Runs	Highest Inns	100s	50s	Average	Catches
1931	v. NZ	1	1	0	3	3	0	0	3.00	0
1932	v. India	1	2	0	68	54	0	1	34.00	0
1932–33	v. Australia	3	5	2	184	83	0	2	61.33	0
1932–33	v. NZ	2	2	0	36	36	0	0	18.00	0
1937	v. NZ	2	3	0	114	74	0	1	38.00	1
1938	v. Australia	4	6	2	407	216*	1	1	101.75	3
1938–39	v. SA	5	8	0	653	243	3	2	81.62	3
1939	v. WI	2	4	1	75	34	0	0	25.00	0
Totals		20	31	5	1,540	243	4	7	59.23	7

CENTURIES (45)

102	for Lancashire v. New Zealanders at Liverpool, 1931.
100	for Lancashire v. Warwickshire at Old Trafford, 1931.
159	for Lancashire v. Kent at Old Trafford, 1932.
153	for Lancashire v. All India at Liverpool, 1932.
152	for Lancashire v. Yorkshire at Bradford, 1932.
148	for Lancashire v. Middlesex at Old Trafford, 1932.
103	for Lancashire v. Gloucestershire at Cheltenham, 1932.
176	for Lancashire v. Cambridge University at Cambridge, 1933.
157*	for Lancashire v. Sussex at Old Trafford, 1934.
143	for Lancashire v. Oxford University at Oxford, 1934.
120*	for Lancashire v. Northamptonshire at Blackburn, 1934.
107	for Lancashire v. Leicestershire at Leicester, 1934.
100*	for Lancashire v. Worcestershire at Worcester, 1934.
208*	for Lancashire v. Northamptonshire at Northampton, 1935.
113	for Lancashire v. Sussex at Old Trafford, 1935.
111	for Lancashire v. Sir Julien Cahn's XI, at West Bridgford, 1935.
177	for Lancashire v. Glamorgan at Old Trafford, 1936.
132*	for Lancashire v. Northamptonshire at Northampton, 1936.
123*	for Lancashire v. Nottinghamshire at Trent Bridge, 1936.
119	for Lancashire v. Northamptonshire at Old Trafford, 1936.

Signifies not out.

CENTURIES (45)—*continued*

322	for Lancashire v. Sussex at Hove, 1937.
266	for Lancashire v. Essex at Old Trafford, 1937.
164	for Lancashire v. Glamorgan at Blackpool, 1937.
150	for Lancashire v. Derbyshire at Old Trafford, 1937.
132	for Lancashire v. Nottinghamshire at Old Trafford, 1937.
291	for Lancashire v. Hampshire at Southampton, 1938.
216*	for England v. Australia at Trent Bridge, 1938 (First Test).
177	for Lancashire v. Nottinghamshire at Old Trafford, 1938.
140	for Lancashire v. Nottinghamshire at Trent Bridge, 1938.
125 113* }	for Lancashire v. Warwickshire at Edgbaston, 1938.
122	for Lancashire v. Hampshire at Old Trafford, 1938.
104	for Lancashire v. Surrey at the Oval, 1938.
222	for Lancashire v. Derbyshire at Old Trafford, 1939.
159	for Lancashire v. Leicestershire at Leicester, 1939.
154	for Lancashire v. Nottinghamshire at Trent Bridge, 1939.
140	for Lancashire v. Glamorgan at Cardiff, 1939.
154	for North v. South at Harrogate, 1947.
127	for The Rest v. M. Leyland's XI, at Harrogate, 1947.

In Australia
102   for M.C.C. v. Tasmania at Launceston, 1932–33.

In South Africa

243	for England v. South Africa at Durban, 1938–39 (Third Test).
158	for M.C.C. v. Griqualand West at Kimberley, 1938–39.
117	for England v. South Africa at Johannesburg, 1938–39 (First Test).
102	for M.C.C. v. N.E. Transvaal at Pretoria, 1938–39.
100	for England v. South Africa at Johannesburg, 1938–39 (First Test).

PARTNERSHIPS

E. Paynter shared in the following large partnerships:

First Wicket
268   with C. Washbrook for Lancashire v. Sussex at Hove, 1937.
215   with C. Washbrook for Lancashire v. Nottinghamshire at Trent Bridge, 1939.
213   with C. Washbrook for Lancashire v. Leicestershire at Leicester, 1939.

Second Wicket
231   with G. E. Tyldesley for Lancashire v. Cambridge University at Cambridge, 1933.
208   with J. Iddon for Lancashire v. Leicestershire at Old Trafford, 1936.

Third Wicket
306   with N. Oldfield for Lancashire v. Hampshire at Southampton, 1938.
271   with N. Oldfield for Lancashire v. Sussex at Hove, 1937.
242   with W. R. Hammond for England v. South Africa at Durban, 1938–39.

Fourth Wicket
236   with G. E. Tyldesley for Lancashire v. Sussex at Old Trafford, 1935.
227   with G. E. Tyldesley for Lancashire v. Northamptonshire at Peterborough, 1934.
222   with W. R. Hammond for England v. Australia at Lord's, 1938.
(*This is the record fourth-wicket stand for England v. Australia.*)
220   with G. E. Tyldesley for Lancashire v. Leicestershire at Leicester, 1934.

Fifth Wicket
206   with D. C. S. Compton for England v. Australia at Trent Bridge, 1938.
(*This is the record fifth-wicket stand for England v. Australia.*)

With C. Washbrook, Paynter in 1937 for Lancashire v. Nottinghamshire at Trent Bridge shared a century first-wicket partnership in each innings: 108 and 126 unbeaten.

In bowling during his first-class career, E. Paynter took 30 wickets for an average of 13.71.

Signifies not out.

PAYTON, Wilfred Richard Daniel, died at Beeston, near Nottingham, on May 2, 1943, aged 61. From 1905 to 1930 he helped his county with steadily increasing value during a long period when Nottinghamshire stood out as an exceptionally strong side. Starting modestly in 1905, he became the regular number five in the batting order, and after the First World War he rivalled W. Whysall for preference as the most consistent run-getter in the team. In 1923 he scored 1,379, with an average of 45.96, and in 1926 did still better with 1,743 runs, average 48.41, in county matches, 133 being the highest of his six three-figure innings.

Twice he assisted Nottinghamshire to win the Championship—in 1907 under A.O. Jones and in 1929 when A.W. Carr was captain. A strained thigh handicapped Payton during this second triumph with which he was associated, but he came out second in the averages to Whysall, his batting at the age of 46 earning high praise; he did especially well against Lancashire at Trent Bridge, making 169, the highest score of his career, during which he hit 39 centuries. Payton and George Gunn were then the only remaining members of the side who helped to carry off the championship 22 years before. Next season, 1930, illness, as in some previous seasons, handicapped Payton, but he maintained his form in this his benefit year, which practically ended his first-class cricket, for he played little in 1931 and then retired.

Altogether he scored 22,132 runs for the county with an average of 34.36. Of rather frail build, Wilfred Payton batted in excellent style with a wide range of well-controlled strokes, and he fielded admirably. Usually steady in defence and orthodox stroke play, he could score freely when time was important. In 1919 at Huddersfield he hit 63 out of 78 in 55 minutes off the Yorkshire bowlers, and next season he made 50 out of 70 in 48 minutes at Worksop against Derbyshire. His son, the Rev. W. E. G. Payton, played for the county and got his Blue at Cambridge in 1937.

PEACEY, The Rev. Canon John Raphael, who died on October 31, 1971, aged 75, played as a batsman for Sussex in 1920 and 1921 after being in the XI at St. Edmund's School, Canterbury.

PEACH, Charles William, died at Coxheath, near Maidstone, on February 27, 1977, aged 77. After being for many years one of the mainstays of the bowling of the Mote, Maidstone, he was tried for Kent against York-shire at Headingley in 1930 and caused some stir by taking six for 93 in the two innings, his victims including Sutcliffe and Leyland twice each. He did some useful work in the later matches and finished the season with 29 wickets at 25.86. However, his action was regarded with suspicion and, although he was never no-balled, two matches in 1931 concluded his first-class career. He bowled right-arm, on the quick side of medium, and could produce a sharp off-break.

PEACH, Frederick George, who died on January 15, 1965, aged 83, made occasional appearances as an amateur for Derbyshire between 1907 and 1925. He played in 16 matches for the county in 1920, scoring 186 runs, average 12.40, and hitting his highest innings, 61 not out against Warwickshire at Edgbaston. He had been Mayor of Burton-on-Trent. He was unrelated to F. G. Peach, the present editor of the *Derbyshire County Cricket Year Book*.

PEACH, Herbert Alan, who died on October 8, 1961, two days after his 71st birthday, was a more than useful all-rounder for Surrey from 1919 to 1931, in which period he scored 8,709 runs, average 23.61, and took 785 wickets for 26.38 runs each. His best season as a strong-hitting batsman was that of 1920 when he hit 913 runs, including 200 not out against Northamptonshire at Northampton. On that occasion he shared a sixth-wicket stand of 171 in 42 minutes with P. G. H. Fender, who obtained 113 not out in the same time. Against Essex at Leyton in 1925, he scored 109 in 85 minutes. As an untiring medium-paced bowler able to spin the ball, he did best in 1923 when his wickets numbered 83 at 23.15 apiece, and the following season he enjoyed the satisfaction of dismissing four Sussex batsmen with following balls at the Oval, finishing with an analysis of eight wickets for 60. A first-rate fieldsman in any position, he held 167 catches. While Surrey coach from 1935 to 1939 he was responsible for the "discovery" of the Bedser twins.

PEAKE, The Rev. Edward, a fast bowler of considerable renown in the '80s, died on January 4, 1945, aged 84. After two years in the Marlborough XI he got his Oxford Blue in 1881 and played three times against Cambridge, his best performances in the University matches at Lord's being seven wickets for 147 runs in 1882 and next year six for 46, but each time Oxford were beaten by seven wickets, Cambridge being very strong at the period with the three Studds, Hon. M. B.

Hawke and C. Aubrey Smith in the side. In 1888 he twice helped Gloucestershire to beat the Australians—by 257 runs at Clifton and by eight wickets at Cheltenham. Peake, right-arm, contrasted well with Woof, slow left, and Roberts, fast left, and the amateur dismissing some of the best batsmen did valuable work in gaining the victories. Altogether in first-class cricket he was credited with 114 wickets at 21.94 runs apiece. He also played for Berkshire.

PEARCE, Henry George, who died on March 27, 1936, in Philadelphia, was a good fast bowler and useful batsman. He toured West Indies in 1909 and four years later for Gentlemen of Philadelphia took seven Australian wickets for 57 runs, among his victims being E. R. Mayne and H. L. Collins. In 1914 he visited England with the Merion club, and besides taking 35 wickets at 10 runs apiece he played an innings of 92 not out. He was an honorary life member of Incogniti, against whom in 1920 he dismissed D. R. Jardine, G. O. Shelmerdine and J. S. F. Morrison at the small cost of 13 runs. Born on April 21, 1886, he was nearly 50 years of age.

PEARCE, Percy (familiarly known as "Peter"), who from 1874 to 1898 was ground superintendent at Lord's, died suddenly at Hither Green, on Tuesday, August 22, 1911. He was born on September 2, 1843, at Shipley, Sussex. For some time he was gaining experience in the making and upkeep of lawns under the direction of Mr. Sydney Ford, of Leonardslee, Sussex. The first cricket ground of which he had charge was the present county ground at Brighton. On November 9, 1874, Pearce was appointed to Lord's, being the successful applicant out of over 400 candidates. About this period the condition of Lord's must have been very bad. The *Saturday Review* in its report of the University match of 1873 said: "We must add in conclusion that very little can be said in favour of the wickets provided for this match. There has not been a single good wicket at Lord's as yet this season.... It is almost an insult to common sense to suppose that a club with an income of £10,000 a year cannot find the means of covering half a dozen acres with turf adapted to the game of cricket.... There are other clubs in London whose committees can provide wickets for any number of great matches, on which cricketers may play without any fear of their teeth being knocked down their throats, or their arms being disabled." Pearce went to Lord's in the winter of 1874, and a new order

of things soon came to pass. The *Field* reporting the Gentlemen v. Players match of 1876, said: "There is a certain amount of novelty attached to the idea of a cricket ground being 'too good' for the purpose of a great match, yet such an idea is entertained by the Marylebone club, and Pearce has orders not to improve it further.... Better wickets than those of Monday were not needed, and to their condition the heavy scoring may in a large degree be attributed." The *Standard* of June 27, 1876, speaking of the University game, said: "Time was when a good wicket at Lord's was the exception, but now, happily—thanks to Pearce, the groundsman—the playing portion of the arena is in faultless condition, and a batsman can concentrate his energies on the defence of his 'timber' without, as formerly, having any misgiving as to his personal safety." Pearce's death was due to syncope, and the funeral took place on August 26, 1911, at Ladywell Cemetery. He left a widow, three sons, and a daughter. His eldest son, a promising cricketer who had played for the Sussex Colts, and had wonderful records in India, was killed in the South African War.

PEARCE, Thomas Alexander, died in hospital at Tunbridge Wells on August 11, 1982, aged 71. He was three years in the Charterhouse XI and, after playing a number of matches for Kent in 1930 and 1931, won a regular place in the side in 1932, when he scored 581 runs with an average of 24.13, his highest score being 83 against Northamptonshire at Tunbridge Wells: he and Ames put on 194 for the seventh wicket "by brilliant cricket." At the end of the season he went out to join his father's business in Hong Kong, but reappeared in the county side when home on leave in 1937 and 1946. Captured in the siege of Hong Kong, he spent the rest of the War as a prisoner, and it was therefore no mean performance when in his third match in 1946 he made 106 in two and three-quarter hours against Northamptonshire at Northampton. This was his only hundred in first-class cricket. A natural games-player, who had been in the racquets pair at school and a scratch golfer, he relied largely on the typical racquets player's off-side strokes, and county bowlers soon found ways of keeping him relatively quiet, though he was a prolific scorer in club cricket. To Kent his main value was his glorious fielding in any position, a more important consideration than it would be in these days when the average age is so much lower. He was for many years a leading figure in cricket in

Hong Kong and after his retirement to England he served on the Kent committee and was president in 1978. Altogether for Kent he scored 1,177 runs with an average of 17.05.

PEARCE, Sir William, who was born in 1853 and died at Walmer, Kent, on August 24, 1932, played a few innings for Kent and subsequently assisted Essex when a second-class county.

PEARE, William George, who died at St. Luke's, Cork, on November 16, 1979, aged 74, was a fast-medium bowler and useful batsman who played seven matches for Warwickshire in 1926, but, meeting with little success, abandoned professional cricket and took a job with Dunlop. It was while working for them that he played as an amateur for M.C.C. v. Gentlemen of Ireland in 1936.

PEARSE, Alan A., who died on June 14, 1981, aged 67, played occasionally for Somerset from 1936 to 1938 as an amateur. In nine matches his batting average was 5.79 and his highest score 20 against Kent in his first innings for the county.

PEARSE, Charles Ormerod Cato, who died at Durban on May 7, 1953, aged 68, was a member of the South African touring team in Australia in 1910–11, taking part in three Test matches, and narrowly missed selection for the tour of England in 1912. A stylish batsman and useful change bowler, he played at intervals for Natal from 1905 to 1924.

PEARSON, Frederick, who died on October 11, 1963, aged 83, played as an all-round professional for Worcestershire from 1900 to 1926, hitting 18,737 runs, average 24.23, taking 823 wickets for 29.38 runs each and holding 151 catches. Born at Mitcham, Surrey, "Dick" Pearson attracted attention in 1900 when, while qualifying for Worcestershire, he earned a match-analysis of 10 wickets for 98 runs against the West Indies team captained by R. S. A. Warner, brother of Sir Pelham. An opening batsman, he scored the first of his 22 County Championship centuries the following season, and hit the highest of them, 167 against Glamorgan at Swansea, in 1921 when heading the county averages with 1,498 at 36.53 an innings. Six times he exceeded 1,000 runs in a season and in 1923, when 43, he achieved the "cricketers' double," this being the one summer in which he dismissed 100 batsmen. For some years after the First World War he and F. Root between them virtually comprised the Worcestershire attack.

PEARSON, Harry Eyre, who played three times for Yorkshire in 1878 and twice in 1880, died at Sheffield on July 8, 1903, and was buried at Intake on July 11. He was born on August 7, 1851, at Attercliffe, near Sheffield. *Scores and Biographies* (xiv–696) described him as "an excellent slow, originally fast, round-armed bowler, with (1878) a great 'local reputation,' and an average batsman, fielding generally at cover-point or long-leg." In the five matches in which he assisted Yorkshire he scored 36 runs, with an average of nine, and obtained seven wickets at a cost of 18.85 runs each.

PEARSON-GREGORY, Thomas Sherwin, who died on November 25, 1935, aged 84, was in the Rugby XI of 1869 when C. K. Francis, after taking seven wickets for 25 runs and doing the hat-trick in Marlborough's first innings, dismissed all his opponents at a cost of 15 runs—an astonishing performance giving him a match record of 17 wickets for 40 runs. For several years T. S. Pearson—his name before adding Gregory—played regularly at Lord's when M.C.C. and Middlesex put very strong sides in the field. One of his best innings was 121 for M.C.C. against Sussex in 1880. Ten years later he assisted Leicestershire, his native county—he was born at Barnwell on June 20, 1851—and in 1902 he was the Nottinghamshire president. Over 6ft. tall T. S. Pearson hit hard in good free style and bowled slow round-arm. At Oxford he failed to get his Blue but he played in many representative matches including some for England in the Canterbury Week. Adept at all court games he was champion of racquets at Rugby and in 1875 he played real tennis for Oxford against Cambridge.

PEATE, Edmund, the most famous slow bowler of his day, died on March 11, 1900, at Newlay, near Leeds. Though he had long since ceased to take part in first-class cricket—dropping out of the Yorkshire XI at the beginning of the season of 1887—he was quite a young man. He was born at Holbeck on March 2, 1856. His career was exceptionally brilliant while it lasted, but very short. Earning a place in the Yorkshire team in 1879 he rose in the following season to the top of the tree, and there he remained until the end of 1884, succeeding Alfred Shaw as the representative slow-bowler of England. There ought to have been many more years of good work before him, but he put on weight to a great extent, and in the summer of 1886 it became evident that his day was over. Without using a harsh word, it may fairly be said that he would have lasted longer if he had ordered his life more carefully. He never entirely lost his skill as a bowler, and even up to the last year or two he was successful in club cricket in and around Leeds. At his best he was a great bowler. As to that there cannot be two opinions, though it is true that he was fortunate at the outset of his career in playing in very wet seasons. He did not set store on a big break, but on most wickets he could make the ball do enough to beat the bat, and his pitch was a marvel of accuracy. He has had brilliant successors in the Yorkshire XI in Peel and Rhodes, but many batsmen—W. L. Murdoch among the number—who met him in his prime are of opinion that as a left-handed slow bowler he has never been equalled. The immediate cause of his death was pneumonia, but his health had been in a bad state for some time.

Some of his best performances with the ball were:

6 wickets for 14 runs, Yorkshire v. Middlesex, at Huddersfield, 1879.
5 wickets for 11 runs, Yorkshire v. Derbyshire, at Derby, 1880.
14 wickets for 130 runs, Yorkshire v. Sussex, at Brighton, 1881.
14 wickets for 77 runs, Yorkshire v. Surrey, at Huddersfield, 1881.
8 wickets for 71 runs, England v. Australia, at the Oval, 1882.
8 wickets for 57 runs, Shaw and Shrewsbury's XI, at Sydney, 1882.
6 wickets for 12 runs, Yorkshire v. Derbyshire, at Derby, 1882.
8 wickets for 32 runs, Yorkshire v. Middlesex, at Sheffield, 1882.
8 wickets for   5 runs, Yorkshire v. Surrey, at Holbeck, 1883.
5 wickets for 17 runs, Yorkshire v. Notts, at Sheffield, 1883.
6 wickets for 13 runs, Yorkshire v. Gloucestershire, at Moreton-in-Marsh, 1884.
10 wickets for 51 runs, North of England v. the Australians, at Manchester, 1884.
10 wickets for 45 runs, Yorkshire v. Derbyshire, at Huddersfield, 1885.
6 wickets for 17 runs, England v. Shaw's Australian XI, at Lord's, 1885.
9 wickets for 21 runs, Yorkshire v. Sussex, at Huddersfield, 1886.

In all first-class matches in 1882 he obtained 214 wickets at a cost of 2,466 runs.

He first represented the Players against the Gentlemen in 1881, and took part in the matches for six years, bowling in 11 matches (21 innings), 3,227 balls for 996 runs, and 39 wickets, average 25.53.

PECHELL, Capt. C. A. K., who soon after the outbreak of the War in South Africa was killed at Mafeking in 1899, was a member of the Eton XI in 1888. He will be remembered as one of the slowest left-handed bowlers ever seen at Lord's.

PEDDER, Frederick, who died at Moonah, near Hobart, on March 5, 1926, aged 85, played in representative matches for Tasmania, one of these being against the English team of 1873–74.

PEDEN, Mrs Margaret, who died in 1981, was a founder member of the Australian Cricket Council. In 1937 she captained the first Australian women's team to tour England, and she maintained her interest and support for the game, especially in her home state of New South Wales, until her death.

PEEBLES, Ian Alexander Ross, who died on February 28, 1980, aged 72, was for a short time one of the most formidable bowlers in the world and one of the few who could make Bradman look fallible. A tall man with a beautifully easy run-up and a high action, which gave him a particularly awkward flight, he bowled leg-breaks and googlies, and in an age of fine leg spinners he was, for a while, the equal of any.

The start of his career was unusual. Coming south from Scotland in the hope of getting a chance in the cricket world, he was engaged as secretary at the Aubrey Faulkner School of Cricket and so impressed Faulkner himself (to whose coaching he always acknowledged a great debt) and also Sir Pelham Warner that, when difficulty was found in raising a good enough Gentlemen's side against the Players at the Oval in 1927, he was given a place. On this occasion he bowled Sandham, but that was his only wicket; nor was he more successful later in the season at the Folkestone and Scarborough festivals. However, that winter he was sent with the M.C.C. side to South Africa; ostensibly he went as secretary to the captain, but bowled well enough to secure a place in the first four Tests and, without doing anything spectacular, made it clear that his possibilities had not been overestimated. In 1928 he played a few matches for Middlesex, but it was in 1929 that he really came to the fore, taking 120 wickets at just under 20 runs each and being one of three amateurs to take 100 wickets for the county that season—a unique performance. In 1930 he was up at Oxford, for whom he took 70 wickets, 13 of them against Cambridge; then, after taking six wickets (including Hobbs, Sutcliffe and Leyland) for 105 for the Gentlemen v. the Players, he was picked for the fourth Test at Old Trafford. Here, as soon as Peebles came on, Woodfull, who was well set, became acutely uncomfortable, on one occasion leaving a ball which just went over his middle stump; Bradman, coming in, was all but bowled first ball by Peebles, who then had him dropped in the slips and finally caught at slip for 14. The first three balls Kippax received from Peebles produced three confident but unsuccessful appeals for lbw. For such bowling three for 150 was a wholly inadequate reward. In the final Test at the Oval six for 204 may not look much, but in an Australian total of 695 it was better than anyone else. That winter Peebles went again with M.C.C. to South Africa and both there and against New Zealand in the following summer he was one of the most effective bowlers. Already, though, the amount of bowling he had had to do in matches, followed by countless hours in the nets in winter, was affecting him; his leg-break was losing its venom, he was becoming increasingly dependent upon his googly, and his great days were passing, though he was picked for the last Test in 1934, an invitation which he had to refuse owing to injury. When, after several seasons of intermittent appearances, he returned to regular County Cricket in 1939 to captain Middlesex, Peebles was really no more than a change bowler, and though he played occasionally until 1948, the loss of an eye in a wartime air-raid had, to all intents and purposes, ended his serious cricket career.

After his playing days were over he entered the wine trade and also became a notable cricket writer and journalist. When writing of players he had played with or seen, he was in the top class; to a deep knowledge of the game he added rare charm and humour. For any student of cricket history over the last 60 years, his many books are compulsory and delightful reading.

PEEL, Robert, who died at Morley on August 12, 1941, aged 84, was one of the finest all-round cricketers of any time. Primarily he was a bowler, the second in the remarkable succession of slow left-handers—Edmund Peate, Peel, Wilfred Rhodes and Hedley Verity—who rendered such brilliant service to Yorkshire over a period of 60 years. Born at Churwell, near Leeds, on February 12, 1857, "Bobby" Peel first played for his county in 1882, when Yorkshire were singularly rich in bowling talent, so that he had to wait several years before gaining real distinction. Still, being a capital fieldsman, especially at cover-point, and a punishing left-handed batsman, he kept his place in the team, and when Peate's connection with the county ceased in unhappy circumstances Peel came to the fore. For nine seasons, with his fine length, easy action and splendid command of spin, this sturdily built left-hander regularly took over 100 wickets for Yorkshire, his county total amounting to 1,550 at an average cost of 15 runs each. He was often a match-winner. In 1887 he took five Kent wickets for 14 runs in an innings and, with 43 runs in a low-scoring match, helped largely in a victory by four wickets. In the same season 11 Leicestershire wickets fell to him for 51 runs at Dewsbury, five in the first innings for four runs. A year later he took eight Nottinghamshire wickets in an innings for 12 runs, while in 1892 five wickets for seven runs in an innings and eight for 33 in the match against Derbyshire at Leeds was a startling performance. He did even better in 1895 against Somerset, 15 wickets falling to him in 36 overs for 50 runs, nine for 22 in one innings causing a sensation. At Halifax in 1897, a month before his county career ended, Peel dismissed eight Kent men in an innings for 53 runs, his match average showing 11 for 85; this performance gave Yorkshire an innings victory with 103 runs to spare in two days. Peel's full return in bowling in first-class cricket was 1,754 wickets at 16.21 runs apiece.

He did some remarkable things in Test matches with Australia, against whom he played for England 20 times. At Sydney in 1894, Australia, set to get 177, hit off 113 of the runs for the loss of two wickets before stumps were drawn on the fifth day. The result then appeared a foregone conclusion, but strong sunshine followed heavy rain during the night. Peel slept through the storm. Astounded when he saw the drying pitch, he said to the English captain, "Mr. Stoddart, gie me t' ball," and with "Johnny" Briggs, the Lancashire left-hander, also at his best, the remaining eight batsmen were disposed of for 53 runs. So England gained an extraordinary win by 10 runs after facing a total of 586, then a record for these Tests, the previous best being Australia's 551 at the Oval in 1884. Peel's analysis in the fourth innings was six for 67. Peel also enjoyed a large share in winning the rubber match of that tour. He took seven wickets, scored 73 in a stand for 152 with A. C. MacLaren, and following a grand partnership for 210 by Albert Ward, of Lancashire, and J. T. Brown, of Yorkshire, the two best scorers in England's first innings hit off the runs, the victorious total being 298 for four wickets. In 1896 at Kennington Oval, with conditions very difficult for batsmen, he and J. T. Hearne got rid of Australia for 44. Peel's share in the victory by 66 runs was eight wickets for 53 runs, and his last innings analysis six wickets in 12 overs for 23 runs—some revenge for getting "a pair." Hearne's figures showed 10 wickets for 60. That was the last match in which W. G. Grace led England to success over Australia.

Besides his great achievements as a bowler, Peel scored over 11,000 runs for Yorkshire, hitting 10 centuries. His highest innings was 226 not out against Leicestershire in 1892, and four years later he obtained 210 not out in a Yorkshire score of 887 against Warwickshire at Edgbaston, a total which remains a county match record. Peel and Lord Hawke, who added 292 for the eighth wicket, F. S. Jackson and E. Wainwright all reached three figures in that innings—then a record, four centuries in an innings. In 1889, the year in which the over was increased from four balls to five, Peel put together 158 in the Yorkshire second innings at Lord's, but yet was on the losing side, a brilliant 100 not out in 80 minutes by T. C. O'Brien taking Middlesex to victory by four wickets with 10 minutes to spare. Yielding 1,295 runs for 36 wickets, the game produced a record aggregate for a match in England at the time.

Peel went four times to Australia, in 1884–85, 1887–88, 1891–92 and 1894–95, and in Test matches with Australia he took 102 wickets for less than 17 runs each. He also figured in Players' teams against the Gentlemen from 1887 to 1897, taking in those games 48 wickets at a cost of 16 runs apiece.

He scored 1,206 runs and took 128 wickets in all matches in 1896, the year before his remarkable career came to an end. Sent off the field by Lord Hawke during a game at Bramall Lane and suspended for the remainder of the 1897 season, he was not seen again in the Yorkshire team. He did, however, appear for an England XI against Joe Darling's Australian side at Truro two years later, taking five wickets. His benefit match at Bradford in 1894 realised £2,000.

PEGLER, Sidney James, who died in South Africa on September 10, 1972, aged 84, was a very fine spin bowler. He appeared in 16 Tests against England and Australia, taking 47 wickets for 33.44 runs apiece. He toured England in 1912, when he took 29 wickets in six Tests in the triangular tournament, and in 1924 when *Wisden* stated: "How the side would have got on without Pegler it is painful to think and he was not one of the original choices." Pegler returned to England in 1951 as manager of Dudley Nourse's side. They won only eight matches, but 900,000 saw them play and the tour produced a record profit of £17,500—£6,000 more than the 1947 side.

PEIRCE, Lieut.-Col. Harold Ernest ("Joe"), C.B.E., J.P., a vice-president of Surrey County C.C., who died aged 87 on November 12, 1979, was a generous financial benefactor to sport, and to cricket in particular. Lord's Taverners and the National Playing Fields Association both benefited by over £15,000 from a function organised on his 80th birthday. Earlier he purchased the Addiscombe C.C. ground, where he spent a lifetime as player and official, and put it in trust for the club. His ashes were scattered on the square.

PELHAM, Anthony George, who died on March 9, 1969, aged 57, distinguished himself for Eton in 1930, his one year in the XI, when, with skilfully varied medium-pace bowling against Harrow at Lord's, he dismissed seven batsmen for 21 runs in the first innings and four for 23 in the second. During that season and the next he played in 10 matches for Sussex and in 1933 appeared briefly for Somerset. The following year he got his Blue for Cambridge. He was grandson of the Hon. F. G. Pelham—later the fifth Earl of Chichester—a Cambridge Blue from 1864 to 1867, who also played for Sussex.

PELLEW, Clarence Edward ("Nip"), died in Adelaide on May 9, 1981, aged 87. The last survivor but one of Warwick Armstrong's great Australian side of 1921, which was perhaps the first to set the winning of the Tests above all other considerations, he stood out from the rest as having more the traditional approach of the English amateur. Flaxen-haired and seldom wearing a cap, he was an attacking batsman, a matter of some importance when Tests in England were confined to three days. He was a fine straight-driver and a great exponent of the off-drive played slightly late to send the ball between cover and third man; he was also a competent player off his legs and a splendid runner between the wickets. But though he made two 100s in the 1920–21 series and for his career in Sheffield Shield cricket had an average of 39.50, it is as an outfield that he is chiefly remembered. Credited with being able to run the 100 yd. in 10.2 seconds and to throw a cricket ball over 100 yd., he might well, after sprinting 40 yd. round the boundary save not one run but two or three, so swiftly did he get rid of the ball. In any discussion of the world's greatest outfields, he must be a candidate for a place.

After showing promise for South Australia in 1913–14 and making 97 against New South Wales in 1914–15, he went to the War and it was not until 1919, when he was a member of the A.I.F. side in England, that he really became prominent. Starting with 105 not out against Cambridge University in his first match, he made 1,260 runs with an average of 38, including four centuries. Returning to Australia he made 271 in four and three-quarter hours against Victoria, equalling a record set up by George Giffen 30 years before. In 1920–21 he played in four of the five Tests, scoring 115 in just over three hours in the second and hitting brilliantly in the third to get 104 in two hours. After this he was a trifle disappointing as a batsman in England in 1921, failing to reach 1,000 runs, but even so he was never omitted from the Test side. That was the end of his regular first-class career but, reappearing for South Australia in a few matches in 1928–29, he showed what a loss his premature retirement had been. From 1930 to the War, and again from 1958 to 1970, he was South Australia's state coach. Several members of his family had played for South Australia, and it was from one of them, J. H. Pellew, a very useful performer, that he inherited the nickname of "Nip."

PENN, Capt. Eric Frank (4th Grenadier Guards), born in London on April 17, 1878, was killed in action in France on October 18, 1915. As a member of the Eton XI of 1897 he scored 195 runs with an average of 15.00 and took 12 wickets for 18.08 runs each. Against Harrow he made 0 and 22 and obtained two wickets in the first innings for 46 runs. In 1899 and 1902 he played for Cambridge against Oxford, scoring 43 runs in his three innings and taking one wicket at a cost of 113 runs. In 1902 he played an innings of 51 not out v. All Ireland on the Cambridge ground. He visited America in 1898 as a member of Mr. P. F. Warner's team, and the same year

was elected a member of the M.C.C. Owing to service in the South African War, he did not play in first-class cricket in 1900 and 1901. His name will be found in Norfolk matches, commencing in 1899. He was the eldest son of Mr. William Penn, and nephew of Messrs. Frank and Alfred Penn, and of Messrs. Frederick, Lennard and Graham Stokes, all of whom have played for Kent.

PENN, Frank, the famous Kent batsman of a generation back, died on December 26, 1916, at his home, Bifrons, near Canterbury. Though little or nothing had been seen of him in the cricket field for 35 years he was far indeed from forgotten. Born at Lewisham on March 7, 1851, Mr. Penn had a short but very brilliant career, ranking for several years among the finest batsmen of his day. He had a free, commanding style, and combined strong defence with splendid hitting. Stepping out of ordinary club cricket into first-class matches, he was, from the beginning, thoroughly at home in his new surroundings. He began to play for Kent in 1875, and in the following year he was seen at Lord's for the first time, scoring 44 and 35 for M.C.C. against Yorkshire. No doubt was felt as to his class. Indeed he made such an impression that he was picked for Gentlemen against Players in 1876, both at the Oval and Lord's. Thenceforward he was in the front rank. Unfortunately, his health gave way just when he was at the height of his fame. In the season of 1881 he was attacked by an affection of the heart and, being forbidden to run, had perforce to give up the game. Among those who helped Lord Harris to re-establish Kent cricket no one did better work than Mr. Penn. His best year for the county was 1877 when he made 857 runs in 24 innings—three times not out—with an average of 40. He made many big scores for Kent, the highest being 160 against Surrey, at Maidstone in 1878; 148 against Surrey, at the Oval in 1877; and 135 against England, at Canterbury in 1877. Perhaps the innings of his life, however, was 134 at Lord's, for M.C.C. against Cambridge University, in 1879, when he treated A. G. Steel's bowling as it had never been treated before. He had finished with cricket before Test matches became frequent, but it was his privilege to play for England against Australia at the Oval in September, 1880, in the first of the long series of contests in this country. Scoring 23 and 27 not out, he made the hit that gave England a victory by five wickets in that memorable game, cutting George Palmer for four. Now that he is dead the only survivors of the England XI of 1880 are Lord Harris and Mr. A. P. Lucas. Mr. Penn was a member of Lord Harris's team in Australia in 1878–79. He appeared eight times for Gentlemen v. Players, batting well, but without any conspicuous success. His best score was 52, at the Oval in 1876. As a batsman, Mr. Penn had one advantage over many of his contemporaries. Learning ˙ the game against bowlers not devoted to the "off theory" he knew the joy of real leg hitting. He could hit as hard to square leg as William Oscroft. He was president of the Kent County Club in 1905.—S.H.P.

PENN, Frank, Jnr., who died on April 23, 1961, aged 76, played in three matches for Kent in 1904 and 1905. For Household Brigade against the Royal Artillery in 1906 he scored innings of 101 and 123 not out.

PENTECOST, J., the old Kent wicket-keeper, died at St. John's Wood on February 23, 1902, aged 42, after a long illness. For some time he had been a member of the ground staff at Lord's. In 1892 the match between Kent and Surrey, at Tonbridge, was set apart as a benefit to him. Pentecost was obliged to abandon the game sooner than would ordinarily have been the case, owing to failing eyesight. He was born on October 15, 1859.

PENTELOW, John Nix, a great authority and a prolific writer on the game, died at Carshalton Beeches, Surrey, on July 5, 1931, aged 59. He was a frequent contributor to *Cricket*, of which he was editor and proprietor from January, 1912, Lillywhite's *Annual* and *The Cricketer* and to *Wisden*. Among his best-known publications are: *England v. Australia* (two editions); *Australian Team of 1899*, *Cricket's Guide to Cricketers*, *Who's Who In the Cricket World*, *Australian Cricket Teams in England* and *Historic Bats*. He was born at St. Ives, Huntingdonshire, on March 26, 1872.

PEPALL, G., who died on January 8, 1953, aged 76, played occasionally for Gloucestershire when Dr. W. G. Grace was at his best. Pepall, a fast bowler, achieved his best performance at Bristol in 1896 when he took five Yorkshire wickets for 63 runs. His victims included F. S. Jackson, J. T. Brown, R. Moorhouse and E. Wainwright.

PERCIVAL, John Douglas, died in hospital at Roehampton on March 5, 1983, aged 80. After heading the Radley batting averages in

1918, when he was under 16, he was in the Westminster XI in the next three years and captain in 1921. With a good defence and strong on the leg side, he seemed to have a bright future. However, at Oxford, though he had a trial for the University and played for Gloucestershire against them in 1923, he was never seriously in the running for a Blue. His batting style and even his mannerisms were modelled closely on D. J. Knight, from whom he had learnt much of his cricket.

PERCY, Robert Henry Gilbert, who died at Johannesburg on August 31, 1948, aged 63, played occasionally for Griqualand West from 1906 to 1923, latterly keeping wicket. Against Orange Free State at Bloemfontein in December 1922, besides scoring 53, he dismissed six opponents, three caught and three stumped.

PEREIRA, The Rev. Edward, died on February 25, 1939, aged 72. Educated at Oratory School, Birmingham, of which he became headmaster, he took great interest in cricket. A good all-round player himself, he helped his boys by buying a ground at Edgbaston for the school. He played for Warwickshire occasionally in 1886, 1895, and 1896 without doing anything noteworthy; but his few appearances suggested that he would have been valuable if able to give time to County Cricket.

PERKINS, Henry, so well known to all classes of cricketers as secretary of the Marylebone club, died on May 6, 1916, at his home, Ormskirk, New Barnet. Born at Sawston, Cambridgeshire, on December 10, 1832, he was in his 84th year, and had survived nearly all the contemporaries of his early days in the cricket field. He went from Bury St. Edmunds Grammar School to Cambridge, and played once against Oxford at Lord's, scoring five and 27 in 1854. Mr. Perkins never rose to fame as a player, but he was a hard-hitting bat, a fearless fieldsman, and, following the fashion of his time, he bowled lobs. It was his privilege to take part in many a good match at Southgate when Mr. John Walker and his brothers provided the best club cricket that could be seen in England. He played for Cambridgeshire in the great days of Hayward, Carpenter and Tarrant, and tried hard, but without success, to keep the County Club going when he became hon. secretary—1866 to 1868. To the end of his life he was fond of recalling a famous match between Cambridgeshire and Surrey at the Oval in 1861. He was in at the finish with Alfred Diver, Cambridgeshire winning by two wickets. In that match Hayward, Carpenter and Julius Caesar all made 100s. Mr. Perkins did not become a personage in the cricket world until he succeeded Mr. FitzGerald at Lord's. He became secretary of the M.C.C. in October, 1876, and ruled —an easy-going autocrat—until the end of 1897. About the great things that happened at Lord's during his long period of office—most important of all the appearance of the first Australian XI in 1878—a substantial volume could be written. Even after the time for retirement had come he was constantly at the old ground—he was one of the M.C.C. auditors to the day of his death—and it always struck me that in those later years he liked particularly to talk to men who had known him in his days of power. No one could meet him without being struck by his personality and strength of character. He had a wonderful memory for cricket, and to the end it remained unimpaired. Almost the last time I saw him I happened to make a slip as to the age of an old Cambridge Blue and he corrected me on the instant. I believe I am right in saying that, though full of admiration for many modern men, he thought the famous Billy Buttress the most difficult of all slow bowlers. Concerning that eccentric genius he could tell many good stories. He had his foibles—all his friends knew them—but scores of famous cricketers to whom the pavilion at Lord's was a holy place will retain pleasant and kindly thoughts of Henry Perkins.—S.H.P.

PERKINS, Thomas Toswill Norwood, who died at Tonbridge on July 20, 1946, aged 75, was a prolific scorer for St. John's School, Leatherhead, from 1884 to 1887. In his last year he played six three-figure innings, the highest being 238 against St. Bartholomew's Hospital, and at Blackheath against Proprietary School he did the hat-trick twice. He played for Cambridge in 1893–94, receiving his Blue from F. S. Jackson, and with him were K. S. Ranjitsinhji, A. O. Jones, an England captain, H. Gay, the wicket-keeper who went to Australia in 1894, James Douglas, a splendid bat for Middlesex, and C. M. Wells, who played Rugby for England at half-back. Oxford were beaten by 266 runs. Always welcome in the Kent XI when available, he made 109 at Trent Bridge in 1903, and scored heavily for Band of Brothers and M.C.C. He appeared for Gentlemen against Players at the Oval in 1894. Subsequently he played for Hertfordshire and Wiltshire. On entering the scholastic profession he found less time for serious cricket.

A powerful soccer player, he was in the Cambridge XI from 1892 to 1895. Perkins captained the side in 1894, and his dash at centre-forward together with the grand defence of L. V. Lodge at full-back brought about a surprise win over a great Oxford XI which included W. J. Oakley, C. B. Fry and G. O. Smith at Queen's Club on turf frozen hard.

PERKS, Reginald Thomas David, who died on November 22, 1977, aged 66, was by many good judges considered an underestimated bowler. In 1939 he had played twice for England, in the notorious timeless Test at Durban and against the West Indies at the Oval, and had performed respectably without meeting with spectacular success. He was then 28. When cricket was resumed he was 35 and had missed the years when a bowler of his type would naturally be in his prime. Now he was perhaps just past it and had moreover Bedser to compete with.

A tall man who made full use of his height, he bowled fast-medium right-hand, swinging the ball both ways, and was very steady, a great trier, endlessly cheerful and quite tireless. A left-handed bat, he started as a poor player but made himself into a useful tail-end hitter. Born at Hereford, he first appeared for Worcestershire in 1930 and his first victim was Jack Hobbs. By 1931 he had made a sufficient reputation to be picked for the Players at Lord's. He continued to play for the county until 1955 and, when he retired, had taken more wickets for them than any other bowler, 2,143 at an average of 23.73. In all first-class cricket his tally was 2,233 and in 16 consecutive seasons he had taken over 100 wickets.

The respect in which he was held was shown when in his last season he was appointed the first professional captain of Worcestershire. Later he was a valuable and outspoken member of the committee. He had no warmer admirer than his old county captain, Lord Cobham, who only a couple of months before his own unexpected death, hearing of Perks's illness, drove at once 25 miles through the snow to visit him.

Perks twice performed the hat-trick— against Kent at Stourbridge in 1931, and against Warwickshire at Edgbaston in 1933— and twice he took nine wickets in an innings— against Glamorgan at Stourbridge, 1939, and against Gloucestershire at Cheltenham, 1946.

PERRIN, Percival Albert, the famous Essex batsman, best known in recent years as a member of the Test selection committee of which he was elected chairman in 1939, died at his home at Hickling, Norfolk, on November 20, 1945, after a long illness, aged 69. Essentially a natural cricketer, Perrin improved his skill both in stroke play and defence until he became a very consistent scorer and a real personality whom spectators watched with interest and admiration. Without any training except honest knowledge of batting gained in club cricket at Tottenham, Perrin first appeared for Essex in 1896 when less than 20 years of age. No trial could have been more severe, for he faced at the Oval such notable bowlers as Tom Richardson, the fast bowler then at his best, Bill Lockwood and Tom Hayward—that season top of the Surrey bowling averages. In an uphill fight Perrin scored 52. Almost as a coincidence he finished his active cricket career with 51 against Oxford University at Colchester in 1928, when, 52 years old, he reappeared in the Essex side as captain, though he practically retired three years earlier.

Always reliable, he scored over 1,000 runs in 18 different seasons, and altogether made 29,709 runs at an average of 35.96. He played 66 three-figure innings, four times making a century twice in a match, and in 1903 was credited with a hundred in three consecutive innings. Next year he dwarfed all his other efforts by putting together 343 not out, but a total of 597 at Chesterfield did not suffice to save Essex, Derbyshire, thanks to G. A. Olliviere (229 and 92), winning by nine wickets. Such was the force of his strokes, mainly drives, that there were 68 fours in that magnificent display, a remarkable achievement, for, by comparison, A. C. MacLaren hit no more than 62 fours in his record 424 made at Taunton in 1895.

Over 6ft. in height Percy Perrin, "Peter" to his intimate friends, largely relied on forward play until acquiring knowledge of the wiles of the best spin bowlers and then he used defensive back strokes with power enough to earn runs and continued to increase his value as a consistent batsman of high quality. Regularly going in first wicket down, he often met the full brunt of a hostile attack. In that first season by making 50 when F. L. Fane and Carpenter failed he helped largely towards a six wickets victory over Yorkshire, the Champion County. With his first century, 139 at Edgbaston, Perrin then made his aggregate the best for Essex, and only H. G. Owen, the captain, had a better average. Next to him as a dangerous opponent was Charles McGahey, also 6ft. tall, and the "Essex Twins" compelled respect from all county rivals. Both of powerful physique they kept fieldsmen in front of the wicket very busy and in matter of style Perrin was the superior. As proved when first tried in County Cricket Perrin showed to special advantage against fast bowlers who often put three or four fieldsmen in the deep in the effort to check the Essex giant's driving. While his batting was of a quality often described as faultless, one defect in his cricket hindered his progress to representative cricket. Often he was described as "the best batsman who never played for England" and the explanation was—inability to field with any spark of speed. Heavy on his feet, he could not move quickly to the ball, and this deficiency, though he would hold any catch within his long reach, prevented him from ever appearing in a Test match or for Gentlemen against Players.

Of quiet, even retiring disposition, Percy Perrin possessed a keen knowledge of the game with clever appreciation of a player's ability. Of this merit advantage was taken by his election to the selection committee of which he became chairman in 1939 when Sir Pelham Warner resigned. With him were Brian A. Sellers, A. J. Holmes and M. J. Turnbull. The Glamorgan captain fell a War victim in August 1944, and, consequently, the Yorkshire and Sussex 1939 captains were the two survivors of the committee when the visit from India was in preparation.

PERSHKE, Flight-Lieut. W. J., who got his Blue for Oxford when a Freshman in 1938, was killed in January 1944, aged 26. After heading the Uppingham averages with 36.38 and taking 31 wickets, he scarcely realised expectations at the University, but against Glamorgan his fast bowling accounted for eight batsmen, so helping largely in a victory by 10 wickets, and earning him a place in the side at Lord's. The match with Cambridge was drawn owing to high scoring, Pershke, who took three wickets for 54, doing some of the best bowling. In a match at Lewes in 1940 for a Sussex XI against an R.A.F. XI he took six wickets for 25, being mainly responsible for victory by 15 runs over a side including W. R. Hammond and L. E. G. Ames.

PERSSE, Major Henry Wilford, M.C. (Royal Fusiliers). Wounded twice. Military Cross. Died of wounds June 28, 1918. Hampshire 1905–09 (then going abroad). Was quite a useful bowler for the county.

PETERS, E. A., of the South Australian XI in 1898–99, died in September, 1903.

PETTIFORD, Jack, who died in Sydney on October 11, 1964, aged 44, was a member of the Australian Services team of 1945 who did so much towards the recovery of cricket in England after the Second World War. He appeared in two of the "Victory Tests" and also played for the Royal Australian Air Force in which he was a Flying Officer. He assisted New South Wales in 13 Sheffield Shield matches before returning to England where he took part in League cricket with Nelson and Oldham. In 1954 he joined Kent as a professional, heading the county's batting averages in his first season, and continued with them until 1959. His best innings was 133 against Essex at Blackheath in 1954, and, twice exceeding 1,000 runs, he altogether scored 7,077 runs in English first-class cricket, average 25.64. With leg-breaks, he took 295 wickets at a cost of 31.37 runs each.

PFEIFFER, Capt. C. W. Knowles, who died on March 14, 1951, played cricket for Essex and Devon and also managed M.C.C. matches for a number of years. He served on the committee which formed the London Playing Fields Association and was a member of the England Hockey selection committee from 1904–06.

PHILIPSON, Hylton, died in London after a long illness, on December 4, 1935, in his 70th year. Born on June 8, 1866, at Tynemouth, he went to Eton and gaining a place in the XI as a batsman in 1883, he subsequently kept wicket besides going in first. In his third year he scored 141 against Winchester; 53 and 27 against Harrow. Illness prevented Philipson from playing cricket in 1886, but next year he got his Blue at Oxford, and in 1889 he captained the XI instead of W. W. Rashleigh, who was studying for the Church. He played his highest innings of 150 in 1887 for Oxford against Middlesex, taking part in a seventh-wicket stand of 340 with K. J. Key, who scored 281.

Philipson created such an impression as wicket-keeper at Oxford that he played for the Gentlemen both at Lord's and the Oval in 1887. In these two games, the Gentlemen were very strong, and the Players had exactly the same XI, all of whom played against Australia in England except Bates, who took part in the tour which brought back the Ashes by beating W. L. Murdoch's team twice in three matches. Bates contributed largely towards the triumph by taking 13 wickets for 102 runs in the second engagement. Included in this performance was the hat-trick, Bates having as his victims three great batsmen: P. S. McDonnell, George Giffen and G. J. Bonnor. That was in January, 1883.

Philipson was in G. F. Vernon's team which went to India in 1889, and he paid two visits to Australia. On the first occasion, in the winter of 1891, Gregor MacGregor was chief wicket-keeper in Lord Sheffield's side, but three years later, when A. E. Stoddart took his first team to Australia, Philipson, after the opening Test, was preferred to L. H. Gay, and figured prominently in a memorable rubber which ended with England winning the fifth and deciding match by six wickets. When 297 were wanted for victory, Albert Ward, Lancashire, and J. T. Brown, Yorkshire, made 210 for the fourth partnership.

These facts tell of Philipson's class. He was one of the very best wicketkeepers. Standing close to the stumps for most bowlers, he took the ball with easy grace and certainty. As a batsman he did not fulfil his early promise, but when in form he showed strong defence and could hit freely in front of the wicket. He played occasionally for Middlesex until 1898, and then for Northumberland, his native county.

While most famous as a cricketer, "Punch" Philipson held a prominent place in many other games. He earned the title of Racquets Champion at Eton and represented Oxford against Cambridge both at Racquets and in the Tennis singles and doubles. He beat Percy Ashworth for the Racquets Amateur Championship in 1891. C. Wreford-Brown gave him his Association football Blue as full-back in 1889; so altogether Philipson played for Oxford against Cambridge at four ball games.

A contemporary and racquets partner considered Philipson the best "all rounder" he ever knew at Eton.

Lord Hawke, of Eton and Cambridge, the M.C.C. treasurer and former Yorkshire captain, paid this tribute:

"Everyone loved 'Punch'. I was very fond of him. He was a little after my time, but I know he was a very fine wicket-keeper and a great success in Australia. He was up against MacGregor. Comparisons are odious, but if it hadn't been for MacGregor, Philipson would have played in many more representative matches. He was a lovable personality."

PHILLIPS, Frank Ashley, who died on March 5, 1955, aged 81, played in three University matches for Oxford late in the last century. After being in the XI at Rossall for three years from 1889, he gained a Blue in 1892 and, though passed over in the following season, in 1894 and 1895. With the cut and the drive his best strokes, he was a free-scoring batsman, though not specially strong in defence, a fine deep fieldsman and useful medium-pace bowler. His best performance against Cambridge was in 1894 when, hitting 78, he helped C. B. Fry in a fifth-wicket partnership of 137. In 1892 he played for Essex, then a second-class county, and from 1894 he assisted Monmouthshire, the county of his birth, until in 1897 he began an association with Somerset which lasted until 1911.

His highest innings for Somerset was 163 against Sussex at Taunton in 1899 when, in a game yielding 1,293 runs for the loss of 26 wickets, he and C. A. Bernard put on 171 for the third wicket. Phillips bore a handsome part in the one defeat of Yorkshire on their way to the County Championship in 1901. Against the bowling of Hirst, Rhodes and Haigh, Somerset were dismissed at Leeds for 87 but, facing first innings arrears of 238, they built up a total of 630, of which Phillips's share was 122, and triumphed by 279 runs. In 1895, he was a member of Frank Mitchell's team which visited America. A schoolmaster by profession, he served in both the Boer War and the First World War, when he was awarded the D.S.O., and for a time was an assistant District Commissioner in Southern Nigeria.

PHILLIPS, Harry, the veteran Sussex wicket-keeper, died at Hastings on July 4, 1919, in his 75th year. He was born at Hastings on October 14, 1844, and lived all his days in the town. It was Phillips' misfortune to be a little overshadowed by wicket-keepers more gifted than himself. He was first-rate—wonderfully nimble and clever—but not quite equal to Pooley and Pinder at the start of his career or in later years to Pilling and Sherwin. For this reason he was largely restricted to County Cricket. The M.C.C. picked him for the Players at Lord's in 1873—a choice he abundantly justified—but his only other appearances against the Gentlemen were in John Lillywhite's benefit match on the old Brighton ground in 1871 and at Hastings in 1891—the year curiously enough in which he took leave of public cricket. Coming out for Sussex in 1868 he kept wicket for the county right on until 1888. In the following year he played in a few matches and in 1891 he played once. As a wicket-keeper he was physically well equipped. He was ambidextrous and, for a man of

his short stature, he had very long arms. His success was at times astonishing. For Sussex against Surrey at the Oval in 1872 he caught five batsmen and stumped five, and against Kent at Brighton in 1884 he caught three and stumped five. These were the most conspicuous of many remarkable feats. Phillips had small pretensions as a batsman—his average for Sussex during his whole career works out at a trifle over 11—but he enjoyed one day of greatness. For Sussex against the Australians at Brighton in July, 1884, he played an innings of 111, he and Mr. G. N. Wyatt putting on 182 runs for the eighth wicket. The fact of his making such a score against Spofforth, Palmer, Giffen, Boyle, W. H. Cooper, and Midwinter bewildered the good people of Brighton, but it is safe to say that no one was quite so astonished as Phillips himself. He played very well, but Spofforth and Palmer were stale and dispirited, England having beaten Australia in a single innings on the previous day at Lord's. Phillips was always the cheeriest of cricketers. No day was long enough to damp his good spirits.—S.H.P.

PHILLIPS, James, a brother of Henry Phillips, the famous wicket-keeper, died on January 31, 1905, at Hastings, where he was born on September 26, 1849. He came into prominence by means of an innings of 103 for the Sussex Colts against Nine Gentlemen and Three Players of Sussex, at Brighton, on June 1, 1871, and the same season witnessed his debut in County Cricket. Between 1871 and 1886 he appeared for Sussex in 67 matches, scoring 1,801 runs in 122 completed innings, average 14.76. His highest score was 89 against Hampshire, at Brighton, in 1882, when he and Mr. W. Newham, who scored 101, added 185 runs together for the sixth wicket. He never appeared in a Gentlemen v. Players match, but in 1878 was chosen to assist the Players against the First Australian team at the Oval. This, as students of the game will readily recall, was the match in which the late E. Barratt took all 10 of the Australians' wickets in an innings without bowling down a single one. Phillips, too, had good reason to remember the match with gratification, for, although he was on the losing side (the Australians winning a close game by eight runs), his scores of 19 not out and 14 were the highest in each innings of the Players. He was the author of an interesting pamphlet on Hastings cricket.

PHILLIPS, James, who was born at Port Adelaide in South Australia on September 1,

1860, and died at Burnaby, Vancouver, on April 21, 1930, will be remembered more for his work as an umpire than for anything he accomplished as a player. To Phillips more than anyone else is due the credit for stamping out throwing in first-class cricket. Going out to Australia to act as umpire with A. E. Stoddart's team in 1897–98, he twice no-balled Ernest Jones, the fast bowler, whose delivery when visiting this country with Harry Trott's team in 1896 was condemned as unfair, and the courageous action of Phillips found many imitators. Throwing on English cricket grounds had for a long time been allowed to go on unchecked but in 1898 C. B. Fry was no-balled by West at Trent Bridge, by Phillips himself at Brighton and by Sherwin at Lord's, while a new Warwick-shire bowler, Hopkins, came under the ban of Titchmarsh at Tonbridge. A storm of controversy was aroused after F. R. Spof-forth, in a letter to the *Sporting Life* in 1897, suggested that the best way would be to legalise throwing and in one season it would bring about its own cure. However, as a result of Phillips's example, speedy and satis-factory action was taken by the captains of the first-class counties who at a meeting at Lord's in December, 1900, arrived at an agreement to deal strongly with the matter in the following summer. Then, in a match between Lancashire and Somerset at Old Trafford, Phillips no-balled Mold 16 times. A strong agitation was got up on Mold's behalf but owing to the fact that the Lanca-shire fast bowler had been condemned as unfair by the county captains at their famous meeting—by a majority of 11 to one—this was systematically ignored. The M.C.C. committee in the following December issued a circular to all the county secretaries in which was expressed the hope that the County Cricket executives would, in future, decline to play bowlers with doubtful de-liveries. Thereafter English bowling was more uniformly fair and above suspicion than in any season during the previous 25 years and, eventually, throwing practically disappeared.

Phillips was a good medium-pace bowler, a fairly useful batsman and a smart field at cover-point. He came to England in 1888 and joined the ground staff at Lord's, appearing for Middlesex between 1890 and 1898 and for many years journeying between England and Australia. For a time he was engaged as coach at Christchurch, in New Zealand, and whilst there played an innings of 110 not out for Canterbury v. Wellington in 1898–99. In the course of his career with Middlesex,

Phillips made 1,091 runs and took 216 wick-ets for just over 22 runs each. Among his bowling feats were: seven wickets for 20 runs (Victoria v. New South Wales at Melbourne in 1890–91); 13 for 117 (Middlesex v. Sussex at Lord's in 1895), and 13 for 187 (Middlesex v. Gloucestershire on the same ground in 1896). In the course of a week's cricket for M.C.C. at Lord's in 1888 he took 16 of Scarborough's 20 wickets and dismissed four Notts Castle men in four balls. His benefit match was Middlesex v. Australians at Lord's in 1899.

PHILLIPS, Leslie Jack, died at Woodford Wells on April 22, 1979, aged 80. A useful bat and slow left-arm bowler, he played a few games for Essex between 1919 and 1922.

PICKERING, William Percival, an old Cam-bridge Blue, famous as a cover-point in the days when fielding was considered of as much importance as batting and bowling, died on August 16, 1905, at Vancouver, British Columbia, at the age of 85. From 1834 to 1838 he was in the XI at Eton, where he was christened "Bull" Pickering, to distin-guish him from his brother E.H., who greatly distinguished himself in the cricket field in after years. Mr. Pickering was the Eton captain in his last two seasons, and even as a schoolboy he won fame as a magnificent field. His batting and fielding gained him a place in the Cambridge XI in 1840 and 1842, and twice afterwards he represented the Gentlemen at Lord's, while for four years he played occasionally for Surrey. The critics were unanimous in saying that he was the greatest cover-point of his time, and those among them who had an opportunity of seeing the Rev. Vernon Royle, who was undoubtedly the best cover-point of more recent times, bracketed the two men as equally good. Mr. Pickering was a Surrey man, and one of the original members of the County C.C.; he was also one of the original members of I Zingari. At the meeting at the Horns Tavern, Kennington, in October, 1845, when the Surrey County C.C. was formed, he stated that its object was "to give the cricketers of Surrey an opportunity of proving that they inherited or retained much, if not all, the strength of play for which their forefathers in the game had been so dis-tinguished." His career as a cricketer ended in 1852 as far as England was concerned, but in Canada, his new home, he played regu-larly until 1857, taking part in all the matches against the United States. It was chiefly through his efforts that George Parr's team visited Canada in 1859. He returned to England for a few years, during which he served on the committee of the M.C.C., but Canada again claimed him. For some years before his death he was in the service of the Canadian Pacific Railway. It will interest collectors of cricket literature to know that he wrote a little book entitled *Cricket Wrinkles*, and dedicated to the boys of a Toronto school. This notice of Mr. Pickering appeared in *The Field*. Mr. "Bull" Pickering was not the only cricketing member of his family, for his elder brother, Mr. Edward Hayes Pickering, played for Eton in 1824–25–26, for Cambridge in 1827 and 1829, and for the Gentlemen against the Players from 1836 until 1844, whilst a nephew, Mr. F. P. U. Pickering, was a member of Mr. R. A. FitzGerald's team which visited America in 1872. Mr. W. P. Pickering was born at Clapham, in Surrey, on October 25, 1819.

PICKETT, Henry, once so well known as a fast bowler for Essex and the M.C.C., came to a sad end. He disappeared on September 27, 1907, and his body was discovered on the beach at Aberavon on October 3. Not until the end of December, however, was his fate known, some articles found in his clothes proving his identity. Born on March 26, 1862, he was in his 46th year. For several seasons he was a valuable member of the Essex team. His best piece of work for the county was done in a match against Leicestershire at Leyton in 1895—the year in which Essex took part for the first time in the championship. At a cost of 32 runs he took all 10 wickets in Leicestershire's first innings. Despite his fine performance, however, Essex lost the game by 75 runs. After he retired from first-class cricket he was for some time coach at Clifton College.

PIERCE, Michael, who died in Sydney on February 4, 1913, at one time gave promise of making a name for himself as a player, being a sound bat and good field and a slow bowler who kept a good length and could make the ball break both ways. By far his greatest feat was to take eight wickets for 111 and five for 154 for New South Wales v. South Australia, at Adelaide, in December, 1892. Subsequently he settled in Queensland, but represented that State only once—against the English team in 1894–95, when he did nothing of note.

PIGG, Herbert, the well-known Hertfordshire cricketer, died suddenly in Manitoba on June 8, 1913. He was born at Buntingford, Hertfordshire, September 4, 1856, and appeared for his native county from 1876 to 1897, having previously assisted Northamptonshire in 1874 and 1875. As a member of the Cambridge XI of 1877 he did practically nothing against Oxford, scoring only a couple of runs in his two innings and having nine runs scored off him without taking a wicket. Subsequently he took part in the Hastings Week with success, making seven and 59 and taking eight wickets for 125 for South v. Australians in 1886, and in two Gentlemen v. Players matches, in 1889 and 1891, scoring 54 for twice out and obtaining 12 wickets for 13.66 runs each.

PIGGOT, Julian Ito, who died on January 23, 1965, aged 76, played occasionally for Surrey from 1910 to 1913, hitting 84 against Oxford University at the Oval in 1910. As a batsman, he was in the Cheltenham XI from 1904 to 1907.

PIGOT, James Poole Maunsell, who died in Dublin on July 20, 1980, aged 79, was a member of a well-known Dublin cricket family. He played as a forcing right-handed batsman and leg-break bowler in two matches for Dublin University against Northamptonshire in 1924 and 1925, scoring 50 on the latter occasion. He also played three times for the Europeans in the Madras presidency match between 1926 and 1930. In 1923 he scored 194 for Phoenix C.C. in a Senior League match in Dublin, still a club record in that competition. His brother, D. R. Pigot, represented Ireland between the Wars, as did his nephew, also D. R., more recently.

PIKE, Arthur, who kept wicket several times for Notts, in the mid-'90s, died at Keyworth, his native place, on November 15, 1907, after a long illness. He was born on December 25, 1862, and learnt his cricket with the Keyworth C.C., of which he continued a member for almost 30 years, although in the '80s he joined the Notts Commercial club and afterwards accepted an engagement at Leyland. His best wicket-keeping seasons—he succeeded Sherwin and was followed by Oates—were 1896 and 1897, his record in the former year being 27 caught and seven stumped and in the latter 23 caught and 12 stumped. He scored freely when set, his highest innings being 66 v. Middlesex at Trent Bridge in 1896, 54 v. Surrey at the Oval the same year, and 50 v. Warwickshire at Edgbaston in 1894. His engagement at

Lord's dated back to 1895, and after his retirement from County Cricket he frequently umpired in the great matches.

PILCH, George Everett, a member of the famous Norfolk cricketing family, died at Cringleford on September 12, 1979, aged 67. Between 1935 and 1946 he did useful work for the county as a bowler and was later a great help to it on the administrative side.

PILKINGTON, Charles Carlisle, the second of three brothers who played for Eton, died at The Manor, South Warnborough, on January 8, 1950, aged 73. During four years in the Eton XI he scored 427 runs, average 32.84, in the matches with Harrow and Winchester, and when captain in 1895 he took five wickets for 30 runs in Harrow's second innings. Getting his Oxford Blue as a Freshman, he helped to beat Cambridge by four wickets in his only inter-University match, which made cricket history by influencing the change in the follow-on rule to *optional.* Cambridge, led by Frank Mitchell, copying the example set three years before when F. S. Jackson was captain, gave away 12 extras, three balls being bowled deliberately to the boundary, in order to prevent the follow-on. Cambridge began badly in their second innings after a tremendous uproar all round the ground and a critical demonstration by M.C.C. members in the pavilion. Oxford were set to score 330 in the last innings, and they won by accomplishing the heaviest task ever performed at that time in the University match. P. F. Warner, G. J. Mordaunt and H. K. Foster were out for 60 runs before Pilkington helped G. O. Smith to add 84; H. D. G. Leveson Gower, the Oxford captain, did still better by staying while 97 were put on, and the runs were obtained for the loss of six men, G. O. Smith, 132, leaving when only two were required for victory. Pilkington averaged over 36 for Oxford that season. He gave up first-class cricket when on the Stock Exchange, but in 1901 for Silwood Park he took all 10 R.M.C. wickets for 25 runs at Sandhurst. I saw that 1896 game at Lord's and remember vividly all that happened.—H.P.

PILKINGTON, Hubert Carlisle, youngest of three brothers who played cricket for Eton, died after two operations in a Hertfordshire nursing home on June 17, 1942. A first-rate batsman with admirable style, he enjoyed the highly acclaimed distinction of scoring a hundred when first appearing at Lord's—101 against Harrow in 1896. In three matches for Eton against Harrow he made 239 runs, average nearly 48. Eton were not fortunate at that time, and H. C. Pilkington, after taking part in two drawn games with Harrow, led the side in a match that ended in defeat by nine wickets, despite his good work as opening batsman.

Getting his Oxford Blue in 1899 as a Freshman, he scored 93 in the second innings against Cambridge, and next season his 87 and 45 were prominent in an encounter memorable for the batting of R. E. Foster, whose 171 was then the highest score in a match between the Universities. He excelled at the Eton football games and at Fives. He was president of the Eton Society, 1897–98.

Becoming a member of the London Stock Exchange in 1902, H. C. Pilkington found little time for first-class cricket, but played occasionally for Middlesex. During the last War he became an officer in a Guards machine-gun regiment. Born on October 25, 1879, at Woolton, Lancashire, he passed away in his 63rd year.

PILLING, William, who kept wicket for Lancashire in one match in 1891, died at Stretford, Manchester, on March 27, 1924, aged 66. He was brother of Richard Pilling.

PINCH, Frank B., who died on October 9, 1961, aged 70, enjoyed the distinction of hitting 138 not out on his debut in first-class cricket for Glamorgan against Worcestershire at Swansea in 1921, the year that the Welsh county entered the Championship competition. That season he scored 321 runs, average 22.92, but he did not repeat that success in his next five years with Glamorgan.

PINDER, George, who had been in bad health for some little time, died on January 15, 1903, at Hickleton, in his 62nd year. Inasmuch as he dropped out of first-class cricket more than 20 years ago, he was only a name to the present generation of players, but lovers of the game, whose recollections go back to the '70s, will remember him as one of the finest wicket-keepers we ever had. To very fast bowling he was perhaps the best of all, but in this connection something could be said for Tom Plumb. In a match at Lord's in 1870, George Freeman, then at the height of his fame as a fast bowler, was given his choice between the two men and selected Plumb, but it must have been a nice point. Pinder came out for Yorkshire in 1868, and played regularly for the county until 1880, after which year he gave place to the late

Joseph Hunter. It may safely be said that no wicket-keeper ever had harder work to do. In his young days Pinder had to stand up to Freeman, Emmett, Allen Hill, and Ulyett, and wickets then, all over the country, were by no means so perfect as they are today. The faster the bowling, however, the better Pinder acquitted himself. Against slow and medium pace bowling he was—perhaps from lack of practice—less brilliant than Pooley. It is interesting to recall the fact that when Blackham came to this country in 1878 with the first Australian XI and astonished everyone by his skill, Pinder and Pooley were still playing for their counties, and the late Richard Pilling had just come forward for Lancashire. The modern practice of standing back to fast bowling was then very rarely indulged in, and wicket-keepers earned greater distinction than they do now. Pinder was a useful, hard-hitting batsman, and occasionally bowled lobs with success. He was a tall, spare man, and was not lacking in the keen sense of humour characteristic of so many of the old Yorkshire players.

PIPER, W. J., who died in July, 1940, combined his duty as cricket correspondent of the *Derby Daily Telegraph* with that of honorary scorer when Derby re-entered the first-class championships in 1895. For many years he attended all the Derbyshire matches at home and when on tour, earning wide popularity by his uniform and obliging manner in giving information required by colleagues. When journalistic work confined him largely to the office, he had to give up scoring for the County Club, but he always retained a keen interest in the game and seldom missed a home match.

PITON, John Henry, who died at Johannesburg on July 20, 1942, was one of the best-known early South African cricketers. A useful batsman and clever lob bowler, he played for Transvaal "odds" teams against the English touring teams of 1888–89, 1891–92 and 1898–99. He was a member of the Transvaal team that beat Kimberley in April 1890, and in the first Currie Cup match played, and next season at Johannesburg, in the second of the series, he took seven wickets for 82 and six for 122. The match produced 1,402 runs, Kimberley beating Transvaal by 58 on the seventh day. He also played for Natal in the Currie Cup and continued club cricket for many years.

PITT, Thomas Alfred, who died at Northampton on April 23, 1957, aged 63, played

for Northamptonshire in 1934 and 1935, taking 43 wickets for just over 26 runs each. Of medium-pace, he kept a good length and made the ball turn a little either way. A pilot in the R.F.C. during the First World War, he served with the R.A.F. in the Second.

PLATT, George J. W., who died at Old Hill, Birmingham, on April 14, 1955, aged 73, played occasionally as a medium-paced bowler for Surrey from 1906 to 1914. In 1909 at the Oval, he took five wickets for 40 in the Somerset second innings, the last four in 16 deliveries for 11 runs. His best season was that of 1910 when in 13 county games he dismissed 43 batsmen for 19.65 runs each. After the First World War he became professional to Old Hill C.C., doing good work as off-break bowler, and later played for West Bromwich Dartmouth before taking up the position of head groundsman and coach at Worcester which he held until his retirement in 1952.

PLATTS, John, the well-known Derbyshire cricketer—one of the best all-round players possessed by the county in its early days—died on August 6, 1898. He was in his 50th year having been born on December 6, 1848. A tragic interest attached to the start of Platts' career as a cricketer, as it was a ball bowled by him in the M.C.C. and Notts match at Lord's in 1870 that caused the death of George Summers. At that time a very fast bowler, Platts afterwards lessened his pace and the catastrophe made such a painful impression upon him that it is said he never in subsequent years could play, with any pleasure, at Lord's ground. After dropping out of active work in the cricket field he became one of the regular county umpires.

PLAYER, Allen Shrewsbury, who died on November 17, 1962, aged 69, played for Auckland in 27 first-class matches between 1919 and 1929. A bowler of medium pace, he took 89 wickets, average 26.83, his best analysis being six wickets for 38 runs against Canterbury at Christchurch in 1926–27.

PLOWDEN, Sir Henry Meredyth, died at Ascot in January, 1920, in his 80th year, having for some time been in failing health. He was born in Bengal on September 26, 1840. Sir Henry appeared in first-class cricket so long ago, and went out to India so early in his life, that his career belonged to a very distant part, but in his day he was a prominent figure at Fenner's and Lord's. He was in the Harrow XI in 1858, and in the Cambridge XI from 1860 to 1863, inclusive, being captain in his last two years. His fame as a cricketer, though he was quite a useful bat, rested on his slow bowling, his off-break—not by any means so common a gift in the early '60s as it became in later years—proving deadly on slow wickets. He had pleasant recollections of all his big matches at Lord's except the last. Thanks largely to his bowling Harrow beat Eton in one innings in 1858—he took three wickets for 29 runs and six for 49—and Cambridge beat Oxford in 1860, 1861, and 1862. Fortune changed in 1863 when Oxford won by eight wickets, but Sir Henry always contended that winning the toss went far towards losing the game. Three innings and a bit were completed on the first day under very difficult conditions, but the pitch had improved when Oxford went on batting the next morning with about 60 to get, F. G. Inge, who is, I believe, still alive, quickly settled the matter by hitting up 48 not out. Sir Henry was very proud of his XI in 1862—by far the best Cambridge side of those days—and in Mr. W. J. Ford's book he wrote most entertainingly about the various players. The side which included the Hon. C. G. Lyttelton (now Lord Cobham), A. W. T. Daniel, Robert Lang, the Hon. T. de Grey, M. T. Martin, H. W. Salter, W. Bury, and Clement Booth had not a weak point, and against Oxford at Lord's Lang's fast bowling was irresistible. Cambridge played seven matches that year and won five of them. They were beaten by Buttress's bowling in their opening game against the professionals engaged at Fenner's. After leaving Cambridge Henry Plowden played a little for Hampshire in 1865 and then his career in first-class cricket ended. Taking his B.A. at Cambridge in 1863 he was called to the Bar in 1866 and not long afterwards he went to India. He was Government Advocate at Lahore 1870–77 and Judge of the Chief Court in the Punjab from 1877 to 1894. On his return to England he was as keenly interested as ever in cricket—more especially Harrow and Cambridge cricket—and right on until 1914 he was a constant attendant at Lord's. I never met Sir Henry but he very kindly put me in the way of getting some valuable information about John Wisden for the *Almanack* of 1913. For Cambridge against Oxford he took in 1860 six wickets for 29 runs and two for 15; in 1861 he met with no success and had 34 runs scored from him; in 1862 he took one wicket for 11 runs and two for 38; and in 1863—the only time he was on the losing side—seven wickets for 25 runs and one wicket for 37. He never appeared for Gentlemen v. Players.— S.H.P.

Some of his best performances were as under:

Took 8 wkts. in inns. for 14—Gents. of South v. XI Players of South, at Southampton	1865
Took 6 wkts. for 6 runs—Camb. Univ. v. Players engaged at Cambridge, at Cambridge	1862
Took 3 wkts. in 3 balls—Camb. Univ. v. M.C.C. and Ground, at Cambridge ..	1862
Scored 60—Camb. Univ. v. Old Cambridge Men, at Cambridge	1861
Scored 69—Camb. Univ. v. Cambridge Town club, at Cambridge	1861
Scored 80—Gents. of Hampshire v. Gents. of Sussex, at Brighton	1865

PLUMB, Tom. The death took place on March 29, 1905, of the once-famous wicket-keeper Tom Plumb. For some years he had been in very poor circumstances, and he passed away in the workhouse at Northampton. Born on July 26, 1833, he was in his 72nd year. To the present generation he was only a name, but cricketers whose memories go back as far as 1870 will remember him as a worthy rival of Pooley and the late George Pinder. His misfortune was that he did not belong to a leading county, his opportunities in first-class cricket being in consequence much restricted. It was always a disputed point whether he or George Pinder was the finer wicket-keeper to fast bowling. In a match at Lord's in 1870, between the United North and the United South XIs, the late George Freeman—then in his prime, and beyond question the best fast bowler of the day—was given his choice between the two men, and selected Plumb. Twice at least—in 1868 and 1869—Plumb appeared in the big match of the Canterbury Week, and fairly divided honours with Pooley. The match in 1868—between the North of the Thames and the South of the Thames—was a memorable one, the North winning by 58 runs, though W. G. Grace scored 130 and 102 not out for the South. For the winners the Rev. Joseph McCormick (now Canon McCormick) made 137 and 27; R. A. H. Mitchell, 22 and 90; and Plumb, one and 67. Plumb appeared in the Gentlemen v. Players match at Lord's in 1869.

PLUNKET, The Fifth Baron (William Lee Plunket), who was born on December 19, 1864, died in London on January 24, 1920. Whilst Governor of New Zealand, 1904–10, he presented a Shield bearing his name, which is competed for annually by the chief cricket associations of the Dominion.

POIDEVIN, Dr. L. O. S., whose death occurred in Sydney on November 18, 1931, was a thoroughly sound and watchful, if not particularly attractive batsman, being quite content, however long he had been at the wicket, to play the good ball but rarely failing to punish anything loose. He had already made a name in New South Wales cricket when he came to England to study medicine. At that time Australia as well as England were very rich in first-class batsmen, and Poidevin did not enjoy the distinction of making a mark in Test cricket, but in the Australian season of 1901 he took part in what then was the record score for an innings. New South Wales put together 918 and his 140 not out was the fifth century obtained, the others being 168 by Syd Gregory, 153 by M. A. Noble, 119 by R. A. Duff and 118 by Frank Iredale. South Australia were beaten by an innings and 605 runs, one of the most overwhelming victories ever obtained in cricket. This score has twice been excelled by Victoria with 1,059 against Tasmania at Melbourne and again four seasons later in December, 1926, with 1,107 against New South Wales at Melbourne.

First assisting London County Poidevin qualified for Lancashire and during the seven seasons—1902 to 1908—he scored 5,925 runs with an average of nearly 30 an innings. In his first season in County Cricket—1904— he helped Lancashire to carry off the Championship, his contribution to the side's efficiency being 865 runs with an average of 34. Next year Poidevin headed the Lancashire averages with 44 and the highest aggregate of 1,376 runs, his personal success being the more remarkable as it surpassed the efforts of such great batsmen as J. T. Tyldesley, Mr. R. H. Spooner, Mr. A. C. MacLaren and John Sharp who followed in the order named. That summer, in the course of a fortnight at the end of June, he made 122 against Somerset at Taunton, 168 not out against Worcestershire at Worcester and 138 against Sussex at Manchester.

Poidevin batted in a style typical of Australian cricket of that era. Of moderate build, he had a very strong defence and he made runs steadily all round the wicket by orthodox strokes. A good field anywhere, he occasionally bowled slows with some success. Born on November 5, 1876, he had at the time of his death just completed his 55th year.

POLLARD, David, was found dead in his bed in Huddersfield on March 26, 1909. He was born at Comus Lepton on August 7, 1835, and in 1865 played for Yorkshire against Surrey at Sheffield. *Scores and Biographies* (ix—25) said of him: "He is an average batsman, a middle-paced, high, round-armed bowler, and in the field is generally short-slip." From 1864 to 1871 he was engaged by the Yorkshire Gentlemen's club at York, and subsequently coached at Winchester and Harrow. In his earlier days he was connected with Lascelles Hall cricket, and for many years was a familiar figure at the Scarborough Festival.

POLLARD, Marjorie, O.B.E., who died on March 21, 1982, aged 81, was a foremost figure in the fight for the establishment and recognition of women's team games. She was a founder member of the Women's Cricket Association, the first official reporter of women's cricket in the national press and the first woman radio commentator on the game. For 20 years she produced and edited the magazine *Women's Cricket.* She was herself a fine all-round player and a shrewd captain. Her O.B.E., awarded in 1965, was for services to sport.

PONSONBY, Cecil Brabazon, who died in London on May 11, 1945, aged 53, played for Worcestershire from 1911 to 1928. He went to Eton and Oxford, but was not in either XI.

PONSONBY, Col. Sir Charles, Bart., who died at Woodstock on January 28, 1976, at the age of 96, had the remarkable distinction of having been a member of I Zingari for 78 years. At the time of his death he was the oldest living member. He was a nephew of Sir Spencer Ponsonby-Fane, one of the founders of the club and its first governor.

SIR SPENCER PONSONBY-FANE

The Right Hon. Sir Spencer Cecil Brabazon Ponsonby-Fane, P.C., G.C.B., sixth son of the fourth Earl of Bessborough, was born in Cavendish Square on March 14, 1824, and died at Brympton, Yeovil, on December 1, 1916, in his 92nd year. He was a nephew by marriage of the famous Lord Frederick Beauclerk, and brother of the sixth Earl of Bessborough, who did so much for Harrow cricket, and assumed the additional name of Fane in 1875 upon inheriting Brympton from Lady Georgina Fane. He was by far the most interesting link with past cricket, seeing that he had visited Lord's for over 80 years (the last time being in 1913) and had always been in the closest touch with the game. As a boy of 15 he had played for the M.C.C. in 1839, although it was not until May 14, 1840, that he was elected a member of the club on the proposal of Mr. Aislabie, seconded by Lord Paget. His term of membership was without parallel in the history of the M.C.C., and during it he occupied almost every office possible, except the presidency, which he declined several times. He served on the committee 1866–68, 1870–73, and 1875–78; was treasurer from 1879 until his death; and a trustee from 1900 until the end of his long life. It will, perhaps, be owing to the fact that he was responsible for the unrivalled collection of paintings, engravings, prints, etc., being made at Lord's that he will be chiefly remembered. His experiences in this matter he related in a short contribution to the second edition of the M.C.C. *Catalogue*, published in 1912. He did so much for the club as to merit fully the honour bestowed on him by the committee in 1896, when they asked him to sit to Ouless for his portrait, which now hangs in the Long Room of the pavilion. In 1845, with his brother and Mr. J. Loraine Baldwin, he founded I Zingari, of which he was the hon. secretary and deeply loved, though autocratic, governor. For over 50 years he was a very familiar figure at Canterbury, either as a player or an Old Stager or both, and now that he is dead the Rev. Sir Emilius Laurie, Bart.—the famous Emilius Bayley of other days—is the only survivor of all the cricketers who took part in the first Festival, that of 1842. As a player Sir Spencer was very useful in his younger days. *Scores and Biographies* described him as "A free and lively hitter, forward and to leg. Also a good field, generally long-leg, middle wicket or point. Is remarkably quick between wickets, but has run himself and partner out very frequently." He was a member of the original committee of the Surrey County C.C., and played for the county in 1844, 1848, and 1853. He assisted the Gentlemen against the Players from 1851 until 1858. In important matches his chief scores were as follows:

54	Gentlemen of England v. Gentlemen of Kent, at Canterbury			..	1849
67	Gentlemen of England v. Gentlemen of Kent, at Canterbury			..	1850
76	M.C.C. and Ground v. Sussex, at Lord's	..	..	..	1853
89	I Zingari v. Gentlemen of Kent, at Canterbury		..	..	1856
108	Gentlemen of England v. Gentlemen of Kent and Sussex, at Canterbury		..	1856
57	M.C.C. and Ground v. Sussex, at Lord's		..	..	1858

Since 1890 he had been president of the Somerset County C.C. When in congenial society he was full of most entertaining reminiscences, and it is much to be regretted that he could never be induced to give his experiences to the world. A man who could claim to have played with William Ward and to have been a regular *habitué* of Lord's for over 80 years would have had a most interesting story to tell. His contributions to the literature of the game were all too few, and by far the best is his Introduction to *Lord's and the M.C.C.*, the volume published in 1914 in commemoration of the club's completion of 100 years' tenure of their present ground. By Sir Spencer's death Sir John Leslie, first Bart., the oldest cricket Blue, becomes the oldest member of the M.C.C., and the only surviving original member of I Zingari; he was elected to the M.C.C. on May 31, 1841. Apart altogether from cricket, Sir Spencer's career was a noteworthy one. He entered the Foreign Office in 1840; was Private Secretary to Lord Palmerston, the Earl of Clarendon and Earl Granville; Attaché at Washington 1846–47; Comptroller of the Lord Chamberlain's Office until 1901;

Gentleman Usher to the Sword; and Bath King of Arms since 1904. He also brought from Paris the treaty which ended the Crimean War.—F.S.A.C.

PONTIFEX, Sir Charles, K.C.I.E., born on June 5, 1831, died at South Kensington on July 27, 1912. In 1851 and 1853 he played for Cambridge v. Oxford, but was too ill to do so in 1852, when his side could muster only 10 men. In 1851 he obtained 10 wickets, and in 1853, when captain, was second in the batting averages to A. R. Ward. He was a good batsman and an excellent left-hand medium-paced bowler. In 1851 he scored 61 for Gentlemen of England v. Gentlemen of Sussex at Brighton, and in the following year made his first appearance for the Gentlemen of Kent. Playing once for the B.B. against a Garrison team at Canterbury he dismissed Alfred Lubbock, then at his best, for a pair of spectacles. Sir Charles, who had been a member of the M.C.C. since 1870, was one of the best tennis players of his day at Cambridge.

PONTIFEX, Dudley David, died on September 27, 1934, aged 79. A useful batsman for Surrey he did best in 1881, when he came out fifth in the batting list with an aggregate of 303 runs and an average of 18. Probably his most valuable innings was against Nottinghamshire at the Oval in July that season when, going in first, he scored 89 and helped materially towards a Surrey victory by an innings and 22 runs. Born at Bath on February 12, 1855, Mr. Pontifex also played for Somerset.

POOL, C. J. T., who died at Epsom on October 13, 1954, aged 78, did fine work as a batsman for Northamptonshire from the time they attained first-class status in 1905 until 1910. In 1905 he headed the county's averages, his 110 against Hampshire being the one century obtained for Northamptonshire during the season, and remained a consistent and attractive run-getter until he retired from the first-class game. His best summer was that of 1909, when he scored 796 runs, average 22.12. He hit the highest of his four three-figure innings at Worcester in 1906 when Northamptonshire, after following on 165 behind Worcestershire, won by 41 runs thanks largely to his 166, made without chance in three hours. Sound in defence, he neglected few scoring chances and was specially strong in on-side strokes. He was also a good hockey player.

POOLEY, Edward, the once-famous Surrey wicket-keeper, died in Lambeth Infirmary on July 18, 1907. He had for a long time been in very poor circumstances and was often compelled to seek the shelter of the workhouse. Born on February 13, 1838, he was in his 70th year. All through his cricket career it was generally supposed that he was born in 1843 and the real date of his birth was only made known by himself in his interview in *Old English Cricketers*. It seems that when he determined to take up cricket professionally his father thought that he would have a better chance if he knocked a few years off his age. Thus, though regarded at the time as quite a young player, he was over 23 when in May, 1861, he played at the Oval for a team of Surrey Colts against the Gentlemen of the Surrey club with Hayes and Heartfield. At that time his future fame as a wicket-keeper was unthought of, and presumably he was tried for his batting. Playing on the same side were Harry Jupp and the still surviving J. Bristow. In 1862 Pooley was engaged as one of the bowlers at the Oval, but his regular connection with the Surrey XI did not begin until about 1865. In the meantime he played for Middlesex, making his

first appearance at Lord's for that county against the M.C.C. on July 25, 1864. The match was a memorable one inasmuch as Grundy and Wootton got Middlesex out in the first innings for a total of 20. The story of how he came to succeed Tom Lockyer is graphically told by himself in *Old English Cricketers*. He said, "My introduction to wicket-keeping would be about the year 1863. Old Tom Lockyer's hands were bad, and the ground being fiery he could not take his usual place behind the sticks. Mr. F. P. Miller, the Surrey captain, was in a quandary as to who should relieve him, so I, saucy-like, as usual, went up to him and said, 'Mr. Miller, let me have a try.' 'You? What do you know about wicket-keeping? Have you ever kept wicket at all?' was Mr. Miller's remark. 'No, never, but I should like to try,' I replied. 'Nonsense,' said he, and when just at that moment H. H. Stephenson came up and remarked, 'Let the young 'un have a go, sir,' Mr. Miller thereupon relented. I donned the gloves, quickly got two or three wickets, and seemed so much at home that Tom Lockyer was delighted, and said I was born to keep wicket and would have to be his successor in the Surrey team. What he said came true."

In 1866, Pooley established his position as one of the leading professionals of the day and thenceforward he remained a member of the Surrey XI for 17 years, finally dropping out in 1883. His great days as a wicket-keeper date from the time of the late James Southerton's connection with Surrey in 1867. The two men helped each other enormously. Southerton's slow bowling with a pronounced off-break was then something comparatively new and while batsmen were learning to play him the wicket-keeper naturally had great chances. It is safe to say that no wicket-keeper then before the public could have assisted Southerton to the extent that Pooley did. He was quick as lightning and with all his brilliancy very safe. Partly from lack of opportunity he was not quite so good as Pinder or Tom Plumb to very fast bowling, but to slow bowling he was in his day supreme. Two or three pages of *Wisden* could easily be filled with details of his doings, but it is sufficient to say here that the record of the greatest number of wickets obtained in a first-class match still stands to his credit after an interval of nearly 40 years. In the Surrey v. Sussex match at the Oval in July, 1868, he got rid of 12 batsmen, stumping one and catching five in the first innings and stumping three and catching three in the second. Curiously enough Southerton was in the Sussex team in this match, players in those days being allowed to play for two counties in the same season if qualified by birth for one and by residence for the other. The rule was changed just afterwards and Southerton threw in his lot with Surrey. Apart from his wicket-keeping Pooley was a first-rate bat, free in style, with fine driving power and any amount of confidence. He made many good scores and would without a doubt have been a much greater run-getter if he had not been so constantly troubled by damaged hands. During the Canterbury Week of 1871 he played an innings of 93 when suffering from a broken finger. Of the faults of private character that marred Pooley's career and were the cause of the poverty in which he spent the later years of his life there is no need now to speak. He was in many ways his own enemy, but even to the last he had a geniality and sense of humour that to a certain extent condoned his weaknesses.

POORE, Brig.-Gen. Robert Montagu, who during one season was the most prolific scorer in England, died on July 14, 1938, aged 72. He used to relate that he did not take seriously to cricket before going to India as a Lieutenant in the 7th Hussars. Then he studied textbooks on the game while playing in Army matches. From 1892 to 1895 when A.D.C. to Lord Harris, then Governor of Bombay, he averaged 80 for Government House. Going to South Africa, better opportunities came for finding his true ability when facing the formidable bowlers under the command of Lord Hawke. He hit up 112 at Pietermaritzburg and at Durban, when Fifteen of Natal were set to get 228, he scored 107, being mainly responsible for the local side winning by five wickets; these were the only 100s scored against the touring team of 1895–96. He also appeared for South Africa in the three Test matches without distinguishing himself more than did some others in badly beaten XIs.

In the course of a few months in Natal he scored 1,600 runs, including nine separate 100s, so that when returning to England in 1898 at the age of 32, Major Poore was ready for first-class cricket. On a soft wicket at Lord's he scored 51 and helped appreciably in an innings victory for M.C.C. over Lancashire. He averaged 34 for 11 Hampshire matches and next season he became the most sensational batsman in the country, his doings being described as phenomenal. Making a late start he scored in two months—June 12 to August 12—1,399 runs

for Hampshire with an average of 116.58. Major Poore hit seven centuries, two against Somerset at Portsmouth, and in his next innings another off the Lancashire bowlers at Southampton; he also scored exactly 100 runs in two innings against the Australians. In 21 first-class innings he made 1,551 runs, average 91.23—a figure not exceeded until Herbert Sutcliffe averaged 96.96 in 1931. The return with Somerset at Taunton was specially noteworthy, Major Poore scoring 304 and with captain E. G. Wynyard (225) adding 411 in four hours 20 minutes—the English record for the sixth wicket. Chosen for the Gentlemen against the Players at both the Oval and Lord's, Poore did little. Military duty took him back to South Africa before the end of the season, and after occasional appearances his County Cricket ceased in 1906, but so well did he retain his form and activity that in 1923, when 57 years old, he hit three consecutive centuries during a tour of M.C.C. in the West Country. His 304 stood as a Hampshire record for 38 years, being surpassed in 1937 by R. H. Moore with 316 against Warwickshire at Bournemouth.

6ft. 4in. in height, of massive frame with powerful limbs, Major Poore when at the top of his form used his long reach with great effect in driving, his strokes between the bowler and cover point going with such speed over the turf that fieldsmen, no matter how placed, could not prevent him from scoring freely. Before becoming accustomed to English wickets, he played forward more in defence for smothering the ball than as a hitter, but his drive ripened to one of the most powerful ever known.

A versatile sportsman, Major Poore was one of the finest swordsmen in the Army, taking the highest honours at the Military Tournament. A first-rate polo player he also twice won the West of India Lawn Tennis Championship, a feat he repeated in Matabeleland, and was in his regimental shooting team. His exceptional physical powers were demonstrated in his wonderful 1899 season; during a fortnight in June he played in the winning team of the Inter-Regimental Polo Tournament, won the best-man-at-arms mounted event at the Royal Naval and Military Tournament and scored three consecutive centuries for Hampshire, 104 and 119 not out against Somerset and 111 against Lancashire.

POPE, Dudley Fairbridge, the well-known Essex batsman, was killed on September 8, 1934, when his car and a motor lorry collided at Writtle, near Chelmsford. Another car driven by Peter Smith, the Essex bowler, with whom Pope was going to Walton-on-the-Naze for the weekend, had passed a little way ahead. Smith heard the crash and when he came back found that Pope had been killed instantly. Previously associated with Gloucestershire for three seasons—1925, 1926 and 1927—Pope first appeared in Essex in 1930 and proved of great value. With an aggregate of 1,224 runs and an average of 34, he enjoyed a highly successful season. During the following summer he scored 342 fewer runs but made some very useful scores. Last season for the third time consecutively Pope obtained over 1,000 runs, getting 1,640 with an average of 34, and put four centuries to his credit. A very restrained batsman, Pope showed special defensive skill under difficult conditions. Against Surrey at the Oval in 1930, when Essex required 342 runs to escape the follow-on, he and Sheffield, going in first, made a great stone-walling effort. The two players kept up their wickets for three hours and a half while scoring 113 runs, thus ensuring a draw. A very good field, Pope could throw the ball from long distances direct to the wicket-keeper's hands. He was most popular both on and off the field. Pope played hockey for Brentham. Born at Barnes in Surrey on October 28, 1908, Pope was 25 years of age.

POPE, Frederick, who died in May, 1961, aged 76, was father of G. H. Pope, the Derbyshire and England fast bowler and batsman. He was for many years grounds-man at Edgbaston, headquarters of Warwickshire.

POPE, Dr. Rowland James, who died at Sydney on July 27, 1952, aged 88, was a frequent visitor to England with Australian teams, though not as a playing member. Born on February 18, 1864, he was educated at Hutchins School, Hobart, Tasmania, gaining a place in the XI as a batsman and bowler of lobs, and he later played for Sydney University. Subsequently, while studying medicine, he was in the Edinburgh University side. In 1884–85, after hitting 170 not out for Melbourne Zingari against Richmond, he represented New South Wales in two matches against Victoria, and he appeared for a Combined XI of Australia and for his State against Alfred Shaw's team. An M.D. and F.R.C.S. of Edinburgh and an ophthalmic specialist, he became a member of M.C.C. in 1887.

PORCH, Robert Bagehot, who died on October 29, 1962, aged 87, was probably the last survivor of those who took part in the historic match at Taunton in 1895 when A. C. MacLaren played his innings of 424 for Lancashire against Somerset. This was then easily the highest individual score in first-class cricket, the previous best being 344 by W. G. Grace for M.C.C. against Kent at Canterbury in 1876, and MacLaren's record stood until W. H. Ponsford hit 429 for Victoria against Tasmania at Melbourne in the Australian season of 1922–23. A useful batsman who drove well, "Judy" Porch was in the Malvern XI in 1893 and 1894, heading the averages in the second year. He went up to Oxford without gaining a Blue and played occasionally as an amateur for Somerset from 1895 to 1910, his appearances being limited by his duties as a master at Malvern. In all, he scored 659 runs, average 15.32, his highest innings being 85 not out against Essex at Taunton in 1895. As a great believer in the importance of fielding, his maxim was: "Save six fours when the other side is batting, and you have 24 to your name before you get off the mark, though it's not in the score-book." He was president of the Malvernian Society.

PORTER, The Rev. Albert Lavington, who died at Tiverton, Devon, on December 14, 1937, aged 73, played for Somerset and Hampshire. He was at Marlborough College and Cambridge University.

PORTER, George, who was born at Spondon, near Derby, on December 3, 1861, died at his native place on July 15, 1908, after a long and painful illness caused by sunstroke. After fulfilling many engagements in Lancashire he was tried for Derbyshire in 1881, but, not meeting with much success, did not again appear in County Cricket until 1888. He then quickly made his place in the XI secure, and for several seasons was one of the best bowlers on the side. He delivered the ball at a good pace and at times was very effective. In 1895, his best season, he took 78 wickets in first-class matches for 16.74 runs each. Against Lancashire at Derby he took five wickets for one run upon going on for the third time and thereby brought success to his side by 63 runs. The same season (1895) he credited himself with the highest score of his career in a great match—93 against Notts at Trent Bridge. In 1891, when Surrey were the Champions, he took 10 wickets for 121 runs in the match at the Oval and thereby had a very prominent share in a memorable victory by 10 wickets. He played his last first-class match in 1896, and afterwards took to umpiring. Porter was 6 ft. 2 in. in height and weighed 14 st. 3 lb.

PORTER, The Rev. James, D.D., died at Peterhouse Lodge, Cambridge, on October 2, 1900, aged 72. Master of Peterhouse, Cambridge. For many years treasurer of the Cambridge University C.C., and did much towards acquiring Fenner's Ground.

PORTMAN, Francis John, who died of typhoid fever on May 2, 1905, at the early age of 27, was educated at Radley and Oxford, but did not play against Cambridge. He appeared, however, both for Berkshire and Somerset.

POSTHUMA, C. J., who died in Holland in December, 1939, aged 71, was mainstay of the Dutch teams which visited England in 1892, 1894, 1901 and 1906. A medium to fast left-hand bowler, he used off-break with a slower ball. On the invitation of W. G. Grace he played for London County for a season. During his long career (1884–1926) he took over 2,000 wickets. During the First World War, Posthuma earned the gratitude of cricketers among the British soldiers and marines interned in Holland by organising cricket matches for them.

POSTLES, Alfred J., died early in August, 1976, aged 73. A good bat, he captained Auckland in three seasons when they won the Plunket Shield. He had been president of the Auckland Cricket Association and of the New Zealand Cricket Council and also a member of the New Zealand Board of Control.

POTTER, Joseph, who was born at Northampton on January 13, 1839, and died there on June 2, 1906, had a curious career. In succession he played for Northamptonshire, Kent, Surrey, Wiltshire, and then Northamptonshire again. He was a fair batsman and a useful right-hand medium-paced bowler; for Surrey, in 1880, he took 78 wickets at a cost of 16 runs each. For several years he was coach at Marlborough College, and from 1892 to 1897 an umpire in first-class matches.

POTTER, Thomas Owen, who played for Lancashire against Surrey at Edge Hill in 1866, died at Hoylake, in Cheshire, on April 27, 1909, aged 64. That was his only appearance for the county, and he scored 39 and 0. His brother, Mr. W. H. Potter, assisted Lancashire in 1870.

POUGHER, Arthur Dick, born at Leicester, on April 19, 1865, died at his native place on May 20, 1926, aged 61. An excellent all-round cricketer, he will be recalled chiefly as a capital medium-pace bowler with a high delivery and a break-back, combined with skilful variation of pace. His most memorable feat was in taking five wickets without a run in 15 balls for M.C.C. against the Australians at Lord's in June, 1896, the latter being dismissed for 18: one man was absent ill, and the last six wickets went down with the total unchanged. Among many other good performances with the ball by Pougher the following are worthy of mention:

13 for 54	(including 6 for 10), Leicestershire v. Surrey, at Leicester ..	1886
	(He and Rylott bowled unchanged)	
7 for 8	Leicestershire v. Warwickshire, at Edgbaston	1886
Hat-trick	M.C.C. v. Cambridge University, at Lord's	1887
8 for 81	Leicestershire v. Essex, at Leicester	1887
6 for 14	Shrewsbury's team v. Queensland Eighteen, at Brisbane ..	1887–88
10 for 71	Leicestershire v. Australians, at Leicester	1888
	(The county won by 20 runs)	
6 for 15	Leicestershire v. Derbyshire, at Leicester	1888
6 for 13	Leicestershire v. Essex, at Leyton	1888
13 for 104	Leicestershire v. Surrey, at Leicester	1888
	(He and Rylott bowled unchanged)	
8 for 115	Leicestershire v. Warwickshire, at Leicester	1890
	(The other two men were run out)	
13 for 41	(Including 8 for 18), Leicestershire v. M.C.C., at Lord's ..	1890
8 for 52	Leicestershire v. M.C.C., at Lord's	1891
	(He did the hat-trick)	
8 for 48	Leicestershire v. Essex, at Leyton	1892
5 for 15	Leicestershire v. Surrey, at Leicester	1893
13 for 86	Leicestershire v. Hampshire, at Leicester	1893

14 for	84	Leicestershire v. Hampshire, at Southampton	..	..	1893
		Unchanged with J. T. Hearne, M.C.C. v. Kent, at Lord's		..	1894
7 for	17	Leicestershire v. South Africans, at Leicester	..	..	1894
14 for	89	(Including 8 for 60), Leicestershire v. Essex, at Leyton		..	1894
8 for	40	Leicestershire v. Surrey, at Leicester	..	..	1894
9 for	34	England v. Surrey, at the Oval	..	.. ..	1895
8 for	85	Leicestershire v. Yorkshire, at Leicester	..	.. ..	1895
		Unchanged with J. T. Hearne, Earl de la Warr's XI v. Australians, at Bexhill	.. ..	.. ..	1896
8 for	151	M.C.C. v. Worcestershire, at Lord's	..	.. ..	1900

In games of less note he took 11 wickets for 18 runs for R. G. Barlow's XI v. XXII of Blackpool and District in 1889, and (in conjunction with F. Martin, of Kent) obtained eight wickets in nine balls for Mr. W. W. Read's team v. XXII of the Country Clubs at Cape Town in 1891–92, each player taking four in succession. In a 12-a-side match, too, at Streatham in July, 1892, whilst playing for M.C.C. v. Streatham he took all 11 wickets for 37 runs.

For Leicestershire he made many good scores, including 109 v. Essex at Leyton in 1894, 102 not out v. Warwickshire at Leicester and 114 v. Derbyshire at Derby in 1896, and 104 v. Surrey and 106 v. Yorkshire, both at Leicester, in 1899. From 1887 until 1909 he was a member of the M.C.C. ground staff at Lord's, and he took part in two tours overseas, visiting Australia with Shrewsbury's team in 1887–88 and South Africa with Mr. W. W. Read's in 1891–92. His only appearance for the Players was at the Oval in 1895. He received reward for his service to the game in two benefit matches—Leicestershire v. Yorkshire at Leicester in 1900 and Middlesex v. Kent at Lord's in 1910. For many years he had kept the Old Cricket Ground Hotel, Aylestone Park, Leicester.

POULIER, Hilton E., who died in Melbourne on May 6, 1979, aged 70, was Ceylon's leading fast bowler 50 years ago. At the age of 20 he was picked for All-Ceylon against Harold Gilligan's side in 1929 when he had the distinction of dismissing Frank Woolley, and he was a member of the All-Ceylon side which toured India under C. H. Gurrasekara in 1932–33, the first Ceylon overseas tour.

POWELL, Adam Gordon, who died at his home in Sandwich on June 7, 1982, aged 69, was regarded by some good judges as one of the outstanding English wicket-keepers of his time. A pupil of Strudwick, to whom he always acknowledged a great debt, he stood up to all but the fastest bowlers and was so neat and quiet, making the whole job look so simple, that it was easy to underestimate him. He was also a useful attacking bat: with beautiful wrists, a lovely cover drive and an effective golf-shot over mid-on, he was particularly good against fast bowling. When Essex beat Yorkshire at Southend by an innings in 1934, he contributed 62 not out and had an unfinished partnership of 113 in 90 minutes with Peter Smith for the ninth wicket. In the next year he scored 47 against Larwood and Voce: on this occasion his partner, an England batsman, was inclined to leave to him the playing of Larwood.

After three years in the Charterhouse side he went up to Cambridge, but got his Blue only in his third year, 1934: many thought he should have had it earlier. Between 1932 and 1937 he played frequently for Essex and in 1935 went as one of the two wicket-keepers with E. R. T. Holmes's M.C.C. side to Australia and New Zealand: unfortunately he missed much of the tour with a sprained ankle. His county career ended when in 1937 the doctors forbade him to play serious first-class cricket. In 1939 he appeared for Suffolk and captained them in 1946 when they won the Minor Counties Championship for the first time. He continued for many years to play club cricket and also to represent M.C.C. and Free Foresters in first-class matches. He was a member of the M.C.C. sides to Canada in 1937 and 1951 and also toured Egypt with Hubert Martineau's XI.

POWELL, Albert James, who died in Liskeard on February 15, 1979, aged 85, played one match for Worcestershire in 1921.

POWELL, Archie, who died on December 27, 1963, aged 95, played for Gloucestershire Colts and, when catching W. G. Grace at cover point, was reputed to be the only newspaperman ever to dismiss the Doctor for a "duck." Powell contributed articles on cricket and Rugby football to the *Daily Mail* for 40 years. A Bristol journalist, he was a director of the *Western Daily Press*.

POWELL, Ernest Ormsby, born at Liverpool on January 19, 1861, died at Stafford on

March 28, 1928, aged 67. A good and successful bat and an excellent cover-point, he gained his colours at Charterhouse in 1878 and in the next two seasons captained the side. During his third season in the XI, when he scored 66 v. Westminster, he had an average of 28.33. Although he appeared at Cambridge for the Freshmen, Seniors and the Sixteen, playing several good innings, and was tried for the University in 1883, he did not obtain his Blue. After assisting Surrey in four matches in 1882, he played for Hampshire, and in 1884 made 140 v. Somerset at Southampton and 99 v. Surrey at the Oval. Another good innings of his was 89 for M.C.C. v. Cambridge University at Lord's. He was in the scholastic profession, and had been headmaster of Stafford Grammar School.

POWELL, W. A., who died on January 1, 1954, aged 68, played occasionally for Kent in the last few seasons before the First World War.

POWYS, Walter N., the famous fast left-handed bowler, died at his residence, Queen's Walk, Nottingham, on January 8, 1892. He was in his 43rd year, having been born on July 3, 1849. He was privately educated, and went up to Pembroke College, Cambridge, appearing in the University match in 1871, 1872, and 1874. In these three matches he took 24 Oxford wickets at a cost of 153 runs, but his fame chiefly rests on his performance in the match of 1872, when he obtained 13 wickets. In that year he played for the Gentlemen against the Players at Lord's. For some time Mr. Powys had faded out of first-class cricket, but in his day he was one of the best amateur fast bowlers in England. Owing to failing health he was advised to take a trip to America, but he returned invalided, and died while still in the prime of life.

POWYS-KECK, Capt. Horatio James, who died in London on January 30, 1952, aged 79, was educated at Malvern, but did not gain a place in the XI. He played a few games for Worcestershire. As a member of the Oxford University Authentics XI he toured India and Burma in 1902–03.

POYNTON, Dr. Frederick John, died at Bath on October 29, 1943, aged 74. An admirable bat at Marlborough, he made 30 and 47 against Rugby at Lord's in the 1886 match, when C. W. Bengough, by going on to bowl twice at each end in the same innings, broke Law 14. This infringement, which caused the Law to be altered, was mentioned in 1943 *Wisden* in regard to S. A. P. Kitcat. Poynton, highest Marlborough scorer in an effort to get 233 runs for victory, was batting with his captain when the incident occurred. Rugby won by 36 runs after a splendid struggle. Poynton played for Somerset from 1891 to 1896 when free from medical duties, and in 1893 he took part in another match that aroused much discussion. On a very wet Thursday morning it was decided that play was impossible; but the weather turned fine, many people came to Taunton to see the Australians, and to avoid disappointment the Somerset authorities overruled the umpires and play began late in the afternoon. Poynton's highest score for Somerset was 57 at Hove in 1895.

POYNTZ, E. S. Massy, died on December 26, 1934. A member of the Haileybury XI in 1901, Mr. Poyntz made his first appearance for Somerset in 1905 and played regularly for the county until the outbreak of the War, being captain in 1913 and 1914. He made a few appearances in 1919. An enterprising batsman, he hit the ball hard and was an excellent fielder. In his first season with Somerset he played in five matches, scoring 307 runs with a highest score of 89 and an average of 34.31. After this promising start he did little of note until 1910 when he made 352 runs in 10 matches, while the next summer he scored 597 runs in 14 games. In 1914 his aggregate reached 642 runs, but he averaged only 18.34. It was during his captaincy that J. C. White, the famous left-hand slow bowler, was discovered. Mr. Poyntz played under S. M. J. Woods and John Daniell, whom he succeeded.

POYNTZ, Col. H. S., who died on June 22, 1955, aged 77, played occasionally for Somerset between 1904 and 1910. His best performance was at Beckenham in his first season when he scored 85 and 48. Kent won the match thanks to the all-round success of J. R. Mason, who, besides hitting 126, took 10 wickets for 180 runs. Poyntz was also a good Association footballer and captained the Army in 1907. He fought in the Boer War and in the First World War in which he was awarded the D.S.O. and twice Mentioned in Dispatches.

PRATT, Richard, who died on October 10, 1982, aged 86, had a few trials for Derbyshire as a batsman in 1923 and 1924, but met with no success. He could also keep wicket.

PRATT, Ronald C. E., who died on June 1,

1977, aged 49, played for Surrey from 1952 to 1959. A tall left-handed batsman who played in spectacles, he could never get an assured place in the very strong side of those days and finally left to take a job in insurance. His best performances were 90 against Kent at the Oval in 1953, when he and Clark put on 250 in four hours for the fourth wicket, and 120 against Cambridge University at Guildford in 1956, on which occasion he helped Stewart to add 255. A fine slip, he caught six catches against Sussex at Hastings in 1956. His brother, D. E. Pratt, also played for the county.

PRATT, William Ewart, who died at Leicester during 1974 when approaching 80, played a number of times for Leicestershire as a batsman in 1920 and 1921. His highest innings, 29 not out against Sussex at Leicester in 1921, enabled the county to win by three wickets. Set 259 to get, they lost seven wickets for 172 and then J. H. King and Pratt hit off the remaining runs.

PREECE, Cecil Arthur, who died on November 11, 1966, aged 77, played as a professional for Worcestershire from 1920 to 1924. At a period when the county were far from strong, he headed the bowling averages in 1920 when taking with slow-medium deliveries 42 wickets at 30.11 runs each. He never again did as well, though against Warwickshire at Edgbaston in 1924 he performed the hat-trick. He achieved occasional good work as a batsman, his best season being that of 1921, when he hit 505 runs, average 17.66. His highest innings was 69 for the Sussex bowling at Worcester in 1922.

PREECE, Charles Richard, who played for Worcestershire between 1920 and 1929, died at Oldbury in the West Midlands on February 2, 1976, aged 87. During his playing career his initials were given as C. A. which later led to such confusion that his death was reported in *Wisden*, 1967, on the demise of a certain Cecil Arthur Preece. There is no question that Charles Richard Preece was the Worcestershire slow-medium bowler who appeared for them after the First World War. In the possession of his son is the ball with which C. R. Preece performed the hat-trick against Warwickshire at Edgbaston in 1924. Back in those days the county was far from strong, and in 1920 C. R. Preece headed the bowling averages with 42 wickets at 30.11 each. His highest innings was 69 against Sussex at Worcester in 1922. For 20 years he was groundsman at Chance Bros.,

Smethwick. In 1967 he suffered the handicap of a leg amputation.

PRENTICE, Frank Thomas, died at Headingley on July 10, 1978, after a long illness, aged 66. Born at Knaresborough, he was spotted by Herbert Sutcliffe while playing for Yorkshire Second XI in 1931, and as there seemed little chance of a place in the Yorkshire side he qualified for Leicestershire. He was a valuable member of their team from 1934 to 1951. A right wrist, badly broken during the War, slightly handicapped him in later years. None the less, his most successful season was his last regular one, in 1949, when he scored 1,742 runs with an average of 38.71, and made his highest score, 191 v. Nottinghamshire at Loughborough. After this season he decided to concentrate on his business, and in 1950 played in only 13 matches. Four appearances as an amateur in 1951 concluded his first-class career, but he never lost his interest in the game and in recent years had done some coaching in South Africa. In his whole career he scored 10,997 runs with an average of 27.70, including 17 centuries, took 117 wickets, and held 75 catches.

PRENTICE, Leslie Roff Vincent, who died at Harrold, Bedfordshire, on August 13, 1928, aged 41, appeared on a few occasions for Middlesex. He hailed from Sydney, Australia.

PREST, E. P., who died in mid-June, 1903, at the age of 73, was a member of the Cambridge XI of 1850, playing that year against Oxford, in the last Varsity match played at Oxford. He was educated at Eton and Trinity College, Cambridge, and was called to the Bar in 1855.

PREST, Harold Edward Westray, who died on January 5, 1955, aged 64, gained his Blue at Cambridge for cricket, golf and Association football early in the century. In the Malvern XI for three years before going to the University, he headed the batting averages in 1908 with 174 not out his best innings, and *Wisden* stated: "It is doubtful whether Prest had a superior as a batsman among the schoolboys of the year. He plays in excellent style, with a full quiver of fine forcing strokes anywhere except behind point. He is a fine field into the bargain."

He played against Oxford as a Freshman in 1909, when he scored 54 and shared in a sixth-wicket partnership of 94 with J. F. Ireland. His other University match was that of

1911, when he made six and 16. In the second innings he fell to a magnificent wide return catch with the left hand by P. R. Le Couteur off a full-blooded drive. Le Couteur did much to win the match for the Dark Blues by taking in that innings eight wickets for 99 runs. Prest played a little for Kent between 1909 and 1911. In the last season he distinguished himself with an innings of 133 not out in two and a half hours against Somerset at Taunton, taking part in stands of 108 with F. H. Huish and 128 with D. W. Carr. This was his only century in first-class cricket.

PRESTON, Harry J., who died suddenly while watching television on April 23, 1964, aged 77, played for Kent as a professional in a few matches between 1907 and 1913 and also represented Scotland while coaching there. He afterwards became groundsman at the Central Cricket Ground, Hastings, and assisted the Priory C.C. when well over 60. He retired when, following an accident with a mowing machine, his right hand was amputated.

HUBERT PRESTON
By Neville Cardus
Born on December 16, 1868, Hubert Preston died on August 6, 1960, aged 91. He spent the greater part of his life reporting cricket and Association football. He helped in the preparation of Wisden *from 1895 to 1951, being Editor for the last eight years.*

When I entered the Press Box at Lord's some 40 years ago, Hubert Preston sat next to Sydney Pardon at the end of the front row, near the steps leading to the exit. It was a different Press Box then, far different from the large place of accountancy which today is metallic during the summers with typewriters. I doubt if Sydney Pardon would have allowed anybody to use a typewriter in his presence at Lord's or any other cricket ground.

I didn't dare go into the Lord's Press Box during my first season as a cricket writer for the *Manchester Guardian*. I was shy, provincially raw. I wrote my reports sitting on the Green Bank. I wrote them on press telegram forms, and at close of play handed them in at the telegraph office under the clock at the Nursery End.

One afternoon, Hubert Preston saw me as I sat on the Green Bank scribbling my message. "Why don't you come into the Press Box?" he said, in his own brisk, rapidly articulated way. He took me by the arm and led me up the steep iron steps. The tea interval wasn't over yet. Preston introduced me to Sydney Pardon, who then introduced me to the other members of the Press Box, some of them life-members—Stewart Caine, Harry Carson, Frank Thorogood and others. Each made a courteous bow to me; it was like a *levée*. Pardon pointed to a seat in the back row. In time, he assured me, I would graduate to a front place among the elect.

Hubert Preston was, with Pardon and Stewart Caine, the most courteous and best-mannered man ever to be seen in a Press Box on a cricket ground. Stewart Caine would actually bow to me and give me precedence into a gentlemen's lavatory. Hubert's deafness was the reason why, now and again, the aristocratic Pardon was obliged to raise his voice. Pardon once apologised to me for an occasional voice crescendo. "You know," he said, "Hubert is quite sensationally deaf." At the Oval, a match was beginning on a superlative wicket in the 1930s, a shaven lawn, reduced into an anaesthetic condition by a 10-ton roller. As we watched, we made our several comments on this batsman's paradise. "Not fair to bowlers." "Ought to be stopped, this doping." "Bound to be a draw—no life in the pitch." "Not fair to bowlers—doped—killin' the game" and so on.

Hubert, unable to hear a word of all this, sat concentrating on the cricket. Then he spoke: "This wicket is playing funny already. J. T. Hearne would have 'em all out before lunch. Too much water in the preparation." What is more, Hubert's prophecy, uttered in the silence surrounding him, was soon proven right. The wicket *did* very soon help the bowler.

Hubert was so modest, so reticent of his own talents and history, that not until his death did I learn from the obituary notices that his first job in London as a journalist was with my own paper, *The Guardian*. Or that he farmed for some time in Canada, from 1893 to 1895. Or that he had played cricket on the sacrosanct turf of Lord's and had performed the hat-trick there, for the Press v. The Authors. Or that he had played soccer for Lyndhurst v. The Royal Arsenal, forerunners of *the* Arsenal.

He was naturally a man of few words because of his deafness. But his sparkling eyes could talk. I have seen him chastise a poor stroke on the field of play by means of a facial expression far more eloquent than any word, written or oral. He was alive in every nerve and muscle. If responsive life had departed from his ears, the more sharply

vital his other faculties seemed to grow. In
no sense did he become an "old man." And
though he extolled the great players of the
past, he was, to the end of his career as a
cricket journalist, quick to recognise young
talents of quality. Almost to the last hours of
a life extending from December 16, 1868, to
August 6, 1960, he remained mentally active
and curious. He was apparently tireless, and
a continuous enjoyer of good health. His
only stay in a hospital as a patient was the
last two days of his life.

As a boy, cricket was at his shoulders
temptingly. He began his education at a
preparatory school overlooking Kennington
Oval. Later he was a student at the City of
London School. He joined Pardon's Cricket
Reporting Agency in 1895 and was in active
and faithful service for this same agency until
1951. In those days there was no radio to
spread far and wide the latest cricket scores.
The work of the Cricket Reporting Agency,
responsible for the Press Association's sporting news, was comprehensive and exhaustive. But nothing could exhaust Hubert. He
saw dynasty succeed unto dynasty at cricket—Grace and Shrewsbury, "Ranji" and
Trumper, right down the historic line, Abel,
Hayward, Hobbs and Tyldesley, until the
Bradman sunset. His life was full and happy.
And he had the happy knowledge in his
period of heavily accumulated years of
knowing that his son was carrying on the
good work of his life, as Editor of his beloved
Wisden. He was loved as a man and a
gentleman. And he was respected by his
colleagues as a craftsman.

E. Eden writes: "H. P.", as all his friends
knew him, was celebrated all over Great
Britain as a journalist who, whether reporting cricket or football, wrote what he meant
and meant what he wrote. He never really
liked the modern tendency towards speed as
opposed to accuracy, about which he was
meticulous to a degree; and, among his
idiosyncrasies, he insisted always that ped-
estrians should walk on the right-hand side of
the pavement! When I first worked with him
42 years ago, he used an old-fashioned ear-
trumpet. As they became available, he
adopted electrical hearing-aids which occasionally led to mildly awkward situations.
For instance, when a change of battery was
needed, it became necessary to roar at
"H. P." to make him hear. When, without
one's knowledge, he attached a fresh battery, a few words above normal tones would
evoke the sharp rebuke: "There's no need to
shout, my boy, I'm not deaf!"

Even late in life he liked to talk about his

footballing exploits, and many a less heavily
built colleague suffered something of a shaking when he illustrated forcibly "how we
used to charge 'em in the old days." Despite
his handicap, he served for a time in the East
Surrey Regiment during the First World War
and inwardly he was intensely proud of the
fact that he was an Honorary Freeman of the
City of London though he rarely mentioned
it.

Unfortunately, H. P. was not spared to
learn of the exciting Test tie in Brisbane. The
finish of that match would have given him
much pleasure for he was the leading cam-
paigner for the last over to be played out in a
close finish irrespective of whether a wicket
fell or not. I quote the following extract from
his "Notes by the Editor," page 68 of the
1947 Wisden:

The newly arranged "Laws of Cricket,"
which will not come into force as finally
approved until the 1948 season, clarify some
details, and make one change which is specially pleasing to me. The "last over" of a
match shall be played to a finish at the
request of either captain. I first urged this in
my Notes in the 1944 edition of Wisden, and
each subsequent year emphasised the possible unfairness to the fielding side, so I may
take some credit for bringing about this
alteration which makes the balance even in a
close finish on time.

Other tributes:
Sir John Hobbs: "We became great friends
almost as soon as I gained a footing in first-
class cricket. We had a common attraction
because our birthdays fell on the same day,
he being my senior by 14 years. The players
looked up to Hubert Preston as a genuine
cricket reporter who knew the game and
always did us justice."
Ronald Aird, secretary of M.C.C.: "I remember him since the early '20s. He was
always so courteous and helpful over the
business which we did together. His work for
cricket with Wisden will live for all time and
was a great contribution to the game. I am
very grateful for having known him so well."
A. H. H. Gilligan: He was a familiar figure
to us all in those far-off days when I used to
play County Cricket and whether we got 0 or
plenty he always had a smile and a word of
encouragement. If there was criticism it was
always constructive."
Ian Macartney: "He played a long innings
with very little public recognition. The vivid
and concise reporting of Wisden taught a
generation of youngsters—the striplings of
1920—how to write their own language, far
better than any formal English lesson, with-

out wasting words and space. The whole match was brought to life in a few lines. Gibbon and Macaulay had plenty of time to spread themselves, but S. H. Pardon and his successors are among the masters of English prose."

Leslie Deakins, secretary of Warwickshire County C.C.: "Cricket is deeply indebted to him for his achievements on its behalf over a very long lifetime. His journalistic talents gave pleasure to those thousands of Englishmen who regularly follow the game. He could truly reflect with the late Charles Fry that his had been 'Life Worth Living'."

PRESTON, John, who died in Birmingham on February 16, 1913, aged 74, played a few times for Warwickshire in 1882 and 1883, when past his prime. He soon dropped out of the side, but attended the Edgbaston ground whenever a county match was in progress there.

PRESTON, Peter R., who died in hospital at Wellington, New Zealand, in October, 1960, aged 24, following injuries received at cricket practice, was one of Wellington's most promising all-round sportsmen. He played for Wellington College Old Boys at cricket and Rugby football and also represented Wellington at cricket.

PRETTY, Dr. Harold C., who died at his home at Kettering on May 31, 1952, aged 76, achieved some noteworthy performances during a brief career in big cricket. On his first appearance in a first-class game, against Nottinghamshire at the Oval in 1899, he helped Surrey to victory by an innings and 85 runs by hitting 124. Upon joining Northamptonshire in 1906 he punished the Derbyshire bowling at Derby for 200, which, scored out of 280 in 200 minutes, included 35 fours. Born on October 23, 1875, he was a strong, punishing batsman and a very good fieldsman, generally at third man. He also represented Surrey at Rugby football.

PRICE, A.B. Seaman David, reported missing, presumed killed, after an action at sea on July 6, 1942, played regularly for Western Province teams from 1934 to 1940. A useful spin bowler, he also fielded with dash and certainty.

PRICE, Vincent Ramo, who died suddenly on May 29, 1973, aged 78, was in the Bishop's Stortford College XI before going up to Oxford, for whom he played in the University match from 1919 to 1922, being captain in 1921. A fast-medium out-swing bowler, he attracted attention in the first first-class match to be played after the First World War when taking 14 wickets for 112 runs for Oxford against Gentlemen of England, but, lacking accuracy in length, he never again met with anything like this success. He took part in one game for Surrey in 1919. As a Rugby footballer, he played against Cambridge as full-back in 1919 and as a powerful centre in 1920 and 1921.

PRICE, Walter (Notts), died September 4, 1894. Though never in the front rank of professional players, Walter Price was in his day a useful all-round cricketer. Born at Ruddington on October 9, 1834, he was very late in coming before the public, as it was not until 1867 that he was first tried in the Colts' match at Trent Bridge. He was drafted into the Notts XI in 1869, and played pretty regularly for them until June 1870, his last match being against Yorkshire. Both at Lord's and the Oval in 1870 he appeared for the Players against the Gentlemen, but only as a substitute. One of the best things he ever did for Notts was in the remarkable match against Surrey at the Oval in 1869, when Notts won the game within a quarter of an hour of time after a draw had seemed almost inevitable. On that occasion Price scored 57 and 14 not out. He joined the ground staff at Lord's in 1868, and remained in the service of the M.C.C. until 1876, when he succeeded the late Alfred Diver as coach at Rugby. On leaving Rugby he returned to Lord's, and was on the ground staff at the time of his death. A North and South match was played for his benefit at Lord's in 1887, but unfortunately for him, rain had spoiled the wicket, and the game was finished off in one day. In the latter part of his career Price was one of the M.C.C.'s regular umpires.

PRICE, William Frederick Frank, the former Middlesex and England wicketkeeper and Test match umpire, died in hospital on January 12, 1969, aged 66. A skilled performer behind the stumps, Fred Price held 648 catches and brought off 316 stumpings during a first-class career extending from 1926 to 1947. In 1937 he set up a record, since equalled but not surpassed, when he took seven catches in the Yorkshire first innings at Lord's.

After the match, a lady approached Price with congratulations upon his feat. "I was so thrilled with your performance, Mr. Price," she said, "that I nearly fell over the balcony." With mock gravity, Price responded:

"If you had, madam, I would have caught you as well!"

For so many years contemporary with L. E. G. Ames, 47 times capped for England, Price appeared in only one Test match, against Australia at Headingley in 1938, making two catches in the first innings. Twice he toured abroad, with the Hon. F. S. G. Calthorpe's M.C.C. team in 1929–30, when he was sent to the West Indies as replacement for the injured Major R. T. Stanyforth, and with Sir Theodore Brinckman's side in South America in 1937–38. Price developed into a distinctly useful batsman and often opened the innings for his county. In all he scored 6,666 runs, average 17.35, three times reaching three figures. He narrowly failed to obtain two centuries in the game with Kent at Lord's in 1934, scoring 92 and 107. The previous summer, when he made his highest innings, 111 off the Worcestershire bowling at Dudley, he and E. H. Hendren (301 not out) engaged in a fifth-wicket partnership of 332.

Fearless as an umpire from 1950 to 1967, Price created a sensation when he three times no-balled G. A. R. Lock, the Surrey and England left-arm slow bowler, for throwing against V. S. Hazare's India touring team at the Oval. In the same season on the same ground when the Yorkshire batsmen, struggling to avoid defeat from Surrey, were being subjected to continuous barracking by the crowd, Price lay on the ground at square-leg until the noise subsided. "I did so," he explained afterwards, "because three times there were catcalls just as the batsman was about to play the ball. That is not my idea of British sportsmanship and under the Laws of 'fair and unfair play' I will not tolerate such things on any ground, Lord's included, where I am umpiring." He officiated in eight Test matches.

F. S. Lee, the former Somerset player and Test umpire, who often "stood" with Price, paid him this tribute: "He was very conscientious, a very good umpire and a brilliant wicket-keeper, especially on the leg-side."

PRICHARD, Major Hesketh Vernon Hesketh, D.S.O., M.C., F.R.G.S., F.Z.S., born in India on November 17, 1876, died at Gorhambury, near St. Albans, on June 14, 1922. He learned his cricket at Fettes and afterwards played successfully for Hampshire, M.C.C., the Gentlemen and other prominent teams. As a fast bowler he was most useful, his deliveries getting up very quickly from the pitch. For Hampshire he obtained 222 wickets for 23.11 runs each, and he was probably at his best in 1904 when,

in all first-class matches, he took 106 wickets for an average of 21.92. He assisted the Gentlemen in 1903 and two following seasons, and took part in a couple of tours, visiting the West Indies with Lord Brackley in 1904–05 and America as a member of the M.C.C. team in 1907. When Kent were set 131 to win v. M.C.C. at Lord's in 1904, Hesketh Prichard took six wickets for 23 runs, the innings closing for 97. Half the side were out for 12, and he dismissed C. H. B. Marsham, Hardinge and Murrell without a run between them. For Hampshire he claimed 13 wickets for 78 runs v. Derbyshire at Southampton in 1905, and six for 18 v. Worcestershire at Worcester in 1912. For M.C.C. v. Gentlemen of Philadelphia at Haverford in 1907 he did the hat-trick. He was well known as a traveller and author, and during the War carried out responsible duties and was twice Mentioned in Dispatches.

PRIDE, Tom, who was born on July 23, 1864, died at Canobie, on February 16, 1919. A very useful batsman and fine wicket-keeper, he appeared in three matches for Yorkshire in 1887 and 1888 and also, more often, for Perthshire. In 1894 he played an innings of 201 for York v. Beverley. At the time of his death he was headmaster of Canobie School. Pride was in nearly every respect a first-rate wicket-keeper but his hands would not stand the strain of three-day matches. When playing against Sussex at Brighton he made a great impression.

PRIDHAM, Major C. H. B., late of the Duke of Wellington's Regiment, died at East Sheen, Surrey, on April 9, 1952, aged 68. Severely wounded in the First World War, he played for many years under considerable difficulty, chiefly for Somerset Stragglers. He was author of *The Charm of Cricket Past and Present*.

PRIDMORE, Major Reginald G. (R.F.A., Howitzer). M.C. Killed March 13, 1918, aged 31. Hertfordshire XI; Warwickshire XI.

PRIESTLEY, Sir A., died on April 10, 1933. A member of the M.C.C., he was not particularly prominent in the game itself. In 1896 when he took out a team to the West Indies, something of a stir was caused in cricket circles for another team under Lord Hawke visited the West Indies at the same time. Sir Arthur Priestley's team was invited by Barbados and Jamaica; Lord Hawke took out a side at the invitation of Demerara;

Trinidad was ready to welcome both parties. An amalgamation was proposed, but the plan did not work. Neither team clashed in any way, but Priestley's, which looked the stronger because it included A. E. Stoddart, S. M. J. Woods and R. C. N. Palairet, was beaten five times. He was born on November 9, 1865.

PRIESTLEY, Lance-Corp. Donald Lacey (Artists' Rifles), born at Tewkesbury on July 28, 1887; killed November 18, 1917. Played for Tewkesbury Grammar School, Tewkesbury, and Gloucestershire.

PRIESTLEY, Hugh William, M.C., who died on January 6, 1932, was educated at Uppingham and Cambridge University. He played for Buckinghamshire and in some first-class matches for M.C.C. in 1911.

PRINGLE, Donald, was killed in a car crash on October 4, 1975, on his way back from a match in Nairobi, in which he had taken six for 16. He was 43. An opening bowler, he was one of the East African side in England last summer. He was unable, owing to injury, to play in the Prudential Cup match against New Zealand, but played against England, without, however, much success. Born in Lancashire, he had been playing for Kenya, where he was a landscape consultant, for 17 years.

PRIOR, Charles Bolingbroke Leathes, who died in January, 1964, aged 80, played a little for Norfolk in 1906 and 1907 and was hon. secretary to the County Club for 12 years from 1909. A solicitor, he was Official Receiver for Norwich and Norfolk from 1922 to 1937 and a Norwich magistrate from 1940 to 1957.

PRITCHARD, David Edward, who died on July 4, 1983, aged 90, scored six centuries for South Australia, including 119 against the 1928–29 M.C.C. team. For nearly 50 years his 327 not out for Port Adelaide against Sturt stood as the highest individual score in Adelaide district cricket.

PRITCHETT, G. E. B., who died in London on November 27, 1920, aged 53, was formerly a well-known member of the Hertfordshire XI. He had been a member of the M.C.C. for 25 years, and also played for Incogniti. He was born on March 13, 1867.

PROMNITZ, Henry Louis Ernest, who died at King William's Town on September 7,

1983, aged 79, played twice for South Africa, against England in 1927–28. Like bowlers of more modern times, such as Iverson of Australia and the West Indian, Ramadhin, his spin was difficult to fathom, the off- and leg-breaks being frequently misread. Also like Iverson and Ramadhin, he was a poor fielder, which may have accounted for his playing in only two Test matches. In the first of them, at Johannesburg, he finished England's first innings with five for 58 in 37 overs after the score at one time had been 230 for one. In his second Test, at Cape Town, he took three for 56 in 30 overs in England's second innings. His eight Test wickets included Hammond, Sutcliffe, Ernest Tyldesley, Wyatt and Stevens. Between 1924–25 and 1936–37 he played at different times for Border, Griqualand West and Orange Free State, taking 150 first-class wickets at 23.80.

PUDDEFOOT, Sydney C., who died in a Southend hospital on October 4, 1972, aged 77, played as a professional in a few matches for Essex in 1922 and 1923. Better known as an Association football centre-forward, he played in three "Victory" Internationals after the First World War when with West Ham United. After a spell with Falkirk, he joined Blackburn Rovers and was capped twice for England in 1926. He also found a place in football League representative sides in 1925 and 1926. Puddefoot gained an F.A. Cup winners medal in 1928 when Blackburn Rovers beat Huddersfield Town at Wembley, 3–1.

PUGH, John Geoffrey, who died suddenly on February 12, 1964, while on holiday in Barbados, aged 60, was in the Rugby XI from 1920 to 1922, being captain in the last year when he appeared four times for Warwickshire. In 1921, when he was one of the outstanding school batsmen of the season, he headed the Rugby averages with 1,034 runs at 73.85 an innings, showing special strength in leg-side strokes. He was uncle of C. T. M. Pugh, of Gloucestershire.

PULLAN, Cecil Douglas Ayrton, who died on June 24, 1970, aged 59, was in the Malvern XI for three years from 1927. He headed the batting averages in 1928 with 61.60, his highest innings being 147 not out against Repton. "Plug" Pullan played for Worcestershire in 1935 and 1938.

PULLE, John, who died in 1982 at the age of 70, represented Ceylon against the Australians, who were on their way to England, in both 1934 and 1938. A forthright opening batsman and a good captain, he spent much of his life in England.

PULLEN, William Wade Fitzherbert, died at Southampton on August 9, 1937, aged 71. First playing for Gloucestershire in 1882 when 16 years of age he scored 71 at Cheltenham against Yorkshire. He made his highest county score, 161, two years later on the same ground when Middlesex were the visitors. His perfect innings, notable for admirable style and free, safe hitting, was the best score for Gloucestershire that season. Although continuing to show good form until 1891 Pullen never fulfilled his early promise. In 1881 he played for Somerset against Hampshire, neither county then being first-class, and, when a Professor of Engineering at Cardiff College, he assisted Glamorgan in 1895. In a match at Alveston in 1888 Pullen, 184, and Dr. E. M. Grace (160) made 311 for Thornbury's first wicket.

PULLIN, Alfred W. ("Old Ebor"), the well-known sporting journalist, died on June 23, 1934, when travelling to Lord's for the Test match. Aged 73, Mr. Pullin was one of the foremost authorities on cricket and football in English journalism. In the early '90s when newspapers began to devote space to sport Mr. Pullin soon built up a reputation with the followers of the games he helped to foster. Nurtured in Rugby football, he never rose to fame, though he played three-quarter back for Cleckheaton and afterwards acted as referee for the Yorkshire Union.

These experiences stood him in good stead when he came to travel all over the kingdom as the football writer of the *Yorkshire Post* and *Yorkshire Evening Post*. For nearly 40 years he never missed a Rugby International match in which England was engaged. Similarly, in cricket he was fortunate in accompanying the Yorkshire team all over the country. His writings were at all times discriminative, informative and voluminous. His contributions to his own papers over a term of 40 years averaged two columns a day during the summer and at least one column a day during the winter. Mr. Pullin was the author of several books on cricket, including *Old English Cricketers, Alfred Shaw, Cricketer,* and *The History of Yorkshire County Cricket from 1903 to 1923.*

In a foreword to this book, Lord Hawke referred to Mr. Pullin as "the non-playing member of the county team." He added, "His criticisms on our side form an invaluable guide to the captain, his enthusiasm is contagious, but never allows his judgment to become unbalanced, whilst his eloquent writings on cricket have gone to every part of the world in which there are lovers of the game ... I feel bound to say to the esteemed author of this book—'Well done, thou faithful friend.'"

About 10 years ago recognition was paid to him as a leading writer on cricket by the inclusion of his name among the cricket immortals in *Wisden's Cricketers' Almanack.* His right to be there was generally acknowledged for, along with Sydney Pardon and Stewart Caine, successive editors of *Wisden,* he was regarded as among the greatest authorities on the game.

PULLIN, Charles King, died at Bristol on April 2, 1894. By the sudden death from congestion of the lungs of Charles Pullin English cricket was deprived of one of the best umpires of the present generation. Born on November 3, 1838, Pullin first came into prominence with the Gloucestershire County Club, standing umpire on all occasions for the XI until the system of appointing neutral umpires was brought into force some few years back. Thoroughly impartial, quick and firm in giving his decisions, and possessing a perfect knowledge of the game, Pullin was a model umpire, and it will be hard indeed to replace him.

PUTTOCK, Eric C., who died on December 14, 1969, aged 69, played as an amateur in four matches for Sussex in 1921.

PYCROFT, The Rev. James, who died on March 10, 1895, at Brighton, aged 82, will be remembered for all time as the author of *The Cricket Field.* In the course of his long life he wrote much about the game to which he was devoted, but *The Cricket Field* is emphatically the work upon which his fame will rest. A good cricketer himself in his Oxford days, he played at Lord's in 1836 in the second of the long series of matches between the two Universities, among those who took part in the same game being Lord Bessborough, then the Hon. Frederick Ponsonby, Mr. R. Broughton, and Mr. C. G. Taylor. The University match was first played in 1829, and became an annual fixture in 1838. Knowing cricket thoroughly, Mr. Pycroft was certainly one of the best writers on the game. He was, if we may judge from some of his works, a little inclined to think that the great men of the Fuller Pilch and Alfred Mynn era were superior to any of their successors, but this perhaps unconscious prejudice in favour of the cricketers of his young days does not make his pages any the less entertaining. He was for about 30 years on the committee of the Sussex club, and retained to the last a lively interest in Sussex cricket.

QUAIFE, Bernard William, died at Bridport on November 28, 1984, aged 85. A son of the famous Willie Quaife, he played for Warwickshire in 48 matches between 1920 and 1924, almost all of them with his father. Only George Gunn and his son can have played more often together in the Championship. In 1922, when they were batting against Derbyshire, the unique spectacle was witnessed of the Bestwicks, father and son, bowling to the Quaifes. However, Bernard Quaife met with only modest success for Warwickshire and except in 1923, when he made 99 not out against Northamptonshire at Edgbaston, he could never keep a regular place in the side. So he moved to Worcestershire, for whom he did yeoman service for 10 seasons during which they were gradually working their way up from the bottom of the table. Twice he scored 1,000 runs. Usually he got some 900 by solid and consistent rather than brilliant batting and he made three hundreds, the highest being 136 not out against Glamorgan at Worcester in 1928. Moreover, when in 1929 the side lacked a wicket-keeper, he took over the job, although he had had no previous experience in the position in first-class cricket. Such "made" wicket-keepers are rarely a success, but he was an exception. Improving year by year, he was always adequate and at his best he could keep very well indeed. He continued to play, always as an amateur, until 1937 when, in the absence of the captain, the Hon. C. J. Lyttelton, through illness, he captained the side for most of the season. By now Buller had taken over the wicket-keeping, a number of young batsmen had appeared and he retired. In the course of his career he increased his repertory of strokes and, while always primarily a sound bat, who was particularly valuable when the ball was turning, he had strokes all round the wicket and was especially good at the leg-glance. When not required to keep wicket, he was a fine outfield. In all first-class cricket he scored 9,594 runs with an average of 20.03.

QUAIFE, Frank C., who died on August 27, 1968, was professional at Eastbourne College from 1946 to 1963. A slow left-arm bowler, he played in two matches for Sussex in 1928.

QUAIFE, Walter, elder brother of W. G. Quaife, who died at his home at Norwood, Surrey, on January 18, 1943, aged 78, was an opening batsman of much ability, possessed of excellent style and attractive hitting power. Born at Newhaven on April 1, 1864, he first appeared for Sussex in 1884, and continued to assist his home county until half-way through the summer of 1891, when, questioned by the committee as to whether he was qualifying for Warwickshire, he refused all information and was consequently dropped from the side. He made 3,306 runs for Sussex with an average of nearly 19, highest score 156 not out against Gloucestershire at Brighton in 1890. In this most disastrous season for Sussex—11 of 12 championship engagements ending in defeat—he headed the batting averages. In 1893 he turned out for Warwickshire—at that time one of seven teams competing for the second-class counties championship. He at once showed himself an acquisition, making 756 runs with an average of 31, helped Warwickshire reach first-class rank in 1895, when he headed the averages with 37, and kept his place in the XI for eight years, dropping out early in 1901. For Warwickshire during those seasons he scored 6,316 runs, averaged 26, and put together 10 three-figure innings, of which the highest was 144 against Gloucestershire in 1899. He finished his county career with Suffolk in 1905. Three times he appeared for the Players against the Gentlemen and thoroughly justified his selection, scoring 42 not out and 59 at the Oval in 1889, 55 on the same ground in 1895, and 40 not out at Lord's in 1890. Although of only moderate height, he was 4 in. taller than his brother William.

QUAIFE, William George, a leading Warwickshire player when they won the County Championship in 1911, died after a short illness at his home at Edgbaston on October 13, 1951, aged 79. An exceptionally skilful batsman and splendid field, despite his lack of inches and slight physique, he first appeared for the county in 1893 and enjoyed a great career lasting until 1928. He earned the special distinction of beginning his career with the county with an innings of 102 not out and finishing it also with a century, 115 against Derbyshire in his one appearance for the XI in 1928. In all, Quaife made 35,836 runs for the county and hit 72 centuries in first-class cricket. In 25 seasons he exceeded 1,000 runs and on four occasions reached a score of over 200, with 255 against Surrey at the Oval in 1905 the highest.

Particularly sound in defence, Quaife played with a very straight bat and, if careful rather than enterprising, was always stylish and attractive to watch. Born at Newhaven on March 17, 1872, he enjoyed the advantage of being coached in his early years by Alfred Shaw. After appearing in one match for Sussex, he, together with his brother Walter, decided to qualify for Warwickshire. So commenced an association with the Midland county which extended over 35 seasons.

William Quaife speedily established himself as a capable member of the side. Against Surrey at the Oval in 1913 he made 124 and 109, and twice, in 1901 and 1913, he hit three separate 100s in succession. In 1898 he played six consecutive innings without once losing his wicket while making 471 runs. His best summer was that of 1905, when his aggregate amounted to 2,060 and his average to 54. He played for England against Australia twice in 1899, and in 1901–02 went to Australia with A. C. MacLaren's team, for whom his best performance was in the third Test match at Adelaide, where he scored 68 and 44. He assisted Players against Gentlemen 11 times between 1897 and 1913.

As a fieldsman, especially at cover-point, Quaife had few superiors and he bowled leg-breaks with considerable success, but in his early years his delivery of the ball was so open to suspicion that in 1900 the county captains passed a resolution that he, in company with several others, should not be allowed to bowl in competition matches. This decision did not receive the support of M.C.C., and Quaife, possibly altering his methods, bowled with such effect that during his career he took 928 wickets. He was the first Warwickshire professional to receive two benefits, the first in 1910 and the second in 1927 when he was the oldest player in first-class cricket. Though this latter match was ruined by rain, cricket being limited to 90 minutes, he received a cheque for £917. Following his retirement, he engaged in business as a cricket bat manufacturer. A frequent visitor to the Edgbaston ground, he described the Championship-winning side of 1951 as one of the best-balanced ever to represent the county.

QUENTIN, The Rev. George Augustus Frederick, born at Kirkee, India, on November 3, 1843, died at St. Leonards-on-Sea on May 6, 1928. Described in *Scores and Biographies* as "A good batsman and a fast round-armed bowler," he was a member of the Shrewsbury XI of 1866. Subsequently ill-health handicapped him, and he made no mark in

the game whilst at Oxford. In 1874, however, he played for Gloucestershire v. Yorkshire at Sheffield.

QUINN, Neville A., the South African cricketer, died suddenly at Kimberley on August 5, 1934, at the age of 26. Quinn played for Griqualand West. A left-hand medium-paced bowler, he toured England with the South African team in 1929, finishing second in the bowling averages to H. G. Owen-Smith. In the first innings of the third Test at Leeds he took six wickets for 92 runs, and for the season headed the South African averages with 65 wickets at 23.89 runs apiece. In a dry summer he found his swerve effective, but could not make the ball get up straight on our turf wickets as he did on matting in South Africa. A moderate batsman he scored only 200 runs in 22 innings. He visited Australasia with the South African team in 1931–32, finishing second to A. J. Bell in the bowling averages for Test matches with 13 wickets for 512 runs. He headed the bowling figures in all first-class matches taking 42 wickets for just under 24 runs per wicket. Bradman had a high opinion of his capabilities.

QUINTON, Brig.-Gen. Francis William Drummond, born in India on December 27, 1865, died on November 4, 1926, aged 60. A free and effective hitter, and a good field at a distance from the wicket, he was in the Marlborough XI in 1882 and 1883, and in that of Woolwich the two following years. In his matches against Rugby he scored 43 not out and one, 39 and five. He had played for Devon as early as 1882, and later he performed well for Hampshire, and against Leicestershire, at Leicester, in 1895, made a score of 178. The highest innings of his career, however, was 216 not out in a match between Royal Artillery and Royal Inniskilling Fusiliers, on May 17, 1892.

QUINTON, J. M., who died by his own hand on December 22, 1922, played in a few matches for Hampshire between 1894 and 1899. He was born on May 12, 1874.

RADCLIFFE, Sir Everard Joseph Reginald, Bt., who died on November 23, 1969, aged 85, played for Yorkshire from 1909 to 1911. A native of Tiverton, Devon, he was one of only five players born outside Yorkshire who have appeared for the county in the 20th century. In his first two seasons, he served as joint captain with Lord Hawke, upon whose retirement he took over for one year. He scored altogether 828 runs, average 10.89.

He also took two wickets for 67 runs each—though he always claimed that this should have been three. In *The History of Yorkshire Cricket*, he wrote that he was convinced that he got R. H. Spooner lbw when the England batsman had made 199 of his 200 not out for Lancashire at Old Trafford in 1910!

RADCLIFFE, George, who died at his Dukinfield home on October 27, 1951, at the age of 74, was the first player to score 1,000 runs in a season of Central Lancashire League cricket. He remains the only amateur to have performed the feat, which he achieved in 17 innings for Stalybridge C.C. in 1915. A neat, compact opening batsman and a grand stroke-player, Mr. Radcliffe earned a reputation as one of the finest cricketers to hail from the North Cheshire area. He represented Cheshire at the age of 17 and in 1903 he qualified for Lancashire. He failed to do justice to his ability in first-class cricket, however, and after six years as a Lancashire professional he returned to Stalybridge, with whom his name will be always chiefly associated. He captained the club for many years and at the time of his death was president and a life member.

RADCLIFFE, Octavius Goldney, a contemporary of W. G. Grace in the Gloucestershire XI, died at Cherwell, near Colne, on April 13, 1940, aged 81. A very steady batsman, he often opened the innings and could force the game when in the mood. At the Oval in 1884 he made 101 for Somerset before throwing in his lot with the neighbouring county. Another fine display was 104 not out at Lord's against Middlesex, and in 1889 he scored 101 not out against Kent at Canterbury. Equally good was his 116 against Lancashire at Old Trafford in 1891. In 1888 at Clifton he played specially well in scoring 99 off the Australian bowlers, and during these seasons he was so dependable that W. G. Grace took him to Australia with the side organised by Lord Sheffield in the autumn of 1891. Unfortunately Radcliffe failed to find his form at any period of the tour and did not play in one of the three matches against Australia. He appeared for Gentlemen against Players at the Oval in 1886 and at Hastings in 1889. Altogether in first-class cricket he averaged 22 runs an innings for an aggregate of 5,496 runs, and met with considerable success as a rather slow bowler. To such an extent could he adapt himself to the needs of the occasion that for Wiltshire against M.C.C. at Swindon in 1894 he batted 55 minutes without scoring,

while in a match of less importance he hit four sixes and a four off an over of lobs from E. M. Grace at Alverton. He played for Wiltshire, the county of his birth, in 1884, and captained that county after giving up first-class cricket. At Dunstable against Bedfordshire in 1895 he did one of his best bowling performances—five wickets for 11 runs.

RAE, Edward, who introduced the game into Russian Lapland, died at Birkenhead on June 26, 1923, aged 76.

RAIKES, The Rev. George Barkley, who died on December 18, 1966, aged 93, was an Oxford Blue at both cricket and Association football. In the cricket XI at Shrewsbury from 1889 to 1892, he was captain and headed the batting averages in the last three years. He played in the University matches of 1894 and 1895 without achieving anything of note and from 1890 to 1897 he assisted Norfolk. From 1900 to 1902 he appeared for Hampshire, finishing second in the county averages in the first year, when he hit 77 from the Yorkshire bowling at Portsmouth. In 1904 he returned to Norfolk. "Ginger Beer," as, because of his initials, he was known to his intimates, was also a useful medium-paced bowler on occasion. He liked to tell the story of the time that he was invited to play for Nottinghamshire, but was compelled to decline because he was captain of Norfolk. As a footballer, he kept goal for Shrewsbury from 1890 to 1892; became a Corinthian in 1894; was in the Oxford side in 1894 and 1895 and in 1895 and 1896 gained four "full" International caps for England.

RAIKES, Thomas Barkley, died on March 2, 1984, at Rickinghall Superior, Norfolk, aged 81. Three years in the Winchester XI and captain in 1921, he headed the bowling averages in 1920 with 50 wickets at 12.41 and again in 1921 (when he was also second in the batting averages) with 60 at 16.07. Going up to Oxford, he took five for five in the first innings of the Freshman's match and had bowled 57 balls before a run was scored off him. He was immediately drafted into the Varsity side and although an unfair number of catches was dropped off him he finished the season with 40 wickets at an average of 20.72. He bowled particularly well at Lord's, where his analysis of 44-19-65-3 in a Cambridge total of 403 for four declared represented better work than many more spectacular feats.

At this point it seemed that he might well

At this point it seemed that he might well take his place among the leading bowlers of the day. Strongly built, he could bowl accurately for long periods at a brisk medium, with plenty of swerve and spin and some subtle variations of pace. The off-break with which he bowled in this Varsity match that fine batsman C. E. Fiddian-Green is said to have pitched almost outside the mown area of the wicket. Unfortunately this promise was never fulfilled. He found the pleasure of life at Oxford too alluring, rapidly put on weight and was never again really fit enough for a first-class bowler. In 1923 he was dreadfully expensive and kept his place only on reputaton and lack of competition. In 1924 he did rather better and took nine for 38 in the second innings against the Army, but in 1925 he finally lost his place in a side which was desperately short of class bowling. Besides playing for Oxford he had for some years been a member of the Norfolk side, but on going down he went abroad and played no more serious cricket. He will be remembered as a bowler of great possibilities which he lacked the dedication to develop.

RAMSBOTHAM, Col. Wilfrid Hubert, who died in London on November 7, 1978, aged 89, was in the Uppingham XI in 1905, 1906 and 1907, being second in the batting averages in his first year and heading them in his last two. He did not get a Blue at Cambridge, but between 1908 and 1910 played a few games for Sussex.

RANDALL, William Richard, of the Winchester XI of 1867, died at Cronody, Bridgend, on January 27, 1930, aged 80. He was in the Winchester XI of 1867 when he made the highest score in the side's first innings against Eton. He was a capital field at long-leg, his throwing-in being splendid, and he played some County Cricket for Glamorgan.

RANDELL, Alfred Charles, who died at Sydney on September 13, 1958, aged 74, played for Western Australia, whom he represented on the Australian Board of Control from 1946 to the time of his death.

RANDELL, Rolland Henry, who died at King William's Town, South Africa, on October 22, 1978, at the age of 92, made his début in 1906–07 for Border as a batsman/wicket-keeper and played until 1925–26. He scored 71 against M.C.C. in 1913–14. He practised as an attorney, which limited his first-class appearances.

RANDON, Charles, an elder brother of F. Randon, the Notts and Leicestershire fast bowler, was born at Stapleford, in Notts, on February 6, 1840, and died at Hathern on May 2, 1910. In *Scores and Biographies* (ix—12) he was described as "An excellent fast bowler, a fair bat, and in the field generally in the slips." He accepted many engagements, and it was not until 1874 that he made his first appearance for Leicestershire.

RANGNEKAR, Khandu Moneshwar, who died in Bombay on October 11, 1984, aged 67, was an attractive left-handed batsman who scored 2,548 runs for Maharashtra, Bombay and Holkar in the Ranji Trophy with an average of only just under 50. The largest of his first-class hundreds were 217 for Holkar against Hyderabad in 1950 and 202 for Bombay against Maharashtra in 1940. Chosen for India's tour of Australia in 1947–48, he played in three Test matches but had a disappointing tour. He had hit 102 and 17 not out on his first-class debut, for Maharashtra against Western India, at Poona in 1939–40, and in all first-class matches, from 1939 until 1964, he made 4,602 runs, average 41.45, including 15 centuries, and took 21 wickets at medium pace. A vice-president of the Indian Board of Control, he also became President of the Bombay Cricket Association.

RANJI, L., who died at Rajkot on December 20, 1948, following a long illness, was an elder brother of the late Lala Amarsingh. As a fast bowler, he achieved considerable success for the Hindus in the Bombay Quadrangular tournament and he made one Test appearance against D. R. Jardine's side in the contest at Bombay, December 1932. Six years later he came to England with a Rajputana team. He took 96 wickets in all first-class matches during his career.

RANSFORD, Vernon Seymour, who died at Melbourne on March 19, 1958, the day before his 73rd birthday, was an attractive left-handed batsman and fine deep fieldsman for Australia and Victoria. He first appeared for his State in 1903–04 and between then and 1925–26 he scored 4,350 runs for them, including 12 centuries, average 37.24. Against New South Wales at Sydney in 1908–09 he hit a century in each innings, 182 and 110, and almost made three in successive innings against the same opponents, for he put together 94 in the first meeting at Melbourne.

He took part in 20 Test matches for Australia, 15 of them in his own country and five when touring England with M. A. Noble's team, scoring 1,211 runs. In England he overcame strange conditions so successfully that he hit 143 not out in the Test match at Lord's and headed the Australian Test figures with an average of 58.83. In all matches that season, 1909, he registered 1,783 runs, average 43.48, and his six three-figure innings included the highest of his career—190 against M.C.C. at Lord's. From 1939 to 1957 he held the post of secretary to the Melbourne C.C.

RAPHAEL, Lieut. John Edward (King's Royal Rifles and A.D.C. to the G.O.C. of a Division), born at Brussels April 30, 1882; died of wounds June 11, 1917. Merchant Taylors, 1898, etc.: captain two years; Oxford v. Cambridge 1903–04–05. Surrey XI, 1903, etc., and captain for a time in 1904. Member of M.C.C. since 1906.

The news that John Raphael was dead caused sorrow to a very wide circle of friends. Though he never gained quite the place as a batsman that his deeds as a schoolboy had suggested, he was in the cricket field and still more in the world of Rugby football a distinct personality. Everything he did created more than ordinary interest, his popularity as a man, apart from his ability, counting for much. At Merchant Taylors he had a brilliant record. He was in the XI for five years—1897 to 1901. In 1898 as a boy of 16 he headed the batting with an average of 23 and, being quite a good school bowler, took 32 wickets at a cost of less than nine runs each. Thenceforward his school career was one long success. He was third in batting in 1899—average 27—and first in bowling with 51 wickets for just under 15 runs each. Then in 1900 he had a great season. At the top of the list both in batting and bowling he scored 962 runs with an average of 43, and took 68 wickets. His highest innings was 152 not out. He finished up at school in 1901 with nothing short of a triumph. Again first in batting he scored 1,397 runs with an average of 69, and as a bowler he was second, 76 wickets falling to him. He and J. Dennis made 326 together without being parted against Kennington Park, their scores being 175 not out and 135 not out respectively. Naturally great things were expected of Raphael when he went up to Oxford, but as a cricketer he began with a setback. From some cause, after making 47 not out in the Freshmen's match, in 1902, he showed such poor form that he never had any chance of gaining his Blue. As a matter of fact he was not tried in a single first-class

match. In 1903 his prospects while Oxford played at home were equally dismal. However, he got on well for Surrey against Oxford at the Oval, and was given a trial for the University against Sussex at Brighton. Seizing his opportunity he played a fine innings of 65, when no one else could do much against the Sussex bowlers, and two days before the match with Cambridge at Lord's Mr. Findlay gave him his colours. As in the case of Lord George Scott for Oxford and the late Eustace Crawley for Cambridge in 1887, the last choice proved the batting success of his side. Raphael scored 130 on the first day and laid the foundation of Oxford's victory. His innings did not start well, but it was brilliant in its later stages. In the drawn match of 1904 Raphael only made 12 and 25 against Cambridge, but in the sensational match the following year—won in brilliant style by Cambridge after it had at one point seemed any odds against them—he played perhaps the best innings of his life. With a score of 99 he only failed by a single run to rival Yardley's feat of getting two 100s in the University match. In Surrey cricket Raphael never became a power, but he often played well for the county and when—as the last of various captains—he took charge of the team in 1904 he proved quite a capable leader. Raphael's weakness as a batsman was that he relied too exclusively upon forward play. His method—at any rate when he had to contend against first-rate bowling—demanded an easy wicket. His bowling seemed to leave him after his schooldays.

At the game of Rugby football Raphael earned much distinction as a three-quarter back, playing for England in nine matches—against Scotland and against Wales in 1902, 1905, and 1906; against Ireland in 1902; and against New Zealand and France in 1906. A beautiful kick, a brilliant field, and possessed of a good turn of speed, he was a fine natural player, even if his special qualities did not always make for success as one of a line of four three-quarters in international encounters. He accomplished great things for the Old Merchant Taylors, and gaining his Blue as a Freshman at Oxford in 1901, not only appeared for his University against Cambridge on four occasions, but only once failed to secure a try.

In a by-election at Croydon he stood as Liberal candidate but did not succeed in entering Parliament.—S.H.P.

RASHLEIGH, Jonathan, who was born on January 7, 1820, died on April 12, 1905. He was in the Harrow XI of 1836, but, owing to illness, did not appear at Lord's. In 1842 he was in the Oxford side which was defeated by Cambridge by 162 runs, the winners receiving 81 extras in totals of 139 and 180.

RASHLEIGH, Canon William, died at Balcombe, Sussex, on February 13, 1937, when nearly 70 years of age. He played in the Tonbridge School XI from 1882 to 1885. In 1884 he averaged 64, thanks mainly to innings of 160 against Lancing and 203 against Dulwich. Next year, when captain, he averaged 63. Going up to Oxford he distinguished himself as a Freshman by getting his Blue and joining with K. J. Key in a stand for 243 which remains a first wicket record for the University match. This happened in the second innings of Oxford who were all out for 304, no one else reaching double figures and nine wickets going down for 61—a curious coincidence in figures, as in the Cambridge first innings the last six wickets fell for 61 runs. So this splendid stand came between two collapses and it caused the greater enthusiasm at Lord's because both batsmen distinguished themselves in feats at that time unparalleled. Key's 143 was then the highest score hit in a University match and Rashleigh's 107, which ended with the total 257, was the first 100 by a Freshman for either University in the great match. Also it was the first time that two batsmen reached 100 in one innings of a University match. The stand lasted no more than two hours 50 minutes and both batsmen were out when forcing the game. Oxford won by 133 runs, a success they followed with victory by seven wickets but when Rashleigh captained the XI in 1888 the result was a draw, owing to bad weather, and the same thing occurred when Rashleigh played his fourth match under H. Philipson.

Born at Farningham on March 7, 1867, Rashleigh naturally was called upon for Kent, and from 1885 to 1901 he proved of great service to his county. Taking part in 98 matches he scored 4,041 with an average of 24. Altogether in first-class cricket he played nine three-figure innings—two for Oxford, seven for Kent—the highest being for Kent against Middlesex at Tonbridge in 1896, when he scored 163 out of 201 in two hours and a half.

Because of his freedom Rashleigh seldom began well but otherwise he possessed all the essentials of a great batsman. Absolutely orthodox in style he scored readily by perfect timing of the off-side forward stroke made with such grace and ease at the full stretch of his reach that the pace at which the ball sped along the turf to the boundary astounded the fieldsmen. He hit the half-volley with tremendous power, and invariably with a straight bat. His cut was delightful, and he used his supple wrists in strong back play while on slow wickets he could pull and hit to leg besides jump in and drive. In fact, Rashleigh, as nearly as anyone has done, deserved the description of the perfect batsman, because of admirable style and free use of all the strokes.

A capable Rugby footballer he played full back against Cambridge in 1887 and 1888, Oxford losing both matches. Of medium height he was sturdily built. After occupying posts at Uppingham and Tonbridge as assistant master, he took Holy Orders in 1892. He was a Minor Canon of Canterbury Cathedral from 1903 to 1912, rector of St. George's, Canterbury, from 1912 to 1916, and subsequently vicar of Horton Kirby, Kent, and Ridgmont, Bedfordshire.

RATCLIFFE, George, who died at Nottingham on March 7, 1928, was a good bat of the forcing type and a useful change bowler. He appeared for Derbyshire in 1887 and two following seasons.

RAVEN, R. O., who died on April 4, 1936, aged 51, showed great promise as a batsman at Wellingborough Grammar School, but did not fulfil expectations. His best season for Northamptonshire was 1920 when captain, his average being 18.68. He also led the county XI in 1921.

RAWLENCE, Col. John Rooke, O.B.E., who died in hospital at Ascot on January 17, 1983, aged 67, played two matches for Hampshire in 1934 and in the second, against Nottinghamshire at Southampton, made 38 and helped Creese put on 60 for the seventh wicket in just over half an hour. He had headed the Wellington College averages in 1933. Later he played for the Army.

RAWLIN, E. R., who played occasionally for Yorkshire from 1927 to 1936, died on January 11, 1943, aged 43.

RAWLIN, John Thomas, born at Greasborough, near Rotherham, in Yorkshire, on November 10, 1857, died at his native place on January 19, 1924, aged 66. In addition to being a fast-medium bowler with a high delivery and a little break both ways, he was a hard-hitting batsman who scored freely when set. He played for Yorkshire in five matches between 1880 and 1885, was a member of the M.C.C. ground staff 1887–1911, and took 631 wickets for Middlesex between 1889 and 1909. In 1887–88 he visited Australia with Mr. G.F. Vernon's team, and in 1892, 1895, and 1896 appeared for the Players. Four times he took as many as eight wickets in an innings for Middlesex—for 64 runs v. Somerset at Taunton in 1891, for 52 v. Yorkshire at Leeds in 1892, for 29 v. Gloucestershire at Bristol in 1893, and for 50 v. Yorkshire at Sheffield in 1894. He also obtained seven at a cost of 18 runs v. Notts at Lord's in 1895, and with J.T. Hearne bowled unchanged throughout v. Sussex at Hove in 1892 and v. Surrey at the Oval four years later. For M.C.C. v. Notts at Lord's in 1891 he had an analysis of four for eight. Two benefit matches, at Lord's, were given to him, Middlesex contending with Somerset in 1896 and with Sussex in 1911. His highest score for the county was 100 v. Surrey at Lord's in 1899.

RAWLINSON, Elisha Barker, who died in Australia on February 17, 1892, was never in the front rank of English professionals, but at one time he was well known in connection with Yorkshire cricket. Born at Yeadon, near Leeds, on April 10, 1837, he was nearing the completion of his 55th year at the time of his death. He was, in his best day, a very good all-round man, but it was more to his batting than anything else that he owed his place in first-class XIs. He was a fast round-arm bowler, and used to field either at point or cover point. For six years, from 1870 to 1875 inclusive, he was professionally attached to the Leeds Clarence club. He first appeared at Lord's for the Colts of England against the M.C.C. in May 1867, a match in which the late George Summers was also seen at headquarters for the first time. Rawlinson's name will be found in the Yorkshire XI in 1869 and 1870.

RAWSON, Col. Herbert Rawson, who was born at Mauritius on September 3, 1852, died in a nursing home in London on October 18, 1924. He was educated at Wallace's (Cheltenham) and Westminster, and in 1873 played in one match for Kent, catching one and stumping three of the 13 wickets lost by W.G. Grace's XI at Gravesend. The next year he was invited to play in the Canterbury Week, but was unable to do so as he was ordered abroad with his regiment.

RAYNOR, Kenneth, who died at Salisbury, Rhodesia, on April 15, 1973, aged 86, was in the Ipswich Grammar School XI and after-

wards played for Suffolk and, in 1923, for Leicestershire. At Oxford, he was a Harlequin and gained Blues at hockey and Association football.

RAYNOR, Samuel, who played for Derbyshire a few times in 1891, died at Heanor in the second week of September, 1907. Being unable to obtain a regular place in the side he qualified for Worcestershire, with which county he was associated for some years.

READ, E.G., who died in March, 1921, at the age of 46, was educated at St. Edmund's School, Oxford, and was a most useful wicket-keeper and batsman. He played on a few occasions for Hampshire (by birth) and Sussex (by residence), and scored heavily for the Worthing and Heathfield clubs, his highest innings for the latter being 224 not out. He was a nephew of Dr. Russell Bencraft.

READ, John Maurice, nephew of the famous H.H. Stephenson, was born at Thames Ditton on February 9, 1859, and died in Winchester Hospital, after a long illness, on February 17, 1929, aged 70. During his career, which extended from 1880 to 1895, he ranked among the best professional players and obtained all the chief honours which the cricket field had to offer. He earned his place in the Surrey XI when first tried, and maintained his form to the end of his career for, in order to take an appointment on the Tichborne estate, he retired after a season in which he made 1,031 runs with an average of 31. Always an enterprising player, Maurice Read had some unorthodox strokes, but these were natural to a forcing batsman of his style. He hit the ball hard in defence and could cut and keep down his off-drive with masterly ease. A rather fast bowler, he occasionally did useful work with the ball before George Lohmann and Jack Beaumont, under John Shuter's captaincy, made Surrey tremendously strong. In the deep field and at third man he was brilliant, having remarkably sure hands in picking up and catching, besides being quick in getting to the ball.

He first played for England at the Oval in 1882, when Spofforth's bowling won Australia the sensational victory by seven runs. He was still in England's best side in 1890, when he appeared in the Test matches at the Oval and Lord's, the Manchester fixture owing to rain being abandoned without a ball bowled; and he also played at Lord's in 1893. He took a large share in winning the 1890 match at the Oval, when the Surrey authorities could not get together a fully representative XI. On a bowler's pitch Australia were dismissed for 92 and 102, so England, after getting 100, wanted 95 to win. W. G. Grace, Shrewsbury, W. Gunn, and W. W. Read fell before Turner and Ferris for 32 runs, but Maurice Read who made 35, and James Cranston, the left-handed Gloucestershire amateur, took the score to 83. Yet eight men were out for 93, and the finish was dramatic. After five maiden overs had been sent down, Sharpe, the Surrey bowler, hit a ball to Dr. Barrett at cover point, and Gregor MacGregor, responding to the call, both batsmen were in the middle of the pitch when Dr. Barrett returned so wide that the two runs needed for victory were scored.

Maurice Read went to Australia four times—in the winters of 1884, 1886, 1887, and 1891—taking part in 11 Test matches. His last trip was with Lord Sheffield's team captained by W. G. Grace. The Test match at the Oval in 1893 was played for Maurice Read's benefit. His chief innings were:

130	Players v. Australians, at the Oval	.. ..	1882
113*	Surrey v. Gloucestershire, at the Oval	.. ..	1883
186*	Surrey v. Somerset, at the Oval	.. ..	1885
186	Surrey v. Australians, at the Oval	.. ..	1886
	(He and Abel added 241 for fourth wicket.)		
109	South v. Australians, at Gravesend	.. ..	1886
109	Surrey v. Yorkshire, at Bradford	.. ..	1888
103	Surrey v. Derbyshire, at the Oval	.. ..	1889
136	Surrey v. Oxford University, at the Oval	.. ..	1889
135	Surrey v. Gloucestershire, at the Oval	.. ..	1890
135	Surrey v. Yorkshire, at Sheffield	.. ..	1891
106	England v. New South Wales, at Sydney	.. ..	1891–92
131	Surrey v. Leicestershire, at Leicester	.. ..	1892
108	Surrey v. Derbyshire, at the Oval	.. ..	1893
131	Surrey v. Hampshire, at the Oval	.. ..	1895

Signifies not out

This last score was made in his last innings for Surrey, when 36 years of age. In all matches, first-class and second-class, for the county he made 13,058 runs with an average of 26 and took 78 wickets for 22 runs each. For the Players, between 1882 and 1895, he scored 546 runs (average 22), in Test matches v. Australia 447 (average 18), and in all first-class cricket 14,010 (average 27). After his retirement from great matches he kept up the game in Hampshire, but, although qualified to do so by residence, never appeared for that county. In several seasons he averaged over 100 runs an innings for Tichborne Park. Among the many large scores he obtained for that side were 202 v. Incogniti in 1897, 256 v. Cheriton in 1900, 216 v. Incogniti the same season, and 245 not out v. Royal Navy in 1901.

READ, Reginald John, a right-arm medium-paced bowler who took 184 wickets, average 25.56, for Canterbury (N.Z.), died at Christchurch on March 1, 1974, aged 87. He made his first appearance for New Zealand when 41, against the Melbourne C.C. side in 1927–28 and he also played in two "Tests" against the visiting Australians led by V. Y. Richardson in 1927–28. It was said that only his age counted against his selection for the 1927 New Zealand team that toured England. His best performance was seven for 35 and seven for 24 for Canterbury against Southland, then a first-class side, in 1920–21.

READ, W. W. died on January 6, 1907. Born on November 23, 1855, he was in his 52nd year. The following figures will be valuable as a permanent record.

MR. W. W. READ'S HUNDREDS IN IMPORTANT MATCHES

	Against			Score	Ground				Year
(a)	For England (4).								
	Australia	..	..	117	.. Oval	..	..	..	1884
	New South Wales	..	..	119	.. Sydney	..	..	..	1887–88
	South Australia	..	...	183	.. Adelaide	..	..	..	1887–88
	Victoria	..	..	142*	.. Melbourne	..	..	..	1887–88
(b)	For the Gentlemen (2).								
	Australians	..	..	109	.. Lord's	..	..	..	1888

Signifies not out.

MR. W. W. READ'S HUNDREDS IN IMPORTANT MATCHES—*continued*

Against	Score	Ground	Year
Players	159	.. Oval	1885

(c) For W. W. Read's XI (1).

W. G. Grace's XI	128	.. Reigate	1893

(d) For the South (1).

Australians	102*	... Brighton	1886

(e) For Surrey (38).

Against	Score	Ground	Year
Cambridge Univ. (2). ..	114	.. Oval	1886
	244*	.. Oval	1887
Derbyshire (4)	123	.. Derby	1885
	109	.. Oval	1885
	115	.. Oval	1886
	145	.. Derby	1887
Essex (3)	143	.. Oval	1885
	214*	.. Leyton	1885
	129	.. Leyton	1888
Gloucestershire (3)	135	.. Clifton	1884
	120	.. Clifton	1886
	107	.. Cheltenham	1882
Hampshire (2)	168	.. Oval	1883
	102	.. Oval	1890
Kent (4)	106	.. Maidstone	1876
	160	.. Maidstone	1881
	117	.. Oval	1882
	100	.. Oval	1887
Lancashire (3)	127	.. Manchester	1883
	247	.. Manchester	1887
	147*	.. Manchester	1893
Leicestershire (2)	162*	.. Oval	1884
	157*	.. Oval	1886
Middlesex	115	.. Oval	1889
Notts	135	.. Oval	1885
Oxford Univ. (2)	118	.. Oxford	1887
	338	.. Oval	1888
Scotland	156	.. Edinburgh	1892
Sussex (6)	163	.. Oval	1885
	101	.. Brighton	1885
	171	.. Oval	1888
	112	.. Brighton	1892
	196*	.. Oval	1892
	111	.. Brighton	1895
Warwickshire	112	.. Oval	1896
Yorkshire (3)	140	.. Oval	1877
	103	.. Oval	1888
	161	.. Oval	1894

(f) For Surrey, Gentlemen of (4).

Against	Score	Ground	Year
Notts, Gentlemen of	160	.. Reigate	1885
Parsees	132	.. Oval	1888
Philadelphia,	105	} .. Oval	1889
Gentlemen of (2).	130		

The two hundreds hit against the Gentlemen of Philadelphia in 1889 were made in one match.

In successive innings against Derbyshire bowling, Mr. Read scored 123, 109, 115 and 145. His scores of 247 and not out 244 were made in consecutive innings in 1887.

Signifies not out.

MR. W. W. READ'S BATTING AVERAGES IN FIRST-CLASS MATCHES

Year			Inns	Not Out	Highest Score	Total	Average
1873	..	..	4	0	39	56	14.00
1874	..	..	4	0	16	20	5.00
1875	..	..	10	2	98	247	30.87
1876	..	..	17	3	106	588	42.00
1877	..	..	11	0	140	399	36.27
1878	..	..	15	3	80	278	23.16
1879	..	..	6	0	53	123	20.50
1880	..	..	12	0	93	306	25.50
1881	..	..	30	1	160	931	32.10
1882	..	..	35	1	117	882	25.94
In Australia			11	0	75	291	26.45
1883	..	..	39	6	168	1,573	47.66
1884	..	..	46	3	135	1,256	29.20
1885	..	..	42	0	163	1,880	44.76
1886	..	..	46	3	120	1,825	42.44
1887	..	..	36	2	247	1.615	47.50
In Australia			13	2	183	610	55.45
1888	..	..	41	2	338	1,414	36.25
1889	..	..	33	1	115	805	25.15
1890	..	..	48	2	94	1,169	25.41
1891	..	..	36	0	77	831	23.08
In S. Africa		..	1	0	40	40	40.00
1892	..	..	37	5	196*	1,088	34.00
1893	..	..	46	4	147*	1,377	32.78
1894	..	..	37	3	161	824	24.34
1895	..	..	34	1	111	767	23.24
1896	..	..	43	5	112	863	22.71
1897	..	..	16	4	86*	291	24.25
Totals	..		749	53	338	22,349	32.11

Signifies not out.

REDDICK, Tom Bockenham, died in Cape Town on June 1, 1982, aged 70. Born in Shanghai, he had a varied and unusual career as player and coach, spread over half a century. After showing unusual promise as an all-rounder while on the staff of G. A. Faulkner's cricket school in London, he appeared twice for Middlesex in 1931, while still in his teens; but although his Championship appearances extended over nearly two decades he had only two full seasons of County Cricket. Both were for Nottinghamshire, whom he joined in 1946 as player-coach after war service with the RAF. One of the mainstays of a weak side he scored more runs (994) in 1946 than anyone except Keeton and Harris, playing one specially good fighting innings of 131 against Lancashire. In the following year he made 1,206 runs; captaining the side for the first time, against Kent, he scored 139, sharing in a fifth-wicket partnership of 244 with Winrow. After that he spent almost all his cricketing life in South Africa, appearing for Western Province in the Currie Cup and making a great reputation in the coaching field. After returning to England for two summers as chief coach to Lancashire, he settled permanently in the Cape, where his flair as a teacher of the game unearthed and developed the talents of countless young players who later made their mark, Basil D'Oliveira among them. A main reason for Reddick not having played more first-class cricket for England was his engagement by Sir Julien Cahn, for whom he played from 1930 to 1939, scoring over 1,500 runs in three successive seasons in a competitive environment. A man of charm, modesty and wit, Reddick for many years wrote a weekly column for the *Cape Times*. In 1979 he had published an autobiography, *Never Cross a Bat*.

REDFEARN, James, who died on March 10, 1916, aged 79, played for Victoria v. New South Wales at Sydney in February, 1863. He was described as "Good bat and very powerful hitter; good in the field."

REDGATE, Oliver, died at Nottingham on

May 11, 1913, in his 50th year. He played a few times for Notts in 1891, 1892, and 1894, but never realised expectations. In club cricket, however, he was to be feared.

REDMAN, Jack, died at Salisbury on September 24, 1981, aged 55. Born at Bath, he played for Somerset, first as an amateur and later as a professional, from 1948 to 1953, but only in two seasons, 1951 and 1952, did he appear at all frequently. A fast-medium right-arm swinger, he took in 1951, 50 wickets at 33.76 apiece and in 1952 33, at 35.36. It will be seen that, though a whole-hearted trier, he was expensive, and after 1952, deciding that there was no future for him as a professional, he retired and went into business, playing however a match or two as an amateur in 1953. He had enjoyed one day of special glory, when, against Derbyshire at Frome in 1951, he took seven for 23 in the first innings. Occasionally he made useful scores in the tail, his highest being 45 against Essex at Brentwood in 1951. Between 1958 and 1964 he made a few appearances for Wiltshire and in 1962 played an innings of 112 against Somerset Second XI.

REED, The Rev. Francis, who was born at Ottery St. Mary, in Devon, on October 24, 1850, and played frequently for Somerset between 1870 and 1884, died in London on April 12, 1912. It was said of him: "Is a good average batsman, bowls middle-paced round armed, and fields generally at short slip." In 1878 he made 55 v. Hertfordshire at Barnard's Heath, St. Albans, and in 1884 carried out his bat for 57 against Hampshire at Southampton. He was educated privately and at Oxford.

REEDMAN, John C., born on October 9, 1867, died at Adelaide on March 25, 1924, aged 56. He was an effective but not a graceful batsman, a useful change bowler, and a really great fieldsman, being a sure catch, covering much ground and having a splendid return to the wicket. He never toured England, but for some years he enjoyed a big reputation in his own country. For South Australia, which State he captained on a few occasions, he scored 113 v. Victoria at Adelaide in March, 1894, and took 13 wickets for 149 runs (seven for 54 and six for 95) against the same side in 1904–05. At Sydney in March, 1899, when playing for The Rest v. The Australian XI, he made 51 in his first innings and 108 in his second. On his only appearance in a Test match he scored 17 and four: that was at Sydney in 1894–95, when England, after going in against a total of 586,

won by 10 runs. For many years Reedman coached at St. Peter's College, Adelaide, and captained the North Adelaide C.C. He was also in quite the front rank as a footballer. By occupation he was a postman.

REES, "Eddie" L., at one time an active member of the Glamorgan County and Cardiff Clubs, died at St. Mellons on October 13, 1911, aged 46. His forte was fast bowling.

REES, Robert Blackie, who died at Bowmans Green, Hertfordshire, on September 20, 1966, aged 84, was a leg-break bowler of English birth who, between 1909 and 1913, took 57 wickets for South Australia in Sheffield Shield matches at an average cost of 27.92 runs each. He later returned to England and played for West Kent and Free Foresters.

REES, W. L., a cousin of W. G. Grace, died at Gisborne, New Zealand, on May 13, 1912, aged 76. A good all-round cricketer, he played for Victoria v. New South Wales in 1857, 1858 and 1865, and later on a few occasions for Auckland. He was chosen captain of the East Melbourne C.C. upon the formation of that club over 50 years ago, and in his early days in New Zealand defeated single-handed an XI in Auckland. He was a Member of Parliament in the Dominion, and once made a stone-walling speech of about 20 hours.

REESE, Daniel, who died at Christchurch on June 12, 1953, aged 74, was one of the best-known cricketers and businessmen in New Zealand. First playing for Canterbury in 1895, when 16, he visited Australia in 1898–99 with the first touring team to leave New Zealand, and for 14 years from 1907 he was captain of Canterbury and of New Zealand. In all first-class matches he scored as a forcing left-handed batsman 3,186 runs and with slow-medium bowling took 196 wickets. He went as a draughtsman to Australia in 1900 and during three years there played for Melbourne. In 1903, when visiting England, he took part in four matches with Dr. W. G. Grace for London County, and in 1906 appeared eight times for Essex, scoring 70 and 20 in the game with the West Indies. His long playing career ended in 1921, to which point he was probably the best left-handed batsman produced by New Zealand. He afterwards served as member of the Management Committee and President of the New Zealand Cricket Council.

REESE, T. W., one of the best fieldsmen in

New Zealand around 1900, died on April 13, 1949, aged 81. He played in 22 representative matches between 1887–88 and 1907–08, and appeared for Canterbury against teams from this country in 1902–03 and 1906–07. He was also a cricket author and wrote the history of New Zealand cricket from 1841 to 1933.

REEVES, William, a very useful bat and bowler for Essex and in recent years one of the best of the first-class umpires, died after an operation on March 24, 1944, aged 67. Born at Cambridge, he joined the ground staff at Leyton, where his life centred, for he married into the family of E. C. Freeman, head groundsman. A free, hard-hitting batsman and right-arm bowler of medium pace, Reeves fielded keenly and altogether accomplished much useful work for Essex from 1897 to 1921. Altogether he scored 6,603 runs, average 16.63, took 595 wickets at an average cost of 27.93, and held 116 catches. His best bowling season was 1904, when 106 wickets fell to him at 26 runs apiece. Next year, when he did his best batting with 1,174 runs, average 29.35, he scored 135 against Lancashire in two hours and 101 against Surrey—both at Leyton. In 1906 his only other century for Essex, 104 against Sussex, was a dashing performance, he and C. P. Buckenham (68) making 163 for the eighth wicket in 70 minutes. Another, noteworthy effort came in 1919, when he and G. M. Louden, the fast bowler, put on 122 for the last Essex wicket against Surrey. All these efforts were at Leyton, where also he twice severely punished the powerful Yorkshire attack, and with 71 out of 90 in 50 minutes in 1905, with Charles McGahey as partner, helped in a total of 521. The champions had to follow-on and only just escaped defeat with three wickets in hand, Ernest Smith, who stayed an hour without getting a run, being not out with Lord Hawke. Some of his best bowling performances also were achieved at Leyton, then regarded as a batsman's paradise. In the course of 11 balls he took the last five Derbyshire wickets without conceding a run in 1901. Six years later he and Walter Mead bowled unchanged through both innings of Nottinghamshire, who won a low-scoring game by only seven runs and went on to carry off the Championship without suffering defeat.

A member of the Lord's ground staff for many years, he played in some good matches for M.C.C., and at Lord's in 1920 he dismissed five Nottinghamshire batsmen for 13 runs. Recently Bill Reeves took part in the special Easter coaching class for schoolboys at Lord's, but the present generation knew him best as an admirable umpire who stood in many Test matches. In this capacity he often gave evidence of his caustic humour. Once when a batsman protested that he was not out, Reeves retorted, "Weren't you? Wait till you see the papers in the morning." To a bowler notorious for appealing, he remarked, "There's only one man who appeals more than you do." "Oh, who's that?" asked the bowler. "Dr Barnardo," replied Reeves.

REID, Alexander Bernard John, died suddenly in Cape Town on March 7, 1977, at the age of 61. He was a fairly regular choice as wicket-keeper for Western Province in the first five years after the War and also a useful tail end batsman. His highest score was 81 against North-Eastern Transvaal in 1939–40 but his batting is chiefly remembered for his defiance of Ray Lindwall during the Australian tour of 1949–50.

REID, Allan, who died at Cape Town on October 31, 1948, aged 71, was a member of the South African team which toured England in 1901. A punishing batsman, he scored 710 runs, average 23.66, in all matches, his highest innings being 77 not out made in 70 minutes against Kent. He played regularly for Western Province from 1897 to 1909, and in Currie Cup matches averaged 17.07 with an aggregate of 461 runs. His brother, Norman Reid, played for South Africa in 1921.

REID, Norman, who died at Cape Town in tragic circumstances in June, 1947, aged 56, played in one Test match for South Africa, against Australia at Cape Town in 1921, when he scored 11 and six and took two wickets. A useful all-rounder for Western Province from 1920 to 1923, he gained his international cap mainly through brilliant fielding, usually at cover point. His most notable performance in first-class cricket was 81 not out for Western Province v. Orange Free State in 1921–22. An Oxford Rugby Blue of 1912 and 1913, he was awarded the D.S.O. and M.C. during the First World War.

RELF, Albert Edward, one of the best all-round cricketers of his time and an extremely popular man, shot himself on March 26, 1937. The cause for such a sad act was attributed to poor health and depression due to the serious illness of his wife; he died a wealthy man.

After making a name with Norfolk, Albert Relf played first for Sussex, the county of his birth, in 1900, when in his 26th year, and he was one of the mainstays of his side 21 years later, when, at Horsham, he scored 153 against Leicestershire. After the War, owing to his coaching duties at Wellington, where he succeeded his father, he could not play regularly until the school holidays. In 1921 he came out second in the batting and first in the bowling averages; he took his benefit match and finished his county career.

In first-class matches for Sussex, Relf scored 18,089 runs with an average of 27.32 and took 1,584 wickets at 21.10 runs apiece. He was nearly 40 when he was included in *Wisden*'s Five Cricketers of the Year, his figures for 1913 season, in which he earned the distinction, being 1,846 runs, average 32, and 141 wickets at 18 runs apiece.

In his first season for Sussex, Relf shone chiefly as a batsman, but his bowling gradually improved and in 1903 he headed the county averages. His work created such an impression that he was picked for the first team which toured Australia under the auspices of the M.C.C. The very powerful side captained by P. F. Warner won the rubber, and Relf in the first Test helped R. E. Foster in a ninth wicket stand of 115.

On his return to England, Relf displayed his true form and from that time never looked back. He was very unfortunate in not being chosen more than once to play against Australia in England. On this occasion, at Lord's in 1909, he took five wickets for 85 runs in an innings of 350. In the ordinary course of events he would have been picked for England in the three subsequent matches, but S. F. Barnes stepped into the team at Leeds and another right-handed bowler of medium pace was not required. Relf went to South Africa in the winters of 1905 and 1913 and also appeared in Gentlemen and Players matches.

Few bowlers were so difficult to play on a wicket the least bit crumbled. Taking a short run with an easy, natural delivery, Relf possessed perfect command of length and could keep an end going all day without fatigue. He spun the ball very quickly off the pitch. Relf always looked first-rate as a bowler, but his style of batting gave rather a false idea of his powers. No one seeing him for the first time would think him capable of scoring hundreds in high class company, for in defence he let the ball hit the bat in a way not impressive to the eye. Yet season after season he made as many runs as men who looked greatly superior. Relf was a brilliant fieldsman in the slips, and so a great all-round cricketer.

RELF, Robert Richard, who died at Reading on April 28, 1965, aged 81, played as a boy for Berkshire before qualifying for Sussex, whom he assisted as a professional all-rounder from 1905 to 1924, being one of three brothers to play for the county. He then returned to his native county, with whom he continued until the age of 63. As an all-rounder he scored 13,433 runs, including 22 centuries for Sussex, average 28.15, took 283 wickets for 28.04 runs each, and altogether held 278 catches. Capable of stern defence, he was a highly consistent run-getter who hit well all round the wicket, with the drive probably his best stroke. His highest innings for the county was 272 not out, when he carried his bat through an innings of 433 against Worcestershire at Eastbourne in 1909, and he exceeded 200 on two other occasions. Six times he hit more than 1,000 runs in a season—from 1908 to 1913—his best year being 1912 when in all matches he reached an aggregate of 1,804, average 32.21. He played for Players against Gentlemen at Folkestone in 1925, scoring 73.

His career with Sussex ended on an unfortunate note. Against Surrey at the Oval in 1924, he fielded while Surrey scored four runs, when rain stopped cricket. During the break, P. G. H. Fender, the Surrey captain, objected to the inclusion of Relf in the Sussex XI on the grounds that he had played for Berkshire the previous season and thus broke his qualification. Relf was withdrawn from the side, his place being taken by J. H. Parks.

He later enjoyed great success for Berkshire, and never more so than in the 1924 Minor Counties' Challenge match with Northumberland. He hit 100 in the first innings and followed by taking nine wickets for four runs apiece. From 1942 to 1960, Relf served as coach and groundsman at Leighton Park School, Reading, where his services were highly esteemed. Previously he was cricket coach to Charterhouse and Westminster.

REMNANT, Ernest R., who died on March 18, 1969, aged 88, played as a professional for Hampshire from 1908 to 1922, scoring in that time 2,850 runs, average 17.27, taking 170 wickets with left-arm slow bowling at a cost of 27.36 runs apiece and holding 60 catches. His one century was 115 not out against Kent at Southampton in 1911. On seven occasions he dismissed five batsmen in an innings, his best analysis being eight wickets for 61 runs in the first innings of Essex at Colchester in 1921. When his county career ended, he became assistant coach at

Harrow. Son of G. H. Remnant, of Chilham, the old Kent player, he was an expert wood carver and his home at Harrow contained a vast amount of panelling executed by him and depicting incidents in the Battle of Hastings.

REMNANT, George Henry, who died in February, 1941, aged 92, was the oldest living Kent professional cricketer and a friend of Charles Dickens. Born at Rochester on November 20, 1848, he made the first of 42 appearances for his county at the age of 20. His best score for Kent was 62 against Hampshire at Canterbury in 1877, but in minor cricket he hit 238 and 211 not out for Chilham Castle. He was a magnificent fieldsman. As a young man, Remnant played in the village team at Gad's Hill, Higham. He used to relate how, when playing in the meadow adjoining the house where Charles Dickens lived, he drove a ball into the back of a trap in which sat the novelist's children and their governess. The pony bolted; Remnant dropped his bat, dashed in pursuit, and checked the runaway before any harm could be done.

RENNY-TAILYOUR, Col. Henry Waugh, born in Missouri North-West Provinces, on October 9, 1849, died at Newmanswell, Montrose, on June 15, 1920. He was in the Cheltenham XI in 1867 and played in 19 matches for Kent between 1873 and 1883, making 694 runs (average 23.93) with 124 v. Lancashire at Maidstone in 1874 as his highest score. He was an excellent all-round player, and could hit very hard, but was not seen in great matches as frequently as his skill entitled him. In 1873 and two following years, however, he assisted the Gentlemen against the Players at Prince's. In minor matches his scoring was very heavy. For Royal Engineers v. Civil Service at Chatham in 1880 he scored 331 not out (out of 498 made whilst in) in 330 minutes, hitting an eight, a seven, two sixes, four fives, and 21 fours. At Chatham, in 1875, he made 285 not out for Royal Engineers v. Royal Artillery, and in 1882 at Thornton (Scotland) 240 for Strathmore v. St. Lawrence, in the latter match adding 370 for the second wicket with J. M. Ramsay (142). For I Zingari v. Gentlemen of Kent at Canterbury in 1873 he bowled 40 balls for five runs and five wickets, and in the corresponding match of the following year took four wickets for 12 runs. When in Scotland he played occasionally for Aberdeenshire. As an Association footballer he obtained great distinction, representing

Scotland against England in 1872–73 and being one of the forward line when the Royal Engineers won the F.A. Cup in 1874–75.

REVILL, Thomas Frederick, died in hospital at Mansfield on March 29, 1979, aged 86. A left-handed bat, he made a number of appearances for Derbyshire between 1913 and 1920, his highest score being 65 not out against Northamptonshire in 1919. His son, Alan, was for many years a valuable member of the Derbyshire side.

REYNOLDS, Frederick Reginald, born at Bottisham, Cambridgeshire, on August 7, 1834, died at Chorlton-cum-Hardy on April 18, 1915, aged 80. *Scores and Biographies* said of him: "As a batsman he does not excel, hitting at everything with but small defence. He is, however, a superior fast and straight round-armed bowler, with a break-back from the off, and with an easy delivery." In his later years he took to lobs. After filling various engagements he played in turn for the United and All England XIs, as well as for Cambridgeshire and Lancashire. In 1861 he went to Manchester, and for 48 years was manager of the Old Trafford ground, retiring in December, 1908, with a pension of £100 a year. In 1870 the match at Manchester between Lancashire and Surrey was played for his benefit, but the financial result was disappointing, the game lasting only 10 hours. On his occasional appearances for Lancashire between 1865 and 1874 he scored 304 runs with an average of 6.75 and took 94 wickets at a cost of 19.21 runs each. Playing for the A.E.E. v. XXII Gentlemen of Sussex at Brighton in 1859, he took nine wickets for 40 runs in the first innings and six for 15 in the second; for United E.E. v. Fifteen of M.C.C. and Ground at Lord's in 1863, eight for 49 second innings and 15 for 126 in the match.

REYNOLDS, H., Notts, died April 21, 1894. Reynolds, who was born on January 6, 1847, was in his day a very good batsman, but it cannot be said that he ever approached the first rank. He was seen to special advantage for England against Kent and Gloucestershire in the Canterbury Week of 1874.

RHODES, Albert Ennion Grocott ("Dusty"), died at his home at Barlow, near Chesterfield, on October 18, 1983, aged 67. Born in Cheshire, he came into the Derbyshire side in 1937 and showed great promise as an all-rounder, scoring 363 runs with an average of 21.35 and taking 25 wickets at 27.72.

Originally a leg-spinner, he was now bowling fast-medium out-swingers with a long run which put an undue strain on a slight physique. Indeed, his record throughout his career suggests that he was never sufficiently robust to be a genuine all-rounder: in the seasons in which he scored runs his bowling usually suffered and vice versa. Thus in 1938, while he made 916 runs at an average of 27.75, he took only 18 wickets and in 1939, when his batting was disappointing his bowling was less expensive; in any case the county's bowling was then so strong that he was only used as a change. By 1946 things were very different: most of the pre-war bowlers had gone and Rhodes was used freely both as an opener and a leg-spinner. Not surprisingly his bowling in this dual role was expensive, his 75 wickets being obtained at 29.90 and not surprisingly, too, he met with little success as a bat. Thereafter he concentrated on leg-breaks and googlies, but though he had considerable powers of spin and might at any time take valuable wickets, he never attained consistent accuracy. However, he performed the hat-trick five times, a number which only three bowlers have exceeded. By far his best season with the ball was 1950, when he took 130 wickets at 22.19. In 1951 he was very expensive but none the less was selected for the M.C.C. tour of India and Pakistan that winter. The opening matches showed that his spin, though costly, might be valuable and it was a blow to the side when he had to return home before the first Test for an operation. In 1952 he had a good season, taking 83 wickets at 24.95. This was almost the end of his career, though he played in a few matches in 1953 and 1954. Since the War he had been regarded largely as a bowler, but in 1949 he again showed what a good bat he could be, scoring 1,156 runs with an average of 25.68. Significantly that year his 66 wickets cost 38.62 each. In all he made in first-class cricket 7,363 runs with an average of 18.98, including four centuries, and took 661 wickets at 28.83. A determined batsman, he had a sound defence but was also a powerful off-side player and could score fast. Against Nottinghamshire at Ilkeston in 1949 he made a hundred before lunch. His highest score was 127 against Somerset at Taunton in the same season. From 1959 to 1979 he was a first-class umpire and stood in eight Tests. He had also coached at both Oxford and Cambridge. He was father of Harold Rhodes, the England fast bowler.

RHODES, Arthur Cecil, who died on May 21, 1957, aged 50, played for Yorkshire from 1932 to 1934, taking 107 wickets, average 28.28, with fast-medium bowling and, by forcing methods, scoring 917 runs, average 17.93. Among his performances was the taking of nine Gloucestershire wickets for 117 runs in the match at Sheffield in 1933, in which season he hit his highest first-class score, 64 not out against Leicestershire at Leicester. He was well known in Yorkshire and Lancashire League cricket.

WILFRED RHODES – YORKSHIRE PERSONIFIED
Born at Kirkheaton, West Riding, October 29, 1877.
Died near his home in Dorset, July 8, 1973.
He had been blind since 1952.
by Sir Neville Cardus

Wilfred Rhodes was Yorkshire cricket personified in the great period of the county's domination, shrewd, dour, but quick to seize opportunity. For Yorkshire he scored more than 30,000 runs, averaging 30 an innings: for Yorkshire he took 3,608 wickets at 16 runs each. When he was not playing for Yorkshire, in his spare time, so to say, he played for England and amassed 2,000 runs, average 30, and took 127 wickets, at the cost of 26.96 apiece. In his first Test match he was last in the batting order, and at Sydney in the 1903–04 rubber he took part in the most persistent and prolific Test match last-wicket partnership to this day; he helped R. E. Foster to add 130 for the 10th wicket, his share 40 not out. Eight years afterwards he went in first for England at Melbourne, and against Australia he was the partner of Hobbs in the record first-wicket stand of 323.

His career is already legendary; it does indeed read like a fairy tale. He was not 21 years old when he first bowled for Yorkshire in a match against M.C.C. at Lord's. In the first innings he accounted for Trott and Chatteron; in the second for Trott, Chatteron, C. P. Foley, and the Hon. J. R. Tufton—six wickets for 63, a modest beginning, true. But at the season's end he had established himself as the greatest slow left-hand bowler in England with 154 wickets, average 14.60.

During the period in which Rhodes and Hobbs opened every England innings by prescriptive right, Rhodes put aside his bowling. In the Australian rubber of 1911–12 he contributed only 18 overs. But then the War came, reducing the Yorkshire attack. In 1919 Yorkshire needed again the spin and flight of Rhodes, so he picked up his bowling arts exactly where years before he had laid them down, picked them up as though he had not lost touch for a moment. He headed the bowling averages of 1919, 164 wickets, average 14.42 in 1,048 overs. He was nearly 42 by the calendar. In 1902 he had gone in last for England at Kennington Oval when 15 runs were wanted to beat Australia; George Hirst, with whom he always opened Yorkshire's attack, was holding the wicket at the other end. England won by one wicket.

Twenty-four years afterwards, Rhodes in his 49th year was recalled to the England XI and was one of the main causes of Australia's defeat and England's emergence from years in the wilderness. On this, his last appearance for England, Rhodes took the wickets of Woodfull, Ponsford, Richardson (twice), Collins, and Bardsley for 79 runs. He had probably lost by then much of his old quick vitally fingered spin: but as he explained to me: "If batsmen thinks as I'm spinnin' them, then I am"—a remark metaphysical, maybe, but to the point. At Sydney, in December, 1903, on the shirt-fronted polished Bulli soil pitches of that distant halcyon day of batsmen, Australia scored 485, and the might of Australia's champions commanded the crease—Trumper, Hill, Duff, Armstrong, Gregory. Rhodes bowled 48 overs for 94 runs, five wickets. It was on this occasion that Trumper, most brilliant of all batsmen, alive or dead, made his famous remark to Rhodes—"for God's sake, Wilfred, give me a minute's rest."

Rhodes could not turn the ball on the Australian grounds of half a century ago. He prevailed by length, variations of flight, but chiefly by unceasing accuracy of pitch, always demanding close attention from the batsman, the curving arc through the air, the ball dropping on the same spot over by over, yet not on quite the same spot, each over in collusion with the rest, every ball a decoy, some balls apparently guileless, some artfully masked—and one of them, sooner or later, the master ball. He was economical in action, a few short strides, then a beautifully balanced sideways swing of the body, the arm loose and making a lovely arch. He could go on for hours; the rhythm of his action was in its easy rotation, hypnotic, lulling his victims to the tranced state in which he could work his will, make them perform strokes contrary to their reason and intention. Batsmen of Rhodes's heyday frequently succumbed to his bait for a catch in the deep field. David Denton had safe hands at long-on; and the score-sheets of the period repeated day by day the rubric—"c Denton b Rhodes." In rainy weather, "c Tunnicliffe b Rhodes" was familiar proof that Wilfred was at work on a "sticky" pitch, for Tunni-

cliffe was the best slip fielder of the century, a long giant with a reach into infinity.

Rhodes really was a slow bowler, not quick and low flight to the pitch, after Lock's manner. At the end of his career he proudly maintained that "Ah were never hooked and Ah were never cut," a pardonable exaggeration considering the proportion of truth in it. Rhodes seldom pitched short. "Best ball on a 'sticky' pitch is a spinnin' half-volley," such was his doctrine. And he bowled to his field with the precision of high mathematics. Ernest Tyldesley once told me that he often had no alternative but to play at least three balls an over, on a batsman's wicket, straight to mid-off, an inch off the spot where Rhodes had planted mid-off.

Rhodes made himself into a batsman by practice and hard thinking. He was one of the first batsmen to adopt the full-fronted stance, left shoulder pointing to forward leg. But it is a mistake to suppose that his batting was perpetually dour and parsimonious in strokeplay. In the Test match against the Australians at Lord's in 1912, England had first innings on a rain-damaged pitch. *Wisden* relates that Rhodes, with Hobbs as company, "so monopolised the hitting that his share of 77 runs amounted to 52." On the whole and naturally enough, Rhodes distrusted the romantic gesture. One day in conversation with him, I deplored the absence in modern cricket of the cut. "But it were never a business stroke," he maintained.

While he was actively engaged in the game he was not a man given to affability. He was known as a "natterer" on the field; and to natter in the North of England means to talk naggingly, mostly to oneself, with the intention of being overheard. At Old Trafford in the '30s Lancashire reached a total of 500 against Yorkshire. The Lancashire captain, Leonard Green, was about to take the bowling of Rhodes when the score was 499. Green was sure in his mind that a total of 500 would never again, or not for decades, be achieved by Lancashire against Yorkshire. He therefore determined that come what may he would himself score the 500th run. So he blocked a ball from Rhodes, then ran like the wind. The ball was picked up by Emmott Robinson at silly-point, and hurled to the bowler's end, where it struck Rhodes on the wrist even as Green got home by the skin of his teeth. And in all the scurry and excitement Wilfred was heard to mutter, while he retrieved Robinson's violent throw, "There's somebody runnin' up and down this wicket. Ah don't know who it is, but there's somebody runnin' up and down this wicket."

He was a great player, one of the greatest in cricket's history, not only for his all-round performances denoted by the statisticians: nearly 40,000 runs scored in 37 seasons and 4,184 wickets taken. He was great because his cricket was redolent and representative of Yorkshire county. In his old age he lost his eyesight and found his tongue. He accepted his affliction philosophically, and consoled himself by a flow of genial chatter never before heard from him. He attended cricket as long as his health would permit. With an acquired sense he was able to follow the play. "He's middlin' the ball right." But it was his delight in his last years to recall the old days. I asked him what he thought of Ranjitsinhji. "He were a good bat were 'Ranji.' But I always fancied myself getting him leg before doin' that leg glance of his." I tried again. "What did you think of Trumper?" "'E were a good bat were Victor." There was no advance of a "good" bat in Wilfred's vocabulary of praise. Once, though, he let himself go. I asked him his opinion of Sidney Barnes as a bowler. "The best of 'em today is half as good as Barnie." He intended this as a compliment to the champions of today.

I last saw him as his daughter, Muriel, and her husband Tom Burnley, led him out of Trent Bridge at the close of play of a Test match. More than 50 years ago he had first played for England, on this same ground, in 1899, when he was 21. Now he was going home to Canford Cliffs, Bournemouth, white stick in hand, arm in arm with his son-in-law, his face ruddy after hours sitting and listening to cricket, and whether he knew it or not, himself a permanent part of the game's history and traditions.

WILFRED RHODES — CAREER AT A GLANCE
Compiled By STANLEY CONDER

BATTING AND BOWLING

In England	Matches	Inns.	Not Outs	Runs	Highest Inns	100's	Average	Runs	Wkts	Average	5 wkts. in Inns	Catches
1898	33	41	9	557	78	0	17.40	2,249	154	14.60	12	18
1899	34	49	12	432	81*	0	11.67	3,062	179	17.10	12	22
1900	35	42	11	655	79	0	21.12	3,606	261	13.81	24	11
1901	37	45	13	854	105	1	26.68	3,797	251	15.12	25	24
1902	37	46	14	490	92*	0	15.31	2,801	213	13.15	19	20
1903	36	51	9	1,137	98*	0	27.07	2,813	193	14.57	16	20
1904	36	47	4	1,537	196	2	35.74	2,829	131	21.59	9	23
1905	38	52	8	1,581	201	2	35.93	3,085	182	16.95	15	44
1906	37	62	3	1,721	119	3	29.16	3,018	128	23.57	8	39
1907	33	47	1	1,055	112	1	22.93	2,757	177	15.57	13	20
1908	36	57	4	1,673	146	3	31.56	1,855	115	16.13	6	12
1909	37	59	7	2,094	199	5	40.26	2,241	141	15.89	12	25
1910	34	59	4	1,465	111	1	26.63	1,671	88	18.98	6	15
1911	36	64	5	2,261	128	5	38.32	2,817	117	24.07	7	27
1912	37	58	5	1,597	176	2	30.13	1,165	53	21.98	2	29
1913	36	64	4	1,953	152	4	32.71	1,882	86	21.88	4	29
1914	31	49	2	1,377	113*	2	29.29	2,157	118	18.27	5	36
1919	32	46	10	1,237	135	1	34.36	2,365	164	14.42	11	30
1920	34	45	5	1,123	167*	1	28.07	2,123	161	13.18	12	33
1921	32	47	10	1,474	267*	3	39.83	1,872	141	13.27	8	27
1922	37	46	8	1,511	110	4	39.76	1,451	119	12.19	6	28
1923	37	48	8	1,321	126	2	33.02	1,547	134	11.54	9	35
1924	38	50	7	1,126	100	1	26.18	1,576	109	14.45	6	22
1925	37	43	9	1,391	157	2	40.91	1,134	57	19.89	0	17
1926	33	36	3	1,132	132	1	34.30	1,709	115	14.86	6	15
1927	35	37	7	577	73	0	19.23	1,731	85	20.36	2	8
1928	33	28	6	579	100*	1	26.31	2,258	115	19.63	9	20
1929	30	32	9	617	79	0	26.82	1,870	100	18.70	6	15
1930	26	29	8	418	80*	0	22.75	1,395	73	19.10	1	9

*Signifies not out.

WILFRED RHODES — CAREER AT A GLANCE—*continued*

In Australia	Matches	Inns.	Not Outs	Runs	Highest Inns	100's	Average	Runs	Wkts	Average	5 wkts. in Inns	Catches
1903–04 ..	14	18	7	239	49*	0	21.72	1,055	65	16.23	7	14
1907–08 ..	17	27	8	929	119	2	48.89	1,069	31	34.48	1	8
1911–12 ..	14	24	4	1,098	179	4	54.90	234	0	—	0	11
1920–21 ..	12	19	0	730	210	2	38.42	479	18	26.61	1	6
In South Africa												
1909–10 ..	14	22	2	579	77	0	28.95	535	21	25.47	1	12
1913–14 ..	17	24	3	731	152	1	34.80	662	31	21.35	0	26
In West Indies												
1929–30 ..	9	12	7	129	36	0	25.80	947	39	24.28	2	5
In India												
1921–22 ..	2	2	0	339	183	2	169.50	103	19	5.42	3	1
1926–27 ..	1	1	1	13	13*	0	—	73	3	24.33	0	0
All First-Class												
Matches ..	1,107	1,528	237	39,802	267*	58	30.83	69,993	4,187	16.71	286	756

Batting—Mode of Dismissal: Bowled 405, caught 683, lbw 144, stumped 20, hit wicket 1, run out 38. Total 1291.
Bowling—How wickets were taken: Bowled 901, caught 2400, lbw 495, stumped 373, hit wicket 18. Total 4187.
In his career W. Rhodes sent down 184,890 balls (2748.4 5-ball overs, and 28,524.2 (6-ball overs) of which 9438
were maiden overs (1925 5-ball overs, and 8413 6-ball overs).

COUNTY CHAMPIONSHIP MATCHES

Season	Matches	Inns	Not Outs	Runs	Highest Inns	100s	Average	Runs	Wkts	Average	5 wkts. in Inns	Catches
1898 ..	26	30	8	472	78	0	21.45	1,745	126	13.84	11	14
1899 ..	23	35	9	359	81*	0	13.80	2,021	129	15.66	9	16
1900 ..	26	29	7	400	79	0	18.18	2,532	206	12.29	20	6
1901 ..	27	31	7	522	53	0	21.75	2,664	196	13.59	20	20
1902 ..	22	24	5	299	92*	0	15.73	1,748	140	12.48	12	8
1903 ..	26	37	6	751	79*	0	24.22	2,105	143	14.72	12	12
1904 ..	26	35	2	1,082	196	2	32.78	2,070	104	19.90	8	17
1905 ..	26	35	4	1,117	201	2	36.03	1,986	126	15.76	10	35
1906 ..	28	46	3	1,431	119*	2	33.27	2,036	91	22.37	6	32
1907 ..	25	34	1	891	112	1	27.00	2,314	141	16.41	12	14
1908 ..	27	43	1	1,412	146	3	33.61	1,295	78	16.60	3	5
1909 ..	24	40	2	1,351	199	3	35.55	1,635	107	15.28	11	19
1910 ..	28	49	4	1,282	111	1	28.48	1,384	77	17.97	6	7
1911 ..	27	48	3	1,606	125	2	35.68	2,260	93	24.30	6	20
1912 ..	20	32	4	965	176	2	34.46	808	37	21.83	1	17
1913 ..	28	49	4	1,531	152	3	34.02	1,560	62	25.16	2	23
1914 ..	27	44	1	1,176	113	1	27.34	1,965	110	17.86	5	35
1919 ..	25	34	8	890	135	1	34.23	1,764	142	12.42	11	23
1920 ..	27	36	3	949	167*	1	28.75	1,846	143	12.90	11	30
1921 ..	24	33	6	1,184	267*	3	43.85	1,488	117	12.71	7	19
1922 ..	30	36	6	1,181	110	4	39.36	1,068	84	12.71	5	25
1923 ..	31	38	5	1,023	126	2	31.00	1,353	120	11.27	8	31
1924 ..	30	37	5	826	100	1	25.81	1,085	81	13.39	4	18
1925 ..	32	35	7	1,234	157	2	44.07	928	52	17.84	0	15
1926 ..	26	28	3	1,022	132	1	40.88	1,388	100	13.88	5	14
1927 ..	30	32	6	481	44	0	18.50	1,546	77	20.07	2	7
1928 ..	28	23	4	542	100*	1	28.52	1,995	103	19.36	9	6
1929 ..	24	27	7	543	79	0	27.15	1,464	85	17.22	6	14
1930 ..	19	20	5	337	80*	0	22.46	858	42	20.42	0	8
Totals ..	762	1,020	136	26,859	267*	38	30.38	48,911	3,112	15.71	222	520

*Signifies not out.

FOR YORKSHIRE AGAINST TEAMS IN ENGLAND

	Matches	Inns	Not Outs	Runs	Highest Inns	100s	Average	Runs	Wkts	Average	5 wkts. in Inns	Catches
Derbyshire ..	46	55	8	1,299	157	2	27.63	2,221	189	11.75	11	35
Essex ..	58	70	12	2,048	132	5	35.31	3,595	264	13.61	18	29
Glamorgan ..	16	9	2	321	110	1	45.85	496	41	12.09	3	14
Gloucestershire	47	57	3	1,227	110	1	22.72	2,669	240	11.12	22	33
Hampshire ..	45	56	8	1,599	135	2	33.31	2,631	44	18.27	8	28
Kent ..	54	83	8	1,574	101	1	20.98	2,971	164	18.11	12	32
Lancashire ..	57	86	15	1,892	107	1	26.64	3,937	228	17.26	14	33
Leicestershire	50	62	10	2,253	267*	5	43.32	3,274	227	14.42	14	44
Middlesex ..	55	85	9	1,970	126	2	25.92	4,447	223	19.94	18	33
Northamptonshire	34	45	6	1,436	140	3	36.82	1,729	141	12.26	10	41
Nottinghamshire	55	80	8	2,039	176	2	28.31	3,857	231	16.69	17	36
Somerset ..	43	55	10	1,737	201	5	38.60	2,510	196	12.80	15	33
Surrey ..	55	80	12	1,663	107	1	24.45	4,425	231	19.15	17	33
Sussex ..	51	72	10	2,307	199	4	37.20	4,149	197	21.06	15	30
Warwickshire ..	58	79	11	1,988	81	0	29.23	3,874	256	15.13	17	43
Worcestershire	38	46	4	1,506	196	3	35.85	2,126	140	15.18	11	23
Totals	762	1,020	136	26,859	267*	38	30.38	48,911	3,112	15.71	222	520

OTHER MATCHES FOR YORKSHIRE

	Matches	Inns	Not Outs	Runs	Highest Inns	100s	Average	Runs	Wkts	Average	5 wkts in Inns	Catches
Cambridge Uni.	25	35	6	752	102	1	25.93	1,784	137	13.02	9	22
Oxford University	3	3	1	32	24*	0	16.00	221	7	31.57	0	0
M.C.C. ..	43	63	6	1,707	128	5	29.94	2,871	157	18.28	10	21
Lancashire ..	2	3	1	163	105*	1	81.50	116	9	12.88	1	1
Surrey ..	1	1	1	41	41*	0	—	120	7	17.14	1	0
Sussex ..	1	1	0	9	9	0	9.00	68	5	13.60	0	0
As Champion County												
v. Rest of England	8	15	2	439	96	0	33.76	688	21	32.76	2	4
England XI ..	2	3	1	62	36	0	31.00	160	6	26.66	1	0
Rest of England	2	3	0	41	26	0	13.66	221	6	36.83	0	1
C.I. Thornton's XI	5	9	3	129	35*	0	21.50	576	25	23.04	2	1
Australians ..	15	20	2	562	108	1	31.22	916	49	18.69	2	9
South Africans	8	13	2	258	54	0	23.45	679	32	21.21	1	4
New Zealanders	1	1	0	2	2	0	2.00	29	4	7.25	0	0
West Indians ..	3	4	0	19	14	0	4.75	122	7	17.42	0	0
Gents. of Ireland	1	1	0	10	10	0	10.00	64	4	16.00	0	1
All Ireland ..	1	1	0	13	13	0	13.00	88	9	9.77	1	2
Totals ..	121	176	25	4,239	128	8	28.07	8,723	485	17.98	30	66

OTHER MATCHES

	Matches	Inns	Not Outs	Runs	Highest Inns	100s	Average	Runs	Wkts	Average	5 wkts in Inns	Catches
Players v. Gents	39	60	12	1,296	82	0	27.00	2,086	103	20.25	4	23
North v. South	8	12	2	329	93	0	32.90	673	38	17.71	4	5
Rest of England v. Champion County	8	10	4	243	78	0	40.50	344	18	19.11	0	6
For Other Teams	45	66	15	1,322	121	1	25.92	2,680	137	19.56	8	31
Totals ..	100	148	33	3,190	121	1	27.73	5,783	296	19.53	16	65

*Signifies not out.

BATTING AND BOWLING ON ENGLISH GROUNDS

Ground	Matches	Inns	Not Outs	Runs	Highest Inns	100s	Average	Runs	Wkts	Average	5 wkts in Inns	Catches
Bath	7	8	3	270	115*	1	54.00	357	36	9.91	4	6
Blackheath ..	1	1	0	15	15	0	15.00	40	2	20.00	0	0
Bournemouth	8	9	1	325	106	1	40.62	442	18	24.55	0	5
Bradford ..	90	124	17	3,028	126	4	28.29	6,055	405	14.95	34	57
Bray ..	2	3	0	31	12	0	10.33	64	4	16.00	0	1
Bristol ..	13	17	1	403	110	1	25.18	837	79	10.59	7	10
Bristol (Fry's Grd.)	1	1	0	3	3	0	3.00	55	2	27.50	0	2
Cambridge ..	24	33	6	738	102	1	27.33	1,729	130	13.30	9	22
Canterbury ..	4	8	1	173	95	0	24.71	279	18	15.50	1	5
Cardiff	6	3	0	40	34	0	13.33	58	4	14.50	0	5
Catford	3	5	0	36	18	0	7.20	189	19	9.94	1	1
Cheltenham ..	4	6	0	58	25	0	9.66	247	32	7.71	4	1
Chesterfield ..	12	16	2	365	82*	0	26.07	475	41	11.58	1	8
Derby	9	9	1	228	69	0	28.50	451	43	10.48	2	4
Dewsbury ..	29	41	2	1,310	135	2	33.58	1,948	152	12.81	13	32
Dover ..	4	6	0	105	53	0	17.50	90	3	30.00	0	1
Dublin ..	1	1	0	13	13	0	13.00	88	9	9.77	1	2
Dudley ..	1	1	0	13	13	0	13.00	41	8	5.12	1	0
Eastbourne ..	3	4	0	62	35	0	15.50	261	18	14.50	2	0
Edgbaston ..	31	37	10	1,015	81	0	37.59	1,926	135	14.26	11	17
Glossop ..	2	2	0	1	1	0	0.50	155	15	10.33	1	1
Gloucester ..	5	6	0	201	72	0	33.50	160	22	7.27	1	4
Harrogate ..	29	37	9	1,403	176	5	50.10	1,813	108	16.78	8	23
Hastings ..	14	18	6	379	93	0	31.58	1,301	66	19.71	8	13
Headingley	88	124	14	3,096	267*	7	28.14	5,592	361	15.49	29	50
Hove ..	24	35	4	1,078	199	2	34.77	1,971	94	20.96	7	17
Huddersfield	29	33	3	1,081	140	2	36.03	1,300	108	12.03	8	29
Hull ..	37	44	4	1,054	105*	1	26.35	1,633	97	16.83	6	24
Ilkeston ..	1	2	1	9	7*	0	9.00	—	—	—	0	0
Kettering ..	1	1	0	55	55	0	55.00	10	2	5.00	0	0
Leicester ..	26	31	3	1,145	152	3	40.89	1,821	118	15.43	8	21
Leyton ..	27	34	7	882	132	2	32.66	1,677	117	14.33	8	15
Liverpool ..	1	2	0	58	58	0	29.00	78	8	9.75	1	1
Lord's ..	71	105	11	2,408	121	1	25.61	4,853	215	22.57	12	33
Maidstone ..	6	12	2	239	68	0	23.90	390	19	20.52	2	4
Northampton	16	22	3	734	110	0	38.63	920	75	12.26	5	18
Old Trafford ..	34	51	12	1,160	94*	0	29.74	2,235	114	19.60	7	22
Oxford ..	3	3	1	32	24*	0	16.00	221	7	31.57	0	0
Portsmouth ..	7	8	1	279	98	0	39.85	507	25	20.28	2	2
Reigate ..	1	2	0	10	5	0	5.00	95	10	9.50	1	2
Scarborough ..	83	124	22	2,825	128	5	27.69	5,656	299	18.91	15	42
Sheffield ..	105	149	22	3,508	146	3	27.62	6,802	415	16.39	21	70
Southampton ..	8	11	3	250	58*	0	31.25	520	23	22.60	0	6
Southend ..	2	2	0	11	10	0	5.50	117	12	9.75	0	0
Stourbridge ..	1	1	0	51	51	0	51.00	—	—	—	0	2
Swansea ..	1	1	0	4	4	0	4.00	80	8	10.00	1	2
Taunton ..	12	16	2	503	201	1	35.92	978	70	13.97	6	11
The Oval ..	59	86	20	1,968	96	0	29.81	4,089	158	25.87	6	42
Tonbridge ..	5	9	2	126	31*	0	18.00	382	19	20.10	2	2
Trent Bridge ..	31	41	6	1,192	83	0	34.05	2,208	128	17.25	8	22
Tunbridge Wells	4	6	0	145	53	0	24.16	242	10	24.20	1	4
Uttoxeter ..	1	2	1	56	33	0	56.00	77	4	19.25	0	1
Weston-super-Mare	2	3	0	126	100	1	42.00	77	9	8.55	1	1
Worcester ..	18	23	2	715	196	2	34.04	1,244	66	18.84	5	10
Totals ..	1,007	1,379	205	35,015	267*	47	29.82	64,836	3,960	16.37	271	673

Signifies not out.

BATTING AND BOWLING ON AUSTRALIAN GROUNDS

Ground	Matches	Inns	Not Outs	Runs	Highest Inns	100s	Average	Runs	Wkts	Average	5 wkts in Inns	Catches
Adelaide	10	14	3	549	210	1	49.90	537	10	53.70	0	7
Brisbane	7	9	2	373	162	1	53.28	261	9	29.00	0	6
Hobart	3	3	1	227	119	2	113.50	81	5	16.20	0	4
Launceston	3	5	3	81	39	0	40.50	127	0	—	0	2
Melbourne	15	25	4	692	179	1	32.95	773	50	15.46	6	14
Perth	2	2	1	36	32	0	36.00	115	7	16.42	0	0
South Melbourne	1	1	1	105	105*	1	—	90	3	30.00	0	0
Sydney	16	29	4	933	119	2	37.32	853	30	28.43	3	6
Totals	57	88	19	2,996	210	8	43.42	2,837	114	24.88	9	39

BATTING AND BOWLING ON SOUTH AFRICAN GROUNDS

Ground	Matches	Inns	Not Outs	Runs	Highest Inns	100s	Average	Runs	Wkts	Average	5 wkts in Inns	Catches
Bloemfontein	1	1	0	68	68	0	68.00	24	0	—	0	4
Cape Town	5	9	2	155	35*	0	22.14	149	6	24.83	0	6
Durban	5	8	0	235	64	0	29.37	243	11	22.09	1	5
East London	2	3	0	79	35	0	26.33	41	1	41.00	0	3
Johannesburg	8	14	1	547	152	1	42.07	461	16	28.81	0	12
King Williams Town	1	2	0	67	38	0	33.50	41	5	8.20	0	1
Maritzburg	1	1	0	1	1	0	1.00	34	4	8.50	0	0
Pietermaritzburg	1	1	0	14	14	0	14.00	5	1	5.00	0	0
Port Elizabeth	3	4	1	63	31	0	21.00	68	4	17.00	0	4
Pretoria	2	1	0	1	1	0	1.00	124	2	62.00	0	2
Vogelfontein	2	2	1	80	56*	0	80.00	7	2	3.50	0	1
Totals	31	46	5	1,310	152	1	31.95	1,197	52	23.01	1	38

BATTING AND BOWLING ON WEST INDIES GROUNDS

Ground	Matches	Inns	Not Outs	Runs	Highest Inns	100s	Average	Runs	Wkts	Average	5 wkts in Inns	Catches
Bridgetown	2	2	1	50	36	0	50.00	234	6	39.00	0	2
Georgetown	3	3	2	19	10*	0	19.00	403	16	25.18	1	3
Kingston	2	3	2	33	14	0	33.00	133	7	19.00	0	0
Port of Spain	2	4	2	27	11	0	13.50	177	10	17.70	1	0
Totals	9	12	7	129	36	0	25.80	947	39	24.28	2	5

BATTING AND BOWLING ON INDIAN GROUNDS

Ground	Matches	Inns	Not Outs	Runs	Highest Inns	100s	Average	Runs	Wkts	Average	5 wkts in Inns	Catches
Bombay	2	2	0	339	183	2	169.50	103	19	5.42	3	1
Patalia	1	1	1	13	13*	0	—	73	3	24.33	0	0
Totals	3	3	1	352	183	2	176.00	176	22	8.00	3	1

FOR M.C.C. AGAINST TEAMS IN AUSTRALIA

	Matches	Inns	Not Outs	Runs	Highest Inns	100s	Average	Runs	Wkts	Average	5 wkts in Inns	Catches
Australian XI	3	4	0	45	34	0	11.25	129	3	43.00	0	2
New South Wales	8	14	3	567	119	2	51.54	373	14	26.64	2	4
North Tasmania	1	1	0	39	39	0	39.00	54	0	—	0	1
Queensland	4	5	2	328	162	1	109.33	132	6	22.00	0	4
South Australia	6	6	2	349	210	1	87.25	240	5	48.00	0	3
Tasmania	5	7	4	269	119	2	89.66	154	5	30.80	0	5

*Signifies not out.

FOR M.C.C. AGAINST TEAMS IN AUSTRALIA—continued

	Matches	Inns	Not Outs	Runs	Highest Inns	100s	Average	Runs	Wkts	Average	5 wkts in Inns	Catches
Victorian XI ..	1	1	1	105	105*	1	—	90	3	30.00	0	0
Victoria ..	7	10	3	226	66	0	32.28	339	29	11.68	4	5
Western Australia	2	2	1	36	32*	0	36.00	115	7	16.42	0	0
Totals ..	37	50	16	1,964	210	7	57.76	1,626	72	22.58	6	24

FOR M.C.C. AGAINST TEAMS IN SOUTH AFRICA

	Matches	Inns	Not Outs	Runs	Highest Inns	100s	Average	Runs	Wkts	Average	5 wkts in Inns	Catches
Border ..	1	1	0	20	20	0	20.00	41	1	41.00	0	3
Border District	1	2	0	59	35	0	29.50	—	—	—	0	0
The Border ..	1	2	0	67	38	0	33.50	41	5	8.20	0	1
Cape Province	1	1	0	5	5	0	5.00	54	4	13.50	0	2
Eastern Province	1	1	0	31	31	0	31.00	—	—	—	0	0
Natal ..	4	5	0	114	64	0	22.80	116	12	9.66	1	0
Orange Free State	1	1	0	68	68	0	68.00	24	0	—	0	4
The Reef ..	1	2	1	80	56*	0	80.00	—	—	—	0	0
XI of Transvaal	1	—	—	—	—	—	—	7	2	3.50	0	1
Transvaal ..	6	8	1	278	76*	0	39.71	447	14	31.92	0	5
Western Province	3	5	1	73.	35*	0	18.25	125	6	20.83	0	2
Totals ..	21	28	3	795	76*	0	31.80	855	44	19.43	1	18

FOR M.C.C. AGAINST TEAMS IN THE WEST INDIES

	Matches	Inns	Not Outs	Runs	Highest Inns	100s	Average	Runs	Wkts	Average	5 wkts in Inns	Catches
Barbados ..	1	1	0	36	36	0	36.00	80	3	26.66	0	0
British Guiana	2	1	1	9	9*	0	—	214	12	17.83	1	2
Jamaica ..	1	1	0	14	14	0	14.00	94	5	18.80	0	0
Trinidad ..	1	2	1	19	11	0	19.00	106	9	11.77	1	0
Totals ..	5	5	2	78	36	0	26.00	494	29	17.03	2	2

MATCHES AGAINST TEAMS IN INDIA

	Matches	Inns	Not Outs	Runs	Highest Inns	100s	Average	Runs	Wkts	Average	5 wkts in Inns	Catches
Europeans v. Hindus	1	1	0	156	156	1	156.00	44	7	6.28	1	1
Europeans v. Parsis	1	1	0	183	183	1	183.00	59	12	4.91	2	0
Patiala v. M.C.C.	1	1	1	13	13*	0	—	73	3	24.33	0	0
Totals ..	3	3	1	352	183	2	176.00	176	22	8.00	3	1

BATTING AND BOWLING IN TEST CRICKET

	No. of Tests	Inns	Not Outs	Runs	Highest Inns	100s	Average	Runs	Wkts	Average	5 wkts in Inns	Catches
v. Australia ..	41	69	14	1,706	179	1	31.01	2,616	109	24.00	6	36
v. South Africa	13	22	2	568	152	1	28.40	356	8	44.50	0	21
v. West Indies	4	7	5	51	14*	0	25.50	453	10	45.30	0	3
Totals ..	58	98	21	2,325	179	2	30.19	3,425	127	26.96	6	60

AGGREGATES OF BATTING AND BOWLING

	No. of Tests	Inns	Not Outs	Runs	Highest Inns	100s	Average	Runs	Wkts	Average	5 wkts in Inns	Catches
In England ..	24	35	11	727	98	0	30.29	1,419	67	21.17	3	22
In Australia ..	20	38	3	1,032	179	1	29.48	1,211	42	28.83	3	15
In South Africa	10	18	2	515	152	1	32.18	342	8	42.75	0	20
In West Indies	4	7	5	51	14*	0	25.50	453	10	45.30	0	3
Totals ..	58	98	21	2,325	179	2	30.19	3,425	127	26.96	6	60

* Signifies not out.

W. Rhodes shared in 17 century stands in Test cricket during his career, as follows:

For the First Wicket
323	With J. B. Hobbs v. Australia at Melbourne, 1911–12
221	With J. B. Hobbs v. South Africa at Cape Town, 1909–10
159	With J. B. Hobbs v. South Africa at Johannesburg, 1909–10
147	With J. B. Hobbs v. Australia at Adelaide, 1911–12
141	With A. E. Relf v. South Africa at Johannesburg, 1913–14
133	With J. B. Hobbs v. South Africa at Durban, 1913–14
112	With J. B. Hobbs v. Australia at Lord's, 1912
107	With J. B. Hobbs v. Australia at the Oval, 1912
100	With J. B. Hobbs v. South Africa at Johannesburg, 1913–14

For the Second Wicket
127	With J. W. Hearne v. Australia at Melbourne, 1911–12
124	With R. H. Spooner v. South Africa at Lord's, 1912
113	With H. Makepeace v. Australia at Melbourne, 1920–21
102	With G. Gunn v. Australia at Melbourne, 1911–12

For the Third Wicket
152	With C. P. Mead v. South Africa at Johannesburg, 1913–14
104	With C. B. Fry v. Australia at the Oval, 1909

For the Sixth Wicket
113*	With F. S. Jackson v. Australia at Trent Bridge, 1905

For the Tenth Wicket
130	With R. E. Foster v. Australia at Sydney, 1903–04

BATTING AND BOWLING IN TEST MATCHES ON ENGLISH GROUNDS

Ground	No. of Tests	Inns	Not Outs	Runs	Highest Inns	100s	Average	Runs	Wkts	Average	5 wkts in Inns	Catches
Edgbaston ..	2	2	2	53	38*	0	—	34	8	4.25	1	2
Headingley ..	2	4	0	45	16	0	11.25	96	6	16.00	0	1
Lord's ..	5	5	0	114	59	0	22.80	246	9	27.33	0	0
Old Trafford ..	4	6	3	133	92	0	44.33	274	17	16.11	1	7
Sheffield ..	1	2	2	14	7*	0	—	96	6	16.00	1	1
The Oval ..	7	11	3	265	66	0	33.12	427	10	42.70	0	9
Trent Bridge ..	3	5	1	103	39*	0	25.75	246	11	22.36	0	2
Totals ..	24	35	11	727	92	0	30.29	1,419	67	21.17	3	22

BATTING AND BOWLING IN TEST MATCHES ON AUSTRALIAN GROUNDS

Ground	No. of Tests	Inns	Not Outs	Runs	Highest Inns	100s	Average	Runs	Wkts	Average	5 wkts in Inns	Catches
Adelaide ..	4	8	1	200	59	0	28.57	297	5	59.40	0	4
Melbourne ..	8	15	1	466	179	1	33.28	434	21	20.66	2	9
Sydney ..	8	15	1	366	69	0	26.14	480	16	30.00	1	2
Totals ..	20	38	3	1,032	179	1	29.48	1,211	42	28.83	3	15

BATTING AND BOWLING IN TEST MATCHES ON SOUTH AFRICAN GROUNDS

Ground	No. of Tests	Inns	Not Outs	Runs	Highest Inns	100s	Average	Runs	Wkts	Average	5 wkts in Inns	Catches
Cape Town ..	2	4	1	82	77	0	27.33	24	0	—	0	4
Durban ..	3	5	0	136	44	0	27.20	166	4	41.50	0	5
Johannesburg ..	4	7	0	270	152	1	38.57	138	4	34.50	0	9
Port Elizabeth	1	2	1	27	27	0	27.00	14	0	—	0	2
Totals ..	10	18	2	515	152	1	32.18	342	8	42.75	0	20

Signifies not out.

BATTING AND BOWLING IN TEST MATCHES ON WEST INDIAN GROUNDS

Ground	No. of Tests	Inns	Not Outs	Runs	Highest Inns	100s	Average	Runs	Wkts	Average	5 wkts in Inns	Catches
Bridgetown ..	1	1	1	14	14*	0	—	154	3	51.33	0	2
Georgetown ..	1	2	1	10	10*	0	10.00	189	4	47.25	0	1
Kingston ..	1	2	2	19	11*	0	—	39	2	19.50	0	0
Port-of-Spain ..	1	2	1	8	6*	0	8.00	71	1	71.00	0	0
Totals ..	4	7	5	51	14*	0	25.50	453	10	45.30	0	3

Mode of dismissal in Test matches: Bowled 17, caught 43, lbw 10, stumped 2, run out 5. Total 77.
How wickets have been taken in Test matches: Bowled 25, caught 85, lbw 11, stumped 5, hit wicket 1. Total 127.
In Test cricket W. Rhodes sent down 8,226 balls, and he bowled 364 maiden overs.
Against Australia at Melbourne in 1903–04 he took 15 wickets for 124 runs, seven wickets for 56 in the first innings and eight for 68 runs in the second innings.
W. Rhodes is the oldest player ever to have played in a Test match, being over 52 years when he played for England v. West Indies in 1929–30.

CENTURIES (58)

105	Yorkshire v. M.C.C. at Scarborough, 1901
107	Yorkshire v. Surrey at Bradford, 1904
196	Yorkshire v. Worcestershire at Worcester, 1904
108	Yorkshire v. Somerset at Harrogate, 1905
201	Yorkshire v. Somerset at Taunton, 1905
119	Yorkshire v. Leicestershire at Leicester, 1906
115*	Yorkshire v. Somerset at Bath, 1906
109	Yorkshire v. M.C.C. at Scarborough, 1906
112	Yorkshire v. Leicestershire at Leicester, 1907
105*	M.C.C. v. A. Victorian XI at South Melbourne, 1907–08
119	M.C.C. v. Tasmania at Hobart, 1907–08
122	Yorkshire v. Leicestershire at Harrogate, 1908
140	Yorkshire v. Northamptonshire at Huddersfield, 1908
146	Yorkshire v. Worcestershire at Sheffield, 1908
114	Yorkshire v. Essex at Headingley, 1909
101	Yorkshire v. Kent at Huddersfield, 1909
199	Yorkshire v. Sussex at Hove, 1909
101	Yorkshire v. M.C.C. at Scarborough, 1909
108	Yorkshire v. Australians at Sheffield, 1909
111	Yorkshire v. Sussex at Hove, 1910
100	Yorkshire v. Derbyshire at Sheffield, 1911
125	Yorkshire v. Sussex at Headingley, 1911
128	Yorkshire v. M.C.C. at Scarborough, 1911 (first innings)
115	Yorkshire v. M.C.C. at Scarborough, 1911 (second innings)
121	England v. The Rest at Lord's, 1911
102	M.C.C. v. Tasmania at Hobart, 1911–12
179	England v. Australia at Melbourne, 1911–12
119	M.C.C. v. New South Wales at Sydney, 1911–12 (first innings)
109	M.C.C. v. New South Wales at Sydney, 1911–12 (second innings)
107	Yorkshire v. Lancashire at Bradford, 1912
176	Yorkshire v. Nottinghamshire at Harrogate, 1912
110	Yorkshire v. Gloucestershire at Bristol, 1913
152	Yorkshire v. Leicestershire at Leicester, 1913
110	Yorkshire v. Northamptonshire at Northampton, 1913
102	Yorkshire v. Cambridge University at Cambridge, 1913
152	England v. South Africa at Johannesburg, 1913–14

Signifies not out.

CENTURIES (58)—*Continued*

113	Yorkshire v. Sussex at Bradford, 1914
105*	Yorkshire v. Lancashire at Hull, 1914
135	Yorkshire v. Hampshire at Dewsbury, 1919
167*	Yorkshire v. Nottinghamshire at Headingley, 1920
162	M.C.C. v. Queensland at Brisbane, 1920–21
210	M.C.C. v. South Australia at Adelaide, 1920–21
102*	Yorkshire v. Essex at Leyton, 1921
267*	Yorkshire v. Leicestershire at Headingley, 1921
104*	Yorkshire v. Northamptonshire at Northampton, 1921
156	Europeans v. Hindus at Bombay, 1921–22
183	Europeans v. Parsis at Bombay, 1921–22
108*	Yorkshire v. Essex at Harrogate, 1922
110	Yorkshire v. Glamorgan at Headingley, 1922
106	Yorkshire v. Hampshire at Bournemouth, 1922
105	Yorkshire v. Middlesex at Headingley, 1922
102	Yorkshire v. Essex at Dewsbury, 1923
126	Yorkshire v. Middlesex at Bradford, 1923
100	Yorkshire v. Somerset at Weston-super-Mare, 1924
157	Yorkshire v. Derbyshire at Headingley, 1925
114*	Yorkshire v. Somerset at Harrogate, 1925
132	Yorkshire v. Essex at Leyton, 1926
100*	Yorkshire v. Worcestershire at Worcester, 1928

EXCEPTIONAL BOWLING ANALYSES

6 for 24 Yorkshire v. Essex at Bradford, 1898
7 for 24 Yorkshire v. Somerset at Bath, 1898 (first innings)
6 for 21 Yorkshire v. Somerset at Bath, 1898 (second innings)
5 for 25 Yorkshire v. Leicestershire at Dewsbury, 1898
7 for 24 Yorkshire v. Surrey at Bradford, 1898
9 for 28 Yorkshire v. Essex at Leyton, 1899 (first innings)
6 for 28 Yorkshire v. Essex at Leyton, 1899 (second innings)
6 for 16 Yorkshire v. Gloucestershire at Bristol, 1899
8 for 38 Yorkshire v. Nottinghamshire at Trent Bridge, 1899
5 for 11 Yorkshire v. Somerset at Bath, 1899
9 for 24 C. I. Thornton's XI v. Australians at Scarborough, 1899
7 for 20 Yorkshire v. Worcestershire at Bradford, 1900
8 for 23 Yorkshire v. Hampshire at Hull, 1900
8 for 28 Yorkshire v. Essex at Harrogate, 1900
7 for 32 Yorkshire v. Derbyshire at Derby, 1900
7 for 20 Yorkshire v. Gloucestershire at Hull, 1901
6 for 4 Yorkshire v. Nottinghamshire at Trent Bridge, 1901
6 for 27 Players v. Gentlemen at Hastings, 1901
7 for 24 Yorkshire v. Middlesex at Bradford, 1902
5 for 22 Yorkshire v. Gloucestershire at Headingley, 1902
8 for 26 Yorkshire v. Kent at Catford, 1902
7 for 17 England v. Australia at Edgbaston, 1902
6 for 15 Yorkshire v. M.C.C. at Lord's, 1902
5 for 4 Yorkshire v. Worcestershire at Huddersfield, 1903
5 for 20 Yorkshire v. Gloucestershire at Sheffield, 1903
5 for 21 Yorkshire v. Essex at Sheffield, 1903
6 for 24 Yorkshire v. M.C.C. at Scarborough, 1903
5 for 6 M.C.C. v. Victoria at Melbourne, 1903–04
6 for 27 Yorkshire v. Hampshire at Headingley, 1904
6 for 9 Yorkshire v. Essex at Huddersfield, 1905
6 for 16 Yorkshire v. Cambridge University at Cambridge, 1905
6 for 22 Yorkshire v. Derbyshire at Glossop, 1907

*Signifies not out.

EXCEPTIONAL BOWLING ANALYSES—*Continued*

6 for 19 North v. South at Scarborough, 1907
6 for 17 Yorkshire v. Leicestershire at Leicester, 1908
6 for 29 Yorkshire v. Essex at Leyton, 1909
5 for 5 Yorkshire v. Derbyshire at Bradford, 1910
6 for 29 Yorkshire v. Surrey at Headingley, 1911
6 for 16 Yorkshire v. Derbyshire at Chesterfield, 1911
7 for 19 Yorkshire v. Derbyshire at Headingley, 1914
5 for 16 Yorkshire v. Warwickshire at Edgbaston, 1919
5 for 20 Yorkshire v. Essex at Dewsbury, 1920
5 for 16 Yorkshire v. Northamptonshire at Bradford, 1920
6 for 28 Yorkshire v. Worcestershire at Sheffield, 1920
8 for 39 Yorkshire v. Sussex at Headingley, 1920
7 for 24 Yorkshire v. Derbyshire at Derby, 1920
7 for 26 Europeans v. Hindus at Bombay, 1921–22
7 for 33 Europeans v. Parsis at Bombay, 1921–22
5 for 24 Yorkshire v. Gloucestershire at Bristol, 1922
6 for 13 Yorkshire v. Sussex at Hove, 1922
5 for 12 Yorkshire v. Warwickshire at Edgbaston, 1922
5 for 24 Yorkshire v. Worcestershire at Dudley, 1922
6 for 27 Rest of England v. R.A.F. at Eastbourne, 1922
6 for 23 Yorkshire v. Nottinghamshire at Headingley, 1923
7 for 15 Yorkshire v. Gloucestershire at Bristol, 1923
5 for 20 Yorkshire v. Cambridge University at Cambridge, 1923
6 for 25 Yorkshire v. Derbyshire at Huddersfield, 1924
6 for 22 Yorkshire v. Cambridge University at Cambridge, 1924
6 for 29 Yorkshire v. Somerset at Huddersfield, 1926
6 for 20 Yorkshire v. Gloucestershire at Dewsbury, 1927
9 for 39 Yorkshire v. Essex at Leyton, 1929
7 for 35 Yorkshire v. Cambridge University at Cambridge, 1930

W. Rhodes has taken 10 or more wickets in a match on 68 occasions, the chief of which are as follows–
15 for 56 Yorkshire v. Essex at Leyton, 1899
15 for 124 England v. Australia at Melbourne, 1903–04
14 for 68 Yorkshire v. Essex at Harrogate, 1900
14 for 192 Yorkshire v. Gloucestershire at Bradford, 1900
14 for 66 Yorkshire v. Hampshire at Hull, 1900
14 for 141 Yorkshire v. Gloucestershire at Bristol, 1901
14 for 211 Yorkshire v. Worcestershire at Worcester, 1903
14 for 139 Yorkshire v. Northants, at Northampton, 1911
14 for 77 Yorkshire v. Somerset at Huddersfield, 1926
13 for 45 Yorkshire v. Somerset at Bath, 1898
13 for 103 Yorkshire v. Gloucestershire at Cheltenham, 1900
13 for 96 Yorkshire v. Leicestershire at Leicester, 1901
13 for 152 Yorkshire v. Lancashire at Bradford, 1903
13 for 118 Lancashire and Yorkshire v. Rest at Hastings, 1903
13 for 108 Yorkshire v. Lancashire at Bradford, 1909
12 for 70 Yorkshire v. Sussex at Bradford, 1898
12 for 86 Yorkshire v. Gloucestershire at Hull, 1901
12 for 134 Yorkshire v. Middlesex at Lord's, 1901
12 for 182 Yorkshire v. Somerset at Taunton, 1901
12 for 159 Players v. Gentlemen at Hastings, 1901
12 for 195 Yorkshire v. Essex at Bradford, 1902
12 for 58 Yorkshire v. Gloucestershire at Headingley, 1902
12 for 52 Yorkshire v. Kent at Catford, 1902
12 for 128 Yorkshire v. Warwickshire at Edgbaston, 1904
12 for 130 Yorkshire v. Somerset at Taunton, 1907
12 for 115 Yorkshire v. Leicestershire at Dewsbury, 1909
12 for 80 Yorkshire v. Essex at Leyton, 1929

BOWLING UNCHANGED THROUGH A COMPLETED MATCH

1900 Rhodes (11 for 36) and Haigh (7 for 49) Yorkshire v. Worcestershire at Bradford
1901 Rhodes (6 for 37) and Hirst (12 for 29) Yorkshire v. Essex at Leyton
1903 Rhodes (7 for 55) and Haigh (12 for 52) Yorkshire v. Cambridge University
     at Sheffield
1903 Rhodes (10 for 81) and Hirst (10 for 67) Yorkshire v. Surrey at the Oval
1904 Rhodes (10 for 39) and Haigh (10 for 49) Yorkshire v. Hampshire at Headingley
1907 Rhodes (8 for 71) and Hirst (11 for 44) Yorkshire v. Derbyshire at Glossop

NINE WICKETS IN AN INNINGS

9 for 28 Yorkshire v. Essex at Leyton, 1899
9 for 24 C. I. Thornton's XI v. Australians at Scarborough, 1899
9 for 39 Yorkshire v. Essex at Leyton, 1929

EIGHT WICKETS IN AN INNINGS

8 for 38 Yorkshire v. Nottinghamshire at Trent Bridge, 1899
8 for 43 Yorkshire v. Lancashire at Bradford, 1900
8 for 23 Yorkshire v. Hampshire at Hull, 1900
8 for 72 Yorkshire v. Gloucestershire at Bradford, 1900
8 for 28 Yorkshire v. Essex at Harrogate, 1900
8 for 68 Yorkshire v. Cambridge University at Cambridge, 1900
8 for 53 Yorkshire v. Middlesex at Lord's, 1901
8 for 55 Yorkshire v. Kent at Canterbury, 1901
8 for 26 Yorkshire v. Kent at Catford, 1902
8 for 61 Yorkshire v. Lancashire at Bradford, 1903
8 for 87 Yorkshire v. Worcestershire at Worcester, 1903
8 for 68 England v. Australia at Melbourne, 1903–04
8 for 90 Yorkshire v. Warwickshire at Edgbaston, 1905
8 for 92 Yorkshire v. Northamptonshire at Northampton, 1911
8 for 44 Yorkshire v. Nottinghamshire at Bradford, 1919
8 for 39 Yorkshire v. Sussex at Headingley, 1920
8 for 48 Yorkshire v. Somerset at Huddersfield, 1926
W. Rhodes performed the hat-trick once—against Derbyshire at Derby in 1920

OUTSTANDING BOWLING ANALYSES

	Balls	Maidens	Runs	Wickets
Yorkshire v. Nottinghamshire at Trent Bridge, 1901 ..	47	4	4	6
Yorkshire v. Derbyshire at Bradford, 1910 ..	28	2	5	5
Yorkshire v. Gloucestershire at Gloucester, 1921 ..	198	26	19	3
Europeans v. Hindus at Bombay, 1921–22 ..	165	16	26	7
Yorkshire v. Nottinghamshire at Trent Bridge, 1929 ..	210	29	11	0
Yorkshire v. Gloucestershire at Bristol, 1930 ..	162	16	21	4
Yorkshire v. Lancashire at Headingley, 1930 ..	264	32	19	1

W. Rhodes in his first five seasons in first-class cricket took 1,058 wickets.

LARGE WICKET PARTNERSHIPS SHARED IN BY W. RHODES

For First Wicket
323   With J. B. Hobbs, England v. Australia at Melbourne, 1911–12
221   With J. B. Hobbs, England v. South Africa at Cape Town, 1909–10
211*   With J. B. Hobbs, M.C.C. v. Transvaal at Johannesburg, 1913–14
207   With J. B. Hobbs, M.C.C. v. Natal at Durban, 1909–10

For Second Wicket
368   With A. C. Russell, M.C.C. v. South Australia at Adelaide, 1920–21
206   With F. E. Woolley, M.C.C. v. Tasmania at Hobart, 1911–12
202*   With G. H. Hirst, Yorkshire v. Somerset at Bath, 1906

Signifies not out.

LARGE WICKET PARTNERSHIPS SHARED IN BY W. RHODES—*continued*

For Third Wicket
152   With C. P. Mead, England v. South Africa at Johannesburg, 1913–14
147   With J. W. Rothery, Yorkshire v. Sussex at Hove, 1909

For Fourth Wicket
266   With B. B. Wilson, Yorkshire v. Sussex at Bradford, 1914
160   With E. Oldroyd, Yorkshire v. Leicestershire at Sheffield, 1922

For Fifth Wicket
276   With R. Kilner, Yorkshire v. Northamptonshire at Northampton, 1921
170   With R. Kilner, Yorkshire v. Derbyshire at Headingley, 1925

For Sixth Wicket
229   With N. Kilner, Yorkshire v. Leicestershire at Headingley, 1921
210   With J. Hardstaff, Snr., M.C.C. v. Tasmania at Hobart, 1907–08

For Seventh Wicket
254   With D. C. F. Burton, Yorkshire v. Hampshire at Dewsbury, 1919
247   With P. Holmes, Yorkshire v. Nottinghamshire at Trent Bridge, 1929
170   With J. Iremonger, England v. The Rest at Lord's, 1911
157   With Biart, Europeans v. Parsis at Bombay, 1921–22

For Eighth Wicket
191*   With G. G. Macaulay, Yorkshire v. Essex at Harrogate, 1922
161   With E. Smith, Yorkshire v. M.C.C. at Scarborough, 1901
152   With J. W. Rothery, Yorkshire v. Hampshire at Portsmouth, 1904
151   With Lord Hawke, Yorkshire v. Somerset at Taunton, 1905

For Ninth Wicket
173   With S. Haigh, Yorkshire v. Sussex at Hove, 1902
162   With S. Haigh, Yorkshire v. Lancashire at Old Trafford, 1904

For Tenth Wicket
130   With R. E. Foster, England v. Australia at Sydney, 1903–04

* Signifies not out.

RHODES, William, who played once for Yorkshire in 1911, died on August 5, 1941, aged 56.

RHYS, Hubert Ralph John, who died in hospital on March 18, 1970, aged 72, enjoyed the distinction of hitting a century—149—for Free Foresters against Cambridge University at Fenner's in 1929 when making his first-class debut. In the XI at Shrewsbury in 1914 and 1915, he was captain in the second year and in 1929 and 1930 he played as an amateur in a few matches for Glamorgan.

RICE, Reginald William, died at Bedford on February 11, 1938, in his 70th year. Born at Tewkesbury, he played for Gloucestershire in 1890, three years before being given his Oxford Blue by L. C. H. Palairet.

Both Universities were very strong at that time. C. B. Fry, G. J. Mordaunt and H. D. G. Leveson Gower were in the Oxford XI besides the brothers Lionel and R. C. N. Palairet, while Cambridge, captained by F. S. Jackson, now Sir Stanley, included K. S. Ranjitsinhji, A. O. Jones, James Douglas, A. J. L. Hill, E. C. Streatfeild, C. M. Wells and L. H. Gay. Cambridge won by 266 runs.

This was the match in which C. M. Wells gave away eight runs by bowling wides in order to frustrate the apparent desire of Oxford to follow-on so that Cambridge would have to bat last. This incident and a repetition three years later brought about the change in the law placing the question of the follow-on at the option of the side who, having batted first, held a lead authorising them to enforce the law.

A steady batsman with admirable defence, Rice played for Gloucestershire until 1903 and when at his best he often opened the innings with W. G. Grace. He made some centuries, but never played a more valuable innings than his 82 not out at Bath in 1900. Going in first with 210 runs wanted for victory, Rice was missed in the slips when the game was a tie, the ball went to the boundary and Gloucestershire won by one wicket six minutes from time. The next highest score in the match was 66 by Lionel Palairet for Somerset, Rice's captain at Oxford.

After being a master at Forest School, Rice continued his scholastic career at Bedford and played for the county. He had a curious experience at Bury St. Edmunds in 1909 against Suffolk. The game was a tie with three Bedfordshire wickets to fall. Rice was indisposed and, though coming from his hotel, he did not have an opportunity to make the winning hit. All three wickets fell at one total and the match was a tie.

RICE, Father William Ignatius, O.S.B., M.A., who died at Douai Abbey on April 22, 1955, aged 72, was Headmaster of Douai School from 1915 to 1952. In his younger days he played for Warwickshire during the summer holidays and for some years enjoyed the distinction of being the only monk whose cricket performances were chronicled in *Wisden*.

RICHARDS, Lieut.-Col. Arthur Carew, was born on February 2, 1865, and died at Nottingham on November 9, 1930, aged 65. He was in the Eton XI in 1881 and two following years, and in his matches against Harrow and Winchester scored 118 runs besides taking 16 wickets. He became quite a good batsman of vigorous methods and he could also bowl a useful slow ball and field well at short-slip. He played occasionally for Hampshire and took part in much military cricket. In an inter-company game of the 2nd Hampshire Regiment at Barberton, South Africa, in October 1901, he made 101 not out and 185, scoring altogether 286 out of 311 from the bat. No one else could make more than two in the first innings (through which he carried his bat), nor more than six in the second. He also took eight wickets in his opponents' first innings.

RICHARDS, Cyril James Ridding, who was born on July 14, 1870, died on October 27, 1933. Educated at Lancing and Oxford, where he did not get his Blue, he played a little for Hampshire from 1889 to 1895.

RICHARDS, The Right Rev. Dr. Isaac, died at Christchurch, New Zealand, on May 10, 1936, aged 77. Born in Lincolnshire in 1859, he was educated at Taunton and Oxford where he was captain of the Exeter College Cricket XI. Going to Auckland he played for the local club and Dunedin; also in representative matches against touring sides. He was a sound batsman and reliable wicket-keeper. Curate at St. Paul's, Truro, before going to New Zealand, be became Anglican Bishop of Dunedin, an office he held for 14 years.

RICHARDS, Walter, born at Balsall Heath, September 28, 1865; died at Hollywood, near Birmingham, October 14, 1917. Warwickshire 1883–96. Best scores: 120 not out v. Yorks, at Edgbaston, 1889; 113 not out v. Hampshire, at Edgbaston, 1889; and 102 not out v. Cheshire, at Edgbaston, 1890. A stylish bat and fine field. It was a misfortune for Richards that he played most of his cricket before Warwickshire became a first-class county. Well-known as an excellent umpire in later years.

RICHARDSON, Alfred Graham, had his best season in England in 1897 when he scored 371 runs with an average of 21 for Gloucestershire. Born on July 24, 1874, he went to King's School, Canterbury, and appeared in Cambridge University trial games before playing in turn for Bedfordshire, once for Somerset and for Gloucestershire. He batted well for Orange Free State during several seasons from 1904. Headmaster at Umtata High School from 1917, he died there on December 17, 1934, aged 60.

RICHARDSON, Arthur J., a noted Australian Test cricketer of the '20s, died in his native Adelaide on December 23, 1973, aged 85. A tall, dark lean figure who wore glasses, Richardson was an extremely competent opening batsman who also bowled off breaks at medium pace. He played in nine Tests for Australia, all against England, between 1924 and 1926, and he hit one century at Headingley in 1926.

He first made his presence felt against M.C.C. when A. C. MacLaren took a side of amateurs reinforced by two professional bowlers, A. P. Freeman and H. Tyldesley, to New Zealand. They played in Australia on the way there and back. In the first engagement Richardson scored 150 and in the return match he hit a hundred before lunch—a feat never before performed in Australia—and went on to make 280, still the highest individual score for any State side against M.C.C.

In the famous match at the Oval in 1926, when A. P. F. Chapman captained England for the first time and recaptured the Ashes, England were caught on a sticky wicket, yet Hobbs and Sutcliffe batted through the two and a half hours before lunch on the third day and during the crucial one and a half hours from noon till lunch when the wicket was at its worst. Hobbs, dreading that H. L. Collins might put on Gregory, pretended to be in difficulties to encourage Collins to keep on Richardson, who was turning the ball towards his cluster of five short leg fieldsmen. Hobbs made 100 and Sutcliffe 161 and the timeless Test was finished in four days with England winning by 289 runs.

For South Australia, Arthur Richardson scored 3,755 runs, average 45.79, and his 117 wickets on those perfect pitches cost 39.41 runs each. Later he played a little for Western Australia besides appearing for Bacup in the Lancashire League. Arthur and Victor Richardson, who were unrelated, engaged in several big partnerships for South Australia.

RICHARDSON, Arthur Walker, who died in a nursing home at Ednaston on July 29, 1983, will be remembered as the captain under whom Derbyshire won the Championship in 1936, at a time when this was regarded as the prerogative of the "big six." After many vicissitudes, including a period when they were relegated to second-class status, Derbyshire had reached rock bottom in 1920 when they suffered the indignity of losing all their matches except one in which not a ball was bowled. For the change in their fortunes in the next 16 years they owed much to successive captains. G. M. Buckston for one season in 1921, G. R. Jackson for nine and then, for the last six, Richardson. He had a side rich in bowling, which he managed shrewdly, among other things seeing to it that Copson, who was to mean so much to the team in the future, was not overbowled at the start of his career. He did much also by his own enthusiasm and warm personality. A solid and slightly ungainly batsman, he scored mainly on the leg, but by determination and courage and keeping sensibly within his own limitations, he played many useful innings. By far his best season was 1932, when he scored 1,258 runs with an average of 29.95 and made the highest score of his career, 90 against Nottinghamshire at Ilkeston. In all, between 1928 and 1936, he made 3,982 runs with an average of 19.05. He was also a good mid-off. He had been in the Winchester XI in 1925 and had played an innings of 117 against Harrow, putting on 295 for the second wicket with E. Snell. His son, G. W.

Richardson, later represented Derbyshire with some success.

RICHARDSON, Charles Augustus, who died at Waipara, North Canterbury, on August 17, 1949, aged 85, scored the first hundred for New Zealand in a representative match.

Born in Sydney, New South Wales, he represented that state on several occasions before going to New Zealand in 1897. Within a few days of his arrival he turned out for Wellington and, scoring 77, helped to beat Canterbury by an innings and 20 runs. In 1900 he made 133 for Wellington against Otago and shared with F. Midlane in a fourth wicket stand of 207. The same year he represented New Zealand against the Melbourne C.C. at Christchurch and stayed four hours for 114 not out.

Richardson captained New Zealand against Lord Hawke's touring team in 1903, but scored only 44 runs in four innings. His last appearance for Wellington was against M.C.C. in 1906–07.

RICHARDSON, Henry, who died in March, 1940, aged 83, was a prominent bowler for Nottinghamshire some 50 years ago. He shared the honours in attack with Attewell, Shacklock and Flowers in 1889, when Nottinghamshire, Lancashire and Surrey were bracketed at the top of the Championship competition. Richardson took 53 wickets at 11.41 in 13 matches, the full programme consisting of 14 fixtures. Medium-paced, with both off and leg break, he kept an accurate length, seldom yielding runs readily. Occasionally he batted well when going in late, and at the Oval in 1887 he made 54 not out.

Before appearing first for his county in 1887, Richardson played for Gloucester, Newport and Liverpool clubs. In 1886 he took 149 wickets at seven runs apiece for Liverpool, and so earned a place in the North and South match at Lord's on the following Whit Monday, when the chief bowlers were engaged with their counties. He and J. T. Rawlin dismissed the South twice for an aggregate of 143. Richardson, bowling throughout both innings, disposed of nine batsmen for 64 runs, and the North XI won by six wickets in a day. This performance secured Richardson a place in the Nottinghamshire XI. Altogether for the county Richardson dismissed 139 batsmen at an average cost of less than 14 runs. He joined the ground staff at Lord's in 1889, and received a benefit in 1919.

RICHARDSON, Henry Adair, died at his

home in St. John's Wood on September 16, 1921. Born in London on July 31, 1846, he was in his 76th year. Mr. Richardson dropped out of first-class cricket while still a young man, and was only a name to the present generation. Old cricketers will remember him as a brilliant batsman, who for one season was quite in the front rank. He learnt the game at Tonbridge, he and the late J. W. Dale, if I am not mistaken, first making Tonbridge famous as a cricket school. In his last year in the XI he made scores of 157 and 150, going up to Cambridge with a big reputation. Still he did not get his Blue as a Freshman. He was in the Cambridge XI in 1867, 1868, and 1869, and, though meeting with no success as a batsman, was on the winning side in all three years against Oxford at Lord's. In 1868 he reached his highest point. It was his great season. He was the chief run-getter for a fine Cambridge team, heading the batting with an average—very high in those days—of 38. Early in the year he scored 97 and 51 for Sixteen of Trinity College against the United South of England XI, and against Surrey at the Oval he played an innings of 143 that remains historical. James Southerton was then in the first flush of his fame as a slow bowler, his pronounced off-break being almost as much dreaded as the googlies of the South African bowlers nearly 40 years later. Mr. Richardson treated Southerton as he had never been treated before, and gave a dazzling display of hitting. The innings gained him his place for Gentlemen against Players both at Lord's and the Oval. He failed at Lord's, but at the Oval he made 55. Like his contemporary, W. B. Money, and F. E. R. Fryer, who immediately followed him in the Cambridge XI, he was not half the batsman at Lord's that he was at Fenner's and the Oval. Without being great, Mr. Richardson was a good wicket-keeper, and in the University match in 1869 he got rid of six men—three stumped and three caught. Curiously enough the Oxford wicket-keeper, the late W. A. Stewart, was even more successful, catching six and stumping two. Mr. Richardson was an excellent billiard player—one of the best amateurs of his day—but he met more than his match in W. W. Rodger of Oxford.—S.H.P.

RICHARDSON, John Maunsell, who played for Harrow in 1864 and 1865, and for Cambridge in the three following years, died in London on January 22, 1912, in his 66th year. He was born at Limber, near Caistor, in Lincolnshire, on June 12, 1846, and was an all-round sportsman, excelling at racquets,

the long jump and hurdles, fencing, hunting and riding in addition to cricket. *Scores and Biographies* (viii–391) said of him: "Is an excellent batsman, a splendid field, generally at a distance from the wicket, and can bowl slow round-armed well. He promised to turn out a first-rate cricketer, had he only continued the game." According to the Hon. Spencer Lyttelton, he anticipated the glide, which is now almost universal. Among Mr. Richardson's contemporaries at Harrow were C. F. Buller, W. B. Money, M. H. Stow, and A. N. Hornby. He made 29 and 24 in his two matches with Eton, who were beaten on each occasion by an innings. Proceeding to Cambridge, he obtained his Blue as a Freshman, but, although he was on the winning side in two of his three matches with Oxford, he made only 42 runs in six innings. In the field, especially at cover-point, his work was admirable. He played little serious cricket after leaving the University, but his name will occasionally be found in Lincolnshire, Quidnuncs, I Zingari, and Na Shuler matches. Playing once for the Jockeys against the Press he scored 188. Mr. W. Richardson, who played for Harrow in 1863, was his brother, and Mr. H. G. Southwell, of the School XI in 1848 and 1849, his father-in-law. Mr. J. M. Richardson, who was one of the best gentlemen jockeys ever seen, rode the winner of the Liverpool Grand National in 1873 and 1874. An excellent portrait of Mr. Richardson, whose reminiscences of the Eton v. Harrow match appeared in the *Daily Telegraph* in 1908, was published in *Baily's Magazine* of November, 1889.

RICHARDSON, Leslie Walter, who died in Hobart on November 1, 1981, aged 70, was one of seven members of the same family who played for Tasmania, the others being his four brothers, his father and an uncle.

RICHARDSON, Samuel, who played for Derbyshire in the '70s of last century and for 16 years was assistant secretary of the County C.C., died in Madrid in March, 1938, at the advanced age of 93. A little man, he earned some fame as a wicket-keeper and batsman. He also was secretary of the Derby County Football Club.

RICHARDSON, Tom, whose tragic end caused such a painful shock to his friends, was born at Byfleet, August 11, 1870; died at St. Jean d'Arvey, July 2, 1912. He will live in cricket history as perhaps the greatest of all fast bowlers. Among the only men who can be placed with him are George Freeman, John Jackson, and William Lockwood. Many famous batsmen, among them Ranjitsinhji, contend that on his good days Lockwood was more difficult to play than Richardson, but for consistent excellence there was no comparison between the two bowlers. While he was at his best—from 1893 to 1897 inclusive—Richardson scarcely knew what it was to be out of form. Allowing for the excellence of the wickets on which he had to bowl, it is quite safe to say that his work during those five years has never been surpassed. Too much was exacted from him, but he ought not to have gone off as soon as he did. He began to lose efficiency before he was 28, and though for a year or two longer he did brilliant things he was never again his old self. A great increase in weight rather than hard work was responsible for his comparatively early decline. Looking at the matter in the light of after events, it was no doubt a misfortune that he paid a second visit to Australia. When in the autumn of 1897 he went out with Mr. Stoddart's second team, he was at the top of his form and the height of his fame, having just completed a wonderful season's bowling. In English first-class cricket in 1897 he took 273 wickets for less than 14½ runs each. One remembers that when Mr. Stoddart's team sailed from Tilbury, Maurice Read was full of forebodings as to the effect the tour might have on Richardson's future, thinking that a winter's rest after his strenuous labours would have been far better for him than Test matches on Australian wickets. After Richardson came home his falling off was plain for everyone to see. He took 161 wickets in first-class matches in 1898, but his bowling had lost its superlative quality, and only in two or three matches at the end of the season—notably against Warwickshire at the Oval—was he the old Richardson of the previous year. He continued to assist Surrey for several seasons, playing for the county for the last time in 1904. After that he lived for a time at Bath and appeared once at least in the Somerset XI, but he had become very bulky in figure, and his day for serious cricket was over.

In his prime Richardson had every good quality that a fast bowler can possess. Lithe and supple in figure he combined with his splendid physique an inexhaustible energy. While he kept his weight down to reasonable limits no day was too long for him. There have been faster bowlers—W. N. Powys, 40 years ago, and C. J. Kortright and Ernest Jones, the Australian, in our own day—but for sustained pace through a long innings he

perhaps never had an equal. Pace, however, was only one of his virtues. It was his pronounced off-break in combination with great speed that made him so irresistible. He took a long run up to the wicket and kept his hand very high at the moment of delivery. Purely a fast bowler, he did nearly all his best work on dry, run-getting wickets. A firm foothold was so essential to him, that he was far less effective after heavy rain than off-break bowlers of less pace, such as Spofforth and Charles Turner. Still, when the ground was dry on the surface and soft underneath he could be very deadly. One recalls a Surrey and Notts match at the Oval that began under these conditions. Mr. J. A. Dixon won the toss for Notts and, as it happened, practically lost the game before luncheon. Richardson on that August Bank Holiday was literally unplayable, fizzing off the pitch and breaking back five or six inches at his full pace.

As regards sustained excellence Richardson never did anything better than his wonderful effort in the last innings of the England v. Australia match at Manchester in 1896. After having made England follow on the Australians were left with 125 to get to win. They won the match by three wickets, but it took them three hours to get the runs. It was said at the time that during those three hours Richardson did not send down one really bad ball. He took six wickets and would have won the game if Briggs or Jack Hearne had given him any effective help. In the Test match at Lord's in the same season he did one of his finest performances, he and George Lohmann getting the Australians out on a perfect wicket for a total of 53. Richardson in that innings bowled 11 overs and three balls for 39 runs and six wickets. As contradictory statements have been made on the point, it is only right to say that at the outset of his career the fairness of Richardson's delivery gave rise to a great deal of discussion. When he came out for Surrey in 1892 his action was condemned by, among others, the late W. L. Murdoch, and when in the Whit Monday match at Trent Bridge in 1893 he gained for Surrey an easy victory over Notts, half the Notts XI expressed a positive opinion that he threw his very fast ball. However, he soon learned to straighten his arm, and little or nothing more in the way of adverse criticism was heard. Like a wise man, Richardson in his great days treated himself as a bowler pure and simple. He once scored 60 against Gloucestershire at the Oval, but he never took his batting seriously. His business was to get wickets and, with that end in view, he kept himself fresh, seldom staying in long enough to discount his bowling. He was one of the pre-eminent cricketers of his generation.

RICHARDSON'S BOWLING IN FIRST-CLASS CRICKET

Season			Balls	Runs	Wickets	Average
1892	..	..	1,173	602	29	20.74
1893	..	..	4,969	2,680	174	15.40
1894	..	..	4,683	2,024	196	10.32
1894–95 (in Australia)			3,554	1,616	69	23.42
1895	..	..	8,451	4,170	290	14.37
1896	..	..	8,282	4,015	246	16.32
1897	..	..	8,019	3,945	273	14.45
1897–98 (in Australia)			3,110	1,594	54	29.51
1898	..	..	6,119	3,147	161	19.54
1899	..	..	5,085	2,505	98	25.56
1900	..	..	5,999	2,949	122	24.17
1901	..	..	7,810	3,697	159	23.25
1902	..	..	5,305	2,607	106	24.59
1903	..	..	5,568	2,732	119	22.95
1904	..	..	787	446	9	49.55
1905	..	..	78	65	0	—
Totals	..	..	78,992	38,794	2,105	18.42

EIGHT OR MORE WICKETS IN AN INNINGS

Wkts	Runs			Season
10 for	45	Surrey v. Essex, at the Oval	..	1894
9 for	47	Surrey v. Yorkshire, at Sheffield	.. ..	1893
9 for	49	Surrey v. Sussex, at the Oval	.. ..	1895
9 for	70	Surrey v. Hampshire, at the Oval	..	1895
8 for	28	Surrey v. Warwickshire, at the Oval	..	1898
8 for	32	Surrey v. Cambridge University, at the Oval	.. ..	1894
8 for	36	Surrey v. Derbyshire, at Derby	.. ..	1893
8 for	40	Surrey v. Cambridge University, at Cambridge		1894
8 for	49	Surrey v. Kent, at Beckenham	.. ..	1897
8 for	52	Surrey and Sussex v. England, at Hastings		1898
8 for	52	England v. Queensland, at Brisbane	.. ..	1894–95
8 for	54	Surrey v. Leicestershire, at Leicester	.. ..	1892
8 for	82	Surrey v. Leicestershire, at the Oval	.. ..	1896
8 for	90	Surrey v. Essex, at Leyton	..	1900
8 for	91	Surrey v. Gloucestershire, at Clifton	.. ..	1895
8 for	94	England v. Australia, at Sydney	.. ..	1897–98
8 for	99	Surrey v. Yorkshire, at Leeds	.. ..	1897
8 for	108	Surrey v. Yorkshire, at the Oval	.. ..	1897
8 for	117	Surrey v. Essex, at Leyton	.. ..	1892

THIRTEEN OR MORE WICKETS IN A MATCH

15 for	83	Surrey v. Warwickshire, at the Oval	..	1898
15 for	95	Surrey v. Essex, at the Oval	.. ..	1894
15 for	113	Surrey v. Leicestershire, at the Oval	..	1896
15 for	154	Surrey v. Yorkshire, at Leeds	.. ..	1897
15 for	155	Surrey v. Hampshire, at the Oval	.. ..	1895
15 for	172	Surrey v. Essex, at Leyton	.. ..	1892
14 for	102	Surrey v. Kent, at Beckenham	.. ..	1897
14 for	145	Surrey v. Notts, at Nottingham	.. ..	1893
14 for	161	Surrey v. Warwickshire, at Edgbaston	..	1895
14 for	185	Surrey v. Essex, at Leyton	.. ..	1900
13 for	61	Surrey v. Gloucestershire, at Cheltenham	..	1894
13 for	99	Surrey v. Notts, at Nottingham		1894
13 for	131	Surrey v. Somerset, at the Oval	.. ..	1896

THIRTEEN OR MORE WICKETS IN A MATCH—*Continued*

13 for	134	Surrey v. Yorkshire, at Bradford	..	..	1895
13 for	135	Surrey v. Worcester, at the Oval	..	..	1903
13 for	141	Players v. Gentlemen, at Hastings	..	..	1897
13 for	152	Surrey v. Somerset, at Taunton	..	..	1895
13 for	193	Surrey v. Middlesex, at Lord's	..	..	1897
13 for	244	England v. Australia, at Manchester		..	1896

BOWLING UNCHANGED THROUGH TWO COMPLETED INNINGS

With Smith (F.E.)	Surrey v. Gloucestershire, at the Oval	1894
With Lohmann	Surrey v. Derbyshire, at Derby	1895
With Hayward	Surrey v. Leicestershire, at Leicester	1897

For Surrey v. Leicestershire, at Leicester, in 1897, he took 12 wickets for 20 runs and the match was completed in a day.

In first-class cricket, Richardson took 2,104 wickets for 18.43 runs each. In 14 Test matches, all against Australia, he obtained 88 for 25.22 runs apiece, and in Gentlemen v. Players matches 63 at a cost of 20.71 each.

RICHARDSON, Thomas Haden, born at Tutbury on July 4, 1865, died at his native place on December 10, 1923. He played for Staffordshire and, in 1895, for Derbyshire.

RICHARDSON, Victor York, who died on October 29, 1969, aged 75, was a noted all-round Australian sportsman for, besides taking part in 19 Test matches between 1924 and 1935, he represented his country at baseball and played for South Australia at cricket, baseball and golf. He also won a State tennis title, was prominent at lacrosse and basketball and was a first-rate swimmer.

As a cricketer, he attracted most attention by his remarkable fielding, his speed, agility and eminently safe hands making him prominent in any position. In batting, he was noted for forceful methods and during his career he scored 10,714 runs, average 37.59. He hit 27 centuries. He was at his best in driving and hooking. His highest innings was 231 for South Australia, whom he captained for some years, against A. P. F. Chapman's M.C.C. team at Adelaide in 1928; he reached three figures twice in the Sheffield Shield game with New South Wales at Sydney in 1924 and failed by only four runs to repeat the feat off the Queensland bowling at Brisbane in 1930. His biggest Test score was a spectacular 138 against A. E. R. Gilligan's 1924–25 England side at Melbourne, during which he achieved the rare feat of hooking H. Larwood, the Nottinghamshire fast bowler, for six.

Richardson played in all five Test matches of the "body-line" tour of D. R. Jardine's England team in 1932–33, he (83) and W. M. Woodfull (67) sharing an opening stand of 133 in the fourth Test at Brisbane. He was vice-captain to Woodfull in England in 1930 and led the unbeaten Australian team in

South Africa in 1935–36. In both these tours his batting proved something of a disappointment, though he made centuries against Leicestershire and Northamptonshire in 1930.

After retiring from active participation in cricket, "Vic" became a radio commentator of the game. His partnership "on the air" with Arthur Gilligan on the occasions of England visits proved immensely popular in Australia.

RICHARDSON, William Alfred, born on August 22, 1866, died at Sydney, N.S.W., January 3, 1930, aged 63. He was a stylish right-handed batsman, a useful fast bowler, and a brilliant field. In matches for New South Wales against Victoria he made 59 not out at Sydney in 1888–89 and 76 at Melbourne in 1895–96, and took four wickets for 18 runs at Sydney in 1887–88.

RICHARDSON, William Ethelbert, who died suddenly on November 5, 1971, aged 76, was in the Liverpool College XI before he played as an amateur fast bowler in a few matches for Worcestershire between 1926 and 1928. He also appeared for M.C.C. Free Foresters and Worcestershire Gentlemen. As a Rugby footballer, "Ritchie" assisted Moseley, Kidderminster and Bromsgrove, whom he captained. In 1924, he represented North Midlands against the All Blacks.

RICHES, Norman Vaughan Hurry, died in hospital on November 6, 1975, at the age of 92. He was a batsman who, had he in his prime played for a first-class county and been able to devote his time to the game, must have been a candidate for Test matches. He had the natural ability, the technique and the temperament. He first played for Glamorgan in 1901 and in the next 19 years scored heavily in the Minor Counties Championship (in 1911 he made 1,015 runs with an average of 92), but it was only on their promotion in 1921 when he was 38 that his first-class career really began.

Even then 1921 was his only full season. He managed to play a number of times each year until 1929 and, as he grew older, there were those who suggested that he was deliberately picking his matches in order to avoid the stronger bowling sides and particularly the sides which possessed really fast bowlers. These insinuations must have been silenced when in 1928 at the age of 45 he "picked" the Lancashire match at Old Trafford. That year Lancashire were Champions for the third time running: McDonald was still a great fast bowler and he and Dick Tyldesley were perhaps the most formidable combination in the country. Riches's answer was a superb second innings of 140. After 1929 he played little, though his final appearance was not until 1934.

It will be seen that he was seldom in full practice. Moreover he was usually the only batsman of real class in a very weak side. In the circumstances his record over these 13 years of 4,419 runs with an average of 33.99 is remarkable and gives some idea of what he might have accomplished 20 years earlier. He combined an impenetrable defence on the worst of wickets with intense power of concentration and yet at the same time was by no means a slow scorer—certainly a far quicker one than the average spectator realised. At the beginning of his innings his runs came mainly in ones and twos on the leg side, but he had in fact a full range of strokes, was very quick on his feet and fast between the wickets and was always looking for a chance to score. He was a master of the tactical single designed to bring about a rearrangement of the field, and, having achieved this object, took particular pleasure in putting the next ball into the gap created.

Another stroke, characteristic also of Arthur Shrewsbury and Harry Altham, was to lift the ball over the heads of the infieldsmen with just sufficient strength to clear them and secure two runs. The opposition thus found it extremely difficult to peg him down and it is small wonder that at times he would reduce bowlers to impotent fury. Indeed he regarded it as his duty to establish his ascendancy over them. He was a thorough cricketer, a beautiful field whether in the covers or the deep and a competent wicket-keeper, though, being a dentist, he was reluctant to keep except in an emergency for fear of damaging his hands. He captained Glamorgan in 1921 and in 1929 shared the captaincy with J. C. Clay. Later he was for 16 years the county's vice-chairman.

CAREER FIGURES IN ALL FIRST-CLASS CRICKET

Matches	Inns	Not Outs	Runs	Highest Inns	100s	Average	Catches	Stumpings
105	180	13	5,800	239*	9	34.73	42	5

CENTURIES (9)

177*	For Glamorgan v. Leicestershire at Leicester, 1921	
128	For Glamorgan v. Worcestershire at Worcester, 1922	
170	For Glamorgan v. Derbyshire at Swansea, 1924	
187*	For Wales v. M.C.C. at Lord's, 1925	
114	For Wales v. Ireland at Llandudno, 1925	
239*	For Wales v. Ireland at Belfast, 1926	
136	For Glamorgan v. Derbyshire at Pontypridd, 1926	
159	For Glamorgan v. Warwickshire at Cardiff, 1928	
140	For Glamorgan v. Lancashire at Old Trafford, 1928	

Signifies not out

RICHMOND, Thomas Leonard, who died on December 30, 1957, aged 65, was a prominent slow bowler for Nottinghamshire between 1912 and 1928. During his career in first-class cricket he took 1,158 wickets, average 21.24. The number of runs he scored exceeded his total of wickets by no more than 406, so that when he scored 70 in a last wicket partnership of 140 in 65 minutes with S. J. Staples against Derbyshire at Worksop in 1922 the general surprise may readily be imagined. The batting skill he displayed in this his highest innings was not repeated and it is as a skilful leg-break bowler who did not allow occasional heavy punishment to upset him that he will be remembered.

In one or two appearances in the county side before the First World War he accomplished little, but afterwards he became one of the best bowlers of his type in the country. He dismissed more than 100 batsmen in each of eight seasons, his best being that of 1922 when his 169 wickets cost him 13.48 runs each and exceeded the Nottinghamshire record of 163 set up by T. Wass in 1907. Among his most notable performances were: nine wickets for 21 in Hampshire's second innings at Nottingham in 1922; nine for 19 (three for nine and six for 10) in the match with Leicestershire at Trent Bridge and 14 for 83 (seven for 30 and seven for 53)—all in one day—against Gloucestershire at Cheltenham in 1925; 13 for 76 v. Leicestershire at Nottingham in 1920; 13 for 107 v. Essex at Leyton in 1922, and 13 for 165, including a hat-trick, v. Lancashire at Nottingham in 1926. For Pudsey St. Lawrence in 1920 he disposed of all 10 Lowmoor batsmen in an innings for 39 runs. "Tich" Richmond played in one Test match for England, against Australia at Trent Bridge in 1921, taking two wickets for 86 runs.

RICKETTS, George William, born at Allahabad, in India, on June 2, 1864, died in London on June 16, 1927, aged 63. He could hit with great power—his height was 6ft. 5in.—and was a good field at point. At Winchester he played in the XI in 1881, 1882, and 1883, appearing each year against Eton, and in the school sports won the 100 yd. and the high jump and threw the best ball. He also played racquets for Winchester. At Oxford he obtained his Blue in 1887. For his University against Lancashire, at Liverpool, that year he made 92 out of 126 in an hour and a half. The same season also he appeared in three matches for Surrey, and in the autumn of 1891 was a member of Lord Hawke's team which visited America. He had served on the Committee of the M.C.C. In 1909 he married the widow of Mr. E. H. Buckland. Since 1914 he had been Recorder of Portsmouth and since 1920 a Bencher of the Inner Temple. He unsuccessfully contested Winchester as a Liberal in January and December, 1910.

RICKETTS, James (Lancashire), who died in June 1894, will be chiefly remembered by cricketers of the present day for the extraordinary success that attended his first appearance in a county match. Playing for Lancashire against Surrey in June 1867, he went in first and took out his bat for 195. The hopes excited by this wonderful performance, however, were far from being realised, and though on some subsequent occasions Ricketts did fairly good work for Lancashire his career as a whole was a sad disappointment. He was 52 years of age at the time of his death, having been born in 1842.

RIDDING, The Rev. Charles Henry, elder brother of Messrs. Arthur and William Ridding, died at Kneller Court, Fareham, on March 13, 1905. He will always be remembered as a splendid wicket-keeper and long-stop, never using pads or gloves. He was, in addition, a good steady batsman. He played for Winchester in 1842 and 1843, for Oxford against Cambridge in 1845–49, and for the Gentlemen v. Players from 1848 to 1853. He scored 33 and 26 against Cambridge in 1848, and 27 not out and 14 the following year. Owing to his profession—the Church—he was obliged to discontinue the game much earlier than he otherwise would have done. In the Gentlemen v. Players match at Lord's in 1849 he performed the extraordinary feat of stumping Hillyer off the terrific bowling of Mr. Harvey Fellows. His principal scores in important matches were 75 for Oxford University v. Cowley, at Oxford, in 1847; 63 for Oxford University v. Clapton, at Clapton, in 1846; 63 for Gentlemen of Hampshire v. Gentlemen of Sussex, at Brighton, in 1858; and 53 for Oxford University v. Cowley, at Oxford, in 1848. He was born at Winchester on November 26, 1825, was 5ft. 5½in. in height and weighed 10st. 9lb. His name will be found in the Oxfordshire XI from 1859 to 1864, and in that of Hampshire from 1861 to 1865. He occasionally played under the assumed name of Charles.

RIDLEY, Arthur William, one of the finest all-round players of his day, died suddenly at his home, 92 Eaton Place, on August 10, 1916. Mr. Ridley was a first-rate batsman of the true Eton type, a superb field in whatever place he chose to fill, and a capital lob bowler. As an amateur lob bowler he was nearly the last of a long line that included V. E. Walker, T. C. Goodrich, E. T. Drake, W. M. Rose, and W. B. Money. Almost his only successor was Jephson. The professional lob bowlers ended practically with Walter Humphreys. Ridley had not so much spin as some of the men named, but he had excellent judgment, and was quick to find out a batsman's weak points. In fielding his own bowling he was brilliant indeed, fearing nothing. Ridley was in the Eton XI in 1870 and 1871, and in the Oxford XI from 1872 to 1875. He played a very fine innings of 117 against Harrow in 1871, but in his four matches against Cambridge he scored only 61 runs in seven innings, once not out. Captain of the Oxford team in 1875, he won a sensational match against Cambridge at Lord's by six runs. Cambridge had gone in to get 175, and with seven wickets down the score reached 161, or only 14 to win, H. M. Sims and W. S. Patterson being well set. At this point Mr. Ridley put himself on with his lobs, and with his first ball he bowled Patterson. G. Macan was next in, and amid great excitement seven runs were added. Then a very fine catch at long on got rid of Sims. A. F. Smith, the last Cambridge man, had to face Ridley, and the situation proved too much for him. He stopped two balls, but the third clean bowled him, and the match was over. That was the greatest day of Ridley's cricket life. Except the two runs' victory for Cambridge in 1870, when F. C. Cobden did the hat trick, there has never been such a finish to the University match.

During his career Mr. Ridley did many brilliant things in the cricket field. His highest innings in first-class matches was 136 for Middlesex against Surrey at Lord's in 1883, but perhaps his best was 103 for Gentlemen against Players at Lord's in 1876. He played for Hampshire from 1875 to 1878 and for Middlesex from 1882 to 1885. In Gentlemen and Players matches he scored 491 runs with an average of 24.55 and took 19 wickets. Though good enough for any XI he was never picked for England against Australia. For the Gentlemen of England against the Australians at Lord's in 1884, however, he played an innings of 68—the highest score on the side. He was born at Newbury, Berkshire, on September 11, 1852.—S.H.P.

RIDLEY, G. V. N., who died on November 12, 1953, aged 57, was a member of the Executive Committee of Essex County C.C. from 1929 until his death. He made a few appearances for the county during three seasons from 1924, his best innings being 54 against Gloucestershire at Colchester. He was a Justice of the Peace.

RIGHTON, Edward Grantham, who played as an amateur for Worcestershire in four matches from 1911 to 1913, died in Evesham Hospital on January 3, 1964, aged 79. His best innings was 48 against Leicestershire at Worcester in 1911.

RILEY, Harry, who was born at Thackley on August 17, 1875, and died on November 6, 1922, at Bradford, had been an excellent left-hand medium-paced bowler. He appeared a few times for Yorkshire in 1895 and 1900, but with little success. In Bradford and Lancashire League cricket, however, he obtained hundreds of wickets, taking 840 in eight seasons in the latter organisation's matches.

RILEY, Martin, died in June 1899, aged 48. Though never reaching the front rank, Mr. Riley was in his day an extremely good free hitting batsman. He was at his best about the end of the '70s and appeared occasionally in the Yorkshire XI.

RILEY, Gunner William, (attached R.G.A.), born at Newstead, August 11, 1886; killed by a shell splinter in Belgium, August 9, 1917. His early cricket was played for Newstead Colliery C.C.; first match for Notts in 1909. Left-hand slow-medium bowler. Did good work in 1911. He promised well, but never came up to expectation in County Cricket. In 1911 he took 47 wickets for Notts in Championship matches, but they cost just over 23½ runs each. Played very little County Cricket in 1914, appearing for Oldfield Uttoxeter C.C. In his two games v. Longton he took nine wickets for nine runs, and all 10 for 31—19 out of a possible 20. When he and Alletson (189) added 152 for the 10th wicket of Notts v. Sussex at Brighton, in 1911, in 40 minutes, Riley's share was 10 not out.

RILEY, William Nairn, who died at Hove on November 20, 1955, aged 62, gained a Blue as opening batsman for Cambridge in 1912 when the Light Blues, following a tie on the first innings, beat Oxford in an exciting struggle by three wickets. The result might have been even closer had not G. E. V. Crutchley, after reaching 99 not out in the first Oxford innings, been compelled to retire from the match owing to measles. From 1911 to the outbreak of the First World War in 1914, Riley, who was educated at Worcester Grammar School, appeared for Leicestershire with no special distinction except in 1913. That season he scored 521 runs, average 22.65, and registered a hard-hit century against Yorkshire at Leicester. Actually he obtained 100 out of 141, at one point 60 out of 72 in 40 minutes, punishing G. H. Hirst for 24 in an over. In the same match he brought off a remarkable right-hand catch in the long field when dismissing M. W. Booth. He was a vice-president of Sussex.

RINGROSE, William, well known on cricket grounds as the Yorkshire scorer and held in high esteem by all who came in personal touch with him, died at his home at Crossgates, Leeds, on September 14, 1943, aged 72. In his official capacity he scored the first-wicket record of 555 made by Herbert Sutcliffe and Percy Holmes at Leyton in June 1932, and was on duty at Hove on September 1, 1939, when the only County Cricket concluded that day, before the crisis stopped first-class cricket, brought victory to Yorkshire by nine wickets over Sussex in James Parks' benefit match. The bowling analysis of the Sussex second innings, showing the last performance by Hedley Verity—six overs, one maiden, nine runs, seven wickets—written by Ringrose, was kept by Major Brian Sellers, and found in his blazer pocket at Lord's when the sad news of Captain Verity's death was announced. Besides these historic events, Ringrose placed on paper many remarkable performances during the seasons from 1923 to 1939. Yorkshire started and finished that period as champion county and altogether took chief honours 10 times, with Ringrose chronicling in the score-book all that happened.

He brought practical knowledge to bear on this work, having played for the county occasionally from 1901 to 1906, and would have found more opportunities to show his worth but for the presence of Sir Stanley Jackson, George Hirst, Wilfred Rhodes and Schofield Haigh in the Yorkshire XI during those years. In 1905, his best season, he took 73 wickets at 19 runs apiece, excelling against the Australians at Bradford by dismissing nine men at a cost of 76 runs in the first innings. Described as one of the first bowlers to develop the "out-swinger," Ringrose said that this ball led to a fieldsman being placed in the "gully." Bowled at the stumps and swinging away it caused batsmen much trouble. Among other bowlers who profited by his advice was William Bowes, so valuable to Yorkshire for several seasons before the Second World War. Before playing for Yorkshire, Ringrose was on the staff of the Liverpool club at Aigburth, and after finishing his county experience he enjoyed marked success in Scotland for several years.

RIPPON, Albert Dudley Eric, who died on April 16, 1963, aged 70, opened the innings with his twin brother, A. E. S. Rippon, for Somerset between 1914 and 1920. A patient amateur batsman, he scored 1,043 runs, average 20.05. In making the first of his two centuries, he carried his bat for 105 against Sussex at Bath in 1914 though lame and having to employ a runner. When hitting 134

from the Essex bowling at Leyton in 1919, he shared with his brother in a partnership of 144. Troubled by the effects of a wound received in the First World War, he played only one innings in 1920 and never appeared afterwards.

RIPPON, Arthur Ernest Sydney, who died on April 13, 1966, aged 73, played as an amateur for Somerset between 1914 and 1937. At his best a brilliant batsman, on a number of occasions he opened the innings for the county with his twin brother, A. D. E. Rippon. In all, Arthur Rippon hit 3,833 runs, including six centuries, for an average of 20.17 and he held 46 catches. One of his best innings was that at Portsmouth in 1928, when he scored 112 and he and A. Young (92) made 197 in less than two and a half hours for the first wicket. J. C. White taking six wickets for 35 in the Hampshire second innings, Somerset triumphed in an innings with 28 runs to spare.

RITCHIE, Lieut.-Col. David Maudsley, who died at Stevenage on September 10, 1974, aged 82, played in one match for Lancashire in 1924 against Northamptonshire at Liverpool. He was in the Loretto XI.

ROACH, Flight-Sergt. W. A., a left-hand opening batsman from Western Australia, who appeared in the two 1944 Whitsuntide matches at Lord's for Australia, was shortly afterwards killed during operations against the enemy. He was 29.

ROBBINS, Victor Clark, who died at Durban on June 16, 1947, aged 56, played for Natal from 1920 to 1927, making 571 runs, average 24.82, in the Currie Cup Tournament, his highest score being 80 v. Transvaal in 1923–24. In January 1925 he took part in one of the unofficial Test matches against S. B. Joel's team.

ROBERTS, Albert William, who died in Clyde, N.Z., on May 13, 1978, aged 68, was a member of the 1937 New Zealand side in England. Regarded at the outset of his career simply as a bat, he owed his place in the first Test against Harold Gilligan's team in 1929–30 to a couple of useful innings at a crisis for Canterbury against the tourists. Two years later he played in both Tests against the South Africans in New Zealand and in the first made 54. However by 1937 he had developed into a good medium-pace opener who could swing the ball and get considerable pace from the pitch. Unfortunately that summer shoulder trouble, and later a damaged finger, took the life out of his bowling and left it for the most part merely negative. Even so, with 62 wickets at 26 runs each and 510 runs with an average of 22.50, he was an extremely useful member of the side, especially as he was a brilliant slip. Moreover he had a way of getting runs when they were wanted; in the Lord's Test he made 66 not out and at the Oval 50, both very valuable innings which left him at the top of the Test match batting averages. The second Test he had missed through injury. His highest score during the season was 82 v. Sussex. He was no stylist, but had a strong defence and could hit hard in front of the wicket. In all in his five Tests spread over seven years he scored 248 runs with an average of 27.55.

ROBERTS, Christopher Paul, was killed by a fall when climbing in Borrowdale on June 9, 1977, aged 25. Born at Cleethorpes, he played a few times for Lincolnshire in 1971 and 1972 and once for Worcestershire in 1974. He was a right-hand batsman and a medium-pace bowler.

ROBERTS, Desmond, who died on January 11, 1968, aged 72, was educated at St. Bees where he was in the XI. He played on occasion for Surrey Second XI and took part

in several first-class matches for M.C.C. In 1920 he toured America with the Incogniti and during a stay in that country captained Hollywood C.C. for five years.

ROBERTS, Capt. Francis Bernard (Rifle Brigade), born at Anjini Hill, near Nasik, India, on May 20, 1882, fell in action on February 8, 1916. He was in Rossall XI in 1898 and three following years, and during his last three seasons performed thus:

1899	259 runs (average 19.92) and 33 wickets (average 14.12)	
1900	314 runs (average 24.07) and 59 wickets (average 13.08)	
1901	287 runs (average 26.09) and 27 wickets (average 24.51)	

In each of these years he took most wickets, and in batting was first in 1899 and second in each of the other seasons. At Cambridge he obtained his Blue for cricket and hockey, and he played against Oxford in 1903, scoring only 0 and one and taking six wickets for 153 runs; Oxford won by 268 runs. Earlier in the year, when appearing for Next Sixteen v. First Twelve, he had played an innings of 71 and obtained eight wickets for 52. Later he assisted Gloucestershire and gained many successes. Among his best scores for the county were:

103*	v. Essex, at Bristol	1908
88 } 129 }	v. Surrey, at Bristol	1909
157	v. Worcestershire, at Cheltenham	1910
154*	v. All India, at Bristol	1911
138	v. Worcestershire, at Cheltenham	1911

Signifies not out.

In 1909, when he played 10 innings, he headed the Gloucestershire averages with 40.60 in Championship matches. In the game v. Surrey, at Bristol, in 1906, he and Dennett bowled unchanged throughout, the latter taking 15 wickets for 88 runs, including all 10 in the first innings for 40. Mr. Roberts, who had played occasionally for Oxfordshire, may be summed up as a good batsman and field and a very useful right-handed fast bowler. He always played in glasses. His brother, Mr. A. W. Roberts, has also assisted Gloucestershire.

ROBERTS, Frederick G., the fast left-hand bowler, died in Bristol on April 7, 1936, aged 74. Born on April 1, 1862, Fred Roberts was a member of the Gloucestershire XI from 1887 to 1903. In the course of 250 matches

for the county he took 940 wickets for just over 21 runs apiece. In 1901 he dismissed 118 batsmen at an average of under 23 runs, and two years later when he really finished his active career, he at times showed his best form, 79 batsmen falling to him at a cost of less than 16 runs each. He made one appearance in 1905.

Roberts accomplished many notable performances but did nothing better than on his first appearance for the county at Dewsbury, where he took seven wickets in each Yorkshire innings for an aggregate of 171 runs. It was then written of him that "he was able to get a lot of work on the ball both ways." He bowled 138 overs in the match, which Yorkshire won by 70 runs within 10 minutes of time, thanks to Wade, who, after rain had made the pitch treacherous, took six wickets for 18 runs. In 1891 at Brighton, Roberts took 12 Sussex wickets for 59 runs, seven for 16 in the second innings. Twelve years later at Bristol, he and Dennett, slow left-hand, bowled throughout both of Surrey's innings, Roberts claiming 11 wickets for 93 runs and being largely responsible for a fine victory by 18 runs.

G. L. Jessop has described how Roberts made the ball swerve and it is a noteworthy fact that this fast left-handed bowler played for 10 seasons before a batsman was given out leg-before to him.

Although possessing little skill as a batsman, Roberts often proved very useful by keeping up his end in case of emergency. In 1897 at Bristol, when nine Gloucestershire wickets had fallen for 63 runs before the Lancashire attack, he helped F. H. B. Champain put on 74 and he was not out seven when the Oxford Blue was caught for 97. Six years later, also at Ashley Down, Roberts stayed while W. S. A. Brown hit the Sussex bowlers so freely that 104 runs came before the amateur was out for 155. Roberts had 11 for his share of the runs added by this stand.

Appointed a first-class umpire in 1906, Roberts "stood" regularly in County Cricket matches until the end of the 1914 season. Following the long stoppage of County Cricket by the War, Roberts officiated again in 1919, but then his active career on the field closed.

ROBERTS, Henry Edmund, who died on June 28, 1963, aged 73, played as a professional for Sussex from 1911 to 1925. A fast bowler, he took during that time 340 wickets for 24.27 runs each and hit 2,312 runs, average 13.21, besides holding 66 catches. His most successful season with the ball was that of 1922, when he and Maurice Tate, bowling unchanged, disposed of Yorkshire, the eventual Champions, at Hove for 42. Each bowler took five wickets for 20 runs. "Curly" Roberts hit his highest innings against Worcestershire on the same ground in 1920, he and G. Stannard sharing in a partnership of 209. In 1914, too, he shone as a batsman when scoring 62 of a last-wicket stand of 112 with Albert Relf (175 not out) from the Lancashire bowling at Eastbourne.

ROBERTS, Thomas Webb, a well-known cricketer in Ceylon, died during 1976 at the age of 96. In 1908 he made 70 against an M.C.C. side which included the amateurs returning from the Australian tour. Educated at Harrison College, Barbados, and Hertford College, Oxford, he made 51 in the Freshman's match in 1898 and 54 in the Seniors' match in 1899, but was never tried for the University.

ROBERTS, William B., died suddenly at Bangor, North Wales, on August 24, 1951, at the age of 36, after a relapse following an operation several months before. A left-arm slow bowler of considerable ability and a most likeable personality, Roberts first appeared for Lancashire in 1939. He came into national prominence in war-time cricket and played in three of the 1945 Victory matches against the Australians. When County Cricket resumed in 1946 he took 123 wickets in all matches. Though not so successful in 1947 (81 wickets), he failed by only one to claim a hundred victims in the following season when his performances included six for 73 (with a spell of five for 29) for Lancashire against Don Bradman's Australian side at Old Trafford. He obtained 71 wickets in 1949, but by this time two other left-arm bowlers, M. Hilton and R. Berry, were challenging for places in the county XI, and in 1950 he did not play in any county games. Nevertheless he gave splendid assistance to Lancashire Second XI, for whom he took 71 wickets, before joining West Bromwich Dartmouth in the Birmingham League. Unfortunately his health broke and he played little more cricket. Lancashire recognised his loyal services by awarding him a testimonial which realised £3,000.

ROBERTSON, G. P., who was in the Oxford XI in 1866, died in Australia in the spring of 1895. Mr. Robertson had lived in the Colonies for many years, and held a far more prominent place in Australia than he ever did in English cricket, playing several times for Victoria against New South Wales, and in 1873 captaining the Eighteen of Victoria that beat Mr. W. G. Grace's XI at Melbourne in a single innings.

ROBERTSON, W. R., died in June, 1938, aged 76. He played for Victoria in 1884–85 against Alfred Shaw's team, scoring 33 for once out and taking eight wickets in the match for 82 runs. Wilfred Flowers, of Nottinghamshire, dismissing eight men for 88 in Victoria's second innings, helped the Englishmen to win by 118 runs. For the Combined XI of Australia, beaten by 10 wickets at Melbourne, Robertson got only two runs and was unsuccessful with the ball. He did not play for the full strength of Australia in the other three matches—all five were eventually included as "Tests." Robertson went to America in 1888 and, returning to Australia after 10 years, played in minor cricket for several seasons.

ROBERTSON, William, at one time probably the best bowler in New Zealand, died in April, 1912. For many years he played with marked success for Canterbury and Southland, his best feat perhaps being to take 13 wickets for 163 for Canterbury v. Wellington at Christchurch in 1894–95. He was nothing of a bat, but was in great request as a coach.

ROBERTSON, William Parish, died on May 7, 1950, at Debden, near Saffron Walden, aged 70. In the Harrow XI from 1896 to 1898, he went to Cambridge and gained a Blue in 1901. A fast-scoring, attractive batsman, he subsequently played for Middlesex up to 1914. In 1914 he scored 580 runs, average 38.66, in Championship matches, including 130 against Nottinghamshire at Trent Bridge. He toured America in 1899 under K. S. Ranjitsinhji.

ROBERTSON-GLASGOW, Raymond Charles, who died suddenly on March 4, 1965, aged 63, was both a distinguished player and a celebrated cricket writer. In the Charterhouse XI in 1918 and 1919, he did specially well as opening batsman and fast-medium bowler in the second year, when he scored 537 runs, average 38.36, and took 44 wickets for 18.52 runs each, including six for 90 against Winchester. Going up to Oxford, he gained a Blue as a Freshman and played against Cambridge for four years from 1920 to 1923. He appeared for Somerset with varying frequency from 1920 to 1937 and played five times for Gentlemen v. Players between 1924 and 1935.

In all first-class cricket he scored 2,083 runs, average 12.93, dismissed 464 batsmen at a cost of 25.74 runs each and held 79 catches. After his schooldays, he was better known as a tall bowler able to swing the ball appreciably, and he achieved such notable performances for Somerset as nine wickets for 38 runs in the first innings of Middlesex at Lord's in 1924; seven for 56 and seven for 50 against Sussex at Eastbourne and six for 60 and five for 87 against Gloucestershire at Bristol in 1923 and five for 47 and five for 37 against Warwickshire at Weston-super-Mare in 1930. That he did not altogether lose his batting skill he showed in 1928 when, opening the Somerset innings with A. Young, he shared in stands of 160 against Essex at Knowle and 139 against Worcestershire at Taunton in following matches. His highest

innings was 80 from the Hampshire bowling at Taunton in 1920.

He was known to his host of friends as "Crusoe," a nickname which came to him as the outcome of a match between Somerset and Essex. C. P. McGahey, the Essex and England amateur, was in and out so rapidly that the next batsman, who had not been watching the play at the time, asked what had happened. "First ball," explained McGahey, "from a chap named Robinson Crusoe."

Of considerable personal charm, an infectious laugh, and possessing an infallible sense of humour which found its way into his writings when he became cricket correspondent in 1933 for *The Morning Post*, "Crusoe" was popular wherever he went. He later wrote for *The Daily Telegraph*, *The Observer* and *The Sunday Times*, contributed a number of articles to *Wisden* and was the author of many books, including *Cricket Prints*, *More Cricket Prints*, *46 Not Out*—an autobiography—*Rain Stopped Play*, *The Brighter Side of Cricket*, *All In The Game* and *How To Become A Test Cricketer*.

His stories regarding the game he loved were many and various, but never ill-natured. One against him concerned the occasion when he was in the Pavilion at Lord's during the match following the University game of 1922. A friend introduced him to a certain celebrated Pressman who, as was his wont, paid little attention to his name. When the friend left them, the Pressman, endeavouring to make conversation, enquired: "Did you see Chapman's wonderful innings in the Varsity match?" For once "Crusoe" was speechless. A. P. F. Chapman had hit a brilliant 102 for Cambridge, a big proportion of his runs coming at the expense of Robertson-Glasgow, who sent down 43.1 overs for 97 runs and did not take a wicket!

ROBERTSON-WALKER, James, born in Edinburgh on November 10, 1850, died in London after a long illness on March 21, 1927, aged 76. *Scores and Biographies* said of him: "Is a hard hitter, fields well at short-slip, but is principally noted for his fast round-armed bowling, which is, at times, very destructive." He was in the XI at Edinburgh Academy, but not in that of Oxford, and his fame rests on what he did for Middlesex. Between 1878 and 1891 he took 295 wickets for the county for 21.91 runs each, among his best figures being six for 22 v. Surrey in 1878, four for eight v. Yorkshire in 1879, eight for 48 v. Nottinghamshire in

1881, five for 20 v. Surrey in 1885, and seven for 35 v. Nottinghamshire in 1886. Against the first Australian team at Lord's in 1878 he obtained three wickets in four balls. He also appeared for Scotland in representative matches, and twice assisted the Gentlemen against the Players. He had served on the Committee of the M.C.C., of which club he had been a member since 1876.

ROBINS, Robert Walter Vivian, who died at his home near Lord's on December 12, 1968, aged 62, will live in history as one of the most dynamic all-round cricketers of his time. In three of his four years in the XI at Highgate School he headed both batting and bowling averages, being captain in the last, 1925, when, with an innings of 206 and seven wickets for 54 runs against Aldenham his outstanding performance, he scored 816 runs, average 62.76, and dismissed 60 batsmen for 15.18 runs apiece. He also captained the Highgate football XI. In 1925, while still at school he made his first appearance for Middlesex, for whom he played irregularly until 1950. In all first-class cricket, he hit 13,940 runs, average 26.45, and took 946 wickets at 23.59 runs each—figures which do not convey his true worth.

From an early age, "Robbie" was taught the rudiments of the game by his father, a Staffordshire player, and as a boy he assisted East Molesey C.C. He attributed his success to "an indefatigable, patient male parent," but, whatever the reason, he always displayed an aggressively enterprising attitude to the game, whether in batting, bowling, fielding, particularly at cover point, or in captaincy, which made him immensely popular with spectators and frequently swayed the course of a match.

He got his Blue as a Freshman at Cambridge in 1926 purely as a batsman, scoring 37 and 21 not out. In the next season's University match he hit 55 and 41, sending down only one over; but in 1928 he not only put together innings of 53 and 101 not out, but took eight wickets for 151 runs, almost bringing success over Oxford. That gained him a place in the Gentlemen's team against the Players for the first of numerous occasions. Impatient of dull cricket, Robins wasted few scoring opportunities as a batsman, employing his nimble footwork and flexible wrists to the full, especially in cutting and driving. His example transformed a hitherto drab Middlesex side when he took over the captaincy from 1935 to 1938. He also led the county in 1946, 1947—when they carried off the Championship—and 1950.

In his first full season for them, 1929, he achieved his only "double," scoring 1,134 runs, including one century, and taking 162 wickets, but more than once he came near repeating that feat. He took part in 19 Test matches for England, being captain in the home series with New Zealand in 1937, and in these he made 91 runs, average 22.75, and took eight wickets for 21.62 runs each. His highest innings in a Test was 108, when runs were sorely needed, against South Africa at Old Trafford in 1935, and his best bowling analysis six wickets for 32 runs against the West Indies at Lord's in 1933. His one major tour abroad was to Australia in 1936–37, when he was vice-captain under G. O. Allen. Unfortunately he broke a finger of the right hand at fielding practice in the first week of the tour with the result that he could not spin the ball and achieved small bowling success. At the age of 45, he captained the M.C.C. team which visited Canada in 1951, meeting with considerable all-round success.

As a bowler of leg-breaks and googlies, Robins could not always command a good length; but though he sometimes came in for punishment, he was always capable of producing a telling delivery. Twice he did the hat-trick for Middlesex: against Leicestershire in 1929 and against Somerset in 1937, both at Lord's. At Trent Bridge in 1930, he bowled Sir Donald Bradman with a googly to which that famous batsman did not offer a stroke and virtually won the game for England. One recalls, too, an occasion at Lord's when Robins, arriving late through business claims, put himself on to bowl directly he took the field. Nottinghamshire at that time were making runs comfortably, with F. W. Stocks, the left-hander, well set. The last ball of an over from Robins pitched so near the end of the popping crease on the batsman's off-side that he completely ignored it. To his astonishment, the ball turned almost at right-angles and hit the stumps! No wonder that "Robbie" doubled up with laughter.

As a Test team selector, Robins served from 1946 to 1949 and again in 1954 and was chairman of the Committee from 1962 to 1964. He began this latter period by issuing an ultimatum to first-class cricketers: "Play aggressively at all times; otherwise you will not be chosen for England." It cannot be said that this produced precisely the results desired, but at least it relieved Test cricket of some of the stagnation which threatened its popularity at the time. Robins also ably filled the position of manager of the M.C.C. team in the West Indies in 1959–60.

As an Association footballer, he displayed

much of the same dash which distinguished him on the cricket field. He played on the right wing for Cambridge in the University matches of 1926, 1927 and 1928, being captain in the second season, and he appeared with credit for that celebrated amateur club, the Corinthians. He also took part in League football with Nottingham Forest.

Tributes included:

S. C. Griffith: "Walter was one of the most dynamic cricketers with whom I played. His tremendous enthusiasm and deep knowledge of the game and its history made him the complete cricketer. As an administrator he always proved extremely helpful."

I. A. R. Peebles: "I think that he was the most enthusiastic and joyous cricketer I played with. In addition he possessed an unparalleled knowledge of the game."

D. J. Insole: "Walter's death is a sad blow. He was the greatest exponent ever of 'brighter cricket,' though never for its own sake, but because he believed such cricket achieved greater success. As a selector his judgment of a player was excellent."

A. W. Flower (Middlesex C.C. Secretary): "Mr. Robins was still a member of the county's General and Cricket Committees. He was a wonderful character, a dynamic personality both on and off the field."

ROBINSON, Arthur, died at Northampton on February 11, 1945, aged 76. He played cricket, Rugby football and hockey for his county, and for several seasons was a highly successful full-back for the Northampton R.F.C.

ROBINSON, Canon Cyril Deason, a notable South African wicket-keeper, died at Kearsney, Natal, on August 26, 1948, aged 75. He never played in a Test match, but was reserve wicket-keeper and vice-captain of the strong South African team that toured England in 1907 under P. W. Sherwell. Born at Durban on July 18, 1873, he played against W. W. Read's English team of 1891-92 while still at school. Proceeding to England, he played in several matches for Cambridge University in 1895 and 1896, but failed to obtain his Blue. He appeared for Buckinghamshire and was a member of Frank Mitchell's team which visited America in 1895. On returning to South Africa, he frequently kept wicket for Natal sides until the First World War, and, as late as January 1923, captained the Natal Northern Districts XI that opposed the M.C.C. team.

ROBINSON, C. W., who first represented

Wellington in 1911-12, died on May 22, 1948, aged 55. A fast bowler, he was a member of the 1913-14 New Zealand team, and played in some Service matches in England during the First World War.

ROBINSON, Lieut.-Col. Douglas Charles, who died on July 30, 1963, aged 79, played for Gloucestershire from 1905 to 1926, being captain in the last three years. In all matches, he hit 4,239 runs, average 16.95, and brought off 173 catches and 44 stumpings. He kept wicket for Marlborough in 1901 and appeared for Essex before joining Gloucestershire, for whom his best season was that of 1925 when he scored 838 runs, average 18.62. Only once did he reach three figures, when in 1912 he obtained 150 not out from the Worcestershire bowling at Worcester. He played six times for Gentlemen v. Players between 1912 and 1919 and was a member of the Gentlemen team who beat the Australian Imperial Forces by an innings and 133 runs at Lord's in 1919.

ROBINSON, Edward, who died on September 3, 1942, at Clifton, Bristol, aged 79, played one match for Yorkshire in 1887, scoring 23. He settled in Bristol when married and was a familiar figure in Gloucestershire sporting circles.

EMMOTT ROBINSON
Born on November 16, 1883, and died on November 17, 1969, played for Yorkshire from 1919 to 1931 and afterwards became a first-class umpire.

An appreciation by
Neville Cardus

Emmott Robinson was as Yorkshire as Ilkley Moor or Pudsey. He was the personification of Yorkshire cricket in one of its greatest periods, the '20s, when the county appeared to look forward towards winning the Championship by a sort of divine right. He came to first-class cricket in his late 30s—and "thrive he did though bandy."

Statistics tell us little of his essential self; in 12 seasons he scored 9,444 runs and took 892 wickets. Many cricketers have surpassed these figures; few have absorbed the game, the Yorkshire game, into their systems, their minds, nerves and bloodstreams, as Emmott did. Yorkshire cricket was, for him, a way of living, as important as stocks and shares.

With Rhodes he established the unwritten Constitution of Yorkshire cricket, the skipper content to serve in a consultative capacity. Nowadays we hear much of the supposition to the effect that first-class cricket in recent years has become "more scientific" than of yore. To speak the truth, there are few players of our latest "modern" times who would not seem to be as innocent as babes talking tactics and know-how in the company of Rhodes and Emmott.

It was these two shrewd men who evolved—with rival competition from Makepeace and Co. in Lancashire—the protective philosophy: how to close a game up, how to open it out, how to stifle the spin on a "sticky" wicket with the "dead" bat. "Loose grip on top of 'andle," said Emmott.

The shrewdness, humour, uninhibited character of North of England life was marvellously revealed and fulfilled in Yorkshire v. Lancashire matches of the '20s. Gates closed at noon; 30,000, even 40,000, partisan spectators watching. Watching for what? "Bright cricket"? Not on your life.

"We've won the toss." Harry Makepeace would announce in the Lancashire professionals' dressing-room. "Now lads, no fours before lunch." And Emmott Robinson was already polishing the new ball, holding it up to the light of day, as though investigating an egg. He bowled outswingers, for in his heyday the lbw rule rendered inswing more or less harmless. He swung the ball from middle and leg, compelling a stroke of some sort.

He was shocked if anybody "wasted new ball." After he had bowled the first over, he would personally carry the new ball, in cupped hands, to the bowler at the other end.

At Bradford in 1920, he took nine wickets in an innings against Lancashire. At a crisis for Yorkshire too! Lancashire needed only 52 to win, six wickets in hand. Then Emmott turned the game round violently. For some reason or other, I did not, in my report of the match, praise Emmott in generous enough language. I was not a convert to seam bowling in those days; and am not a bigoted convert yet. When Emmott next met me he said, "Ah suppose if Ah'd tekken all 10 Lanky's wickets, tha'd have noticed me."

As a batsman he exploited pad-play to perfection. Remember that the lbw law of Emmott's halcyon years permitted a batsman to defend with his pads a ball pitching outside the off stump. If any young greenhorn, batting for Yorkshire or Lancashire, were to be bowled by an off break, he received severe verbal chastisement. "What dos't think thi pads are for?" was Emmott's outraged inquiry.

Emmott was one of the pioneer students of the "green wicket" and its habits. One day,

at Headingley, rain soaked the field, then the sun shone formidably. After lunch Emmott and Rhodes walked out to inspect the pitch. Arrived there, Rhodes pressed the turf with a forefinger and said, "It'll be sticky at four o'clock, Emmott." Whereat Emmott bent down and also pressed the turf with a forefinger. "No, Wilfred," he said, "half-past."

These grand Yorkshiremen in general, and Robinson in particular, never were consciously humorous. Emmott was a terribly serious man. He could not, as Freddie Trueman did, play for a laugh. One summer at Lord's, Yorkshire got into dire trouble against Middlesex. During a tea interval I ran into Emmott. "Hey dear," he growled, "fancy, just fancy Yorkshire getting beat by Middlesex. And wheer *is* Middlesex? Is it in Lundin?" A far reaching question; because London swamps county boundaries and identities. We know what county means in Yorkshire and Lancashire.

Emmott merged his ability as cricketer into the Yorkshire XI entirely; by sheer power of will he added a technical stature which, elsewhere, might not have amounted to much. A celebrated Indian batsman, introduced to Rhodes in Rhodes's wonderful blind old age, said he was honoured to meet so "great a cricketer." "Nay," said Wilfred, "Ah never considered myself a Star. I were just a good utility man."

Thus might Emmott have spoken; no part, no individual, was greater than the part of any Yorkshire team. "Aye," Emmott once reminded me, "and we are all born and bred Yorksheer. And in thy county, tha's tekken in Ted McDonald. A *Tasmanian*, mind you," as though a Tasmanian was beyond the pale.

He maintained an average of round about 24 while compiling more than 9,000 runs in his years of active service. The point about his use of the bat, aided and abetted by the broadest pads procurable, is that every stroke he ventured to make was part of a plan, designed to win the match for Yorkshire or save it.

I imagine that in all his days in the sun and rain, his keen eyes were as constantly on the clock as on the score-board. But, in the field, crouching close to the bat, he missed nothing. A lordly batsman who could hit asked Emmott to move away a little, for the sake of self-preservation. "Thee get on with thi laikin', and Ah'll get on with mine," retorted Emmott—and for the benefit of the uninitiated I herewith translate: "laikin'" means playing; "get on with thy playing."

As I write this tribute to Emmott Robinson, with as much affection as admiration, I am bound in fairness to memory of him, to recount an incident at Old Trafford in 1927. The wicket prepared in those days, for the Lancashire and Yorkshire match, was a batsman's sleeping bed stuffed with runs. Match after match was unfinished—none the less, a grim fight for first-innings points (78,617 rabid Lancastrians and Yorkshiremen paid to watch the Lancashire v. Yorkshire match at Old Trafford in 1926, no fours before lunch.

Over after over did Emmott resist on this occasion in time and space, when he was, with Rhodes, salvaging his county. Suddenly, for no reason, in fact, as he later admitted, against all reason, he indulged in a most elegant late-cut towards third man. So transfixed was he by this stroke that he stood there contemplating it. And when he emerged from the realm of aesthetic contemplation to the world of unescapable reality, Wilfred Rhodes was on his doorstep and was run out. Consequently Yorkshire lost. "Fancy," he said sorrowfully to me (years after), "fancy. What could Ah'ave been thinkin' about? Me and mi cuts! But, mind you, Wilfred should never 'ave come runnin' down the pitch. Runs didn't matter with game in that sta-ate. They counted for nowt." He was an economist. Must not waste new ball.

One Saturday Yorkshire batted all day at Lord's, scoring 350 or thereabouts. Sunday morning was drenching, a thunderstorm cleared up by noon, followed by dazzling sun. In Hyde Park near four o'clock I came upon Robinson and Rhodes. "A lovely afternoon," I said to them, in greeting. "Aye," snapped Emmott, "and a sticky wicket waastin' at Lord's."

He was richly endowed by native qualities of character, and gave himself, heart and soul and with shrewd intelligence, to Yorkshire cricket. That's why he is remembered yet; that's why no statistics can get to the value of him. The score-board cannot reflect human nature, Yorkshire human nature, in action. He was not named Emmott Robinson for nothing.

ROBINSON, G. E., an Oxford Blue 1881 to 1883, died on November 30, 1944, at Acton, near Newcastle, Staffordshire. Born on March 13, 1861, he was 83 years old. He bowled fast left hand with a natural break back. Mr. Dover Betham advised me of his death, which removes all doubt as to M. C. Kemp being the oldest living University Blue. Contemporary with Robinson at Oxford, Kemp kept wicket for Kent until 1895. Kemp was born on September 7, 1861.

ROBINSON, J. Sandford, died at Worksop Manor, on April 21, 1898. Born on February 4, 1868, he had only recently completed his 30th year. The immediate cause of death was a fall from his horse, but he had for some time been more or less out of health. His sudden death at such an early age was a great shock to his large circle of friends. Educated at Harrow and Cambridge Mr. Robinson, despite strenuous efforts, did not succeed in getting into the XI either at school or the University, but he played with considerable success for Notts, being at his best for the county in 1892. He had the pleasure that year of taking part in two memorable matches—one against Middlesex, at Lord's, and the other against Surrey, at the Oval, on the August Bank Holiday. At Lord's he scored 72, and with a catch at the wicket off Attewell's bowling, gave Notts a single innings victory within four minutes of time. This was the match in which Sherwin's bowling changed the whole position after a draw had seemed inevitable. A free attractive batsman, Mr. Robinson gave promise at one time of greater things in the cricket field than he ever achieved.

ROBINSON, John James, who died on January 3, 1959, aged 86, was a "double Blue" for Cambridge. He played cricket against Oxford at Lord's in 1894 and took part as a forward in the University Rugby football match in 1892. He also played Rugby for Yorkshire and for England, gaining four International caps.

ROBINSON, Lieut.-Col. P.G., D.S.O., D.L., J.P., who died at Queen Charlton, Somerset, on January 30, 1951, aged 68, played occasionally for Gloucestershire between 1904 and 1921. His highest score was 66. He was captain of the Clifton College XI in 1900.

ROBINSON, Theodore, who died on October 4, 1959, aged 93, played in a few matches for Somerset between 1892 and 1894. He was a member of a cricketing family who from 1878 onwards fielded a Robinsons XI in an annual match against Flax Bourton.

ROBINSON, Commander Vivian John, RN (retired), who died at Warminster on February 28, 1979, aged 81, was a member of the famous Backwell House family who for many years regularly produced their own XI, and a younger brother of D. C. Robinson, who captained Gloucestershire. A useful batsman and fast-medium bowler, he appeared for Gloucestershire against Oxford University in 1923.

ROBSON, Charles, died on September 27, 1943, in his 85th year. After playing a little for Middlesex, he was actively associated with Hampshire from 1891 to 1906, captaining the county in four seasons, 1889 to 1902. A useful wicket-keeper, he went to America with K. S. Ranjitsinhji's team in 1899, and in 1901–02 was deputy to A. A. Lilley for A. C. MacLaren's side in Australia. Then 42 years of age, he did not play in any Test match. In 1903 he appeared for Gentlemen against Players at the Oval. Often playing a good innings, he scored 52 out of 113 added with Captain J. G. Greig for Hampshire against Lancashire at Liverpool in 1901. Greig scored 296 without being dismissed in a match that was always an uphill fight for his side, and, thanks to his efforts, was drawn. Tall and of robust build, Robson hit hard besides showing skill in defence.

ROBSON, Ernest, born at Chapel Allerton, in Yorkshire, on May 1, 1871, died at Bristol, after an operation, on May 23, 1924. He had played for Somerset as recently as 1923 and had been placed on the Umpire's list for 1924, so that his death came as a great shock. A most useful all-round cricketer, he could hit freely and well, was a capital right-hand medium-paced bowler, and worked hard in the field. After appearing for Cheshire from 1891 to 1893, he qualified for Somerset, a county he began to assist in 1895 though not regularly until a year later. Among his chief innings for the latter county were 104 v. Surrey at the Oval in 1900; 163 not out v. Oxford University at Oxford and 102 v. Hampshire at Taunton, both in 1901; 103 and 85 not out v. Gloucestershire at Taunton in 1909, and 111 v. Worcestershire at Worcester in 1921, when aged 50. He was probably at his best as a batsman in 1899 when, in all first-class matches, he scored 1,048 runs with an average of 31.75. In Somerset's match with Middlesex at Weston-super-Mare in 1922, the latter declared and lost by two wickets: off the second ball of what would in any case have been the last over of the match Robson made the winning hit by sending a ball from Hearne (J.W.) out of the ground for six, a feat for which he received an anonymous gift of £50. As a bowler he was responsible for many very

good performances. Against the Australians at Taunton in 1896 he took six wickets for 22 runs, and in the corresponding match at Bath in 1909 eight for 35. He also claimed 14 for 96 v. Derbyshire at Taunton in 1914, five for 14 v. Hampshire at Bath in 1898, four for eight v. Kent at Taunton in 1902, four for 10 v. Yorkshire on the same ground the same year, four for 12 v. Derbyshire at Taunton in 1913 and seven for 19, also against Derbyshire, at Bath in 1919. He did the hat-trick v. Hampshire at Bath in 1898 and v. Yorkshire at Taunton in 1902, while as far on as 1919, when in his 49th year, he bowled unchanged with Mr. J. C. White through both innings of Derbyshire at Derby. At one period during the match with Sussex at Hove in 1897 he bowled 50 balls without a run being made off him. At Bridgwater on November 2, 1919, he was presented with a cheque for £178 subscribed in recognition of his valuable services to Somerset cricket, the presentation being made by S. M. J. Woods. In 1905 he was given the match with Worcestershire at Taunton for his benefit, and in August 1922 the game against the same county on the same ground was played on behalf of his family.

ROCHDALE, Baron, C. B., who died on March 24, 1945, aged 78, at Lingholm, Keswick, earned fame as an admirable batsman for Cambridge University and Lancashire 50 years ago when George Kemp—knighted in 1909, he became a peer in 1913. He learned cricket at Mill Hill School before going to Shrewsbury where he played in the school XI from 1882 to 1884. Starting at Cambridge with 100 in the Freshmen's match he gained his Blue in a strong side captained by the Hon. M. B. Hawke (afterwards Lord Hawke) in 1885. With useful scores of 29 and 26 he helped in a victory by seven wickets over Oxford at Lord's, but fared less well next year, when Cambridge lost by 133 runs. That, however, was his best season in first-class cricket, for he headed the Cambridge averages with 31, and excelled against Yorkshire, with 125 in the follow-on at Fenner's where the county lost a stirring match by 26 runs, while in the return at Sheffield his 103 was the highest innings in the match, which Yorkshire won by seven wickets. Unable to play for Cambridge in 1887 he re-appeared next season when he averaged 30.9, but did little in a drawn University match.

In 1885 for Lancashire he played a grand innings of 109 against Yorkshire, scoring the runs out of 156 without giving a chance in an uphill struggle. For Gentlemen of England against Australians in 1886 at Kennington Oval his 83 was the next highest score to 148 by W. G. Grace, and only S. P. Jones, with 151 for the Australians, did better in a drawn match. Such brilliant performances were intermittent and George Kemp failed to repeat this form during his few subsequent appearances for Lancashire, but he retained his interest in the County Club as a Vice-President. Of good height and build he batted in splendid style, with special power in front of the wicket strokes, and fielded very well at mid-off.

He played for Cambridge in the Lawn Tennis Doubles in 1886 and excelled in Trinity College Athletic Sports. He enjoyed all outdoor pursuits until very late in life, notably game shooting. Mentioned in Dispatches when serving with Imperial Yeomanry in South Africa, 1900–02, he also commanded a Battalion of the Lancashire Fusiliers in the First World War, and altogether was a Territorial officer for over 30 years. From 1929 he was Lord Lieutenant of Middlesex. As a Liberal Unionist he was M.P. for the Heywood Division from 1895 for 10 years and in two elections in 1910 held his seat as a Liberal.

ROCK, Dr Harry Owen, who died in Sydney on March 10, 1978, aged 81, had a unique career. His six first-class matches, spread over three Australian seasons, 1924 to 1927, produced 758 runs with an average of 94.75; his four Sheffield Shield matches 560 runs, average 112. In his first match for New South Wales he scored 127 and 27 not out, and in his next 235 and 51: then room had to be found for Collins, Bardsley, Taylor, Andrews and Kelleway and he was omitted! Two more Sheffield Shield matches and one against Western Australia, in which he scored 151, with a Test Trial match in 1926–27 completed his career. Qualifying as a doctor and practising in Newcastle, he was lost to Australian cricket: otherwise he must surely have ranked among the great. Though slightly built, he was a tremendous driver and had a wonderful gift of placing the ball and a basic soundness of technique which enabled him, as an opening batsman, to score at a great pace without taking undue risks. He was a son of C. W. Rock, the Cambridge Blue and Warwickshire player.

RODGER, Sir John Pickersgill, K.C.M.G., who was born in London on February 12, 1851, died in London on September 19, 1910, a few days after his return from seven years' service as Governor of the Gold Coast. He was in the Eton XI in 1869 and 1870 and in the latter year was described as "A good sound bat, though his style is peculiar; may generally be depended on for runs; slow in the field, but much improved." In his four Public School matches he made 116 runs in six innings and on three occasions was on the winning side. He did not obtain his Blue at Oxford, and his connection with Kent was restricted to a single match—with M.C.C., at Canterbury, in 1870. Mr. W. W. Rodger, who played occasionally for Kent, was his elder brother.

RODWELL, John, who played for Leicestershire in three matches in 1878, scoring 38 runs in six innings, died in March, 1911. He will be remembered chiefly on account of the sensational catch he made on the boundary which dismissed Frank Allan in the first innings of the Australians.

ROE, William Nichols, died in a London nursing home after an operation on October 11, 1937. A very well-known figure in the world of cricket from the time that he played with great success for the Clergy Orphan School, Canterbury, until last summer, when at the age of 76 he regularly attended Lord's and the Oval, W. N. Roe maintained his close connection with the game unbroken.

For his school in 1878 he scored 1,095 runs, including four 100s, with an average of 57. Next year he took all 10 Chartham Asylum wickets for 16 runs, and in three seasons for the school 292 wickets fell to him at eight runs each. Going to Magdalene College, Cambridge, he received his Blue in 1883 from C. T. Studd, but, though on the winning side, he did not get a run and the Oxford wickets were shared by his captain and C. Aubrey Smith. He was famous already for the highest score then on record, having made 415 not out when, on invitation, he completed the Emmanuel Long Vacation Club XI in a game against Caius Long Vacation Club in 1881. W. N. Roe got these runs out of 708 for four wickets in five hours. This was in reply to a score of 100 and Caius gave up the match rather than continue on the third day. So close was his concentration on the game that he counted all his runs and on this occasion he challenged the scorer with having given him one less than his total.

He played for Somerset in 1879 before leaving school, and his first experience of County Cricket was being bowled by W. G. Grace, as he said, "neck and crop." He followed E. Sainsbury as captain of Somerset in 1889 and played intermittently for the county of his birth until 1899, his highest score being 132 against Hampshire at Bath in 1884. He also made hundreds against Devon, Middlesex, Sussex and Surrey, all at Taunton.

Always ready to talk cricket, W. N. Roe told how when playing for Cambridge at Old Trafford it was so cold that the fieldsmen could not hold catches. Nash, the Lancashire professional, was missed off every ball of an over from R. C. Ramsay. C. T. Studd bowled the next ball, and "a catch came to me at mid-off, the crowd began to boo and I felt certain I should not make the catch, but by great good fortune the ball stuck!"

A stylish batsman with excellent defence, and a resolute hitter all round the wicket, he bowled medium pace and was a safe fieldsman, usually in the deep. W. N. Roe was a master at Elstree School from 1883 to 1900, and helped to make Elstree Masters famous in club cricket. These traditions were maintained when he went with the Rev. Vernon Royle to Stanmore Park School.

ROGERS, Stuart Scott, who died suddenly on November 6, 1969, aged 46, captained Somerset and also acted as secretary from 1950 to 1952. Educated at Highgate, he became captain of the XI. His first season for Somerset, in which he hit 1,030 runs, was his best, but he was generally a useful batsman, strong in driving and pulling. He took 107 not out, the highest innings of his first-class career, off the bowling of A. D. Nourse's South African team at Taunton in 1949 and, in hitting 102 not out against Northamptonshire at Glastonbury in 1952 in H. Gimblett's benefit match, registered his second 50 in half an hour. A Chindit in the Second World War, Rogers assisted Middlesex Club and Ground before joining Somerset.

ROLLER, Charles Trevor, who was born at Clapham Common on February 28, 1865, died at Eastbourne in November, 1912. He was in the Westminster XI in 1881 and 1882, and in 1886 played for Surrey v. Middlesex at Lord's, scoring 14 and one, and in both matches v. Essex, making four at the Oval and 10 not out and seven not out at Leyton. In his last year at Westminster it was said of him: "Having a good reach, plays forward straight, hard, and well-timed; rather slow between wickets. Good long-stop."

ROLLER, William Eyton, Vice-President of the Club, who played for Surrey in their great days of the '80s when they won the Championship six years running, died at his London home on August 27, 1949, aged 91. He was one of the finest all-round cricketers who, going to Cambridge, was never tried for the University. A high-class batsman, free in method and having many strokes at his command, he also possessed considerable skill as a medium pace bowler with a high delivery. Born at Clapham on February 1, 1858, he was educated at Westminster and in that XI in 1873 had the only double figure average.

Over 6ft. high and weighing nearly 13 st., he first appeared for Surrey in 1881, but although he was seen in his county's ranks in 1890, his really active career, owing to injuries and impaired health, did not extend beyond seven seasons. He established himself as a class player on the occasion of Surrey's match with Lancashire at the Oval in 1883. The Lancashire bowlers included Briggs, Crossland, Barlow, Watson and Nash, and Surrey—set 234 to make to win—lost seven wickets for 122. The game looked as good as over, but on K. J. Key—afterwards Surrey's captain—joining Roller, 56 of the 112 runs then required were obtained overnight and the remaining 56 next morning. The performance of the two young batsmen stood out as one of the best of the season. Against Sussex at the Oval in 1885 he scored 204 and did the hat-trick and in the return encounter at Brighton he made 144. In 1887 at Old Trafford, when Surrey put together a total of 557, Roller made 120 and W. W. Read 247, the two batsmen sharing in a third wicket partnership of 305. Altogether he scored 3,822 runs for the county with an average of nearly 22 and took 188 wickets for 19 runs each. Roller assisted the Gentlemen against Players twice at Lord's and once at the Oval and in 1885 and 1886 toured the United States and Canada with E. J. Sanders' team, acting as captain of the side in the latter year. In addition to his ability as a cricketer he was a fine swimmer and Association football player. Surrey members and visitors to the pavilion at the Oval will remember him by the striking portrait which hangs in the Long Room of him going out to bat.

ROMANS, George, died suddenly at Bedminster on January 2, 1946, aged 69. Playing for Gloucestershire from 1899 to 1903, he scored 218 runs, average 13.62, and was at one time a member of the County C.C. Council. Rugby full-back for Gloucester, he captained the side from 1901 to 1905, and appeared for the county.

ROME, David Audley Moberley, who died as the result of a fall at the Oval on May 20, 1970, aged 60, appeared occasionally for Middlesex between 1931 and 1933. A son of Brigadier-General C. S. Rome, who captained Harrow in 1893, he was in the XI of that school from 1926 to 1929, being captain in the last year when he scored 74 and 27 not out against Eton, 90 against Winchester and headed the batting averages with 69.25. Going up to Cambridge, he did not gain a Blue. He later played for Surrey Second XI, Harrow Wanderers, I Zingari and the Free Foresters. For many years until his death, he was a member of the Surrey County Committee.

ROMNEY, Francis William, who died on January 28, 1963, aged 89, played for Worcestershire before they attained first-class status in 1889 and occasionally in 1900. Educated at Malvern, he was in the XI.

ROOT, Charles Frederick, who died in the Royal Hospital, Wolverhampton, on January 20, 1954, aged 63, was celebrated as a leading exponent of "leg-theory" bowling. Born in Derbyshire on April 16, 1890, Fred Root, as he was always known, served for a time on the Leicestershire ground staff before commencing his first-class career with the county of his birth in 1910. After five seasons of moderate success as an orthodox bowler came the First World War, and in 1921 Root joined Worcestershire.

With his new county he changed his style, bowling fast-medium in-swingers on the leg stump with five fieldsmen stationed on the leg-side close to the batsman. So successful did these tactics prove that from 1923 onwards he took over 100 wickets in nine successive seasons, eight times heading the county averages. His best year was 1925 when, with 219 victims, average 17.21, he set up a record for a Worcestershire bowler. That achievement earned him a special testimonial fund in the county. In 1926, for North of England at Edgbaston, he startled the cricket world by dismissing seven of H. L. Collins's Australian team in an innings for 42 runs. This gained him a place in the England team in three of the Test matches. Rain ruined the first, at Nottingham, but in the other two Root bowled well without repeating his earlier devastating form. In the fourth Test at Old Trafford, he gained these figures: 52 overs, 27 maidens, 84 runs, four wickets.

Three times in his career Root took nine wickets in an innings—for 23 runs against Lancashire in 1932, for 40 runs against Essex in 1924, both at Worcester, and for 81 against Kent at Tunbridge Wells in 1930, when he disposed of three batsmen in four balls. He was also a batsman of no mean ability and in 1928 he completed the "cricketers' double," scoring 1,044 runs and taking 118 wickets. Altogether before his retirement from first-class cricket in 1933 he took 1,512 wickets for 21.11 runs each, scored 8,089 runs, average 15.37, and held 219 catches. Afterwards he played in Lancashire League cricket for a time, acted as coach to Leicestershire and as cricket correspondent of a national newspaper. In 1937 he wrote a book, *A Cricket Pro's Lot,* in which he expressed admirably the point of view of the professional player.

ROPER, Edward, who was born at Richmond, Yorkshire, in April, 1851, died in a Liverpool nursing home after an operation for appendicitis, on April 27, 1921, aged 70. In 1867 he obtained a place as a fast bowler in the Clifton XI, among his contemporaries being Messrs. E. F. S. Tylecote and J. A. Bush. Subsequently he played a few times for Lancashire between 1876 and 1886 and for Yorkshire between 1878 and 1880, his highest score for the former being 65 v. Kent at Manchester in 1884 and for the latter 68 v. Middlesex at Lord's in 1878. For many years he was Secretary of the Liverpool C.C., and he was also Vice-President of the Lancashire County C.C. A splendid organiser, he got together thousands of teams for the Sefton and Liverpool Clubs. He was the author of *A Sportsman's Memories,* a posthumous work.

ROSE, William Molyneux, died on January 13, 1917. During the stress of the war the death of the once-famous lob bowler passed unnoticed. When the ordinary announcement appeared on the front page of *The Times* no one connected with the sporting papers seems to have identified the cricketer. Writing last summer about the English team in Canada I assumed that Mr. Rose was still alive and was kindly put right on the matter by his brother. Mr. W. M. Rose will be remembered chiefly for the part he played in the memorable tour of R. A. Fitz-Gerald's side in 1872. He bowled with extraordinary success, taking, so Lord Harris makes out, 136 wickets for less than three and a half runs apiece. In the second innings of the match against XXII of Montreal he took all 19 wickets credited to the bowlers, two men being run out. For the Canadian and American batsmen of those days he and Arthur Appleby were altogether too much. Against batsmen of a much bigger class Mr. Rose enjoyed a triumph in the Canterbury Week of 1871. He played in all three matches and took 25 wickets. It was no fault of his that the South beat the North, for in the second innings of the South eight wickets fell to him for 71 runs, among his victims being C. I. Thornton, G. F. Grace, W. H. Hadow, Jupp, Alfred Lubbock, and I. D. Walker. At that time, Mr. Rose must have been about the best bowler in England. V. E. Walker was no longer a force to be reckoned with, R. C. Tinley had dropped out of the Notts XI, W. B. Money had lost his skill, amd A. W. Ridley in 1871 was just leaving Eton for Oxford. Mr. Rose, who did not get into the XI while at Eton, was born in London on September 20, 1842. One must not forget to add that though a lob bowler he played cricket in glasses.—S.H.P.

ROSEBERY, Sixth Earl of, who died on May 30, 1974, aged 92, was a cricketer, soldier, politician and administrator of distinction. When Lord Dalmeny, he was in the Eton XI of 1900, scoring 52 against Harrow and 55 against Winchester. In 1901 he turned out for Buckinghamshire, took part in two matches for Middlesex the following season and began playing for Surrey in 1903. He took over the Surrey captaincy in 1905 and held the post until 1907. Both his centuries for the county were made at the Oval in 1905, against Leicestershire and Warwickshire. While hitting the first, he drove fiercely during a stand for the sixth wicket of 260 with J. N. Crawford. That season was the first for Surrey of J. B. Hobbs and Lord Dalmeny was always proud of the fact that he awarded that great batsman his cap after two games.

He succeeded to the title of Lord Rosebery when his father, a former Prime Minister, died in 1929, and became President of Surrey from 1947 to 1949. It was thanks to his approach to the Prince of Wales in 1905 that the County Club adopted the Prince of Wales's feathers as their crest. For many years Lord Rosebery was a celebrated figure in the world of horse racing.

In 164 innings in first-class cricket he scored 3,551 runs, average 23.05.

He left £9,650,986 net.

ROSS, Hamilton, who died at his birthplace, Grenada, British West Indies, on March 29, 1938, aged 90, played for Somerset and was a prolific scorer for Incogniti, Lansdown and M.C.C. He made 101 for Gentlemen against Players of Sussex at Hove in 1869; in 1871, hit six centuries, ranging from 107 to 188; in

1876, 11 centuries; in 1877, nine centuries; while in 1883 he played four consecutive three-figure innings in the course of 10 days. That year he headed the Marylebone Club averages with 59. He hit up 216 for Somerset against Emeriti in 1879 and on August 31, 1876, in a match between Shanklin and Ryde visitors, he made 291. These performances were all exceptional in those days even if the bowling and fielding were inferior on some occasions. He kept wicket efficiently.

ROSSER, John, who died in Queensland in January, 1926, was a free bat and excellent field, but did not meet with much success in matches of note: he played first for Victoria and later for Queensland. From 1879 until 1884 he assisted the South Melbourne C.C. and in the 1882–83 season averaged 60 for the club for 12 innings. In the match against St. Kilda on January 27 and February 3, 1883, he scored 192 and with J. Slight (279) made 395 for the first wicket.

ROTHERHAM, Hugh, died on February 24, 1939, when nearly 78 years of age. He finished three years in the Uppingham XI as captain in 1879 and next year, when 19, he played for the Gentlemen at Lord's. Over 6ft. in height he took a long run and bowled very fast, right round arm. He met with marked success, clean bowling five Players at a cost of 41 in the first innings and dismissing three in the second innings. His victims were Ulyett, Bates, Scotton, Alfred Shaw, Fred Morley and Barlow, all England players. Thanks to his success the Players followed-on and were beaten by five wickets. He appeared for the Gentlemen on several occasions and was prominent in a tie match at the Oval in 1883. After taking six wickets for 41 in the first innings he made 13 not out, so helping the Gentlemen to a lead of 32. In a great final struggle, he joined A. P. Lucas and 23 runs brought the scores level before he was bowled by Peate, the Yorkshire and England slow left hander. A. P. Lucas carried his bat through the innings of 149 for 47. Rotherham played in a few matches for Warwickshire when business permitted before going to Australia. He was a brilliant three-quarter in the Coventry Fifteen.

ROTHERY, James William, born at Staincliffe on September 5, 1877, died in Leeds Hospital on June 3, 1919, as the result of wounds received whilst serving with the East Kent Regiment. He played for Yorkshire from 1903 until 1910, his highest innings being 161 v. Kent at Dover in 1908, 134 v.

Derbyshire at Chesterfield in 1910, and 118 v. Hampshire at Bournemouth in 1905.

ROUGHT-ROUGHT, Rodney Charles, died suddenly in London on May 5, 1979, after an accident, aged 71. When he went up to Cambridge he had already made a considerable name in Minor County cricket, having headed the Norfolk bowling averages in 1929 with 59 wickets at 12.94. Taking seven for 36 in the first innings against Middlesex in his second match, he naturally made his Blue secure and headed the University averages in 1930 with 43 wickets at 18.93. In 1931 he lost his form and his place in the side but next year regained both, and he and Farnes were a formidable pair. Rought-Rought's greatest asset was his ability to make the ball lift sharply off a length. One of three brothers who for many years did great service for Norfolk, he himself continued to take many wickets for the county up to 1939, besides being a valuable hitter in the lower half of the order. In all, over a career for Norfolk with lasted 13 years, he took 462 wickets at 15 runs each. His younger brother obtained his Blue at Cambridge in 1937.

ROUND, The Right Hon. James, P.C., who was born at Colchester on April 6, 1842, died at Birch Hall, Essex, on December 24, 1916. He was educated at Eton, where he was in the XI in 1860 with R. A. H. Mitchell and the Hon. C. G. Lyttelton, being then regarded as a first-rate long-stop, a useful lob-bowler and a steady and painstaking batsman. Against Harrow he scored 0 and 20 and v. Winchester five and 22. Whilst at Oxford he developed into the best amateur wicket-keeper of the day and led the Christ Church XI: curiously enough, however, he did not receive his Blue, although while still in residence he was chosen for the Gentlemen v. Players match at Lord's. Of his four appearances against the Players decidedly the most successful was that at the Oval in 1867, when, besides scoring 29, he caught three men and stumped two and allowed only one bye in a total of 249: altogether he had a hand in the downfall of eight wickets during the innings. On the Magdalen Ground, in 1867, he scored 142 for Southgate v. Oxford University. For many years he appeared with success for Essex, and until the close of the season of 1882 was Treasurer of the County C.C. He had been a member of the M.C.C. since 1865, and served on the Committee from 1869 until 1871. For 38 years he represented East and North-East Essex in the House of Commons.

ROWBOTHAM, Joseph (Yorkshire), born in Little Sheffield, July 8, 1831, died December 22, 1899. Height 5ft. 6½in., weighed 10st. 7lb., but (in 1874) 14½st. His runs were obtained (says *Scores and Biographies*) "in a fine, free, manly style." (v – 162). Also "In the field he is very fine and can take any place, but excels especially at long stop, as wicket-keeper, or at point." In July, 1873, the match, Yorkshire v. Gloucestershire at Sheffield, was set apart as a benefit for him, and proved a "bumper." Rowbotham was a fine, punishing player in front of the wicket, and was considered by the late James Southerton to be the best Yorkshire batsman of his day. His best scores in first-class matches were 101 for Yorkshire against Surrey at the Oval in 1869; 100 for Yorkshire v. Notts at Sheffield in the same year, and 113 for Yorkshire v. Surrey at the Oval in 1873.

ROWE, Ernest Fentiman, born January 27, 1866. Captained the XI while at Felsted School, and played for Essex in 1892. He died after an operation April 14, 1918. He was a younger brother of the better-known Mr. F. E. Rowe, of Marlborough and Essex.

ROWE, Francis Erskine, born at Hartford End, Felsted, on November 30, 1864, died at Littlehampton on May 17, 1928. He was in the Marlborough XI in 1881 and two following years, being captain in 1882 and 1883. In his five Public School matches—three against Rugby and two against Cheltenham—his highest score was 67 v. Cheltenham in 1883. Although a good average batsman and field at point, he did not obtain his Blue for Cambridge. He played for both Essex and Berkshire, and at Leyton in July, 1892, made 129 against Surrey.

ROWLANDS, William Henry, who died suddenly at Bristol on June 30, 1948, aged 64, played for Gloucestershire from 1901 to 1928 and captained the side in his last two seasons. He scored 3,248 runs in first-class matches, average 16.48. In his best year, 1921, his aggregate reached 1,014, average 22.04.

ROWLEY, Alexander Butler, J.P., D.L., one of the famous cricket brotherhood, died at Dover on January 10, 1911. Born at Manchester on October 3, 1837, he had completed his 73rd year. He was educated at Rossall, and was one of the first cricketers of note turned out by that school. In *Scores and Biographies* (vi–243) it is said of him: "Bats right-handed, hitting with great freedom, and has made some excellent scores in capital style, beginning to play when quite young at Manchester, and being a pupil (at cricket) of the famous Thomas Hunt. Bowls left round-armed, rather slow and twisting, and has been pretty successful in that department of the game also... In the field he was generally short-leg... Height, 5ft. 11in., and weight 11st." In addition to appearing for Lancashire, he took part occasionally in North v. South matches and assisted the Gentlemen against the Players four times between 1859 and 1863. In the last-mentioned matches he proved singularly unsuccessful as a bowler, but he scored 156 runs with an average of 26, making 47 and six not out at the Oval in 1859 and 37 and 23 at Lord's in the following year. Mr. A.B. Rowley took a prominent part in the formation of the Lancashire County C.C., and from 1874 to 1879 was President of the Club.

ROWLEY, Edmund Butler, who died on February 8, 1905, in Manchester, was born in that city on May 4, 1842. He was the fourth of seven cricketing brothers, the most famous of whom was Mr. A.B. Rowley. *Scores and Biographies* says (x–64): "Is a fine free hitter, and has made excellent scores in the North, though he has not often appeared South. In the field he is generally short-slip." He learnt his cricket at Rossall School and assisted Lancashire from 1864 until 1880, during which period he played 134 innings for the county, scoring 1,665 runs with an average of 13.21. After handing over the captaincy of the team to Mr. A.N. Hornby, he continued to take the greatest possible interest in everything connected with Lancashire cricket, and served on the County Committee until his death. His most notable feat was an innings of 219 for the Gentlemen of Lancashire against the Gentlemen of Yorkshire, at Manchester, in July, 1867. At the Oval in 1862, when only 20 years of age, he made two splendid scores of 61 and 70 for the Gentlemen of the North against the Gentlemen of the South, and in the same year he was chosen to assist in the Gentlemen v. Players match at the Surrey ground. By profession he was a solicitor.

ROWLEY, Ernest Butler, who died on October 4, 1962, aged 92, was up to the time of his death the oldest living Lancashire cricketer. A member of a family prominent in the County Club since 1873, he was never officially appointed captain, but led the side on occasion. He appeared in 15 matches be-

tween 1893 and 1898, scoring 537 runs, average 28.60, his highest score being 65.

ROWNTREE, Richard William, who died in Auckland on June 16, 1968, aged 84, played as wicket-keeper for New Zealand against V.S. Ransford's Australian team in 1920–21. Born at Leyburn, Yorkshire, he appeared for the county's Second XI in 1904. After a serious illness, he emigrated to New Zealand, where he gained a high place among wicket-keepers. Between 1914 and 1931, he took part in 33 first-class matches, all but two for Auckland, and dismissed 93 batsmen. Standing close up to the wicket, he was specially skilled in stumping, by which means he disposed of 38 of his victims.

ROYLE, George Murray, was born at Nottingham on January 9, 1843, and died at Fern Lodge, Sherwood Rise, on February 26, 1910. His early cricket was played with the Nottingham Commercial C.C., for which he scored 10 and 100 not out against the Australian Aboriginal team of 1868. His first match for the county was against Gloucestershire at Trent Bridge in 1871, and his last against Surrey at the Oval 10 years later. Mr. Haygarth said of him: "Is a batsman above the average, and excels in the field at long-leg, and at mid-wicket off." He was devoted to the game all his life, and although business prevented him from playing as often as was desired, he served on the County Committee for 16 years.

ROYLE, The Rev. Vernon Peter Fanshawe Archer, born at Brooklands, Cheshire, on January 29, 1854, died at Stanmore Park School, Middlesex, of which he was headmaster, on May 20, 1929, after a short illness, aged 75. The brilliant fielding of Royle at cover-point for Oxford in the University match of 1876 brought him into special prominence, and when he went to Australia with Lord Harris's team in the winter of 1878–79 he earned high praise, particularly by his fine play in a match with Victoria at Melbourne, when, fielding at cover point, he made five catches. He was in the XI at Rossall School at the age of 16, and before going up to Brasenose College, Oxford, he played for Lancashire in 1873. Mr. Royle played regularly for the county until his duties as a master at Elstree School obliged him to give up first-class cricket. Altogether, he scored 1,423 runs, with an average of 16.31. The end of the season of 1878 found him with second place in the Lancashire batting averages, and he was always a fast run-getter when well set. Standing 5ft. 9in., he got well over the ball, and played in good style, often hitting with plenty of power. Starting by bowling fast, he developed some talent for slow bowling, and in the second innings against Cambridge in 1875 he took four of the best wickets in the memorable game which Mr. A. W. Ridley's bowling won for Oxford by six runs.

It was, however, for his brilliant fielding that Royle will be chiefly remembered. He was ambidextrous, very quick on his feet and smart in return, preventing many a run which would have been successful against a less expert fieldsman. Tom Emmett's famous remark to a brother Yorkshireman, who called to him for a sharp run when Royle was at cover point, was a practical tribute to the fieldsman's excellence: "Woa, mate, there's a policeman," called Emmett, and there was no more attempt at a sharp run. Besides doing creditably at Association football, Mr. Royle won the 100yd. race when he was captain of Rossall School in 1872. Last year he was elected president of the Lancashire County Club. He was a master at Elstree from 1879 to 1899, and while holding that position was ordained and served for some years as curate of Aldenham. He played for the Gentlemen v. Players in 1882, and scored 31. The highest innings of his life was 205 for Gentlemen of Cheshire v. Staffordshire Borderers, at Chelford, in July, 1874. For a short period he was headmaster of Elstree, and in 1901 he became head of Stanmore Park Preparatory School. He was married and left four sons, one of whom, J. S. Royle, was in the Harrow XIs of 1906 and 1907.

RUBIE, Lieut.-Col. Claude Blake, C.B.E., E.D., died on November 3, 1939, after an operation, aged 51. He was the appointed manager of the cricket team that would have toured India during the winter had not the war intervened. A well-known member of M.C.C., he used to keep wicket occasionally for Sussex.

RUDD, George Edward, who died at Leicester on September 16, 1921, aged 55, had played for and captained the Leicestershire XI. For a time, too, he was Hon. Secretary of the County Club. He was the father of Mr. G. B. F. Rudd.

RUDSTON, Horace, who died in April, 1962, aged 82, played as a professional for Yorkshire from 1902 to 1907. Of the 609 runs he scored for the county, average 20.30, he obtained 269 in 1904 when he put together

innings of 164 and 69 in the match with Leicestershire at Leicester. He took part in an eventful game at Bristol in 1906. Set to get 234 to beat Gloucestershire, Yorkshire lost half the side for 119, but Rudston and E. Smith put on 66 and looked to have brought victory within range when Rudston, square cutting G. Jessop, had the misfortune to hit his wicket. That cost Yorkshire the match—and the Championship—by one run.

RUGGLES-BRISE, Major-General Sir Harold Goodeve, K.C.M.G., C.B., M.V.O., born at Finchingfield, near Braintree, in Essex, on March 17, 1864, died in London on June 24, 1927, aged 63. He was a batsman with a free style, hitting well to the off, a good field at cover-point and mid-off, and could bowl a useful medium-paced ball. He was in the Winchester XI in 1880 and two next years, being captain of the side in 1882, when Eton were beaten by an innings and 20 runs. He was an Oxford Blue of 1883, and the same season he made the first of his appearances for Essex. He was younger brother of Sir E. J. Ruggles-Brise, of the Eton teams of 1875 and 1876, and played much military cricket both at home and abroad. Since 1884 he had been a member of the M.C.C.

RUNDELL, Joseph U., who was father of Mr. P. D. Rundell of the South Australian XI, died on January 7, 1922. He himself, being a good all-round cricketer, played occasionally for the State, but most of his cricket was for the Hindmarsh and Port Adelaide side.

RUSHBY, Thomas, who died in a Surrey hospital on July 13, 1962, aged 80, was a celebrated medium-paced bowler for Surrey between 1903 and 1921. Twice he headed the Surrey averages, in 1914 with 103 wickets for 19.14 and in his last season when dismissing 59 batsmen for 18.84 apiece, and during his career he took 954 wickets, average 20.58. The best performance of a bowler who never lost his enthusiasm was the taking of all 10 wickets in 17.5 overs for 43 runs in the first innings of Somerset at Taunton in 1921. In 1907 at the Oval he (six wickets for 67 runs) and J. N. Crawford (11 for 63) bowled unchanged during the two innings of Sussex who, disposed of for 43 and 90, lost to Surrey by an innings and 94 runs. Never highly regarded as a batsman, Rushby hit 1,227 runs, average 7.90, and he held 60 catches.

RUSHTON, Frank, who died in Bolton Royal Infirmary on October 15, 1975, aged 69, was a fast-medium swinger who, after some good performances for the Second XI, played for Lancashire in six matches in 1928 and 1929. Later he had a long and highly successful career, first for Royton in the Central Lancashire League and then for 17 seasons with Eagley in the Bolton League.

RUSSEL, John Somerville, who died suddenly at Aberdeen on September 12, 1902, was born at Edinburgh, on March 19, 1849, and was therefore in his 54th year at the time of his death. His boyhood was spent in his native city, his early education being received at the Royal High School. In July, 1870, he made his first appearance at Lord's, assisting the North of Ireland against M.C.C., though what qualification he possessed to figure on the side of the former is hard to understand. He was an excellent batsman when at his best. His style was not attractive, but his on-drives were hard and all along the ground, and his late cuts sharp and well timed. In the field, he excelled at point. He played in numberless matches for the M.C.C., and assisted Northumberland for several years, being a merchant at Newcastle-on-Tyne. In June, 1882, he appeared for the M.C.C. against Leicestershire, at Lord's, this being the match in which Barnes (266) and Midwinter (187) added 454 runs together for the third wicket. Two years later he assisted the M.C.C. against Yorkshire, at Lord's, and proved the highest scorer in the first innings with 33, made against the bowling of Peel, Preston, Bates, Peate, Ulyett, and Emmett. The match was a notable one, inasmuch as Gunn (203) and Barnes (140 not out) added 330 runs in partnership for the fourth wicket, so lengthy a stand being then a much rarer occurrence than it is now. Mr. Russel assisted in other matches which have become historic—the one at Lord's, in 1885, between the M.C.C. and Ground and Rutland, in which the former made 643 for eight wickets in their second innings, and that between the M.C.C. and Ground and Wiltshire, in 1888—also at Lord's—in which the premier club obtained a total of 735 for nine wickets, which still ranks as the highest ever hit at headquarters. In the Rutland match Mr. Russel made only 31 (the Rev. P. Hattersley-Smith obtained 132, and Mr. F. W. Maude 141), but against Wiltshire he scored 196 runs for the first wicket in partnership with Mr. E. Sainsbury (180), before he was hurt and obliged to retire altogether from the game with a total of 54 to his credit.

Probably, his most notable performance was accomplished in the M.C.C. match against Somerset, at Lord's, in 1882, in which he scored 56 and 83, in each innings making more runs than any other two men put together. In minor cricket, he was a prolific run-getter, and made large scores all over the country. His highest innings was 168 for M.C.C. and Ground against Hampstead, at Lord's, in 1879. When Mr. Henry Perkins resigned the secretaryship of the Marylebone Club, Mr. Russel put up for election, but, as he withdrew at the last moment, no poll was necessary.

RUSSELL, Albert Charles, who died in Whipps Cross Hospital on March 23, 1961, aged 73, was the first English batsman to hit a century in each innings of a Test match. This he did against South Africa at Durban in 1923 when he scored 140 and 111 and played a leading part in England's rubber-winning victory by 109 runs. The performance was the more remarkable because "Jack" Russell, as he was generally known, "had," Wisden recorded at the time, "to battle against illness; when he started his second innings he ought to have been in bed rather than on the cricket field."

Son of Tom Russell, for many years Essex wicket-keeper, "Jack" was born near the county ground at Leyton. He assisted Essex from 1908 to 1930 and in all matches during that time he scored 27,546 runs, including 71 centuries, average 41.73, obtained 285 wickets with slow bowling for 27.17 runs each and brought off 292 catches, principally in the slips, where he excelled. A master of on-side strokes, he occasionally drove well to the off and, though not specially attractive to watch, he became, once he established himself in the Essex XI in 1913, one of the most dependable batsmen in the game. Thirteen times he exceeded 1,000 runs in a season and five times, in 1920, 1921, 1922, 1925 and 1928, passed 2,000. His best year was 1922, when he put together an aggregate of 2,575—the highest of all batsmen—including nine centuries, for an average of 54.78.

His highest innings was 273 against Northamptonshire at Leyton in 1921, but that which he considered his best was in the previous summer at Lord's against Middlesex, that season's Champions, when he hit 197 and he and L. C. Eastman added 175 for the ninth wicket after eight men had been dismissed for 184. Besides his Test match feat, he twice scored two separate hundreds in a match for Essex—115 and 118 v. Surrey at the Oval in 1922 and 131 and 104 v.

Lancashire at Liverpool in 1928—and he enjoyed the distinction of hitting centuries against every first-class county, Australia, South Africa and the West Indies. Twice for his county he shared in a three-figure opening partnership in each innings of a game, 191 and 104 with F. Loveday v. Lancashire at Leyton in 1921 and 122 and 140 with the Rev. F. H. Gillingham v. Surrey at the Oval in 1927. Russell took part in 16 stands of 200 or more for Essex, the biggest being 263 with D. F. Pope against Sussex at Hove in 1930.

Russell played 10 times for England, scoring 135 not out in his first against Australia at Adelaide in 1920; 101 at Manchester and 102 not out at the Oval during the disastrous Test series of 1921. In five appearances for Players against Gentlemen, his largest and best innings was 162 at Lord's in 1922. First a coach and then a groundsman following his retirement from first-class cricket, he was among those professional players granted honorary membership of the M.C.C.

RUSSELL, Alfred Isaac, who died on August 20, 1961, aged 94, played as wicket-keeper and batsman for Hampshire before they acquired first-class status. For over 70 years, 50 of them as chairman, he was associated with the Deanery C.C., whom he had captained. He liked to relate how once he caught an Essex batsman behind the wicket, threw the ball into the air and loudly appealed. "Not out," said the umpire. "I won't be rushed."

RUSSELL, Lord Charles, died June 20, 1894. One of the most venerable and respected members of the Marylebone Club passed away with the death of Lord Charles Russell. Born in Dublin on February 10, 1807, he made his first appearance at Lord's in a small match on June 15, 1837, between the Earl of Chichester's side and Mr. B. Aislabie's side. His interest in the leading club, which thus commenced when he was only 20 years of age, lasted throughout the rest of his long life. Lord Charles Russell came prominently before modern cricketers on the occasion, in 1879, of the public presentation at Lord's of a testimonial to Mr. W. G. Grace; he then, in a long and eloquent speech, paid perhaps the best tribute to Mr. Grace's powers that the great cricketer has ever received. A half-brother of the famous Earl Russell, Lord Charles was for many years Serjeant-at-Arms in the House of Commons.

RUSSELL, Major Leonard G., of St. Cross,

Winchester, who died on April 8, 1946, aged 90, as the result of a street accident, was hon. secretary of Green Jackets C.C. for 50 years. In his young days he played for Hampshire.

RUSSELL, Thomas Marychurch, born at Lewisham, in Kent, on July 6, 1868, died at Leyton on February 28, 1927, aged 58. He played on the Leyton ground as a boy, and had the satisfaction of being in the side that earned promotion to first rank in 1895. He had then been tried as wicket-keeper several times, and he secured a regular place in the Essex side, remaining their chief wicket-keeper until 1905. If he never quite reached the highest standard he had to take Mr. C. J. Kortright at his fastest; Harry Pickett, well above medium pace; and Walter Mead and Mr. F. G. Bull, both spin-bowlers who made the ball turn considerably. Essex finished third in the Championship in 1897, and were equal to beating the strongest counties for several seasons. During this time Tom Russell was the regular wicket-keeper and also a useful batsman, with his best season 1896, when he averaged 23. He scored 110 v. Surrey at Leyton that year and 139 v. Derbyshire at Derby in 1900. In the Essex v. Kent match at Canterbury in 1901 he caught two men and stumped four in an innings, and in the game with the same county at Leyton in 1899 he caught eight. He joined the ground staff at Lord's in 1894, and remained with the Marylebone Club until 1926, when, after several seasons as a first-class umpire, illness compelled him to retire. In 1905 the Essex v. Middlesex match at Leyton had been given to him for his benefit. Russell was of a rather reserved disposition but extremely popular. He was the father of A. C. Russell, the Essex and England player.

RUSSELL, William, a member of the Glamorgan XI for nine years, died at Cowbridge, South Wales, on March 8, 1908, in his 41st year. His highest score for the county was 143 against Berkshire at Cardiff in 1899. In 1894 and 1895 he appeared on four occasions for Middlesex Second XI.

RUTHERFORD, Arnold Page, who died on July 23, 1980, aged 87, was three years in the Repton XI as a batsman and captain in 1911, and in 1912 played in one match for Hampshire.

RUTHERFORD, J. S., who played for Hampshire in 1913, died on April 14, 1943.

RUTTER, Edward, born at Hillingdon, near

Uxbridge, on August 3, 1842, died at Shepperton-on-Thames on February 4, 1926, aged 83. While a free right-handed batsman, he will be better remembered as a slow round-armed bowler with much break. At Rugby, where he was coached by Alfred Diver, he was in the XI in 1859 and two following years, among his contemporaries being C. Booth, B. B. Cooper, and G. P. Robertson. In the one match against Marlborough during his time—that of 1860—Rutter took six wickets in the first innings and three in the second. He appeared for Middlesex from 1862 until 1876, and against Kent at Gravesend in 1868 had an analysis of 11 for 123. It was for the county that he also obtained his highest score in a match of note—64 v. Oxford University at Prince's in 1872. One incident in his career that he was fond of recalling was that, when playing for the Veterans against M.C.C. in one of the Centenary games at Lord's in 1887, he clean bowled W. G. Grace for 24 with the first ball he sent down. He was for very many years a most prominent member of the Free Foresters as well as their Hon. Secretary, and for that club did many noteworthy things. Against Southgate on the latter's ground in July, 1868, he took as many as 17 wickets for 161 runs, although one man was run out; in the match with Gentlemen of Notts, at Beeston in August, 1871, he obtained all 10 wickets for 99; and when, aged nearly 52, he carried out his bat for 41 against Mr. C. T. Hoare's XI at Bignell, in July, 1894, he and the Rev. J. H. Savory (125) put on 165 for the 10th wicket. For Hillingdon v. I Zingari in August, 1869, he took seven wickets in the first innings and 10 in the second, the game being 12-a-side and one batsman being run out. For over 50 years he had been a member of the M.C.C. and the Middlesex County C.C., and had served on the Committee of both clubs. He was the author of *Cricket Memories*. Although known mainly in connection with cricket, Mr. Rutter was leader of football at Rugby in 1861. Late in the '60s he played for Richmond and rendered especially useful service by his skill in dropping goals with the left foot. He was a member of the first Committee of the Rugby Union to whom was entrusted the drafting of the laws of the game.

RUTTER, Ronald Howard, who died on August 8, 1974, after a long illness, was a noted fast bowler in the Tonbridge XI before he left his mark on Buckinghamshire cricket. He took five or more wickets on 26 occasions. But his personal highlight came against Oxfordshire at High Wycombe in 1932 when he spent only three-quarters of an hour scoring 106, which remains the fastest century for Buckinghamshire.

RYAN, Frank, who died at Leicester on January 6, 1954, aged 65, was one of the best slow left-arm bowlers of his day. Tall, with a high easy action, he not only spun the ball considerably but maintained admirable accuracy. Born in New Jersey, U.S.A., on November 14, 1888, he came to England at an early age and was educated at Bedford Grammar School. Following service in the Royal Flying Corps during the First World War, he began his first-class cricket career with Hampshire in 1919, but after two seasons turned to Lancashire League cricket before joining Glamorgan in 1923. With his arrival the Welsh county's attack increased in effectiveness, and in 1924, when dismissing 120 batsmen for 14.58 runs each, Ryan enjoyed his most successful season. Among his feats that summer were six wickets for 17 and six for 48 v. Somerset at Taunton; six for 46 and five for 18 v. Leicestershire and four for 69 and six for 40 v. Lancashire, both at Swansea. In 1927, by taking nine wickets for 95 runs, he played a big part in the defeat in a single innings at Swansea of Nottinghamshire—a sensational result which enabled Lancashire to snatch the County Championship. Before leaving Glamorgan in 1931, Ryan brought his aggregate of wickets to 1,000 at an average cost of 21.20. He later took part in South Wales League, Yorkshire Council and Lancashire League cricket.

RYAN, Capt. James H. A., M.C. (1st Liverpool Regiment) was killed in France on September 25, 1915, aged 23. He was not in the XI whilst at Wellingborough Grammar School, but played once or twice for Northamptonshire in 1913 and 1914, in the latter year making 41 v. Somerset on the Northampton ground. He appeared also for Sandhurst and Aldershot Command, his right-hand fast bowling proving very useful. He had received the Military Cross and been Mentioned in Dispatches.

RYDER, Jack, who died at the age of 87 on April 3, 1977, had been taken ill two days after the Centenary Test, at which he was the oldest ex-player present. Much though he accomplished, his career was a trifle disappointing. Competing with a number of great players, he was merely a good one, whose place was never quite secure and who fell below the incredibly high standards of his contemporaries in fielding. In his first season for Victoria, 1912–13, he took 30 wickets at 15.40 and it seemed that a new star had arisen. He also had a batting average of 33. Bowling fastish right-hand, he ran the ball away and could also make it lift. In the next season his wickets cost more, but he did one outstanding all-round performance, taking seven for 88 in the first innings against South Australia and scoring 36 not out and 105. In 1914–15 his batting average rose to 85, but his eight wickets cost him 28.62 runs each.

When cricket was resumed after the War, it was clear that his bowling promise was not going to be fulfilled. Thenceforward, he was only a change, used on his tours in England to relieve the leading bowlers in the lesser matches: in Tests against England his 13 wickets cost 48.66 apiece. Nevertheless he played in all five Tests against Douglas's side in 1920–21, though his highest score was only 52 not out and his average 18.85. Doubtless his innings of 54 and 105 in the second match for Victoria against the Englishmen kept him his place in the last two Tests. But it must have been a disappointment when in England that summer he did not get a place in a single Test.

Against Arthur Gilligan's side in 1924–25 a bad back put him out of consideration for the first two Tests, but in the third, coming in at 119 for six, he made 201 in six and a half hours, a remarkable effort of concentration for one who was primarily an attacker, and followed it with 88 in the second innings. In fairness it must be said that the English bowling was gravely depleted: Tate, Gilligan and later Freeman were off the field and Woolley was handicapped by a weak knee. Freeman, as tough a little man as ever stepped on to a cricket field, fainted with pain when one of Ryder's on-drives which he was attempting to catch hit him on the wrist.

In England in 1926 Ryder was again a disappointment: he had a respectable record for the whole tour, but did little in the Tests. Nevertheless in 1928–29 he was made captain against Chapman's side. Few men can have had a more difficult assignment. Collins, Bardsley, Macartney, Taylor and Mailey had retired. Arthur Richardson was in England and Gregory and Kelleway broke down in the first Test and played no more. Under the circumstances the surprise was not that Australia should lose the series 4–1 to a strong side, but that they should recover so quickly as to regain the Ashes in England in 1930. For their failure in Australia no blame could be attached to Ryder. He simply had not the material nor was he well served by

the selectors: he himself made 492 runs with an average of 54.66, including a century in the third Test. After this, considerable surprise and some resentment was caused when he was omitted from the 1930 team for England. No doubt his co-selectors (he was himself now a selector) felt that, if he went, he must be captain and that for that Woodfull was the better choice.

Ryder continued to play for Victoria until 1931–32, captained an unofficial Australian side on a tour of India in 1935–36 and was a selector again from 1946 to 1970. He also did much to help young players. Standing over 6ft, he was almost entirely a front-of-the-wicket player with an immensely powerful drive. He was certainly more effective in Australia than in England. His highest score was 295 against New South Wales in 1926 when Victoria compiled the record total of 1,107.

RYDER, Rowland Vint, who died at his home in Birmingham on September 1, 1949, aged 76, was associated with Warwickshire County C.C. for nearly 50 years, the greater part of that time as secretary. Born at Wetherby, Yorkshire, on March 11, 1873, he spent most of his early life in Staffordshire assisting his father in a printing business and the production of a local newspaper. When 20 he twice appeared for Staffordshire and he played a good deal of club cricket before, in 1895, he became assistant secretary to Warwickshire. Seven or eight years later he succeeded Mr. William Ansell in the secretaryship, a position he held until he retired in 1944. His efforts on behalf of cricket in general and of the interests of the County Club in particular were indefatigable. It was upon his proposal that, in 1920, the starting days for all county matches were changed from Mondays and Thursdays to Saturdays and Wednesdays. When the finances of the County Club became very precarious, he organised special appeals in 1903 and 1904 which realised over £3,000 and in 1906 he made a personal canvass of Birmingham and suburbs that resulted in an increase of 600 in membership. Besides being granted honorary life membership of Warwickshire, when he retired he received a testimonial comprising a cheque for £1,608 and an inscribed silver salver.

For the 1936 *Wisden* he wrote an article under the heading "Trials of a County Secretary" in which he stated that more than 200 players passed through the club's books during his term of office. He mentioned also an entry in the Minutes of 1897 which contained the following: "It was decided that on account of the heavy expenses already incurred in connection with next year's ground staff an engagement could not be offered W. Rhodes, of Huddersfield."

RYE, George Joseph, enjoyed a long career for Norfolk from 1878 to 1895. During those 18 seasons he scored 1,112 runs and took 264 wickets, among the opposing sides being Essex, Derbyshire, Hampshire, Leicestershire and Northamptonshire. When still playing well he started umpiring, and until 1931 was on the list of Minor Counties umpires. For 40 years he acted as coach to Norwich Grammar School. He died at his daughter's house at Norwich on January 6, 1943, aged 86. Accurate length with slow to medium-paced spin delivery enabled Rye to keep batsmen on the defensive. When F. E. Lacey made 323 not out for Hampshire in 1887—still the highest score in a Minor County match—Rye bowled 33 overs, 14 maidens, for 77 runs and four wickets. Against Essex at Norwich in 1883 his figures read: 51 overs, 20 maidens, 69 runs, five wickets.

RYLANCE, Harry, secretary of the Lancashire County Club from the year 1921, died on January 22, 1932, from pneumonia. Born at Newton-le-Willows on September 15, 1884, Mr. Rylance, while still a boy, showed considerable aptitude for both cricket and football and, when only 14 years of age, secured a place in the Newton club team for which he rendered fine service as batsman and bowler. He joined the staff at Old Trafford in 1905, fulfilled a number of engagements as cricket coach, acted during the latter part of the First World War as assistant to Mr. Matthews his predecessor as secretary and, for two seasons, performed the duties of scorer to the County Club. At Association football, Mr. Rylance was generally associated with the post of goalkeeper. On giving up actual play, he became a referee and progressed so steadily in that capacity that he officiated in League games and Cup-ties, among the contests of which he was given control being the semi-final tie for the Association Cup between Chelsea and Aston Villa at Sheffield in 1920. Quiet in manner but firm of purpose, Mr. Rylance was deservedly popular both as Lancashire County Secretary and as a football referee.

RYLE, The Rev. J. C., born at Macclesfield, May 10, 1816; died at Lowestoft, June 10, 1900, aged 84. For many years Bishop of Liverpool. His religious works, pamphlets, could be numbered by the hundred. For two years, 1833 and 1834, he assisted Eton against Harrow and Winchester, scoring seven and three and 21 and one against the former school, and 20 and 11 and 26 and 0 against the latter. He was contemporary at Eton with J. H. Kirwan and C. G. Taylor. He was in the Oxford XIs of 1836 and 1838. But little is known of his style of batting or mode of bowling, as no biography is given of him in *Scores and Biographies*, but from a perusal of old scores it is apparent that he was generally successful both with bat and ball.

RYLOTT, Arnold, born at Grantham on February 18, 1840, died of pneumonia at Sandy, in Bedfordshire, on April 17, 1914, aged 74. *Scores and Biographies* said of him: "Is a right-handed batsman, but a fast left round-armed bowler; fields in no particular place, and has on various occasions distinguished himself in matches of note." He was rather late in coming to the fore, being 30 when he played his first match at Lord's. In 1872 he was engaged at Lord's, subsequently becoming head of the ground staff. In 1875 he became qualified for Leicestershire, and for that county he appeared for many years.

Rylott received two benefit matches—Leicestershire v. M.C.C. and Ground, at Leicester, in 1889, and North v. South, at Lord's, in 1891. He was the author of the book of verse entitled *Our Bobby Rylott when a Boy.*

SADLER, James, who died at Chiddingfold, in Surrey, where the family had been settled for some centuries, on November 21, 1924, in his 97th year, was, like his father and grandfather, a life-long lover of the game. In his early days he had been invited to play for the county, but he preferred to restrict his activities to local matches in the West Surrey district. His death caused many interesting links with the past to be severed. He was, it is believed, the last survivor of the Shillinglee team which dismissed the Second Royal Surrey Militia without a run on August 13, 1855. For over 20 years he knew the great William Beldham well, and as a small child he had met Tom Walker, another member of the famous Hambledon XI, who died as long ago as 1831.

SADLER, Thomas, who died at Chiddingfold on September 29, 1915, aged 80, was about 60 years ago a well-known all-round cricketer in West Surrey. He had declined an invitation to play for Surrey. He was the founder of the Chiddingfold Hunt.

SAINSBURY, Edward, died suddenly at Weston-super-Mare on October 28, 1930, in his 80th year, having been born at Bath on July 5, 1851. He was in the Sherborne Cricket XI of 1866 and became captain of Somerset in 1886, appearing for Gloucestershire by residence for the first time in 1891. He played many fine innings for the Lansdown Club, Bath.

SAINSBURY, Francis John, who died at Bath, on April 30, 1919, aged 72, played occasionally for Essex and later for Somerset, his best innings for the latter county being 54 v. Hampshire at Bath in 1881. For nearly 20 years he was Captain of the Lansdown C.C., of which his father had been one of the founders in 1824. He was a sound batsman and could bowl lobs. He was elder brother of Mr. E. Sainsbury, of Clifton, Somerset and Gloucestershire.

SALE, Edward V., who died at Devonport, Auckland, on November 23, 1918, was a very good batsman and a useful wicket-keeper. In strictly first-class cricket his highest innings were 121 for Auckland v. Otago at Auckland in 1909–10 and 100 not out for New Zealand v. Australians at Auckland in 1913–14.

SALE, Richard, who died on September 7, 1970, aged 81, was in the Repton XI from 1906 to 1908 and gained his Blue at Oxford in 1910. Between 1908 and 1912, he assisted Derbyshire. He was for many years a master at Shrewsbury, where he did much for the school cricket. His son, Richard, a member of the Repton XI in 1937 and 1938, was an Oxford Blue in 1946 and also appeared for Derbyshire.

SALMON, Gordon Hedley, died at Exmouth on June 13, 1978, aged 83. He played a good deal for Leicestershire from 1913 to 1924 as a batsman. So badly wounded in his left arm during the First World War that it was doubtful whether he would ever be able to play again, he recovered sufficiently to do much useful work for the county, though he was never able to play regularly. His highest score was 72 v. Glamorgan at Swansea in 1921. From 1940 to 1946 he was Leicestershire's representative at Lord's.

SALTER, George F., who died at Chichester on August 15, 1911, in his 78th year, was a useful cricketer in his younger days, but will also be best remembered as the scorer for many years of the Sussex County C.C. His one match for the county was against Kent at Margate in 1864, when he scored 15 and four not out.

SALTER, Malcolm Gurney, who died on June 15, 1973, aged 86, was in the Cheltenham XI from 1902 to 1906, being captain in the last three years. He gained a Blue at Oxford in 1909 and 1910 and from 1907 to 1925 appeared for Gloucestershire.

SAMPSON, Richard King, who died on July 12, 1927, aged 67, played in one match for Sussex—v. Nottinghamshire at Trent Bridge in 1886. In his first innings he was bowled for two by a ball from Flowers which sent a bail 39yd.; in his second he batted an hour for five runs.

SAMSON, Lieut. Oswald Massey (R.G.A.), died of wounds September 17, 1918, aged 37. Cheltenham XI; Oxford XI 1903, when he scored eight and 32 not out against Cambridge at Lord's; Somerset XI.

SANDERS, Wilfred, who died in a Nuneaton hospital after many years of ill-health in May, 1965, aged 55, played for Warwickshire as a professional medium-pace bowler between 1928 and 1934. In all first-class cricket he took 117 wickets for 39.85 runs apiece. Though rarely achieving much with the bat, he hit 64 against Nottinghamshire at Edgbaston in 1936 and in the same summer, also at Birmingham, scored 54 in a partnership of 128 with F. R. Santall (105 not out)—a last-wicket record for Warwickshire.

SANDERSON, Gerald Barry, who died on October 10, 1964, aged 83, was in the Malvern XI as a batsman from 1898 to 1900. His first-class career was both curious and brief. In 1901 he played for Warwickshire against London County at the Crystal Palace ground, being run out 0; in 1923, while serving for many years as a master at Malvern, he turned out for Worcestershire against Northamptonshire at Worcester, again being run out, this time for 16.

SANDFORD, The Venerable Ernest Grey, M.A., Archdeacon of Coventry, and formerly Archdeacon and Canon Residentiary of Exeter, died at Exmouth on March 8, 1910. He was born at Dunchurch, in Warwickshire, on August 16, 1839, and must be regarded as one of the most accomplished all-round cricketers ever produced by Rugby. Whilst batting was his forte, his wicket-keeping and slow underhand bowling were also of a very high standard. Ill-health, unfortunately, handicapped him severely and in consequence his career as a player was a very short one. He was coached by John Lillywhite and Alfred Diver, and played his first match for the School in September, 1852, when only 13 years of age; he did not, however, appear again in the XI until 1854. Matches with Marlborough were not started until 1855, but Sandford remained long enough at the school—he was captain in 1856 and two following years—to appear in three of them. In the game of 1856 he played a wonderful not-out innings of 88—one of the finest public school displays ever seen at Lord's. The only other double-figure score on the side was 11 by A. Helme. In the following year he was only slightly less prominent, playing an innings of 58 and taking eight wickets. Among his contemporaries at Rugby were T. W. Wills, W. H. Bullock, C. T. Royds and M. T. Martin. Proceeding to Oxford, Sandford obtained his Blue as a Freshman, and in the same season (1859) was asked to assist the Gentlemen against the Players at Lord's. The Gentlemen were over-matched, but Sandford—still under 20 years of age—made 28 and 13 against Wisden, Willsher, and Jackson. Ill-health kept him out of the University match in 1860, and in the following year he took part in the match only after Cambridge had consented to allow him the services of a runner. As it happened, he scored only nine and three, and Cambridge won by 133 runs. Of Archdeacon Sandford it may truly be said that he possessed that amount of genius for the game which would have made him a great player in any age.

SANDHAM, Andrew, who died in hospital on April 20, 1982, aged 91, might, had things turned out differently, have been for years a regular and successful Test match batsman. It was his misfortune that, slow to develop, owing partly to the great pressure for places as batsmen in the Surrey side, partly to the First World War, he was over 30 when he first came into serious consideration, and by then his rival as Hobbs's partner was Sutcliffe. By the time Hobbs retired from international cricket Sandham was too old to be his replacement. And so he will be remembered as a wonderful servant of Surrey and as Hobbs's partner for the county for 15 years.

His career began as long ago as 1911 when in his first match he made 53 against Cambridge and in his second 60 against Lancashire, creating a great impression. None the less in 1912 he had only one match for the county. In 1913 he scored 196 against Sussex, adding 298 with Harrison for the sixth wicket, and one might have supposed that this would have made his place secure, but a month later he was dropped for D. J. Knight, who had just left Malvern, and in 1914 he appeared in only five matches. Even in 1919 he was dropped for some matches, but an innings of 175 not out against Middlesex at the beginning of August at last ensured him a regular place, which he retained until 1937 when, having made a century against Sussex at Hove in the last match of the season, he left it to the Surrey Committee to announce his retirement. By then he had made in all first-class matches 41,284 runs with an average of 44.83, including 107 centuries. Twenty times he had exceeded a thousand runs, two of these occasions being on tours abroad, and his 219 for Surrey in 1934 is still the highest score made for a county against the Australians.

His first Test match was against Australia at the Oval in 1921, when he made a useful 21 at No. 5. In 1922–23 he went to South Africa, where he played in all five Tests as an opener, but did little, although taking the tour as a whole he was the most consistent bat on the side, and in 1924 he played twice against South Africa, scoring 46 in his only innings. That winter he was a member of Arthur Gilligan's side in Australia. Hobbs and Sutcliffe were now in their prime as an opening pair and Sandham in his two Tests, going in lower down, met with no success. Finally in 1929–30 he went to West Indies and played innings of 152 at Bridgetown and 325 at Kingston. These matches were classified as Tests only at a later date: at the time they were called Representative matches and in fact only one of the English team played in the Tests in England in the following summer. So, unluckily, he never had the chance of opening for England with Hobbs. To Surrey, Hobbs and Sandham meant what Hobbs and Sutcliffe did to England. They put up 100 for the first wicket 63 times, their highest partnership being 428 against Oxford University in 1926. Sandham was the ideal partner, content to stay there and let Hobbs take the applause and as much of the bowling as he wanted. When, against Somerset at Taunton in 1925, Hobbs, having equalled W. G.'s number of centuries in the first innings, had a chance of beating it in the second, Sandham saw to it that he got the bowling, thus sacrificing a possible hundred for himself. He was the least selfish of players.

He had formed his style in his early days by watching Tom Hayward, much of whose skill on the leg side he had inherited, and he perfected it by association with Hobbs. Like many small men he was quick on his feet and a fine and fearless hooker; this, with his mastery of the cut, in which he always made full use of such height as he had, made him a particularly good player of fast bowling. Of his other strokes perhaps the best was a square drive. He was also a magnificent outfield with a fast and low return, whose value was even greater in the days when the whole area of the Oval was used more often than it is now.

His services to Surrey did not end with his playing career. From 1946 to 1958 he was their coach and then for another 12 years their scorer. An Honorary Member at the Oval since 1961 and a Vice-President since 1979, he continued to watch the play there until the end of his life. He was also an Honorary Member of M.C.C. A quiet man with a great sense of humour, who set himself and expected of others a high standard of behaviour, he was much respected.

SANDMAN, Donald McKay, who died in Christchurch on January 29, 1973, aged 84, was one of New Zealand's most versatile sportsmen. As a good batsman and leg-break bowler, he played cricket for New Zealand in 1910, 1914, and 1921 and for 17 years assisted Canterbury in the Plunket Shield tournament. He was a half-back in the New Zealand Army Rugby football team which toured South Africa in 1919 and turned out for South Island in 1921. He also excelled at billiards, hockey, badminton, boxing, lawn tennis, bowls and rifle shooting.

SANDS, John, who died at his residence, The Wickets, Dallington, Sussex, on December 24, 1902, aged 80, was born at Mountfield, Sussex, on November 22, 1822. He had been coach at Stourbridge, in Worcestershire, and Harrow, and for 25 years was engaged by the Drumpelier Club, Glasgow. A few years before his death, and when almost an octogenarian, he took six wickets for three runs in a village match. When Kent played Sussex, at Tunbridge Wells in 1858, Sands fielded substitute for one of the Kent players, who had met with an accident, and made four brilliant catches during the innings. On September 20 and 21, 1877, the match between XXII of Drumpelier and District and the United South of England XI was played for his benefit.

SANKEY, Arthur, born at Stoney Stanton on June 18, 1845, died on June 1, 1922. He was a sound steady batsman and a good fieldsman. His best performance for Leicestershire was in the first innings of the match with the Australians in July, 1878, when he scored 70 and, with John Wheeler (60), made 113 for the first wicket. The county led by 63 on the first innings but were beaten by eight wickets, the Australians making 210 for the loss of Charles Bannerman (133) and W. L. Murdoch upon going in the second time. The match marked the opening of the old county ground at Aylestone, which had been laid out at a cost of £16,000.

SANKEY, Charles, who died at Cimiez on April 19, 1927, aged 84, was a very useful cricketer, left-handed, who played some county cricket for both Leicestershire and Suffolk. After being an Assistant Master at Marlborough, he was for 11 years Headmaster of King Edward's School, Bury St. Edmunds, and subsequently—1890–1905—a Harrow Master.

SANKEY, Thomas, died at Blackpool Grammar School, Lancashire, on May 23, 1910, aged 53. He was born at Bilston, in Staffordshire, and played occasionally for his native county, Shropshire, Oxfordshire, Buckinghamshire, and Berkshire, and in one season made four hundreds in succession. He was the founder of the Blackpool Cricket Week in 1904.

SANTALL, Frederick Reginald, died at his home in Cheltenham on November 3, 1950, at the age of 47. He made his debut for Warwickshire against Yorkshire in May 1920, and became a professional in 1923. From that time until County Cricket was suspended on the outbreak of war in 1939 Santall remained a regular member of the side. He made more than 16,000 runs, including a highest score of 201 not out against Northamptonshire at Peterborough in 1933. On that occasion he reached 100 in 80 minutes, 150 in 110 minutes, and 201 in 165 minutes. Santall could always be relied upon to keep a game alive with his powerful driving and he was a useful medium-paced right-arm change bowler. As a fieldsman he excelled, and his total of catches—265— were bettered for Warwickshire only by Croom and W. G. Quaife. Santall received a benefit in 1935. After leaving Warwickshire he coached at Wrekin College and Oratory School, Reading, before accepting a similar post at Dean Close School, Cheltenham.

SANTALL, Sydney, who died at his home at Bournemouth on March 19, 1957, aged 83, rendered valuable service to Warwickshire as a right-arm medium-pace bowler from 1892 to 1914. From 1894, when the county attained first-class status, until the outbreak of the First World War he took 1,219 wickets, average 24.41, and held 150 catches. He appeared for Northamptonshire as an amateur before going on trial to Warwickshire in 1892 and he remained, first as player and then as coach, until 1920.

He was also a useful batsman, and in his first-class career he scored 6,561 runs, average 15.58. His best season as an all-rounder was probably that of 1905, when he dismissed 94 batsmen at a cost of 24.59 runs each and obtained 685 runs, including his highest score—67 against Hampshire at Southampton—average 22.83. On four occasions he headed the Warwickshire bowling figures, his greatest success with the ball occurring in 1907 when he took 100 wickets, average 16.79. In that season he numbered among his performances seven wickets for 38 runs v. Leicestershire at Coventry; eight for 72 v. Yorkshire at Sheffield and seven for 77 v. P. W. Sherwell's South African team at Edgbaston. Other good analyses were seven for 39 v. Lancashire at Liverpool and eight for 32 v. Essex at Edgbaston in 1898; eight for 23 v. Leicestershire at Edgbaston in 1900 and eight for 44 v. Somerset at Leamington in 1908, when Warwickshire, after being 86 behind on the first innings, dismissed their opponents for 93 and won by 161 runs. His son, F. R. Santall, who died in 1950, played for many years as a batsman for Warwickshire.

SARAVANAMUTTU, Lieut.-Col. S., who died suddenly at Colombo on July 17, 1957, aged 59, was President of the Board of Control for Cricket in Ceylon. While a schoolboy at St. Thomas's, he hit 121 against St. Anthony's, Kandy, in 38 minutes, the fastest century scored in Ceylon. He captained the Tamil Union Club for eight years, played in the European–Ceylonese Test series and for Ceylon against New Zealand, M.C.C. and Australia, being captain on two occasions. He figured with some success in the University trials at Cambridge from 1921 to 1923 without getting a Blue. He held the M.B.E.

SAREL, Major W. G. M., whose death occurred in April, 1950, at the age of 74, was a good, stylish batsman who played for Surrey, Kent, Sussex, Northumberland and Trinidad, but his appearances in inter-County Cricket were limited and mostly made for Surrey, for whom he scored 1,143 runs at an average of 22.41. From 1919 to 1922 he was the Sussex secretary, and in 1919 he hit 103 at Hove against Oxford University. Afterwards Major Sarel became well known as a golf club secretary, first at Beaconsfield and then at the Berkshire club.

SATHASIVAM, Mahadevan, the most gifted and stylish batsman of Sri Lanka, died of a heart attack in 1977, at the age of 62, in Colombo. He had a style of his own and his stroke play had perfect poise and power. Against Madras for Ceylon at the Chepauk Grounds, Madras, in 1947, he scored 215, a ground record until eclipsed by Joe Hardstaff (jnr.) of Nottinghamshire fame several years later. Against Lal Amarnath's Indian team of 1945, he played a stylish innings of 111 at the Colombo Oval. Against the 1950 Commonwealth side led by L. Livingston, he made 98 at the Colombo Oval for Ceylon. He held the unique distinction of having captained three countries in cricket against visiting English and Australian teams—Sri Lanka, Singapore and Malaysia.

SAUNDERS, Dyce Willcocks, the "G.O.M." of Canadian cricket, was born at Guelph, Ontario, on March 22, 1862, and died in London on June 12, 1930, aged 68. *Scores and Biographies* records: "He was a batsman above the average, having a sound, strong, upright style, and was an excellent wicket-keeper." He was educated at Trinity College School, Port Hope, where he led the XI in 1879, and for some years he captained the Toronto C.C. He played for Canada in many representative matches, against both the United States and visiting English teams, and when he toured this country with the Gentlemen of Canada in 1887 he scored 613 runs with an average of 23. Keeping up the game well, he came over again 35 seasons later as a member of Mr. Norman Seagram's team, being then in his 61st year.

SAUNDERS, John Victor, born on February 3, 1876, died under an operation in Melbourne on December 21, 1927, in his 52nd year. He will be remembered chiefly as a member of the Australian team of 1902, which toured England and South Africa under Darling's captaincy. He came over with a big reputation as a left-handed slow bowler, and, favoured as he was by a wet season, met with considerable success. In all matches he obtained 127 wickets for just over 17 runs apiece, and in the four Test matches in which he took part he dismissed 18 men at a cost of rather more than 26 runs per wicket. On turf which suited him he was undoubtedly a difficult bowler. Delivering the ball from a good height and getting on an appreciable amount of spin, his big break made him at times quite deadly, but his action was open to criticism. In the Test match at Sheffield, when Australia played better all-round cricket than England and won by 143 runs, Saunders obtained five wickets for 50 in the first innings, but had 68 runs hit off 12 overs in the second innings without dismissing anybody. At Manchester, where Australia won a remarkable match by

three runs, Saunders, on a ruined pitch, had much to do with the victory. Eight runs were wanted when Tate, the last man, joined Rhodes, and, having scored a four from the first ball he received from Saunders, he was bowled by the fourth which came with the bowler's arm and kept low. The Oval match was the one in which G. L. Jessop played his great innings of 104 after half the England side were out for 48. Saunders took four wickets in the second innings, the first three falling to him for 10 runs, but Darling undoubtedly kept him on too long, and he came in for severe punishment when Jessop was hitting in such terrific fashion. During the tour Saunders' most noteworthy bowling performance was in the second match against Surrey at the Oval when he took six wickets for nine runs. Among his best performances on Australian wickets were:

6 for 71, Victoria v. South Australia, at Melbourne	..	..	..	..	1899–1900
6 for 90, Rest v. Australian team, at Sydney	..	..	..	..	1899–1900
6 for 70, Victoria v. New South Wales, at Melbourne	..	..	..	..	1901–01
11 for 130, (including 6 for 57), Victoria v. New South Wales, at Sydney	..	..	..	..	1901–02
13 for 194, (including 8 for 106), Victoria v. South Australia, at Adelaide		..	..	..	1902–03
12 for 262, (including 7 for 122), Victoria v. New South Wales, at Sydney		..	..	..	1905–06
10 for 143, Victoria v. South Australia, at Adelaide		..	..	..	1906–07
6 for 61, Victoria v. New South Wales, at Sydney		..	..	..	1907–08
6 for 76, Victoria v. New South Wales, at Sydney		..	..	..	1909–10

In Test matches against England he obtained 64 wickets for 25.32 runs each, and against South Africa, 15 for 11.73 apiece. One of his analyses at Johannesburg was seven for 34. After making his last appearance for Victoria he settled in New Zealand and played in representative games for Wellington.

SAVIGNY, J. H., who was found dead on the banks of the Lefroy River, where he had gone fishing, at Bishopsbourne, near Launceston, on February 11, 1923, was for several years one of the leading batsmen of Tasmania. He was aged 56 at the time of his death. For Launceston against Cornwall in December, 1901, he made 106 in his first innings and 153 in his second. When he scored 164 not out v. England at Launceston in 1903–04, he and O. H. Douglas made 202 together for the first wicket. This was his best feat in first-class cricket, and he hit 21 fours and was missed when 33 during the five hours his innings lasted.

SAVILE, George, who was born at Methley, near Leeds, on April 26, 1847, died at Tetbury, in Gloucestershire, on September

4, 1904. He was in the Rossall XIs of 1864, 1865, and 1866, being captain the last two years, and played for Cambridge in 1867 and 1868, but against Oxford in 1868 only. His highest score in first-class cricket was 105 for Cambridge University against the M.C.C., at Fenner's, in 1868, when he made his runs off the bowling of Grundy, Wootton, Farrands, T. Hearne, Biddulph, and Mr. A. J. Wilkinson. He appeared occasionally in the Yorkshire XI between 1867 and 1874, but not so frequently as could have been wished. It has been recorded of him that, when playing in a match in Hertfordshire, in 1874, he hit a ball a distance of 135yd.

SAVILLE, Capt. Clifford Allen (East Yorks. Regiment), killed in a raid November 8, 1917, aged 25. Played for Middlesex 1914. Born February 5, 1892. He played in three matches for Middlesex in the season of 1914, but met with little success, scoring only 57 runs in five innings.

SAVILLE, Stanley Herbert, who died in an Eastbourne nursing home after a long illness on February 22, 1966, aged 76, gained his Blue as a batsman for Cambridge in four years from 1911 to 1914, being captain in the last season. He met with little success in the University matches, but he hit 101 against Free Foresters in 1913 and 141 not out from the Army bowling the following summer. He was in the Marlborough XI of 1907 and played a few times for Middlesex before and after the First World War. A fine hockey player at inside-right, "Sammy" Saville captained England and won 37 International caps at a time when matches were fewer than they are today. He had been President of the Hockey Association since 1951.

SAWYER, Charles Montague, who died on March 30, 1921, aged 65, was for many years a member of the Broughton C.C. and in 1884 played for Lancashire in one match. As a Rugby footballer he was one of the most brilliant three-quarters Lancashire ever had. In 1880 he played for England v. Scotland and in 1881 against Ireland.

SCANLON, Edmund, who died at Newtown (N.S.W.) on January 9, 1916, played for New South Wales v. Victoria at Melbourne in December, 1877, when, going in last, he scored 25. He was a good batsman and wicket-keeper.

SCHILIZZI, Stephen, who died on July 18, 1961, aged 89, was President of Northamptonshire County C.C. from 1929 to 1938. A millionaire and an old Harrovian, he did much to finance the club in the years between the two World Wars.

SCHNEIDER, Karl J., who died at Adelaide on September 5, 1928, of heart failure, had had a brief but brilliant career. Although very short, he was in quite the first flight of left-handed batsmen. He had not many strokes, but his footwork was excellent and he could hit hard: in addition a brilliant outfield, he could also bowl a useful slow ball. For four years he appeared in the Xavier College XI, at Melbourne, and for a little while he was also at Melbourne University. In club matches for the Melbourne C.C. in 1921–22 his average was 134.66, and during his last season in first-class cricket—1927–28,—his figures were 10—0—143—520—52.00. When Victoria totalled 1,059 against Tasmania in 1922–23 he made 55, assisting Ponsford, who set up a new record in scoring 429, to add 164 for the seventh wicket. Subsequently his chief triumphs were obtained for South Australia during the seasons 1926–27 and 1927–28, when he scored 146 and 108 v. New South Wales, 107 v. West Australia, 143 v. Victoria, and 114 v. Queensland. First with A. J. Richardson and later with G. W. Harris, he proved himself a splendid man to open the innings. Against Victoria at Melbourne in 1927–28 he and Harris figured in first wicket stands of 89 and 138. Just a year ago he took part in the Australian tour of New Zealand, where he continued to display capital form. In the match with Canterbury he scored 138, he and Oldfield, who made 137, pulling round the game by adding 229 together after six wickets had fallen for 135.

SCHULTZ, Sandford Spence, who died on December 17, 1937, aged 80, was in the Uppingham XI of 1873 and four years later was given his Cambridge Blue by W. S. Patterson. From 1877 to 1882 he appeared occasionally for Lancashire. He went to Australia in 1878–79 under Lord Harris for the tour which originated in an invitation from the Melbourne club to the Gentlemen of England. By arrangement, Tom Emmett and George Ulyett, the two Yorkshire fast bowlers, were included because suitable amateurs were not available, but the team lacked slow bowling. The one match played against Australia, represented by David Gregory's XI who were in England during the previous summer, was lost by 10 wickets, F. R. Spofforth taking 13 wickets for 110 runs. Schultz, scoring 20, helped to save the innings defeat.

A fast round-arm bowler, good bat and smart slip fieldsman, Schultz was very prominent in club cricket. He took nine wickets, one man being run out, in an innings for Orleans Club against Bexley in 1882 and for Uppingham Rovers against United Services at Portsmouth in 1887 he scored 286—a noteworthy performance 50 years ago. Mr. Schultz, who changed his name to Storey late in life, was concerned in one exceptional incident. Mr. Leveson Gower, in *Recollections of Oxford Cricket* in last year's *Wisden*, mentioned a match with Gentlemen of England in 1881, begun on the Christchurch ground, and, because of the bumpy state of the pitch, re-started a few hours later in The Parks. Mr. Edmund Peake, in a letter to *The Times* last July, explained: "The fast bowler (I blush to say it) committed such havoc as would have made him famous in these days. The Gentlemen refused to continue and the match was begun all over again in The Parks. One batsman—S. S. Schultz—was out first ball each time. Twice first ball in one innings —a record." Mr. A. J. Webbe will remember the match.

SCHWARZ, Major R. O. (Eighth K.R.R.C.) **M.C.** Died of influenza, in France, November 18, 1918.

Major Schwarz, as everyone knows, was famous as a slow bowler. Few men did so much to establish the reputation of South African cricket. He learnt the game in England and played for Middlesex before going to South Africa. In those early days, however, he did not make any mark. His fame began when he returned to his country with the South African team of 1904. Studying very carefully the method of B. J. T. Bosanquet, he acquired, and afterwards carried to a high standard, the art of bowling off breaks with, to all appearance, a leg-break action. He did very well in 1904, but his success that year was only a foretaste of far greater things to come. In the brilliant tour of 1907 he and Vogler and G. A. Faulkner raised South African cricket to the highest pitch it has ever reached. He was less successful than his two comrades in the Test matches against England, but for the whole tour he was easily first in bowling, taking 143 wickets at a cost of 11½ runs each. He proved rather disappointing in Australia, and in the Triangular Tournament in this country in 1912 he failed. Before going to South Africa Schwarz was an International half-back at Rugby football, playing against Scotland in 1899 and against Wales and Ireland two seasons later. He also played for Cambridge against Oxford in 1893. He was born on May 4, 1875, and was educated at St. Paul's School. Inasmuch as he always made the ball turn from the off and had no leg break Schwarz was not in the strict sense of the word a googly bowler, and was in this respect inferior to his colleagues Vogler and Faulkner. Still, when at his best, he was a truly formidable opponent, his accuracy of length in the season of 1907, in combination with such a big break, being extraordinary.

The writer of the obituary notice in *The Times* said: "Personally 'Reggie' Schwarz was a man of exceptional charm, and his untimely death will bring real sorrow to his hosts of friends in many parts of the world. He had the great gift of absolute modesty and self-effacement. No one meeting him casually would ever have guessed the renown he had won in the world of sport. Quiet, almost retiring, in manner; without the least trace of 'side'; and with a peculiarly attractive voice and way of speaking, Schwarz impelled and commanded the affection even of acquaintances. During his years in South Africa he was secretary to Sir Abe Bailey—a post which his social gifts enabled him to fill

with remarkable success. Before coming to Europe for service in France, he had won distinction in the campaign in German South-West Africa. All who knew him knew that at the first possible opportunity he would be in the field in France, quietly and unostentatiously devoting all his gifts—gifts that were bound to ensure his success as an officer—to the service of his country. He had been wounded twice." S.H.P.

SCORER, Reginald Ivor, died on March 19, 1976, after a long illness, aged 84. Between 1921 and 1926 he played 29 matches for Warwickshire, his chief performance being an innings of 113 against Hampshire at Birmingham in 1921 in a high-scoring match. He was also a useful fast-medium change bowler. During the War he did much to keep cricket going in the Midlands by promoting Festivals and in the course of this became the first person to use the Public Address system at cricket matches. A keen Rugby footballer he served 16 years on the Rugby Union committee.

SCOTT, Andrew, one of South Australia's leading bowlers three decades ago, died at Ngoorla, Adelaide, on October 8, 1907, aged 56. In the match at Adelaide in November, 1874, between Eighteen of South Australia and XI of Victoria he obtained 10 wickets for 73 runs, and that season (1874–75), when playing for North Adelaide, headed the Association bowling averages with 52 wickets at a cost of 4.05 runs each.

SCOTT, The Ven. Avison Terry, born at Cambridge on July 18, 1848, died in a London nursing-home on June 18, 1925, aged 76. He was above the average as a batsman and whilst at Brighton College—he was in the XI from 1864 until 1867, being captain his last year—he distinguished himself by playing a not-out innings of 140 against Lancing College in 1865. Obtaining his Blue for Cambridge, he played against Oxford in 1870 and 1871, in the former year scoring 45 and 0 in "Cobden's Match" which Cambridge won so sensationally by two runs. The same season he played an innings of 202 for Cambridge Long Vacation against Peripatetic Clowns. At various times he appeared for Cambridgeshire, Gentlemen of Sussex and Norfolk, and for Cambridgeshire against the University in May, 1868, he scored 76 in his first innings and 75 in his second. Whilst at Cambridge he won the pole-jump before it became an event in the University Sports, and he was one of the founders of the Royal Ashdown Forest Golf Club. He became Vicar of St. James's, Tunbridge Wells, in 1886, and since 1906 had been Archdeacon of Tonbridge.

SCOTT, Lord George William Montagu-Douglas, O.B.E., third son of the sixth Duke of Buccleuch, died on February 24, 1947, aged 80. After playing for Eton in 1884–85, he got his Blue at Oxford, and made history in the 1887 match with Cambridge by scoring 100 and 66, at that time the highest individual aggregate in a University match. He was the last choice, filling a vacancy caused by the inability of C. Wreford Brown to play owing to an injured hand. He was missed three times in the first innings, but his second display was the most brilliant of the match, which Oxford won by seven wickets. Next year, when the match, though extended to four days, was drawn because of bad weather, Scott scored 32, highest for his side; and in 1889, when Cambridge won by an innings and 105 runs, thanks to S. M. J. Woods taking 17 wickets, his efforts were 37 not out and nine, again the best for Oxford. He played once for Gentlemen against Players, and also for Middlesex, without reproducing his early Oxford form. Sound in defence, Lord George Scott drove with special freedom in attractive style; he fielded well in the deep.

SCOTT, Dr Henry James Herbert, died on September 23, 1910, at Scone, New South Wales, where he had for many years practised as a medical man. He was born at Toorak, near Melbourne, on December 6, 1858. Scott's career in first-class cricket lasted less than 10 years, beginning in February, 1878, at Sydney, when he played in his first big match—Victoria v. New South Wales—and ending with the tour in England in 1886. In his young days he was a fast bowler, but his reputation as a cricketer was gained entirely as a batsman. He began to be talked about in 1882, and an innings of 114 not out that he played against New South Wales at Melbourne in the season of 1883–84 was the main cause of his being given a place in the Australian team that came to England in 1884. He had a very successful tour, scoring 102 against England at the Oval in the memorable match in which Australia ran up a total of 551, and getting, among other good scores, 75 and 31 not out against England at Lord's, 82 not out against the Gentlemen at Lord's, 79 against Gloucestershire at Clifton, and 65 against Gloucestershire at Cheltenham. He stood third to

Murdoch and Percy McDonnell in the batting, with an aggregate of 973 runs and an average of over 22. It was a misfortune for Scott that he should have been chosen by the Melbourne Club to captain the team they sent to England in 1886. Under happier circumstances he might have got on well, but fortune was against him. Quarrels began among the players during the opening match at Sheffield Park, and Scott had neither the strength of character nor the experience as a leader that the difficulties of his position demanded. He did himself justice as a batsman, scoring 1,289 runs with an average of just under 22, but as a captain he had anything but a pleasant time. His best score during the tour was 123 against Middlesex, at Lord's. In an innings of 67 not out against Yorkshire at Sheffield he hit in one over of four balls from Saul Wade 22 runs—a six, a four, and two sixes. When the tour was over he stayed behind in England to finish his medical studies, and on his return to Australia cricket saw no more of him.

SCOTT, John Gordon Cameron, C.I.E., one of six Sussex players who scored a century on first appearing for the county, died on March 21, 1946. This fine display was against Oxford University at Eastbourne in July 1907, when he and Joe Vine (72) put up 163 for the first wicket in 110 minutes. Scott did not give a chance in his 137 and was eighth out at 285; the next highest score was 21. In a few other matches for Sussex he experienced little success. Captain of the Marlborough XI in 1906, he went to Cambridge and showed good form in a Seniors' match but did not get his Blue.

SCOTT, Major K. B., M.C., was killed in August, 1943, aged 28, when serving with the West Kent Regiment. A medium-paced right-hand bowler, he used the in-swinger with effect when at Winchester, particularly in 1934, and also batted well, but at Oxford, where he was Golf captain, he was described as a "surprise selection" for the 1937 XI which beat Cambridge by seven wickets—the first success for the Dark Blues since 1931. Scott's contribution to the triumph at Lord's was 10 runs. Of that team, Sub Lieut. E. J. H. Dixon and Sub Lieut. M. H. Matthews previously lost their lives in the war, and Major T. G. L. Ballance was killed after gaining the M.C.

Scott played for Sussex against his University in 1937 and in five Championship matches without ever reproducing his best school form.

SCOTT, O. C., who died at Kingston, Jamaica, on June 16, 1961, aged 67, played for Jamaica and in eight Test matches for the West Indies. A batsman and slow leg-break bowler, "Tommy" Scott toured England in 1928, playing in two Test matches. When visiting Australia in 1930–31, he took part in all five Tests and in the first at Adelaide he finished the Australian innings by dismissing four batsmen in nine deliveries without cost. In first-class cricket he scored 1,322 runs, average 22.40, and took 203 wickets for 28.70 runs each.

SCOTT, The Hon. Osmund, third son of the late Earl of Eldon, died in London, September 9, 1948, aged 72. Played sometimes for Gloucestershire.

Played golf for England v. Scotland in the first international match at Hoylake 1902, and for a few years after. In 1905 at Prestwick he lost to Gordon Barry in the final of the Amateur Golf Championship.

SCOTT, Robert Strickland Gilbert, who died after an operation at Peasmarsh, Sussex, on August 26, 1957, aged 48, was a former Oxford Blue. After three seasons from 1926 to 1928 in the XI at Winchester, where he was captain in the last year, he went up to Oxford, appearing with much success against Cambridge in 1931. In that game A. T. Ratcliffe set up a record for the University match by hitting 201 in the Cambridge first innings—a record which lasted only one day, for in the Oxford reply the Nawab of Pataudi scored 238. Despite Ratcliffe's big innings, Scott, bowling above medium-pace, took six wickets for 64 runs in a total of 385 and in the second innings helped further towards victory by eight wickets when dismissing two men for 23. He played in one game for Sussex that season and for the next two years was a regular member of the county side. In 1932, when the health of K. S. Duleepsinhji broke down and Scott captained the team in several games, he hit 559 runs, average 20.70, including 116 out of 169 (seven sixes, 11 fours) in a hundred minutes, and took 54 wickets, average 20.31. He also played in a Test Trial match. The following summer he took 113 from the Hampshire bowling at Horsham. The end of his first-class career came when his father died in 1933. He figured prominently in Sussex affairs and became High Sheriff of the county.

SCOTT, Stanley Winckworth, who died on December 8, 1933, was a prominent figure in Middlesex cricket and when contemporary with Walter Read, A. E. Stoddart, Lionel Palairet and H. T. Hewett stood out as one of the best batsmen in the country. Born in Bombay, on March 24, 1854, he played for Middlesex by residence. Educated at Streatham School and Brentwood School, he learned his cricket on Streatham Common, but did not get into the Middlesex XI until 24 years of age. At once showing himself a batsman of more than ordinary ability, he improved so much that in 1882, 1885 and 1886, he headed the county batting averages, his average in the last-mentioned season being 37.10. In 1892, he did particularly well, coming out first in batting with an average of 39, and, hitting up 224 against Gloucestershire, achieved what at that time was a rare distinction. Chosen that year for the Gentlemen both at Lord's and at the Oval, he on each occasion did himself full justice. At Lord's in the first innings he scored 60, and at the Oval 80 in the second, the latter effort being made against such great bowlers as Lohmann, Peel, Lockwood and William Barnes. After 1893, however, Stanley Scott, due to the claims of his business on the Stock Exchange, had to give up the game; otherwise he undoubtedly would have earned still greater renown. His powerful build and large dark moustache made him easily recognised on the field. Playing in a fine attractive style, and getting most of his runs in front of the wicket, he was especially brilliant on the off-side. He also appeared for Herefordshire and in minor cricket was always a great run-getter.

SCOTT, Verdun John, who died suddenly at Devonport, New Zealand, on August 2, 1980, played in 10 Tests for New Zealand between 1946 and 1952, and was a member of the side which toured England in 1949. Though overshadowed by Sutcliffe and Donnelly, he was one of their most dependable batsmen, scoring 1,572 runs with an average of 40.30 and making four hundreds. A big man, he had hardly any backlift and was no stylist, but he was very strong in the arms and his strokes travelled deceptively fast. He was an ideal foil to Sutcliffe as an opening partner and their value can be gauged from the fact that in the Tests of 1949 they took part in partnerships of 122 at Leeds, 89 at Lord's and 121 at the Oval. His highest Test score was against West Indies in 1952 when he saved the side with an innings of 84 in rather over four hours. For Auckland in the Plunket Shield he was a heavy scorer.

SCOTT, Dr. William Jernan, who died at

Windsor on July 19, 1920, aged 56, played in three matches for Middlesex in 1894 and 1895, but made only 12 runs in five innings. For the Second XI of the county, however, he did better, scoring 56 v. Kent Second XI at Lord's in 1894 and 68 in the corresponding match of the following year. He had played successfully for Kensington Park, M.C.C., Incogniti, and Windsor Home Park, his best performance being an innings of 107 for M.C.C. v. Warwickshire at Lord's in 1895.

SCOTTON, William, (Notts), who died by his own hand on July 9, 1893, was born on January 15, 1856, and was thus in his 38th year. For some time previous to his tragic end he had been in a very low, depressed condition, the fact that he had lost his place in the Notts XI having, so it was stated at the inquest, preyed very seriously upon his mind. Scotton played his first match at Lord's for Sixteen Colts of England against the M.C.C. on May 11 and 12, 1874, scoring on that occasion 19 and 0. He was engaged as a groundsman by the M.C.C. in that year and 1875, and after an engagement at Kennington Oval returned to the service of the M.C.C., of whose ground staff he was a member at the time of his death. His powers were rather slow to ripen, and he had been playing for several years before he obtained anything like a first-rate position. At one period of his career, however, and more particularly during the seasons of 1884 and 1886, he was beyond all question the best professional left-handed batsman in England. In 1884 he scored 567 runs for Notts in 13 matches, with an average of 31.9; in 1885, 442 runs in 14 engagements, with an average of 22.2; and in 1886, in county fixtures only, 559 runs, with an average of 29.8. Though he several times made higher scores, his finest performance was undoubtedly his innings of 90 for England against Australia at Kennington Oval in August, 1884. The match, as cricket readers will readily remember, resulted in a draw, Australia scoring 551 and England 346 and 85 for two wickets. In England's first innings, Scotton went in first, and was the ninth man out, the total when he left being 332. During a stay of five hours and three quarters he played the bowling of Spofforth, Palmer, Boyle, Midwinter, and George Giffen without giving the slightest chance, and but for his impregnable defence it is quite likely that England would have been beaten. Up to a certain time he received very little assistance, but when W. W. Read joined him, 151 runs were put on for the ninth wicket. Against the Australian

team of 1886 Scotton played two remarkable innings in company with Mr. W. G. Grace, the two batsmen scoring 170 together for the first wicket for England at the Oval, and 156 for Lord Londesborough's XI at Scarborough. Scotton's score at the Oval was only 34, but at Scarborough he made 71. Scotton paid three visits to Australia, going out with Shaw and Shrewsbury's teams in 1881, 1884 and 1886. In the three tours he averaged respectively in the 11-a-side matches, 20.8, 17.3, and 10.13. Few left-handed men have ever played with so straight a bat or possessed such a strong defence, but he carried caution to such extremes that it was often impossible to take any pleasure in seeing him play.

SEABROOK, Frederick James, died in hospital on August 7, 1979, aged 80. A member of the Haileybury XI in 1916 and 1917, he began to play for Gloucestershire in 1919. Going up to Cambridge at much above the ordinary age he won his Blue in 1926 as an opening batsman and played three years against Oxford, being captain in 1928. By 1928 he had become a most consistent scorer, was second in the Cambridge averages with 39.83, and for the whole season had a record of ·1,406 runs at 40.17. He continued to play for Gloucestershire in the school holidays until 1935. In the course of his career he scored eight centuries, the highest of them 136 for Gloucestershire v. Glamorgan in 1928. He was for many years a master at Haileybury and for some 20 years was in charge of cricket there.

SEAGRAM, Phillip Froude, who was born at Waterloo, Canada, came to London and was a victim of an air raid on March 8, 1941. He played cricket for Ridley, where he studied at the College, for Waterloo and Toronto from 1933 to 1939. Seagram proved himself a good batsman, but when visiting England in 1936 with the team brought over by the Hon. R. C. Matthews he averaged only 14, with a highest score of 26 not out. He took 21 wickets at 15.53 runs apiece. In August 1937 the M.C.C. for the first time sent out a team to Canada, 13 amateurs being captained by G. C. Newman, the Oxford Blue and Middlesex batsman. Against them Seagram played a capital innings of 66 for Toronto.

SEALY, James Edward Derek, who died in Trinidad on January 3, 1982, aged 69, was something of an infant prodigy. When he first played for West Indies, against England at Bridgetown in 1929–30, he was 17 years

122 days, at the time the youngest-ever Test cricketer. He still is the youngest to have played for West Indies. He was to become more than a very good, quick-footed batsman, occasionally bowling effectively at medium pace and twice (against England in 1939) keeping wicket in Test matches. He epitomised the natural cricketing ability of so many West Indians, his cap at a rakish angle, the bat seeming to be an extension of himself, often smiling, always friendly. As a boy, in his first Test match, he was placed in the order between Headley and Constantine and scored 58 against an England attack which included Voce, Rhodes and Stevens. In Australia in 1930–31 he had a disappointing tour and was not chosen to go to England in 1933. In 1934–35, by when he was 22, he averaged 45 in the four Test matches against R. E. S. Wyatt's England team, only Headley, with whom he added 202 for West Indies' third wicket at Kingston in the fourth Test match, doing better. In England in 1939 he made his highest first-class score, 181 in three and a half hours against Middlesex at Lord's, although more was expected of him as a batsman than he achieved. "Sealy," wrote *Wisden*, "not unlike Headley in appearance at the wicket, and somewhat similar in forcing tactics, showed less ability to score when playing back, but he gave some attractive displays." In 1941–42, for Barbados against Trinidad in Bridgetown, he had a large share in a remarkable record, taking eight wickets for eight runs as Trinidad were bowled out for 16 on a sticky wicket. After the War, having moved to Trinidad, he made no particular impact on West Indian cricket. He continued, however, to bring happiness wherever he went. In 11 Tests he scored 478 runs (average 28.11), with a highest score of 92 against England at Port-of-Spain in 1934–35, and took three wickets for 94 runs. His overall first-class record was 3,831 runs at an average of 30.40 and 63 wickets at 28.60 apiece.

SEARLE, James, died at Sydney on December 28, 1936, aged 75. He was a fine wicket-keeper for New South Wales just before the Sheffield Shield Competition was founded. While taking part in a trial match at Sydney he collided with a fence, fracturing his leg, but although giving up active cricket, he did valuable work as coach for public schools and New South Wales Cricket Association. In his early days he played for the Redfern club with F. R. Spofforth.

SECCULL, Arthur William, a member of the first South African team that visited England in 1894, died at Johannesburg on July 20, 1945, aged 76. During that tour Seccull scored 355 runs, average 15.10, his highest innings being 63 against Glamorgan. He took only four wickets at a cost of 42.30 each in first-class matches, but in South Africa he often bowled well and in March 1896 dismissed two batsmen for 37 runs in the third representative match against Lord Hawke's touring side at Cape Town. He played inter-provincial cricket regularly from 1887 to 1899, his highest score being 64 for Transvaal against Western Province.

SECRETAN, H. H., for many seasons a member of the Canterbury (N.Z.) team, died at Canterbury on June 16, 1911. In his last big match—against Auckland—he scored 75, but perhaps his best innings, taking into consideration the bowling against which it was played, was his 35 for Canterbury v. Murdoch's team of 1882.

SEDDON, Dudley Cecil, a representative player for New South Wales at cricket between 1926 and 1929 and as a fine Rugby League centre, died in Sydney on April 18, 1978, at the age of 75. Best known in more recent years for his work as a cricket administrator, Seddon acted as a N.S.W. selector for 20 years from 1947 and was an Australian selector from 1954 until replaced by Neil Harvey in 1967. "Snow" Seddon was a stalwart of the Petersham Club and, in four Sheffield Shield appearances, he scored 185 runs at an average of 27.85. But it was the enthusiasm and thoroughness with which he moved far and wide to seek out junior cricket talent that was the forte of this gentlemanly and well-liked member of the Sydney cricket fraternity.

SEITZ, John Arnold, who died on May 1, 1963, aged 79, was a Rhodes Scholar from Victoria and gained a Blue at Oxford in 1909. Returning to Melbourne, he took up teaching. In 1910 he made his first appearance for Victoria and scored a century in each of the matches with South Australia in 1911–12. In 1947 he was elected President of the Victoria Cricket Association, a position he held until he died. He was made a Companion of the Order of St. Michael and St. George in 1949. From 1936 until he retired in 1948, he was Director of Education for Victoria.

SELBY, John, (Notts), died on March 11, 1894. Born in Nottinghamshire on July 1,

1849, John Selby first came prominently before the public in the season of 1870, and for a number of years after that was a regular member of the Notts XI, assisting the county during the period of its greatest success. He played regularly down to the end of the season of 1886, but only made one appearance in 1877, from which time his connection with first-class cricket ceased. It is to be feared that in his later days he was anything but successful or prosperous. Indeed it is probable that the stroke of paralysis which ended his life in his 45th year was partially due to a criminal charge brought against him in Nottingham of which he was acquitted. In his day Selby was undoubtedly a first-class batsman. He was probably at his best in the seasons of 1872 and 1878. In the latter year he headed the Notts figures, in a very wet summer, with an aggregate of 577 and an average of 27.10, and scored for the Players against the Gentlemen at Lord's 88 and 64. Indeed, he and George Ulyett were that year the most successful professional batsmen in England. A professional runner of great merit, Selby during his early years in the Notts XI was an outfield of exceptional speed and brilliancy. He visited Australia in 1876–77 with James Lillywhite's team, and went out again with Shaw and Shrewsbury's XI in 1881–82.

SELBY, William, father of John Selby, and once a well-known Notts cricketer, died at Nottingham on January 29, 1892, in his 71st year. He had been for a long time connected with the ground staff at Trent Bridge, and in his day was a fairly good player. He was contemporary with Clarke, Redgate, Davies, George Parr and others of the old school who helped to make Notts famous before the County Club was established.

SELINCOURT, Hugh de, author of many delightful books about cricket, died at his home near Pulborough, Sussex, on January 20, 1951. He was 72. Educated at Dulwich and University College, Oxford, Mr. de Selincourt was for some years dramatic, then literary critic for London newspapers before he decided to devote his career to writing. Although his works were not confined to cricket, and there is no evidence that he was a specially accomplished player himself, he was perhaps best known for such tales as *The Cricket Match, Over* and *More Over*. These revealed particularly his love for cricket of the village-green variety.

SELLERS, Arthur, prominently connected with the Yorkshire County C.C. for 52 years, died on September 25, 1941, at Keighley, aged 71. He played for Yorkshire from 1889 to 1899, but only during two seasons—1892 and 1893—could he give much time to first-class cricket because of the call of business. In helping to raise Yorkshire to the championship for the first time, he came third in the 1893 averages, only J.T. Brown and John Tunnicliffe, who became such a great pair of opening batsmen, being above him, and there was little difference in their figures. Sellers excelled with two centuries, 105 at Lord's against Middlesex and 103 against Somerset at Sheffield. Only one other first-class county hundred was scored for Yorkshire that summer. Perhaps the most notable performance by Arthur Sellers was in June 1895, in the match celebrating the jubilee of I Zingari. The Gentlemen of England required 172 runs for victory, and Sellers, 70, and W.G. Grace, 101, hit off the runs in an hour and three-quarters. Sellers played each of these fine innings as opening batsman. Admirable in style, he used his height—6ft.—in forward play and driving, and his forcing strokes showed perfect timing. He fielded with dash and precision, usually in the deep. A vice-president of the County Club and chairman of the Yorkshire selection committee for many years, Arthur Sellers retained these offices until his death. Heredity in cricket had proof in the ability of his son, Arthur Brian Sellers, captain of Yorkshire from 1932; father and son afford the only instance of such relations each scoring 1,000 runs in a season for the county.

SELLERS, Arthur Brian, M.B.E., who died at his home near Bingley on February 20, 1981, aged 73, was one of the most effective county captains of this century. The great Yorkshire XIs of the 1920s, immensely powerful in batting, bowling and fielding, were for the most part weak in captaincy, but strong enough to triumph in spite of this. Sellers came into the side in 1932, without any previous first-class experience — when the official captain, F.E. Greenwood, found himself unable to play as much as he had hoped—and acting as captain in 25 matches he did not lose one. From the first he made it clear that, experienced or inexperienced, he was in charge and that what he said must be done. He could talk to the professionals in their own language and never minced his words, and after some initial dissatisfaction they became attached to him. Moreover other counties, however often they might be beaten, began to enjoy playing against Yorkshire, which had not always been the case. The cricket would be stern and tough but it would be good-humoured, and there were no longer the distasteful incidents arising from indiscipline, which had tended to mar their matches a few years earlier.

Sellers was captain from 1933 to 1947 and in those nine seasons led Yorkshire six times to the Championship. Had he been a better player, he would have made a captain of England in this country: whether he had the tact necessary to captain a touring side is more doubtful. His career figures of 9,273 runs with an average of 23 do not look much, but it needed a crisis to bring the best out of him and crises in his Yorkshire sides were rare. Typically, the first of his four hundreds was against the Australians in 1934, when Sutcliffe had had to retire from the match owing to an injury. Another was against Kent in 1937, when, coming in at 48 for five, he made 109. His highest score was 204 against Cambridge University in 1936. As a fieldsman he was in the top class, especially close to the wicket, and if he was sometimes criticised for placing key players in dangerous positions, he never shunned these positions himself. He played for the Gentlemen at Lord's in 1937.

Between 1938 and 1955 he was several times an England selector, and, until his retirement in 1972, was a leading member of the Yorkshire committee, where, while he rendered great service, his outspokenness also tended to involve him in storms, culminating in a major one in 1971 when Boycott was appointed to replace Close as captain. Sellers's father had been a prominent Yorkshire batsman in the 1890s, and was later Chairman of the county's selection committee.

SEN, Probir, who died in Calcutta on January 27, 1970, aged 43, kept wicket for India in 14 Test matches between 1947 and 1952, taking part in two tours abroad—in Australia in 1947–48 and England in 1952. He made his first-class debut when 17 in 1943 for Bengal, whom he later captained, and also played for Calcutta University. Before retiring in 1958, he helped in the dismissal of 125 men and as a right-handed batsman hit 2,461 runs in first-class cricket, average 23.66. His highest innings was 168 against Bihar at Jamshedpur in 1950–51, he and J. Mitter putting on 231 for the ninth Bengal wicket. He had also represented East Bengal at Association football and hockey.

SENANAYAKE, Dudley Shelton, who died on April 13, 1973, aged 61, was a free-scoring batsman and agile fieldsman when at St. Thomas's College, Ceylon, where his father, D. S. Senanayake, had also been a member of the cricket team. His father became Ceylon's first Prime Minister. Going to England, Dudley took part in trials at Cambridge and appeared for Indian Gymkhana. At home, he played for Sinhalese S.C., being a consistent scorer in club cricket. Even when he was Prime Minister of Sri Lanka, he captained Cambridge in the local "Oxford v. Cambridge" match.

SERJEANT, Sir David Maurice, M.D., born at Ramsey, Hampshire, January 18, 1830, died at Camberwell, January 12, 1929, within a few days of entering upon his 100th year. As far back as August, 1850, he was a member of the XXII of Peterborough side which beat the All England XI by 13 wickets. In that game he scored five and five, being caught by Felix off Martingell in the first innings and bowled by Wisden in the second. Clarke, Hillyer and Alfred Mynn also bowled. Going to Australia whilst still a young man, Sir David opened the innings for Victoria in each of the first two matches ever played against New South Wales—at Melbourne in March, 1856, and at Sydney in January, 1857. To the end of his long life he took the deepest interest in cricket, and as recently as 1926 was among those who welcomed the Australians on their arrival in London. He was the author of *Australia: Its Cricket Bat, Its Kangaroo, Its Farming, Fruit and Flowers*.

SESHA CHARI, Kilvidi, born in Madras, January 2, 1875; died of pneumonia, at Calcutta, January 25, 1917. Best wicket-keeper India ever produced. Came to England with the All-India team in 1911.

SETON-KARR, Walter Scott, born on January 23, 1822, died at Auchinskeoch, Dalbeattie, on November 22, 1910, aged 88. Entering Rugby School in 1836, he formed one of the XI in the first match ever played between the School and the M.C.C.—at Lord's in June, 1840, when he scored four and 10 and took two wickets. Among his companions in the XI on that occasion were three subsequent Oxford Blues, Messrs. W. S. Townshend and the brothers G. E. and Thomas Hughes. Mr. Seton-Karr was a godson of Sir Walter Scott.

SEVERN, Arthur, an opening batsman for Derbyshire in 1919 and 1920, died on January 10, 1949, aged 55. He joined the nursery staff at Derby in 1914, and after war service with the Coldstream Guards played regularly in 1919. In this season he enjoyed one very successful match, against Leicestershire at Leicester, where he scored 73 and 52 not out. In 1920, however, he severed his connection with Derbyshire after playing only six innings and went to live at Stainforth, near Doncaster.

SEVERN, Dr Clifford Brill, who died in California in February, 1981, aged 90, was a pioneer of cricket in Southern California. One of the founders, in 1931, of the Hollywood Cricket Club, he was an Honorary Member of the M.C.C. For more than half a century he worked hard to keep cricket in America alive.

SEWELL, The Rev. Arthur, died at Cambridge on November 13, 1947, in his 107th year. Radley XI 1859 and 1860. Rowed in the eight. At the time of his death was the oldest clergyman of the Church of England, the oldest Radleian and the oldest member of Oxford University. Chaplain of the Order of St. John of Jerusalem since 1871. Assistant Master at Malvern 1866–71. Actively engaged in Church work until 1935.

SEWELL, Cyril Otto Hudson, who died at Bexhill on August 19, 1951, was born at Pietermaritzburg, Natal, on December 19, 1874. He was only 19 years of age when he visited England as a member of the first South African side in 1894. Despite his youth and lack of experience in representative cricket, he made most runs, 1,038 (average 30.52) on the tour, hitting 170 v. Somerset at Taunton and 128 v. Derbyshire at Derby. Later he came to live in England and he assisted Gloucestershire periodically from 1895 to 1919. He captained the county in 1913 and 1914, and was secretary from 1912 to 1914, succeeding Mr. G. L. Jessop in both offices. He toured Canada and the United States with P. F. Warner's team in 1898. Sewell will be remembered as a hard-hitting, attractive batsman and a magnificent off-side fieldsman. During the First World War he served as a Major in the Oxfordshire and Bucks Regiment, previously having been with the 5th Gloucesters.

SEWELL, Edward Humphrey Dalrymple, well known for many years as a cricket and Rugby football journalistic reporter, died on September 21, 1947, aged nearly 75. Born in India, where his father was an Army officer, he was educated at Bedford Grammar School, captaining the cricket and Rugby teams and playing for Bedfordshire County. In a curiously varied life he returned to India as a civil servant, and his very powerful hitting enabled him to make many big scores at an exceptional rate of scoring. The first batsman in India to make three consecutive hundreds, he also twice exceeded 200. Sometimes he enjoyed the advantage of having Ranjitsinhji for captain. Coming back to England, he joined the Essex County Club as a professional and met with considerable success, notably in 1904 at Edgbaston, where, with Bob Carpenter, he shared in an opening stand of 142. He used to relate that the partnership lasted only 65 minutes—he was first out for 107; but, as he added, "They didn't give prizes for the fastest century in those days." The time was given officially as 80 minutes. In 1904, for London County, captained by W. G. Grace, he played his highest innings in first-class cricket, 181, against Surrey at Crystal Palace; one of his on-drives off Lockwood measured 140yd. He punished moderate bowling in matches of minor class with merciless severity. Whitgift School suffered especially when, at Croydon for M.C.C., he hit up 142 out of 162 in 50 minutes, and again at the Oval, where for Wanderers he hit three sixes and 19 fours while scoring 108. After being a coach at the Oval, he became hon. secretary to the Buckinghamshire Club and played for the county as an amateur. He bowled medium pace with marked effect against any batsmen but the best, and fielded with dash and certainty. During recent years he attended every match of importance at Lord's, having a regular seat in the Long Room, where he was often the centre of discussions on the game he loved and knew so thoroughly. He gave practical evidence of this in several books— *From a Window at Lord's, The Log of a Sportsman* and *Who Won the Toss* being the best known. He played Rugby football for Blackheath and Harlequins; put the shot 37ft. and threw the cricket ball 117yd. at athletic sports meetings.

SEWELL, J. J., died at Pietermaritzburg on June 8, 1897. Born on February 10, 1844, he was only in his 54th year. Inasmuch as he left England for the Cape 30 years ago, Mr. J. J. Sewell was quite unknown to the present generation, but his former fame as a batsman was vividly brought to mind by the doings for the South African team in 1894, and afterwards for Gloucestershire of his son, Mr. C. O. H. Sewell. Cricketers whose experience goes back to the '60s will remember Mr. J. J. Sewell, first as the most brilliant Marlborough batsman of his day, and later as a valuable member of the Middlesex XI, when at the start of the County Club's existence, the home matches were played at the Cattle Market Ground at Islington. At the Oval in 1866 he played, against Surrey, an innings of 166, which is still referred to by those who saw it as something quite exceptional in the way of free hitting. After the season of 1867 Mr. Sewell settled at the Cape, and was thenceforth lost to English cricket. The news of his illness last spring caused his son to leave England for Pietermaritzburg, and the announcement of his death appeared soon afterwards.

SEWELL, Robert Page, who played frequently for Essex some 10 or 12 years ago, died at Surbiton on February 7, 1901. He was a very good batsman, and above the average as a bowler.

SEYMOUR, Charles Read, who died at Winchester on November 6, 1934, was in his 80th year having been born on February 6, 1855. He failed to find a place in the Harrow XI but, a batsman of more than average skill and a smart point, he played for M.C.C. and for Hampshire from 1880.

SEYMOUR, James, an indispensable member of the great Kent XIs before the First World War, was born at Brightling, in Sussex, on October 25, 1879, and died at Marden on September 30, 1930, aged 50. He played for Kent through long residence at Pembury. Like Humphreys, whose name is inevitably associated with his own, he never rose to the highest standard of representative cricket for in his day that standard was very high but as a county player he was in the highest class. In August during any of Kent's halcyon years, when room had to be found for so many great amateur players, it must have been almost impossible to decide on what actually was Kent's best team, but Seymour could never be left out. He was not a classic batsman—even in those days his stance was too modern—but he possessed many strokes both skilful and attractive. His flash past cover-point was a thing of special delight, and if he did not always appear sure of himself in playing fast bowling, he was a wonderfully watchful player of the ball on a turning wicket. As a slip fieldsman he ranked with the greatest in that position, the combination of Huish, Seymour, J. R. Mason, R. N. R. Blaker, and K. L. Hutch-

ings behind the wicket being one difficult to surpass. Whilst fielding there he caught six South Africans in an innings at Canterbury in 1904. He never took part in a Test and appeared in only three Gentlemen v. Players matches, in the first of which—at the Oval in 1913—he made 80 in his second innings. In 1900 he was engaged to play for the London County C.C. and an innings of 66 not out which he made in that year for Kent Club and Ground against Gravesend gained for him the offer of a place on the ground staff at Tonbridge. There he developed his skill considerably through the coaching of the late Capt. W. McCanlis. His first season as a regular member of the Kent team was in 1902 and from then until 1927 he was a regular member of the side. When in 1906 Kent won the County Championship, he scored 1,096 runs and was the leading professional batsman of the XI and in 1913 had a great season, finishing up with an aggregate of 2,088 runs and an average of 38. He scored 53 centuries during his career and twice made a three-figure innings in each innings of a match—against Worcestershire at Maidstone in 1904 and against Essex at Leyton in 1923. He played a great innings against Hampshire at Tonbridge in 1907, his 204 setting up a new record for Kent, and twice subsequently again exceeded the second hundred, scoring 218 not out v. Essex at Leyton in 1911 and 214 against the same county at Tunbridge Wells three years later. Only Woolley and Hardinge had played more three-figure innings for Kent and in all matches for the county, including those in the American tour of 1903, he scored 27,064 runs with an average of 32. His benefit was against Hampshire at Canterbury in 1920, and arising from it was the case—brought to the House of Lords—that established the right of the cricket benefit, unless guaranteed by contract, to be free from tax. After he had dropped out of first-class cricket he accepted an engagement as coach at Epsom College. He was brother of John Seymour who played for Sussex.

SEYMOUR, John, who died on December 2, 1967, aged 84, played as a professional for Sussex for four years from 1904 before joining Northamptonshire, whom he served from 1908 to 1919. In all first-class cricket he scored 3,430 runs, average 17.06; took with right-arm bowling of medium pace 107 wickets for 26.42 runs each and held 97 catches. Going to Northamptonshire primarily as a bowler, he developed into a useful batsman. His one century was a highly valuable effort.

Going in at Blackwell in 1913 when Northamptonshire had lost six wickets to the Derbyshire bowlers for 112 runs, he hit 136 out of 206, including one five and 21 fours in two hours 10 minutes and was not out when the innings closed. Northamptonshire won the match by nine wickets. John was the brother of James Seymour, of Kent.
CORRECTION. In the 1969 edition, Obituary, 1967, wrongly described John Seymour as a medium-pace right-arm bowler. He did, in fact, bowl slow left-arm.

SHACKLOCK, Frank, who died at Christchurch, New Zealand, on May 3, 1937, aged 75, played for the Nottinghamshire XI from 1886 to 1893. Nearly 6ft. tall, he bowled fast right-hand, sometimes round the wicket, with a slinging action which made the ball swing away. He was considered particularly difficult because of this pronounced swerve from leg, varied with an off-break that came very quickly from the turf.

Shacklock belonged to an old Kirkby-in-Ashfield family, but was born in Derbyshire and played for both counties before receiving a professional engagement in Scotland where he did some remarkable performances. For Lasswade he took all 11 wickets in a 12-a-side match against Edinburgh University and all 10 against Loretto.

Frank Shacklock began first-class cricket by failing to score in either innings when making a solitary appearance for Nottinghamshire in 1883, but in the same match five M.C.C. wickets for 48 was a performance indicating bowling ability. During the next two seasons he appeared for Derbyshire with considerable success, particularly when he dismissed eight Yorkshire men for 45 runs at Derby in 1885—13 in the match for 132. On four other occasions he took eight wickets in an innings, his best analysis being at Lord's in 1887, when M.C.C. batsmen scored only 32 runs off him.

He became most prominent in 1889 when 80 wickets fell to him at 14 runs apiece. Nottinghamshire then tied with Surrey and Lancashire for the Championship. Shacklock was on the ground staff at Lord's for several seasons doing useful work for M.C.C. and he was in the Players XI of 1889. In 1893 at Trent Bridge he took four Somerset wickets with successive balls and in the innings eight for 46.

Although unreliable with the bat, Shacklock played some valuable innings at a time when runs did not come easily. At Clifton in 1887 against Gloucestershire his 71 included three square-leg hits out of the ground and

his partnership with Arthur Shrewsbury, not out 119, contributed largely to victory by an innings and 65 runs. In the follow-on, W. G. Grace carried his bat through the innings for 113. After losing his form, Shacklock emigrated to New Zealand, where he proved a valuable coach.

SHAKESPEARE, Wing-Commdr. William Harold Nelson, O.B.E., M.C., A.F.C., President of the Worcestershire County C.C., died on July 10, 1976, at the age of 83. Between 1919 and 1931 he played intermittently for the county scoring 789 runs with an average of 19.72. Worcestershire were then very weak and some of Shakespeare's performances suggested that he would have been valuable if he could have played regularly. His highest score was 62 not out v. Glamorgan in 1924, when he and Preece added 79 for the ninth wicket in half an hour. In the following year he and G. E. B. (now Sir George) Abell put on 111, also for the ninth wicket, v. Middlesex at Lord's, Shakespeare's share being 56. Working in London, he scored heavily for Brondesbury for many years.

SHALDERS, William A., born February 10, 1880; died at Cradock, Cape Province, March 18, 1917. Griqualand West XI; Transvaal XI; played for South Africa in Test matches v. England and Australia. Was a member of the teams that came to England in 1904 and 1907. Without being one of the stars of the famous South African side in 1907, Shalders was a very useful bat. He played an innings of 108 against Hampshire, and came out sixth on the list for the whole tour, getting 747 runs in 22 matches, with an average of just under 22. His best scores in the three Test games were 31 and not out 24 at the Oval. For the 1904 team he had an excellent record, scoring 842 runs and averaging 27. As his biggest innings was 81 his figures meant very consistent work.

SHARDLOW, Bertie (Bert), who died in hospital on April 30, 1976, after a long illness, did wonderful work as a slow left-hander for Staffordshire between 1936 and 1957, taking in that time 558 wickets. No less a judge than Sydney Barnes reckoned that, had he accepted one of several offers which he received to qualify for a first-class county, he might well have played for England; but it was 1947 before he clearly established himself as an outstanding bowler and at 37 he naturally felt he was safer to stick to his trade as a boat carpenter. Apart from his bowling he was a useful bat and had played a number of times for representative Minor County teams.

SHARP, Aubrey Temple, who died in Leicester after a motor-car accident on February 15, 1973, aged 83, played for Leicestershire as an amateur from 1908 to 1934. He scored 5,263 runs, average 25.06, and brought off 61 catches. He turned out in matches during the Second World War when over 50. As captain in 1921, he headed the batting figures with 814 runs, including four of his eight centuries, average 40.70. In 1911 at Chesterfield, he and Major G. H. S. Fowke put on 262 for the sixth wicket—still a record for the county, Sharp playing his highest innings, 216. He was a solicitor.

SHARP, John, who died on January 27, 1938, enjoyed an unparalleled career in cricket and football. As a professional with Everton, he took part in two final ties for the Football Association Cup and was on the winning side in 1906. He helped England beat Ireland in 1903, in 1905 was in the XI victorious over Scotland and he became a director of the Everton Club. When still in his football prime as an outside right, he played in three cricket Tests against the Australian team of 1909, scoring 105 at the Oval, the only century for England in that series. The Oval match was made historic by Warren Bardsley getting 136 and 130—the first batsman credited with two centuries in a Test and the only Australian who has met with such success. From 1899 to 1914 Sharp was a regular member of the Lancashire XI and played in all the matches of 1904 when the Championship was won without defeat being suffered. After the War he appeared as an amateur and captained the side from 1923 to 1925 when he retired. In 1924 he was on the England Test selection committee with H. D. G. Leveson Gower and John Daniell — so completing a unique set of honours.

Born at Hereford on February 15, 1878, John Sharp showed exceptional batting ability when 14 years of age by scoring 208 not out against Ledbury, but for Lancashire he did best as a bowler for some time. Short and thick-set he put a lot of power behind the ball and, if not very fast, he kept up a good pace with off-break and lift. In 1901 he took 112 wickets at 22.43 each, and with 883 runs, average 25.22, he was the one notable all-rounder in his county XI. Nine batsmen fell to him in an innings at Worcester and ten years later at Derby he took five wickets for 14 runs. Another good performance with the

ball was seven Middlesex wickets for 25 at Lord's in 1909, six men being dismissed by him in the course of four overs and two balls. Altogether for Lancashire Sharp took 448 wickets at 26.22 runs apiece. His batting figures are much more impressive—20,829 runs for the county and 22,715 all told, average nearly 32 in each case, while his first-class centuries numbered 38, the highest being 211 against Leicestershire at Old Trafford in 1912. On that occasion A. H. Hornby, then the Lancashire captain, helped Sharp add 245 for the eighth wicket in two hours and a half.

Always good to watch, Sharp scored freely to the off by hard drives and cuts, while, like most short batsmen, he pulled with plenty of power. Brilliant fielding, usually at cover point, completed John Sharp's cricket equipment and a bright cheerful disposition helped him as captain; yet an error in judging a catch influenced his retirement from first-class cricket. This happened when Cecil Parkin was taking his benefit at Old Trafford in 1925. Middlesex won the toss and John Sharp, fielding at short-leg, missed H. W. Lee off the first ball. An opening partnership of 121 between Lee and J. W. Hearne ensued and Middlesex won decisively. Sharp was greatly upset by the attitude of some of the crowd over the dropped catch, and he threatened never again to play at Old Trafford. The Lancashire Committee persuaded him to change his decision, but at the end of the season Sharp sent in his resignation.

In 1913 John Sharp was given a benefit which realised £1,679 and in 1936 he was made an honorary life member of the Lancashire County Club.

SHARP, General Sir John Aubrey Taylor, K.C.B., M.C., died suddenly in Oslo on January 15, 1977, aged 59. A son of the former Leicestershire captain, A. T. Sharp, he was in the Repton XI as a batsman in 1936 and between 1937 and 1946 played occasionally for Leicestershire. For Cambridge University v. Essex in 1939 he made top score, 36, in the first innings, but failed to get his Blue.

SHARPE, The Rev. Charles Molesworth, died on June 25, 1935, in his 84th year, having been born on September 6, 1851, at Codicote, Hertfordshire. Educated privately, he went to Jesus College, Cambridge, and got his Blue in 1875. A slow round-arm bowler with tremendous break, which was described at the time as "very deceptive," he met with marked success when first appearing at Lord's against M.C.C. and a week later he took five wickets for 89 runs in Oxford's first innings and six for 66 in the second; but in a great finish Cambridge were beaten by six runs. As Sharpe made 35 runs for once out in a low scoring match, he was unfortunate to be on the losing side. The same season he appeared once for Yorkshire, but bowled without success and scored only 15. He played for Hertfordshire from 1884 to 1890. He was in the Cambridge Association Football XI of 1874 and 1875. Curate in turn at Sheffield, Huddersfield and Tankersley, he was Vicar of Elsecar, Barnsley, from 1888 to 1922.

SHARPE, John William, the old Surrey and Nottinghamshire fast-medium right-hand bowler, died on June 19, 1936, at Ruddington, the place of his birth, aged 69. His father, Samuel Sharpe, played for Nottinghamshire and John Sharpe received trials for the Colts against the county at Trent Bridge. On one occasion, he took four wickets for five runs, but there was not room for him in the very powerful Nottinghamshire XI of those days and so Sharpe qualified at Kennington Oval. Playing for Surrey from 1889 to 1893, he took 462 wickets at 13.81 runs each in all matches for the county. His best year was 1890, when altogether 179 wickets fell before him at just over 12 runs apiece. Next season in the match with Middlesex at the Oval, he dismissed nine men for 47 in the first innings and five for 50 in the second. Against Lancashire at Old Trafford in 1890 and next year against Somerset at the Oval, he and Lohmann bowled unchanged through both innings. In 1890 he played for England against Australia at the Oval, and in the autumn of 1891 he went to Australia with the team organised by Lord Sheffield. Sharpe bowled specially well on hard pitches and could make the ball break from the off to a remarkable degree for a man of such pace; his extra fast "yorker" was deadly. Although handicapped by the loss of his right eye, Sharpe was a smart field and often proved a useful batsman, notably on his first appearance for Surrey, when he helped George Lohmann put on 149 runs for the last wicket against Essex. Later in the season he and Beaumont, going in number 11, made 118 together. After returning from Australia Sharpe lost his form and, though he appeared for Nottinghamshire in 1894, his first-class career practically ceased when he left Surrey. At that time, Surrey were exceptionally strong; from 1887 to 1895,' they only

once fell from first place in the County Championship.

SHARPE, Samuel, born at Ruddington, Notts, on January 13, 1839, died at his native place on November 5, 1924. In 1868 he appeared in two matches for his county, scoring 29 runs with an average of 9.66. Later he became associated with the Rock Ferry C.C., for whose first XI he played for 22 years. He was father of J. W. Sharpe, the well-known Notts and Surrey cricketer.

SHAW, Alfred, after a long illness, died at his home, Gedling, near Nottingham, on January 16, 1907. In him there passed away one of the greatest figures in modern cricket. His connection with the game lasted more than 40 years, only ending in 1905, when, despite shattered health, he managed somehow to get through his duties as one of the umpires in county matches. It was felt, however, that he no longer possessed the strength for the work, and when the county captains met at Lord's to select the umpires for the following season, his name was omitted from the list. Born at Burton Joyce on August 29, 1842, Alfred Shaw played his first match at Lord's in 1864 for the Colts of England against the M.C.C. and Ground. The Colts were beaten by 10 runs, but Shaw did great things, taking 13 wickets and dividing the honours of the game with the late William Oscroft, who, also appearing at Lord's for the first time, scored 51 and 76. Both men were at once given places in the Notts XI, and in the following year Alfred Shaw had the distinction of being picked for Players against Gentlemen, both at Lord's and the Oval. In this early part of his career Shaw's bowling was faster than in later years, and he was essentially an all-round man. Indeed, so good was his batting that in the Gentlemen and Players' match at the Oval in 1866 he made a score of 70. His great days began about 1870 or 1871. With a decrease of speed he got far more spin and break on the ball, and from 1872 to 1880 he was, beyond all question, the best slow bowler in England. After his first trip to Australia he was laid aside in the season of 1877 by a severe attack of bronchitis, but otherwise his success was uninterrupted. After being on the M.C.C.'s ground staff from 1865 to 1867, inclusive, he had a year with the All England XI, but in 1870 he returned to Lord's, and for the M.C.C. and Notts most of his best work was done. His position as the leading bowler of his day once established he paid less regard to batting, contending that no bowler who wished to remain for any length of time at his best ought to get many runs. For his self-denial in this respect he was well rewarded, his form with the ball being uniformly good until he was close upon 40 years of age.

Of all his feats, perhaps the most remarkable was accomplished in a match at Lord's in 1875, between Notts and the M.C.C. In the M.C.C.'s second innings he sent down 41 overs and two balls for seven runs and seven wickets, bowling out, among other batsmen, W. G. Grace, A. W. Ridley, C. F. Buller, and Lord Harris. On May 27, 1878, he played for the M.C.C. at Lord's in the sensational match against the first Australian XI, and it was no fault of his that the club suffered a nine wickets' defeat, he and the late Fred Morley getting the Australians out for a total of 41. A little over two years later Shaw appeared for England against Australia at the Oval in the first Test match ever played in this country. After 1880 his bowling began to show some falling off, and in the great match at the Oval in 1882 England's slow bowler was Peate. In the meantime the only regrettable incident of Shaw's career had occurred, he being one of the prime movers in the strike of the Notts professionals in 1881. The quarrel was made up before the end of the season, but it left some feeling of soreness behind. Shaw continued to play for Notts for some years longer, dropping out of the XI in 1887. Though he was at that time a man of 45, it was probably a mistaken policy on the part of the Notts committee to dispense with his services. He had great influence over the other Notts professionals, and for that reason, together with his long experience and fine knowledge of the game, was most valuable as captain. When a few years later the fortunes of Notts had declined, a member of the team was heard to say very sorrowfully, "We never went down the hill while we had Shaw with us." That the veteran had a good deal of cricket left in him was proved when he afterwards played, under the residential qualification, for Sussex. Time had robbed him of much of his spin, but his bowling was still wonderfully steady. However, he soon found the strain of county cricket too much for him at his age, and, without any formal farewell, he retired from the active pursuit of the game, and in due course took up umpiring.

As a bowler Alfred Shaw placed his chief reliance on accuracy of pitch. In this respect he has never been surpassed. When in his prime he could keep up his end for hours, without ever becoming short or getting in any way loose. In being able to get through so much work he was greatly helped by his delivery, which, from the beginning of his career to its close, was beautifully easy and natural. When the ground helped him, he broke back a good deal, but he never set much store on a big break, always arguing that the most dangerous ball was the one that did just enough to beat the bat. Unlike most of the present-day bowlers, he regarded the off theory as more or less a waste of time, preferring to keep on the wicket and trust to variations of pace and elevation to deceive the batsmen. It may be interesting here to quote W. G. Grace's opinion of him. In his book on cricket Mr. Grace says: "The great power of his bowling lay in its good length and unvaried precision. He could break both ways, but got more work on the ball from the off; and he was one of the few bowlers who could very quickly cause a batsman to make a mistake if he was too eager to hit. An impatient batsman might make two spanking hits in succession off him, but he would not make a third. Shaw was sure to take his measure and get him in a difficulty. On a good wicket, when batting against him, I did not find it difficult to play the ball; but I had to watch him carefully, and wait patiently before I could score."

In Shaw's great day scores were by no means so big as they are now, and as compared with the doings of even the best of his successors his figures seem very wonderful. To give only one example, he took in 1880 177 wickets in first-class matches for less than nine runs apiece. It must be said, however, that at that time batsmen had not acquired anything like their present ability to get runs on wickets spoilt by rain. The arts of "pulling" and "hooking" have made a great advance during the last quarter of a century. Still, Shaw contended that even modern batsmen would not have dared to pull so much if the bowling had been as steady in length as it was in his time. In conjunction with James Lillywhite and the late Arthur Shrewsbury, Shaw, beginning in the winter of 1881–82, took four teams to Australia. The first three trips answered very well, but the fourth venture—in 1887–88—resulted in financial disaster, another English XI, with the late Mr. G. F. Vernon as captain, touring Australia at the same time. The Melbourne Club was responsible for the visit of Mr. Vernon's side, and they, like Shaw and Shrewsbury, suffered heavily in pocket. Shaw went to Australia for the last time as manager of Lord Sheffield's XI in 1891–92, and discharged a difficult task with unfailing tact and judgment. It was through Lord Sheffield that he first became associated with Sussex cricket, being engaged while still a member of the Notts XI to coach the young Sussex players.

SHAW, David Bruce, born on August 15, 1907, died of pneumonia on December 31, 1925, at the early age of 18. A member of the Marlborough College XI of 1925, he took part in the sensational finish of the match with Rugby at Lord's. He was the slow bowler of the team and he went in to bat last when his side were a long way behind and half an hour remained for play. He and F. G. Philpott, however, stayed together and saved the match. Just over a month before his death, Shaw was given his Rugby football Fifteen colours.

SHAW, The Right Rev. Edward Domett, Bishop of Buckingham, died at Marlow on November 5, 1937, aged 77. From Forest School he went to Oriel College, Oxford, and got his Blue in 1882. Second in the averages to C. F. H. Leslie he made 63 and four at Lord's in the match which Cambridge, who included the three Studds, Lord Hawke, F. E. Lacey and C. Aubrey Smith, won by seven wickets. An opening batsman with sound defence and good style in stroke play, E. D Shaw did a notable performance in the opening match of the Australians' tour in 1882. Oxford faced a total of 362, and they fared badly but Shaw carried his bat for 78 in a total of 189. The Australians won by nine wickets, H. H. Massie following his highest innings in England, 206, by making 46 not out. Shaw played for Essex, Middlesex, Hertfordshire and Buckinghamshire. A fast medium paced bowler, he took nine wickets in an innings of 17 for which 12 of M.C.C. were dismissed by Wooburn House in 1886. Two of his sons were in the Marlborough XI before joining the Army: both were killed in the First World War.

SHAW, George Bernard, who died in a car accident in South Australia in August, 1984, aged 52, took 26 wickets for Glamorgan between 1951 and 1955 with his off-spinners at 27.15 apiece. He was not a batsman.

SHAW, James, who was born at Linthwaite on March 12, 1866, died at Armley on January 22, 1921. In four matches for Yorkshire in 1896 his slow left-handed bowling accounted for 16 wickets for 18.18 runs each.

SHAW, Vero Kemball (afterwards Shaw-Mackenzie), who appeared in the Kent XI from 1875 to 1878, was born at Belgaum, Bombay, on January 14, 1854, and died at Hastings on December 18, 1905. He was in the Haileybury XI of 1870 and 1871, and played for Cambridge against Oxford in 1876. He was a good batsman and field and a useful fast left-handed bowler. His highest score for his county was 74 v. Surrey, at Maidstone, in 1876.

SHEEPSHANKS, Ernest Richard, was killed on December 31, 1937, while acting as special correspondent to Reuter's with the insurgent forces in Spain. Born on March 22, 1910, he met his tragic end when 27. Very prominent in every respect at Eton, he was President of "Pop," captain of cricket, and a member of the Association football and Fives teams.

A first-rate batsman, he was in the Eton XI of 1927 before being captain. He used his feet cleverly and possessed excellent judgment in stroke-play and admirable defence. He saved Eton from the probability of a follow-on against Winchester in 1927 when, after the fall of nine wickets for 108, he and R. H. R. Buckston, the present Derbyshire captain, put on 144 for the last stand, exactly clearing off the arrears. Sheepshanks scored 116, hitting with remarkable freedom until the follow-on was saved; then he trod on his wicket.

In the following season, he helped Eton to victory by 28 runs over Harrow—a fine performance considering that Eton were 108 behind on the first innings. Sheepshanks and I. Akers-Douglas added 149 for the third wicket in the second innings, Sheepshanks, despite the handicap of a damaged hand, scoring 69.

At Cambridge he took part in the Freshmen's match in 1929 and the Seniors' matches of 1930 and 1931, but did not play for the University. In 1929 he appeared in the Yorkshire XI.

SHEFFIELD, Edward James, who died on April 28, 1971 aged 62, was a professional fast-medium in-swing bowler for Surrey from 1930 to 1932. He did specially well in 1931 when heading the county bowling averages with 57 wickets at 18.47 runs each. In 1933, he gained a place in the Kent side for four Championship matches without meeting with much success before recurring back trouble compelled his retirement. For a few years he acted as coach to Dudley, the Birmingham League club.

SHEFFIELD, Third Earl of, Henry North Holroyd, Viscount Pevensey, Baron Sheffield of Dunsmore, Meath, Baron Sheffield of Roscommon, in Ireland, and Baron Sheffield, of Sheffield, Yorkshire, was born in London on January 18, 1832, and died at Beaulieu on April 21, 1909. By his death Sussex lost the best supporter of cricket they ever had. When the fortunes of the county were at a low ebb he engaged Alfred Shaw and William Mycroft to coach young Sussex players of promise, thereby benefiting the game in the county to a very great extent. His liberality, in fact, was almost unbounded. Unlike Lord Harris he never gained fame as a player, but in 1856, when Viscount Pevensey, was considered good enough to play for the Gentlemen of Sussex against the Gentlemen of Kent. He was President of the County Club from 1879 until 1897, and was re-elected to the position in 1904, when he made an additional donation to the Club of £100. In the winter of 1891–92, entirely at his own expense, he took an English team to Australia, chiefly in order that the Australian public might have another opportunity of seeing W. G. Grace. The visit benefited the game in Australia enormously, and to commemorate the trip Lord Sheffield presented a trophy, known as the Sheffield Shield, for competition between Victoria, South Australia, and New South Wales. His private ground at Sheffield Park was opened in 1846 and no charge was ever made for admission. Five of the Australian teams opened their tours there, as did the South African team of 1894. Lord Sheffield had been a member of the M.C.C. since 1855.

SHELTON, Albert William, a close follower and strong supporter of cricket, died at his home in Nottingham on September 10, 1938, aged 75. Taken ill, when packing his bag preparatory to making his customary visit to Scarborough for the Festival, he never rallied. An estate agent, he was a leading authority on housing and town planning. Apart from professional duties, his chief interest was cricket; and particularly the Nottinghamshire County Club to which he belonged, as member, committeeman, and president, during more than 50 years of his busy life. Mr. Shelton and Mr. J. A. Dixon, captain of the county XI for many seasons last century, shared the distinction of being elected honorary life members of the Committee. Mr. Shelton wrote the history of the Trent Bridge ground for last year's *Wisden* and preferred that his share in arranging for purchasing and improving the ground should not be mentioned. He used to recall memories of all the Australian visiting teams from personal knowledge as a spectator, and in this historical vein he was mainly instrumental in collecting the cricket curiosities and library in the Trent Bridge pavilion. Always considerate for the welfare of professional players, he was pioneer in the insurance of benefit matches against interference by weather.

SHENTON, J. C. L., who died on January 26, 1900, was well known in connection with the Clapton Club. He played for Middlesex v. Kent, at Gravesend, in August, 1888.

SHEPHERD, James Stevens Fraser, who died at Dunedin on July 11, 1970, aged 78, represented New Zealand in five matches in the early '20s. An attractive batsman possessing a variety of strokes, he generally opened the innings for Albion C.C. and for Otago. He made his debut for Otago in 1912–13 and in his first match after the First World War hit a brilliant 146 against Canterbury. In 1923–24 he scored 307 runs, average 51.16, in three Plunket Shield games, sharing with R. W. de R. Worker in partnerships of 154 and 155 in the fixture with Wellington.

SHEPHERD, Thomas F., who died in Kingston Hospital on February 13, 1957, aged 66, was one of Surrey's great batsmen at a period after the First World War when the county were richly endowed with run-getters and a place in the side was extremely difficult to command. Between 1919 and 1932, when he retired and became head groundsman and coach to Wandgas C.C.—a post he held until his death—Shepherd hit 18,719 runs, including 42 centuries, average 39.82, in first-class cricket, took 441 wickets, average 30.81, with medium-pace bowling, and, generally fielding in the slips, held 268 catches.

His rise to fame was sensational. In 1920 he provided almost the entire batting strength of the Second XI. He hit 236 from the Essex Second XI bowling at Leyton and altogether scored 709 runs, average 101.28. As he also took 38 wickets, average 15.50, he headed both sets of averages. These performances literally forced Surrey to give him a regular position in the Championship team, and he seized his opportunity with such avidity that in each of 11 successive seasons he exceeded 1,000 runs. In 1921 he distinguished himself by hitting 212 against Lancashire at the Oval and 210 not out against Kent at Blackheath—then known as

"The Surrey Graveyard"—in following innings and he obtained 1,658 runs, including six centuries, in Championship fixtures, average 51.81. He did even better in 1927, putting together eight scores of three figures, with 277 not out against Gloucestershire at the Oval the highest. In the course of his innings which, the biggest of his career, occupied four and three-quarter hours, he and A. Ducat put on 289 in two and three-quarter hours for the fourth wicket. Shepherd's aggregate that summer reached 2,145, average 55.00, of which 1,681 were registered in competition matches. The previous season he hit two separate centuries in a match—121 and 101 not out from the Leicestershire attack at the Oval.

Born at Headington Quarry, near Oxford, Shepherd played for his village team at the early age of 11. A player of imperturbable temperament, he suited his methods to the conditions and the state of the game, for while he could pull and hit to the off with exhilarating power, he was capable of considerable patience. He appeared in Test trial matches and for Players against Gentlemen, but, so great was the competition during his time, he never played for England.

SHEPHERD, William, who died at Tooting on May 27, 1919, was in his 78th year. He was born at Kennington on August 9, 1841, and had a brief connection with the Surrey XI, playing regularly in 1864, but failing to keep his place in the following season. In 1864, when Surrey had a wonderful season—the only match they lost was against Fourteen of Hampshire—Shepherd bowled uncommonly well, and made up to some extent for the absence of Caffyn. Bowling left-hand medium pace with a decided twist he had such a peculiar delivery that he was sometimes called the "corkscrew" bowler. Against Sussex at Brighton he took eight wickets in one innings for 42 runs. After dropping out of the Surrey XI he does not seem to have played any first-class cricket, but in 1868 he went round England with the Australian Aboriginal team. In 1872 he was appointed coach and ground-keeper at Dulwich College. This post he retained for a number of years, turning out many excellent pupils. In his old age, right up to the outbreak of the War, he was constantly to be seen at the Oval. To the day of his death he used to recall with great pride that at the crisis of the memorable match between Surrey and Notts at Trent Bridge in 1864 he stopped a yorker from Jackson. He went in last, Mr. Dowson being at the other end, and

Surrey won by one wicket.—S.H.P.

SHEPPARD, R. A., who died on January 28, 1953, aged 83, played for Surrey as an all-rounder in two seasons at the start of the century. In nine matches in 1904 he scored 316 runs, average 24.30, his highest innings being 82 against Derbyshire at Derby, and with slow bowling took 16 wickets, average 27.93. He was educated at Whitgift.

SHEPSTONE, George Harold, a free hitter and good fast bowler, died at Johannesburg on July 3, 1940, aged 63. Born at Pietermaritzburg on April 8, 1876, he was educated at Repton, and played in the XI in 1892–93. On returning to South Africa, he took part in two representative matches at Johannesburg: in March 1896 against Lord Hawke's first English team, and in February 1899 against the second team taken to South Africa by the Yorkshire captain, his scores being 21, nine, eight and 0. In 1904 he came to England with the team captained by Frank Mitchell, but played little owing to illness. Shepstone appeared for Transvaal from 1898 to 1905, his highest score being 104 against Griqualand West at Cape Town in April 1898.

SHERIDAN, Edward ("Ned") Orwell, born in New South Wales on January 3, 1842, died at Brisbane on November 30, 1923, aged 81. He played for his native State for some years, taking part in nine matches v. Victoria, and later did good service for the game in Brisbane, where he settled in 1883.

SHERIDAN, Robert Owen, of the Philadelphia C.C., was born in Philadelphia on May 18, 1885, and died there in January, 1912. He intended visiting England with the side the club sent last year.

SHERMAN, Tom, one of the oldest of professional cricketers, died in Croydon Hospital of pneumonia on October 10, 1911. As he was born – at Mitcham, in Surrey – on December 1, 1827, he was in his 84th year at the time of his death. *Scores and Biographies* (iii–417) said of him: "Is one of the fastest round-armed bowlers there has ever been, and for some seasons he was very successful in the Surrey XI, being also a fine field. Bats in good style, but is too impatient, often running in at the ball and trying to make it a 'half-volley.' " His first match for Surrey was in 1847 and his last in 1870, and in all matches for the county he obtained 229 wickets and scored 422 runs with an average of 6.91. When the South beat the North at

Tunbridge Wells in 1855, he and John Lilly-white, bowling unchanged throughout, dismissed the North for 77 and 74, Sherman taking eight of the wickets for 71 runs. But his greatest feat was to obtain six wickets for 16 runs for Surrey and Sussex against England at Lord's three years earlier. After his great days Sherman coached at several colleges and schools, including Harrow, Eton, Winchester and Rugby, and to the close of his long life continued to take a great interest in the game. He belonged to a cricketing family, both his father (James Sherman) and an uncle (John Sherman) having played in their time for Surrey. It may be of interest to recall that the latter was born at Crayford, in Kent, on October 14, 1783, and that his father – old Tom's grandfather, that is – was fetched away from a cricket match for the event. The name was originally Shearman.

SHERWELL, Noel Benjamin, who was killed while skiing at Flims, Switzerland, on December 29, 1960, aged 56, was the finest amateur wicket-keeper of his day and the best ever produced by Tonbridge School. In the Tonbridge XI from 1920 to 1922, he was one of four brothers who got their colours for the school. As captain in his last year, he headed the batting figures with 745 runs, including three centuries, average 53.21, caught 15 batsmen and stumped 16. *Wisden* of the time described him as a fine cricketer, an excellent captain and a first-rate, sound and punishing batsman. Going up to Caius College, Cambridge, he received his Blue as a Freshman in 1923 and also played against Oxford in the two following years. Though he did not meet with the same success as a batsman as during his school-days, he developed in wicket-keeping, standing right up when taking the bowling of G. O. Allen, who later played for England, at his fastest. In 1925 Sherwell was one of four members of that year's Cambridge team to play for Gentlemen against Players at Lord's. The others were K. S. Duleepsinhji, E. W. Dawson and H. J. Enthoven. In 1926 he took part in one game for Middlesex. He served with the R.A.F.V.R. during the Second World War and was awarded the O.B.E. in the 1946 New Year's Honours List. He was a solicitor.

C. T. Bennett, Cambridge captain of 1925, writes: "The tragedy of Ben's untimely death is mourned by all, particularly by those who played in his company. As a wicket-keeper, like G. E. C. Wood, he never blinded his slip fieldsmen and gave the experienced and tactful advice that only the great can dis-

pense. As a man and a friend, *semper idem*."

SHERWELL, Percy William, captain of the South African side which visited England in 1907 and played the first series of Tests in this country, died at Bulawayo, Southern Rhodesia, on April 17, 1948. Born on August 17, 1880, at Isipingo, Natal, he was 67 years old. Brought to England in childhood, he was educated at Bedford County School and Royal School of Mines, Camborne. He played for Cornwall before going to the Transvaal, where he obtained an important position in the mining industry. This work interrupted his cricket after 1907, but altogether he captained South Africa in 13 Test matches; five against England in 1905–06, four being won, three next year against England, who won at Leeds, the other two being drawn. Of five against Australia, 1910–11, South Africa won the match at Adelaide by 38 runs, but lost the other four. In these encounters Sherwell caught 22 men and stumped 16; in two of the matches against Australia he allowed only four byes, all off one ball, in four innings while 1,479 runs were scored and only when Australia scored 578 in an innings he conceded only four byes.

In his first Test match, the memorable occasion at Johannesburg in January 1906 which resulted in victory for South Africa, he went in last and with A. D. Nourse steadily knocked off the 45 runs then wanted to win, South Africa gaining their first victory over England. Sherwell's share was 22.

Another last wicket stand, 94 with A. E. Vogler, helped South Africa to a great triumph at Cape Town by an innings and 16 runs, but by far his best batting performance was at Lord's in July 1907. Because of the uncertain form of his side, Sherwell promoted himself to opening batsman and after being run out he gave a great display when South Africa followed-on, scoring 115 out of 153 before he played on after an hour and three-quarters of glorious batting. The late cut was his best stroke in a chanceless display. To quote 1947 *Wisden*—Sherwell was "Strong to captain, to keep the wicket and the England fielders on the run."

He was on the Selection Committee that chose the South African touring teams of 1907, 1912, and 1924 and, as N. S. Curnow added in his valuable information, Sherwell was South African lawn tennis singles champion in 1904 and represented his country against England in 1908–09.

SHERWIN, Mordecai, the famous Notts

wicket-keeper, died at Nottingham on July 3, 1910, in his 60th year. He was born at Kimberley, Notts, on February 26, 1851. He played his first match for Notts in August 1876, and took part in some of the later fixtures in the following season, but it was not until 1880 that he became the regular wicket-keeper of the XI. From 1880 he held his position without a break down to the end of the season of 1893, after which the Notts Committee, for some not very obvious reason, dropped him. He became a member of the M.C.C.'s ground staff in 1877, and retained his engagement for a quarter of a century. The M.C.C. gave him the Middlesex and Somerset match on Whit Monday 1894, but the result was disappointing, the game ending on the second afternoon. Among the English wicket-keepers of his day Sherwin had scarcely a superior, except Pilling and Mr. MacGregor. A very bulky man of great physical power, he could stand any amount of work, and his strong fleshy hands did not often suffer damage. He was inclined to show off a little for the benefit of the crowd, but this after all was a small fault. He was at all times one of the cheeriest of cricketers. Although he took part several times in Gentlemen and Players' matches he only once kept wicket in a Test match in England, playing at Lord's in 1888, when Turner and Ferris gave Australia a victory on a ruined pitch. At different times the Hon. Alfred Lyttelton, Pilling, Mr. E. F. S. Tylecote, and Mr. MacGregor stood in his way. Sherwin only paid one visit to Australia, being a member of Shaw and Shrewsbury's team in the winter of 1886–87. He had no pretensions as a batsman, but he often made runs when they were wanted, and as a bowler one memorable achievement stands to his credit. In a Notts v. Middlesex match at Lord's in 1892, when the regular bowlers were tired out, he went on as a last hope and took two of the last five Middlesex wickets for nine runs, helping Notts to win the match within four minutes of time. In his young days Sherwin was a good man at Association football, keeping goal for Notts County. During the 16 seasons for which he played for Notts he stumped 110 batsmen and caught 365, his record year by year being as follows:

				Ct.	Stmpd.
1876	..	..	..	6	2
1877	..	..	..	7	3
1880	..	..	..	11	3
1881	..	..	..	16	7
1882	..	..	..	18	11
1883	..	..	..	23	10
1884	..	..	..	26	10
1885	..	..	..	34	11
1886	..	..	..	24	9
1887	..	..	..	39	11
1888	..	..	..	24	8
1889	..	..	..	26	8
1890	..	..	..	33	4
1891	..	..	..	19	5
1892	..	..	..	32	2
1893	..	..	..	22	6
				360	110

SHIELDS, Major John, who died on May 11, 1960, aged 78, played as wicket-keeper for Leicestershire from 1906 to 1914, being captain from 1911 to 1913. He appeared for Gentlemen against Players at Lord's and the Oval in 1909. Though seldom shining as a batsman, he hit 63 from the Hampshire bowling at Southampton in 1913.

SHILTON, John, the Warwickshire bowler, died in September, 1899, at the early age of 42. He was born on September 18, 1857. Though his career was cut short by a breakdown in health, Shilton will always be remembered as one of the players who did most to bring the Warwickshire XI to the front. At his best he was a first rate left handed bowler, slow to medium pace. Bowling with a very high and very easy action, he combined plenty of spin with accuracy of pitch, and during his early years in the Warwickshire XI he was brilliantly successful. Apart from his bowling, he was a very useful bat. When his health failed, through severe attacks of asthma and bronchitis, he was sent to South Africa, but no permanent cure could be effected, and when he came home again his cricket career was obviously over. Shilton was personally quite a character, but though he had his faults, this is not the place in which to dwell upon them. By birth a Yorkshireman, he was first at Lord's in 1883 for the Colts of the North against the Colts of the South. He took six wickets for 20 runs, but his success was overshadowed by that of G. P. Harrison, who in the second innings of the Southern team took nine wickets—all clean bowled—for 14 runs.

SHINDE, Sadashiv G., who died in Bombay on June 22, 1955, aged 31, played in seven Test matches for India between 1946 and 1952. A slow leg-break and googly bowler, he toured England in 1946 and 1952 without much success. His best performance in a Test match was in the first England innings at New Delhi in 1951–52, when he took six wickets for 91 runs.

SHINE, Eustace Beverley, C.B., who died at his home at New Milton, Hampshire, on November 11, 1952, will always hold a place in cricket history as the fast bowler who bore a leading part in bringing about an important alteration in the law governing the follow-on. Born at Port of Spain, Trinidad, on July 9, 1873, he was educated at King Edward VI School, Saffron Walden, and Selwyn College, Cambridge, where he got his Blue in 1896 and the following year. It was in the first of his appearances against Oxford that Shine became involved in an incident which had far-reaching results. By quarter to four on the second day, Oxford stood 131 behind the Cambridge first innings total of 319 with only one wicket to fall. Then, to quote *Wisden* of the time, the Cambridge captain, Frank Mitchell, "by palpably giving away runs to prevent his opponents from following-on, forced the M.C.C. to reconsider the whole question" of a much-criticised law.

"Shine sent down three balls—two of them no-balls—to the boundary for four each. These 12 runs deprived Oxford of the chance of following-on and immediately afterwards the Dark Blues innings closed for 202, or 117 behind. As they left the field the Cambridge XI came in for a very hostile demonstration at the hands of the public, and inside the pavilion matters were still worse, scores of' members of the M.C.C. protesting in the most vigorous fashion against the policy that Frank Mitchell had adopted." In the end Oxford, set 330 to get, won by four wickets. At that time Law 53 read: "The side which goes in second shall follow their innings if they have scored 120 runs less than the opposite side in a three days' match, or 80 runs in a two days' match." In 1900 the law was altered, making the enforcing of the follow-on optional to the side who led by 150 on the first innings in a three-day match. After his University days Shine played occasionally for Kent between 1896 and 1899. When making his highest score (49) against Warwickshire at Tonbridge in 1897, he and F. Marchant (144 not out) added 158 for the ninth wicket in an hour. In all Shine took 129 wickets, average 24.14. A man of charming personality, he served with the Board of Agriculture from 1900 until he retired in 1933.

SHIPMAN, Alan Wilfred, who died, aged 79, on December 12, 1979, after years of ill-health, rendered valuable service to Leicestershire from 1920 to 1936, scoring 13,605 runs with an average of 23.26, including 15 centuries, and taking 597 wickets at 25.37.

At first he was regarded almost entirely as a bowler, but by 1925, when he scored his first century, his powers of defence had created such an impression that he had been promoted to go in first, a position he retained until back trouble caused his premature retirement 11 years later. Like many others so promoted, Shipman remained solid and unexciting, scoring chiefly to leg, but he was reliable and there could be no question of his value. His highest score, 226 v. Kent at Tonbridge in 1928, took seven hours, but it turned an apparently certain defeat into an honourable draw and almost into a glorious victory. As a brisk medium-pace bowler, he had neither the physique nor the action to achieve greatness, but, for a Leicestershire side which was generally strong enough to save him from being over-bowled, he did much good work. His most notable all-round performance was against Worcestershire at Kidderminster in 1929, when he followed five for 30 by making 183, all on the first day of the match. After his retirement he kept a pub at Ratby, his native place, emerging for one season in 1947 to coach at Tonbridge.

SHIPMAN, William, a very good bowler and useful batsman for Leicestershire from 1908 to 1914, died on August 26, 1943, at Ratby, his home, aged 57. In 1911, his most successful season, he took 100 wickets in championship matches at 25.61 apiece and averaged 16.27 with the bat, his best display, 69 out of 93 in 70 minutes, being in an uphill struggle against Warwickshire at Hinckley. He bowled fast right-hand with off-break and showed to most advantage on hard turf. He often lacked effective help, but once at least, this misfortune did not spoil his work. In 1910 at the Oval he took nine wickets for 83 runs, hitting the stumps six times, and so enabled Leicestershire to atone for a poor first innings and win by 63 runs, Surrey suffering their second defeat at the Oval in their last match of the season. Strangely enough, in the second dismissal of Surrey Shipman did not earn any reward.

In 1909 he did the hat-trick against Derbyshire. Twice he excelled against Yorkshire; in 1910 at Leeds he took their first five wickets for 12 runs, and Jayes dismissed seven men for 87 runs in the second innings, the two fast bowlers being mainly responsible for a victory by 259 runs—Leicestershire's first triumph over Yorkshire in a championship match. Next year, at Leicester, Shipman got rid of seven opponents for 73, and with King, the slow right-hander—eight wickets for 17—brought about the defeat of Yorkshire by an innings and 20 runs, the only win for Leicestershire that season. The War brought his County Cricket career to an end, though he played once in 1921. Altogether he took 367 wickets, average 27.26, and scored 2,479 runs, average 14.18. Shipman joined Todmorden, the Lancashire League Club, in 1914, and afterwards played for Smethwick in the Birmingham League.

SHIRLEY, William Robert De La Cour, who died on April 25, 1970, aged 69, was in the Eton XI from 1917 to 1919, taking part in the one-day games with Harrow and Winchester in the first two years and in the big match at Lord's in the last. He got his Blue at Cambridge in 1924, when he helped T. C. Lowry's team to beat Oxford by nine wickets. A useful batsman and bowler, he played for Hampshire from 1922 to 1925. His highest innings for the county was 90 from the Glamorgan bowling at Southampton in 1922. That season he played in the extraordinary match at Edgbaston where Hampshire, dismissed for 15 in the first innings and compelled to follow on 203 behind, hit up 521 and in the end triumphed over Warwickshire by 155 runs.

SHORROCKS, Sergt. Ernest, (Royal Fusiliers), killed in July, 1916, played in one match for Somerset in 1905—v. Lancashire, at Taunton—scoring 0 and 16 not out, and taking two wickets for 60 runs. He was a well-known Somerset Rugby footballer.

SHORTING, Wilfrid Lionel, died at Hastings late in 1982, aged 78. He played occasionally for Worcestershire as a batsman between 1922 and 1926, but his highest score was only 27.

SHOTTON, William, died during the last week of May, 1909, aged 68. He was born at Lascelles Hall on December 1, 1840, and made his first appearance at Lord's in May, 1867, when he played for Colts of England against M.C.C. and Ground. *Scores and Biographies* (x–19) describes him as: "A good batsman, a middle-paced round-armed bowler, and a fielder at point." He played in two matches for Yorkshire, the first in 1865 and the other not until 1874, and made only 13 runs in his four innings. He was prominently associated with Lascelles Hall cricket in its halcyon days.

SHOUBRIDGE, Thomas, died on October 22, 1937, aged 68. Over 40 years ago he was one of the best bowlers on Merseyside and played for Liverpool and District against Yorkshire in 1890. Though not very successful in his match he clean bowled Lord Hawke with "one out of the bag," a delivery which even now lingers in the memory of at least one spectator. Sussex born, he played for his county at Old Trafford in 1890 when Lancashire scored 246 for two wickets and, having declared, dismissed their visitors on a treacherous pitch for 35 and 24. Shoubridge bowled 13 overs for 25 runs, an example of length under bad bowling conditions. After a blank Monday the match was played out on two afternoons. With a round-arm delivery, Shoubridge made the ball keep low. A. T. Kemble often stood back to him though capable of stumping batsmen off Mold's lightning deliveries.

SHREWSBURY, Arthur. As everyone interested in cricket is aware, Arthur Shrewsbury shot himself on the evening of May 19, 1903. Illness which he could not be induced to believe curable, together with the knowledge that his career in the cricket field was over, had quite unhinged his mind, and those who knew him best—Alfred Shaw among the number—had for some little time before the tragic end came been apprehensive of suicide.

It may fairly be claimed for Shrewsbury that he was the greatest professional batsman of his day. He had strong rivals in William Gunn, Abel, George Ulyett, Barnes, and, more recently, Hayward, but, looking at his career as a whole, he would, by the majority of critics, be given the first place. There was never any doubt about his class, for even when in 1873, as a lad of 17, he came up to Lord's to play for the Colts of England against the M.C.C., it was confidently stated at Nottingham that he was sure to develop into a crack batsman. Like other young Notts players of those days, he had, to a certain extent, modelled his style on that of the late Richard Daft, and to this fact can be attributed the ease and finish of his method. He played from the first like one who had little left to learn, and only needed experience. He was given a place in the Notts XI in 1875, and in a season of wet weather and small scores he came out fourth in the county's batting, averaging 17, with an aggregate of 313 runs. His highest innings was only 41, but he played in such fine form as to justify all that had been said in his favour. The following year he made his first great success, scoring 118 against Yorkshire, at Trent Bridge, and in May, 1877, he made 119 at the Oval for the Players of the North against Gentlemen of the South, this being his first big innings on a London ground. Thenceforward he was recognised as one of the leading professional batsmen in England.

The turning point in Shrewsbury's career was his first visit to Australia in the winter of 1881–82. He went out in bad health, but came home, physically speaking, a new man, the sea voyages and the warm climate having done wonders for him. In 1882, in the August Bank Holiday match at the Oval, he played an innings of 207 against Surrey—the first of his many scores of over 200 in big matches—and from that time he met with ever-increasing success, his highest point being reached in 1887, when in first-class cricket he scored 1,653 runs, with the wonderful average of 78. Eight times that season he obtained over a hundred, his highest score being 267 at Trent Bridge against Middlesex. He was absent from English cricket in 1888, being engaged in managing a football team in Australia, but he was back again in the Notts XI in 1889, and played on without interruption until the end of the season of 1893. In 1894, partly by reason of indifferent health, he was not seen in first-class matches, but he reappeared for Notts in 1895, and, as everybody knows, went on playing regularly until the close of the season of 1902. In that year his form for a man of 46 years of age was astonishingly good, and for the first time in his life—against Gloucestershire, at Nottingham—he made two separate hundreds in one match.

Among his many great innings he always thought himself that absolutely the best was his 164 for England against Australia, at Lord's, in 1886. The wicket on the first day varied in pace, owing to rain, in a most puzzling way, and one famous member of the Australian XI said frankly that he should not have thought it possible under the conditions that prevailed for any batsman to obtain such a mastery over the bowling. The innings, however, great as it was, could scarcely have been finer than his 106—also at Lord's—for England against Australia in 1893, when he and F. S. Jackson triumphed over Charles Turner's bowling on a wicket rendered extremely difficult by rain and sun. In Gentlemen and Players matches Shrewsbury was conspicuously successful, scoring over a hundred twice at Lord's and twice at the Oval. As a batsman he had a style of back play peculiarly his own, and his judgment of the length of bowling was almost unequalled. It was said of him that he seemed to see the ball closer up to the bat than any other player.

More than that, there was such an easy grace of style and such a suggestion of mastery in everything he did that, whether he scored slowly or fast, his batting, to the true judge of cricket, was always a delight. Excepting of course W. G. Grace, it may be questioned if we have ever produced a more remarkable batsman. On sticky wickets he was, by universal consent, without an equal in his best seasons, his defence being so strong and his patience so inexhaustible. Personally, Shrewsbury was a man of quiet, retiring disposition, and while very proud of the place he had won in the cricket-field, always modest when speaking of his own doings.

SHREWSBURY, Arthur, Jun., nephew of the famous Arthur Shrewsbury. Born at Nottingham July 4, 1874; died at Nottingham, October 6, 1917. Played in three matches for Notts in 1892, and against Sussex at Brighton made 13 not out and 31 not out.

SHREWSBURY, William, an elder brother of Arthur Shrewsbury, was born at New Lenton on April 30, 1854, and died at Fiskerton on November 14, 1931, in his 78th year. A good batsman, without attaining to anything approaching the excellence of his famous brother, he played in a few matches for Notts in the '70s, making his first appearance for the county at Lord's in 1875, in the game in which Alfred Shaw in the second innings bowled 166 balls for seven runs and seven wickets. William Shrewsbury's highest score for Notts was 34 against Lancashire at Trent Bridge in 1876. At Lord's that year for Colts of Notts and Yorkshire against Colts of England he put together a score of 88. While he met with little success in County Cricket, he played many long innings in local club matches.

SHUKER, Abraham, a steady batsman who rendered good service to Derbyshire for a number of years, died at Tunstall on February 11, 1909. He was born at Stockton, in Shropshire, on July 6, 1848, and was educated at Cambridge, where he just failed to secure his Blue. His highest score in a match of note was 86 against Sussex at Brighton in 1882.

SHULDHAM, Walter Frank Quantock, who died after a long illness on February 7, 1971, aged 78, played occasionally for Somerset between 1914 and 1924. He was in the Marlborough XI from 1909 to 1911.

SHUTER, John. The sudden death on July 5,

1920, at his home at Blackheath, of John Shuter came as a shock to the general body of cricketers. On the previous Friday he was at the Oval and to all appearances in good health. His intimate friends knew, however, that the attack of haemorrhage that killed him was not the first of the kind from which he had suffered. It was in September, 1919, when Mr. Findlay went to Lord's, that he took up the post of secretary to the Surrey Club. He was, perhaps, a little too old for such an onerous position, but everyone hoped he had several years of work before him. Any way it was only fitting that he should to the end have been closely associated with Surrey cricket. His name will be remembered as long as the Surrey Club exists, as it was under his leadership that Surrey won back the first place among the counties in 1887, and enjoyed for the next five seasons a period of unexampled success. John Shuter belonged to Surrey by birth—he was born at Thornton Heath on February 9, 1855—but living at Bexley he was in his young days connected with club cricket in Kent. He was in the Winchester XI in 1871, 1872, and 1873, being captain and the best bat in the team in his last year. In 1873 he played a fine innings of 52 but it was only in 1871 that he had the good fortune to be on the winning side. It was in that year and 1870 that G. S. Raynor—anticipating modern bowlers—demoralised the Eton batsmen by his bewildering swerve. After leaving Winchester John Shuter played in a county match for Kent—against Lancashire at Maidstone—in 1874, and in the following year he played for the county XI against the Kent Colts at Catford Bridge. However, his potential value as a batsman was not realised, and after a time he threw in his lot with Surrey, playing in three matches for his native county in 1877. No success rewarded him that year, but in 1878 he took a very decided step to the front, and left no doubt as to his class.

To the end of his life Mr. Shuter recalled with some pride—he was talking about the matter last summer—that when the Australians were seen for the first time at the Oval he scored 39 against Spofforth. I remember the occasion very well, for some of the Australians—flushed with the triumph over the M.C.C. at Lord's—said in their innocence that Shuter was the best bat in England! I am not quite sure when Mr. Shuter became permanently captain of Surrey—the books are rather vague on the point, but he was, I think, firmly installed when the great revival began in 1883. From that time the improvement went on almost without check.

The season of 1886, marked by a double victory over the Australians, saw Surrey practically as good a side as Notts, and in 1887 came the full reward of long continued effort. For the first time since 1864 Surrey stood at the top of the tree. Mr. Shuter had long before this made himself a first-rate captain and he had a splendid XI under his command, George Lohmann's bowling and W. W. Read's batting being of course the main elements of strength. Once on top Surrey did not look back until 1893. They were first in 1888, tied with Lancashire and Notts in 1889, and were first in 1890, 1891, and 1892. Then came a change of fortune in 1893, but as some compensation for falling behind in purely County Cricket, Surrey won both their matches with the Australians. After the season of 1893, Mr. Shuter, to everyone's regret, was compelled by stress of business to resign the captaincy of the XI. He was succeeded by Mr. K. J. Key and as all lovers of cricket will remember Surrey under their new leader won the championship in 1894, 1895, and 1899.

In thinking of John Shuter as the Surrey captain one is apt to forget what a fine batsman he was—good enough for any XI. For so short a man—he stood only 5ft. 6in.—he had a singularly graceful style, and his punishing power on the off side was remarkable. He did not care for averages or personal glory. His one idea was to win the match for his side. Among all his doings in the cricket field there was nothing he recalled with keener pleasure than a fight against time in a match between the M.C.C. and the Australians at Lord's in 1890. The M.C.C. were left with only 111 to get, but they had to beat the clock as well as the Australians, 85 minutes remaining for play. W. G. Grace took Shuter in with him and, with Turner and Ferris bowling, 32 runs were scored in a quarter of an hour. In an hour the match was over, the M.C.C. winning by seven wickets. Mr. Shuter played nine times for Gentlemen v. Players, but little or no success rewarded him, his best score being 41, and his aggregate of runs in 15 innings only 182. All his best work was done for Surrey. He played once for England against Australia—at the Oval in 1888. In the long years between his resignation of the captaincy and his appointment in 1919 as secretary of the club Mr. Shuter was always in closest touch with Surrey cricket. I find from Bat v. Ball that he made nine scores of over a hundred for Surrey. The first was 110 against Sussex at Brighton in 1879, and the last 117 against Essex at the Oval in 1890. His best score against the Australians was 71 for the Gentlemen of England at Lord's in 1888.—S.H.P.

SHUTER, Leonard Allen, elder brother of the late Mr. John Shuter, was born at Thornton Heath, in Surrey, on May 15, 1852, and died at Eastbourne on July 13, 1928. A fairly attractive batsman, he could also field well at cover-point and bowl with either hand—slow left or fast right. He appeared in 37 matches for Surrey between 1876 and 1883, making 1,040 runs with an average of 16.50. His highest scores—both against Kent at the Oval—were 89 in 1877 and 65 in 1879. He had been a member of the M.C.C. since 1877 and of the Surrey County C.C. a year longer.

SIBBLES, Frank Marshall, who died after a long illness on July 20, 1973, aged 69, helped Lancashire win the County Championship in three successive years from 1926 to 1928 and also in 1930 and 1934. Born at Oldham, he became a member of Werneth C.C. at the age of seven and after experience in the Central Lancashire League, became a member of the ground staff at Old Trafford in 1925. Originally a batsman, he developed into a natural off-break bowler able also to cut the ball. Altogether, until a painful and persistent elbow trouble ended his playing career in 1937, he took 932 wickets at around 22 runs each and held 164 catches.

Among his best performances were eight wickets for 24 runs against Somerset at Weston-super-Mare and five wickets for eight runs against Essex. At Buxton in 1932 he dismissed three Derbyshire batsmen in four balls.

After the Second World War, in which he rose from the ranks to Major, he did much able service as an administrator for Lancashire. Elected to the General Committee in 1950, he served on the committee responsible for team selection and the welfare of players and was its chairman for two years.

In 1937, Sir Neville Cardus wrote of Sibbles in *The Guardian*: "There is nothing cheap or spectacular about Sibbles. I doubt if I have ever heard him appeal: he even asks the umpire, puts a question to him, instead of stating a fact. A nicer mannered cricketer never wore flannels. He has the gift of modesty and his upright way of carrying himself and his crinkled hair (they call him "Top" in the Lancashire side) seem entirely in keeping with the style of his play."

SIDES, F. W., a free-hitting left-handed batsman for Victoria, after playing during several seasons for Queensland, was killed in September, 1945, while a sergeant on active service with a Commando unit against the Japanese in Salamana, aged 29. In each of the last two seasons before the War he averaged over 34 by consistently good cricket. According to Australian statistics, Sides scored 859 runs, average 42.95, for Victoria in representative matches, his highest innings being 121 against Western Australia at Perth in 1939.

SIDNEY, Thomas Stafford, K.C., Attorney-General, Leeward Islands. Died in Liverpool November 16, 1917, aged 54. Author of *'W.G.' up to date*, published at Ootacamund in 1896. Member of M.C.C. since 1888.

SIDWELL, Thomas Edgar, who died on December 8, 1958, aged 70, kept wicket for Leicestershire between 1913 and 1933, his total of 551 catches and 127 stumpings constituting a record for the county. A sound batsman, he enjoyed his best season in 1928 when he scored 1,153 runs, average 29.56, and hit two of his three centuries. He retired from County Cricket in 1931, but played in several matches two seasons later when his successor, P. Corrall, was badly hurt. He never lost his love for the game and took part in two club matches last summer.

SIEDLE, Ivan Julian ("Jack"), who died in Durban on August 24, 1982, aged 79, was South Africa's oldest surviving Test cricketer at the time of his death. He had the unique distinction of scoring the first century on a turf pitch in South Africa in both a Currie Cup match and a Test match. The first, 114 for Natal against Border at Durban, was in December, 1926. The second was at Newlands in Cape Town in 1930–31 when he and Bruce Mitchell shared a record first-wicket partnership of 260 against England, Siedle making 141, his one Test century. A right-handed opening batsman, solid and watchful, he made his first-class debut for Natal on the day after he turned 19, scoring six and eight against the 1922–23 M.C.C. team. In 1924–25 he appeared in three unofficial Tests against S. B. Joel's English team, scoring 52 in the final match. In 1926–27 he and J. F. W. Nicolson shared in a first-wicket stand of 424 for Natal against Orange Free State at Bloemfontein, a record to this day. Nicolson scored 252 not out, Siedle 174. Siedle's 265 not out, also for Natal against Orange Free State, in 1929–30 was the highest score made in the Currie Cup until J. E. Cheetham's 271 not out for Western Province against Orange Free State in 1950–51, a figure passed within five days by E. A. B. Rowan (277 not out for Transvaal against Griqualand West). Siedle's first Test match was against England at Durban in 1927–28, but he was dropped after scoring 11 and 10 as H. W. Taylor's opening partner. Selected for the 1929 tour of England, he finished second in the batting averages, totalling 1,579 runs at an average of 35.88 with centuries against Leicestershire and Yorkshire. He missed two of the five Tests through injury. In his first full home series, against England in 1930–31, he scored 384 runs (average 42.66). Unavailable for the 1931–32 tour of Australia, he made his second trip to England in 1935, starting in fine form and becoming the first member of the side to reach 1,000 runs, these including three successive hundreds—against Surrey, Oxford University and M.C.C. In the third of them he carried his bat for 132 not out in a total of 297. He was less successful in the Tests, one of which he missed through injury. Against the all-conquering Australian team in South Africa in 1935–36 he was second to A. D. Nourse in both Test average and Test aggregate. That was the finish of his Test career, and at the end of the 1936–37 season, after successive scores of 105, 111 and 207, he retired. His 17 first-class centuries included three of over 200. In all first-class matches he scored 7,730 runs with an average of 40.05. In 18 Tests he made 977 runs at an average of 28.73. He was a fine all-round fielder and had a wide range of strokes. His son John (J.R.) hit a century on his debut in first-class cricket, for Western Province against Eastern Province in 1955–56.

SIEVERS, Maurice, who died in a Melbourne hospital on May 1, 1968, following a heart attack, aged 56, played as a fast-medium bowler and useful batsman for Victoria from 1934 to 1941. He took 92 wickets for the State at a cost of 35.81 runs each and hit 1,540 runs, average 28.00. In 1936–37 he played in three Test matches for Australia against G. O. Allen's England side, heading his country's averages with nine wickets for 17.88 runs apiece. He achieved his best performance in his third Test when, on a "glue-pot" pitch at Melbourne, he dismissed five batsmen for 21 runs in the first innings. Australia won the game by 365 runs, and, as they also triumphed in the next two Tests, retained the Ashes after losing the first two fixtures of the series.

SIEVWRIGHT, R. W., one of the best-known personalities in Scottish cricket, died on July 12, 1947, aged 65. While batting for Arbroath United against Perthshire he collapsed with a heart seizure and died at the crease. He was president of the club with which he had been associated for 47 years. Arthur, one of two sons playing in the match, was his father's partner at the time of the tragic occurrence. The match was abandoned. A slow bowler, he played for Scotland from 1912 to 1929, six times against Australia, twice against South Africa, twice against Ireland, as well as against Oxford, Surrey, Northamptonshire, Australian Imperial Forces, M.C.C., and Middlesex. Against Australia at Edinburgh in 1912 he captured six wickets for 60 runs, with C. G. Macartney among his victims. In 1921 against the Australians he took seven wickets in two matches, and Warren Bardsley paid "Sievy," as he was known wherever cricket was played, the compliment of describing him as one of the best spin bowlers he had ever encountered. In May 1936 at Lochlands he took all the Aberdeenshire wickets for 16 runs.

SILCOCK, Frank, died at Ongar, on May 26, 1897. He was born on October 2, 1838, and was thus in his 59th year. Silcock was in his day a first-rate all-round cricketer, and would no doubt have taken a much higher position if he had had the good fortune to be associated with a leading county. He was at his best about 1868–69, doing splendid work in these two seasons for Players against Gentlemen. In 1869 the two matches were peculiarly interesting, the Gentlemen winning by 17 runs at the Oval, and by three wickets at Lord's. At the Surrey ground Silcock shone as a batsman, and at Lord's he bowled so finely that the Gentlemen were very hard pushed to get the 98 runs required in the last innings. Silcock bowled 124 balls for 35 runs and five wickets, bowling A. N. Hornby, Alfred Lubbock, I. D. Walker, and E. M. Grace, and getting W. G. Grace caught at the wicket by Tom Plumb. Silcock was a fine steady batsman, very correct and upright in method, and as a bowler he belonged to a school that has now almost passed away. Bowling at a good pace he delivered the ball a little below the shoulder, and got on a deal of bias from the leg-side. Silcock was a prominent member of the United South of England XI and did a lot of bowling for the team in company with Southerton, Willsher and James Lillywhite. He was coach at Uppingham when Mr. C. E. Green was at school, and years afterwards played side by side with that gentleman in the Essex XI, when the now famous County Club was struggling to make a name. No professional cricketer was more respected. His health had been failing for some little time before his death, but at the complimentary banquet to Mr. C. E. Green after the cricket season of 1896, he was one of the guests.

SIME, His Honour William Arnold, C.M.G., M.B.E., died at Wymeswold, Leicestershire, on May 5, 1983, aged 74. Four years in the XI at Bedford School, in 1928, when he was captain, he made two centuries for Bedfordshire. He did not get a Blue at Oxford, but continued to play with success for Bedfordshire and captained them in 1934. In 1935 he transferred to Nottinghamshire, but made only occasional appearances until 1947 when he was appointed captain, a position he held until 1950. He proved a useful member of the side and made in all 2,328 runs with an average of 19.98, besides taking occasional wickets as a slow left-hander: he was also a good field. His outstanding performance and his only century was an innings of 176 not out against Sussex at Hove in 1948. This took him six hours, a contrast to his usual methods, but it secured a victory for his side, who had lost three for 33 when he went in in the first innings. More typical perhaps was his 58 not out against Surrey at Trent Bridge in 1949, made in 37 minutes and including three sixes: Nottinghamshire, set to get 206 in two hours, got them in 97 minutes. It may be noted that in this time Surrey bowled 36.3 overs. Sime was also a first-class rugger player, who appeared in an England trial, and a good golfer. Later he was Recorder of Grantham and in 1972 was appointed a Circuit Judge. However, he did not lose touch with cricket, being President of Nottinghamshire in 1975–77 and lately President of the XL Club.

SIMMS, Harry Lester, died on June 8, 1942, aged 54. For Sussex and Warwickshire he was a valuable player. When first playing he was a dashing, uncertain bat and moderate field, while his bowling was negligible, but after returning from a long stay in India he showed astonishing improvement, particularly as a bowler. He often batted admirably, fielded well, and at times his fastish bowling was deadly. In 1912 in all matches he scored 1,099 runs and took 110 wickets, being the only amateur, besides R. A. Faulkner of South Africa, to achieve the double that season of the Triangular Tournament, when

wet weather spoiled a lot of matches. That year Simms played twice for Gentlemen against Players. At the Oval he did little, but in a drawn match at Lord's he scored 22 and took seven wickets. He gave a remarkable display of hitting against Nottinghamshire at Hove, scoring 126, the fifth individual hundred in the match, in 85 minutes, and in the course of four overs getting 64 runs; there were 10 sixes in his spectacular innings. After the last War he played occasionally for Warwickshire and regularly in Birmingham League cricket. He played golf splendidly.

SIMPSON, Edward Thornhill Beckett, an Oxford Blue in 1888, whose best effort was 82 against Gentlemen of England, died on March 20. 1944, at Wakefield, aged 77. He failed to get into the Harrow XI, but the Blue was recommendation enough for him to play a little for Yorkshire during the seasons 1889 to 1891—fine fielding helped him to find favour; he did little with the bat.

SIMPSON, Gerald Amyatt, who died on February 22, 1957, aged 70, took part in a few first-class matches for Kent in 1929 and 1930 after spending his early manhood in the Argentine. For many years he captained Kent Second XI; he led the Club and Ground team until he was 63, and he played for the Band of Brothers and the St. Lawrence clubs. A hard-hitting batsman, he was also a splendid fieldsman close to the wicket. As a member of the Committee, he rendered long service to Kent. During the First World War he served in the Royal Artillery and was wounded in France.

SIMPSON, Capt. Harold Benjamin, who was born on January 27, 1879, died suddenly in March, 1924, at Chelveston, near Higham Ferrers. Whilst still in the Wellingborough School XI he appeared for Northamptonshire, but he assisted the county on only a few occasions altogether. Against the Australian team of 1905 he made 25 in his first innings and 44 in his second.

SIMPSON-HAYWARD, G. H., who died on October 2, 1936, aged 61, was one of the last underhand bowlers in first-class cricket. He seldom flighted the ball like the ordinary lob bowler and did not often use spin from leg. In fact he was quite unusual with the speed at which he could make the ball, delivered with low trajectory, break from the off. Going from Malvern to Cambridge, he did not get his Blue and not until 1902 did he play much for Worcestershire. He met with most success in 1908 when 68 wickets fell to him at an average of 18.61. Also a very useful forcing batsman, he hit up 105 out of 140 in 80 minutes against the University at Oxford and then took six wickets for 13 runs. He played for the Gentlemen at Lord's that summer without emulating the success of D. L. A. Jephson, who with his lobs in 1899 dismissed six of the Players for 21. One big performance in the best class cricket stands to Simpson-Hayward's name. Going to South Africa with Mr. H. D. G. Leveson Gower's team in 1909, he took 23 wickets at 18.26 runs each in the five Tests, and in the first at Johannesburg his first innings analysis was six for 43. The matting wickets just suited his exceptional power of spinning the ball. His all-round ability stood out against the Australians at Worcester in 1909, when he was highest scorer for the county with 51 and took six wickets for 132 in a total of 389. A very good Association football full back, before adding Hayward to his name, he played against Oxford from 1896–98.

SIMS, Sir Arthur, who died at East Hoathly, Sussex, on April 27, 1969, aged 91, shared with V. T. Trumper against Canterbury at Christchurch in 1913–14 an eighth-wicket partnership of 433 which still stands as a world's record in first-class cricket. Playing for an Australian team which he got together and took on a New Zealand tour, Sims took out his bat for 114 and Trumper scored 293, the second highest innings of his career. Of Lincolnshire birth, Sims was taken to New Zealand when three years old. Returning to England to start a meat-importing business, he frequently turned out for Dr. W. G. Grace's team and upon his last appearance made 127 not out. For many years New Zealand representative at the Imperial Cricket Conference, he was a life member of the M.C.C. and patron of the London New Zealand C.C. He was a celebrated philanthropist.

SIMS, James Morton, who died on April 27, 1973, aged 68, was in his day a splendid legbreak and googly bowler and a more than useful batsman for Middlesex. He had been county scorer for a number of years and his death occurred while he was staying at a Canterbury hotel on the night preceding a game with Kent there. Making his debut for Middlesex in 1929, he retired from County Cricket in 1952 and between those years he took 1,572 wickets at an average cost of 24.90 runs each and scored over 9,000 runs, including four centuries. He afterwards had

charge of the county Second XI and served as coach until taking over the post of scorer.

Originally regarded mainly as a batsman, often opening the innings, Jim Sims developed into an all-rounder and particularly after the Second World War was relied upon chiefly for his bowling. Eight times he dismissed over 100 batsmen in a season and in 1939, with 159 victims at 20.30 runs each, he was the most prolific wicket-taker in English first-class cricket. For East against West at Kingston-upon-Thames in 1948 he enjoyed the distinction of taking all 10 wickets—for 90 runs—in an innings, a feat he went close to performing 15 years earlier at Old Trafford when disposing of nine Lancashire batsmen for 92 runs. He achieved the hat-trick for Middlesex at the expense of A. Melville's South African team at Lord's in 1947 and in 1933 sent back three Derbyshire batsmen in the course of four balls at Chesterfield.

In his book, *Cricket Prints* the late R. C. Robertson-Glasgow wrote: "Jim Sims can unbuckle the most difficult googly in the game today." How highly this tall, lean, genial cricketer was held in the esteem of the Middlesex authorities was illustrated by their granting him two benefits in five seasons. The first in 1946 was seriously affected by rain.

He toured Australasia under E. R. T. Holmes in 1935–36 and under G. O. Allen the following winter when, though doing well in other matches, he proved costly on the hard pitches, in the two Tests for which he was called upon. He also played once each for England against South Africa, in 1935, and India, in 1936, both in England.

A humorous man, who never tired of telling stories about the game in words spoken from the side of his mouth, he was popular wherever he went. Many of them concerned his idol "Patsy" Hendren. One regarding Sims was about the occasion when Harold Larwood, on a fiery pitch, was making the ball fly in a somewhat terrifying manner. Sims, unusually quiet, was awaiting his turn to bat when Hendren asked him: "Feeling nervous, Jim?" Said Sims: "Not exactly nervous, Patsy: just a trifle apprehensive."

On one occasion after dismissing a capable batsman with a googly, he remarked confidentially to the nearest fieldsman: "I'd been keeping that one warm all through the winter."

Tributes to Sims included: J. M. Brearley (Middlesex captain): "Jim helped a lot of us young players and I suppose there is no one in the side who has not benefited from his help and advice. He was a great chap to have around and everybody will miss him terribly."

L. E. G. Ames (Kent secretary-manager): "I knew Jim for between 40 and 50 years and toured with him in Australia. I would say that he was one of the great characters of the game."

SINCLAIR, James Henry, who died at Yeoville on February 23, 1913, was born on October 16, 1876. One of the first men who made South African cricket famous, he came into prominence during the tour of Lord Hawke's team in South Africa in the winter of 1898–99. In that tour the Englishmen played 17 matches, of which they won 15 and drew two. A couple of defeats at Matjesfontein and Cape Town were suffered in scratch games outside the regular programme. Little in the cricket of the South African players at that time suggested the rapid development that followed, but Sinclair met with brilliant success. Playing for South Africa at Johannesburg in February, 1899, he scored 86, and at Cape Town in April he did even better, playing a brilliant innings of 106, and taking nine wickets—six for 26 runs and three for

63. These two matches established his reputation as the best all-round man in South Africa. Coming to England with the South African team in 1901, he fulfilled expectations as a bowler, but his batting was disappointing. Despite his great hitting powers he made only 742 runs during the tour, with an average of 19.5. On his next visit to England, with the South African team in 1904, Mr. Sinclair again bowled very well, taking 100 wickets, but it became evident that as a batsman he was little more than a big hitter. His last visit to England was with the famous side of 1907. This time he was not wanted much as a bowler, being quite overshadowed by Schwarz, Vogler, Faulkner, and Gordon White. In batting, too, he had quite a modest record, but on occasions his hitting was tremendous, notably in a remarkable match against Sussex at Brighton. The South Africans won by 39 runs after starting the game with a paltry score of 49. In their second innings they made 327, Sinclair hitting up 92 out of 135 in an hour and 40 minutes. As a bowler Sinclair, at his best, was excellent, combining a nice variety of pace with a very high delivery. Among his best feats with the ball in this country may be mentioned:

7 for 32	London County v. Derbyshire, at the Crystal Palace	1901
7 for 98 } 13 for 153 }	South Africans v. Surrey, at the Oval	1901
7 for 54	South Africans v. Yorkshire, at Harrogate	1901
7 for 20 } 13 for 73 }	South Africans v. Gloucestershire, at Clifton	1901
8 for 69	South Africans v. Oxford University, at Oxford	1904
7 for 75	South Africans v. Gloucestershire, at Bristol	1904

In Test matches against England and Australia he made 1,069 runs, with an average of 23.23, and took 63 wickets at a cost of 31.68 runs each. His hundreds were 106 v. England at Cape Town in 1898–99, and 101 and 104 v. Australia, at Johannesburg and Cape Town respectively, in 1902–03. In making the last-mentioned score he hit 10 sixes and eight fours. In February, 1897, he scored 301 not out for Villagers v. Roodeport, at Johannesburg, an innings which still ranks as the record for South Africa.

SINCOCK, Harold, who died in Adelaide on February 3, 1982, aged 74, played twice for South Australia as a leg-spinner and forceful batsman in 1929–30, the first of his appearances being against A. H. H. Gilligan's visiting M.C.C. team. In his nine overs in the match he took four wickets for 72 runs. His son, David, played three times for Australia as a left-arm wrist spinner. Another son,

Peter, also made five appearances for South Australia.

SINGH, Lieut.-Col. Kanwar Shumshere, died in New Delhi on May 12, 1975, aged 95. A member of the Rugby XI in 1896, he had a trial for Cambridge in 1901 and played three matches for Kent that year and one the next, showing much promise. A batsman with a strong defence and a fine field, he made top score, 45, in the first innings against Worcestershire, and against Surrey at the Oval he helped Murrell to add 115 in 55 minutes for the seventh wicket. He entered the Indian Medical Service, and at the time of his death was the oldest surviving Kent cricketer.

SKEET, Challen Hasler Lufkin, who died after a long illness on April 20, 1978, aged 82, will be remembered as one of the great fieldsmen of his time and also for one notable innings, which helped to decide the County

Championship. Four years in the XI at St Paul's, he headed the batting averages in his last two years and in his last, 1914, the bowling averages as well. A fastish slinger, he never bowled seriously later. A solid bat rather than a stroke player, after a good trial for Oxford in 1919, he got his Blue in 1920 in a particularly strong side, partly as the reward of some consistent scoring, but even more so for his superlative fielding, especially at cover or in the outfield. As R. .C. Robertson-Glasgow said, he had "a throw that would have satisfied Sydney."

After the University match, he became a regular member of the Middlesex side, but 15 innings had produced only 168 runs when it came to the second innings of the last match (Sir Pelham Warner's last county match for Middlesex) against Surrey at Lord's, on which the championship hung. Middlesex were 73 behind on the first innings, and, when Skeet and Lee went in on the second evening with 40 awkward minutes to play out time the odds against Surrey losing must have been considerable. In fact both batsmen made centuries, Skeet 106, the first wicket did not fall until after lunch next day, when the score was 208, and Middlesex won a sensational victory and the championship.

C. H. L. SKEET
CAREER FIGURES — BATTING

Season	Matches	Inns	Not Outs	Runs	Highest Inns	Average	Catches
1919	6	10	2	120	41	15.00	2
1920	18	31	5	563	106	21.65	11
1922	9	14	3	262	61	23.81	6
Totals	33	55	10	945	106	21.00	19

CENTURY

106 for Middlesex v. Surrey at Lord's, 1920.

Going out to the Sudan, Skeet was soon lost to first-class cricket, a few matches for Middlesex in 1922 concluding his career. Of one catch in particular Sir Pelham used to talk. At Edgbaston G. A. Rotherham hit Lee higher than Sir Pelham had ever seen a ball hit: he thought it must rival the famous blow off which G. F. Grace caught Bonner at the Oval in 1880, and the Rev. E. F. Waddy felt sure there must have been snow on the ball when it descended. Skeet had to run 20yd. and then wait almost half a minute before it arrived safely in his hands.

SKELDING, Alexander, who died at Leicester on April 17, 1960, aged 73, stood as a first-class umpire from 1931 to 1958. He began his cricket career as a very fast bowler with Leicestershire in 1905, but, because he wore spectacles, was not re-engaged at the end of the season. He then joined Kidderminster in the Birmingham League and achieved such success that in 1912 the county re-signed him and he continued with them until1929. His best season was that of 1927, when he took 102 wickets, average 20.81. Altogether he dismissed 593 batsmen at a cost of less than 25 runs each. One of the most popular personalities in the game, he always wore white boots when umpiring and he was celebrated for his sense of humour. It was his custom at the close of play to remove the bails with an exaggerated flourish and announce: "And that concludes the entertainment for the day, gentlemen."

"Alec" was the central figure in many amusing incidents. Once in response to an appeal for run out, he stated: "That was a 'photo-finish' and as there isn't time to develop the plate, I shall say not out." In another match a batsman who had been celebrating a special event the previous evening was rapped on the pad by a ball. At once the bowler asked: "How is he?" Said Alec, shaking his head sadly: "He's not at all well, and he was even worse last night." Occasionally the joke went against Alec. In a game in 1948 he turned down a strong appeal by the Australian touring team. A little later a dog ran on to the field, and one of the Australians captured it, carried it to Skelding and said: "Here you are. All you want now is a white stick!"

Asked in his playing days if he found spectacles a handicap, Alec said: "The specs are for the look of the thing. I can't see without 'em and on hot days I can't see with 'em, because they get steamed up. So I bowl on hearing only and appeal twice an over."

One of his most cherished umpiring memories was the giving of three leg-before decisions which enabled H. Fisher of Yorkshire to perform a unique hat-trick against Somerset at Sheffield in 1932. "I was never more sure that I was right in each case," he said afterwards, "and each of the batsmen agreed that he was dead in front."

SKINNER, Alan Frank, who died in the West Suffolk Hospital on February 28, 1982, aged 68, did much useful work for Derbyshire between 1931 and 1938. Captain of the Leys School side in 1931, he had trials for the county that year and the next without achieving much, but in 1933, his second year at Cambridge, who had not yet given him a match, he scored 788 runs with an average of 28. Next year he did have a trial for Cambridge but failed to get his Blue: however, in all first-class matches he made 1,019 runs with an average of 27.54, including the only century of his career, 102 for Derbyshire against Gloucestershire at Gloucester. From 1935 to 1938 his opportunities were more limited, but in 1935 his 550 runs and an average of 36.66 suggested what he might have done had he been able to devote his whole time to the game. Though he watched the ball carefully, he was a good stroke-player and could be the most attractive bat on the side, equally prepared to open or to go in lower down. He was also a fine slip. On a number of occasions he captained the county. After the War his first-class cricket was confined to one match for Northamptonshire in 1949. Later he was for many years Clerk to the West Suffolk County Council. His younger brother, David, captained Derbyshire in 1949.

SLACK, James, who died at Ipswich, Queensland, on September 17, 1903, was one of the pioneers of cricket in those parts. He made the first score of a hundred in Queensland.

SLATEM, John James, died at Johannesburg on March 20, 1941, aged 68. A regular member of Transvaal teams from 1894 to 1905, he made 728 runs, average 28, in first-class matches; highest score 154.

SLATER, Archie G., died July 22, 1949, at Bacup, Lancashire, aged 58. The son of a former Derbyshire player, he was a sound all-rounder and appeared for the same county at times from 1907 to 1933. He scored 5,982 runs at an average of 19.05, and took 502 wickets for 21.08 each. He interspersed spells in County Cricket with periods during which he played in League cricket, both in the Bradford League and the Lancashire League. Although a reliable batsman, Slater will be best remembered for his steady right-hand medium-pace bowling. His last season for Derbyshire, 1932, proved his best in this direction for he claimed 106 wickets at an average of 16.07. Among several notable bowling feats he took eight wickets for 24 against West Indies for Derbyshire at Derby in 1928.

SLATER, Harry, who died on November 20, 1916, played occasionally for Derbyshire between 1882 and 1887. He was a useful fast bowler, and a fair bat and field. Three of his sons have appeared in County Cricket.

SLATER, Herbert, who died on December 2, 1958, aged 77, played in five matches for Derbyshire in 1907. A good batsman and an excellent fielder, he scored many runs in club cricket.

SLATER, William Drake, who died at Otley on May 4, 1930, aged 83, was the last surviving member of the Yeadon team which played the Australians in 1878. For two seasons he was associated with the well-known Casey's clown cricketers who travelled from one end of the country to the other.

SLATTER, William H., born September 12, 1851, died in Harrow Hospital on August 16, 1929, aged 77. Son of the better-known "Steevie" Slatter, he was engaged at Lord's for 57 years, originally as a pavilion dressing-room attendant in 1863, and working his way up to become clerk of works. His reminiscences were published in a private circulation pamphlet, in 1914, entitled *Recollections of Lord's and the Marylebone Cricket Club.* Some idea of the changes which time wrought during his long association with the ground can be gauged from the fact that he could recall seeing wild rabbits there. He designed and built the luncheon arbours surrounding the practice-ground.

SLIGHT, James, born at Geelong, in Victoria, on November 17, 1855, died on December 10, 1930, aged 75. He was educated at South Melbourne Grammar School and was a member of the Australian team of 1880 which, under the captaincy of W. L. Murdoch, toured England and New Zealand. When at his best he was a batsman with a sound defence and a free style but impaired health, which necessitated an operation, handicapped him whilst in this country. He took part, however, in the first Test ever played here—at the Oval. His fielding at point and long-on was always good. For many years he played for the South Melbourne C.C. and, when he scored 279 for that club against St. Kilda in the early part of 1883, his first-class wicket stand with J. Rosser (192) produced 395 runs.

SMAILES, Thomas Francis, who died in a Harrogate hospital on December 1, 1970, aged 60, did admirable work for Yorkshire as a professional right-arm medium pace bowler and an enterprising left-handed batsman from 1932 to 1948. He had been in poor health for several years. Yorkshire won the County Championship seven times during Frank Smailes's first-class career, in which he took 802 wickets for them for 20.72 runs each and hit 5,683 runs, average 19.19. In each of four seasons he took over 100 wickets, achieving the "cricketers' double" in 1938, when he hit the highest of his three centuries—116 against Surrey at Sheffield. That summer, too, he was an outstanding figure for Yorkshire in the game at Bramall Lane which, but for rain, would in all probability have brought victory over D. G. Bradman's Australians. When A. B. Sellers sent the Australians in to bat on rain-affected turf, Smailes dismissed six batsmen in 29 overs for 92 runs and in the second innings he took four wickets for 45. As a result, his name figured among the 13 from which England were to choose their team for the third Test at Old Trafford, but rain prevented any play in the match. Smailes's only Test appearance was against India at Lord's in 1946.

His command of length and ability to make the ball "move" played a big part in a number of fine bowling performances. Chief of these was the taking of all 10 Derbyshire wickets for 47 runs—following first-innings figures of four for 11—at Sheffield in 1939. He enjoyed great success against Glamorgan at Hull the summer before, his analyses reading: six wickets for 35 runs—all in 37 deliveries at a cost of 17 runs—for 68. In 1936 he disposed of seven Worcestershire batsmen in an innings for 24 runs at Headingley and obtained four for 26 and six for 36 in Yorkshire's meeting with the Indian touring side. He served in the Royal Artillery during the Second World War, reaching the rank of captain.

SMALL, Joe A., who died on April 26, 1958,

aged 75, played in the first Test match between England and the West Indies at Lord's in 1928, his score of 52 in the second innings being the highest for the West Indies in the game. This tall, loose-limbed all-rounder, who did much fine work for Trinidad, hit 595 runs, average 18.59, in the tour, his highest innings being 106 not out against the University at Oxford, and with off-breaks dismissed 50 batsmen for 28.88 runs each. He also toured England in 1923, averaging 31.04 for 776 runs, including innings of 94 and 68 in the match against Lancashire at Old Trafford, but took only 19 wickets, average 33.47. Altogether Small, who was a splendid slip fieldsman, scored 2,995 runs, average 25.50, and took over 100 wickets.

SMART, Cyril Cecil, died on May 21, 1975, aged 75. Between 1920 and 1922 he played in 45 matches for Warwickshire, but his highest score was 59 and his nine wickets cost him 56.44 runs each. Nor was he much more successful during a number of appearances for Glamorgan between 1927 and 1933. It was only in 1934 at the age of 36 that he achieved anything of note and from then to the outbreak of the War he was a most valuable member of the county side. In those six seasons he scored 7,416 runs with an average of 32.72 and made nine centuries, his powerful driving making a welcome contrast to the more sedate methods of other members of the side. He was moreover a splendid all-round field and a useful change leg-break bowler. His highest score was 151 not out against Sussex at Hastings in 1935, but more notable than this was his 114 not out against the South Africans the same year. Following on 259 behind, Glamorgan were 114 for nine. At this point Smart and D. W. Hughes, who was making his first appearance for the county, put on 131 unfinished for the last wicket in an hour and with the help of rain saved the match.

He is perhaps more widely remembered for hitting G. Hill of Hampshire, an offspinner, for 32 in one over at Cardiff in 1935, at that time a record number off a genuine six-ball over in first-class cricket. (When Alletson scored 34 off an over from Killick in his famous innings at Hove, he was aided by two no-balls.) Even now the feat has only once been surpassed—when Sobers hit six sixes in one over off Nash at Swansea in 1968. Smart returned to the Glamorgan side in 1946, but at 48 could not produce his old form and that was his last season. He and his elder brother Jack, the Warwickshire wicket-keeper, were both born in Wiltshire; their father was for years one of the mainstays of the Wiltshire side.

SMART, John Abbott (Jack), died at his home at Bulkington, Warwickshire, on October 3, 1979, aged 88. Playing his first match for Warwickshire in 1919 as an attacking batsman who might pick up an occasional wicket with his off-spin, he had by 1923 secured a more or less regular place in the side. However, the return to the staff of Parsons, the engagement of Croom and Norman Kilner, and the rapid improvement of Wyatt and Santall, meant that he was relegated to spare man. It was not until "Tiger" Smith's retirement at the end of 1930 that his real chance came, and for six seasons he was the county's regular wicket-keeper. In 1932, with 79 dismissals, he established what is still a Warwickshire record. As a batsman he was purely an attacker and frequently played a valuable innings when runs were wanted. From 1937 to 1948 he was a first-class umpire and to the end of his life was often seen at Edgbaston.

SMITH, Alfort, who was born at Bank Lane, near Bury, in Lancashire, on July 7, 1846, died at Glossop on December 21, 1908. *Scores and Biographies* (x–294) described him as: "A good average batsman, and in the field often wicket-keeper." He played occasionally for Lancashire between 1867 and 1871 and frequently for Derbyshire from 1873 until 1880. Soon after he made his place in the latter side secure he resolved to dispense with the services of Frost as long-stop, and accordingly stood up to the bowling of William Mycroft, George Hay, and Hickton, who required careful watching on the indifferent wickets of the '70s.

SMITH, Alfred Farrer, who was born at Birstall on March 7, 1847, died at Ossett in January, 1915. Between 1868 and 1874 he played in 29 matches for Yorkshire, making 692 runs with an average of 14.72, his highest score being 89 v. Notts, at Huddersfield in 1873. A year later he made 99 for Players of North v. Gentlemen of South at Prince's. He was described as "A fine batsman, having excellent defence, with plenty of hit... Is also a good field at cover-point and can bowl fast round-armed." Owing to business reasons he retired from first-class cricket at the age of 27, but afterwards was nominated a county umpire.

SMITH, Sir Archibald Levin, was born at Salt Hill, Chichester, August 27, 1836, and died at Wester Elchies House, Aberlour, Morayshire, October 20, 1901. *Scores and Biographies* (viii–319) says of him, "Plays occasionally for the M.C.C., bats steadily, fields anywhere, and bowls fast underhand, with a curious 'windmill' delivery." He was educated at Trinity College, Cambridge, and became a barrister of the Inner Temple in 1860. In 1879 he was appointed to be a junior Counsel to the Treasury, and in 1883 became a Judge of the High Court. In June, 1892, he became a Lord Justice of Appeal, and Master of the Rolls at the latter end of 1900, when he succeeded the present Lord Chief Justice (Lord Alverstone). In 1857, 1858, and 1859, he rowed in the Cambridge boat against Oxford. On the last occasion the Light Blues sank; Smith could not swim, being the only member of the two crews ignorant of the art, but was saved by a lifebuoy thrown to him by the umpire. Sir A. L. Smith frequently assisted the Gentlemen of Sussex, and in July, 1862, when appearing for them, played an innings of 95 against the Midland Counties Diamonds, at Brighton. He was above the average as a cricketer, although he did not gain a place either in the Cambridge or the Sussex XI. There can be no doubt that his death was considerably hastened by the tragic death of his wife, who was drowned in the Spey, near Aberlour, on August 26, 1901, the eve of her husband's 65th birthday. Sir A. L. Smith was President of the Marylebone Club in 1899, and the author, in *The Walkers of Southgate,* of the chapter entitled: "Reminiscences: by an old friend of the Walkers."

SMITH, Arthur, born at Hurstpierpoint on May 26, 1851, died at Amberley, in Sussex, on March 8, 1923. He was younger brother of the late Mr. C.H. Smith, and himself played in 20 matches for Sussex between 1874 and 1880, scoring 91 runs with an average of 3.95 and taking 63 wickets each. His bowling was left-hand medium-paced with considerable break. He was not in the XI whilst at Brighton College.

SMITH, Arthur Frederick, died on January 18, 1936. Born on May 13, 1853, he went to Harrow and Wellington schools and played for Middlesex before getting his Blue at Cambridge in 1875. He appeared occasionally for the county until 1877. A useful batsman, he was a fine field, usually at long leg. A good athlete before going to South Africa, he helped to form the Kimberley

Golf Club. He retired from De Beers Company about 10 years ago.

SMITH, B. C., for 20 years a member of the Northamptonshire team, helping to raise the county from second-class rank, died at Northampton, aged 83, on November 29, 1942. A wicket-keeper of considerable ability, he often caused trouble as a batsman late on the list. He played only two seasons in first-class cricket, 1905 and 1906, and the next year became an umpire on the first-class list.

SMITH, Cedric Ivan James, known universally as "Big Jim" Smith, died at his home near Blackburn on February 8, 1979, aged 72. Born at Corsham, he played for Wiltshire from 1926 until 1933, but, having been on the staff of Lord's since 1926, came to the notice of the Middlesex authorities, who persuaded him to qualify for them. To the general public he was at that time unknown and his first season, 1934, was a triumph. With 172 wickets at an average of 18.88, he came sixth in the first-class bowling averages and played for the Players at Lord's. That winter he was a member of the M.C.C. side to the West Indies, a great honour for a player with so little first-class experience. He played in all the Tests on his tour and gave some sensational displays of hitting. His only other Test match was against New Zealand at Old Trafford in 1937. He continued as a very valuable member of the Middlesex side until 1939, and in his six seasons for the county he took 676 wickets at 17.75. Standing 6 ft. 4 in. and immensely strong, he had the cardinal virtue of bowling at the stumps and revelled in long spells of bowling.

Yet fine bowler and fieldsman that he was, he will surely be remembered most as a batsman whose entry always roused a hum of excitement. His principal stroke (perhaps his only one!) was to advance the left foot approximately in the direction of the ball and then swing with all his might. If the ball was well up (and the foot on the right line) it went with a low trajectory an astonishing distance. Against Gloucestershire at Bristol in 1938 he reached 50 in 11 minutes; disregarding one instance which the connivance of the bowlers rendered farcical, this is a record for first-class cricket. Against Kent at Maidstone in 1935 his 50 took 14 minutes. In comparison to these herculean feats, his one century, 101 not out against Kent at Canterbury in 1939, was a sedate performance, taking 81 minutes! He added 116 for the last

wicket with Ian Peebles, his own share being 98.

SMITH, Charles—he was always known as C. H. Smith, though he had only one Christian name—died at Henfield on March 12, 1909, in his 71st year. He was born at Albourne, Hurstpierpoint, on August 31, 1838, and played in 63 matches for Sussex between 1861 and 1874. His highest scores were 95 v. Surrey at the Oval in 1864, when he and G. Wells (82) added 159 together for the third wicket, and 94 v. Hampshire at Brighton in the following year. In the match with Surrey at the Oval in 1866 he went in first and carried his bat through the innings for 47. *Scores and Biographies* (ix–118) says of him: "Height, 5ft. 8½in., and weight, 10st. 7lb. (or 11st.). Has been a very successful batsman in the matches in which he has assisted his county, and fields anywhere near the wicket, though generally mid-wicket-off." For several years he was joint Hon. Secretary of the Sussex County C.C. At one time he was in business in Brighton as a wine merchant, ill-health preventing him from following the medical profession for which he was intended. His uncle, Mr. Alfred Smith, played for Sussex between 1841 and 1852, his brother, Mr. Arthur Smith, from 1874 to 1880, and his son, Mr. C. L. A., who played first in 1898, was captain of the county XI.

SMITH, Charles, who was born at Calverley, near Leeds, in Yorkshire, on August 24, 1861, died at his native place on May 2, 1925, aged 63. He was a useful batsman and a capital and plucky wicket-keeper, and, after appearing in one match for Yorkshire in 1885, assisted Lancashire from 1893 until 1902. In all first-class games in 1895 he caught 51 men and stumped 25, and two years later caught 47 and stumped 21: altogether he obtained 399 wickets—296 caught and 103 stumped. His highest innings in first-class cricket was 81 for Lancashire v. Sussex at Manchester in 1895. In July, 1903, the Lancashire v. Essex match at Old Trafford was given to him and Cuttell for their benefit.

SMITH, Sir Charles Aubrey, C.B.E., famous in the world of cricket before making a name on the stage and becoming a universal favourite on the films in comparatively recent years, died on December 20, 1948, aged 85, at Beverly Hills, California. Born in London on July 21, 1863, the son of a doctor, C. A. Smith went to Charterhouse School and bowled with such success that it came as no surprise that he gained his Blue at Cambridge when a Freshman in 1882. Four times he played at Lord's against Oxford and, by a remarkable series of coincidences, all of these matches ended with a decisive margin of seven wickets, Cambridge winning three of these interesting encounters. In the 1884 match which Oxford won, C. A. Smith was not out 0 in each innings and took two wickets for 65 runs, but in the other three games he showed his worth. In 1883 he helped C. T. Studd dismiss Oxford for 55 and in the second innings he took six wickets for 78 and Oxford just equalled the Cambridge total 215. He made four catches in the match. His last effort for the Light Blues brought six wickets for 81. His captains were the three brothers Studd and the Hon. M. B. Hawke.

He played for Sussex from 1882 until 1896, with varying regularity, and was captain from 1887 to 1889. For Gentlemen at Lord's in 1888 he and S. M. J. Woods dismissed the last four players for one run scored after A. G. Steel handed the ball to Smith. Each of the Cambridge fast bowlers took two of these wickets and Gentlemen won by five runs. In the match Woods took 10 wickets for 76 and C. A. Smith five for 36.

In the previous winter he went to Australia, captaining the side organised by Shaw and Shrewsbury, and in 1888–89 he captained the first English side which went to South Africa. Major R. G. Wharton, the Australian, was manager. All the matches were against "odds" except two engagements called "English Team v. XI of South Africa," but some years afterwards given the description "Tests." During the tour C. A. Smith took 134 wickets at 7.61 each, a modest achievement compared with the 290 wickets at 5.62 credited to John Briggs, the Lancashire left-hander. Smith stayed in South Africa for a time in partnership with M. P. Bowden, of Surrey, a member of the team, as stockbrokers. During this period he captained Transvaal against Kimberley in the first Currie Cup match in April 1890, so initiating a competition which has done much to raise the standard of cricket in South Africa.

Among C. A. Smith's best bowling performances were five wickets for eight runs for Sussex against the University at Cambridge in 1885, and seven for 16 against M.C.C. at Lord's in 1890. A hard-hitting batsman, he scored 142 for Sussex at Hove against Hampshire in 1888.

Over 6ft. tall, he made an unusual run-up to deliver the ball and so became known as "Round The Corner" Smith. Sometimes he started from a deep mid-off position, at others from behind the umpire, and, as described by W. G. Grace, "it is rather startling when he suddenly appears at the bowling crease."

He maintained his love for cricket to the end. Until a few years ago he captained the Hollywood side and visited England for the Test matches, the last time as recently as 1947, when South Africa were here.

He was knighted in 1944 in recognition of his support of Anglo-American friendship.

A very good Association outside-right, he played for Old Carthusians and Corinthians.—H.P.

SMITH, Charles James Edward, an elder brother of H. E. Smith of the 1907 South African team, died at Johannesburg on March 27, 1947, aged 74. He played for Transvaal from 1894 to 1904. Against the Australian team of 1902 he scored 58 and 71 not out for Transvaal Fifteen, and in the three Test matches made 106 runs, average 21.20, including 45 at Cape Town.

SMITH, Charles John, born in London on January 19, 1849, died on May 8, 1930, aged 81. *Scores and Biographies* summed him up thus: "As a batsman he possesses an excellent style, and is a good free hitter, is a capital field anywhere, and bowls fast round-armed, being altogether an energetic and useful cricketer." In 1866 he was a member of one of the best sides Harrow ever had: that year they beat Eton by an innings and 136 runs, Cobden and Money bowling with great effect. He was unable to play at Lord's the next year as about a fortnight before the match he cut his foot severely on a concealed scythe in jumping a ditch. His County Cricket was confined to a few appearances for Middlesex.

SMITH, Charles Lawrence Arthur, who died at Henfield, Sussex, on November 22, 1949, aged 79, played for Sussex from 1898 to 1911. A son of C. H. Smith, also a Sussex cricketer, he first played for the county when captain of Brighton College. In 1906 he took over the Sussex captaincy for the remainder of the season after C. B. Fry was hurt in the second game, and also led the side in the 1909 season. A sound right-hand batsman, he scored 5,778 runs, average 19.72, for Sussex.

SMITH, Denis, died suddenly at Derby on September 12, 1979, aged 72. Born at

Somercotes on January 24, 1907, he played for Derbyshire from 1927 until 1951. He was then appointed county coach in succession to Harry Elliott, making a solitary appearance in 1952 in an emergency and finally ending his 44-year connection with the club in 1971, though he was quietly scouting until last year. By 1930 he had developed into a reliable left-handed batsman, scoring 83 and 105 in Payton's benefit match at Trent Bridge. In the next match, his 107 at the Oval was largely responsible for Derbyshire's first victory against Surrey for 26 years. At this time he was opening the innings, and although he dropped down the order at times over the years, he is best remembered as an opener. His ability in this direction was to bring something rare to Derbyshire—success. In four consecutive seasons, Derbyshire were twice third, runners-up in 1935 (which from a playing point of view was a better year than 1936) and champions in 1936.

Tall and elegant in style, he approached the artistry of Frank Woolley, though not possessing the fluency of the Kent player. Usually attractive to watch, Smith's forcing shots were well executed, being severe on anything over-pitched, especially on middle or leg stump, and his runs came at a good rate. Throughout most of the '30s his usual opening partners were Storer or Alderman—the latter an almost perfect foil to Smith's aggression—and they could be relied on to give the side a sound start. Consistent batting in the early weeks of 1935 gained him Test recognition in two matches against South Africa, when he shared in stands of 52 and 128 at Headingley with scores of 36 and 57, followed by 35 and a failure at Old Trafford.

He scored over 2,000 runs that year, becoming one of *Wisden*'s Five, and exceeded 1,000 runs on 12 occasions—a county record, as was his aggregate of 20,516 runs and his 30 centuries. He played for the Players at Lord's in 1935 and in the second innings scored 78 out of 112 for The Rest against the Champion County when no other player reached double figures. This was the last such match to be played, so he was denied the honour of appearing for both sides in successive years when Derbyshire won the Championship in 1936. He toured Australia and New Zealand in the winter of 1935–36 with the M.C.C. under the captaincy of Errol Holmes. No Tests were played but in the representative matches against New Zealand his average was over 43, and he shared in stands of 239 with J. H. Parks against Otago and 204 with W. Barber against Queensland.

Following his 189 against Yorkshire at Chesterfield in the opening match of 1935, an innings he considered marked the turning point of his career, came his highest score of 225 versus Hampshire on the same ground, when he sustained a broken rib which caused his absence from the first Test that year. In 1937 he made 202 not out at Trent Bridge. During the War, he played in the Bradford League and took up wicket-keeping, acting in this capacity for Derbyshire for part of 1946 and 1947 until the arrival of George Dawkes. His usual place in the field was first slip, and it was not unknown for him to bowl an over or two of right-arm medium pace. As county coach he was hard to please, and no doubt he chastened some with his blunt approach. But when words of praise did fall from his lips, the pupil knew they were truly earned.

DENIS SMITH
CAREER FIGURES

Season	Matches	Inns	Not Outs	Runs	Highest Inns	100s	50s	Average	Catches
In England									
1927	3	2	0	1	1	0	0	21.88	0
1928	7	11	0	175	58	0	1	34.76	3
1929	18	24	3	336	46	0	0	0.50	7
1930	20	35	2	975	107	2	6	15.90	9
1931	30	47	4	1,281	131	2	5	16.00	23
1932	29	48	4	1,551	111	3	11	29.54	13
1933	27	48	5	941	129*	1	4	29.79	39
1934	29	49	3	1,599	131	4	5	35.25	31
1933	27	48	5	941	129*	1	4	21.88	29
1934	29	49	3	1,599	131	4	5	34.76	31
1935	31	61	6	2,175	225	2	14	39.54	24
1936	31	51	5	1,421	169	2	9	30.89	22

Signifies not out.

DENNIS SMITH CAREER FIGURES—*Continued*

Season	Matches	Inns	Not Outs	Runs	Highest Inns	100s	5s	Average	Catches
1937	29	50	3	1,914	202*	5	8	40.72	28
1938	28	45	1	1,234	122	3	5	28.04	21
1939	30	55	5	1,597	132	2	8	31.94	24
1946	24	42	3	1,391	146	2	7	35.66	32
									(+ 4 st)
1947	19	31	5	952	79	0	7	36.61	30
1948	24	38	0	1,076	107	1	6	28.31	22
1949	22	37	2	1,033	89	0	9	29.51	25
1950	22	39	6	1,117	122*	1	5	33.84	20
									(+ 1 st)
1951	12	20	3	337	56	0	2	19.82	6
1952	1	2	0	26	16	0	0	13.00	0
In Australia and New Zealand									
1935–36	11	18	3	711	165	2	2	47.40	10
Totals	447	753	63	21,843	225	32	114	31.65	379
									(+ 5 st)

Bowling: Smith took 20 wickets for 735 runs, average 36.75; 5 wkts in an innings once.

CENTURIES (32)

In England (30)

All of Denis Smith's 30 centuries in England were scored for Derbyshire

105	v. Nottinghamshire at Ilkeston, 1930.
107	v. Surrey at the Oval, 1930.
131	v. Essex at Leyton, 1931.
108	v. Hampshire at Chesterfield, 1931.
103*	v. Hampshire at Southampton, 1932.
107*	v. Middlesex at Derby, 1932.
111	v. Essex at Leyton, 1932.
129*	v. Northamptonshire at Northampton, 1933.
126	v. Surrey at the Oval, 1934.
120	v. Sussex at Buxton, 1934.
131	v. Gloucestershire at Gloucester, 1934.
125	v. Surrey at Ilkeston, 1934.
189	v. Yorkshire at Chesterfield, 1935.
225	v. Hampshire at Chesterfield, 1935.
106	v. Surrey at the Oval, 1936.
169	v. Leicestershire at Oakham, 1936.
158	v. Yorkshire at Sheffield, 1937.
140*	v. Hampshire at Chesterfield, 1937.
121	v. Leicestershire at Chesterfield, 1937.
104	v. Northamptonshire at Chesterfield, 1937.
202*	v. Nottinghamshire at Trent Bridge, 1937.
110	v. Lancashire at Ilkeston, 1938.
122	v. Kent at Tonbridge, 1938.
113	v. Gloucestershire at Burton upon Trent, 1938.
123	v. Worcestershire at Chesterfield, 1939.
132	v. Worcestershire at Dudley, 1939.
140	v. Surrey at Derby, 1946.
146	v. Nottinghamshire at Trent Bridge, 1946.
107	v. Somerset at Taunton, 1948.
122*	v. Yorkshire at Bradford, 1950.

In Australia and New Zealand (2) for M.C.C.

109	v. Queensland at Brisbane, 1935.
165	v. Otago at Dunedin, 1935.

*Signifies not out.

SMITH, Douglas, who died at Grahamstown, South Africa, on August 16, 1949, aged 75, made a few appearances for Somerset and Worcestershire and also played for Glamorgan, then a second-class county, from 1895 to 1904. In first-class cricket he scored 556 runs, averaging 11.12.

SMITH, Ernest, who died on April 11, 1945, aged 75, was a very capable all-round cricketer for Oxford University and Yorkshire. After two years in the Clifton College XI he got his Blue at Oxford in 1890 and next year also played against Cambridge. He fared only moderately in the University matches at Lord's, but his free batting and fast bowling often proved valuable, as he made full use of his height and weight. A schoolmaster, he was a welcome member of the Yorkshire XI during vacations from 1888 to 1907, and, in the absence of Lord Hawke, he occasionally captained the side. Altogether for Yorkshire he scored 4,787 runs, average 20.81, and took 284 wickets at 23.87 runs apiece. A versatile batsman he usually scored fast, once making 70 out of 76 against M.C.C. at Oxford, while at Hastings in 1891 he scored 154 for North against South, he and C. E. de Trafford adding 254 in 105 minutes. He gave a very different display at Leyton in 1905, staying an hour without scoring and taking out his bat, so saving Yorkshire when a heavy defeat from Essex seemed inevitable. He made many runs at Eastbourne and in 1912 on the Saffrons ground he scored 164 not out for H. D. G. Leveson-Gower's XI against Cambridge University. At the age of 53 he hit up 160 for Eastbourne against Uppingham Rovers. One of his best bowling performances was for Oxford University in 1890, 13 Lancashire wickets falling to him for 146 runs; and once for Elstree Masters he took 17 wickets in a match.

SMITH, Ernest, who died in hospital on January 2, 1972, aged 83, played for Yorkshire as a professional fast-medium left-arm bowler between 1914 and 1926, taking 46 wickets at an average cost of 23.69. He achieved considerable success in League cricket, possessing mounted cricket balls presented by Rotherham Town C.C. for taking all 10 Notts Ramblers' wickets for 33 runs in 1908, this feat including a hat-trick, and by Ossett C.C. for dismissing 116 batsmen in the 1920 season.

ERNEST JAMES SMITH
Born February 6, 1886
Died August 31, 1979
by Rowland Ryder

The death of Ernest James ("Tiger") Smith

marks the end of an era in cricket. He had played with and against W. G. Grace; he had kept wicket for England against Australia before the First World War; and his connection with Warwickshire spanned no fewer than 75 years. He was the oldest living Test cricketer up to the time of his death.

Ernest James Smith—for over 70 years he had been known as "Tiger", although a few Warwickshire associates called him Jim—was born in Benacre Street, Birmingham; a street which has now disappeared, that area of Birmingham having been replaced by a series of ring roads, underpasses and flyovers near the centre of the city. But it used to be about a mile from the Edgbaston ground, and, four months after "Tiger" Smith was born, Warwickshire played their first match at Edgbaston.

In 1902 Edgbaston became a Test match venue, and on May 31, thanks to Wilfred Rhodes, England bowled Australia out for 36. Young Smith was working at Cadbury's then, and two years later he offered his services to Warwickshire as a wicket-keeper, although he had lost the tips of two fingers in a works accident.

He was taken on, and in 1904 played his first match for Warwickshire against the South African tourists. Right up to the end of his life he remembered the names of the South African side that came over in the googly summer of 1904, and he would rattle them off with reminiscent delight: Shalders, Tancred, Hathorn, Frank Mitchell, Sinclair, Llewellyn, Schwartz, White, S. J. Snooke, Halliwell and Kotze. Wisden referred to him simply as Smith, and although he played in two other games there is no reference to him in the Warwickshire report for 1904.

For a time he was seconded to the M.C.C. It was during this period that he met W. G. Grace, and played in several matches for and against Grace's London County XI. "Do you know what he'd do if he thought you weren't any good?" chuckled "Tiger." "He'd go out and buy a rabbit and put it in your cricketing bag." While he was on the ground staff, "Tiger's" duties sometimes included bowling to George Robey in the nets.

When Smith returned to Edgbaston he was apprenticed to "Dick" Lilley, who had also worked at Cadbury's before joining Warwickshire. Lilley himself, who played in 35 Test matches, 32 of them against Australia, had been for many years an opponent and close friend of J. McC. ("Old Jack") Blackham, generally considered to be the first of the great modern wicket-keepers.

"Tiger" Smith was therefore fortunate in

his apprenticeship to this craft within a craft, for he was to learn from the greatest contemporary exponent in England, and indirectly from Blackham. By the year 1910 he was coming into his own, playing in 19 of Warwickshire's 20 matches. "More than a word of praise is due to Smith," ran the Warwickshire report in *Wisden*, "who, called on to fill the vacancy created by Lilley's retirement from wicket-keeping, acquitted himself with every credit."

The next year, 1911, proved to be the most remarkable in Warwickshire's history. Under the inspiring captaincy of F.R. Foster, the side, near the bottom of the table halfway through the season, eventually won 13 matches out of 20 and caused a cricket sensation by carrying off the Championship honours. Foster's part in this achievement was outstanding, but "Tiger" Smith himself did remarkably well, with 40 catches and five stumpings in Championship matches; 11 of his victims were off Foster's bowling. It was said that he was the only wicket-keeper who could take the left-arm bowling of Foster, whose amazing swing and speed off the pitch rendered him as much a problem to his own wicket-keepers as to the opposing batsmen. And this was during a period when there were a number of county wicket-keepers of Test match calibre playing regularly. In addition to Smith, there were Strudwick of Surrey, Huish of Kent, Dolphin of Yorkshire, Murrell of Middlesex, Humphries of Derbyshire, Buswell of Northamptonshire, Butt of Sussex, Oates of Nottinghamshire, and Brown of Hampshire—when he wasn't bowling!

Even more exciting for the young "Tiger" Smith—he was 25 in 1911—than the winning of the Championship was the 1911–12 tour of Australia, when he was chosen as understudy to Strudwick. In the event it was Smith who kept wicket in all the Test matches, except the first; probably because he could take Foster better and read his signals to the wicket-keeper—one of which, a change in step during the run up, to indicate the slower ball, was spotted by an Australian tram conductor.

England lost the first Test. The turning point of the series was perhaps Barnes' opening spell of four wickets for one run in five overs in Australia's first innings of the second Test. In this innings Smith took three catches. England won the series 4–1 and Smith had eight catches and one stumping in his four Tests. Informed opinion has it that he excelled himself in the second Test. "Well, you'd got to be good at Melbourne,

with 40,000 people watching you", he reminisced.

In the third Test Smith stumped the left-handed Clem Hill first ball off Foster's bowling when Hill was attempting a glide. P.F. Warner described the execution of this pre-arranged stratagem as "one of the technical masterpieces of the game." Smith always contended that he did it again in the second innings, with Hill out by "about 12 inches," but the umpire thought otherwise and Hill went on to make 98.

During the ill-fated, rain-ridden Triangular Tournament of 1912, "Tiger" Smith played in all six Tests involving England, and he played in one more Test against South Africa in 1913. In the last two seasons before the First World War he kept to the brilliant bowling of Percy Jeeves during the latter's brief meteoric career for Warwickshire.

When cricket was resumed after the war "Tiger" Smith was 33. He continued to play for Warwickshire until 1930. His wicket-keeping was never less than competent, and he became a sound, attacking, opening batsman. Two amazing games he played in during this period were against Hampshire in 1922 and Sussex in 1925.

In the first of these games, Hampshire were dismissed for 15 in their first innings. Following on 207 behind, they made 520 and won the match easily. Had "Tiger" stopped a ball on the leg side that went for four byes and had another fielder held a catch—the ball went through his hands and travelled to the boundary—Hampshire would have been all out for seven in their first innings.

In the Sussex match, Warwickshire were set 391 to win in just under five hours and scored 392 for one in four hours and a quarter. All three Warwickshire batsmen made centuries: J.H. Parsons (now Canon J.H. Parsons) 124, "Tiger" Smith 139 not out and the Hon. F.S.G. Calthorpe 109 not out. Although this was not his highest score for Warwickshire— he made 177 against Derbyshire in 1927 and 173 against Kent the following year—"Tiger" always considered this innings against Sussex was the best he ever played.

In 1930 Smith retired as a player and went on the list of first-class umpires, standing in several Test matches. There was a brief period of coaching at Worcester; he was an air-raid warden during the Second World War, and in 1946 he became senior coach at Edgbaston, a position he filled with distinction until Tom Dollery succeeded him in 1955. "Tiger," now 69, continued to supervise the indoor cricket school, where he was still taking an active part up to 1970.

By the mid-1950s he had become almost a legendary figure. "The gatemen are beginning to know me now!" was one of his favourite quips. "Is 'Tiger' watching?" members would ask one another during the course of the day's play. More often than not he *was* watching, from his seat in the corner of the players' dining-room. Often he would be joined by his team-mates of the '20s: Norman Kilner, "Danny" Mayer, Jack Parsons, George Paine, Jack Smart; sometimes W. H. Ashdown, the great Kent cricketer of that period, would join the party from his home in Rugby.

It wasn't only with the players of the past that "Tiger" Smith discussed the game in its myriad facets. Cricketers from many counties—especially, says Leslie Deakins, since the death of C. B. Fry in 1956—would come to "Tiger" with their batting problems. "Let's see you in the middle first," he would say, and afterwards he would diagnose the trouble. Almost invariably, because of high intelligence, experience, and a knowledge of bone and muscle structure acquired in his First World War experience with the St John Ambulance Brigade, plus that indefinable intuitive flair that only the truly gifted teacher commands, he would put his finger on what was wrong and indicate the remedy. In very recent years Mike Brearley has been one of those who testified to "Tiger" Smith's remarkable powers in this direction.

He was a big, robust man, tall for a wicket-keeper, with a wonderful agility in his prime. He had more than a little in common with that "kind and manly Alfred Mynn" of a former generation. Always a fighter, he had a razor-sharp sense of humour and loved "the rigour of the game." "It was 'Good morning!' before we started and 'How's that!' for the rest of the day," he said of one hard-fought contest.

Once he was asked who was the best captain he had served under and he replied: "Well, any captain's a good one if you're winning." After reflection he added that F. S. G. Calthorpe was the happiest captain he had known.

He loved thinking about cricket, and in particular about the craft of wicket-keeping. In assessing Bert Oldfield and Dick Lilley as the greatest wicket-keepers who have ever played, he referred to "an enthusiasm greater even than dedication." He was too modest to claim that attribute for himself, but others would claim it for him.

When Field-Marshal Slim spoke of the Birmingham spirit of "resilience, adaptability and a cheerful refusal to lie down under difficulties," he had summed up "Tiger" Smith in a nutshell. The 17-year-old boy from Benacre Street who had lost the tip of two fingers in a works accident, and who asked the Edgbaston authorities for a job as wicket-keeper, possessed these qualities in good measure. Which was why he played for England at the age of 25.

CAREER AT A GLANCE
BY A. H. WAGG

Season	Matches	Inns	Not Outs	Runs	Highest Inns	Average	100s	50s	Catches	Stumpings
1904	3	4	3	19	11*	19.00	0	0	4	1
1905	6	6	1	60	24	12.00	0	0	13	1
1906	2	2	2	10	7*	—	0	0	3	0
1907	1	1	0	0	0	00.00	0	0	1	1
1908	6	9	2	64	16*	9.14	0	0	13	3
1909	11	17	0	181	35	10.64	0	0	22	4
1910	19	31	6	306	39*	12.24	0	0	42	10
1911	23	40	6	827	113	24.32	1	3	43	5
1911–12	7	9	0	124	47	13.77	0	0	16	2
1912	33	54	2	991	134	19.05	1	6	48	10
1913	23	43	0	971	89	22.58	0	5	58	10
1913–14	8	8	2	146	36	24.33	0	0	6	1
1914	25	42	6	768	89	21.33	0	6	45	3
1919	16	28	2	556	72	21.38	0	2	27	7
1920	28	49	6	769	80	17.88	0	3	39	13
1921	24	46	0	733	100	15.93	1	1	35	14
1922	29	51	2	1,303	116	26.59	2	4	29	9
1923	26	46	2	917	65	20.84	0	5	32	12
1924	26	44	2	913	104	21.77	1	3	34	5
1925	27	51	4	1,477	149	31.42	3	8	46	9
1925–26	11	17	0	489	73	28.76	0	3	8	4

CAREER AT A GLANCE—*Continued*

Season	Matches	Inns	Not Outs	Runs	Highest Inns	Average	100s	50s	Catches	Stumpings
1926	31	40	3	514	48	13.89	0	0	41	9
1927	30	45	3	1,292	177	30.76	4	2	42	8
1928	24	39	1	1,194	173	31.42	2	4	20	9
1929	29	49	0	1,354	142	27.63	2	6	28	2
1930	28	43	0	1,019	132	23.69	3	2	27	4
Totals	496	814	55	16,997	177	22.39	20	63	722	156

TEST MATCHES

Season	Matches	Inns	Not Outs	Runs	Highest Inns	Average	Catches	Stumpings
1911–12 v. Australia	4	5	0	47	22	9.40	9	1
1912 v. Australia	3	4	1	22	14*	7.33	3	0
1912 v. South Africa	3	4	0	35	13	8.75	4	2
1913–14 v. South Africa	1	1	0	9	9	9.00	1	0
Totals	11	14	1	113	22	8.69	17	3

CENTURIES (20)

All of E. J. Smith's 20 centuries were scored for Warwickshire

113	v. Surrey at Edgbaston, 1911
134	v. Hampshire at Coventry, 1912
100	v. Worcestershire at Worcester, 1921
115	v. Worcestershire at Stourbridge, 1922
114	v. Hampshire at Southampton, 1922
104	v. Hampshire at Edgbaston, 1924
134	v. Leicestershire at Leicester, 1925
139*	v. Sussex at Edgbaston, 1925
149	v. Leicestershire at Coventry, 1925
101*	v. Nottinghamshire at Edgbaston, 1927
132	v. Middlesex at Lord's, 1927
177	v. Derbyshire at Edgbaston, 1927
132	v. Kent at Coventry, 1927
108	v. Nottinghamshire at Coventry, 1928
173	v. Kent at Edgbaston, 1928
109	v. Gloucestershire at Edgbaston, 1929
142	v. Yorkshire at Edgbaston, 1929
124	v. Essex at Edgbaston, 1930
132	v. Gloucestershire at Edgbaston, 1930
126	v. Glamorgan at Swansea, 1930

* Signifies not out

BEST WICKET-KEEPING PERFORMANCES

8 dismissals in a match

ct 5 st 3	Warwickshire v. Northamptonshire at Edgbaston	..	..	1927
ct 7 st 1	Warwickshire v. Worcestershire at Edgbaston	..	..	1930

7 dismissals in a match

ct 6 st 1	Warwickshire v. Northamptonshire at Edgbaston	..	..	1912
ct 5 st 2	Warwickshire v. Lancashire at Old Trafford	..	..	1920

SMITH, Frank Ernest, who played in the great days of Surrey under John Shuter and K. J. Key, died at Sedbergh, Yorkshire, where he lived since his retirement from coach at the school, on December 3, 1943, aged 71. Born at Bury St. Edmunds, he obtained a trial at the Oval on the recommendation of C. Baldwin, a Surrey professional also of Suffolk birth, and when qualified by residence played from 1893 to 1896 and made subsequent appearances, while playing also for the London County

Club under W. G. Grace. A rather slow left-handed bowler, he afforded the perfect contrast to Tom Richardson and William Lockwood, then in their prime, and such success did they achieve that, thanks mainly to them, Surrey were champions in 1894 and 1895. Smith enjoyed by far his most successful season in 1894, when his average showed 95 wickets at 13.90 apiece and the three bowlers took 270 wickets between them in championship matches and 414 in all matches; seven other bowlers claimed only 58 victims between them. At Cheltenham Smith twice dismissed W. G. Grace, and against Gloucestershire at the Oval, where Surrey also won by an innings, he and Tom Richardson bowled unchanged, equally sharing the wickets, Smith's 10 costing 71 runs and Richardson's 99. In 1895 Richardson stood out by himself with 237 wickets, Smith deteriorating to a modest 40 at 24 runs apiece in championship matches and he never recovered his ability of 1894. Frank Smith spent many winters coaching in South Africa with Western Province club and Wanderers of Johannesburg.

SMITH, Frederick, who had a somewhat extended trial in the Yorkshire XI in 1902 and had lately been associated as a three-quarter back with the Bramley Football Club, died on October 21, 1905. He caught cold a week before through travelling back to Nelson in wet clothes after playing for Bramley, and pneumonia quickly set in. A left-handed batsman, Smith took part in 12 matches for Yorkshire in 1903, scoring 292 runs with an average of 16. This was a very fair record for a new man, but as he did not play in 1904, except in a few Second XI matches, he was presumably not thought good enough for a regular place in the county team. His best scores for Yorkshire were 55 against Kent at Leeds, and 51 against Somerset at Bradford. He was born at Yeadon on December 18, 1880, and at the time of his death was qualifying for Lancashire.

SMITH, The Rev. Gerald Hyde, who died at Ickham, near Canterbury, on October 16, 1927, aged 87, had played for both Staffordshire and Northamptonshire. An all-round sportsman, he was Rector of Wickhambreaux, in Kent, for over 40 years.

SMITH, Gilbert Osbert, who died on December 6, 1943, aged 71, at his home at Lymington, Hampshire, earned higher fame at Association football than at cricket, but he captained both XIs at Charterhouse and

became a double Blue at Oxford. During a short cricket career he earned lasting fame as the hero in a record performance by Oxford in the University match of 1896. Left to get 330 runs, the XI, captained by H. D. G. Leveson Gower, gained a glorious victory; the feat of making so many runs surpassing anything previously accomplished in University contests. G. O. Smith, going in second wicket down, scored 132 and with only two wanted gave an easy catch to slip when attempting the winning hit. Apart from this wonderful accomplishment the match lives in cricket history because it produced similar incidents to those of 1893, Cambridge again conceding runs so as to avoid making the batting side follow-on. As the outcome of each of these occurrences in University matches the M.C.C. altered law 53 by increasing the margin of runs involving a follow-on first from 80 to 120, and then making it optional with a lead of 150.

Cambridge won when F. S. Jackson allowed C. M. Wells to bowl so as to give away extras; but three years later success did not attend the scheme of Frank Mitchell, the captain, and E. B. Shine, the fast bowler, who sent down two no-balls and a wide, all of which went to the boundary. Cambridge batted again 117 ahead, but were so unnerved by the hostile attitude of the crowd and the loudly expressed criticism in the pavilion, with shouts of "Play the game" and "It's not cricket," that six of their strong batting side fell for 61 runs. Rain stopped play when Cambridge were improving, and after a considerable downpour the pitch rolled out well in the morning. Oxford made a good beginning to a task regarded as impossible in those days, and, thanks mainly to G. O. Smith, the runs were obtained, Oxford winning by four wickets. As "G. O." scored 37 in his first innings and made 51 not out and two in the 1895 match he showed himself admirably fitted for the big occasion. I saw those matches and all that happened in 1896 comes fresh to my memory, including the many opinions expressed in a long correspondence in *The Times.*

H. D. G. Leveson Gower, the Oxford captain who gave G. O. Smith the last place in his XI for the 1896 match, when told that "G. O." was dead, said that "Joe" was a good bat. "I persuaded him to play against the Australians for Surrey at the Oval. Always modest, 'G. O.' said, "I'm not good enough, I'll make two noughts;' and sure enough he did." Unable to find much time for County Cricket, he seldom appeared for Surrey, but having joined A. T. B. Dunn,

W. J. Oakley and other noted players of games as a master at Ludgrove School, he assisted Hertfordshire when free from duty. He became headmaster of the school in February 1902.

In his third season in the Charterhouse cricket XI G. O. Smith scored 168 not out against Old Carthusians; next year, when captain for the second time, he excelled with 229 against Westminster at Godalming and 109 at Wellington. A free scorer, he cut beautifully and got power into his drives by perfect timing; in fact admirable right-hand batting. He also bowled well and at cover-point he used safe hands and returned the ball accurately to the wicket-keeper. Nearly 5ft. 11in. in height and of slim build, he moved gracefully with quickness in all he did.

Going straight into the Oxford Association XI with R. J. Salt from Charterhouse, where they played together on the right wing, G.·O. Smith was put in the centre and earned the description, which lasts to the present time, of being the best centre-forward in the annals of the game. He helped Oxford win three out of four University matches and finished as captain. Playing first for England in 1894 during his brilliant Oxford career, "G. O." was capped 20 times and captained England in the 1898–99 series of internationals, all of which were won, that with Ireland by 13 goals to two—an international record aggregate. He led Corinthians when they became first holders of the Sheriff of London Charity Shield, and scored the winning goal in a great match with Aston Villa at Crystal Palace in November 1899.—H.P.

SMITH, Harry, the Gloucestershire professional, died on November 12, 1937, aged 46. He succeeded Jack Board as wicket-keeper in 1914, and did good service until illness checked his career in 1932. After an unexpected return to the side in 1935 he retired and was for a time coach to the county colts. Besides being a reliable wicket-keeper he was a sound batsman and in 1928 played for England against West Indies at Lord's. Against Hampshire at Southampton in 1919 he made 120 and 102 not out. A noteworthy incident occurred in that match. Pothecary, the last Hampshire batsman, played a ball from Parker into the top of his pad, shook it into Smith's hands, and was given out "caught" contrary to Law 33B which declares in such a case that the ball becomes "dead."

SMITH, Haydon Arthur, died at his birth-place, Groby, four-and-a-half miles from Leicester, on August 7, 1948, from heart failure, aged 47. A tall right-arm fast bowler, he made the fullest use of his height, and besides causing the ball to move either way he was quick off the pitch. After assisting Ratby Town in the South Leicestershire League, he was recommended to the county by W. Shipman and made his debut in first-class cricket in 1925. He took 1,076 wickets, average 25.90, and scored 4,603 runs. His best year was 1935 when he obtained 150 wickets, costing 19 runs apiece. One of his finest performances occurred in 1934 when he took six Yorkshire wickets for 39 and Leicestershire gained their first victory over the northerners for 23 years. In his early days he showed promise as an unorthodox bats-man, but on changing his style, he met with less success, and so he decided to concentrate on bowling, although he remained a useful hitter. Later Smith became coach and groundsman at Ashby Grammar School.

SMITH, Horace Clitheroe (Clyde), I.S.O., O.B.E., who died at Hobart on April 6, 1977, in his 85th year, lived long enough to hear the news of Tasmania's admission to the Inter-state Sheffield Shield Competition—an event he had canvassed for most of the 50 years span during which he was a member of the Australian Board of Cricket Control. A man of many parts in Tasmanian Government, community and sporting life, Clyde Smith was Chairman of the Tasmanian Cricket Association for 35 of the 52 years he served on its Committee of Management. After early success as a batsman at Queen's College, Smith starred with the South Hobart Club—on one occasion scoring a century for his School in the morning and the Club in the afternoon. While a State player and Captain, he won the fielding trophy in the match against H. L. Collins' Australian XI in Hobart. First elected to the Australian Cricket Board as long ago as 1919, Smith managed the Australian team which toured New Zealand in 1960.

SMITH, John, who died on November 26, 1898, was closely associated with Derbyshire cricket, and played a good deal for the County Club in its early days. He was in his 57th year.

SMITH, John, for 14 years (1883–1897) professional cricketer for Worcestershire, and afterwards groundsman, died at Worcester on February 12, 1909, aged 75. He was born at Yeadon, in Yorkshire, on March 23, 1833, and played for his native county twice in

1865, when he made 28 runs in three innings and took six wickets for 72 runs. In 1865, 1866, and 1869 he appeared occasionally for Lancashire. *Scores and Biographies* (viii–301) says of him: "He is a left-handed batsman, and also a fast left round-armed bowler, fielding generally at short-slip or point. Height 5ft. 11in., and weight 12st." He was father of Douglas Smith (Somerset and Worcestershire) and of W. Smith (Wiltshire).

SMITH, Langford D., who died in Dunedin on November 1, 1978, aged 63, was a left-hand bat and a slow left-arm bowler who played for Otago from 1934–57 and also represented South Island. Later he was well-known as a selector and broadcaster.

SMITH, Lewis A., who died in October, 1978, aged 65, played occasionally for Middlesex between 1934 and 1937 and later appeared for Northamptonshire in 1947; against the South Africans he took four for 55, and then, going in at number 11 when the game appeared over, he helped to add 76 for the last wicket, scoring 55.

SMITH, O'Neill Gordon, who died in hospital at Stoke-on-Trent on September 9, 1959, aged 26, following injuries received in a motor-car accident in which two other West Indies players, G. Sobers and T. Dewdney, were also involved, took part in 26 Test matches between 1955 and 1959, scoring 1,331 runs, including four centuries, average 31.69. His death came as a heavy blow to the West Indies, for much had been hoped from him against P. B. H. May's M.C.C. team last winter.

Smith's interest in cricket began at the age of seven and, such was his rapid advance, he gained a place in the team at St. Alban's School, Jamaica, when nine and became captain inside three years. Later at Kingston College he progressed still further, but not until 1955 did he first appear for Jamaica. This was against the visiting Australians and he gave full evidence of his quality by playing an innings of 169, he and A. P. Binns putting on 277 for the sixth wicket. That performance earned him a place in the opening Test match and, by hitting 104 in the second innings, he joined the list of men who obtained a century on Test debut. His success in three other Tests in the series was limited—indeed, he was dismissed for 0 and 0 in the second— but, with characteristic cheerfulness, he did not allow setbacks to deter him and from 1956, when he toured New Zealand, his place in the team was firmly established.

He learned to curb his natural desire to hit at practically every ball, though he never lost his punishing powers, and in England in 1957 he took 161 in the Edgbaston Test, becoming the only batsman to register a century on first appearance against both Australia and England. In the third meeting with England at Trent Bridge he made his highest Test score, 168, doing much to rescue the West Indies from what had seemed a hopeless position. "Collie" Smith was also a useful off-break bowler, having turned from pace to spin after watching J. C. Laker during the M.C.C. tour of 1948. During the summers of 1958 and 1959 he achieved marked all-round success as professional to Burnley in the Lancashire League.

His body was taken to Jamaica where it was estimated that about 60,000 people attended the funeral.

Tributes to Smith included:

Sir Kenneth Blackburne, Governor of Jamaica: "The name of Collie Smith will long live as an example not only of a fine cricketer, but also of a great sportsman. He will provide inspiration for our youth in the future."

J. F. Dare, President of the West Indies Board of Control: "He was one of a diminishing band who play a game for the game's sake and he had a great future before him."

F. C. M. Alexander, West Indies and Jamaica captain: "His passing is a tremendous loss to those of us who came to realise what a wonderful spirit of cricket he was."

S. C. Griffith, Assistant-Secretary of M.C.C.: "His death came as a terrible blow to all cricketers in England who have the future of the game at heart."

SMITH, R. P. The death occurred at his residence, Staunton Grange, Newark, on Monday May 1, 1899, of Mr. R. P. Stevens, better known to the last generation of cricketers as R. P. Smith, captain of the Derbyshire XI. Mr. Smith was a native of Sawley, Derbyshire, and in his early days gained distinction in various branches of sport, being an excellent football player, oarsman, and hurdle racer. He was also one of the best shots in Derbyshire, and a bold rider to hounds. It was as a cricketer, however, that his great reputation was made. He appeared for Derbyshire in the first match ever played by the county, namely, that against Lancashire in 1871. On that occasion he made 17 runs, and it is a curious fact that he was the third Derbyshire player taking part in that match who died within nine months, the other two being Mr. John Smith and Platts. Mr. R. P. Smith was the hero of many fine performances for Derbyshire, being a splendid batsman and a brilliant field at point, in which position he made many catches off Mycroft's bowling. He was at his best in 1875, when, in addition to heading the Derbyshire's averages, he had the honour of taking part in some of the representative matches of the year, and met with conspicuous success. As a batsman he depended chiefly on back play, and never appeared to make the most of his reach. He watched the ball very closely, and had many fine strokes on the off side. As a captain he was somewhat lacking in judgment, but there can be no two opinions as to the value of his services to Derbyshire cricket at a time when the county was none too rich in high class batsmen. The one thing that possibly stood in the way of his achieving the highest distinction was a somewhat indolent temperament. About the time of his retirement from the captaincy, 14 or 15 years back, he came into a big fortune, and settled down to the life of a country gentleman in Notts, taking the name of Stevens. He had, at the time of his death, just completed his 50th year.

SMITH, Sydney Gordon, who died in Auckland on October 25, 1963, aged 82, was a capital left-handed all-rounder. He played for Trinidad, where he was born, and in 1901–02 distinguished himself by taking 16 wickets at a cost of 85 runs for a Combined West Indies XI against R. A. Bennett's team of English amateurs at Trinidad. Touring England with H. B. G. Austin's West Indian team in 1906, he headed both batting and bowling averages for all matches. He scored 1,107 runs, average 33.54, and with slow bowling of excellent length dismissed 116 batsmen for 19.31 runs each. Against Northamptonshire he gained a match-record of 12 wickets for 99 runs and the following season began qualifying by residence for that county. From 1909 to 1914, playing as an amateur, he rendered them splendid service, becoming captain in 1913, when G. A. T. Vials fell ill, and the following summer.

From his first full season he brought about a tremendous rise in the fortunes of Northamptonshire for whom he became the first batsman to reach 1,000 runs. He achieved the "cricketers' double" in 1909, 1913, and 1914. Generally a hard-hitting batsman, specially strong in cutting, driving and leg-side strokes, he could offer the soundest of defences when the situation demanded such tactics. His highest innings was 204 against Gloucestershire at Northampton in 1910.

Twice he performed the hat-trick, at the expense of Leicestershire at Leicester in 1912 and when taking four Warwickshire wickets with following deliveries at Edgbaston in 1914. He frequently appeared for Gentlemen against Players and met with marked success with A. F. Somerset's M.C.C. team in the West Indies in 1910–11. After the First World War, he played for Auckland and represented New Zealand against the Australians in 1920–21, M.C.C. in 1922–23 and New South Wales in 1923–24. He continued playing until he was in his 50s. Smith was one of the "Five Cricketers Of The Year" in the 1915 edition of *Wisden*.

SMITH, William, who played for London County Club under W. G. Grace, and profited so much by his captain's coaching that in 1901 he averaged over 64, died in North Devon in April, 1942, aged 66. He won the match with M.C.C. at Lord's by four wickets with a splendid 61 not out, Walter Mead and Albert Trott being foremost in a powerful club attack. W. Smith scored 79 in the match without being dismissed. W. G. Grace in that engagement, finished in two days, took 13 wickets for 110 runs—seven for 30 in the club's first innings. At Crystal Palace Smith made 143, highest score in a total of 578 against Cambridge University, who were beaten by an innings and 73 runs, Ranjitsinhji claiming six wickets for 53 in the Cambridge second innings and so contributing towards the defeat of his old University. W. Smith also played for Oxfordshire in the second-class County Championship, and that season headed their averages with 43.80. He did not maintain anything like that form, but again headed the Oxfordshire averages with 36.16 in 1904.

SMITH, William C., the former Surrey slow bowler, died on July 15, 1946, aged 68. Extreme thinness brought him the affectionate nick-name of "Razor," and he lived up to the description by getting much "cut" on the ball, while the off-break brought most of the 1,061 wickets, which he took at an average cost of 17.45, during a career which might have lasted more than from 1900 to 1914 but for his frail physique and weak heart—the cause of his death, which occurred at Surridge's, the firm with whom he was associated for many years. Owing to this weakness he seldom played through a full season, but when equal to the strain of much work he seldom failed, and, if helped by the state of the pitch, carried all before him.

In 1909 he and Rushby dismissed Yorkshire for 26, the smallest total ever recorded by that county. Kent were champions that year. In 1905, when the Australians won by 22 runs, 12 wickets fell to Smith for 124 runs, and he earned identical figures for Surrey against the touring side of 1909. Most success came to him in 1910, when he was credited with 247 wickets at 13.06 each. Colin Blythe of Kent did next best with 175. In County Championship matches he took 215 wickets at 12.56 apiece—most help coming from W. Hitch with 83 at 21.54 apiece, and he bowled more than twice as many overs as any one of his colleagues sent down. Against Northamptonshire at the Oval he returned astounding figures: 14 wickets at a cost of 29 runs in 28 overs and a ball: he also scored 31 not out, only Ducat, with 67, making more runs in that match.

Accurate length, deceptive flight and swerve from leg helped to make him extremely difficult. It was said at the time that for Surrey no slow bowler could be compared to Smith since James Southerton, some 50 years before. He was honoured deservedly with a place in the Players' XI at Lord's that season.

SMITHSON, Gerald A., who died suddenly on September 6, 1970, aged 43, played for Yorkshire in 1946 and 1947, his highest innings for the county being 169 against Leicestershire at Leicester in the second year. Conscripted as a "Bevin Boy" in the mines after the War, he received special permission, after his case had been debated in the House of Commons, to tour the West Indies with the M.C.C. team of 1947–48, taking part in two Test matches. His picture appeared in *Wisden* 1948, page 38. In 1951 he joined Leicestershire, with whom he remained for six seasons, of which his best was that of 1952 when, by attractive left-hand batting and the aid of two centuries, he hit 1,264 runs, average 28.08. He afterwards served as coach, first at Caterham School and then at Abingdon School, and between 1957 and 1962 he also assisted Hertfordshire.

SMITHSON, Sam, at one time a well-known club cricketer in the Heavy Woollen District, died at Bright's Cottage, Heckmondwike, on December 11, 1911, aged 71. His *forte* was fast bowling, and in the match between the U.S.E.E. and Twenty of Batley in June, 1876, he bowled W. G. Grace with the first ball he sent down.

SMOKER, George, who died on September 7, 1966, aged 85, played for Hampshire early

in the century as a professional fast-medium bowler. His best performance for the county was in 1907, when he disposed of seven South African batsmen for 35 runs. Next year he became professional to New Brighton, who made him a life member in 1961; in 1910 he achieved the feat unique in the Liverpool area of scoring 1,085 runs and taking 109 wickets for fewer than nine runs apiece. After gaining a cap for Cheshire, he saw service with Colne and Birkenhead Park and as coach to Birkenhead School and Wallasey C.C.

SNAITH, John Collis, best known as author of *Willow the King*, and many novels, died at Hampstead on December 8, 1936. An all-round cricketer of considerable ability, he played twice for Nottinghamshire in 1900, scoring 21 at Lord's against M.C.C. and 18 at Trent Bridge against West Indies. He took four wickets in the two innings of West Indies, among his victims being C. A. Ollivierre, a remarkable batsman. For Authors against the Rev. E. Stogden's XI at Elstree in 1902 Snaith took all 10 wickets for 32 runs, and in 1914 he made 156 not out for Skegness against Cossall Colliery; he and Clarke, also a Nottinghamshire man, the club professional, added 340 runs for the second wicket. Snaith played for Notts Amateurs and often appeared in the county Second XI.

SNEDDEN, Andrew Nesbit Colin, who died at Auckland on September 27, 1968, aged 76, captained New Zealand in several representative matches against overseas sides, his first-class career finishing before New Zealand were granted Test status. A capable all-rounder, he played for Auckland from 1909 to 1928, averaging over 30 with the bat, and taking altogether nearly 100 wickets with his medium-pace bowling. He toured Australia in 1913–14, and after the war captained New Zealand against V. S. Ransford's Australian side in 1920–21 and against the M.C.C. in 1922–23. His highest score was 139 against Hawke's Bay in 1920–21 when he also took five for 13. For most of the period between 1922 and 1937 he was a member of the New Zealand Selection Committee.

SNELL, Arthur Patrick, died at Brighton on July 26, 1937, aged 67. In the Halleybury XI in 1888 and captain next year, he played in the Cambridge Freshmen's match in 1890 and occasionally for Essex.

SNOOKE, Stanley Delacourtte, who died at Cape Town on April 4, 1959, aged 80, did not meet with the same success as a cricketer as his brother S. J. His one Test appearance was against England at the Oval in 1907. He did not score, but brought off two good catches.

SNOW, Samuel C., who died at Venezuela on September 8, 1931, represented British Guiana in the Inter-colonial cricket competitions held between Barbados, British Guiana and Trinidad. He also played for Jamaica.

SNOWDEN, Alexander William, who played for Northamptonshire from 1931 to 1939, died in hospital on May 7, 1981, aged 67. First appearing for the county before he was 18, after being in the XI at King's School, Peterborough, he showed promise in the next two seasons, but in 1934 surpassed all he had done before by scoring 105 in three and three-quarter hours against the Australians. First in and last out, he gave only one chance. This was the highlight of his career, although later in the season he took part in what may well be some kind of record. At Edgbaston, Warwickshire declared part way through the second morning at 429 for nine and Snowden and Bakewell came out to open at 12.45. They put up 119, but, even so, Northamptonshire made only 164 and they were on the way to the wicket again at half past four. When they were separated at six o'clock, they had scored 121. Snowden's share of these partnerships was 57 and 42. That year, for the only time, he reached 1,000 runs. He never quite fulfilled his promise.

In the nets at the beginning of 1935 the Northamptonshire captain, W. C. Brown, was injured and, until G. B. Cuthbertson took over in June, Snowden had to captain the side. Although he won the toss in his first 10 matches, he was not a success: he had insufficient confidence in himself and the side rather lost confidence in him. The experience had a disastrous effect on his form and in 30 innings his highest score was only 29. Thereafter he played only spasmodically, though his last appearance was not until 1939 and in 1937 he made the highest score of his career, 128 against Lancashire at Old Trafford. In all he scored 4,343 runs for the county with an average of 18.10.

Naturally left-handed, he had originally been a left-hand bat but was forced by a master to change to right-hand "because a left-hander wastes so much time." It may be that this helped to restrict the freedom of his strokes. Short and stockily built, he combined an endless patience with a sound defence, scoring mainly on the leg. He also made himself into a fine short leg. His father had

been a considerable benefactor to the County Club and was one of those who helped to save it in the financial crisis of 1931.

SNOWDEN, Arthur Owen, who died suddenly on May 22, 1964, aged 79, played in one match for Kent in 1911, against the All-Indian touring team. In the Rugby XI from 1901 to 1903, he was captain in the last year. A free batsman and slow left-arm bowler, he did specially well in the annual matches with Marlborough. In 1901 he scored 20 and 78 and took six wickets for 82 runs; next year he made 16 and 41 and took nine for 88, and in 1903 he hit 23 and took 10 for 75. He went up to Oxford, but did not gain a Blue, though he hit 54 for the University against a Gentleman of England XI got together and including Dr. W. G. Grace in 1905. He was latterly librarian to Kent County C.C.

SOAMES, William Aldwin, born at Brighton on July 10, 1850, died in London on December 27, 1916. He was in the Brighton College XI in 1868 and three following years and in 1875 appeared in three matches for Sussex. His experience in County Cricket was unfortunate, for he failed to score in four consecutive innings—v. Hampshire at Brighton and v. Gloucestershire at Cheltenham. *Scores and Biographies* said of him: "Is a good average bat and fields well at long-leg or cover-point." He had been a member of the M.C.C. since 1874.

SOLBÉ, Edward Phillip, who died at West Bridgford, Nottingham, on December 28, 1961, was a prominent schoolboy batsman during the First World War and he made a few appearances for Kent between 1921 and 1924, scoring 321 runs for the county, average 16.86. Solbé spent four seasons in the Tonbridge School XI, 1917–20, being captain in his final year. A very slow starter, he was a sound bat and hit hard when well set. In 1920, when Tonbridge met I Zingari, Solbé and T. E. S. Francis put on over 300 for the second wicket and in the same year Solbé made 195 v. Westminster and 66 not out against Clifton at a critical period, an innings *Wisden* described as being worth many a hundred.

SOLBÉ, Frank de Lisle, who died in January 1933, at Bickley, was born at Chefoo on June 1, 1871. He had the rare experience of being a member of two Public School XIs—of Dulwich College in 1887 and 1888, and of Blair Lodge in 1889 and 1890. A free and attractive batsman, he did splendid service for Bickley Park, but achieved no great distinction on a few appearances for Kent in 1891, 1892, and 1898. He was the father of the Tonbridge and Kent amateur, E. P. Solbé.

SOMERS, Lieut.-Col. Lord, K.C.M.G., D.S.O., M.C., who kept closely in touch with cricket from his Charterhouse days, died on July 14, 1944, when 57 years old, at Eastnor Castle, Herefordshire. In 1904 he scored 115 not out for Charterhouse, helping to beat Westminster at Godalming and showing himself a determined batsman at a crisis. He also made 95 and 28 against Haverford College. Poor health handicapped him then, but he averaged 68.50 in six innings. He appeared occasionally in the seasons 1923 to 1925 for Worcestershire, making 42 against Derbyshire; he could not give much time to cricket in the field but was a Vice-President of the County Club and President of M.C.C. in 1936. Besides his Army activities in the First Life Guards, with whom he distinguished himself in the First World War, he succeeded Lord Baden-Powell as Chief Scout. After gaining popularity as Governor of Victoria, he was Acting Governor-General of Australia, and when visiting Melbourne he was received enthusiastically by the large crowd at a Test match.

SOMERS-COCKS, Arthur, a Manchester man by birth, died at Barbados on February 9, 1923, aged 54. His early education was received at Manchester Grammar School, and whilst at Oxford he was a member of the Oriel XI and played in the Seniors' match, but did not obtain his Blue. In February, 1892, however, he represented his University at Association football. At cricket he was a splendid field at slip and a useful medium-to-fast bowler. For Barbados between 1894–95 and 1901–02 he obtained 52 wickets for 1,002 runs, and against A. Priestley's team in 1896–97 performed the hat-trick. When R. S. Lucas's team scored 369 in 1894–95 he had an analysis of seven for 99, while two years later, at Kingston, he took five wickets for 19 runs against Jamaica. His most successful season was probably that of 1896–97, during which he obtained 137 wickets for less than 11 runs each. He was a schoolmaster by profession, and became Headmaster of Harrison College, Barbados.

SOMERSET, Arthur William Fitzroy, who died on January 8, 1937, at Castle Goring, near Worthing, was President of Sussex County Club in 1936. Born at Chatham on September 20, 1865, he was in the Welling-ton XI in 1871 and captain in 1872. A useful fast bowler, besides a sound, hard-hitting batsman, he became a good wicket-keeper. After eight years in Australia he returned to England in 1881 and for about 20 years captained the Gentlemen of Sussex. He made infrequent appearances for Sussex between 1892 and 1905.

Three times he went to West Indies with touring sides, captaining the M.C.C. teams there in 1910–11 and 1912–13. During this last tour, when scoring 55 not out against Barbados at Bridgetown, he assisted W. C. Smith in a last-wicket stand of 167. Against West Indies at Lord's in 1900, he scored 118 for M.C.C. An excellent Rugby football forward, he played for Richmond and was a heavyweight boxer of some class.

SONDES, Second Earl, George Edward Milles, died in London on October 1, 1907, in his 47th year as the result of an operation necessitated by pleurisy contracted during the South African War. He was born at Lees Court, Faversham, on May 11, 1861, and played his first match at Lord's, for Eton against Harrow, in July, 1880. Mr. Haygarth described him as a good and steady batsman, and added that in the field he took no place in particular. He did not obtain his Blue at Cambridge, but appeared for Kent four times in 1882 and twice in 1884, scoring 119 runs in seven completed innings with an average of 17. In his second county match—against Sussex at Gravesend—he opened the innings with Lord Harris (176) and, scoring 82, helped to make 208 for the first wicket. In a match at Huntingdon in July, 1881, when playing for Mr. A. E. Fellowes' XI against Huntingdonshire, he played an innings of 123 and, in partnership with Mr. W. F. Forbes (331), scored 404 for the first wicket. In 1891 he was President of the Kent County C.C., and in the autumn of the same year visited America as a member of Lord Hawke's team. Last Easter a report of his death was circulated, the result being that several obituary notices of him appeared. Lord Sondes, who played for the county whilst Viscount Throwley, was a membe᠎ of a family which has been intimately associ᠎ :d with Kent cricket for over a century.

SOUTER, Vernon John, died at Elsternwick, Victoria, on July 17, 1915, aged 21. He was a very promising left-hand batsman and right-hand medium-paced bowler with a high delivery, who had played for Elsternwick in the sub-District Association and the St. Kilda C.C. In 1913–14 and 1914–15 he had been tried in the Victorian XI, in the former season making 55 v. Tasmania at Hobart, and in the latter 57 v. Queensland at Brisbane.

SOUTHERN, Commdr. John Dunlop, R.N., who died on February 7, 1972, aged 72, was in the Marlborough XI in 1916 and 1917, being captain in the second year. He assisted Derbyshire from 1919 to 1934 and in his first match for the county made 43, the top score, when they beat the Australian Imperial Forces side in 1919.
CORRECTION. Commdr. John Dunlop Southern was stated in the 1973 edition to have been in the Marlborough XI in 1916 and 1917. This should have been the Malvern XI.

SOWDEN, Abram, born on December 1, 1853, died at Heaton, Bradford, on July 5, 1921, aged 67. Between 1878 and 1887 he appeared in nine matches for Yorkshire, scoring 140 runs with an average of 11.66. He played for Bingley from 1875 to 1893 and for Bradford from 1893 to 1901. His best performance was to score 221 for Bradford v. Scarborough at the age of 45, while two years later he played successive innings of 157 v. Sheffield and 121 not out v. Dewsbury.

SOWTER, Unwin, one of the founders of the Derbyshire County C.C. in 1870, died at Derby on April 14, 1910. He was born at Derby on April 22, 1839, and was educated at Derby School. *Scores and Biographies* (xi–429) says of him: "Is a good batsman, and fields well, generally at point." He played for Derbyshire from 1871 until 1876, and for many years afterwards was a vice-president of the County Club and a member of the Committee.

DE SOYRES, The Rev. John, Rector of St. John the Evangelist's, St. John's, New Brunswick, who died suddenly on February 3, 1905, while undergoing an operation, was a great lover of cricket. He was born in Somerset in 1849, and educated at Brighton College and at Gonville and Caius College, Cambridge, where he had a most distinguished career. He went out to New Brunswick in 1888, and had made for himself a reputation as the most distinguished preacher in Eastern Canada. He was a nephew of Edward Fitzgerald, the translator of *Omar Khayyam.*

SPALDING, Albert Goodwill, born at Byron, Illinois, on September 2, 1850, died at Point Loma, California, on September 9, 1915. A famous base-baller, he brought a team to England in 1874 which played seven cricket matches, winning four and drawing three. In the early '80s he was a member of the Chicago C.C. XI. He was the head of a well-known American sporting outfitter's firm bearing his name.

SPARROW, Henry, who died at Wornbourn, Dudley, in February, 1919, aged 95, played for Warwickshire and Worcestershire XIs as far back as 1839. He rode to hounds from the age of six until he was 80.

SPENCER-SMITH, The Rev. Orlando, born at Brooklands, Hampshire, on December 17, 1843, died at Swanwick Glen, Southampton, on November 23, 1920. He was in the Eton XI of 1861 and obtained his Blue for Oxford five years later, when his batting—he scored 30 in Oxford's second innings—contributed to the Cambridge defeat by 12 runs. On his only appearance against Harrow he scored 21 and 44 and took six wickets for 64, his bowling being slow round-arm. He played for Hampshire in 1864 and 1866.

SPENS, Major-General James, C.B., C.M.G., was born in India on March 30, 1853, and died on June 19, 1934, aged 81. In the Haileybury XI of 1868 and 1869. Captain Spens he then was, played for the Army at Lord's in 1877 scoring 54 and 47 against The Bar who included such famous cricketers as C. J. Ottaway, T. S. Pearson, C. K. Francis, R. D. Walker, and E. Bray. He scored heavily in Army cricket and for United Services against Nondescripts at Portsmouth on August 9, 1882, he hit up 386. First playing for Hampshire in 1884 he began by making 60 but he could not give much time to cricket when Hampshire became a first-class county. Above medium height and of good physique Spens was a free hitter, a clever medium-paced round-arm bowler and a very smart cover-point. He played Racquets for Haileybury and the Army, besides competing for The Amateur Championship at Queen's Club.

SPICER, Peter A., who was killed in a motor-car accident on August 15, 1969, aged 30, played as a left-handed batsman and slow bowler for Essex, taking part in 15 Championship games in 1962 and 1963. He attracted attention when making his debut, his first scoring-stroke in an innings of 80 against Somerset at Taunton being a six. He had been coaching in the Netherlands in 1969.

After leaving Essex, he played with distinction for Wanstead C.C.

SPIERS, Felix William, who died in Paris on May 31, 1911, aged 79, was one of the founders of the well-known firm of Spiers and Pond. Messrs. Spiers and Pond were originally the proprietors of a popular restaurant in Melbourne, and thinking that it would be a profitable speculation to get a good English cricket team to go out to Australia, made the arrangements whereby H. H. Stephenson took a side out in 1861–62. The tour was an immense success, the first day's takings, in fact, paying the whole expenses of the trip. Having made a fortune out of their venture, Messrs. Spiers and Pond came to London and established themselves at Ludgate Hill.

SPILLER, William John, who died on June 9, 1970, aged 83, gained the distinction as an amateur of hitting the first century for Glamorgan after they acquired first-class status in 1921—104 against Northamptonshire at Northampton. He played in a few matches for the county in the two following seasons. Better known as a centre three-quarter for Cardiff, he earned 10 Rugby International caps for Wales between 1910 and 1912, helping his country to carry off the Triple Crown and the International Championship in the 1910–11 season.

SPILLMAN, George, who played occasionally for Middlesex a quarter of a century ago, died at Brighton on April 18, 1911, aged 53. As he did not take part in County Cricket until 1886, he was rather late in coming to the front, for he was born in London on October 24, 1857. His appearances for Middlesex were limited to 10 matches, in which he scored 430 runs with an average of 23.88. At Lord's in June 1886 he scored 86 and 14 v. Yorkshire, 63 and 39 v. Gloucestershire, and 87 v. the Australians. He was also a wicket-keeper above the average, and at one time a good boxer. His early cricket was played in Sussex, chiefly with the old Brighton, Lewes Priory, Chichester and Hastings clubs. In those days he was an amateur, and his name will be found occasionally in Gentlemen of Sussex and United South of England teams. Later he assisted many clubs in the London district, and, on the recommendation of Robert Thoms, was tried for Middlesex. For some seasons he was engaged as cricket coach at a school in Jersey, and it was whilst going out there eight or nine years ago that he fell down the cabin stairs of a passenger steamer. The accident, inasmuch as it necessitated the amputation of his right leg, brought his connection with the game to a close. Spillman was educated at a Kensington school—which has also been attended by Messrs. Bernard Pauncefote and A. O. Whiting, both old Blues—and King's College, London. It was some time after his father's death that he made cricket a profession.

SPINKS, Edwin Frederick, who died in Orsett Hospital, Essex, on October 19, 1982, played in two matches for Essex as a professional in 1926. An opening bowler, he played in club cricket for Colchester and East Essex.

SPOFFORTH, Frederick Robert, one of the most remarkable players the game has ever known, was born at Balmain, Sydney, on September 9, 1853, and died at Ditton Hill Lodge, Ditton Hill, Surbiton, Surrey, on June 4, 1926, aged 72. From his earliest days cricket had the greatest possible fascination for him, and whilst still quite a small boy at Eglington College, Sydney, he determined, through seeing the success met with by George Tarrant, of Cambridge, to become as fast a bowler as possible. Later he studied the methods of Southerton and Alfred Shaw, and resolved, if possible, to combine the styles of all three men. He had played with success in good class matches before he ever bowled a ball in England, but his great days may be said to date from May 27, 1878, when he had so much to do with the wonderful victory gained, in the course of a single day, by D. W. Gregory's team over a very strong M.C.C. side at Lord's. From that day forward, Spofforth was always regarded as a man to be feared, even by the strongest teams. He probably never did anything better than to take 14 wickets for 90 runs in the Test match at the Oval in 1882, when Australia gained their first success—by seven runs—in an international game on English soil. It is to be regretted that when he came over with the teams of 1878 and 1880 so few 11-a-side matches were played, for he was presumably then at about his best, and his energies were expended for the most part in mowing down wickets in games against odds. For the former side he obtained 764 wickets at a cost of 6.08 runs each, and for the latter 763 for 5.49 apiece. These figures include his doings in the Colonies and (in 1878) in America.

Spofforth was a member of the Australian teams of 1878, 1880, 1882, 1884, and 1886, and for them he performed the following feats:

19 for 108	v. Fifteen of New South Wales, at Sydney	..	..	..	1877–78
17 for 125	v. Eighteen of South Australia, at Adelaide	..	..	..	1877–78
14 for 25	v. XXII of Southland, at Invercargill	..	..	..	1877–78
15 for 41	v. XXII of Wellington, at Wellington	..	..	..	1877–78
22 for 59	v. XXII of Hawke's Bay, at Napier	..	..	..	1877–78
22 for 68	v. XXII of Auckland, at Auckland	..	..	..	1877–78
10 for 20	v. M.C.C., at Lord's (including the hat-trick)	..	..		1878
13 for 134	(including 9 for 53) v. Lancashire, at Manchester	..	..		1878
20 for 64	v. Eighteen of New York, at Hoboken	..	..		1878
17 for 66	v. XXII of Ontario, at Toronto	..	..	..	1878
19 for 84	v. Eighteen of South Australia, at Adelaide	..	..		1878–79
13 for 110	v. England, at Melbourne (including the hat-trick)	..	..		1878–79
16 for 112	v. Fifteen of Victoria, at Melbourne	..	..	..	1879–80
13 for 85	v. Derbyshire, at Derby	..	..	..	1880
17 for 77	v. Eighteen of Northants (with given men), at Northampton	..		1880
17 for 96	v. Fifteen of South Australia, at Adelaide	..	..	..	1880–81
10 for 19	v. XXII of Southland, at Invercargill	..	..	..	1880–81
20 for 65	v. XXII of Wellington, at Wellington	..	..	..	1880–81
22 for 60	v. XXII of Hawke's Bay, at Napier	..	..	..	1880–81
13 for 113	(including 9 for 51) v. Somerset, at Taunton	..	..		1882
14 for 90	v. England, at the Oval	..	..	..	1882
14 for 58	(including 8 for 11), v. Scotland, at Glasgow	..	..		1882
5 for 15	v. Shaw's XI, at Holbeck	..	..	..	1882
10 for 12	v. Eighteen of New York, at Hoboken	..	..	..	1882
14 for 37	(including 7 for 3) v. An England XI, at Aston	..	..		1884
13 for 123	v. Players, at Sheffield	..	..	..	1884
7 for 16	v. Middlesex, at Lord's	..	..	..	1884
14 for 96	v. Players, at the Oval	..	..	..	1884
13 for 85	v. Camb. Univ. Past and Present, at Hove	..	..		1884
Hat-trick	v. South, at the Oval	..	..	..	1884
15 for 36	v. Oxford University, at Oxford	..	..	..	1886
7 for 19	v. North, at Manchester	..	..	..	1886

After settling in England:

15 for 81	Derbyshire v. Yorkshire, at Derby	..	..		1889
14 for 114	(including 9 for 56) Derbyshire v. Leicestershire, at Derby	..		1890
8 for 74	M.C.C. v. Yorkshire, at Scarborough	..	..	..	1896

In Tests against England he obtained 94 wickets for 18.41 runs each. In his own country he represented both New South Wales and Victoria, the former by birth and the latter by residence, and in really big cricket, both at home and abroad, took 1,146 wickets with an average of 13.55.

Below are the records of his most noteworthy seasons:

			Balls	Runs	Wickets	Average
Australia 1877–78	..	..	1,379	499	58	7.74
England 1878	..	..	3,018	1,259	109	11.55
Australia 1878–79	..	..	1,274	634	52	12.18
Australia 1879–80	..	..	1,546	688	49	14.04
England 1880	..	..	968	396	46	8.60
Australia 1880–81	..	..	2,075	852	84	10.14
England 1882	..	..	6,395	2,282	188	12.13
Australia 1882–83	..	..	1,766	700	33	21.21
England 1884	..	..	6,364	2,732	218	12.53
Australia 1884–85	..	..	1,216	469	25	18.76
Australia 1885–86	..	..	741	274	18	15.22
England 1886	..	..	3,726	1,528	89	17.16

The summary of his bowling in good matches during the whole of his career was:

In Australia	..	..	13,140	5,515	385	14.32
In England	..	..	24,101	9,917	750	13.22
In America	..	..	259	107	11	9.72
Totals	..	..	37,500	15,539	1,146	13.55

MOST NOTEWORTHY SEASONS—*Continued*

In 11-a-side games he bowled unchanged throughout as follows:

With E. Evans, New South Wales v. Victoria, at Sydney	..	..	..	1875–76
With G. E. Palmer, Australia v. Rest, at Melbourne	..	..	..	1880–81
With H. F. Boyle, Australians v. Somerset, at Taunton	..	..	..	1882
With H. F. Boyle, Australians v. Scotland, at Glasgow	..	..	..	1882
With G. E. Palmer, Australians v. Yorkshire, at Bradford	..	..	..	1884
With G. E. Palmer, Australians v. Middlesex, at Lord's	..	..	..	1884
With T. W. Garrett, Australians v. Oxford Univ., at Oxford	..	..	..	1886

In minor matches he naturally did many very remarkable things. Thus, in an up-country game in Australia, in 1881–82, he bowled down all 20 wickets of his opponents; for the Australian team of 1878 he took nine wickets in 20 balls against Eighteen of Hastings, and for that of 1880, 12 in 18 against Eighteen of Burnley; while twice for Hampstead he obtained all 10 wickets in an innings of Marlow on his opponents' ground—for 20 runs in 1893, and for 14 a year later. In the game of 1893, his day's figures were 17 for 40. When he made his first appearance for Hampstead he was in his 38th year, yet he took as many as 951 wickets for the club for seven and a half runs each. In 1894 he claimed 200 wickets for the side for an average of 5.90.

SPOONER, Archibald Franklin, who died on January 11, 1965, aged 79, was younger brother of R. H. Spooner, the Lancashire and England batsman. In the Haileybury XI of 1901 and 1902, A. F. Spooner also played as an amateur for Lancashire from 1906 to 1909. His best and highest innings for the county was at Leyton in 1908 when, despite a nasty blow on the knee, he hit 83 out of a total of 195. That season he scored 450 runs, average 16.07, and *Wisden* said of him: "He had much of his brother's grace and style, but speaking generally was only a partial success."

SPOONER, Reginald Herbert, who died in a Lincoln nursing home on October 2, 1961, aged 80, played for England at both cricket and Rugby football. One of the most stylish opening batsmen in the history of cricket, he possessed a variety of strokes equalled by few even in The Golden Era to which he belonged. A tall, slim right-handed batsman, he drove with special skill to the off, often at the expense of fast bowlers, and strong wrists enabled him to invest his strokes with surprising power when playing back. In a first-class career for Lancashire dating from 1899 to 1923, he scored 13,681 runs, average 36.28, hitting 31 centuries, five of them of 200 or more, and as an impeccable cover-point held 132 catches.

He established a high reputation as an all-round sportsman when at Marlborough. In the big match with Rugby at Lord's in 1898 he put together an innings of 139 and the following season, when captain, he made 69 in the first innings and 198 in three and a half hours in the second. In this latter season he headed the Marlborough batting figures with 926 runs, average 71.23, and in addition took, with slow spinners, 25 wickets for 15.28 runs each. Not surprisingly he was invited to play for the county of his birth upon leaving school and on his first appearance, against Middlesex at Lord's in 1899 when 18 years of age, he hit 44 and 83 from an attack including Albert Trott at his best.

For the next three years, half of which time was spent on military duty in South Africa during the War, he was lost to cricket, but he returned to Lancashire in 1903 and showed that his skill had not been impaired by absence when punishing the Nottinghamshire bowlers at Trent Bridge for 247, at that time the highest innings ever hit against them. His other scores of 200 were: 215 v. Essex at Leyton in 1904; 240 v. Somerset at Bath in 1906; 200 not out v. Yorkshire at Old Trafford in 1910 and 224 v. Surrey at the Oval in 1911, in which season, with the aid of seven centuries, he reached his highest aggregate, 2,312, average 51.37. Both in the big innings against Nottinghamshire and when facing the same opponents on the same ground in 1905, when hitting 164, he got to three figures before lunch. With A. C. MacLaren (204) he (168) shared an opening partnership of 368 against Gloucestershire at Liverpool in 1903, which still stands as a Lancashire record.

Spooner played 10 times for England in England between 1905 and 1912 and in his first match against South Africa at Lord's in 1912 hit 119. He accepted an invitation to captain M.C.C. in Australia in 1920–21, but injury compelled him to withdraw and thenceforward he was not often seen in the field. He played on 17 occasions for Gentlemen v. Players. These included the match at Lord's in 1906 when, though Arthur Fielder took all 10 Gentlemen wickets in the first innings for 90 runs, an innings of 114 by Spooner and devastating fast bowling by N. A. Knox (seven wickets for 110) took the amateurs to victory by 45 runs. At the Oval in 1911, Spooner obtained 190 against the Players, he and P. F. Warner (91) putting on 208 for the third wicket.

As a centre three-quarter, Spooner played Rugby football for Liverpool and he represented England against Wales at Swansea in the 1902–03 season.

SPOTTISWOODE, William Hugh, born in London on July 12, 1864, died suddenly of heart failure at Llandrindod Wells on August 20, 1915. He was not in the XI whilst at Eton, but was a good batsman and captained the Balliol team at Oxford. He played for Kent three times in 1890, his highest score being 37 against Yorkshire. At times his lobs were very successful.

SPROT, Edward Mark, an all-round sportsman of much ability, died on October 8, 1945, at his home at Farnham, Surrey, aged 75. Born in Scotland and educated at Harrow he made a name in Army cricket before playing first for Hampshire in 1898 and in company with many noted soldiers (among them Captain E. G. Wynyard, Major R. M. Poore, Colonel J. G. Grieg—giving their rank at that time), he helped to raise Hampshire to such a good standard that during his captaincy they reached fifth place in the County Championship. He held the reins from 1903 until 1914, and under his lead Hampshire invariably played attractive cricket with enterprise and enthusiasm. Himself a fine free hitter with zest for the forcing game, Captain Sprot, for a man of medium physique put plenty of power into his strokes, made in free style that meant quick run-getting when he was at the crease.

In first-class cricket he scored 12,251 runs, including 13 hundreds, averaging 28.55 an innings, and with slowish bowling took 54 wickets, besides holding 208 catches. Clearly a valuable man for any county, and as captain in 1918 at Southampton he aroused admiration and astonishment by declaring the innings closed when Hampshire, with a wicket to fall, were 24 behind their visitors, Northamptonshire, at lunch time on the third day, after rain had hindered the progress of the match. By this action he saved the interval between the innings and he soon put

on Phillip Mead, little known as a bowler. Six wickets for 18 runs fell to Mead's left-hand slows. Hampshire wanted no more than 86 runs for victory and when A. C. Johnston was out at three, Sprot hit up 62 in less than an hour, two sixes and eight fours being characteristic of his determined aggression. Alec Bowell was the watchful partner in gaining a victory which *Wisden* described as "without parallel, which makes a unique incident in the history of the game." Sprot saw the possibility of victory by dismissing the opposition on a drying pitch and went for runs with the success described—a splendid example of "dynamic" cricket which Sir Stanley Jackson's Committee had asked for in first-class cricket of the future.

When serving with the Shropshire Light Infantry in 1899 Sprot, with Colonel J. Spens, won the Army Racquets Challenge Cup. An admirable golf player, a sure shot and clever fisherman, Sprot found billiards the most fascinating indoor recreation, and on a strange table in Cairo he won a 200 up game from the opening left by his opponent on starting the play.

SPRY, Edward, who died at Bristol on November 19, 1958, aged 77, played as a slow leg-break bowler for Gloucestershire between 1899 and 1909, taking 149 wickets, average 28.97. His most successful season was that of 1902, when he dismissed 60 batsmen at a cost of 21.66 each, and his best analysis was eight wickets for 52 runs in the first innings of Warwickshire at Bristol in 1903. A useful batsman, he scored 1,447 runs, average 11.13, his highest innings being 76 against Nottinghamshire at Trent Bridge in 1903. His father was groundsman at Bristol.

SPURWAY, The Rev. Edward Popham, Rector of Heathfield, Taunton, died on February 11, 1914, aged 50. He played only twice for Somerset, but frequently for the Wellington C.C. and the Somerset Stragglers.

SPURWAY, The Rev. Francis Edward, who died at Hale, near Taunton, on December 30, 1980, aged 86, played fairly frequently for Somerset as a wicket-keeper from 1920 to 1929. He had been in the XI at King's School, Bruton, and several members of his family had played for the county.

SPURWAY, Capt. R. P., who at one time played pretty regularly for Somerset, died early in December 1898. Born on July 16, 1866, he was only in his 33rd year.

SQUIRES, Harry Stanley, the Surrey cricketer, died on January 24, 1950, in Richmond Royal Hospital as the result of an illness brought about through a virus in the blood. He was in his 41st year. On leaving school when 16, Squires began a business life in a City stockbroker's office, but, contrary to his father's wishes, he always wanted to take up cricket as a profession. He spent his leisure time receiving lessons from Aubrey Faulkner, the South African Test player, and he joined Faulkner's coaching staff when a member of Richmond C.C.

Leading county cricketers noticed his ability, and in 1928 and 1929 he appeared for Surrey as an amateur. His debut in first-class cricket was against Middlesex at Lord's. In 1930 he realised his ambition when Surrey gave him a contract as a professional, and no more popular player wore the Surrey colours.

A perfect stylist, Squires was a model batsman for boys to copy. He possessed a rich abundance of strokes, and best of all was his drive through the covers. He never appeared to impart any force into his batting; correct timing and supple wrists sent the ball speeding to the boundary. He was a grand fielder, notably in the deep and at cover. As a slow bowler he specialised in off-breaks, although in later years to suit his county's needs he turned to the leg variety.

Throughout his cricket career Squires wore glasses. During the war he served with the R.A.F., reaching the rank of Flying Officer. After spending two years in the Hebrides he returned to this country wearing contact lenses, which he used for boxing, squash, Rugby and Association football as well as cricket.

Between 1928 and 1949 Squires scored over 19,000 runs in first-class cricket and hit 37 centuries. His highest innings was 236 for Surrey against Lancashire at the Oval in 1933. He took his benefit in the Middlesex match at the Oval in 1948. He was at the top of his form in the summer preceding his death, when he made 1,785 runs with an average of 37.18.

During the winter Squires kept himself fit playing golf, and only a week or two before his fatal illness began he won the 27 hole foursome handicap in the Croydon and District Alliance competition at Shirley Park for his club, Fulwell. He was partnered by W. J. Cox, the former British Ryder Cup golfer. Born at Kingston-on-Thames on February 22, 1909, Squires was a licensee at Hampton Hill. He left a widow and three children.

Paying a tribute to Squires, Mr. H. D. G. Leveson Gower, former president and chairman of Surrey, whose connection with the club covered over 50 years, said: "Squires was an extremely good player, probably better than most people imagined. Often he scored runs when others failed. He was a great example to other professional cricketers. It is because of players like Squires that the profession to which they belong incites so much admiration."

STANDING, Michael Frederick Cecil, C.B.E., who died on December 1, 1984, aged 74, was the first commentator from the BBC to report cricket. Obviously in the 50 years since then, apart from mechanical improvements, broadcasting technique has profited from experience, but even so he will be remembered as a very good commentator with a pleasant delivery and a good working knowledge of his subject: he was himself a keen and regular club cricketer, a useful opening bowler, who played a good deal for the Free Foresters and the Butterflies. For cricket broadcasting he did a splendid pioneering job.

STANLEY, H. T., (Somerset), born August 20, 1873; died (whilst assisting the British cause in the South African War) at Hekpoort, September 16, 1900. A most useful batsman, his defence against all kinds of bowling and on all kinds of wickets being very good. He twice, in 1899, scored over 200 runs in an innings in minor matches, namely 212 not out for M.C.C. and Ground v. United Services, on June 5, and 201 not out for E. A. V. Stanley's XI v. Bridgwater Amateurs, on August 3. He made 127 for Somerset v. Gloucestershire, at Gloucester, in June, 1899, this being his only three figure innings in first-class matches.

STANNARD, George, who died in a Brighton hospital on June 25, 1971, aged 78, played as a professional for Sussex from 1914 to 1926. "Joe," as he was generally known, scored 1,437 runs, average 13.42, by far his best innings being 114 at Hove in 1920, when he and H. E. Roberts (124 not out) mastered the Worcestershire bowling so completely that they added 209 runs in 95 minutes.

STANNING, John, born October 10, 1877, was killed in a motor accident in Kenya Colony on May 19, 1929, aged 51. For Rugby against Marlborough, in 1894, he played an innings of 152 not out, and brought his school career to a close with a batting average of 28. Going up to Cambridge, he failed to secure his Blue until 1900. Against the M.C.C., he scored 120, and in the University match hit 20 and 60, obtaining 554 runs for Cambridge during the season with an average of 27. Playing for Lancashire between 1900 and 1903, he had an aggregate of 845 runs in all first-class matches during his career. He also played some cricket for Cheshire, and in 1902–03 was a member of Lord Hawke's team which visited New Zealand and Australia.

STANTON, John Lothian, who died on June 27, 1973, was in the Marlborough XI before playing in a few matches for Gloucestershire in 1921 and 1922.

STANYFORTH, Lieut.-Col. Ronald Thomas, who died on February 20, 1964, aged 71, was a well-known amateur wicket-keeper. He did not get a place in the XI at Eton, nor did he gain a Blue at Oxford, but he soon gained prominence in Army cricket and in 1928 played in three matches for Yorkshire. In 1926 he toured South America with P. F. Warner's M.C.C. team and next winter led the M.C.C. side who toured South Africa, sharing the rubber. He took over the captaincy when illness compelled the original choice, G. R. Jackson, of Derbyshire, to withdraw. In the four Test matches in which he took part—he missed the last through injury—he made seven catches and brought off two stumpings. Though he achieved little in batting, *Wisden* described him as "a capable captain and a strong and popular personality." He also toured the West Indies under the Hon. F. S. G. Calthorpe in 1929–30, but met with early injury and did not play again, W. F. Price being sent out as replacement. Altogether in first-class matches he accounted for 73 batsmen, 58 caught and 15 stumped. He was a trustee of M.C.C. at the time of his death.

STAPLES, Arthur, who died on September 9, 1965, aged 66, was a valuable professional all-rounder for Nottinghamshire from 1924 to 1938. His brother, S. J. Staples, also played for the county. A steady batsman and medium-paced bowler, Arthur seven times exceeded 1,000 runs in a season and he hit 10 centuries. In dismissing 64 batsmen in 1929, he helped materially in the winning of the county title by Nottinghamshire. His best seasons as an all-rounder were those of 1932

when, with the aid of three centuries, he registered 1,265 runs and took 51 wickets, and 1933 (1,251 runs, 67 wickets). In the 1932 match against Northamptonshire at Kettering his 67 included a nine, five being from a stroke that stopped short of the ring and J. E. Timms overthrew to the boundary. He also played Association football, keeping goal for Mansfield Town and Bournemouth.

STAPLES, Samuel James, died on June 4, 1950, after being in poor health for some months. When Staples, who was born at Newstead Colliery on September 18, 1893, ended his cricketing career with Nottinghamshire after a connection with the County Club extending over 18 years, he had taken 1,400 wickets. Medium-paced, with a rather shuffling, jumpy run, he bowled "cutters" an excellent length for long spells, with ability to make the ball break either way. On hard pitches he kept down runs, and was specially effective on turf which helped him, making the ball turn sharply from the off when bowling round the wicket. In 1932 at Southampton he enjoyed the distinction of dismissing, at a cost of 21 runs, all 10 Hampshire batsmen in an innings. He was a splendid fieldsman, and as a batsman low in the order did good work, his highest innings being 110 against Surrey at the Oval in 1923. He toured South Africa in 1927–28 with the M.C.C. team led by Captain R. T. Stanyforth, appearing in three Test matches, and went to Australia with A. P. F. Chapman's side the following winter, but was compelled by rheumatism to return home without taking part in a single game. In 1939 he became coach to Hampshire, and he served for one season, 1949, on the list of first-class umpires, but owing to ill-health he resigned both these positions.

STAUNTON, The Rev. Harvey (Chaplain to the Forces), of Staunton Hall, Notts, died on service in Mesopotamia, January 14, 1918, aged 45. Selwyn Coll. (Camb.) XI; Notts county XI, 1903–04–05. To Notts people he was perhaps best known as a member of the County Cricket team, for whom he played fairly regularly from 1903 to 1905, inclusive. A batsman of the punishing type, his highest innings was against Middlesex at Trent Bridge in 1904, when he scored 78, and one of the notable features of his brief career in County Cricket occurred at Gravesend in a match with Kent. More than one of the Notts batsmen had had a blow on the body from the fast bowling of Fielder, and Mr. Staunton was violently struck on the knee by an extra speedy ball. His revenge was to despatch the four succeeding deliveries to the boundary!

STEAD, Barry, died on April 7, 1980, aged 40. Born at Leeds, he was a fast-medium left-arm bowler who made a sensational first-class debut, taking seven for 76 for Yorkshire v. the Indians in 1959. However, so strong at the time was the Yorkshire bowling that he only appeared once more for them before moving to Nottinghamshire for whom he played from 1962 to 1976. He got his cap in 1969 when he took 83 wickets at an average of 23.83. His best season was 1972 when his 98 wickets cost 20.38 each. He had a benefit in 1976. In all for Nottinghamshire he took 604 wickets at 28.04. A left-handed batsman who delighted in hitting sixes, his highest score was 58 for Nottinghamshire v. Gloucestershire in 1972. He also played for Northern Transvaal. He died after a long illness and is much missed by his fellow players with whom he was extremely popular.

STEDMAN, Fredk., born March 4, 1872; killed accidentally on the railway at Bray, Co. Wicklow, February 5, 1918, Surrey wicket-keeper. Engaged for 10 years on the Woodbrook Ground, Ireland. Stedman was quite a good wicket-keeper for Surrey, but he could not keep his place for long when the more gifted Strudwick came on the scene.

STEEL, Allan Gibson, died in London on June 15, 1914. The greatest of all Marlborough cricketers, he was in the college XI from 1874 to 1877 inclusive, being captain in his last two years. He was in the great Cambridge XIs of 1878, 1879, 1880, and 1881, being captain of the team in 1880, and playing under the Hon. Ivo Bligh (now Earl of Darnley) in 1881. In the Gentlemen and Players matches at Lord's and the Oval he appeared 18 times. He was not especially successful in these matches as a batsman, his highest score being 76, and his average 25; but he had a wonderful record as a bowler, taking 99 wickets for something over 15 runs apiece. Mr. Steel played nine times for England against Australia in England—at the Oval in 1880 and 1882; at Manchester, Lord's, and the Oval in 1884; at Manchester, Lord's, and the Oval in 1886; and at Lord's in 1888. He was captain in 1886 when England won all three matches, and also at Lord's in 1888 when the bowling of Turner and Ferris won the game for Australia. He also played in four Test matches in Australia in the season of 1882–83 for the England team captained by Ivo Bligh. Twice in his 13 international matches Mr. Steel made over a hundred, scoring 148 at Lord's in 1884 and 135 not out at Sydney in February, 1883. Mr. Steel was born at Liverpool on September 24, 1858.

Mr. Steel's hundreds in first-class cricket:

118	Cambridge University v. Surrey, at the Oval	1880
106*	M.C.C. & Ground v. Yorkshire, at Scarborough	1881
171	Gentlemen of England v. Cambridge University, at Cambridge ..	1882
135*	England v. Australia, at Sydney	1882–83
134	M.C.C. & Ground v. Australia, at Lord's	1884
148	England v. Australia, at Lord's	1884
105	Lancashire v. Surrey, at Manchester	1887

Signifies not out.

For Lancashire he scored 1,929 runs (aver. 29.67) and took 238 wkts. (aver. 12.57)
For Gentlemen v. Players he scored 610 (aver. 25.41) and took 99 wkts. (aver. 15.36)
For Cambridge v. Oxford he scored 184 runs (aver. 30.66) and took 38 wkts. (aver. 9.00)
For England v. Australia he scored 600 runs (aver. 35.29) and took 29 wkts. (aver. 20.86)
In first-class cricket he scored 6,759 runs (aver. 29.25) and took 781 wkts. (aver. 13.50)

STEEL, Lieut. Allan Ivo (Coldstream Guards), son of A. G. Steel; killed October 8, 1917, aged 25. Eton XI, 1910–11; Middlesex, 1912. Calcutta C.C. Member of M.C.C. since 1912. A good slow bowler at Eton, Steel had obviously modelled his style on that of his famous father. His school records were excellent—42 wickets with an average of 12.71 in 1910, and 47 wickets with an average of 14.53 in 1911. He fairly divided honours with Fowler in 1910 on the whole season's work, and took the other two wickets when Fowler, with eight wickets for 23 runs, beat Harrow in such sensational fashion at Lord's. Steel was improving fast as a batsman when he left Eton, and would no doubt have developed considerably if he had gone to Cambridge instead of taking up a business appointment in India.

STEEL, Douglas Quintin, a member of the famous Lancashire family of which "A. G." was the most illustrious, died on December 2, 1933, at Upton, Cheshire. He was a member of the Uppingham School XI for five seasons—1871 to 1875—and led the side in the last two years. At this time, Uppingham, thanks to the excellent work of their coach, H. H. Stephenson, were very strong, among Mr. Steel's contemporaries being his brother A. G., A. P. Lucas, W. S. Patterson, S. S. Schultz and H. T. Luddington—all Cambridge Blues. D. Q. Steel was in the Cambridge XI for four years—1876 to 1879—and batted very well in the first two years. His career for Lancashire extended from 1876 to 1886. His only century in first-class cricket was 158 for Cambridge University v. Surrey at the Oval in 1877.

STEEL, Ernest Eden, youngest of the four brothers who played for Lancashire, died on July 14, 1941, at Southport, aged 77. After doing well in the Marlborough XI, 1880 and 1881, as free batsman and slow bowler, he appeared occasionally in the county side, but poor health and absence abroad prevented him from playing much first-class cricket. In 1901, after an interval of 13 seasons, he re-appeared for Lancashire and proved useful. Next season his deceptive flight bowling earned 44 wickets, his average of 18.93 being second to S. Webb's, though Barnes was the most destructive bowler for Lancashire. In 1904 he scored 62 for Gentlemen against Players at the Oval, but he never approached the special standard of A. G. Steel, of high fame for Cambridge, Lancashire and England. Nor was E. E. so good as D. Q., the senior and first of the brothers, who got Cambridge Blues; A. G., the other Blue, followed two years after D. Q., and was captain in 1880 when Cambridge gained their third consecutive victory over Oxford. Each helped in three wins, twice being in the same XI.

STEEL, Harold Banner, who died at Burnham, Somerset, on June 29, 1911, was one of the seven sons of the late Mr. Joseph Steel, and was born at South Hill Grove, Liverpool, on April 9, 1862. Of the seven brothers—T., A. J., F. J., D. Q., A. G., H. B., and E. E.—as many as six were actively identified with the game, and in June 1884, four of them assisted Lancashire against Surrey at Liverpool. Mr. H. B. Steel received his early education at Uppingham, but leaving there at the Borth crisis (in 1875), was, like Mr. F. D. Gaddum, who proceeded to Rugby, not in the XI. He was transferred to Repton, for whom he played in 1879 and 1880, heading the batting averages each season, in the former with 20.27 and in the latter with 26.36. In his second year as a member of the side he scored 61 against Malvern and 58 v. Uppingham. Among his contemporaries were Messrs. H. J. and W. A. J. Ford. Mr. Steel was a very powerful hitter, and obtained an unusually large proportion of his runs by boundary hits. He was seen but seldom, however, in county matches, preferring good-class club cricket, of which he played a very great deal on behalf of the Liverpool C.C., the Uppingham Rovers, the Quidnuncs, Hoi Pepneumonoi (which he founded), etc. For Lancashire he scored 765 runs with an average of 22.50, his first appearance for the county being in 1883 and his last in 1896. His highest scores were 100 v. Surrey at the Oval and 77 v. Kent at Maidstone, both made in 1884. At one time he was also a fair change bowler, and he could keep wicket. It is not generally known that a relationship exists between the Steel and Studd brotherhoods.

STEELE, David Aubrey, died on March 25, 1935, aged 65. Born on June 3, 1869, he first played for Hampshire when a second-class county in 1887 and between 1895 and 1906 he met with considerable success in first-class cricket. A free bat, with stubborn defence at times, he never quite realised expectations, his average for an aggregate of 3,448 runs being 14.13. Bowling fairly fast right hand with a low delivery, he took 136 wickets at 30 runs each. He sometimes kept wicket, sharing the duties at one time with Captain E. G. Wynyard and Mr. Charles Robson. At Southampton in 1897 when all the Hampshire XI bowled against Warwickshire, Wynyard and Steele each did successful stumping.

STEELE, Frederick, born in London on May 14, 1847, died on January 22, 1915, in his 68th year. He was no batsman, but useful as a left-handed fast bowler. He played for Middlesex between 1877 and 1879, taking 34 wickets for 18.09 runs each. Among his analyses for the county were three for 10 v. Yorkshire at Lord's in 1877, five for 22 v. Gloucestershire at Lord's in 1879, eight for 93 v. Oxford University at Lord's in 1879, and four for 28 v. Surrey at the Oval in 1879.

STEPHENS, Frank G., who died on August 9, 1970, aged 81, played for Warwickshire between 1907 and 1912 and was, with his twin brother, the late George W. Stephens, a member of the team who carried off the Championship for the first time in the county's history in 1911. Both brothers played for Rossall and for Moseley and each served on the Warwickshire Committee.

STEPHENSON, Edwin, the once famous Yorkshire wicket-keeper, died in July, 1898. Born on June 5, 1832, he had just entered his 67th year. Though he had dropped out of the recollection of present day cricketers, Stephenson was in his time a very noted player, keeping wicket for Yorkshire before George Pinder was heard of, and sharing the honours of many a match in the '60s with George Anderson, Roger Iddison, Slinn, Hodgson, Rowbotham and George Atkinson. Over and above his skill as a wicket-keeper he was a good hard hitting bat, and was perhaps as safe a run-getter as anyone in the Yorkshire team of those days except Anderson, Rowbotham and Iddison. He was a member of the first English team that visited Australia, under H. H. Stephenson's captaincy, in 1861–62. It should be mentioned that though he was always spoken of as Edward Stephenson his Christian name was Edwin. In his later days he unfortunately fell into very poor circumstances.

STEPHENSON, H. H., the once famous Surrey cricketer, died on December 17, 1896, at Uppingham, where for nearly a quarter of a century he had been coach at the school. In that position he was conspicuously successful, among the many fine players he helped to train being A. P. Lucas, W. S. Patterson, D. Q. Steel, G. MacGregor, G. R. Bardswell, and C. E. M. Wilson. Stephenson began to play for Surrey about 1854, and took his benefit at the Oval in 1871, when he retired from the active pursuit of the game. He was a first-rate bat, a good wicket-keeper, and during his first few seasons, a most effective bowler—rather fast with a big break from the off. As a batsman he perhaps reached his highest point in 1864—the last year until 1887 in which Surrey stood first among the counties. Apart from his merits as a player and a coach, Stephenson will be remembered as captain of the first English XI that went to Australia, the visit being paid in the winter of 1861–62. He was born at Esher on May 3, 1833, and was certainly one of the most popular cricketers of his day.

STEPHENSON, John Stewart, died suddenly at Horsham on October 7, 1975, aged 71. He was four years in the Shrewsbury XI and in the fourth, when he was captain, scored 778 runs with an average of 70.72. He played for Yorkshire from 1923 to 1926, being awarded his cap, and for Oxford in 1925 and 1926. For Yorkshire his highest innings was 60 against Hampshire and for Oxford 72 against H. D. G. Leveson Gower's XI, both in 1926, but undoubtedly his two most notable innings were 45 for Oxford against the Australians in the same year and a month or two later 52 in the second innings of the Varsity match, which nearly won his side a sensational victory. A magnificent figure of a man, he made full use of his height when batting and was a good back-player and a fine driver. He was also one of the best mid-offs of his day. After 1926 he played little cricket of any kind. All games came naturally to him: he was four years in the Oxford soccer side as a back, captaining them in two Varsity matches, and played for three years in the golf side. He was also an outstanding player of Eton Fives. From 1928 to 1937 he was a master at Lancing, where he ran the cricket for some years.

STEPHENSON, Lieut.-Col. John William Arthur, D.S.O., died at his home at Pulborough on May 20, 1982, aged 73. If there were more cricketers like him, there would always have been fewer empty grounds. There could never, when he was in action, be a dull moment; nor, as far as he was concerned, would there be a slow over-rate. Whatever he was doing he was the very personification of energy and enthusiasm. Bowling brisk fast-medium seamers with a high action and a full follow-through, he seemed almost to hurl himself down the pitch after the ball. He could move it both ways, making it come off the ground at a remarkable pace. He was a serviceable attacking batsman in the lower half of the order and, as R. C. Robertson-Glasgow put it, "ran three when the book said two" and "was dangerous for a partner with short legs or a weak heart." A brilliant and untiring fielder, he never took a rest whether bowling or not, and he was popularly supposed to go to bed with his fingers wrapped round a cricket ball.

Originally playing for Buckinghamshire, he started to appear for Essex in 1934 and his first big performance was against the South Africans at Southend in the following year when, deputising for H. D. Read, who was resting for the Oval Test, he took seven for 66 and three for 44. But the feat for which he will always be remembered was to take nine for 46 in the first innings for the Gentlemen at Lord's in 1936, one of the most notable bowling performances by an amateur in the history of the match. After this he must have been a serious candidate for G. O. Allen's team to Australia in the following winter and there were those who thought that he should have been preferred to Copson, who, with Allen himself, Farnes and Voce in the side, was really superfluous. Stephenson continued to play when his military duties allowed until 1939, and in that year he was one of three amateurs who shared the Essex captaincy between them. The War virtually ended his serious cricket, though he did play one match for Worcestershire in 1947. He would never have lingered on once he found his energy and activity gradually abating. In later years he played much golf in a style peculiarly his own, giving equal enjoyment to himself and his friends, putting one-handed back-hand from any part of the green and holing, if not a proportion that would have satisfied a champion, at least as many as more orthodox players in his own class. It was no surprise to learn from tributes after his death what a splendid and inspiring leader he had shown himself in the war and how much his men had liked him. In all first-class cricket he scored 2,582 runs with an average of 21.34 and took 311 wickets at 23.99.

STEVENS, George, who died at his home at Gaywood, Norfolk, on March 28, 1957, aged 89, played cricket with and against the brothers E. M. and W. G. Grace. In 15 matches for Norfolk from 1905 to 1911, "Pro" Stevens scored 257 runs and, with left-arm medium-pace bowling, took 27 wickets. His best performance with the ball was six wickets for 56 runs against Suffolk in 1909. Born at Bognor, Sussex, he served as professional to Lynn Town C.C. before becoming groundsman at King Edward VII School, King's Lynn, a post he held for 41 years. Dr. E. M. Grace once wrote of Stevens: "No one knows better how to prepare a first-class cricket pitch," and also praised him as an all-rounder.

STEVENS, Greville Thomas Scott, who died on September 19, 1970, aged 69, was beyond question one of the outstanding amateurs of his time. A fine batsman and bowler of leg-breaks and googlies, he came to the fore when in the XI at University College School from 1917 to 1919. He attracted special attention in the last year with an innings of 466 in a house match, and

that season he was accorded the signal honour for a schoolboy of inclusion in the Gentlemen's team against the Players at Lord's.

Middlesex readily appreciated his worth and they called upon his services in 1919. Upon his debut in first-class cricket, he took 10 Hampshire wickets at Lord's for 136 runs, and the next summer he helped Middlesex to win the County Championship. Not surprisingly, he gained his Blue as a Freshman at Oxford in 1920 and he remained a valued member of the University side for the following three years, being captain in 1922. In 1923 he bore a major part in an overwhelming Oxford victory in an innings with 227 runs to spare over Cambridge. Caught on a pitch affected by sunshine after heavy rain, the Light Blues were dismissed in their first innings for 59, Stevens taking six wickets for 20 runs. That season, too, he shone brightly as a batsman, hitting 182—his highest innings—for Oxford against the West Indies and 122 for the Gentlemen at Lord's.

Stevens took part in 10 Test matches for England. He helped them regain the Ashes from H. L. Collins's Australians in 1926; visited South Africa with small success in 1922 and 1927 and played twice in the West Indies in 1929, when he took 10 wickets for 195 runs in the first of the representative games.

A batsman who, considering his short back-lift, hit with surprising power, he twice exceeded 1,000 runs in a season and in all first-class cricket registered 10,361 runs, including 12 centuries, at an average of 29.69, took 676 wickets for 26.55 runs each and, as a superb fieldsman close to the wicket, held 200 catches. He would doubtless have far eclipsed this record had he been able to spare more time from business for cricket.

STEWART, Dr. Haldane Campbell, an attractive batsman for Kent when finding time for County Cricket, died on June 16, 1942, aged 74. From 1892 to 1903 he was always a welcome member of the side, and he scored 2,846 runs in first-class cricket with an average of 22.76. He was a fine fieldsman. At Lord's in 1897 he made 142 against M.C.C., and played for Gentlemen against Players at Hastings in 1897. In 1903 he went with the Kent team to America. A prolific scorer for Blackheath, he showed to special advantage in an innings of 203 not out against Granville, Lee. A noted musician, H. C. Stewart was at different times a master at Lancing, Wellington, and Tonbridge schools, and was organist of Magdalen College, Oxford, from 1919 to 1938.

STEWART-MORGAN, William Guy, who died in a Carmarthen hospital on July 27, 1973, aged 65, was in the XI at Christ's College, Brecon, before going up to Cambridge, where he was 12th man for the University. He appeared for Glamorgan between 1927 and 1938. Better known as a Rugby footballer, he gained prominence as W. G. Morgan, playing against Oxford from 1926 to 1929 and being captain in the last year. As a skilful centre, he also gained eight caps for Wales between 1927 and 1930, and played for Swansea and Guy's Hospital. His uncle was the legendary Dr. Teddy Morgan.

ST. HILL, Edwin Lloyd, who died at Withington, Lancashire, on May 21, 1957, aged 51, played as a medium-paced bowler for Trinidad and for the West Indies against the Hon. F. S. G. Calthorpe's M.C.C. touring team in 1930. On the occasion of St. Hill's second representative match appearance, George Headley set up a record by scoring a century in each innings. From 1943 to 1951, St. Hill played in Central Lancashire League cricket.

STILL, Robert S., who introduced roundarmed bowling into Australia in a match between the Australian and Victoria clubs at Sydney in March, 1843, died in July, 1907, aged 85. All his early cricket was played in New South Wales, and he kept up the game for many years after settling in Tasmania. He was a good all-round cricketer. He visited England in 1878 and witnessed the triumph of the Australians in their match with the M.C.C. at Lord's.

STINCHCOMBE, Frederick William, died at Worksop on September 19, 1984, aged 54. A right-hand bat, but a left-arm bowler, he played a few times for Nottinghamshire in 1950 and 1951. His four wickets cost him 134.75 runs each, but in 1951 he scored 48 against Kent at Trent Bridge. He was engaged in the Bassetlaw League.

STOCKS, Francis Wilfred, born at Market Harborough, December 10, 1873, died at Framlingham College, of which he was headmaster, May 21, 1929, aged 55. A useful batsman and a keen field, his chief asset, however, was left handed, medium-paced bowling. He had an easy delivery, and on

ground which gave him any assistance was very difficult to play. After being at Lancing and Denstone, he obtained his Blue for Oxford, playing against Cambridge in 1898 and 1899. In 1899 he performed two of the best bowling feats of his career, taking eight wickets for 22 for the University v. A. J. Webbe's XI and 13 for 120 (including eight for 56) for Leicestershire v. Worcestershire, at Leicester. He visited America with P. F. Warner's team in 1897, and assisted the Gentlemen against the Players at the Oval in 1898 and 1899, taking five wickets in the former match and seven in the latter. He represented Oxford at hockey as well as at cricket.

STOCKTON, Sir Edwin, died on December 4, 1939, aged 66. Hon. treasurer of Lancashire for six years from 1919 immediately after the First World War, he became president for two seasons and then chairman of the committee until 1932. He retained his keen interest in Lancashire cricket as a Vice-President. Sir Edwin advocated the inclusion of one or two professionals on the England selection committee but disapproved of suggestions for County Cricket on Sundays. Yet, he frequently entertained visiting teams for big matches by taking them for a Sunday trip by boat up the Manchester Ship Canal and a return from Liverpool by train. He gained no special reputation on the field of play.

STOCKWIN, Alfred, who died suddenly on the County Cricket Ground at Northampton on May 15, 1922, aged 70, was a Sheffield man by birth, and a good medium-paced bowler and a steady bat. He had been associated with the Northamptonshire County C.C. as professional and groundsman for 51 years, and had prepared every wicket used on the County Ground since its opening.

STODDART, A. E., one of the greatest of batsmen, died by his own hand on Saturday, April 3, 1915, shooting himself through the head. A brilliant career thus came to the saddest of ends. Mr. Stoddart was born at South Shields on March 11, 1863, and had thus completed his 52nd year. Curiously enough, considering the great fame he won, he did not take to cricket seriously until 22 years of age, when he became associated with the Hampstead Club, and showed such form, scoring no fewer than five separate hundreds for that team, that before the end of the season of 1885 he had been tried for

Middlesex. From 1886 to 1898, except for the summer of 1888, when he was engaged playing Rugby football in Australia and New Zealand, Mr. Stoddart proved a tower of strength to Middlesex in batting, keeping up his skill so well that in 1898—his last full season in County Cricket—he averaged 52. He soon became a popular idol at Lord's, his batting, in conjunction with that of T. C. O'Brien, making the Middlesex matches far more attractive than they had ever been before his day.

He turned out only once for Middlesex in 1899, and twice in the following year, but in his last match for the county—against Somerset at Lord's—he put together a score of 221, the highest of his career in first-class cricket. Among his most famous innings were 215 not out against Lancashire at Manchester in 1891 and 151 for England against the M.C.C. at Lord's in 1887, when he and Arthur Shrewsbury raised the total to 266 for the first wicket. In 1886, for Hampstead against the Stoics, he played an innings of 485—at that time the highest individual score on record.

On four occasions Mr. Stoddart paid visits to Australia, first in 1887, as a member of G. F. Vernon's team, when he averaged 32. Four years later he formed one of the side taken out by Lord Sheffield, his average then amounting to 37. In 1894–95, and again in 1897–98, he himself took a team out to Australia. The first of these undertakings resulted in England winning the rubber after two victories had been gained by each country, but the second proved a big disappointment, no fewer than four of the five Test matches ending in favour of Australia. Still, in the two tours associated with his leadership, Mr. Stoddart came out well with averages of 51 and 34. In the fifth match in the tour of 1894–95, which decided the rubber in England's favour, J. T. Brown played a memorable innings of 140, and Albert Ward scored 91. As a Test match player in this country, Mr. Stoddart achieved no special distinction. He took no part in those games in 1890, and although he played in all three matches three years later, making 83 at the Oval, his only other appearances for England at home were at Lord's and Manchester in 1896.

A splendid batsman to watch, Mr. Stoddart had all strokes at his command, but was especially strong in driving and hitting on the leg side. Again and again he proved his greatness by his ability to make runs under conditions which found other batsmen at fault, his play, both on fiery and on soft wickets, being quite exceptional. As a special instance of his power on fiery wickets one recalls a superb innings of 91 for Middlesex against Surrey at the Oval in 1892. The Oval was not in good order that year, and Lockwood's bowling needed some facing. Stoddart, however, did not mind a bit. Two or three times he hit to the boundary balls that got up as high as his head. Almost equally good was his batting, when in with W. G. Grace, against Richardson and Mold in the Gentlemen and Players match at Lord's in 1895. In the early part of his career he proved a useful change bowler, and anywhere in the field he was both brilliant and safe. In his early seasons for Middlesex he had onerous work to do on the off-side when George Burton was bowling, but he was never known to flinch.

Mr. Stoddart was one of the very few men who have represented their country at Rugby football as well as at cricket. Between 1886 and 1893 he took part in 10 international Rugby matches, and would certainly have played in more but for the fact that in two of the intermediate seasons England, owing to a dispute with the other Unions, had no International matches. He appeared twice against Scotland, three times against Ireland, and four times against Wales, while in 1889 he played against the Maories. A splendid runner, with plenty of pace and dodging ability, and not above jumping over an opponent on occasion, he was a great three-quarter—possessed of a very fine pair of hands—a brilliant kick, and a player full of resource.

It was a memorable drop-kick against a gale of wind he made that, giving Middlesex victory over Yorkshire by a goal to four tries, led to the rules of the game being altered. At that time a goal counted more than any number of tries. Mr. Stoddart captained England against Wales in 1890, when, on a muddy swamp at Dewsbury, Wales, scoring a try to nothing, gained their first victory over England. Another famous match in which he took part was that at Cardiff in 1893, when, after England had established a commanding lead, Wales finished in great form, and, under the method of scoring then in vogue, succeeded in snatching a win by one point. It may be questioned whether any two players ever enjoyed a better understanding than Alan Rotherham, at half, and Andrew Stoddart at three-quarter. Certainly the combination of these two men formed one of the brightest features of the Rugby game in the '80s.   C.S.C.

A. E. STODDART IN THE CRICKET FIELD
BATTING AVERAGES IN FIRST-CLASS MATCHES

Year			Innings	Times not out	Most in an innings	Total runs	Average
1885	..	..	8	0	79	149	18.62
1886	..	..	24	1	116	640	27.82
1887	..	..	28	0	151	799	28.53
Australia		..	15	0	94	459	30.00
1888	..	..	Absent in Australia				
1889	..	..	35	2	78*	817	24.75
1890	..	..	45	1	115	845	19.20
1891	..	..	32	1	215*	857	27.64
Australia		..	12	0	134	450	37.50
1892	..	..	47	2	130	1,403	31.17
1893	..	..	50	1	195*	2,072	42.28
1894	..	..	39	0	143	1,174	30.10
Australia		..	18	1	173	870	51.17
1895	..	..	43	0	150	1,622	37.72
1896	..	..	50	2	127	1,671	34.81
West Indies		..	17	2	153*	677	45.13
1897	..	..	21	0	109	650	30.95
Australia		..	11	0	40	205	18.63
1898	..	..	26	4	157	1,038	47.18
1899	..	..	5	0	44	78	15.60
America		..	3	1	74	193	96.50
1900	..	..	11	1	221	402	40.20
In America		..	3	1	74	193	96.50
In Australia		..	56	1	173	1,975	35.90
In England		..	464	15	221	14,217	31.66
In West Indies		..	17	2	153*	677	45.13
Totals		..	540	19	221	17,062	32.74

HIS SCORING IN TEST MATCHES

		Date of First Match	Innings	Times not out	Most in an innings	Total	Average
In Australia	..	1887–88	21	1	173	731	36.55
In England	..	1893	9	1	83	265	33.12
Totals	..	1887–88	30	2	173	996	35.57

A. E. STODDART'S HUNDREDS IN FIRST-CLASS CRICKET (28)

Score	For	Against	Ground	Season
116	Middlesex	Kent	Gravesend	1886
151	England	M.C.C. & Ground	Lord's	1887
116	Gents. of England	I Zingari	Scarborough	1887
115	South	North	Lord's	1890
†215*	Middlesex	Lancashire	Manchester	1891
134	England	Australia	Adelaide	1891–92
130	Middlesex	Notts	Lord's	1892
†195* } 124 }	Middlesex	Notts	Lord's	1893
125	Middlesex	Surrey	Lord's	1893
127	C. I. Thornton's XI	Australians	Scarborough	1893
148	Gents. of England	Notts	Nottingham	1894
149	England	Queensland	Brisbane	1894–95

Signifies not out
†*Signifies carried bat through completed innings*

A. E. STODDART'S HUNDREDS IN FIRST-CLASS CRICKET (28) — *Continued*

Score	For	Against	Ground	Season
173	England	Australia	Melbourne	1894–95
150	Middlesex	Somerset	Lord's	1895
131	Middlesex	Kent	Lord's	1895
100	Middlesex	Yorkshire	Lord's	1896
121	Middlesex	Somerset	Lord's	1896
109	Middlesex	Lancashire	Manchester	1896
127	Middlesex	Kent	Lord's	1896
153*	A. Priestley's Team	St. Vincent	Bridgetown	1896–97
108*	A. Priestley's Team	Queen's Park	Port-of-Spain	1896–97
100	A. Priestley's Team	Jamaica	Kingston	1896–97
143	A. Priestley's Team	Jamaica	Kingston	1896–97
109	Middlesex	Somerset	Taunton	1897
138	Middlesex	Notts	Lord's	1898
157	Middlesex	Leicestershire	Leicester	1898
221	Middlesex	Somerset	Lord's	1900

* Signifies not out
† Signifies carried bat through completed innings

HIS LONG PARTNERSHIPS FOR THE FIRST WICKET

Score		Season
266 Stoddart (151) and Shrewsbury (152): England v. M.C.C. and Ground, Lord's *(Lord's Centenary Match)*	.. .. ..	1887
228 Stoddart (125) and T.C. O'Brien (113): Middlesex v. Surrey, Lord's *(Middlesex followed-on, 179 behind, and won by 79)*	.. .. ..	1893
218 Stoddart (100) and H. B. Hayman (152): Middlesex v. Yorkshire, Lord's	.. .. ..	1896
205 Stoddart (116) and A. J. Webbe (103): Middlesex v. Kent, Gravesend	.. .. ..	1896

In three consecutive innings which opened together against the Australians in 1893, Stoddart and "W. G." scored 120, 114, & 151 for the first wicket.

In August, 1896, Stoddart and J. Douglas made over 150 for the first wicket of Middlesex three times in a fortnight.

FIRST-CLASS CRICKET NOTABILIA

1885—His debut for Middlesex, and his first appearance in first-class cricket—v. Yorkshire, at Sheffield. Going in first, he scored three and 21: he also bowled 12 balls for seven runs and no wickets, and made a catch. Middlesex won by 49 runs.

1886—Middlesex v. Notts, at Nottingham. Stoddart batted three hours 20 minutes on a difficult wicket for 32, the highest score of the match. During the Middlesex innings of 168 as many as 92 maiden overs were bowled.

1887–88—Visited Australia as a member of the late G. F. Vernon's team.

1887–88–v. New South Wales, at Sydney. Of the 74 runs scored for the first wicket with Abel (88) he made 55.

1890—On a difficult wicket in second innings of South v. North, at Lord's, Stoddart got 115 of the 169 runs scored during the 140 minutes he was batting, making not the slightest mistake. The runs were obtained off Attewell. Peel, Briggs, and William Barnes. At one period of his innings he scored 50 while "W.G." made three.

1891—Middlesex v. Yorkshire, at Lord's. Stoddart obtained spectacles—c Wainwright b Peel, 0; b Peel, 0.

1891–92—Visited Australia as a member of the late Earl of Sheffield's team.

1893—Middlesex won by Notts, at Lord's. Stoddart scored 195 not out and 124, carrying his bat through the first innings and being sixth out in the second. This was the first occasion on which a batsman had obtained two separate hundreds in a first-class match at Lord's since 1817.

1893—At the end of the season Stoddart was presented with an elegant silver bowl on an ebonised stand thus inscribed: "Presented to Andrew Ernest Stoddart by the Middlesex County C.C. in appreciation of his splendid cricket for the county in 1893." In the bowl itself are recorded his scores—three figures, each of them—against Notts and Surrey, and his total runs and averages for Middlesex in 1893.

1894–95—A. E. Stoddart took a team to Australia for the first time.

1895—Middlesex v. Surrey, at the Oval. Stoddart scored 75 and 67. In his first innings he was given out stumped, but the bail was not dislodged. (His innings was, of course, continued.) In his second innings a ball from Smith (F. E.) hit his wicket hard without removing a bail.

1896–97—Visited the West Indies with A. Priestley's team.

1897—Elected vice-captain of the Middlesex XI, a position he resigned at the end of 1898.

1897–98—Took a team to Australia for the second time. This was his fourth, and last, visit to that country.

1899—In the autumn visited America as a member of K. S. Ranjitsinhji's team.

1900—His last appearance for Middlesex—v. Somerset, at Lord's, Hearne's (J. T.) benefit match. He made 12 and 221, his highest innings in first-class cricket.

1900—South v. North, Lord's. Stoddart made four catches in the second innings of the North, although only seven wickets fell.

PERFORMANCES FOR THE HAMPSTEAD C.C.

Year	Innings	Times not out	Most in an innings	Total runs	Average	Runs	Wickets	Average
1885	19	3	185	1,097	68.56	†	51	†
1886	21	1	485	1,671	83.55	†	72	†
1887	17	5	275	1,862	155.16	434	42	10.33
1888	Absent in Australia							
1889	16	2	144	874	62.42	587	66	8.89
1890	12	2	97*	418	41.80	393	44	8.93
1891	24	1	153*	979	42.56	921	105	8.77
1892	18	2	132	1,053	65.81	773	80	9.66
1893	7	2	210	558	111.60	90	13	6.91
1894	11	1	226*	649	64.90	205	37	5.54
1895	9	2	134*	340	48.57	256	26	9.84
1896	2	1	122	126	126.00	43	5	8.60
1897	9	2	127	527	75.28	414	38	10.89
1898	8	1	75*	336	48.00	410	32	12.81
1899	17	4	163	1,363	104.84	716	60	11.90
1900	14	2	145	864	72.00	493	62	7.95
1901	12	1	109	551	50.09	398	20	19.90
1902	12	1	108	535	48.63	280	16	17.56
1903	1	0	3	3	3.00	79	2	39.50
1907	2	1	100*	106	106.00	—	—	—
Totals	231	34	485	13,912	70.61	{ — 6.492	123 648	— 10.01

* Signifies not out
† No analysis kept

MINOR CRICKET NOTABILIA

1886—Playing for Hampstead v. Stoics, at Hampstead, on August 4h, A. E. Stoddart scored 485—of 811 obtained whilst in—in six hours 10 minutes, this being then the highest innings on record. His hits were an eight (four from an overthrow), three fives, 63 fours, 20 threes, 36 twos, and 78 singles, and except for a very difficult chance to mid-on when 421 made no mistake. He was caught eventually from a miss-hit. With J. G. Q Besch (98) he added 214 for the second wicket, and with E. Swift (92) 383 for the fourth in about three hours. Despite the fact that the bowling was good throughout—only one wide was delivered, and not a single no-

ball during the six hours and a quarter the innings of 813 for nine wickets lasted—the scoring was always fast. At lunch the total was 370 for three wickets, made in two hours and a half, and runs were obtained throughout at an average rate of 130 an hour.

1886—In three consecutive innings in five days Stoddart scored 790 runs, making 485 for Hampstead v. Stoics, at Hampstead, on August 4; 207 for Hampstead v. Blackheath at Hampstead, on August 7; and 98 for Middlesex v. Gloucestershire, at Gloucester, on August 9.

1887—In six days, during the Hampstead Week (July 25 to 30) he made 900 runs in six innings, three times not out:—21 v. M.C.C. and Ground, 205 v. Ne'er-do-Weels, 275 not

out v. London Scottish, 55 v. Clapham
Wanderers, 114 not out v. A. D. Slade's XI,
and 230 not out v. Old Finchleians.

1887–88—G. F. Vernon's Team v. Eighteen Melbourne Juniors, at Melbourne, December 9, 10, 12. Batting just over six and a
quarter hours, and hitting 24 fours, Stoddart
contributed 285 to the total of 556, this being
then the highest innings obtained for an
English team in Australia. He made 125 for
the first wicket with Abel (38) and added 215
for the fourth with Peel (95), gave six distinct
chances and eventually played-on.

1892—In consecutive innings for Hampstead this year he made 126 v. Crystal Palace
at Hampstead on July 21, 117 v. Hendon at
Hampstead on July 22, 104 and 17 not out v.
Bournemouth at Bournemouth on July 25,
26, and 103 and 23 not out v. Hampshire
Hogs at Southampton on July 27, 28.

1896–97—In *all* matches for A. Priestley's
team in the West Indies Stoddart scored
1,079 runs (average 53.95) and took 104
wickets (average 7.85).

1899—In consecutive innings for Hampstead he made 154 v. South Hampstead on
August 7, 126 not out v. Gnats on August 9,
130 v. London and Westminster Bank on
August 12, and 163 v. West Herts. C. and G.
on August 16. All the scores were made at
Hampstead.

In Minor Cricket Stoddart made 68 scores
of a hundred.

STODDART, W. Bowering, died on January
8, 1935, aged 63. A slow leg break bowler he
played occasionally for Lancashire, and in
1898 at Scarborough for Gentlemen against
Players and for M.C.C. against Australians.
Captain of the Liverpool cricket and Rugby
football teams, he was a member of the
Lancashire C.C. Committee. A strong forward, he played Rugby for Lancashire and
for England in all the 1897 internationals. He
was born on April 27, 1871.

STOGDON, John Hubert, who played for
Harrow, Cambridge University and Middlesex, died on December 17, 1944, aged 68.
In 1894 against Eton he made the highest
score in each innings (32 and 19), and next
year, when captain, he played a brilliant
innings of 124, the third highest hit in the big
schools match at headquarters. Stogdon
never showed his best form at Lord's against
Oxford, and he met with only small success
when appearing occasionally in County Cricket, but he possessed splendid style, using his
height to the full extent in playing forward
and driving. Almost as a coincidence,

T. G. O. Cole, who first played for Harrow
when J. H. Stogdon was captain, died on
December 15, 1943. Very good at racquets,
Stogdon, with A. S. Crawley, won the Public
Schools Cup in 1895, while he and E. Garnett won the racquets doubles for Cambridge
against Oxford in 1897. A son of J. H.
Stogdon, J. W. Stogdon, played for Harrow
in 1928 and 1929.

STOKES, Frederic, who was born at Greenwich on July 12, 1850, and died at Baughurst,
Basingstoke, on January 7, 1929, aged 78,
was a good batsman and long stop and could
bowl a very fast ball. He was in the Rugby XI
of 1867, played for Kent five times between
1871 and 1875, and assisted the Gentlemen
against the Players in 1873 and 1874. On his
first appearance for his county—v. Lancashire at Gravesend—he scored 65 and 38. He
was one of three brothers who played for
Kent, and he married a sister of Mr. Frank
Penn, the famous batsman, who assisted
England against Australia at the Oval in
1880. One of the most famous of Rugby
football forwards, Mr. Stokes captained the
England Fifteen against Scotland in 1871–
72–73 in the first three matches between the
two countries.

STOKES, Graham, born at Greenwich on
March 22, 1858, died at Blackheath on
December 19, 1921. He was younger brother
of Messrs. Frederic and Lennard Stokes and
played for Kent once in 1880 and three times
in 1881.

STOKES, Leonard, who died on May 3,
1933, was educated at Bath and played in a
few matches for Kent in 1877 and 1880,
though his highest score was only 17. In club
cricket, however, he showed fine hitting
powers and on one occasion played an innings of 224. He was much more successful at
Rugby football; a fine three-quarter, he
played for England when 19 years old and
continued his International career for seven
consecutive seasons—1875 to 1881. During
his five years captaincy of Blackheath the
Club enjoyed the most brilliant period in its
history. From 1886 to 1888 he was President
of the Rugby Union.

STONE, Major Charles Cecil, who died at
Eastbourne on November 11, 1951, aged 86,
was in the Uppingham XI of 1883 and
played occasionally for Leicestershire as an
all-rounder from 1884 to 1896. He visited the
West Indies with A. Priestley's team in 1896–
97.

STONE, James, Hampshire wicket-keeper and first-class umpire, died at Maidenhead on November 15, 1942, aged nearly 64. First tried for Hampshire in 1900, he found a regular place in the county XI as wicket-keeper in 1902, and did valuable service, both behind the stumps and as batsman, until 1914 when war broke out. In three seasons, 1911–1913, his record exceeded a thousand runs. He did specially well in 1912, and helped to beat the Australians by eight wickets, the first victory by Hampshire over an Australian team. Directly after this fine performance Yorkshire visited Southampton, and Stone enjoyed the most successful benefit of any Hampshire professional up to that time. He went in first and helped C. B. Fry add 109 for the third wicket, Yorkshire being hard pressed until Hirst and Haigh caused a second innings collapse. Short, but strongly built, Stone was a smart, unobtrusive wicket-keeper and a steady batsman. After leaving Hampshire he played for Glamorgan, and then acted as a first-class umpire from 1925 to 1934. Altogether in first-class cricket he scored over 10,000 runs with an average of 22.

STOPS, John Faulkner, who died at Northampton on June 4, 1944, aged 68, showed to advantage at cricket, golf, lawn tennis and especially Rugby football, at which he appeared for East Midlands, while he played hockey for Northamptonshire and Midland Counties. After getting his cricket and Association football colours at Wellingborough School, he played in the County Cricket XI.

STORER, Harry, a brother of the well-known wicket-keeper, died in the first week of May 1908 of consumption at the early age of 38. He played for Derbyshire on a few occasions in 1895, his highest score being 35 against Leicestershire at Derby. As an Association footballer he gained much distinction, and played for Liverpool in two of the memorable English Cup semi-finals with Sheffield United.

STORER, William, born at Butterley Hill, Derbyshire, January 25, 1868; died at Derby, March 5, 1912. Though he had dropped out of first-class matches for some time Storer was only in his 45th year. Derbyshire has perhaps never produced a more remarkable player. Storer came into great prominence as a wicket-keeper in 1893, when chosen for the M.C.C. in their second match that season with the Australians, the way he kept to Mr. Kortright's terrific bowling causing quite a sensation. He remained at his best for several seasons, and was picked for England against Australia at Nottingham in 1899. In the meantime he developed into a first-rate batsman, making, among many big scores, 100 and 100 not out for Derbyshire against Yorkshire at Derby in 1896. In that year he scored 1,091 runs for Derbyshire, and headed the batting with the splendid average of 57. He was almost as successful for his county in 1898, when his average was 50. It is worthy of mention that in 1898 he was picked for the Players against the Gentlemen at Lord's for his batting alone—Lilley being the wicket-keeper—and with scores of 59 and 73 more than justified his selection. He went to Australia in the winter of 1897–98 as chief wicket-keeper for the second team taken out by Mr. Stoddart. In first-class cricket he made 12,999 runs, average 28.82; highest score, 216 not out v. Leicestershire, at Chesterfield in 1899. In first-class cricket he took 232 wickets for 34 runs each.

STORY, Col. William Frederick, C. B., whose death took place on December 1, 1939, at the age of 87, always took a keen interest in cricket, though in recent years he may have been better known as an owner of racehorses. Born at Stockport in April, 1852, he played cricket for Nottinghamshire several times in 1878 and 1879; a batsman above the average, he bowled fast round-arm, and excelled as a wicket-keeper, being one of the first stumpers to dispense with the services of a long-stop. He was President of the County Club in 1929 when Nottinghamshire carried off the Championship, chiefly through the fast bowling of Larwood and Voce, for the first time for 22 years.

STRACHAN, George, who 30 years ago was one of the finest all-round players in the world, died from fever in January, 1901, whilst in charge of one of the concentration camps in the Transvaal. *Scores and Biographies* (xi–95) says of him: "Is a capital batsman, being a quick and lively hitter, and on several occasions has made excellent displays. As a field, at long-leg or cover-point, he is not to be excelled, indeed, many have pronounced him to be the best out in those positions ... He is also a pretty good slow round-armed bowler." From 1872, until 1880, he assisted the Gentlemen in their matches against the Players, and at the Oval, in 1875, he performed the extraordinary feat of bowling 39 balls for no runs and five wickets. In his early days he appeared for Gloucestershire, Surrey and Middlesex, and it was the desire to see him properly qualified for Surrey that led to the formulation of a regular system of qualification for County Cricket in 1873. He assisted Surrey from 1872 until 1875, and again from 1877 until 1880, generally captaining the side, but afterwards appeared in the ranks of Gloucestershire, for which county he possessed a birth qualification, having been born at Prestbury, near Cheltenham, November 21, 1850. He was educated at Cheltenham, and captained the cricket and football teams, besides representing the College at racquets.

STRATFORD, Alfred Hugh, who was born at Kensington on September 5, 1853, died at Newark, New Jersey, on May 2, 1914. He was in the Malvern XI in 1871 and two following years, and played occasionally for Middlesex between 1877 and 1880. For the former in 1873 he made 703 runs with an average of 32.40, scoring 149 v. Cotswold Magpies and 120 v. Rev. H. Foster's XI, and took 62 wickets for under 13 runs each. *Scores and Biographies* said of him: "A good and free hitter, and his bowling is slow and twisting, breaking both ways, being very difficult to operate against at times. In the field he is excellent, generally taking coverpoint or long-leg." His highest score in first-class cricket was 55 not out v. Gloucestershire at Clifton in 1879, and his best feat with the ball was to take five wickets for 12 runs for M.C.C. and G. v. Yorkshire at Lord's in 1879. In 1876 he took 17 wickets out of 20 for Incogniti v. Ealing, on the Ealing ground, and 18 out of 20 (besides making a catch) for Kensington Park v. Bickley Park at Notting Hill. Whilst in America he played with success for Winnipeg, Pittsburgh, New York and Newark, and when appearing for New York Eighteen against the Australians in 1893 scored 25, the only double-figure, in his side's first innings. Mr. Stratford was famous at Assocation football in the early days of the game. He played for the Wanderers when they won the cup in 1876, 1877, and 1878.

STRAUSS, Major Sarel Stephanus François, died suddenly at Pretoria on March 6, 1946, aged 53, while batting in a cricket match between two military teams. Best known as a South African Rugby international, he played cricket a few times for Griqualand West in Currie Cup and other matches in the years 1920 to 1922.

STREATFEILD, Edward Champion, an accomplished left-handed batsman, a smart slip fieldsman and a capital medium-pace bowler with plenty of break and variety, was born at Hatfield in Surrey on June 16, 1870, and died on August 22, 1932, at the age of 62. He stood over 6ft. in height. Educated at Charterhouse, he was in the XI there from 1885 to 1888 and captain during his last two years. In the match of 1888 against Westminster he took eight wickets for 26 and nine for 41—17 in all for less than four runs apiece. Going up to Cambridge he obtained his Blue as a Freshman and played four times against Oxford, putting together in 1892 an innings of 116 and taking in all 17 Oxford wickets for 12 runs apiece. His biggest score in first-class cricket was 145 for Cambridge University (Past and Present) at Leyton against the Australian team of 1890. He hit so brilliantly that he made the runs in 110 minutes. He appeared for Surrey occasionally between 1890 and 1892, for the Gentlemen at Lord's in 1891 and twice for the Gentlemen at the Oval. In company with W. Shelmerdine he won the Public Schools' Racquets Cup in 1888 and in 1891 and 1892 he obtained his Blue for Association football. A schoolmaster after he came down from Cambridge, he afterwards received, under the Board of Education, an appointment as Inspector of Schools.

CORRECTION: In the obituary notices in the 1933 issue of the *Almanack* Mr. E. C. Streatfeild was referred to as a left-handed batsman. Actually he batted and bowled right hand.

STREATFEILD-MOORE, Alexander McNeill, a member of the Streatfeild family, so well known in Kent, died on December 30, 1940, aged 77. Elder brother of E. C. Streatfeild—a splendid all-round cricketer—he assumed by royal licence the name of Streatfeild-Moore in 1885. After two years in the Charterhouse XI, he became in 1883 captain of Sandhurst, and against R.M.A., Woolwich, he scored 118 not out. He played for Kent occasionally in the years 1885 to 1888. A free-hitting bat with good style, he was a useful slow bowler and a brilliant fieldsman.

STREET, Alfred Edward, who died at Budleigh Salterton on February 18, 1951, aged 80, played for Surrey from 1892 to 1898, scoring 1,304 runs, average 22.48. A useful cricketer and a friend of W. G. Grace, he might have played more regularly for the county had not Surrey during this period been specially rich in batting talent. Born at Godalming on July 7, 1871, "Jim" Street was the son of the former Surrey fast bowler, James Street. On his first appearance he created a most favourable impression by helping Hayward in a stand of 95 against the Australians touring side of 1893, and in 1895 he hit 161 not out from the Leicestershire bowling at Leicester. Twice he was concerned in "tie" matches. In 1894, when Surrey carried off the County Championship, they "tied" with Lancashire at the Oval, Street distinguishing himself by scoring 48 in a first innings of 97. Then, during a long career as a first-class umpire, during which he stood in an England v. Australia Test match, he became involved in a controversy because of what *Wisden* then described as "a regrettable incident." In the match with Somerset at Taunton in 1919 the scores stood level with one Sussex wicket to fall and the remaining batsman, Heygate, crippled with rheumatism. It was understood at the start of the innings that Heygate would not be able to bat, but as some doubt existed as to whether he would be able to go in a Somerset player appealed to Street on the ground that the two minutes time limit had been exceeded. Street thereupon pulled up the stumps and the match was officially recorded as a "tie." This incident gave rise to much discussion and was at length referred to the M.C.C., who upheld Street's decision.

STREET, Francis Edward, born at Hampstead on February 16, 1851, died at Armidale, New South Wales in June, 1928. *Scores and Biographies* said of him "A promising bat and good field, generally taking long-leg or cover-point." He was in the Uppingham XI in 1868 and played for Kent three times in 1875 and once in 1877. For some years he appeared for the Uppingham Rovers, and he also took part in club cricket for Beckenham and Chislehurst.

STREET, Lieut. Frank (Royal Fusiliers), killed on July 7, 1916, aged 46, was in the Westminster XI in 1888 and 1889, when he performed thus: 1888, 266 runs (average 20.46) and 38 wickets (average 16.39); 1889, 224 runs (average 18.66) and 22 wickets (average 15.04).

In 1888 he was first in batting and second in bowling, and in 1889 (when captain) second in batting and third in bowling. In the latter year it was said of him: "A good bat, with an extremely pretty style, and a steady bowler." At Oxford he obtained his Blue for Association football, but not for cricket. Later he played with success for Essex, and in 1899, when he averaged 30.66, scored 76 v. Leicestershire at Leicester and 60 v. Hampshire at Southampton.

STREET, George Benjamin, the well-known Sussex wicket-keeper, was killed at Portslade on April 24, 1924. He was riding a motorcycle and, in endeavouring to avoid a lorry at a cross-roads, crashed into a wall and died immediately. Born at Charlwood, in Surrey, on December 6, 1889, he was in his 35th year at the time of his death. He made his first appearance for Sussex in 1909, but did not assist the team regularly until 1912, when he became Butt's successor. He had fairly established his reputation when the War came and put a stop to cricket for four years. He might not have gone much further ahead in the cricket world, but he was at his best in his last season (1923) and could safely have reckoned on many more years of play. He joined the M.C.C.'s England team in South Africa in the winter of 1922–23, being cabled for when a broken finger disabled Livsey. He played in the third of the five Test matches, but was left out of the remaining two, Brown being given the preference. In the game with Fifteen of the Orange Free State, he caught four men and stumped three. As a batsman for the side, Street turned a few opportunities to good account. He was often a useful run-getter for Sussex, and, in 1921, he hit up a score of 109 against Essex at Colchester. In first-class cricket in England he caught 304 men and stumped 115, total 419, thus:

Year	Caught	Stumped	Total
1909	5	0	5
1910	3	1	4
1911	3	1	4
1912	23	16	39
1913	32	10	42
1914	58	15	73
1920	25	13	38
1921	30	8	38
1922	54	25	79
1923	71	26	97
Total	304	115	419

He was not seen in the cricket-field in 1919, not being demobilised. Six times he obtained as many as five wickets in the course of an innings—v. Lancashire in 1914, v. Warwickshire in 1921, v. Gloucestershire and Northamptonshire in 1922, and v. Worcestershire and Middlesex in 1923. In the match with Worcestershire at Hastings in the last-mentioned year he caught seven men and stumped one.

STREET, James, whose death occurred at Godalming on September 17, 1906, dropped out of first-class cricket nearly 30 years ago, so he was merely a name to the present generation, but he did excellent work as a fast bowler for Surrey in the early '70s. Born at Cranleigh on March 10, 1840, he made his first appearance at Lord's in 1863, assisting a team of Colts and Professionals, who had never played at Lord's or the Oval, against the Marylebone Club. In the same XI were John Smith of Cambridgeshire, a great batsman, and one of the finest fieldsmen of his day—Tom Bignall of Notts, and Frank Silcock, the famous bowler who, after assisting several counties in turn, finished his career with Essex. The notes on the match, in *Scores and Biographies*, state that "His Royal Highness the Prince of Wales arrived soon after the commencement of the play on the first day, and remained for a short time. It was his *first* visit to the 'old spot.'" Street bowled for Surrey in 1864, with Mortlock, Griffith, and Shepherd, but it was four years later, before he found a regular place in the team, and then, in company with James Southerton, he regularly opened the attack. From 1870 to 1875 he never once failed to take over 50 wickets in first-class cricket—no mean achievement in those days of small programmes—and although his career seemed to have closed with the season of 1876, Surrey fell upon evil days to summers later, and Street, although 38 years of age, turned out again and took over 20 wickets. Although spoken of as a good free hitter, his best score was 50 against Middlesex at the Oval in 1870. So accurate was he in his bowling that, it is stated, he sent down for Surrey in 1875 no fewer than 3,043 balls, of which only one was a wide. Street, after his active days as a cricketer, umpired in first-class matches for several years. Without ever ranking as a great bowler, he did sound and skilful work for Surrey in the days between the famous years of that county and the revival in the middle of the '80s under Mr. John Shuter.

STRICKER, Louis Anthony, who died at Capetown on February 5, 1960, aged 75, played as opening batsman for Transvaal and took part in 13 Test matches for South Africa against England and Australia between 1909 and 1912. His Test record was 342 runs in 24 innings, average 14.25. For Transvaal against H. D. G. Leveson Gower's M.C.C. Team in 1910, he (101) and J. W. Zulch (176) scored 215 together in two hours 20 minutes, which then constituted a record for the first wicket against a touring team in South Africa.

STRUDWICK, Herbert, who died suddenly on February 14, 1970, a few days after his 90th birthday, held the world record for most dismissals in a career by a wicket-keeper. One of the greatest and assuredly one of the most popular players of his time, he helped to get rid of 1,493 batsmen, 71 of them in Test matches, and he established another world record which still stands by holding 1,235 catches. His stumpings numbered 258. He set up a third record in 1903 when taking 71 catches and bringing off 20 stumpings, but Fred Huish, of Kent, surpassed this eight years later.

Strudwick figured regularly behind the stumps for Surrey for 25 years and, becoming scorer afterwards, served the county altogether for 60 years. He played 28 times for England between 1911 and 1926 during the period when Australia and South Africa were their only Test match opponents and would doubtless have been chosen more often had he not been contemporary with A. A. Lilley, of Warwickshire, a better batsman. Four times he toured Australia, in 1903–04, 1911–12, 1920–21 and 1924–25 and visited South Africa with M.C.C. in 1909–10 and 1913–14. In addition, he was a frequent member of Players teams against Gentlemen. For England at Johannesburg in 1913–14, he dismissed seven South African batsmen in the match. His best performance in a single innings was six catches against Sussex at the Oval in 1904 and in a match eight victims (seven caught, one stumped) against Essex at Leyton in 1904.

No more genuine sportsman, in every sense of the word, than the teetotal, non-smoking Strudwick ever took the field for Surrey. An idol of the Surrey crowd, he was always ready to proffer helpful advice to young players. He never appealed unless sure in his own mind that a batsman was out, and such was his keenness to save runs that he was frequently known to chase a ball to the boundary. Sir H. D. G. Leveson Gower, the former Oxford, Surrey and England captain, once wrote: "When you walk on to a certain cricket ground and you find Strudwick behind the wicket, you feel that you will not only get full value for your money, but you will participate in the cheerfulness that his presence always lends to the day."

In an article, "From Dr. Grace to Peter May", in the 1959 *Wisden*, hailed by the critics as one of the best published by "The Cricketers' Bible" for many years, "Struddy", as he was affectionately known throughout the cricket world, described how hard was life as a professional cricketer in his younger days. Then, one dare not stand down because of injury for fear of losing a place in the side and consequent loss of pay. Compared with that of today, the equipment of wicket-keepers was flimsy and the men behind the stumps took a lot of punishment, especially as, on the far from perfect pitches, it was difficult to gauge how the ball would come through. The article mentioned that F. Stedman, Strudwick's predecessor in the Surrey side, habitually protected his chest with a South Western Railway timetable stuffed into his shirt, and on one occasion, after receiving a more than usually heavy blow, he remarked to a nearby team-mate: "I shall have to catch a later train to-night. That one knocked off the 7.30!"

It is of interest to note that a lady set "Struddy" on the path to becoming the world's most celebrated wicket-keeper. As a choir-boy at Mitcham, his birth-place, he took part in matches under supervision of the daughter of the vicar, a Miss Wilson. Then about 10 years old, Strudwick habitually ran in from cover to the wicket to take returns from the field. Observing how efficiently he did this, Miss Wilson once said: "You ought to be a wicket-keeper." From that point, Strudwick became one.

Not in the ordinary way regarded as much of a batsman, he hit 93 in 90 minutes, easily his largest innings, against Essex at the Oval in 1913, when he and H. S. Harrison shared an eighth-wicket partnership of 134. In the second Test match at Melbourne during the Australian tour of J. W. H. T. Douglas's 1920–21 team, he distinguished himself with innings of 21 not out and 24.

Honours bestowed upon "Struddy" included honorary membership of M.C.C. in 1949 and life membership of Surrey, whose oil-paintings of celebrities in the Long Room at the Oval include one of him.

Tributes to Struckwick included:
A. E. R. Gilligan, under whose captaincy he played in Australia: "Not only was he a magnificent wicket-keeper, but he set a fine example of the rest of the side, always being first to be ready to play. He was 100 per cent in every way."

Wilfred Rhodes, Yorkshire and England: "Struddy was above all a wonderful man and a great player. I telephoned him just before his 90th birthday and we had a long chat over old days. I went with him on his first M.C.C. tour to Australia in 1903–04 and then to South Africa. We were great friends."

S. C. Griffith, M.C.C. Secretary and a former England wicket-keeper: "This wonderful man and great cricketer taught me, when 14, all I ever knew about wicket-

keeping at the cricket school he helped to run in South London. He was the best coach I have ever known and from that time I always numbered him among my dearest friends. Apart from his ability, he was one of the outstanding figures and personalities of the game."

Herbert Sutcliffe, Yorkshire and England: "He was first of all a gentleman and a sportsman and in his capabilities as fine a player as Bertie Oldfield, the great Australian wicket-keeper. I played both with and against Struddy and rated him absolutely first-class in every way."

STUBBERFIELD, Henry, died at Brighton, February 14, 1918. Though well remembered by many old cricketers, Stubberfield had outlived most of his early contemporaries. Born at Brighton, on March 16, 1835, he played his first match at Lord's in 1858, appearing for Sussex against the M.C.C. A right-handed fast bowler, he met with great success, taking seven wickets for 50 runs in the club's second innings and winning the match. The Sussex team included John Wisden, John Lillywhite, Jimmy Dean, Mr. E. Napper, Charles Ellis, and James Southerton, whose fame as a slow bowler came some years later. Stubberfield had a long career for Sussex, and without being first-rate was a very useful bowler. When his days as an active cricketer were over he acted as umpire, and up to the time of the outbreak of the War in 1914 he was a familiar figure at the Brighton Ground.

STUBBINGS, James, who played occasionally for Derbyshire between 1880 and 1893, died suddenly at Huddersfield on July 17th, 1912. He was born at Whitwell, near Chesterfield, on April 27, 1856, and was a good fast round-armed bowler. Against Lancashire at Manchester in 1880 he took five wickets for 51, and v. Surrey at the Oval in 1892 four for 24. For 27 years he was professional to the Huddersfield C.C.

STUDD, Arthur Haythorne, a member of the famous brotherhood, died in London on January 26, 1919, aged 55. He was a member of the Eton XI in 1882 and 1883, and in his matches v. Harrow and Winchester made 137 runs each. Unlike his brothers, he did not play much first-class cricket after leaving Eton.

STUDD, Charles Thomas, the youngest and most famous of three brothers all of whom played for Eton, Cambridge University and

Middlesex, was born at Spatton, Northamptonshire, on December 2, 1860, and died at Ibambi in the Belgian Congo on July 16, 1931. Each of the three brothers enjoyed the distinction of captaining the Cambridge XI— G.B. in 1882, C.T. in 1883 and J.E.K. in 1884. J.E.K., the eldest—Lord Mayor of London in 1929—left Eton in 1877 but did not go up to Cambridge until 1881. All three figured in the Eton XI of 1877 and also in the Cambridge XI of 1881 and 1882.

A great batsman, a fine field and a high-class bowler, C.T. Studd developed his powers so rapidly that, while still at Cambridge, he was in the best XI of England. He possessed a fine upright style in batting and was particularly strong on the off-side. He bowled right-hand rather above medium pace and, tall of build, brought the ball over from a good height.

In 1882 he made 118 for Cambridge University and 114 for the M.C.C. against probably the strongest bowling Australia ever sent to this country, the side including, as it did, Spofforth, Palmer, Boyle, Garratt and Giffen. That year he also scored 100 at Lord's for Gentlemen against Players, yet he finished the season ingloriously at Kennington Oval with the memorable match which England lost by seven runs. Bowled by Spofforth in the first innings without scoring he, in the second innings, despite the two hundreds he had hit against the Australians earlier in the summer, went in 10th and, when the end came just afterwards, was not out 0. For all that he ranked high amongst the best of the all-round cricketers of his time—particularly during his years at Cambridge where he had a batting average of 30 in his first season and one of 41 for the next three summers. In 1882, moreover, he took 48 wickets for the University at 16 runs apiece and in 1883 40 at 14 runs apiece, while in his last three years at Cambridge he obtained against Oxford at Lord's 27 wickets for less than 12 runs each. For Middlesex his best seasons were 1882 and 1883. In the former year he had a batting average of 23 and obtained 58 wickets at an average cost of 14 runs and, in the latter, his batting improved to 51 runs an innings and his bowling resulted in 56 wickets for 17 runs each. Among his bowling performances were:— four wickets for eight runs when assisting Middlesex against Surrey at the Oval in 1880, eight wickets for 40 runs (Cambridge against Lancashire) at Manchester in 1882, eight wickets for 71 runs (Middlesex v. Gloucestershire) at Cheltenham in 1882 and 13 wickets for 147 runs (Gentlemen of England

v. Cambridge University, at Cambridge in 1884. He was a member of the team taken out to Australia in the winter of 1882–83 by the Hon. Ivo Bligh. This side, if beaten by Australia, won two matches out of three against the men who had visited England in the previous summer and so were acclaimed as having brought back the Ashes.

Unhappily for English cricket C.T. Studd was not seen in the field after 1884. Feeling a call for missionary work, he went out to China in connection with the China Inland Mission and there remained from 1885 to 1895. Invalided home, he engaged in missionary work in England and America and after 1900 with the Anglo-Indian Evangelization Society. Later on the state of the multitudes of the Belgian Congo, which had not been touched by any missionary agency, made such strong appeal to him that he went out to that uncivilised region and, despite numerous illnesses and many hardships, devoted the remainder of his life to missionary work there.

STUDD, Edward John Charles, who died at Folkestone on March 1, 1909, was born at Tirhoot, in India, on February 13, 1849, and was a member of the well-known cricketing family, being elder half-brother of Messrs. J.E.K., G.B., C.T., A.H., H.W., and R.A. Studd. He was in the Cheltenham XI of 1866 and had been a member of the M.C.C. since 1871. His first match at Lord's was for M.C.C. and Ground v. XXII Colts of Middlesex, in May, 1879. Playing against Oxford University at Oxford in 1885 he scored 110 and 44 for M.C.C. and 60 for Gentlemen of England. He was a good hitter and fine field, and made several high scores for the Incogniti. His career as a cricketer would in all probability have been a distinguished one had he been able to play regularly, but his residence for 16 years in India, where he was an indigo planter, prevented him from keeping up the game. Mr. Studd's height was 6ft. and weight 14st.

STUDD, George Brown, died on February 13, 1945, aged 85. The second eldest of three famous cricketing brothers, Sir J.E. Kynaston Studd and C.T. Studd being the others, all of whom played for both Eton and Cambridge, and established a record by captaining the University in consecutive years. Born at Netheravon House, near Amesbury, Wiltshire, on October 20, 1859, G.B. Studd got his Colours for Eton in 1877 when he scored 32 and 23 against Harrow and 54 against Winchester. He fared less well in the following year, but going up to Cambridge he got his Blue as a Freshman and appeared in the University match four times. Against Oxford in 1880 he made 38 and 40, and two years later, when captain of the Light Blues, he played a great innings of 120, which was the seventh three-figure score, and, at the time, the second highest in University matches. True to Eton form he showed special skill and power in driving, notably to the off, and in the field saved many runs by sure picking up, but did not always hold a catch. He enjoyed his best season for Cambridge in 1881, in which year and the following summer all three brothers were in the University XI. In 1882 he made 819 runs in first-class matches—a big achievement in those days—and put together for the Cambridge Long Vacation Club 289 in a grand display of forcing cricket. In the autumn G. B. and C. T. Studd went with the team taken out to Australia by the Hon. Ivo Bligh (afterwards Earl of Darnley) which brought back the Ashes by defeating W. L. Murdoch's team in two out of three matches, but G. B. failed to produce his best form. He assisted Middlesex occasionally from 1879 to 1886.

During his last two years at Cambridge he represented the University against Oxford in the tennis match—both singles and doubles. He was called to the Bar, but owing to a severe illness was compelled to winter abroad and did not practise. Like his brother C. T., G. B. Studd became a missionary, first in India and China, but from 1891 onwards at Los Angeles, California.

Altogether six brothers Studd played in the Eton XI; those besides the three seniors who captained Cambridge—J. E. K., G. B., and C. T.—were A. H., H. W., and R. A. The youngest of the six, R. A., got his Blue in 1895. An elder half-brother E. J. C., who played in the Cheltenham XI in 1866, died in 1909. C. T. Studd died in 1931, J. E. K. Studd on January 14, 1944. G. B. was the last survivor of the 1879 University match.

As written in last year's *Wisden* of Sir J. E. K. Studd, the three brothers helped Cambridge to beat by six wickets the Australian team which won the Ashes match by seven runs. The opening stand of 106 by G. B. (48) with J. E. K. (68) largely accounted for the splendid victory by Cambridge, but C. T. Studd, scoring 118 and 17 not out, after taking eight wickets, contributed still more to the triumph. G. B. played for Past and Present of Cambridge, who that season beat the Australians by 20 runs at Portsmouth, and altogether in 10 innings against that 1882 team he averaged 25.20.

STUDD, Brigadier-General Herbert William, who died on August 8, 1947, aged 76, was the fifth of six brothers, all of whom played in the Eton XI, the most distinguished being G. B., C. T., and J. E. K., who captained Cambridge in that order in consecutive years. He played a little County Cricket for Middlesex and Hampshire. Reginald Augustus Studd, youngest of the brothers who got his Cambridge Blue, and played for Hampshire, died in 1947.

STUDD, Sir John Edward Kynaston, Bart., O.B.E., the eldest but the last of three brothers who captained Cambridge in consecutive seasons, gained high renown in other walks of life before passing on at the age of 85 on January 14, 1944. Altogether six brothers Studd played in the Eton XI, besides the three Cambridge captains, being G. B., C. T., and J. E. K., and the youngest of them, R. A., got his Blue at Cambridge in 1895, while an elder half-brother, E. J. C., played for Cheltenham in 1866. G. B. captained Cambridge in 1882, and now of the three he alone survives, C. T., most famous in the cricket world, having died in 1931. All three were in the Cambridge XI of 1881 when Oxford won by 135 runs, and the next year they helped in a revenge victory by seven wickets with G. B. in command, a result exactly repeated under C. T. in 1883; but strange to relate Oxford turned the tables by the same margin when J. E. K. led the Light Blues.

At Eton, J. E. K. Studd was never on the losing side in the big school matches with Harrow and Winchester, but in these seasons his best score was 52 against Winchester in 1877. After two years in business J. E. K. went up to Cambridge and was four years in the XI without doing much in the University match, his aggregate for eight innings reaching only 100, but in 1882 he and his brothers took a large share in defeating by six wickets the great Australian side who later in the season beat England at Kennington Oval by seven runs. J. E. K. scored 6 and 66, G. B. 42 and 48, C. T. 118 and 17 not out. When Cambridge batted a second time requiring 165 runs for victory, the two elder brothers put up 106, the first appearance of three figures on the telegraph board against an Australian side in England without a wicket falling.

After leaving Cambridge, J. E. K. Studd played occasionally for Middlesex, but gave his time to business and the Polytechnic, of which he was President from 1903 until his death. Knighted in 1923, Sir Kynaston became Lord Mayor of London in 1928 and was created Baronet at the end of his official year. When President of M.C.C. in September 1930 he gave a banquet at Merchant Taylors' Hall to the Australian team captained by W. M. Woodfull.

Canon F. H. Gillingham, the old Dulwich College and Essex batsman, in his address at the Memorial Service in St. Paul's Cathedral, said that after coming down from Cambridge Kynaston Studd realised that games were but a preparation for sterner duties, and in his presence it was easier for men to be good and harder to be bad. He made such rapid progress in the life of the City that he became the leading citizen of this Empire. "Everything he touched he lifted up."

As a Merchant Taylor and Fruiterer and a high officer in the Masonic world, Sir Kynaston exercised his splendid influence in the quietest manner, with benevolence a leading feature in his character.

STUDD, Reginald Augustus, who died on February 3, 1948, aged 74, was the youngest of six brothers of distinction in Eton cricket. Three of them captained Cambridge in this order, G. B., C. T., J. E. K. consecutively, 1882 to 1884, and were all in the 1882 side which beat Oxford by seven wickets at Lord's, a margin which was repeated five times in the next seven years, Oxford winning two of these games. R. A. Studd played for Cambridge in 1895, when a very powerful Oxford XI suffered defeat by 134 runs. He appeared occasionally for Hampshire and went to America in September 1895 with a side captained by Frank Mitchell, then Cambridge Captain elect.

SUGDEN, Herbert Edward, who played twice for Derbyshire in 1882, scoring nine and one v. Australians and 0 and three v. Lancashire, died at Bradford on May 14, 1913, aged 50.

SUGG, Frank Howe, who died on May 29, 1933, was born at Ilkeston on January 11, 1862. A fine enterprising batsman, especially strong in driving and square-leg hitting, and a brilliant outfield, who not only covered a lot of ground but possessed a very safe pair of hands, he had the experience—very unusual in modern days—of playing for three different counties. He appeared for Yorkshire in 1883, for Derbyshire—his native county—in 1884, 1885 and 1886, and for 13 seasons subsequently, having qualified by

residence, he assisted Lancashire. While doing little as a member of the Yorkshire team, he rendered capital service to Derbyshire, running second in the averages one year to L. C. Docker, and in another to W. Chatterton, while amongst his scores was one of 187 against Hampshire at Southampton. His great work, however, was accomplished for Lancashire. Standing 6ft. high, he possessed very quick sight and, if his methods tended to make him a poor starter, no one was more likely on a bad wicket to turn the fortunes of a game. Altogether for Lancashire he scored 10,375 runs with an average of 26. He played in 1896 an innings of 220 against Gloucestershire and on five other occasions exceeded 150, his hundreds in first-class cricket numbered 16 in all. In the game with Somerset at Taunton in 1899, he and G. R. Baker hit up 50 runs off three consecutive overs, Sugg, in one of these, registering five fours. Sugg appeared several times for the Players against the Gentlemen and in 1888 took part in Test matches against Australia at the Oval and at Manchester. His recollections of these two games must have been very happy, for at the Oval, where he made 31, the Australians were dismissed for 80 and 100, England winning in a single innings, and at Manchester, where he scored 24, Australia's totals were 81 and 70, and again England triumphed with an innings to spare. Some time after the close of his career Sugg officiated as an umpire in first-class matches. Lancashire gave him their match with Kent at Old Trafford in 1897 as a benefit. Frank Sugg was equally good at Association football and he gained fame with Sheffield Wednesday, Derby County, Burnley and Bolton Wanderers, being captain of the first three teams. Such was his versatility in sport that, besides his prowess at cricket and football, he excelled as a long distance swimmer and joined with Burgess and Heaton in swims; he held the record for throwing the cricket ball; reaching the final of the Liverpool Amateur Billiards Championship; won prizes all over the country for rifle shooting, bowls, and putting the shot, and was famed as a weight lifter.

SUGG, Walter, who died in May, 1933, was a good free-hitting batsman and a magnificent field at cover-point. Although not built on such generous lines as his more famous brother, Frank, and while not so successful, he had a good eye and flexible wrists, and generally looked to be the better batsman. From 1884 until 1902 he played for Derbyshire every season with the exception of that of 1885. Contemporary with Chatterton, Davidson, Bagshaw, Joseph Hulme, Storer and S. H. Evershed, he played one of his best innings for Derbyshire against the South Africans at Derby in 1894. Derbyshire were put in to bat after H. H. Castens, the South African captain, won the toss, but they scored 325, Walter Sugg hitting up 121 before he was run out. Altogether in first-class matches he scored 3,471 runs with an average of 18.36. His benefit match, the Yorkshire fixture at Chesterfield in 1898 is still talked about. On that occasion Brown and Tunnicliffe eclipsed all previous records in important cricket with a first-wicket partnership of 554, that stood as a record until two other Yorkshire batsmen—Sutcliffe and Holmes—beat it with a stand of 555 against Essex at Leyton in 1932. Prior to assisting Derbyshire Sugg, in 1881, appeared in one match for Yorkshire. He was born at Ilkeston on May 21, 1860.

SULIN, Thomas Richard, captain of I Zingari C.C., of Natal, died by his own hand at Lord's Cricket Ground, Durban, on July 30, 1912. He was 32 years of age.

SULLEY, Joseph, born on May 28, 1850, died on February 14, 1932 in his 82nd year. He figured in only two matches for Notts, the first being the 1887 game with Surrey at the Oval, which was largely instrumental in the Southern County gaining the Championship. Scotton being unable to play through rheumatism, the side was completed by Sulley. A left-handed bowler, Sulley secured six wickets for 106 runs but Surrey, set 205 to win, got home by four wickets after five had gone down for 127. In February 1871, Sulley won the Sheffield Shrovetide Handicap of 204yd. off the 73yd. mark.

SULLIVAN, Dennis, who died in Harold Wood Hospital, Essex, on December 28, 1968, aged 81, kept wicket for Surrey in 1920. Seeing little prospect of a place in the first team while H. Strudwick, the England player was still available, he joined forces with Glamorgan, for whom he played from 1925 to 1927. In all first-class matches he held 92 catches and brought off 56 stumpings.

SULLIVAN, Joseph Hubert Baron, who died on February 8, 1932, appeared in the Yorkshire XI in 1912. Educated at Rossall, he went up to Cambridge but did not get a Blue. He was born on September 21, 1890.

SUSSKIND, Bernard Victor, who died at

Johannesburg on January 1, 1954, aged 59, played for Orange Free State from 1921 to 1926, his highest score being 102 against Griqualand West at Bloemfontein in 1924–25. Like his elder brother, M. J. Susskind, who toured England with H. W. Taylor's South African team in 1924, he was educated at the University College School, where he was in the XI in 1909 and 1910.

SUSSKIND, Manfred J., collapsed and died on July 9, 1957, aged 66, at the Johannesburg Stock Exchange, of which he was a member for 30 years. Educated at University College School and Cambridge University, he played in a few games for Middlesex before returning home and assisting Transvaal, for whom he obtained 2,595 runs, average 49.90, in Currie Cup matches, hitting six centuries. He and H. B. Cameron set up a Transvaal record when adding 207 for the sixth wicket against Eastern Province in 1926–27. In 1924 "Fred" Susskind, as he was always known, was one of H. W. Taylor's South African team in England, playing in all five Test matches. He was second in the Test batting averages with 268 runs, average 33.50, and in all games scored 1,469 runs, including two centuries, average 32.64. A tall batsman, he was often cramped in style and his proneness to pad-play caused a good deal of criticism during the tour.

HERBERT SUTCLIFFE
Born at Summerbridge, near Harrogate, November 24, 1894.
Died at Crosshills, January 22, 1978.
By J. M. Kilburn

Herbert Sutcliffe was one of the great cricketers and he brought to cricket as to all his undertakings an assurance and capacity for concentration that positively commanded success. His technical talent matched his character and his achievements were therefore on the highest plane.

In a career extending from 1919 to 1939 Herbert Sutcliffe scored more than 50,000 runs and averaged 52. He never knew a season of failure, except by the standard of his own astonishing peaks, and at the zenith of his career he scored 16,255 runs in five years as a measure of mastery in all conditions and over the world's best bowling of the time.

The First World War delayed his entry into County Cricket until he was 24 years old when, after demobilisation from a commission in the Green Howards, he was given a place in the Yorkshire side. His quality was never in doubt and by the end of the 1919 season he had scored five centuries in an aggregate of 1,839 runs. He had also established a first-wicket partnership with Percy Holmes. For 14 years these two batsmen opened the innings for Yorkshire, representing a partnership of unparalleled success in which they put up a hundred on 74 occasions. Equally happy was Sutcliffe's Test match association with J. B. Hobbs, for this became the most accomplished of all opening partnerships. Sutcliffe's good fortune, however, was only in the presentation of opportunity. Seizure of it was his own merit and with one partner or another he constructed 145 first-wicket century stands.

His artistry and efficiency in difficult conditions became legendary in his lifetime, with his centuries against Australia at the Oval in 1926 and at Melbourne in 1929 as historic examples. Matches against Lancashire stirred him to nine centuries. His defensive patience and skill became a byword, yet at need his hitting was brilliant in the extreme. Against Northamptonshire at Kettering he met spin on the sticky wicket with an innings of 113 which included 10 sixes. At Scarborough against the fast bowling of Farnes and Nichols, Sutcliffe took his personal score from 100 to 194 in 40 minutes. His 100th first-class century was the 132 he hit in less than two hours at Bradford when Yorkshire were hurrying to defeat Gloucestershire.

Courage and concentration were his basic attributes. No prospect daunted him, no difficulty dismayed him, no crisis upset him. He was an artist of the dead bat and an uncompromising hooker of fast bowling. He sought solution to his batting problems by taking them as they came, one at a time. He never allowed the present to be influenced by the alarms of the past or fears for the future. In the means and manner of his performances he raised enormous prestige for himself throughout the cricketing world. He was admired and respected wherever he played and by his refusal to depreciate his own value he raised the status of his profession.

He took the supplementary rewards of his distinction with polished grace and unfailing consideration for colleagues. Herbert Sutcliffe the individual always made it clear that he was Herbert Sutcliffe inseparable from Yorkshire and England. he was as punctilious in acknowledgment of obligations as he was single-minded towards the immediate task in hand.

After the retirement of A. W. Lupton in 1927, Sutcliffe was offered the Yorkshire captaincy as a professional player. Although he was on tour in South Africa when the invitation came he appreciated the possibility of divided opinions and with characteristic diplomacy declined the appointment, giving assurance of his willingness to play under any captain.

During his playing days he founded and developed a sports outfitting business, now directed by his elder son. After his retirement from the field he took a managerial appointment in the paper trade. He showed himself as successful in commerce as in cricket and for the same reasons of application and reliability. His repayment to the game which had given him so much was service on the Yorkshire committee, as an England selector, and as sponsor for many good causes in cricket. Though he was born in Summerbridge, Sutcliffe was a Pudsey native in cricket association. There, as a schoolboy, he began League cricket and from there he advanced to the county, but neither Pudsey nor any other nursery could have claimed Herbert Sutcliffe as a typical product. He was a Yorkshireman in his loyalty and training, but he was cosmopolitan in approach and outlook. His manner fitted Lord's as expressively as it fitted Leeds.

Immaculate, alert, brisk of movement, serene in repose, he carried his character with a clear label wherever he appeared. His off-drive wore a silk hat and his hook was a ready response to the aggressive intent of any bumper. His defensive play was the reduction of risk to the minimum and his self-confidence was unshakable.

In his first-class career he scored 149 centuries. He shared with Holmes a partnership of 555 for Yorkshire, and with Hobbs a partnership of 283 for England against Australia.

Second in the nominal batting order, Herbert Sutcliffe was second to none in steadfastness on all occasions. He was esteemed for accomplishment, he was acclaimed for his unfailing resolution. His name will always stay in the headlines.

Other tributes

Sir Leonard Hutton: "Herbert and Jack Hobbs were my boyhood heroes. My first innings with Herbert was a most wonderful experience for me, an uncapped Yorkshire player. A young player could not have wished to receive more encouragement than I did on that occasion. He was correct in all he did, on and off the field, but never so ambitious that he forgot he was playing a team game. Herbert was the finest hooker of the short-pitched ball that I have seen. Don Bradman was the finest puller in front of square, but Herbert hit the ball up behind square to perfection. He was at his best playing against Lancashire and Australia when every run had to be earned. I had known Herbert as long as I had known my parents and my brothers. He led me through my early days of doubts and indecision to the promised land."

Bill Bowes: "Herbert was born at Summerbridge but will always be associated with Pudsey where he learned cricket and played for a local team. He had his county trial when he was 18, but the outbreak of the First World War, in which he served with the Sherwood Foresters and the Green Howards, interrupted his career. He was in his 30th year before being selected for England and he was an immediate success. He never did anything mean or underhand. His personality had the same characteristics as his batting. He was reliable. He was the first to admit that he had not the same ability as Jack Hobbs, Wally Hammond, or Sir Len Hutton, but he had concentration and the will to harness his ability. As a result he was England's most successful batsman of all time. He was a magnificent judge of a single and a magnificent hooker of bouncers. During his long association with Percy Holmes, his county partner, they were involved in only 22 runs out—slightly more than one a season."

Sir Donald Bradman: "I was very sorry to hear of his death. He was a great player and he had the best temperament of any cricketer I ever played with or against."

Harold Larwood: "Herbert Sutcliffe, needed some getting out. He was a great battler for England and for Yorkshire. He never gave his wicket away—unless he was satisfied he had made enough already. With

Percy Holmes he formed just about the finest opening partnership I bowled against. I got him out cheaply a few times, but he scored a few hundreds against my bowling, so I reckon we ended up just about square."

Brian Sellers: "We played together for eight years from when I was elected captain in 1932 and it was not an easy job to fill. I had never played first-class cricket and I was to skipper a side of real professionals who knew their job from A to Z. It was then I really got to know Herbert and he was of great help to me. Later we served together on the county committee for over 21 years. Very few people realise what a great fellow he was. He was always courteous, kind and considerate, and he helped many people in many ways. He was also an astute businessman, brimful of confidence and concentration. You *never* saw him untidy; always chest out and chin up. Apart from being one of the all-time greats in our wonderful game, he was a great gentleman and was known as such throughout the cricket world."

The late R. C. Robertson-Glasgow wrote of Herbert Sutcliffe: "[He] was the serenest batsman I have known. Whatever may have passed under that calm brow—anger, joy, disagreement, surprise, relief, triumph—no outward sign was betrayed on the field of play. When I first saw him, in 1919, he was a debonair and powerful stylist. As you bowled opening overs to the later Sutcliffe you noticed the entire development of every defensive art; the depressingly straight bat, the astute use of pads (as with Hobbs), the sharp detection of which out-swinger could be left; above all, the consistently safe playing down of a rising or turning ball on leg stump, or thighs."

CAREER AT A GLANCE

In England

Season	Inns	Not Outs	Runs	100s	Average	Other Inns over 50	Ducks	Catches
1919	45	4	1,839	5	44.85	7	1	22
1920	45	3	1,393	4	33.16	7	2	14
1921	43	2	1,235	0	30.12	8	3	16
1922	48	5	2,020	4	45.95	12	1	20
1923	60	6	2,220	3	41.11	15	1	24
1924	52	8	2,142	6	48.68	9	5	20
1925	51	8	2,308	7	53.67	7	4	36
1926	47	9	2,528	8	66.52	12	0	33
1927	59	6	2,414	6	56.13	11	1	25
1928	44	5	3,002	13	76.97	13	1	15
1929	46	4	2,189	9	52.11	8	1	17
1930	44	8	2,312	6	64.22	13	2	21
1931	42	11	3,006	13	96.96	9	0	20
1932	52	7	3,336	14	74.13	8	3	26

HERBERT SUTCLIFFE CAREER AT A GLANCE—*continued*

In England

Season	Inns	Not Outs	Runs	100s	Average	Other Inns over 50	Ducks	Catches
1933	52	5	2,211	7	47.04	6	2	35
1934	44	3	2,023	4	49.34	12	2	21
1935	54	3	2,494	8	48.90	12	0	19
1936	53	7	1,532	3	33.30	6	4	21
1937	54	5	2,162	4	44.12	11	1	22
1938	50	7	1,790	5	41.62	8	2	12
1939	29	3	1,416	6	54.46	1	1	7
1945	1	0	8	0	8.00	0	0	0

In Australia and New Zealand

1924–25	18	0	1,250	5	69.44	4	1	6
1928–29	16	0	852	2	53.25	5	0	4
1932–33	21	1	1,342	5	64.04	6	1	4

In South Africa

1927–28	23	3	1,030	2	51.50	9	1	4

In Jamaica

1935–36	4	0	81	0	20.25	0	0	4
Total	1,087	123	50,135	149	52.00	219	40	468

SUMMARY

			Inns	Not Outs	Runs	100s	Average
Test matches	..	..	84	9	4,555	16	60.73
Gentlemen v. Players	..	..	28	5	1,113	2	48.39
County matches	..	..	721	74	32,814	100	50.71
Other matches	..	..	254	35	11,653	31	53.21
Total	..	..	1,087	123	50,135	149	52.00
In England	..	..	1,005	119	45,580	135	51.44
Abroad	..	..	82	4	4,555	14	57.69
Total	..	..	1,087	123	50,135	149	52.00

INNINGS BY INNINGS IN TEST CRICKET

Date		Innings	Runs	Average
1924	(SA)	64, 122, 83, 29*, 5	303	75.75
1924–25	(A)	59, 115, 176, 127, 33*, 59, 143, 22, 0	2,734	81.55
1926	(A)	13*, 82, 26, 94, 20, 76, 161	472	78.66
1927–28	(SA)	102, 41*, 29, 99, 25, 8, 37, 3, 51, 23	418	46.44
1928	(WI)	48, 54, 63	165	55.00
1928–29	(A)	38, 32, 11, 58, 135, 64, 17	355	50.70
1929	(SA)	26, 114, 100, 10, 37, 4, 9, 104, 109*	513	64.12
1930	(A)	29, 58*, 32, 28*, 74, 161, 54	436	87.20
1931	(NZ)	117, 109*	226	226.00
1932	(I)	3, 19	22	11.00
1932–33	(A)	194, 1*, 52, 33, 9, 7, 86, 2, 56	440	55.00
1933	(NZ)	0, 24	24	12.00
1933	(WI)	21, 20	41	20.50
1934	(A)	62, 24, 20, 63, 69*, 38, 28	304	50.66
1935	(SA)	61, 3, 38	102	34.00

*Signifies not out.

INNINGS BY INNINGS IN TEST CRICKET—*continued*

			Tests	Inns	Not Outs	Runs	Average
v. Australia	..	..	27	46	5	2,741	66.85
v. South Africa		..	17	27	3	1,336	55.66
v. West Indies	..	..	5	5	0	206	41.20
v. New Zealand	..	..	4	4	1	250	83.33
v. India	..	.. ..	1	2	0	22	11.00
Total	..	.. ..	54	84	9	4,555	60.73

CENTURIES IN TEST CRICKET

16: at Lord's (2) 122 (1924), 100 (1929); at The Oval (5) 161 (1926), 109* and 104 (1929), 161 (1930), 117 (1931); at Manchester (1) 109* (1931); at Birmingham (1) 114 (1929); at Sydney (2) 115 (1924), 194 (1932); at Melbourne (4) 176 and 127 (1925), 143 (1925), 135 (1929); at Johannesburg (1) 102 (1927).

Catches in Test Cricket—23

WHERE THE CENTURIES WERE MADE

In England (135)
The Oval 14, Scarborough 14, Sheffield 12, Bradford 11, Lord's 9, Leeds 8, Birmingham 7, Hull 7, Dewsbury 5, Leicester 5, Manchester 5, Cambridge 4, Nottinghamshire 4, Leyton 3, Northampton 3, Bournemouth 2, Brighton 2, Gloucester 2, Huddersfield 2, Portsmouth 2, Southend 2, Worcester 2, Bristol 1, Derby 1, Dover 1, Eastbourne 1, Folkestone 1, Hastings 1, Kettering 1, Neath 1, Oxford 1, Peterborough 1.

In Australia (10)
Melbourne 4, Sydney 3, Adelaide 2, Perth 1.

In South Africa (2)
Johannesburg 1, Kimberley 1.

In Tasmania (2)
Hobart 1, Launceston 1.

Sutcliffe scored hundreds on 40 different grounds—32 in England and eight abroad. He was most successful on two widely different grounds—the Oval (large) and Scarborough (small).

TWO HUNDREDS IN ONE MATCH

Innings	For	Against	Ground	Date
176 127	England	Australia	Melbourne	1925
107 109*	Yorkshire	M.C.C.	Scarborough	1926
111 100*	Yorkshire	Nottinghamshire	Nottingham	1928
104 109*	England	South Africa	The Oval	1929

FIFTY AND HUNDRED IN ONE MATCH

Innings	For	Against	Ground	Date
103 78	Yorkshire	Middlesex	Lord's	1919
124 50*	Yorkshire	Rest of England	The Oval	1925
59 115	England	Australia	Sydney	1924
76 161	England	Australia	The Oval	1926
71 131	Yorkshire	Surrey	The Oval	1926
107 50*	Players	Gentlemen	Lord's	1926

Signifies not out.

FIFTY AND HUNDRED IN ONE MATCH—*Continued*

Innings		For	Against	Ground	Date
95	135	Yorkshire	Lancashire	Leeds	1927
58	135	England	Australia	Melbourne	1929
161	54	England	Australia	The Oval	1930
76	150	Yorkshire	Essex	Dewsbury	1930
173	59	Yorkshire	Sussex	Brighton	1930
83	132	Yorkshire	Gloucestershire	Bradford	1932
96	110*	North	South	Manchester	1932
138	56	Yorkshire	Surrey	Bradford	1937

CENTURIES (149)

For Yorkshire (112)

v. Leicestershire (1): 234*, 212, 200, 189, 187, 174, 129, 119, 109, 105.

v. Essex (9): 313, 255, 194, 166, 150*, 133*, 129, 125, 108*.

v. Lancashire (9): 195, 165, 140, 135, 135, 132, 126, 122, 106.

v. Surrey (9): 232, 203, 176, 138, 131*, 129, 123, 114, 101*.

v. Warwickshire (8): 205, 205, 153*, 142, 130, 129, 109, 102.

v. Middlesex (7): 235, 202, 177, 175, 120*, 104, 103.

v. Hampshire (6): 131, 116, 112, 107, 104*, 100.

v. Nottinghamshire (6): 169, 135, 111, 110*, 107, 100.

v. Glamorgan (5): 147*, 135*, 132*, 121, 121.

v. Northamptonshire (5): 150, 145, 113, 107*, 104.

v. Sussex (5): 270, 228, 173, 160, 122*.

v. Gloucestershire (4): 134, 132, 118, 110.

v. Somerset (4): 213, 183, 139, 136.

v. Worcestershire (4): 200*, 187, 138, 112.

v. Derbyshire (3): 182, 138, 111.

v. Kent (3): 230, 174, 110.

v. M.C.C. (7): 171, 109*, 108, 107, 107, 102*, 101.

v. Cambridge University (4): 173*, 152, 108, 105.

v. Rest of England (2): 124, 114*.

v. South Africans (1): 113.

v. Oxford University (1): 125*.

Other Matches (37)

England v. Australia (8): 194, 176, 161, 161, 143, 135, 127, 115.

England v. South Africa (6): 122, 114, 109*, 104, 102, 100.

England v. New Zealand (2): 117, 109*.

M.C.C. v. Tasmania (2): 188, 101.

M.C.C. v. South Australia (2): 154, 122.

M.C.C. v. Combined XI (1): 169.

M.C.C. v. New South Wales (1): 182.

M.C.C. v. Griqualand West (1): 100.

Players v. Gentlemen (2): 120, 107.

North v. South (2): 131, 110.

England v. The Rest (2): 227, 101.

Rest of England v. Lancashire (2): 139, 136.

H. D. G. Leveson Gower's XI v. New Zealanders (1): 126.

H. D. G. Leveson Gower's XI v. All India (2): 106, 102.

M.C.C. Australian Team v. H. D. G. Leveson Gower's XI (1): 119*.

C. I. Thornton's XI v. M.C.C. South African Team (1): 111.

Rest of England v. Lord Cowdray's XI (1): 119.

DOUBLE CENTURIES (17)

313 Yorkshire v. Essex at Leyton (1932).

270 Yorkshire v. Sussex at Leeds (1932).

255 Yorkshire v. Essex at Southend (1924).

235 Yorkshire v. Middlesex at Lord's (1925).

234* Yorkshire v. Leicestershire at Hull (1939).

232 Yorkshire v. Surrey at the Oval (1922).

230 Yorkshire v. Kent at Folkestone (1930).

228 Yorkshire v. Sussex at Eastbourne (1928).

227 England v. The Rest at Bristol (1927).

213 Yorkshire v. Somerset at Dewsbury (1924).

Signifies not out.

212 Yorkshire v. Leicestershire at Leicester (1935).
206 Yorkshire v. Warwickshire at Dewsbury (1925).
205 Yorkshire v. Warwickshire at Birmingham (1933).
203 Yorkshire v. Surrey at the Oval (1934).
202 Yorkshire v. Middlesex at Scarborough (1936).
200* Yorkshire v. Worcestershire at Sheffield (1935).
200 Yorkshire v. Leicestershire at Leicester (1926).

* Signifies not out.

555 FOR ONE WICKET

On June 16, 1932, cricket history was made at Leyton when Yorkshire met Essex. Winning the toss, the Yorkshiremen took first innings, and Holmes and Sutcliffe began a patnership which lasted for seven and a half hours. During this time the famous Yorkshire pair scored 555 runs, thus beating by one run the record for any wicket set up in 1898 by two other Yorkshiremen, J. T. Brown and J. Tunnicliffe.

The latter made their runs in 305 minutes compared with 450 minutes required by Holmes and Sutcliffe, but it must be remembered that Chesterfield—the ground where Brown and Tunnicliffe made history—is a small one compared with Leyton. Moreover, in 1898 the Derbyshire attack was much weaker than the Essex bowling in 1932.

Sutcliffe's share of the new record was 313, made without a chance, and—as in 1898—the partnership ended only when one of the batsmen made a present of his wicket to the opposition. In 1898 Brown threw away his wicket; in 1932 Sutcliffe followed his example.

Holmes's and Sutcliffe's record stood until February 1977, when it was surpassed by the opening stand of 561 by the Pakistanis Waheed Mirza (324) and Mansoor Akhtar (224*) for Karachi Whites v. Quetta.

NOTES

In eight consecutive English seasons (1925–32) and on four overseas tours, Sutcliffe never failed to average more than 50 runs per innings. During this period his average ranged from 51.50 in South Africa in 1927–28 to 96.96 in England in 1931.

On 16 occasions Sutcliffe shared partner-

ships for the first wicket exceeding 250 runs—11 times with P. Holmes, three times with Hobbs, and twice with Hutton.

Holmes and Sutcliffe scored 100 or more runs for the first wicket 74 times. In all first-class cricket Sutcliffe helped to score 100 for the first wicket on 145 occasions.

On 11 occasions Hobbs and Sutcliffe scored 100 or more runs for England's first wicket in Test matches.

During one period of 24 months—May 1931 to May 1933—Sutcliffe scored 7,687 runs, including 32 hundreds and 22 other innings over 50. His average for this period was 79.24.

In Yorkshire matches Sutcliffe is credited with many remarkable performances and records, of which the following may be noted:

His aggregate—38,561 runs—is greater than that of any other Yorkshire batsman, D. Denton with 33,608 runs being the nearest.

Sutcliffe shared 38 partnerships exceeding 200 runs in Yorkshire matches—19 with P. Holmes, five with M. Leyland, three each with Hutton and E. Oldroyd, two with W. Barber, D. Denton and A. Mitchell, and one each with R. Kilner and A. Wood.

For Yorkshire Sutcliffe carried his bat through the innings six times—v. Essex (1920), v. Hampshire (1932), v. Rest of England (1933), v. Worcestershire (1934), v. Glamorgan (1936), and v. Oxford University (1939).

Holmes and Sutcliffe scored a hundred or more in each innings of a match twice—105 and 265 (unfinished) v. Surrey at The Oval (1926), and 184 and 210 (unfinished) v. Nottinghamshire at Nottingham in 1928.

In five seasons—1925, 1928, 1932, 1935 and 1937—Sutcliffe scored more than 2,000 runs in Yorkshire matches.

On 98 occasions Sutcliffe shared a first-wicket partnership of 100 runs or more for Yorkshire—69 times with P. Holmes, 15 with L. Hutton, six with A. Mitchell, four with M. Leyland, twice with W. Barber, and once each with P. A. Gibb and E. Robinson.

In his first season (1919) Sutcliffe headed the Yorkshire batting averages.

In Australia in 1924–25 J. B. Hobbs and Sutcliffe scored more than 100 runs for England's first wicket in three consecutive innings. On the third occasion they batted a whole day without being parted, scoring 283 runs.

Sutcliffe was the only cricketer who played regularly in each of the 21 inter-war seasons. He scored more than 1,000 runs in each.

In Test matches v. Australia Sutcliffe averaged 66.85 runs per innings—16.60 runs per innings more than his average for Yorkshire.

Towards the end of his life, Sutcliffe suffered from arthritis and he was bedridden in hospital at Harrogate in 1974 when he celebrated his 80th birthday. In the same year he lost his wife Emma, aged 75. Later he went to St. Anne's nursing home, Crosshills, where he died.

His son, William Herbert Hobbs Sutcliffe, to whom he gave his own name and that of his England partner, played as an amateur for Yorkshire for 10 years from 1948, and captained the county in 1956 and 1957. He is now chairman of the Yorkshire Cricket Committee.

SUTHERLAND, David, who died on October 6, 1971, aged 99, was one of the last surviving men who saw the Hon. Ivo Bligh's England team in 1882–83. He played for Victoria in the closing years of the last century and in hitting 180 against Tasmania, shared a second-wicket partnership of 206 with W. H. McCormack which remains a record. In 11 innings for the State he scored 516 runs. He was a member of the Melbourne C.C. for over 80 years.

SUTTHERY, Arthur Melbourne, who played for Cambridge against Oxford in 1887, died on May 15, 1937, aged 73. Born on March 25, 1864, at Clifton Reynes, in Buckinghamshire, he was in the Uppingham Second XI before going to Oundle School. He played occasionally for Northamptonshire when at Oundle, and in later years for Devon and Shropshire. A free-hitting batsman, fast medium bowler and smart fieldsman he was a valuable all-round player. His best season was in 1887 when scores of 72 against Surrey and 72 against M.C.C. came before his 73 and 21 against Oxford. He played for the Gentlemen at the Oval and next year he appeared in several representative XI's against the Australians.

SWAIN, William, at one time a well-known Yorkshire cricketer, died at East Brisbane on October 5, 1910. He was born at Burley near Otley, on September 8, 1830, and had therefore just completed his 80th year. In *Scores and Biographies* (viii–300) it is said of him: "Bats in good style, is a nice field, either at point or long-stop, while his bowling is round-armed, fast or slow. On July 11, 1853, he played perhaps the most extraordinary single-wicket match on record with John Barrett, at Otley, the ball all through

the contest not once touching the bat, and on October 11, 1861, he beat at single wicket an XI (very inferior, however) of the Burley Club." Swain accepted many engagements and was for some years a tailor in Halifax. Later he opened a sports outfitter's shop in Bradford, and eventually settled in Queensland. As recently as September 1908, a match (in which he himself took part) was played in Brisbane for his benefit. He took the greatest interest in the game to the end, and in May last contributed some reminiscences of King Edward's connection with cricket to a local newspaper. In his younger days he was of a poetical turn of mind, and produced several cricket verses.

SWALWELL, Major Reginald Sawdon, born on June 25, 1873, died at Sunningdale on September 20, 1930, in his 58th year. A batsman of some ability, he never played regularly in first-class cricket but he appeared several times for Yorkshire Second XI, Dorset and Worcestershire, as well as for M.C.C. For Yorkshire Second XI in 1901 he carried his bat through the innings for 109 v. Surrey Second XI at the Oval and a year later scored 100 against the same side at Harrogate. Among other good performances may be mentioned his 57 for Worcestershire v. Oxford University at Oxford in 1908 and 72 for M.C.C. v. Cambridge University at Lord's in 1921.

SWAMY, V. N., who died at Dehra Dun on May 1, 1983, was a medium-paced bowler who played in one Test match against New Zealand at Hyderabad in 1955–56. He opened the bowling, without taking a wicket, and did not bat. Swamy played for Services in the Ranji Trophy, taking 58 wickets at 19.98 apiece. His best performance was six for 29 against East Punjab in 1954–55

SWAN, John James, born at Oadby, near Leicester, on September 24, 1848, died at Maidstone on February 22, 1924. Between 1870 and 1876 he appeared in 32 matches for Surrey, scoring 637 runs with an average of 11.79 and taking two wickets for 41.50 runs each. Against Sussex at the Oval in 1874 he played an innings of 62. He was a useful batsman, bowled medium-pace, and generally fielded at long-stop or mid-on.

SWIFT, J. S., who died on February 28, 1926, aged 74, was at one time regarded as one of the fastest run-getters in Victoria, in addition to being a good wicket-keeper and a sure field generally. In his two matches against New South Wales he scored 39 runs in three completed innings. In club cricket—chiefly with the Melbourne, South Melbourne, Yarra Bend and Kew Asylum Clubs—he was much more successful. During the season of 1877–78 he made five hundreds in succession, and for the Asylum team, which he captained, he scored 1,200 runs with an average of 92.30.

SWINFORD, Capt. Thomas, late in H.M.'s 98th Regiment (North Staffordshire), born at Margate on May 9, 1839, died at Eastbourne on January 23, 1915. He was educated at Blackheath Proprietory School, and played for Kent four times in 1874, scoring 89 runs with an average of 11.12, his highest innings being 50 v. Lancashire at Manchester. He was a good batsman and long-stop.

SWINSTEAD, George Hillyard, R.I., who died at Hampstead on January 16, 1926, was a well-known batsman in Metropolitan cricket circles, especially for the Hampstead C.C. He had played for Middlesex 2nd XI, and was the author of a pamphlet entitled "The New Cricket." An artist of repute, he designed several cricket *menu* cards much prized by collectors.

SWIRE, S. H., who had for 36 years been Hon. Secretary of the Lancashire County Club, died at Southport, after a long illness, on December 29, 1905. Though never a prominent cricketer, he played occasionally for Lancashire in the early days of the XI. He was born on January 3, 1939.

SYED HASSAN SHAH, who died on September 28, 1957, aged 67, following a car accident at Multon, played for about nine years in the Bombay Quadrangular Tournament, captaining the Muslims on two occasions. Educated at Government College, Lahore, and M.A.O. College, Alligarh, he later took the Civil Engineering course in England.

SYMONDS, Harry G., who died at Cardiff on January 1, 1945, aged 55, played for Glamorgan both in minor and first-class cricket, from 1921 to 1929. For 12 years he was racing manager to the Cardiff Arms Park Greyhound Racing Company.

SYREE, Dr. Anton Hugh, born at Port Currie, Cape of Good Hope, on October 21, 1859, died at Cannock, in Staffordshire, on February 3, 1924, of strychnine self-administered. He was in the XI at St. John's School,

Leatherhead, and played for Kent in one match in 1879. He was above the average as a batsman, bowled slows and generally fielded at cover-point.

TABOR, Alfred, born at Trent, in Middlesex, on February 24, 1850, died at Eastbourne on December 16, 1925. *Scores and Biographies* said of him: "As a batsman, he is a steady and careful player, remaining a long while at the wickets for his runs, while in the field he is good everywhere. He took great pains while at Harrow, and paid every attention to his instructors, improving rapidly under able tuition." He was a member of the Harrow XI in 1868, when, by his innings of 38 (top score) and 14, he contributed much to his side's success over Eton by seven wickets. In 1866–67 he was in the School Football XI. He did not obtain his Blue for Cambridge, although quite a useful player, but, appearing for Middlesex against Surrey at the Oval in 1872, he scored seven and 42. His career in important cricket was very short, as from 1873 until 1890 he was coffee-planting in Ceylon. For many years he scored well for Dikoya and Up-Country teams, and he also captained the Ceylon sides which visited Calcutta in 1884–85 and played Mr. G. F. Vernon's team in 1889–90. He was brother of Mr. R. M. Tabor of the Eton XI of 1864 and of Mr. A. S. Tabor who played three years (1869–71) for Eton and three (1872–74) for Cambridge.

TABOR, Arthur Sydney, born at Trent, in Middlesex, on November 9, 1852, died in London on October 14, 1927, aged 74. At Eton he was in the XI in 1869 and two following years, but although he was, even then, recognised as a batsman of much merit, his scores in the Public School matches were, with one exception, very small. It is on account of what he did for Cambridge that he will chiefly be remembered. Obtaining his Blue as a Freshman, he played three times against Oxford. In the match of 1872 he and his fellow-Etonian, G. H. Longman—both Freshmen—made 104 together for the first wicket in an hour and three-quarters, Tabor's score being 50. A year later he scored three and 45, and in 1874 made 52 and 0, the former innings, played on difficult ground, being the highest in the match for either side. It was in 1874 that he made his only appearance—at Prince's—for the Gentlemen. He played occasionally for Middlesex in 1872 and the next two years, and once for Surrey in 1878, but his form in those games was very disappointing. R. M. Tabor, who played in 1864, and Alfred Tabor, of the Harrow XI of 1868, were his brothers. For 30 years, 1891–1920, he was headmaster of Cheam School.

TAGART, Noel Dugley, of the Clifton XI of 1896 and two following years, died at Molyneux Park, Tunbridge Wells, on October 8, 1913, at the early age of 34. He was a good batsman, a fine field at point and occasionally of use as a change bowler. He averaged 31 for Clifton in 1896, 19 in 1897, and 44 in 1898, when he was captain. In the last-mentioned year he scored 103 v. Incogniti, and 54 and 51 v. Cheltenham. He did not succeed in obtaining his Blue at Cambridge, and in the few matches in which he subsequently appeared for Gloucestershire, did not succeed in making more than 28 in an innings.

TAIT, James, who died on February 1, 1966, aged 69, was masseur at Kennington Oval for 36 years. An injury during boyhood ended "Sandy" Tait's athletic aspirations and he turned his attention to ministering to the hurts of others. From 1916 to 1924 he served with Crystal Palace F.C. and later with Dulwich Hamlet and Kingstonian F.C.s. After joining Surrey he attended to England players and to those of some touring teams when they visited the Oval. A banjo-player and a humorist, he kept the Surrey players in good spirits in the dressing-room and when travelling. His father played at left-back in the Tottenham Hotspur F.A. Cup-winning team of 1901.

TAIT, J. R., who died at Bristol on April 13, 1945, aged 58, was born in Scotland, but went to Swansea early in life and became well known as a cricket umpire in Bristol and Glamorgan, for which county he appeared with fair success. Mr. A. E. Brown, secretary of Glamorgan, stated that "J. R. Tait played in our first first-class county game against Sussex at Cardiff in 1921, which we won by 23 runs; he scored 31 in first innings, and 96 in the second. He last played in 1926 and altogether, in 81 innings, scored 1,495 runs, highest score 96, average 18.69. An aggressive batsman; and when he made runs the spectators were thrilled. Properly coached he might have been a very great player."

TALBOT, Ronald Osman, who died in Auckland on January 5, 1983, at the age of 79, toured with the New Zealand team to England in 1931 as a forceful right-handed batsman and a medium-paced bowler. In his best innings of the tour – 66 against M.C.C. at Lord's (his county's first appearance there) – he made one of the biggest straight drives, high on to the pavilion, seen on the ground. The first of his three first-class 100s was in his debut match – for Otago against Canterbury at Dunedin in 1922–23. An all-round sportsman, he excelled at squash, golf, bowls and athletics, and he played Rugby for Canterbury.

TALLON, Donald, who died in Brisbane on September 7, 1984, aged 68, was a great wicket-keeper. Unlucky not to be chosen to tour England in 1938 – his omission caused quite a stir – he had to wait until after the War, in which he did Army service, to become established in the Australian side. Unusually tall for a wicket-keeper (5ft. 10½in.) and very slim, he yet crouched low behind the stumps. He was a man of few words (partly, perhaps, because his hearing was not good) and of quick, neat movement of the gloves. Born in Bundaberg on the Queensland coast, he made his first appearance against an English side for a Queensland Country XI at Toowoomba in 1932–33, when he was 16. He stumped Sutcliffe. He first played for Queensland a year later and was still only 19 when he scored 193 for Queensland against Victoria at Brisbane in 1935–36, the highest of his nine first-class hundreds. He was Queensland's leading batsman that year, with 503 runs at an average of 55.88. By the outbreak of war he had equalled E. Pooley's long-standing world record of 12 victims in a match (it has yet to be beaten) for Queensland against New South Wales at Sydney, this in the 1938–39 season. He had six in each innings, catching nine of them and stumped three. Seven dismissals in an innings for Queensland against Victoria at Brisbane a month later was also, at that time, a world record, though shared with several others.

The first of Don Tallon's 21 Tests were Australia's first after the War, against New Zealand at Wellington in March, 1946 (it was not granted Test status until 1948), his first victim came from a stumping off O'Reilly. Having made the wicket-keeping place his own against England in 1946–47, and established what was then a record 20 victims in the series, he was an integral part of Bradman's brilliant 1948 side in England, being equally at home whether keeping to the speed of Lindwall and Miller or the spin of Johnson, McCool and Ring. He had wonderful timing behind the stumps and exceptionally fast hands when it came to taking off the bails. Perhaps his most famous catch was at the Oval in 1948, when he dived down the leg side to dismiss Hutton for 30. He caught an authentic leg-glance left-handed and at full stretch – "a great finish to Australia's splendid performance", wrote *Wisden*, Hutton being the last man out and England's total a mere 52. Tallon came to England again in 1953, but he was 37 by then and no longer quite the supreme craftsman he had been. Having played in the first Test, he gave way to Langley.

His rugged, weathered features helped to make him seem a typical Australian to many English cricket followers. In the few years after the War he was looked upon almost with awe. Bradman was of the opinion that as a wicket-keeper he was the equal of the great Oldfield, to whose coaching Tallon acknowledged a considerable debt. Lindwall and Miller both rate Tallon as the best they ever saw. His unavailability to tour South Africa in 1949–50 deprived him of one full series, but his Test victims numbered 58 (50ct, 8 st). All told he claimed 432 first-class victims, no fewer than 129 of them being stumped, Australian cricket at that time being well endowed with leg-break bowlers. Tallon's batting record in Tests was disappointing, partly no doubt because in such a strong and all-conquering Australian side runs were seldom needed from him. His best Test was his 92 against England at Melbourne in 1946–47, when he and Lindwall added 154 for the eighth wicket. In first-class cricket he scored 6,034 runs (average 29.18), in Test cricket 394 runs (average 17.13).

TANCRED, Augustus Bernard, eldest member of the well-known South African brotherhood, died at Cape Town on November 23, 1911, after an operation. He was born at Port Elizabeth in 1865, and educated at St. Aidan's College, Grahamstown. For about 10 years he was undoubtedly the finest batsman in South Africa, and in club cricket met with remarkable success, his best remembered feat being to score 132 and 103 not out for Eclectic v. Union at Pretoria in 1896–97. For South Africa against England at Cape Town in March, 1889, he carried his bat through the innings of 47 for 26, being the only player to reach double figures against Briggs, Ulyett, and Fothergill. His defence was very strong, and he was a good field at point. In 1894 he was asked to visit England as a member of the first South African team, but was unable to do so owing to the claims of business.

TANCRED, Louis J., the famous Transvaal and South African cricketer, died at Johannesburg, on July 30, 1934, aged 58. He was well known in England for he made four visits with representative teams, in 1901, 1904, 1907, and 1912. On his last tour he took over the captaincy from Frank Mitchell in three of the six Test matches which his team played against England and Australia in the Triangular tournament. Possessed of abundant patience, Tancred was an excellent opening batsman for he could wear down the bowling for other players to punish. He also hit powerfully and though a pronounced crouch spoilt his style he was especially good against fast bowling. During his trip to England in 1907 he was handicapped for a long time through illness and was only at his best during the last 10 days of the tour. His highest score in a Test match was 97, at Johannesburg, against Australia in 1902, when J. Darling's team visited South Africa on the way home from England. His aggregate in 26 innings against England and Australia was 530 with an average of 21.20.

TANCRED, Vincent, a brother of Messrs. A.B. and L.J. Tancred, the well-known South African cricketers, shot himself at Johannesburg on June 3, 1904, being then but 29 years of age. He was a good all-round cricketer, useful as batsman, bowler, and wicket-keeper, and was among the reserves for the team which visited England summer 1902. He played for South Africa and the Transvaal against Lord Hawke's team in 1898–99, and for the Transvaal against the Australians in 1902.

TANDY, John Hubert, who died at Cape Town on August 26, 1954, aged 71, played a few times for Transvaal between 1909 and 1914. A member of the South African Test Selection Committee from 1927 to 1936, he was manager of the team which toured Australasia in 1931–32, and also served as a Border representative on the South African Rugby Football Board. In the First World War, "Sass" Tandy won the M.C. in France and in the Second was awarded the O.B.E.

TANNER, Arthur Ralph, who died suddenly on August 16, 1966, aged 77, was an exceptionally good fieldsman close to the wicket. As an amateur for Middlesex between 1920 and 1929, he held 53 catches besides taking 71 wickets with slow bowling and scoring 764 runs.

TAPSCOTT, George Lancelot, died at Kimberley on December 13, 1940, aged 61. A hard-hitting batsman, he scarcely fulfilled the promise given in an innings of 106 for Griqualand West against Natal in March 1911. In the following December, by brilliant hitting he scored 111 in 70 minutes and 60 for the Rest of South Africa against Transvaal; but he failed to gain selection for the South African team that toured England in 1912. When the England team under J. W. H. T. Douglas visited South Africa in 1913–14, Tapscott played in the first Test match, but scored only four and one, and was not called upon again, though he continued to bat and bowl with considerable success for Griqualand West until 1923, when he gave up first-class cricket because of knee trouble. His brother, L. E. Tapscott, also played for South Africa.

TAPSCOTT, Lionel Eric, one of three brothers, L. G., N. V., and L. E. who all played in cricket of class, had the unusual distinction of representing South Africa both at lawn tennis and cricket. Born on March 8, 1889, L. E. first played for Griqualand West in 1911. His highest innings in Currie Cup matches was 102. Twice he played against England in Test matches making 50 not out at Johannesburg in February, 1923. A sparkling batsman and a fielder without a superior in South Africa he was in the running for a place in the 1924 team that visited England. Known as "Doodles" he was very popular. He died at Cape Town on July 7, 1934.

TARBOX, Charles Victor (Percy), died in hospital on June 15, 1978, aged 84. Between 1921 and 1929 he scored 5,824 runs for Worcestershire with an average of 15.87 and took 375 wickets at 35.25. These figures do not look much, but they represent valuable service to a county which was never far from the bottom of the table and Tarbox was always picking up a few wickets and making useful scores. A medium-pace right-hand bowler, he never fulfilled the promise of his first season when, in the second innings against Somerset at Worcester, he took seven for 55 and, in the return at Taunton in the two innings, 10 for 158. His two highest scores and his only centuries were 109 in 1927 v. Nottinghamshire at Trent Bridge and 103 not out in 1925 v. Warwickshire at Edgbaston. In 1929 he lost his form so badly that he was not re-engaged, but he later played with considerable success for Hertfordshire, the county of his birth.

TARILTON, P. H. ("Tim"), who died at Kingston, Jamaica, in February, 1953, aged 68, was a member of the West Indies team who toured England under the captaincy of H. B. G. Austin in 1923. In that year Tarilton, a strong-driving batsman, scored 554 runs, average 21.30, with 109 not out against Nottinghamshire his best innings. He was the first West Indies batsman to put together an innings of over 300, hitting 304 not out against Trinidad in the first first-class match played in the Caribbean Islands following the First World War. In partnership with G. Challenor in 1927 he scored 292 against Trinidad, which remained a record for the first wicket in West Indies cricket until A. Rae and J. Stollmeyer hit 355 from the Sussex bowling at Hove in 1950. In all first-class cricket Tarilton scored 2,742 runs, average 39.17.

TARRANT, Frank A., the Australian all-round cricketer who made a great name with Middlesex in the years preceding the First World War, died at Melbourne on January 29, 1951, aged 69. Once a ground bowler at Melbourne earning 30 shillings a week, Tarrant, who was related to George Tarrant, the noted Cambridgeshire fast bowler of the 1860s, became a noted cricketer and wealthy sportsman. He played for Middlesex from 1903 to 1914 and occasionally for Victoria, Australia. Between the First and Second World Wars he made a large income from buying and selling racehorses in both India and Australia, and there were many Indian princes among his friends. Tarrant came to England unheralded, joined the ground staff at Lord's, and when two years later—in 1905—he became qualified to play in the County Championship for Middlesex, he had already built up a reputation. This was soon enhanced.

He was rated the best all-round cricketer in England in 1907, and for eight consecutive seasons, until 1914, accomplished the double of scoring 1,000 runs and taking 100 wickets. In 1907 his figures were 1,552 runs and 183 wickets, and in 1911 he scored 2,030 runs and took 111 wickets. In England he scored altogether 15,903 runs with an average of nearly 36, and obtained 1,335 wickets for less than 18 runs apiece. He played 17 times for Players v. Gentlemen. Five times Tarrant took nine wickets in an innings and he hit four scores of 200 or over in England, including 250 not out for Middlesex against Essex at Leyton in 1914.

This was a remarkable match and yielded Middlesex one of the biggest victories on record. Sent in by J. W. H. T. Douglas on a wet pitch, Middlesex scored 464 before declaring with only one wicket down. Tarrant, number two, batted five hours and 20 minutes for his highest score in first-class cricket. J. W. Hearne scored 106 for Middlesex and then took seven wickets in each of the Essex innings, which ended for 172 and 235, at a total cost of 146 runs.

In the winter of 1907–08 Tarrant paid a visit to his homeland, and while there played against the English team led by A. O. Jones. Tarrant scored 81 and 65 for Victoria against the tourists and 159 for A Victorian XI. He also made some good scores in Inter-State games, including 206 for Victoria against New South Wales at Sydney. When, after the First World War, Tarrant re-settled in Australia, he played for Victoria in the winter of 1924–25 with a fair amount of success, then, after an unsuccessful appearance for the State the following season, did not play again in first-class cricket. Under the auspices of the Maharajah of Patiala he took an Australian team to India in the winter of 1935–36.

When Tarrant first played for Middlesex there was much adverse criticism as to the importation of cricketers by the county, but this was soon forgotten when he showed his delightful qualities. He was a most enthusiastic cricketer and obviously enjoyed every moment of a game whether batting, bowling or fielding. As a batsman he was, at times, apt to exercise undue caution, but he always had a fine cut at his command and gradually developed powers of scoring on the on-side. A left-handed bowler, from slow to medium pace, he naturally excelled when the turf helped him, and on a damaged pitch there was no one more likely than Tarrant to go through a side. He was a safe catch in the slips, and in his prime a player who would not have been out of place in any XI. He never played in a Test match because of the rules governing international cricket.

TATE, Edward, who died on January 4, 1953, aged 75, served Malvern College for 50 years as cricket professional and manager of the college store. Known affectionately to Malvernians, both masters and boys, as "Father," he played as a medium-pace bowler for Hampshire from 1898 to 1902. In 1898, when taking 35 wickets for 27.94 runs each, he enjoyed the satisfaction of dismissing five such batsmen as J. T. Brown, J. Tunnicliffe, F. S. Jackson, D. Denton and Lord Hawke for 83 runs in the Yorkshire first innings at Huddersfield. Later in the same season, when taking eight Somerset wickets for 51 runs on a crumbling pitch at Bournemouth, he bore the leading part in a win by nine runs for Hampshire, who were 115 behind on the first innings. The last seven of these wickets fell to him for 25 runs. Tate also appeared for Devon before and after the First World War, in which he served with the Royal Artillery in France.

TATE, Frederick, died on April 24, 1935, aged 90 years, having been born on June 6, 1844, at Lyndhurst. He bowled fast round-arm and was a safe field, usually in the slips or at point. In his first match for Hampshire against Lancashire at Old Trafford on July 21, 1870, he took six wickets for 63 runs. A. N. Hornby scored 132 and Lancashire won by 10 wickets. W. Hickton took all 10 wickets, when Hampshire followed-on, at a cost of 46 runs. In Hampshire's first innings Hickton took four wickets for 27. After four seasons with Trinity College, Cambridge, as coach, Tate in 1873 began a long engagement with the Richmond club, Surrey, where he lived for many years.

TATE, Frederick William, died at Burgess Hill, Sussex, on February 24, 1943, aged 75. He first played for Sussex in 1888, and not until 1905 did his career end. Subsequently he went to Derby as coach to the County C.C. and in 1921 to Trent College as professional coach. Two of his three sons played county cricket, Maurice, so well known with Sussex and England, and C. L. Tate, who played for Derbyshire and Warwickshire.

A slow to medium-paced right-hand bowler, with easy action and good command of length, Fred Tate took over 100 wickets in five different seasons. His great year came when he was 35, 180 wickets falling to him for less than 16 runs apiece in 1902. His full record in first-class cricket shows 1,324 wickets at an average cost of 21 runs apiece. He accomplished many good performances. When Hampshire were a second-class county he took nine wickets for 24 runs, and at Leicester in 1902 he again got nine wickets in an innings at a cost of 73 runs. Perhaps his best achievement that year at Lord's was when against Middlesex he dismissed 15 men for 68 runs in a day. Other exceptional feats were five wickets for one run against Kent at Tonbridge in 1888 and seven for 17 against Gloucestershire at Bristol in 1891; and in 1901 he did the hat-trick against Surrey at the Oval. This was his benefit year and the match against Yorkshire at Hove brought him £1,051.

In his best season, 1902, Tate played against the Gentlemen at Lord's and for

England in the fourth Test against Australia at Old Trafford—one of the most dramatic struggles in the history of cricket, Australia winning by three runs after astonishing changes of fortune and incidents that I still can see clearly. Rain-drenched ground influenced the last-minute preference of Tate over George Hirst, and to the last choice fell the lot of being the central figure in a fielding error and in the final scene. Quite recently Len Braund, whom I met by chance, told me that when Joe Darling, the Australian captain, a left-handed batsman, and S. E. Gregory changed ends during an over he wanted Lionel Palairet, fielding at square-leg, as customary when Braund bowled for Somerset, to cross the ground. A. C. MacLaren, the England captain, sent Tate to the position, although he invariably fielded slip or near the wicket for Sussex—never in the deep. At once Darling lifted a catch and Tate dropped it—an absolute disaster for England, 48 more runs coming before the fourth wicket fell at 64. Unquestionably this, the only stand of the innings, determined the issue of the tensely close struggle. In this second innings of Australia Tate bowled five overs, and took two wickets for seven runs. Next day, on a very treacherous pitch, England, striving to hit off 124 runs before a threatening storm burst, lost their ninth wicket with eight wanted for victory. Rain then interrupted the game for three-quarters of an hour before Tate joined Rhodes and edged the next ball to the leg boundary: but the fourth ball he received from Saunders bowled him, and so finished the memorable match with a victory that gave Australia the rubber, no matter what might happen in the last encounter at the Oval. A few minutes later torrents of rain fell and washed us all back to Manchester.—H.P.

TATE, Maurice William, "Chubby" to his many friends and admirers, died at his home at Wadhurst, Sussex, on May 18, 1956, aged 61. Only three weeks earlier he had umpired the opening match of the Australians' tour against the Duke of Norfolk's XI at Arundel.

Maurice Tate was the son of Fred Tate, the Sussex and England cricketer whose name will ever be associated with the 1902 Test at Old Trafford, which England lost by three runs. Fred Tate missed a vital catch and was last out when England wanted only four runs to win. In his reminiscences, published in 1934, Maurice Tate wrote that his father's greatest ambition was to see his son playing for England and retrieving his own tragic blunder. How well the son atoned for

the father's misfortune! Maurice Tate began as a slow off-break bowler and had been playing some years before he developed his fast-medium action which gave him a deceptive swerve and tremendous pace off the pitch. He was probably the first bowler deliberately to use the seam and many of the best batsmen of the day regarded him as the most dangerous bowler they had ever played against.

He will be remembered as one of the greatest-hearted bowlers in the game—and one of cricket's most lovable and colourful personalities. He was an inveterate fun-maker and wherever he went he found new friends. He could go on bowling for hours, keeping an immaculate length and seeming to enjoy every moment of the game. A large and amiable man, with many of the characteristics of the true rustic, his broad grin and large feet were a "gift" to contemporary cartoonists.

Between 1912 and 1937, when he retired from the game, Tate took 2,784 wickets at an average cost of 18.12 runs. A. E. R. Gilligan, his old county and England captain, told of his "conversion" when, reviewing the history of Sussex cricket in the 1954 *Wisden*, he wrote:

"Tate, I must say at once, was the greatest bowler our county has produced. Curiously, when I first played for Sussex, Maurice used the same run-up and style of delivery as his father—a slow bowler! A sheer piece of luck caused Maurice to change his methods. Sussex had batted very badly in 1922, and when we had a day off the whole team practised at the nets. Maurice Tate bowled me several of his slow deliveries, then down came a quick one which spreadeagled my stumps. He did this three times. I went up to him and said: 'Maurice, you must change your style of bowling immediately.' My hunch paid. In the next match against Kent at Tunbridge Wells, Maurice, in his new style as a quick bowler, was unplayable. He took three wickets in four balls and eight in the innings for 67. That was the turning-point in his career.

"In the Test trial at Lord's in 1923, he took five wickets without a run being scored from him after the Rest had made 200 for four wickets. They were out for 205. The following year Maurice and I bowled out South Africa at Birmingham for 30—a day neither of us will ever forget. I was fortunate to take six for seven runs, and Maurice captured the other four for 12. In the second innings we shared nine wickets and England won by an innings. The tide flowed for Sussex bowlers about that time, for we had previously dismissed Surrey for 53 at the Oval, and in the Whitsuntide match at Lord's had disposed of Middlesex in their second innings for 41.

"Maurice was a member of my 1924–25 M.C.C. team to Australia and on this tour he beat Arthur Mailey's record of 36 wickets in a Test series by taking 38. He bowled Mailey out to gain his 37th success! Besides being a great bowler, Maurice was a hard-hitting batsman with a wealth of strokes. He scored 17,518 runs (average 24.19) for the county and took 2,223 wickets (average 16.34). For seven consecutive seasons he did the 'double' and in 1929 he took over 100 wickets for the county alone and scored more than 1,000 runs in first-class cricket. In fact, with the exception of 1933 when a damaged foot kept him out of the last three matches (he had taken 99 wickets), he never failed to take over 100 wickets for Sussex.

"In 1953 Alec Bedser beat Tate's Test record by taking 39 wickets in a series, and many times since I have been asked how I compare Bedser with Maurice. My answer is: 'They are two very great bowlers.' Having said that, I still think that Maurice Tate just stands out as the superior bowler of the two, bearing in mind the strength of the Australian batting in the 1924–25 series. But it is a very close thing indeed and one must not forget that Bedser had to contend with Bradman between 1946 and 1948."

Tate played in 20 consecutive Test matches against Australia and represented England in a further 19 Tests against South Africa, India and the West Indies. In all he took 155 Test wickets—a feat excelled only by A. V. Bedser and S. F. Barnes.

Tate was so consistently successful as a bowler that the quality of his batting is now often overlooked. Yet he was one of the best all-rounders of his generation. He scored 100 not out against South Africa in the Lord's Test in 1929. Eight times he completed the cricketers' double of 1,000 runs and 100 wickets in a season—and in 1923, 1924, and 1925 his "bag" of wickets topped 200. Fourteen times he took over 100 wickets in a season.

As a batsman, his best season was 1927, when he scored 1,713 runs, including five centuries. In 1922 he was the best all-rounder in the country, taking 118 wickets and scoring only 22 short of his 1,000. In 1921 he shared with Bowley a second-wicket partnership of 385 against Northamptonshire—a Sussex record.

Tate was the first professional ever to captain Sussex—the honour later fell to James Langridge—and after his retirement he was elected an honorary life member of the County C.C. He was also one of the former professionals similarly honoured by M.C.C. in 1949.

When he retired from first-class cricket, Tate took over the licences of several Sussex inns and for a number of years coached the boys of Tonbridge School.

Tributes included the following:

Capt. C. B. Fry: "Tate was a very great cricketer indeed. He could make the ball swing away very late outside the off-stump, and even the best batsmen were often beaten by him. He could make the ball rear off the pitch like a snake striking. He was even more successful in Australia than in this country—in fact, he ranks with S. F. Barnes as the most successful bowler England has ever sent there."

Sir John Hobbs: "Maurice was one of the greatest bowlers of all time. It is difficult to find words to praise him sufficiently. I know from experience how difficult it was to play against him."

A. E. R. Gilligan: "His death has come as a great shock to everybody in Sussex, and in fact the whole of the cricket world. Not only was Maurice a great bowler; he was a very great sportsman. He played cricket for the real joy and fun of it. It was his life."

E. ("Patsy") Hendren: "I doubt whether we shall ever see the like of Maurice again. He was a great bowler and a great character. How they loved him in Australia! As a bowler he made the batsman play at five balls out of six. He was the finest fast-medium bowler I ever played with or against."

S. C. Griffith: "He was the best bowler of his type I have ever kept wicket to. If the modern field-placing had been in vogue when he was playing, I feel sure he would have taken hundreds more wickets. Often batsmen would get an inside edge which now would almost certainly mean a catch at short-leg. In Maurice's day, the ball used to run harmlessly down the leg-side."

Herbert Strudwick: "He was the best length bowler I ever kept wicket to and the best bowler of his pace I ever knew. There was not a quicker bowler off the wicket. I class him with Sidney Barnes and F. R. Foster as the three best bowlers I ever kept to."

TAYLER, Albert Chevallier, born on April 5, 1862, died in London on December 20, 1925, aged 63. A well-known artist, he will be remembered by followers of the game on account of his series of drawings entitled *The Empire's Cricketers,* published in 1905.

TAYLER, Charles J., who died on April 3, 1958, aged 77, played in three matches for Gloucestershire in 1900 and 1901 and for many years assisted Cheltenham. At one time the Tayler family fielded a complete side and took part in a number of games.

TAYLER, Herbert William, died at Dawlish on April 17, 1984, aged 96. An Old Wellingburian, he played twice for Gloucestershire in 1914 in the Cheltenham Festival, and thanks to an innings of 43 not out against Sussex he headed their batting averages for the season. After the War he played a few times for Glamorgan, his last appearance being in 1927. His highest score for them was 44 against Nottinghamshire at Swansea in 1926, on which occasion he and Mercer added 56 in 15 minutes for the ninth wicket.

TAYLOR, Alfred Daniel, who was born in London on July 30, 1872, died at Hove, in Sussex, on March 8, 1923. He was a well-known writer on the game and at the time of his death possessed the largest library on cricket which had ever been collected. Among his best-known books were *The Catalogue of Cricket Literature*—a model compilation and the standard work on the subject—*Annals of Lord's and History of the M.C.C.*, histories of the Hastings and Cheltenham festivals, and (published posthumously) *The Story of a Cricket Picture* (the well-known Kent v. Sussex engraving published by Mason). He was also the author of several books and pamphlets on the game in Sussex which will prove most valuable when the history of that county's cricket comes to be written. He was known as "The Cricketologist", a title conferred on him by the late G. R. Sims.

TAYLOR, Charles James, who died in August, 1960, aged 79, played as a fast-medium bowler for Staffordshire and in a few matches for Warwickshire in 1908 and 1909.

TAYLOR, Claude Hilary, who died on January 27, 1966, aged 61, achieved fame in 1923 when he became the first Freshman in history to hit a century in the University match. From 1918 to 1922 he was in the XI at Westminster, rendering splendid service as a solid, stylish batsman with an eminently straight bat and as a leg-break and googly bowler. In his last season at school, when *Wisden* said of him that he had "strong claims to be considered the best all-round school cricketer of the year," he headed the batting averages at 47.00 and was top of the bowling with 41 wickets for 12.73 runs each. Going up to Oxford, he got his Blue in 1923 and, with an innings of 109, bore a big part in the overthrow of Cambridge by an innings and 227 runs. He played in the University matches of the following three seasons without achieving anything like the same success. First playing for them in 1922 when at school, Taylor assisted Leicestershire until 1927, putting together four three-figure scores, the highest of which was 123 against Hampshire at Southampton in 1924—the only century obtained for the county that summer. After the Second World War, he appeared for Buckinghamshire. He was a master at Eton for many years and joint-author with D. H. Macindoe, another Oxonian and Eton master, of *Cricket Dialogue*.

TAYLOR, Dr. Clifford John, F.R.C.S., L.S.A., who died at Chatham after a long illness on November 10, 1952, aged 76, played in a few matches for Gloucestershire at the end of last century. He liked to relate how, in 1899, when he dismissed K. S. Ranjitsinhji in a match against Sussex, the famous batsman called to him: "Well bowled, young 'un!" After qualifying at Edinburgh University, Taylor practised medicine in London and Chelmsford before going to Chatham in 1910. In the First World War he served with the R.A.M.C. in Egypt and Palestine.

TAYLOR, Dan, who was born in Durban on September 22, 1852, died in October, 1927, aged 75. He was a great worker for the game in Natal, and a good all-round cricketer. He played against more than one English team, and in 1889–90 captained the Natal side which toured Cape Colony. Mr. H. W. Taylor, who has captained South Africa, is one of his sons.

TAYLOR, Donald Dougald, died on December 5, 1980, aged 57. Playing for Auckland from 1946 to 1961, he appeared three times for New Zealand in Tests, against England in 1946–47, against West Indies at Wellington in 1955–56, when he made 43 and 77, and in the final match of that series, which produced New Zealand's first Test victory. However, he is best remembered for his opening partnerships of 220 and 286 with Ben Sutcliffe for Auckland against Canterbury in 1948–49, the only instance of two players putting up 200 in each innings of a first-class match. Taylor's own share was 99 and 143. After this he was perhaps unlucky not to be picked for the tour of England in 1949. Instead, he came over and qualified for Warwickshire, but though he played some useful innings for them, notably 90 not out in as many minutes against Nottinghamshire at Trent Bridge in 1951, he could never command a regular place. He returned to New Zealand after the season of 1953. A neat, attractive, stroke-playing batsman, in all first-class cricket he scored 3,734 runs with an average of 23.63.

TAYLOR, Edmund Juskin, died on December 25, 1936, and was buried on the 82nd anniversary of his birthday, December 31. When playing for Rugby against Marlborough at Lord's in 1871 he was described as "a capital batsman; an active and excellent fieldsman, generally taking cover point or long stop." In 1876 he averaged 16 for Gloucestershire and appeared occasionally in the very strong team of those days when W. G. Grace was in his prime.

TAYLOR, Edward Fairfax, who was long actively identified with the Oatlands Park C.C., died in February, 1902. He was born in London, July 10, 1845, and was therefore in his 57th year at the time of his death. He was educated at Marlborough, and was for the long period of 37 years a clerk in the House of Lords. He appeared twice for Surrey— against Middlesex, at the Oval in 1865, and against the M.C.C., at the same ground two years later. In the former match he scored one and 15, and took six wickets for 87 runs, bowling C. F. Buller for 0 in the first innings.

TAYLOR, Frank, died on August 16, 1936, aged 81. Born at Rochdale on May 4, 1855, he played for Clifton College, scoring 98 not out against Cheltenham in 1872 and 60 in the same engagement next season, when he made 33 not out against M.C.C. at Lord's, the game being left drawn when Clifton wanted 12 runs for victory with three wickets in hand. For Gloucestershire that season he scored 41 runs in three matches and then played County Cricket for Lancashire, his total runs for 74 innings being 1,326, average nearly 20. 6ft. 2in. in height, he was a free hitter with good style and a smart fieldsman, usually at long slip and long on.

TAYLOR, F. H., who died on December 6, 1963, aged 73, played as an amateur in a few matches for Derbyshire between 1908 and 1911. He was brother of W. T. Taylor, secretary to the County C.C. for over 50 years.

TAYLOR, Col. Francis Pitt Stewart, C.M.G., R.A.S.C., who was born on June 15, 1869, died at East Cowes on December 22, 1924. He was in the Marlborough XI of 1887, when he was described as "a useful wicketkeeper and liable to get runs." He played against both Cheltenham and Rugby. In the First World War he gained the Cordon of the White Eagle of Serbia and Officer of the Crown of Italy. His C.M.G. was received in 1917, and he retired from the Army in 1919.

TAYLOR, Herbert Wilfred, who died in Cape Town on February 8, 1973, aged 83, was one of South Africa's foremost batsmen. In a career extending from 1909 to 1935, he scored 13,105 runs in first-class cricket at an average of 41.87 and hit 30 centuries. Coached by George Cox, the Sussex bowler, when a boy at Michaelhouse School, Durban, "Herbie" Taylor developed at an early age. Strong in defence and a master of back-play, he possessed a variety of polished strokes which earned him 42 caps for South Africa and the position of captain of his country in 1913 at the age of 24. He was also captain against Australia in 1921 and against England in 1922 and 1924. On the last occasion, though meeting with small success in the Test matches, he headed the South African averages with 1,925 runs, including four centuries, average 41.84.

He obtained seven three-figure scores in Test cricket, all of them against England, but only one of them in England when he made 121 at the Oval in 1929 and he and H. G. Deane established a record for the South African fourth wicket by adding 214. In all Tests he registered 2,936 runs, average 40.77, his highest innings being 176 at Johannesburg in 1922–23. He met with great success in Currie Cup fixtures, in which he scored 3,226 runs in 58 innings at an average of 58.65 and reached 12 centuries, the largest of which was 250 not out for Natal against Transvaal at Johannesburg in 1912–13.

Almost to the end of his days, "Herbie" after his retirement spent Sunday mornings coaching schoolboys. His opinions were highly respected and his criticisms of players, from boys to men of international class, greatly valued. He lived close to the famous Newlands ground.

During the First World War he served in the Royal Field Artillery and the Royal Flying Corps—forerunner of the Royal Air Force—and was awarded the Military Cross. In the early days after the end of hostilities he played Rugby football as a three-quarter for Blackheath.

TAYLOR, John, who was born at Pudsey on April 2, 1850, died at Boston Spa on May 27, 1924. A steady, useful batsman and a good field, he played in nine matches for Yorkshire in 1880 and 1881, scoring 107 runs with an average of 8.91.

TAYLOR, John Edward, who was born at Kennington on April 9, 1824, and died in Farnborough Hospital, Kent, on July 13, 1929, aged 105, saw the first game ever played at the Oval—in 1845. His wife died at the age of 103 after 68 years of married life.

TAYLOR, John Morris, who died in a Sydney hospital following a heart attack on May 12, 1971, aged 75, was a polished batsman and a brilliant fieldsman at cover point who played in 20 Test matches for Australia between 1920 and 1926—18 against England and two in South Africa in 1921-22. He toured England with the 1921 and 1926 Australian teams, exceeding 1,000 runs on each tour, and he was a member of the Australian Imperial Forces side in England in 1919. After proving an outstanding boy cricketer at Newington College, Sydney, he served with an artillery unit in the First World War while still in his teens. He hit 108 against A. E. R. Gilligan's team in the first Test at Sydney in 1924–25, he and A. A. Mailey adding 127 runs together, which remains a record for the last wicket for Australia in a Test with England. In 21 matches for New South Wales in the Sheffield Shield, he scored 1,299 runs, highest innings 180, average 39.36. He was elected a life member of the New South Wales Cricket Association.

TAYLOR, Malcolm L., died in hospital at Wimborne on March 14, 1978, after a short illness, aged 73. Making his first appearance for Lancashire in 1924, he was by 1926 arousing high hopes. The county's batting at that time was immensely powerful, but for the most part desperately dull and Lancashire supporters looked back wistfully to the days of MacLaren, J. T. Tyldesley and Spooner. It was to their school rather than that of his contemporaries that Taylor belonged. A left-hander, he was a beautiful stylist with a wide range of strokes, which he delighted in using, and he had been instructed by his coach, J. T. Tyldesley, that he ought never to allow a fast bowler to bowl to him without a man out straight. It will be remembered that as late as 1904 in the Badminton volume on cricket, when Tyldes-ley was in his prime, the plan of a field set for a fast bowler shows a man by the screen. But though he did fairly well and was for a season or two a regular member of the side, Taylor never fulfilled his promise. He never acquired the soundness in defence necessary to support his attacking powers and moreover towards the end of his time he took to batting in spectacles. His highest score and his only century was 107 not out against Oxford in 1930. At the end of 1931 he left the county and went as coach to Canford, where he learnt tennis and taught that as well as cricket and remained until 1969. From 1934 to 1948 he made many runs for Dorset. He was a man who everywhere won the affection and respect of those with whom he came in contact.

TAYLOR, Reginald Marshall, D.F.C., who died in Johannesburg in January 1984, aged 74, played regularly for Essex between 1931 and 1939. A forcing right-hand batsman with plenty of strokes, and a slow left-arm bowler, he was also a good slip fielder. On his day his chinamen and googlies were effective; when it was not his day the hook shot, which he played compulsively, was often his undoing. Returning to Essex in 1946, after war service with Bomber Command, he shared with D. R. Wilcox in a stand of 263 for Essex's eighth wicket against Warwickshire, turning an impending follow-on into an innings victory. Wilcox made 134 and Taylor 142. Soon afterwards he emigrated to South Africa, where he became captain of the Wanderers Club in Johannesburg. In all first-class matches he scored 6,755 runs (average 20.60) and took 92 wickets (average 31.88). Of his five hundreds the highest was 193 against Sussex at Colchester in 1938. At Taunton in 1946 he took seven for 99 in Somerset's first innings, his best analysis.

TAYLOR, Tom Lancelot, who died on March 16, 1960, aged 81, was president of Yorkshire from 1948 until the time of his death. He played for Cambridge from 1898 to 1900, being captain in the last year. In the 1898 University match he scored 70 and 15, followed with two and 52 not out the next season and in 1900 hit 74 and 29 not out. For Yorkshire between 1899 and 1906, he registered 3,951 runs, including eight centuries, average 35.27. He also played hockey for Cambridge for four seasons, being captain in one of them, and as a lawn tennis player won, with Sidney Watson, the Yorkshire doubles championship in 1922 and 1923 and, with Miss Willans, the mixed doubles title in

1924. In 1901, Taylor was one of *Wisden's* Five Cricketers of the Year.

TAYLOR, William Henry, who was associated for many years with the management of Lord's Hotel, died at St. John's Wood on September 30, 1911, aged 55. He was the author of *History of Kilburn Cricket*, and was a great lover and keen student of the game.

TAYLOR, Lieut.-Col. William Herbert, who died on May 26, 1959, aged 72, played for Worcestershire from 1909 to 1922. He captained the county in 1914 and again in 1919 when Worcestershire took no part in the Championship competition. Over 6ft. tall, "Bill" Taylor scored 1,778 runs, average 11.62, and with fast bowling took 160 wickets, average 35.83. He was a member of the county committee at the time of his death. For many years he was joint Master of the Croome Hunt.

TAYLOR, William Thomas, who died at Breadsall on August 17, 1976, in his 92nd year, was the oldest surviving Derbyshire player at his death, having first appeared in 1905 and again in 1906 and 1910. He was better known as secretary of the Derbyshire C.C., serving from August 4, 1908, until December 31, 1959—a period of 51 years and 149 days, thus exceeding that of the previous longest-serving county secretary, A. J. Lancaster of Kent, by 17 months.

When appointed, the Derbyshire Cricket Guide described him as "An enthusiastic worker of a firm but courteous disposition who is likely to prove a successful official, combining the advantages of a good business training with an intimate knowledge of cricket and cricketers"—a forecast which proved to be entirely correct. He saw the club through many vicissitudes, but no problem was too great for him.

In his early years Will Taylor frequently travelled with the XI to away matches, acting as scorer and substitute. He served in the First-World War, reaching the rank of captain before he was badly wounded. In the middle '20s he was offered the Lancashire secretaryship, but Derbyshire was always his county. Had Guy Jackson been able to lead the M.C.C. side to South Africa in 1927–28 he would have been the manager. After retiring in 1959 he was appointed to the committee, and was hon. secretary from 1962 to 1972 when he finally left the scene, though his interest was as keen as ever. Few men have done so much for cricket.

TEAPE, Charles Ashley, who was born at Blackheath in 1844, died in London on August 1, 1925, aged 81. He was a member of the Eton XI of 1863, playing against both Harrow and Winchester, being described then as "A difficult bowler on his day, and an improving bat. No field." He was tried for Oxford University but did not receive his Blue, and in 1872 he played for both Middlesex (v. Surrey at Prince's) and the Gentlemen of Kent. He was brother of the Etonian, Mr. A. S. Teape, the Oxford Blue of 1863–65.

TEESDALE, Hugh, who died on March 31, 1971, aged 85, was in the Winchester XI in 1904 and 1905 and gained his Blue at Oxford in 1908 when, though suffering from a badly damaged thumb, he helped with a defensive innings to enable the Dark Blues to beat Cambridge by two wickets. As an opening batsman of marked soundness, he played two specially noteworthy innings for the University in matches with the Gentlemen of England. In the game at Oxford he scored 108, he and T. Bowring (228) sharing a stand of 338 for the first wicket, and at Eastbourne he hit 149 of a partnership of 237 with the Hon. C. N. Bruce, later Lord Aberdare. In 1906 and 1908 Teesdale made a few appearances for Surrey.

TENNANT, Hector Norman, who was born at Hobart Town, in Tasmania, on April 6, 1842, died at 2, Harewood Place, Hanover Square, W., on April 16, 1904. He was educated at Merchiston Castle and Loretto, and was chiefly identified with the M.C.C. and I Zingari. On a few occasions he assisted Lancashire. He was a useful batsman, and in the Canterbury Week of 1870 made a score of 61 for I Zingari against the Gentlemen of Kent. Like his two younger brothers, Messrs. W. M. and J. T. Tennant, he was a fine sprint runner. At the time of his death he was secretary to the Empire Theatre in London. Height 5 ft. 9¾ in.; weight 11 st. 8 lb.

TENNYSON, the Third Baron (Lionel Hallam Tennyson), who died at Bexhill-on-Sea on June 6, 1951, aged 61, was a grandson of the poet and succeeded his father in the title in 1928. Intimately identified with Hampshire cricket from 1913 to 1936, he captained the county team for 14 years from 1919 onwards. During his career he scored 16,828 runs, average 23.63, including 19 centuries. His highest innings was 217 against the West Indies at Southampton in 1928, when, after the fall of five Hampshire wickets for 88, he and J. Newman (118) shared in a partnership of 311.

While never a really dependable batsman, he was, at his best, a splendid hitter and represented in a striking way the spirit of adventure on the cricket field. He knew no fear, and the more desperate the position the more likely was he to accomplish something brilliant. Gregory and McDonald, the famous Australian fast bowlers who frightened so many of our professional batsmen in 1921, held no terrors for him. He scored 74 not out in the second innings of the Test match at Lord's that year and was chosen to succeed J. W. H. T. Douglas as captain of England in the three remaining contests with Australia. At Leeds, while fielding in the first Test of this series, he damaged his hand badly enough to have justified him in forgoing his innings. That course made no appeal to him. Wearing a basket guard, he duly went in to bat and, though suffering great pain with every contact of bat and ball, faced Gregory and McDonald in such plucky and resourceful fashion that he made 63 and 36. Altogether he played nine times for England, appearing in all five Tests when touring South Africa with J. W. H. T. Douglas's side in 1913–14. He also took several teams to India, the West Indies and South Africa.

Born on November 7, 1889, Tennyson went to Eton and, as a fast bowler, gained a place in the XI in 1907 and 1908. Three years later he entered the Army as a subaltern in the Coldstream Guards, transferring 12 months later to the Rifle Brigade, with whom he served in the First World War, being three times wounded and twice Mentioned in Dispatches. By the time he began to play for Hampshire his powers as a bowler had largely deserted him. On the other hand, he developed as a batsman, and in the summer of 1913 he and Lieut. C. H. Abercrombie, who lost his life in the Battle of Jutland, scored so well that the achievements of the two young men went a long way to make up for the loss of the services of C. B. Fry. On his first appearance in first-class cricket, for M.C.C. against Oxford University at Lord's, Tennyson scored 110 in the second innings, and he hit centuries against Essex at Leyton and Nottinghamshire at Trent Bridge. When County Cricket was resumed in 1919, he followed E. M. Sprot as Hampshire captain and, although his batting remained an uncertain quantity, he gave many a fine display of free hitting. Such power did he put into his strokes that on one occasion at Southampton he drove a ball from Fairservice, of Kent, over the pavilion into an adjoining garden, a

distance of almost 140 yd. He gave another example of fierce hitting when, against Gloucestershire on the same ground in 1927, he scored 102 not out in 55 minutes.

Under his inspiring leadership, Hampshire accomplished some remarkable performances, the most notable being that in the match with Warwickshire at Birmingham in 1922. Then Hampshire, after being dismissed for 15, followed-on, put together a total of 521 and gained an extraordinary victory by 155 runs. Later in the same season, in a game against Yorkshire on a most difficult pitch at Bradford, where the average score was less than nine, he went in first and knocked up 51 out of 64, a fearless display which decided the issue.

His funeral took place during the first Test match between England and South Africa at Trent Bridge, and play was stopped for a brief period as a tribute to his memory.

TERRY, The Rev. Francis W., who was born at Wells, Somerset, in 1863, died at Mimico, Ontario, on October 5, 1936. In 1882 at Taunton, he scored 22 and 77 not out for Somerset against M.C.C. He played in the Oxford Freshmen's match in 1881, and for Merton College made many centuries but failed to get his Blue. Going to Canada, he played several times against United States and in 1895 scored 111 in the representative match. During 1892, he scored 1,509 runs in all matches which stood as a Canadian record until 1935. He accomplished an extraordinary performance at London, Ontario, on July 4, 1895, when playing for Ontario Hospital against Forest Club, he scored 130 not out in a total of 149. There were six extras, one score of eight, nine men making five runs between them. Mr. Terry hit 27 fours in this wonderful display. He also took two wickets for 18 runs, with his right-hand medium-pace bowling, stumped one man and caught another—altogether enjoying a large share in a victory by an innings and 45 runs. Mr. George W. Harvey, the scorer in this match, supplied these details.

THACKRAY, Richard, who was killed in an accident at a mine near Johannesburg on May 18, 1944, aged 38, played several times for Griqualand West in the Currie Cup tournament of 1926–27 and against the M.C.C. team during the following season.

THAIN, Caryl, who died on September 24, 1969, aged 74, was the then president of Surrey County C.C. A former honorary treasurer, he had served on the committee for 40 years.

He played in one match for Surrey in 1923, against Glamorgan at Cardiff.

THAYER, Harry Chapman, who died at Haverford on August 3, 1936, aged 63, was one of five brothers who played in the Merion Club First XI. Between 1882 and 1917, he scored 5,500 runs for the club, with an average of 21. He appeared against several touring teams and in 1897, by scoring 35 and 44, he helped materially in beating P. F. Warner's side by six wickets. He played for United States against Canada, visited Bermuda, and in 1897 came to England with the Gentlemen of Philadelphia, his highest innings being 59 at the Oval against the full strength of Surrey. A famous college football player, he was full-back in the All-America team of 1892.

THEOBALD, Canon the Rev. Charles, born on July 4, 1831, died at Chichester on January 27, 1930, in his 99th year. A good bat and smart field at cover-point and long-leg, he was in the Winchester XI of 1848, playing at Lord's against both Harrow and Eton. In the following season, when he was possibly the side's best batsman, he was kept out of the game by an injured foot. He did not obtain his Blue for Oxford for, being one of 16 children, the expense of joining the Magdalen Club, membership of which was then considered almost essential to obtain such distinction, could not be afforded. Canon Theobald lived to become the oldest Wykehamist and the oldest public school cricketer.

THEWLIS, Herbert, born on August 31, 1865, died at Lascelles Hall on November 22, 1920. In 1888 he played occasionally for Yorkshire, scoring 78 runs with an average of 11.14. In League cricket he made many large scores, playing successfully with Holbeck Eagley in the Bolton league, and finally with his old club, Lascelles Hall, in the Huddersfield league.

THEWLIS, John (Yorkshire), born at Kirkheaton, January 30, 1828, died at Manchester in December, 1899. *Scores and Biographies* (vii–273) says: "A good and steady batsman, also an excellent long-stop. He broke his leg in his own house at Lascelles Hall, May 17, 1869, and was unable to play that season, but resumed the game with success in 1870." Yorkshire v. Gloucestershire at Sheffield, in July, 1875, was his benefit match. Height 5 ft. 7 in., weight 10 st. to 10 st. 7 lb. He and Luke Greenwood in a match for Lascelles Hall v. Todmorden, at

Todmorden, once added over 200 runs for the last wicket. Possibly his greatest triumph was at the Oval in 1868 in the Surrey v. Yorkshire match when he scored 103, and his nephew, Ephraim Lockwood (whose first appearance it was for the county), 91, the two scoring 176 for the first wicket. Eleven Thewlises once played on a side in a match at Chickenley. John Thewlis only appeared once for the Players v. Gentlemen—at the Oval in 1868—when he scored, four and six, being 40 years of age at the time.

THOMAS, Albert E., who died in Kidderminster Hospital on March 21, 1965, aged 71, accomplished much good work as a professional medium-paced bowler for Northamptonshire between 1919 and 1933. Accurate in length, he made the ball swing either way and during his career he dismissed 832 batsmen for 25.52 runs each. A useful lower-order batsman, he scored 4,835 runs, average 13.31, his highest innings being 84 against Worcestershire at Worcester in 1930, and he held 116 catches. He attracted attention in 1920 when, at Bradford, he obtained nine wickets for 30 runs in the Yorkshire first innings, conceding only six runs while taking the last seven. Among a number of other good analyses were seven wickets for 44 in the first Lancashire innings at Old Trafford in 1928; 10 for 54 in the match with Glamorgan at Kettering in 1924 and 10 for 67 against the same opponents at Northampton the following year, and 10 for 61 against Sussex at Kettering in 1930. He also performed the hat-trick at the expense of Leicestershire at Northampton in 1927. His most successful summer was that of 1928 when in all matches he took 101 wickets for 25.36 runs apiece and represented Players v. Gentlemen at Lord's. He was chosen for the Players at Folkestone in the same season and again in 1930, when he hit 74 not out and he and G. S. Boyes (95 not out) put on 140 in an unbroken last-wicket partnership. Thomas lost some of his effectiveness during his last two seasons with the county, following an operation on the elbow of his bowling arm, but for some years afterwards he did well in Birmingham League cricket.

THOMAS, Frank E., born on April 5, 1877, died at Bristol on May 20, 1924, aged 47. He could cut and hit well, was a useful medium-paced right-handed bowler and a good field. As a member of the Clifton College XIs of 1894 and 1895—he was captain the latter year—he was contemporary with C. L. Townsend and John Daniell. With the bat he did comparatively little, but in his second year he headed the bowling averages with a record of 27 wickets for 13.09 runs each. Between 1901 and 1906 he assisted Gloucestershire, but not regularly, his best season being his last, when he scored 138 v. Nottinghamshire at Trent Bridge and 111 v. Sussex at Cheltenham. In 1903 he had made 116 against Lancashire at Bristol.

THOMAS, Percy Francis, who wrote about cricket during the last 40 years as "H.P.T." and "Hippo-Pott-Thomas," died at Cricklewood on October 13, 1931. Born on May 27, 1866, at Woolwich, he was the author of several booklets, the best known being a series on *Early Cricket*, which already rank as classics. He was a learned student of cricket lore and a man of much humour.

THOMPSON, George Joseph, died on March 3, 1943, at Bristol in his 67th year. To him largely belonged the credit of raising Northamptonshire to the first class in 1905, and he was recognised as the greatest player the county ever produced. After playing in the Wellingborough Grammar School XI, Thompson, when 17 years of age, appeared first for the county in 1895, before Northamptonshire ranked in the second-class competition. When that advance was made Thompson in 1901 and again in 1902 took over 100 wickets and in batting averaged 36. In 1903, with 92 wickets for 10 runs apiece and 33 as batting average, he played a big part in bringing Northamptonshire to the head of the competition. He attained to greater heights in the following summer with 99 wickets for 11 runs each and a batting average of 42. Having won 10 matches out of 12 and drawing the others, Northamptonshire in the ensuing winter were received into the first-class circle and in 1905 entered the senior county competition. Prior to that memorable occurrence Thompson, in 1900, put together 125 for Players against Gentlemen at Scarborough, and in the winter of 1902–03 was a member of the team captained by Lord Hawke but led on the field by P. F. Warner. In New Zealand the side won all 18 matches, Thompson playing a notable part in the success with 177 wickets for six runs apiece. At Adelaide in South Australia's first innings he took nine wickets for 85. Two years later, when one of Lord Brackley's side in the West Indies, Thompson batted consistently and took 126 wickets at 10 runs each. So good was his form that he played for England against Australia at Birmingham in 1909, but he bowled only four

overs in a low-scoring match, George Hirst and Blythe sharing the 20 Australian wickets. Next winter he went to South Africa with the team captained by H. D. G. Leveson Gower, and with 33.37 was second to Hobbs in the batting averages, besides taking 23 wickets in the five Test matches, of which three were lost, the rubber going to South Africa. Throughout the tour Thompson showed consistent form without doing anything exceptional.

In the course of a great career which really ended with the First World War, during which he was wounded, Thompson, in about 10 full seasons of first-class cricket, took 1,437 wickets for less than 20 runs apiece and scored 11,398 runs, average 22. Eight times between 1905 and 1913 over 100 wickets fell to him, 126 in 1905, 136 in 1906, 127 in 1907, and 163 at 14 runs each in 1909 being his best achievements. He continued to play occasionally until 1922, and his full record in first-class cricket showed 1,595 wickets at 18.80 and 12,015 runs, average 22.0, while he held 226 catches. In 1906 and 1910 he did the "double." Right-hand both with bat and ball, he bowled well above medium pace, commanded an accurate length, brought the ball off the ground with plenty of life and spin, and when helped at all by the pitch got up very awkwardly, as the Gentlemen realised at the Oval in 1905, six wickets in the second innings falling to him for 59 runs. As a batsman he possessed strong defence and considerable hitting power. After retiring from first-class cricket Thompson became coach in turn at Rugby School, Clifton College and Stowe School.

THOMPSON, Henry, hon. secretary of Incogniti, died on August 8, 1941, at Sevenoaks, after an operation, aged 54. He played occasionally for Leicestershire in the seasons 1908, 1909, and 1910. Beginning with 15 and 72—the highest score in his side's second innings against Derbyshire—he suggested success in championship cricket, but he failed to maintain anything like this form.

THOMPSON, Herbert S., an old Sydney Grammar School boy, and a great lover of the game, died on March 2, 1907, in his 53rd year. He collapsed suddenly whilst walking towards the pavilion on the conclusion of his innings in a match at Concord Park, and died two hours later.

THOMPSON, Nat., one of the most famous players in the early days of Australian cricket, died on September 2, 1896, in his 59th year. Nat. Thompson had a long and brilliant career, playing for New South Wales in inter-Colonial matches for fully 20 years. He was a fine bat and wicket-keeper, and if the Australians had paid their first visit to England a little earlier than 1878, he would no doubt have been included in the team. He was indeed asked to become a member of Gregory's XI, but was not able to undertake the trip.

THOMS, Robert. For some time before he passed away on June 10, 1903, there had been such very bad accounts of Bob Thoms's health that no one was at all surprised when the announcement of his death appeared in the papers. It had been known for some months there was no chance of his recovery, but less than two months before his death he had so much to say about cricket and his mind was still so bright that it did not seem as if the end were quite so near. He broke up very rapidly at the finish, and died after one final rally. In him there has gone a remarkable and interesting personality. No one had a more thorough knowledge of cricket, or could speak with greater authority about all the leading players of the last 60 years. Ambitious of being a public cricketer himself, he came out at Lord's when Fuller Pilch was the best bat in England, and it was his privilege to watch the triumphs of George Parr, Hayward, Carpenter, Richard Daft, Jupp, Tom Humphrey, E. M. Grace, W. G. Grace, and all the other great run-getters down to Ranjitsinhji and C. B. Fry. Even in the season of 1902 he saw Victor Trumper bat at the Hastings Festival, and complimented him on his splendid innings of 120 against the South of England. Thoms always looked at cricket with the eyes of a young man, and was quite free from the fault—so common among men who live to a great age—of thinking that all the good things belonged to the past. This freshness of mind prevented his talk about cricket from ever becoming prosy or flat. In his last years as an umpire—he gave up after the season of 1900—he was just as enthusiastic in his praise of fine work with bat or ball as he would have been 40 years ago. To Middlesex cricket, with which he was closely associated from the formation of the County Club in the '60s, he was always devoted, and nothing cheered him up more in his last illness than visits from Mr. V. E. Walker and Mr. A. J. Webbe. He was never tired of referring to the Middlesex XI in the days when V. E. Walker was captain, and was very proud of the fact that he stood umpire in every first-class match played on the old Cattle Market ground at Islington. Right up to the end he had a singularly retentive memory, and when in congenial company he would tell numberless stories about the Walkers, C. F. Buller, and A. W. T. Daniel. In those distant days, of course, the modern system had not been adopted, and each county always appointed its own umpire.

The Graces, as cricketers, had no more fervent admirer than Thoms, and he was fond of saying that if W. G. Grace had not been such a marvellous bat he would have been the best slow bowler in England, his head work being so remarkable and his command of length so perfect. Of E. M. Grace's all-round capabilities, too, and especially his fielding at point, Thoms would never weary of talking. Among modern bowlers he, in common with most good judges, placed Spofforth first, while fully recognising the great qualities of Palmer, Turner and George Lohmann. As to the bowlers of his younger days, he thought very highly indeed of Hillyer and John Wisden. Curiously enough the present writer never heard him speak of Buttress, the famous but unfortunately too thirsty leg-breaker, who has been described by more than one distinguished cricketer of the past as absolutely the most difficult bowler England ever produced. Buttress's sovereign gift was his power of bowling a deadly leg-break with a real control over his pitch. He got so much spin on the ball that, according to Mr. Henry Perkins, the man who tried to play him without gloves on was almost certain to have the skin knocked off his knuckles.

In dress, manner and appearance Thoms belonged essentially to the '60s, looking exactly like the photographs of some of the players of those days. He had a keen sense of humour, and told his cricket stories in a short, crisp way peculiarly his own. It was to be regretted that he did not, during the throwing controversy, bring the weight of his authority to bear on the side of fair bowling, but the traditions of his youth were too strong for him, and he always shrank from the task. However, in a quiet way he made his influence felt, plainly telling the leading amateurs that if they wanted to rid the game of an evil they all admitted they must act for themselves and not throw the whole onus on the umpires. Moreover, he was the means of some audacious young throwers dropping out of County Cricket, his kindly method being to get them employment in other directions. Though cricket was the main interest of his life Thoms was a good all-round sportsman, taking as a young man a keen delight in foot racing and the prize ring. He was a good runner himself, and could, so it is said, do 100 yd. in 10.5 sec. Of anything he took up he was bound to be a good judge, his perception of excellence amounting to an absolute gift. He often talked about putting into book form his 60 years' experience of the cricket field, but whether he ever seriously commenced the task one cannot say.

THOMSON, Arthur Alexander, who died in hospital near Lord's on June 2, 1968, aged 74, was one of the best-known and best-loved writers on cricket. "A.A." or "Tommy" was born at Harrogate on April 7, 1894, and educated at Harrogate Grammar School and King's College, London. His early thoughts of entering the scholastic profession were interrupted by the First World War, when he joined the West Yorkshire Regiment and served in France and Mesopotamia. His early boyhood in Yorkshire had formed the subject of his brilliant autobiographical novel, *The Exquisite Burden* (1935), re-issued in 1963. He wrote nearly 60 books in all, including plays, novels, verse, humour and travel books, and in 1953, with *Cricket My Pleasure*, there began his long series of cricket books in which his buoyant philosophy of the game, with all its comedy and character, shone through in rich prose and mellow phrases. There then followed *Cricket My Happiness* (1954), *Pavilioned in Splendour* (1956), *The Great Cricketer* (a biography of Dr. W.G. Grace) (1957 and 1968), *Odd Men In* (1958), *Hirst and Rhodes* (1959), *Cricket Bouquet* (1961), *Cricket: The Golden Ages* (1961), *Hutton and Washbrook* (1963), *Cricket: The Great Captains* (1965), *Cricket: The Wars of the Roses* (1967), and *Cricketers of My Times* (1967). He also contributed some delightful articles to *Wisden*. Probably no cricket author since Sir Neville Cardus was in his prime had a closer following. Cricket, he once declared, gave him more unalloyed pleasure over a longer period than any single thing.

He had an enormous sense of fun and a perpetual twinkle in his eye, and when, in 1958, he started writing cricket for *The Times*, and then rugger in the winter, his presence in press-boxes throughout the country could guarantee a warm fund of stories, all told with an expressive fervour, that made up for any deficiencies on the field. As an after-dinner speaker at cricket gatherings he was one of the most original

and popular of the last decade, and since 1963 he had been president of the Cricket Society. During the Second World War he worked first at the Air Ministry and then as a lecturer with the Ministry of Information. In the 1966 Birthday Honours List, he was awarded the M.B.E. for services to sports writing.

THOMSON, Ernest Alfred Charles, secretary of the Club Cricket Conference, which he founded in 1915, died in a nursing home on April 11, 1941, after a long illness which kept him away from the annual meeting for the first time for 26 years. From 35 clubs at its inception, the Conference grew into the greatest cricket organisation in the world. Mr. Thomson assisted in founding the National Playing Fields Association in 1925 and for two years acted as hon. secretary of the Open Spaces Bill Committee. Born at Woodford, Essex, in 1872, he was grandson of John William Thomson, who planned the Crystal Palace grounds and reorganised Kew Gardens. At the age of nine Thomson played cricket on Mitcham Green and appeared for such clubs as Townley Park and Heathfield. Besides cricket—his great love—he played Association football, hockey, lawn tennis, bowls and golf, and he also found time for athletics, cycle racing and boxing. A journalist by profession, he edited *Hockey World*.

THORNTON, Albert J., a brother of R.T. and W.A. Thornton, but in no way related to C.I. Thornton, died in London on June 14, 1931, aged 75. A good and free hitter and a useful lob bowler, he played a good deal of cricket for Devon (in 1874), Gentlemen of Hampshire, Sussex and Kent. Playing for Sussex in 1880, and in the following season, Mr. Thornton afterwards appeared in the Kent XI and between 1884 and 1891 he took part in 23 matches, his highest innings being 137 against Sussex at Hove in 1887. He went to America with E.J. Sanders' team in 1885 and 10 years later was a member of the side that visited Portugal under T. Westray.

THORNTON, Charles Inglis, born at Llanwarne, Herefordshire, on March 20, 1850, died suddenly in London on December 10, 1929, aged 79. With his death there passed a great personality in the history of cricket. He had long given up active participation in the game, but in his day he was one of the biggest—if not actually the mightiest of all time—of hitters. To the present generation he was only a name, but in the memories of those who, like Lord Harris and Mr. A.J.

Webbe, were his contemporaries, his famous deeds must remain firmly implanted. He went to Eton in 1861, to the Rev. G. R. Dupuis's house, and was in the XI in 1866, 1867, and 1868, being captain in his last year. He also played in Oppidan and Mixed Wall and Field XIs, won the school Fives and was Keeper in 1867 and 1868, and won the Double Raquets and Putting the Weight in 1868, and Throwing the Cricket Ball in 1867. Going up to Trinity College, Cambridge, he played in the XI four times from 1869, being captain in 1872, the year that Cambridge, thanks to a fine innings of 130 by W. Yardley and some effective bowling of W. N. Powys, beat Oxford in an innings. Thornton was on the winning side for Cambridge three times out of four. The year that Oxford won was in 1871, when S. E. Butler took all 10 wickets in the first innings of Cambridge. Thornton also played from 1867 onwards for Kent, and a little for Middlesex in the middle '70s. To him more than to anybody else was due the success of the annual Scarborough Festival. He was largely instrumental in starting it, and although he had long given up cricket he never lost his interest in the famous Week, even until last season. To mark the esteem in which he was held and to recognise his services to the Scarborough Festival, which had then been in existence a quarter of a century, he was, in 1894, presented with a silver loving-cup subscribed for by the members of the Scarborough C.C. He received another presentation in 1921 and was also given the freedom of the borough.

Like many others of his day, Thornton always regarded cricket more as a game than as a serious business. Adventurous by nature, he felt that in cricket he could indulge this spirit to the full. Whenever he was captain he liked going in first. Individual in style, he jumped quickly to the ball in making his magnificent drives, and in this respect differed from the famous Australian hitters, Bonnor, McDonnell and Lyons, all of whom were fast-footed. In his brilliant career he put together many scores of 100 in remarkable time, and the length of some of his drives were enormous. It is on record, for instance, that in the North v. South match at Canterbury in 1871, he hit a ball from W. M. Rose a strictly measured 152 yd., while at the practice nets at Hove the same year he sent it 168 yd. 2 ft. and 162 yd. Playing against Harrow at Lord's in 1868, he drove the ball over the old pavilion, and at the Oval he accomplished the same feat, while it is noted that at Canterbury he hit V. E. Walker out of the ground each ball of an over. The over

then consisted of four balls.

A good story is told of him when, visiting the neighbourhood of Oakham School and going to the cricket ground, he was asked to play as a substitute. Nobody at the time knew who he was, but they had reason to before the day was out, for in the second innings he scored 188 out of 216 in two hours, sending the ball out of the ground 13 times. Hitting the ball out of the ground was a feat he always took a delight in accomplishing. On one occasion at Scarborough, off the bowling of A. G. Steel, he drove a ball over a four-storeyed house into the adjoining street, called Trafalgar Square.

To slow bowlers Thornton was a terror, and on James Southerton, in particular, he was generally very severe. He often threatened to hit Southerton out of the Oval, and at length succeeded. As the ball sailed over the fence Thornton dropped his bat, put his hands on his hips, and laughed uproariously, saying, "I told you I would do it, Jim." Southerton shook his head, and replied, "Quite right, Mr. Thornton, but I shall get you out." And get him out he did. As a matter of fact he hit Southerton twice over the pavilion, once over the scoring-box, and also for a two in a four-ball over, and, altogether, he hit out of three sides of the Oval. Once, in a match between Kent and Notts, Thornton hit a ball back to Shaw, who, although knocked off his feet, held it and thus brought off a marvellous catch. In the power and consistency of his driving, Thornton was by himself constantly bringing off hits that have become more or less historic in the game. As showing the difference between cricket in his days and now, he took part, in six seasons for Kent, in only 18 matches. Still, in 34 innings he got three 100s. Probably his finest exhibitions in the latter part of his career were a couple of 100s at Scarborough for the Gentlemen of England against I Zingari. In the game of 1866, he made 107 out of 133 in 70 minutes in 29 hits—eight sixes, 12 fours, two twos and seven singles. A. G. Steel was among the bowlers on that occasion. Thornton stood 6 ft. and had rather sloping shoulders, so that he was admirably proportioned for the batting style he loved.

In business Thornton was in the timber trade for 35 years, and retired in 1912. A keen motorist, he was also extremely fond of travelling, having been all through Japan, Siberia, and Russia. When the War broke out he was in Berlin, and was very nearly caught. In his book, *East and West and Home Again*, he described a trip round the world. He had been a member of the M.C.C. and of the Orleans club for 50 years. He married Fanny, daughter of Mr. Charles Dowell, of Croydon, but left no children.

THORNTON, Dr. George, who died in London on January 31, 1939, occasionally played for Yorkshire and Middlesex before going to South Africa. Born at Skipton, Yorkshire, on December 24, 1867, he was educated at Skipton Grammar School, and took his degree at Edinburgh University. When the South African War broke out, Dr. Thornton was one of the first medical men to volunteer. He was made head of the Government Hospital at Pretoria, and spent nine years in South Africa. During this time he appeared for Transvaal, and for South Africa at Johannesburg in the first match Australia played in South Africa in October, 1902, when Joe Darling's team were on the way home from England.

Left-handed, with both bat and ball, he was at his best in 1895 when for Middlesex he averaged 31 and took 23 wickets. He bowled with deadly effect against Gloucestershire at Lord's. The fifth man tried, he bowled W. G. Grace, who had scored 169, and in the last innings he took all five wickets that fell at a cost of 20—making nine for 72 in the match. Strangely enough in the corresponding fixture next season he gave by far his best batting display—161—and Middlesex won by an innings and 77 runs. He was not wanted as a bowler.

THORNTON, James Richard, born on January 11, 1861, died at Burgess Hill on March 1, 1916. He appeared in one match for Sussex in 1881, and again in 1883, making 67 runs with an average of 16.75 and taking one wicket for 30 runs.

THORNTON, John, who died at Myrtoon, Camperdown, on December 15, 1919, aged 85, played for Victoria against New South Wales at Sydney in 1858–59 and in Melbourne a year later. He was a good long-stop. He joined the Melbourne C.C. in 1858 and was the oldest member of the club.

THORNTON, Richard Thornton ("Parson"), born at Folkestone on March 28, 1853, died at Eastbourne on May 30, 1928, aged 75. A brother of Messrs. A. J. and W. A. Thornton, he was a free-hitting bat and could bowl both slow-round and lobs. With the latter he was very successful indeed in club games. His earliest experience of County Cricket was for Devon, and for

Dorset and Wiltshire sides, but in 1881 he played in the first of his 46 matches for Kent. With 79 against Surrey at the Oval in 1885 as his highest score, he made 1,495 runs for the last-mentioned team with an average of 21.66. When he visited America with Mr. E. J. Sanders' team in 1885 he played an innings of 107 against Philadelphia, and when a Philadelphian side came to England four years later he scored 111 at their expense for M.C.C. at Lord's. Among his many large innings in club games were 201 not out for Sidmouth, 207 for Blue Mantles, and 200 not out for Mote Park. In 1895 he went to Portugal with Mr. T. Westray's team. In a match at Southborough he once made hits for seven and eight off consecutive balls from Mr. A. F. J. Ford. He and D. D. Pontifex, both of whom wore spectacles, made 222 together for the first wicket of Incogniti v. Gentlemen of Sussex at Hove in 1885. Whilst at Oxford Mr. Thornton obtained his Blue for Association football, but not for cricket.

THORNTON, Walter Alfred, brother of Messrs. R. T. and A. J. Thornton, was born in London on February 23, 1858, and died at Kidderminster on February 2, 1915. He has been described as "A fast but erratic bowler, a hard hitter and a sure field." In 1874 and next two seasons he was in the Winchester XI, in 1876 making 31 not out and 22, in totals of 74 and 67, v. Eton: he was the highest scorer in each innings and in his first carried his bat through. In 1879 and three following years he was in the Oxford XI, but in his four matches v. Cambridge made only 86 runs in eight innings, and took but five wickets for 126 runs. He also played for Devonshire, and at Southampton in 1880 played an innings of 122 not out. He once hit Mr. David Buchanan for 20 runs (six, four, six, four) off a four-ball over. In strictly first-class cricket his highest score was 70 for Oxford University v. M.C.C. and Ground, at Oxford, in 1879.

THORPE, Charles, who died on May 5, 1953, aged 70, played as a batsman in several matches for Northamptonshire shortly before the First World War.

THURLOW, Hugh Motley, who died on December 3, 1975, aged 72, came into prominence by taking six for 60 for Queensland against Victoria in December 1929; in the course of doing this he broke Woodfull's finger and put him out of action for the rest of the season. After this he did useful work for several seasons for his State as a fast bowler and in 1932 was picked for the fourth Test against South Africa, a match in which O'Reilly made his first appearance for Australia. Thurlow, who opened the bowling, failed to get a wicket and did not play in a Test match again.

TILLARD, Charles, who was in the Repton XI from 1866 to 1870, played twice for Cambridge in matches which Oxford won, and who appeared occasionally for Norfolk from 1868 and Surrey from 1874, died at Bathford, near Bath, on March 10, 1944, aged nearly 93. Bowling fast round-arm and very straight, as noted in *Scores and Biographies*, he did some remarkable performances. In 1870 for Repton he took 17 Uppingham wickets—15 bowled; and in 1873 at Lord's, when Cambridge lost by three wickets, he accounted for all seven Oxford batsmen who fell in the last innings, bowling six and catching the other. In a match at Kennington Oval in June 1874 between University players and other Gentlemen of England not Blues he clean bowled the most notable pair of opening batsmen of that time—W. G. Grace and A. N. Hornby. He was a hard hitter and fielded well, generally at cover-point. Born at Wimbledon, on April 18, 1851, Charles Tillard was the oldest surviving University Blue except F. A. MacKinnon, who played in the 1870 match. After leaving Cambridge he became a master at Cheltenham College.

TILLEY, Eric Warrington, died at Leicester on December 1, 1977, aged 63. Born in Derbyshire, he had a few trials for Leicestershire as a fast-medium bowler in 1946 but, after dismissing Alderman with his first ball in first-class cricket, accomplished little.

TIMMS, John Edward, who died at his home in Buckingham on May 18, 1980, aged 73, rendered splendid service to Northamptonshire from 1925 to 1949. When he retired he had scored more runs for the county than any other batsman, though he never quite took the place in the cricket world that many had expected. He lacked consistency, and apart from one appearance in a Test trial, in 1932, he remained purely a county player. A member of the Wellingborough XI in 1924, he played originally as an amateur but turned professional in 1927. Short and slightly built, he was a natural cricketer, quick on his feet and severe on the short ball. At the start of his career he was apt to be lackadaisical in the field, but spurred on by his captains he

developed into a fine cover point, a not unworthy successor to the great Fanny Walden. At slow-medium, Timms was a rather expensive change bowler, who had no great belief in his own ability, so that when, in 1938, he took six for 18 v. Worcestershire and nearly brought about his county's first win in the Championship since 1935, it caused some surprise. In all he scored 20,384 runs for Northamptonshire with an average of 25.07, his highest innings being 213 v. Worcestershire at Stourbridge in 1934. His 149 wickets cost 44.42 each. Later he combined a post as professional and greenkeeper at the Buckingham Golf Club with coaching cricket at Bloxham School.

TINDALL, E., born March 31, 1851, died at Tempe, Sydney, N.S.W., on January 15, 1926, aged 74. He was a useful batsman and a good right-hand medium-paced bowler with a high delivery. Among his best figures for New South Wales were six for 31 v. Victoria in 1877–78 and six for 89 v. Lord Harris's team a year later—in each case at Sydney. Against Victoria at Melbourne in 1879–80 he played an innings of 52.

TINDALL, The Rev. Henry Charles Lenox, a great runner and well-known cricketer, died on June 11, 1940, at Peasmarsh, Sussex, aged 77. Although a good all-round cricketer— useful bat with sound style, fast bowler and dashing fieldsman—Tindall failed to get his Blue at Cambridge at a time when University cricket was very strong. He appeared occasionally for Kent without doing much, but was prominent in Sussex club cricket. Among many good performances, especially for South Saxons, he took all 10 wickets at a cost of only 25 runs for Hastings Rovers against Rye in 1906. In the Hastings Festival of 1894 he appeared for Gentlemen against Players. He set up a quarter-mile record in 1889 by winning the Amateur Championship in 48¼ seconds, and also won the half-mile in one minute 56 seconds. In 1886 he won the 100 yd. and quarter-mile in the University sports, and for several years was prominent at all distances from 100 to 1,000 yd. At the private schools at Hurst Court, Ore, and High Croft he found many cricketers of promise. An originator of the Rye Golf Club, he became chairman of the committee.

TINDALL, Sidney Maguire, born at Margate on February 18, 1867, died in Sydney Hospital on September 19, 1922, of a fractured skull sustained in falling from a moving tram near the Hotel Australia. Like his brother, the Rev. H. C. L. Tindall, he was educated at Dane House School, Margate. He was a free and plucky batsman and a fine outfield, covering much ground. His first match for Lancashire was in 1894, and one of his best, though not his highest, innings for the side was 49, played at a most critical time, in the tie-match with Surrey at the Oval in 1894. Subsequently he played several times for the London County C.C. Going to Australia in 1911, he succeeded Major B. J. Wardill as secretary of the Melbourne C.C., a position he held only for a short time. At one time he was one of the best hockey players in England.

TINLEY, Robert Crispin, who died on December 11, 1900, at Burton-on-Trent, was only a name to the present race of players, but he held a very high place among the cricketers of a past generation. He was a very fair bat, often by free hitting getting a few runs when they were most wanted, and as a field at point he divided honours with Robert Carpenter in the days when the annual match between the All-England and United All-England XIs was the event of the season at Lord's. His fame, however, rested not upon his fielding or batting, but upon his remarkable skill as a lob bowler. His success during a number of seasons for the All-England XI against local XXIIs was extraordinary, and he took an immense number of wickets when he went out to Australia in 1863 with George Parr's famous team. Alfred Shaw, who came out as a colt for Notts while Tinley was still a member of the county XI, thinks that he never saw so good a lob bowler; but Canon McCormick, whose experience goes back further, holds a different opinion, ranking Tinley below V. E. Walker and one or two others.

Lob bowling is so little cultivated in these days that since the decline of Walter Humphreys we have had no one of any class except Mr. Jephson, but in Tinley's time things were different, and cricketers not very far advanced in middle age can recall the deeds not only of V. E. Walker, but of the Rev. E. T. Drake, the late Mr. T. C. Goodrich of the Free Foresters, and, to come down a little later, Mr. W. M. Rose and Mr. W. B. Money. Prior to the rise of Walter Humphreys, perhaps the last really good lob bowler was Mr. A. W. Ridley. Tinley made his first appearance at Lord's for Notts against England in 1853. Born on October 25, 1830, he was in his 71st year at the time of his death. He had, we believe, been for a considerable time an invalid. Tinley played

his first match for Notts, being then a lad of 16, against an England XI at Nottingham in August, 1847, the match being for T. Barker's benefit and his last against Surrey at Nottingham in July, 1869. He made his first appearance for the Players against the Gentlemen at Lord's in 1858, and appeared for the Players for the last time at Lord's in 1864. In this latter match he did not have an opportunity of bowling, Willsher and Tarrant being unchanged through both innings of the Gentlemen. He only took part in three Gentlemen and Players matches, scoring 31 runs in four innings, and taking five wickets for 46 runs. Several pages could be filled with details of his performances against XXIIs, but it must suffice to say that he is said to have taken in all matches—first-class and against odds—303 wickets in 1860, 186 in 1861, and 351 in 1862. A North v. South match was played for his benefit at Nottingham in June, 1875, the profit accruing to him being just over £406. Originally he was a very fast round-arm bowler, but after playing for some few seasons he took to the lob bowling which he carried to such perfection.

TINSLEY, A., who like his brother, H. J. Tinsley, played for both Yorkshire and Lancashire, died during 1933. Born at Malton, Yorkshire, on March 13, 1867, he appeared for Yorkshire in one match during 1887 but afterwards turned out for Lancashire, whom he assisted from 1890 to 1895. He finished sixth in the batting list of 1892 with an aggregate of 403 in county games. In the match with Sussex at Manchester in 1894, he and Briggs added 97 in an hour; the following season he batted admirably in making 65 against Nottinghamshire at Nottingham. Tinsley assisted Staffordshire some years afterwards.

TITCHMARSH, Charles Harold, born at Royston, Hertfordshire, on February 18, 1881, died, following a stroke, at his native place, on May 23, 1930, in his 50th year. Educated at the Nonconformist College at Bishop's Stortford, he was in the XI for two years. Although short of stature, he possessed a neat style of batting and strong defence, having, moreover, most of the scoring strokes at his command. He made most of his runs in front of the wicket. He was a remarkably consistent batsman who, if he had played for a first-class county, would assuredly have acquired a great reputation. He was also much above the average as a wicket-keeper. He played for the Gentlemen against the Players at the Oval in 1921 and

1925, but these were almost the only two big games in which he took part. Hertfordshire was his first county and he remained faithful to it all through his cricket life. He first played for Hertfordshire in 1906 and had an average of 44 that year. He had a bad season in 1909, and in 17 innings scored only 141 runs, but after that there were no more failures and in 1914 he had an average of 67. When cricket was resumed after the War he continued to do great things for Hertfordshire and in his last season, 1929, had an average of 51 with a highest innings of 169. In all matches in 1913 he actually scored 4,016 runs and included among his scores that year were 21 centuries. In 1922–23 he formed one of the party that toured Australasia under the leadership of A. C. MacLaren. During his career he made well over 100 three-figure scores, the first of them in 1897, at the age of 16.

TITCHMARSH, Valentine Adolphus, one of the best umpires of recent years, died of locomotor ataxy at St. Albans on October 11, 1907. He was born at Royston, in Cambridgeshire, on February 14, 1853, but was always associated with Hertfordshire cricket. *Scores and Biographies* (xiv–82) described him as "An excellent batsman, and a successful fast round-armed bowler, while in the field he takes no particular place ... He is a left-handed batsman, but bowls and fields right. Beginning his cricket as an amateur, he subsequently, commencing in 1880, appeared as a professional." About that time Hertfordshire possessed some very good players in William Hearn, Titchmarsh, Hughes, Pearce, and Messrs. C. and H. Pigg, and in 1879 beat Sussex in the only two matches ever arranged with that county. Titchmarsh had a great deal to do with the two successes mentioned, for at Hitchin he took 10 wickets for 35 runs and at Brighton 13 for 60. Two years before, in the match with Essex at Hitchin, he had taken all 10 wickets in the first innings for 33 runs and five in the second for 44. For a few years he was engaged as a bowler at Oxford, but in 1885 became a member of the ground staff at Lord's and remained so until his death. His all-round cricket was always of great use in club and ground matches. His most notable performance was in June, 1892, when on successive days he took all 10 wickets in an innings against Sherborne School, and scored 101 not out against Rossall. In 1906 the proceeds of the Middlesex v. Somerset match at Lord's were set apart as a benefit for him by the M.C.C. in order to mark the club's appreciation of his services for over 20 years, but although between 10,000 and 12,000 spectators were present on the opening day the match scarcely proved so attractive as had been hoped and anticipated.

TITLEY, Uel Addison, who died on November 11, 1973, aged 67, appeared for the XI while at Rugby, but did not get his colours. He went up to Cambridge and for some years afterwards held an appointment in Brazil. He wrote on cricket for some years for *The Times*, but was better known as the Rugby correspondent for that newspaper. His excellent style and occasional flashes of humour earned him great respect in the football world, but his biggest achievement was the compilation of the *History of the Rugby Football Union* published in their centenary year, 1971. His unusual first name was given by his father, Samuel Titley, who said: "Everybody calls me Sam. The boy can have the other half."

TOBIN, W. A., who played for Victoria against New South Wales at Melbourne, in 1880–81, died in Australia in the middle of January, 1904. He was educated at Stonyhurst, and was a good all-round player. In 1878, whilst still at school, he played an innings of 49 for Eighteen of Keighley and District against the first Australian team.

TOLHURST, Edward Keith, who died at Melbourne in 1982, aged 86, played first-class cricket for Victoria as a batsman in 1930–31, his best score being 63 against G. C. Grant's touring West Indians. In 1930 he toured Canada and the U.S.A. in a team captained by Arthur Mailey and which included Bradman. He was closely connected with the Melbourne C.C., finally as an honorary life member.

TOLLEY, Robert, who rendered good service to Nottinghamshire cricket in the '70s, died at his residence, Ruislip, Mapperley, on January 2, 1901. *Scores and Biographies* (x–6) sums him up as follows: "He is a good batsman, bowls fast and slow round-armed." His first match for Nottinghamshire was against Gloucestershire, at Clifton, in 1871, and his last against Gloucestershire, at Trent Bridge, in 1878. His highest scores for his county were 54 v. Gloucestershire, at Nottingham, in 1871, and 53 in the corresponding fixture of 1877. He was born at Nottingham on March 14, 1849, and was, therefore, in his 52nd year at the time of his death.

TOMKINS, Eric Feltham, who died on July 20, 1980, had a few trials for Northamptonshire as a batsman in 1920 and 1921, his highest score being 50 not out against Leicestershire at Leicester in 1920. He was better known as a hard-working half-back in the strong Northampton Town football team before and after the First World War. By profession he was a schoolmaster at Rushden.

TOMKINSON, Sir Geoffrey Stewart, who died on February 8, 1963, aged 81, played in two matches for Worcestershire early in the century and became president of the County C.C. in 1956. In the Winchester XI of 1900, he went up to King's College, Cambridge, for whom he rowed and played cricket, Rugby and Association football; but after leaving the University he found the claims of the family carpet-making business so strong that he played little more cricket until he was past 40. Then he appeared regularly for Kidderminster, once scoring 200 not out inside two hours in a Birmingham league game. A founder of Kidderminster R.F.C., he was captain from 1921 to 1924 and played in a match at the age of 63 when a side was a man short.

TOMLIN, William, who was born at Leicester on September 16, 1867, died of cancer at his native place on May 11, 1910, at the early age of 42. He was one of the best batsmen who ever appeared for Leicestershire, but his career as a county player was rather short, extending only from 1887 to 1899. His best seasons were 1894 and 1895, when he headed the county's batting averages. His finest innings was probably his 106 not out against Richardson's bowling in the match with Surrey at the Oval in 1895, when his batting enabled Leicestershire to gain a victory which some effective bowling by Woodcock had rendered possible. His highest score for the county was 140 against M.C.C. and Ground at Lord's in 1894.

TOMLINSON, William James Vincent, who died at Elsing, Norfolk, on May 16, 1984, aged 82, had a fine all-round record as captain of Felsted in 1920, heading both the batting and bowling averages, and being given a good trial for Derbyshire in August took five for 53 against Sussex at Hove in his first match, thereby raising hopes which he never quite fulfilled. In the next two seasons he frequently made useful scores for the county, notably 64 and 44 against Worcestershire at Worcester in 1922, but his bowling

was disappointing. Nor did he make much mark at Cambridge. However, in 1923, nine for 68 in the Seniors' match secured him a good trial and seven for 34 in the two innings against Sussex at Hove, coupled with an innings of 51, won him his Blue. A match or two for Derbyshire that year and the next concluded his first-class career. He was a medium-paced right-arm bowler with an easy action and a hard-hitting batsman. He became a well-known prep school master.

TOMPKIN, Maurice, who died in a Leicester hospital on September 27, 1956, aged 37, was one of the best and most popular cricketers ever to play for Leicestershire, for whom he was senior professional. He underwent an internal operation a week before his death. A tall, polished batsman specially strong in driving, Tompkin was also a first-rate deep fieldsman. George Geary discovered him in junior cricket and he first played for the county in 1938, since when he hit in all first-class matches 19,927 runs, average 31.83.

In every season except the first after the War, during which he served in the Royal Air Force, he completed 1,000 runs and in 1955 enjoyed the best summer of his career, scoring 2,190 runs, average 37.11, including an innings of 115 for the Players at Lord's. In the same match C. H. Palmer, his county captain, hit 154 for the Gentlemen. That form earned Tompkin a place in the M.C.C. "A" team which toured Pakistan the following winter, but on his return he complained of pains in the back and abdomen and, thus handicapped, he made only 635 runs last season.

Of his 31 centuries, 29 were obtained for Leicestershire, the highest being 186 against Pakistan at Leicester in 1954. To him also belonged the distinction, against Middlesex at Leicester in 1952, of reaching a century in each innings of a match, a feat achieved by only four other Leicestershire players. He received as his benefit the game with Lancashire at Leicester in 1954. Not a ball was bowled, but fortunately Tompkin had insured the match. An Association footballer of class, he appeared as inside- or outside-right for Leicester City, Bury and Huddersfield Town.

TONGE, Lieut.-Col. William Corrie, D.S.O., died on May 2, 1943, after a long illness, aged 81. A very good batsman, he captained Cheltenham College in his third season, 1880, in the XI, and was tried for Gloucestershire while still at school. Two years afterwards he played for Sandhurst, and from 1895 he appeared for Norfolk, being an officer in the county regiment.

TOOGOOD, Thomas, who died in September, 1953, aged 81, was in his youth among the best slow-medium spin bowlers in the Bristol district. For a long time grounds-man and professional to Clifton C.C., he was for 12 years assistant coach at Clifton College and between 1906 and 1914 made a few appearances for Gloucestershire.

TOONE, Sir Frederick Charles, who was born on June 25, 1868, and died at Harrogate on June 10, 1930, at the age of 62, achieved no distinction as a player but as an organiser he stood supreme. His love for the game in its highest tradition—of which he was the stoutest upholder—was immense. A master of detail, he thought of everything, and the fact that he went three times to Australia as manager of the teams sent out by M.C.C. since the War clearly showed the extent to which he enjoyed the confidence of the ruling body of the game. To manage a touring side with success calls for various strong traits of character. Fred Toone had them all in abundance. Firm in principle, particularly where the interests of the men in his charge were concerned, he was courteous in manner, easy of address, and invariably tactful and obliging. Small wonder, therefore, that wherever he went in Australia he was always popular. He was secretary of the Leicestershire County C.C. from 1897 to 1902 and of Yorkshire from 1903 until his death. The professionals of the latter county who had benefits during his regime all had cause to remember him, his work in making these successful being really wonderful. That of the late Roy Kilner produced £4,016. The Yorkshire County C.C. Year Book, which he edited, was a model compilation of its kind. In his younger days he was a very good runner, and for some seasons he played Rugby football regularly for the Leicester club. On his return to England from the last Australian tour he received the honour of knighthood from the King in recognition of his great work in helping to promote the best relations between the Commonwealth and the Mother Country. In January, 1927, he was presented with a testimonial of £3,500. To the last issue of *Wisden* he contributed an article on "Australian Tours and their Management."

TOONE, John William, born at Halifax, in Yorkshire, in 1872, died in New York City on September 1, 1927. As a fast bowler he

was for some years a very prominent figure in the game in Jamaica, and in that island's match against Mr. R. S. Lucas's team in 1894–95 he took 13 wickets for 80 runs.

TOPPIN, Charles, born at Penrith, Cumberland, on August 9, 1864, died at Great Malvern on June 8, 1928. He was in the Sedbergh XI for six years, 1878 to 1883 inclusive, being captain his last season. Playing first for his University in 1885, Toppin helped Cambridge to win by seven wickets, his bowling in the first innings, when he dismissed seven men at a cost of 51 runs, giving Cambridge an advantage that was never lost. He was on the losing side in the next two years, Key and W. Rashleigh getting 100s for Oxford in 1886, and Lord George Scott, the last choice, hitting up 100 and scoring 66 when Oxford wanted 148 to win in 1887. For St. John's College v. Emmanuel College in May, 1884, he played an innings of 232. Subsequently he took part in County Cricket for Cumberland and Worcestershire, and in 1885 and 1886 appeared for the Gentlemen against the Players at the Oval. A fast right-hand bowler, Toppin owed his success mainly to keeping on the wicket, and, when finding a length, his straight bowling required a lot of stopping. When playing for Cumberland, the county of his birth, he took 16 wickets for 48 runs in a match against Northumberland at Carlisle in July, 1885, and three years later for the M.C.C. he took 14 Radnorshire wickets, his analysis in the first innings being remarkable—eight for 18. He was a sure catch at slip, and a smart fieldsman at cover-point or in the long field. In 1899 he took part in a short tour in Holland. On leaving Cambridge, Mr. Toppin went as a master to Malvern College, where he remained for 42 years. He helped to develop many of the fine cricketers who played for the College, and became famous in more important cricket. Among those who passed through his hands at Malvern were C. J. Burnup, the brothers Day, the Fosters, P. H. Latham, G. H. Simpson-Hayward, W. H. B. Evans, W. S. Bird, F. T. Mann, D. J. Knight, N. E. Partridge, G. B. Legge and E. R. T. Holmes.

TOPPIN, John Fallowfield Townsend, who died suddenly on November 22, 1965, aged 65, was a member of the Winchester XI in 1917 and 1918, taking five wickets for 38 runs against Eton in the second year. He played in one match for Worcestershire in 1920. He was the elder brother of C. G. Toppin, who also assisted Worcestershire, and nephew of

S. H. and A. P. Day, of Kent. Their father was C. Toppin, who "made" Malvern cricket.

TORRENS, William Matt, who died on February 18, 1931, was in the Harrow XI of 1886 and 1887. Wicket-keeping was his forte. During the season of 1890 he played in four games for Kent. He was born at Hayes on October 19, 1869.

TOSETTI, Gilbert, born on August 1, 1879, died at Eldoret, Ussin Gishu Plateau, British East Africa, on April 16, 1923. He will be recalled as a former member of the Essex team, for which his best performance was an innings of 132 not out, made in three and three-quarter hours, against Lancashire at Manchester in 1902. He was brother of the late Major Douglas Tosetti, who fell in action in March, 1918, whilst serving with the Royal Berkshire Regiment.

TOULMIN, Evelyn Murraugh O'Brien, who died in Paris on January 7, 1945, aged 66, played a little for Essex after leaving King's School, Oxford. CORRECTION. The reference to Mr. E. M. O'Brien Toulmin, *Wisden*, 1946, should have read King's School, Canterbury, where he was the best all-round player before going to Magdalen College, Oxford. He did little in Freshmen's and Trial matches at the University.

TOWELL, Edgar Freemantle, who died on June 2, 1972, aged 70, played as an amateur all-rounder for Northamptonshire from 1923 to 1934. A left-hander, he scored 1,199 runs and, with medium to fast bowling, took 101 wickets.

TOWNLEY, Reginald Colin, who died in Hobart on May 3, 1982, aged 76, was a well-known Tasmanian cricketer who later became a member of the Tasmanian House of Assembly and, for six years, Leader of the Opposition. A right-handed batsman and leg-spin bowler, he played 16 times for Tasmania between 1926–27 and 1935–36, scoring only 175 runs but taking 36 wickets at an average of 35.42. His last match for Tasmania was against South Australia, when in 20 overs he took three for 169, including the wicket of Bradman, caught and bowled for 369.

TOWNSEND, Charles Lucas, who died at his home at Stockton-on-Tees on October 17, 1958, aged 81, was a right-arm slow bowler and left-handed batsman for Gloucestershire between 1893 and 1909. It is not too much to say that towards the close of the 1895 season, when a youth of 18, he was the most remarkable amateur bowler since A. G. Steel carried all before him in 1878. Such was the amount of spin that Townsend imparted to the ball that even the most experienced of batsmen found themselves in difficulties with his leg-breaks. In Gloucestershire matches with Nottinghamshire in 1895 he took at Trent Bridge 16 wickets for 122 runs and at Cheltenham 13 for 110. Against Yorkshire at Cheltenham he obtained 15 wickets, and against Sussex at Bristol, Surrey at Clifton and Somerset at Taunton 12 wickets fell to him on each occasion. Though he played in only one game until late in July, he dismissed 131 batsmen at a cost of 13 runs each.

During the next two years, without quite maintaining his bowling skill, he took 113 wickets in 1896 and 92 in 1897 and materially enhanced his reputation as a batsman. In 1898 he reached the height of his career, for after winning the match with Middlesex at Lord's by his bowling, he played a series of splendid innings. As soon as he left off making 100s, he bowled almost as finely as in that memorable 1895 season. Altogether that year he hit 1,270 runs, average 34, and took 145 wickets, average 20.

The summer of 1899 saw him one of the great batsmen of the day, for he scored 2,440 runs, averaged 51, put together nine centuries—including one for Gentlemen v. Players—and was chosen for England against Australia at Lord's and the Oval. He had then lost some of his talent as a bowler; yet he obtained 101 wickets that year. In the autumn he visited Australia with a team led by K. S. Ranjitsinhji and in 1900 he registered 1,662 runs. Never afterwards could he afford much time for cricket, his practice as a solicitor and a subsequent appointment as Official Receiver at Stockton demanding so much of his attention. All the same, he enjoyed a memorable triumph in 1909 when scoring 129 out of 169 in two hours against the Australians at Cheltenham.

A son of Frank Townsend, a leading member of the Gloucestershire team when the Graces were at their zenith, Charles Townsend gained a place in the Clifton College XI at the age of 15. The next season, 1893, he took nine wickets out of 10 against Cheltenham and a year later against Cheltenham performed the hat-trick, taking 12 wickets in all, and played an innings of 55. He made his first appearance for Gloucestershire before he was 17. His highest innings were 224 not out v. Essex in 1899 and 214 against Worcestershire in 1906. Although he had only half a dozen full seasons, he hit 9,390 runs in first-class cricket, average 30, and took 725 wickets, average 24.

Townsend figured in a notable hat-trick against Somerset at Cheltenham in 1893 when W. H. Brain stumped three men of successive balls sent down by him. It remains the only instance of its kind in first-class cricket.

TOWNSEND, Frank, died in King's College Hospital after an operation, on December 25, 1920. Mr. Townsend's death—he had long been in failing health—brought back recollections of the great days of Gloucestershire cricket. There has never been anything quite like those old matches at Clifton and Cheltenham. Many fine players helped the Graces to take Gloucestershire to the top of the tree and Frank Townsend was one of the best of them—a fine, free-hitting bat, an untiring field, and on occasions a useful bowler with his lobs. An original member of the County Club he took part in the first county match, against Surrey at Bristol, in 1870, and he went on playing for over 20 seasons. During all that time he kept up his form so well that so late as 1888 he scored 66 and 92 against the Australians at Clifton. His highest score was 136 against Sussex at Cheltenham in 1873. He was as keen and enthusiastic a cricketer as the Graces themselves, and devoted to W. G. Not long after his retirement he had the satisfaction of seeing his son, Charles Townsend, do great things for Gloucestershire, but, except in 1895, not for anything like such a successful side as the old XI. It is worth remembering that, beginning in 1870, Gloucestershire did not lose a match at home until the first Australian team beat them at Clifton in 1878. Frank Townsend was picked by the Surrey committee for Gentlemen against Players at the Oval in 1874 and in his first innings made 59—the top score for his side. Naturally anxious to do himself justice he played with unusual caution against some splendid bowling by Allen Hill—then at his very best. Frank Townsend was born on October 17, 1847, being a year and three months older than W. G. Grace.—S.H.P.

TOWNSHEND, The Rev. Canon William, died on July 19, 1923, at Kirkby Mallory Rectory. Mr. Townshend was a batsman who scarcely fulfilled the high hopes entertained of him in his schooldays. At Rossall he was, with good reason, regarded as the best bat

the school had produced barring F. W. Wright. In 1867 when Rossall met the Old Rossalians he caused quite a sensation by getting two separate 100s—a feat never accomplished before except by W. Lambert in 1817—his scores being 100 and 146. For all that he was on the beaten side, the Old Rossalians—for whom F. W. Wright, the captain, made 123 not out and 36—winning by three wickets. At Oxford Mr. Townshend was in the XI in 1870, 1871, and 1872, taking part in three of the most memorable of the University matches at Lord's. His scores were 0 and one; 22 and six; and 20 and 0. Three times in six innings he was beaten by the tremendous pace of W. N. Powys' bowling. Mr. Townshend was in the Rossall XI four years—1865 to 1868, being captain in 1867 and 1868. His great year for the school was 1867 when, according to *Scores and Biographies*, he made 1,179 runs in 20 innings, three of them not out, giving an average of 69. In succession he scored 100 and 146 v. Old Rossalians, 104 v. Bury, 81 v. Eccles, and 136 v. Cheshire. He assisted Herefordshire between 1878 and 1881, and Leicestershire in 1883 and 1884. He was born at Sehore, Bhopal, in central India, on November 16, 1849.—S.H.P.

TOZER, Dr. C. J., who died in Sydney on December 21, 1920, was one of the best of the younger generation of Australian batsmen. For New South Wales Colts against those of Victoria in 1912–13 he scored 83, 80 and 63, and in the same season made 78 not out v. Queensland and 54 v. West Australia. In the season before his death he scored 51 and 103 for New South Wales against Queensland at Brisbane.

TRACEY, William, a slow leg-break bowler, who had played with success against English teams in Australia, died at Newcastle (N.S.W.), on October 14, 1912, at the age of 73. Against Lillywhite's side in December, 1876, he took four wickets in the first innings and six in the second.

TRAFFORD, The Hon. Charles Edmund de, captain of Leicestershire from 1890 to 1907 and a friend and contemporary of W. G. Grace, died at Sibbertost, near Market Harborough, on November 12. 1951. "C. E.," who was 87, was born at Trafford Park, Manchester, at the time when the Old Trafford ground belonged to his father, Sir Humphrey. After playing one game for Lancashire, he moved south, and assisted M.C.C. before joining Leicestershire in

1888. Altogether during his first-class career, which was extended by occasional appearances until 1920, he made nearly 10,000 runs.

TRAILL, William Frederick, who was born at Lewisham, in Kent, on January 7, 1838, died on October 3, 1905. He was educated at Merchant Taylors' School and at Oxford, and was in the latter XI in 1858 and two following years. Against Cambridge in 1860 he took 11 wickets for 53 runs—six for 35 and five for 18—but Oxford lost a low-scoring game by three wickets. He appeared on a few occasions for the Gentlemen against the Players between 1859 and 1867, and assisted Kent 11 times—in 1860, 1861, 1862, 1863, and 1866. His debut in inter-county cricket—against Sussex at Tunbridge Wells in 1860—was a very successful one, seeing that he scored 49 runs in the only innings he had, and obtained eight wickets for 68. *Scores and Biographies* (vi–48) says of him: "A capital round-armed bowler, middle-paced, with an easy delivery.... Also an excellent batsman, and fields well."

TRASK, William, died at Frome on June 24, 1949, aged 89. Learning his cricket at Sherborne where he was in the XI in 1877, he played intermittently for Somerset from 1882 to 1900. Standing nearly 6ft. and weighing 12 st. 7 lb., he was a steady batsman and reliable slow bowler. While bowling at Wells in 1879, he dislocated a knee.

TREGLOWN, Lieut.-Col. Claude Jesse Helby, M.C., died at Worthing on May 7, 1980, aged 87. He played fairly frequently for Essex from 1922 to 1928, sometimes opening the innings. His highest Championship score was 72 not out v. Kent at Tunbridge Wells in 1923. He also appeared for Norfolk and Sussex Second XI.

TREMLETT, Maurice Fletcher, died at Southampton, where he had lived since he retired from first-class cricket, on July 30, 1984, aged 61. Born at Stockport, he was living in Somerset when he joined their staff in 1938. It was not, however, until the opening match of 1947, against Middlesex at Lord's, that he got a place in the county side. His start was sensational: he took three for 47 and five for 39 and, though he batted at number 10, it was only a sensible little innings of 19 not out at the crisis that enabled his side to beat by one wicket that year's County Champions. Naturally he kept his place to the end of the season and if, admittedly in a year of high scoring, his

wickets were slightly expensive, he did much good all-round work.

However, it was his bowling that really aroused hopes. Tall and strongly built, with a good action, he could move the ball and looked as if with a bit more pace he might develop into the fast bowler for whom England was desparately looking. At the end of the season he was a member of the partly experimental side which M.C.C. sent to the West Indies, but, though he played in three of the Tests, he was a failure: he was bottom of the batting averages for the tour and his 10 wickets cost 70 runs apiece. None the less, after a good season in 1948, in which he took eight for 31 against Glamorgan at Weston-super-Mare, he went under F. G. Mann to South Africa in the following winter, but there too, apart from innings of 105 and 63 not out against Natal Country Districts, he accomplished little and did not play in the Tests. In 1949 he scored 1,000 runs for the first time and was still bowling well, but in 1950 he suddenly lost all control of the ball – the trouble had begun in South Africa in 1948–49 – and from then on was never more than a change bowler.

Nor, although in 1951 he scored over 2,000 runs, was he ever a sufficiently consistent batsman to be a candidate for England in that capacity alone. A tremendous straight driver, he was always fun to watch and continued for the rest of the decade to be an important member of the Somerset side, especially when in 1956 he became the first professional to be appointed their captain. In those days professional captains were not taken for granted, and he had his difficulties, coming in for some criticism, but he proved himself on the whole a good choice and in 1958 led them to the highest place they had ever occupied in the Championship, third. He resigned the captaincy after 1959, and after a few matches in 1960 retired to take a job with Guinness. He had a benefit in 1956. In all first-class cricket he scored 16,038 runs with an average of 25.37 and took 351 wickets at 30.63. The highest of his 16 centuries was 185 at Northampton in 1951. In recent years his son, Tim, has been a member of the Hampshire XI.

TREMLIN, Bert, who died on April 12, 1936, aged 58, played for Essex from 1900 until 1919 before retiring. He was then a useful coach and in 1923 and 1924 was on the list of first-class umpires. A medium-paced right-hand bowler, he had to wait for vacancies in the Essex XI, which included P. A. Perrin, C. McGahey, J. W. H. T. Douglas,

Buckenham, and Walter Mead, but he became a regular member of the side in 1905. Tremlin then in all matches took 99 wickets at 27.16 apiece, but not until 1914, when 36, did he show to most advantage with 101 wickets at 26 runs each, and an aggregate of 416 runs—average nearly 21. Then the War intervened.

TRENERRY, William Leo, M.C., who died on September 4, 1975, aged 82, was one of the few surviving members of the Australian Imperial Forces side of 1919. An adaptable batsman, who frequently went in first, he scored 961 runs with an average of 28.26 and a highest score of 82 against Lancashire. These figures show his consistency, but they do not show how often he came to the rescue when runs were badly needed. His leg-breaks, bowled as an occasional change, were not very successful. His first-class cricket virtually ended with this tour, but he was well known in club cricket in Sydney.

TRESAWNA, Henry, who died on May 24, 1968, aged 90, enjoyed a long and distinguished career as one of Cornwall's outstanding cricketers. He played for the county from 1898 to 1934, captaining the side from 1905 until he retired. In all he scored 6,814 runs for the county, average 23.10, and took 100 wickets at 18.25 runs apiece. A great character and a fine sportsman, he was immensely popular and got the best out of his players.

TRESTRAIL, Major Alfred Ernest Yates, D.S.O., T.D., who played for Somerset in 1905, died suddenly at New Milton, Hampshire on February 5, 1935, aged 59. He went to Amersham Hall School, and Christ's College, Cambridge. He served in the 15th Batt. Cheshire Regiment.

TREVOR, Arthur Hill, Commissioner of the Board of Control, was born at Calcutta on November 14, 1858, and died suddenly on September 27, 1924, at Elvanfoot, Lanarkshire, where he was spending his holiday. He was a sound, free-hitting batsman and a good field, taking no particular place, though often long-field or long-stop. In 1877 he was in the Winchester XI, and in the match with Eton scored 41 and 14. Obtaining his Blue for Oxford in 1880, he played against Cambridge in that year and the next, making 18 and four, 41 and 40. He commenced playing for Sussex in 1880, and on his first appearance for the county—against Kent at Hove—scored 28 and 103. Unfortunately,

but little was seen of him in first-class cricket after he left the University, and his appearances for Sussex were restricted to a dozen matches between 1880 and 1882, in which he obtained 480 runs and averaged 20.86. In 1881 he represented the Gentlemen against the Players both at Lord's and Hove. On August 4, 1882, he scored 338 for Orbans Club v. Rickling Green at Twickenham, he and the late Mr. G. F. Vernon adding 603 runs whilst together for the second wicket. Three years later he scored 203 for the Earl of Northesk's XI against the Green Jackets.

TREVOR, Major-General Francis Charles, died at the Army and Navy Club on March 26, 1914, aged 82. He was an auditor of the M.C.C. from 1895 until 1913.

TRIM, John, who died in hospital in British Guiana on November 12, 1960, aged 45, played in four Test matches for the West Indies. A right-arm fast-medium bowler, he gained his first Test match honours on the strength of a good performance for British Guiana, for whom he made his debut in 1944, against G. O. Allen's M.C.C. team in 1947–48 when at Georgetown he earned analyses of four wickets for 68 runs and five for 36. He toured India in 1948 and Australia in 1951. In all he took 18 Test wickets, average 16.16.

TRITTON, Edward William, who died at the end of November, 1901, was born in London, on August 3, 1844. Mr. Tritton was in the Eton XI in 1862 and 1863, and among a very strong group of Eton batsmen at that time had no superior, except Alfred Lubbock. In 1863 he scored 130 against Winchester, and 91 and 58 against Harrow. On leaving school he went to Oxford and played in the XI from 1864 to 1867, inclusive. It can hardly be said that he quite realised the expectations formed of him at Eton, but he was one of the best bats in the famous XIs captained by Mr. R. A. H. Mitchell in 1864 and 1865. In the latter season he played a magnificent innings of 114 for Oxford against the M.C.C. at Lord's, the club bowlers including Wootton, Grundy, Alfred Shaw, S. C. Voules and R. D. Walker. In County Cricket he assisted both Surrey and Middlesex. For many years before his death, nothing had been seen of him in the cricket field.

TROLLOPE, W. S., died in October, 1895. Born on July 31, 1854, Mr. Trollope was only in his 42nd year, and his early death was a great grief to a large circle of friends. Educated at Westminster, where he distinguished himself at cricket, Mr. Trollope made a few appearances in the Surrey XI, and without doing anything remarkable, revealed abilities as an all-round player which would have repaid cultivation had circumstances admitted of his devoting more time to first-class matches. He was closely connected with the Streatham club, and was a member of the Surrey committee.

TROTT, Albert Edwin, shot himself at his lodgings, Denbigh Road, Willesden Green, on July 30, 1914. He had been very ill for some time without hope of recovery and, finding the monotony of life in hospital intolerable, he thought a pistol shot the best way out. His death, in his 42nd year, was indeed a tragedy. At his best, Albert Trott was one of the greatest all-round men of his time. The misfortune was that he declined in skill so soon after reaching his highest point. There is nothing unkind in the statement that he ought to have had a much longer career. Born in Melbourne on February 6, 1873, he sprang into fame by reason of his splendid cricket against Mr. Stoddart's England XI in the winter of 1894–95. At that time he was the most promising young cricketer in Australia. Against the Englishmen in 11-a-side matches he scored 331 runs in nine innings and took 19 wickets. His greatest success was gained in the Test match at Adelaide in which he scored 38 and 72, both times not out, and took in the last innings of the game eight wickets for 43 runs. In the fourth Test match of the tour, played at Sydney, he scored 86 not out, but on a bad wicket his bowling was not required. It was taken for granted in this country that Albert Trott would come to England with the team captained by his brother in 1896 but, for some reason which has never been properly explained, he was not selected. Having been thus passed over by his own people, he came to England on his own account and, as everyone knows, qualified in due course for Middlesex. While qualifying for the county he played for the M.C.C., and in 1897 he had a record of 48 wickets for just over 14 runs each. In 1898 he began to play for Middlesex. Injuring his hand very badly in May, he lost a month's cricket and could not, when he started playing, do himself justice. However, when the injury had healed he lost no time in asserting himself, he and J. T. Hearne bowl-

ing in such irresistible form that in August Middlesex won eight matches out of nine and drew the other. In the whole season Trott took for Middlesex 102 wickets.

Following this good beginning, Trott went to the top of the tree, 1899 and 1900 being his greatest years. It would have been hard indeed in those two seasons to find a better all-round man. In first-class matches in 1899 he scored 1,175 runs and took 239 wickets, and in 1900 his figures came out at 1,337 runs and 211 wickets. Thanks to his bowling, his hard hitting, and brilliant fielding, and also his strong personality, he became for the time more popular at Lord's than any other professional. In those days his bowling was extraordinarily good and quite individual. Appreciably lower in delivery than most Australian bowlers, he had plenty of spin, but he depended less on break than upon an endless variety of pace. He rarely bowled two balls alike, and he could whip in his yorker at a tremendous speed. A long and very bright career seemed before him, but, unhappily, he soon began to fall off. Even in 1901, though he took 176 wickets, he was not quite the man he had been, and from that time he steadily declined. Becoming heavy and muscle-bound, he could no longer bowl the extra fast ball that had been so deadly, and batsmen ceased to fear him. In 1902–03–04 he still bowled well, but after 1904 he was only a shadow of his former self. In his benefit match against Somerset at Lord's on Whit Monday, 1907, he came out with a last flash of greatness, taking four wickets in four balls, and finishing the game by doing the hat-trick a second time in the same innings. This was a feat without precedent in first-class cricket. Trott played for Middlesex for the last time in 1910. His active career as a cricketer over, he became one of the county umpires, giving up the work early last season. His health was then so bad that he could go on no longer. One fact in Trott's career must not be forgotten. He was the only batsman who ever hit a ball over the present pavilion at Lord's. The great hit was made off Noble's bowling in a match between the M.C.C. and the Australians in 1899. Near the wicket, Trott was one of the best fieldsmen of his day, few catches that could be reached escaping his capacious hands. Appended are Trott's records in first-class cricket in England from 1898 to 1907.

Year					Runs	Average		Wickets	Average
1898	..	..	..	..	482	20.08	..	130	17.94
1899	..	..	..	..	1,175	22.03	..	239	17.09
1900	..	..	..	..	1,337	23.87	..	211	23.33

TROTT, Albert Edwin—*Continued*

Year				Runs	Average		Wickets	Average
1901	..	..	..	880	20.46	..	176	21.78
1902	..	..	..	941	19.60	..	133	21.67
1903	..	..	..	604	17.76	..	105	19.32
1904	..	..	..	747	16.97	..	108	23.82
1905	..	..	..	428	13.80	..	62	27.80
1906	..	..	..	952	25.05	..	62	25.67
1907	..	..	..	549	14.44	..	96	16.67

His 100s in first-class cricket were as follows:

101*	Lord Hawke's team v. Transvaal, at Johannesburg	.. ..	1899
164	Middlesex v. Yorkshire, at Lord's	.. ..	1899
123	Middlesex v. Sussex, at Lord's	.. ..	1899
112	Middlesex v. Gloucestershire, at Lord's	.. .. ..	1900
102	Rest v. Surrey and Sussex, at Hastings	.. .. ..	1900
112	Middlesex v. Essex, at Lord's	.. ..	1901
103	Middlesex v. Somerset, at Lord's	.. ..	1902
103	Middlesex v. Gloucestershire, at Lord's	.. .. ..	1903

Signifies not out.

Some of his best bowling feats will be found interesting:

Eight or more wickets in an innings

10 for 42	Middlesex v. Somerset, at Taunton	.. .. ..	1900
8 for 43	Australia v. England, at Adelaide	.. .. ..	1895
8 for 47	Middlesex v. Gloucestershire, at Clifton	.. ..	1900
8 for 53	M.C.C. v. Oxford University, at Lord's	..	1897
8 for 54	Middlesex v. Essex, at Lord's	.. .. ..	1901
8 for 64	C. I. Thornton's XI v. Yorkshire, at Scarborough	..	1899
8 for 83	Middlesex v. Notts, at Nottingham	.. .. ..	1898
8 for 84	An England XI v. Yorkshire, at Lord's	.. ..	1901
8 for 91	Middlesex v. Lancashire, at Lord's	.. .. ..	1899
8 for 115	Middlesex v. Sussex, at Lord's	.. .. ..	1901

Thirteen or more wickets in a match

15 for 187	Middlesex v. Sussex, at Lord's	.. .. ..	1901
13 for 88	Middlesex v. Gloucestershire, at Clifton	.. .. ..	1900
13 for 125	Middlesex v. Leicestershire, at Lord's	.. ..	1899
13 for 140	Middlesex v. Surrey, at Lord's	.. .. ..	1899
13 for 140	Middlesex v. Notts, at Lord's	.. .. ..	1901
13 for 170	M.C.C. v. Philadelphians, at Lord's	.. .. ..	1897
13 for 170	An England XI v. Yorkshire, at Lord's	.. ..	1901
13 for 178	Middlesex v. Notts, at Nottingham	.. .. ..	1898
13 for 183	C. I. Thornton's XI v. Yorkshire, at Scarborough	..	1899
13 for 213	Middlesex v. Lancashire, at Lord's	.. .. ..	1900

TROTT, Fred, a younger brother of G. H. S. and A. E. Trott, died at Glasgow in the last week of March, 1921. For a little time he was engaged at Lord's and played a few times for Middlesex Second XI, but in 1906 went to Scotland as professional to the Peebles County C.C., with whom he remained for eight years, two as professional and six as an amateur. He was a very useful all-round player. After the War he was engaged by the Clydesdale C.C. as groundsman and coach.

TROTT, George Henry ("Harry") Stevens, born August 5, 1866; died at Melbourne,

November 12, 1917. Came to England in 1888, 1890, 1893, and 1896.

Australia has produced greater cricketers than Harry Trott, but in his day he held a place in the front rank of the world's famous players. He was a first-rate bat, a fine field at point, and his leg-breaks made him a very effective change bowler. Four times he came to England—first in 1888, again in 1890 and 1893, and, finally, in 1896, when he had the honour of captaining the team. As a leader in the field he perhaps gained even more distinction than as an all-round player. Ranjitsinhji considered him a better captain than

Darling, and beyond that praise could hardly go. The personal popularity that Harry Trott enjoyed in 1896 wherever he went was remarkable. One is inclined to think that no Australian captain, before or since, was liked so much by his opponents. By sheer force of character he overcame the disadvantages involved in lack of education, and won the warm regard of men with whom, apart from the comradeship of the cricket field, he had nothing in common. In managing his team he owed much to his equable temper and innate tact. Knowing all the little weaknesses and vanities of the men under his command, he believed in a policy of kindly encouragement. Never outwardly disturbed by the state of the game, he could inspire even the most despondent with something of his own cheerfulness. He played cricket in the best possible spirit, taking victory and defeat with the same calm philosophy.

No better loser was ever seen than Harry Trott at the end of the Test match at the Oval in 1896. It was the disappointment of his life, as the result decided the rubber in England's favour, but he was full of praise for the way in which Peel and J. T. Hearne had made the most of a horribly difficult wicket. In the England match at Lord's the same season Trott played his finest innings, he and Sydney Gregory enabling Australia to make a most creditable fight in face of overwhelming odds. Against Tom Richardson's bowling on a wicket of lightning pace Trott trusted to the strength of his back play and was justified by success. His method recalled the way in which Daft and Bob Carpenter used to withstand the fastest bowling at Lord's on the much rougher wickets of the early '60s. Trott made 143 and Gregory 103, the two batsmen putting on 221 runs for the fourth wicket in Australia's second innings. Trott's play was almost flawless, but the Englishmen felt certain that Hayward caught him in the slips with his score at 61. Perhaps next to this 143 the best innings Trott ever played in this country was his 92 against England at the Oval in 1893. Trott, who had been in ill-health for some time before his death, was the elder brother of the late Albert Trott, who for many years played so brilliantly for Middlesex.—S.H.P.

G. H. S. TROTT IN FIRST-CLASS CRICKET

		BATTING						BOWLING			
	Season	Inns.	N.O.	Highest	Runs	Aver. Score		Balls	Runs	Wkts	Aver.
Aust.	1885–86	4	2	54*	97	48.50	..	414	160	7	23.85
Aust.	1886–87	11	2	29*	116	12.88	..	1,038	421	12	35.08
Aust.	1887–88	14	1	30	106	8.15	..	1,367	687	26	26.42
Eng.	1888	65	2	83	1,212	19.23	..	2,015	1,145	48	23.83
Aust.	1888–89	13	0	172	507	39.00	..	1,150	436	25	17.44
Aust.	1889–90	7	1	72	228	38.00	..	859	379	18	21.05
Eng.	1890	65	1	186	1,273	19.89	..	995	610	23	26.52
Aust.	1890–91	8	1	81	161	23.00	..	150	98	2	49.00
Aust.	1891–92	11	0	23	85	7.72	..	601	359	11	32.63
Aust.	1892–93	8	1	70*	304	43.42	..	360	179	2	89.50
Eng.	1893	59	2	145	1,437	25.21	..	1,906	1,141	60	19.01
Amer.	1893	5	0	58	117	23.40	..	200	106	5	21.20
Aust.	1893–94	8	0	54	132	16.50	..	897	395	18	21.94
Aust.	1894–95	21	1	152	630	31.50	..	1,578	806	41	19.65
Aust.	1895–96	10	0	66	306	30.60	..	630	346	7	49.42
Eng.	1896	54	5	143	1,297	26.46	..	1,699	928	44	21.09
Amer.	1896	6	0	55	90	15.00	..	398	178	11	16.18
Aust.	1896–97	8	0	104	323	40.37	..	480	285	6	47.50
Aust.	1897–98	18	0	92	463	25.72	..	1,678	803	29	27.68
Aust.	1900–01	2	0	22	39	19.50	..	242	177	8	22.12
Aust.	1903–04	10	0	59	268	26.80	..	484	306	13	23.53
Aust.	1904–05	1	0	26	26	26.00	..	48	27	0	—
Aust.	1907–08	2	0	30	34	17.00	..	198	155	5	31.00
New Zealand	1912–13	3	61	188	37.60	..	—		109	27.25	
	Totals	418	22	186	9,439	23.83	..		10,236	425	24.08

Signifies not out

Note: Only matches on even terms included in the cases of the English and American tours; in New Zealand only the matches with the provinces. Defective bowling analysis in one of these prevents completion of "Balls" column.

Serious illness practically ended Trott's career after the Australian season of 1897–98.

TROUGHTON, Lieut.-Col. Lionel Holmes Wood, a notable figure in Kent cricket circles, died on August 31, 1933. He was born at Seaford, Sussex, on May 17, 1879. A member of the Dulwich College XI in 1897, he played for Kent Second XI in 1900, but did not appear for the county side until 1907. His two most successful seasons for Kent were 1914, when he scored 776 runs and hit up 104 against Oxford University, and 1921 when he obtained 761 runs. He followed Mr. E. W. Dillon as captain of Kent in 1914 and held the leadership until 1923 when he succeeded the late Tom Pawley as general manager of the county club—a post he held at the time of his death. Although never a very prominent batsman, Mr. Troughton often batted with resolution and was a capable captain. Accompanying the M.C.C. side to the Argentine under the captaincy of Mr. A. C. Mac-Laren in 1911–12 he played an innings of 112 not out v. Combined Camps at Buenos Aires.

TROUGHTON, Medhurst Albert, who died at Kensington on January 1, 1912, was a fine batsman and field and a useful slow underhand bowler. Between 1864 and 1873 he appeared for Kent in 39 matches, scoring 981 runs with an average of 15.57, and taking 10 wickets at a cost of 21.80 runs each. His highest innings for the county was 87 v. Yorkshire at Gravesend in 1865, but for the Gentlemen of Kent he twice exceeded 100, making 116 at Brighton in 1865 and 130 at Gravesend in 1867, each time against the Gentlemen of Sussex. In 1873 he scored 206 not out for Gentlemen of Mid-Kent v. South Norwood, and this ranked as the highest innings of his career. For Kent against Surrey at the Oval in 1865, he took five wickets for 70 in a total of 368. He was born at Milton, near Gravesend, on December 25, 1839, and had been a member of the M.C.C. since 1872.

TROUNCER, Charles Albert, who died on March 13, 1938, in Anglesey, aged 71, failed to get his Blue at Cambridge but played a few times in 1888 for Surrey—then Champion County.

TROUP, Capt. Frank Colin, who died at Murray Bridge, near Adelaide, in South Australia on January 19, 1924, was in the Cheltenham XI of 1913, when he had a batting average of 11.09. He appeared for Gloucestershire in two matches in 1914 and one in 1921. He was the only son of Major W. Troup.

TROUP, Major Walter, a prominent member of the Gloucestershire XI at different times from 1887 to 1911, died in January, 1940, aged 71. He appeared first for the county when 17 and still at a private school at Clifton. A very sound batsman, he often opened the innings with W. G. Grace, and he contributed 180 to Gloucestershire's 634 against Nottinghamshire at Bristol in 1898; during that season he also scored 176 and 100; when he helped W. G. put up 169 at Taunton against Somerset, his own contribution reached 127. Finishing second to W. G. Grace in the county batting, Troup averaged 38 for an aggregate of 968 runs. Troup became county captain next year when W. G. Grace ceased his connection with Gloucestershire, but was in office only one season before returning to India—the place of his birth. Altogether Troup scored 3,250 runs at an average of 26 an innings in first-class cricket. He played for the Gentlemen at Scarborough in 1898 and at the Oval in 1902.

Of small build, he was strong in defence and extremely patient, sometimes avoiding any attempts at scoring. More than once he batted about an hour for a single run. It is recorded that at Liverpool in 1888 he withstood the Lancashire attack altogether for 95 minutes and yet "bagged a brace." Despite all his care he was stumped in the first innings and leg-before-wicket in the second, each time to the cunning bowling of Briggs. Under favourable conditions he showed skill in stroke play but was always a slow scorer. He fielded well at cover-point. After being on the staff under Lord Harris at Poona, he was District Superintendent of Police in North-West Provinces. In the First World War he became a captain in the Royal Flying Corps and he retired from the Army in 1920.

TRUBSHAW, Ernest, J.P., D.L., at one time a member of the Glamorganshire XI, died at Llanelli on September 3, 1910, at the age of 65.

TRUEMAN, Geoffrey, who died in Sydney on June 28, 1981, kept wicket for New South Wales and came near to playing for Australia in the early '50s. Of the 82 dismissals, including 20 stumpings, in which he shared in his three seasons of state cricket, 18 were off Richie Benaud. He was a member of two Sheffield Shield winning sides—in 1951–52 and 1953–54.

TRUMBLE, Hugh, died at Melbourne on August 14, 1938, aged 71. Improving almost beyond belief each succeeding time he came to England, Hugh Trumble has been very properly placed among the most accomplished of Australian bowlers. Exceptionally tall, he made the most of his height by bringing the ball over at the full extent of his right arm so that "flighting," a new term since, his days, came in the natural delivery. Length, with either leg- or off-break, and pace slightly varied to medium were the means employed by Trumble and experience enabled him to deceive the best batsmen on perfect pitches while, given any help from the state of the turf, he was deadly. After doing moderately in 1890, when Turner and Ferris were in their prime, he stood out as a front rank bowler in 1893 and his other three tours, at similar intervals, increased his reputation in England. Such consistent form did he show that his figures in the four tours after his quiet start read—123 wickets at 16.39; 148 at 15.81; 142 at 18.43; and 140 at 14.27. His success in 1899 was not confined to bowling, for he scored 1,183 runs with average 27.51, so proving himself quite as valuable an all-rounder as M. A. Noble, particularly as he was a fine slip fieldsman.

Trumble in matches against England had the unequalled record in these Tests of 141 wickets at 20.88 each and a batting average of nearly 20 for an aggregate of 838 runs. When A. C. MacLaren led England in 1901–02, Trumble took 28 wickets; in the following summer 26 at 14.26 and against the first official M.C.C. team captained by P. F. Warner in the winter of 1903–04 his return for the Tests was 24 wickets at 16.58. Only Trumble has done the hat-trick twice against England, each at Melbourne in the last two tours mentioned. His best Test performances were 12 wickets for 89 at the Oval in 1896; 10 for 128 at Manchester, when Australia won by 3 runs; and 12 for 173 also in 1902 at the Oval where England won by one wicket, these three matches being among the most remarkable between the two countries. In England's first innings at the Oval in 1902, he dismissed A. C. MacLaren, L. C. H. Palairet, J. T. Tyldesley, T. Hayward, L. C. Braund, G. L. Jessop, G. H. Hirst and A. A. Lilley—eight wickets—at a cost of only 65 runs. He also bowled unchanged while England were getting the 263 runs required for victory.

For Victoria in Sheffield Shield matches, Trumble took 159 wickets at 20.67 and scored 1,150 runs, average 22.54. For some 20 years Trumble was secretary of the Melbourne C.C. where his knowledge of the game and happy spirit made him universally popular.

TRUMBLE, John William, who played for Victoria and Australia, died in Melbourne after a long illness on August 17, 1944, aged 80. By comparison with his famous brother Hugh, John Trumble accomplished little, but he was a useful all-round player. In seven Test matches against England he scored 243 runs with an average of 20.2 and took 10 wickets at 22.2 apiece. He first played for Victoria in 1884, and for them made 486 runs and took 52 wickets. He bowled with a good high delivery and was noted for accurate length. He came to England with the team captained by H. J. H. Scott in 1886, but never showed form up to the standard of his colleagues. England were superior in every way that season and won all three Test matches, two of them very easily by an innings with many runs to spare. A solicitor by profession, he retained a close connection with cricket and was one of the oldest members of the Melbourne club.

A letter from him on "Cricket Reform" to *The Times* was reprinted in *Wisden*, 1927. It dealt specially with the over-preparation of pitches, particularly in Australia.

TRUMAN, 2nd Lieut. T. A. (A.S.C.), died of pneumonia and peritonitis on September 13, 1918. Played a few times for Gloucestershire.

VICTOR THOMAS TRUMPER

Victor Trumper died at Sydney on June 28, 1915. Of all the great Australian batsmen Victor Trumper was by general consent the best and most brilliant. No one else among the famous group, from Charles Bannerman 39 years ago to Bardsley and Macartney at the present time, had quite such remarkable powers. To say this involves no depreciation of Clem Hill, Noble, or the late W. L. Murdoch. Trumper at the zenith of his fame challenged comparison with Ranjitsinhji. He was great under all conditions of weather and ground. He could play quite an orthodox game when he wished to, but it was his ability to make big scores when orthodox methods were unavailing that lifted him above his fellows.

For this reason Trumper was, in proportion, more to be feared on treacherous wickets than on fast, true ones. No matter how bad the pitch might be from the combined effects of rain and sunshine, he was quite likely to get 50 runs, his skill in pulling good-length balls amounting to genius. Of this fact our English bowlers had convincing evidence day after day during the season of 1902. Trumper paid four visits to this country—in 1899, 1902, 1905, and 1909—but it was in 1902 that he reached his highest point.

In that summer of wretched weather he scored 2,570 runs in 35 matches for the Australian team, with the wonderful average, in the circumstances, of 48. He was as consistent as he was brilliant, and did not owe his average to a few exceptional scores. Of 11 innings of over 100, the biggest was 128. Trumper did not again touch the same level in this country. He played very well in 1905 and 1909, but he was no longer preeminent. He was fifth in the averages in 1905, and in 1909 he was overshadowed by Bardsley and Ransford. In the latter year, however, he was now and then seen at his best, notably against England at the Oval, when he played D. W. Carr's googlies with perfect ease, and in the second match against the M.C.C. at Lord's. When he came here first, in 1899, he jumped at once into the front rank, playing a splendid innings of 135 (not out) against England at Lord's, and scoring 300 (not out) against Sussex at Brighton. His innings at Lord's was in itself sufficient to prove that Australia had found a world's

batsman. Nothing could have been better.

His career culminated when the South Africans visited Australia in the season of 1910–11. He then recovered his finest form, and on the beautiful wickets at Melbourne, Adelaide, and Sydney the "googly" bowlers had no terrors for him. In the five Test matches he scored 662 runs, with an average of 94. It was agreed on all hands that he had not played so well since his trip to England in 1902. Under all conditions Trumper was a fascinating batsman to watch. His extreme suppleness lent a peculiar grace to everything he did. When he was hitting up a big score batting seemed quite an easy matter. He took so many liberties, however, and scored from so many good balls, that in order to do himself justice he had to be in the best possible health and condition. The strokes with which he drove even the best bowlers to despair demanded a marvellous union of hand and eye. His game at its highest point of excellence could only be played by a young man.

Trumper was the most popular Australian cricketer of his time. A match played for his benefit—between New South Wales and the Rest of Australia—at Sydney in February, 1913—produced in gate-money and donations nearly £3,000. Born on November 2, 1877, Trumper was in his 38th year. He had been in bad health for some little time, and the latest accounts of his condition received in this country were so discouraging as to prepare his friends for the worst. He died of Bright's disease. Trumper was never spoilt by success in the cricket field. When his name was in everyone's mouth he remained as modest and unaffected as on the day he first set foot in England.—S.H.P.

BATTING AVERAGES IN FIRST-CLASS MATCHES

Year			Innings	Times not out	Most in an Innings	Total Runs	Average
1894–95	..	..	4	1	11	22	7.33
1897–98	..	..	10	0	68	192	19.20
1898–99	..	..	15	1	292*	873	62.35
1899	..	..	48	3	300*	1,556	34.57
1899–1900		..	10	0	208	721	72.10
1900–01	..	..	7	0	230	458	65.42
1901–02	..	..	18	0	73	486	27.00
1902	..	..	53	0	128	2,570	48.49
1902–03 (S. Af.)	..		8	1	70	307	43.85
1902–03	..	..	9	0	178	446	49.55
1903–04	..	..	21	3	185	990	55.00
1904–05	..	..	4	0	81	198	49.50
1904–05 (N.Z.)	..		5	1	172	436	109.00
1905	..	..	47	1	110	1,667	36.23
1905–06	..	..	6	0	101	250	41.66

BATTING AVERAGES IN FIRST-CLASS MATCHES—*Continued*

Year			Innings	Times not out	Most in an Innings	Total Runs	Average
1906–07	..	..	3	0	11	23	7.66
1907–08	..	..	19	0	166	797	41.94
1908–09	..	..	1	0	0	0	—
1909	..	..	45	2	150	1,435	33.37
1909–10	..	..	1	0	105	105	105.00
1910–11	..	..	20	2	214*	1,246	69.22
1911–12	..	..	20	3	113	583	34.29
1912–13	..	..	13	3	201*	843	84.30
1913–14	..	..	5	0	32	107	21.40
1913–14 (N.Z.)		..	10	0	293	839	83.90
In Australia	..	..	186	13	292*	8,340	48.20
In England	..	..	193	6	300*	7,228	38.65
In N.Z.	..	..	15	1	293	1,275	91.07
In S. Africa	..	..	8	1	70	307	43.85
Totals	..	..	402	21	300*	17,150	45.01

His doings in the very wet season of 1902 were extraordinary, for not once was he dismissed without a run, and he had not even one not-out innings to assist him. Only Shrewsbury, who scored 1,250 runs and was not out seven times, was above him in the averages.

TRUMPER'S HUNDREDS IN FIRST-CLASS CRICKET

For Australia, in Australia (6):
  v. England, 185*, 113, 166, 113
  v. South Africa, 159, 214*

For Australia, in England (19):
  v. Cambridge University, 128, 133
  v. Derbyshire, 113
  v. England, 135*, 104
  v. XI of England, 113, 150
  v. Essex, 109 and 119
  v. Gloucestershire, 104, 125, 108
  v. M.C.C. and Ground, 105
  v. Oxford University, 121
  v. XI Players, 127
  v. South, 120
  v. Surrey, 101
  v. Sussex, 300*
  v. Worcestershire, 110

For Australia, in New Zealand (3):
  v. Canterbury, 293
  v. New Zealand, 172
  v. Southland, 211

For New South Wales (15):
  v. Australia, 105, 126*
  v. New Zealand, 253
  v. Queensland, 208
  v. South Australia, 165, 178, 135, 201*
  v. Tasmania, 292*
  v. Victoria, 230, 130, 101, 119, 142, 138

Forty-three such innings in all. His two 100s against Essex were made in one match in 1902, during which season he obtained 11 centuries. The same year he scored 105 and 86 in a match with M.C.C. and Ground at Lord's. Trumper also made 218 not out for Australia v. Fifteen of the Transvaal, at Pretoria in 1902–03.

TRUMPER'S SCORING IN TEST-MATCH CRICKET

	Innings	Times not out	Most in an Innings	Total Runs	Average
1899 (in England) ..	9	1	135*	280	35.00
1901–02 (v. England)	10	0	65	219	21.90
1902 (in England) ..	8	0	104	247	30.87
1902–03 (in S. Africa)	6	1	70	239	47.80
1903–04 (v. England)	10	1	185*	574	63.77
1905 (in England) ..	8	1	31	125	17.85
1907–08 (v. England)	10	0	166	338	33.80
1909 (in England) ..	9	1	73	211	26.37
1910–11 (v. S. Africa)	9	2	214*	661	94.42
1911–12 (v. England)	10	1	113	269	29.88
In Australia	49	4	214*	2,061	45.80
In England	34	3	135*	863	27.83
In S. Africa	6	1	70	239	47.80
Against England ..	74	5	185*	2,263	32.79
Against S. Africa ..	15	3	214*	900	75.00
Totals	89	8	214*	3,163	39.04

Signifies not out

FIRST-CLASS CRICKET NOTABILIA

Trumper's first century in first-class cricket was 292 not out for New South Wales v. Tasmania, at Sydney, in 1898–99. He and F. A. Iredale (196) added 258 for the sixth wicket.

Whilst scoring 300 not out v. Sussex, at Brighton, in 1899, he took part in three stands of over 100, adding 178 for the second wicket with J. Worrall (128), 211 for the third with S. E. Gregory (173) and 106, without separation, with J. Darling (56 not out), after the fall of the fourth.

The same season he scored 62 runs out of 80 in 50 minutes in the Test match at Sheffield.

For New South Wales v. South Australia, at Sydney, in 1902–03, Trumper (178) and the late R. A. Duff (132) scored 298 for the first wicket.

In the first innings of New South Wales v. Victoria on the same ground the same season, the pair obtained 267 ere a wicket fell. In the second innings Trumper, for the first time in 78 innings in first-class cricket, was dismissed without a run.

For New South Wales v. Victoria, at Sydney, in 1903–04, Trumper and Duff made 113 for the first wicket in the first innings and 119, without being separated, for the first wicket in the second, winning the match by 10 wickets. Trumper's scores were 53 and 53 not out; Duff's 67 and 62 not out.

For Australia v. New Zealand, at Wellington, in 1904–05, Trumper (172) and C. Hill (129) added 269 for the sixth wicket in 107

minutes. At one period they put on 100 in 35 minutes.

In scoring 108 for Australians v. Gloucestershire, at Bristol, in 1905, Trumper obtained all his runs before lunch on the first day.

On the second afternoon of the Australians' match v. Northamptonshire, at Northampton, in 1905, Trumper (68) and W. W. Armstrong (122) added 90 without being parted in 35 minutes for the seventh wicket.

In the second innings of Australians v. Oxford University, at Oxford, in 1905, Trumper and R. A. Duff scored 30 runs off two consecutive overs, the former obtaining 12 off N. R. Udal and Duff·18 off E. G. Martin.

In making 101 out of 139 in 57 minutes, on a wicket favouring the bowlers, for New South Wales v. Victoria, at Sydney, in 1905–06, Trumper gave perhaps the most brilliant display of his career. He hit a six and 18 fours, and reached 64 out of 78 in 31 minutes, and 73 out of 90 in 40 minutes.

For New South Wales v. Victoria, at Melbourne, in 1906–07, Trumper scored 119 out of 150 in 101 minutes. He obtained 62 runs out of 81, and completed his 100 out of 124 in an hour and a half.

He scored 20 runs (five fours) off an over from G. Hazlitt for New South Wales v. Victoria, at Melbourne, in 1907–08.

Whilst making 150 for Australians v. An England XI, at Blackpool, in 1909, Trumper added 93 for the sixth wicket in 35 minutes with M. A. Noble (36) and 45 for the seventh in 10 minutes with A. J. Hopkins (21 not out) for the seventh. Three-quarters of an hour's play thus produced 138 runs.

For New South Wales v. South Africans, at Sydney, in 1910–11, Trumper (70 and 78) and W. Bardsley (70 and 45) made over 100 together in each innings for the first wicket—122 in the first and 121 in the second.

Trumper made 159 out of 237 in 171 minutes for Australia v. South Africa at Melbourne in 1910–11.

In 1911–12 he scored 58 out of 77 in 57 minutes for New South Wales v. Victoria, at Melbourne.

For New South Wales v. Victoria, at Sydney, in 1912–13, Trumper (138) and E. P. Barbour (146) added 270 together for the eighth wicket.

Trumper (293) and A. Sims (184 not out) put on 433 for the eighth wicket of Australians v. Canterbury, at Christchurch, in 1913–14.

In first-grade cricket in Australia—playing for Paddington from 1896–97 to 1908–09 and for Gordon from 1910–11 to 1914–15, Trumper scored 8,946 runs with an average of 69.

TRUMPER, Victor (Jun.), the only son of his legendary father, died in Sydney on August 31, 1981, at the age of 67. A fast out-swing bowler, with few pretensions to batting, he played for New South Wales in 1940–41, though not in the Sheffield Shield, which was suspended for the duration of the Second World War.

TRYON, Lieut., of the Grenadier Guards, died in South Africa, from enteric fever, in the third week of April, 1901. He played occasionally for Northamptonshire in 1898, making 61 against the Surrey Second XI. He was the only son of the late Sir George Tryon, who went down in the *Victoria*, off Tripoli, in June, 1892. He was born on October 22, 1878, and was thus only in his 23rd year at the time of his death.

I have been requested to state that Lieutenant Tryon, who died in South Africa in 1901, was a nephew, not a son, of the late Admiral Tryon.—S.H.P.

TUCKER, K. H., who died in Wellington on December 1, 1939, aged 64, was one of New Zealand's ablest all-round cricketers. A steady batsman with many strokes, he also bowled cleverly; first leg-breaks, then off theory, and he fielded well at cover-point. Against Lord Hawke's team in the winter of 1902 he scored 86 for Wellington, and for New Zealand 56, 67 and 21. Five years later against the M.C.C. amateur side he saved

Wellington with an innings of 50 not out, but was not so successful for New Zealand who lost the first Test by nine wickets but won the second by 56 runs.

TUCKETT, Lindsay Richard, who died in June, 1963, aged 78, played for South Africa against England in one Test match in 1914. Though best known as a bowler, he helped to establish a world batting record in 1925–26 when, playing for Orange Free State, he shared in a three-figure stand for the last wicket in each innings against Western Province. In the first innings he and L. G. Fuller put on 115 and in the second F. Caulfield helped him add 129. Known as Len, he was the father of Lindsay who played nine times against England in the Tests of 1947–48 and became president of the Orange Free State Cricket Union and Test selector.

TUCKWELL, B. J., died at Wellington on January 2, 1943. Well known in cricketing circles in Victoria, where he was born, he played for the State team against P. F. Warner's 1903–04 England side. Going to New Zealand, he gained a place in the team that toured Australia in 1913–14, and did well in the minor matches with 84 at Maitland v. Northern Districts and 63 and 44 at Goulburn v. Southern Districts. In New Zealand he played for both Otago and Wellington and also for representative New Zealand teams. A stylish bat, excelling in crisp cuts both square and late, he often made useful scores and did good service as an excellent slip fieldsman.

TUDOR, Brig. Claud Lechmere St. John, C.B.E., M.C., died at Halton, Oxford, on August 3, 1977, aged 88. Educated at Eastbourne College, he played a few times for Sussex in 1910 and 1911 and in his second match made 116 against Oxford. He was the last survivor of the match in which Alletson played his famous innings at Hove in 1911. Later he played for and captained the Army. His younger brother also played for Sussex: they were cousins of another Sussex cricketer, Lieut.-Col. G. S. Grimston, who was later the county's secretary.

TUDOR, Lieut.-Col. Roland Grimston, who died on October 11, 1973, aged 82, was in the Eastbourne College XI before playing for Sussex on occasion between 1912 and 1919.

TUFNELL, Carleton Fowell, died on May 26, 1940, aged 84. He left Eton when 16 without a chance of getting into the XI, but played for Cooper's Hill from 1876 to 1878, being captain in the last two seasons. A useful batsman and medium-paced bowler, he played in a few matches for Kent in 1878 and 1879 before going to India. In May 1884 a report reached England of his death at Simla.

TUFNELL, Col. Neville Charsley, whose death at the age of 64 occurred on August 3, 1951, was in the Eton XI in 1905-06-07. When he went up to Cambridge he quickly established a reputation as a talented wicket-keeper, gaining a place in the University teams of 1909–10. While still at Cambridge he toured South Africa with the M.C.C. team of 1909–10 and deputised for Strudwick of Surrey, injured, in the fifth Test match at Cape Town. Tufnell also toured New Zealand with E. G. Wynyard's team in 1906–07. He kept wicket for the Gentlemen at Lord's and played for Surrey between 1907 and 1922.

TUKE, Dr. Charles Molesworth, born at Chiswick on May 23, 1857, died on January 24, 1925, after a long illness, aged 67. In *Scores and Biographies* (xiv – 100) it was said of him: "Is a very fast round-armed bowler 'with a whip from the wrist'; an average bat, and fields generally at short slip or cover-point." In 1882 he appeared, though not with much success, in seven matches for Middlesex.

TUNNICLIFFE, John, who died at Westbury Park, Bristol, on July 11, 1948, when nearly 82 years of age, could be described as the most conspicuous of the many professionals of high repute and ability who played for Yorkshire during the long period in which Lord Hawke held command. Born on August 26, 1866, "Long John of Pudsey," his familiar and affectionate name, was approaching 25 years of age when he reached county status and from 1891 to 1907 he helped to raise Yorkshire to their greatest strength, the Championship coming to them seven times while Tunnicliffe was in the side.

Helped by his height—6 ft. 2 in.—he made his name by big hitting, but soon found restraint necessary against clever bowlers, and with more experience he could mould his methods according to the needs of the moment. Then he used his long reach more as a defender than as a forcing batsman. Height and long arms enabled Tunnicliffe to bring off catches at short slip that would have been impossible for most fieldsmen.

As shown in the *Yorkshire Year Book*, he scored 20,109 runs with an average of 26.84 and made 22 centuries for the county. Twice he and J. T. Brown, of Driffield, set up a first-wicket partnership record. In July, 1897, at Sheffield the Sussex attack yielded 378 runs before a wicket fell; next month Abel and Brockwell for Surrey at the Oval against Hampshire just beat that, but in 1898 at Chesterfield the Yorkshire pair put together 554 against Derbyshire and this remained the best stand until 1932, when Sutcliffe and Percy Holmes went one better at Leyton for Yorkshire against Essex, Sutcliffe, 313, giving away his wicket just as Brown did 34 years before.

Tunnicliffe's share of the Chesterfield stand was 243, his highest score in first-class cricket. I saw that match and recall clearly Lord Hawke waiting all the first day with his pads on while 503 runs were scored and he did not bat until Brown completed 300, with 51 runs added. What a difference to Yorkshire's experience last year on the same ground, where they fell for 44, their lowest score of the season!

Altogether Tunnicliffe took part in 26 opening stands of three figures, 19 of them with Brown, notable efforts being 139 and 147, which gave Yorkshire a victory by 10 wickets at Lord's in 1896 after A. E. Stoddart and H. B. Hayman had opened the match with 218 for Middlesex.

He made over 1,000 runs in a season for Yorkshire 13 times, his highest aggregate being 1,672 in 1898, and held no fewer than 575 catches in first-class cricket, twice taking seven in a match. The *County Annual* credits him with 678 catches for Yorkshire and adds that he kept wicket in 1891 and 1892, stumping nine and catching seven batsmen in six games. His benefit match against Lancashire in 1903 at Bradford brought him £1,750. He several times took part in matches for Players against Gentlemen.

After giving up County Cricket Tunnicliffe became coach at Clifton College in 1908 and was elected a member of the Gloucestershire county committee, while his son W. G. Tunnicliffe was secretary of the Gloucestershire club from 1921 to 1935.—H.P.

MAURICE TURNBULL
Born March 16, 1906.
Killed in action, August 5, 1944
By J. C. Clay

Major Maurice Joseph Turnbull, Welsh Guards, was killed in action near Montchamp in Normandy on August 5, 1944. He was 38. During an attack his company got cut off, and while making a reconnaissance he was shot through the head by a sniper and killed instantaneously.

"Maurice was such a grand person. So often have I seen him go into action and never have I seen him rattled. He was always the same: quiet, confident, thinking always of his men and disregarding all danger to himself. A really great person." This extract from a letter written from France is a straightforward appreciation of him as a soldier; there are other and sometimes more fulsome tributes paid to him. But I choose this one because it also exactly describes his leadership of Glamorgan in the days of peace, and shows that in his greatest Test of all he did not alter his style but played his own game to the end.

His Achievements

Maurice Turnbull played cricket for England and Rugby football and hockey for Wales; he also held the South Wales Squash Racquets Championship. He captained Cambridge at cricket, was a member of the Test match selection committee, and captain and secretary of the Glamorgan club since 1930. He was top scorer in his first innings for Glamorgan (40 v. Lancashire in 1924) and was again top scorer in his last innings (156 v. Leicestershire, 1939). In between those dates he made, in first-class cricket, nearly 18,000 runs, averaging 30 per innings, 29 centuries, and held over 300 catches.

These are the bare statistics; as he was only 33 when the War broke out, they are formidable achievements fully entitling him to the position he held in the public estimation—a very prominent games-player. But to those of us who knew him well mere facts and figures do him scant justice. A great player he may have been, but an astute brain made him an even greater captain—the best of his generation who never captained England—and there is little doubt that he would have become one of the game's foremost administrators. And finally, what a grand fellow.

He Started Young

I first met Maurice in July, 1924, when as a boy of 17, fresh from many triumphs at Downside, he came down to play against Lancashire at Swansea. In the nets at Cardiff the day before, he batted so badly that he wondered if he ought not to stand down. Luckily he played, and by making 40 in the first innings and 16 in the second he contributed very largely to a Glamorgan victory—a sensation in those days. The wicket was never easy (153 was the highest total of the four innings), but he faced that celebrated trio of bowlers, McDonald, Parkin and R.

Tyldesley, all at their best, with the assurance of one accustomed to meet them regularly and with success. It was not a case of novice's luck, but of sound and mature judgment worthy of one double his age. Which encourages me to believe that, when a year or so later he sent for the majestic wine waiter of a London hotel and administered a rebuke on the quality of the claret, he was probably quite right!

Maurice, in fact, was something of an infant prodigy, but, unlike so many of them, he did not fade out after a year or two of glorious life: he became a celebrity in 1924 and remained one to the finish. 1925 found him still at Downside, and that it was almost unfair to ask schoolboys to bowl to him is shown by his figures—1,400 runs, average 95. In 1926 he went up to Cambridge, got his Blue, and also his first century for Glamorgan. In 1927 he was unable to play owing to injury, and he hardly recovered his best form in 1928. But in 1929 he captained Cambridge and scored 1,000 runs for them with an average of 50. And here the carefree days of youth ended, for in 1930 he took over the captaincy of Glamorgan.

What He Did For Glamorgan

Glamorgan became a first-class county in 1921, but, except for one good season and one or two sensational victories, failed to live up to that high-sounding title. The side sadly lacked a regular captain, and by the close of the 1929 season, during which it had no less than seven leaders, it resembled a bedraggled flock without a shepherd. Moreover, no public likes seeing its side beaten too frequently: the English are annoyed while the Welsh are hurt, but both show their displeasure in the same way—they stay away. It is not surprising, therefore, to find that Glamorgan, with little tradition and a very small membership, were in dire financial trouble.

At this unpropitious moment Maurice took charge, comforted perhaps by the knowledge that any change he could bring about was almost bound to be for the better. And change there was, not only in the playing results but in the whole atmosphere: and this better spirit enabled the club to overcome the financial disaster which was shortly to face it.

Noteworthy success did not come all at once, but by linking Monmouthshire with Glamorgan, running a Minor Counties side, and going all out to encourage local talent, he not only found players but widened the interest; and earned his reward in 1937 when Glamorgan won 13 matches in all and finished seventh in the County Championship.

With all due respect, the general public is not frightfully interested in the doings of Boards of Control, committees and secretaries; it is far more concerned with what happens on the field of play between 11.30 and 6.30. But Maurice's administrative achievements were so great that they must be referred to here.

Briefly, then, Glamorgan at the end of 1932 were in debt to the tune of about £5,000, and as something drastic had to be done, and quickly, an appeal was launched. Now Glamorgan knew all about appeals to the sporting public—it had lived on them since 1921—but nothing like the one organised by Maurice ever happened before. Whereas a faithful few contributed time and again, on this occasion nobody was left out; every town and every village was encouraged to run a dance or similar function, and to each of these Turnbull made a point of going. If the figures were known, the number of miles he danced for Glamorgan might be favourably compared with the number of runs scored by some of the side! Anyhow, this big effort realised £3,500 and, maybe, gave him valuable ideas, for whenever subsequently funds ran low he found means to supplement them.

He was indeed a most efficient secretary: always on the job, and his suggestions were based on practical knowledge and experience. He went all out, successfully, for an increased membership and paid great attention to the comfort of the spectators. In short, by 1939 he converted a shambling, shamefaced, bankrupt into a worthy and respected member of society with a bank balance of £1,000.

Batting: A Gay Adventure

For a batsman who appeared in nine Tests and held for many years what amounted to a standing invitation for the Gentlemen v. Players, an average of 30 is moderate enough: honest toilers with no great gifts have attained better figures. The reason is that Maurice never made runs unnecessarily; he seldom indulged in those large, average-raising, but meaningless, innings which with everything in the batsman's favour might have been played by almost anybody who could bat at all. An innings by him invariably had some definite effect on the game, and he was at his best when others were failing or when runs were required at a pace to beat the clock. He always looked a class batsman and was always attacking the bowler.

In his early days an on-side player, he soon developed all the recognised strokes and a few of his very own, which, though they did not appeal to the purist, were extremely good value for the ordinary spectator and poison to the bowler. Contrary to some belief, bowlers do not enjoy being hit any more than a fox enjoys being hunted; but if they must receive punishment, let it be correctly administered and according to the book. I only bowled against him once: it was most disquieting!

From all of which it can be gathered that an innings by him was a delight to watch; it contained that element of impudence and unorthodoxy which added spice to the rather stolid pudding of accepted county batsmanship.

It is difficult to state with certainty which were his best seasons or his best innings, but his appearances in Tests were between 1930 and 1936, when he played against South Africa, five times, and New Zealand, once, abroad; and against New Zealand, West Indies and India in England. His most noteworthy innings, looked at in retrospect, was perhaps his double century (one of three he made altogether) against Larwood and Voce at Cardiff in the last match of 1932 season. Three months later this celebrated pair, bowling in exactly the same way, were causing a rumpus in Australia. In the same year, on a crumbling Swansea wicket, against Parker and Goddard, and incidentally the clock, he played a magnificent match-winning innings of 119 which enabled Glamorgan to win with 10 minutes to spare.

Was There A Better Captain?

I say "No;" but with the reservation that it is only human to get to appreciate highly that which you see often and at its best. Which may account, incidentally, for any element of truth in the cheap gibe that a cricketer must play for a "fashionable" county or do well at Lord's to gain official recognition. But he certainly was very good and must have been near to being selected to lead England: he did actually captain one of the sides in a Test trial match.

Above all things Maurice was a "quiet" captain: there was no fuss, no gesticulating, no shouting on the field. He never got rattled or irritable and always contrived to make the bowlers feel that, although the scoreboard said otherwise, they were really doing pretty well. A grand "boss" to work for: I always bowled much better for him than I ever did for myself or anybody else. As with his batting, he never played for safety, but so sound was his judgment that decisions which appeared almost foolhardy at the time turned out to have been extremely well-calculated risks.

Needless to say, the professionals thought the world of him; and well they might, for nobody kept their interests more at heart or gave them sounder advice. The result was that he always got the best out of what was really a moderate side and did not have to contend seriously with those petty grievances and squabbles which may arise. For cricketers, like other public entertainers, can grow temperamental. Those who are not playing well, or are "out of luck" as it is politely called, become moody or depressed; others, while welcoming favourable notices, are deeply wounded by any hint of adverse criticism.

The example he set in the field, of course, accounted largely for his beneficial influence. He could field anywhere, but short-leg was his real position: the risks he ran and the catches he caught there had to be seen to be believed. Sometimes he literally picked the ball off the defensively held bat and at others he would hang on to red-hot drives although standing but a few yards away from the batsman. Such efforts inspired the bowler and convinced the luckless batsman that there was indeed no justice in the world. "Quiet, confident, thinking always of his men"—yes, it is a good description.

He Will Be Missed

Maurice was so closely identified with sport that his name will always be associated with it. Yet he had views and interests which covered a far wider field. He was very well read, he appreciated good music, and could talk knowledgeably on a variety of subjects, and always with a subtle sense of humour in which he abounded. With M. J. C. Allom he wrote *The Book of the Two Maurices* and *The Two Maurices Again*, giving accounts of their tours in New Zealand and South Africa. These books contain some descriptive writing which is remarkable when compared to the utilitarian accounts of cricket tours to which we are accustomed.

He will be sadly missed—by sport generally, by cricket in particular; but most of all by his friends. As one of them—and, when you have knocked about England together as much as he and I did, you get to know each other pretty well—I say farewell to a fine player, a great sportsman and a grand fellow.

The news of his death came through while Glamorgan were fulfilling one of their wartime fixtures at Cardiff Arms Park, the scene of his first century and many subsequent triumphs. And, as the crowd stood in respectful silence, perhaps the more imaginative or sentimental among them may have pictured for a fleeting instant the well-known figure out there on the field, and derived some small measure of comfort. For Glamorgan were carrying on: and he would have wished that.

TURNER, Brig. Arthur Jervois, C.B., C.M.G., D.S.O. and Croix de Guerre, who died at Graffham, Sussex, on September 8, 1952, aged 74, was born at Mussorie, India, one of several cricketing sons of Major J. T. Turner, who, with other members of the Hong Kong cricket team, lost his life in the wreck of the *Bokhara* in 1892 when returning from a match with Shanghai. An all-rounder, A. J. Turner was educated at Bedford Modern School, where he gained a place in the XI in 1892 when 13. He played four seasons for the school, being captain in 1895. For Woolwich and the Army he also earned a reputation as a cricketer, and after occasional appearances for Bedfordshire he assisted Essex between 1897 and 1910. In his first season of first-class cricket he hit 40 and 111 against Yorkshire at Huddersfield. He played for Gentlemen v. Players at the Oval in 1898 and was invited for the Lord's match the following summer, but because of military duties could not accept. Besides his cricketing abilities, Turner was an excellent Rugby footballer and played for Blackheath and Kent. He served with the Royal Artillery in the South African War and, while on the General Headquarters Staff in France during the First World War, was four times Mentioned in Dispatches.

TURNER, Charles Thomas Biass, a bowler ranking with the best ever produced by Australia, and by many who played against him considered without superior, died on New Year's Day, 1944, in Sydney, aged 81. Records that stand to his name tell of his work with the ball, but it is remarkable that in the first set of photographs that appeared in *Wisden* he is holding a bat and wearing pads in company with his colleague J. J. Ferris, grasping a ball in his left hand. Chosen with G. A. Lohmann, of Surrey, Robert Peel, of Yorkshire, John Briggs, of Lancashire, and S. M. J. Woods, of Cambridge University and Somerset—himself an Australian—the two members of the team captained by P. S. McDonnell fully deserved the honour, for they practically dominated every match in which they played on this their first visit to England. In a season when bowlers accomplished wonderful things, almost beyond belief in these days, Turner took 314 wickets at 11.12 runs apiece and Ferris 224 at 14.10 each—G. H. S. Trott coming next with 48 at 23.41. In nine matches against specially chosen sides, three representing England, 70 wickets fell to Turner and 41 to Ferris, seven others claiming only 23 between them. The habit prevailed at that time of relying upon two or three bowlers on a side for the chief work of the season and McDonnell carried this custom to the extreme limit, but of the other specialists picked by C. F. Pardon, Lohmann for Surrey was almost as supreme with 253 wickets at 10.69, Beaumont, with 59, giving most help in carrying off the championship in this year of bowlers' triumphs mainly on rain-affected pitches.

To have seen these masters of the art at the Oval is a pleasant recollection, and not one of them creates a happier memory than Turner in his rather long rhythmic run and beautiful right-arm action without any effort to make the most of his medium height—5 ft. 9 in. He delivered the ball almost facing square down the pitch, and, added to his off-break with slightly varied pace about fast-medium, was ability to turn the ball from leg, send down a fast yorker, and, above all, to get quick lift from the turf. As sufficient evidence of Turner's skill, Sir Stanley Jackson said in last year's *Wisden*, "I always regarded Charles Turner as the best medium-paced bowler I ever played against"—and he could gather an opinion as he scored 91 at Lord's and 103 at the Oval in the Tests in 1893, when Turner, on his third and last visit to England, fell from his greatest achievement to 149 wickets at 14 each, after 215 at 12 in 1890.

Turner earned fame in the 1886–87 season against Arthur Shrewsbury's team. After taking 13 wickets for 54 runs for New South Wales, he in his first Test match dismissed six batsmen for 15 runs, England being all out for 45, which remains the lowest total by England against Australia. He excelled again for New South Wales with 14 wickets for 59, clean bowling Shrewsbury for nought in each innings. In the following season, when Shrewsbury again captained a side in Australia, Turner for New South Wales took 10 wickets for 45 and 16 for 79. G. F. Vernon led another team in Australia at that time, and against the Combined England sides Turner claimed 12 wickets for 87, but, thanks to Peel and Lohmann, the visitors beat Australia by 126 runs. Altogether in 1887–88 Turner took 106 wickets at 13.59 apiece, and his record of being the only bowler to take 100 wickets in first-class cricket in a season in Australia still stands.

So expectations were rife and at once we knew in England that no one had overrated "The Terror." Turner and Ferris routed side after side, actually disposing of England at Lord's for 53 and 62 and steering Australia to victory by 61 runs. Ten wickets for 63 was Turner's share at the expense of very powerful batting, as shown in the other two Tests played on hard turf and both won by England with an innings to spare. Turner also gave early proof of his batting ability, for in the third victory of the tour, each gained in two days, he played a dashing innings of 103 at the Oval and then, taking nine wickets for 101 runs, was chiefly instrumental in beating Surrey, the Champion County of the year, by an innings and 154 runs. Checks were bound to occur when so many strong teams were opposed, but at Lord's Turner returned an average of 11 Middlesex wickets for 59 runs in a low-scoring match, and whenever helped by the state of the turf he did wonders. Twelve wickets for 64 runs at Old Trafford against North of England; 11 for 76 at Liverpool; 11 for 64 at Leicester, where the county won a sensational match by 20 runs—thanks to Pougher, 10 for 91, and Arnall-Thompson, nine for 65; then 13 for 46 at Derby and 13 for 48 at Stoke against an England XI in the course of five days. In the first innings of the Stoke match Turner bowled seven men and got two leg-before, the other being run out. So he paved the way for that big performance in the first meeting with England at Lord's. Ten wickets for 46 against Yorkshire and 10 for 59 against Kent also may be cited, and still more extraordinary was his greatest return, 17 wickets for 50 runs against an England XI, at Hastings in August. In the two innings Turner hit the stumps 14 times, got two men l.b.w., and one stumped—further wonderful proof of how he did beat the bat. When Turner, owing to indisposition, was compelled to rest, Gloucestershire beat the Australians by 257 runs, and altogether nine of the last 11 matches were lost without marring the wonderful work of Turner and Ferris.

Such performances tell of the conditions that so often helped these two consistent bowlers, who repeated their excellence in 1890, if inevitably not quite so deadly. Exact figures show best how they shared the attack and the honours in these two tours, their wickets being equal on the second visit when W. L. Murdoch last led an Australian team.

1888	Matches	Overs	Maidens	Runs	Wickets	Average
Turner	39	2,589.4	1,222	3,492	314	11.12
Ferris	40	2,222.2	998	3,101	220	14.10
1890						
Turner	35	1,651.1	724	2,725	215	12.60
Ferris	35	1,685.4	688	2,838	215	13.20

(Four balls to the over was the rule in 1888, five in 1890.)

In 1893 Turner again headed the Australian bowling figures with 160 wickets at 13.76 each; Hugh Trumble, 123 at 16.39, and George Giffen, 148 at 17.89, affording more help than when Ferris, who at this time was playing for Gloucestershire, fairly shared the honours.

By comparison, the figures of W. J. O'Reilly, the best Australian bowler in the 1938 tour, are interesting: 709.4 overs, 215 maidens, 1,726 runs, 104 wickets, 16.59 average. Six balls an over certainly; and he complained of over-work.

Altogether in 17 Test matches—all against England—Turner took 101 wickets at 16.53 runs apiece in the course of 10 years. This average just beats Robert Peel's 102 wickets at 16.81 and far surpasses the next best Australian record, 141 at 20.88 by Hugh Trumble in 32 Tests.

In all first-class matches Turner is credited with 1,061 wickets at 13 runs each, as mentioned in *Scores and Biographies*.

After some years in the Australian Joint Stock Bank, Turner was associated with other business, and when he left Sydney for Queensland in 1897 his first-class cricket career ended.—H.P.

TURNER, Cyril, who died on November 19, 1968, aged 66, played as a professional all-rounder for Yorkshire from 1924 to 1946. As a left-handed batsman he obtained 6,117 runs, average 26.14, and with right-arm spin bowling took 173 wickets at a cost of 30.75 runs each. He did not gain a regular place in the county XI until 1934, but thereafter proved a sound and valuable addition to the batting strength. His first full season was his most successful, for he scored 1,153 runs. He hit both his centuries, 130 v. Somerset at Bath and 115 not out v. Hampshire at Bournemouth, in 1936. From 1952 until ill-health forced him to retire in 1960, he acted as scorer for Yorkshire.

TURNER, Dr. James William Cecil, who died on November 29, 1968, aged 82, played occasionally for Worcestershire between 1911 and 1921. His highest innings was 106 against Northamptonshire at Northampton in his last season. For some years he was treasurer of the Cambridge University C.C.

TURNER, John Alfred, who was born at Leicester on April 10, 1863, died on July 23, 1924. He was a steady and safe batsman, a good fast bowler, and a capital field, generally taking cover-point. Before going to Uppingham, he was at Mill House School, Leicester, where he and Mr. H. T. Arnall (afterwards Arnall-Thompson) were the chief bowlers. In 1880 and two next years he was in the Uppingham XI, being captain in 1882, and, obtaining his Blue for Cambridge as a Freshman, played four times (1883 to 1886) against Oxford. In the inter-University matches his scores were small, but in other games for Cambridge he played some large innings, including 109 v. Mr. A. J. Webbe's XI in 1885 and 174 v. Mr. C. I. Thornton's a year later. He assisted Leicestershire from 1883 until 1892, visited the United States and Canada with Mr. E. J. Sanders' teams of 1885 and 1886, and in the last-mentioned season took part in the Gentlemen v. Players match at the Oval. His career in important cricket would doubtless have been longer had he not lost the sight of an eye in January, 1893, whilst playing racquets.

TURNER, Montague, died at Woodcroft, Cuckfield, Sussex, on January 25, 1908. He was born at Acton, in Middlesex, on September 21, 1843, and was educated at Cheltenham, where he was in the XI in 1860. For some years he was one of the best wicket-keepers in England, and on 52 occasions he appeared for Middlesex, his first match being against M.C.C. and Ground at Lord's in 1863 and his last against Surrey on the same ground 15 years later. In the match against Notts, at Prince's in 1875 he caught six and stumped three, a number of wickets he had obtained four years earlier, when he caught four and stumped five when assisting the Gentlemen of England against Oxford University on the Magdalen ground. Playing for the Gentlemen against Cambridge University at Fenner's in 1876, he caught three and stumped five and also played an innings of 51. His highest innings in first-class cricket was 82 for Middlesex v. Oxford University at

Prince's in 1876, when Oxford, going in against a total of 439, made 612, every player on the side reaching double figures and W. H. Game, with 141, being highest scorer. In the match between Oxford University and Gentlemen of England at Oxford in 1870, the former, going in first, curiously lost their first four wickets in the same manner, the score-sheet reading:

Mr. A. T. Fortescue st Turner b Buchanan 1
Mr. W. H. Hadow st Turner b Buchanan   6
Mr C. J. Ottaway not out   24
Mr. B. Pauncefote st Turner b Buchanan 0
Mr. E. F. S. Tylecote st Turner b Buchanan 0

Two years later, in the Gentlemen of South's first innings against Players of the South at the Oval, Mr. Turner scored only four runs while Mr. C. I. Thornton made 63. He appeared twice for the Gentlemen against the Players—at Brighton in 1871 and at the Oval in the following year. Mr. Turner, a solicitor by profession, had been a member at Lord's since 1869, and had served on the committees of the M.C.C. and the Middlesex County C.C.

TURNER, Capt. Noel Vernon Cyril, who died on June 13, 1941, aged 54, at Hungerford Park, Berkshire, showed to advantage in the Repton XI from 1903 to 1905, and played sometimes for Nottinghamshire from 1906 to 1913, when A. O. Jones was captain and the strong side included John Gunn, George Gunn, J. Hardstaff senior, J. Iremonger and W. Payton. Turner averaged 23.36 for nine matches in 1907, the year Nottinghamshire were absolutely Champion County for the first time since 1886. Tom Wass and Hallam in that season of triumph did nearly all the bowling, taking between them 298 wickets, while only 42 fell to six other bowlers in competition matches. Turner kept goal for Corinthians and played for England against Belgium in the amateur international match of 1920.

TURNER, Major Robert Harrison Tom, M.C., died on September 13, 1947, aged 58. Played for Repton and a little for Nottinghamshire.

TURNER, Lieut.-Col. Walter Martin Fitz-Herbert, R.A., died suddenly at Harrow, on February 1, 1948, aged 66. Wellington captain in 1897. A good bat. Played occasionally for Essex, 1899–1923, scoring 2,017 runs, average 28.01. Younger brother of A. J. Turner.

TWINING, Richard Haynes, C.B.E., who died on January 3, 1979, aged 89, had had close associations with Lord's for over 70 years. Three years in the Eton XI and captain in 1909, he then played four years for Oxford, captaining them in 1912. Between 1910 and 1914 he made a few appearances for Middlesex, but was so severely wounded in the First World War that for a long time he was on crutches and it seemed that his serious cricket must be over. By 1919, however, though handicapped still by lameness, he had recovered sufficiently to reappear for the county and to make 100 for the Free Foresters against Cambridge. He continued to play for Middlesex, when business permitted, until 1928, and in his last season made 121 against Sussex at Lord's. The innings of his life was in the Surrey match at Lord's in 1921. If Surrey won, they became champions; otherwise, Middlesex retained the title. When Surrey led by 137 on the first innings, the odds were definitely on them, and they were still favourites when Middlesex went in to make 322 to win. But a second-wicket stand of 277 in four hours 10 minutes between Twining, who scored 135, and Jack Hearne settled the issue and Middlesex won by six wickets. Off the field he did great work for cricket. First serving on the M.C.C. committee in 1933, he was president in 1964, a trustee from 1952 to 1969, and on retiring from this became the second Life Vice-President in the history of the club, the first having been Sir Pelham Warner. From 1950 to 1957 he was president of Middlesex.

TWISLETON-WYKEHAM-FIENNES, The Rev. The Hon. Wingfield Stratford, born at Adlesthorp, in Gloucestershire, on May 1, 1834, died at Broughton Castle, Banbury, on October 10, 1923, in his 90th year. He was the fourth son of Frederick, 16th Baron Saye and Sele. *Scores and Biographies* (iv–289) said of him: "Is a sharp quick hitter and bowls round-armed of a moderate speed with a pretty delivery." In his four Public School matches for Winchester in 1851 and 1852 against Harrow and Eton he made 63 runs in eight innings and took 15 wickets. Obtaining his Blue for Oxford in 1856, he appeared three times against Cambridge, scoring 47 runs in five innings and taking 14 wickets. His best bowling feat in a match of note was to take eight wickets in an innings for 56 runs against M.C.C. and Ground at Oxford in 1856, but for XXII of Hungerford Park v. the England XI in 1854 he had an analysis of nine for 23 in a total of 70, his victims including Julius Cæsar, Anderson, Parr,

Caffyn, H. H. Stephenson and Guy. For I Zingari v. Liverpool in 1860 he made 20 not out and 109 not out, the only other double-figure score in the second innings being 21 by Capt. F. H. Bathurst; he claimed 109 of the 160 made from the bat. In another match at Liverpool he took five wickets with consecutive balls. His County Cricket was played for Herefordshire and Oxfordshire. His elder brother, Mr. C. B., was also in the XI whilst at Winchester.

TWYMAN, George, born at Canterbury on November 15, 1862, died at Godalming in 1919. He made many large scores for the St. Lawrence C.C. and played in one match for Kent in 1887. He was a steady batsman and generally fielded at mid-off.

TYE, John, who was born at Bulwell, Nottinghamshire, on July 10, 1848, died at Brighouse in the last week of November, 1905. *Scores and Biographies* described him as "a good hard hitter, and a very fast and bumpy round-armed bowler." In 1874 he appeared on a few occasions for Derbyshire, and it was not until 1876 that he assisted his native county. He played for Nottinghamshire six times in 1877, and twice in 1878 and 1881. His highest score was 48 v. Gloucestershire, at Clifton, in 1876, and his best bowling performance nine wickets for 101 v. Lancashire, at Manchester, the same year. For nearly a quarter of a century he had been connected with the Brighouse club.

TYLDESLEY, Ernest, of Lancashire and England, died at his home at Rhos-on-Sea on May 5, 1962, aged 73.

Neville Cardus wrote in *The Guardian*:

Ernest Tyldesley, one of the most accomplished batsmen ever to play for Lancashire, was born in Lancashire, brother of one of the three greatest professional batsmen in the game's history. As a boy he played for Roe Green, which in a way was a Tyldesley club; for the famous "J.T.T." learned his cricket on the same village green. J. T. Tyldesley kept a more than brotherly eye on Ernest but turned the other way when he saw the youngster's cross-bat. "J.T.T." also tended to bring his bat along a line beginning at third man. "A straight bat's all right to a straight ball," said "J.T.T." one day, "but there are not many runs to be made by straight pushing." "J.T.T." never pushed; but Ernest seldom began an innings without one or two anxious or tentative thrusts. Once he had "seen" the ball he could be as brilliant and as punitive as he was defensively sound.

"J.T.T." was a genius, and it is to Ernest's credit that, though on his entrance into Lancashire cricket he had to survive a disheartening comparison, he never lost faith. "J.T.T.," of course, constantly encouraged him. "Some day," he said, "he'll be a better bat than ever I was." Ernest certainly scored a few more runs in his career than came from the broadsword of his brother. Between 1909 and 1936 Ernest scored 38,874, average 45.46; "J.T.T.'s" portion was, between 1895 and 1932, 37,807, average 40.69.

In style they were more than different. Ernest's batting was always courteous; in his most aggressive moods, when he would hook fast bowling vividly, he rarely suggested militancy or the ruthless slayer of bowling. "Johnny" was usually on the kill... If a maiden over were bowled at him, "J.T.T." would gnaw a glove at the end of it. He had, with Macartney, no patience with a good attack; he felt the necessity of falling on it and demolishing it without delay. Ernest was more patient. But when the situation called for valiance Ernest could go into battle with chivalric manners concealing ruthless and belligerent purpose.

In the Test match of 1921 at Old Trafford he was the first England cricketer that year really to treat the conquering attack of Armstrong with contumely. In 1925 at Kennington Oval he played one of the most tremendously incisive, powerful, merciless, and gallant innings I have ever seen. At close of play on the second day Lancashire were apparently at Surrey's mercy. Four wickets had fallen, with 117 still needed to escape defeat by an innings. Hitch began the Surrey attack next morning at a hair-raising pace. He employed five slips. In a quarter of an hour four of those slips had been moved to the leg and on sides—defensively. Tyldesley's hooking was savage and daring: he hooked from his eyebrow. His hits to the off were no less swift and exacting. In five hours he scored 236 without a shadow of error. Lancashire saved the game easily.

Ernest's experiences in Test cricket were peculiar, making strange reading these days when all manner of inglorious Miltons are asked, almost on bended knees, to bat for England. In 1921 Tyldesley played for England at Nottingham against the ferocious McDonald and Gregory attack. He made 0 and seven, knocked out second innings by Gregory, bowled off his cheek-bone. He was recalled for the Old Trafford Test, when he scored 78 not out, and for the fifth Test at Kennington Oval where he made a pleasant 39. Not until 1926 was he again asked to play for England against Australia at Old Trafford in the fourth Test of the rubber. He scored 81; and was dropped for the concluding game of the same rubber.

He was taken to Australia, one of Chapman's team of 1928–29, but was entrusted with only one Test, in which he made 31 and 21. He was never again chosen for the England XI against Australia. So, in five opportunities against the strongest cricket power, his record was, and remains, 0, seven, 78 not out, 39, 81, 31, and 21. In South Africa, in the Test matches there of the 1927–28 rubber, he headed England's averages—65 an innings for 520 runs, with these scores: 122, 0, 87, 78, 62 not out, 42, eight, 100, and 21. And South Africa's attack was then composed of Nupen, Morkel, Vincent, Bissett, and Hall.

In 1928 Tyldesley amassed 3,024 runs in the season, average 79.57. In 1926, when he was only once picked for the England XI (and scored his 81), he made four centuries in successive innings, with a season's aggregate of 2,826, average 64.22, only Hobbs and Sutcliffe his statistical peers. Yet he could not hold a place in the England side. In his career he reached the century 102 times, and twice he scored two centuries in the same match.

Figures alone will give some idea to posterity of his quality. Like his brother, he had the answer to unpleasant wickets. His great cricket in South Africa was achieved on matting, against Nupen spinning viciously. In fact, he preferred a turning ball to the one that came straight through quickly enough to find a slight clink in the armour—the bat just a little out of the straight. But those of us who saw him play and knew him off the field as a friend will remember his batsmanship not only for its skill, resource, and plenty, but mainly because it was so like the man himself—modest yet firm of character, civilised in all its called-for action. He was, in a word, a gentlemanly babuean who, when he needed to assert his authority, never exceeded the privileges of class and manners.

His cricket was part and parcel of a Lancastrian of quiet charm, having a modesty that concealed the tough fibre in him of Lancashire. A year or two ago, a painful stage of his broken health, George Duckworth went to visit him at his home. "And how are you, Ernest?" "Well, George, I was at the specialist's yesterday, and he says my eyes are in a bad way. And I've had awful pains in my thighs, and my chest's been giving me jip." Then he paused, before adding, "But, mind you, George, there's nothin' the matter with me!"

That's the Lancashire man for you, all over. We'll not forget him.

TYLDESLEY, Harry, one of four brothers from Westhoughton who have played for Lancashire, died at Morecambe on August 30, 1935, aged 42. Harry Tyldesley was on the ground staff at Old Trafford for many years and occasionally appeared for the county without doing anything of note. Unable to get a regular place in the county XI, he played for several league clubs.

TYLDESLEY, James Darbyshire, born at Ashton-in-Makerfield on August 10, 1889, died in a nursing home at Bolton whilst under an anaesthetic on January 31, 1923. An elder brother of Richard Tyldesley, he was tried for Lancashire as a fast bowler in 1910, but did not become a regular member of the side until two years later. He did the hat-trick against Derbyshire at Manchester in 1920 and v. Worcestershire on the same ground in 1922, at one period of the latter game taking five wickets for nine runs. His three 100s for the county were all made at Old Trafford—101 not out v. Warwickshire in 1919, 112 v. Surrey in 1921, and 112 not out v. Leicestershire in 1922. Against Yorkshire at Sheffield, in 1914, he carried out his bat for 62 and took eight wickets. In September 1921 a match was played between Lancashire and the Bolton league for the benefit of his family.

TYLDESLEY, John Thomas, one of England's greatest batsmen, who had been in weak health for some years, died on November 27, 1930. On the morning of his death he was putting on his boots before going to his business at Deansgate, Manchester, when he collapsed and died. He had carried on his duties as coach at Old Trafford until the end of the summer. Born at Roe Green, Worsley, on November 22, 1873, he was just 57 years of age at the time of his death. Tyldesley received his early training in Lancashire club cricket—a very stiff school—and was a well-equipped batsman when he first appeared for Lancashire in 1895. In his second match he scored 152 not out against Warwickshire on the Edgbaston ground—the scene of many triumphs for him in subsequent years. He did nothing else of much note that summer—he was not given a trial until the middle of July—but two years later he made over 1,000 runs, and he achieved that performance for 19 consecutive seasons. Four times he scored over 2,000 runs, and in 1901 he had an aggregate of 3,041, his innings including nine separate centuries, eight of which were made for Lancashire, and his average being 55. In two seasons—1897 and 1904—he played three successive innings of 100, and on three occasions he made two separate 100s in the same match. These scores were 106 and 100 not out for Lancashire against Warwickshire in 1897, 121 and 100 not out in a North and South match in 1900, and 136 and 101 for Lancashire against Hampshire in 1910. His highest innings—all for his county—were:

295*	v. Kent, at Manchester	..	..	..	..	..	..	1906
272	v. Derbyshire, at Chesterfield	..	..	..	..	..	..	1919
253	v. Kent, at Canterbury	..	..	..	..	..	..	1914
250	v. Notts, at Trent Bridge	..	..	..	..	..	..	1905
249	v. Leicestershire, at Leicester	..	..	..	..	..	..	1899
248	v. Worcestershire, at Liverpool	..	..	..	..	..	..	1903
243	v. Leicestershire, at Leicester	..	..	..	..	..	..	1908
225	v. Notts, at Trent Bridge	..	..	..	..	..	..	1904
221	v. Notts, at Trent Bridge	..	..	..	..	..	..	1901
210	v. Somerset, at Bath	..	..	..	..	..	..	1904
210	v. Surrey, at the Oval	..	..	..	..	..	..	1913
209	v. Warwickshire, at Edgbaston	..	..	..	..	..	..	1907
200	v. Derbyshire, at Manchester	..	..	..	..	..	..	1898

Signifies not out.

Altogether in the course of his brilliant career he scored 37,803 runs in first-class matches with an average of nearly 41 and made 86 separate centuries. He played frequently in Gentlemen v. Players matches and in 1901 made 140 at Lord's. He also took a leading part in Test match cricket between 1899 and 1909, appearing for England in 16 games in this country and going out to Australia with A. C. MacLaren's team in 1901–02 and with the M.C.C.'s side two years later. In England he made three 100s against Australia, scoring 138 at Birmingham in 1902 (after the side had started in disastrous fashion), 100 at Leeds in 1905, and 112 not out at the Oval in the latter year. In all he scored 1,661 runs in Test matches with an average of 30. Tyldesley was a member of the team Lord Hawke took out to South Africa in the winter of 1898–99. He scored 742 runs during the tour with an average of 32. Among his innings was one of 112 in a Test match at Cape Town. There were few batsmen more attractive to watch than John Tyldesley. He was exceptionally quick on his feet and so always appeared to have plenty of time in which to make his strokes. Essentially a batsman of enterprise, when he went forward to the ball it was nearly always to hit. He also possessed a very strong defence and had at his command practically all the strokes in the game. His ability to adapt himself to circumstances was emphasised in a Test match at the Oval in 1905, when Armstrong, bowling well outside the leg stump with an off-break, reduced to impotence a number of batsmen, but not Tyldesley, who drew back and cut him. One of the best of outfieldsmen, he was very fast, picked the ball up cleanly, and had a very accurate return, in addition to being a very sure catch.

His benefit match, against Yorkshire at Manchester in 1906, yielded a profit of £3,105. Ernest Tyldesley, the Lancashire batsman, was a younger brother of John Tyldesley.

TYLDESLEY, Richard Knowles, youngest and only survivor of four brothers, all of whom were on the Old Trafford ground staff and played for Lancashire, died at his home, Little Hulton near Bolton, on September 17, 1943, aged 45. His father, J. D. Tyldesley, a Westhoughton club professional, taught his sons cricket, and "Dick" reached a high standard. Constant practice at the nets in boyhood brought perfection in length, and with experience he mastered spin, varied pace and other artifices which brought him a trial for Lancashire in 1919 when county matches after the First World War were restricted to two days. His skill as a slow bowler increased like his bulk, and he gradually gained renown as a slow bowler of the heaviest build in County Cricket, looking older than his years but carrying his weight with remarkable ease while toiling for long spells without tiring. Above medium height, he flighted the ball naturally and used the top spinner in a way often earning the umpire's agreement with the leg-before appeal. His leg-break, expected by batsmen rather than operative, turned little if at all under normal conditions but, given a responsive pitch, Dick Tyldesley could be devastating, though length, adjusted to a batsman's ability, was his most effective means of attack.

Regularly from 1922 his victims numbered at least 100 a season, and he showed little if any deterioration in 1931 when the Lancashire committee could not concede to his request for an engagement for a definite period at a fixed salary of £400 a year, no matter whether he could play or not; and his association with the county ceased.

In 1923 he took 106 wickets in Championship matches at 15 runs apiece. Next season, when the South Africans toured England, Tyldesley appeared to considerable advantage in four of the five Test matches, but his most brilliant achievement was six wickets for 18 runs at Leeds, where, thanks to him and Parkin, Yorkshire were dismissed for 33 and beaten by 24 runs.

This form gained Tyldesley a place in the side which visited Australia in the following winter under A. E. R. Gilligan, but he met with little success on the "shirt-front" wickets, and played against Australia only in the Test match at Melbourne, being dismissed for one and 0, and sending down 37 overs for 136 runs without getting a wicket.

In 1930 Dick Tyldesley played for England against Australia at Nottingham, where England triumphed, and at Leeds in a drawn match, dismissing seven batsmen at an average of 33 runs in the two encounters, but was not called upon again. He headed his county's bowling with 121 wickets at 14.73 each, and Lancashire were Champion County for the fourth time in five seasons, the first of these successes coming in 1926 after an interval of 22 years when A. C. MacLaren captained the side. He was again the most effective bowler for Lancashire in 1931 with a record of 116 wickets at a fraction under 16 runs each, but his county dropped to sixth place; and that ended his county career. During several seasons he enjoyed considerable success with the bat, and in 1922 he hit up 105 against Nottinghamshire at Old Trafford.

Parkin and Dick Tyldesley did some remarkable performances besides the triumph at Leeds. In 1924 they shared the wickets in both innings at Old Trafford for Lancashire against the South Africans, Tyldesley's figures being seven for 28 and five for 50; they were unchanged against Warwickshire, 10 wickets falling to Tyldesley for 103 runs. In that season he dismissed five Leicestershire batsmen, three clean bowled and the other two leg-before-wicket, in five maiden overs—all he bowled in the innings. Another fine performance was seven Northampton-

shire wickets for six runs at Aigburth. Against the same county at Kettering in 1926 he dismissed eight men for 15 runs. Also a unique performance stands to his credit at Derby in 1929, when he dismissed two men with the last two balls of one innings and two more with the first two deliveries he sent down in the second innings.

Altogether in first-class cricket he took 1,513 wickets at 17.15 runs apiece, scored 6,424 runs, average 15.04, and held 328 catches—mostly at short-leg. For Lancashire his record showed 1,447 wickets, a number exceeded only by John Briggs and Arthur Mold. After giving up County Cricket, Tyldesley helped Nantwich to win the North Staffordshire and District League Championship twice, and he did good service for Accrington, whom he joined in 1934.

In 1930 his benefit match, when Surrey visited Old Trafford, realised £2,027, although it clashed with England v. Australia at Trent Bridge where Tyldesley was engaged. At different periods Dick Tyldesley shared in the Lancashire bowling honours with Cecil Parkin and E. A. McDonald, the Australian—and now all three are dead: McDonald passed away in 1937, Parkin three months before Richard Tyldesley.

So much doubt has prevailed as to the relationship of the six Tyldesleys who played for Lancashire that it is opportune to emphasise that the brothers John Thomas, who died in 1930, and Ernest, both famous batsmen and England Test players, belonged to a Worsley family and were not related to the four Westhoughton professionals; these were:

William K. Tyldesley, a batsman. Killed in 1918 during the First World War while a lieutenant in the North Lancashire Regiment. Obituary 1919 *Wisden*.

James Darbyshire Tyldesley, a fast bowler and good batsman; played first for Lancashire in 1910, died in 1923. Obituary 1924 *Wisden*.

Harry Tyldesley, died in 1935. Played first for the county in 1914, at Derby on July 11, when two pairs of Tyldesley brothers figured in the Lancashire XI; that season the Lancashire averages included five Tyldesleys. Harry toured with A. C. MacLaren's team in the winter of 1922 and headed the bowling averages both in Australia and New Zealand. Obituary 1936 *Wisden*.

Richard Tyldesley, the youngest, the subject of this obituary.

TYLDESLEY, Lieut. W. K. (Loyal North Lancashire Regiment), born 1887; killed

April 25, 1918. Lancashire: first match, 1908. Highest score 152 v. Derbyshire at Derby.

TYLECOTE, Edward Ferdinando Sutton, one of the best batsmen wicket-keepers of all time, died at Hunstanton on March 15, 1938, aged 88. He showed such exceptional form as a boy that he was in the Clifton College XI five years, finishing as captain in 1868. That summer he made the then record score of 404 during three spells of two hours each for Modern v. Classical, carrying his bat through an innings of 630. He got his Blue at Oxford as a Freshman and his second experience against Cambridge was in the "Cobden match." Next year he led the Dark Blues to victory by eight wickets, but in his second season as captain, Cambridge won by an innings and 166, William Yardley setting up a record with his second 100 in University matches. Mr. Tylecote was the oldest living University captain.

When a mathematical tutor at Royal Military Academy, Tylecote played for Kent and perhaps his best performance for the county was a perfect not out 100 against the 1882 Australian team, when T. W. Garrett and G. E. Palmer were carrying all before them. W. H. Patterson, the present chairman of the Kent county committee, played a fine second innings in the same match. Tylecote also assisted Bedfordshire, the county of his birth.

Tylecote went to Australia at the end of the 1882 season with the Hon. Ivo Bligh's team which won two out of three matches against W. L. Murdoch's touring side. He scored 66 in the deciding encounter which gave the Englishmen the rubber. Played for his wicket-keeping in the 1886 matches against Australia at Lord's and the Oval he helped in two victories, each by an innings. He appeared several times for the Gentlemen against the Players during a period of 16 years, ending with that of 1886 when, though 37 years of age, he was probably at his best behind the stumps. He showed exceptionally fine form against the Players at Lord's in 1883, his 107 being a faultless display of two and a half hours' stylish batting, notable for offside strokes made with delightful ease. He was only the sixth batsman to hit a century at Lord's for the Gentlemen, the first having been William Ward in 1825.

When keeping wicket he stood close up unless the bowling was exceptionally fast. By his quiet, unobtrusive taking of the ball under the difficult conditions of rough wickets he was very reliable both in catching and stumping. He was one of the first wicket-keepers who dispensed with a long stop. Two brothers of E. F. S. Tylecote, C. B. L. and H. G., both good cricketers, died within a few days of each other in March, 1935, aged 88 and 82 respectively; like E. F. S. both captained the Clifton XI and H. G. was in the Oxford XI, 1874–77.

TYLECOTE, Henry Grey, died at Oxford on March 8, 1935. Born on July 24, 1853, he was in his 82nd year. Mr. Tylecote was in the Clifton College XI from 1870 to 1873, being captain in his last two seasons, and he played for Oxford against Cambridge at Lord's in the next four years. A sound, patient batsman and a round-arm medium-paced bowler, he kept wicket in his first years in the Oxford side but on his last appearance against the Light Blues he enjoyed a large share in his side's victory by taking nine wickets for 122 runs. Scoring 39 he helped F. M. Buckland in a stand of 142 for the seventh wicket which turned the game and Oxford won by 10 wickets.

Henry Tylecote played for the Gentlemen against the Players at Prince's Ground in 1877 and two years later for South against North at the Oval, the match being for the benefit of James Southerton, father of the late editor of the *Almanack*. Mr. Tylecote was the last survivor of those who took part in that game. Between the years 1876 and 1883 Henry Tylecote played for Bedfordshire and subsequently for Hertfordshire. He gained prominence in athletic sports by his prowess at throwing the cricket ball and as a half-mile and mile runner. In 1877 he finished second in the mile to the Cambridge representative. Henry Grey was the youngest of three brothers of whom Mr. E. F. S. Tylecote played for England against Australia at Lord's and the Oval in 1886 and toured Australia with the England team in 1882–83. E. F. S. Tylecote played for Oxford against Cambridge from 1869 to 1872, being captain of the Dark Blues in his last two seasons.

The captains in the 1877 match were A. J. Webbe, still president of Middlesex county, and W. S. Patterson, who after leaving Cambridge played for Lancashire and retains a close interest in the game. They are the only two survivors of the Gentlemen and Players match that same year at Lord's. All the Players are dead. Patterson took a leading part in a remarkable victory by one wicket. When the Players batted first he dismissed seven men for 58 runs. Thanks to 12 runs by him, going in No. 9, the Gentlemen led by six. Two wickets for 55 was then Patterson's share in dismissing the Players for 148. Although W. G. Grace scored 41, the Gentlemen wanted 46 when Patterson, going in last this time, joined G. F. Grace. Against wonderfully accurate bowling the runs were got slowly, Fred Grace with a four and a single winning "The Glorious Match," as it was called, by one wicket.

TYLER, Edwin James, born at Kidderminster, October 13, 1866; died at Taunton, January 21, 1917. Tyler will always be remembered for the share he had in securing Somerset's promotion to first-class rank in 1891, and his effective bowling in the seasons that immediately followed, when Somerset, with S. M. J. Woods and Lionel Palairet at their best, had such a strong and attractive team. In his own style Tyler was a remarkable left-handed bowler. So slow was his pace that unless he had had a good head and great command of length first-rate batsmen would have hit him all over the field. As it was he made even the best batsmen respect him, and on occasions he did great things.

Though never ranking with Rhodes and Blythe he had a highly successful career. On the question of his delivery there is no need to say very much. It was fortunate for him that he came out at a time when great laxity prevailed with regard to throwing. He was too slow to hurt anybody, and so his action, though often talked about, passed muster for many years. Had he appeared after the captains of the first-class counties had taken the matter of unfair bowling into their own hands, things might not have gone so pleasantly for him. One may say this without doing him any injustice. Many offenders, 10 times worse than Tyler, were allowed to pursue their evil courses quite unchecked until the hour of reform arrived. Tyler played much of his early cricket for the Kidderminster club, and for two years—1885 and 1886—he was in the Worcestershire XI, bowling with marked success in 1885. Then came his connection with Somerset and his fame as a slow bowler. Personally Tyler was very popular, his genial nature gaining him friends wherever he went.—S.H.P.

Bowling for Somerset in Second-class days:

Year	Overs	Maidens	Runs	Wickets	Average
1888	471.2	206	752	74	10.00
1889	405.4	130	814	67	12.14
1890	669.1	249	1,192	126	9.00

Bowling for Somerset in First-class Cricket:

1891	479.4	123	1,156	57	20.00
1892	656.1	191	1,548	101	15.00
1893	944.1	333	1,873	106	17.00
1894	800.4	256	1,551	95	16.00
1895	1,085.3	251	2,800	124	22.00
1896	841	195	2,309	76	30.00
1897	797	184	2,132	91	23.00
1898	763.3	156	2,134	86	24.00
1899	617	110	1,716	68	25.00
1900	477.3	97	1,542	58	26.58

Only occasionally later for Somerset.

Some of Tyler's chief bowling feats (for Somerset unless otherwise stated):
(a) Eight or more wickets in an innings:

Wkts Runs			
8 for 23	v. Essex, at Taunton		1888
8 for 47	v. Warwickshire, at Bath		1888
9 for 33	v. Notts, at Taunton		1892
8 for 51	v. Sussex, at Taunton		1895
10 for 49	v. Surrey, at Taunton		1895
8 for 72	v. Gloucestershire, at Bristol		1896
8 for 218	v. Gloucestershire, at Bristol		1898
8 for 42	v. Middlesex, at Lord's		1899

(b) Thirteen or more in match:

15 for —	v. Essex, at Taunton		1888
13 for 124	v. Warwickshire, at Edgbaston		1890

E. J. TYLER'S BOWLING FEATS—*Continued*

14 for 98	..	v. Glamorgan, at Cardiff	1890
13 for 92	..	v. Devon, at Taunton	1890
14 for 80	..	H. T. Hewett's Twelve v. Camb. Univ. Twelve, at Cambridge	1892
15 for 96	..	v. Notts, at Taunton	1892
15 for 95	..	v. Sussex, at Taunton	1895
13 for 91	..	v. Surrey, at Taunton	1895
14 for 247	..	v. Yorkshire, at Taunton	1895
14 for 122	..	v. Gloucestershire, at Bristol	1896
13 for 163	..	v. Surrey, at the Oval	1897
14 for 235	..	v. Lancashire, at Taunton	1898
13 for 135	..	v. Hampshire, at Bath	1900

(c) Four or more wickets for three runs or less each:

5 for 9	..	v. Warwickshire, at Taunton	1890
7 for 16	..	v. Devon, at Taunton	1890
6 for 17	..	v. Glamorgan, at Lansdown	1890
5 for 10	..	v. Gloucestershire, at Cheltenham	1891

(d) Unchanged through both completed innings:

With S. M. J. Woods	v. M.C.C. and G., at Lord's	1889
With Nichols	.. v. Staffordshire, at Stoke	1890
With Nichols	.. v. Hampshire, at Taunton	1890

TYLER, Fred, a former Northamptonshire player, died at Northampton on October 15, 1930, aged 76.

TYSON, Cecil, appeared at a somewhat advanced age—32—in the Yorkshire XI, and met with startling success. In his opening match he set up a record for the county by scoring a century on his first appearance—exactly 100 not out. He followed with 80, also not out, in Yorkshire's second innings, but such a phenomenal feat did not prove the forerunner of big things. In fact, Tyson played in only two more first-class matches after his triumph at Southampton against Hampshire in 1921, making 29 against the Australians and 23 off the Lancashire bowlers after failure in the first innings. Yorkshire were then, as usual, very powerful, and Tyson was not young enough to fill occasional vacancies whilst training for a permanent place in the side. He joined a South Wales club with the idea of qualifying for Glamorgan, but in 1926 he returned to Yorkshire club cricket. He died at his home at Whitwood, near Leeds, on April 4, 1940, aged 51.

TYSSEN, The Rev. Charles Amhurst Daniel, died on Christmas Day, 1940, aged 84, and was buried at Cheriton on New Year's Day. He played for Harrow, and in the 1875 match with Eton helped to save his side from defeat. Harrow followed-on and lost six men before Tyssen joined Chater, and they played out time, Tyssen making 39. In a match for Harrow against M.C.C. he scored 20 in a total of 31 and was not out. Twenty years later, 1896, Tyssen played for Authors' club against the Press club at Lord's and went in first with Dr. Conan Doyle; there was a prolonged stand on sodden turf while drizzling rain fell. Tyssen scored 97 and Conan Doyle 101 not out. J. M. Barrie took part in the match, which was drawn. A photograph of the teams grouped in front of the pavilion appeared in *Black and White*.

UBSDELL, George, died at the Palatine Hotel, Ganton, near Liverpool, on October 15, 1905. Born at Southampton on April 4, 1845, he was for many years a prominent member of the Hampshire XI. *Scores and Biographies* says of him (ix–378): "Is an excellent hitter to all parts of the field, especially to the off, bowls round-armed, middle-paced, and is also a capital wicket-keeper." In the match at Southampton, in August, 1865, between Hampshire and Surrey, he caught one and stumped five off the latter in a single innings, the Surrey total realising only 37. After relinquishing first-class cricket, Ubsdell was for 12 years groundsman of the Liverpool C.C., at Aigburth. Height, 5 ft. 6 in.; weight, 10 st.

UDAL, Geoffrey Francis, died on December 5, 1980, aged 72. A fast bowler, he played once for Middlesex in 1932 and twice for Leicestershire in 1946, though without success. In 1946 it was discovered that he had been bowling with a fractured rib. He was a grandson of the Hon. J.S. Udal, who did so much for cricket in Fiji.

UDAL, John Symonds, who was born near Birmingham, on November 10, 1848, died suddenly in London on March 13, 1925, aged 76. A very useful all-round cricketer, he obtained his colours whilst at Bromsgrove School, and later played for Dorset, Somerset, M.C.C., Richmond, Free Foresters and Incogniti, but he did not succeed in securing his Blue for Oxford. In 1873 he was invited by "W.G." to accompany his team to Australia, but he was unable to do so. In 1894–95 he captained a Fiji team in New Zealand, and he did much to encourage the game whilst Attorney-General of Fiji and, later, Chief Justice of the Leeward Islands. In 1869 he became a member of the M.C.C., and he had served on the Committee and also been an auditor of the club. He was father of Mr. N.R. Udal, of Winchester, Oxford University and Dorset.

ULLATHORNE, Charles Edward, was born at Hull, April 11, 1845, and died at Manchester in May, 1904. He appeared for Yorkshire from 1868 to 1875, playing 50 innings with an average of 7.21. Ullathorne was a splendid field, especially at cover-point, where he saved any number of runs. In 1874 he played an innings of 59 for Yorkshire United v. Derbyshire, having to contend with the bowling of Mycroft, Platts, and Tye. In the second innings of Yorkshire v. Notts, at Nottingham, in 1869, he batted 50 minutes for one run. The Yorkshire County C.C. granted £20 to his widow, who had been left in somewhat straitened circumstances.

ULYETT, George, died on Saturday evening, June 18, 1898. He was only in his 47th year, his last season in the Yorkshire XI being 1893. His health had been failing for some time, but the immediate cause of death was an acute attack of pneumonia, contracted at Bramall Lane during the Yorkshire and Kent match. Yorkshire has always been rich in first-rate cricketers, but a finer player than Ulyett the county has never produced. He was for years the best bat in the team, and even if he had not been able to get a run he would have been worth his place for his bowling and fielding. His career for the county extended over a period of 20 years, his first appearance in the XI dating back to July, 1873. It was seen at once that a player of remarkable gifts had been discovered, and before very long he was at the top of the tree. To begin with, if one

remembers rightly, he was played as much for his fast bowling as for his batting. One talent, however, developed to a much greater extent than the other, and in two or three seasons he was quite as good a bat as Ephraim Lockwood, who, when Ulyett came out, was the bright particular star of the Yorkshire XI. Once having established his position Ulyett never looked back. There was no doubt about his class as a batsman after his first visit to Australia with James Lillywhite's team in the winter of 1876–77, and from that time until 1891 he was always in the front rank. Of course, like other great batsmen, he did much better in some seasons than others, but he never lost his place as a representative cricketer. A peculiar interest attaches to the tour of James Lillywhite's team—not, in some respects, very brilliant—as it was then that the Australians first ventured to play an English XI on even terms. Thanks to a wonderful innings of 165 by Charles Bannerman, Australia won the first match, but in the return the Englishmen had their revenge, Ulyett's batting deciding the fortunes of the game. It was the fine play they showed that season that led the Australians to pay their first visit to England, a momentous chapter in the history of modern cricket being thus opened.

At home Ulyett, of course, played many times for England against Australia, and in two memorable encounters at Lord's he contributed in a very marked degree to England's success. The first of the two matches was in 1884, when A.G. Steel scored 148—the innings of his life. On the Tuesday afternoon the Australians, with a balance of 150 runs against them, went in for the second time. The wicket had not worn well, and Peate, bowling from the Nursery end, had the batsmen from the first in obvious difficulties. After a little time, however, to everyone's surprise, Lord Harris took him off and gave Ulyett the ball. Never was a captain better justified by results. The broken places on the pitch which had made Peate difficult rendered Ulyett well-nigh irresistible. Bowling his fastest, and repeatedly breaking back several inches, he had one of the strongest of all Australian teams at his mercy. At the drawing of stumps that evening four men were out for 73, and the next morning the Australians were all out for 145, England winning the match by an innings and five runs. Ulyett took seven wickets in 39 overs and a ball, and had only 36 runs hit from him. It was on that eventful Tuesday afternoon that Ulyett caught and bowled Bonnor in a way that no one who was present will ever forget. Bonnor's mission was to knock the fast bowler off, and he did his best. He drove a half-volley with all his force, but the ball—travelling faster than an express train—went into Ulyett's right hand instead of to the boundary. Bonnor wandered disconsolately back to the pavilion, and the England players gathered round Ulyett, curious, perhaps, to know what manner of man he was, and anxious to congratulate him on his escape from imminent danger. One can remember, even now, the look of wonder on the faces of A. G. Steel and Alfred Lyttelton. Ulyett himself was very modest about the matter. Complimented on the catch, when the day's play was over, he said simply that if the ball had hit his fingers instead of going into his hand he should have played no more cricket that season.

The other England match was in 1890. England had much the stronger side, and won in the end by seven wickets, but on the first day there was a period of great anxiety. The ground had suffered a good deal from rain, and after the Australians had been put out for 132, England lost W. G. Grace, Shrewsbury, W. W. Read and Gunn—the four best bats on the side—for 20 runs. Turner and Ferris were bowling their best, and the outlook was, to say the least, cheerless. However, Maurice Read and Ulyett saved the side from collapse. They put on 72 runs in an hour and a half, and next morning Ulyett carried his own score to 74. That was the highest innings he ever played for England against Australia in this country, and, curiously enough, he never appeared for England again. The Yorkshire authorities would not let him off for the Oval match in 1890, and when the Australians paid us their next visit, in 1893, his star had waned.

Of Ulyett's doings for Yorkshire and in the Gentlemen and Players matches a column could easily be written. He was at his very best for his county in the season of 1887, when he and Louis Hall did great things. The one brilliancy itself, the other a miracle of patience, they were an ideal pair to start an innings. It is a moot point whether bowlers were the more disturbed by Ulyett's hitting or by Hall's unwearying defence. Some preferred to bowl at Ulyett because he hit at so many balls that there was always a chance of getting him out. Alfred Shaw for one never despaired of seeing him caught if the ground was large enough to allow of the outfields being placed very deep. To say that Ulyett was the greatest batsman Yorkshire ever possessed would scarcely be exceeding the

truth, but Lockwood in the past and F. S. Jackson in the present must in fairness be classed with him.

UPHAM, Ernest Frederick, of Wellington, New Zealand, died on October 23, 1935, aged 62. A medium-fast bowler, he took over 1,000 wickets in club and representative cricket. Against the M.C.C. team of amateurs who toured New Zealand in the winter of 1906, he took six wickets for 78 in one innings for Wellington, and in the second of two Test matches, by dismissing six men for 84 in the England team's first innings, he helped appreciably in a victory, by 56 runs.

UTLEY, The Rev. Richard Peter Hugh, O.S.B., who died suddenly at Ampleforth College, on August 28, 1968, aged 62, was in the Ampleforth XI from 1922 to 1924, doing much splendid work as a fast bowler and heading the batting averages in the last year. He played for Hampshire in 1927 and 1928. Of medium height and bowling from an economical run-up, he appeared only occasionally in the first summer but in the next rendered excellent service by taking 59 wickets at 23.27 runs each. His best performances were the taking of 12 Warwickshire wickets for 140 runs in the match at Bournemouth and six for 70 in the first innings of Middlesex at Lord's. A product of Cranwell, he became a pilot and played cricket for the Royal Air Force. After entering the Church he commanded for 30 years the Cadet Force at Ampleforth, where he was a housemaster, and was in charge of cricket from 1936 to 1955.

VALENTINE, Bryan Herbert, M.C., who died on February 2, 1983, aged 75, was a gifted athlete to whom most games came naturally. At Repton he won the public schools lawn tennis with the great H. W. Austin; at Cambridge he got a soccer Blue as a brilliant forward and later he became a scratch golfer. But, happily, it was to cricket that he really devoted himself and he never made the mistake, which so many talented players have made, of being satisfied with what he could achieve without study and effort. He was three years in the Repton XI, but after a splendid season in 1925, his last was spoilt by illness and injury. After a year spent in duels with the examiners, he made 114 (retired) in 75 minutes in the Freshmen's match at Cambridge in 1928, but it was not until 1929 that he got a Blue and even then his place was in doubt until the last match at Fenner's, when, against an unusually strong

Free Foresters bowling side, which included M. J. C. Allom, R. J. O. Meyer, C. S. Marriott, M. Falcon and A. G. Doggart, he scored 101 in 85 minutes. Meanwhile, he had been playing for Kent since 1927, but with only moderate success, and it was not until 1931 that he made his place secure. At this period he was just a promising county cricketer with beautiful strokes, capable of playing a brilliant innings and stronger on the leg than most of his type, but distinctly suspect in defence. By the mid-'30s he had become far sounder, had learned to watch the turning ball and was a potential England player, and this without curbing his instinct to attack. His average rate of scoring throughout his career is said to have been some 50 runs an hour. He was particularly adept at on-driving, with a full swing of the bat, the numerous off-spinners and in-swingers encouraged by the new lbw law. However, English batting was strong at this time and his Test cricket was confined to the tours of India in 1933–34 and South Africa in 1938–39. In India he came third in the batting, and at Bombay in the first Test made 136 in under three hours. In South Africa consistent batting brought him an average of 45.38 and in the second Test, at Cape Town, he made 112 in two hours, 40 minutes. In the previous summer he had made the highest score of his career, 242 for Kent against Leicestershire at Oakham.

After serving in the War, winning the M.C. and being severely wounded, he returned to captain the county from 1946 to 1948, when he retired from first-class cricket. He had already captained frequently in the absence of A. P. F. Chapman and in 1937 had shared the captaincy with R. T. Bryan. A post-war England captain, who played under Valentine, whom he had not previously met, for an M.C.C. side years after his retirement, said regretfully, "What fun County Cricket must have been when men like that were captain!" And, of course, he was right. Valentine took his cricket seriously enough, as the story of his career shows, and was as keen as anyone to win, but he never forgot that cricket is a game and as such he enjoyed it himself and did all he could to see that others enjoyed it too, including the spectators. In a friendship of over 50 years I myself never saw him anything but cheerful and usually laughing. His own account of his mild away-swingers is typical. He used to say that Chapman had occasionally given him the new ball "because no one else ever gets the shine off so quickly for 'Tich'." As a fieldsman he was in the top

class, equally good on the boundary or close to the wicket. President of Kent in 1967 and for many years on the committee, he remained in close touch with the county and will be widely missed. In all first-class cricket he scored 18,306 runs with an average of 30.15 and made 35 centuries.

VAN DER BIJL, Pieter Gerhart Vintcent, who died on February 16, 1973, aged 65, played in five Test matches for South Africa in 1938–39. This included the "timeless" match which, after 10 days, had to be left drawn to enable the Englishmen to catch their liner home. In that game Van der Bijl scored 135 and 97, sharing opening stands of 131 and 191 with A. Melville, his captain, and in the series he hit 460 runs, average 51.11. Educated at Bishop's, Cape Town, he won a Rhodes scholarship to Oxford and gained a Blue in 1932. Though he did well enough for the University in other games, he failed to come off in the University match.

VAN MANEN, Hugo, who died on January 2, 1983, captained Holland between the Wars and again after the Second World War, being the most prolific Dutch batsman of his day. From 1945 to 1955 he was president of the Netherlands Cricket Association.

VARACHIA, Rashid, who died in Johannesburg on December 11, 1981, aged 66, had been president of the South African Cricket Union since its formation as the non-racial controlling body of South African cricket in September, 1977. A highly successful businessman, born in Bombay, he was previously president of the South African Cricket Board of Control (S.A.C.B.O.C.), administering Indians and Coloureds. Latterly he had worked under the handicap of a heart condition but had travelled the world, frail of body but intensely sincere of purpose, putting South Africa's claims for a return to international cricket. He withstood many rebuffs and was even amused when, because of his connection with South African cricket, the Australian government refused him a visa to visit Sydney where his son lived. At first he was frustrated not so much by his lack of success in approaches to the I.C.C. but by the ignorance of South Africa shown by representatives of some member-countries and by their unwillingness to learn more about it or even discuss it. His last rebuff, in July, 1981, was a heavy blow for one of fragile health to bear.

VASSALL, Gilbert Claude, of high fame as an Association football outside-right and a long jumper, was a useful all-round cricketer without attaining to the front rank. After leaving Charterhouse he scored freely for Oriel College matches at Oxford, but during his four years at the University, 1896–99, the Dark Blues were very strong at cricket, and Vassall gave his chief attention to athletics and football. He played occasionally for Somerset in 1902, 1903, and 1905, but made few runs, and his fast bowling met with little success. Becoming a master at Dragon School, Oxford, soon after completing his undergraduate days, he refused invitations to go elsewhere and died joint headmaster of the preparatory school on September 19, 1941, aged 65.

VAUGHTON, Roland William, a widely known figure in Adelaide sporting and hotel circles, died there on January 5, 1979, aged 64. While still at school, "Roly" Vaughton played first-grade cricket and football and was South Australian wicket-keeper on a number of occasions between the eras of the late C. W. Walker and the advent of G. R. A. Langley. He was also a top-grade baseball catcher and, as state coach, directed South Australia to successive wins in three inter-state series. A warm-hearted mine host of the well-known King's Head Hotel, Roly typically provided a handsome donation to the Shield players' sponsor fund on the last visit he made to the Adelaide Oval.

VEAL, Major Charles Lewis, who died on June 1, 1929, aged 52, was in the Repton XI of 1894, and had played for Middlesex Second XI and Glamorgan.

VENN, W. Horace, who died in hospital at Coventry on November 23, 1953, aged 61, appeared as opening batsman for Warwickshire from 1919 to 1922. Strong in defence, with a stiff fore-arm forcing stroke, he scored most of his runs in front of the wicket. Born on July 4, 1892, he played 32 innings for the county in 1920, scoring 553 runs, average 17.28, his highest innings being 115 in two hours and a half against Kent at Catford.

VERELST, Harry William, born July 2, 1846, died April 5, 1918. Mr. Verelst was in his schooldays one of the most prominent Rugby batsmen, being in the school XI in 1864 and 1865. He was quite at his best in 1865 when he scored 84 and 23 not out against Marlborough at Lord's, and had a big share in Rugby's victory by nine wickets.

R. G. Venables and the late Bernard Paunceforte were in the Rugby XI that year, Venables taking 13 of the Marlborough wickets. Mr. Verelst was seldom seen in first-class cricket, but he played twice for Yorkshire, and at the old Cattle Market Ground, Islington, in 1867, he scored 78 for Gentlemen of the North against Gentlemen of the South. For many years he was closely associated with the Free Foresters.

HEDLEY VERITY
Born May 18, 1905; died of wounds received in action, July 31, 1943
By R. C. Robertson-Glasgow

Capt. Hedley Verity, the Green Howards, died of wounds a prisoner of war in Italy on July 31, 1943, some two months after his 38th birthday. He had been reported wounded and missing, and the news of his death came on September 1, exactly four years after he had played his last match for Yorkshire and, at Hove, taken seven Sussex wickets for nine runs in one innings, which finished County Cricket before the War.

He received his wounds in the Eighth Army's first attack on the German positions at Catania, in Sicily. Eye-witnesses, who were a few yards from Verity when he was hit, have told the story. The objective was a ridge with strong points and pillboxes. Behind a creeping barrage Verity led his company forward 700 yd. When the barrage ceased, they went on another 300 yd. and neared the ridge, in darkness. As the men advanced, through corn 2 ft. high, tracer-bullets swept into them. Then they wriggled through the corn, Verity encouraging them with "Keep going, keep going." The moon was at their back, and the enemy used mortar-fire, Very lights and fire-bombs, setting the corn alight. The strongest point appeared to be a farmhouse, to the left of the ridge; so Verity sent one platoon round to take the farmhouse, while the other gave covering fire. The enemy fire increased, and, as they crept forward, Verity was hit in the chest. "Keep going," he said, "and get them out of that farmhouse." When it was decided to withdraw, they last saw Verity lying on the ground, in front of the burning corn, his head supported by his batman, Pte. Thomas Reynoldson, of Bridlington. So, in the last grim game, Verity showed, as he was so sure to do, that rare courage which both calculates and inspires.

His Bowling Art
Judged by any standard, Verity was a great bowler. Merely to watch him was to know that. The balance of the run-up, the high

ease of the left-handed action, the scrupulous length, the pensive variety, all proclaimed the master. He combined nature with art to a degree not equalled by any other English bowler of our time. He received a handsome legacy of skill and, by an application that verged on scientific research, turned it into a fortune. There have been bowlers who reached greatness without knowing, or, perhaps, caring to know just how or why; but Verity could analyse his own intentions without losing the joy of surprise and describe their effect without losing the company of a listener. He was the ever-learning professor, justly proud yet utterly humble.

In the matter of plain arithmetic, so often torn from its context to the confusion of judgment, Verity, by taking 1,956 wickets at 14.87 runs each in 10 years of first-class cricket, showed by far the best average during this century. In the recorded history of cricket the only bowlers of this class with lower averages are: Alfred Shaw, 2,072 wickets at 11.97 each; Tom Emmett, 1,595 wickets at 13.43 each; George Lohmann, 1,841 wickets at 13.73 each; James Southerton, 1,744 wickets at 14.30 each. It might be argued that during the period 1854 to 1898, covered by the careers of these cricketers, pitches tended to give more help to the bowler than they did during Verity's time. Verity, I know, for one, would not have pressed such a claim in his own favour. He never dwelt on decimals; and, while he enjoyed personal triumph as much as the next man, that which absorbed his deepest interest was the proper issue of a Test match with Australia or of an up-and-down bout with Lancashire; and if, in his country's or county's struggle towards victory, he brought off some recondite plot for the confounding, of Bradman or McCabe or Ernest Tyldesley or Edward Paynter, well, then he was happy beyond computing.

Notable Feats

Yet his bowling achievements, pressed into but overflowing the 10 years of his career, were so rich and various that they here demand some concentrated notice:

He played in 40 Test matches, taking 144 wickets at 24.37 runs each. He took 100 wickets in Test cricket in a shorter period than any other English bowler.

He is the only cricketer who has taken 14 wickets in a day in a Test match, this feat being performed against Australia at Lord's in the second Test, 1934. During this match, he took 15 wickets for 104 runs, thus sharing with Wilfred Rhodes, his Yorkshire prede-cessor, the honour of taking most wickets in an England v. Australia match.

Twice he took all 10 wickets in an innings; in 1931, against Warwickshire at Headingley, Leeds, for 36 runs in 18.4 (6-ball) overs, six maidens; in 1932, on the same ground, against Nottinghamshire, for 10 runs in 19.4 (6-ball) overs, 16 maidens—a world record in first-class cricket for the fewest number of runs conceded by a bowler taking all 10 wickets in an innings, and it included the hat-trick.

Against Essex at Leyton, in 1933, he took 17 wickets in one day, a record shared only by C. Blythe and T. W. Goddard.

In each of his nine full English seasons he took at least 150 wickets, and he averaged 185 wickets a season; thrice consecutively (1935–36–37) he took over 200 wickets. His average ranged from 12.42 to 17.63. He headed the first-class English bowling averages in his first season (1930) and in his last (1939), and never came out lower than fifth.

How He Began

Verity was born at Headingley, but passed his 25th birthday before he played for Yorkshire, in 1930, the year that W. Rhodes retired. Some of his earlier seasons were spent in playing as an amateur for Rawdon in the Yorkshire Council; for Accrington in the Lancashire league; and for Middleton in the Central league. He was then, as always afterwards when allowed, an all-rounder. As a batsman, his height, reach, concentration and knowledge of what to avoid raised him distinctly from the ruck of mediocrity; but, whereas his bowling included grace, his batting had only style. The former was nature embellished by art; the latter was art improved by imitation.

As a bowler, Hedley Verity stands, and will stand, with his illustrious predecessors in the Yorkshire attack: Edmund Peate (1879–87), Robert Peel (1882–99), Wilfred Rhodes (1898–1930)—the dates indicate the time of their respective playing careers—but Verity was not a slow left-hander in the accepted sense, and he used to reject comparison with Rhodes so far as method was concerned, saying: "Both of us are left-handed and like taking wickets; let's leave it at that."

Verity's mean pace was what is called slow-medium; on fast pitches, often about medium; and he would send down an inswinging yorker of an abrupt virulence not unworthy of George Hirst.

Naturally, on wet or crumbled or sticky pitches, he reduced pace and tossed the leg-spinner higher, but even here his variety of pace and of angle of delivery was remarkable. He was a born schemer; tireless, but never wild, in experiment; as sensitive in observation as a good host, or as an instrumentalist who spots a rival on the beat; the scholar who does not only dream, the inventor who can make it work.

Comparison of Giants

Just how good a bowler was he? In relation to rivals in his own craft but of an earlier day, such a question is useless except to amuse an idle hour or to excite an idle quarrel. We can only say that, in his own short time, he was the best of his kind. In England, day in and day out, he may never have quite touched the greatness of Robert Peel, Colin Blythe or Wilfred Rhodes. In Australia, neither in 1932–33 or 1936–37, did he perplex their batsmen quite as J. C. White perplexed them in 1928–29, but, as a workman-artist, he will take some beating. H. B. Cameron, that fine wicket-keeper-batsman of South Africa, playing against Yorkshire in 1935, hit him for three fours and three sixes in one over; but very rarely did a batsman survive a liberty taken with Verity. He had, besides, a wonderful skill in restoring the "rabbits," early and with little inconvenience, to the hutch.

If a touchstone of Verity's greatness be needed, there is D. G. Bradman, the most inexorable scorer of runs that cricket has yet seen, whose Test match average against England stands at 91.42 in 46 innings. I think it was Verity who kept that average under 150. He was one of only three or four bowlers who came to the battle with Bradman on not unequal terms (*haud impar congressus!*); and Bradman was reported as saying: "I think I know all about Clarrie (Grimmett), but with Hedley I am never sure. You see, there's no breaking-point with him."

Beating the Best

Verity timed his blows. In the fifth Test match, at Sydney, early in 1933, Australia, 19 runs behind on the first innings, lost Victor Richardson for 0. Woodfull and Bradman added 115; Larwood, injured, had left the field—and that particular Larwood never came back—then Verity deceived Bradman in flight, bowled him for 71 and went on to take five for 33 in 19 overs and win the match. In the earlier Tests, amid the fast bowling and the clamour, not much had been heard of Verity, except as a rescuing batsman. But, when the last pinch came, there he was to relieve the weary line; very Yorkshire.

Verity never allowed the opinion that Bradman was less than a master on damaged pitches, refusing to stress the evidence of his own triumph at Lord's in 1934 (Bradman c and b Verity 36; c Ames b Verity 13) and referring to Bradman's two innings of 59 and 43 in 1938 against Yorkshire at Sheffield. "It was a pig of a pitch," he said, "and he played me in the middle of the bat right through." Maybe Verity's opinion of Bradman was heightened by a natural generosity in its giver, but on this matter I think that Verity had reason to know best.

As an all-round fielder, Verity was no more than sound, but to his own bowling, or at backward point, he sometimes touched brilliance; and there sticks in the memory the catch that he made at Lord's in 1938, when McCabe cut one from Farnes crack from the bat's middle.

Opened England Batting

As a batsman for Yorkshire, Verity was mostly kept close to the extras. His build and reach suggested power and freedom, but it remained a suggestion; and he was analogous to those burly golfers who prod the tee-shot down the middle to a prim 180 yd. A casual observer might have mistaken Verity for Sutcliffe a little out of form, for he seemed to have caught something of that master's style and gesture, and, like Sutcliffe, he could be clean bowled in a manner that somehow exonerated the batsman from all guilt. He never quite brought off "the double," though in 1936 he took 216 wickets and scored 855 runs. But he had the sovereign gift of batting to an occasion. In the 1936–37 visit to Australia, G. O. Allen could find no opening pair to stay together, so he sent in Verity with C. J. Barnett in the fourth Test, at Adelaide, and they put up partnerships of 53 and 45. Not much, perhaps; but the best until then. In all Test matches, his batting average was close on 21; nearly three units higher than his average in all first-class cricket.

Verity had the look and carriage of a man likely to do supremely well something that would need time and trouble. His dignity was not assumed; it was the natural reflection of mind and body harmonised and controlled. He was solid; conscientious, disciplined; and something far more. In all that he did, until his most gallant end, he showed the vital fire, and warmed others in its flame. To the spectator in the field he may have seemed, perhaps, a little stiff and aloof; but among a known company he revealed geniality, wit, and an unaffected kindness that will not be forgotten.

There was no "breaking-point" with Verity; and his last reported words: "Keep going," were but a text on his short and splendid life.

HEDLEY VERITY WITH THE BALL

ALL FIRST-CLASS MATCHES

Season					Runs	Wickets	Average
1930	..	..	..	..	795	64	12.42
1931	..	..	..	..	2,542	188	13.52
1932	..	..	..	..	2,250	162	13.88
1932–33 (Australia)	..	..	..	..	698	44	15.86
1932–33 (New Zealand)	..	..	..	..	64	1	64.00
1933	..	..	..	..	2,553	190	13.43
1933–34 (India)	..	..	..	..	1,180	78	15.12
1934	..	..	..	..	2,645	150	17.63
1935	..	..	..	..	3,032	211	14.36
1936 (Jamaica)	..	..	..	..	360	16	22.50
1936	..	..	..	..	2,847	216	13.18
1936–37 (Australia)	..	..	..	..	1,043	38	27.44
1937	..	..	..	..	3,168	202	15.68
1938	..	..	..	..	2,476	158	15.67
1938–39 (South Africa)	..	..	..	..	937	47	19.93
1939	..	..	..	..	2,509	191	13.13
Total	..	..	..	..	29,099	1,956	14.87

COUNTY CHAMPIONSHIP MATCHES

Season					Runs	Wickets	Average
1930	..	..	..	..	595	52	11.44
1931	..	..	..	..	1,703	138	12.34
1932	..	..	..	..	1,856	135	13.74
1933	..	..	..	..	1,826	153	11.93
1934	..	..	..	..	1,210	79	15.31
1935	..	..	..	..	2,196	161	13.63
1936	..	..	..	..	1,942	153	12.69
1937	..	..	..	..	2,270	157	14.45
1938	..	..	..	..	1,523	111	13.72
1939	..	..	..	..	2,095	165	12.69
Total	..	..	..	..	17,216	1,304	13.20

BOWLING SUMMARY

In ENGLAND

			Runs	Wickets	Average
Yorkshire (County Championship)	..	..	17,216	1,304	13.20
Yorkshire (other matches)	..	..	..	4,150	254	16.33
Tests (v. Australia)	..	..	..	930	38	24.47
Tests (v. South Africa)	..	..	..	250	12	20.83
Tests (v. West Indies)	..	..	..	207	9	23.00
Tests (v. New Zealand)	..	..	..	166	6	27.66
Tests (v. India)	..	..	..	228	15	15.20
Gentlemen v. Players	..	..	..	515	27	19.07
Other first-class matches	..	..	..	1,155	67	17.23

In AUSTRALIA

			Runs	Wickets	Average
Tests	..	..	..	726	21	34.57
Other first-class matches	..	..	..	1,015	61	16.80

BOWLING SUMMARY—*Continued*

In SOUTH AFRICA

	Runs	Wickets	Average
Tests	552	19	29.05
Other first-class matches	385	28	13.75

In NEW ZEALAND

	Runs	Wickets	Average
Tests	64	1	64.00

In INDIA

	Runs	Wickets	Average
Tests	387	23	16.82
Other first-class matches	793	55	14.41

In JAMAICA

	Runs	Wickets	Average
First-class matches	360	16	22.50
Total	29,099	1,956	14.87

10 WICKETS IN AN INNINGS
10 for 36	Yorkshire v. Warwickshire, at Leeds	..	..	..	1931
10 for 10	Yorkshire v. Nottinghamshire, at Leeds	..	..	..	1932

9 WICKETS IN AN INNINGS
9 for 60	Yorkshire v. Glamorgan, at Swansea	..	..	..	..	1930
9 for 44	Yorkshire v. Essex, at Leyton	..	..	..	..	1933
9 for 59	Yorkshire v. Kent, at Dover	..	..	..	..	1933
9 for 12	Yorkshire v. Kent, at Sheffield	..	..	..	..	1936
9 for 48	Yorkshire v. Essex, at Westcliff	..	..	..	..	1936
9 for 43	Yorkshire v. Warwickshire, at Leeds	..	..	..	..	1937
9 for 62	Yorkshire v. M.C.C., at Lord's	..	..	..	..	1939

8 WICKETS IN AN INNINGS
8 for 33	Yorkshire v. Glamorgan, at Swansea	..	..	..	1931
8 for 39	Yorkshire v. Northamptonshire, at Northampton	..	..	1932
8 for 47	Yorkshire v. Essex, at Leyton	..	..	..	1933
8 for 43	England v. Australia, at Lord's	..	..	..	1934
8 for 28	Yorkshire v. Leicestershire, at Leeds	..	..	..	1935
8 for 56	Yorkshire v. Oxford University, at Oxford	..	..	..	1936
8 for 40	Yorkshire v. Worcestershire, at Stourbridge	..	..	..	1936
8 for 42	Yorkshire v. Nottinghamshire, at Bradford	..	..	..	1936
8 for 80	Yorkshire v. Sussex, at Eastbourne	..	..	..	1937
8 for 43	Yorkshire v. Middlesex, at Kennington Oval	..	..	..	1937
8 for 38	Yorkshire v. Leicestershire, at Hull	..	..	..	1939

17 WICKETS IN A MATCH
17 for 91	Yorkshire v. Essex, at Leyton	..	..	..	1933

15 WICKETS IN A MATCH
15 for 104	England v. Australia, at Lord's	..	..	..	1934
15 for 38	Yorkshire v. Warwickshire, at Bradford	..	..	..	1936
15 for 129	Yorkshire v. Oxford University, at Oxford	..	..	..	1936
15 for 100	Yorkshire v. Essex, at Westcliff	..	..	..	1936

14 WICKETS IN A MATCH
14 for 54	Yorkshire v. Glamorgan, at Swansea	..	..	..	1930
14 for 83	Yorkshire v. West Indies, at Harrogate	..	..	..	1933
14 for 78	Yorkshire v. Hampshire, at Hull	..	..	..	1935
14 for 132	Yorkshire v. Sussex, at Eastbourne	..	..	..	1937
14 for 92	Yorkshire v. Warwickshire, at Leeds	..	..	..	1937
14 for 68	Yorkshire v. Glamorgan, at Bradford	..	..	..	1939

BOWLING SUMMARY—*Continued*

13 WICKETS IN A MATCH

13 for 83	Yorkshire v. Hampshire, at Bournemouth	..	..	..	1930
13 for 97	Yorkshire v. Warwickshire, at Leeds	..	..	..	1931
13 for 145	Yorkshire v. Sussex, at Hove	..	..	..	1931
13 for 102	Yorkshire v. Northamptonshire, at Leeds	..	..	..	1933
13 for 97	Yorkshire v. Leicestershire, at Leeds	..	..	..	1935
13 for 107	Yorkshire v. Hampshire, at Portsmouth	..	..	..	1935
13 for 88	Yorkshire v. Worcestershire, at Stourbridge	..	..	..	1936

12 WICKETS IN A MATCH

12 for 117	Yorkshire v. Glamorgan, at Swansea	..	..	..	1930
12 for 74	Yorkshire v. Nottinghamshire, at Leeds	..	..	..	1932
12 for 53	Yorkshire v. Derbyshire, at Hull	..	..	..	1933
12 for 137	Yorkshire v. Kent, at Dover	..	..	..	1933
12 for 96	Yorkshire v. M.C.C., at Lord's	..	..	..	1935
12 for 114	Yorkshire v. Leicestershire, at Hull	..	..	..	1939
12 for 85	Yorkshire v. M.C.C., at Lord's	..	..	..	1939

11 WICKETS IN A MATCH

11 for 69	Yorkshire v. Derbyshire, at Leeds	..	..	..	1932
11 for 74	Yorkshire v. Essex, at Dewsbury	..	..	..	1933
11 for 92	Yorkshire v. Middlesex, at Lord's	..	..	..	1933
11 for 153	England v. India, at Madras	..	..	..	1933–34
11 for 73	Yorkshire v. Middlesex, at Leeds	..	..	..	1935
11 for 111	Yorkshire v. Glamorgan, at Swansea	..	..	..	1936
11 for 90	Yorkshire v. Nottinghamshire, at Bradford	..	..	..	1936
11 for 181	Yorkshire v. M.C.C., at Scarborough	..	..	..	1937
11 for 88	Yorkshire v. Cambridge University, at Cambridge	..	..	1938
11 for 66	M.C.C. v. Griqualand West, at Kimberley	..	..	..	1938–39

HEDLEY VERITY WITH THE BAT

ALL FIRST-CLASS MATCHES

Season				Innings	Not Outs	Runs	Highest Innings	Average
1930	..	..	..	14	3	164	32	14.90
1931	..	..	..	25	6	234	28	12.31
1932	..	..	..	33	7	494	46	19.00
1932–33 (Australia)	..	..	17	3	300	54*	21.42
1932–33 (New Zealand)	..	..			(did not bat)		
1933	..	..	..	42	6	620	78*	17.22
1933–34 (India)	..	..	..	18	4	384	91*	27.42
1934	..	..	..	41	11	520	60*	17.33
1935	..	..	..	45	8	429	35	11.59
1936 (Jamaica)	..	..	..	4	0	195	101	48.75
1936	..	..	..	41	14	855	96*	31.66
1936–37	..	..	..	22	2	180	31	9.00
1937	..	..	..	37	14	335	76	14.56
1938	..	..	..	34	11	385	45*	16.73
1938–39 (South Africa)	..	..	12	2	245	39	24.50
1939	..	..	..	30	15	263	54	17.53
Complete batting figures		..		415	106	5,603	101	18.13

Signifies not out.

COUNTY CHAMPIONSHIP MATCHES

Season					Innings	Not Outs	Runs	Highest Innings	Average
1930	..	..	..	..	11	2	133	32	14.77
1931	..	..	..	..	18	3	183	28	12.20
1932	..	..	..	..	25	4	384	36*	18.28
1933	..	..	..	..	36	3	572	78*	17.33
1934	..	..	..	..	22	4	309	38	17.16
1935	..	..	..	..	28	3	256	35	10.24
1936	..	..	..	..	29	9	535	89	26.75
1937	..	..	..	..	24	9	229	76	15.26
1938	..	..	..	..	20	5	176	41	11.73
1939	..	..	..	..	27	13	248	54	17.71
Total	..	..	..		240	55	3,025	89	16.35

In all Yorkshire matches Verity scored 3,883 runs, average 17.89.

* Signifies not out

OUTSTANDING ACHIEVEMENTS

1. During his career (1930–39) Hedley Verity took 1,956 wickets at a cost of 14.87 runs apiece; scored 5,603 runs, average 18.13; and made 238 catches.

2. Verity played in 40 Test matches, taking 144 wickets for 24.37 runs each, and scoring 669 runs at an average of 20.90.

3. Verity took 100 wickets in Test cricket in a shorter period than any other English bowler.

4. He is the only cricketer who has taken 14 wickets in a day in a Test match, this feat being accomplished against Australia at Lord's in 1934. During this match he took 15 wickets for 104 runs, thus sharing with Wilfred Rhodes, his Yorkshire predecessor, the honour of taking most wickets in an England v. Australia match.

5. Twice Verity took all 10 wickets in an innings. His 10 wickets for 10 runs for Yorkshire against Nottinghamshire at Leeds in 1932 is a world record for the fewest number of runs conceded by a bowler taking 10 wickets, and it included the hat-trick. Full analysis was 19.4–16–10–10. In his last three overs he took seven wickets for three runs. The next best average recorded for 10 wickets is 10 for 18 runs by G. Geary for Leicestershire against Glamorgan at Pontypridd in 1929. In seven other innings Verity took nine wickets.

6. Against Essex at Leyton in 1933, 17 wickets fell to him in one day—a record shared with Colin Blythe and Tom Goddard.

7. Verity started County Championship cricket at Hull on May 31, 1930, against Leicestershire, taking in the match eight wickets, four for 15 runs in the second innings; and finished at Hove on September 1, 1939, the last day of County Cricket before war began, with this remarkable analysis: 6–1–9–7. His first-class debut for Yorkshire was in a friendly against Sussex on May 21, 1930.

8. In each of his nine full English seasons he took at least 150 wickets, and his average was 185 wickets per season; three times consecutively he took over 200 wickets in a season (1935–36–37).

9. In each of his 10 seasons of first-class cricket Verity's average ranged from 12.42 to 17.63, in 1930 and 1934 respectively. He headed the English bowling averages in his first season, a feat which he accomplished again in 1939, and he never came out lower than fifth, twice being second, five times third, and once fifth. In his nine full English seasons his wickets ranged from 150 to 216.

10. In 1936, Verity took his 100th wicket in first-class cricket as early as June 19—a record for a Yorkshireman, though J. T. Hearne (Middlesex) in 1896 took his 100th wicket on June 12. In 1931, C. W. L. Parker (Gloucestershire) equalled this, and next day A. P. Freeman (Kent) completed 100 wickets.

11. Verity bowled 766 balls in two innings at Durban in the final Test match against South Africa in March, 1939—a record number of balls by one bowler in a match. This match was the longest ever played— drawn after 10 days.

12. Verity scored only one century in first-class cricket—for Yorkshire against Jamaica

at Sabina Park, Jamaica, in 1936.

13. At Adelaide, in January, 1937, he opened the batting with C. J. Barnett, and scored 19 out of 53 for the first wicket, the best start to an innings for England in the first four Tests of that rubber.

14. Verity's best all-round season was in 1936, when he took his greatest number of wickets, 216; and made his highest aggregate of runs, 855.

15. During Verity's 10 years Yorkshire won the County Championship seven times; in six of these seasons Brian Sellers led the team.

The Best Bowler this Century

According to the list in 1940 *Wisden* of bowlers who have taken 1,500 wickets, Hedley Verity, with 1,956 wickets in 10 years at 14.87 each, showed by far the best average during this century, and in the history of cricket the only bowlers of this class showing lower averages are:

Alfred Shaw, 2,072 wickets at 11.97 in 34 years.

Tom Emmett, 1,595 wickets at 13.43 in 23 years.

George Lohmann, 1,841 wickets at 13.73 in 15 years.

James Southerton, 1,744 wickets at 14.30 in 22 years.

As the careers of these four famous professionals extended from the year 1854, when Shaw began, to 1898, when Lohmann finished, their remarkable records were achieved during an era when bowlers received far more help from the pitches than was the case during the period in which Verity earned such great reward for his skill.

Four Great Yorkshiremen

Of slow left-handers comparable with Verity as England players, his three predecessors of similar type in the Yorkshire XI stand out:

Edmund Peate (1879–87), 1,063 wickets at 13.86.

Robert Peel (1882–99), 1,754 wickets at 16.21.

Wilfred Rhodes (1898–1930), 4,188 wickets at 16.71.

Hedley Verity (1930–39), 1,956 wickets at 14.87.

These four Yorkshiremen excelled through a period of 61 years.

Other Notable Exponents

Other slow left-handers of this category in chronological order have been:

John Briggs, Lancashire (1879–1900), 2,200 wickets at 16.10.

Colin Blythe, Kent, killed in the First World War on November 8, 1917, aged

38 (1899–1914), 2,506 wickets at 16.81.

C. W. L. Parker, Gloucestershire (1903–35), 3,278 wickets at 19.48.

Frank E. Woolley, Kent (1906–38), 2,068 wickets at 19.86.

J. C. White, Somerset (1909–37), 2,358 wickets at 18.56.

AN AUSTRALIAN APPRECIATION
By Don Bradman

The present War has already taken heavy toll of gallant men who, after faithfully serving their countries on the cricket field in peacetime, have laid down their lives for a greater cause. Of those who have fallen, Hedley Verity was perhaps the most illustrious, and from the Dominion of Australia I feel it my sad duty to join with cricketers of the Motherland in expressing sorrow that we shall not again see him on our playing fields.

It could truthfully be claimed that Hedley Verity was one of the greatest if not *the* greatest left-hand bowler of all time. Most certainly he could lay just claim to that honour during the 1918–39 period. No doubt his Yorkshire environment was of great assistance for left-hand bowling seems to be in the blood of Yorkshiremen. It is one of their traditions and inalienable rights to possess the secrets of the art.

Although not a young man from a cricketing standpoint when the call came, Verity was little if any beyond the zenith of his powers. He was always such a keen student of the game, and his bowling was of such a type, that brains and experience played perhaps a greater part in his successes than natural genius.

Although opposed to him in many Tests, I could never claim to have completely fathomed his strategy, for it was never static nor mechanical.

Naturally he achieved his most notable successes when wickets were damp. Nobody privileged to witness that famous Test at Lord's in 1934 (least of all the Australian batsmen) will forget a performance to which even the statistics could not do justice. But it would be ungenerous to suggest that he needed assistance from the wicket, as his successful Australian tours will confirm. The ordinary left-hander who lacks the vicious unorthodox finger-spin of the Fleetwood-Smith variety needs uncommon ability to achieve even moderate success in Australia, yet Verity was the foundation stone of England's bowling in both countries during his era.

Apart from his special department of the game, Verity could also claim to be a remarkably efficient fieldsman close to the wicket where safe hands and courage are greater attributes than agility. Add this to the fact that once he opened a Test match innings for England, not without success, and we have a fairly general picture of a really fine player.

Those of us who played against this swarthy, capless champion (I never remember having seen him wear a cap) probably appreciated his indomitable fighting spirit even more than his own colleagues. We knew, when war came, that he would plainly see his duty in the same way as he regarded it his duty to win cricket matches for Yorkshire no less than England.

During our association together I cannot recall having heard Verity utter a word of complaint or criticism. If reports of his final sacrifice be correct, and I believe they are, he maintained this example right to the end.

His life, his skill, his service all merited the highest honour, and with great sorrow I unhesitatingly pay humble tribute to his memory.

YORKSHIRE CAPTAIN'S TRIBUTE

By Major A. B. Sellers

My association with Hedley began during my first game for Yorkshire Second XI at Middlesbrough in June, 1930. Being new to that type of cricket, I kept a careful eye on what was going on and the fellows with whom I was playing. Our "skipper," Brigadier R. C. Chichester-Constable, D.S.O., duly introduced me to all the team, and my first impressions of Hedley were that he was a very quiet type of man who did not say very much but had a great sense of humour.

At that time he played for the First XI when Rhodes was not available, and at the end of the season he topped the English bowling averages. There was nothing in his conversation to lead anyone into thinking that he had ever played for the First team. However, as the game progressed I kept my eye on him and found him to be quite casual about everything he did. There was no fuss; he just got on with the game. An occasional appeal to the umpire; if it was refused he made no signs whatsoever as to what he thought about it.

I came away from that game thinking that there was a man who would not be driven by anyone into doing anything that he did not want to do, and how true that turned out to be. When I became "skipper" of the First XI I found that Hedley would work hard all day and every day in his own little way, no fuss or hurry or rush. If you studied his bowling

action closely, that gave you an insight to his character—steady, even, coupled with determination.

I look back upon my cricketing days with Hedley and find that he never really changed from the Hedley I first met at Middlesbrough on that June day. His advice was sound and good. He was prepared to sit and talk with anyone on most subjects, and of course, like most of us, would talk cricket all day and all night. His bowling always improved, and, as we all know, he played for England so often that he became an automatic choice like Hobbs and Sutcliffe in their day.

His character and disposition never changed amidst all his many triumphs; he just remained Hedley Verity. On many occasions, in order to win a match, I turned to him and said, "Well Hedley, everything depends on you." That was sufficient; although he might be very tired indeed, his determination to help the side win was something to wonder at. If I had given him a direct order, a lot of that determination would not have come to the fore. It was not his nature to be ordered about, although he never gave any outward sign of resentment. His answer was to keep going along in his own sweet way. He knew what he could and what he could not do.

Hedley lost his life playing a game of war, and I can guarantee that as he lay wounded on the battlefield in Sicily the grim determination to go forward prevailed more than ever before. His death draws a line under his name and the finish to a remarkable cricket career. England and Yorkshire lose a great player and I a great friend. I feel honoured to have met and played with him.

VERNON, Augustus Leveson, born at Clifton, Bristol, on September 20, 1836, died at Hilton Park, Wolverhampton, on December 9, 1925, aged 89. A right-handed batsman and a left-handed medium-paced bowler, he played for Essex, Suffolk, Staffordshire, M.C.C. and I Zingari. For over 60 years he had hunted with the South Staffordshire and the Albrighton Hounds.

VERNON, G. F., who died at Elmina, West Africa, on August 10, 1902, was scarcely one of the great batsmen of his day, but he had a long and distinguished career in the cricket field. Born in June, 1856, he made his first appearance at Lord's as a member of the Rugby XI in 1873, and so recently as 1897 he took part in first-class matches, making scores of over 50 against both the Universities. For many years he played regularly for

Middlesex, and for that county and the M.C.C. the greater part of his best work was done. He was a splendid natural hitter, and his quickness of eye made up to some extent for his defect in never playing with quite a straight bat. Coming to the front in 1878, he held a prominent place for 12 seasons or more, and even when he gave up first-class cricket he could hit nearly as hard as ever. Clean, powerful driving was always the best feature of his play. Of all the matches in which he took part for Middlesex, perhaps the most remarkable was the one with Yorkshire, at Lord's in 1889. Middlesex won by four wickets, T. C. O'Brien scoring 100 not out in 80 minutes, and playing, by general consent, the innings of his life. In order to win the game Middlesex had to score at the rate of nearly 80 an hour for just over three hours and a half—a tremendous task against Yorkshire's bowling. When the sixth wicket fell Vernon became O'Brien's partner, 83 runs having then to be made in three-quarters of an hour. O'Brien went on hitting in tremendous style, and the match was won 10 minutes before time. We remember very well Mr. Vernon's amusement at a statement in one of the reports of the game that he, in helping O'Brien, had scored slowly. He was slow by comparison, but as a matter of fact he made 30 runs in 35 minutes. His recollections of another and still more famous match at Lord's were far less agreeable, as he was a member of the M.C.C. team that on May 27, 1878, went down before the first Australian XI for scores of 33 and 19. He himself failed to get a run in either innings, being out both times to Spofforth's bowling.

Acting in conjunction with the Melbourne club, Mr. Vernon took a team to Australia in the winter of 1887-88. Unfortunately Shaw and Shrewsbury took an XI out at the same time, and the financial result all round was disastrous in the extreme. The Melbourne club were said to have lost £4,000 by their enterprise, and Alfred Shaw has stated that he and Shrewsbury found themselves £2,400 to the bad. Such a fatal blunder as to send two English XIs to the colonies in the same season will assuredly never be repeated. From the cricket point of view, Mr. Vernon's side did wonderfully well, only losing one of their matches. For one special occasion towards the end of the season the two English XIs joined forces, and had the satisfaction of beating Australia by 126 runs.

Mr. Vernon, five years before he took his own team to Australia, went out to the colonies as a member of the XI captained by the Hon. Ivo Bligh, now Lord Darnley. For that side—very rich in batsmen, though they did not all come off—he was to some extent an emergency, only playing in four of the seven 11-a-side matches. His best score in half a dozen innings was 24 against New South Wales; but, as he went in either ninth or 10th, and on one occasion last, he did not have much chance of showing what he could do. In the matches against odds he had better opportunities, and obtained an average of 20, but his best score was only 41. In his young days Mr. Vernon was a prominent Rugby football player, appearing for England against Scotland in 1878 and 1880, and against Ireland in 1878, 1880, and 1881.

VIALS, George Alfred Turner, who died on April 26, 1974, aged 87, was in the XI at Wellingborough and played as an amateur for Northamptonshire from 1904 to 1922. He was captain from 1911 to 1913 and later became president from 1956 to 1968. In first-class cricket he hit 3,808 runs, average 18.30, his highest innings being 129, and held 98 catches. He also played Association football for Northampton Town and represented the county at hockey.

VILJOEN, Kenneth George, who died in Johannesburg on January 21, 1974, aged 63, played in 27 Test matches for South Africa between 1930 and 1947. A fine batsman, who suited his methods to the needs of the occasion, and an outstanding deep fieldsman, he took part in Currie Cup cricket for Western Province and Orange Free State from 1926 to 1947, scoring 2,658 runs, average 59.06. In all first-class cricket he hit 23 centuries, the highest being 215 for Griqualand West v. Western Province at Kimberley in 1929-30. His best home season as a run-getter was that of 1936-37 when he scored 743 runs at an average of 92.87.

In Test cricket, he registered two three-figure scores while scoring 1,365 runs, 124 against England at Old Trafford in 1935—the year in which, under H. F. Wade, South Africa gained their first Test win on English soil—and 111 v. Australia at Melbourne in 1931-32. He visited England a second time in 1947, distinguishing himself by taking 205 not out from the Sussex bowling at Hove. After his playing career ended, he managed South African teams in Australia and New Zealand in 1952-53 and 1963-64 and in England in 1955. He became president of the South African Cricket Association.

VINE, Joseph, one of the best and most popular among many Sussex professionals possessing similar characteristics, died on April 25, 1946, aged 70. Below medium height and strongly built, he could bat for long hours, field in the deep with rare speed and certainty, and bowl slow leg-breaks without tiring. His aggregate of 25,169 runs, average 29.92, and 683 wickets at 29.99, give an idea of the work he got through from 1896 to 1922; and seldom can anyone have equalled his appearance in 421 consecutive matches for Sussex, a number extended to 503 with only one absence from a match against Oxford.

Joe Vine might have been more prominent in representative cricket but for the role he usually undertook of subduing himself to the needs of a steady batsman as partner to C. B. Fry and the still more brilliant K. S. Ranjitsinhji. How well he and Fry succeeded as an opening pair is proved conclusively by their putting up three figures 33 times. In 1901 Vine scored 1,190 runs and took 113 wickets, the first "double" done for Sussex.

Born on May 15, 1875, he ripened as a cricketer rather slowly, and though good in every sense from his start in first-class cricket at 21, he did not earn the highest honours until 1911, when he toured Australia with the team, captained by J. W. H. T. Douglas, which won four of the Test matches. Vine played in two of these, and in the fifth contest at Sydney he and Frank Woolley set up a seventh-wicket record for England against Australia by making 143. Vine, No. 8 in the batting order, claimed only a modest 36; Woolley, who went in No. 7, took out his bat for 133, his first century against Australia.

Originally a forcing batsman, Vine curbed his natural instincts while in company with brilliant hitters, but as late as 1920 he gave evidence of hitting powers in his biggest innings by scoring 202 in five hours against Northamptonshire at Hastings. This, compared with 55 not out and 57 for which he batted over seven hours in 1901 at Hove, conveys a correct idea of his versatility. Perhaps his best bowling performance was in that same season of his special all-round ability when, at Trent Bridge, he opened the attack and took 15 wickets for 161 runs.

Soon after retiring from County Cricket Joe Vine became coach at Brighton College, an office he held for many years.

VINTCENT, Charles Henry, an Old Carthusian, who died at George, Cape Province, on September 28, 1943, played in the two representative matches against the first English team that visited South Africa during the winter of 1888–89. Both ended in easy victories for the English XI captained by C.

Aubrey Smith. Three years later he played in one match against the side captained by W. W. Read, the XI of South Africa again suffering a heavy defeat. Left-handed both as batsman and bowler, Vincent was a good all-round cricketer; his best performance was to score 87 and take nine wickets in a match for 105 runs for Eighteen of Kimberley against Aubrey Smith's team. He frequently bowled well in the inter-district "champion bat" tournaments that preceded the Currie Cup competitions, but did little in the matches eventually included in the statistics as "Tests." Born at Mossel Bay, Cape Colony, on September 2, 1866, he was educated at Charterhouse, where he was in the XI 1882–84.

VIVIAN, Henry Gifford, who died in Auckland on August 12, 1983, aged 70, was only 18 years 267 days when, as a left-handed all-rounder of much natural ability, he played in the first of his seven Tests for New Zealand. That was at the Oval in 1931, and, besides taking the wickets of Sutcliffe and Ames, he was top scorer, in New Zealand's second innings, with 51. His record on that tour (1,002 runs and 64 wickets) included centuries against Oxford University and Yorkshire. At Wellington in 1931–32, against South Africa, he scored 100 (his only Test century) and 73, the highest score in each innings. On his second tour to England, in 1937, he opened New Zealand's innings in the three Test matches, three times reaching 50. A charming person and welcoming host, he had been only 22 when appointed to the captaincy of Auckland. By the time a back injury ended his first-class career and confined him to the game's administration—he did not play after the Second World War—he had scored 4,443 runs (average 34.71), including six centuries, the highest of them 165 for Auckland against Wellington in 1931–32, and taken 223 wickets. He also played with success in the late '30s for Sir Julien Cahn's XI. His son, Graham, played five times for New Zealand between 1964 and 1972.

VIZARD, Walter Oswald, born at Bellary, India, November 16, 1861, died in London on January 10, 1929, aged 67. He was in the Clifton College XI in 1879 and two next years, being captain in 1880 and 1881, and having a batting average of 36 in his third season. In 1882 he began to assist Gloucestershire, but he played only occasionally for the side.

VIZIANAGRAM, The Rajkumar of, Sir Gajapatairaj Vijaya Ananda, who died in Benares, Northern India, on December 2, 1965, aged 59, captained the Indian team in England in 1936. He showed his strength of character before the first Test match by sending home as a disciplinary measure India's most successful all-rounder, L. Amarnath, who had scored more runs than anyone and hit two centuries in the game against Essex at Brentwood. In three matches against England, "Vizzy," as he was known in the cricket world, scored only 33 runs, his highest innings being 19 not out at Lord's. On the whole tour, however, his aggregate reached 600, including 60 from the University bowling at Oxford, average 16.21. Three times he was elected president of the Board of Control for Cricket in India. He was a member of the Indian Legislative Assembly.

VOCE, William (Bill), who died at Nottingham on June 6, 1984, aged 74, is largely thought of in these days as the junior in one of the great bowling partnerships, Larwood and Voce, and for the contribution that he made to the "bodyline" attack in Australia in 1932–33. Although he was somewhat slower than Larwood, his line, from left-arm over the wicket, and the steeper bounce that he obtained from his height, made him formidable enough and the batsmen got no relief when facing him. His job in that 1932–33 series was to maintain the pressure and he did it nobly, taking, besides, 15 wickets in four matches: he missed the fourth Test owing to injury. The controversy which this tour excited and the amount that has been written since has diverted attention from his performances in the first two Tests in 1936–37. No English side in this century had had such a bad press before the tour started: it was popularly regarded as having no chance whatever. Its captain, G. O. Allen, the third fast bowler on the previous trip, had been irredeemably opposed to bodyline and had refused to bowl it: it is worth recording that he himself had by orthodox methods taken eight for 131 in the third Test. So before the selection of the team was completed the Chairman arranged a meeting between Allen and Voce at which Allen insisted on an undertaking being given that bodyline tactics would not be employed. Voce demurred at first, but finally agreed to fall in with his captain's wishes and throughout the tour bowled over the wicket to an off-side field. In the first Test he took six for 41 and four for 16: Australia lost by 322 runs and the critics were confounded. The second was even more sensational. Allen declared (a step almost unprecedented in a timeless Test) at

426 for six in order to get Australia in on a wet wicket, and with the seventh ball of the first over Voce had O'Brien, a left-hander, caught at slip: from the next ball Bradman was caught at short-leg. A maiden followed and off the second ball of his next over McCabe was caught. Australia were three wickets down for one run and Voce had taken them all in four balls. The side was out for 80 and, though they got 324 in their second innings, they lost by an innings, Voce's figures being four for 10 and three for 66. In addition Chipperfield had been missed off his bowling in the first innings. In this match the weather had helped England, in the next it helped Australia, who won by 365 runs. Voce was in no way to blame: though his six wickets cost him 169 runs, he maintained, according to *Wisden*, "his concentration and deadliness right throughout both innings."

Unfortunately, at this stage of the tour Voce's back gave out. Allen was strongly opposed to playing him in the fourth Test. He reckoned that no fast bowler can give of his best unless he is completely sound, and he hoped by resting Voce to have him fit for the fifth Test. However, he was overruled by the selection committee. England again lost: Voce took one wicket only which cost him 135 runs. Nor was he up to form in the last Test when Australia, scoring 604, won by an innings. He took three for 123, giving him a record for the series of 26 wickets at 21.53. During this tour a close and life-long friendship had arisen between Voce and his captain. Years later he told Allen that he now reckoned that bodyline had been wrong, but that, from loyalty to his old friend Larwood, he was not prepared to say anything on the subject to the press. This sidelight on his character helps to explain why he was so widely respected when, after his playing days were over, he coached first at Trent Bridge and later for many years for M.C.C. at Lord's and elsewhere.

After starting work in a colliery when 14, Voce was noticed in local cricket by Fred Barratt, the Nottinghamshire fast bowler, and engaged on the county staff in 1926. Success in the Second XI brought him a trial for Nottinghamshire in June 1927, against Gloucestershire at Trent Bridge. He seized it by taking five for 36 and followed this a few weeks later with six for 39 against Essex. Strong though the county's bowling was, he kept his place for the rest of the season and finished with 37 wickets at 27.18. At this time he was an orthodox slow left-armer, though in the later matches he sometimes lowered his arm slightly and bowled swingers. In 1928 he definitely settled to bowl fast-medium and many felt that England had lost a great slow left-armer. That may well be true, but it is certain that they had gained a great fast one. After heading the Nottinghamshire averages in 1929 and having a big part in winning them the Championship, he went that winter with M.C.C. to the West Indies and played with considerable success in what were then called Representative matches and have since been canonised as Tests. There was, in fact, simultaneously an M.C.C. side playing Tests in New Zealand and the two teams between them contained only five men who played in the Tests against Australia in 1930. On this tour Voce bowled mainly fast, but his chief success was in Trinidad where, moderating his pace to medium on the matting, he took 12 for 110 against the island and 11 for 119 in the Test. In the Tests in South Africa in the next winter, he took 23 wickets, more than any other bowler on either side, and, after representing England at home against New Zealand in 1931 and India in 1932, he was picked for Jardine's Australian tour. Despite their success there, neither he nor Larwood was selected to play against Australia in England in 1934 and, as Jardine himself had refused to be considered, there was much the same indignation in many quarters as in 1984: it was felt that owing to diplomatic considerations England were fielding something considerably less than their best team. Cricitism increased when at Trent Bridge in August Voce took eight for 66 against the tourists and was accused of bouncing the ball at them unnecessarily.

Before the 1935 season started both he and Larwood asked M.C.C. not to pick them for any of the Tests. However, midway through 1936 Voce again made himself available if wanted, and, picked for the third Test against India, bowled well without any luck at all: it was this performance that made him a certainty for the side to Australia that winter. With that tour, through no fault of his own, his best days ended. In 1937, after playing in the first Test against New Zealand, he damaged a knee and had to have a cartilage removed, which finished his cricket for the season. In 1938 he was much troubled by synovitis and his wickets were expensive, and he thus shares with J. N. Crawford and D. R. Jardine the distinction of being a great England cricketer who never appeared against Australia in a Test in England. In 1939 he was given a benefit, and modern readers may be surprised to hear that this produced only £980. In 1946 he was 37 and it could hardly be expected that, after six

seasons away from serious cricket, he would be the bowler he had been, especially as he was still in the forces and not regularly available. None the less, four for seven in a Test trial won him a place in the second Test against India and also in the side for Australia in the autumn. The selection was a mistake: the beautiful action remained, the venom had gone, and he now bowled in those whom once he would have bowled out. Moreover his knee still troubled him, and in June 1947 he resigned from the county side. However, appointed their coach, he continued to play occasionally in a crisis till 1952.

In his earlier days as a fast bowler he bowled round the wicket. On his first tour of Australia he used to bowl round for five or six overs while the shine lasted and then switch to bodyline, bowled over the wicket. To left-handers he used a normal field, but bowled a generous allowance of bouncers. On Allen's tour he bowled almost entirely over the wicket. In England after his Australian tours he bowled over or round according to circumstances. But his cricket by no means ended with his bowling. A tall, very strong man, he could hit immensely hard and soon became a dangerous batsman who made four hundreds in first-class cricket and in 1933 scored over 1,000 runs. Against Glamorgan at Trent Bridge in 1931 he made 129 in 75 minutes, having reached his 100 in 45 minutes. He was also a splendid field and a fine thrower with a very loose arm. In all first-class matches he scored 7,583 runs with an average of 19.19 and took 1,558 wickets at 23.08 apiece. In 27 Tests his figures were 98 wickets at 27.88.

VOGLER, Albert Edward Ernest, whom R. E. Foster and many other great batsmen regarded as the best bowler in the world in the year 1907, died on August 10, 1946, aged 69. Born at Swartwater, near Queenstown in Cape Colony, on November 28, 1876, he spent his boyhood at Durban, and made a name for himself at cricket with the Natal team at Johannesburg in November, 1903. Going to live in Pretoria, he decided in 1905 to adopt cricket as a profession, and came to England with the intention of qualifying for Middlesex. He obtained an engagement on the M.C.C. ground staff, and in his second year at Lord's bowled on several occasions for the M.C.C. with brilliant success. The idea of Vogler qualifying for Middlesex aroused some feeling in 1906, the metropolitan county having already two colonial players, Albert Trott and Frank Tarrant.

Happily, any friction which might have arisen disappeared, Sir Abe Bailey finding a position for him.

Returning home, Vogler played for South Africa in the five Tests against the team sent out under the leadership of P. F. Warner; the Englishmen suffered defeat in four of the games. In 1907 Vogler came here as one of the most famous bowling combinations that ever appeared for South Africa. The team lost by 53 runs the only Test match brought to a definite issue, but there could be no question about the exceptionally formidable attack which included four googly bowlers in Vogler, R. O. Schwartz, G. A. Faulkner and Gordon White, as well as Nourse and Sinclair. During the tour Vogler in first-class matches took 119 wickets for less than 16 runs each—and scored 723 runs with an average of 21.

At his best Vogler reached the highest class as a bowler. Delivering the off-break with a leg-break action, while depending chiefly upon the leg-break, he became exceptionally difficult and deceptive by the skill with which he used the reverse break and his variations of pace. Scarcely any batsman claimed that he could detect differences in Vogler's delivery of either the googly or the leg-break. Vogler also mixed the off-break with a ball which came straight through at greater pace, and occasionally sent down a most deceptive slow yorker. A bowler of infinite resource, he could keep going for a long time without losing length.

Strangely enough, considering the height to which he attained in 1907, Vogler accomplished little afterwards. One of the South African team that visited Australia in 1910–11, his batting average in first-class matches was only nine, and in 21 innings he captured no more than 31 wickets at a cost of nearly 39 runs each. Associated with various Scottish, Irish and English clubs, Vogler, in the year of the Triangular Tournament—1912—when South African and Australian teams visited England, appeared at Bray against his fellow countrymen as a member of the Woodbrook Club and Ground XI.

VORRATH, W., a representative Otago cricketer, died on June 7, 1934, in his 30th year. During the season 1927–28 he represented Otago in all its matches including the game against the Australian team. His best score was 103 not out against Wellington in the Plunket Shield match. A good Rugby footballer with the Union club he afterwards joined the Rugby League in which code he represented Otago.

VOSS, R., died November 16, 1900. Played three times for Surrey in 1883, and once in 1886.

VOULES, The Rev. Stirling Cooksley, died in London on May 6, 1923. Entering the Church just after he left Oxford in 1866, Mr. Voules had rather a brief career in first-class cricket, but he never lost his interest in the game and almost to the end of his long life he was frequently seen at Lord's. He was born at Middle Chinnock in Somerset on January 4, 1843. Educated at Marlborough, he was in the XI for four years—1859–62—and had an excellent record. Indeed among the Marlborough cricketers of his time he was no doubt the best all-round man—a free-hitting batsman, a good fast bowler and a capital field. He played for the first time at Lord's in 1859 for Marlborough against the M.C.C. and by scoring 33 and taking four wickets in a one-day match gave clear proof of his ability. Whilst still at Marlborough, he played for Gentlemen of the South against Gentlemen of the North at the Oval in 1862. Going up to Oxford he gained his Blue as a Freshman, and had the very rare experience of being on the winning side in the big match at Lord's for four years in succession. It was to the victory in 1863 that Voules chiefly contributed, taking seven wickets—five of them bowled down—in Cambridge's second innings at a cost of only 26 runs. Voules's own scores in the four matches were small—24 and 21 were the best—but in 1864 he stayed in with R. A. H. Mitchell at a very critical time and helped to turn the fortunes of a game that had seemed likely to be won for Cambridge by T. S. Curteis's splendid bowling. Mr. Voules was picked for Gentlemen v. Players at Lord's in 1863 and 1864 but found himself each year on a hopelessly beaten side. On the wickets at Lord's in those two seasons the Players' fast bowlers were irresistible. Mr. Voules played for the Eighteen Veterans against the Gentlemen of M.C.C. in the Centenary Week at Lord's in 1887, scoring 29 and 22 not out.—S.H.P.

WADDINGTON, Abram, who died at Scarborough after a long illness on October 28, 1959, aged 66, rendered splendid service to Yorkshire as a fast-medium left-arm bowler from 1919 to 1927. During that time he took in all first-class cricket 857 wickets for 19.75 runs each, hit 2,529 runs, average 12.90, and held 217 catches. A forthright character, "Abe" Waddington possessed in marked degree that first essential to a bowler of his type—accuracy of length—and this, allied to an easy action, ability to make the ball swerve and pace from the pitch, enabled him to dismiss 100 or more batsmen in six of his nine seasons. His total of wickets reached 100 in his first summer with the county, when he did much to help Yorkshire win the County Championship, as he did in four successive years from 1922 to 1925.

His most successful season as a bowler was that of 1920, when he took 141 wickets, average 16.72. Northamptonshire were his bright particular victims, for at Bradford he earned figures of six wickets for 24 runs in the first innings and five for 30 in the second, and at Northampton, where he and E. Robinson bowled unchanged in both innings, six for 30 and seven for 18—including a hat-trick and four wickets in five balls. Other remarkable feats of 1920 were the dismissal of seven Warwickshire batsmen for 21 runs at Harrogate and analyses of five for 48 and seven for 25 against Leicestershire at Hull. In 1921 at Harrogate against Northamptonshire, when he and Robinson again bowled unchanged, his record was six for 21 and three for 40; but his most startling achievement was seven Sussex wickets in seven overs, four of them maidens, for six runs on helpful turf at Hull in 1922. His first four successes came before he conceded a run. A useful batsman, he reached his highest innings in his last season, making such use of an early "life" that he hit 114, his only century, from the Worcestershire bowling at Leeds. He and G. G. Macaulay added 163 in 85 minutes.

Waddington toured Australia with J. W. H. T. Douglas's M.C.C. team of 1921. He did not come-off in the two Test matches in which he played, but did well in games against odds. In the fixture with a Ballarat Sixteen he took eight wickets for 15 runs and against a Benalla and District Sixteen 10 for 31 and six for 69. He headed the bowling averages for all matches. He was a keen and skilful golfer and at one time was an amateur goal-keeper with Bradford City.

WADDY, The Rev. Ernest Frederick, who died at Evesham, where he was Vicar of The Littletons, on September 23, 1958, aged 77, played for New South Wales in the days of Victor Trumper, M. A. Noble and S. E. Gregory. In 1904-05 he headed the Inter-State batting averages with figures of 70.20 and a highest innings of 129 not out against South Australia. In 1908 he hit 107 not out and 57 from the bowling of A. O. Jones's M.C.C. team and acted as 12th man in the final Test match. His 308 for Melbourne against Sydney in 1904 was the biggest score ever hit in Australian Inter-University cricket. He came to England in 1915, becoming a master at Rugby, and from 1919 to 1922 appeared in some matches for Warwickshire, scoring 995 runs, average 23.87. He was top of that county's averages with 54.66 in 1921 when hitting 109 not out against Middlesex at Lord's.

WADE, Herbert Frederick, who died in Johannesburg on November 22, 1980, aged 75, after a long illness, captained South Africa in all his 10 Test matches, five in England in 1935 and five against Australia in South Africa in 1935-36. He was made captain more for his qualities of leadership than for his batting ability, though he was one of the most effective South African batsmen of his time. The fact that he had played League cricket in Yorkshire (for whom he played Rugby football) was also a point in favour when it came to appointing a captain to England in 1935. The previous South African side, to Australia and New Zealand in 1931-32, had been led by H. B. Cameron, a contemporary of Wade's at Hilton College, Pietermaritzburg, and his vice-captain in England. As leader of the first South African side ever to win a Test match in England, Wade's place in South African Test history is secure. His own main contribution to that series, other than as a captain of "unostentatious efficiency" (*A History of Cricket,* Altham and Swanton), was his unbeaten 32 at Headingley when England was pressing hard for a victory to level the series. In all first-class matches on the tour he scored 1,042 runs at an average of 28.94, including centuries against Cambridge University, Nottinghamshire and Glamorgan. For the strong Natal side of the 1930s, he was very consistent (1,912 runs, average 44.46), with a highest score of 190 against Eastern Province at Pietermaritzburg in 1936-37. Determined but unassuming, he earned the respect of all his players. His younger brother, W. W. (Billy), played 11 times for South Africa between 1938-39 and 1948-49, besides becoming a Test umpire.

WADE, Saul, was born on February 8, 1858, and died in November, 1931, in his 74th year. A valuable member of the Yorkshire county team between 1886 and 1890, he figured in 92 matches for the county, scoring 2,029 runs with an average of 17 and a highest of 103 (not out) against Leicestershire in 1889 and taking 207 wickets at a cost of 16 runs apiece. In the match against the Australians at Bramall Lane, Sheffield, he was, with 19 wanted to win, punished by the tourists' captain, H. J. H. Scott, to the extent of 22 in the over of four balls, viz., six, four, six, and six. Wade, who bowled very slowly, with a big break from the off, had to use a wet ball on that occasion.

WADSWORTH, Kenneth John, died in Nelson, N.Z., on August 19, 1976, aged 29. He had been New Zealand's regular keeper since 1969, playing in 33 Tests, the last of them against India at Wellington in February, 1976: in these he dismissed 95 batsmen and made over a thousand runs. He toured England in 1969 and 1973. As a keeper, he was always brilliant and as time went on became more consistent: perhaps even when he died he had not reached his best. He was primarily an aggressive bat, whose impetuosity often cost him his wicket, but he could defend doggedly enough when the situation demanded. His highest Test innings was 80 against Australia at Melbourne in 1974: in the same season he made a century against them in the one-day Test at Christchurch.

At Kingston, Jamaica, in 1972, coming in to join Turner at 108 for five, he helped to put on 220, still a New Zealand Test record for the sixth wicket. Above all he was a determined cricketer who loved winning, meant to win and was sure he could, and who equally hated losing. His outlook was more typical of an Australian or a Yorkshireman than a New Zealander and this made him proportionately more valuable to his side, who found his courage and confidence an inspiration. His early death is a tragic loss not only to New Zealand cricket but to world cricket in general.

WAINWRIGHT, Edward, the famous Yorkshire cricketer, after a long illness, passed away at Sheffield on October 28, 1919. A very fine batsman, a deadly bowler on a wicket which gave him any assistance, and an excellent field, he had no small share in the many triumphs which attended the Yorkshire team during the 14 years he was a member of the side. Coming out in the season of 1888, he soon showed that he was a player out of the common by putting together an innings of 105 against the Australians at Bradford. For some seasons afterwards he met with only a moderate share of success as a batsman, but in 1892 he fairly established himself as one of the leading professionals of the day, heading the Yorkshire bowling averages, and running second to Ernest Smith in batting. His great years in run-getting were 1897, when he had an aggregate of 1,612, and 1899, when he totalled 1,541 runs. Altogether, in the course of his career, he played 20 three-figure innings for Yorkshire, his highest being 228 against Surrey, at the Oval, when he and George Hurst put on 340 runs for the seventh wicket.

Prominent as he was as a batsman, Wainwright's claim to fame will probably rest more upon his achievements in bowling. Right hand rather slow, he could always impart a lot of spin to the ball, and on a sticky wicket his off-break was formidable indeed. Had his command of length been as strong as his spin and break he might have ranked as one of the greatest of bowlers. He was rather lacking in variety of device, and when the ground was fast and true batsmen did not find him difficult to play. Altogether he took over 1,000 wickets for Yorkshire, his best season being in 1894, when in first-class matches he obtained 166 wickets for less than 13 runs apiece. Among his great feats was the taking of five Sussex wickets in seven balls at Dewsbury in 1894. Four years earlier, at Sheffield, in a match against Staffordshire, he accomplished the feat of taking all 10 wickets in an innings. In 1897 he enjoyed the distinction not only of scoring 1,612 runs, but of securing 101 wickets.

Wainwright played for England against Australia at Lord's in 1893, and four years later formed one of the team that A. E. Stoddart took to Australia. The side proved very disappointing, losing four of the five Test matches, and Wainwright achieved little worthy of his reputation beyond an innings of 105 against South Australia. There was every reason to pick him for the team, but Australia did not suit him at all. It was literally months before he made a score of 50, and on the beautiful wickets at Sydney and Melbourne his bowling was so harmless that no purpose was served by putting him on. In the 11-a-side matches he took one wicket in 72 overs at a cost of 249 runs, and during the whole tour only 13 wickets fell to him. The contrast to his brilliant form at home was bewildering. His career really finished in 1901, when Yorkshire, unbeaten in the previous summer, won 20 matches out of 27 and suffered only one defeat. A benefit awarded him in 1898 realised £1,800. Born at Tinsley, near Sheffield, in 1865, Wainwright was 54 years of age.

THREE-FIGURE INNINGS FOR YORKSHIRE (21)

105	v. Australians, at Bradford	1888
104	v. Sussex, at Sheffield	1892
122	v. Leicestershire, at Bradford	1892
107	v. Durham, at Darlington	1892
107	v. Warwickshire, at Edgbaston	1894
126	v. Warwickshire, at Edgbaston	1896
145	v. Sussex, at Bradford	1896
100	v. Gloucestershire, at Bristol	1897
171	v. Middlesex, at Lord's	1897
118*	v. Hampshire, at Southampton	1897
104*	v. Sussex, at Sheffield	1897
103	v. Notts, at Dewsbury	1897
182	v. Worcestershire, at Worcester	1898
153	v. Leicestershire, at Leicester	1899
228	v. Surrey, at the Oval	1899
100	v. Kent, at Tonbridge	1899
116	v. Kent, at Catford	1900
109	v. Somerset, at Taunton	1900
117	v. England XI, at Scarborough	1900
108*	v. Derbyshire, at Glossop	1901
116	v. South Africans, at Harrogate	1901

Signifies not out

He also scored 105 for England (Stoddart's Team) v. South Australia, at Adelaide, in 1897–98.

Wainwright himself considered his *best* innings to have been his 182 on the Worcester ground in 1898. Yorkshire, set 269 to win, won by three wickets, but (apart from Wainwright's large contribution) the only double-figure scores were 26 by Mr. Hugh Barber, 20 by Moorhouse, and 18 by Brown, of Darfield. It was a remarkable personal triumph.

In *all* matches for Yorkshire he made 12,768 runs (average 21.93) and took 1,173 wickets (average 17.24).

EIGHT OR MORE WICKETS IN AN INNINGS

10 for 31	Yorkshire v. Staffordshire, at Sheffield	1890
8 for 33	Yorkshire v. Warwickshire, at Edgbaston	1891
8 for 49	Yorkshire v. Middlesex, at Sheffield	1891
9 for 66	Yorkshire v. Middlesex, at Sheffield	1894
8 for 34	Yorkshire v. Essex, at Bradford	1896

THIRTEEN OR MORE WICKETS IN A MATCH

13 for 38	Yorkshire v. Sussex, at Dewsbury	1894
14 for 77	Yorkshire v. Essex, at Bradford	1896

FOUR WICKETS OR MORE FOR THREE RUNS OR LESS EACH

4 for 3	Yorkshire v. Warwickshire, at Sheffield	1889
4 for 9	Yorkshire v. Middlesex, at Lord's	1891
5 for 5	Yorkshire v. Durham, at Sunderland	1891
5 for 14	Yorkshire v. Essex, at Dewsbury	1892
4 for 8	Yorkshire v. Lancashire, at Manchester	1893
6 for 18*a* 7 for 20*b* 13 for 38*c*	Yorkshire v. Sussex, at Dewsbury	1894

a signifies 1st inns., *b* 2nd., and *c* both.

BOWLING UNCHANGED THROUGH BOTH COMPLETED INNINGS

With Peel, for Yorkshire v. Sussex, at Dewsbury   1894

CONSECUTIVE BALLS

5 in 7 balls for 0 runs, Yorkshire v. Sussex, at Dewsbury   1894

CONSECUTIVE BALLS—*Continued*

In all first-class matches he took 104 wickets in 1892, 119 in 1893, 166 in 1894, 102 in 1896, and 101 in 1897. In the last-mentioned year he also scored 1,612 runs.

In all matches for Yorkshire in 1892 he made 1,206 runs and took 124 wickets.

WAIT, Owen John, died on April 26, 1981, aged 54. A successful bowler in the Dulwich College XI, he got his Blue at Cambridge in 1949, when he headed the bowling averages. In 1950, suffering from a doubtful leg, he lost his form and his place, but returned to the side in 1951, when he had the splendid record of 44 wickets at 19.65 and against Sussex at Hove took six for 18. In 1950 and 1951 he played a few times for Surrey. Standing 6ft. 4in. tall, he bowled fast medium with a high action, largely in-swingers. Becoming a schoolmaster, for years he ran the cricket at Mill Hill and was also active in the selection of representative school sides in the holidays. In 1977 he was elected to the M.C.C. Committee.

WAKE, W. R., who died on Saturday, March 14, 1896, will be remembered as an occasional member some years back of the Yorkshire county XI. Without ever taking a high place, he was a useful, hard-hitting batsman. He was in his 44th year, and at the time of his death was Registrar of the Sheffield County Court.

WAKEMAN, Edward Maltby, born on November 19, 1846, died at Coton Hall, Bridgnorth, on March 18, 1926, aged 79. In 1865, when he was in the Eton XI, it was said of him: "A good bat, with rather too much flourish; a good field, and successful with lobs at times." Against Winchester he took five wickets for 52 in a total of 242, and against Harrow three for 43 in one of 248. He played for both Shropshire and Worcestershire.

WALCOTT, Leslie Arthur, was the oldest surviving West Indian Test player until his death in Barbados on February 28, 1984, at the age of 90. His one appearance for West Indies was against England at Bridgetown in 1929–30, when in a high-scoring match he scored 24 (run out) and 16 not out and took one wicket (George Gunn's) for 32 runs in eight overs. A right-hand batsman and off-spin bowler, he played for Barbados in the inter-colonial tournament from 1925 until 1936, his highest score being 73 not out for the island against the 1929–30 M.C.C. team. Until 1981 he was a regular visitor to the Kensington Oval in Bridgetown. He was unrelated to Clyde Walcott, the great West Indian batsman.

WALDEN, Fred, popularly known to cricket and soccer enthusiasts as "Fanny," died at Northampton on May 3, 1949, at the age of 61. As a first-class cricketer for Northamptonshire, a Test match umpire and an England footballer, Walden was a remarkable figure; he stood only 5ft. 2in. high, but proved himself a skilful batsman, a right-winger of uncanny dribbling powers, and an umpire of repute. A native of Wellingborough, Walden, who was born on March 1, 1888, played for Northamptonshire between 1910 and 1929. At times, considering his lack of inches, he hit with surprising strength, and he scored several fine centuries. As befitted a footballer, he excelled in the field and few surpassed him as a cover-point. Altogether he scored 7,462 runs, average 18.74, took 114 wickets costing 37.03 each, and held 126 catches. After his playing career ended, Walden was put on the first-class umpires' list. He soon earned recognition, and stood in several Tests, including the historic encounter between England and Australia at the Oval in 1938 when Hutton made the world record Test score of 364. Walden was known in the cricket world before the last War as much by the peculiar touring car in which he travelled from ground to ground as by his small stature. He shared in the triumphs of Tottenham Hotspur F.C. after the First World War—although injury prevented his appearance in the F. A. Cup Final of 1921—and he gained caps against Scotland in 1914 and Wales in 1922. Before and after assisting Tottenham, he helped Northampton Town F.C.

WALKDEN, George Godfrey, born on March 10, 1883, died in Derby Infirmary on May 17, 1923, as the result of a motor-cycling accident near Risley. His name will be found in the Derbyshire XI in 1905 and 1906.

WALKER, Ashley, born at Bradford, in Yorkshire, on June 22, 1844, died at Harrold, Buckinghamshire, on May 26, 1927, aged 82. He batted in good style and was a free scorer, and he also bowled a useful slow ball and fielded well at long-leg and cover-point. He learned his cricket at Westminster School, where he was in the XI in 1860 and the next two years, and upon going up to Cambridge obtained his Blue in 1864. In 1865 his form for the University was good, for, besides carrying out his bat for 38 in the first innings against Oxford, he made 65 v. M.C.C. at Cambridge and 56 v. Surrey at the Oval. Between 1863 and 1870 he appeared in nine games for Yorkshire and he also played a few times for Staffordshire. During the 25 years of his service abroad in the Department of Public Education he did much for cricket in Ceylon, especially at Royal College. In 1885 he captained a Ceylon team in Madras and a year later led another which visited Bombay.

WALKER, Flying Officer Charles W., the South Australian wicket-keeper, failed to return to England after a flight over Germany in the autumn of 1942. He was 33. As a player Walker reached his best form at the peak of Oldfield's career, and, though touring England with the 1930 and 1938 Australian teams, he never appeared in a Test match. Born at Hindmarsh (S.A.) on February 19, 1909, Walker was only just 20 when he stumped five and caught three in his first big match for South Australia against New South Wales in March 1929. His form against A. H. H. Gilligan's side in 1929–30 went further to prove his ability, particularly in bringing off amazing catches and stumpings on the leg side. A neat cricketer, he was a useful batsman and often opened the innings for his State. When hostilities broke out, he became an air-gunner, and during leave in England he was always welcome at cricket grounds; in fact he kept wicket in several games for the R.A.F.

WALKER, Flight-Lieut. David Frank, Oxford University captain in 1935 and the most successful batsman who ever played for Norfolk, lost his life during operational duties in February, 1942, and was buried at Trondheim, Norway. He played three seasons in the Uppingham XI, 1930 to 1932. Only one match was lost when he was captain in his last two years. By far the best bat, he headed the averages each season, and made 224 not out against Shrewsbury in 1932, the next best score being 39, and he averaged 78. Twice he played for The Rest against Lord's Schools. Going up to Oxford, he started his University career in such fine form that he made a hundred (retired) in the Freshmen's match, and, after 67 against Yorkshire, he carried his bat through the innings against Gloucestershire, scoring 107 not out. His first innings in The Parks produced 394 runs for three times out. At Lord's, on a rain-damaged pitch against Kenneth Farnes, Jahangar Khan, R. S.

Grant and H. J. Human, he held out for two hours and 40 minutes, scoring 46 before being sixth out at 117. In his typical display under adverse conditions he showed admirable defence, and he accomplished nothing better for Oxford. He finished his University career captain of the losing side at Lord's, after taking part in two drawn games with Cambridge. He also played hockey for Oxford.

David Walker found greater opportunities for showing his batting ability when appearing for Norfolk, and developed from a patient defender into a brilliant exponent of many strokes. When a schoolboy in 1931 he stayed in four hours against Kent Second XI, and his 73 not out was the best score for Norfolk that season. Altogether in nine seasons for Norfolk he obtained 4,034 runs with an average of 62, and hit 13 centuries, the highest being 217 against Northumberland in 1939. He invariably began each season for Norfolk in splendid form: in 1933 with 179, 71 and 139; in 1934 with 157, 190 and 95, while in 1938 he played consecutive innings of 57, 101 not out, 167, 7, 65, 27 not out and 158. In 1933, when Norfolk finished head of the second-class counties and the challenge match was cancelled because Yorkshire Second XI, the winners, were found to have an inferior record to Wiltshire's, David Walker averaged 85.22 in all games for the county. This figure he surpassed next year with 93. Seven times he headed the Norfolk averages, and in three seasons he was the best batsman in the Second-Class Counties competition. He took part in three record partnerships for Norfolk: first wicket, 323 with H. E. Theobald, v. Northumberland in 1939; second wicket, 218 with W. J. Edrich, v. Lincolnshire in 1934; third wicket, 221 with J. C. Thistleton-Smith, v. Kent Second XI in 1936.

In April 1939 he went to Egypt with H. M. Martineau's team, and in 10 matches scored 716 runs, the highest aggregate, average 55, and with his slow left-hand spinners headed the bowling averages—17 wickets for 208 runs. After leaving Oxford he was appointed Cricket Master at Harrow, which he left in September 1939 for an educational post under the Sudan Government. He joined the R.A.F. in South Africa, training in Rhodesia, before returning to England in August 1941. He was married three months before his disastrous flight, when 28 years of age.

WALKER, Flight-Lieut. Donald Frederick, R.A.F.V.R., who was killed during a flight over Germany on the night of June 17, 1941, and buried in Holland, was one of Hampshire's most promising batsmen. Born on August 15, 1912, he went to King's College School, Wimbledon, where he developed into a very good cricketer. A left-handed batsman, he averaged 30.62 in 1928 and in his last year he headed the batting with 23.20, besides proving useful with the ball. A brilliant fieldsman, he also could keep wicket. He was good enough for a trial in the Surrey Second XI in 1933, but his home was at Bournemouth and, having attracted attention by scoring 1,000 runs and taking 100 wickets one season in club cricket, he was persuaded to turn professional and joined the Hampshire staff. Playing first for the county in 1937, he soon showed his skill, and took part in a record fifth-wicket stand for Hampshire, 235 being added in company with G. Hill, who also got his first 100 in County Cricket. Altogether that season Walker scored 847 runs, and next year he made 925. He surpassed this in 1939 with 1,117 runs, including three centuries; average 29.39. Only Arnold and Bailey were above him. Sound in defence, with unlimited patience, Walker brought off good strokes all round the wicket and generally gave every indication of a successful career. A strong

Rugby football player, he captained the Dorset County team and also captained an R.A.F. side. This Walker of Hampshire must not be confused with David Frank Walker, who went to Uppingham, got his Blue as a Freshman, captained Oxford University in 1935, and was prominent in the Norfolk County XI.

WALKER, George Glossop, who was born at Harthill Grange, in Yorkshire, on June 14, 1860, died on January 11, 1908, at Whitwell, in Derbyshire, where he had been for many years a farmer on the estate of the Duke of Portland. Originally a slow bowler, he later took to delivering the ball (left-handed) at a great pace, and it was as a fast bowler that he obtained his numerous triumphs in County Cricket. He was often erratic and short and frequently got up quickly off the pitch, being at times a very awkward bowler to play. His first match for Derbyshire was against Yorkshire on the Derby ground in 1881, and his last against Lancashire at Manchester in 1898. For some years he captained the team, and it was no fault of his that only a small amount of success attended their efforts, for he was a splendid worker and popular with all. Some of his best performances with the ball for Derbyshire were as follows:

7 for 105	..	(in an innings of 451), v. Notts, at Derby	..	..	..	1885
4 for 11 ⎱ 6 for 26 ⎰	..	v. M.C.C. and Ground, at Lord's	..	..	..	1886
7 for 38 ⎱ 5 for 75 ⎰	..	v. Surrey at Derby	..	..	..	1886
5 for 31	..	v. M.C.C. and Ground, at Lord's	..	..	..	1888
7 for 53	..	v. Leicestershire, at Leicester ..	..	..	..	1890
6 for 5	..	v. Essex, at Derby	..	..	..	1890
5 for 19 ⎱ 3 for 22 ⎰	..	v. Norfolk, at Derby	..	..	..	1890
4 for 13 ⎱ 5 for 45 ⎰	..	v. Hampshire, at Southampton	..	..	..	1893
5 for 24	..	v. Lancashire, at Derby	..	..	..	1894

As a batsman Mr. Walker was a lively and energetic hitter, but he did not possess sufficient guard on his wicket. His highest score in first-class cricket was 66 for Derbyshire v. Surrey at the Oval in 1884, which was made at a time when runs were much wanted. He was invited to assist the Gentlemen against the Players at Lord's in 1888 and 1894 but declined on each occasion. In the latter year, however, he twice took part in representative cricket, appearing for North v. South in Wood's benefit at the Oval and for Gentlemen v. Players on the same ground.

WALKER, I. D., born January 8, 1844, died July 6, 1898. On the morning of July 6, two days before the Eton v. Harrow match, I. D. Walker passed away at his brother R. D. Walker's house in Regent's Park. Very few people except some of his most intimate friends, and the school at Harrow knew that he was ill, so suddenly was he taken from us. Indeed it was only with difficulty that he was persuaded on June 29—as he was feeling ill—to leave Harrow and come to his brother's with the intention of returning for the Harrovian match on July 2, in which he hoped to play, and captain the side as he had done for so many years. No one who was present at the Eton v. Harrow match can ever forget the sadness of the scene—the flags floating half-mast high, and the genuine grief that was expressed on all sides—for though perhaps there may have been cricketers who have had more friends than I. D. Walker, no cricketer could have so many dear and close friends. Those who had the privilege of his friendship came almost entirely from the cricket field, Harrow men being the most numerous. Throughout his long career he was wonderfully successful; four years in the Harrow XI; twice captain; and then for 20 years he played for Middlesex, being captain for a great part of that time; in the Gentlemen v. Players match, and indeed all the important matches. He founded the Harrow Wanderers in 1870, and from that date until the time of his death, with the exception of one year, 1885, he played continuously for them. It was entirely due to him that the tour has been such a success for so many years, and those who were fortunate enough to be asked by him to play will never forget his unvarying kindness and the trouble he took to make them happy. We may safely say that devoted as he was to County Cricket, Harrow cricket was the thing dearest to his heart, and when he retired from first-class matches after the season of 1884, he gave up the whole of his time to coach the boys at his old school. After the loss of Lord Bessborough and Mr. Grimston, Harrow has indeed been fortunate in having the services of such a successor for the last 10 years, for not only did he bring the cricket up to a very high standard, but he gained the love and affection of the boys to an extraordinary degree. To Harrovians and Middlesex cricketers his loss is irreparable and indeed to the whole cricketing world, for he played the game throughout his career in the most chivalrous spirit, and it is impossible to estimate the value of his example.

For the foregoing tribute I am indebted to one of the late Mr. Walker's closest friends and I may perhaps be permitted to supplement this personal note on the famous cricketer with a brief biographical sketch, only slightly altered, that I wrote when the announcement of his death appeared:

With Harrow and Middlesex cricket Mr. I. D. Walker's name will be associated as long as the national game retains its popularity. He was captain of the Harrow XI in 1862 and 1863, and had even then played for Middlesex, the formation of the County Club being, as everyone knows, chiefly due to the Walkers. All the sons in the family played cricket, but only four became famous—John, who died in 1885, V. E., R. D., and I. D. It is, perhaps, a fair criticism to say that V. E. was the finest all-round player, and I. D. the best bat. Gradually improving after he left Harrow, Mr. I. D. Walker jumped to the top of the tree in 1868, in which year he had, by general consent, no superior as a batsman, except Mr. W. G. Grace. It was in 1868 that he played his greatest innings of 165 for the Gentlemen at the Oval, an innings which, after an interval of 30 years, is referred to in enthusiastic terms by everyone who had the pleasure of seeing it. No one but Mr. Grace, it may be mentioned, has ever made a bigger score for Gentlemen against Players, either at the Oval or Lord's. Like all other batsmen, I. D. Walker had his good and bad seasons, but he kept up his form wonderfully well, and even so late as 1883 he did one of the biggest things of his career, he and the Hon. Alfred Lyttelton, for Middlesex against Gloucestershire at Clifton, scoring 324 runs together for the second wicket. Mr. Walker made 145 and Lyttelton 181. It is recorded that after the luncheon interval the two batsmen put on 226 runs in an hour and three-quarters. It is never safe to be dogmatic on anything connected with cricket, but one may question whether such an extreme rate of run-getting has ever been sustained for so long a time in a first-class match. Be this as it may, however, the hitting was altogether exceptional in quality. Mr. Walker scored 552 runs for Middlesex in 1883 with an average of 34, and though he had been before the public for more than 20 years, no one outside his immediate circle of friends knew that his career in big matches was nearing its close. However, he made up his mind that the season of 1884 should be his last, and he kept to his resolve, handing over the captaincy of the Middlesex XI after 1884 to Mr. A. J. Webbe. He said at the time that he thought he could bat nearly as well as ever, but that he knew he was falling off in the field. Perhaps he was wise to retire while his powers were so little impaired, but the county team did not seem itself without him. He was the last of the Walkers, and the Walkers had made Middlesex cricket.

As a batsman, I. D. Walker was essentially a punishing player. Probably no one could hit harder on the off-side. He had one stroke which, if not peculiar to himself, has been possessed by very few batsmen. Shaping as if for an orthodox drive, he would often send the ball over cover-point's head to the boundary. The hit was too much in the air to be pretty to look at, but unless a fieldsman had been placed out deep it was safe, and the ball nearly always went to the ring. Sometimes against left-handed bowlers the hit would go as far back as third man, looking then to those not familiar with Mr. Walker's style of play to be quite a fluke. As pointed out in Mr. Grace's book on cricket, one of the other batsmen noted for this particular hit was H. H. Massie, the fastest run-getter in the great Australian team of 1882. Like many Harrow batsmen, I. D. Walker stood at the wicket with his legs rather wide apart, but he made full use of his height, his style being quite different to that of A. J. Webbe and W. H. Hadow. He depended on driving for most of his runs, but could score all round the wicket. Though it is considerably more than 20 years ago, one recalls a tremendous hit of his at Lord's which went through the billiard-room window, and would assuredly have found its way into St. John's Wood Road, if there had been nothing to stop it. In the field Mr. Walker almost invariably stood mid-off, and in his young days no one in that position surpassed him. He was an extremely good underhand bowler but when his brother V. E. was on the same side, as was almost invariably the case in his earlier days, his services were seldom required. Later on when he himself acted as captain in important matches, he was always diffident about putting himself on. When he could be persuaded to bowl he was most successful, as the records of the Harrow Wanderers' tours will bear testimony. After he retired from the captaincy of the Middlesex XI a presentation was made to him in the Pavilion at Lord's, the chief spokesman on the occasion being Lord George Hamilton. Even at this distance of time I have a vivid recollection of Mr. Walker's speech in returning thanks to his cricket comrades, in whose delightful society, he said, all the pleasantest hours of his life had been passed. Much more could be written, but it may suffice to say that one of the most notable figures in modern cricket has passed from among us. Born on January 8, 1844, Mr. Walker was in his 55th year. The funeral on Monday, July 11, drew to Southgate Churchyard a notable band of cricketers. Whichever way one looked familiar faces were to be seen. Cricket of a bygone time was represented by Harvey Fellows, Canon McCormick, R. A. H. Mitchell, and C. E. Green, and not far from them stood such great players of the present day as A. E. Stoddart, A. C. MacLaren, F. G. J. Ford and G. Macgregor. These two generations were, if one may say so, united by the presence of A. N. Hornby, A. J. Webbe, and A. P.

Lucas, three batsmen who, though their early fame dates back a long time, are still playing first-class cricket. Among others present were the Rev. J. E. C. Welldon, E. E. Bowen, the Hon. Alfred Lyttelton—personal friend, and President of the M.C.C.—Lord Harris, C. W. Alcock (officially representing the Surrey Club) and quite a number of past and present Middlesex players—E. Rutter, Stanley Scott, C. T. Studd, P. F. Warner, and Sir T. C. O'Brien. Professional cricket at the present time seemed to be represented only by J. T. Hearne. George Hearne, senior, who played for Middlesex in old days at the Cattle Market Ground was there, but his better known brother, the veteran Tom Hearne, was prevented by feeble health from being present. The body was laid to rest in the family vault of the Walkers, which stands just outside the west front of Southgate Church. Wreaths had been sent by cricketers and Cricket Clubs from all parts of the country, a prominent place being of course given to the one from the Marylebone Club. The coffin bore the simple inscription: "Isaac Donnithorne Walker. Born January 8, 1844. Died July 6, 1898." — S.H.P.

WALKER, Jack, who collapsed and died on May 29, 1968, aged 54, kept wicket in one match for Kent, against Essex at Gravesend, in 1949. He played on a number of occasions for the Second XI. For 16 years he assisted Gravesend C.C. and was chairman of Cobham C.C. for 21 years.

WALKER, James George, died on March 24, 1923, at Nether Auchendrane, Ayr, in his 64th year. Without ever rising to quite the front rank Mr. Walker was an excellent batsman of the defensive school. Though he went up to Oxford from Loretto with a considerable reputation it was not until his third year at the University that he gained his Blue. Playing against Cambridge at Lord's in 1882 and 1883 he was on the losing side in both years, but in 1883 he played a very good second innings of 51. It was his misfortune to be associated with two XIs of far less than average strength. Fate was not kind to him in the big match as in his four innings he was twice run out. After leaving Oxford he kept his place in first-class cricket for several years, playing for Middlesex from 1886 to 1890. His best year for the county was 1886 when he was clearly at the top of his form. Among other good innings he scored 67 in the match in which Middlesex nearly brought off a sensational victory against the Australians. I gather from *Bat v. Ball* that his only hundred in first-class matches was 111 for the Zingari against the Gentlemen of England at Scarborough in 1885, but he twice got very near to three figures in 1888, scoring 99 not out for the Gentlemen of England against Oxford University at Oxford and 97 for Middlesex against Gloucestershire at Lord's. Mr. Walker was a batsman pure and simple. He did not bowl and I cannot recall him as more than an ordinary good field. He excelled at Rugby football, playing three times for Oxford against Cambridge—1879, 1880, and 1881—and getting his International cap for Scotland against England in 1882 and against Wales in 1883. A man of great wealth, he was born at Glasgow on October 9, 1859.—S.H.P.

WALKER, The Rev. John Spencer Mullins, who died at Hove on November 19, 1953, in his 101st year, played in the Lancing cricket XIs of 1870 to 1872 and in the Association football teams of 1867 to 1872. Known as "The Father of Sussex Football," he was one of a committee of three boys who in 1871 gave the Association code a trial in place of a game played only at Lancing. He was the oldest living old boy of the school. He played for Clapham Rovers in the F.A. Cup Semifinal at Kennington Oval in 1874, when four spectators saw the victory of Oxford University by 1–0, and he became the first President of the Sussex F.A. in 1881. For 13 years after graduating at Oxford he was assistant master at Lancing, and later spent 30 years as Vicar of Amport St. Mary, Hampshire, before retiring to Hove in 1935.

WALKER, Livingston, died on October 10, 1940, aged 61. A good club cricketer, he showed to such advantage with the London County XI under W. G. Grace that he twice found a place in the 1900 Surrey team, and became captain in 1903 at a time when high-class amateurs were scarce at Kennington Oval. Very popular and familiarly known as "Livy," he went to Shanghai and so was lost to County Cricket.

WALKER, Capt. Neil Alexander McDonald, who died on August 10, 1960, aged 65, played for Derbyshire against the New Zealanders in 1931 and against Kent at Gravesend five years later, when he captained the side.

WALKER, Roger, though far better known in connection with Rugby football than cricket—he played four times for England against Scotland and once against Ireland—died at Reading on November 11, 1919, at the age of 73. He took a keen interest in the summer game and was for years a member of the M.C.C. During the War he did much to prevent the club's tour of matches against the Sussex schools from falling through. He was a life-long friend of Mr. A. N. Hornby, and played once or twice for Lancashire in 1874 and 1875.

WALKER, Russell Donnithorne, died on March 29, 1922. He had been very ill for some time, but the end came quite suddenly just when he seemed to be rallying and was not without hope of watching one more season's cricket at Lord's. Born on February 13, 1842, he had received many congratulations on completing his 80th year.

Mr. A. J. Webbe writes: "The passing of Russie Walker has closed a wonderful chapter of English cricket, for he was the last of the famous brothers who will always be remembered as having played the game in the best and most chivalrous spirit.

The Walkers of Southgate founded the Middlesex County C.C., and until 'I.D.' retired in 1884 the XI was always captained by one of the brothers. After that V. E. and R. D. followed each other as Presidents of the club, so that we may say that Middlesex cricket was run by the family from 1864, when it was started, until the commencement of 1922. Russie was two years in the Harrow cricket and football XIs, and also won the Champion Racquet. He then proceeded to B.N.C., Oxford, and was five years in the University XI, also representing Oxford in the single and double Racquet contests. For several years he played for the Gentlemen v. the Players, and, of course, for Middlesex county, though he retired from first-class cricket far too soon, actually making a century in almost his last county match—against Surrey at the Oval, when the match resulted in a tie.

Present-day cricketers will hardly believe that he faced the fastest bowlers—faster than any we have at the present moment—unarmed with either pads or gloves and, strange to say, he was never seriously hurt.

As a racquet and tennis player he was quite at the top of the tree. In both these games, as in his cricket, he played in a most peculiar style, but with great effect. He simply revelled in unorthodoxy. He certainly attained a higher eminence at racquets than he did at tennis, and often said he regretted not having taken up the latter game earlier. It was a great treat in the old days of Prince's

Club, in Hans Place, to see him play a single, as he did frequently, with Punch Fairs, the champion racquet player, from whom he used to receive three aces.

He was also a wonderful Whist player, but I fancy he never became equally good at Bridge. He was a very fine Billiard player and frequently had one of the professionals to play on his small pocket table at North Villa, Regent's Park.

Indeed, he took a keen interest in almost every game up until the very last hour of his life, and the handicap of his long illness seemed if anything to add to his keenness. He struggled up to Lord's—he was a trustee of the M.C.C.—to attend the Committee meetings, both of M.C.C. and of the Middlesex C.C., and to witness the matches all through the summer of 1921. The absence of his bath chair, which used to be drawn up in front of the Players' dressing room, was greatly noticed last summer. The Middlesex professionals and his old friends had many a pleasant chat there with him.

It seems strange that neither he nor any of the seven brothers were married. A partial explanation of this is, I think, their wonderful attachment to each other. Never was there a more united family, and Russie was idolised up to the end of his long life by his numerous nephews and nieces—his five sisters were all married, but alas, there was not one to perpetuate the family name. No one had more friends, though, of course, he had outlived most of them: his friendship once gained was wonderfully strong and true, and those friends who, like the writer, had survived him, will treasure his memory to the end of their lives.

He was one of the most generous of men, but, like his brothers, he had a horror of his name appearing in any subscription list, and insisted on remaining anonymous.

Besides his interest in games he was fond of music of the best kind, in former days never missing the concerts which were termed 'Monday Pops.' In fact, he was all his life a constant attendant of the best concerts and operas. To recall these performances and the numerous great performers that he had met and heard was a great joy to him, and his memory was never at fault."

To what Mr. Webbe has written one may add as a matter of record that Mr. Walker was in the Harrow XI in 1859 and 1860, and in the Oxford XI from 1861 to 1865, he being the last man who played five times in the University match. A rule was passed in 1865 that no one should play for more than four years. Mr. Walker met with little success as a batsman against Cambridge, his best score being 42 in 1861. In the five matches nine wickets fell to his innocent-looking but rather deceptive slow bowling. He had pleasanter recollections of his two matches against Eton. In 1859, when Harrow won in a single innings, he scored 28 and took six wickets, getting rid of R. A. H. Mitchell for 10 and 0, and in the drawn game in 1860 he took five wickets for 37 runs and two for 60. It was often said of him that his style of batting could be neither described nor imitated. It was entirely his own. He assisted the Gentlemen against the Players in 10 matches between 1863 and 1868, and had a batting average—very good in those days—of 24. His best score was 92 at the Oval in 1865. He made 63 in his second innings at Lord's in 1866, when the Gentlemen were beaten, after a fine fight, by 38 runs, and in the same year he scored 52, when the Gentlemen followed on and gained their first victory at the Oval.—S.H.P.

WALKER, Thomas, born on April 3, 1854, died at Leeds on August 29, 1925, aged 71. For over 40 years he was well known in club cricket in Yorkshire and he took part in eight matches for the county in 1879 and in six in 1880, making, however, only 179 runs with an average of 8.95. He was the founder of the old Leaminton C.C. and had much to do with bringing Robert Peel forward as a slow bowler. Until August 18, 1879, he played as an amateur.

WALKER, V. E. The death at Southgate on January 3, 1906, after a brief illness, of Mr. Vyell Edward Walker, removed from among us one of the most famous of cricketers. Mr. Walker's career as an active player ended long ago, but his interest in the game remained as keen as ever to the last, and almost daily during the season he was to be seen at Lord's. The fifth of the seven brothers Walker—all of them cricketers—he was born on April 20, 1837, and was thus in his 69th year. He played his first match at Lord's for Harrow against Winchester in 1853, and made such rapid progress that he was picked for Gentlemen against Players when only 19 years of age. His position as one of the leading cricketers of the day was already secure when in 1859, for England against Surrey, at the Oval, he did the biggest thing of his whole career, scoring 20 not out and 108, and taking with his lobs 14 wickets—all 10 in the first innings and four in the second. Thenceforward he was quite at the top of the tree as an all-round player, having no rival among amateurs until E. M. and W. G. Grace in turn appeared on the scene. He was at his best, both as batsman and bowler, down to 1866, and went on playing for several years longer, giving up first-class cricket, if we remember rightly, after the season of 1877. Ten years later he returned to the field for one special occasion, captaining the Veterans against the M.C.C. during the M.C.C.'s Centenary Week at Lord's in 1887. Mr. Walker was in every sense of the word an all-round cricketer, as, apart from his batting, his lob bowling, and his splendid fielding, he was, on the admission of all who played with or against him, the very best captain of his time. No point in the game escaped him, and many stories have been told of his skilful generalship in Middlesex matches.

He was one of the founders of the Middlesex Club, early in the '60s, and regularly captained the XI until, as his powers began to wane, he gave up the post to his youngest brother, Mr. I. D. Walker, who died in 1898. In the early days of Middlesex cricket, when the matches were played on the old Cattle Market ground at Islington, the Walkers practically ran the County Club. The support accorded by the public was not great, but the cricket could scarcely have been keener. When the Cattle Market ground had to be given up to the builders, Middlesex, after a tentative experiment at Lillie Bridge, played for some years at Prince's ground, Hans Place, and then, in 1877, came to the arrangement—still in force—with the Marylebone Club to play all their home matches at Lord's. County Cricket 40 years ago was a small thing compared with what it is now, but the Middlesex XI were very proud of taking the first place in 1866. In that season they played eight county matches, and won six of them, the only defeat being against Cambridgeshire at the Cattle Market. It was one of Mr. Walker's best years, and in a couple of single innings' victories over Surrey he had a notable share, scoring 79 at Islington and 74, not out, at the Oval. Encouraged by success, Middlesex ventured to play England at Lord's in 1867, but the result was disastrous, the batting of Alfred Lubbock and W. G. Grace giving the England team an easy victory. Mr. Walker became president of the Middlesex County Club in 1898, and retained the post for the rest of his life. He was one of the trustees of the Marylebone Club, and filled the office of president in 1891.

To Mr. Walker's varied gifts as a cricketer many of the men who played side by side with him in his best days bear testimony, all agreeing as to his skill as a captain and the exceptional excellence of his fielding and lob bowling. Writing in Mr. Bettesworth's book, *The Walkers of Southgate*, Canon McCormick said, "I think that V. E. was the best slow bowler I ever played after old Clarke, who bowled faster than V. E. as a rule. V. E. and W. B. Money were, perhaps, nearer each other in style than any other two bowlers of the time. I never think that Money had full justice done to him. V. E. was better than he in both judgment and the way in which he fielded his own bowling; they neither of them tossed the ball in the air as much as other bowlers, such as A. W. Ridley and E. T. Drake, who were both very good indeed. V. E.'s difficulty chiefly lay in his deceptive variation of pace. He was a splendid judge of a batsman's abilities, and very quickly found out his weak spots. He did not concern himself with averages; his one leading idea was to get a man out. I have seen all the modern lob-bowlers, including Humphreys, and the only conclusion I can come to is that there is no accurate, well-paced lob-bowling now." Mr. Edward Rutter, his companion in many a Middlesex match, was particularly impressed by the catches he made from his own bowling. He said of him, "He was a most formidable customer as a bowler, and he was the most athletic fellow that I ever saw in the cricket field. I have seen him catch a man behind the batsman's wicket near short-leg, which shows as well as anything I can think of what a lot of ground he covered. It did not matter to him how hard the ball was driven back to him; if it was within reach he made a catch of it with either hand." Apart from the Surrey and England match in 1859, Mr. Walker twice took all 10 wickets in one innings—for Gentlemen of Middlesex against Gentlemen of Kent at Maidstone in 1864, and for Middlesex against Lancashire at Manchester in 1865. He is also said to have performed the feat once in a minor game. With regard to the Surrey and England match, Mr. Walker was fond of recalling the fact that the not-out man in Surrey's first innings—Julius Caesar—was missed off his bowling. As a batsman Mr. Walker was more graceful in style than any of his brothers, and was essentially an on-side player. Though very modest when speaking of his own deeds in the cricket field, he remembered with some pride that he made top score against the late George Freeman, when that greatest of purely fast bowlers caused such a sensation in a North and South match at the Oval in 1869.

Of the many famous matches in which Mr. Walker took part it would be easy to write several pages without in any way exhausting the subject. Two of the most memorable—Gentlemen v. Players and Surrey v. England—were played at the Oval in 1862. The Gentlemen and Players match, after a tremendous fight, was left drawn, the Players at the finish having two wickets to fall and wanting 33 runs to win. H. H. Stephenson and George Anderson were the not-outs, and Tom Lockyer had still to go in. Of the Players' XI on that occasion William Caffyn—now in his 79th year—is the only survivor, but four or five of the Gentlemen are still living. The late Mr. John Walker—eldest of the seven brothers—headed the Gentlemen's score with 98 and 10. The Surrey and England match of 1862—the last in which Surrey met England's full strength—is, even after the lapse of more than 44 years, vividly remembered. England scored 503—a total until then not equalled in first-class matches—and Willsher was no-balled by John Lillywhite for bowling over the shoulder. Lillywhite's action caused a great stir, and led to the alteration of Law 10 in 1864. One of the kindliest of men, Mr. Walker had numberless friends in the cricket world, and his death leaves a gap that can never be filled. Of the seven brothers Mr. Russell D. Walker, the sixth, is the only one now living.

WALL, Thomas Wheelbourne, who died in Adelaide on March 26, 1981, was Australia's fast bowler from 1929 to 1934. In that time he played in nine Tests in Australia, where his 37 wickets cost him 25 runs each, and nine in England, in which he took 19 at 56 runs each. In fact, in both his tours to England, in 1930 and 1934, he was expensive in all matches, his total for the two seasons being 98 wickets at an average of 30, though it is only fair to say that in 1934 he was handicapped by a bad leg. Doubtless he could get more pace and bounce in Australia: still, it was his ability to swing the ball away that made Bradman pronounce him "The finest fast bowler I ever played with the new ball" (he was ever prepared to bowl into the wind to help it swing) and one would have expected him to be more effective in England. Apart from his bowling he was a fair short-leg and a number 11 who could take some moving at a crisis.

Standing over 6 ft., he took a run of 27 paces, then regarded as the longest in the world: bowling with a high arm and good action he was accurate both in length and direction. He was unlucky in not having in Tests a fast bowler as his regular partner at the other end. He first played for Australia in his second season of state cricket, in the last Test against England in 1928–29 when, with five for 66 in the second innings, he had much to do with his side's only victory in the series. At Old Trafford in 1930, coming on for his second spell with 100 up for no wicket, he dismissed Hobbs, Sutcliffe and Hammond for six runs in the course of four overs. But perhaps his most famous feat was for South Australia against New South Wales at Sydney in 1932–33, when in the first innings, without any assistance from the pitch but with a strong breeze to help him, he took 10 for 36. No bowler had previously taken all 10 wickets in the Sheffield Shield: moreover the first four batsmen were Fingleton, Brown, Bradman and McCabe. If he will not be remembered as one of the great bowlers, he was always, however things were going, a whole-hearted trier and in these tempestuous times many will look back nostalgically to one whom Ray Robinson described as "the most gentlemanly of all fast bowlers."

WALL, William, who died at Southport on April 18, 1922, aged 68, played for Lancashire v. Derbyshire at Derby in 1877, scored 17 not out and 0. He was one of three brothers who had assisted the county, and was born on January 8, 1854.

WALL, William Henry, who was born at Eastnor, near Ledbury, on July 29, 1844, died at Bacup on September 24, 1914. He was the first professional to play for Gloucestershire, and was described as "a good average batsman, a middle-paced round-armed bowler, and fields well, generally at mid-on or short-leg." He was engaged by many clubs at different times and for 13 years was coach at Rugby School, retiring in 1906.

WALLACH, Benjamin, who died at Johannesburg on May 25, 1935, aged 61 years, was reserve wicket-keeper to E. A. Halliwell in the South African team that visited England in 1904. He also played occasionally for London County.

WALLER, George, who died on December 9, 1937, aged 73, in a Sheffield Nursing Home, played occasionally for Yorkshire from 1893 to 1896. At different times he was engaged by the Wrexham, Lowerhouse, Burnley, Middlesborough and Sheffield United Clubs. In 1896 in Yorkshire Council matches he scored 2,000 runs and took 198 wickets. A good Association football player he was in the Sheffield Wednesday XI who lost the F.A. Cup final tie to Blackburn Rovers by the then record margin of six goals to one. As player and trainer he was with Sheffield United 40 years before retiring in 1930.

WALLROTH, Conrad Adolphus, born at Lee, in Kent, on May 17, 1851, died at Compton, near Godalming, on February 22, 1926, aged 74. He was a steady batsman with good style and an excellent field, especially at long stop. As a member of the Harrow XI of 1870, he scored 30 and 0 v. Eton, and during the three years, 1872 to 1874, that he played for Oxford he made 15 and one, 0 and four, and 44 against Cambridge. He was probably at his best in 1873 when he played an innings of 109 for the University v. Middlesex at Prince's and scored 72 not out and 40 for Sixteen of Brasenose College against the United North of England XI. His County Cricket was very restricted, but he appeared for Kent in 1872 and for Derbyshire in 1879.

WALMSLEY, Edgar, a member of the Surrey County Club Committee, and very well known at the Oval because of his great size—height 6ft., weight 24st. as he admitted—died on September 1, 1948, aged 60. He played with W. G. Grace when London County Club was no longer first-class.

WALMSLEY, Walter Thomas, who died suddenly in New Zealand on February 25, 1978, aged 61, was a much travelled Australian all-round cricketer who made good use of limited opportunities, including the establishment of long standing records in Queensland and Tasmania while embarking on a successful coaching career. After early years spent with the Sydney Western Surburbs Club, Walmsley gained further experience in Lancashire League before transferring to Tasmania as the coach of its Northern area. Walmsley scored 180 against the 1948 Indian touring side, this remaining as a State record for International matches. None the less valuable was a long unbeaten defensive innings of 41 which staved off Tasmania's defeat in Hobart two months later at the hands of the powerful 1948 Australian team, then en route to England.

Transferring to Brisbane as official QCA coach in the 1948–49 season, Walmsley became a valuable member of the Queensland Sheffield Shield team, his well flighted

leg spinners gathering 95 wickets. In addition, he still holds the State's ninth and 10th wicket partnerships—the former being 152 scored with the late Wally Grout against N.S.W. in 1956–57 and the last wicket stand with fellow spin bowler John Freeman against the same State a year later. A deeply dedicated cricketer. Walmsley effectively carried his experience into coaching duties in which he showed marked ability to impart the basic principles to his many charges in a most infectious manner. After transferring to reside in New Zealand, Wal Walmsley frequently returned to Australia to attend Test series—often accompanied by some members of his large family of children—his last visit being the January 1978 Australia v. India Test match at the Sydney Cricket Ground.

WALSH, George, who played for Lancashire in 1875 and 1877, died at the end of May. 1904.

WALSH, John (Jack) Edward, who died at Newcastle, New South Wales, on May 20, 1980, aged 67, was for some years one of the most dangerous, if not the most consistent, bowlers in the world, though as an Australian resident in England he never played in a Test. Born in Sydney, he had in 1937 acquired a sufficient reputation in his native state to be invited over to play for Sir Julien Cahn and to qualify for Leicestershire. In three seasons for Sir Julien's XI he took nearly 600 wickets, meanwhile playing occasionally as an amateur for Leicestershire, and in 1938, when he headed their bowling averages, taking seven for 46 against Northamptonshire. In 1946 he joined the Leicestershire staff and for the next 10 years was one of the mainstays of the side. A left-arm bowler with tremendous powers of spin, he was of the Fleetwood-Smith type—chinamen and googlies. In fact he had two googlies; one which could be easily detected, to lull the batsman into a sense of security, when he would unleash the other, which was calculated to deceive even the greatest batsmen. In all for Leicestershire he took 1,127 wickets at an average of 24.25, his best season being 1948 when he took 174 at 19.56. Apart from his bowling he was a good slip and a left-hand batsman of great power with a full range of strokes, who would have scored many more runs had he restrained his passion for straight drives into the pavilion. When he played his highest innings—106 in 95 minutes against Essex at Loughborough in 1948—82 of his runs came in boundaries;

seven sixes and 10 fours. In 1952 he performed the double of 1,000 runs and 100 wickets. Outside County Cricket he represented the Players at Lord's in 1947. Retiring from first-class cricket at the end of 1956, he captained Leicestershire Second XI in 1957 and was for a time the county's assistant coach. Later he coached both in Tasmania and Scotland.

WALSINGHAM, Baron—in his cricket days the Hon. T. de Grey—died on December 3, 1919, in his 77th year. He was born in London on July 29, 1843. Though he played for Norfolk as late as 1868, he did not keep up his cricket very seriously after his University days. He was in the Eton XI in 1860 and 1861, and though overshadowed by R. A. H. Mitchell in both years and by the Hon. C. G. Lyttelton (now Lord Cobham) in 1860, he was one of the school's trusted batsmen, always going in first. In the big school matches he was never on the losing side, Eton beating Winchester in both his years, and drawing both games with Harrow at Lord's. His best score in the four matches was 30 not out against Winchester in 1861. Going up to Cambridge he gained his Blue as a Freshman and was thus a member of H. M. Plowden's famous XI in 1862—by far the strongest side sent up to Lord's by Cambridge in those far-off days. More than that, he had a share in the eight wickets victory over Oxford, scoring 20 and 22 not out. He played again in the University match in 1863, and it was no fault of his that Oxford won this time by eight wickets, as out of totals of 65 and 61 he made 12 and 24. The wicket was very dead on the first day and Cambridge suffered by getting first innings. On a much-improved pitch the next day Oxford had an easy task. The Hon. T. de Grey should have appeared a third time against Oxford, in 1864—he played against Surrey in a memorable draw at the Oval—but rheumatism prevented him. In 1865 he played in three of Cambridge's trial matches, but not at Lord's. I learn from the late Mr. W. J. Ford's book that he had an excellent record as a batsman for Cambridge, his average for four years being 32, 22, 24, and 17. Sir Henry Plowden says of him in Mr. Ford's book: "Tommy de Grey, now Lord Walsingham, was among the finest fields of the day, especially at cover-point. As a batsman he had as much confidence as any one. His defence was very strong; his amusement to have two or three bowlers going at once in practice, with a fourth stump on the off side to encourage them." In 1863 the Hon. T. de Grey had the honour of being chosen for Gentlemen v. Players at Lord's, but Tarrant and Jackson were a little too good for him; he was bowled for two and eight. Apart from cricket he was at one time the best game shot in England. His record of 1,070 grouse to his own gun in one day in August, 1888, has, I believe, never been equalled. He was still more famous for his wonderful collection—by far the finest in the world—of micro-lepidoptera (the smaller butterflies and moths). He presented the whole collection in 1910 to the Natural History Museum at South Kensington.—S.H.P.

WALTERS, Francis Henry, born on February 9, 1866, died at sea off Bombay early in June 1922. He was a good, and generally a free, batsman, but he was not seen at his best during his visit to England in 1890. Against Surrey, at the Oval, however, he played a very steady and valuable innings of 53 not out, but speaking generally, he never mastered the slow wickets in this country. His chief successes were gained on the Sydney ground where he scored 122 for Combined Australia v. the 1888 Australian Team (who had Turner to bowl for them) in 1888–89, 106 for Victoria v. New South Wales in 1890–91, 112 for Victoria v. New South Wales in 1891–92, and 150 for New South Wales v. Queensland in 1895–96. The last-mentioned innings was the first he ever played for N.S.W. In all matches in which he took part between Victoria and New South Wales—he appeared for both States—he made 700 runs with an average of 28.00. For years he did very great things in Melbourne club cricket, and his doings in first-class matches, were, therefore, on the whole disappointing.

WARBURTON, Leslie, who died at Gloucester on February 11, 1984, aged 73, had the very rare distinction of being called up out of League cricket, in 1936, to play in a Test trial, between North and South, at Lord's. However, to quote *Wisden*, his bowling "caused little trouble", and going in at number seven between Hardstaff and Verity, he failed to score. He was born at Haslingden and was a member of the town's Lancashire League side at 16. Two years later he scored the first of many centuries he was to make for League clubs, in the North, and at 19 he made his first-class debut for Lancashire against Surrey at the Oval, scoring 74 in his first innings. But he preferred the safe career of a bank clerk to that of a full-time cricketer. For more than 20 years he acted as professional for various League clubs in Lancashire and Yorkshire. For Littleborough in the Central Lancashire League he scored 1,000 runs and took 100 wickets in a season. Altogether he made six appearances for Lancashire, all as an amateur.

WARD, Albert, a prominent Lancashire and England batsman 50 years ago, died on January 6, 1939, at his home in Bolton, aged 73. In 1886 Albert Ward played a few times for Yorkshire, the county of his birth, but, having qualified for Lancashire by residence, he at once proved himself worth a regular place in first-class cricket. Starting in 1889 against M.C.C. at Lord's, he scored 95 for once out and soon afterwards showed his liking for the game at Headquarters by making 114 not out and helping largely towards a victory by an innings and 67 runs over Middlesex. He finished second in the batting averages with 29 and was always valuable in the side that finished level with Nottinghamshire and Surrey at the top of the Championship. He remained a source of strength to Lancashire batting for 14 years. He was the first professional who reached a four figure aggregate for Lancashire in a season's county matches and nine times consecutively in first-class fixtures he made over 1,000 runs a season, his best record being 1,790 runs in 1895 with an average of 42. Altogether for Lancashire he obtained 14,698 runs, average 30.95. These were remarkable figures at that time.

Possessing the ideal temperament for an opening batsman—cool, patient, and persevering—he carried his bat through an innings on five occasions and for England against Australia he accomplished some of his best performances.

After scoring 222 in four innings for Lancashire and North of England off the Australian bowlers he made 55 in England's one innings of 483 at the Oval in 1893 and, going out with A. E. Stoddart's XI in the autumn of 1894, he took a conspicuous part in winning the rubber. Australia began the first encounter at Sydney by putting together 586—then the record for these matches—and England, despite 75 by Ward and consistent batting, had to follow-on. Ward, as usual, going in first, again received capable support and scored 117 towards a total of 437. Australia, before the drawing of stumps, got 113 while losing two batsmen and wanted only 64 runs for victory but, after a night's rain, Peel and Briggs took the remaining eight wickets for 53 runs and England snatched a sensational victory. Eng-

land won the second Test, Ward with 30 and 41 doing his share, but under unfavourable conditions they were dismissed for small scores. Two victories for Australia squared the rubber. In the final struggle England, set to make 297, lost Brockwell and Stoddart for 28 runs but J. T. Brown, of Yorkshire, joined Ward in a wonderful stand which put on 210 and practically decided the issue, England winning by six wickets. Brown scored 140 in brilliant style and Ward followed a first innings of 32 with 93. Altogether during the tour Ward made 916 runs, the highest aggregate in first-class matches, with an average of 41.

Seeing that Albert Ward maintained his form for Lancashire it was strange that he was not called upon again for England, particularly for the next tour in which Australia won the Test series by four to one.

Standing 6ft. high Ward used his long reach in irreproachable defence and, while essentially careful, he drove with plenty of power and cut well. Besides being a fine outfield, where he seldom dropped a catch, he bowled slows which got valuable wickets when the regular bowlers were mastered. He used to say "they get so mad at being beaten by a cock-a-doodler like me." Among his victims when in their prime were C. L. Townsend, Arthur Shrewsbury, George Hirst and C. B. Fry. In fact he was one of the early freak bowlers before the description "googly" was invented.

Albert Ward took his benefit in August 1902 when Yorkshire visited Lancashire. Over 24,000 people paid at the gates on the first day, and the total amount realised by the match was £1,739, although rain prevented play on the last day. Albert Ward was dismissed in an unusual way when Derbyshire were at Old Trafford in 1899. In playing a ball from Davidson he broke his bat; a piece of wood knocked off the leg bail and he was out for 72 "hit wicket."

WARD, The Rev. C. G., who died on June 27, 1954, aged 78, played occasionally for Hampshire at the turn of the century, and later appeared for Lincolnshire and Hertfordshire.

WARD, The Rev. Edward Ewer Harrison, of Cambridge, prominent in the "Cobden" match of 1870, died on March 25, 1940, at his home at Gorleston, Norfolk, aged 92. His death five days before that of A. C. Bartholomew, of Oxford, left F. A. MacKinnon, Chief of the Scottish Clan of Morayshire, the oldest living Cambridge Blue. Mr. MacKinnon, who also played in the 1870 match, now holds seniority among University as well as International cricketers. He went to Australia in 1878 with the team captained by Lord Harris, and took part in the only representative match of the tour, which Dave Gregory's XI won by 10 wickets. H. C. Maul, who died on October 10, aged 90, was another member of that side, but did not play in the game which long afterwards was classed as a "Test." Mr. A. J. Webbe, number three for England in that match, was 86 in January, 1941; he passed away in February.

Born on July 16, 1847, at Timworth Hall, Suffolk, in the family of Harrison, "E. E." adopted the surname Ward after leaving Bury St. Edmund's School, where Mr. J. H. Marshall, a Cambridge Blue of 1859, taught him spin and length.

So well did young Harrison master control of his left-hand medium-paced bowling that, despite somewhat moderate physique and indifferent health, he accomplished long spells of success bowling in University and County Cricket. Making the ball go with his arm, he often pitched well to the off and hit the leg stump, delivery from little higher than the shoulder helping this natural flight—so awkward for right-handed batsmen—quite different to imparted swerve with high delivery.

When talking of his University experiences, Mr. Ward used to say: "I was never robust, and knew my own strength and weakness, and always wanted to be my own captain. During Oxford's second innings in the 'Cobden' match there was a stand after I had taken the second and third wickets, and I asked to be given a rest. My captain agreed, and when I was put on again I soon took four more wickets."

In an interview at Mulbarton Rectory with an *Eastern Daily Press* representative some 20 years ago, Mr. Ward fully described Cobden's feat, about which many varying descriptions have appeared. This may be accepted as authentic.

"From the first ball a run was made by Hill, and the match stood two to tie, three to win, and three wickets to go down. One hundred pounds to one on Oxford was offered and taken. The second ball hit to cover-point, a hard catch which Bourne managed to hold. Two more wickets were left—Stewart's and Belcher's. Cobden's third ball bowled Belcher off his pads. Stewart, the last man, was deadly pale and nervous when he walked past me, padded and gloved. A dead silence came over the players and spectators. Cobden crammed his cap on his head, rushed up to the bowling crease, and bowled what I have always thought was a plain long hop. Anyhow, the bails flew, and amid a scene of the wildest excitement Cambridge won by two runs!"

The Hon. Robert Lyttelton, in the Badminton Library account of the match, did justice to Ward's share in the victory. He wrote: "The unique performance of Cobden has unduly cast in the shade Mr. Ward's performance in the second innings. It was a good wicket and Oxford had certainly on the whole a good batting XI. Yet Mr. Ward bowled 32 overs for 29 runs and got six wickets, and of these five were certainly the best batsmen in the side. He clean bowled Messrs. Fortescue, Pauncefote, and Tylecote, and got out in other ways Messrs. Ottoway, Townshend, and Francis. It is hardly too much to say that in this innings Mr. Ward got the six best wickets and Mr. Cobden the four worst. In the whole match Mr. Ward got nine wickets for 62 runs, and this again, let it be said, on an excellent ground."

Ward was doubtful about playing in the 1871 match, which, curiously enough, made further University cricket history. S. E. Butler took all 10 wickets in the Cambridge first innings, another record. The Dark Blues won by eight wickets. Owing to illness Ward wanted to stand down, but his captain, "Bill" Yardley, of high renown, would not hear of this. That Ward's knowledge of himself was sound came true, for, though bowling 36 overs (four balls each) at a cost of only 38 runs, he did not get a wicket.

When playing for Suffolk, Ward met with much success. At Bury he once scored 46 out of 60 for the last wicket after dismissing six men cheaply, and in 1872 he took 13 M.C.C. wickets for 46 runs. He became Secretary of the Suffolk County Club on its revival in 1876, and, as a prominent member of the side, excelled against Norfolk that year, taking 11 wickets at Bury, and in 1877 returning this extraordinary analysis:

	O	M	R	W
First innings ..	21	18	7	5
Second innings ..	8	7	3	

Thirteen I Zingari wickets once fell to him for 47.

Mr. Ward gave 59 years of service to the Church of England, holding appointments in Suffolk, Northumberland, Yorkshire, Derbyshire and Norfolk, his last living being at Mulbarton, where he ministered for 24 years before resigning in 1931.

WARD, Frank A., who died in March, 1974, aged 65, was an accomplished leg-spinner who had the misfortune to be in action at the same time as two of Australia's best exponents of the art, Clarrie Grimmett and Bill O'Reilly. Consequently, his Test appearances were limited to four matches, all against England, three in Australia in 1936 and one on the 1938 tour. He took 92 wickets at an average of 19.27 on that trip, but with O'Reilly on hand gained a place in only the first Test, at Nottingham. He failed to take a wicket in a total of 658 for eight declared which included a double hundred by Paynter and single centuries from Barnett, Compton and Hutton.

Ward did best on his first Test appearance, taking six for 102 in 46 overs during England's second innings at Brisbane. Then he served his country well in the third game at Melbourne with dogged work as a nightwatchman which preceded a partnership of 346 by Bradman and Fingleton. This was the beginning of a recovery which took Australia from two games down to win the series three – two.

Beginning his career in similar fashion to Bradman by playing for the St. George Club in Sydney before moving to Adelaide, Ward took 120 wickets for South Australia in 28 Shield matches, and 187 wickets in all matches for the State side. Oldfield described him as a unique bowler who flighted the ball with great skill. "It was sheer delight to keep wicket to him" was the tribute paid by Australia's greatest stumper.

WARD, H. F., the well-known Hampshire cricketer, died at Winchester, on June 6, 1897. He had played for Hampshire against Lancashire on May 20, and the news of his death caused a painful sensation in cricket circles. In him, Hampshire lost a cricketer who had already done much and from whom a great deal more had been expected. Mr. Ward first appeared for Hampshire in 1894, the season in which Warwickshire, Derbyshire, Essex and Leicestershire were promoted, and Hampshire for the moment left out in the cold. He quickly gave proof of his value as a batsman, and in his Hampshire averages at the end of the summer he came second to Captain Wynyard. In 11 innings—twice not out—he scored 383 runs with an average of 42. In 1896, Hampshire, like the other promoted counties, took part in the Championship Competition and finished 10th on the list. The players, taking them all through, did very well, but Mr. Ward disappointed his friends only getting an average of 18 in 14 matches, with an aggregate of 508

runs. Still he did well on occasions, scoring 63 against Sussex at Brighton; 51 against Warwickshire at Birmingham, and 71 against Somerset at Taunton. In 1896, when Hampshire stood eighth among the counties Mr. Ward got on better, scoring 675 runs with an average of 24. Twice during the season he had the satisfaction of playing three-figure innings, on the Southampton ground, scoring 113 against Derbyshire, and 100 against Essex. Mr. Ward was a batsman of excellent powers, and his untimely death was a loss, not only to Hampshire, but to the whole cricket world as well. He was in his 25th year.

WARD, Humphrey Plowden, died at Thornton-le-Dale, Yorkshire, on December 16, 1945, aged 47. In the Shrewsbury XI 1916–17, he got his Oxford Blue in 1919 and 1921. A good batsman, he averaged over 32 in 1921, his best innings being 103 against H. D. G. Leveson Gower's XI at Eastbourne; he and W. G. Lowndes made 218 for the fourth wicket in 90 minutes. At Lord's his 68 was the highest aggregate for Oxford, and Cambridge won by an innings and 24 runs. He played once for Yorkshire in 1920. Association Blue 1919 and 1920.

WARD, Leslie Maynard, who died at Bideford on January 12, 1981, aged 72, was an off-spinner of slightly more than average pace. He played one match for Warwickshire, against Leicestershire in 1930, his single victim being W. E. Astill. He spent much of his life in Australia.

WARD, Merrik de Sampajo Cecil, died on February 13, 1981, aged 72. A hard-hitting left-handed bat and an accurate medium-pace left-arm bowler, he was in the Eton XI in 1926 and 1927 and played occasionally for Hampshire between 1927 and 1929. In County Cricket he met with little success apart from an innings of 48 against Kent in 1928.

WARD, Thomas Alfred, the South African wicket-keeper, was accidentally electrocuted when working at the West Springs Gold Mine on February 16, 1936. He came to England in 1912 and 1924 and if not so brilliant as Halliwell and Sherwell, who preceded him, or Cameron, he maintained a high standard of excellence. During that period he kept wicket in 23 Test matches, the first being at Old Trafford against Australia in the triangular tournament, and was thoroughly reliable. A dogged batsman with strong defence, he scored in Test cricket 459 runs with an average of 13.90. Going in first, he made 64 at Johannesburg in February, 1923, against the England side captained by F. T. Mann, and in 1924 at Old Trafford he again opened the innings well by scoring 50. When the Australian Imperial Forces team visited South Africa on the way home in 1919 Ward scored 62 not out at Johannesburg in the first of two representative matches. He was in the Transvaal XI from 1909 to 1927, and in all first-class matches scored 1,651 runs with an average of 15.43. Born on August 2, 1887, he died in his 49th year.

WARD, William, who died at Birmingham on December 13, 1961, aged 87, played for Warwickshire in a few matches in 1895 and 1896. He opened the bowling at Edgbaston in 1896 when Yorkshire put together a total of 887. This stood as a record in English first-class cricket until England reached 903 for seven wickets against Australia at the Oval in 1938 and remains the highest in a county match. F. S. Jackson, with 117, E. Wainwright, 126, R. Peel, 210 not out, and Lord Hawke, 166, provided the first instance of four batsmen obtaining centuries in the same innings. All the Warwickshire team except A. Law shared the bowling, Ward's figures being 62–11–175–2. The only surviving member of that Warwickshire XI is Mr. J. Ernest Hill, now aged 94.

WARDALL, Thomas Arthur, who died in December, 1932, at the age of 69, having been born on April 19, 1863, played in all 65 matches for Yorkshire between 1884 and 1894. A batsman above the average, he bowled right hand slows and against Surrey in 1893 at Sheffield he took four wickets for six runs in the first innings and five for 13 in the second. For Yorkshire v. Staffordshire at Hull in 1892 he figured with David Hunter in a last-wicket partnership of 153. In all he scored 2,009 runs for the northern county (average 20) and hit four centuries. After leaving County Cricket he appeared in Lancashire club games for Colne and subsequently Nelson and was coach at Rossall School until a few years back.

WARDEN, Jehangir Sorabji, one of the best all-round cricketers the Parsis ever had, was born at Bombay on January 13, 1885, and died there on January 16, 1928, aged 43. He came to the front as a slow left-handed bowler with a big break, and he developed into quite a good bat. In 1911 he toured England with the All India team making 928 runs with an average of 22.09 and taking 94 wickets for 20.42 runs each. In the game with Northumberland at Newcastle-on-Tyne, which the county won by one wicket, he scored 116 and 11 and had analyses of three for 85 and eight for 88. In the Quadrangular Tournaments in Bombay he invariably made his presence felt with bat or ball, if not with both, and in such cricket he made 528 runs with an average of 40.61 and took 48 wickets for 12.25 apiece. When he carried out his bat for 115 against the Hindus in 1912, the next highest score in the total of 183 was only 15; and when he made 85 v. Mohommedans in 1912, he and H. D. Kanga (150) added 209 together for the third wicket. Among his many good bowling figures for the Parsis in great matches were:

6 for 11, v. Bombay Presidency, at Bombay	..	..	..	..	1907
11 for 86 (including 6 for 21) v. Bombay Presidency, at Poona	..	..	..		1908
12 for 96 (including 7 for 40), v. Bombay Presidency, at Bombay	..	..	..		1911
7 for 37, v. Mohommedans, at Bombay	..	..	..	..	..	1916
12 for 112 (including 7 for 44), v. Mohammedans, at Bombay	..	..	..		1921

For Jorah Bajan v. Customs, at Calcutta, in 1920, he took five wickets with the first five balls of the match. He was the author of *Knotty Cricket Problems Solved*.

WARDILL, Major Benjamin Johnson, born at Everton, Liverpool, October 15, 1842; died at Melbourne, October 17, 1917. Secretary to Melbourne C.C., 1878 to 1910, when he retired owing to ill health; in 1878 there were only 400 members, but in 1910 between 5,000 and 6,000. He was Manager of the Australian teams in England in 1886, 1899, and 1902. Went to Australia at age of 19, and in his young days was a useful cricketer. Played for XXII of Victoria v. Parr's Team at Melbourne, and kept wicket for Victoria and the Melbourne C.C. For Victoria v. Sixteen of Tasmania, in 1865–66, he caught two and stumped two. Played for the Australians in 1886 v. XI of the South of England at Hastings and scored 17. He did much to popularise rifle shooting in Australia, and was himself a splendid shot. Was one of the Victorians who visited Wimbledon in 1876 on their way to compete at the first Rifle Competition at Creedmore, U.S.A., during the Philadelphia Exhibition. Major Wardell was very fond of England, and came here more than once on visits after the tour of 1902. As manager for the Australians he had rather a trying experience in 1886, when the players did not get on well together, but he thoroughly enjoyed his subsequent trips.

WARING, Seth, died at Keighley on April 17, 1919, aged 80. He played in one match for Yorkshire in 1870, scoring nine runs. He was born on November 4, 1838.

SIR PELHAM WARNER
by A. W. T. Langford

Known affectionately as "Plum" Warner and the "Grand Old Man" of English cricket, died at West Lavington, near Midhurst, Sussex, on January 30, 1963. He was 89.

When I was a small boy my father purchased a second-hand copy of *Cricket Across the Seas* by P. F. Warner at the modest price of sixpence.

It was my first cricket book and I devoured every word of it; indeed I almost knew the book by heart. I imagined myself playing bridge with F. L. Fane on the voyage out to New Zealand—the book was an account of the tour of Lord Hawke's team in New Zealand and Australia: I enjoyed the scenery and I was horrified by A. D. Whatman, one of the wicket-keepers of the team, being so engrossed in a book, *The Three Years' War* by Christian de Wet, during the match against Otago that he did not watch the cricket at all. A wicket fell, and a companion nudged the bookworm, appraising him of the fact. He sauntered into the pavilion, padded up—and returned to his book. Another wicket fell, another nudge, and Whatman strolled out to the wicket. He played the first ball, but no doubt still thinking of the book he played all over the second one and there was a crash of timber. The book had won! I never forgave Whatman for that episode.

I had entered a new world, but never in my wildest dreams did I think that I was destined to spend well over 30 supremely happy years in the closest possible contact with the author as his assistant on *The Cricketer*.

In the 1921 *Wisden* Sydney Pardon wrote "There have been many greater cricketers than Pelham Warner but none more devoted to the game. Nothing has ever damped his enthusiasm. Whether winning or losing he has always been the same."

With that verdict I imagine few, if any, students of the game will disagree, but in his prime, and in good health, Pelham Warner was a very fine batsman indeed as his record, especially against the redoubtable Yorkshire XIs of his era, testifies.

Pelham Francis Warner was born in the island of Trinidad in the West Indies on October 2, 1873, and he died on January 30, 1963. His father, Charles William Warner, C. B., for many years Attorney General of Trinidad, was born two days before the Battle of Trafalgar, so father and son between them saw warships develop from the three deckers of Nelson's time to the present day atomic submarine—an astounding thought.

Excluding the handicap of ill health Sir Pelham had a remarkably happy life and received virtually every honour the game has to offer, on and off the field.

He often used to relate that his first recollections of cricket were of batting on a marble gallery at his home, The Hall, Port of Spain, Trinidad, to the bowling of a black boy who rejoiced in the name of Killebree (Humming Bird). At 13½ he came to England, but before that he had three years at Harrison College, Barbados, and at 13 had gained a place in the First XI.

On May 20, 1887, he paid his first visit to Lord's to see M.C.C. play Sussex. On August Bank Holiday he saw the Oval for the first time, and the following month he entered Whitelaw's House at Rugby where he was in the XI for four years, being captain in 1892. He had the good fortune to be coached by that amusing character Tom Emmett, who taught him to play back in the right way and how to attack the half volley, saying "if you come to her, come. You may as well be stumped by two feet as by one inch."

Sir Pelham never tired of recalling his Rugby days, and so vividly did he portray his contemporaries that I almost felt that I knew them personally, particularly a certain Sam Slater, a useful bowler, who laughed his way through five years at Rugby. It was at Rugby that Pelham developed into Plum.

Going up to Oxford, where he was at Oriel, he did not get his Blue until his third year when his captain, G. J. Mordaunt, said to him "Plum, I think you would look very nice in a dark blue cap." Influenza had interfered with his prospects during his first two summers. He was not particularly successful in his two University matches, making 22 and four in 1895, and 10 and 17 in 1896, being run out in each innings. The 1896 match was memorable for Cambridge giving away 12 extras to prevent Oxford following on (compulsory in those days) and for G. O. Smith's superb 132 which enabled Oxford to make 330 for six and win by four wickets.

It was in 1894 that Sir Pelham made his

debut for Middlesex, playing against Somerset at Taunton on August 6, 7 and 8. He scored six and four and Middlesex won an exciting game by 19 runs. Curiously enough his last innings against Somerset at Taunton was also six. His next match was against Gloucestershire and W. G. arrived on the ground wearing a morning coat over white flannel trousers and a black hat, half topper and half bowler—a wonderful sartorial effort.

Sir Pelham took his Bar final examination in 1896, and in subsequent years he often stated in his speeches that "I am by courtesy my learned friend." It was one of my great privileges to lunch with him on numerous occasions in the Inner Temple and to be fascinated by the brilliant conversation.

The whole course of his life was altered by Lord Hawke's invitation to tour the West Indies, and on January 13, 1897, he began the first of many journeys across the seas. As it happened the opening match was against Trinidad and he had the distinction of scoring 119, the first hundred that had ever been scored in the Island in an important match. Scores of black men rushed across the ground at the end of his innings shouting out "I taught you, Mr. Pelham. You play well, Sir; we are proud of you."

On his return from the West Indies, he made his first hundred in a first-class match at his beloved Lord's—108 not out against Yorkshire. This was the first of many fine innings against Yorkshire, and he was justifiably proud of his record against that county; indeed he rarely failed against them, as a perusal of the records will show. Furthermore, he had a sincere affection for many of the Yorkshire players, particularly Hirst and Haigh, who were inseparable friends. David Hunter, the old Yorkshire wicket-keeper, paid him a splendid compliment when he said "Ah, Mr. Warner, you play Wilfred (Rhodes) better than anyone else." This remark was made when Sir Pelham was batting against Yorkshire on a very false wicket at Bradford. He scored 48 in a total of 87.

Sir Pelham owed a great deal to Lord Hawke and he had an intense admiration and affection for "The Baron," whose "Is it quite the same Plum who left us in September? Has England discovered a great leader?" uttered after the triumphant 1903–04 tour, had a life-long influence on him. As Sir Pelham wrote in Long Innings, flattery like this is intoxicating wine. I well remember his grief when he learnt of Lord Hawke's death.

The visit to the West Indies with Lord Hawke's team had infected him with the travel bug and in 1897, at the age of 23, he took a side to America. It was on this tour that he first met J. B. King who was the first of the right arm in-swing bowlers and one of the greatest bowlers of all time. It was also on this tour that the following verses appeared in a long poem about the team:

At one end stocky Jessop frowned
The human catapult
Who wrecks the roofs of distant towns
When set in his assault
His mate was that perplexing man
We know as Looshun Gore
It isn't spelt at all that way
We don't know what it's for

In the spring of 1898 he toured Portugal with T. Westray's side. At the end of the season he led another team to America and included Canada, and in December sailed for South Africa as a member of Lord Hawke's team, scoring 132 not out in the first Test match at Johannesburg.

Back from South Africa, and feeling very fit, he played one of the finest innings of his life when he scored 150 against Yorkshire at Lord's and by now had established himself as one of the leading batsmen in the country. He more than maintained his improved form in the 1900 season which he began with 83 and 69 for M.C.C. against Yorkshire, 114 for Middlesex against Sussex and 146 for Middlesex against Lancashire. In this match a nasty blow on the left shin from Mold kept him out of cricket for the next three weeks, and when he went to play for the touring West Indies side against Leicestershire, incidentally making 113, a ball from Woodcock, almost as fast as Mold, struck him on his injured shin and he was laid up once more. But for these injuries he would almost certainly have played for the Gentlemen v. Players at Lord's. As it was he scored five centuries for Middlesex and in 18 matches for the county made 1,335 runs, average 44.50. Wisden enthused over his skill in playing fast bowling.

In 1901 Sir Pelham was chosen for the Gentlemen at Lord's—and a successful debut it was. He helped C. B. Fry to put on 105 in the first innings for the opening partnership, and in the second innings his 48 was top score for the Gentlemen.

He was a great advocate for retention of Gentlemen v. Players and in his preface to "Gentlemen v. Players, 1806–1949" he wrote "I am indeed fortunate to have lived to attempt to give some sort of history of an historic match which began long before Test matches were dreamed of, and which I pray, and believe, will never die out." Mercifully, he died before the decision was made to call all players "cricketers" which, of course, meant the termination of "the historic match."

The year 1902 saw Sir Pelham once more on his travels, this time as captain of Lord Hawke's team to New Zealand and Australia, Lord Hawke himself being unable to go at the last minute owing to the illness of his mother. This tour, although in many ways only of minor importance—many of the New Zealand matches being against odds—was destined to have a far-reaching and historic influence on the future of cricket. While the team were playing in Australia at the conclusion of the New Zealand fixtures it was suggested that he should bring out the next side to Australia (it was the custom in those days for tours to be privately organised). He replied "Ask the M.C.C. They are the proper body." And thus it came about that the M.C.C. took over the organisation of official overseas tours.

When it was announced that Sir Pelham had been appointed captain of the first M.C.C. touring team, F. S. Jackson having stated that he was not available, there was considerable criticism as at the time he had not played in a Test match in England, and A. C. MacLaren was considered by many as the only possible choice. However, all was well in the end, and although MacLaren, Fry, Ranji and Jackson were not available, all the best professionals were able to accept and Sir Pelham had the assistance of the following players: R. E. Foster, B. J. T. Bosanquet, A. A. Lilley, G. H. Hirst, W. Rhodes, L. C. Braund, J. T. Tyldesley, H. Strudwick, E. G. Arnold, A. E. Relf, A. Fielder and A. E. Knight. One well-known critic of the time wrote that "when they return beaten five–love they will be more than ever the laughing stock of cricketing England."

Contrary to this critic's doleful prediction England won the rubber 3–2, Bosanquet's googlies playing a prominent part in the success. Clem Hill went so far as to state that if England had not had Bosanquet Australia would have won the rubber. In the fourth Test, which decided the fate of the Ashes, Bosanquet had a second innings analysis of six for 51. Apart from captaining the side with the greatest possible skill Sir Pelham played his part well as a batsman, helping Hayward in opening stands of 122 at Melbourne and 148 at Adelaide.

On his return from Australia he was honoured with a place on the M.C.C. commit-

tee, and a year later he was appointed captain of the first M.C.C. side to tour South Africa. It was a good but by no means a representative team and South Africa won 4–1 after a titanic struggle in the first Test at Johannesburg where South Africa triumphed by one wicket and beat England for the first time in a Test match. To his dying day I do not think he ever quite forgave that most accurate of bowlers, A. E. Relf, for sending down a full toss to leg to P. W. Sherwell when the scores were level. South Africa had a wonderful array of googly bowlers at that time—R. O. Schwarz, G. A. Faulkner, A. E. Vogler and G. C. White—and Sir Pelham, as he frankly admitted, was unable to cope with them on the matting wickets.

Back in England, he soon regained his best form, and the following season, the very wet one of 1907, found him missing top place in the averages by only a fraction, C. B. Fry making 1,449 runs, average 46.74, against his 1,891 runs, average 46.12. He considered the best innings he ever played on a good wicket was his 149 against Surrey at the Oval that season, the opposing bowlers being N. A. Knox, W. Lees, J. N. Crawford and T. Rushby. At lunch on the first day he was 115 not out. He and J. Douglas put on 232 for the first wicket in two and a half hours!

He succeeded G. MacGregor in the captaincy of the Middlesex side in 1908 and held the position until his retirement at the end of the 1920 season. The summer of 1908 was an outstanding one for him, his Middlesex record being 1,298 runs, average 54.08, including five centuries, but perhaps his greatest performance that year was his 64 not out in a total of 95 for M.C.C. on a sticky wicket against a Yorkshire attack consisting of Hirst, Rhodes, Haigh and Newstead. He considered this his best innings on a bad wicket, and M.C.C. evidently concurred as they presented him with two bats in appreciation.

Duodenal trouble worried him during the 1909 summer, but he was selected for the Old Trafford Test against Australia—his first Test in England—and scored nine and 25 in a drawn game which was played on a slow wicket.

The summers of 1910 and 1911 were fine ones for Sir Pelham who in the latter year not only scored over 2,000 runs for the first time in his life, but when playing for England against the Champion County, Warwickshire, reached the highest score of his career, 244. He hit 35 fours and batted for five hours and 20 minutes. This great innings was the prelude to his second visit to Australia as captain of an M.C.C. team. This time he had with him J.W.H.T. Douglas, F.R. Foster, W.Rhodes, J.B. Hobbs, H. Strudwick, J.W. Hitch, S.P. Kinneir, E.J. Smith, G.Gunn, J. Iremonger, S.F. Barnes, C.P. Mead, J.Vine, F.E. Woolley and J.W. Hearne. Five of the team were under 25 when they left England and Hitch was only four months over that age.

In the first match of the tour against South Australia he scored 151, but it was, alas, the only innings he played on the tour as he was struck down by a serious illness. England won the series 4–1 with what many people consider the strongest side that has ever visited Australia. Douglas took over the captaincy, but from his sick bed Sir Pelham had considerable influence on the strategy of the campaign.

He had recovered sufficiently from his illness to begin playing in 1912, and on May 23 he scored 126 for the M.C.C. Australian Touring XI against The Rest of England, at Lord's. The Rest, strongly represented, were defeated by an innings and 10 runs which confirmed the strength of the touring side. His early good form gained him a place in the England XIs which met Australia and South Africa in the Lord's Tests—it was the Triangular Tournament season—but the exertion of his early successes was too much for him, and before the end of June he dropped out of cricket for the rest of the season.

He was able to play fairly regularly in 1913, making 987 runs for Middlesex with an average of 41.12. The county would probably have won the County Championship in 1914 if war had not been declared on August 4. He made no big score that season, but *Wisden* said that "he played very well in several matches."

During the First World War he served with the Inns of Court, spent some time at the War Office with the rank of Captain attached to General Staff and then in 1916 went into the King Edward VII Hospital for Officers for an operation. After six months' sick leave he served with Col. John Buchan in the Department of Information at the Foreign Office. Another six months and he was again very ill and on March 21, 1918, he had to resign his commission on account of his health.

When County Cricket was resumed in 1919 he was then 45 and found the hours of play, 11.30 to 7.30 on the first day, and 11 to 7.30 on the second, too much for him and, as he put it, by the middle of July he was a "dead dog" and he seriously thought of resigning the Middlesex captaincy, but A.J.

Webbe, for whom he had great admiration, persuaded him to continue, and as events proved 1920 was to be his *annus mirabilis*.

At the beginning of the season Middlesex were not rated as very serious contenders for the Championship, and by the end of July were apparently out of the running, but, beginning with the Sussex match at Hove on July 31, they won their last nine matches and the Championship was theirs. Two of the matches were desperately close affairs, Kent being beaten at Canterbury by five runs and Yorkshire at Bradford by four runs. Surrey were due at Lord's on August 28, 30, and 31, and it was necessary for Middlesex to win to finish as Champions.

It was only after a tremendous struggle that Middlesex succeeded by 55 runs. C.H.L. Skeet and H.W. Lee scored hundreds for the winners, and G.T.S. Stevens, then only 19, had a grand match with scores of 53 and 21 not out and five wickets for 61 in Surrey's second innings. But Sir Pelham himself had a rare triumph. He batted for nearly four and a half hours to make 79, top score in the first innings when matters were going none too well for his county, and in his very last innings for Middlesex at Lord's he was 14 not out when he declared, leaving Surrey to make 244 in three hours and seven minutes. Valuable as his batting was, and especially in this match, it was, to quote *Wisden* once again "his skill as a captain that made his final season memorable."

During the whole of his first-class career Sir Pelham scored 29,028 runs with an average of 36.28. He hit 60 centuries and exceeded 1,000 runs in 14 seasons.

His retirement from first-class cricket did not mean the end of his touring. In 1926–27 he led the M.C.C. team which visited South America, playing seven matches in the Argentine, one at Montevideo, one at Valparaiso and one at Lima. The team included Lord Dunglass, later Lord Home and now, as I write, Sir Alec Douglas-Home, Prime Minister, and created a tremendous amount of good will. The matches were reported in the South American press, one account saying that the veteran captain was "eliminado" at slip. As he was fond of saying, there was no disputing that dismissal. A year later he captained M.C.C. for the last time on an overseas tour, taking a strong side to Holland. It was the jubilee of The Hague club, founded in 1878.

In 1932–33 he went to Australia as joint manager with R.C.N. Palairet of the M.C.C. team captained by D.R. Jardine. Bodyline cast a shadow over the tour. He was completely opposed to this type of bowling; indeed he had objected to it as long ago as 1910 when W. B. Burns bowled it for a few overs for Worcestershire against Middlesex at Lord's, but he never allowed his opposition to interfere with his admiration for Jardine as a man and as a leader. History has of course proved that Sir Pelham was right, and in 1937 his outstanding services to cricket, both on and off the field, were recognised by a knighthood.

Shortly before the Second World War started he went to Denmark with an M.C.C. team captained by G. C. Newman, but as he was nearly 66 he naturally took no active part in the cricket.

It has already been stated that he was honoured with a place on the M.C.C. committee in April 1904. He served on and off for virtually the rest of his life. In 1926 he was appointed Chairman of the Selection committee composed of P. Perrin and A. E. R. Gilligan in addition to himself, and to his great delight England regained the Ashes after their memorable win in the fifth Test at the Oval. He was appointed chairman again in 1931, the two other members of the committee being P. Perrin and T. A. Higson. I suppose it would be difficult to think of three men who were so dissimilar in character yet they worked splendidly together even if Higson occasionally "let fly," and they built up the fine team which won 4–1 in Australia 1932–33.

Sir Pelham was also chairman of the Selectors in 1935, 1936, 1937, and 1938. The South Africans were here in 1935, and for the first time they succeeded in winning a Test match in England, defeating us at Lord's by 157 runs. Sir Pelham that year again had the assistance of Perrin and Higson, with R. E. S. Wyatt, who was appointed captain, co-opted. The selection of the England team for the Lord's Test produced the longest Selection Committee meeting of Sir Pelham's long experience. He, Perrin and Higson wanted to play R. W. V. Robins; Wyatt was emphatic in urging T. B. Mitchell of Derbyshire. After an all-day sitting the Selectors with great reluctance gave way to Wyatt and Mitchell played. In a comparatively low scoring match he bowled 53 overs for 164 runs and took only three wickets. It took Sir Pelham a long time to get over that match—if he ever did.

During the Second World War he was appointed Deputy Secretary of M.C.C. He threw himself heart and soul into his work and before long was arranging splendid matches for a harassed public and responded

nobly, eagerly seizing the opportunity of seeing some of their favourites playing once again.

He retired from his secretarial duties at Lord's in September, 1945, and two years later he sailed with G. O. Allen's M.C.C. side to the West Indies. I do not think it is any secret that some of the younger members of the team were a little apprehensive about having an elderly gentleman touring with them. But his tact, courtly charm and old world manners soon put everyone at their ease, and when the tour was over the players said how pleased they were to have had him with them.

He told me he was fearful that the great honour of being President of M.C.C. might elude him, for as he often said "I'm a delicate old dog and will not be here much longer." It is therefore not difficult to picture his delight, and relief, when on May 3, 1950, he was nominated President by H.R.H. the Duke of Edinburgh. In point of fact His Royal Highness was unable to be present, and Lord Cornwallis, President in 1947, presided in his absence. When he began to make the announcement he got no further than "Sir Pel—" when there was an unprecedented scene, the cheering which followed lasting for several minutes. It was indeed an unforgettable moment. He was 76 years and seven months old when he was nominated, and only one older man had been made President—Stanley Christopherson who beat Sir Pelham by a year. He had been President of Middlesex from 1937 to 1946.

In 1950 he was Chairman of the Committee which selected F. R. Brown's team to tour Australia that winter, and three years later, in November, 1953, the M.C.C. gave a dinner in the Long Room to celebrate his 80th birthday. In 1958 a new grandstand built at Lord's was named after him. There was still one final honour to come to him. In May 1961 he became the first life Vice President of M.C.C.

When Lord Hawke took a team to the West Indies in 1897 he was asked by H. V. L. Stanton ("Wanderer" of *The Sportsman*) if he could arrange for somebody to send back accounts of the matches to be played by his team. Lord Hawke turned to Sir Pelham and said "Plummy, you're last from school. Why shouldn't you do it?" He did and that began his career as one of the outstanding writers on the game.

Sir Pelham in fact provided the account of that tour for the *Wisden* of 1898, and in 1911 he contributed a short article for the Almanack entitled *Our Young Cricketers*. His

Twilight Reflections, which appeared in the 1955 Wisden, was an extensive survey of the game as well as a critical analysis which contained much advice on problems which still confront us.

During his long life he wrote, or edited, the following books: *Cricket in Many Climes*, *Cricket Across the Seas*, *How we recovered the Ashes*, *With M.C.C. in South Africa*, *England v. Australia (1911–12 Tour) Cricket Reminiscences*, *Boys' Book of Outdoor Games and Pastimes* (with others), *Imperial Cricket*, *Book of Cricket* (numerous editions), *Cricket* (Badminton Library, revised edition, 1920, with others), *Story of the Ashes* (Morning Post, 1920), *My Cricketing Life*, *Fight for the Ashes 1926*, *Oxford and Cambridge at the Wicket* (with F. S. Ashley-Cooper), *Cricket Between Two Wars*, *Fight for the Ashes 1930*, *Lord's 1787–1945*, *Gentlemen v. Players 1806–1949*, and *Long Innings*. He was also Cricket Correspondent for the *Westminster Gazette*, *The Morning Post* and *The Daily Telegraph*. With his first-class career over, he became Editor of *The Cricketer* when the magazine was founded in 1921, and retained that position until 1962 when he was succeeded by his son, John Warner. I think it is correct to state that when he was appointed it was thought he would be largely a figurehead, but on the contrary he threw himself wholeheartedly into his duties and maintained his enthusiastic interest in the magazine until his death.

In the earlier years he wrote many articles for *The Cricketer*. Often he would discuss a topic, and I would then rough it out. After that we had a session in which we would endeavour to add polish. It was great fun, and I spent many hours with him on this kind of work.

From 1921 to 1932 he wrote regularly for *The Morning Post*. Early in 1933, under the strain of the Bodyline controversy, he cabled the paper and certainly, but quite unwittingly, gave the Editor, H. A. Gwynne, and the Sports Editor, Tom Hodder, the impression that he did not wish to continue as their Cricket Correspondent. There was little time for *The Morning Post* to find another correspondent and they could hardly be blamed for appointing R. C. Robertson-Glasgow—an excellent choice.

Subsequently, Sir Pelham explained that the cable had been misinterpreted, but by then it was too late as *The Morning Post* had committed themselves with Mr. Robertson-Glasgow. Happily the matter ended with Mr. Gwynne and Sir Pelham still the best of friends.

As a result of this unfortunate misunderstanding Sir Pelham was invited to write for *The Daily Telegraph*, and after all these years it may not be out of place to state that he was rather less happy with *The Telegraph* than *The Post*. Possibly they did not quite understand his approach to the game he loved so dearly. For example, when he wrote about Bowes they altered his copy to the "bespectacled" Bowes, and when Bradman was mobbed by girls at Worcester he received a wire: "Send 500 words Bradman and the girls." It would be difficult to imagine anyone less suited to write a "story" of that nature. He thought the whole thing was a joke, put the wire in his pocket, and took no action. As my boyhood was spent in Sussex I saw very little of Sir Pelham as an active player, and my only real recollection is of seeing him lead Middlesex on to the field at Hove, wearing of course a Harlequin cap which he renewed every two years. As the years passed I got to know him most intimately and to my dying day I shall treasure memories of his great encouragement and countless kindnesses to me. His one fault was that he was too generous with his praise. Thirty years ago the use of Christian and nicknames was not nearly so common as it is today and therefore I shall always remember with pride the day when he said "Why don't you call me by my cognomen?"

Until the outbreak of war he visited *The Cricketer* office virtually every morning. His visits did on occasion interfere with work as he delighted in discussing the previous day's play, and if he had been to a show overnight he was quite capable of giving more or less word for word what Harry Lauder, for example, had said at the Palladium—Scottish accent and all. He was, too, very fond of Western films and I can hear him saying, with a twinkle in his eyes, "Stick 'em up, Baby." He was no mean mimic, and he was especially good at imitating Lord Harris, who had a habit of stroking his cheek when a difficult point was being discussed in committee—"We--ll, Warner, there may be something in what you say." He loved animals, and on one occasion he thought he was paying our then secretary a great compliment when he told her she had eyes just like his spaniel's. She was not amused.

It is, I know, only stating the obvious to say that cricket predominated in Sir Pelham's thoughts, but he was a great patriot, believing passionately in the British way of life and had made a study of Naval and Military history. He delighted in listening to Service debates at Westminster, and one of the happiest experiences of his life was when Admiral Jellicoe asked him to take passage with him in H.M.S. *New Zealand* to Egypt at the beginning of 1919. But, of course, cricket always came first, and I think this story told to me by Lady Warner was typical of his devotion to the game. Some years ago, they, with some friends, were admiring the beauties of a charming little French church. Suddenly, Sir Pelham left the party by the altar and strode off down the aisle towards the west door with a rather grim expression on his face. When he rejoined the party Lady Warner said to him "Whatever is the matter, Pelham?" (She never called him Plum.) "Oh, nothing, it is just as I thought, the length of the cricket pitch."

He had a great admiration for youth, and he was a remarkably fine judge of a young player, which reminds me of an argument he had with his old friend, the one and only Gerry Weigall, at the Folkestone Festival many years ago. Weigall contended, perhaps with a good deal of reason, that Middlesex were unduly favoured by having the pick of young players at Lord's without any expense to themselves, while Kent had to pay wages to any young cricketer while he was qualifying. To bring home his points Weigall would take off the inevitable straw hat and bang it with his fist before putting it on again. This happened many times as the argument developed to the delight of the rest of us at the tea table. At the end of it all, Sir Pelham said, almost with tears in his eyes, "I can see, my dear Gerry, that you don't want Middlesex to have any young players at all."

And now a recollection of one of the most entertaining two hours I have ever had in my life. I was at Sir Pelham's flat and just as I was leaving he said "Don't go, Charlo (C. B. Fry) is coming." Well, Fry arrived and for the next two hours I was spellbound. He never ceased talking, he took off his jacket, he played imaginary strokes, he danced around the room, in fact he did everything. Every now and again Sir Pelham tried to get a word in, but every time he did Fry held up his hand in an imperious manner and said "Plum, be quiet" and off he went again. It was all highly entertaining. The following morning when Sir Pelham came to *The Cricketer* office he said in a most doleful manner "Do you know Charlo spoke for 45 minutes last night before he would let me get a word in," which when one comes to think of it was no mean feat as Sir Pelham was a great talker himself.

On June 7, 1904, he married Agnes Blyth, by whom he had two sons and a daughter, at the Parish Church of St. Marylebone. Lord Hawke was best man, and Field Marshal Lord Roberts signed the register. (Subsequently he was an enthusiastic supporter of Lord Roberts' campaign for National Service.) Many years later as a result of frequent visits to the Warner home I got to know Lady Warner extremely well—and the better I knew her the more I admired her. For the last 10 years of her life she was a chronic invalid, being confined to her bed for long periods at a time, but never once did I hear her grumble, and she maintained the keenest possible interest in the events of the day. She was a remarkably brave and patient woman, and I can see her now lying in bed and watching the television, preferably a sporting event. She was a fine judge of cricket, and did not W. H. Patterson once say, "If you cannot have Warner on the Selection Committee you should ask his wife"

She was present at the famous Eton and Harrow match of 1910—Fowler's match—and with Eton apparently well beaten she turned to a friend and said, "I shall not send my boy to Eton as they cannot play cricket," and then left Lord's for her home in Kent as the end seemed so near. When she reached Caring she found a telegram awaiting her: "Better send him Eton won by nine runs." On another occasion she told me how she used to amuse Sir Pelham when he was recovering from his serious illness in Australia by picking up odd *Wisdens* and asking him what he had scored in a particular match. Almost invariably he answered correctly.

On Friday March 8, 1963, his ashes were scattered at Lord's near the Warner stand close to the spot where he had hit his first four for Rugby v. Marlborough in 1889. It was my very great privilege to be present on a most impressive occasion. The wind blew hard during the ceremony, but the sun was shining. Directly we returned to the pavilion it poured with rain. I could not help thinking that dear old Plum had been favoured to the very end.

WARNER, Robert Stewart Aucher, K.C., who captained the first West Indies team that visited England in 1900, died at Nynehead Court, Taunton, on December 1, 1944, aged 85. A very useful batsman, he unfortunately contracted malarial fever when getting accustomed to cricket in England. He played a very good innings of 53 not out at Trent Bridge without revealing the form associated with his brother, Sir Pelham Warner—14 years his junior. In fact at 41 he was rather old to undergo the fatigue of continuous cricket, but he will remain in history as a keen lover and supporter of the game in West Indies. To quote *The Times*, he was a direct descendant of Sir Thomas Warner, who founded the first English colony, St. Kitts, in West Indies. Aucher Warner left Trinidad in 1922, but retained his close connection with the colony by writing in 1934 a book, *Sir Thomas Warner, a Chronicle of his Family*, and also by founding the Trinidad Cocoa Planters Association. Educated in Trinidad and at Oriel College, Oxford, he was called to the Bar, Inner Temple, in 1882, and he followed in the steps of his father as Solicitor-General and Attorney-General of Trinidad.

WARREN, Arnold R., born at Codnor, Derbyshire, on April 2, 1875, died there on September 3, 1951. Becoming a regular Derbyshire player in 1902, he appeared for the county until 1920, obtaining 939 wickets for 24.55 runs each. One of the fastest right-arm bowlers of his time—he stood over 6ft.— Warren achieved his best performance on a wet, soft pitch at Welbeck in 1904, when, of the 18 Nottinghamshire wickets which fell, he took 15 for 112 runs—eight for 69 and seven for 43. During that season he dismissed 101 batsmen at an average cost of 22.18 in Derbyshire matches alone, becoming the first player to achieve the feat for the county. He also took over 100 wickets in 1906 and 1908.

In 1905 he played for England in the third Test match against Australia at Leeds, and in the first innings he took five wickets for 57, numbering among his victims Victor Trumper, M. A. Noble, W. W. Armstrong and J. Darling. The ball used on that occasion was mounted and presented to him. In Warren's own opinion his best performance was against Leicestershire at Ashby-de-la-Zouch in 1912. On turf which did not help bowlers, Leicestershire, needing 180 to win, were put out for 97, Warren dismissing seven batsmen for 52.

A batsman described as "useful," he hit his one century (123) in 1910 against Warwickshire at Blackwell, where he and J. Chapman (165), coming together with 111 needed to avoid an innings defeat, put on 283 in less than three hours and established a world's ninth wicket record which still stands.

WASHER, Arthur, who represented Canterbury against Otago in the '80s, died at Christchurch (N.Z.) on November 12, 1910. On the day of his death he had umpired in a local match.

WASHINGTON, William Arthur Irving, born at Mitchell Main on December 11, 1879, died at Wombwell on October 20, 1927, aged 47. A left-handed batsman of unusual promise, he appeared in 45 matches for Yorkshire in 1900 and 1902, making 1,290 runs with an average of 23.03. In 1902, when he played an innings of 100 not out against Surrey, at Leeds, he scored 1,022 runs and averaged 27.62. That, as it happened, was the last season in which he was seen in first-class cricket. Ill-health handicapped him, and, although he wintered at Torquay and in South Africa, he was unable to gain sufficient strength to enable him to resume play. He was a member of the team which dismissed the Australians for 23 at Leeds in 1902.

WASS, Tom, who died at Sutton-in-Ashfield on October 27, 1953, aged 79, was on his day one of the most effective bowlers of his time. Born in Sutton-in-Ashfield, a village once the most productive nursery for Nottinghamshire cricketers, on December 26, 1873, he gained an early reputation as a fast bowler in local cricket. Following a spell as a professional with Edinburgh Academicals he joined Liverpool C.C., and, becoming qualified by residence for Lancashire, was offered a place on the staff at Old Trafford. This Wass, originally a miner, declined, and instead gave his services to his native county, for whom he made a first-class debut in 1897. Not until the following season, however, did his county career really begin, and thereafter he progressed from strength to strength.

Ability to make the ball turn from leg rendered him specially dangerous to batsmen, and no bowler of his pace was a greater menace on slow pitches. Before he gave up first-class cricket in 1920 he took 1,679 wickets, a Nottinghamshire record. In 1907 he played a leading part in helping Nottinghamshire to carry off the County Championship without suffering defeat, dismissing in that season 163 batsmen at a cost of 14.28 runs each. It was remarkable that in view of his many successes "Topsy" Wass was never chosen for England, but he appeared three times for Players against Gentlemen, at Lord's in 1908 and at the Oval in 1904 and 1908.

Twice he took 16 wickets in a match, and on each occasion performed the feat in the course of a single day. The first was against Lancashire at Liverpool in 1901, when his figures were eight for 25 and eight for 44; the second against Essex at Trent Bridge in 1908, his analyses then being eight for 29 and eight for 74. In the first innings of Essex he at one time took six wickets for nine runs, including the hat-trick. Twice, against Surrey at the Oval in 1902 (for 91 runs) and against Derbyshire at Blackwell in 1911 (for 67 runs) he dismissed nine batsmen in an innings, and he took eight wickets in an innings no fewer than 16 times. The best of these latter performances was eight for 13 at the expense of Derbyshire at Welbeck in 1901. At Lord's in 1907 he gained the remarkable analysis of six wickets for three runs, his victims including J. H. King, F. A. Tarrant and L. C. Braund. A moderate fieldsman, Wass also accomplished little in batting, though in 1906 at Derby he hit, with the aid of four missed catches, an innings of 56, he and J. W. Day adding 98 for the ninth wicket and so enabling Nottinghamshire to recover from a breakdown against A. W. Warren.

Generally of kindly character, Wass could be stubborn when roused. The story used to be told of how he once arrived at the Oval for a match accompanied by his wife and was told by the gateman that the lady would not be allowed in without payment. "Oh," said Wass grimly. "If this beggar doan't coom in, this beggar"—indicating himself—"doan't play!" Mrs. Wass was admitted without further argument.—E. E.

WATERMAN, Leonard William, died suddenly after a heart attack at Brisbane on January 1, 1952, in his 56th year. A capable wicket-keeper and lusty batsman, his chief claim to fame was his catching of O. W. Bill and D. G. Bradman off the aboriginal fast bowler, E. Gilbert, without either batsman scoring. This occurred in his first Sheffield Shield match for Queensland v. New South Wales in November 1931. He represented his State in four Sheffield Shield matches, dismissing 11 batsmen (7 c., 4 st.).

WATHEN, Arthur Cave, died on March 14, 1937, in his 96th year. Educated at Blackheath Proprietary School, he played for Kent a few times in 1863 and 1864.

WATHEN, William Hulbert, who died on March 29, 1913, played for Kent against Sussex at Brighton in 1863, scoring five and 38. He was born at Streatham on May 5, 1836, and educated first at Brighton College and afterwards at Rugby, but was not in either XI. He was a moderate batsman, and sometimes obtained wickets, though at a somewhat heavy cost, and generally fielded

in the slips. For Gentlemen of Kent v. Gentlemen of Sussex at Brighton in 1863 he scored 53, and in the corresponding match of 1855 took five wickets for 21 runs. For many years he played regularly for the West Kent C.C.

WATKINS, Bert Thomas Lewis, died in December 1982, aged 80. In 1932 he had a good trial for Gloucestershire, who were trying to find a replacement for H. Smith as wicket-keeper, and in 1937 again came into the side when Smith's successor, Hopkins, a far better bat than Watkins, broke a finger. He made his last appearance for the county in 1938. Unfortunately he was slightly uncertain in taking the spinners, in whom much of the bowling strength of the side lay at that period.

WATLING, Walter Herbert, a Melbourne man by birth, died at Randfontein, South Africa, on December 19, 1928, aged 64. His first-class cricket was played for South Australia, and his two highest innings for the side were both against Victoria—54 at Adelaide in 1883–84 and 58 at Melbourne in 1884–85. He maintained his interest in the game after settling in South Africa, and was one of the first to advocate the provision of turf wickets on the Wanderers' ground at Johannesburg.

WATSON, Alec, who died at Manchester on Tuesday, October 26, 1920, played, as everyone will remember, a prominent part in Lancashire cricket for more than 20 years, being one of the mainstays of the XI when A. N. Hornby was captain. No other Scotsman has ever held such a place in professional cricket. Born at Coatsbridge on November 4, 1844, Watson owed his connection with Lancashire to an engagement in 1869 at Rusholme. Two years later he played his first county match against Cheshire in 1871, and his career lasted until 1893, when the Lancashire committee thought it well to leave him out of the team. He was asked to play again in 1898, but the chance of starting afresh at the age of 54 did not tempt him. Watson was first and last a county cricketer. Though he bowled for the Players at Lord's in 1877, his appearances in representative matches were few, and he never went to Australia. Here one must touch on rather delicate ground. Watson was one of the best and most successful slow bowlers of his generation—he took 1,529 wickets for Lancashire with an average of 11.60—but there is no hiding the fact that all through his career the fairness of his delivery was freely questioned. In the rather bitter controversy on the subject of Lancashire bowling that raged for several seasons—1882 to 1885 inclusive—he was not subjected to the unsparing criticism meted out to Crossland and Nash, but many cricketers had very decided views as to his methods. There was a great deal of throwing in English cricket in the '80s, and a lot of grumbling about it, but though Kent in 1885 cancelled their return match with Lancashire the evil was not properly dealt with until, years afterwards, the county captains took the matter into their own hands. When the day of reform came Watson had finished with first-class cricket, so it is impossible to say how he would have fared. Apart from the question of his deliv-

ery, not a word could be said against Watson. He was a thorough cricketer, and everyone liked him. The special virtue of his bowling lay in the combination of extreme accuracy of pitch and a formidable off-break. Those who thought his delivery unfair supported their view by pointing out how well, for a slow bowler, he could keep his length against the wind. There can be no doubt that his delivery was the cause of his not being picked for travelling XIs. Even when throwing was rampant here—I can remember seeing three grievous offenders in a Gentlemen and Players match at Lord's—Shaw and Shrewsbury were careful not to take to Australia any bowler whose action could be questioned.—S.H.P.

Below are Watson's most notable feats set out in detail.

EIGHT OR MORE WICKETS IN AN INNINGS:

9 for 117	Lancashire v. Derbyshire, at Manchester	1874
8 for 43	Lancashire v. Cheshire, at Nantwich	1892

THIRTEEN OR MORE WICKETS IN A MATCH:

14 for 49	England v. M.C.C. and G., at Lord's..	1877
13 for 62	Lancashire v. Kent, at Manchester	1887
15 for 68	Lancashire v. Cheshire, at Nantwich	1892

FOUR OR MORE WICKETS FOR THREE RUNS OR LESS EACH:

5 for 13	Lancashire v. Surrey, at the Oval	1873
4 for 12	Lancashire v. Derbyshire, at Derby	1875
7 for 10	England v. M.C.C. and G., at Lord's..	1877
4 for 11	Lancashire v. Kent, at Maidstone	1877
5 for 10	England v. M.C.C. and G., at Lord's..	1878
6 for 18	Lancashire v. Kent, at Manchester	1880
4 for 8	Lancashire v. Gloucestershire, at Manchester	1881
6 for 8	Lancashire v. M.C.C. and G., at Lord's	1886
7 for 15	Lancashire v. Derbyshire, at Manchester	1886
6 for 12	North v. Australians, at Manchester	1886
7 for 20	Lancashire v. Sussex, at Manchester	1887
4 for 10	Lancashire v. Derbyshire, at Manchester	1888
6 for 17	Lancashire v. Derbyshire, at Derby	1888
5 for 15	Lancashire v. Leicestershire, at Manchester	1889
6 for 5	Lancashire v. Warwickshire, at Edgbaston	1890
5 for 7a		
4 for 6b	Lancashire v. Sussex, at Manchester	1890
9 for 13c		

a 1st innings.   b 2nd innings.   c Both innings.

BOWLING UNCHANGED THROUGH BOTH COMPLETED INNINGS:

With

McIntyre (W.)	Lancashire v. Derbyshire, at Derby	1872
McIntyre (W.)	Lancashire v. Surrey, at Manchester	1873
McIntyre (W.)	Lancashire v. Surrey, at the Oval	1873
McIntyre (W.)	Lancashire v. Derbyshire, at Manchester	1876
McIntyre (W.)	Lancashire v. Derbyshire, at Derby	1876
McIntyre (W.)	Lancashire v. Notts., at Manchester	1877

BOWLING UNCHANGED THROUGH BOTH COMPLETED INNINGS—*Continued*

With

Barlow	Lancashire v. Derbyshire, at Derby ..	..	..	..	1883
Peate	North v. Australians, at Manchester ..	..	..	..	1886
Briggs	Lancashire v. Cheshire, at Stockport ..	..	..	..	1886
Briggs	Lancashire v. Leicestershire, at Manchester ..	..	..	..	1889
Briggs	Lancashire v. Sussex, at Manchester ..	..	..	..	1890
Mold	Lancashire v. Yorkshire, at Huddersfield ..	..	..	..	1890

OTHER FEATS

For XXII of Birmingham (with two given men), v. North of England XI, at Aston, he took eight for 56 in first innings and nine for 37 in second 1872

For Manchester v. Liverpool, at Liverpool, he took all 10 wickets for 24 in first innings and seven in the second 1883

For Lancashire v. XXII Colts he took 11 for 27 1889

For Lancashire v. XXII of Manchester he took 12 for 20 1890

WATSON, Lieut. Col. Arthur Campbell, D.S.O., who died at Shermansbury, Horsham, on January 16, 1952, aged 67, was in the Uppingham XI of 1901. From 1922 until 1928 he played for Sussex as a hard-hitting batsman. Against Northamptonshire at Hove in 1922, when batting number 10, he scored 111 out of 168 in 85 minutes, giving only one chance—when 90. He hit two sixes, one five and 13 fours. Later he played on occasions for Essex. He served in the South African War in 1902 and in India and Egypt during the First World War.

WATSON, Arthur Kenelm, who died at Harrow on January 2, 1947, aged 79, played for Harrow in 1884 and 1885. In his second match against Eton he played a great innings of 135, and with Eustace Crawley added 235 for the second wicket in two hours and three-quarters. Harrow won by three wickets within two minutes of time. He was awarded the Ebrington Cup for fielding. An Oxford Blue in 1889, he failed in a disastrous match at Lord's, Cambridge winning by an innings and 105 runs; he was also disappointing for Middlesex before playing in turn for Norfolk and Suffolk. He was a master at Rugby School.

WATSON, Darsie, who died on November 19, 1964, aged 75, was a capital all-rounder when in the Rugby XI from 1905 to 1907. He was captain in the last year. *Wisden* described him as "a natural batsman with no nerves and a wonderful eye." Against Marlborough at Lord's he enjoyed special success, for in his three games against them he scored 357 runs—highest innings 108 in 1907—at an average of 71.40 and took 20 wickets for just over 13 runs apiece. He played in one match for Sussex in 1920, against Essex at Hove.

WATSON, Frank, who died on February 1, 1976, in hospital at Warrington, aged 76, was a batsman whom spectators of 50 years ago will, unless they were fervent Lancashire supporters, remember as one of whom they wished to see as little as possible, but there could be no doubt of his value to the county. He could drive the overpitched ball and was a good hooker, but usually gave the impression that his main object was to stay there, and stay there he did and the runs came. Between 1920 and 1937 he scored 23,596 runs with an average of 36.98 and made 50 centuries.

Five times in this period Lancashire were champions and they were seldom far off it and to these successes Watson was a notable contributor. He was an equally unwelcome sight to the opposition coming in in his early days second wicket down when they were already jaded after bowling for two or three hours to Makepeace, Hallows and Ernest Tyldesley or later in his career opening with Hallows or Hopwood. His most prolific season was 1928 when in county matches he scored 2,403 runs, average 68.25, and made nine centuries including 300 not out, then a record for Old Trafford, against Surrey in Hallows's benefit.

The competition in those days for places in the England side for batsmen was very strong and his representative cricket was confined to one appearance for the Players at Lord's and an occasional Test Trial. Apart from his batting he was a useful medium-pace in-swinger, who took over 400 wickets in all and had a rare knack of breaking tiresome partnerships, and a good first slip. His career was shortened by a bad blow in the eye by a ball from Bowes. Though the sight was not in the end affected, his confidence against the quicker bowlers clearly was and he was only 37 when he dropped out of the side.

WATSON, George, who died on November 26, 1937, at Scarborough at the advanced age of 93, was a member of the town club for 60 years. In 1869 he played in the first match arranged by C. I. Thornton at Scarborough and in 1880 he captained the Eighteen of Scarborough and District side who beat the Australians by 90 runs.

WATSON, George Sutton, who died on April 1, 1974, aged 66, was in the Shrewsbury XI in 1924 and 1925, heading the batting averages in the second year. In 1929 and the following season he made occasional appearances as an amateur for Kent. In 1935 he became a professional with Leicestershire, for whom he played until 1950, as an attacking batsman and first-rate fieldsman, and later served as professional at Cranleigh School. He gained two England amateur International caps at Association football before turning professional with Charlton Athletic.

WATSON, Harold, who died on March 14, 1969, aged 81, played as a professional fast-medium bowler for Norfolk before and after the First World War. Making his first appearance in 1910, he altogether took 384 wickets, average 17.23. His best season was that of 1922, when he dismissed 59 batsmen for 14.37 runs each, and he helped his county to win the Minor Counties' Championship in 1910 and 1913. He performed the hat-trick against Hertfordshire at Cheshunt in 1920, earning a first-innings analysis of seven wickets for 27 runs. On the ground staff at Lord's, he played for M.C.C. and in 1913 enjoyed the distinction of bowling F. E. Woolley, the great Kent and England left-hand batsman, with his first delivery in first-class cricket. Watson was also a useful hard-hitting batsman. He was at one time coach at the R.N.C. Dartmouth, Bishop's Stortford College and Perse School and later served as head porter at Trinity College, Cambridge.

WATSON, The Rev. Thomas Herman, who died on February 15, 1944, aged 63, at Singleton, near Blackpool, where he was vicar for 24 years, played in Freshmen and Seniors matches at Cambridge, but only once for the University—in 1903. In the Freshmen's Match in 1901 he took six wickets for 74 runs in an innings. In 1904 he appeared once for Warwickshire, but did not fulfil his early promise shown when at St. Bees School, Cumberland.

WATT, Alan Edward, a noted fast bowler and fearsome hitter who played for Kent between 1929 and 1939, died in Pembury Hospital on February 3, 1974, aged 66. He kept the Star Inn at Matfield. Born at Limpsfield Chart, near Westerham, Watt went to Westerham School and was a bulldog breed of cricketer. In first-class cricket he scored 4,079 runs, average 13.60, and he took 609 wickets at 28.81 runs apiece, but mere figures could not convey the delight he gave as he approached the batting crease. In those days Watt formed a trio with "Big" Jim Smith (Middlesex) and Arthur Wellard (Somerset) famed for hitting sixes.

Watt excelled with the straight drive and the pull. For his highest score, 96 against M.C.C. at Lord's in 1932, he went in number 10, and hit one six and 14 fours, all in 65 minutes. Against Leicestershire at Maidstone in 1933 he struck 89 out of 124 in 55 minutes, including four sixes and 11 fours. In that historic finish at Dover in 1937 when Kent set a record, which still stands, by scoring 219 in 71 minutes to beat Gloucestershire, Watt, 39 not out, gave such an amazing display that the last 51 runs came in 10 minutes and Watt finished the contest with a straight six out of the ground. In 1937, also, at Folkestone, for Over Thirty against Under Thirty, he hit 77 in 35 minutes, striking four sixes and five fours.

Tall and strong, Watt entered the Kent side when Tich Freeman was at his zenith and between 1928 and 1935 and for eight consecutive seasons took at least 200 wickets each year, so Watt was not required to do much more than see the shine off the ball. His best season with the ball was in 1937 when he took 108 wickets for 27.09 runs each. After Freeman retired, Watt and Leslie Todd formed a very effective opening attack during the four summers that preceded the war.

R. C. Robertson-Glasgow wrote: "Alan Watt of Kent is a cricketer for all the day. He is never known to tire, never willingly relieved of his bowling which comes very sharply from the pitch. He can swing the ball awkwardly late from leg, does not pitch just a little short for safety and fields to his own bowling with a fierce agility that is a joy to watch. He is impervious to rain. Such a man was born to be a hitter. Coming in at number 10, he hit me five or six times from the middle wicket to the square leg boundary. Suddenly, he played a relatively calm stroke, missed, and was stumped. This was difficult to understand. I asked the square leg umpire what had happened. 'Well, you see,' he answered, 'he had both feet off the ground at once'."—N.P.

WATT, John, a very good bowler in his younger days, when he represented Tasmania, died at Hobart on November 14, 1918. He was born on February 16, 1858.

WATTS, Edward Alfred, was found dead in his home at Cheam on May 2, 1982. He was 70. Coming out for Surrey as an amateur in 1933, he immediately showed how valuable he was going to be if he could play regularly, scoring 318 runs with an average of 39.75 and taking 28 wickets at 24.85. In 1934 he joined the staff and with 928 runs and 91 wickets made it clear that he had not been overestimated: moreover, against the powerful Yorkshire attack at Bradford he made 123 in under two hours, with four sixes and 14 fours. His only other century for the county, 116 not out against Hampshire at Bournemouth in 1936, also took less than two hours. He continued as an essential member of the side up to the War, heading the bowling averages in 1938 with 114 wickets in county matches at 17.69 and in 1939 taking 10 for 67 in the second innings against Warwickshire at Edgbaston. After the War he was less effective, but continued to give useful assistance when required. He retired at the end of 1949, having received a benefit. Later he ran a sports shop. A strongly built man, he bowled fast-medium, could swing the ball both ways and got plenty of life off the wicket: to these gifts he added a shrewd bowling brain. He was a good striker of the ball, particularly through the covers, and a reliable slip. He was a brother-in-law of Alf Gover. All told he scored 6,158 runs at an average of 21.41 and took 729 wickets at 26.06 apiece.

WATTS, George Herbert, a former Surrey and Cambridgeshire wicket-keeper, died at Cambridge on April 22, 1949, aged 82. Watts retained a connection with Cambridge University for much of his life, for he was born in the pavilion at Fenner's where his father, Weller Watts, was groundsman. After his retirement from play he acted as University umpire. Although he played very little for Surrey, Watts did very well for Cambridgeshire as wicket-keeper, hard-hitting batsman and fast bowler. In 1899 he scored 212 for Cambridgeshire against M.C.C. at Cambridge.

WAUGH, Alec, brother of Evelyn, died in Florida on September 3, 1981, aged 83. A great lover of cricket, he was "Bobby South-cott" in A. G. Macdonnell's *England, their England,* and for 50 years seldom missed a Test match at Lord's.

WAUGH, H.P., who died in a London hospital on December 13, 1954, aged 56, played occasionally as opening batsman for Essex. Specially good in cutting, he scored 128 against Glamorgan at Leyton in 1928, he and J.A. Cutmore sharing in an opening partnership of 161. From 1934 he appeared for Suffolk, being captain for five years until the start of the Second World War, scoring 1,515 runs and, with fast-medium bowling, taking 84 wickets. He played for Minor Counties and Club Cricket Conference in representative matches.

WAZIR ALI, Major Syed, the former Indian Test match cricketer, died in Karachi on June 17, 1950, aged 46, after an operation for appendicitis. Elder brother of S. Nazir Ali, another Test player, Wazir Ali appeared in seven Test matches—all against England. He toured England in 1932 and 1936 and played against England in India in 1933. A fine batsman with a keen eye and a wide range of powerful strokes, Wazir Ali hit six hundreds during the 1932 tour and scored 1,725 runs in all matches. On his second visit to England he was handicapped by a finger injury. He missed a month's cricket, but although unable to do himself justice he hit the highest score for the Indians during the tour—155 not out against an England XI at Folkestone. He led the Indian team which won matches against visiting Australian sides in India in 1935 and 1936.

WEAVER, Frederick Charles, who died at Limpley Stoke, Wiltshire, on December 29, 1949, aged 70, was very prominent in West Country club cricket, scoring over 35,000 runs and taking more than 5,000 wickets. Three times he won the "Gully" bat for the best record in club cricket. He played in a few matches for Gloucestershire when G. L. Jessop succeeded W. G. Grace as captain, doing little, though in 1900 he appears in the averages as the head of the county bowling with eight wickets at 16.75 each; but in four innings he scored only four runs: C. J. Kortright at Leyton dismissed him for a "brace of ducks."

WEBB, Lieut.-Commdr. Arthur Geoffrey Gascoigne, Secretary of Leicestershire from 1933 to 1939, died at Oakham on April 6, 1981, aged 84. Born near Sittingbourne, he played for Kent Second XI in 1922 and occasionally for Leicestershire between 1933 and 1938. He had also appeared for the Navy and for Nigeria. A left-hand bat, he could also, if required, keep wicket.

WEBB, The Rev. Charles Johnstone Bourne, who died on November 18, 1963, aged 88, was in the Radley XI from 1891 to 1893, being captain in the last year. He played in two matches for Middlesex in 1902 and later assisted Dorset.

WEBB, George, an old time Wellington, New Zealand, representative cricketer, died on June 7, 1934, aged 78. Born in Ireland he came to Wellington in the middle '70s. He was a free batsman, driving particularly well and a fast round-arm bowler of the old-fashioned type. He represented Wellington against the Australian teams of 1878 and 1880 and played in a few other representative games, the last in 1897.

WEBB, Sidney, who was born at Brompton, in Middlesex, on February 1, 1874, died at Ilford on April 4, 1923. For a few seasons he was successful as a right-hand medium-paced bowler, but it cannot be said that he ever took quite the place in the game that seemed likely. He played for Middlesex in 1897 and 1898, and in his first match for the county—against Notts at Trent Bridge—took 10 wickets for 101 runs, seven of them in the first innings for 56. Between 1899 and 1903 he appeared for Lancashire, and among his various feats for that side may be mentioned his seven for 12 runs v. Hampshire at Manchester in 1900, eight for 36 v. M.C.C. at Lord's and seven for 17 v. Kent, both in 1902. Altogether he took 270 wickets for Lancashire for 18.59 runs each. Twice he bowled unchanged through both innings of his opponents—v. Hampshire in 1900 and v. Kent a year later, in each case at Old Trafford. He joined the ground-staff at Manchester in June, 1897, after engagements at Newport (Mon.) and with Somerset County (a year and a half) at Taunton.

WEBBE, Alexander Josiah, of high renown in Harrow, Oxford University and Middlesex cricket, died on February 19, 1941, at his home, Fulvens Farm, Abinger Hammer, Surrey, aged 86. Born on January 16, 1855, he had not been seen on a cricket field in active pursuit of the game in an important fixture for over 40 years, but during all that time he still exercised much influence at Lord's as President of Middlesex and member of the Marylebone Club Committee, to which he was first elected in 1886.

Like the Walkers before him, he first made his name in Harrow cricket, and was a member of the XI from 1872 to 1874, finishing as captain of the School XI when, in the big match at Lord's, notwithstanding his personal contributions of 77 and 80, Eton were victorious by five wickets. Going up to Trinity College, Oxford, Webbe got his Blue as a Freshman, and on his first appearance against Cambridge he made 55, the highest score in the match, and 21, so helping materially in a narrow victory by six runs. As evidence of his popularity and excellence as a cricketer, he was twice captain of Oxford, and, when first the leader, his side won handsomely by 10 wickets, he and his brother, H. R. Webbe, hitting off 47 runs needed for victory. It is of special interest to recall that he and W. S. Patterson, the Cambridge captain, both played that year for Gentlemen against Players at Lord's, in what was described as "the glorious match," which the Gentlemen won by one wicket when everybody present anticipated a triumph for the Players. W. S. Patterson and A. J. Webbe were the last survivors of the 22 engaged in that game, and after Patterson passed away in October 1939, A. J. Webbe remained as the oldest living University captain.

Another very interesting episode during his early period at Oxford was that in 1875 he played for the Gentlemen at Lord's and, going in first, helped W. G. Grace make 203 in the opening stand, his share being 65; "the champion" scored 152. Writing in his book, W. G. Grace said of that occasion, "In a sticky-wicket season, batting suffered, but one young player, Mr. A. J. Webbe, came to the front with a rush; when we put on 203 runs his defence and patience were perfect." Those attributes expressed by the greatest of batsmen fairly described some of Webbe's characteristics at the wicket.

Webbe also started playing for Middlesex during his first year at Oxford when 20 years of age, and his success in the strongest company still serves as an example of how the best schoolboy cricketers in those days quickly reached the front rank. In every particular a great batsman, he possessed skill in defence, with untiring patience and remarkable power in stroke play. True to type, like many Harrow batsmen of the period, he stood at the wicket with legs wide apart, a position well suited to playing back in defence or cutting—something like the posture adopted and made memorable in later years by Gilbert Jessop, "the Croucher." Webbe cut splendidly, both square and late,'used the "Harrow drive," now known as the hit through "the covers," and placed the ball to the on or hit to leg with perfectly timed strokes. In fact, an admirable exponent of the batsman's art. Of middle height and good build, his early stamina had proof in an innings of 299 not out for Trinity College against Exeter; also in 1875 he made his first hundred in important cricket, 120 for the University against Gentlemen of England.

Ripening to maturity, Webbe got more runs as pitches became less favourable to bowlers, and in 1887 he enjoyed his best season, scoring 1,244 runs, with an average of 47, his highest innings being 243 not out against Yorkshire at Huddersfield; 192 not out at Canterbury off the Kent bowlers was another highly meritorious display. When set he exemplified what Robertson-Glasgow now calls a "Difficult Target." Altogether in first-class cricket, A. J. Webbe scored 11,761 runs, with an average of 23.75, as given in Sir Home Gordon's *Form at a Glance*.

Lord Harris accepting an invitation from the Melbourne Club for a team of Amateurs to visit Australia in the autumn of 1878, A. J. Webbe was one of the chosen. The impossibility of finding amateur bowlers able to go necessitated the inclusion of Tom Emmett and George Ulyett of Yorkshire. By no means representative of England, the side lost the one match against Australia. The death of A. J. Webbe leaves as the only survivor of that touring team F. A. Mackinnon, head of the clan Mackinnon, who has maintained his interest in Kent, his cricketing county, by going to the Canterbury Festival regularly up to 1939.

Free to give practically all his time to cricket, A. J. Webbe kept up his close connection with the game, as known to the public, for nearly 70 years—from his presence in the Harrow XI to his resignation of the Middlesex Club presidency in 1937; and even to the last, as a trustee of M.C.C., he held an honoured place in cricket.

Besides his first-class activities, A. J. Webbe, on leaving school, went on the annual tours of Harrow Wanderers, under the lead of I. D. Walker, and he took teams to Oxford and Cambridge each season. After captaining Oxford Harlequins for several years, he was elected president of the club. For such sides he used to bowl medium pace, but really his skill was confined to batsmanship and fielding. Good everywhere, he excelled in the deep, and some magnificent catches stand to his credit.

At other games A. J. Webbe ranked high.

He represented Oxford twice at racquets in the doubles, and in 1888 he won the tennis silver racquet at Lord's. Added to his fondness for games and skill in their practice, he served on hospital committees and in many ways helped to relieve the troubles and sufferings of people less fortunate than himself.

Tributes to A. J. Webbe

Sir Pelham Warner, who succeeded Mr. A. J. Webbe as President of Middlesex in 1937, wrote directly after the loss of his old captain:

"I played my first match for Middlesex under his captaincy at Taunton in August 1894 and, among the many happy things which cricket has brought me, am glad to remember that I was in the XI when he played his last match for Middlesex at Worcester in July 1909—his only appearance for the county that season. He saved us from impending defeat by playing a splendid innings of 59 not out, half the total made on a very difficult wicket. After that, when in turn he was hon. secretary and president of Middlesex, it was easy to know where to go for encouragement and sympathy; this attitude towards successive captains he maintained to the end of his life. Mr. F. T. Mann, Mr. Nigel Haig, Mr. R. W. V. Robins, Mr. H. J. Enthoven and Mr. I. A. R. Peebles will fully endorse this.

Just as the Walkers made Middlesex cricket, 'Webbie' continued in their tradition. No county captain ever had a more helpful and understanding supporter. We may count ourselves a very lucky band. Webbe was the soul of Middlesex cricket. He was a fine leader, kindness itself, with a rare charm of manner, and no one ever had a more loyal and truer friend. To 'lame dogs' and in the troubles which from time to time befall cricketers he was a veritable champion. He lived to a great age and his passing was to be expected, but none the less one feels that a landmark has been removed and that something very tangible and visible has gone out of one's life. He fully earned almost every honour that cricket can give—for he was a great cricketer—and Lord's will not be the same without him to hundreds of others besides myself."

Mr. A. J. H. Cochrane, an Oxford Blue in 1885, 1886, and 1888, who played for Derbyshire, and remains, at the age of 77, in close touch with first-class cricket, writes:

"I am glad to pay a brief tribute to the memory of A. J. Webbe, as one among the many devoted friends who lament him, not only as a famous cricketer, but as a man whose long life was full of kindly deeds and kindly thoughts. His death breaks a line with the heroic past, for as an admiring small boy I watched him play in the early '80s, when I. D. Walker's Middlesex champions came north in August, and their matches at Nottingham or Sheffield were the great events of the summer holidays. I remember an innings of his against Yorkshire in 1882—the light was bad and the wicket, ruined by rain, was exactly suited to the left-hand slows of Peate who, that season, was the best bowler in England. Middlesex, with a splendid batting side, had to get something like 140 to win, and lost by 20 runs. 'Webbie' went in first and, while his gifted colleagues failed one after the other, carried out his bat for 62. His watchfulness and correct timing were remarkable, and he never made a mistake or looked like getting out.

At Oxford a few years later I came to know him, for he brought down teams against us every summer. He always seems to me to have been the central figure of any match or gathering at which we met, as much for his personal characteristics as for his cricket reputation. In the field his keenness knew no bounds, making him impetuous and somewhat impatient in his comments, which, while a little disturbing to strangers, were a source of amusement to his acquaintances. At that date, half a century ago, first-class amateurs had more time than they have to-day for minor engagements, and Harlequin or Harrow Wanderers tours formed what I am sure 'Webbie' found an enjoyable part of his summer campaign. I once played for the Harlequins with him at Woolwich, where our hospitable hosts regarded him as a well-known and welcome guest. On these festive occasions he had more opportunities of bowling than in county games, and he was very fond of bowling. He was not at all a bad change either and often got a wanted wicket.

During the last 40 years, brought together by other associations as well as cricket, I got to know 'Webbie' well. We met by appointment whenever I went to Lord's during the summer, and I always envied him his memory for faces, among the crowds of all ranks and ages, who saluted him with affection. He and his wife used to stay with us in the country, and we delighted in their visits. Our long talks wandered over many subjects, past and present; we spoke of old comrades and old opponents; and his judgments, mellowed no doubt by increasing years, were always charged with that charity which is the greatest of virtues."

Mr. J. T. Hearne, who played for Middlesex from 1888 for over 20 years and, in 1920, had the rare distinction for a professional of being elected to the Committee of his County Club, writes of his old captain:

"It would be impossible for me to express in words the high esteem in which Mr. A. J. Webbe was held by me and how greatly I feel his loss. The whole of my cricket life has been very happy and I have played under many fine captains, but to me he was the best of them all, and I look back on the period of years when playing under his leadership as the most zestfully happy time of all. Ever ready with encouragement, at the same time giving such advice as to inspire one with absolute confidence in his judgment of the game, he could only succeed in getting the best out of one. Added to all this was his wonderfully kind nature, and it was my good fortune to realise quite early that I had in him a true friend to whom I could appeal both on and off the field; a friendship most highly valued which, by many an act of kindness, remained unbroken up to the time of his lamented death. I can in no way overstate how truly I revere the memory of so great a friend.

Two incidents in matches I have never forgotten. Mr. Webbe and I have often spoken of them through the years. Quite early in the '90s when playing Lancashire at Lord's, little Johnny Briggs was making a lengthy stand against us when, after several changes, Mr. Webbe put himself on to bowl—a rare occurrence—I believe at the Nursery end. I was fielding orthodox 'third man,' but was brought up to what is now known as 'the gully,' and had the satisfaction of catching Briggs off him in his first over. I vividly remember his delight at having broken up a dangerous partnership.

The other happened when we were playing Yorkshire at Bradford. Rain had driven us to the pavilion, and the usual precaution of 'stringing off the pitch' had been taken, with two policemen placed on guard. After some delay and all of us sitting in front of the dressing room, Mr. Webbe was the first to notice that the two guards had absent-mindedly stepped over the rope and were patrolling side by side down the pitch, and, as captain, he shouted at them from the pavilion to 'get off'!

WEBBER, Lieut. Henry (South Lancashire Regiment), of Horley, Surrey, and a J. P. for the county, was killed in action on July 21, 1916, aged 68. He was in the Tonbridge School XI 50 years before, among his contemporaries being Mr. J. W. Dale, and later played for Pembroke College, Oxford. He had been a member of the M.C.C. since 1872. He made his first hundred in 1863 and as recently as August 6, 1904, when 56 years of age, made 209 not out for Horley v. Lowfield Heath, at Horley, in three hours after a full round of golf in the morning. His pluck and patriotism in insisting on being given a commission at his advanced age were much admired.

WEBBER, Roy, who died suddenly on November 14, 1962, aged 48, was a celebrated cricket statistician. An accountant before serving with the Royal Air Force in the Second World War, he afterwards decided to turn a long-standing hobby into a profession. Besides acting for many years as official cricket scorer for the B.B.C. he was joint editor of the Playfair Cricket Monthly, the author of a number of books, chiefly of cricket records, and was in turn a contributor to the *News Chronicle* and the *Daily Mail*.

WEDEL, George, who died on April 16, 1981, aged 80, was a useful bowler for Gloucestershire between 1925 and 1929. In 1926 he showed considerable promise as a leg-spinner, taking 30 wickets at an average of 20.66 and finishing second in the county's bowling averages. His best analysis in that season was four wickets for four runs in seven overs against Northamptonshire, against whom, in 1929, he also made his highest first-class score of 53. He was a left-handed batsman. His appearances after 1926 were too infrequent for him to fulfil the hopes he had raised. His first first-class victim was Herbert Sutcliffe. As a bowler he was somewhat after the style of Dick Tyldesley: not much break and came through quick. He was also a very good fielder. Wedel was hon. secretary of the Gloucestershire Gypsies, besides, at different times, being captain, secretary, chairman and president of the Stroud club.

WEEDING, Thomas Weeding, better remembered by cricketers as T. W. Baggallay, was born in London on June 11, 1847, and died at Addlestone, in Surrey, on December 19, 1929, aged 82. As a batsman he hit freely and well, making the most of his height—6ft. 3½in.—and was an excellent wicket-keeper. A member of the Marlborough XI in 1863 and the two following years, he played each season against Rugby and Cheltenham. Owing to his profession he was unable to take part in much first-class cricket, but he appeared occasionally for Surrey between 1865 and 1874 and in the match with Cambridge University, at Cambridge, in the last-mentioned year scored 82.

WEIGALL, Gerald John Villiers, one of the best-known personalities connected with the game, died on May 17, 1944, aged 73. Troubled by illness from the outbreak of war, he passed away in a Dublin hospital.

After three years in the Wellington College XI "Gerry" Weigall—his pet name from early years—received his Cambridge Blue from Gregor MacGregor in 1891, and next season under F. S. Jackson kept his place in the batting order as number three, scored 63 not out when his side collapsed and 25 in the follow-on against Oxford, who won by five wickets.

A very smart field at cover-point, he was always welcome in the Kent XI from 1891 to 1903. In his first county match he played a good innings of 73 against Warwickshire at Edgbaston. A stubborn defender with "good" cutting power, he usually batted low on the list after his University days and often pulled the game round. His best score for Kent was 138 not out at Maidstone in 1897 against the Philadelphians; at Cambridge for Emmanuel College against Peterhouse in 1891 he made 265—the highest innings he ever played. He was in the Gentlemen's XI at Scarborough in 1900.

Altogether in first-class cricket he scored 6,212 runs, with an average of nearly 20. For some years from 1923 he coached the young players at Tonbridge and captained Kent Second XI; he also coached Yorkshire "Colts" for a time. He went to America with Kent in 1903, and in Argentine for an M.C.C. side in 1926 he averaged 26.29. With Free Foresters he visited Germany in 1920.

A stickler for orthodox batting, "Gerry" Weigall used to amuse and delight all comers in the Pavilion at Lord's with his portrayal of the correct "follow through" in the off-drive and of his stylish cut with a borrowed bat, stick or umbrella. Seldom did he miss a Kent match, and at Canterbury "Gerry" Weigall could be described as part of the Festival.

He represented Cambridge against Oxford at racquets after being champion at Wellington, and took a prominent part in popularising squash—excelling in that very hard game until approaching 70 years of age.

WEIGHELL, The Rev. William Bartholomew, who was born at Cheddington, Buckinghamshire, on June 21, 1846, died on October 24, 1905. He was a very good fast round-armed bowler, and in the first over he ever delivered at Lord's—for Cambridge University v. M.C.C. and Ground, in 1866— he bowled down the wickets of Mr. W. Nicholson, Grundy, and Mr. C.F. Buller with consecutive balls. He was educated at Bedford Grammar School and Cambridge, and in 1866, 1868, and 1869, played against Oxford. His fielding was very good indeed, and his batting often effective; his highest score was 197 for Brighton v. Horsham in 1876. He assisted Sussex 13 times between 1868 and 1878, and appeared for Norfolk in 1882 and 1883.

WELCH, T. H. G., who captained the Trinity College, Dublin, XI, and played for Northamptonshire, died in December, 1936, aged 77. A schoolmaster, he delighted in teaching his boys cricket. He was a good footballer, oarsman and runner.

WELFORD, James W., who died in Glasgow on January 17, 1945, aged nearly 76, was best known as a full back in partnership with Robert Chatt when Aston Villa won the F.A. Cup in 1895, but he was a good cricketer. A native of Barnard Castle he played for Durham County from 1891, heading the batting averages in 1895, and making 153 against Staffordshire. Then he became qualified for Warwickshire and in 1896 averaged 23 for 11 matches, scoring his best innings, 118, at Leicester in May, the home county winning, after a great struggle, by one wicket. That was the extent of his first-class cricket, and he did not appear again for Durham.

WELLARD, Arthur William, died peacefully in his sleep on December 31, 1980, aged 77. In a career extending from 1927 to 1950 he scored 12,575 runs with an average of 19.73 and took 1,614 wickets at 24.35— figures which suggest a valuable county all-rounder. In fact he was more than that. Though he was a good enough opening bowler to be selected in that role for a Test against Australia, and once took nine for 117 in an unofficial Test in India, it is as a batsman that he will be chiefly remembered. In the course of his career he hit some 500 sixes, thus accounting for a quarter of the runs he made. But he was no mere slogger; he had a sound defence and was, for one of his type, remarkably consistent. His record was not boosted by large innings. He made only two hundreds, his highest score being 112 against Lancashire at Old Trafford in 1936. A tall, strong man, he bowled fast-medium with a vicious break-back, and a

large number of his victims were clean-bowled. For variety in a second spell, or when the pitch was taking spin, he could bowl just as efficiently slow off-breaks round the wicket. He was a fine field anywhere close in. Above all, whatever he was doing he was an indefatigable trier.

Born at Southfleet, near Gravesend, he originally played for Bexley and as early as 1921 took six for 21 against Kent Club and Ground. When the sides next met in 1926, he took five for 36. But despite this, and although he headed the Bexley batting and bowling averages for three years, Kent were not interested and tradition has it that, when he asked whether there was any chance of a trial for them, he was told he had much better be a policeman. It was Arthur Haywood, late of the Kent staff and then professional at Taunton School, who suggested that he should approach Somerset and he started to qualify for them in 1927. That year and the next he showed promising form against the touring side, and in his first full season, 1929, he took 131 wickets at 21.38. For the next few years, owing largely to elbow trouble, his bowling was disappointing, but in 1933 he did the double, a feat he repeated in 1935 and 1937. A good example of what he could do was the Hampshire match at Portsmouth in 1933. Coming in when six wickets were down for 38, he made 77 out of 94, took seven for 43, made 60 in the second innings and then took three more wickets for 66. In 1936 he hit Armstrong of Derbyshire, a slow left-armer, for five sixes off consecutive balls: he had already taken nine wickets in the match and his 86 in 62 minutes brought his side a one-wicket victory. In 1938 he again hit five consecutive sixes, this time off Frank Woolley, being dropped just in front of the screen off the sixth ball. On this occasion his scores were 57 and 37 and he took 13 for 115; so again he had much to do with his side's victory. These feats, at that time unparalleled, were both performed on the small ground at Wells.

In 1937 he played in the Test at Old Trafford against New Zealand without any particular success and in 1938 was in the side against Australia at Lord's. On this occasion he certainly bowled well and in the second innings made 38 vital runs, including a pulled drive for six off McCabe on to the grandstand balcony. When he joined Compton at 142 for seven, an Australian victory was possible: when he was out at 216 for eight, the match was safe. This was his last Test, but he was due to go to India in the winter of 1939–40 had war not intervened. He had already been a member of Lord Tennyson's unofficial side there in 1937–38 and had had a successful tour. After the War he continued for another four seasons to be a valuable member of the Somerset side, finally dropping out in 1950.

WELLDON, James Turner, born at Felsted, Chelmsford, on August 3, 1847, died at Ashford, in Kent, on February 6, 1927, aged 79. A good bat and an active field at cover-point and long-leg, he played for Kent three times in 1867 and once in 1869. Whilst at Tonbridge, of which school his father was for many years headmaster, he was captain of the XI.

WELLS, Cyril Mowbray, a former Cambridge cricket and Rugby football Blue, died on August 22, 1963, aged 92. A member of the Dulwich XI from 1886 to 1890, inclusive, he was captain in the last year and when going up to Cambridge got his Blue as a Freshman. He played three times against Oxford and though achieving little in batting, he bore a big part in victory by 266 runs in 1893 when taking seven wickets for 66 runs. In that game he was concerned in a memorable incident that in all probability led to an alteration a few years later in the law governing the follow-on.

At that time the side 80 runs behind on first innings had to follow on and in this match Oxford, in reply to a total of 182, lost nine wickets for 95 when T. S. B. Wilson and W. H. Brain became associated. Three more runs were added, taking Oxford to within 84 of the Cambridge score, when a consultation between the batsmen suggested that the Dark Blues, in order that Cambridge might bat last on a pitch likely to crumble, intended to throw away their remaining wicket. Sensing the drift of the conversation, Wells decided to frustrate the plan. He immediately bowled a no-ball wide to the boundary and followed a little later with a round-arm delivery that also reached the ring, thus destroying Oxford's chance of following on. This action led to M.C.C. increasing the deficit which meant a follow-on from 80 to 120, but when, three years later, E. B. Shine, in very similar circumstances, gave away 12 runs to prevent Oxford from following their innings, further consideration of the question became necessary. So in 1900 the Law was amended, leaving the side leading by 150 with the option of enforcing the follow-on.

Wells assisted Surrey as an amateur from 1890 to 1893 but appeared for Middlesex, the county of his birth, from 1895 to 1909. He represented Gentlemen v. Players in 1892, 1893, and 1901. A free-hitting batsman, he also bowled right-arm slow-medium with a deceptive delivery. He generally bowled off-breaks, but sometimes employed the leg-break and took many wickets with a ball which went straight through.

Wells played for Cambridge in the University Rugby matches of 1891 and 1892, first as full-back and then as half-back, and was half-back for England in six matches between 1893 and 1897. He also appeared for the Harlequins and Middlesex.

WELLS, George, better known to the cricketers of his day as "Tiny" Wells, died on January 23, 1891, in the 60th year of his age. He was born on November 2, 1831. Wells was probably one of the shortest men who ever acquired a reputation in the cricket field. It would be an exaggeration to say that he was ever quite a first-rate player, but for a number of seasons he batted with considerable success, being associated with both Sussex and Middlesex. It was a peculiarity of his batting that he took his guard close to the stumps, and then came forward to meet the ball. He was a member of the first English team that went to Australia, under the captaincy of H. H. Stephenson, in the season of 1861–62.

WELLS, Joseph, who played for Kent in 1862 and 1863, died at Liss, in Hampshire, on October 20, 1910. He was born at Red-leal, Penshurst, in Kent, on July 14, 1828, and was therefore in his 83rd year at the time of his death. *Scores and Biographies* (vii – 243) says of him: "Height 5ft. 8½in., and weight about 10st. 7lb. (or 11st). Bowls very fast round-armed, with a low delivery; but did not appear for his county until he was about 34 years of age... As a bat he does not excel, and fields generally at short-slip." He will always be remembered for his great feat in the match between Kent and Sussex on Box's ground at Brighton in June, 1862, when, in the first innings of Sussex, he bowled down the wickets of Dean, Mr. S. Austin Leigh, Ellis and Fillery with consecutive balls. In 1856 he was responsible for the revival of the Bromley C.C., while from 1857 to 1869 he was engaged at Chislehurst by the West Kent Club, from 1870 to 1872 by Bickley Park, and afterwards by Norwich Grammar School. He was the father of H. G. Wells, the famous novelist, and a nephew of Timothy Duke, the noted bat and ball maker of Penshurst.

WELLS, Lionel Seymour, a brother of Mr. C. M. Wells, was born on February 3, 1870, and, after practising at the Oval, died in the Pavilion on April 26, 1928, aged 58. A useful forcing batsman and slow bowler, he played occasionally for Middlesex between 1898 and 1905 as well as for the now defunct London County C.C. In London club cricket he was associated with the Wanderers and the Crystal Palace C.C.

WELLS, William, the Northamptonshire fast bowler, died on March 18, 1939, aged 58. He did his best work from 1908 until the War started in 1914, subsequent to which he enjoyed most success in 1921, when his 70 wickets averaged 18.44, and in 1924 with 61 wickets at 13.29 apiece—his least expensive season. In 1910 he performed a hat-trick against Nottinghamshire, his victims being George Gunn, John Gunn and Payton. Always playing on the weaker side, he occasionally showed to advantage with the bat and in 1923 he averaged nearly 26 in Championship matches.

WELMAN, F. T., died at South Ascot on December 30, 1931. Born on February 19, 1849, he assisted in turn Somerset and Middlesex. As a batsman he was not particularly successful but he was quite a high-class wicket-keeper—one of a brilliant sequence associated with the western county.

WENMAN, William, the second of the five sons of the famous Edward Gower Wenman, was born at Benenden on May 22, 1832, and died at Souris, in Manitoba, on November 23, 1921, aged 89. His name will be found in the Kent XI in 1862 and two following years. He was a free-hitting batsman, and kept up the game in Canada until his 75th year.

WENSLEY, Albert Frederick, who died on June 17, 1970, aged 72, rendered excellent service to Sussex as a professional all-rounder from 1922 to 1936. In that time he took with medium-pace bowling 1,135 wickets for 26.42 runs each and hit 10,735 runs, average 20.40. He achieved the "cricketers' double" in 1929 when scoring 1,057 runs and dismissing 113 batsmen. In each of four other years he took 100 wickets and against Middlesex at Lord's in 1935 he performed the hat-trick. The best bowling analysis of his career was nine Otago wickets for 36 runs at Auckland in 1929–30. In 1925 at Hove, he and M. W. Tate bowled unchanged through both Glamorgan innings. How economical Bert Wensley's bowling could be was illustrated by his figures against Derbyshire at Chesterfield in 1928: 32 overs, 20 maidens, 21 runs, 0 wicket.

In that season he made the highest of his five centuries, 140 against Glamorgan at Eastbourne. Three times he completed 1,000 runs in a summer for the county. Strong in driving and pulling, he hit 120 in 110 minutes against Derbyshire at Horsham in 1930, when he and H. W. Parks, in putting on 178 for the ninth wicket, established a Sussex record which still stands. A very reliable fieldsman near the wicket, he twice held five catches in an innings and in the second innings of Warwickshire at Edgbaston in 1932 he had a hand in the dismissal of nine of the ten batsmen, returning bowling figures of six wickets for 73 runs.

Wensley's benefit match at Hove in 1936 came near to causing a cessation of fixtures with Nottinghamshire. With five minutes of the extra half hour remaining, Sussex were left to get nine runs to win. They scored seven from the first over. Then slight rain began and, after appealing to the umpires, G. F. H. Heane, the Nottinghamshire captain, led his players from the field, the game being left drawn.

On September 5 of that same year, 1936, Wensley and W. H. Ashdown played a match against XI of the Isle of Oxney before 2,000 spectators. They put out the XI for 153 runs in 24.4 overs and then Ashdown and Wensley made 186 before Wensley was out for 96 leaving Ashdown 83 not out made in 36.4 overs. It commemorated the centenary of the match played by E. G. Wenman and Richard Mills of Benenden, Kent, who defeated 11 chosen players of the Isle of Oxney at Wittersham on September 4 and 5, 1834.

WENYON, H. J., who played occasionally for Middlesex from 1921 to 1923, died in July, 1944. His one innings of note was 51 not out against Warwickshire in the first county match at Lord's in 1922; strangely enough he did not appear again for Middlesex that season.

WEST, George H., died on October 6, 1896, at his residence, Champion Hill, aged 45. After many years service on the staff of *The Field*, he became cricket correspondent of *The Times* in 1880, a post which he retained to the day of his death. Owing, however, to failing health, he was not, during the last season or two, seen so often at Lord's or the Oval as in former years. At one time— beginning at the end of the '70s—Mr West was editor of *Wisden's Almanack*.

WEST, John Edward, born at Stepney on November 18, 1861, died in London on March 14, 1920. He was a useful medium-paced bowler, could hit hard and fielded well, and for a few seasons kept wicket. Between 1885 and 1896 he scored 1,092 runs for Middlesex with an average of 11.37 and took 76 wickets for 24.29 runs each; as wicket-keeper he caught 34 and stumped 30. His highest scores were 83 v. Gloucestershire at Lord's in 1888 and 67 against the same county in 1885. In the match with Kent at Lord's in 1886 he took six wickets for 31 runs in the first innings and three for 27 in the second. For over 20 seasons he was a member of the ground staff at Lord's and for several years umpired in first-class matches.

WEST, Leslie Harold, who died suddenly on November 12, 1982, aged 77, at a cricket dinner, had a trial for Essex as a professional in 1928. A stylish batsman, he made many runs later in club cricket, first for Ilford and then for Wanstead, and after his retirement he did wonderful work in coaching and inspiring young players.

WEST, William Arthur John, a popular member of the ground staff at Lord's for many years and a first-class umpire, sometimes "standing" in Test matches, died on February 22, 1938, aged 75. After playing as an amateur for Northamptonshire, he turned professional in 1886 and was engaged at the Oval for two seasons. Then he joined the M.C.C. staff and continued to assist Northamptonshire until 1891 when he helped Warwickshire, the county of his birth, his best performance with the ball being five wickets for seven runs against Cheshire. All these counties were at that time second-class. Over 6 ft. tall and powerfully built, "Bill" West was a fast bowler and hard hitter. In the '80s he excelled as an amateur boxer, winning the Queensberry Cup in 1884, and next year the Amateur Boxing Association heavyweight cup.

WESTBROOK, Keith Raymond, who died in Tasmania on January 20, 1982, aged 94, was at that time the second-oldest surviving Australian first-class cricketer. Two of his great-uncles played in the first first-class match ever played in Australia. A right-handed batsman he scored 35 and 25 in his one game for Tasmania, against Victoria in 1910.

WESTELL, William Thomas, who was born at St. Albans on December 13, 1854, and died at his native place on May 25, 1924,

after having been confined to his bed for 10 months, was a good all-round cricketer who played for Hertfordshire first as an amateur and later as a professional for 20 years. He was a dashing batsman—he made 49 hundreds in all kinds of cricket—a fair change bowler and a good field. For some years his 188 against Essex at St. Albans in 1884 remained the highest score hit for his county. He was son of William Westell, and at one time he, his father and two uncles were playing together for Hertfordshire. Later he acted as coach at Aldenham, Bedford Grammar School and Winchester, and among the famous players whom he trained was Mr. A. O. Jones. For a time he was Hon. Secretary of the St. Albans C.C., and he played his last game for the club in 1914.

WESTLEY, Roger Bancroft, who was master-in-charge of cricket at Haileybury, died on May 12, 1982, aged 35. In 1969, when his brother, Stuart, got a Blue, he played in five matches for Oxford without success. The two provide one of the comparatively few instances of twins appearing together in first-class cricket. They were educated at Lancaster Grammar School.

WESTMORLAND, 13th Earl of (Anthony Mildmay Julian Fane), born on August 16, 1859, died at Hove on June 9, 1922. He was not in the XI while at Eton, but was very fond of the game and arranged many interesting matches at his seat, Apethorpe. As Lord Burghersh, he played occasionally for Northamptonshire.

WHALLEY-TOOKER, E., died on November 23, 1940, aged 77, and his passing removed a link with the old Hambledon club, renowned as a cradle of cricket some 150 years ago. The Broad Halfpenny ground has been ploughed up for farm land, and Whalley-Tooker, a descendant of a member of the original Hambledon club, set about the task of securing the field for cricket again. It was got into condition for a match in July 1925 between Winchester College, then given the possession of the land, and Hambledon. Mr. Whalley-Tooker captained the side representing Hambledon and led his team to victory.

WHATELEY, Major Ellis George, who died on September 4, 1969, aged 87, was in the Eton XI in 1900 and 1901. In the first year, although he took five wickets for 59 runs in the second innings, he was on the losing side against Harrow, who got home by one wicket. The next season, when he was captain, he played innings of 45 and 40, but again Harrow won, this time by 10 wickets. He played for Somerset in 1904 and in later years for Hertfordshire and Middlesex Second XI.

WHEAT, Arthur, B., who died on May 20, 1973, aged 75, was associated with Nottinghamshire County Cricket for over half a century, first as wicket-keeper and then as scorer. He joined the staff in 1922 after gaining something of a reputation in the Notts and Derby League with Jacksdale who, during his three seasons with them, won the Championship three times and the Cup twice. He was first choice for Nottinghamshire during the heyday of that celebrated pair of fast bowlers, Larwood and Voce. When his playing career ended in 1947, he became county scorer and held the position for 26 years, in which time he scored for England in every Test match at Trent Bridge. He was the longest serving scorer for a first-class county. This likeable little man went into the mines upon leaving school, spent most of the Second World War years in that occupation and returned underground every winter. In 1972 he received a presentation to mark his 50 years' service to the County Club.

WHEATLEY, Jack Brian, who died at Sellescombe, Sussex, on April 29, 1982, aged 78, appeared for Middlesex against Oxford University in 1925 and then in 1928 played in seven matches for the county, making 62 against Worcestershire at Lord's in the first of them but doing little later. A batsman who played straight and was a good driver, he was also a useful slow left-arm bowler. He had been in the XI at St. Paul's School but did not get a Blue at Oxford.

WHEATLEY, John, who died at Waimate, New Zealand, on April 20, 1962, aged 102, was the oldest Canterbury cricketer. Going to New Zealand from Australia when 16, he played in representative games for Canterbury from 1882 to 1906, his highest innings at a time when pitches were far from good being 53 against Queensland in 1897. For some years he was the sole New Zealand selector.

WHEELER, Cecil, the Hon. Treasurer of the Warwickshire County C.C., died at Edgbaston on February 13, 1930, aged 68. He took part in the formation of the club and figured occasionally in the county XI between 1888 and 1890.

WHEELER, John, the well-known Leicestershire cricketer and one of the most respected members of the ground staff at Lord's, died at Sutton Bonnington, Nottinghamshire, on September 22, 1908. He was born at Sutton Bonnington—or, according to another account, at Leicester—on December 9, 1844, and appeared for Nottinghamshire Colts from 1863 until 1872. Accepting several engagements—from 1870 to 1875 he was with the Phoenix Park Club in Dublin—his career in County Cricket was naturally seriously interfered with and only twice, in 1873 and 1877, did he appear for Notts, his opponents on each occasion being Yorkshire at Trent Bridge. Meanwhile he had appeared for Leicestershire, and against M.C.C. and Ground at Lord's in 1876 had scored 59 and 38 not out, Morley being one of the bowlers opposed to him. Two years later he performed the feat of his career, making 60 and 65 against the first Australian team, who had Spofforth, Allan, Garrett, and Boyle to bowl for them. A. Sankey, who scored 70, helped Wheeler to make 113 for the county's first wicket in the first innings, and, although the Australians eventually won by eight wickets, owing to a rousing innings of 133 by Charles Bannerman in the final stage of the game, the match was a triumph for the pair named, and especially for Wheeler. In the same year Wheeler was offered a position on the ground staff at Lord's which he accepted and retained without a break until his death. He continued to appear for Leicestershire, however, until 1892, when he was in his 48th year. At the Oval in 1885 he played an innings of 107 against Surrey, the next highest score on the side being 12 by Warren. After retiring from County Cricket Wheeler took to umpiring and invariably gave the greatest satisfaction. He was granted two benefit matches, one by his county and the other by the M.C.C., the former being Leicestershire v. Derbyshire on the Leicester ground in 1892 and the latter between M.C.C. and Ground v. Notts at Lord's in the following May. He was a sound batsman, a fast round-armed bowler, and a good field at mid-off or at the wicket. In the match between Leicestershire and Warwickshire at Edgbaston in 1890 he made three catches in the first innings and four in the second.

WHELDON, George Frederick, who was born at Langley Green, near Birmingham, on November 1, 1871, died at Worcester on

January 14, 1924. He was a good batsman and wicket-keeper, and appeared for Worcestershire in both its second-class and first-class days. He scored 100 v. Hampshire at Bournemouth in 1900, 112 v. Somerset at Worcestershire in 1903 and 103 v. Leicestershire at Leicester in 1904. In the last mentioned year he was in very good form behind the wicket, and caught six men in the match with Hampshire at Southampton and repeated the feat v. Oxford University at Oxford. Commencing in 1910, he appeared later for Carmarthenshire. He was a member of the Aston Villa football team which won the English Cup and the League Championship 1896–97, and the League Championship in 1898–99 and 1899—1900, and he also represented England v. Ireland in 1897, and v. Scotland, Wales and Ireland in 1898.

WHISTLER, General Sir Lashmer Gordon, who died in Cambridge Military Hospital, Aldershot, on July 4, 1963, aged 64, played for Harrow in the second of the season's "unofficial" one-day war-time matches with Eton in 1916. He scored eight and 25 and brought off two catches. At one time it looked as though this match would not take place. Breaking bounds and other offences had resulted in half-holidays at Harrow being suspended. What was described as "a quite unpardonable comment" upon this decision was written across the school rules in the yard and as the miscreant could not be discovered, the match was cancelled. Only at a late hour on the night before the game did the headmaster yield to urgent representations and give permission for the team to travel to Eton. The whole-day holiday to the rest of the school was stopped.

WHITAKER, Edgar Haddon, O.B.E., who died at his home at Roehampton on January 5, 1982, was editor of *Wisden Cricketers' Almanack* from 1940 to 1943. He was Chairman of J. Whitaker and Sons, publishers of *Whitaker's Almanack* and from 1938 to 1978 of *Wisden*.

WHITBY, Hugh Owen, died on October 14, 1934, aged 70, having been born on April 12, 1864. A very good fast right-hand bowler with an easy action he went from Leamington College to Oxford and got his Blue as a Freshman in 1884. In four matches against Cambridge, three of which he helped to win, Whitby took 20 wickets at an average of 20.30 apiece. More notable than anything he did in the University engagements were the leading part Whitby enjoyed in beating the

very powerful Australian team of 1884 by seven wickets. W. L. Murdoch's side late in the season scored 551 at the Oval against England—a total that stood as a record for a Test match in this country until 1899 when England made 576—eclipsed in 1930 by Australia's 695. These figures make the performance of Whitby as a Freshman all the more remarkable. After beating in a single innings a strong XI got together by Lord Sheffield the Australians went to Oxford and, batting first, were dismissed for 148, Whitby taking eight wickets for 82 runs. Oxford secured a lead of 61, thanks mainly to a brilliant 92 by T. C. O'Brien, and then got their visitors out for 168; E. W. Bastard with five wickets for 44, and H. V. Page two for 16 doing better this time than Whitby with two for 55. M. C. Kemp, the Oxford captain, scored 63 not out in knocking off the runs required for victory. It may be recalled that Cambridge beat Murdoch's previous side in 1882 by six wickets, these being the only occasions when either University has defeated an Australian XI. In 1886 when the Australians, nothing like so good at batting, were dismissed for 70 and 38, on a rain-ruined pitch, Whitby had a record in the match of nine wickets for 35 runs; but F. R. Spofforth took 15 Oxford wickets for 36 runs and the Australians won the game by 25 runs. Mr. Whitby assisted Warwickshire in a few matches in the seasons 1884 to 1889 and went to America in 1885 with a side captained by Mr. E. J. Sanders. For many years a master at Tonbridge School until his retirement in 1919 Mr. Whitby maintained a close interest in cricket and was a popular figure in the pavilion at Lord's until a few months before his death.

WHITE, Sir Archibald Woollaston, 4th Bart., who died in a nursing home on December 16, 1945, aged 68, was in the Wellington XI 1894–96. He captained Yorkshire from 1911 to 1914, leading the team to the County Championship in 1912, the only time this distinction came to Yorkshire between 1908 and 1919. He scored 1,457 runs for the county, average 14.57.

WHITE, Edward Albert, born at Yalding on March 16, 1844, died in London on May 3, 1922. He was not in the XI while at Marlborough, but played for Kent in 29 matches between 1857 and 1875. He was a good hitter and possessed strong defence. His highest score for the county was 81 v. Surrey at Canterbury in 1861, but at Brighton in 1866 he made 96 for Gentlemen of Kent v.

Gentlemen of Sussex. In the second innings of the match with Lancashire at Gravesend in 1871 he finished his innings with 25 singles, making altogether 39 singles in a score of 55. He was a cousin of Mr. L. A. White, of the Kent XI of 1869.

WHITE, Gordon C., the well-known South African cricketer, died of wounds in October, 1918. Born on February 5, 1882, he was in his 37th year. Gordon White did much to establish the fame of South African cricket, but in England he never quite came up to the reputation he enjoyed at home as a batsman. He came here in 1904 and 1907, and visited us for the third time with the team that took part in the Triangular Tournament in 1912. In the tour of 1904 he scored in all matches 937 runs with an average of 30, his highest innings being 115 against Notts at Trent Bridge. For the great team of 1907, though he scored 162 not out against Gloucestershire at Bristol, he was disappointing as a batsman, the soft wickets being quite unsuited to his fine off-side hitting, but he bowled his leg breaks with marked success, taking 72 wickets at a cost of just under 13 runs each. In 1912 he did not do himself justice as a batsman, and as a bowler he failed. He took part in five of the half-dozen Test matches, his best score being 59 not out in the drawn game against Australia at Nottingham. When getting runs, Gordon White always looked to be a first-rate batsman, his style of play being very free and attractive.

WHITE, Harry, head groundsman at Lord's for 26 years before retiring on pension at the end of the 1936 season, died on December 19, 1943, at his home at Luton, aged 74. He performed the difficult task of preparing "natural" pitches with marked skill. The M.C.C. committee would not allow the use of "dope," but White contrived to keep the turf fit to withstand the wear of three-day matches throughout each season, and the centre for Test matches was his special pride. In 1926 during the England and Australian match he overcame a severe trial. On the Monday morning part of the ground, including a narrow strip across the middle of the pitch, was saturated with water from the hose, turned on in some way that always remained a mystery. By careful drying White and his staff got the ground in order so satisfactorily that the game was resumed only 10 minutes late. Played in perfect weather, that match produced 1,052 runs while 18 wickets fell. A greater cause for worry was

the plague of "leather jackets" during the 1934 winter. With the help of Austin Martin, of the Oval, and his son, who eventually succeeded Harry White at Lord's, this trouble was dealt with satisfactorily. Harry White played regularly for Hertfordshire from 1894, and after a modest start became the best all-round player for the county, taking many wickets each season and scoring freely for a side that often showed marked weaknesses. In 1909, when he finished County Cricket, he headed the batting averages with 37.58 and made the only century for Hertfordshire, while his bowling earned 93 wickets at just over 12 runs apiece, Coleman, his chief helper, taking 40 at 16.90 each. Bowling medium-pace right-hand, White was very good on sticky wickets.

WHITE, John Cornish, who died on May 2, 1961, aged 70, was one of England's best slow left-arm bowlers. Educated at Taunton School, where he was a prominent member of the XI, he first appeared for Somerset in 1909 when 17, but not until four years later did he gain the regular place in the side which he held until he retired from first-class cricket in 1937. From 1919 onwards he regularly took 100 wickets a season and in 1929 and 1930 he completed the "cricketer's double." During his career he dismissed 2,361 batsmen at a cost of 18.58 runs each, hit 12,152 runs, average 17.89, and brought off 389 catches.

"Farmer" White, son of a cricket-loving farmer, enjoyed special success in matches with Worcestershire, against whom he took 16 wickets for 83 runs in one day at Bath in 1919 and, at Worcester two years later, disposed of all 10 batsmen in an innings for 76 runs. For his success, White relied more upon flight, consistent accuracy of length and variation of pace than upon spin, and a strong constitution enabled him to bowl economically for long spells.

Never more than when touring Australia as vice-captain under A. P. F. Chapman in 1928–29 did he demonstrate his powers of endurance. He played his part in an overwhelming England win by 675 runs in the opening Test at Brisbane where, with sunshine following rain during the night, he took four wickets in 6.3 overs for seven runs. In the fourth meeting with Australia, which ended in favour of England at Adelaide by 12 runs, he performed with such untiring skill in boiling heat that he sent down a total of 124 overs and five balls and took 13 wickets for 256 runs. Owing to the illness of Chapman, he captained England in the last match of the rubber which, lasting eight days, was the longest Test in history to that time, and in which the team suffered their one reverse of the tour.

M. A. Noble, the former Australian captain, paid a great tribute to the bowling of White on that tour. He wrote: "One of the most tireless workers with muscle and brain that this or any other England team has ever possessed... On bad, worn and good wickets alike, White was always able to call the tune and compel the batsmen to dance to it... To my mind, the only man who truly and actually won the Ashes was the capable, modest, unassuming sportsman, Jack White."

Altogether White played in 15 matches for England from 1921 to 1930, including a tour of South Africa in 1930–31. He captained his country in three Tests against South Africa in England in 1929. He also served for a time as a Test Selector and in 1960 became President of Somerset. Fond of all sports, he lost an eye following a shooting accident.

WHITE, Lieut.-Col. Lionel Algernon, died at Tunbridge Wells on June 25, 1917. He played in four matches for Kent in 1869, his best score in eight innings being 34. Joining the 53rd Shropshire Regiment in 1869 he retired from the Army with the rank of Lieut.-Col. in 1892. He was born at Wateringbury on November 9, 1850, and was educated at St. Paul's School, London.

WHITE, Montague Eric, who died on June 21, 1970, aged 62, played occasionally as a professional fast bowler for Worcestershire from 1931 to 1934. He took 66 wickets for the county at an average cost of 31.60. He later served as professional to Birkenhead Park C.C.

WHITE, Brig. William Nicholas, C.B., D.S.O., who died on December 27, 1951, aged 72, was in the Malvern XIs of 1896 and 1897. He played for Hampshire from 1907 to 1914 and also for the Army, scoring in first-class cricket 3,045 runs, average 26.70. A good Association footballer, he captained the Army in 1901 and 1902, and was chairman of the Army F.A.

WHITEHEAD, Lieut. George William Edendale (R.F.A., attached R.A.F.), born 1895, killed on October 17, 1918. Among the many public school cricketers lost during the War perhaps none, except John Howell of Repton, had better prospects of winning distinction at the game than George White-head. In the Clifton College XI for four years—he was captain in 1913 and 1914—he had a brilliant record at school. Starting in 1911 he was third in batting with an average of 33, and in the following year he did still better, playing a remarkable innings of 259 not out against Liverpool and averaging 41. Moreover he took 14 wickets with a fairly good average. Against Cheltenham he played a first innings of 63. In his two years as captain he was conspicuously successful, heading the batting in both seasons with averages of 46 in 1913 and 40 in 1914. He also bowled well, especially in 1914, when he took 36 wickets for a trifle over 13 runs apiece. He played three times at Lord's for Public Schools against the M.C.C., and in 1914 he was given a couple of trials for Kent.

An old Cliftonian writes:

"George Whitehead was a perfect flower of the public schools. He was not limited to athletics only, great though he was in this respect. Intellectually he was far above the average, and was as happy with a good book as when he was scoring centuries. His ideals were singularly high and though gentle and broad-minded, he always stood uncompromisingly for all that was clean. So modest was he, that strangers sometimes failed to realise his worth. He insisted on being transferred to the Royal Air Force from the R.F.A., fully appreciating the risks, because he knew of his country's then urgent need of air-men and so he died, greatly patriotic. Clifton has lost more than 500 of her sons in the War. She is proud of every one of them, but of none more than of this very perfect gentleman."

WHITEHEAD, Harry, a very good bat for Leicestershire from 1898 to 1922, died on September 16, 1944, within three days of completing 69 years. If rather cramped in style, a symptom of weakness in many of his county colleagues, he was when set difficult to dismiss, as many bowlers discovered with some surprise. Statistics in Sir Home Gordon's *Form at a Glance* show that he averaged 23.07 for an aggregate of 15,112 runs— no mean figures for a man accustomed to face adversity with one of the least successful counties. As an opening batsman Whitehead earned considerable renown, notably in 1906 at Worcester, when he and C. J. B. Wood hit up 380, establishing for Leicestershire a first-wicket record still unbeaten, and making the way for their county's highest total, 701 for four wickets. In the return at Leicester he again excelled with 139 in a total of 382 which brought his county an innings victory—a six and 21 fours showed that he could punish bowlers when master of the situation. But he was apt to fail, and in that season he totalled no more than 776, average 26.75. Three times in a season his aggregate reached four figures, the highest being 1,116, average 29.36, in 1913, when he was 38 years of age. In 1919, when County Cricket was resumed, he played comparatively little but showed consistent form with an average of 35.50 for 426 runs.

WHITEHEAD, James George, died at Mowbray, Cape Town, on January 23, 1940, aged 63. He bowled fast-medium left-hand for Western Province from 1904 to 1921, except just before the First World War, when he played for Griqualand West. In all first-class matches he took 118 wickets at an average cost of 18.88.

WHITEHEAD, Lees, at one time a member of the Yorkshire XI, died of pneumonia on November 22, 1913, at West Hartlepool. Born on March 14, 1864, he was in his 50th year. When he came out for Yorkshire in 1889, Whitehead showed considerable promise as a fast bowler, taking 52 wickets for the county that season in all matches. However, he did not improve on his early performances, and though associated with Yorkshire for a number of years, he could only be described as a useful cricketer. He often travelled with the team as 12th man—a thankless position. It is likely that if connected with a weaker county than Yorkshire, Whitehead would have taken a higher place in the cricket world. He was not quite good enough for the brilliant company in which he found himself; still he was always a capable bat and bowler.

WHITEHEAD, Stephen James, who was born at Enfield, in Middlesex, on September 3, 1862, died at Small Heath, Birmingham, on June 9, 1904, the day following the conclusion of the match at Edgbaston between Warwickshire and Essex, the proceeds of which had been set apart as a benefit for Richards and himself. So sudden and unexpected was his death that he visited the ground during the match, apparently in his usual health. He played for Warwickshire, and in all first-class matches in 1894 obtained 73 wickets at a cost of 17.13 runs each. At various times during his career he fulfilled engagements at Oxford, Malvern, and Rugby.

WHITEHOUSE, Lieut. Peter Michael William, of the 13th Frontier Force, I.A., was killed in November, 1943, aged 26. For Marlborough from 1933 to 1935 he showed good all-round form, though used mostly for his right-hand medium-pace bowling, his action and length being admirable. He started at Oxford in 1936 with not out scores of 50 and 91 in the only innings he played for the University, but did not get his Blue until 1938, when he made 36 and 26 not out against Cambridge, his second display helping to avoid defeat. He averaged nearly 38, with a top score of 72, and took 21 wickets in this his last season for Oxford, and played a little for Kent without revealing his form.

WHITESIDE, John Parkinson, wicket-keeper for Leicestershire from 1894 to 1905, died on March 8, 1946, at his home at Leicester aged 84. After playing a little for Lancashire, he qualified for Leicestershire when a member of the M.C.C. staff, which he joined in 1889, and was with the Midland county when raised to the first class in 1894. Although small and rather frail, he was particularly good in taking Woodcock, who bowled very fast, usually round the wicket. In 1901 at Leicester he stumped the first four Essex batsmen to be dismissed; these successes were off Geeson, a slow bowler who turned the ball a lot. A moderate batsman, Whiteside's average never amounted to 12, but in the home match with Warwickshire in 1896 he held out and made five runs while Woodcock, 46, enjoyed the chief share in obtaining the 47 runs wanted to win when they, the last pair, came together. He received a benefit at Lord's, where he was very popular.

WHITESIDES, Thomas, who died at Hobart in the first week of October, 1919, aged 84, was formerly a well-known figure in Tasmanian cricket. It was on his proposal, on February 1, 1866, that the Southern Tasmanian Cricket Association was formed, and he was elected hon. secretary and, later, hon. treasurer of the body. He played for the old Derwent Club, and in February, 1862, played an innings of 50 for XXII of Tasmania against the England team taken out by H. H. Stephenson. He represented Tasmania several times and kept up his cricket until about 1886–87.

WHITFELD, Herbert, who was born at Lewes on November 25, 1858, died at Chailey on May 6, 1909. *Scores and Biographies* (xiii 598) says of him: "Possesses an excellent style with good defence and power of hitting, and has already (1877) made some capital scores. He is a right-handed batsman, but bowls left round-armed middle-paced, and fields generally at long-slip." He was in the Eton XI in 1875 and two following years, being captain in his last. In the matches with Harrow and Winchester he made the following scores:

Year	v. Harrow	v. Winchester
1875	6*	18
1876	15	13
1877	63* and 19*	65

Signifies not out.

He also took five wickets in the six matches for 73 runs. Proceeding to Cambridge, he at once gained his Blue, and played against Oxford four times, being on the winning side on three occasions: in the four games he scored 122 runs with an average of 17.42. Between 1878 and 1885 he played for Sussex, and, with 80 against Yorkshire at Brighton in 1884 as his highest score, made 1,411 runs with an average of 21.37. During 1884, when he captained the side, Sussex won nine of their 16 engagements and drew two. In 1881 he appeared in James Lillywhite's benefit match at Brighton between Gentlemen and Players which, after being a tie on the first innings, was won by the Players by one run. Mr. Whitfeld had been a member of the M.C.C. since 1878 and also belonged to I Zingari. His brother, Mr. F.D. Whitfeld, played for Sussex in 1878 and a nephew, Mr. G.A. Whitfeld, in 1908. Mr. Herbert Whitfeld was an all-round athlete, and appeared for Cambridge in the mile race, at Association Football, and (with the Hon. Ivo Blythe) in the tennis doubles.

WHITFIELD, H.E.P., for some years a prominent player with South Australia, died from blood poisoning on January 14, 1937, aged 33, six days after he had captained East Torrens against Sturt. He played twice for South Australia against A.P.F. Chapman's team, but did little. In the following season he scored 68 and 20 for J. Ryder's team against W.M. Woodfull's XI and his batting form gave promise of a visit to England, but his fast-medium bowling, delivered from a good height, met with only moderate success. Business limited his appearances in first-class cricket and his highest score for his State was 91 in an aggregate of 977 runs spread over several seasons; average 24; his 57 wickets cost 36 runs apiece.

WHITING, Charles Percival, who died suddenly on January 14, 1959, aged 70, played as a fast bowler in a few matches for Yorkshire between 1914 and 1920.

WHITINGTON, Richard Smallpiece, who died in Sydney on March 13, 1984, aged 71, was a Sheffield Shield cricketer for South Australia before becoming a prolific producer of cricket books. In England he may be best remembered as Captain R.S. Whitington, a member of A.L. Hassett's Australian team that met "England" in the Victory "Tests" of 1945, his opening partner being Flight Sergeant J.A. Workman. "Whitington, often troubled by hay fever, displayed a beautiful square cut and hooked well", wrote *Wisden*. He was not, however, a naturally attacking batsman. When Hassett's same team played a series of matches in India, on their way home to Australia, Whitington scored 155 in the Representative match in Calcutta. For South Australia he made three Sheffield Shield hundreds and scored 1,728 runs at 30.86. Of his 20 cricket books, several were written in conjunction with K.R. Miller, with whom he had played in the Victory "Tests". He also wrote biographies of W.J. O'Reilly, Ray Lindwall, Lindsay Hassett, Victor Richardson and Miller himself, and he assembled the distinguished *Illustrated History of Australian Cricket*. Poker-faced and peripatetic, he was as likely to turn up at a Test match in Johannesburg as in Melbourne, and he was internationally read as a journalist as well as in his many books.

WHITRIDGE, William Oswald, who died in Adelaide on February 12, 1919, aged 65, was a very successful bowler with the Norwood C.C. of South Australia. He appeared for his State in the first match arranged (against odds) with Victoria, the latter winning by 15 runs. In a game between the same sides in 1875 – 76 his analyses were eight for 10 and three for 14, the Victorians being dismissed for 29. He edited three issues of the *South Australian Cricketers' Guide*, and one year was President of the Australian Cricket Council.

WHITTAKER, David, a player well known in cricket circles in Lancashire, was found drowned in the canal at Rishdon, on December 17, 1901. He appeared on a few occasions for Lancashire, and was a useful left-handed bat and bowler. He played 10 years for Rishdon, seven years for Enfield, and seven years for Ramsbottom. At the time of his death he was 45.

WHITTINGTON, Thomas Aubrey L., died on July 17, 1944, aged 63. A very good bat, he headed the Glamorgan averages with 44.23 in 1908, and in 1911 did still better with 45.88, while his consistent form was shown in 1910 when he scored most runs for the county, 600, and averaged 42.85. When Glamorgan received first-class status in 1921, Whittington found run-getting less easy, but he captained the side for two seasons before being succeeded in 1924 by Mr. J. C. Clay. Prior to 1915 Mr. Whittington acted as hon. secretary for several years.

WHITTY, William James, who died on January 30, 1974, aged 87, was the last surviving member of the Australian team who visited England under M. A. Noble in 1909. In that tour Whitty took 77 wickets for 20.42 runs each. He again visited England with S. E. Gregory's side of 1912, when his victims numbered 100 and cost 18.08 runs each.

In 14 Test matches against England and South Africa from 1909 to 1912, Whitty, a left-arm bowler above medium pace, obtained 65 wickets, average 21.12, his chief performance being the dismissal of six batsmen for 17 runs at Melbourne in 1910–11 when South Africa, facing the task of scoring 170 to win, were disposed of for 80. In all first-class cricket he took 525 wickets, 154 of them for 32.64 runs apiece in 37 Sheffield Shield appearances for South Australia. He was previously with New South Wales for one season.

WHITWELL, Joseph Fry, born on February 22, 1869, at Saltburn-on-Sea, Yorkshire, died on November 6, 1932, aged 63. Educated at Uppingham School, where he was a member of the XI from 1883 to 1887 and captain in his last year, he proved himself to be a good bat and an excellent medium-paced bowler. He appeared for Yorkshire in two matches in 1890 but then threw in his lot with Durham and when this county carried off the Second-Class Championship honours in 1901, acted as captain of that unbeaten team and headed the batting statistics with an average of 35.

WHITWELL, William Fry, died in April, 1942, aged 74. During four seasons in the Uppingham XI he was useful both with bat and ball. When captain in 1886, he went in first, and a year later he made 181 for Redcar against Middlesbrough in the Cleveland Cup final tie. Born at Saltburn-on-Sea, he played in 10 matches for Yorkshire in 1890, scoring

few runs but taking 25 wickets at 20.72 runs apiece. Most of his County Cricket was for Durham, and his fast bowling often proved devastating. In a 12-a-side match against I Zingari he took 16 wickets for Gentlemen of Durham; against Warwickshire in 1891 at Stockton-on-Tees his figures showed 12 wickets for 55 runs, and in 1895 at Sunderland eight Lincolnshire batsmen fell to him for 18 runs. In 1900 he took part in the Gentlemen and Players match at Scarborough. He toured America with Lord Hawke's team in 1894, and in the match against Philadelphia at Havenford his first innings analysis read four wickets for 14, and he headed the bowling averages for the tour with 18 at 6.12. Above medium height and strongly built, he put much energy into his attack and fielded with dash at cover-point or mid-off.

WHYSALL, William Wilfred, who had reached the height of his fame last season, died in hospital at Nottingham on November 11, 1930. About a fortnight earlier he had fallen on a dance floor and injured his elbow. Septicaemia set in and, although a blood transfusion was performed, he passed away. Born at Woodborough, Nottinghamshire, on October 31, 1887, he was only 43 years of age at the time of his death. He matured slowly as a cricketer, and not until 1908 was he invited to join the ground staff at Trent Bridge. Two seasons later he made 140 for Notts Second XI, at Trent Bridge against Staffordshire, who had Sydney Barnes to bowl for them. While a useful wicket-keeper, he played for the county as a batsman and, though first tried for Nottinghamshire in 1910, he did not realise expectations until 10 years later when, after the long break due to the War, he resumed his place in the side. From that time he forged ahead rapidly until he became the most reliable batsman in the XI, a position he held unchallenged last summer when he headed the averages with 47.84 for an aggregate of 1,866. During five consecutive summers he had an aggregate of over 2,000 runs in first-class matches and in 1929 he made 2,716 runs. Whysall possessed unlimited patience and a defence most difficult to penetrate. He could bring off all the strokes known to a modern batsman, and, when really set, his pulling and off-driving were very sure. During the summer of 1921 Whysall became the recognised opening batsman with George Gunn and, altogether, the pair took part in 40 first-wicket three-figure stands for the county. He was a capable catch in the slips. On the strength of his ability as a wicket-keeper as well as a batsman, he secured a place as deputy to Strudwick in the M.C.C. team that toured Australia under the captaincy of A.E.R. Gilligan in the winter of 1924–25, but it was for his batting that he played in three of the Test matches, scoring 186 runs with an average of 37.20. When England lost the third Test match by 11 runs, he was the highest scorer with 75 in the great effort to gain victory. His form, although always consistent, did not earn him a place in another Test match until last August, when at the Oval he had the disappointing experience of being dismissed for 13 and 10 in the prolonged struggle which resulted in Australia recovering the Ashes. He was accorded a benefit in 1926, when Yorkshire visited Trent Bridge. In all first-class matches he scored 51 centuries, eight of them last season, with 248 against Northamptonshire as his highest. In four consecutive matches for his county in 1924, he scored 61 and 150 not out v. Hampshire, seven and 138 v. Northamptonshire, 151 and 23 not out v. Kent, and 131 v. Worcestershire, while last year four of his hundreds were made in successive innings.

WICKHAM, Prebendary Archdale Palmer, died on October 13, 1935, aged 79, having been born on November 5, 1855, at Holmwood in Surrey. When playing for Marlborough against Rugby at Lord's in 1873 he went in first, but A.J. Webbe gave him his Blue at Oxford as wicket-keeper in the 1878 XI. During a long period as priest at Norwich and in Suffolk he played for Norfolk, while after becoming Vicar of Martlock he played for Somerset from 1891, being one of several capable wicket-keepers who appeared for the county. His figure behind the stumps with feet wide apart, legs straight, hands on his brown pads and wearing a Harlequin cap, lives in the memory as a notable figure of the Taunton ground when S.M.J. Woods captained a very strong Somerset XI. In his University match at Lord's, which the particularly powerful Cambridge XI, captained by the Hon. Edward Lyttelton, won by 238 runs, he caught such noted batsmen as A.P. Lucas and the Hon. Ivo Bligh, who brought back the Ashes from Australia and afterwards became the eighth Lord Darnley and President of M.C.C. A.G. Steel took 13 wickets for 73 runs in the match and scored 44 not out in the Cambridge first innings. Mr. Wickham never tired of relating one remarkable experience. He kept wicket at Bristol in May, 1895, for Somerset against Gloucestershire, when W.G. Grace in scoring 288—his 100th century—allowed only four balls to pass his bat. In the innings of 474, Wickham conceded only four byes.

WIDDOWSON, Sam Weller, born at Hucknall Torkard on April 16, 1851, died at Beeston on May 9, 1927, aged 76. *Scores and Biographies* said of him: "An average batsman, a fast round-armed bowler, and fields in no particular place." He appeared for Nottinghamshire in two matches in 1878. A well-known athlete, he was appointed in 1873 as captain of the Nottingham Forest Football Club, and he played against Scotland at Hampden Park in March, 1880.

WIGGINTON, Searson Harry, who died in Bulawayo on September 15, 1977, aged 68, played for Leicestershire from 1930 to 1934. Educated at Wyggeston School, he was by 1934 showing distinct promise as a bat and in August that year made 120 not out against Worcestershire at Leicester, his only century for the county. At the end of the season he left them for a job at Paisley and then, after being for a time coach at Taunton School, went in 1947–48 to be coach to the Rhodesian Cricket Association.

WILCOX, Denys R., who died at Westcliff-on-Sea on February 6, 1953, aged 42, formerly captained Dulwich, Cambridge University and Essex. A prominent all-rounder for Dulwich from 1926 to 1929, he headed the batting averages in the last three years, and in 1929, when scoring 1,025 runs, average 64.06, obtained a record aggregate for the school. A stylish right-hand batsman, he first appeared for Essex in 1928, two years before going to Cambridge, where he gained a Blue in three seasons from 1931, being captain in 1933. In the 1932 match with Oxford he hit 157, the highest innings of his career.

His duties as headmaster of a preparatory school, which numbered among its pupils T.E. Bailey, the Essex and England all-rounder, limited his opportunities for taking part in first-class cricket when he went down from the University, but he became joint captain of Essex from 1933 to 1939. His biggest score for the county was 134 against Warwickshire at Southend in 1946, when he and R.M. Taylor put on 263—a record for the eighth Essex wicket. In 1937, when making 1,250 runs, average 46.40, he hit 104 and 129 in the match with Kent at Chalkwell Park. In all first-class matches he scored 8,392 runs. When his first-class career ended he did much to assist in the Essex coaching scheme.

WILD, Frederick, the well-known Notts cricketer, died in February, 1893. Wild was born on August 28, 1847, and was thus in his 46th year at the time of his death. He first gained a place in the Notts XI in the year 1868, and played regularly for the county down to the end of the season of 1879. Very little was seen of him in Nottingham matches in 1880, but his services were called into frequent requisition during the schism of 1881. With that season his career as a county cricketer closed, but he retained his position on the ground staff at Lord's as long as he lived. At his best, Wild was certainly a first-class batsman, and he would probably have enjoyed still greater success than he did if the death of Biddulph had not compelled him to become wicket-keeper to the Notts XI. The injuries to his hands that he was constantly sustaining handicapped him considerably in batting. He was in particularly good form about 1872, during which season he played an innings of 104 for Notts against Gloucestershire at Trent Bridge. This was the first 100 ever scored for Notts at Nottingham, but, curiously enough, Selby, in the same innings, made 128 not out. A collection was made for the two players, Selby receiving £17 and Wild £13. Another fine performance of Wild's was in the M.C.C. and Cambridge University Match at Lord's in 1877, when he largely helped to win the game for the club by scoring in the last innings 104 not out. Wild was, perhaps, never a first-rate wicket-keeper, but in his match between the M.C.C. and Cambridge he did an extraordinary piece of work which is constantly referred to in the Pavilion at Lord's, stumping Alfred Lyttelton in the most brilliant fashion on the leg side from W. N. Powys's fast bowling. It is also worthy of note that he was a member of the Marylebone Club team in the memorable game with the Australians, on May 27, 1878, which ended in one day, and established the reputation of Australian cricket in England.

WILD, Harold, a right-hand batsman and bowler, died at Glossop on August 8, 1977, aged 86, having been born at Hatfield on February 3, 1891. He joined the Derbyshire staff in 1913 and played in 32 matches up to the end of the 1920 season. His highest score was 68 against Warwickshire at Edgbaston in 1919.

WILKIE, Daniel, born in Melbourne, December 1, 1843, died about June, 1917. One of the most genial of men. Slow underhand bowler. Captain of the Melbourne University XI. Made the first 100 ever hit for the East Melbourne C.C. Captain of East Melbourne 1861–75. Played for Victoria v. New South Wales. For Victoria v. Sixteen of Tasmania, at Launceston, 1865–66, his analyses were seven wickets for 15 runs and 11 for 12— altogether 18 for 27. Later played for the St. Kilda C.C. He was the best known of four cricketing brothers.

WILKINSON, Anthony John Anstruther, who was born at Mount Oswald, Durham, on May 28, 1836, died on December 11, 1905. He was educated at Shrewsbury and Cambridge, but never played in the University XI, although he afterwards assisted both Middlesex and Yorkshire. He possessed splendid defence, and, without making any very large scores, often rendered his side great service by wearing down the bowling. In the match between Cambridge University and the Gentlemen of England, at Cambridge, in 1871, though he only scored 19, he stayed in with Mr. W. G. Grace, while 103 runs were made for the Gentlemen's first wicket. In 1867 he scored 75 not out for M.C.C. and Ground v. Surrey, at the Oval, while in a representative match his highest innings was 62 for Gentlemen of the South v. Gentlemen of the North, at Nottingham, in 1862. Among other good scores he made may be mentioned 94 for Gentlemen of Yorkshire v. M.C.C. at Lord's, 84 not out for Gentlemen of Middlesex v. Gentlemen of England at Islington, and 59 for Middlesex v. Lancashire at Manchester, all in 1865; and 53 for Yorkshire v. Surrey at the Oval, in 1867. In 1865 he assisted the Gentlemen against the Players at the Oval. As a very slow round-armed bowler he often proved successful.

WILKINSON, Cyril Theodore Anstruther, who died on December 16, 1970, aged 86, was in the Blundell's School XI before he played for Surrey between 1909 and 1920. He captained the county when they won the Championship in 1914 and again in the first two seasons following the First World War, in which he saw military service. *Wisden* said of him in 1914: "He proved himself a real leader, keeping the side under firm control and managing the bowling with sound judgement." He scored in all first-class matches 1,173 runs, average 25.32, his highest innings being 135 in less than two hours against Middlesex at the Oval and, as an occasional bowler, took 23 wickets for 31.47 runs each. A great club cricketer, he turned out every

August in the Sidmouth XI for whom, in 1953 at the age of 69, he hit 50 and took all 10 wickets against the Nondescripts. As a hockey player, he represented England, whom he captained, and appeared for Great Britain in the 1920 Olympic Games. He was Registrar of the Probate and Divorce Registry from 1936 to 1959.

WILKINSON, Col. William Alexander Camac, D.S.O., M.C., G.M., who died at Storrington on September 19, 1983, aged 90, was a soldier of great gallantry in two wars and a cricketer who overcame a serious handicap to become one of the most consistent batsmen of his day in a high class of club cricket and indeed, when the opportunity offered, in first-class cricket. A legendary character whose outspokenness knew no close season, he was no respecter of persons; yet he is seldom mentioned by anyone who knew him without genuine affection. Leaving Eton too young to have been in the XI and finishing his school education in Australia, where his father, an old Middlesex cricketer, was in practice as a doctor, he went up to Oxford and got his Blue in his third year, 1913, largely on the strength of an innings of 129 in an hour and a half against M.C.C. in which, *Wisden* says, "he hit with delightful freedom all round the wicket." In 1914 he had a poor season and lost his place. He had also represented Oxford twice in the hurdles. In the War he was shot through the right hand and narrowly avoided amputation. As it was, though he could put his hand on the bat it had little strength. His beautiful cutting, however, remained as much a feature of his play as his skill on the leg. Despite his handicap he was not a slow scorer. Almost as remarkable as his batting was his fielding. Though much of the work on his right side had to be done back-handed by his left hand, he was never reckoned a liability in the field.

For years he was a regular member of the Army side, which he often captained, and most of his other cricket was played by the Household Brigade, Eton Ramblers, I Zingari, Harlequins, Free Foresters and other clubs. He never played for a first-class county, though he appeared for Sussex XI before the First World War, but he was constantly to be found in first-class matches for M.C.C. or Free Foresters and played too in the Folkestone Festival and for the Gentlemen at the Oval. His scoring in these matches right up to 1939 suggested that he would not have been out of place in County Cricket. More solid evidence was provided when he went as a member of A. C. MacLaren's side to Australia and New Zealand in 1922–23. On this tour he scored 689 runs with an average of 28.70, his highest score being 102 against Canterbury. On this occasion he added 282 with A. P. F. Chapman in two and a quarter hours. Even after the Second World War he continued to make runs in club cricket and he himself believed that the century which he made in his last innings was the 100th of his career. In any case it was a fitting finale to the career of a brave and determined man.

WILKINSON, Dr. W. C., who died early in 1946, played for Middlesex occasionally in 1881, when he headed both sets of averages, and in 1882.

WILKINSON, William Herbert, who died on June 6, 1961, aged 80, played as a left-handed batsman for Yorkshire from 1905 to 1910. His best season was that of 1908 when, as the most consistent of the county's batsmen, he scored 1,282 runs, average 28.48, and helped Yorkshire to win the County Championship without suffering defeat. Though he hit only one first-class century, 103 against Sussex at Sheffield in 1909, he twice narrowly missed the distinction, reaching 99 at Leicester in 1908 and 95 not out at Nottingham in 1910. From 1910 to 1953, when he retired, he was professional with Mitchell and Butlers of Birmingham.

WILLES, The Rev. E. H. L., died on September 9, 1896. Mr. Willes was in the Winchester XI in 1848, and in the Oxford XI in 1852, 1853, and 1854. On some few occasions also he played for Kent. He is described as having been a free bat, a useful fast bowler, and a good field. His connection with first-class cricket ceased when he went into the Church.

WILLIAMS, Arnold Butler, born at Swansea, Glamorgan, on January 6, 1870, died at Wellington, N.Z., on August 20, 1929, aged 59. He went to New Zealand in 1881 and learned his cricket at Otago High School. At first a very steady bat, he developed into a good hitter, and he was also a brilliant wicket-keeper. His later cricket of note was played for Wellington, for whom he scored 163 v. Canterbury in 1896–97 and 100 v. M.C.C. in 1906–07. At Christchurch in 1896 he made 73 in his second innings for Fifteen of New Zealand v. the Australians— probably the most meritorious display of his career. At Wellington in February, 1898, he made two separate 100s in one game, 114 and 105, for Midland against Wellington.

WILLIAMS, Benjamin Huntsman, was killed in Rhodesia on August 3, 1978, when the vehicle in which he was travelling came under a rocket attack from terrorists. He is the first first-class cricketer to have lost his life in the present conflict. Huntsman Williams, a left-arm fast-medium bowler, won Rhodesian Nuffield and South African Schools' Caps in 1961 and 1962 and, while still a schoolboy, played for Rhodesian Country Districts against the visiting New Zealand team in 1961–62, taking four wickets for 89 in the first innings. He made his first-class debut in 1966–67 and was a regular member of the Rhodesian team in 1969–70 when he took four wickets for 56 against Transvaal in Salisbury, his best analysis. Thereafter he played no more. His total career covered eight first-class matches. Born in Bulawayo on June 10, 1944, he was 34.

WILLIAMS, Lieut.-Col. Dyson Brock, who died in London on April 18, 1922, aged 40, appeared on a few occasions for Glamorganshire.

WILLIAMS, Herbert Reginald Hewett, D.S.O., who died on November 4, 1974, aged 74, was in the Charterhouse XI in 1917 and 1918 and kept wicket a number of times for Essex in 1919 and 1920.

WILLIAMS, Col. Leoline, D.S.O., O.B.E., died on February 29, 1984, aged 83. Never in the XI at Winchester, he played for Sussex from 1919 to 1930, but only in 1926 and in 1930, when he was second in their batting averages, could he find time for more than an occasional game. Meanwhile in 1922 he had appeared under a birth qualification for Gloucestershire. In County Cricket his highest score was 106 not out for Sussex against Essex at Southend in 1926, but he also made two centuries for the Army, both against the RAF at the Oval; 107 in 1930 and 103 in 1931. An attractive bat, who could also keep wicket adequately if required, in all first-class cricket he scored 1,440 runs with an average of 22.86. His brother, P. V. Williams, also played for Sussex and the Army.

WILLIAMS, Lewis Erskine Wyndham, who died on April 24, 1974, aged 73, was in the Oratory School XI before playing for Glamorgan in a few matches from 1928 to 1930. "Tip" Williams will best be remembered in Welsh club cricket circles as joint founder in 1926 of the South Wales Hunts C.C., of which he was captain, chairman and, last year, president.

WILLIAMS, The Rev. P. (Winchester, Oxford University, and Nottinghamshire) died on November 18, 1899. Played for Winchester, at Lord's, in the Public School matches of 1840, 1841, and 1842, his highest scores being 28 not out v. Harrow in 1842, and 22 v. Eton in 1841. Also assisted Oxford v. Cambridge in 1844, 1845, 1846, and 1847. Also played for Nottinghamshire.

WILLIAMS, Richard Harry, died in December 1982, aged 81. A left-hander who often went in first, he played for Worcestershire from 1923 to 1932. A record of 713 runs with an average of 11.14 does not look much, but he played some useful innings. The highest, 81 against Nottinghamshire at Trent Bridge in 1926, was made largely off change bowlers when the match was dead, but in the corresponding match the year before he had scored 56 going in first, the highest score in a total of 161, and in 1928 against Yorkshire at Worcester he made 76 not out. True, the total was 402, but there were no easy runs in those days against the Yorkshire bowling.

WILLIAMS, Robert Graham, M.B.E., who died in Adelaide on August 31, 1978, aged 67, was a member of the strong Australian Services team which, in the course of the 1945 English season—and particularly the Victory Tests against England—played an important part in bringing back such immediate and enthusiastic interest in first-class cricket after the Second World War. Although just repatriated, and showing the effects of four and a half years as a prisoner of war in German hands, Williams immediately impressed in the first Test with a hard-hit 53, including 11 fours, and two early wickets with the smooth fast-medium bowling that gained him 53 wickets in Australian first-class cricket. A prominent playing member of Adelaide's East Torrens club, he topped the South Australian grade figures in 1936–37 with a bowling average of 8.95, the best since pre-First World War days. During his incarceration, which followed his aircraft being shot down in North Africa in 1941, Williams devoted much time and patience to teaching over 30 blind or partially blind prisoners braille and touch typing, for which he was awarded his M.B.E. He played little after the War, when he built up important business associations within the Australian wool industry.

WILLIAMS, ROBERT JAMES, who died of a heart attack in Durban on May 14, 1984, aged 72, was a notable all-round sportsman who had a Springbok rugby trial besides touring England in 1935 as second wicket-keeper with H. F. Wade's successful South African side. Although he never played in a Test match, he was a fairly regular member of the Natal side between 1930 and 1950, catching 76 batsmen and stumping 56. His early schooling was in England, where he accepted, for a while, a business appointment after the 1935 tour.

WILLIAMS, William, who died at his home at Hampton Wick on April 14, 1951, aged 90, was a fine all-round sportsman. Born on April 12, 1860, he was a member of M.C.C. from 1900. In the seasons of 1885 and 1886 he appeared as wicket-keeper for Middlesex, and after an absence of 14 years returned to the county side as a bowler of leg-breaks, playing occasionally until 1905. During the winter of 1896–97 he toured the West Indies with Mr. Arthur Priestley's team and, with 67 wickets at an average cost of 9.62, finished second in the bowling averages to A. E. Stoddart. He often assisted M.C.C. and was credited with taking 100 or more wickets in a season in all matches for 55 years. In his last summer as a player, he turned out at the age of 74 for M.C.C. against the House of Lords and, after dismissing Lord Dalkeith, Lord Tennyson and Major L. George for 16 runs, was presented by the Marylebone Club with the ball. A good story is told of when, at the age of 65, he visited the West Indies during the tour of the Hon. F. S. G. Calthorpe's M.C.C. team in 1925–26. In Georgetown he challenged a West Indian friend against whom he played 30 years before to a single-wicket match for £25 a side. Winning the toss, Williams severely punished his opponent's bowling, completed a century and declared. Then, with a googly, he bowled his exhausted victim first ball.

Apart from his cricket, "Billy" Williams, as he was known to everyone for many years, was celebrated as the man who, in the early part of the century when a member of the Middlesex County Rugby Union Committee, ended a long search for a suitable site for a National Rugby Union ground by discovering a cabbage field of 10 acres which has since developed into the famous Twickenham enclosure. For a long time the ground, later extended to 18 acres, was known to Rugby football as "Billy Williams's cabbage patch." Formerly a player for the Harlequins R.F.C., he was a Rugby referee

for 21 years. An hon. member of the Wimbledon Park Golf Club, he played a daily round until his last illness, and was a regular attendant at Lord's and at Rugby matches in the London area, particularly Richmond.

WILLINGDON, The Marquess of, P.C., G.C.S.I., G.C.M.G., G.C.I.E., G.B.E., formerly Mr. Freeman-Thomas, who died on August 12, 1941, aged 74, played in the Eton XI three seasons, being captain in 1885. Going up to Cambridge, he obtained his Blue as a Freshman and played against Oxford four times. He did nothing of note in either the big school games or the University matches at Lord's, but at Cambridge in 1887 he scored a brilliant 114 against Yorkshire at Fenner's and headed the University averages with 40.2. From 1886 to 1890 he appeared occasionally for Sussex, and in 20 county matches he made 738 runs with an average of nearly 20. He adopted the surname of Freeman-Thomas in 1892 and so became Mr. Freeman Freeman-Thomas before entering Parliament as member for Hastings. As Governor of Bombay and of Madras, he did much to further the interests of cricket in India before being appointed Viceroy. In 1924 he was raised to the Peerage.

WILLIS, Carl Bleackley, born on March 23, 1893, at Daylesford, died on May 11, 1930, aged 37. Educated at Wesley College, Melbourne, and Melbourne University, playing in the XI of both, he was a stylish bat and a very good outfield. As a member of the A.I.F. team of 1919 he was very successful, making four hundreds in scoring 1,652 runs in first-class matches with an average of 41 and being first among those who played regularly. His most meritorious innings was doubtless his 96 v. An England XI at Scarborough. His highest scores were 156 not out v. Leicestershire, when he and C. E. Pellew added 261 for the fifth wicket, 129 not out v. Worcestershire when, with Pellew again as partner, he helped to put on 301 (unseparated) for the fifth wicket in two hours and 40 minutes, 130 v. Notts, when he and Oldfield added 169 for the ninth, and 127 v. Sussex. For the same team during its visit to South Africa he made 94 v. Western Province. His first big success was to play an innings of 168 for Victorian Colts against New South Wales Colts at Melbourne in 1912–13, and later he made 111 for A.I.F. v. Victoria in 1919–20, 133 for the Rest v. The Australian Team at Sydney in 1921–22, and 100 for Victoria v. New South Wales, also at Sydney, in 1924–25. During the tour of the Victorian team in

New Zealand in 1924–25 he scored 104 against Canterbury at Christchurch.

WILLIS, Henry, who was born on March 17, 1841, and died at Horton Lodge, Epsom, on September 29, 1926, aged 85, played for Surrey v. Yorkshire, at the Oval in 1868. For some years he captained the Epsom XI.

WILLS, Arnold Cass Lycett, died on February 28, 1978, aged 71. A member of the Harrow XI in 1925, when he was second in both the batting and the bowling averages, he did not get a trial at Cambridge, but between 1926 and 1929 played several valuable innings for Northamptonshire. In his first match v. Leicestershire at Northampton, coming in at 75 for six, he made 47 and helped Judd to add 110. Next year his innings of 68 contributed largely to his county beating the first New Zealand touring side.

WILLS, Sidney George, who died at Bristol on October 7, 1977, aged 76, was picked as a batsman for Gloucestershire against Kent at Bristol in 1927, but the match was abandoned without a ball being bowled.

WILMOT, William, who died on May 19, 1957, aged 84, played occasionally for Derbyshire between 1897 and 1901. An excellent wicket-keeper, he was unfortunate to be contemporary with W. Storer and J. Humphries.

WILSON, A. Cracroft, who played for Canterbury against Otago as far back as 1864— the first occasion upon which the two provinces met—died in Christchurch, N.Z., in the middle of January 1911.

WILSON, Arthur Keith, who died at his home on November 8, 1977, aged 83, played for Sussex from 1914 to 1934. A member of the Brighton College XI in 1911, in his first innings for the county he made 78 not out v. Northamptonshire; in his last match, after an absence of nine years from the side, he scored 69 v. Kent. In 1919 he made his only century, 134 v. Northamptonshire. A good bat and an especially skilful cutter, he took hundreds of wickets in minor cricket with slow flighted leg-breaks, which were particularly formidable to schoolboys. Indeed, one cricket master installed a bowling machine specifically to teach his pupils to play Keith Wilson. For a time he was Chairman of the County C.C. and during the Second World War did wonderful work in keeping cricket going on the county ground.

WILSON, Benjamin B., who died on September 17, 1957, aged 77, played as opening batsman for Yorkshire between 1906 and 1914 and later coached at St. Peter's School, York, and at Harrow. During his first-class career he scored 6,454 runs, including 15 centuries, for an average of 27.69. His highest innings was 208 against Sussex at Bradford in 1914, when he put together an aggregate of 1,605 runs—his best—and altogether he exceeded 1,000 runs in a season five times. Yet, as illustrated by references to him in *Wisden* by that excellent judge Sydney H. Pardon, he rarely showed his real capabilities and this led to his services being dispensed with by the county following the First World War. Of him in 1909 Mr. Pardon wrote: "Playing in excellent style, he had everything in his favour, but for some reason that one is quite unable to explain, his success made him unduly cautious"; next year: "If he would only give free play to his natural ability, he might soon be first-rate"; and the following season: "Possessing every physical advantage, he is at his best a very fine hitter, but he is apt for no reason whatever to subside into laborious slowness. He ought by this time to have been Tunnicliffe's successor, but he cannot be considered as more than a partial success." Had Wilson given full rein to his natural skill in driving and cutting, he might well have earned himself a place among the great men of Yorkshire cricket.

WILSON, The Right Rev. Cecil, D.D., died on January 20, 1941, aged 80. After three years in the Tonbridge XI, being captain in 1879, he could not accept an offered Blue at Cambridge because of an engagement to travel abroad, but he proved himself a fine batsman for Kent. During the seasons 1882 to 1890 he played in 28 matches for the county with an average of 22.23. In the Canterbury Week of 1882 he excelled against the Australians. He stopped a bad collapse by helping E. F. S. Tylecote (100 not out) add 125 for the eighth wicket; when Kent followed-on 85 behind, he went in first and scored 50. He again did well at Canterbury in 1886, making 127 against Yorkshire, and with George Hearne (117) taking part in a third-wicket stand for 215. After Wilson's dismissal the last seven wickets fell to Emmett and Bates for 31 runs. Yet Kent won by six wickets—so completing a most successful Festival, for they had beaten the Australians in the Bank Holiday match by 10 wickets. Standing 5ft. 11in. tall, Cecil Wilson drove hard and scored rapidly when set. He could field anywhere and earned a reputation for fast, accurate returns to the wicket-keeper. His elder brother, Leslie Wilson, played for Kent from 1883 to 1897.

After important work with the Melanesian Mission, following service in the Church at Portsea, and Bournemouth, Dr. Wilson became Archdeacon of Adelaide, and in 1917 Bishop of Bunbury, Western Australia, where he retained office for 20 years before retiring.

WILSON, Charles Geldart, who died at Roseneath, Victoria, Australia, on June 28, 1952, aged 84, was for many years a prominent personality in New Zealand sport. Born at Ballarat, Victoria, "Gillie" Wilson played as an attractive, forceful batsman for Victoria, and in New Zealand appeared for Southland, Otaga, South Island and Wellington. In all cricket in New Zealand, where from 1902 he was manager of a business firm for many years, he scored 6,585 runs, average 30.48. At one time he was chairman of the Southland Cricket Association and President of the Southland Rugby Union.

WILSON, The Rev. Clement Eustace Macro, Prebendary of Bishopshull in Lichfield Cathedral, who died on February 8, 1944, aged 68, at Colverhall, Shropshire, of which he was Vicar, stood out supreme in the Uppingham XI some 50 years ago. After a moderate start in 1891, he profited so much from the supervision of H.H. Stephenson, most famous of coaches, that in 1893 he scored 722 runs, including 117, 145, and 183 not out consecutively. In the last effort against Repton he carried his bat through the innings. He averaged 90.25 that season and 44.2 when captain. He also headed the bowling averages in 1893. Gaining his Cambridge Blue as a Freshman, he finished four years in the XI as captain. He progressed in excellence, 35, 80, 77, and 115 being his best efforts in the four successive matches against Oxford at Lord's. It is interesting to recall that E. Rockley Wilson scored a hundred (118) in the 1901 University match, the only instance of two brothers accomplishing this for Cambridge, while H.K. Foster, with 121 in 1895, and R.E. Foster, 171 in 1900, set up a similar record for Oxford—all four innings being played in the course of seven years. From 1896 to 1899 Clem Wilson played a little for Yorkshire, averaging 25.60 for 10 completed innings, his best score being 91 not out against Kent at Canterbury in 1897, the highest innings in the match. The calls of Church prevented him continuing first-class

cricket. He toured South Africa with a team captained by Lord Hawke in the winter of 1898. Besides his ability as a batsman, Clem Wilson bowled medium pace and possessed the exceptional craft of being able to use with effect either arm. In 1895 at the Oval Abel and Holland mastered the Cambridge attack, and Wilson ended a stand of 306 for the third wicket by holding a return catch when bowling left-hand.

WILSON, Ernest Frederick, who died on March 3, 1981, aged 73, was one of several professional batsmen who might have made a name with other counties but were unable to secure a place in the tremendously strong pre-war Surrey batting sides. Having played an innings of 240 in three and a half hours for the Second XI against Devon at the Oval in 1928, he was given a trial for the county at Northampton and scored 99. Surrey declared at 530 for nine. The Northamptonshire bowling, never at that period strong (it was the first of three consecutive innings in which they fielded out to totals of over 500), was in the absence of Jupp, Thomas and Clark, so perhaps Wilson's success was not taken very seriously. At any rate, it was his only game for the side that season. In 1929 he had a good trial and scored 660 runs with an average of 25.42, his outstanding performance being 110 against Kent at Blackheath, the only century of his career, in the course of which he put on 154 in 95 minutes for the fifth wicket with P.G.H. Fender. Afforded another fair trial in 1930 he was disappointing and for the next few years appeared only spasmodically, playing occasionally a good innings but never really fulfilling his promise. Some had seen in him the successor to Sandham. He watched the ball well, had a good defence and scored mainly in front of the wicket. Perhaps his fielding did not help: he had a safe pair of hands, but was a slow mover. His last appearance was in 1936. In all matches for Surrey he made 2,516 runs with an average of 23.30.

WILSON, Evelyn Rockley, who died at Winchester on July 21, 1957, aged 78, was one of the best amateur slow right-arm bowlers of his time. Educated at Rugby, he was in the XI for three years from 1895, heading both batting and bowling figures when captain in 1897. With a highest innings of 206 not out, he averaged 51.11 in batting and he took 31 wickets for 14.93 runs each. Before he gained his Blue at Cambridge, whom he represented against Oxford in four matches from 1899 to 1902, he scored a century against his University for A. J. Webbe's XI. In the University match of 1901 he hit 118 and 27 and took five wickets for 71 runs and two for 38, and in that of 1902, when captain, he played a noteworthy part in victory by five wickets for the Light Blues by taking five wickets for 23 and three for 66.

He made a brief appearance for Yorkshire in 1899, but when, on going down from Cambridge, he became a master at Winchester, a position he held for 40 years, he preferred to engage in club cricket during the school holidays, his stated reason being that he preferred to play in three matches a week rather than two. He did, however, go to America with B. J. T. Bosanquet's side in 1901; with the team of English amateurs who visited the West Indies in 1902, when he stood first in the bowling averages with 78 wickets for less than 11 runs each, and with the M.C.C. to Argentina in 1912.

A suggestion that Wilson might use his residential qualification for Hampshire led to him being pressed into service once again by Yorkshire when over 40 years of age, but, whatever the reason, there could be no doubt as to his immense value to the county during the closing weeks of each season. In 1913 he made his only century for Yorkshire, 104 not out against Essex at Bradford, in the course of which he claimed to have hit the only six obtained by skying a ball directly over the wicket-keeper's head, but it was as a bowler that he achieved his best work. He met with such success in 1920 that he took 64 wickets for 13.84 runs apiece, being fourth in the English averages. This brought him a place in J. W. H. T. Douglas's M.C.C. team who, the following winter, toured Australia. Wilson played in his only Test match during that tour, of which *Wisden* of the time reported: "A good deal of friction was caused by cable messages sent home to the *Daily Express* by Mr. E. R. Wilson. This led to a resolution passed at the annual meeting of the Marylebone Club in May deprecating the reporting of matches by players concerned in them."

Among Wilson's best performances was that in the match with Middlesex at Bradford in 1922 when, in the second innings, he sent down 44 overs, 22 of them maidens, for 62 runs and six wickets. He and A. Waddington shared in a last wicket stand of 53 for Yorkshire, but all the same Middlesex won an exciting struggle by four runs. Wilson was the first bowler to perform the hat-trick for Gentlemen against Players, which he did at Scarborough in 1919. Altogether in first-class cricket he took 385 wickets, average 21.66,

and scored 3,033 runs, average 18.94.

Immaculate length and cleverly disguised variation of pace made Wilson difficult to punish. His own explanation of his success was typically whimsical. "I have always been a lucky bowler," he said, "as my best ball has been the ball which broke from the off when I meant to break from leg. I bowled far more of these as a man of 40 than as a young man." Another example of this slightly built, diffident cricketer's sense of humour was provided at the nets at Winchester when to a somewhat inept boy batsman he said: "My dear boy, you must hit one ball in the middle of your bat before you meet your Maker." He will always be remembered by the vast number of Wykehamists who enjoyed the benefit of his advice and of whom several gained cricket fame. His elder brother, C. E. M. Wilson, also captained Cambridge.

WILSON, Frederic Bonhote, who died on January 19, 1932, was born on September 21, 1881. In his younger days himself a wonderful natural player of any ball game, he devoted his life after leaving Cambridge to journalism, to which he brought not only an unsurpassed knowledge of his subjects but also a light and kindly touch. His counsel and advice to young players, generously and modestly offered, was that of the expert, and equally his opinion carried great weight with older and more experienced players.

His criticism, although ample, was always that of an open-hearted man, full of good fun and amazingly quick in perception. To him W. G. Grace, with whom he at one time played a great deal of cricket, was a hero and an inspiration, but that never prevented him from appreciating and enjoying modern worth. He had an old-world courtesy to his elders, knew to the finest point what was right and what was wrong, was as courageous as a lion, and withal was the jolliest, wittiest person for whom the heart of man could ask.

When a boy at Elstree, he at once made his mark as possessing an eye and a power of wrist well above the ordinary and, going on to Harrow, he did all that a boy could do to win credit for his school. He played in the cricket matches against Eton at Lord's in 1899 and 1900 and in both those years represented his school at racquets and fives. In the game with Eton in 1900, making 79 and 24, he contributed largely to Harrow's victory by one wicket. Going up to Cambridge he did little in 1902 but in the following season he scored seven and 42 against Oxford and in 1904, when captain, he made 46 and seven in the University match. He played for Cambridge at tennis in the Doubles in 1902 and 1903 and in the Singles in the latter year, while at racquets—the game at which he particularly excelled—he represented his University in the Singles in 1903 and the Doubles in both 1902 and 1903. After coming down from Cambridge he kept up his cricket for a time with the London County Club at the Crystal Palace where he developed his greatest friendship with W. G. Grace. On the outbreak of war he joined the R.N.V.R. and later on, when holding a commission in the Royal Fusiliers, was wounded. Associated in his earliest days, as a journalist, with the *Daily Mirror* he reported games in a racy style of his own and after the war was identified with *The Times* for which it was his legitimate pride that he contributed accounts of no fewer than 20 different kinds of games.

WILSON, Geoffrey, who died on November 29, 1960, aged 65, captained Yorkshire from 1922 to 1924. He was in the Harrow XI for three years from 1912 to 1914, enjoying special success in the match with Eton at Lord's in 1913 when he played a splendid innings of 173. After taking two and a half hours to reach 50, he hit so brilliantly all round the wicket that he added a further 123 runs in just over 90 minutes. In the big match next year he made 65 and 58. After serving with the Royal Marine Artillery in the First World War, he went to Cambridge, where he received a Blue in 1919. In that season he made his debut for Yorkshire. Though he rarely achieved much in batting for the county, Yorkshire carried off the Championship in each of his three years of captaincy. He toured Australia and New Zealand with A. C. MacLaren's M.C.C. team of 1923, scoring 430 runs, average 39.09. At Melbourne, where the Englishmen, dismissed for 71 in the first innings, went in again 546 behind Victoria, Wilson and W. W. Hill-Wood dispelled any danger of defeat by batting throughout the last day and sharing an unbroken first-wicket partnership of 282.

WILSON, George A., who died at Abbots Langley, Herts., on March 3, 1962, aged 84, played as a fast bowler for Worcestershire in the early part of the century. In first-class matches between 1899 and 1906, he took 732 wickets at a cost of 24.06 runs each. In 1899, the year that Worcestershire were accorded first-class status, he dismissed eight Yorkshire batsmen for 70 runs on the opening day of the season. Though inconsistent, he three times took over 100 wickets in a summer, his

best record being 120, average 22.95, in 1901. His swerve and ferocious pace made him a menace on fast pitches not entirely true. His most remarkable analysis was eight wickets for 30 runs in the Somerset first innings in 1905 at Taunton, where his match-figures were 15 for 142.

WILSON, George Lindsay, who was born at Melbourne on April 27, 1868, died at his native place on March 9, 1920. He was educated at the Scotch College, Melbourne, and Brighton College, Sussex, being in the latter XI in 1884 and three following years. He headed the batting averages in 1886 and 1887 with 59.63 and 54.06 respectively, and was captain in his last year. Between 1887 and 1895 he appeared in 54 matches for Sussex, scoring 2,042 runs with an average of 21.95 and taking 27 wickets for 59.11 runs each. His chief scores were 105 v. Gloucestershire at Brighton in 1893, 117 and 92 in the return at Bristol, and 174 v. Oxford University at Brighton in 1895. In making the last-mentioned score, he and Marlow (130) obtained 303 together for the first wicket. In 1890 Mr. Wilson secured his Blue for Oxford and in his matches against Cambridge made 0 and 20 in his first year and 0 and 53 in 1891. Possessed of good height, he hit well all round the wicket and was an excellent field.

WILSON, Henry, professional to the Kidderminster Club, died from tumour on the brain at Kidderminster on August 13, 1906. He was born in Yorkshire, and made his first appearance for Worcestershire in the match against Lancashire at Manchester in 1904. He was a useful all-round cricketer.

WILSON, Herbert G., born on January 9, 1864, died at Winnipeg on January 16, 1925. An effective bowler at his best, he took 39 wickets for 65 runs while on tour with the Winnipeg C.C. in 1887, and in 1895 played for Canada v. United States. He was a member of the Expedition for the relief of General Gordon at Khartoum in 1884 and also a Klondyke pioneer.

WILSON, Herbert L., died suddenly on March 15, 1937, at his home near Eastbourne. Born on June 27, 1881, he played first for Sussex in 1913, when the fine form that made him the best Suffolk batsman during the previous season, with an average of 57.66, was revealed against the best county bowlers. With a highest innings of 109 against Gloucestershire at Hove—one of four centuries in a remarkable match which Sussex won by 470 runs—Wilson scored 1,341 runs, average 31.18, Albert Relf alone doing better. If not reproducing such consistent ability Wilson enjoyed a second good season and after the War he captained the county XI for three years. During his term as leader Wilson raised the standard of Sussex fielding which A. E. R. Gilligan brought to a still higher pitch of excellence. Grace of style and free hitting in front of the wicket made Wilson very good to watch and it was regrettable that he did not start first-class cricket at an earlier age than nearly 32. A slow right-hand bowler he occasionally ended a stubborn stand. Altogether he played for Sussex during six seasons, scoring in first-class matches 5,752 runs, average 25.67, and taking 23 wickets at a cost of 50.86 runs apiece. He played in the 1920 Gentlemen and Players match at the Oval.

WILSON, John, died at Sheffield in November, 1931, in his 74th year, having been born at Pitsmoor, Sheffield, on June 20, 1858. An excellent lob bowler, he played for Yorkshire in eight matches between 1887 and 1893, his best scores being 62 v. Warwickshire, at Edgbaston, and 70 v. Cheshire, at Stockport—both in 1877. He had a batting average of 15 and took 24 wickets for 12 runs each.

WILSON, Major John Philip, who died on October 3, 1959, aged 70, played in a few matches for Yorkshire in 1911 and 1912. Educated at Harrow and Cambridge University, he was at one time well known as an amateur steeplechase jockey and he rode Double Chance to victory in the 1925 Grand National.

WILSON, Leslie, died on April 17, 1944, aged 85. While at school at Tonbridge, like so many other noted Kent batsmen, he learned the brightest and most graceful way of making runs, with the natural result that he was welcome in the county XI whenever business permitted from 1883 to 1897. Cuts and drives to either side of the wicket made by perfect timing marked every innings of any length that he played. Always looking for runs, he sometimes erred in rashness or he might have reached higher prominence in the cricket world. As it was, he scored 3,507 runs—average 20.47—and seldom failed. In 1889 he came first in the Kent averages with 36—a high figure in those days—for an aggregate of 360, and the highest score of his first-class career, 132 at Canterbury against Gloucestershire.

WINCH, Richard Foord, born at Cranbrook, Kent, on April 4, 1853, died at Crondall, in Hampshire, on June 6, 1927, aged 74. Although he played occasionally for Northamptonshire, he will be remembered chiefly for two bowling feats he performed for Oundle School while a master there. At Northampton on July 2, 3, 1879, he bowled down all the 10 wickets in the first innings of the Gentlemen of Northants, and on the Oundle ground on June 2, 1881, he was similarly successful at the expense of Kettering.

WINDSOR-CLIVE, Lieut. The Hon. Archer, second son of Lord Plymouth, died on September 1, 1914, of wounds received at Mons while serving with the 3rd Batt. Coldstream Guards. He was born at Hewell Grange, Worcestershire, on November 6, 1890, and was in the Eton XI in 1908 and 1909. In the former season he scored 10 and 38 v. Harrow, and 105—a sound innings—v. Winchester; in the latter, 14 and one v. Harrow, and 44 v. Winchester. Proceeding to Cambridge he scored 12 and took seven wickets for 49 runs in the Freshmen's match in 1910, but did not obtain his Blue. He was a good batsman and a useful medium-paced left-handed bowler. In 1908 his name will be found in the Glamorganshire XI.

WINLAW, Squadron-Leader Roger de Winton Kelsall, the Cambridge cricket and Association Blue, was killed on active service on October 31, 1942. He made a name at Winchester, being four years in the cricket XI 1928–31, captain in the last two seasons. His best year was 1930, when he headed both batting and bowling averages. Scoring 85 and 33 in the Freshmen's match, he got his Blue in 1932, and was in the Cambridge XI three times, all the matches against Oxford being drawn. He batted splendidly in 1934, being second to J. H. Human in the averages with 977 runs, average 57.47, and hit five centuries, the highest being 161 not out against Essex at Fenner's. At Cardiff, against Glamorgan, his two separate 100s, 108 and 109 not out, came as an outstanding achievement. The other centuries were at Fenner's—104 against Yorkshire and 103 against Free Foresters. In the University match he made 56 and 12 not out. He played in nine county engagements for Surrey that season, scoring 341 runs, average 28.41, and his full aggregate amounted to 1,330, average 42.90. A very good display was his 91 against Sussex at the Oval, and he was not out five when

Surrey won by eight wickets. In the Middlesex match he took part in a thrilling finish and stood out as the hero of a rare struggle. Scoring 61 in the first innings, he helped R. J. Gregory in a stand that stopped a bad start, and Surrey gained a lead of 175. In an uphill fight, Middlesex played grandly on the third day, and setting their opponents to get 117 for victory, dismissed six men for 43, and Winlaw, struck on the head by a ball from Jim Smith, retired. Garland-Wells hit a dashing 45, and the total rose to 104 before the ninth wicket fell. Then Winlaw resumed. A bye was snatched as the last ball of an over went to the wicket-keeper, so that Brooks could face the bowling. As it happened, he fell hurt by a ball from Smith, a nasty blow; but, recovering, he drove the next two balls to the boundary and Surrey won by one wicket. Except in 1934, Winlaw played for Bedfordshire from 1931. Captain in 1935, he led the side admirably and headed the averages with 85 for an aggregate of 425. Next year, thanks to team work, they rose to fourth in the second-class County Championship—their best season for 31 years. Winlaw set the example of brilliant fielding, in which he excelled generally at mid-off, though his batting fell off badly. Winlaw recovered his form next year, but others were less consistent, and there came a further decline in 1939, when Winlaw finished with an average of 27.45. He played three times in the University Association match on the right wing, being captain in his last year. Before joining the Royal Air Force, Winlaw was a master at Harrow, where he was held in the highest repute by the scholars and all who knew him. It was a sad coincidence that R. G. Tindall, his Winchester colleague in the 1930 XI, was killed early in the year. They were opposed in the University matches of 1933 and 1934, Tindall being a double Blue at Oxford. In the same plane, tragedy also overtook another and more famous Old Wykehamist, C. T. Ashton.

WINROW, Harry F., who died in South Africa in August, 1973, aged 57, played as a left-handed all-rounder for Nottinghamshire from 1946 to 1951. In his first full season, 1947, he enjoyed considerable success, scoring 1,073 runs—including his highest innings, 204 not out against Derbyshire at Trent Bridge—for an average of 44.70 and taking with slow bowling 56 wickets at a cost of 38.42 each. Though he lost form in bowling after that, he remained a very useful batsman for a county then strong in run-getting. In all he obtained 4,769 runs during

his brief career. Going to South Africa, he engaged in coaching and became President of the Cricket Umpires' Association. He was also a selector for the Border Cricket Union.

WINSER, Legh, who died in Australia on December 20, 1983, aged 99, was at the time the oldest living Sheffield Shield cricketer. Born in Cheshire and educated at Oundle, he played for Staffordshire from 1906 to 1908, keeping wicket to S. F. Barnes, at the time perhaps the world's deadliest bowler. Emigrating to South Australia in 1909, Winser was soon keeping wicket for that state. By 1913 he had become a strong candidate for a place in the Australian team to South Africa, a tour that was, in fact, cancelled because of the onset of war. After giving up cricket he achieved eminence as an amateur golfer, winning the Championship of South Australia eight times and the Australian Amateur Championship once. At the time of the Bodyline tour, in 1932–33, he was secretary to the Governor of South Australia, Sir Alexander Hore-Ruthven (afterwards the Earl of Gowrie). Hore-Ruthven being in England at the time, Winser was intimately concerned with the exchange of cables between the Australian Board of Control and M.C.C. when, after ugly scenes in the Adelaide Test match, the future of the tour, indeed of the special relationship between the United Kingdom and Australia, were put in jeopardy. In his later years, spent at Barwon Heads, near Geelong in Victoria, he regularly beat his age at golf, on one occasion by no fewer than 11 strokes: when 87 he played the 18 holes of the Barwon Heads links in 76 strokes.

WINSLOW, O. E., who died on October 13, 1896, in his 47th year, was at one time a member of the Sussex XI, and a very brilliant batsman.

WINSTONE, Alick, who died on March 29, 1963, aged 84, played as a professional for Gloucestershire under the captaincy of G. L. Jessop between 1906 and 1909, scoring 975 runs, average 12.66. His highest innings was 58 against Hampshire at Bournemouth in 1907.

WINTER, Gerald Esdale, born in London on November 29, 1876, died there on January 17, 1923. He was a capital hard-hitting batsman and a useful lob-bowler, and played for Winchester in 1895, for Cambridge in 1898 and 1899, and for Middlesex in 1900. His best feats in matches of note were performed for the University. Against Sussex at Hove in 1898 he took 10 wickets for 93 runs and scored 80 out of 108 in less than 70 minutes, and the same season made 142 against Liverpool and District. A year later, while playing against Surrey at the Oval, he claimed 84 of the 89 runs added with E. R. Wilson for the third wicket. In 1898 he visited America as a member of P. F. Warner's team.

WINTERBOTHAM, James Percival, who died at Cheltenham on December 2, 1925, aged 42, was a useful slow left-handed bowler with spin and break. During the four years that he played for Cheltenham College—1899 to 1902—he obtained 187 wickets for 16.49 runs each. In 1900 he did the hat-trick v. Old Cheltonians, in 1901 had analyses of six for 60 and nine for 49 in the match with Marlborough, and in the following season took five wickets for five runs against Marlborough, who were dismissed in their first innings for 19. He captained the XI and was in the Cheltenham College Rugby Fifteen. At Oxford he played for the Freshmen and Seniors and was tried for the University, but did not obtain his Blue. On a few occasions, commencing in 1902, he appeared for Gloucestershire, and represented the county at hockey and golf. He was wounded in the First World War while serving as Captain in the 5th Batt. Gloucestershire Regiment. By profession he was a solicitor.

WINTERTON, Edward Turnour, Fifth Earl of, was born at Shillinglee Park, near Petworth, in Sussex, on August 15, 1837, and died there suddenly on September 5, 1907. As Viscount Turnour he played in the Eton XI of 1855 with fair all-round success. He appeared in five matches for Sussex between 1862 and 1867, and also assisted Norfolk on a few occasions. Mr. Haygarth described him as: "A good hard hitter, a fast round-armed bowler, and in the field generally cover-point and cover-slip." His highest innings in a match of note was 96 for Gentlemen of Sussex v. Gentlemen of Kent, at Brighton in 1867. In 1884 he was President of the M.C.C.

WISHART, Kenneth L., who died suddenly in Georgetown in October, 1972, aged 64, was a leading cricket administrator in the West Indies, being Guyana's representative on the West Indies Board from 1949 until he retired early in 1971. He was also President of the Guyana Cricket Association. He played as opening batsman for the West Indies against England at Georgetown in 1934, scoring 52 not out in a first-innings total of 184.

WISTER, William Rotch, "The Father of American Cricket," died at Saunderstown, Rhode Island, on August 21, 1911, in his 84th year. He was one of the promoters of the Philadelphia C.C., and played for the United States against Canada in 1859. Throughout his life he was a great enthusiast of the game, and even participated in it when the Germantown C.C. celebrated its 50th anniversary—in 1904. His *Reminiscences of Cricket in Philadelphia before 1861* is a valuable contribution to the history of the game in America. He was born on the Wister Estate, Germantown, on December 7, 1827.

WODEHOUSE, Sir Pelham Grenville, the famous novelist who died in hospital on Long Island on February 14, 1975, at the age of 93, had been a member of the Dulwich College XI in 1899 and 1900. He was godfather of M. G. Griffith, the late Captain of Sussex.

WOMERSLEY, Dale, who was in the Marlborough XI in 1878 with A. G. Steel, and afterwards played for Essex, died in August, 1942, aged 82. Of medium height, but strongly built, he batted well and fielded smartly—usually at cover-point.

WOOD, Arthur, who died on April 2, 1973, aged 74, played for Yorkshire from 1927 until 1946 and was first choice as wicketkeeper between 1927 and 1939. He helped in the dismissal of 848 batsmen—603 caught and 245 stumped—and, a useful batsman, scored 8,579 runs for the county at an average of 21.13. His best season as a run-getter was that of 1935 when he hit 1,087, average 36.23, and put together the only century of his career, 123 not out off the Worcestershire bowling at Bramall Lane.

He gained his first Test cap a few days before his 40th birthday and I had something to do with him receiving the honour. While reporting a match at Lord's, I was sent a message in the Press Box from Sir Pelham Warner, then chairman of the England Selectors, asking me to go to the Pavilion to see him. This I did and Sir Pelham told me that he was worried because Leslie Ames was indisposed and unable to play at the Oval. He asked me if I could recommend a wicket-keeper-batsman as replacement. At once I suggested Wood and, sure enough, he got the place. That was the match against Australia in which Len Hutton hit his record-breaking 364. Wood got 53, but the score had exceeded 500 by the time he went in. Noted for his sense of humour, he said when congratulated upon his batting success: "I was always good in a crisis."

Most celebrated of the stories about Wood concerned the game at Sheffield in 1935 when H. B. Cameron, the South African wicket-keeper, punished the Yorkshire and England slow left-arm bowler, H. Verity, for 30 runs in one over. At the end of that over, Wood told Verity: "You've got him in two minds. He doesn't know whether to hit you for six or four."—E.E.

WOOD, Arthur Hardy, died on July 12, 1933, aged 89. Born on May 25, 1844, he was educated at Eton but did not get a place in the XI, and for some years was best known in the hunting field as secretary of the Hampshire Hunt and in 1884 became Master of the Hounds. He first played for Hampshire in 1868 and captained the XI for three seasons beginning in 1883. In 1886 he was elected President of the County Club and remained a vice-president until his death. He was also a vice-president of the Sussex County Club and, for many seasons recently when a member of the committee, was a very good friend to the young professionals. Standing 6ft. high Mr. Wood is described as having been an excellent batsman and capable fieldsman, usually at "mid-wicket-off." He also kept wicket for Hampshire—then a second-class county.

WOOD, Arthur Machin, died in Philadelphia on August 25, 1947, aged 86. Played for Notts in 1878 and Derbyshire in 1879 before going to United States, where he became one of the best batsmen for Gentlemen of Philadelphia who visited England in 1897, 1903, and 1908.

WOOD, Cecil John Burditt, a former Leicestershire captain and secretary, who died at Leicester in June, 1960, aged 84, held the unique distinction of carrying his bat through two completed innings of a first-class match and scoring a century in each. He performed the feat for Leicestershire against Yorkshire at Bradford in 1911, and totalling 107 not out and 117 not out, was on the field for the whole of the game. A sound and watchful batsman, but still a stylist, Wood carried his bat on 13 other occasions, altogether hit 34 centuries for Leicestershire—during a career spanning 27 years from 1896 to 1923—and totalled almost 24,000 runs.

He was born at Market Harborough on December 21, 1877, and, educated at Wellingborough, gained a place in the school XI when only 13 years of age. A coal merchant by trade, he played as an amateur for Northamptonshire in a few matches during 1895 and the following season commenced his long association with Leicestershire. At first he represented them as a professional, but later he returned to his amateur status and captained the county in 1914, 1919, and 1920. His most successful seasons were 1900 when he obtained 1,841 runs (average 39) and 1901 when he scored 2,033 runs (average 41). In 1906 he recorded his highest score, 225, against Worcestershire at Worcester and together with H. Whitehead (174) shared a first wicket partnership of 380 which is a Leicestershire record.

Wood played for the Gentlemen four times in their annual match with the Players at the Oval, and in 1901—a notable year in his career—he took part in two century stands with W. G. Grace, for London County against Surrey at Crystal Palace. Wood scored 66 and 70 and W. G. 71 and 80. In the first innings the pair scored 131 together and in the second 142. In addition to possessing remarkable powers as a defensive batsman, Wood was a good fielder and useful change bowler. At Loughborough in 1914, bowling slow right-arm, he took five wickets for six runs against Surrey. As a boy he also showed promise as a footballer and assisted Leicester Fosse—now Leicester City—as a half-back. In later life he became secretary to Leicestershire County C.C. and as a cricketer and administrator altogether served the county for 47 years.

WOOD, George Edward Charles, who died on March 18, 1971, aged 77, was a brilliant amateur wicket-keeper for Cheltenham, Cambridge and for England in three Test matches with South Africa in 1924. He stood right up to the stumps for the fastest bowlers in his day. He was in the school XI from 1910 to 1912, leading the side in the last year. He gained his Blue in his second season at Cambridge in 1914 and again after the First World War in 1919 and in 1920, when he captained one of the strongest XIs ever fielded by the Light Blues. In three appearances against Oxford, he hit 195 runs for an average of 39.00.

Three times he played for the Gentlemen against the Players at Lord's and in 1920 he was invited to tour Australia with J. W. H. T. Douglas's M.C.C. team, but had to decline. He took part in a few matches for Surrey Second XI in 1913 and for Kent Second XI the following season and from 1919 to 1927 played occasionally for Kent in Championship matches. He was a member of the team of amateurs got together by A. C. MacLaren who created a sensation in 1921 at Eastbourne by overcoming by 28 runs the hitherto unconquerable Australian touring team under the captaincy of W. W. Armstrong. A forcing batsman, he registered his one first-class century off the Free Foresters' bowling at Fenners in 1919.

A natural games player, Wood got a Rugby Blue as a wing threequarter in 1919 and also represented his University at hockey.

WOOD, Henry. After a long illness, from which there was never the slightest hope of recovery, Harry Wood, as he was always called, died on April 30, 1919. He was the third of the four wicket-keepers who have helped to sustain the fame of Surrey cricket for 70 years, following Tom Lockyer and Pooley and being in his turn succeeded by Strudwick. Of the four Wood was the least gifted, but he did an immense amount of work and was painstaking to a degree. The Surrey committee paid him a handsome compliment when they picked him to keep wicket for England against Australia at the Oval in 1888 and he justified their choice, being seen at his very best in the big match. Apart from that one occasion his reputation rested almost entirely on his doings in county cricket. Born at Dartford on December 14, 1854, he was ambitious in his young days as a cricketer to play for his native county, but the Kent authorities did not realise what a good wicket-keeper he was likely to be and let him slip out of their hands. He played in a few odd matches for Kent, but never secured a regular place in the XI. It was an engagement as ground keeper to the Streatham club that enabled him to qualify for Surrey. He made his first appearance for Surrey in 1884—just when Surrey cricket was reviving—and kept wicket for the team right until 1899. He thus shared in all Surrey's triumphs under the leadership of Mr. John Shuter, and afterwards of Mr. K. J. Key. Keeping to Bowley, Beaumont, George Lohmann and Sharpe, and then—a far more onerous task—to Lockwood and Tom Richardson, he had a trying time of it even on the Oval wickets and his hands often suffered terribly, but he took it all as part of the day's work, and was not often heard to complain. Except when his hands were very bad he was seldom away from his post, but I remember one occasion when his absence involved disaster. He was too unwell to play against Lancashire at the Oval in 1888 and faulty wicket-keeping undoubtedly cost Surrey the match—their only defeat in the Championship that season. Wood was not first-rate as a batsman, but he was an uncommonly good man to go in, as he did for Surrey, ninth or even 10th on the order. Thanks to his nerve and good hitting he could generally be counted on for a fair share of runs. His greatest triumph as a batsman was an innings of 134 not out for the English team v. South Africa at Cape Town in 1891–92. For years after he had ceased to play Wood was one of the county umpires.—S.H.P.

WOOD, The Rev. Hugh, died at Whitchurch Vicarage, Aylesbury, on July 31, 1941, aged 86, leaving the captain, the Hon. and Rev. Edward Lyttelton, who passed away in January, 1942, as the last survivor of the Cambridge XI which beat the Australian team of 1878 at Lord's by an innings and 72 runs. A slow left-hand bowler, Wood was not put on in this match, A. G. Steel and P. H. Morton bowling unchanged in Australia's first innings and A. F. J. Ford helping them with one wicket when the touring team followed-on. Wood did not get his Blue that year, but in 1879 at Lord's he took four wickets for 46, sharing the honours of the first Oxford dismissal with A. G. Steel, who then scored 64, highest innings of the match, and when Oxford batted again got rid of seven men for 23, making his match record 11 wickets for 69 runs. A. F. J. Ford took the other three wickets that innings, and with three slip catches off Steel helped largely in the victory by nine wickets. This result gave Cambridge a lead of 22 victories to 21 by Oxford in the series of University encounters. Mr. Wood played for Yorkshire in 1879 and 1880, taking 10 wickets at 21 runs apiece and averaging 10.40 in 15 innings as a right-handed batsman.

WOOD, Sir John Barry, K.C.I.E., K.C.V.O., C.S.I., was born on April 27, 1870, and died on February 10, 1933. He was a member of the Marlborough College XI in 1887, 1888, and 1889, leading the side in the last two years. Tried for Oxford University in 1891 he obtained his Blue the following year, and in 1892 and 1893, he took 53 wickets for the University with his lob bowling, but in the latter year he was very expensive. He was a good field and often batted quite well. Although in 1890 he played for Warwickshire, then a second-class county, he gave up first-class cricket after his Oxford days.

WOOD, John J. (Hickory), Author of *The Cricket Club of Red Nose Flat*, died at Purley, Surrey, on August 25, 1913, aged 54.

WOOD, Lieut.-Col. M.D., D.S.O. (West Yorkshire Regiment), officially reported wounded and missing at Gallipoli on August 22, 1915, now believed killed on that date, was in the Sandhurst XI in 1892, and played later in much regimental cricket and occasionally for Hampshire.

WOODCOCK, Arthur, the well-known Leicestershire fast bowler, died (as the result of poison self-administered) at Billesdon, on May 14, 1910. He was born at Northampton on September 23, 1865, but when only a few months old was taken into Leicestershire, where he learned the game and spent the greater part of his life. In 1887 he accepted an engagement with the Mitcham C.C., of Surrey, and the form he showed while there was so good that Mr. Alcock, upon being asked to recommend a player as coach at Haverford College, at once mentioned him, the result being that he entered upon the engagement in 1888 and retained it until 1894. The vacation enabled him to play in England from July to September, but it was not until 1889 that he was invited to assist Leicestershire. He played in only one match that year, but appeared more frequently in the following season, when, in consecutive matches against Essex and Warwickshire, he took 17 wickets for 201 runs. During the next two years he appeared for the side as often as his American engagement permitted and how much Leicestershire's promotion to the first-class was due to his bowling is a matter of history. In 1895 he became a member of the ground staff at Lord's, and during that season took 102 wickets in first-class matches for a fraction over 19 runs each. That, as it happened, was his most successful year. He continued to appear for Leicestershire regularly for a few more seasons, but knee trouble handicapped him severely and in 1903 he dropped out of the side. Woodcock possessed a splendid physical development, and at one time was, C. J. Kortright alone excepted, the fastest bowler in England. As a batsman he was poor, but he enjoyed one pronounced success, making 62 not out at Old Trafford in 1898 against the bowling of Mold, Cuttell, and Briggs. After dropping out of County Cricket he continued to play for the M.C.C., and, in a match against Lewes Priory on the Dripping Pan, Lewes, in 1908, bowled a bail off the wicket 149 ft. 6 in., sending it over a 14-ft. bank and a wall on the boundary. Among his many good performances with the ball the following were perhaps the best:

8 for 67 } 7 for 69 }	Leicestershire v. Notts, at Leicester	1894
8 for 111	(in 1st inns.) Leicestershire v. Warwickshire, at Leicester ..	1895
3 for 48 } 6 for 44 }	Leicestershire v. Surrey, at the Oval	1895
8 for 66 } 5 for 66 }	M.C.C. and Ground v. Kent, at Lord's	1897
13 for 125	Leicestershire v. M.C.C. and Ground, at Lord's	1897
5 for 44 } 9 for 28 }	Leicestershire v. M.C.C. and Ground, at Lord's	1899

In a minor match at Uppingham in 1894 he bowled down all 10 wickets in an innings when playing for Uppingham v. the President's XI of Past and Present.

WOODFULL, William Maldon, who collapsed and died while playing golf on a course near Brisbane on August 11, 1965, aged 67, played as opening batsman in 35 Test matches for Australia and captained them in 25. Known as "The Rock" because of his imperturbable temperament, he possessed immensely strong defence and great patience. Yet, though the backlift of his bat was very short indeed, his weight and strength of wrist enabled him to score at a faster rate than many a more attractive player.

During a Test career extending from 1926 to 1934, he hit 2,300 runs for an average of 46.00, the highest of his seven centuries being 161 against South Africa at Melbourne in 1931–32. He shared nine three-figure stands in Test matches, three with his fellow-Victorian, W. H. Ponsford, during the tour of England in 1930—162 at Lord's, 159 at the Oval and 106 at Old Trafford. In all first-class cricket he hit 49 centuries, the highest of which was 284 for an Australian XI against a New Zealand XI at Auckland in 1927–28. Three times he toured England and on each occasion he well exceeded 1,000 runs. In 1926, after making 201 against Essex at Leyton in his first innings on English soil, he headed the batting figures with an aggregate of 1,809 (eight centuries), average 58.35; in 1930, as captain, he made 1,435 runs (six centuries), average 57.36, and four years later when again leading the side 1,268 runs (three centuries), average 52.83.

For Victoria, Bill Woodfull registered 16 centuries, of which the biggest was 275 not out from the bowling of A. P. F. Chapman's M.C.C. team at Melbourne in 1928–29. His most prolific opening partnership for the State was 375 with Ponsford against New South Wales in 1926–27 at Melbourne.

Woodfull led Australia against D. R. Jardine's team during the notorious "body-line" tour in Australia in 1932–33. Though he achieved little against this menacing form of bowling in the first two Test matches, four innings bringing him no more than 43 runs, he displayed such grit and determination in the remaining three that he put together innings of 73 not out, 67, and 67.

He achieved distinction in another field. He was headmaster of Melbourne High School and in the New Year's Honours list of 1963, he received the O.B.E. for his services to education.

His quiet, unassuming demeanour won him respect and affection from team-mates and opponents alike, and tributes to him included:

R. W. V. Robins (former Middlesex and England captain): "As a man he was very kindly and as a batsman he had a wonderful defence. Only once did I have the distinction of getting him out—at Lord's in the second Test in 1930. By then he had made 155 and I think he fell through sheer exhaustion!"

H. Sutcliffe (former Yorkshire and England opening batsman): "First-class as a man and a great fighter. As a batsman he always took such a lot of getting out and as a captain he was a fine leader."

Sir Donald Bradman (former Australian captain): "He was a great gentleman, a fine citizen and an ornament to the game of cricket."

WOODHEAD, Frank Ellis, who played a little for Yorkshire from 1892 to 1894, died at Huddersfield, his native town, on August 25, 1943, aged 75. He averaged 11.72 for 11 completed innings. Going up to Cambridge from Loretto, where he created a record average when captain, he appeared in the Freshmen's match of 1889 but was never in the running for a Blue. For Huddersfield in the West Riding league he did well as batsman and bowler, George Hirst, of Yorkshire and England fame, holding a high opinion of his all-round ability. Proficient at most games, he excelled as a wing three-quarter until a knee injury compelled him to give up Rugby football. Three times he won the Amateur Golf Championship of Wales, and of Yorkshire four times. He played cricket for touring teams in Canada and Holland.

WOODHOUSE, W. H., a useful batsman, who played for Yorkshire in 1884–85, died on March 4, 1938, aged 80.

WOODMAN, Reginald George, died on May 20, 1980, aged 84. He played two matches for Gloucestershire in 1925 as a batsman, but without success.

WOODROFFE, 2nd Lieut. Kenneth Herbert Clayton (6th Batt. Rifle Brigade, attached 2nd Welsh Regiment), was born at Lewes on December 9, 1892, and was killed in action near Neuve Chapelle on May 9, 1915. In 1909 and three following seasons he was in the Marlborough XI, being captain in 1912, and he played for Cambridge in 1913 and 1914, obtaining his Blue as a Freshman. Mr. F. B. Wilson, writing of him in *Wisden* for 1912, said: "He is really fast, and can make the ball turn from the off on nearly any wicket. His action is a high and easy one, and, being tall, he often makes the ball get up very quickly. Moreover, what is most important, missed catches do not appear to worry him unduly, and he keeps on trying all the time." He headed the Marlborough bowling in 1910 and 1911, and in 1912 was second to R. D. Busk. In his three matches v. Rugby—he did not play in the 1910 game, which Rugby won easily—he took 21 wickets for 14.95 runs each, and on his two appearances in the University match obtained seven for 14.85 apiece. In 1912 he appeared for Hampshire against the South Africans, and two years later assisted Sussex in a couple of games and in the match with Surrey at the Oval almost pulled off the match by taking six wickets for 43 runs. He had been Mentioned in Dispatches.

WOODS, Arthur Phillips (Bobby), who died at Balgowan, Natal, on October 15, 1950, aged 46, played regularly for Natal from 1925 to 1934. A fast-medium bowler and useful batsman low in the order, he took 85 wickets for Natal, average 21.03, and scored 617 runs, average 19.90. His highest score was 93 against Western Province at Cape Town in 1929–30.

WOODS, Samuel Moses James, one of the most famous and popular of athletes, a splendid cricketer and a great Rugby football forward, was born at Glenfield near Sydney on April 14, 1867, and died on April 30, 1931, at Taunton. A player of grand physique, cheery disposition, and unflinching courage, he was generally at his best against the strongest and never knew when he was beaten. Although essentially an all-rounder and a most efficient and inspiring captain, it is on his bowling that his fame will chiefly rest. He was fast and accurate and had at his command not only a deadly yorker but also a slow ball which was as formidable and deceptive as any he sent down. Unquestionably he reached a measure of excellence which entitled him to a place among the great fast bowlers of all time.

Essentially a forcing batsman Woods drove tremendously hard especially to the on. He used his reach, great strength and sure eye to hit at the pitch of the ball without leaving his crease. Often he knocked the most accurate bowlers off their length and he could cut any short ball with a swing of his massive shoulders and arms, sending the ball at tremendous speed past cover-point. While Woods preferred the fast-scoring game he could, in case of need, adopt a sound, correct method and then he excelled in off-side driving. As with age his effectiveness with the ball declined he used the bat to greater purpose. His highest scoring season was 1895 when he made 1,405 runs with an average of 34. This he surpassed four years later with a record of 40 an innings.

He received his early education at Sydney Grammar School and Royston College, Sydney, and at the latter institution showed such ability as a bowler that in 1883 he took 70 wickets for five runs each and on one occasion obtained seven wickets in seven balls.

He came to England in 1884 and went to Brighton College where he and G. L. Wilson stood out as two of the best Public School cricketers of the season. In the following summer for Brighton College Woods obtained 78 wickets for seven and a half runs apiece, getting 14—all bowled—in the match with Lancing College, and, in addition to achieving so much as a bowler, showed no little ability as a hard-hitting batsman while, later on, he developed into a brilliant field at cover-point or extra mid-off and a sure catch. He began to play regularly for Somerset in 1887 but a year earlier had figured at Portsmouth in a match between the fifth Australian team and a side got together by G. N.

Wyatt, a prominent amateur who appeared first for Gloucestershire, afterwards for Surrey and finally for Sussex. While reaching double figures in each innings and taking two wickets, Woods accomplished nothing of much note on that occasion, but on going up to Cambridge in 1888 he, in the course of very few weeks, made himself certain of his Blue. For four years he appeared for the University and, during that period, secured 190 wickets for less than 15 runs apiece, while in the four encounters with Oxford at Lord's, of which three were won and one drawn, he obtained 36 wickets for something under nine runs each. Cricket has presented no more exhilarating sight than the University match of those days with Woods bowling his hardest and Gregor MacGregor keeping wicket in that famous player's masterly fashion.

Woods did little as a batsman against Oxford, but in his last year when Cambridge—set 90 to make to win—had lost eight wickets for 89, he went in and hit the first ball he received to the boundary. He was Cambridge captain in 1890 when the Light Blues proved victorious by seven wickets.

Although earning great fame as a bowler at Cambridge and repeatedly chosen to assist Gentlemen against Players—he and F. S. Jackson bowled unchanged in the match of 1894 and were mainly instrumental in gaining a single innings victory over the professionals—Sam Woods' career was essentially identified with Somerset, for whom he appeared from 1886 to 1907, acting as captain in 1894 and taking over the duties of secretary until 1923. His biggest score was one of 215 which he hit against Sussex at Hove in 1895, the total meanwhile being increased by 282 in two hours and a half. Three years later, on the same ground, he made 143 out of 173 in two hours and a quarter off the Sussex bowlers.

Among his many bowling feats, in addition to his great performances for Gentlemen v. Players, was the taking of all 10 wickets for 69 runs in an innings for Cambridge against C. I. Thornton's XI—15 wickets in the match for 88 runs—at Cambridge in 1890. Two years earlier in a contest against another side got together by C. I. Thornton he performed the hat-trick, and in 1891 at the Oval against Surrey he obtained 14 wickets for 11 runs each.

He played for the Australians in this country several times in 1888 and participated in several tours abroad, going to America in 1891 and to South Africa in 1896–97 with teams led by Lord Hawke, to the West Indies with a side captained by Sir A. Priestley and to America again in 1899 when Ranjitsinhji was in control.

In the course of his career he made 19 100s—18 of these for Somerset—scored in all 15,499 runs with an average of 23 and took 1,079 wickets for 20 runs apiece. Over six feet in height, he weighed in his cricket days 13½ st.

His career as a Rugby football player naturally did not extend over so many years as his cricket life, but he attained the highest honours at the winter game, playing for Cambridge against Oxford in 1888 and in the two following years and being "capped" for England 13 times in the days when there were only three international encounters each season. Four times he played against Scotland between 1890 and 1895, five times against Ireland and four times against Wales. Tremendously strong and very fast, he possessed all the qualities necessary and, in his quickness in breaking away, was, after Frank Evershed, one of the most famous of wing forwards in the comparatively early days of the Rugby game. He also played Rugby for Somerset and appeared at Association football for Sussex. In the War he served in the Somerset Light Infantry and in the Devon Regiment.

WOODWARD, Joseph, who died at Aston, Birmingham, on December 31, 1926, aged 73,had played for both Warwickshire and Worcestershire, and forthe former county at Lichfield in 1882 obtained seven wickets in an innings against Staffordshire.

WOODWARD, Kenneth Alexander, who died at Charlton Kings, Cheltenham, on December 24, 1950, aged 76, was a member of the Harrow XI of 1892 and 1893. He went to University College, Oxford, but did not gain a Blue. Afterwards he played for Herefordshire and Derbyshire. Served in the Royal Marine Engineers during the First World War.

WOOF, William Albert, the old Gloucestershire slow left-hand bowler, died at Cheltenham on April 4, 1937, aged 77. Born at Gloucester on July 9, 1859, he was educated at Bedford Grammar School with the intention of becoming an engineer. He played for the Gloucestershire Colts in 1878 and took five wickets for 78 runs, among his victims being W. G. and G. F. Grace. When tried for the county, he failed and next year, accepting an engagement on the ground staff at Old Trafford, he decided to make cricket his career. Then A. N. Hornby persuaded him to change his pace from fast to slow with very

beneficial effect. W. G. Grace, hearing of this, got him a post as bowler at Cheltenham College and in 1882 recommended him for the ground staff at Lord's where he made a name in M.C.C. matches and remained for four seasons. Appointed coach at Cheltenham in 1885 he retained the position until 1925 and on his retirement he received £1,200 as a testimonial from past and present Cheltonians.

Altogether in first-class cricket Woof took 752 wickets at less than 17 and a half runs apiece. His best seasons were 1884, when he dismissed 116 men for 18 runs each, and 1885, when 100 wickets fell to him at an average cost of less than 18 runs. After this, owing to his duties at Cheltenham, he could not give much time to help his county until the vacation, and he retired from first-class cricket in 1894, but four years later for East Gloucestershire he took seven M.C.C. wickets for 28 runs.

Very clever in keeping a length Woof got on a lot of spin for the break back, while, without change of action, he made the ball go with his arm quickly off the pitch; on drying turf he was deadly. Against the Australians in 1886 at Cheltenham he took nine wickets for 76 (seven for 32 in the second innings); but F. R. Spofforth, with 10 for 106, helped the team captained by H. J. H. Scott to win by 26 runs.

Other notable performances were 14 wickets for 97 against Nottinghamshire at Clifton in 1890, six wickets for 14 runs for M.C.C. against Kent at Lord's in 1882, and five for 13 for M.C.C. at Trent Bridge in 1883. In this match against Nottinghamshire Woof and Rylott at one period at the start of the county's first innings sent down 64 balls without a run being scored from the bat, while six wickets fell. Woof dismissed William Barnes, Flowers, both England players, and Shacklock in the course of five balls. After retiring as a player Woof for a time was on the first-class umpires list.

Among the many fine cricketers coached at Cheltenham by Woof were five brothers Champain, four of whom played for Gloucestershire, E. I. M. Barrett, Hampshire, A. H. Du Boulay, Kent and Gloucestershire, and, more recently, K. S. Duleepsinhji. Woof was buried at Cheltenham College Chapel, the Dean of Hereford conducting the service.

WOOLF, Louis Sydney, who played for Victoria against New South Wales in 1877, and lived to be the oldest representative of his State, died in August, 1942. For South

Melbourne he was prominent in club cricket, and played also for his University. A barrister, he often appeared for the Bar against the Army—popular matches in Australia early this century.

WOOLLEY, Claude N., who died at Northampton on November 3, 1962, aged 76, played as opening batsman for Northamptonshire from 1911 to 1931, scoring 15,353 runs for them, average 24.76, taking with slow-medium bowling 352 wickets, average 32.98, and holding 134 catches. Of his 13 centuries, the highest was 204 not out against Worcestershire at Northampton in 1921. He spent two years with Gloucestershire before joining Northamptonshire. Remarkably similar in appearance to his younger brother, Frank, the Kent and England left-handed allrounder, "Dick," as he was generally known, twice carried his bat through an innings, for 59 against Sussex at Hastings in 1925 and for 38 against Yorkshire at Bradford four years later. Oddly enough, he was in each case dismissed for nought in the second innings. He played once for Players against Gentlemen, in the rain-ruined game at the Oval in 1922. His best bowling performance was at Bristol in 1926, when he followed an innings of 90 by taking five Gloucestershire wickets for 11 runs. He did the hat-trick against Essex at Northampton in 1920. After retiring from County Cricket, he became a first-class umpire until 1949, standing in the England v. Australia Test match at Lord's in 1948. Once in 1946, when umpiring in a match between Warwickshire and Nottinghamshire, he had the unusual experience of officiating from the bowler's end for each over until a substitute arrived to replace his colleague, G. Beet, who had been taken ill en route from Manchester. He was a groundsman at the County Ground at Northampton from 1949 until last summer.

FRANK WOOLLEY
Born at Tonbridge, Kent, May 27, 1887, died in Halifax, Nova Scotia, October 18, 1978
By Norman Preston

Frank Edward Woolley, who died aged 91, was beyond doubt one of the finest and most elegant left-handed all-rounders of all time. In a first-class career extending from 1906 to 1938 he hit 58,969 runs—a total exceeded only by Sir Jack Hobbs—including 145 centuries, to average 40.75; he took 2,068 wickets for 19.85 runs each, and he held 1,015 catches, mainly at slip, a record which remains unsurpassed.

Even more impressive than the number of runs Woolley amassed was the manner in which he made them. Standing well over 6ft., he was a joy to watch. He played an eminently straight bat, employed his long reach to full advantage, and used his feet in a manner nowadays rarely seen. His timing of the ball approached perfection and he generally dealt surely with all types of bowling. Master of all the strokes, he was at his best driving, cutting, and turning the ball off his legs. He was described by Sydney Pardon as the cleanest driver since F. G. J. Ford, but he often started badly and there was something wanting in his defence. As a bowler he made good use' of his height and bowled with a graceful easy swing.

As a small boy he was always to be found on the Tonbridge cricket ground, and his natural ability as batsman and bowler attracted so much attention that, in 1903, he was engaged to take part in the morning practice and play in a match or two in the afternoon if required. In the following year he became a regular member of the Tonbridge ground staff, which in those days was the official Kent nursery. When given his first chance in the Kent XI in 1906, he was almost unknown to the public, and his all-round form in his third match, against Surrey at the Oval, came as nothing less than a revelation. To begin with, he took three Surrey wickets, clean bowling Hayward, Hayes, and Goatly. He then made 72, and when Surrey batted again he took five wickets for 80 runs. Finally he scored 23 not out, helping to win a wonderful game for Kent by one wicket. The match established his reputation.

When Frank Woolley announced his retirement in 1938, I spent an afternoon with him at his home in Hildenborough where he talked about "My happy cricket life." In his first season with Kent they won the County Championship for the first time, and altogether between 1906 and 1913 they were top four times. Now let Woolley speak for himself as he told his story to me.

"Those were the great days when plenty of amateurs could spare time for cricket. I do not believe there are so many good players in the game now as before the [First World] War. In the old days we were probably educated in cricket in a far more serious way than now. For the purpose of giving the younger people my idea of the difference, I will put up Walter Hammond, England's captain, as an example. Before 1914 there were something like 30 players up to his standard and he would have been in the England team only if at the top of his form. I make these remarks without casting the slightest reflection on Hammond. He is a grand player and one of the greatest all-round cricketers since the War—in fact, the greatest.

"I doubt whether English cricket has really recovered from the effects of the War. You see, we missed half a generation and since then young men have found many other ways of occupying their leisure hours. Still, I believe it is only a passing phase and cricket will one day produce an abundance of great players."

Unfortunately for cricket, within a year England was plunged into another war, and in my opinion the game in this country has only just shown signs of getting on its feet again with a stream of fine young players coming through, notably in the county of Kent. But to return to the Woolley interview as he saw the game 40 years ago.

"There is little wrong with the game itself. Just a question of the way it is played. It is amazing how the public steadfastly refuse to attend the third day of a match when so often the last day produces the best and most exciting cricket.

"Touching on a personal subject I have been asked if I can explain why I was dismissed so many times in the '90s'. The statisticians inform me that I was out 35 times between 90 and 99 and I am also told that I am credited with 89 ducks. With regard to those '90s', I can honestly say that with me it was never a case of the 'nervous 90s'. Lots of times I was out through forcing the game. We were never allowed to play for averages in the Kent side or take half an hour or more to get the last 10 runs under normal conditions. We always had to play the game and play for the team. It is a Kent tradition.

"As a matter of fact I consider the two finest innings I ever played were in the second Test against Australia in 1921 when I was out for 95 and 93. I don't think I ever worked harder at any match during my career to get runs as I did then, nor did I ever have to face in one game such consistently fast bowlers as the Australian pair, Gregory and McDonald. Square cuts which ordinarily would have flashed to the boundary earned only two, and I believe that those two innings would have been worth 150 apiece in a county match.

"I was not depressed when they got me out. I have always taken my dismissals as part of the game. In the first innings I was in the '80s' when I was joined by the last man, Jack Durston. It was my own fault completely that I lost my wicket. Mailey bowled me a full toss to the off; I walked down the pitch, stepping to the on to force the ball past extra cover, I missed it, and that fine wicket-keeper, H. Carter, eagerly accepted the opportunity to stump me. I was rather unlucky in the second innings when again I fell to Mailey. The ball stuck in his hand and dropped half-way on the leg side. I hit it pretty plumb between square leg and mid-on and just there was standing 'Stalk' Hendry. As I made the shot he jumped in the air and up went his right hand. The ball hit him, I think, on the wrist, and he lost his balance. The ball went up 10ft. and as he was lying on the ground it fell in his lap and he caught it. He was the only man on the leg side and I think the shot would have carried for six. It was a marvellous catch.

"It is often argued that left-handed batsmen have an advantage compared with the right-handers. I do not agree. When the turf is worn the right-hand leg-break bowlers and left-arm slow bowlers are able to pitch the ball into the footholes of the bowlers who have operated at the other end. Right-handed batsmen can let these balls hit their pads, but the left-handers must use their bats. Perhaps the new [1937] lbw rule has not helped us there, but the amended law does not worry me, though in my opinion it has not improved the game. As for further extending the lbw rule I think it would make a farce of the game.

"In many quarters surprise was expressed that at the age of 51 I went in number one. Until then I had never been in first regularly, though I had always preferred that place. Beginning as a bowler made Kent place me four or five in the order, and moreover the county were always rich in opening batsmen. Consequently my wish to start the innings was denied until 1938.

"Because Kent have experienced their bad times against fast bowling [there were very few bouncers in those days] the cry has gone round that we cannot play the fast men, but I think if you search the records you will also find that Kent have hit a tremendous lot of runs off fast bowling. Again I must emphasise that Kent always endeavour to play sporting cricket, and trying to make runs off that type of bowling must sometimes have contributed to our downfall. It was never a policy of the Kent team that the pitch *must* be occupied all day after winning the toss.

"I cannot let this opportunity pass without placing on record how much I have enjoyed my cricket with Kent. If I was a youngster starting as a batsman I think I should like to play always at the Oval, but the Kent grounds, with their natural decorations of beautiful trees, members' tents flying their own colours and bedecked with flowers, lend the right tone to cricket."

After his retirement from the field, Woolley was elected a life member of M.C.C. and Kent, and also to the county committee. He was quite active into his late 80s and in January, 1971, flew to Australia to watch the last two Tests. Nine months later, in Canada, he married for a second time, his first wife having died 10 years earlier. His second bride was Mrs. Martha Morse, an American widow.

R. L. Arrowsmith writes:

Frank Woolley was a slow left-arm bowler with a beautiful action who took over 2,000 wickets and was at one time perhaps the best of his type in the world. He caught during his career far more catches than anyone else, except wicket-keepers, yet it is as a batsman that he is primarily remembered. Few now alive have seen a player who approached him in ease and grace, and his average rate of scoring has been exceeded only by Jessop and equalled by Trumper. His philosophy was to dominate the bowler. "When I am batting," he said, "*I* am the attack." I was lucky enough to see him innumerable times. Obviously I often saw him out for small scores, but I never saw him in difficulties. If a ball beat him, the next would probably go for four or six.

This was made possible not only by his wonderful eye and sense of timing but by his range of strokes at his command and no preference for one over another. Like W.G., he simply employed the one the occasion demanded. Each of these strokes could be commended to a young player as the perfect example of how to do it. In defence, too, his back stroke, certainly in his maturer years, was a model of soundness. All types of bowler came alike to him personally, but, if he saw his partner in trouble, he would make it his business to "settle" the bowler responsible.

At Tunbridge Wells in 1924, he came in at 29 for two to join George Wood, who was in grievous difficulties with Tate, then at his best. As he passed Wood, he said: "Push a single, Mr. Wood, and leave me to deal with Chubby." The single was duly obtained and Tate's next two balls were driven for four. Great trier though he was, Tate, always demonstrative, flung the ball down, exclaiming, "I can't bowl to this chap." Wood, a useful though not great ball, went on to make 49, Woolley made 87, and together they put on 103 out of a total of 190. Though Kent won by 200 runs, it is not fanciful to suggest that those two early fours had a considerable effect on the course of the match.

At Folkestone in 1928, an England XI required 286 to beat the West Indies. There was a bit of feeling in the air, and the three fast bowlers, Francis, Constantine, and Griffith, set out to intimidate the batsmen. Lee and Hammond were quickly out and Wyatt, though struggling with typical determination, was acutely uncomfortable. Woolley, as if unconscious of any trouble, set about the bowlers from the start and hit them to every corner of that large ground. Never have I seen fast bowling so massacred. He scored 151 in three hours, Wyatt compiled a gallant 75, and against all the odds the England side won by four wickets. Years later Constantine said it was the worst hammering he ever received.

The feelings of an opposing captain on such occasions were succinctly expressed by Woodfull: "He made the game look so untidy." It appeared as if the wrong bowlers were on and the fieldsmen all in the wrong places. One can see why Woolley could be a far greater menace to the opposition than players with higher averages, and why 40 years after his retirement he is mentioned in print more than any other batsman of his time except Bradman. And if some statistically minded reader says, "But wouldn't he have been a greater player had he exercised a bit more caution?" I am sure that all who saw him, and, even more, all who played with him would answer firmly, "No."

FRANK E. WOOLLEY—CAREER AT A GLANCE

By STANLEY CONDER

BATTING

	Matches	Inns	Not Outs	Runs	Highest Inns	100s	Avge
In England							
1906	16	26	1	779	116	1	31.16
1907	27	43	1	1,128	99	0	26.85
1908	30	46	3	1,286	152	2	29.90
1909	32	39	0	1,270	185	2	32.56

FRANK E. WOOLLEY—CAREER AT A GLANCE
BATTING—*continued*

	Matches	Inns	Not Outs	Runs	Highest Inns	100s	Avge
In England							
1910	31	47	2	1,101	120	3	24.46
1911	30	47	2	1,700	148*	6	37.77
1912	35	49	5	1,827	117	2	41.52
1913	29	45	6	1,760	224*	4	45.12
1914	31	52	2	2,272	160*	6	45.44
1919	20	27	1	1,082	164	3	41.61
1920	31	50	3	1,924	158	5	40.93
1921	31	50	1	2,101	174	6	42.87
1922	33	47	3	2,022	188	5	45.95
1923	33	56	5	2,091	270	5	41.00
1924	34	49	2	2,344	202	8	49.87
1925	29	43	4	2,190	215	5	56.15
1926	32	50	3	2,183	217	6	46.44
1927	31	41	2	1,804	187	5	46.25
1928	36	59	4	3,352	198	12	61.03
1929	35	55	5	2,804	176	11	56.08
1930	29	50	5	2,023	120	5	44.95
1931	34	51	4	2,301	224	5	48.95
1932	35	52	2	1,827	146	1	36.54
1933	28	48	1	1,633	198	5	34.74
1934	33	56	1	2,643	176	10	48.05
1935	32	56	0	2,339	229	6	41.76
1936	32	58	3	1,532	101	1	27.85
1937	29	52	0	1,645	193	3	31.63
1938	29	52	3	1,590	162	2	32.44
In Australia							
1911–12	14	18	4	781	305*	2	55.78
1920–21	13	20	2	619	138	1	34.38
1924–25	10	17	0	737	149	2	43.35
1929–30	4	7	0	425	219	2	30.61
In South Africa							
1909–10	13	21	2	353	69	0	18.57
1913–14	18	23	1	595	116	1	27.04
1922–23	12	19	1	551	115*	1	30.61
In New Zealand							
1929–30	8	11	1	355	132	1	40.75
All first-class matches	979	1,532	85	58,969	305*	145	40.75

Signifies not out.

BATTING—Mode of Dismissal: Bowled 406, caught 779, lbw 172, stumped 39, hit wicket 7, run-out 44. Total 1,447

BOWLING AND FIELDING

	Matches	Runs	Wkts	Avge	5 wkts/ Inns	Catches
In England						
1906	16	887	42	21.11	0	6
1907	27	623	21	29.66	0	22
1908	30	1,355	80	16.93	2	19

FRANK E. WOOLLEY—CAREER AT A GLANCE
BOWLING AND FIELDING—*continued*

	Matches	Runs	Wkts	Avge	5 wkts/ Inns	Catches
In England						
1909	32	1,399	72	19.43	2	24
1910	31	1,973	136	14.50	11	33
1911	30	1,814	85	21.34	6	19
1912	35	1,802	126	14.30	10	31
1913	29	1,542	83	18.57	4	34
1914	31	2,432	125	19.45	8	24
1919	20	2,196	128	17.15	12	24
1920	31	2,633	185	14.23	15	44
1921	31	2,697	167	16.14	11	34
1922	33	2,995	163	18.37	13	37
1923	33	1,938	101	19.18	6	49
1924	34	1,749	81	21.59	3	38
1925	29	1,610	65	24.76	4	32
1926	32	1,347	36	37.41	0	38
1927	31	794	29	27.37	0	39
1928	36	981	34	28.85	1	37
1929	35	1,133	50	22.66	0	38
1930	29	530	16	33.12	0	31
1931	34	110	1	110.00	0	24
1932	35	76	2	38.00	0	32
1933	28	117	3	39.00	0	16
1934	33	212	6	35.33	0	38
1935	32	42	1	42.00	0	44
1936	32	185	7	26.42	0	34
1937	29	785	31	25.32	2	38
1938	29	525	22	23.86	2	22
In Australia						
1911–12	14	503	17	29.58	0	14
1920–21	13	1,051	31	33.90	0	12
1924–25	10	549	13	42.23	0	10
1929–30	4	270	7	38.57	0	8
In South Africa						
1909–10	13	466	17	27.41	0	24
1913–14	18	717	33	21.72	1	28
1922–23	12	448	23	19.47	2	14
In New Zealand						
1929–30	8	580	29	20.00	2	4
All first-class matches	979	41,066	2,068	19.85	117	1,015

BOWLING—How wickets were taken: Bowled 495, caught 1,177, lbw 201, stumped 190, hit wicket 5. Total 2,068

BATTING AND BOWLING IN TEST CRICKET
BATTING

	Tests	Inns	Not Outs	Runs	Highest Inns	100s	Avge
v. Australia	32	51	1	1,664	133*	2	33.28
v. South Africa	26	37	5	1,354	154	3	42.31
v. New Zealand	5	8	1	235	80	0	33.57
v. India	1	2	0	30	21	0	15.00
Totals	64	98	7	3,283	154	5	36.07

Signifies not out.

BOWLING AND FIELDING

	Tests	Runs	Wkts	Avge	5 wkts/ Inns	Catches
v. Australia	32	1,555	43	36.16	1	36
v. South Africa	26	999	27	37.00	2	27
v. New Zealand	5	261	13	20.07	1	0
v. India	1	—	—	—	-	0
Totals	64	2,815	83	33.91	4	63

LARGE WICKET PARTNERSHIPS SHARED IN BY F. E. WOOLLEY

For 1st wicket
204   with A. E. Fagg, Kent v. Worcestershire, at Tonbridge, 1938.

For 2nd wicket
262   with H. T. W. Hardinge, Kent v. Warwickshire, at Tunbridge Wells, 1928.
260   with A. E. Fagg, Kent v. Northamptonshire, at Northampton, 1934.
255   with H. T. W. Hardinge, Kent v. Derbyshire, at Chesterfield, 1929.
239   with H. T. W. Hardinge, Kent v. Yorkshire, at Tonbridge, 1929.
228   with H. T. W. Hardinge, Kent v. Hampshire, at Folkestone, 1929.
224   with W. H. Ashdown, Kent v. Yorkshire, at Bradford, 1931.
219   with A. E. Fagg, Kent v. Surrey, at Blackheath, 1934.
218   with A. E. Fagg, Kent v. Somerset, at Taunton, 1934.
213   with H. T. W. Hardinge, Kent v. Gloucestershire, at Gloucester, 1928.
211   with A. E. Fagg, Kent v. Hampshire, at Southampton, 1936.
206   with W. Rhodes, M.C.C. v. Tasmania, at Hobart, 1911–12.
204   with P. V. F. Cazalet, Kent v. Oxford University, at Oxford, 1928.
202   with A. Sandham, M.C.C. v. New South Wales, at Sydney, 1924–25.
202   with J. W. Hearne, England XI v. South Africans, at Folkestone, 1929.

For 3rd wicket
283   with H. T. W. Hardinge, Kent v. South Africans, at Canterbury, 1924.
280   with J. Seymour, Kent v. Lancashire, at Dover, 1922.
273   with H. T. W. Hardinge, Kent v. Hampshire, at Southampton, 1922.
264   with J. W. Hearne, M.C.C. v. Tasmania, at Hobart, 1911–12.
253   with H. T. W. Hardinge, Kent v. Lancashire, at Dover, 1926.
245   with R. E. S. Wyatt, England v. South Africa, at Old Trafford, 1929.
243*   with E. Hendren, Rest of England v. Champion County, at the Oval, 1926.
220   with B. H. Valentine, Kent v. Surrey, at Tunbridge Wells, 1938.
210   with H. Seymour, Kent v. Oxford University, at Oxford, 1913.

For 4th wicket
296   with K. L. Hutchings, Kent v. Northamptonshire, at Gravesend, 1908.
265   with M. J. Turnbull, M.C.C. v. New South Wales, at Sydney, 1929–30.
233   with K. L. Hutchings, Kent v. Sussex, at Hastings, 1910.
211   with A. F. Bickmore, Kent v. Hampshire, at Southampton, 1920.
200   with S. H. Day, Kent v. Worcestershire, at Canterbury, 1914.
200   with J. C. Hubble, Kent v. Warwickshire, at Edgbaston, 1921.

For 5th wicket
277   with L. E. G. Ames, Kent v. New Zealanders, at Canterbury, 1931.
241*   with D. W. Jennings, Kent v. Somerset, at Tunbridge Wells, 1911.

For 10th wicket
235   with A. Fielder, Kent v. Worcestershire, at Stourbridge, 1909.
      (Still an English record.)

Signifies unbroken partnership

LARGE WICKET PARTNERSHIPS SHARED IN BY F. E. WOOLLEY—*Continued*

F. E. Woolley shared in 12 century stands in Test cricket:

For 2nd wicket
142   with J. B. Hobbs v. South Africa, at Lord's, 1924.

For 3rd wicket
245   with R. E. S. Wyatt v. South Africa, at Old Trafford, 1929.
145   with E. Hendren v. Australia at Lord's, 1926.
121*   with E. Hendren v. South Africa at Lord's, 1924.

For 4th wicket
100   with F. L. Fane v. South Africa, at Cape Town, 1909–10.

For 5th wicket
113   with P. F. Warner v. South Africa, at Lord's, 1912.
111   with J. W. Hearne v. South Africa, at Headingley, 1912.
104   with C. P. Mead v. South Africa, at Port Elizabeth, 1913–14.

For 6th wicket
124   with F. T. Mann v. South Africa, at Johannesburg, 1922–23.
106   with M. Leyland v. South Africa, at Headingley, 1929.

For 7th wicket
143   with J. Vine v. Australia, at Sydney, 1911–12.

For 9th wicket
128   with A. P. Freeman v. Australia, at Sydney, 1924–25.

Signifies unbroken partnership

CENTURIES (145)

116   Kent v. Hampshire, at Tonbridge, 1906.
152   Kent v. Northamptonshire, at Gravesend, 1908.
105   Kent v. Somerset, at Taunton, 1908.
117   Kent v. Surrey, at Blackheath, 1909.
185   Kent v. Worcestershire, at Stourbridge, 1909.
120   Kent v. Middlesex, at Lord's, 1910.
102   Kent v. Somerset, at Taunton, 1910.
117   Kent v. Sussex, at Hastings, 1910.
148   Kent v. Gloucestershire, at Cheltenham, 1911.
108   Kent v. Hampshire, at Canterbury, 1911.
104   Kent v. Somerset, at Tunbridge Wells, 1911.
148*   Kent v. Somerset, at Tunbridge Wells, 1911.
108*   Kent v. Sussex, at Hove, 1911.
119   Kent v. Worcestershire, at Maidstone, 1911.
133*   England v. Australia, at Sydney, 1911–12.
305*   M.C.C. v. Tasmania, at Hobart, 1911–12.
117   Kent v. Worcestershire, at Dudley, 1912.
101   M.C.C. Australian XI v. the Rest, at Lord's, 1912.
105   Kent v. Hampshire, at Portsmouth, 1913.
101*   Kent v. Somerset, at Taunton, 1913.
177   Kent v. Surrey, at Blackheath, 1913.
224*   Kent v. Oxford University, at Oxford, 1913.
116   M.C.C. v. Transvaal, at Johannesburg, 1913–14.
120   Kent v. Gloucestershire, at Maidstone, 1914.
111*   Kent v. Gloucestershire, at Gloucester, 1914.

* *Signifies not out*

CENTURIES (145)—*continued*

101	Kent v. Lancashire, at Canterbury, 1914.
147	Kent v. Leicestershire, at Catford, 1914.
117	Kent v. Leicestershire, at Ashby de la Zouch, 1914.
160*	Kent v. Worcestershire, at Canterbury, 1914.
134	Kent v. Hampshire, at Bournemouth, 1919.
107	Kent v. Sussex, at Hove, 1919.
164	Rest of England v. Champion County, at the Oval, 1919.
133	Kent v. Essex, at Dover, 1920.
158	Kent v. Hampshire, at Southampton, 1920.
150	Kent v. Northamptonshire, at Maidstone, 1920.
139*	Kent v. Sussex, at Horsham, 1920.
105	M.C.C. Australian team v. C. I. Thornton's XI, at Scarborough, 1920.
138	M.C.C. v. New South Wales, at Sydney, 1920–21.
174	Kent v. Gloucestershire, at Maidstone, 1921.
103	Kent v. Leicestershire, at Leicester, 1921.
103	Kent v. Middlesex, at Lord's, 1921.
109	Kent v. Nottinghamshire, at Trent Bridge, 1921.
149	Kent v. Warwickshire, at Edgbaston, 1921.
111	Kent v. Worcestershire, at Tonbridge, 1921.
188	Kent v. Hampshire, at Southampton, 1922.
155	Kent v. Lancashire, at Dover, 1922.
123	Kent v. Leicestershire, at Gravesend, 1922.
102*	Kent v. Somerset, at Tonbridge, 1922.
100	Kent v. Surrey, at the Oval, 1922.
115*	England v. South Africa, at Johannesburg, 1922–23.
136*	Kent v. Leicestershire, at Maidstone, 1923.
270	Kent v. Middlesex, at Canterbury, 1923.
106*	Kent v. Somerset, at Weston-super-Mare, 1923.
138	Kent v. Yorkshire, at Tonbridge, 1923.
107	Kent v. Oxford University, at Oxford, 1923.
117*	Kent v. Essex, at Leyton, 1924.
101	Kent v. Hampshire, at Canterbury, 1924.
141	Kent v. Leicestershire, at Leicester, 1924.
117	Kent v. Sussex, at Tunbridge Wells, 1924.
108	Kent v. Sussex, at Hastings, 1924.
176	Kent v. South Africans, at Canterbury, 1924.
134*	England v. South Africa, at Lord's, 1924.
202	Rest of England v. Champion County, at the Oval, 1924.
123	England v. Australia, at Sydney, 1924–25.
149	M.C.C. v. New South Wales at Sydney, 1924–25
176	Kent v. Gloucestershire, at Cheltenham, 1925.
215	Kent v. Somerset, at Gravesend, 1925.
118	Kent v. Sussex, at Canterbury, 1925.
136	Kent v. Warwickshire, at Edgbaston, 1925.
104	Rest of England v. Champion County, at the Oval, 1925.
137	Kent v. Lancashire, at Dover, 1926.
106	Kent v. Leicestershire, at Maidstone, 1926.
217	Kent v. Northamptonshire, at Northampton, 1926.
114	Kent v. Nottinghamshire, at Trent Bridge, 1926.
104	Kent v. Sussex, at Hastings, 1926.
172*	Rest of England v. Champion County, at the Oval, 1926.
187	Kent v. Derbyshire, at Chatham, 1927.
101	Kent v. Essex, at Leyton, 1927.
106*	Kent v. Northamptonshire, at Northampton, 1927.
141*	Kent v. M.C.C., at Folkestone, 1927.
125	Kent v. New Zealanders, at Canterbury, 1927.
198	Kent v. Derbyshire, at Maidstone, 1928.

* Signifies not out.

CENTURIES (145)—*Continued*

102*   Kent v. Essex, at Leyton, 1928.
107   Kent v. Gloucestershire, at Gloucester, 1928.
151   Kent v. Lancashire, at Old Trafford, 1928.
160   Kent v. Leicestershire, at Tonbridge, 1928.
128   Kent v. Sussex, at Tunbridge Wells, 1928.
120   Kent v. Sussex, at Hastings, 1928.
156   Kent v. Warwickshire, at Tunbridge Wells, 1928.
100   Kent v. Oxford University, at Oxford, 1928.
125   Kent v. M.C.C., at Folkestone, 1928.
141*   Players v. Gentlemen, at Folkestone, 1928.
151   An England XI v. West Indians, at Folkestone, 1928.
155   Kent v. Derbyshire, at Chesterfield, 1929.
118   Kent v. Essex, at Leyton, 1929.
119   Kent v. Gloucestershire, at Canterbury, 1929.
117   Kent v. Hampshire, at Folkestone, 1929.
176   Kent v. Middlesex, at Lord's, 1929.
108   Kent v. Somerset, at Tonbridge, 1929.
131   Kent v. Yorkshire, at Tonbridge, 1929.
142   Kent v. M.C.C., at Folkestone, 1929.
154   England v. South Africa, at Old Trafford, 1929.
111   England XI v. South Africans, at Folkestone, 1929.
106   Rest of England v. Champion County, at the Oval, 1929.
132   M.C.C. v. Otago, at Dunedin, 1929–30.
146   M.C.C. v. South Australia, at Adelaide, 1929–30.
219   M.C.C. v. New South Wales, at Sydney, 1929–30.
103   Kent v. Lancashire, at Dover, 1930.
110   Kent v. Surrey, at Blackheath, 1930.
109   Kent v. Surrey, at the Oval, 1930.
120   Kent v. Sussex, at Folkestone, 1930.
119   Kent v. Yorkshire, at Headingley, 1930.
108   Kent v. Lancashire, at Old Trafford, 1931.
168   Kent v. Northamptonshire, at Tonbridge, 1931.
103*   Kent v. Warwickshire, at Folkestone, 1931.
188   Kent v. Yorkshire, at Bradford, 1931.
224   Kent v. New Zealanders, at Canterbury, 1931.
146   Kent v. Glamorgan, at Swansea, 1932.
161   Kent v. Derbyshire, at Canterbury, 1933.
131   Kent v. Leicestershire, at Maidstone, 1933.
108   Kent v. Middlesex, at Gravesend, 1933.
198   Kent v. Somerset, at Tunbridge Wells, 1933.
136   England XI v. West Indians, at Folkestone, 1933.
172   Kent v. Essex, at Gravesend, 1934.
124   Kent v. Gloucestershire, at Tunbridge Wells, 1934.
122   Kent v. Hampshire, at Folkestone, 1934.
104   Kent v. Northamptonshire, at Dover, 1934.
176   Kent v. Northamptonshire, at Northampton, 1934.
101   Kent v. Nottinghamshire, at Canterbury, 1934.
121   Kent v. Somerset, at Taunton, 1934.
132   Kent v. Surrey, at Blackheath, 1934.
104   Kent v. Worcestershire, at Tonbridge, 1934.
106   Kent v. Yorkshire, at Headingley, 1934.
110   Kent v. Gloucestershire, at Bristol, 1935.
105   Kent v. Lancashire, at Gravesend, 1935.
229   Kent v. Surrey, at the Oval, 1935.
157   Kent v. Sussex, at Hastings, 1935.
172   Kent v. Sussex, at Tunbridge Wells, 1935.
117   Kent v. M.C.C., at Folkestone, 1935.

Signifies not out.

CENTURIES (145)—*Continued*

101	Kent v. Hampshire, at Southampton, 1936.
100	Kent v. Gloucestershire, at Dover, 1937.
193	Kent v. Somerset, at Dover, 1937.
114	Kent v. Surrey, at Blackheath, 1937.
162	Kent v. Sussex, at Tunbridge Wells, 1938.
136	Kent v. Worcestershire, at Tonbridge, 1938.

* Signifies not out.

EXCEPTIONAL BOWLING ANALYSES

6 for 8	Kent v. Middlesex, at Lord's, 1908.
5 for 17	Kent v. Surrey, at Blackheath, 1908.
7 for 9	Kent v. Surrey, at the Oval, 1911.
7 for 25	Kent v. Essex, at Gravesend, 1912.
6 for 21	Kent v. Nottinghamshire, at Trent Bridge, 1912.
5 for 20	England v. Australia, at the Oval, 1912.
5 for 20	Players v. Gentlemen, at Lord's, 1920.
8 for 22	Kent v. Gloucestershire, at Maidstone, 1921.
7 for 20	Kent v. Northamptonshire, at Dover, 1921.
6 for 21	Kent v. Essex, at Leyton, 1923.
5 for 14	Kent v. Northamptonshire, at Gravesend, 1924.

F. E. Woolley took 10 or more wickets on 28 occasions, the chief of which were:

14 for 91	Kent v. Warwickshire, at Edgbaston, 1922.
13 for 123	Kent v. Middlesex, at Canterbury, 1922.
12 for 122	Kent v. Gloucestershire, at Gloucester, 1914.
12 for 129	Kent v. Lancashire, at Old Trafford, 1919.
12 for 61	Kent v. Sussex, at Tonbridge, 1919.
12 for 128	Rest of England v. Champion County, at the Oval, 1921.
12 for 105	Kent v. Essex, at Leyton, 1923.

BOWLING UNCHANGED THROUGH A COMPLETED MATCH

1910   Woolley (8 for 91) and Blythe (11 for 95) Kent v. Yorkshire at Maidstone.
1912   Woolley (9 for 58) and Blythe (11 for 56) Kent v. Nottinghamshire at Canterbury.

EIGHT WICKETS IN AN INNINGS

8 for 52   Kent v. Sussex, at Hastings, 1910.
8 for 22   Kent v. Gloucestershire, at Maidstone, 1921.
8 for 52   Kent v. Warwickshire, at Edgbaston, 1922.

NOTES

F. E. Woolley performed the hat-trick once—against Surrey at Blackheath in 1919.

Twice Woolley completed 100 before lunch—against Surrey at Blackheath in 1930 and against Derbyshire at Canterbury in 1933.

F. E. Woolley in the Test match England v. South Africa at Headingley in 1929 scored 83 and 95 not out.

In his 98 Test innings, he had 13 "ducks" but never a "pair."

His 154 v. South Africa at Old Trafford in 1929 was scored in 165 minutes, during which time he and R. E. S. Wyatt put on 245 runs for the third wicket.

In 1929 he scored four consecutive centuries as follows: 155 v. Derbyshire at Chesterfield, 108 v. Somerset at Tonbridge, 131 v. Yorkshire at Tonbridge, and 117 v. Hampshire at Folkestone.

He scored over 2,000 runs in 13 seasons, and did the double on eight occasions.

For England v. Australia at the Oval in 1912 he had a match analysis of 104 balls, four maidens, 49 runs, 10 wickets.

Woolley made every score between 0 and 111, both inclusive, during his career.

Woolley played in 52 consecutive Test matches—a record only equalled later by P. B. H. May.

WOOSNAM, Maxwell, who died on July 14, 1965, aged 72, was one of the greatest all-round amateur sportsmen of his day. He captained Winchester in 1911, his second season in the XI, at cricket and golf. In 1911, when *Wisden* described him as one of the School players of the year, he hit 144 and 33 not out for a Public Schools XI against M.C.C. at Lord's. Going up to Cambridge, he did not get a Blue for cricket, though he was 12th man in the 1912 match against Oxford, but he represented the University at Association football, captaining the side in 1914, lawn tennis and real tennis. An outstanding centre-half, "Max" played football for the Corinthians, with whom he was on tour in Brazil when the First World War broke out. After Army service, he played for three years for Manchester City, whom he captained, and in 1922 became one of the few amateurs to gain an England cap in a full international when he was chosen as captain against Wales. At lawn tennis, he and R. Lycett won the doubles at Wimbledon in 1921 when he also captained the British Davis Cup team in America. At Antwerp in 1920 he won an Olympic Gold Medal as partner to O. G. N. Turnbull in the men's doubles and a silver medal in the mixed doubles. He later did much good work for the International Lawn Tennis Club of Great Britain.

WOOTTON, George, the famous Notts bowler of years gone by, died at Ruddington on June 15, 1924. Born at Clifton, Nottinghamshire, on October 16, 1834, he was thus in his 90th year. Inasmuch as George Wootton gave up cricket when he retired from Lord's after the season of 1873 he was only a name to the present generation, but old cricketers will remember him as one of the most successful left-handed bowlers of his day. He played his first match for Notts in 1861 and was in the XI until 1871, but though always a valuable member of the team he did not as a bowler for his county approach the feats of Jackson, J. C. Shaw, Alfred Shaw and Morley. His fame rests on what he did for the M.C.C., and more especially the M.C.C. at Lord's. Learning the game before the law was altered, he bowled with a round arm action, and without being very fast, was well above medium pace. In his early days the wickets at Lord's—rough, rather bare, and sometimes not too carefully rolled—presented difficulties with which modern batsmen rarely or never have to contend. I do not think that Wootton, though irreproachable in length and quite untiring, was a very difficult bowler on other grounds, but at Lord's for several years he was a veritable terror. Perhaps his comparatively low delivery helped him, but from all I can read no one ever bowled so many shooters. It was no uncommon experience for a batsman to get two of them in an over of four balls. No wonder R. A. H. Mitchell said that playing Wootton at Lord's was his sorest trial in the cricket field. Jimmy Grundy found Lord's in the first half of the '60s just as much to his liking as Wootton did, and in combination the two bowlers did wonderful things. Some variations of form in 1864, due wholly to differences in the grounds, were astounding. Mitchell's Oxford XI hit up a total of 439 against Grundy and Wootton at Oxford, but in the second innings of their return match at Lord's the two bowlers rattled them out for an ignominious total of 44. Again, in the same season Wootton and Grundy bowled Middlesex out for 20 at Lord's, but a week later, at the long-since-demolished Cattle Market ground at Islington, the county scored 411 against them. George Wootton took all 10 wickets in an innings for the All-England XI against Yorkshire in 1865, but with regard to that feat, the fact is generally overlooked that Yorkshire put a very poor side into the field, George Anderson, Iddison and Rowbotham, for some reason, being away. No professional attached to the M.C.C.'s ground staff at Lord's was ever better liked than Wootton, and it was entirely at his own wish that he retired in 1873—the year in which he had his benefit. He was then under 40, but he preferred farming to cricket. Still, in his retirement, he did not wholly lose his interest in the game. In 1921 he was present at the Test match at Trent Bridge and watched the play without wearing glasses.—S.H.P.

WOOTTON, James, a slow left-handed bowler of high skill, died in February, 1941, aged 80. By clever use of flight he made up for moderate height—5 ft. 6 in.—and sometimes sent down a surprise ball of unexpected speed. For Kent he took 628 wickets at 16.90 runs each. After playing for the county of his birth from 1880 to 1890, Wootton became coach at Winchester College, and when the first-class counties were increased to 14 in 1895 Hampshire were glad to use him, but his old skill had gone and he did little of note when occasionally appearing. He joined the staff at Lord's in 1884 and remained attached to the M.C.C. until 1890.

Among some of his best performances were: 13 wickets for 84 runs against Lancashire at Gravesend in 1883, 14 for 162 runs against Sussex at Hove in 1886, and in the same summer 13 wickets for 64 against Lancashire at Maidstone, while at Gravesend in 1888 he took five Middlesex wickets for eight runs. In 1894 he was given the Kent match with Surrey at Catford as a benefit. More memorable than his doings in County Cricket were two achievements at Canterbury against Australian sides. In 1884 Wootton helped Kent to win by 96 runs. Seven wickets fell to him in the match for 93 runs, three for 21 in the last innings. Alec Hearne, the present Kent scorer, did even better, with five wickets for 36 in the first innings—seven for 66 altogether. Stanley Christopherson, the fast bowler who played for England that year at Lord's and is now president of M.C.C., enjoyed a share in Kent's victory with three wickets for 12 runs in the final collapse. That was the only match against a county which W. L. Murdoch's third team lost. In 1886 the touring team, captained by H. J. H. Scott, were outplayed and defeated at Canterbury by 10 wickets. Wootton played a notable part in Kent's triumph, dismissing five men in each innings; he sent down 83 overs and two balls (four to the over) at a total cost of 100 runs. Alec Hearne, on this occasion, claimed four wickets for 37 runs, and George Hearne three in the first innings for 19 runs, the three professionals sharing the honours in twice dismissing the Australians after Kent had been put in to bat on a pitch soaked by heavy rain.

WORDSWORTH, The Right Rev. Charles, Bishop of St. Andrews, died on December 5, 1892. Dr. Wordsworth was a double Blue at Oxford in 1829, rowing in the eight in the first boat race against Cambridge, and playing in the XI in the first cricket match.

WORKMAN, James Allen, died suddenly on his way home from work on a London bus on December 23, 1970, aged 53. A most popular figure in London club cricket circles, Jim Workman, born in Australia, served with the Royal Australian Air Force in England and played in four of the five Victory Tests in 1945. He was a solid opening batsman and his top score in those matches, 63 at Sheffield, took him three and three-quarter hours. He came back to England after the War, coached the B.B.C. cricketers and ran the Australia House cricket team besides coaching regularly at weekends at Alf Gover's school in Wandsworth. He was a member of M.C.C. and Surrey.

WORMALD, Major John, M.C. who died on November 14, 1957, aged 75, was in the Eton XI in 1899 and the following year. A sound batsman, he scored 326 runs in 1899, average 29.63. From 1910 to 1912 he played in a few matches for Middlesex and subsequently he assisted Norfolk. He hit 61 against Yorkshire at Lord's in 1910 and he equalled that score against Sussex on the same ground the following season. He was awarded the M.C. while serving with the King's Royal Rifle Corps in France during the First World War.

WORRALL, John, died in Melbourne on November 17, 1937, aged 74. An excellent batsman for Victoria, he came to England in 1888 with the team captained by P. S. McDonnell and failed to show his proper form, but on his second visit, 11 years later, he was Australia's regular opening partner for his captain, Joseph Darling. A damaged knee kept Worrall out of several matches but he averaged 45 in four tests and scored altogether 1,202 runs. His 76 against England at Leeds on a rain-affected pitch was a forcing innings of special merit. He got the runs out of 95 in 75 minutes; his first three partners failed to score but he punished every loose ball and hit 14 fours. When Australia won at Lord's by 10 wickets, the only match of the five Tests brought to a definite issue, he scored 18 and 11 not out. He made centuries at Bradford, Leicester and Hove and took a conspicuous part in winning a remarkable match at Cambridge. On the last morning the Australians exactly equalled the University's total of 436; then dismissed their opponents for 122 and Darling and Worrall hit off the runs against time, the last 74 coming in 28 minutes. He was brilliant in the field.

For Victoria, Worrall played many fine innings and for Carlton against Melbourne University in 1896 he hit up 417 not out, the total, 922, then being the highest ever recorded officially in any match.

For many years Mr. Worrall wrote on cricket for Melbourne newspapers.

SIR FRANK WORRELL
Born in Barbados, August 1, 1924
Died in Jamaica, March 13, 1967
Knighted for his services to cricket, 1964
By Sir Learie Constantine

Sir Frank Worrell once wrote that the island of Barbados, his birthplace, lacked a hero. As usual, he was under-playing himself. Frank Maglinne Worrell was the first hero of the new nation of Barbados and anyone who doubted that had only to be in the island when his body was brought home in mid March of 1967.

Or in Westminster Abbey when West Indians of all backgrounds and shades of opinion paid their last respects to a man who had done more than any other of their countrymen to bind together the new nations of the Caribbean and establish a reputation for fair play throughout the world. Never before had a cricketer been honoured with a memorial service in Westminster Abbey.

Sir Frank was a man of strong convictions, a brave man and it goes without saying, a great cricketer. Though he made his name as a player his greatest contribution was to destroy for ever the myth that a coloured cricketer was not fit to lead a team. Once appointed, he ended the cliques and rivalries between the players of various islands to weld together a team which in the space of five years became the champions of the world.

He was a man of true political sense and feeling, a federalist who surely would have made even greater contributions to the history of the West Indies had he not died so tragically in hospital of leukaemia at the early age of 42, a month after returning from India.

People in England can have little idea of the problems of West Indian cricket. It is not a question of a few countries bordering each other coming together in a joint team. Jamaica is 1,296 flying miles from Barbados, and Georgetown in Guyana 462 miles from Bridgetown in Barbados.

Before that wonderful tour of Australia in 1960–61, Barbadians would tend to stick together and so would the Trinidadians, Jamaicans and Guyanans. Worrell cut across all that. Soon there were no groups. Just one team.

He told his batsmen to walk if they were given out. When Gary Sobers appeared to show his dissent with a decision, he reprimanded him. After that, everyone walked as soon as the umpire's finger went up.

So when half a million Australians lined the streets of Melbourne in their ticker tape farewell to Worrell and his men, they were not only paying a final tribute to the team's great achievements, they were recognising the capacity and potential of equals both on and off the turf.

Sir Frank started life in Barbados, worked and lived in Trinidad and died in Jamaica after doing much useful work at the University of the West Indies there. He incurred enmity by leaving his birthplace but he did not care much for insularity, cant and humbug.

He saw the many diverse elements of the West Indies as a whole, a common culture and outlook separated only by the Caribbean Sea. This is why he upset certain people in Barbados when he wrote to a newspaper there criticising the island for having the cheek to challenge the rest of the world to celebrate independence.

Worrell was strongly criticised for this action, bitterly in fact in some quarters. But being attacked did not worry him. He always had the courage to say what he felt about every issue he thought vital to the well-being of the islands.

Sadly, the news that he was dying came through as Barbados played the Rest of the World XI. But Worrell held no rancour against his homeland. He had bought a piece of land there and had intended to retire there eventually.

This willingness to speak out often got him into trouble, even at school. Cricket had come naturally to him as it does to most youngsters in the West Indies, particularly Barbados. More so with him because he was born in a house only a few yards away from the Empire cricket ground. He and his friends used to set up stumps on the outfield and play nearly all day in the holidays.

At Combermere School he fell foul of a master who accused him of hogging the crease and not letting his colleagues bat.

He was to write later: "I was unfortunate enough to have been under an endemic psychological and mental strain throughout my school days. So much so that by the time I reached the fourth form I was suffering from a persecution complex.

"These were the days when child psychology was not a subject demanded of applicants to teachers' posts. Indeed, the majority of masters did not have the experience of raising families of their own. There was no allowance for the original point of view."

Worrell was a pupil who always had an original point of view. Also, as it was becoming clear at this time, he was a cricketer with an original talent. He soon made the Barbados team and records began to flow from his bat as he moved up the order from number eleven (yes, that is where he began his career!).

He shared a partnership of 502 with John Goddard in 1943–44 and an unfinished 574 with Clyde Walcott in 1945–46. Typically he dismissed both. "The conditions were loaded in our favour," he said. "I wasn't all that delighted about it."

In 1947 he tired of living in Barbados. His mother had moved to New York and his father was away at sea most of the time so he moved to Jamaica. English people will be surprised to learn that many of Worrell's fellow Bajans have never forgiven him for this "betrayal". When will they ever learn?

He established an international reputation against the 1947–48 England touring side and at the end of that tour took the step that made him a batsman for all seasons and all wickets. He signed as professional for the Central Lancashire League side Radcliffe for a fee of £500 a year.

It was a good year to enter League cricket. The Central Lancashire League was a cricket academy and the young, talented player was bound to improve by the experience. Playing in neighbouring clubs were Bill Alley, Jock Livingston, Ray Lindwall, Cecil Pepper, Clyde Walcott, Everton Weekes, Vinoo Mankad and Dattu Phadkar.

I have always held that League cricket makes a cricketer, not only as a player but as a man. There is much to learn in the field of human relations from the kind, friendly and warm people of the North of England. Frank brought his fiancée, Velda, over and their marriage was another settling influence on him.

Worrell was not just living for the present —as I regret is the case with some of our cricketers—but he was thinking of the future. He took a course at Manchester University and qualified in economics, his chosen subject.

The flag on Radcliffe Town Hall was at half mast on the day of his death. He married his wife, Velda, at Radcliffe, and their daughter was born there. Such was the esteem in which he was held by Radcliffe that in 1964 a street near the cricket ground was named Worrell Close.

The 1950 tour of England was a triumph for him and he topped the Test batting averages with 539 runs at an average of 89.83. His best Test score of 261 was made in this season, at Trent Bridge.

Norman Yardley, the England captain of the time, told me it was impossible to set a field to him. Place the fieldsmen straight and he beat them on the wide. Place them wide and he would beat them straight.

I am not one for averages myself. I am more concerned with how a batsman made his runs and not what his average was at the end of the series. Sir Neville Cardus has written of Sir Frank that he never made a crude or an ungrammatical stroke. I agree with that. Worrell was poetry.

While Walcott bludgeoned the bowlers and Weekes dominated them, the stylist Worrell waved them away. There was none of the savage aggression of a Sobers in his batting. He was the artist. All three "Ws" were geniuses but Worrell was my favourite because he had more style and elegance. He had all the strokes and the time and capacity to use them without offence to the eye, without ever being hurried.

He was never seen playing across the line. That is why he never hooked. Players and Pressmen agreed that even when he ducked beneath a bouncer, he did so with a lack of panic and great dignity. And remember he had Lindwall and Miller to contend with!

The tour to Australia in 1951–52 was not such a success as the 1950 tour of England. Worrell himself said this was because there were too many factions in the side and John Goddard, previously showered with advice, was not helped this time by the seniors.

When Worrell took over the captaincy nine years later, he was to heed the lessons of this dismal tour. The return series in the West Indies in 1955 was again a disappointment for Worrell; he scored only 206 runs. The 1957 tour of England was a further let down. Clearly the West Indies authorities had to change their policy of always appointing a white man to captain the side.

The break was made in 1960 when Worrell, the only candidate with the outstanding qualities to do this gigantic repair job, was asked to lead the side in Australia. Everyone knows the story of that tour and how much it did to restore the good name of cricket after the "bumper" rows, "slow over rates" disputes and other ills which had been afflicting the international game.

Back in Jamaica, Worrell was acclaimed and rightly so. He was appointed Warden of the University College of the West Indies and also a Senator in Parliament.

The Indians were the next tourists to the West Indies and it was typical of the man that when their captain, Nari Contractor, was seriously injured by a blow on the head, Worrell was one of the donors of blood which saved his life.

It was not generally known that Worrell, the 13th West Indies captain, was a superstitious man. During the 1951 tour of Australia he was bowled first ball by Geoff Noblet. Determined to make a fresh start in the second innings, he changed every stitch of clothing, fitting himself out in a completely new gear and walked to the wicket hoping that by discarding his old clothes he would change his luck. Not a bit of it! He was out for another first baller!

As he came in, crestfallen, Clyde Walcott, the next batsman, said with a laugh: "Why do I have to face a hat-trick every time I follow you?"

His finest hours in England came in 1963 when he led the West Indies to more glory. By this time he had slowed up in the field and his figure was well in excess of Miss World proportions. He was 38 (age I mean) and no longer the player he had been. He was a tired man and often told me so.

But his influence over the side as captain was such that it was unthinkable to rest him in any of the Tests. He bowled a few shrewd medium pacers with his deceptively easy delivery and when the crisis was on in the Lord's Test, the greatest Test of all times as it was called by the critics, he helped Butcher to add 110 on the Saturday afternoon. The following Monday morning the second innings collapsed.

Asked if Worrell was worried about this, another player replied: "No, he is asleep." Sir Frank had this ability to drop off at any time, particularly when there was a batting collapse. After his death, I wondered whether this had something to do with his illness which was obviously affecting him at this time, though no one knew that he was not a fit man.

As Wes Hall prepared for the final over which could have won or lost the Lord's Test, Worrell went to him with some advice. What was he saying? Bounce them? Bowl 'em straight? No, none of the obvious things. Sir Frank said calmly: "Make sure you don't give it to them by bowling no balls." Worrell was the calmest man at Lord's that day and trust him to think of a highly pertinent point which Hall, in his excitement, may have overlooked!

He announced his retirement at the end of this tour which was a triumph of leadership, technical skill and adaptability. The following year Her Majesty the Queen knighted this complete Cricketer, Philosopher and Captain. It was a fitting end to an unforgettable career but there was one more job for him to do—manage the West Indies side against the 1965 Australian tourists.

He had groomed Sobers well for the captaincy and theirs was an unbeatable partnership. At last the West Indies were the undisputed champions in their truly national sport.

Throughout his life, Sir Frank never lost his sense of humour or his sense of dignity. Some nasty things were said and written during that 1965 tour but Sir Frank was ever

the diplomat. He lost no friends, made no enemies yet won more respect. He would always come up with a smile and a loud laugh. West Indians really laugh their laughs. And Sir Frank laughed louder than most of us.

He was a happy man, a good man and a great man. The really tragic thing about his death at the age of 42 was that it cut him off from life when he still had plenty to offer the islands he loved. He was only at the beginning. Or was it that the opportunity came to him a bit too late?

Other tributes:

S. C. Griffith (Secretary of M.C.C.): "Ever since I first saw him play during the M.C.C. tour of the West Indies, I have thought of Frank Worrell as a great and impressive batsman and a very useful bowler. Even more than that, I have been impressed by his ever growing stature as leader of cricketers, by his tolerance and understanding and by the contribution he was making to the game. He was a great friend of mine and like countless other cricketers I shall miss him more than I can say."

P. B. H. May: "The game has lost a personality we all admired. He was one of the greatest of the long line of Barbadian cricketers. One associated him with his two colleagues, Weeks and Walcott, but I regard him as the most accomplished of the trio."

Sir Donald Bradman: "His name is for ever shrined on the Frank Worrell Trophy which Australia is proud to have created for permanent competition between our two countries. Players of his calibre are rare. Not only was he a truly great and stylish batsman, he was also a fine thinker with a broad outlook."

Richie Benaud: "He was a great leader of men and one of the finest cricketers on and off the field in the history of the game. It is difficult to realise that the indolent drawl, the feline grace known all over the world are no more. Few men have had a better influence on cricket."

Ian Johnson: "He was easily the greatest captain of modern times. He brought West Indies cricket to the top and set a wonderful example to world cricket."

Alan Barnes (Secretary, Australian Board of Control): "His name is indelibly linked with the finest traditions of cricket throughout the world and particularly in the hearts of all Australian cricket lovers."

E. R. Dexter: "His reputation as a cricketer is beyond dispute. I found him one of the best captains I have seen or played against."

F. S. Trueman: "He was one of the nicest people I ever played against."

J. M. Kilburn: "Cricket was always distinguished in the presence of Worrell—Sir Frank. His knighthood was a personal honour to a cricketer of rare quality and an acknow-ledgement that West Indian cricket had reached the highest level in the world. In his captaincy he won esteem and affection by the calm demeanour in which he cloaked firmness and shrewd tactics. His serenity smoothed ruffled feathers and diminished crises."

SIR FRANK WORRELL IN FIRST-CLASS CRICKET

		Matches	Inns.	Not Outs	Runs	Highest Inns.	Average	Runs	Wickets	Average
1941–42	In West Indies	4	7	2	134	48	26.80	300	15	20.00
1942–43	In West Indies	2	4	1	322	188	107.33	110	1	110.00
1943–44	In West Indies	2	3	1	347	308*	173.50	145	10	14.50
1944–45	In West Indies	4	7	0	325	113	46.42	293	8	36.62
1945–46	In West Indies	1	2	1	271	255*	271.00	77	2	38.50
1946–47	In West Indies	2	4	1	148	67*	49.33	223	7	31.85
1947–48	In West Indies	7	10	4	568	131*	94.66	466	11	42.36
1949–50	In India, Pakistan and Ceylon	17	26	4	1,640	223*	74.54	611	26	23.50
1950	In England	22	31	5	1,775	261	68.26	970	39	24.87
1950–51	In India and Ceylon	22	33	3	1,900	285	63.33	1,186	39	30.41
1951	In England	2	3	0	88	52	29.33	2	0	—
1951–52	In Australia and New Zealand	12	22	4	872	160*	48.44	583	28	20.82
1952	In England	1	2	0	97	62	48.50	—	—	—
1952–53	In West Indies	6	10	1	446	237	49.55	283	7	40.42
1953	In England	2	4	0	83	37	20.75	52	5	10.40
1953–54	In India	11	16	0	833	165	52.06	659	24	27.45
1953–54	In West Indies	4	8	1	334	167	47.71	193	2	96.50
1954	In England	2	3	1	116	74	58.00	52	1	52.00
1954–55	In West Indies	7	13	0	378	100	29.07	443	8	55.37
1955	In England	2	4	0	178	100	44.50	185	6	30.83
1957	In England	19	34	9	1,470	191*	58.80	949	39	24.33
1958	In England	2	3	0	173	101	57.66	66	1	66.00
1959	In England	1	2	0	79	54	39.50	63	3	21.00
1959–60	In West Indies	5	7	1	395	197*	65.83	252	6	42.00
1960–61	In Australia	12	22	3	818	82	43.05	748	22	34.00
1961	In England	2	3	0	46	29	15.33	141	6	23.50
1961–62	In West Indies	6	8	3	403	98*	80.60	178	4	44.50
1963	In England	18	23	2	522	74*	24.85	480	13	36.92
1963–64	In West Indies	5	6	1	158	73	31.60	260	9	28.88
1964	In England	5	6	1	106	42	21.20	164	7	23.42
		207	326	49	15,025	308*	54.24	10,134	349	29.03

TEST MATCHES

		Matches	Inns.	Not Outs	Runs	Highest Inns.	Average	Runs	Wickets	Average
v. England	..	25	42	6	1,979	261	54.97	1,211	28	43.25
v. Australia	..	14	28	0	918	108	32.78	997	30	32.23
v. New Zealand	..	2	3	1	233	100	116.50	81	2	40.50
v. India	..	10	14	2	730	237	60.83	384	9	42.66
		51	87	9	3,860	261	49.48	2,673	69	38.73

*Signifies not out.

WORSLEY, Arthur Edward, who died on August 10, 1969, aged 86, was in the Malvern XI at the turn of the century. He played for Northamptonshire before they became a first-class county and in 1905, the year they were elevated to the County Championship competition.

WORSLEY, Francis, died in a London hospital on September 15, 1949. He was best known as producer of the radio variety programme "Itma," but in his younger days he played cricket for Glamorgan during seasons 1922 and 1923, and always retained his love for the game. Worsley was educated at Brighton College and Oxford and formerly held a scholastic appointment.

WORSLEY, William, born at Wandsworth, died at Accrington on November 14, 1918. Lancashire league cricket—Accrington and Church—1893–1903; Lancashire XI, 1903–13. During his connection with the Lancashire XI, which extended over 11 seasons Worsley proved himself a very useful wicketkeeper but he never rose to the first class.

WORSLEY, Col. Sir William Arthington, Bart., who died on December 4, 1973, aged 83, was president of Yorkshire County C.C. since 1960. He was in the Eton XI in 1908 and 1909, being top scorer with 42 against Harrow in the first year and afterwards played much Army and club cricket. He became captain of Yorkshire in 1928 and 1929, and although he achieved little as a batsman—he scored 733 runs at an average of 16.28—the county were only twice beaten under his leadership. When he was president of M.C.C. in 1962, he visited India when E. R. Dexter's M.C.C. team were touring there. While serving with the Green How-

ards in the First World War, he was wounded and taken prisoner. His daughter, the Duchess of Kent, conferred an honorary degree of Doctor of Laws upon him at Leeds University in 1967.

WORTHINGTON, Thomas Stanley, who died in hospital on September 1, 1973, aged 68, while on holiday at King's Lynn, was a fine all-rounder for Derbyshire between 1924 and 1947. He took part in nine Test matches for England, five of them when a member of G. O. Allen's team in Australia in 1936–37. He distinguished himself at the Oval in 1936 when scoring 128, he and W. R. Hammond (217) adding 266 and setting up a fourth-wicket record against India.

During his career, Stan Worthington, as he was always known, scored as a firm-hitting right-handed batsman 19,221 runs, average 29.07; hit 31 centuries—two in the same match against Nottinghamshire at Ilkeston in 1938; with bowling of splendid length at above medium pace, took 682 wickets at a cost of 29.22 runs apiece and held 326 catches.

Unlike several Derbyshire players of his time, he did not begin his working life as a miner. At the age of 17 he became an electrician with the Bolsover Colliery Company and achieved much success for their cricket club in the Bassetlaw league. He did not play for the county with any regularity until 1926, but soon proved his value. He hit a glorious 133 against Essex at Chesterfield in 1928, completing his century in 100 minutes, and in that year he reached 1,000 runs for the first of 10 seasons.

When his first-class career ended, he played for Northumberland and in Lancashire league cricket and for 10 years served as chief coach to Lancashire County C.C., at Old Trafford.

T. S. WORTHINGTON
BATTING

	Inns	Not Outs	Runs	Highest Inns	100s	Aver.
1924	2	0	12	12	0	6.00
1925	6	1	49	20	0	9.80
1926	37	4	669	84	0	20.27
1927	33	2	801	98	0	25.83
1928	45	6	1,164	133	3	29.84
1929	47	3	1,031	72	0	23.43
1929–30	15	0	370	125	1	24.66
1930	43	2	803	83	0	19.58
1931	38	7	649	60*	0	20.93
1932	44	3	1,386	129	2	33.80

Signifies not out

BATTING—*Continued*

	Inns	Not Outs	Runs	Highest Inns	100s	Aver.
1933	48	6	1,243	200*	2	29.59
1934	46	1	1,196	154	2	26.57
1935	42	2	1,357	126	2	33.92
1936	45	3	1,734	174	5	41.28
1936–37	25	1	571	89	0	23.79
1937	49	6	1,774	238*	4	41.25
1937–38	18	2	530	82	0	33.12
1938	41	2	1,573	121	5	40.33
1939	42	4	1,045	119	2	27.50
1946	29	1	559	147*	1	19.96
1947	25	3	705	130	2	32.04
Totals	720	59	19,221	238*	31	29.07

BOWLING

	Inns	Runs	Wkts	Aver.	5 wkts in Inns	Catches
1924	2	98	3	32.66	0	0
1925	6	99	5	19.80	0	0
1926	37	1,723	57	30.22	1	22
1927	33	1,236	49	25.22	1	17
1928	45	2,027	67	30.25	3	24
1929	47	2,093	89	23.51	5	20
1929–30	15	801	30	26.70	0	6
1930	43	1,727	59	29.27	2	22
1931	38	1,444	58	24.89	1	16
1932	44	1,660	54	30.74	1	20
1933	48	1,378	50	27.56	0	25
1934	46	1,666	59	28.23	1	27
1935	42	969	23	42.13	0	23
1936	45	727	23	31.60	0	21
1936–37	25	346	4	86.50	0	10
1937	49	372	10	37.20	0	18
1937–38	18	426	18	23.66	0	7
1938	41	146	7	20.85	1	18
1939	42	—	—	—	—	12
1946	29	279	3	93.00	0	9
1947	25	717	14	51.21	0	9
Totals	720	19,934	682	29.22	16	326

CENTURIES (31)

For Derbyshire (27)

v. Leicestershire (5) 147*, 130, 121, 106, 102.
v. Nottinghamshire (5) 126, 110*, 108, 108, 103.
v. Sussex (3) 238*, 133*, 119.
v. Hampshire (2) 154, 121.
v. Lancashire (2) 103, 101.
v. Northamptonshire (2) 147, 104.
v. Yorkshire (2) 135, 102.
v. Essex (1) 133.
v. M.C.C. (1) 101.
v. Oxford University (1) 174.
v. Surrey (1) 107.
v. Warwickshire (1) 163.
v. Worcestershire (1) 200*.

*Signifies not out.

CENTURIES—*Continued*

Other matches (4)
England v. India (1) 128.
M.C.C. Australian XI v. Rest of England (1) 156*.
M.C.C. v. Auckland (1) 125.
Players v. Gentlemen (1) 129.

Against Nottinghamshire at Ilkeston in 1938 he scored a century in each innings, 110* and 103.

BATTING IN TEST CRICKET

	Matches	Inns	Not Outs	Runs	Highest Inns	100s	Aver.
v. Australia	3	6	0	74	44	0	12.33
v. India	2	2	0	215	128	1	107.50
v. N.Z.	4	3	0	32	32	0	10.66
Totals	9	11	0	321	128	1	29.18

BOWLING IN TEST CRICKET

	Matches	Runs	Wkts	Aver.	Catches
v. Australia	3	78	0	—	3
v. India	2	52	1	52.00	3
v. N.Z.	4	186	7	26.57	2
Totals	9	316	8	39.50	8

Signifies not out.

WREFORD BROWN, Charles, the amateur footballer and Soccer legislator who played first-class cricket between 1886 and 1889, died at his home in London on November 26, 1951, aged 85. A free hitter, a slow bowler with a break either way and a good field at mid-off, Wreford Brown captained Charterhouse, and in 1887 he would have been in the Oxford team against Cambridge but for an accident. He occasionally assisted Gloucestershire, the county of his birth, and he visited America with Lord Hawke's team in 1891. As a soccer player, Wreford Brown achieved fame as a centre-half, although he could fill any position. He captained Oxford against Cambridge in 1889 and gained four caps for England, one when he led his team to notable victory against Scotland in Glasgow in 1898. He helped Old Carthusians and Corinthians. He became vice-president of the Football Association and for many years was chairman of the F.A. International Selection committee. He kept in trim even when undertaking legislative duties, and at 60 he turned out for Corinthians against Eton. Wreford Brown, who was a solicitor, made many trips abroad with F.A. teams as member in charge, and a good tale is told of him in this connection. A fine chess player, his keenness for the game led him into an embarrassing situation during one visit to the colonies. On arrival he was greeted by an old friend, a high officer of the home Association, also an enthusiastic chess player. All tour matters forgotten for the moment, the pair slipped off to a little café for a game, and there they stayed for several hours oblivious of the fact that officials were searching in vain for them and that the lunch of welcome had to go on without them.

WREFORD-BROWN, Capt. Oswald Eric (Northumberland Fusiliers), who died of wounds on July 7, 1916, aged 38, was in the Charterhouse XI in 1894 and two following years, being captain in 1896. In Public School matches his highest innings was 47 v. Wellington in his last season. Subsequently he played for Old Carthusians, Free Foresters and—only once or twice— Gloucestershire.

WRIGHT, Albert Charles, who died in Westminster Hospital on May 26, 1959, aged 63, played for Kent from 1921 to 1931. He had been ill for some time. A right-arm bowler considerably above medium pace, he took 596 wickets for the county at a cost of

24.32 runs each, among his best performances being six for 29 against Middlesex at Blackheath in 1926 and a precisely similar analysis against Somerset at Taunton the following season. In each of these summers his total of victims exceeded 100. Against Warwickshire at Edgbaston in 1925, he performed the hat-trick. A hard-hitting batsman, Wright obtained 3,258 runs, average 12.97, his highest innings being 81 against Essex at Gravesend in 1924, when he and A. L. Hilder, who hit 103 in his first county match, shared in an eighth-wicket stand of 157, a record for the county. He also brought off 122 catches.

WRIGHT, Charles William, died at Melton Mowbray on January 10, 1936, aged 72. A very good bat and wicket-keeper at Charterhouse, he got his Blue at Cambridge as a Freshman in 1882 and played four times against Oxford, his captains being the three Studds and Lord Hawke. In those matches he scored 292 runs with an average of 48. His innings of 102 in 1883 was faultless and attracted so much attention that the Cambridge authorities presented him with a medal. Born at Harewood, Yorkshire, Charles Wright when quite young went with his parents to Wollaton in Nottinghamshire, and before he was 13 played cricket at Trent Bridge, where he was fortunate to receive coaching by the leading county professionals, to whom he was much indebted. He first appeared for Nottinghamshire in 1881 and played intermittently with the county until July, 1899. A very steady bat, he usually went in first, and when wickets fell fast his defence often averted a complete collapse. For a scratch XI at Stoke-on-Trent in 1890 against the Australians he went in first, scored 26 out of 60 and, in the second innings, carried out his bat for seven in a total of 51. A year later when Nottinghamshire fell at Lord's before M.C.C. for 21, he was last out for five, the top score, only 15 runs coming from the bat. In the second innings of this match he made 39 out of 69, but the county were beaten in a day by an innings and 37 runs. On treacherous pitches, his strong back play enabled him to keep up his end against the best bowlers. In 1883 he played for the Gentlemen against Players at Lord's and the Oval. The loss of the sight of one eye in a shooting accident no doubt influenced Mr. Wright to give up active participation in the game comparatively early in life, but his interest in cricket remained unabated. Treasurer of the Nottinghamshire club for many years and a trustee

since 1900, Charles Wright was always closely in touch with his county's cricket. He went on four tours; with teams captained by Lord Hawke—to America and Canada in 1891 and 1894; to India in the winter of 1892, and to South Africa three years later.

WRIGHT, Edward Campbell, died on July 28, 1947, aged 73. Clergy Orphan School, Canterbury. Played for Oxford in 1897; also a little for Kent and Gloucestershire. For 35 years assistant master at Christ's Hospital, Horsham.

WRIGHT, Capt. and Brigade Major Egerton Lownes (Oxfordshire and Bucks. Light Infantry; General Staff Officer, Third Grade), born November 15, 1885, killed May 11, 1918. E. L. Wright had quite a brilliant career as a cricketer, being four years in the Winchester and four years in the Oxford XI. In his first season for Winchester in 1901, being then a boy of 16, he played an innings of 113 against Eton, and came out second in the college batting with an average of 34. In 1902 he was by no means so successful, but in 1903 he averaged 24 and in 1904 he finished up splendidly with an average of 50, and with an innings of 53 not out had a big share in beating Eton by eight wickets. He was captain in his two last years. At Oxford he began well, heading the batting in 1905 with an average of 31 and scoring 95 and 26 against Cambridge at Lord's. The following year he was not quite so good, but he again came off at Lord's, playing a brilliant second innings of 79. In 1907 and again in 1908 he was captain of the XI. The side had a very bad season in 1907, only winning one match out of nine, but Wright himself with an average of 30 was second to G. N. Foster in batting. Against Cambridge he scored four and 48. He finished up badly as a batsman at Oxford in 1908, being lower on the batting list than in any of his previous seasons. Still he had the satisfaction of seeing Oxford beat Cambridge by two wickets, and had something to do with the victory, scoring 37 in the last innings. He was tried for the Lancashire XI, and apart from cricket won his Blue at Oxford for Association football.

WRIGHT, Ernest V., a fair batsman in the Wellingborough XI in 1910 and 1911, who played twice for Northamptonshire in 1919, died at Kettering on December 16, 1977, aged 84. His two younger brothers, Stephen and Richard, both played for the county, as did three cousins, B., N.E. and P.A.

WRIGHT, The Rev. Frank Wynyard, born at Woodstock, in Oxfordshire, on April 6, 1844, died at Eastbourne on February 5, 1924. Living until nearly 80, F. W. Wright retained to the end the keenest interest in cricket. His own career, so far as first-class matches were concerned, finished nearly half a century ago. While still a young man he settled down to scholastic work at Eastbourne and remained there for the rest of his life. His was a case of a batsman who did not quite fulfil the abundant promise of his youth. Seldom has a schoolboy made a more vivid impression. He got his colours at Rossall as a boy of 14 and, though never captain, was in the XI five years. In 1861 he hit up a score of 198 not out for Present v. Past at Rossall and had an average for the season of 72. Then in 1862 he jumped into fame. For XXII of the school against the All-England XI he scored, with Willsher, Jackson and Tarrant bowling at him, 41 and 10, and later in the summer he was seen twice at Lord's in first-class matches. He played first for Gentlemen of the North against Gentlemen of the South, and next for North v. South in Grundy's benefit match. Scores were small at Lord's in those days, and for a lad of little more than 18 his innings of 50 for the North was looked upon as something wonderful. It caused quite a sensation and was regarded as one of the events of the season. Going up to Oxford with a big reputation, F. W. Wright was on the winning side against Cambridge at Lord's, under Mitchell's captaincy, in 1863–64–65, but except for a modest score of 27 in his last year he contributed nothing to the three victories. While he was at Oxford he took part in the famous tie match at Trent Bridge between Fourteen Free Foresters and Notts. In that game he played, perhaps, the innings of his life, driving Jackson straight out of the ground for six and knocking up a score of 64 in half an hour. Between 1864 and 1875 he appeared occasionally for Lancashire, and in 1869 played an innings of 120 not out against Sussex at Old Trafford. Nothing was seen of him in first-class cricket after he settled at Eastbourne, but for some time he must have kept up his batting, as in 1876, for Masters v. Colleges and Schools, he scored 307 not out in less than four hours, and in the following year 206 for Devonshire Park against Reigate. He was a son of the Rev. F. B. Wright, who was in the Oxford XI in 1829.—S.H.P.

WRIGHT, Capt. Harold (6th Loyal North Lancashire Regiment), died in London on September 13, 1915, of wounds received in the Dardanelles on July 28, aged 31. He was in the Mill Hill School XI in 1899 and two following years, being captain in 1901, when he had a batting average of 23.30, among his scores that season being 61 v. Wellingborough Grammar School, 51 v. Royal Naval School, and 47 v. Bedford Modern. He was an excellent club cricketer, and captain of the Leicester Ivanhoe C.C. In 1914 he appeared in six matches for Leicestershire, scoring 111 runs with an average of 13.87. His highest innings was 29 v. Hampshire at Leicester, and in the match between the same sides earlier in the year, at Southampton—his second game for the county—he had carried his bat through the innings for 26. Since 1913 he had been a member of the M.C.C.

WRIGHT, Henry, who since 1866 had been custodian of the Bramall Lane ground, died at Sheffield on November 28, 1893, having completed his 71st year on November 15. Though a familiar figure to all cricketers who have visited Sheffield, Wright, as an active player, was unknown to the present generation. His name will be found in the Sheffield club team as far back as 1843. He represented North against South at Lord's in 1855, and once during his career had the distinction of being chosen for the Players against the Gentlemen. In his day he was a fairly good bat, a tolerably successful bowler, and an extremely fine field at point. During his long connection with the Sheffield ground he won the regard of all with whom he was brought in contact.

WRIGHT, Henry Fitzherbert, died at Ashbourne, Derbyshire, on February 23, 1947, aged 76. He was in the Eton XI 1889, and played occasionally for Derbyshire from 1891 to 1905. Unionist M.P. for North Herefordshire, 1912–18.

WRIGHT, James, who died on August 20, 1961, aged 88, played in seven matches for Derbyshire between 1898 and 1905. His highest innings was 53 not out against Hampshire at Southampton in the first season.

WRIGHT, Leslie, who died in London on January 6, 1956, aged 52, played for Worcestershire from 1925 to 1933. Of Durham birth, he served as professional to Stourbridge before joining Worcestershire, for whom he scored 5,735 runs, average 19.44, and took 76 wickets. Twice he exceeded 1,000 runs in a season, scoring 1,395 in 1928 and 1,134 in 1930. He scored five centuries, the highest being 134 against Northamptonshire at Northampton in 1930. When he hit his maiden 100, 111 against Hampshire at Portsmouth in 1926, he and M. F. S. Jewell (103) shared in an opening partnership of 181. At one time he played Association football in the Worcester league, scoring 40 goals in a season from the centre-forward position. In recent years, Wright had been in charge of a remand home at Mitcham, Surrey.

WRIGHT, Levi George, who died at Derby on January 11, 1953, four days before his 91st birthday, was one of the finest batsmen who ever appeared for Derbyshire. Probably a better player at the age of 40 than at any other period of his career, he will be best remembered for his work as a fieldsman at point. Never standing more than four or five yards from the bat, he brought off many brilliant catches.

Born at Oxford on January 15, 1862, Wright was a batsman well worth watching, though possessing no particular grace of style. Like most cricketers who learned the game before hooking and pulling came into general vogue, he played forward a lot and scored chiefly on the off-side. Strong in defence, he displayed a good deal of enterprise considering that during the whole of his career he so regularly found himself battling for a side that was nearly always struggling. First playing for Oxford City, he went to Derby as an assistant schoolmaster in 1881, appearing for Derby Midland. A year later began that association with Derbyshire which, apart from the summers of 1885 and 1886, went on without interruption until he retired at the end of the season of 1909.

His biggest scores were 195 against Northamptonshire in 1905 and 193 against Nottinghamshire in 1901, both at Derby. On five other occasions for the county he exceeded 140. He followed his score of 195 with 176 and 122 against Warwickshire at Edgbaston, so enjoying the satisfaction of playing three successive three-figure innings. Four times he represented Gentlemen against Players, and, with 1901 his best year when he registered 1,482 runs, average 32, he scored in all 15,155 runs, average 26. He was also an able Association footballer, and after giving up cricket took to bowls, a game he continued until the late '80s.

Of his fielding, E. M. Grace used to relate how on one occasion when a batsman kept poking at the ball and cocking it up, Wright crept in closer and closer until he was only a yard or so away from the striker. Soon the fieldsman thought he saw his chance of a catch. He made a grab and the crowd cheered, but it was the bat he held, not the ball!

WRIGHT, Nicholas Edward, who died at Corby on May 20, 1974, aged 73, played in eight matches for Northamptonshire in 1921 and 1922. He was in the Wellingborough XI for three seasons, 1918–20, when altogether he scored 441 runs, average 20.45, and he took 60 wickets for 23.76 runs each. He was believed to be the last surviving Wright, nine of whom appeared for the county. His brothers were Bertie and Philip Alan (Bill), the brothers Ernest, Stephen, Richard and Albert were cousins. R.C.B. and A.J.B. were unrelated to that family. He umpired and scored in the Weldon, Kettering and Rockingham districts up to a week before his death.

WRIGHT, Philip Alan, who died in hospital after a short illness on December 21, 1968, aged 65, was in the Wellingborough XI before gaining a Blue as a Freshman at Cambridge in 1922. He helped to beat Oxford with an innings to spare by taking five wickets for 54 runs in the big match at Lord's. With five wickets in seven overs for five runs against Lancashire at Fenner's—twice he disposed of two men with following deliveries—he obtained 52 wickets for the Light Blues at a cost of 17.26 runs each. He could not produce his true form the next season and came in for punishment from Oxford; but he again did well at the expense of Lancashire at Fenner's with six first-innings wickets for 79. The following summer he returned to his best and, with two wickets for 21 runs and six for 49 in the University match, did much to bring success for Cambridge by nine wickets. He also dismissed six Sussex batsmen at Fenner's for 77 runs and he headed the University bowling figures with 56 wickets at an average cost of 15.85. An opening bowler of medium pace who employed a certain amount of spin with good effect and bowled an admirable length, he assisted Northamptonshire as an amateur from 1921 to 1929. In 1925, his one full season with the county, he took 100 wickets for 24.62 runs apiece. On seven occasions that summer he obtained five or more wickets in an innings, with his chief performance six for 65 runs against Nottinghamshire at Northampton, and he also hit 83, far and away his highest score from the Dublin University bowling at Kettering. In all first-class cricket "Bill," as he was known, took 343 wickets, average 23.55. Both his brothers, B. and N.E., also played for the county as well as three other brothers Wright who were cousins.

WRIGHT, Col. Thomas Yates, who died in February, 1964, aged 95, was the first man to hit a score of 200 in first-class cricket in Ceylon. Of Lancashire birth, he went to the island in 1899 and became one of the best all-round sportsmen there, excelling at cricket, Rugby football, hockey and polo. He played cricket for the Matale and Kandy Sports club and for Up Country from 1893 to 1919. He assisted Ceylon against several touring teams. From 1920 to 1925 he was a member of the Legislative Council.

WRIGHT, Walter, one of the first bowlers capable of swerving the ball to an appreciable extent, died at Leigh, Lancashire, on March 22, 1940, aged 84. Born at Hucknell, he played for Nottinghamshire from 1879 to 1886, for Kent from 1888 to 1899, and finished a long and varied career on the first-class cricket field as umpire. Bowling left-hand above medium pace, with good control of length, he used to trouble most batsmen at the start of an innings. His swerve, then almost a novelty, and speed from the turf rendered him extremely difficult, and he accomplished some remarkable performances. At Trent Bridge, he once dismissed six Yorkshiremen for 10 runs, and five M.C.C. wickets fell to him for one run on the same ground. During eight seasons when comparatively few first-class county matches were played, he took 193 wickets for Nottinghamshire at 18 runs apiece. His association with the county of his birth ended through some dispute over remuneration for a match with the Australian team of 1886. He then qualified for Kent, and for 12 years enjoyed much success, chiefly when sharing the attack with "Nutty" Martin, another left-hander of less pace. Before the ground was levelled, these two went through many sides at Moat Park, Maidstone. Wright, with the slope favouring his swerve, made the ball go very fast down-hill; Martin, using the left-hander's natural break-back, afforded a marked contrast—a leg-break to the right-handed batsman. Altogether for Kent, Walter Wright took 725 wickets at less than 20 runs each. Two notable performances against Middlesex, at Canterbury and Lord's, were identical—13 wickets for 106 runs in each match. On a third occasion 13 wickets fell to him, this time at a cost of 150 runs, when Nottinghamshire visited Maidstone in 1895.

In 1880 a team of Canadians lost their best man, a deserter from the Horse Guards, and Wright was engaged to play for them. In his first match he scored 80 runs and took 14 wickets, but payment being uncertain in an ill-starred venture, Wright soon left the team and the tour broke down in mid-season. His ability as a right-handed batsman was shown in 1883, when, in the match with Gloucestershire, he was sent in shortly before time on the first evening, withstood the attack throughout the next day, and when the innings closed on the third morning he remained unbeaten with 127 runs to his credit. For Mote Park in 1887 he scored 237 against Free Foresters.

During his period as umpire, Wright officiated in the match at Taunton when James Phillips, standing at square leg, no-balled Tyler for doubtful delivery. Disagreeing with his colleague, Wright would not allow more than the regulation number of balls (four) to the over. At a time when single-wicket matches were popular, Wright in 1885 opposed 11 men and won very easily; he made 61 runs and dismissed his opponents in each innings for six.

In his young days, thanks to his quickness off the mark, he was an excellent field. His sprinting powers were demonstrated when he won the Sheffield Handicaps in 1880 and 1881—races which were stopped eventually because of the extensive betting with which they were associated. At one time he was considered to be the second fastest runner in the world at 130 yd.

After his long spell in first-class cricket, Walter Wright turned out for Berkshire in 1904, and for some years was coach at Radley College. He also acted as trainer to Association football clubs.

WRIGLEY, Arthur, who died in a Stockport hospital on October 30, 1965, aged 53, was well known as a cricket statistician. After service with the Royal Air Force, he became, as a slow right-arm bowler and forceful batsman, a member of the Lancashire ground staff before, in 1934, he took up the post of scorer for the B.B.C., which he held until his death.

WRIGLEY, Samuel, died at Northampton in January, 1927, at the age of 71. He had kept wicket for Northants and for some years was an umpire in Minor County matches.

WROTTESLEY, Arthur, Third Baron Wrottesley, died at 6, Herbert Crescent, Chelsea, on December 28, 1910. He played in the famous Rugby School v. M.C.C. match in June, 1841, immortalised in *Tom Brown's School Days*, taking six wickets in the first innings and four in the second. From this fact he is supposed to be identical with the character Johnson depicted in that book. He was born in London on June 17, 1824, and was educated at Rugby and Oxford.

WYATT, Col. Francis Joseph Caldwell, who died on May 5, 1971, aged 88, was in the Glenalmond XI before playing in 10 matches for Hampshire between 1906 and 1919. He took 44 wickets for the county at an average of 19.22. In 1906–07 he appeared for Orange Free State.

WYATT, George Nevile, born at Chumparum, in India, on August 25, 1850, died at Clifton, Bristol, on February 16, 1926, aged 75. He was a good, free batsman, an excellent field at long-leg and cover-point, and a useful medium-paced change bowler. While at Cheltenham, where he was in the XI in 1869, he was coached by James Lillywhite, senr., and when captain of Sandhurst, in 1870, he scored 62 and nine v. Woolwich at Lord's. After playing for Gloucestershire—1871–75—he went to India for three years with his Regiment, and, on his return, appeared for Surrey in 1877 and 1879, and in 40 matches for Sussex between 1883 and 1886. The great event of his career was to play an innings of 112 against the Australians at Hove in 1884, when he and Harry Phillips (111) put on 182 together for the eighth wicket. Other good scores made by him for Sussex were 62 v. Nottinghamshire at Trent Bridge in 1883 and 65 v. Surrey at Hove two years later. On his one appearance for the Gentlemen v. Players—at Prince's in 1875—he made 0 and 11.

WYNNE, Owen E., who opened South Africa's batting in six Tests but never came to England, was lost at sea on July 13, 1975, yachting with his wife, his son and two friends. He was 56. Before the War he played for the Transvaal and in the first season after made 200 not out for them against the Border. He then moved to Western Province and, playing for them against F. G. Mann's M.C.C. side in 1948 in the first match of their tour, scored 108, and followed this a week later by making 105 against them for Cape Province. This naturally gained him a place in the Test side, but after his four innings in the first two Tests had produced only 17 runs, he was perhaps lucky to be picked for the third. In this he made 50 and

44 and was then dropped for the last two Tests, a decision which, without knowing the reasons, one is in no position to criticise.

Next season he began with innings of 35 (out of a total of 84) and 20 for a South African XI v. the Australians, being the only batsman to face Lindwall with confidence, and after failing against them for Western Province, again made his Test place secure with an innings of 138 against them for another South African XI: this innings took him nearly six hours. However, his best score in six innings was 33 and he was again dropped.

Taking to farming, he then disappeared from first-class cricket, but in 1958 played one more season for Western Province and, scoring 75 in his first innings, and later making 141 against the Transvaal, showed how much South Africa had lost by his early retirement. A solid rather than a brilliant bat, he was primarily an on-side player.

WYNYARD, Major Edward George, D.S.O., died at the age of 75, at The Red House, Knotty Green, Beaconsfield, Bucks, on October 30, 1936. Born in India on April 1, 1861, Major Wynyard was educated chiefly at Charterhouse School. He enjoyed a distinguished career in the Army, mainly in the East, before retiring in 1903. He served in the First World War in different staff appointments.

Over 6 ft. in height and finely built, Wynyard was a brilliant player of most games, and excelled on the cricket field, where his commanding figure could not escape attention. In his Hampshire days he usually wore an I Zingari cap of polo shape balanced at the military angle with a strap under the chin. A splendid forcing batsman he played many fine innings, and in 1899 in company with Major R. M. Poore he scored 225 out of 411 added for Hampshire's sixth wicket against Somerset at Taunton, a record stand for the sixth wicket by English batsmen. The runs were made in four hours, 20 minutes, and Major Poore finished with 304. Major Wynyard bowled lobs and in this match he took five wickets for 38 runs.

He went to New Zealand in the autumn of 1906 as captain of the M.C.C. touring team, but in the third match he snapped a tendon in his leg and returned home. He captained an M.C.C. amateur team who went to America at the end of our 1907 season. Twice he was compelled to decline invitations to accompany England teams to Australia. He toured South Africa in 1905 and 1909 with the teams led by P. F. Warner and H. D. G. Leveson Gower.

From the time when Hampshire became a first-class county in 1895, Major Wynyard scored 7,572 runs with an average of 34. He excelled in 1894 with an average of 66. Two years later he was in the England XI which beat Australia at the Oval by 66 runs, the Colonials being dismissed by Peel and J. T. Hearne for 44 in the fourth innings. That was the last match in which W. G. Grace led England to victory.

Major Wynyard played his last first-class match in 1912 for M.C.C. against Oxford University, but was regular in his visits to Lord's where, for a time, he assisted in the management. As he appeared first for Hampshire at Lord's against M.C.C. in 1878, his playing career extended over 35 years. He used to say that he made 150 centuries in all kinds of cricket of which he kept a record.

While on service in India, Major Wynyard played many big innings and in one match scored 123 and 106, both not out. When home on leave in 1887, he made 233 for Incogniti against Phoenix Park at Dublin.

A fine, free hitter, Major Wynyard used a great variety of strokes, especially those in front of the wicket. He had a grand drive, a powerful hook, a good cut, back strokes of a forcing description and a rare pull in making which he dropped to his right knee and drove the ball on the half-volley over mid-on. He developed also a special method of hitting left-handed bowling over cover-point in most effective fashion. While he could field admirably anywhere, he excelled at slip and at mid-on.

A splendid Association forward, he played in the Old Carthusian XI who won the Football Association Cup in 1881 by beating Old Etonians in the Final Tie at Kennington Oval.

WYNYARD, W. T., died on March 15, 1938, at Wellington. He played both for Wellington and Auckland against visiting teams from New South Wales over 50 years ago. His best score was 62 for Auckland against the Fijians in 1895. Besides being a free and attractive batsman, he was an excellent fieldsman. A member of the Native football team which toured England in 1888–89, he showed brilliant form at centre three-quarter back. His father, Col. Wynyard of the 57th Regiment, went out from England to quell the Waikato Native War. He was related to Major E. G. Wynyard of Hampshire.

YALLAND, Lieut. W. S., who was killed in action on October 25, 1914, played once for Gloucestershire in 1910. Although a very useful cricketer, he did not obtain a place in the XI while at Clifton. He was born in 1889, and served in the Gloucestershire Regiment.

YARDLEY, William, whose sudden death occurred at Kingston on October 28, 1900, will be remembered as one of the greatest cricketers of his day. After showing brilliant promise at Rugby he was in the Cambridge XI from 1869 to 1872, inclusive, and it is safe to say that Cambridge never possessed a more brilliant batsman. It was his distinction to make, in 1870, the first 100 ever hit in the University match. His score was exactly 100 and, as all lovers of cricket will remember, Cambridge in the end won the match by two runs, Mr. F. C. Cobden performing the hat trick after a victory for Oxford had appeared inevitable. In 1872 Mr. Yardley scored 130 against Oxford, and his feat of twice getting 100 in the University match remains to this day unique. He played more or less regularly for Kent between 1868 and 1877, and for Gentlemen against Players at Lord's in every year from 1869 to 1874. At the Oval he played for the Gentlemen twice and at Prince's once. Altogether he scored in nine Gentlemen and Players matches 435 runs, with the fine average of 36. Few batsmen, either of his own day or any other time, have been better worth looking at than Mr. Yardley, his style being free and commanding and his hitting brilliant in the extreme. He thought himself that the finest innings he ever played was 73 for South against North at Prince's on a very difficult wicket in May, 1872. It is no flattery to say that in 1870, 1871, and 1872, his only superior as a batsman was Mr. W. G. Grace. In those days when he and Mr. Grace played on the same side they always had a small wager on their scores and, long after he had retired from first-class cricket, Mr. Yardley was fond of recalling the fact that in the Gentlemen and Players match at Lord's, in 1871, he beat the great man in both innings. Mr. Yardley was in his young days a good tennis and racquets player. His name was at one time associated with the theatre almost as prominently as it was with cricket. He was part author of *Little Jack Shepherd*, one of the famous Gaiety burlesques, and more recently he helped to write *The Passport*, an amusing farce which still has life in it. He produced other pieces for the stage both alone and in collaboration, and he was for some time a dramatic critic. He was born in Bombay on June 10, 1849.

YARNOLD, Hugo, who died on August 13, 1974, aged 57, served Worcestershire with great loyalty as a wicket-keeper from 1938 to 1955 and then helped the game as a whole from 1959 as an umpire. He was returning home from officiating in the Northamptonshire v. Essex match at Wellingborough when his car was in collision with an eight-wheel lorry in Leamington.

This little man with a big heart took his chance when an accident brought the premature retirement of Syd Buller, with whom in later years he was to stand in the white coat. Once in the Worcestershire side he became a permanent fixture, helping in the dismissal of 695 batsmen, 462 of them caught, 233 stumped. He also scored 3,741 runs, average 10.45.

In his best seasons, 1949, 1950, and 1951, Yarnold had a hand in 110, 94 and 95 wickets respectively, and during the last of those three years he entered the record books with six stumpings in an innings, as well as one catch, playing against Scotland at Broughty Ferry. His high percentage of stumpings—as big as 47 against 63 catches in 1949—was attributable to his uncanny understanding with Roly Jenkins, whose leg breaks delivered from a crab-like action were not easy to "take".

Yarnold's character shone through in his last four years as a player when he overcame the handicap of the removal of both knee caps. His steadfastness helped again as an umpire, winning him recognition in three Tests, one against Pakistan in 1967 and two against Australia the following year.

YATES, Major Humphrey William Maghull, who died at Johannesburg on August 21, 1956, aged 73, figured for some years in Army cricket in England as a dashing batsman and brilliant out-fielder. He played a few times for Hampshire from 1910 to 1913, but his highest first-class innings was 97 for the Army against the Royal Navy at Lord's in 1920. He continued to play when going to South Africa and took part in good class club cricket when past 60. He became scorer to the Transvaal Cricket Union and acted in this capacity for all Test and other important matches in Johannesburg from 1945 to 1956.

YEADON, James, who kept wicket for Yorkshire in four matches in 1888, was born at Yeadon on December 11, 1861, and died there on May 30, 1914.

YEOMAN, William Farquhar, who died at Cape Town on February 2, 1944, aged 58, was one of South Africa's earliest Rhodes scholars. He appeared in the Oxford Freshmen's match in 1905, but was not tried for the University side. On returning to South Africa he played for Western Province in three Currie Cup tournaments, scoring 457 runs with an average of 26.88, his highest score being 86 against Transvaal at Durban in March, 1911. An arm wound in the First World War ended his active cricket, but he was for some years one of the Western Province selection committee.

YONGE, George Edward, one of the best-known cricketers in England 60 years ago, died on December 27, 1904. As he was born at Eton as far back as July 4, 1824, he was in his 81st year at the time of his death. He was in the Eton XI in 1841–42–43, and in that of Oxford in 1844–45–46–47–48. *Scores and Biographies* (iii–40) says of him: "Is a fine and very fast round-armed bowler, exceedingly straight, and with a beautiful easy delivery, always keeping *both* his feet behind the bowling crease."

YORKE, Gerald Joseph, who died on April 29, 1983, aged 81, was in the Eton XI in 1918 and 1919 and in 1920 played against Winchester, but did not play at Lord's. A strong hitter, he made one appearance for Gloucestershire in 1925. His father had also played for the county.

YOUNG, Sir Alfred Karney, prominent in cricket at Rochester, who played for Kent once in 1887 and again in 1890, died at Cape Town, where he was a resident magistrate, on January 5, 1942, aged 76. A sound, steady batsman, he showed special skill in placing the ball off his legs and late cutting.

YOUNG, Archibald, who has been described as one of the finest cricketers Somerset ever produced, died at Bath on April 2, 1936, aged 45. He had been ill for some years and retired from County Cricket at the end of the 1933 season. Appointed to the first-class umpires list, Young never officiated owing to his health which, it is believed, had been adversely affected during four years' service in France. Though first called upon by Somerset in 1911, Young met with little success until 1921. An enterprising batsman, he always hit the ball hard, excelling with strokes in front of the wicket and the cut. He fielded smartly in the slips and was a good right-hand slow bowler. Bath, his birthplace, was the scene of his highest score—198 against Hampshire in 1924. He did best work as an all-rounder in his last season when he scored 951 runs and took 90 wickets. "Tom"

Young, as he was generally called, overcame the handicap of periodical illness with splendid courage.

YOUNG, Harding Isaac, who died in hospital on December 12, 1964, aged 88, played as a professional all-rounder for Essex from 1898 to 1912. His death escaped general notice at the time. Born at Leyton, he achieved prominence in minor cricket while serving in the Royal Navy and the excellence of his bowling in the nets at Leyton attracted the attention of Mr. C. E. Green. So much so, indeed, that Mr. Green bought Young out of the Service to play for Essex. From this originated the nickname "Sailor" by which he was known in the cricket world.

Easily Young's best season was that of 1899 when, besides making 607 runs, he took 139 wickets at a cost of 21 runs each with left-arm bowling of medium pace from a good height and with what was described as "a deceptive curl". That summer, W. G. Grace's last in Test cricket, Young played in two matches for England against Australia, heading his country's Test bowling averages with 12 wickets for 21.83 runs apiece. In addition, he bore an outstanding part in the overthrow of the Australians by 126 runs at the hands of Essex at Leyton. In the first innings he obtained four wickets for 42 runs and in the second disposed of seven batsmen for 32, resulting in the dismissal of the touring team for 81. This was one of only three reverses suffered by J. Darling's side during the tour. Of "Sailor's" feat at Leyton, *Wisden* recorded: "He was practically unplayable, pitching outside the off-stump and turning in six or eight inches with his arm."

He twice represented Players against Gentlemen, in 1899 at the Oval where, in scoring 81—his highest innings—he helped T. W. Hayward to add 135 for the last wicket and took seven wickets for 141 runs, and in 1900 at Scarborough. He also toured the West Indies with the M.C.C. team of 1910–11. He earned a match analysis of 15 wickets for 154 runs against Warwickshire at Edgbaston in 1899, eight of them for 54 in the second innings, and on three other occasions dismissed 10 or more men in a match. During the "Indian summer" of his career, he performed his only hat-trick, against Leicestershire at Leyton in 1907, his full analysis being four wickets for six runs.

For a long time on the ground staff at Lord's, and often turning out for M.C.C., he served as a first-class umpire from 1921 to 1931 and until a very late age engaged in school coaching.—L.F.N.

YOUNG, John H., who played a few times for Derbyshire in 1899, 1900, and 1901, died on August 2, 1913, aged 37. He was born at Melbourne, near Derby, on July 2, 1876, and began his professional career with a year's engagement at Old Trafford. His best score for his county was 42 v. Leicestershire, at Derby, in 1900. Subsequently he accepted engagements at Southport, Bootle, and Chard.

YOUNG, John Villiers, who died in hospital at Eastbourne on September 3, 1960, aged 76, was in the Eastbourne College XI from 1901 to 1904, being captain in the last two years. A fine all-rounder, he scored 947 runs and took 63 wickets in 1903. To him belonged an unusual distinction, for he played in the 1906 Cambridge Freshmen's match and in the 1907 Oxford Freshmen's match, becoming both a Cambridge Crusader and an Oxford Authentic. He played in three matches for Sussex in 1908. He was the brother of R. A. Young, the celebrated Cambridge University, Sussex and England batsman.

YOUNG, Richard Alfred, who died on July 1, 1968, aged 82, was one of the few spectacled players to represent England at both cricket and Association football. He established a high reputation as a wicket-keeper and batsman while in the XI at Repton from 1901 to 1904, heading the averages in 1902 when *Wisden* described him as "out and away the best batsman" at the school. He captained the side in the last two seasons. A consistent and reliable batsman, strong on the leg-side and in driving to the off, he gained a Blue as a Freshman at Cambridge in 1905 and also played in the University matches of the following three seasons. In 1906 he distinguished himself by hitting 150 against Oxford out of a total of 360, being first in and last out when, with wickets falling fast, he began to take risks. In 1907 and again in 1908, when captain, he occupied first place in the University batting figures. He enjoyed the honour in 1907–08 of being chosen as a member of the M.C.C. team which toured Australia under A. O. Jones, taking part in two Test matches. From 1905 to 1925 he assisted Sussex as an amateur, his highest innings for the county being 220 in a total of 611 against Essex at Leyton in 1905. In all first-class cricket he scored 6,502 runs, including six centuries, for an average of 28.76, and he brought off 82 catches behind the wicket and 23 stumpings.

A clever and speedy outside-right, Young

also represented Cambridge at Association football and was a noted player for the famous Corinthians. He earned an amateur cap against Hungary and also played for the Amateur F.A. against France. For over 30 years he was mathematics and cricket master at Eton until retiring in 1951.

YOUNG, The Rev. Wilfred Alec Radford, died at Kimcote Rectory, near Rugby, March 19, 1947, aged 79. Played for Harrow 1883–85, and occasionally for Somerset.

ZULCH, J. W., Sen., who died at Johannesburg on July 26, 1912, was the father of J. W. Zulch, who visited Australia in 1910–11, and was himself a good cricketer. He took part in the first Currie Cup tournament.

ZULCH, John William, for some years one of South Africa's leading batsmen, was found dead in bed on May 19, 1924, at Umkomaas (Natal), where he had gone to recoup his health after a nervous breakdown. He was born in the Lydenburg District, Transvaal, on January 20, 1886, and so was only 37 years of age at the time of his death. His education was received at Green and Sea Point High School, Cape Town, and his earliest big success on the cricket field was an innings of 180 for Pretoria v. Potchefstroom. He was a great batsman, having many strokes and a strong defence, and a good field, but he never visited England. He toured Australia, however, in 1910–11, and played innings of 150 at Sydney and 105 at Adelaide in the Test matches. His first really big game was in 1905–06 for Pretoria against England, but he did not begin to come to the front until three years later. In Test matches against both Australia and England he commenced 32 innings, was twice not out and, with the 150 mentioned as his highest effort, scored 985 runs with

an average of 32.83. (In one of the games with Australia—at Johannesburg in 1921–22—he was dismissed in an unusual manner, a splinter from his bat being removed by a ball from E. A. Macdonald and dislodging a bail.) When he made 106 not out for Transvaal v. England at Pretoria in 1909–10, he and L. A. Stricker (101) put up 215 for the first wicket. Twice in the Tests of 1913–14, too, he and H. W. Taylor were responsible for excellent opening partnerships, the pair making 153 together at Johannesburg and 129 at Port Elizabeth: Zulch's innings were respectively 82 and 60 and Taylor's 70 and 87. In the Test at Cape Town four seasons earlier Zulch had carried his bat through the innings for 43. In other great matches in his native land he scored 112 not out for Transvaal v. Border at Cape Town in 1908–09—he and A. Difford (91) made 190 for the first wicket, 168 for H. D. G. Leveson-Gower's XI v. Rhodesia at Bulawayo in 1909–10, and 135 for South Africa v. Australia Imperial Forces at Johannesburg.in 1919–20. In his seven innings while on tour with a Transvaal XI in 1920–21, he made six and 64 v. Border, 171 v. Grahamstown, 124 v. Eastern Province, 76 v. Graaff Reinet, and 185 and 125 v. Orange Free State, thus averaging 107.28.

ZULFIQAR, Ali, who died in Pakistan on October 12, 1968, aged 26, was a talented off-break bowler and capable tail-end batsman. Earlier in the year he played in the first two Tests against the Commonwealth XI at Multan, where he took eight wickets, and at Lahore. Educated at West Pakistan Agricultural University, he came to the fore as a cricketer in the Ayub Zonal tournament of 1964–65 when, for Lahore Board, he scored 285 runs and dismissed 15 batsmen. His side lost in the Final to Karachi by an innings and 91 runs.